MOVIES ON TV
AND
VIDEOCASSETTE
1992–1993

Conceived and Edited by
Steven H. Scheuer

BANTAM BOOKS
NEW YORK · TORONTO · LONDON · SYDNEY · AUCKLAND

MOVIES ON TV AND VIDEOCASSETTE 1992–1993

A Bantam Nonfiction Book
Original Bantam edition / November 1958
Ninth revised edition / November 1981
Tenth revised edition / December 1983
Eleventh revised edition / December 1985
Twelfth revised edition / December 1987
Thirteenth revised edition / February 1989
Fourteenth revised edition / December 1989
Fifteenth revised edition / November 1990
Sixteenth revised edition / November 1991

ISBN 0-553-29147-5

Published simultaneously in the United States and Canada

PRINTED IN THE UNITED STATES OF AMERICA

RAD   0 9 8 7 6 5 4 3 2 1

Guide to alphabetization:

The reviews in *Movies on TV and Videocassette* are alphabetized in letter order, ignoring punctuation and word breaks. Just think of each title as one long string of letters: *Total Recall* comes before *To the Devil . . . a Daughter, Shocker* before *Shock to the System, A,* and *Woman's Secret, A,* before *Woman Times Seven.*

Numbers are alphabetized as if spelled out—look for *10 Violent Women* between *Ten to Midnight* and *Ten Wanted Men.* However, sequels which have the same title followed by "Part 2" or the equivalent are listed in chronological order. We feel it would be pretty dumb to list *Rocky IV* ahead of *Rocky III* even if "four" would normally precede "three."

In the cases of films beginning with "Mister," "Doctor," "Saint," and other often-abbreviated words, you'll find them under the correct official movie title, so check under "Mr.," "Dr.," and "St." as well.

Articles at the beginning of English language titles (The, A, An) are not included as part of the title for purposes of alphabetization and are accordingly moved to the end of the title: *Hunt for Red October, The* will be found under "H." For titles in a foreign language, however, articles are kept at the beginning— *Les Miserables* will be found under "L".

Key to ratings:

****	Excellent! Entertaining and a great cinematic achievement.
***½	Very Good. But just this side of paradise.
***	Above Average. Thoroughly satisfying.
**½	Average. You won't be wasting your time.
**	Fair. Falls short of the mark.
*½	Poor. Tired formula, overblown epics, and the like.
*	Awful. You'll be sorry.
½	Abysmal. People got paid for making these!?!

A dagger (†) at the end of a review indicates that the film is available on videocassette as of publication.

The symbol (MTV) in a review means made for television and (MCTV) means made for cable television originally.

THE ASSOCIATE EDITORS

JOHN GOUDAS, Senior Editor, who authored many of the reviews of movies made for TV included in this edition, is a syndicated columnist for "TV Key," which covers all aspects of television from prime time to soap operas. He interviews the top stars in show business, and has served as a guest host on Steven H. Scheuer's "All About TV." Mr. Goudas helped write the books *The Television Annual* and *Movie Blockbusters*, he represented the U.S. on the international jury at the Banff (Canada) TV Festival, and was a member of the committee for the International Emmy Awards.

ROBERT J. MONDZAK, Senior Editor, is a graduate of Hunter College in New York City with a degree in film and theater, and he is the recipient of honorary awards in playwriting and video production. He is a contributor to the nationally syndicated "TV Key" newspaper column, and is currently writing a screenplay.

MICHAEL CALLERI, Senior Editor, divides his time between his native Buffalo and Los Angeles. A graduate of the State University of New York at Buffalo with a degree in English and Film, he is the author of two screenplays and has written about movies for more than ten years.

LINDA SANDAHL, Associate Senior Editor, is an editor and writer on movie and entertainment subjects who has contributed to many earlier editions of *Movies on TV and Videocassette*. She lived in London for several years, and is the author of the book *Rock Films*.

MARY BOSS, Associate Editor, studied film criticism at the University of Paris/Sorbonne, and works in film production and distribution.

ABOUT THE EDITOR

STEVEN H. SCHEUER is the author of numerous critically acclaimed books about motion pictures and television, including *The Movie Book*, a pictorial history of world cinema, *Who's Who in Television & Cable*, and *The Television Annual*. His most recent work is *The Complete Guide to Videocassette Movies*.

Mr. Scheuer is also the editor and publisher of "TV Key," a widely syndicated daily newspaper column. He has contributed to many magazines including *TV Guide*, and he lectures throughout the world on motion pictures, television, and home video. In the spring of 1991 Mr. Scheuer gave a month-long series of lectures and seminars on American television in China at Beijing University. He is considered one of the most knowledgeable media critics in the country.

He is the executive producer and moderator of the award-winning weekly TV series "All About TV," seen on public television stations and on the cable network The Learning Channel. "All About TV" is the only television program in the United States dealing candidly with television itself. It is distributed overseas via the United States Information Agency. For several years Mr. Scheuer served as the television critic of the CBS Radio Network.

Mr. Scheuer is a native New Yorker and a graduate of Yale University. He has done postgraduate work at the London School of Economics and Political Science, and has taught college and university courses on the history of American television. He is a member of the Communications Media Committee of the American Civil Liberties Union, The Society of Fellows of the Aspen Institute for Humanistic Studies, The Royal Television Society, and the International Institute of Communications, and has served as a vice president of International Film Seminars.

Mr. Scheuer participates in many sports and was a nationally ranked squash tennis player.

of Lifetime; the helpful staff at Bender, Goldman & Helper; Danny Kopels of Magnum Video; Claudia Harris of Turner Network Television; Warren Betts of IVE; Jane Ayer of Universal/MCA; Michael Finnegan and Susan Edwards of Warner Bros. Video; Fritz Feldman and Marilu Eagles of RCA/Columbia Home Video; Steve Grenyo and Joanna Ney of the New York Film Festival; the staff of Clein, Feldman and White; Judy McGuinn and Susan Prestine of Virgin Vision; Bruce Lynn, Wynn Lowenthal, Renee Furst, Lauren Hyman, and everyone we've inadvertently overlooked.

We continue to be grateful for the work done by reviewers who contributed to earlier editions of the book: We offer continuing thanks to Myron Meisel, William Wolf, Mark Harris, Charles Derry, and Michael Faust.

In this 34th year of *Movies on TV and Videocassette*, I leave you with the words of the late Winthrop Sergeant, the music critic of the *New Yorker* for more than two decades:

"The critic's function is not to lay down incontrovertible laws or pronounce absolute truths. It is to reflect his personal taste, for what it is worth, and try to stimulate his readers into accepting or rejecting it according to their own lights."

This is demonstrably true of the much newer art of motion pictures, arguably the most pervasive and influential art of our time. Sergeant's concerns and point of view toward his music criticism remain the tenets we endorse unreservedly as guidelines for film criticism.

Good reading, and more important, HAPPY VIEWING!

New York City
October 1991

STEVEN H. SCHEUER

video store. As much as we struggle to keep the video daggers current, it is inevitable that the day after the book goes to press (no matter how late we try to stretch the deadline), we will learn of another collection of classic films being released on video. And although we have indicated over 400 new video releases this year, by the time you read this there will be a few dozen more that we haven't noted. So, don't take our word as final—check with your neighborhood video store, or investigate the many mail-order firms that specialize in more obscure films.

We are grateful to a large number of people who contributed to this latest edition of *Movies on TV and Videocassette*.

Lynne Arany and her staff at Ink Projects (with a special thanks to Michael Yawney) diligently supervised the complex composition of this work.

Special thanks are also due to the always reliable Donna Janosik (a wiz on the computer), and to the invaluable contributions of Mary Hinckley, Ed Grant, and Maggie Soffel of Nova Works.

We would also like to extend a warm token of appreciation to those who provided information and access to screenings and review tapes, as well as moral and technical support, including: Joe DeMarco, Jeanmarie Henry, Joseph N. Ventre, Cindy Abbott, Michael Early, Mae Woods, Bonnie MacFadyen, Allison Montante, Sandi and Tommy Tang, Doug Smith of WIVB-TV; Doug Young of WGR Radio; Patricia Thompson of *Film Canada Yearbook*; Rick Szykowny of *The Humanist* magazine; Patricia Ward Biederman of *The Los Angeles Times*; Penny Costigan of Twentieth Century Fox; Sue Cohen of Universal Pictures; Bruce Stern of Stern Advertising/Warner Brothers; Michele Maheux and the staf of the Toronto Film Festival; Lynn LaRocca and Beth Kobland of Allied Advertising; Sherry Natkow of Cinema Specialties; David Koester of *Buffalo Night-Life* magazine; Steven Parkansky, Michelle Kij, Dennis Sullivan, Sal Ciffa, Maynard Pettit, and Lisa Szymanek of General Cinema Corporation; and Patrick Dahn, Mike Kostyszyn, Jim Maisano, and Dan Prygon of American Multi Cinema.

We would also like to extend further thanks to Hali Simon of CBS; Helen Manasian and Paul Reader of USA Cable Network; Matt Messina of NBC; Janice Gretemeyer of ABC; Patrick McFarland and Marlea Willis of Arts and Entertainment; Tobe Becker and Nancy Lesser of HBO; Karen Gault of Cinemax; Kat Stein of Showtime; Les Schecter and Associates of American Playhouse/PBS; Steve Savage of Fox Lorber Home Video; Andrew Blau of Monarch Home Video; Joan-Ellen Delaney of Fox Broadcasting Company; Alex Wagner, Abby Gans, and Lee Fryd made for television releases of the last year as possible. Then, as in prior years, we concentrated on three general areas:

• Foreign films, possibly the single strongest growth area in the home video market right now, as distributors begin to realize the potential of this vastly untapped market.

• Older movies (including silent films), which are now being shown on cable TV, and are also available on home video.

• Obscure, unusual, and otherwise worthy or notable movies, which are now available on home video as well.

In other words we think you will find that, besides being the original reference for home viewing, this 1992–1993 edition of *Movies on TV and Videocassette* is the most complete guide of its type available. If the movie you are looking up is not in our pages, in all likelihood you would not be able to find it anyway, or, you really wouldn't want to.

Film buffs and the more discerning among you will appreciate the wealth of lore, trivia, and inside information included in many hundreds of these reviews. In what film did Betty Grable sub for the ailing Alice Faye and break through to stardom? What film costarred Kurt Russell and Goldie Hawn fifteen years before *Swing Shift?* In what movie did Jimmy Durante first perform his signature song "Inka Dinka Doo"? You can find the answers to these cosmic film questions and many more in the pages which follow.

We have added hundreds of alternate titles to help save you from wasting your time on a movie you've already seen under another name. We have also tried to note important changes in the television and video versions of movies, an increasingly difficult task as movies are shortened and even sped up in order to cram them into briefer time slots and onto shorter tapes.

Conversely, we have also noted when a film has been restored to its original form. The colorization furor seems to be dying down, although it is probably too much to hope that it will go away completely. Sadly, great black and white beauties will continue to show up in their new colors.

A general word of warning: Some feature length movies on videocassettes are now turning up with commercials in them—a truly obnoxious and annoying development for those of us who prefer to watch movies on cassette to avoid the advertisements on television and the popcorn crunchers who always seem to be sitting next to you at the local movie house!

And, a word on our video dagger (†) found at the end of reviews to indicate that a film is available on home video. As in the past, our rule has been to include the dagger when the movie is *readily* available through standard outlets such as your local

Preface

For the three decades that I have produced this book, I have had a special goal: To provide concise, honest, useful information for the selective viewer about movies on television. Alfred H. Barr, the founding director of the Museum of Modern Art in New York City, once defined his task as the "... resolute distinction of quality from mediocrity." That has been precisely my task as well!

In the past, old favorites, or notable new movies screened at a film festival, would not be reviewed here since it was unlikely that they would be showcased on American television. Now, however, thanks largely to cable television and videocassette, there has been an explosion in what is available for public viewing: old movies, new movies, American, and foreign made.

While industry analysts say that the growth of the videocassette market has leveled off, that just means it is holding its own at the astounding rate of one hundred new releases on videocassette each month! And there are other choices for the viewer at home as well. The cable networks continue to expand.

As this edition goes to press, American television is about to undergo an even more dramatic change: A truly staggering increase in the channel capacity of many cable franchises. New communications technology, including fiber optics, will allow new cable systems (such as the Queens, New York system built by Time Warner) to offer a minimum of one hundred and fifty channels. Many cable TV experts expect the number to exceed three hundred channels in the next few years. Because many of these will be "Pay Per View" channels, it is more important than ever before that movie lovers at home have first-class, reliable information to help make an informed decision about the movie they are about to plunk down real money to watch. *Movies on TV and Videocassette* is gearing up to help in this new viewing climate.

This year, with the addition of over 400 new entries, my staff and I were once again faced with having to decide which movies to add and which to "leave on the cutting room floor." We decided, of course, to add as many of the theatrical and

For Alida:

My miraculously wise and beloved savior, an increasingly and deservedly "Big Potato."

MOVIES ON TV
AND
VIDEOCASSETTE

TV Movie Reviews and Ratings

Aaron Loves Angela (1975)**½ Irene Cara, Kevin Hooks, Moses Gunn, Robert Hooks, Ernestine Jackson. Heart-warming variation of the Romeo and Juliet theme as a black boy and a Puerto Rican girl become star-crossed lovers. (Dir: Gordon Parks, Jr., 98 mins.)†

Aaron Slick from Punkin Crick (1952)** Alan Young, Robert Merrill, Dinah Shore, Guy Mitchell. A city slicker tries to fleece a poor widow out West. Tedious musical comedy. (Dir: Claude Binyon, 95 mins.)

Aaron's Way (MTV 1988)*½ Merlin Olsen, Belinda Montgomery, Jessica Walter. Squeaky-clean family fare about an Amish couple who picks up the family and moves to California in order to help their daughter-in-law harvest her grapes. Enough "culture-clash" jokes to last a lifetime. (Dir: Noel Nosseck, 96 mins.)

Abandoned (1949)**½ Dennis O'Keefe, Gale Storm, Raymond Burr, Jeff Chandler. Sensationalized drama centering around baby-adoption rackets and how a determined girl and a newspaper man help to crack them. (Dir: Joe Newman, 79 mins.)

Abandon Ship (1957)*** Tyrone Power, Mai Zetterling, Lloyd Nolan. Tense drama about the fate of twenty-six survivors of a luxury liner disaster crammed into a lifeboat that can only hold twelve safely. (Dir: Richard Sale, 100 mins.)

Abbott and Costello Go to Mars (1953)** Bud Abbott, Lou Costello, Mari Blanchard. For the duo's fans: slapstick and double talk routines are emphasized in this silly space comedy about an accidental trip to Venus. (Dir: Charles Lamont, 77 mins.)

Abbott and Costello in Hollywood (1945)** Bud Abbott, Lou Costello, Frances Rafferty. Bud and Lou run a barbershop in Hollywood; the usual, with lots of clowning. (Dir: S. Sylvan Simon, 83 mins.)†

Abbott and Costello in the Foreign Legion (1950)** Bud Abbott, Lou Costello, Patricia Medina. The boys don Foreign Legionnaires' duds in this moderately funny farce about intrigue amid the sand dunes of Algiers. (Dir: Charles Lamont, 80 mins.)

Abbott and Costello Meet Captain Kidd (1952)** Bud Abbott, Lou Costello, Charles Laughton, Fran Warren. Standard A&C nonsense, as the boys go after Captain Kidd's treasure with the pirate in hot pursuit. (Dir: Charles Lamont, 70 mins.)†

Abbott and Costello Meet Dr. Jekyll and Mr. Hyde (1953)**½ Bud Abbott, Lou Costello, Boris Karloff. Abbott and Costello fans will enjoy this comedy-horror film with them playing a couple of American detectives in London during the late 1800s. (Dir: Charles Lamont, 76 mins.)†

Abbott and Costello Meet Frankenstein (1948)***½ Bud Abbott, Lou Costello, Lon Chaney, Bela Lugosi. Horror-film parody, with Chaney as the Wolfman and Lugosi as the Count. The antics tend to be side-splitting. (Dir: Charles Barton, 83 mins.)†

Abbott and Costello Meet the Invisible Man (1951)** Bud Abbott, Lou Costello, Nancy Guild. A lightweight farce in which Abbott and Costello play detectives hired by a unique client—an invisible man. (Dir: Charles Lamont, 82 mins.)

Abbott and Costello Meet the Keystone Kops (1955)*** Bud Abbott, Lou Costello, Fred Clark, Lynn Bari. A&C are in the movie business circa 1912 this time. In between pies in the face, there's a wild chase complete with the famous Keystone Kops. Mack Sennett makes a guest appearance. (Dir: Charles Lamont, 80 mins.)

Abbott and Costello Meet the Killer (1949)** Bud Abbott, Lou Costello, Boris Karloff. A silly excursion into murder and mirth with the comedy team as a pair of amateur sleuths who almost get themselves killed. (Dir: Charles Barton, 94 mins.)†

Abbott and Costello Meet the Mummy (1955)** Bud Abbott, Lou Costello, Marie Windsor. Bud and Lou are treasure hunters in this yarn about Egyptian tombs and the crooks who want to get their hands on a hoard of gold and jewels. (Dir: Charles Lamont, 90 mins.)

Abby (1974)** Carol Speed, William Marshall, Terry Carter, Austin Stoker, Juanita Moore. A minister's wife is in need of some ministering when Satan possesses her. Fairish blaxploitation thriller that rips off *The Exorcist* rather handily. (Dir: William Girdler, 92 mins.)

Abdication, The (Great Britain, 1974)*½ Liv Ullmann, Peter Finch, Cyril Cusack, Paul Rogers. Ineffective historical epic concerning the abdication of Queen Christina in 17th-century Sweden and her subsequent conversion to Catholicism in Rome, where she falls in love with a cardinal. (Dir: Anthony Harvey, 103 mins.)

Abduction, The (1975)*½ Gregory Rozakis, Judith-Marie Bergan, David Pendleton, Leif Erickson, Dorothy Malone, Lawrence Tierney. Although based on a book written before Patty Hearst had her coming-out party with the Symbionese Liberation Army, the film's attempt to cash in on the Hearst case is poorly disguised. (Dir: Joseph Zito, 100 mins.)†

Abduction of Karl Swenson, The (MTV

1987)*½ Tracy Pollan, Joe Don Baker, M. Emmet Walsh, Ronny Cox. Dull TV film about the strange incident in which a biathalon athlete was kidnapped by two mountain men who believed in the caveman ethic. (Dir: Stephen Gylenhaal, 104 mins.)

Abduction of Saint Anne, The (MTV 1975)**½ E. G. Marshall, Robert Wagner, Lloyd Nolan. A young girl is reputed to have healing powers, and the Catholic Church wants to have her miracles certified. But there's a hitch...she's being held a virtual prisoner in her gangland father's estate. (Dir: Harry Falk, 72 mins.)†

Abductors, The (1957)**½ Victor McLaglen, Fay Spain. Fairly interesting true life crime tale about Lincoln's grave. (Dir: Andrew McLaglen, 80 mins.)

Abductors, The (1972)* Cheri Caffaro, William Grannell, Richard Smedley. Female superagent Caffaro battles an international ring of white slavers. Sequel to *Ginger* is even more sleazy and violent. Followed by *Girls Are For Loving*. (Dir: Don Schain, 88 mins.)†

Abdullah's Harem—See: **Abdulla the Great**

Abdulla the Great (Great Britain-Egypt, 1956)** Gregory Ratoff, Kay Kendall, Sydney Chaplin, Alex D'Arcy. Dated satire of Egypt's King Farouk (who threatened to sue if the film was released) with Ratoff as the monarch pursuing English model Kendall, blithely ignorant that his people are on the brink of revolution. Ratoff (who also produced and directed) hams it up, though his Russian accent is out of place in these Arab surroundings. Originally 105 mins. AKA: **Abdullah's Harem**. (89 mins.)†

Abe Lincoln in Illinois (1940)**** Raymond Massey and Ruth Gordon star in this moving, wonderfully acted version of Robert E. Sherwood's Broadway play about the 16th President's life, his ill-fated love for Ann Rutledge, and his marriage to Mary Todd. (Dir: John Cromwell, 110 mins.)†

Able's Irish Rose (1946)* Joanne Dru, Richard Norris, Michael Chekov, Eric Blore. Unconvincing version of the smash hit play, which was considered outdated when it played to packed houses in the twenties. Sentimental slapstick comedy spares no ethnic slurs in detailing the tribulations of an Irish girl married to a Jewish boy. (Dir: A. Edward Sutherland, 96 mins.)

Abilene Town (1945)*** Randolph Scott, Ann Dvorak, Rhonda Fleming. The marshal of Abilene has his hands full separating the cattlemen from the homesteaders in 1870. Fast, well-produced western. (Dir: Edwin Marin, 89 mins.)†

Abismos de Pasion—See: **Wuthering Heights** (1954)

Abominable Dr. Phibes, The (Great Britain, 1971)*** Vincent Price, Joseph Cotten, Terry-Thomas, Virginia North. The king of camp horror, Vincent Price, is at it again with great style. Stalking amid gothic backdrops, he plays a mad doctor out to polish off a surgical team he believes did in his wife. (Dir: Robert Fuest, 93 mins.)†

Abominable Snowman of the Himalayas, The (1957)**½ Forrest Tucker, Peter Cushing, Maureen Connell. Better than average horror–sci-fi yarn about an expedition in search of the legendary man-beast. (Dir: Val Guest, 85 mins.)

A Bout de Souffle—See: **Breathless** (1959)

About Face (1952)** Gordon MacRae, Eddie Bracken, Phyllis Kirk. Cadet musical with lavish production numbers. This is a remake of *Brother Rat* with tunes added. (Dir: Roy Del Ruth, 94 mins.)

About Last Night... (1986)**½ Rob Lowe, Demi Moore, Jim Belushi, Elizabeth Perkins. David Mamet's acerbic play *Sexual Perversity in Chicago* is given a dose of unneeded optimism on celluloid. Lowe and Moore are excellent as a couple whose one night stand turns into a serious and ultimately doomed relationship, but the romantic clichés used to solve the couple's problems dispel the film's realistic feeling. (Dir: Edward Zwick, 113 mins.)†

About Mrs. Leslie (1954)**½ Shirley Booth, Robert Ryan. When a tycoon dies and leaves a boarding house owner some money, her secret love affair is recalled. Unadorned soap opera, compensated for by fine acting. (Dir: Daniel Mann, 104 mins.)

Above and Beyond (1952)*** Robert Taylor, Eleanor Parker. An absorbing subject well handled. Robert Taylor gives a nicely etched performance as the officer who piloted the plane which dropped the atom bomb on Hiroshima. (Dirs: Melvin Frank, Norman Panama, 122 mins.)

Above Suspicion (1943)**½ Joan Crawford, Fred MacMurray, Basil Rathbone. Fast-moving chase melodrama with Fred and Joan trying to aid the British secret service while they honeymoon in Paris. (Dir: Richard Thorpe, 90 mins.)

Above the Law (1988)**½ Steven Seagal, Henry Silva, Pam Grier, Sharon Stone. A tough cop, equipped only with martial arts expertise and CIA training from Vietnam, uncovers a conspiracy involving the CIA, drugs, explosives, a Senate committee, and Central American refugees. (Got that?) A formula picture, but one with spirit. (Dir: Andrew Davis, 97 mins.)†

Above Us the Waves (Great Britain, 1956)*** John Mills, John Gregson, Donald Sinden, James Robertson Justice. Taut, stiff-upper-lip WWII submarine chase with a superior cast. Look for Anthony Newley in a small part as an engineer. (Dir: Ralph Thomas, 92 mins.)†

Abraham Lincoln (1930)** Walter Huston, Una Merkel, Kay Hammond, Hobart Bosworth. Creaky biography was pioneering director D. W. Griffith's first talkie; Huston is excellent. Script by Stephen Vincent Benét. (85 mins.)†

Abroad with Two Yanks (1944)*** Dennis O'Keefe, William Bendix, John Loder, Helen Walker. Two wacky Marines turn Australia inside out in their escapades over a girl. Wild, frequently hilarious comedy. (Dir: Allan Dwan, 80 mins.)†

Absence of Malice (1982)*** Paul Newman, Sally Field, Bob Balaban, Melinda Dillon, Luther Adler, Barry Primus. Newman is in top form as a man falsely implicated in the disappearance of a labor leader; the film is entertaining and thought-provoking. Excellent cast. (Dir: Sydney Pollack, 116 mins.)†

Absent-Minded Professor, The (1961)**½ Fred MacMurray, Nancy Olson, Tommy Kirk, Ed Wynn, Keenan Wynn. The kids should get a kick out of this vintage Disney production. It's all simple-minded fun as MacMurray bumbles his way through the title role, where his accidental discovery of a formula makes his old Model T Ford fly. (Dir: Robert Stevenson, 104 mins.)†

Absinthe—See: **Madame X** (1929)

Absolute Beginners (Great Britain, 1986)*** Eddie O'Connell, David Bowie, Anita Morris, Ray Davies, Sade, James Fox, Patsy Kensit. A mesmerizing story of alienated youths viewed against a backdrop of race riots in 1950s England. Good ideas and characters abound, but director Julien Temple is too busy breaking the participants into song and dance to exploit them fully. Still, the abundantly happy energy and surreal symbolism cover most of the faults. (107 mins.)†

Absolute Strangers (MTV 1991)*** Henry Winkler, Richard Kiley, Karl Malden, Patty Duke, Audra Lindley, Jennifer Hetrick, Doris Belak. Compelling drama based on a true story. After a car accident leaves his pregnant wife (Hetrick) in a coma, Winkler decides she has a better chance for survival if she has an abortion. What he doesn't expect are the legal ramifications and the pro-life groups who exploit the case for their own ends. Powerful story enhanced by the top-notch cast. (Dir: Gilbert Cates, 96 mins.)

Absolution (Great Britain, 1981)½ Richard Burton, Dai Bradley, Dominic Guard, Billy Connolly, Andrew Keir. Burton put another dent in his reputation with this inert tale of a schoolmaster under the thumb of a student with a predilection for pranks that get out of hand. (Dir: Anthony Page, 95 mins.)†

Abyss, The (Belgium, 1988) *** Gian Maria Volonte, Jean Bouise, Philippe Leotard, Sami Frey, Anna Karina, Marie-Christine Barrault, Marie-France Pisier. Superior production values and photography highlight story about a 16th-century Flemish physician and alchemist who wanders Europe fleeing the Inquisition, who have charged him with dissidence and bisexuality. Outstanding ensemble acting and riveting atmosphere overcome the film's staginess. (Dir: Andre Delvaux, 110 mins.)

Abyss, The (1989)** Ed Harris, Mary Elizabeth Mastrantonio, Michael Biehn, Todd Graff, John Bedford Lloyd, Leo Burmester, Kimberly Scott. The crew of an oil rig is called upon to investigate a nuclear sub disaster; director James Cameron is fine at the heavy-metal action, but his pacing and storyline are abysmal. Oscar winner for visual effects. (135 mins.)†

Acapulco Gold (1978)* Marjoe Gortner, Robert Lansing, Ed Nelson, John Harkins, Randi Oakes. The title's the name of a drug prized by smugglers in this tedious if scenic adventure that will not give you a cinematic high. (Dir: Burt Brinckerhof, 105 mins.)

Accatone! (Italy, 1961)*** Franco Citti, Franca Pasut, Silvana Corsini, Paola Guidi, Adele Cambria. A brutal slice of neorealism. Citti plays a Roman ne'er-do-well who tries to get by on his charm and is then motivated by love to change his wastrel ways. Interesting feature debut by Pier Paolo Pasolini. (120 mins.)†

Accent on Youth (1935)**½ Herbert Marshall, Sylvia Sidney, Phillip Reeds, Holmes Herbert, Donald Meek, Lon Chaney, Jr. Witty and enjoyable adaptation of the popular Samson Raphaelson play about a secretary who falls in love with her middle-aged boss, a playwright. Remade as *But Not For Me*. (Dir: Wesley Ruggles, 77 mins.)

Acceptable Risks (MTV 1986)** Brian Dennehy, Cicely Tyson, Kenneth McMillan, Christine Ebersole, Beah Richards, Richard Gilliland. This problem drama calculatedly plays on our fears of the accidents possible at a chemical plant. The cast doesn't rise above the built-in hysteria. (Dir: Rick Wallace, 104 mins.)

3

Access Code (1988)½ Martin Landau, Michael Ansara, MacDonald Carey, Michael Durrell, Marcia Mueller, Michael Napoli. Confusing, senseless political thriller about CIA efforts to stop a terrorist organization trying to invade the computer systems of the U.S. military. Reportedly, this was never finished, with key scenes left unfilmed, but what the heck, put it out on video and *someone* will rent it. (Dir: Mark Sobel, 88 mins.)†

Accident (Great Britain, 1967)*** Dirk Bogarde, Stanley Baker, Jacqueline Sassard. A fascinating, if uneven, study of a married college professor who becomes involved with one of his attractive female students. (Dir: Joseph Losey, 105 mins.)†

Accidental Tourist, The (1988)***½ William Hurt, Geena Davis, Kathleen Turner, Amy Wright, Bill Pullman, David Ogden Stiers, Ed Begley, Jr. Diluted but still compelling adaptation of Anne Tyler's novel about stodgy travel writer Hurt, who gets a new lease on life from an eccentric dog trainer (Oscar winner Davis). Full of marvelously quirky characters and details. (Dir: Lawrence Kasdan, 120 mins.)†

Accidents Will Happen (1939)**½ Ronald Reagan, Sheila Bromley, Gloria Blondell, Dick Purcell. Trim programmer about an above-board insurance investigator who puts a premium on honesty and exposes a phony accident payoff scam. (Dir: William Clemens, 62 mins.)

Accursed, The (1958)**½ Donald Wolfit, Robert Bray. A fairly interesting mystery involving the guests of a onetime colonel of the Resistance forces at the annual reunion held at his home. (Dir: Michael McCarthy, 78 mins.)

Accused, The (1948)*** Loretta Young, Robert Cummings, Wendell Corey. Schoolteacher accidentally kills an amorous student and tries to cover her crime. Well-made drama. (Dir: William Dieterle, 101 mins.)

Accused, The (1988)*** Jodie Foster, Kelly McGillis, Leo Rossi. Foster's Oscar-winning performance far outclasses the exploitative nature of this film. Based on a true story of a waitress who brought criminal charges against onlookers who cheered while she was raped, the film is melodramatically directed by Jonathan Kaplan (*Project X*). Still, Foster is a must-see. (110 mins.)†

Accused of Murder (1956)** Vera Ralston, David Brian. Homicide officer falls for a nightclub singer suspected of killing a gangland lawyer. Ordinary mystery. (Dir: Joseph Kane, 80 mins.)

Ace Eli and Rodger of the Skies (1973)*½ Cliff Robertson, Pamela Franklin, Eric Shea, Bernadette Peters. Robertson is a barnstorming pilot in rural Kansas who flies with son Rodger, who's 11 years old and the more mature of the duo. Written by Steven Spielberg. (Dir: "Bill Sampson" [John Erman], 92 mins.)

Ace High (Italy, 1968)**½ Eli Wallach, Brock Peters, Kevin McCarthy. Occasionally interesting spaghetti western which spoofs the genre. Wallach plays a sly bandit in Mexico, who gets the loot no matter what obstacles are in his way. (Dir: Giuseppe Colizzi, 120 mins.)†

Ace in the Hole—See: **Big Carnival, The**

Ace of Aces (1933)*** Richard Dix, Elizabeth Allan, Ralph Bellamy, Bill Cagney, Joe Sauers (Sawyer). Strongly felt and unusually thoughtful World War I melodrama, with Dix a pacifistic artist goaded into military service by his fiancée and embittered by his combat experiences. (Dir: J. Walter Ruben, 76 mins.)†

Aces High (Great Britain, 1976)*** Malcolm McDowell, Simon Ward, Peter Firth, Christopher Plummer, Ray Milland. A competent remake of *Journey's End*, the old story about WWI aerial combat, with the young squadron leader (McDowell) sending men to fight and perhaps to die. (Dir: Jack Gold, 103 mins.)

Acorn People, The (MTV 1981)*** Ted Bessell, Cloris Leachman, LeVar Burton, Dolph Sweet. A tale set at a summer camp for severely handicapped kids seen through the eyes of a bleeding-heart camp counselor and his associates. At first the show is not easy to take but the kids grow on you and so do the counselors. (Dir: Joan Tewkesbury, 104 mins.)

Acqua e Sapone (Italy, 1985)*½ Carlo Verdone, Natasha Hovey, Florinda Balkan, Fabrizio Bracconeri. Poor romantic comedy about a milquetoast tutoring an American model in Rome and falling for her despite her ambitious mother's career plans for her. (Dir: Carlo Verdone, 105 mins.)†

Across 110th Street (1972)** Anthony Quinn, Anthony Franciosa, Yaphet Kotto. Violent crime drama shot in Harlem. Infighting among the Mafia and small-time hoods regarding a theft of syndicate cash amounting to close to a half a million. (Dir: Barry Shear, 102 mins.)†

Across the Bridge (Great Britain, 1957)*** Rod Steiger, David Knight. Crooked tycoon on the lam from Scotland Yard is cornered in Mexico. Considerable suspense; good performances, especially Steiger's. (Dir: Ken Annakin, 103 mins.)

Across the Great Divide (1976)*** Robert Logan, George Flower, Heather Rattray. An unusually well done children's film. Two spunky orphans have plenty of adventures and hardships en route to their new home in Oregon in the old West. (Dir: Stewart Raffill, 89 mins.)†

Across the Pacific (1942)*** Humphrey Bogart, Mary Astor, Sydney Greenstreet. John Huston's directing magic and a fine cast make this a taut spy melodrama. (Dir: John Huston, 97 mins.)

Across the Wide Missouri (1951)**½ Clark Gable, Ricardo Montalbán, Adolphe Menjou, John Hodiak, J. Carroll Naish. An unusual western set in the 1820s. Clark Gable plays a trapper married to an Indian girl. (Dir: William Wellman, 78 mins.)

Act, The (1984)*½ Robert Ginty, Sarah Lagenfeld, Nick Surovy, Jill St. John, Eddie Albert, Pat Hingle. Muddled satire of union corruption and politics, with lawyer Ginty caught in the middle. Incongruously pleasant song score by John Sebastian only adds to the confusion. (Dir: Sig Shore, 94 mins.)†

Action for Slander (Great Britain, 1938)**½ Clive Brook, Ann Todd, Margaretta Scott, Arthur Magetson, Percy Marmont, Francis L. Sullivan. Interesting British social melodrama, as Brook struggles to prove his innocence when he is falsely accused of cheating at cards. (Dir: Tim Whelan, 83 mins.)†

Action In the North Atlantic (1943)***½ Humphrey Bogart, Raymond Massey. Forget that it was originally war propaganda, relax and enjoy this exciting dramatic tribute to the Merchant Marines. (Dir: Lloyd Bacon, 127 mins.)

Action Jackson (1987)**½ Carl Weathers, Craig T. Nelson, Vanity, Sharon Stone. Weathers is "Action," a Harvard Law School graduate and all-around tough guy who works as a Motown cop; Nelson is his quarry, a fat cat intent on infiltrating the automobile union with his own stooges. Better-than-average, thanks to the cartoonlike violence. (Dir: Craig R. Baxley, 95 mins.)†

Action Man (France, 1966)**½ Jean Gabin, Robert Stack, Margaret Lee, Suzanne Flon. An aging, bored business magnate, once a major crook, hooks up with an American opportunist to commit one last big crime. Gabin is his usual wonderfully crusty, blasé self. (Dir: Jean Delannoy, 95 mins.)

Action of the Tiger (1957)**½ Van Johnson, Martine Carol, Herbert Lom. Routine adventure yarn with all the clichés intact—an American adventurer on foreign soil meets a glamorous lady with dangerous plans. (Dir: Terence Young, 92 mins.)

Action U.S.A. (1989)**½ Barri Murphy, Gregory Scott Cummins, William Hubbard Knight, William Smith, Cameron Mitchell. Girl sees her boyfriend murdered by mobsters, who then set out after her to make sure she won't talk. Unmemor-

able but entertaining Texas chase movie, with enough stunts and crashing cars for those who enjoy such things. (Dir: John Stewart, 89 mins.)†

Act of Love (1953)*** Kirk Douglas, Dany Robin. American soldier has a tragic affair with a poor girl in occupied Paris. Powerful love story, excellently acted, filmed in France. (Dir: Anatole Litvak, 105 mins.)

Act of Love (MTV 1980)**½ Ron Howard, Robert Foxworth, Mickey Rourke. Howard shows another side of his acting ability in this sentimental drama about the mercy killing of a paralyzed family member. (Dir: Jud Taylor, 104 mins.)

Act of Murder, An (1948)***½ Fredric March, Edmond O'Brien, Florence Eldridge. Judge is tried for the mercy killing of his wife. Grim and unrelenting, but finely done drama. AKA: **Live Today for Tomorrow.** (Dir: Michael Gordon, 91 mins.)

Act of Passion—See: **Lost Honor of Kathryn Beck, The**

Act of the Heart (Canada, 1970)*** Genevieve Bujold, Donald Sutherland, Bill Mitchell. An often moving, superbly acted entry that is marred by a preposterous ending. Young former farm girl arrives in Montreal and falls in love with a priest while developing a case of religious hysteria. (Dir: Paul Almond, 103 mins.)

Act of Vengeance (1974)** Jo Ann Harris, Peter Brown, Jennifer Lee, Steve Kanaly, Lada Edmund. A sick movie, but a competently made action pic, nonetheless. Five women team up to snare a sadistic rapist-killer. AKA: **Rape Squad.** (Dir: Bob Keljan, 90 mins.)†

Act of Vengeance (MCTV 1986)**½ Charles Bronson, Ellen Burstyn, Wilford Brimley, Hoyt Axton, Ellen Barkin, Joseph Kell. Bronson plays Joseph Yablonski, the United Mine Workers officer who unnerves the big union boys when he sets his cap for the presidency. Based on real-life characters, this dramatization still manages to come across like fiction. (Dir: John MacKenzie, 110 mins.)†

Act of Violence (1948)*** Van Heflin, Janet Leigh, Robert Ryan. Well acted and directed but routine melodrama about a guy who betrayed his buddies in a Nazi prison camp. (Dir: Fred Zinnemann, 82 mins.)

Act of Violence (MTV 1979)*** Elizabeth Montgomery, James Sloyan, Sean Frye. Ms. Montgomery in a provocative tale about mugging in a big city. Liz plays the liberal, protected divorcée who experiences a change of attitude after she is attacked one night. (Dir: Paul Wendkos, 104 mins.)

Act One (1963)*** George Hamilton, Jason

Robards, Eli Wallach. If you have never read Moss Hart's sentimental, best-selling autobiography about his youthful love affair with the Broadway theater, this watered-down film version will entertain you. (Dir: Dore Schary, 110 mins.)

Actors and Sin (1952)*** Edward G. Robinson, Eddie Albert, Marsha Hunt. Two stories by Ben Hecht: "Woman of Sin," a hilarious Hollywood burlesque about a child who writes a great screenplay, and "Actor's Blood," a drama of a beautiful actress whose strange death implicates many people. All in all, an entertaining package. (Dir: Ben Hecht, 86 mins.)

Actor's Revenge, An (Japan, 1963)***½ Kazuo Hasegawa, Fujiko Yamamoto, Ayako Wakao, Ganjiro Nakamura. A 19th-century kabuki theater *onnagate* (female impersonator) seeks revenge on the men who murdered his parents. Complex, fascinating tale of opposites, especially male/female and illusion/reality. Hasegawa is magnificent playing characters of both sexes. (Dir: Kon Ichikawa, 113 mins.)

Actress, The (1953)*** Spencer Tracy, Jean Simmons, Teresa Wright, Anthony Perkins. Thoroughly enjoyable screen version of Ruth Gordon's play, *Years Ago*. Tracy and Simmons shine brilliantly as father and daughter. (Dir: George Cukor, 91 mins.)

Ada (1961)*** Susan Hayward, Dean Martin. Guitar-playing sheriff is persuaded to run for governor, but his attraction to a good-time girl threatens his political career. Juicy melodrama. (Dir: Daniel Mann, 109 mins.)

Adalen 31 (Sweden, 1969)*** Peter Schildt, Roland Hedlund, Martin Widerberg, Marie de Geer. Director Bo Widerberg's beautiful, perceptive drama played out against the background of a real event in Swedish history—the 1931 strike in the town of Adalen. Focuses on one family, whose working father is a strike leader. (115 mins.)

Adam (MTV 1983)*** Daniel J. Travanti, JoBeth Williams. The agonizing ordeal, based on a true story of Florida parents whose child vanishes. Parental grief and anger are followed by an assault on Washington to change the laws about disappearing kids. Travanti runs the gamut as the shattered father and is nicely supported by Williams, playing an angry, numbed mother. Disturbing and timely. Sequel: *Adam: His Song Continues*. (Dir: Michael Tuchner, 99 mins.)

Adam and Evelyne (Great Britain, 1949)** Stewart Granger, Jean Simmons, Edmund Styles, Raymond Young, Wilfred Hyde-White. Star chemistry is the main attraction in this melodramatic romance

between a gambler and his ward, who thinks he's a stockbroker. (Dir: Harold French, 92 mins.)

Adam at 6 A.M. (1970)*** Michael Douglas, Joe Don Baker, Lee Purcell. Douglas is a hip California college professor who starts questioning his lifestyle. His odyssey brings him to Missouri, where he meets a variety of "just plain folks" who eventually let him down. (Dir: Robert Sheerer, 100 mins.)†

Adam Had Four Sons (1941)*** Ingrid Bergman, Warner Baxter, Susan Hayward, Fay Wray, Richard Denning. Family governess looks after four children after the mistress of the house dies. Well-acted drama. (Dir: Gregory Ratoff, 81 mins.)†

Adam: His Song Continues (MTV 1986)**½ Daniel J. Travanti, JoBeth Williams, Richard Masur, Martha Scott, Paul Regina, Lindsey Amelio. A sequel to the stirring 1983 drama with Travanti and Williams back as Adam's parents, John and Reve Walsh; the plot's about John Walsh becoming a full-time lobbyist for children's rights. (Dir: Robert Markowitz, 104 mins.)

Adam's Rib (1949)**** Spencer Tracy, Katharine Hepburn, Judy Holliday, Jean Hagen, Tom Ewell, David Wayne. One of the best of the Tracy-Hepburn cycle, written by Garson Kanin and Ruth Gordon. Tracy is an assistant D.A. in New York prosecuting a woman accused of shooting her husband, while wife Hepburn defends her. Ewell and Holliday do well as the husband and wife—but the show belongs to Tracy and Hepburn. (Dir: George Cukor, 101 mins.)†

Addict—See: **Born to Win**

Addicted to His Love (MTV 1988)*½ Barry Bostwick, Polly Bergen, Colleen Camp, Erin Gray, Linda Purl, Dee Wallace Stone. Bostwick plays an unctuous ladies' man who works his way into the hearts of four trusting women. Their lighthearted revenge scheme, involving Camp as a "Southern Belle," is the film's only virtue. (Dir: Arthur Allan Seidelman, 96 mins.)

Adding Machine, The (Great Britain-U.S., 1969)**½ Phyllis Diller, Milo O'Shea, Billie Whitelaw. Erratic film version of Elmer Rice's brilliant expressionist play. An overworked accountant murders his boss when he learns he is to be replaced by a machine. (Dir: Jerome Epstein, 100 mins.)

Addition—See: **L'Addition**

Address Unknown (1944)*** Paul Lukas, Carl Esmond. Businessman in Germany embraces the Nazi cause, but his partner in America has his revenge. Interestingly produced drama. (Dir: William Cameron Menzies, 72 mins.)

Adios Amigo (1975)** Fred Williamson, Richard Pryor, Thalmus Rasulala, James L. Brown, Mike Henry. A pallid western comedy with a mostly black cast. Williamson wrote, directed, produced, and stars as the patsy to con man Pryor. (87 mins.)†

Adios Sabata (Italy, 1971)**½ Yul Brynner. Another violent, grotesque—but engaging spaghetti western. Brynner plays the tough hombre out to get a $1 million bag of gold dust from a villainous Austrian colonel. (Dir: Giancarlo Parolini, 106 mins.)

Admirable Crichton, The—See: **Paradise Lagoon**

Admiral Was a Lady, The (1950)** Edmond O'Brien, Wanda Hendrix, Rudy Vallee. Four ex-GIs living on their wits meet an ex-Wave, vie for her hand. Mild, amusing comedy. (Dir: Sidney Salkow, 87 mins.)†

Adolescent, The (France, 1978)**½ Simone Signoret. Jeanne Moreau's second film as a director shows a considerable advance in technical skill, though the project is a hackneyed one about a young girl's coming of age during a rural summer just before WWII. (90 mins.)

Adorable Julia (France, 1962)** Lilli Palmer, Charles Boyer, Jean Sorel. Glamorous actress of the London stage embarks on one last fling with a younger man, soon regrets it. Based on a Somerset Maugham play, it is flat when it should have bubbled. (Dir: Alfred Heidenmann, 94 mins.)

Adrift (Czechoslovakia, 1969)***½ Rade Markovic, Milena Dravic, Paula Pritchett, Josef Kroner. Allegorical tale about a happily married fisherman who rescues a beautiful amnesiac from a river, and is overcome by her beauty and need to be cared for. A simple story filled with tension born of obsession and desire; one of the seminal works of the Czech New Wave. (Dir: Jan Kadar, 108 mins.)

Adulteress, The (France, 1958)**½ Simone Signoret, Raf Vallone, Sylvie. Somewhat simple story of a woman who kills her husband for her lover, and the ensuing blackmail by a young sailor. Saved by the acting of Miss Signoret. (Dir: Marcel Carne, 106 mins.)

Adulteress, The (1973)* Tyne Daly, Eric Braden, Greg Morton, Lynn Roth. A woman and her impotent husband think they've found a way to keep their marriage together when they hire a gigolo to take care of the wife's sexual needs. That Daly went on from this garbage to TV stardom is quite a feat. (Dir: Norbert Meisel, 88 mins.)†

Advance to the Rear (1964)**½ Glenn Ford, Stella Stevens, Melvyn Douglas. Civil War comedy about a band of Union Army goldbricks who are transferred to the wild and wooly West. (Dir: George Marshall, 97 mins.)

Adventure (1945)*½ Clark Gable, Greer Garson, Joan Blondell. Much publicized postwar film is one big fizzle. Romance of a sea-going bum and a shy librarian is as disappointing a film as either of its stars ever appeared in. (Dir: Victor Fleming, 125 mins.)

Adventure for Two—See: **Demi-Paradise, The**

Adventure in Baltimore (1948)** Robert Young, Shirley Temple. Minister's daughter has modern views for the 1900 period, keeps her father in hot water by sticking by them. Mild, slow little comedy-drama. (Dir: Richard Wallace, 89 mins.)

Adventure in Diamonds (1940)**½ George Brent, Isa Miranda. Beautiful jewel thief is promised a pardon if she will help an English officer trap the rest of the gang. Pleasant melodrama. (Dir: George Fitzmaurice, 76 mins.)

Adventure in Manhattan (1936)**½ Jean Arthur, Joel McCrea. Well-played but routine tale about a criminologist who is sure that a master criminal, believed dead, is alive and involved in thefts. (Dir: Edward Ludwig, 73 mins.)

Adventure Island (1947)** Rory Calhoun, Rhonda Fleming, Paul Kelly, John Abbott, Alan Napier. Low-budget remake of *Ebb Tide*. Smugglers and their innocent passengers are shipwrecked on a South Seas island ruled by a madman. (Dir: Peter Stewart, 66 mins.)

Adventure of Sherlock Holmes' Smarter Brother, The (1975)*** Gene Wilder, Madeline Kahn, Marty Feldman, Dom DeLuise. Impressive comedy by Gene Wilder who, in addition to starring in this low-brow slapstick romp, also wrote and directed it. He plays Sigi Holmes, Sherlock's younger brother, who's sleuthing for a music hall singer (Kahn). (91 mins.)†

Adventurers, The (1970)* Bekim Fehmiu, Candice Bergen, Olivia de Havilland, Anna Moffo. Harold Robbins's sex-filled saga of a poor boy who grew up to be an international playboy reached the screen with all its soap-opera ingredients intact. (Dir: Lewis Gilbert, 171 mins.)

Adventures Beyond Belief—See: **Neat and Tidy**

Adventures in Babysitting (1987)** Elisabeth Shue, Keith Coogan, Anthony Rapp, Maia Brewton, Calvin Levels. After being stood up by her boyfriend, a teenage girl takes a babysitting job that leads her to a series of adventures in Chicago. Unfortunately, there's no real sense of danger about them, and the comedy elements aren't very strong, but there is a great scene in a blues club. (Dir: Chris Columbus, 99 mins.)†

Adventures of a Private Eye (Great Britain,

7

1977)* Christopher Neil, Suzy Kendall, Diana Dors, Jon Pertwee. Bumbling assistant private eye tries to solve a case on his own. Most of his investigations seem to land him in the beds of housewives whose husbands come home at the wrong time. (Dir: Stanley Long, 74 mins.)†

Adventures of a Young Man (1962)** Richard Beymer, Paul Newman, Dan Dailey, Arthur Kennedy, Susan Strasberg. Devotees of Hemingway's works will find a great deal wrong with this film based on his short stories on the life of his fictional hero, Nick Adams. Beymer is awful in the title role. AKA: Hemingway's Adventures of a Young Man. (Dir: Martin Ritt, 145 mins.)

Adventures of Baron Munchausen, The (Germany, 1943)***½ Hans Alber, Wilhelm Bendow, Marina Ditmar, Michael Bohnen. (Germany was in the midst of WWII, but propaganda minister Goebbels wanted an extravaganza to celebrate the 25th anniversary of UFA studios. He got it.) Photographed in magnificent color and filled with eye-popping sets and costumes, this fantasy is as full of fun as any great adventure can be. AKA: Munchausen. (Dir: Josef von Baky, 134 mins.)†

Adventures of Baron Munchausen, The (1988)**½ John Neville, Eric Idle, Sarah Polley, Oliver Reed, Robin Williams, Valentina Cortese, Uma Thurman, Jonathan Pryce, Sting. Megamillion-dollar epic based on the tall tales of the infamous 18th-century Baron offers consistently brilliant special effects that quickly overwhelm the viewer. Director Terry Gilliam (*Brazil*) has a bountiful imagination, but little control over it. (125 mins.)†

Adventures of Barry McKenzie, The (Australia, 1972)** Barry Crocker, Barry Humphries, Peter Cook, Spike Milligan. A cartoonish comedy based on a comic strip about a transplanted Aussie in Great Britain (a distasteful location, since he cannot abide the English). Sequel: *Barry McKenzie Holds His Own*. (Dir: Bruce Beresford, 114 mins.)

Adventures of Buckaroo Banzai, The (1984)**½ Peter Weller, John Lithgow, Ellen Barkin, Jeff Goldblum, Christopher Lloyd. A sporadically funny pop culture item that mixes movie genres and changes tones so rapidly the audience may be left behind. When physicist Buckaroo Banzai (Weller) accidentally frees some evil aliens from the eighth dimension, he and his scientist cohorts have to set things straight. (Dir: W. D. Richter, 103 mins.)†

Adventures of Bullwhip Griffin, The (1967)*** Roddy McDowall, Suzanne Pleshette, Karl Malden, Harry Guardino, Richard Haydn. Disney comedy-adventure has a

mild-mannered servant learning how to be his own master out on the wild frontier. (Dir: James Neilson, 110 mins.)†

Adventures of Captain Fabian (1951)*½ Errol Flynn, Micheline Presle, Vincent Price. Sea captain saves a servant girl from a murder charge, but she is bent on revenge. Slipshod costume adventure, wooden and dull. (Dir: William Marshall, 100 mins.)†

Adventures of Don Juan (1948)** Errol Flynn, Viveca Lindfors. Title notwithstanding, this is just another "swashbuckler" with Errol as the great Don Juan. (Dir: Vincent Sherman, 110 mins.)†

Adventures of Don Quixote, The (MTV 1972)**½ Rex Harrison, Frank Finlay, Rosemary Leach. Acceptable television adaptation of the great 17th-century Cervantes novel about the frustrated scholar who dreams of knighthood. (Dir: Alvin Rakoff, 120 mins.)

Adventures of Ford Fairlane, The (1990)* Andrew Dice Clay, Lauren Holly, Wayne Newton, Priscilla Presley, Ed O'Neill. Crude and sexist. Clay acts—if you can call it that—the part of a "rock and roll detective" investigating the murder of a disk jockey. He's built a career around smarmy behavior, but on screen his routine is boring, sophomoric, and embarrassing. The direction and story are amateurism personified. (Dir: Renny Harlin, 104 mins.)†

Adventures of Freddie—See: **Magnificent Magical Magnet of Santa Mesa**

Adventures of Frontier Fremont, · **The** (1976)**½ Dan Haggerty, Denver Pyle. A tinsmith in the 1830s gets tired of his lot in St. Louis and decides to head for the hills and the simple life. (Dir: Richard Freidenberg, 106 mins.)†

Adventures of Gallant Bess (1948)** Cameron Mitchell, Audrey Long. Rodeo performer captures a wild mare, enters it for prize money. Ordinary outdoor drama. (Dir: Lew Landers, 73 mins.)

Adventures of Goopy and Bagha, The (India, 1968)**½ Tapan Chatterjee, Robi Ghosh, Santosh Dutta. Director Satyajit Ray's first movie made for children (written by his grandfather) is a whimsical fantasy about roaming musicians who are granted wishes by a spirit. Filled with music, romance, farce, and even a pair of magic slippers. (132 mins.)

Adventures of Hajji Baba, The (1954)*½ John Derek, Elaine Stewart. How a barber longing for adventure finds it when he rescues the daughter of the caliph. It's played straight, which makes this Arabian Nights tale even funnier. (Dir: Don Weis, 110 mins.)

Adventures of Hercules, The (Italy, 1984)* Lou Ferrigno, Milly Carlucci, Sonia

Vivani. Sequel to the 1983 *Hercules* (actually, both were made at the same time), with Herc on a mission from Zeus to recover his stolen thunderbolts. More of the same silliness, though Sybil Danning is missed. (Dir: "Lewis Coates" [Luigi Cozzi], 89 mins.)†

Adventures of Huckleberry Finn (1939)** Mickey Rooney, William Frawley, Walter Connolly. Strictly for the youngsters is this flavorless adaptation of the Mark Twain story. (Dir: Richard Thorpe, 110 mins.)†

Adventures of Huckleberry Finn, The (1960)**½ Tony Randall, Eddie Hodges, Judy Canova, Archie Moore, Andy Devine. In this version of the Mark Twain classic, the Twain atmosphere is occasionally captured by a good cast. (Dir: Michael Curtiz, 107 mins.)

Adventures of Huckleberry Finn, The (MTV 1981)** Kurt Ida, Dan Monahan, Brock Peters, Forrest Tucker. New faces Kurt Ida and Dan Monahan star as Huck Finn and Tom Sawyer in still another presentation of Mark Twain's classic. (Dir: Jack Hively, 104 mins.)†

Adventures of Ichabod and Mister Toad, The (1949)*** Composed of two separate cartoon films. The first is an adaptation of "The Wind in the Willows." Superbly animated, this funny featurette concerns the courtroom trial of Toad, who's falsely accused of car theft. The second half is a broad version of "The Legend of Sleepy Hollow," with a climactic pursuit by the Headless Horseman an impressive highlight. Released separately on video. (Dirs: Jack Kinney, Clyde Geronimi, James Algar, 68 mins.)†

Adventures of Marco Polo (1938)**½ Gary Cooper, Sigrid Gurie, Basil Rathbone. Sprawling adventure film with extravagant production detail, but somewhat of a miss as entertainment. (Dir: Archie Mayo, 101 mins.)

Adventures of Mark Twain, The (1944)*** Fredric March, Alexis Smith. Biographical sketch of America's great humorist falls short of its goal and cannot be ranked with the great screen biographies. More informative than entertaining. (Dir: Irving Rapper, 130 mins.)

Adventures of Mark Twain, The (1985)** Voices of James Whitmore, Chris Ritchie, Gary Krug, Michele Mariana. Filmed in the Claymation animation process, this film details the high-flying adventures of Tom Sawyer, Huck Finn, and Becky Thatcher who're accompanied on a balloon ride by Mark Twain, who spins some of his favorite yarns along the way. (Dir: Will Vinton, 90 mins.)†

Adventures of Martin Eden, The (1942)*** Glenn Ford, Evelyn Keyes, Claire Trevor.

A seaman struggles to become a successful author. Well-done drama based on Jack London's novel. (Dir: Sidney Salkow, 87 mins.)

Adventures of Michael Strogoff (1937)*** Anton Walbrook, Akim Tamiroff. In 1870, a messenger of the Czar imperils his life to warn of invading hordes. Crammed full of action, this Jules Verne story should satisfy the most demanding adventure fan. (Dir: George Nicholls, Jr., 90 mins.)

Adventures of Milo and Otis, The (Japan, 1986)**½ Dudley Moore contributes a silly narration to this meandering live-action children's story of a puppy and kitten who become lost in the forest, meeting other animals and eventually raising their own litters. (Dirs: Masanori Hata, Kon Ichikawa, 76 mins.)†

Adventures of Nellie Bly, The (MTV 1981)** Linda Purl, Gene Barry, John Randolph. Playing America's first well-known female journalist, Purl struggles with her male-dominated newspaper, and covers the plight of sweatshop workers in New York. (Dir: Henning Schellerup, 104 mins.)†

Adventures of Nick Carter, The (MTV 1972)** Robert Conrad, Shelley Winters, Broderick Crawford, Dean Stockwell. A famous private eye of the early 1900s. Flavor of the era is nicely captured in this glossy production, but it's familiar gangster stuff. (Dir: Paul Krasny, 72 mins.)

Adventures of Picasso, The (Sweden, 1978)*** Gosta Ekman, Hans Alfredson, Margaretha Krook, Per Oscarsson, Bernard Cribbins, Wilfred Brambell. Mad farce bears about as much relation to the real Picasso as *Young Einstein* did to the inventor, though in the end it's both more respectful and funnier, too. British comics Cribbins and Brambell are a hoot in drag as Gertrude Stein and Alice B. Toklas. Originally 110 mins. (Dir: Tage Danielsson, 88 mins.)†

Adventures of Rabbi Jacob, The—See: **Mad Adventures of Rabbi Jacob, The**

Adventures of Robin Hood, The (1938)**** Errol Flynn, Olivia de Havilland, Basil Rathbone, Claude Rains. The quintessential swashbuckler! Flynn is dashing as the legendary folk hero who robs from the rich and gives to the poor. The superb Technicolor film is overflowing with breathtaking adventures in Sherwood Forest and Nottingham Castle as Robin Hood matches wits with King John and attempts to return King Richard to his throne. (Dirs: William Keighley, Michael Curtiz, 106 mins.)†

Adventures of Robinson Crusoe (Mexico, 1954)**** Dan O'Herlihy, Jaime Fernandez. Splendid adaptation of the

Defoe classic starring the superb O'Herlihy. Even when using a realistic plot, director Luis Buñuel manages to introduce surrealist subtleties: the erotic fanatasies of Crusoe as he constructs a scarecrow to chase birds away from his wheat crop; the moment when Friday discovers women's clothing in Crusoe's plunder from the sunken ship. (90 mins.)

Adventures of Sadie, The (Great Britain, 1955)*** Joan Collins, Kenneth More. Curvaceous Joan Collins is stranded on a tropic island with three males and the situation becomes hilarious. Hermione Gingold is seen briefly, and she's funny. (Dir: Noel Langley, 88 mins.)

Adventures of Sherlock Holmes (1939)*** Basil Rathbone, Nigel Bruce, Ida Lupino. Holmes stops the attempt to steal the Crown Jewels of England. Good Holmes mystery, well made and exciting. (Dir: Alfred Werker, 85 mins.)†

Adventures of Tartu (Great Britain, 1943)**½ Robert Donat, Valerie Hobson, Glynis Johns. Based on an actual WWII incident (also the basis of *The Foreman Went to France*), this thriller stars Donat as a British agent who helps the Czech resistance destroy a secret Nazi weapon. AKA: **Tartu.** (Dir: Harold S. Bucquet, 103 mins.)†

Adventures of the American Rabbit, The (1986)**½ A mild-mannered rabbit is groomed for super-rabbitdom, but first he has to defeat a pack of jackals. Cute dialogue; colorful animation style and a story that hops along nicely down the bunny trail. (Dirs: Fred Wolf, Nobutaka Nishizawa, 85 mins.)†

Adventures of the Queen (MTV 1975)** Robert Stack, Ralph Bellamy, David Hedison, Bradford Dillman, Lara Parker. It's the old bomb plot, set on a cruise ship, with a whiz-bang explosion, dazzling fire-and-rescue number. (Dir: David Lowell Rich, 100 mins.)

Adventures of the Wilderness Family (1975)*** Robert Logan, Susan Damante Shaw. A convincing piece of family fare. A beleaguered family, led by a disillusioned construction worker, jettisons their urban existence for living off the land. (Dir: Stewart Raffill, 101 mins.)†

Adventures of Tom Sawyer, The (1938)***½ Tommy Kelly, May Robson, Victor Jory. This flawed David O. Selznick production is probably the best Twain on screen—a crime that ought to be remedied. The early Technicolor is interesting, with James Wong Howe doing some fascinating lighting experiments in the cavern scenes. (Dir: Norman Taurog, 93 mins.)†

Adventures of Tom Sawyer, The (1973)—See: **Tom Sawyer** (MTV 1973)

Adventuress, The (Great Britain, 1947)****

Deborah Kerr, Trevor Howard. An Irish lassie, traditionally hating the English, unwittingly becomes the tool of Nazi agents. Thoroughly delightful comic thriller, with Kerr giving a charming performance. AKA: **I See a Dark Stranger.** (Dir: Frank Launder, 98 mins.)†

Adversary, The (India, 1970)***½ Dhritiman Chatterjee, Jayashree Roy, Krishna Bose, Kalyan Chatterjee. An intellectual youth is forced by his father's death to leave the university and work in crowded, polluted Calcutta to support his family. One of director Satyajit Ray's best films. AKA: **Siddharta and the City.** (100 mins.)

Advice to the Lovelorn (1933)**½ Lee Tracy, Sally Blane, Sterling Holloway. Well-acted but trite story of a reporter who's made lovelorn editor and, in spite of himself, is a sensation at the job. (Dir: Alfred L. Werker, 62 mins.)

Advice to the Lovelorn (MTV 1981)** Cloris Leachman, Joe Terry, Kelly Bishop. Newspaper tale with Leachman running an advice column to the lovelorn is moderately interesting. (Dir: Harry Falk, 104 mins.)

Advise and Consent (1962)***½ Henry Fonda, Walter Pidgeon, Charles Laughton, Don Murray, Lew Ayres, Gene Tierney, Franchot Tone, Burgess Meredith. Absorbing, excellently acted drama of Washington politics; slick and glossy, in the better sense of the words. Taken from Allen Drury's prize-winning novel, it concerns the appointment of a controversial figure as Secretary of State by the President, and the various machinations for and against this appointment. (Dir: Otto Preminger, 139 mins.)†

Aeroblcide—See: **Killer Workout**

Aerograd (U.S.S.R., 1935)***½ Semyon Shagaida, Serei Stolyarov, Stepan Shkurat. Russian workers battle Japanese saboteurs, in one of the great Soviet films of the 1930s, a passionate work filled with patriotic propaganda, extraordinary images and brilliant editing. AKA: **Frontier.** (Dir: Alexander Dovzhenko, 81 mins.)

Affair, The (MTV 1973)**½ Natalie Wood, Robert Wagner, Bruce Davison. An old-fashioned love story with some modern twists. An insulated lyricist of 30-plus who had polio as a kid, has her first love affair. (Dir: Gilbert Cates, 74 mins.)†

Affair In Havana (1957)**½ John Cassavetes, Raymond Burr, Sara Shane. The actors make this somewhat melodramatic opus palatable. It's a love story, triangle-fashion, and the setting adds to the mood of the film. (Dir: Laslo Benedek, 80 mins.)

Affair In Mind, An (Great Britain, 1988)*** Stephen Dillon, Amanda Donohoe, Matthew Marsh, Jean-Laurent Cochet. Six months after their one-night stand, a novelist is drawn into a plot by a mystery woman to kill her brutish husband. (Dir: Colin Luke, 88 mins.)†

Affair in Trinidad (1952)**½ Glenn Ford, Rita Hayworth, Valerie Bettis. Intrigue and romance in the tropics with Rita Hayworth cast as a valuable pawn in the deadly game of espionage. (Dir: Vincent Sherman, 98 mins.)†

Affair to Remember, An (1957)*** Cary Grant, Deborah Kerr, Cathleen Nesbitt, Richard Denning. Romantic affair about a shipboard encounter that weathers some heartaches and finally leads to true love. As the lovers who agree to rendezvous in six months' time but are separated by fate, Grant and Kerr make a captivating duo in this three-hanky soap opera. (Dir: Leo McCarey, 115 mins.)†

Affair with a Stranger (1953)*** Jean Simmons, Victor Mature. Successful playwright and wife plan to divorce, but manage to solve their problems. Well-acted romantic drama. (Dir: Roy Rowland, 89 mins.)

Affairs in Versailles (France, 1954)**½ Claudette Colbert, Gerard Philippe, Orson Welles. Sacha Guitry's colorful and ambitious film about the court affairs and naughty intrigues during the time of Louis XIV. Good cast but film is overdone and lacks continuity. (Dir: Sacha Guitry, 152 mins.)

Affairs of Annabel, The (1938)**½ Lucille Ball, Jack Oakie, Ruth Donnelly, Bradley Page, Fritz Feld. A bubbly B movie about a dizzy movie star and her anything-for-an-item publicist who propels her into the national consciousness in unusual ways. Sequel: *Annabel Takes a Tour.* (Dir: Ben Stoloff, 73 mins.)†

Affairs of Cellini (1934)*** Fredric March, Constance Bennett, Frank Morgan, Fay Wray. Stylish diversion set during the Renaissance. An artist-mountebank falls in love with a Duchess whose husband has a yen for a luscious artists' model. Superb direction keeps this tale of riven infidelities spinning along with effortless charm. (Dir: Gregory La Cava, 80 mins.)

Affairs of Dobie Gillis, The (1953)**½ Debbie Reynolds, Bobby Van, Bob Fosse. Light comedy with musical numbers about the young and their carefree antics. (Dir: Don Weis, 73 mins.)

Affairs of Martha, The (1942)**½ Marsha Hunt, Richard Carlson, Spring Byington. A maid turns a small town upside down by writing a book about her employers. Diverting comedy. (Dir: Jules Dassin, 66 mins.)

Affairs of Susan, The (1945)**½ Joan Fontaine, Dennis O'Keefe, George Brent. Occasionally amusing, but overdone, romantic comedy about an actress who changes character to match the requirements of her suitors. (Dir: William A. Seiter, 110 mins.)

Affectionately Yours (1941)** Rita Hayworth, Merle Oberon, Dennis Morgan. Forced, weak little comedy about a man trying to woo back his ex-wife. (Dir: Lloyd Bacon, 90 mins.)

African Queen, The (1951)****Katharine Hepburn, Humphrey Bogart, Robert Morley, Theodore Bikel. John Huston's wonderful comedy-adventure, set on an African river in 1914, is a timeless delight, thanks to the odd-couple casting of Bogart as the grimy, grizzled mailboat captain Charlie Allnut, and Hepburn as the prim English missionary he must bring upriver as World War I breaks out. Bogart won an Oscar for his wry, charismatic turn. Huston's direction (from a script he co-wrote with James Agee) is remarkably efficient, disguising the story's contrivances and allowing the two stars to shine. (103 mins.)†

African Treasure (1952)*½ Johnny Sheffield, Laurette Luez, Lyle Talbot, Smoki Whitfield, Arthur Space. Skimpy "Bomba" series entry. Bomba's animal pals help him foil some geologists who smuggle diamonds. (Dir: Ford Beebe, 70 mins.)

Africa Screams (1949)*½ Bud Abbott, Lou Costello, Frank Buck. Bud and Lou on safari for diamonds in darkest Africa. Pretty weak slapstick. (Dir: Charles Barton, 80 mins.)†

Africa—Texas Style (1966)**½ Hugh O'Brian, John Mills, Tom Nardini. Authentic African locales add to this otherwise slow-moving adventure about a cowboy who hunts and tames wild game. The photography is splendid, lensed in Kenya. (Dir: Andrew Marton, 106 mins.)†

After Dark, My Sweet (1990)*** Jason Patric, Rachel Ward, Bruce Dern, George Dickerson, James Cotton. An ex-boxer flees from the confines of a mental institution only to become involved in a haphazard kidnapping scheme. Top-notch adaptation of Jim Thompson's seamy novel. (Dir: James Foley, 114 mins.)†

After Hours (1985)*** Griffin Dunne, Rosanna Arquette, Teri Garr, Linda Fiorentino, John Heard, Catherine O'Hara, Cheech & Chong. A casual date turns into a terrifying, funny nightlong odyssey through the rain-drenched streets of New York's Soho in Martin Scorsese's quirky paranoid comedy. You'll relish the deft structuring of Joseph Minion's script and the comic turns by the supporting cast. (Dir: Martin Scorsese, 97 mins.)†

After Midnight (1989)*½ Jillian McWhirter, Pamela Segall, Ramy Zeda, Marc McClure, Billy Ray Sharkey. Anthology of horror stories, tied together as a discussion by a college psychology class of what frightens them. A combination of extreme boredom and extreme violence. (Dirs: Ken and Jim Wheat, 90 mins.) †

After Midnight With Boston Blackie (1943)** Chester Morris, Ann Savage, Cy Kendall, George E. Stone, Richard Lane. Wisecracking sleuth uncovers some stolen gems. Par for the series. (Dir: Lew Landers, 64 mins.)

After Office Hours (1935)**½ Clark Gable, Constance Bennett, Stuart Erwin, Billie Burke. Fast-moving newspaper drama with comic overtones. Gable is an editor, Bennett a music critic. (Dir: Robert Z. Leonard, 74 mins.)

After Pilkinton (Great Britain, 1988)*** Miranda Richardson, Bob Peck, Barry Foster. A stuffy young Oxford professor finds his life rearranged when a girl he hasn't seen since childhood shows up and requests his help in disposing of a corpse. Richardson is the whole show in this dryly British tale of obsession. (Dir: Christopher Morahan, 100 mins.) †

After School (1988)** Sam Bottoms, Renée Coleman, Edward Binns, James Farkas, Page Hannah, Robert Lansing. Heavy-handed morality tale about a priest, preparing for a televised debate with an atheist, who falls in love with one of his students. (Dir: William Olson, 89 mins.) †

Aftershock (1990)*½ Jay Roberts, Jr., Elizabeth Kaitan, Christopher Mitchum, Richard Lynch, John Saxon, Michael Berryman, Russ Tamblyn. Emissary from another planet is sent to seek advice on how we've avoided nuclear war, but arrives just at the end of WWIII. Mostly chases and fights, with some preaching about the need for peace and understanding. (Dir: Frank Harris, 91 mins.) †

After the Fall of New York (France-Italy, 1985)½ Michael Sopkiw, Valentine Monnier, Anna Kanakis, Edmund Purdom. Lousy post-nuclear melodrama. (Dir: Martin Dolman, 95 mins.) †

After the Fox (U.S.-Great Britain-Italy, 1966)**½ Peter Sellers, Britt Ekland, Victor Mature. Funny tale about an ingenious convict (Peter Sellers) who gets involved in moviemaking in order to cover a big caper. Victor Mature plays an American has-been movie star and he hams it up all the way for the film's biggest laughs. Neil Simon wrote the script and Vittorio De Sica directed. (103 mins.) †

After the Promise (MTV 1987)*½ Mark Harmon, Diana Scarwid, Rosemary Dunsmore. Widower Harmon loses custody of his children to an evil babysitter in this TV movie inspired by a real incident. (Dir: David Greene, 96 mins.) †

After the Rehearsal (Sweden, 1984)*** Ingrid Thulin, Erland Josephson, Lena Olin.

An intense, esoteric film from Ingmar Bergman. Fans of the Swedish director will be enthralled by Bergman's opinions about the creative process, the perils of romantic love, and the symbiotic relationship between the two. (72 mins.) †

After the Shock (MCTV 1990)*** Rue McClanahan, Jack Scalia, Yaphet Kotto, Scott Valentine. Well-made, fact-based dramatization about the immediate aftermath of the 1989 San Francisco-Oakland earthquake. Unnerving documentary approach incorporates actual news footage covering the catastrophe. (Dir: Gary Sherman, 96 mins.) †

After the Thin Man (1936)*** William Powell, Myrna Loy, James Stewart. Second in the series is again a delight thanks to smooth acting, glib dialogue, and top production. Detective story is incidental to the fun. (Dir: W. S. Van Dyke, 113 mins.) †

Against a Crooked Sky (1975)** Richard Boone, Stewart Peterson, Jewel Blanch, Geoffrey Land, Henry Wilcoxon. A sturdy but resolutely conventional oater about a kid trying to retrieve his sister from some injuns. (Dir: Earl Bellamy, 89 mins.) †

Against All Flags (1952)** Errol Flynn, Maureen O'Hara, Anthony Quinn. Flynn the dauntless officer vs. Quinn the brazen Caribbean pirate in a thoroughly routine adventure yarn. (Dir: George Sherman, 84 mins.) †

Against All Odds (Spain-West Germany-U.S.-Great Britain, 1968)*½ Christopher Lee, Richard Green, Shirley Eaton, Maria Rohm. One of the worst Fu Manchu "thrillers." Even the Brazilian location photography is lifeless. Sequel: *Castle of Fu Manchu*. AKA: **Blood of Fu Manchu** and **Kiss and Kill**. (Dir: Jess Franco, 92 mins.) †

Against All Odds (1984)**½ Jeff Bridges, Rachel Ward, James Woods, Richard Widmark, Dorian Harewood, Alex Karras. Ward is an elusive heiress who brings out the lust in disgruntled football player (Bridges) and big-time bookie (Woods). Director Taylor Hackford is at his best filming sensual love scenes, but is unable to keep the complicated plot coherent. (125 mins.) †

Against the Wind (Great Britain, 1948)***½ Simone Signoret, Jack Warner. British agents parachute into occupied France to aid the resistance movement in their fight against the Nazis. Tense, exciting war melodrama, well done. (Dir: Charles Crichton, 95 mins.)

Agatha (Great Britain, 1979)**½ Dustin Hoffman, Vanessa Redgrave, Timothy Dalton. This exercise in mystification suggests a solution to the unsolved disappearance of mystery novelist Agatha

Christie after she was jilted by her caddish husband (Timothy Dalton); but the solution is simply not very interesting. (Dir: Michael Apted, 98 mins.)†

Agatha Christie's A Caribbean Mystery—See: Caribbean Mystery, A

Agatha Christie's Dead Man's Folly—See: Dead Man's Folly

Agatha Christie's Murder in Three Acts—See: Murder in Three Acts

Agatha Christie's Murder Is Easy—See: Murder Is Easy

Agatha Christie's Murder With Mirrors—See: Murder With Mirrors

Agatha Christie's Ordeal by Innocence—See: Ordeal by Innocence

Agatha Christie's Sparkling Cyanide—See: Sparkling Cyanide

Agatha Christie's 13 at Dinner—See: 13 at Dinner

Agency (Canada, 1982)** Robert Mitchum, Lee Majors, Saul Rubinek, Valerie Perrine, Anthony Parr, Alexandra Stewart. Muddled thriller about brainwashing over the airwaves. (Dir: George Kaczender, 94 mins.)†

Agent 8¾ (Great Britain, 1964)** Dirk Bogarde, Sylva Koscina, Robert Morley. Spyspoof. Bogarde plays a rather witless guy, out of a job, who's sent to Czechoslovakia on U.S. "business." Finds himself embroiled in international espionage. AKA: **Hot Enough for June.** (Dir: Ralph Thomas, 98 mins.)

Agent for H.A.R.M. (1965)** Mark Richman, Wendell Corey. Secret agent is assigned to protect the life of a defecting scientist. Routine Iron Curtain cloak-and-dagger melodrama. (Dir: Gerd Oswald, 84 mins.)

Age of the Earth (Brazil, 1980)**½ Jece Valadao, Mauricio Do Valle, Ana Maria Magalhaes, Norma Benguel. Director Glauber Rocha's last film, an angry discourse on politics and religion using complex images of festivals, folk dances, men and women heatedly debating important issues, all wildly contrasted via bludgeonlike editing. Not for all tastes. (158 mins.)

Age-Old Friends (MTV 1989)*** Hume Cronyn, Vincent Gardenia, Tandy Cronyn, Esther Rolle. Gardenia is fit as a fiddle but showing signs of Alzheimer's disease; Cronyn has chronic arthritis, but a keen mind. Living in a retirement home, the two friends present a united front until Gardenia's mental health is threatened. Two fine performances. (Dir: Allan Kroeker, 90 mins.)†

Agent on Ice (1986)* Tom Ormeny, Clifford David, Louis Pastore, Matt Craven. Everyone's out to kill a former CIA agent, including his ex-bosses and a Mafia big shot who's supposed to be dead. (Dir: Clark Worswick, 97 mins.)†

Agnes of God (1985)**½ Jane Fonda, Anne Bancroft, Meg Tilly. This adaptation of the prize-winning play about an unbalanced nun who's accused of killing her newborn infant works well intermittently; tantalizing its audience with symbolistic clues one minute—yet ringing with a sense of Hollywood superficiality the next. Makes a fine vehicle for actresses; Bancroft as a sardonic mother superior and Tilly as her naive protégée, both Oscar nominated. (Dir: Norman Jewison, 99 mins.)†

Agony and the Ecstasy, The (1965)**½ Charlton Heston, Rex Harrison. The agony refers to Michelangelo's troubles during the painting of the Sistine Chapel, but there's a lot of historical inaccuracies along the way in this overblown account. (Dir: Carol Reed, 140 mins.)†

Aguirre, the Wrath of God (West Germany, 1972)**** Klaus Kinski, Ruy Guerra, Helena Rojo. Fascinating intellectual epic about a half-crazed 16th-century conquistador intent on discovering the fabled city of El Dorado. As the visionary explorer subjects his men to certain death, the film confronts us with disturbing issues about imperialism and religious zeal. (Dir: Werner Herzog, 95 mins.)†

A-Haunting We Will Go (1942)** Stan Laurel, Oliver Hardy, Sheila Ryan, Elisha Cook, Jr., Willie Best. Slapstick comedy involving a magician and a coffin. Not the boys' best, but fair fun. (Dir: Alfred L. Werker, 69 mins.)

Ah, Wilderness (1935)***½ Lionel Barrymore, Mickey Rooney, Wallace Beery. O'Neill's poignant, warm story of a boy breaking through the shackles of adolescence in 1906 receives an excellent screen treatment. (Dir: Clarence Brown, 100 mins.)

Aida (Italy, 1954)**½ Sophia Loren, Lois Maxwell. Colorful version of Verdi's opera. Aida is sung by Renata Tebaldi. (Dir: Clemente Fracassi, 96 mins.)

Ain't Misbehavin' (1955)**½ Rory Calhoun, Piper Laurie, Jack Carson. Mildly amusing comedy about a sexy chorine (Miss Laurie) who marries a millionaire tycoon and then has to learn how to get along in high society. Every girl should have Piper's problems! (Dir: Edward Buzzell, 82 mins.)

Air America (1990)* Mel Gibson, Robert Downey, Jr., Nancy Travis, Lane Smith. Not even a buzz of believability exists in this inane tale about the antic adventures of two renegade CIA pilots ferrying cargo during the Vietnam War. Disagreeable revisionist history. (Dir: Roger Spottiswoode, 113 mins.)†

Air Cadet (1951)** Stephen McNally, Gail Russell. Another routine drama about the training of a group of jet air cadets,

13

and how they finally turn into flying aces. (Dir: Joseph Pevney, 94 mins.)

Air Force (1943)*** John Garfield, Arthur Kennedy, Faye Emerson. Another exciting war story about an army plane which takes off for the Pacific, December 6, 1941. Again, forget the propaganda, and watch an exciting film. (Dir: Howard Hawks, 124 mins.)†

Air Mail (1932)**½ Pat O'Brien, Ralph Bellamy, Gloria Stuart. Brash pilot causes trouble at an airport. (Dir: John Ford, 83 mins.)

Airplane (1980)*** Robert Hays, Leslie Nielsen, Kareem Abdul Jabbar, Lloyd Bridges, Peter Graves, Julie Hagerty, Robert Stack. A hilarious parody of disaster films of the '50s, which were unintentionally funny even then. (Dirs: Jim Abrahams, David Zucker, Jerry Zucker, 88 mins.)†

Airplane II: The Sequel (1982)**½ Robert Hays, Julie Hagerty, Chad Everett, Peter Graves, William Shatner. This time it's a space shuttle. Sight gags aplenty liven up doings at the airport, and many are funny. (Dir: Ken Finkleman, 85 mins.)†

Airport (1970)*** Burt Lancaster, Dean Martin, Helen Hayes, Jacqueline Bisset, Jean Seberg, Van Heflin, Maureen Stapleton, George Kennedy, Dana Wynter, Lloyd Nolan, Barbara Hale. Entertaining box-office hit. Hayes is memorable as an unlikely stowaway who highlights this film set in a bustling metropolitan airport, beset not only with tracking her down, but by the madness of a passenger whose attaché case holds a bomb. (Dir: George Seaton, 137 mins.)†

Airport 1975 (1974)** Charlton Heston, Karen Black, George Kennedy, Efrem Zimbalist, Jr., Helen Reddy, Sid Caesar. A tacky successor to *Airport*. Heston plays an airline troubleshooter whose derring-do involves transferring from a helicopter to the cockpit of a disabled 747 being flown by stewardess Karen Black. (Dir: Jack Smight, 106 mins.)†

Airport '77 (1977)** Jack Lemmon, Lee Grant, Brenda Vaccaro, George Kennedy, James Stewart, Joseph Cotten, Olivia de Havilland, Darren McGavin, Christopher Lee. For this flight, art-magnate Stewart has converted a jumbo jet to transport his friends and his art treasures to the opening of his Palm Beach museum. Disaster strikes when hijackers take over the plane and crash it into the ocean. (Dir: Jerry Jameson, 113 mins.)†

Airport '79—See: **Concorde—Airport '79, The**

Air Raid Wardens (1943)*½ Stan Laurel, Oliver Hardy, Edgar Kennedy, Donald Meek. This slapstick had some minor appeal when it was first shown because of its timely subject. Today it's only for

the team's fans. (Dir: Edward Sedgwick, 67 mins.)

Airwolf (MTV 1984)** Jan-Michael Vincent, Ernest Borgnine, Alex Cord, Belinda Bauer. The series' pilot about a high-tech plane, which the Russians want and the super-pilot sent to thwart its theft. (Dir: Donald Bellisario, 98 mins.)

A. K. (France, 1985)***½ Director Chris Marker's important documentary about Akira Kurosawa and his crew during the filming of *Ran*. Shot on the awesomely beautiful slopes of Mount Fuji, the film includes a telling interview with Kurosawa about his directorial style and his relationship with his crew, as well as insight into Marker's own politics of the cinema. (75 mins.)

Akahige—See: **Red Beard**

Akira Kurosawa's Dreams (Japan, 1990)***½ Akira Terao, Mieko Harada, Chishu Ryu, Martin Scorsese. Eight uneven self-contained segments comprise writer-director Akira Kurosawa's interpretation of his dreams, which touch on subjects as diverse as Asian mysticism and ecology. The film is both solemn and exhilarating; Kurosawa is examining the specter of death and the power of creativity. Filmmaker Scorsese plays artist Vincent van Gogh in the fifth episode, *Crows*. Takao Saito and Masaharu Ueda's cinematography is magnificent. Some wonderful episodes intermingled with lesser segments. AKA: **Dreams**. (Dir: Akira Kurosawa, 120 mins.)†

Aku Aku (1959)*** Generally interesting documentary despite the amateurish camerawork, as Thor Heyerdahl, of "Kon-Tiki" fame, explores Easter Island and makes some fascinating discoveries. (No director credited, 60 mins.)

Aladdin (Italy, 1986)*½ Bud Spencer, Danny Spencer, Luca Venantini. Teenager discovers Aladdin's lamp in a junk store and finds the genie still eager to grant his every wish. Made in Miami by an Italian company, which explains the incomprehensible accents (especially spaghetti-western star Spencer as the genie). But given the silly dialogue, it hardly matters. (Dir: Bruno Corbucci, 95 mins.)†

Alakazam the Great (1961)*** Nice little cartoon feature about a smart monkey who fancies himself brighter than humans until he learns otherwise. Originally Japanese-made; voices heard include Jonathan Winters, Frankie Avalon, Dodie Stevens. (Dir: Lee Kresel, 84 mins.)†

Alambrista! (1978)*** Domingo Ambriz, Linda Gillin, Ned Beatty, Trinidad Silva. Director Robert M. Young's examination of Mexican farmworkers who enter the United States illegally to find work is direct and forceful. (110 mins.)

Alamo, The (1960)*½ John Wayne, Richard Widmark, Laurence Harvey, Chill Wills, Richard Boone, Carlos Arruza, Frankie Avalon, Patrick Wayne, Linda Cristal. Wayne produced, directed and played Col. Davey Crockett in this splashy, simpleminded reenactment of the famous clash between our outnumbered soldiers and the Mexican army. (192 mins.)†

Alamo Bay (1985)** Amy Madigan, Ed Harris, Ho Nguyen, Donald Moffat. A tendentious disappointment from renowned director Louis Malle. He and his screenwriters have drained all the juice out of this slanted examination of a Texas community unable to cope with Vietnamese refugees who outdo the locals in the fishing industry. The refugees are saintly; the red necks are beastly; the end result is overdone. (105 mins.)†

Alamo: Thirteen Days to Glory, The (MTV 1987)**½ James Arness, Lorne Greene, Alec Baldwin, Brian Keith, David Ogden Stiers. This retelling of the Alamo saga should keep western fans engrossed, even though the small screen necessarily diminishes the scope of the battle scenes. (Dir: Peter Werner, 156 mins.)

Alamut Ambush (Great Britain, 1986)** Terrence Stamp, Michael Culver. Special agent Stamp is the target of a fanatical terrorist who's trying to halt secret peace negotiations in the Middle East. Sequel to *Cold War Killers* has a better story and peppier pace, but is still predictable and uninspired. (Dir: Ken Grieve, 94 mins.)†

Alaska Seas (1954)** Robert Ryan, Gene Barry, Jan Sterling, Brian Keith. Ex-jailbird is given a chance by his former partner in an Alaskan salmon cannery, but joins a gang of robbers. Lukewarm remake of *Spawn of the North*. (Dir: Jerry Hopper, 78 mins.)

Albino (West Germany-South Africa, 1976)* James Faulkner, Christopher Lee, Trevor Howard, Horst Frank, Sybil Danning. Tiresome chase melodrama set in Africa, with an ex-policeman in pursuit of the albino terrorist whose men killed his fiancée. Danning is bumped off early and Lee and Howard contribute little to the story, so don't expect star power. (Dir: Juergen Goslar, 85 mins.)†

Albuquerque (1948)** Randolph Scott, Barbara Britton. Typical western centered around the nephew who revolts against his uncle's ways. (Dir: Ray Enright, 89 mins.)

Al Capone (1959)*** Rod Steiger, Fay Spain, Martin Balsam. An excellent performance by Steiger raises this drama

several notchese the average fare. The setting is the Prohibition era in Chicago when Capone controlled everything. (Dir: Richard Wilson, 104 mins.)†

Alcatraz: The Whole Shocking Story (MTV 1980)*** Michael Beck, Art Carney, Ronny Cox, Alex Karras, Richard Lynch, Will Sampson, Telly Savalas. A compelling, no-frills prison drama about Clarence Carnes, the youngest man ever sentenced to the impenetrable fortress Alcatraz. Ignoring the claim that Alcatraz is breakout proof, Carnes desperately spends his sentence trying out escape plans. (Dir: Paul Krasny, 200 mins.)

Alchemist, The (1985)½ Robert Ginty, Lucinda Dooling, John Sanderford. The story of this supernatural horror flick is barely there—the first half unexplained; the second uninteresting. Even the effects aren't scary and the Evil One, the alchemist himself, graces the screen for only a scant ten minutes. (Dir: James Amante, 84 mins.)†

Alexa (1988)*½ Christine Moore, Kirk Baily, Ruth Collins, Tom Voth. Low-budget story of a New York City prostitute trying to decide whether to get out of "the business" is more serious than the usual exploitation product. Unfortunately, it's also much more boring. (Dir: Sean Delgado, 80 mins.)†

Alexander Hamilton (1931)**½ George Arliss, Doris Kenyon, Alan Mowbray, Dudley Diggs. Stagey, creaky melodrama from the early days of sound, enjoyable mainly for Arliss' humorous performance. Mowbray makes a convincing George Washington. (Dir: John Adolphi, 73 mins.)†

Alexander Nevski (Russia, 1938)**** Nikolai Cherkassov. Sergei Eisenstein, Russia's greatest director, used all his cinematic magic to tell the epic tale of Prince Nevsky and his heroic stand against German invaders during the 13th century. (112 mins.)†

Alexander the Great (1956)*** Richard Burton, Fredric March, Claire Bloom. Lavish spectacle. Burton is brilliant in several of his major scenes as the famous Greek out to conquer the world. (Dir: Robert Rossen, 141 mins.)†

Alexander: The Other Side of Dawn (MTV 1977)**½ Eve Plumb, Leigh McCloskey. Good-looking Alexander (Leigh McCloskey) hustles women and men on Hollywood Boulevard because he can't land a job. (Dir: John Erman, 106 mins.)

Alexander's Ragtime Band (1938)***½ Tyrone Power, Alice Faye, Don Ameche, Ethel Merman. Sentimental story following the careers of some performers from 1911 to 1938 serves as a nice excuse for 26 Irving Berlin all-time hits. (Dir: Henry King, 105 mins.)

Alexandria—Why? (Egypt, 1978)***½ Mohsen Mohiedine, Farid Shawki, Ezzat El Alayli, Naglaa Fathi. A love song to the movies. War rages in North Africa in 1943, but a boy who cares more about films is preoccupied by the success of his school play. Story about people going about their daily lives while madness swells nearby at the front is filled with great humor and a devotion to American cinema. (Dir: Youssef Chahine, 125 mins.)

Alex and the Gypsy (1976)*½ Jack Lemmon, Genevieve Bujold, James Woods. Lemmon is a cynical middle-aged bailbondsman who's smitten with an aggressive, nubile gypsy. Unendurable! (Dir: John Korty, 99 mins.)

Alex in Wonderland (1970)**½ Donald Sutherland, Ellen Burstyn, Federico Fellini, Jeanne Moreau, Paul Mazursky. Director Paul Mazursky's film is a failure, but many parts are worth seeing. Sutherland plays a director who has one hit behind him and doesn't know what to do next. Neither, apparently, did Mazursky, evidently suffering from Fellini-on-the-brain. (109 mins.)

Alex: The Life of a Child (MTV 1986)***½ Bonnie Bedelia, Craig T. Nelson, Gennie James, Danny Corkill. Touching and gripping drama based on the true life story by sportswriter Frank Deford about his daughter's valiant bout with cystic fibrosis. (Dir: Robert Markowitz, 104 mins.)

Alfie (Great Britain, 1966)***½ Michael Caine, Shelley Winters, Millicent Martin, Vivien Merchant, Shirley Anne Field, Denholm Elliott, Julia Foster. This is the film which catapulted Michael Caine to stardom and his performance as an unscrupulous womanizing male is excellent. Alfie is a lecher and he lets you know it right from the start (Caine's talking to the audience really works). The romantic excursions are honestly portrayed. (Dir: Lewis Gilbert, 114 mins.)†

Alfie Darling (Great Britain, 1975)** Alan Price, Jill Townsend, Paul Copley, Joan Collins, Rùla Lenska. Inferior sequel; singer Price is charming but limited in the role made famous by Michael Caine. AKA: **Oh, Alfie.** (Dir: Ken Hughes, 99 mins.)†

Alfred Hitchcock Presents (MTV 1985)**½ Kim Novak, John Huston, Tippi Hedren, Steve Bauer, Melanie Griffith, Annette O'Toole, Ned Beatty, Bianca Rose. Four updated episodes from the TV series. Of the quartet, "The Man from the South," about a bet over a cigarette lighter, is the most fun. (Dirs: Steve De Jannatt, Fred Walton, Joel Oliansky, Randa Haines, 104 mins.)

Alfred the Great (1969)* David Hemmings,

Michael York, Prunella Ransome. Idiotic treatment of the 9th-century King Alfred of Wessex, who, according to this text, tried valiantly and nobly to unite all of England. (Dir: Clive Donner, 122 mins.)

Alfredo, Alfredo (Italy, 1973)*** Dustin Hoffman, Stefania Sandrelli, Carla Gravina. A first-rate domestic comedy by Pietro (*Divorce Italian Style*) Germi about a milquetoast bank clerk who's lucky enough to escape one bad marriage but unfortunate enough to end up in another no-win situation. Hoffman contributes an amusing, relaxed performance. (97 mins.)

Algiers (1938)*** Charles Boyer, Hedy Lamarr, Sigrid Gurie, Joseph Calleia, Gene Lockhart, Alan Hale, Johnny Downs. The story of Pepe LeMoko, the crook who sought refuge from the police in the Casbah of North Africa; perhaps Boyer's most famous role. (Dir: John Cromwell, 100 mins.)†

Alias a Gentleman (1948)** Wallace Beery, Tom Drake, Dorothy Patrick, Gladys George, Leon Ames, John Qualen, Sheldon Leonard, Jeff Corey. When oil is discovered on the property of farmer Beery, his shady acquaintances try to horn in on his new wealth by passing off a moll as his long-lost daughter. Typical Beery vehicle, broadly sentimental comedy. (Dir: Harry Beaumont, 76 mins.)

Alias Boston Blackie (1942)**½ Chester Morris, Adele Mara. While doing a benefit show for prisoners, Blackie runs into a jail break and a man bent on revenge. (Dir: Lew Landers, 67 mins.)

Alias Jesse James (1959)*** Bob Hope, Rhonda Fleming, Wendell Corey. Eastern insurance company sends its worst agent out West to protect a client, who turns out to be the notorious outlaw. Diverting Hope spoof. (Dir: Norman McLeod, 92 mins.)

Alias Nick Beal (1949)***½ Ray Milland, Thomas Mitchell, Audrey Totter. Honest district attorney is sidetracked in his crime crusade by a mysterious stranger. Absorbing fantasy with fine performances. (Dir: John Farrow, 93 mins.)

Alias Smith & Jones (MTV 1971)*½ Pete Deuel, Ben Murphy. The best thing about this tale of two young outlaws seeking amnesty from the Governor is the freewheeling performance by Pete Deuel. (Dir: Gene Levitt, 104 mins.)

Ali Baba and the Forty Thieves (1943)**½ Maria Montez, Jon Hall. Lad brought up by outlaws fights a Mongol tyrant to regain his rightful place on the throne. Juvenile but lively costume fantasy; pretty good fun. (Dir: Arthur Lubin, 87 mins.)

Ali Baba Goes to Town (1937)**½ Eddie Cantor, Tony Martin, June Lang, Gypsy

Rose Lee, Roland Young. Another musical Cantor romp, with Eddie in the time of the Arabian Nights. The usual monkey business, plus a young Martin's fine singing. (Dir: David Butler, 81 mins.)

Alibi Ike (1935)*** Joe E. Brown, Olivia de Havilland, William Frawley, Ruth Donnelly. Good Joe E. Brown baseball comedy loosely based on the Ring Lardner story. (Dir: Ray Enright, 73 mins.)

Alice (1990)**** Mia Farrow, Alec Baldwin, Blythe Danner, Judy Davis, William Hurt, Keye Luke, Joe Mantegna, Bernadette Peters, Cybill Shepherd, Gwen Verdon. Farrow plays a wealthy, bored, shopoholic Manhattanite who dreams of meeting Mother Teresa and whose husband is a self-righteous adulterer. Her life is forever changed when she visits a kindly, mysterious Asian herbalist-hypnotist, wonderfully played by Luke in his final screen appearance, who gives her unusual powders and powers. The entire cast sparkles in this gentle adult fantasy about self-discovery and self-fulfillment from writer-director Woody Allen. The comedy premise is slight, but the payoff is magical. (Dir: Woody Allen, 106 mins.)†

Alice Adams (1935)**** Katharine Hepburn, Fred MacMurray, Fred Stone, Evelyn Venable, Frank Albertson. A glorious adaptation of Tarkington's novel of the middle-class wallflower yearning for a way out of her social straitjacket. George Stevens's meticulous direction evokes the stifling small town atmosphere of the book's haves and have-nots. Hepburn rarely found roles that utilized her mannerisms and angular beauty as effectively. (99 mins.)†

Alice Doesn't Live Here Anymore (1974)**** Ellen Burstyn, Kris Kristofferson, Alfred Lutter, Jodie Foster, Diane Ladd, Harvey Keitel, Vic Tayback, Billy Green Bush, Valerie Curtin. Memorable, poignant comedy-drama about a 35-year-old widow who finds her identity while being obliged to cope with the harsh reality of economic survival. Burstyn deservedly won an Academy Award for her portrait of an itinerant ex-housewife turned waitress-singer trying to support herself and her 12-year-old son. The basis of the TV series "Alice." (Dir: Martin Scorsese, 112 mins.)†

Alice Goodbody (1974)*½ Sharon Kelly, Daniel Kauffman, Arem Fisher, Norman Field. An innocent waitress hired for a small part in a movie about Julius Caesar becomes the film's star through a series of accidents and assignations. Innocuous sex comedy. AKA: **Gosh!** (Dir: Tom Scheuer, 80 mins.)†

Alice in the Cities (West Germany, 1977) ***½ Rudiger Vogeler, Yella Rottlander, Elizabeth Kreuzer. A world-weary photographer gets saddled with a genial little girl and gradually loses his apathetic attitude. A good introduction to director Wim Wenders's style, this beautiful black-and-white film favors authentic emotion over sentimentality. (110 mins.)†

Alice in Wonderland (1933)**½ W. C. Fields, Charlotte Henry, Gary Cooper, Jack Oakie, Cary Grant. Ambitious film version of the classic fantasy; but lovers of the book will not find the film satisfactory. (Dir: Norman McLeod, 80 mins.)

Alice in Wonderland (Great Britain, 1950)**½ Carole Marsh, Pamela Brown, Bunin Puppets. Combination of live action and puppets is interesting, faithful to Lewis Carroll's book, but the film is rather disjointed. (Dir: Dallas Bower, 83 mins.)

Alice in Wonderland (1951)*** Animated. Though not as popular when first released as Disney's other animated features, it has grown steadily in favor. Wonderfully entertaining, and children will never forget that Cheshire Cat! (Dirs: Clyde Geronimi, Hamilton Luske, Wilfred Jackson, 75 mins.)†

Alice in Wonderland (MTV 1986)*½ Telly Savalas, Red Buttons, Jayne Meadows, Imogene Coca, Martha Raye. Producer Irwin Allen, that master of disasters, trashes Lewis Carroll, leaving few survivors in the all-star cast. The rampant mugging and flavorless songs qualify this as a disaster. (Dir: Harry Harris, 208 mins.)

Alice, or, the Last Escapade (France, 1977)**½ Sylvia Kristel, Charles Vanel, Thomas Chabrol, Marcel Dalio. Director Claude Chabrol's mystery designed as a *hommage* to Lewis Carroll's *Through the Looking Glass.* There's a weird old man, a spooky house, a faithful servant, and a very beautiful Kristel fleeing her marriage only to end up lost in a storm and seeking shelter. (93 mins.)

Alice's Adventures in Wonderland (Great Britain, 1972)** Peter Sellers, Fiona Fullerton, Ralph Richardson. Star-studded but listless version of the Lewis Carroll classic. (Dir: William Sterling, 100 mins.)†

Alice's Restaurant (1969)***½ Arlo Guthrie, Pat Quinn, James Broderick. Director Arthur Penn's film is loose, episodic, and deeply felt. Based on Guthrie's hit record, it recounts his arrest for littering and brief induction into the U.S. Army. Offbeat and warmly funny. (111 mins.)†

Alice Sweet Alice (1976)*** Linda Miller, Paula Sheppard, Brooke Shields, Lillian Roth. Put together on a Woolworth budget and shot in suburban New Jersey, this sleeper broaches more serious moral issues than most American films even dream of. This thriller concerns a little girl suspected of killing her sister. AKA:

17

Holy Terror and **Communion**. (Dir: Alfred Soles, 108 mins.)†

Alice to Nowhere (Australia, 1986)** John Waters, Rosey Jones, Steve Jacobs, Ebsen Storm. A woman and two guides fight for their lives against jewel thieves and the elements in the sprawling Australian outback. There's not enough plot to justify the three and one-half hour running time of this Australian made-for-TV movie. (Dir: John Power, 210 mins.)†

Alien (1979)**** Sigourney Weaver, Tom Skerritt, Yaphet Kotto, John Hurt, Veronica Cartwright, Harry Dean Stanton. A group of space explorers on a routine mission are tricked into bringing an extremely adaptable alien life form on board. Most of the crew pays for this mistake with their lives in a film notable for its special effects and relentless suspense. (Dir: Ridley Scott, 117 mins.)†

Alienator (1989)** Ross Hagen, Jan-Michael Vincent, John Phillip Law, Teagan Clive, Dawn Wildsmith, P. J. Soles, Robert Clarke, Robert Quarry. Distaff version of *The Terminator*, with an escapee from a prison spaceship stalked by a female android that doesn't mind blasting away innocent bystanders in the pursuit of her quarry. Campy thrills. (Dir: Fred Olen Ray, 93 mins.)†

Alien Contamination (Italy, 1980)** Ian McCulloch, Louise Monroe, Martin Mase. Ridiculous Italian horror movie, with laughable effects and dialog, and music by Dario Argento's band Goblin. (Dir: "Lewis Coates" [Luigi Cozzi], 85 mins.)†

Alien Dead (1982)* Buster Crabbe, Ray Roberts, Linda Lewis. A meteorite strikes Florida and turns teens on a boat into zombies. Strictly from poverty; Crabbe's last movie, and what a way to go out. (Dir: Fred Olen Ray, 89 mins.)†

Alien Factor, The (1978)** Don Liefert, Tom Griffith, Richard Dyszel. A trio of monsters from outer space land near Baltimore and terrorize the locals. Not bad if you consider that this was made by amateurs. Some imaginative special effects. (Dir: Donald M. Dohler, 82 mins.)†

Alien from L.A. (1987)* Kathy Ireland, Thom Matthews, Don Michael Paul, Linda Kerridge. Inane comedy-fantasy about a shy L.A. girl who falls into a hole in the ground and discovers a lost kingdom under the earth's surface. Overly stylized and pretentiously directed. (Dir: Albert Pyun, 87 mins.)†

Alien Nation (1988)**½ James Caan, Mandy Patinkin, Terence Stamp. In 1992 L.A., tough cop Caan teams up with outer space immigrant Patinkin to investigate murders in the alien community. Great allegorical sci-fi premise involving rac-

ism is wasted in a film that, after some clever early scenes, sinks into formula cop/buddy clichés. (Dir: Graham Baker, 89 mins.)†

Alien Predators (U.S.-Spain, 1987)* Dennis Christopher, Martin Hewitt, Lynn-Holly Johnson, Luis Prendes. Skylab falls to Earth with nasty alien beings attached, and the audience falls asleep from the flaccid writing, direction, and uninspired acting. (Dir: Deran Serafian, 90 mins.)†

Alien Prey (Great Britain, 1983)*½ Barry Stokes, Sally Faulkner, Glory Annan. A pair of lesbian lovers at a secluded country cottage are joined by a visitor, an extra-terrestrial scouting Earth for food. Guess what they eat on his planet? Odd but unsuccessful combination of sex and sci-fi. (Dir: Norman J. Warren, 85 mins.)†

Aliens (1986)***½ Sigourney Weaver, Michael Biehn, Paul Reiser, Bill Paxton, Jenette Goldstein, Lance Henriksen, Carrie Henn. Effective sequel to *Alien* has Ripley returning to fight the deadly monster accompanied by a band of battle-hungry space marines. A special video edition has 17 mins. of footage cut before the film's initial release. (Dir: James Cameron, 137 mins.)†

Aliens Are Coming, The (MTV 1980)** Tom Mason, Melinda Fee, Eric Braeden. Another rip-off of *Invasion of the Body Snatchers*, with a smidgen of *The Man Who Fell to Earth* thrown in. Outer space creatures take over earthlings when they can no longer make a go of it on their own planet. (Dir: Harvey Hart, 100 mins.)†

Alien Seed (1989)** Erik Estrada, Heidi Paine, Steven Blade. Estrada plays a murderous government scientist on the trail of a woman who has been impregnated by aliens with a baby who will save the Earth from its woes. Sci-fi runs out of ideas before the standard shoot-em-up ending. (Dir: Bob James, 88 mins.)†

Aliens from Spaceship Earth (1977)*½ Donovan, Lynda Day George. Another pseudo-documentary *Chariots of the Gods*–type exploration of the notion that great men in history were in fact visitors from outer space. (Dir: Don Como, 107 mins.)†

Alien Terror—See: **Sinister Invasion**

Alien Thunder (Canada, 1973)** Donald Sutherland, Kevin McCarthy, Chief Dan George. The Mounties always get their man, but R.C.M.P. Sutherland has difficulties trailing an Indian accused of murder. (Dir: Claude Fournier, 90 mins.)

Alien Warrior (1985)*½ Brett Clark, Pamela Saunders, Reggie DeMorton, Nelson Anderson. A vigilante from another planet comes to Earth to help clean up the streets of crime. Low-budget rip-off of

Death Wish and *Superman*, a not very appealing combination. AKA: **King of the Streets.** (Dir: Edward Hunt, 100 mins.)†

Alien Women (Great Britain, 1969)*½ Robin Hawdon, Yutte Stensgaard, James Robinson Justice, Charles Hawtry, Dawn Addams. Like *Barbarella*, this sci-fi comedy about a special agent fighting a society of amazonian aliens was adapted from an adult comic strip, resulting in a leaden sex farce. AKA: **Zeta One.** (Dir: Michael Cort, 86 mins.)†

Ali, Fear Eats the Soul (West Germany, 1974)***½ Brigitte Mira, El Hedi Ben Salem, Barbara Valentin, Irm Hermann. A German widow marries an Arab thirty years her junior as their passion erupts despite the difference in age and the racial prejudice against their pairing. An unflinching and perceptive portrait of contemporary German society with strikingly unsentimental performances that transform familiar material. (Dir: Rainer Werner Fassbinder, 94 mins.)†

Alison's Birthday (Australia, 1979)** Joanne Samuel, Lou Brown. Family's celebration of daughter's 19th birthday gets wild when she discovers her relatives are devil worshippers. Script doesn't take plot anywhere but into predictability. (Dir: Ian Coughlan, 99 mins.)†

Al Jennings of Oklahoma (1951)* Dan Duryea, Gale Storm, Dick Foran. A lawyer-turned-bandit, Al Jennings, goes to Oklahoma to go legit but pulls one more job and gets caught. Fair western drama. (Dir: Ray Nazarro, 79 mins.)

All About Eve (1950)**** Bette Davis, Gary Merrill, Anne Baxter, George Sanders, Celeste Holm, Thelma Ritter, Marilyn Monroe, Hugh Marlowe, Gregory Ratoff. Mankiewicz's jaundiced look at the show biz battle zone better known as Broadway is probably the summit of Hollywood moviemaking; it's as finely crafted an entertainment as we're likely to see. Eve insinuates herself into the good graces of some generous theater folk. What gives this cynical high comedy its emotional resonance and depth, however, is the poignance with which Davis plays Margo Channing, the just-turned-forty actress who's a living monument to enormous talent and volcanic temperament. (Dir: Joseph Mankiewicz, 138 mins.)†

All-American, The (1953)** Tony Curtis, Lori Nelson, Richard Long, Mamie Van Doren, Stuart Whitman. Stilted drama about college football hero Curtis, who quits after the death of his parents but makes a comeback at a snooty Ivy League school. (Dir: Jesse Hibbs, 80 mins.)

All American Boy, The (1973)** Jon Voight, Carol Androsky, Anne Archer. Voight skillfully plays an alienated boxer who desperately wants to leave his town, but does not want to commit himself to anything or anyone. Some nice touches scattered along the way, but clumsy. (Writer-Dir: Charles Eastman, 118 mins.)

Allan Quartermain and the Lost City of Gold (1986)*½ Richard Chamberlain, Sharon Stone, James Earl Jones, Henry Silva, Robert Donner. Silly follow-up to *King Solomon's Mines* with the same leads. Cardboard cutout adventure. (Dir: Gary Nelson, 110 mins.)†

All-Around Reduced Personality—Outtakes, The (West Germany, 1978)*** Helke Sander, Joachim Baumann, Frank Burckner, Eva Gagel. Single mother struggles to balance demands of work and family in charming study of the failure of capitalist and socialist segments of Berlin to provide affordable housing and suitable jobs. Humorous, sometimes grim, but sensitive film. (Dir: Helke Sander, 98 mins.)

All Ashore (1953)** Mickey Rooney, Dick Haymes, Peggy Ryan. Same old musical about three sailors on leave and their adventures. (Dir: Richard Quine, 80 mins.)

All at Sea (Great Britain, 1958)***½ Alec Guinness, Irene Browne. An often hilarious comedy about a seasick skipper, who finds himself in charge of one of the most unusual vessels ever seen. (Dir: Charles Frend, 83 mins.)

All Creatures Great and Small (MTV 1974)*** Simon Ward, Anthony Hopkins, Brian Stirner, Freddie Jones, Lisa Harrow. Nicely textured autobiographical period piece about the salad days of an English veterinarian. Persuasively acted character study; followed by *All Things Bright and Beautiful.* (Dir: Claude Watham, 92 mins.)

All Dogs Go to Heaven (1989)**½ Voices of Burt Reynolds, Dom De Luise, Judith Barsi, Vic Tayback, Charles Nelson Reilly, Melba Moore, Loni Anderson. Disappointing animated tale with an all-canine cast, centering on an ex-con mutt who returns to earth after a premature death. The story meanders, the well-known voices are distracting, and the songs . . . you'd think Burt would have learned his lesson in *At Long Last Love.* (Dir: Don Bluth, 85 mins.)†

Allegheny Uprising (1939)*** John Wayne, Claire Trevor, George Sanders, Brian Donlevy, Moroni Olsen, Chill Wills. Rousing pre-Revolutionary War actioner. The colonists grapple with a hard-nosed British commander who treats the Yanks as if they were ripe for exploitation. Exciting workmanlike epic; no surprises but satisfying. (Dir: William Seiter, 81 mins.)†

Allegro Non Troppo (Italy, 1977)***½ This tongue-in-cheek send-up of Disney's

Fantasia also manages to skewer the pretensions of symphony orchestras (in live action sequences) and practically all of western civilization (in the animated sequences). The animation style is bright and modern, and the content is outrageous and sometimes risque. (Dir: Bruno Bozzetto, 85 mins.)†

Alley Cat (1982)*½ Karin Mani, Robert Torti, Britt Helfer, Michael Wayne, Timothy J. Cutt. Billie is just your average single girl, but when her Gramps and Gram are attacked on the streets, she uses her handy martial arts skills to clean up the city. (Dir: Edward Victor, 82 mins.)†

All Fall Down (1962)**½ Eva Marie Saint, Warren Beatty, Karl Malden, Angela Lansbury. Wild lad with a way with women is attracted to a girl in town for a visit. Implausible drama, generally well acted. (Dir: John Frankenheimer, 110 mins.)

All God's Children (MTV 1980)**½ Richard Widmark, Ned Beatty, Ossie Davis, Ruby Dee, Trish Van Devere. Dramatic impact of an important and topical issue—forced busing to achieve racial equality in education—squandered by a screenplay wasting time on phony plot distractions. (Dir: Jerry Thorpe, 104 mins.)†

All Good Citizens (Czechoslovakia, 1968)***½ Vladimir Mensik, Radoslav Brozobohata, Pavel Pavlovsky. Life and violent death in a Czech village between 1945 and 1968. The deaths are linked to the subjugation of the peoples of Moldavia by the Soviets. Filled with satire and drama, this is a brilliant look at man's desire to be free. Director Vojtech Jasny was named Best Director at Cannes, after which the film was banned in Czechoslovakia and he was forced to flee to West Germany. AKA: **All My Good Countrymen**. (126 mins.)

All Hands on Deck (1961)*½ Pat Boone, Buddy Hackett, Barbara Eden, Dennis O'Keefe. A predictable service comedy with songs, long on corny dialogue and a ridiculous plot. (Dir: Norman Taurog, 98 mins.)

All I Desire (1953)*** Barbara Stanwyck, Richard Carlson, Maureen O'Sullivan, Richard Long. An actress who left her husband and children years before returns to their small-town home for a reconciliation. Touching, well-acted soap opera, with the sparkle of intelligence and humor. (Dir: Douglas Sirk, 79 mins.)

Alligator (1980)*** Robert Forster, Robin Riker, Perry Lang, Jack Carter, Michael Gazzo, Dean Jagger, Sydney Lassick. Pity the poor orphaned gator unceremoniously flushed down the toilet when it was no longer baby-cute. But every alligator will have his day; and when growth hormones are dumped into the sewers, our peripatetic hero grows up fast and wanders the urban jungle. John Sayles's witty, scary script is a model for fright-night specials; and the film is rare among horror films in that it develops a central romance with depth, intelligence and humor. (Dir: Lewis Teague, 94 mins.)†

Alligator Eyes (1991)*** Annabelle Larsen, Roger Kabler, Mary McLain, Allen McCullough, John MacKay. Audacious drama about a blind woman so independent and clever that she can walk unaided alongside a busy highway and convince friends she has sight. Film's shift into psychodrama and sexual hijinks is awkwardly handled, but the drama remains fascinating. (Dir: John Feldman, 101 mins.)†

Alligator People, The (1959)* Beverly Garland, Lon Chaney, Bruce Bennett. Scientist gives a wounded man serum taken from an alligator, and the poor guy starts turning into one. (Dir: Roy Del Ruth, 74 mins.)

All in a Night's Work (1961)*** Shirley MacLaine, Dean Martin, Cliff Robertson. When a tycoon dies under mysterious circumstances, his nephew inherits the empire. Sophisticated comedy, brightly paced, pleasant performances. (Dir: Joseph Anthony, 94 mins.)

All Mine to Give (1957)**½ Glynis Johns, Cameron Mitchell. Long, sad saga of a brave pioneer family and their hardships in early Wisconsin. Good performances give some spark to the tale. (Dir: Allen Reisner, 102 mins.)†

All My Darling Daughters (MTV 1972)**½ Robert Young, Raymond Massey, Eve Arden. Enjoyable family fare finds Robert Young playing the kindly father, watching his four daughters marry in a single ceremony. (Dir: David Lowell Rich, 72 mins.)

All My Good Countrymen—See: **All Good Citizens**

All My Sons (1948)*** Edward G. Robinson, Burt Lancaster, Howard Duff. Wealthy man's son accuses him of war profiteering. Frequently gripping, based on Broadway play by Arthur Miller. Well acted. (Dir: Irving Reis, 94 mins.)

All My Sons (MTV 1986)*** Aidan Quinn, James Whitmore, Michael Learned, Joan Allen, Zeljko Ivanek. Superior adaptation of Arthur Miller's shattering play, set during World War II. A family refuses to accept that their eldest son, long missing overseas, may be dead. When his girlfriend comes to visit, the lid is blown off of the calm surface of their lives. Overt staginess is the only minor drawback of this powerful presentation. (Dir: John Power, 110 mins.)†

Allnighter, The (1987)* Susanna Hoffs, DeDee Pfeiffer, Joan Cusack, John Terlesky, James Anthony Shanta, Pam Grier, Michael Ontkean. A teen-tease flick about three college roommates in pursuit of immediate romantic gratification. (Dir: Tamar Simon Hoffs, 92 mins.)†

All Night Long (Great Britain, 1962)*** Patrick McGoohan, Betsy Blair, Paul Harris, Richard Attenborough. *Othello* in a modern jazz background. An ambitious drummer sets out to discredit a top jazzman by compromising his wife. Some fine swingin' music by top players such as Brubeck, Dankworth, Mingus, etc. (Dir: Michael Relph, 95 mins.)

All Night Long (1981)***½ Gene Hackman, Barbra Streisand, Dennis Quaid, Diane Ladd. Offbeat comedy with Streisand as an unfulfilled married lady having an affair with a virile teenager (Quaid). Gene Hackman, an executive reduced to managing an all-night pharmacy, is Quaid's dad, and when Gene meets Barbra all hell breaks loose. It's a wacky comedy played with a refreshing off-center viewpoint.(Dir: Jean-Claude Tramont, 87 mins.)†

All of Me (1934)**½ Fredric March, Miriam Hopkins, George Raft. A society girl learns the true meaning of love from the selfless devotion she sees in a gangster's moll. Dated, but the performances are worth watching. (Dir: Jones Flood, 75 mins.)

All of Me (1984)*** Steve Martin, Lily Tomlin, Victoria Tennant, Richard Libertini. Delightful fantasy comedy. Martin stars as a lawyer who, through a metaphysical mixup, must share half of his body with a recently deceased, pampered, rich woman (Tomlin). Martin's schizoid comedy routines are priceless. (Dir: Carl Reiner, 93 mins.)†

Allonsanfan (Italy, 1974)***½ Marcello Mastroianni, Mimsy Farmer, Lea Massari, Laura Betti. Betrayal is the theme as an Italian nobleman turns in the leader of a revolutionary society after the 1816 Restoration in France. The central point of duplicity is contrasted with the confusion of the times and the disorganization of the people opposed to monarchy. An angry film by directors Paolo and Vittorio Taviani that has only recently come into its own. (100 mins.)†

Allotment Wives (1945)** Kay Francis, Paul Kelly, Otto Kruger. Con women led by socialite Francis prey on soldiers to collect their pay. Better acted than the dopey script deserves. (Dir: William Nigh, 83 mins.)

All Over Town (1937)** Olsen & Johnson, Mary Howard. Two nutty vaudevillians get tangled in a murder case. Slapstick

for those who like the O&J brand of laughs. (Dir: James W. Horne, 62 mins.)†

All Quiet on the Western Front (1930)**** Lew Ayres, Louis Wolheim. The reactions of young German soldiers to the utter calamity of warfare. A film classic, its dated technique doesn't interfere with its great power. (Dir: Lewis Milestone, 130 mins.)†

All Quiet on the Western Front (MTV 1979)***½ Richard Thomas, Ernest Borgnine, Ian Holm, Donald Pleasence, Patricia Neal. Remarque's classic novel about WWI from the German point of view. This retelling, as seen through the eyes of the young, idealistic student-turned-soldier, is very good indeed. (Dir: Delbert Mann, 155 mins.)†

All Screwed Up (Italy, 1973)***½ Luigi Diberti, Lina Polito, Isa Danieli. Excellent minor comedy directed by Lina Wertmuller, shorter than usual on big ideas but more concrete in their development. About a group of young people who come to the big city and industrialized urban living. (105 mins.)†

All's Fair (1989)* George Segal, Sally Kellerman, Robert Carradine, Jennifer Edwards, Jane Kaczmarek, Lou Ferrigno. What can you say about a movie with a cast like this in which Lou Ferrigno does the best acting? Awful comedy about corporate wives who organize a weekend war-games team to compete with their husbands. (Dir: Rocky Lane, 89 mins.)†

All That Heaven Allows (1955)*** Jane Wyman, Rock Hudson, Agnes Moorehead, Conrad Nagel, Virginia Grey. A lonely widow risks social disapproval when she falls in love with a gardener. Absorbing soap opera, beautifully directed. (Dir: Douglas Sirk, 89 mins.)

All That Jazz (1979)***½ Roy Scheider, Jessica Lange, Ann Reinking, Ben Vereen, Cliff Gorman. One of the most imaginative contemporary musicals, this innovative reworking of Fellini's *8½* chronicles the near-fatal heart problem which plagued director Bob Fosse. Roy Scheider gives the performance of his life as the arrogant, egotistical chain-smoking director Joe Gideon who encounters "Death" (Jessica Lange) and relives his past inequities. The musical numbers, as can be expected, are extraordinary. An ironic and fitting testament to a master choreographer and a talented director. (Dir: Bob Fosse, 119 mins.)†

All That Money Can Buy—See: **Devil and Daniel Webster, The**

All the Brothers Were Valiant (1953)**½ Robert Taylor, Stewart Granger, Ann Blyth. Two strong-willed New England whaling captains come to grips when one decides to go after lost treasure rather than blubber. (Dir: Richard Thorpe, 95 mins.)

All the Fine Young Cannibals (1960)** Natalie Wood, Robert Wagner, Susan Kohner, Pearl Bailey, George Hamilton. Muddled soap opera about a headstrong girl who is loved by one lad but marries another. (Dir: Michael Anderson, 112 mins.)

All the Gold in the World (France, 1961)*** Bourvil, Philippe Noiret, Colette Castel, Annie Fratellini. Land developers want to build a high-priced health resort on a farm supposed to contain a miraculous spring, but the farm's owner won't sell. Bourvil plays three roles in this city mouse–country mouse comedy, directed in typically whimsical fashion by René Clair. (100 mins.)

All the Kind Strangers (MTV 1974)**½ Stacy Keach, Samantha Eggar, John Savage, Robby Benson. This tale of quiet terror begins with photographer-journalist Keach giving a young boy a ride to his secluded farmhouse.... There, he meets the rest of the kids and a young woman (Eggar) whom they call mother. (Dir: Burt Kennedy, 72 mins.)†

All the King's Horses (1935)*½ Carl Brisson, Mary Ellis. In one of those mythical kingdoms, a visiting film star is mistaken for the husband of a noblewoman. Tired operetta. (Dir: Frank Tuttle, 87 mins.)

All the King's Men (1949)**** Broderick Crawford, Joanne Dru, John Ireland, Mercedes McCambridge, John Derek, Shepherd Strudwick, Anne Seymour. This political cautionary tale about the rise and fall of a senator-of-the-people has lost little of its power over the years. Maverick writer-director Robert Rossen created a fluid screen version of Robert Penn Warren's novel, inspired by the career of Huey Long. Oscars for Best Picture, Best Actor, and Best Supporting Actress. (109 mins.)†

All the Marbles (1981)*** Peter Falk, Vicki Frederick, Laurene Landon, Burt Young, Tracy Reed, Susan Mechsner. You don't have to be a fan of lady wrestling to enjoy this film about a small-time promoter and his two gorgeous "California Dolls," the tag team he's leading into the big time. Falk is at his funniest as the wheeler-dealer with ambition instead of a heart. (Dir: Robert Aldrich, 113 mins.)†

All the President's Men (1976)**** Dustin Hoffman, Robert Redford, Jason Robards Jr., Jane Alexander, Martin Balsam, Jack Warden. One of the triumphs of this spellbinding political thriller about the Watergate is that the audience is fascinated and involved, despite the fact that we already know who the villain is, and

that he will be captured by the posse but never brought fully to justice. The astonishingly high level of the ensemble acting is extraordinary. (Dir: Alan J. Pakula, 136 mins.)†

All the Right Moves (1983)** Tom Cruise, Craig Nelson, Lea Thompson, Charles Cioffi. This naturalistic drama has all the right moves as far as production design goes, but dramatically it's unconvincing. Story of a high school athlete hoping to win a scholarship in order to escape a small-town existence has the simplistic tone of a TV problem drama. (Dir: Michael Chapman, 113 mins.)†

All the Rivers Run (Australia, 1964)** Sigrid Thornton, John Waters. A spirited and self-reliant woman marries a riverman and becomes the owner and captain of her own boat in turn-of-the-century Australia. Picturesque location and pleasant performances. (Dirs: George Miller, Pino Amento, 274 mins.)†

All These Women (Sweden, 1964)**½ Bibi Andersson, Carl Billquist. Director Ingmar Bergman's first film in color is disappointing. A critic makes a deal with a concert cellist to write his autobiography if the cellist will play the critic's compositions. (Dir: Ingmar Bergman, 80 mins.)

. . . All the Way, Boys (Italy, 1973)** Terence Hill, Bud Spencer, Cyril Cusack, Michel Antoine. The co-stars of *My Name Is Trinity* return in this broad comedy as pilots of a shabby South American airline who crash in the jungle. Dumb slapstick saved only by the (limited) appeal of Hill and Spencer. (Dir: Giuseppe Colizzi, 105 mins.)†

All the Way Home (1963)*** Jean Simmons, Robert Preston, Pat Hingle, Aline MacMahon, Michael Kearney. Based on James Agee's Pulitzer Prize–winning novel about the death of the head of a family in rural America during the early 1900s and its effects upon his small son. Acting is uneven, but much of it is poignant and moving. (Dir: Alex Segal, 103 mins.)

All the Young Men (1960)**½ Alan Ladd, Sidney Poitier, James Darren, Glenn Corbett, Mort Sahl. All the young men are types you met in so many other war films set in Korea. (Dir: Hall Bartlett, 87 mins.)

All Things Bright and Beautiful (Great Britain, 1978)*** John Alderton, Lisa Harrow, Colin Blakely. One of several films based on the autobiographical books of James Herriot, a vet in the magnificent north Yorkshire dales. Low-key, gentle, well acted. (Dir: Eric Till, 94 mins.)

All This and Heaven, Too (1940)*** Bette Davis, Charles Boyer, Barbara O'Neil.

Ornate, superbly acted version of Rachel Field's fact-based bestseller about the notorious murder of the Duchess of Praslin. (Dir: Anatole Litvak, 143 mins.)†

All Through the Night (1942)*** Humphrey Bogart, Conrad Veidt, Peter Lorre, Judith Anderson, Jackie Gleason, Phil Silvers. Sheer fun and games, with Bogart breaking up a Nazi spy ring. (Dir: Vincent Sherman, 107 mins.)

All Together Now (MTV 1975)**½ Bill Macy, Jane Withers, John Rubinstein, Glynnis O'Connor. A family of four orphans decides to go it alone with their older brother at the head of the household, and they have to convince their relatives they can make it. (Dir: Randal Kleiser, 72 mins.)

All You Need Is Cash—See: Rutles, The— All You Need Is Cash

Almos' a Man (1977)*** LeVar Burton, Madge Sinclair, Robert DoQuol, Christopher Brooks, Gary Goodrow. Unflashy version of Richard Wright's short story about a fifteen-year-old boy whose desire for independence leads him into some manageable problems. Sensitive tale set in the deep South of the 1930s is part of the American Short Story series, hosted by Henry Fonda. (Dir: Stan Lathan, 51 mins.)†

Almost a Man (Italy, 1966)*** Jacques Perrin, Lea Padovani, Gianni Garko, Francesca De Seta. Perrin is terrific as a young writer who contemplates suicide because of artistic and personal failures. He is committed to an asylum but flees, returning to his hometown to reflect on his life. (Dir: Vittorio De Seta, 100 mins.)

Almost an Angel (1990)* Paul Hogan, Elias Koteas, Linda Kozlowski, Charlton Heston. Plodding comedy-drama about a petty thief (Hogan) who awakens in a hospital room after a chat with God (Heston). Meandering, relentlessly unfunny, and wretchedly acted by all involved, this is the kind of manipulative treacle that gives religion a bad name. (Dir: John Cornell, 96 mins.)†

Almost Angels (1962)**½ Peter Weck, Hans Holt, Fritz Eckhardt. A moderately entertaining music-filled film about members of the Vienna Boys Choir. This sentimental "boys will be boys" comedy-drama is well made, but the cynical had better get a schmaltz innoculation first. (Dir: Steve Previn, 93 mins.)†

Almost Perfect Affair, An (1979)*** Keith Carradine, Monica Vitti, Raf Vallone, Dick Anthony Williams. Pleasant light romance against the backdrop of the Cannes Film Festival. Carradine is an innocent abroad who has an affair with the wife of a producing magnate (Vallone). (Dir. Michael Ritchie, 93 mins.)†

Almost Summer (1978)*** Bruno Kirby, Lee Purcell, John Friedrich, Didi Conn, Tim Matheson. The best teen pic in a long time. The writing is astute and witty, the story (crooked politics in a student council election) engrossing, and the acting full of conviction and subtlety. Martin Davidson directs gracefully. (88 mins.)

Almost You (1985)** Griffin Dunne, Brooke Adams, Karen Young, Josh Mostel, Joe Silver, Spalding Grey. Muddled film on modern relationship malaise. The cloudy plot features a love triangle involving Manhattanites Dunne, Adams, and Young. The boredom and confusion of the characters is all too well instilled in the viewer. (Dir: Adam Brooks, 96 mins.)†

Aloha, Bobby and Rose (1975)* Paul Le Mat, Diane Hull, Martine Bartlett. Bobby's a garage mechanic; Rose works in a carwash office. He kills a liquor store clerk in a hold-up that was meant to be a joke. (Dir: Floyd Mutrux, 89 mins.)†

Aloha Means Goodbye (MTV 1974)* Sally Struthers, James Franciscus, Joanna Miles, Henry Darrow. Boring suspense yarn. A teacher is singled out to become a heart-transplant donor because of her rare blood type. (Dir: David Lowell Rich, 100 mins.)

Aloha Summer (1988)*½ Chris Makepeace, Yuji Okumoto, Don Michael Paul, Sho Kosugi. Teen tripe with a message of racial brotherhood about the antics of a group of lunkhead multiracial surfers in Hawaii. Nice kung fu sequence choreographed by chopsocky champ Kosugi. (Dir: Tommy Lee Wallace, 96 mins.)†

Aloïse (France, 1975)***½ Isabelle Huppert, Delphine Seyrig, Marc Eyraud, Francois Chatelet. Beautifully framed, filmed, and acted biography of the Swiss artist Aloïse, whose primitive paintings were all created during forty years spent in a mental institution, where she was sent after protesting WWI. Huppert and Seyrig, playing Aloïse at different ages, both give sterling performances. (Dir: Liliane De Kermadec, 120 mins.)

Aloma of the South Seas (1941)*½ Dorothy Lamour, Jon Hall. Native king goes to American college and returns in time to stop rebellion in this trashy sarong saga. (Dir: Alfred Santell, 77 mins.)

Alone in the Dark (1982)* Martin Landau, Jack Palance, Erland Van Lidth, Donald Pleasence. Three escaped mental patients invade a shrink's house, pushing him to violence. The film's schizophrenic, too, mixing horror and comedy unsuccessfully. (Dir: Jack Sholder, 93 mins.)†

Alone in the Neon Jungle (MTV 1988)*½ Suzanne Pleshette, Danny Aiello, Jon Tenney, Joe Morton. An evocative title for a run-of-the-mill TV movie. Chief of police Aiello handpicks tough gal Pleshette to ferret out the dirty cops in a rough precinct. (Dir: Georg Stanford Brown, 96 mins.)

Alone on the Pacific (Japan, 1963)***½ Yujiro Ishihara, Kinuyo Tanaka, Ruriko Asaoko. A young man sails a 19-foot yacht across the Pacific Ocean from Osaka to San Francisco. Stirring and satisfying, based on a true story. (Dir: Kon Ichikawa, 104 mins.)

Along Came a Spider (MTV 1970)**½ Suzanne Pleshette, Ed Nelson. A young widow goes to incredible lengths to prove that a prof. was responsible for her husband's death. (Dir: Lee Katzin, 72 mins.)

Along Came Jones (1945)*** Gary Cooper, Loretta Young, Dan Duryea. A mild-mannered cowpoke is mistaken for a notorious killer, nearly gets killed by both sides of the law. Humorous, enjoyable western. (Dir: Stuart Heisler, 90 mins.)†

Along the Great Divide (1951)**½ Kirk Douglas, Virginia Mayo, Walter Brennan. Slow-paced but interesting western drama about the capture and return to justice of an escaped criminal. Excellent desert photography. (Dir: Raoul Walsh, 88 mins.)†

Alouette, Je Te Plumerai (France, 1988)*** Claude Chabrol, Valerie Allain, Fabrice Luchini. Director Chabrol gets a chance to ham it up in this comedy-drama as an aging con man who allows a young couple to "adopt" him, thinking that he's rich and will leave them his fortune. (Dir: Pierre Zucca, 98 mins.)

Alpha Beta (Great Britain, 1973)***½ Albert Finney, Rachel Roberts. Lacerating drama, based on the British hit play by E. A. Whitehead. Superb performances by the two stars as they torment and torture each other during the course of a rotting marriage. (Dir: Anthony Page, 67 mins.)

Alphabet City (1984)*½ Vincent Spano, Kate Vernon, Michael Winslow, Zohra Lampert, Jami Gertz. Young drug kingpin Spano has to get through one more night before "retiring" from his criminal lifestyle. Unsurprising. (Dir: Amos Poe, 85 mins.)†

Alphabet Murders, The (Great Britain, 1966)** Tony Randall, Anita Ekberg, Robert Morley. An overly coy attempt to bring Agatha Christie's shrewd master sleuth, Hercule Poirot, to the screen in the person of Tony Randall. (Dir: Frank Tashlin, 90 mins.)†

Alpha Caper, The (MTV 1973)**½ Henry Fonda, Larry Hagman, Leonard Nimoy, James McEachin. A knowledgeable probation officer, forced to retire, uses ex-cons to heist a huge shipment of gold ingots. (Dir: Robert Lewis, 90 mins.)

Alphaville (France, 1965)*** Eddie Constantine, Anna Karina, Akim Tamiroff. Witty, stylish fantasy about a troubleshooter sent to a futuristic city where the dictator has a race of robots doing his bidding. Visually, director Jean-Luc Godard's most striking early film. (100 mins.)†

Alsino and the Condor (Nicaragua, 1983)**** Dean Stockwell, Alan Esquivel, Carmen Bunster, Alejandro Parodi, Delia Casanova. A powerful, evocative film that depicts war-torn Nicaragua before the revolution through the eyes of Alsino, an introverted twelve-year-old peasant boy who dreams of flying above the jungle like a bird. (Dir: Miguel Littin, 89 mins.)†

Altered States (1980)*** William Hurt, Blair Brown, Charles Haid, Bob Balaban. Hurt's screen debut as an ambitious scientific researcher who creates a monster—himself—in this extravagant, entertaining head trip directed by the ever-excessive Ken Russell. Russell's flair for the bizarre proves a boon to the movie, since he steamrolls over most of the scientific mumbo-jumbo and gets right to the point—Hurt's hallucinatory experiences inside a sensory deprivation tank and his terrifying physical transformation. (100 mins.)†

Alvarez Kelly (1966)*** William Holden, Richard Widmark, Janice Rule. Two-fisted acting by Widmark and Holden and the colorful setting of the Civil War make this a must for devotees. Southern guerrilla officer Widmark decides to rustle some 2,500 head of cattle for his side, and meets up with Alvarez Kelly (Holden). (Dir: Edward Dmytryk, 116 mins.)†

Always (1986)*** Henry Jaglom, Patrice Townsend, Melissa Leo. Filmmaker Henry Jaglom reunited with his ex-wife, actress Patrice Townsend, for this relationship comedy in which the two hash out their differences while their friends wallow in their own private neuroses; some uneasy truths are revealed. (Dir: Henry Jaglom, 105 mins.)†

Always (1989)**½ Richard Dreyfuss, Holly Hunter, Brad Johnson, John Goodman, Audrey Hepburn, Keith David. Pleasant but wholly unnecessary remake of *A Guy Named Joe*. Dreyfuss plays a recently deceased devil-may-care bush pilot called back from the Great Beyond to oversee and encourage the relationship between his former girlfriend (Hunter) and an awkward young flier (Johnson). A sunny tone is sustained by the amiable presence of the leads and Hepburn's brief appearance as Dreyfuss's guardian angel. But there's not even a glimmer of substance, which is presumably what Spielberg intended. (121 mins.)†

Always a Bride (Great Britain, 1953)*** Peggy Cummins, Terence Morgan. Stuffy Treasury official gets mixed up with a confidence ring, including an attractive blonde. Light, laughable romantic comedy. (Dir: Ralph Smart, 83 mins.)

Always Goodbye (1938)** Barbara Stanwyck, Herbert Marshall, Ian Hunter, Cesar Romero, Lynn Bari, Binnie Barnes. Soap opera story of a woman who gives up her illegitimate child for adoption and then, several years later, tries to get the youngster back. (Dir: Sidney Lanfield, 75 mins.)

Always In My Heart (1942)**½ Walter Huston, Kay Francis, Gloria Warren, Sidney Blackmer. A man comes home after a long, unjust prison stretch and wins his daughter's love although she does not know his true identity. (Dir: Jo Graham, 92 mins.)

Always Leave Them Laughing (1949)**½ Milton Berle, Virginia Mayo. Milton is well cast as a comedian who rides to the top on everybody's jokes. Bert Lahr is wonderful in some old sketches. (Dir: Roy Del Ruth, 116 mins.)

Always Remember I Love You (MTV 1990)*** Patty Duke, David Birney, Stephen Dorff, Richard Masur, Joan Van Ark. A truly touching drama that works on your heartstrings without being the least bit phony. A sixteen-year-old boy (Dorff) discovers he has been adopted; but more than that, he learns that he was kidnapped, unbeknownst to his adoptive parents. The boy seeks his real parents. The finale of this well-played tearjerker will wrench your emotions. (Dir: Michael L. Miller, 96 mins.)

Amadeus (1984)***** Tom Hulce, F. Murray Abraham, Elizabeth Berridge, Roy Dotrice, Charles Kay, Jeffrey Jones. Winner of eight Academy Awards. This lavishly mounted screen version of the Broadway hit about the musical prodigy Mozart was expanded and restructured by playwright Peter Shaffer with the assistance of director Forman. Beautifully photographed on location in Czechoslovakia, the film's based on the premise that the one man capable of fully appreciating Mozart's genius, Salieri, was so insanely jealous of his talents he was driven to poisoning his gifted but childish rival composer. (Dir: Milos Forman, 158 mins.)†

Amarcord (Italy-France, 1973)**** Magali Noel, Bruno Zanin, Luigi Rossi. A joyous, beautiful film. Federico Fellini's semi-autobiographical look back at life in the Italian provinces in the 1930s under Mussolini. The screen is filled with an unending succession of dazzling, remarkable images which few other living directors can match. Screenplay by Fellini and Tonino Guerra. (127 mins.)†

Amateur, The (Canada, 1982)** John Savage, Christopher Plummer, Marthe Keller, Arthur Hill, Ed Lauter. Computer technologist stalks three terrorists behind the Iron Curtain. It appears that the trio killed his girlfriend who was taken hostage in a raid on an American consulate in Munich. Starts well but bogs down. (Dir: Charles Jarrott, 111 mins.)†

Amateur Hour—See: **I Was a Teenage TV Terrorist**

Amateur Night (1985)* Dennis Cole, Allen Kirk, Geoffrey Duel. Silly amorphous comedy about contestants battling each other in a talent competition at a world-famous nightclub. (Dir: Eddie Beverly, Jr., 91 mins.)†

Amateur Night at the Dixie Bar and Grill (MTV 1979)***½ Henry Gibson, Tanya Tucker, Candy Clark. Engaging melodrama set in a Dixie roadhouse which focuses on the crowd that hangs out there and the help that serves them booze and small talk. Director Joel Schumacher, who also wrote the deft yarn which has moments of parody—as well as moments of homage to Altman's *Nashville*—skillfully guides a uniformly good cast. (104 mins.)

Amazing Colossal Man, The (1957)** Glen Langan, Cathy Downs. Atomic effects make a guy grow and grow and grow. Science-fiction script drags. (Dir: Bert Gordon, 80 mins.)

Amazing Dobermans, The (1976)** James Franciscus, Barbara Eden, Fred Astaire, Jack Carter, Billy Barty. More doggie hijinks about a fast talker whose prize pooches go to work for Uncle Sam and help bust up a gang of no-goodniks. (Dirs: David and Byron Chudnow, 94 mins.)†

Amazing Dr. Clitterhouse (1938)***½ Edward G. Robinson, Claire Trevor, Humphrey Bogart. Entertaining, amusing story of a psychiatrist who becomes a crook to study the criminal mind. (Dir: Anatole Litvak, 90 mins.)

Amazing Grace (1974)* Moms Mabley, Slappy White, Stepin Fetchit, Rosalind Cash, Butterfly McQueen. Moms Mabley was a funny raunchy nightclub comedienne long popular with black audiences, but she's absurdly cast as a God-fearing, harmless old lady. (Dir: Stan Lathan, 99 mins.)

Amazing Grace and Chuck (1987)*** Jamie Lee Curtis, Alex English, William Peterson, Gregory Peck, Lee Richardson, Joshua Zuehlke, Frances Conroy. Engaging Americana about a youngster who puts his principles into practice by giving up Little League baseball in order to make a one-boy protest against nuclear weapons. In Frank Capra-esque fashion, professional athletes soon jump on the kid's antinuke bandwagon and world leaders snap to attention. (Dir: Mike Newell, 96 mins.)†

Amazing Howard Hughes, The (MTV 1977)*** Tommy Lee Jones, Ed Flanders, James Hampton, Tovah Feldshuh, Lee Purcell. An engrossing study of the puzzling eccentric who had an eye for Hollywood beauties but really preferred airplanes and gadgets to people. The movie becomes an account of a deteriorating human in need of psychiatric help, but rich enough to indulge in his eccentricities. (Dir: William Graham, 210 mins.)†

Amazing Mr. Blunden, The (Great Britain, 1972)*** Laurence Naismith, James Villiers, David Lodge, Lynne Frederick, Diana Dors. A widow and her two children move into an old house still occupied by the ghost of its previous owner, who solicits their help in solving a hundred-year-old mystery. Good family film, neither too scary for kids nor condescending to adults. (Dir: Lionel Jeffries, 100 mins.)†

Amazing Mrs. Holliday, The (1943)**½ Deanna Durbin, Edmond O'Brien, Barry Fitzgerald. A silly comedy with dramatic overtones about an American schoolteacher and a group of refugee children. (Dir: Bruce Manning, 96 mins.)

Amazing Mr. Williams, The (1939)**½ Melvyn Douglas, Joan Blondell, Clarence Kolb, Ruth Donnelly. A murder-romance, with interesting chemistry between Douglas and Blondell. (Dir: Alexander Hall, 80 mins.)

Amazing Mr. X, The (1948)**½ Turhan Bey, Lynn Bari, Cathy O'Donnell, Richard Carlson, Donald Curtis. Some dollops of cynicism lend forcefulness to this dated shocker about a fake spiritualist who's out to bilk a widow of her fortune with the cooperation of her scheming spouse. AKA: **The Spiritualist.** (Dir: Bernard Vorhaus, 78 mins.)†

Amazing Transparent Man, The (1960)* Douglas Kennedy, Marguerite Chapman, James Griffith, Ivan Triesault. A mad scientist creates an invisible thief in order to snatch some radioactive stuff, but the crook disappears into his own life of crime. (Dir: Edgar G. Ulmer, 58 mins.)†

Amazing Transplant, The (1970)½ Juan Fernadez, Linda Southern, Larry Hunter. Amazing as it is, thanks to a plot twist straight from exploitation heaven and a lot of distinctly unerotic sex scenes. A series of murders result from a man's desire to be as popular with the ladies

as his dead friend was—thus the highly irregular organ transplant of the title. (Dir: "Louis Silverman" [Doris Wishman], 78 mins.)†

Amazon Jail (1985)* Elisabeth Hartmann, Mauricio Do Valle, Sondra Graffi. A gaggle of babes-in-rags escape a jungle prison only to be captured by a satanist's men. The girls' dresses remain at half-mast throughout; some interesting dance numbers and stupid plot twists. (Dir: Osvaldo de Oliveira, 94 mins.)†

Amazons (MTV 1984)** Tamara Dobson, Stella Stevens, Jack Scalia, Madeline Stowe, Jennifer Warren. Warren and Stevens belong to a secret organization of voluptuous vigilantes who kill undesirable men they believe don't deserve to live any longer. (Dir: Paul Michael Glaser, 99 mins.)†

Amazon Women on the Moon (1987)*** Michelle Pfeiffer, Rosanna Arquette, Griffin Dunne, Steve Guttenberg, Ed Begley, Jr., Steve Allen, Ralph Bellamy, Howard Hesseman, Lou Jacobi, Arsenio Hall, Sybil Danning, Carrie Fisher, Paul Bartel, Henry Silva, Russ Meyer, Andrew Dice Clay. All-star collection of satirical spoofs provides hit-and-miss hilarity. The most inspired lunacy involves a celebrity roast staged at a man's funeral. Several extra skits are included in broadcast TV showings; one features Dick Miller and Jenny Agutter. (Dirs: Joe Dante, Carl Gottlieb, Peter Horton, John Landis, Robert K. Weiss, 85 mins.)†

Ambassador, The (1984)*** Robert Mitchum, Ellen Burstyn, Rock Hudson, Fabio Testi, Donald Pleasence. Reasonably complex suspenser about an American ambassador who must cope with the flare-up of the Israeli-Palestinian conflict as well as the extracurricular activities of his wife. Smart performances and an adroit blend of topical issues and thrills. (Dir: J. Lee Thompson, 90 mins.)†

Ambassador's Daughter, The (1956)**½ Olivia de Havilland, John Forsythe, Myrna Loy, Adolphe Menjou. GI in Paris falls for ambassador's daughter. Strained comedy isn't as funny as it might have been. (Dir: Norman Krasna, 102 mins.)

Amber Waves (MTV 1980)***½ Dennis Weaver, Kurt Russell, Mare Winningham, Fran Brill. Moving drama transcends the soap opera overtones of the plot. Russell creates a credible portrait of a brash New York model thrown into the raw world of Midwest wheat harvesting, in contrast to the strong-willed yet surprisingly worldly farmer, perfectly played by Weaver. (Dir: Joseph Sargent, 104 mins.)

Ambush (1950)** Robert Taylor, Arlene Dahl, John Hodiak. Routine. An Indian scout draws a special mission which makes him a hero. Some good action sequences. (Dir: Sam Wood, 88 mins.)

Ambush at Cimarron Pass (1958)** Scott Brady, Margia Dean, Clint Eastwood. The title tells the story of this typical juvenile western. (Dir: Jodie Copelan, 73 mins.)

Ambush at Tomahawk Gap (1953)*** John Hodiak, John Derek, David Brian. Offbeat western about four ex-convicts who band together to find some buried stolen money. Exciting climax. Good performances by all. (Dir: Fred Sears, 73 mins.)

Ambush Bay (1966)**½ Hugh O'Brian, Mickey Rooney, James Mitchum. A familiar WWII drama about two-fisted Marines in the Philippines on a special mission; well played by O'Brian and Rooney. (Dir: Ron Winston, 109 mins.)

Ambushers, The (1967)* Dean Martin, Senta Berger. The obligatory number of fistfights and available femmes. As a gumshoe star, Dean's a fine crooner! (Dir: Henry Levin, 102 mins.)†

Ambush Murders, The (MTV 1982)**½ James Brolin, Dorian Harewood, Alfre Woodard, Robert Denison. Harewood is the black activist accused of murdering white police officers in a predominantly black town. Who will defend the accused? It's all a little too pat, yet the cast overcomes some of the obstacles. (Dir: Steven Hilliard Stern, 104 mins.)†

Amelia Earhart (MTV 1976)*** Susan Clark, John Forsythe, Stephen Macht, Susan Oliver. She delivers the goods again as the much-publicized Amelia Earhart, America's heroine of the '20s and '30s who loved to fly but hated performing as a celebrity. (Dir: George Schaefer, 162 mins.)

America (1924)***½ Neil Hamilton, Carol Dempster, Erville Alderson, Lionel Barrymore. Worthwhile but flawed D. W. Griffith-produced spectacle about the American Revolution. Must-see for Griffith admirers; was initially twice its present length. (92 mins.)

America, America (1963)**** Stathis Giallelis, Lou Antonio, John Marley. Written, produced and directed by Elia Kazan, this is an eloquent tribute to Kazan's forebears, and to generations of immigrants who struggled to pursue the American dream. *America* focuses on one young Greek boy who works his way to the U.S. in the late 1890s. (174 mins.)

America at the Movies (1976)*** Originally produced by the American Film Institute for the American Bicentennial celebration, this clip-filled collage is fun for the nondiscriminating who'll want to see favorite film scenes flying by at a rapid clip. (Designed by James Silke, 116 mins.)†

American, The (France, 1969)*** Jean-Louis Trintignant, Simone Signoret, Francoise Fabian, Marcel Bozzuffi. Trintignant returns to his French village after twelve years in the U.S. and finds life there has changed. Bittersweet little film filled with superb performances and directed by co-star Bozzuffi, best known to American audiences as the French drug kingpin in *The French Connection*. AKA: L'Americain. (80 mins.)

Americana (1981)** David Carradine, Barbara Hershey, Michael Greene. Meandering post-Vietnam adjustment drama about a former soldier who tries to get a carousel to work, as small town life goes spinning by him. (Dir: David Carradine, 91 mins.)†

American Anthem (1986)*½ Mitch Gaylord, Janet Jones, Tiny Wells, Michael Pataki, Patrice Donnely, John Aprea. Music and muscles are what hold this very flimsy plot together. The story revolves around Steve (Mitch Gaylord) and his father (John Aprea) who continuously tells him that he is a Big Nothing, so he discovers the exciting world of gymnastics and proves his worth. Seeing Olympic Gold Medalist Gaylord act is like watching a beefcake poster struggling to come to life. (Dir: Albert Magnoli, 110 mins.)†

American Blue Note (1989)*** Peter MacNichol, Carl Capotorto, Tim Guinee, Charlotte d'Amboise, Trini Alvarado, Zohra Lampert. Salad-days story of a month in the career of a young jazz band in the early sixties. Comedy-drama has an easy charm that should appeal to all, even non–jazz buffs. AKA: Fakebook. (Dir: Ralph Toporoff, 96 mins.)

American Boy (1978)*** Kinetic filmmaker Martin Scorsese made this minimalist profile of his friend Steven Prince shortly after *Taxi Driver*, in which Prince played the role of the talkative gun salesman. The setup is simple—Scorsese simply shows Prince telling a string of choice anecdotes all relating to his different personas: homosexual, junkie, Neil Diamond's road manager (!), and, in the film's most riveting tale, killer. (55 mins.)

American Boyfriends (Canada, 1989)** Margaret Langrick, John Wildman, Jason Blicker. Sequel to *My American Cousin* moves the characters into the sixties. Result: yet another coming-of-age-in-the-sixties movie, with autobiographical validity but little else to distinguish it from scores of others. (Dir: Sandy Wilson, 100 mins.)†

American Christmas Carol, An (MTV 1979)** Henry Winkler, David Wayne, Chris Wiggins. In this incarnation, Winkler is weighted down with makeup as old Mr. Slade (alias Scrooge), and the time and place have been switched to the Depression years in New England. The flashbacks are the only time the story comes alive. (Dir: Eric Till, 104 mins.)†

American Dream, An (1966)**½ Stuart Whitman, Janet Leigh, Eleanor Parker. Uneven film version of Norman Mailer's offbeat novel. Parker, as the hero's bitter drunken ex-wife, makes the first few scenes memorable, but Whitman is inadequate as the tough TV commentator whose attacks on the Mafia have brought him a death warrant. (Dir: Robert Gist, 103 mins.)

American Dream, The (MTV 1981)*** Stephen Macht, Karen Carlson, Michael Hershewe, Hans Conried. Promising pilot for a series that never materialized. Typical middle-class American family from suburbia moves to a racially integrated neighborhood in Chicago, adopting a new set of problems but becoming more closely knit in the process. (Dir: Mel Damski, 78 mins.)†

American Dreamer (1984)** JoBeth Williams, Tom Conti, Giancarlo Giannini. For winning a writing competition, a discontented housewife goes to Paris, where, after an accident, she wakes up believing she's the dauntless heroine of her favorite novels. Her madcap adventures lack that certain "je ne sais quoi," style-wise. (Dir: Rick Rosenthal, 104 mins.)†

American Dreamer, The (1971)**½ Our man Dennis Hopper at the height of his gonzo genius. This indulgent exercise in documentary profiles Mr. Hopper as he edits *The Last Movie*; the filmmakers get him to philosophize at length, and put him in a room with a dozen women to see what will happen(!). (Dirs: L. M. Kit Carson, Lawrence Schiller, 93 mins.)

American Drive-In (1987)*½ Emily Longstreth, Pat Kirton, Rhonda Snow, Joel Bennett. One night at a small-town drive-in (where the movie just happens to be the filmmakers' previous effort, *Hard Rock Zombies*) featuring teen romance, goofy adults, gang violence, and revenge. Too much of too many elements, and not enough of anything good. (Dir: Krishna Shah, 92 mins.)†

American Empire (1942)**½ Richard Dix, Leo Carrillo, Preston Foster, Francis Gifford, Guinn Williams. During the antebellum period, two pals build up a beef business in Texas. Old-fashioned oater with Dix overcoming cattle rustlers and brandishing his movie star profile to denote heroic status. (Dir: William McGann, 82 mins.)†

American Flyers (1985)**½ Kevin Costner, David Grant, Rae Dawn Chong, Alexandra Paul, Janice Rule. Above-average inspirational sports film in which bicyclist brothers put their best feet forward for

the toughest bicycle race in America (even though for one, it will be the last race). Unfortunately, despite flashes of humor in the screenplay and superbly photographed competition sequences, this bicycle course has been pedaled over once too often. (Dir: John Badham, 114 mins.)†

American Friend, The (West Germany-France, 1977)*** Dennis Hopper, Bruno Ganz. Wim Wenders has developed a cult following for this film about people operating outside the law. An art smuggler (Hopper) and a German craftsman kill a man, and that murder binds them in friendship. (Dir: Wim Wenders, 127 mins.)†

American Geisha (MTV 1986)** Pam Dawber, Richard Narita, Robert Ito, Stephanie Faracy, Beulah Quo, Dorothy McGuire. Pam Dawber plays the American intrigued by the geisha way of life, learning their rites and having a love affair with a Kabuki actor. (Dir: Lee Philips, 104 mins.)

American Gigolo (1980)**½ Richard Gere, Lauren Hutton, Hector Elizondo. Sleek, shiny, and superficial, this film helped make a star of Gere, who plays a first-class male whore who finds true love after falling for a politician's wife. Unfortunately, he's also accused of murdering a client, and his occupation doesn't help his case. The sexual chemistry of Gere and Hutton, and the memorable rock score, helped make this a hit. (Dir: Paul Schrader, 117 mins.)†

American Gothic (1988)* Rod Steiger, Yvonne DeCarlo, Michael J. Pollard. A truly horrific comedy with the biggest laughs coming at the expense of Steiger and DeCarlo, two performers who put their pride in check when they agreed to appear as the parents of a trio of warped psychos. (Dir: John Hough, 90 mins.)†

American Graffiti (1973)***½ Ronny Howard, Cindy Williams, Charlie Martin Smith, Richard Dreyfuss, Mackenzie Phillips, Candy Clark. A perceptive film about growing up in a small town environment in the early sixties and how teenagers use their automobiles in modern courtship rites. This refreshing portrait of adolescent hijinks and rites of passage was the unofficial inspiration for the TV series "Happy Days." (Dir: George Lucas, 110 mins.)†

American Guerrilla in the Philippines, An (1950)** Tyrone Power, Micheline Presle. American naval officer joins forces with Filipino patriots in WW II. Usual adventure story, slowed down by love angle. Filmed in the South Pacific. (Dir: Fritz Lang, 105 mins.)

American Harvest (MTV 1987)** Wayne Rogers, Fredric Lehne, Earl Holliman,

Mariclare Costello. Earnest if all-too-familiar tale of the plight of the American farmer given a personal twist with the addition of two feuding families. (Dir: Dick Lowry, 104 mins.)

American Hot Wax (1978)***½ Tim McIntire, Fran Drescher, Laraine Newman, Chuck Berry, Jerry Lee Lewis. Director Floyd Mutrux has accomplished what many have claimed and few have evoked: the poetry of experience represented by rock and roll. Alan Freed's landmark Brooklyn concert is the focal point. (91 mins.)

American in Paris, An (1951)***½ Gene Kelly, Leslie Caron, Oscar Levant, Nina Foch, Georges Guetary. This Oscar-winning film musical written by Alan Jay Lerner, with a George & Ira Gershwin score, and Gene Kelly's brilliant, ambitious choreography, is a must. Leslie Caron made her film debut in this story about an American ex-GI (Kelly) who stays in Paris after WWII to make it as an artist. (Dir: Vincente Minnelli, 113 mins.)†

Americanization of Emily, The (1964)*** James Garner, Julie Andrews, Melvyn Douglas. Paddy Chayefsky's skillful screenplay is adapted from William Bradford Huie's book about a navy officer whose main job during WWII is to supply his superiors with a variety of the creature comforts, including girls. Julie Andrews gives a beguiling portrayal of a British war widow who can't help falling in love with him. Entertaining, and if you listen, the film actually has something pertinent to say. (Dir: Arthur Hiller, 117 mins.)†

American Justice (1986)*½ Gerald McRaney, Jameson Parker, Jack Lucarelli, Wilford Brimley, Jeannie Wilson. The stars of TV's "Simon and Simon" appear in a big screen release that looks exactly like a small screen movie. Two good guys pool their bravery to battle crooked cops who force illegal immigrants from Mexico into prostitution. (Dir: Gary Grillo, 95 mins.)†

American Madness (1932)*** Walter Huston, Pat O'Brien, Constance Cummings. The first film fully in the patented Capra style—with its spark of contemporary urgency, the masses of crowds arrayed against the decent individual working for their benefit. Huston incarnates rectitude without stuffiness as the town banker. (Dir: Frank Capra, 81 mins.)

American Nightmare(1986)—See: **Combat Shock**

American Nightmare (1984)*½ Lawrence S. Day, Lora Staley, Neil Dainard, Michael Ironside, Alexandra Paul. Young man searches for his runaway sister in the big bad city, and encounters all the evils of Sodom and Gomorrah (as well as the obligatory psycho killer) along the way. Exploitation with pretensions of social significance a la *Hardcore*. (Dir: Don McBrearty, 87 mins.)†

American Ninja (1985)** Michael Dudikoff, Steve James, Judie Aronson, Guich Koock. Brutal martial arts opus. A real life nephew of his Uncle Sam battles a swarm of high-kicking villains single-handedly in the Philippines. (Dir: Sam Firstenberg, 95 mins.)†

American Ninja 2: The Confrontation (1987)*** Michael Dudikoff, Gary Conway, Steve James, Larry Poindexter. Heroic Joe Armstrong (Dudikoff) and his sidekick Curtis Jackson (James) journey to the Caribbean to find out why so many Marines have vanished; it turns out an archfiend needs them for his proposed army of superninjas. Lots of violence and even élan: high-spirited fun. (Dir: Sam Firstenberg, 100 mins.)†

American Ninja 3: Blood Hunt (1989)*½ David Bradley, Steve James, Marjoe Gortner, Michele Chan. Tired follow-up replaces Dudikoff with Bradley as the hero fighting Gortner's evil plan to hatch a deadly virus for use in germ warfare. Sidekick James is the only reason to watch this. (Dir: Cedric Sundstrom, 90 mins.)†

Americano, The (1954)**½ Glenn Ford, Frank Lovejoy. Texas cowboy gets mixed up with bandits in Brazil. Good cast helps this below-the-equator western. (Dir: William Castle, 85 mins.)†

American Pop (1981)** Voices of Ron Thompson, Marya Small, Jerry Holland, Lisa Jane Persky, Jeffrey Lippa, Roz Kelly. Director Ralph Bakshi's attempt to tell through animation the history of American popular songs, from the turn of the century to new wave rock, is a trivial exercise in pointless indulgence. (98 mins.)

American Romance, An (1944)*** Brian Donlevy, Ann Richards, Walter Abel, John Qualen. Donlevy is excellent in this strong World War II drama of American roots. The story tells of the rise of an illiterate young immigrant to wealth and power between the turn of the century and WWII. (Dir: King Vidor, 122 mins.)

American Soldier, The (West Germany, 1970)*** Karl Scheydt, Elge Sorbas, Magarethe von Trotta, Rainer Werner Fassbinder. An early R.W. Fassbinder film about a mob hit man and his milieu that both pays tribute to, and dissects, the classic Hollywood gangster picture. The strikingly detached style of acting makes it seem as if all the characters have seen too many of these films and have started living them out. (80 mins.)

American Success Company, The (1979)** Jeff Bridges, Belinda Bauer, Ned Beatty, Steven Keats, Bianca Jagger, John Glover. Director William Richert followed up his clever *Winter Kills* with a cryptic fable about how to succeed in business. Jeff Bridges plays a wimpy but ambitious corporate underling who's married to the boss's shrewish daughter. He adopts a tough-guy alter ego in order to get back at them, and the results are more beneficial than he'd ever have imagined. Screenplay by Richert and Larry Cohen. AKA: **Success.** (90 mins.)

American Tail, An (1986)**½ Voices of Cathianne Blore, Dom DeLuise, John Finnegan, Phillip Glasser, Christopher Plummer, Nehemiah Persoff. Cutesy cartoon fable featuring splendid animation, but the charm is vitiated by bland storytelling and flavorless songs. Aimed at very young audiences, the film relates the travails of sweet little Feivel the Mouse, who's separated from his family after they escape persecution in Russia to find freedom in America. (Dir: Don Bluth, 80 mins.)†

American Tragedy, An (1931)*** Phillips Holmes, Sylvia Sidney, Frances Dee. Josef von Sternberg's version of Theodore Dreiser's novel emphasizes personal, emotional causes of the tragedy over social ones, thereby obliterating Dreiser's perspective. (95 mins.)

American Werewolf in London, An (1981)**½ David Naughton, Griffin Dunne, Jenny Agutter, John Woodvine. Naughton is an American student backpacking it through Europe one night when he's attacked on the moors one night and turns into a werewolf. The story is old hat but Naughton's charm and the transformation scenes work well. (Dir: John Landis, 98 mins.)†

Americathon (1979)* John Ritter, Harvey Korman, Nancy Morgan. An alleged satire aimed at big business. The U.S. holds a telethon in order to save Uncle Sam from imminent bankruptcy. Forced and unfunny. (Dir: Neal Israel, 85 mins.)†

Amin—the Rise and Fall (Kenya, 1981)**½ Joseph Olita, Geoffrey Keen. A ragged, unsubtle but often powerful film depicting the life and violent times of the despot Idi Amin. (Dir: Sharad Patel, 101 mins.)†

Amityville Horror, The (1979)*½ James Brolin, Margot Kidder, Rod Steiger, Don Stroud. Rackety claptrap in a house possessed by demons. Brolin and Kidder are the middle-class couple whose Long Island home goes haywire. (Dir: Stuart Rosenberg, 117 mins.)†

Amityville II: The Possession (1982)* Burt Young, Rutanya Alda, Diane Franklin. Unsuspecting family moves into a house inhabited by the Devil, who proceeds to enter the body of the older son and compel him to murder his family. (Dir: Damiano Damiani, 104 mins.)†

Amityville III (1983)*½ Tony Roberts, Tess Harper, Candy Clark, Robert Joy. Derivative tale of still another family in a haunted house is so inept that ghosts everywhere may start haunting moviegoers who frequent these flicks. AKA: **Amityville 3: The Demon.** (Dir: Richard Fleischer, 93 mins.)†

Amityville 3: The Demon—See: **Amityville III**

Amityville Curse, The (Canada, 1990)*½ Kim Coates, Dawna Wightman, Helen Hughes, David Stein, Jan Rubes. Routine horror tale follows a generic *Amityville* formula: new family moves into a haunted Long Island house where a priest was murdered a decade ago, have trouble with evil spirits. (Dir: Tom Berry, 91 mins.)†

Amityville: The Evil Escapes (MTV 1989)**½ Patty Duke, Jane Wyatt, Frederic Lehne, Brandy Gold. Duke works hard as the latest occupant of the unfriendly house, whose daughter falls under the control of its malevolence. As scare films go, give this one a B for structure, pace, and performance. (Dir: Sandor Stern, 96 mins.)

Among the Living (1941)**½ Albert Dekker, Susan Hayward, Frances Farmer, Harry Carey. Man is wrongfully accused when his insane twin brother escapes and commits murder. (Dir: Stuart Heisler, 68 mins.)

Among the Living Dead (France, 1971)*½ Christina von Blanc, Howard Vernon, Britt Nichols, Paul Muller. Woman visiting the villa of her late uncle for the reading of his will gets a cold reception from his other relatives, who are just as dead as Unk. Murky foreign shocker has a few moments, depending on which of several re-edited versions you see. AKA: **Virgin Among the Living Dead.** (Dir: Jess Franco, 90 mins.)†

Amorous Adventures of Moll Flanders, The (Great Britain, 1965)*** Kim Novak, Richard Johnson, George Sanders. Daniel Defoe's classic tale about a gorgeous 18th-century female who stops at nothing to achieve money and social position comes off as a poor man's *Tom Jones* but it's fun all the same. Superb costumes and atmospheric settings. (Dir: Terence Young, 126 mins.)

Amorous Mr. Prawn, The (Great Britain, 1962)**½ Joan Greenwood, Cecil Parker, Ian Carmichael, Dennis Price. General about to retire hasn't enough money, so while he's away his wife converts his HQ into a vacation spot for salmon fishermen. Mildly amusing comedy. (Dir: Anthony Kimmins, 89 mins.)

Amos (MTV 1985)*** Kirk Douglas,

Elizabeth Montgomery, Pat Morita, James Sloyan, Ray Walston, Dorothy McGuire. Douglas shines as an old baseball coach who finds himself confined to a nursing home where strange things are happening. There are some surprises in this Gray Power mystery story that should keep you intrigued. (Dir: Michael Tuchner, 104 mins.)†

Amsterdam Kill, The (1978)**½ Robert Mitchum, Bradford Dillman, Keye Luke, Leslie Nielsen, Richard Egan. Drug traffic drama, with Mitchum as a narc busted for embezzling to support a habit of his own. The film opens with some well-tempoed plotting before losing itself in pointless, arbitrary action sequences. (Dir: Robert Clouse, 93 mins.)†

Amsterdamned (Holland, 1988)**½ Huub Stapel, Monique van de Ven, Hidde Maas. Don't get too close to those canals—they're home to a surly skindiver prone to attacking anyone who wanders into his reach. Silly as it sounds, a few good action scenes and lots of Dutch scenery make it a change of pace. (Dir: Dick Maas, 114 mins.)†

Amy (1981)*** Jenny Agutter, Barry Newman, Kathleen Nolan, Chris Robinson, Margaret O'Brien, Nanette Fabray. Pleasing Disney adventure about an independent-minded woman who turns her back on marriage to find fulfillment as a teacher in a school for the handicapped. Neither preachy nor sentimental; ideal family fare. (Dir: Vincent McEveety, 100 mins.)†

Amy Prentiss: Baptism of Fire (MTV 1974)** Jessica Walter, William Shatner, Peter Haskell. The pilot for a series about a woman chief of detectives played by Jessica Walter. (Dir: Jeffrey Hayden, 72 mins.)

Ana and the Wolves (Spain, 1972)*** Geraldine Chaplin, Jose Vivo, Jose Marie-Prada, Fernando Fernan-Gomez. An English governess becomes the ultimate female fantasy of three sexually rabid sons of the hideously mean-spirited woman for whom she works. Director Carlos Saura's anti-Franco allegory (each boy represents an aspect of that repressive regime) passed Franco's censors because they thought it simply absurd. Chaplin is wonderful as a kind of politically abused Cinderella. (100 mins.)

Anastasia (1956)*** Ingrid Bergman, Yul Brynner, Helen Hayes. Absorbing drama of an amnesiac girl in Germany who may or may not be the daughter of Czar Nicholas II of Russia. Excellently acted, won Miss Bergman her second Oscar award. (Dir: Anatole Litvak, 105 mins.)

Anastasia: The Mystery of Anna (MTV 1986)*** Amy Irving, Olivia de Havilland, Edward Fox, Rex Harrison, Omar Sharif, Jan Niklas, Susan Lucci, Claire Bloom. By now everyone knows the story of the woman who claimed she was the Grand Duchess Anastasia, daughter of the last Czar of Russia. However, this four-hour miniseries also recreates the events leading to the slaughter of Czar Nicholas's family. (Dir: Marvin Chomsky, 208 mins.)

Anatomist, The (Great Britain, 1961)**½ Alastair Sim, George Cole. Gruesome story of a Scots doctor who procures bodies for his medical experiments. Good cast, good fare for thriller fans. (Dir: Leonard William, 73 mins.)

Anatomy of a Marriage (France-Italy, 1964)** Marie-Jose Nat, Jacques Charrier. A failed marriage from two points of view. Overlong, superficial, but intermittently interesting. (Dir: Andre Cayatte, 112 mins.)

Anatomy of a Murder (1959)***½ James Stewart, Lee Remick, Ben Gazzara, Joseph Welch, Arthur O'Connell, Eve Arden, George C. Scott, Murray Hamilton. Michigan lawyer defends an Army lieutenant on a murder charge after the man's wife had been raped. Engrossing fare. (Dir: Otto Preminger, 160 mins.)†

Anatomy of an Illness (MTV 1984)**½ Ed Asner, Eli Wallach, Millie Perkins. An account of editor-lecturer Norman Cousins's winning battle against a painful disease using laughter, vitamin C, and determined cheer. Cousins's decision to fight the illness with the mind instead of drugs is a well-told story, although not particularly suited to visual drama. (Dir: Richard T. Heffron, 98 mins.)

Anatomy of a Seduction (MTV 1979)**½ Susan Flannery, Jameson Parker, Rita Moreno. An older woman–younger man love affair is explored in this glossy soap opera, with a couple of moments of genuine emotion. Flannery heads the cast as a beautiful 40-year-old divorced mother who takes up with her best friend's 20-year-old son. (Dir: Steven Hilliard Stern, 104 mins.)†

Anatomy of the Syndicate—See: **Big Operator, The**

Anchors Aweigh (1945)*** Gene Kelly, Frank Sinatra, Kathryn Grayson, Dean Stockwell, Jose Iturbi. Even director George Sidney can't mix audacity and simple lack of taste to put over all of this MGM musical about two sailors on leave; but Sinatra and Kelly manage to sell a bit of it, especially when Sinatra sings and Kelly dances with Jerry the cartoon mouse. (140 mins.)†

And Baby Makes Six (MTV 1979)**½ Colleen Dewhurst, Warren Oates. Dewhurst plays Mother Earth splendidly. Her Anna, a middle-aged mother with grown children, is pregnant. Loving husband doesn't want another child; Anna, who does, is strong, loving, the family peacemaker—in short, the ideal mom. Sequel: *Baby Comes Home*. (Dir: Waris Hussein, 104 mins.)†

And Baby Makes Three (1949)** Robert Young, Barbara Hale. Foolish comedy about a recently divorced couple who discover that they are to be parents. Good performances. (Dir: Henry Lewis, 83 mins.)

Anderson's Angels—See: **Chesty Anderson, U.S. Navy**

Anderson Tapes, The (1971)*** Sean Connery, Dyan Cannon, Martin Balsam, Alan King. Lively, suspenseful crime caper with a gimmick. Thief plans to rob an entire Fifth Avenue apartment house. Exciting; the acting is uniformly good. Director Sidney Lumet uses New York locations well. (98 mins.)†

Andersonville Trial, The (MTV 1970)***½ Martin Sheen, William Shatner, Buddy Ebsen, Richard Basehart, Cameron Mitchell. Superb drama recreating MacKinlay Kantor's Pulitzer Prize–winning book about the notorious Civil War prison camp in Georgia where nearly 15,000 Union soldiers died. Director George C. Scott has fashioned a realistic and gripping account of the war-crimes trial of the camp's administrators. (150 mins.)†

And God Created Woman (France, 1957)**½ Brigitte Bardot, Curt Jurgens, Jean-Louis Trintignant. B.B. was an immediate hit in this tale of a family of sexually preoccupied men who openly and understandably lust after her. (Dir: Roger Vadim, 92 mins.)†

And God Created Woman (1988)** Rebecca De Mornay, Vincent Spano, Frank Langella, Donovan Leitch. Not a remake of the Bardot sensation, but a vehicle for the charms of De Mornay. She plays a sleek ex-con who carries on an affair with a paunchy senatorial candidate (Langella) while married to a solid respectable sort. Roger Vadim is as incompetent a director as ever; Rebecca does have a singularly erotic presence despite the weaknesses in the script. (100 mins.)†

And Hope to Die (France, 1972)* Robert Ryan, Jean-Louis Trintignant, Aldo Ray. Trintignant is being pursued by gypsies when he meets Ryan, who is a father figure for a gang of mental misfits. (Dir: Rene Clement, 99 mins.)†

And I Alone Survived (MTV 1978)**½ Blair Brown, David Ackroyd. True story about a gutsy young lady who survived an air crash in the Sierra Nevadas. (Dir: Billy Graham, 104 mins.)†

... And Justice for All (1979)**½ Al Pacino, Jack Warden, John Forsythe, Christine Lahti, Jeffrey Tambor. Pacino rises above the melodramatics here with a fine performance as a struggling Baltimore lawyer forced to defend a cold-hearted judge (Forsythe) on a rape charge. Pacino effectively conveys his frustration at the "unjust" legal system, where the innocent are jailed and the guilty are set free. (Dir: Norman Jewison, 118 mins.)†

And Millions Will Die (1973)** Richard Basehart, Susan Strasberg, Leslie Nielsen. Adventure yarn supplies some suspense as a team of scientists try to unearth a dead madman's plan to destroy Hong Kong. (Dir: Leslie Martinson, 104 mins.)

And No One Could Save Her (MTV 1973)** Lee Remick, Milo O'Shea. Dublin locations highlight this tale. A wealthy American woman comes to Ireland looking for her husband, who has disappeared. (Dir: Kevin Billington, 74 mins.)

And Nothing but the Truth (Great Britain, 1984)*** Glenda Jackson, Jon Finch, Kenneth Colley, James Connelly. A bristling British drama indicting the corporate structure that inhibits television reporters from presenting complete and "objective" news reporting. A sound and well-rounded treatment, and the film does not opt for easy answers or happy endings. (Dir: Karl Francis, 90 mins.)†

And Now for Something Completely Different (1972)*** Graham Chapman, John Cleese, Eric Idle, Terry Jones, Michael Palin, Carol Cleveland, Connie Booth. A collection of skits from Monty Python's Flying Circus which dares to insult the British Army, Her Majesty, guidance counselors, and baby carriages. Deemed a threat to social order and public gravity, the film has one irretrievable drawback—it ends. (Dir: Ian MacNaughton, 89 mins.)†

And Now Miguel (1966)*** Pat Cardi, Michael Ansara, Guy Stockwell. Young son of a sheepherder tries to prove that he's old enough to go along on grazing treks. Refreshing entertainment for all the family. (Dir: James Clark, 95 mins.)

And Now My Love (France, 1975)***½ Marthe Keller, Andre Dussolier, Charles Denner. Another bit of froth by France's cockeyed optimist, director Claude Lelouch. Can a Jewish princess with Marxist ideas and a lumpen individualist with bourgeois aspirations fall in love and live happily ever after? (121 mins.)†

And Now the Screaming Starts (Great Britain, 1973)**½ Peter Cushing, Herbert Lom, Patrick Magee, Stephanie Beacham. A curse involving a severed hand hangs heavy over the pregnant bride of the lord of a British manor house. Veteran horror director Roy Ward Baker creates a suitable Gothic mood. (91 mins.)†

And Now Tomorrow (1944)**½ Loretta Young, Alan Ladd. Corny story about a romance between a deaf girl and her doctor. (Dir: Irving Pichel, 85 mins.)

And Quiet Flows the Don (U.S.S.R., 1958)*** Ellina Bystritskaya, Pytor Glbov, Zinaida Kirienko. A small Russian village is the setting for this visual ode to life during and after WWI. The character studies are strong, and director Sergei Gerasimov stages some grand action sequences, including a Cossack charge that is as good as any ever filmed. (107 mins.)

Andrei Rublev (U.S.S.R., 1966)**** Anatoly Solonitsin, Ivan Lapikov, Nikolai Grinko, Nikolai Sergeyev. Director Andrei Tarkovsky's masterpiece, a film about the legendary 15th-century icon painter that explores the deeper role of an artist caught up in the social and political turmoil of his times. Co-written by Tarkovsky and Andrei Konchalovsky, the film is shot in both black and white and color, with sweeping camera movement and stunning performances. A must-see! (185 mins.)†

Andrews' Raiders—See: **Great Locomotive Chase, The**

Androcles and the Lion (1952)*** Alan Young, Jean Simmons, Victor Mature, Robert Newton, Maurice Evans. Hardly Shaw at his best, but the combination of physical comedy and epigrammatic discourse is stimulating. A superb ensemble give the maximum in droll line readings. (Dir: Chester Erskine, 98 mins.)†

Android (1984)**½ Klaus Kinski, Don Opper, Brie Howard. Imaginative low-budget sci-fi about a human clone who exhibits more humanity than many of the real people he meets. If only his creator hadn't tampered with him, he might not have picked up some of mankind's less endearing traits. (Dir: Aaron Lipstadt, 81 mins.)†

Andromeda Strain, The (1971)***½ James Olson, Arthur Hill, Kate Reid, David Wayne. Excellent sci-fi tale based on the popular novel by Michael Crichton. A remote spot in New Mexico is contaminated when a satellite crashes there and a team of four top scientists fight to discover a solution. Interesting throughout. (Dir: Robert Wise, 130 mins.)†

And Soon the Darkness (Great Britain, 1970)** Pamela Franklin, Michele Dotrice. Two British girls are alone on a bicycle holiday in France. When one girl is missing, the other girl panics. The buildup is breathtaking, but with no definitive denouement the film fizzles into disappointment. (Dir: Robert Fuest, 98 mins.)†

And So They Were Married (1936)*** Melvyn Douglas, Mary Astor, Edith Fellows, Jackie Moran, Dorothy Stickney, Donald Meek. Single parents Douglas and Astor fall in love, but are broken up by their kids—who then change their minds and struggle to get the duo back together. Warm comedy with a light touch. (Dir: Elliott Nugent, 74 mins.)

And So They Were Married (1944)*** Simone Simon, James Ellison. Screwball comedy about a girl who finds that too many keys to her apartment had been given out during wartime and the romantic complications that ensue. Watch for Robert Mitchum in a bit role. AKA: **Johnny Doesn't Live Here Anymore.** (Dir: Joe May, 79 mins.)

And the Angels Sing (1944)**½ Betty Hutton, Fred MacMurray. Story of some singing sisters and the band leader who discovers them. Routine musical but Betty sings one of her biggest hits, ''My Rocking Horse Ran Away.'' (Dir: George Marshall, 96 mins.)

And Then There Were None (1945)**** Barry Fitzgerald, Walter Huston, June Duprez, Louis Hayward, Judith Anderson. Based on an Agatha Christie thriller, this mystery blends equal parts humor and suspense into an entertaining yarn in which diverse characters are lured to a remote island, with lethal results. (Dir: Rene Clair, 98 mins.)†

And the Sea Will Tell (MTV 1991)*** Richard Crenna, Rachel Ward, Hart Bochner, Susan Blakely, Diedre Hall, James Brolin. A gripping, grisly murder story based on a real-life incident. Richard Crenna plays famed attorney Vincent Bugliosi, who takes on the defense of a woman accused of conspiracy and murder, along with her lover. Flashbacks flesh out what happened and the case plays out like a mystery story. (Dir: Paul Wendkos, 192 mins.)

And the Ship Sails On (Italy, 1984)*** Barbara Jefford, Freddie Jones, Janet Suzman. Director Federico Fellini's dazzling visual style is full of surprises; a memorial cruise in honor of a deceased diva is interrupted by a motley bunch of Serbian refugees. (128 mins.)†

And the Wild, Wild Women (Italy, 1960)*** Anna Magnani, Giulietta Masina. This Italian film drama about a women's prison is altered for this dubbed version but it still has two of Italy's great film stars to make it worthwhile. (Dir: Renato Castellani, 85 mins.)

Andy (1965)**½ Norman Alden, Ann Wedgeworth. Mentally retarded son of Greek immigrants struggles to communicate with people. Some powerful moments, deserves credit for trying. (Dir: Richard Sarafian, 86 mins.)

Andy and the Airwave Rangers (1989)*½ Randy Josselyn, John Franklin, Jessica Puscas. Babysitter and his little sister

33

are imprisoned in a fantasyland inside their television set by an evil wizard. Ripoff of *The Wizard of Oz* by way of *Labyrinth*, featuring lots of footage recycled by producer Roger Corman from his 1983 *Space Rangers*. AKA: **Andy Colby's Incredible Video Adventure**. (Dir: Deborah Brock, 75 mins.)†

Andy Colby's Incredible Video Adventure —See: **Andy and the Airwave Rangers**

Andy Hardy series. A dated, somewhat charming portrait of American family life that was not much of a reflection of contemporary realities during the WWII years. The unsophisticated series, a favorite of MGM bigwig Louis B. Mayer, began with *A Family Affair* (1937) and ended with *Andy Hardy Comes Home* (1958). In addition to the titles reviewed below, fans will want to see: *The Courtship of Andy Hardy, The Hardys Ride High, Judge Hardy and Son, Judge Hardy's Children, Life Begins for Andy Hardy, Love Laughs at Andy Hardy, Out West with the Hardys,* and *You're Only Young Once.*

Andy Hardy Comes Home (1958)**½ Mickey Rooney, Pat Breslin. Andy Hardy is all grown up and a successful lawyer when he returns to his home town. Andy Hardy film fans will get a kick out of seeing the cast reunited. (Dir: Howard Koch, 80 mins.)

Andy Hardy Gets Spring Fever (1939)**½ Mickey Rooney, Lewis Stone, Cecilia Parker, Fay Holden, Ann Rutherford, Sara Haden. Mild amusement from the Hardy clan as Andy develops a crush on his drama teacher. (Dir: Woody Van Dyke, 85 mins.)

Andy Hardy Meets a Debutante (1940)**½ Mickey Rooney, Judy Garland. Mickey is still chasing attractive MGM starlets in this one. Good Andy Hardy comedy. (Dir: George Seitz, 86 mins.)

Andy Hardy's Blonde Trouble (1944)** Mickey Rooney, Lewis Stone. Andy's college days are complicated by a pair of luscious blonde co-eds who happen to be twins. (Dir: George Seitz, 107 mins.)

Andy Hardy's Double Life (1942)** Mickey Rooney, Lewis Stone. Andy goes to college in this one. The only important thing about this one is that one of Andy's flirtations is newcomer Esther Williams. (Dir: George Seitz, 92 mins.)

Andy Hardy's Private Secretary (1941)**½ Mickey Rooney, Lewis Stone. Andy gets out of high school in this one and his secretary is played by a lovely newcomer with a delightful voice named Kathryn Grayson. (Dir: George Seitz, 101 mins.)

And Your Name Is Jonah (MTV 1979)*** Sally Struthers, James Woods, Jeffrey Bravin. A heartbreaking, sometimes poignant story about a seven-year-old deaf child originally diagnosed as mentally retarded. (Dir: Richard Michaels, 104 mins.)

Andy Warhol's Bad (1976)*** Carroll Baker, Perry King, Susan Tyrrell. A delightfully gross comedy with Baker as a housewife who's head of a gang of assassins for hire: all spacy ingenues. Not for all tastes, and quite slick compared to early Warhol galleries of grotesquery, but if approached in the right spirit the film evokes high comedy in the lowest depths. Directed by the able Jed Johnson. (105 mins.)

Andy Warhol's Dracula (Italy-France, 1974)**½ Udo Kier, Joe Dallesandro, Vittorio De Sica, Arno Juerging. Count Dracula travels from Rumania to Italy in search of virgins' blood in this campy, sexy, and gory version of the vampire legend. Stud Dallesandro is on the scene to save the virgins by deflowering them. Some sources suggest that this and *Andy Warhol's Frankenstein* were directed by Antonio Margheriti, with credited director Paul Morrissey serving a supervisory function. AKA: **Blood for Dracula**. (106 mins.)

Andy Warhol's Frankenstein (Italy-Germany-France, 1973)* Udo Kier, Joe Dallesandro, Monique Van Vooren. While the mad Baron is putting together (limb by limb) a male zombie to mate with his female creature, his sex-starved wife is keeping Dallesandro very busy in the castle's bedchambers. Typical Warhol camp, but at times too revolting and gruesome even for the strongest stomachs. Shot in 3D. AKA: **Flesh for Frankenstein**. (Dir: Paul Morrissey, 94 mins.)

Andy Warhol's Women—See: **Women in Revolt**

Angel (1937)** Marlene Dietrich, Herbert Marshall, Melvyn Douglas. A diplomat's wife has an affair with a stranger and then meets him again. This one will disappoint you. (Dir: Ernst Lubitsch, 90 mins.)

Angel (Ireland, 1984)—See: **Danny Boy**

Angel (1984)** Donna Wilkes, Dick Shawn, Cliff Gorman, Susan Tyrrell. How many teenage honor students do you know who are hookers? This troubled teen has more trouble than worrying about her former clients showing up at the senior prom. Soon, many of the ladies of the night are being bumped off. Will Angel be next? Not to be taken too seriously, but a must-see for exploitation fans. Sequel: *Avenging Angel* (Dir: Robert Vincent O'Neil, 93 mins.)†

Angel III: The Final Chapter (1988)* Mitzi Kapture, Maud Adams, Mark Blankfield, Richard Roundtree, Dick Miller. The former prostitute goes back on the streets to rescue her sister. Rotten. (Dir: Tom DeSimone, 99 mins.)†

Angela (Canada, 1977)** Sophia Loren, Steve Railsback, John Huston, John Vernon. Modern day Oedipus tale. Loren discovers her young lover is really her son, whom she believed was killed as a baby by Mafia chieftain Huston. (Dir: Boris Sagal, 100 mins.)†

Angel and the Badman (1946)***½ John Wayne, Gail Russell, Harry Carey, Irene Rich. A notorious gunslinger is reformed by the love of a Quaker girl. Western has action, fine scenery, and a good plot; superior entertainment of its type. (Dir: James Edward Grant, 100 mins.)†

Angel, Angel, Down We Go (1970)*½ Jennifer Jones, Charles Aidman, Holly Near, Roddy McDowall, Lou Rawls. A camped-up slice of decadence. This lurid saga deals with a sexy ne'er-do-well who seduces an entire family, although his attentions can prove to be fatal. AKA: Cult of the Damned. (Dir: Robert Thom, 103 mins.)

Angel at My Table, An (New Zealand, 1990)*** Kerry Fox, Alexian Keogh, Karen Ferguson, Iris Churn. A celebration of survival in the face of tragedy. Director Campion's adaptation of Janet Frame's autobiographies is a poignant and humorous study of a woman who, because of a quirk of fate, spent eight years in a mental home. Originally shown on New Zealand television. (Dir: Jane Campion, 150 mins.)

Angel Baby (1961)*** Salome Jens, George Hamilton, Mercedes McCambridge. Effective drama about the tent-circuit evangelists who travel through small towns preaching salvation for sinners. Jens is impressive as a mute who miraculously gets her voice back and falls in love with the young preacher who she thinks is responsible. (Dir: Paul Wendkos, 97 mins.)

Angel City (MTV 1980)*** Ralph Waite, Paul Winfield, Mitch Ryan. The lives of West Virginia mountain folk working the fields of Florida are a series of misfortunes and deceptions, including cruel labor contracts. (Dir: Philip Leacock, 104 mins.)†

Angel Dusted (MTV 1981)**½ Jean Stapleton, Arthur Hill, John Putch, Darlene Craviotto, Percy Rodrigues. Jean Stapleton is hard to resist as a worried, understanding, frightened mom whose boy goes berserk after an encounter with angel dust. (Dir: Dick Lowry, 104 mins.)

Angèle (France, 1934)*** Orane Demazis, Fernandel, Henri Poupon. Marcel Pagnol, author of the novels and plays on which *Jean de Florette, Manon of the Spring* and *Fanny* were based, wrote and directed this recently rediscovered melodrama about a provincial farm girl who runs away from her domineering father to the big city. Fans of the above films are sure to enjoy it. (150 mins.)†

Angel Face (1952)**½ Jean Simmons, Robert Mitchum, Herbert Marshall. A moody study in perverse psychology (immeasurably enhanced by Jean Simmons's icy elegance here). She plays a beautiful woman whose outward appearance masks her murderous impulses. (Dir: Otto Preminger, 90 mins.)

Angel from Texas, An (1940)**½ Jane Wyman, Ronald Reagan, Eddie Albert. Occasionally cute, Grade B comedy about the yokels who take the city slickers. (Dir: Ray Enright, 69 mins.)

Angel Heart (1987)***½ Mickey Rourke, Robert De Niro, Lisa Bonet, Charlotte Rampling. Disturbing thriller has a Brooklyn private eye hired by a mysterious stranger (De Niro) to collect a debt. His search takes him to Louisiana voodoo country where he uncovers some unsettling truths. (Dir: Alan Parker, 113 mins.)†

Angel in Exile (1948)*** John Carroll, Adele Mara. Crooks plan to hide stolen gold in a small town and then "discover" it, but the townspeople look upon the gold as a miracle. Good melodrama. (Dirs: Allan Dwan, Philip Ford, 90 mins.)

Angel in Green (MTV 1987)*½ Bruce Boxleitner, Susan Dey, Milo O'Shea. Ludicrous romance. All-around good-gal nun Dey has a fling with Special Forces captain Boxleitner on a South Sea island during a rebel insurrection. (Dir: Marvin J. Chomsky, 96 mins.)

Angel in My Pocket (1969)**½ Andy Griffith, Lee Meriwether. A midwestern town's many problems become Reverend Andy's personal responsibilities. TV faces in the supporting cast include Jerry Van Dyke, Kay Medford, and Edgar Buchanan. (Dir: Alan Rafkin, 105 mins.)

Angel Levine, The (1970)** Zero Mostel, Harry Belafonte. A black angel comes to earth to redeem an aging Jew who has lost his faith. Overdrawn performances, abundance of supersentimentality. (Dir: Jan Kadar, 104 mins.)

Angel of Death (1987)* Christopher Mitchum, Susan Andrews, Fernando Rey, Howard Vernon, Dora Doll. Nazi hunter battles an evil plot by war criminal Josef Mengele to turn South America into the Fourth Reich. Atrocious nonsense. (Dir: "A. Frank Drew White" [Jess Franco], 90 mins.)†

Angel of H.E.A.T. (1982)** Marilyn Chambers, Stephen Johnson, Mary Woronov. Chambers exits the green door and steps into Bond territory with this trashy but fun spy comedy. (Dir: Myrl A. Schreibman, 93 mins.)†

Angel of Vengeance—See: War Cat

Angelo, My Love (1983)*** Angelo Evans, Michael Evans, Ruthie Evans, Tony Evans, Steve Tsingonoff. Charming neo-realism about the life of a young gypsy in New York City. Fascinating portrayal of a side of New York that very few people are aware of. (Dir: Robert Duvall, 115 mins.)†

Angel on My Shoulder (1946)*** Paul Muni, Claude Rains, Anne Baxter. A deceased gangster makes a deal with the Devil to return to earth. Enjoyable fantasy. (Dir: Archie Mayo, 101 mins.)†

Angel on My Shoulder (MTV 1980)** Peter Strauss, Richard Kiley, Barbara Hershey. A remake of the superior '46 Paul Muni movie. Strauss plays a '40s gangster who is executed and comes back to earth today in the body of a look-alike D.A. (Dir: John Berry, 104 mins.)†

Angel on the Amazon (1948)*½ George Brent, Vera Ralston, Brian Aherne. Constance Bennett. After crash landing in the jungle, a pilot falls in love with a beautiful girl with a mysterious (and lengthy) past. Far-fetched, badly acted. (Dir: John Auer, 86 mins.)

Angels' Alley (1948)** Bowery Boys, Mary Gordon, Frankie Darro, Nestor Paiva, Gabriel Dell. A good deal of the movie portrays the Mahoneys' family life; and Slip's Mama (Mary Gordon) makes us feel right at home. Unfortunately, the storyline about Slip taking the rap for his cousin doesn't ring true. (Dir: William Beaudine, 67 mins.)

Angels from Hell (1968)*½ Tom Stern, Arlene Martel, Ted Markland, Stephen Oliver. Brutal, mindless action pic about a vet who uses his combat experience to form a rebel band and battle the cops. (Dir: Bruce Kessler, 86 mins.)†

Angels Hard as They Come (1971)*** Scott Glenn, Charles Dierkap, Gary Busey, Janet Wood. Leaders of two Hell's Angels clubs clash in a ghost town populated by hippies in director Joe Viola's mythic story of bikers on the run, framed by references to the 19th-century American West. Produced and co-written by Jonathan Demme. Busey's film debut. (90 mins.)

Angels in Disguise (1949)**½ Bowery Boys, Gabriel Dell, Bernard Gorcey. Slip relates how he and Sach were in hot pursuit of the Loop Gang who shot their pal, Gabe. (Dir: Jean Yarbrough, 63 mins.)

Angels in the Outfield (1951)***½ Paul Douglas, Janet Leigh, Keenan Wynn. Enjoyable comedy fantasy about a baseball team and an orphan who sees angels. (Dir: Clarence Brown, 99 mins.)

Angels of Darkness (Italy, 1957)*½ Linda Darnell, Valentina Cortesa, Giulietta Masina, Anthony Quinn. Three prostitutes are evicted from the bordello where they were living and go on to find greater miseries. Depressing and unpleasant. (Dir: Giuseppe Amato, 84 mins.)

Angels of the City (1989)**½ Kelly Galindo, Cynthia Cheston, Michael Ferrare, Lawrence-Hilton Jacobs. Two coeds venture into the seamy side of L.A. for a sorority prank and witness a brutal shooting, making them the killers' next target. Action exploitation with some novel elements, a respectable directing debut for co-star Lawrence-Hilton Jacobs. (89 mins.)†

Angels of the Streets (France, 1943)*** Jany Holt, Renée Fauré, Sylvie, Mila Parely. The first film from director Robert Bresson. Fauré is a young novitiate who tries to redeem a paroled murderer for the Catholic church. Filled with the religious and existential touches that would become the hallmark of Bresson's later work. (73 mins.)

Angels One Five (Great Britain, 1952)*** Jack Hawkins, Michael Denison. Story of the Royal Air Force in the dark days of 1940. Authentic, well-made war drama. (Dir: George O'Ferrall, 98 mins.)

Angels Over Broadway (1940)***½ Rita Hayworth, Douglas Fairbanks, Jr., Thomas Mitchell. Good performances and top-notch Ben Hecht screenplay make this story about a group of oddballs in a Broadway cafe fascinating viewing. (Dirs: Lee Garmes, Ben Hecht, 80 mins.)†

Angels Wash Their Faces (1939)**½ Ann Sheridan, Dead End Kids. Mildly entertaining sequel to Angels with Dirty Faces. (Dir: Ray Enright, 90 mins.)

Angels' Wild Women (1972)* Kent Taylor, Regina Carrol, Maggie Bemby, Ross Hagen, Vicki Volante. Nearly plotless amalgam of motorcycle and hippie movie clichés involving a bevy of biker babes and the desert commune of an evil guru. Some clever photography, but this makes little sense even by director Al (Dracula vs. Frankenstein) Adamson's minimal standards. AKA: Rough Riders. (85 mins.)†

Angels with Dirty Faces (1938)***½ James Cagney, Pat O'Brien, Humphrey Bogart, Ann Sheridan, Huntz Hall, Leo Gorcey, Billy Halop. Exciting story of two men whose roots were in the same gutter. One becomes a priest; the other, a killer. (Dir: Michael Curtiz, 97 mins.)†

Angel Unchained (1972)*½ Don Stroud, Luke Askew, Larry Bishop, Tyne Daly, Aldo Ray, Bill McKinney. Bikers and hippies team up to fight nasty redneck types. No doubt intended as a sincere plea for brotherhood of the counter cultures. Chain it up. (Dir: Lee Madden, 92 mins.)

Angel Who Pawned Her Harp, The (Great Britain, 1954)**½ Diane Cilento, Felix Aylmer, Jerry Desmonde, Alfie Bass. Whimsical British social comedy-fantasy depends entirely on the beauty and charm of Cilento, totally believable as an angel who comes to Earth to study human behavior. (Dir: Alan Bromly, 76 mins.)

Angel Wore Red, The (1960)** Ava Gardner, Dirk Bogarde, Joseph Cotten. A serious attempt to mount a love story against the turmoil of the Spanish Civil War of the 1930s. Disappointing despite a fairly literate script and earnest performances. Bogarde plays a Catholic priest who gives up his beliefs and returns to the everyday world. (Dir: Nunnally Johnson, 99 mins.)

Angi Vera (Hungary, 1978)**** Veronika Papp, Tamas Dunai, Erzsi Pasztor, Eva Szabo. Searing indictment of the oppressive intellectual and moral climate in a Communist society. That this film was made in Hungary, about the repressive nature of the Communist party structure and activities there three decades earlier, makes it all the more powerful. Focuses on an upwardly mobile 18-year-old girl trying to climb the political ladder in the Stalinist regime in '48. (Dir: Pal Gabor, 96 mins.)

Angry Breed, The (1969)* Jan Sterling, James MacArthur, William Windom. Incredible plot concerning a returned Vietnam veteran who wants to be an actor. (Dir: David Commons, 89 mins.)

Angry Harvest (Poland, 1985)*** Armin Mueller-Stahl, Elisabeth Trissenaar, Wojtech Pszoniak. Powerful drama about a farmer during WWII, who encounters an escaped Jew after she jumps from a death train, then hides her in his cellar. Sexually repressed, the farmer falls in love with her, and keeps her as his prisoner. (Dir: Agnieszka Holland, 102 mins.)†

Angry Hills, The (Great Britain, 1959)**½ Robert Mitchum, Gia Scala, Stanley Baker. Based on a Leon Uris novel, this tale concerns the Greek Resistance during WWII. (Dir: Robert Aldrich, 105 mins.)

Angry Red Planet, The (1960)*½ Gerald Mohr, Les Tremayne, Nora Hayden. Spaceship returning from Mars meets with disaster (Dir: Ib Melchoir, 94 mins.)†

Angry Silence, The (Great Britain, 1960)*** Richard Attenborough, Michael Craig, Pier Angeli, Bernard Lee, Laurence Naismith, Brian Bedford, Oliver Reed. Effective but propagandistic antiunion drama about one man who becomes a pariah because he defies a union's strike decision. (Dir: Guy Green, 95 mins.)

Angst—See: Fear (1955)

Anguish (Spain, 1988)**½ Zelda Rubinstein, Michael Lerner, Talia Paul, Angel Jove. Unusual horror drama begins as a straightforward psycho film, which turns out to be a film being watched by an audience that finds itself stalked by a madman. Overwrought and silly, but with a number of compelling ideas and scary moments. (Dir: Bigas Luna, 91 mins.)†

Animal Behavior (1988)* Karen Allen, Armand Assante, Holly Hunter, Josh Mostel, Richard Libertini. Perfectly awful romantic comedy that looks to have been edited with kitchen scissors. Allen is grating as a frigid researcher in the title subject whose heart warms to nerdy musician Assante; Hunter is equally shrill in a supporting role. (Dir: "H. Anne Riley" [Jenny Bowen, Kjehl Rasmussen], 90 mins.)†

Animal Crackers (1930)*** The Four Marx Brothers, Margaret Dumont. Worth watching just to see Groucho strut his way through "Hooray for Captain Spaulding." Wacky screenplay by Morrie Ryskind, based on the hit Broadway musical he wrote with George S. Kaufman. (Dir: Victor Heerman, 98 mins.)†

Animal Farm (Great Britain, 1954)** This animated version of Orwell's satire on Soviet history tends to emphasize the old-maid aspects of his leftward criticism, while banalizing his marvelous imagery. Strictly from *Cliff Notes*. (Dirs: John Halas, Joy Batchelor, 75 mins.)†

Animal House—See: National Lampoon's Animal House

Animal Kingdom, The (1932)*** Leslie Howard, Ann Harding, Myrna Loy, Neil Hamilton, William Gargan. Play by Philip Barry. Comedy-drama adapted from a Philip Barry play follows one of his favorite themes, as a idealistic publisher man is torn between an honest bohemian artist and a wealthy beauty, making a marriage that he comes to regret. (Dir: Edward H. Griffith, 85 mins.)

Animals, The (1971)** Henry Silva, Keenan Wynn, Michele Carey. A schoolteacher goes after the gang of desperadoes who raped her, with the aid of a helpful Apache. Raunchy western that reworks the standard "revenge" plotline, with a script by character actor Dick Bakalyan. (Dir: Ron Joy, 86 mins.)

Animals Are Beautiful People (South Africa, 1975)*** A rewarding documentary with lots of interesting tidbits and humorous asides. Its attitude toward all God's creatures is summed up in the title, but the footage is sufficiently sharp to keep the film from becoming too cute. By the director of *The Gods Must Be Crazy*. (Dir: Jamie Uys, 92 mins.)†

Animalympics (1979)**½ Voices of Gilda Radner, Billy Crystal, Harry Shearer. Cartoon take-off of the Olympics with animals taking part in various sporting events. Good for toddlers; but suffers from a surfeit of cuteness. (Dir: Steven Lisberger, 80 mins.)†

Anna (Italy, 1951)** Silvana Mangano, Raf Vallone, Vittorio Gassman. Nightclub singer who has become a nun thinks over the reason for her doing so. (Dir: Alberto Lattuada, 95 mins.)

Anna (1987)*** Sally Kirkland, Paulina Porizkova, Robert Fields, Gibby Brand, John Robert Tillotson. A wonderfully acted drama about an aging Czech movie star (Kirkland) who comes to the U.S. to find stateside stardom and instead ends up having her life and reputation swindled by a beautiful, struggling young actress (Porizkova). Original and absorbing look at the vagaries of fame, thanks to Kirkland's stunning performance and a screenplay that's both touching and witty. (Dir: Yurek Bogayevicz, 95 mins.)†

Anna and the King of Siam (1946)***½ Irene Dunne, Rex Harrison, Linda Darnell, Lee J. Cobb, Gale Sondergaard, Mikhail Rasumny. Non-musical basis for *The King and I*, with Harrison and Dunne exuding as much charm and star-power as Yul Brynner and Deborah Kerr in the musical film of '56. John Cromwell's direction is attentive to nuance; the charm of the story and the central relationship carry the film along. (128 mins.)

Annabel Takes a Tour (1938)*** Lucille Ball, Jack Oakie, Ruth Donnelly, Bradley Page, Ralph Forbes. A slightly higher quotient of laughs here than in the original *Affairs of Annabel*. Ball once again portrays a scatterbrained screen star tangling with her overly zealous press agent. (Dir: Lew Landers, 66 mins.)

Anna Christie (1930)*** Greta Garbo, Charles Bickford, Marie Dressler. This is where Garbo first spoke, saying "Gif me a viskey, ginger ale on the side, and don't be stingy, baby." The Eugene O'Neill play was always a pain, with the tag phrase "that old debbil sea" incanted almost as often as the words "pipe dream" in *The Iceman Cometh*. Slow but well acted by Garbo and the rest. (Dir: Clarence Brown, 90 mins.)†

Anna Karenina (1935)*** Greta Garbo, Fredric March, Basil Rathbone, Maureen O'Sullivan, Freddie Bartholomew. Tolstoy's story of an illicit romance in the imperial court of Russia is splendidly acted; a bit heavy in dialogue for modern tastes but Garbo compensates for a lot of things. (Dir: Clarence Brown, 95 mins.)†

Anna Karenina (Great Britain, 1948)**½ Vivien Leigh, Ralph Richardson. Tolstoy's immortal classic of the life and loves of a lady in old Russia. Elaborately produced, well-acted drama. (Dir: Julien Duvivier, 110 mins.)

Anna Karenina (MTV 1985)**½ Jacqueline Bisset, Christopher Reeve, Paul Scofield. The people and production values are handsome, but these trappings smother the story's grand passion. Reeve displays his elegant profile as lover Count Vronsky. Bisset has better luck as the smitten Anna giving up her son for her count, but the most compelling reason to watch is a rare screen appearance by Paul Scofield, portraying Anna's betrayed husband Karenin. (Dir: Simon Langton, 104 mins.)†

Anna Lucasta (1958)**½ Eartha Kitt, Sammy Davis, Jr. The hit Broadway show about a loose woman who tries to go straight when she falls for a sailor. The play starred an all-black cast, as does this film version. (Dir: Arnold Laven, 97 mins.)

Annapolis Story (1955)** John Derek, Diana Lynn. Two brothers, both midshipmen at Annapolis, vie for the same girl. Familiar. (Dir: Don Siegel, 81 mins.)†

Anna to the Infinite Power (1984)**½ Dina Merrill, Martha Byrne, Mark Patton. A standard, competently made shocker about supernatural forces at work on a twelve-year-old girl. (Dir: Robert Wiemer, 88 mins.)†

Anne of Green Gables (1934)*** Anne Shirley, Helen Westley, Tom Brown. A young girl begins to grow up when she must go live with her aunt in rural Nova Scotia. Entertaining version of the popular children's book by L. M. Montgomery. Sequel: *Anne of Windy Poplars*. (Dir: George Nicholls, Jr., 79 mins.)

Anne of Green Gables (Made for Canadian TV, 1985)**** Megan Follows, Colleen Dewhurst, Richard Farnsworth, Schuyler Grant. Enchanting adaptation of the children's classic. Follows is impossible to resist as Anne ("with an 'E'"), a dreamy young orphan who is adopted by a stern farm woman (Dewhurst) and her kindly brother (the impeccable Farnsworth). Anne's uncanny ability to charm even the stodgiest of her elders will prove captivating to viewers young and old, as will the breathtaking Canadian scenery. (Dir: Kevin Sullivan, 197 mins.)†

Anne of the Indies (1951)**½ Jean Peters, Louis Jourdan, Debra Paget. Lady pirate comes to the aid of a French ex-naval officer. Smart direction and some fast action; good fare for adventure devotees. (Dir: Jacques Tourneur, 81 mins.)

Anne of the Thousand Days (Great Britain, 1969)*** Richard Burton, Genevieve Bujold, Irene Papas, Anthony Quayle. Effective historical drama about England's King Henry the Eighth and his legendary romance with Anne Boleyn, quite wonderfully acted by Genevieve Bujold. (Dir: Charles Jarrott, 146 mins.)†

Anne of Windy Poplars (1940)**½ Anne Shirley, James Ellison, Henry Travers, Patric Knowles, Slim Summerville. In this sequel to *Anne of Green Gables,* our heroine copes with various trials as a new young teacher in a small town. (Dir: Jack Hively, 88 mins.)

Anne Trister (Canada, 1986)*** Albane Guilhe, Louise Marleau, Lucie Laurier, Guy Thauvette. The death of a young woman's father begins a downward emotional spiral that causes her to examine her religion (Judaism), her work (artist) and her sexuality; she leaves her male friend and falls in love with an older woman. Director Lea Pool has made a convincing, personal film about sorrow, loss, and change. (115 mins.)

Annie (1982)**½ Aileen Quinn, Carol Burnett, Albert Finney, Bernadette Peters, Tim Curry, Ann Reinking, Geoffrey Holder. Big, splashy screen version of the Broadway hit. Aileen Quinn as Annie comes across as much too showbiz oriented to make us truly care what happens to her. It's all there—the music, lyrics, and optimism that made "Annie" a comic strip tradition. (Dir: John Huston, 128 mins.)†

Annie Get Your Gun (1950)*** Betty Hutton, Howard Keel, Keenan Wynn. Film version of the hit Broadway musical, relating the story of sharpshooter Annie Oakley. The Irving Berlin tunes are great and the production lavish. (Dir: George Sidney, 107 mins.)†

Annie Hall (1977)**** Woody Allen, Diane Keaton, Shelley Duvall, Tony Roberts, Colleen Dewhurst, Christopher Walken. This is a marvelous film, directed and co-authored by Woody Allen. Our redheaded hero Alvy Singer has been in analysis for fifteen years, loves New York, and falls in love with Diane Keaton. Woody and co-author Marshall Brickman fire off an enormous number of comic salvos; the one-liners and the sight gags pay off brilliantly. A joy from start to finish! (94 mins.)†

Annie Oakley (1935)*** Barbara Stanwyck, Preston Foster, Melvyn Douglas, Pert Kelton, Andy Clyde. A modest, pleasant star vehicle for Stanwyck, with a soupçon of something extra by director George Stevens. As usual with Stevens, the plot (about the famous sharpshooter's romance) goes by the wayside, though individual sequences are memorable. (88 mins.)†

Annihilator, The (MTV 1986)** Mark Lindsay Chapman, Susan Blakely, Lisa Blount. An innocent fugitive on the run learns that airplane passengers have been transformed into alien "Dynamitards" (who look like their human selves). Violent sci-fi. (Dir: Michael Chapman, 104 mins.)

Annihilators, The (1985)½ Christopher Stone, Andy Wood, Lawrence Hilton-Jacob, Gerrit Graham, Paul Koslo. A group of Vietnam vets teach hapless citizens how to fight against urban sleaze-balls. (Dir: Charles Sellier, Jr., 87 mins.)†

Anniversary, The (Great Britain, 1968)**½ Bette Davis, Sheila Hancock. Mama Davis (with an eyepatch, no less) celebrates her anniversary, even though her husband has been dead for 10 years. Davis has a field day. (Dir: Roy Ward Baker, 95 mins.)

Ann Jillian Story, The (MTV 1988)**½ Ann Jillian, Tony Lo Bianco, Viveca Lindfors, George Touliatos. Jillian plays herself in a biopic that's half glitz and half affecting drama. The glitz surrounds her romance with an amorous, middle-aged cop (Lo Bianco in an unlikely romantic role); the emotion appears in the second half, which covers her mastectomy. (Dir: Corey Allen, 96 mins.)†

Ann Vickers (1933)** Irene Dunne, Bruce Cabot, Walter Huston, Conrad Nagel, Edna May Oliver. One of those assembly line unwed-mother flicks of the '30s. Dunne sucks back her tears as a female prison warden, and whose self-sacrifice nets her a noble judge by the windup. (Dir: John Cromwell, 72 mins.)†

Anonymous Venetian, The (Italy, 1970)**½ Tony Musante, Florinda Balkan, Toti Del Monte. The beauty of Venice steals the show in this tearjerker about an estranged couple who spend a single day together in that city recalling the ups and downs of their marriage. (Dir: Enrico Maria Salerno, 93 mins.)

A Nos Amours (France, 1983)**½ Sandrine Bonnaire, Dominique Besnehard, Maurice Pialat, Evelyn Ker. Disturbing but slow-paced tale about troubled adolescence. Burdened by a hellish home life, Suzanne (Bonnaire) is a young woman who, after talking herself into not being able to fall in love, falls into relentless promiscuity. (Dir: Maurice Pialat, 103 mins.)†

Another Country (Great Britain, 1984)***½ Rupert Everett, Colin Firth, Anna Massey. Absorbing drama based on the events that led to the treason and defection to Moscow by British spy Guy Burgess. It describes the unhappy boarding school existence of an upper-class homosexual whose humiliation, as the result of an indiscretion with another student, causes his radical conversion to Marxism. (Dir: Marek Kanievska, 90 mins.)†

Another Dawn (1937)**½ Errol Flynn, Kay Francis, Ian Hunter, Frieda Inescourt.

Married Francis must choose between husband and Flynn. Soapy exotic romance, replete with typhoons, love and mood music. (Dir: William Dieterle, 73 mins.)

Another Day (Hungary, 1982)***½ Jadwiga Jankowska-Cieslak, Grazyna Szapolowska, Jozef Kroner. After the Hungarian revolt of 1956, two female journalists fall in love, shattering their marriages and emotionally crippling their husbands. Director Karoly Makk, Hungary's elder cinema statesman, makes a plea for tolerance and against violence in this courageous, brilliant exploration of politics and sexuality. (109 mins.)

Another 48 HRS. (1990)**½ Eddie Murphy, Nick Nolte, Brion James, Kevin Tighe, Bernie Casey. Only the billing has changed in this sequel to *48 HRS.* that's more like a remake. There's still some boisterous fun from the team of Nolte and Murphy, but the film seems like a calculated attempt by talented filmmakers to make easy money by Giving the People What They Want. (Dir: Walter Hill, 95 mins.)†

Another Language (1933)*** Helen Hayes, Robert Montgomery, Louise Closser Hale, John Beal, Henry Travers, Margaret Hamilton. Biting social drama with a terrific performance from Hayes as a girl who marries into a snobbish family ruled by Hale. Donald Ogden Stewart and Herman J. Mankiewicz adapted the script from a play by Rose Franken. (Dir: Edward H. Griffith, 77 mins.)

Another Man, Another Chance (France-U.S., 1977)**½ James Caan, Genevieve Bujold, Jennifer Warren, Susan Tyrrell. Talented director Claude Lelouch comes a cropper in this muddled, pretentious yarn set in the American West in the 1870s. Caan, playing a widower whose wife has been raped and slain, meets Bujold, the young French widow of a murdered photographer. (128 mins.)†

Another Man's Poison (Great Britain, 1952)**½ Bette Davis, Gary Merrill. A blackmailer enters the scene with proof that a woman has murdered her husband, and forces her to do his bidding. Fairly interesting melodrama, good cast. (Dir: Irving Rapper, 89 mins.)

Another Part of the Forest (1948)*** Fredric March, Ann Blyth, Dan Duryea. Lillian Hellman's absorbing story of the Hubbard family, a band of ruthless Southern industrialists who hated each other but loved money. Prequel to *The Little Foxes*. (Dir: Michael Gordon, 107 mins.)

Another Thin Man (1939)*** William Powell, Myrna Loy. Not as sharp as the earlier efforts, but Powell and Loy were and still are the most delightful of screen sleuths. A guy who dreams of deaths

before they happen is causing the trouble in this one. (Dir: W. S. Van Dyke II, 105 mins.)†

Another Time, Another Place (Great Britain, 1958)** Lana Turner, Barry Sullivan, Sean Connery. Soapy stuff about a lady correspondent during World War II who engages in a hopeless love affair with a married man and suffers a breakdown when he's killed. (Dir: Lewis Allen, 98 mins.)

Another Time, Another Place (Great Britain, 1984)** Phyllis Logan, Giovanni Mauriello, Paul Young. A wartime romance full of travelogue scenery and subdued passions. A Scottish housewife wed to a dour older man risks her reputation when she has an affair with an Italian prisoner of war. The film's so resolutely commonplace and slow moving that our sympathies for this star-crossed pair are never fully engaged. (Dir: Michael Radford, 101 mins.)†

Another Woman (1988)*½ Gena Rowlands, Mia Farrow, Ian Holm, Blythe Danner, Martha Plimpton, John Houseman, Sandy Dennis, Gene Hackman, Betty Buckley. If Woody Allen the "Serious Director" has any fans left, this spiteful depiction of angst-ridden New York gentiles should drive them away. Why does Allen feel compelled to make dour movies about people he obviously despises? (81 mins.)†

À Nous la Liberté (France, 1931)**** Raymond Cordy, Henri Marchand, Rolla France. A delightful romp about freedom in an industrial state. Chaplin borrowed the assembly line gags for *Modern Times*; it's a tribute to both artists that the scene is equally inspired in both films. (Dir: Rene Clair, 97 mins.)†

Antarctica (Japan, 1983)*** Ken Takakura, Masako Natsume. Earnest nature drama about a Japanese scientific expedition that makes the difficult decision to leave behind its sled dogs after being told a relief team will pick them up soon. Animal lovers will be gripped by this exploration of man's relationship to his beloved companions, even though the unfortunate voice-over narration makes the film less compelling than it should have been. (Dir: Koreyoshi Kurahara, 112 mins.)†

Anthony Adverse (1936)**½ Fredric March, Olivia de Havilland, Claude Rains, Gale Sondergaard, Louis Hayward. The sprawl at least adds some vitality to the tired best-seller format. March is properly dashing as the 19th-century adventurer. (Dir: Mervyn LeRoy, 136 mins.)†

Anthropophagus—See: **Grim Reaper, The**

Antigone (Greece, 1960)***½ Irene Papas, Manos Katrakis, Maro Kontou, Nikos Kazis. Papas dominates this Greek tragedy as Antigone, condemned to death for defying a royal order against burial for her two dead brothers. Director George Tzavellas uses flashbacks, gripping images and a narrative voice over to create a cinematic equivalent for the traditional Greek chorus and messenger. (93 mins.)†

Antonio and the Mayor (MTV 1975)*** Diego Gonzales, Gregory Sierra. Howard Rodman's offbeat, touching little drama of the 1920s, filmed in Mexico, is the story of a bright Mexican boy who infuriates the mayor of his village because of his ability to handle a bicycle that the mayor can't manage. This simple morality tale takes its time in the telling, capturing the flavor of village life and building slowly to an emotional, tearjerking finale. (Dir: Jerry Thorpe, 72 mins.)

Antonio das Mortes (Brazil, 1969)***½ Mauricio Do Valle, Odete Lara, Othon Bastos, Hugo Carvana. Director Glauber Rocha was forced out of Brazil after he made this radical outcry against oppressive landowners who exploit and abuse the peasant class. Filled with demands for change and using strong images of Brazilian cultural traditions, this is one of the great political films. (95 mins.)

Antonio Gaudí (Japan, 1984)***½ Director Hiroshi Teshigahara (*Woman in the Dunes*) recounts his twenty-five-year obsession with the art of famed architect Antonio Gaudí in this stirring, visually breathtaking exploration of Gaudí's Barcelona masterworks. (97 mins.)†

Ants—See: It Happened at Lakewood Manor

Any Number Can Play (1949)*** Clark Gable, Alexis Smith, Wendell Corey. Well done drama about a gambler who faces a series of crises in a matter of a few hours. Good cast supports Gable in this fast-moving story. (Dir: Mervyn LeRoy, 103 mins.)

Anyone Can Play (Italy, 1967)** Ursula Andress, Virna Lisi, Marisa Mell, Claudine Auger, Brett Halsey, Jean-Pierre Cassel. Mediocre comedy about four women trying to solve their varied sex-related problems. Co-written by Ettore Scola; originally 110 mins. (Dir: Luigi Zampa, 88 mins.)

Any Second Now (MTV 1969)*** Stewart Granger, Lois Nettleton, Katy Jurado, Joseph Campanella, Tom Tully. Nifty TV suspense yarn about a woman whose life is in jeopardy, after her straying husband learns that she's got the goods on his infidelity. (Dir: Gene Levitt, 97 mins.)

Anything Can Happen (1952)*** Jose Ferrer, Kim Hunter. Delightfully played comedy about an immigrant who accustoms

himself to America and finds himself a wife. (Dir: George Seaton, 107 mins.)

Anything for Love—See: 11 Harrowhouse

Anything Goes (1936)**½ Bing Crosby, Ethel Merman. The original Porter score makes this watered-down production moderately entertaining. "You're the Top" number with Ethel is the limit. (Dir: Lewis Milestone, 100 mins.)

Anything Goes (1956)**½ Bing Crosby, Donald O'Connor, Jeanmaire, Mitzi Gaynor. Musical comedy co-stars in Europe try to sign a leading lady for their show. The film needs more sparkle. Great Cole Porter score. (Dir: Robert Lewis, 106 mins.)

Anything to Survive (MTV 1990)*** Robert Conrad, Matthew Le Blanc, Ocean Hellman, Emily Perkins. Raw emotion and horrific human combine in this fact-based dramatization. After their boat sinks in the brutally cold seas of Alaska, a man and his three children fight to survive on a small island. A series of heartbreaking miscalculations compounds their problems as their health deteriorates. Compelling. (Dir: Zale Dale, 96 mins.)

Any Wednesday (1966)*** Jane Fonda, Jason Robards, Jr., Dean Jones. The successful Broadway comedy about a kept girl, her married lover, his wife, and an out-of-town salesman who acts as a catalyst, comes to the screen improved, thanks to Miss Fonda's bright performance. (Dir: Robert Miller, 109 mins.)†

Any Which Way You Can (1980)*** Clint Eastwood, Sondra Locke, Geoffrey Lewis, Ruth Gordon, William Smith. Sequel to *Every Which Way But Loose*, featuring the same popular characters, including Clyde the orangutan. (Dir: Buddy Van Horn, 105 mins.)†

Anzio (1968)** Robert Mitchum, Peter Falk, Arthur Kennedy, Robert Ryan. Fabricated account of the decisive World War II battle of the Italian campaign. (Dir: Edward Dmytryk, 117 mins.)†

Apache (1954)**½ Burt Lancaster, Jean Peters. A peace-seeking Indian, forced to turn renegade in this action-filled western. (Dir: Robert Aldrich, 91 mins.)†

Apache Ambush (1955)** Bill Williams, Richard Jaeckel. Action-filled but routine western—hero fights unreconstructed Confederate soldiers, Mexican banditos, and, of course, the Apaches. (Dir: Fred Sears, 70 mins.)

Apache Drums (1951)** Stephen McNally, Coleen Gray. Familiar western fare. A gambler with a bad reputation who shows he's made of sterner stuff when the chips are down. (Dir: Hugo Fregonese, 75 mins.)

Apache Rifles (1964)** Audie Murphy, Michael Dante, Linda Lawson. Cavalry captain struggles to bring peace when the Apaches go on the warpath. (Dir: William Witney, 92 mins.)

Apache Territory (1958)** Rory Calhoun, Barbara Bates. A group of survivors of an Indian attack led to safety by a brave cowboy. (Dir: Ray Nazarro, 75 mins.)

Apache War Smoke (1952)** Gilbert Roland, Robert Horton. Indians, cavalry, stage-coaches, and romance. Familiar. (Dir: Harold Kress, 65 mins.)

Aparajito (The Unvanquished) (India, 1958)**** An Indian cast brilliantly performs this artistic masterpiece of a boy's growth to manhood, the second in a trilogy of features made by Satyajit Ray. For the discriminating viewer, a must-see. (Dir: Satyajit Ray, 113 mins.)

Apartment, The (1960)**** Jack Lemmon, Shirley MacLaine, Fred MacMurray, Ray Walston, Jack Kruschen, Edie Adams, David Lewis, Joan Shawlee. Director Billy Wilder's bitterly funny view of modern urban morality won the Oscar as the best film of its year. A young wheeler-dealer "lends" his apartment to senior executives who wish to do a bit of cheating on the side. Witty adult fare. (125 mins.)†

Apartment for Peggy (1948)*** Jeanne Crain, William Holden, Edmund Gwenn. Dated story about married vets struggling to get through college. Warm, humorous and charming. (Dirs: Henry Koster, George Seaton, 98 mins.)

Apartment Zero (1989)**** Colin Firth, Hart Bochner, Liz Smith, Dora Bryan. Murderous politics and sexual repression get a workout in this superb film about cinema owner Firth and assassin Bochner, whose lives mesh in Buenos Aires. Both actors shine while challenging script by directors Martin Donovan and David Koepp explores the gamut of human sexuality and evil. Witty touches of movie lore (including a great trivia game) and quirky characters abound, as film gives dark new meaning to the term "death and transfiguration." Video version runs 114 mins. (122 mins.)†

Ape, The (1940)*½ Boris Karloff, Gertrude W. Hoffman, Henry Hall, Maris Wrixon. Karloff monkeys around with an ape in order to save a girl's life. (Dir: William Nigh, 62 mins.)

Ape Man, The (1943)*½ Bela Lugosi, Louise Currie, Wallace Ford, Henry Hall. Lugosi makes a monkey of himself as he plays a mad scientist shooting up with ape injections. (Dir: William Beaudine, 64 mins.)†

Ape Woman, The (France-Italy, 1964)*** Ugo Tognazzi, Annie Girardot. Comic, cynical, poignant story of a sideshow freak and the man who marries and exploits her. A softened ending has been substituted for the original stark one. (Dir: Marco Ferreri, 97 mins.)

Apocalypse Now (1979)***½ Martin Sheen, Marlon Brando, Robert Duvall, Dennis Hopper, Frederic Forrest. Intended to be the definitive film epic about war in general, and the hell of the Vietnam War in particular, this flawed masterpiece does have some of the most remarkable scenes ever photographed, especially a helicopter attack on a Vietcong village with a soundtrack blaring Wagner's "Ride of the Valkyries." The protagonist is a U.S. Army captain (Sheen) assigned dangerous mission of running down a renegade Green Berets colonel (Brando) who has taken refuge in the Cambodian jungles. (Dir: Francis Ford Coppola, 153 mins.)†

Apology (MCTV 1986)*** Lesley Ann Warren, Peter Weller, George Loros, John Glover, Jimmy Ray Weeks. A fine cast and a new story twist make this suspense thriller above-average entertainment. Set in New York Soho's slick art community, the plot concerns a distressed innovative artist whose artistic experiment goes haywire when a psychotic killer confesses his crimes into her answering machine. (Dir: Robert Bierman, 100 mins.)†

Appaloosa, The (1966)** Marlon Brando, Anjanette Comer, John Saxon. A wronged buffalo hunter meets with adversity at every turn. The story has Brando pitted against a Mexican bandit, and their many confrontations become tiresome long before the shoot-out at the finale. (Dir: Sidney J. Furie, 98 mins.)†

Applause (1929)**½ Helen Morgan, Joan Peers. Innovative early talkie about a burlesque star who almost forsakes her daughter for success. (Dir: Rouben Mamoulian, 87 mins.)

Apple, The (1980)½ Catherine Mary Stewart, Allan Love, George Gilmore, Grace Kennedy, Joss Ackland. A poor excuse for a musical; set in 1994. Bibi and Alphie write a love song for the "worldwide annual song festival." Unfortunately for this happy couple, their efforts are sabotaged by a rock promoter and his henchmen. (Dir: Menahem Golan, 90 mins.)

Apple Dumpling Gang, The (1975)** Bill Bixby, Susan Clark. A story for kids about a trio of orphans who find a huge gold nugget in a seemingly tapped-out mine during the 1870s. (Dir: Norman Tokar, 104 mins.)†

Apple Dumpling Gang Rides Again, The (1979)*½ Don Knotts, Tim Conway, Tim Matheson, Jack Elam, Henry Morgan, Ruth Buzzi. Even the kids may not care for this mirthless Disney sequel, again featuring those two inept bandits

Conway and Knotts. (Dir: Vincent McEveety, 89 mins.)†

Applegates, The—See: **Meet the Applegates**

Apple Pie (1975)** Tony Azito, Brother Theodore, Ruth Kaplan. Free-form comedy about a crime boss, played in most unlikely fashion by Azito as a self-obsessed weirdo who guides us on a tour of his past. Never-released movie features brief appearances by Calvert DeForest (alias Larry "Bud" Melman), Veronica Hamel, and Irene Cara. (Dir: Howard Goldberg, 90 mins.)†

Appointment, The (1969)* Omar Sharif, Anouk Aimee. Mawkish and melodramatic yarn with the stolid Sharif marrying model Aimee, against his friend's warning that she's been a lady of the night. (Dir: Sidney Lumet, 100 mins.)

Appointment for Love (1941)*** Charles Boyer, Margaret Sullavan, Reginald Denny. Marital mix-ups get a big play in this sometimes clever, sometimes silly comedy-romance. (Dir: William Seiter, 89 mins.)

Appointment in Berlin (1943)*** George Sanders, Marguerite Chapman, Gale Sondergaard, Onslow Stevens, Alan Napier. Englishman poses as a Nazi radio commentator to get valuable information for the Allies. Good spy melodrama. (Dir: Alfred E. Green, 78 mins.)

Appointment in Honduras (1953)** Glenn Ford, Ann Sheridan, Zachary Scott. Adventurer goes on a dangerous trek through the jungles. Melodrama moves slowly and has banal plot. (Dir: Jacques Tourneur, 79 mins.)

Appointment With a Shadow (1958)** George Nader, Joanna Moore, Brian Keith. Alcoholic reporter is given a chance at a big story, finds himself target for a killer. Undistinguished crime melodrama. (Dir: Joseph Pevney, 72 mins.)

Appointment With Danger (1951)*** Alan Ladd, Phyllis Calvert, Jack Webb. Post office investigator gets some aid from unexpected sources while foiling a mail robbery. Good crime melodrama. (Dir: Lewis Allen, 88 mins.)

Appointment With Death (1988)** Peter Ustinov, Lauren Bacall, John Gielgud, Piper Laurie, Hayley Mills, Carrie Fisher, Jenny Seagrove, David Soul. Traveling in Jerusalem, Agatha Christie's Belgian detective Hercule Poirot (Ustinov, for the sixth time) probes the murder of a shrewish widow with a long list of enemies. A threadbare production and an easily guessed ending make this a disappointment, despite amusingly hammy turns by the almost all-star cast. (Dir: Michael Winner, 102 mins.)†

Appointment With Fear (1985)*½ Michele Little, Douglas Rowe. Another serial killer, another maniac detective, another

movie disowned by its director (hence billing for the fictional "Alan Smithee") equals another good night to go to bed early. (Dir: "Alan Smithee" [Ramzi Thomas], 96 mins.)†

Appointment With Murder (1948)*½ John Calvert, Catherine Craig, Lyle Talbot, Jack Reitzen. The Falcon, here an insurance investigator, seeks out stolen paintings in Hollywood and Italy. (Dir: Jack Bernhard, 67 mins.)

Apprenticeship of Duddy Kravitz, The (Canada, 1974)***½ Richard Dreyfuss, Randy Quaid, Joseph Wiseman, Jack Warden, Denholm Elliott, Micheline Lanctot. An exuberant, hilarious, sometimes sad film. Richard Dreyfuss is excellent playing a hustling Jewish teenager on the make in Montreal. (Dir: Ted Kotcheff, 121 mins.)†

Apprentice to Murder (1988)** Donald Sutherland, Chad Lowe, Mia Sara. Busy Mr. Sutherland stars as a small-town doctor with supernatural powers who takes on the demon-next-door. When you watch Don's stirring performance, remember: so what if the actual movie's bad, next month's Sutherland picture might be good. (Dir: R. L. Thomas, 94 mins.)†

Approaching Omega (1983)*** Harry Hart-Browne, Steve Griffin, Robin Fuentes, Jacquelyn Hyde, Nita Talbot. Unconventional story of mountaineering backpackers who play mind games with each other as they ascend to the peak. Rich comedy of words and relationships features '50s star Talbot in dream sequence. (Dir: John Dorr, 103 mins.)†

April Fools, The (1969)** Jack Lemmon, Catherine Deneuve, Sally Kellerman, Jack Weston, Charles Boyer, Myrna Loy. Unsatisfying romantic comedy. Lemmon falls in love with his boss's beautiful wife (Miss Deneuve), and gets in and out of improbable messes. (Dir: Stuart Rosenberg, 95 mins.)†

April Fool's Day (1986)** Jay Baker, Deborah Foreman, Deborah Goodrich, Ken Olandt, Griffin O'Neal, Amy Steel. An April foolish horror spoof about some collegians who are systematically bumped off à la *Friday the 13th* on a deserted island. Chills and chuckles don't mix, but the scare scenes are dexterously set up. (Dir: Fred Walton, 90 mins.)†

April in Paris (1953)**½ Doris Day, Ray Bolger, Claude Dauphin. A chorus girl named "Dynamite" (Doris, of course) invited to Paris Arts Festival (by mistake) as the representative of the American Theater. (Dir: David Butler, 101 mins.)

April Love (1957)**½ Pat Boone, Shirley Jones, Arthur O'Connell. A young man arrives on a farm in Kentucky and immediately is up to his blue jeans in romance and song. (Dir: Henry Levin, 99 mins.)

April Morning (MTV 1988)** Tommy Lee Jones, Robert Urich, Chad Lowe, Susan Blakely, Meredith Salenger, Rip Torn. Based on Howard Fast's novel, this is a personal saga of the American Revolutionary War, detailing a young man's traumatic transition to manhood on the eve of the battle at Lexington and Concord. (Dir: Delbert Mann, 96 mins.)

April Showers (1948)**½ Jack Carson, Ann Sothern, Robert Alda, S. Z. Sakall. The old vaudeville backstage theme receives an undistinguished treatment in this musical. (Dir: James Kern, 94 mins.)

A Propos De Nice (France, 1930)***½ Director Jean Vigo's witty and influential documentary about life in the Riviera resort city of Nice. Vigo experiments with montage, contrasting the status of rich and poor in the tradition of Russian documentarian Dziga Vertov. Photographed by Boris Kaufman (Vertov's brother). (45 mins.)

Aquarians, The (1970)**½ Ricardo Montalban, Jose Ferrer, Tom Simcox, Kate Woodville. A team of deep sea laboratory scientists stumble upon a group of opportunists bent on salvaging a wrecked vessel with a cargo of poison nerve gas. (Dir: Don McDougall, 102 mins.)

Arabella (Italy, 1967)** Virna Lisi, Margaret Rutherford, James Fox, Terry-Thomas. Mild romantic comedy set in Italy in the 1920s. Virna Lisi tries to extract money from men in order to help her aunt pay off taxes dating back to 1895. (Dir: Mauro Bolognini, 105 mins.)

Arabesque (1966)**½ Gregory Peck, Sophia Loren, Alan Badel, Kieron Moore. A contrived, not altogether successful chase melodrama with handsome Greg Peck and beautiful Sophia Loren amid lavish international settings. A language expert (Peck) unwillingly gets involved in intrigue. (Dir: Stanley Donen, 104 mins.)†

Arabian Adventure (Great Britain, 1979)**½ Christopher Lee, Milo O'Shea, Oliver Tobias, Puneet Sira, Emma Samms, Peter Cushing. Although not in a league with Korda's *Thief of Bagdad*, this far-from-big budget pic is directed with a flair for high adventure. A wicked caliph seeks ultimate power through a magical rose. (Dir: Kevin Connor, 98 mins.)

Arabian Nights (1942)** Maria Montez, Jon Hall, Sabu. Corny but elaborately produced spectacle about the days of dancing slave girls, tent cities, and the Caliph of Baghdad. (Dir: John Rawlins, 86 mins.)

Arabian Nights (Italy, 1974)***½ Ninetto Davoli, Franco Citti, Franco Merli, Ines Pellegrini. Ten stories from *A Thousand and One Nights*, beautifully filmed in Nepal, Yemen, and Eritrea. Final and most successful segment of director Pier Paolo Pasolini's medieval trilogy has a wonderfully exotic, almost hallucinogenic quality. (155 mins.)†

Arachnophobia (1990)** Jeff Daniels, Harley Jane Kozak, John Goodman, Julian Sands, Stuart Pankin, Brian McNamara. Billed as a *Thrillomedy*, this is standard monster insect fare about a vampire spider on the prowl in a picture postcard village. The movie looks terrific, but its plot, with tired writing, is rehashed fifties giant bug material. (Dir: Frank Marshall, 103 mins.)†

Archer's Adventure (Australia, 1985)**½ Brett Climo, Robert Coleby, Nicole Kidman. In 19th-century Australia, a young horsetrainer's apprentice sets out on the impossible task of taking a horse across 600 miles of unknown terrain in order to enter it in a race. Based on a true story; overlong, but good family viewing nonetheless. (Dir: Denny Lawrence, 120 mins.)†

Archie: To Riverdale and Back Again (MTV 1990)*½ Christopher Rich, Lauren Holly, Karen Kopins, Sam Whipple, Gary Kroeger, David Doyle. Live-action update of the perennially fatuous comic strip is no improvement, with the gang as thirtysomethings back together for a high school reunion. (Dir: Dick Lowry, 97 mins.)

Arch of Triumph (1948)** Charles Boyer, Ingrid Bergman, Charles Laughton. A refugee doctor and a girl with a past in Paris, just before the Nazis take over. From Remarque's novel. Long, rather emotionless drama. (Dir: Lewis Milestone, 120 mins.)†

Arch of Triumph (MTV 1985)**½ Lesley-Anne Down, Anthony Hopkins, Donald Pleasence. Remake of the 1948 film about love in Paris before the Nazis moved in. (Dir: Waris Hussein, 104 mins.)

Are Husbands Necessary? (1942)** Ray Milland, Betty Field. Contrived, forced farce about the problems of newlyweds. Rarely funny, often embarrassing. (Dir: Norman Taurog, 75 mins.)

Arena (1953)** Gig Young, Polly Bergen. Story of cowboys competing for prizes in the Tucson rodeo—but there's not much story. Ordinary stuff. (Dir: Richard Fleischer, 70 mins.)

Are Parents People? (1925)*** Betty Bronson, Adolphe Menjou, Florence Vidor. Delightfully acted silent social comedy, as a teenage girl strives to reconcile her quarreling parents. A light classic. (Dir: Malcolm St. Clair, 60 mins.)†

Are You in the House Alone? (MTV 1978)*½ Blythe Danner, Kathleen Beller, Tony Bill, Robin Mattson. This predictable thriller about a terrorized coed plays on everyone's fear of being stalked in an empty house. (Dir: Walter Grauman, 104 mins.)†

Are You There? (Great Britain, 1930)****
Beatrice Lillie. A comic masterpiece
that contains one of the most excruciatingly funny scenes ever recorded on
film—the great Lady Peel (Lillie) wooing
a recalcitrant suitor while swirling a huge
chain of beads. AKA: **Exit Laughing.**
(Dir: Hamilton MacFadden, 57 mins.)

Are You with It? (1948)*** Donald O'Connor, Olga San Juan. Mathematician leaves
his job and joins a traveling carnival.
Cute and pleasant musical, with some
good work by O'Connor. (Dir: Jack
Hively, 90 mins.)

Argentine Nights (1940)** Ritz Brothers,
Andrew Sisters. Three madcaps and an
all-girl orchestra sail for Argentina to
play at a resort there. Pretty mild whacky
musical. (Dir: Albert S. Rogell, 74 mins.)

Aria (Great Britain, 1987)** John Hurt,
Buck Henry, Anita Morris, Beverly
D'Angelo, Bridget Fonda. Ten directors
each take a crack at creating a film
around a different aria, with results ranging from stylish to (more often) insipid,
emphasizing sex, satire, and snappy visuals. Best: Franc Roddam's lush imagining of "Tristan and Isolde" as a teen
love-and-death melodrama in Vegas.
(Dirs: Robert Altman, Bruce Beresford,
Bill Bryden, Jean-Luc Godard, Derek
Jarman, Franc Roddam, Nicolas Roeg,
Ken Russell, Charles Sturridge, Julien
Temple, 100 mins.)†

Arise My Love (1940)*** Claudette Colbert,
Ray Milland, Walter Abel, Dennis
O'Keefe, Dick Durcell. Important, near-
ly forgotten comedy-melodrama, with
Colbert and Milland as two American
reporters in Europe as WWII impends.
Backdrops include the Spanish Civil War
and the sinking of the *Athenia*. Billy
Wilder and Charles Brackett wrote the
script. (Dir: Mitchell Leisen, 113 mins.)

Aristocats, The (1970)*** The voices of
Eva Gabor, Phil Harris, Maurice Chevalier. A mama cat and three of her babies
are kidnapped and left in the country by
a mean butler. Pleasant animated family
fare. (Dir: Wolfgang Reitherman, 78
mins.)

Arizona (1940)**½ William Holden, Jean
Arthur. Western gal has trouble when
her rivals have her wagon trains attached. Some fine action scenes; but it's
just too darn long. (Dir: Wesley Ruggles,
122 mins.)

Arizona Bushwhackers (1968)** Howard
Keel, Yvonne DeCarlo, Scott Brady,
John Ireland. Standard western has a
gunslinger-spy (Howard Keel) town-
taming during the Civil War. (Dir: Lesley
Selander, 86 mins.)

Arizona Mission—See: **Gun the Man Down**

Arizona Raiders (1965)* Audie Murphy,
Michael Dante, Buster Crabbe. Audie

Murphy plays a former Confederate soldier who joins the newly formed Arizona Rangers. Partially based on the 1951
The Texas Rangers. (Dir: William Witney,
88 mins.)†

Arizona Ripper, The—See: **Bridge Across
Time**

Arkansas Traveler, The (1938)*** Bob
Burns, Jean Parker, Lyle Talbot, Fay
Bainter, John Beal, Irvin S. Cobb. People who like folksy comedy should love
this. Plenty of warm chuckles as a wandering printer comes to a small town
and saves the local paper. (Dir: Alfred
Santell, 85 mins.)

Armed and Dangerous (1986)**½ John Candy, Eugene Levy, Robert Loggia, Kenneth
MacMillan, Meg Ryan, Brion James,
Jonathan Banks, Don Stroud, Steve
Railsback. Unadventurous comic romp
for Candy and Levy. They're both quite
droll as reluctant night watchmen who
must redeem themselves by exposing
corruption in the security guard business. (Dir: Mark L. Lester, 88 mins.)†

Armored Attack—See: **North Star, The**

Armored Car Robbery (1950)***½ Charles
McGraw, William Talman. Four participants in an armored car robbery kill a
cop. Tough, exciting, extremely well-
made melodrama. (Dir: Richard Fleischer,
67 mins.)†

Armored Command (1961)** Howard Keel,
Tina Louise, Earl Holliman. Routine war
film with a romance thrown in. Predictable. (Dir: Byron Haskin, 99 mins.)†

Army Brats (Holland, 1984)*½ Akkemay,
Frank Schaafsma, Geert De Jong, Peter
Faber. A career army officer and his
wife, fed up with the shambles their
impossible children have made of their
lives, declare all-out war. (Dir: Ruud
van Hemert, 103 mins.)†

Army in the Shadows, The (France,
1969)**** Lino Ventura, Simone Signoret, Jean-Pierre Cassel, Claude Mann,
Christian Barbier. A great cast rises to
the occasion in this powerful and tragic
look at the French Resistance during
WWII. Exciting, moving, and thought
provoking. (Dir: Jean-Pierre Melville,
143 mins.)

Arnelo Affair, The (1947)** John Hodiak,
George Murphy, Frances Gifford, Eve
Arden, Dean Stockwell. A woman whose
husband takes her for granted seeks solace in the arms of a man who turns out
to be—a murderer! (Dir: Arch Oboler,
86 mins.)

Arnold (1973)**½ Stella Stevens, Roddy
McDowall, Elsa Lanchester, Farley
Granger, Shani Wallis, Victor Buono. A
strange, fitfully amusing all-star horror
parody. Stella marries a corpse in this
quirky comedy and her dead hubby soon

45

has a slew of graveyard companions for company. (Dir: Georg Fenady, 100 mins.)†

Around the World in 80 Days (1956)**** David Niven, Shirley MacLaine, Cantinflas. Delightful rendition of the Jules Verne tale. Phileas Fogg (Niven) bets his London club that he can do it in 80 days, and away we go. An odds-on favorite all the way. (Dir: Michael Anderson, 170 mins.)†

Around the World Under the Sea (1966)** David McCallum, Brian Kelly, Marshall Thompson, Lloyd Bridges. Scientists explore the ocean deep to determine the cause of tidal waves and such. Strictly for kids. (Dir: Andrew Marton, 117 mins.)†

Arousers, The (1970)* Tab Hunter, Nadyne Turner, Roberta Collins. A flaccid sex thriller in which poor Tab battles a sexploitative script with a sensitive performance and loses. Those expecting kinky sex or suspense of any kind will remain non-aroused by this drab tale about a man whose cure for impotence is to kill women. AKA: **Sweet Kill.** (Dir: Curtis Hanson, 90 mins.)†

Arrangement, The (1968)**½ Kirk Douglas, Faye Dunaway, Deborah Kerr, Richard Boone. Uneven treatment of Elia Kazan's novel about the search for meaning by a successful ad agency exec, and the resistance he encounters from those closest to him. (Dir: Elia Kazan, 127 mins.)†

Arrest Bulldog Drummond (1938)*** John Howard, Heather Angel, H. B. Warner, Reginald Denny, E. E. Clive, Jean Fenwick, George Zucco. Solid series entry. The inventor of a super weapon sought by international agents is slain, and B.D.'s in pursuit of the bad guys. (Dir: James Hogan, 60 mins.)†

Arrivederci, Baby! (1966)*** Tony Curtis, Rosanna Schiaffino. An amusing comedy about a money-hungry young man who keeps discarding guardians and wives for their fortunes. (Dir: Ken Hughes, 105 mins.)

Arrogant, The (1987)½ Sylvia Kristel, Gary Graham, Leigh Wood, Joe Condon. Motorcyclist Graham, on the road after taking an axe to his father-in-law, picks up hitchhiker Kristel and spends the rest of the movie boring her (and us) with his inane existential philosophy. An inept, hilariously stupid and pretentious mess; the title must apply to producer-writer-director Philippe Blot for having the nerve to expect people to pay to see this. (87 mins.)

Arrowhead (1953)**½ Charlton Heston, Jack Palance, Katy Jurado. Trouble in the Southwest when a Cavalry unit attempts to sign a peace treaty with the Apaches. Well-made but routine western. (Dir: Charles Warren, 105 mins.)

Arrow in the Dust (1954)** Sterling Hayden, Coleen Gray. Wagon train dependent on one strong man—this time it's Sterling Hayden and he's a cavalry trooper who impersonates a major. (Dir: Lesley Selander, 80 mins.)

Arrowsmith (1931)***½ Ronald Colman, Helen Hayes, Richard Bennett, Myrna Loy. From Sinclair Lewis's novel about dedicated medical researcher (Colman) who remains true to his ideals despite the loss of his beloved wife (Hayes) and the temptation of a rich girl's love (Loy). An absorbing film drama, thanks to an exceptional screenplay by Sidney Howard and John Ford's intelligent direction. (108 mins.)†

Arruza (1971)***½ Carlos Arruza, Manuel Arruza, Carlos Arruza, Jr. Sterling documentary based on the career of bullfighter Carlos Arruza. Best for fanciers of this violent sport, but an exemplary piece of filmmaking nonetheless. (Dir: Budd Boetticher, 73 mins.)†

Arsenal (U.S.S.R., 1929)*** Semyon Svashenko, Mikola Nademsky. Ukranian director Alexander Dovzhenko's highly symbolic examination of his homeland's struggles to rise from a feudal society to its involvement and battles during the revolutionary changes that wracked Russia and the Ukraine. Shot in neorealist documentary style, it is now considered a major early work of the international cinema. (99 mins.)†

Arsenal Stadium Mystery, The (Great Britain, 1939)**½ Leslie Banks, Greta Gynt, Ian Maclean, Anthony Bushell. Scotland Yard investigates a murder that took place during the most important soccer match of the season. Interesting as a reflection of nearly extinct stiff-upper-lip tradition. (Dir: Thorold Dickinson, 85 mins.)

Arsène Lupin Returns (1938)** Melvyn Douglas, Warren William, Virginia Bruce, Monty Woolley. This MGM sequel teams the interesting pair of Douglas and William as the gentleman thief and the detective who pursues him. (Dir: George Fitzmaurice, 81 mins.)

Arsenic and Old Lace (1944)***½ Cary Grant, Priscilla Lane, Josephine Hull, Jean Adair, Raymond Massey, Peter Lorre, Jack Carson, James Gleason, Edward Everett Horton. A funny hit play and the number one comedy director in Hollywood add up to a madcap classic. Lorre's giggling, guzzling Dr. Einstein and the two delightful maiden aunts steal every scene. (Dir: Frank Capra, 116 mins.)†

Arthur (1981)*** Dudley Moore, Liza Minnelli, John Gielgud, Geraldine Fitzgerald, Jill Eikenberry, Stephen Elliott. Dudley Moore is a millionaire playboy who spends his time in the pursuit of women, wine, and song (more or less in that order) and is taken to task by everyone but his loyal butler, played with unerring wit and timing by John Gielgud (he won an Oscar for this performance, and rightly so). (Dir: Steve Gordon, 97 mins.)†

Arthur 2: On the Rocks (1988)* Dudley Moore, Liza Minnelli, Paul Benedict, Geraldine Fitzgerald, Cynthia Sikes, John Gielgud. Taking place several years after the first film, this sodden sequel details how Arthur loses his fortune. Full of poorly conceived plot expediencies, repetitive bits, and a complete contempt for those of us who don't have $750,000,000. Minnelli is given nothing to do; the other characters are the only people who can find Moore's antics genuinely funny. (Dir: Bud Yorkin, 110 mins.)†

Arthur's Hallowed Ground (Great Britain, 1984)**½ Jimmy Jewel, Jean Boht, David Swift, Michael Elphick. Master cinematographer Freddie Young made his directorial debut (at the age of 82!) in this quaint but minor film about an elderly man struggling to save something very important to him—a cricket field. (84 mins.)†

Arthur the King (MTV 1985)*½ Malcolm McDowell, Dyan Cannon, Candice Bergen, Edward Woodward, Lucy Gutteridge, Joseph Blatchely, Rupert Everett. A costume piece combining the serious and the hokey. McDowell plays a straightforward King Arthur surrounded by weirdos like Bergen's Morgan Le Fay and Dyan Cannon as an American observer who falls down a Stonehenge hole to relive the days of Camelot. (Dir: Clive Donner, 156 mins.)

Artists and Models (1937)*** Jack Benny, Ida Lupino, Gail Patrick. Jack runs a down-and-out advertising agency, and if he can find the right model, he lands a big account. Plenty of specialty numbers performed by Martha Raye, Connee Boswell, and Louis Armstrong. (Dir: Raoul Walsh, 97 mins.)

Artists and Models (1955)*** Dean Martin, Jerry Lewis, Shirley MacLaine, Dorothy Malone. Artist lands a big job doing comic strips, inspired by his goofy partner's dreams. Some fun, but it goes on too long. (Dir: Frank Tashlin, 109 mins.)†

Artists and Models Abroad (1938)**½ Jack Benny, Joan Bennett. Some witty lines make this musical sparkle, but it's mainly a chance to see the high fashion styles that thrilled women in 1938. (Dir: Mitchell Leisen, 90 mins.)

Art of Crime, The (MTV 1975)**½ Ron Leibman, Jose Ferrer, David Hedison, Jill Clayburgh. Writers Martin Smith and Bill Davidson, basing their material on the novel *Gypsy in Amber*, dip into gypsy culture and reveal interesting tidbits on the art of fooling the antique-buying public. A slick and slightly different product. (Dir: Richard Irving, 72 mins.)

Art of Love, The (1965)**½ James Garner, Dick Van Dyke, Elke Sommer, Angie Dickinson. Deciding that dead artists are the only ones who sell well, a painter and his buddy decide to fake a suicide. (Dir: Norman Jewison, 98 mins.)

Arthur Rubinstein—Love of Life (1975)**** A beguiling portrait of the great pianist near retirement, musically supple and anecdotally engrossing. François Reichenbach and S. G. Patris directed this Oscar-winning documentary. (91 mins.)

Ashanti (Switzerland, 1979)*½ Michael Caine, Peter Ustinov, Rex Harrison, William Holden, Beverly Johnson, Kabir Bedi. Action-filled nonsense. Caine and his black wife (Johnson) are members of a World Health Organization medical team in Africa when she's kidnapped by slave trader Ustinov. AKA: *Ashanti: Land of No Mercy*. (Dir: Richard Fleischer, 117 mins.)†

Ashes (Poland, 1965)***½ Daniel Olbrychski, Pola Raksa, Boguslaw Kierc, Piotr Wysocki. Director Andrzej Wajda leaves the safety of his personal films for this black-and-white wide-screen epic about Polish patriots who fought for Napoleon, hoping to establish freedom and stability in their native land. Filled with sweeping images and grand battle scenes, an urgent cry for Polish individuality and sovereignty. Released in the U.S. at 160 mins. (233 mins.)

Ashes and Diamonds (Poland, 1958)**** Zbigniew Cybulski. This film, based on a controversial postwar Polish novel, is about the last day of war and the first day of peace in Warsaw, and the mixed-up loyalties and emotions of a young Polish partisan. (Dir: Andrzej Wajda, 104 mins.)†

Ash Wednesday (1973)½ Elizabeth Taylor, Henry Fonda, Helmut Berger. Liz Taylor undergoes a facelift in a vain attempt to retain her youth. Her pain is nothing compared to what the audience goes through. (Dir: Larry Peerce, 99 mins.)†

As Is (MCTV 1986)**½ Robert Carradine, Jonathan Hadary, Colleen Dewhurst, Allan Scarfe, Joanna Mills. On the New York stage, William Hoffman's *As Is* was a powerful story about a newly published author (Robert Carradine) who gets stricken with AIDS and his photographer lover (Jonathan Hadary) who sticks by him. Unfortunately, this TV adaptation suffers from a startlingly hollow performance by Carradine. (Dir: Michael Lindsay-Hogg, 86 mins.)†

Ask Any Girl (1959)**½ David Niven, Shirley MacLaine, Gig Young. An attractive cast of expert screen comics adds stature to this featherweight story about the plight of the single girl in the big city. (Dir: Charles Walters, 98 mins.)

As Long as They're Happy (Great Britain, 1955)**½ Jack Buchanan, Janette Scott. Englishman's daughter swoons for a visiting American crooner. Amusing. (Dir: J. Lee Thompson, 76 mins.)

Asphalt Jungle, The (1950)**** Sterling Hayden, Sam Jaffe, Marc Lawrence, Jean Hagen, Louis Calhern, James Whitmore, Marilyn Monroe. Director John Huston's theses of collective effort and nihilist failure were never more starkly dramatized than in this genre-creating caper film. Uniformly well acted by a nonpareil gallery of small-bracket losers; Lawrence was never better. (Dir: John Huston, 112 mins.)†

Asphyx, The (Great Britain, 1972)*** Robert Powell, Robert Stephens, Jane Lapotaire. Not a bad little thriller, with a premise that's certainly unusual. A Victorian scientist (Stephens) discovers that death can occur only when a spiritlike creature called the asphyx escapes from the body. He decides to trap the asphyx and thus create eternal life. (Dir: Peter Newbrook, 99 mins.)†

Assam Garden, The (Great Britain, 1985)*** Deborah Kerr, Madhur Jaffrey, Alec McCowen, Zia Mohyeddin, Anton Lesser. A sensitive character study which touches on British and Indian relations as it examines the power structure between the gentry and their servants. Slow going, but Kerr's performance (her first screen role in fifteen years) as the Englishwoman refurbishing her garden in her husband's memory with the help of an Indian woman recalls her best screen work. (Dir: Mary McMurray, 92 mins.)

Assassin (MTV 1986)** Robert Conrad, Robert Webber, Karen Austin, Richard Young, Jonathan Banks. It's the man vs. robot plot again, only the late model robots are becoming tougher to destroy. A dogged Conrad stalks Young's menacing mechanical man. (Dir: Sandor Stern, 104 mins.)

Assassin, The (1989)** Nicholas Guest, Xander Berkeley, Sam Melville. Two cops—a sensitive alcoholic and a tough street veteran—battle terrorists in Mexico City. Standard buddy-cop entry, with the emphasis on action instead of wisecracks. (Dir: John Hess, 91 mins.)†

Assassin, The (1961)—See: **Ladykiller of Rome, The**

Assassination (1987)*½ Charles Bronson, Jill Ireland, Stephen Elliott, Jan Gan Boyd. Shoddy Bronson action pic for fans only. Chuck plays the National Chief of Security and he's assigned to secure the safety of the First Lady (Ireland). (Dir: Peter Hunt, 88 mins.)†

Assassination Bureau, The (Great Britain, 1969)*** Oliver Reed, Diana Rigg, Telly Savalas, Curt Jurgens, Beryl Reid. Rigg is on assignment for a London newspaper as she gets the goods on a professional outfit headed by ambivalent hero Reed. Together they smash villains Jurgens and Savalas, while escaping fates worse than death in Reid's Parisian House of Pleasure. Too much pseudo-Victorian whimsy, but just the right amount of Rigg. (Dir: Basil Dearden, 106 mins.)

Assassination of Trotsky, The (Great Britain-France-Italy, 1972)**½ Richard Burton, Alain Delon, Romy Schneider. Delon plays the murderer hired to kill Trotsky, the Russian revolutionary, who lives in a total fortress, but is still defenseless because of his humanitarian ideology. An oddity, laced with symbolism and psychological insight. (Dir: Joseph Losey, 103 mins.)†

Assault (Great Britain, 1971)** Suzy Kendall, Frank Finlay, Freddie Jones, James Laurenson, Lesley-Anne Down. Teacher at a girls' school plagued by an unseen murderer offers herself as a decoy to help trap the killer. Pretty tame, especially compared to more recent slasher films. A young Lesley-Anne Down plays one of the schoolgirls. AKA: **In the Devil's Garden** and **The Creepers.** (Dir: Sidney Hayers, 91 mins.)†

Assault, The (The Netherlands, 1987)*** Derek de Lint, Marc van Uchelen, Monique van de Ven, John Kraaykamp. A WWII survivor traces the incidents that led to the extermination of his family. The opening scenes depicting wartime life have a gripping power; the later scenes, set against the background of various postwar events, have considerably less impact. Academy Award for Best Foreign Film. (Dir: Fons Rademakers, 149 mins.)†

Assault and Matrimony (MTV 1987)*½ Jill Eikenberry, Michael Tucker, John Hillerman, Michelle Phillips. Real-life spouses Tucker and Eikenberry have fun as a married couple who decide to sever the ties that bind with murder. Spirited nonsense. (Dir: Jim Frawley, 96 mins.)

Assault of the Killer Bimbos (1988)*½ Christina Whitaker, Elizabeth Kaitan, Nick Cassavetes, Griffin O'Neal. Go-go girls on the lam from a murder they didn't commit run into mobsters and surf bums. Dopey comedy with some scattered laughs. (Dir: Anita Rosenberg, 81 mins.)†

Assault of the Party Nerds (1989)*½ Richard Gabai, Michelle McClellan (Bauer), Linnea Quigley, Troy Donohue. The last four members of a college fraternity plan to hold a party to bring in new members, while the local jock frat and their girlfriends plot against them. Silly video fodder. (Dir: Richard Gabai, 79 mins.)†

Assault of the Rebel Girls (1959)* Errol Flynn, Beverly Aadland, John MacKay, Jackie Kackler. Flynn narrates and appears as himself in his last film, a wooden, pseudo-documentary tribute to the rebel troops of Fidel Castro. Aadland, Flynn's seventeen-year-old mistress, plays an American beautician who joins Cuban women smuggling weapons from Florida to help out their soldier boyfriends. An embarrassment for Flynn, who is also credited with writing this turkey. AKA: **Attack of the Rebel Girls** and **Cuban Rebel Girls**. (Dir: Barry Mahon, 66 mins.)†

Assault on Agathon (Great Britain-Greece, 1976)* Nico Minardos, Nina Van Pallandt, John Woodvine, Marianne Faithful. Overplotted story of British and American agents working to prevent a revolutionary leader from overthrowing the Greek government. Edited down from twice this length, and it shows. (Dir: Laslo Benedek, 96 mins.)†

Assault on a Queen (1966)* Frank Sinatra, Virna Lisi, Tony Franciosa. Foolish story about a group of con men who get together to rob the Queen Mary on the high seas with a reconverted German U-boat. (Dir: Jack Donohue, 106 mins.)

Assault on Paradise—See: **Maniac** (1978)

Assault on Precinct 13 (1976)*** Austin Stoker, Darwin Joston, Laurie Zimmer. First-rate paranoia, third-rate motivation in this exceedingly violent reworking of Howard Hawks's *Rio Bravo* set in a police station in a forsaken neighborhood of Los Angeles. For all the frank borrowings, the film is genuinely reimagined by writer-director John Carpenter (*Halloween*) as an urban horror film. (Dir: John Carpenter, 91 mins.)†

Assault on the Wayne (MTV 1971)*½ Leonard Nimoy, Lloyd Haynes, William Windom. A commander discovers some of his submarine crew are working for a foreign power. (Dir: Marvin Chomsky, 74 mins.)

Assignment K (Great Britain, 1968)** Stephen Boyd, Camilla Sparv, Michael Redgrave, Leo McKern, Jeremy Kemp. Spies and counterspies all over Europe, with an intrepid British intelligence agent played for a patsy. (Dir: Val Guest, 97 mins.)

Assignment Kill Castro—See: **Kill Castro**

Assignment Munich (MTV 1972)**½ Roy Scheider, Richard Basehart, Lesley Ann Warren, Robert Reed. Pilot for the TV series "Assignment Vienna." Scheider stars as Jake Webster, a worldly guy who runs a bar in Munich and does odd jobs for the American military division connected with Interpol. (Dir: David Lowell Rich, 104 mins.)

Assignment Outer Space (West Germany, 1961)*½ Archie Savage, Rik von Nutter, Gabriela Farinon, Dave Montresor, Alan Dijon. An Alpha II spaceship run by an electronic brain gets out of control and threatens to destroy earth. (Dir: "Anthony Davies" [Antonio Margheriti], 70 mins.)†

Assignment—Paris (1952)**½ Dana Andrews, Marta Toren, George Sanders. A reporter is captured and imprisoned when he comes into possession of some important microfilm. (Dir: Robert Parrish, 85 mins.)

Assignment to Kill (1968)*½ Patrick O'Neal, Joan Hackett, Herbert Lom. Contrived, boring melodrama. Private eye is hired to investigate possible big time corporate fraud in Switzerland. (Dir: Sheldon Reynolds, 102 mins.)

Assisi Underground, The (1984)** Ben Cross, James Mason, Maximillian Schell. Average anti-Nazi adventure about the attempts of the Catholic Church to rescue hundreds of Jews from certain extermination during the 1943 occupation of Italy by German troops. A four-hour version shows on cable TV. (Dir: Alexander Ramati, 105 mins.)†

Associate, The (France-West Germany, 1982)*** Michel Serrault, Claudine Auger, Catherine Alric. Realizing that his lackluster personality has kept his business from growing, a man invents a fictitious partner. But the ruse succeeds too well, causing more problems than it solved. Funny French comedy buoyed by *La Cage aux Folles* star, Serrault. (Dir: René Gainville, 94 mins.)†

As Summers Die (MCTV 1986)** Scott Glenn, Bette Davis, Jamie Lee Curtis, Penny Fuller, Beah Richards, Ron O'Neal, John McIntire. This plays like like a seamy B movie about Southern decadence from the fifties. Curtis is sexy as the heroine, involved with a nonconformist lawyer unimpressed by her great wealth. (Dir: Jean-Claude Tramont, 87 mins.)†

As the Sea Rages (1960)*½ Maria Schell, Cliff Robertson. Crude plot mars this story of Yugoslavian refugees. (Dir: Horst Haechler, 74 mins.)

Astonished Heart, The (Great Britain, 1950)**½ Noel Coward, Margaret Leighton, Celia Johnson. Married psychiatrist falls for an old friend, the affair leading to tragedy. Overdone drama. (Dirs: Anthony Darnborough, Terence Fisher, 92 mins.)

Astounding She Monster (1957)* Robert Clarke, Marilyn Harvey. Dull, inept science fiction yarn about a very tall female creature from another planet. (Dir: Ronnie Ashcroft, 59 mins.)†

Astronaut, The (MTV 1972)**½ Monte Markham, Susan Clark. After an astronaut dies during a Mars landing, space officials use the old masquerade trick, hoping to deceive the world with a double. (Dir: Robert Michael Lewis, 72 mins.)

Astro-Zombies, The (1968)* Wendell Corey, John Carradine, Tom Pace, Tura Satana. Mad scientist (operating on a low budget) creates artificial man. Astro-awful! AKA: Space Zombies and Space Vampires. (Dir: Ted V. Mikels, 94 mins.)†

Asylum (Great Britain, 1972)*** Peter Cushing, Herbert Lom, Richard Todd, Barbara Parkins. A chilling quartet of tales are told to a visiting doctor at an asylum. Entertaining. Written by Robert Bloch. (Dir: Roy Ward Baker, 88 mins.)†

As You Desire Me (1931)*** Greta Garbo, Melvyn Douglas, Erich von Stroheim, Owen Moore, Hedda Hopper. An amnesia victim falls in love again with her former husband, after much travail. Star chemistry keeps this extremely odd story humming. Garbo looks astonishing in a platinum wig. From a play by Luigi Pirandello. (Dir: George Fitzmaurice, 71 mins.)†

As You Like It (Great Britain, 1936)***½ Laurence Olivier, Elisabeth Bergner, Felix Aylmer. The art direction, as is its wont, overpowers the Shakespeare in this overmounted production, which is nonetheless notable for the Viennese-accented Rosalind of gamine Bergner and a young Olivier as Orlando, the classic goof. (Dir: Paul Czinner, 97 mins.)†

As Young as You Feel (1951)** Monty Woolley, Thelma Ritter, David Wayne, Jean Peters, Marilyn Monroe, Constance Bennett. Zany family and their madcap shenanigans. It doesn't come off despite the starring line-up. (Dir: Harmon Jones, 77 mins.)

Atame!—See: Tie Me Up! Tie Me Down!

At Close Range (1986)*** Sean Penn, Christopher Walken, Mary Stuart Masterson, Candy Clark, Millie Perkins, Christopher Penn. Disturbing, bloody tale based on a true story about two teenage punks who fall prey to their evil criminal father (Walken). The acting is of the highest caliber, but director James Foley's showy camerawork sometimes serves as a distraction. (111 mins.)†

At Gunpoint (1955)**½ Fred MacMurray, Dorothy Malone. A good cast and good production make this western drama entertaining. A peaceful man who does his duty as a citizen stalked by a band of outlaws. (Dir: Alfred Werker, 81 mins.)†

Athena (1954)** Jane Powell, Debbie Reynolds, Edmund Purdom, Vic Damone. Lawyer falls for a pretty miss, meets her family, a bunch of health nuts. Musical tried for a different angle and missed. (Dir: Richard Thorpe, 96 mins.)

Atlanta Child Murders, The (MTV 1985) ***½ Calvin Levels, Rip Torn, Martin Sheen, Jason Robards, Jr., Morgan Freeman, Ruby Dee, James Earl Jones, Gloria Foster, Paul Benjamin. Superb docudrama about the killings that terrified the city of Atlanta. The film was the center of controversy due to scriptwriter Abby Mann's intimation that the accused Wayne Williams may not have been the guilty party. Uniformly well acted, the film is brimming with fascinating details about police investigative techniques as well as being a heartbreaking glimpse at the pain of a city coping with crimes too heinous to comprehend. (Dir: John Erman, 260 mins.)

Atlantic Adventure (1935)**½ Nancy Carroll, Lloyd Nolan, Harry Langdon, Arthur Hohl, E. E. Clive. Reporter gets involved in skullduggery aboard an oceanliner. Fairly entertaining melodrama. (Dir: Albert Rogell, 68 mins.)

Atlantic City (1944)** Constance Moore, Brad Taylor, Jerry Colonna. An idea man and his girl build an enterprise out of some useless swampland. Just fair. (Dir: Ray McCarey, 87 mins.)

Atlantic City (1981)**** Burt Lancaster, Susan Sarandon, Robert Joy, Michel Piccoli, Kate Reid, Hollis McLaren. A stunning, brilliantly acted film. The scene is the title town, where the glory days have gone to seed and a new dawn of opportunism is breaking. The drama focuses on a series of losers and fools, pursuing their fantasies and facing the harsh dangers of the ruthless real world. The supple screenplay is by playwright John Guare. (Dir: Louis Malle, 105 mins.)†

Atlantis, the Lost Continent (1961)** Anthony Hall, Joyce Taylor. Dopey costume adventure tale about a mythical lost continent in the days of the Roman Empire. (Dir: George Pal, 90 mins.)

At Long Last Love (1975)½ Burt Reynolds, Cybill Shepherd, Madeline Kahn, Eileen Brennan, Duilio Del Prete, John Hillerman. Inane musical, clumsily directed, written, and produced by Peter Bogdanovich. Burt Reynolds, miscast as a wealthy playboy of the Art Deco set, sings poorly, and Cybill Shepherd as his vis-a-vis dances with bovine splendor. (115 mins.)

At Mother's Request (MTV 1987)*** Stefanie Powers, Doug McKeon, John Woods, E. G. Marshall, Frances Sternhagen. A compact, unsettling version of the notorious Frances Schreuder murder case done in a straightforward, B-movie fashion that perfectly suits the sleazy material. Unsubtly acted, but chilling as social climber Schreuder tries to loosen her father's grasp on his wallet by murderous means. (Dir: Michael Tuchner, 208 mins.)

Atoll K—See: **Utopia**

Atom Age Vampire (Italy, 1961)½ Alberto Lupo, Susanne Loret. Scientist restores beauty to a scarred entertainer with serum taken from dead women, which means he has to kill more to keep her that way. Unintentionally funny horror thriller. (Dir: Anton Giulio Majano, 87 mins.)†

Atomic Café, The (1982)**** Training films, news clips, and musical hits like "Atomic Love" by Little Caesar capsulize the spirit of twenty years of official government planning, probing, promoting, and propagandizing about The Bomb. This chilling examination of what the American government's propaganda machine churned out to a gullible public is one of the finest feature-length documentaries of the decade. (Dirs: Kevin Rafferty, Jayne Loader, Pierce Rafferty, 88 mins.)†

Atomic City, The (1952)*** Gene Barry, Lydia Clarke, Milburn Stone. Son of a physicist is kidnapped. Suspenseful melodrama with an unusual locale, thoughtful script, nice performances. (Dir: Jerry Hopper, 85 mins.)

Atomic Kid, The (1954)** Mickey Rooney, Robert Strauss, Elaine Davis. Guy survives an atomic blast but becomes radioactive. Fair comedy. (Dir: Leslie Martinson, 86 mins.)†

Atomic Man, The (1956)** Gene Nelson, Faith Domergue. A reporter and his girl stumble on a mystery concerning a shady scientist. (Dir: Ken Hughes, 78 mins.)

Ator, the Fighting Eagle (1983)* Miles O'Keeffe, Sabrina Siani. Musclebound warrior must crush an evil empire and save his gorgeous damsel in distress. (Dir: David Hills, 98 mins.)†

Ator, the Invincible—See: **Blademaster, The**

Atragon (Japan, 1964)*½ Tadao Takashima, Yoko Fujiyama. Creatures from a submerged continent rise to the surface to cause all kinds of mischief. (Dir: Inoshiro Honda, 85 mins.)

At Sword's Point (1952)*** Cornel Wilde, Maureen O'Hara. The sons of the Three Musketeers save their queen from intrigue. Lively costume melodrama. (Dir: Lewis Allen, 81 mins.)†

Attack (1956)**** Jack Palance, Eddie Albert. Enormously moving drama of cowardice and heroism during the Battle of the Bulge in WWII. Excellent cast and good script. One of the finest antiwar movies ever made and a much underrated effort of director Robert Aldrich. (107 mins.)

Attack and Retreat (U.S.S.R.-Italy, 1964)**½ Arthur Kennedy, Peter Falk, Tatiana Samilova. Sprawling World War II story of Italian soldiers and their experiences on the Russian front. (Dir: Giuseppe De Santis, 156 mins.)

Attack Force Z (Australia-Taiwan, 1980)**½ John Philip Law, Sam Neill, Mel Gibson, Chris Haywood, John Waters. A World War II story, set in the South Pacific, which doesn't waste too much time on character development but gets to the heart of the action. An Australian troupe is detached to pick up survivors from a plane crash behind enemy lines. (Dir: Tim Burstall, 84 mins.)†

Attack of the Beast Creatures (1985)½ Robert Nolfi, Julia Rust, Robert Lengyel. Survivors of a shipwreck are stranded on an island with the doll-sized maneaters of the title. A must for the so-bad-it's-good crowd. (Dir: Michael Stanley, 82 mins.)†

Attack of the Crab Monsters (1957)*½ Richard Garland, Pamela Duncan. Another sci-fi film about monsters unearthed by the H-Bomb tests, fallout in the Pacific. (Dir: Roger Corman, 70 mins.)

Attack of the 50-Ft. Woman (1958)½ Allison Hayes, Yvette Vickers, William Hudson, Roy Gordon. She was more woman than any man could handle! Poor Nancy Archer (Hayes) is a rich clinging vine and her adulterous hubby Harry wants to have her committed. Nutty 50s sci-fi trash extravaganza has to be seen to be believed. (Dir: Nathan Juran, 66 mins.)†

Attack of the Giant Leeches (1959)* Ken Clark, Yvette Vickers, Bruno VeSota. Routine horror tale about outsized leeches attacking girls in a Florida swamp. AKA: **The Giant Leeches**. (Dir: Bernard L. Kowalski, 62 mins.)†

Attack of the Killer Tomatoes! (1978)*½ David Miller, George Wilson, Sharon Taylor, Jack Riley. Spoof of horror pix in which seemingly ordinary objects (guess what) become sinister menaces. Sequel: *Return of the Killer Tomatoes.* (Dir: John de Bello, 87 mins.)†

Attack of the Mushroom People (Japan, 1964)*** Akiro Kubo. Dumb Japanese horror. A group of holiday-goers run aground on an island; starved, some

51

dine on unknown fungi, and learn that you are what you eat. (Dirs: Inoshiro Honda, Giji Tsuburaya, 89 mins.)

Attack of the Puppet People (1958)*½ John Agar, June Kenny. Silly horror film about a doll manufacturer who makes some rather unique products. (Dir: Bert I. Gordon, 79 mins.)

Attack of the Rebel Girls—See: Assault of the Rebel Girls

Attack on Fear (MTV 1984)*½ Paul Michael Glaser, Linda Kelsey, Kevin Conway, Barbara Babcock. This drama based on a true story misses the mark. Glaser and Kelsey are miscast as married journalists who crusade to turn a small-town newspaper into a *New York Times*. (Dir: Mel Damski, 104 mins.)

Attack on Terror: The FBI versus the Ku Klux Klan (MTV 1975)**½ Rip Torn, George Grizzard. Compelling recreation of the 1964 murder of three civil-rights workers in Mississippi. The movie romanticizes the real performance of the FBI in the Deep South during the '50s and '60s, but it's still worth seeing. Originally shown in two parts as a four-hour drama. (Dir: Marvin Chomsky, 215 mins.)

Attack on the Iron Coast (Great Britain, 1968)**½ Lloyd Bridges, Andrew Keir, Sue Lloyd, Mark Eden. Commandos attempt a daring raid on German installations during World War II. Competently handled. (Dir: Paul Wendkos, 89 mins.)

At the Circus (1939)**½ The Marx Brothers, Margaret Dumont, Florence Rice, Kenny Baker, Eve Arden. The Marx Brothers in unmistakable decline. Groucho has his moments, as always, singing of "Lydia the Tattooed Lady," and he and Dumont have their act down to a stylized duet of sublime interplay. (Dir: Edward Buzzell, 87 mins.)†

At the Earth's Core (Great Britain, 1976) **½ Doug McClure, Peter Cushing, Cy Grant. Follow-up to *The Land That Time Forgot*. Occasionally entertaining blend of fantasy, humor, and chills based on the novel by Edgar Rice Burroughs. Cushing bores through to the center of the earth. (Dir: Kevin Connor, 90 mins.)†

Attic, The (1979)*** Carrie Snodgress, Ray Milland, Rosemary Murphy, Ruth Cox, Francis Bay, Marjorie Eaton. A domineering father stops at nothing to control his mousey daughter whom he bullies and badgers into caring for him in his wheelchair. Not frightening, but a chilling, nicely shaded psychological study. (Dir: George Edwards, 97 mins.)†

Attica (MTV 1980)**** George Grizzard, Charles Durning, Henry Darrow, Morgan Freeman, Anthony Zerbe. This gripping docudrama is about the unnecessary slaughter at Attica prison in 1971 after Governor Nelson Rockefeller sent in the New York state troopers. The writer and director had to make changes demanded by the network—one of which made the film less critical of Rockefeller—but it remains a searing, powerful indictment. (Dir: Marvin Chomsky, 104 mins.)†

Attic: The Hiding of Anne Frank, The (MTV 1988)**½ Mary Steenburgen, Paul Scofield, Huub Stapel, Eleanor Bron, Victor Spinetti. A new slant on the well-known story. Steenburgen is the personification of bravery and dedication as Miep Gies, the woman who helped shelter the Frank family. Although the details are familiar, it all seems brand new, thanks to the fine cast. (Dir: John Erman, 96 mins.)

Attila (France-Italy, 1955)*½ Anthony Quinn, Sophia Loren, Irene Papas. Attila the Hun, scourge of the Roman Empire, takes over Europe with a hunting party and piously does an about-face when met by Pope Leo I and his tabernacle choir. Schmaltz. (Dir: Pietro Francisci, 83 mins.)

At War with the Army (1950)** Dean Martin, Jerry Lewis, Polly Bergen. Sergeant tries to get a dumb PFC to help him out of some girl trouble. Despite the fact that this farce shot Martin & Lewis to fame as a screen comedy team, it doesn't happen to be terribly funny. (Dir: Hal Walker, 93 mins.)†

Audience, The (Italy, 1971)*** Enzo Jannacci, Ugo Tognazzi, Claudia Cardinale, Vittorio Gassman, Michel Piccoli, Alain Cluni. Satirical tale of a young man who goes to Rome in hopes of getting a message to the Pope. Biting anticlerical story about rigid bureaucracy. (Dir: Marco Ferreri, 114 mins.)†

Audrey Rose (1977)* Marsha Mason, Anthony Hopkins. Unscary drivel about reincarnation, ploddingly directed. Another rip-off of *The Exorcist* gambit and it fails, as another girl has nightmares and is seized by forces of the devil, tra la la.... (Dir: Robert Wise, 113 mins.)†

Au Hasard Balthazar (France, 1966)**** Anne Wiazemsky, François Lafarge, Philippe Asselin, Nathalie Joyaut. One of writer-director Robert Bresson's most enchanting and accessible works tells the story of the life cycle of a gentle donkey. The animal pulls plows and carriages, is ridden by children, turns a mill wheel, and works in a circus. Its death on a hillside, as sheep look on, is one of cinema's magical moments. Bresson has created a wonderful parable about the beauty of love and devotion and the willingness to please. It's a simple film that stirs the soul. (Dir: Robert Bresson, 95 mins.)

Auntie Mame (1958)***½ Rosalind Russell, Coral Browne, Roger Smith, Fred Clark,

Forrest Tucker, Peggy Cass. Everyone's favorite madcap relative proves that life's a banquet and most poor suckers are starving to death! Although the film slavishly follows the form of the play, complete with blackouts, Russell's comic cyclone of a performance supplies enough centrifugal force to keep a dozen comedies in motion. (Dir: Morton DaCosta, 143 mins.)†

Aunt Mary (MTV 1979)*** Jean Stapleton, Martin Balsam, Harold Gould, Dolph Sweet, Anthony Cafiso. A true "you can do anything you want" story, based on the experiences of Baltimore's Mary Dobkin (a chipper old maid who coaches a sandlot baseball team). (Dir: Peter Werner, 98 mins.)

Au Revoir Les Enfants (Good-bye, Children) (France, 1987)***½ Gaspard Manesse, Raphaël Fejtö, Francine Racette. Louis Malle's haunting, understated memoir of occupied France, set in a wintry Catholic boarding school, probes the relationship between a young student and his reserved new classmate whose Jewish identity is kept secret by the monks trying to protect him from the Gestapo. (104 mins.)†

Aurora (MTV 1984)**½ Sophia Loren, Daniel J. Travanti, Philippe Noiret. Loren stars as a widow with a blind son in need of an operation seeking help from former lovers. Okay melodrama. (Dir: Maurizio Ponzi, 104 mins.)

Author! Author! (1982)**½ Al Pacino, Dyan Cannon, Tuesday Weld, Alan King, Bob Dishy, Bob Elliott, Ray Goulding. Often lame comedy with a few funny one-liners. Al Pacino plays a playwright and father, trying to make a home for his son, and four other children who are offsprings from his wife and her various ex-husbands. (Dir: Arthur Hiller, 110 mins.)†

Autobiography of Miss Jane Pittman, The (MTV 1974)**** Cicely Tyson, Richard Dysart, Odetta, Michael Murphy, Collin Wilcox. One of the best movies ever made for TV. Cicely Tyson won an Emmy award for her triumphant performance as a 110-year-old woman who was an ex-slave, and lived to take part in a civil rights demonstration in 1962. Adapted from Ernest J. Gaines's novel. (Dir: John Korty, 102 mins.)†

Autumn Afternoon, An (Japan, 1962)***½ Chisu Ryu, Shima Iwashita, Shinichiro Mikami, Keiji Sada. Director Yasujiro Ozu's last film is a majestic story of an aging widower who marries off his last daughter, only to find himself lonelier than he has ever felt. As sensitive, beautiful, and rewarding as all of Ozu's best work. (115 mins.)

Autumn Leaves (1956)**½ Joan Crawford,

Cliff Robertson, Lorne Greene, Vera Miles, Ruth Donnelly. Crawford is fine as a middle-aged spinster who is romanced by a mentally unstable young man prone to fits of violence (Robertson). The material could go tawdry at any point, but doesn't. (Dir: Robert Aldrich, 110 mins.)†

Autumn Sonata (Sweden, 1978)**** Ingrid Bergman, Liv Ullmann, Lena Nyman. Director Ingmar Bergman painfully evokes the cruelty of unforgiveness, with Ullmann the resentful daughter trying, futilely, to settle old scores with her self-absorbed mother, a concert pianist of international rank, played with uncommon candor by Ingrid Bergman. (97 mins.)†

Avalanche (1978)*½ Rock Hudson, Mia Farrow, Robert Forster, Jeanette Nolan. A Rocky Mountain avalanche spoils the fun for denizens at a posh winter resort. (Dir: Corey Allen, 89 mins.)

Avalanche Express (1979)* Robert Shaw, Lee Marvin, Maximilian Schell, Linda Evans, Joe Namath. Shabbily constructed melodrama about CIA agents and their efforts to secure information on a biological warfare scheme from a defecting KGB agent. (Dir: Mark Robson, 88 mins.)

Avalon (1990)**** Armin Mueller-Stahl, Aidan Quinn, Elizabeth Perkins, Kevin Pollak, Joan Plowright, Lou Jacobi, Elijah Wood, Leo Fuchs, Israel Rubinek. Affectionate, poignant portrait of four generations of a Baltimore Jewish immigrant family. Much of the film is centered around family get-togethers, especially holiday meals, and Mueller-Stahl (in an exquisite performance) is the focus of the family's unity, which is strained by petty squabbles, the rise of the suburbs, and the introduction of television. The film's comedy is gentle, and its cinematography and production values are superb. *Avalon* is the name of the apartment building where the five brothers made their first home. (Dir: Barry Levinson, 127 mins.)†

Avanti! (1972)*** Jack Lemmon, Juliet Mills. Not one of director Billy Wilder's best, but entertaining nevertheless. A successful businessman goes to Italy to arrange for the return of his tycoon-father's body, only to discover dad died with his mistress of long standing. (144 mins.)

Avengers, The—See: **Day Will Dawn, The**

Avenging Angel (1985)* Betsy Russell, Rory Calhoun, Susan Tyrrell. Dopey exploitation flick. Angel returns to the streets she used to walk—in order to waste the killer of her policeman savior. Trashes the meager virtues of the original schlocker. (Dir: Robert Vincent O'Neil, 88 mins.)†

Avenging Conscience, The; Or, Thou Shall Not

Kill (1914)*** Lillian Gish, Henry B. Walthall. A psychological drama from D. W. Griffith, based on Edgar Allan Poe's *The Tell-Tale Heart*, this silent classic stars Walthall and Gish as the poet and his inspiration. Ambitious and fascinating. (Dir: D. W. Griffith, 78 mins.)†

Avenging Force (1986)** Michael Dudikoff, Steve James, John P. Ryan, James Booth, Bill Wallace, Karl Johnson. A secret agent battles a white supremacist group in this fist-flying, gun-popping action pic. (Dir: Sam Firstenberg, 103 mins.)†

Avenging Godfather (1979)* Rudy Ray Moore, Carol Speed, Lady Reed, Jimmy Lynch. Silly vintage blaxploitation. The original title was *Disco Godfather*, and you can't get any more seventies than that. (Dir: J. Robert Wagoner, 93 mins.)†

Aviator, The (1985)*½ Christopher Reeve, Rosanna Arquette, Jack Warden, Sam Wanamaker, Marcia Strassman, Tyne Daly, Scott Wilson. Dull attempt at an old-fashioned Hollywood romance about a dashing pilot and a spoiled rich girl. (Dir: George Miller, 96 mins.)†

Aviator's Wife, The (France, 1981)**½ Phillipe Marlaud, Marie Riviere, Anne-Laure Meury, Matthieu Carriere. When a man spots his lover with a former beau, he puffs up with jealousy and trails the flyer around Paris. Overdone romantic comedy. (106 mins.)

Awakening, The (1956)***½ Anna Magnani, Eleonora Rossi-Drago. A heartwarming and touching film. A nun becomes attached to a little boy who has run away from his mother. (Dir: Mario Camerini, 97 mins.)

Awakening, The (Great Britain, 1980)*½ Charlton Heston, Susannah York, Jill Townsend, Stephanie Zimbalist. Several unintended laughs cannot save this sleep-inducer about an archaeologist who uncovers an ancient Egyptian tomb. (Dir: Mike Newell, 105 mins.)†

Awakening of Candra, The (MTV 1983)*½ Blanche Baker, Cliff De Young, Richard Jaeckel, Jeffrey Tambor. A sleep-inducing pic about a bride who's kidnapped on her honeymoon. (Dir: Paul Wendkos, 104 mins.)†

Awakenings (1990)***½ Robert De Niro, Robin Williams, Julie Kavner, Ruth Nelson, Penelope Ann Miller, John Heard, Anne Meara, Judith Malina, Richard Libertini, Dexter Gordon, Max von Sydow. Engrossing, deeply moving account of actual events surrounding the administering of the drug L-dopa to patients in vegetative states, which results in their awakening from their virus-induced sleeping sickness. Penny Marshall directs without any flourishes. There are some wonderful comic and touching moments, but it's occasionally a bit pedantic. Powerhouse cast. De Niro got an Oscar nomination as the primary patient, but Williams, portraying the remarkable author-doctor Oliver Sacks, is also superb. (Dir: Penny Marshall, 121 mins.)†

Away All Boats (1956)**½ Jeff Chandler, George Nader, Julia Adams. Overproduced naval war drama; outrageous displays of heroics. (Dir: Joseph Pevney, 114 mins.)†

Awful Dr. Orloff, The (Spain, 1962)* Howard Vernon, Conrado Sammartin, Diana Lorys. Mad doctor kidnaps beautiful women. Orloff is awful. (Dir: Jess Franco, 95 mins.)

Awful Truth, The (1937)**** Cary Grant, Irene Dunne, Ralph Bellamy, Cecil Cunningham. Screwball comedy straight up; a divorcing couple discover that they need each other in spite of it all. Delicious and hilarious. (Dir: Leo McCarey, 90 mins.)†

Ay, Carmela! (Spain-Italy, 1990)*** Carmen Maura, Andres Pajares, Gabino Diego, Maurizio Di Razza, Miguel A. Rellan. Oscar nominee for Best Foreign Film. A traveling acting troupe entertains forces on both sides of the Spanish Civil War in order to survive. Maura's star turn energizes the film's politics. (Dir: Carlos Saura, 103 mins.)†

Aziza (Tunisia, 1980)***½ Yasmine Khlat, Raouf Ben Amor, Dalila Ramez, Mohammed Zinet. An orphaned girl learns independence. Compassionate film details the changing role of women in Arab society. (Dir: Abdel-Latif Ben Ammar, 90 mins.)

Babar: The Movie (Canada, 1989)**½ Voices of Gordon Pinsent, Gavin Magreth, Elizabeth Hanna. Inoffensive feature-length adaptation of the classic childrens' stories about the gentle elephant king is good for young kids. (Dir: Alan Bunce, 79 mins.)†

Babbitt (1934)*** Guy Kibbee, Aline MacMahon, Claire Dodd. They lost the bite of the Sinclair Lewis novel, but the performances, especially Mr. Kibbee's, help you forget the weak adaptation. (Dir: William Keighley, 74 mins.)

Babe (MTV 1975)*** Susan Clark, Alex Karras. Babe Didrikson Zaharias was one of the greatest female athletes of all time, and it was inevitable that a movie would be made about her life. Two solid performances by Clark, as Babe, and Karras, as her husband George Zaharias. Worth watching. (Dir: Buzz Kulik, 106 mins.)

Babe Ruth Story, The (1948)** William

Bendix, Claire Trevor, Charles Bickford. Sentimental, mediocre biography of the mighty Babe. Run-of-the-mill. (Dir: Roy Del Ruth, 106 mins.)†

Babes in Arms (1939)*** Mickey Rooney, Judy Garland, Charles Winninger, Guy Kibbee. Delightful though doctored version of the Rodgers and Hart musical hit about children of vaudeville parents who grow up to see vaudeville die. (Dir: Busby Berkeley, 97 mins.)†

Babes in Bagdad (1952)* Paulette Goddard, Gypsy Rose Lee. Ridiculous burlesque of Arabian Nights epics; weak all around. (Dir: Edgar Ulmer, 79 mins.)

Babes in Toyland—See: **March of the Wooden Soldiers**

Babes in Toyland (1961)**½ Tommy Sands, Annette Funicello, Ann Jillian, Ray Bolger. A colorful version of the Victor Herbert classic about the magical adventures of the people in Toyland. As produced by the Disney folks, it's light and tuneful, but lacking the heart, humor, and suspense of the original version with Laurel and Hardy. (Dir: Jack Donahue, 105 mins.)†

Babes in Toyland (MTV 1986)* Drew Barrymore, Richard Mulligan, Pat Morita, Eileen Brennan, Keanu Reeves, Jill Schoelen. Lousy version of Victor Herbert's operetta; Barrymore plays a tyke transported into a storybook village that must be liberated from the evil Barnaby, who has designs on Miss Mary (Schoelen). The muzak-al score of Leslie Bricusse is an insult to elevators and supermarkets everywhere. (Dir: Clive Donner, 144 mins.)

Babes on Broadway (1941)**½ Mickey Rooney, Judy Garland. Young hopefuls on Broadway. Only the musical numbers merit any attention. (Dir: Busby Berkeley, 118 mins.)†

Babes on Swing Street (1944)** Ann Blyth, Leon Errol, Peggy Ryan, Andy Devine, Kirby Grant. Passable Grade B musical: a bunch of youngsters try to open a nightclub to pay dues to a music school. (Dir: Charles Gould, 69 mins.)

Babette's Feast (Denmark, 1987)**** Stéphane Audran, Birgitte Federspiel, Bodil Kjer, Jarl Kulle. A moving, flawlessly constructed adaptation of an Isak Dinesen tale about a French exile (Audran) who finds refuge working for two elderly sisters in a Danish fishing village in 1871. Masterful in every aspect. Academy Award winner for Best Foreign Film. (Dir: Gabriel Axel, 102 mins.)†

Babette Goes to War (France, 1959)** Brigitte Bardot, Jacques Charrier, Hannes Messemer, Ronald Howard. Bardot is at the peak of her beauty in this otherwise flat war comedy about a French refugee

lass sent by the British as a smoke screen to relax Nazi troops while they kidnap a German general. Too bad the movie doesn't match Bardot's power. (Dir: Christian-Jaque, 106 mins.)

Baby, The (1973)**½ Anjanette Comer, Ruth Roman, Marianna Hill, Suzanne Zenor, David Manzy. Starting out as a social document about a kinky family and a dedicated welfare worker, this develops into a full-fledged horror film. Comer becomes interested in Baby, fully grown but with the mind of an infant. (Dir: Ted Post, 86 mins.)†

Baby Blue Marine (1976)*½ Jan-Michael Vincent, Glynnis O'Connor, Katherine Helmond. A young man washed out of boot camp returns to his small California home town and claims to be a war hero. Idealized characters, vacuously played. (Dir: John Hancock, 89 mins.)

Baby Boom (1987)*** Diane Keaton, Sam Shepard, Harold Ramis, Sam Wanamaker, James Spader. Keaton is charming as an unrepentant yuppie who is suddenly confronted with nonfinancial responsibility in the form of a baby left to her by a dead cousin. (Dir: Charles Shyer, 103 mins.)†

Babycakes (MTV 1989)*** Ricki Lake, Craig Sheffer, John Karlen. Overweight mortuary attendant, feeling love has passed her by, makes a no-holds-barred attempt at winning the man of her dreams. Based on the German film *Sugarbaby*, this is an appealing comedy-drama with a fine turn by Lake (*Hairspray*). (Dir: Paul Schneider, 96 mins.)

Baby Cat (France, 1983)* Julie Margo, Felix Marten, Corinne Carson. Mistress of a rich businessman plots her own kidnapping so that she and her other boyfriend can extort a fat ransom from the sugar daddy. Soft-core sleaze, badly dubbed in English. (Dir: Pierre Unia, 76 mins.)

Baby Doll (1956)***½ Carroll Baker, Eli Wallach, Karl Malden, Mildred Dunnock, Lonny Chapman, Rip Torn. Tennessee Williams's tale about a child bride, her possessive but foolish husband, and a stranger who dupes them. Works brilliantly most of the time, thanks to Elia Kazan's direction and a good cast. (114 mins.)†

Baby Face (1933)*** Barbara Stanwyck, George Brent, Donald Cook, Douglass Dumbrille, Margaret Lindsay. Remarkable performance by Stanwyck as the ultimate pre-Code gold digger, hopping up the social ladder from bed to bed. (Dir: Alfred E. Green, 70 mins.)†

Baby Face Harrington (1935)*** Charles Butterworth, Una Merkel, Nat Pendleton, Eugene Pallette, Donald Meek, Claude

Gillingwater. Extremely funny gangster spoof directed by Raoul Walsh, of all people, along the lines of *Three Men on a Horse*. Butterworth, as a mild-mannered clerk, and Pendleton, as an inept hood, have scenes together that are truly hilarious. (Dir: Raoul Walsh, 61 mins.)

Baby Face Harry Langdon (1925-26)*** Harry Langdon. Two shorts from the once-famous but now nearly forgotten silent clown, scripted by Frank Capra, who began his career as one of Langdon's gag men. Includes *Saturday Afternoon* and *Lucky Stars*. Well worth seeing. (60 mins.)†

Baby Face Nelson (1957)*** Mickey Rooney, Carolyn Jones, Cedric Hardwicke. Action-crammed story of stickups, bank robberies, ruthless killings, and prison breaks. (Dir: Don Siegel, 85 mins.)

Baby Girl Scott (MTV 1987)**½ John Lithgow, Mary Beth Hurt, Linda Kelsey. What happens when parents have a premature baby that only technology can keep alive? It's a nightmare as they battle doctors for the right to let their child die. Superb performances, but depressing. (Dir: John Korty, 104 mins.)

Baby, It's You (1982)*** Vincent Spano, Rosanna Arquette, Joanna Merlin, Jack Davidson, Nick Ferrari, Tracy Pollan, Matthew Modine, Robert Downey, Jr., Fisher Stevens. Director John Sayles has fashioned an accurate and poignant portrait of the youth of the late sixties and their coming of age during those turbulent times. Arquette and Spano are excellent as two high school kids who come from opposite sides of the tracks but are attracted to each other. The narrative follows the pair through her college days and his Miami adventures as a waiter-singer. (105 mins.)†

Baby Love (Great Britain, 1969)** Linda Hayden, Keith Barron. A sleazy tale about a nymphet who uses her wiles and body to sexually enslave a household. (Dir: Alastair Reid, 98 mins.)†

Baby M (MTV 1988)*** JoBeth Williams, John Shea, Robin Strasser, Bruce Weitz, Anne Jackson, Dabney Coleman. This miniseries was quickly produced after the actual events it dramatizes; nevertheless, it stands as a quality production, which has the good faith to present the issue it explores—that of surrogate motherhood—in an objective manner. Williams plays Mary Beth Whitehead, the celebrated surrogate mother who decided she wanted to keep her baby daughter. (Dir: James Steven Sadwith, 192 mins.)

Babymaker, The (1970)**½ Barbara Hershey, Sam Groom, Collin Wilcox-Horne. A young, free-spirited girl agrees to bear a child, fathered by the husband of a childless

couple. Offbeat drama, successful most of the way. (Dir: James Bridges, 107 mins.)†

Baby...Secret of the Lost Legend (1985)*** William Katt, Sean Young, Patrick McGoohan. A couple (Katt and Young) decide to adopt an orphan—only it's a dinosaur whose dad has been killed and whose mom has been kidnapped. The bouncing baby brontosaurus is an adorable creation and audiences will be held rapt by the helpful humans trying to reunite Baby with his parent. (Dir: B. W. L. Norton, 95 mins.)†

Baby Sister (MTV 1983)** Ted Wass, Phoebe Cates, Pamela Bellwood, Efrem Zimbalist, Jr., Virginia Kiser. Soapy, sappy romantic drama involving a troubled girl who falls for her sister's boyfriend...and lots of tragedy, crazed drug dealers, dirt from the past, and illicit trysts. (Dir: Steven Hilliard Stern, 104 mins.)

Babysitter, The (MTV 1980)**½ William Shatner, Patty Duke Astin, Stephanie Zimbalist, Quinn Cummings. A troubled married couple (superbly played by Shatner and Astin) hire an attractive teenager to take care of their house and younger daughter. Shortly thereafter, the babysitter takes over the family with spellbinding effect and eventually tries to kill them. (Dir: Peter Medak, 104 mins.)†

Baby Take a Bow (1934)**½ Shirley Temple, James Dunn, Claire Trevor, Alan Dinehart. The darling of the Depression had her first top-lined role here and enchanted audiences as a pouty-lipped Pollyanna who helps her pop overcome the stigma of a prison record. (Dir: Harry Lachman, 76 mins.)†

Baby, the Rain Must Fall (1965)** Lee Remick, Steve McQueen, Don Murray. Soggy drama of a noble wife who tries to live with her moody, guitar-twanging, hotheaded husband. (Dir: Robert Mulligan, 100 mins.)†

Bachelor and the Bobby-Soxer, The (1947)*** Cary Grant, Myrna Loy, Shirley Temple, Rudy Vallee. Sparkling comedy with artist Grant, the object of a crush from teenage Temple, "sentenced" by the girl's older sister to be her escort until she gets over him. Grant uses his seductive physical grace to the hilt as the overage escort in juvenile settings. Loy matches him in the ability to rip out dialogue at a precision-drill clip, and the interaction between them sparkles. (Dir: Irving Reis, 95 mins.)†

Bachelor Apartment (1931)**½ Lowell Sherman, Irene Dunne, Mae Murray, Norman Kerry. A man-about-town has had too many girlfriends; sly and amusing, thanks to star and director Sherman.

This is also a rare chance to see Murray, a great silent star. (77 mins.)

Bachelor Bait (1934)**½ Stuart Erwin, Rochelle Hudson, Pert Kelton. Breezy, early George Stevens-directed comedy about a civil servant who starts a marriage brokerage and ends up entangled in the complications. (75 mins.)†

Bachelor Father (1930)**½ Marion Davies, Ralph Forbes, C. Aubrey Smith, Ray Milland. An elderly rake decides to meet his illegitimate grown-up children. Pre-Production Code farce was considered extremely risqué in its time. Charmingly played, especially by Davies. (Dir: Robert Z. Leonard, 90 mins.)

Bachelor Flat (1962)**½ Terry-Thomas, Tuesday Weld, Richard Beymer. A shy professor is caught in a romantic complication with a forthright teenager. Amusing. (Dir: Frank Tashlin, 91 mins.)

Bachelor in Paradise (1961)*** Bob Hope, Lana Turner, Paula Prentiss, Jim Hutton. Author upsets a suburban community when he moves in to write about life there. Pleasing comedy. (Dir: Jack Arnold, 109 mins.)

Bachelor Mother (1939)***½ Ginger Rogers, David Niven, Charles Coburn. Delightful comedy directed by Garson Kanin, with Rogers as recipient of an abandoned baby. Of course, nobody believes that one, but the store owner's son (Niven) is most understanding. Remade as *Bundle of Joy* (1956). (81 mins.)†

Bachelor Party, The (1957)*** Don Murray, E. G. Marshall, Jack Warden, Carolyn Jones, Patricia Smith, Larry Blyden. Once shocking but still compelling slice of social realism from Paddy Chayefsky's sensitive pen. On the eve of his marriage, a bookkeeper is treated to a stag party where despair rather than merriment prevails. With a brilliant Oscar-nominated performance by Jones as a love-starved party girl. (Dir: Delbert Mann, 93 mins.)

Bachelor Party (1984)*½ Tom Hanks, Tawney Kitaen, Adrian Zmed, George Grizzard. A minor little comedy in which a bridegroom throws one of those rowdy prenuptial affairs, much to the chagrin of both his fiancée and her father. (Dir: Neal Israel, 106 mins.)†

Back at the Front (1952)**½ Tom Ewell, Harvey Lembeck, Mari Blanchard. Bill Mauldin's wacky GI creations—Willie and Joe—find themselves back in uniform and in trouble with the M.P.'s. (Dir: George Sherman, 87 mins.)

Back Door to Heaven (1939)*** Wallace Ford, Aline MacMahon, Stuart Erwin, Kent Smith, Van Heflin, Jimmy Lydon. Undeservedly obscure social problem drama about delinquency and its causes. Impact builds forcefully, as poverty inexorably leads a youth to lawbreaking. (Dir: William K. Howard, 85 mins.)

Backdraft (1991)** Kurt Russell, William Baldwin, Scott Glenn, Jennifer Jason Leigh, Rebecca DeMornay, Donald Sutherland, Robert De Niro. Large-scale drama about contemporary Chicago firemen has good special effects but gets lost in the smoke with a dull brother vs. brother storyline. Weak performances hamper film, but De Niro, as an arson investigator, and Sutherland, as an arsonist, both shine. (Dir: Ron Howard, 138 mins.)†

Backfire (1950)** Gordon McRae, Edmond O'Brien, Virginia Mayo, Dane Clark, Viveca Lindfors, Ed Begley. Murky postwar mystery about the hunt for a missing man, framed for murder by a gangster whose gal he was messing with. (Dir: Vincent Sherman, 91 mins.)

Backfire (France, 1964)**½ Jean-Paul Belmondo, Jean Seberg, Gert Frobe. Good comedy and action. Smuggler Belmondo tries to transport a car to Lebanon. (Dir: Jean Becker, 97 mins.)

Backfire (1988)** Keith Carradine, Karen Allen, Jeff Fahey, Dinah Manoff. Cheating wife Allen wants to kill her husband, Fahey. Her plans are set awry when his past begins to catch up with him. Overheated *noir* update tries yet again to substitute empty style for a novel plot. (Dir: Gilbert Cates, 91 mins.)†

Back from Eternity (1956)**½ Robert Ryan, Anita Ekberg, Rod Steiger. Fair remake of *Five Came Back*. Plane forced down in the jungle can return to safety with only five passengers. (Dir: John Farrow, 97 mins.)†

Back from the Dead (1957)** Peggie Castle, Arthur Franz, Marsha Hunt. The actors try very hard with this supernatural tale about a nice girl who is suspected of being a fiend. (Dir: Charles Marquis, 79 mins.)

Background to Danger (1943)**½ George Brent, Brenda Marshall. Spy story set in Turkey. Bad guys Peter Lorre and Sydney Greenstreet make it a treat. (Dir: Raoul Walsh, 80 mins.)

Backlash (1956)**½ Richard Widmark, Donna Reed. Two people set out to solve the mystery surrounding an Apache massacre of five people—two of whom were never identified. (Dir: John Sturges, 84 mins.)

Back Roads (1981)**½ Sally Field, Tommy Lee Jones, David Keith, Miriam Colon. Field plays a hooker, Jones a footloose guy she takes up with on a journey from Mobile to California. Not credible enough to be taken seriously, and not funny enough to make the grade as comedy. (Dir: Martin Ritt, 94 mins.)†

Back Street (1932)**½ Irene Dunne, John Boles, George Meeker, ZaSu Pitts. This first sound filming of the novel by Fannie Hurst is well acted by Irene Dunne as a "kept woman," but will seem excessively sentimental by today's standards. (Dir: John M. Stahl, 89 mins.)

Back Street (1941)*** Charles Boyer, Margaret Sullavan, Richard Carlson. Incandescent lead performances elevate this soap opera about a married man and his "back street" wife. Based on Fannie Hurst's novel. (Dir: Robert Stevenson, 89 mins.)

Back Street (1961)** Susan Hayward, John Gavin, Vera Miles. Third version of the tearful tale of love on the sly. Not up to the previous versions. (Dir: David Miller, 107 mins.)†

Back to Bataan (1945)*** John Wayne, Anthony Quinn. American colonel forms a guerrilla army in the Philippines to fight the Japanese. Well made, exciting war drama. (Dir: Edward Dmytryk, 95 mins.)†

Back to God's Country (1954)** Rock Hudson, Marcia Henderson, Steve Cochran. Adventure yarn about a couple who face tremendous obstacles. Takes place in Canada. (Dir: Joseph Pevney, 78 mins.)

Back to School (1986)***½ Rodney Dangerfield, Sally Kellerman, Burt Young, Keith Gordon, Robert Downey, Jr., Paxton Whitehead, Terry Farrell. Riotously funny comedy in which Rodney decides to go to college along with his kid. Self-made man Rodney buys his way into the Ivy League establishment and becomes the big party man on campus before learning that doing things the hard way is best. Hilarious sight gags and one-liners. (Dir: Alan Metter, 90 mins.)†

Back to the Beach (1987)*** Frankie Avalon, Annette Funicello, Lori Loughlin, Tommy Hinkley, Connie Stevens. Good-natured reunion for those *Beach Party* teenagers, Frankie and Annette, now cast as parents. (Dir: Lyndall Hobbs, 90 mins.)†

Back to the Future (1985)*** Michael J. Fox, Christopher Lloyd, Lea Thompson, Crispin Glover, Marc McClure, Wendy Jo Sperber. Teenager travels back in time aboard a nuclear-powered DeLorean to 1955, where he meets his parents as high-schoolers. With the help of a mad scientist, he tries to unite his youthful parents in matrimony before he ceases to exist. A madcap comedy with lots of zingy one-liners and exaggerated characterizations. (Dir: Robert Zemeckis, 115 mins.)†

Back to the Future, Part II (1989)** Michael J. Fox, Christopher Lloyd, Lea Thompson, Thomas F. Wilson, Charles Fleischer, Flea, Joe Flaherty. All stops are pulled out for this impressive but unsatisfying sequel, with Fox playing three different

characters (on-screen at the same time!) in the year 2015 before spending the bulk of the movie in an alternate 1985 and back in 1955. Intricate plot sets up some astounding state-of-the-art visual effects. (Dir: Robert Zemeckis, 107 mins.)†

Back to the Future, Part III (1990)*** Michael J. Fox, Mary Steenburgen, Christopher Lloyd, Lea Thompson, Thomas F. Wilson, Elisabeth Shue, Richard Dysart. Entertaining and imaginative third installment to this delightful series finds Fox traveling back in time to the Wild West to save the life of his eccentric scientist companion (Lloyd). The blending of fantasy and western genres works beautifully and benefits from eye-popping special effects. (Dir: Robert Zemeckis, 118 mins.)†

Backtrack (1969)**½ Neville Brand, Doug McClure, Peter Brown, William Smith, Fernando Lamas, Rhonda Fleming, Ida Lupino, Royal Dano, James Drury. McClure is on his way to Mexico when he stops to help Texas Rangers find a gang of train robbers. Nonstop fights and plenty of colorful characters elevate this one a bit. (Dir: Earl Bellamy, 95 mins.)

Backwoods Massacre (1980)*½ Melanie Verlin, Lawrence Tierney, John Amplas. John Russo, who co-wrote the original *Night of the Living Dead*, wrote and directed this thriller about a runaway girl captured by a family of Satanists. AKA: **Midnight**. (88 mins.)†

Backyard (1986)**** A moving autobiographical exploration by filmmaker Ross McElwee of his strained relationship with his father. McElwee captures the real essence of people, conflict, the way words hurt, and how some folks just get under one's skin. A beautiful, oddly loving relationship. (87 mins.)†

Bad—See: **Andy Warhol's Bad**

Bad and the Beautiful, The (1952)***½ Kirk Douglas, Lana Turner, Dick Powell, Gloria Grahame, Walter Pidgeon, Barry Sullivan. Excellent drama about ambition and success in Hollywood. One ruthless producer, superbly played by Kirk Douglas, touches and affects the lives of many people. Gloria Grahame won an Oscar. (Dir: Vincente Minnelli, 118 mins.)†

Bad Bascomb (1945)** Wallace Beery, Margaret O'Brien. Run-of-the-mill western which is only good in the scenes where little Margaret tames outlaw Beery. (Dir: Sylvan Simon, 110 mins.)

Bad Blood (New Zealand, 1987)**½ Jack Thompson, Carol Burns, Dennis Lill. True story of a failed farmer with a paranoid delusion that his neighbors were responsible for his problems, who went berserk and murdered seven people.

Thompson gives a strong performance in a film that may be a little unclear to American audiences not familiar with the incident. (Dir: Mike Newell, 104 mins.)†

Bad Blood (1989)—See: **Woman Obsessed, A**

Bad Boy (1949)*** Audie Murphy, Lloyd Nolan. The head of a boys' rehabilitation ranch makes a man of a youth considered to be a hopeless criminal. Good melodrama. (Dir: Kurt Neumann, 86 mins.)

Bad Boys (1983)***½ Sean Penn, Reni Santoni, Jim Moldy, Esai Morales, Eric Gurry. *Bad Boys* is a sometimes effective, extremely disturbing look at the treatment of delinquent youths. Penn conveys the anger and hostility of someone sliding into crime, yet there is always the hint that his life could become more constructive if only someone could reach him. (Dir: Richard Rosenthal, 123 mins.)†

B.A.D. Cats, The (MTV 1980)* Asher Brauner, Steve Hanks, Jimmie Walker, Vic Morrow. Junky pilot film. The B.A.D. (Burglary Auto Detail) Cats destroy cars and property as they chase gold thieves and auto theft wiz Jimmie Walker. (Dir: Bernie Kowalski, 78 mins.)

Bad Company (1931)**½ Ricardo Cortez, Helen Twelvetrees, John Garrick, Frank McHugh, Edgar Kennedy, Harry Carey. Sharp flick about a manipulative gangster with designs on the innocent sister of his enemy. Directed by the underrated Tay Garnett. (75 mins.)

Bad Company (1972)***½ Jeff Bridges, Barry Brown. Brown plays a youth on the run in the Civil War West, whose misadventures form the basis of the film. A fine script meshes humor, action, and insight in order to present a picture of an immature generation forced to grow up to survive. (Dir: Robert Benton, 91 mins.)†

Bad Day at Black Rock (1954)**** Spencer Tracy, Robert Ryan, Anne Francis, Ernest Borgnine, Lee Marvin, John Ericson, Walter Brennan. An excellent cast enhances this powerful story about a well-guarded town secret and the stranger who uncovers it. (Dir: John Sturges, 81 mins.)†

Bad Dreams (1988)*½ Jennifer Rubin, Bruce Abbott, Richard Lynch, Harris Yulin. The sole survivor of a Jonestown-like cult massacre awakens from a coma 13 years later, only to be haunted by the spirit of the cult's evil guru. Half-baked horror whose visual slickness is at odds with the cheap nature of its storytelling. (Dir: Andrew Fleming, 84 mins.)†

Bad for Each Other (1954)** Charlton Heston, Lizabeth Scott, Dianne Foster.

Wealthy socialite tries to convince young doctor to practice among the town's exclusive clientele. Dull soap opera. (Dir: Irving Rapper, 80 mins.)

Badge of Marshal Brennan (1957)** Jim Davis, Arleen Whelan. An outlaw is mistaken for the new marshal in town and thereby hangs the plot. (Dir: Albert C. Gannaway, 76 mins.)

Badge of the Assassin (MTV 1985)*** James Woods, Yaphet Kotto, Alex Rocco, Steven Keats, Larry Riley, Pam Grier, Rae Dawn Chong. A look back at an incident when militant blacks killed cops to express their discontent. James Woods and Yaphet Kotto play the prosecuting attorney and the black detective determined to seek justice; their intensity keys this retelling of a turbulent chapter of history. (Dir: Mel Damski, 104 mins.)†

Badge 373 (1973)* Robert Duvall, Verna Bloom, Henry Darrow, Eddie Egan. Screenplay by Pete Hamill, based on the adventures of real-life cop Eddie Egan. (Dir: Howard W. Koch, 116 mins.)†

Bad Girl (1931)**½ Sally Eilers, James Dunn, Minna Gombell, William Pawley. A young couple face the hardships of married life after she becomes unexpectedly pregnant. The film won an Oscar for its director, neglected master Frank Borzage. (90 mins.)

Bad Girls—See: **Les Biches**

Bad Guys (1986)** Adam Baldwin, Mike Jolly, Michele Nicastro, Ruth Buzzi. Two cops trade in pounding a beat for taking a pounding on mats in the not-so-glamorous world of wrestling. Expect to be half-nelsoned and pummeled with sight gags, insult humor, and over-the-top acting. (Dir: Joel Silberg, 86 mins.)†

Bad Influence (1990)** Rob Lowe, James Spader, Lisa Zane, Christian Clemenson. Devilesque nasty-boy Lowe teaches milquetoast stockbroker Spader a few tricks about sex and revenge, but eventually demands a price. David Koepp's script (which borrows heavily from his much better *Apartment Zero*) never lives up to plot's promise, and director Curtis Hanson is too busy aping Hitchcock to repair the damage. Spader and Clemenson, who's terrific as his paranoid pothead brother, are the film's only merits. (90 mins.)†

Bad Jim (1990)**½ James Brolin, Richard Roundtree, John Clark Gable, Harry Carey, Jr., Rory Calhoun, Ty Hardin, Pepe Serna. A supporting cast of veteran western stars decorates this enjoyable Old West story about three bank robbers who carry out their thefts while pretending to be Billy the Kid and his gang. Light on plot, but still recommended to western fans starved for something new. (Dir: Clyde Ware, 90 mins.)†

Badlanders, The (1958)**½ Alan Ladd, Ernest Borgnine, Katy Jurado. A remake of *Asphalt Jungle* on horseback as Ladd and Borgnine plan a big gold robbery. Good action. (Dir: Delmer Daves, 83 mins.)

Bad Lands (1939)**½ Noah Beery, Jr., Robert Barrat, Guinn Williams, Andy Clyde, Robert Coote. Slightly off-beat western with more than a passing resemblance to *The Lost Patrol*, about a posse lost in the Arizona desert. Unusual cast. (Dir: Lew Landers, 70 mins.)

Badlands (1974)**** Sissy Spacek, Martin Sheen, Warren Oates. A remarkable directorial debut by Terrence Malick, who also wrote and produced this meticulous film about two young lovers who go on a killing spree in the 1950s before being apprehended. Based on the real-life killing spree of Charles Starkweather and Caril Fugate. (95 mins.)†

Badlands of Dakota (1941)**½ Broderick Crawford, Robert Stack. When his brother marries the girl he loves, an ordinary guy turns outlaw. (Dir: Alfred E. Green, 74 mins.)

Bad Lord Byron (Great Britain, 1949)** Dennis Price, Mai Zetterling, Joan Greenwood, Linden Travers, Ernest Thesiger, Wilfred Hyde-White. Stiff version of the life of the notorious rake and poet. Unlike the subject it lacks humor, and the cast is largely wasted. (Dir: David Macdonald, 85 mins.)

Bad Luck (Poland, 1960)*** Bogumil Kobiela, Maria Ciesielska, Barbara Kwiatkowski, Aleksander Dzwonkowski. Director Andrzej Munk's last film is an affectionate tale of Poland's history from the 1930s to the 1950s as reflected in the melancholy story of a middle-aged inmate who tells the warden about the miseries of his life. Both sad and funny, a keen example of the Polish film community's struggle against bureaucracy and conformity. (158 mins.)

Bad Manners (Canada, 1984)½ Martin Mull, Karen Black, Anne DeSalvo. A grotesque comedy about a wealthy couple who adopt an urchin from an orphanage, but all his orphan buddies conspire to spring him from his gilded cage. (Dir: Bobby Houston, 85 mins.)†

Badman's Country (1958)** George Montgomery, Neville Brand, Buster Crabbe. Pat Garrett forsakes retirement to team with Wyatt Earp and Buffalo Bill (Malcolm Atterbury) to snare outlaws led by Butch Cassidy. Routine western. (Dir: Fred Sears, 68 mins.)

Badman's Territory (1946)*** Randolph Scott, Ann Richards. Marshal has to put up with the most notorious outlaws in the West in a territory outside the control of the government. Good western. (Dir: Tim Whelan, 97 mins.)

Bad Medicine (1985)*½ Steve Guttenberg, Alan Arkin, Julie Hagerty, Bill Macy, Curtis Armstrong, Julie Kavner. A puerile comedy that never lives up to its premise—surely a comedy about American doctors-to-be who couldn't make a U.S.A. medical school and must resort to studying in a banana republic should have resulted in funnier situations than this. (Dir: Harvey Miller, 96 mins.)†

Badmen of Missouri (1941)*** Dennis Morgan, Jane Wyman, Arthur Kennedy. Exploits of the infamous Younger brothers. (Dir: Ray Enright, 71 mins.)

Bad News Bears, The (1976)*** Walter Matthau, Tatum O'Neal, Vic Morrow, Joyce Van Patten, Brandon Cruz, Jackie Earle Haley. Sparkling comedy. A former minor-league ballplayer who presently cleans swimming pools signs on to coach a team with lots of enthusiasm, but little skill. His solution is to recruit the meanest spitball pitcher in the state, an 11-year-old girl. (Dir: Michael Ritchie, 105 mins.)†

Bad News Bears Go to Japan, The (1978)*½ Tony Curtis, Jackie Earle Haley, Tomisaburo Wakayama. Curtis's adept portrayal of a talent agent out to exploit the famous kids' baseball team is the only notable aspect of this forgettable film. (Dir: John Berry, 91 mins.)†

Bad News Bears in Breaking Training, The (1977)** William Devane, Clifton James, Jimmy Baio, Chris Barnes. The first lackluster sequel to the box-office hit about a team of young baseball misfits. This one, which takes the Bears to the Houston Astrodome, lacks the cast and quality of the original. (Dir: Michael Pressman, 103 mins.)†

Bad Ronald (MTV 1978)**½ Scott Jacoby, Kim Hunter, Pippa Scott. Macabre little tale about a young boy living in a secret room in an old Victorian house and slowly going mad. (Dir: Buzz Kulik, 72 mins.)†

Bad Seed, The (1956)*** Nancy Kelly, Patty McCormack, Eileen Heckart. The macabre stage hit is faithfully brought to the screen, chills intact, except for a trumped-up Hollywood ending. Nancy Kelly goes through a series of hysterical scenes as the mother of a six-year-old murderess, excellently portrayed by Patty McCormack. (Dir: Mervyn LeRoy, 129 mins.)†

Bad Seed, The (MTV 1985)** Carrie Wells, Blair Brown, David Carradine, Lynn Redgrave, David Ogden Stiers. Remake of the '50s movie based on the hit play. This one has watered down the terror of a young child who turns out to be a cold-blooded killer when things don't go her way. (Dir: Paul Wendkos, 104 mins.)

Bad Sleep Well, The (Japan, 1960)*** Toshiro Mifune, Takeshi Kato, Masayuki Mori. More stylish than similarly plotted American films, this crime thriller delves into corporate corruption, Japanese style. Given Kurosawa's mastery of the medium, it's more involving than "The Yakuza" if you're in the mood for crime oriental style. (Dir: Akira Kurosawa, 135 mins.)

Bad Son, A (France, 1980)***½ Patrick Dewaere, Yves Robert, Brigitte Fossey, Claire Maurier. Young Frenchman returns home to Paris after serving time in a U.S. jail for dealing drugs. His readjustment and fight against drug addiction are the heart of this excellent story, keenly acted, about average people overwhelmed by disorienting problems. (Dir: Claude Sautet, 110 mins.)

Bad Taste (New Zealand, 1988)*** Peter Jackson, Pete O'Herne, Mike Miett, Terry Potter. If you thought *The Evil Dead* was outrageous, wait 'til you see this one. Man-eating aliens, looking for stock for their chain of intergalactic fast-food restaurants, battle a squad of government commandos. The *ne plus ultra* of gore humor will have you howling with disbelief every other minute. Needless to say, *not* for all tastes, but a must for horror and special effects buffs. (Dir: Peter Jackson, 103 mins.)

Bad Timing: A Sensual Obsession (Great Britain, 1980)***½ Art Garfunkel, Theresa Russell, Harvey Keitel. A profoundly disturbing erotic drama about the oppressive relationship between a psychologist and a troubled young woman. The tension between the two is paralleled by director Nicolas Roeg's exceptional visual flourishes. (123 mins.)

Bagdad (1949)** Maureen O'Hara, Paul Christian, Vincent Price. The British-educated daughter of a tribal leader of the desert returns to her people after her father is murdered. (Dir: Charles Lamont, 82 mins.)

Bagdad Cafe (West Germany, 1988)*** Marianne Sagebrecht, CCH Pounder, Jack Palance. Warm affectionate story of a rotund German woman who parts from her husband somewhere on a road in Nevada and winds up finding a home at a roadside gas-station–cafe. Director Percy Adlon (*Sugarbaby*) fashions a perfectly charming group of oddballs to populate *Bagdad*, with Palance a standout as a friendly silk-shirted painter. Sagebrecht stands at the center of it all, giving a sympathetic, beautifully understated performance. (91 mins.)

Bahama Passage (1942)*½ Madeleine Carroll, Sterling Hayden. 'A' picture offers "C" entertainment in this hack tale of a lady who tames a bronze heman in the Bahamas. (Dir: Edward Griffith, 83 mins.)

Bail Jumper (1990)**½ Eszter Balint, B. J. Spalding, Tony Askin, Joie Lee. Peculiar comedy about a pair of thieves whose new love affair is continually interrupted by a string of natural disasters. Not for all tastes, but the movie to see if you've ever wanted to see Staten Island destroyed by a tidal wave. (Dir: Christian Faber, 96 mins.)

Bail Out at 43,000 (1957)** John Payne, Karen Steele, Paul Kelly. Routine flying film about pilots and their affairs. (Dir: Francis Lyon, 73 mins.)

Bait (1954)** Hugo Haas, Cleo Moore, John Agar. Haas is an old prospector married to a sexy blonde, trying to kill his partner. (Dir: Hugo Haas, 80 mins.)

Bait, The (MTV 1973)** Donna Mills, Michael Constantine, William Devane, Arlene Golonka. Miss Mills plays a policewoman acting as bait to catch a demented murderer. (Dir: Leonard Horn, 73 mins.)

Baja Oklahoma (MCTV 1988)**½ Lesley Ann Warren, Peter Coyote, Swoozie Kurtz, William Forsythe. Slow-moving but pleasant tale of a good ol' Texas gal who works by day as a barmaid, and dreams of being a famous country songwriter. (Dir: Bobby Roth, 105 mins.)

Baker's Wife, The (France, 1938)**** Raimu, Ginette Laclerc, Charles Moulin, Robert Vattier, Robert Brassa. A truly great actor (Raimu) in a profoundly poignant movie. The story is simplicity itself—about cuckoldry in rural France. Some villagers want to stop the baker's wife's adultery when it affects the quality of her husband's bread-making. (Dir: Marcel Pagnol, 124 mins.)

Balalaika (1939)** Nelson Eddy, Ilona Massey. Pretentious, dull operetta set in Russia during World War I about the time of the Revolution. (Dir: Reinhold Schunzel, 102 mins.)

Balboa (MTV 1982)** Tony Curtis, Carol Lynley, Jennifer Chase, Chuck Connors, Lupita Ferrer, Sonny Bono, Catherine Campbell, Cassandra Peterson, Martine Beswicke, Henry Jones. Feature version of a never-shown miniseries about power, sex, and corruption among the rich. As familiar as it sounds; we give it an extra half-star for the slightly bizarre cast. (Dir: James Polakof, 93 mins.)

Balcony, The (1963)*** Shelley Winters, Peter Falk, Lee Grant, Leonard Nimoy. Uneven but frequently interesting adaptation by screenwriter Ben Maddow of French author Jean Genet's disturbing symbolic play about life in a Parisian brothel. (Dir: Joseph Strick, 84 mins.)

Ballad in Blue—See: **Blues for Lovers**

Ballad of a Soldier (U.S.S.R., 1960)****
Vladimir Ivashov, Shanna Prokorenko, Antonia Maximova. This is a hauntingly beautiful story of a young Russian soldier's attempts to get home to see his mother during a leave from the Army during World War II; unspoiled by any propaganda whatever. Excellent example of Soviet filmmaking, a simple story that gains emotional resonance through the strength of its images and unaffected technique. Wonderfully directed and photographed. (Dir: Grigori Chukhrai, 89 mins.)†

Ballad of Andy Crocker, The (MTV 1969)***
Lee Majors, Joey Heatherton. A Vietnam war hero comes home to find nothing but disappointment and despair. His sweetheart has married another guy and his motorcycle repair business has been run into the ground by his lazy partner. (Dir: George McCowan, 73 mins.)

Ballad of Cable Hogue, The (1970)***½
Jason Robards, Jr., Stella Stevens, David Warner. Director Sam Peckinpah's ambitious, romantic elegy about capitalism and the old west. Robards is a worn-out prospector who talks to God. Stevens plays a prostitute who takes up with Robards, and Warner plays a disturbed preacher. (121 mins.)†

Ballad of Gregorio Cortez, The (1983)***
Edward James Olmos, Tom Bower, James Gammon. This true story deals with a Mexican cowhand who becomes the victim of prejudice in Texas. After a series of Spanish-English language misunderstandings, he ends up killing a local sheriff and is pursued by the Texas Rangers. (Dir: Robert Young, 99 mins.)†

Ballad of Josie, The (1968)*½ Doris Day, Peter Graves, George Kennedy, William Talman, Andy Devine, Audrey Christie. A raucous, forced comedy in which Doris's rancher neighbors lose sleep worrying while she raises sheep. (Dir: Andrew V. McLaglen, 102 mins.)

Ballad of Nareyama, The (Japan, 1984)***
Ken Ogata, Sumiko Sakamoto, Tonpei Hidari, Tukejo Aki. A stark viewing experience about life on the subsistence level for poverty-stricken farmers in 19th-century Japan. This sad ballad reaches the summit of its power in a scene in which an old woman climbs a mountaintop to prepare herself for death, thus removing one of her overburdened clan's burdens. (Dir: Shohei Imamura, 130 mins.)

Ballad of the Sad Cafe, The (U.S.-Great Britain, 1991)***½ Vanessa Redgrave, Keith Carradine, Cork Hubbert, Rod Steiger, Austin Pendleton, Beth Dixon. Exceptional film version of Carson McCullers' novella and Edward Albee's play about picaresque Southerners and a wild battle of the sexes. Well-made and superbly acted drama is directorial debut of Simon Callow. Not for everyone, but worth a look. (Dir: Simon Callow, 100 mins.)†

Ball of Fire (1941)***½ Barbara Stanwyck, Gary Cooper, Oscar Homolka, Henry Travers, S. Z. Sakall. A perfect cast and a crackling script (by Charles Brackett and Billy Wilder) make this a classic '40s comedy. A gangster's moll hides out with a group of unworldly professors. (Dir: Howard Hawks, 111 mins.)†

Baltimore Bullet, The (1980)**½ James Coburn, Bruce Boxleitner, Omar Sharif, Ronee Blakely, Michael Lerner. A vulgar tale of two hustlers (Coburn and Boxleitner) on the road, trying to set up a big game with legendary gambler Sharif. (Dir: Robert Ellis Miller, 103 mins.)†

Bambi (1942)***½ Animated. A children's classic, beautifully done by Walt Disney's Studios. Story of a fawn's life and his forest friends. From the book by Felix Salten. (Dirs: David Hand, Perce Pearce, 69 mins.)†

Bambole (France-Italy, 1965)** Monica Vitti, Elke Sommer, Franco Rossi, Gina Lollobrigida. Mundane quartet of stories on Italian life. AKA: **Four Kinds of Love.** (Dirs: Mauro Bolognini, Franco Rossi, Luigi Comencini, Dino Risi, 111 mins.)

Bamboo Prison, The (1954)*** Robert Francis, Brian Keith, Dianne Foster. A young sergeant is accused of collaborating with the Communists during the Korean War. (Dir: Lewis Seiler, 80 mins.)

Bamboo Saucer, The (1968)*½ John Ericson, Lois Nettleton, Dan Duryea, Nan Leslie, Bob Hastings. Laughable sci-fi, a combination Red Scare Picture and UFO Paranoia flick. The Yanks and Soviets team up to investigate a flying saucer which may have ties to Red China. (Dir: Frank Telford, 100 mins.)†

Banacek (MTV 1972)**½ George Peppard. Pilot for the detective series finds Banacek investigating the disappearance of an armored truck with a million-dollar-plus gold cargo. (Dir: Jack Smight, 104 mins.)

Banana Monster, The—See: **Schlock**

Bananas (1971)***½ Woody Allen, Louise Lasser, Howard Cosell, Carlos Montalban. Woody runs off to South America and becomes a revolutionary leader, in the only American film within memory that makes it clear that J. Edgar Hoover really was a black woman. So many of the jokes and sight gags are hilarious it doesn't matter—and probably can't be helped—that a few of them bomb out. (Dir: Woody Allen, 82 mins.)†

Bananas Boat, The (Great Britain, 1975)* Doug McClure, Hayley Mills, Lionel

Jeffries, Dilys Hamlett, Warren Mitchell. Nonsensical nautical comedy about a seafarer's adventures in Cuba and his long-suffering girl's efforts to get him to tie the knot. (Dir: Sidney Hayers, 101 mins.)†

Bande à Part—See: **Band of Outsiders**

Bandido (1956)**½ Robert Mitchum, Ursula Thiess, Zachary Scott. American adventurers cross the border into Mexico during the revolt of 1916 to sell weapons. (Dir: Richard Fleischer, 92 mins.)

Bandit of Sherwood Forest (1946)** Cornel Wilde, Anita Louise, Jill Esmond, Henry Daniell. The son of Robin Hood comes to the aid of the Queen. Elaborate but uninspired. (Dirs: George Sherman, Clifford Sanforth, 86 mins.)

Bandits (France, 1987)** Jean Yanne, Marie-Sophie Lelouch, Patrick Bruel. Proper young lady finds that her long-absent father has been in prison. She thinks of him as a sort of gentleman bandit, but learns otherwise when he is released. Not one of director Claude Lelouch's better efforts; he seems more concerned with close-ups of his female star (whom he married after filming) than with the story. (108 mins.)

Bandits, The (Mexico, 1967)*½ Robert Conrad, Jan-Michael Vincent, Roy Jenson, Pedro Armendariz, Jr. A trio of bandits are rescued by Mexican outlaws so they can find a hidden treasure. (Dirs: Robert Conrad, Alfredo Zacharias, 89 mins.)†

Bandits of Corsica (1953)** Richard Greene, Paula Raymond, Raymond Burr. Twins overthrow a villainous tyrant in Corsica. Humdrum costume melodrama, based on Dumas's *Corsican Brothers*. (Dir: Ray Nazarro, 82 mins.)

Band of Angels (1957)**½ Clark Gable, Yvonne DeCarlo, Sidney Poitier. Gable in the role of a New Orleans gentleman with a past. Sidney Poitier easily walks off with the acting honors as an educated slave. (Dir: Raoul Walsh, 127 mins.)

Band of Outsiders (France, 1964)***½ Sami Frey, Claude Brasseur, Anna Karina. One of Godard's more entertaining opuses. He adroitly mixes philosophical observations with musical numbers in this gangster fable about bungling burglars. AKA: **Bande à Part** (Dir: Jean-Luc Godard, 97 mins.)

Band of the Hand (1986)** Stephen Lang, Michael Carmine, Lauren Holly. Five of Miami's scurviest street trash are reformed, and return to the city cesspool to rid Miami of Vice. Mundane thriller. (Dir: Paul Michael Glaser, 109 mins.)†

Bandolero! (1968)*½ James Stewart, Dean Martin, Raquel Welch. Offbeat casting, with James Stewart and Dean Martin as two robbers, doesn't overcome the familiarity of this big-scale western. (Dir: Andrew V. McLaglen, 106 mins.)†

Band Wagon, The (1953)**** Fred Astaire, Cyd Charisse, Jack Buchanan, Nanette Fabray, Oscar Levant. A delightful musical with a wealth of familiar Dietz and Schwartz tunes, and Astaire in top form. The plot on which the musical numbers are conveniently hung involves the trials and tribulations of a Broadway show. (Dir: Vincente Minnelli, 112 mins.)†

Bang Bang Kid, The (U.S.-Spain-Italy, 1968)*** Guy Madison, Sandra Milo, Tom Bosley. Tight comedy approach to absurd tale of a feudal westerner who gets his comeuppance when a robot incites his people to insurgency. (Dir: Stanley Prager, 90 mins.)†

Bang, Bang, You're Dead (Great Britain, 1967)*½ Tony Randall, Senta Berger, Terry-Thomas, Herbert Lom, Wilfrid Hyde-White. Limp spy spoof about double agents and triple crosses, etc., in Marrakesh. (Dir: Don Sharp, 92 mins.)

Bang the Drum Slowly (1973)***½ Robert De Niro, Michael Moriarty, Vincent Gardenia, Heather MacRae, Phil Foster. De Niro is touching as an average baseball player dying of Hodgkin's Disease, who wants to play just one more season. Moriarty shines as his friend and teammate. (Dir: John Hancock, 98 mins.)†

Bang! You're Dead (Great Britain, 1954)**½ Jack Warner, Derek Farr, Veronica Hurst, Anthony Richmond. Young boy shoots a man in rural England and is tracked down by police. AKA: **Game of Danger**. (Dir: Lance Comfort, 88 mins.)

Banjo Hackett (MTV 1976)**½ Don Meredith, Ike Eisenmann, Jennifer Warren, Chuck Connors. Meredith becomes an 1880s horse trader with a good heart, whisking his nephew out of an orphanage with the intention of giving the boy a prize mare. (Dir: Andrew McLaglen, 103 mins.)

Banjo on My Knee (1936)**½ Joel McCrea, Barbara Stanwyck, Walter Brennan. Story of the folks who live along the banks of the Mississippi. (Dir: John Cromwell, 80 mins.)

Bank Dick, The (1940)**** W. C. Fields. One of the genuinely great movie comedians has a field day in this still wonderfully funny romp. As a reward for accidentally capturing a bank robber, Egbert Sousé is made a bank guard. (Dir: Eddie Cline, 74 mins.)†

Banker, The (1989)**½ Robert Forster, Duncan Regehr, Shanna Reed, Jeff Conaway, Leif Garrett, Richard Roundtree, Teri Weigel, Deborah Richter, E. J. Peaker. Corporate banker Spalding Osbourne (with a name like that, you'd have to be a banker) moonlights as a crossbow-wielding serial killer. Typical

63

slasher stuff enlivened by a familiar cast, led by Forster as the cop on the job. (Dir: William Webb, 95 mins.)†

Bank Shot, The (1974)* George C. Scott, Joanna Cassidy, Clifton James. A limp crime-caper comedy which strains for laughs. A collection of losers execute a bank heist (they actually uproot a small bank and drive it away). Based on the novel by Donald E. Westlake. (Dir: Gower Champion, 83 mins.)

Bannerline (1951)** Keefe Brasselle, Sally Forrest, Lionel Barrymore. Routine newspaper story about an aggressive small town reporter who tries to launch a one-man campaign against corruption. (Dir: Don Weis, 86 mins.)

Banning (1967)*½ Robert Wagner, Jill St. John, James Farentino, Anjanette Comer. Young men earn their living as golf pros. Watching is as tiring as walking eighteen holes around Banning's course. (Dir: Ron Winston, 102 mins.)

Banyon (MTV 1971)**½ Robert Forster, Anjanette Comer, Jose Ferrer, Darren McGavin. A tough John Garfield–type private-eye hero (Robert Forster) who drinks tea instead of booze, and plays it cool with the ladies, can hardly keep up with the killings after a hood is released from prison. (Dir: Robert Daly, 100 mins.)

Barabbas (Italy, 1962)**½ Anthony Quinn, Silvana Mangano, Arthur Kennedy, Jack Palance, Ernest Borgnine. Lavish spectacle concerning the thief whom Jesus replaced on the cross; his life in the mines, his victories as a gladiator. Far superior to the usual run of its kind. (Dir: Richard Fleischer, 134 mins.)†

Barbarella (France-Italy, 1968)**½ Jane Fonda, Milo O'Shea, Marcel Marceau. Far-out science fiction comic strip about a 41st-century astronaut. You can't help but be impressed by the resourcefulness of the special-effects crew and the various ways that were found to tear off what few clothes Jane seemed to possess. (Dir: Roger Vadim, 98 mins.)†

Barbarian, The (1933)**½ Ramon Novarro, Myrna Loy, Reginald Denny, C. Aubrey Smith, Edward Arnold, Hedda Hopper. Slight to the point of silliness, this exotic romance concerns a tourist in Egypt falling for her guide. The stars give it what interest it has, and it does contain Loy's famous nude swimming scene. Written by Anita Loos. (Dir: Sam Wood, 82 mins.)

Barbarian and the Geisha, The (1958)** John Wayne, Sam Jaffe. Confused historical drama about Townsend Harris, first U.S. Ambassador to Japan, and his adventures in the East. (Dir: John Huston, 105 mins.)†

Barbarians, The (1987)* Peter Paul, David Paul, Richard Lynch, Eva La Rue, Virginia Bryant. Two siblings separated by a cruel fate are reunited ten years later to thwart Kodar, the villain who had imprisoned them and kidnapped their queen. Stultifying. (Dir: Ruggero Deodato, 87 mins.)†

Barbarosa (1982)*** Willie Nelson, Gary Busey, Isela Vega, Gilbert Roland, Danny De La Paz, George Voskovec. A 19th-century fable about rites of passage and comradeship in the old west. Australian director Fred Schepisi and cinematographer Ian Baker effectively use the majestic Rio Grande landscape as a backdrop for the relationship of a legendary outlaw and the young farm lad he befriends. (90 mins.)†

Barbary Coast (1935)** Joel McCrea, Edward G. Robinson, Miriam Hopkins. Drama about the tough Barbary Coast during the late 1800s. Two fine supporting performances by Walter Brennan and Brian Donlevy. (Dir: Howard Hawks, 100 mins.)†

Barbary Coast, The (MTV 1975)**½ William Shatner, Dennis Cole, Lynda Day George, John Vernon. Shatner plays an undercover agent skulking about San Francisco's muddy streets of iniquity. Hokum amidst fairly gaudy surroundings. (Dir: Bill Bixby, 100 mins.)

Barbary Coast Gent (1944)** Wallace Beery, Binnie Barnes, John Carradine. Beery fans may enjoy this routine western about a con man who tries to be good. (Dir: Roy Del Ruth, 88 mins.)

Bare Essence (MTV 1982)**½ Genie Francis, Bruce Boxleitner, Linda Evans, Lee Grant, Joel Higgins, Donna Mills, Tim Thomerson. Women's-magazine fare about the not-so-sweet smell of success in the cutthroat Perfume Business. Tyger, a spunky Californian, deals with catty older ladies and preening males in New York's salons while learning about love, rejection and how to avoid common scents. (Dir: Walter Grauman, 200 mins.)

Barefoot Contessa, The (1954)*** Humphrey Bogart, Ava Gardner, Rossano Brazzi, Edmond O'Brien. The life and times of an unhappy glamour girl: her beginnings, her rise to stardom, her loneliness, her tragedy. Splendid production and cast, occasional witty dialogue—but too talky, often obscure drama. (Dir: Joseph L. Mankiewicz, 128 mins.)†

Barefoot Executive, The (1971)*** Kurt Russell, Joe Flynn, Harry Morgan, Wally Cox. Walt Disney spoofs TV ratings with an amiable comedy for kids about a chimpanzee who is able to predict programs with good ratings. (Dir: Robert Butler, 96 mins.)†

Barefoot in the Park (1967)***½ Robert Redford, Jane Fonda, Charles Boyer, Mildred Natwick, Herb Edelman. Neil

Simon's Broadway smash hit survived the transfer to the big screen reasonably well. Benefits from Robert Redford, who repeats his Broadway role, and Jane Fonda, who does not, setting up Manhattan housekeeping with more ideas than money. (Dir: Gene Saks, 104 mins.)†

Barefoot Mailman, The (1951)**½ Robert Cummings, Terry Moore, Will Geer. Genial confidence man and a school girl try to swindle some yokels with shady railroad stock. (Dir: Earl McEvoy, 83 mins.)

Barfly (1987)*** Mickey Rourke, Faye Dunaway, Alice Krige, Jack Nance, J.C. Quinn, Frank Stallone. A raucous comic-drama from the pen of Charles Bukowski, bard of beer and broads. Rourke, trying on a character part for the first time, is slovenly yet appealing as the boozer who hides his literary activities from the other bar insects. His pursuit by a ritzy publisher (Krige) may seem unlikely, but his relationship with a female down-and-outer (played by Dunaway, always at her dingy best) is right on target. (Dir: Barbet Schroeder, 100 mins.)†

Barkleys of Broadway, The (1948)*** Fred Astaire, Ginger Rogers, Oscar Levant. Fred and Ginger are together again in this delightful, though not first-rate, film about the battles of a theatrical couple when one wants to abandon musicals for drama. (Dir: Charles Walters, 109 mins.)†

Bar Mitzvah Boy (Great Britain, 1976)***½ Jeremy Steyn, Maria Charles, Adrienne Posta. One of the most popular BBC-produced dramas, this mounting of Jack Rosenthal's play is about a boy who runs away on the day of his bar mitzvah. (Dir: Michael Tuchner, 75 mins.)

Barnaby and Me (Australia, 1977)**½ Sid Caesar, Juliet Mills, Sally Boyden, John Newcombe. Pleasant tale of a con man who falls for beautiful woman whose daughter has a pet koala. The kid falls for the guy long before her mom, and he is enchanted by the koala and turns over a new (eucalyptus) leaf. (Dir: Norman Panama, 90 mins.)†

Barn of the Naked Dead (1973)* Andrew Prine, Manuella Thiess, Sherry Alberoni. Low-budget horror perversity about a Nevada nut case with a barn full of tortured women and a mutant father wandering the desert. The director is actually Alan Rudolph, and the only reason to watch this is to marvel at how much better he got after his association with Robert Altman. AKA: **Terror Circus.** (Dir: "Gerald Cormier," 86 mins.)†

Barnum (MTV 1986)**½ Burt Lancaster, Hanna Schygulla, John Roney. The biographical film has Lancaster playing the old P.T. recalling his life in flashbacks.

The show is a bit uneven, but we all love a con man and Barnum's coup in presenting Tom Thumb and Jenny Lind, and the creation of the famed circus are hard to resist. (Dir: Lee Phillips, 104 mins.)†

Barocco (1978)*** Isabelle Adjani, Gerard Depardieu, Marie-France Pisier, Claude Brasseur, Jean Claude Brialy. Subdued but engrossing contemporary *noir* with Adjani drawn to the hood who killed her boxer boyfriend (both played by Depardieu). By turns disturbing and alluring, the film boasts beautiful photography by Bruno Nuytten and Adjani at her most entrancing. (Dir: André Techine, 110 mins.)

Baron and the Kid, The (MTV 1984)**½ Johnny Cash, Greg Webb, June Carter Cash, Claude Akins. Cash sticks to formula, becoming an alcoholic, cheating pool shark who sees the light, and then discovers his pool-hustler son is bent on repeating dad's mistakes. (Dir: Gary Nelson, 104 mins.)†

Baron Blood (Italy, 1972)*½ Joseph Cotten, Elke Sommer, Massimo Girotti. Ghastly ghost story, many gruesome murders. AKA: **Torture Chamber of Baron Blood.** (Dir: Mario Bava, 90 mins.)†

Baroness and the Butler, The (1938)** William Powell, Annabella, Helen Westley, Joseph Schildkraut, Nigel Bruce. A politician masquerades as a lady's butler—or is it the other way around? Underscripted whimsy; Powell is wasted, and French import Annabella (in her Hollywood debut) hadn't quite mastered English. (Dir: Walter Lang, 75 mins.)

Baron Munchausen (Czechoslovakia, 1961)*** Milos Kopecky, Jana Brejchova, Rudolf Jelinek, Karel Hoger. From the maker of *The Fabulous Jules Verne,* a similar combination of live action and animation is used to relate some of the more preposterous adventures of the infamous liar. Not really for kids, who probably won't get much of what's going on. AKA: **The Fabulous Baron Munchausen.** (Dir: Karel Zeman, 80 mins.)†

Baron of Arizona, The (1950)** Vincent Price, Ellen Drew. The story of James Addison Reavis, who once tried to swindle the government out of Arizona Territory by means of a fantastic scheme. Based on fact. (Dir: Samuel Fuller, 97 mins.)

Barracuda (MTV 1978)** Wayne David Crawford, Jason Evers, Roberta Leighton. Fair drama about the pollution of a river in a small Florida community. (Dir: Harry Kerwin, 93 mins.)†

Barren Lives—See: **Vidas Secas**

Barretts of Wimpole Street, The (1934)*** Norma Shearer, Fredric March, Charles Laughton. The romance of Elizabeth

Barrett and Robert Browning, despite the tyrannical opposition of her father, is given a respectful treatment by director Sidney Franklin and producer Irving Thalberg. (110 mins.)

Barretts of Wimpole Street, The (Great Britain, 1957)****½** Jennifer Jones, William Travers, John Gielgud. Sensitive but dull remake of the luminous love story between Elizabeth Barrett and Robert Browning. (Dir: Sidney Franklin, 105 mins.)

Barricade (1939)****** Alice Faye, Warner Baxter, Charles Winninger, Arthur Treacher, Keye Luke. Chinese civil war rages tangentially in the background; Faye and Baxter are thrown together in an embassy. In old movie fashion, war and revolution are just devices to bring romantics together. (Dir: Gregory Ratoff, 71 mins.)

Barrier (Poland, 1966)******* Jan Nowicki, Joanna Szczerbic, Tadeusz, Zygmunt Malonowicz. Surreal yet satisfying satire of everyday Polish life by director Jerzy Skolimowski. His script follows a dejected medical student on a search for the meaning of life. (83 mins.)

Barry Lyndon (Great Britain, 1975)*****½** Ryan O'Neal, Marisa Berenson, Patrick Magee, Hardy Kruger, Michael Hordern. Stanley Kubrick's tenth feature film is a lavish, visually ravishing adaptation of the Thackeray novel. Lyndon, passive but likable Irish lad, becomes a socially fashionable peer after his marriage to a rich widow (Berenson, who is exquisitely photographed at every turn). O'Neal's unemotional stoicism lends itself well to the role of the naive fledgling who learns quickly how to become a successful opportunist. (185 mins.)†

Barry McKenzie Holds His Own (Australia, 1975)****** Barry Crocker, Barry Humphries, Donald Pleasence, Roy Kinnear, John Le Mesurier, Tommy Trinder. Sequel to *The Adventures of Barry McKenzie* is equally loud, vulgar, and silly, as the ultimate Ozzie hero goes up against evil vampire Count Plasma (Pleasence). The Australian slang is confoundingly thick, but the raucous slapstick alone raises guffaws. Originally 120 mins. (Dir: Bruce Beresford, 93 mins.)†

Bartleby (Great Britain, 1970)*****½** Paul Scofield, John McEnery. Updating of Herman Melville's novella redefines the character of Bartleby as a symbol of modern, alienated man who is slowly giving up. Paul Scofield plays the boss who has empathy with Bartleby, but must fire him. The acting is superb. (Dir: Anthony Friedman, 79 mins.)

Bashful Elephant, The (1962)****** Molly Mack, Kai Fisher, Helmut Schmidt, Buddy Baer. Hungarian orphan girl, accompanied by

pet dog and elephant (!?) tries to find foster parents in Austria. Acceptable children's fare for the most part, except for a peculiar subplot about an extramarital affair being carried on by one of the prospective new parents. (Dirs: Dorrell and Stuart McGowan, 82 mins.)

Basic Training (1986)***** Ann Dusenberry, Rhoda Shear, Angela Ames, Will Nye, Walter Gotell. Farcical comedy about a savvy Secretary of Defense who proves that a woman's place is in the Pentagon by outsmarting the Russian bigwigs and the American top brass. Filmed in 1983. (Dir: Andrew Sugarman, 91 mins.)†

Basileus Quartet (Italy, 1984)******* Pierre Malet, Hector Alterio. This is an intricately plotted chamber drama about the effect of an ensemble violinist's death on his co-players. When the remaining members take on a young man to revive the quartet, each man finds his life changed by this young, talented musician. An intriguing treatise on the themes of aging and unrequited love—these themes are played together here with few false notes. (Dir: Fabio Carpi, 118 mins.)†

Basket Case (1982)****½** Kevin Van Hentenryck, Terri Susan Smith, Beverly Bonner, Robert Vogel. A one-of-a-kind low budget horror flick that runs the gamut from the sublime (imaginative concept and tart black humor) to the ridiculous (some of the worst amateur acting this side of Edith Massey). A boy is surgically separated from his freakish Siamese twin, but their fraternal bonds are not so easily broken; the siblings avenge themselves on the doctors who performed the surgery. (Dir: Frank Henelotter, 91 mins.)†

Basket Case 2 (1990)******* Kevin Van Hentenryck, Annie Ross, Kathryn Meisle, Heather Rattay, Jason Evers, Ted Sorel. Duane and his mutant bro Belial return in a refreshingly brain-damaged sequel with higher production values than its predecessor and a greater variety of garish monstrosities. This time the twins are brought into a community of "special people" run by the notorious but caring Dr. Freak (Ross) and threatened by a tabloid reporter. Good, gruesome fun. (Dir: Frank Henenlotter, 89 mins.)†

Bastard, The (MTV 1978)****½** Andrew Stevens, Lorne Greene, Patricia Neal, Barry Sullivan, Olivia Hussey, William Daniels, Kim Cattrall, Eleanor Parker. Lush historical epic. Originally shown in two parts, this film concerns Philip Kent, whose search for his birthright leads him from Europe to America, circa the Revolutionary War. (Dir: Lee H. Katzin, 200 mins.)

Bat, The (1958)***½** Vincent Price, Agnes Moorehead. Ineffective chiller about a smart dowager who foils a killer in a spooky mansion. (Dir: Crane Wilbur, 80 mins.)†

Bataan (1943)*** Robert Taylor, Thomas Mitchell. Good story of the heroes who endured one of our early World War II defeats. A grim reminder and a realistic melodrama. (Dir: Tay Garnett, 114 mins.)†

Bates Motel (MTV 1987)* Bud Cort, Lori Petty, Kerrie Keane, Jason Bateman, Gregg Henry, Moses Gunn. Norman Bates, Hitchcock's mama's boy and murderer bequeaths his famous motel to a fellow mental patient (Cort) who reopens the tourist trap for business. This amateurish mixture of spoof, suspense and pathos is haphazardly structured and abysmally written. (Dir: Ken Topolsky, 104 mins.)

Bathing Beauty (1944)**½ Esther Williams, Red Skelton, Basil Rathbone, Harry James, Xavier Cugat. Songwriter Skelton wants to retire with fiancée Williams, but his publisher (Rathbone) schemes to break them up. Brilliant color; flashy musical numbers. (Dir: George Sidney, 101 mins.)

Batman (1966)**½ Adam West, Burt Ward, Lee Meriwether, Frank Gorshin, Burgess Meredith, Cesar Romero. The dynamic duo's arch enemies team up to rub out the caped crusaders and control the world. (Dir: Leslie Martinson, 105 mins.)†

Batman (1989)**½ Jack Nicholson, Michael Keaton, Kim Basinger, Robert Wuhl, Michael Gough, Billy Dee Williams, Pat Hingle, Jack Palance, Tracey Walter. Box office blockbuster is visually overwhelming but dramatically negligible. Director Tim Burton recreates Gotham City as a nightmarish vision of the worst of New York. But the story is strictly kid stuff, as Batman (underplayed by Keaton) battles the Joker (overplayed by Nicholson). An enormous disappointment, especially when viewed on TV or video, where it loses most of its striking visual splendor. (126 mins.)†

Bat People, The (1974)** Stewart Moss, Marianne McAndrew, Michael Pataki, Paul Carr. A low-budget, sci-fi thriller that may have a happy ending, depending on your point of view. Dr. Beck is bitten by a bat on his honeymoon, starts acting strangely and, finally, turns into a bat. (Dir: Jerry Jameson, 95 mins.)†

Battered (MTV 1978)*** Karen Grassle, LeVar Burton, Mike Farrell, Joan Blondell, Howard Duff. Stories of three abused wives are interwoven in this realistic drama co-written by Grassle. Pulls no punches in its depictions of these emotional horrors. (Dir: Peter Werner, 100 mins.)†

Batteries Not Included (1987)**½ Hume Cronyn, Jessica Tandy, Frank McRae, Elizabeth Pena. Solid family fare (cynics beware) about a group of five people who fight against the demolition of their tenement home, and eventually receive aid from (Spielberg produced it—take a guess) cute, friendly aliens. Tandy and Cronyn lend some credibility to this fluff. (Dir: Matthew Robbins, 106 mins.)†

Battle at Apache Pass (1952)**½ John Lund, Jeff Chandler. Jeff Chandler repeats his characterization of the Indian Chieftain Cochise, which he originated in the film *Broken Arrow*, in this rousing western adventure. (Dir: George Sherman, 85 mins.)

Battle Beneath the Earth (Great Britain, 1968)** Kerwin Mathews, Viviane Ventura. Absurd yarn about a planned invasion of the U.S. by the Chinese through a maze of underground tunnels dug beneath major cities and defense centers. (Dir: Montgomery Tully, 92 mins.)†

Battle Beyond the Stars (1980)*** Robert Vaughn, John Saxon, Richard Thomas, George Peppard. Decent sci-fi entry about a young man's quest in space to recruit mercenaries to prevent a ruthless ruler from obliterating the planet Akir. The amiability of the script and the direction makes this an honestly enjoyable film. (Dir: Jimmy T. Murakami, 104 mins.)†

Battle Beyond the Sun (1963)* Edd Perry, Andy Stewart, Bruce Hunter, Arla Powell. Canny low-budget producer Roger Corman revamped a 1959 Russian space flick into this 1963 American sci-fi offering. Two groups clash over visiting rights to the Red Planet; the film's not worth fighting over. (Dir: Thomas Colchart, 75 mins.)†

Battle Circus (1953)** Humphrey Bogart, June Allyson. Love amid the holocaust of war serves as the plot line in this maudlin drama. Trite script and uninspired performances. (Dir: Richard Brooks, 90 mins.)

Battle Cry (1954)**½ Van Heflin, Aldo Ray, Nancy Olson, Tab Hunter, Mona Freeman, Dorothy Malone. A star-filled picturization of Leon Uris's adventure-packed tale of a bunch of marines during WWII. There are multiple subplots, all involving romance. (Dir: Raoul Walsh, 149 mins.)†

Battle Flame (1959)** Scott Brady, Elaine Edwards. Brady plays a lieutenant who meets his former love when he is wounded (you guessed it—she's a nurse). (Dir: R. G. Springsteen, 78 mins.)

Battleforce—See: **Great Battle, The**

Battle for the Planet of the Apes (1973)** Roddy McDowall, Claude Akins, John Huston. Last film in the series brings it full circle. The plot, for those who still care, is another case of crass human beings vs. the more intelligent simians. (Dir: J. Lee Thompson, 86 mins.)†

Battleground (1949)**½ Van Johnson, John

Hodiak, Ricardo Montalban, James Whitmore, George Murphy. Although a critical and commercial success, this story of the Battle of the Bulge has only intermittent patches of strong direction and forceful dialogue. James Whitmore's quiet authenticity stands out in his first showy role. (Dir: William Wellman, 118 mins.)

Battle Hell (Great Britain, 1957)*** Richard Todd, Akim Tamiroff. A fine film about the daring escape of a British ship which has run aground in the Yangtze River during the Chinese Civil War. (Dir: Michael Anderson, 113 mins.)†

Battle Hymn (1957)**½ Rock Hudson, Anna Kashfi, Dan Duryea, Don DeFore, Martha Hyer, Jock Mahoney. Well-filmed but slow and self-righteous true story of an Army chaplain who tries to help Korean orphans. Hudson is not at his best in such a heavy role. (Dir: Douglas Sirk, 108 mins.)

Battle of Algiers (Italy-Algeria, 1967)**** Brahim Haggiag, Jean Martin. Director Gillo Pontecorvo recreated the events leading up to the Algerians' independence from France without using actual newsreel footage, but imparting to the film a quality of astonishing realism. Pontecorvo's triumph includes his sympathetic handling of *both* sides of this agonizing, brutal struggle for independence. A masterpiece. (123 mins.)†

Battle of Austerlitz (France, 1960)** Leslie Caron, Jack Palance, Vittorio De Sica, Claudia Cardinale. Lavishly produced story of Napoleon and his ambitions as ruler. Badly marred by excessive cutting. (Dir: Abel Gance, 73 mins.)†

Battle of Britain (Great Britain, 1969)** Michael Caine, Laurence Olivier, Trevor Howard. All the cliché characters from the war movies of the '40s are back. As for the actual fighting of the Battle of Britain, it's squeezed in as a break from the melodrama of the one-dimensional story line. (Dir: Guy Hamilton, 130 mins.)†

Battle of El Alamein, The (Italy-France, 1968)**½ Frederick Stafford, Ettore Manni, George Hilton, Robert Hossein, Michael Rennie. Lots of action and a good plot enhance this tale of Rommel's defeat late in '42. (Dir: Giorgio Ferroni, 105 mins.)†

Battle of Elderbrush Gulch, The (1913); and **Musketeers of Pig Alley** (1912)**** Lillian Gish, Mae Marsh, Robert Harron. Video compilation with two of director D. W. Griffith's greatest shorts, made before he moved on to what are now thought of as feature-length films. Though preceding better-known masterpieces such as *Birth of a Nation*, both films offer gripping stories in a powerful, confident style. Essential viewing for anyone interested in film, and great entertainment. (60 mins.)†

Battle of Neretva, The (Yugoslavia-U.S.-Italy-West Germany, 1969)** Yul Brynner, Sergei Bondarchuk, Curt Jurgens, Sylva Koscina, Hardy Kruger, Franco Nero, Orson Welles. Tale of Yugoslavians facing a 1943 invasion by the Germans and Italians. When cut for American release, it lost much of its impact and coherence. Still, it won an Oscar nomination for Best Foreign Film. (Dir: Veljko Bulajic, 102 mins.)†

Battle of Rogue River (1954)** George Montgomery, Martha Hyer. Indians and the admittance of Oregon as a state. Average. (Dir: William Castle, 70 mins.)

Battle of the Bulge (1965)** Henry Fonda, Robert Ryan, Robert Shaw, Telly Savalas, Pier Angeli. Muddled WWII film. The performances are secondary to the battle scenes, and they're nothing special. (Dir: Ken Annakin, 162 mins.)†

Battle of the Commandos (Italy, 1969)**½ Jack Palance, Curt Jurgens, Diana Lorys, Tomas Hunter. Shades of *The Guns of Navarone:* Palance leads a commando raid against a giant German cannon near D-Day landing site. AKA: **Legion of the Damned.** (Dir: Umberto Lenzi, 94 mins.)†

Battle of the Coral Sea (1959)** Cliff Robertson, Gia Scala, Teru Shimada, Patricia Cutts. Robertson is a submarine officer who is captured by the Japanese and escapes from an island. (Dir: Paul Wendkos, 100 mins.)

Battle of the Mareth Line—See: Great Battle, The

Battle of the Sexes, The (Great Britain, 1960)** Peter Sellers, Robert Morley, Constance Cummings, Jameson Clark. This comedy, though unsuccessful, has many points of interest as it wavers between banal farce and piquant satire. Sellers plays the worm who turns Morley, his gout-ridden, sybaritic boss, and Cummings is a career woman executive on the rise. (Dir: Charles Crichton, 88 mins.)†

Battle of the Villa Fiorita, The (1965)** Maureen O'Hara, Richard Todd, Rossano Brazzi. When their mother runs off with her lover her children try to get her back with pater. (Dir: Delmer Daves, 111 mins.)

Battle of the Worlds (Italy, 1961)*½ Claude Rains, Bill Carter, Maya Brent, Umberto Orsini. Scientist races to explode a hostile planet as it hurtles toward earth. (Dir: "Anthony Dawson" [Antonio Margheriti], 84 mins.)†

Battleship Potemkin—See: Potemkin

Battleshock—See: Woman's Devotion, A

Battlestar Galactica (TV, 1978)** Lorne Greene, Richard Hatch, Dirk Benedict, Maren Jensen. Designed as TV's answer to *Star Wars*, this is the series' premiere episode that was later released theatrically. A sci-fi blockbuster about a huge spacecraft which escapes destruction by human-hating robots, the Cyclons. (Dir: Richard A. Colla, 152 mins.)†

Battle Stations (1956)** William Bendix, Richard Boone, John Lund. A naval aircraft carrier during WWII. (Dir: Lewis Seller, 90 mins.)

Battle Taxi (1954)** Sterling Hayden, Arthur Franz. Young officer learns the value of the helicopter rescue service in Korea. (Dir: Herbert Strock, 80 mins.)

Battletruck—See: **Warlords of the 21st Century**

Battle Zone (1952)** John Hodiak, Linda Christian, Stephen McNally, Martin Milner. Wartime adventure set in Korea, with two Marine photographers competing for Ms. Christian when not dodging bullets. (Dir: Lesley Selander, 82 mins.)

Battling Bellhop, The—See: **Kid Galahad** (1937)

Battling Hoofer, The—See: **Something to Sing About**

BAT 21 (1988)**½ Gene Hackman, Danny Glover, Jerry Reed. Downed in Viet Cong territory, a middle-aged officer must rely on his wits and radio contact with a helicopter pilot to escape. No great shakes, except for the solid professionalism of Hackman and Glover. (Dir: Peter Markle, 100 mins.)†

Bawdy Adventures of Tom Jones, The (Great Britain, 1976)** Nick Henson, Trevor Howard, Terry-Thomas, Arthur Lowe, Georgia Brown, Joan Collins, Jeremy Lloyd. Lowbrow musical version of Henry Fielding's classic novel is a poor substitute for the Albert Finney-Tony Richardson *Tom Jones*, though taken on its own merits it offers some laughs. (Dir: Cliff Owen, 89 mins.)†

Baxter (Great Britain, 1972)**½ Patricia Neal, Jean-Pierre Cassel, Britt Ekland, Scott Jacoby, Lynn Carlin. Moving drama of a boy's breakdown after his parents divorce. The acting is remarkably sensitive, especially Scott Jacoby in the title role. (Dir: Lionel Jeffries, 105 mins.)

Baxter (France, 1990)*** Lisa Delamare, Jean Mercure, François Driancourt. Unsentimental satire about Baxter, a half-civilized bull terrier who observes humankind with an ironic eye. He lives with, in turn, an elderly lady, a young couple, and a troubled teen as we see his perspective on their problems. Unusual and well worth seeing. (Dir: Jerome Bolvin, 82 mins.)

Bay Boy, The (Canada, 1985)** Liv Ullmann, Kiefer Sutherland, Peter Donat. A teen yearns to become a man in 1930s Nova Scotia. Fine period atmosphere and acting, marred by needless brutality. (Dir: Daniel Petrie, 107 mins.)†

Bay Coven (MTV 1987)*½ Pamela Sue Martin, Tim Matheson, Barbara Billingsley, Woody Harrelson. Not-too-chilling thriller about a couple who suspect that their neighbors are members of a witches' coven. (Dir: Carl Schenkel, 96 mins.)

Bay of Angels (France, 1962)*** Jeanne Moreau, Claude Mann, Paul Guers, Henri Nassiet. Light and airy film about a compulsive gambler who finds love with a bank clerk. Moreau makes this worthwhile. (Dir: Jacques Demy, 85 mins.)

Bay of Blood (Italy, 1971)**½ Claudine Auger, Luigi Pistilli, Claudio Volonte, Isa Miranda. Greed for a prime piece of isolated lakeside property inspires a series of murders. Not one of director Mario Bava's best, though the (purposely?) overdone denouement compensates for a lot of the tedium. AKA: **Last House on the Left Part II** (even though it has no relation to the Wes Craven film) and **Twitch of the Death Nerve**. (85 mins.)†

Bayou—See: **Poor White Trash**

Baywatch: Panic at Malibu Pier (MTV 1989)*½ David Hasselhoff, Parker Stevenson, Shawn Weatherly, Billy Warlock, Monte Markham, Richard Jaeckel. The adventures of lifeguards at a Malibu beach; primarily an excuse for displays of beef- and cheesecake. (Dir: Richard Compton, 96 mins.)

Beach Ball (1965)* Edd Byrnes, Chris Noel, Robert Logan. Sunbaked beach boys and girls in a familiar story about a musical group who needs money to keep the band going. (Dir: Lennie Weinrib, 83 mins.)

Beach Blanket Bingo (1965)**½ Frankie Avalon, Annette Funicello, Deborah Walley, Paul Lynde, Linda Evans. Beach adventure with the typical muscle-bound boys and the bikini-clad girls. (Dir: William Asher, 98 mins.)†

Beach Boys: An American Band, The (1985)*** The Beach Boys. The rock and roll group with the happiest sound of all bands sings about a sun-filled, carefree lifestyle that didn't reflect the offstage turmoil of its members. But this documentary is primarily a good-natured celebration of a musical sound that delivered good vibrations to its many fans and still does. (Dir: Malcolm Leo, 103 mins.)†

Beachcomber, The (Great Britain, 1938) ***½ Charles Laughton, Elsa Lanchester. Man of a shiftless disposition becomes respectable when a lady missionary sets out to reform him. Delightful comedy-drama based on Somerset Maugham's story. (Dir: Erich Pommer, 90 mins.)†

Beachcomber, The (1955)**½ Robert Newton, Glynis Johns. Bum meets missionary's sister on a tropical island and his life is changed. Overacted, but absorbing film. (Dir: Muriel Box, 82 mins.)

Beaches (1988)** Bette Midler, Barbara

Hershey, John Heard, Spalding Gray, Lanie Kazan. Soap opera about the life-long friendship of two women. Midler all but pushes Hershey right out of the movie, even in the latter's death scenes! For fans of Bette and of overwrought tearjerkers only. (Dir: Garry Marshall, 120 mins.)†

Beach Girls, The (1982)** Debra Blee, Val Kline, Jeana Tomasina, Adam Roarke. Innocuous beach party movie, with little plot to speak of, but lots of silly jokes and an attractive cast. Dumb but enjoyable. (Dir: Pat Townsend, 91 mins.)†

Beachhead (1954)**½ Tony Curtis, Frank Lovejoy, Mary Murphy. Four Marines are assigned to locate Jap mine fields off Bougainville. Routine. (Dir: Stuart Heisler, 89 mins.)

Beach House (1982)* Ileana Seidel, John Cosola, Kathy McNeil, Richard Duggan, Spence Waugh, Paul Anderson. Slobs and snobs are stuck together in the same New Jersey beach house, but patch up their differences in time for the big dance. With no gross-out scenes, no sex, and characters with names like Snooky, Nudge, and Googy. (Dir: John Gallagher, 75 mins.)†

Beach Party (1963)** Dorothy Malone, Robert Cummings, Harvey Lembeck, Frankie Avalon. Cummings has some good moments as a professor studying teenage dating habits in this sand and surf musical. (Dir: William Asher, 101 mins.)†

Beach Patrol (MTV 1979)*½ Christine Delisle, Richard Hill, Jonathan Frakes. Routine police story. Christine Delisle is a member of a special California police team who patrols the beaches in dune buggies. (Dir: Robert Kelljan, 90 mins.)

Beach Red (1967)*** Cornel Wilde, Rip Torn, Burr De Benning. Sincere and frequently moving. A group of Marines tries to capture a Japanese-held island near the Philippines. (Dir: Cornel Wilde, 105 mins.)

Beaks, the Movie (1987)*½ Christopher Atkins, Michelle Johnson. Pair of reporters connect a string of seemingly random attacks by birds into a larger bird-against-man conspiracy. Despite the goofy title, not a spoof of Hitchcock's *The Birds*, just a bad rip-off. AKA: **Birds of Prey**. (Dir: René Cordona, Jr., 86 mins.)†

Bear, The (1984)** Gary Busey, Cynthia Lake, Carmen Thomas, Harry Dean Stanton, Jon-Erik Hexum, Steve Greenstein. Flaccid biopic about Paul "Bear" Bryant, the legendary coach of the U. of Alabama. Busey growls convincingly as the coach, but the script is an incomplete forward pass. (Dir: Richard C. Sarafian, 112 mins.)

Bear, The (France, 1988)*** Good family film about an orphaned baby bear and the huge kodiak bear that "adopts" it. Not a Disney throwaway, this was made over several years with a huge budget and top French talent; it's the rare movie of its type that adults can enjoy as well simply for its accomplishment. (Dir: Jean-Jacques Annaud, 95 mins.)†

Bear Island (Canada-Great Britain, 1979)*½ Vanessa Redgrave, Donald Sutherland, Richard Widmark, Christopher Lee, Lloyd Bridges. Boring Alistair Maclean adaptation about a U.S. meteorological team on a barren Arctic island which once housed a German submarine base and a cache of gold. (Dir: Don Sharp, 118 mins.)†

Beast, The (1988)*** George Dzunda, Jason Patric, Steven Bauer. Effective war film, with plenty of parallels to Vietnam, set in Afghanistan during the Soviet occupation. The crew of a Russian tank, under a fanatical commander, wends its way through the desert while pursued by Afghani fighters bent on vengeance. (Dir: Kevin Reynolds, 109 mins.)†

Beast from the Haunted Cave, The (1960)*½ Sheila Carol, Michael Forrest, Frank Wolff. The performances of the actors are better than the script, but not as good as the beast's. (Dir: Monte Hellman, 65 mins.)†

Beast from 20,000 Fathoms, The (1953)**½ Paul Christian, Paula Raymond, Cecil Kellaway, Donald Woods, Lee Van Cleef. Radiation from an atom-bomb test in the Arctic thaws out a prehistoric rhedosaurus that slouches toward the Big Apple. Exceptional special effects by Ray Harryhausen. (Dir: Eugene Lourie, 80 mins.)

Beast In the Cellar, The (Great Britain, 1971)*½ Beryl Reid, Flora Robson, John Hamill, T. P. McKenna. A basement-quality thriller about two sisters secreting their demented brother away in the cellar. (Dir: James Kelley, 87 mins.)†

Beastmaster, The (1983)* Marc Singer, Tanya Roberts, Rip Torn. A demented high priest enslaves an ancient people and demands they sacrifice their young children. Singer and Roberts strut their gorgeous bodies through this campy movie on their way to stopping villain Torn. Strictly for beefcake fans. (Dir: Don Coscarelli, 120 mins.)†

Beast Must Die, The (Great Britain, 1975)**½ Calvin Lockhart, Peter Cushing, Charles Gray, Anton Diffring, Marlene Clark. Unusual combo of horror genre and an Agatha Christie mystery in which a big game hunter plans a hair-raising weekend by gathering at his large estate several guests—one of whom is a were-wolf. (Dir: Paul Annett, 93 mins.)†

Beast of Hollow Mountain (1956)**½ Guy Madison, Patricia Medina. A routine western with a bit of science fiction.

Interesting. (Dir: Edward Nassour, 79 mins.)

Beast of Morocco (1967)* William Sylvester, Diane Clare, Alizia Gur. Drivel about a man obsessed with a woman who turns out to be a vampire. (Dir: Frederic Goode, 86 mins.)

Beast of the City, The (1932)*** Walter Huston, Jean Harlow, Jean Hersholt, Tully Marshall, John Miljan. The granddaddy of "Dirty Harry." A police captain stoops to bending the law in his zeal to catch a particularly slippery criminal. None of the usual MGM sugarcoating here. (Dir: Charles Brabin, 87 mins.)

Beasts Are in the Streets, The (MTV 1978)** Carol Lynley, Dale Robinette. Carol Lynley plays a veterinarian at a wildlife park where the huge animals escape, menacing the populace. If you like shots of rhinos chasing down automobiles, tune in. (Dir: Peter Hunt, 104 mins.)

Beast with a Million Eyes (1956)*½ Paul Birch, Lorna Thayer, Dona Cole, Chester Conklin. Trite science fiction horror yarn with ridiculous plot developments involving a multi-orbed creature who preys on animals. Anyone for a Paul Birch film festival? (Dir: David Kramarsky, 78 mins.)

Beast with Five Fingers, The (1946)**½ Peter Lorre, Robert Alda, Andrea King. This story of a pianist's severed hand running amok has some fine images, and a good performance by Lorre, but it drags a lot. Luis Buñuel denied the popular rumor that he worked on parts of this film. (Dir: Robert Florey, 88 mins.)

Beast Within, The (1982)* Bibi Besch, Ronny Cox, Paul Clemens. A woman is raped by a foul monster, and when their progeny reaches puberty, his beastly nature surfaces. This kid will never make it as student council president. (Dir: Philippe Mora, 90 mins.)†

Beat, The (1988)* John Savage, David Jacobson, William McNamara. Absolutely awful drama about a poetry-spouting young man who changes the lives of a group of inner-city teens. Obscure and pretentious. (Dir: Paul Mones, 98 mins.)†

Beat Generation, The (1959)*½ Mamie Van Doren, Steve Cochran, Ray Danton. Psychopath gets his kicks assaulting housewives. Pretty sick stuff. AKA: **This Rebel Age.** (Dir: Charles Haas, 93 mins.)

Beat Girl (Great Britain, 1959)**½ David Farrar, Noelle Adam, Christopher Lee. A real archival find, a 1959 British teenpic. Including Adam Faith (later the road manager of *Stardust*), and introducing Gillian Hills as an angry teenager whose resentment of her attractive stepmother has made her determined to destroy her father's happy marriage. (Dir: Edmond T. Greville, 92 mins.)

Beatlemania (1981)½ Ralph Castelli, Mitch Weissman. Wretched, horrible, and (worst of all) unnecessary film version of the hit Broadway show which provided an "incredible simulation" of the Beatles in concert. (Dir: Joseph Manduke, 86 mins.)†

Beatrice (France, 1988)**½ Julie Delpy, Bernard Pierre Donnadieu, Monique Chaumette, Nils Tavernier. This harrowing drama, set in 14th-century France, details the emotional and physical brutalization suffered by a young woman at her father's hands. An overlong study in sustained misery from the director of the far better *Round Midnight* and *A Sunday in the Country*. Also available on video in a 132 min. version as **The Passion of Beatrice**. (Dir: Bertrand Tavernier, 128 mins.)†

Beat Street (1984)** Rae Dawn Chong, Jon Chardiet, Guy Davis. The first mainstream, all-breakin', all-rappin', all-graffiti movie! The plot concerns a record-scratching DJ, a breakdancer, and a subway painter with conflicts about going straight or continuing his life of vandalism. (Dir: Stan Lathan, 102 mins.)†

Beat the Devil (1954)**½ Humphrey Bogart, Jennifer Jones, Gina Lollobrigida, Peter Lorre, Robert Morley. Director John Huston's satiric thriller was so offbeat that it didn't die at the box office—it never even breathed. But it's a funny movie that spoofs the spy thriller genre in tricky, interesting ways, and Jones, Lorre, and Morley are quite hilarious. However, Bogart doesn't seem to get the joke. (92 mins.)†

Beau Brummell (1925)*** John Barrymo, Mary Astor, Willard Louis, Irene Rich, Carmel Myers. Barrymore was at his screen peak when he starred in this handsome period d piece as the famous womanizer with a grudge against the social order. Eighteen-year-old Astor became a star here as Brummell's lost love. The tearjerker ending is movie sentimentalism at its best. (Dir: Harry Beaumont, 117 mins.)†

Beau Brummell (1954)*** Elizabeth Taylor, Stewart Granger, Peter Ustinov. Superbly photographed and excellently played adventure-drama about the exploits of one of England's most colorful figures. (Dir: Curtis Bernhardt, 111 mins.)

Beau Geste (1939)***½ Gary Cooper, Ray Milland, Robert Preston, Brian Donlevy, J. Carroll Naish, Albert Dekker, Susan Hayward. Foreign Legion classic is brought to the screen with a superlative cast, and director William Wellman brings off the set pieces with impressive flair. Cooper, Milland, and Preston are the brothers Geste, though the film is easily stolen by Donlevy's martinet and Naish's informer. (120 mins.)

Beau Geste (1966)** Doug McClure, Guy

Stockwell, Telly Savalas. Another go-round for this yarn concerning brothers in the Foreign Legion. Pretty slack retelling. (Dir: Douglas Heyes, 103 mins.)

Beau James (1957)*** Bob Hope, Vera Miles, Paul Douglas, Alexis Smith. Hope stars as the dapper Mayor James Walker, in the life and times of New York's favorite politician and gay blade of the dizzy decade of the 1920s. Good entertainment. (Dir: Melville Shavelson, 105 mins.).

Beau Père (France, 1981)*** Patrick Dewaere, Ariel Besse, Nicole Garcia. What could have been another exploitation film of a serious subject—child sexuality—French style—is handled throughout with restraint and charm. A fourteen-year-old girl chooses to live with her mother's lover after her mother is killed in a car accident. (Dir: Bertrand Blier, 120 mins.)†

Beauties of the Night (France, 1952)***½ Gina Lollobrigida, Gerard Philippe, Martine Carol. A whimsical and charming fantasy. A struggling young composer takes refuge in a dream world. AKA: **Les Belles-de-Nuit.** (Dir: René Clair, 84 mins.)

Beautiful Blonde from Bashful Bend, The (1949)**½ Betty Grable, Cesar Romero, Rudy Vallee, Hugh Herbert, Margaret Hamilton. Director Preston Sturges's last Hollywood film hasn't the brashness or the inventiveness of his earlier masterworks. Grable is a saloon canary who shoots a sheriff and hides out as a schoolmarm. (77 mins.)†

Beautiful but Dangerous (Italy, 1958)*½ Gina Lollobrigida, Vittorio Gassman, Robert Alda. Operatic hijinks of 1900. Clichés come and go, but Miss Lollobrigida looks ravishing in her turn-of-the-century gowns. (Dir: Robert Z. Leonard, 103 mins.)

Beautiful but Deadly—See: **Don Is Dead, The**

Beauty and the Beast (France, 1946)**** Josette Day, Jean Marais. A lavish, surrealistic film of great interest. Cocteau's wild imagination never lets up as he follows the heroine through her unconventional love story with the Beast. Brilliant. (Dir: Jean Cocteau, 90 mins.)†

Bebo's Girl (Italy, 1964)**½ Claudia Cardinale, George Chakiris, Marc Michel. Cardinale shines in this romance about a village girl and a former war hero who is now wanted by the police. (Dir: Luigi Comencini, 106 mins.)

Because of Him (1946)*** Deanna Durbin, Franchot Tone, Charles Laughton, Helen Broderick, Stanley Ridges, Donald Meek. Comedy, songs and romance as playwright Tone and actress Durbin haggle over his new play. Laughton steals the movie as a hammy Broadway star, as perfect a bit of casting as you'll ever find. (Dir: Richard Wallace, 88 mins.)

Because of You (1952)**½ Loretta Young, Jeff Chandler. A woman serves a prison term for being an accessory to a crime and is determined to pick up the pieces of her life when she is paroled. (Dir: Joseph Pevney, 95 mins.)

Because They're Young (1960)**½ Dick Clark, Tuesday Weld. New high school teacher asks for trouble when he takes an active interest in the destinies of his pupils. (Dir: Paul Wendkos, 102 mins.)

Because You're Mine (1952)*** Mario Lanza, James Whitmore, Doretta Morrow, Paula Corday, Dean Miller. A drafted opera singer falls for the sister of his tough Army sergeant. One of Lanza's pleasanter vehicles. (Dir: Alexander Hall, 103 mins.)

Becket (Great Britain, 1964)**** Richard Burton, Peter O'Toole, John Gielgud, Donald Wolfit, Pamela Brown, Martita Hunt, Felix Aylmer. About the remarkable 12th-century Englishman, Thomas Becket, and his turbulent relationship with King Henry II of England. Based on the wonderful play by Frenchman Jean Anouilh. A thrilling pageant and a valuable history lesson. Sumptuously costumed and flawlessly directed by Peter Glenville. (148 mins.)†

Becky Sharp (1935)*** Miriam Hopkins, Cedric Hardwicke, Frances Dee, Billie Burke, Alison Skipworth. Old movie buffs will enjoy this as a star vehicle for Miriam Hopkins, who has a field day as the sharp-witted mercenary who climbs the ladder of social success without worrying about whom her hoopskirts are knocking out of the way. (The first full-length Technicolor film ever made.) (Dir: Rouben Mamoulian, 83 mins.)†

Bed and Board (France-Italy, 1970)***½ Jean-Pierre Leaud, Claude Jade, Hiroko Berghauer. One of director François Truffaut's most glowing commentaries on life and love, and the fourth in his partly autobiographical series which began with Antoine Doinel (Leaud) in *The 400 Blows*. (Then came *Love at Twenty* and *Stolen Kisses*.) His true love (Jade) has now become Antoine's wife and the film covers the first few years of their marriage. (95 mins.)

Bedazzled (Great Britain, 1967)*** Peter Cook, Dudley Moore, Eleanor Bron, Raquel Welch. A comedy based on the Faustian legend. It doesn't all work, but the jokes, both visual and verbal, are hurled at a rapid nonstop pace, and enough of them are sufficiently inventive and outrageous to reward any enterprising viewer. (Dir: Stanley Donen, 107 mins.)†

Bedeviled (1955)** Anne Baxter, Steve Forrest. Muddled melodrama about a young American preparing for the clergy and his encounter with a femme fatale in Paris. (Dir: Mitchell Leisen, 85 mins.)

Bedford Incident, The (1965)*** Richard Widmark, Sidney Poitier, James MacArthur, Martin Balsam. The dilemma which arises aboard a U.S. Navy destroyer after an unidentified submarine is discovered in the North Atlantic. Widmark's performance plus a fine production should hold your attention. (Dir: James Harris, 102 mins.)†

Bedknobs and Broomsticks (1971)**½ Angela Lansbury, David Tomlinson, Roy Smart, Andy O'Callaghan. This Disney fantasy about an apprentice witch foiling an invasion by Nazis in World War II mixes live action and animation with mixed results. The cartoon sequences, with a fast-moving animal soccer match and musical interlude underwater, are among the best animation Disney artists have ever done. (Dir: Robert Stevenson, 117 mins.)†

Bedlam (1946)*** Boris Karloff, Anna Lee, Ian Wolfe. A girl risks her life to reform the mental institutions in England in the 17th-century. Well-made, strong horror thriller. (Dir: Mark Robson, 79 mins.)†

Bed of Roses (1933)*** Constance Bennett, Joel McCrea, Pert Kelton, Franklin Pangborn, John Halliday. Little-known, acerbic comedy about the early years of the Depression. (Dir: Gregory La Cava, 67 mins.)

Bedroom Eyes (1986)**½ Kenneth Gilman, Dayle Haddon, Barbara Law. Stockbroker Harry Ross (Gilman) discovers a penchant for voyeurism that eventually makes him a murder suspect. Though it's marred by lapses of logic, this decent comic thriller could signal the arrival of a new subgenre—lighthearted yuppie porn. (Dir: William Fruet, 90 mins.)†

Bedroom Eyes II (1989)** Wings Hauser, Kathy Shower, Linda Blair, Jane Hamilton. Spurred by his wife's philandering, stockbroker Hauser has a fling with Blair, whose death makes both cheating spouses murder suspects. Minor suspenser keeps you guessing. (Dir: Chuck Vincent, 85 mins.)†

Bedtime Story, A (1933)**½ Maurice Chevalier, Helen Twelvetrees, Edward Everett Horton, Baby LeRoy. Chevalier seems pretty uneasy as a devil-may-care bachelor landed with an abandoned infant, but Baby Leroy is a real scene stealer. (Dir: Norman Taurog, 82 mins.)

Bedroom Window, The (1987)** Steve Guttenberg, Elizabeth McGovern, Isabelle Huppert, Paul Shenar, Carl Lumbly, Wallace Shawn, Frederick Coffin, Brad Greenquist. An effective foray into Hitchcock territory, but ultimately it falls apart due to assorted red herrings and implausibilities in character reactions. While carrying on an illicit affair with his boss's wife, Guttenberg insists on reporting an assault his married lover had witnessed but is too fearful to testify about. As the plot thickens, he pretends he was the one who saw the crime, but the Good Samaritan finds himself implicated in a series of rape murders and has to prove his innocence. (Dir: Curtis Hanson, 111 mins.)†

Bed Sitting Room, The (Great Britain, 1969)*** Rita Tushingham, Sir Ralph Richardson, Spike Milligan, Sandy Nichols. Surreal comedy about the survivors of an atomic war which has wiped out most of the world. Though episodic, it remains wickedly inventive. (Dir: Richard Lester, 91 mins.)

Bedtime for Bonzo (1951)**½ Ronald Reagan, Diana Lynn, Walter Slezak. Silly comedy has some appeal. Professor Reagan experiments with a chimp. (Dir: Frederick de Cordova, 83 mins.)†

Bedtime Story (1941)***½ Fredric March, Loretta Young. Actress wants to retire, but her playwright-husband has other ideas. Sparkling comedy. (Dir: Alexander Hall, 85 mins.)

Bedtime Story (1964)**½ Marlon Brando, David Niven, Shirley Jones. Wolfish GI and a smooth con man vie for the affections of a visiting soap queen in Europe. Provides some moments of fun. Remade as *Dirty Rotten Scoundrels*. (Dir: Ralph Levy, 99 mins.)†

Beer (1985)* Loretta Swit, Rip Torn, Kenneth Mars, David Alan Grier, Saul Stein, William Russ, Dick Shawn. Unbeerable comedy. An ad agency lands in the black after a campaign that hypes beer as the ultimate macho accoutrement. You'll need a case of Budweiser to get through this. (Dir: Patrick Kelly, 83 mins.)†

Bees, The (1978)* John Saxon, John Carradine, Angel Tompkins, Claudio Brook. Silly film about killer bees traveling from South America and now arriving at the U.S. The little insects are indestructible and very intelligent, unlike the story. (Dir: Alfredo Zacharias, 83 mins.)†

Beethoven's Nephew (France-West Germany, 1985)** Wolfgang Reichmann, Dietmar Prinz, Jane Birkin, Nathalie Baye, Mathieu Carrière. One wonders when Beethoven ever had time to compose his immortal symphonies while watching this overwrought period piece in which the great master (Reichmann) relentlessly pursues the task of being a guardian for his long-haired nephew. Talented director Paul Morrissey did a good deal of research for this project, but despite his passion he still seems out of his depth and allows Reichmann to devour the scenery in whole chunks. (103 mins.)†

Beetlejuice (1988)*** Alec Baldwin, Geena Davis, Catherine O'Hara, Jeffrey Jones, Winona Ryder, Michael Keaton, Sylvia Sidney. A wacky, wonderful fantasy in which a sweet young couple (Baldwin and Davis) dies and returns to their house as ghosts, only to find that an obnoxious family has moved in. Keaton is hilarious as a bizarre "bio-exorcist" they call upon to drive the intruders from their home, but the real star is the film's oddball look and tone, courtesy of *Pee-Wee's Big Adventure* director Tim Burton. A visual and comic delight. (96 mins.)†

Before and After (MTV 1979)**½ Patty Duke Astin, Bradford Dillman, Barbara Feldon. Astin is terrific as a pudgy married woman and mother who sees her marriage disintegrating right before her girdle. Wisecracking and self-deprecating, she finally embarks on a diet and exercise routine, eventually emerging as a new, trim, confident person. (Dir: Kim Friedman, 104 mins.)

Before I Hang (1940)**½ Boris Karloff, Evelyn Keyes, Bruce Bennett, Edward Van Sloan. Hokey B movie with Boris registering solidly on the goosebump scale with his interpretation of a mad scientist whose experiment with a serum goes awry. (Dir: Nick Grinde, 71 mins.)†

Before Stonewall (1985)**** A passionate look at America's gay and lesbian communities since the roaring twenties. This documentary is an examination of gay liberation as both a social and political process, and it employs an amazing variety of archival footage gleaned from both pro- and anti-gay points of view. (Dirs: Greta Schiller, Robert Rosenberg, 87 mins.)

Before the Revolution (France, 1964)***½ Adriana Asti, Francesco Barilli. An astonishing film about European politics and Marxism. One of the most surprising things about it is that Bernardo Bertolucci was only twenty-two when he directed this richly textured drama. Asti is outstanding as a neurotic young aunt suffering from guilt complexes. Original screenplay by Bertolucci. Loosely based on Stendhal's *The Charterhouse of Parma*. (112 mins.)

Before Winter Comes (Great Britain, 1969)**½ David Niven, Topol, Anna Karina. Comedy about the use of democratic or autocratic means in dispatching prisoners East and West after WWII; a multilingual con man gets into the action. (Dir: J. Lee Thompson, 108 mins.)

Beg, Borrow or Steal (MTV 1973)**½ Michael Cole, Michael Connors, Kent McCord. Offbeat heist film. Handicapped buddies find it rough staying legit, and decide to execute a robbery. (Dir: David Lowell Rich, 72 mins.)

Beggarman, Thief (MTV 1979)**½ Jean Simmons, Andrew Stevens, Glenn Ford, Lynn Redgrave, Tovah Feldshuh, Bo Hopkins, Anne Francis. In this glittering follow-up to the wildly successful miniseries "Rich Man, Poor Man," the Jordache family continues to wallow in their soapsuds and champagne bubbles in the 1960s. (Dir: Lawrence Doheny, 200 mins.)

Beggars of Life (1928)*** Wallace Beery, Louise Brooks, Richard Arlen, Edgar "Blue" Washington. There's no better evidence of Brooks' transcendent beauty than the fact that she remains attractive even while disguised as a boy for a good deal of this silent film about a girl on the run who encounters the "hobo" lifestyle firsthand. Some good cliffhanger action, and advanced visual effects by director William Wellman, following up his classic *Wings*. (90 mins.)

Beggar's Opera, The (Great Britain, 1953)***½ Laurence Olivier, Dorothy Tutin, Daphne Anderson, Hugh Griffith. A most interesting film of John Gay's 17th-century operetta of Macheath the highwayman, who is on the lam and torn between the loves of two women. Absorbing and unusual. (Dir: Peter Brook, 94 mins.)

Beginning, The (Made for Canadian TV, 1973)**½ Keir Dullea, Barry Morse. Derived from the TV series "Starlost." A trio of individuals find that the "world" they know is actually just a compartment on a space-ark populated by similarly confused human beings. AKA: **Starlost: The Beginning**. (Dir: Harvey Hart, 96 mins.)

Beginning of the End, The (1957)*½ Peter Graves, Peggie Castle. Giant grasshoppers menace the world this time. (Dir: Bert Gordon, 74 mins.)

Beginning or the End, The (1947)**½ Brian Donlevy, Robert Walker. Ambitious film which strives to tell the story of the first A-Bomb. Too many clichés. (Dir: Norman Taurog, 112 mins.)

Beguiled, The (1971)***½ Clint Eastwood, Geraldine Page, Elizabeth Hartman. Director Don Siegel's Civil War gothic horror tale is one of his best films, containing what is probably Eastwood's finest performance as a wounded Union soldier taking refuge in a girls' school under the knowing hand of mistress Page. At first the women go into a sexual panic reminiscent of the nuns in *Black Narcissus*, but there's no doubt that for all of Eastwood's tattered swagger, he is more the prey than the hunter. Evocative, frightening (but not violent), the film springs out of the best of Bierce and Poe—an art film in the most entertaining sense of the term. (109 mins.)†

Behave Yourself (1951)**½ Farley Granger, Shelley Winters, Margalo Gilmore, William Demarest, Lon Chaney, Jr., Sheldon Leonard, Marvin Kaplan, Allen Jenkins, Elisha Cook, Jr., Hans Conreid. Granger and Winters adopt a stray dog, but wish they hadn't when they meet its criminal owners. Sporadically amusing comedy. (Dir: George Beck, 81 mins.)†

Behind Enemy Lines (MTV 1985)*** Hal Holbrook, Ray Sharkey, David McCallum, Tom Isbell, Anne Twomey. A good WWII adventure film. The edge-of-your-seat plot involves a mission to annihilate a Norwegian scientist who may be a Nazi collaborator. (Dir: Sheldon Larry, 104 mins.)†

Behind Locked Doors (1948)*** Richard Carlson, Lucille Bremer. Investigator goes to a sanitarium where a missing judge is being held captive. Suspenseful, well-acted thriller. (Dir: Budd Boetticher, 61 mins.)

Behind the Badge—See: Killing Affair, A (1977)

Behind the Cellar Door—See: Revenge

Behind the Eight Ball (1942)**½ Ritz Brothers, Carole Bruce. Zany trio come to grips with a killer in a summer theater. Entertaining musical mystery; some good laughs. The Ritzes could be brilliant at times. (Dir: Edward Cline, 60 mins.)

Behind the Front (1926)**½ Wallace Beery, Raymond Hatton, Richard Arlen, Mary Brian, Chester Conklin. Army comedy features Beery and Hatton tumbling in and out of trouble. The granddaddy of a whole genre. (Dir: A. Edward Sutherland, 60 mins.)†

Behind the High Wall (1956)*½ Tom Tully, Sylvia Sidney. Worn-out prison escape plot is warmed up once more. (Dir: Abner Biberman, 85 mins.)

Behind the Korean Airliner Tragedy—See: Tailspin: Behind the Korean Airliner Tragedy

Behind the Mask (1932)** Boris Karloff, Jack Holt. The Secret Service combats a well-organized dope ring. Dated but entertaining. (Dir: John Francis Dillon, 70 mins.)

Behind the Rising Sun (1943)*** Tom Neal, Margo, Robert Ryan. Japanese publisher alienates his son with his extreme political views. Well-acted war drama. (Dir: Edward Dmytryk, 89 mins.)†

Behold a Pale Horse (1964)** Gregory Peck, Anthony Quinn, Omar Sharif. Renegade loyalist continues to harass the Spanish regime; police captain sees a chance to trap him. Vague, cloudy, slow. (Dir: Fred Zinnemann, 118 mins.)†

Behold My Wife (1935)*½ Sylvia Sidney, Gene Raymond. Offensive little "comedy" about a young man who marries an Indian to spite his family. (Dir: Mitchell Leisen, 78 mins.)

Being, The (1983)* Martin Landau, Jose Ferrer, Dorothy Malone, Ruth Buzzi, Rexx Coltrane. Another monster born of nuclear waste terrorizes an Idaho town. (Dir: Jackie Kong, 79 mins.)†

Being There (1979)*** Peter Sellers, Melvyn Douglas, Shirley MacLaine, Jack Warden, Richard Dysart, Richard Basehart. Based on Jerzy Kosinski's novel about a man who lives behind the walls of a Washington, D.C., house with its garden and TV (which is always on). When he's forced to enter the real world, this simple soul becomes, by a series of delightful ironies, the toast of the town by spouting meaningless jargon he's picked up from the tube. Peter Sellers gives one of his finest performances as the untutored victim of environmental isolation. (Dir: Hal Ashby, 107 mins.)†

Bejewelled (Great Britain, MTV 1991)** Emma Samms, Denis Lawson, Jean Marsh, Jerry Hall, Dirk Benedict. Weak Disney offering as Samms travels to England to place the family jewels in a museum, only to become lost on the journey. Youngsters may be amused. (Dir: Terry Marcel, 96 mins.)

Bela Lugosi Meets a Brooklyn Gorilla (1952)½ Bela Lugosi, Duke Mitchell, Sammy Petrillo, Charlita, Muriel Landers. Two bumbling idiots find themselves lost in a jungle where Bela rules the roost with his sinister behavior. Witless horror parody. AKA: The Boys from Brooklyn. (Dir: William Beaudine, 74 mins.)†

Believe In Me (1971)* Michael Sarrazin, Jacqueline Bisset, Allen Garfield. Botched drama about a drug addict whose girlfriend also becomes hooked on speed. (Dir: Stuart Hagmann, 90 mins.)

Believers, The (1986)*** Martin Sheen, Helen Shaver, Richard Masur, Harley Cross, Jimmy Smits, Robert Loggia. A genuinely effective film about the supernatural that starts off with a *Blue Velvet*-type tragedy-invades-suburbia opening, and closes with a re-enactment of the Abraham and Isaac story from the Bible. Sheen and Shaver acquit themselves admirably as the non-believers who are forced by circumstances to change their mind, but it is director John Schlesinger's riveting visual style that provides the focus here, lending a menacing quality to N.Y.C. streets. (100 mins.)†

Belizaire, The Cajun (1986)**½ Armand Assante, Gail Youngs, Michael Schoeffling. A thick, atmospheric chunk of Cajun folklore. Assante makes a swaggering heroic figure as a cagey Cajun who defends himself and the rights of his people against their Louisiana neighbors. (Dir: Glen Pitre, 105 mins.)†

Bell, Book & Candle (1959)*** James Stewart, Kim Novak, Jack Lemmon, Ernie Kovacs. This wacky B'way play is delightfully brought to the screen. Zany characters include a whimsical warlock, a high priestess of magic, and Ernie Kovacs as an eccentric author. It's fun all the way! (Dir: Richard Quine, 106 mins.)†

Bellboy, The (1960)**½ Jerry Lewis, Alex Gerry. Madcap misadventures of a bungling bellboy at a posh Florida hotel, and that's it—no plot, just a series of Lewis-oriented gags. (Dir: Jerry Lewis, 72 mins.)†

Bellboy and the Playgirls, The (U.S.-West Germany, 1962)* June Wilkinson, Gigi Held, Louise Lawson, Lori Shea. Nudie movie featuring an aspiring detective spying on a hotel full of models is noteworthy only as the directorial debut of Francis Ford Coppola, who merely added a few color scenes to a 1958 German film. (Dir: Fritz Umgelter, 94 mins.)†

Belle de Jour (France-Italy, 1967)**** Catherine Deneuve, Jean Sorel, Genevieve Page, Michel Piccoli. A remarkably beautiful film by director Luis Buñuel. A frigid young housewife decides to spend her midweek afternoons as a prostitute. Buñuel's familiar obsessions with anticlericism and hypocritical society, and a preoccupation with erotica, are all here. Comments on our sexual fantasies and hang-ups are humorous and perceptive. Based on Joseph Kessel's novel. (100 mins.)

Belle of New York, The (1952)**½ Fred Astaire, Vera-Ellen, Marjorie Main, Alice Pearce, Keenan Wynn. Turn-of-the-century comedy about a stage door Johnny who falls in love. The dancing's the thing and Astaire and Vera-Ellen make a good team. (Dir: Charles Walters, 80 mins.)

Belle of the Nineties (1934)**½ Mae West, Roger Pryor, John Mack Brown, Katherine De Mille, Duke Ellington and his Orchestra. Amusing satire on life in the Gay Nineties. Song, "My Old Flame," by Arthur Johnston and Sam Coslow. (Dir: Leo McCarey, 75 mins.)

Belle of the Yukon (1944)** Gypsy Rose Lee, Randolph Scott, Dinah Shore. Dance hall in the Yukon country. Mild Alaskan melodrama with music. (Dir: William Seiter, 84 mins.)

Belles-de-Nuits, Les—See: **Beautles of the Night**

Belles of St. Trinian's (Great Britain, 1954)*** Alastair Sim, George Cole, Joyce Grenfell, Hermione Baddeley. An enormously popular version of Ronald Searle's schoolgirl cartoons, in which the bankrupt institution (presided over by Sim in drag)

plays host to little darlings who play the horses, terrorize the natives, and indulge in assorted grotesqueries. (Dir: Frank Launder, 89 mins.)†

Belles on Their Toes (1952)**½ Jeanne Crain, Myrna Loy, Debra Paget, Jeffrey Hunter. Sequel to *Cheaper by the Dozen*. Some funny scenes involving the further adventures of the large Gilbreth family. (Dir: Henry Levin, 89 mins.)

Belle Starr (1941)**½ Gene Tierney, Randolph Scott, Dana Andrews. Tierney isn't exactly a raunchy outlaw, but then this isn't exactly the story of the real Belle Starr. Your basically absurd Hollywood laundry job. (Dir: Irving Cummings, 87 mins.)

Belle Starr (MTV 1980)**½ Elizabeth Montgomery, Cliff Potts, Michael Cavanaugh, Gary Combs. The talented Ms. Montgomery is Belle Starr, the bandit lady with an itch to steal cattle and rob trains alongside the James boys, the Youngers, and the Daltons. (Dir: John Alonzo, 104 mins.)

Belle Starr's Daughter (1948)**½ George Montgomery, Ruth Roman, Rod Cameron. Outlaw queen's offspring is bent on avenging her mother's death; but the youngster isn't all that bad. Neither is the film. (Dir: Lesley Selander, 86 mins.)

Bell for Adano, A (1945)***½ John Hodiak, William Bendix, Gene Tierney, Richard Conte, Glenn Lagan, Harry Morgan. John Hersey's story of the American occupation of a small Italian town is beautifully brought to life on the screen. Believable and sensitively handled. (Dir: Henry King, 103 mins.)

Bellissima (Italy, 1951)**½ Anna Magnani, Walter Chiari, Tina Apicella. Seriocomic neo-realist tale of a determined mother struggling to get her pretty child into the movies. Worth watching but not entirely enjoyable. (Dir: Luchino Visconti, 100 mins.)†

Bell Jar, The (1979)** Marilyn Hassett, Julie Harris, Anne Jackson, Robert Klein. A young girl's trip to the big city, won in a magazine short story contest, hastens her mental collapse. Sylvia Plath's tragic, autobiographical novel has no real cinematic potential, but this soppy-yet-well-intentioned adaptation may serve as a good introduction to its themes, a sort of Cliff Notes drama. (Dir: Larry Peerce, 107 mins.)†

Bellman and True (Great Britain, 1988)**½ Bernard Hill, Kieran O'Brien, Richard Hope, Frances Tomelty. Good performances by Hill and O'Brien highlight this drama about a computer expert forced to help engineer a bank heist, and the thirteen-year-old son in his charge. A familiar caper plot and parenting dilemmas are combined with unusual, often fresh results. (Dir: Richard Loncraine, 112 mins.)†

Bells, The (1926)*** Lionel Barrymore, Fred Warren, Boris Karloff. Barrymore stars in the silent film version of a play that was one of Sir Henry Irving's standbys; a respected burgomaster is haunted by a secret from his past. Remarkable historic document. (Dir: James Young, 92 mins.)†

Bells (Canada, 1980)** Richard Chamberlain, John Houseman, Sara Botsford, Barry Morse, Gary Reineke, Robin Gammell. Gimmicky technological thriller that taps into a few good scare scenes. Chamberlain tracks down a psycho who kills with lethal jolts of electricity over the wires, and finds a high-level conspiracy that is far less interesting than Ma Bell's former monopoly. Released in shorter form as *Murder by Phone* (79 mins.). We call it "Reach Out and Kill Someone." (Dir: Michael Anderson, 94 mins.)

Bells Are Ringing (1960)***½ Judy Holliday, Dean Martin, Fred Clark, Eddie Foy, Jr., Jean Stapleton, Frank Gorshin, Ruth Storey. Delightful musical with a fine score and an ample serving of comedy socked across by the indispensable Judy Holliday. In this, her last film role, Judy displays her comic finesse as a meddling telephone answering service operator who listens in on the conversations of her clients. Like a fairy godmother with good connections, she butts in and changes everyone's lives for the better. (Dir: Vincente Minnelli, 127 mins.)†

Bells of St. Mary's, The (1945)*** Bing Crosby, Ingrid Bergman, William Gargan, Henry Travers, Ruth Donnelly. Priest and Mother Superior make plans to entice a wealthy skinflint to build them new surroundings. Sequel to *Going My Way*. Still entertaining. (Dir: Leo McCarey, 126 mins.)†

Belly of an Architect, The (Britain, 1987)**½ Brian Dennehy, Chloe Webb, Serge Fantoni, Lambert Wilson. Handsomely filmed, thematically murky tale of a successful architect obsessed with the work of a forgotten French architect, his wife's infidelity, her impending pregnancy, and his own incipient stomach cancer. (Dir: Peter Greenaway, 108 mins.)

Beloved Enemy (1936)*** David Niven, Brian Aherne, Merle Oberon. Well-done drama about people caught in the Irish Rebellion. Good cast. (Dir: H. C. Potter, 90 mins.)

Beloved Infidel (1959)**½ Gregory Peck, Deborah Kerr, Eddie Albert, Herbert Ruddy, Phil Ober. The story of F. Scott Fitzgerald's last years as a Hollywood scenarist, and his torrid love affair with columnist Sheila Graham, becomes a super-charged soap opera. (Dir: Henry King, 123 mins.)

Beloved Rogue, The (1927)**** John Barrymore, Conrad Veidt, Marceline Day. A lovely medieval story boasting a captivating performance by Barrymore as François Villon and breathtaking photography. (Dir: Alan Crosland, 99 mins.)

Below the Belt (1980)*** Regina Baff, Shirley Stoler, Dolph Sweet, Mildred Burke, John C. Becher. Filmed on a shoestring, this is a generally engrossing tale of a waitress who trades in slinging hash for slinging her opponents around the wrestling ring in an attempt to improve her lot in life. An interesting study of people living on the fringes of society, with the local color and carnival-like atmosphere of the wrestling world exceedingly well captured. (Dir: Robert Fowler, 98 mins.)

Be My Valentine or Else!—See: **Hospital Massacre**

Ben (1972)* Lee Harcourt Montgomery. Tasteless sequel to "Willard," the box-office success about killer rats. (Dir: Phil Karlson, 95 mins.)†

Bend of the River (1952)*** James Stewart, Rock Hudson, Arthur Kennedy. Sprawling western adventure. Stewart and Kennedy are pitted against each other in this tale of big men in the big country. (Dir: Anthony Mann, 91 mins.)†

Beneath the Planet of the Apes (1970)**½ James Franciscus, Charlton Heston, Maurice Evans, Linda Harrison, Kim Hunter. First sequel picks up where original left off. Astronaut Franciscus is sent on a rescue mission, and things really get hairy. Mutated humans living "beneath" the planet are featured. Followed by *Escape from the Planet of the Apes*. (Dir: Ted Post, 108 mins.)†

Beneath the Twelve-Mile Reef (1953)**½ Robert Wagner, Terry Moore, Gilbert Roland. Fine underwater photography in this adventure about Greek sponge divers. (Dir: Robert Webb, 101 mins.)†

Beneath the Valley of the Ultravixens (1979)**½ Francesca (Kitten) Natividad, Ann Marie, Ken Kerr, Stuart Lancaster. The wonderful world of director Russ Meyer, where "bountiful buxotics" and their impotent male counterparts try to find sexual fulfillment in Smalltown, U.S.A. Meyer's lewdest comedy to date retreads some of his older characters and plotlines; big-time film reviewer Roger Ebert (who says he really hates it when women get exploited on screen) wrote the bouncy screenplay. (93 mins.)†

Bengal Brigade (1954)** Rock Hudson, Arlene Dahl, Ursula Thiess. A wronged British officer in the Bengal troops in

India sets out to clear his reputation. Miss Dahl is exquisite. (Dir: Laslo Benedek, 87 mins.)

Bengazi (1955)** Richard Conte, Mala Powers, Richard Carlson. Police inspector tries to locate stolen war surplus goods. Hackneyed. (Dir: John Brahm, 78 mins.)

Ben Hur (1925)*** Ramon Navarro, Francis X. Bushman, May McAvoy, Betty Bronson, Carmel Myers. A silent film classic. Ramon Navarro wins the chariot race in the mammoth 1925 production of the Roman epic, based on Lew Wallace's best-selling novel. A major international success at the time and it still holds up well. (Dir: Fred Niblo, 116 mins.)†

Ben-Hur (1959)***½ Charlton Heston, Stephen Boyd, Haya Hayareet, Hugh Griffith, Martha Scott, Jack Hawkins. Spectacular screen version of the celebrated novel about the conflict between the Jews and the Romans in Jerusalem during the lifetime of Jesus. The film is meticulously produced and there are numerous sequences of awesome proportions, especially the chariot race. (Dir: William Wyler, 217 mins.)†

Benlker Gang, The (1984)**½ Andrew McCarthy, Jennie Dundas, Danny Dintantro, Charles Fields. Eighteen-year-old orphan McCarthy, who makes a living ghostwriting an advice column, helps his younger friends at the orphanage discourage potential parents who would adopt them and take them away from their friends. Cute but not cutesy, surprisingly good. (Dir: Ken Kwapis, 87 mins.)†

Benjamin (France, 1968)*** Michele Morgan, Catherine Deneuve, Pierre Clementi. Elegantly photographed adventures of a dashing young rake and his conquests in 18th-century France. (Dir: Michel Deville, 100 mins.)

Benji (1974)*** Patsy Garrett, Allen Fiuzat, Cynthia Smith, Peter Breck. Benji outshines his human supporting players. Simple story has the hound saving two kids from kidnappers and earning a place in their grateful parents' home. (Dir: Joe Camp, 89 mins.)†

Benji, the Hunted (1987)**½ Benji, Frank Inn, Nancy Francis. Strictly for kids. Braving the wilderness, the savvy canine plays adoptive parent and rescues some adorable orphaned cougar cubs. (Dir: Joe Camp, 93 mins.)†

Benny and Barney: Las Vegas Undercover (1977)*½ Jack Cassidy, Terry Kiser, Timothy Thomerson. Routine cops-and-kidnappers yarn. Benny and Barney are two ex-cops performing as singers. (Dir: Ron Stalof, 86 mins.)

Benny Goodman Story, The (1956)**½ Steve

Allen, Donna Reed. Typical Hollywood version of a bandleader's life and loves. Harry James, Gene Krupa, and others make guest appearances. (Dir: Valentine Davies, 116 mins.)†

Benny's Place (MTV 1982)*** Lou Gossett, Cicely Tyson, David Harris, Bever-Leigh Banfield, Anna Maria Horsford. Lou Gossett is superb as a proud black man who created his own space both in his job as a repairman in a factory and in his private life as the ageless dude who can out-drink and out-wrestle the younger guys, until time catches up with him. (Dir: Michael Schultz, 104 mins.)

Benson Murder Case, The (1930)**½ William Powell, Natalie Moorhead, Eugene Palette, Paul Lukas. One of those Old Dark House whodunits as Philo Vance uses his arsenal of crime detection tricks to flush out Mr. Benson's murderer. (Dir: Frank Tuttle, 65 mins.)

Ben Turpin Rides Again* Ben Turpin. Three silent comedy shorts from the Keystone studios starring the cross-eyed clown. Includes *The Daredevil, Yukon Jake,* and *The Eyes Have It.* (40 mins.)†

Berkeley in the 60s (1990)*** Mario Savio, Todd Gitlin, Huey Newton, Barry Melton, Allen Ginsberg. Enjoyable though undemanding documentary chronicling the Free Speech Movement that arose on the UCLA campus in the early '60s. Mainly archive films and interviews with little analysis, but fascinating all the same. (Dir: Mark Kitchell, 117 mins.)

Berkeley Square (Great Britain, 1933)***½ Leslie Howard, Heather Angel, Irene Browne. One of the best romantic fantasies of the '30s, greatly aided by a stylish performance from Howard, who plays a dapper transatlantic commuter who hobnobs with persons dead for more than a century. (Dir: Frank Lloyd, 87 mins.)

Berlin Affair, The (MTV 1970)**½ Darrin McGavin, Fritz Weaver, Claude Dauphin, Brian Kelly. Ex-spy is blackmailed into a contract for the murder of his best friend. Good performances and West German locations dress up a second-rate story. (Dir: David Lowell Rich, 104 mins.)

Berlin Affair, The (Italy-West Germany, 1985)** Gudrun Landgrebe, Kevin McNally. Tale of obsessed love against the backdrop of Nazi Germany. Elegant but slow-moving and obvious. (Dir: Liliana Cavani, 119 mins.)†

Berlin Alexanderplatz (Made for German TV, 1983)**** Gunter Lamprecht, Hanna Schygulla, Elisabeth Trissenaar. Director Rainer Werner Fassbinder's 15-hour film based on a well-known German novel about life in Berlin between the world wars. Despite its length, the film's sense of composition is rich and the director commands our attention throughout. (921 mins.)

Berlin Express (1948)***½ Merle Oberon, Robert Ryan. Allied group in Europe battle a band of Nazi fanatics. Exciting, well-written spy thriller. (Dir: Jacques Tourneur, 86 mins.)†

Berlin, Symphony of a Great City (Germany 1927)***½ A great silent documentary with its own orchestral score looks at one day in the life of the Berlin of 1927; unusual and fascinating. (Dir: Walter Ruttman, 53 mins.)†

Berlin Tunnel 21 (MTV 1981)**½ Richard Thomas, Horst Bucholtz, Ute Christensen, Jose Ferrer. A slow-starting but interesting escape drama set in East and West Berlin during the Cold War. A group of characters plan to escape by digging an elaborate tunnel complex under the Berlin Wall. (Dir: Richard Michaels, 184 mins.)†

Bermuda Affair (Great Britain, 1956)**½ Kim Hunter, Gary Merrill. Grim but interesting film about the disintegration of a marriage. (Dir: Edward Sutherland, 88 mins.)

Bermuda Depths, The (MTV 1978)*½ Leigh McCloskey, Connie Sellecca, Burl Ives, Julie Woodson. An emotionally disturbed young man (McCloskey) returns to Bermuda, where he grew up, to get to the bottom of his father's mysterious death and encounters a beautiful underwater siren (Sellecca). (Dir: Tom Kotani, 104 mins.)

Bernardine (1957)** Pat Boone, Terry Moore, Janet Gaynor, Richard (Dick) Sargent, Dean Jagger, James Drury, Natalie Schafer. Teenagers' tribulations; Boone and buddies fantasize about the perfect girl, who moves into town in the person of Moore. Weak stuff, though Pat is actually quite good. Gaynor's last film appearance. Ronnie Burns, who plays Griner, is the son of George Burns and Gracie Allen. (Dir: Henry Levin, 95 mins.)

Berry Gordy's The Last Dragon—See: The Last Dragon

Berserk! (1968)** Joan Crawford, Ty Hardin, Judy Geeson. Circus nonsense as Joan Crawford takes to the big top in a murder yarn with practically no surprises, just unintended laughs. (Dir: Jim O'Connolly, 96 mins.)†

Bert Rigby, You're a Fool (1989)**½ Robert Lindsay, Anne Bancroft, Corbin Bernsen, Robbie Coltrane, Cathryn Bradshaw. Writer-director Carl Reiner's showcase for the talents of Broadway musical star Lindsay (*Me and My Girl*) is a disappointment, though passable TV fodder. Lindsay plays a coal miner with dreams of stardom who gets a shot at Hollywood when he wins an amateur dance contest. (95 mins.)†

Beryl Markham: A Shadow on the Sun (MTV 1988)**½ Stephanie Powers, Claire Bloom, Peter Bowles, Brian Cox, Frederic Forrest. A courageous and glamorous real-life heroine is profiled in this uneven biopic. Whether flying the Atlantic solo or carrying on romances with men of wealth and taste, Markham led a fascinating life, and Powers does her best to evoke her spirit. (Dir: Tony Richardson, 192 mins.)

Best Boy (1979)**** Academy Award–winning documentary of Philly Wohl, 52-year-old retarded cousin of filmmaker Ira Wohl, is deeply moving and impressive. Made over a span of more than three years, following the friendly Philly's relations with his elderly parents (both now deceased) and his efforts to learn simple tasks. (Dir: Ira Wohl, 104 mins.)†

Best Defense (1984)½ Dudley Moore, Eddie Murphy, Kate Capshaw, Helen Shaver. A topical but irresponsible "comedy" concerning the adventures of both the inventor of a supertank (Moore) and the army officer (Murphy) who must man it in Kuwait. Feeble-minded toward world issues, insulting to third world nations, and unfunny as satire. (Dir: Willard Huyck, 94 mins.)†

Best Foot Forward (1943)*** Lucille Ball, June Allyson, William Gaxton. Lively, entertaining adaptation of the musical about a boy who induces a screen star to be his date at the military-school prom. (Dir: Edward Buzzell, 95 mins.)†

Best Friends (1982)**½ Burt Reynolds, Goldie Hawn, Ron Silver, Barnard Hughes, Audra Lindley, Jessica Tandy. Can two Hollywood screenwriters who have been living together for five years survive marriage? That's the thin premise of this uneven but ingratiating comedy featuring Reynolds and Hawn. These two stars work well together, but the script by Valerie Curtin and Barry Levinson (it's based on their lives) never gets beyond the good idea stage. (Dir: Norman Jewison, 116 mins.)†

Best House in London, The (Great Britain, 1969)*½ David Hemmings, Joanna Pettet, George Sanders, Dany Robin. When risqué farce is ineptly handled, it becomes very boring indeed, as happens here in this tale of government big shots frequenting a house of pleasure. (Dir: Philip Saville, 105 mins.)

Best Kept Secrets (MTV 1984)**½ Frederic Forrest, Patty Duke Astin, Peter Coyote, Meg Foster. When a patrolman's wife finds that her husband has been turned down for a promotion because of her previous indiscretions and her current activity in helping refugees from El

Salvador, she fights back. (Dir: Jerrold Freedman, 104 mins.)†

Best Little Girl in the World, The (MTV 1981)*** Jennifer Jason Leigh, Charles Durning, Jason Miller, Eva Marie Saint. Uncommonly good "disease-of-the-week" TV movie, concerning a young girl's bout with anorexia nervosa. Ms. Leigh and the entire cast deliver exceptional performances. (Dir: Sam O'Steen, 96 mins.)†

Best Little Whorehouse in Texas, The (1982)** Burt Reynolds, Dolly Parton, Dom DeLuise, Charles Durning, Jim Nabors, Robert Mandan. Disappointing, mostly lethargic version of the Broadway musical. Reynolds and Parton lack chemistry together, the direction by Colin Higgins is flat, and the film about efforts to close down the Texas institution known as the Chicken Ranch comes alive only occasionally through some of the song and dance numbers. (114 mins.)†

Best Man, The (1964)***½ Cliff Robertson, Henry Fonda, Lee Tracy. Based on Gore Vidal's perceptive and outspoken play, it deals with the hot-and-heavy fight between two leading contenders of the Presidential nomination of their party. Excellent performances from Robertson and Fonda as the political rivals, and a tour de force by Tracy in the role of an ex-President. One of the best American movies about politics. (Dir: Franklin Schaffner, 102 mins.)†

Best of Everything, The (1959)*** Hope Lange, Stephen Boyd, Suzy Parker, Diane Baker, Joan Crawford, Brian Aherne, Robert Evans, Martha Hyer, Louis Jourdan. A trashy, sexist, and very watchable soap opera. Ingenuous Baker gets seduced by a philandering playboy, talented Lange ends up renouncing her promotion in order to redeem a handsome alcoholic, and failed actress Parker gets a bad case of *l'amour fou* over a fickle stage director. Best is Crawford's gilt-edged cameo as a living example of why women weren't supposed to trade in sewing baskets for briefcases. (Dir: Jean Negulesco, 121 mins.)

Best of the Best (1989)** Phillip Rhee, Eric Roberts, James Earl Jones, Sally Kirkland, Christopher Penn, Louise Fletcher, John P. Ryan. Routine martial arts drama in the *Karate Kid* mold. To get vengeance on the Korean karate master who killed his brother in the ring, Rhee joins the American national team. No cliché is left unturned. (Dir: Bob Radler, 95 mins.)†

Best of Times, The (1986)** Robin Williams, Kurt Russell, Pamela Reed, Holly Palance, Donald Moffat. Wimpy bank vice president Williams, whose life has been all downhill ever since he dropped the pass that would have won the football game against his high school's archrivals 14 years ago, decides that he can recapture himself (and the town) by replaying the game. Lots of rah-rah but no sis-boom-bah. (Dir: Roger Spottiswoode, 104 mins.)†

Best Place to Be, The (MTV 1979)** Donna Reed, Efrem Zimbalist, Jr., Betty White, Timothy Hutton. Glossy, sudsy woman's show, produced by Ross Hunter, brings Ms. Reed out of retirement to play a protected widow forced to discover what life is all about. (Dir: David Miller, 202 mins.)

Best Seller (1987)***½ James Woods, Brian Dennehy, Victoria Tennant. Taut, expertly made thriller that casts Woods as a crafty hit man and Dennehy as the Wambaugh-like cop-turned-novelist whom Woods enlists to write his life story. The complicated interplay between the two characters, involving suspicions, secrets, and, ultimately, friendship, makes *Best Seller* as competent a character study as it is an edge-of-the-seat action picture. (Dir: John Flynn, 95 mins.)†

Best Things in Life Are Free, The (1956)**½ Gordon MacRae, Sheree North, Dan Dailey, Ernest Borgnine. MacRae, Borgnine, and Dailey portray the hit songsmiths DeSylva, Brown, and Henderson. It's the tunes that make up the best part of the film. Songs include: "Good News," "Sonny Boy," "Sunnyside Up," and "Birth of the Blues." (Dir: Michael Curtiz, 104 mins.)

Best Way, The (France, 1976)*** Patrick Dewaere, Patrick Bouchitey. A tale of two young counselors at a boys' summer camp circa '60—athletic Dewaere, sensitive Bouchitey, and their involved relationship. Dramatic insights and sardonic humor maintain interest. (Dir: Claude Miller, 85 mins.)

Best Way to Walk, The—See: **Best Way, The**

Best Years of Our Lives, The (1946)**** Fredric March, Myrna Loy, Dana Andrews, Harold Russell, Hoagy Carmichael, Teresa Wright, Virginia Mayo, Gladys George, Roman Bohnen. One of Hollywood's best: three men return home after WWII and must readjust—to civilian life, to their families, to their own changed selves. Expertly crafted and beautifully acted, the film won and deserved many Oscars and remains contemporary for a more cynical America several wars later. (Dir: William Wyler, 172 mins.)†

Bethune, The Making of a Hero (Canada-China-France, 1990)***½ Donald Sutherland, Helen Mirren, Helen Shaver, Harrison Liu, Anouk Aimee, Ronald Pickup. Fascinating biographical film about Canadian physician Norman Bethune, who crusaded for socialized medicine in Depression-era Montreal, treated the wounded during the Spanish civil war, but was most famous for bringing modern medical care to China during its invasion by a million Japanese soldiers in 1938. Well directed by Phillip Borsos, the movie contains an intense performance by Sutherland as the legendary doctor. (Dir: Phillip Borsos, 115 mins.)

Betrayal (MTV 1978)**½ Lesley Ann Warren, Rip Torn, Richard Masur, Ron Silver. A true story, of a psychiatrist who had an affair with a patient in the name of therapy, becomes a sudsy movie. (Dir: Paul Wendkos, 104 mins.)†

Betrayal (Great Britain, 1982)**½ Ben Kingsley, Jeremy Irons, Patricia Hodge. Harold Pinter adapted this examination of a love triangle from his play, retaining one unusual theatrical device—the story is told backwards, tracing the paths of infidelity and deceit from their ends to their origins. The result is presented with all the pregnant pauses and pretentiousness that are Pinter trademarks. (Dir: David Jones, 95 mins.)†

Betrayed (1944)***½ Kim Hunter, Dean Jagger, Robert Mitchum. One of the best "surprise" films ever made. Suspenseful melodrama of a wife whose husband of a few days is suspected of murder. AKA: **When Strangers Marry.** (Dir: William Castle, 67 mins.)

Betrayed (1954)** Clark Gable, Lana Turner, Victor Mature, Louis Calhern, Wilfred Hyde-White, Ian Carmichael, Anton Diffring. Spy melodrama with suspected Nazi collaborator Turner given a chance to prove her loyalty by undertaking a mission in German-occupied Holland. (Dir: Gottfried Reinhardt, 108 mins.)

Betrayed (1988)** Debra Winger, Tom Berenger, John Heard, Betsy Blair, John Mahoney, Richard Libertini. Disappointing film from director Costa-Gavras obscures an important social issue in steamy melodrama. Winger plays a government agent assigned to infiltrate a middle-American white supremacist group; Berenger is a good-ol'-boy bigot who becomes the object of her passion. (123 mins.)†

Betrayed by Innocence (MTV 1986)*½ Barry Bostwick, Lee Purcell, Cristen Kauffman, Paul Sorvino, Isaac Hayes. A film director sacrifices his seemingly happy marriage for a brief affair with a young girl who turns out to be a minor. The young lady's father is a cop who raises the issue of statutory rape. (Dir: Elliot Silverstein, 104 mins.)†

Betsy, The (1978)**½ Laurence Olivier, Robert Duvall, Katharine Ross, Tommy Lee Jones. Tame hokum about a car-manufacturing dynasty presided over by a lascivious, power-hungry Olivier. Based on Harold Robbins's potboiler, the screenplay would embarrass most soap opera writers, but Olivier and a top-notch cast throw themselves into it with abandon. (Dir: Daniel Petrie, 119 mins.)†

Betsy's Wedding (1990)** Alan Alda, Molly Ringwald, Madeline Kahn, Joe Pesci, Dylan Walsh, Anthony LaPaglia, Bibi Besch, Ally Sheedy, Burt Young, Joey Bishop, Nicholas Coster, Catherine O'Hara. Bride-to-be Ringwald's dream of a small funky wedding gets derailed in writer-director-star Alda's dopey film which sinks in a storm of silly clichés and comic-opera subplot about the mob. The entire cast is excellent, especially LaPaglia as a hood with style and class. (90 mins.)†

Better Late Than Never (MTV 1979)**½ Harold Gould, Strother Martin, Harry Morgan, Victor Buono, Donald Pleasence. Old folks revel in a retirement home under the leadership of a spry and canny newcomer. Diverting fare, a bit farfetched. (Dir: Richard Crenna, 104 mins.)†

Better Late Than Never (Great Britain, 1982)** David Niven, Art Carney, Maggie Smith, Kimberley Partridge, Catherine Hicks, Lionel Jeffries. Ne'er-do-wells Carney and Niven compete for the affections of a ten-year-old heiress who will decide which of the two is her grandfather. Fine cast struggles with a disappointingly flat script from writer-director Bryan Forbes. (95 mins.)†

Better Off Dead (1985)*** John Cusack, Diane Franklin, David Ogden Stiers, Curtis Armstrong, Kim Darby, Daniel Schneider, Amanda Wyss. Imaginative, often funny teen comedy about sad sack Cusack, depressed by his girlfriend's leaving him for the ski team captain. Nothing new plotwise, but mix of low-key gags and broadly caricatured characters keep this peppy until a disappointingly conventional windup. (Dir: Savage Steve Holland, 98 mins.)†

Better Tomorrow, A (Hong Kong, 1986)*** Chow Yun-fatt, Leslie Cheung, Ti Lung. Hong Kong's biggest box-office success to date and a splendid introduction to a cinema filled to overflowing with emotionally ripe melodrama, broad comedy, and explicit, impeccably choreographed violence. The Warner Bros.–like plot concerns the rift between two brothers, one a cop, the other a crook, and the latter's honorable cohort, played by the charismatic Yun-fatt. (Dir: John Woo, 95 mins.)

Better Tomorrow III, A—See: **Love and Death In Saigon**

Betty Blue (France, 1986)*** Jean Hugues-Anglade, Beatrice Dalle, Gerard Darmon, Consuelo de Havilland. Tender and flamboyant romance. A young man is drawn

81

out of his shell by a free-spirited but mentally unhinged woman in this visually expressive film. (Dir: Jean-Jacques Beineix, 117 mins.)†

Betty Ford Story, The (MTV 1987)**½ Gena Rowlands, Josef Sommer, Nan Woods, Concetta Tomei, Jack Radar. Ex-First Lady Betty Ford's real-life dilemmas (her bouts with alcohol and drug addiction and breast cancer) should make for inspirational viewing, especially with a talent like Rowlands cast in the central role. Instead, this TV movie is clichéd in approach, with banal dialogue and one-dimensional characters (except for Betty). (Dir: David Greene, 104 mins.)

Between Friends (MTV 1983)*** Carol Burnett, Elizabeth Taylor. A sleek updating of 1940s women's pictures like *Old Acquaintance*, this intimate melodrama is enhanced by the rapport between Taylor and Burnett. Taylor is a divorcée unsure about remarrying an unappealing but wealthy tycoon, while Burnett, another divorcée, handles her mid-life crisis with a series of one-night stands. As their friendship blossoms, the two women's feeling for each other changes both of them for the better. (Dir: Lou Antonio, 100 mins.)†

Between Heaven and Hell (1956)**½ Robert Wagner, Terry Moore, Broderick Crawford. War tale about a group of less than exemplary soldiers. Wagner plays a spoiled Southerner who learns things the hard way. (Dir: Richard Fleischer, 93 mins.)

Between Midnight and Dawn (1950)** Edmond O'Brien, Gale Storm, Mark Stevens. Two cops love the same gal; a mobster kills one off. Routine. (Dir: Gordon Douglas, 90 mins.)

Between the Darkness and the Dawn (MTV 1985)** Elizabeth Montgomery, Dorothy McGuire, Karen Holland, Michael Goodwin, Karen Grassle. Montgomery plays a thirty-seven-year-old woman who comes out of a twenty-year coma trying to catch up with life. (Dir: Peter Levin, 104 mins.)

Between the Lines (1977)***½ John Heard, Lindsay Crouse, Jeff Goldblum, Jill Eikenberry, Gwen Welles, Bruno Kirby, Stephen Collins, Marilu Henner, Michael J. Pollard, Lewis J. Stadlen, Lane Smith, Douglas Kenney, Southside Johnny and the Asbury Jukes. An appealing, perceptive comedy about the problems and pressures of publishing a youth-oriented antiestablishment weekly newspaper. Marvelous ensemble acting from the cast. Sardonic, skillful screenplay by Fred Barron. (Dir: Joan Micklin Silver, 101 mins.)†

Between Two Brothers (MTV 1982)** Pat Harrington, Michael Brandon, Helen Shaver. The question of guilt between two brothers—one a successful lawyer, the

82

other a resentful sibling running the family paint business—is explored with moderate success. In this domestic drama Harrington and Brandon play the dueling brothers, while Shaver is the lawyer's wife who discovers Harrington's possible involvement in burglaries. (Dir: Robert Lewis, 104 mins.)

Between Two Women (1944)** Van Johnson, Lionel Barrymore, Gloria DeHaven, Keenan Wynn, Keye Luke, Alma Kruger. Lots of cases for Dr. Red Adams (Johnson) as he helps a woman with an eating disorder and also comforts the switchboard operator who's targeted for surgery. (Dir: Willis Goldbeck, 83 mins.)

Between Two Women (1986)*** Farrah Fawcett, Colleen Dewhurst, Michael Nouri, Bridgette Anderson, Steven Hill, Danny Corkill. A stunning performance by Dewhurst highlights this domestic drama. Colleen Dewhurst plays Farrah's nerve-wracking mother-in-law who suddenly has to rely on her daughter-in-law's strength when she suffers a stroke. (Dir: Jon Avnet, 104 mins.)†

Between Two Worlds (1944)**½ John Garfield, Edmund Gwenn, Eleanor Parker. Second and weaker version of Sutton Vane's play *Outward Bound*. People who don't know they're dead, sailing to meet their destiny. (Dir: Edward Blatt, 112 mins.)

Between Us Girls (1942)** Diana Barrymore, Robert Cummings, Kay Francis, John Boles, Andy Devine. Francis falls for Boles, persuades her twenty-year-old daughter Barrymore to pretend to be twelve so as not to give away Mom's age. Lighthearted romance doesn't get what it needs from the uncharismatic Barrymore. (Dir: Henry Koster, 89 mins.)

Beulah Land (MTV 1980)** Lesley Ann Warren, Paul Rudd, Meredith Baxter-Birney, Hope Lange, Michael Sarrazin, Martha Scott, Eddie Albert, Don Johnson, Dorian Harewood. Picked-over *Gone with the Wind* clone: a Dixie belle hangs onto her plantation, leering Yankees pillage and blunder, and the cornpone accents rise and fall. (Dirs: Virgil Bogel, Harry Falk, 267 mins.)†

Beverly Hills Bodysnatchers (1989)*½ Vic Tayback, Frank Gorshin, Art Metrano, Rodney Eastman. Combine mad doctor Gorshin, mortician Tayback and mobster Metrano with a serum that brings dead bodies back to life and what do you get? In this case, a mess. If that synopsis doesn't strike you as funny, neither will anything else in the movie. (Dir: Jon Mostow, 85 mins.)†

Beverly Hills Brats (1989)* Burt Young, Martin Sheen, Terry Moore, Peter Billingsly, Ramon Sheen. Feeling unappreciated by his rich parents, a teen stages his own kidnapping to get some attention. Feeble comedy is so lacking in mirth that you start wondering if it was designed to lose money for a tax break. (Dir: Dimitri Sotirakis, 91 mins.)†

Beverly Hills Cop (1984)**½ Eddie Murphy, Judge Reinhold, John Ashton, Lisa Eilbacher, Ronny Cox. Uneven but entertaining cop story about a fast-talking Detroit policeman (Murphy) who comes to Beverly Hills to avenge the death of his best friend. With razor-edged Murphy placed in the chichi California town, this comedy-drama should have been funnier. Unfortunately, the plot is reminiscent of vigilante movies, and the final shootout is unpleasantly violent. At least an ensemble of talented actors keep the comedy fresh and offbeat. (Dir: Martin Brest, 105 mins.)†

Beverly Hills Cop 2 (1987)** Eddie Murphy, Judge Reinhold, Jurgen Prochnow, Ronny Cox, John Aston, Brigitte Neilsen, Dean Stockwell, Allen Garfield, Paul Reiser. Brash sequel to the smash hit, with Murphy going through the motions as Alex Foley, the smart-ass Detroit cop showing the Beverly Hills Boys how to enforce the law. For Murphy's fans, this is sure-fire; for others, this kind of movie-making is the filmic equivalent of slam dancing. (Dir: Tony Scott, 102 mins.)†

Beverly Hills Cowgirl Blues (MTV 1985)** Lisa Hartman, James Brolin, David Hemmings, Irena Ferris, Lane Smith. Sexy Lisa is a Wyoming cop after a murderer in Beverly Hills. James Brolin plays her Beverly Hills counterpart unable to keep up with Ms. Hartman. (Dir: Corey Allen, 104 mins.)

Beverly Hills Madam (MTV 1986)*½ Faye Dunaway, Louis Jourdan, Melody Anderson, Donna Dixon, Marshall Colt, Rod McCary. This is merely an excuse for girl-watching, as beautiful, scantily clad females prance across the screen under the watchful eye of Madame Faye. (Dir: Harvey Hart, 104 mins.)

Beverly Hills Vamp (1989)** Eddie Deezen, Britt Ekland, Tim Conway, Jr., Jay Richardson, Michelle Bauer, Robert Quarry. Young filmmakers trying to make connections in L.A. connect with vampire Ekland instead. Dopey parody is loaded with Hollywood in-jokes (a few of them good), and Deezen's Jerry-Lewis-on-speed routine either strikes you funny or gives you a severe headache. (Dir: Fred Olen Ray, 90 mins.)†

Beware, My Lovely (1952)**½ Ida Lupino, Robert Ryan. Young war widow is menaced by a sinister handyman. Suspenseful. (Dir: Harry Horner, 77 mins.)†

Beware of a Holy Whore (Germany, 1971)**½ Eddie Constantine, Hanna Schygulla, Margarethe von Trotta, Lou Castel, Rainer Werner Fassbinder. Life on the set of a Fassbinder film, as seen by the director himself. Very little footage gets shot, but there are affairs, tantrums, and all sorts of anguish. (Dir: Rainer Werner Fassbinder, 110 mins.)

Beware of Blondie (1950)** Penny Singleton, Arthur Lake, Adele Jergens, Douglas Fowley. Dagwood is left in charge of his boss's construction company. Fair comedy. (Dir: Edward Bernds, 66 mins.)

Beware! The Blob (1972)*½ Robert Walker, Godfrey Cambridge, Shelley Berman. Plays better for laughs than terror. A frozen, shapeless mass thaws, grows, and goes on a rampage. (Dir: Larry Hagman, 88 mins.)

Bewitched (1945)**½ Phyllis Thaxter, Edmund Gwenn. Generally interesting psychological melodrama about a girl with a split personality. (Dir: Arch Oboler, 65 mins.)

Beyond, The—See: **7 Doors of Death**

Beyond a Reasonable Doubt (1956)***½ Dana Andrews, Joan Fontaine, Sidney Blackmer, Shepperd Strudwick, Arthur Franz. Grim, shadowy, obscure melodrama of a writer who frames himself for murder on circumstantial evidence to expose the "system." The plot twists rather unconvincingly, but the dark ambiance has a gripping quality. (Dir: Fritz Lang, 80 mins.)

Beyond Atlantis (U.S.-Philippines, 1973) *½ John Ashley, Sid Haig, Patrick Wayne, George Nader, Vic Diaz, Lenore Stevens. The lame-brain plot involves an attempt to loot precious pearls from a tribe of ancient island people whose leader has mating plans for one of the plunderers. (Dir: Eddie Romero, 89 mins.)†

Beyond Evil (1980)*½ John Saxon, Lynda Day George, Michael Dante, Janice Lynde, David Opatoshu. Another entry in the possession sweepstakes, with an archetypal cast. The spirit of a woman who murdered her husband tries to possess the body of one of the new owners of her house. (Dir: Herb Freed, 93 mins.)†

Beyond Glory (1948)**½ Alan Ladd, Donna Reed. West Point drama has some good moments but many of its scenes away from the Academy are boring. (Dir: John Farrow, 82 mins.)

Beyond Good and Evil (1984)*½ Dominique Sanda, Erland Josephson, Robert Powell, Virna Lisi. Like the same director's *The Night Porter*, the film's pronounced interest in sex will appeal to prurient tastes. It's based on the life of Lou Andreas-Salome, who was mistress to both Nietzsche and the intellectual doctor Paul Ree. (Dir: Liliana Cavani, 106 mins.)

Beyond Mombasa (Great Britain, 1957)** Cornel Wilde, Donna Reed, Leo Genn. Mediocre adventure film set in Africa. (Dir: George Marshall, 100 mins.)

Beyond Reason (1977)* Telly Savalas, Laura Johnson, Diana Muldaur, Marvin Laird, Bob Basso. A film to mortify the intellect. Savalas's directorial debut was never released theatrically; it deals with a shrink who's on the verge of losing his mind. (Dir: Telly Savalas, 83 mins.)†

Beyond Reasonable Doubt (New Zealand, 1980)**½ David Hemmings, John Hargreaves, Martyn Sanderson, Grant Tilly, Diana Rowan. True story of a man convicted of crimes he didn't commit. Film explores the initial detective work and the later demands by the public to know how such a miscarriage of justice occurred. Hemmings is chilling as venomous cop. (Dir: John Laing, 127 mins.)†

Beyond the Bermuda Triangle (MTV 1975)* Fred MacMurray, Sam Groom, Donna Mills. Flat-footed yarn about people mysteriously disappearing off the Florida coast. (Dir: William A. Graham, 78 mins.)

Beyond the Blue Horizon (1942)*½ Dorothy Lamour, Richard Denning. Childish sarong saga has Dotty out to prove she is the rightful heir to something. A good film is definitely not her legacy. (Dir: Alfred Santell, 76 mins.)

Beyond the Door (U.S.-Italy, 1975)½ Juliet Mills, Richard Johnson, David Colin, Jr. The wife of a San Francisco record producer is about to give birth to a demon child. If you think it sounds just like a combination of *Rosemary's Baby* and *The Exorcist*, you're absolutely right. (Dir: Oliver Hellman, 97 mins.)†

Beyond the Door: II (Italy, 1979)*½ Daria Nicolodi, John Steiner, David Colin, Jr., Ivan Rassimov. Better than the first *Beyond the Door*—due to Mario Bava's stylish direction—but still a possession clinker. This time, a deceased daddy possesses his boy in order to wreak revenge on his wife. Sort of a satanic version of "Hamlet." (92 mins.)†

Beyond the Doors (1983)* Gregory Allen Chatman, Riba Meryl, Bryan Wolf, Stuart Lancaster. Did you know that Janis Joplin, Jimi Hendrix, and Jim Morrison were all killed as part of a secret CIA plot? If you believe that, you'll probably go for the awful impersonations of those stars offered in this inane attempt at a conspiracy movie. (Dir: Larry Buchanan, 117 mins.)†

Beyond The Fog—See: *Horror on Snape Island*

Beyond the Forest (1949)*** Bette Davis, Joseph Cotten, Ruth Roman, David Brian, Dona Drake. Two masters of hysteria, Davis and director King Vidor, combine for a hurricane of frenzy. The movie is fiercely trashy but is made impressive by Davis's bravura intensity and Vidor's almost mystical apprehension of his star's

excesses. Close to good art, and definitely great camp. (96 mins.)†

Beyond the Law (Italy, 1967)*½ Lee Van Cleef, Antonio Sabato, Lionel Stander, Bud Spencer. An overcooked spaghetti western featuring wincing Van Cleef as an outlaw who becomes sheriff so he can pull off a big job. (Dir: Giorgio Stegani, 85 mins.)†

Beyond the Law (1968)*** Rip Torn, George Plimpton, Norman Mailer, Jose Torres, Beverly Bentley. Tough, frequently absorbing film is offbeat, original moviemaking. It's Mailer's version, and vision, of a modern big city police lieutenant (Mailer) and his interrogations in the course of a single evening. (Dir: Norman Mailer, 110 mins.)

Beyond the Limit (1983)*½ Richard Gere, Michael Caine, Bob Hoskins. Based on Graham Greene's *The Honorary Consul*, this convoluted thriller boasts a minimum of thrills and contains an intricate plot that doesn't transfer well to film. Gere plays a physician whose father is a political prisoner in Paraguay. Complicating matters are a kidnapping plot which goes awry and a romantic triangle involving Gere's mistress, who's the wife of an alcoholic consul (Caine). (Dir: John Mackenzie, 103 mins.)†

Beyond the Next Mountain (1987)* Alberto Issaac, Bennett Ohta. Trite but true story about a devout tribesman from northeast India who translated the New Testament into his native tongue. The wooden acting is not likely to win many converts. (Dirs: Rolf Forsberg, James Collier, 98 mins.)†

Beyond the Poseidon Adventure (1979)*½ Michael Caine, Sally Field, Telly Savalas, Peter Boyle, Shirley Jones, Jack Warden. Disappointing sequel. Some good moments, however, as the two crews race to loot the half-sunken *Poseidon* of its treasures. (Dir: Irwin Allen, 114 mins.)†

Beyond Therapy (1987)* Glenda Jackson, Jeff Goldblum, Julie Hagerty, Tom Conti, Christopher Guest. Adaptation of Christopher Durang's play about a neurotic Manhattan couple and their meddling headshrinkers. Filmed in Paris by director Robert Altman, this comedy's rhythm is all wrong. (93 mins.)†

Beyond the Stars (1989)** Martin Sheen, Christian Slater, Robert Foxworth, Sharon Stone, Olivia d'Abo, F. Murray Abraham. Plodding story of young Slater, who wants to be an astronaut and meets one (Sheen) who teaches him about dreams, disappointments—and a secret discovery brought back from the moon. AKA: *Personal Choice*. (Dir: David Saperston, 94 mins.)†

Beyond the Time Barrier (1960)*½ Robert

Clarke, Darlene Tompkins. Air Force pilot crashes through the time barrier into the future, finds the Earth in a pretty sad state. (Dir: Edgar Ulmer, 75 mins.)†

Beyond the Valley of the Dolls (1970)*** Edy Williams, Marcia McBroom, Cynthia Myers, Michael Blodgett, Dolly Reed. A female rock band hits the big time in swingin' L.A. Soft-core pioneer director Russ Meyer made his Hollywood debut with this hip parody of soap operas effectively destroying Jacqueline Susann's *Valley* rock flicks, drug pics, and his own tongue-in-cheek adult films. Film critic Roger Ebert wrote the script, which includes such gems as "This is my happening: and it's freaking me out!" (109 mins.)†

Beyond the Walls (Israel, 1985)**½ Arnon Zadak, Muhamad Bakri. This Academy Award nominee for Best Foreign Film is an exciting but rather obvious prison drama. Fortunately, the political subtext adds interest as Arabs and Jews, long accustomed to opposing each other, unite against their common captor. (Dir: Uri Barbash, 103 mins.)†

Beyond Tomorrow (1940)*** Richard Carlson, Jean Parker, C. Aubrey Smith, Harry Carey, Charles Winninger, Maria Ouspenskaya. A lovely fable about three rich men sharing their good fortune with two have-nots. Pleasing yuletide fare. (Dir: Edward Sutherland, 84 mins.)†

Be Yourself (1930)** Fanny Brice, Robert Armstrong, Harry Green, Gertrude Astor. Fanny plays a nightclub chanteuse who pines for a boxer with tear-jerking results. (Dir: Thornton Freeland, 77 mins.)

B.F.'s Daughter (1947)*½ Barbara Stanwyck, Van Heflin, Charles Coburn. J.P. Marquand's novel about an heiress's marriage to an economics professor is boring, poorly paced, and uninteresting. (Dir: Robert Z. Leonard, 108 mins.)

Bhowani Junction (Great Britain, 1956)**½ Ava Gardner, Stewart Granger, Bill Travers. Drama mixing love with political intrigue. Ava Gardner plays an Anglo-Indian girl who is torn between her loyalty for the British and the Indians. (Dir: George Cukor, 110 mins.)

Bible, The...In the Beginning (U.S.-Italy, 1966)*** George C. Scott, Ava Gardner, Peter O'Toole, Franco Nero. Elaborate production trappings and some good acting spark this otherwise predictable Hollywood retelling of the Bible stories. The story of Abraham and Sarah (Scott and Gardner) is the best-acted section of the film, and comes closest to intimate human drama in an otherwise spectacular film of enormous proportions. (Dir: John Huston, 174 mins.)†

Bicycle Thief, The (Italy, 1949)**** Enzo Staiola, Lamberto Maggiorani. Tragic story of a poor man whose needed bicycle is stolen, and his search through Rome with his small son to find the thief. Superbly directed by Vittorio De Sica, a touching, heart-gripping drama. Won the Oscar for Best Foreign Film. (90 mins.)

Big (1988)*** Tom Hanks, Elizabeth Perkins, Robert Loggia, John Heard, Jared Rushton. A twelve-year-old boy is changed, via a carnival booth, into Tom Hanks and proceeds to make his fortune in the toy business. A terrific vehicle for Hanks, who displays an entrancing quality of innocence and playful awkwardness. More a movie about childhood than a movie for children, the film's best audience would seem to be tired executives who long to act like kids. The scene where Hanks and his boss (Loggia) dance to "Chopsticks" on a huge keyboard is a classic. (Dir: Penny Marshall, 102 mins.)†

Bigamist, The (1953)*** Edmond O'Brien, Joan Fontaine, Ida Lupino. Businessman married to a career woman is discovered to have another wife in another city. (Dir: Ida Lupino, 80 mins.)

Big Bad Mama (1974)*² Angie Dickinson, William Shatner, Tom Skerritt. A Depression-era gang of bank robbers. A mother turns to a life of crime in order to escape the dire poverty she has known all her life. (Dir: Steve Carver, 85 mins.)†

Big Bad Mama II (1987)* Angie Dickinson, Robert Culp, Danielle Brisebois, Julie McCullogh, Jaff Yahger. A late-in-coming sequel to the 1974 exploitation drama brings Dickinson back as the pistol-packing matriarch on a crime spree, while her now-teenage daughters miss no opportunity to frolic in the nude. A bad career move for all concerned. (Dir: Jim Wynorski, 85 mins.)†

Big Bang, The (1989)*** James Toback, Don Simpson, José Torres, Eugene Fodor, Darryl Dawkins. Who are we, how did we get here, what are we doing while we're here and why? Filmmaker James Toback, who has some very definite theories along those lines, poses these questions to a diverse group of people, most of whom haven't previously given them much thought. Some of the answers are insightful, others less so, but the film as a whole is consistently provocative. (Dir: James Toback, 81 mins.)

Big Beat, The (1958)** William Reynolds, Gogi Grant. Musical with pop tunes and a thin background story about the record business. (Dir: Will Cowan, 85 mins.)

Big Bet, The (1985)* Lance Sloane, Kim Evenson, Sylvia Kristel. High school nerd makes a bet that he can have sex with an attractive new student within a week's time, seeks advice from sexy new neighbor Kristel on how to do so. Vulgar comedy whose only aim is to undress its female stars as often as possible. (Dir: Bert I. Gordon, 90 mins.)†

Big Bird Cage, The (1972)*½ Anitra Ford, Pam Grier, Sid Haig, Candice Roman, Vic Diaz. Sloppy follow-up to *The Big Doll House*, with a heavily parodistic tone. Haig and Grier team up to mastermind a prison break. (Dir: Jack Hill, 88 mins.)†

Big Black Pill, The (MTV 1981)** Robert Blake, JoBeth Williams, Neva Patterson, James Gammon, Veronica Cartwright, Edward Winter. Blake tries for another series with this TV movie about Joe Dancer, a gumshoe suspected of murder. Some hard-boiled sleuthing and a pre-stardom JoBeth Williams make this routine "Pill" easier to swallow. (Dir: Reza Badiyi, 100 mins.)

Big Blue, The (France, 1988)** Jean-Marc Barr, Rosanna Arquette, Jean Reno. Obscure, often pretentious tale of a French deep-sea diver who has an unusually strong connection to the sea and its inhabitants. Some beautiful underwater photography, but the script is (dare we say it) waterlogged. (Dir: Luc Besson, 119 mins.)†

Big Boodle, The (1957)** Errol Flynn, Pedro Armendariz, Gia Scala. Counterfeiters pass phony bills in a casino in Havana. (Dir: Richard Wilson, 83 mins.)

Big Bounce, The (1969)* Ryan O'Neal, Leigh Taylor-Young, Lee Grant, James Daly, Van Heflin. Muddled crime melodrama. Action for action's sake, and virtually nonexistent character motivation. (Dir: Alex March, 102 mins.)

Big Boy (1930)*** Al Jolson, Claudia Dell. As weird and tasteless as it looks to modern eyes, Jolson is memorable in blackface as a devoted Negro servant who becomes a champion jockey. Film ends with a short concert segment with Jolson out of character, promising *not* to sing *Sonny Boy*—apparently everyone was sick of it by this time! (Dir: Alan Crosland, 69 mins.)

Big Brawl, The (1980)** Jackie Chan, Jose Ferrer, Kristine de Bell, Mako. A combination martial arts picture and gangster yarn with the expected brawling energy and a cast that knows how to get their kicks. (Dir: Robert Clouse, 95 mins.)†

Big Broadcast, The (1932)*** Bing Crosby, Burns & Allen, Stuart Erwin. Often amusing musical-comedy spoof of the then high-riding radio industry. Bing first displayed the naturalness that was to make him one of the biggest all-time stars in this film. (Dir: Frank Tuttle, 78 mins.)

Big Broadcast of 1936, The (1935)**½ Burns & Allen, Jack Oakie, Ethel Merman. Big revue with some good moments and many weak ones. (Dir: Norman Taurog, 97 mins.)

Big Broadcast of 1937, The (1936)**½ Jack Benny, George Burns, Gracie Allen, Martha Raye, Shirley Ross, Benny Goodman and his Orchestra, Leopold Stokowski and his Symphony Orchestra. Entertaining variety show which provides a fair satire on the radio industry. (Dir: Mitchell Leisen, 100 mins.)

Big Broadcast of 1938, The (1938)*** W. C. Fields, Dorothy Lamour, Bob Hope, Shirley Ross. Fields's golf and billiards routines plus Bob and Shirley singing "Thanks for the Memory" are all this film offers—but it's enough. (Dir: Mitchell Leisen, 100 mins.)

Big Brown Eyes (1936)***½ Cary Grant, Joan Bennett, Walter Pidgeon. Delightful detective yarn with bright dialogue and marvelous teamwork by Grant as a detective and Bennett as his girlfriend who helps him ensnare some crooks. (Dir: Raoul Walsh, 77 mins.)

Big Bus, The (1976)** Joseph Bologna, Stockard Channing, Rene Auberjonois, Lynn Redgrave, Ruth Gordon. This parody of disaster pics is so self-conscious that it misses the comic mark. The usual nuts sign on for the first nuclear-powered bus trip from New York to Denver. (Dir: James Frawley, 88 mins.)†

Big Business (1988)**½ Bette Midler, Lily Tomlin, Fred Ward, Edward Herrmann, Daniel Gerroll, Mary Gross. Midler and Tomlin each play a set of identical twins in this high-pitched, often very funny farce. When the rural Bette and Lily encounter their counterparts, predictable complications, close calls, and mistaken identities ensue. The film spends way too much time establishing its tangled premise, and the jokes and sight gags never pay off as well as they should, but Tomlin's subtle character work and Midler's unmatchable brassiness are delights. (Dir: Jim Abrahams, 91 mins.)†

Big Bust-Out, The (1973)* Vonetta McGee, Monica Taylor, Linda Fox, Gordon Mitchell. Tedious exploitation picture about black women who escape from prison only to land in the clutches of a white slavery gang. Worthless, no fun on any level. (Dir: Richard Jackson, 75 mins.)†

Big Cage, The (1933)** Clyde Beatty, Wallace Ford. Trainer Beatty decides to put lions and tigers in the same cage and it takes the whole film to build to this big moment. (Dir: Kurt Neumann, 76 mins.)

Big Caper, The (1957)** Rory Calhoun, Mary Costa. Crooked couple decide to mend their ways after a taste of small town friendliness, but the gang has other ideas. (Dir: Robert Stevens, 84 mins.)

Big Carnival, The (1951)**** Kirk Douglas, Jan Sterling, Porter Hall, Bob Arthur. Terrific drama. Grim tale of a big city reporter who capitalizes on a disaster to ride himself back to the big time. Unrelenting in its cynicism, superb performances. AKA: *Ace in the Hole.* (Dir: Billy Wilder, 112 mins.)

Big Cat, The (1949)*** Preston Foster, Lon McCallister, Forrest Tucker. City lad in the mountain country aids in the tracking down of a killer cougar. Exciting outdoor story. (Dir: Phil Karlson, 76 mins.)†

Big Chill, The (1983)***½ William Hurt, Kevin Kline, Mary Kay Place, JoBeth Williams, Glenn Close, Tom Berenger, Jeff Goldblum. Seven college pals gather at the funeral of a friend who has just committed suicide. Examining their careers and their friendships, they come to terms with their past and the suicide. Ensemble acting and a sparkling screenplay by director Lawrence Kasdan highlight the film. (106 mins.)†

Big Circus, The (1959)**½ Victor Mature, Red Buttons, Rhonda Fleming. Sprawling film about behind-the-scenes big top activities. Tough circus boss has his hands full with performers and their problems. (Dir: Joseph Newman, 109 mins.)

Big City, The (1937)**½ Spencer Tracy, Luise Rainer, Charley Grapewin, Janet Beecher, Eddie Quillen, William Demarest, Regis Toomey. Corruption in the taxi business causes trouble for honest hack Tracy. Glossy and overproduced by MGM, with a distasteful antiunion bias, but the stars are worth watching. (Dir: Frank Borzage, 80 mins.)

Big City (1947)*½ Margaret O'Brien, Danny Thomas, Robert Preston. An orphan is jointly adopted by a Catholic, Protestant, and Jew. Talky, sentimental hokum. (Dir: Norman Taurog, 103 mins.)

Big City Blues (1932)*** Joan Blondell, Eric Linden, Guy Kibbee, Lyle Talbot, Humphrey Bogart, Ned Sparks, J. Carrol Naish. Country boy comes to the city to make good, falls in love with Blondell. Ordinary story given warmth and feeling by director LeRoy and a fine cast. (Dir: Mervyn LeRoy, 65 mins.)

Big Clock, The (1948)*** Ray Milland, Charles Laughton, Maureen O'Sullivan, Elsa Lanchester. Suspenseful drama about a man who follows a murderer's clues and finds they lead directly to him. Top mystery entertainment. (Dir: John Farrow, 75 mins.)

Big Combo, The (1955)***½ Cornel Wilde, Richard Conte, Jean Wallace. A good *film noir* crime drama about policemen and their battle with the syndicate. (Dir: Joseph Lewis, 89 mins.)†

Big Country, The (1958)*** Gregory Peck, Charlton Heston, Carroll Baker, Jean Simmons, Burl Ives (Oscar winner), Charles Bickford. Director William Wyler's large-scale anti-western has some sweep and persuasiveness despite its overly studied avoidance of genre conventions. Peck is a Pacific sea captain who comes home with his bride to meet discord on the range. He faces opposition from his competitor in love (Heston), his adversary in business (Ives), and his skeptical father-in-law (Bickford). (165 mins.)†

Big Crime Wave, The (Canada, 1986)**½ John Paizs, Darrel Baran, Eva Covacs. Suburban girl befriends her family's new boarder, a quiet young man trying to write "the ultimate color crime movie." Movie buffs will appreciate the many imaginative genre parodies, but the rest of the film seems to have been constructed as an afterthought to hold those bits together. (Dir: John Paizs, 80 mins.)†

Big Cube, The (Mexico-U.S., 1969)** Lana Turner, George Chakiris, Dan O'Herlihy. Uninspired melodrama. A stepdaughter resents her stepmother and tries to do away with her. (Dir: Tito Davison, 91 mins.)

Big Deal on Madonna Street, The (Italy, 1958)**** Marcello Mastroianni, Vittorio Gassman, Renato Salvatori, Carla Gravina, Rossana Rory. A motley gang of bungling crooks makes a mess of trying to rob a pawn shop. Film buffs think this is among the funniest films ever made and they're dead right. (Dir: Mario Monicelli, 91 mins.)†

Big Doll House, The (1971)** Judy Brown, Roberta Collins, Pam Grier, Sid Haig. The first of producer Roger Corman's immortal "women in cages" features shot in the Philippines. Its plotline has become a B-movie staple: a group of chesty women get tortured in a hellhole prison, and then break out with machine guns blazing. The straightforward mixture of cheesy humor, soft-core S&M, and fast-paced action made it the model for countless American, Italian, and South American imitations. (Dir: Jack Hill, 93 mins.)†

Big Easy, The (1986)*** Dennis Quaid, Ellen Barkin, Ned Beatty, John Goodman, Ebbe Rose Smith, Charles Ludlam, Marc Lawrence, Lisa Jane Persky. Entertaining oddball tale in which a cocky cop courts the attention of a desirable D.A.'s official who's sent to investigate crooked police practices. Although the film resolves all the issues about police corruption too neatly, the central romance is played with vigor and breezy charm. (Dir: Jim McBride, 108 mins.)†

Big Fisherman, The (1959)**½ Howard Keel, Alexander Scourby, Susan Kohner, John Saxon, Martha Hyer, Herbert Lom. Set in the early days of Christianity, the story of Simon called Peter, also known as the Big Fisherman, unfolds with predictable pageantry and uplifting sermonizing. (Dir: Frank Borzage, 166 mins.)

Big Fix, The (1978)**½ Richard Dreyfuss, Bonnie Bedelia, Susan Anspach, John Lithgow, F. Murray Abraham. A drama about a Cal-Berkeley University-bred private eye who is still a "revolutionary" of the '60s at heart. Bonnie Bedelia graces any movie she's in, but Dreyfuss confuses star power with an overkill of actor's tricks. (Dir: Jeremy Paul Kagan, 108 mins.)†

Big Foot (1970)* Christopher Mitchum, Joi Lansing, John Carradine, John Mitchum, Lindsay Crosby, Ken Maynard, Joy Wilkerson, Doodles Weaver, Haji. The skinniest, least frightening version of Bigfoot ever seen on screen skulks though the Northwest forests in search of human breeding partners. (Dir: Robert Slatzer, 94 mins.)†

Bigfoot (MTV 1987)**½ Colleen Dewhurst, James Sloyan, Joseph Maher. Rather entertaining family fare; not in the same tacky league as all those big-screen Bigfoot feature films. Two youngsters are appropriated by Mr. and Mrs. Sasquatch while they're out camping with their mom and dad. (Dir: Dan Huston, 104 mins.)

Bigfoot, the Mysterious Monsters (1975)* Peter Graves. Clumsy compilation of so-called eyewitness reports about legendary creatures such as the Loch Ness Monster, the Abominable Snowman, the Kyoto Lizard, and various bigfoot monsters. (Dir: Robert Guenette, 76 mins.)

Big Gamble, The (1961)** Stephen Boyd, Juliette Greco, David Wayne. An Irishman, his bride, and a meek cousin seek their fortune on the Ivory Coast. Pretty mild stuff. (Dir: Richard Fleischer, 100 mins.)

Bigger Splash, A (Great Britain, 1974)*** Artist David Hockney is the subject of fascinating documentary by director Jack Hazan. Colorful Hockney is a natural as he becomes subject instead of painting one. Film centers around Hockney's life and work in Los Angeles. (105 mins.)†

Bigger Than Life (1956)***½ James Mason, Barbara Rush, Walter Matthau. An uncommonly brilliant melodrama which tells the story of an average schoolteacher who develops a monster-sized superiority complex when he becomes hooked on a wonder drug (cortisone). Filmmaker Nicholas Ray transformed this otherwise standard tale of addiction into

a compelling exhibition of the Nietzschean hiding inside the common middle-class citizen. Mason is remarkable as the afflicted teacher. (95 mins.)

Biggest Bundle of Them All, The (U.S.-Italy, 1967)** Robert Wagner, Raquel Welch, Edward G. Robinson. A group of bumbling kidnappers abducts an exiled American hood living in Italy. (Dir: Ken Annakin, 110 mins.)

Biggles—Adventures in Time (Great Britain, 1988)*½ Neil Dickson, Alex Hyde-White, Fiona Hutchison, Peter Cushing. Flat, unimaginative fantasy about a businessman who travels back in time (don't ask how) to join forces with WWI pilot Biggles to defeat the Germans. Lifeless and mechanical, especially for American audiences. (Dir: John Hough, 92 mins.)†

Big Guy (1939)** Jackie Cooper, Victor McLaglen. Prison warden captured by convicts becomes a criminal himself. (Dir: Arthur Lubin, 78 mins.)

Big Hand for the Little Lady, A (1966)*** Joanne Woodward, Henry Fonda, Jason Robards, Jr., Charles Bickford, Burgess Meredith. Clever, well-played yarn; Fonda and wife arrive in Laredo during an annual big-stakes poker game, and before you can shuffle a deck, Fonda is in the game. (Dir: Fielder Cook, 95 mins.)†

Big Hangover, The (1950)**½ Elizabeth Taylor, Van Johnson. Sometimes funny comedy about a lawyer who has a peculiar drinking problem. Johnson tends to mug more than is necessary. (Dir: Norman Krasna, 82 mins.)

Big Heat, The (1953)***½ Glenn Ford, Gloria Grahame, Lee Marvin, Carolyn Jones, Jocelyn Brando, Jeanette Nolan. Excellent police drama with top performances. Glenn Ford, as an ex-cop, cracks the underworld hold on a city with the help of a mobster's moll played by Gloria Grahame. Lee Marvin excels as a sadistic killer. (Dir: Fritz Lang, 90 mins.)†

Big House, The (1930)*** Robert Montgomery, Chester Morris, Wallace Beery, Lewis Stone. Desperate convicts try prison break. This early example of prison melodrama is still entertaining. (Dir: George Hill, 88 mins.)

Big House, USA (1955)*** Broderick Crawford, Ralph Meeker. The FBI is called in to track down a brutal kidnap gang. Strong crime melodrama. (Dir: Howard Koch, 82 mins.)

Big Jack (1949)**½ Wallace Beery, Marjorie Main, Richard Conte. Fast moving comedy-drama about a renegade bandit and his misadventures with a young doctor he saves from an angry mob. Beery's last film. (Dir: Richard Thorpe, 85 mins.)

Big Jake (1971)** John Wayne, Richard Boone, Maureen O'Hara. Tall-in-the-saddle John Wayne rides to the rescue of his kidnapped grandson. A western that tries to be a comedy. (Dir: George Sherman, 110 mins.)†

Big Jim McLain (1952)** John Wayne, Nancy Olson, James Arness. The setting is Hawaii and Wayne, as a special agent, arrives on the scene to investigate a report about a ring of terrorists. (Dir: Edward Ludwig, 90 mins.)

Big Knife, The (1955)*** Jack Palance, Ida Lupino, Wendell Corey, Shelley Winters, Rod Steiger. A Hollywood star tries to break with a grasping producer. Well acted. (Dir: Robert Aldrich, 111 mins.)

Big Knife, The (MTV 1988)** Peter Gallagher, Betsy Brantley, Nehemiah Persoff. Clifford Odets's play, which castigated the Hollywood star system, is dated, to say the least, but given an earnest reading by a well-selected cast. Gallagher sets the right tone as a star who tries to fight the system but learns that there are no winners when one tangles with the Hollywood hierarchy. (Dir: John Jacobs, 120 mins.)

Big Land, The (1957)**½ Alan Ladd, Virginia Mayo, Edmond O'Brien. Cattleman and wheat growers combine to have a railroad built near their land. Doesn't blaze any new trails. (Dir: Gordon Douglas, 92 mins.)

Big Leaguer (1953)** Edward G. Robinson, Vera-Ellen, Jeff Richards. Routine baseball film centering on the bush leagues. (Dir: Robert Aldrich, 70 mins.)

Big Lift, The (1950)**½ Montgomery Clift, Paul Douglas. Factual story of the Berlin Airlift filmed on the spot. (Dir: George Seaton, 120 mins.)

Big Meat Eater (Canada, 1983)**½ George Dawson, Andrew Gillies, Big Miller. Aliens use a butcher shop as their base to exploit earth in this spaced-out Canadian cult comedy (with songs, yet). (Dir: Chris Windsor, 82 mins.)†

Big Mo—See: **Maurie**

Big Mouth, The (1967)** Jerry Lewis, Harold J. Stone, Susan Bay. The big mouth is after diamonds and the gangsters are after Jerry. (Dir: Jerry Lewis, 107 mins.)†

Big Night, The (1951)*** John Barrymore, Jr., Preston Foster. A young kid goes looking for the man who mercilessly beat his father, intending to kill him. Moody, grim drama has a lot to recommend it. (Dir: Joseph Losey, 75 mins.)

Big One, The: The Great Los Angeles Earthquake (MTV 1990)**½ Joanna Kerns, Dan Lauria, Bonnie Bartlett, Lindsay Frost, Brock Peters. Disaster movies usually spend lots of time building character before getting down to the action and here's another typical effort. Kerns is a seismologist who has a hard time convincing officials that a major quake is going to hit L.A. When it strikes an eight on the Richter scale, be prepared for a showcase of masterful special effects. (Dir: Larry Elikann, 192 mins.)†

Big Operator, The (1959)*½ Mickey Rooney, Steve Cochran, Mamie Van Doren, Mel Torme, Ray Danton. A crooked union boss terrorizes an upstanding worker who threatens to expose his racket; little Mickey is the tough, crooked leader. AKA: **Anatomy of the Syndicate**. (Dir: Charles Haas, 90 mins.)

Big Parade, The (1925)**** John Gilbert, Renee Adoree, Hobart Bosworth, Claire McDowell, Karl Dane. A silent film classic and one of the great war movies, this film balances the drama of ordinary souls whose lives are altered by World War I with sweeping battle sequences that are among the most harrowing ever captured on celluloid. A stirring, impassioned war epic. (Dir: King Vidor, 126 mins.)†

Big Picture, The (1989)*** Kevin Bacon, Emily Longstreth, J.T. Walsh, Jennifer Jason Leigh, Michael McKean. Warm but satirical comedy about the Hollywood hit machine. Plenty of cameo appearances (John Cleese, Martin Short, Eddie Albert, June Lockhart, Elliott Gould, Roddy McDowall) help hold your interest. (Dir: Christopher Guest, 99 mins.)†

Big Pond, The (1930)**½ Maurice Chevalier, Claudette Colbert. Enterprising Frenchman combines business and pleasure to win a girl. Creaky but the star quality shines through. (Dir: Hobart Henley, 75 mins.)

Big Red (1962)**½ Walter Pidgeon, Gilles Payant. Show horse escapes while on his way to be sold, goes in search of the little boy he loves. OK fare for the kids. (Dir: Norman Tokar, 89 mins.)†

Big Red One, The (1980)***½ Lee Marvin, Mark Hamill, Bobby DiCicco, Robert Carradine, Kelly Ward. Director Samuel Fuller's most personal film profoundly comprehends the effect of war on men. Story of a squad (WWII, Europe) headed by an anonymous sergeant (Marvin) and his four "horsemen" who survive the war over the bodies of the "wetnose" replacements who facelessly arrive and die. (113 mins.)†

Big Ripoff, The (MTV 1975)**½ Tony Curtis, Brenda Vaccaro, Larry Hagman, Roscoe Lee Browne. Curtis stars as a stylish con man hired by a millionaire to recover a huge ransom paid to kidnappers. (Dir: Dean Hargrove, 72 mins.)

Big Risk, The (France-Italy, 1960)** Jean-Paul Belmondo, Lino Ventura, Marcel

89

Dalio. Slow story of a thief on the run with his two children who gradually realize they'd be better off if Papa gave himself up. (Dir: Claude Sautet, 111 mins.)

Big Rose: Double Trouble (MTV 1974)** Shelley Winters, Barry Primus, Michael Constantine, Joan Van Ark. Unsold pilot for a series featuring Winters and Primus as a pair of private detectives. (Dir: Paul Krasny, 78 mins.)

Big Score, The (1983)*½ Fred Williamson, Richard Roundtree, Nancy Wilson, Ed Lauter, John Saxon. A typical entry in the once-thriving blaxploitation market. A narcotics cop is suspected of going crooked. (Dir: Fred Williamson, 85 mins.)†

Big Shakedown, The (1934)** Bette Davis, Glenda Farrell, John Farrell, Ricardo Cortez, Adrian Morris. A slight Warner Bros. tale about a wife who can't abide her hubby's decision to team up with a gangster. (Dir: John Francis Dillon, 64 mins.)

Big Shots (1987)** Ricky Busker, Darius McCrary, Robert Joy, Robert Prosky, Jerzy Skolimowski, Paul Winfield. Brainless kid stuff about the criminal life of two preteens, one a suburban white boy and the other a savvy black kid. (Dir: Robert Mandel, 90 mins.)†

Big Show, The (1961)** Esther Williams, Cliff Robertson, Nehemiah Persoff, Robert Vaughn. Son takes the rap for domineering circus father's negligence, returns from prison to find forces working against him. (Dir: James Clark, 113 mins.)

Big Sky, The (1962)*** Kirk Douglas, Dewey Martin, Elizabeth Threatt, Buddy Baer, Steven Geray, Jim Davis, Arthur Hunnicutt. Adventures of a keelboat expedition to establish a new trading post in 1830. Lengthy, rather tame frontier melodrama. (Dir: Howard Hawks, 122 mins.)†

Big Sleep, The (1946)**** Humphrey Bogart, Lauren Bacall, Martha Vickers, John Ridgely, Regis Toomey, Elisha Cook, Bob Steele, Dorothy Malone. A near-masterpiece directed by Howard Hawks, full of corruption, annihilation, and efficient wit. Bogart is a tough private eye, Bacall a shady society broad whose nymphomaniac sister sucks her thumb. The atmosphere is like a chronic hangover, with action and scenes mostly there for their own sake. The plot is impossible to follow; even scripter William Faulkner had problems adapting Raymond Chandler's novel. (114 mins.)†

Big Sleep, The (Great Britain, 1978)* Robert Mitchum, Sarah Miles, Richard Boone, Candy Clark, John Mills, Joan Collins, James Stewart. Unbelievably awful remake of the 1946 classic of murder and

mayhem. The setting has been changed to modern London, and the once daring elements have been made overexplicit. (Dir: Michael Winner, 99 mins.)†

Big Steal, The (1949)*** Robert Mitchum, Jane Greer, William Bendix, Patric Knowles, Ramon Novarro. Sharp thriller concerning Mitchum in one long chase through Mexico. Teaming up later with Greer, he chases Knowles who, in turn, is being chased by Bendix—for a large bundle of money. At first a bit confusing, but when the reason for the chase becomes clear, the interest is strong. (Dir: Don Siegel, 71 mins.)

Big Store, The (1941)*** The Marx Brothers, Margaret Dumont, Douglass Dumbrille, Tony Martin. Far too conventional in its comedy for much of its length, but this largely pallid Marx Brothers feature (their last for MGM) has some passages of devilishly good whimsy. (Dir: Charles Reisner, 80 mins.)†

Big Street, The (1942)**½ Henry Fonda, Lucille Ball, Barton MacLane, Eugene Palette, Agnes Moorehead. Busboy falls for a crippled nightclub singer. Sentimental but colorful Damon Runyon drama. (Dir: Irving Reis, 88 mins.)†

Big Time (1988)*** A concert film featuring music from beat-cabaret-funk-jazz-bebop-whatever singer-songwriter Tom Waits's theatrical show "Frank's Wild Years," staged by Chicago's Steppenwolf Theater Company. Visually reminiscent of Laurie Anderson's *Home of the Brave*, though more cinematic, this can really only be recommended to those with some familiarity with Waits and his peculiar, individual music. (Dir: Chris Blum, 90 mins.)†

Big T.N.T. Show, The (1966)**½ David McCallum, Joan Baez, Ike and Tina Turner, Bo Diddley, The Ronettes, The Lovin' Spoonful, Ray Charles. Some terrific acts in this attempt to follow up the success of *The T.A.M.I. Show*. Whether you like soul, rock 'n roll, or rhythm and blues, you can enjoy several peak performances. Some of these performances are in the video *That Was Rock*. (Dir: Larry Peerce, 93 mins.)†

Big Top Pee-wee (1988)*** Paul Reubens (Pee-wee Herman), Kris Kristofferson, Valeria Golino, Penelope Ann Miller, Susan Tyrrell. The silver screen's oldest youngster has a circus appear in his very own backyard in this bright, amusing vehicle. There are a few weak spots but aside from this, the film has a colorful array of good-natured show folk and farm animals. (Dir: Randal Kleiser, 86 mins.)†

Big Town (1947)*½ Philip Reed, Hillary Brooke. Newspaper editor and a girl reporter manage to solve a series of murders. Mediocre melodrama. (Dir: William C. Thomas, 60 mins.)

Big Town, The (1987)** Matt Dillon, Diane Lane, Tommy Lee Jones, Bruce Dern, Lee Grant, Tom Skerritt. Flashy trash, with whiz-kid gambler Dillon choosing between a "good girl" (Suzy Amis) with a baby, and a "bad girl" (Lane) married to his chief rival (Jones). The only elements surviving the morass of clichés and feigned "attitudes" are Lane's strip number and Dern's peculiar cameo as a blinded deal-maker. (Dir: Ben Bolt, 110 mins.)†

Big Trail, The (1930)*** John Wayne, Marguerite Churchill, Tyrone Power, Sr., Ian Keith, Ward Bond. Epic western of a Missouri-to-Oregon wagon trek casts Wayne in his first starring role as the scout. The Wayne philosophy is much in evidence, and the dirty villain is played by Tyrone Power, Sr., father of the famed star, in his last role. (Dir: Raoul Walsh, 110 mins.)†

Big Trees, The (1952)**½ Kirk Douglas, Eve Miller, Patrice Wymore, Edgar Buchanan. Rugged adventure tale filled with outdoorsy action. A greedy lumberman tries to cut a giant redwood forest down to size but he's won over by the local Quakers. (Dir: Felix Feist, 89 mins.)†

Big Trouble (1986)*** Alan Arkin, Peter Falk, Beverly D'Angelo, Valerie Curtin, Robert Stack, Charles Durning, Paul Dooley, Richard Libertini. Lighter-than-air goofball comedy sustained by a brilliant comedic ensemble. Insurance salesman Arkin plays a doting papa worried about how to send his musical genius triplets to Yale. After he toys with a larcenous scheme à la *Double Indemnity*, he is then led down the garden path by a con man (Falk) who has no end of inventive ways of raising tuition money. (Dir: John Cassavetes, 93 mins.)†

Big Trouble in Little China (1986)*** Kurt Russell, Kim Cattrall, Victor Wong, Dennis Dun, Kate Burton, James Hong. A rip-roaring combination of spectacular martial arts numbers, imaginative oriental fantasy, and highly eccentric characters. Russell (doing a John Wayne impersonation) plays a bumbling truck driver who gets in big trouble when he ventures to the underground Chinatown domain of Lo-Pan, a 2,000-year-old sorcerer. (Dir: John Carpenter, 100 mins.)†

Big Wednesday (1978)** Jan-Michael Vincent, Gary Busey, William Katt. Three surfing pals hold a reunion in order to test themselves on the big wave, the ultimate challenge. (Dir: John Milius, 125 mins.)†

Big Wheel, The (1949)**½ Mickey Rooney, Thomas Mitchell. Hot-shot auto racer

nearly causes tragedy. Excellent Indianapolis racing scenes. (Dir: Edward Ludwig, 92 mins.)

Bikini Beach (1964)**½ Frankie Avalon, Annette Funicello, Martha Hyer. Familiar beach movie. Some drag strip racing is thrown in. (Dir: William Aster, 100 mins.)†

Bikini Genie—See: **Wildest Dreams**

Bill (MTV 1981)***½ Mickey Rooney, Dennis Quaid, Largo Woodruff. Mickey Rooney gives an enormously satisfying performance as a retarded fellow coping with life after 44 years in a mental institution. This is a heartwarming drama, based on a true story, about a young Iowa filmmaker (Dennis Quaid) who extends his hand to Bill, gets him jobs, and makes him feel like he's part of the family. (Dir: Anthony Page, 104 mins.)†

Bill and Ted's Excellent Adventure (1989) *½ Keanu Reeves, Alex Winter, George Carlin. The title lies. Monument to institutionalized stupidity about two valley dudes who get to travel through history to do research for their history project. Reeves and Winter are appealingly clownish, but the movie is dumb beyond belief. (Dir: Stephen Herek, 90 mins.)†

Bill Cosby Himself (Canada, 1983)**½ A live one-man show filmed during Cosby's 1981 show in Ontario. (Dir: Bill Cosby, 99 mins.)†

Billie (1965)** Patty Duke, Jim Backus, Warren Berlinger. Family comedy about a young miss who's a wizard in all athletic endeavors. Her prowess on the track field makes her unpopular with the boys. (Dir: Don Weis, 87 mins.)

Billionaire Boys Club (MTV 1987)**½ Judd Nelson, Frederic Lehne, Raphael Sbarge, John Stockwell, Ron Silver. Absorbing telepic, based on real events, about a group of despicable young men, headed by Nelson, who start out manipulating rich kids' investments in the commodities market, and end up murdering a slick con man (Silver). (Dir: Marvin Chomsky, 192 mins.)

Billion Dollar Brain (Great Britain, 1967)** Michael Caine, Karl Malden, Ed Begley, Françoise Dorleac, Oscar Homolka. Secret agent Palmer, crossing and double-crossing the enemy in Finland. (Dir: Ken Russell, 111 mins.)

Billion Dollar Hobo, The (1978)**½ Tim Conway, Will Geer, John Myhers, Victoria Carroll. Mild kid comedy has bungling drifter (or drifting bungler) Conway sole heir to the fortune of Geer, who insists that Conway must prove himself by retracing Geer's steps as a hobo during the Depression. (Dir: Stuart McGowan, 96 mins.)†

Billion Dollar Threat, The (MTV 1979)** Dale Robinette, Patrick MacNee, Ralph

Bellamy. James Bond should sue! The agent is an American, but his derring-do follows the Bond mode, down to an adversary who threatens to pierce the Earth's ozone layer. (Dir: Barry Shear, 104 mins.)

Bill of Divorcement, A (1932)*** John Barrymore, Katharine Hepburn, Billie Burke. Dated in style and substance, but breathtakingly acted; a veteran returns to his unprepared family after years in a mental institution, just as his beloved wife is planning to marry again. Barrymore's power and depth of feeling are riveting. Hepburn's first film role shows her a natural star; and Billie Burke gives a lovely, much-underrated performance. (Dir: George Cukor, 76 mins.)

Bill of Divorcement, A (1940)** Maureen O'Hara, Adolphe Menjou, Fay Bainter, Herbert Marshall, Dame May Whitty, Patric Knowles, C. Aubrey Smith. Thin remake of the classic melodrama, not a patch on the 1932 version. (Dir: John Farrow, 74 mins.)†

Bill: On His Own (MTV 1983)**½ Mickey Rooney, Dennis Quaid, Helen Hunt. This TV-movie sequel finds Rooney, once again, capturing the feelings of a retarded man trying to be self-sufficient. However, the emphasis is more on a college student's (Hunt) endeavor to educate him, which drags the story out without adding dramatic substance. (Dir: Anthony Page, 104 mins.)†

Billy Budd (Great Britain, 1962)***½ Peter Ustinov, Robert Ryan, Terence Stamp, Melvyn Douglas. Well-produced film based on Herman Melville's classic allegorical tale of treachery in the 18th-century British navy. Ustinov directed and adapted from the Broadway play. (Dir: Peter Ustinov, 112 mins.)†

Billy Galvin (1986)**½ Karl Malden, Lenny Von Dohlen, Joyce Van Patten, Toni Kalem, Alan North, Keith Szarabajka. Working class realism predominates as a blue-collar daddy wants a better life for his son, who's determined to don Papa's hard hat and enter the exciting world of construction. This drama's not badly constructed and the cast couldn't be better, but nothing about the script or direction is out of the ordinary. (Dir: John Gray, 94 mins.)†

Billy Jack (1971)*** Tom Laughlin, Delores Taylor, Clark Howat, Bert Freed. Interesting drama about youth vs. the Establishment. Laughlin stars as Billy Jack, an idealistic young Indian who is committed to aiding a "freedom school" after the young students are harassed by bigots. Some of it is dated and simplistic, but it's involving anyway. Sequels: *The Trial of Billy Jack* and *Billy Jack*
92

Goes to Washington. (Dir: Tom Laughlin, 112 mins.)†

Billy Jack Goes to Washington (1977)*½ Tom Laughlin, Delores Taylor, E. G. Marshall, Sam Wanamaker, Lucie Arnaz, Dick Gautier, Pat O'Brien. Seldom-seen final sequel (thus far) to *Billy Jack* is a remake of *Mr. Smith Goes to Washington*, with the peaceful-but-deadly B.J. sent to Washington to fight a planned nuclear plant. Not as bad as you might think, but too pedantic and humorless. (Dir: "T. C. Frank" [Tom Laughlin], 155 mins.)

Billy Liar (Great Britain, 1963)*** Tom Courtenay, Julie Christie, Mona Washbourne. The Hall-Waterhouse farce has had seemingly indestructible life in its many incarnations over the years—on stage, in print, in movies, and on television. The plot follows the day-to-day life of an average Walter Mittyesque dreamer (Courtenay). (Dir: John Schlesinger, 96 mins.)†

Billy: Portrait of a Street Kid (MTV 1977)**½ LeVar Burton, Ossie Davis, Michael Constantine. Burton offers an honest and at times touching performance as a sullen kid caged in by the ghetto. (Dir: Steven Gethers, 112 mins.)

Billy Rose's Diamond Horseshoe (1945)**½ Betty Grable, Dick Haymes, Phil Silvers, William Gaxton, Margaret Dumont. Grable plays a nightclub singer, this time in love with medical student Haymes, in this comedy-drama directed and written by George Seaton. Tongue-in-cheek writing and a showy production. (104 mins.)

Billy Rose's Jumbo (1962)*** Doris Day, Stephen Boyd, Jimmy Durante, Martha Raye. It was a great spectacle in the '30s when Billy Rose's musical extravaganza, with book by Ben Hecht and Charles McArthur and music and lyrics by Rodgers and Hart, opened at the Hippodrome Theatre. The film version isn't nearly as impressive, but the cast performs with verve and the musical numbers are staged brilliantly by Busby Berkeley. (Dir: Charles Walters, 125 mins.)

Billy the Kid (1930)*** Johnny Mack Brown, Wallace Beery, Kay Johnson, Karl Dane, Roscoe Ates. Shot in actual locations where Billy the Kid lived, this is a handsome-looking western made in a widescreen process that would only find popularity decades later. The plot concerns Pat Garrett and Billy the Kid, whom Pat allows to escape; the film's affecting despite Vidor's difficulties with taming the widescreen process to suit his purposes. (Dir: King Vidor, 90 mins.)

Billy the Kid (1941)**½ Robert Taylor, Brian Donlevy. Good western adventure based on the life of the famous outlaw. (Dir: David Miller, 95 mins.)

Billy the Kid vs. Dracula (1966)* Chuck Courtney, John Carradine, Melinda Plowman. The gunslinger wants to reform and settle down, only to find his gal's uncle is old vampire Drac himself. (Dir: William Beaudine, 72 mins.)†

Billy Two Hats—See: **Lady and the Outlaw, The**

Biloxi Blues (1988)**½ Matthew Broderick, Christopher Walken, Mary Mulhern. Ably adapted version of the second of Neil Simon's autobiographical trilogy of plays which began with *Brighton Beach Memoirs*. In this installment, Broderick is Eugene Jerome, a sensitive young writer who goes through basic training and loses his virginity during the final year of WWII. At points, *Biloxi* is simply another "boot camp comedy," but it benefits from some amusing moments and Walken's wonderful turn as a silently loony drill instructor. (Dir: Mike Nichols, 109 mins.)†

Bimini Code (1984)½ Vickie Benson, Kristal Richardson, Frank Alexander, Rosanna Simanaitis. Two well-endowed ladies running a diving operation get involved with kidnappers and international spies from California to Bimini Island. (Dir: Barry Clark, 104 mins.)†

Bingo Long Traveling All-Stars and Motor Kings, The (1976)*** Billy Dee Williams, James Earl Jones, Richard Pryor. High-spirited, charming tale of a barnstorming black baseball team of 1939, who have abandoned the Negro National League in favor of lighting out on their own. Good blend of show business and the struggle for survival. (Dir: John Badham, 111 mins.)†

Biography of a Bachelor Girl (1935)*** Ann Harding, Robert Montgomery, Edward Everett Horton, Edward Arnold, Una Merkel, Donald Meek. Snappy and interesting comedy of the havoc wreaked when an actress writes her memoirs. Screenplay by Anita Loos. (Dir: Edward Griffith, 82 mins.)

Bionic Showdown, The: The Six Million Dollar Man and the Bionic Woman (MTV 1989)** Lee Majors, Lindsay Wagner, Richard Anderson, Martin E. Brooks, Robert Lansing. Majors and Wagner return to tussle once more with superpower villainy. A few novel ideas dress up the old plotting about assassins, and the actors deliver their dialogue with straight faces. (Dir: Alan J. Levi, 96 mins.)

Bionic Woman, The (MTV 1975)* Lindsay Wagner, Lee Majors, Richard Anderson, Monica Randall, Bob Sullivan. Pilot for the "Six Million Dollar Man" spin-off featuring Wagner as a tennis pro who almost dies in an accident but is revived and turned into a bionic do-gooder. Watch it and be amazed we survived the seventies with any functioning brain cells at all. (Dir: Richard Moder, 96 mins.)†

Birch Interval (1976)*** Eddie Albert, Rip Torn, Ann Wedgeworth, Susan McClung, Anne Revere. Sensitive, "uplifting" tale of a troubled family in Pennsylvania around 1947: a young girl (McClung) goes to live with relatives in the Pennsylvania Amish country and has some painful learning experiences. (Dir: Delbert Mann, 103 mins.)

Bird (1988)***½ Forest Whitaker, Diane Venora, Michael Zelniker. Clint Eastwood's perceptive portrait of jazz legend Charlie Parker comes up perfect in every department. Clint's direction is tight, visually evoking the smoky nightclubs and seedy hotel rooms that Parker inhabited; Forest Whitaker does a virtuoso turn as Parker, ably supported by Venora as his weary wife; and finally, there is Parker's music (slightly augmented for the film's soundtrack) which eloquently demonstrates how a musician who led a troubled private life was able to ultimately transfigure his existence. (160 mins.)†

Birdman of Alcatraz (1962)**** Burt Lancaster, Karl Malden, Thelma Ritter, Betty Field, Neville Brand, Telly Savalas, Edmund O'Brien, Hugh Marlowe. Gripping true story of convict Robert Stroud, who became an expert on birdlife while serving time for murder. Superior adult drama. (Dir: John Frankenheimer, 147 mins.)†

Birdmen, The (MTV 1971)*** Doug McClure, Richard Basehart, Chuck Connors, Max Baer. Tense, prisoner-of-war drama. This junior-grade "great escape" yarn is based on a WWII incident in Germany. (Dir: Philip Leacock, 78 mins.)

Bird of Paradise (1932)**½ Dolores Del Rio, Joel McCrea, Skeets Gallagher, John Halliday. This South Seas romancer is an unconvincing drama, but director King Vidor shoots with an eye for sensual detail and exotic eroticism. McCrea is the adventurer who marries native princess Del Rio, and there is some nonsense about sacrifices to the volcano god. (80 mins.)†

Bird of Paradise (1951)*** Louis Jourdan, Debra Paget, Jeff Chandler, Everett Sloane. White man come to island. Native princess have eyes for him. Gods get angry. Volcano erupt. And the only method of lava stoppage at the time was for the princess-in-residence to jump into the volcano. Silly, but endearing; and everyone looks pretty. (Dir: Delmer Daves, 100 mins.)

Bird on a Wire (1990)*½ Mel Gibson,

Goldie Hawn, David Carradine, Bill Duke, Stephen Tobolowsky, Joan Severance, Harry Caesar. Awful "package deal" movie fails to combine the stocks-in-trade of Gibson (fast-paced action laced with sex and sarcastic dialogue) and Hawn (predictable slapstick and ridiculous scripting). As ex-lovers who haven't seen each other in fifteen years, the now-odd couple is unwillingly reunited on the run from murderous Carradine. (Dir: John Badham, 110 mins.)†

Birds, The (1963)*** Tippi Hedren, Rod Taylor, Suzanne Pleshette, Veronica Cartwright, Jessica Tandy. Virtually every character in *The Birds* is somewhat isolated and lonely, which gives this film resonance and urgency as Melanie Daniels, a bored socialite, comes into the lives of a widower, his widowed mother, his lonely daughter, and his estranged ex-fiancée in Bodega Bay. What do the birds represent? Why do they attack? Hitchcock gives no answers in this ambiguous film filled with images of incredible beauty and violence. (Dir: Alfred Hitchcock, 120 mins.)†

Birds and the Bees, The (1956)** George Gobel, Mitzi Gaynor, David Niven. Millionaire innocent is snared by a lady card sharp. Remake of *The Lady Eve*. (Dir: Norman Taurog, 94 mins.)

Birds Do It (1966)** Soupy Sales, Tab Hunter, Arthur O'Connell. A Cape Kennedy janitor enters an off-limits room and finds after coming out that he is irresistible to women and that he can fly. (Dir: Andrew Marton, 95 mins.)

Birds in Peru (France, 1968)* Jean Seberg, Maurice Ronet, Pierre Brasseur, Danielle Darrieux. Pointless, pretentious study of a frigid blonde's attempts to be satisfied sexually, played out amidst a landscape of contrived symbols and one-dimensional characters. (Dir: Romain Gary, 95 mins.)

Birds of a Feather—See: La Cage Aux Folles

Birds of Prey (MTV 1973)** David Janssen. Airwatch pilot who chases bank robbers. Unusual aerial footage. (Dir: William Graham, 78 mins.)†

Birds, the Bees and the Italians, The (Italy-France, 1965)***½ Virni Lisi, Nora Ricci, Gastrone Moschin, Alberto Lioncello. Three tales of sex, love, and marriage from the inimitable Italian point of view of director Pietro Germi (*Divorce, Italian Style*). Hilarious musical-beds romp was an international hit and Golden Palm winner at Cannes. (115 mins.)

Bird with the Crystal Plumage, The (1970)**½ Tony Musante, Suzy Kendall. Slick murder mystery; Musante witnesses a near-murder and becomes obsessed in his amateur sleuthing. (Dir: Dario Argento, 98 mins.)†

Birdy (1984)*** Matthew Modine, Nicholas Cage, John Harkins, Sandy Baron. This puzzling and intriguing antiwar film will not appeal to everyone, but it's worth a look. Modine is remarkable playing "Birdy," a man obsessed with birds who becomes emotionally and physically scarred in Vietnam, while Cage plays the best friend who helps him through the traumatic aftermath of the war. An adaptation of William Wharton's 1978 cult novel. (Dir: Alan Parker, 120 mins.)†

Birgit Haas Must Be Killed (France, 1981)*** Philippe Noiret, Jean Rochefort, Lisa Kreuzer, Bernard Le Coq. Complicated suspenser that works beautifully as a character study and only slightly less effectively as a thriller. A conscienceless policeman (Noiret) plans the perfect set-up; he encourages a patsy (Rochefort) to become involved with a former terrorist but sneakily plans to snuff her out and pin the crime on the poor dupe. (Dir: Laurent Heynemann, 105 mins.)

Birthday Party, The (Great Britain, 1968)*** Robert Shaw, Dandy Nichols. Stimulating, well-acted version of Harold Pinter's enigmatic play. A boarder in a British seaside dwelling is taken away by two strangers, who've come to give him a birthday party. (Dir: William Friedkin, 127 mins.)

Birth of a Nation, The (1915)**** Lillian Gish, Henry B. Walthall, Mae Marsh. This silent classic directed by D. W. Griffith made the full-length feature film a commercial reality. President Woodrow Wilson described the film as ". . . writing history with lightning," and its impressive achievement hasn't diminished with time. Griffith's Civil War epic recreates both battle scenes and the Reconstruction period; some intimate family scenes, such as the Little Colonel's return from the War, are among the most moving reunion scenes ever committed to film. (157 mins.)†

Birth of the Beatles (MTV 1979)*½ Stephen MacKenna, Rod Culbertson, John Altman. Fans of the Fabs will be turned off by this monstrously lame telepic, which (like *John and Yoko*) puts a Hollywood luster on the early, rough-edged days of the band. (Dir: Richard Marquand, 96 mins.)

Birth of the Blues (1941)***½ Bing Crosby, Mary Martin. Minor story of a trumpet player who supposedly organized the first Dixieland jazz band. A delightful score and good performances. (Dir: Victor Schertzinger, 85 mins.)

Biscuit Eater, The (1940)***½ Billy Lee, Cordell Hickman, Helene Millard, Richard Lane. The story of an interracial friendship between two boys who try to make a champion out of an unwanted dog. This endearing adaptation of James Streets's story is considered one of the finest B pictures ever made. (Dir: Stuart Heisler, 83 mins.)

Biscuit Eater, The (1972)** Johnny Whitaker, Lew Ayres, Godfrey Cambridge. Disney story about a boy and his dog. Two youngsters try to train a mutt into a champion bird dog. (Dir: Vincent McEveety, 90 mins.)

Bishop Misbehaves, The (1935)*** Edmund Gwenn, Maureen O'Sullivan, Lucille Watson, Reginald Owen. Cute comic mystery has a clergyman tracking thieves through London's dangerous Limehouse district. Depends for its charm on the wonderful cast. (Dir: E. A. Dupont, 86 mins.)

Bishop Murder Case, The (1930)** Basil Rathbone, Leila Hyams, Roland Young, George Marion. Creaky Philo Vance mystery concerns a chess piece, not a cleric. The early sound technique is dreadful, and the humorless script doesn't help. (Dir: Nick Grinde, 91 mins.)†

Bishop's Wife, The (1947)*** Cary Grant, Loretta Young, David Niven, Monty Woolley. Amusing comedy fantasy; an angel comes to Earth to aid in the lives of some pleasant people including Monty Woolley, who steals each scene he's in. (Dir: Henry Koster, 108 mins.)†

Bitch, The (Great Britain, 1979) ½ Joan Collins, Kenneth Haigh, Ian Hendry. With her tired bag of acting tricks, Joan plays a schemer who toys with the crime world to rebuild her one-woman disco empire. A tasteless farrago in which Collins treats every line, even "Hello," as an innuendo and stares at every available male with an unbridled lust Mae West would have deemed excessive. Only for campaholics who delight in the misfortunes of aging actresses. (Dir: Gerry O'Hara, 93 mins.)†

Bite, The—See: Curse II: The Bite

Bitter Sweet (Great Britain, 1933)*** Anna Neagle, Fernand Graavey (Gravet), Esme Percy, Miles Mander, Kay Hammond. Noel Coward's nostalgic operetta about a woman's tragic love for a gambler is given a heartfelt, grand treatment. The score includes some of Coward's most beautiful songs; well worth seeing. (Dir: Herbert Wilcox, 93 mins.)

Bite the Bullet (1975)*** Gene Hackman, James Coburn, Candice Bergen. Written, directed, and produced by Richard Brooks. An unconventional, entertaining western about the cruel endurance horseraces that were customary in the West between 1880 and 1910. Coburn and Hackman are marvelous. (Dir: Richard Brooks, 131 mins.)†

Bitter Harvest (MTV 1981)*** Ron Howard, Art Carney, Richard Dysart. Scary, uncomfortable, life-on-the-farm story based on a true incident. Everything goes wrong for a young dairy farmer, frantically looking for reasons why his herd is sick and dying. Howard is splendid as the panicky, gutsy farmer who battles bureaucracy, before discovering a fat-soluble chemical in his dairy feed. (Dir: Roger Young, 104 mins.)†

Bitter Reunion (France, 1959)*** Gerard Blain, Jean-Claude Brialy. A reunion of two childhood friends after ten years of separation. Excellent performances. (Dir: Claude Chabrol, 105 mins.)

Bitter Rice (Italy, 1950)*** Silvana Mangano. Italian film, with English dialogue very poorly dubbed. About workers in the rice fields who toil for grain. Earthy, shocking drama. (Dir: Giuseppe De Santis, 107 mins.)

Bitter Sweet (1940)*** Jeanette MacDonald, Nelson Eddy, George Sanders, Herman Bing. A bowdlerization of Noël Coward's show. It's one of the most worthwhile MacDonald-Eddy vehicles, but what's interesting in the film comes from the original material, which has been gutted. (Dir: W. S. Van Dyke, 92 mins.)†

Bittersweet Love (1976)** Lana Turner, Robert Lansing, Celeste Holm, Robert Alda, Scott Hylands, Meredith Baxter-Birney. An old-fashioned, sudsy family melodrama with a modern plot twist. Soon after their honeymoon, a young couple discover, to their horror, that they are half-brother and sister. (Dir: David Miller, 92 mins.)†

Bitter Tea of General Yen, The (1933)***½ Barbara Stanwyck, Nils Asther, Walter Connolly. Although not one of director Frank Capra's better-known films, this Occidental-Oriental romance is one of his most deeply felt movies. Stanwyck is drawn to a Chinese warrior, who holds her captive; the film is strikingly sensual and daring for its time. (89 mins.)

Bitter Tears of Petra von Kant, The (West Germany, 1972)***½ Margit Carstensen, Hanna Schygulla. A morose, elegant film about unrequited love between two lesbians. The protagonist is a top fashion designer who brutalizes her worker-slave, Marlene, and talks of why her two marriages failed. Written and directed by Rainer Werner Fassbinder. (124 mins.)†

Bitter Victory (1958)*** Richard Burton, Curt Jurgens, Ruth Roman. An interesting personal drama played out against a background of the African campaign during WWII. Jurgens is quite effective as a commander who fears he is losing his nerve and Burton, in the less colorful role of a young captain under Jurgens's command, adds to the drama. (Dir: Nicholas Ray, 83 mins.)

Bizarre, Bizarre (France, 1937)***½ Michel Simon, Louis Jouvet, Françoise Rosay, Jean-Louis Barrault, Jean-Pierre Aumont. Superb comedy, scripted by Jacques Prevert and directed by Marcel Carne. Michel Simon plays an English mystery writer with a block, and the best French farceurs of the age all gang up on him. AKA: **Drole de Drama.** (109 mins.)

Bizet's Carmen—See: Carmen (1984)

BJ and the Bear (MTV 1978)*½ Claude Akins, Greg Evigan. Silly series pilot about a guitar-playing trucker (Evigan) who travels around with a pet chimp. (Dir: John Peyser, 104 mins.)

B. J. Lang Presents—See: **Manipulator, The**

Black and White in Color (France-Africa, 1976)***½ Jacques Spiesser, Jean Carmet, Catherine Rouvel. Surprise Oscar winner as Best Foreign Film. A first film by director Jean-Jacques Annaud, who wrote the screenplay with Georges Conchon, it examines the reactions of two groups, one French and one German, stationed in West Africa at the outbreak of WWI. Its perceptive look at patriotism contains truths which can't be overlooked. Filmed in Africa. (91 mins.)†

Black Angel (1946)*** Dan Duryea, June Vincent, Peter Lorre, Broderick Crawford. Absorbing mystery, with Vincent trying to clear her husband of an unjust murder charge. Imaginative directing produces a chilling atmosphere. (Dir: Roy William Neill, 80 mins.)

Black Angels (1970)* Des Roberts, John King III, Linda Jackson, James Whitworth. Member of a black motorcycle gang passes for white and infiltrates an enemy gang. Casting a real biker gang as one of the warring clubs may add this violent movie some authenticity, but it doesn't make it any more interesting. AKA: **Black Bikers from Hell.** (Dir: Laurence Merrick, 92 mins.)†

Black Arrow, The (1948)*** Louis Hayward, Janet Blair. Above average swashbuckler. Set around England's famous War of the Roses. (Dir: Gordon Douglas, 76 mins.)†

Black Bart (1948)** Yvonne DeCarlo, Dan Duryea. Daring road agent falls for a dancing beauty. Good cast in an unexceptional western. (Dir: George Sherman, 80 mins.)

Blackbeard, The Pirate (1952)**½ Robert Newton, Maureen O'Hara, William Bendix. The notorious pirate with a price on his head holds a girl captive as he seeks a fortune. Overdone pirate melodrama, but some good moments. (Dir: Raoul Walsh, 99 mins.)†

Blackbeard's Ghost (1967)*½ Peter Ustinov, Dean Jones, Suzanne Pleshette. Comedy-fantasy about a bumbling ghost is labored and tedious. Ustinov mugs throughout as a notorious pirate who stops a hotel from becoming a casino. (Dir: Robert Stevenson, 107 mins.)†

Black Beauty (1946)** Mona Freeman, Richard Denning, Evelyn Ankers, Terry Kilburn, Arthur Space. A sweet, somewhat perfunctory adaptation of the beloved children's tale. A little girl tries to recover her missing colt back in Victorian England. (Dir: Max Nosseck, 74 mins.)†

Black Beauty (Great Britain, 1971)**½ Mark Lester, Walter Slezak, Peter Lee Lawrence, Ursula Glas. More faithful to the book than the '46 version, this kiddie pic traces the history of a horse who's reunited with its young owner after a long separation. For the preadolescent horsey set. (Dir: James Hill, 106 mins.)†

Black Belly of the Tarantula, The (Italy-France, 1972)* Giancarlo Giannini, Claudine Auger, Barbara Bouchet, Barbara Bach. Investigator Giannini hunts for a killer who uses a knife dipped in spider venom. The type of thing that Dario Argento does well but seldom works in less capable hands. The Ennio Morricone score, however, is fine as always. (Dir: Paolo Cavara, 88 mins.)†

Black Bikers from Hell—See: **Black Angels**

Black Bird, The (1975)**½ George Segal, Stephane Audran, Lionel Stander, Signe Hasso, Elisha Cook. Occasionally funny updated parody of *The Maltese Falcon.* Film-trivia buffs please note that Elisha Cook, Jr. is back playing the same role. Lee Patrick again plays Spade's secretary. (Dir: David Giler, 98 mins.)†

Blackboard Jungle, The (1955)*** Glenn Ford, Anne Francis, Vic Morrow, Louis Calhern, Sidney Poitier, Richard Kiley, Warner Anderson, Paul Mazursky, John Hoyt, Jamie Farr. This satisfying melodrama has had a little of the stuffing knocked out of it over the years. (Today's teen punks on and off the screen make the delinquents here seem like boy scouts having a bad day.) Still, this remains a pungent tale about a committed teacher trying to educate, while receiving an education in criminal behavior from some of his charges. Expertly adapted from Evan Hunter's novel. (Dir: Richard Brooks, 101 mins.)†

Black Book, The (1949)*** Robert Cummings, Arlene Dahl. Both forces during the French Revolution are after possession of a secret diary containing vital information. Lively, exciting costume adventure; good cast, crammed full of action. (Dir: Anthony Mann, 84 mins.)

Black Caesar (1973)** Fred Williamson,

Art Lund, Julius Harris, Gloria Hendry, D'Urville Martin. A black gangster saga along the lines of *Little Caesar*. Tough and tawdry. (Dir: Larry Cohen, 92 mins.)

Black Camel (1931)** Warner Oland, Sally Eilers, Bela Lugosi, Victor Varconi, Robert Young, Dwight Frye. Charlie Chan investigates the murder of a starlet who had killed her director. (Dir: Hamilton McFadden, 71 mins.)

Black Castle, The (1952)** Richard Greene, Boris Karloff, Stephen McNally, Lon Chaney, Jr., Paula Corday. Sinister castles, unscrupulous counts, and strange happenings. (Dir: Nathan Juran, 81 mins.)†

Black Cat, The (1934)***½ Boris Karloff, Bela Lugosi, David Manners, Jacqueline Wells (Julie Bishop). Lugosi engages in a battle of wills with satanist Karloff in an eerie old castle where "even the phones are dead." Some may view the proceedings as high camp, but this is undoubtedly the best joint vehicle the two horror greats ever had. This is primarily due to the extraordinary mood of stylized menace created by the stark modernist decor and the haunting Expressionist images of German emigré director Edgar G. Ulmer. (70 mins.)

Black Cat, The (1941)*** Broderick Crawford, Hugh Herbert, Basil Rathbone, Gale Sondergaard. A real estate promoter and a goofy antique collector intrude upon the reading of a will in a gloomy old mansion. Neat mixture of comedy and shudders. (Dir: Albert Rogell, 70 mins.)

Black Cat, The (Italy, 1981)** Patrick Magee, Mimsy Farmer, David Warbeck, Al Cliver. Gothic horror with only the slightest connection to the Edgar Allan Poe story that "inspired" it. Magee succeeds in contacting dead spirits, who wreak their evil on a small town via the titular tabby. Lacking the extreme gore of director Lucio Fulci's better-known zombiethons. (91 mins.)

Black Cauldron, The (1985)**½ Voices of Grant Bardsley, Freddie Jones, John Hurt, John Byner. Disney cartoon that pits a young pig keeper against the malefic Horned King, who wishes to use a magical cauldron to unleash an army of undead warriors. The imagery is incredible to behold, but this type of story has been done with a lot more animation and coherency than here. (Dirs: Ted Berman, Richard Rich, 80 mins.)

Black Christmas (Canada, 1975)** Olivia Hussey, John Saxon, Keir Dullea, Margot Kidder. Suspense yarn begins intriguingly but becomes predictable. Hussey plays a college student whose sorority sisters are being killed off and whose ex-boyfriend may be the killer. AKA: **Silent Night, Evil Night,** and **Stranger in the House**. (Dir: Bob Clark, 100 mins.)†

Black Dragons (1942)*½ Bela Lugosi, Joan Barclay, Clayton Moore, George Pembroke. A Poverty Row propaganda flick which uses Lugosi for name value only. Bela's out to settle the score against a sextet of Nipponese spies, the recipients of plastic surgery that perfectly transformed them into average-looking Americans, the better to spy on Uncle Sam. AKA: **Black Dragon.** (Dir: William Nigh, 61 mins.)

Black Eagle (1988)** Sho Kosugi, Jean-Claude Van Damme, Doran Clark. CIA agent Kosugi battles bad guy Van Damme, who has stolen a top-secret weapon. Chop socky fans attracted by the presence of two of the genre's top stars won't be disappointed, although Kosugi and Van Damme could have had more scenes together. (Dir: Eric Karson, 94 mins.)†

Blackenstein (1973)½ John Hart, Ivory Stone, Liz Renay. Possibly the worst blaxploitation film ever made, and definitely the worst variation on the Frankenstein legend. Wounded in Vietnam, poor Eddie permits the innovative Doctor Stein to perform experimental surgery, but the medic's assistant has the hots for Eddie's chick, so he replaces Eddie's DNA injection, thus unleashing Blackenstein. (Dir: Willam Levey, 87 mins.)†

Black Flowers for the Bride—See: Something for Everyone

Black Fox, The (1962)*** Unusually interesting documentary of Hitler and his rise to power, paralleled by the Goethe fable of Reynard the Fox, symbol of political ruthlessness. Different. Narration by Marlene Dietrich. (Dir: Louis Clyde Stoumen, 89 mins.)

Black Friday (1940)**½ Boris Karloff, Stanley Ridges, Bela Lugosi, Anne Nagel, Anne Gwynne. Interesting B movie horror item in which Boris transplants a hoodlum's brain into the skull of a mild-mannered professor, who understandably exhibits some pronounced behavioral changes. (Dir: Arthur Lubin, 70 mins.)

Black Fury (1935)*** Paul Muni, Karen Morley, William Gargan, Barton MacLane, John Qualen. A simple Pennsylvania miner is driven to desperate action by the corruption around him. Muni is powerful, as always, and Morley gives an affecting performance as his troubled girl friend. (Dir: Michael Curtiz, 95 mins.)†

Black Gestapo, The (1975)* Rod Perry, Charles P. Robinson, Phil Hoover, Ed Cross, Lee Frost. During the Watts riots, a vigilante group forms to clean out the bad elements in black neighborhoods, but one of the group's leaders takes the rackets over himself. Violent blaxploitation with a veneer of social responsibility. (Dir: Lee Frost, 88 mins.)†

Black Girl (Senegal-France, 1969)***½ Mbissine Therese Diop, Anne-Marie Jelinck. A remarkable directorial effort by the African novelist Ousmane Sembene, who also wrote the screenplay, based on his book about a young black girl from Dakar hired to be a maid in France. Chronicles the unhappy life of an unsophisticated girl trying to cope with an alien culture. (60 mins.)

Black Gold (1947)*** Anthony Quinn, Katherine De Mille. An Indian gives permission to drill for oil on his property to obtain money enough to raise horses. Excellent performances turn this into an interesting drama. (Dir: Phil Karlson, 90 mins.)

Black Hand (1950)**½ Gene Kelly, J. Carrol Naish, Teresa Celli. Interesting drama about the activities of the Mafia or Black Hand as it was known at the turn of the century. (Dir: Richard Thorpe, 93 mins.)†

Black Hole, The (1979)** Maximilian Schell, Tony Perkins, Yvette Mimieux, Robert Forster, Ernest Borgnine. Our valiant troupe of explorers tangles with a Black Hole and an insane doctor who's commandeered a spacecraft which he has controlled for 20 years with his private army of robots. (Dir: Gary Nelson, 97 mins.)†

Black Horse Canyon (1954)**½ Joel McCrea, Mari Blanchard. A group of people try to recapture a wild stallion who has taken to the hills. (Dir: Jesse Hibbs, 81 mins.)

Black Jack (France-Great Britain-Spain, 1950)*½ George Sanders, Patricia Roc, Agnes Moorehead, Herbert Marshall, Marcel Dalio. Pedestrian saga of drug smugglers operating in the French Riviera, headed by socialite Moorehead. Sad to see this cast and director Julien Duvivier (who also wrote and produced) wasting their time here. AKA: **Captain Black Jack.** (103 mins.)†

Black Jack (1972)* Brandon DeWilde, Keenan Wynn, Georg Stanford Brown. Unfunny comedy about air piracy that became DeWilde's last film. AKA: **Wild in the Sky.** (Dir: William T. Naud, 87 mins.)

Black Klansman, The (1966)*½ Richard Gilden, Rima Kutner. After his daughter is killed in a Ku Klux Klan bombing, a light-skinned Negro infiltrates the Klan, seeking revenge. Melodrama has good intentions, little else. (Dir: Ted V. Mikels, 88 mins.)†

Black Knight, The (Great Britain, 1954)** Alan Ladd, Patricia Medina. Fast but disappointing tale of knighthood in the days of King Arthur. (Dir: Tay Garnett, 90 mins.)

Black Legion (1936)**½ Humphrey Bogart, Ann Sheridan, Dick Foran, Erin O'Brien Moore. Honest worker is duped into joining a terrorist Ku Klux Klan-type organization. (Dir: Archie Mayo, 83 mins.)

Black Like Me (1964)**½ James Whitmore, Clifton James, Roscoe Lee Browne. Based on fact. A writer poses as a Negro by chemically changing the color of his skin. (Dir: Carl Lerner, 107 mins.)†

Black Magic (1944)—See: **Meeting at Midnight**

Black Magic (1949)** Orson Welles, Nancy Guild. The evil plans of Cagliostro the magician are thwarted. Heavy melodrama. (Dir: Gregory Ratoff, 105 mins.)†

Blackmail (Great Britain, 1929)***½ Sara Allgood, Anny Ondra, Cyril Ritchard. A Scotland Yard detective story that is director Alfred Hitchcock's first sound film, and marks the brilliant young Hitchcock as a major talent. (78 mins.)†

Black Mama, White Mama (U.S.-Philippines, 1972)* Sid Haig, Pam Grier, Margaret Markov, Lynn Borden. A *Defiant Ones* variant about a black prostie and a white revolutionary who escape from jail and then disguise themselves as nuns. (Dir: Eddie Romero, 87 mins.)

Black Marble, The (1980)*** Paula Prentiss, Robert Foxworth, Harry Dean Stanton, Barbara Babcock, John Hancock, Judy Landers, James Woods. A welcome change of pace for policeman-turned-novelist Wambaugh. This romantic comedy concerns a lady cop smitten with her partner, a castles-in-the-air type who has trouble coping with the daily grind of police work. (Dir: Harold Becker, 113 mins.)†

Black Market Baby (MTV 1977)** Linda Purl, Desi Arnaz, Jr., Bill Bixby, Jessica Walter. A college girl nearly loses her baby to an unorthodox adoption agency in this ultramelodramatic TV movie. (Dir: Robert Day, 96 mins.)

Black Moon (France-West Germany, 1975)**½ Cathryn Harrison, Alexandra Stewart, Joe Dallesandro. An ambiguous, sometimes irritating allegory with some captivating moments. Trying to escape a civil war between the sexes, a young girl (a sort of Alice in Wonderland for our times) encounters assorted bizarre adventures. (Beautifully photographed by Sven Nykvist.) (Dir: Louis Malle, 92 mins.)

Black Moon Rising (1985)*** Tommy Lee Jones, Robert Vaughn, Linda Hamilton. A mean, lean adventure machine, this film has a labyrinthine plot, but the special effects and glistening cinematography propel it forward. Jones is a thief who has to dodge his employers (government agents), once he is robbed of the secret documents he stole for them. (Dir: Harley Cokliss, 100 mins.)†

Black Narcissus (Great Britain, 1947)***½ Deborah Kerr, Flora Robson, David Farrar, Sabu, Jean Simmons, Kathleen Byron. This one involves a man's man who sets the hearts of nuns in a Himalayan convent aflutter. The fox-in-the-henhouse theme is piquantly realized in ravishing color, but one might wonder what this perverse intelligence is all about. (Dirs: Michael Powell, Emeric Pressburger, 99 mins.)†

Black Orchid, The (1959)**½ Sophia Loren, Anthony Quinn, Ina Balin. Gangster's widow tries to overcome barriers when she falls in love again. Weepy drama. (Dir: Martin Ritt, 95 mins.)

Black Orpheus (France-Portugal, 1959)**** Breno Mello, Marpessa Dawn. Excellent film based on the Orpheus-Eurydice legend. Updated and played against the colorful background of carnival time in Brazil, complete with dancing, lovemaking, and black witchcraft. A hauntingly beautiful score. Oscar as Best Foreign Film. (Dir: Marcel Camus, 98 mins.)†

Blackout (Canada, 1978)*½ Jim Mitchum, June Allyson, Ray Milland, Belinda Montgomery, Jean-Pierre Aumont. Set in Manhattan during the second big power blackout, but made in Canada, this violent actioner has a decent cast to offset its excessive brutality. (Dir: Eddy Matalon, 90 mins.)†

Blackout (MCTV 1985)**½ Keith Carradine, Kathleen Quinlan, Gerald Hiken, Richard Widmark, Michael Beck. Murder mystery with all the stock ingredients. Joe Steiner (Richard Widmark) is a retired cop determined to find the murderer of the Vinson family; Keith Carradine plays an amnesiac with a mysterious past. (Dir: Douglas Hickox, 98 mins.)†

Black Pearl, The (1977)** Gilbert Roland, Mario Custodio, Carl Anderson, Perla Cristal. Scott O'Dell's novel has been turned into a pleasant enough feature for children. Story of a Mexican boy's discovery of a fabulous black pearl, guarded by a deadly manta ray, is marred by inadequate special effects. (Dir: Saul Swimmer, 96 mins.)

Black Peter (Czechoslovakia, 1964)***½ Ladislav Jakim, Pavla Martinkova. Czech teenager isn't making much headway with his girl friend or his new job of store detective in a supermarket. Co-authored by director Milos Forman. He has a keen eye for the hesitancies and insecurity of adolescents. (85 mins.)

Black Pirate, The (1926)***½ Douglas Fairbanks, Sr., Billie Dove, Donald Crisp.

Exciting silent movie swashbuckler with the athletic swagger of Fairbanks and the sweeping action sequences sprawling all over the screen. (Dir: Albert Parker, 94 mins.)†

Black Pirate, The (Italy, 1961)** Ricardo Montalban, Vincent Price. Buccaneer, campaigning for an end to the slave trade, is condemned to death, but escapes to vanquish the true villain. AKA: **Rage of the Buccaneers.** (Dir: Mario Costa, 90 mins.)

Black Rain (1989)***½ Michael Douglas, Andy Garcia, Ken Takakura, Kate Capshaw, Yusaku Matsuda, Tomisaburo Wakayama. Director Ridley Scott's films are always a feast for the eyes, and this one is no exception. The plot—about a corrupt N.Y. police detective (Douglas) in Osaka looking to recapture an escaped killer and bust a powerful crime organization—is familiar (the final sequences bring to mind *The Yakuza*), but Scott's stylishly complex visuals and rollercoaster pacing are overpowering. Douglas exudes a grizzled charm, while Takakura and Garcia are winning as his Japanese and American sidekicks. Veteran Japanese actor Wakayama has a brief but chilling scene as the local mob leader. (126 mins.)†

Black Rain (Japan, 1989)**** Yoshiko Tanaka, Kazuo Kitamura, Etsuko Ihihara, Shoichi Ozawa. The effects of the nuclear attack on Hiroshima are seen five years later in a family, now living in a rural village, who want to have their daughter married. But exposure to the lingering effects of radiation have lessened her value. Shohei Imamura, one of Japan's most important filmmakers, directs with a style that, on the surface, seems to derive from Ozu, but his examination of a traditional Japanese family in the postwar era is distinctively his own. (123 mins.)†

Black Rainbow (1989)*** Rosanna Arquette, Jason Robards, Tom Hulce, Mark Joy. A father-and-daughter duo who perform tricks of clairvoyance at small-town carnivals find their lives in danger when the daughter starts receiving messages from spirits of people who aren't dead—yet. North Carolina locations lend polish to this intelligently written thriller. (Dir: Mike Hodges, 113 mins.)†

Black Raven, The (1943)*½ George Zucco, Wanda McKay, Noel Madison, Bob Randall, Charlie Middleton, Glenn Strange, I. Stanford Jolley. An out-of-the-way country inn is the setting for more different plots (involving thievery, vengeance, romance, and of course, murder) than should be crammed into a movie that only runs for about one hour. This Poverty Row cheapie is finished before you can get bored. (Dir: Sam Newfield, 64 mins.)†

Black Rodeo (1972)**½ Muhammad Ali, Woody Strode. Documentary of black rodeo held in New York. (Dir: Jeff Kanew, 87 mins.)

Black Room, The (1935)*** Boris Karloff, Marian Marsh, Robert Allan, Edward Van Sloan. Superb chiller from a story by Robert Louis Stevenson; Karloff is excellent as twin brothers, one kindly and the other criminally insane. (Dir: Roy William Neill, 67 mins.)†

Black Room, The (1982)* Stephen Knight, Cassandra Gaviola, Jim Stathis, Linnea Quigley. Siblings lure victims into their house with promises of sexual delights, using them instead as unwilling blood transfusion donors. Static horror yawner. (Dirs: Elly Kenner, Norman Thaddeus Vane, 87 mins.)†

Black Rose, The (1950)** Cecile Aubrey, Tyrone Power, Orson Welles, Jack Hawkins, Herbert Lom. Good action scenes and lots of phony local color enliven this saga of a Saxon warrior on oriental travels in the 13th century—a good time to go abroad. (Dir: Henry Hathaway, 120 mins.)

Black Roses (1988)*½ John Martin, Ken Swofford, Sal Viviano, Julie Adams, Carmine Appice. The old folks who protested a heavy-metal concert in a small town are right this time—this band really is in cohorts with the devil, and wants to take the local kids with them. The monsters outweigh the music, but not by much in this lightweight effort. (Dir: John Fasano, 83 mins.)†

Black Sabbath (Italy, 1964)*** Boris Karloff, Mark Damon, Susy Andersen. Boris acts as M.C. and performs in the third of a trio of terror tales: "The Wurdalak," "A Drop of Water," and "The Telephone." Above average. (Dir: Mario Bava, 99 mins.)†

Black Scorpion, The (1957)**½ Richard Denning, Carlos Rivas, Mara Corday. When a volcano erupts in Mexico, a giant scorpion rises from the earth to spread destruction in this better-than-usual horror thriller. (Dir: Edward Ludwig, 88 mins.)

Black Shield of Falworth, The (1954)**½ Tony Curtis, Janet Leigh. Swashbuckling adventure set in medieval times. (Dir: Rudolph Mate, 99 mins.)

Black Sister's Revenge—See: **Emma Mae**

Black Sleep, The (1956)** Basil Rathbone, Akim Tamiroff, Lon Chaney, Jr., Bela Lugosi, John Carradine. Scientist uses a drug that brings on a sleep resembling death. Fair horror thriller. (Dir: Reginald Le Borg, 81 mins.)

Blacksnake (1973)* Anouska Hempel, David Warbeck, Percy Herbert, Milton

100

McCollin, Thomas Baptiste, Bernard Boston, Dave Prowse. One of filmmaker Russ Meyer's rare departures from his distinctive sex extravaganzas, this unpleasantly violent tale of vicious slaveowners in the Old South is presumably meant as a parody, though it's not nearly as funny as *Mandingo*. Meyer himself apparently doesn't like it—he markets his own movies on videotape, and this one isn't available. AKA: ~~Sweet Suzy, Slaves~~. (82 mins.)

Black Stallion, The (1979)**** Kelly Reno, Mickey Rooney, Teri Garr, Clarence Muse. Walter Farley's 1941 children's classic comes magically to life. The wonderful story of a loving young boy and a black Arabian stallion who survive a shipwreck and life on a rugged island. Mickey Rooney renders an outstanding (and remarkably restrained) performance as the wise old trainer. Beautiful photography. One of the finest children's films ever made. (Dir: Carroll Ballard, 125 mins.)†

Black Stallion Returns, The (1983)** Kelly Reno, Teri Garr, Allen Goorwitz, Jodi Thelen. Disappointing sequel is not the usual slapdash ripoff, but an adaptation of another one of nineteen Walter Farley books. Don't look for screen versions of the other seventeen, though, because this horse opera, notably weak in the stretch, is a flop. (Dir: Robert Dalva, 100 mins.)†

Black Sunday (Italy, 1961)*** Barbara Steele, John Richardson, Andrea Checchi. Witch returns from her grave to seek revenge after being burned at the stake. Atmospheric horror thriller still packs a punch. (Dir: Mario Bava, 83 mins.)

Black Sunday (1977)*** Robert Shaw, Bruce Dern, Marthe Keller, Fritz Weaver. The Arab guerrilla terrorist organization Black September plans to intimidate America by blowing up the Super Bowl while the President is in attendance. Exciting shootout between police helicopters and the loonies who've stolen the Goodyear blimp. Based on the best-selling suspense novel by Thomas Harris. (Dir: John Frankenheimer, 145 mins.)†

Black Swan, The (1942)*** Tyrone Power, Maureen O'Hara, George Sanders. Swashbuckling pirate tale adapted from Sabatini's novel. Great for kids and for adventure-minded adults. (Dir: Henry King, 85 mins.)

Black Tuesday (1954)*** Edward G. Robinson. Condemned killer masterminds his escape from the death house. Good gangster film. (Dir: Hugo Fregonese, 80 mins.)

Black Water Gold (MTV 1970)** Keir Dullea, Ricardo Montalbán, Bradford Dillman. Beautiful Bahama location. Story is a mish-mash about sunken treasure, etc. (Dir: Alan Landsburg, 75 mins.)

Blackwell's Island (1939)**½ John Garfield, Rosemary Lane, Victor Jory, Leon Ames. A reporter pursues a mobster, even having himself thrown into prison when he learns that the jailed thug is now behind prison corruption. Crime drama with energetic star performances. (Dir: William McGann, 71 mins.)

Black Whip, The (1956)** Hugh Marlowe, Coleen Gray, Angie Dickinson, Shela Wooley. A dance hall girl is suspected of being in cahoots with an outlaw in this sluggish western. (Dir: Charles Marquis Warren, 77 mins.)

Black Widow (1954)**½ Van Heflin, George Raft, Ginger Rogers, Gene Tierney, Peggy Ann Garner. Interesting whodunit. An ambitious girl comes to the big city and ends up being murdered. Through a series of flashbacks, the pieces are fitted into the puzzling murder case by detective George Raft. (Dir: Nunnally Johnson, 94 mins.)

Black Widow (1987)*** Debra Winger, Theresa Russell, Sami Frey, Dennis Hopper, Nicol Williamson, Terry O'Quinn, James Hong, Diane Ladd, Lois Smith, Mary Woronov, Rutanya Alda. A sleek, stylish thriller. Tired of being a desk jockey, a Justice Department investigator becomes obsessed with a case involving a perpetual widow with an addiction to murdering her wealthy mates soon after the nuptials. Although there's the usual red herring here and there, the film draws fascinating parallels between the two women's obsessions (one with crime-solving; the other with getting away with murder). (Dir: Bob Rafelson, 100 mins.)†

Black Windmill, The (1974)** Michael Caine, Janet Suzman, Donald Pleasence, Delphine Seyrig. Espionage potboiler loses steam midway. A British agent's son is kidnapped as part of a bigger plan to discredit him. (Dir: Don Siegel, 106 mins.)†

Black Zoo (1963)** Michael Gough, Jeanne Cooper, Virginia Grey. Proprietor of a private zoo turns murderer. (Dir: Robert Gordon, 88 mins.)

Blacula (1972)**½ William Marshall, Vonetta McGee, Emily Yancy, Thalmus Rasulala. This film has a certain style to it if you like horror films. It tells the story of an African prince who is turned into a vampire by the original Count Dracula. Two hundred years later he turns up in Los Angeles. (Dir: William Crain, 92 mins.)†

Blade (1973)**½ John Marley, Jon Cypher, Kathryn Walker, William Prince, John Schuck, Rue McClanahan. A psychotic woman-hater is stalked by the

New York cops. (Dir: Ernest Pintoff, 90 mins.)†

Blade in Hong Kong (MTV 1985)**½ Terry Lester, Keye Luke, Anthony Newley, Leslie Nielsen, Nancy Kwan, Mike Reston, Ellen Regan. Terry Lester, from "The Young and the Restless," tears through the streets of Hong Kong to fend off bad guys pursuing his beloved adopted Chinese father (Keye Luke). (Dir: Reza Badiyi, 104 mins.)†

Blademaster, The (1984)* Miles O'Keeffe, Chen Wong, Lisa Foster, Charles Borromel. O'Keeffe flexes and ripples once again in this nonsensical adventure set in mythical times. AKA: *Ator, the Invincible.* (Dir: David Hills, 92 mins.)†

Blade Runner (1982)**** Harrison Ford, Rutger Hauer, Sean Young, Edward James Olmos, Joanna Cassidy, Daryl Hannah. Superbly crafted sci-fi, which invests a remarkable storyline with a distinctive *noir*-ish visual style and the seventies high-tech look. Ford is a "blade runner" (bounty hunter) out to terminate four escaped androids who are thought to be dangerous. Impeccable in every detail, from casting to scripting to the unforgettable look at a future where machines have a truer sense of soul than humans do. Extra footage added on video. (Dir: Ridley Scott, 122 mins.)†

Blame It on Rio (1984)** Michael Caine, Joseph Bologna, Valerie Harper, Michelle Johnson, Demi Moore. Two men, one about to be divorced (Bologna) and one on the verge of considering it (Caine), vacation in Rio de Janeiro with their teenage daughters. The samba sounds, hot sands, and the well-endowed Johnson seduce Caine, who has an affair with his friend's daughter. The film stumbles over the new morality rather than mining it for laughs. Remake of the French *One Wild Moment.* (Dir: Stanley Donen, 110 mins.)†

Blame It on the Night (1984)** Nick Mancuso, Byron Thames, Leslie Ackerman, Dick Bakalyan, Red Ludwick. Blame it on the routine rock-of-ages script (original story by Mick Jagger) about the generation gap between a pop music star and his conservative little sonny boy. Tiresome even with all the rock music scene atmosphere thrown in. (Dir: Gene Taft, 85 mins.)†

Blanche Fury (Great Britain, 1948)**½ Valerie Hobson, Stewart Granger. Grasping girl about to marry her uncle's son carries on an affair with a steward, resulting in murder. Hard-breathing costume drama is heavy, but nicely acted, tastefully produced. (Dir: Marc Allegret, 93 mins.)

Blancheville Monster (Spain, 1963)**½ Joan Hills, Richard Davis. Young girl is terrorized in a spooky castle as an ancient family legend says her life must be sacrificed. (Dirs: Albertó de Martino, Martin Herbert, 89 mins.)

Blaze (1989)**½ Paul Newman, Lolita Davidovitch, Robert Wuhl, Jeffrey De-Munn. Writer-director Ron Shelton's biography of Earl K. Long turns the three-term Louisiana governor and folk hero into a political Gabby Hayes. Crusty Newman is full of spit 'n' vinegar and just plain adorable, but Davidovitch lacks the sultry vamping bawdiness needed to play showgirl stripper Blaze Starr. Long's love for Starr is sweet, but he wasn't quite the civil rights martyr the script would have you think. Look for the real Blaze in a cameo. (120 mins.)†

Blaze of Noon (1947)**½ William Holden, Anne Baxter. Drama about a pilot in love with the sky who gets married. Plays like a corny B movie, but the kids may like its air scenes. (Dir: John Farrow, 91 mins.)

Blazing Forest, The (1952)** John Payne, Susan Morrow, William Demarest. A dull story of the big men who fell the big trees for big stakes. As the title implies, there is a big forest fire sequence. (Dir: Edward Ludwig, 90 mins.)

Blazing Saddles (1974)*** Cleavon Little, Gene Wilder, Harvey Korman, Madeline Kahn, Alex Karras, Slim Pickens, Mel Brooks. A wildly funny "western." Little and Wilder try to save a small frontier town from the heartless governor (Brooks) and his cronies. Some of the jokes are sophomoric, but they keep coming so fast, you'll forget the clinkers. (Dir: Mel Brooks, 93 mins.)†

Blazing Stewardesses—See: **Texas Layover**

Blessed Event (1932)*** Lee Tracy, Dick Powell, Emma Dunn. Good dialogue and an amusing performance by Tracy make this story of a Broadway gossip columnist entertaining. (Dir: Roy Del Ruth, 83 mins.)

Bless the Beasts and Children (1971)**½ Billy Mumy, Barry Robins, Miles Chapin, Ken Swofford. Glendon Swarthout's novel is the basis of this interesting if not totally successful story about a group of problem boys from an expensive ranch-camp who set out to free some captive buffalo earmarked to be shot for sport. (Dir: Stanley Kramer, 106 mins.)†

Blind (1987)*** One of a series of documentaries by noted filmmaker Frederick Wiseman about the educational process at the Alabama School for the Deaf and Blind, where impaired students as young as five are taught living skills along with standard classes. Wiseman doesn't interview or question, but simply records life at the school; as a result, some segments go nowhere, but many

more are poignant and deeply revealing. (132 mins.)

Blind Date—See: **Chance Meeting** (1959)

Blind Date (1934)**½ Ann Sothern, Paul Kelly, Neil Hamilton, Mickey Rooney, Jane Darwell. Nice performances in this light romantic story of a girl choosing between two suitors. (Dir: Roy William Neill, 71 mins.)

Blind Date (1984)**½ Joseph Bottoms, Kirstie Alley, James Daughton, Lana Clarkson, Keir Dullea. American ad man Bottoms is accidentally blinded after witnessing a murder in Athens, but a computer implant restores enough of his sight to help him track the killer. Greek writer-director Nico Mastorakis is better at the latter, but knows how to entertain. (99 mins.)†

Blind Date (1987)** Kim Basinger, Bruce Willis, John Larroquette. Blind dates have a tendency to go awry, but this dinner date between Walter Davis (Willis) and Nadia Gates (Basinger) propels the hardworking Walter into a disastrous series of events that leave him jobless, carless, intoxicated, and inculpated. (Dir: Blake Edwards, 95 mins.)†

Blinded by the Light (MTV 1980)** Kristy McNichol, James Vincent McNichol, Anne Jackson, Michael McGuire. The subject is brainwashing in religious cults. However, this script only taps a small number of the fascinating, disturbing issues involved. (Dir: John Alonzo, 104 mins.)

Blind Faith (MTV 1990)**½ Robert Urich, Joanna Kerns, Dennis Farina, Joe Spano. Real-life story about a New Jersey insurance salesman with a pretty wife and three fine boys who murders his spouse for a local bimbo. Robert Urich is customarily leaden as the family man revealed as a selfish whiner. Another tale from the author of *Fatal Vision*. (Dir: Paul Wendkos, 192 mins.)

Blind Fear (Canada, 1989)**½ Shelly Hack, John Lagedijk, Kim Coates, Heidi Von Palleske, Jan Rubes. Replay of *Wait Until Dark*, with Hack as a blind employee of a deserted Maine lodge turning the tables on a trio of murderous gangsters in hiding there. Viewers will be rewarded by some nifty plot twists toward the end. (Dir: Tom Berry, 87 mins.)†

Blindfold (1966)*** Rock Hudson, Claudia Cardinale, Jack Warden. Psychologist is contacted by a security officer to treat a mentally disturbed scientist, which involves the headshrinker in an international plot. Enjoyable suspense. (Dir: Philip Dunne, 102 mins.)

Blind Fury (1989)*** Rutger Hauer, Brandon Call, Terrance O'Quinn, Lisa Blount, Meg Foster, Nick Cassavetes, Rick Overton, Randall "Tex" Cobb, Sho Kosugi. Blind Hauer tracks the murderers who have kidnapped his best friend's young son. What the bad guys don't know is that Hauer was trained in the martial arts by the Vietnamese to compensate for the loss of his sight. Westernized adaptation of Japan's popular "Zatoichi" character is played broadly, though it stops short of parody. (Dir: Phillip Noyce, 85 mins.)†

Blind Husbands (1919)**** Erich von Stroheim, Fay Wray. Superb film stars von Stroheim (who also directed) as a dashing officer enticing a bored wife into an affair. Truly sophisticated drama, brilliantly filmed and acted. (98 mins.)†

Blind Justice (MTV 1986)*** Tim Matheson, Mimi Kuzyk, Philip Charles MacKenzie, Tom Atkins, Lisa Eichorn. The nightmare of being fingered as a rapist-killer because you resemble the actual culprit is explored in this interesting drama. Tim Matheson conveys the right amount of disbelief as the victim whose personal life is all but destroyed. (Dir: Rod Holcomb, 104 mins.)†

Blind Man's Bluff—See: Cauldron of Blood

Blind Rage (Philippines, 1983)* D'Urville Martin, Leo Fong, Tony Ferrer, Dick Adair, Darnell Garcia, Charles Davao, Leila Hermosa. Five blind criminals attempting to rob a bank of five million dollars. (Dir: Efren C. Pinion, 81 mins.)†

Blind Spot (1947)*** Chester Morris, Constance Dowling. Writer on a drunk is accused of the murder of his publisher. Well-done mystery. (Dir: Robert Gordon, 73 mins.)

Blind Trust (Canada, 1987)**½ Marie Tifo, Pierre Curzi, Jacques Godin. A grim, intelligent crime drama about an undercover cop and an ex-con involved in a plot to pull off a fake robbery for the government. Fine acting by a cast of unfamiliar faces lends the film an air of authenticity. AKA: **Pouvoir Intime.** (Dir: Yves Simoneau, 88 mins.)†

Blind Vengeance (MCTV 1990)**½ Gerald McRaney, Lane Smith, Marg Helgenberger. Good performances highlight this tense psychological revenge drama. Slowly mounted tale builds gradually as a father seeks his own style of justice after his son is viciously murdered by a group of white supremacists. (Dir: Lee Philips, 92 mins.)

Blind Witness (MTV 1989)**½ Victoria Principal, Paul LeMat, Stephen Macht, Matt Clark, Tim Choate. Principal's pluck and gusto almost saves this routine story. She plays a blind woman, the sole witness to her husband's brutal murder at the hands of burglars. (Dir: Richard Colla, 96 mins.)

Bliss (Australia, 1985)**½ Barry Otto, Lynette Curran, Helen Jones, Miles Buchanan. An advertising big shot passes away for a few minutes, but returns with a vengeance, only to live through a hell on earth before attaining his personal nirvana. The convoluted cleverness of the screenplay obfuscates rather than illuminates, but it deserves credit for being different. (Dir: Ray Lawrence, 111 mins.)†

Bliss of Mrs. Blossom, The (Great Britain, 1968)*** Far-out farce about a bored wife (Shirley MacLaine) of a brassière manufacturer (Richard Attenborough) and how she stashes away a lover (James Booth) in the attic. Slyly amusing, once the spirit of the thing makes itself evident; amazingly, it's based on fact. Good fun. (Dir: Joe McGrath, 93 mins.)

Blithe Spirit (Great Britain, 1945)***½ Rex Harrison, Constance Cummings, Kay Hammond, Margaret Rutherford. Enchanting, astringent supernatural farce, from the play by Noël Coward. A widower (Harrison) remarries and finds himself haunted by the slinky ghost of his first wife (Hammond). Delightful performances by an expert cast; fascinating color effects by Ronald Neame. Good fun. (Dir: David Lean, 96 mins.)

Blob, The (1958)** Steve McQueen, Anita Corseaut. Gooey glob of ooze flops down from outer space and devours people. Adolescent sci-fi thriller doesn't have much except young McQueen's performance, yet many people have a nostalgic soft spot for this movie. (Dir: Irvin Yeaworth, 85 mins.)†

Blob, The (1988)*** Kevin Dillon, Shawnee Smith, Donovan Leitch, Joe Seneca. High-powered remake of the '58 cult thriller about an amorphous creature terrorizing a town. Updated special effects make this a Blob the way it oughta be. (Dir: Chuck Russell, 94 mins.)†

Blockade (1938)***½ Henry Fonda, Madeleine Carroll. An adventuress meets and loves a member of the Loyalist forces in Civil War–torn Spain. Well made, excellently acted. (Dir: William Dieterle, 90 mins.)

Block Busters (1944)**½ Leo Gorcey, Huntz Hall, Gabriel Dell, Billy Benedict, Frederick Pressel. No blockbuster, but a pleasant Bowery Boys entry with surprisingly sensitive interaction between the boys and a young Frenchman on the baseball diamond plus some zany comic moments at a costume party. (Dir: Wallace Fox, 60 mins.)

Blockheads (1938)*** Laurel & Hardy. Twenty years after the war ends, Stan is still guarding the trenches in France unaware that the fighting is over. When discovered, he returns to civilian life, rejoins Oliver, and they both get into another mess. Delightful. (Dir: John G. Blystone, 55 mins.)†

Blockhouse, The (Great Britain, 1973)** Peter Sellers, Charles Anavour, Per Oscarsson, Jeremy Kemp. Claustrophobic yarn about workmen trapped in an underground bunker after Allies land at Normandy on D-Day. If the setting doesn't drive you crazy, this dreary film will. Great cast, though. (Dir: Clive Rees, 90 mins.)†

Blonde Blackmailer (Great Britain, 1958)* Richard Arlen, Constance Leigh, Susan Shaw, Vincent Ball. After serving a rap for murder, an innocent man is released and sets out to prove his innocence. (Dir: Charles Deane, 58 mins.)

Blonde Bombshell (1933)*** Jean Harlow, Lee Tracy, Franchot Tone, Frank Morgan, Pat O'Brien. Raucous Hollywood comedy about a movie star, with snappy line readings and not-too-sluggish direction from Victor Fleming. Harlow and Tracy are well matched in this screwy farce—vintage racy, since it was made just before the Code lowered the boom. Loaded with tangy bits and players. AKA: **Bombshell** (91 mins.)†

Blonde Crazy (1931)**½ James Cagney, Joan Blondell, Louis Calhern, Guy Kibbee, Ray Milland. Sharp and unusual crime story has small-time con artists taking on the big players. Meanders a bit, but fast and entertaining. (Dir: Roy Del Ruth, 79 mins.)

Blonde Dynamite (1950)** Bowery Boys, Gabriel Dell, Adele Jergens, Lynn Davies. While Louie vacations, the Boys use his sweet shoppe as a base for a male escort service. (Dir: William Beaudine, 66 mins.)

Blonde Ice (1949)** Leslie Brooks, Robert Paige, Walter Sande, John Holland, James Griffith. Socialite Brooks, hungry for attention and titillated by scandal, murders a series of husbands and lovers. Obscure, lurid thriller never delivers. (Dir: Jack Bernhard, 73 mins.)†

Blonde Venus (1933)** Marlene Dietrich, Cary Grant, Herbert Marshall. This bizarre combination of campy excess and a soap opera plot tried to turn Dietrich into a long-suffering mother figure. She sacrifices herself to Cary Grant (if you call that a sacrifice) in order to pay the hospital bills for her ultra-proper husband (Marshall). The highlight is Dietrich warbling the tune "Hot Voodoo" in a gorilla suit. (Dir: Josef von Sternberg, 97 mins.)†

Blondie series. Follow the exploits of bumbling Dagwood Bumstead, his helpful spouse, Blondie, their kids Cookie and Alexander and their indispensable dog, Daisy, through 28 films beginning in 1938 and ending with *Beware of Blondie* (1950). Today these movies, based on the still popular Chic Young comic strip, play like TV sitcoms, so it's not so surprising that "Blondie" also became a TV series with Arthur Lake and Pamela Britton in 1957 and again with Will Hutchins and Pat Harty in 1968. Besides the films listed below, series titles include: *It's a Great Life, Footlight Glamour, Leave It to Blondie, Life with Blondie,* and *Beware of Blondie.*

Blondie (1938)**½ Penny Singleton, Arthur Lake, Larry Simms, Jonathan Hale. Snappy comedy, first one in the series based on the popular comic strip. Blondie and Dagwood have problems paying off their furniture installments when he gets stuck with a loan shark's note. (Dir: Frank R. Strayer, 80 mins.)

Blondie Brings Up Baby (1939)**½ Penny Singleton, Arthur Lake, Larry Simms. A salesman tells Blondie that Baby Dumpling has a high IQ, so he's enrolled in school. Good share of laughs in this series comedy. Well done. (Dir: Frank R. Strayer, 70 mins.)

Blondie for Victory (1942)** Penny Singleton, Arthur Lake, Larry Simms. Blondie joins the war effort with a vengeance, which causes Dagwood to pose as a GI. Fair comedy in the series. (Dir: Frank Strayer, 70 mins.)

Blondie Goes Latin (1941)**½ Penny Singleton, Arthur Lake, Tito Guizar, Ruth Terry. The Bumsteads are on the way to South America for a business deal with some frantic byplay on shipboard. A good musical as well as an up-to-standard entry in the series. (Dir: Frank Strayer, 69 mins.)

Blondie Goes to College (1942)** Penny Singleton, Arthur Lake, Janet Blair, Larry Parks. Blondie and Dagwood decide to go to college, concealing their marriage. Series comedy moves more slowly than some others but is still fair fun. At the end of this one Dagwood learns he's to become a father again. (Dir: Frank Strayer, 74 mins.)

Blondie Has Servant Trouble (1940)*** Penny Singleton, Arthur Lake, Arthur Hohl, Jonathan Hale. The Bumsteads spend a weekend at a supposedly haunted house with two sinister servants. Very funny at times—neat combination of family comedy and mystery. (Dir: Frank Strayer, 70 mins.)

Blondie Hits the Jackpot (1949)* Penny Singleton, Arthur Lake, Lloyd Corrigan. Dagwood muffs a big construction deal, finds himself serving hard labor on the construction gang. Slapstick replaces fun. Below par. (Dir: Edward Bernds, 66 mins.)

Blondie in Society (1941)*** Penny Singleton, Arthur Lake, William Frawley. Dagwood's in the dog house when he accepts a Great Dane as payment for a loan and Blondie enters it in a dog show. Series comedy has more laughs than many higher-budgeted shows. Good fun. (Dir: Frank Strayer, 75 mins.)

Blondie in the Dough (1947)** Penny Singleton, Arthur Lake, Hugh Herbert. Dagwood flubs a deal for a radio station, while Blondie catches the attention of a cookie manufacturer. Standard. (Dir: Abby Berlin, 69 mins.)

Blondie Johnson (1933)**½ Joan Blondell, Chester Morris, Allen Jenkins, Claire Dodd, Mae Busch, Sterling Holloway. Blondell rises from prostitute to first lady of crime. Interestingly directed, well acted. (Dir: Ray Enright, 67 mins.)

Blondie Knows Best (1946)**½ Penny Singleton, Arthur Lake, Shemp Howard. Dagwood gets himself in hot water when he has to impersonate his boss to corner a client. Amusing series comedy, with a funny bit by Shemp Howard as a process server. (Dir: Abby Berlin, 69 mins.)

Blondie Meets the Boss (1939)**½ Penny Singleton, Arthur Lake, Jonathan Hale. Dagwood loses his job and Blondie takes his place at the office. Second in the series, keeps up the fast moving amusement set by its predecessor. (Dir: Frank Strayer, 80 mins.)

Blondie of the Follies (1932)**½ Marion Davies, Robert Montgomery, Billie Dove, Jimmy Durante, James Gleason, Zasu Pitts. Hearst's sweetheart plays a girl from a poor neighborhood who breaks into the big time—the follies and playboy boyfriend Montgomery—thanks to a childhood friend. It's hard to imagine that this odd mixture of half-baked tragedy and flibbertigibet dialogue was ever intended to be taken seriously by an audience. (Dir: Edmund Goulding, 97 mins.)

Blondie on a Budget (1940)*** Penny Singleton, Arthur Lake, Rita Hayworth. Blondie wants a fur coat, Dagwood wants to join the Trout Club; complications become even more clouded when Dagwood's ex-girlfriend enters the picture. Enjoyable series comedy has good gags, the presence of Hayworth at her most glamorous. (Dir: Frank Strayer, 73 mins.)

Blondie Plays Cupid (1940)**½ Penny Singleton, Arthur Lake, Glenn Ford. En route to a vacation, Blondie and Dagwood help out an eloping couple. Pleasant comedy in the series, with the added attraction of Ford in his salad days. (Dir: Frank Strayer, 68 mins.)

Blondie's Anniversary (1947)** Penny Singleton, Arthur Lake, Adele Jergens, William Frawley. Dagwood inadvertently gives Blondie the wrong package for her anniversary present, which means more trouble. (Dir: Abby Berlin, 75 mins.)

Blondie's Big Deal (1949)** Penny Singleton, Arthur Lake, College Lyons. Dagwood invents a fireproof paint, but is double-crossed by unscrupulous competitors. Fair comedy. (Dir: Edward Bernds, 66 mins.)

Blondie's Big Moment (1946)** Penny Singleton, Arthur Lake, Jerome Cowan, Anita Louise. Exit "Mr. Dithers," enter "Mr. Radcliffe," as Dagwood gets a new boss and is promptly in hot water. Fair series comedy—around this time, it shows signs of wear. (Dir: Abby Berlin, 69 mins.)

Blondie's Blessed Event (1942)*** Penny Singleton, Arthur Lake, Hans Conried. When the strain of Blondie's expectant motherhood begins to show on Dagwood, he's sent to a Chicago convention, where he encounters an impoverished arty playwright. (Dir: Frank Strayer, 75 mins.)

Blondie's Hero (1950)*½ Penny Singleton, Arthur Lake, William Frawley, Joseph Sawyer. Dagwood finds himself in the Army Reserve Corps and victimized by a real tough sergeant. (Dir: Edward Bernds, 67 mins.)

Blondie's Holiday (1947)** Penny Singleton, Arthur Lake, Grant Mitchell. Blondie gets Dagwood in a financial jam when he's required to pay all expenses for a class reunion. Average. (Dir: Abby Berlin, 67 mins.)

Blondie's Lucky Day (1946)** Penny Singleton, Arthur Lake, Robert Stanton. Dagwood is fired, so he and Blondie set up their own business. Fair comedy in the series. (Dir: Abby Berlin, 75 mins.)

Blondie's Reward (1948)** Penny Singleton, Arthur Lake, Chick Chandler, Frank Jenks. Dagwood buys a swamp instead of the property he was supposed to purchase. Mild comedy in the series. (Dir: Abby Berlin, 67 mins.)

Blondie's Secret (1948)** Penny Singleton, Arthur Lake, Thurston Hall. While waiting for Dagwood so they can start their postponed vacation, Blondie chances upon some counterfeit money. (Dir: Edward Bernds, 68 mins.)

Blondie Takes a Vacation (1939)**½ Penny Singleton, Arthur Lake, Donald MacBride. The Bumsteads take over a rundown resort hotel and try to put it on a paying basis. Chucklesome comedy in the series, some good laughs. (Dir: Frank Strayer, 70 mins.)

Blood Alley (1955)** John Wayne, Lauren Bacall, Anita Ekberg. He-man adventurer John Wayne fights off Chinese Communists single-handed and still finds time for Lauren Bacall. Anita Ekberg, disguised in this one, plays a refugee clad in burlap. Strictly for the undiscriminating. (Dir: William Wellman, 115 mins.)

Blood and Black Lace (Italy, 1964)** Cameron Mitchell, Eva Bartok. Grisly shocker concerning some mysterious murders of fashion models. Not for the squeamish. (Dir: Mario Bava, 88 mins.)†

Blood and Orchids (MTV 1986)*** Kris Kristofferson, Jane Alexander, Madeline Stowe, William Russ, Matt Salinger, Sean Young. A febrile courtroom drama whose scandal sheet crime story works better than the romantic subplots. Sensing a cover-up, cop Kristofferson doggedly pursues the truth about a case involving four local Hawaiians who've been railroaded on rape charges so the gentry can camouflage a scandal. (Dir: Jerry Thorpe, 208 mins.)

Blood and Roses (France, 1961)** Mel Ferrer, Annette Vadim, Elsa Martinelli. Jealous girl's body becomes possessed, commits murders as a vampire. Colorful backgrounds and photography can't overcome a hazy plot. (Dir: Roger Vadim, 74 mins.)

Blood and Sand (1922)*** Rudolph Valentino, Lila Lee, Nita Naldi. The story of a bullfighter trying to choose between a good woman and a bad one is dated and corny, but Rudolph Valentino's Latin lover magnetism still pulls it off. (Dir: Fred Niblo, 80 mins.)†

Blood and Sand (1941)*** Tyrone Power, Nazimova, Anthony Quinn, Linda Darnell, Rita Hayworth. Director Rouben Mamoulian concentrates more on color and spectacle than on drama in this remake of the Ibáñez chestnut. Power is always a bit ridiculous doing Latins, but the color photography is something to see. (123 mins.)†

Blood Arrow (1958)** Scott Brady, Phyllis Coates. Gunfighter is hired to take medical supplies through rough country. A not-bad idea, but routine production. (Dir: Charles Marquis Warren, 75 mins.)

Blood Bath—See: **Track of the Vampire**

Bloodbath at the House of Death (Great Britain, 1984)*½ Kenny Everett, Pamela Stephenson, Vincent Price, Gareth Hunt, Graham Stark. Broad spoof of horror movies set in an old mansion where Price and his satanic cult plan to relive a hundred-year-old sacrifice. Price's hamming is the only redeeming feature; the rest is straight from the "Carry On" school of Brit humor. (Dir: Ray Cameron, 92 mins.)†

Blood Beach (1981)* John Saxon, David Huffman, Marianna Hill. Teenagers are being eaten by something living underneath the sand in this silly horror pic. Is it Frankie and Annette seeking revenge against a new generation of beach bunnies? Watch this and you'll want to commit surf-icide. (Dir: Jeffrey Bloom, 89 mins.)†

106

Blood Beast from Outer Space—See: **Night Caller from Outer Space**

Blood Beast Terror, The (Great Britain, 1968)** Peter Cushing, Robert Flemyng, Wanda Ventham, Vanessa Howard. A bloodcurdler. A young woman on the prowl delivers a kiss of instant and horrifying death. (Dir: Vernon Sewell, 88 mins.)†

Bloodbrothers (1978)***½ Richard Gere, Paul Sorvino, Tony Lo Bianco. Powerfully acted drama of the tensions tearing a working-class family apart; strong and well done. (Dir: Robert Mulligan, 116 mins.)†

Blood Creature—See: **Terror Is a Man**

Blood Demon, The—See: **Torture Chamber of Dr. Sadism**

Blood Diner (1987)½ Rick Burks, Carl Crew, Roger Dauer. Atrocious, amateurish schlock about two demented brothers who plan a "blood buffet" at the title eatery. One of those films that tries to be bad, and boy, does it succeed! (Dir: Jackie Kong, 90 mins.)†

Bloodeaters—See: **Toxic Zombies**

Blood Feast (1963)½ Thomas Wood, Connie Mason, Mel Arnold. A milestone in drive-in history, this first "gore" film has extremely cheap gross-out effects, acting that's so bad it's other-worldly, memorably inane music, and a ridiculous plot about a crazed Egyptian caterer who carves up young girls to pay homage to his favorite goddess. (Dir: Herschell Gordon Lewis, 75 mins.)†

Blood Feast (Mexico, 1972)* Hugo Stiglitz, Anjanette Comer, Zulma Faiad, Gerardo Cepeda. Madman lives in a castle where he keeps hundreds of man-eating cats. Originally 92 mins. AKA: **Night of 1,000 Cats**. (Dir: René Cardona, Jr., 83 mins.)†

Blood Feud (Italy, 1979)**½ Sophia Loren, Marcello Mastroianni, Giancarlo Giannini. Director Lina Wertmuller never follows through on any of her ideas—political, cinematic, sexual—and it's apparent that her directionless energy is flagging of its own accord. The result is a standard Italian comedy about a Sicilian widow wooed by a lawyer and a gangster. (100 mins.)†

Blood Feud (MTV 1983)***½ Robert Blake, Cotter Smith, Ernest Borgnine, Forrest Tucker, Brian Dennehy, Danny Aiello. The well-made story of the decade of hostility that existed between Robert F. Kennedy and Teamsters President Jimmy Hoffa. It's not only an excellent re-creation of recent political history, but engrossing drama as well. (Dir: Michael Newell, 199 mins.)

Blood Fiend—See: **Theatre of Death**

Bloodfist (1989)** Don Wilson, Joe Mari Avellana, Riley Bowman, Vic Diaz. World Kickboxing Champion Wilson makes his bid for Chuck Norris–Jean Claude Van Damme status in this Roger Corman production that will satisfy both diehard martial arts fans and casual thrill seekers. The standard revenge-for-a-dead-brother plot doesn't get in the way of the nonstop flying feet. (Dir: Terence H. Winkless, 86 mins.)†

Blood for Dracula—See: **Andy Warhol's Dracula**

Blood Frenzy (1986)* Wendy MacDonald, Tony Montero. Which of the six patients at a desert group therapy weekend is killing the others? What's on the other channel? (Dir: Hal Freeman, 91 mins.)†

Blood From the Mummy's Tomb (Great Britain, 1972)**½ Michael Carreras, Andrew Keir, Valerie Leon, Hugh Burden, James Villiers. Based on Bram Stoker's "Jewel of the Seven Stars," this reincarnation chiller was badly done as *The Awakening* (1980). Here, a comely woman is possessed by the spirit of Queen Tana, an Egyptian ruler not happy to have had her rest disturbed by tomb-breaking archaeologists. (Dir: Seth Holt, 94 mins.)

Blood Hook (1986)* Mark Jacobs, Ann Todd, Don Winters. At a fishing festival five vacationing college kids encounter a bizarre group of fishing fanatics and a killer who'd rather catch tourists than fish. In the finale, hero and villain face off for a battle to the death—with fishing poles. Dopey mystery dozes until its gory ending, but it's too little, too late. (Dir: James Mallon, 85 mins.)†

Blood Hounds of Broadway (1952)**½ Mitzi Gaynor, Scott Brady, Mitzi Green, Marguerite Chapman, Michael O'Shea. A comedy with music in the *Guys and Dolls* tradition, but not nearly as effective. Miss Gaynor plays a hillbilly who comes to the city and turns into a curvaceous Broadway babe. (Dir: Harmon Jones, 90 mins.)

Bloodhounds of Broadway (1988)*** Matt Dillon, Julie Hagerty, Randy Quaid, Madonna, Rutger Hauer, Jennifer Grey, Esai Morales, Ethan Phillips, Anita Morris. Barely-released but entertaining adaptation of several Damon Runyon stories about various lowlife Manhattanites on New Year's Eve, 1928. The script successfully captures Runyon's distinctive style, while the production effectively re-creates New York nightlife at the end of the Roaring Twenties. William S. Burroughs has a funny cameo appearance. (Dir: Howard Brookner, 101 mins.)†

Blood in the Face (1991)*** Powerful documentary about some of America's most repulsive citizens—the Ku Klux Klan, American Nazi Party, and the Aryan Nations—alleges a systematic campaign of hate by America's extreme radical right, and examines these groups from the inside. (Dirs: Anne Bohlen, Kevin Rafferty, James Ridgeway, 75 mins.)†

Bloodline (1979)½ Audrey Hepburn, James Mason, Ben Gazzara, Omar Sharif, Romy Schneider, Beatrice Straight, Gert Frobe. Tedious thriller about an heiress to an international pharmaceutical empire who, after the suspicious death of her father, heads the firm and lives in fear of her own life. (Dir: Terence Young, 116 mins.)†

Blood Mania (1970)* Peter Carpenter, Maria de Aragon, Vicki Peters, Alex Rocco, Reagan Wilson. Chiller Theater garbage; one of those "greed does not pay" shockers about a woman who kills daddy only to find that she's not slated for his moolah anyway. (Dir: Robert O'Neil, 88 mins.)†

Blood Money (1933)*** George Bancroft, Frances Dee, Judith Anderson, Chick Chandler, Blossom Seeley. Bustling drama about crime world denizens. A bail bondsman tries to step out with the swells, but his jealous partner wants him to keep his mitts off a certain carefree debutante. Flashy and lively. Lucille Ball has a bit part. (Dir: Rowland Brown, 65 mins.)

Blood Money (1988)—See: **Clinton and Nadine**†

Blood of a Poet, The (France, 1930)*** Enrico Ribero, Lee Miller, Jean Desbordes. A landmark film, Cocteau's first, written and narrated by him. *Poet* is constructed as a series of episodic, enigmatic, frequently autobiographical imaginary events, revelations, and transformations. Cocteau fills the screen with an unending collage of remarkable allegories and images. (Dir: Jean Cocteau, 53 mins.)†

Blood of Dracula (1957)* Sandra Harrison, Louise Lewis. Wicked girls' school teacher puts one of her students under a vampire's curse. Curse is right. (Dir: Herbert L. Strock, 68 mins.)

Blood of Dracula's Castle (1967)½ John Carradine, Paula Raymond, Robert Dix. Amusingly awful "blood-sucker" about a vampiric couple who keep a well-stocked blood bank of young women chained in their cellar. The thirsty duo is understandably dismayed when faced with eviction. (Dir: Al Adamson, 84 mins.)†

Blood of Fu Manchu—See: **Against All Odds** (1968)

Blood of Heroes, The (1990)** Rutger Hauer, Joan Chen, Vincent Phillip D'Onofrio, Anna Katarina, Delroy Lindo. Bloody futuristic sports fantasy which finds Hauer running a team of "juggers," scarred warrior-athletes who compete in football-like contests that have two teams scrambling to get a dog's head on a stake.

Petite Chen is sadly miscast as a ambitious young woman who wants to be a champ in the game. The action sequences are full of spirited mayhem and sports movie clichés, but the dramatic interludes are dull and ponderous. Originally 102 mins. (Dir: David Webb Peoples, 90 mins.)†

Blood of Others, The (MCTV 1984)*½ Jodie Foster, Michael Ontkean, Sam Neill, Stephane Audran, Lambert Wilson. This bloodless made-for-cable film concentrates on a bland romance between Foster, a fledgling fashion designer who joins the French resistance in World War II, and Ontkean, a politically active advocate of worker's rights. Based on Simone de Beauvoir's 1946 novel about moral responsibility. (Dir: Claude Chabrol, 177 mins.)†

Blood of the Condor (Bolivia, 1969)***½ Marcelino Yanahuaya, Benedicta Mendoza Huanca, Vincente Salinas. A Quechua Indian chief discovers that American medical workers in his country are sterilizing native women to keep the population down. An angry, shocking film that presaged a greater political awareness in Bolivia and went on to become an international sensation. (Dir: Jorges Sanjines, 74 mins.)

Blood of the Man Beast—See: **House of the Black Death**

Blood of the Man Devil—See: **House of the Black Death**

Blood of the Vampire (Great Britain, 1958)**½ Sir Donald Wolfit, Barbara Shelley. Vampire is restored to life and continues his bloodcurdling ways. Gory but reasonably fast-moving shocker. (Dir: Henry Cass, 87 mins.)†

Blood on Satan's Claw (Great Britain, 1970)*** Patrick Wymark, Linda Hayden, Barry Andrews. Rural England circa 1670 is the setting for witch trials and an atmosphere of suspense. Better-than-average horror. Not for the squeamish. (Dir: Piers Haggard, 93 mins.)†

Blood on the Arrow (1965)*½ Dale Robertson, Martha Hyer, Wendell Cory, Ted DeCorsia, Elisha Cook, Jr. Young survivor of an Apache attack is taken in by the wife of a trader who is involved with outlaws. Sub-par western that depicts Indians as bloodthirsty savages. (Dir: Sidney Salkow, 91 mins.)

Blood on the Moon (1948)**½ Robert Mitchum, Walter Brennan, Robert Preston, Barbara Bel Geddes. Murky, violent postwar western. (Dir: Robert Wise, 88 mins.)†

Blood on the Sun (1945)*** James Cagney, Sylvia Sidney. In prewar Japan, an American newspaperman foresees the threat to democracy posed by the ruling warlords, who try to silence him. Fast-paced,

suspenseful melodrama. Plenty of Cagney action. (Dir: Frank Lloyd, 94 mins.)†

Blood Orgy of the She-Devils (1973)½ Lila Zaborin, Victor Izay, Tom Pace. A coven of mod-looking witches are responsible for a series of odd deaths in this slightly psychedelic, low-budget wonder. High point is the séance sequence in which the evil high priestess channels the spirits of both an American Indian and her prim Aunt Jessica! (Dir: Ted V. Mikels, 78 mins.)†

Blood Rage (1983)* Louise Lasser, Mark Soper. Lasser is pathetic doing "Mary Hartman" shtick in this slasher movie about a young killer whose twin is blamed for the crime. When the innocent boy escapes from a mental hospital, his brother starts a new series of murders. AKA: **Nightmare at Shadow Woods.** (Dir: John M. Grissmer, 83 mins.)†

Blood Red (1989)** Eric Roberts, Giancarlo Giannini, Dennis Hopper, Burt Young, Carlin Glynn, Lara Harris, Julia Roberts, Elias Koteas, Frank Campanella, Aldo Ray, Susan Anspach, Horton Foote, Jr. Lackluster tale of family passions and feuds set one hundred years ago in California wine country. Siblings Eric and Julia Roberts play a few scenes together. Made in 1986. (Dir: Peter Masterson, 91 mins.)†

Blood Relations (Canada, 1989)*½ Jan Rubes, Lydie Denier, Kevin Hicks. Father, son, and son's girlfriend try to bump each other off in competition for the family fortune. Mediocre mystery-thriller with a particularly disappointing ending. (Dir: Graeme Campbell, 88 mins.)†

Blood Shack—See: **Chooper, The**

Blood Simple (1984)*** John Getz, Frances McDormand, Dan Hedaya, M. Emmet Walsh. Praised for its black humor, this twangy yarn about a couple scheming to murder the woman's husband (who may or may not end up dead) and the slimy detective hired (who may or may not be on the husband's side) is complicated and usually dazzling. (Dir: Joel Coen, 97 mins.)†

Blood Song (1982)** Donna Wilkes, Frankie Avalon, Richard Jaeckel, Antoinette Bower, Dane Clark. Avalon is surprisingly good as a mad killer whose progress is "followed" by teenager Wilkes in nightmarish visions. (Dir: Alan J. Levi, 90 mins.)†

Bloodsport (MTV 1973)*** Ben Johnson, Larry Hagman, Gary Busey. Johnson charges this truthful, direct drama with tension in the role of a small-town worker who sees nothing but big-time gridiron glory for his hot-shot high-school-star son. (Dir: Jerrold Freedman, 78 mins.)

Blood Sport (MTV 1986)**½ William Shatner, James Darren, Heather Locklear,

Don Murray, Kim Miyori, Henry Darrow. The "T. J. Hooker" crew goes to Hawaii to protect a senator from "threatening terrorists." (Dir: Vincent McEveety, 104 mins.)

Bloodsport (1987)**½ Jean-Claude Van Damme, Donald Gibb, Leah Ayres, Forest Whitaker. Martial arts adventure with American soldier Van Damme competing in the Kumite, an outlawed martial arts competition in Hong Kong. Pretty hokey, but great for those who love the sound of breaking bones. (Dir: Newt Arnold, 97 mins.)†

Bloodstone (1988)** Brett Stimely, Rajni Kanth, Anna Nicholas, Charlie Brill. Ex-cop and his wife, honeymooning in India, become unwilling participants in the hunt for a stolen ruby. Exotic location photography enlivens a stale plot. (Dir: Dwight Little, 91 mins.)†

Bloodsuckers (Great Britain, 1970)** Patrick Mower, Peter Cushing, Patrick Macnee, Imogen Hassall, Johnny Sekka, Madeline Hinde, Edward Woodward, Alex Davion. Oxford don in Greece falls under the spell of a woman who seduces him into vampirism. Potentially interesting approach, viewing vampires as non-supernatural psychotics suffering from sexual impotence, was lost in studio tampering that resulted in director Hartford-Davis removing his name from the credits. Cushing is wasted in an insignificant role. (Dir: "Michael Burrowes" [Robert Hartford-Davis], 87 mins.)†

Blood Suckers, The—See: Dr. Terror's House of Horrors

Bloodsucking Freaks (1976)½ Seamus O'Brien, Niles McMaster, Louie DeJesus, Viju Krim, Alan Dellay. Tawdry "horror" comedy set at a Grand Guignol-type theater in Manhattan. Of course, all the "fake" tortures presented on stage turn out to be real, and they're not nearly as bad as the ones that take place backstage. Even fans of this debased genre will be appalled; the parodic tone only serves to make the violence even more misanthropic. AKA: The Incredible Torture Show. (Dir: Joel M. Reed, 88 mins.)†

Bloodthirsty Butchers (1969)½ John Miranda, Jane Helay, Berwick Kaler. Cheapjack version of the Sweeney Todd story, with very little gore (despite the title) and a lot of time-filling subplots. Another must-to-avoid from Staten Island director Andy Milligan, whose films give new meaning to the term "low budget" (he supposedly spent only $7,000 on this one). (79 mins.)†

Blood Ties (MCTV 1986)**½ Brad Davis, Vincent Spano, Tony Lo Bianco, Maria Conchita Alonso, Michael V. Gazzo. A brutal melodrama about an innocent American architect (Davis) who's blackmailed by the Mafia into murdering an anti-mob judge in Italy (a distant cousin of his) in exchange for the life of his kidnapped father. (Dir: Giacomo Battiato, 122 mins.)†

Blood Vows: The Story of a Mafia Wife (MTV 1987)**½ Joe Penny, Melissa Gilbert, Talia Shire, Eileen Brennan, Tony Franciosa. A young orphan (Gilbert) marries a handsome lawyer (Penny) only to discover she's in the Mafia now. (Dir: Paul Wendkos, 104 mins.)

Blood Wedding (Spain, 1981)**½ Antonio Gades, Christina Joyas, Juan Antonio Jiminez, Pilar Cardenas, Carmen Villena. Director Carlos Saura lyrically captures the Spanish ballet master Antonio Gades and his troupe dressing, rehearsing, and finally, performing in a barren, sunlit studio. Unfortunately, there is not a trace of Garcia Lorca's play in this film. Without the legendary dramatist's distinctive prose, this uncomplicated ballet resembles a hundred other tragic love tangos. (72 mins.)†

Bloody Mama (1970)*** Shelley Winters, Pat Hingle, Robert De Niro. Tough crime saga about Ma Barker and her brood of disturbed sons will be appreciated by some, dismissed by others. It's a brutal, machine-gun-paced account of the criminal rise and fall of the Barker brood. (Dir: Roger Corman, 92 mins.)†

Bloody New Year (Great Britain, 1986)** Suzy Aitchson, Mark Powley, Catherine Roman. Six teens trapped on deserted island discover seemingly abandoned hotel decorated for New Year's Eve. To their dismay they find it inhabited by ghostly presences. Dreary horror movie has a few imaginative special effects. (Dir: Norman J. Warren, 93 mins.)†

Bloody Wednesday (1985)**½ Raymond Elmendorf, Pamela Baker. To recover from a nervous breakdown, a man is set up as caretaker of a vacant hotel, where real and imaginary terrors only make his condition worse. Tale of a man's descent into madness is unpredictable from scene to scene, though final failure to tie plot elements together is frustrating. Written and produced by veteran screenwriter Philip Jordan. (Dir: Mark Gilhuis, 97 mins.)†

Bloomfield—See: Hero, The

Blossoms in the Dust (1941)** Greer Garson, Walter Pidgeon, Marsha Hunt, Fay Holden. What might have been a strong, noble subject—the founding of an orphanage by a woman who has lost her husband and child—founders in the glossy, phony MGM treatment. (Dir: Mervyn LeRoy, 100 mins.)†

Blown Away—See: Necessity

Blowing Wild (1953)**½ Barbara Stanwyck, Gary Cooper, Anthony Quinn. Power-crazy gal tries to gain control in Mexican oil fields. Well done but hardly worth the trouble. (Dir: Hugo Fregonese, 90 mins.)†

Blow Out (1981)***½ Nancy Allen, John Travolta, John Lithgow, Dennis Franz, Peter Boyden. A razzle-dazzle thriller from director Brian DePalma. He blows the ending, but until then the film is an enthralling, visually fascinating tale of a politician's death, an attempt at cover-up, and a horror film soundman's determination to prove what really happened and save a girl involved from a stalking killer. (107 mins.)†

Blow-Up (Great Britain–Italy, 1966)***½ David Hemmings, Vanessa Redgrave, Sarah Miles, Verushka. Director Michelangelo Antonioni's fascinating psychological puzzler of the young photographer who believes he's an accidental witness to a murder. (The small screen won't help clarify the filmmaker's intent.) Viewers may find the story baffling, but they'll be held spellbound by incandescent Redgrave and the photographer's nightmarish world. (111 mins.)†

Blue (1968)* Terence Stamp, Joanna Pettet, Karl Malden, Ricardo Montalban. Western oddity about a surly American raised by the Mexicans. A peculiar blend of sagebrush and psychology. (Dir: Silvio Narizzano, 113 mins.)

Blue Angel, The (Germany, 1930)**** Marlene Dietrich, Emil Jannings. The first film collaboration between director Josef von Sternberg and Dietrich. Reeks with the atmosphere of decay and sexuality. Jannings plays the professor who tries to stop his students from visiting nightclub singer Dietrich and ends up succumbing to her plump charms. The professor is a repressed little prig whose first sexual encounter results in his total destruction. A riveting performance by Dietrich, which made her a European star and prompted her invitation to Hollywood. (90 mins.)†

Blue Angel, The (1959)**½ May Britt, Curt Jurgens. Nowhere near as good as the original, but those who aren't familiar with the Dietrich opus will probably enjoy it. (Dir: Edward Dmytryk, 107 mins.)

Blue Bayou (MTV 1990)*** Alfre Woodard, Keith Williams, Mario Van Peeles, Elizabeth Ashley, Maxwell Caufield, Bibi Besch. Drama about a black attorney learning the ropes in the world of New Orleans' old money, written by "L.A. Law" creator Terry Louise Fisher. Could have been more focused—there's just too much going on at once—but the case is above average. (Dir: Karen Arthur, 96 mins.)

Bluebeard (1944)*** John Carradine, Jean

Parker. A puppeteer who strangles girls as a sideline falls for a beautiful dress shopowner, which is his downfall. Suspenseful thriller. Carradine is restrained, very good. (Dir: Edgar Ulmer, 73 mins.)†

Bluebeard (1963)—See: Landru

Bluebeard (1972)*½ Richard Burton, Virna Lisi, Joey Heatherton, Raquel Welch, Nathalie Delon. A sloppy black comedy with some lively moments provided by an attractive supporting cast of victims—all of whom succumb to Burton's courtly killer. Admittedly, some of the intentional humor works, but none of it is as much fun as watching Heatherton's hyperactive show girl trying to emote opposite Burton, who performs like a battery-operated actor in immediate need of new Duracells. (Dir: Edward Dmytryk, 125 mins.)†

Bluebeard's Eighth Wife (1938)** David Niven, Gary Cooper, Claudette Colbert. Highly problematical Ernst Lubitsch-directed comedy, in which the emotions are uncharacteristically inelegant. Cooper is an American millionaire who runs through wives until he meets determinedly emasculating Colbert, who wants to keep him, whatever the price in sexual humiliation. (85 mins.)

Bluebeard's Ten Honeymoons (Great Britain, 1960)** George Sanders, Corinne Calvet. George Sanders is so suave that he could probably get away with multiple murders as he does in this modern version of Bluebeard. (Dir: W. Lee Wilder, 93 mins.)

Blueberry Hill (1988)** Carrie Snodgress, Jennifer Rubin, Margaret Avery. Nostalgic drama set in the fifties, with Snodgress consumed by the memory of her dead husband while daughter Rubin learns the truth about her father from jazz singer Avery. Good music, but you'll find few thrills on this *Blueberry Hill*. (Dir: Strathford Hamilton, 87 mins.)†

Blue Bird, The (1940)**½ Shirley Temple, Spring Byington. Maeterlinck's classical fantasy about a little girl's search for true happiness receives an elaborate screen treatment. (Dir: Walter Lang, 88 mins.)†

Blue Bird, The (U.S.–U.S.S.R., 1976)* Elizabeth Taylor, Cicely Tyson, Jane Fonda, Ava Gardner. A disappointing remake of the Shirley Temple fantasy. (Dir: George Cukor, 99 mins.)

Blue City (1986)* Ally Sheedy, Judd Nelson, David Caruso, Anita Morris, Paul Winfield, David Caruso, Scott Wilson. Ross MacDonald mystery redone as a Brat Pack vehicle. Nelson plays a rebellious old man of 23 who returns home to investigate his father's murder with the full blessing of the local police. (Dir: Michelle Manning, 83 mins.)†

Blue Collar (1978)*** Richard Pryor, Yaphet Kotto, Harvey Keitel. Screenwriter Paul Schrader directed this downbeat tale of workday oppression. The union squeezes from one side, the bosses from another, and three auto workers are caught in the contradictions of capitalism. Intelligent and well observed. (114 mins.)†

Blue Country (France, 1978)*** Brigitte Fossey, Jacques Serres. Written and directed by Jean-Charles Tacchella as a follow-up to his enormously successful *Cousin, Cousine*. The leads are a couple who try to retain their independence while carrying on a lengthy love affair; some of the scenes are marvelous. (104 mins.)

Blue Dahlia, The (1946)*** Alan Ladd, Veronica Lake, Doris Dowling, William Bendix, Hugh Beaumont, Howard da Silva. A caustic murder melodrama full of that postwar disillusionment that the Hollywood *film noir* exhibited. When Ladd returns to hearth and home, he finds it occupied by other men, thus making Alan a prime suspect when his trampy wife is iced. Glamorous Lake stands by Ladd, and their screen chemistry enlivens this sharp thriller. (Raymond Chandler's only movie writing done directly for the screen.) (Dir: George Marshall, 96 mins.)

Blue Denim (1959)**½ Carol Lynley, Brandon de Wilde. Another one about misunderstood youth and the consequences of premature love. Well acted but says nothing especially profound. (Dir: Philip Dunne, 89 mins.)

Blue DeVille (MTV 1986)½ Jennifer Runyon, Kimberly Pistone, Mark Thomas Miller, Robert Prescott, Toni Sawyer, Noel Conlon, Nicole Mercurio. Horrendous young-adult pic that plays like a music video whose slim plotline was inexplicably padded out to feature length. A gutsy broad persuades her timid pal to forget about her engagement and cut loose on the open road. (Dir: Jim Johnson, 104 mins.)

Blue Gardenia (1953)**½ Anne Baxter, Richard Conte, Ann Sothern. Slick, but slow moving mystery-drama about a girl wrongly accused of murder and her efforts to prove her innocence. Good performances. (Dir: Fritz Lang, 90 mins.)

Bluegrass (MTV 1988)*½ Cheryl Ladd, Brian Kerwin, Anthony Andrews, Shawnee Smith. Miniseries tailored for Ladd has her playing a horse breeder who encounters, and overcomes, all sorts of obstacles on the road to the Kentucky Derby. (Dir: Simon Wincer, 192 mins.)

Blue Hawaii (1961)**½ Elvis Presley, Joan Blackman, Angela Lansbury. Returning soldier takes a job with a tourist agency against his parent's wishes, makes good. Pretty pictures do not always a movie

make—but this one also has good songs and Presley. (Dir: Norman Taurog, 101 mins.)†

Blue Iguana, The (1988)* Dylan McDermott, Jessica Harper, James Russo, Pamela Gidley, Tovah Feldshuh, Dean Stockwell. Excruciating spoof of the private eye genre, "south of the border" sagas, Sergio Leone westerns, and just about anything else that writer-director John Lafia happened to think of. McDermott is a bounty hunter sent down to South America by two oddball IRS agents (Feldshuh and Stockwell) to break into a bank that launders money. (90 mins.)†

Blue Knight, The (1973)***½ William Holden, Lee Remick, Sam Elliott, Joe Santos, Jamie Farr, Vic Tayback. Superior TV film based on the Joseph Wambaugh best-seller. Even in this truncated version (cut down from miniseries length) Holden's full-bodied performance makes this something special. He plays Bumper Morgan, a vet cop who, en route to retirement, spends his last days on the force trying to find a prostitute's killer. (Dir: Robert Butler, 103 mins.)

Blue Knight, The (MTV 1975)**½ George Kennedy, Alex Rocco, Glynn Turman, Verna Bloom. George Kennedy plays Joseph Wambaugh's Bumper Morgan tracking down a cop-killer while making human contact on the street. (Dir: J. Lee Thompson, 73 mins.)†

Blue Lagoon, The (Great Britain, 1948)** Jean Simmons, Donald Houston. Boy and girl are shipwrecked on a tropic isle, grow to maturity and love each other. Picturesque scenery doesn't overcome the weakness of the tale; moderate adventure drama. (Dir: Frank Launder, 101 mins.)

Blue Lagoon, The (1980)* Brooke Shields, Christopher Atkins, Leo McKern, William Daniels. Two kids discover love and sex while shipwrecked on a tropical island. Like an R-rated movie for children, this insipid film inspired less curiosity about the birds and the bees than it did disgust over the teasing peek-a-boo courtship of the two leads. This is the cleanest, most thinly disguised soft-core porn flick ever made. (Dir: Randal Kleiser, 104 mins.)†

Blue Lamp, The (Great Britain, 1950)*** Jack Warner, Dirk Bogarde. A young recruit nabs a robber after he has killed a fellow policeman. Glorifying the British bobby, this is exciting as well as having an authentic documentary-like flavor. (Dir: Basil Dearden, 84 mins.)

Blue Light, The (Germany, 1932)*** Leni Riefenstahl, Max Holzboer, Mathias Wieman, Beni Fuhrer. A painter is in love with a young girl believed to be a witch because only she knows the secret way to the top of a dangerous mountain

111

peak. Using natural mountain settings, film is simple, romantic, and shot with a keen eye for detail. This was actress Riefenstahl's directorial debut; it brought her to the attention of Adolph Hitler, who asked her to make films glorifying the Nazi party. (77 mins.)†

Blue Lightning, The (MTV 1986)** Sam Elliott, Rebecca Gilling, John Meillion, Robert Coleby, Max Phipps. Elliott goes all the way to Australia to be overshadowed by aerial highway chases and aerial shootouts over a valuable blue opal. (Dir: Lee Philips, 104 mins.)

Blue Max, The (1966)**½ George Peppard, Ursula Andress, James Mason. Overblown World War I flying epic that is at its best during some superbly photographed and staged aerial battle sequences featuring vintage planes. George Peppard is well cast as a fastidious German pilot who is eager to become a war ace. (Dir: John Guillermin, 156 mins.)†

Blue Money (Great Britain, 1984)**½ Tim Curry, Debby Bishop, Billy Connolly, Dermot Crowly, Frances Tomelty. Curry, who's been underutilized since *The Rocky Horror Picture Show,* gets to show off his many talents here as a London cabdriver with dreams of stardom who accidentally comes into possession of a suitcase of mob money. (Dir: Colin Bucksey, 82 mins.)†

Blue Monkey (Canada-U.S., 1987)** Steve Railsback, Susan Anspach, Gwynyth Walsh, John Vernon, Joe Flaherty. No monkeys here, just a ten-foot insect that terrorizes a hospital. Plays like a fifties monster flick, with a good opening and climax. (Dir: William Fruet, 98 mins.)†

Blue Murder at St. Trinian's (Great Britain, 1958)**½ Alastair Sim, Joyce Grenfell, Terry-Thomas. Foolish comedy about a jewel thief hiding from the law in a girls' school. The events leading to his eventual capture are pure slapstick. The delightful cast of performers are at the script's mercy, but Sim still gets his share of laughs. (Dir: Frank Launder, 88 mins.)

Blueprint for Murder, A (1953)** Joseph Cotten, Jean Peters. Contrived "perfect crime" melodrama which may keep some viewers guessing as to whether the beautiful Miss Peters is guilty or not. (Dir: Andrew Stone, 76 mins.)

Blues Brothers (1980)** John Belushi, Dan Aykroyd, Carrie Fisher, Cab Calloway, John Candy, Aretha Franklin. A tiresome, noisy chase film featuring the characters Belushi and Aykroyd made famous on "Saturday Night Live." While director John Landis always reverts to wholesale destruction when things get slow, the film is made bearable by musical interludes from soul greats James

Brown, Aretha Franklin, and Ray Charles. (130 mins.)†

Blues Busters (1950)*** Huntz Hall, Phyllis Coates. This one is all Huntz Hall—Sach discovers he has a singing voice, becomes a swoonin' crooner. One of the best of the Bowery Boys series. (Dir: William Beaudine, 67 mins.)

Blues for Lovers (Great Britain, 1965)** Ray Charles, Tom Bell, Mary Peach, Dawn Addams. Dull melodrama about a blind boy's friendship with a blind American jazz musician. Jazz-pianist Ray Charles performs well enough in his screen debut, but the music is best—an attractive mixture of American jazz and English-ballad blues. AKA: **Ballad in Blue.** (Dir: Paul Henreid, 89 mins.)†

Blues in the Night (1941)*** Priscilla Lane, Richard Whorf, Betty Field, Lloyd Nolan, Elia Kazan. A wonderful score by Harold Arlen and Johnny Mercer, plus an occasionally moving plot about a traveling jazz band add up to good entertainment. With a little more work this could have been a great motion picture. (Dir: Anatole Litvak, 88 mins.)

Blue Skies (1946)*** Bing Crosby, Fred Astaire, Joan Caulfield. Bing, Fred and 20 Irving Berlin tunes add up to pleasant entertainment about a dancer and nightclub owner wooing the same girl. (Dir: Stuart Heisler, 104 mins.)

Blue Skies Again (1983)*½ Harry Hamlin, Mimi Rogers, Kenneth McMillan, Dana Elcar. A spunky female wants to break the baseball gender barrier. . . . Strike one is the ridiculous plotting. Strike two is the uninspired direction. Strike three is the unconvincing acting of the cast. Strikeout! (Dir: Richard Michaels, 110 mins.)†

Blue Steel (1990)**½ Jamie Lee Curtis, Ron Silver, Clancy Brown, Elizabeth Peña, Louise Fletcher, Philip Bosco. Murderous Wall St. trader Silver develops a deadly obsession for rookie N.Y.C. policewoman Curtis in this slickly directed but ludicrously plotted urban cop thriller. The film loses ground rapidly as it charts the course of Silver's insane killing spree, depicting him as a virtually indestructible force of nature spouting incomprehensible psychobabble. (Dir: Kathryn Bigelow, 102 mins.)†

Blue Sunshine (1976)*** Zalman King, Mark Goddard, Robert Walden, Deborah Winters, Charles Siebert. Must viewing for Fright Night afficionados. Falsely accused of some senseless, brutal murders, an innocent man races to find the motives of the real killer. In this upsetting and violent shocker, he discovers the murderers are suffering from a flashback syndrome related to a psychedelic drug from the LSD-conscious sixties. A terrifying film about losing control. (Dir: Jeff Lieberman, 97 mins.)†

Blue Thunder (1983)*** Roy Scheider, Malcolm McDowell, Candy Clark, Daniel Stern, Warren Oates. This exhilarating, well-crafted adventure stars Roy Scheider as a Vietnam-vet-turned-cop whose traumatic blackouts don't keep him from test-piloting and then stealing the title character—a fearsome, gadget-laden police helicopter. Filled with striking aerial photography, accomplished supporting performances, and salty, knowing dialogue. (Dir: John Badham, 110 mins.)†

Blue Veil, The (1951)**½ Jane Wyman, Charles Laughton, Joan Blondell. Young woman thwarted by love finds happiness in being a children's nurse. Long, tearful drama. (Dir: Curtis Bernhardt, 114 mins.)

Blue Velvet (1986)*** Kyle MacLachlan, Isabella Rosselini, Laura Dern, Dennis Hopper, Dean Stockwell. The surprise cult hit of the eighties. It's a curious film which mixes a potent satire of American mediocrity with the malevolence of *film noir*. The contrived plotline follows a wimpish young man who discovers a nightmare world of decadence and sex hidden right in the heart of his own small town. The clincher is Dennis Hopper's full-tilt incarnation of town psycho Frank Booth. And even he is upstaged briefly by Stockwell, as "suave" Ben. (Dir: David Lynch, 120 mins.)†

Blue Water, White Death (1971)***½ Underwater-photography buffs and adventurers of all ages will not want to miss this exciting odyssey in search of a Great White Shark, also known as White Death. (Dir: Peter Gimbel, 100 mins.)

Blue, White and Perfect (1941)**½ Lloyd Nolan, Mary Beth Hughes. Detective Michael Shayne gets in the war effort by chasing foreign agents who've been stealing industrial diamonds. Good B film. (Dir: Herbert I. Leeds, 78 mins.)

Blue Yonder, The (MCTV 1985)*** Peter Coyote, Huckleberry Fox, Art Carney, Joe Flood, Dennis Lipscomb. A spunky young boy goes back to the 1920s to meet his grandfather. The two hit it off so well that their attachment causes them to challenge the course of history. AKA: **Time Flyers**. (Dir: Mark Rosman, 104 mins.)†

Bluffing It (MTV 1987)** Dennis Weaver, Janet Carroll, Michelle Little. The very serious issue of illiteracy is given the standard TV-movie treatment. Weaver never quite gets under the skin of Jack Duggan, a factory foreman whose inability to read or write is embarrassingly discovered later in life. (Dir: James Sadwith, 96 mins.)†

Blume in Love (1973)***½ George Segal, Susan Anspach, Kris Kristofferson, Marsha Mason, Shelley Winters. Wry, affecting comedy-drama about a husband unable to let go of his ex-wife. Writer-director Paul Mazursky is on target in capturing the middle class facing the breakdown of their institutions. (115 mins.)†

BMX Bandits (Australia, 1983)** John Ley, David Argue, Nicole Kidman, James Lugton, Angelo D'Angelo. Cheery but inane adventure about small fry bikers foiling crooks; geared to cash in on the BMX biking craze. (Dir: Brian Trenchard-Smith, 90 mins.)

Boarding House (1984)½ Hawk Adley, Kalassu, Alexandra Day, Joel Riordan, Brian Buderlin. Amateurish shocker that looks like it was made over a weekend. Nubile young women in a California boarding house fall victim to a telekinetic killer, with plenty of badly executed special effects. (Dir: John Wintergate, 85 mins.)†

Boarding School (West Germany, 1978)** Nastassja Kinski, Carolin Ohrner, Marion Kracht, Gerry Sundquist, Veronique Delbourg. Girls and boys from neighboring boarding school scheme to get together in this rather innocent movie that tends to show up on late-night cable and the "adult" aisle of video stores. (Dir: Andre Farwagi, 100 mins.)†

Boardwalk (1979)**½ Lee Strasberg, Ruth Gordon, Janet Leigh, Eli Mintz, Joe Silver. Drama with comic and violent overtones about an elderly Jewish couple, Gordon and Strasberg, who are about to celebrate their 50th anniversary. The wife is dying of cancer, their grown children have problems, and their life is being threatened by a street gang, in this Coney Island setting. (Dir: Stephen Verona, 98 mins.)

Boat, The—See: **Das Boot**

Boat Is Full, The (Switzerland, 1981)*** Tina Engel, Martin Walz, Curtis Bois. Despite the plethora of World War II holocaust films, director Markus Imhoof's understated work deserves attention. This heartrending tale of that horrifying time in recent history depicts the Swiss people's attitudes towards Jewish refugees and the racial prejudice on a more comprehensible level. (101 mins.)†

Boatniks, The (1970)**½ Phil Silvers, Norman Fell, Mickey Shaughnessy, Robert Morse. Another Walt Disney comedy about bumbling crooks and lovable kooks. This time Morse is the adorable coast guard officer who must pursue a trio of vaudevillian jewel robbers. (Dir: Norman Tokar, 104 mins.)†

Boat People (Hong Kong-China, 1983)*** Cora Miao, Lam Chi-Cheung. A photojournalist on a visit to Vietnam tours Danang, where he's shown a group of happy children playing, by the official Tourist Council. Afterwards, the reporter sees a different and terribly harsh

113

reality. An emotionally gripping look at the pitiable living conditions of the boat people in Communist Vietnam. (Dir: Ann Hui, 106 mins.)

Bob and Carol and Ted and Alice (1969) ***½ Elliott Gould, Dyan Cannon, Natalie Wood, Robert Culp. Paul Mazursky's directorial debut was a shrewd blend of satire and commercial calculation, a mixture of sharp gags and mushy sentiment. When the film works, it works very well; when it doesn't, it dies. Gould and Cannon were better attuned to the spirit of the enterprise than Wood and Culp. (105 mins.)†

Bobbie Jo and the Outlaw (1976)*½ Marjoe Gortner, Lynda Carter, Jesse Vint, Merrie Lynn, Belinda Belaski, Gerrit Graham. Two of screendom's most resistible personalities team up in this unappealing rip-off of *Bonnie and Clyde* about two crumb-bums on a robbery-murder spree. (Dir: Mark L. Lester, 89 mins.)†

Bobbikins (Great Britain, 1960)**½ Max Bygraves, Shirley Jones. Young couple are amazed to discover their 14-month baby talking like an adult, and giving stock market tips too. Pleasant fantasy has some chuckles, clever manipulating of baby to give the effect of speech. (Dir: Robert Day, 89 mins.)

Bobby Deerfield (1977)**½ Al Pacino, Marthe Keller. An all-consuming love story between a maladjusted race car driver (Pacino) and a wealthy, terminally ill jet-setter (Keller). The pace is tedious, but Pacino and Keller make the most of the material under Sydney Pollack's careful direction. (124 mins.)†

Bobby Ware Is Missing (1955)**½ Neville Brand, Arthur Franz. An offbeat drama about the search for a young teenage boy who has an accident and doesn't come home. (Dir: Thomas Carr, 66 mins.)

Bob le Flambeur (France, 1955)*** Roger Duchesne, Isabelle Corey, Daniel Cauchy. Flawed but pleasant pastiche of American *film noir* and heist films like *Rififi*. Director Jean-Pierre Melville has re-created these genres with great care and affection. (97 mins.)†

Bob Mathias Story, The (1954)**½ Bob Mathias, Ann Doran. Low-budget, entertaining biography of the decathlon champ of the 1948 and 1952 Olympics. (Dir: Francis Lyon, 80 mins.)

Bobo, The (Great Britain, 1967)** Peter Sellers, Britt Ekland, Rossano Brazzi. Sellers plays an inept matador who can land a singing job, providing he's able to seduce a courtesan (Ekland). (Dir: Robert Parrish, 105 mins.)†

Boccaccio '70 (Italy, 1962)***½ Sophia Loren, Anita Ekberg, Romy Schneider. Three naughty tales—"The Temptation of Dr. Antonio," with Ekberg as a post-

er come to life in a satire on prudishness; "The Job," with Schneider as a discontented wife; and "The Raffle," with Loren as the big prize in a love lottery. Sexy and funny escapist fare. (Dirs: Federico Fellini, Luchino Visconti, Vittorio De Sica, 165 mins.)

Body and Soul (1947)**** John Garfield, Lilli Palmer, Anne Revere, Hazel Brooks, William Conrad, Joseph Penny. A guy from the slums battles his way to the top of the fight racket, only to learn that the crooked way isn't necessarily the best. Hard-hitting melodrama, crisp and rugged, with some excellent prizefight sequences. Palmer is near-perfect; Garfield gives his best performance. (Dir: Robert Rossen, 104 mins.)†

Body and Soul (1981)½ Leon Isaac Kennedy, Jayne Kennedy, Peter Lawford, Michael V. Gazzo, Peter Lang, Kim Hamilton, Muhammad Ali. Kennedy casts himself as an amateur boxer anxious to make it to the top and to avoid all the corruptive influences on the way. (Dir: George Bowers, 100 mins.)†

Body Chemistry (1990)**½ Marc Singer, Lisa Pescia, Mary Crosby, David Kagen, Joseph Campanella. Director of a sexual research lab is seduced by an overly enthusiastic colleague who refuses to take "no" for an answer. Sound familiar? Blatant rip-off of *Fatal Attraction* but fine anyway, unless you're a copyright lawyer. (Dir: Kristine Peterson, 87 mins.)†

Body Count—See: 11th Commandment, The

Body Disappears, The (1941)** Jane Wyman, Jeffrey Lynn. Daffy little forced comedy in the *Topper* tradition but not in the same league. (Dir: Ross Lederman, 72 mins.)

Body Double (1984)*½ Craig Wasson, Deborah Shelton, Dennis Franz, Melanie Griffith, Gregg Henry, Guy Boyd. While apartment sitting, a man suffering from claustrophobia (a replacement for the dizziness in Hitchcock's *Vertigo*) begins spying on a luscious neighbor (a steal of the plot of *Rear Window*) as she dances nude in front of her window. Or is he seeing double? Brian DePalma's responsible for directing, co-producing, and co-writing this semi-pornographic bit of voyeurism. (114 mins.)†

Body Fever (1969)½ Carolyn Brandt, Bernard Fein, Gary Kent, Ray Dennis Steckler. Another brilliantly awful effort from producer-director-scripter-photographer-star Ray Dennis Steckler, the usual mix of demented humor, tepid acting, and unconventional plotting. In this discount *noir*, a ramshackle private eye searches for a tall, mysterious female (Brandt, of course) and a cache of stolen drugs. Steckler's parboiled narration supplies the real laughs here. (78 mins.)

Body Heat (1981)*** William Hurt, Kathleen Turner, Richard Crenna, Ted Danson, J. A. Preston, Mickey Rourke. A sexy movie with a plot that will keep you guessing until the end. Murder, greed, and lust come into sharp focus as a sensuous woman crosses the path of a lawyer who's barely making ends meet. (Dir: Lawrence Kasdan, 113 mins.)†

Body of Evidence (MTV 1988)*½ Margot Kidder, Barry Bostwick, Tony Lo Bianco. Lackluster *Suspicion* revamp has Kidder unsure about her police pathologist hubby (Bostwick) who may or may not be a pathological killer. (Dir: Roy Campenella II, 96 mins.)

Body Rock (1984)*½ Lorenzo Lamas, Vicki Frederick, Cameron Dye, Michelle Nicastro, Ray Sharkey. Nothing more than a series of noisy music videos loosely strung together by a third-rate plot. Lamas, of "Falcon Crest," is badly cast in the role of a hardened ghetto kid destined for fame. (Dir: Marcelo Epstein, 93 mins.)†

Body Shop—See: **Doctor Gore**

Body Slam (1986)*½ Dirk Benedict, Tanya Roberts, Roddy Piper, Captain Lou Albano, Barry Gordon, Charles Nelson Reilly, Billy Barty, the Tonga Kid (Sam Fatu). Any hour of professional wrestling on TV has far more laughs and unpredictable action than this lackluster comedy. (Dir: Hal Needham, 90 mins.)†

Body Snatcher, The (1945)***½ Boris Karloff, Bela Lugosi, Henry Daniell. A doctor is blackmailed by a villainous coachman when he wishes to stop securing bodies for medical research in Scotland of the 19th century. For horror fans, this is one of the best; for others, a good and chilling version of Robert Louis Stevenson's tale. (Dir: Robert Wise, 77 mins.)†

Boeing-Boeing (1965)** Tony Curtis, Jerry Lewis. A pair of calculating Romeos figure out an elaborate plan involving a bachelor pad with airline stewardesses coming and going. (Dir: John Rich, 102 mins.)

Bofors Gun, The (Great Britain, 1968)***½ Grim sessions at a British army camp in postwar Germany, with a superb performance by Nicol Williamson as a misfit Irish soldier. (Dir: Jack Gold, 106 mins.)

Boggy Creek II (1984)*½ Cindy Butler, Chuck Pierce, Charles B. Pierce, Jimmy Clem, Serene Hedin. This creeky follow-up to writer-producer-director Charles B. Pierce's *Legend of Boggy Creek* is a fictional story of a college professor who takes three students into Southern swampland to search for the half-human Boggy Creek monster. (91 mins.)

Boggy Creek II (1989)** Charles B. Pierce, Cindy Butler, Chuck Pierce. Pseudo-documentary sequel to *Legend of Boggy Creek* details what happens to a professor and his three students when they make the mistake of looking for a Bigfoot-like beastie in a Texarkana swamp. (Dir: Charles B. Pierce, 93 mins.)†

Bogie—The Last Hero (MTV 1980)** Kevin O'Connor, Kathryn Harrold, Ann Wedgeworth. A fan magazine view of the life and loves of Humphrey Bogart. (Dir: Vincent Sherman, 104 mins.)†

Bohemian Girl, The (1936)** Stan Laurel, Oliver Hardy, Antonio Moreno, Jacqueline Wells, Darla Hood, Mae Busch, James Finlayson, Thelma Todd. Stan and Ollie aren't at their best as gypsies in this plot-bound adaptation of the once-popular operetta. Todd's last film is far from her most memorable appearance. (Dir: James W. Horne, 74 mins.)†

Bold and the Brave, The (1956)***½ Mickey Rooney, Wendell Corey, Don Taylor. Better than average war film with many touches of comedy, the best being a "crap game" sequence in which Mickey Rooney is marvelously funny. (Dir: Lewis Foster, 87 mins.)

Bolero (1934)** George Raft, Carole Lombard, Frances Drake, Ray Milland, Sally Rand. An ambitious nightclub dancer sacrifices love for success. The charismatic cast enlivens this dated story somewhat. (Dir: Wesley Ruggles, 85 mins.)

Bolero (1982)*** James Caan, Robert Hossein, Nicole Garcia, Geraldine Chaplin. Sprawling musical epic about succeeding generations spanning France, America, and Russia, and going from pre–World War II to the present. Director Claude Lelouch, a romantic at heart, has painted a broad canvas of relationships, family histories, love stories, tragedy, and irony. (173 mins.)†

Bolero (1984)½ Bo Derek, George Kennedy, Andrea Occhipinti, Ana Obregon. Even voyeurs and die-hard Bo fans will want to doze after a reel of her adventures as a 1920s college student pining desperately to lose her virginity. (Dir: John Derek, 106 mins.)†

Bomba series. Johnny Sheffield grew up from playing Boy and into portraying teenage Bomba in this action series based on Roy Rockwood's children's books about a jungle boy. Besides the films reviewed below, fans of this likeable low budget adventure series will want to catch: *The Lion Hunters, African Treasure, 'Safari Drums, The Last Volcano, The Golden Idol, The Killer Leopard,* and *Lord of the Jungle.*

Bomba and the Elephant Stampede (1951)**½

Johnny Sheffield, Donna Martell, Edith Evanson, Martin Wilkins. Best of the Bomba series. The jungle hero battles greed as two ivory collectors kill elephants without regard for the law, not to mention basic jungle courtesy. (Dir: Ford Beebe, 71 mins.)

Bomba and the Hidden City (1950)*½ Johnny Sheffield, Sue England, Paul Guilfoyle, Smoki Whitfield. Below-average jungle exploits about Bomba's aiding an orphan and battling the Big Cheese ruler of the Hidden City. (Dir: Ford Beebe, 71 mins.)

Bomba and the Jungle Girl (1952)** Johnny Sheffield, Karen Sharpe, Walter Sande, Suzette Harbin. Standard Bomba-esque adventure about the jungle orphan's search for information about his real parents. (Dir: Ford Beebe, 70 mins.)

Bomba on Panther Island (1949)** Johnny Sheffield, Allene Roberts, Lita Baron, Charles Irwin. Bomba must destroy a panther that the superstitious natives think is a god. (Dir: Ford Beebe, 76 mins.)

Bomba the Jungle Boy (1949)*½ Johnny Sheffield, Peggy Ann Garner, Onslow Stevens, Charles Irwin. First in the series of Bomba's adventures, strictly for the nursery set. (Dir: Ford Beebe, 65 mins.)

Bombardier (1943)*** Pat O'Brien, Randolph Scott. Men are trained for missions in the flying fortresses in raids over Japan. Good war melodrama, well done. (Dir: Richard Wallace, 99 mins.)†

Bombay Talkie (India, 1970)**½ Shashi Kapoor, Jennifer Kendall, Zia Mohyeddin. A complex protracted study of a self-destructive American woman in search of herself. The film is more fascinating for its glimpses into the Indian film industry than it is for its delineation of a love triangle out of control. (Dir: James Ivory, 105 mins.)†

Bombers B-52 (1957)** Natalie Wood, Karl Malden, Efrem Zimbalist, Jr. So-so romance and airplane drama. Malden plays Natalie's father who opposes her seeing Col. Zimbalist. (Dir: Gordon Douglas, 106 mins.)

Bombshell—See: **Blonde Bombshell**

Bonanza: The Next Generation (MTV 1988)** John Ireland, Gillian Greene, Michael Landon, Jr., Robert Fuller, John Amos. It's back to the Ponderosa as Ben Cartwright's brother meets up with the progeny of Little Joe and Hoss. (Dir: William F. Claxton, 96 mins.)

Bonfire of the Vanities, The (1990)*½ Tom Hanks, Bruce Willis, Melanie Griffith, Morgan Freeman, John Hancock, Kim Cattrall. Hopelessly inept adaptation of Tom Wolfe's caustic satire, written by Michael Cristofer and directed by Brian De Palma as if they completely missed the point of the source novel. The only things hot in this emotionally cold movie are the camera movements, a dizzying display that ultimately stresses the emptiness of the project. Hanks is woefully miscast as the WASP caught in the political cesspool over the hit-and-run injury of an impoverished black youth. His mistress is Griffith, who is forced to act in a vacuum. (Dir: Brian De Palma, 125 mins.)†

Bonjour Tristesse (1958)*** Deborah Kerr, David Niven, Jean Seberg, Mylene Demongeot. Director Otto Preminger transformed Françoise Sagan's incisive novelette into a masterpiece of ambiguity, with a piercing yet compassionate moral stance. Seberg, the young daughter of a Riviera sybarite (Niven, at his best), comes of age one summer while ridding her father's house of a threatening influence, the warm and mature Kerr. (94 mins.)

Bonnie and Clyde (1967)**** Warren Beatty, Faye Dunaway, Estelle Parsons, Gene Hackman, Michael J. Pollard. Magnificent film version of the story of Bonnie Parker and Clyde Barrow, the tough, psychotic young bank robbers who terrorized the Midwest in the early 1930s. A perceptive film, quite stunningly directed by Arthur Penn. Beatty, who also produced this exciting, well-written gangster classic, is brilliant as the impotent hoodlum Barrow. The film established Dunaway as a major screen personality, and Parsons won an Academy Award for her supporting role as Clyde's sister-in-law. (Dir: Arthur Penn, 111 mins.)†

Bonnie Parker Story, The (1958)** Dorothy Provine, Richard Bakalyan. Blood-spattered story of the infamous gal desperado of the public enemy era of the 1930s. Some fast action, otherwise second rate. (Dir: William Whitney, 80 mins.)

Bonnie Scotland (1935)**½ Laurel & Hardy, June Lang. Trip to Scotland for inheritance leads somehow to India. A funny sequence in which the two are on a cleanup detail is the film's highlight. (Dir: James Norne, 80 mins.)†

Bon Voyage (1962)**½ Fred MacMurray, Jane Wyman. Features MacMurray and Wyman as the parents of a family that takes their first trip abroad. (Dir: James Neilson, 130 mins.)†

Bon Voyage, Charlie Brown (And Don't Come Back!) (1980)***½ A new "Peanuts" animated feature from the studio of Lee Mendelson and Bill Melendez. The latter directed, as always, and of course Mr. Schulz does the inimitable writing. Droll fun for the kids. (70 mins.)†

Bonzo Goes to College (1952)** Maureen O'Sullivan, Edmund Gwenn. Sequel to

Bedtime for Bonzo, the zany comedy that introduced the misadventures of the mischievous chimp known as Bonzo. (Dir: Frederick de Cordova, 80 mins.)

Boogens, The (1982)*** Rebecca Balding, Fred McCarren, Jeff Harling, Anne-Marie Martin. A mine blast frees some subterranean beasties who have been sealed up since 1912. The film wisely withholds glimpses of these fiends until the climactic moments, and the scare scenes are set up with consummate skill. (Dir: James L. Conway, 95 mins.)

Boogey Men, The (1980)* Suzanna Love, Ron James, John Carradine, Nicholas Love, Raymond Boyden. Derivative, confused low-budget shocker about a haunted mirror. Features one of the most contrived "creative murders" in horror film history. (Dir: Ulli Lommel, 83 mins.)†

Boogie Man Will Get You, The (1942)*** Boris Karloff, Peter Lorre, Jeff Donnell, Maxie Rosenbloom, Larry Parks. A delightful spoof of horror movies. Karloff and Lorre, as crackpot scientists, try to create a "superman" but with the highest motives: they want to aid the war effort. (Dir: Lew Landers, 66 mins.)

Book of Love (1991)*** Chris Young, Keith Coogan, Aeryk Egan, Josie Bissett, Tricia Leigh Fisher. Pleasant coming-of-age comedy about a newly divorced man reminiscing about his favorite time as a teenager, the years 1955–56. The cast is fresh, Young is especially appealing in the lead role, and Robert Shaye directs with a genuine fondness for the era. The movie avoids many of the pitfalls of the genre; it's harmless fun. Included are 32 wonderful songs from the period. Written by William Kotzwinkle from his novel, *Jack in the Box*. (Dir: Robert Shaye, 87 mins.)†

Boom! (U.S.-Great Britain, 1968)*½ Elizabeth Taylor, Richard Burton, Noël Coward. A coarse, dying millionairess who forms an unholy alliance with a stranger known as the "Angel of Death" (Burton). (Dir: Joseph Losey, 113 mins.)

Boomerang (1947)**** Dana Andrews, Jane Wyatt, Lee J. Cobb. Elia Kazan's brilliant direction, an outstanding cast, and a fascinating story of a prosecuting attorney who didn't believe the state's case. This semidocumentary based on an actual case is topflight screen entertainment. (88 mins.)

Boom in the Moon (Mexico, 1945)* Buster Keaton, Angel Grassa, Fernando Sotto, Virginia Serret. Keaton was at the nadir of his career when he appeared in this Mexican comedy as a schnook who is "volunteered" for a moon launch. Unseen until it was resurrected for video; only for completists forewarned to be disappointed. (Dir: Jaime Salvador, 83 mins.)†

Boom Town (1940)*** Clark Gable, Spencer Tracy, Hedy Lamarr, Claudette Colbert, Lionel Atwill, Chill Wills, Frank Morgan. A good cast in a rousing tale about a pair of roughnecks who strike it rich in the oil fields. Entertaining and exciting although not a first-rate film. (Dir: Jack Conway, 116 mins.)

Boost, The (1988)* James Woods, Sean Young, John Kapelos. Ridiculous antidrug diatribe with insecure Woods taking to cocaine for professional courage and wife Young soon following. Just say no to this one. (Dir: Harold Becker, 95 mins.)†

Boots Malone (1952)*** William Holden, Johnny Stewart. Fast paced racetrack story with good performances. William Holden plays a somewhat shady character with a good heart. (Dir: William Dieterle, 103 mins.)

Border, The (1982)**½ Jack Nicholson, Harvey Keitel, Valerie Perrine, Warren Oates, Elpidia Carrillo, Shannon Wilcox. Typical action yarn with a face-off between the hero (Nicholson), a border guard who wants to stay honest, and the sellouts who are ripping off the Mexicans. (Dir: Tony Richardson, 107 mins.)†

Border Heat—See: **Deadly Stranger**

Border Incident (1949)**½ Ricardo Montalbán, George Murphy, Howard Da Silva. Interesting drama about "wetbacks" and murder. Montalban effectively plays an immigration agent who is used as a decoy to break up a large "slave trading" market. (Dir: Anthony Mann, 92 mins.)

Borderline (1950)** Fred MacMurray, Claire Trevor, Raymond Burr, Roy Roberts. A policewoman goes undercover as a chorus girl to crack a ring of drug smugglers. Uncertain melodrama waivers between seriousness and farce, is successful at neither. (Dir: William A. Seiter, 88 mins.)

Borderline (1980)*½ Charles Bronson, Bruno Kirby, Burt Remsen, Ed Harris. Routine action drama starring Bronson as a Border patrol officer searching for a murderer who is roaming between Mexico and California. (Dir: Jerrold Freeman, 97 mins.)†

Border Radio (1987)** Chris D., Luanna Anders, Chris Shearer, John Doe, Dave Alvin. Semi-improvised movie about rock musicians hiding out in the desert from a club owner they've robbed. Good music by X (whose guitarists play supporting parts) and others. (Dirs: Allison Anders, Dean Lent, Kurt Voss, 85 mins.)†

Border River (1954)** Yvonne DeCarlo, Joel McCrea, Pedro Armendariz, Howard Petrie. Fair western drama with action and colorful characters. Set during the last days of the Civil War, McCrea is cast as a Confederate captain who goes to Mexico to buy guns. (Dir: George Sherman, 80 mins.)

Border Street (Poland, 1948)***½ Maria Broniewska, Mieczyslawa Cwiklinska, Jerzy Leszcynski, Wladyslaw Godik. Memorable, powerful story shows the effects of Nazism on different characters living in the Warsaw ghetto, culminating in the uprising of 1943. Occasionally melodramatic but quite effective. (Dir: Aleksander Ford, 101 mins.)†

Bordertown (1935)**½ Paul Muni, Bette Davis, Eugene Pallette. Muni looks properly seedy as a degenerate lawyer who gets involved with more than he can handle when he tangles with the bored wife of a local businessman. Though the film is turgid, there is a fair amount of mood and sexual tension, and the result is fairly engrossing. (Dir: Archie Mayo, 100 mins.)

Borgia Stick, The (MTV 1966)** Don Murray, Inger Stevens, Barry Nelson, Fritz Weaver. Far-fetched story of two pawns in a super-crime syndicate who try to break with the organization. First half is interesting, giving a unique interpretation of modern-day gangsterism. (Dir: David Lowell Rich, 100 mins.)

B.O.R.N. (1989)* Ross Hagen, P. J. Soles, Hoke Howell, William Smith, Russ Tamblyn, Amanda Blake, Clint Howard, Dawn Wildsmith. Hagen (who also directed) tries to rescue his three daughters from the clutches of the Body Organ Replacement Network, which acquires organs for transplants from not-always-willing donors. You're more likely to find this a B.O.R.E. (90 mins.)†

Born Again (1978)½ Dean Jones, Anne Francis, Dana Andrews, Raymond St. Jacques, George Brent. Squeaky clean biopic about former presidential advisor, Chuck Colson, who found God after the Watergate investigation landed him in trouble with the law. (Dir: Irving Rapper, 110 mins.)

Born American (1986)½ Mike Norris, Steve Durham, David Coburn, Thalmus Rasulala, Albert Salmi. Derivative action bunk about three strapping Americans who playfully bust into the Soviet Union and have slightly more trouble getting out. What did these guys think—that they were embarking on a panty raid of the Ukraine? (Dir: Renny Harlin, 95 mins.)†

Borneo (1937)*** Still-fascinating documentary made by Martin and Osa Johnson, who spent their lives exploring unknown parts of this planet. On the South Seas island of Borneo, they introduce us to sights never before seen, including primitive native rituals and an assortment of bizarre animals. (76 mins.)†

Born Free (Great Britain, 1966)***½ Bill Travers, Virginia McKenna. A treat for the whole family. Even if you don't particularly care for films about animals, you'll be won over by the touching tale of Elsa, the lion cub raised in captivity, who then must learn to fend for herself in the jungle wilds of Kenya. Bill Travers and Virginia McKenna play a game warden and his wife who supervise the retraining of Elsa when they find out she's too big to remain a pet and might be shipped to the confinement of a zoo. (Dir: James Hill, 96 mins.)†

Born in East L.A. (1987)**½ Richard "Cheech" Marin, Daniel Stern, Paul Rodriguez. Cheech took his Springsteen song parody and transformed it into a pleasant vehicle picture. The plot involves his mistaken deportation to Mexico with a carload of illegal immigrants and his weird exploits in attempting to make it back to East L.A. (Dir: Richard "Cheech" Marin, 87 mins.)†

Born Innocent (MTV 1974)**½ Linda Blair, Joanna Miles, Kim Hunter. Blair plays a runaway teenager facing the cruelties of a juvenile detention home. Though the subject matter may put many people off, the hardy should find merit in Joanna Miles's portrayal of the home's understanding teacher and Miss Blair's capable handling of the unfortunate youngster. (Dir: Donald Wrye, 100 mins.)†

Born Killer (1988)**½ Ty Hardin, Ted Prior, Fritz Matthews, Adam Tucker, Francine Lapensee. A friendly weekend war game in the woods turns serious when the players come up against escaped convicts. Implausible but sometimes inventive adventure with a rare appearance by Hardin. (Dir: Kimberley Casey, 89 mins.)†

Born Losers (1967)* Tom Laughlin, Elizabeth James, Jane Russell. A young girl is terrorized by a gang of thugs, until a wandering half-breed helps her out. Incredibly unpleasant biker film which featured the debut of the "Billy Jack" character which later brought Laughlin to prominence. Laughlin directed under the pseudonym T. C. Frank. (112 mins.)†

Born of Fire (1986)* Peter Firth, Susan Crowley, Stefan Kalipha, Oh-Tee. British flutist Firth and mysterious astronomer Crowley go to Turkey to battle a satanic, bald-headed "Master Musician" who spews fire from his eyes and mouth and controls the fate of mankind with the flute. Handsome location photography can't overcome pseudo-religious nonsense. (Dir: Jami Dehlavi, 84 mins.)†

Born on the Fourth of July (1989)**** Tom

Cruise, Raymond J. Barry, Caroline Kava, Willem Dafoe, Kara Sedgwick, Abbie Hoffman, Tom Berenger. Oscar-winning director Oliver Stone pulls no punches in this powerful movie based on Vietnam War veteran Ron Kovic's memoirs about his service and tragic paralysis. Kovic's screenplay details the horrors of both war and rehabilitation. Stone's camera pushes the audience into the action and pummels it with a relentless depiction of a young man's dissatisfaction with the war, his family, country, and religion. Cruise is brilliant as Kovic; entire cast is strong in a film that demands to be seen. (144 mins.)†

Born to Be Bad (1950)*** Joan Fontaine, Robert Ryan, Zachary Scott. Ruthless female hides behind an innocent exterior, but eventually reveals her true self. Fashionable romantic drama. (Dir: Nicholas Ray, 94 mins.)

Born to Be Sold (MTV 1981)** Lynda Carter, Harold Gould, Philip Sterling, Ed Nelson. Lynda Carter plays a social worker fighting an illegal baby adoption ring almost single-handedly. An important subject is trivialized. (Dir: Burt Brinckerhoff, 104 mins.)

Born to Dance (1936)** Eleanor Powell, James Stewart, Buddy Ebsen, Reginald Gardiner, Virginia Bruce. Powell (wind her up and she taps) dominates a musical that comes alive in its musical numbers but is otherwise lame. Cole Porter wrote the songs, including "I've Got You Under My Skin" and "Easy to Love." The plot is sailor-meets-girl. (Dir: Roy Del Ruth, 105 mins.)†

Born to Kill (1947)*** Lawrence Tierney, Claire Trevor, Audrey Long, Walter Slezak, Elisha Cook, Jr., Philip Terry. B movie bad guy Tierney has a field day here in this *noir*-ish item. He marries one sister (Long) but yearns to stray with her sexy sister (Trevor). If that weren't enough to keep him busy, he's also a murderer. Cold-blooded, cynical, and engrossing. (Dir: Robert Wise, 92 mins.)

Born to Race (1988)* Joseph Bottoms, Marla Heasley, Marc Singer, George Kennedy. Auto-racing adventure set at a North Carolina stock car rally, with Bottoms and Italian Heasley trying to protect her new engine design from thieves prior to the race. Stillborn. (Dir: James Fargo, 90 mins.)†

Born to Sing (1941)** Virginia Weidler, Leo Gorcey, Ray McDonald, Sheldon Leonard, Margaret Dumont. Gorcey and pals save a composer from suicide and help him regain his stolen score. The entire movie was designed merely as a frame to stage the song "Ballad for Americans," which (as staged and directed by Busby Berkeley) is by far the

best thing here. (Dir: Edward Ludwig, 82 mins.)

Born to Win (1971)*** George Segal, Karen Black, Paula Prentiss, Hector Elizondo, Robert De Niro. A real downer with moments of brilliance and humor due to Czech-born Ivan Passer's direction of a superb cast. The portrayal of the Big Apple drug culture is harrowing and Segal is astonishing as a heroin-addicted former hairdresser whose fast lane lifestyle engulfs him. AKA: **Addict**. (90 mins.)†

Born Yesterday (1951)***½ Judy Holliday, William Holden, Broderick Crawford. Excellent movie version of the B'way success. Judy Holliday copped an Oscar for her hilarious performance as Billie, the dumb blonde to end all dumb blondes. Witty dialogue and top performances by all. (Dir: George Cukor, 103 mins.)†

Borrowers, The (MTV 1973)*** Eddie Albert, Tammy Grimes, Judith Anderson, Dennis Larson. A pleasant fable for young and old. A little boy who has come to convalesce at his great-aunt Sophie's house is overwhelmed with loneliness until he makes a marvelous discovery. Under the floorboards of the house, a fascinating family of tiny little people have made their home. (Dir: Walter C. Miller, 78 mins.)

Borsalino (France-Italy, 1970)*** Jean-Paul Belmondo, Alain Delon, Mirielle Darc. A French tribute to the gangster films of the Hollywood 1930s. Belmondo and Delon, teamed together for the first time, play two small-time hoodlums on the make. The main virtue of the film is not the familiar story, but the costumes, settings, and musical backdrop which really do capture the look and mood of the period. (Dir: Jacques Deray, 126 mins.)

Boss (1974)** Fred Williamson, D'Urville Martin, R.G. Armstrong. Blaxploitation western with bounty hunter Williamson setting himself up as the law in a small town terrorized by a bad guy with a hefty price on his head. Humorous touches make it better than most Williamson vehicles. (Dir: Jack Arnold, 90 mins.)†

Boss, The (1956)*** John Payne, William Bishop, Doe Avedon. A power-hungry politician takes over a city in the U.S. with frightening results. John Payne gives one of the best performances of his career. (Dir: Byron Haskin, 89 mins.)

Boss's Son, The (1978)*** Asher Brauner, Henry G. Sanders, James Darren, Rita Moreno, Piper Laurie. A somewhat pampered boy starts to work in his father's carpet-manufacturing business as a delivery trucker and learns some of the contradictions between privilege and labor. A small, very independent film, faltering on story points yet dealing with recognizable human situations with compassion. (Dir: Bobby Roth, 102 mins.)†

Boss's Wife, The (1986)*½ Daniel Stern, Arielle Dombasle, Fisher Stevens, Melanie Mayron, Lou Jacobi, Martin Mull, Christopher Plummer. Wafer-thin comedy about a stockbroker who has to weigh his integrity against improving his opportunities for advancement by sleeping with the boss's wife. Pointless. (Dir: Ziggy Steinberg, 83 mins.)†

Boston Blackie series. The former jewel thief turned one-man crime deterrent preferred to do his detective work without police interference. Based on Jack Boyle's 1910 book, the series benefited from a welcome reliance on humor that's kept it fresh over the years. It later made the transition to TV as a series with Kent Taylor in 1951. In addition to the films reviewed below, check the following entries: *Meet Boston Blackie, One Mysterious Night, Alias Boston Blackie, Phantom Thief, Trapped by Boston Blackie,* and *Close Call for Boston Blackie.*

Boston Blackie and the Law (1946)*½ Chester Morris, Trudy Marshall. Blackie is suspected of helping a gal escape from prison. Juvenile film. (Dir: D. Ross Lederman, 69 mins.)

Boston Blackie Booked on Suspicion (1945)** Chester Morris, Lynn Merrick. Blackie gets mixed up with counterfeit rare books and murder. (Dir: Arthur Dreifuss, 66 mins.)

Boston Blackie Goes Hollywood (1942)**½ Chester Morris, Forrest Tucker, George E. Stone. Blackie's after crooks who are after a valuable diamond. (Dir: Michael Gordon, 68 mins.)

Boston Blackie's Chinese Venture (1949)** Chester Morris, Maylia, Richard Lane. Once again, someone gets murdered and the police lay the blame for a Chinese laundry owner's death on Blackie. (Dir: Seymour Friedman, 59 mins.)

Boston Blackie's Rendezvous (1945)**½ Chester Morris, Steve Cochran, Nina Foch. Blackie chases after a homicidal maniac bent on killing a girl. Suspenseful melodrama. (Dir: Arthur Dreifuss, 64 mins.)

Bostonians, The (Great Britain, 1984)*** Christopher Reeve, Vanessa Redgrave, Madeline Potter, Jessica Tandy, Linda Hunt, Nancy Marchand, Wallace Shawn. An extremely literate, if inordinately languid, version of Henry James's opinions on the feminist movement. Verena, an inexperienced girl, becomes the prize in a tug-of-war between Olive (Redgrave), a spinster who wants her to embrace the women's movement, and Basil (Reeve), a Southern gent who wants to wed Verena. (Dir: James Ivory, 120 mins.)†

Boston Strangler, The (1968)**½ Tony

Curtis, Henry Fonda. Despite its lapses, this is a reasonably absorbing screen treatment of Gerold Frank's best-selling account of the Boston murders of a group of women, allegedly committed by a schizophrenic plumber named Albert De Salvo. Curtis is convincing as the deranged De Salvo and Fonda adds to the credibility of director Richard Fleischer's documentary-like approach. (120 mins.)†

Botany Bay (1953)** Alan Ladd, James Mason, Patricia Medina. Unjustly convicted man suffers aboard a convict ship bound for Australia, under the wheel of a cruel captain. Fancy but undistinguished costume melodrama. (Dir: John Farrow, 94 mins.)

Bottom of the Bottle (1956)**½ Van Johnson, Joseph Cotten, Ruth Roman, Jack Carson. Melodrama all the way—Van Johnson is an escaped convict. He invades his brother's (Joseph Cotten) comfortable world and asks for help. (Dir: Henry Hathaway, 88 mins.)

Boudu Saved from Drowning (France, 1932)*** Michel Simon, Charles Grandval, Marcelle Hainia, Severine Lerczynska. An unsweetened comedy of manners, class, and morals written and directed by Jean Renoir, who adapted an Anatole France short story for this film. This fable about the antisocial bum rescued from the Seine and his effect on those who shelter him was remade and prettied up as *Down and Out in Beverly Hills.* (87 mins.)†

Boulevard Nights (1979)**½ Richard Yniguez, Danny de la Paz. A Chicano kid has trouble avoiding gang life. Despite some tangy ethnic detail, there isn't an unpredictable moment in this film. (Dir: Michael Pressman, 102 mins.)†

Bound for Glory (1976)***½ David Carradine, Ronny Cox, Melinda Dillon. A generally excellent biography of Woody Guthrie, one of America's greatest folksingers. Woody's left-wing politics have been toned down somewhat in this, the first major screen story of how Woody left his dust-devastated Texas home in the '30s to find work, and discovered the oppression, suffering, and strength of the working people of America during the Great Depression. (Dir: Hal Ashby, 147 mins.)†

Bounty, The (1984)*** Anthony Hopkins, Mel Gibson, Laurence Olivier, Edward Fox. This third go-round for Fletcher Christian and Capt. Bligh tips the scales in favor of Bligh. As the sailors defy their captain and eventually settle on Pitcairn Island after setting him adrift at sea, audiences may be held more by the breathtaking Tahiti photography than by the central drama. Not based on the

1935 and 1962 films, but adapted from Richard Hough's book *Captain Bligh*. (Dir: Roger Donaldson, 130 mins.)†

Bounty Hunter, The (1954)** Randolph Scott, Dolores Dorn. For Randolph Scott fans—he's a bounty hunter this time, out to capture three criminals. (Dir: Andre de Toth, 79 mins.)

Bounty Hunter, The (1989)*½ Robert Ginty, Bo Hopkins, Loeta Waterdown, Melvin Holt. Unexceptional revenge tale with Ginty versus crooked small-town sheriff Hopkins over an investigation into the death of his Vietnam War buddy. (Dir: Robert Ginty, 90 mins.)†

Bounty Man, The (MTV 1972)** Clint Walker, Richard Basehart, Margot Kidder. It's the same old story—a man sets out to find the varmint who caused his wife's death, and falls in love in the process. (Dir: John Llewelyn-Moxey, 72 mins.)

Bourne Identity, The (MTV 1988)*** Richard Chamberlain, Jaclyn Smith, Yorgo Voyagis, Donald Moffat, Anthony Quayle, Denholm Elliott. Robert Ludlum's thriller, set in the world of international espionage, is excellently adapted. A man suffering from amnesia is washed up on a beach, and must piece together his true identity from his fragmented memory. Is he indeed a world-famous terrorist? (Dir: Roger Young, 192 mins.)

Bowery, The (1933)***½ George Raft, Wallace Beery, Jackie Cooper, Pert Kelton, Fay Wray. An excellent turn-of-the-century saloon drama, drawn from director Raoul Walsh's childhood memories, including Steve Brodie's (Raft's) historic leap from the Brooklyn Bridge. (110 mins.)

Bowery at Midnight (1943)*½ Tom Neal, Bela Lugosi, Wanda McKay. Poverty Row production about a slippery killer eluding capture in the N.Y.C. Bowery. (Dir: Wallace Fox, 63 mins.)

Bowery Boys series. Those lovable urchins from B movies got their cinematic start playing young hoodlums in the prestigious film version of Sidney Kingsley's tenement drama *Dead End*. The road to Bowery stardom was a rather circuitous one thereafter. After Sam Goldwyn dumped their contracts due to their unruly behavior, the then-named "Dead End Kids" (Billy Halop, Leo Gorcey, Huntz Hall, Bobby Jordan, Gabriel Dell, and Bernard Punsley) starred in films at Warner Bros. and then gravitated to Universal to appear as the *Little Tough Guys*, but not all the kids appeared in each entry. Afterwards, Monogram studios employed various kids in their East Side Kid series while the Tough Guy films were still being ground out. In 1946, in *Live Wires*, the Bowery Boys, with Gorcey as Slip and Hall as Sach, first made their bow. The Dead

End Kids flicks include: *Dead End, Crime School, Angels with Dirty Faces, They Made Me a Criminal, Hell's Kitchen, Angels Wash Their Faces*, and *On Dress Parade*. Regarded as the weakest of the lot, the Little Tough Guy movies include: *Little Tough Guy, Call a Messenger, You're Not So Tough, Give Us Wings, Hit the Road, Mob Town, Tough as They Come, Mug Town*, and *Keep 'Em Slugging*, as well as some serials not reviewed by us. The East Side Kids (with Gorcey as Muggs and Hall as Glimpy) starred in: *East Side Kids, Boys of the City, That Gang of Mine, Pride of the Bowery, Flying Wild, Bowery Blitzkrieg, Spooks Run Wild, Mr. Wise Guy, Let's Get Tough, Smart Alecks, 'Neath Brooklyn Bridge, Kid Dynamite, Clancy Street Boys, Ghosts on the Loose, Mr. Muggs Steps Out, Million Dollar Kid, Follow the Leader, Block Busters, Bowery Champs, Docks of New York, Mr. Muggs Rides Again*, and *Come Out Fighting*. The Bowery Boys movies are: *Live Wires, In Fast Company, Bowery Bombshell, Spook Busters, Mr. Hex, Hard-Boiled Mahoney, News Hounds, Bowery Buckaroos, Angels Alley, Jinx Money, Smugglers Cove, Trouble Makers, Fighting Fools, Hold That Baby, Angels in Disguise, Master Minds, Blonde Dynamite, Lucky Losers, Triple Trouble, Blues Busters, Bowery Batallion, Ghost Chasers, Let's Go Navy, Crazy Over Horses, Hold That Line, Here Come the Marines, Feudin' Fools, No Holds Barred, Jalopy, Loose in London, Clipped Wings, Private Eyes, Paris Playboys, Bowery Boys Meet the Monsters, Jungle Gents, Bowery to Bagdad, High Society, Spy Chasers, Jail Busters, Dig That Uranium, Crashing Las Vegas, Fighting Trouble, Hot Shots, Hold That Hypnotist, Spook Chasers, Looking for Danger, Up in Smoke, In the Money*.

Bowery Batallion (1951)** The Bowery Boys are up to their necks in slapstick hokum. (Dir: William Beaudine, 69 mins.)

Bowery Blitzkrieg (1941)*½ A boxing tournament the Bowery Way. Leo Gorcey is the centerpiece; Huntz Hall isn't given nearly enough to do. (Dir: Wallace Fox, 62 mins.)

Bowery Bombshell (1946)**½ The Boys pose as mobsters when Sach is implicated in a robbery. (Dir: Phil Karlson, 65 mins.)

Bowery Boys Meet the Monsters, The (1954)*** A family of mad scientists want Sach and Slip as, respectively, a primary brain donor and an alternate brain donor for their strange experiments. A vampy vampiress, a man-eating plant, and an excellent supporting cast made this the series' highest grossing film. (Dir: Edward Bernds, 65 mins.)

Bowery Buckaroos (1947)*½ Average Bowery Boys comedy. (Dir: William Beaudine, 66 mins.)

Bowery Champs (1944)**½ Muggs (Leo Gorcey) is a copyboy who aspires to be a reporter. (Dir: William Beaudine, 62 mins.)

Bowery to Bagdad (1955)** The Bowery Boys delve into fantasy—and come up empty, or should we say heavy-handed. (Dir: Edward Bernds, 64 mins.)

Bowery to Broadway (1944)**½ Maria Montez, Turhan Bey, Jack Oakie. As the title suggests, this is a show business movie about the rise of a singing star (Maria Montez) and her two lovable producers. Maria Montez? Singing? (Dir: Charles Lamont, 94 mins.)

Boxcar Bertha (1972)*** David Carradine, Barbara Hershey, Barry Primus. Often interesting drama, based on a book, *Sister of the Road*. About a woman labor organizer in Arkansas during the violence-filled Depression era of the early '30s. Rabble-rousing union man (Carradine) fights the railroad establishment aided by the remarkable real-life character Boxcar Bertha (Hershey). (Dir: Martin Scorsese, 88 mins.)†

Boy (Japan, 1969)***½ Tetsuo Abe, Fumio Watanabe, Akiko Koyama. Startling, true story about parents who train ten-year-old son to be hit by cars so they can collect money in order to live. Acting, wide-screen color photography, and director Nagisa Oshima's keen psychological insight made this an extraordinary international sensation. (97 mins.)†

Boy and His Dog, A (1975)*** Susanne Benton, Don Johnson, Jason Robards, Jr. Based on Harlan Ellison's sci-fi classic, this cult movie is about the aftermath of the Big Bomb—the world becomes divided into two camps, grubby looters and some middle class citizens who live in a town buried five miles underground. (Dir: L. Q. Jones, 87 mins.)†

Boy and the Pirates, The (1960)** Charles Herbert, Susan Gordon, Murvyn Vye. Strictly for the young tots. A long dream sequence in which a boy imagines he's involved with pirates and buried treasure. (Dir: Bert Gordon, 82 mins.)

Boy Cried Murder, The (Great Britain-Germany-Yugoslavia, 1966)**½ Veronica Hurst, Phil Brown, Fraser MacIntosh. Boy with a vivid imagination witnesses a murder, but nobody will believe him. Remake of *The Window* still carries some effective suspense. (Dir: George Breakston, 86 mins.)

Boy, Did I Get a Wrong Number (1966)*½ Bob Hope, Elke Sommer, Phyllis Diller. Hope's a small-town real estate agent who gets involved with a visiting sex queen (Sommer). Boy, did they make the wrong movie. (Dir: George Marshall, 99 mins.)†

Boy Friend, The (Great Britain, 1971)**½ Twiggy, Christopher Gable, Moyra Fraser, Tommy Tune, Glenda Jackson. Director Ken Russell, master of grotesque, pays tribute to the genre where the surreal is commonplace: the musical comedy. The result is a high-spirited and (as always with Russell) excessive put-on and take-off of Sandy Wilson's hit twenties musical. The picture seesaws between a ramshackle production of *The Boy Friend* being put on in Portsmouth (and watched by a ritzy Hollywood director) and the big-budget Busby Berkeley dreams of the participants. Never again will Russell's work be so . . . well, charming. With a priceless appearance by Jackson. Rereleased in 1988 with restored footage. (Dir: Ken Russell, 137 mins.)†

Boyfriends and Girlfriends (France, 1987) *** Emmanuelle Chaulet, Sophie Renoir, Anne-Laure Meury. A charming trifle from director Eric Rohmer, noted for his appealing relationship comedies. Two women meet and discuss their crushes and affairs, as the boyfriend of one drifts to the other. AKA: L'Ami de Mon Amie and My Girlfriend's Boyfriend. (102 mins.)†

Boy from Oklahoma, The (1954)*** Will Rogers, Jr., Nancy Olson. Will Rogers, Jr. has more acting ability than his famous father displayed in his early films. In this charming western comedy-drama, he is cast as a quiet, peace-loving sheriff of a town called Bluerock, which is run by a group of desperadoes. (Dir: Michael Curtiz, 88 mins.)

Boy in Blue, The (Canada, 1986)** Nicolas Cage, Cynthia Dale, Christopher Plummer, David Naughton, Melody Douglas. A standard biopic about Canadian scull champion Ned Hanlan who turned his back on bootlegging and a blue-collar marriage in order to row his way to fame. (Dir: Charles Jarrott, 98 mins.)†

Boy in the Plastic Bubble, The (MTV 1976)**½ John Travolta, Robert Reed, Diana Hyland. A fascinating subject is given a fairly sensitive airing in this story about a boy, born with immunity deficiencies, who grows up in a special plastic-bound controlled environment. (Dir: Randal Kleiser, 106 mins.)†

Boy Meets Girl (1938)*** Pat O'Brien, Marie Wilson, James Cagney. Slightly antiquated today but still a delightful spoof of the movie business. Forerunner of hundreds of imitations. (Dir: Lloyd Bacon, 90 mins.)

Boy Named Charlie Brown, A (1970)**½ The famous comic strip, "Peanuts," which has inspired endless TV specials, serves as the basis for this full-blown, fairly charming animated theatrical feature. (Dir: Bill Melendez, 85 mins.)†

Boy Next Door, The—See: **To Find a Man**

Boy on a Dolphin (1957)**½ Alan Ladd, Sophia Loren, Clifton Webb. The best things about this adventure film are great location shots and the physical beauty of Sophia Loren. The plot about the discovery of a sunken work of art offers no surprises. (Dir: Jean Negulesco, 113 mins.)

Boys, The (Great Britain, 1962)**½ Richard Todd, Robert Morley, Jess Conrad. Four teenagers go on trial for murder and robbery. (Dir: Sidney Furie, 82 mins.)

The Boys (MTV 1991)*** James Woods, John Lithgow, Joanna Gleason, Eve Gordon. A touching tearjerker based on the real-life writing team of William Link and Richard Levinson (creators of *Columbo*), who worked together for more than 20 years. Written by Link (played by Lithgow), the film serves as a tribute to Levinson (Woods), who died of lung cancer that might have been caused by his friend's chain-smoking. The performances by the two leads couldn't be better. (Dir: Glenn Jordan, 96 mins.)

Boys from Brazil, The (1978)**½ Gregory Peck, Laurence Olivier, Uta Hagen, Rosemary Harris. Director Franklin Schaffner gives Ira Levin's gimmicky thriller the big treatment; Olivier is brilliant as the hero modeled, loosely, on Nazi-hunter Simon Wiesenthal. (123 mins.)†

Boys from Brooklyn, The—See: **Bela Lugosi Meets a Brooklyn Gorilla**

Boys from Syracuse, The (1940)*** Joe Penner, Allan Jones, Martha Raye. Two sets of twins cause confusion and havoc in ancient Greece. Entertaining musical comedy based on the Broadway show. Fine Rodgers and Hart songs. (Dir: A. Edward Sutherland, 73 mins.)

Boys in Company C, The (1978)* Stan Shaw, Andrew Stevens, James Canning, Michael Lembeck. This was virtually the first film produced by a major Hollywood studio (Columbia) about the Vietnam War. It's a special pity, then, that it is such a foul-mouthed, stereotypical saga of life and combat in the paddies of Nam in 67–68. (Dir: Sidney J. Furie, 125 mins.)†

Boys in the Band, The (1970)*** Cliff Gorman, Laurence Luckinbill, Kenneth Nelson, Leonard Frey. Mart Crowley has adapted his own acclaimed, award-winning play about a gay birthday party, retaining much of the qualities of pathos, bitchiness, loneliness, and jealousy that so enriched the play. Under William Friedkin's generally sensitive guiding hand, *Boys* is often hilarious and builds to a powerful climax. (Dir: William Friedkin, 118 mins.)†

Boys Next Door, The (1986)**½ Charlie Sheen, Maxwell Caulfield, Patti D'Arbanville, Christopher MacDonald, Paul Dancer, Hank Garrett. Bleak character study of two punks who, knowing their future holds little promise, vent their rage in a senseless murder spree. (Dir: Penelope Spheeris, 91 mins.)†

Boys' Night Out (1962)*** Kim Novak, James Garner, Tony Randall, Howard Duff, Howard Morris. Entertaining comedy about executives who want a little fun and scheme to lease an apartment for their shenanigans. Kim Novak is a college student doing research in s-e-x who is their prime target. (Dir: Michael Gordon, 115 mins.)

Boys of the City (1940)** Leo Gorcey, Bobby Jordan, "Sunshine Sammy" Morrison, David Gorcey, Forest Taylor. Sequel to *East Side Kids*; the plot involves the murder of a judge in a semi-haunted house. (Dir: Joseph H. Lewis, 63 mins.)

Boys' Ranch (1946)**½ Butch Jenkins, James Craig. Highly recommended for the youngsters is this cute story about delinquents who are given a chance to reform by working on a cattle ranch. (Dir: Roy Rowland, 97 mins.)

Boys' Town (1938)*** Spencer Tracy, Mickey Rooney. Story of Father Flanagan's Boys' Town and how his motto, "There is no such thing as a bad boy," is almost destroyed by an incorrigible youngster is too sentimental but is still rewarding film fare. Tracy won an Oscar. (Dir: Norman Taurog, 90 mins.)†

Boy Ten Feet Tall, A (Great Britain, 1963)*** Edward G. Robinson, Fergus McClelland, Constance Cummings, Harry H. Corbett. Nice family entertainment, thanks to the exotic locale and a good human interest story of a young lad trying to cross Africa alone to reach his aunt. (Dir: Alexander Mackendrick, 88 mins.)

Boy Who Could Fly, The (1986)***½ Lucy Deakins, Jay Underwood, Bonnie Bedelia, Fred Savage, Colleen Dewhurst. Melancholy fantasy that confronts its characters' pain without condescending to children or insulting adults' intelligence. A young boy becomes autistic after his parents' death in a plane crash and thereafter demonstrates the ability to fly. (Dir: Nick Castle, 114 mins.)†

Boy Who Drank Too Much, The (MTV 1980)**½ Scott Baio, Lance Kerwin, Ed Lauter, Mariclare Costello. Teen idol Baio is a high school hockey star who turns to alcohol when things get too much for him. (Dir: Jerrold Freedman, 100 mins.)

Boy Who Talked to Badgers, The (MTV 1975)**½ Christian Juttner, Carl Betz, Salome Jens. Disney adventure about a lost six-year-old boy who survives out on the prairie thanks to a friendly badger. (Dir: Gary Nelson, 100 mins.)

Boy with Green Hair, The (1948)*** Pat O'Brien, Dean Stockwell. War orphan becomes an outcast when he finds his hair has suddenly turned green. Fanciful message drama. (Dir: Joseph Losey, 82 mins.)†

Braddock: Missing in Action III (1988)* Chuck Norris, Roland Harrah III, Aki Aleong. Chuck follows in the footsteps of the great god Stallone—he co-wrote this outing in which he ventures back into Vietnam to retrieve his Amerasian kid. He let his brother Aaron direct. (What generosity! You'd never see Frank Stallone directing a *Rambo*.) (Dir: Aaron Norris, 101 mins.)†

Brady's Escape (U.S.-Hungary, 1984)**½ John Savage, Kelly Reno, Ildiko Bansagi, Laszo Mensaros. During WWII, a U.S. captain parachutes into Nazi-occupied territory and is rescued by some Ciskos, European cowboys. A cowboy back in the states, the captain proves himself riding the Magyar range, and the cowboys help him plan his escape, along with that of an orphan boy he's befriended. (Dir: Pal Gabor, 96 mins.)†

Brady Girls Get Married, The (MTV 1981)** Robert Reed, Florence Henderson, Ann B. Davis, Maureen McCormick, Barry Williams, Christopher Knight, Eve Plumb, Mike Lookinland. Everyone's grown-up and two of the girls—Marcia and Jan—are actually getting married. Pilot for the series "Brady Brides" is strictly for fans (and you know who you are). (Dir: Peter Baldwin, 104 mins.)

Brain, The (1971)—See: **Brain of Blood**

Brain, The (1988)*½ Tom Breznahan, Cindy Preston, David Gale. A psychologist develops a giant brain which he uses to take over the minds of innocent TV viewers. No, it's not a comedy, though it sure sounds like one. Would-be throwback to fifties sci-fi takes itself far too seriously to be any fun. (Dir: Edward Hunt, 85 mins.)†

Brain Damage (1971)—See: **Brain of Blood**

Brain Damage (1988)** Rick Herbst, Jennifer Lowry, Gordon MacDonald. Bizarre, blackly comic horror film about a young man and the parasite that enslaves him through injections of a blue drug. From the writer-director of *Basket Case*, this is a similarly twisted tale that's enjoyable only if you're not squeamish. (Dir: Frank Henenlotter, 94 mins.)†

Brain Dead (1990)*½ Bill Pullman, Bill Paxton, Bud Cort, Nicholas Pryor, Patricia Charbonneau, George Kennedy. A neurologist examining the delusions of an insane scientist is pulled into the man's nightmarish world. Thin plot excuse for

a movie that piles on too many horrific elements, leaving viewers confused and unsatisfied. (Dir: Adam Simon, 85 mins.)†

Brain Eaters, The (1958)** Joanna Lee, Edwin Nelson, Alan Frost, Leonard Nimoy, Jody Fair. Some tingles here as the creepy crawlers suck the brains right out of you. Not as bad as the title suggests and you'll spot a pre-Spock Nimoy and Joanna Lee, "Tanna" of *Plan Nine from Outer Space*. (Dir: Bruno Ve Sota, 60 mins.)

Brain from Planet Arous, The (1958)* John Agar, Joyce Meadows. Outer space being captures the body of a young scientist, takes over his will. No brains necessary to skip this one. (Dir: Nathan Juran, 71 mins.)†

Brainiac, The (Mexico, 1963)* English-dubbed. Abel Salazar. Hokey horror thriller about an evil baron who returns from the dead to seek revenge. (Dir: Chano Urveta, 70 mins.)†

Brain of Blood (1971)½ Kent Taylor, Grant Williams, Regina Carroll, Angelo Rossitto, John Bloom, Reed Hadley, Vicki Volante, Zandor Vorkov. Mad scientist is hired by a dying foreign dictator to transplant his brain into a strong new body. But the usual problems result in the usual hulking, murderous monster. More inane stupidity from the maker of *Dracula vs. Frankenstein*. AKA: **Brain Damage** and **The Brain**. (Dir: Al Adamson, 83 mins.)†

Brainsnatchers, The—See: **Man Who Changed His Mind, The**

Brainstorm (1965)**½ Jeffrey Hunter, Anne Francis, Viveca Lindfors. Nicely played suspense yarn about a pair of lovers who work out a plan to get rid of the lady's husband. (Dir: William Conrad, 114 mins.)

Brainstorm (1983)**½ Christopher Walken, Natalie Wood, Louise Fletcher, Cliff Robertson. Special-effects wizard Douglas Trumbull directed this technological thriller about a device that enables one to experience someone else's thoughts and experiences. The device is great, but the plot is hokey, with the usual banal military types using the machine for their own purposes. (106 mins.)†

Brain That Wouldn't Die, The (1963)½ Jason Evers, Adele Lamont, Leslie Daniel, Virginia Leith. Surgeon manages to keep his fiancée's head alive after she has been decapitated in an accident, searches for a body to go with it. Grisly thriller is a favorite of bad movie lovers. (Dir: Joseph Green, 81 mins.)†

Brainwash—See: **Circle of Power**

Brainwashed (Germany, 1961)** Curt Jurgens, Claire Bloom. A German aristocrat is imprisoned by the Nazis and struggles to keep his sanity. Good performance cannot overcome the static nature of the tale. (Dir: Gerd Oswald, 102 mins.)

Brainwaves (1982)**½ Keir Dullea, Suzanna Love, Vera Miles, Tony Curtis, Nicholas Love. A young woman, thrown into a coma in a car accident, is revived through electrical restoration of her brain impulses, only to have terrifying flashbacks to a murder. An intriguing low-budget sci-fi thriller, whose execution isn't quite up to its best ideas. (Dir: Ulli Lommel, 81 mins.)†

Bramble Bush, The (1960)** Richard Burton, Barbara Rush, Jack Carson, Angie Dickinson. Small-town sinful dramatics reminiscent of *Peyton Place* as a doctor returns home to find all sorts of physical, mental, and moral complications. (Dir: Daniel Petrie, 105 mins.)

Branded (1950)**½ Alan Ladd, Mona Freeman, Charles Bickford. Crooks pick a wanderer to pose as heir to a wealthy rancher. Leisurely western needs more pace, but has a story that holds the interest. (Dir: Rudolph Mate, 104 mins.)†

Brand New Life (MTV 1989)*½ Barbara Eden, Don Murray, Shawnee Smith, Jenny Garth. Rich California lawyer marries a divorced waitress with three kids, and the usual adjustment difficulties ensue. Despite the title, just the same old stuff. (Dir: Eric Laneuville, 96 mins.)

Brand New Life, A (MTV 1973)***½ Cloris Leachman, Martin Balsam, Mildred Dunnock, Gene Nelson, Marge Redmond, Wilfred Hyde-White. Among the best made-for-TV films. Honest, touching, thoroughly human story about a couple, married for 18 years (she's going to be 41 and he'll be 46), who discover they are about to become parents for the first time. Cloris Leachman has never been better, and her performance earned her an Emmy. (Dir: Sam O'Steen, 74 mins.)

Brannigan (Great Britain, 1975)**½ John Wayne, Richard Attenborough. John Wayne in London town! He's an Irish cop from Chicago who journeys to London to bring back a criminal who has fled there. (Dir: Douglas Hickox, 111 mins.)†

Brasher Doubloon, The (1947)** George Montgomery, Nancy Guild, Florence Bates, Conrad Janis, Fritz Kortner. *The High Window* is disappointingly adapted into the weakest film of any of his books. This mystery about a rare coin short changes detective thriller fans. (Dir: John Brahm, 72 mins.)

Brass (MTV 1985)** Carroll O'Connor, Lois Nettleton, Larry Atlas, Samuel E. Wright, Jimmy Baio, Anita Gilette. Carroll O'Connor stars as New York City's Chief of Detectives in this pilot that didn't make the grade for CBS. (Dir: Corey Allen, 104 mins.)†

Brass Bottle, The (1964)** Tony Randall, Burl Ives, Barbara Eden. Oops! The one about the inferior man who finds an old lamp with a genie in it. Although Barbara Eden of "I Dream of Jeannie" is in the cast, it's Burl Ives who plays the helpful spirit. (Dir: Harvey Keller, 89 mins.)

Brass Legend, The (1956)** Hugh O'Brian, Raymond Burr, Nancy Gates. Sheriff O'Brian tracks down and shoots it out with desperado Burr. (Dir: Gerd Oswald, 79 mins.)

Brass Target (1978)*½ Sophia Loren, John Cassavetes, George Kennedy, Max von Sydow, Robert Vaughn, Edward Herrmann, Bruce Davison, Patrick McGoohan. A star-filled cast in a protracted musing about the events leading up to General Patton's alleged assassination in Germany after WWII. Paging George C. Scott. (Dir: John Hough, 111 mins.)

Bravados, The (1958)** Gregory Peck, Joan Collins, Stephen Boyd. Rambling western about a man bent on revenge for his wife's murder. Peck is as stoic as ever and Joan Collins is beautiful but rides a horse badly. (Dir: Henry King, 98 mins.)†

Brave and the Beautiful, The—See: **Magnificent Matador, The**

Brave Bulls, The (1951)**** Mel Ferrer, Anthony Quinn, Miroslava. Superb screenplay about the life, both private and public, of a famed matador. Probing photography makes it a penetrating study. Performances are top caliber, except for Mel Ferrer—even Ferrer is not as dull as usual. (Dir: Robert Rossen, 108 mins.)

Brave Little Toaster, The (1987)**½ Voices of Jon Lovitz, Tim Stack, Timothy Day. Oddball animated kiddie fare about a group of household appliances that set off in search of their owner. Cute, but weird. (Dir: Jerry Rees, 89 mins.)

Brave New World (MTV 1980)** Julie Cobb, Bud Cort, Keir Dullea, Ron O'Neal. Aldous Huxley's influential and controversial British novel about a controlled society 600 years from now receives a production with little of the impact of the original story. (Dir: Burt Brinkerhoff, 152 mins.)

Brave One, The (1956)*** Michel Ray, Rodolfo Hoyos. Young boy is attached to his pet bull, runs away to Mexico City to find the beast when he's sold. Charming drama won an Oscar for original story—and original it is. Good entertainment. Written by Dalton Trumbo. (Dir: Irving Rapper, 100 mins.)†

Brave Warrior (1952)** Jon Hall, Michael Ansara. History gets in the way of the action in this western set in the time of

125

the War of 1812. (Dir: Spencer Bennet, 73 mins.)

Bravos, The (MTV 1971)*½ George Peppard, Peter Duel, Pernell Roberts. Dull western concerning an Army officer sent to command a small fort after the Civil War. (Dir: Ted Post, 110 mins.)

Brazil (Great Britain-U.S., 1985)*½ Jonathan Pryce, Katherine Helmond, Ian Holm, Bob Hoskins, Robert De Niro. A lumbering, overpraised satire set in a *1984*-like future, all of whose inventiveness seems to have gone into the production design. You'll know where this futuristic comedy is going after the first five minutes and it goes there and goes there and . . . (Dir: Terry Gilliam, 130 mins.)†

Bread and Chocolate (Italy, 1974)***½ Nino Manfredi, Anna Karina. A deliciously witty, insightful, and deeply compassionate comedy about the frustrations of Everyman trying to better his lot in life—in this case an uneducated workingman from Naples who arrives in condescending Switzerland and becomes simultaneously a waiter, a resident alien, an illegal immigrant, and an inspired comic hero. Deftly directed by Franco Brusati. (86 mins.)

Breaker! Breaker! (1977)½ Chuck Norris, George Murdock, Terry O'Connor, Don Gentry. Chuck Norris stars in this inept revenge drama incorporating the CB craze. (Dir: Don Hulette, 86 mins.)†

Breaker Morant (Australia, 1980)***½ Edward Woodward, Jack Thompson, John Waters, Charles Tingwell. Careful, well-acted reconstruction of a famous British court-martial during the Boer War, *Breaker* depends on an audience perceiving the heroes as simple men caught in an ambiguous situation to gain any emotional credence. Whether they have done wrong or are simply political fodder for the Empire is too simple a reduction of the historical events, but that reduction is the turf staked out by this award-winner. Despite hedging the important questions, the film has rich performances, and the dramatic effects are wrenching. (Dir: Bruce Beresford, 107 mins.)†

Breakfast at Tiffany's (1961)**** Audrey Hepburn, George Peppard, Patricia Neal, Buddy Ebsen, Mickey Rooney. Daffy screwball comedy romance with a stylish verve that set the standard for sophistication in the sixties. Hepburn is an irresistible Holly Golightly perfectly suggesting the frightened child inside the playgirl who chases away the "Mean Reds" by high-tailing it over to Tiffany's. As a comedy-romance, the film's sublime, with melancholy Mancini music setting the mood and George Axelrod's witty script keeping the sentimentality

in check. (Dir: Blake Edwards, 115 mins.)†

Breakfast Club, The (1985)*** Emilio Estevez, Anthony Michael Hall, Judd Nelson, Molly Ringwald, Ally Sheedy. A perceptive, sensitive portrait of the difficulties of teen years, this nonexploitative teen picture chronicles one afternoon in which five "types" are kept in detention. All the performers are at the top of their form and, for once, director-scripter John Hughes creates a focused work. (97 mins.)†

Breakheart Pass (1976)** Charles Bronson, Richard Crenna, Ben Johnson, Jill Ireland. Tedious action yarn about a series of unexplained murders aboard a troop-transport train. (Dir: Tom Gries, 95 mins.)†

Breakin' (1984)** Adolfo Quinones, Michael Chambers, Lucinda Dickey. Filmed on location in L.A. and designed to cash in on the break dance craze. The plot keeps hopping as a street-wise street-dancing trio wins favor with the mainstream dance world. (Dir: Joel Silberg, 87 mins.)†

Breakin' 2: Electric Boogaloo (1984)** Lucinda Dickey, Adolpho (Shabba-Doo) Quinones, Michael (Boogaloo Shrimp) Chambers, Susie Bono. In this cheerful, but naive revamp of those "let's-put-on-a-show" musicals, a rich, college-bound student (Dickey) joins some underprivileged youths in saving a community center from being converted into a shopping mall. (Dir: Sam Firstenberg, 94 mins.)†

Breaking Away (1979)**** Dennis Christopher, Dennis Quaid, Barbara Barrie, Paul Dooley, Daniel Stern, Jackie Earl Haley. A breath of cinematic fresh air about four Indiana working-class teenagers looking for a sense of direction after graduating from high school. Shot entirely in Bloomington, Indiana, this charming, tender film follows Dave Stoller's (Christopher's) dogged efforts to become a champion Italian bike racer. This engaging yarn benefits from the believable characters in Steve Tesich's Academy-Award–winning screenplay, and the talented performers who bring them to life. (Dir: Peter Yates, 99 mins.)†

Breaking Glass (Great Britain, 1980)**½ Phil Daniels, Hazel O'Connor, Jon Finch, Jonathan Pryce. The premiere attempt by big studios to co-opt punk rock failed for good reasons: a) its *Star Is Born* story-line had little to do with the music, and b) the punk kids were too busy living it in the streets to see it in the theaters. (Dir: Brian Gibson, 104 mins.)†

Breaking Home Ties (MTV 1987)** Jason Robards, Eva Marie Saint, Doug McKeon, Erin Gray, Claire Trevor. Based on a Norman Rockwell painting, this coming-of-age-cum-terminal-disease drama concerns young McKeon, who encounters the "real world" of college, just as his mom (Saint) contracts leukemia. Good performances by the leads. (Dir: John Wilder, 96 mins.)

Breaking In (1989)**** Burt Reynolds, Casey Siemaszko, Sheila Kelley, Lorraine Toussaint, Albert Salmi, Harry Carey. Working from a script by John Sayles, the wonderfully quirky Scottish director Bill Forsyth (*Local Hero*) elicits the best performance Burt Reynolds has given in years, as an aging burglar who takes on a young partner. Flawless all around, this gentle comedy is a real treat. (91 mins.)†

Breaking Point (MTV 1989)** Corbin Bernsen, Joanna Pacula, John Glover, David Marshall Grant, Lawrence Pressman. Prior to the end of WWII, a U.S. intelligence officer is captured by the Germans, who attempt to pry information out of him by convincing him that they are Americans as well and that he has been in a coma for two years. Lackluster remake of *36 Hours*. (Dir: Peter Markle, 90 mins.)†

Breaking Point, The (1950)***½ John Garfield, Patricia Neal, Phyllis Thaxter, Juano Hernandez, Wallace Ford. The first attempt to do a straight version of Hemingway's potboiler *To Have and Have Not*. Almost totally neglected by film historians, this may be the best Hemingway adaptation ever filmed. Garfield arguably gives his most rounded performance as the charter boat owner who gets involved with criminals, and director Michael Curtiz never elicited more thematic values than he did in this story of loyalty, moral commitment, and adventure. Remade in '58 as *The Gun Runners*. (97 mins.)

Breaking the Sound Barrier (Great Britain, 1952)***½ Ralph Richardson, Ann Todd, Nigel Patrick. An aircraft manufacturer endures personal grief in his quest to produce a plane that can travel faster than the speed of sound. Truly marvelous aerial drama with a stirring story, superb performances, breathtaking photography. (Dir: David Lean, 115 mins.)

Breaking Up (MTV 1978)**½ Lee Remick, Granville Van Dusen. Competent, sensitive account of how one woman (Remick) struggles to put her life back together after her fifteen-year marriage ends. (Dir: Delbert Mann, 96 mins.)

Breaking Up Is Hard to Do (MTV 1979)*** Ted Bessell, Jeff Conaway, Billy Crystal, Robert Conrad, Tony Musante. Probing, honest, and often engrossing look at six male friends, all involved in show biz, who share a beach house one summer—the summer of their discontent. (Dir: Lou Antonio, 198 mins.)†

Break of Hearts (1935)*** Katharine Hepburn, Charles Boyer. Female musician falls in love with an orchestra leader. Good romantic drama. (Dir: Philip Moeller, 80 mins.)

Breakout (Great Britain, 1959)**½ Richard Todd, Richard Attenborough, Michael Wilding, Dennis Price. Attenborough and Wilding head a fine cast which adds zest to the plot about a group of British POWs in an Italian prison camp planning an escape. AKA: **Danger Within.** (Dir: Don Chaffey, 99 mins.)

Breakout (MTV 1971)** James Drury, Woody Strode, Red Buttons, Kathryn Hays. Prison drama takes a different twist as bank robber Drury becomes thwarted in various escape plans. (Dir: Richard Irving, 100 mins.)

Breakout (1975)* Charles Bronson, Robert Duvall, Jill Ireland, John Huston. Charles Bronson is, as usual, a stoic superhero, as he plays a helicopter pilot who engineers the escape of a falsely accused prisoner from a Mexican prison. (Dir: Tom Gries, 96 mins.)†

Breakthrough (1950)** David Brian, Frank Lovejoy, John Agar. Run-of-the-mill glory-drenched war story with time out for occasional romance. (Dir: Lewis Seller, 91 mins.)

Breakthrough (1981)** Richard Burton, Robert Mitchum, Rod Steiger, Curt Jurgens, Klaus Loewitsch. Despite an all-star cast, this is a routine WWII adventure. It's the closing days of the war and Hitler's army has become disillusioned; Burton's soldier is dispatched to contact American forces and try to negotiate a cease-fire. (Dir: Andrew McLaglen, 115 mins.)†

Breathless (France, 1959)**** Jean Seberg, Jean-Paul Belmondo, Daniel Boulanger. Not only the key film in the French *nouvelle vague*, but the first by this era's greatest filmmaker, Jean-Luc Godard. Featuring Belmondo in his screen debut as a befuddled French gangster. Godard cast Seberg as the quintessential American, epitomizing seductiveness in our society. AKA: **A Bout de Souffle.** (89 mins.)†

Breathless (1983)** Richard Gere, Valerie Kaprisky, Art Metrano. Pointless, emptyheaded remake of Jean-Luc Godard's 1959 groundbreaker about a small-time hood and his whirlwind affair with a beautiful foreign student is all the more disappointing because it occasionally shows real promise. (Dir: Jim McBride, 105 mins.)†

Breath of Scandal, A (1959)** Sophia Loren, Maurice Chevalier, John Gavin. Young American in Vienna rescues a princess, falls for her, is hampered by court protocol. Stale romance despite pretty costumes, production. (Dir: Michael Curtiz, 98 mins.)

Breed Apart, A (1984)** Rutger Hauer, Powers Boothe, Kathleen Turner, Donald Pleasence, John Dennis Johnston, Brion James. Was this movie magically hatched on the shelf of a video store? It's not terrible, just terribly ordinary considering the talents assembled. Pleasence is a demented egg collector who pays financially strapped mountain climber Boothe to steal two rare eggs from Hauer, a conservationist-recluse, even though that theft will wipe out a species of eagle. (Dir: Philippe Mora, 101 mins.)†

Breezy (1973)** William Holden, Kay Lenz, Roger C. Carmel, Marj Dusay. Sudsy, romantic film about a weary, middle-aged man (Holden) who regains his lust for life through an affair with a "flower child" (Lenz). (Dir: Clint Eastwood, 108 mins.)

Brenda Starr (MTV 1976)*½ Jill St. John, Jed Allan, Victor Buono. Lightweight spoof features Jill St. John as comic-strip newspaper reporter Brenda Starr. She tracks down a group of voodoo extortionists from Los Angeles to the jungles of Brazil. (Dir: Mel Stuart, 72 mins.)

Brewster McCloud (1970)*** Bud Cort, Sally Kellerman, Michael Murphy, William Windom, Shelley Duvall, Rene Auberjonois, Stacy Keach, Margaret Hamilton. Following the success of *M*A*S*H*, director Robert Altman was able to fully unleash his comic imagination with this oddball comedy, about a boy searching for the secret of flight. (104 mins.)

Brewster's Millions (1945)**½ Dennis O'Keefe, June Havoc. Young man inherits a million dollars, but has to spend it in two months in order to claim an even larger fortune. Amusing comedy. (Dir: Allan Dwan, 79 mins.)†

Brewster's Millions (1985)** Richard Pryor, John Candy, Lonette McKee, Pat Hingle, Hume Cronyn, Tovah Feldshuh, Yana Nirvana. A bush league bozo must spend 30 million dollars in order to collect an even larger fortune. Candy and Pryor are million dollar comics, but this script is strictly poverty row. (Dir: Walter Hill, 97 mins.)†

Brian's Song (MTV 1971)**** James Caan, Billy Dee Williams. Beautifully adapted true story about Brian Piccolo, the Chicago Bears football player who shared a unique friendship with teammate Gale Sayers before cancer claimed Piccolo's life at the age of 26. For a tale dealing with death, this film is bursting with life, particularly in the impeccable, perfectly matched performances of Caan, as the warm and witty Piccolo, and Williams, as the more serious Sayers. (Dir: Buzz Kulik, 71 mins.)†

128

Bribe, The (1949)** Robert Taylor, Ava Gardner, Charles Laughton, Vincent Price. Corny, cheap melodrama about the government agent chasing crooks in the Caribbean who falls in love with the seductive wife of one of the bad men. (Dir: Robert Z. Leonard, 98 mins.)

Bride, The (1985)**½ Jennifer Beals, Sting, Clancy Brown, David Rappaport, Anthony Higgins, Verushka, Quentin Crisp. The problem here is that the feminist reconception of the Monster Bride is not as emotionally rich as the subplot involving the Frankenstein monster's adventures with an enterprising dwarf, once the reconstructed creature flees his master's laboratory. (Dir: Franc Roddam, 118 mins.)†

Bride and the Beast, The (1958)½ Charlotte Austin, Lance Fuller, Johnny Roth, Steve Calvert, William Justine, Slick Slavin. The new bride of a big-game hunter has the hots for someone else—the gorilla that hubby keeps in a cage. A little hypnotic investigation shows that she was a gorilla herself in a past life! Edward D. Wood, Jr. wrote this howler. (Dir: Adrian Weiss, 78 mins.)†

Bride Came C.O.D., The (1941)*** James Cagney, Bette Davis. Cagney and Davis dig all the laughs possible out of the script and succeed in making it funny. Plot is all in the title with Cagney as the flying delivery boy and Bette as the bride. (Dir: William Keighley, 92 mins.)

Bride Comes Home, The (1935)**½ Claudette Colbert, Fred MacMurray, Robert Young. Routine romantic triangle comedy, well played by its stars. (Dir: Wesley Ruggles, 85 mins.)

Bride for Sale (1949)**½ Claudette Colbert, Robert Young, George Brent. Head of an accounting firm finds his ace female tax expert is marriage-minded, so he persuades his handsome friend to go to work on her. Romantic comedy acted by old masters, even if the material is thin. (Dir: William D. Russell, 87 mins.)

Bride Goes Wild, The (1948)**½ Van Johnson, June Allyson, Hume Cronyn. Van, who hates kids, has to get Butch Jenkins to pose as his son, and the result is an occasionally amusing farce. (Dir: Norman Taurog, 98 mins.)

Bride in Black, The (MTV 1990)**½ Susan Lucci, David Soul, Finola Hughes. Susan Lucci has never had a better showcase, playing a shy woman who works in a Brooklyn deli. Into her life comes a dashing suitor and, after a whirlwind courtship, they marry only to have tragedy invade their happiness. Her husband is gunned down on the steps of the church on their wedding day and his widow sets out to find out why. (Dir: James Goldstone, 96 mins.)

Bride of Frankenstein, The (1935)**** Boris Karloff, Colin Clive, Elsa Lanchester, Ernest Thesiger, Valerie Hobson, Dwight Frye, Una O'Connor. Probably the most *delightful* monster movie ever made, though it has its share of real feeling too. The elegantly wicked Dr. Praetorious enlists the monster's aid to force Dr. Frankenstein to build a woman. Indescribably stylish, witty, and grotesque; nothing remotely like it has ever been made since. (Dir: James Whale, 90 mins.)†

Bride of Re-Animator, The (1990)** Jeffrey Combs, Bruce Abbott, Claude Earl Jones, Fabiana Udenio, David Gale, Kathleen Kinmont, Mel Graves. Sequel to cult hit *Re-Animator* offers buckets of blood but not much believability in oft-told tale of scientist seeking to create life from spare body parts. (Dir: Brian Yuzna, 97 mins.)†

Bride of the Monster (1955)½ Bela Lugosi, Tor Johnson, Tony McCoy, Loretta King, Harvey Dunne. A perky reporter who must have overdosed on Lois Lane comics almost ends up mated with a grotesque creature belonging to Bela. Hilarious Woodian weirdness. (Dir: Edward Wood, Jr., 69 mins.)

Bride of Vengeance (1948)** Paulette Goddard, John Lund, Macdonald Carey. Cesare Borgia sends his sister to eliminate an opposing ruler, but she falls for him. Overstuffed costume drama. (Dir: Mitchell Leisen, 91 mins.)

Bridesmaids (MTV 1989)**½ Shelley Hack, Sela Ward, Brooke Adams, Stephanie Faracy. Former high school pals are reunited as bridesmaids in their friend's wedding, an occasion to share secrets and memories. Soap opera all the way, with Adams a standout in a good cast. (Dir: Lila Garrett, 96 mins.)

Brides of Dracula, The (Great Britain, 1960)**½ Peter Cushing, David Peel, Martita Hunt, Freda Jackson. A vampire with an unusual ally seeks victims in 19th-century England. An above-average Hammer horror flick; atmospheric and entertaining. (Dir: Terence Fisher, 85 mins.)

Brides of Fu Manchu, The (Great Britain, 1966)** Christopher Lee, Douglas Wilner, Marie Versini. Lee is back playing the ominous Fu Manchu, who this time has scientists working feverishly on a monster ray gun. Followed by *Vengeance of Fu Manchu*. (Dir: Doug Sharp, 94 mins.)

Bride Walks Out, The (1936)**½ Barbara Stanwyck, Gene Raymond, Robert Young, Ned Sparks, Helen Broderick, Willie Best, Billy Gilbert, Hattie McDaniel. Social comedy of newlyweds trying to survive on a budget, but the husband doesn't want the wife to work. A look at standards *long* discarded. (Dir: Leigh Jason, 81 mins.)

Bride Wore Black, The (France, 1967)*** Jeanne Moreau, Jean-Claude Brialy, Charles Denner. An entertaining murder melodrama, dedicated to Alfred Hitchcock. Moreau is out to revenge the death of her bridegroom. (Dir: François Truffaut, 107 mins.)

Bride Wore Boots, The (1946)** Barbara Stanwyck, Robert Cummings. Nonsensical comedy about a girl who loves horses but her groom does not. (Dir: Irving Pichel, 86 mins.)

Bride Wore Red, The (1937)** Joan Crawford, Franchot Tone, Robert Young, Billie Burke, Reginald Owen. Director Dorothy Arzner wrings some feminist issues out of this otherwise tired MGM soap opera. A peasant girl seeks a chance to marry rich and aristocratic. (103 mins.)†

Bridge, The (West Germany, 1959)**** Fritz Wepper, Volker Bohnet. One of the most powerful antiwar films ever made. Taut direction by Swiss director Bernhard Wicki. Based on a true story about a group of German youths killed two days before the end of WWII in Europe, in a hopeless attempt to stall the Allied advance before the Nazi regime surrendered. (Dir: Bernhard Wicki, 100 mins.)

Bridge Across Time (MTV 1985)*½ David Hasselhoff, Stepfanie Kramer, Randolph Mantooth, Adrienne Barbeau, Clu Gulager. Silly show about Jack the Ripper loose in Arizona's Havasu Lake, home of the London Bridge. AKA: **The Arizona Ripper.** (Dir: E. W. Swackhamer, 104 mins.)

Bridge at Remagen, The (1969)**½ George Segal, Robert Vaughn, Ben Gazzara, Bradford Dillman, E. G. Marshall. Based on fact, an account of the efforts by Allied soldiers to commandeer an important tactical bridge from German hands before it's destroyed. (Dir: John Guillermin, 116 mins.)†

Bridge of San Luis Rey, The (1944)**½ Lynn Bari, Francis Lederer, Alla Nazimova, Louis Calhern, Akim Tamiroff, Blanche Yurka. Ambitious but, ultimately, failed attempt to film Thornton Wilder's elusive novel. The story investigates the accidental deaths of five people. (Dir: Rowland V. Lee, 85 mins.)†

Bridge on the River Kwai, The (Great Britain, 1957)**** William Holden, Alec Guinness, Jack Hawkins, Sessue Hayakawa. Mammoth, magnificent war drama directed by David Lean, a superb motion picture; about a hardened, resolute British officer, captive of the Japanese, who drives his men to build a bridge as therapy, and the attempt of an escaped prisoner to demolish it. Performances, production, script all deserve the highest praise. (161 mins.)†

Bridger (MTV 1976)** James Wainwright, Sally Field, Dirk Blocker, Ben Murphy, John Anderson, William Windom. Typical action pic about the real-life James Bridger, a mountain man who helped chart a trail through the Rockies to California. Subsequently edited down to 78 mins. (Dir: David Lowell Rich, 104 mins.)

Bridges at Toko-Ri, The (1954)***½ William Holden, Grace Kelly, Fredric March, Mickey Rooney. Jet pilot takes off on a dangerous mission during the Korean conflict, while his wife waits patiently for his return. Based on James Michener's book, filmed professionally, powerfully, with fine performances. (Dir: Mark Robson, 110 mins.)†

Bridge Too Far, A (1977)**½ Robert Redford, Ryan O'Neal, Gene Hackman, Laurence Olivier, Sean Connery, Liv Ullmann, James Caan, Dirk Bogarde, Anthony Hopkins. *A Bridge Too Far* is a movie much, much too long. This mammoth production, costing $25 million, re-creates the disastrous Allied parachute push into the Netherlands in September '44. Based on the exhaustive book by Cornelius Ryan, this epic becomes exhausting. (Dir: Richard Attenborough, 175 mins.)†

Bridge to Silence (MTV 1989)**½ Lee Remick, Marlee Matlin, Michael O'Keefe, Candace Brecker, Josef Sommer. Deaf actress Matlin speaks aloud and with sign language in this interesting drama tailored for her. She plays a married woman and mother whose life is completely disrupted when her husband is killed in an auto accident. Her mother, played with a surprising edge by Remick, adds to her grief by taking over her life. (Dir: Karen Arthur, 96 mins.)

Bridge to the Sun (1961)*** Carroll Baker, James Shigeta. Based on Gwen Terasaki's autobiography, this compelling drama relates the difficulties of a young woman married to a Japanese diplomat during World War II, victim of suspicion and animosity from her husband's government. (Dir: Etienne Perier, 113 mins.)

Brief Encounter (Great Britain, 1946)**** Celia Johnson, Trevor Howard. Superb transcription of Noël Coward's drama; a mature married woman finds the beginnings of an affair with a chance acquaintanceship, unknown to her husband. Sensitively directed, finely acted. The love scenes between Johnson and Howard are among the most touching ever filmed. (Dir: David Lean, 85 mins.)†

Brief Encounter (MTV 1974)** Richard Burton, Sophia Loren, Jack Headley. The two leads go through the motions in this petrified TV adaptation of the Noël Coward classic. (Dir: Alan Bridges, 76 mins.)

Brief Vacation, A (Italy, 1975)**** Florinda Bolkan, Renato Salvatori, Daniel Quenaud. This final film from director Vittorio De Sica should find favor with Marxists and feminists alike. A production line worker struck by lung disease is sent to a state sanitorium where, free from the usual social pressures and exposed to new ideas brought to her by other women, she has time to think through the various aspects of her oppression. Although entertaining, the film moves ruthlessly to a bitter ending. (106 mins.)

Brigadoon (1954)*** Gene Kelly, Cyd Charisse, Van Johnson. This is not our favorite MGM musical, despite the stars, the artwork of Cedric Gibbons and Preston Ames, the fine Lerner-Loewe score, and the directorial presence of Vincente Minnelli. The film—about two Americans on holiday in Scotland who discover a magical village on the one day each century that it comes to life—is curiously uninspired given the delightful premise. Fun, but not thrilling. (108 mins.)†

Brigand, The (1952)**½ Anthony Dexter, Jody Lawrance, Anthony Quinn. Anthony Dexter plays a dual role in this predictable adventure film about intrigue in the Spanish royal court. (Dir: Phil Karlson, 94 mins.)

Brigham Young, Frontiersman (1940)**½ Dean Jagger, Tyrone Power, Linda Darnell. Interesting but not particularly exciting story of the Mormons and Brigham Young's struggle to find a place to live. (Dir: Henry Hathaway, 114 mins.)

Bright Eyes (1934)*** Shirley Temple, James Dunn, Jane Withers, Judith Allen, Lois Wilson. As factions wage a custody battle over little Shirley, Miss Curly Top is engaged in her own battles with brattish Jane Withers in a breezy vehicle that gives Shirley a chance to dispense childlike wisdom, charm the pants off straight-laced elders, and sing "On the Good Ship Lollipop." Bright-eyed! (Dir: David Butler, 83 mins.)†

Bright Leaf (1950)**½ Gary Cooper, Lauren Bacall, Patricia Neal. A fine cast tells the story of one man's rise to wealth in the early days of tobacco growing. Well acted but a bit overlong. (Dir: Michael Curtiz, 110 mins.)

Bright Lights (1935)*** Joe E. Brown, Ann Dvorak, William Gargan, Patricia Ellis, Arthur Treacher, William Demerest. Wonderful vehicle for Brown, a classic backstage story of a comic acrobat whose success goes to his head. Completely charming. (Dir: Busby Berkeley, 83 mins.)

Bright Lights, Big City (1988)** Michael J. Fox, Kiefer Sutherland, Phoebe Cates, Swoosie Kurtz, Frances Sternhagen, Dianne Wiest, Jason Robards, John Houseman. Fox is miscast in this adaptation of Jay McInerney's popular book detailing the cocaine-addled life of a young Manhattanite. The script (also by McInerney) gives Fox numerous travails to endure, but the movie never gives us a reason to care, and it soon becomes deadening rather than involving. (Dir: James Bridges, 110 mins.)†

Brighton Beach Memoirs (1986)**½ Blythe Danner, Bob Dishy, Jonathan Silverman, Judith Ivey, Jonathan Silverman, Judith Ivey. Homogenized film version of Neil Simon's smash Broadway hit. What we're left with is a semiautobiographical domestic comedy about the trials and tribulations of the Jerome family as seen from the adolescent viewpoint of the young Neil Simon. For Simon fans primarily; otherwise it's like a Norman Rockwell painting of delicatessen life. (Dir: Gene Saks, 108 mins.)†

Brighton Rock—See: Young Scarface

Brighton Strangler, The (1945)**½ John Loder, June Duprez. Unusually good B picture about an actor who plays a murderer, and ends up taking his part too seriously. (Dir: Max Nosseck, 67 mins.)

Bright Road (1953)** Dorothy Dandridge, Robert Horton, Harry Belafonte. New fourth-grade teacher takes an interest in a lad who is antagonistic. Story of a black youngster and his teacher has sincerity but lacks that necessary spark. (Dir: Gerald Mayer, 68 mins.)

Bright Victory (1951)*** Arthur Kennedy, Peggy Dow. Touching film about the crisis-laden rehabilitation of a WWII soldier who is blinded in battle. Arthur Kennedy gives one of the best performances of his career as the victim and Peggy Dow is perfect as the understanding girl who finally gives him the courage he needs to go on. (Dir: Mark Robson, 97 mins.)

Brighty of the Grand Canyon (1967)** Joseph Cotten, Dick Foran. Brighty is a mule who befriends an old prospector (Foran) who has discovered a mother lode of gold. The Grand Canyon steals the film from the mule. (Director: Norman Foster, 89 mins.)†

Brimstone (1949)*** Rod Cameron, Adrian Booth, Walter Brennan. Undercover marshal tangles with a cattleman who has turned outlaw with his sons. (Dir: Joseph Kane, 90 mins.)

Brimstone and Treacle (Great Britain, 1983)*** Sting, Denholm Elliott, Joan Plowright. A bizarre, well-acted comedy-drama about a handsome young drifter who gradually takes over the lives of a middle-class British couple and their com-atose daughter. Sting, formerly of the rock group The Police, proves himself an actor of considerable virtuosity. (Dir: Richard Loncraine, 85 mins.)†

Bringing Up Baby (1938)**** Katharine Hepburn, Cary Grant, Barry Fitzgerald, Charlie Ruggles, May Robson. This Howard Hawks-directed classic is perhaps the screwiest of the '30s screwball comedies. Features Grant as an absentminded paleontologist beleaguered by a persistently kooky Hepburn (and her pet leopard, Baby). (102 mins.)†

Bring Me the Head of Alfredo Garcia (1974)**½ Warren Oates, Isela Vega, Gig Young, Robert Webber, Kris Kristofferson, Helmut Dantine. Oates is quite affecting as an American caught up in the kind of metaphorically evil Mexico best realized by Orson Welles in *Touch of Evil*. The director's gift for violence hasn't deserted him, but his understanding of basic scriptwriting logic has in this uneven tale of a two-bit piano player who could make a fortune selling Señor Garcia's noggin to a wealthy landowner. Brutal and bizarre. (Dir: Sam Peckinpah, 112 mins.)†

Bring Me the Head of Dobie Gillis (MTV 1988)**½ Dwayne Hickman, Bob Denver, Connie Stevens, Sheila James, Steve Franken. Besides having the best title of any of the recent slew of "reunion" TV movies, this breezy farce successfully revives the wonderfully silly dialogue and cartoonlike characters of the original series. Although credited to the great humorist Max Shulman (who wrote the original "Dobie" stories), the plotline, which has Thalia (Stevens) returning to town to offer a bounty for Dobie's murder, smacks of *The Visit* by Durrenmatt (see separate entry). (Dir: Stanley Z. Cherry, 96 mins.)

Bring on the Girls (1945)**½ Eddie Bracken, Veronica Lake, Sonny Tufts. Minor little musical about a man who inherits a fortune and joins the Navy to avoid gold-digging females. (Dir: Sidney Lanfield, 92 mins.)

Bring on the Night (Great Britain, 1985)*** Sting, Omar Hakim, Darryl Jones, Kenny Kirkland, Branford Marsalis. Well-received documentary that slices a small segment out of the life of Sting, the charismatic rock performer and former lead singer with The Police. This deifying documentary has its bonuses, like the footage of Sting's recent jazz-flavored concerts, but fans of Sting will be just as enthralled by the behind-the-scenes looks at his personal life. (Dir: Michael Apted, 97 mins.)†

Bring Your Smile Along (1955)**½ Keefe Brasselle, Frankie Laine, Constance Towers. Frankie Laine fans will enjoy this musical romance about a female high school teacher who writes lyrics for her composer boyfriend's music. (Dir: Blake Edwards, 83 mins.)

Brink of Life (Sweden, 1957)** Eva Dahlbeck, Ingrid Thulin, Bibi Andersson, Max von Sydow, Erland Josephson, Gunnar Sjoberg. Lesser-known, depressing Ingmar Bergman film about three women in a hospital maternity ward, each enormously uncertain about the course she is taking. An interesting sidelight to Bergman's more famous films of this era, featuring most of the performers who functioned as Bergman's repertory troupe. (82 mins.)†

Brink's Job, The (1978)**½ Peter Falk, Peter Boyle, Allen Goorwitz, Warren Oates. Director William Friedkin mixes his customary harsh location grittiness with loutish humor in this recreation of the famous '50 Boston heist. (118 mins.)†

Brink's: The Great Robbery (MTV 1976)** Darren McGavin, Cliff Gorman, Jenny O'Hara, Leslie Nielsen, Carl Betz. Lengthy recreation of the famous 1950 Boston robbery which took years to solve. (Dir: Marvin Chomsky, 102 mins.)

Britannia Hospital (Great Britain, 1983)* Graham Crowden, Leonard Rossiter, Joan Plowright, Malcolm McDowell, Mark Hamill. Theoretically the third in the trilogy begun by *If . . .* and *O Lucky Man!*, this offbeat, offbase satire actually places Mick Travis (McDowell) in a very minor supporting role as a TV reporter. Instead the film goes for broad farce, throwing in crabby doctors, angry protestors, and a mad scientist whose final invention is a lot like this film: it doesn't work. (Dir: Lindsay Anderson, 116 mins.)†

British Agent (1934)*** Kay Francis, Leslie Howard, William Gargan, Philip Reed, Walter Byron, J. Carroll Naish, Halliwell Hobbes. Spiffy intrigue with a secret agent good guy losing his heart to the Mata Hari of the Ukraine. Francis's smoldering allure could easily drive patriots to treason, so it's easy to buy this glossy escapism. (Dir: Michael Curtiz, 81 mins.)

British Intelligence (1940)**½ Boris Karloff, Margaret Lindsay, Maris Wrixon, Holmes Herbert. It won't surprise anybody to learn that the butler actually did it in this convoluted spy story, since he's played by Karloff! (Dir: Terry Morse, 62 mins.)

Broadcast News (1987)**** William Hurt, Holly Hunter, Albert Brooks, Joan Cusack, Lois Chiles, Jack Nicholson (cameo). A funny, wonderfully insightful examination of network television news, abetted by a terrific screenplay by writer-director James L. Brooks and faultless perform-

ances. Hurt plays a handsome anchorman who doesn't fully understand the news he reads, Hunter is enchanting as his driven, unwillingly smitten producer, and Brooks steals his scenes as a supercompetent but unphotogenic newsman who can't stand to see Hurt's undeserved success. On a par with *Network* as a caustic, knowing study of the showbizzing of TV news. (131 mins.)†

Broadminded (1931)**½ Joe E. Brown, Ona Munson, William Collier, Jr., Bela Lugosi, Thelma Todd. Brown is hired to play chaperon to rich brat Collier. Funny script by Bert Kalmar and Harry Ruby, with amusing bits by Todd and Lugosi (as her Latin American lover!). (Dir: Mervyn LeRoy, 65 mins.)

Broadway (1942)*** George Raft, Janet Blair, Broderick Crawford. George Raft plays himself in this entertaining period piece of the speakeasy era, gangsters, and bootleggers. (Dir: William Seiter, 91 mins.)

Broadway Bad (1933)**½ Joan Blondell, Ricardo Cortez, Ginger Rogers. Blondell effective as a chorus girl who, when slandered by her husband, uses the publicity to get ahead. Stylish melodrama. (Dir: Sidney Lanfield, 61 mins.)

Broadway Bill (1934)*** Warner Baxter, Walter Connolly, Myrna Loy, Helen Vinson, Lynne Overman. Runyonesque racetrack comedy, breezily directed by Frank Capra in his positive, wisecracking, all-American style. Good performances; young Myrna is lovely. Story by Mark Hellinger. A remake, also directed by Capra, was called *Riding High*. (103 mins.)

Broadway Danny Rose (1984)*** Woody Allen, Mia Farrow, Nick Apollo Forte. A black-and-white small-scale gem from Allen. Damon Runyon's spirit infuses this tale of a small-time agent and the would-be talents who employ him. These dropouts from lounge acts and amateur acts never give up, and neither does Danny, whose faith in them gives the film emotional resilience. Sweet-tempered and full of laughs. (Dir: Woody Allen, 86 mins.)†

Broadway Drifter, The (1927)**½ George Walsh, Dorothy Hall, Bigelow Cooper, Arthur Donaldson. Enjoyably silly light melodrama about a playboy whose father cuts off his allowance, forcing him to get a job—in a girls' gymnasium! Designed to show off Walsh's admittedly remarkable physique. (Dir: Bernard McEveety, 90 mins.)†

Broadway Gondolier (1935)**½ Dick Powell, Joan Blondell, Adolphe Menjou, Louise Fazenda, William Gargan, Joe Sawyer, the Mills Brothers. Cabbie Powell is hired to impersonate a singing gondolier on the radio. Typical Warner's musical introduced the hit song "Lulu's Back in Town." (Dir: Lloyd Bacon, 98 mins.)

Broadway Limited (1941)** Dennis O'Keefe, Victor McLaglen, Marjorie Woodworth, Patsy Kelly, ZaSu Pitts. Showbiz hopefuls stage a publicity stunt on the famous train. Nothing special. (Dir: Gordon Douglas, 74 mins.)

Broadway Melody, The (1929)** Anita Page, Bessie Love, Charles King. This was billed as the first full-length all-talking, all-singing, all-dancing musical. Two sisters suffer behind the scenes, but learn the show must go on. Winner Best Film Academy Award 1929. (Dir: Harry Beaumont, 104 mins.)†

Broadway Melody of 1936, The (1935)*** Jack Benny, Robert Taylor, Eleanor Powell. Benny's a columnist, loosely modeled on Winchell (weren't they all?), who's lambasting Taylor's vain producer. A top-rate score, Powell's dancing, and the old reliable show-biz plot are perfectly blended in an entertaining musical. (Dir: Roy Del Ruth, 103 mins.)

Broadway Melody of 1938 (1937)*** Judy Garland, Robert Taylor, George Murphy, Eleanor Powell, Sophie Tucker, Buddy Ebsen. A likable musical that appeals despite the big production, particularly with ingratiatingly low-key performers like Ebsen. The story revolves around Powell, that smiling dancing machine, with Taylor and Murphy as the love interests. Garland made the strongest impression with her rendition of "Dear Mr. Gable (You Made Me Love You)." (Dir: Roy Del Ruth, 110 mins.)†

Broadway Melody of 1940 (1940)***½ Fred Astaire, Eleanor Powell, George Murphy, Frank Morgan, Ian Hunter. Astaire and Powell, in their only teaming, dominate this entertaining musical with a strong Cole Porter score (including "Begin the Beguine"). Astaire is in a rivalry with Murphy (no contest), and the plot is a tad of a nuisance, but the dance numbers are good and there are plenty of them. (Dir: Norman Taurog, 101 mins.)†

Broadway Musketeers (1938)**½ Margaret Lindsay, Ann Sheridan, Marie Wilson, John Litel. Three women, friends since their days in an orphanage, try to make a go of it in N.Y.C. Remake of the far superior melodrama *Three on a Match*, necessarily sterilized, since the original was pre-Code. Still a good story, though. (Dir: John Farrow, 62 mins.)

Broadway Rhythm (1943)**½ Gloria De Haven, Ginny Simms, Ben Blue, George Murphy. Some good individual numbers by people like Lena Horne but generally just a lavish piece of nothing. (Dir: Roy Del Ruth, 114 mins.)

Broadway Serenade (1939)*½ Jeanette MacDonald, Lew Ayres, Ian Hunter, Frank Morgan. MacDonald has her first starring role as a solo performer, but the film's burdened with overdone production numbers and a weak story of a vaudeville marriage jeopardized when the wife's career takes off. (Dir: Robert Z. Leonard, 111 mins.)

Broadway to Hollywood (1933)**½ Alice Brady, Frank Morgan, Jackie Cooper, Eddie Quillan, Madge Evans, Mickey Rooney. Showbiz melodrama of a family of entertainers. Hackneyed but well done, with plenty of star cameos and musical numbers. (Dir: Willard Mack, 85 mins.)

Brock's Last Case (MTV 1973)**½ Richard Widmark, Henry Darrow. This pilot film about a New York detective quitting the force to raise oranges in California is rather entertaining. Everything goes wrong for the retired cop; still he manfully springs his Indian foreman loose from a murder rap. (Dir: David Lowell Rich, 100 mins.)

Broken Angel (MTV 1988)*½ William Shatner, Susan Blakely, Roxanne Biggs, Erika Eleniak. Big Bill acts the concerned dad in this sermonizing melodrama. When his daughter is missing, he goes on the prowl and finds she's a member of a nasty drug-dealing gang. (Dir: Richard T. Heffron, 96 mins.)

Broken Arrow (1950)**½ James Stewart, Jeff Chandler, Debra Paget, Will Geer. The most successful of the westerns with red men as heroes. Chandler (who won an Oscar nomination) plays Cochise, who makes a blood brother of Indian agent Stewart. It's less than rousing, but it does make you feel warm and liberal. (Dir: Delmer Daves, 93 mins.)†

Broken Blossoms (1919)**** Lillian Gish, Richard Barthelmess, Donald Crisp. D. W. Griffith classic love story of a young woman and a Chinese gentleman can still tug at the heartstrings. Griffith allowed Gish and Barthelmess to play the romantic duo with realistic enthusiasm. Crisp, one of Hollywood's most distinguished character actors, is hateful and menacing as Gish's vicious exprizefighter father. (89 mins.)†

Broken Commandment—See: **The Sin**

Broken Lance (1954)** Spencer Tracy, Richard Widmark, Robert Wagner, Earl Holliman, Jean Peters, Katy Jurado, E. G. Marshall, Eduard Franz. This remake of Joseph L. Mankiewicz's *House of Strangers* as a western, with Tracy performing well as the tyrannical papa riding hard on three rebellious sons, unaccountably won Philip Yordan the

Oscar for Best Story. The movie is overheated and without conviction. (Dir: Edward Dmytryk, 96 mins.)†

Broken Lullaby (1932)*** Lionel Barrymore, Nancy Carroll, Phillips Holmes, ZaSu Pitts, Tom Douglas. Soldier who killed a man in World War I tries to make amends for the deceased's family. Dated but still powerful drama; caused a sensation at the time. AKA: **The Man I Killed.** (Dir: Ernst Lubitsch, 77 mins.)

Broken Promise (MTV 1981)*** Melissa Michaelson, Chris Sarandon. Five youngsters, left stranded by their parents, are separated, going to different foster homes. However, twelve-year-old Patty, the family leader, battles against the bureaucracy to keep the brood together. (Dir: Don Taylor, 104 mins.)

Broken Rainbow (1986)***½ Narrated by Martin Sheen. Heartbreaking Academy Award–winning documentary about the plight of thousands of Indians who are fighting relocation from their homes in Arizona. (Dir: Mario Florio, 70 mins.)

Broken Vows (MTV 1987)**½ Tommy Lee Jones, Annette O'Toole, M. Emmet Walsh, Milo O'Shea, David Groh. Jones is a priest working in a ghetto area who is beginning to doubt his effectiveness. After giving last rites to a murder victim, he takes up with the dead man's girl in order to find the killers. (Dir: Jud Taylor, 104 mins.)

Bronco Billy (1980)*** Clint Eastwood, Sondra Locke, Geoffrey Lewis, Scatman Crothers, Sam Bottoms. A winsome comedy about a small-bracket Wild West show presided over by Eastwood's sappy prince of delusion, but the results are more often screwy than screwball. Eastwood swings wide for his laughs, but the film has a coherence of vision that makes it more satisfying as a whole than in its parts. (Dir: Clint Eastwood, 116 mins.)†

Bronco Buster (1952)**½ Scott Brady, John Lund, Joyce Holden. Some good touches in this unassuming yarn about a champ rodeo rider who takes a young hopeful in hand and trains him. (Dir: Budd Boetticher, 90 mins.)

Bronk (MTV 1975)** Jack Palance, Henry Beckman, Tony King, David Birney, Joseph Mascolo, Joanna Moore, Chelsea Brown. A pilot for the series. When his partner dies in the midst of a drug investigation, a trustworthy cop has to fight both City Hall and the Mob to arrive at the truth. (Dir: Richard Donner, 74 mins.)

Bronte Sisters, The (France, 1979)*** Isabelle Adjani, Marie-France Pisier, Isabelle Huppert, Pascal Greggory, Patrick Magee. Three fine actresses have a field day in this intriguing biography of the three writers whose lives were every bit as interesting as the fiction they created. (Dir: Andre Techiné, 115 mins.)

Brood, The (Canada, 1979)*** Samantha Eggar, Oliver Reed, Art Hindle, Cindy Hinds, Nuala Fitzgerald. A repellent but resonant horror film that might have been that rarity—a modern-day horror classic—if some of the script's loopholes had been filled in. A psychiatrist experiments with ridding his patients of their psychoses by enabling them to give birth to physical manifestations of their rage. One especially hate-ridden patient delivers a brood of murderous children who begin attacking all her perceived enemies. (Dir: David Cronenberg, 91 mins.)†

Brother, Can You Spare a Dime? (Great Britain, 1975)*** An unusual documentary collage about the Depression Era in America, using contemporary film and newsreel footage, made by Australian Philippe Mora. Definitely worth seeing. (Dir: Philippe Mora, 103 mins.)†

Brother from Another Planet, The (1984)*** Joe Morton, Darryl Edwards, Dee Dee Bridgewater, John Sayles, David Strathaim. A quietly charming comedy-fantasy that echoes *E.T.*, *The Man Who Fell to Earth*, and *Being There*. A black extraterrestrial (Morton) crashes on Ellis Island and is then pursued by two alien bounty hunters in Harlem. (Dir: John Sayles, 110 mins.)†

Brotherhood, The (1968)**½ Kirk Douglas, Alex Cord, Irene Pappas, Susan Strasberg. Highly charged drama about the passions and intrigues of an Italian family connected with the Mafia. Douglas, complete with dark hair and handlebar moustache, gives a very strong performance as a syndicate leader who has to run away to Sicily after killing his younger brother's father-in-law. (Dir: Martin Ritt, 96 mins.)†

Brotherhood of Justice, The (MTV 1986)** Keanu Reeves, Lori Loughlin, Kiefer Sutherland, Joe Spano, Darren Dalton, Evan Mirand. Vigilantism, high-school style. A group of bright students take it upon themselves to form a vigilante group to control the low-life elements who have contributed to the deterioration of their school. (Dir: Charles Braverman, 104 mins.)

Brotherhood of Satan (1971)**½ Strother Martin, L. Q. Jones. Martin has a field day in this devil-go-round horror movie set in the Southwest. A local coven needs only one more possessed child to continue their Satan-filled activities. (Dir: Bernard McEveety, 92 mins.)†

Brotherhood of the Bell, The (MTV 1970)**½ Glenn Ford, Rosemary Forsyth, Dean Jagger, Maurice Evans, Will

Geer, William Conrad, Dabney Coleman. Professor Ford loses his young wife, his father, all his possessions, and his reputation in a battle to expose a secret college alumni group whose political machinations have gotten out of control. (Dir: Paul Wendkos, 100 mins.)

Brotherhood of the Rose (MTV 1989)*** Peter Strauss, Robert Mitchum, David Morse, Connie Sellecca. Agents Strauss and Morse are marked for termination by Mitchum, the CIA boss who recruited them from orphanages, when they stumble across his plot for world domination. Violent, fast-moving spy yarn. (Dir: Marvin J. Chomsky, 192 mins.)

Brotherhood of the Yakuza, The—See: **Yakuza, The**

Brother John (1970)** Sidney Poitier, Beverly Todd, Will Geer, Bradford Dillman. Here's a lesser Poitier effort. He plays an angel who returns to his hometown in Alabama to see how the folk are faring in this day and age of hate and violence. (Dir: James Goldstone, 94 mins.)†

Brotherly Love (Great Britain, 1970)*** Peter O'Toole, Susannah York, Michael Craig, Harry Andrews, Brian Blessed. Unhappy tale of a Scottish nobleman's descent into insanity. O'Toole is brilliant as the unbalanced peer; York is fine as his abnormally beloved sister. (Dir: J. Lee Thompson, 112 mins.)

Brotherly Love (MTV 1985)***½ Judd Hirsch, Karen Carlson, George Dzundza. Hirsch does double-duty playing lookalike brothers with the bad twin out to dust off his better half. Ernest Tidyman's script is all menace, as the diabolical plotting of this psychopath unfolds with edge-of-the-seat suspense. (Dir: Jeff Bleckner, 104 mins.)†

Brother Orchid (1940)***½ Edward G. Robinson, Ann Sothern, Humphrey Bogart, Donald Crisp. Hysterically funny film about a gangster who takes refuge in a monastery and learns some things about life. You'll have a lot of fun with this one especially if you happen to catch it after exposure to some of the rough gangster pictures of the era. (Dir: Lloyd Bacon, 91 mins.)

Brother Rat (1938)***½ Eddie Albert, Wayne Morris, Priscilla Lane, Ronald Reagan, Jane Wyman. Side-splitting comedy about life in a military school. A tremendous hit on Broadway and equally good in this screen version. Remade as a musical, *About Face* (1952). (Dir: William Keighley, 90 mins.)

Brother Rat and a Baby (1940)** Eddie Albert, Jane Wyman, Ronald Reagan. Good performances don't help this weak script cash in on the success of *Brother Rat*. (Dir: Ray Enright, 87 mins.)

Brothers (1977)* Vonetta McGee, Bernie Casey, Ron O'Neal, Renny Roker. Self-righteous film about the relationship between Angela Davis and convict George Jackson. Loaded with agitprop and overheatedly written and directed. (Dir: Arthur Brown, 105 mins.)

Brothers in Law, The (Great Britain, 1957)**½ Richard Attenborough, Ian Carmichael, Terry-Thomas, Jill Adams, John Le Mesurier. Bumbling young lawyer Attenborough beats the system in this funny satire of the complex British legal profession; players make it fun. (Dir: Roy Boulting, 94 mins.)

Brothers Karamazov, The (1958)**½ Yul Brynner, Maria Schell, Lee J. Cobb, Claire Bloom, William Shatner. Handsomely mounted drama, based on Dostoyevsky's classic. The cast is very good, particularly Lee Cobb. Film is overlong and episodic. Fans of the book will probably find fault with director Richard Brooks's screenplay, but it's still better than most adaptations. (146 mins.)†

Brothers Karamazov, The (U.S.S.R., 1968)***½ Mikhail Ulianov, Lionella Pyrieva, Kirill Lavrov, Andrei Myahkov. Dostoyevski's novel about the effect a father's murder has on his three sons is brought to the screen in a meticulously faithful, sweeping, wide-screen epic, filled with great performances and lavish sets. Oscar-nominated film was completed by stars Ulianov and Lavrov after the death of director Ivan Pyriev during shooting. (220 mins.)

Brothers Rico, The (1957)**½ Richard Conte, Dianne Foster. Fairly well-done crime drama with good performances by the principals. Plenty of action. Remade as TV movie *The Family Rico*. (Dir: Phil Karlson, 100 mins.)

Brother Sun, Sister Moon (1973)**½ Alec Guinness, Graham Faulkner, Judi Bowker, Valentina Cortese. OK, it is sappy spiritual platitudinizing, but the production values are sumptuous and sedulous, which compensates for the story about St. Francis of Assisi. One of those pleasant, dumbfounding works spawned full bloom from a mutant strain of flower children. Songs by Donovan. (Dir: Franco Zeffirelli, 121 mins.)†

Broth of a Boy (Great Britain, 1959)*** Barry Fitzgerald, Tony Wright, June Thorburn. Entertaining comedy about a TV producer who discovers the oldest man in the world, tries to get him on his video show. (Dir: George Polleck, 77 mins.)

Browning Version, The (Great Britain, 1951)**** Michael Redgrave, Jean Kent,

Nigel Patrick. An extraordinarily brilliant and moving performance by Michael Redgrave in the title role makes this Terence Rattigan story a memorable film about a stuffy professor of English at a boys' school who learns of his wife's affair with another teacher as he prepares to leave the school for another teaching post. (Dir: Anthony Asquith, 90 mins.)

Brubaker (1980)**½ Robert Redford, Yaphet Kotto, Jane Alexander, Morgan Freeman, Murray Hamilton. Redford stars as a loner-hero, an idealistic warden who attempts to reform prison conditions only to torpedo his own efforts for the sake of an obscure moral principle. Based on the experiences of Thomas O. Murlan, dismissed as superintendent of the Arkansas State Penitentiary in 1968 after his humane prison reforms embarrassed then Gov. Winthrop Rockefeller. (Dir: Stuart Rosenberg, 130 mins.)†

Brushfire (1962)* John Ireland, Everett Sloane, Jo Morrow. Melodramatic account of guerrilla skirmishes in Vietnam reflects the naive American dogma of the times. (Dir: Jack Warner, Jr., 80 mins.)

Brute Force (1947)***½ Burt Lancaster, Yvonne DeCarlo, Howard Duff, Ann Blyth, Hume Cronyn. Expertly made prison drama. Prisoners plan to pull off a prison break and get even with a sadistic guard captain. (Dir: Jules Dassin, 98 mins.)

Brute Man, The (1946)** Rondo Hatton, Jane Adams, Tom Neal, Jan Wiley, Donald MacBride. Football player, disfigured in an accident, seeks revenge on those he holds responsible. But his heart melts for a blind pianist who can't see his ugliness. Last film and only starring appearance for Hatton, who died that year of the acromegaly that produced his distorted features. (Dir: Jean Yarbrough, 58 mins.)†

B.S. I Love You (1971)**½ Peter Kastner, Jo Anna Cameron, Louise Sorel, Joanna Barnes, Gary Burghoff. Saucy little flick spotlighting an ad man (Kastner) lost among the spice of life—a fiancée, an eighteen-year-old temptress and her mother, his boss (Barnes). (Dir: Steven Stern, 99 mins.)

Bubble, The (1966)** Michael Cole, Deborah Walley, Johnny Desmond, Vic Perrin. Honeymooning couple become trapped in a rural town covered by a giant bubble and filled with zombielike citizens. Vague sci-fi drama designed to show off a short-lived 3-D process. Originally 112 mins. AKA: **Fantastic Invasion of Planet Earth, The**. (Dir: Arch Obler, 91 mins.)

Buccaneer, The (1938)*** Fredric March,

Francisca Gaal, Akim Tamiroff, Walter Brennan. Although this isn't one of C. B.'s better known epics, this swashbuckler about Jean Laffite fighting the British in 1812 is fast-paced and spectacular. (Dir: Cecil B. DeMille, 124 mins.)

Buccaneer, The (1958)*** Yul Brynner, Inger Stevens, Charlton Heston, Charles Boyer, Claire Bloom. Jean Lafitte the pirate comes to the aid of Andy Jackson during the War of 1812. Generally good performances and lavish production make this good big-scale adventure stuff. (Dir: Anthony Quinn, 120 mins.)†

Buchanan Rides Alone (1958)*** Randolph Scott, Craig Stevens, Jennifer Holden. Rugged western with strong plot, good cast and generally far more entertaining than usual western film fare. (Dir: Budd Boetticher, 78 mins.)

Buck and the Preacher (1972)*** Sidney Poitier, Harry Belafonte, Cameron Mitchell, Ruby Dee. Poitier and Belafonte work well together, but the mood is odd. Starts as drama, mood lightens and becomes more entertaining. The duo play escaped slaves heading west, and Cameron Mitchell plays the sly villain. Poitier's first directorial effort. (102 mins.)†

Buckaroo Banzai—See: **Adventures of Buckaroo Banzai Across the Eighth Dimension, The**

Buck Benny Rides Again (1940)**½ Jack Benny, Ellen Drew. Routine comedy that employed Jack's radio character Buck Benny. (Dir: Mark Sandrich, 82 mins.)

Bucket of Blood, A (1959)**½ Dick Miller. Barboura Morris. Far-out sculptor gets a macabre idea on how to improve his artwork. Sick, sick, sick horror-comedy that's interesting, in a repulsive way. Screenplay by Charles Griffith, who wrote *Little Shop of Horrors* (1960). (Dir: Roger Corman, 66 mins.)†

Buck Privates (1941)*** Abbott & Costello, the Andrews Sisters, Shemp Howard. This film certified Abbott and Costello as topflight stars, and although there isn't a fresh joke in the movie, the recycled burlesque routines are still funny. (Dir: Arthur Lubin, 84 mins.)†

Buck Privates Come Home (1947)** Abbott & Costello, Tom Brown. Ex-GIs take care of a French war orphan. Typical A & C slapstick. (Dir: Charles Barton, 77 mins.)

Buck Rogers in the 25th Century (1979)* Gil Gerard, Erin Gray, Pamela Hensley. Revamped tongue-in-cheek story of the comic strip hero who wakes up in the 25th century amidst voluptuous females and sinister villains. (Dir: Daniel Haller, 88 mins.)†

Bud and Lou (MTV 1978)*** Buddy Hackett, Harvey Korman, Michele Lee,

Robert Reed. A sad but revealing biopic. The backstage lives and tumultuous careers of the famous comedy team of Abbott and Costello, beginning with their burlesque and vaudeville days, through their successful movie career. (Dir: Robert C. Thompson, 104 mins.)†

Buddies (1985)**½ Geoff Edholm, David Schachter. A poignant low-budget drama about a young man who volunteers his spare time as a "buddy" to help care for a dying person with AIDS. (Dir: Arthur J. Bressan, Jr., 81 mins.)

Buddy, Buddy (1983)** Jack Lemmon, Walter Matthau, Paula Prentiss. Boring, boring! This Americanized version of the French *A Pain in the A*-- features Matthau as an impatient hitman who meets a whiny Lemmon, distressed over the breakup of his marriage. (Dir: Billy Wilder, 96 mins.)†

Buddy Holly Story, The (1978)***½ Gary Busey, Don Stroud, Charles Martin Smith, Bill Jordan, Maria Richwine, Conrad Janis, Dick O'Neill. Another Hollywood biopic, this time about the innovative rocker who died in an airplane crash in 1959 at the ripe old age of 22. The power of this Hollywood "musical docudrama" is due to the riveting and galvanizing performance by Gary Busey portraying Holly in the late '50s. Busey is himself a part-time rock musician. He's full-time fabulous in this one. (Dir: Steve Rash, 114 mins.)†

Buddy System, The (1984)**½ Richard Dreyfuss, Susan Sarandon, Nancy Allen, Jean Stapleton, Wil Wheaton. A slight but agreeable romantic trifle about two people who're afraid to commit themselves after being burned by unsatisfying affairs. Opting for friendship instead of passion, the couple nonetheless fall in love, provoking a few laughs and some facile sentiment along the way. (Dir: Glenn Jordan, 110 mins.)†

Buffalo Bill (1944)**½ Joel McCrea, Maureen O'Hara, Linda Darnell, Anthony Quinn, Thomas Mitchell. One of the first epic westerns in color, this is a biographical spectacle without much drama. (Dir: William Wellman, 90 mins.)†

Buffalo Bill and the Indians or Sitting Bull's History Lesson (1976)***½ Paul Newman, Joel Grey, Shelley Duvall, Geraldine Chaplin, Burt Lancaster, Kevin McCarthy, Harvey Keitel. Robert Altman's eccentric, ambitious, flawed but invariably interesting Bicentennial offering, a visually stunning celebration of his understandable conviction that the business of America is and has been, for a long time, show business! Screenplay by Altman and Alan Rudolph presents a different version of William F. Cody's exploits during the Presidency of Grover Cleveland than you have seen in Hollywood films before. (125 mins.)†

Buffet Froid (France, 1980)*** Gerard Depardieu, Bernard Blier, Jean Carmet. A consummate dark comedy. Boiling the absurdist plot down isn't easy, but we can assure you that it concerns Depardieu's relation to a murder in a metro station, his wife's subsequent murder, the man who committed them both (Carmet), and a gruff old police inspector (Blier). Top-flight abnormality, from the director who gave us *Menage*. (Dir: Bertrand Blier, 95 mins.)

Bug (1975)** Bradford Dillman, Joanna Miles, Richard Gilliland. What happens when a biology professor mates cockroaches with pyrokinetic insects that emerge from an earthquake rift in a small Western town? Well, if he's Dillman he gets foot-long, man-eating bugs that kill female victims. (Dir: Jeannot Szwarc, 101 mins.)†

Bugles in the Afternoon (1952)*** Ray Milland, Helena Carter. Fast-moving cavalry western about an officer who is demoted but rejoins the service as a private and goes on to become a hero. (Dir: Roy Rowland, 85 mins.)†

Bugle Sounds, The (1941)**½ Wallace Beery, Marjorie Main, Lewis Stone, George Bancroft, Henry O'Neill, Donna Reed, Guinn Williams, William Lundigan. Veteran Cavalry sergeant is at odds with the new mechanized Army. Satisfying comedy-drama with the then-popular team of Beery and Main. (Dir: S. Sylvan Simon, 101 mins.)

Bugs Bunny/Road Runner Movie, The (1979) *** Animated compilation of some of the best Warner Bros. cartoons, whose excellence is acknowledged by any serious cartoon fancier. Bugs himself, in new footage, hosts the selection of madcap examples of Chuck Jones's work, featuring Daffy Duck, Porky Pig, Elmer Fudd, Pepe Le Pew, and the inimitable Road Runner vs. Coyote shorts. Produced and directed by Chuck Jones. (97 mins.)†

Bugs Bunny, Superstar (1975)*** Even those who have never been fans of Warner Brothers' classic cartoons made between 1940 and 1948 will be entranced by the artistry of the "old-fashioned," realistic animation technique, as well as the ageless wisecracking humor. (Dir: Larry Jackson, 90 mins.)†

Bugsy Malone (Great Britain, 1976)** Jodie Foster, Scott Baio, Martin Lev. If you want to see a gangster musical in which all the parts are played by kids, then this film's for you. Otherwise, you may have trouble enjoying this cloying concoction, which isn't helped by Paul Williams songs, nor by most of the children, who seem to be playing dress-up, rather than acting. (Dir: Alan Parker, 93 mins.)†

Bulldance—See: **Forbidden Sun**

Bulldog Drummond series. Herman Cyril McNeile's detective character (introduced in 1920) was particularly well suited to the action series format; Capt. Hugh ("Bulldog") Drummond, the former pride of the British army, had too much adventure in his blood to settle comfortably into civilian life. The silky-voiced Ronald Colman got this series off to a rousing start with *Bulldog Drummond* (1929); and all subsequent entries, even the lower budget ones, strived to be the same kind of briskly paced mystery lark. Fans of the devil-may-care crime smasher should catch the films reviewed below and also: *Calling Bulldog Drummond, Arrest Bulldog Drummond, The Challenge* (1947), *13 Lead Soldiers,* and the later revivals *Deadlier Than the Male* and *Some Girls Do.* (Other series entries exist, including some silent films, but were not included due to their rarity.)

Bulldog Drummond (1929)***½ Ronald Colman, Joan Bennett, Lilyan Tashman. Colman's mellifluous voice and urbane manner may not have suggested the Bulldog Drummond of the printed page, but he certainly made the role all his own onscreen. Bulldog aids a lady whose uncle has been kidnapped by phony psychiatrists. (Dir: F. Richard Jones, 80 mins.)†

Bulldog Drummond at Bay (1947)*½ Ron Randell, Anita Louise, Pat O'Moore. The famous sleuth after valuable diamonds and a murderer. Mediocre mystery. (Dir: Sidney Salkow, 70 mins.)

Bulldog Drummond Comes Back (1937)**½ John Barrymore, John Howard, Reginald Denny, J. Carroll Naish, Louise Campbell. Howard is a comedown from Colman as Drummond. Naish is the villain, and Campbell the girl on whom Drummond has his eye. (Dir: Louis King, 64 mins.)†

Bulldog Drummond Escapes (1937)** Ray Milland, Heather Angel, Sir Guy Standing, Porter Hall, E. E. Clive. Drummond battles a gang of crooks trying to swindle a woman out of her inheritance. Not one of the best of the series—Milland seems strained in the role. (Dir: James Hogan, 65 mins.)†

Bulldog Drummond in Africa (1938)**½ John Howard, Heather Angel, H. B. Warner, J. Carroll Naish, Reginald Denny, E. E. Clive, Anthony Quinn. Diverting entry in which Bulldog shows Scotland Yard how to get their crimes solved. His fiancée involves him in a mystery after she does some amateur sleuthing of her own. (Dir: Louis King, 60 mins.)†

Bulldog Drummond's Bride (1939)** John Howard, Heather Angel, H. B. Warner, Reginald Denny, Eduardo Ciannelli, Elizabeth Patterson. Does marriage mean the end of the crime-solving road when Bulldog finally weds his long-suffering fiancée? (Dir: James Hogan, 55 mins.)†

Bulldog Drummond's Peril (1938)**½ John Howard, John Barrymore, Louise Campbell, Reginald Denny, E. E. Clive. Drummond's wedding plans are postponed when he sets on the trail of a diamond counterfeiter. The plot is too confusing, but Howard and Barrymore work well together. (Dir: James Hogan, 66 mins.)†

Bulldog Drummond's Revenge (1937)**½ John Howard, John Barrymore, Louise Campbell, E. E. Clive, Reginald Denny. The formula to a new secret explosive is Drummond's quarry in this fast-paced, enjoyable entry in the series. (Dir: Louis King, 60 mins.)†

Bulldog Drummond's Secret Police (1939)**½ John Howard, Heather Angel, H. B. Warner, Leo G. Carroll, Reginald Denny. Generally snappy programmer in which Bulldog reminisces about his past adventures (lots of flashbacks from other series entries) when not pursuing the mad killer. (Dir: James Hogan, 55 mins.)†

Bulldog Drummond Strikes Back (1934)**** Ronald Colman, Loretta Young, C. Aubrey Smith, Warner Oland. An excellent comedy-suspense film that holds up well today. One of the best of the series. You won't find this detective yarn at all dull. (Dir: Roy Del Ruth, 83 mins.)

Bulldog Jack (Great Britain, 1935)*** Ralph Richardson, Jack Hulbert, Claude Hulbert, Fay Wray. Semi-classic mild British comedy-thriller about a playboy who poses as Bulldog Drummond when the real man is sidelined with an injury; the dandy catches the thieves and rescues the girl. (Dir: Walter Forde, 73 mins.)

Bull Durham (1988)*** Kevin Costner, Susan Sarandon, Tim Robbins, Trey Wilson, Robert Wuhl. A delightfully romantic comedy that spotlights two of America's favorite pastimes—baseball and sex. Sarandon plays a woman utterly obsessed with the sport who each season takes a promising player and gives him the benefit of her experience. But when she tags "Nuke" LaLoosh (Robbins), a pitcher with "a million-dollar arm and a five-cent head," his assigned mentor (played by Costner in his liveliest performance) decides to intercede. Altogether a charming film which will endear even those completely put off by baseball; although it occurs much later than expected, Sarandon and Costner do strike sparks as a screen couple. (Dir: Ron Shelton, 108 mins.)†

Bullet for a Badman (1964)** Audie Murphy, Darren McGavin, Ruta Lee. Ex-

ranger is menaced by an outlaw who threatens to kill him for marrying his ex-wife. (Dir: R. G. Springsteen, 80 mins.)

Bullet for Joey, A (1955)** Edward G. Robinson, George Raft. Ex-gangster is hired to kidnap a scientist. Routine melodrama. (Dir: Lewis Allen, 85 mins.)

Bullet for Pretty Boy, A (1970)* Fabian Forte, Jocelyn Lane, Astrid Warner, Adam Roarke. A beach-blanket biography of gangster Pretty Boy Floyd, played by former pop star Fabian as a nice guy who just found himself in an unfortunate situation. Ludicrous. (Dir: Larry Buchanan, 88 mins.)

Bullet for the General, A (Italy, 1967)** Gian-Maria Volonte, Klaus Kinski. Italians play Pancho Villa and his men during the Mexican Revolution, as an American agent infiltrates the Mexican army in an attempt to arrest the notorious bandit "El Chuncho." (Dir: Damiano Damiani, 115 mins.)†

Bullet Is Waiting, A (1954)**½ Rory Calhoun, Jean Simmons, Stephen McNally, Brian Aherne. Suspense when a lawman and his prisoner are marooned with an old man and his daughter. Melodrama begins well, falls off as it progresses. (Dir: John Farrow, 90 mins.)

Bulletproof (1988)* Gary Busey, Darlanne Fluegel, Henry Silva, Thalmus Rasulala, L. Q. Jones. Brain-dead action adventure. When Communist forces capture an American super-tank and appear poised to invade, only one man can stop them. (Dir: Steve Carver, 96 mins.)†

Bullets or Ballots (1936)*** Edward G. Robinson, Joan Blondell, Humphrey Bogart. Good racketeering story with customary tough guy performance by Robinson. (Dir: William Keighley, 77 mins.)

Bullfighter and the Lady (1951)***½ Robert Stack, Joy Page, Gilbert Roland. American sportsman visiting in Mexico is intrigued by bullfighting, gets a matador to help him become one. Absorbing drama of the bullring, with suspenseful ring scenes, fine performances. (Dir: Budd Boetticher, 87 mins.)†

Bullfighters, The (1945)** Stan Laurel, Oliver Hardy, Margo Woods, Richard Lane. Stan has a dual role as himself and an arrogant matador, which naturally leads the boys into the ring with a bull. Not one of their best. (Dir: Mal St. Clair, 61 mins.)†

Bullies (Canada, 1986)** Jonathan Crombie, Janet Laine-Green, Stephen Hunter. Predictable, violent revenge thriller that pits a clean-cut new family in town against a sadistic clan that holds the entire community in its grip. Very brutal. (Dir: Paul Lynch, 96 mins.)†

Bullitt (1968)*** Steve McQueen, Robert Vaughn, Jacqueline Bisset. Excellent chase finale would make this film worthwhile by itself but it has more to recommend it . . . not the least being Steve McQueen's aggressive performance as a tough, modern-day police detective involved in the middle of Mafia dealings and political intervention. Well directed by Peter Yates. (113 mins.)†

Bullwhip (1958)**½ Guy Madison, Rhonda Fleming. Guy Madison accepts a shotgun wedding to avoid the gallows in this western, which seems a fair exchange, especially when the bride is lovely Rhonda Fleming. (Dir: Harmon Jones, 80 mins.)†

Bump In the Night (MTV 1991)*** Meredith Baxter-Birney, Christopher Reeve, Wings Hauser, Geraldine Fitzgerald, Shirley Knight. Absorbing drama tackles two diverse but damaging personal problems—alcoholism and pedophilia. Baxter-Birney is a celebrated investigative reporter caught in the throes of alcoholism. Her young son is picked up by a convicted pedophile (Reeve), who pretends to be a friend of the boy's father. Acting honors are shared by Baxter-Birney and Reeve. (Dir: Karen Arthur, 96 mins.)

Bundle of Joy (1956)**½ Debbie Reynolds, Eddie Fisher. Love and songs amid a big department store setting in this light and occasionally amusing comedy. Debbie's cute and Eddie sings. Remake of old Ginger Rogers comedy *Bachelor Mother*. (Dir: Norman Taurog, 98 mins.)†

Bunker, The (MTV 1981)** Anthony Hopkins, Richard Jordan, Piper Laurie, Susan Blakely. A disappointing, overly long drama about Adolf Hitler's final days in a Berlin bunker. Hopkins gives an unconvincing performance as Hitler, the deteriorating leader refusing to admit defeat. (Dir: George Schaffer, 104 mins.)

Bunny Lake Is Missing (1965)**½ Laurence Olivier, Keir Dullea, Carol Lynley, Noël Coward. Mystery-drama: Lynley goes through one nightmare after another as a harried young mother who enlists the aid of Scotland Yard to find her missing daughter. (Dir: Otto Preminger, 107 mins.)

Bunny O'Hare (1971)*½ Bette Davis, Ernest Borgnine, Jack Cassidy. Embarrassing farce about aging bank robbers who make up to look like hippies to stage their holdups and make their getaway on a motorcycle. (Dir: Gerd Oswald, 92 mins.)

Bunny's Tale, A (MTV 1985)** Kirstie Alley, Cotter Smith, Deborah Van Valkenburgh, Diana Scarwid. Gloria Steinem's real-life experiences as an undercover Playboy bunny for a magazine article are transformed into a feminist statement passing for entertainment. While being a Playboy bunny may not be the best job in the world, this exposé portrays them as slave-like sex objects who must endure constant humiliation. (Dir: Karen Arthur, 104 mins.)

Buona Sera, Mrs. Campbell (1968)*** Gina Lollobrigida, Peter Lawford, Shelley Winters, Phil Silvers. A diverting comedy premise, well directed by old pro Melvin Frank. Gina, an Italian mother of a lovely young daughter, has been getting checks from 3 former WWII American romances; each thinks he is the child's father. Some twenty years later, the Air Force veterans come back for a squadron reunion and the fun starts. (111 mins.)

'Burbs, The (1989)*** Tom Hanks, Bruce Dern, Corey Feldman, Rick Ducommun, Brother Theodore, Henry Gibson, Gale Gordon, Dick Miller. Delightfully goofy comedy about a trio of bored suburbanites convinced that their secretive new neighbors are up to no good. Director Joe Dante's best since *Gremlins*. (93 mins.)†

Burden of Dreams (1982)*** Werner Herzog, Klaus Kinski, Claudia Cardinale, Mick Jagger, Jason Robards. This documentary follows West German film director Herzog to the middle of the South American jungle where he attempted the seemingly impossible—to make a movie about a 19th-century Irishman called "Fitzcarraldo," who wanted to build an opera house in the middle of the Amazon jungle. (Dir: Les Blank, 95 mins.)†

Bureau of Missing Persons (1933)**½ Bette Davis, Pat O'Brien, Lewis Stone, Glenda Farrell. Supposed inside story of Missing Persons Bureau never stays in one direction, and gets lost itself. Comedy portion is much more entertaining than dramatic segment. (Dir: Roy Del Ruth, 73 mins.)

Burglar, The (1957)*½ Jayne Mansfield, Dan Duryea, Martha Vickers, Peter Capell, Mickey Shaughnessy. Set in Philadelphia and Atlantic City, the story deals with Duryea and Mansfield as members of a gang of jewel thieves, and Vickers who belongs to another gang trying to hijack the expensive loot. (Dir: Paul Wendkos, 90 mins.)

Burglar (1987)** Whoopi Goldberg, Bob Goldthwait, G. W. Bailey, Lesley Ann Warren. Goldberg plays a San Francisco bookseller moonlighting as a cat burglar in this predictable comedy-drama. Goldthwait gets most of the laughs as her close-to-the-edge confederate. Based on the *Burglar* books of Lawrence Block. (Dir: Hugh Wilson, 98 mins.)†

Burglars, The (France-Italy, 1971)**½ Jean-Paul Belmondo, Omar Sharif, Dyan Cannon. Above-average heist film. Belmondo is the head crook who steals a fortune in emeralds; Sharif is the dishonest and sadistic policeman out to get the jewels for himself; and Cannon is a woman whose loyalties waver between the two of them. (Dir: Henri Verneuil, 120 mins.)

Buried Alive (Italy, 1980)* Kiernan Canter, Cinzia Monreale, Franca Stoppi. Extremely gory Italian thriller about a young taxidermist (his latest project is the body of his first wife), with subplots of necrophilia and incest. It's a favorite of *Gore Gazette;* otherwise, the sole redeeming factor is music by Goblin. (Dir: "Joe D'Amato" [Arstide Massaccesi], 90 mins.)†

Buried Alive (MCTV 1990)*** Tim Matheson, Jennifer Jason Leigh, William Atherton, Hoyt Axton, Jay Gerber. The plot about the scheming oversexed wife enticing her lover to help murder her husband has been done to death, but this clever black comedy effectively revives it with a twist when the supposedly dead (and none-too-happy) husband crawls out of his grave. Good performances, witty script. (Dir: Frank Darabont, 96 mins.)†

Burke and Wills (Australia, 1986)*** Jack Thompson, Nigel Travers, Greta Scacchi. True story of glory-seeking Irishman Robert Burke, who led a doomed trek across the uncharted continent of Australia in 1860 accompanied by a train of men, wagons, horses, and camels. Overlong, and the loss of widescreen on television lessens the film's atmosphere, but still compelling. (Dir: Graeme Clifford, 140 mins.)†

Burmese Harp, The—See: **Harp of Burma**

Burn! (France-Italy, 1970)*** Marlon Brando. Ambitious film about an island in the Caribbean during the mid-19th century, but made in Italy by the Italian director Gillo Pontecorvo, who directed the remarkable *Battle of Algiers*. Story concerns the troubled course of a slave revolt and a small island's battle for nationhood while brutalized and exploited by a succession of colonial powers. AKA: **Queimada**. (112 mins.)†

Burndown (South Africa, 1989)*½ Peter Firth, Cathy Moriarty, Hal Orlandini, Hugh Rouse. Dreary combination of murder mystery and antinuke themes, as a small-town sheriff and big-city reporter investigate murders that seemed to be tied to a nuclear power plant, now shut down. (Dir: James Allen, 87 mins.)†

Burning, The (1981)½ Brian Matthews, Leah Ayres, Brian Backer, Larry Joshua. Another *Friday the 13th* rip-off. Some campers encounter a deranged caretaker who seeks revenge for the torching some kids gave him years ago. (Dir: Tony Maylem, 90 mins.)

Burning Bed, The (MTV 1984)*** Farrah Fawcett, Paul LeMat, Richard Masur, James Callahan. True story of a battered housewife who, at wits' end, sets fire to her ex-husband rather than take another beating. Compelling drama. (Dir: Robert Greenwald, 104 mins.)†

Burning Bridges (MTV 1990)** Meredith Baxter-Birney, Nick Mancuso, Derek de Lint, Lois Chiles, Elizabeth Wilson. Housewife unhappily facing middle age has an affair with her doctor, which she insists on confessing to her husband. Reversal of the usual TV movie formula strives for realism with Baxter-Birney's able performance, but the situations and characters don't ring true. (Dir: Sheldon Larry, 96 mins.)

Burning Cross, The—See: **The Klansman**

Burning Hills, The (1956)*½ Natalie Wood, Tab Hunter. Trite western drama with Tab and Natalie as a pair of young lovers who fight for happiness against a ruthless cattle baron's young son. (Dir: Stuart Heisler, 94 mins.)

Burning Rage (MTV 1984)** Barbara Mandrell, Tom Wopat, Eddie Albert, Bert Remsen, John Pleshette, Carol Kane. Country music's Mandrell and "Dukes of Hazzard'''s Wopat play do-gooders battling a greedy mine owner (Albert) in an Appalachian coal town. (Dir: Gil Cates, 104 mins.)†

Burning Secret (1988)*** Klaus Maria Brandauer, Faye Dunaway, David Eberts, Ian Richardson. Brandauer's acting makes this gloomy story watchable. He plays a mysterious aristocrat who befriends a boy undergoing treatment at an Austrian clinic in 1919. But is his friendship real, or is he using the boy to get to his mother (Dunaway)? (Dir: Andrew Birkin, 107 mins.)†

Burnt Offerings (1976)* Oliver Reed, Karen Black, Burgess Meredith, Eileen Heckart, Bette Davis. Horrendous! When Miss Black and hubby Reed rent a summer house, they're faced with a number of surprises, none of which seem credible. (Dir: Dan Curtis, 106 mins.)†

Burn, Witch, Burn (Great Britain, 1962)*** Janet Blair, Peter Wyngarde. Professor's wife becomes obsessed with witchcraft, is convinced she must die in his place. Well-made supernatural thriller gets good direction helping the plot through its more farfetched phases. (Dir: Sidney Hayers, 90 mins.)

Burroughs (1984)***½ Upfront, lively documentary about the life and work of American writer William Burroughs. Filmmaker Howard Brookner spent four years capturing the essence of the iconoclastic author, revealing fresh details

about his acceptance of drugs and alcohol, his homosexuality, his wife Joan whom he accidentally shot to death, and his moneyed family's ostracism of him at an early age. Best scenes feature Burroughs reading from his own works and commenting on life and love. (86 mins.)†

Bury Me an Angel (1971)*½ Dixie Peabody, Terry Mace, Clyde Ventura, Dan Haggerty, Gary Littlejohn. Female biker sets out to find her brother's killer. Nothing here lives up to the movie's advertising, which promised a "howling hellcat humping a hot steel hog on a roaring rampage of revenge." Those inspired by the presence of a female star and writer-director to look for any feminist message will be disappointed. (Dir: Barbara Peeters, 86 mins.)†

Bush Christmas (Australia, 1947)*** Chips Rafferty. Some school kids run afoul of a couple of thieves on Christmas Day. Highly unusual drama, depicting Yuletide life Down Under. Recommended. (Dir: Ralph Smart, 80 mins.)

Bushido Blade (1980)**½ Richard Boone, Toshiro Mifune, James Earl Jones. In 19th-century Japan, the fabled Bushido Blade is stolen by three samurai opposed to giving it to the U.S.A. as a gift. When three American naval officers are sent to retrieve the sword, they face impending peril. (Dir: Tom Kotani, 92 mins.)

Business as Usual (Great Britain, 1988) ** Glenda Jackson, John Thaw, Cathy Tyson. Well-intentioned but unmoving true story about sexual harassment in the workplace, starring Jackson as a woman fired from her job when she complains about her boss's lechery toward another employee. Cardboard villains lessen the impact. (Dir: Lezli An-Barrett, 92 mins.)†

Bus Is Coming, The (1971)***½ Mike Simms, Stephanie Faulkner, Morgan Jones. Impressive, intelligent low-budget independently produced drama. Made by a group of blacks faced with the issue of school integration in a small California town. (Dir: Horace Jackson, 107 mins.)†

Bus Riley's Back in Town (1965)** Ann-Margret, Michael Parks, Janet Margolin. Youth returns to his home from the Navy determined to make good, resumes an affair with an old flame from the high-rent district. Plodding drama. (Dir: Harvey Hart, 93 mins.)

Bus Stop (1956)*** Don Murray, Arthur O'Connell, Marilyn Monroe, Betty Field, Eileen Heckart. Critics began to recognize Monroe's acting talent in this version of the William Inge play. This small-scale romance between a galoot of a cowboy and an untalented club singer has its tender moments, despite some overly raucous comedy situations. (Dir: Joshua Logan, 96 mins.)†

Busted Up (Canada, 1986)*½ Paul Coufos, Irene Cara, Tony Rosato, Frank Pellegrino, Stan Shaw. A small-time boxer and a gym owner stand up to the mobsters who are trying to force them out so that they can build a health club. (Dir: Conrad E. Palmisano, 91 mins.)†

Buster (Great Britain, 1988)**½ Phil Collins, Julie Walters, Larry Lamb. Collins makes an auspicious acting debut as the one suspect in the Great Train Robbery of 1963 who evaded police capture. But his performance is subsumed by the movie's dreary touting of the virtues of home and family. (Dir: David Green, 93 mins.)†

Buster and Billie (1974)*** Jan-Michael Vincent, Joan Goodfellow. An uneven but perceptive story about high school students in 1948 rural Georgia. Goodfellow is touching as the acquiescent town tramp who finally falls for Buster, played with strength and charm by Vincent. (Dir: Daniel Petrie, 100 mins.)†

Buster Keaton: A Hard Act to Follow (Made for British TV, 1987)*** A reverent, in-depth look at one of the screen's comic geniuses. We follow Buster from his early vaudeville days through his triumphs, downfall, and eventual rediscovery in the 1950s. An entertaining slice of film history. (Dirs: David Gill, Kevin Brownlow, 180 mins.)

Buster Keaton Festival (1922)**** Three of his greatest shorts, *The Boat, The Frozen North,* and *The Electric House,* make up this collection, all comedy classics. (Dir: Buster Keaton, 75 mins.)†

Buster Keaton Rides Again and The Railroader (Canada, 1965)***½ Absolutely priceless compilation of Keaton's last short, made for Canada's National Film Board, and a loving documentary about him that was filmed simultaneously with it, giving a very rare glimpse of the star at work and play. (89 mins.)†

Buster Keaton Scrapbook (1922)**** Buster Keaton, Joe Roberts, Mal St. Clair. Three more of the great comic's classic shorts: *The Pale Face, Daydreams,* and *The Blacksmith,* all endlessly hilarious. (Dir: Buster Keaton, 60 mins.)†

Buster Keaton Story, The (1957)** Donald O'Connor, Ann Blyth, Rhonda Fleming, Peter Lorre. Screen biography of the brilliant movie comedian disregards facts flagrantly, presents an almost totally false impression of Hollywood and its brilliant subject. O'Connor tries hard, is responsible for what little success the film has. (Dir: Sidney Sheldon, 91 mins.)

Buster Keaton TV Scrapbook*** This tape contains Keaton's appearance on the '50s TV show *This Is Your Life,* with Donald O'Connor, and an episode of his own TV series. A must for Keaton fans. (60 mins.)†

Busting (1973)*** Elliott Gould, Robert Blake, Allen Garfield. Commendable attempt to realistically portray the seamy lives of two Los Angeles vice-squad cops. Gould and Blake are the cynical detectives, forced to arrest (or "bust") the small-time addicts and hookers instead of the real kingpins of organized crime because their police department superiors are getting paid off by the big guys. (Dir: Peter Hyams, 92 mins.)

Bustin' Loose (1981)*** Richard Pryor, Cicely Tyson, Robert Christian, Alphonso Alexander, Janet Wong. Pryor is very funny as an ex-con who is pressed into service to drive a busload of orphaned problem kids cross-country to the state of Washington. The kids are hellions, but Pryor is a match for them. (Dir: Oz Scott, 94 mins.)†

Busy Body, The (1967)**½ Sid Caesar, Robert Ryan, Anne Baxter. Fairly funny comedy about bumbling gangsters has Sid Caesar in a role which seems tailored for Jerry Lewis. (Dir: William Castle, 90 mins.)

Butch and Sundance: The Early Days (1979)*** William Katt, Tom Berenger, Jeff Corey, John Schuck, Jill Eikenberry. Muted retrospective imagining of the buddies before the events for which they were immortalized in *Butch Cassidy and the Sundance Kid.* Katt and Berenger struggle manfully with characters that are based on other actors' personalities (Newman and Redford); they acquit themselves respectably. A film of humor, steady style, and intimations of maturity in search of something resembling a subject. (Dir: Richard Lester, 110 mins.)†

Butch Cassidy and the Sundance Kid (1969)***½ Paul Newman, Robert Redford, Katharine Ross. An appealing anti-western directed with great flair by George Roy Hill. Newman and Redford give such ingratiating performances that it's easy to overlook some shortcomings in the original screenplay by William Goldman based on two legendary bank and train robbers who clowned their way through much of the 1890s before fleeing to South America. Graced with a catchy musical score including the award-winning tune "Raindrops Keep Fallin' on My Head." (112 mins.)†

But I Don't Want to Get Married! (MTV 1970)**½ Herschel Bernardi, Shirley Jones, Brandon Cruz, Nanette Fabray, June Lockhart, Tina Louise. Comedy with two things going for it—a fairly good script, and Bernardi as a recent widower who is seen as a prize catch by women in his age bracket. (Dir: Jerry Paris, 72 mins.)

Butley (Great Britain, 1974)*** Alan Bates, Susan Engel, Jessica Tandy, Richard O'Callaghan. Originally an American Film Theater presentation, this is a respectable screen translation of Simon Gray's acerbic serio-comedy about a self-centered professor trying to juggle the various loves in his life. Superb performance by Bates. (Dir: Harold Pinter, 127 mins.)†

But Not for Me (1959)**½ Clark Gable, Carroll Baker, Lilli Palmer. Middle-aged Broadway producer is chased by a young secretary, who doesn't think the difference in age matters. Remake of *Accent on Youth* starts promisingly, loses steam as it progresses. (Dir: Walter Lang, 105 mins.)†

Butterfield 8 (1960)**½ Elizabeth Taylor, Laurence Harvey, Mildred Dunnock, Dina Merrill, Betty Field, Eddie Fisher. Elizabeth Taylor won her first Oscar for her portrayal in this melodrama based on John O'Hara's best-seller about a misguided gal who lets herself go whenever a man enters the scene. Miss Taylor has given far better performances, but there's a glamorous aura about the slick yarn and Laurence Harvey cuts a good romantic figure as Liz's once-in-a-lifetime love. (Dir: Daniel Mann, 109 mins.)†

Butterflies Are Free (1972)*** Goldie Hawn, Edward Albert, Eileen Heckart. The funny and credible Broadway play has been turned into an entertaining film. Goldie Hawn is perfectly cast as a fledgling actress who stumbles into the life of self-sufficient blind boy Edward Albert. Enter the boy's over-protective but genuinely loving mother, brilliantly played by Oscar-winner Heckart, and doubts creep into the relationship. (Dir: Milton Katselas, 109 mins.)†

Butterfly (1982)* Stacy Keach, Pia Zadora, Orson Welles, Lois Nettleton, Edward Albert. Second-rate James Cain novel about backwoods incest becomes a perfectly awful film that you watch with fascination just to see how bad it can become. Pia Zadorable and the supporting cast get through it astonishingly, without smirking. (Dir: Matt Cimber, 108 mins.)†

Butterfly Affair, The (France-Italy, 1970)** Henri Charriere, Georges Arminel, Leroy Haynes, Claudia Cardinale, Stanley Baker. Charriere, whose life story was the basis of the movie *Papillon* (that's French for butterfly), wrote and stars in this heist film about thieves plotting to steal $2 million worth of diamonds in Venezuela. The theft and the behind-the-scenes tensions are pretty familiar

stuff. An abbreviated video version runs 75 mins. (Dir: Jean Herman, 100 mins.)†

Butterfly Revolution, The—See: **Summer Camp Nightmare**

Buy and Cell (1988)*½ Robert Carradine, Michael Winslow, Malcolm McDowell, Lise Cutter, Roddy Piper, Randall "Tex" Cobb, Ben Vereen. Stockbroker Carradine, framed for a stock swindle and sent to prison, gets even from within by carrying on his business with the help of his fellow convicts. The title's the cleverest thing about this otherwise obvious comedy. (Dir: Robert Boris, 95 mins.)†

Buying Time (Canada, 1989)** Jeff Schultz, Page Fletcher, Laura Cruikshank, Dean Stockwell. Two young friends are blackmailed by the police into helping trap the mobsters who murdered their other buddy. Only Stockwell's performance as a manipulative cop lifts this a bit out of the ordinary. (Dir: Mitchell Gabourie, 97 mins.)†

Buy Me That Town (1941)**½ Lloyd Nolan, Albert Dekker, Sheldon Leonard. Comedy about some gangsters who save a town from bankruptcy by using the jail as a refuge for people wanted in other states. Potentially first-rate, but only occasionally amusing. (Dir: Eugene Forde, 70 mins.)

Bwana Devil (1954)*½ Robert Stack, Barbara Britton. Silly jungle film originally made in 3-D is just a bore without visual trickery. (Dir: Arch Oboler, 79 mins.)

By Candlelight (1934)**½ Paul Lukas, Elissa Landi, Nils Asther, Dorothy Revier. Lively bedroom farce with a butler posing as his employer to gain a lady's favors. (Dir: James Whale, 70 mins.)

By Dawn's Early Light (MTV 1990)*** Martin Landau, Powers Boothe, Rebecca De Mornay, James Earl Jones, Darren McGavin, Rip Torn, Peter MacNichol, Jeffrey DeMunn. Plausible and frightening nuclear thriller compares favorably to *Fail Safe* and other sixties films on the subject. A nuclear missile from an unknown source in the Middle East strikes the Soviet Union, and the countdown to global annihilation begins. (Dir: Jack Sholder, 100 mins.)†

By Design (Canada, 1981)** Patty Duke Astin, Sara Botsford, Saul Rubinek, Sonia Zimmer. A gay fashion designer decides she wants to be a mother despite the shock waves her decision will cause. Not designed that carefully by the director. (Dir: Claude Jutra, 88 mins.)†

Bye Bye Baby (Italy, 1988)** Carol Alt, Jason Connery, Brigitte Nielsen, Luca Barbareschi. Comic sexual round robin involving nurse Alt, her conniving husband, a young doctor, and a billiards champion. A bit better than you'd expect, though too much depends on your desire to gaze at models Alt and Nielsen. (Dir: Enrico Oldoini, 80 mins.)†

Bye, Bye Birdie (1963)**½ Dick Van Dyke, Janet Leigh, Ann-Margret, Maureen Stapleton, Paul Lynde, Bobby Rydell, Ed Sullivan. A clumsy but cheerful musical spoof of Elvismania, adapted from the Broadway hit about the hysteria surrounding a teen singing idol's last appearance before his Army induction. The pleasant score, which includes "I've Got a Lot of Living to Do" and "Put on a Happy Face," compensates for the occasional missteps into low comedy. (Dir: George Sidney, 111 mins.)†

Bye Bye Blues (Canada, 1989)*** Rebecca Jenkins, Michael Ontkean, Luke Reilly, Stuart Margolin, Robyn Stevan, Kate Reid. Woman whose husband is lost and possibly dead in WWII joins an up and coming jazz band. Flavorful period piece with feminist overtones. (Dir: Anne Wheeler, 118 mins.)

Bye Bye Braverman (1968)***½ George Segal, Jack Warden, Alan King, Godfrey Cambridge. Warm-hearted attempt by director Sidney Lumet to create a comedy on the mores of would-be Jewish intellectuals in New York City. Focuses on a day when a group of friends attend Braverman's funeral. (94 mins.)

Bye Bye Brazil (Brazil, 1980)*** Jose Wilker, Betty Faria. Carlos Diegues's lush travelogue on modern-day Brazil traverses sufficiently variegated terrain to keep its thin saga of a traveling carnival troupe engaging. There are grand theatrical flourishes to the threadbare show-biz of the Lord Gypsy and his Salome, Queen of the Rhumba. The naïveté of the young couple who join up with them is a bit tiresome, though Diegues's view of his native land is never sentimental. (Dir: Carlos Diegues, 110 mins.)†

By Love Possessed (1961)**½ Lana Turner, Efrem Zimbalist, Jr., Thomas Mitchell, Jason Robards, Jr., George Hamilton. Wealthy attorney realizes his domestic life is not all it should be, is drawn into an affair with the equally lonely and discontented wife of his crippled partner. Controversial novel made into a lackluster film. (Dir: John Sturges, 115 mins.)

By the Light of the Silvery Moon (1953)*** Doris Day, Gordon MacRae. Songs, dances, and a good amount of nostalgia enrich this turn-of-the-century musical comedy. Doris and Gordon make sweet music together. (Dir: David Butler, 102 mins.)

Cabaret (1972)**** Liza Minnelli, Joel Grey, Michael York, Helmut Griem,

Marissa Berenson. A knockout. One of the most brilliant musicals ever made and certainly the definitive version of Christopher Isherwood's 1939 book about life in pre–WWII Berlin. Its handling of the political material during the time of Hitler's rise to power is done with style and integrity. Bob Fosse's direction is inspired throughout. (124 mins.)†

Cabinet of Caligari (1962)½ Glynis Johns, Dan O'Herlihy, Dick Davalos. Impeccably dressed Johns runs desperately through a mental institution, pausing only for badly filmed dream sequences. An aberration! (Dir: Roger Kay, 105 mins.)

Cabinet of Dr. Caligari, The (Germany, 1919)*** Werner Krauss, Conrad Veidt, Lil Dagover, Friedrich Feher. The earliest and purest German Expressionist film features a scary plotline about a carnival hypnotist (Krauss) who uses his somnambulist (Veidt) for evil doings. The heavy stylization is still striking, particularly in the surprise resolution. (Dir: Robert Wiene, 69 mins.)†

Cabin in the Cotton (1932)**½ Richard Barthelmess, Bette Davis, Henry B. Walthall, Dorothy Jordan, Tully Marshall. A poor sharecropper is almost brought to ruin when he starts to run with rich-bitch Southern belle Davis (in her best early performance). The film's attitudes are severely dated, but the sadistic twinge in director Michael Curtiz's style holds up remarkably well. (77 mins.)

Cabin in the Sky (1943)*** Eddie Anderson, Ethel Waters. For his first shot at directing, Vincente Minnelli was given a throwaway MGM property with an all-black cast. Anderson gets his one great chance to act and perform, and he is ably matched by Waters as the woman who helps him choose God over Satan. (99 mins.)†

Cabiria—See: **The Nights of Cabiria**

Cable Car Murder, The (MTV 1971)**½ Robert Hooks. Well-made San Francisco cops-and-robbers film features a '70s style murder story. Inspector Louis Van Alsdale (Hooks) takes on the Establishment over the murder of a shipping magnate's son. (Dir: Jerry Thorpe, 78 mins.)

Caboblanco (1980)*½ Charles Bronson, Jason Robards, Jr., Dominique Sanda, Simon MacCorkindale, Fernando Rey, Denny Miller. Any resemblance to *Casablanca* is purely intentional and totally undeserved. Bronson plays a surly barkeep, and a colorful bunch floats in and out of his establishment when they're not searching for a cache of gold. (Dir: J. Lee Thompson, 87 mins.)†

Cactus (Australia, 1986)**½ Isabelle Huppert, Robert Menzies. European woman vacations in Australia where she has an accident that may cost her her eyesight. Her loving relationship with a blind cactus grower opens her eyes to facing her emotional problems squarely and coming to terms with her impairment. Technically brilliant, but the film never elicits our full sympathy for the unfocused central character. (Dir: Paul Cox, 95 mins.)†

Cactus Flower (1969)**½ Walter Matthau, Ingrid Bergman, Goldie Hawn. Disappointing adaptation of the Broadway hit comedy despite an Oscar-winning debut by Goldie Hawn. Matthau plays a dentist who is having an affair with Goldie, while not admitting to himself that he really loves his nurse (Bergman). (Dir: Gene Saks, 103 mins.)†

Caddie (Australia, 1976)** Helen Morse, Takis Emmanuel, Jack Thompson. The tribulations of a middle-class woman evicted from her home by her philandering husband and her efforts to support her children as a barmaid. Should have had more punch than this. (Dir: Donald Crombie, 107 mins.)†

Caddy, The (1953)** Dean Martin, Jerry Lewis, Donna Reed. Jerry's a golf hopeful who's afraid of crowds. Not the team's best. (Dir: Norman Taurog, 95 mins.)†

Caddyshack (1980)**½ Chevy Chase, Ted Knight, Rodney Dangerfield, Bill Murray. Comedy set in an exclusive country club should have been better. However, Murray's running battle with oversized gophers borders on the surreal, and there are a number of equally hilarious moments scattered throughout, mainly from Rodney Dangerfield. (Dir: Harold Ramis, 90 mins.)†

Caddyshack II (1988)*½ Jackie Mason, Dyan Cannon, Robert Stack, Dina Merrill, Chevy Chase, Dan Aykroyd. The original had no plot but enough scattered laughs to compensate; this sequel has neither. Mason is relied on to carry far too much of the film, although Chase and Aykroyd manage to be thoroughly annoying with the brief screen time they have. (Dir: Allan Arkush, 103 mins.)†

Cadence (1991)** Charlie Sheen, Martin Sheen, Ramon Estevez, Larry Fishburne. Life in a 1965 army work camp as directed by veteran actor Martin Sheen (his directorial debut). Rebellious soldier (Charlie) is sent to a stockade run by an authoritative sergeant (his dad, Martin) and a wimpy warden (his brother, Ramon). Flawed drama has a positive note on racial harmony. (Dir: Martin Sheen, 97 mins.)†

Cadillac Man (1990)*** Robin Williams, Tim Robbins, Pamela Reed, Fran Drescher, Zack Norman, Anabella Sciorra, Lori Petty. Williams is superb as a Queens car salesman with an overbooked love life and a precarious career. Those and other troubles come to a boil when a confused young man (Robbins) crashes into Williams's showroom and holds everyone hostage at gunpoint. (Dir: Roger Donaldson, 97 mins.)†

Caesar and Cleopatra (Great Britain, 1945)*** Vivien Leigh, Claude Rains, Stewart Granger. Bernard Shaw's intellectual joke about the aging Roman conqueror and the beautiful but slightly addle-brained beauty of the Nile. Some of the Shavian wit has been preserved, but there are dull stretches. (Dir: Gabriel Pascal, 127 mins.)†

Café Express (Italy, 1980)**½ Nino Manfredi, Adolfo Celi, Vittorio Mezzogiorno. Mediocre Italian import takes place on a train, and concerns a nice guy (Nino Manfredi) selling coffee to passengers illegally. (Dir: Nanni Loy, 89 mins.)†

Café Metropole (1937)*** Tyrone Power, Loretta Young, Adolphe Menjou. Amusing comedy about a young man who is forced to pose as a prince in order to make good on a gambling debt. The phony prince, played by Tyrone, is ordered by his creditor to woo and win an heiress, played by Loretta. (Dir: Edward H. Griffith, 83 mins.)

Café Society (1939)**½ Madeleine Carroll, Fred MacMurray, Shirley Ross. Spoiled society girl marries a reporter on a bet and learns all about love. Typical '30s comedy, well played and sprightly. (Dir: Edward H. Griffith, 84 mins.)

Cage, The—See: **Mafu Cage, The**

Cage, The (1989)* Lou Ferrigno, Reb Brown, Michael Dante, Marilyn Tokuda. Exploitation action about "cage fighting," in which two men battle to the death while locked in a steel cage. (Dir: Lang Elliott, 101 mins.)†

Caged (1950)***½ Eleanor Parker, Hope Emerson, Jan Sterling. Gripping drama of women's prison. Eleanor Parker runs the gamut from young innocent bystander sentenced for theft to hard and bitter convict. Hope Emerson, as the cruel police matron, equals Parker's great performance. Remade as *House of Women* (1962). (Dir: John Cromwell, 91 mins.)

Caged Fury (1984)* Bernadette Williams, Jennifer Laine, Taffy O'Connell. Women held prisoner by the Vietnamese are brainwashed and turned into assassins. Philippines-made potboiler that even fans of the women-in-prison genre should keep locked up. (Dir: Cirio H. Santiago, 84 mins.)†

Caged Fury (1990)** Erik Estrada, Richie Barathy, Roxanna Michaels, Ty Randolph, Paul Smith, James Hong, Michael Parks,

Jack Carter, Ron Jeremy. Clichéd but lively women's prison movie with Michaels as the innocent midwestern girl who comes to Hollywood seeking stardom and instead lands in prison as part of a white slavery scheme. (Dir: Bill Milling, 95 mins.)†

Caged Heart, The—See: L'Addition

Caged Heat (1974)*** Juanita Brown, Roberta Collins, Erica Gavin, Barbara Steele. Assigned to turn out another "women's prison" picture for producer Roger Corman, director Jonathan Demme instead came up with this imaginative B movie that renovated the entire genre. Sure, there's the standard "caged" plotline, where a woman is innocently imprisoned and corrupted behind the walls, but how many other exploitation features have exciting breakout action, Barbara Steele in a wheelchair, a fine John Cale score, and surrealist dream sequences? (83 mins.)†

Caged in Paradise (1989)** Irene Cara, Peter Kowanko, Paula Bond, Joseph Culp, Big John Studd. Women on a prison island, with a sci-fi twist: The island is surrounded by lasers, preventing anyone from taking too lengthy a swim. Cara is the obligatory innocent subject to nameless cruelties and dangers. (Dir: Mike Snyder, 90 mins.)†

Caged Women (Italy-France, 1984)*½ Laura Gemser, Gabriele Tinti, Lorraine de Selle. Sex'n'violence vehicle for Italo exploitation star Gemser as a reporter investigating conditions in a women's prison. Nastier than most of the women-in-prison genre. From the director of *Night of the Zombies*. (Dir: "Vincent Dawn" [Bruno Mattei], 96 mins.)†

Cage of Gold (Great Britain, 1950)**½ Jean Simmons, David Farrar, Herbert Lom. An old flame, who's a scoundrel, returns to blackmail a girl now happily married. (Dir: Basil Dearden, 83 mins.)

Cage Without a Key (MTV 1975)**½ Susan Dey, Michael Brandon, Sam Bottoms. The theme of this film—how a poorly run juvenile detention home can turn teenagers into hardened criminals—is strengthened by firm direction that avoids sensationalism. Dey plays a naïve youngster, making the transition into a tough little punk, thanks to her fellow inmates. (Dir: Buzz Kulik, 100 mins.)

Cagney & Lacey (MTV 1981)** Loretta Swit, Tyne Daly, Al Waxman. Swit and Daly star as a pair of cops elevated into plainclothes work. But the ladies have to prove themselves at home, in the precinct, and on the street, and must outwit their peers by solving a diamond broker murder. (Dir: Ted Post, 104 mins.)

Cahill: U.S. Marshal (1973)*½ John Wayne, Gary Grimes, George Kennedy, Neville

Brand. Tiresome attempt to flesh out the usual Wayne-western plots by saddling him with two sons who get involved with bank robbers and murderers because Daddy isn't home enough to guide their moral upbringing. (Dir: Andrew V. McLaglen, 102 mins.)†

Cain and Mabel (1936)**½ Marion Davies, Clark Gable, Guy Kibbee. Showgirl Davies meets Gable, and surprise! They fall in love. It's a hackneyed story, but it gives you a chance to see Miss Davies's considerable charm. (Dir: Lloyd Bacon, 90 mins.)

Caine Mutiny, The (1954)*** Humphrey Bogart, Jose Ferrer, Van Johnson, Fred MacMurray, Lee Marvin, E. G. Marshall. An all-star cast effectively brings this tale of a modern mutiny to the screen. Bogart is a standout as Captain Queeg, the skipper of the *Caine*. (Dir: Edward Dmytryk, 125 mins.)†

Caine Mutiny Court-Martial, The (MTV 1988)*** Eric Bogosian, Jeff Daniels, Brad Davis, Peter Gallagher, Michael Murphy. This version of the Wouk play about the prosecution of a wartime rebellion against an unbalanced captain succeeds by not overly venerating its source. Without theatrics, the story slowly grabs you. Good work by Bogosian as the defense attorney who lets Queeg (Davis, effectively prissy and self-righteous) destroy himself. (Dir: Robert Altman, 96 mins.)

Cairo (1942)** Jeanette MacDonald, Robert Young, Ethel Waters, Mona Barrie. Silly, romantic MacDonald vehicle about an actress suspected of being a Nazi spy by a newspaper reporter (Young). (Dir: W. S. Van Dyke II, 101 mins.)

Cal (Great Britain, 1984)*** Helen Mirren, John Lynch, Donal McCann, John Kavenhagh. A young Irish Roman Catholic (Lynch) is recruited into Irish Republican Army terrorist activities and falls in love with the widow (Mirren) of an executed Protestant policeman. Though somber and depressing, the film is skillfully done, bringing much needed insight into a topical and complex situation. (Dir: Pat O'Connor, 102 mins.)†

Calamity Jane (1953)***½ Doris Day, Howard Keel, Allyn Ann McLerie, Phil Carey. A sunny musical comedy about the dynamic first lady of the American frontier. Day has a field day as the rough-and-tumble Calamity who makes up in big-heartedness what she lacks in refinement. (Dir: David Butler, 101 mins.)†

Calamity Jane (MTV 1984)**½ Jane Alexander, Frederic Forrest, David Hemmings. Ms. Alexander's "Calamity" is not the tomboy next door as depicted in previous movies and musicals, but a grimy, gritty, independent woman who prides herself on being able to compete with men on an equal basis. (Dir: James Goldstone, 104 mins.)†

Calamity Jane and Sam Bass (1949)*½ Yvonne DeCarlo, Howard Duff. Mediocre western about the two celebrated figures of the wild and woolly West. Miss DeCarlo overacts throughout, and the rest of the cast underplay as if they were afraid of her. (Dir: George Sherman, 85 mins.)

Calcutta (1947)**½ Alan Ladd, Gail Russell, June Duprez, William Bendix. Old-fashioned intrigue as Ladd tries to get even when his buddy's bumped off. Standard, but compact and satisfying. (Dir: John Farrow, 83 mins.)

Calendar Girl Murders, The (MTV 1984)**½ Robert Culp, Tom Skerritt, Barbara Parkins, Sharon Stone. Who's killing those girlie magazine centerfolds? If you enjoy girl watching and a minor mystery, tune in. (Dir: William A. Graham, 104 mins.)

California (1947)*** Ray Milland, Barbara Stanwyck, Anthony Quinn. Rip-roaring western set in early California when greedy men did not want the territory to become a state. (Dir: John Farrow, 97 mins.)

California Conquest (1952)**½ Cornel Wilde, Teresa Wright, Alfonso Bedoya. Spanish Californians, under Mexican rule, almost end up in the hands of the Russians in this fast paced western drama. (Dir: Lew Landers, 79 mins.)

California Dreaming (1979)* Seymour Cassel, Glynnis O'Connor, Dennis Christopher. Senseless updating of the sixties beach flicks. Mopey Christopher is a sweet young kid from Chicago, and he yearns to achieve California surf set status. (Dir: John Hancock, 92 mins.)†

California Girls (1981)* Al Music, Lantz Douglas, Mary McKinley. Feeble plot (California radio station sponsors beauty contest) is little more than an excuse for nonstop shots of babes in bikinis set to a Top Forty soundtrack. (Dir: William Webb, 83 mins.)†

California Girls (MTV 1985)** Robbie Benson, Martin Mull, Martha Longley, Charles Rocket, Doris Roberts. Standard wish fulfillment with Robbie Benson playing a disenchanted guy from New Jersey who travels to California looking for the idealized golden California girl. (Dir: Rick Wallace, 104 mins.)

California Gold Rush (MTV 1981)**½ Robert Hays, John Dehner, Henry Jones, Gene Evans, Ken Curtis. Cast saves this picture about a newly built town besieged by greedy gold prospectors. Robert Hays strikes the right chord as an ambitious young writer who heads west to follow the gold rush. (Dir: Jack B. Hively, 104 mins.)†

California Kid, The (MTV 1974)**½ Martin Sheen, Vic Morrow, Michelle Phillips, Stuart Margolin. Sheen and Morrow are pitted against each other throughout this tense drama about a sheriff who is a one-man judge, jury, and executioner in dealing with speeders on the highway. (Dir: Richard Heffron, 72 mins.)

California Split(1974)***½ Elliott Gould, George Segal, Ann Prentiss, Gwen Welles. The title is western-slang jargon for cutthroat high-low poker. Robert Altman has fashioned here one of his most entertaining, compelling, and powerful films. Gould and Segal work beautifully together as two parasitical gamblers, and the scenes in the poker parlor capture the compulsive quality of the frenzied souls down on their luck. (111 mins.)

California Straight Ahead (1937)** John Wayne, Louise Latimer, Tully Marshall. John is an ambitious young truck driver trying to prove that trucks can get the goods there faster than railroads. (Dir: Arthur Lubin, 67 mins.)

California Suite (1978)***½ Michael Caine, Maggie Smith, Jane Fonda, Alan Alda, Walter Matthau, Elaine May, Richard Pryor, Bill Cosby. An all-star cast in an excellent adaptation of Neil Simon's play by Simon himself. Four stories about guests at the Beverly Hills Hotel are intertwined, the best being the bittersweet relationship between actress Smith and her gay antique dealer husband Caine. (Dir: Herbert Ross, 103 mins.)†

Caligula (1980)½ Malcolm McDowell, Peter O'Toole, Teresa Ann Savoy, Helen Mirren, Sir John Gielgud, Guido Mannar. Sickening mixture of hard-core pornography and gore amid corny dramatics and lavish sets allegedly depicting ancient Rome. Writer Gore Vidal and director Tinto Brass understandably told producer Bob Guccione to remove their names from the credits. (156 mins.)†

Call a Messenger (1939)** Billy Halop, Huntz Hall, William Benedict. Billy Halop tries to keep himself and his sister on the straight and narrow in this nicely paced but routine programmer. (Dir: Arthur Lubin, 65 mins.)

Callaway Went Thataway (1951)*** Fred MacMurray, Dorothy McGuire, Howard Keel. Funny film about a western hero whose career is revitalized by TV showings of his early films. (Dirs: Norman Panama, Melvin Frank, 81 mins.)

Call Her Mom (MTV 1972)*½ Connie Stevens, Van Johnson, Charles Nelson Reilly, Jim Hutton, Gloria De Haven. College campus show with Stevens as a peppery fraternity housemother. Mixing 1970 college problems with an early

147

1950s atmosphere, the show attempts a spoof, but lands with a thud. (Dir: Jerry Paris, 73 mins.)

Call Her Savage (1932)**½ Clara Bow, Monroe Owsley, Thelma Todd. Fast-paced comeback for the troubled Bow, a wow here as a young woman who doesn't know that her wild nature is the result of her being half-Indian. Inanely racist melodrama was a bomb then, though it's fun now in an antiquated way. (Dir: John Francis Dillon, 88 mins.)†

Call Him Mr. Shatter (Great Britain-Hong Kong, 1976)*½ Stuart Whitman, Ti Leung, Lily Li, Peter Cushing, Anton Diffring. Weak spy-cum-kung-fu movie casts Whitman as an international hit man on assignment in Hong Kong. (Dir: Michael Carreras, 90 mins.)†

Callie and Son (MTV 1981)** Lindsay Wagner, Jameson Parker, Dabney Coleman, Joy Garrett, Michelle Pfeiffer, John Harkins. Long-winded Texas yarn about a naïve waitress who becomes a Dallas power broker. (Dir: Waris Hussein, 156 mins.)†

Calling Bulldog Drummond (Great Britain, 1951)**½ Walter Pidgeon, Margaret Leighton. Drummond comes out of retirement and with the aid of a police-woman smashes a crime ring. (Dir: Victor Saville, 80 mins.)

Calling Doctor Death (1943)*** Lon Chaney, Patricia Morison. Effective little thriller, with Chaney as a distinguished doctor whose wife has a yen for other fellows. When the cheating wife is murdered, there are suspects aplenty. (Dir: Reginald Le Borg, 63 mins.)

Calling Dr. Gillespie (1942)** Lionel Barrymore, Donna Reed, Phil Brown, Nat Pendleton, Alma Kruger. No Dr. Kildare here. Just an extra slice of Lionel Barrymore's ham as Gillespie takes on a new protégé interested in psychiatry as a madman stalks Blair General. (Dir: Harold S. Bucquet, 82 mins.)

Calling Dr. Kildare (1939)**½ Lionel Barrymore, Lew Ayres, Laraine Day, Nat Pendleton, Lana Turner. Here, Kildare works the out-patient department of a big city hospital where he gets a crash course in practical patient care. (Dir: Harold S. Bucquet, 86 mins.)

Calling Homicide (1956)**½ William Elliot, Kathleen Case. Cop investigating the death of a fellow policeman uncovers blackmail in a modeling school. Neat little mystery merits praise for achievement on a small budget. (Dir: Edward Bernds, 61 mins.)

Calling Philo Vance (1940)*½ James Stephenson, Margot Stevenson, Henry O'Neill, Martin Kosleck. Lackluster revamping of *The Kennel Murder Case* with the added topical kick of some

WWII spying tossed in. (Dir: William Clemens, 62 mins.)

Call It a Day (1937)*** Ian Hunter, Freida Inescort, Olivia de Havilland, Anita Louise, Roland Young, Bonita Granville, Peggy Wood. Unexpectedly delightful comedy of one day in the life of a middle-class British family whose members are unexpectedly struck by spring fever. An unknown gem. (Dir: Archie Mayo, 89 mins.)

Call It Murder (1934)*½ Humphrey Bogart, Sidney Fox, Henry Hull. Top-billed, Bogart only plays a supporting part. A jury foreman, responsible for sending a woman to the electric chair, has his beliefs tested when a similar circumstance occurs within his family. AKA: Midnight. (Dir: Chester Erskine, 74 mins.)†

Call Me (1988)*½ Patricia Charbonneau, Patti D'Arbanville, Sam Freed, Boyd Gaines, Steven McHattie. Confused erotic thriller. The tension starts (or is supposed to start) when an obscene phone call plunges Charbonneau into a world of drug deals, corrupt cops, and disconnected lust. (Dir: Sollace Mitchell, 95 mins.)†

Call Me Anna (MTV 1990)**½ Patty Duke, Jenny Robertson, Ari Meyers, Karl Malden, Howard Hesseman, Deborah May, Millie Perkins. Patty Duke's autobiographical account of her rise in show business as a child actress and her lifelong bout with manic depression. It's an honest and brave retelling, but the book is much better. (Dir: Gilbert Cates, 96 mins.)

Call Me Bwana (Great Britain, 1963)**½ Bob Hope, Anita Ekberg, Edie Adams. Hope chased by foreign agents once more as he tries to recover a lost capsule. Hope springs eternal and he has some good gags. (Dir: Gordon Douglas, 103 mins.)

Call Me Madam (1953)***½ Ethel Merman, Donald O'Connor, George Sanders, Billy De Wolfe, Walter Slezak, Vera-Ellen. Snappy stage musical about the free-wheeling Washington "hostess with the mostess." The tunes are fine, the production colorful; Merman fans will be in heaven, of course. (Dir: Walter Lang, 117 mins.)

Call Me Mister (1951)**½ Betty Grable, Dan Dailey, Danny Thomas, Dale Robertson. Dailey was always playing song-and-dance men who had to make up with their wives, and if he made the sinful life plausible, he also made it wholesome, usually because the wife was Grable. Set in Japan during what is tactfully not referred to as "the occupation." (Dir: Lloyd Bacon, 95 mins.)

Call Northside 777 (1947)***½ James

Stewart, Lee J. Cobb, Richard Conte, Helen Walker, E. G. Marshall. Exciting, fast-paced story of a newspaperman who proves a man innocent by probing an eleven-year-old case history. A bit implausible toward the end but you'll like it. (Dir: Henry Hathaway, 111 mins.)

Call of the Flesh, The (1931)*** Ramon Novarro, Dorothy Jordan, Renée Adorée, Ernest Torrance. Old-fashioned but enjoyable early musical stars the multitalented Novarro, who dances, juggles, and sings up a storm as a young Spanish cabaret singer with operatic aspirations. Several excellent operatic numbers including an aria from Massenet's *Manon* AKA: **The Singer of Seville.** (Dir: Charles Brabin, 90 mins.)

Call of the Wild (1935)*** Clark Gable, Loretta Young, Jack Oakie, Reginald Owen, Frank Conroy. Ingratiating version of the Jack London classic, altered to accommodate the romantic interest of virile Gable and scrumptious Young. (Dir: William Wellman, 100 mins.)

Call of the Wild (1972)** Charlton Heston, Michele Mercier, Maria Rohm, Rik Battaglia. Rugged action tale based on Jack London's classic. Weakest of the three adaptations reviewed here. (Dir: Ken Annakin, 100 mins.)†

Call of the Wild (MTV 1976)*** John Beck, Bernard Fresson, John McLiam, Donald Moffat. Gripping version of the Jack London adventure novel about gold fever in the Yukon of 1903, with a script by James Dickey. As in the book, the real star is Buck, the sled dog, who struggles against the selfish greed of the prospectors as well as against the forces of nature. (Dir: Jerry Jameson, 100 mins.)†

Call Out the Marines (1942)**½ Edmund Lowe, Victor McLaglen. Two thickheads round up foreign agents. Funny comedy, boisterous and bawdy. (Dirs: Frank Ryan, William Hamilton, 67 mins.)

Call to Danger (MTV 1973)**½ Peter Graves. Slick outing by ''Mission: Impossible'' writer-producer Laurence Heath, featuring Graves as a Justice Department sleuth, who retrieves a mobster kidnapped by thugs during crime hearings held in Washington. (Dir: Tom Gries, 73 mins.)

Call to Glory: JFK (MTV 1985)** Craig T. Nelson, Cindy Pickett, C. Thomas Howell. This TV movie involves the characters from the cancelled TV series ''Call to Glory'' during the days preceding and following the assassination of President Kennedy. (Dir: Peter Levin, 104 mins.)

Caltiki, the Immortal Monster (Italy, 1960)** John Merivale. Archaeologists and corpses of Mayans from the seventh century come to grips. The kids who like their chills on the wild side might enjoy this one. (Dir: Robert Hampton, 76 mins.)

Came a Hot Friday (New Zealand, 1985)*** Peter Bland, Philip Gordon, Billy T. James. A lightweight con man comedy set in 1949 about two racetrack touts who run various scams while not using their wiles on every woman within reach. Blessedly free of pretensions, this old-fashioned caper film ambles along pleasantly and delivers its laughs with a refreshingly jaunty air. (Dir: Ian Mune, 100 mins.)†

Camel Boy, The (Australia, 1984)*** Voices of Barbara Frawley, Ron Haddrick, John Meillon, Michael Pate. Animated feature about an Arab boy who treks across the Great Victoria desert with his grandfather, a camel driver. Good animated characters combined with real-life Australian settings make this one to bring home for the family. (Dir: Yoram Gross, 78 mins.)†

Camelot (1967)** Richard Harris, Vanessa Redgrave, David Hemmings, Franco Nero. Disappointing but opulent, well-acted version of the Lerner and Loewe musical about the Knights of the Round Table. Joshua Logan's plodding direction of this $15 million epic is relieved by the magnetic performances of Harris and Redgrave, with the latter displaying her special magical brand of beauty, femininity, and strength. (179 mins.)†

Cameron's Closet (1988)** Cotter Smith, Mel Harris, Scott Curtis, Chuck McCann, Leigh McCloskey, Tab Hunter. As a result of his father's joint experiments in psychokinetics and demon worship, a boy becomes the gateway into this world for a monster. Tense atmosphere is spoiled by disappointing special effects (by the usually reliable Carlo Rambaldi). (Dir: Armand Mastroianni, 87 mins.)†

Camila (Argentina-Spain, 1984)***½ Susu Pecoraro, Imanol Arias, Hector Alterio, Elena Tasisto. An impassioned true tale about a Catholic Argentine woman who runs afoul of her repressive government and her Church, when both of those institutions take action against her love affair with a priest. Political points are scored incidentally; the film concentrates on a torrid love story that heats up the screen with a passion that is palpable. (Dir: Maria Luisa Bemberg, 105 mins.)†

Camille (1936)**** Greta Garbo, Robert Taylor, Lionel Barrymore, Henry Daniell, Elizabeth Allan, Laura Hope Crews. Garbo shines as Marguerite Gautier, the courtesan who finds true love and then sacrifices it for the sake of her callow beloved. She is sublime as the bountiful

149

free spirit who gives as generously of her purse as she does her heart. As the youthful swain Armand, Taylor is, if anything, more beautiful than Garbo (but not remotely in her league). (Dir: George Cukor, 108 mins.)†

Camille (MTV 1984)**½ Greta Scacchi, Colin Firth, John Gielgud, Denholm Elliott, Ben Kingsley. Decent remake of the Greta Garbo 1936 classic. (Dir: Desmond Davis, 104 mins.)

Camille 2000 (1969)** Daniele Gaubert, Eleanora Rossi-Drago, Nino Castelnuovo, Philippe Forquet. Classic Dumas *fils* tale goes erotic as this Camille, dying of what seems to be a venereal disease instead of tuberculosis, sleeps with every earl in the court (and a few Bobs and Johns too), all the while lusting for her true love, Armand. Cheap sets and bad acting add camp value. (Dir: Radley Metzger, 115 mins.)†

Camille Claudel (France, 1989)*** Isabelle Adjani, Gerard Depardieu, Laurent Crevill, Alain Cluny. Biography of the unheralded French sculptress who began as aide and mistress to Auguste Rodin and spent the last decades of her life in an asylum. Even at this length (it originally ran 174 mins.), film seems to have missed details, concentrating instead on visualizing the visceral appeal of sculpture. But Oscar nominee Adjani (in a role reminiscent of *The Story of Adelle H.*) and Depardieu make it a watchable, if overlong, biopic. (Dir: Bruno Nuytten, 149 mins.)†

Camorra: The Naples Connection (Italy, 1985)**½ Angela Molina, Francisco Rabal, Harvey Keitel, Vittorio Squillante. Director Lina Wertmuller says no to drugs in this violent and complicated tale of Italian mothers taking the fight against organized crime into their own hands. Sensationalistic and lurid, charged with Wertmuller's passion, though the film's mounting body count wearies the viewer. (106 mins.)†

Camouflage (Poland, 1976)*** Piotr Garlicki, Zbigniew Zaasiewicz. Pointed satire about the bureaucratic infighting and failed dreams plaguing college faculty members at a linguistics seminar; the film deftly takes swipes at communism as well. (Dir: Krzysztof Zanussi, 106 mins.)

Campbell's Kingdom (Great Britain, 1957)*** Dirk Bogarde, Stanley Baker. Young landowner battles a crooked contractor. Typical western plot transplanted to Canada—still plenty of action, elaborate production values. (Dir: Ralph Thomas, 102 mins.)

Camp on Blood Island, The (Great Britain, 1958)*** Carl Mohner, André Morell. Fair drama with horror overtones. Pris-

oners try to escape from a Japanese camp during WWII. (Dir: Val Guest, 81 mins.)

Campus Man (1987)** John Dye, Steve Lyon, Kim DeLaney, Kathleen Wilhoite, Miles O'Keeffe, Morgan Fairchild, John Welsh. A fast-talking business student talks his handsome athlete pal into posing for a beefcake calendar, which results in the jock being yanked off the diving team. Tame teen comedy. (Dir: Ron Casden, 94 mins.)†

Canadian Pacific (1949)**½ Randolph Scott, Jane Wyatt. A surveyor fights all odds to get the railroad through the wilderness. Outdoor melodrama has enough action to receive a passing grade. (Dir: Edwin L. Marin, 95 mins.)

Canary Murder Case, The (1929)**½ William Powell, Louise Brooks, James Hall, Jean Arthur. Powell made his Philo Vance debut here. A Broadway entertainer is strangled, and Philo has additional murders on his hands before he figures out whodunit. An artifact, but a classy-looking one, and Powell's work hasn't dated. (Dir: Malcolm St. Clair, 82 mins.)

Can-Can (1960)**½ Frank Sinatra, Shirley MacLaine, Maurice Chevalier, Juliet Prowse, Louis Jourdan. Lawyer protects a café owner when she's accused of presenting the Can-Can, a supposedly lewd dance. Although musical fans will be entertained, this Cole Porter musical lumbers across the screen with emphasis upon the razzle dazzle. Unfortunately, the score isn't one of his best and the script lacks true wit. (Dir: Walter Lang, 131 mins.)

Cancel My Reservation (1972)* Bob Hope, Eva Marie Saint, Ralph Bellamy, Forrest Tucker, Keenan Wynn. Talky, moribund comedy about a talk show host who becomes entangled in a murder case in Arizona. Hope's one-liners die a slow death, and the cast performs as if it were doing penance. (Dir: Paul Bogart, 99 mins.)†

Candidate, The (1972)***½ Robert Redford, Melvyn Douglas, Peter Boyle, Karen Carlson, Allen Garfield. Refreshing, earnest, and quite entertaining. Redford as the vacuous U.S. Senate candidate who gradually becomes aware of his vacuity—not too many steps ahead of the audience, but way ahead of the voting public—turns in one of his best performances. Many of those involved, including director Michael Ritchie and screenwriter Jeremy Larner, were in real political campaigns during the late '60s, and they've captured some of the look and feel of such campaigns. (109 mins.)†

Candles at Nine (Great Britain, 1944)*½ Jessie Matthews, John Stuart, Beatrix Lehmann, Reginald Purdell. Greedy relatives try to cheat a young singer out of her inheritance while she is fulfilling the one condition of her uncle's will—that she live for one month in his spooky old house. Creaky British mystery complete with a song from popular music hall star Matthews. (Dir: John Harlow, 84 mins.)†

Candleshoe (1977)** Jodie Foster, David Niven, Helen Hayes. Unexceptional detective yarn about a junior miss hunting for treasure in an English estate. (Dir: Norman Tokar, 101 mins.)†

Candy (1968)* Ewa Aulin, Richard Burton, Charles Aznavour, James Coburn, Marlon Brando, Ringo Starr, Walter Matthau. More novelty than entertainment when Brando, Matthau, Burton, Coburn, and Starr all pursue Ewa Aulin as the befuddled young girl who can't understand what the fuss is all about. Sort of like sitting through a two-hour cartoon in "Playboy." (Dir: Christian Marquand, 113 mins.)

Candy Mountain (Switzerland-Germany, 1988)** Kevin J. O'Connor, Harris Yulin, Bulle Ogier. Slow-moving story of a young musician (O'Connor) who sets out to make a name for himself by finding a master guitar maker (Yulin). Brief appearances by several noted singers—David Johansen, Tom Waits, Dr. John, and Leon Redbone—provide the film's only bright spots; O'Connor doesn't have the charisma needed to sustain this downbeat "road movie." (Dirs: Robert Frank, Rudy Wurlitzer, 91 mins.)†

Can Ellen Be Saved? (MTV 1974)**½ Kathy Cannon, Michael Parks. Young girl gets caught up with a religious group who live and work on a commune until her worried parents enlist help. (Dir: Harvey Hart, 72 mins.)

Can Heironymus Merkin Ever Forget Mercy Humppe and Find True Happiness? (Great Britain, 1969)*½ Anthony Newley, Joan Collins, Milton Berle, George Jessel. X-rated, surreal tale about an entertainer (Newley) reaching a mid-life crisis, which makes him relive his torrid past. Sometimes clever, sometimes dull ego trip that was written, directed, and produced by Newley. (117 mins.)

Cannery Row (1982)*** Nick Nolte, Debra Winger, M. Emmet Walsh, Audra Lindley. A feisty girl (Winger) and a marine biologist (Nolte) fight their feelings for each other while the colorful inhabitants of Cannery Row (romanticized prosties and low-lifes) play matchmaker. A colorful, stylish journey through Steinbeck's stories "Cannery Row" and "Sweet Thursday." (Dir: David Ward, 120 mins.)†

Cannibal Attack (1954)** Johnny Weissmuller, Judy Walsh, David Bruce, Bruce Cowling. Complicated Jungle Jim pic

about cannibals selling cobalt to villainous foreign powers. (Dir: Lee Sholem, 69 mins.)

Cannibal Girls (Canada, 1973)** Eugene Levy, Andrea Martin, Ronald Ulrich, Randall Carpenter. Horror parody with two of SCTV's finest helping flesh out the tongue-in-cheek scenario. A couple find themselves in a strange restaurant where one of them may be on the menu. (Dir: Ivan Reitman, 84 mins.)

Cannibal Holocaust (Italy, 1979)½ Francesca Ciardi, Luca Barbareschi, Robert Krerman. Pretty much the nadir of the subgenre of Italian gross-out horror movies. Made on location in Africa, this film pretends to be documentary footage shot by greedy American filmmakers who prompt natives to commit atrocities on camera. With footage of animals being killed and people tortured, this is definitely one to keep away from the kids (and everyone else). (Dir: Ruggero Deodato, 95 mins.)†

Cannibal Women in the Avocado Jungle of Death (1988)**½ Shannon Tweed, Adrienne Barbeau, Bill Maher, Barry Primus. Parody of "Indiana Jones"–type adventure movies with anthropologist Tweed investigating the lost tribe of Piranha Women, a bunch of feminist maneaters (literally). Plenty of literary "in" jokes and campy humor enliven this talky low-budget production. (Dir: J.D. Athens, 89 mins.)†

Cannon (MTV 1971)**½ William Conrad, Vera Miles, Keenan Wynn, Earl Holliman, Barry Sullivan. Conrad stars as a private investigator who travels to New Mexico to solve a war buddy's murder. (Dir: George McCowan, 99 mins.)

Cannonball (1976)**½ David Carradine, Bill McKinney, Veronica Hamel, Gerrit Graham. The reward is $100,000 to the driver reaching New York first on a race from Los Angeles. Exciting and action-packed, it should appeal to those who enjoy this type of vehicular violence. Martin Scorsese has a small role as a mafioso. (Dir: Paul Bartel, 93 mins.)†

Cannonball Run (1981)½ Burt Reynolds, Roger Moore, Dom DeLuise, Farrah Fawcett, Dean Martin, Sammy Davis, Jr., Jack Elam, Adrienne Barbeau, Jackie Chan. Yahoo comedy about a cross-country auto race appears to have been produced simply to give Reynolds and every Hollywood friend he had a chance to pal around. They seem to have had fun, but it's not contagious to the viewer. (Dir: Hal Needham, 90 mins.)†

Cannonball Run II (1984) ½ Burt Reynolds, Dom DeLuise, Shirley MacLaine, Marilu Henner, Dean Martin, Sammy Davis, Jr., Susan Anton, Catherine Bach, Jim Nabors, Ricardo Montalban, Frank Sinatra. More of the same, with an endless parade of cameos by more third-rate "celebrities" than we're willing to list here making this look like an SCTV parody of *It's a Mad, Mad, Mad, Mad World.* One more sequel, *Speed Zone,* was yet to come. (Dir: Hal Needham, 108 mins.)†

Cannon for Cordoba (1970)**½ George Peppard, Giovanna Ralli, Raf Vallone, Peter Duel. It's Peppard vs. the banditos as he heads a contingent of soldiers safeguarding the Texas border in 1912. Routine, but action-packed and energetic. (Dir: Paul Wendkos, 104 mins.)

Canon City (1948)*** Scott Brady, Jeff Corey, Whit Bissell. Exciting true story of an escape from the Colorado prison told in semidocumentary style and filmed where it happened. (Dir: Crane Wilbur, 82 mins.)

Can She Bake a Cherry Pie? (1983)** Karen Black, Michael Emil, Michael Margotta. A rambling character comedy that urban sophisticates may appreciate. Others will find this overly precious and tedious. The performers are capable in this tale of a movie-loving man and a would-be songstress who hang out in cafes and grow to appreciate each other. (Dir: Henry Jaglom, 90 mins.)†

Can't Buy Me Love (1987)*½ Patrick Dempsey, Amanda Peterson, Courtney Gains. Nerdish Dempsey gives fox Peterson $1,000 to date him for a month in order to upgrade his image. Originally titled *Boy Rents Girl,* this one's for Poverty Row. (Dir: Steve Rash, 94 mins.)†

Canturbury Tale, A (Great Britain, 1944)*** Eric Portman, Dennis Price, Sheila Sim, Esmond Knight, Charles Hawtry. A deep strain of patriotism animates this seemingly simple story of a variety of people in a village near Canturbury Cathedral during WWII; the camera lingers on the pastoral beauty and timeless way of life threatened by the Nazis. Many strange touches from the writing-producing-directing duo of Michael Powell and Emeric Pressburger. (124 mins.)

Canterbury Tales, The (Italy, 1971)*** Pier Paolo Pasolini, Hugh Griffith, Laura Betti, Tom Baker, Ninetto Davoli, Josephine Chaplin, Jenny Runacre. Selected tales from Chaucer, with emphasis on the Merchant and the Wife of Bath. Part of director Pasolini's medieval trilogy (in between *The Decameron* and *The Arabian Nights*), it has his stamp of aggressive bawdiness—so much that it was declared obscene by the Italian courts. (109 mins.)†

Canterville Ghost, The (1944)*** Charles Laughton, Robert Young, Margaret O'Brien. Amusing little whimsy about a cowardly ghost who can only be released from his haunting chores when a descendant performs a deed of bravery. Laughton is wonderful as the ghost. (Dir: Jules Dassin, 96 mins.)

Canterville Ghost, The (MTV 1986)**½ Sir John Gielgud, Ted Wass, Andrea Marcovicci, Alyssa Milano. Middling remake featuring Milano as the girl who encounters a spooky ancestor (Gielgud in a truly spirited turn). Tries to be scary, but the plot contrivances get in the way. Screenplay co-written by mystery novelist Sue Grafton. (Dir: Paul Bogart, 96 mins.)†

Can't Help Singing (1944)**½ Deanna Durbin, Robert Paige. Strong-willed girl trails her sweetheart west. Pleasant but uneven costume musical. Jerome Kern tunes help. (Dir: Frank Ryan, 89 mins.)

Can't Stop the Music (1980)*½ The Village People, Valerie Perrine, Bruce Jenner, Barbara Rush. Compulsively watchable for its awful, sunny crassness. Subject and stars are the Village People, a gay disco group for straights. (Dir: Nancy Walker, 118 mins.)†

Canyon Crossroads (1955)**½ Richard Basehart, Phyllis Kirk. Uranium prospectors are beset by crooks when they make a strike. Interesting western with a modern touch. (Dir: Alfred L. Werker, 84 mins.)

Canyon Passage (1946)*** Dana Andrews, Susan Hayward, Brian Donlevy. Good western. Dana loves Susan, who is his buddy Brian's fiancée. There's an Indian battle and, of course, Donlevy obligingly dies to let Dana kiss Susan. (Dir: Jacques Tourneur, 99 mins.)

Can You Feel Me Dancing? (MTV 1986)** Justine Bateman, Roger Wilson, Jason Bateman, Max Gail, Frances Lee McCain, Susan Rinnell. Predictable tale about a blind girl endeavoring to lead a normal life despite her family's oversolicitousness. (Dir: Michael Miller, 104 mins.)

Can You Hear the Laughter? The Story of Freddie Prinze (MTV 1979)*** Ira Angustain, Kevin Hooks, Julie Carmen. Screen biography of the Puerto Rican comic who rose from the barrio to superstardom in TV in a short time, and then took his life. (Dir: Burt Brinkerhoff, 106 mins.)†

Cape Canaveral Monsters, The (1960)½ Scott Peters, Linda Connell. Two people survive a traffic accident only to be turned into fiends who communicate with extraterrestrials. From the director of *Robot Monster,* though not quite *that* bad. (Dir: Phil Tucker, 71 mins.)

Cape Fear (1962)*** Gregory Peck, Robert Mitchum, Polly Bergen. Brutal tale of a revenge-seeking convict preying upon the sensibilities of the lawyer who sent him to prison. Excellent performances, with a brilliant study in sadism by Mitchum as the meanie. (Dir: J. Lee Thompson, 105 mins.)†

Caper of the Golden Bulls (1967)*** Stephen Boyd, Yvette Mimieux, Walter Slezak, Vito Scotti, Clifton James. Ex-criminal Boyd is blackmailed into aiding in a jewel heist during the famous running of the bulls in Pamplona, Spain. Location footage and a taut climax overcome a slow beginning. (Dir: Russell Rouse, 104 mins.)†

Capital News (MTV 1990)** Lloyd Bridges, Mark Blum, Christian Clemson, Kurt Fuller, Kathryn Harrold, Wendell Pierce, Daniel Roebuck, William Russ, Helen Slater, Jenny Wright, Beah Richards. Interesting characters and stock situations at a fictitious Washington, D.C. newspaper. Pilot for a large-ensemble show spends much time setting the series up and therefore isn't completely satisfying viewed as a separate movie. (Dir: Mark Tinker, 96 mins.)

Capone (1975)** Ben Gazzara, Susan Blakely, John Cassavetes. Gazzara plays Capone with imagination and a case of hypertension. Excessive shootouts and violence. (Dir: Steve Carver, 101 mins.)

Caprice (1967)** Doris Day, Richard Harris, Ray Walston, Jack Kruschen. Pure escapist film fare. The plot involves espionage, complete with double agents, undercover men, and a line-up of international villains. (Dir: Frank Tashlin, 98 mins.)

Capricorn One (1978)*** James Brolin, Elliott Gould, Sam Waterston. Imaginative adventure flick about a mission to Mars by the U.S. space program that turns out to be faked. (Dir: Peter Hyams, 127 mins.)†

Captain America (MTV 1979)* Reb Brown, Heather Menzies, Len Birman. The Marvel comic book hero, Captain America, tested the TV waters and sank. Steve Rogers (Brown) follows in the footsteps of his famous crime-fighting dad, thanks to the super-steroid FLAG—"full latent ability gain." (Dir: Rod Holcomb, 104 mins.)†

Captain Black Jack—See: **Black Jack** (1950)

Captain Blood (1935)***½ Errol Flynn, Olivia de Havilland, Lionel Atwill, Basil Rathbone, Ross Alexander. Exciting adaptation of the Sabatini adventure story. This was Mr. Flynn's first major starring picture and he was happily welcomed by critics and fans. Pass up the colorized version. (Dir: Michael Curtiz, 99 mins.)†

Captain Boycott (Great Britain, 1947)***½ Stewart Granger, Kathleen Ryan, Cecil Parker. When a landowner in Ireland threatens his tenants with eviction, the farmers decide to fight. Lusty historical melodrama moves with speed, has fine performances. (Dir: Frank Launder, 92 mins.)

Captain Carey, U.S.A. (1950)**½ Alan Ladd, Wanda Hendrix, Francis Lederer. OSS agent returns to Italy after WWII to track down the man who had betrayed him to the Nazis. Fairly competent; also includes the Oscar-winning best song "Mona Lisa." (Dir: Mitchell Leisen, 85 mins.)

Captain Caution (1940)** Victor Mature, Louise Platt, Bruce Cabot. A girl takes over her father's ship and battles the British during the War of 1812. Lots of action here, and if you don't blink you'll see Alan Ladd in a small role. (Dir: Richard Wallace, 85 mins.)

Captain China (1949)** John Payne, Gail Russell, Jeffrey Lynn. Payne tries to clear himself of false charges that have cost him his captaincy. More than the usual share of exciting sea storms for action fans. (Dir: Lewis Foster, 97 mins.)

Captain Eddie (1945)**½ Fred MacMurray, Lynn Bari. Famous aviator's life is used as an excuse for a routine sentimental comedy-drama covering most of this century. Rickenbacker's story is pleasant enough. (Dir: Lloyd Bacon, 107 mins.)

Captain from Castile (1947)** ½ Tyrone Power, Jean Peters, Lee J. Cobb, Cesar Romero, Thomas Gomez, Alan Mowbray, Barbara Lawrence, George Zucco, Marc Lawrence. Overlong, color adventure saga starring Power as an ambitious man out to strike it rich in the New World. A lot of spectacle and a ground-breaking score by Alfred Newman are the compensations. (Dir: Henry King, 140 mins.)

Captain Fury (1939)*** Brian Aherne, Paul Lukas, Victor McLaglen. A brave soldier of fortune fights the villainous heads of early Australia's penal colony. Rousing action film, highly enjoyable. (Dir: Hal Roach, 90 mins.)

Captain Hates the Sea, The (1934)**½ John Gilbert, Walter Connolly, Victor McLaglen, Helen Vinson. Among the passengers on a cruise are a sea-hating skipper, a tippling reporter, cops, and crooks. Snappy comedy with some screwball touches. (Dir: Lewis Milestone, 92 mins.)

Captain Horatio Hornblower (Great Britain, 1951)***½ Gregory Peck, Virginia Mayo. Sprawling sea saga about the British captain of the Napoleonic wars—his naval victories and his loves. From the novel by C. S. Forester. Robust, exciting, colorful. (Dir: Raoul Walsh, 117 mins.)

Captain Is a Lady, The (1940)** Charles Coburn, Beulah Bondi. Well-acted but minor comedy about an old man who insists on being with his wife in an old ladies' home. (Dir: Robert B. Sinclair, 63 mins.)

Captain January (1936)** Shirley Temple, Guy Kibbee. Shirley is an orphan again and the mean old law is trying to take her away from her wonderful guardian. (Dir: David Butler, 75 mins.)†

Captain Kidd (1945)** Charles Laughton, Randolph Scott, Barbara Britton, Reginald Owen, John Carradine, Gilbert Roland. A ''Yo-ho-ho and a bottle of rum'' pirate flick. The famous Captain Laughton hams it up with gusto, but the film lacks action and vigor. (Dir: Rowland V. Lee, 89 mins.)

Captain Kronos: Vampire Hunter (1974)*** Horst Janson, John Carson, Caroline Munro, Shane Briant. Writer-director Brian Clemens translates the stylish panache of his ''Avengers'' series to the dashing exploits of a Nordic vampire killer. Fantastic swordplay and black humor abound as Kronos takes on a group of the life-draining monsters, headed by his undead fencing foe. (91 mins.)†

Captain Lightfoot (1955)**½ Rock Hudson, Barbara Rush. Beautifully filmed period adventure about rebellion in Old Ireland of the 1800s. Rock Hudson fits his adventurer's role to a T and Miss Rush offers fine feminine support. (Dir: Douglas Sirk, 90 mins.)

Captain Nemo and the Underwater City (Great Britain, 1970)**½ Robert Ryan, Chuck Connors, Nanette Newman. There are enough spurts of action and wondrous sights to keep this nautical children's tale fairly entertaining. Ryan is Captain Nemo, whose underwater empire is visited by shipwrecked people, including a U.S. Senator (Connors) and a feminist (Miss Newman). (Dir: James Hill, 106 mins.)

Captain Newman, M.D. (1963)*** Gregory Peck, Tony Curtis, Angie Dickinson, Eddie Albert, Bobby Darin. Interesting drama of an air-force psychiatrist whose duty is to his patients first, the military brass second. Well-done vignettes are used as a substitute for any strong plotline, with some good performances helping considerably. (Dir: David Miller, 126 mins.)†

Captain Pirate (1952)** Louis Hayward, Patricia Medina, John Sutton, Ted de Corsia, George Givot. More about Captain Blood, the doctor-turned-pirate. Colorful, conventional action tale. (Dir: Ralph Murphy, 85 mins.)

Captain Scarlett (1953)** Richard Greene, Lenora Amar, Nedrick Young, Manolo Fabregas. Standard grade-B swashbuckler finds young rebel fighting royal tyranny with the help of a runaway princess in post-Napoleonic France. (Dir: Thomas Carr, 75 mins.)†

Captains Courageous (1937)*** Spencer Tracy, Freddie Bartholomew, Lionel Barrymore, Mickey Rooney, Melvyn Douglas.

Rudyard Kipling's story of a spoiled rich boy who falls overboard from an ocean liner and gets picked up by fishermen who teach him humility and the value of honest toil. Director Victor Fleming couldn't overcome the embalming impulses of MGM studio style. Tracy, with a thick Portuguese accent, somehow won the Oscar for Best Actor. (116 mins.)†

Captains Courageous (MTV 1977)**½ Karl Malden, Jonathan Kahn, Johnny Doran. More faithful to Kipling, but lacks the excitement of the '37 film. (Dir: Harvey Hart, 104 mins.)

Captain Sinbad (1963)*** Guy Williams, Heidi Bruhl, Pedro Armendariz, Abraham Sofaer, Bernie Hamilton. Top-notch special effects dominate this colorful, monster-filled fairy tale. Simple but entertaining plot of Sinbad's brave mission to save a beautiful princess who, among other misfortunes, is nearly squashed by an elephant. (Dir: Byron Haskin, 85 mins.)

Captains of the Clouds (1942)*** James Cagney, Dennis Morgan. Some good moments in this fairly exciting melodramatic salute to the RCAF. Cagney may be a bum for the first few reels but he literally comes through with flying colors at the end. (Dir: Michael Curtiz, 113 mins.)

Captain's Paradise, The (Great Britain, 1953)**** Alec Guinness, Celia Johnson, Yvonne DeCarlo. A ferry-boat captain between Gibraltar and Algiers establishes the perfect formula for living by having two wives, one in each port, of opposite personalities. Another merry Guinness romp; delightful comedy, adult, witty, grand fun. (Dir: Anthony Kimmins, 80 mins.)†

Captain's Table, The (Great Britain, 1959)**½ John Gregson, Peggy Cummins. Captain of a cargo vessel is given a trial command of a luxury liner, with the expected comic complications resulting. (Dir: Jack Lee, 90 mins.)†

Captive (Great Britain, 1987)** Irina Brook, Oliver Reed. A young heiress is taken from her daddy's stifling influence and ''liberated'' by a trio of international radicals. An arty exercise in terrorist chic. (Dir: Paul Mayersberg, 103 mins.)†

Captive City, The (1952)*** John Forsythe, Joan Camden. A fearless newspaper editor and his wife are threatened when they intend to expose a gangland syndicate. Suspenseful, intelligent crime melodrama. (Dir: Robert Wise, 91 mins.)

Captive Girl (1950)*½ Johnny Weissmuller, Buster Crabbe, Anita Lhoest, Rick Vallin, John Dehner. Jungle Jim finds the legendary leopard woman and thwarts villains diving for a cache of gold at the bottom of the Lagoon of Death. (Dir: William Berke, 73 mins.)

Captive Heart, The (Great Britain, 1946)***½ Michael Redgrave, Rachel Kempson. Czech officer posing as a British officer killed in action writes to his wife from a concentration camp, and they fall in love with each other through the letters. Finely done war drama, excellent in every way. (Dir: Basil Dearden, 86 mins.)

Captive Rage (1988)* Oliver Reed, Robert Vaughn, Claudia Udy. Low budget sex-and-sadism spectacle with South American Generalissimo Reed kidnapping a plane of co-ed cuties and demanding the release of his drug-dealing son by the U.S. as ransom. Plenty of torture and counter-torture on display for violence voyeurs. (Dir: Cedric Sundstrom, 92 mins.)†

Captive Wild Woman (1943)** Acquanetta, John Carradine, Milburn Stone. Mad doctor transforms an orangutang into a beautiful girl. (Dir: Edward Dmytryk, 61 mins.)

Capt. Sirocco—See: **Pirates of Capri, The**

Capture, The (1950)*** Lew Ayres, Teresa Wright. In Mexico a man unjustly becomes a fugitive. Good melodrama, well acted. (Dir: John Sturges, 91 mins.)

Captured (1933)*** Leslie Howard, Douglas Fairbanks, Jr., Paul Lukas, Margaret Lindsay. Unusual, thoughtful story of soldiers in a German POW camp during WWI; well acted and well produced. (Dir: Roy Del Ruth, 72 mins.)

Capture of Grizzly Adams, The (MTV 1982)** Dan Haggerty, Kim Darby, Noah Beery, Keenan Wynn, June Lockhart, Chuck Connors. That lovable bewhiskered fugitive returns in this telefilm that attempted to tie up the loose ends left by the cancellation of the TV show. The Griz comes out of hiding to see to the fate of his orphaned niece. (Dir: Don Kessler, 96 mins.)

Car, The (1977)* James Brolin, Kathleen Lloyd, John Marley, John Rubinstein. Possessed by the devil, a customized luxury sedan terrorizes a New Mexico town. (Dir: Elliot Silverstein, 95 mins.)

Caravaggio (Great Britain, 1986)*** Nigel Terry, Sean Bean, Garry Cooper. Excessive but imaginative biopic seeking to convey the essence of Caravaggio's striking artwork. Made on a shoestring, the director dabbles in anachronisms and also imposes a homosexual interpretation on the proceedings, depicting the artist's murder of his male model as the result of a lover's spat. (Dir: Derek Jarman, 93 mins.)

Caravan (1934)**½ Loretta Young, Charles Boyer, Phillips Holmes, Jean Parker, Eugene Pallette, C. Aubrey Smith, Charles Grapewin, Noah Beery. Operetta tells the story of an unlikely romance between a princess and a wanderer, with an unusual cast of players. (Dir: Erik Charrell, 101 mins.)

Caravans (1978)** Anthony Quinn, Jennifer O'Neill, Michael Sarrazin, Christopher Lee, Barry Sullivan. Plodding '40s-type adventure made in Iran, takes place in '48. O'Neill is an American senator's daughter who has joined Quinn's nomadic Kochi tribe. It's up to young diplomat Sarrazin to get her back. Based on James Michener's long novel. (Dir: James Fargo, 127 mins.)

Caravan to Vaccares (Great Britain-France, 1975)* David Birney, Charlotte Rampling, Michel Lonsdale, Marcel Bozzuffi. American ne'er-do-well Birney is hired by mysterious Lonsdale to escort a gypsy (Bozzuffi) to America. Rampling is along to provide an occasional double entendre in this second-rate thriller from an Alistair MacLean novel. (Dir: Geoffrey Reeve, 99 mins.)†

Carbine Williams (1952)*** James Stewart, Jean Hagen, Wendell Corey. Based on fact, this is an engrossing personal drama of the man who invented and improved the Carbine Rifle for use by the Armed Forces. Stewart is effective in the lead role. (Dir: Richard Thorpe, 92 mins.)

Carbon Copy (1981)*½ George Segal, Jack Warden, Denzel Washington. Limp comedy about a Jewish businessman who is at the peak of his life when a son turns up—the son is black so you can just about write the script from that point on. (Dir: Michael Schultz, 92 mins.)†

Cardiac Arrest (1980)** Garry Goodrow, Mike Chan, Maxwell Gail. Weird murder mystery, made in 1975, boasts decent performances but no production values as a nut case brings up the mortality rates in San Francisco and beheads his victims for good measure. (Dir: Murray Mintz, 90 mins.)†

Cardinal, The (1963)*** Tom Tryon, Carol Lynley, John Huston, Romy Schneider. Handsomely produced if episodic saga about the personal life and religious career of a dedicated young Catholic priest who rises to the lofty position of cardinal. Tom Tryon is very attractive as the young cleric, but he plays his role in too stoic a fashion. (Dir: Otto Preminger, 175 mins.)†

Cardinal Richelieu (1935)*** George Arliss, Maureen O'Sullivan, Edward Arnold, Cesar Romero. The plots and intrigues of the wily cardinal, the power behind the throne of France. An Arliss acting field day. Elaborate production, fun to watch. (Dir: Rowland V. Lee, 83 mins.)

Care Bears Adventure in Wonderland, The (Canada, 1987)**½ Voices of Bob Dermer, Eva Almos, Dan Hennessy. Enjoyable cartoon feature for young kids.

The Bears take a cue from Lewis Carroll and try to persuade Alice to stand in for a princess who's been snatched away by an evil wizard. Appropriately sunny songs by John Sebastian. (Dir: Raymond Jafelice, 75 mins.)†

Care Bears Movie, The (1985)**½ The voices of Mickey Rooney, Georgia Engel. Sprightly animated fantasy about two orphans befriended by the Care Bears and an Evil Spirit angling to wipe out all feeling from the world. Songs by John Sebastian and Carole King. (Dir: Arna Selznick, 75 mins.)†

Care Bears Movie 2, The: A New Generation (1986)** Voices of Chris Wiggins, Hadley Kay, Alyson Court, Debbie Allen, Stephen Bishop. This time the plush meddlers intervene when Dark Heart starts indoctrinating little campers with a bad attitude. (Dir: Dale Schott, 77 mins.)†

Career (1959)**½ Tony Franciosa, Dean Martin, Shirley MacLaine, Carolyn Jones. Dark drama of a determined actor who will do anything to succeed. Interestingly directed but overwrought. (Dir: Joseph Anthony, 105 mins.)

Career Opportunities (1991)* Frank Whaley, Jennifer Connelly, Dermot Mulroney, Jenny O'Hara, Barry Corbin, John Candy. Writer-producer John Hughes delves into familiar teen territory in this tedious tale about a sweet young guy who gets a job as a watchman in a department store. Smarmy, sexist, and silly. (Dir: Bryan Gordon, 85 mins.)†

Carefree (1938)*** Fred Astaire, Ginger Rogers, Ralph Bellamy, Luella Gear. Psychiatrist attempting to help a lawyer and his fiancée, falls for her. Not up to the Astaire-Rogers standard, but still a good musical. (Dir: Mark Sandrich, 83 mins.)†

Careful, He Might Hear You (Australia, 1984)***½ Wendy Hughes, Nicholas Gledhill, Robyn Nevin, John Hargreaves. An emotionally devastating film about a sensitive lad who becomes the prize in a no-holds-barred custody battle between his two aunts. Exceptionally perceptive. (Dir: Carl Schultz, 166 mins.)†

Caretaker, The—See: **Guest, The**

Caretakers, The (1963)*½ Robert Stack, Joan Crawford, Polly Bergen, Janis Paige. The plight of a young woman who suffers a nervous breakdown and is treated at a mental hospital. Touchy subject needs careful handling, which it doesn't get here. (Dir: Hall Bartlett, 97 mins.)

Carey Treatment, The (1972)**½ James Coburn, Jennifer O'Neill, Skye Aubrey, Regis Toomey. Director Blake Edwards's interesting but muddled medical murder story in which hip pathologist Coburn

clears a buddy charged with a messy abortion. AKA: **Emergency Ward**. (100 mins.)

Cargo to Capetown (1950)**½ Broderick Crawford, Ellen Drew, John Ireland. Personal drama gets in the way of the action in this adventure film about two tanker tramps in love with the same girl. (Dir: Earl McEvoy, 80 mins.)

Caribbean (1952)** John Payne, Arlene Dahl, Cedric Hardwicke. Mild adventure yarn about the days of pirates, land grants, and the slave trade in the Caribbean. (Dir: Edward Ludwig, 97 mins.)

Caribbean Mystery, A (MTV 1983)*** Helen Hayes, Barnard Hughes, Cassie Yates, Swoosie Kurtz, Maurice Evans, Jameson Parker. Helen Hayes makes a perfect Miss Marple, Dame Agatha's amateur sleuth, and she's up to her knitting in murder while vacationing in the Caribbean. AKA: **Agatha Christie's A Caribbean Mystery**. (Dir: Robert Lewis, 104 mins.)

Caribe (Canada, 1988)** John Savage, Kara Glover, Stephen McHattie, Maury Chaykin. British agent Savage and beautiful tough gal Glover seek an ex-CIA agent who is masterminding an illegal arms ring in Belize. The attractive scenery may inspire you to plan your next vacation rather than pay attention to the plot. (Dir: Michael Kennedy, 89 mins.)†

Caribou Trail, The (1950)**½ Randolph Scott, "Gabby" Hayes, Bill Williams. Up in Canada in the 1890s, a cattleman turns to gold prospecting while searching for land. (Dir: Edwin L. Marin, 81 mins.)

Carleton-Browne of the F. O.—See: **Man in a Cocked Hat**

Carly's Web (MTV 1987)*½ Daphne Ashbrook, Cyril O'Reilly, Vincent Baggetta, Peter Billingsley. A Justice Department clerk pushes for heroine status by exposing corrupt individuals. A pilot for a lightly comic action series that never materialized. (Dir: Kevin Inch, 96 mins.)

Carmen (Spain, 1983)***½ Laura del Sol, Antonio Gades. Flamenco-flavored tale about a dance company performing the story of the hot-blooded factory girl who taunts the men in her life. Before they know it, the dancers find their roles are taking over their lives offstage. (Dir: Carlos Saura, 99 mins.)†

Carmen (France-Italy, 1984)***½ Julia Migenes-Johnson, Placido Domingo, Ruggero Raimondi. The familiar Bizet music is gloriously sung and presented in this satisfying screen treatment of the opera. Filmed by a director best known for grim realism, the oft-told tale, of the Spanish vixen who ruins the life of a guard who saves her from prison, packs dramatic force that's equal to the music. AKA: **Bizet's Carmen** (Dir: Francesco Rosi, 152 mins.)†

Carmen Jones (1954)*** Dorothy Dandridge, Harry Belafonte, Pearl Bailey. The story of the femme fatale "Carmen," adapted by Oscar Hammerstein II updating the Bizet music, and directed by Otto Preminger. Despite some faults, it packs quite a bit of power. Well sung by dubbed voices for the principals. (105 mins.)

Carnaby, M.D. (Great Britain, 1966)** Leslie Phillips, James Robertson Justice, Shirley Ann Field. Sixth entry in the "doctor" series has Justice once again playing Sir Lancelot Spratt trying to train a young doctor. AKA: **Doctor In Clover.** (Dir: Ralph Thomas, 95 mins.)

Carnal Knowledge (1971)*** Jack Nicholson, Arthur Garfunkel, Ann-Margret, Candice Bergen. A chillingly accurate and cynical account of the sexual mores and hang-ups of American males over two decades. Nicholson and Garfunkel are Amherst college students in the late '40s who share a dormitory room and a blonde virgin from nearby Smith (Bergen). (Dir: Mike Nichols, 97 mins.)†

Carnegie Hall (1947)*** Marsha Hunt, William Prince, Frank McHugh. Director Edgar G. Ulmer has a budget above poverty row for once in this concert film with musical performances set against the story of an immigrant cleaning woman whose son becomes a concert pianist. Music by Bruno Walter, Leopold Stokowski, Arthur Rubenstein, Jascha Heifetz, Lily Pons, Risë Stevens, and the New York Philharmonic—and for filler, Ezio Pinza, Jan Peerce, Harry James, and Vaughn Monroe. (134 mins.)

Car 99 (1935)*** Fred MacMurray, Guy Standing, Ann Sheridan. Good police drama involving a huge manhunt which is snarled when the master criminal destroys the police radio system. (Dir: Charles Barton, 70 mins.)

Carnival In Flanders (France, 1935)***½ Louis Jouvet, Françoise Rosay, Jean Murat, Pierre Labry. After the cowardly male villagers run off, the women left behind keep the occupation troops occupied. A historic fable rendered with enchanting accuracy in sets and costumes and high-spirited charm in the performances. (Dir: Jacques Feyder, 95 mins.)†

Carnival of Blood (1971)½ Earle Edgerton, Judith Resnick, Burt Young. Unwatchable movie about maniacal murders at Coney Island; most of the running time consists of characters sitting around (inside, not at the amusement park, which would at least have been scenic) talking about what's going on. Young's film debut, if that's worth an evening's rental to you. Not released until 1976. (Dir: Leonard Kirman, 87 mins.)†

Carnival of Fools—See: **Death Wish Club**

Carnival of Souls (1962)*** Candace Hilligoss, Frances Feist. A low-budget horror film that succeeds admirably in creating an eerie, haunting atmosphere. The oft-copied storyline concerns a young woman who survives a car crash and is subsequently plagued by odd blackouts and visions of zombie-like beings. You won't easily forget it. (Dir: Herk Harvey, 84 mins.)†

Carnival Rock (1957)** Susan Cabot, Brian Hutton, David J. Stewart, Dick Miller, Iris Adrian, Jonathan Haze, Ed Nelson. *Blue Angel* set in a carnival. Watch it only for the music by the Platters, David Houston, and the Shadows. (Dir: Roger Corman, 75 mins.)†

Carnival Story (1954)**½ Anne Baxter, Steve Cochran, George Nader. Tragedy ensues when two men love a beautiful carnival high-diving star. Heavy-handed drama; good performances. (Dir: Kurt Neumann, 95 mins.)†

Carny (1980)*** Jodie Foster, Gary Busey, Robbie Robertson, Meg Foster. The friendship of two men is disrupted when a runaway waif seeks shelter in their carnival. While it's adept at conjuring up the seamy sideshow atmosphere, it's less successful in satisfactorily putting across the love triangle. (Dir: Robert Kaylor, 106 mins.)†

Caroline? (MTV 1990)**½ Stephanie Zimbalist, Pamela Reed, George Grizzard, Patricia Neal, Dorothy McGuire. Fourteen years after she was presumed killed in a plane crash, a young woman reappears at the home of her widowed and remarried father—just in time to collect a sizable inheritance. The "Is-she-or-isn't-she?" part of the story fortunately gives way to a more interesting subplot about the woman's influence on her neglected step-siblings. (Dir: Joseph Sargent, 96 mins.)

Carousel (1956)*** Gordon MacRae, Shirley Jones. Tastefully produced version of the fantasy *Liliom*, with the Rodgers and Hammerstein evergreen score. Concerns the marriage of a swaggering carnival barker and a shy girl, and the tragic consequences when he takes drastic steps to provide for their child. (Dir: Henry King, 128 mins.)

Carpenter, The (Canada, 1987)** Wings Hauser, Lynn Adams, Pierce Lenoir. Recuperating from a nervous breakdown in a new, unfinished house, a woman is protected from attackers by a mysterious carpenter who only works at night.

Low-key horror with an unusually restrained Hauser. (Dir: David Wellington, 87 mins.)†

Carpetbaggers, The (1964)**½ Carroll Baker, George Peppard, Lew Ayres, Elizabeth Ashley, Alan Ladd, Martha Hyer. Compulsively watchable Harold Robbins trash compactor about a disagreeable rich young man on the corporate make, with subplots about booze, Hollywood, and broads. (Dir: Edward Dmytryk, 150 mins.)†

Carpool (MTV 1983)** Harvey Korman, Peter Scolari, T. K. Carter, Stephanie Faracy. Ragged comedy good for occasional chuckles when four losers stumble across a million dollars in cash and can't decide whether to keep the loot or return it. (Dir: E. W. Swackhamer, 104 mins.)

Carrie (1952)*** Jennifer Jones, Laurence Olivier, Eddie Albert, Miriam Hopkins. This adaptation of Dreiser's *Sister Carrie* has good casting, with Olivier turning in one of his richest screen performances as the man who ruins himself for the upwardly mobile Carrie (Jones). (Dir: William Wyler, 118 mins.)†

Carrie (1976)***½ Sissy Spacek, Piper Laurie, William Katt, Amy Irving, John Travolta, Betty Buckley. Stylish thriller about a sheltered highschool girl who discovers she has telekinetic powers. Spacek is excellent as the eccentric girl with a fanatically religious mother (played to the hilt by Laurie). Carrie is invited as a joke to the high-school prom by one of the most popular, handsome boys in the school; when her dream-come-true turns into a nightmare she turns on her powers, bringing havoc and destruction. The finale is pure Grand Guignol. Eerie and entertaining. (Dir: Brian DePalma, 97 mins.)†

Carrier, The (1985)** Gregory Fortescue, Steve Dixon, N. Paul Stevenson, Patrick Butler. Weird movie about residents of a small town ravaged by a plaguelike disease reduced to warfare against each other. Presumably meant as an allegory about AIDS, this often inept low-budget movie gets an extra star for sheer strangeness; you won't be bored. (Dir: Nathan J. White, 95 mins.)†

Carrington, V.C.—See: **Court Martial**

Carry On series. This British cavalcade of low humor and slapstick was sufficiently energetic and amusing to find favor in the U.S. Many of these British comedies featuring the "Carry On" crew seemed like extended TV sketches, but some like *Carry on Nurse* were fine blends of bawdiness and physical comedy. Besides the films below, fans of the series should catch *Follow That Camel.*

Carry On at Your Own Convenience (Great

Britain, 1971)*½ Sidney James, Kenneth Williams, Joan Sims, Charles Hawtrey. The "Carry On" gang barely gasps along in this weak comedy about a strike at a toilet factory. Flush with double entendres. (Dir: Gerald Thomas, 86 mins.)†

Carry On Behind (Great Britain, 1975)* Elke Sommer, Kenneth Williams, Joan Sims, Bernard Bresslaw, Jack Douglas, Kenneth Connor, Liz Fraser, Peter Butterworth. Inept archaeologists open a dig at a holiday camp. One of the last of the series, which by this time had become almost entirely preoccupied with juvenile sex jokes. (Dir: Gerald Thomas, 90 mins.)†

Carry On Cabby (Great Britain, 1963)** Sidney James, Hattie Jacques. A taxi-cab company competes against a rival that's owned by the boss's neglected wife. (Dir: Gerald Thomas, 91 mins.)

Carry On Camping (Great Britain, 1970)*½ Sidney James, Kenneth Williams, Joan Sims. This time the company of "Carry On" actors make light of counterculture youths on an outing. Lamer than usual. (Dir: Gerald Thomas, 89 mins.)

Carry On Cleo (Great Britain, 1965)**½ Amanda Barrie, Sidney James, Kenneth Connor. Corned-up takeoff on the Cleopatra legend. (Dir: Gerald Thomas, 92 mins.)†

Carry On Constable (Great Britain, 1960)** Sidney James, Eric Barker, Kenneth Connor. Group of bungling police rookies manage to gum up the works but redeem themselves. (Dir: Gerald Thomas, 86 mins.)

Carry On Cowboy (Great Britain, 1967)**½ Sidney James, Kenneth Williams, Jim Dale. Mild hilarity as a sanitary engineer is mistaken for the brave sheriff who was killed en route to cleaning up the town of bad guys. (Dir: Gerald Thomas, 94 mins.)†

Carry On Cruising (Great Britain, 1962)** Sidney James, Kenneth Williams, Kenneth Connor, Liz Frazer. Skipper of a Mediterranean cruising ship is inflicted with a group of inept crewmen gumming up the works. One moth-eaten slapstick gag after another, but this lowbrow comedy manages to keep afloat. (Dir: Gerald Thomas, 89 mins.)†

Carry On Doctor (Great Britain, 1968)** Frankie Howerd, Jim Dale, Kenneth Williams, Barbara Windsor. Fans of the series will be in stitches; others will be unamused by the skinny plot concerning the fight over a weight-reduction formula. (Dir: Gerald Thomas, 95 mins.)†

Carry On Emmanuelle (Great Britain, 1978)*½ Suzanne Danielle, Kenneth Williams, Kenneth Connor. Substandard series entry about the French ambassador's wife who "carries on" with most of the men in London while her husband experiences impotency problems. (Dir: Gerald Thomas, 88 mins.)†

Carry On England (Great Britain, 1976)* Kenneth Connor, Windsor Davies. During WWII the captain of an antiaircraft fleet proves a klutz when it comes to keeping his crew shipshape. (Dir: Gerald Thomas, 89 mins.)

Carry On Henry VIII (Great Britain, 1972)** Kenneth Williams, Joan Sims, Charles Hawtrey, Barbara Windsor. The much-married Henry VIII and his ribald court get some prime-ribbing from the "Carry On" crew. The jokes are old enough to have originated at Henry's court, so maybe that's why this film plays so well. (Dir: Gerald Thomas, 90 mins.)

Carry On Jack—See: **Carry On Venus**

Carry On Loving (Great Britain, 1970)* Kenneth Williams, Sidney James. The subject is sex, but nobody has any; the talk about it is boring, too. (Dir: Gerald Thomas, 88 mins.)

Carry On Nurse (Great Britain, 1959)** Kenneth Connor, Shirley Eaton, Wilfrid Hyde-White. Fun and games in an English hospital—and that's all there is to it. (Dir: Gerald Thomas, 90 mins.)†

Carry On Regardless (Great Britain, 1961)** Sidney James, Kenneth Connor, Joan Sims, Liz Frazer. Head of an employment agency assigns various bunglers to jobs. Sheer persistence makes some of the ancient gags in this broad farce seem occasionally amusing. (Dir: Gerald Thomas, 86 mins.)

Carry On Sergeant (Great Britain, 1958)**½ William Hartnell, Bob Monkhouse, Shirley Eaton. Tough sergeant about to retire wants his last platoon to be a crack one—but the members are mostly cracked. All the old army routines are crammed into this first entry in the long-running series. (Dir: Gerald Thomas, 88 mins.)

Carry On Spying (Great Britain, 1964)**½ Kenneth Williams, Barbara Windsor, Bernard Cribbins. B.O.S.H. Security Headquarters sends some inept agents to Vienna to combat the villainous activities of S.T.E.N.C.H.—which gives you the idea of the subtle humor involved here. (Dir: Gerald Thomas, 88 mins.)

Carry On Teacher (Great Britain, 1959)**½ Ted Ray, Kenneth Connor, Joan Sims. Dean of a private school wants a better position, but his students and classmates wish him to stay, so they sabotage a scheduled inspection to make him look bad. (Dir: Gerald Thomas, 86 mins.)

Carry On TV (Great Britain, 1961)*½ Bob Monkhouse, Kenneth Connor. Tepid farce, not really one of the "Carry On" series. Advertising promoter goes to extremes to launch a new toothpaste. AKA: **Dentist on the Job** and **Get On with It!** (Dir: C. M. Pennington Richards, 88 mins.)

Carry On, Up the Jungle (Great Britain, 1970)*½ Frankie Howerd, Sidney James, Joan Sims. Another in the series: this one parodies jungle safaris, Tarzan, assorted other African gags. Cruder than usual. (Dir: Gerald Thomas, 89 mins.)

Carry On up the Khyber (Great Britain, 1968)*** Sidney James, Kenneth Williams, Charles Hawtrey. Back in the days when Queen Victoria occupied India, scandal erupts when the locals demand to know whether the fearsome Scottish Devils Regiment have anything on underneath their kilts. Consistently amusing. (Dir: Gerald Thomas, 87 mins.)*

Carry On Venus (Great Britain, 1963)**½ Bernard Cribbins, Juliet Mills, Kenneth Williams. More royal messing up as a bunch of deadheads nearly manage to upset the Royal Navy. AKA: **Carry On Jack.** (Dir: Gerald Thomas, 91 mins.)

Carson City (1952)**½ Randolph Scott, Raymond Massey, Lucille Norman. Railroad engineer fights those who don't want the thing built. Well-made western. (Dir: Andre de Toth, 87 mins.)

Cars That Ate Paris, The (Australia, 1974)**½ Terry Camilleri, John Meillon, Melissa Jaffa. A black comedy lark that doesn't quite sustain itself but shows flashes of the director's gift for unsettling an audience. In Paris, Australia, the locals make a buck by causing traffic accidents and selling the spare parts. AKA: **The Cars That Eat People.** (Dir: Peter Weir, 91 mins.)†

Carter's Army (MTV 1970)**½ Stephen Boyd, Robert Hooks, Susan Oliver, Richard Pryor, Moses Gunn. Often interesting feature which benefits greatly from the fine performance by Hooks as the lieutenant in charge of an all-black outfit during WWII. (Dir: George McCowan, 72 mins.)

Carthage in Flames (France-Italy, 1960)**½ Anne Heywood, Jose Suarez, Pierre Brasseur, Daniel Gelin. Carthaginian warrior rescues a young slave girl during the Third Punic War, and she eventually is instrumental in avenging his death. (Dir: Carmine Gallone, 96 mins.)†

Cartier Affair, The (MTV 1984)**½ Joan Collins, David Hasselhoff, Telly Savalas. Chic caper film which relies heavily on the charm of its co-stars. Joan is TV star Cartier Rand, and David is an ex-con who becomes her secretary as part of a deal with crime lord Savalas. (Dir: Rod Holcomb, 104 mins.)†

Cartouche (France, 1964)*** Jean-Paul Belmondo, Claudia Cardinale. Generally amusing swashbuckling spoof, with the athletic Mr. Belmondo as a sort of Gallic Robin Hood. Cardinale is pretty, the pace is fast. (Dir: Philippe de Broca, 115 mins.)

Carve Her Name with Pride (Great Britain, 1958)**** Virginia McKenna, Paul Scofield. Inspiring true story of Violette Szabo, who braved death while working for the French Resistance in World War II. Excellent performances from McKenna and Scofield. (Dir: Lewis Gilbert, 116 mins.)

Car Wash (1976)** Richard Pryor, Franklin Ajaye, Irwin Corey. The title tune helped make this series of sketches in search of a movie into a box-office hit. Some talented comics live through a day in the life of a car wash, and some good, dirty fun results. (Dir: Michael Schultz, 97 mins.)†

Casablanca (1942)**** Humphrey Bogart, Ingrid Bergman, Paul Henreid, Conrad Veidt, Claude Rains, Peter Lorre, Dooley Wilson, Sydney Greenstreet, S. Z. Sakall. A timeless classic that doesn't age as time goes by, this thrilling wartime romance and propaganda piece has taken on the aura of a myth. As owner of Rick's Place, a hangout for anti-Nazis, Nazis, motley opportunists, and assorted hangers-on, uncommitted outsider Bogart beefs about looking out for number one but cannot fight his freedom-loving impulses. When his former inamorata picks his gin joint out of all the places in the world to walk into, passion erupts, but Bogie realizes that compared with WWII, their feelings don't amount to a hill of beans. An incandescent love story and adventure yarn shored up by an impressive rogues' gallery of displaced persons in supporting roles. (Dir: Michael Curtiz, 102 mins.)†

Casablanca Express (Italy, 1989)**½ Jason Connery, Francesco Quinn, Jinny Steffan, Glenn Ford, Donald Pleasance. The sons of Sean Connery and Anthony Quinn lay to rest any charges of nepotism in this adventure about a Nazi plot to murder Winston Churchill in 1942. Standard wartime suspense done with some panache. (Dir: Sergio Martino, 84 mins.)†

Casanova (1976)—See: **Fellini's Casanova**

Casanova (MTV 1987)** Richard Chamberlain, Faye Dunaway, Sylvia Kristel, Hanna Schygulla, Toby Rolt, Frank Finlay, Ornella Muti, Kenneth Colley, Roy Kinnear. In this latest retelling of the Casanova legend, Richard Chamberlain dons the mantle of the Giacomo-of-all-trades and the enchanter of the opposite sex. The emphasis is on mannered comedy, and Chamberlain and the cast ham it up. (Dir: Simon Langton, 156 mins.)

Casanova and Co.—See: **Some Like It Cool**

Casanova Brown (1944)**½ Gary Cooper, Teresa Wright. College professor, whose marriage has been annulled, finds

that he's a father as he is about to marry again. Fairly amusing comedy, but could have been better. (Dir: Sam Wood, 94 mins.)

Casanova's Big Night (1954)** Bob Hope, Joan Fontaine, Basil Rathbone, Vincent Price. Hope as a tailor's apprentice who poses as the great lover and finds himself in the middle of court intrigue. Not on a par with other Hope farces—some laughs, but too much tedium in between. (Dir: Norman Z. McLeod, 86 mins.)†

Casanova '70 (Italy-France, 1965)*** Marcello Mastroianni, Virna Lisi, Michele Mercier, Marisa Mell. Attractive wolf has psychological difficulty with his love affairs, becoming even more complicated when he meets the real love for him. The sexiest of Mastroianni's films still has some good laughs, and he's always a joy to behold. (Dir: Mario Monicelli, 113 mins.)

Casbah (1948)**½ Yvonne DeCarlo, Tony Martin, Peter Lorre. Another version of the saga of Pepe LeMoko, the criminal who hides from the law in the Casbah section of Algiers, until the love of a woman forces him to the outside world and his doom. (Dir: John Berry, 94 mins.)

Case Against Brooklyn, The (1958)** Darren McGavin, Maggie Hayes. A hard-hitting but fictionalized account of one rookie cop's attempt to single-handedly break a big gambling syndicate in Brooklyn. (Dir: Paul Wendkos, 82 mins.)

Case Against Mrs. Ames, The (1936)**½ Madeleine Carroll, George Brent, Arthur Treacher, Alan Baxter. Entertaining story of an acquitted woman who offers an attorney a large sum of money if he can prove her guilty. Well-acted drama. (Dir: William A. Seiter, 85 mins.)

Case Closed (MTV 1988)*½ Charles Durning, Byron Allen, Marc Alaimo. Standup comic Allen co-wrote, produced, and stars in this routine comedy as a young police detective who links up with a retired cop to solve three murders and a jewel heist. Mildly funny but senseless. (Dir: Dick Lowry, 96 mins.)

Case of Deadly Force, A (MTV 1986)*** Richard Crenna, John Shea, Lorraine Touissant, Frank McCarthy, Tom Isbell. This true story centers around the shooting by Boston police of an innocent man whom they mistook as a robber. While the police investigation wraps up the case claiming "self-defense," widow Touissant tenaciously proves the truth. (Dir: Michael Miller, 104 mins.)

Case of Dr. Laurent, The (France, 1957)***½ Jean Gabin, Nicole Courcel. An excellent French film about a country doctor who is a dedicated man with an abundance of compassion for his patients. (Dir: Jean-Paul Chanois, 92 mins.)†

Case of Libel, A (MTV 1985)*** Ed Asner, Daniel J. Travanti, Gordon Pinsent. Rousing courtroom drama based on Louis Nizer's book about a case of libel in 1954. It involves two famous journalists—Quentin Reynolds, a war correspondent dramatized as Dennis Corcoran (Gordon Pinsent) and Westbrook Pegler, a conservative newspaper columnist portrayed as Boyd Bendix by Travanti. (Dir: Eric Till, 90 mins.)†

Case of Mrs. Loring, The (Great Britain, 1959)** Julie London, Anthony Steel. Provocative theme poorly handled. Wife realizing her husband is sterile submits to artificial insemination and loses her husband in the process. AKA: **A Question of Adultery.** (Dir: Don Chaffey, 86 mins.)

Case of Rape, A (MTV 1974)***½ Elizabeth Montgomery, William Daniels, Cliff Potts, Ronny Cox. A provocative, controversial subject is treated with candor in this fine dramatization about a married woman who is raped twice by the same young man, and then suffers indignities and personal loss when she goes to court. The script introduces little-publicized legal facts about rape cases which will surprise you, and the ending does not make any compromises. (Dir: Boris Sagal, 104 mins.)

Case of the Black Cat, The (1936)**½ Ricardo Cortez, Harry Davenport, June Travis, Jane Bryan. One of the more watchable entries in the Perry Mason series. An old man makes a fatal mistake when he changes his will. (Dir: William McGann, 66 mins.)

Case of the Curious Bride, The (1935)** Warren William, Margaret Lindsay, Donald Woods, Claire Dodd. Allen Jenkins, Wini Shaw. Perry Mason is dragged into a case involving a woman who's being blackmailed by her husband—only he's supposed to be dead. (Dir: Michael Curtiz, 80 mins.)

Case of the Hillside Stranglers, The (MTV 1989)**½ Richard Crenna, Dennis Farina, Billy Zane, Tony Plana, Karen Austin. Frustration is the key word in this true story of the search for serial killers who stalked Los Angeles in the early eighties. Crenna is very believable as the detective who won't give up until he sends crazy cousins Zane and Farina to prison for the grisly murders of ten women. (Dir: Stephen Gethers, 96 mins.)

Case of the Howling Dog, The (1934)** Warren William, Mary Astor Allen Jenkins, Grant Mitchell, Helen Trenholme. Average Perry Mason outing in which Perry needs the wisdom of Solomon when two men each claim the same

woman as his wife. (Dir: Alan Crosland, 75 mins.)

Case of the Lucky Legs, The (1934)** Warren William, Genevieve Tobin, Patricia Ellis, Lyle Talbot, Barton MacLane. Perry Mason pursues a crooked beauty contest promoter who keeps the money for himself. (Dir: Archie Mayo, 77 mins.)

Case of the Stuttering Bishop, The (1937) *½ Anne Nagel, Ann Dvorak, Donald Woods, Linda Perry. Inferior mystery with Perry Mason (Woods) trying to ascertain whether a certain woman is an heiress or a fake. (Dir: William Clemens, 70 mins.)

Case of the Velvet Claws, The (1936)** Warren William, Claire Dodd, Wini Shaw, Gordon Elliott, Addison Richards. Perry Mason has to postpone his honeymoon when he gets charged with murder. (Dir: William Clemens, 63 mins.)

Casey's Shadow (1978)*** Walter Matthau, Alexis Smith, Robert Webber, Murray Hamilton. Appealing sentimental comedy-drama about quarter-horse raising. Matthau is almost the whole show as the opportunistic horse trainer who would just about sacrifice his three young sons' affections if he could come up with a winner. (Dir: Martin Ritt, 116 mins.)†

Cash (Great Britain, 1933)** Robert Donat, Wendy Barrie, Edmund Gwenn. Poorly constructed social comedy with the usual ex-playboy earning his own living for the first time. Unfortunately, the fine cast can't do without a script. AKA: **For Love Or Money** and **If I Were Rich.** (Dir: Zoltan Korda, 73 mins.)†

Cash McCall (1959)**½ Natalie Wood, James Garner, Nina Foch, Dean Jagger, E. G. Marshall. The best-selling novel about big business and the people who play at it. Glossily produced. (Dir: Joseph Pevney, 102 mins.)

Casino (MTV 1980)* Mike Connors, Robert Reed, Lynda Day George, Barry Sullivan, Gary Burghoff. Hackneyed drama starring Connors as a macho gambler whose $14 million cruise ship is being plagued by saboteurs on its maiden voyage. (Dir: Don Chaffey, 104 mins.)

Casino Murder Case (1935)**½ Paul Lukas, Rosalind Russell, Alison Skipworth, Ted Healy, Donald Cook. Lukas brought his own brand of continental polish to playing Philo Vance. This case involves a series of mysterious deaths in a strange household. (Dir: Edward L. Marin, 85 mins.)

Casino Royale (Great Britain, 1967)**½ Peter Sellers, Ursula Andress, David Niven. An overblown, lavish production with an array of big-name guest stars such as William Holden, Charles Boyer, Deborah Kerr, Orson Welles, Jean-Paul Belmondo, and Woody Allen. It's a spoof of all the James Bond spy adventures and there are more Bonds than you can keep track of—but what the picture really needs is Sean Connery and he's conspicuously missing. (Dirs: John Huston, Ken Hughes, Robert Parrish, Joe McGrath, Val Guest, 100 mins.)†

Cassandra (1987)** Tessa Humphries, Shane Briant, Kit Taylor. Woman, haunted by the murder of her mother when she was a child and now dreaming of real murders, makes a startling discovery when she returns to her childhood home. Slow-moving, overpopulated suspense story. (Dir: Colin Eggleston, 94 mins.)†

Cassandra Crossing, The (1977)* Sophia Loren, Burt Lancaster, Martin Sheen, Richard Harris, Ava Gardner. A stupid disaster yarn about beautiful people aboard a train, possibly carrying a deadly virus. The all-star cast suffers through the long ride that is taking them to Poland via a route over an old, rickety bridge, which is less rickety, however, than this story. (Dir: George Pan Cosmatos, 125 mins.)†

Cass Timberlane (1947)**½ Spencer Tracy, Lana Turner, Zachary Scott. One of Sinclair Lewis's weakest novels receives a sincere adaptation and is fairly good commercial screen fare. Story is about a respectable midwestern judge who marries a beautiful immature bride and has trouble keeping pace with her youth. (Dir: George Sidney, 119 mins.)

Cast a Dark Shadow (Great Britain, 1957) **½ Dirk Bogarde, Margaret Lockwood. Scoundrel after cash marries a woman—object: matrimony, then murder. Unevenly paced thriller has some good suspense, sturdy performances. (Dir: Lewis Gilbert, 84 mins.)

Cast a Giant Shadow (1966)**½ Kirk Douglas, Senta Berger, Angie Dickinson, Topol. Highly romanticized but interesting tale about the Israeli-Arab conflict in the days when Israel first became a state. Douglas is cast as Col. Marcus, the legendary American soldier who helps shape up Israel's fighting force in 1948. There's action galore, and even a love story, plus cameo roles by John Wayne, Frank Sinatra, and Yul Brynner. (Dir: Melville Shavelson, 142 mins.)†

Castaway (Great Britain, 1986)**½ Oliver Reed, Amanda Donohoe, Georgina Hale. Intriguing but protracted character study about a sexually frustrated middle-aged man who advertises for a beautiful wife with whom he can retire to a tropical paradise. (Dir: Nicolas Roeg, 118 mins.)†

Castaway Cowboy, The (1974)*** James Garner, Vera Miles. Amiable family fare which bears the authentic stamp of Disney quality. James Garner is a Texan who finds himself in Hawaii in 1850 where

162

he gives in to the pleadings of a widow and her charming son to turn their farm into a cattle ranch. (Dir: Vincent McEveety, 91 mins.)†

Castaways on Gilligan's Island, The (MTV 1979)* Bob Denver, Alan Hale, Jr., Jim Backus. A sequel to the TV movie, *Rescue From Gilligan's Island*, this opus chronicles the "castaways'" rescue attempts and ends with the Gilligan crew buying the island and turning it into a resort. (Dir: Earl Bellamy, 78 mins.)

Castle, The (Switzerland-West Germany, 1968)***½ Maximilian Schell, Cordula Trantow. Generally absorbing adaptation of Franz Kafka's uncompleted novel about a land surveyor who comes to a village, and can't make contact with the people in "the castle" who control the town. A graphic study of man in hopeless conflict with bureaucracy. (Dir: Rudolf Noelte, 93 mins.)†

Castle in the Desert (1942)** Sidney Toler, Arleen Whelan, Richard Derr, Douglass Dumbrille, Victor Sen Yung, Henry Daniell. Average Charlie Chan mystery. A fortress yields its secrets to Charlie when he's invited by a rich couple to their desert castle to ascertain who killed one of their guests. (Dir: Harry Lachman, 62 mins.)†

Castle Keep (1969)**½ Burt Lancaster, Peter Falk, Patrick O'Neal. Offbeat, well-produced WWII story set in a Belgian castle where a great many art treasures are kept. Lancaster is the Major who has to hold off a German attack from the castle, and he comes to grips with the Count (Jean-Pierre Aumont), who can't stand by and see the priceless art be destroyed. (Dir: Sydney Pollack, 105 mins.)

Castle of Evil (1966)* Scott Brady, Virginia Mayo, David Brian, Lisa Gaye, Hugh Marlowe. A robot becomes disgruntled at the reading of his late creator's will, and starts sending the surviving heirs off to their eternal reward. A pitifully shabby horror flick. (Dir: Francis D. Lyon, 81 mins.)†

Castle of Terror (Italy, 1963)** Barbara Steele, Georges Rivière. Man makes a bet that he can spend the night in a castle from which no living soul has ever returned. Dubbed horror thriller has its share of creepy moments, along with some ridiculous ones. (Dir: Anthony Dawson, 77 mins.)

Castle of the Living Dead (Italy-France, 1964)**½ Christopher Lee, Gaia Germani, Philippe Leroy, Antonio de Martino, Donald Sutherland. Evil Count Draco (Lee, of course) experiments with raising the dead. Generally dull Euro-horror picks up toward the end thanks to some scenes shot by an uncredited

Michael Reeves. Sutherland's debut. (Dir: "Herbert Wise" [Warren Keifer, Luciano Ricci], 90 mins.)†

Castle on the Hudson (1940)**½ John Garfield, Ann Sheridan, Pat O'Brien, Burgess Meredith. Of course the acting is top drawer, but you've seen this tired old prison movie plot a million times. Remake of *20,000 Years in Sing Sing* (1933). (Dir: Anatole Litvak, 77 mins.)

Cast the First Stone (MTV 1989)**½ Jill Eikenberry, Richard Masur, Elizabeth Ruscio, Joe Spano, Lew Ayres, Holly Palance. Small-town teacher is fired and persecuted for keeping her child, the result of a rape. Acting, writing, and direction make a difference here, with the sensitive director John Korty getting the best out of Eikenberry as a former novice nun who is both too naive and strong willed for her own good. (96 mins.)

Casual Sex? (1988)**½ Lea Thompson, Victoria Jackson, Andrew Dice Clay. A sex comedy with a decidedly female perspective; some moments are fresh and funny, others fall flat. Thompson and Jackson search for Mr. Right in a resort/health spa, and come out reappraising their respective attitudes toward sex. Clay steals the film as a guido-on-the-make with a tender side, the "Vin Man." (Dir: Genevieve Robert, 90 mins.)†

Casualties of War (1989)** Michael J. Fox, Sean Penn, Thuy Thu Le, Don Harvey, John Leguizamo. Courageous but failed retelling of actual Vietnam War incident in which a squadron of American soldiers kidnapped, raped, and murdered a Vietnamese girl. Le is extraordinary as abused girl, but too much pseudo-philosophizing about guilt, innocence, and friendship bogs film down. Penn overacts wildly, while Fox is so weak as the squad's conscience that the result is like *Andy Hardy Goes to War*. Screenplay by David Rabe from Daniel Lang's 1969 *New Yorker* article. (Dir: Brian DePalma, 113 mins.)†

Casualty of War, A (MTV 1990)*** Shelly Hack, David Threlfall, Alan Howard, Bill Bailey. Frederic Forsyth fans won't be disappointed by this adaptation of one of his stories. Retired agent is called back to duty to investigate rumors that Libya is supplying arms to the IRA. Top-billed Hack is along to provide window dressing, but the rest of the cast is convincing. (Dir: Tom Clegg, 96 mins.)†

Cat! (1966)**½ Roger Perry, Peggy Ann Garner, Barry Coe. Youngsters may like this outdoor tale of a boy who makes friends with a wildcat that eventually saves him from a rustler. Pleasantly done.

AKA: **The Cat.** (Dir: Ellis Kadison, 87 mins.)†

Catamount Killing, The (1974)*** Horst Bucholz, Ann Wedgeworth, Chip Taylor, Louise Clark. A claustrophobic small town is a breeding ground for crime. It's replete with restless cops and repressed lovers, and foul play is in the air. A juicy potboiler. (Dir: Krzysztof Zanussi, 93 mins.)†

Cat and Mouse (France, 1975)*** Michele Morgan, Jean-Pierre Aumont, Serge Reggiani. One of director Claude Lelouch's better efforts. Reggiani happily mugs his way through the part of a Paris police inspector on the trail of a murderer. (107 mins.)†

Cat and the Canary, The (1927)*** Laura LaPlante, Tully Marshall, Creighton Hale, Flora Finch. Original silent version of the classic tale about a young woman who inherits a spooky old house. Wonderfully expressive acting and clever special effects made this an important work in American movie history. (Dir: Paul Leni, 75 mins.)†

Cat and the Canary, The (1939)*** Bob Hope, Paulette Goddard, Gale Sondergaard, John Beal, Douglass Montgomery. Deliberately antiquated horror story about a girl who is willed her uncle's estate provided she meets certain conditions. Spoofs the genre without sacrificing mystery. (Dir: Elliott Nugent, 72 mins.)

Cat and the Canary, The (Great Britain, 1978)*** Michael Callan, Carol Lynley, Wendy Hiller, Wilfrid Hyde-White, Olivia Hussey, Edward Fox, Honor Blackman. Well-acted traditional English thriller, with chicanery rampant over a disputed will. The action takes place on an unsurprisingly dark and stormy night in a resourcefully photographed manor house. (Dir: Radley Metzger, 98 mins.)†

Cat and the Fiddle, The (1934)*** Ramon Novarro, Frank Morgan, Jeanette MacDonald. Charming, visually inventive version of the Jerome Kern-Oscar Hammerstein operetta. An aspiring young singer is waylaid in her love for a temperamental composer by her big break. (Dir: William K. Howard, 90 mins.)

Cat Ballou (1965)*** Lee Marvin, Jane Fonda, Michael Callan, Dwayne Hickman, Tom Nardini. A very funny offbeat western yarn with a magnificent comedy performance by Lee Marvin as a has-been gunslinger who is called back into duty to do away with a look-alike villain. Marvin plays both roles and won an Oscar. (Dir: Elliot Silverstein, 96 mins.)†

Catch As Catch Can (Italy, 1967)** Vittorio Gassman, Martha Hyer. Moderately bawdy satire features Gassman as a billboard advertising model being harassed by every sort of beast and bug. Improbable

163

"bugging" is overdone—satire of advertising/political idolization is better—but Gassman is finally overcome by the endless situations. (Dir: Franco Indovina, 95 mins.)†

Cat Chaser (1989)*** Peter Weller, Kelly McGillis, Charles Durning, Frederic Forrest. A Miami hotel owner who served in the U.S. army in Santo Domingo is drawn back into those days by an affair with a woman who is married to the head of that country's secret police. Sex, double-crosses, and murder abound in this Elmore Leonard tale, directed in prime *noir* style by Abel Ferrara. (90 mins.)†

Catcher, The (MTV 1972)*½ Michael Whitney, Jan-Michael Vincent, Tony Franciosa, David Wayne. Former policeman turns to contemporary bounty hunting, i.e., looking for lost persons for cash rewards. (Dir: Allen H. Miner, 100 mins.)

Catch Me If You Can (1989)** Matt Lattanzi, Loryn Locklin, M. Emmet Walsh, Geoffrey Lewis. A high school class president trying to raise money to keep her school from being torn down teams up with a drag racer who needs money to continue his career. Blandly inoffensive drama. (Dir: Stephen Sommers, 105 mins.)†

Catch the Heat (1988)* Tiana Alexandra, David Dukes, Rod Steiger, John Hancock. Martial arts stuff with undercover agent Alexandra stalking a Brazilian drug dealer who has a novel way of getting drugs into the U.S.—he implants them in the breasts of exotic dancers. Catch a few winks instead. (Dir: Joel Silberg, 90 mins.)†

Catch-22 (1970)***½ Alan Arkin, Martin Balsam, Richard Benjamin, Arthur Garfunkel, Jack Gilford, Bob Newhart, Anthony Perkins, Jon Voight. Joseph Heller's black comedy about war and all it really means to the common man has been turned into a flawed masterpiece. Heller's antiwar crusade against war profiteers is set in Italy during WWII, and his gallery of lunatic characters is vividly brought to life by a wonderful cast headed by Arkin as the very sane Yossarian who tries desperately to be certified mad so that he can stop flying missions. (Dir: Mike Nichols, 120 mins.)†

Cat Creature, The (MTV 1973)** Stuart Whitman, Meredith Baxter, Gale Sondergaard, Kent Smith, John Carradine. Unexciting tale of prowling cats, Egyptian curses, and reincarnation. (Dir: Curtis Harrington, 73 mins.)

Cat Creeps, The (1946)*½ Noah Beery, Jr., Paul Kelly, Lois Collier, Douglass Dumbrille, Rose Hobart. Second-rate mystery, with supernatural overtones. The

spirit of a corpse supposedly lives on in the body of a cat. Poorly done. (Dir: Erle C. Kenton, 58 mins.)

Catered Affair, The (1956)*** Bette Davis, Ernest Borgnine, Debbie Reynolds, Rod Taylor, Barry Fitzgerald. This is one of those big-screen adaptations of "little-people" dramas that were to give social realism a bad name. However, this adaptation of Paddy Chayefsky's TV play is skillful, and Richard Brooks's direction dignifies the material with visual coherence. Davis is cast against type as a Bronx housewife who attempts to mount a bigger wedding for her daughter than her taxi driver husband (Borgnine) can afford. (93 mins.)†

Cat from Outer Space, The (1978)** Ken Berry, Sandy Duncan, Harry Morgan. Harmless kiddie comedy about a feline named Jake from another world, with a collar that gives him extraordinary powers. (Dir: Norman Tokar, 103 mins.)†

Cat Girl (1958)** Barbara Shelley, Kay Callard. Beauty suddenly turns feline, murders result. British-made and cheap, but Shelley is better than the material. (Dir: Alfred Shaughnessy, 69 mins.)

Catherine & Co. (France-Italy, 1975)*½ Jane Birkin, Patrick Dewaere, Jean-Pierre Aumout. Lame, tame sex farce about a working girl who takes the oldest profession seriously by forming a company and enjoying the pleasures of capitalism. Originally 99 mins. (Dir: Michel Boisrond, 84 mins.)

Catherine the Great (Great Britain, 1934)**½ Elisabeth Bergner, Douglas Fairbanks, Jr. The Empress of Russia is forced into a marriage that she does not wish, with resulting unhappiness. Elaborate but heavy, slow historical drama. AKA: **Rise of Catherine the Great**. (Dir: Paul Czinner, 100 mins.)†

Catholics (MTV 1973)***½ Trevor Howard, Cyril Cusack, Martin Sheen. Splendid adaptation of Brian Moore's novel about simple worship in an ancient Irish monastery, threatened by increasing permissiveness in the Mother Church. A memorable performance by Trevor Howard, as the wise, wistful abbot of the institution. Superior. (Dir: Jack Gold, 100 mins.)†

Cathy's Curse (France-Canada, 1976)* Alan Scarfe, Randi Allen, Beverly Murray, Roy Witham, Linda Koot. Young girl is possessed by the malevolent spirit of her aunt, who died when she was her age. Tame, padded rip-off of *The Exorcist*. (Dir: Eddy Matalon, 90 mins.)†

Cathy Tippel (The Netherlands, 1975)**** Monique van der Ven, Rutger Hauer, Eddie Brugman. The family of a free-spirited girl forces her into prostitution to support them in 1881 Amsterdam. A worthy resurrection of early 20th-century social fiction; exhibits detail, wit, and conscience. AKA: Keetje Tippel; Katie's Passion. (Dir: Paul Verhoeven, 104 mins.)†

Catlow (Great Britain, 1971)**½ Yul Brynner, Richard Crenna, Leonard Nimoy. Unpretentious action western as Brynner plays a post–Civil War outlaw-drifter hunted down by friend and marshal Crenna. (Dir: Sam Wanamaker, 101 mins.)

Cat on a Hot Tin Roof (1958)**** Elizabeth Taylor, Paul Newman, Burl Ives, Jack Carson, Judith Anderson. One of Tennessee Williams's most powerful studies of a southern family is successfully filmed by adaptor-director Richard Brooks. Taylor gives a very fine performance as the wife of a former hero (Newman), who is dominated by his father and has taken to drink. Newman is very good, and Ives masterfully recreates his stage portrayal of massive "Big Daddy." Potent drama. (108 mins.)†

Cat on a Hot Tin Roof (MCTV 1984)*** Jessica Lange, Tommy Lee Jones, Rip Torn, Kim Stanley, Penny Fuller, David Dukes. Tennessee Williams's searing drama about vixen Maggie the Cat and her endless plotting to get her petulant husband Brick in her bed is given a thoughtful reading, with material cut from the 1958 film version restored. (Dir: Jack Y. Hofsiss, 150 mins.)†

Cat People (1942)***½ Simone Simon, Kent Smith, Tim Conway. Man marries a strange girl possessed with a dreadful spell passed on from her ancestors. Superior horror thriller, intelligently written and directed. (Dir: Jacques Tourneur, 73 mins.)†

Cat People (1982)** Nastassia Kinski, Malcolm McDowell, Annette O'Toole, John Heard, Ruby Dee, Ed Begley, Jr., Scott Paulin. Classy-looking but ultimately silly tale of a brother and sister who turn into panthers as a result of their strange family tree. (Dir: Paul Schrader, 118 mins.)†

Cat's Eye (1985)*** Drew Barrymore, Candy Clark, Robert Hays, Alan King, James Woods, Kenneth McMillan, James Naughton. Horror anthologies are not easy to pull off, but this trio of Stephen King yarns should keep fans of the macabre purring contentedly. (Dir: Lewis Teague, 94 mins.)†

Cat's Paw, The (1934)*** Harold Lloyd, Una Merkel, Nat Pendleton, Warren Hymer, J. Farrell MacDonald, Samuel S. Hinds. In this wild and weird comedy, Harold is a missionary's son, brought up in China, who comes to the U.S. to make good, with the guidance of the eighth-century Chinese poet Li Po, whom he quotes (with complete accuracy) incessantly! He ends up reforming a corrupt city government by very original means; well worth seeing. Originally 101 mins. (Dir: Sam Taylor, 90 mins.)

C.A.T. Squad (MTV 1986)**½ Joseph Cortese, Steven James, Jack Youngblood, Patricia Charbonneau, Bradley Whittford. Slick action drama about a group of highly trained government agents assigned to high priority secret missions. (Dir: William Friedkin, 104 mins.)

C.A.T. Squad: Python Wolf (MTV 1988)**½ Joe Cortese, Jack Youngblood, Steve James, Deborah Van Valkenburgh, Miguel Ferrer. The second outing for the Counter Assault Tactical Squad abounds in clichés, but it also has some very exciting violent moments and one stunning plot twist that will be familiar to fans of Friedkin's theatrical work. R-rated video version contains extra footage. (Dir: William Friedkin, 96 mins.)

Cattle Annie and Little Britches (1980)**½ Amanda Plummer, Burt Lancaster, Diane Lane, John Savage, Rod Steiger. Offbeat western about a pair of outlaw groupies who trail their down-at-the-heels heroes and make them restore their legend. Plummer is very impressive in her film debut. (Dir: Lamont Johnson, 95 mins.)

Cattle Drive (1951)**½ Joel McCrea, Dean Stockwell. Interesting western with good performances by McCrea and Stockwell as a saddle worn cowhand and a young upstart, respectively, who team up on a cattle drive and become fast friends. (Dir: Kurt Neumann, 77 mins.)

Cattle Empire (1958)**½ Joel McCrea, Gloria Talbott. Another western tale in which the hero is believed to be a renegade but turns out all right after all, but done with finesse. Better than average. (Dir: Charles Marquis Warren, 83 mins.)

Cattle King (1963)*½ Robert Taylor, Joan Caulfield, Robert Loggia, William Windom. Strife and blazing guns in a tired western about fence-rights conflicts between cattlemen and farmers. Set in Wyoming, 1880s. (Dir: Tay Garnett, 88 mins.)

Cattle Queen of Montana (1954)** Barbara Stanwyck, Ronald Reagan. When her pop is murdered, a lone gal fights an unscrupulous land grabber. Not very believable western. (Dir: Allan Dwan, 88 mins.)†

Cattle Town (1952)** Dennis Morgan, Phil Carey, Rita Moreno. The cowboys and the farmers should be friends, but they aren't—so Morgan comes along to set things right. (Dir: Noel Smith, 71 mins.)

Cat Women of the Moon (1953)½ Victor Jory, Marie Windsor, Sonny Tufts. So bad it looks like an unclaimed work by Edward Wood, Jr. Spacemen encounter more than black holes and meteors in outer space: they find an underground empire on the moon—populated by a bevy of voluptuous females played by the "Hollywood Cover Girls." AKA: **Rocket to the Moon**. (Dir: Arthur Hilton, 64 mins.)†

Caught (1949)*** James Mason, Barbara Bel Geddes, Robert Ryan. Model marries neurotic millionaire, is unhappy until a young doctor comes to her aid. Good melodrama, well acted. (Dir: Max Ophuls, 88 mins.)†

Caught in the Draft (1941)***½ Bob Hope, Dorothy Lamour. The Army may have changed since 1941, but this picture about a draft-dodging movie star who is finally caught and placed in the Army is grand fun. (Dir: David Butler, 82 mins.)

Cauldron of Blood (Spain, 1967)*½ Boris Karloff, Viveca Lindfors, Jean-Pierre Aumont. In one of his final roles, Karloff plays a blind sculptor who uses human bones for his art. Not scary, quite dull. AKA: **Blind Man's Bluff** and **Children of Blood**. (Dir: Edward Mann, 95 mins.)†

Cause for Alarm (1951)** Loretta Young, Barry Sullivan. This overdramatic story about a woman being terrorized by her husband who suspects her of infidelity is like an expanded TV show. (Dir: Tay Garnett, 74 mins.)

Cavalcade (1933)*** Diana Wynyard, Clive Brook, Una O'Connor, Margaret Lindsay. Elegant adaptation of Noël Coward's play traces the Marryot family from 1899 to 1932. Rich characterizations bring alive the sorrows and triumphs which befall the family during World War I and the Depression. (Dir: Frank Lloyd, 110 mins.)

Cavegirl (1985)½ Daniel Roebuck, Cindy Ann Thompson. A prehistoric comedy that's primitive in technique. A nerd gets transplanted back in time for some lame-brain sexist adventures; it's no surprise that this clod fits in so well with the neanderthals. (Dir: David Oliver, 85 mins.)†

Cave-In! (MTV 1983)**½ Dennis Cole, Susan Sullivan, Leslie Nielsen, Julie Sommars, Ray Milland. Another formulaic Irwin Allen–produced disaster epic: Take a cast of "types" (headed here by park ranger Cole), put them in deadly peril and let us see how they squirm their way out of danger. Good effects despite the obviously low TV-movie budget. (Dir: Georg Fenady, 96 mins.)

Caveman (1981)*** Ringo Starr, Dennis Quaid, Shelley Long, Jack Gilford, John Matuszak. A prehistoric comedy, the brainchild of Carl Gottlieb, who directed and co-wrote the script with Rudy deLuca (all fifteen words of dialogue). Silly, lighthearted, and often hilarious. Ringo invents rock 'n' roll with real rocks, and one unexpected scene-stealer is the most charming dinosaur you'll ever see! (94 mins.)†

Cave of Outlaws (1951)²* Macdonald Carey, Alexis Smith. Routine western about hidden gold and the lengths men go to uncover the secret hiding place. (Dir: William Castle, 75 mins.)

Cave of the Living Dead (West Germany-Yugoslavia, 1964)* Adrian Hoven, Karin Field, Erika Remberg, Wolfgang Preiss, John Kitzmiller. Village professor is really a vampire who keeps a bevy of female vampires in the cave beneath his castle, releasing them periodically to feed on the villagers. Tiresome horror movie. (Dir: Akos von Ratony, 89 mins.)†

Cavern, The (1965)**½ John Saxon, Brian Aherne, Rosanna Schiaffino. World War II adventure about six men and a woman trapped in a German munitions dump. Tensions are high, death is near, and escape remote. (Dir: Edgar G. Ulmer, 100 mins.)

C.C. and Company (1970)*½ Joe Namath, Ann-Margret, William Smith, Jennifer Billingsley, Teda Bracci, Sid Haig. Ann-M and Joe N. compete for cleavage space and bad acting honors in a sophomoric bike-a-thon in which Joe pits his brawn against B-movie bad guy Smith. (Dir: Seymour Robbie, 88 mins.)†

Cease Fire (1984)** Don Johnson, Lisa Blount, Robert F. Lyons, Richard Chaves, Rick Richards, Chris Noel. A Viet vet (and this film that features him) suffers from bouts of delayed stress syndrome. Something awful happened to this soldier and his buddy over in Nam, and they now experience flashbacks that understandably frighten their loved ones. The film's delayed stress has to do with the fact that it was held up for release until the fortuitous moment of Don Johnson's stardom on "Miami Vice." (Dir: David Nutter, 95 mins.)†

Ceiling Zero (1935)***½ James Cagney, Pat O'Brien. The planes may look like antiques but this is still as exciting an aviation story as today's filmmakers can produce at supersonic speeds. (Dir: Howard Hawks, 95 mins.)

Celebration Family (MTV 1987)*½ Stephanie Zimbalist, James Read, Diane Ladd, Ed Begley, Jr. A young couple unselfishly take in what they call the "family that nobody wanted." When they are accused of neglect, the syrup flows. (Dir: Robert Day, 96 mins.)

Céleste (West Germany, 1981)***½ Eva Mattes, Jurgen Arndt, Norbert Wartha, Wolf Euba, Joseph Manoth. Based on Celeste Albaret's memoirs, this biography follows the relationship of writer

Marcel Proust and Céleste, his housekeeper, an uneducated farm girl who lovingly cared for the middle-aged homosexual until his death. Exquisitely photographed, sincerely detailed and filled with a witty and understanding sensitivity of the characters and their time. (Dir: Percy Adlon, 107 mins.)†

Celia (Australia, 1988)*** Rebecca Smart, Nicholas Eadie, Maryanne Fahey, Victoria Longley. A nine-year-old girl's disappointments and small griefs lead to a surprising climax in this film that has misleadingly been sold as a horror story. The stifling atmosphere of a 1950s suburb is well evoked. (Dir: Ann Turner, 102 mins.)†

Céline and Julie Go Boating (France, 1974)**** Dominique Labourier, Juliet Berto, Bulle Ogier, Marie-France Pisier, Barbet Schroeder. Director Jacques Rivette's masterwork is a fantastic adventure in literature and cinematic sleight of hand. Céline, a magician, takes Julie, a librarian, to an odd house where she sometimes watches the young daughter of the widower who resides within with two women. The visitors are then caught up in the drama of the house and its residents. Based on stories by Henry James, the film is weirdly funny and rich in expressive language and images. A great film! (192 mins.)

Cell 2455, Death Row (1955)**½ William Campbell, Kathryn Grant. Based on Caryl Chessman's book about his life in prison and the events leading up to it. Frank and sometimes effective. (Dir: Fred F. Sears, 80 mins.)

Cemetery High (1987)½ Debi Thibeault, Karen Nielsen, Lisa Schmidt, Simone. The makers of *Psychos in Love* return with an equally stupid followup about female vigilantes who kill "male slimeballs." Little more than a lame in-joke preserved on film, which is too precious a commodity to waste on such drivel as this. (Dir: Gorman Bechard, 80 mins.)†

Census Taker, The—See: **Husbands, Wives, Money and Murder**

Centennial Summer (1946)*** Linda Darnell, Jeanne Crain, Constance Bennett, Walter Brennan, Cornel Wilde. About a family in Philadelphia in 1876 during the Centennial Exposition. A respectable imitation of *Meet Me in St. Louis*, well directed by Otto Preminger, who one might have thought ill suited for this fluff. Pleasant Jerome Kern-Oscar Hammerstein songs. (102 mins.)

Central Airport (1934)*** Richard Barthelmess, Sally Eilers, Tom Brown, John Wayne. Swift-paced aerial adventure has a daredevil pilot losing his airline job and barnstorming around the world. Wonderfully acted, with some unusual and effective montage by director Wellman, who was an experienced pilot himself (as was Barthelmess). (Dir: William Wellman, 72 mins.)

Central Park (1932)**½ Joan Blondell, Wallace Ford, Guy Kibbee, Henry B. Walthall. Depression-plagued boy and girl meet in New York's Central Park and share varied adventures. A fascinating look at the city in the early '30s, with much location footage. In the film's climax a lion escapes from Central Park Zoo and rampages through New York! (Dir: John Adolphi, 61 mins.)

Ceremony, The (Great Britain, 1964)** Sarah Miles, Laurence Harvey, Robert Walker, Jr., John Ireland. A try for suspense, with efforts to spring a criminal from a Tangier prison. Harvey stars and directs—one task too many, for this cinema ceremony. Good moments offset by uneven treatment. (105 mins.)

Certain Fury (1985)* Tatum O'Neal, Irene Cara, Peter Fonda, Moses Gunn, George Murdoch. Sort of a distaff *The Defiant Ones*, but only the credulous would take this fugitive-flick seriously. O'Neal, an illiterate prostitute, and Cara, a good girl who's temporarily strayed from good citizenry, get mistaken as accomplices to two cuckoo convicts whose courtroom breakout wipes out half the metropolitan police force. Unintentionally funny. (Dir: Stephen Gyllenhaal, 88 mins.)†

Certain Sacrifice, A (1985)½ Jeremy Pattinosh, Madonna. A painfully tedious journey into the depths of the steamy New York underworld. Even if you are a Madonna wanna-be, think twice about watching this. (Dir: Stephen John Lewicki, 60 mins.)†

Certain Smile, A (1958)**½ Rossano Brazzi, Joan Fontaine, Bradford Dillman, Christine Carere. Françoise Sagan's novel about a young girl's adventures in affairs of the heart with a suave, middle-aged Frenchman (played by Brazzi as if he were remembering all the early Boyer films) and a rebellious youth (played by Dillman as if he never saw an early Boyer film) is given a sumptuous production that spills all over with the beauty of the French Riviera. (Dir: Jean Negulesco, 104 mins.)

César (France, 1936)**** Raimu, Crane Desmazis, Pierre Fresnay. Director-writer-producer Marcel Pagnol ends his trilogy with a culminating masterpiece. (*Fanny* (1932) and *Marius* (1931) were the others.) Marius returns to Marseilles after a twenty-year absence to find the child he left with Fanny. The emotional impact is overwhelming. (117 mins.)†

Cesar and Rosalie (France, 1972)*** Yves Montand, Romy Schneider, Sami Frey. Sincere and mature love story with Schneider as the beautiful Rosalie, a woman torn between an aging lover (Montand) and a younger, more romantic man (Frey). (Dir: Claude Sautet, 100 mins.)†

C'est La Vie (France, 1990)*** Nathalie Baye, Julie Bataille, Candice Lefranc, Richard Berry, Jean-Pierre Bacri. From the director of *Entre Nous* and *Pepper-mint Soda*. A poignant, perceptive, accurate, and often humorous look at a family splitting up from the perspective of the young daughter. A family summer holiday at the beach is torn apart by a mother's decision to divorce. Get out your hankie. (Dir: Diane Kurys, 97 mins.)

Chad Hanna (1940)** Henry Fonda, Dorothy Lamour, Linda Darnell, Guy Kibbee. Overlong drama of a young man who joins the circus in the 19th century. The cast of fine actors has little to do. Color. (Dir: Henry King, 86 mins.)

Chadwick Family, The (MTV 1974)**½ Fred MacMurray, Kathleen Maguire. MacMurray is the editor and publisher of a newspaper, thinking of moving to Chicago to head a new national magazine. Crises in his family call for a last-minute change of plans. (Dir: David Lowell Rich, 78 mins.)

Chained (1934)**½ Joan Crawford, Clark Gable, Stuart Erwin. Star-powered little love triangle. And you'll know before the first reel that Joan will end up with Gable. (Dir: Clarence Brown, 71 mins.)

Chained Heat (U.S.-West Germany, 1983)**½ Linda Blair, John Vernon, Sybil Danning, Tamara Dobson, Stella Stevens. A follow-up to the women's prison hit *The Concrete Jungle* with plenty of violence, and sex-tease action. Not exactly a triumph of the genre. (Dir: Paul Nicolas, 95 mins.)†

Chain Lightning (1950)**½ Humphrey Bogart, Eleanor Parker, Raymond Massey. Good shots of air action but unfortunately pilot Bogart lands and fights a losing battle with a hackneyed script. (Dir: Stuart Heisler, 94 mins.)

Chain Reaction, The (Australia, 1980)**½ Steve Bisley, Anna-Maria Winchester, Ross Thompson. In this slick thriller from down under, a married couple are thrown into a world of terror after being contaminated with radioactivity. (Dir: Ian Barry, 87 mins.)†

Chairman, The (Great Britain, 1969)** Gregory Peck, Anne Heywood, Arthur Hill. Picture if you will Peck behind the Chinese bamboo curtain on a spy mission, with an explosive device sewn into his head ready to be detonated. Farfetched? Yes, indeed. (Dir: J. Lee Thompson, 102 mins.)

Chalk Garden, The (Great Britain, 1964)***½ Deborah Kerr, Hayley Mills, John Mills, Edith Evans. Tender story of a governess who tries to provide the love her charge, a disturbed sixteen-year-old girl, needs so badly. Sensitively written and directed, with fine performances by all. (Dir: Ronald Neame, 106 mins.)†

Challenge, The (1947)**½ Tom Conway, June Vincent, Richard Stapley. Conway investigates the death of an old skipper. (Dir: Jean Yarbrough, 68 mins.)

Challenge, The (MTV 1970)** Darren McGavin, Mako, Broderick Crawford, James Whitmore, Skip Homeier, Paul Lukas, Sam Elliott, Adolph Caesar. Action picture masquerading as a think piece; two soldiers battle *mano a mano* on an unclaimed island. Good cast, slight material. (Dir: Alan Smithee, 96 mins.)

Challenge, The (1982)**½ Scott Glenn, Toshiro Mifune, Donna Kei Benz. A drifter, convincingly played by Glenn, is paid to take a sword from the United States to Japan, and finds himself caught in a feud between two brothers. (Dir: John Frankenheimer, 112 mins.)†

Challenge for Robin Hood, A (Great Britain, 1967)*** Barrie Ingham, Leon Greene. Yet another recounting of the fun and games in Sherwood Forest, but this retelling is better than most. (Dir: C. M. Pennington-Richards, 85 mins.)

Challenge of a Lifetime (MTV 1985)**½ Penny Marshall, Jonathan Silverman, Richard Gilliland. Marshall is delightful in this light drama about a divorced woman in a mid-life slump, who decides to enter sport's most grueling competition—the triathlon. (Dir: Russ Mayberry, 104 mins.)

Challenger (MTV 1990)*** Karen Allen, Barry Bostwick, Julie Fulton, Richard Jenkins, Brian Kerwin, Joe Morton, Peter Boyle, Lane Smith. Accurate and thoroughly absorbing recreation of the preparations leading up to the flight and tragic explosion of the 1986 *Challenger* mission, in which seven astronauts perished. (Dir: Glenn Jordan, 144 mins.)

Challengers, The (MTV 1969)** Darren McGavin, Sean Garrison, Nico Minardos, Susan Clark. Standard car-racing drama with a triangular love story between two racers and an heiress. (Dir: Leslie Martinson, 99 mins.)

Challenge to Be Free (1976)* Mike Mazurki, Vic Christy, Jimmy Kane, Fritz Ford. The law keeps hounding a fur trapper in the frozen wastelands of the Arctic, but you know those fur trappers; they just gotta be free. (Dir: Tay Garnett, 88 mins.)†

Challenge to Lassie (1949)**½ Edmund Gwenn, Donald Crisp, Lassie. Good family picture starring the famous collie.

Veteran actors Edmund Gwenn and Donald Crisp make the somewhat sentimental story ring true. (Dir: Richard Thorpe, 76 mins.)†

Chamber of Fear (U.S.–Mexico, 1968)* Boris Karloff, Juissa, Carlos East, Isela Vega. Mad scientist feeds humans to a living rock, which thrives on a substance secreted by frightened women. One of four Mexican movies for which Karloff shot separate footage in Hollywood just before his death; he's hardly in this junk, which is a blessing to his memory. AKA: **Fear Chamber** and **Torture Zone**. (Dirs: Juan Ibanez, Jack Hill, 85 mins.)†

Chamber of Horrors (1966)** Patrick O'Neal, Suzy Parker. Horror film fans may enjoy this opus about a mass killer loose in Baltimore of the 1880s. All others will probably laugh at the wrong places. (Dir: Hy Averback, 99 mins.)

Champ, The (1931)*** Wallace Beery, Jackie Cooper, Irene Rich. Director King Vidor's sentimental story of a washed-up boxer and his doting son living the happy lowlife in Tijuana. Rich's performance is accomplished as the mother who has abandoned them. Beery shared an Oscar with Fredric March. (Dir: King Vidor, 87 mins.)†

Champ, The (1979)**½ Jon Voight, Faye Dunaway, Ricky Schroder, Joan Blondell. Update of the classic four-hankie tale of a broken-down fighter, his adoring son, and the ex-wife who wants custody of the boy she never really knew. (Dir: Franco Zeffirelli, 121 mins.)†

Champagne Charlie (Great Britain, 1944)*** Tommy Trinder, Betty Warren, Stanley Holloway, Jean Kent. Lively musical of the British music halls in the 1860s, with Trinder as an aspiring performer who wins success with the title song (a huge hit in the last century). Classic routines are lovingly re-created in this charming film. (Dir: Alberto Cavalcanti, 107 mins.)

Champagne for Caesar (1950)***½ Ronald Colman, Celeste Holm, Vincent Price. An unemployed genius gets on a quiz show and proceeds to take the sponsor for all he's worth. Rollicking comedy never lets up for a minute! (Dir: Richard Whorf, 99 mins.)†

Champagne Murders, The (France, 1967)** Anthony Perkins, Maurice Ronet, Stephane Audran, Yvonne Furneaux. Is the eccentric playboy a murderer as well? Seems that way, but you never know. Too many other things are unclear in this Gallic-made whodunit, wherein director Claude Chabrol dallies by the wayside too long. (98 mins.)

Champagne Waltz (1937)*** Fred MacMurray, Gladys Swarthout. Jazz musi-

cian incurs the wrath of a Viennese waltz enthusiast, but all is well at the end because of the old man's pretty granddaughter. Good musical. (Dir: A. Edward Sutherland, 100 mins.)

Champ for a Day (1953)*** Alex Nicol, Audrey Totter. Prize fighter investigates the disappearance of his manager. Good melodrama has some unusual plot twists. (Dir: William Seiter, 90 mins.)

Champion (1949)***½ Kirk Douglas, Arthur Kennedy, Lola Albright, Ruth Roman, Marilyn Maxwell. Douglas punched his way to stardom as the boxing heel in this rather free adaptation of Ring Lardner's mordant short story. When Douglas socks his crippled younger brother (Kennedy), we cringe, but we also cheer the slugging of a sanctimonious scrounge. (Dir: Mark Robson 99 mins.)†

Champions (Great Britain, 1983)**½ John Hurt, Ben Johnson, Edward Woodward. After being diagnosed as having cancer, an English jockey, Bob Champion, underwent chemotherapy and rode again to win the Grand National Steeplechase. Another in the long line of sports-conquers-all films, but Hurt makes the plucky horseman into a likable heroic figure. (Dir: John Irvin, 115 mins.)†

Champions: A Love Story (MTV 1979)*** James Vincent McNichol, Joy LeDuc, Tony LoBianco. Uneven but touching tale of puppy love against a backdrop of amateur skating competitions. Better acted than most made-for-TV films. Toward the end, the film gets bogged down in sentiment. (Dir: John A. Alonzo, 104 mins.)

Chance at Heaven (1933)**½ Ginger Rogers, Joel McCrea, Marion Nixon, Andy Devine, Lucien Littlefield, Betty Furness. A small-town boy is torn between two girls; nice star performances make this one. (Dir: William A. Seiter, 70 mins.)

Chance Meeting (Great Britain, 1959)**½ Hardy Kruger, Stanley Baker, Micheline Presle. Painter is arrested for a girl's murder although he insists he's innocent. Good performances in a mystery that never grips as it should. AKA: **Blind Date**. (Dir: Joseph Losey, 95 mins.)

Chance of a Lifetime, The (1943)** Chester Morris, Jeanne Bates, Eric Rolf, Richard Lane, George E. Stone, Lloyd Corrigan. Boston Blackie asks for trouble when some prisoners are paroled in his custody. Average crime story in the Boston Blackie series. (Dir: William Castle, 65 mins.)

Chances (1931)**½ Douglas Fairbanks, Jr., Rose Hobart, Anthony Bushell. Two British officers fall for the same girl. Tender, interesting story, well acted and directed. (Dir: Allan Dwan, 72 mins.)

Chances Are (1989)** Robert Downey, Jr.,

Cybill Shepherd, Ryan O'Neal, Mary Stuart Masterson, Joe Grifasi. Clumsy romantic fantasy about a college student who "remembers" that he is the reincarnation of a murdered lawyer when the mother of the girl he is romancing turns out to be his past-life wife. Slight material has OK performances but is way too long. (Dir: Emile Ardolino, 110 mins.)

Chance to Live, A (MTV 1978)** David Cassidy, Gloria De Haven, Anne Lockhart. Pilot for the short-lived series "Man Undercover" casts Cassidy as an undercover cop who poses as a high school student to ferret out drug pushers. (Dir: Corey Allen, 104 mins.)

Chandler (1971)*½ Warren Oates, Leslie Caron, Gloria Grahame, Mitchell Ryan. Muddled detective story. Warren Oates drags his way through the plot as a security guard setting out to trail Leslie Caron, who is linked to an important underworld figure. (Dir: Paul Magwood, 88 mins.)

Chandu the Magician (1932)*½ Edmund Lowe, Bela Lugosi, Irene Ware, Henry B. Walthall. Inferior B movie in which mystically powered Bela endeavors to save the world from a deadly ray. (Dirs: Marcel Varnel, William Cameron Menzies, 70 mins.)

Chanel Solitaire (U.S.-France, 1981)** Marie-France Pisier, Timothy Dalton, Rutger Hauer, Karen Black, Brigitte Fossey. Melodramatic treatment of how Coco Chanel managed to overcome her poor orphan background, eventually conquering the fashion world. (Dir: George Kaczender, 120 mins.)†

Changeling, The (Canada, 1979)** George C. Scott, Trish Van Devere, Melvyn Douglas. Scott is a musician seeking a retreat, but the house he moves to is haunted by the spirit of a dead child. Some spooky atmosphere but predictably scripted and overlong. (Dir: Peter Medak, 113 mins.)†

Change of Habit (1970)** Elvis Presley, Mary Tyler Moore. Presley plays a doctor, no less, who heads a clinic in a poor section of town, and Miss Moore plays one of a trio of nuns who offer their services to help out Presley's cause in this mild film. (Dir: William Graham, 93 mins.)†

Change of Heart (1943)**½ Susan Hayward, John Carroll, Eve Arden, Melville Cooper, Gail Patrick, Walter Catlett. Forgettable but charming trifle with young Hayward quite fetching as a budding songwriter who gets ripped off. Good Jule Styne-Harold Adamson score and look for Dorothy Dandridge performing. AKA: **Hit Parade of 1943.** (Dir: Albert S. Rogell, 90 mins.)

Change of Mind (1969)** Raymond St. Jacques, Susan Oliver. Absurd premise—the brain of a prominent white DA, dying of cancer, is transplanted into the body of a black listed as virtually DOA after an auto accident—gets a mounting here. Too farfetched. (Dir: Robert Stevens, 103 mins.)

Change of Seasons, A (1980)** Shirley MacLaine, Anthony Hopkins, Bo Derek, Michael Brandon, Mary Beth Hurt. MacLaine's intelligent performance as the betrayed wife of a philandering professor is the only bright spot in this insincere, conventional romantic comedy. Noel Black began directing, but was replaced during shooting. (Richard Lang, 102 mins.)†

Chan Is Missing (1982)*** Wood Moy, Marc Hayashi, Laureen Chew, Judy Mihei, Peter Wang, Presco Tabios. Two Oriental taxi drivers try to track down a friend named Chan who has vanished with $2,000 worth of borrowed money in a film made for only ten times that amount. Shot in San Francisco's Chinatown, this is the first feature-length American film produced entirely by an Asian-American cast and crew. (Dir: Wayne Wang, 80 mins.)

Chant of Jimmie Blacksmith, The (Australia, 1978)*** This film chronicles the rampage by a half-breed aboriginal at the turn of the century. Based on a novel by Thomas Keneally, it seeks both epic sweep and ironic comment and does middling well with each. Much of the character detail is excitingly individual, and director Fred Schepisi creates an effective, large canvas. (122 mins.)

Chapayev (U.S.S.R., 1934)*** Boris Bobochkin, Boris Blinov, Barbara Miasnikov. Directors Sergei Vasiliev and Georgi Vasiliev (no relation) drew on their own experience in the Russian Revolution to make this stirring account of a Soviet hero, an illiterate who rose to the rank of general. There's a minimum of revolutionary preaching in this realistic, entertaining film, a popular hit in the U.S.S.R. (100 mins.)†

Chaplin Revue, The (1958)**** Charlie Chaplin, Edna Purviance, Syd Chaplin. A compilation of his best silent comedy shorts, assembled by Chaplin himself, including *A Dog's Life* (1918), *Shoulder Arms* (1918), and *The Pilgrim* (1923). With added sound effects and a rather obtrusive score composed by Chaplin. (119 mins.)†

Chapman Report, The (1962)**½ Jane Fonda, Efrem Zimbalist, Jr., Claire Bloom, Glynis Johns, Shelley Winters. The best-selling novel inspired by the Kinsey Report on the sexual mores of suburban women is brought to the screen as a glossy soap opera. Of the group, Claire Bloom delivers the best performance as a tragic nymphomaniac. (Dir: George Cukor, 125 mins.)

Chapter Two (1979)*** James Caan, Marsha Mason, Valerie Harper, Joseph Bologna. Neil Simon has adapted his Broadway play for the screen. The first portion is snappy and entertaining as a widowed writer and a divorcée, neither ready for a new relationship, meet and find themselves overwhelmingly attracted to each other. But when the sparring and romancing gives way to the emotional upheaval involved in the man's guilt about loving another, the film sags. (Dir: Robert Moore, 124 mins.)†

Charade (1963)**** Cary Grant, Audrey Hepburn, Walter Matthau, James Coburn, George Kennedy, Ned Glass. As slick and sophisticated as its two charming stars, with a delightful Hepburn as the nervous Reggie, who meets the debonair Grant about the same time that her husband is murdered. It seems her late spouse swindled some cronies out of a quarter of a million dollars in gold. Now they think she knows where the loot is stashed. The ensuing game of "charade" and hidden identity is played out with wit and menace amid the marvelous European settings. (Dir: Stanley Donen, 114 mins.)†

Charge at Feather River, The (1953)** Guy Madison, Vera Miles, Frank Lovejoy. Just another western adventure—originally made in 3-D but without it the gimmicks misfire. (Dir: Gordon Douglas, 96 mins.)

Charge of the Lancers (1954)** Paulette Goddard, Jean-Pierre Aumont. Mediocre adventure pic about a gypsy girl and an officer set during the Crimean War. (Dir: William Castle, 80 mins.)

Charge of the Light Brigade, The (1936)***½ Errol Flynn, Olivia de Havilland, David Niven, Donald Crisp, Henry Stephenson, Patric Knowles. A splendid gung-ho adventure, with Flynn romancing de Havilland before the fatal assault. The climactic sally is a supreme example of Hollywood craft. (Dir: Michael Curtiz, 115 mins.)†

Charge of the Light Brigade (Great Britain, 1968)***½ Trevor Howard, Vanessa Redgrave, David Hemmings, John Gielgud. Director Tony Richardson's withering, stimulating polemic about the stupidity and brutality of the military mind, and societies that not only condone but also glorify war. Superlatively acted by an all-star cast. Excellent animated sequences done by Richard Williams. (116 mins.)

Chariots of Fire (Great Britain, 1981)***½ Ben Cross, Ian Charleson, Nigel Ha-

vers, Nick Farrell, Alice Krige, Ian Holm, Sir John Gielgud, Lindsay Anderson, Patrick Magee. A thrilling, poignant drama based on a true story of two members of Britain's 1924 Olympic team, Harold Abrahams, a Jew running to prove himself in the face of the subtle hostility he found in his British environment, and Eric Liddell, a deeply religious man who refused to run on the Sabbath. Occasionally heavy-handed in the use of slow motion and the reliance upon speech-making dialogue, but otherwise engrossing, impressively acted, and impeccably costumed and designed to convey the sense of the period. 1981 Academy Award winner for Best Picture. (Dir: Hugh Hudson, 123 mins.)†

Chariots of the Gods (1974)*** Broken Egyptian pyramids, gutted Incan and Mayan metropolises, weed-covered Biblical sites—this well-made *Chariot* bumps down many roads advancing Erich von Daniken's popular theories about the extra-terrestrial origins of mankind's great feats. (Dir: Harald Reinl, 98 mins.)†

Charlene (1981)***½ Filmmaker Ross McElwee's remarkable, insightful documentary study of an extraordinary, complex woman who writes and teaches poetry to young people. From the maker of *Sherman's March*. (83 mins.)†

Charles & Diana: A Royal Love Story (MTV 1982)**½ David Robb, Caroline Bliss, Margaret Tyzack, Christopher Lee. At the height of the frenzy over the royal marriage of Prince Charles and Lady Diana Spencer, the networks jumped on the bandwagon and made films about the pair's courtship and marriage. This is the better version. (Dir: James Goldstone, 104 mins.)

Charles Dead or Alive (Switzerland, 1968)***½ François Simon, Marcel Robert. Watch manufacturer drops out of his materialistic lifestyle and takes up with a young couple who show him how to live again. Fine testament of modern angst, with a disturbing but inevitable ending, as time runs out for the unlikely social dropout. (Dir: Alain Tanner, 110 mins.)

Charleston (MTV 1979)* Martha Scott, Lynne Moody, Delta Burke, Patricia Pearcy, Richard Lawson. Wilted magnolias and melodrama set in the post–Civil War South, which will remind "you all" of a dozen other such movies, with Burke as the Scarlett O'Hara clone. (Dir: Karen Arthur, 104 mins.)

Charley and the Angel (1973)** Fred MacMurray, Cloris Leachman, Harry Morgan, Kurt Russell, Kathleen Cody. An odd-looking angel (Morgan) tells an earthbound father (MacMurray) that his days are numbered. Add to this yarn a bunch of gangsters and the usual comic she-nanigans, and you have a light yet agree-able movie from the Disney people. (Dir: Vincent McEveety, 93 mins.)†

Charley Hannah (MTV 1986)**½ Robert Conrad, Shane Conrad, Christian Conrad, Joan Leslie, Red West. Robert Conrad's sons Shane and Christian co-star as a street kid and a rookie cop respectively, and macho Robert plays a cop who kills a boy by mistake and spends the rest of the film making amends by becoming a substitute father for another street kid. (Dir: Peter H. Hunt, 104 mins.)

Charley's Aunt (1941)*** Jack Benny, Kay Francis. Perennial comedy about the man who poses as an old lady to help his roommate out of a jam is a good vehicle for Jack. (Dir: Archie Mayo, 81 mins.)

Charley Varrick (1973)***½ Walter Matthau, Joe Don Baker, Andy Robinson, Sheree North, John Vernon. Very slick, entertaining crime yarn sparked by Matthau's deft performance as a crop-duster pilot who dabbles in bank rob-bing on the side. Matthau specializes in small bank heists until he accidentally steals some Mafia funds and thereby hangs the storyline—a good one that will keep you going until the end. (Dir: Don Siegel, 111 mins.)†

Charlie and the Great Balloon Chase (MTV 1981)*½ Jack Albertson, Moosie Drier, Adrienne Barbeau, John Reilly, Slim Pickens. A spry senior citizen and his grandson travel across the country in a hot air balloon. (Dir: Larry Elikann, 104 mins.)†

Charlie Bubbles (Great Britain, 1968)***½ Albert Finney, Liza Minnelli, Colin Blakely, Billie Whitelaw. Tantalizing, offbeat movie. Finney is wonderfully resourceful in creating the image of a man of modest circumstances who is catapulted out of his station and into fame, fortune, and an excessive bore-dom he cannot bear. (Dir: Albert Finney, 91 mins.)

Charlie Chan series. In many ways, the best loved of all movie series heroes, the inscrutable sage began life in Earl Derr Biggers's books, starting with *House Without a Key* in 1925. Although a few silent versions were filmed, Chan was most memorably personified during the talkies by Warner Oland and Sidney Toler, and less memorably by Roland Winters (not forgetting that Ross Martin and Peter Ustinov also played the man of many sayings). (Note: only one print exists of the first Chan talkie, *Behind That Curtain* [1929], in which Charlie is a supporting character.) In addition to the fortune-cookie mysteries reviewed below, fans should check out *Black Camel, The Chinese Cat, Dark Alibi, Dan-*

172

gerous Money, Murder over New York, Dead Men Tell, Castle in the Desert, Meeting at Midnight, Shadows over Chinatown, The Feathered Serpent, The Golden Eye, The Chinese Ring, The Red Dragon, The Scarlet Clue, Sky Dragon, and *Happiness is a Warm Clue (The Return of Charlie Chan).*

Charlie Chan and the Curse of the Dragon Queen (1981)*½ Peter Ustinov, Richard Hatch, Lee Grant, Angie Dickinson, Brian Keith, Roddy McDowall, Rachel Roberts. This slapstick update has some inven-tive gags, for the most part staged with the timing a hair off. Ustinov barely attempts to create the Chan character, and the focus is entirely on his young grandson, a comic bumbler with good intentions. (Dir: Clive Donner, 97 mins.)†

Charlie Chan and the Trap (1947)*** Sidney Toler, Mantan Moreland, Tanis Chand-ler. A bevy of chorus cuties start pointing accusing fingers at each other when the youngest member of the troupe is gar-rotted. Chan's confident sleuthing, some secret passageways, and the pervasive air of mistrust among the suspects keep this mystery hopping. (Dir: Howard Bretherton, 68 mins.)

Charlie Chan at Monte Carlo (1937)*½ Warner Oland, Keye Luke, Virginia Field. Faults: lack of "ancient Chinese prov-erbs," lack of romantic interest, lack of coherent clues. (Dir: Eugene Forde, 71 mins.)

Charlie Chan at the Circus (1936)** Warner Oland, Keye Luke. Big Oland and his big Chan brood frolic at the Big Top. Their fun is interrupted by a three-ring murder mystery perpetrated by a man in an ape suit. (Dir: Harry Lachman, 72 mins.)

Charlie Chan at the Olympics (1937)*** Warner Oland, Katherine deMille. One of the more exciting of Chan's capers, this one sees him chasing an airplane guidance system from Honolulu to the Berlin Olympics via U.S. Navy ship, airplane, and—no kidding—the *Hinden-burg.* (Dir: H. Bruce Humberstone, 71 mins.)

Charlie Chan at the Opera (1936)*** Warner Oland, Boris Karloff. One of the better Chan mysteries. The inscrutable one finds that high culture and low-down murder are not incompatible. (Dir: Bruce Hum-berstone, 66 mins.)†

Charlie Chan at the Race Track (1936)**½ Warner Oland, Keye Luke. This Chanfest moves at a gallop as a big-time horse owner solicits Charlie's help in subverting equine dopers on a transport ship and later in L.A. (Dir: H. Bruce Humber-stone, 70 mins.)

Charlie Chan at the Wax Museum (1940)* Sidney Toler, Victor Sen Yung. Chan pursues an archfiend fond of hiding out in a wax museum and performing plastic surgery on criminals. (Dir: Lynn Shores, 63 mins.)†

Charlie Chan at Treasure Island (1939)*** Sidney Toler, Cesar Romero. The hood in this one: Zodiac, a manic mystic who makes a mint in blackmail. The bait: the airboard suicide of one of Chan's writer friends. The launch: the then-tropical Treasure Island (San Francisco Fair). The verdict: smooth sailing. (Dir: John Larkin, 72 mins.)

Charlie Chan Carries On (1931)**½ Warner Oland, John Garrick. This shipboard mystery about Charlie solving a wealthy American's murder on a world cruise reaches port in satisfying fashion. (Dir: Hamilton MacFadden, 69 mins.)

Charlie Chan (Happiness Is a Warm Clue) (MTV 1971)* Ross Martin, Rocky Gunn, Virginia Ann Lee. Misguided campy revival, brings the Oriental detective out of retirement to solve some less-than-inscrutable mysteries on board a yacht. Martin rarely evokes the mystique created by former Chans, Warner Oland and Sidney Toler. (Dir: Leslie Martinson, 97 mins.)

Charlie Chan in Egypt (1935)**½ Warner Oland, Rita Hayworth, Stepin Fetchit. Tutmania with Chan, in an above-average entry in the long-running series. (Dir: Louis King, 65 mins.)

Charlie Chan in Honolulu (1938)** Sidney Toler, Phyllis Brooks, Victor Sen Yung. Toler's first Chan assignment (after the death of Warner Oland) is blissfully familiar: after a dockside murder, Chan ties up the boat and eventually the murderer. (Dir: H. Bruce Humberstone, 67 mins.)

Charlie Chan in London (1934)**½ Warner Oland, Drue Leyton, Ray Milland. Though more restricted in geography than some others in the series, Oland was at his aphoristic best in this country home crime-crusher. (Dir: Eugene Forde, 79 mins.)

Charlie Chan in Panama (1940)**½ Sidney Toler, Jean Rogers. Disguised as a hat-blocker, Toler tries to block a plot to blow up the Panama Canal. When released it was topical and entertaining; now it's merely entertaining—but it remains one of the better of the Toler Chan pics. (Dir: Norman Foster, 67 mins.)

Charlie Chan in Paris (1935)**½ Warner Oland, Mary Brian, Erik Rhodes. A Chan mystery set in the City of Lights. The solution to the murders involves disguises. (Dir: Lewis Seiler, 71 mins.)†

Charlie Chan in Reno (1939)**½ Sidney Toler, Ricardo Cortez, Phyllis Brooks. A divorce-seeker is murdered, and Toler eventually wrests custody of the culprit. (Dir: Norman Foster, 70 mins.)

Charlie Chan in Rio (1941)*** Sidney Toler, Mary Beth Hughes. Colorful mystery that cashes in on the exotic Rio background as Chan joins forces with the Brazilian police to solve a tricky case. (Dir: Harry Lachman, 60 mins.)†

Charlie Chan in Shanghai (1935)** Warner Oland, Irene Harvey, Charles Locher, Jon Hall, Keye Luke. The Chinese detective assays Shanghai drug haunts. Middling. (Dir: James Tinling, 70 mins.)

Charlie Chan in the City of Darkness (1939)**½ Sidney Toler, Lynn Bari, Lon Chaney, Jr., Leo G. Carroll. A combo mystery-propaganda piece as the Shanghai Sherlock Holmes gets involved with espionage while reminiscing with old army pals in Paris. (Dir: Herbert Leeds, 75 mins.)

Charlie Chan in the Secret Service (1944)** Sidney Toler, Gwen Kenyon. Chan is dispatched to the home of a dead inventor to uncover his murderer and some stolen plans. Monogram Studios unwove Toler and the Chan label from 20th Century-Fox but failed to stitch a well-knit product. (Dir: Phil Rosen, 65 mins.)

Charlie Chan on Broadway (1937)*** Warner Oland, Keye Luke, Joan Marsh. Charlie is in the Big Apple sleuthing his way through nightclubs, the Mob scene, and gossip columns in one of the best Chan pics. (Dir: Eugene Forde, 68 mins.)

Charlie Chan on the Docks of New Orleans (1948)** Roland Winters, Virginia Dale, Mantan Moreland. Wily Charlie investigates some murders in which the *modus operandi* is poison emitted through radio tubes. AKA: **Docks of New Orleans.** (Dir: Derwin Abrahams, 64 mins.)

Charlie Chan's Chance (1932)**½ Warner Oland, Alexander Kirkland. Alliterative Chan caper features Charlie working with Scotland Yard no-talents in undermining a criminal mastermind. (Dir: John Blystone, 73 mins.)

Charlie Chan's Courage (1934)*½ Warner Oland, Drue Leyton. Most of the courage exudes from Oland, because a lesser man would have dropped dead in terror at the atrocious script: he hangs around a ranch disguised as a Chinese servant in order to solve a jewelry theft and murder mystery. (Dir: George Hadden, 70 mins.)

Charlie Chan's Greatest Case (1933)**½ Warner Oland, Heather Angel. The title's claim is a tad excessive. More lighthearted and pleasant than many Chan mysteries, this one follows Oland on the trail of the murderer of a bawdy bachelor. (Dir: Hamilton MacFadden, 70 mins.)

Charlie Chan's Murder Cruise (1940)** Sidney Toler, Marjorie Weaver. Boats, like trains, are good settings for deduction—several Chan mysteries could have had the same title as this one. A Scotland Yard detective dies in Honolulu and Toler boards a cruise for clues in the case. (Dir: Eugene Forde, 75 mins.)

Charlie Chan's Secret (1936)**½ Warner Oland, Rosina Lawrence. At an estate where everyone including the butler could have murdered the magnate's son, Oland plays dumb in order to draw out the culprit. (Dir: Gordon Wiles, 71 mins.)†

Charlie Chaplin Carnival (1916)**** Contains *The Vagabond, The Fireman,* and *Behind the Screen,* the last a particular gem with Chaplin working as a stagehand at a Sennett-like studio. (80 mins.)†

Charlie Chaplin Cavalcade (1916)**** Three shorts—*One A.M., The Floorwalker,* and *The Rink*—all among Chaplin's best. (60 mins.)†

Charlie Chaplin's Keystone Comedies, Volumes 1–5 (1912–16)***½ Charlie Chaplin, Mabel Normand, Fatty Arbuckle, Edgar Kennedy. Five video collections, each containing several short Chaplin comedies made at Mack Sennett's Keystone Studios, home of the famous Kops and cradle of some of the greatest silent comics. These are not Chaplin's best work; his own independent two-reelers were far subtler and more refined than these knock-down farces. But they provide an invaluable look at Chaplin in the process of perfecting his art.

Vol. 1: *Making a Living, Kid Auto Races, A Busy Day, Mabel's Married Life, Laughing Gas, The New Janitor.* (59 mins.)†

Vol. 2: *His Trysting Place, Getting Acquainted, The Fatal Mallet.* (60 mins.)†

Vol. 3: *Caught In a Cabaret, The Masquerader, Between Showers.* (59 mins.)†

Vol. 4: *His Million-Dollar Job, Caught In the Rain, Mabel's Busy Day, The Face On the Barroom Floor.* (54 mins.)†

Vol. 5: *The Rounders, Mabel's Strange Predicament, Tango Tangles, The Star Boarder.* (57 mins.)†

Charlie Chaplin: The Early Years, Vols. 1–4 (1916–20)**** Charlie Chaplin, Mack Swain, Edna Purviance, Syd Chaplin. Here Chaplin came into his own, with more control over his two-reelers and more time to produce them. Also featuring his stock company of players, including the entrancingly awkward Purviance and Chaplin's half-brother Syd.

Vol. 1: *The Immigrant, The Count, Easy Street.* (62 mins.)†

Vol. 2: *The Pawnshop, The Adventurer, One A.M.* (61 mins.)†

Vol. 3: *The Cure, The Floorwalker, The Vagabond.* (63 mins.)†

Vol. 4: *Behind the Screen, The Fireman, The Rink.* (63 mins.)†

Charlie Chase and Ben Turpin (1917–24)*** A pair of two-reelers by Chase and one by Turpin make up this collection from Keystone Studios: *All Wet, Publicity Pays* and *A Clever Dummy.* (67 mins.)†

Charlie Chase Festival (1923–26)***½ Terrific shorts by a forgotten comedy great, Charlie Chase, whose persona was like an older Harold Lloyd. His Everyman caught up in events beyond his control was never at a loss for an inventive solution, even if it usually made matters worse. This compilation includes: *Long Fliv the King, Stone Goods, Fighting Fluid, The Ten-Minute Egg, Young Oldfield,* and *At First Sight.* (70 mins.)†

Charlie Cobb: Nice Night for a Hanging (MTV 1977)** Clu Gulager, Ralph Bellamy, Blair Brown, Stella Stevens. Gulager is an 1880s western private eye named Charlie Cobb, who is taken for a greenhorn by everyone when he turns up with a rancher's daughter. The prodigal daughter isn't exactly welcomed by the rancher's second wife, a lady with a murderous scheme. (Dir: Richard Michaels, 100 mins.)

Charlie McCarthy, Detective (1939)** Edgar Bergen, Robert Cummings, Constance Moore, Louis Calhern, Edgar Kennedy. Nightclub entertainers are involved in the murder of a publisher. Unlikely mixture of mystery and below par Bergen comedy. (Dir: Frank Tuttle, 78 mins.)

Charlie's Angels (MTV 1976)*½ Kate Jackson, Farrah Fawcett-Majors, Jaclyn Smith, David Doyle, David Ogden Stiers, Bo Hopkins. Three beautiful, well-coiffed detectives use their wiles in solving the murder of a wealthy wine grower. The popular TV series followed. (Dir: John Llewellyn Moxey, 78 mins.)

Charlotte's Web (1973)*** Heartwarming animated version of children's classic by E. B. White about a pig who's afraid he's going to be turned into bacon, and a spider who saves him through her magic web. The voices, all marvelous, include Debbie Reynolds, Paul Lynde, Henry Gibson, and Agnes Moorehead. For the whole family. (Dirs: Charles Nichols, Iwao Takamoto, 93 mins.)†

Charly (1968)*** Cliff Robertson, Claire Bloom, Lilia Skala. The superlative Academy Award–winning performance of Cliff Robertson playing a mentally retarded bakery worker is reason enough to see this one. The rest of the film is appreciably less successful, including a questionable romance between Charly (Robertson) and a bright, beautiful woman (Bloom) after surgery has drastically improved Charly's I.Q. (Dir: Ralph Nelson, 103 mins.)†

Charming Sinners (1929)** Ruth Chatterton, Clive Brook, Mary Nolan, William Powell, Florence Eldridge. Slow-moving emotional drama, as Brook betrays wife Chatterton, who is determined to get revenge. Based on *The Constant Wife* by W. Somerset Maugham. (Dir: Robert Milton, 85 mins.)

Charro! (1969)½ Elvis Presley, Ina Balin, Lynn Kellogg, Paul Brinegar, Victor French. Elvis on the Range! Swivel Hips looks saddle sore in this cloddish western about a former outlaw who's accused of pilfering a cannon. (Dir: Charles Marquis Warren, 98 mins.)†

Chartroose Caboose (1960)** Molly Bee, Ben Cooper, Edgar Buchanan. A sugary and sentimental tale (with musical numbers added) about an old railroader who takes in stray people in trouble. (Dir: William "Red" Reynolds, 75 mins.)

Chase, The (1966)** Marlon Brando, Jane Fonda, Robert Redford, E. G. Marshall, Angie Dickinson, James Fox, Miriam Hopkins, Janice Rule, Robert Duvall. Despite a fine cast, a screenplay that bears Lillian Hellman's name, though others were involved, and the directorial talents of Arthur Penn, this story about sex and sin in a small Texas town is an unending compendium of clichés. Producer Sam Spiegel kept interfering with and overruling Penn during production, and the final jumbled film is evidence of various unresolved points of view. (135 mins.)†

Chase (MTV 1973)½ Mitchell Ryan, Reid Smith. A Jack Webb police show pilot about a specialized mobile unit formed to handle tough cases. (Dir: Jack Webb, 78 mins.)

Chase (MTV 1985)*½ Jennifer O'Neill, Robert S. Woods, Richard Farnsworth. Jennifer O'Neill plays a no-nonsense lawyer who comes back to her hometown and takes on a highly controversial case that pits her against old friends and lovers. (Dir: Rod Holcomb, 104 mins.)†

Chase a Crooked Shadow (Great Britain, 1958)**½ Anne Baxter, Richard Todd. Performances make up for the inconsistencies in this drama. Baxter becomes the victim of a diabolical plot set up to do her out of her sizable inheritance. (Dir: Michael Anderson, 87 mins.)

Chasing Dreams (1981)** David G. Brown, John Fife, Jim Shane, Matthew Clark. OK story of a young man torn between trying to keep up the family farm and a chance to play professional baseball. The video packaging, which plays up a bit appearance by Kevin Costner and tries to make this look like another *Field of Dreams*, is extremely misleading. (Dirs: Sean Roche, Therese Conte, 96 mins.)†

Chastity (1969)* Cher, Tom Nolan, Barbara London. Sophomoric nonsense about a forlorn girl trying to find both her own identity and a little love and affection in the bargain. Banal script written and produced by Sonny Bono for his then wife. (Dir: Alessio De Paola, 85 mins.)

Chatahoochee (1989)** Gary Oldman, Dennis Hopper, Frances McDormand, Pamela Reed, Ned Beatty, M. Emmet Walsh. Exposé, based on a true story, of horrendous conditions in a rural southern mental institution in the 1950s, as experienced by a sane man who wound up in one. The cast members are all as good as you might expect, but the script is maddeningly unfocused, with a comic interlude involving a bank robbery that destroys the entire film. (Dir: Mick Jackson, 103 mins.)†

Chato's Land (Great Britain-Spain, 1972)*½ Charles Bronson, Jack Palance, Richard Basehart, Jill Ireland. Violence-ridden western in which a half-breed stays one step ahead of a bloodthirsty posse in New Mexico circa 1873. (Dir: Michael Winner, 110 mins.)†

Chattanooga Choo Choo (1984)** George Kennedy, Barbara Eden, Melissa Sue Anderson, Joe Namath, Clu Gulager. Inoffensive comedy nonsense about a man who must take the legendary train on one last run to claim an inheritance. (Dir: Bruce Bilson, 90 mins.)†

Chatterbox (1943)**½ Judy Canova, Joe E. Brown. A timid radio cowboy goes to a dude ranch, where he becomes a hero with the aid of the ranch's handy girl. Amusing. (Dir: Joseph Santley, 76 mins.)

Che! (1969)½ Omar Sharif, Jack Palance. A notably asinine bit of Hollywood claptrap allegedly depicting the Cuban Revolution, with a focus on Che Guevara. Everyone connected with it deserves censure. (Dir: Richard Fleischer, 96 mins.)

Cheap Detective, The (1978)**½ Peter Falk, Ann-Margret, Eileen Brennan, Sid Caesar, Stockard Channing, James Coco, Dom DeLuise, John Houseman. This Neil Simon comedy offers an unending series of puns and gags based on *Casablanca*, *The Maltese Falcon*, and *The Big Sleep*. Falk, DeLuise, and Houseman are fun to watch in their impersonations, respectively, of Humphrey Bogart, Peter Lorre, and Sydney Greenstreet. (Dir: Robert Moore, 92 mins.)†

Cheaper by the Dozen (1950)*** Clifton Webb, Jeanne Crain, Myrna Loy. Heartwarming and funny comedy drama about a very large family ruled by Papa Webb. Nostalgic and corny at the same time. One of Webb's best performances. Followed by *Belles on Their Toes*. (Dir: Walter Lang, 85 mins.)

Cheaper to Keep Her (1980)* Mac Davis,

175

Tovah Feldshuh, Jack Gilford, Art Metrano, Ian McShane, Rose Marie, Priscilla Lopez. Better to avoid it. Gumshoe Mac hires himself out to stop the husbands of divorcées from holding back alimony. (Dir: Ken Annakin, 92 mins.)†

Cheat, The (1931)*½ Tallulah Bankhead, Irving Pichel, Harvey Stephens, Jay Fassett, Arthur Hohl. Woman accepts money from an Oriental-type villain, and later he demands repayment. Corny melodrama. (Dir: George Abbott, 65 mins.)

Cheaters, The (1945)*** Joseph Schildkraut, Billie Burke. A broken-down ham actor comes to a household of snobs at Christmastime, makes human beings of them. Delightful comedy-drama, excellently acted. (Dir: Joseph Kane, 87 mins.)

Checkered Flag or Crash (1977)* Joe Don Baker, Susan Sarandon, Larry Hagman. Routine car-racing story set in the Philippines. (Dir: Alan Gibson, 104 mins.)

Checking Out (1989)*½ Jeff Daniels, Melanie Mayron, Michael Tucker, Kathleen York, Ann Magnuson. Misfired black comedy. Daniels sent into a midlife frenzy after his best friend's sudden death. (Dir: David Leland, 93 mins.)†

Check Is in the Mail, The (1986)* Brian Dennehy, Anne Archer, Hallie Todd, Chris Herbert, Dick Shawn, Nita Talbot. Woefully inadequate comedy about a frustrated consumer who wages a one-man war against overspending. (Dir: Joan Darling, 91 mins.)†

Cheech and Chong's Next Movie (1980)*** Richard "Cheech" Marin, Tommy Chong, Evelyn Guerrero, Betty Kennedy, Sy Kramer. Los Guys have never gone further, and have rarely been funnier, than in this goofily haphazard vehicle which begins when Cheech's cousin (played by Cheech himself with a Southern Fried Texan accent) comes to visit. (Dir: Tommy Chong, 99 mins.)†

Cheech and Chong's Nice Dreams (1981)** Cheech Marin, Thomas Chong, Evelyn Guerrero, Stacy Keach, Dr. Timothy Leary. The usual random silliness, with the duo playing themselves and a pair of rich Arabs. (Dir: Thomas Chong, 110 mins.)†

Cheech and Chong's Still Smokin' (1983)½ Cheech Marin, Thomas Chong, Hans von In't Veld. Cheech and Chong, playing themselves, venture to Amsterdam for a film festival. Their worst movie, a cheap excuse to use some bad footage of them in a live performance. (Dir: Thomas Chong, 97 mins.)†

Cheech and Chong's The Corsican Brothers (1984)*½ Cheech Marin, Thomas Chong, Roy Dotrice, Shelby Fiddis. The Corsican Brothers is more like it. Their talents are expanded here in a send-up of

swashbucklers. (Dir: Thomas Chong, 87 mins.)†

Cheerleaders, The (1972)½ Stephanie Fondue, Denise Dillaway, Richard Meatwhistle. Junk like this is what gave drive-ins a bad name. A shy teenager joins the cheerleading squad at Amorosa High so that she can, uh, "gain experience." Even fans of trash movies will hate this. (Dir: Paul Glicker, 76 mins.)†

Cheers for Miss Bishop (1941)*** Martha Scott, William Gargan. The story of the long life span of a midwest schoolteacher, her loves, sorrows. Heartwarming drama, excellently acted, written. (Dir: Tay Garnett, 95 mins.)†

Cheetah (1989)** Keith Coogan, Lucy Deakins, Collin Mothupi. Predictable Disney tale of American boy and girl compelled to live with scientist parents in Africa. The teens befriend a young African, adopt a cheetah, and whine about missing MTV. Talk about ugly Americans; these unappreciative brats never get excited about exploring new land and its culture. (Dir: Jeff Blyth, 84 mins.)†

Chernobyl: The Final Warning (U.S.-U.S.S.R., MCTV 1991)**½ Jon Voight, Jason Robards, Sammi Davis. Frightening story about the Ukrainian nuclear plant explosion at Chernobyl in 1986. Ernest Kinoy's script combines real-life facts and a fictional account of what happened to some of the workers and their families. An important subject that helps us understand the ramifications of one of the worst nuclear accidents of our time. Flawed but not uninteresting. AKA: Final Warning. (Dir: Anthony Page, 96 mins.)†

Cherry, Harry, and Raquel (1969)*** Linda Ashton, Charles Napier, Larissa Ely. Russ Meyer is the adult film world's Eisenstein, and there's no better example of his frenetic editing than this softcore saga of a small town sheriff and his two busty girlfriends. Campily scripted by Tom Wolfe, who certainly knew the Right Stuff when he saw it. (Dir: Russ Meyer, 71 mins.)†

Cherry 2000 (1986)** Melanie Griffith, David Andrews, Tim Thomerson, Ben Johnson. Sci-fi adventure with tracker Griffith leading yuppie Andrews into an outlaw-controlled desert to find a replacement part for his damaged love robot. Some good satire early on, but soon settles into formula chases. (Dir: Steve de Jarnatt, 93 mins.)†

Chess Players, The (India, 1977)*** Richard Attenborough, Saeed Jaffrey. An allegorical study of the British Raj in 1856, the film contrasts the chess rivalry of two bickering friends with the power play of a British general to take over a local government. (Dir: Satyajit Ray, 129 mins.)

Chesty Anderson, U.S. Navy (1975)** Shari Eubank, Dorri Thomson, Rosanne Katon, Marcie Barkin, Fred Willard, Frank Campanella, Scatman Crothers, Dyanne Thorne, Ushi Digard, Betty Thomas. Mild service comedy about the adventures of four WAVEs searching for a kidnapped girl. AKA: **Anderson's Angels.** (Dir: Ed Forsyth, 88 mins.)†

Cheyenne—See: **Wyoming Kid, The**

Cheyenne Autumn (1964)***½ Richard Widmark, Carroll Baker, Karl Malden, James Stewart. Director John Ford came up with a winner in this epic retelling of a true incident in frontier history. It's about the migration of a tribe of half-starved Cheyenne Indians from their barren reservation in Oklahoma to their home ground in Wyoming. The treacherous journey tests the Cheyenne's courage and stamina, and their trek is further endangered as the Cavalry sets out to prevent their exodus. (160 mins.)†

Cheyenne Social Club, The (1970)*½ James Stewart, Henry Fonda, Shirley Jones. The only lure here is the appeal of Stewart and Fonda playing a couple of middle-aged cowboys who take up residence at the "Cheyenne Social Club," which is, in reality, a frontier bordello. (Dir: Gene Kelly, 103 mins.)†

Chicago Calling (1952)** Dan Duryea, Mary Anderson. A man hears that his estranged wife and daughter have been injured in a motor accident, is unable to contact them via telephone. Slim story, but plenty of human interest in this drama, practically a one-man show by Duryea. (Dir: John Reinhardt, 74 mins.)

Chicago Confidential (1957)**½ Brian Keith, Beverly Garland. Hollywood seems to think that there should be a motion picture about every city in the United States with the tag "confidential" after it. This is one of them. Crime exposés, gangster war lords, etc. (Dir: Sidney Salkow, 74 mins.)

Chicago Deadline (1949)**½ Alan Ladd, Donna Reed, Arthur Kennedy. Routine newspaper yarn about crusading reporter who gets involved with murder and the underworld. Remade as TV feature *Fame Is the Name of the Game* (1966). (Dir: Lewis Allen, 87 mins.)

Chicago Joe and the Showgirl (1990)** Kiefer Sutherland, Emily Lloyd, Patsy Kensit, Keith Baland. Dull thriller, based on a real crime spree by American G.I. and his English girlfriend in 1944. The realistic atmosphere is well conveyed but it is hard to be interested in these vapid criminals or their inept exploits. (Dir: Bernard Rose, 103 mins.)†

Chicago Syndicate (1955)** Dennis O'Keefe, Abbe Lane, Paul Stewart. Unbelievable drama about one man's attempt to smash the ten-billion-dollar crime network of the "Chicago Syndicate." (Dir: Fred F. Sears, 90 mins.)

Chicken Chronicles, The (1977)**½ Phil Silvers, Ed Lauter, Steve Guttenberg, Lisa Reeves, Gino Baffa. A sometimes interesting look at affluent southern California society through the eyes of a group of well-to-do teenagers. The main characters work after school at a fast-food shop (run by Phil Silvers, excellent in a semi-serious role). (Dir: Francis Simon, 92 mins.)†

Chicken Every Sunday (1949)**½ Dan Dailey, Celeste Holm, Alan Young. As homespun as a sampler and as nostalgic as blueberry pie cooling off on the window sill. Plot involves a small-town dreamer (Dailey) who's always going to strike it big and always ends up losing his shirt. (Dir: George Seaton, 91 mins.)

Chicken Ranch (1982)*** Straightforward, discomfiting documentary about Nevada's famed legal brothel suffers from poor quality in sound and editing and becomes depressing to watch as one realizes the hatred professional prostitutes (many of whom were abused and battered) generally have for their clients. Ironically, the inspiration for the feel-good musical *Best Little Whorehouse in Texas*. (Dirs: Nick Broomfield, Sandi Sissel, 84 mins.)†

Chief Crazy Horse (1955)**½ Victor Mature, Suzan Ball, John Lund. An interesting yarn about one of the greatest Indian chiefs of all time—Crazy Horse, well played by athletic Victor Mature. The plot concerns his alliance with a cavalry major and their eventually necessary parting. (Dir: George Sherman, 86 mins.)

Chikamatsu Monogatari (Japan, 1954)**** Kazuo Hasegwa, Kyoko Kagawa, Eitara Shindo. One of the great films of postwar Japanese cinema. A merchant wife and a romantic young clerk flee the protection and influence of shoguns and find themselves lost in a mercenary society. Breathtaking cinematography and extraordinary performances celebrate this timeless historical love story. AKA: **Crucified Lovers, The** (Dir: Kenji Mizoguchi, 110 mins.)

Child Bride of Short Creek (MTV 1981)*** Conrad Bain, Christopher Atkins, Diane Lane, Kiel Martin, Helen Hunt. Offbeat, well-made drama based upon a 1950s raid on Arizona polygamists. Conrad Bain is the sect leader who plans to marry a fifteen-year-old, only to be thwarted by his son, a Korean War vet (Christopher Atkins). (Dir: Robert Lewis, 104 mins.)†

177

Child in the House (Great Britain, 1956)*** Phyllis Calvert, Eric Portman, Mandy Miller, Stanley Baker. Intelligent drama of a youngster from a broken home and the change she brings into the lives of her aunt and uncle. (Dirs: Cy Endfield, Charles de la Tour, 88 mins.)

Child Is Born, A (1940)**½ Jeffrey Lynn, Geraldine Fitzgerald. Remake of *Life Begins* is well done but the maternity hospital drama is still too morbid and heavy to be called entertaining. (Dir: Lloyd Bacon, 79 mins.)

Childish Things—See: Tale of the Cock

Child Is Waiting, A (1963)*** Burt Lancaster, Judy Garland, Steven Hill, Gena Rowlands. Frequently gripping story of a music teacher and a psychologist on the staff of a school for retarded children. Poignant, despite some weak spots in script and direction. (Dir: John Cassavetes, 102 mins.)†

Child of Glass (MTV 1978)** Steve Shaw, Katy Kurtzman, Barbara Barrie, Biff McGuire, Nina Foch, Anthony Zerbe, Olivia Barash. When his family moves into an old New Orleans mansion, a young boy discovers a ghost whose death has to be solved before she can rest. (Dir: John Erman, 93 mins.)†

Children, The (1980)* Gale Garnett, Gil Rogers, Martin Shaker, Tracy Griswold. Nuclear contamination gives kiddies the power to zap you with a hot flash you won't live to talk about. Only for those who find suburban children terrifying under any circumstances. (Dir: Max Kalmanowicz, 89 mins.)†

Children in the Crossfire (MTV 1984)*** Charles Haid, Karen Valentine, Julia Duffy, David Hoffman. A charming TV movie about Protestant and Catholic kids from Belfast in America for the summer. The plot concerns how the youngsters are exposed to easy-going American families, and how the Americans react to the kids' attitudes about their homeland. An upbeat sequel to the 1972 *A War of Children*. (Dir: George Schaefer, 104 mins.)

Children Nobody Wanted, The (MTV 1981)**½ Fred Lehne, Michelle Pfeiffer, Matt Clark, Noble Willingham, Anne Haney. Based on a real story about a young college student who bucked all odds to become a foster parent at the age of 21. (Dir: Richard Michaels, 104 mins,)

Children of a Lesser God (1986)*** William Hurt, Marlee Matlin, Piper Laurie, Philip Bosco. This award-winning theatrical piece about a dedicated teacher (Hurt) obsessed with making a proud deaf woman cope with the hearing world is superbly acted. The film flounders a bit on the device of Hurt having to verbalize all of the nonspeaking actress's dialogue. Best Actress Oscar went to Matlin. (Dir: Randa Haines, 119 mins.)†

Children of An Lac, The (MTV 1980)*** Shirley Jones, Ina Balin, Beulah Quo. Compelling drama based on the real-life evacuation and airlift of 219 Vietnamese orphans from the An Lac ("Happy Place") orphanage in Saigon just before the city fell to the Communists in April 1975. (Dir: John Llewellyn Moxey, 104 mins.)†

Children of Blood—See: Cauldron of Blood

Children of Chaos (France, 1988)**½ EmmanueIle Béart, Robert Hossein, Patrick Catalifo. Well-intentioned but vague drama about a program to rehabilitate young petty criminals and drug abusers via an acting workshop. Feminist writer-director Yannick Bellon is adept at showing the pressures faced by young people, but the plot never rises above standard melodrama. (98 mins.)

Children of Divorce (MTV 1980)** Barbara Feldon, Stacy Nelkin, Christopher Ciampa, Billy Dee Williams, Olivia Cole. The kids of three households of divorced parents commiserate with each other to try to understand what has happened to their lives. A good cast helps the story along but the segmented plotting detracts. (Dir: Joanna Lee, 104 mins.)†

Children of Paradise (France, 1945)**** Jean Louis Barrault, Arletty, Pierre Brasseur, Maria Casares. Universally praised as a masterwork, this romantic film is about the tragic love of a mime for a glamorous woman of easy virtue. It captures the flavor of theatrical life, both the excitement felt in the gallery and the emotional upheaval emanating from the wings. This is one of the great French postwar classics. (Dir: Marcel Carne, 188 mins.)

Children of Rage (Great Britain-Israel, 1975)*** Helmut Griem, Olga Georges-Picot, Cyril Cusack, Simon Ward. Talky but worthy look at the issues behind Palestinian terrorism, as seen by an Israeli doctor at a refugee camp. (Dir: Arthur Allen Seidelman, 106 mins.)†

Children of Sanchez, The (1978)** Anthony Quinn, Dolores Del Rio, Katy Jurado. Slow-moving drama of Mexican laborer Quinn's attempts to keep his many offspring, some illegitimate, together. (Dir: Hall Bartlett, 126 mins.)†

Children of the Corn (1984)** Peter Horton, Linda Hamilton, R. G. Armstrong. Is there anything Stephen King has written that won't be turned into a film? A young couple stumbles across a rural cult in which human sacrifices are harvested for a bloodthirsty god. Vegetarians be forewarned. (Dir: Fritz Kiersch, 93 mins.)†

Children of the Damned (Great Britain, 1964)**½ Ian Hendry, Barbara Ferris. Here's the sequel to the infinitely superior *Village of the Damned*. The menacing children with the strange luminous eyes set their target as the destruction of the world. (Dir: Anton M. Leader, 90 mins.)

Children of the Lotus Eaters—See: **Psychiatrist, The: God Bless the Children**

Children of the Night (MTV 1985)**½ Kathleen Quinlan, Nicholas Campbell, Mario Van Peebles, Lar Park-Lincoln, Wally Ward. Another sad teenage prostitute story, seen through the eyes of a young sociologist (Kathleen Quinlan) who provides a home for abused kids. (Dir: Robert Markowitz, 104 mins.)

Children of Times Square, The (MTV 1986)**½ Howard Rollins, Jr., Joanna Cassidy, Branden Douglas, Larry B. Scott, Jason Bernard, David Ackroyd. A 14-year-old boy from a suburban family heads for the Times Square area of New York City; doesn't take long for him to be recruited into a ring of adolescent drug runners. Joanna Cassidy is the victim's mother, who sets out to find her son before it's too late. (Dir: Curtis Hanson, 104 mins.)

Children Shouldn't Play with Dead Things (1972)* Alan Ormsby, Anya Ormsby, Valerie Mauches, Jane Daly, Jeffrey Gillen. A group of cloddish aspiring filmmakers accidentally bring the dead back to life. They should have revived this imaginative but overly silly script. (Dir: Benjamin [Bob] Clark, 85 mins.)†

Children's Hour, The (1962)**½ Audrey Hepburn, Shirley MacLaine, James Garner, Miriam Hopkins, Fay Bainter, Karen Balkin, Veronica Cartwright. Mildly engrossing remake of *These Three*, Lillian Hellman's play about ruinous gossip. The director of the original film, William Wyler, obviously wanted to do a more faithful version, but his direction here is overstated, with pregnant pauses all over the place. Lacks the punch of the original, despite MacLaine's intriguing performance. (107 mins.)†

Child Saver, The (MTV 1988)** Alfre Woodard, Mario Van Peebles, Deon Richmond. Woodard stars as a career woman who tries to help out a seven-year-old street kid (Richmond) break away from a drug dealer (Van Peebles). Solid, streetwise drama. (Dir: Stan Lathan, 96 mins.)

Child's Cry (MTV 1986)*** Lindsay Wagner, Peter Coyote, Taliesin Jaffe, Guy Boyd, Gerald S. O'Loughlin. Heartwrenching drama starring Lindsay Wagner as a dedicated social worker out to get

to the bottom of a young boy's psychological scars. (Dir: Gilbert Cates, 104 mins.)

Child's Play (1972)*** James Mason, Robert Preston, Beau Bridges. Is Mr. Malley (James Mason) paranoid? Is there really a conspiracy against him by the boys of St. Charles boarding school? Direction is atmospheric, and creates the obligatory demonic and suspenseful mood. Acting is exemplary, led by Preston as the teacher suspected of leading the conspiracy. (Dir: Sidney Lumet, 100 mins.)

Child's Play (1988)*** Catherine Hicks, Chris Sarandon, Brad Dourif, Alex Vincent. Spiffy horror thriller with psycho Dourif transferring his soul into a doll, then seeking vengeance on those who killed him. Director Tom Holland *(Fright Night)* demonstrates careful pacing, starting out slowly and leaving the good stuff for the end. (87 mins.)†

Child's Play 2 (1990)* Alex Vincent, Jenny Agutter, Gerrit Graham, Brad Dourif, Grace Zabriskie. Inevitable sequel is short on logic but strong on gore. Devil doll Chucky is madder than Rambo as he continues to terrorize poor little Vincent. Only for hardcore horror fans. (Dir: John Lafia, 84 mins.)†

Child Stealer, The (MTV 1979)***½ Beau Bridges, Blair Brown, David Groh. The subject of a divorced parent abducting his children from his ex-wife is given honest, compelling treatment. (Dir: Mel Damski, 104 mins.)

Child Under a Leaf (Canada, 1974)*½ Dyan Cannon, Joseph Campanella, Donald Pilon. Dyan adores her lover; but she's been married so long she can't break the habit, and she keeps talking about what she should do until you're numbed by her indecisiveness. (Dir: George Bloomfield, 88 mins.)

Chiller (MTV 1985)**½ Michael Beck, Beatrice Straight, Paul Sorvino, Laura Johnson. Pretty fair scare movie, something TV usually bungles. Given a neatly structured plot, director Wes Craven makes the most of this unsettling thriller in which a cryogenically frozen body comes back to life to conduct a reign of terror. (104 mins.)

Chilly Scenes of Winter (1982)*** John Heard, Mary Beth Hurt, Gloria Grahame, Peter Riegert, Kenneth McMillan. Originally released with a different ending as *Head over Heels*, this touching adaptation of the novel by Ann Beattie (who appears briefly as a waitress) finds Heard painfully smitten with beguiling married co-worker Hurt. Director Joan Micklin Silver, who helmed *Hester Street*, coaxes wonderful performances from her cast. (99 mins.)†

179

Chimes at Midnight (Spain-Switzerland, 1967)*** Orson Welles, Jeanne Moreau, John Gielgud. Welles's most successful attempt at transferring Shakespeare to the screen. The epic tale of the loyal fat knight, Falstaff, is marred by some technical inadequacies, but is strikingly acted and directed with great visual authority. (Dir: Orson Welles, 115 mins.)

China Clipper (1936)*** Pat O'Brien, Beverly Roberts. Well-acted and written story of the first flight of Pan American's China Clipper. Sticks to the facts and avoids the clichés of air stories. (Dir: Raymond Enright, 100 mins.)

China Cry (1990)* Julia Nickson Soul, Russell Wong, James Shigeta, France Nuyen. Dull, ludicrous drama about the persecution of Christians in Mao's China. Features firing squads and government-sanctioned torture of pregnant women. Only Wong's performance, as a young man torn between Church and State, merits attention. (Dir: James F. Collier, 103 mins.)†

China Gate (1957)** Gene Barry, Angie Dickinson, Nat King Cole. A contrived bit of action concerning France's troubles in Indo-China. (Dir: Samuel Fuller, 97 mins.)†

China Girl (1987)*** James Russo, Sari Chang, Richard Panebianco, David Caruso. Remarkably slick low-budget effort which sets *Romeo and Juliet* in a contemporary gang milieu, and successfully avoids being an ersatz *West Side Story.* In this case, the lovers in question, and their gang-oriented older brothers, hail from Little Italy and Chinatown. (Dir: Abel Ferrara, 88 mins.)†

China Is Near (Italy, 1967)*** Elda Tattoli, Glauco Mauri. An uneven yet occasionally brilliant film from the talented young Italian director Marco Bellocchio. Story concerns the affairs of an Italian politician's family, and most of it is a satire on left-wing Italian politics, with a few darts thrown at Italian sexual mores. (108 mins.)

China Lake Murders, The (MCTV 1990)** Tom Skerritt, Michael Parks, Nancy Everhard, Lauren Tewes, Bill McKinney, J. C. Quinn. Stressed-out cop Parks takes a vacation in a small California desert town where, still in uniform, he pulls drivers off the road and murders them senselessly. Skerritt is wasted as the local policeman in this binge of gratuitous violence. (Dir: Alan Metzger, 96 mins.)†

China Rose (MTV 1983)*** George C. Scott, Ali MacGraw, David Snell, Michael Biehn. Intriguing, if slow-moving, drama about an American businessman (Scott) who is searching for his son's
180

grave in China. With the aid of an interpreter (McGraw), Scott's innocent odyssey turns into a nightmarish series of events dealing with drug traffickers in Hong Kong. (Dir: Robert Day, 104 mins.)

China Seas (1935)*** Clark Gable, Jean Harlow, Wallace Beery, Rosalind Russell. A rousing melodrama about pirates in the China Seas trying to defeat Captain Gable. The stars give a good account of themselves in this entertaining adventure story. (Dir: Tay Garnett, 89 mins.)†

China Syndrome, The (1979)***½ Jane Fonda, Jack Lemmon, Michael Douglas, Peter Donat, Scott Brady, Wilford Brimley. Fonda, Lemmon, and Douglas (who also doubled as producer) all contribute excellent performances in this suspense thriller about a near-disastrous accident at a nuclear power plant and the subsequent cover-up by the top brass. The tension is taut throughout, with an exciting climax. (Dir: James Bridges, 123 mins.)†

Chinatown (1974)**** Jack Nicholson, Faye Dunaway, John Huston, Diane Ladd, Perry Lopez, John Hillerman. Excellent crime drama, set in the Los Angeles of the thirties; Nicholson is superb as a small-time private eye who stumbles on a big case which involves graft over valuable land and water rights, murder, incest, and other intriguing elements. They're all put in their proper place by writer Robert Towne in an intricate, entertaining screenplay. Sequel: *The Two Jakes* (Dir: Roman Polanski, 130 mins.)†

China Venture (1953)**½ Edmond O'Brien, Barry Sullivan, Jocelyn Brando. WWII adventure story about two officers and a navy nurse who try to rescue an admiral held captive by Chinese guerrillas. (Dir: Don Siegel, 83 mins.)

Chinese Boxes (Great Britain-West Germany, 1984)*** Will Patton, Gottfried John, Adelheid Arndt, Robbie Coltrane. American Patton, on the verge of leaving West Berlin, is drawn into a complex series of troubles beginning with the death of a drug runner. Director Christopher Petit (who wrote this along with L. M. Kit Carson) uses thriller conventions as a jumping-off point for a Wim Wenders–like exploration of alienation. (87 mins.)†

Chinese Ring, The (1947)*½ Roland Winters, Warren Douglas, Victor Sen Yung. For true Chan fans, this Charlie may be the Winters of their discontent. Penetrating the mystery of a Chinese princess's murder, Chan flushes out various venal types who were out to nab money the princess was going to use to buy U.S. planes. (Dir: William Beaudine, 67 mins.)

Chinese Roulette (West Germany, 1976)*** Margit Carstensen, Ulli Lommel, Anna Karina, Macha Meril, Volker Spengler. Knowing that her parents are both having affairs, a crippled girl cons all four partners into spending a weekend at the same country home. One of director Rainer Werner Fassbinder's most jaundiced looks at sex and love. Michael Ballhaus's ever-moving camera adds to the nasty fun of this gorgeously photographed, sharply written story. (86 mins.)

Chipmunk Adventure, The (1987)*** Voices of Ross Bagdasarian, Jr., Janice Karman, Dody Goodman, Susan Tyrrell, Frank Welker. Fooled by a pair of nogoodniks, the Chipmunks get mixed up in a diamond smuggling scheme as they sail around the world in a balloon race. Smooth sailing throughout with catchy tunes and a welcome avoidance of icky sentimentality. (Dir: Janice Karman, 76 mins.)†

Chip Off the Old Block (1944)*** Donald O'Connor, Ann Blyth. Teenager goes through misunderstandings with the young daughter of a musical comedy star. Neat, breezy comedy with music. (Dir: Charles Lamont, 82 mins.)

Chisum (1970)**½ John Wayne, Forrest Tucker, Christopher George, Ben Johnson. Slam-bang action western with tall-in-the-saddle John Wayne as a cattle baron fighting off the treacherous land barons. (Dir: Andrew V. McLaglen, 118 mins.)†

Chitty, Chitty, Bang, Bang (Great Britain, 1968)**½ Dick Van Dyke, Sally Ann Howes, Anna Quayle. This $10-million production does provide a few laughs for the kids, but it's pretty sophomoric most of the way and bogged down by some really terrible songs. The car-star does eventually get airborne, though the picture itself never takes off. (Dir: Ken Hughes, 142 mins.)†

Chloe in the Afternoon (France, 1972)***½ Bernard Verley, Zouzou, Françoise Verley, Françoise Fabian, Beatrice Romand. The conclusion of writer-director Eric Rohmer's cycle of *Six Moral Fables*. A featherweight, beautifully crafted look at monogamous marriage and the foibles of imperfect man. (97 mins.)†

Chocolat (France, 1988)***½ Issach de Bankole, Giulia Boschi, François Cluzet. A young Frenchwoman recalls her childhood in colonial Africa, just prior to the withdrawal of European settlers. Most of the movie's meaningful and poignant moments occur in the faces and reactions of the characters rather than in their words. Subtle, beautifully directed. (Dir: Claire Denis, 105 mins.)†

Chocolate Soldier, The (1941)*** Nelson Eddy, Risë Stevens. Score from "The Chocolate Soldier," plus plot of Molnar's "The Guardsman," tempered with good debut performance of Miss Stevens, adds up to a nice package for operetta fans. (Dir: Roy Del Ruth, 102 mins.)†

Chocolate War, The (1989)** John Glover, Ilan Michael-Smith, Wally Ward. At a boys' school controlled by an ambitious monk and a clan of student fascists, one student upsets the system by refusing to take part in a fund-raising chocolate sale. Teens who enjoyed the popular novel may enjoy this low budget adaptation, but most adults will find it obvious and dreary. (Dir: Keith Gordon, 100 mins.)†

Choice, The (MTV 1981)**½ Susan Clark, Mitchell Ryan, Jennifer Warren. A turgid drama about a mother who finds her daughter caught in almost the same dilemma which she recently faced herself. Should her pregnant daughter have an abortion in order to maintain her relationship with her lover? (Dir: David Greene, 104 mins.)†

Choice of Arms (France, 1983)*** Yves Montand, Catherine Deneuve, Gerard Depardieu. This French *film noir* is worth seeing for the high-voltage trio of Deneuve, Depardieu, and Montand. After years of a shady existence as a mobster, Montand plans to retire to Ireland with his mistress. A monkey wrench is thrown in his plans when violent-tempered Depardieu breaks out of jail with one of Montand's old pals. (Dir: Alan Corneau, 117 mins.)†

Choices (1981)** Paul Carafotes, Victor French, Lelia Goldoni, Dennis Patrick, Val Avery. Mawkish inspirational drama about a sports enthusiast who wants to play football despite his deafness. (Dir: Silvio Narizzano, 90 mins.)

Choices (MTV 1986)*** George C. Scott, Jacqueline Bisset, Melissa Gilbert, Laurie Kennedy, Steven Flynn. The ongoing debate about abortion serves as the basis for a drama that confronts the issues, pro and con. Scott is a sixty-two-year-old man whose daughter (Gilbert) announces she is pregnant and intends to have an abortion. (Dir: David Lowell Rich, 104 mins.)

Choices of the Heart (MTV 1983)*** Melissa Gilbert, Martin Sheen, Mike Farrell, Helen Hunt. Caring drama, performed with beguiling energy and skill by Gilbert as Jean Donovan, the American missionary murdered three years ago in El Salvador. Apart from being a political indictment, it's a finely etched portrait of a headstrong woman who discovers meaning to her life among the peasants of wartorn Central America. (Dir: Joseph Sargent, 104 mins.)

Choirboys, The (1977)**½ Perry King,

Don Stroud, James Woods, Randy Quaid, Charles During, Lou Gossett, Jr., Tim McIntyre, Blair Brown, Burt Young. Dark-humored comedy-drama about L.A. police who periodically meet for "choir practice"—wild binges to let them release their tensions. Many found this offensive, but it's based on a novel by ex-detective Joseph Wambaugh, who knows whereof he speaks when he talks about cops. (Dir: Robert Aldrich, 119 mins.)†

Choke Canyon (1986)** Stephen Collins, Nicholas Pryor, Janet Julian, Lance Henriksen, Bo Svenson. The not-to-be-taken-seriously plot involves a dedicated physicist whose sound-energy experiment (undertaken in the hopes of saving the Earth's energy supply) can only be carried out at Choke Canyon at the exact moment Halley's comet is passing by. (Dir: Chuck Bail, 94 mins.)†

C.H.O.M.P.S. (1979)* Wesley Eure, Valerie Bertinelli, Conrad Bain, Chuck McCann, Red Buttons. Strictly for kids. A young genius invents a bionic dog designed to be the best home protection device. (Dir: Don Chaffey, 89 mins.)†

Chooper, The (1971)½ Carolyn Brandt, Ron Haydock, Jason Wayne. Actress Brandt (playing herself, if anyone cares) inherits a ranch possessed by the spirit of an Indian god of vengeance. Low-budget weirdness has the feel of a glorified home movie, with acting to match. Mercilessly padded, but great fun for Z-movie aficionados. AKA: **Blood Shack**. (Dir: Ray Dennis Steckler, 69 mins.)†

Choose Me (1984)**** Genevieve Bujold, Lesley Ann Warren, Keith Carradine, Rae Dawn Chong, John Larroquette. An eccentric, sometimes erotic, always perceptive adult comedy. A free-loving bar owner (Warren) works out her problems with the help of a radio show sex therapist (Bujold) who meddles in others' romances while repressing her own libido. A sexy but slightly strange drifter (Carradine) pursues them both, proposes marriage, and alters both women's lives. A unique, dreamy meditation on sexual longings. (Dir: Alan Rudolph, 114 mins.)†

Chopper Chicks In Zombletown (1990)** Jamie Rose, Catherine Carlen, Kristina Loggia, Don Calfa, Martha Quinn. Yet another spoof of horror movies, this one pitting a pack of female bikers against a town full of zombies created by mad doctor Calfa (the best thing in the movie). Some laughs for horror buffs along with a lot of cheap jokes. (Dir: Dan Hoskins, 89 mins.)

Chopping Mall (1986)** Kelli Maroney, Tony O'Dell, John Terlesky, Russell Todd, Karrie Emerson, Barbara Crampton. Hor-

ror film about malfunctioning security robots that attack a group of teenagers in a shopping mall gets, uh, mechanical after awhile. AKA: **Killbots**. (Dir: Jim Wynorski, 76 mins.)†

Chords of Fame (1983)**½ Documentary about the work and life of the late Phil Ochs, one of the more political singers to emerge from the folk music boom of early '60s. Interviews with his contemporaries, including Abbie Hoffman, Jerry Rubin, Pete Seeger, Oscar Brand, Tom Paxton, Dave Van Ronk, and others (many of whom perform Ochs's songs) make this a must-see for anyone interested in '60s folk music in general, but there's too little footage of Ochs himself, and actor Bill Burnett's impersonation of him is unsatisfying. (Dir: Michael Korolenko, 88 mins.)

Chorus Line, A: The Movie (1985)** Michael Douglas, Alyson Reed, Justin Ross, Cameron English, Blane Savage, Vicki Frederick, Terrence Mann, Audrey Landers, Gregg Burge, Janet Jones. A flat-footed filming of Broadway's longest-running hit, directed with a conspicuous lack of energy by Richard Attenborough. He has absolutely no feeling for the musical-drama pacing or for the raw, desperate drive of young dancers that made the show work on stage. Justin Ross and Cameron English exhibit star quality, but nominal star Michael Douglas is charmless as the show's director. (117 mins.)†

Chorus of Disapproval, A (Great Britain, 1988)** Jeremy Irons, Anthony Hopkins, Prunella Scales, Jenny Seagrove, Patsy Kensit, Alexandra Pigg, Lionel Jeffries. A shy, recently widowed Brit joins an amateur theatrical company in order to meet people. The people he meets, however, are married women more interested in playing around than playacting. Adaptation of an Alan Ayckbourn comedy is well acted but misdirected by action specialist Michael Winner. (99 mins.)†

Chosen, The (1978)—See: **Holocaust: 2000**

Chosen, The (1981)***½ Maximilian Schell, Rod Steiger, Robby Benson, Barry Miller, Hildy Brooks, Ron Rifkin, Val Avery. Lovely movie, dealing with friendship, values, and change, with an authentic Brooklyn setting during World War II. Film focuses on the friendship of two teenagers, one a Hasidic youth isolated by the constraints placed upon him by his father, a rabbi, the other the son of a professor, journalist, and Zionist and part of the wider world denied his friend. Based on Chaim Potok's celebrated novel. (Dir: Jeremy Paul Kagan, 108 mins.)†

Chosen Survivors (1974)**½ Jackie Cooper, Bradford Dillman, Alex Cord, Richard Jaeckel, Diana Muldaur. How would you feel if you'd been chosen to survive atomic desolation way under the ground, only to find out that some of your fellow survivors happened to be vampire bats? Good enough to drive you batty for awhile. (Dir: Sutton Roley, 99 mins.)

Christiane F. (West Germany, 1981)**½ Natja Brunckhorst, Thomas Haustein, David Bowie. Cynical, violent, brutally realistic drama about teenage junkies, based on the real life story of a thirteen-year-old girl who turned to prostitution to support her heroin habit. Despite a style that is by turns moralistic and exploitative, its relentless attention to the horrifying details of addiction has an undeniable power. (Dir: Ulrich Edel, 124 mins.)†

Christina (Canada, 1974)*½ Barbara Parkins, Peter Haskell, James McEachin, Marlyn Mason. A lame thriller. A gorgeous lady (Parkins) approaches an unemployed engineer (Haskell) with a proposition that he become her husband for a fee of $25,000. (Dir: Paul Krasny, 98 mins.)†

Christine (1983)**½ Keith Gordon, John Stockwell, Harry Dean Stanton. This Stephen King yarn about a murderous car certainly has a few miles on it. Luckily, Gordon excels as the shy teen whose personality is transformed by the evil domination of his auto. (Dir: John Carpenter, 116 mins.)†

Christmas Carol, A (1938)*** Reginald Owen, Gene Lockhart. Sincere, well-acted adaptation of the Dickens classic. (Dir: Edwin L. Marin, 70 mins.)†

Christmas Carol, A (Great Britain, 1951)***½ Alastair Sim, Kathleen Harrison. The best-known version of the classic Dickens tale of miser Scrooge who was turned into a human being by the spirit of Yuletide. Well done. (Dir: Brian Desmond Hurst, 86 mins.)†

Christmas Carol, A (MTV 1984)*** George C. Scott, Edward Woodward, Frank Finlay, David Warner, Susannah York. An absolutely delightful rendering of the famous Dickens yarn about the skinflint Scrooge. Scott is a perfect Ebeneezer Scrooge, playing all the shadings of the character, creating a memorable portrait. (Dir: Clive Donner, 104 mins.)

Christmas Coal Mine Miracle, The—See: **Christmas Miracle in Caulfield U.S.A.**

Christmas Comes to Willow Creek (MTV 1987)*½ John Schneider, Tom Wopat, Kim Delaney. A reunion of the stars of "The Dukes of Hazzard" casts them as feuding brothers who are counted on to deliver Christmas goodies to an Alaskan town. No Catherine Bach, and bad country music to boot. (Dir: Richard Lang, 96 mins.)†

Christmas Eve—See: **Sinner's Holiday**

Christmas Eve (MTV 1986)*** Loretta Young, Arthur Hill, Ron Liebman, Trevor Howard, Patrick Cassidy, Charles Frank, Season Hubley, Kate Reid, Deborah Richter. Trite storyline is redeemed by Young. She portrays a wealthy woman who initiates a reunion with the three grandchildren whom her son had driven away years before. (Dir: Stuart Oper, 104 mins.)

Christmas Evil—See: **You Better Watch Out**

Christmas Gift, The (MTV 1986)** John Denver, Jane Kaczmarek, Edward Winter. Denver plays an architect who encounters a town that seems unaffected by time (sort of a Brigadoon with snow peaks), and he and his daughter fall under the town's mysterious spell, so that he now must oppose his employer's plans for development. Sappy Americana. (Dir: Michael Pressman, 104 mins.)

Christmas Holiday (1944)*** Deanna Durbin, Gene Kelly. Nice girl marries a ne'er-do-well whose weakness turns him to crime. Sordid tale receives classy direction, good performances to make it above average. (Dir: Robert Siodmak, 92 mins.)

Christmas in Connecticut (1945)**½ Barbara Stanwyck, Dennis Morgan, Sydney Greenstreet, Reginald Gardiner. Occasionally funny farce about a newspaper columnist who is instructed by her boss to have a war hero as her family's guest for Christmas dinner. Of course, she has no family…and by that thread the film hangs. (Dir: Peter Godfrey, 101 mins.)†

Christmas in July (1940)**** Dick Powell, Ellen Drew. Guy mistakenly thinks he has won a coffee slogan contest, starts buying everything on credit. Hilarious comedy, written and directed by Preston Sturges with an unerring hand. (70 mins.)†

Christmas Kid, The (U.S.-Spain, 1966)**½ Jeffrey Hunter, Louis Hayward, Gustavo Rojo, Perla Cristal. Offbeat western short on action, but tries to develop a decent character study. Hunter, born on Christmas Day and attended by three wise men (a mayor, a judge, and a doctor), grows up wild because his father rejects him. (Dir: Sidney Pink, 87 mins.)

Christmas Lilies of the Field (MTV 1979)**½ Billy Dee Williams, Maria Schell, Fay Hauser, Judith Piquet, Lisa Mann. An acceptable follow-up to *Lilies of the Field*, with Williams as Homer Smith, the itinerant workman with a soft heart. Returning to the chapel he built for the nuns fifteen years earlier, Homer is persuaded to construct an orphanage. (Dir: Ralph Nelson, 104 mins.)†

Christmas Memory, A—See: Trilogy

Christmas Miracle in Caufield U.S.A. (MTV 1977)* Mitch Ryan, Kurt Russell, Andrew Prine, John Carradine, Don Porter. The tight-fisted miner-owner (Porter), who doesn't maintain safety precautions, is the villain in this caved-in yarn about troubles in a coal town at Christmastime. AKA: **The Christmas Coal Mine Miracle.** (Dir: Jud Taylor, 104 mins.)†

Christmas Star, The (MTV 1986)**½ Ed Asner, Rene Auberjonois, Jim Metzler, Susan Tyrrell, Fred Gwynne. Saccharine tale of a con man who dons a Santa Claus suit as a disguise, and then can't bear to disappoint two kids who think he's the real item. (Dir: Alan Shapiro, 104 mins.)

Christmas Story, A (1983)***½ Melinda Dillon, Darren McGavin, Peter Billingsley. An utterly beguiling, perfect little Christmas picture. Based on the nostalgic writings of humorist Jean Sheperd, this "story" is about young Ralphie, whose only goal in life is to get a certain BB air rifle for Christmas. The excellent sense of period detail and the letter-perfect casting is surprising, considering that this precious bit of Christmas cheer was directed by the man who had previously given us *Porky's*. (Dir: Bob Clark, 98 mins.)†

Christmas to Remember, A (MTV 1978)***½ Jason Robards, Jr., Eva Marie Saint, George Parry, Joanne Woodward. Robards is in top form playing a cantankerous, ailing old Minnesota Depression farmer who is angry with God for taking his son away in WWI and treats his city-bred grandson with derision. A moving script and splendid acting turn this into quality fare. (Dir: George Englund, 104 mins.)†

Christmas Tree, The (France-Italy, 1969)** William Holden, Virna Lisi, Brook Fuller, Bourvil. A strained lunge for the tear ducts, in a tale of a father's attempt to make the last days happy for his son, dying of leukemia. AKA: **When Wolves Cry.** (Dir: Terence Young, 110 mins.)*

Christmas Wife, The (MCTV 1988)***½ Jason Robards, Julie Harris. Two of America's greatest actors star as a pair of lonely strangers who make a contract to spend Christmas together. A poignant, offbeat delight about love in the later years. (Dir: David Jones, 75 mins.)†

Christmas Without Snow, A (MTV 1980)*** Michael Learned, John Houseman, Calvin Levels. Offbeat film for the holiday season. A church choir is rehearsing Handel's "Messiah," and we get to know the singers during rehearsals. Learned's di-

vorced woman and Levels's ghetto college student are the most intriguing characters. (Dir: John Korty, 96 mins.)†

Christopher Columbus (Great Britain, 1949)**½ Fredric March, Florence Eldridge. Lavish but empty production concerning the attempts of the explorer to get permission from the Spanish court to sail to the New World. Very slow, talky, dull. (Dir: David MacDonald, 104 mins.)

Christopher Strong (1933)*** Katharine Hepburn, Colin Clive, Billie Burke, Helen Chandler. A superior feminist drama from 1933, directed by the sole female Hollywood director of that era, Dorothy Arzner. Hepburn is perfectly cast as the aviatrix hemmed in by the competing demands of love and career. (77 mins.)†

Christ Stopped at Eboli (Italy, 1979)***½ Gian Maria Volonte, Irene Papas, Paolo Bonicelli, Lea Massari, Alain Cluny. Extraordinary but demanding film about antifascist Carlo Levi, who went into exile in the mid 1930s. The film recounts how he acclimatized himself to life in a remote Italian village. AKA: **Eboli.** (Dir: Francesco Rosi, 120 mins.)†

Chrome and Hot Leather (1971)**½ William Smith, Tony Young, Marvin Gaye, Kathy Baumann. An ex-Green Beret enlists his army buddies to help him get revenge on the biker gang that killed his girlfriend. Not bad, though singer Marvin Gaye's acting debut doesn't come to much. (Dir: Lee Frost, 91 mins.)

Chronicle of Anna Magdalena Bach, The (West Germany, 1967)***½ Gustav Leonhardt, Christiane Lang, Paolo Carlini. Near-documentary account of the daily life of Johann Sebastian Bach taken from the writings of his second wife. Classic example of minimalist cinema is famous for its detailed concert scenes, historical authenticity, still landscapes and static camera work. (Dir: Jean-Marie Straub, 93 mins.)

Chubasco (1968)**½ Richard Egan, Christopher Jones, Susan Strasberg, Ann Sothern, Simon Oakland, Audrey Totter. Inconsequential but absorbing drama about a young man's estrangement from his employer when he marries the man's daughter. (Dir: Allen Miner, 100 mins.)

Chu Chu and the Philly Flash (1981)** Carol Burnett, Alan Arkin, Jack Warden, Danny Aiello, Adam Arkin, Danny Glover, Sid Haig. Contrived comedy about two lost souls who pull themselves out from behind the eight ball after they pick up a briefcase filled with government papers worth a lot to several people. (Dir: David Lowell Rich, 100 mins.)†

Chuck Berry: Hail! Hail! Rock 'n' Roll (1987)*** Chuck Berry, Keith Richards,

Linda Ronstadt. That reelin' and rockin' genius, Chuck Berry, is candidly profiled and saluted by peers and protégés in this wonderful documentary. Included are fascinating details about Berry's early days, and a high-energy concert which stands as a perfect, all-inclusive celebration of this pioneering duckwalker. (Dir: Taylor Hackford, 118 mins.)†

C.H.U.D. (1984)**½ John Heard, Kim Greist, Daniel Stern, Christopher Curry. C.H.U.D. stands for "Cannibalistic Humanoid Underground Dwellers" in this tongue-in-cheek horror yarn. Hot on C.H.U.D.'s trail are a photographer (Heard), and a Bowery priest (Stern). TV prints feature extra footage, including a diner scene featuring John Goodman as a cop. (Dir: Douglas Cheek, 90 mins.)†

C.H.U.D. II: Bud the C.H.U.D. (1989)*½ Brian Robbins, Bill Calvert, Tricia Leigh Fisher, Gerrit Graham, Robert Vaughn. Lame sequel is played strictly for laughs, and gets very few. Graham hamming it up as the titular zombie is funny, but otherwise this *C.H.U.D.* is a dud. Padded out by cameos from such minor lights as Bianca Jagger, Larry Linville, Jack Riley, Norman Fell, June Lockhart, and Rich Hall. (Dir: David Irving, 84 mins.)†

Chuka (1967)** Rod Taylor, John Mills, Luciana Paluzzi, Ernest Borgnine, James Whitmore, Louis Hayward. A formula wild western with a veteran desperado keeping soldiers and injuns from slaughtering each other as best he can. (Dir: Gordon Douglas, 105 mins.)

Chump at Oxford, A (1939)*** Laurel & Hardy. Young love abetted by two American nitwits. Excellent Laurel & Hardy film. (Dir: Alfred J. Goulding, 63 mins.)†

Cimarron (1931)** Richard Dix, Irene Dunne, Estelle Taylor. Dated, epic western about the Cravat family settling the Oklahoma prairie. Only western film to win a Best Film Oscar. (Dir: Wesley Ruggles, 130 mins.)†

Cimarron (1960)*** Glenn Ford, Maria Schell, Anne Baxter, Arthur O'Connell. Director Anthony Mann's remake of the Edna Ferber novel, originally filmed in 1931. The protagonists are a carefree survivor of the Old West (Ford) and his civilizing wife (Schell). (140 mins.)

Cimarron Kid, The (1951)** Audie Murphy, Yvette Dugay. Routine western fare with Audie Murphy playing an ex-con who tries to go straight against tremendous odds. (Dir: Budd Boetticher, 84 mins.)

Cincinnati Kid, The (1965)*** Steve McQueen, Edward G. Robinson, Joan Blondell, Rip Torn, Ann-Margret, Tuesday Weld. McQueen, in the title role, is an itinerant card shark who travels from one big game to the next. Fine performances by McQueen and Robinson. Their confrontation in a superbly staged card game finale is a highlight. Director Norman Jewison has a good eye for detail and the film evokes the Depression period, in which the story is set. (113 mins.)†

Cinderella (1950)*** Superb animation and a bright score highlight this Disney animated version of the fairy tale. Augmenting the romance of the poor girl capturing a prince are the mandatory fairy godmother as well as an assortment of cartoon mice. (Dirs: Wilfred Jackson, Hamilton Luske, Clyde Geronomi, 75 mins.)†

Cinderella (1977)** Cheryl Smith, Kirk Scott, Brett Smiley, Sy Richardson, Yana Nirvana, Marilyn Corwin. The world may not exactly have been clamoring for a soft-core musical version of the fairy tale, but here it is anyway. Cheerfully dirty-minded adaptation isn't quite camp but close to it, as the performers give their all delivering ridiculous dialogue, bad jokes, and absurd songs. Fun, if you're of a mind. Followed by *Fairy Tales*. (Dir: Michael Pataki, 94 mins.)†

Cinderella Jones (1946)** Joan Leslie, Robert Alda. Silly triviality about a pretty scatterbrain who must marry an intelligent man to gain a million-dollar legacy. (Dir: Busby Berkeley, 88 mins.)

Cinderella Liberty (1973)*** James Caan, Marsha Mason. Good performances by Caan, as a sailor with a sense of responsibility, and Mason, as an unorthodox bar girl with a street-toughened 11-year-old whose black sailor father ran away before his birth. (Dir: Mark Rydell, 117 mins.)†

Cinderfella (1960)** Jerry Lewis, Anna Maria Alberghetti, Ed Wynn. The fairy tale adapted to suit the talents of Lewis. A misguided venture—tasteless, ornately dull musical fantasy. (Dir: Frank Tashlin, 91 mins.)†

Cindy (MTV 1978)*** Charlaine Woodward, Scoey Mitchill, Mae Mercer. The Cinderella fairy tale, with a black cast of principals, is reset in Harlem, circa '43. (Dir: William Graham, 104 mins.)

Cinema Paradiso (Italy-France, 1989)**** Philippe Noiret, Jaques Perrin, Salvatore Cascio, Agnese Nano. Moviegoing as a way of life is celebrated in this warm and tender story of a wise old projectionist's influence on the life of a small town Italian boy. Noiret makes an indelible impression as the embodiment of the magic that young Toto experiences while watching classic American, Italian, and French movies. A poignant tribute to the churchlike picture palaces of times

185

gone by, and the distinctive power of the movies that makes us want to live our dreams. Oscar winner, Best Foreign Language Film. Originally 155 minutes. (Dir: Giuseppe Tornatore, 123 mins.)†

Circle of Children, A (MTV 1977)***½ Jane Alexander, Rachel Roberts, David Ogden Stiers, Nan Martin. Luminous adaptation of Mary McCracken's novel about a financially poor, spiritually rich private school for emotionally disturbed children. The most talented of the understanding teachers is Helga, unschooled, but a "therapeutic genius," who inspires an affluent suburban woman to volunteer at the school. (Dir: Don Taylor, 100 mins.)

Circle of Danger (Great Britain, 1951)*** Ray Milland, Patricia Roc. American returns to Europe to investigate the mysterious death of his brother during World War II. Interesting melodrama keeps the viewer in suspense. (Dir: Jacques Tourneur, 86 mins.)

Circle of Deceit (West Germany, 1982)*** Hanna Schygulla, Bruno Ganz, Jerzy Skolimowski. A complex and detached film about the face of war in Lebanon. A journalist, whose assignments often take him to areas of strife, has trouble returning to hearth and home after his stint in civil war-torn Beirut. Ostensibly a study of man's incapacity for commitment, the film's observations on Lebanon are almost documentary-like in their accuracy and make the film a richer experience. (Dir: Volker Schlondorff, 108 mins.)

Circle of Deception (Great Britain, 1961)**½ Bradford Dillman, Suzy Parker. Intelligence agent is assigned a dangerous mission in Germany, is captured and spills the beans. War melodrama has a suspenseful twist but doesn't bring it off too well. However, it has its moments. (Dir: Jack Lee, 100 mins.)

Circle of Iron (1979)**½ David Carradine, Jeff Cooper, Christopher Lee, Roddy McDowall, Eli Wallach. A Kung Fu fantasy shot in Israel, better produced than the usual chop-'em-sock-'em flicks. (Dir: Richard Moore, 102 mins.)†

Circle of Power (1983)*** Yvette Mimieux, Christopher Allport, Cindy Pickett, John Considine. An "executive-development training" center in a lavish estate in the woods turns into a hell for a young, unsuspecting couple when they are psychologically and physically abused in the sadistic program. A frightening comment on pop therapy, corporate ambition, and peer pressure. Originally released as *Mystique*. AKA: **Brainwash.** (Dir: Bobby Roth, 103 mins.)

Circle of Two (Canada, 1980)*½ Richard

Burton, Tatum O'Neal, Kate Reid. O'Neal surprisingly overshadows Burton in this nonsensical film which tells of the love between a sixty-year-old artist and a sixteen-year-old schoolgirl. (Dir: Jules Dassin, 105 mins.)†

Circle of Violence: A Family Drama, A (MTV 1986)** Tuesday Weld, Geraldine Fitzgerald, Peter Bonerz, River Phoenix. This problem drama dealing with parental abuse has its heart in the right place, but loses dramatic momentum before the halfway mark. Elderly Fitzgerald comes to live with her daughter, Weld, at the time Tuesday is going through a trial separation from her husband; tensions rise and Tuesday loses control. (Dir: David Greene, 104 mins.)

Circuitry Man (1990)**½ Jim Metzler, Dana Wheeler-Nicholson, Vernon Wells, Lu Leonard. Well-acted, low-budget science-fiction thriller with wit. Set in a post-apocalypse subterranean world, a beautiful blond bodyguard (Wheeler-Nicholson) will be granted freedom if she makes a risky delivery of computer drug chips. Aiding her is a love-struck android (Metzler). Moderately exciting chase fantasy. (Dir: Steven Lovy, 93 mins.)†

Circus, The (1928)**** Charles Chaplin, Merna Kennedy, Betty Morrissey. Marvelous sight gags and glimpses of the Chaplin genius in this little-known film. The characters are right out of the melodramas of the time, wicked father, an ailing daughter, etc. Original story and song written by Chaplin, who produced and directed. (60 mins.)†

Circus Clown (1934)*** Joe E. Brown, Dorothy Burgess, Patricia Ellis, Tom Dugan, William Demarest. Another good vehicle for Brown in a double role as a young man who longs to join the circus as a clown, and his own disapproving father. The setting also provides Brown a chance to demonstrate his breathtaking acrobatic abilities. (Dir: Ray Enright, 63 mins.)

Circus of Fear (Great Britain, 1967)** Leo Genn, Christopher Lee, Suzy Kendall, Cecil Parker, Eddi Arent. Robbery clues lead to a circus, where the bodies begin to pile up. Involved plot, but enough red herrings strewn along the way to interest mystery fans. AKA: **Psycho Circus.** (Dir: John Moxey, 65 mins.)†

Circus of Horrors (Great Britain, 1960)**½ Anton Diffring, Erica Remberg. Well-done horror film about a plastic surgeon who finds temporary shelter from flight in a traveling circus. (Dir: Sidney Hayers, 89 mins.)†

Circus of Love (West Germany, 1954)** Eva Bartok, Curt Jurgens. Mediocre carnival melodrama of a woman caught between emotions for two men. An

English-language version (*Carnival Story*) was made simultaneously, and some of the stars of the American version (Anne Baxter, Steve Cochran) appear here as extras. (Dir: Kurt Neumann, 93 mins.)

Circus World (1964)**½ John Wayne, Claudia Cardinale, Rita Hayworth. Wayne is the head of a combination Wild West and circus show which is in financial straits, and if that isn't enough plot, there are two or three romantic involvements thrown in. Don't expect much and you'll enjoy it. (Dir: Henry Hathaway, 135 mins.)†

Cisco Pike (1971)**½ Gene Hackman, Kris Kristofferson. Narcotics agent (Hackman) blackmails a washed-up rock star (Kristofferson) into dealing $10,000 worth of Acapulco Gold. (Dir: Bill L. Norton, 94 mins.)

Citadel, The (Great Britain, 1938)**** Robert Donat, Rosalind Russell, Rex Harrison, Ralph Richardson. Cronin's novel about a young dedicated Scots physician who almost loses his way in life is a brilliantly acted gem which improves on the book. (Dir: King Vidor, 113 mins.)†

Citizen Kane (1941)**** Orson Welles, Joseph Cotten, Dorothy Comingore, Ruth Warrick, Everett Sloane, Agnes Moorehead, George Coulouris. Orson Welles called RKO Studios, where he made his directorial debut, "the best toy train set a boy ever had," and *Citizen Kane* was the first outpouring of Welles's playful enthusiasm for filmmaking. Decades later, many critics and scholars continue to call it the greatest American film ever made; certainly, it remains unequalled for its dazzling cinematic inventiveness which fills every frame. Welles used little-known actors from New York's Mercury Theater to tell the story of the tumultuous personal and professional life of a newspaper magnate (not-so-loosely based on William Randolph Hearst, whose cronies tried to keep the film from release). From the opening shots to the last, Welles's genius, wit, imagination and command of the medium make his first film not only a cinematic milestone but superb entertainment. Herman Mankiewicz co-wrote the screenplay with Welles. (119 mins.)†

Citizens Band—See: **Handle with Care**

City, The (MTV 1971)*½ Anthony Quinn, E. G. Marshall, Robert Reed, John Larch, Skye\Aubrey, Pat Hingle. Quinn stars as the responsible, crusading, and hardworking veteran mayor of an unnamed urban metropolis. Pilot for the series. (Dir: Daniel Petrie, 104 mins.)

City, The (MTV 1977)** Robert Forster, Don Johnson, Ward Costello, Jimmy Dean, Mark Hamill, Susan Sullivan. A failed pilot from the stable of producer Quinn Martin. L.A. detective Forster works in tandem with buddy Johnson to track down a weirdo who wants to destroy a country-western singer. Fairly predictable, with Dean stealing scenes as the frightened singer. (Dir: Harvey Hart, 72 mins.)†

City Across the River (1949)**½ Stephen McNally, Thelma Ritter, Anthony (Tony) Curtis. Irving Shulman's explosive book on juvenile delinquency in Brooklyn, *The Amboy Dukes*, makes a tough movie. (Dir: Maxwell Shane, 90 mins.)

City Beneath the Sea (1953)**½ Robert Ryan, Anthony Quinn, Mala Powers. Two-fisted adventure about big men in the big business of treasure hunting beneath the sea. (Dir: Budd Boetticher, 87 mins.)

City Beneath the Sea (MTV 1971)**½ Stuart Whitman, Robert Wagner, Richard Basehart. This Irwin-Allen-produced sci-fi film is about an undersea city in the year 2053. When its co-creator returns under Presidential orders, he faces a fistful of crises during shipments of gold and nuclear H-128 from Fort Knox. (Dir: Irwin Allen, 99 mins.)

City for Conquest (1940)*** James Cagney, Ann Sheridan, Arthur Kennedy, Elia Kazan, Donald Crisp. Sentimental story of a boxer who goes blind making sacrifices for his brother. There's a lot of corn here but it's well seasoned and expertly served. (Dir: Anatole Litvak, 101 mins.)

City Girl (1984)*** Laura Harrington, Joe Mastroianni, Carole McGill, Peter Reigert, Colleen Camp, Rosanne Katon. Pleasantly un-clichéd look at the professional and romantic life of a young woman, played with flaws intact by Harrington. (Dir: Martha Coolidge, 85 mins.)

City Heat (1984)**½ Burt Reynolds, Clint Eastwood, Jane Alexander, Madeline Kahn, Rip Torn, Tony Lo Bianco, Irene Cara. What seemed like a sure-fire casting coup—pairing Reynolds and Eastwood in a Prohibition era gangster film—doesn't come off. (Dir: Richard Benjamin, 97 mins.)†

City in Fear (1972)—See: **Place Called Today, A**

City in Fear (MTV 1980)** Robert Vaughn, David Janssen, Perry King, Susan Sullivan. When a psychotic killer terrorizes Los Angeles, reporter Janssen sensationalizes the story to sell more papers. (Mickey Rourke made his debut here.) (Dir: Jud Taylor, 104 mins.)†

City Killer (MTV 1984)** Heather Locklear, Gerald McRaney, Terrence Knox, Todd Sussman, John Harkins. Contrived suspense drama about a psychopath whose lust for Locklear turns him into the self-proclaimed "love bomber," terrorizing an entire city as a show of affection. (Dir: Robert Lewis, 104 mins.)†

City Lights (1931)**** Charlie Chaplin, Virginia Cherrill, Florence Lee. Perhaps Chaplin's greatest comedy, which means that it is one of the great works in the history of cinema. The last of Chaplin's silent films, thanks to Chaplin's refusal to make this a talkie after he had been preparing it for two years. Touching and hilarious tale of the "Little Tramp" who falls in love with a blind flower girl and gets money for an operation to restore her sight. Written and directed by Chaplin.(90 mins.)†

City Limits (1985)**½ Darrell Larson, John Stockwell, Kim Cattrall, Rae Dawn Chong, Robby Benson, James Earl Jones, John Diehl. Flashily designed action pic with a good cast, particularly Larson. Otherwise, this is a teenybopper foray into typical post-Apocalyptics. After a devastating plague reduces the population, some biker gangs battle to be top dog. (Dir: Aaron Lipstadt, 85 mins.)†

City of Bad Men (1953)**½ Dale Robertson, Jeanne Crain, Richard Boone, Lloyd Bridges. Outlaws ride into Carson City and plan to rob the proceeds from the Corbett-Fitzsimmons prizefight. (Dir: Harmon Jones, 82 mins.)

City of Fear (1959)**½ Vince Edwards, John Archer, Lyle Talbot. An escaped convict steals a metal container he believes is filled with heroin but actually contains a dangerous radioactive powder. Neatly made on a small budget. (Dir: Irving Lerner, 81 mins.)

City of Sadness, A (Taiwan, 1989)**** Tony Leung, Hsin Shu-fen, Chen Sownyung, Kao Jai, Li Tien-lu. Epic tale of one family, an old man and his four sons, set in Taiwan 1945, the year that the Japanese occupation ended—and the Chinese occupation began. Winner of the Golden Lion award at the Venice Film Festival, this richly rewarding humanistic film is long, but provides an evening well spent. (Dir: Hou Hsiaohsien, 155 mins.)

City of the Walking Dead (Italy-Spain, 1980)*½ Hugo Stiglitz, Laura Trotter, Francisco Rabal, Mel Ferrer, Sonia Viviani. More Euro-gore, this time with an ecological message as radiation leaks produce an ever-growing horde of zombies. AKA: **Nightmare City.** (Dir: Umberto Lenzi, 92 mins.)†

City of Women (Italy, 1980)*** Marcello Mastroianni, Ettore Manni, Anna Pruncal. Director Federico Fellini outshouts the women's movement with his own hysterical brand of cinematic rhetoric. The paper-thin plot has Marcello, the perennial Fellini-surrogate, wandering into a feminist convention and a millionaire's sin palace, which sets off a series of wonderfully extravagant fantasies. (138 mins.)†

City on a Hunt (1953)** Lew Ayres, Sonny Tufts. Routine mystery, innocent victim of a murder charge uncovering the real culprit. San Francisco background. AKA: **No Escape.** (Dir: Charles Bennett, 76 mins.)

City on Fire (Canada, 1979)*½ Barry Newman, Susan Clark, Shelley Winters, Ava Gardner, Leslie Nielsen, Henry Fonda. Nothing new here except perhaps for the fact that Montreal doubles for an American city. An oil refinery on fire causes the entire city to be endangered by flames. (Dir: Alvin Rakoff, 101 mins.)†

City Streets (1931)** Gary Cooper, Sylvia Sidney, Paul Lukas, William Boyd, Guy Kibbee. Story by Dashiell Hammett. No need to comment on this routine gangster film, as the curious will want to see a 1931 Gary Cooper playing "the Kid." (Dir: Rouben Mamoulian, 82 mins.)

City That Never Sleeps (1953)*** Gig Young, Mala Powers. Policeman nearly strays off the straight and narrow because of a café entertainer. Well made crime melodrama with some good performances. (Dir: John H. Auer, 90 mins.)

Civilization (1916)*** J. Barney Sherry, Enid Markey, Howard Hickman, George Fisher. Producer-director Thomas H. Ince was one of D. W. Griffith's only rivals in the early years of the film industry. This epic was planned as a major antiwar statement; unfortunately for Ince, it was released just as America's participation in WWI became inevitable. The allegorical plot has a devastating war break out between mythical nations, and in the end Christ returns to plead for peace on earth. A remarkable document, and a gripping drama. (102 mins.)†

Clair de Femme (France, 1979)*** Yves Montand, Romy Schneider, Romolo Valli, Heinz Bennent. Director Costa-Gavras tackles a love story, and there are no better screen lovers around today than Yves Montand and Romy Schneider as two people whose relationship helps heal their previous emotional wounds. From a novel by Romain Gary. (105 mins.)

Claire's Knee (France, 1970)***½ Jean-Claude Brialy, Aurora Cornu, Laurence de Monaghan, Beatrice Romand. A sophisticated, literate gem. Brialy plays a Frenchman who has the enormous good fortune to spend the summer dallying with three enchanting women on the shores of Lake Geneva. A film full of grace and gossamer joys. (Dir: Eric Rohmer, 103 mins.)†

Clairvoyant, The (Great Britain, 1934)**½ Claude Rains, Fay Wray, Jane Baxter, Ben Field. Claude Rains is good in this otherwise ordinary tale about a soothsayer who predicts the future. Lacks tension. AKA: **The Evil Mind.** (Dir: Maurice Elvey, 73 mins.)

Clairvoyant, The (1985)**½ Perry King, Kenneth McMillan, Elizabeth Kemp. Some of the material borders on the salacious, which is a shame because the director has a talent for instilling tension where you least expect it. A bizarre, seemingly unrelated series of murders baffle the police until a psychic is called in; then her life is in danger, too. AKA: **The Killing Hour.** (Dir: Armand Mastroianni, 97 mins.)†

Clambake (1967)**½ Elvis Presley, Shelley Fabares, Will Hutchins, Bill Bixby, Gary Merrill. *Prince and the Pauper* plot finds rich kid Presley switching places with a ski instructor at a Miami Beach hotel. (Dir: Arthur H. Nadell, 100 mins.)†

Clancy Street Boys (1943)**½ Leo Gorcey, Huntz Hall, Bobby Jordan. Another East Side Kids entry. The pacing of this comic visit from Muggs's Uncle Pete is fairly snappy and gives the regular characters a chance to show off their comedic talents. (Dir: William Beaudine, 66 mins.)

Clan of the Cave Bear, The (1985)** Daryl Hannah, Pamela Reed, James Remar. Fans of the book may be perturbed by this filmization, but others in the mood to watch a Cro-Magnon orphanette become the first feminist warrior in prehistory may want to join this clan. Not as terrible as you might think. (Dir: Michael Chapman, 100 mins.)†

Clara's Heart (1988)*½ Whoopi Goldberg, Neil Patrick Harris, Kathleen Quinlan, Michael Ontkean, Spalding Gray. Maudlin drama about the relationship between Jamaican housekeeper Whoopi and her charge, young Harris, whose parents are on the brink of divorce. Whoops, Whoopi! (Dir: Robert Mulligan, 108 mins.)†

Clarence, the Cross-Eyed Lion (1965)**½ Marshall Thompson, Betsy Drake. Clarence can't focus on his prey when hunting, and he is taken to the Study Center for Animal Behavior in Africa, where he becomes a pet of the daughter of a doctor. Basis for the TV show *Daktari*. (Dir: Andrew Morton, 98 mins.)

Clash by Night (1952)**½ Barbara Stanwick, Robert Ryan, Paul Douglas, Marilyn Monroe. Stark Clifford Odets drama of a fishing boat skipper and his lonely wife who becomes involved in an affair with his best friend. Good performances,

some good scenes, but never quite makes it. (Dir: Fritz Lang, 105 mins.)†

Clash of the Titans (Great Britain, 1981)**½ Laurence Olivier, Harry Hamlin, Judi Bowker, Burgess Meredith, Sian Phillips, Maggie Smith, Claire Bloom. A jazzed-up version of the story of the ancient Greek hero Perseus, the mortal son of Zeus. A perfect vehicle through which special-effects wizard Ray Harryhausen can show his stuff. (Dir: Desmond Davis, 118 mins.)†

Class (1983)* Rob Lowe, Jacqueline Bisset, Cliff Robertson, Andrew McCarthy. An Ivy League Lothario loses his virginity to a pick-up who turns out to be his schoolmate's mother. (Dir: Lewis John Carlino, 100 mins.)†

Class Action (1991)*** Gene Hackman, Mary Elizabeth Mastrantonio, Colin Friels, Donald Moffat, Jan Rubes. Solid cast, especially Hackman and Rubes, adds luster to this courtroom drama with a twist: Father and daughter are arguing the two sides of a case involving an automaker's negligence. Routine plot picks up near the end. (Dir: Michael Apted, 109 mins.)†

Classified Love (MTV 1986)*½ Michael McKean, Dinah Manoff, Stephanie Faracy, Franc Luz, Paula Trueman. Three coworkers at a New York ad agency turn to the personal columns to infuse their love life with new potentials. Clichés abound. (Dir: Don Taylor, 104 mins.)

Class of '44 (1973)** Gary Grimes, Jerry Houser, Oliver Conant, William Atherton. A disappointing sequel to the much better *Summer of '42*, with the same three boys—Hermie, Oscay and Benjie—now a little older and graduating from high school. Benjie disappears early, off to war, while the others go on to college—fraternity hazings, cheating on exams, proms, etc. (Dir: Paul Bogart, 95 mins.)†

Class of Miss MacMichael, The (Great Britain, 1978)*½ Glenda Jackson, Oliver Reed, Michael Murphy, Rosalind Cash. Clumsy comedy about a London trade school attended by problem students, staffed by problem teachers and ruled by uncaring principal Reed. (Dir: Silvio Narizzano, 93 mins.)†

Class of 1984 (1982)** Perry King, Roddy McDowall, Timothy Van Patten, Al Waxman. Violent, nasty updating of *The Blackboard Jungle*, with dedicated, straight-arrow teacher King and vicious teen punks in a decrepit urban high school. Look for a young Michael J. Fox. (Dir: Mark L. Lester, 93 mins.)†

Class of 1999 (1990)** Bradley Gregg, Traci Lind, Malcolm McDowell, Stacy Keach, Pam Grier, John P. Ryan, Joshua Miller. Follow-up to *Class of 1984*. Keach has an enjoyably gonzo turn as a white-wigged albino scientist who introduces three androids into the faculty of principal McDowell's embattled school. Familiar trash. (Dir: Mark L. Lester, 98 mins.)†

Class of Nuke 'Em High (1986)*½ Janelle Brady, Gilbert Brenton, Robert Prichard. A faulty nuclear reactor causes bizarre mutations among students at a nearby high school. (Dirs: Richard W. Haines, Samuel Weil, 84 mins.)†

Class of Nuke 'Em High Part 2: Subhumanoid Meltdown (1991)* Brick Bronsky, Lisa Gaye, Leesa Rowland, Trinity Loren. Overblown comic nightmare sequel about melting mutants, a mad female scientist with a beehive hairdo, and a 30-foot squirrel on the rampage. Incoherent mess. (Dir: Eric Louzil, 95 mins.)†

Class of '63 (MTV 1973)***½ Joan Hackett, James Brolin. Joan Hackett delivers a stunning performance as the unhappy wife who meets her old campus flame. What could be soap-opera material about a jealous husband and a wandering wife becomes an absorbing conflict played abainst fraternity foolishness. (Dir: John Korty, 73 mins.)†

Class Reunion—See: **National Lampoon's Class Reunion**

Claudelle Inglish (1961)** Diane McBain, Arthur Kennedy, Will Hutchins. Novel by Erskine Caldwell about a teenager, a sharecropper's daughter, who drives men mad, eventually comes to a sad end. Miss McBain and her director try to make something of it, to little avail—pretty drab. (Dir: Gordon Douglas, 99 mins.)

Claudia (1943)*** Dorothy McGuire, Robert Young. If you've never seen Rose Franken's almost classical story of a child bride who grows up, you're in for a treat. Funny but not hilarious, sentimental but not corny. A delightful story. (Dir: Edmund Goulding, 91 mins.)

Claudia and David (1946)**½ Dorothy McGuire, Robert Young. Not as delightful as *Claudia*, but this sequel about her baby and life in suburban Connecticut is easy to take. (Dir: Walter Lang, 78 mins.)

Claudine (1974)***½ James Earl Jones, Diahann Carroll, Lawrence Hinton-Jacobs. Charming, skillful comedy-drama about two attractive people in love. Jones and Carroll are delightful together in this film about Harlem residents and how they cope with poverty and ghetto life. A welcome relief from the spate of black super-stud movies. (Dir: John Berry, 94 mins.)

Clean and Sober (1988)*** Michael Keaton, Kathy Baker, Morgan Freeman, M. Emmet Walsh. Hotshot real estate salesman Keaton checks into a drug and alcohol

detoxification program in order to avoid the police, and eventually realizes that he really does have a problem with addiction. A mixed bag; some fine acting and quietly effective scenes nearly compensate for Keaton's underwritten character and a few too many clichés. (Dir: Glenn Gordon Caron, 124 mins.)†

Clean Slate—See: **Coup de Torchon**

Clear All Wires (1933)*** Lee Tracy, Benita Hume, Una Merkel, James Gleason, Alan Edwards. Sharp and speedy vehicle for fast-talking Tracy casts him as an unethical foreign correspondent trying to get out of bolshevik Russia. (Dir: George Hill, 78 mins.)

Clear and Present Danger, A (MTV 1970)*** Hal Holbrook, E. G. Marshall, Joseph Campanella. The pilot film for "The Senator" TV series starring Hal Holbrook. His performance, plus a thoughful script about air pollution, should keep your interest. (Dir: James Goldstone, 99 mins.)

Cleo from 5 to 7 (France, 1962)**½ Corinne Marchand, Dorothea Blanck. Two hours in the life of a beautiful but spiritually empty singer who anxiously awaits a doctor's report on her health. Some critics found this artistic, others will think it merely arty. (Dir: Agnes Varda, 90 mins.)

Cleo/Leo (1989)*½ Jane Hamilton (Veronica Hart), Scott Baker, Ginger Lynn Allen, Kevin Thomsen. Sexist pig Leo is reincarnated as Cleo and experiences the same sexual harassments he used to dish out. (Dir: Chuck Vincent, 94 mins.)†

Cleopatra (1934)*** Claudette Colbert, Warren William, Henry Wilcoxon. Lavishly produced, this Cecil B. DeMille spectacular nonetheless works on a more intimate level than most epics as it entails the affairs of the Queen of the Nile and her Roman lovers. Colbert plays Cleo as a saucy coquette, which helps lighten the traditionally heavy plotting which ruins most big budget spectacles. (101 mins.)†

Cleopatra (1963)**½ Elizabeth Taylor, Richard Burton, Rex Harrison. As a spectacle, this elaborate production has few equals, but as an historical drama it leaves something to be desired. Miss Taylor is a feast for the eyes and some of the drama is interesting, particularly those scenes with Harrison, who gives a superb performance. (Dir: Joseph L. Mankiewicz, 243 mins.)†

Cleopatra Jones (1973)**½ Tamara Dobson, Shelley Winters, Bernie Casey, Brenda Sykes, Esther Rolle, Antonio Fargas. Cleopatra Jones is the slick, karate-chopping government agent trying to crack a drug ring in this violent thriller. Watch for Shelley Winters as a butch leader of a gang—definitely one of her most bizarre characterizations. (Dir: Jack Starrett, 89 mins.)†

Cleopatra Jones and the Casino of Gold (1975)** Tamara Dobson, Stella Stevens, Tanny, Albert Popwell, Norman Feld. Uneven sequel to *Cleopatra Jones*. Again we find Tamara Dobson as the brave and sexy agent in her mission to wipe out the drug trade, this time in Hong Kong. (Dir: Chuck Bail, 94 mins.)†

Climax, The (1944)** Boris Karloff, Susanna Foster. Silly melodrama. Crazy doctor (Karloff, of course) thinks an opera singer is a girl who has been dead for years. He plots a twisted revenge. (Dir: George Waggner, 86 mins.)

Climb an Angry Mountain (MTV 1972)** Barry Nelson, Fess Parker. Filmed around Mount Shasta country, lawman Parker, a widower who raises his kids on a ranch, reluctantly goes after a local Indian on the run for a murder rap. (Dir: Leonard Horn, 97 mins.)

Clinic, The (Australia, 1985)* Chris Haywood, Simon Burke, Gerda Nicolson, Rona MacLeod. Alleged comedy about the never-ending fun to be sampled at an Australian V.D. clinic. Aesthetically, the film's a social disease. (Dir: David Stevens, 93 mins.)†

Clinton and Nadine (MCTV 1988)** Andy Garcia, Ellen Barkin, Morgan Freeman, Michael Lombard. A small-time bird smuggler (Garcia), seeking to avenge his brother's murder, stumbles on to an illegal arms sales conspiracy in this fast-moving but muddled action caper. (Dir: Jerry Schatzberg, 108 mins.)†

Clipped Wings (1953)** Bowery Boys, Todd Karns, June Vincent, Philip Van Zandt, Bernard Gorcey, Fay Roope. While visiting an Air Force base, the Boys try to find out why a friend has been held for treason and inadvertently enlist in the Air Force. (Dir: Edward Bernds, 65 mins.)

Clive of India (1935)*** Ronald Colman, Loretta Young, Cesar Romero, C. Aubrey Smith, Francis Lister. Stately epic about the British Empire's adventures in exotic India, decked out with the usual mangling of history and *de rigueur* romance. Not extraordinary, but smoothly acted and opulently produced; Colman made the perfect storybook hero. (Dir: Richard Boleslawski, 90 mins.)

Cloak and Dagger (1946)*** Gary Cooper, Lilli Palmer, Robert Alda. University professor works on a secret mission for the OSS inside Germany. Loosely constructed but tense espionage melodrama, well acted. (Dir: Fritz Lang, 106 mins.)†

Cloak and Dagger (1984)*** Henry Thomas, Dabney Coleman, Michael Murphy, John McIntire, Jeanette Nolan. A tightly scripted thriller about a boy with an overly active imagination who comes face-to-face with real espionage; Coleman is cleverly cast as both the boy's unbelieving father, and his imaginary hero, Jack Flash. (Dir: Richard Franklin, 101 mins.)†

Clock, The (1945)***½ Robert Walker, Judy Garland, James Gleason, Lucille Gleason, Keenan Wynn. Glowing, loving film by Judy's then-husband Vincente Minnelli, has a slight plot about a soldier and a working girl who meet, fall in love, and marry during his 24-hour leave. The performances are pure star quality. (90 mins.)†

Clockmaker, The (France, 1974)***½ Philippe Noiret, Jean Rochefort, Jacques Denis. An astonishing, perceptive first feature film directed by former critic Bertrand Tavernier and based on a novel by Georges Simenon. Protagonist is a watchmaker in Lyon who is mortified to learn that his grown-up son has committed a political murder, though the son is not politically involved. Noiret is remarkable playing the watchmaker, inspecting and analyzing the developments as if he were looking through his magnifying glass. (100 mins.)

Clockwise (Great Britain, 1986)*** John Cleese, Alison Steadman, Stephen Moore. A clock-watching academic makes a wrong move and a lifetime of perfect punctuality goes right out the window. Slow in spots, but the cast's impeccable timing keeps the laughter ticking away. (Dir: Christopher Morahan, 96 mins.)†

Clockwork Orange, A (Great Britain, 1971)***½ Malcolm McDowell, Patrick Magee, Adrienne Corri. A shattering political allegory about a loathsome, violent antihero in a modern society where gangs of young punks run amok and peaceful citizens are imprisoned in their own homes. Produced, written, and directed by Stanley Kubrick, based on the novel by Anthony Burgess, *Clockwork* is loaded with fascinating images, and a sterling performance by McDowell. (135 mins.)†

Clone Master (MTV 1978)*** Art Hindle, Ralph Bellamy, Robyn Douglas. John D. F. Black, one of our better mystery writers, not only dramatizes the act of cloning, but considers how clones—all of them being alike—can go through an identity crisis. This mystery-science fiction entry merits a look because of its script, production, and stars. (Dir: Don Medford, 104 mins.)

Clones, The (1973)** Michael Greene, Gregory Sierra. A strange sci-fi thriller that tries, without much luck, for laughs.

(Dirs: Paul Hunt, Lamar Card, 94 mins.)†

Clonus Horror, The (1979)*½ Dick Sargent, Paulette Breen, Keenan Wynn, Tim Donnelly, Peter Graves. A breeding facility creates clones of the mighty and powerful so that once one of their vital parts stops functioning, it can be replaced, thus perpetuating them forever. (Dir: Robert Fiveson, 90 mins.)†

Close Call for Boston Blackie, A (1946)*½ Chester Morris, Lynn Merrick, Richard Lane, Frank Sully, George E. Stone, Russell Hicks. Blackie's accused of murder but we know he's innocent. (Dir: Lew Landers, 60 mins.)

Close Call for Ellery Queen (1942)** William Gargan, Margaret Lindsay, Ralph Morgan, Edward Norris. Ellery figures out who murdered a millionaire in this one. OK whodunit. (Dir: James P. Hogan, 67 mins.)

Close Encounters of the Third Kind (1977) **** Richard Dreyfuss, François Truffaut, Melinda Dillon, Teri Garr, Cary Guffey, Bob Balaban. Exhilarating sci-fi fantasy about friendly aliens touching base with specially selected earthlings. Suspense and humor blend as Dreyfuss and several others disobey government orders to rendezvous with the extra-terrestrials. The climactic landing of the mother ship is very uplifting. **Close Encounters: The Special Edition** features a little extra footage. (Dir: Steven Spielberg, 137 mins.)†

Closely Watched Trains (Czechoslovakia, 1966)***½ Vaclav Neckar, Jitka Bendova. Gentle, touching film about a shy sexually inexperienced train dispatcher during the period of the German occupation throughout World War II. Made during a period of increasing artistic freedom in Czechoslovakia, this comedy-drama shows how the decent instincts in people can survive during difficult times. (Dir: Jiri Menzel, 89 mins.)†

Close My Eyes (Great Britain, 1991)*** Alan Rickman, Clive Owen, Saskia Reeves, Karl Johnson. Powerful drama, unflinching in its frank treatment of incest. A single, womanizing brother (Owen) and married sister (Reeves) consummate their stirring desire with a passionate sexual affair, while her husband (Rickman) suspects infidelity. Mature subject, well directed and acted. (Dir: Stephen Poliakoff, 105 mins.)

Closet Land (1991)** Madeleine Stowe, Alan Rickman. Highly stylized, minimalist two-character drama about a woman author of children's books who is imprisoned and tortured in this offbeat but pretentious and unoriginal allegory about censorship and fascism. Produced by Ron Howard's Imagine Entertainment; written and directorial debut by Radha

Bharadwaj. (Dir: Radha Bharadwaj, 95 mins.)†

Close to My Heart (1951)**½ Gene Tierney, Ray Milland, Fay Bainter. Soap opera plot about a couple who adopt the baby of a convicted murderer and prove there's nothing in heredity. Well acted by a good cast. (Dir: William Keighley, 90 mins.)

Clouded Yellow (Great Britain, 1951)*** Jean Simmons, Trevor Howard. Secret service agent, demoted to cataloguing butterflies, aids a girl wrongly accused of murder. Mystery begins slowly but picks up as it progresses to a suspenseful climax. (Dir: Ralph Thomas, 96 mins.)

Clouds Over Europe—See: **Q Planes**

Cloud Waltzing (MCTV 1987)**½ Kathleen Beller, François Eric Gendron. This escapism with a continental flair involves a beautiful journalist falling for a sexy, rich French vintner whom she was interviewing. (Dir: Gordon Fleming, 120 mins.)†

Clown, The (1953)*** Red Skelton, Jane Greer, Tim Considine. If you're a Red Skelton fan, you might be surprised to see him act in this one—a drama about a comedy performer who loses his wife through divorce and almost loses his son's love. Remake of *The Champ*, 1931. (Dir: Robert Z. Leonard, 89 mins.)†

Clowns, The (Italy-France, 1971)**½ Mayo Morin, Lima Alberti, Alvaro Vitali, Gasparmo. Three rings of spectacle, slapstick, and sensation invade the screen in this piece from the master Italian director Federico Fellini. Clowns race to and fro in a fantasy circus world of Fellini's youth which is approached as a documentary-within-a-film. (90 mins.)†

Club Havana (1946)*½ Tom Neal, Margaret Lindsay, Don Douglas. An unconvincing drama set in a fashionable Latin nightclub. Lindsay attempts suicide and Tom Neal—as a young doctor on his first call—comes to the rescue. (Dir: Edgar G. Ulmer, 62 mins.)

Club Life (1987)* Tony Curtis, Dee Wallace Stone, Michael Parks, Tom Parsekian, Jamie Barrett, Pat Ast, Yana Nirvana. Flashy but lifeless action-flick about a motorcyclist who comes to the Big City and winds up as a bouncer in a disco owned by tough-guy philosopher Curtis. (Dir: Norman Thaddeus Vane, 93 mins.)†

Club Med (MTV 1986)*½ Jack Scalia, Linda Hamilton, Patrick Macnee. Aimless excursion about the young, rich set who gravitate to the Mexican resort of Ixtapa Club Med. (Dir: Bob Giraldi, 104 mins.)†

Club Paradise (1986)** Robin Williams, Peter O'Toole, Rick Moranis, Twiggy, Jimmy Cliff, Andrea Martin. An island's snobs are pitted against the slobs at an ex-fireman's ramshackle resort. (Dir: Harold Ramis, 95 mins.)†

Clue (1985)*½ Eileen Brennan, Tim Curry, Madeline Kahn, Christopher Lloyd, Michael McKean, Martin Mull, Lesley Ann Warren, Colleen Camp, Lee Ving. A cast of wonderfully appealing comic performers can't help ignite this gimmick picture, which brings us a three-dimensional adaptation of the famous board game. Three different versions, each with a different conclusion, were released initially; now all three endings are tacked onto the film. (Dir: Jonathan Lynn, 87 mins.)†

Cluny Brown (1946)***½ Jennifer Jones, Charles Boyer. Pleasant comedy, superbly acted and directed, about the turbulent career of a plumber's niece and a Czech refugee in England during the war. A satirical spoof of the first order. (Dir: Ernst Lubitsch, 100 mins.)

C'mon, Let's Live a Little (1967)* Bobby Vee, Jackie De Shannon, Eddie Hodges, Patsy Kelly, John Ireland, Jr., Kim Carnes. Silly musical about on-campus life. (Dir: David Butler, 85 mins.)

Coach (1978)* Cathy Lee Crosby, Michael Biehn, Keenan Wynn. Sex and sports mix in this tepid comedy involving a gorgeous woman coach of a high school basketball team. (Dir: Bud Townsend, 100 mins.)†

Coach of the Year (MTV 1980)**½ Robert Conrad, Red West, David Hubbard, Daphne Maxwell. Macho man Conrad delivers a warm, genuine performance as a Vietnam paraplegic, a former football star who tries to coach kids behind bars. (Dirs: Don Medford, Andy Sidaris, 104 mins.)

Coal Miner's Daughter (1980)*** Sissy Spacek, Tommy Lee Jones, Beverly D'Angelo, Levon Helm, Phyllis Boyens. Writer Tom Rickman and director Michael Apted wisely concentrate on the atmosphere and the characters, content to let the plot tag along. Spacek's incarnation of country singer Loretta Lynn shows remarkable emotional range and consummate control in this smoothly crafted biography. Quietly observant and warm. (125 mins.)†

Coast to Coast (1980)** Dyan Cannon, Robert Blake. An unbelievable cross-country odyssey. Dyan escapes from an asylum where her nasty husband had her locked up, and hitches a ride with burly Robert Blake, who's on the run because his truck is about to be repossessed. (Dir: Joseph Sargent, 95 mins.)

Cobra (1986)* Sylvester Stallone, Brigitte Nielsen, Andrew Robinson, Val Avery, Art La Fleur, Reni Santoni. Slick stuff that takes the fascist ideals of *Dirty Harry* to extremes as cop Stallone trails a group of axe-wielding serial killers. (Dir: George P. Cosmatos, 87 mins.)†

Cobra Woman (1944)**½ Maria Montez, Jon Hall, Sabu, Lois Collier, Mary Nash, Edgar Barrier, Lon Chaney, Jr. Forties camp with Montez as a good sister and the wicked twin whose throne she wants to reclaim. Lots of giggles as M.M. does her phallic Cobra dance with a live cobra. (Dir: Robert Siodmak, 70 mins.)

Cobweb, The (1955)***½ Richard Widmark, Lauren Bacall, Charles Boyer, Gloria Grahame, Susan Strasberg, John Kerr, Lillian Gish. A stellar cast brings William Gibson's dramatic novel about a modern mental institution to the screen with conviction. Gish and Boyer are standouts. (Dir: Vincente Minnelli, 124 mins.)

Coca-Cola Kid, The (Australia, 1985)*** Eric Roberts, Greta Scacchi, Bill Kerr, Max Gillies. An intense American advertising executive will stop at nothing to saturate the Australian outback with the world's most popular soft drink in this deliciously offbeat satire. Roberts shows an unexpected humorous flair as the ad man, while Scacchi radiates sexuality as a secretary bent on seducing him. (Dir: Dusan Makavejev, 94 mins.)†

Cocaine and Blue Eyes (MTV 1983)** O. J. Simpson, Eugene Roche, Candy Clark, Keye Luke, Cliff Gorman. While searching for a girl named "Blue Eyes," a macho San Francisco detective stumbles upon a cocaine-smuggling operation that points to a wealthy family. (Dir: E. W. Swackhamer, 104 mins.)

Cocaine Fiends, The (1936)* Noel Madison, Lois January, Sheila Manner, Dean Benton. Mob pusher turns a young girl and her brother on to the evils of cocaine in this absurd, preachy morality tale. Lacks the campiness that made *Reefer Madness* an underground hit. (Dir: William A. O'Connor, 68 mins.)†

Cocaine: One Man's Seduction (MTV 1983)*** Dennis Weaver, Karen Grassle, Pamela Bellwood, James Spader, David Ackroyd. A convincing contemporary drama on the temptations and dangers that accompany the "chic" use and abuse of cocaine. A high-powered and successful realtor turns to cocaine as a release, refusing to admit to his increasing dependency on the drug. (Dir: Paul Wendkos, 104 mins.)†

Cocaine Wars (1986)** John Schneider, Kathryn Witt, Federico Luppi, Royal Dano. When the girlfriend of drug enforcement agent Schneider is kidnapped by a South American cocaine empire, he must singlehandedly crack the crack business. Familiar plot and acting that never rises above daytime TV level turn this violent Roger Corman–produced picture into another tiresome *Rambo* clone. (Dir: Hector Olivera, 82 mins.)†

Cockeyed Cavaliers (1934)*** Bert Wheeler, Robert Woolsey, Thelma Todd, Noah Beery, Sr, Franklin Pangborn, Snub Pollard, Billy Gilbert. Wheeler and Woolsey vehicle set in just about the unlikeliest era imaginable for the boys, Restoration England! And it turns out to be one of their best comedies, as they pose as doctors for King Charles II. Nonstop jokes from a great ensemble. (Dir: Mark Sandrich, 72 mins.)†

Cockeyed Cowboys of Calico County, The (1970)** Dan Blocker, Nanette Fabray, Jack Cassidy, Mickey Rooney, Wally Cox, Marge Champion, Jim Backus, Jack Elam. Lame comedy western. Blocker's a blacksmith whose attempts to secure a mail-order bride net him a saloon hostess substitute (Fabray). (Dir: Ranald Mac Dougall, 99 mins.)

Cockeyed Miracle, The (1946)** Frank Morgan, Keenan Wynn, Audrey Totter. Cockeyed little fantasy about a couple of ghosts trying to straighten out those they left behind is completely dependent on the cast. (Dir: Sylvan Simon, 81 mins.)

Cockeyed World, The (1929)**½ Victor McLaglen, Edmund Lowe, Lily Damita, Stuart Erwin, El Brendel. First sequel to *What Price Glory?*, with marine sergeants Flagg and Quirt up to their usual troublemaking from Russia to South America. Energetic comedy-musical lacks the depth and punch of their first teaming. (Dir: Raoul Walsh, 118 mins.)†

Cockleshell Heroes (Great Britain, 1955)*** Jose Ferrer, Trevor Howard. Tense suspense tale about one of the most dangerous missions of WWII. "Operation Cockleshell" is the name given to the canoe invasion by a handful of volunteers of an enemy-held French port in order to destroy a group of battleships. (Dir: Jose Ferrer, 110 mins.)

Cocktail (1988)* Tom Cruise, Bryan Brown, Elisabeth Shue, Lisa Banes, Kelly Lynch. Empty excuse for a movie, as Manhattan bartender Cruise learns that true love is worth more than money. The actor's charm is relied upon to the exclusion of anything else in the film, such as plot or characterization. Eighties big-studio moviemaking at its worst. (Dir: Roger Donaldson, 100 mins.)†

Cocktail Molotov (France, 1981)*** Elise Caron, Philippe Lebas, Françoise Cluzet. Comedy about a 17-year-old French girl coming of age in the turmoil of the late '60s. Three students travel from Paris to Venice in the spring of 1968, become involved with some half-hearted anarchists, and find that the revolution has
194

started without them at home. Charming, sentimental, and funny. (Dir: Diane Kurys, 100 mins.)

Cocoanuts, The (1929)*** The Four Marx Brothers, Margaret Dumont, Kay Francis, Oscar Shaw. The Marxes' first film, made on a soundstage in New York. Technically, it creaks, but it contains some of their great routines ("Why a duck?"). (Dirs: Joseph Santley, Robert Florey, 96 mins.)†

Cocoanut Grove (1938)** Fred MacMurray, Harriet Hilliard, Ben Blue, Eve Arden. Unknown swing band from Chicago makes the grade in a Hollywood nightclub. "Ozzie and Harriet" fans will enjoy seeing a 1938 version of Harriet Hilliard Nelson, while MacMurray plays the saxophone (his preacting profession). (Dir: Alfred Santell, 85 mins.)

Cocoon (1985)*** Don Ameche, Wilford Brimley, Gwen Verdon, Brian Dennehy, Steve Guttenberg, Tahnee Welch, Hume Cronyn, Maureen Stapleton, Jessica Tandy. After making a splash with *Splash*, director Ron Howard returns to the ocean for this affable sci-fi fantasy. Aliens return to Earth for their compatriots who have been dormant on the ocean floor for eons. Something in these cocoons has the power to regenerate senior citizens nearby. (Dir: Ron Howard, 118 mins.)†

Cocoon: The Return (1988)*½ Don Ameche, Wilford Brimley, Courtney Cox, Hume Cronyn, Jack Gilford, Steve Guttenberg, Maureen Stapleton, Elaine Stritch, Jessica Tandy, Gwen Verdon, Tahnee Welch, Brian Dennehy. Crass sequel plays like a string of outtakes from the original movie, as the oldsters return from outer space for a few days on Earth. A shameful ripoff. (Dir: Daniel Petrie, 116 mins.)†

Code Name: Diamond Head (MTV 1977)*½ Roy Thinnes, France Nuyen, Zulu, Ward Costello, Don Knight. Here's another pilot that didn't sell. Roy Thinnes is an American agent on the trail of a European thief. (Dir: Jeannot Szwarc, 90 mins.)†

Code Name: Emerald (1985)** Ed Harris, Eric Stolz, Max von Sydow, Horst Bucholz, Helmut Berger. Stolid World War II adventure about an intrepid hero who has to save the Allies' plans for D-Day after an American soldier falls into the hands of the Axis powers. (Dir: Jonathan Sanger, 95 mins.)†

Code Name: Foxfire (MTV 1985)** Joanna Cassidy, Sheryl Lee Ralph, John McCook, Henry Jones. This launched a short-lived series about a seductive super agent. Hoping to clear her good name after being falsely imprisoned, she tackles a dangerous assignment involving a stolen rocket and her ex-lover. (Dir: Corey Allen, 99 mins.)†

Codename: Kyril (MCTV 1988)*** Edward Woodward, Ian Charleson, Denholm Elliott, Joss Ackland. An espionage drama that takes some time getting off the ground, but once it does, it's fascinating to watch. Charleson is Kyril, a KGB agent who discovers he's a sacrificial lamb in a game of high-powered intrigue. Woodward plays the arch-villain with lip-smacking relish. (Dir: Ian Sharp, 192 mins.)

Code Name Trixie—See: **Crazies, The**

Codename: Wild Geese (1986)* Lewis Collins, Lee Van Cleef, Ernest Borgnine, Klaus Kinski, Mimsy Farmer. Second sequel to *The Wild Geese* offers more mindless brutal adventures about the mercenary set, for whom war is business. (Dir: Anthony Dawson, 101 mins.)†

Code of Silence (1985)*** Chuck Norris, Henry Silva, Bert Remsen. This fast-paced flick marked a step up for Norris from the usual martial arts fare and broadened his appeal in the strong silent Eastwood-Bronson tradition. Norris portrays a cop who must fight both internecine drug rivalries as well as a cover-up in the police department. (Dir: Andy Davis, 102 mins.)†

Code of Vengeance (MTV 1985)**½ Charles Taylor, Charles Haid, Keenan Wynn, Erin Gray, Chad Allen, Lenka Peterson. Murder, dope-peddling, and even some gun-running occupies our hero, Dalton. No one really knows who Dalton is or where he comes from, but he certainly is a hero to a woman out to avenge her brother's murder. AKA: **Dalton: Code of Vengeance I.** (Dir: Richard Rosenthal, 104 mins.)

Code Red (MTV 1981)*½ Lorne Greene, Andrew Stevens, Sam J. Jones. Pilot for the rotten series about a family of dedicated firefighters with Lorne Greene as the patriarchal head of the clan. (Dir: J. Lee Thompson, 78 mins.)

Coffee, Tea or Me? (MTV 1973)**½ Karen Valentine, John Davidson, Michael Anderson, Jr. This lighthearted comedy leans heavily on the perkiness of Valentine as a stewardess leading a double life, commuting between two husbands in Los Angeles and London. (Dir: Norman Panama, 90 mins.)

Coffy (1973)** Pam Grier, Booker Bradshaw, Robert Doqui, Allan Arbus, Sid Haig. Pam Grier, the dazzling actress who should have become the screen's first black female superstar, once again battles substandard blaxploitation material. She plays a nurse pretending to be a junkie in order to find the creeps who hooked her sister on drugs. (Dir: Jack Hill, 91 mins.)†

Cold Comfort (Canada, 1989)*** Maury Chaykin, Margaret Langrick, Paul Gross. Businessman is rescued from a blizzard by a passing trucker, who takes him home as a gift for his nubile young daughter. Black comic weirdness based on a cult theater piece, a strong directing debut for veteran Canadian cinematographer Vic Sarin. (92 mins.)†

Cold Feet (1984)*** Griffin Dunne, Marissa Chibas, Blanche Baker. A contemporary romantic comedy that you'll warm up to. When a TV writer's marriage to a self-absorbed neurotic falls apart, he falls for a caring research scientist who's just survived a failed affair. (Dir: Bruce Van Dusen, 96 mins.)†

Cold Feet (1989)**½ Keith Carradine, Sally Kirkland, Tom Waits, Bill Pullman, Rip Torn, Kathleen York. Offbeat western comedy written by Tom McGuane about three petty thieves thrown together by a search for hidden emeralds. Not for all tastes, but a change of pace. Look for McGuane and Jeff Bridges in cameos. (Dir: Robert Dornhelm, 91 mins.)†

Cold Front (Canada, 1989)** Martin Sheen, Michael Ontkean, Kim Coates, Beverly D'Angelo. U.S. agent Sheen and Canadian Mountie Ontkean team up to stop a terrorist who, not satisfied with political assassinations, murders the wives of his victims first. Thriller might have been better with a bigger budget; as is, it's rather tepid. (Dir: "Paul Bnarbic" [Allan S. Goldstein], 96 mins.)†

Colditz Story (Great Britain, 1957)*** John Mills, Eric Portman. Offbeat comedy-drama about British prisoners of war in a German castle fortress (WWII). Excellent performance by Eric Portman. (Dir: Guy Hamilton, 97 mins.)†

Cold Night's Death, A (MTV 1973)*** Eli Wallach, Robert Culp. Strange forces disrupt experiments being made on monkeys in a snowbound mountain lab. Could the culprit be the Abominable Snowman? Takes its time building up the dilemma, but it's worth hanging on for the unpredictable solution. (Dir: Jerrold Freedman, 73 mins.)

Cold Room, The (MCTV 1984)**½ George Segal, Amanda Pays, Anthony Higgins, Warren Clarke. Writer Segal is trying to mend his relationship with his daughter when they meet in West Berlin. When she discovers a young man in a secret chamber behind furniture in her hotel room, they are plunged into a nightmarish series of unexplained incidents. (Dir: James Dearden, 115 mins.)†

Cold Steel (1988)* Brad Davis, Sharon Stone, Adam Ant. Davis is a cop out to avenge his father's brutal murder who becomes involved with a psycho with a grudge. A plot so thin, dialogue so predictable, and acting so mediocre that one might figure the title describes the canister which this film should never have left. (Dir: Dorothy Ann Puzo, 90 mins.)†

Cold Sweat (France-Italy, 1971)** Charles Bronson, Liv Ullmann, James Mason, Michael Constantine, Jill Ireland. A trim Richard Matheson tale gets beefed up here to fit the framework of a Bronson film. He plays an American in Paris who gets swept up in the seamy world of drug trafficking. (Dir: Terence Young, 94 mins.)†

Cold Turkey (1971)*** Dick Van Dyke, Pippa Scott, Tom Poston. Uneven but often funny comedy about a small midwestern town trying to win a 25 million dollar reward if everyone in the town will go "cold turkey" for thirty days, i.e., give up smoking cigarettes. (Dir: Norman Lear, 102 mins.)†

Cold War Killers (Great Britain, 1986)** Terence Stamp, Michael Culver. British operative Stamp investigates the mystery of a recently recovered aircraft that vanished thirty years earlier, bearing a cargo that the KGB would still like to find. The title suggests more excitement than this talky, tedious spy drama delivers. Sequel: *Alamut Ambush*. (Dir: William Braine, 85 mins.)†

Cold Wind in August, A (1961)***½ Lola Albright, Scott Marlowe, Herschel Bernardi. A very moving drama of a lonely burlesque stripper in her thirties and her friendship with a 17-year-old boy which turns into a love affair. Albright, under the sensitive directorial hand of Alexander Singer, gives a beautifully shaded, poignant performance playing the stripper searching for affection. (80 mins.)

Cole Justice (1989)**½ Carl Bartholomew, Keith Andrews, Nick Zickefoose, Mike Wiles. Schoolteacher Justice, a fan of classic western films, decides to emulate their vigilante methods in cleaning up his town. Star Bartholomew, who also directed, loves westerns as well, and sprinkles this tribute with scenes from some of the classics. (91 mins.)†

Cole Younger, Gunfighter (1958)** Frank Lovejoy, James Best. Tough western about the notorious gunslinger, Cole Younger. (Dir: R. G. Springsteen, 79 mins.)

Collector, The (1965)***½ Samantha Eggar, Terence Stamp. Veteran director William Wyler has fashioned an interesting psychological drama of John Fowles's bestselling novel about a maniacal plan executed by a psychotic young Englishman. The young man, well acted by Stamp, kidnaps beautiful art student (Eggar) and keeps her captive in the cellar of his country home. The film builds considerable tension, and the two stars are mesmerizing throughout. (119 mins.)†

Collector's Item (Italy, 1987)** Tony Musante, Laura Antonelli, Florinda Balkan. When a chance meeting reunites Musante and Antonelli fifteen years after their affair, she and her daughter hold him captive in their apartment to make sure he doesn't get away again. Kinky tale of sexual obsession has the benefit of the alluring Ms. Antonelli, but the choppy script is hard to follow. (Dir: Giuseppe Patroni Griffi, 99 mins.)†

Colleen (1936)**½ Ruby Keeler, Dick Powell, Jack Oakie. Typical Powell musical. Hugh Herbert's portrayal of an eccentric millionaire is the only redeeming feature. (Dir: Alfred E. Green, 100 mins.)

College (1927)*** Buster Keaton, Anne Cornwall, Grant Withers, Snitz Edwards. Egghead Keaton tries to win his college sweetheart by becoming a sports hero—in the process he tries every sport possible. Not quite as unified or elegant as most of his films, but still hilarious. (Dir: James W. Horne, 65 mins.)†

College Coach (1933)**½ Dick Powell, Ann Dvorak, Pat O'Brien, Hugh Herbert, Lyle Talbot, Donald Meek. Forceful and different story of corruption in college athletics, very unusual at a period which usually produced slick, rah-rah sports stories. (Dir: William Wellman, 75 mins.)

College Confidential (1960)* Steve Allen, Jayne Meadows, Walter Winchell, Mamie Van Doren. Another producer-director Albert Zugsmith's crude commercial opuses spiced with sex and violence. This time the action takes place in a small town where Prof. Steve Allen's classroom is filled with such atypical college types as Mamie Van Doren, Conway Twitty and Ziva Rodann. (91 mins.)

College Holiday (1936)**½ Jack Benny, Burns & Allen. Plot is a bit too silly for even Jack, George, and Gracie. Something about a bankrupt hotel, a genetics expert, and the inevitable variety show that saves the hotel. (Dir: Frank Tuttle, 87 mins.)

College Humor (1933)**½ Bing Crosby, Jack Oakie, Burns & Allen. Fine cast, some good fun in this campus comedy but most of it is routine, especially the big football game finale. (Dir: Wesley Ruggles, 84 mins.)

College Swing (1938)*½ Martha Raye, Burns & Allen, Bob Hope, Ben Blue, Betty Grable, Jackie Coogan, Jerry Colonna. You've read the cast. Now we dare you to watch this classic example of a bad 1938 film musical. Gracie Allen comes off the best. (Dir: Raoul Walsh, 86 mins.)

Collision Course (1987)**½ Pat Morita, Jay Leno, Chris Sarandon, Ernie Hudson, John Hancock, Al Waxman, Soon-Teck Oh, Randall "Tex" Cobb. Imagine *Red Heat* with Morita and Leno instead of Schwarzenegger and Belushi. (That may take a little work.) Japanese detective Morita is aided by Detroit cop Leno in tracking down a stolen experimental car. Not as funny as it might have been, but an agreeable buddy-cop entry anyway. (Dir: Lewis Teague, 96 mins.)†

Colonel Blimp—See: **Life and Death of Colonel Blimp, The**

Colonel Effingham's Raid (1945)*** Charles Coburn, Joan Bennett. A retired Southern colonel decides to use his military background to straighten out a town. Good comedy thanks to Coburn. (Dir: Irving Pichel, 70 mins.)†

Colonel Redl (Hungary-West Germany-Austria, 1985)*** Klaus Maria Brandauer, Armin Mueller-Stahl, Gudrun Landgrebe. The director and star of the Oscar-winning *Mephisto* reunite to explore the life of Col. Alfred Redl, a high-ranking intelligence agent in the Austro-Hungarian Empire, who committed suicide on the eve of World War I. This fictionalized treatment of his life pits his homosexuality, peasant birth, and possible Jewish origins against the strictures of the aristocratic military society he desperately yearns to be accepted into. There is less substance than there might appear to be, but plenty of style, and Brandauer brings life to what might otherwise have been a cipher. (Dir: Istvan Szabo, 144 mins.)†

Colorado Territory (1949)***½ Joel McCrea, Virginia Mayo, Dorothy Malone, Henry Hull, John Archer. Smashing western remake by director Raoul Walsh of his own *High Sierra*. McCrea is the outlaw who escapes from prison and sets out to commit one last robbery. (94 mins.)

Color Me Blood Red (1965)* Don Joseph, Candi Conder, Elyn Warner. A highstrung artist wants to find a new shade of red for his abstract paints, and discovers that blood substitutes nicely for oils. Some very trusted camp humor punctuates this, the third of H.G. Lewis's immortal "gore" trilogy. AKA: **Model Massacre**. (Dir: Herschell Gordon Lewis, 74 mins.)†

Color Me Dead (U.S.-Australia, 1969)** Tom Tryon, Carolyn Jones, Patricia Connolly, Rick Jason. Ragged remake of the semiclassic *D.O.A.* A man suffering from fatal poisoning has just enough time to hunt down his killer. (Dir: Eddie Davis, 97 mins.)†

Color of Money, The (1986)*** Paul Newman, Tom Cruise, Mary Elizabeth Mastrantonio, Helen Shaver, John Turturro. Knockout follow-up to *The Hustler* finds Fast Eddie Felson (an Oscar-winning performance by Newman) grooming a naïve young protégé (a solid performance by Cruise) to be a top pool shark. The filming of the pool sequences is varied and exciting, the atmosphere is perfectly caught, and the acting is standout all around. However, there are script weaknesses in the film's latter half. (Dir: Martin Scorsese, 119 mins.)†

Color Purple, The (1985)***½ Whoopi Goldberg, Danny Glover, Rae Dawn Chong, Margaret Avery, Oprah Winfrey. A beautifully made and acted adaptation of Alice Walker's prize-winning novel about a black woman, who's cruelly separated from her sister and who endures a lifetime of brutalization by men before finding the courage to free herself. Most of it comes across as being a tear-jerker, about oppression, but the film's constant violence and expert performances are riveting. (Dir: Steven Spielberg, 155 mins.)†

Colors (1988)**** Sean Penn, Robert Duvall, Maria Conchita Alonso, Randy Brooks, Grand Bush. Powerful, disturbing film about gang warfare in ethnic L.A. Unlike the *Dirty Harry* school of tough-cop flicks, *Colors* gives its brutal violence a real context, and also supplies us with characters we can care about and identify with. Duvall is an aging cop with a few months to go until his pension; Penn is his hard-assed rookie partner. Director Dennis Hopper has done a marvelous job of playing off of Penn's volatile public persona, while also giving Duvall the best role he's had since *Tender Mercies*. From the crisp cinematography by Haskell Wexler to the surprisingly eclectic soundtrack, and the casting of real L.A. gang members, all the elements are uniformly excellent. Video version runs 127 mins. (120 mins.)†

Colossus of New York, The (1958)*½ John Baragrey, Otto Kruger, Robert Hutton, Mala Powers. A father transplants his late genius-son's gray matter into a robot who subsequently behaves like neither a scientist nor a gentleman. Like something *Mad* magazine might dream up as a joke. (Dir: Eugene Lourie, 70 mins.)

Colossus of Rhodes, The (France-Spain-Italy, 1961)** Rory Calhoun, Lea Massari, Georges Marchal, Angel Aranda, Mabel Karr. Better than usual spear-and-sandal effort. Lots of action as heroes try to destroy a huge statue guarding the port of Rhodes. (Dir: Sergio Leone, 128 mins.)

Colossus: The Forbin Project (1970)**½

197

Eric Braeden, Susan Clark, William Schallert. Computer runs amok, pits wits against scientists in attempt to take over. Intelligent story, adequately told. AKA: **The Forbin Project.** (Dir: Joseph Sargent, 100 mins.)†

Colt .45—See: **Thundercloud**

Column South (1953)** Audie Murphy, Joan Evans, Robert Sterling. Slow-moving Civil War yarn with Murphy playing a young cavalry officer who averts an all-out Navajo uprising. (Dir: Frederick de Cordova, 85 mins.)

Coma (1978)*** Genevieve Bujold, Michael Douglas, Elizabeth Ashley, Rip Torn, Richard Widmark. Robin Cook's best-selling chiller makes a good, suspenseful, and satisfying film. Don't let logic cloud your senses; just sit back and watch Dr. Genevieve Bujold unearth a diabolical business that stems from many young patients dying on the operating table at a metropolitan hospital. (Dir: Michael Crichton, 112 mins.)†

Comanche (1956)** Dana Andrews, Linda Cristal, Kent Smith. Indians raid a Mexican town and kidnap the daughter of a Spanish aristocrat, among others. Cavalry Scout Andrews has a rough time before he convinces chief that he is on a peace mission. (Dir: George Sherman, 87 mins.)

Comancheros, The (1961)*** John Wayne, Stuart Whitman, Ina Balin, Lee Marvin, Nehemiah Persoff. Generally enjoyable big-scale western about a ranger who infiltrates a gang supplying guns and firewater to the Indians. (Dir: Michael Curtiz, 107 mins.)†

Comanche Station (1960)*** Randolph Scott, Nancy Gates. Lawman guides a woman and three desperadoes through hostile Indian country. These Scott westerns are usually better than average, and this one is no exception; well made and exciting. (Dir: Budd Boetticher, 74 mins.)

Comanche Territory (1950)** Maureen O'Hara, Macdonald Carey. Another retelling of the adventures of famed Jim Bowie and his encounter with the Apaches. (Dir: George Sherman, 76 mins.)

Combat Academy—See: **Combat High**

Combat High (MTV 1986)* Keith Gordon, Wally Ward, Jamie Farr, Dick Van Patten, Robert Culp, John Ratzenberger, Richard Moll. TV revamp of *Police Academy*; here a bunch of hell-raising teenagers are sent to a military academy to straighten out. AKA: **Combat Academy.** (Dir: Neal Israel, 104 mins.)†

Combat Killers (1980)*½ Paul Edwards, Marlene Dauden, Claude Wilson, Leopold Salcedo. American troops in the Philippines face as much danger from the

Japanese as from their own commander, who doesn't mind risking his men's lives for his own glory. No-nonsense war movie looks like it was made in 1950 rather than 1980. (Dir: Ken Loring, 96 mins.)†

Combat Shock (1986)** Ricky Giovinazzo, Nick Nasta, Veronica Stork. Not a good film, but there are infrequent flashes of power in this tale about a Viet vet coping with guilt over his deformed child whose plight was the result of his dad's exposure to Agent Orange. AKA: **American Nightmare.** (Dir: Buddy Giovinazzo, 90 mins.)†

Combat Squad (1953)** John Ireland, Lon McCallister, Hal March. During the Korean War, a young, frightened boy finds the courage to become a man in the eyes of his buddies. Familiar war story. (Dir: Cy Roth, 72 mins.)

Come and Get It (1936)*** Joel McCrea, Frances Farmer, Walter Brennan. Good drama based on Edna Ferber's tale of the lumber country and the people who toil in it. The cast does well with Oscar winner Brennan the standout. (Dirs: William Wyler, Howard Hawks, 99 mins.)†

Come and See (USSR, 1987)**½ Aleksei Kravchenko, Olga Mironova. A young boy's view of the German invasion of Russia in WWII. Wonderful film technique augments this remembrance of a painful past. (Dir: Elem Klimov, 142 mins.)

Comeback, The (Great Britain, 1978)* Jack Jones, Pamela Stephenson, David Doyle, Bill Owen. Jones plays a singer who gets mixed up with a series of gruesome murders. Overlong, and not especially frightening. (Dir: Pete Walker, 100 mins.)†

Come Back Charleston Blue (1972)** Godfrey Cambridge, Raymond St. Jacques, Jonelle Allen. Detectives Coffin Ed Johnson and Grave Digger Jones return in this sequel to the amusing *Cotton Comes to Harlem*. Unfortunately, the gritty frivolity that made *"Cotton"* a joy is missing in this opus concerning the fight between the black and white gangs that hope to control the Harlem heroin trade. (Dir: Mark Warren, 100 mins.)

Comeback Kid, The (MTV 1980)**½ John Ritter, Susan Dey, Rod Gist. Ritter is Bubba Newman, a flashy ex-minor-league pitcher who lands a job coaching dispirited kids. Ritter is charming playing a basically unattractive character, but the story turns syrupy. (Dir: Peter Levin, 104 mins.)†

Come Back, Little Sheba (1952)*** Shirley Booth, Burt Lancaster, Terry Moore. Splendid performance by Shirley Booth, who won an Oscar, as a slatternly middle-aged housewife, and an equally effective one by Lancaster as her alcoholic husband in this absorbing adaptation of the hit play by William Inge. Emotionally searing drama of an unhappy marriage. (Dir: Daniel Mann, 99 mins.)†

Come Back to Me—See: **Doll Face**

Come Back to the Five and Dime, Jimmy Dean, Jimmy Dean (1982)*** Karen Black, Sandy Dennis, Cher, Sudie Bond, Kathy Bates, Marta Heflin. Director Robert Altman has worked wonders with this screen translation of a meretricious play about a 1975 reunion of a James Dean fan club from the fifties; the bargain-basement dramatics provide golden opportunities for the cast. (109 mins.)†

Comeback Trail, The (1974)** Chuck McCann, Buster Crabbe, Robert Staats, Ina Balin, Joe Franklin, Henny Youngman. Low-budget, nostalgic farce has schlockmeisters McCann and Staats hiring has-been cowboy star Crabbe in hopes he will pass away before they finish filming to collect the insurance. (Dir: Harry Hurwitz, 80 mins.)

Come Blow Your Horn (1963)*** Frank Sinatra, Tony Bill, Molly Picon, Lee J. Cobb, Barbara Rush. Neil Simon's Broadway comedy about a Jewish family in New York City is successfully brought to the screen with Sinatra well cast as a playboy and Tony Bill as his hero-worshipping younger brother. (Dir: Bud Yorkin, 112 mins.)

Comedians, The (U.S.-France; 1967)**½ Richard Burton, Elizabeth Taylor, Peter Ustinov, Alec Guinness, Paul Ford, Lillian Gish, James Earl Jones, Raymond St. Jacques. Graham Greene's novel of unrest in Haiti, transferred to the screen, is interesting but the splendid cast is hampered by Peter Glenville's sluggish direction, and a script that dwells too long on unnecessary detail. (160 mins.)

Comedy Company, The (MTV 1978)** Jack Albertson, Lawrence-Hilton Jacobs, Michael Brandon. The film tries to duplicate the atmosphere of the best known comedy clubs, but fails. (Dir: Lee Philips, 104 mins.)

Comedy of Terrors, The (1964)*** Vincent Price, Peter Lorre, Boris Karloff, Basil Rathbone. An outstanding cast of veteran horror stars have fun spoofing the type of film they used to work in. The story concerns a funeral home and a unique scheme for garnering more business. (Dir: Jacques Tourneur, 111 mins.)

Come Fill the Cup (1951)*** James Cagney, Phyllis Thaxter, Gig Young. James Cagney in another fine performance as an alcoholic ex-newspaper reporter and his struggle to reconstruct his shattered life. Fine performances throughout. (Dir: Gordon Douglas, 112 mins.)

Come Fly with Me (U.S.-Great Britain; 1963)** Dolores Hart, Hugh O'Brian, Karl Malden, Pamela Tiffin, Lois Nettleton. Typical empty romantic yarn about a trio of airline hostesses, and the objects of their affection: a pilot, a titled jewel thief, and a Texas millionaire (what else)! (Dir: Henry Levin, 109 mins.)

Come Live with Me (1941)** James Stewart, Hedy Lamarr. Hedy marries Jimmy to avoid being deported. If you can't guess how it ends you haven't seen many movies. (Dir: Clarence Brown, 86 mins.)

Come Next Spring (1956)*** Ann Sheridan, Steve Cochran, Walter Brennan, Sonny Tufts. Arkansas man returns home to his wife and family after eight years of wandering. Touching drama with excellent performances, a good script. (Dir: R. G. Springsteen, 92 mins.)

Come-On, The (1956)** Anne Baxter, Sterling Hayden, John Hoyt, Jesse White. Anne's a calculating gal mixed up in homicide. Naturally her nobler emotions get the better of her. Shoddy melodrama redeemed by Baxter's brio in an atypical role. (Dir: Russell Birdwell, 83 mins.)

Come Out Fighting (1945)** East Side Kids, Addison Richards, June Carlson. The Kids have two new gang members—a girl and the son of a judge. (Dir: William Beaudine, 62 mins.)

Comes a Horseman (1978)*** Jane Fonda, James Caan, Jason Robards, Jr., George Grizzard, Jim Davis, Richard Farnsworth. Uneven, but often compelling "modern" western, set in Montana right after WWII, in which easygoing cowpoke Caan teams up with tough but vulnerable rancher Fonda to beat off bad cattle baron Robards, who knows that there's oil on her land. Farnsworth, the former stuntman, earned an Oscar nomination for his beautiful portrayal of a gentle old cowhand. (Dir: Alan J. Pakula, 119 mins.)†

Come See the Paradise (1990)**½ Dennis Quaid, Tamlyn Tomita. A flawed, but still worthwhile film about the treatment of American Japanese during World War II. Although the film does not fit together in places, and we are left with too many loose ends, it bears attention. A rare and honest look at the internment camps and a stunning performance by Tomita. Quaid is adequate but not brilliant. (Dir: Alan Parker, 132 mins.)

Come September (1961)*** Rock Hudson, Gina Lollobrigida, Sandra Dee, Bobby Darin. Splendid Italian scenery grafted to a frothy little comedy plot about a millionaire who discovers his caretaker is using his villa as a hotel when he's away. (Dir: Robert Mulligan, 112 mins.)

Come Spy with Me (1967)** Troy Donahue, Valerie Allen, Albert Dekker. Silly spy spoof with nice Jamaican locales. (Dir: Marshall Stone, 85 mins.)

Come to the Stable (1949)*** Loretta Young, Celeste Holm, Elsa Lanchester, Regis Toomey, Hugh Marlowe, Mike Mazurki. Warm, human story about two French nuns and their efforts to build a children's hospital in America. Young and Holm, both nominated for Oscars, play the nuns with taste and charm. (Dir: Henry Koster, 94 mins.)

Comet over Broadway (1938)** Kay Francis, Ian Hunter, John Litel, Donald Crisp. Famous actress sacrifices all to return to her family. Just another sudsy drama. (Dir: Busby Berkeley, 65 mins.)

Comfort and Joy (Scotland, 1984)*** Bill Peterson, Eleanor David, C. P. Grogan, Alex Norton. A Scottish D.J. becomes involved in the local ice cream war in an attempt to alleviate his loneliness after his girlfriend deserts him. (Dir: Bill Forsyth, 106 mins.)†

Comfort of Strangers, The (1991)***½ Christopher Walken, Natasha Richardson, Rupert Everett, Helen Mirren. Creepy and darkly erotic tale, set within mysterious, yet alluring Venice, may recall the frightening *Don't Look Now*. Two lovers (Everett and Richardson) on vacation are wooed by a bizarre married couple (Walken and Mirren) with strange intentions. Director Schrader has mounted a handsomely perverse mood piece, from a witty screenplay by Harold Pinter that lingers in the mind. (Dir: Paul Schrader, 105 mins.)†

Comic, The (1969)***½ Dick Van Dyke, Mickey Rooney, Michele Lee, Cornel Wilde. Fine, incisive portrait by Dick Van Dyke of a silent-film comedian. Authentic Hollywood atmosphere, hilarious scenes blended with pathos. (Dir: Carl Reiner, 94 mins.)†

Comic, The (1985)* Steve Munroe, Bernard Plant. In a futuristic police state, an aspiring comic kills a popular entertainer in order to get a chance to perform. (Dir: Richard Driscoll, 90 mins.)†

Comic Book Confidential (Canada, 1988) *** Documentarian Ron Mann turns his attention to comic books. Through interviews with their creators (Harvey Pekar, William M. Gaines, Robert Crumb, Will Eisner, Lynda Barry, and more), he posits the independent "underground" comics as the vanguard of modern social criticism. (90 mins.)

Comic Magazine (Japan, 1987)**½ Yuya Uchida, Yumi Asou, Hiromi Go, Beat Takeshi. Scurrilous hit-and-miss satire about "kamikaze journalism" in Japan. This film follows the exploits of a Japanese TV reporter out to serve up as much scandal as the public can possibly digest. (Dir: Yojiro Takita, 120 mins.)

Comin' at Ya! (Italy, 1981)½ Tony Anthony, Gene Quintano, Victoria Abril, Gordon Lewis. A ragout western that throws all sorts of 3-D gimmicks into a preposterous storyline. An ersatz gunslinger that covers new dimensions—in stupidity. (Dir: Ferdinando Baldi, 91 mins.)

Coming Apart (1969)** Rip Torn, Lois Markle, Viveca Lindfors, Sally Kirkland. A New York City psychiatrist (Torn) records his own mental collapse on film. (Dir: Milton Moses Ginsberg, 110 mins.)

Coming Attractions—See: *Loose Shoes*

Coming Home (1978)*** Jon Voight, Jane Fonda, Bruce Dern, Robert Carradine, Penelope Milford, Robert Ginty. This deeply moving movie is an unusually touching love story, while also being a powerful anti-Vietnam War statement. Voight plays a paraplegic veteran who, after returning to a veterans hospital in the States, gradually falls in love with another man's wife (Fonda). Voight and Fonda won Oscars. (Dir: Hal Ashby, 128 mins.)†

Coming Out of the Ice (MTV 1982)*** John Savage, Willie Nelson, Francesca Annis, Ben Cross, Peter Vaughan. Somber, well-made TV drama based on the real life story of Victor Herman, an American who spent most of his life in Russia, first as an honored athlete, then as a prisoner in Siberia. (Dir: Waris Hussein, 104 mins.)†

Coming Out Party, A (Great Britain, 1962)*** James Robertson Justice, Leslie Phillips. Crusty radar expert is captured and imprisoned by the Germans and devises a daring escape from prison camp. World War II story played for comedy. (Dir: Ken Annakin, 90 mins.)

Coming-Out Party, The (1933)** Frances Dee, Gene Raymond, Alison Skipworth, Nigel Bruce. Debutante Dee falls in love with a jazz musician (ludicrously played by Raymond), much to her snooty family's dismay. (Dir: John G. Blystone, 79 mins.)

Coming to America (1988)**½ Eddie Murphy, Arsenio Hall, John Amos, James Earl Jones, Madge Sinclair, Shari Headley, Louie Anderson. Murphy stars as an African prince who journeys to the Big Apple in search of a wife in this sticky-sweet outing. Murphy does rate in a number of smaller roles (including an old Jewish barbershop kibitzer), and his first-ever interpretation of a character with humility allows his charm to keep the show afloat. (Dir: John Landis, 115 mins.)†

Comin' Round the Mountain (1951)** Bud Abbott, Lou Costello, Dorothy Shay. The feudin', fussin', and a fightin' gets an added slapstick touch as A&C head for them there hills in this cornball comedy about hillbilly hostility. (Dir: Charles Lamont, 77 mins.)

Command, The (1953)** Guy Madison, Joan Weldon, James Whitmore. The first CinemaScope western. Formula Cavalry vs. Indians plot about a medic who takes over a fighting outfit. (Dir: David Butler, 120 mins.)

Command Decision (1949)*** Clark Gable, Walter Pidgeon, Van Johnson. Interesting insight into the emotions of military brass who send men to their deaths to win battles. Fine cast does very well in this adaptation of the Broadway hit. (Dir: Sam Wood, 112 mins.)†

Command 5 (MTV 1985)** Stephen Parr, Sonja Smits, Wings Hauser, John Matuszak. *The Dirty Dozen* minus seven ... the same old plot about an "elite" group of law enforcers who operate without restrictions. (Dir: E. W. Swackhamer, 104 mins.)

Commando (1985)*** Arnold Schwarzenegger, Rae Dawn Chong, Dan Hedaya, Alyssa Milano. A nifty entertainment, thrill-packed and funny. The climax is too brutal in a commonplace way, but overall, the Fabulous Torso provides ripples of laughter and ripples of muscles in equal measure. (Dir: Mark L. Lester, 90 mins.)†

Commando Invasion (1987)* Michael James, Gordon Mitchell, Pat Vance, Ken Watanabe, Carol Roberts. Marine captain leads a squadron into Vietcong territory to find the leader responsible for ambushing his last command. (Dir: John Gale, 88 mins.)†

Commando Squad (1987)* Brian Thompson, Kathy Shower, William Smith. When special U.S. agent Thompson is captured by Texas drug kingpin Smith, fellow agent (and ex-lover) Shower loads up with more weapons than the Six-Day War and goes to his rescue. No thrills here. (Dir: Fred Olen Ray, 90 mins.)†

Commandos Strike at Dawn, The (1942)*** Paul Muni, Anna Lee. When the Nazis invade Norway, partisans resist and pave the way for a commando raid. Occasionally exciting war drama. (Dir: John Farrow, 98 mins.)

Commissar (U.S.S.R., 1967)*** Nonna Mordukova, Rolan Bykov. Banned by Soviet censors after it was completed, this remarkable feature about anti-Semitism and the Russian bureaucracy was unseen until 1988. Set in 1922, it tells the story of a strict by-the-rules commissar who, needing to hide her pregnancy, is put up with a family of Jewish peasants. Filled with audacious,

unforgettable images. (Dir: Alexander Askoldov, 110 mins.)

Common Ground (MTV 1990)***½ Jane Curtin, Richard Thomas, C. C. H. Pounder, James Farrentino, Erika Alexander, Georgia Emelin. Intelligent examination of racial tensions caused by Boston's school busing program in the '60s and '70s as seen by three different families. Seldom is a made-for-TV movie so fair to all points of view on such an explosive issue. Felicitously adapted from J. Anthony Lukas's Pulitzer Prize-winning book of the same name. (Dir: Mike Newell, 192 mins.)

Common Law Cabin (1967)**½ Adele Rein, Babette Bardot, Ken Swofford, Alaina Capri, Jack Moran, Franklin Bolger. Passions boil at an out-of-the-way Colorado fishing retreat, where an escaped bank robber hides out with the guests. More straightforward than other Russ Meyer movies, which isn't necessarily a good thing. AKA: **How Much Loving Does a Normal Couple Need?** (70 mins.)†

Common Threads: Stories From the Quilt (1989)***½ Powerful Academy Award-winning feature documentary about the giant quilt that is made up of panels created in memory of the tens of thousands of men, women, and children who have died of AIDS-related illnesses. Contains interviews with people with AIDS, including movie historian Vito Russo, and their families and friends, some of whom are shown fashioning pieces of the quilt. Movingly captures the emotionally charged moment when the quilt is put on display in Washington, D.C. Narrated by Dustin Hoffman with original music by Bobby McFerrin. (Dirs: Robert Epstein, Jeffrey Friedman, 79 mins.)†

Communion—See: Alice Sweet Alice

Communion (1989)** Christopher Walken, Lindsay Crouse, Joel Carlson, Frances Sternhagen. Based on novelist Whitley Streiber's book in which he claimed that he and members of his family were periodically "borrowed" by aliens, the movie is more domestic psychodrama than sci-fi. Unsatisfactory by any standard. (Dir: Philippe Mora, 103 mins.)†

Companions in Nightmare (MTV 1968)**½ Melvyn Douglas, Gig Young, Anne Baxter, Dana Wynter, Patrick O'Neal. An interesting made-for-TV feature which starts out promisingly, but reverts to melodrama. Various types undergoing group therapy become suspects when one of their kind is murdered. (Dir: Norman Lloyd, 99 mins.)

Company of Killers (1970)**½ Van Johnson, Ray Milland, John Saxon, Diana Lynn. Above-average thriller about a man being harassed by a newspaperman and later the police, after having muttered in a fit of delirium that he is a hired killer. (Dir: Jerry Thorpe, 86 mins.)

Company of Strangers, The (Canada, 1990)***½ Alice Diabo, Constance Garneau, Winifred Holden, Cissy Meddings, Mary Meigs, Catherine Roche, Michelle Sweeney, Beth Webber. Director Cynthia Scott's first feature is a charming and thoroughly winning story about eight elderly women stranded in the country when their tour bus breaks down. Filled with memories and joy. AKA: **Strangers in Good Company.** (Dir: Cynthia Scott, 101 mins.)

Company of Wolves, The (1985)*** Angela Lansbury, David Warner, Sarah Patterson, Brian Glover, Graham Crowden. A fanciful embroidering of fables, sexual symbolism, and mysterious happenings in a storybook forest village. As eerie tales are told by Granny (a memorably persnickety comic creation by Lansbury), her ingenuous Red Riding Hood-type granddaughter encounters wolves in many disguises. (Dir: Neil Jordan, 95 mins.)†

Competition, The (1980)**½ Lee Remick, Richard Dreyfuss, Amy Irving, Sam Wanamaker. Overly romantic yarn about two young pianists participating in a prestigious competition. The predictable romance between the two contestants takes a backseat to the piano sequences. (Dir: Joel Oliansky, 129 mins.)†

Compleat Beatles, The (1982)*** Entertaining look at the Beatles. While this magical mystery tour of their career is sketchy, we are treated to music clips extending from their first U.S. concert through their 1969 film *Let It Be*. (Dir: Patrick Montgomery, 120 mins.)†

Compromising Positions (1985)*** Susan Sarandon, Edward Herrmann, Raul Julia, Judith Ivey, Mary Beth Hurt, Ann DeSalvo, Joe Mantegna, Josh Mostel. A comic mystery set in the wonderful world of suburbia which loses steam early on. The cast, however, make the best of it, led by Sarandon as a housewife and former reporter who conducts her own investigation into the mysterious death of a womanizing dentist. (Dir: Frank Perry, 98 mins.)†

Compulsion (1959)*** Dean Stockwell, Bradford Dillman, Orson Welles, E. G. Marshall, Martin Milner. Unrelenting account of the murder trial of two twisted youths for a "thrill" murder, based on the Loeb-Leopold case of the '20s. Has a horrific fascination, a bravura performance by Welles as the defense lawyer; but remains a rather cold, detached film. (Dir: Richard Fleischer, 103 mins.)

Computercide (MTV 1982)* Joseph Cortese, Tom Clancy, Susan George, David Huddleston, Donald Pleasence.

Poor proposed pilot for a series about the last private eye in the world, circa the late twentieth century, and his search for a missing scientist. (Dir: Robert Michael Lewis, 104 mins.)

Computer Wore Tennis Shoes, The (1970) **½ Kurt Russell, Cesar Romero, Joe Flynn, William Schallert, Alan Hewitt. A light, frothy comedy which should appeal mostly to kids. Russell is a college student who somehow gets plugged into the college's big computer. (Dir: Robert Butler, 90 mins.)†

Comrade X (1940)*** Clark Gable, Hedy Lamarr. Cute, slapstick anti-Russian comedy in the *Ninotchka* vein but not half as good. Hedy's a Russian street car conductor and Clark's an American newspaperman. (Dir: King Vidor, 90 mins.)

Conan the Barbarian (1982)** Arnold Schwarzenegger, James Earl Jones, Max von Sydow, Sandahl Bergman, Ben Davidson, Cassandra Gaviola. Visually stunning but slow paced, ludicrously overwrought adventure story set in the "Hyborean Age" when men were men and the likes of Schwarzenegger were on the side of justice. The bodybuilder stars as a young man out to seek revenge for his father's murder by the evil Thulsa Doom and to learn "the riddle of steel." (Dir: John Milius, 129 mins.)†

Conan the Destroyer (1984)**½ Arnold Schwarzenegger, Grace Jones, Wilt Chamberlain, Sarah Douglas. Colorful account of a virgin princess being plotted against by an evil queen. A note of humor is added to the proceedings, thanks to Arnold's camp heroics and Jones's eccentric presence. (Dir: Richard Fleischer, 103 mins.)†

Concealed Enemies (MTV 1984)***½ Edward Herrmann, John Harkins, Peter Riegert. A riveting docudrama, originally shown in four parts on PBS's "American Playhouse," about the famed Alger Hiss–Whittaker Chambers spy case and the red-baiting atmosphere that surrounded it. Herrmann (Hiss) and Harkins (Chambers) head a fine cast, performing sensitively in the thought-provoking script. (Dir: Jeff Bleckner, 240 mins.)

Concert for Bangladesh (1972)*** Bob Dylan, Ravi Shankar, George Harrison, Eric Clapton, Leon Russell. Straightforward film record of the historic benefit concert at Madison Square Garden in August 1971. (Dir: Saul Swimmer, 99 mins.)†

Concorde—Airport '79, The (1979)* Alain Delon, Susan Blakely, Robert Wagner, Sylvia Kristel, Cicely Tyson, Martha Raye, Charo, George Kennedy, Eddie Albert, John Davidson. Ruthless tycoon

Wagner wants to destroy the aircraft so that his dirty dealings won't be revealed by his mistress Blakely, a top newscaster. (Dir: David Lowell Rich, 123 mins.)†

Concrete Angels (Canada, 1986)**½ Joseph DiMambro, Luke McKeehan, Omie Craden, Dean Bosacki. In 1964 Toronto, a group of juvenile delinquents hope to improve their lot by forming a band and auditioning for a contest to choose the opening act for a local appearance by the Beatles. Unlike the usual *American Graffiti*-type nostalgia, this doesn't look back with rose-colored glasses, though it sometimes seems to go out of its way to be coarse. The acting is amateurish, but the film is well made and original. (Dir: Carlo Liconti, 97 mins.)†

Concrete Beat (MTV 1984)** Darlanne Fluegel, John Getz, Kenneth McMillan. Deadly serious drama about a newspaperman who is part crusader and part idealist. He takes up the cause of a woman accused of killing her child. (Dir: Robert Butler, 104 mins.)†

Concrete Cowboys, The (MTV 1979)* Jerry Reed, Tom Selleck, Morgan Fairchild, Ray Stevens, Barbara Mandrell. Low-caliber slapstick opus about the exploits of two country boys turned detectives searching for a missing singer is full of gimmicks. (Dir: Burt Kennedy, 104 mins.)

Concrete Jungle, The (Great Britain, 1960)** Stanley Baker, Sam Wanamaker, Margit Saad. Hoodlum pulls a racetrack robbery and goes to prison after burying the loot. His attempts to retrieve it fail due to some double-crossing. (Dir: Joseph Losey, 86 mins.)

Concrete Jungle, The (1982)** Jill St. John, Tracy Bregman, Barbara Luna. Another excuse for male chauvinists to ogle prison babes in their revealing outfits. An innocent girl is unjustly imprisoned, but the film is really about penitentiary pulchritude. (Dir: Tom De Simone, 99 mins.)†

Condemned! (1929)**½ Ronald Colman, Ann Harding, Dudley Digges, Louis Wolheim. The penal colony of Devil's Island is made to look like a French resort in this early talkie about a handsome convict (Colman) falling in love with the warden's wife (Harding). Corny but still entertaining. (Dir: Wesley Ruggles, 86 mins.)

Condemned of Altona, The (1963)*** Sophia Loren, Maximilian Schell, Fredric March, Robert Wagner. Confused but interesting drama based on a play by Jean-Paul Sartre, which tells the story of a strange family living in postwar Germany. March builds ships, and his son (Schell) is a madman living in the attic of their estate wearing his Nazi officer's uniform. (Dir: Vittorio De Sica, 114 mins.)

Condominium (MTV 1979)* Dan Haggerty, Steve Forrest, Ralph Bellamy, Pamela Hensley, Dane Clark, Elinor Donohue, Stuart Whitman. TV disaster movie with special effects that even the makers of low-budget Japanese horror flicks would have rejected on grounds of tackiness. The source of all the trauma: a tidal wave. (Dir: Sidney Hayers, 195 mins.)

Condor (MTV 1986)** Ray Wise, James Avery, Wendy Kilbourne. Another unsold pilot. This adventure is set in the popular movie year of 2001 as a top agent of an international security detail is assigned an attractive android as his partner. (Dir: Virgil Vogel, 104 mins.)

Condorman (1981)**½ Michael Crawford, Oliver Reed, Barbara Carrera, James Hampton. An amusing adventure yarn with Crawford as a cartoonist who becomes involved with CIA and KGB agents and various other espionage characters. He calls upon his cartoon creation, Condorman, to get him out of more than one tight spot. (Dir: Charles Jarrott, 90 mins.)†

Conduct Unbecoming (Great Britain, 1975)*** Michael York, Richard Attenborough, Trevor Howard, Stacy Keach, Susannah York. The film is an actor's holiday and the cast is excellent. About a scandal in a British officers' mess in Northwest India circa 1878, and their notions about honor, women, and civility. Unfortunately, once the mystery is revealed it seems rather silly. (Dir: Michael Anderson, 107 mins.)

Code of Silence—See: **Trouble in the Sky**

Coney Island (1943)*** Betty Grable, Cesar Romero, George Montgomery. Betty is at her leggy best in this gay, though routine, musical set in the turn of the century. George and Cesar fight over Betty's affections. Remade as *Wabash Avenue*. (Dir: Walter Lang, 96 mins.)

Confession (1937)*** Kay Francis, Basil Rathbone, Jane Bryan, Ian Hunter, Donald Crisp. The best film in director Joe May's undistinguished American career, a soaper in which Francis is tried for the murder of concert pianist Rathbone. (86 mins.)

Confession, The (France, 1970)**** Yves Montand, Simone Signoret. Emotionally shattering drama which stands as one of the most powerful and intellectually compelling anti-Communist films ever made. Montand, giving one of the most restrained performances of his career, depicts a top party bureaucrat tortured and dehumanized by his beloved Communist party leaders into giving a false confession. (Dir: Costa-Gavras, 138 mins.)

Confessions of a Married Man (MTV 1983)** Robert Conrad, Jennifer Warren, Ann Dusenberry, Lance Guest, Mary Crosby. Conrad faces the mid-life crazies by seeking solace and stimulation in the arms of a younger woman. A subtle portrait of a man caught in a whirlwind of expectations. (Dir: Steve Gethers, 104 mins.)

Confessions of a Nazi Spy (1939)*** Edward G. Robinson, Francis Lederer. Well-done propaganda melodrama about a weak link in the Nazi spy network. Dated but for all its flag waving speeches, still a grim reminder. (Dir: Anatole Litvak, 102 mins.)

Confessions of an Opium Eater (1962)** Vincent Price, Linda Ho, Richard Loo, June Kim. In this trashy cult favorite Price—always dressed in black—plays an adventurer involved with runaway slave girls and a tong war in 19th-century San Francisco. Bizarre. AKA: Souls for Sale. (Dir: Albert Zugsmith, 85 mins.)

Confessions of a Police Captain (Italy, 1971)**½ Martin Balsam, Franco Nero, Marilu Tolo. Balsam gives a fine performance in this occasionally heavy-handed film about a policeman's fight to bring in criminals who seem above the reach of the law. (Dir: Damiano Damiani, 92 mins.)†

Confessions of Boston Blackie (1941)*** Chester Morris, Harriet Hilliard, Richard Lane. In this snappy entry, B.B. not only apprehends the killer of a man slain at an art auction, he also finds time to break up a painting scam in Manhattan. (Dir: Edward Dmytryk, 65 mins.)

Confessions of Felix Krull (Germany, 1958)*½ Horst Buchholz, Lisa Pulver. The amours and experiences of a young opportunist. Better things could have been done with Mann's novel, but the results are satisfactory. (Dir: Kurt Hoffman, 107 mins.)

Confessions of Tom Harris—See: Tale of the Cock

Confidential Agent (1945)*** Charles Boyer, Lauren Bacall, Peter Lorre. Exciting intrigue adventure with the Spanish Civil War as background in this slick adaptation of a Graham Greene story. (Dir: Herman Shumlin, 118 mins.)

Confidentially Connie (1953)** Van Johnson, Janet Leigh, Walter Slezak, Louis Calhern. Teacher in a small Maine college is thrown into the middle of a terrific uproar, all because his wife loves steaks, which come high. (Dir: Edward Buzzell, 71 mins.)

Confidentially Yours (France, 1984)**½ Fanny Ardant, Jean-Louis Trintignant. Somehow we expect more from a director like François Truffaut than this mellow re-creation of Hollywood mystery movies. A secretary remains loyal to her

boss who's accused of murder; she sets out to prove his innocence. Ardant has an infectious smile as the Roz Russell-esque girl Friday, and mystery lovers may be amused by the proceedings. (111 mins.)†

Confidential Report—See: Mr. Arkadin

Confirm or Deny (1941)**½ Don Ameche, Joan Bennett. War correspondent finds love in a London blackout and it mixes up his whole life. Some excitement but a bit dated. (Dir: Archie Mayo, 73 mins.)

Conflagration—See: Enjo

Conflict (1945)*** Humphrey Bogart, Alexis Smith, Sydney Greenstreet. Humphrey kills his wife in this one and spends most of the film in a battle of wits with Greenstreet who tries to break the perfect alibi. Without the fine cast it would be a routine melodrama. (Dir: Curtis Bernhardt, 86 mins.)

Conflict of Wings (Great Britain, 1954)*** John Gregson, Muriel Pavlow, Kieron Moore. The RAF wants to use a small island as site for testing rockets, but the townspeople prefer to let the birds which have nested there for generations remain. Pleasant comedy-drama. (Dir: John Eldridge, 84 mins.)

Conformist, The (Italy-France-West Germany, 1970)**** Jean-Louis Trintignant, Stefania Sandrelli, Dominique Sanda. A fascinating study of decadence and Fascism during Mussolini's reign in Italy in 1938, based on the novel by Alberto Moravia, adapted and directed by Bernardo Bertolucci. Brilliantly captures the mood, texture, and look of the 1930s, and it's extraordinarily well acted. Trintignant plays a philosophy professor reflecting on his past life. (115 mins.)†

Congo Crossing (1956)** Virginia Mayo, George Nader, Peter Lorre. A predictable tale of fugitives from the law who congregate in a West African city where extradition laws are not practiced. (Dir: Joseph Pevney, 85 mins.)

Congo Maisie (1940)*** Ann Sothern, John Carroll, Rita Johnson, Shepperd Strudwick, E. E. Clive. While stranded in the Darkest Continent Maisie keeps the natives from getting restless. A breezy remake of Red Dust. (Dir: H. C. Potter, 70 mins.)

Congratulations, It's a Boy (MTV 1971)**½ Bill Bixby, Diane Baker, Jack Albertson, Ann Sothern. Comedy-drama about an over-thirty-five swinger who is visited by a seventeen-year-old lad claiming to be his son. (Dir: William A. Graham, 78 mins.)

Congressman, The—See: Deputy, The

Conjugal Bed, The (Italy, 1963)**** Ugo Tognazzi, Marina Vlady. The original title translation for this was The Queen Bee, which explains all. It's about a forty-year-old bachelor who marries a virtuous young girl who—literally—loves him to death. Funny, ribald comedy-drama. (Dir: Marco Ferreri, 90 mins.)

Connecticut Yankee in King Arthur's Court, A (1949)*** Bing Crosby, Rhonda Fleming, Cedric Hardwicke. The Mark Twain tale of a blacksmith who is transported back to the time of King Arthur, uses modern methods to overcome obstacles. Lavish musical fits Crosby like a glove; good fun. (Dir: Tay Garnett, 107 mins.)†

Connecticut Yankee in King Arthur's Court, A (MTV 1989)**½ Keshia Knight Pulliam, Michael Gross, Jean Marsh, Emma Samms, Whip Hubley, René Auberjonois. Updated version of the Mark Twain story still delivers a cheery bounce, with Pulliam as the American who falls off a horse in Connecticut and wakes up in sixth-century Camelot. Solid family fare—colorful and, surprisingly, not too syrupy. (Dir: Mel Damski, 96 mins.)

Connecting Rooms (Great Britain, 1971)** Bette Davis, Michael Redgrave, Alexis Kanner. Geritol opera exploring relationships within a British boardinghouse. Davis plays a street musician, Redgrave is a former schoolmaster, and Kanner is the rambunctious youth who comes between them. (Dir: Franklin Gollings, 103 mins.)

Connection, The (1962)*** William Redfield, Warren Finnerty, Roscoe Lee Browne, Barbara Winchester. Arty innovative movie about a documentary maker who gets too involved with his subject, a circle of strung-out jazz musicians. The film we're watching is the film he's "making"—as he's talked into trying heroin himself. (Dir: Shirley Clarke, 103 mins.)†

Connection, The (MTV 1973)**½ Charles Durning, Ronnie Cox, Zohra Lampert, Dennis Cole, Dana Winter. If you like tough, hard-boiled New York characters who have hearts of gold you'll enjoy the lead in this film. Durning's casual acting style fits his character in a tale concerning a daring hotel robbery, and a deal between the crooks and the insurance companies. (Dir: Tom Gries, 73 mins.)†

Conquered City (Italy, 1962)**½ David Niven, Ben Gazzara, Martin Balsam, Michael Craig. After the Nazis are chased from Athens, a British major is ordered to hold a hotel to prevent a cache of arms from falling into the hands of Greek rebels. (Dir: Joseph Anthony, 91 mins.)

Conqueror, The (1956)½ John Wayne, Susan Hayward, Pedro Armendariz, Agnes Moorehead, William Conrad. Listed in the book *The Fifty Worst Films of All Time*, this prestigious production relates the adventures of Genghis Khan (Wayne) the Mongol warrior who conquered the world as well as the heart of the Princess Bortai (Hayward). Ironically, it was later discovered that this

Hollywood folly had tragic overtones. The film was made near an atomic test site and many of those connected with the film have died of cancer. (Dir: Dick Powell, 112 mins.)†

Conqueror Worm, The—See: **Witchfinder General**

Conquerors, The (1932)**½ Richard Dix, Ann Harding, Edna May Oliver, Guy Kibbee, Donald Cook. Panoramic view of the growth of the Old West, with Dix founding a banking empire and keeping it alive through the years. Strongly directed by William Wellman. (86 mins.)†

Conquest (1937)*** Greta Garbo, Charles Boyer, Reginald Owen, Leif Erickson, Dame May Whitty. Amiably secondrate, though the performances of Boyer and Garbo are detailed and observant, and Maria Ouspenskaya etches one of her most effective bits. This dramatization of the relationship of Napoleon and Marie Walewska of Poland is probably the most creditable of the collaborations between Garbo and her favored director, Clarence Brown. (112 mins.)†

Conquest (Italy-Spain-Mexico, 1983)*½ Jorge Rivero, Andrea Occhipinti, Sabrina Siani. Violent, gory sword and sorcery epic pitting warriors Ilias and Maxz against a beautiful demon bent on world conquest. Music by Claudio Simonetti, formerly of Goblin, who scored Dario Argento's films. (Dir: Lucio Fulci, 92 mins.)†

Conquest of Cochise (1953)** John Hodiak, Robert Stack, Joy Page. Mediocre Cowboys and Indians yarn hampered greatly by miscasting of John Hodiak as Cochise. (Dir: William Castle, 80 mins.)

Conquest of Space (1955)**½ Eric Fleming, Walter Brooke, Phil Foster. Army space explorers set out to make a landing on Mars. Clever production effects by George Pal, along with a rather bloodless narrative. (Dir: Byron Haskin, 80 mins.)†

Conquest of the Planet of the Apes (1972)*** Roddy McDowall, Don Murray, Ricardo Montalban. The fourth of the big box-office "ape" films. The time is 1990 and the apes are being used as slaves. One of the best of the series. Next was *Battle for the Planet of the Apes*. (Dir: J. Lee Thompson, 86 mins.)†

Conrack (1974)*** Jon Voight, Paul Winfield, Madge Sinclair, Hume Cronyn. A gentle, moving story about a young white schoolteacher who goes to help a group of culturally deprived black youngsters on an island off the coast of South Carolina. Voight is convincing as he gradually reaches the children with his stories and activities. (Dir: Martin Ritt, 106 mins.)†

Consenting Adult (MTV 1985)*** Marlo Thomas, Martin Sheen, Barry Tubbs, Talia Balsam. Laura Z. Hobson's intelligent and heartfelt novel about a controversial subject has been turned into a commendable TV drama. Thomas and Sheen are the upper-middle-class parents who are devastated when their golden boy of a son announces that he is a homosexual. (Dir: Gilbert Cates, 104 mins.)†

Consequence, The (West Germany, 1977)***½ Jurgen Prochnow, Ernst Hannawald, Walo Luond, Edith Volmann. A homosexual actor jailed for his relationship with a minor falls in love with prison guard's son. Tense, sensitive film attacks both prejudice and a society which uses prison system as means of persecution. A superb performance by Prochnow, who worked again with director Wolfgang Peterson in *Das Boot*. (100 mins.)

Consolation Marriage (1931)**½ Irene Dunne, Pat O'Brien, John Halliday, Myrna Loy. Dunne and O'Brien make an interesting and effective team in this slightly off-beat romantic comedy of two jilted lovers who find happiness with each other. (Dir: Paul Sloane, 82 mins.)

Conspiracy of Hearts (Great Britain, 1960)*** Lilli Palmer, Sylvia Syms. Group of nuns hide Jewish children from the Nazis. Well-done drama, keeps the suspense pretty much on high throughout. (Dir: Ralph Thomas, 116 mins.)

Conspiracy of Love (MTV 1987)*½ Robert Young, Drew Barrymore, Elizabeth Wilson, Glynnis O'Connor. Saccharine story of a grandpa (Young) who's so full of charm and vigor that his tomboy granddaughter just can't resist idolizing him. Sensible Mom breaks the two up, but it's not long before...You can guess the rest. (Dir: Noel Black, 96 mins.)

Conspiracy of Terror (MTV 1975)*½ Michael Constantine, Barbara Rhoades. Pilot for a police-mystery series. A husband and wife team of detectives are confronted by a cult of weirdos while investigating a series of unexplained deaths in a small community. (Dir: John Llewellyn Moxey, 104 mins.)

Conspiracy: The Trial of the Chicago 8 (MCTV 1987)***½ Robert Carradine, Peter Boyle, David Clennon, Elliott Gould, David Kagen, Michael Lembeck, Robert Loggia. Excellent, imaginative re-creation of the 1969 conspiracy trial of the Chicago 8, charged with inciting a riot at the 1968 Democratic National Convention. To present this trial, one of the key historical events of the sixties, writer-director Jeremy Kagan has interspersed commentary by the actual participants, speaking now with the hindsight of the 1980s. (120 mins.)†

Conspirator (1949)**½ Elizabeth Taylor, Robert Taylor. Interesting but not altogether engrossing drama about a beautiful girl who discovers the alarming fact that her new husband, a British army officer, is working with the Communists. (Dir: Victor Saville, 85 mins.)

Conspirators, The (1944)** Hedy Lamarr, Paul Henreid. Routine intrigue melodrama which is bogged down by gimmicks and contrivances. (Dir: Jean Negulesco, 101 mins.)

Constant Husband, The (Great Britain, 1955)*** Rex Harrison, Margaret Leighton, Kay Kendall. Man about to be wed discovers he has already been married—seven times. Amusing, well-acted comedy. (Dir: Sidney Gilliat, 88 mins.)

Constant Nymph, The (1943)**½ Joan Fontaine, Charles Boyer, Alexis Smith, Charles Coburn. A poor young musician must choose between two wealthy sisters; one loves him, the other doesn't. Seems like an easy choice! The performances are fine in this romance. (Dir: Edmund Goulding, 112 mins.)

Consuming Passions (Great Britain, 1988)*½ Vanessa Redgrave, Jonathan Pryce, Tyler Butterworth, Freddie Jones, Prunella Scales, Sammi Davis. Based on a play by Michael Palin and Terry Jones, this offbeat outing tries too hard (unsuccessfully) to make like the raucous British comedies of the sixties. It tells the story of a young man (Butterworth) who accidentally adds a secret ingredient to his boss's chocolate product—dead bodies. The top-flight supporting cast can't help. (Dir: Giles Foster, 100 mins.)†

Contagion (Australia, 1987)** John Doyle, Nicola Bartlett, Roy Barrett, Nathy Gaffney, Pamela Hawksford. Real estate agent traveling through the outback stops at an isolated mansion whose mysterious owner makes him a devilish deal: money and sexual pleasures beyond his imagining if he can prove he deserves them—by committing murder. Well-produced suspense-horror movie fails by getting too deep into its reality-vs.-illusion subtheme at the expense of the story. (Dir: Karl Zwicky, 90 mins.)†

Contempt (France-Italy, 1963)**** Brigitte Bardot, Jack Palance, Fritz Lang, Michael Piccoli, Georgia Moll. A masterpiece about an Italian filming of "The Odyssey," with Piccoli as scriptwriter, Lang as director, and Palance as an American producer, each with his own interpretation of the Greek classic. Action centers on the breakup of dramatist Piccoli's marriage to Bardot. (Dir: Jean-Luc Godard, 103 mins.)†

Contest Girl (Great Britain, 1965)*** Janette Scott, Ian Hendry, Edmund Purdom. Nicely acted and directed exposé of the beauty-contest racket, as a pretty typist enters a contest, and finds herself caught up in a whirl of deceit and disappointments. (Dir: Val Guest, 82 mins.)

Continental Divide (1981)** John Belushi, Blair Brown. An agreeable romantic comedy, but Belushi and Brown aren't temperamentally suited to be the Hepburn and Tracy of the '80s. A hard-nosed journalist invades the mountain retreat of a reclusive scientist devoted to preserving wildlife. (Dir: Michael Apted, 103 mins.)†

Contra Conspiracy (1990)*½ Michael Williams, Tom Maher, Blake Bahner, Robert Beal, Vickie Stephenson. Movie crew shooting at an isolated desert location are attacked as a practice exercise by CIA-backed mercenaries. Odd idea for an action story, with the film crew using special effects materials to ward off their attackers. (Dir: Tom DeWeir, 87 mins.)†

Contract (Poland, 1980)**** Leslie Caron, Maja Korowska, Tadeuz Lomnicki, Magda Jarowszowna. Memorable comedy about a shaky wedding involving a nose-to-the-grindstone careerist and his incipient bride, both of whom are suffering from a case of nuptial cold feet. Not recommended for those headed for the altar, this acerbic satire is the other side of the picture-book romances typified by films like *Father of the Bride*. Superb ensemble work. (Dir: Krzysztof Zanussi, 114 mins.)

Contract on Cherry Street (MTV 1977)*** Frank Sinatra, Verna Bloom, Harry Guardino, Martin Balsam. Sinatra's TV-movie debut turns out to be a good one. He plays an angry, frustrated New York police inspector who begins cleaning out the mob with his own men after a buddy is killed. (Dir: William A. Graham, 156 mins.)

Control (MCTV 1987)** Burt Lancaster, Kate Nelligan, Ben Gazzara, Kate Reid, Erland Josephson, Andrea Occhipinti, Ingrid Thulin. Slow-paced survival drama about an experiment on the psychological effects of life in a nuclear fallout shelter. (Dir: Giuliano Montaldo, 90 mins.)†

Conversation, The (1974)**** Gene Hackman, John Cazale, Allen Garfield, Cindy Williams. A shattering mystery-drama shot in San Francisco about surveillance and wiretapping in America, produced, written, and directed by Francis Ford Coppola. Bugging expert (Hackman) becomes uneasy about the contents of a tape he made, and what it will be used for. Hackman is marvelous as the guilt-ridden Catholic wire tapper trying to keep his sanity. Not a false note in this

disciplined, chilling knockout. (113 mins.)†

Conversation Piece (Italy-France, 1975)*** Burt Lancaster, Silvana Mangano, Helmut Berger, Claudia Cardinale. One of director Luchino Visconti's most revealing works. Lancaster plays a retired professor, a man of intellect confronted with his absurdity when he befriends a group of young hedonistic leeches. Some of the performances are too broad, but this is a rewarding experience. (122 mins.)

Convicted (1950)*** Glenn Ford, Broderick Crawford, Dorothy Malone. Prison life gets a candid look in this good screenplay about a prisoner and his personal relationship with a warden's daughter. (Dir: Henry Levin, 91 mins.)

Convicted (MTV 1986)*** Lindsay Wagner, John Larroquette, Carroll O'Connor. Larroquette stars as a man wrongly accused of rape and sent to prison. Wagner plays his devoted wife who leaves no stone unturned to prove her husband's innocence during a five-year nightmare. Based on a true story, this TV film avoids excesses and makes for sound drama. (Dir: David Lowell Rich, 104 mins.)

Convicted: A Mother's Story (MTV 1987)**½ Ann Jillian, Kiel Martin, Gloria Loring, Fred Savage. Vivacious Ann Jillian is a strange casting choice for the central role in this lowbrow melodrama of an unemployed mom who embezzles money from her job for her no-good boyfriend, and ends up going to jail for it. (Dir: Richard T. Heffron, 104 mins.)†

Convicts Four (1962)**½ Ben Gazzara, Stuart Whitman, Sammy Davis, Jr., Vincent Price. True story of a prisoner who is rehabilitated through his love for painting. Starts off well, soon becomes cloudy in motivation, uncertain in treatment. (Dir: Millard Kaufman, 105 mins.)

Convoy (1978)** Kris Kristofferson, Ali MacGraw, Ernest Borgnine. A CB epic about a trucking caravan that keeps on the move after insulting a sheriff. Lots of smash-ups as the trucks fight the National Guard and head for Mexico. (Dir: Sam Peckinpah, 111 mins.)†

Coogan's Bluff (1968)** Clint Eastwood, Lee J. Cobb, Susan Clark, Don Stroud. Fast-paced, familiar detective story with Clint Eastwood playing a western sheriff who arrives in New York City to nab a hood convicted of murder. (Dir: Don Siegel, 100 mins.)†

Cook & Peary: The Race to the North Pole (MTV 1983)**½ Rod Steiger, Richard Chamberlain, Diane Venora, Michael Gross. Chamberlain and Steiger are the famous Arctic explorers locked in cold-blooded competition to be the first to reach the North Pole. (Dir: Robert Day, 104 mins.)

Cook, the Thief, His Wife and Her Lover, The (Netherlands-Holland-France, 1989)***½ Richard Bohringer, Michael Gambron, Helen Mirren, Alan Howard, Tim Roth. Writer-director Peter Greenaway this time refers to violent Jacobean melodrama for his distinctive brand of cinematic puzzle-making. (Pay particular attention to color schemes.) The sexual, criminal, and gastronomical activities of the titular quartet may be extreme for viewers unfamiliar with Greenaway, but fans will relish the elegant perversity. (124 mins.)†

Cookie (1989)**½ Peter Falk, Dianne Wiest, Emily Lloyd, Michael V. Gazzo, Brenda Vaccaro, Adrian Pasdar, Lionel Stander, Jerry Lewis. A colorful group of familiar faces, well cast down to the smallest of roles, make the most of this Runyonesque gangster comedy about rambunctious teen Lloyd who gets to know her mobster father Falk by working as his driver. The script by Nora Ephron and Alice Arlen is unusually thin, but features some memorably eccentric characters. (Dir: Susan Seidelman, 93 mins.)†

Cool and the Crazy, The (1958)**½ Scott Marlowe, Gigi Perreau, Dick Bakalyan, Dick Jones. Souped-up tale about a reform school no-goodnik who leads high schoolers down the primrose path to drug habits. Like cool, like crazy—like campy. (Dir: William Witney, 78 mins.)

Cool Blue (1989)** Woody Harrelson, Hank Azaria, Ely Pouget, Sean Penn, John Diehl. Struggling L.A. artist has a one-night stand with the woman of his dreams, then spends the rest of the movie trying to find her again. Somewhat pretentious satire of the City of Angels, enlivened briefly by a funny cameo from Penn. (Dirs: Mark Mullin, Richard Shepard, 89 mins.)†

Cool Breeze (1972)* Thalmus Rasulala, Judy Pace, Raymond St. Jacques. Substandard heist drama based, like so many others, on John Huston's *The Asphalt Jungle*. (Dir: Barry Pollack, 101 mins.)

Cooley High (1975)**½ Glynn Turman, Lawrence-Hilton Jacobs, Garrett Morris. A series of comic-strip incidents about inner-city high school life. A masterful performance by Turman. (Dir: Michael Schultz, 107 mins.)†

Cool Hand Luke (1967)*** Paul Newman, George Kennedy, Strother Martin, Dennis Hopper. Taut, honest drama greatly aided by Stuart Rosenberg's direction and a controlled and artful performance by Paul Newman as a gutsy prisoner on a chain gang. Matching Newman's stunning acting is George Kennedy's Academy Award-winning performance as the bru-

tal leader of the chain-gang crew. (126 mins.)†

Cool Million (MTV 1972)**½ James Farentino, John Vernon, Barbara Bouchet. Expensively mounted pilot which introduces Jefferson Keyes (Farentino), a slick operator whose investigating talents command a flat fee of $1 million. (Dir: Gene Levitt, 104 mins.)

Cool Ones, The (1967)*½ Roddy McDowall, Deborah Watson, Gil Peterson, Glen Campbell, Robert Coote. A marginal musical in which a publicist plays cupid for a rising songbird and a warbler on the skids. Overbaked lampoon of the music biz with lots of guest spots for relief. (Dir: Gene Nelson, 95 mins.)

Cool World, The (1964)***½ Gloria Foster, Hampton Clanton, Carl Lee, George Burke. A powerful film with outstanding direction by Shirley Clarke. A semi-documentary look at the horrors of ghetto slum life filled with drugs, violence, human misery, and a sense of despair due to the racial prejudices of American society. (105 mins.)

Coonskin (1975)** Voices of Barry White, Charles Gordone, Scatman Crothers. Cartoon feature by Ralph Bakshi *(Heavy Traffic, Fritz the Cat)*, wanders far afield in a poorly constructed script. But it boasts first-rate animation in several sequences. AKA: **Streetfight**. (Dir: Ralph Bakshi, 89 mins.)

Cop (1988)** James Woods, Lesley Ann Warren, Charles Durning, Charles Haid. Woods almost rises above this ridiculously plotted thriller, in which every plot twist hinges on coincidence. He plays a hard-bitten detective searching for a psycho who's been brutally murdering women for a decade. (Dir: James B. Harris, 110 mins.)†

Copacabana (1947)** Groucho Marx, Carmen Miranda, Andy Russell, Steve Cochran, Gloria Jean, Louis Sobol. Groucho the eternal anarchist and Carmen the perpetual whirling dervish fail to enliven this with any of their considerable comic drive. Playing a shifty agent with only one client, Groucho gets the bombshell two different jobs in the same place. Busy but routine. (Dir: Alfred E. Green, 92 mins.)†

Copacabana (MTV 1985)*** Barry Manilow, Annette O'Toole, Joseph Bologna. Manilow's pop hit adapted for TV, and the results are pleasantly diverting. The plot, as in the song, concerns a show girl named Lola (the fetching Ms. O'Toole), and a jealous gangster named Rico. (Dir: Waris Hussein, 96 mins.)

Cop and the Girl, The (West Germany, 1986)*½ Jurgen Prochnow, Annette Von Klier. Tough, embittered cop falls in love with a street-smart runaway teen

208

who is wanted by the police. He helps her escape, but by opening up his calloused heart he seals his own doom. Heavy-handed melodrama is more concerned with *Miami Vice*–type visuals than its story. (Dir: Peter Keglevic, 95 mins.)†

Cop Au Vin (France, 1984)***½ Jean Poiret, Stephané Audren, Michel Bouquet, Jean Topart. Stylish thriller about rural villager Audran, who lives with her postman son and refuses to sell her property to a real estate syndicate. Poiret is wonderful as the detective who arrives to investigate the murder of one of the syndicate's members. Director Claude Chabrol is in top form. Sequel: *Inspector Lavardin.* (109 mins.)

Copenhagen's Psychic Loves— See: *Psychic, The*

Cop Hater (1958)**½ Robert Loggia, Gerald O'Loughlin. Mild melodrama about a cop killer. Based on an Ed McBain novel. Routine acting and direction, but the finale is fine. New York locations are used to good advantage. (Dir: William Berke, 75 mins.)

Cop Killers—See: *Corrupt*

Cop-Out (Great Britain, 1968)** James Mason, Geraldine Chaplin, Bobby Darin, Paul Bertoya, Ian Ogilvy. Routine courtroom drama. Mason is coaxed out of retirement to defend his daughter's innocent boyfriend on a murder charge. (Dir: Pierre Rouve, 95 mins.)

Copper Canyon (1950)** Ray Milland, Hedy Lamarr, Macdonald Carey. Gunman helps Civil War vets build new homes in the untamed West. (Dir: John Farrow, 83 mins.)

Cops and Robbers (1973)***½ Cliff Gorman, Joe Bologna. A cleverly plotted, adroitly executed comedy caper film which boasts a pair of excellent performances by Gorman and Bologna as two cops who decide to pull one big robbery and retire. (Dir: Aram Avakian, 99 mins.)

Cops and Robin, The (MTV 1978)** Ernest Borgnine, John Amos, Michael Shannon. Borgnine and Amos as two policemen who work with a robot cop (Shannon). The "future cop" is assigned to protect a little girl whose mother is set to testify against a mobster. (Dir: Allen Reisner, 104 mins.)

Corey: For the People (MTV 1977)**½ John Rubinstein, Eugene Roche, Frank Campanella. Pretty fair lawyer pilot with Rubinstein as a feisty assistant D.A. investigating the shooting of a doctor by his wife, who claims self-defense. (Dir: Buzz Kulik, 78 mins.)

Corky (1971)** Charlotte Rampling, Robert Blake, Patrick O'Neal. A routine version of the country boy who wants to make it big as a stockcar racer. AKA: **Lookin' Good.** (Dir: Leonard Horn, 88 mins.)

Corleone (Italy, 1985)*½ Giuliano Gemma, Francisco Rabal, Claudia Cardinale. Two boyhood friends in Sicily fight the criminal landowners who control the lives of the peasants. One organizes politically for the Communists; the other joins the mobsters to fight from within. Confusing and slow paced (though it is well dubbed for a change). (Dir: Pasquale Squitieri, 115 mins.)†

Cornbread, Earl and Me (1975)**½ Moses Gunn, Bernie Casey, Rosalind Cash, Madge Sinclair. A little more inventiveness might have pushed this predictable but beautifully acted message flick into a higher sphere. As it is, the tragedy grips us superficially as a talented ghetto boy is gunned down senselessly before he can attend college. (Dir: Joe Manduke, 95 mins.)†

Cornered (1945)*** Dick Powell, Micheleine Cheirel, Walter Slezak. Airman goes seeking those responsible for the death of his French wife during the war. Excellent drama, fast, tough, fine performances. (Dir: Edward Dmytryk, 102 mins.)†

Corn Is Green, The (1945)*** Bette Davis, John Dall, Joan Lorring, Rhys Williams, Nigel Bruce. Davis was, if anything, a bit too young for the part of the idealistic schoolmistress who finds one lad in a Welsh mining village with the spark of creativity to seek finer things in life. She gives her customary careful performance, although Dall steals the picture as the student distrustful of the accoutrements of learning. (Dir: Irving Rapper, 114 mins.)†

Corn Is Green, The (MTV 1979)*** Katharine Hepburn, Ian Saynor, Bill Fraser, Anna Massey. Hepburn may be a bit mannered, but her portrayal captures the nuances of a woman who will not be deterred from her goals. The production, shot on-location in north Wales, adds greatly to the atmosphere of the touching story. (Dir: George Cukor, 104 mins.)

Coroner Creek (1948)** Randolph Scott, Marguerite Chapman, George Macready, Sally Eilers, Edgar Buchanan. Randy is out to avenge his gal's death. Fortunately, he meets Miss Chapman and after completing his business has a new gal to marry. (Dir: Ray Enright, 93 mins.)

Corpse Came C.O.D., The (1947)** George Brent, Joan Blondell. Grade B mystery about a couple of Hollywood reporters out to solve some movieland murders. (Dir: Henry Levin, 87 mins.)

Corpse Grinders, The (1971)* Sean Kenney, Monika Kelly, Sanford Mitchell. Sleazy cat food makers corner the market when they add human corpses to their recipe, even after the mix results in killer kitties. A favorite of bad-movie buffs that doesn't live up to its reputation, though the cardboard corpse grinding machine and the sight of the "victims" trying to hold the supposedly ferocious felines to their throats evoke a few chuckles. (Dir: Ted V. Mikels, 73 mins.) †

Corpse Vanishes, The (1942)**½ Bela Lugosi, Luana Walters, Tristram Coffin, Elizabeth Russell. Fairly creepy programmer with Bela at his sinister best. Here he goes hunting for a beauty treatment for his wife—only he doesn't pick up Oil of Olay. Soon some blushing brides aren't around to enjoy their wedding receptions as Bela nabs them to freshen up his wife. (Dir: Wallace Fox, 64 mins.) †

Corridor of Mirrors (Great Britain, 1948)*** Edana Romney, Eric Portman. A girl marries a mysterious man who lives in the past, but their happiness is shattered by murder. Well-done melodrama holds the attention. (Dir: Terence Young, 96 mins.)

Corridors of Blood (Great Britain, 1962)** Boris Karloff, Betta St. John, Christopher Lee. Surgeon in 19th-century London seeks the key to an anesthetic, but becomes a narcotics addict in doing so. Passable horror thriller, with Karloff giving a good performance. (Dir: Robert Day, 87 mins.) †

Corrupt (Italy, 1984)** Harvey Keitel, John Lydon, Sylvia Sidney. Study of a warped bond between a tough, corrupt cop (Keitel) and a weird young man (Lydon) strives so hard to be "intense" that it winds up unintentionally hilarious. Lydon's deadpan line-readings and lack of acting skill won't be a bitter pill for his fans to swallow, but poor Harvey's just wasting his energy. AKA: **Cop Killer.** (Dir: Roberto Faenza, 99 mins.) †

Corruption (Great Britain, 1968)** Peter Cushing, Sue Lloyd, Kate O'Mara. Intriguing but one-dimensional story of plastic surgeon who atones for his guilt in causing his fiancée to be permanently scarred in an auto accident. The catch—he has to steal glands from strangers! (Dir: Robert Hartford-Davis, 91 mins.)

Corrupt Ones, The (1966)** Robert Stack, Nancy Kwan, Elke Sommer. Everybody hustles after a Chinese medallion holding the key to the treasure. Exotic but familiar adventure tale. (Dir: James Hill, 92 mins.) †

Corsican Brothers, The (1941)**½ Douglas Fairbanks, Jr., Akim Tamiroff, Ruth Warrick. The classic tale of Siamese twin brothers separated at birth but still joined by a mental bond. Lively costume melodrama. (Dir: Gregory Ratoff, 112 mins.) †

Corsican Brothers, The (1984)—See: **Cheech & Chong's Corsican Brothers**

Corsican Brothers, The (MTV 1985)**½ Trevor Eve, Geraldine Chaplin, Nicholas Clay, Olivia Hussey, Jean Marsh, Simon Ward. The old Alexandre Dumas swashbuckler of two brothers caught up in a family vendetta receives a sumptuous production. (Dir: Ian Sharp, 104 mins.)

Corvette K-225 (1943)***½ Randolph Scott, Ella Raines. Canadian naval officer's courage and fighting spirit prevent destruction of a convoy. Excellent war drama with many scenes actually photographed in combat. (Dir: Richard Rosson, 99 mins.)

Corvette Summer (1978)**½ Mark Hamill, Annie Potts, Kim Milford. Young Hamill's beloved, custom-built Corvette is stolen. The film details his adventures in trying to retrieve it in a grown-up hostile world. (Dir: Matthew Robins, 104 mins.)

Cosmic Man, The (1958)* Bruce Bennett, John Carradine, Angela Greene, Paul Langton. Visitor from another planet lands on earth to try to reconcile world differences. (Dir: Herbert Greene, 72 mins.) †

Cosmic Monsters (Great Britain, 1958)** Forrest Tucker, Gaby Andre. Muddled science fiction thriller with the mad scientist and the giant insects and the world in constant danger of complete annihilation. (Dir: Gilbert Gunn, 75 mins.) †

Cotter (1973)** Don Murray, Carol Lynley, Sherry Jackson, Rip Torn. Well-acted but cloudily scripted drama about a rodeo clown who returns home to assess his life after a rodeo accident. (Dir: Paul Stanley, 94 mins.)

Cotton Candy (MTV 1978)**½ Charles Martin Smith, Clint Howard. This teenage tale about highschool kids who form a rock band is a pleasant surprise—simple and honest. (Dir: Ron Howard, 104 mins.)

Cotton Club, The (1984)*** Richard Gere, Gregory Hines, Diane Lane, Lonette McKee, Bob Hoskins, James Remar, Fred Gwynne, Gwen Verdon, Nicolas Cage, Joe Dallesandro. Director Francis Coppola's stylish evocation of the Jazz Age's hottest nightspot follows the exploits of two sets of brothers: the Hines', who attempt to tap their way to the big time, and Gere and Cage, who tap into their own underworld connections. Their lives and the lives of the women they love—including a dazzling songbird (McKee) and an exquisite gangster's moll (Lane)—are only part of the broad, colorful tapestry formed by the film's plotline. Not one of Coppola's master-works, the "Club" still provides a solid evening's entertainment. (127 mins.)†

Cotton Comes to Harlem (1970)*** Godfrey Cambridge, Raymond St. Jacques, Calvin Lockhart, Redd Foxx. Raucous, racy, funny treatment of Chester Himes's fictional black detectives, Grave Digger Jones and Coffin Ed Johnson, and their exploits in Harlem. Grave Digger and Coffin Ed are hot on the trail of a bogus Reverend and his scheme to bilk his people out of money. (Dir: Ossie Davis, 92 mins.)

Couch, The (1962)** Grant Williams, Shirley Knight. Psychotic is released from prison, undergoes treatment, but commits crimes while doing so. Plodding suspense melodrama. (Dir: Owen Crump, 100 mins.)

Couch Trip, The (1988)** Dan Aykroyd, Walter Matthau, Charles Grodin, Donna Dixon. Aykroyd plays a psychiatric patient who turns the tables and somehow impersonates a popular radio psychologist. The film sets up a sharp social satire of psychology, but then abandons it in favor of slapdash farce. (Dir: Michael Ritchie, 97 mins.)†

Counsellor at Law (1933)***½ John Barrymore, Bebe Daniels, Melvyn Douglas. Barrymore is oddly cast as a Jewish lawyer who has educated himself up from poverty, but this is one of the best proofs extant of his acting prowess. (Dir: William Wyler, 82 mins.)

Countdown (1968)**½ James Caan, Robert Duvall. Drama about space shots to the moon may be dated by now, but it has some good moments. If you can be patient through the soap opera of the spacemen's private lives, the finale delivers the goods. (Dir: Robert Altman, 101 mins.)†

Countdown to Looking Glass (MCTV 1984)*** Scott Glenn, Michael Murphy, Helen Shaver, Patrick Watson. Riveting and realistic. In a vivid re-enactment of the domino theory at work, this original drama shows how an international crisis in South America propels the world to the brink of nuclear war—and over the edge, in just nine days. (Dir: Fred Barzyk, 115 mins.)

Count Dracula (Spain-Great Britain, 1971)**½ Christopher Lee, Herbert Lom, Klaus Kinski. In this faithful but dull version of the vampire legend, Lee plays Count Dracula again, this time with white hair and a mustache, and still needing fresh blood to stay young. (Dir: "Jesse Franco" [Jesus Franco], 98 mins.)†

Count Dracula and His Vampire Bride—See: Satanic Rites of Dracula, The

Counter-Attack (1945)**½ Paul Muni, Marguerite Chapman, Larry Parks. Russian paratroopers land behind enemy lines and attack German headquarters. (Dir: Zoltan Korda, 90 mins.)

Counter-Espionage (1942)*½ Warren Williams, Hillary Brooke, Eric Blore, Thurston Hall, Fred Kelsey, Forrest Tucker. The Lone Wolf battles a German spy ring. Humdrum mystery melodrama. (Dir: Edward Dmytryk, 71 mins.)

Counterfeit Traitor, The (1962)***½ William Holden, Lilli Palmer, Hugh Griffith. Suspenseful tale based on fact of a businessman approached by the British to pose as sympathetic to the Nazis, in reality spying for England. Fascinating details of espionage, some tense situations, excellent performances by Holden and Palmer. (Dir: George Seaton, 140 mins.)

Counterpoint (1968)* Charlton Heston, Kathryn Hays, Maximilian Schell. A counterpointless drama set in Belgium during 1944. Heston plays a symphony conductor on a U.S.O. tour who is captured by the Nazis, headed by a music-loving general played by Schell. (Dir: Ralph Nelson, 107 mins.)

Countess Dracula (Great Britain, 1972)** Ingrid Pitt, Nigel Green, Peter Jeffrey, Lesley-Anne Down. Countess Elizabeth Bathory (Pitt) is the beautiful vampire who enjoys bathing in the blood of virgins. The nearby town is in an uproar because naked bodies are popping up everywhere. Mediocre shocker. (Dir: Peter Sasdy, 94 mins.)

Countess from Hong Kong, A (1967)** Marlon Brando, Sophia Loren, Patrick Cargill, Margaret Rutherford. Although the film boasts major talents, it's just another romantic comedy. Most of the action takes place aboard a luxury liner with Sophia as an immigrant stowaway in U.S. diplomat Brando's cabin, and there's a fair amount of boudoir fun and games before the finale. (Dir: Charles Chaplin, 120 mins.)

Countess of Monte Cristo, The (1948)** Sonja Henie, Olga San Juan, Dorothy Hart, Michael Kirby, Arthur Treacher. Mildly amusing comedy with ice-skating star Henie posing as the royal countess in an elegant resort hotel, while her friend (San Juan) becomes her personal maid. (Dir: Frederick de Cordova, 77 mins.)

Count Five and Die (Great Britain, 1958)**½ Jeffrey Hunter, Annemarie Dueringer, Nigel Patrick. American undercover agent works with the British to convince the Germans the Allied landing will be in Holland, thus misleading them. Pretty fair spy thriller. (Dir: Victor Vicas, 100 mins.)

Count of Monte Cristo, The (1934)***½ Robert Donat, Elissa Landi. The classic adventure tale of Dumas about the unjustly imprisoned patriot who makes a spectacular escape during the Napoleonic era. A notable film achievement. (Dir: Rowland V. Lee, 113 mins.)†

Count of Monte Cristo (1961)—See: **Story of the Count of Monte Cristo**

Count of Monte Cristo, The (Great Britain, 1975)**½ Richard Chamberlain, Tony Curtis, Trevor Howard. The old Dumas war-horse trotted out again. Competent, but dated. (Dir: David Greene, 104 mins.)†

Country (1984)**½ Jessica Lange, Wilford Brimley, Sam Shepard, Matt Clark. Well-intended ''issue'' film dominated by Lange's incessant nobility as the farmer's wife who fights for her land after the banks foreclose and her husband falls apart. (Dir: Richard Pierce, 108 mins.)†

Country Girl, The (1954)**** Bing Crosby, Grace Kelly, William Holden. Superlative performances in the Clifford Odets drama about a performer, Crosby, wallowing in self-pity, who has a chance to make a comeback. Crosby gives the performance of his career. Kelly won an Oscar for her efforts. (Dir: George Seaton, 104 mins.)†

Country Gold (MTV 1982)*½ Loni Anderson, Earl Holliman, Linda Hamilton, Cooper Huckabee. Lackluster behind-the-scenes tale dwells on the overworked country music star who wants a rest. Hamilton is quite effective as a simple country girl who double-crosses everyone on her way to the top! (Dir: Gilbert Cates, 104 mins.)

Count the Hours (1953)** Teresa Wright, Macdonald Carey. Ranch worker and wife are accused of murdering ranch owners; he confesses to spare his pregnant wife. Muddled melodrama. (Dir: Don Siegel, 74 mins.)

Count Three and Pray (1955)*** Van Heflin, Joanne Woodward, Raymond Burr. First-rate western drama about a Civil War veteran and his influence on a small town when he becomes a self-ordained minister. (Dir: George Sherman, 120 mins.)

Count Yorga, Vampire (1970)**½ Robert Quarry, Roger Perry, Michael Murphy, Donna Anders. Low-budget but fairly effective update of vampirism, as some young people go down for the Count in modern day Los Angeles. (Dir: Bob Kelljan, 91 mins.)†

Count Your Blessings (1959)**½ Deborah Kerr, Rossano Brazzi, Maurice Chevalier. A slight comedy which totally relies on the trio of stars' charm and attractiveness to carry it off. The plot has a British Miss Kerr sharing a civilized long-distance marriage arrangement with Brazzi until she decides to shorten the gap. (Dir: Jean Negulesco, 120 mins.)

212

Count Your Bullets—See: **Cry For Me, Billy**

Coup de Grace (West Germany-France, 1976)***½ Margarethe von Trotta, Matthias Habich. A complex, often involving parable of the collapse of one order while a new one unfolds, set in Latvia just after WWI. A German army unit is billeted on a formerly opulent but now rundown estate belonging to one of the officers. (Dir: Volker Schlondorff, 96 mins.)†

Coup de Foudre—See: **Entre Nous**

Coup de Tête (France, 1979)*** Patrick Dewaere, France Dougnac, Jean Bouise, Michel Aumont. The late Dewaere is at his best in this rollicking comedy about mores and manners in a small French town crazy for soccer. Funny and poignant. AKA: **Hothead**. (Dir: Jean-Jacques Annaud, 90 mins.)†

Coup de Torchon (France, 1981)***½ Isabelle Huppert, Philippe Noiret, Stéphane Audran, Guy Marchand, Irene Skobline, Eddy Mitchell. Set in equatorial French Africa in the late 1930s, a meek, cowardly government constable (Noiret) can't stop killing after he is pushed too far. A chilling black comedy based on a book by Jim Thompson. AKA: **Clean Slate**. (Dir: Bertrand Tavernier, 128 mins.)

Coupe de Ville (1990)*** Patrick Dempsey, Arye Gross, Daniel Stern, Annabeth Gish, Rita Taggart, Joseph Bologna, Alan Arkin. Sibling rivalry surfaces among three Detroit brothers ordered by their stubborn father to drive the title car to Florida as a present for their mother's birthday. Low-key period piece that warms its way into your heart. (Dir: Joe Roth, 99 mins.)†

Couple Takes a Wife, The (MTV 1972)*** Bill Bixby, Paula Prentiss, Valerie Perrine. Concerns a modern married couple who reach an impasse after nine years of wedded bliss, and try to assert their individuality with the aid of a hired ''wife.'' An adroitly acted, cleverly written teleplay. (Dir: Jerry Paris, 73 mins.)

Courage (MTV 1986)*** Sophia Loren, Billy Dee Williams, Hector Elizondo, Val Avery, Ron Rifkin, Dan Hedaya. A remarkably restrained TV movie based on a true-life tale of a brave woman working as an undercover agent to undermine drug traffickers. Loren is good as the Queens housewife seeking expiation for her guilt over her own son's drug problems. (Dir: Jeremy Kagan, 156 mins.)†

Courage and the Passion, The (MTV 1978)**½ Vince Edwards, Desi Arnaz, Jr., Trisha Noble, Linda Foster, Robert Ginty, Robert Hooks, Don Meredith, Monty Hall. Pilot for a series that never got off the ground. Edwards (who also executive produced) stars as the gruff, hard-bitten but secretly lovable commander of an air force base who's always around to solve the problems of young test pilots. (Dir: John Llewellyn Moxey, 96 mins.)

Courage Mountain (1989)**½ Juliette Caton, Jan Rubes, Charlie Sheen, Leslie Caron, Yorgo Voyagis. Attempt to follow up the classic children's story *Heidi* just proves that they don't write 'em like that anymore. Teenaged Heidi is sent to an Italian boarding school, only to be saved by her soldier boyfriend (a miscast Sheen) when the army takes over at the outset of WWI. (Dir: Christopher Leitch, 96 mins.)†

Courage of Black Beauty (1957)** Johnny Crawford, Diane Brewster, Mimi Gibson, J. Pat O'Malley. Another story about a little boy and his horse. Old hat but good for the kiddies. (Dir: Harold Schuster, 78 mins.)†

Courage of Kavik, the Wolf Dog, The (MTV 1980)** Ronny Cox, Andrew Ian McMillan, John Ireland. A champion sled dog, taken to Seattle by a wealthy fool, makes a 2000-mile trip back to Alaska and his young master. (Dir: Peter Carter, 104 mins.)

Courage of Lassie (1945)**½ Elizabeth Taylor, Frank Morgan. Good Lassie adventure with the famous collie becoming a war hero and then, after discharge, she's as confused as any veteran. (Dir: Fred Wilcox, 92 mins.)

Courageous Dr. Christian, The (1940)** Jean Hersholt, Dorothy Lovett, Tom Neal, Maude Eburne, Vera Lewis. The kindly doctor extends his charitableness by trying to rid his hometown, River's End, of slums. (Dir: Bernard Vorhaus, 67 mins.)

Courageous Mr. Penn (Great Britain, 1941)*** Clifford Evans, Deborah Kerr. The story of William Penn the Quaker, and how he pioneered the American wilderness while seeking religious freedom. Thoughtful, well-acted drama. AKA: **Penn of Pennsylvania**. (Dir: Lance Comfort, 79 mins.)†

Courier, The (Ireland, 1988)** Padraig O'Loingsigh, Cait O'Riordan, Gabriel Byrne. A young man who works as a messenger carries out a revenge plot against a crime lord (Byrne). Instantly forgettable, notable primarily for having a musical score by Declan MacManus (Elvis Costello) and for starring his wife, ex-rocker O'Riordan. (Dirs: Joe Lee, Frank Deasy, 87 mins.)†

Courtesans of Bombay, The (Great Britain, 1984)*** Saeed Jaffrey, Zohra Segal, Kareem Samar. Semidocumentary set in the tenements of Pavanpul, where women support themselves as singers, dancers, and prostitutes. Discreetly made, absorbing and entertaining sociological document. (Dir: Ismail Merchant, 73 mins.)†

Court Jester, The (1956)*** Danny Kaye, Glynis Johns, Basil Rathbone, Angela Lansbury, Cecil Parker, Mildred Natwick. Circus clown gets involved with a band of outlaws trying to overthrow the king. Kaye's comedy is an asset in this pleasing spoof of costume epics. (Dir: Norman Panama, 101 mins.)†

Court Martial (Great Britain, 1955)***½ David Niven, Margaret Leighton. Army major is court-martialed for taking company funds and being AWOL, and he fights against unjust treatment. Finely acted, tightly directed drama maintains interest on high. AKA: **Carrington, V.C.** (Dir: Anthony Asquith, 105 mins.)

Court Martial of Billy Mitchell (1955)***½ Gary Cooper, Rod Steiger, Ralph Bellamy, Charles Bickford. Excellent, true story of one of the most controversial American military leaders of this country. Film concentrates on Billy Mitchell's defiance of military brass when they called him a crackpot for ideas that might have cut World War II in half. A fascinating film. (Dir: Otto Preminger, 100 mins.)†

Court Martial of Jackie Robinson, The (MCTV 1990)*** Andre Braugher, Ruby Dee, Stan Shaw, Daniel Stern, Paul Dooley, Bruce Dern. A little known fact about baseball's Jackie Robinson's life is his court martial trial while serving in the Army during World War II, prompted by an incident on a bus at Fort Hood. Braugher is imposing as Robinson, a man whose idealism broke down many barriers. (Dir: Larry Peerce, 96 mins.)†

Courtney Affair, The (Great Britain, 1947)**½ Anna Neagle, Michael Wilding, Gladys Young, Coral Browne, Michael Medwin. The son of a rich family falls for the scullery maid. Sugary romantic drama. (Dir: Herbert Wilcox, 120 mins.)

Courtship (MTV 1987)** Hallie Foote, Michael Higgins, Amanda Plummer, Rochelle Oliver. Drowsy turn-of-the-century piece about a young woman in love with a man whom her parents (especially her strict father) find unacceptable. Script by Horton Foote (*Tender Mercies*) is not up to his usual standard. (Dir: Howard Cummings, 85 mins.)†

Courtship of Andy Hardy, The (1942)**½ Lewis Stone, Mickey Rooney, Cecilia Parker, Fay Holden, Ann Rutherford, Donna Reed. Judge Hardy enlists Andy's aid in helping out the social life of a client's daughter. (Dir: George B. Seitz, 93 mins.)

Courtship of Eddie's Father, The (1963)*** Glenn Ford, Shirley Jones, Stella Stevens, Ronny Howard. Charming comedy drama about a widower who tries to bring

213

up his motherless son—and vice versa. Nice balance of humor and poignancy. (Dir: Vincente Minnelli, 117 mins.)

Cousin Angelica (Spain, 1974)**** José Luis Lapez Vazquez, Lina Canalejas, Maria Clara Fernandez, Fernando Delgado. A remarkable Carlos Saura film about a middle-aged man (Vazquez) with infantile memories of the Civil War era in Spain. For once, Saura's allegorical bent is under control in this tightly structured, rewarding film about memory and reality. (105 mins.)

Cousin, Cousine (France, 1975)*** Victor Lanoux, Marie-Christine Barrault, Marie-France Pisier. A bubbly French romance about two cousins who tire of their spouses' infidelities and run off together. Scoffing at convention, they engage in a lot of photogenic smooching, to the displeasure of their conventional relatives. (Dir: Jean-Charles Tacchella, 95 mins.)†

Cousins (1989)**½ Ted Danson, Isabella Rossellini, Sean Young, William Petersen, Lloyd Bridges, Norma Aleandro. Pleasant story of cousins by marriage who admit their attraction to each other but refuse to have an affair (even though their spouses are). Remake of the French hit *Cousin, Cousine* is too diffuse, but palatable thanks to an attractive cast and offbeat location filming. (Dir: Joel Schumacher, 110 mins.)†

Cousins, The (France, 1959)***½ Jean-Claude Brialy, Gerard Blain. Director Claude Chabrol has fashioned a marvelous study of the contrasting personalities of two young male cousins, both law students at the Sorbonne. Blain is a country lad with an unsophisticated manner who comes to stay with his egomaniacal and decadent cousin, brilliantly played by Jean-Claude Brialy. (112 mins.)

Covenant, The (MTV 1985)** Jose Ferrer, Jane Badler, Michelle Phillips, Bradford Dillman. Leading his wealthy family into power and possible perdition, Jose Ferrer plays the patriarch of an evil clan (one of Hitler's advisors) wedded to his niece; she, along with her twin sister, carries the genes of wickedness. The cast glowers without letup, but all this supernatural scenery-chewing generates few sparks. (Dir: Walter Grauman, 74 mins.)

Covenant with Death, A (1967)** George Maharis, Laura Devon, Katy Jurado. Muddled, often silly drama about a condemned murderer who is instrumental in another man's death while awaiting execution. (Dir: Lamont Johnson, 97 mins.)

Cover Girl (1944)***½ Rita Hayworth, Gene Kelly, Phil Silvers, Eve Arden, Otto Kruger. A model must decide between a Broadway producer and a Brooklyn nightclub owner. Elaborate Technicolor showcase for Hayworth's beauty becomes an exciting musical, thanks to Kelly's inventive dance sequences. The Jerome Kern-Ira Gershwin score is tuneful, and the use of color makes this a musical classic. (Dir: Charles Vidor, 107 mins.)†

Covergirl (Canada, 1984)** Jeff Conaway, Irena Ferris, Cathie Shirriff, Roberta Leighton. Rich but bored Conaway decides to put his power and money into making aspiring model Ferris a superstar. Unexceptional TV-type exposé of the modeling business. (Dir: Jean-Claude Lord, 93 mins.)†

Cover Girl and the Cop, The (MTV 1989) **½ Dinah Manoff, Julia Duffy, John Karlen, David Carradine. Odd-couple comedy as tough cop Manoff is assigned to protect murder witness Duffy, a glamorous model. Some humorous personality clashes ensue before the predictable finale. (Dir: Neal Israel, 96 mins.)

Cover Girls (MTV 1977)**½ Jayne Kennedy, Cornelia Sharpe, Don Galloway, Vince Edwards, Don Johnson, George Lazenby. One of the more brazen efforts to duplicate the success of "Charlie's Angels," with a pair of fashion models who double as high-tech spies. Kennedy and Sharpe look good, which is all that matters in a product like this. (Dir: Jerry London, 96 mins.)

Covert Action (1980)**½ David Janssen, Arthur Kennedy, Corinne Clears. A former CIA operative (Janssen) retreats to Athens to write an exposé about underhanded CIA activities. Another agent, intent on exposing the CIA, is murdered and Janssen is plunged into real-life intrigue. A competent post-Watergate thriller laced with paranoia about the U.S. government's complicity in CIA pursuits. (Dir: Romolo Guerrieri, 98 mins.)

Cover Up (1949)*** William Bendix, Dennis O'Keefe. An insurance investigator comes to a small town to check on a doctor's death, and finds that nobody wants to talk about it. Nicely turned mystery. (Dir: Alfred E. Green, 82 mins.)

Coward of the County (MTV 1981)**½ Kenny Rogers, Frederic Lehne, Largo Woodruff. Kenny's country preacher is a supporting character to nephew Tommy, labeled a small-town coward for being a pacifist during World War II. Filmed in Georgia, the movie has an authentic rural feel, and good performances from Frederic Lehne and Largo Woodruff. (Dir: Dick Lowry, 104 mins.)†

Cowboy (1958)*** Glenn Ford, Jack Lemmon. Refreshing, generally entertaining western story, based on the experiences of a young Frank Harris—a dude goes west and learns the ways of the range. (Dir: Delmer Daves, 92 mins.)

Cowboy (MTV 1983)** James Brolin, Annie Potts, Randy Quaid, George DiCenzo, Michael Pataki, Ted Danson, Edward Holmes. James Brolin and Ted Danson battle bullies in this contemporary western that sticks close to tradition—bad guys are trying to swindle some land. (Dir: Jerry Jameson, 104 mins.)

Cowboy and the Ballerina, The (MTV 1984)**½ Lee Majors, Leslie Wing, James Booth, Steven Ford, Christopher Lloyd. Leslie Wing is the petite ballerina defecting from a Russian dance company and riding across the U.S. with cowboy Majors. (Dir: Jerry Jameson, 104 mins.)

Cowboy and the Lady, The (1938)** Gary Cooper, Merle Oberon, Walter Brennan. Just what the title suggests—a routine romance between a cowpoke and a rich city girl. Some of the comedy falls flat by today's standards. (Dir: H. C. Potter, 90 mins.)

Cowboys, The (1972)* John Wayne, Slim Pickens, Roscoe Lee Browne, Bruce Dern, Colleen Dewhurst. Another "morality" tale about the Old West in the 1870s. This repellent entry glorifies the turning of young schoolboys into conscienceless killers. (Dir: Mark Rydell, 120 mins.)†

Crack—See: **Strike Force**

Cracked Up (MTV 1987)** Ed Asner, Raphael Sbarge, Kim Delaney, Richard Holden. Asner plays a clergyman whose son goes from high school athlete to crack addict. (Dir: Karen Arthur, 104 mins.)

Cracker Factory, The (MTV 1979)*** Natalie Wood, Perry King, Peter Haskell. Wood's performance as an attractive woman who takes refuge in drink and abrasive action to cover her neurotic needs is a tour de force. The cracker factory of the title is the nickname she gives the psychiatric section of a hospital where she is taken. (Dir: Burt Brinckerhoff, 104 mins.)

Crackers (1984)* Donald Sutherland, Sean Penn, Jack Warden, Wallace Shawn. Based on an amusing Italian film, *Big Deal on Madonna Street*, this update pales in comparison. A troop of bungling safecrackers tries to pull off a heist in a pawnshop in San Francisco. (Dir: Louis Malle, 92 mins.)†

Crack House (1989)*½ Gregg Gomez Thomsen, Jim Brown, Anthony Geary, Cheryl Kay, Richard Roundtree, Angel Tompkins. A young inner-city couple is determined not to make the mistakes of their peers who have died from drugs, but are caught up in that world anyhow.

Depressing exploitation with the thinnest facade of good intentions. (Dir: Michael Fischa, 90 mins.)†

Cracking Up (1983)** Jerry Lewis, Herb Edelman, Zane Buzby. Lewis plays at least ten characters in this alleged laugh riot. Be warned, however, that the hilarity decreases in proportion to the frequency that the gags are repeated. AKA: **Smorgasbord.** (Dir: Jerry Lewis, 90 mins.)†

Crack in the Mirror (1960)** Orson Welles, Juliette Greco, Bradford Dillman. Unpalatable involvements about a team of lawyers defending two plaintiffs in a murder trial, whose lives parallel those of their clients. Not helped by the three main actors playing dual roles, a trick that doesn't come off. (Dir: Richard Fleischer, 97 mins.)

Crack in the World (1965)**½ Dana Andrews, Janette Scott. A science-fiction tale that seems very credible and registers a good amount of suspense. A group of scientists attempting to reach the Earth's core explode some nuclear bombs causing "a crack in the world." (Dir: Andrew Marton, 96 mins.)

Crack-Up (1946)*** Pat O'Brien, Claire Trevor, Herbert Marshall. Art museum curator is framed into thinking he was in a train wreck by art forgers. Involved but successful mystery. (Dir: Irving Reis, 93 mins.)

Cradle Will Fall, The (MTV 1983)**½ Lauren Hutton, Ben Murphy, James Farentino. Fairly suspenseful murder-mystery starring Lauren Hutton as a district attorney marked for death for unknowingly "witnessing" a doctor stuff a body in a car trunk. (Dir: John Llewellyn Moxey, 104 mins.)†

Craig's Wife (1936)*** Rosalind Russell, John Boles, Billie Burke. Pulitzer Prize-winning play about a ruthlessly ambitious middle-class housewife with a compulsion for home over husband achieves some intriguing ambiguities under Dorothy Arzner's direction. Harriet Craig is generally played as a monster, but Arzner and Russell suggest the forces behind her destructive passions without blunting their edge. (80 mins.)†

Cranes Are Flying, The (U.S.S.R., 1959)**** Tatyana Samoilova, Alexei Batalov, Vasily Merkuryev. Profoundly moving, beautifully directed, poignant drama of a Russian girl and her sweetheart who goes away to war. Free of propaganda, the World War II era is adeptly captured. (Dir: Mikhail Kalotozov, 94 mins.)

Crash! (1977)** Jose Ferrer, Sue Lyon, John Ericson, Leslie Parrish, John Carradine. You can't get rid of your wife (Lyon) in a car crash, Jose; she has demonic powers. Try the Exorcistmobile. (Dir: Charles Band, 85 mins.)

Crash (MTV 1978)** William Shatner, Eddie Albert, Adrienne Barbeau. Another plane-crash story based on a real incident. (Dir: Barry Shear, 104 mins.)

Crash Course (MTV 1988)½ Jackee, Tina Yothers, Harvey Korman, Alyssa Milano. Moronic misadventures of a summer driver's ed course flunks in the laughs department. Conceived of as a showcase for thoroughly forgettable sitcom stars. (Dir: Oz Scott, 96 mins.)

Crash Dive (1943)**½ Tyrone Power, Dana Andrews, Anne Baxter. Routine war story of a submarine in the North Atlantic and the officers who love the same girl. Why aren't there ever enough girls to go around? (Dir: Archie Mayo, 105 mins.)

Crashing Las Vegas (1956)** Bowery Boys, Jimmy Murphy, Mary Castle. Sach gets the ability to predict numbers and the Boys are off to Vegas. Leo Gorcey's last film in the series. Standard B movie fare. (Dir: Jean Yarbrough, 62 mins.)

Crash of Flight 401, The—See: **Crash**

Crash of Silence—See: **Mandy**

Crashout (1955)*** William Bendix, Arthur Kennedy. Six convicts make a break for freedom. Familiar but fast melodrama. (Dir: Lewis R. Foster, 91 mins.)†

Crawling Eye, The (Great Britain, 1958)**½ Forrest Tucker, Janet Munro. Another oversized deadly menace; this time a "crawling eye," and once more scientists save the world. Get the Murine! (Dir: Quentin Lawrence, 85 mins.)†

Crawling Hand, The (1963)*½ Peter Breck, Kent Taylor, Rod Lauren, Arline Judge, Allison Hayes. A disembodied horror film. The police put the finger on an astronaut's hand in a series of gruesome murders. (Dir: Herbert L. Strock, 89 mins.)†

Crawling Monster, The—See: **Creeping Terror, The**

Crawlspace (MTV 1972)**½ Arthur Kennedy, Teresa Wright, Tom Harper. Interesting, if not altogether successful, drama, about a middle-aged couple who take in a strange young man prone to violence. (Dir: John Newland, 72 mins.)

Crawlspace (1986)*½ Klaus Kinski, Talia Balsam, Barbara Whinnery, Carol Francis, Sally Brown. If the mere sight of Kinski (who seems to be foaming at the mouth even in repose) slithering around the crawlspace of his apartment building and spying on his intended victims makes you shudder, then don't miss this. (Dir: David Schmoeller, 78 mins.)†

Craze (Great Britain, 1974)*½ Jack Palance, Diana Dors, Julie Ege, Dame Edith Evans, Trevor Howard, Hugh Griffith. Silly, uninteresting horror thriller. A London antique dealer (Palance) is
216

killing women as sacrificial offerings to his hungry idol, Chuku. (Dir: Freddie Francis, 96 mins.)†

Crazies, The (1973)** Lane Carroll, W. C. McMillan, Lloyd Hollar, Wayne Jones. A biological pestilence spreads throughout a Pennsylvania town, and the townsfolk start behaving as if they'd just wandered in from *Night of the Living Dead*. Some chilling moments but mainly it's derivative, hopped-up action moviemaking. AKA: **Code Name Trixie**. (Dir: George Romero, 103 mins.)

Crazy Family, The (Japan, 1986)*** Katsuya Kobayashi, Mitsuro Baisho, Yoshiki Arizono, Yuki Kudo. A corrosive, cartoonish farce about a family who move to a suburban dream palace after years of cramped apartment life. Their new home becomes a battleground where family members are pitted against each other and freeloading relatives and a hungry army of uninvited termites. (Dir: Sogo Ishii, 106 mins.)

Crazy Fat Ethel II (1987)½ Priscilla Alden, Michael Flood, Jane Lambert, Robert Copple. Sequel to *Criminally Insane* consists largely of reused footage from that trash classic, with new shot-on-video footage of Ethel's latest slaughters of anyone who gets between her and her lunch. As Ethel, Alden is like Edith Massey with PMS. (Dir: Nick Philips, 70 mins.)†

Crazy Horse—See: **Friends, Lovers and Lunatics**

Crazy House (1943)**½ Olsen and Johnson, Cass Daley. The two comics arrive in Hollywood to make a movie, form their own company, and all hell breaks loose. Amusing nonsensical comedy. (Dir: Edward F. Cline, 80 mins.)

Crazy Joe (1974)** Peter Boyle, Paula Prentiss, Rip Torn. The ads for this gangster saga about real-life hood Joey Gallo read "Who Was Crazy Joe?" Well, after seeing this film, you might be prompted to answer, "He's one-third imitation Edward G. Robinson, one-third bogus Humphrey Bogart, and one-third warmed-over James Cagney." (Dir: Carlo Lizzani, 100 mins.)

Crazylegs (1953)*** Elroy Hirsch, Lloyd Nolan. Biography of the famous football star has two advantages—"Crazylegs" plays himself, and he's a pretty good actor. (Dir: Francis D. Lyon, 88 mins.)

Crazy Love—See: **Love Is a Dog from Hell**

Crazy Mama (1975)** Cloris Leachman, Stuart Whitman, Ann Sothern, Tisha Sterling. Perhaps the first substantial effort of director Jonathan Demme. Leachman is the murderous mama trying to make ends meet during the Depression. It's a gangster movie, kind of sexy in a campy, arch way. (82 mins.)†

Crazy Moon (Canada, 1986)*½ Kiefer Sutherland, Vanessa Vaughan, Peter Spance. Saccharine romance between a goofy high-school misfit (Sutherland) and the hearing-impaired girl (Vaughan) with whom he falls in love. A tedious rack of clichés. (Dir: Allan Eastman, 90 mins.)†

Crazy Over Horses (1951)**½ Bowery Boys, Ted de Corsia, Allen Jenkins, Bernard Gorcey, Gloria Saunders, Tim Ryan. A stable owner who owes a debt to Louie Dumbrowski (Bernard Gorcey) pays it off with a horse. Above-average entry. (Dir: William Beaudine, 65 mins.)

Crazy People (1990)** Dudley Moore, Daryl Hannah, Paul Reiser, Mercedes Ruehl, J. T. Walsh, Ben Hammer, Floyd Vivino, John Terlesky. Farfetched comedy about adman Moore committed to an asylum after a breakdown in which he devises a series of brutally honest commercials ("Volvos—they're boxy but good"). Film tries to create a screwball atmosphere blending a Preston Sturges-like satire of business with Frank Capra-ish sentiment. The mock commercials are funny, but that's about all that is. (Dir: Tony Bill, 90 mins.)†

Crazy Times (MTV 1981)** Michael Pare, David Caruso, Ray Liotta, Talia Balsam. This TV movie celebrates those innocent days of the '50s, when getting a date was a high priority on every schoolboy's list. (Dir: Lee Philips, 104 mins.)

Crazy World of Julius Vrooder, The (1974)** Timothy Bottoms, Barbara Seagull (Hershey), Lawrence Pressman, George Marshall. Attempt to make a comedy about hospitalized Vietnam War veterans misfires. (Dir: Arthur Hiller, 100 mins.)

Created to Kill—See: **Embryo**

Creation of the Humanoids, The (1962)* Don Megowan, Erica Elliot, David Cross, Frances McCann, Dudley Manlove. In a post-nuke future, androids are created to help the surviving 3 percent of mankind carry on. But would you want your sister to date one? Dull, pompous sci-fi was reportedly Andy Warhol's favorite movie, probably because of the extremely stagey, static presentation. Makeup by Jack Pierce, who created the popular Universal Studios monsters of the thirties; he didn't have much to work with here. (Dir: Wesley E. Barry, 78 mins.)†

Creator (1985)**½ Peter O'Toole, Vincent Spano, Virginia Madsen, Mariel Hemingway, David Ogden Stiers. Boy does this movie have problems, but it also has Peter O'Toole giving one of his most deliciously wry performances as a nutty scientist intent on cloning his deceased wife. Around him are a bunch of eccentric, loveable characters who make the film's lack of logic easy to forgive. (Dir: Ivan Passer, 107 mins.)†

Creature (1985)*½ Stan Ivar, Wendy Schaal, Lyman Ward, Klaus Kinski. Another *Alien* clone. Space miners awaken one of Titan's nastier inhabitants and spend the rest of the film wandering into dark corners of their craft and getting knocked off. (Dir: Bill Mallone, 97 mins.)†

Creature from Black Lake (1976)*½ Jack Elam, Dub Taylor, John David Carson. Low-budget yawner concerning two Chicago anthropology students who journey to a Louisiana swamp to search for an eight-foot, 400-pound creature. (Dir: Joy Houck, Jr., 95 mins.)†

Creature from Galaxy 27—See: **Night of the Blood Beast**

Creature from the Black Lagoon (1954)*** Richard Carlson, Julia Adams. Originally produced in 3-D, this science fiction tale has more than its share of visual gimmicks. The plot, complete with bewildered scientists and love interest, is not innovative, but fans of this genre will enjoy it. (Dir: Jack Arnold, 79 mins.)†

Creature from the Haunted Sea (1961)**½ Anthony Carbone, Betsy Jones-Moreland. Low-budget item turns out to be a spoof of horror thrillers mixing gangsters, fleeing revolutionaries, and a sea beast. Some hip dialogue, good-natured kidding of the genre. (Dirs: Roger Corman, Monte Hellman, 72 mins.)†

Creature of the Walking Dead (1960)*½ Rock Madison, Ann Wells. Descendant of a scientist who sought lasting life finds his grandfather in an ancient laboratory, brings him back to life. Farfetched horror thriller. (Dirs: Fernando Cortes, Jerry Warren, 74 mins.)

Creatures of the Prehistoric Planet—See: **Horror of the Blood Monsters**

Creature Walks Among Us, The (1956)*½ Jeff Morrow, Rex Reason. Low-budget science fiction melodrama—this time the expedition sets out to capture and study a monster known as "The Gill Man." (Dir: John Sherwood, 80 mins.)

Creature Wasn't Nice, The—See: **Spaceship**

Creature with the Atom Brain, The (1955)** Richard Denning, Angela Stevens. Overdone science fiction story about a deported mobster who kills those who testified against him with the aid of a mad scientist. (Dir: Edward L. Cahn, 70 mins.)

Creepers (Italy, 1985)** Jennifer Connolly, Daria Nicolodi, Eleanora Giorgi, Donald Pleasence. Misshapen but passable horror film about a killer menacing a girls' school and an insect-loving young lady who uses some strange powers to defend herself. (Dir: Dario Argento, 83 mins.)†

Creepers, The—See: Assault

Creeping Flesh, The (Great Britain, 1970) **½ Peter Cushing, Christopher Lee, Lorna Heilbron. It's slickly produced and might even provoke a chill or two. The plot, if it can be defined at all, concerns a scientist absolutely obsessed with harnessing the "essence of evil" —an ambitious and lofty dedication. (Dir: Freddie Francis, 89 mins.)†

Creeping Terror, The (1964)½ Vic Savage, Shannon O'Neill, William Thourlby. Laugh-provoking sci-fi "thriller" shot at Lake Tahoe. The flesh-eating creature resembles a leafy carpet. AKA: The Crawling Monster. (Dir: A. J. Nelson, 75 mins.)†

Creeping Unknown, The (Great Britain, 1956)**½ Brian Donlevy, Jack Warner, Margia Dean. Nigel Kneale's popular British television science-fiction serial was the subject of three feature films, of which this was the first. Brian Donlevy plays Dr. Quatermass, who must deal with the scientific and ethical problems of treating an astronaut who has become infected with a rare disease in space, which may be turning him into a malignant alien. Intelligent sci-fi. (Dir: Val Guest, 78 mins.)†

Creepozoids (1987)* Linnea Quigley, Ken Abraham, Richard Hawkins, Michael Aranda. Tiresome, unscary Alien rip-off set in the future. A group of Army deserters take shelter in an abandoned scientific complex and are menaced by a slimy creature. (Dir: David DeCoteau, 71 mins.)†

Creepshow (1982)**½ Hal Holbrook, Adrienne Barbeau, Fritz Weaver, Leslie Nielsen, E. G. Marshall, Carrie Nye. Stephen King and director George Romero grew up reading E.C. comics such as Tales from the Crypt, and they joined forces to make this movie homage, which is alternately scary, gross, dumb, funny, and entertaining. Five stories make up the film, which uses a comic-book intro for each segment. (122 mins.)†

Creepshow 2 (1987)*** Lois Chiles, George Kennedy, Dorothy Lamour, Daniel Beer, Page Hannah. Three more Stephen King stories adapted by the director of the first Creepshow, George Romero. This sequel eschews the comic-book stylization of the original in favor of straight, gruesome thrills. (Dir: Michael Gornick, 92 mins.)†

Crest of the Wave (1954)**½ Gene Kelly, Jeff Richards, John Justin. Interesting but slow-moving war film made in England. Gene Kelly seems miscast in a straight non-dancing role. (Dirs: John and Roy Boulting, 90 mins.)

Cricket, The (Italy, 1983)*½ Virna Lisi, Anthony Franciosa, Clio Goldsmith, Renato Salvatori. Lisi's beauty is the only redeeming quality in this offbeat film about an aging chanteuse. After marrying the owner of a sleazy truckstop/restaurant (a miscast Franciosa), she begins to feel threatened when her virginal daughter moves in. AKA: La Cicada. (Dir: Alberto Lattuada, 90 mins.)†

Cries and Whispers (Sweden, 1972)**** Liv Ullmann, Ingrid Thulin, Harriet Andersson. This shattering drama about the relationships of three sisters in a Swedish manor house was voted the best film of the year by the New York Film Critics. Agnes (Andersson) is dying of cancer, circa 1900, and her older and younger sisters come to her home for the deathwatch. The sense of pain and suffering is portrayed so realistically as to become almost unendurable, and the acting throughout is faultless. The great cinematographer Sven Nykvist is at the top of his form. (Dir: Ingmar Bergman, 94 mins.)†

Crime Against Joe (1956)*** John Bromfield, Julie London. Painter is accused of murder. Compact mystery has some surprises; nice pace. (Dir: Lee Sholem, 69 mins.)

Crime and Passion (1976)½ Omar Sharif, Karen Black, Joseph Bottoms, Bernhard Wicki. The product of six scripters and three scripts. Somehow these scripts were scraped together to tell the tale of a woman whose lover persuades her to marry a tycoon who's not as dumb as he looks. (Dir: Ivan Passer, 92 mins.)†

Crime and Punishment (1935)**½ Edward Arnold, Peter Lorre, Marian Marsh. Hollywood's version of Dostoyevsky's classic novel casts a subtly neurotic Peter Lorre as the haunted student-murderer. Arnold's portrayal of the inspector, who doggedly tracks him down, is overblown. Sternberg's direction is full of flavor and invention. (Dir: Josef von Sternberg, 88 mins.)†

Crime and Punishment (France, 1958)*** Jean Gabin, Robert Hossein. Inspector breaks down the will of a murderer. One of the many versions of this crime tale. (Dir: George Lampin, 108 mins.)

Crime and Punishment, USA (1959)** George Hamilton, Mary Murphy. A good idea that never quite jells and a good deal of blame can be attributed to George Hamilton's stoic performance. As the title suggests, this is an updated version of the classic Crime and Punishment. (Dir: Denis Sanders, 95 mins.)

Crime by Night (1944)**½ Jane Wyman, Jerome Cowan, Faye Emerson, Eleanor

Parker. Private eye on vacation suddenly finds himself investigating an axe murder. (Dir: Geoffrey Homes, 72 mins.)

Crime Club (MTV 1973)** Lloyd Bridges, Victor Buono, Paul Burke, William Devane, David Hedison, Cloris Leachman, Barbara Rush, Martin Sheen. A retired judge forms a crime club to investigate the murder or suicide of a wealthy young man. (Dir: David Lowell Rich, 78 mins.)

Crime Club (MTV 1975)**½ Scott Thomas, Eugene Roche, Robert Lansing, Biff McGuire, Barbara Rhodes, Martine Beswick, M. Emmet Walsh. Members of a private club formed to combat crime try to clear a confessed killer who's really just a misfit looking for fame. Well cast and well made, but predictable nonetheless. (Dir: Jeannot Szwarc, 72 mins.)

Crime Doctor series. Based on the popular radio show, these programmers concerned an ex-gangster who becomes a leading criminologist after an initial bout with amnesia helps him leave his past behind. Also see: *Shadow in the Night, Just Before Dawn,* and *The Millerson Case.*

Crime Doctor (1943)*** Warner Baxter, Margaret Lindsay, John Litel. While in a state of amnesia, a clever crook becomes a gifted criminologist. First in the series. (Dir: Michael Gordon, 66 mins.)

Crime Doctor's Courage, The (1945)** Warner Baxter, Hillary Brooke. Routine mystery about a bride who suspects her hubby is a killer. (Dir: George Sherman, 70 mins.)

Crime Doctor's Diary (1949)*½ Warner Baxter, Lois Maxwell. The once-popular series petered out with this lackluster entry. Baxter looks haggard onscreen as he helps a parolee extricate himself from a frame-up for arson and murder. (Dir: Seymour Friedman, 61 mins.)

Crime Doctor's Gamble, The (1947)** Warner Baxter, Micheline Cheirel. The crime doctor investigates an art theft and murder on a European vacation. (Dir: William Castle, 66 mins.)

Crime Doctor's Manhunt (1946)** Warner Baxter, Ellen Drew, William Frawley. War vet visits the crime doctor with a strange tale; later he's found murdered. (Dir: William Castle, 61 mins.)

Crime Doctor's Strangest Case (1943)**½ Warner Baxter, Lynn Merrick, Reginald Denny. Entertaining whodunit has the crime doctor clearing an innocent man. (Dir: Eugene Forde, 68 mins.)

Crime Doctor's Warning, The (1945)** Warner Baxter, John Litel, Dusty Anderson. Three murders and a cast full of suspects as the good doctor finds the

killer of a luscious model. (Dir: William Castle, 69 mins.)

Crime in the Streets (1956)*** John Cassavetes, James Whitmore, Sal Mineo. A familiar '50s urban street-gang opus. The film is ultimately an unsatisfying drama in spite of a lot of craftsmanship, including some sharp writing by Reginald Rose and the consistently intelligent direction of Don Siegel. (91 mins.)

Crime of Dr. Crespi, The (1935)** Erich von Stroheim, Dwight Frye, Paul Guilfoyle, Harriett Russell. Average revenge melodrama about a man who decides to fix the cad who's making eyes at his beloved. (Dir: John Auer, 63 mins.)†

Crime of Dr. Hallet, The (1938)** Ralph Bellamy, Josephine Hutchinson, William Gargan. A researcher in the jungle seeks a cure for a tropical disease and finds romantic complications. (Dir: S. Sylvan Simon, 68 mins.)

Crime of Innocence (MTV 1985)** Andy Griffith, Ralph Waite, Diane Ladd, Shawnee Smith. Unpleasant fare. Andy Griffith plays a fanatical judge who sends joy-riding kids to jail to teach them a lesson. It's nightmare time behind bars where the youngsters live through a sadistic ordeal. (Dir: Michael Miller, 104 mins.)

Crime of M. Lange, The (France, 1935)**** Jean Lefevre, Jules Berry. A masterpiece directed by Jean Renoir. Monsieur Lange (Lefevre), a writer of pulp fiction, is exploited by his boss, capitalist evil incarnate, Batala (Berry). Lange helps form a publishing cooperative after Batala disappears, saving the firm from ruin. When Batala returns, Renoir constructs a convincing moral argument for his murder. Renoir's irony and taste for paradox flourish, abetted by an excellent Jacques Prévert screenplay. (85 mins.)†

Crime of Passion (1957)**½ Barbara Stanwyck, Sterling Hayden, Raymond Burr. A wife's ambition for her husband leads to murder. (Dir: Gerd Oswald, 84 mins.)

Crime School (1938)**½ Humphrey Bogart, Gale Page, Billy Halop, Bobby Jordan, Leo Gorcey, Huntz Hall. The Dead End Kids go to reform school as the result of an accidental death. Bogart is the new warden who sets out to get the Boys pardoned and to clean up the graft-laden reformatory. (Dir: Lewis Seiler, 86 mins.)

Crimes and Misdemeanors (1989)***½ Martin Landau, Woody Allen, Mia Farrow, Anjelica Huston, Claire Bloom, Alan Alda, Sam Waterston, Joanna Gleason, Jerry Orbach, Caroline Aaron. Writer-director Allen's complex ode to jealousy and one-upsmanship weaves two stories: A distinguished doctor has a

219

mistress who threatens to expose their affair; a documentary filmmaker wants to best his insufferable sitcom-producer brother-in-law. The ensemble cast is superb as they tackle such familiar Allen subjects as family, friendship, love, God, show business, and the more serious topic of murder. (104 mins.)†

Crimes of Passion (1984)*** Kathleen Turner, Anthony Perkins, John Laughlin, Annie Potts, Bruce Davison. This controversial tale of lust is blessed with director Ken Russell's outrageous visual design. Turner plays China Blue—fashion designer by day, prostitute by night. Perkins (echoing Norman Bates) plays a deranged preacher who is obsessed with her. (102 mins.)†

Crimes of the Future (Canada, 1970)**½ Ronald Mlodzik, Jon Lidolt, Tania Zolty, Paul Mulholland. Writer-director David Cronenberg's second feature. In a bleak future when all women have died, scientists and manufacturers seek to create alternate means of sexual release, many of which have unfortunate side effects. Not much plot to speak of, but those interested in Cronenberg's unique *oeuvre* will find this an intriguing presage of what was to come. (63 mins.)

Crimes of the Heart (1986)*** Diane Keaton, Jessica Lange, Sissy Spacek, Tess Harper, Hurd Hatfield, Sam Shepard. Three attractive, eccentric Southern sisters are reunited by their grandfather's failing health and a shooting incident involving the youngest (Spacek). A triumph of ensemble acting, with all three leads delivering enchanting performances that transcend the otherwise thin material. Based on Beth Henley's Pulitzer Prize–winning play. (Dir: Bruce Beresford, 105 mins.)†

Crime Story (MTV 1986)*** Dennis Farina, Stephen Lang, Anthony Denison, Darlanne Fluegel, John Santucci, Bill Smitrovich, William Russ, David Caruso. Tough cops apply muscle in the war between the crime unit and the Mob. Set in the 1960s, the show has a dark, brooding style and is overflowing with period cars, neon honky-tonk spots, and nostalgic rock music. (Dir: Abel Ferrara, 104 mins.)†

Crime Wave (1954)** Sterling Hayden, Gene Nelson, Charles Bronson. Dancer Gene Nelson plays a straight dramatic role in this average cops and crooks "melodrama." (Dir: Andre de Toth, 74 mins.)

Crimewave (1986)*½ Louise Lasser, Paul L. Smith, Brion James, Sheree J. Wilson, Edward R. Pressman, Reed Birney. Offbeat comedy written by Joel and Ethan Coen (*Blood Simple*) and directed by Sam Raimi (*The Evil Dead*). The ridiculous story concerns two rat exterminators on a killing spree in Detroit. (Dir: Sam Raimi, 83 mins.)†

Crime Without Passion (1934)*** Claude Rains, Margo. A lawyer who gets involved in crime tries to clear himself by criminal methods. Rains is superb as the sadistic lawyer and Margo scores in the role of the girl he thinks he's murdered. (Dirs: Ben Hecht, Charles MacArthur, 80 mins.)

Crime Zone (1988)**½ David Carradine, Peter Nelson, Sherilyn Fenn. Sci-fi adventure set in a post-apocalyptic society. Government agent Carradine offers an innocent couple the chance to escape from a bleak desert zone if they'll commit a robbery for him. Stylishly directed on a low budget by Luis Llosa. (93 mins.)†

Criminal Act (1989)* Catherine Bach, Charlene Dallas, Nicholas Guest, John Saxon. Two newspaperwomen chase a rat (the four-legged type) into the basement, where they uncover a nasty new type of urban renewal plot. Indifferently written adventure is a dull waste of time. (Dir: Mark Byers, 93 mins.)†

Criminal Code, The (1931)*** Walter Huston, Constance Cummings, Mary Doran, DeWitt Jennings, John Sheehan, Boris Karloff. Based on the Martin Flavin play, this dated but rousing prison melodrama is graced by Huston's commanding performance and by the muscular direction. A district attorney is put through the wringer when his daughter, a prison warden, falls for a criminal her dad sent up the river. (Dir: Howard Hawks, 96 mins.)†

Criminal Justice (MCTV 1990)*** Forest Whitaker, Jennifer Grey, Rosie Perez, Anthony LaPaglia. Probing drama, which has the look of a documentary. A prostitute is robbed and beaten and an ex-con is blamed. The courtroom scenes are hard hitting as legal aid lawyer LaPaglia goes up against assistant D.A. Grey. A rare examination of the judicial system from several angles. (Dir: Andy Wolk, 90 mins.)†

Criminal Law (1988)* Gary Oldman, Kevin Bacon, Tess Harper, Karen Young, Joe Don Baker. *From the Hip* without the humor, as defense attorney Oldman wins an acquittal for killer Bacon, only to discover that he really is guilty when he brutally kills more young women. The ethical questions raised are interesting, but they're abandoned for cheap shock tactics and ludicrous plot devices. (Dir: Martin Campbell, 117 mins.)†

Criminal Life of Archibaldo de la Cruz, The (Mexico, 1955)**** Ernesto Alonso, Miroslava. Despite nagging limitations of budget and style, this last film from

Luis Buñuel's journeyman period in Mexico is nonetheless a superbly Buñuelian fantasy. A man is obsessed with the notion that as a child he had the power to kill people with his music box, and he lives out his guilt and his power in bizarre and funny ways. AKA: **Rehearsal for a Crime**. (91 mins.)

Criminally Insane (1974)½ Priscilla Alden, Michael Flood, Jane Lambert, C. L. LeFleur. Ethel, a compulsive eater with a foul disposition, comes home after years in an institution and makes up for lost time at the refrigerator, with a butcher knife for anyone who gets in her way. Hilariously straight-faced horror cheapie became a cult item on video, with much of this footage reused in the sequel *Crazy Fat Ethel II*. (Dir: Nick Philips, 61 mins.)†

Crimson Altar, The—See: **Crimson Cult, The**

Crimson Cult, The (1968)* Boris Karloff, Christopher Lee, Barbara Steele. Veteran cast of horror stalwarts does little to enliven this black-magic tale. Karloff shows remarkable patience with such nonsensical dialogue. AKA: **The Crimson Altar**. (Dir: Vernon Sewell, 81 mins.)

Crimson Kimono, The (1959)*** Glenn Corbett, Victoria Shaw, James Shigeta. Director Samuel Fuller's crime melodrama deals bluntly with issues of racism and miscegenation. Graphic and fascinating, but not a major film. (82 mins.)

Crimson Pirate, The (1952)*** Burt Lancaster, Eva Bartok, Nick Cravat, Torin Thatcher, Christopher Lee. Adventure on the high seas with Lancaster buckling every swash in sight. Lancaster and circus acrobat Nick Cravat execute some tricky gymnastics in their effort to overthrow tyranny. (Dir: Robert Siodmak, 104 mins.)†

Crisis (1950)*** Cary Grant, Signe Hasso, Paula Raymond, Ramon Novarro, Jose Ferrer. A bit arid and talky, but an absorbing drama that generates real tension. Grant is an American surgeon dragooned into performing delicate brain work on a dying dictator (Ferrer), and political morality gets an entertaining workout. (Dir: Richard Brooks, 96 mins.)

Crisis at Central High (MTV 1981)***½ Joanne Woodward, Charles Durning, Henderson Forsythe, William Russ. A compelling and ultimately moving "docudrama" recreating the events at Central High School in Little Rock, Ark., during the school year 1957-58. Joanne Woodward shines as the resolute teacher and assistant principal who calmly helped produce a peaceful and enduring solution establishing an integrated school. (Dir: Lamont Johnson, 78 mins.)†

Crisis in Mid-Air (MTV 1979)** George Peppard, Desi Arnaz, Jr., Karen Grassle.

Here we are again in the crisis-ridden airport. The predictable drama is played in the aircraft, in the traffic control center, and on the landing strip. (Dir: Walter Grauman, 104 mins.)

Crisis at Sun Valley (MTV 1981)** Dale Robinette, Taylor Lacher, Bo Hopkins, Tracy Brooks Swope, Ken Swofford, John McIntire, Charles Fleisher. Sequel to *The Deadly Triangle* is actually two episodes of an unsold series about the sheriff at a ski lodge, here investigating mountain-climbing teenagers and a radical conservationist. (Dir: Paul Stanley, 104 mins.)

Criss Cross (1949)***½ Burt Lancaster, Yvonne DeCarlo, Dan Duryea, Tony Curtis, Stephen McNally. Probably the best of director Robert Siodmak's exercises in *film noir*. Lancaster plays a pathetic yet powerful loser whose fatal weakness is his attachment to his treacherous ex-wife (DeCarlo). (87 mins.)†

Critical Condition (1987)*½ Richard Pryor, Rachel Ticotin, Ruben Blades, Joe Dallesandro, Bob Dishy. A convict masquerades as a doctor during a hospital blackout. Another disappointing vehicle for Pryor, whose career will be on the critical list after a few more comedies like this. (Dir: Michael Apted, 90 mins.)†

Critical List (1985)—See: **Terminal Choice**

Critical List (MTV 1978)** Lloyd Bridges, Melinda Dillon, Buddy Ebsen, Barbara Parkins, Robert Wagner, Ken Howard, Pat Harrington. Medical drama featuring Bridges as a candidate for the post of Secretary of Health, battling to preserve his reputation and uncovering a problem involving public health funds. (Dir: Lou Antonio, 192 mins.)

Critic's Choice (1963)**½ Bob Hope, Lucille Ball. Even the expert comedy talents of Hope and Ball can't save this contrived tale about a New York drama critic whose wife writes a play. Based on the Broadway play with the same title, the screen adaptation was altered to suit the talents of the leads but it doesn't really help. (Dir: Don Weis, 100 mins.)

Critters (1986)**½ Dee Wallace Stone, Terrence Mann, Scott Grimes, M. Emmet Walsh, Billy Green Bush, Billy Zane. A *Gremlins* rip-off, but a fairly funny one at that. Some furry fiends from outer space escape a galactic prison and come to Earth to snack up on human beings. (Dir: Stephen Herek, 86 mins.)†

Critters 2: The Main Course (1988)*½ Scott Grimes, Liane Curtis, Don Opper. Those fanged furballs are back on Earth, and once again no one believes the young man (Grimes) who's aware of their existence. Best effect: a faceless alien transforms himself into a Playboy centerfold, complete with staple. (Dir: Mick Garris, 87 mins.)†

"Crocodile" Dundee (Australia, 1986)*** Paul Hogan, Linda Kozlowski, John Meillon, Mark Blum, Michael Lombard. The quintessential Aussie, Hogan, lends his charm to this ingratiating money-maker. In this cornball but disarming comedy-romance, Hogan plays a macho crocodile poacher who takes a New York reporter out on a tour of the outback and is in turn wined and dined in the Big Apple, where he proves more than a match for the locals. (Dir: Peter Faiman, 98 mins.)†

"Crocodile" Dundee II (1988)**½ Paul Hogan, Linda Kozlowski, Charles Dutton. A wealthy Colombian drug dealer finds out that the fair-haired bushman isn't as naïve as he seems when he kidnaps Dundee's main squeeze (Kozlowski) in hopes of regaining an incriminating role of film. Action, and plenty of it, is the order of business here, with Hogan's charismatic personality and winning tongue-in-cheek demeanor registering nicely. (Dir: John Cornell, 111 mins.)†

Cromwell (Great Britain, 1970)*½ Richard Harris, Alec Guinness, Robert Morley, Dorothy Tutin, Frank Finlay, Timothy Dalton, Patrick Magee. Straightforward narrative about the 17th-century civil war which divided England and brought Oliver Cromwell to prominence as a revolutionary. (Dir: Ken Hughes, 139 mins.)†

Crook, The (France-Italy, 1970)***½ Jean-Louis Trintignant, Christine Lelouch. Trintignant plays a criminal out to commit an elaborate kidnapping of a bank employee's son and collect ransom from the bank, which would then profit from the publicity. The plan works until a subtle plot twist. Slick, and cynical. (Dir: Claude Lelouch, 73 mins.)

Crooked Hearts, The (MTV 1972)**½ Rosalind Russell, Douglas Fairbanks, Jr. Miss Russell corresponds with the elegant Mr. Fairbanks via a lonely hearts club and they strike up a romance—each thinking the other is enormously wealthy. (Dir: Jay Sandrich, 74 mins.)

Crooked Road, The (Great Britain, 1964)* Robert Ryan, Stewart Granger, Nadia Gray. Third-rate melodrama, made in Yugoslavia. Ryan plays a newspaperman who almost gets the goods on a Balkan dictator. (Dir: Don Chaffey, 86 mins.)

Crooks and Coronets (Great Britain, 1970)** Telly Savalas, Dame Edith Evans, Warren Oates, Cesar Romero, Harry H. Corbett. Genial but colorless comedy romp about crooks getting sidetracked by their fondness for an old

lady they were supposed to rob. The real grand larceny is the way the priceless Evans steals the film. (Dir: Jim O'Connolly, 106 mins.)†

Crooks Anonymous (Great Britain, 1962)** Julie Christie, Leslie Phillips, Wilfred Hyde-White. Petty thief tries to mend his ways, joins an organization dedicated to the reformation of criminals. Cute idea, mediocre handling. (Dir: Ken Annakin, 87 mins.)

Cross and the Switchblade, The (1970)*½ Pat Boone, Erik Estrada, Jackie Giroux, Jo-Ann Robinson. Weak attempt to deliver a family picture about a priest (Boone) trying to reform a pack of New York hoodlums. (Dir: Don Murray, 108 mins.)†

Cross Country (Canada, 1983)** Richard Beymer, Nina Axelrod, Michael Ironside. Lurid mad-killer movie involving a murdered girl's boyfriend (Beymer) who picks up some kinky hitchhikers while a cop is tracking him down, hoping to pin the crime on him. A mystery journey that goes nowhere. (Dir: Paul Lynch, 95 mins.)†

Cross Creek (1983)**½ Mary Steenburgen, Malcolm McDowell, Rip Torn, Dana Hill, Alfre Woodard, Peter Coyote. Marjorie Kinnan Rawlings (author of *The Yearling*) left behind her husband and her home in the big city to stake out a new life for herself in the Florida Everglades. While the film bio doesn't adequately convey Rawlings's passion for writing, it works as a romanticized look at the woman's struggle to free herself. (Dir: Martin Ritt, 120 mins.)†

Crossed Swords (1954)*½ Errol Flynn, Gina Lollobrigida. Bold adventurer foils a wicked counselor in medieval Italy. (Dir: Nato de Angelis, 84 mins.)

Crossed Swords (Great Britain, 1977)**½ Oliver Reed, Mark Lester, George C. Scott. Acceptable remake of Twain's *The Prince and the Pauper* in the vein of Richard Lester's *Three Musketeers*, with sword in hand and tongue in cheek. (Dir: Richard Fleischer, 113 mins.)

Crossfire (1947)*** Robert Ryan, Robert Mitchum, Robert Young, Gloria Grahame, Sam Levene. This B pic with a social angle deserves credit for it. It's an exciting tale of an anti-Semitic murderer pursued by police. (Dir: Edward Dmytryk, 86 mins.)†

Crossfire (MTV 1975)** James Farentino, Ramon Bieri, John Saxon, Patrick O'Neal, Pamela Franklin, Herb Edelman. Cop Farentino goes undercover into the criminal element to uncover the source of a wave of graft. By-the-book police action dominates this failed pilot. (Dir: William Hale, 72 mins.)

Crossing Delancey (1988)*** Amy Irving,

222

Peter Riegert, Reizl Bozyk, Jeroen Krabbe, Sylvia Miles, Suzzy Roche. A very ethnic slice-of-life romantic comedy with an upwardly mobile Jewish girl (Irving) being fixed up with a down-to-earth man who sells pickles for a living (Riegert) by her doting grandmother. Delightful on the whole, but Riegert's charming character gets far too little to do. (Dir: Joan Micklin Silver, 97 mins.)†

Crossing to Freedom (MTV 1990)**½ Peter O'Toole, Mare Winningham, Susan Woodridge, Michael Kitchen. O'Toole is the whole show (as usual) in this WWII drama. He plays a widower who is talked into helping a pair of children escape to England. (Dir: Norman Stone, 96 mins.)

Cross My Heart (1946)** Betty Hutton, Sonny Tufts. Silly comedy about a girl who rarely tells the truth. The young lady confesses to a murder thinking it will help her boyfriend, but the scheme backfires. Remake of *True Confession*, 1937. (Dir: John Berry, 83 mins.)

Cross My Heart (1987)**½ Martin Short, Annette O'Toole, Joanna Kerns, Paul Reiser. A painfully earnest relationship comedy that deals with two bruised romantics who have a "big date" where they discover the truth about each other and then work past their recriminations to a happy ending. Short and O'Toole do their charming best with the material. (Dir: Armyan Bernstein, 100 mins.)†

Cross My Heart (France, 1990)***½ Sylvain Copans, Nicolas Parodi, Cecilia Rouaud, Delphine Gouttman, Olivier Montiege, Lucie Blossier. Delightful, unsentimental film about children who refuse to tell authorities about the death of a friend's mother and invent a false scenario for him so he won't get sent to an orphanage. (Dir: Jacques Fansten, 105 mins.)

Cross of Fire (MTV 1989)*** John Heard, Mel Harris, David Morse, George Dzunda, Donald Moffat, Kim Hunter. The underrated Heard gets a part worthy of his abilities as David Stephenson, the frighteningly charismatic leader who revitalized the Ku Klux Klan into a powerful political organ in the 1920s. Well-written historical drama. (Dir: Paul Wendkos, 192 mins.)

Cross of Iron (Great Britain-West Germany, 1977)** James Coburn, Maximilian Schell, James Mason, David Warner. Despite some formidable action sequences, notably in the tank battles near the end, this film represents director Sam Peckinpah in decline. The characters are superficial, which is no fault of the good actors. (120 mins.)†

Cross of Lorraine, The (1943)*** Jean-Pierre Aumont, Gene Kelly, Sir Cedric Hardwicke. An exceptionally good anti-Nazi film about a group of Frenchmen who surrender too easily, go to a prison camp and learn how the Nazis really operate. (Dir: Tay Garnett, 90 mins.)

Crossover Dreams (1985)*** Ruben Blades, Shawn Elliot, Tom Signorelli. A crossover production from independent producers who made this colorful film a mainstream hit. A salsa musician is willing to try anything and dump anyone in his striving to break out of the ghetto of Spanish music. (Dir: Leon Ichaso, 86 mins.)†

Crossroads (1942)** William Powell, Hedy Lamarr, Basil Rathbone, Claire Trevor. Suspense film about an amnesia victim who is uncertain of his former life is well played. (Dir: Jack Conway, 84 mins)

Crossroads (1986)** Ralph Macchio, Joe Seneca, Jami Gertz, Robert Judd, Joe Morton. This misbegotten fantasy seems like a revamp of *The Karate Kid*, with a crotchety old musician replacing the wise karate master who guided Macchio's coming-of-age. Halfway through, it becomes a Faustian morality play in which Macchio has to play a mean guitar to save his mentor's soul. (Dir: Walter Hill, 100 mins.)†

Crosswinds (1951)** John Payne, Rhonda Fleming, Forrest Tucker. Payne is the victim of a double cross and other villainous deeds in this average tale of island intrigues. (Dir: Lewis R. Foster, 93 mins.)

Crowd, The (1928)**** James Murray, Eleanor Boardman, Bert Roach, Estelle Clark. Director King Vidor's silent masterpiece about a little man lost in the crowd of day-to-day living. Expressionistic film is essential viewing. (98 mins.)†

Crowded Sky, The (1960)**½ Dana Andrews, Rhonda Fleming, Efrem Zimbalist, Jr., Troy Donahue. This airplane drama will strike you as a bit familiar and rightly so—it is a slightly altered retelling of *The High and the Mighty*. (Dir: Joseph Pevney, 105 mins.)

Crowd Roars, The (1932)*** James Cagney, Joan Blondell, Frank McHugh, Eric Linden, Ann Dvorak, Guy Kibbee. And so will Cagney fans as he portrays a dauntless car racer in this fast-paced melodrama jazzed up with actual footage of famous drivers of the time. Jimmy plays an independent cuss who won't settle down. (Dir: Howard Hawks, 85 mins.)

Crowd Roars, The (1938)**½ Robert Taylor, Frank Morgan, Edward Arnold, Maureen O'Sullivan, Lionel Stander, Jane Wyman. An alcoholic papa induces his son to put up his dukes in the fight game, but sonny boy unfortunately ends up sparring with greedy mobsters and promoters. Lacks punch. (Dir: Richard Thorpe, 92 mins.)

Crowhaven Farm (MTV 1970)**½ Hope Lange, Paul Burke, Lloyd Bochner. Thriller dealing with witchcraft and the supernatural. Hope Lange and Paul Burke inherit a farm, which becomes the setting for some very strange happenings. (Dir: Walter Grauman, 73 mins.)

Crucible, The (France, 1958)***½ Simone Signoret, Yves Montand, Mylene Demongeot. A gripping version of Arthur Miller's memorable play about the Salem witch trials and how a young girl's jealousy caused innocent people to be condemned to death. Miller's play was written as a searing commentary on the evils of McCarthyism in America in the 1950s. This movie was ultimately made in France because the prize-winning playwright was blacklisted in America and blackballed by Hollywood at that time. AKA: **Witches of Salem.** (Dir: Raymond Rouleau, 120 mins.)

Crucible of Horror (Great Britain, 1970)*** Michael Gough, Yvonne Mitchell, Sharon Gurney. Tight, chilling tingler. Mother and daughter plan murder of sadistic father. Ending disappoints. (Dir: Viktors Ritelis, 91 mins.) †

Crucified Lovers, The—See: Chikamatsu Monogatari

Cruel Sea, The (Great Britian, 1953)**** Jack Hawkins, Denholm Elliot, Stanley Baker, Alec McCowen. One of the great war movies. Determined Hawkins, in an emotional performance, commands crew of a British warship in the North Atlantic during WWII. German U-boats provide menace; extraordinary action sequences give power to film's semidocumentary tone. Hopes and fears of Hawkins' men add to an emotional sense of bravery. Well worth seeing. (Dir: Charles Frend, 121 mins.) †

Cruel Story of Youth (Japan, 1960)***½ Yusuke Kawazu, Miyuki Kuwano, Yoshiko Kuga. American culture influences director Nagisa Oshima's masterful tale of bored middle-class teens who extort money from adults, shattering traditional Japanese values. Oshima's expressive hand-held camera mixes with long shots of oppressive settings nearly drained of color, including a leaden sky never pierced by the sun's rays. AKA: **Naked Youth.** (97 mins.)

Cruel Swamp (1956)*½ Carole Matthews, Touch (Mike) Connors, Beverly Garland, Marie Windsor. Three tough babes trudge through a swamp in quest of their hidden stolen loot after they break out of prison. Violent but undistinguished early Roger Corman effort, shot in ten days in Louisiana. AKA: **Swamp Women** and **Swamp Diamonds.** (73 mins.) †

Cruel Tower (1956)*** John Ericson, Mari Blanchard. Drifter takes a job as a steeplejack, incurs jealousy over a girl. Suspenseful melodrama with some hair-raising scenes showing the steeplejacks at their work. (Dir: Lew Landers, 80 mins.)

Cruising (1980)½ Al Pacino, Paul Sorvino, Richard Cox, Karen Allen. Don't pick this one up. Director William Friedkin pussyfoots around the gay subject matter and doesn't even manage to create any suspense. A policeman may or may not be taking on the identity of a killer he's pursuing in a case involving the brutal slayings of homosexuals in New York City. (106 mins.) †

Cruise into Terror (MTV 1978)* Ray Milland, Hugh O'Brien, Lynda Day George, Christopher George. If you cross "Love Boat" with *The Exorcist* you might come up with this TV film. A Caribbean cruise ship runs into bizarre happenings resulting in death when an ancient sarcophagus is found. (Dir: Bruce Kessler, 104 mins.) †

Crusades, The (1935)**½ Loretta Young, Henry Wilcoxon, Ian Keith, Katherine DeMille, C. Aubrey Smith. DeMille epic about the third crusade is lavish, and fairly entertaining. History is twisted a bit too much in favor of romance. (Dir: Cecil B. DeMille, 123 min.)

Crusoe (1989)*** Aidan Quinn, Adé Sapara, Hepburn Graham. Daniel Defoe's *Robinson Crusoe* refashioned as a gentle parable about race relations. There's no Friday here as shipwrecked slave trader Crusoe learns about human dignity through his dealings with the natives. (Dir: Caleb Deschanel, 95 mins.) †

Cry-Baby (1990)*** Johnny Depp, Amy Locane, Susan Tyrell, Polly Bergen, Iggy Pop, Ricki Lake, Traci Lords, Kim McGuire. Follow-up to director John Waters's breakthrough hit *Hairspray* is a splashy parody of '50s juvenile delinquent pictures with nary a hint of Waters's usual acid sarcasm, though it does have an eye-catching look, some amusing send-ups of teen-movie clichés, and a dream cast of camp performers. Waters devotes an inordinate amount of time (and all the musical production numbers) to young lovers Depp and Locane, unwisely slighting the other teens and their wonderfully neurotic parents. (85 mins.) †

Cry Baby Killer (1958)**½ Jack Nicholson, Brett Halsey. Teenager thinks he has killed, holes up in a storeroom with hostages. Alert direction, capable acting. Nicholson's debut. (Dir: Justus Addiss, 62 mins.)

Cry Danger (1951)*** Dick Powell, Rhonda Fleming. Released from prison, a man attempts to prove he was innocent of robbery. Fast, tough melodrama, very good. (Dir: Richard Parrish, 79 mins.) †

Cry for Happy (1961)**½ Glenn Ford, Donald O'Connor, Miyoshi Umeki. Through a misunderstanding a group of Navy men living it up in a geisha house is forced to turn its paradise into an orphanage to cool the brass. Mildly amusing service comedy. (Dir: George Marshall, 110 mins.)

Cry for Help, A (MTV 1975)**½ Robert Culp, Elayne Heilveil, Chuck McCann. Interesting drama about a cynical radio phone-show host. When an 18-year-old girl indicates she's about to do away with herself, a barrage of calls starts a race with the clock to find the potential suicide. (Dir: Daryl Duke, 72 mins.)

Cry for Help, A: The Tracey Thurman Story (MTV 1989)**½ Nancy McKeon, Dale Midkiff, Graham Jarvis, Yvette Heyden. Graphic domestic-violence drama based on a true case that led to a Connecticut law protecting abused wives. A dramatic attack sequence and the subsequent court case maintain interest throughout. (Dir: Robert Markowitz, 96 mins.)

Cry for Love, A (MTV 1980)*** Susan Blakely, Powers Boothe. Hollywood divorcée pops pills and finds her equal in a clever alcoholic. Blakely becomes a convincing bundle of jangled nerves, and Boothe plays the drunk with a flair. A nightmarish dissection of addictive behavior. (Dir: Paul Wendkos, 93 mins.)†

Cry For Me, Billy (1972)**½ Cliff Potts, Xochitl, Harry Dean Stanton, Don Wilbanks. Young gunslinger trying to reform comes to the aid of an Indian girl, the last survivor of a massacre by the U.S. army. Alternately violent and sentimental western with a sympathetic treatment of native Americans. Cinematography by Jorden Cronenworth. AKA: **Count Your Bullets.** (Dir: William A. Graham, 93 mins.)†

Cry for the Strangers (MTV 1982)*½ Patrick Duffy, Cindy Pickett, Lawrence Pressman, Claire Makis, Brian Keith. Muddled mystery in a craggy Pacific coastal town. The plot elements include ghosts, a young boy, violent storms, suspicious deaths, and a visiting psychiatrist and his wife. (Dir: Peter Medak, 104 mins.)

Cry Freedom (1987)**** Kevin Kline, Denzel Washington, Penelope Wilton. A stirring, stunning exploration of how apartheid affects both blacks and whites in South Africa, done on an epic scale but never losing sight of the personal concerns of its characters. Kline plays African newspaper editor Donald Woods, who in 1975 met and befriended black activist Stephen Biko (an excellent performance by Washington). After the police murdered Biko, Woods's pursuit of an inquest led to his persecution by the government. (Dir: Richard Attenborough, 157 mins.)†

Cry from the Mountain (1985)* James Cavan, Wes Parker, Rita Walter, Chris Kidd. Family drama with a heavy religious message, brought to you by the Reverend Billy Graham. A father and son take a camping trip into the Alaskan wilderness, where the father plans to break the news of his impending divorce. There they meet a lonely trapper who lives for his faith. Plot and acting are strictly subservient to the message, which is none too subtle. (Dir: James F. Collier, 78 mins.)†

Cry Havoc (1943)**½ Margaret Sullavan, Ann Sothern, Fay Bainter, Marsha Hunt, Ella Raines, Joan Blondell, Frances Gifford. All-female cast in this occasionally moving war melodrama about women who served tirelessly as nurses at Bataan. (Dir: Richard Thorpe, 97 mins.)

Cry in the Dark, A (1988)***½ Meryl Streep, Sam Neill, Bruce Myles. Another excellent turn from Streep, as an Australian mother accused of murdering her baby. Based on a true story (previously filmed as *Who Killed Baby Azaria?*), the powerful film details the mother's lynching in the press because she isn't properly submissive. (Dir: Fred Schepisi, 121 mins.)†

Cry in the Night, A (1956)** Edmond O'Brien, Natalie Wood, Brian Donlevy, Raymond Burr. A mentally unbalanced man kidnaps the daughter of a policeman, and police try to track them down before it's too late. (Dir: Frank Tuttle, 75 mins.)

Cry in the Wild, A (1990)**½ Jared Rushton, Pamela Sue Martin, Stephen Meadows, Ned Beatty. Generally good nature adventure about a thirteen-year-old boy, the sole survivor of a plane crash, who has to survive in a northern California forest using only his wits. Subplot of the boy's trying to come to grips with his parents' divorce seems like a misguided attempt to modernize an old-fashioned type of tale. Rushton *(Big)* is fine in a demanding role. (Dir: Mark Griffiths, 81 mins.)†

Cry in the Wilderness, A (MTV 1974)**½ George Kennedy, Joanna Pettet, Lee H. Montgomery, Collin Wilcox-Horne. Kennedy plays an Oregon farmer who, bitten by a skunk, locks himself in the barn for fear that he will go mad from rabies and attack his family. Then the river starts to rise. . . . (Dir: Gordon Hessler, 90 mins.)

Cry of Battle (1963)** Van Heflin, Rita Moreno, James MacArthur. Wealthy lad earns his mettle when he joins a guerrilla unit in the Philippines during World War II. War drama never gets out of the routine rut despite local color, fairly effective performances. Filmed near Manila. (Dir: Irving Lerner, 99 mins.)

Cry of the Banshee (Great Britain, 1970)**½ Vincent Price, Elisabeth Bergner, Hugh Griffith. Vincent Price rolls his eyes and snarls in his inimitable fashion in still another chiller-diller horror film.

In this one, he's a British magistrate who dabbles in heinous deeds during his off-hours. (Dir: Gordon Hessler, 87 mins.)†

Cry of the City (1948)*** Richard Conte, Victor Mature, Shelley Winters, Debra Paget. Atmosphere is everything (the script is a drag) in this remake of *Manhattan Melodrama* in which two pals from the slums grow up on opposite sides of the law. Though director Robert Siodmak's films lack lasting impact, his style is striking and effective. (96 mins.)

Cry of the Hunted (1953)**½ Vittorio Gassman, Polly Bergen, Barry Sullivan. Gassman's performance as an escaped convict trudging through the swamps gives some credulity to this otherwise melodramatic yarn about the hunter and the hunted. (Dir: Joseph H. Lewis, 79 mins.)

Cry of the Innocent (MTV 1980)**½ Rod Taylor, Joanna Pettet, Cyril Cusack, Nigel Davenport. A fair action yarn by expert Frederick Forsyth about man whose family is wiped out by a plane crash. (Dir: Michael O'Herlihy, 104 mins.)†

Cry of the Penguins (Great Britain, 1971)*** John Hurt, Hayley Mills, Dudley Sutton, Tony Britton. Unusual film revolving around a self-centered man's study of penguin life in the Antarctic. Doesn't sound like much, but the brash character played by Hurt gives it a lot of zest, and there are fascinating shots of the penguins and their gull adversaries. AKA: **Mr. Forbush and the Penguins.** (Dirs: Al Viola, Roy Boulting, Arne Sucksdorff, 101 mins.)

Cry of the Werewolf (1944)*½ Stephen Crane, Nina Foch, Osa Massen, Fritz Leiber. Nina plays the werewolf and she kills more than her share. Mediocre horror film. (Dir: Henry Levin, 63 mins.)

Cry Panic (MTV 1974)*** John Forsythe, Anne Francis, Earl Holliman. Good mystery. Forsythe accidentally hits and kills a man on a highway, but when he leaves the scene of the accident to call the police, the body disappears. (Dir: James Goldstone, 78 mins.)

Cry Rape! (MTV 1973)** Andrea Marcovicci, Peter Coffield. Based on a true story, this veers away from the rape problem to that of the innocent man wrongly identified in the line-up, and simply becomes a variation on the old mistaken identity plot. (Dir: Corey Allen, 90 mins.)

Crystal Ball, The (1943)** Paulette Goddard, Ray Milland. A gal from Texas takes a job as a fortune-teller's assistant, where she snags her man. Just passable comedy, with the players better than the script. (Dir: Elliott Nugent, 81 mins.)

Crystal Heart (1987)**½ Tawny Kitaen, Lee Curreri, Lloyd Bochner. Rich kid Curreri sets out to win the heart of rock singer Kitaen. The only problem: he has no immune system, and must live in a hermetically sealed glass room because physical contact with another human being will kill him. (Dir: Gil Bettman, 103 mins.)†

Cry Terror! (1958)**½ James Mason, Inger Stevens, Rod Steiger, Angie Dickinson. Crafty criminal forces an electronics expert to aid him in an elaborate extortion plot. Occasionally suspenseful crime drama. (Dir: Andrew L. Stone, 96 mins.)

Cry the Beloved Country (Great Britain, 1951)***½ Canada Lee, Charles Carson. Black Reverend in the back country of South Africa journeys to the city, only to find his people living in squalor, and his son a criminal. Powerful drama. (Dir: Zoltan Korda, 105 mins.)

Cry Tough (1959)**½ John Saxon, Linda Cristal. Only moderately interesting drama about the young juvenile delinquent element which springs up in minority groups due to racial hatred. (Dir: Paul Stanley, 83 mins.)

Cry Uncle (1971)*** Allen Garfield, Madeleine de la Roux, Devin Goldenberg. With his neophyte nephew in tow, an overweight detective tackles a millionaire's blackmail problem. Hilariously tasteless and sleazy parody of the private-eye genre. (Dir: John G. Avildsen, 87 mins.)†

Cry Vengeance (1954)*** Mark Stevens, Martha Hyer. Detective seeks revenge for the murder of his wife and child. Tense crime drama. (Dir: Mark Stevens, 83 mins.)†

Cry Wolf (1947)**½ Errol Flynn, Barbara Stanwyck, Richard Basehart, Geraldine Brooks. Woman has a creepy time when she goes to her late husband's estate to claim her inheritance. Hackneyed thriller. (Dir: Peter Godfrey, 83 mins.)

Cuba (1979)*** Sean Connery, Brooke Adams, Chris Sarandon. Connery plays a security advisor from England who rekindles a love affair with sultry (but married) Adams, while the Batista government crumbles in the background. Adams and Connery simmer in this handsome-looking film. (Dir: Richard Lester, 126 mins.)

Cuban Love Song (1931)** Lawrence Tibbett, Lupe Velez, Jimmy Durante, Ernest Torrence. Tibbett has an outstanding supporting cast—but the energy level is minimal. Story of a marine on leave in Cuba; he returns years later to claim his illegitimate child, whose mother has died. (Dir: W. S. Van Dyke II, 86 mins.)

Cuban Rebel Girls—See: **Assault of the Rebel Girls**

Cuckoos, The (1930)*** Bert Wheeler, Robert Woolsey, June Clyde, Hugh Trevor, Dorothy Lee. One of the better

Wheeler and Woolsey vehicles features the duo as phony fortune-tellers hired to find a kidnapped heiress. Full of wacky situations and musical numbers. (Dir: Paul Sloane, 90 mins.)

Cujo (1983)*** Dee Wallace, Christopher Stone, Daniel Hugh Kelly, Danny Pintauro, Ed Lauter. Although designed with skill, *Cujo*'s bark is worse than its bite. The problem is with the material, about a gentle Saint Bernard turned rabid killer. Unfortunately, the supernatural elements in Stephen King's novel were jettisoned in this screen version. What we're left with is a shaggy dog story with fangs. Still, director Lewis *(Alligator)* Teague generates occasional suspense, and Wallace manages to create a sympathetic heroine. (97 mins.)†

Cul-de-Sac (Great Britain, 1966)*** Donald Pleasence, Lionel Stander, Jack MacGowran, Françoise Dorleac. This grim but often hilarious black comedy is about a namby-pamby innkeeper (Pleasance) and his oversexed young wife. Their domicile is invaded by two aging hoods, who're awaiting orders from their leader. A unique blend of claustrophobia and comedy. (Dir: Roman Polanski, 111 mins.)

Culpepper Cattle Company, The (1972)**½ Gary Grimes, Billy "Green" Bush, Luke Askew, Bo Hopkins. A routine yarn about the "coming of age," in post-Civil War Texas, of a young man who signs on as a cook's helper on a huge cattle drive. (Dir: Dick Richards, 92 mins.)†

Cult of the Cobra (1955)** Faith Domergue, Richard Long. Combination murder mystery-horror film about superstitions and curses. Faith Domergue plays a mysterious woman who has the power to change into a snake. (Dir: Francis D. Lyon, 90 mins.)

Cult of the Damned—See: Angel, Angel, Down We Go

Cult of the Dead—See: Snake People

Cure for Love (Great Britain, 1950)**½ Robert Donat, Renee Asherson. A returning soldier finds romantic complications in his home town. Pleasant comedy. (Dir: Robert Donat, 97 mins.)

Curfew (1988)** Kyle Richards, Wendell Wellman, John Putch, Bert Remsen. Two brothers, jailed for a rape-murder, break out and head for the house of the district attorney who convicted them, torturing his family in revenge. Moderately suspenseful plot is hurt by an over-abundance of violence. (Dir: Gary Winick, 86 mins.)†

Curiosity Kills (MCTV 1990)*** C. Thomas Howell, Rae Dawn Chong, Courtney Cox, Jeff Fahey. Ingredients of Hitchcock's *Rear Window* enhance this tight suspense yarn about an aspiring photographer who suspects his new neighbor is responsible for the suicide of a former tenant. Real-life married couple (Howell and Chong) make an engaging pair of sleuths. (Dir: Colin Bucksey, 86 mins.)†

Curly Top (1935)*** Shirley Temple, John Boles, Rochelle Hudson, Jane Darwell, Arthur Treacher. An orphaned moppet (Shirley) is adopted by a millionaire (Boles) who falls in love with her beautiful sister (Hudson). He also happens to be a songwriter, and Shirley sings "Animal Crackers in My Soup." One of the better Temples. (Dir: Irving Cummings, 74 mins.)†

Curse, The (1987)**½ Wil Wheaton, Claude Akins, Malcolm Danare, Cooper Huckabee. Actor David Keith makes a striking directorial debut in this horror story about a meteorite that crashes into a farm and turns the inhabitants into lunatics. From the same H. P. Lovecraft story previously filmed as *Die, Monster, Die!* AKA: The Farm. (90 mins.)†

Curse II: The Bite (U.S.-Italy-Japan, 1989)*½ Jill Schoelen, J. Eddie Peck, Jamie Farr, Savina Gersak, Bo Svenson, Sydney Lassick. Combination of a bite from a snake in a nuclear testing zone and bad medicine result in a victim's arm turning into a giant snake. Inane plot redeemed slightly by over-the-top special effects. Aside from the same producer, no relation to *The Curse*. AKA: The Bite. (Dir: Fred Goodwin, 98 mins.)†

Curse of Dracula, The (1959)** Francis Lederer, Ray Stricklyn. Still another film about the most famous vampire of them all. This tale takes place in the U.S., but the stock characters are all intact. AKA: The Return of Dracula. (Dir: Paul Landres, 77 mins.)

Curse of Frankenstein, The (Great Britain, 1957)*** Peter Cushing, Christopher Lee, Hazel Court, Robert Urquhart, Valerie Gaunt. The dynamic duo of British horror films, Cushing and Lee, join forces in the initial entry in Hammer Studio's series of Frankenstein films. (Dir: Freddie Francis, 93 mins.)†

Curse of King Tut's Tomb, The (MTV 1980)** Raymond Burr, Eva Marie Saint, Wendy Hiller. Hard to take seriously. Chuckles and terror don't mix, as cobras strike and scorpions attack. Burr in dark makeup, wearing a towel on his head, sets the tone as the scheming villain. (Dir: Philip Leacock, 98 mins.)†

Curse of the Black Widow (MTV 1977)*½ June Allyson, Tony Franciosa, Patty Duke Astin. Lots of TV names—Donna Mills, June Lockhart, Max Gail, Vic Morrow, Sid Caesar, Roz Kelly—do what little they can in this familiar murder mystery in which a series of people are killed in the same bizarre fashion. (Dir: Dan Curtis, 104 mins.) †

Curse of the Cat People, The (1944)*** Simone Simone, Kent Smith. Child whose mother was cursed is regarded as strange by her playmates and parents. Odd little drama has moments of genuine quality. Sequel to *Cat People*. (Dirs: Gunther Fritsch, Robert Wise, 70 mins.) †

Curse of the Crimson Altar—See: **Crimson Cult, The**

Curse of the Crying Woman, The (Mexico, 1960)* Rosita Arenas, Abel Salazar. Young bride finds she has inherited a legacy of terror when she visits the home of her aunt. Ridiculous horror thriller. (Dir: Rafael Baledon, 74 mins.)

Curse of the Demon (Great Britain, 1958) ***½ Dana Andrews, Peggy Cummins. One of the finest horror films ever made. Misty, ominous English locations and a fine cast make this suspenseful and involving. Andrews is a dedicated skeptic investigating a deadly supernatural cult, with unexpected results. (Dir: Jacques Tourneur, 95 mins.) †

Curse of the Evil Spirit—See: **Chooper, The**

Curse of the Faceless Man (1958)* Richard Anderson, Elaine Edwards. Horror-science-fiction story with completely implausible plot twists and amateur acting. (Dir: Edward L. Cahn, 66 mins.)

Curse of the Fly, The (1965)* Brian Donlevy, Carole Gray, George Baker, Michael Graham, Jeremy Wilkins. Rusty thriller finds Brian Donlevy struggling with the intricacies of the fourth dimension and assorted weirdos. (Dir: Don Sharp, 85 mins.)

Curse of the Living Corpse (1964)*½ Roy Scheider, Helen Ware. Messy plot concerns several murders that occur after death of a millionaire. Film and corpse both die quickly. (Dir: Del Tenney, 84 mins.) †

Curse of the Living Dead—See: **Curse of the Living Corpse**

Curse of the Mummy's Tomb, The (Great Britain, 1964)** Terence Morgan, Ronald Howard. Mummy returns to life to commence a reign of terror. Undistinguished horror thriller. (Dir: Michael Carreras, 80 mins.)

Curse of the Pink Panther, The (1983)** David Niven, Ted Wass, Robert Wagner, Capucine, Herbert Lom. Some of the slapstick gags are surprisingly inventive, but the series was running out of steam. David Niven's last performance. (Dir: Blake Edwards, 109 mins.) †

Curse of the Queerwolf (1989)**½ Michael Palazzolo, Kent Butler, Taylor Whitney, Forrest J. Ackerman. Tastelessly funny spoof about a straight hero who becomes a gay werewolf. (Dir: Mark Pirro, 90 mins.) †

Curse of the Undead (1959)** Eric Fleming, Kathleen Crowley, Michael Pate. Intriguing mixture of western and "Dracula"-type horror yarn as a vampire stalks the West. (Dir: Edward Dein, 79 mins.)

Curse of the Voodoo (U.S.-Great Britain, 1965)** Bryant Halliday, Dennis Price, Lisa Daniely. White hunter is the recipient of a curse when he ventures into forbidden territory. Fairish thriller has the asset of some well-constructed suspense scenes. (Dir: Lindsay Shonteff, 77 mins.)

Curse of the Werewolf (Great Britain, 1961)*** Clifford Evans, Oliver Reed. Young lad with questionable antecedents is discovered to be a werewolf. Superior shocker, with more adult ramifications than usual in the plotting. Gruesome, but good. (Dir: Terence Fisher, 91 mins.) †

Curtain Call at Cactus Creek (1950)**½ Donald O'Connor, Gale Storm, Eve Arden, Vincent Price. Amusing romp about a traveling troupe of actors who run into trouble wherever they set up to perform. The melodramas staged by the troupe are the funniest things in the movie. (Dir: Charles Lamont, 86 mins.)

Curtain Rises, The (French, 1938)*** Louis Jouvet, Claude Dauphin, Odette Joyeux, Bernard Blier. Melodramatic plot about jealousy and murder among acting students at the Paris Conservatory is worth seeing both for its capturing of bohemian Paris society and the wonderful performance of Jouvet as a wise professor. (Dir: Marc Allégret, 90 mins.)

Curtains (Canada, 1983)** Samantha Eggar, John Vernon, Linda Thorson. Six actresses spend the weekend at the house of a domineering director who wants them to test for one leading role. Naturally, someone is willing to kill for the part. (Dir: Jonathan Stryker, 89 mins.) †

Curtain Up (Great Britain, 1952)**½ Robert Morley, Margaret Rutherford. Small theater group is plagued by an aunt of the backer, who has written a very bad play. Pleasing comedy that doesn't quite succeed. (Dir: Ralph Smart, 81 mins.)

Curucu, Beast of the Amazon (1956)** John Bromfield, Beverly Garland. Plantation foreman sets out to track down a legendary monster who is terrorizing the natives. (Dir: Curt Siodmak, 76 mins.)

Custer of the West (1968)**½ Robert Shaw, Mary Ure, Robert Ryan. Story of the 7th Cavalry general who was wiped out at Little Big Horn. Made in Spain; sprawling narrative redeemed somewhat by Shaw's thespic capabilities as Custer. (Dir: Robert Siodmak, 146 mins.)

Cut and Run (1986)* Lisa Blount, Leonard Mann, Willie Aames, Karen Black,

Michael Berryman. A lame-brain action-pic about an intrepid reporter and her faithful cameraman checking out a drug ring in the jungles of Latin America. (Dir: Ruggero Deodato, 87 mins.)†

Cutter (MTV 1972)* Peter De Anda, Cameron Mitchell, Barbara Rush, Robert Webber. De Anda plays a low-keyed black private eye who must locate a missing pro football player. Naturally, the syndicate is in on it. (Dir: Richard Irving, 78 mins.)

Cutter and Bone—See: **Cutter's Way**

Cutter's Trail (MTV 1971)* John Gavin, Manuel Padilla, Jr., Marisa Pavan, Beverly Garland, Joseph Cotten. Formula western about U.S. marshal who returns to his town to find it nearly destroyed by Mexican bandits, and vows to track 'em down. (Dir: Vincent McEveety, 104 mins.)

Cutter's Way (1981)***½ Jeff Bridges, John Heard, Lisa Eichhorn, Ann Dusenberry, Stephen Elliott. Director Ivan Passer's offbeat mystery has a pervasive atmosphere of cynicism and disillusionment rarely seen in Hollywood films. Seedy gigolo Bridges uncovers a murderer but doesn't want to get involved. His pal Heard, a crippled Vietnam vet, pursues the wealthy killer in a desperate attempt to salvage his own hated existence. AKA: **Cutter and Bone**. (109 mins.)†

Cutting Class (1989)**½ Donovan Leitch, Jill Schoelen, Brad Pitt, Roddy McDowell, Martin Mull. Above-average slasher movie with a high school setting. Is oddball Leitch behind the series of killings? The suspenseful plot is more carefully worked out than most efforts in this genre. (Dir: Rospo Pallenberg, 90 mins.)†

Cyborg 2087 (1966)* Michael Rennie, Wendell Corey. Cyborgs, beings that are half man and half machine, revolt in the year 2087 and travel back to 1966 to prevent their own creation. (Dir: Franklin Andreon, 86 mins.)

Cycle Savages, The (1969)* Bruce Dern, Melody Patterson, Chris Robinson, Scott Brady. A savage slice of motorcycle madness with Dern at his most bug-eyed. (Dir: Bill Brame, 82 mins.)

Cyclone (1986)* Heather Thomas, Jeffrey Combs, Ashley Ferrare, Martin Landau. The girlfriend of a murdered inventor tries to get his new energy-synthesizing motorcycle to the government, pursued by double agents and other bad guys. No whirlwind of excitement here. (Dir: Fred Olen Ray, 87 mins.)†

Cyclops (1957)*½ Gloria Talbott, James Craig. Jungle search party finds their subject turned into a giant one-eyed monster. Humdrum thriller. (Dir: Bert I. Gordon, 75 mins.)†

Cynthia (1947)** Elizabeth Taylor, Gene Lockhart, George Murphy. Syrupy tale of a sickly girl who proves she's normal and, by so doing, solves everybody's problems. (Dir: Robert Z. Leonard, 99 mins.)

Cyrano de Bergerac (1950)*** Jose Ferrer, Mala Powers, William Prince, Elena Verdugo. The classic play about the soldier of fortune with the oversize proboscis, and of his unrequited love for the beautiful Roxanne. Ferrer won the Oscar for his flamboyant, moving performance, though production short-comings and uninspired casting of other roles detract. (Dir: Michael Gordon, 112 mins.)†

Cyrano de Bergerac (France, 1990)**** Gerard Depardieu, Anne Brochet, Vincent Perez, Jacques Weber, Roland Bertin. A visually ravishing, sumptuous, and altogether wonderful version of Edmond Rostand's classic tearjerker. This most recent film adaptation tells the story of the gallant 17th-century French swashbuckler who hesitates declaring his abiding love for his much younger cousin Roxanne until it is too late. As Cyrano, one of the greatest virtuoso turns in the history of theater, Depardieu is enthralling, deeply moving, and poignant, gracefully bearing his most celebrated schnoz of Pinocchio proportions. Depardieu, a Cyrano for the ages, was nominated for an Academy Award. (Dir: Jean-Paul Rappeneau, 135 mins.)†

Da (1988)***½ Barnard Hughes, Martin Sheen, William Hickey. Heartwarming story of an Americanized Irishman who returns to the old sod for his irascible stepfather's funeral. The day after the event, the old man's ghost turns up, vital and talkative as ever. (Dir: Matt Clark, 102 mins.)†

D.A.—Conspiracy to Kill, The (MTV 1970) *½ Robert Conrad, William Conrad, Belinda Montgomery. Robert Conrad plays a deputy district attorney working on cases from Los Angeles police files. Conrad teams with chief prosecutor William Conrad to unravel murders involving a meek druggist. (Dir: Paul Krasny, 104 mins.)

Dad (1989)***½ Jack Lemmon, Ted Danson, Olympia Dukakis, Kathy Baker, Kevin Spacey, Ethan Hawke, Zakes Mokae, Chris Lemmon. Businessman Danson is forced by guilt to care temporarily for his aging, infirm father (Lemmon, with a terrific makeup job); in the process the two revitalize each other. Based on the William Wharton novel. (Dir: Gary David Goldberg, 117 mins.)†

Daddy (MTV 1987)**½ Dermot Mulroney,

John Karlen, Tess Harper, Patricia Arquette, Danny Aiello. Message movie about high school teens who become parents. Mulroney portrays a teenager who has to abandon his lifetime goal of becoming a musician when he becomes "daddy." (Dir: John Herzfeld, 104 mins.)

Daddy, I Don't Like It Like This (MTV 1978)*** Talia Shire, Burt Young, Doug McKeon. Often perceptive handling of a depressing, downbeat subject. Written by actor Young, who plays the laborer father, it centers on the bickering of a married couple and the effect it has on their young son (McKeon, who gives the film's best performance). (Dir: Adell Aldrich, 104 mins.)

Daddy Long Legs (1955)*** Fred Astaire, Leslie Caron. Delightful musical romance. Debonair Astaire has seldom had a better dancing partner than charming and graceful Caron—their numbers are the film's highlights. The plot borders on modern fairy tale—a French orphan is subsidized by a wealthy bachelor with the stipulation that his identity be kept secret. (Dir: Jean Negulesco, 126 mins.)†

Daddy Nostalgia (France, 1990)*** Dirk Bogarde, Jane Birkin, Odette Laure, Emmanuelle Bataille, Charlotte Kady, Michele Minns. Beautifully realized film about a family coming to terms with the illness of its male parent. Bogarde is wonderful as the man facing his own mortality. (Dir: Bertrand Tavernier, 105 mins.)

Daddy's Boys (1988)* Daryl Haney, Laura Burkett, Raymond J. Barry. Ex-farmer and his two sons go on a crime spree during the Depression. Another movie made by producer Roger Corman in a few weeks simply because he had a leftover set. (Dir: Joe Minion, 85 mins.)†

Daddy's Deadly Darling (1972)* Marc Lawrence, Toni Lawrence, Jesse Vint, Katherine Ross. The owner of a roadside café and a girl on the lam form a partnership: she kills people, he feeds the bodies to his pigs. AKA: **Pigs.** (Dir: Marc Lawrence, 86 mins.)†

Daddy's Dyin' . . . Who's Got the Will? (1990)*** Beau Bridges, Beverly D'Angelo, Tess Harper, Judge Reinhold, Amy Wright, Molly McClure, Keith Carradine, Bert Remsen. Adroit adaptation of Del Shores's play set in a small Texas town, where four squabbling siblings have gathered for the reading of their father's will. He's not quite dead yet, though, so in the meantime they relive old grudges and invent new ones. Strong ensemble cast makes this comedy-drama live. (Dir: Jack Fisk, 95 mins.)†

Daddy's Gone A-Hunting (1969)**½ Carol White, Paul Burke, Scott Hylands. Live-

ly suspense tale. White has her hands full when her ex-lover shows up bent on revenge because she had an abortion during their time together. The mad young man (Hylands) kidnaps the now happily married White's new baby and the chase is on. (Dir: Mark Robson, 108 mins.)†

Daffy Duck's Movie: Fantastic Island (1983)** Fourth compilation of Warner Brothers cartoons (featuring Daffy, Bugs Bunny, Yosemite Sam, Foghorn Leghorn, Speedy Gonzales, Pepe LePew, Tweety, and Sylvester) links ten lesser cartoons with a spoof of TV's "Fantasy Island." Daffy is better as an irksome troublemaker than as a host. (Dir: Friz Freleng, 78 mins.)†

Dagora, the Space Monster (Japan, 1965)* Another monster from outer space. This time the thing even interferes with some gangland operations. Pretty silly. (Dir: Ishiro Honda, 80 mins.)

Dain Curse, The (MTV 1978)**½ James Coburn, Hector Elizondo, Jason Miller, Jean Simmons, Dave Stewart. Dashiell Hammett wrote this mystery yarn fifty years ago. The production is first class, but the story about multiple murders, an alleged family curse, and bogus religious cults only comes alive in spurts. Originally shown as a three-parter, running 312 mins. (Dir: E. W. Swackhamer, 118 mins.)†

Daisy Kenyon (1947)*** Joan Crawford, Dana Andrews, Henry Fonda, Ruth Warrick, Peggy Ann Garner, Martha Stewart. A Cinderella soaper in which career-girl Crawford must choose either Andrews or Fonda. Otto Preminger's subtle direction presents a restrained love triangle. One of Crawford's last vulnerable roles. (99 mins.)

Daisy Miller (1974)*** Cybill Shepherd, Barry Brown, Mildred Natwick, Cloris Leachman, Eileen Brennan. An intelligent, visually stunning but curiously uninvolving adaptation of Henry James's superb novella about expatriate Americans in Europe and a nouveau riche American girl from Schenectady, colliding with European high society circa 1879. (Dir: Peter Bogdanovich, 91 mins.)†

Dakota (1945)**½ John Wayne, Vera Hruba Ralston, Ward Bond, Walter Brennan, Mike Mazurki, Hugo Haas. Middle-grade Wayne vehicle, with rascally railroad companies trying to cheat homesteaders out of their land. (Dir: Joseph Kane, 82 mins.)

Dakota (1987)** Lou Diamond Phillips, Eli Cummins, DeeDee Norton. A pre–La Bamba Phillips stars as a troubled teen on the run from his past who takes a job on a Texas ranch where he learns maturity. Sincere but predictable, the type of thing Disney made in the early sixties. (Dir: Fred Holmes, 97 mins.)†

Dakota Incident (1956)**½ Linda Darnell, Dale Robertson, John Lund. Stagecoach wards off Indian attacks. Fairly good western; good performances. (Dir: Lewis R. Foster, 88 mins.)†

Dakota Lil (1950)**½ George Montgomery, Rod Cameron, Marie Windsor. Secret agent poses as an outlaw, enlists the aid of a beautiful lady forger to trap a bandit gang. (Dir: Lesley Selander, 88 mins.)

Daleks—Invasion Earth 2150 A.D.—See: **Invasion Earth 2150 A.D.**

Dallas (1950)**½ Gary Cooper, Ruth Roman, Steve Cochran. Cooper plays a man who comes to Dallas for revenge, in this moderately entertaining western drama. (Dir: Stuart Heisler, 94 mins.)

Dallas Cowboys Cheerleaders, The (MTV 1979)*½ Laraine Stephens, Jane Seymour, Bucky Dent, Ellen Bry. Corny, flashy melodrama about the inner workings of the Dallas Cowboys Cheerleaders. (Dir: Bruce Bilson, 104 mins.)

Dallas Cowboys Cheerleaders II, The (MTV 1980)* John Davidson, Laraine Stephens, Roxanne Gregory, Patti Ames. Are you dying to know all about the heartaches of the girls who become professional cheerleaders? Well, here's your chance. Tacky sequel. (Dir: Michael O'Herlihy, 104 mins.)

Dallas: The Early Years (MTV 1986)*** David Grant, Dale Midkiff, Molly Hagan, David Wilson, Hoyt Axton, Larry Hagman, Bill Duke, Geoffrey Lewis, Diane Franklin. Best for diehard fans of "Dallas." Compelling saga of the early lives and loves of the inhabitants of Southfork. (Dir: Larry Elikann, 180 mins.)

Dalton: Code of Vengeance—See: **Code of Vengeance**

Dalton: Code of Vengeance II (MTV 1986)** Charles Taylor, Donnelly Rhodes, Karen Lambry, Shannon Stein, Alex Harvey, Belinda Montgomery. A sequel to *Code of Vengeance*, the highly rated pilot film for a proposed series about a Vietnam vet traveling through the U.S. in an odyssey of good deeds. Actually, these are two episodes for the series that never materialized. (Dir: Alan Smithee, 104 mins.)

Daltons Ride Again, The (1945)** Alan Curtis, Lon Chaney, Jr., Kent Taylor, Noah Beery, Jr., Martha O'Driscoll, Jess Barker, Thomas Gomez, Milburn Stone. The outlaw brothers stage their last raid. Routine western. (Dir: Ray Taylor, 72 mins.)

Dam Busters, The (Great Britain, 1955) ***½ Richard Todd, Michael Redgrave. Excellent war drama about one of the most dangerous missions of WWII. (Dir: Michael Anderson, 102 mins.)†

Dames (1934)*** Joan Blondell, Ruby Keeler, Dick Powell, ZaSu Pitts, Hugh Herbert. A good Warner Bros. musical. Pitts adds a little variety; Busby Berkeley did the production numbers, which include "When You Were a Smile on Mother's Lips and a Twinkle in Your Daddy's Eye." (Dir: Ray Enright, 90 mins.)†

Damien—Omen II (1978)** William Holden, Lee Grant, Jonathan Scott-Taylor, Lew Ayres, Sylvia Sidney. The devil is still embodied in Damien, now a 13-year-old boarding school student. Fans of *The Omen* will note that Damien's victims are killed or nearly killed in typically grisly fashion every ten minutes or so. Followed by *The Final Conflict*. (Dir: Don Taylor, 107 mins.)†

Damien: The Leper Priest—See: **Father Damien: The Leper Priest**

Damnation Alley (1977)* Jan-Michael Vincent, George Peppard, Dominique Sanda, Paul Winfield. Bore about the survivors of a nuclear holocaust and their dangerous trek to Albany, where they suspect there is other life. (Dir: John Smight, 91 mins.)†

Damn Citizen (1958)**½ Keith Andes, Maggie Hayes, Gene Evans. Story based on fact of a World War II vet who is given a free hand to clean up crime and corruption in a state police organization. Done in documentary fashion, has a fairly good share of interest. (Dir: Robert Gordon, 88 mins.)

Damned, The (France, 1947)***½ Henri Vidal, Florence Marly, Kurt Kronefeld, Jo Dest, Anne Campion. Thriller about Nazi officers seizing U-boat to flee to South America as WWII nears end, kidnapping a French doctor who becomes hero of exciting, well-crafted story. Best Film, Cannes Festival, 1947. (Dir: René Clement, 105 mins.)

Damned, The (1963)—See: **These Are the Damned**

Damned, The (Italy-West Germany, 1969)*** Dirk Bogarde, Ingrid Thulin, Helmut Griem, Helmut Berger, Charlotte Rampling, Rene Koldehoff. Director Luchino Visconti's excessively operatic view of the rise of Nazism within a social climate of complete decadence. Bogarde and Thulin are corrupt munitions manufacturers done in by the perversions and machinations of young Berger, who does a drag schtick with panache. (155 mins.)†

Damned Don't Cry, The (1950)*** Joan Crawford, David Brian, Steve Cochran. Joan finds herself up to her mink in crime and corruption. Heavy Brian makes the going rougher for her but she knows the "damned don't cry." You might, though. (Dir: Vincent Sherman, 103 mins.)

Damned River (1989)*½ Stephen Shellen, Lisa Aliff, John Terlesky, Marc Poppel,

Louis Van Nierkerk. Four young white-water rafters on vacation in Africa have to fight for their lives when their guide turns against them in this lackluster rip-off of *Deliverance*. (Dir: Michael Schroeder, 95 mins.)†

Damn the Defiant! (Great Britain, 1962)*** Alec Guinness, Dirk Bogarde, Anthony Quayle. Commander of a fighting vessel faces the opposition of his second in command, a sadistic and cruel officer hated by the crew. Salty maritime costume drama with performances of high standard, interest maintained throughout. (Dir: Lewis Gilbert, 101 mins.)†

Damn Yankees (1958)*** Gwen Verdon, Tab Hunter, Ray Walston, Jean Stapleton, Russ Brown, Rae Allen, Shannon Bolin. A pleasant, spiritedly choreographed musical comedy about a baseball buff willing to sell his soul to Satan, so that his home team will have a chance at the pennant and World Series. (Dirs: George Abbott, Stanley Donen, 110 mins.)†

Damon and Pythias (U.S.-Italy, 1962)**½ Guy Williams, Don Burnett, Ilaria Occhini, Liana Orfei. The legend of a friendship between two men in Sicily in 400 B.C. (Dir: Curtis Bernhardt, 99 mins.)

Damsel in Distress, A (1937)**½ Fred Astaire, George Burns, Gracie Allen, Joan Fontaine, Ray Noble. A somewhat stodgy George Gershwin–scored musical set in England. Fontaine is the rather wan lead, playing an heiress Astaire thinks is a chorus girl. Burns and Allen are on hand in abundance, and even get to sing and dance. The songs, including "A Foggy Day" and "Nice Work If You Can Get It," are superb. (Dir: George Stevens, 101 mins.)†

D.A.: Murder One, The (MTV 1969)**½ Howard Duff, Robert Conrad, Diane Baker. A murder mystery in which the D.A.'s office tries to trap an attractive nurse (Diane Baker) suspected of multiple murders. (Dir: Jack Webb, 99 mins.)

Dance, Fools, Dance (1930)*** Joan Crawford, Clark Gable, Cliff Edwards. A society playgirl goes to work as a reporter after the stock market crash and nearly sleeps with a gangland boss to get a story. Tough, exciting gangster/newspaper melodrama finds Crawford and Gable at their liveliest. (Dir: Harry Beaumont, 82 mins.)†

Dance, Girl, Dance (1940)*** Maureen O'Hara, Lucille Ball, Ralph Bellamy. An original screen story by Vicki Baum, directed by Dorothy Arzner. Two girls are rivals in their careers, and in love with the same man. (90 mins.)†

Dance Hall (Great Britain, 1950)**½ Natasha Parry, Jane Hylton, Diana Dors, Petula Clark, Kay Kendall. Four factory girls break away from their squalid lives at night when they hang out at the local dance hall. (Dir: Charles Crichton, 78 mins.)

Dance Hall Racket (1954)½ Lenny Bruce, Honey Harlowe, Timothy Farrell, Sally Marr. An amazing oddball item about an ambitious hoodlum-murderer who owns a dance hall. (60 mins.)†

Dance Little Lady (Great Britain, 1954)**½ Mai Zetterling, Terence Morgan. Ballerina's career is halted by an accident, but she sees her daughter take up where she left off. (Dir: Val Guest, 87 mins.)

Dance of Death (Great Britain, 1968)*** Laurence Olivier, Geraldine McEwan, Robert Lang, Carolyn Jones. A filmed record of Laurence Olivier's farewell theatrical performance as the canny, psychotic captain of the August Strindberg play. (Dir: David Giles, 149 mins.)

Dance of Death—See: **House of Evil**

Dance of Hope (1989)***½ Powerful documentary about life under the right-wing military dictatorship that took over Chile (with U.S. help) in 1973. Eight women talk about their efforts to find family members who have "disappeared" under General Pinochet's rule. (Dir: Deborah Shaffer, 75 mins.)

Dance of the Dwarfs (1983)*½ Peter Fonda, Deborah Raffin, John Amos, Carlos Palomino. *African Queen* rip-off, detailing the relationship between scientist Raffin and grubby helicopter pilot Fonda, turns into a silly horror adventure when they run into a race of small, scaly monsters. AKA: **Jungle Heat.** (Dir: Gus Trikonis, 93 mins.)

Dance or Die (1988)* Ray Kieffer, Rebecca Barrington, Georgia Neu, Jerry Cleary. Wan tale of a Las Vegas choreographer whose addiction gets him into trouble with the mob. Why do we doubt that the name given in the credits is the director's real name? (Dir: Richard W. Munchkin, 81 mins.)†

Dancers (1987)* Mikhail Baryshnikov, Alessandra Ferri, Lynn Seymour. A world-famous ballet star (guess who?) toys with the affections of an innocent ballerina who teaches him a thing or two about unspoiled love. Unbearable except for diehard balletomanes. (Dir: Herbert Ross, 97 mins.)†

Dancers in the Dark (1932)** Miriam Hopkins, Jack Oakie. Dance hall girl with a past tries to prove she really loves a temperamental musician. Time tells on this oldie. (Dir: David Burton, 76 mins.)

Dances With Wolves (1990)**** Kevin Costner, Mary McDonnell, Graham Greene. An altogether remarkable drama and love story, that, to virtually everyone's surprise, was both a huge commercial success while simultaneously achieving overwhelming critical acclaim. Based on a 1986 novel of the same name by Michael Blake, *Wolves* is a pictorially stunning, if overly long saga of an American Civil War lieutenant who is moved to befriend an initially skeptical and hostile tribe of Plains Indians. Costner makes one of the most remarkable directorial debuts in many years. Mary McDonnell is wonderful playing a white woman who has been adopted by her tribe. A truly thrilling buffalo stampede is among the most memorable movie images in many years. Try to see this stunner in a movie theater, *not* on a tiny TV screen. Won seven Oscars, including Best Director and Best Picture. (Dir: Kevin Costner, 190 mins.)†

Dance with a Stranger (Great Britain, 1985)***½ Miranda Richardson, Rupert Everett, Ian Holm, Matthew Carroll. Evocative drama, based on the true story of Ruth Ellis, the last woman executed in Britain. Ellis (Richardson) falls in love with, becomes pregnant by, and eventually murders David Blakeley (Everett), the upper-class ne'er-do-well from whom she could not bear to part, in spite of the physical and emotional abuse he inflicted on her. (Dir: Mike Newell, 101 mins.)†

Dance with Me, Henry (1956)*½ Bud Abbott, Lou Costello, Gigi Perreau. Last Abbott and Costello film. Fun in an amusement park. (Dir: Charles Barton, 79 mins.)

Dancing Co-ed (1939)** Lana Turner, Richard Carlson. Nothing here but Lana Turner in dancing clothes back in 1939 and that should be enough to stir memories in many a red-blooded American male. (Dir: S. Sylvan Simon, 80 mins.)

Dancing in the Dark (1949)*** William Powell, Betsy Drake, Mark Stevens. Powell's delightfully droll performance as an ex-ham turned talent scout gives this musical a big lift. Betsy Drake, as his discovery, is hardly a song-and-dance girl, but no matter—Powell steals the show. (Dir: Irving Reis, 92 mins.)

Dancing In the Dark (Canada, 1986)**½ Martha Henry, Neil Munro, Rosemary Dunsmore, Richard Monette. A slow and studied film about a perfect, terrifyingly meticulous homemaker who wakes up from her subjugation with a vengeance. (Dir: Leon Marr, 96 mins.)†

Dancing Lady (1933)*** Joan Crawford, Clark Gable, Franchot Tone, Fred Astaire. This is the musical in which Fred Astaire made his feature film debut, opposite Crawford, who trips the heavy fantastic with him. Perhaps she's too occupied with having to choose between Gable and Tone as she hoofs her way to

Broadway stardom. Full of clichés, but glamorous and entertaining. (Dir: Robert Z. Leonard, 82 mins.)†

Dancing Masters, The (1943)** Oliver Hardy, Stan Laurel, Trudy Marshall, Robert Bailey, Margaret Dumont. Routine L&H fare. Stan and Ollie have to stay on their toes at their dancing academy when they get mixed up with mobsters. (Dir: Mal St. Clair, 63 mins.)

Dancing Mothers (1926)*** Alice Joyce, Conway Tearle, Clara Bow, Donald Keith. Cheerful social comedy about a mother showing her errant flapper daughter the error of her flighty ways. Great star quality with interesting touches from director Herbert Brenon. (102 mins.)†

Dancing on a Dime (1940)**½ Grace McDonald, Robert Paige, Peter Lind Hayes. Out-of-work performers live in an abandoned theater, try to put on their big show. Likable musical is pleasing fun. (Dir: Joseph Santley, 74 mins.)

Dancin' Thru the Dark (Great Britain, 1990)*** Claire Hackett, Con O'Neill, Angela Clarke, Mark Womack. Slightly stagey but engaging adaptation of a play by Willy Russell (*Educating Rita, Shirley Valentine*). The setting is a Liverpool nightclub on the eve of a wedding, where both the bride and groom, along with friends but unaware of each other's presence, converge for a night of drunken revelry and communal soul-searching. Boisterous comedy-drama. (Dir: Mike Ockrent, 95 mins.)

Dandelions (West Germany, 1974)** Rutger Hauer, Dagmar Lasander. After his drug-abusing wife leaves him, Hauer pours his frustration and anguish into a nonstop carrousel of liquor, bar brawls, and decadent love affairs. Supposedly tragic character is too much of a lowlife to elict sympathy, and the result is a pointless exercise in sleaze. (Dir: Adrian Hoven, 92 mins.)†

Dandy in Aspic, A (Great Britain, 1968)* Laurence Harvey, Mia Farrow. Soggy spy stuff, as a Soviet agent working undercover gets tangled in an inextricable web. Sometimes one wishes that that Spy had never come in from the Cold. (Dirs: Anthony Mann, Laurence Harvey, 107 mins.)†

Dandy, The All-American Girl—See: **Sweet Revenge** (1977)

Danger: Diabolik (Italy, 1968)* John Phillip Law, Marisa Mell, Michel Piccoli, Terry-Thomas. The escapades of an infernally clever thief who continually thwarts the law. (Dir: Mario Bava, 99 mins.)

Danger Down Under (MTV 1988)*½ Lee Majors, Rebecca Gilling, Martin Vaughan.

Majors plays a horse breeder who's determined to raise three sons and achieve financial success at the same time. The Australian scenery is the best part of this humdrum telepic. (Dir: Russ Mayberry, 96 mins.)

Danger in Paradise (MTV 1977)*½ John Dehner, Ina Balin, Cliff Potts. Family dynasty drama set in Hawaii. While Big Daddy (John Dehner) lies dying of a stroke, his young bride (Ina Balin) schemes to sell off choice land to the Mafia. The film, however, is a vehicle for Cliff Potts's character, a hell-raising son. (Dir: Marvin Chomsky, 106 mins.)

Danger in the Skies—See: Pilot, The

Danger Lights (1930)** Louis Wolheim, Robert Armstrong, Jean Arthur, Hugh Herbert, Frank Sheridan, Alan Roscoe. Standard melodrama about two railroad workers vying for the heart of the same woman. Only movie made and shown in "Natural Vision," a wide-screen process that flopped—just like the movie. (Dir: George B. Seitz, 87 mins.)†

Danger—Love at Work (1937)**½ Ann Sothern, Jack Haley, Mary Boland, Edward Everett Horton, John Carradine, E. E. Clive, Elisha Cook, Jr. Interesting players in a romantic comedy from tyro director Otto Preminger. The story pits young lawyer Haley against an eccentric family headed by Boland. (81 mins.)

Dangerous (1935)**½ Bette Davis, Franchot Tone. A young architect tries to bring a great actress back from the gutter to stardom and falls in love with her. Very soapy, especially at the end, but Bette's Oscar-winning performance is worth a look. (Dir: Alfred E. Green, 78 mins.)†

Dangerous Affection (MTV 1987)*½ Judith Light, Jimmy Smits, Rhea Perlman, Audra Lindley. Inferior Witness retread with Light playing a pregnant mother whose young son witnesses a murder. (Dir: Larry Elikann, 96 mins.)

Dangerous Charter (1962)* Chris Warfield, Sally Fraser, Richard Foote, Chick Chandler, Peter Forster. Trio of fishermen investigate when they find a yacht with nothing on it but a corpse. Throw this one back. (Dir: Robert Gottschalk, 76 mins.)†

Dangerous Company (MTV 1982)**½ Beau Bridges, Carlos Brown, Karen Carlson, Jan Sterling, Kene Holiday. Gritty, sometimes effective prison tale. A true story about a pair of convicts who put time in "the hole"—solitary confinement. One endures; the other doesn't. (Dir: Lamont Johnson, 104 mins.)†

Dangerous Corner (1934)*** Melvyn Douglas, Virginia Bruce, Conrad Nagel, Ian Keith, Betty Furness. An unusual, sophisticated suspense drama from a play

234

by J. B. Priestley, about a dinner party where the guests are entangled in a long-ago murder. (Dir: Phil Rosen, 66 mins.)

Dangerous Crossing (1953)**½ Jeanne Crain, Michael Rennie. Mystery drama set on an ocean liner. Crain is cast as a bride whose husband disappears during the first few hours after they set sail. Some suspense and the acting's good. (Dir: Joseph M. Newman, 75 mins.)

Dangerous Curves (1988)** Tate Donovan, Danielle Von Zerneck, Grant Heslov. Two nerds hired to drive a Porsche to its new owner have to win it back after it is stolen. Mild-mannered youth comedy padded out with cameos from Robert Stack, Leslie Nielsen, Elizabeth Ashley, Robert Klein, and Martha Quinn. (Dir: David Lewis, 93 mins.)†

Dangerous Days of Kiowa Jones, The (MTV 1966)** Robert Horton, Diane Baker, Sal Mineo, Nehemiah Persoff. Draggy western about a wandering cowpoke who accedes to the request of a dying lawman to take in two killers. (Dir: Alex March, 83 mins.)

Dangerous Exile (Great Britain, 1957)**½ Louis Jourdan, Belinda Lee. During the Revolution, the small son of Marie Antoinette is secretly smuggled into Wales. Typical over-blown costume drama. (Dir: Brian Desmond Hurst, 90 mins.)

Dangerous Female (1931)** Bebe Daniels, Ricardo Cortez. Earliest version of The Maltese Falcon, with Cortez as private eye Sam Spade after the mysterious black bird and avenging the death of his partner. (Dir: Roy Del Ruth, 90 mins.)

Dangerous Friend, A—See: Todd Killings, The

Dangerous Holiday (1937)**½ Ra Hould, Hedda Hopper, Guinn Williams, Jack La Rue, Grady Sutton, Franklin Pangborn. Parents force son to play violin so he runs away from home. They call out the feds, thinking he's been kidnapped. Best parts of the film are future gossip columnist Hopper and wonderful character actors Sutton and Pangborn. (Dir: Nicholas Barrows, 58 mins.)†

Dangerous Liaisons 1960—See: Les Liaisons Dangereuses

Dangerous Liaisons (1988)*** Glenn Close, John Malkovich, Michelle Pfeiffer, Swoosie Kurtz, Keanu Reeves. Adaptation of the scandalous novel and Broadway hit about 18th-century French aristocrats Close and Malkovich, who derive cruel pleasures from seducing and betraying the young and virtuous. Pfeiffer is rather wan as the married woman on whose virtue they bet, but the two stars sink their teeth into their parts with hammy relish. (Dir: Stephen Frears, 119 mins.)†

Dangerous Love (1988)** Lawrence Monoson, Brenda Bakke, Elliott Gould, Anthony Geary. Innocent computer nerd joins a video dating club and becomes a suspect when a psycho starts killing members. The filmmakers are more ambitious than talented, making this would-be Hitchcockian thriller a disappointment. (Dir: Marty Ollstein, 94 mins.)†

Dangerously Close (1986)** John Stockwell, Cary Lowell, J. Eddie Peck. Artiness runs wild as teen vigilantes terrorize their high school in yet another example of rock-video movie-making. Director Albert Pyun submerges the story's potential with an orgy of pop music, flashy lighting effects, and half-baked Nietzschism. (95 mins.)†

Dangerously They Live (1941)**½ John Garfield, Nancy Coleman, Raymond Massey, Moroni Olsen, Lee Patrick. Propaganda-plus, but Florey's capable direction saves it. When an English lady spy is sidetracked by an auto accident, some American Nazi-sympathizers try to uncover her secrets. Garfield comes to her rescue in a watchable, if standardized, spy thriller. (Dir: Robert Florey, 71 mins.)

Dangerous Mission (1954)** Victor Mature, Piper Laurie, William Bendix, Vincent Price, Dennis Weaver. Girl witnesses a gangland killing, flees to Glacier National Park, with both the crooks and the law after her. (Dir: Louis King, 75 mins.)

Dangerous Money (1946)** Sidney Toler, Victor Sen Yung, Willie Best. More shipboard sleuthing for Charlie Chan and son as they get the goods on a circle of thieves who looted the Philippines prior to the Japanese occupation there. (Dir: Terry Morse, 66 mins.)

Dangerous Moonlight (Great Britain, 1941) **** Anton Walbrook, Sally Gray. Polish pianist flies for the RAF, is implored by his loved one to stick to music. Superb war drama, finely acted, with excellent music sequences ("Warsaw Concerto"). (Dir: Brian Desmond Hurst, 83 mins.)†

Dangerous Moves (Switzerland, 1985)**½ Michel Piccoli, Leslie Caron, Liv Ullmann. At a tense championship match, two chess players' obsessions with the game also affect their personal lives. Oscar for Best Foreign Film. (Dir: Richard Dembo, 96 mins.)†

Dangerous Obsession (Italy, 1986)* Brett Halsey, Corinne Clery, Blanca Marsillach, Stefano Madia. After a surgeon accidentally causes the death of a patient, the dead man's girlfriend kidnaps him. Revenge turns to lust in this Italian film

that was substantially (and sloppily) cut before release to the American video market. (Dir: Lucio Fulci, 79 mins.)†

Dangerous Partners (1945)**½ James Craig, Signe Hasso. Fairly good Grade B chase melodrama with the object in question a mere four million dollars' worth of bonds. (Dir: Edward L. Cahn, 74 mins.)

Dangerous Passion (MTV 1990)**½ Carl Weathers, Billy Dee Williams, Lonette McKee, Elpidia Carrillo. Security expert Weathers finds himself under the power of mob boss Williams, a situation that only gets worse when he falls in love with Williams's wife McKee. Slow-moving thriller saves all the action until the end, but star power carries it until then. (Dir: Michael Miller, 96 mins.)

Dangerous Pursuit (MTV 1990)**½ Alexandra Powers, Brian Wimmer, Gregory Harrison, Scott Valentine. Newly married woman is tracked down by a hired assassin about whom she knows too much. Tense, better-than-average suspense thriller with some good chases and psychological depth. (Dir: Sandor Stern, 96 mins.)

Dangerous Summer, A (Australia, 1981)*½ James Mason, Tom Skerrit, Wendy Hughes, Ray Barrett, Ian Gilmore. Mason plays insurance investigator seeking cause of mysterious fire in Australian casino. Muddled, unintentionally hilarious drama wastes star cast. (Dir: Quentin Masters, 100 mins.)†

Dangerous to Know (1938)*½ Akim Tamiroff, Anna May Wong, Gail Patrick, Lloyd Nolan, Anthony Quinn. Slow drama of a racketeer who loves good music and wants to mix with society. (Dir: Robert Florey, 70 mins.)

Dangerous When Wet (1953)** Esther Williams, Fernando Lamas, Jack Carson. Williams swims the English Channel, supported by her cloyingly eccentric all-American family (William Demarest, Charlotte Greenwood, Barbara Whiting) and encouraged by hubby-to-be Lamas. (Dir: Charles Walters, 95 mins.)†

Dangerous Years (1947)** William Halop, Ann E. Todd, Jerome Cowan, Anabel Shaw, Richard Gaines, Scotty Beckett, Darryl Hickman. Juvenile delinquent Halop is on trial for murder, learns that he's really the D.A.'s son. Fair juvenile-delinquency drama. Look for Marilyn Monroe in a bit part. (Dir: Arthur Pierson, 62 mins.)

Danger Route (Great Britain, 1968)** Richard Johnson, Carol Lynley, Barbara Bouchet, Sylvia Syms, Diana Dors, Maurice Denham, Sam Wanamaker, Harry Andrews. British secret agent is ordered to kill a Russian scientist who has defected to the Americans. Murky espionage thriller wants to be cynical but is merely confusing. (Dir: Seth Holt, 91 mins.)

Danger Within—See: **Breakout** (1959)

Danger Zone, The (1987)*½ Robert Canada, Jason Williams, Cynthia Gray. College girls on their way to Las Vegas run afoul of a drug-dealing motorcycle gang. Tepid thriller. (Dir: Henry Vernon, 90 mins.)†

Daniel (1983)** Timothy Hutton, Amanda Plummer, Mandy Patinkin, Lindsay Crouse, Ellen Barkin. Director Sidney Lumet's earnest and ambitious political tract is based on the notorious Rosenberg case, in which Julius and Ethel Rosenberg were convicted of treason for alleged involvement with a Soviet spy ring. The film fails to move us because it incorporates too many disparate political plot points without fleshing out the characters. (129 mins.)†

Daniel Boone (1936)**½ George O'Brien, Heather Angel, John Carradine, Ralph Forbes, Clarence Muse. A suitably rugged, traditional version of the story of the famous frontiersman. Western star O'Brien is well suited to the title role. (Dir: David Howard, 75 mins.)†

Danny Boy (Great Britain, 1941)** David Ferrar, Wilfrid Lawson, Ann Todd, John Warwick, Grant Tyler. Musical drama about Broadway headliner who returns to England to track down her husband and child, long since abandoned by her. Labored tale about lost love. (Dir: Oswald Mitchell, 67 mins.)†

Danny Boy (Ireland, 1984)*½ Veronica Quilligan, Stephen Rea, Alan Devlin, Peter Caffrey, Honor Heffernan, Lise-Ann McLaughlin. Unbearably arty piece by talented writer-director Neil Jordan (*Mona Lisa*). This grim film about a saxophonist who witnesses a double homicide and goes on a vengeance mission is awash in symbolism and is supposed to reflect the lunatic hostilities transpiring in Northern Ireland. AKA: **Angel**. (92 mins.)†

Danny, the Champion of the World (MTV 1989)**½ Jeremy Irons, Samuel Irons, Cyril Cusack, Robbie Coltrane, Lionel Jeffries, Jean Marsh. Charming family story, set in the English countryside during the mid-'50s, stars Jeremy Irons and his son Samuel as a father and son who share a strong bond. An unscrupulous land speculator tries to buy their little piece of property but they stand fast and won't sell. (Dir: Gavin Millar, 90 mins.)

Dante's Inferno (1935)** Spencer Tracy, Claire Trevor. Tracy plays a clever promoter who builds entertainment attractions, including a gigantic replica of the Inferno which ultimately collapses. The film is most noteworthy for a Spanish

dance sequence which heats things up as danced by Rita Cansino, later known as Rita Hayworth. (Dir: Harry Lachman, 88 mins.)

Danton (France-Poland, 1983)**** Roland Blanche, Gerard Depardieu, Wojciech Pszoniak. Director Andrzej Wajda's political epic is adapted from a play, and it abounds in memorable theatrical set pieces. As anarchy rages among the masses, the steel-willed fanatic Robespierre denounces former comrade Danton, an earthy revolutionary. Danton believes that the forgers of the Revolution have forgotten its original purpose. There are clear parallels between the film and conditions in present-day Poland. (136 mins.)†

Darby O'Gill and the Little People (1959)**½ Albert Sharpe, Janet Munro, Sean Connery, Jimmy O'Dea. Disney presents entertaining Irish folklore. Estate caretaker-storyteller Darby O'Gill (Sharpe) is involved in sundry adventures with the leprechauns. (Dir: Robert Stevenson, 93 mins.)†

Darby's Rangers (1958)** James Garner, Etchika Choureau, Jack Warden, Edward Byrnes, Stuart Whitman. Uneven war drama about a band of heroes led by the hero of them all, Major William Darby. (Dir: William Wellman, 121 mins.)

Daredreamer (1990)*** Tim Noah, Alyce LaTourelle, Adam Eastwood, Michael A. Jackson. Charming musical-comedy about a high school senior whose daydreaming keeps him from graduating. The saccharine ending is a bit much, though. Imaginatively filmed in Seattle. (Dir: Barry Cailler, 108 mins.)

Daring Dobermans, The (1973)** Charles Knox Robinson, Tim Considine, David Moses, Joan Caulfield. A fairly snappy sequel to *The Doberman Gang* as the canine crooks lead a life of crime and try to stay out of the doghouse. (Dir: Byron Chudnow, 90 mins.)†

Daring Game (MTV 1968)**½ Lloyd Bridges, Nico Minardos, Michael Ansara, Joan Blackman, Shepperd Strudwick. Unsold series pilot with an aquatic setting, about a squad of commandos who specialize in underwater cases (and, when they get bored, cases in the air as well). (Dirs: Laslo Benedek, Ricou Browning, 101 mins.)†

Daring Young Man, The (1942)**½ Joe E. Brown, Marguerite Chapman, William Wright, Lloyd Bridges, Arthur Lake. Not one of Brown's better vehicles, but his charm supports the thin story of a 4-F who serves his country anyway by tracking down Nazis on the loose in New York. (Dir: Frank Strayer, 73 mins.)

Dark, The (1979)* William Devane, Cathy Lee Crosby, Vivian Blaine. Gory story of an alien zombie terrorizing Los Angeles also has a psychic theme. (Dir: John Bud Cardos, 92 mins.)†

Dark Alibi (1946)*½ Sidney Toler, Mantan Moreland, Ben Carter. Lackluster Charlie Chan entry. He investigates a case involving three ex-convicts who protest their innocence even though their fingerprints were found all over the robbery site. (Dir: Phil Karlson, 61 mins.)

Dark Angel, The (1935)*** Fredric March, Merle Oberon, Herbert Marshall. Remake of a silent film drama about a pair of lovers whose lives are all but destroyed by blindness. Good performances by the cast. (Dir: Sidney Franklin, 110 mins.)

Dark at the Top of the Stairs, The (1960)*** Robert Preston, Dorothy McGuire, Shirley Knight, Angela Lansbury, Eve Arden. Scrubbed version of William Inge's play is a faithful rendition of one of his better works. Delbert Mann's direction is overly careful and deliberate—Inge plays better with a dash of hysteria. The cast is impeccable. (123 mins.)

Dark Circle (1981)*** An unusual documentary about the secret world of making, testing, and selling of the hydrogen bomb. Directors Judy Irving and Chris Beaver mix interviews with declassified footage to create an interesting search into the mysterious and deadly serious subculture that lives by and for the bomb. (80 mins.)

Dark City (1950)**½ Charlton Heston, Lizabeth Scott, Viveca Lindfors, Jack Webb. Overblown melodrama about a gambler who becomes a target for murder. Good performances by Heston (his first major film) and Jack Webb lift it above routine. (Dir: William Dieterle, 110 mins.)

Dark Command (1940)*** John Wayne, Claire Trevor, Walter Pidgeon, Roy Rogers. After the Civil War, the Southwest is terrorized by Quantrill's raiders, until one man puts a stop to it. Big, actionful western drama, colorful, fine cast. (Dir: Raoul Walsh, 94 mins.)†

Dark Corner, The (1946)*** Mark Stevens, Lucille Ball, Clifton Webb. A detective is neatly framed for murder; well-played and generally interesting melodrama. (Dir: Henry Hathaway, 99 mins.)†

Dark Crystal, The (1982)**½ Jim Henson, creator of the Muppets, has put tremendous ingenuity into creating puppet characters on a scale never before done in films. Production design is superb, the total mood letter perfect. But all of this has been expended on a dippy, very conventional good-versus-evil screenplay. (Dirs: Jim Henson, Frank Oz, 93 mins.)†

Dark Delusion (1947)**½ Lionel Barrymore, James Craig. One of Dr. Gillespie's assistants cures a girl of mental disor-

der. Likable medical drama. (Dir: Willis Goldbeck, 90 mins.)

Darker Side of Terror, The (MTV 1979)*½ Robert Forster, Adrienne Barbeau, Ray Milland. Labeled a thriller, there isn't much to prompt gooseflesh as Robert Forster agrees to assist in an experiment in which he is cloned. (Dir: Gus Trikonis, 104 mins.)

Darker Than Amber (1970)*** Rod Taylor, Suzy Kendall, Theodore Bikel. Tough mystery action with more brawn than brain as Taylor plays author John D. Macdonald's character Travis McGee, who lives on a houseboat in Florida and falls in love with a girl whose life is endangered by some mobsters. (Dir: Robert Clouse, 97 mins.)

Dark Eyes (Italy, 1987)**½ Marcello Mastroianni, Silvana Mangano, Marthe Keller. The main joy of this airy comedy, set at the turn of the century, is the winning performance of Mastroianni as a somewhat eccentric free spirit who is married to an aristocrat but finds true love with a Russian beauty he meets at a health spa. Marcello gets better with age. (Dir: Nikita Mikhalkov, 117 mins.)†

Dark Eyes of London (Great Britain, 1939) **½ Bela Lugosi, Hugh Williams, Greta Gynt. This low-budget horror film has quite a reputation among genre fans and admirers of Lugosi, who plays a proprietor of a home for the blind who is involved in an elaborate plot to murder victims for their insurance. AKA: **The Human Monster.** (Dir: Walter Summers, 73 mins.)†

Dark Habits (Spain, 1983)**½ Cristina S. Pascual, Julietta Serrano, Marisa Paredes, Carmen Maura. In this early comedy by Pedro Almodóvar, the talented director of *Law of Desire* and *What Have I Done to Deserve This?*, a young woman on the run from the law seeks refuge in a convent with some very unusual nuns, including Sisters Manure, Snake, and Sin. A hard-edged, intentionally offensive religious satire, not as original or funny as Almodóvar's later films. (95 mins.)†

Dark Hazard (1934)**½ Edward G. Robinson, Genevieve Tobin, Glenda Farrell, Robert Barrat, George Meeker, Henry B. Walthall, Sidney Toler. Interesting and unusual tale for its time of a compulsive gambler trying to quit, with little assistance or understanding from his wife. Remade as *Wine, Women and Horses.* (Dir: Alfred E. Green, 72 mins.)

Dark Holiday (MTV 1989)**½ Lee Remick, Norma Aleandro, Roy Thinnes, Tony Goldwin. American tourist Remick buys some figurines in Turkey, ends up in a harsh Turkish prison when a customs official suspects her of smuggling valuable artifacts. No *Midnight Express*, but a harrowing true story nonetheless. (Dir: Lou Antonio, 96 mins.)

Dark Horse, The (1932)*** Guy Kibbee, Warren William, Bette Davis, Frank McHugh. Absolutely delightful political farce has a slick campaign manager running dim bulb Kibbee for office. Bright and sparkling. (Dir: Alfred E. Green, 75 mins.)

Dark Intruder (1965)**½ Leslie Nielsen, Judi Meredith. Sleuth steps in to aid the police in solving a mysterious series of murders. OK vest-pocket mystery. (Dir: Harvey Hart, 59 mins.)

Dark Journey (Great Britain, 1937)*** Vivien Leigh, Conrad Veidt, Anthony Bushell, Ursula Jeans. A complicated counter-espionage tale of WWI Sweden and France that's made memorable by the luminous performances of Leigh and Veidt as spy-crossed lovers. (Dir: Victor Saville, 82 mins.)†

Darkman (1990)**½ Liam Neeson, Frances McDormand. Imaginative horror film about a disfigured scientist bent on revenge. He's able to concoct holographic masks that last a short time (each one is different) as he stalks his victims. Neeson is wonderful. (Dir: Sam Raimi, 95 mins.)†

Dark Mansions (MTV 1986)*½ Joan Fontaine, Linda Purl, Paul Shenar, Michael York, Melissa Sue Anderson, Grant Aleksander, Lois Chiles. Joan Fontaine is the matriarch of the Drake shipping family. Enter Linda Purl as a writer hired by Miss Fontaine to chronicle the family's history on their Diamond Jubilee. Linda, as fate would have it, is a dead ringer for York's wife, who either was killed, committed suicide, or died in a freak accident. (Dir: Jerry London, 104 mins.)

Dark Mirror, The (1946)*** Olivia de Havilland, Lew Ayres. A doctor has to figure out which twin sister is normal, and which is a demented murderess. Tight, suspenseful mystery, excellent. (Dir: Robert Siodmak, 85 mins.)†

Dark Mirror (MTV 1984)** Jane Seymour, Vincent Gardenia, Stephen Collins. A remake of the 1946 thriller. Seymour plays the dual role of identical twins, one of whom is accused of murder—but which one? (Dir: Richard Lang, 104 mins.)

Dark Night of the Scarecrow (MTV 1981) **½ Charles Durning, Robert F. Lyons, Claude Earl Jones, Lane Smith, Tanya Crowe. A Halloween tale meant to scare you. A small town's hatred for a retarded man's innocent relationship with a young girl is revealed when the girl is attacked by a guard dog. (Dir: Frank De Felitta, 104 mins.)†

238

Dark of the Night (New Zealand, 1986)** Heather Bolton, David Letch, Margaret Umbers, Suzanne Lee, Gary Stalker. A young woman dealing with the pressures and fears of living in the city for the first time finds terror in a haunted car that she buys. Attempt to combine psychological drama with supernatural trappings just doesn't work, despite some good performances and a few humorous moments. (Dir: Gaylene Preston, 83 mins.)†

Dark of the Sun (Great Britain, 1968)** Jim Brown, Rod Taylor, Yvette Mimieux, Kenneth More. Congo mercenary (Rod Taylor) undertakes a dangerous mission: rescue citizens of a besieged town, and bring back valuable diamonds. Plenty of action helps a threadbare script. (Dir: Jack Cardiff, 101 mins.)

Dark Passage (1947)**½ Humphrey Bogart, Lauren Bacall. Man escapes from San Quentin to prove himself innocent of murdering his wife. Occasionally good but uneven melodrama. (Dir: Delmer Daves, 106 mins.)†

Dark Past (1949)*** William Holden, Lee J. Cobb, Nina Foch. Psychiatrist breaks down the resistance of a desperate killer holding him captive. Remake of *Blind Alley* has plenty of suspense, good performances. (Dir: Rudolph Maté, 75 mins.)†

Dark Places (1976)** Joan Collins, Christopher Lee, Robert Hardy, Herbert Lom, Jane Birkin, Jean Marsh. Lee and Collins play an evil brother and sister out to haunt a family living in a large estate so they can have a hidden fortune all to themselves. (Dir: Don Sharp, 91 mins.)†

Dark Power (1985)* Lash LaRue, Anna Lane Tatum. The spirits of ancient Mexican warriors rise to wreak vengeance on kids partying at the site of their burial grounds. As the local sheriff who comes to the rescue, former cowboy star LaRue and his trademark whip add a little flash to this weary supernatural saga. (Dir: Phil Smoot, 87 mins.)†

Dark Ride, The (1982)** Susan Sullivan, James Luisi, Martin Speer, John Karlen, Hillary Thompson. Dumb story about psychopath who picks up female hitchhikers along California's picturesque highways and rapes and murders them. (Dir: Jeremy Hoenack, 83 mins.)†

Dark Sands (Great Britain, 1937)** Paul Robeson, Henry Wilcoxen, Wallace Ford, Princess Kouka. One of Robeson's lesser pictures; here he plays a corporal, unjustly accused of murder, who deserts and finds refuge with an African tribe. (Dir: Thornton Freeland, 77 mins.)

Dark Secret of Harvest Home (MTV 1978) **½ David Ackroyd, Joanna Miles, Rosanna Arquette, Bette Davis, John Calvin, René Auberjonois, Michael

O'Keefe. A horror story of a New York family settling down in a strange New England village, a community that shuns anything modern—machinery and up-to-date medicine. The eerie aspect of the tale doesn't surface immediately, but the frights are worth waiting for. (Dir: Leo Penn, 200 mins.)†

Dark Side of Innocence, The (MTV 1976)* Joanna Pettet, Anne Archer, John Anderson, Lawrence Casey, Kim Hunter, Gail Strickland. Tedious soap opera, focusing on the daughters of an affluent lumber company man. AKA: **Hancocks, The.** (Dir: Jerry Thrope, 72 mins.)

Dark Side of the Moon, The (1990)** Will Bledsoe, Alan Blumenfield, John Diehl, Robert Sampson, Wendy MacDonald, Joe Turkel. Spaceship on a routine repair mission comes across a seemingly abandoned ship that still houses an evil presence. Sci-fi and the supernatural meet by way of the Bermuda Triangle in this OK entry. (Dir: D. J. Webster, 91 mins.)†

Dark Star (1972)** Dan O'Bannon, Brian Narelle, Dre Pahich. John Carpenter's first feature is a low-budget comedy about bored astronauts who try to pass the time in between bombing missions. Unfortunately, the audience can end up experiencing the same boredom as the characters, due to the incredibly amateurish level of acting. This material was mined more profitably by O'Bannon in his screenplay for *Alien*. (Dir: John Carpenter, 83 mins.)†

Dark Tower (1987)*½ Michael Moriarty, Jenny Agutter, Carol Lynley, Theodore Bikel, Kevin McCarthy. Good cast sinks in this cheap horror production about a skyscraper haunted by the ghost of the architect's dead husband. Credited director "Ken Barnett" is actually veteran Freddie Francis, working far below his abilities here. (91 mins.)†

Dark Victory (1939)**** Bette Davis, George Brent, Humphrey Bogart, Geraldine Fitzgerald, Ronald Reagan, Henry Travers. The best of all the terminal-illness soap operas; fast-stepping social butterfly Davis is transformed by her date with death and becomes determined to meet her demise honorably. Despite a few flaws like Bogart's ludicrous impersonation of an Irish stable-hand, this is a powerful melodrama transformed by Davis into a superior tearjerker. (Dir: Edmund Goulding, 106 mins.)†

Dark Victory (MTV 1976)**½ Elizabeth Montgomery, Michele Lee, Anthony Hopkins. Montgomery stars in passable update of the 1939 melodrama. It now concerns a successful, beautiful television executive who discovers she has a short time to live and falls in love with her doctor. (Dir: Robert Butler, 144 mins.)

Dark Waters (1944)**½ Merle Oberon, Franchot Tone, Thomas Mitchell. A girl returns to her Southern mansion after a shipboard disaster, where she becomes convinced someone is trying to drive her insane. Occasionally suspenseful, generally undistinguished thriller. (Dir: Andre de Toth, 90 mins.)†

Darling (Great Britain, 1965)***½ Julie Christie, Dirk Bogarde, Laurence Harvey. Perceptive, cynical, deftly written portrait of a young London model who decides to climb the social ladder quickly by jumping, in rather unceremonious fashion, in and out of assorted beds. Brilliantly directed by John Schlesinger, imaginatively edited, and featuring the radiant performance of the ravishing Miss Christie, this is a moving, amusing, and honest film. (122 mins.)†

Darling, How Could You (1951)** Joan Fontaine, John Lund, Mona Freeman. Sentimental drama of an imaginative girl whose fantasies nearly wreck her parents' domestic life. Inoffensive but overly sweet, slow-moving. (Dir: Mitchell Leisen, 96 mins.)

Darling Lili (1970)*** Julie Andrews, Rock Hudson, Jeremy Kemp, Lance Percival. WWI is the setting for this charming spoof of the Mata Hari legend. Andrews plays the English music hall star, alias German spy, who must coax secrets from flyboy Hudson. A bit long but far from the disaster critics originally said it was. (Dir: Blake Edwards, 136 mins.)

D.A.R.Y.L. (1985)*** Mary Beth Hurt, Michael McKean, Barret Oliver, Josef Sommer, Kathryn Walker. After a rather special little "boy" changes the lives of a childless couple, the government decides to have this robot-child destroyed. Although predictable, this lightweight fairy tale makes for ideal family viewing. (Dir: Simon Wincer, 99 mins.)†

Das Boot (Germany, 1982)**** Jurgen Prochnow, Herbert Gronemeyer, Klaus Wennemann, Hubertas Bengsch. Dealing with submarine warfare, the film accurately depicts not only the crowding and the grime, but also the harrowing menace of being hundreds of feet below water when the depth charges begin to hammer at the fragile hull. With its grim depiction of the hard work and the cold fear that marked the battles for the North Atlantic, *Das Boot* is an aquatic *All Quiet on the Western Front*. AKA: **The Boat.** (Dir: Wolfgang Petersen, 150 mins.)†

Date with an Angel (1987)*½ Michael E. Knight, Phoebe Cates, Emmanuelle Béart, David Dukes. Nonsensical fluff about an angel who crash-lands and the boy-next-door who befriends her. Lovely Ms. Béart is a vision as the earthbound ethe-

239

real, but the cute scripting doesn't do justice to her exceptional looks, or to poor Phoebe who ends up being the pic's main villain. (Dir: Tom McLoughlin, 105 mins.)†

Date with Judy, A (1948)**½ Elizabeth Taylor, Jane Powell, Wallace Beery. The youngsters may enjoy this juvenile comedy, but outside of some good musical numbers and the sight of Taylor as she reached physical maturity, it's not much of a film. (Dir: Richard Thorpe, 113 mins.)†

Date with the Falcon, A (1941)**½ George Sanders, Wendy Barrie, James Gleason. In the process of locating a missing man, the Falcon ends up kidnapped and accused of murder; luckily his fiancée's used to this sort of thing. Fair entry. (Dir: Irving Reis, 63 mins.)

Daughter of Darkness (MTV 1990)**½ Anthony Perkins, Mia Sara, Jack Coleman, Robert Reynolds. Young woman searching Romania for the father she never knew finds him—along with the rest of his vampire friends. Perkins, in an oddly sympathetic role, gives this otherwise silly thriller some appeal. (Dir: Stuart Gordon, 96 mins.)

Daughter of Dr. Jekyll (1957)* Gloria Talbott, Arthur Shields, John Agar, John Dierkes. Girl thinks she turns into a monster at night. It's Daddy's little girl. Ghastly. (Dir: Edgar Ulmer, 69 mins.)†

Daughter of Horror (1955)*** Adrienne Barrett, Bruno VeSota, Ben Roseman, Richard Barron. Narrated by Ed Mc Mahon. Flawed but fascinating curio that looks like a cross between the German Expressionist films of the 20s and the avant-garde shorts of Maya Deren. The plot involves a young woman waking up, meeting a seamy stranger, and then getting hooked up with an overweight mobster who looks like her wife-beating father, whom she had murdered. A bit slow at times, but filmmaker John Parker deserves commendation for telling a story in purely visual terms. AKA: **Dementia**. (55 mins.)

Daughter of Mata Hari, The—See: **Mata Hari's Daughter**

Daughter of Rosie O'Grady, The (1950)**½ June Haver, Gordon MacRae, James Barton. A gay, tuneful turn-of-the-century musical comedy film. James Barton plays June Haver's father, who forbids her to seek a career on the stage. Look for Debbie Reynolds in a small role as June's sister. (Dir: David Butler, 104 mins.)

Daughter of the Mind (MTV 1969)**½ Gene Tierney, Ray Milland, Don Murray, Ed Asner, John Carradine. Milland is cast as a professor of cybernetics who claims he is visited by his recently killed young

240

daughter's spirit. (Dir: Walter Grauman, 73 mins.)

Daughter of the Streets (MTV 1990)*** Jane Alexander, Roxana Zal, John Stamos, Harris Yulin, Martha Scott. Too-busy single mother Alexander tries to win back daughter Zal who, feeling neglected, has taken to the streets. Hard-hitting drama with two fine performances to offset occasional script thinness. (Dir: Ed Sherin, 96 mins.)

Daughters Courageous (1939)*** John Garfield, Claude Rains, The Lane Sisters. Trying to cash in on the box office success of *Four Daughters*, they assembled the same cast and put them through their paces again. They would have made a sequel but they killed Garfield in the original. Good acting still makes it passable. (Dir: Michael Curtiz, 120 mins.)

Daughters of Darkness (Belgium-France-West Germany-Italy, 1971)*** Delphine Seyrig, Daniele Ouimet, Andrea Rau. Stylish vampire nonsense, with a deluxe high-camp performance by Seyrig as the well-accoutred Bloody Countess who takes on a newlywed couple for her sanguinary lease on life. (Dir: Harry Kumel, 96 mins.)†

Daughters of Destiny (France, 1955)** Claudette Colbert, Michele Morgan, Martine Carol. Triple tale of three women of history and how their fortunes are changed—Queen Elizabeth, Joan of Arc, and Lysistrata. (Dir: Marcel Dagliero, 94 mins.)

Daughters of Joshua Cabe, The (MTV 1972)** Buddy Ebsen, Sandra Dee, Lesley Ann Warren, Karen Valentine, Jack Elam. Moderately entertaining western comedy-drama, with Ebsen as a rancher-trapper who has to come up with three long-lost daughters in order to keep his land when a new homesteaders' law is passed. (Dir: Philip Leacock, 72 mins.)

Daughters of Joshua Cabe Return, The (MTV 1975)** Dan Dailey, Dub Taylor, Ronne Troup, Carl Betz. Passable follow-up to the western comedy-drama. (Dir: David Lowell Rich, 72 mins.)

Daughters of Satan (1972)*½ Tom Selleck, Barra Grant. An alleged intellectual is enticed by a painting of three witches being burned, because one of the witches resembles his wife. (Dir: Hollingsworth Morse, 90 mins.)

David (West Germany, 1979)*** Mario Fische, Eva Mattes, Walter Taub, Torsten Henties. Nazi persecutors burn down synagogue and brand rabbi's head with a swastika, causing his son and daughter to flee. Their flight, and the story of those who aid them, make for a gripping tale about WWII told from West

German point of view. (Dir: Peter Lilienthal, 125 mins.)†

David and Bathsheba (1951)**½ Gregory Peck, Susan Hayward. Typical biblical epic with all the stops pulled—lavish sets, sumptuous costumes, posing actors and wooden dialogue. (Dir: Henry King, 116 mins.†)

David and Lisa (1962)***½ Keir Dullea, Janet Margolin. Sensitively written, beautifully acted touching story of two mentally disturbed youngsters finding happiness and faith. Low-budget sleeper was Academy Award nominee for first-time director Frank Perry. (94 mins.)†

David Copperfield (1935)***½ W. C. Fields, Lionel Barrymore, Edna May Oliver, Basil Rathbone, Roland Young, Freddie Bartholomew. There are enough character epiphanies emergent under George Cukor's direction to make this among the most memorable of Dickens adaptations, though sometimes lapsing into tasteful dullness. Superb performances from a top-notch cast. (133 mins.)†

David Copperfield (Great Britain, 1970)*** Ralph Richardson, Michael Redgrave, Edith Evans. Charles Dickens's novel comes to life with inspired casting in a first-class production. There are flaws in this adaptation, and Dickens purists may object to some of it, but most viewers—young and old alike—will be enthralled. (Dir: Delbert Mann, 100 mins.)

David Harum (1934)**½ Will Rogers, Louise Dresser, Evelyn Venable. More down-home fun from Rogers as he espouses rustic virtues in a heart-warming tale of a wise rancher who sorts out everyone's romantic entanglements as he sees fit. (Dir: James Cruze, 83 mins.)

David Holzman's Diary (1968)*** David Holzman, Eileen Dietz, Louise Levine. An imaginative low-budget black and white independently made feature about movie-making and movie-makers. Written, produced, and directed by Jim McBride on location in New York. (74 mins.)

Davy Crockett and the River Pirates (1956) *** Fess Parker, Buddy Ebsen, Jeff York, Kenneth Tobey, Clem Bevans. A Disney delight originally made for television. First part is a river boat race against Mike Fink; second half pits Davy against the Injuns. Entertaining for kids of all ages. (Dir: Norman Foster, 81 mins.)†

Davy Crockett, King of the Wild Frontier (1955)*** Fess Parker, Buddy Ebsen, Basil Ruysdael, Hans Conreid, Kenneth Tobey. Rousing adventure tale that is actually three spliced-together episodes from Disney's TV program. Parker (the idol of millions of school kids in the 1950s) plays Davy as he makes peace with Chief Red Stick, rids a small town

of no-good varmints, runs for Congress, and joins the fight at the Alamo. (Dir: Norman Foster, 93 mins.)†

Dawn at Socorro (1954)**½ Piper Laurie, Rory Calhoun, David Brian. A good cast and a better than average western plot make this one entertaining. Calhoun plays a gunfighter who's forced to think about his life when his health, if not his trigger finger, starts to slip. (Dir: George Sherman, 81 mins.)

Dawning, The (Great Britain, 1988)*** Anthony Hopkins, Rebecca Pidgeon, Jean Simmons, Trevor Howard, Tara MacGowran. Dreamy young girl in 1920s Ireland becomes an accomplice of stranger-on-the-run Hopkins, not realizing he's an agent of the IRA. Generally apolitical tale serves as a showcase for veteran actors Hopkins, Simmons, and Howard (in his last film); the younger Pidgeon holds her own in this distinguished company. (Dir: Robert Knights, 97 mins.)

Dawn of the Dead (1979)*** Gaylen Ross, Ken Foree, Scott Reiniger, David Emge. Gory, satiric sequel to *Night of the Living Dead*. Four survivors of a zombie plague hole up in a huge shopping center and try to avoid getting malled. (Dir: George A. Romero, 125 mins.)†

Dawn of the Mummy (1981)* Brenda King, Barry Sattels, George Peck, Joan Levy. Gory, awful drama about fashion photography crew doing a shoot in Egypt and disturbing some mummies. Better to have left them, and you, sleeping. For fans of bad acting only. (Dir: Frank Agrama, 88 mins.)†

Dawn Patrol (1933)*** Richard Barthelmess, Douglas Fairbanks, Jr., Neil Hamilton. Better than the Errol Flynn remake. This was Howard Hawks's first sound film, and he captures the camaraderie and death-house humor of the aviators trying to withstand the horrors of war. (112 mins.)

Dawn Patrol (1938)**½ Errol Flynn, Basil Rathbone, David Niven. Exciting tale of the men of Britain's Royal Flying Corps during World War I. (Dir: Edmund Goulding, 120 mins.)†

Dawn: Portrait of a Teenage Runaway (MTV 1976)** Eve Plumb, Bo Hopkins, William Schallert. A film set on Hollywood Boulevard focusing on what may happen to teenagers who come to Hollywood and can't find work. (Dir: Randal Kleiser, 102 mins.)

Dawn Rider (1935)**½ John Wayne, Marion Burns, Yakima Canutt, Denny Meadows (Dennis Moore). Wayne is the Dawn Rider as a cowboy who struggles to avenge his father's murder. Not bad if you like formula westerns. Offers a chance to see legendary stuntman Canutt in an acting role. (Robert N. Bradbury, 53 mins.)†

Day After, The (MTV 1983)*** Jason Robards, Jr., JoBeth Williams, Steve Guttenberg, John Cullum, John Lithgow. A moving and devastating drama about the effects of nuclear war on the citizens of Lawrence, Kansas, not far from Kansas City. One of the most provocative movies ever made for TV. The video version features extra footage. (Dir: Nicholas Meyer, 120 mins.)†

Day and the Hour, The (France-Italy, 1963)*** Simone Signoret, Stuart Whitman, Genevieve Page. Old-fashioned, uneven, melodrama set in Nazi-occupied France during World War II. Signoret's husband has been nailed by the Nazis and she befriends Whitman. (Dir: Rene Clement, 115 mins.)†

Day at the Races, A (1937)***½ The Marx Brothers, Maureen O'Sullivan, Allan Jones, Margaret Dumont. The first sign of the Marx Brothers' decline. Often very good when Groucho is given a free hand, and often very bad when the brothers' antics are sublimated to the dreary plotline. (Dir: Sam Wood, 111 mins.)†

Daybreak (Great Britain, 1946)** Eric Portman, Ann Todd, Maxwell Reed. Downbeat melodrama about an unemployed executioner (sounds depressing already, doesn't it?) with marital difficulties. (Dir: Compton Bennett, 81 mins.)

Day Christ Died, The (MTV 1980)**½ Chris Sarandon, Colin Blakely, Keith Michell, Jonathan Pryce, Barrie Houghton, Hope Lange. Reasonably interesting, well-acted docudrama about the events of the few days before Christ's crucifixion. (Dir: James Cellan Jones, 104 mins.)

Daydreamer, The (1966)*** Cyril Ritchard, Paul O'Keefe, Ray Bolger. A very entertaining animated and live musical adventure. Paul O'Keefe plays a young Hans Christian Andersen who has many adventures with a series of wonderful characters from the Andersen fairy tales. Voices are supplied by such stars as Tallulah Bankhead, Victor Borge, Burl Ives, and Terry-Thomas. (Dir: Jules Bass, 98 mins.)†

Daydreamer, The (France, 1975)**½ Pierre Richard, Bernard Blier, Marie Christine Barrault, Maria Pacome. Pierre Richard wrote, directed, and starred in this comedy about a young man whose apprenticeship at a Paris ad agency leads to bumbling chaos. (90 mins.)

Day for Night (France, 1971)**** François Truffaut, Jacqueline Bisset, Jean-Pierre Léaud, Valentina Cortese, Jean-Pierre Aumont, Alexandra Stewart. Director François Truffaut's joyous, exhilarating comedy, an affectionate satire on the art and madness of making movies. *Day for Night* is a lighthearted, charming beauty, faultlessly acted by Truffaut himself and the rest of a carefully chosen cast. Oscar as Best Foreign Film. (116 mins.)†

Day for Thanks on Waltons' Mountain, A (MTV 1982)** Ralph Waite, Jon Walmsley, Judy Norton-Taylor, Robert Wrightman, Ellen Corby. The further adventures of the dirt poor (but spiritually rich) clan who showed us in the recession-ridden '70s the virtues to be found in a good depression. Decent seasonal fare updates us on what happened to John-Boy (Wrightman) and family after the series concluded. (Dir: Harris, 96 mins.)

Day in the Country, A (France, 1936)**** Sylvie Bataille, George Darnoux, Jane Marken, Jacques Brunius, Gabrielle Fontan. Director Jean Renoir's masterpiece about a family's outing in the countryside and a daughter's sudden love for another picnicker. A scintillating, sensuous, warmly comic tribute to rural France and young love. One of the greatest films ever made. (45 mins.)†

Day It Came to Earth, The (1979)* Wink Roberts, Roger Manning, Bob Ginnaven, Delight DeBruine, George Gobel. Meteor crashes into a lake, revives a drowned gangster (the cement shoes variety) who sets out for revenge. Bad in every aspect. (Dir: Harry Z. Thomason, 89 mins.)†

Day in the Death of Joe Egg, A (Great Britain, 1972)**½ Alan Bates, Janet Suzman, Peter Bowles. What worked exultantly on the stage flounders into kitchen sink rancor. The parents of a spastic child make cruel jokes, and it's really just a black-humored variant on the stiff upper lip. (Dir: Peter Medak, 106 mins.)†

Day Mars Invaded Earth, The (1962)* Marie Windsor, Kent Taylor. A poor man's *Invasion of the Body Snatchers*. Martians replace the family of a space official in order to stop U.S. space exploration. (Dir: Maury Dexter, 70 mins.)

Day of the Animals (1977)* Christopher George, Leslie Nielsen, Michael Ansara. Yarn about how aerosol sprays turn some animals into man-killers. Pointless and repulsive. (Dir: William Girdler, 95 mins.)†

Day of the Bad Man (1958)** Fred MacMurray, Joan Weldon, John Ericson. Circuit judge has to sentence a convicted killer to death and face the rage of the man's brothers. Western goes in for suspense, succeeds in being merely routine. (Dir: Harry Keller, 81 mins.)

Day of the Cobra, The (Italy, 1980)**½ Franco Nero, Sybil Danning, Enio Girolane, Mario Marazana. Hardly working detective is hired to find an old enemy in this intriguing tale of violence. Gor-

242

geous location filming in Genoa provides added incentive to watch. (Dir: Enzo G. Castellari, 95 mins.)†

Day of the Dead (1985)* Richard Liberty, Howard Sherman, Lori Cardille. Dull, talky completion to Romero's "living dead" trilogy has a group of scientists and psychopathic soldiers holed up in an abandoned missile silo by flesh-eating zombies. (Dir: George Romero, 103 mins.)†

Day of the Dolphin, The (1973)** George C. Scott, Trish Van Devere, Paul Sorvino, Fritz Weaver. Misguided fable about the efforts of a dedicated scientist (Scott) to train a dolphin to talk, while simultaneously participating in a counter-intelligence scheme involving political assassination. (Dir: Mike Nichols, 104 mins.)†

Day of the Evil Gun (1968)**½ Glenn Ford, Arthur Kennedy, Dean Jagger, Nico Minardos, (Harry) Dean Stanton. Reasonably suspenseful western about a search for women kidnapped by Apaches. (Dir: Jerry Thorpe, 93 mins.)

Day of the Jackal, The (Great Britain-France, 1973)***½ Edward Fox, Cyril Cusack, Delphine Seyrig. High suspense as an assassin (Fox) is hired by French generals to kill Charles de Gaulle. Intensive manhunt is juxtaposed with Fox's preparation for the killing. Acting and the fine European locations are the highpoints. (Dir: Fred Zinnemann, 141 mins.)†

Day of the Locust, The (1975)***½ Donald Sutherland, Karen Black, Burgess Meredith, William Atherton, Geraldine Page. Memorable, harrowing adaptation of Nathanael West's 1939 novel, a crystallization of his long Hollywood experience as a screenwriter. Atherton is impressive as an impressionable "civilized" young Yale screenwriter trying to cope and succeed in Hollywood. (Dir: John Schlesinger, 140 mins.)†

Day of the Outlaw (1959)** Robert Ryan, Burl Ives, Tina Louise. Outlaws, with their leader seriously wounded and the Cavalry in hot pursuit, take over a western community and terrorize the townspeople (Dir: Andre de Toth, 90 mins.)

Day of the Triffids (Great Britain, 1963)*** Howard Keel, Nicole Maurey, Janette Scott, Kieron Moore. Intelligent dialogue and interesting direction have earned this science fiction film a good reputation. Blinding meteor showers rain seeds upon the earth, which grow into man-eating plants. Good special effects. (Dir: Steve Sekely, 93 mins.)†

Day of the Woman—See: I Spit on Your Grave

Day of Wrath (Denmark, 1943)**** Thorkild Roose, Lisbeth Movin, Sigrid Neiiendam. Combining the subject matter of witchcraft and the temptation of sins of the flesh, the film suggests a double dose of Nathaniel Hawthorne and early Ingmar Bergman. When an old woman is condemned to the stake, she puts a curse on the local pastor whose wife may have some bewitching tendencies of her own. As the wife becomes enamored of her stepson, the film weaves an unforgettable spell of sexual tension and atmospheric suspense. (Dir: Carl Dreyer, 105 mins.)

Day One (MTV 1989)**** Brian Dennehy, David Straithairn, Michael Tucker, Hume Cronyn, Richard Dysart, Hal Holbrook, Barnard Hughes. Compelling docudrama about the Manhattan Project. A provocative history lesson as officials argue whether the bomb should be used against Japan. Special credit to writer David Rintels. (Dir: Joseph Sargent, 144 mins.)

Days and Nights in the Forest (India, 1969)***½ Soumitra Chatterjee, Sharmila Tagore, Shubhendu Chatterjee. Four educated city men spend country holiday meeting villagers and developing relationships with women. Director Satyajit Ray takes aim at British imperialism in romantic comedy that mocks worst aspects of elitism and snobbery. (115 mins.)

Days of Glory (1944)**½ Gregory Peck, Tamara Toumanova. Russian guerrillas beat back the Nazi enemy. Slow-moving war drama. Well acted. Peck's film debut. (Dir: Jacques Tourneur, 86 mins.)†

Days of Heaven (1978)**** Richard Gere, Brooke Adams, Linda Manz, Sam Shepard, Robert Wilke. Superbly photographed work of art (Nestor Almendros and Haskell Wexler) in which the visual images dwarf the simple storyline. Writer-director Terrence Malick, in his second film, achieves a visual quality rarely seen in American films. Set in Texas in 1916 (and shot in Alberta, Canada), it is the story of a group of farmworkers and their relations with the sickly owner of the land. (95 mins.)†

Days of Hell (Italy, 1986)* Conrad Nichols, Kiwaku Harada. The "D" Team, a group of mercenaries with perfect blown-dry hair, is hired to rescue a scientist and his daughter from Afghanistan. Once inside, though, they discover that they are being used as pawns in an international battle over a nerve gas formula. The action is plentiful, but it's too poorly made to be exciting. (Dir: Anthony Richmond, 88 mins.)†

Days of Thrills and Laughter, The (1961)***½ Well-chosen compilation of scenes from silent movie classics, featuring Charlie Chaplin, Laurel and Hardy, the Keystone Kops, Fatty Arbuckle, Douglas

Fairbanks, Pearl White, and more. (Dir: Robert Youngson, 93 mins.)†

Days of Thunder (1990)** Tom Cruise, Robert Duvall, Randy Quaid, Michael Rooker, Nicole Kidman, Cary Elwes. The star, producers, and director of *Top Gun* reunite for this similarly vacuous (if less blatantly fascistic) package about a hotshot stock car racer. Screenwriter Robert Towne (who co-wrote the story with Cruise) was clearly just picking up an easy paycheck. (Dir: Tony Scott, 107 mins.)†

Days of Wine and Roses (1962)***½ Jack Lemmon, Lee Remick, Charles Bickford, Jack Klugman, Jack Albertson. A wrenching story of two ordinary people, who have both become desperate alcoholics. The plot is grim, the acting superb. Powerful and absorbing. (Dir: Blake Edwards, 117 mins.)†

Day the Bookies Wept, The (1939)**½ Joe Penner, Betty Grable, Richard Lane, Thurston Hall. Cabbies come into some money and spend it on a racehorse. It turns out to be a pig in a poke, but they're determined to make it a winner anyway. One of those oddball comedies that looks good on the tube during the wee small hours. (Dir: Leslie Goodwins, 53 mins.)†

Day the Bubble Burst, The (MTV 1982)** Blanche Baker, Franklin Cover, Richard Crenna, Dana Elcar, Robert Hays, Audra Lindley, Bill Macy, Rue McClanahan, David Ogden Stiers, Robert Vaughn, David Clennon. A superficial account of the stock market crash of 1929 seen from the eyes of various characters. Stumbles in its attempt to cover too much ground. (Dir: Joseph Hardy, 156 mins.)

Day the Earth Caught Fire, The (Great Britain, 1962)***½ Edward Judd, Janet Munro, Leo McKern. In the front rank of sci-fi thrillers, this one is almost too realistic for comfort. Nuclear tests at the North and South Poles shift the Earth's orbit, send the planet plummeting toward the sun. (Dir: Val Guest, 90 mins.)†

Day the Earth Moved, The (MTV 1974)** Jackie Cooper, Stella Stevens, Cleavon Little, William Windom, Beverly Garland, Sid Melton, Don Steele. Helicopter pilots try to warn residents of a small town about an impending earthquake, but no one believes them until it's too late. (Dir: Robert Michael Lewis, 72 mins.)

Day the Earth Stood Still, The (1951)***½ Patricia Neal, Michael Rennie, Hugh Marlowe, Sam Jaffe. A surprisingly intense science fiction drama, with excellent production values and just about perfect casting. Rennie is an enlightened spaceman who arrives unexpectedly in

Washington, D.C., to warn Earth people against continuing their violent habits. Thoughtful rather than horrifying, with subtle antifascist hints scattered throughout. (Dir: Robert Wise, 92 mins.)†

Day the Fish Came Out, The (Greece-Great Britain, 1967)* Tom Courtenay, Candice Bergen, Sam Wanamaker, Colin Blakely. Writer-producer-director Michael Cacoyannis (*Zorba the Greek*) lays an eggplant with this limp satire about the military trying to retrieve secret material dropped off near a Greek island. (109 mins.)

Day the Loving Stopped, The (MTV 1981) *½ Dennis Weaver, Valerie Harper, Dominique Dunne, Sam Groom, James Canning. Well-intended slow-moving drama that doesn't avoid the plot pitfalls of other similar stories about the pain visited upon the children of divorce. Clichés abound. (Dir: Daniel Mann, 104 mins.)

Day the Women Got Even, The (MTV 1980)*½ Barbara Rhoades, Georgia Engel, Jo Ann Pflug, Tina Louise, Julie Hagerty. A hokey yarn with some fun in it as housewives gang up on a New York talent agent and his musclemen. (Dir: Burt Brinckerhoff, 104 mins.)

Day the World Ended, The (1956)** Richard Denning, Lori Nelson, Adele Jergens, Mike Connors. After the Big Bomb, a motley crew of seven souls demonstrate human nature at its worst as they strive to survive. (Dir: Roger Corman, 82 mins.)

Day They Robbed the Bank of England, The (Great Britain, 1960)*** Peter O'Toole, Hugh Griffith, Elizabeth Sellars, Aldo Ray. "They" are Irish dissidents, who try the big heist in 1901. Considerable suspense in this yarn. O'Toole shows the promise fulfilled later, portraying the arm of the law. (Dir: John Guillermin, 85 mins.)

Day Time Ended, The (1980)** Jim Davis, Dorothy Malone, Christopher Mitchum, Marcy Lafferty, An illogical sci-fi fantasy about a family caught in a time warp. AKA: **Time Warp.** (Dir: John "Bud" Cardos, 79 mins.)†

Daytime Wife (1939)** Tyrone Power, Linda Darnell, Warren William, Binnie Barnes, Wendy Barrie. Girl takes drastic steps to win back her man. Mildly amusing comedy. (Dir: Gregory Ratoff, 71 mins.)

Dayton's Devils (1968)** Leslie Nielsen, Rory Calhoun, Lainie Kazan, Barry Sadler, Georg Stanford Brown, Hans Gudegast (Eric Braeden). Ex-army colonel Nielsen trains a team of experts in order to pull a $1.5 million heist at a Strategic Air Command base. Routine. (Dir: Jack Shea, 103 mins.)

Day Will Dawn, The (1942)*** Hugh Williams, Griffiths Jones, Ralph Richardson, Deborah Kerr, Roland Culver, Francis L. Sullivan, Finlay Currie. Patriotic

British WWII adventure has dashing Williams as a foreign correspondent seeking out a submarine base in Norway. Very well done. AKA: Avengers, The. (Dir: Harold French, 100 mins.)†

D.C. Cab (1983)**½ Mr. T, Adam Baldwin, Max Gail, Gary Busey, Charlie Barnett. A ramshackle but highly entertaining comedy with music about a decrepit cab company looking for self-respect. (Dir: Joel Schumacher, 104 mins.)†

D-Day, the Sixth of June (1956)*** Robert Taylor, Dana Wynter, Richard Todd. The usual plot of two officers loving one girl, a bit more credible than usual. (Dir: Henry Koster, 106 mins.)†

Dead, The (U.S.-Great Britain-West Germany, 1987)***½ Anjelica Huston, Donal McCann, Helena Carroll, Cathleen Delany, Dan O'Herlihy, Donal Donnelly. Director John Huston's final film is a touching work that proceeds at a leisurely pace and provides for wonderful moments of reverie. Based on James Joyce's story, the slim but meaningful narrative concerns a big dinner party given on the Feast of the Epiphany, and the farewells said at the party's end. Farewells to absent friends, farewells to certainty about love and devotion, and most importantly, farewell to a great filmmaker, one who took chances until the end. (83 mins.)†

Dead and Buried (1981)*** James Farentino, Melody Anderson, Jack Albertson, Nancy Locke Hauser. Campy, entertaining horror thriller. Farentino plays the sheriff, running into more surprises than he can handle when investigating a sudden rash of murders in this bizarre seaside fishing town. (Dir: Gary A. Sherman, 92 mins.)†

Dead-Bang (1989)*** Don Johnson, William Forsythe, Bob Balaban, Tim Reid, Penelope Ann Miller. Director John Frankenheimer's skill with action movies makes this tired script play much better than it should. Johnson stars as a grungy L.A. cop on the track of white supremacists who killed a fellow officer. (109 mins.)†

Dead Calm (1989)*** Sam Neill, Nicole Kidman, Billy Zane. Tense thriller about a couple vacationing on a yacht 1,200 miles from the coast of Australia who pick up the sole survivor of a sinking ship, only to find that he's a psychotic. Intelligently made, except for an idiotic "shock" ending. (Dir: Phillip Noyce, 97 mins.)†

Dead Don't Die, The (MTV 1975)*½ George Hamilton, Ray Millard, Linda Cristel, Joan Blondell, Ralph Meeker, Reggie Nalder. No, sometimes they make TV movies. Robert Bloch wrote this stinker starring Hamilton as a '30s private eye

who uncovers a madman's scheme to create an army of zombies. (Dir: Curtis Harrington, 73 mins.)

Dead Easy (Australia, 1982)**½ Scott Burgess, Rosemary Paul, Max Phipps, Tim McKenzie. Wild car chase a la *The French Connection* saves crime thriller about three young folks taking on the mob from being waste of time. Ludicrous, but somehow it works as a kind of Aussie "Mod Squad." (Dir: Bert Deling, 90 mins.)†

Dead End (1937)***½ Humphrey Bogart, Joel McCrea, Sylvia Sidney, Claire Trevor, Marjorie Main, Gabe Dell, Leo Gorcey, Huntz Hall. A film classic. Based on the successful Broadway play about the slums and the youngsters who fight for survival against their environment. A fine mixture of comedy and social drama. (Dir: William Wyler, 93 mins.)†

Dead End City (1988)*½ Dennis Cole, Greg Cummins, Christine Lunde, Robert Zdar. Gang warfare results in the evacuation of part of Los Angeles, but one family decides to stay and fight for their home. Predictable sci-fi action. (Dir: Peter Yuval, 85 mins.)†

Dead End Drive-In (Australia, 1986)*** Ned Manning, Natalie McCurry, Peter Whitford, Wilbur Wilde. Muscular direction highlights this post-apocalyptic thriller where the masses are kept in internment camps created out of drive-in theaters. (Dir: Brian Trenchard-Smith, 92 mins.)†

Dead Heat (1988)*** Treat Williams, Joe Piscopo, Lindsay Frost, Darren McGavin, Vincent Price. A detective is killed while investigating a supernatural crime ring and comes back as a zombie to catch the killers. A gruesome but enjoyable splatter spoof comedy; how can you not love a horror spoof with a zombie hero named "Roger Mortis"? (Dir: Mark Goldblatt, 84 mins.)†

Dead Heat on a Merry-Go-Round (1966)*** James Coburn, Camilla Sparv. James Coburn is well cast as one of the great con artists of all time. After he manages to win a parole from prison, Coburn sets up an ingenious bank heist, marries a gorgeous girl, impersonates some half-a-dozen characters, robs some wealthy dames, pulls off the bank job. (Dir: Bernard Girard, 104 mins.)†

Dead Kids—See: **Strange Behavior**

Deadlier Than the Male (Great Britain, 1967)**½ Richard Johnson, Elke Sommer, Sylva Koscina. The return of Bulldog Drummond (Johnson) as the hardy sleuth comes up against a pair of beautiful but deadly assassins (Sommer & Koscina). Amusing in a lowbrow bulldog way. (Dir: Ralph Thomas, 101 mins.)

Deadliest Season, The (MTV 1977)**½ Michael Moriarty, Kevin Conway, Meryl

Streep, Andrew Duggan, Patrick O'Neal, Sully Boyar. Provocative drama about the world of professional ice hockey. Moriarty gives a well-rounded performance as the run-of-the-mill hockey player who decides to become a ''goon''— someone who incites mayhem and violence during a game. (Dir: Robert Markowitz, 110 mins.)

Deadline (1980)** Marvin Goldhar, Sharon Masters. Horror novelist feels his easy way of life is disintegrating as he tries to write a new book. The terror of the story comes from the writer's own mind as what he prepares for the novel becomes part of the movie's strange plot about paranoia and reality. An interesting failure. (Dir: Mario Azzopari, 85 mins.)†

Deadline (West Germany, 1987)*½ Christopher Walken, Marita Marschall, Hywel Bennett. Muddled Middle East saga featuring Walken as an enterprising journalist behind the lines in war-torn Beirut. Another jaded-journalist-grows-concerned plot line; no significant points are made. (Dir: Nathaniel Gutman, 99 mins.)†

Deadline at Dawn (1946)**½ Susan Hayward, Bill Williams, Paul Lukas. Suspicion of murdering a woman points to a dancer, taxi driver, or sailor. Confused mystery; some good moments. (Dir: Harold Clurman, 83 mins.)

Deadline, U.S.A. (1952)*** Humphrey Bogart, Kim Hunter, Ethel Barrymore. Engrossing newspaper drama without the usual ''city room'' phoniness. Bogart is excellent as the editor of a large city paper who has to fight the underworld and keep the paper's publisher, superbly portrayed by Barrymore, from throwing in the towel and selling out. (Dir: Richard Brooks, 87 mins.)

Deadlock (MTV 1969)*** Leslie Nielsen, Hari Rhodes. Better-than-average, hard-hitting police drama about racial tensions in the ghetto of a large west coast city. Made as a pilot film for a TV series. (Dir: Lamont Johnson, 99 mins.)

Deadly Affair (Great Britain, 1967)*** James Mason, Simone Signoret, Maximilian Schell, Lynn Redgrave. Engrossing detective drama set amid the world of espionage. James Mason is excellent as a British agent who sets out to uncover the hidden facts behind a British government employee's suicide. Based on the John Le Carre novel *Call for the Dead*. (Dir: Sidney Lumet, 107 mins.)

Deadly Alliance (1978)** Mike Lloyd Gentry, Tony DeFonte, Kathleen Arc, Walter Prince. A pair of low-budget filmmakers become embroiled in the affairs of a secret multinational oil cartel. Pretentious and predictable. (Dir: Paul Salvatore Parco, 90 mins.)†

Deadly Bees, The (Great Britain, 1967)**½ Frank Finlay, Suzanna Leigh. Based on H. F. Heard's horror classic *A Taste for Honey*, this is all about a beekeeper who trains a swarm of giant killer bees, and a young lady who almost becomes a victim. (Dir: Freddie Francis, 85 mins.)

Deadly Blessing (1981)**½ Maren Jensen, Susan Buckner, Lisa Hartman, Ernest Borgnine. A confused but visually arresting thriller set in Pennsylvania Dutch country. Two free-thinking city girls visit their pal, a young widow, whose ultra-religious in-laws want her to sell her farm. (Dir: Wes Craven, 102 mins.)†

Deadly Breed (1989)** William Smith, Addison Randall, Blake Bahner, Joe Vance. Parole officer uncovers a gang of murderous neo-Nazis in the local police force. Violent, rather nasty revenge tale. (Dir: Charles T. Kanganis, 83 mins.)†

Deadly Business, A (MTV 1986)*** Alan Arkin, Michael Learned, Armand Assante. Low-key absorbing drama about a small-time mob official who begins to shy away from Mafia business. (Dir: John Korty, 104 mins.)

Deadly Care (MTV 1987)** Cheryl Ladd, Jason Miller, Jennifer Salt. A problem-drama about a troubled nurse who relies on drink and drugs in order to cope with the pressures of her position. Ladd uses both of her expressions: (1) bland befuddlement and (2) teary-eyed sincerity to enact a role beyond her range in this vain attempt to address a serious social issue. (Dir: David Anspaugh, 104 mins.)

Deadly Companions, The (1961)*** Maureen O'Hara, Brian Keith, Steve Cochran. A gunslinger escorts a dance hall hostess through Apache territory on a perilous journey. Good western with a script above the usual run, expert direction, capable performances. (Dir: Sam Peckinpah, 90 mins.)†

Deadly Darling (Hong Kong, 1985)½ Fonda Lynn, Warren Chan, Bernard Tsui, Cherry Kwok. Two lousy movies for the price of one, this turkey starts out as the story of a television model raped by a rich man who is set free by the courts. She disappears halfway through and the movie turns into the story of a female reporter seeking revenge on a gang who raped her. Incomprehensibly dubbed and edited. (Dir: Karen Yahng, 91 mins.)†

Deadly Deception (MTV 1987)*** Matt Salinger, Lisa Eilbacher, Bonnie Bartlett, Mildred Natwick. Psychological drama about a widower who can't come to terms with his wife's sudden death and the disappearance of his infant son, presumed dead. Well acted, particularly by

Natwick in a brilliant cameo. (Dir: John Llewellyn Moxey, 104 mins.)

Deadly Dream, The (MTV 1971)**½ Lloyd Bridges, Janet Leigh, Carl Betz, Leif Erickson. Bridges wanders through a nightmare world and his own seemingly real one... but which is the real one? The strange film builds interest following Bridges, a brilliant scientist, as he goes slowly mad. (Dir: Alf Kjellin, 72 mins.)

Deadly Dreams (1988)**½ Mitchell Anderson, Juliette Cummins, Xander Berkeley. Horror-mystery with a standard plot about a man haunted by nightmares of his parents' brutal murder. Clever twists and decent low-budget filmmaking make it worth a look. (Dir: Kristine Peterson, 79 mins.)†

Deadly Embrace (1988)* Jan-Michael Vincent, Ty Randolph, Linnea Quigley, Jack Carter. Deadly dull suspense drama with rich businessman Vincent trying to kill his troublesome wife with the help of an attractive young student and plenty of spy devices. Sleazy stuff, cheaply made. (Dir: Ellen Cabot, 89 mins.)†

Deadly Encounter (1975)½ Dina Merrill, Carl Betz, Leon Ames, Susan Logan, Vicki Powers, Steve Potter. Rich businesswoman Merrill invites her friends and associates to a dinner party. As they let their hair down, they expose a parade of dirty business dealings and personal perversions. Ponderously symbolic drama. AKA: **The Meal**. (Dir: R. John Hugh, 90 mins.)†

Deadly Encounter (MTV 1982)**½ Larry Hagman, Susan Anspach, James Gammon, Michael G. Gwynne. Hagman has a ball playing a Sam Spade character, an old war pilot helping his favorite blonde (Susan Anspach) outwit Tucson hoods. (Dir: William A. Graham, 104 mins.)†

Deadly Eyes (1983)**½ Sam Groom, Cec Linder, Sara Botsford. Rodents feed on grain laced with steroids and develop the munchies for human beings. The super rats aren't convincing, but the thrills delivered sometimes are. (Dir: Robert Clouse, 127 mins.)†

Deadly Force (1983)* Wings Hauser, Joyce Ingalls, Paul Shenar, Arlen Dean Snyder. Violent waste of time about a vigilante cop trying to snare another mad killer. (Dir: Paul Aaron, 95 mins.)†

Deadly Friend (1986)*½ Matthew Laborteaux, Kristy Swanson, Michael Sharrett, Anne Twomey, Anne Ramsey. When the robot creation of a young science genius (Laborteaux) is destroyed, and his girlfriend (Swanson) is accidentally killed, the boy decides to bring the girl back to life by implanting the robot's "brain"

in her head. Laughable horror film. (Dir: Wes Craven, 92 mins.)†

Deadly Game, The (MTV 1976)**½ David Birney, Allen Garfield, Walter McGinn, Lane Bradbury. A pilot for a TV series with Birney as Serpico, the famous New York cop who had the nerve to finger corruption within the Police Department. (Dir: Robert Collins, 98 mins.)

Deadly Game, The (MTV 1977)** Andy Griffith, Sharon Spelman, Dan O'Herlihy. Griffith fans will enjoy his easygoing police work as he delves into the mysterious deaths of two old people, caused by the transport of a shipment of deadly chemicals. (Dir: Lane Slate, 104 mins.)

Deadly Games (1982)* Sam Groom, Jo Ann Harris, Steve Railsback, Dick Butkus, Alexandra Morgan. Strange, ineffective horror flick about a series of murders in a small town. AKA: **The Eliminator**. (Dir: Scott Mansfield, 94 mins.)†

Deadly Harvest (MTV 1972)*** Richard Boone, Patty Duke. Interesting chase drama filmed in California's Napa Valley benefits greatly from good performances by Boone and Miss Duke. Boone supplies the tang, playing a taciturn, suspicious old wine-grower who defected from an Iron Curtain country years ago, and is now marked for assassination. (Dir: Michael O'Herlihy, 73 mins.)

Deadly Hero (1976)*** Don Murray, Diahn Williams, James Earl Jones, Lilia Skala, Conchata Ferrell, Treat Williams, Danny DeVito. Cop rescues woman from attack, killing her assailant. But when she begins to suspect his methods and goes to his superiors, she becomes his quarry as well. (Dir: Ivan Nagy, 102 mins.)†

Deadly Hunt, The (MTV 1971)*** Tony Franciosa, Peter Lawford, Anjanette Comer, Jim Hutton. Pretty interesting action movie about killers hired to rub out a wealthy lady in the Vancouver woods. (Dir: John Newland, 78 mins.)

Deadly Illusion (1988)** Billy Dee Williams, Vanity, Morgan Fairchild, John Beck, Joe Cortese. Preposterous private eye stuff about P.I. Williams hired to kill the wife of a Wall Street tycoon, only to find out that murder's not really the name of the game. (Dirs.: Larry Cohen, William Tannen, 90 mins.)†

Deadly Intent (1988)** Lisa Eilbacher, Steve Railsback, Maud Adams, Fred Williamson, Persis Khambatta, Lance Henrickson, David Dukes, Clayton Rohner. Assorted villains battle over a valuable jewel brought back from South America by a man murdered soon after. The all-bad-guy approach is a change of pace, but not so the talky movie as a whole. (Dir: Nigel Dick, 87 mins.)†

Deadly Intentions (MTV 1985)***½ Michael Biehn, Madolyn Smith, Cloris

Leachman, Cliff DeYoung, Morgana King, Jack Kruschen. A chilling drama based on a true story dealing with a psychotic doctor and his maniacal treatment of the woman he marries. (Dir: Noel Black, 196 mins.)

Deadly Intentions ... Again? (MTV 1991)**½ Harry Hamlin, Joanna Kerns, Eileen Brennan, Conchata Ferrell, Fairuza Balk. A continuation of the real-life story of Dr. Charles Raynor (Hamlin) who spent time in prison for the attempted murder of his first wife and then plotted his second wife's murder after being paroled. The story unfolds without too many surprises but the fact that it is based in truth adds a chilling note. (Dir: James Steven Sadwith, 96 mins.)

Deadly Lessons (MTV 1983)* Donna Reed, Larry Wilcox, David Ackroyd, Diane Franklin, Ally Sheedy. Reed stars as the stuffy discipline-minded head of a small, exclusive prep school for girls where the beautiful students are being systematically bumped off. Cheap, sleazy, and unredeeming. (Dir: William Wiard, 104 mins.)

Deadly Mantis, The (1957)** Craig Stevens, William Hopper. Scientist works feverishly to stop a giant mantis heading south from the polar regions. (Dir: Nathan Juran, 78 mins.)

Deadly Messages (MTV 1985)** Kathleen Beller, Michael Brandon. This thriller is short on chills and long on predictability. Beller becomes the target of a mysterious would-be killer. The question is why, and some of the answers are provided by a Ouija board. Ms. Beller's big eyes work overtime as she reacts to a series of terrors. (Dir: Jack Bender, 104 mins.)

Deadly Possession (Australia, 1988)**½ Penny Cook, Arna-Maria Winchester, Liddy Clark, Olivia Hamnet. A student attempts to prove that her ex-husband, accused of a vicious murder, is innocent. Of course, that makes her a target of the real killer. Mystery-thriller marred by a sloppy denouement. (Dir: Craig Lahiff, 99 mins.)†

Deadly Prey (1987)* Ted Prior, David Campbell, Cameron Mitchell, Troy Donahue, Dawn Abraham. Sadistic ex-marine colonel trains his private mercenary army by having them hunt innocent people kidnapped for that purpose. But when they kidnap ex-vet Prior, the tables are turned. Avoid unless you're in a mood to see someone beaten to death with his own severed arm. (Dir: David A. Prior, 88 mins.)†

Deadly Reactor (1989)**½ David Heavener, Stuart Whitman, Darwyn Swalve, Allyson Davis. Sort of a post-nuke spaghetti western, starring writer-director Heavener

248

as a gunfighter who reacts to rather than initiates fights (hence the title). In a bombed-out future, he protects a small town from a vicious biker gang. Clint Eastwood fans take note. (88 mins.)†

Deadly Recruits (1986)** Terence Stamp, Michael Culver, Carmen Du Sautoy, Robin Sachs. British agent Stamp tries to prove that a KGB plot is behind the scandalous ruins of a number of promising young Oxford students. Stodgy spy caper with such a stiff-upper-lip attitude that Stamp hardly ever changes expression. (Dir: Roger Tucker, 92 mins.)†

Deadly Revenge (Italy, 1985)* Rodolfo Ranni, Julio de Grazia, Silvia Montanari. Mild-mannered writer agrees to take over the club of his boyhood friend after he is murdered, then finds himself in trouble with the same mobsters who killed his friend. All talk and no action in this dubbed crime drama. (Dir: Juan Carlos Sesanzo, 90 mins.)†

Deadly Rivals—See: Rivals

Deadly Silence, A (MTV 1989)** Mike Farrell, Heather Fairfield, Bruce Weitz, Charles Haid, Richard Portnow, Sally Struthers. Story of Cheryl Pierson, the high school teenager who hired a classmate to kill her sexually abusive father. Farfield's performance is lifeless, and the movie drags. Haid as Cheryl's father gives the best performance. (Dir: John Patterson, 96 mins.)

Deadly Spygames (1989)** Jack M. Sell, Adrianne Richmond, Troy Donohue, Tippi Hendren. Parody of James Bond–type spy films, with Sell and Richmond (who also wrote and produced) saving the world from a murderous Soviet general. Some amusing bits, many labored ones. Top-billed Donohue and Hendren appear only briefly. (Dir: Jack M. Sell, 86 mins.)†

Deadly Sting (France, 1985)** Henry Silva, Andre Pousse. When the backers who financed the robbery of a shipment of gold bullion cheat organizer Silva out of his cut, he executes an elaborate revenge. Below-average crime story. (Dir: Jean-Claude Roy, 90 mins.)

Deadly Stranger (1988)* Darlanne Fluegel, Michael J. Moore, John Vernon, Ted White. Drifter Moore takes a farm job on Vernon's plantation, helps Mexican laborers stand up to Vernon and crooked union official White. Movie wastes the talents of Fluegel, in a bimbo part as Vernon's scheming mistress, as well as viewers' time. AKA: **Border Heat.** (Dir: Max Kleven, 93 mins.)†

Deadly Strangers (Great Britain, 1975)** Hayley Mills, Simon Ward, Sterling Hayden. Two people with deep secrets meet accidentally on the road and share a ride. It gradually develops that one is an escaped homicidal maniac, but is it the one you suspect? The suspense is contrived, and the ending is ridiculous. (Dir: Sidney Hayers, 93 mins.)†

Deadly Tower, The (MTV 1975)*** Kurt Russell, Ned Beatty, John Forsythe, Richard Yniguez, Pernell Roberts. Based on fact, this is an above-average dramatization of the chilling tale of a young sniper, who climbed up the tower at the University of Texas and fired upon innocent passersby, killing 13 people and wounding 33 others. (Dir: Jerry Jameson, 105 mins.)

Deadly Trackers, The (1973)½ Richard Harris, Rod Taylor, Isela Varga. Director Samuel Fuller tried to turn his short story, "Riata," into a film but was fired from the project. Without his guiding hand, this turns into a terrible, violent revenge drama with Harris on the trail of his wife's murderers. (Dir: Barry Shear, 104 mins.)

Deadly Trap, The (1971)** Faye Dunaway, Frank Langella, Barbara Parkins. Muddled thriller. Dunaway is a troubled wife and mother who appears to be suffering a mental breakdown, but there's more to it than meets the eye. (Dir: Rene Clement, 97 mins.)

Deadly Triangle, The (MTV 1977)** Dale Robinette, Diana Muldaur, Robert Lansing. Dale Robinette stars as a former Olympic downhill skiing champion who takes to the slopes as the sheriff of Sun Valley. Sequel: *Crisis in Sun Valley.* (Dir: Charles S. Dubin, 79 mins.)

Deadly Weapon (1988)**½ Rodney Easton, Kim Walker, Gary Frank, Gary Kroeger, Joe Regalabuto, William Sanderson. Maladjusted teenager, the victim of incessant bullying, has a dream come true when he finds a secret army weapon, an antimatter gun that can blast his enemies away. Some surprising plot turns keep this B movie lively. (Dir: Michael Miner, 90 mins.)†

Dead Man on the Run (MTV 1975)** Peter Graves, Katherine Justice, Pernell Roberts, Diana Douglas. Pilot for an unsold series set in New Orleans with Graves as a government agent who uncovers a political scandal involving a murder. (Dir: Bruce Bilson, 72 mins.)

Dead Man Out (MCTV 1989)*** Ruben Blades, Danny Glover, Tom Atkins. Powerful Death Row tale with psychiatrist Glover assigned to "cure" troubled inmate Blades, in keeping with a Supreme Court ruling that mentally ill prisoners cannot be executed. The script deals thoughtfully with the healer's dilemma—if he succeeds, his patient dies—but see it for Blades's powerful performance. (Dir: Richard Pearce, 86 mins.)

Deadman's Curve (MTV 1978)**½ Richard Hatch, Bruce Davison. A sleeper for rock-and-roll fans, based on the true story of a pair of California kids, Jan and Dean, who became famous in the '60s with a string of surfing song hits. Hatch turns in a sensitive performance as cocky Jan, later crippled by an auto smashup. (Dir: Richard Compton, 104 mins.)†

Dead Man's Eyes (1944)** Lon Chaney, Jr., Paul Kelly, Jean Parker. An artist is accused of murdering a man to obtain his eyes for an operation. Silly story, badly acted, but it almost makes it on bizarreness alone. (Dir: Reginald Le Borg, 64 mins.)

Dead Man's Folly (MTV 1986)**½ Peter Ustinov, Jonathan Cecil, Tim Piggot-Smith, Jean Stapleton, Constance Cummings, Susan Woolridge, Nicollette Sheridan. In his first television performance as the detective Hercule Poirot, Ustinov is everywhere: cajoling, mumbling, playing little tricks, as he ferrets out a murderer on an English estate. It's all very British and easy to figure out, but fans will enjoy the sight of Ustinov quizzing the suspects. AKA: **Agatha Christie's Dead Man's Folly.** (Dir: Clive Donner, 104 mins.)†

Dead Man Walking (1988)** Wings Hauser, Brion James, Pamela Ludwig, Sy Richardson, Jeffrey Combs. Sci-fi set in a postplague future with adventurer Hauser, slowly dying of the disease, stalking the kidnappers of a young woman. Some satirical touches help make it watchable. (Dir: Gregory Brown, 90 mins.)†

Dead Mate (1986)* Elizabeth Mannino, David Gregory, Lawrence Bockus. A waitress at a roadside café is swept off her feet by a stranger, a mortician with a more than friendly interest in his clientele. Horror film has a few intriguing ideas but gets completely out of control before too long. (Dir: Straw Weisman, 93 mins.)†

Dead Men Don't Wear Plaid (1982)*** Steve Martin, Rachel Ward, Reni Santoni, Carl Reiner, George Gaynes, Frank McCarthy. Clever mixture of a contemporary comedy-mystery with old film clips, giving the impression that Steve Martin as a private eye is involved with a panorama of stars, including Bogart, Grant, Stanwyck, Ingrid Bergman, Veronica Lake, and many more. (Dir: Carl Reiner, 89 mins.)†

Dead Men Tell (1941)**½ Sidney Toler, Sheila Ryan, Robert Weldon, Victor Sen Yung. Enjoyable Charlie Chan mystery about a murder during a sea-going treasure hunt involving a treasure map in four pieces. (Dir: Harry Lachman, 60 mins.)

Dead Men Walk (1943)** George Zucco,

Mary Carlisle, Nedrick Young, Dwight Frye. They certainly do. Zucco plays twins—one a fiendish vampire; the other a goody-two-shoes whom the bloodsucking sibling puts the bite on. Eerie when the low budget doesn't show through. (Dir: Sam Newfield, 67 mins.)†

Dead of Night (Great Britain, 1946)**** Michael Redgrave, Googie Withers, Mervyn Johns. A man who has had a strange dream visits in the country, where other guests relate how some dream of theirs has had basis in fact. Fine spine-tingling episodic thriller, a true suspense-rouser. (Dirs: Cavalcanti, Charles Crichton, Basil Dearden, Robert Hamer, 102 mins.)†

Dead of Night (1972)—See: **Deathdream**

Dead of Winter (1986)*** Mary Steenburgen, Roddy McDowall, Jan Rubes, William Russ. A nerve-wracking lady-in-distress thriller that will keep you on edge. Steenburgen plays three parts, including that of an actress so desperate to work she falls for a ploy to lure her to an old dark house where unimaginable horror, involving blackmail and murder, awaits her. Steenburgen's conscienceless hosts are played with campy aplomb by Rubes and McDowall. (Dir: Arthur Penn, 100 mins.)†

Dead People—See: **Messiah of Evil**

Dead Pigeon on Beethoven Street (1972)*** Glenn Corbett, Stephane Audran, Christa Lang, Gary Lockwood. An audacious, violent thriller about a detective breaking up an international blackmail ring. Fuller's driving style covers any loopholes in the plot. (Dir: Sam Fuller, 102 mins.)†

Dead Pit (1989)* Jeremy Slate, Cheryl Lawson, Gregory Foster. Tale of lobotomized zombies and mysterious experiments at a mental institution is the pits indeed. (Dir: Brett Leonard, 95 mins.)†

Dead Poets Society (1989)*** Robin Williams, Robert Sean Leonard, Ethan Hawke, Kurtwood Smith. Williams doesn't overwhelm the story for a change in this melodramatic but effective tale set in a boys' prep school circa 1959. He plays a vivacious English teacher who encourages his students to look beyond their repressive school's rules and enjoy life. (Dir: Peter Weir, 128 mins.)†

Dead Pool, The (1988)**½ Clint Eastwood, Patricia Clarkson, Evan C. Kim, Liam Neeson. The fifth Dirty Harry opus eschews the reactionary righteousness of previous entries and substitutes a typically dopey cop-movie plot. Harry investigates a series of murders tied together by a perverse bet among the members of a movie crew. On the plus side, Eastwood prods the character in a few new

directions. But overall, he's just going through the paces. (Dir: Buddy Van Horn, 91 mins.)†

Dead Reckoning (1947)*** Humphrey Bogart, Lizabeth Scott. Occasionally exciting chase melodrama about a veteran investigating the disappearance of his hero buddy. (Dir: John Cromwell, 100 mins.)†

Dead Ringer (1964)*** Bette Davis, Karl Malden, Peter Lawford. Davis fans will enjoy her histrionics as the proprietress of a saloon who kills her look-alike sister and takes over her home and jewels. It's a cushy position until dead sister's boyfriend catches on, and the plot thickens and thickens. (Dir: Paul Henreid, 115 mins.)

Dead Ringers (Canada, 1988)***½ Jeremy Irons, Genevieve Bujold, Heidi von Palleske. Though lacking the overt horror elements of most of his work, director David Cronenberg's psychological thriller is no less disquieting. Irons plays twin brothers, doctors who run a gynecological clinic and share every experience in life until a woman (Bujold) comes between them. An adult drama marked by two excellent performances from Irons—it's easy to forget that is one actor playing the two roles. (113 mins.)†

Dead Run (France-Italy-West Germany, 1969)**½ Peter Lawford, Countess Ira Furstenberg, Georges Geret. Secret agents from all over the world hunt for a petty thief who has unknowingly snatched a briefcase containing top secret documents. Fair spy spoof. (Dir: Christian-Jaque, 97 mins.)

Dead Solid Perfect (MCTV 1988)*** Randy Quaid, Kathryn Harrold, Corrine Bohrer, Jack Warden. Dan Jenkins co-adapted this screenplay from his novel about the world of professional golf, centering around second-rate pro Quaid. The characters are funny and engaging, and the game has never been presented to better advantage on film. (Dir: Bobby Roth, 95 mins.)†

Deadtime Stories (1986)**½ Scott Valentine, Melissa Leo, Cathryn De Prume, Nicole Picard, Matt Mitler. A somewhat uneven but enjoyable collection of gruesome variations on well-known children's stories. The third segment, a demented revamping of "Goldilocks and the Three Bears" involving a psychotic family and a telekinetic girl, has some hilarious, outrageous slapstick-violence. (Dir: Jeffrey Delman, 82 mins.)†

Dead Zone (1983)**½ Christopher Walken, Brooke Adams, Tom Skerritt, Herbert Lom. An eerie, slightly disappointing translation of a Stephen King thriller. A school teacher (Walken) is injured in a car accident, lapses into a coma. When he wakes up years later, he has developed precognitive powers which he is reluctant to use. (Dir: David Cronenberg, 103 mins.)†

Dealing: Or the Berkeley-to-Boston-Forty-Brick-Lost-Bag-Blues (1972)** Robert F. Lyons, Barbara Hershey, John Lithgow. Based on the novel by Michael and Douglas Crichton dealing with a bored Harvard Law student (Lyons) who moves grass from Berkeley to Boston for dealer Lithgow. No assertion of values makes for little drama. (Dir: Paul Williams, 88 mins.)

Deal of the Century (1983)½ Sigourney Weaver, Chevy Chase, Gregory Hines. A purported satire about a high-pressure salesman selling weapons, including a remote control bomber, to anyone who has the cash. When the product proves faulty, Chevy is ordered to unload the junk on a Latin American dictator. No sale! (Dir: William Friedkin, 98 mins.)†

Dear America: Letters Home from Vietnam (MCTV 1988)**** Voices of Ellen Burstyn, Robert De Niro, Martin Sheen, et al. This collection of authentic letters from GIs at war, read by some of Hollywood's best-known actors and accompanied by a potpourri of sixties rock 'n' roll and documentary footage, is a painful and moving testament to the experience of our soldiers in Vietnam. Unlike a dramatization or a cold factual documentary, this film manages to bring the impact of the war on the young men fighting it into a clear light. (Dir: Bill Couturie, 86 mins.)†

Dear Brat (1951)** Mona Freeman, Billy DeWolfe, Lyle Bettger, Edward Arnold. Fairly congenial but dated sequel to *Dear Ruth*, with Mona lending a helping hand to a reformed criminal. (Dir: William Seiter, 82 mins.)

Dear Brigitte (1965)**½ James Stewart, Glynis Johns. Homey family comedy that doesn't come off as successfully as it should have. Papa Stewart tries to cope with his young son's problem—it seems that he has developed a big crush on Brigitte Bardot and keeps sending her fan letters. (Dir: Henry Koster, 100 mins.)†

Dear Dead Delilah (1972)** Agnes Moorehead, Will Geer, Patricia Carmichael. Grisly thriller shot in Nashville. The heirs to an old southern mansion are being axed to death over a hidden fortune. Moorehead, in her last screen appearance, delivers as the dying matriarch of the family. (Dir: John Farris, 95 mins.)†

Dear Detective (France, 1978)*** Annie Girardot, Philippe Noiret, Paulette Dubost. Comedy and mystery are deftly blended in this entertaining tale of a lady detective who falls in love with an old friend, a professor of Greek, while attempting to solve a series of murders involving the Chamber of Deputies. Both Girardot and Noiret are in top form. Sequel: *Jupiter's Thigh*. AKA: **Dear Inspector.** (Dir: Philippe de Broca, 105 mins.)

Dear Detective (MTV 1979)**½ Brenda Vaccaro, Arlen Dean Snyder, Ron Silver. Brenda plays a police detective sergeant who meets a professor and embarks on an offbeat romance while continuing her investigation of a multiple murder. (Dir: Dean Hargrove, 104 mins.)†

Dear Heart (1965)*** Glenn Ford, Geraldine Page, Angela Lansbury. This is the type of sentimental romance which earns the label of "heartwarming" without even trying too hard. Ford is a salesman who meets and woos spinster postmistress Page in New York City during a convention. (Dir: Delbert Mann, 114 mins.)

Dear Inspector—See: **Dear Detective** (1978)

Dear Maestro (Italy, 1983)*** Michele Placido, Tino Schrinzi, Giuliana De Sio. The town of Chieti is trying to put itself on the map by starting its own symphony orchestra. As the players jockey to be top dog, the director mixes his satire of the locals with an obvious love of his characters. The result is a social comedy blessedly free of condescension. (Dir: Luciano Odorisio, 100 mins.)

Dear Michael (Italy, 1976)***½ Mariangela Melato, Delphine Seyrig, Aurore Clement, Fabio Carpi. Traditional values of a middle-class family are challenged when rebellious son, now out of the country fighting with a revolutionary movement, fathers a child with a carefree young woman. Characters interact exclusively through letters in a complex plot that works thanks to superb acting, writing, and direction. (Dir: Mario Monicelli, 108 mins.)

Dear Mr. Wonderful (West Germany, 1983)*** Joe Pesci, Tony Martin, Ivy Ray Browning. This oddity was produced in West Germany, but it does a creditable job of conjuring up Jersey City, America. The operator of a bowling alley has dreams of becoming a lounge singer, Vegas-style, and he serves as an inspiration to his friends and family. Deliberately low-key, the film is sensitive in a TV drama manner, but there's something appealing about this singing *Marty*. (Dir: Peter Lilienthal, 105 mins.)

Dear Ruth (1947)**½ Joan Caulfield, William Holden. Topical farce of 1947 is now rather obvious comedy about a youngster who has a hot correspondence with a soldier while posing as her older sister. (Dir: William D. Russell, 95 mins.)

Dear Summer Sister (Japan, 1972)*** Hosie Komatsu, Hiromi Kurita, Kei Sato, Akiko Koyama. A Tokyo teenage girl journeys to Okinawa to search for a half-brother she has never known. Explores tense themes of incest, WWII guilt, and the relationship between Japan and Okinawa. (Dir: Nagisa Oshima, 96 mins.)

Dear Wife (1949)*** William Holden, Joan Caulfield, Mona Freeman, Billy DeWolfe. "Dear Ruth" is now married, and her teenage sister launches a campaign to get her husband to the State Senate, which disrupts things. Some good laughs in this cleverly directed domestic comedy. (Dir: Richard Haydn, 88 mins.)

Death Among Friends (MTV 1975)** Kate Reid, John Anderson, A Martinez, Martin Balsam, Jack Cassidy, Paul Henreid, Pamela Hensley, William Smith, Denver Pyle, Lynda Day George, Michael Evans. Unsold pilot for a series about a female homicide detective. Reid is the whole show, and gets no help from a hackneyed plot. AKA: **Mrs. R—Death Among Friends.** (Dir: Paul Wendkos, 76 mins.)

Death and the Maiden—See: Hawkins on Murder

Death at Love House (MTV 1976)*½ Robert Wagner, Kate Jackson, Dorothy Lamour, Sylvia Sidney, Joan Blondell. Clumsy "high-camp." A big Hollywood mansion almost steals the attention from the cast in this tale about a big movie star of the thirties who still has a mysterious hold on the son of one of her lovers. (Dir: E. W. Swackhamer, 72 mins.)†

Deathbed—See: Terminal Choice

Death Before Dishonor (1987)** Fred Dryer, Joanna Pacula, Brian Keith, Sasha Mitchell, Peter Parros, Paul Winfield. The usual heady blend of terrorism, treachery, and torture as a Marine gunnery sergeant gets fighting mad after extremists hijack American weapons and kidnap his commanding officer in the Middle East. (Dir: Terry J. Leonard, 96 mins.)†

Death Be Not Proud (MTV 1975)***½ Arthur Hill, Jane Alexander, Robby Benson. A moving film based on a memoir by John Gunther, in which he wrote about his teenage son's valiant bout with cancer and the effect the boy's unflagging efforts to beat the unbeatable had on his divorced parents. Although this is a story dealing with death, it is not downbeat. (Dir: Donald Wrye, 100 mins.)

Death by Hanging (Japan, 1968)***½ Yon-Do Yun, Kei Sato, Fumio Watanabe, Toshiro Ishido, Masao Adachi. Young Korean worker found guilty of rape is sentenced to death but survives his hanging. Authorities are then forced to reenact the crime after the man loses his
252

memory from the aborted execution. Tense, unsettling film describes executions and death chambers in great detail. Director Nagisa Oshima also explores Japanese persecution of Koreans and obsessive, ritual-bound bureaucracy of his native land. (114 mins.)

Death Car on the Freeway (MTV 1979)**½ Shelly Hack, George Hamilton, Frank Gorshin, Peter Graves, Harriet Nelson, Barbara Rush, Dinah Shore, Abe Vigoda, Morgan Brittany, Sid Haig. As could be expected of anything directed by ex-stuntman Hal Needham, the action scenes are the best part of this routine thriller featuring Hack as a TV newswoman trying to catch a crazed van driver. (96 mins.)

Death Chase (1988) Paul Smith, Jack Starrett, William Zipp, Bainbridge Scott. Innocent jogger unwittingly becomes a player in a private, citywide war game being staged by an evil businessman. Interesting idea suffers from alternately dull and exaggerated execution; the ending is a real letdown. (Dir: David A. Prior, 88 mins.)†

Deathcheaters (Australia, 1976)*** John Hargreaves, Grant Page, Noel Ferrer, Drew Forsythe, Margaret Gerard. Former Vietnam War soldiers of fortune, now movie stuntmen, are hired by the government to retrieve important documents from Asian gang leader. Nonstop excitement and tongue-in-cheek approach to plot makes film an action-adventure winner. (Dir: Brian Trenchard-Smith, 96 mins.)†

Death Cruise (MTV 1974)** Richard Long, Polly Bergen, Edward Albert, Kate Jackson, Celeste Holm. Yarn about a luxury cruise that turns out to be a death ship for five out of six passengers, who all won the trip in a contest. It's well cast, with a surprise ending. (Dir: Ralph Senensky, 72 mins.)†

Death Dive—See: Fer-de-Lance

Deathdream (Canada, 1972)*** John Marley, Richard Backus, Lynn Carlin, Anya Ormsby. A distraught wife wishes that her son hadn't died in Vietnam; her request is horribly fulfilled when he turns up on the family's doorstep with an insatiable need for blood. An emotionally forceful drama that's also quite scary. AKA: **Dead of Night.** (Dir: Bob Clark, 90 mins.)†

Death Game (1977)* Sondra Locke, Colleen Camp, Seymour Cassel, Beth Brickell, Two maniacal young women invade a businessman's home, seduce him, destroy his property, drown his delivery boy in a fish tank, and, in general, make nuisances of themselves. Weird and nasty. (Dir: Peter S. Traynor, 89 mins.)

Death Hunt (1981)** Charles Bronson, Lee Marvin, Andrew Stevens, Angie Dickinson, Carl Weathers, Ed Lauter. Bronson and Marvin fans who like plenty of macho action will get what they want. Based loosely on a real-life character in the '30s. Bronson plays Albert Johnson, who was a trapper in Canada allegedly framed on a murder charge and the object of a gigantic manhunt. (Dir: Peter Hunt, 97 mins.)†

Death In California (MTV 1985)*** Cheryl Ladd, Sam Elliott, Granville Van Dusen, Alexis Smith. The most bizarre murder trial in California history is brought to life with a painstaking production and a well-chosen cast. Ladd plays a rich Beverly Hills woman who becomes entangled with a psychopath (Elliott) after he kills her fiancé, rapes her and extracts a promise that she won't talk to the police. (Dir: Delbert Mann, 196 mins.)

Death In Canaan, A (MTV 1978)**** Stefanie Powers, Paul Clemens, Conchata Ferrell, Tom Atkins. A gripping re-creation of the real-life incident in which young Peter Reilly was accused of brutally murdering his mother in a small Connecticut town in '73. Police brainwashed the confused and frightened lad into signing a confession. The townspeople rallied to Peter's defense, aided by a group of famous people. (Dir: Tony Richardson, 130 mins.)

Death In Small Doses (1957)** Peter Graves, Mala Powers, Chuck Connors. When drug abuse causes accidents among truck drivers, an investigation is started. Pep pill yarn may put you to sleep. (Dir: Joseph M. Newman, 79 mins.)

Death In Venice (Italy, 1971)*** Dirk Bogarde, Bjorn Andresen, Silvana Mangano, Marisa Berenson. It may not be possible to really do full cinematic justice to Thomas Mann's classic, complicated, richly textured novella. But Visconti has assuredly captured the visual quality, the look and feel of Venice circa 1911, a city dying of a secret pestilence. Bogarde plays, with great restraint, an aging, world-famous homosexual composer who has developed an uncontrollable passion for a ravishing young boy (Andresen). (Dir: Luchino Visconti, 130 mins.)†

Death Journey (1975)* Fred Williamson, Bernard Kuby, Heidi Dobbs, D'Urville Martin, Stephanie Faulkner. A vanity picture produced and directed by star Williamson. He's a private eye assigned to take a government witness from one coast to another. Williamson fans might enjoy it, but the rest of us should just send him a mirror. A real lemon. (96 mins.)†

Death Kiss, The (1933)**½ Bela Lugosi, David Manners, Adrienne Ames, John Wray, Edward Van Sloan. Low-budget chiller but creepily atmospheric. It's murder-on-the-movie-set time after an actor is killed while making a film. Interesting for glimpses into studio filmmaking at the time. (Dir: Edward L. Marin, 75 mins.)†

Death Line—See: Raw Meat

Deathmaster, The (1972)½ Robert Quarry, Bill Ewing. Vampire is washed ashore, and a beach gang adopt him as their guru. Tedious variation on the fang-baring theme. (Dir: Ray Danton, 88 mins.)

Deathmoon (MTV 1978)** Robert Foxworth, Joe Penny, Barbara Trentham, France Nuyen. Foxworth tries, but can't overcome the trite predictability of a yarn about the supernatural beliefs of Hawaiian natives. (Dir: Bruce Kessler, 104 mins.)

Death of a Bureaucrat (Cuba, 1966)***½ Salvador Wood, Silvia Planas, Manuel Estanillo, Gaspar De Santelices. Young man is forced to deal with miles of red tape in order to disinter his late uncle, who was buried with his union card (needed so his widow can collect his pension). Bureaucratic spoof with heady touches of Billy Wilder–like satire and slapstick antics. Wildly funny and sharply critical. (Dir: Tomas Gutierrez Alea, 87 mins.)†

Death of a Centerfold: The Dorothy Stratten Story (MTV 1981)*½ Jamie Lee Curtis, Bruce Weitz, Robert Reed. Sordid TV movie about the life and shocking murder of beautiful Playmate Stratten. The cast is adequate, but *Star 80* does it better. (Dir: Gabrielle Beaumont, 96 mins.)†

Death of a Cyclist (Spain, 1955)***½ Licia Bose, Alberto Closas, Carlos Casaravilla, Otello Toso, Bruna Corra. Director Juan Antonio Bardem's most famous work tells story of university professor who, while driving in car with his mistress, hits a bicyclist and leaves him to die in the road. Film expertly contrasts rich and poor classes of Franco's Spain while weaving a strong tale of love and guilt with tragic consequences. (88 mins.)

Death of Adolph Hitler, The (Great Britain, 1972)**½ Frank Finlay, Caroline Mortimer, Ed Devereaux, Ray MacAnnaly, Oscar Quitak. Dramatization of the last days of Hitler's life, spent in his underground bunker listening to news of the fall of Germany. Finlay gives an excellent, nonstereotyped portrayal of the dictator, but the low-key nature of the film may leave viewers unmoved. (Dir: Rex Firkin, 107 mins.)†

Death of a Gunfighter (1969)**½ Richard

Widmark, Lena Horne. This is a slow-moving character study of a small-town marshal (Widmark) who is no longer needed by the townspeople. Though credited to "Allan Smithee," the Director's Guild pseudonym, the film was directed by Robert Totten and Don Siegel. (100 mins.)†

Death of a Salesman (1952)*** Fredric March, Mildred Dunnock, Kevin McCarthy. A forceful filmization of Arthur Miller's Pulitzer Prize–winning play about fading salesman Willy Loman and his emotionally charged relationships with his family. Superb performances and interesting film technique add to its appeal. (Dir: Laslo Benedek, 115 mins.)

Death of a Salesman (MTV 1985)**** Dustin Hoffman, Kate Reid, John Malkovich, Stephen Lang, Charles Durning. This theatrical masterpiece, written by Arthur Miller, is one of the enduring glories of American theater. *Salesman* has been directed by the gifted German filmmaker Volker Schlondorff, who taped this production within the confines of a Broadway-stage set, thereby enhancing the intimacy of this study of the disintegration of a traveling salesman. Flashbacks are adroitly interwoven with current scenes, providing a buildup to the shattering climax. (150 mins.)†

Death of a Scoundrel (1956)** George Sanders, Zsa Zsa Gabor, Yvonne DeCarlo. A silly and obvious drama about a suave scoundrel who lives by his charm. (Dir: Charles Martin, 119 mins.)†

Death of a Soldier (Australia, 1986)**½ Reb Brown, James Coburn, Bill Hunter. Occasionally powerful true story about a murder case in WWII Australia. In 1942, a private stationed near Melbourne murdered three women without apparent motive; yet, instead of being sent to a mental institution he was executed. (Dir: Philippe Mora, 93 mins.)†

Death of Empedocles (West Germany, 1987)*** Stark, doctrinaire adaptation of Hölderlin play about Greek philosopher who created basis for central theme of modern physics. Directors Jean-Marie Straub and Daniele Huillete live up to their penchant for historically detailed and artistically correct dramas in this interpretation of Empedocles' fall from God's favor. (132 mins.)

Death of Her Innocence (1974)** Pamela Sue Martin, Parker Stevenson, Betsy Slade. This nostalgic soap opera about a fancy girls' school in 1955 cast TV's Hardy Boy and Nancy Drew as young lovers before they went on to brief TV fame. AKA: Our Time. (Dir: Peter Hyams, 90 mins.)

Death of Innocence (MTV 1971)**½ Shelley Winters, Tisha Sterling. Playing a Utah mother, Miss Winters arrives in New York with husband to attend daughter's murder trial, certain it's all a mistake. Mom slowly faces the idea her daughter might be guilty. (Dir: Paul Wendkos, 73 mins.)

Death of Mario Ricci, The (Switzerland, 1983)***½ Gian Maria Volonte, Heinz Bennent, Mimsy Farmer, Magali Noel. A Swiss television reporter returns home and interviews a famine expert who lives in the Alps. The famous person is one of the many in the village who harbors a dirty little secret: the truth about the death of an Italian worker. Strange but worth seeing, especially for Volonte's award-winning performance as the journalist. (Dir: Claude Goretta, 101 mins.)

Death of Me Yet, The (MTV 1971)**½ Doug McClure, Darren McGavin, Rosemary Forsyth, Richard Basehart, Meg Foster. McClure stars in this fairly suspenseful telepic as a Soviet agent who runs away to the U.S. and lives as a happily married man when his past catches up with him. (Dir: John Llewellyn Moxey, 78 mins.)

Death of Ocean View Park, The (MTV 1979)*** Mike Connors, Martin Landau, Caroline McWilliams, Diana Canova. Exciting disaster drama about an amusement park which is doomed. The plot centers on a large Fourth-of-July park opening which has been plagued by mysterious, unexplained occurrences. (Dir: E. W. Swackhamer, 106 mins.)

Death of Richie, The (MTV 1977)***½ Ben Gazzara, Robby Benson, Eileen Brennan. Here's a sleeper—a well-made emotional drama about a teenaged drug addict who can't give up the habit. (Dir: Paul Wendkos, 104 mins.)

Death of the Incredible Hulk (MTV 1990)** Bill Bixby, Lou Ferrigno, Elizabeth Gracen, Philip Sterling. Follow-up to the TV show about David Banner, the scientist with the unnerving habit of turning into a raging green monster when he gets stressed out. Banner's new romance is complicated by terrorists, who are after the Hulk formula. Bixby's charm in romantic scenes doesn't offset heavy-handed action portions aimed at the kids and cult devotees of the series. (Dir: Bill Bixby, 96 mins.)

Death on the Freeway (MTV 1979)** Shelley Hack, George Hamilton, Frank Gorshin, Peter Graves. Women must drive for their lives when a vehicle, custom built for murder, attacks them on the road. (Dir: Hal Needham, 104 mins.)

Death on the Nile (1978)***½ Peter Ustinov, Bette Davis, David Niven, Mia Farrow, Angela Lansbury, Maggie Smith, Jane Birkin, Lois Chiles. A top-quality cast and an elegantly constructed screenplay by Anthony Shaffer turn Agatha Christie's murder-mystery into a thoroughly diverting entertainment. Ustinov is a delight in his first portrayal of the fussy, ingenious Belgian sleuth, Hercule Poirot, whose placid Egyptian cruise is rudely interrupted by the murder of a young heiress. (Dir: John Guillermin, 140 mins.)†

Death Penalty (MTV 1980)*** Colleen Dewhurst, David Labiosa, Dana Elcar. A fifteen-year-old Puerto Rican kills two Anglo kids in a playground. Should he get the chair? A lady psychiatrist says no and the prosecution counters. A good, realistic drama. (Dir: Waris Hussein, 104 mins.)

Death Race (MTV 1973)**½ Lloyd Bridges, Doug McClure, Roy Thinnes, Eric Braeden. A good cast fight it out in the dust and sand of this WWII story about Rommel's retreat from El Alamein. (Dir: David Lowell Rich, 90 mins.)

Death Race 2000 (1975)*** David Carradine, Sylvester Stallone, Louisa Moritz, Mary Woronov. A quasi-classic exploitation film, and probably one of the most imitated low-budget works of art of seventies cinema. It works on several levels simultaneously—action, parody, politics, entertainment. The premise of a cross-country road race set in the near future has often been pilfered since, but never rendered with greater verve or density. (Dir: Paul Bartel, 80 mins.)†

Death Ray 2000 (MTV 1981)** Robert Logan, Dan O'Herlihy, Penelope Windust, Ann Turkel, Clive Revill. Superspy T. R. Sloane (Logan) fights wealthy villain Revill, whose deadly gadget holds the world in peril. Tepid James Bond rip-off was the basis for the series "A Man Called Sloane" (which was canceled before this pilot was even aired!) (Dir: Lee H. Katzin, 96 mins.)

Death Rides a Horse (Italy, 1968)*½ Lee Van Cleef, John Phillip Law. Overlong spaghetti western with Van Cleef and Law tracking down a gang of killers for revenge. Trouble brews when Law finds out Van Cleef was part of the gang who killed his parents. (Dir: Giulio Petroni, 114 mins.)

Death Rides the Plains (1944)**½ Bob Livingston, Fuzzy St. John. Out in the Old West some psycho is luring possible buyers to his ranch, where he robs and kills them. Our heroes plan to bring 'im to justice. Average western. (Dir: Sam Newfield, 56 mins.)

Death Ride to Osaka—See: **Girls of the White Orchid**

Deathrow Gameshow**½ John McCafferty, Robin Blythe, Beano, Mark Lasky. Broad comedy about the host of a television game show where condemned prisoners

can win a reprieve or be executed on camera. Naturally, this makes him lots of enemies, from media watchdogs to gangsters whose pals died on the show. Cheaply made movie goes for outrageous humor, scores occasional chuckles. (Dir: Mark Pirro, 78 mins.)†

Death Scream (MTV 1975)**½ Raul Julia, Tina Louise, Cloris Leachman, Art Carney. Effective, updated version of the real-life Kitty Genovese murder in a Queens apartment years ago, in which the victim screamed for help for close to half an hour, fighting off her attacker while no one came to her aid. (Dir: Richard T. Heffron, 100 mins.)

Death Sentence (MTV 1974)**½ Cloris Leachman, Laurence Luckinbill. Leachman tries to overcome the plot's obvious loopholes in this story which has her playing a juror who realizes halfway through a murder trial that her own husband may be the culprit. (Dir: E. W. Swackhamer, 72 mins.)†

Death Ship (Canada-Great Britain, 1980)* George Kennedy, Nick Mancuso, Sally Ann Howes, Kate Reid. A heavy-going thriller about a mysterious ghost ship. The unwary passengers on board soon discover that the vessel was used as a torture chamber by the Nazis, and it needs new victims to stay afloat. (Dir: Alvin Rakoff, 91 mins.)

Deathshot (1973)* Richard C. Watt, Frank Himes, Charles Russell. Tough, trigger-happy plainclothes cops harass junkies and prostitutes connected with an Illinois drug ring, trying to get them to work as informants. Dreary no-budget crime story looks like a bad "Saturday Night Live" parody. (Dir: Mitch Brown, 90 mins.)†

Deathsport (1978)*½ David Carradine, Claudia Jennings, Richard Lynch, David McLean. Weak follow-up to *Death Race 2000*. Death-on-wheels is still man's favorite sport, but this film doesn't approach the violent material with much relish. (Dirs: Henry Suso, Alan Arkush, 82 mins.)†

Death Squad, The (MTV 1974)** Robert Forster, Michelle Phillips, Claude Atkins, Melvyn Douglas, Jesse Vint, Bert Remsen. Forster investigates a group of policeman who take the law in their own hands in this halfbaked TV version of *Magnum Force*. Even a solid cast can't help this one. (Dir: Harry Falk, 96 mins.)

Death Stalk (MTV 1975)** Vic Morrow, Vince Edwards, Anjanette Comer, Carol Lynley, Robert Webber. Crisis drama focuses on two couples enjoying an outdoors vacation riding the rapids in rafts, when they are pounced upon by escaped convicts who abduct the wives. (Dir: Robert Day, 72 mins.)†

Deathstalker (1984)* Richard Hill, Barbi Benton, Richard Brooker. Sword 'n' sorcery saga whose only watchable point is plenty of lithe bodies in skimpy outfits that are ridiculously ill suited to the mayhem at hand. (Dir: John Watson, 80 mins.)†

Deathstalker II: Duel of the Titans (1987)*½ John Terlesky, Monique Gabrielle. Tongue-in-cheek sword 'n' sorcery saga with a cast that talks and acts like California surfer kids. (Dir: Jim Wynorski, 78 min.)†

Deathstalker III: Deathstalker and the Warriors From Hell (1989)* John Allen Nelson, Carla Herd, Terri Treas, Thom Christopher. Third entry features another all-new cast of underclad warriors in an unnamed mythical kingdom. (Dir: Alfonso Corona, 86 mins.)†

Death Takes a Holiday (1934)***½ Fredric March, Evelyn Venable, Kathleen Harrison. Fascinating drama. Mr. March, as Death, decides to assume human form and take a vacation. Interesting, well played, and worth seeing. (Dir: Mitchell Leisen, 90 mins.)

Death Takes a Holiday (MTV 1971)*½ Melvyn Douglas, Yvette Mimieux, Myrna Loy, Monte Markham. Drab remake of the lovely thirties fantasy of how the spectre of Death encounters a life-loving woman on Earth and yearns to possess her. (Dir: Robert Butler, 73 mins.)

Death Trap (1976)—See: **Eaten Alive**

Deathtrap (1982)**½ Michael Caine, Christopher Reeve, Dyan Cannon, Irene Worth, Henry Jones. Michael Caine is Sidney Bruhl, the has-been thriller playwright who announces to his wife, Dyan Cannon, that he intends to murder a young playwright, Christopher Reeve, and steal a new thriller he has authored. (Dir: Sidney Lumet, 116 mins.)†

Death Valley (1982)*½ Paul LeMat, Catherine Hicks, Stephen McHattie, A. Wilford Brimley, Peter Billingsley, Edward Herrmann. Aimless thriller about a little city boy tangling with a deranged cowboy in Arizona. (Dir: Dick Richards, 87 mins.)†

Death Vengeance—See: **Fighting Back** (1982)

Death Warrant (1990)* Jean-Claude Van Damme, Patrick Kilpatrick, Robert Guillaume, Cynthia Gibb. A detective goes undercover in a prison to solve the mystery of dying inmates. He comes face to face with a notorious psycho-slasher known as the Sandman. Van Damme doesn't deliver much kickboxing power. A parade of clichés. (Dir: Deran Sarafian, 89 mins.)†

Deathwatch (France-West Germany, 1980)*** Harvey Keitel, Romy Schneider, Harry Dean Stanton, Max von Sydow. Bizarre sci-fi from the masterful French director Bertrand Tavernier. Sometime in the future, some anything-for-a-story media types implant a camera in a man's brain so they can take footage of a dying woman. (Dir: Bertrand Tavernier, 128 mins.)†

Death Weekend—See: **House by the Lake, The**

Death Wish (1974)** Charles Bronson, Hope Lange, Vincent Gardenia, Stuart Margolin, William Redfield. After his wife is killed and his daughter raped by muggers, a New York businessman becomes a vigilante. This morally questionable premise blazed the trail for dozens of other films about one-man urban crimebusters. Colorfully presented, but a violent, unpleasant movie. (Dir: Michael Winner, 94 mins.)†

Death Wish II (1982)½ Charles Bronson, Jill Ireland, Vincent Gardenia, J. D. Cannon, Anthony Franciosa, Ben Frank. The "II" stands for twice as much blood, twice as many corpses. This time Bronson's moved to L.A. where his bad luck continues with the gang rape and murder of his housekeeper and the suicide of his daughter. (Dir: Michael Winner, 89 mins.)†

Death Wish 3 (1985)* Charles Bronson, Deborah Raffin, Ed Lauter, Martin Balsam. The stoic avenger seems to bring bad luck to all those around him, as assorted rapists, muggers, and murderers attack everyone he knows. (Dir: Michael Winner, 92 mins.)†

Death Wish 4: The Crackdown (1987)*½ Charles Bronson, Kay Lenz, John P. Ryan, Perry Lopez, Paul Kersey, the vigilante architect, is back, and this time he becomes a hired killer pledged to wipe out the drug-peddling scum who killed his girlfriend's daughter. (Dir: J. Lee Thompson, 104 mins.)†

Death Wish Club (1983)** Meredith Haze, Rick Barnes, J. Martin Sellers, Ann Fairchild. Student becomes involved with a stripper and her friends, members of a suicide club. Bizarre drama looks like they made it up as they went along. Some of the footage was reused in the anthology movie *Night Train to Terror*, where it doesn't look much better. AKA: **Carnival of Fools**. (Dir: John Carr, 93 mins.)†

Decameron, The (Italy, 1971)***½ Franco Citti, Ninetto Davoli, Angela Luce, Silvana Mangano, Pier Paolo Pasolini. Pasolini's personal vision of uninhibited sexuality—rather than an attempt to recreate historical truth—is one of the driving forces behind the eight earthy and frolicsome stories from Boccaccio's *Decameron*. Working with a mostly nonprofessional cast, Pasolini presents a satisfying medieval fresco, freely painted with comedy, beauty, and even horror. (107 mins.)†

Decameron Nights (Great Britain, 1953)*** Joan Fontaine, Louis Jourdan, Joan Collins. Author Boccaccio follows his ladylove, tries to win her affection by telling her two spicy tales. Good-natured costume adventure, made in Italy. Pleasant fun. (Dir: Hugo Fregonese, 85 mins.)†

Decay—See: **Rabid**

Deceivers, The (Great Britain, 1988) **½ Pierce Brosnan, Saeed Jaffrey, Sashi Kapoor. Adventure set in 1825 India, with Brosnan in blackface as a British officer infiltrating the Thuggee cult. (Dir: Nicholas Meyer, 112 mins.)†

December Bride (Ireland, 1990)*** Donal McCann, Saskia Reeves, Ciaran Hinds, Patrick Malahide, Brenda Bruce. Absorbing drama explores the emotional conflict a woman faces in a small Irish Presbyterian town at the turn of the century when she falls in love with two men at the same time. Feature debut by director Thaddeus O'Sullivan. (Dir: Thaddeus O'Sullivan, 91 mins.)

Deception (1946)*** Bette Davis, Claude Rains, Paul Henreid. A scrumptious plum pudding of a soap opera. Struggling pianist Bette must choose between her old musician *amour* (Henreid) and the composer (Rains) who's been keeping her in style. Wonderful! (Dir: Irving Rapper, 112 mins.)†

Deceptions (MTV 1985)**½ Stefanie Powers, Barry Bostwick, Brenda Vaccaro, Gina Lollobrigida, Sam Wanamaker, Fabio Testi, Jeremy Brett. Unabashedly old-fashioned, romantic yarn; Powers plays twins—one a depressed housewife and the other a chic jet-setter—who trade places. (Dirs: Melville Shavelson, Robert Chenault, 196 mins.)

Decision at Sundown (1957)***½ Randolph Scott, Karen Steele, John Carroll. Exceptionally good, adult-slanted Scott western. Randy is out for revenge again—but the plot gets a novel twist this time. (Dir: Budd Boetticher, 80 mins.)

Decision Before Dawn (1951)**½ Oskar Werner, Richard Basehart, Gary Merrill. Fine performance by Oskar Werner makes up for the shortcomings of the script of this World War II espionage drama. (Dir: Anatole Litvak, 119 mins.)

Decks Ran Red, The (1958)** James Mason, Dorothy Dandridge, Broderick Crawford, Stuart Whitman. Foolish film about a captain endeavoring to thwart a mutiny engineered by two nasty seamen. (Dir: Andrew L. Stone, 84 mins.)

Decline and Fall of a Bird Watcher (Great Britain, 1968)** Genevieve Page, Colin Blakely, Leo McKern, Robin Philips. This adaptation of one of Evelyn Waugh's biting satires on English manners and mores begins well as the callow hero (Philips) gets a position at a weirdly run boys' school. Thereafter the fun runs downhill quickly. (Dir: John Krish, 113 mins.)

Decline of the American Empire, The (Canada, 1986)*** Pierre Curzi, Remy Girard, Yves Jacques, Dominique Michel, Louise Portal. A group of university teachers and students talk about their sexual lives, first separately, then together at a party, leading to revelation, confrontation, and heartbreak. (Dir: Denys Arcand, 101 mins.)†

Decline of Western Civilization, The (1981)*** Black Flag, The Circle Jerks, X, Fear, Germs. A fascinating look at the L.A. punk subculture circa 1980. If many of the individual bands aren't memorable, the scene is still well encapsulated for posterity by documentary filmmaker Penelope Spheeris. (100 mins.)†

Decline of Western Civilization Part II: The Metal Years, The (1988)*** Aerosmith, Alice Cooper, Ozzy Osbourne, Motorhead, KISS, Metallica. The world of heavy-metal rock music, seen through interviews with members of veteran and upcoming bands and their fans. Good for both diehard metalheads and interested but uninitiated observers; director Penelope Spheeris separates the musicians from the posers. (90 mins.)†

Decoration Day (MTV 1990)*** James Garner, Judith Ivey, Bill Cobbs, Ruby Lee. Garner is a pleasure to watch as a crusty, retired Southern judge who returns to help his childhood friend, a man with angry reasons for not accepting the Medal of Honor. It's a quiet drama with nice little touches. (Dir: Robert Markowitz, 96 mins.)

Decoy for Terror—See: **Playgirl Killer**

Deep, The (1977)** Nick Nolte, Jacqueline Bisset, Robert Shaw, Eli Wallach, Lou Gossett, Jr. Peter Benchley's best-selling follow-up to *Jaws* makes passable screen fare. While scuba diving in Bermuda, Nolte and Bisset run afoul of drug smugglers trying to lay hands on a sunken treasure. (Dir: Peter Yates, 123 mins.)†

Deep Blue Sea, The (Great Britain, 1955)** Vivien Leigh, Kenneth More. Terence Rattigan's play of an emotionally unstable woman's affair with a man beneath her station, cumbersomely adapted for the screen. (Dir: Anatole Litvak, 99 mins.)

Deep Dark Secrets (MTV 1987)*½ James Brolin, Melody Anderson, Pamela Bellwood, Morgan Stevens. Anderson uncovers deep dark secrets about mysterious husband (Brolin) after his disappearance.

Overblown and tedious. (Dir: Robert Lewis, 96 mins.)

Deep End (West Germany-Great Britain, 1970)***½ Jane Asher, John Moulder-Brown, Diana Dors. Intelligent, powerful fable of a young boy's first love. Moulder-Brown epitomizes the adolescent who will not be deterred by the obstacles he faces in courting a nubile bathhouse attendant. (Dir: Jerzy Skolimowsky, 87 mins.)

Deep in My Heart (1954)*** Jose Ferrer, Merle Oberon, Walter Pidgeon. Story of composer Sigmund Romberg serves as a peg on which to hang a host of fancy musical numbers with specialties by Fred Astaire, Gene Kelly, Tony Martin, Rosemary Clooney, and Ann Miller. Topheavy, but good musical entertainment. (Dir: Stanley Donen, 132 mins.)

Deep in the Heart (Great Britain, 1983)**½ Karen Young, Clayton Day, Suzie Humphreys. A violated high-school teacher takes revenge on her assailant. Exposé of America's gun culture takes aim and misses, but deserves credit. (Dir: Tony Garnett, 101 mins.)†

Deep Red (Italy, 1975)**½ David Hemmings, Daria Nocolodi, Macha Meril. A psychic detects a mad killer in the audience of a press conference. She is murdered (with a meat cleaver) and Hemmings tries to find out who did it. A gory, above-average thriller with some classy visual effects. Unfortunately, it's been hacked up by so many different distributors that it is currently impossible to see the complete 118 min. version. AKA: The Hatchet Murders, (Dir: Dario Argento, 98 mins.)†

Deep Six, The (1958)** Alan Ladd, William Bendix, Joey Bishop, Dianne Foster, James Whitmore. Naval lieutenant whose religious beliefs are Quaker loses the respect of his men but regains it through an act of heroism. (Dir: Rudolph Mate, 108 mins.)†

Deep Space (1987)*** Charles Napier, Ann Turkel, Ron Glass, Bo Svenson, Julie Newmar, Anthony Eisley, Peter Palmer. Cheerfully dumb monster movie with square-jawed cop Napier stalking the *Alien*-like monster that killed his partner. (Dir: Fred Olen Ray, 90 mins.)†

DeepStar Six (1989)** Greg Evigan, Nancy Everhard, Taurean Blacque, Miguel Ferrer, Marius Weyers. *Alien* on the ocean floor, as a deep-sea exploration station is menaced by a monster. Dopey fun if you keep your expectations low, though the ending is ridiculous even by these low standards. (Dir: Sean Cunningham, 100 mins.)†

Deep Valley (1947)*** Ida Lupino, Dane Clark. Girl living an unhappy life on a farm is attracted to a convict working on a construction job. Excellently acted drama—grim but good. (Dir: Jean Negulesco, 104 mins.)

Deep Waters (1948)**½ Dana Andrews, Jean Peters, Cesar Romero, Dean Stockwell, Ed Begley, Mae Marsh, Will Geer. Warm and homey tale about two lovers brought together by an orphaned boy in a Maine fishing town. (Dir: Henry King, 85 mins.)

Deer Hunter, The (1978)*** Robert De Niro, Meryl Streep, Christopher Walken, John Cazale, John Savage. This first "epic" treatment of the war in Vietnam is actually a downbeat character study focusing on a group of Russian-American friends from a small town who go to war and come back scarred physically and emotionally. At times, the film appears unnecessarily dilated, but the intensity of the project plus the top-flight cast garnered the film a Best Picture Oscar. (Dir: Michael Cimino, 183 mins.)†

Deerslayer, The (1957)** Lex Barker, Forrest Tucker, Rita Moreno. Passable adaptation of James Fenimore Cooper's exciting tale of adventure in the frontiers of colonial America. (Dir: Kurt Neumann, 78 mins.)

Deerslayer, The (MTV 1978)** Steve Forrest, Ned Romero. James Fenimore Cooper's intrepid Hawkeye and his Indian blood brother return in this adequate remake. (Dir: Dick Friedenberg, 78 mins.)†

Def by Temptation (1990)**½ James Bond 3rd, Cynthia Bond, Kadeem Hardison, Bill Nunn. Divinity student, on the verge of taking his vows, is tempted by a beautiful demon in the evil city of New York. Exemplary low-budget film mixes intelligent horror with a smattering of humor. Handsomely photographed by Ernest Dickerson. (Dir: James Bond 3rd, 95 mins.)†

Defcon 4 (1985)** Tim Choate, Kate Lynch, Lenore Zann, Maury Chaykin, Kevin King. A standard post-apocalypse nightmare. When astronauts who are orbiting the Earth when the "Big Bomb" drops are forced back to earth, one is eaten by cannibalistic teenagers; the other cast members must contend with a horny survivalist and a sadistic ruler with a Neo-Fascist power base. (Dir: Paul Donovan, 87 mins.)†

Defection of Simas Kudirka, The (MTV 1978)**** Alan Arkin, Richard Jordan, Donald Pleasence, Shirley Knight. A powerful dramatic essay about man's unquenchable thirst for freedom. The multitalented Arkin is superb as Soviet seaman Simas Kudirka, who defected to an American coast guard cutter in '70 and was, through a series of stupefying bureaucratic blunders by naval and federal authorities, turned back to the

Russians. (Dir: David Lowell Rich, 104 mins.)

Defector, The (West Germany-France, 1966)**½ Montgomery Clift, Hardy Kruger. Kruger, as the German working for the communists, is constantly in opposition to Clift, the amateur spy on a dangerous mission involving the defection of a Russian scientist to the West. (Dir: Raoul Levy, 106 mins.)

Defending Your Life (1991)**½ Albert Brooks, Meryl Streep, Rip Torn, Lee Grant, Buck Henry, Shirley MacLaine. Satire, Brooks-style, which doesn't deliver belly laughs, and overall is rather disappointing. The uneven story revolves around a yuppie (Brooks) who dies and goes to a pleasant and perfect fantasy city to face judgment for his deeds while alive. There he meets the "love of his death" (Streep) with whom he hopes to spend eternity. (Dir: Albert Brooks, 110 mins.)†

Defense of the Realm (Great Britain, 1985)** Gabriel Byrne, Greta Scacchi, Denholm Elliott. An idealistic young Fleet Street reporter (Byrne) investigates a political scandal that may have links with a large cover-up conspiracy. Journalistic thriller has some good moments. (Dir: David Drury, 96 mins.)†

Defiance (1980)* Jan-Michael Vincent, Art Carney, Danny Aiello, Theresa Saldana. A New York neighborhood can only take so much abuse from gang members destroying property and humiliating the law-abiding locals. (Dir: John Flynn, 103 mins.)†

Defiant Ones, The (1958)**** Tony Curtis, Sidney Poitier, Theodore Bikel, Cara Williams. Provocative, honest racial drama of two escaping chain-gang convicts, white and black, whose differences make their flight more difficult because they are literally chained together. Still packs quite a punch, has superb performances, potent direction. (Dir: Stanley Kramer, 97 mins.)†

Defiant Ones, The (MTV 1985)**½ Robert Urich, Carl Weathers, Barry Corbin, Ed Lauter, Rich Brinkley, Thalmus Rasulala. Remake of the Tony Curtis-Sidney Poitier film classic suffers by comparison, for those familiar with the original. (Dir: David Lowell Rich, 104 mins.)

Degree of Murder, A (West Germany, 1967)*** Anita Pallenberg, Werner Enske, Angela Hillebrecht, Hans P. Wallwachs. Gritty drama of a woman who kills her lover and offers a stranger sex and money to help her dispose of the body. Rolling Stones cohort Pallenberg is perfect as the guiltless amoral woman; Stones guitarist Brian Jones composed the pulsating score shortly before his death. (Dir: Volker Schlondorff, 87 mins.)

Déjà Vu (1985)*½ Jaclyn Smith, Nigel Terry, Claire Bloom, Shelley Winters. Monotonous thriller. Smith does her usual plastic job in a double role—a deceased ballerina and a woman who might be her reincarnation fifty years later. (Dir: Anthony Richmond, 90 mins.)†

Delancey Street: The Crisis Within (MTV 1975)*** Walter McGinn, Carmine Caridi, Michael Conrad, Lou Gossett, Mark Hamill, John Karlen, Leigh French. Well-directed account based on the real-life travels of a man who founded a rehab center for substance abusers and ex-convicts. Strong performances. (Dir: James Frawley, 95 mins.)

Deliberate Stranger, The (MTV 1986)***½ Mark Harmon, Frederic Forrest, George Gizzard, Ben Masters, Glynnis O'Connor, M. Emmet Walsh. Tense retelling of the events surrounding the arrest and conviction of Ted Bundy, the law student turned serial killer who was executed in 1989. (Dir: Marvin J. Chomsky, 192 mins.)

Delicate Balance, A (1973)***½ Paul Scofield, Kate Reid, Katharine Hepburn, Lee Remick, Betsy Blair, Joseph Cotten. An aging, civilized couple try to make living together tolerable, but their haven is invaded by their neighbors, their much-divorced daughter, and the wife's alcoholic sister. (Dir: Tony Richardson, 134 mins.)

Delicate Delinquent, The (1957)*** Jerry Lewis, Darren McGavin, Martha Hyer. Scapegoat Jerry joins the police force and has a hard time proving himself as a rookie cop. One of the better Lewis offerings. (Dir: Don McGuire, 101 mins.)†

Delicious (1931)**½ Janet Gaynor, Charles Farrell, El Brendel, Virginia Cherrill, Mischa Auer. Creaky musical has some nice touches, but depends wholly on Gaynor's charm as an innocent Irish girl who arrives in New York City and falls for rich boy Farrell. (Dir: David Butler, 106 mins.)

Delinquents, The (Australia, 1989)** Kylie Minogue, Charlie Schlatter, Angela Punch-McGregor, Bruno Lawrence. A pair of teenaged lovers in 1950s Queensland endure the usual obstacles to stay together. Minogue and Schlatter are too lightweight to make this melodrama anything but sheer formula. (Dir: Chris Thomson, 101 mins.)

Delinquent Schoolgirls (1984)**½ Michael Pataki, Stephen Stucker, Bob Minor. Silly but suprisingly funny sexploitation feature about three inmates who escape from the institution they're in only to land on the campus of an all-girls' school loaded with neglected young ladies. Pataki is particularly manic as the leader of the trio, a crazed celebrity impressionist. (Dir: Gregory Corarito, 89 mins.)†

Delirium (1979)* Debi Chaney, Turk Cekovsky, Terry Ten Broeck, Barron Winchester. Silly yarn about Vietnam vets organizing a vigilante gang to kill criminals released by courts. Utterly worthless. (Dir: Peter Maris, 86 mins.)†

Deliverance (1972)**** Jon Voight, Burt Reynolds, Ned Beatty, Ronny Cox. James Dickey's novel has been excitingly brought to the screen by director John Boorman. Four businessmen—Voight, Reynolds, Beatty, and Cox—set out on a canoe trip down a wild Georgia river and look forward to nothing more hazardous than riding the rapids, but their adventure becomes a nightmare. Superbly acted by the entire cast, particularly Voight as the sensitive man who finds he wants to release his primitive instincts. (109 mins.)†

Deliver Us from Evil (MTV 1973)*** George Kennedy, Jan-Michael Vincent, Bradford Dillman. Spectacular photography adds to the tale of five men who set out, with the aid of a guide, to spend three days in the Oregon wilderness but end up trying to survive the rugged terrain when their guide is killed. (Dir: Boris Sagal, 90 mins.)

Delivery Boys (1984)* Joss Marcano, Tom Sierchio, Jim Soriero. A trio of pizza delivery boys persevere in their jobs while waiting for a big break-dancing contest. The type of thing that makes you wonder if all the money you spend for cable TV is really worth it. (Dir: Ken Handler, 94 mins.)†

Delphi Bureau, The (MTV 1972)*½ Laurence Luckinbill, Joanna Pettet, Celeste Holm. Luckinbill is an agent for the government with a photographic memory. He searches for a stockpile of weapons, with the usual unforeseen consequences. Trivial. (Dir: Paul Wendkos, 72 mins.)

Delta County, U.S.A. (MTV 1977)*½ Jim Antonio, Jeff Conaway, Robert Hays, Edward Power, Morgan Brittany, Peter Masterson, Joe Penny. All is not placid in a sleepy little Southern town, with duplicity, youthful rebellion, and (especially) lust about to boil over. Too bad they never do. Lurid telefilm with less substance than an average nighttime soap. (Dir: Glenn Jordon, 96 mins.)

Delta Factor, The (1971)½ Christopher George, Yvette Mimieux, Diane McBain. A trashy bore, based on Micky Spillane's novel. Wrongly accused international privateer forced to help a top scientist escape from the clutches of an evil dictator. (Dir: Tay Garnett, 91 mins.)

Delta Force (1986)*½ Chuck Norris, Lee Marvin, Shelley Winters, Martin Bal-

sam, Joey Bishop, Robert Forster, Lainie Kazan, George Kennedy, Susan Strasberg, Hanna Schygulla. Brutal adventure tale whose most interesting achievement lies in persuading the critically acclaimed Schygulla to cheapen her status here. (Dir: Menahem Golan, 129 mins.)†

Delta Force 2 (1990)* Chuck Norris, Billy Drago, John P. Ryan, Richard Jaeckel. The Delta Force, sort of a SWAT team with an attitude, is called upon to flush out a drug kingpin. Boring macho fare uneventfully directed by Chuck's brother Aaron. (Dir: Aaron Norris, 110 mins.)†

Delta Pi—See: **Mugsy's Girls**

Dementia—See: **Daughter of Horror**

Dementia 13 (1963)*** Patrick Magee, William Campbell, Luana Anders. An extremely clever, well-made horror film, one of Coppola's earliest efforts. The inhabitants of a picturesque Irish castle are stalked by an axe-murderer. (Dir: Francis Ford Coppola, 81 mins.)†

Demetrius and the Gladiators (1954)** Susan Hayward, Victor Mature, Richard Egan. A routine sequel to *The Robe*. Action fans might like the scenes in the arena where the gladiators do their stuff. (Dir: Delmer Daves, 101 mins.)†

Demi-Paradise, The (Great Britain, 1943)*** Laurence Olivier, Penelope Dudley Ward, Leslie Henson, Margaret Rutherford, Joyce Grenfell, Miles Malleson, Marjorie Fielding, Felix Aylmer, Wilfred Hyde-White. Panoramic, patriotic British WWII effort, which explores the value of their traditions by looking at them through the eyes of a young Russian engineer. Fine ensemble playing, and Olivier is wonderful. AKA: **Adventure for Two**. (Dir: Anthony Asquith, 115 mins.)†

Demon, The (1976)*** Tony LoBianco, Sandy Dennis, Sylvia Sidney, Richard Lynch, Deborah Raffin. Incredibly bizarre and wildly imaginative horror story about a hippie-type alien playing God and ordering humans to murder. AKA: **God Told Me To**. (Dir: Larry Cohen, 95 mins.)†

Demon Barber of Fleet Street, The (Great Britain, 1936)**½ Todd Slaughter, Eve Lister, Bruce Seton, Stello Rho. Early version of the Sweeney Todd story, starring barnstorming British horror star Slaughter in a delightfully hammy turn as the barber who murders his wealthier clients and sells the bodies to the pie maker next door. Creepy moments. AKA: **Sweeney Todd, the Demon Barber of Fleet Street**. (Dir: George King, 66 mins.)†

Demoniac (France, 1957)***½ Jeanne Moreau, Micheline Presle, Francois Perier. Taut and baffling mystery drama of mistaken identities during WWII in France. Fascinating and suspenseful throughout. (Dir: Luis Saslavsky, 97 mins.)

Demon Lover, The—See: **Devil Master, The**

Demon Murder Case, The (MTV 1983)*** Kevin Bacon, Liane Langland, Charlie Fields, Joyce Van Patten, Eddie Albert. A macabre murder is committed, and the accused blames an "outside spirit" for the stabbing. (Dir: Billy Hale, 104 mins.)

Demon of Paradise (1987)* Kathryn Witt, William Steis, Laura Banks. Limp creature feature about an ancient monster terrorizing a Hawaiian island. Too little monster, too many subplots. (Dir: Cirio H. Santiago, 84 mins.)†

Demonoid, Messenger of Death (1981)** Samantha Eggar, Stuart Whitman, Roy Cameron Jenson, Narciso Busquets. Low-budget horror drama has a few interesting moments, as a disembodied hand with supernatural origins possesses a series of victims. AKA: **Macabra**. (Dir: Alfred Zacharias, 78 mins.)†

Demon Planet, The (Italy, 1965)*½ Barry Sullivan, Norma Bengell. After its sister ship, a spacecraft lands on a strange planet and its crew encounters some bloodthirsty creatures there. Low-grade science-fiction thriller. (Dir: Mario Bava, 86 mins.)

Demon Pond (Japan, 1980)***½ Tustomi Yamazaki, Go Kato, Koji Nanoara. Three people in 1933 Japan become involved with the ancient legend of a haunted pond. Director Masahiro Shinoda creates a spectacular tale of the supernatural. (123 mins.)

Demons (Italy, 1985)** Urbano Barberim, Natasha Hovey, Kurl Zinny. A movie theater being infested with murderous zombies during the showing of a slasher film. Bava's (Mario's son) direction is sleek, but the gore is excessive, and the lack of logic exceeds the carnage. (Dir: Lamberto Bava, 90 mins.)†

Demons 2 (Italy, 1986)½ David Knight, Nancy Brilli. The American release of this zombie sequel has been so hacked up and badly dubbed as to render it unreviewable. Most of the gory special effects have been chopped out, and what's left of the plot is incomprehensible. (Dir: Lamberto Bava, 88 mins.)†

Demon Seed, The (1977)**½ Julie Christie, Fritz Weaver, Gerrit Graham. The premise has a super-computer named "Proteus" trying to mate with the alluring wife of a computer scientist. Sci-fi fans might find solace in the parade of 21st-century inventions. (Dir: Donald Cammell, 94 mins.)†

Demons in the Garden (Spain, 1984)*** Angela Molina, Ana Belin, Encarna Paso, Imanol Arias. Rich family saga, laden with symbolism, set in post-WWII Spain. Best is the radiant Molina as the central character, the adopted daughter who has affairs with both of her stepbrothers (and a child with one). (Dir: Manuel Gutierrez Aragon, 100 mins.)†

Demons of the Mind (Great Britain, 1972)** Paul Jones, Gillian Hills, Robert Hardy, Patrick Magee, Michael Hordern. In 19th-century Austria a baron, convinced that insanity runs in his family, keeps his son and daughter virtual prisoners for fear of what harm they might do. A mess of chases, murders, and horror clichés. (Dir: Peter Sykes, 89 mins.)†

Dempsey (MTV 1983)**½ Treat Williams, Sally Kellerman, Victoria Tennant, Sam Waterston. Pretty fair boxing movie about '20s hero Jack Dempsey, the heavyweight champ. Jack's fists do most of the talking in realistic ring scenes, but the show's texture comes from the details about the boxing world. (Dir: Gus Trikonis, 104 mins.)†

Dempsey and Makepeace (Great Britain, MTV 1985)** Michael Brandon, Glynis Barber, Ray Smith. It's hands-across-the-ocean time as a Serpico-type Yankee from New York is shipped abroad in an exchange program with Scotland Yard. High-tech action without depth or logic. (Dir: Ronald Graham, 104 mins.)

Dentist on the Job—See: **Carry on TV**

Denver and Rio Grande, The (1952)**½ Edmond O'Brien, Sterling Hayden, Dean Jagger. Plenty of rough-house action in this western about two rival railroads battling to see who gets through the Royal Gorge first. (Dir: Byron Haskin, 89 mins.)

Depeche Mode 101 (1989)***½ Fascinating documentary about the British post-punk band Depeche Mode's 1988 U.S. tour. Famed *cinema verité* director D. A. Pennebaker weaves the band's on-stage performances, their personal time together, the adventures of a group of young fans driving cross-country. (117 mins.)†

Deported (1950)**½ Marta Toren, Jeff Chandler, Claude Dauphin. Over-sentimentalized tale of a deported American gangster and his reformation in the hands of a beautiful Italian countess. (Dir: Robert Siodmak, 89 mins.)

Deprisa, Deprisa (Spain, 1981)***½ Jose Antonio Valdelomar, Jesus Arias Aranzeque, Jose Maria Hervas Roldan, Berta Socuellamos Zarco. One of the director Carlos Saura's best. Fast-paced crime thriller about gang of robbers who mix love and murder on the road to disaster. Life imitated art when stars Valdelomar and Aranzeque were arrested in separate criminal incidents as the film was premiering. Best Film, Berlin Festival 1981. (98 mins.)

Deputy, The (Spain, 1978)***½ Jose Sacristan, Maria Luisa San José, Jose L. Alonso. Political thriller centers on a happily married up-and-coming Socialist who has a homosexual affair with a punk young enough to be his son. His wife soon joins the two in a *ménage à trois*, as his complex private life begins to jeopardize his position as a force for change in post-Franco Spain. Disturbing, fascinating film. AKA: **Congressman, The** and **El Diputado.** (Dir: Eloy de la Iglesia, 111 mins.)†

Deranged (1974)*** Roberts Blossom, Cosette Lee, Leslie Carlson, Marcia Diamond, Robert Warner. Low-budget shocker based on the Ed Gein case, which inspired the films *Psycho* and *Texas Chainsaw Massacre.* Blossom portrays the son who loves his mama so much he can't bear to part with her after she dies; and, naturally, he wants her to have some company, too. (Dirs: Alan Ormsby, Jeff Gillen, 82 mins.)

Deranged (1987)* Jane Hamilton, Paul Siederman, Jennifer Delora, Jill Cumer. Thrill-less psychosexual thriller about a woman who kills an intruder and then suffers from visions from her troubled past. Below par. (Dir: Chuck Vincent, 85 mins.)†

Derby (1971)***½ Enlightening, entertaining documentary about the great American pastime, the Roller Derby. (Dir: Robert Kaylor, 91 mins.)†

Derby Day (Great Britain, 1952)*** Anna Neagle, Michael Wilding. Four stories revolving about the big horse race at Epsom. Mildly entertaining package of comedy and drama. (Dir: Herbert Wilcox, 84 mins.)

Der Mud Tod—See: **Destiny** (1921)

Dersu Uzala (U.S.S.R.-Japan, 1974)***½ Maxim Munzuk, Yuri Solomin. A fascinating epic about the struggles of hardy souls to chart the wilderness of Siberia around 1900. Remarkable photography and the performance of Munzuk as an old native hunter carry this most of the way. (Dirs: Akira Kurosawa, Vladimir Arseniev, 140 mins.)†

De Sade (U.S.-West Germany, 1969)*½ Keir Dullea, Senta Berger, Lilli Palmer, Sonja Ziemann, John Huston. Low-grade attempt at serious filmmaking with Dullea and Huston in embarrassing roles as the sadistic Marquis de Sade and his weird uncle. (Dir: Cy Endfield, 113 mins.)

Descending Angel (MCTV 1990)*** George C. Scott, Diane Lane, Eric Roberts, Jan Rubes. A better-than-average cast and an intriguing premise. Scott is a Romanian refugee who has established himself in his community, both as a pillar in Romanian-American activities and with the church. All goes well until a stranger appears and labels Scott a Nazi collaborator. An unfortunately hackneyed finale mars the overall effect. (Dir: Jeremy Kagan, 98 mins.)†

Desert Attack (Great Britain, 1959)*** John Mills, Sylvia Syms, Anthony Quayle. Tank commander has his hands full in North Africa carrying two nurses to safety and combatting a German spy. AKA: **Ice Cold in Alex.** (Dir: J. Lee Thompson, 80 mins.)

Desert Bloom (1986)*** Jon Voight, JoBeth Williams, Ellen Barkin, Annabeth Gish, Allen Garfield. A finely acted, realistic drama about a middle-class family in Las Vegas of the fifties, at the time of the first atomic testing, as seen through the eyes of adolescent Gish. (Dir: Eugene Corr, 106 mins.)†

Deserter, The (Italy-Yugoslavia-U.S., 1970)** John Huston, Richard Crenna, Ricardo Montalbán, Bekim Fehmiu. Army officer is out for revenge after the Apaches mutilated his wife. (Dir: Burt Kennedy, 99 mins.)

Desert Fox, The (1951)***½ James Mason, Jessica Tandy. Exciting war drama about the African campaign of Rommel. James Mason is great as the Nazi general. Good desert photography. (Dir: Henry Hathaway, 88 mins.)†

Desert Fury (1947)** John Hodiak, Burt Lancaster, Lizabeth Scott, Mary Astor. Good cast in confusing melodrama about gambling. Everybody in the film has a shady past, and the result is a shady motion picture. (Dir: Lewis Allen, 75 mins.)

Desert Hawk, The (1950)** Yvonne DeCarlo, Richard Greene, Jackie Gleason. The only interesting thing about this stale tale of an Arabian Nights adventure is Jackie Gleason in the supporting role of Aladdin. (Dir: Frederick de Cordova, 78 mins.)

Desert Hearts (1986)**½ Helen Shaver, Audra Lindley, Patricia Charbonneau, Andra Akers, Gwen Welles, Dean Butler. A sometimes poignant feminist film about a woman seeking a divorce and fulfillment, in Reno, Nevada, 1958. (Dir: Donna Deitch, 97 mins.)†

Desert Hell (1958)*½ Brian Keith, Barbara Hale, Richard Denning. Legionnaires on a dangerous trek are menaced by tribesmen on the warpath. (Dir: Charles Marquis Warren, 82 mins.)

Desert Legion (1953)** Alan Ladd, Arlene Dahl, Richard Conte. Can you imagine Alan Ladd as a French Foreign Legionnaire? This adventure yarn has super heroics and beautiful desert princesses. (Dir: Joseph Pevney, 86 mins.)

Desert Rats, The (1953)*** James Mason, Richard Burton, Robert Newton. Good war drama about the turbulent siege at Tobruk during World War II. James Mason once again effectively portrays Gen. Rommel, "The Desert Fox," leader of the Nazi troops. (Dir: Robert Wise, 88 mins.)

Desert Song, The (1953)** Kathryn Grayson, Gordon MacRae. Kathryn Grayson and Gordon MacRae play the duetting stars of the Romberg operetta about derring-do in the desert. (Dir: H. Bruce Humberstone, 110 mins.)

Desert Warrior (1987)* Lou Ferrigno, Shari Shattuck, Kenneth Peer, Antony East. Combination of all the worst aspects of an Italian gladiator movie and a bad *Mad Max* rip-off, with Ferrigno as a post-nuke hero trying to save pure-blooded Shattuck from being used for purposes of involuntary breeding. (Dir: Jim Goldman, 88 mins.)†

Design for Living (1933)**½ Gary Cooper, Fredric March, Miriam Hopkins. Noël Coward's delightful comedy receives an unsuccessful screen treatment. Story of three "sensible" people involved in a love triangle was too sophisticated for a 1930s movie. (Dir: Ernst Lubitsch, 90 mins.)

Design for Scandal (1941)**½ Rosalind Russell, Walter Pidgeon, Edward Arnold. Some good fun in this comedy about an upstanding lady judge and the scoundrel who sets out to smear her good name. (Dir: Norman Taurog, 85 mins.)

Designing Woman (1957)*** Gregory Peck, Lauren Bacall, Dolores Gray, Sam Levene, Chuck Connors. Miss B. plays a successful dress designer who meets and marries sports writer Peck and the fun begins as each tries to adapt to the other's friends and habits. (Dir: Vincente Minnelli, 117 mins.)

Desire (1936)**** Gary Cooper, Marlene Dietrich, John Halliday, William Frawley, Akim Tamiroff, Zeffie Tilbury, Alan Mowbray. Sparkling comic gem about an international jewel thief (Dietrich) who meets her match in an all-American car designer who believes that rehabilitating beautiful criminals is part of the American Way. This deluxe escapism is graced with the comic sass of producer Ernst Lubitsch and the romantic tenderness that was the trademark of director Frank Borzage. (96 mins.)

Desire (France, 1979)***½ Emmanuelle Riva. A wealthy married man's outwardly straight image belies his inner turmoil as he falls for a young male hustler who leads him into the nightmare world of the dark side of sexuality and involves the staid chap in robbery, prostitution, and physical abuse. Director Dominique Delouche depicts the underbelly of homosexuality without judging,

and manages to create a world where good homosexuals and bad homosexuals exist in a tense bond of mutual understanding. (90 mins.)

Desiree (1954)**½ Marlon Brando, Jean Simmons, Michael Rennie, Merle Oberon. With this elaborately produced historical drama, Mr. Brando adds Napoleon to his list of screen credits. Jean Simmons is vividly beautiful in the title role as Napoleon's love before he becomes Emperor. (Dir: Henry Koster, 110 mins.)†

Desire in the Dust (1960)** Raymond Burr, Martha Hyer, Joan Bennett. Tyrannical landowner with skeletons in his closet sees his political ambitions in jeopardy, tries unscrupulous means to rid himself of his troubles. Lust and desire in a Southern town, a long way from Faulkner. (Dir: William F. Claxton, 102 mins.)

Desire Me (1947)** Greer Garson, Robert Mitchum, Richard Hart, Morris Ankrum, George Zucco. Slow-moving, confusing drama, oddly set in postwar France. Mitchum returns from WWII to wife Garson who, thinking him dead, has married his friend Hart. Garson and Mitchum were totally unsuited to each other, and the studio tampered with the final cut so much that neither director George Cukor (who began the film) nor Mervyn LeRoy (who finished it) would allow their names to appear in the credits. (91 mins.)

Desire Under the Elms (1958)**½ Sophia Loren, Anthony Perkins, Burl Ives. O'Neill's play concerning the passions of a farmer's young son and the wife of the elderly man misses something in its transference to the screen. Some powerful moments, mostly unrelieved gloom. (Dir: Delbert Mann, 111 mins.)†

Desk Set (1957)*** Spencer Tracy, Katharine Hepburn, Gig Young, Joan Blondell, Dina Merrill. Laugh-filled comedy fueled exclusively by the Tracy-Hepburn confrontations. She is head of the reference department of a major broadcaster and he is the efficiency expert sent in to size up the operation for computerization. (Dir: Walter Lang, 103 mins.)†

Despair (West Germany, 1978)*** Dirk Bogarde, Andrea Ferreol, Volker Spengler, Klaus Lowitsch. R. W. Fassbinder's dark, drawn-out film about a Russian immigrant owning a chocolate factory in Germany during the Nazi uprising is illuminated by Bogarde's stunning performance. Laced with penetrating insights, this version of the Nabokov story was written for the screen by Tom Stoppard. (119 mins.)†

Desperado (MTV 1987)** Alex McArthur, Lise Cutter, David Warner, Yaphet Kotto,

Pernell Roberts, Donald Moffat, Dirk Blocker, Robert Vaughn. An assembly-line western written by Elmore Leonard. The plot concerns a Shane-type loner who comes to the aid of a feisty home-steader's daughter, whose land is coveted by some ruthless villains. (Dir: Virgil Vogel, 104 mins.)

Desperado: Avalanche at Devil's Ridge (MTV 1988)**½ Alex McArthur, Rod Steiger, Alice Adair, Lise Cutter, Hoyt Axton. The West's most honest outlaw returns. This time 'round, he's about to be hanged when a rich salt mine mogul (Steiger) steps in to offer him his life in exchange for the recovery of his kidnapped daughter. The unusually intriguing script was written by busy moviemaker Larry Cohen. (Dir: Richard Compton, 96 mins.)

Desperado: Badland's Justice (MTV 1989)** Alex McArthur, John Rhys-Davies, James B. Sikking, Patricia Charbonneau, Gregory Sierra. Continuing his quest to clear his name, Duell McCall runs afoul of bad guys in a mining town. McArthur sits the saddle well and makes an imposing figure, but the tale is old and creaky. (Dir: E. W. Swackhamer, 96 mins.)

Desperadoes, The (1969)* Jack Palance, Vince Edwards, George Maharis, Neville Brand. Violence-drenched tale of a young son trying to break away from his out-law family in the post-Civil War West. (Dir: Henry Levin, 90 mins.)†

Desperate (1947)*** Steve Brodie, Nan Leslie. Truckdriver becomes a fugitive when his vehicle is used in a robbery. Above-average melodrama. (Dir: Anthony Mann, 73 mins.)†

Desperate Chance for Ellery Queen, A (1942)*½ William Gargan, Margaret Lindsay, Charley Grapewin, John Litel. Ellery helps a woman find her missing banker-husband, who was believed dead. Not one of the better entries in the detective series. (Dir: James Hogan, 70 mins.)

Desperate Characters (1971)*** Shirley MacLaine, Kenneth Mars, Gerald S. O'Loughlin, Sada Thompson. Well-written character study of a day in the life of an urban couple who face a decaying New York that they are help-less to change. (Dir: Frank Gilroy, 88 mins.)

Desperate for Love (MTV 1989)**½ Chris-tian Slater, Tammy Lauren, Brian Bloom, Veronica Cartwright. A trio of attractive young actors boost this melodrama about teenage love and tragedy in a small Southern town. (Dir: Michael Tuchner, 96 mins.)

Desperate Hours, The (1955)*** Humphrey Bogart, Fredric March, Martha Scott, Dewey Martin, Gig Young. The sus-pense runs high in this taut drama of three escaped convicts who hole up in the home of a respected family and use them as hostages. (Dir: William Wyler, 112 mins.)†

Desperate Hours (1990)**½ Mickey Rourke, Mimi Rogers, Anthony Hopkins, Kelly Lynch, Lindsay Crouse, Elias Koteas. Effective remake of 1955 clas-sic about a family held hostage is opened up a little too much, reducing the ten-sion and breaking the necessary claus-trophobia. Chaotic ending hurts film, but Rogers as the wife and Crouse as an FBI agent are especially good. (Dir: Michael Cimino, 105 mins.)†

Desperate Intruder (MTV 1983)* Meg Fos-ter, Nick Mancuso, Claude Akins, Robert Hogan, Lisa Jane Persky. Hopelessly sappy, clichéd drama about a blind wom-an and her weekend fling with an es-caped convict at her picturesque beach house. (Dir: Nick Havinga, 108 mins.)

Desperate Journey (1942)**½ Errol Flynn, Ronald Reagan, Raymond Massey. One of the pictures made when Errol was winning the war single-handedly. Today, stripped of its propaganda value, it's a good action story. (Dir: Raoul Walsh, 107 mins.)

Desperate Lives (MTV 1982)**½ Diana Scarwid, Doug McKeon, Helen Hunt, Art Hindle, Sam Bottoms, Diane Ladd. Teenagers take drugs and commit sui-cide in this fairly compelling "message" show. Seen through the perspective of a counselor (Diana Scarwid) and a 14-year-old spaced-out boy (Doug McKeon). (Dir: Robert Lewis, 104 mins.)†

Desperate Living (1977)*** Liz Renay, Mink Stole, Susan Lowe, Edith Massey, Mary Vivian Pearce, Jean Hill. Probably Di-rector John Waters's most outrageous mov-ie; and for the man who made *Pink Flamingos*, that's saying a lot. The sto-ry concerns a housewife and maid who enter a fleabitten fictional kingdom named Mortville. Viewers of any gentility will be mortified by all sorts of tasteless goings-on, but that just makes the mov-ie all the more endearing to the college crowd and camp addicts who cherish Waters's movies. (90 mins.)†

Desperately Seeking Susan (1985)**½ Rosanna Arquette, Madonna, Aidan Quinn, Mark Blum, Robert Joy, Laurie Metcalf. A topsy-turvy, somewhat over-rated, screwball comedy about a bored New Jersey housewife (Arquette) who is mistaken for a New Wave temptress with a contract out on her life. The pacing is much too slack, but the direc-tor's ability to create character comedy often pays off, particularly with the supporting cast. (Dir: Susan Seidelman, 104 mins.)†

Desperate Miles, The (MTV 1975)* Tony

Musante, Joanne Pettet, Jeanette Nolan, Lyn Loring. Simplistic drivel about a serious subject: wounded Vietnam veteran, trying to adjust to the new realities of life, decides to make a 130-mile trip in his wheelchair to prove his worth. (Dir: Dan Haller, 72 mins.)

Desperate Mission (MTV 1971)* Ricardo Montalbán, Slim Pickens, Earl Holliman. Bland tale of a victimized man forced to protect wife of wealthy landowner on her journey. (Dir: Earl Bellamy, 100 mins.)

Desperate Moment (Great Britain, 1953)***½ Dirk Bogarde, Mai Zetterling. Displaced person in Europe is tricked into confessing to a murder he didn't commit, and his girl tries to help track down the guilty party. Exciting, tense melodrama; excellent performances. (Dir: Compton Bennett, 88 mins.)

Desperate Ones, The (Spain-U.S., 1967)** Maximilian Schell, Raf Vallone, Irene Papas, Theodore Bikel, Maria Perschy. OK World War II melodrama. Two Polish brothers escape a Siberian labor camp. (Dir: Alexander Ramati, 104 mins.)

Desperate Search (1953)**½ Howard Keel, Jane Greer, Patricia Medina. Moderately interesting drama about the efforts of a search party to bring back two young survivors of a plane crash in the Canadian mountains. (Dir: Joseph H. Lewis, 71 mins.)

Desperate Siege (1951)**½ Tyrone Power, Susan Hayward. In this routine western, Power and Hayward find themselves in the desperate position of being held prisoners in a remote stagecoach station by a band of outlaws. Remake of *Show Them No Mercy*. AKA: **Rawhide**. (Dir: Henry Hathaway, 86 mins.)

Desperate Teenage Love Dolls (1985)* Jennifer Schwartz, Hilary Rubens, Steve McDonald, Tracy Lea. Shot-on-video junk about an all-girl rock band looking for gigs in Santa Monica. Just because any bozo with a camcorder can make a "movie," do they have to put them in video stores? (Dir: David Markey, 60 mins.)†

Desperate Voyage (MTV 1980)** Christopher Plummer, Cliff Potts, Christine Belford, Lara Parker, Nicholas Pryor, Jonathan Banks. Intriguing premise. Christopher Plummer plays a modern-day pirate who waits for SOS signals and then proceeds to give the troubled seamen anything but help. (Dir: Michael O'Herlihy, 104 mins.)

Desperate Women (MTV 1978)*½ Susan St. James, Dan Haggerty, Ann Dusenberry, Ronee Blakley. Westerns seldom work when played for laughs; that's the case with this silly piece of business about three ladies abandoned in the desert. (Dir: Earl Bellamy, 104 mins.)†

Desperation Rising (1989)* Jason Holt, Tally Lauriti, Nick Cassavetes. Things just go from bad to worse for a stock broker: after a market crash, his wife leaves him, he gets ripped off by a hooker, and mixed up with crack-abusing white slavers. Pretentious attempt at social commentary, produced, written, and directed by star Holt. (83 mins.)†

Destination: America (MTV 1987)** Bruce Greenwood, Joe Pantoliano, Carinne Bohrer, Alan Autry, Henry Kingi, Robert Newman, Rip Torn. A prodigal son returns home and becomes a suspect in his father's murder. (Dir: Corey Allen, 104 mins.)

Destination Gobi (1953)**½ Richard Widmark, Don Taylor. A notch or two above the average heroic war story. Good photography and some solid acting make up for some of the shortcomings of the script. (Dir: Robert Wise, 89 mins.)

Destination Inner Space (1966)*½ Scott Brady, Sheree North, Gary Merrill. Lame science fiction as deep-sea divers remove exotic devices from a craft they have salvaged from the ocean's floor. A strange creature arrives for the finale. (Dir: Francis D. Lyon, 82 mins.)

Destination Moon (1950)*** Warner Anderson, John Archer. An American spaceship takes off to reach the moon. Good detail, imaginative special effects. (Dir: Irving Pichel, 91 mins.)†

Destination Tokyo (1943)** Cary Grant, John Garfield, Alan Hale, Dane Clark, Warner Anderson. Archetypal wartime submarine picture, with Grant as the patrician captain on a mission underwater to Tokyo and Garfield as the rebellious sailor. (Dir: Delmer Daves, 135 mins.)†

Destiny (Germany, 1921)*** Lil Dagover, Bernhardt Goetzke, Walter Fanssen. Director Fritz Lang's first major film is an imaginative fantasy about a young woman trying to fulfill a pact with the grim reaper, who will bring her lover back to life if she can find someone willing to die in his place. Her journeys to three different time periods allowed Lang to utilize the skills he gained working on cliffhanger serials and also to exercise the genius for fantasy that marked his later classic *Metropolis*. AKA: **Der Mude Tod**. (121 mins.)†

Destiny (1944)** Alan Curtis, Gloria Jean. Escaped prisoner takes refuge in a farm owned by a man with a blind daughter. Uneven drama, with some sequences much better than others. Expanded from what was originally a sequence shot for *Flesh and Fantasy*. (Dir: Reginald Le Borg, 65 mins.)

Destiny of a Man (U.S.S.R., 1959)***½ Sergei Bondarchuk, Zinaida Kirienkova,

Pavil Pavilk Boriskin. Magnificent story of the effects of WWII on a Russian soldier who escapes from a German concentration camp and returns home, only to find his family gone. Scenes of war, life in the camps, and the struggles of ordinary Russians all presented with gritty realism. Star Bondarchuk's directorial debut packs a bitter emotional wallop. (98 mins.)

Destiny of a Spy (MTV 1969)**½ Lorne Greene, Rachel Roberts, Anthony Quayle, Patrick Magee. Picturesque, well-acted espionage tale with Lorne Greene as a Russian spy who is taken out of mothballs to complete just one more dangerous mission involving the development of a sophisticated counter-radar system. (Dir: Boris Sagal, 99 mins.)

Destroy All Monsters (Japan, 1969)** Akira Kubo, Jun Tazaki. The Kilaaks want to take over the Earth. To do it Mothra, Manda, Rodan, and even the dreaded Godzilla break their cages and go on the rampage. (Dir: Ishiro Honda, 87 mins.)

Destroyer (1988)** Lyle Alzado, Anthony Perkins, Jim Turner, Deborah Foreman, Clayton Rohner. As a serial killer who survived the electric chair and now haunts his abandoned prison, ex-football player Alzado attacks his role with gusto, but there's too little of him in the time-filler plot about a company shooting a movie in the prison. Perkins is amusing as the company's director. (Dir: Robert Kirk, 94 mins.)†

Destructors, The (1968)** Richard Egan, Patricia Owens, John Ericson, Michael Ansara, Joan Blackman. Third-rate James Bond imitation. Investigation of a factory bombing uncovers plot by enemy agents to steal a laser gun. (Dir: Francis D. Lyon, 97 mins.)

Destructors, The (Great Britain, 1974)* Anthony Quinn, Michael Caine, James Mason. Cliché-packed underworld melodrama with American narcotics chief (Quinn) trying to put an end to Marseilles drug kingpin (Mason). (Dir: Robert Parrish, 89 mins.)

Destry (1954)**½ Audie Murphy, Mari Blanchard. Not altogether successful remake of the Stewart-Dietrich vehicle. Murphy is good as the gunless sheriff, but Mari Blanchard is a bust as a replacement for marvelous Marlene. (Dir: George Marshall, 95 mins.)

Destry Rides Again (1939)**** Marlene Dietrich, James Stewart, Charles Winninger, Brian Donlevy, Una Merkel, Irene Hervey, Billy Gilbert, Jack Carson. A free-wheeling comic western with Stewart in double jeopardy—fighting six-gun justice with his own brand of no-gun peacekeeping and fending off the advances of Frenchie, a sexy saloon gal,

played by Dietrich. She makes a beautiful foil for Stewart's strong, silent lawman in this rip-roaring western odyssey. (Dir: George Marshall, 94 mins.)†

Detective, The (Great Britain, 1954)*** Alec Guinness, Peter Finch, Cecil Parker, Joan Greenwood. Guinness is delightful as a priest who fancies himself a top-flight amateur detective. The picture is not among his best but has some pleasant moments as Father Brown tries to trap an art thief. AKA: **Father Brown, Detective.** (Dir: Robert Hamer, 100 mins.)†

Detective, The (1968)*** Frank Sinatra, Lee Remick, Jack Klugman, Jacqueline Bisset, Ralph Meeker, Robert Duvall, William Windom, Tony Musante, Al Freeman. Screenwriter Abby Mann has written some pungent, realistic dialogue for this well-above-average drama about a hard-bitten New York City police detective investigating a messy murder of a young homosexual. (Dir: Gordon Douglas, 114 mins.)

Detective (France-Switzerland, 1985)**½ Claude Brasseur, Nathalie Baye, Johnny Hallyday, Jean-Pierre Leaud, Alain Cuny, Laurent Terzieff. A tricky riff on the *film noir* genre by innovative director Jean-Luc Godard. A married couple whose life savings are at stake pursue a boxing promoter, who's being crowded by a Mafia kingpin who brings his preschool granddaughter with him on his deadly rounds. In turn, they are all shadowed by Jean-Pierre Leaud as a comically crazed detective, who may be a metaphoric stand-in for the film's director. Best appreciated by Godard's fans. (95 mins.)

Detective Story (1951)*** Kirk Douglas, Eleanor Parker, William Bendix, Horace MacMahon, Lee Grant, George Macready. Douglas gives one of his finest screen performances as a detective whose personal code becomes twisted from dealing with criminals over a number of years. (Dir: William Wyler, 103 mins.)

Detour (1945)*** Tom Neal, Ann Savage. While hitchhiking cross-country, a piano player meets a scheming dame and is innocently involved in sudden death. Well above average, ironic melodrama. (Dir: Edgar G. Ulmer, 69 mins.)†

Detour to Terror (MTV 1980)*½ O. J. Simpson, Arte Johnson, Gerald S. O'Loughlin, Lorenzo Lamas, Kathryn Holcomb. O. J. is a bus driver who faces a hijacking on his way to Las Vegas with a group of tourists. (Dir: Michael O'Herlihy, 104 mins.)

Devi (India, 1960)*** Chabi Biswas, Sharmila Tagore, Soumitra Chatterjee, Karuna Bannerjee. Religious fanatic convinces his daughter-in-law that she is the reincarnation of the goddess Kali. As she becomes revered, her intellectual husband despairs. Symbolic study of the conflict between modern thought and religious tradition. (Dir: Satyajit Ray, 93 mins.)

Devil and Daniel Webster, The (1941)**** Walter Huston, Edward Arnold, James Craig, Anne Shirley, Jane Darwell, Simone Simon. A superb fantasy. A simple farmer sells his soul to the devil in exchange for riches, and requires the aid of the famed lawyer to get it back. Richly textured images and an engaging folksiness are the strong points of this handsome adaptation of Stephen Vincent Benet's American fable. Huston is impeccably roguish as the bearded Scratch, Arnold is the picture of heroic advocacy as his legal adversary, and Simone Simon is bewitching as an unearthly seductress. Running times vary from 85 to 112 mins. AKA: **All That Money Can Buy.** (Dir: William Dieterle, 109 mins.)†

Devil and Max Devlin, The (1981)*½ Bill Cosby, Elliott Gould, Susan Anspach, Julie Budd, Adam Rich. Coy Disney comedy about Gould being sent by the Devil (Cosby) to enlist three souls into Satan's roll book. Gould's too old to keep acting teddy-bearish and Cosby's too self-infatuated for words. (Dir: Steven Hilliard Stern, 96 mins.)†

Devil and Miss Jones, The (1941)*** Jean Arthur, Robert Cummings, Charles Coburn, S. Z. Sakall, William Demarest. Pleasant comedy about a department store tycoon who takes a job, incognito, in his own store. Dated but fun. (Dir: Sam Wood, 92 mins.)†

Devil and Miss Sarah, The (MTV 1971)** Gene Barry, James Drury, Janice Rule, Charles McGraw, Slim Pickens, Logan Ramsey, Donald Moffat. Ineffective fusion of Western and supernatural elements has Barry attempting to draw a young wife under his Satanic influence. Six-guns and pentagrams don't make for an easy marriage. (Dir: Michael Caffey, 72 mins.)

Devil and the Deep (1932)*** Charles Laughton, Gary Cooper, Tallulah Bankhead, Cary Grant. A preposterous, entertaining melodrama about an insane submarine commander (Laughton) who's so jealous of his wife he drives her right into Cooper's arms. Laughton is at his hammiest, which is something to see. (Dir: Marion Gering, 80 mins.)

Devil and the Nun, The (Poland, 1960)*** Lucyna Winnicka, Anna Ciepielewska, Maria Chwalibog. Script, acting, and design are all superior in this story of 17th-century nuns possessed by demons. From the same incident that inspired Ken Russell's *The Devils* as well as works by Aldous Huxley (a novel), John Whiting (a play) and Krzysztof Penderecki (an opera). (Dir: Jerzy Kawalerowicz, 108 mins.)

Devil at 4 O'Clock, The (1961)**½ Spencer Tracy, Frank Sinatra, Kerwin Mathews, Jean-Pierre Aumont. Aging priest and three convicts undertake a perilous rescue mission when a tropic island is threatened by a volcanic eruption. Uneven drama. (Dir: Mervyn Le Roy, 126 mins.)†

Devil Bat, The (1941)*** Bela Lugosi, Suzanne Kaaren, Dave O'Brien. Bela's training an entire army of little bloodsuckers to attack his enemies. Grade B thriller, but you'll be changing into a turtleneck sweater by the time it's over. AKA: **Killer Bat.** (Dir: Jean Yarbrough, 69 mins.)†

Devil Bat's Daughter (1946)** Rosemary La Planche, John James, Molly Lamont, Michael Hale. Ridiculous sequel to *The Devil Bat* has mad doctor's daughter (played by La Planche, Miss America of 1941) trying to clear his name, though she's suspected of having inherited his criminal nature. Stupid but enjoyable. (Dir: Frank Wisbar, 66 mins.)

Devil by the Tail, The (France-Italy, 1969)*** Yves Montand, Maria Schell, Jean Rochefort, Marthe Kelly, Madeleine Renaud. Wonderfully zany comedy about an innkeeper and a mechanic who conspire to sabotage cars of passing motorists who are then forced to stay overnight at her hotel. (Dir: Philippe De Broca, 93 mins.)

Devil Commands, The (1941)**½ Boris Karloff, Richard Fiske, Amanda Duff, Anne Revere. Very good Karloff vehicle, with a great deal of atmosphere and emotional tension supporting what could have been an ordinary melodrama of a mad scientist trying to communicate with the dead. (Dir: Edward Dmytryk, 65 mins.)

Devil Dogs of the Air (1935)*** James Cagney, Pat O'Brien, Margaret Lindsay, Frank McHugh. Jimmy is a cocky kid from Brooklyn who enlists in the Marines and wins the respect and love of his girl. An enjoyable aviation flick. (Dir: Lloyd Bacon, 86 mins.)

Devil Dog: The Hound of Hell (MTV 1978)½ Richard Crenna, Yvette Mimieux, Victor Jory, Ken Kercheval. The family pet, an innocent-enough looking puppy, turns out to be possessed by the devil. Lots of unintended laughs as the devil dog bumps off anyone who doesn't fit into its dog-in-the-manger schemes. (Dir: Curtis Harrington, 104 mins.)†

Devil Doll, The (1936)***½ Lionel Barrymore. Director Tod Browning's terrific horror thriller about the revenge of a man framed for murder by three business rivals. Marvelous, scary special effects. (80 mins.)†

Devil Doll (Great Britain, 1964)**½ Bryant Halliday, William Sylvester, Yvonne Romain. Hypnotist who uses a wooden dummy in his act is suspected by an investigating reporter of having some dire secret. (Dir: Lindsay Shonteff, 80 mins.)†

Devil Goddess (1955)** Johnny Weissmuller, Angela Stevens, Selmer Jackson, William Tannen, Ed Hilton. Jungle Jim leads explorers into the land of a fire-worshipping tribe in order to find a long-lost person. (Dir: Spencer Bennet, 70 mins.)

Devil In Love, The (Italy, 1966)*** Vittorio Gassman, Mickey Rooney, Claudine Auger. Surprisingly entertaining film. Gassman and Rooney are sent as envoys from Archdevil Beelzebub circa 1478 to foment war between Rome and Florence during the Renaissance. Refreshing approach to period farce, exuberant cast make this an amusing outing. (Dir: Ettore Scola, 72 mins.)

Devil In the Flesh (France, 1949)***½ Gerard Philippe, Micheline Presle. Beautifully acted tragic tale of a young student's affair with a mature married woman during World War I. (Dir: Claude Autant-Lara, 110 mins.)

Devil In the Flesh (Italy, 1987)** Maruschka Detmers, Federico Pitzalis, Anita Laurenzi, Alberto di Stasio, Riccardo de Torreruna. An erotic, somewhat inaccessible version of the famous French novel magnificently filmed before in 1947. When her terrorist boyfriend shows signs of latent conformity, a beautiful, unstable lady goes off on a romantic tangent with a teenage boy. On video in R- and X-rated versions. (Dir: Marco Bellochio, 110 mins.)†

Devil In the House of Exorcism—See: **House of Exorcism**

Devil Is a Sissy, The (1936)**½ Mickey Rooney, Jackie Cooper, Freddie Bartholomew. Occasionally entertaining juvenile delinquency story featuring the top three young male stars of the era. (Dir: W. S. Van Dyke, 92 mins.)

Devil Is a Woman, The (1935)***½ Marlene Dietrich, Cesar Romero, Lionel Atwill. Story of an older man who permits himself to be destroyed by the demands of a lovely woman. A bit stilted for modern tastes, but exquisitely photographed and charismatically acted by Marlene. (Dir: Josef von Sternberg, 85 mins.)

Devil Makes Three, The (1952)**½ Gene Kelly, Pier Angeli. American GI in postwar Germany becomes involved in black market smuggling after meeting a nightclub girl. (Dir: Andrew Marton, 90 mins.)

Devil Master, The (1977)½ Jerry Younkins, Ron Hively, Christmas Robbins, Gunnar Hansen, Val Mayerick. Amateurish, laughably awful horror tale about a satanist who calls on the devil to seek revenge on some former members of his cult. AKA: **Demon Lover, The.** (Dir: Donald G. Jackson, 91 mins.)†

Devil on Horseback (Great Britain, 1954)**½ Googie Withers, Jeremy Spencer, John McCallum, Liam Redmond, George Rose, Meredith Edwards, Sam Kydd, Vic Wise. Teenage jockey, a spoiled brat of the highest order, gets his comeuppance in this pleasant comedy about horse racing. Co-produced by noted film historian John Grierson. (Dir: Cyril Frankel, 89 mins.)†

Devil Pays Off, The (1941)*** J. Edward Bromberg, Osa Massen. A civilian agent exposes a shipping magnate about to sell his fleet to a foreign power. Well-made, exciting melodrama. (Dir: John H. Auer, 56 mins.)

Devil, Probably, The (France, 1977)***½ Antoine Monnier, Tina Irissari, Henri De Maublanc. Another morally instructive work from director Robert Bresson. Young man, saddened by the world's physical and intellectual pollution, rejects the entrapments of life and pays a drug-addicted friend to kill him in a cemetery. Spare, poetic autumnal images and existential theme limit potential audience, but if you like thought and grace this film's for you. (95 mins.)

Devil Rides Out, The—See: **Devil's Bride, The**

Devils, The (Great Britain, 1970)***½ Vanessa Redgrave, Oliver Reed, Murray Melvin, Max Adrian. Ken Russell's grotesque historical drama about clerical decadence in seventeenth-century France is a wildly flamboyant, disturbing piece that will offend the devout and delight the non-believer. Hunchbacked nun Redgrave becomes fixated with charismatic priest Reed to the point where she claims he "possesses" her. Extraordinary art direction. (109 mins.)†

Devil's Angels (1967)*½ John Cassavetes, Beverly Adams, Mimsy Farmer, Leo Gordon. Sleazeball movie about outlaw bikers seeking sanctuary, running afoul of the law en route to their leather-and-chrome Shangri-La. (Dir: Daniel Haller, 84 mins.)

Devil's Bride, The (Great Britain, 1968)**½ Christopher Lee, Charles Gray, Nike Arrighi. Above-average horror chiller, with Lee razor-sharp in a switch to the good-guy role—fending off the gathering powers of evil aroused by a group of Satanists. AKA: **The Devil Rides Out.** (Dir: Terence Fisher, 95 mins.)

Devil's Brigade, The (1968)**½ William Holden, Cliff Robertson, Vince Edwards, Michael Rennie, Dana Andrews. Misfit American GIs join efficient Canadian troops for commando tactics during World War II. Competent if familiar heroics. (Dir: Andrew McLaglen, 130 mins.)

Devil's Brother, The (1933)** Laurel and Hardy, Thelma Todd, James Finlayson. L&H trapped in music and whipped-cream sentiments. This operetta suffers from the second-banana roles given the stars by the script—which casts them as servants to a singing lead. AKA: **Fra Diavolo.** (Dirs: Hal Roach, Charles Rogers, 88 mins.)

Devil's Canyon (1953)**½ Virginia Mayo, Dale Robertson. Ex-marshal is sent to prison where he becomes involved with mutineers against his will. (Dir: Alfred L. Werker, 91 mins.)

Devil's Commandment, The—See: **I Vampiri**

Devil's Daughter, The (MTV 1972)* Shelley Winters, Belinda Montgomery, Robert Cornthwaite, Jonathan Frid, Joseph Cotten. Occult hokum about a sweet young girl who tries to buck the odds and avert a marriage to the Prince of Doom. (Dir: Jeannot Szwarc, 74 mins.)

Devil's Disciple, The (Great Britain, 1959)***½ Kirk Douglas, Burt Lancaster, Laurence Olivier. Not the best screen translation of a George Bernard Shaw work, but a rousing good try. Kirk Douglas energetically portrays "Dick Dudgeon," the rebellious and romantic rogue; Burt Lancaster pompously plays a New England pastor; and Olivier makes the most of his few scenes as the British General Burgoyne. (Dir: Guy Hamilton, 82 mins.)

Devil's Doorway, (1950)*** Robert Taylor, Louis Calhern. An Indian veteran of the Civil War returns to find injustice and tragedy for his people, fights to aid them. Well-done western drama takes the Indian's point of view, does a good job of it. (Dir: Anthony Mann, 84 mins.)

Devil's Eight, The (1969)** Christopher George, Ralph Meeker, Fabian. George is a federal agent who enlists the services of a motley crew of prisoners to bust a big moonshining syndicate. (Dir: Burt Topper, 97 mins.)

Devil's Eye, The (Sweden, 1960)*** Jarl Kulle, Bibi Andersson. Bits of the Bergman elegance and insight, snips of humor and captivating paradoxical detail. The Devil gets a sty in his eye and resurrects his captive, Don Juan, to deal with its cause—the irritating chastity of a young woman up on Earth. (Dir: Ingmar Bergman, 90 mins.)†

Devil's General (West Germany, 1956)***½ Curt Jurgens, Marianne Cook. Famous wartime flyer gradually becomes disgusted with the Nazis, and the hopelessness of World War II. Talkative but engrossing drama. (Dir: Helmut Kautner, 119 mins.)

Devil's Hairpin, The (1957)**½ Cornel Wilde, Jean Wallace, Mary Astor. Champion sports car racer's disregard of safety is responsible for the crippling of his brother—he tries to reform. (Dir: Cornel Wilde, 82 mins.)

Devil's Hand, The (1962)* Robert Alda, Linda Christian. Horror film with all the obvious clichés used once again. (Dir: William Hole, Jr., 71 mins.)†

Devil's In Love, The (1933)*** Loretta Young, Victor Jory, David Manners, J. Carrol Naish, Bela Lugosi, Akim Tamiroff. Jory is fine as a Foreign Legion doctor accused of murder, struggling to clear his name. Interesting and unusual. (Dir: William Dieterle, 71 mins.)

Devil's Island (1940)**½ Boris Karloff, Nedda Harrigan, James Stephenson, Adia Kuznetzoff. Good nonhorror vehicle for Karloff as an innocent man condemned to Devil's Island and struggling against the villainous commandant, well played by Stephenson. Originally released in a longer version in 1939, but pulled and reedited when the French government objected to the realistic depictions of prison brutality. (Dir: William Clemens, 62 mins.)

Devil's Messenger, The (1962)*½ Lon Chaney, Jr., Karen Kadler. Satan assigns an attractive girl to perform tasks for him in order that she be admitted to the Dark World. Episodic thriller. (Dir: Curt Siodmak, 72 mins.)†

Devil's Nightmare, The (Italy-Belgium, 1971)**½ Erika Blanc, Jean Servais, Jacques Monseau. Travelers stranded at an accursed castle are stalked by a mysterious woman. Each of the seven victims represents one of the seven deadly sins, and they get their comeuppance while indulging in this formulaic shocker with a few good scares. Originally 95 mins. AKA: **Succubus** and **The Devil Walks at Midnight.** (Dir: Jean Brismee, 87 mins.)†

Devils of Darkness (Great Britain, 1965)*½ William Sylvester, Tracy Reed, Hubert Noel, Carole Gray. A modern-day vampire dabbling in devil-worshipping gives visiting tourists a tour of the local crypts not mentioned in the travel brochures. (Dir: Lance Comfort, 88 mins.)

Devil's Own, The (Great Britain, 1966)***

Joan Fontaine, Kay Walsh, Ingrid Brett. Teacher (Fontaine) at an English private school comes across witchcraft and voodoo rites. Suspense fans will come across more than a few chills. (Dir: Cyril Frankel, 90 mins.)

Devil's Party, The (1938)**½ Victor McLaglen, William Gargan, Paul Kelly, Beatrice Roberts, Frank Jenks, Samuel S. Hinds. Boyhood friends who grew up in the slums have a yearly reunion; when one of them is murdered, the others try to find out why. Off-beat story, very well done. (Dir: Ray McCarey, 65 mins.)

Devil's Playground (1937)**½ Richard Dix, Chester Morris, Dolores Del Rio, Ward Bond. A good teaming of Dix and Morris has them as navy ocean divers fighting over the same woman, the lovely Del Rio. Realistic underwater sequences. (Dir: Eric C. Kenton, 74 mins.)

Devil's Playground, The (Australia, 1976)**½ Arthur Dignam, Nick Tate, Simon Burke. Tale of repression in a Roman Catholic boy's school is a grave, sensitive film about how the students channel their sexual energy, and how the grownups in charge deal with their own stifled sexuality. (Dir: Fred Schepisi, 107 mins.)†

Devil's Rain, The (1975)* Ernest Borgnine, Eddie Albert, Ida Lupino, William Shatner, Keenan Wynn, John Travolta. Satanic shenanigans. Garbled attempt at horror, sports Borgnine as a coven leader back to haunt a western ghost town. (Dir: Robert Fuest, 85 mins.)†

Devil Strikes at Night, The (West Germany, 1957)***½ Claus Holm, Mario Adorf, Hannes Messemer, Anne Marie Duringer. Thriller set in Nazi Germany. Outside investigator looking into the murders of eighty women finds all were strangled by a Gestapo member, but the Nazis cover up the facts and blame the deaths on an innocent minor official. Suspenseful, meticulously crafted film (based on a true case) gives tremendous insight into the workings of the Nazi hierarchy. (Dir: Robert Siodmak, 105 mins.)

Devil's Wanton, The (Sweden, 1949)**½ Doris Svedlund, Birger Malmsten. Director Ingmar Bergman's theory of Hell on Earth, told from the viewpoint of a girl who tries to find happiness with a man deserted by his wife after her lover has had their baby killed. Often more artiness than art; gloomy drama for devotees of the Swedish director. (72 mins.)

Devil's Wedding Night, The (Italy, 1973)** Sara Bay, Mark Damon, Frances Davis. Man searching Transylvania for the ring of the Nibelungen falls under the spell of sexy vampire Bay. (Dir: "Paolo Solvay" [Luigi Batzella], 85 mins.)†

Devil's Widow, The—See: **Tam Lin**

Devil Thumbs a Ride, The (1947)**½ Lawrence Tierney, Ted North, Nan Leslie, Betty Lawford. Driver picks up a hitchhiker, unaware that he's just committed a double murder and won't mind a few more. Standard thriller given a boost by Tierney's rabid performance as the killer. (Dir: Felix Feist, 63 mins.)†

Devil Times Five (1974)** Gene Evans, Sorrell Booke, Shelly Morrison, Leif Garrett. Unmemorable thriller set in a backwoods house where five disturbed children terrorize a family. AKA: **Horrible House on the Hill**. (Dir: Sean McGregor, 90 mins.)†

Devil To Pay, The (1930)*** Ronald Colman, Loretta Young, Frederick Kerr, David Torrence, Myrna Loy. Charming Colman vehicle has him as a devil-may-care young man who wants to settle down when he meets Young. Light and sparkling. (Dir: George Fitzmaurice, 73 mins.)

Devil Walks at Midnight, The—See: **Devil's Nightmare, The**

Devil Within Her, The (Great Britain, 1975)*½ Joan Collins, Eileen Atkins, Donald Pleasence, Ralph Bates, Caroline Munro. Singer-stripper Collins gives birth to a murdering tot after spurning the attentions of a dwarf. AKA: **I Don't Want to Be Born**. (Dir: Peter Sasdy, 90 mins.)†

Devonsville Terror, The (1983)* Donald Pleasence, Suzanna Love, Robert Walker Jr. Sadistic shocker about a witch's curse that catches up with a small town three hundred years later. Wait until you see Pleasence worm his way out of an ailment. (Dir: Ulli Lommel, 82 mins.)†

Devotion (1946)**½ Ida Lupino, Paul Henreid, Olivia de Havilland. The genius of the Brontë sisters receives a Hollywood treatment in this photoplay. Excellent acting rescues the film but they should have called it "Distortion." (Dir: Curtis Bernhardt, 107 mins.)

D.I., The (1957)** Jack Webb, Don Dubbins, Monica Lewis. Webb portrays a very tough marine drill instructor who puts the raw recruits through their paces. (Dir: Jack Webb, 106 mins.)†

Diabolical Dr. Cyclops, The—See: **Dr. Cyclops**

Diabolical Dr. Z, The (Spain-France, 1966)* Mabel Karr, Estella Blain, Fernando Montes. Doctor invents a personality-changing device; after his death, his daughter plots revenge. (Dir: Jesus Franco, 86 mins.)†

Diabolically Yours (France, 1968)*** Alain Delon, Senta Berger, Peter Mosbacher, Claude Preplu. Delon wakes up from a coma and remembers nothing—neither his beautiful wife, his palatial estate nor the years he spent amassing a fortune. His wife and best friend think he's faking. Who's trying to pull the wool over whose eyes? (Dir: Julien Duvier, 94 mins.)†

Diabolique (France, 1955)**** Simone Signoret, Vera Clouzot. Excellent, scary murder mystery, as the mistress of a schoolmaster and his wife plan an elaborate murder. Edge of the seat excitement. (Dir: Henri-Georges Clouzot, 107 mins.)†

Diagnosis: Murder (Great Britain, 1975)**½ Christopher Lee, Jon Finch, Judy Geeson, Jane Merrow. Slow-moving, but very well acted meller about psychiatrist Lee's elaborate plans to do away with his wife. (Dir: Sidney Meyers, 90 mins.)

Dial: Help (Italy, 1988)**½ Charlotte Lewis, William Berger, Marcello Modugno. A British model finds herself pursued by a very strange threat—dead souls who communicate with her via the telephone. Though it has its share of standard horror elements, this odd little item is bigger on sensuality than slashings. (Dir: Ruggero Deodato, 96 mins.)†

Dial Hot Line (MTV 1969)* Vince Edwards, Chelsea Brown, Kim Hunter. Pilot film for the television series "Matt Lincoln" had Vince Edwards heading a "Hot Line," a telephone service for people who need psychiatric aid. (Dir: Jerry Thorpe, 100 mins.)

Dial M for Murder (1954)*** Ray Milland, Grace Kelly, Robert Cummings, John Williams, Anthony Dawson. In this screen version of Frederick Knott's play about a thwarted murder attempt, director Hitchcock ignores the play's single-set restriction, proving that imaginative direction can be cinematic without "going" anywhere. (Dir: Alfred Hitchcock, 105 mins.)†

Dial M for Murder (MTV 1981)** Angie Dickinson, Christopher Plummer, Anthony Quayle, Ron Moody, Michael Parks, Gerry Gibson. Standard TV remake of the Hitchcock film about the perfect crime that hits a few snags. Stick with the original. (Dir: Boris Sagal, 104 mins.)

Dial 1119 (1950)**½ Marshall Thompson, Keefe Brasselle. Good suspense thriller about a bar where a killer keeps a group trapped. (Dir: Gerald Mayer, 74 mins.)

Diamond Earrings, The (France, 1953)**** Charles Boyer, Danielle Darrieux, Vittorio De Sica. An ultimately tragic and always romantic "merry-go-round" about the ironic giving and receiving of a pair of diamond earrings. A masterpiece. AKA: **The Earrings of Madame De.** (Dir: Max Ophuls, 105 mins.)†

Diamond Head (1962)** Charlton Heston, Yvette Mimieux, James Darren, George Chakiris. Charlton Heston is a plantation owner in Hawaii who wants everything his way. His sister (Yvette Mimieux) is equally independent and announces she is going to marry a Hawaiian native (James Darren). (Dir: Guy Green, 107 mins.)†

Diamond Jim (1935)*** Edward Arnold, Binnie Barnes, Jean Arthur. Story of "Diamond Jim" Brady, the millionaire sportsman and man-about-town of the gay nineties. Well-done period drama. (Dir: A. Edward Sutherland, 100 mins.)

Diamond Queen, The (1953)**½ Fernando Lamas, Arlene Dahl, Gilbert Roland. Two soldiers of fortune in India bargain with a treacherous Mogul for a fabulous blue diamond. Routine adventure. (Dir: John Brahm, 80 mins.)

Diamonds (U.S.-Israel, 1976)*½ Robert Shaw, Richard Roundtree, Barbara Seagull (Hershey). In this caper film Shaw plays a dual role—the mastermind behind a gem heist as well as his rival brother. (Dir: Menahem Golan, 106 mins.)†

Diamonds Are Forever (Great Britain, 1971)***½ Sean Connery, Jill St. John, Charles Gray, Bruce Cabot. Terrific escapist James Bond fun. The basic setting is Las Vegas; the quarry is another evil villain who is willing and eager to rule the world. (Dir: Guy Hamilton, 119 mins.)†

Diamond's Edge, The (Great Britain, 1990)**½ Susannah York, Colin Dale, Dursley McLinden, Patricia Hodge. Tongue-in-cheek detective yarn follows the adventures of a teenage private eye and his younger brother as they investigate the shady Fat Man and his mysterious box. Pleasant outing, with a good performance from York as a sexy nightclub singer. (Dir: Stephen Bayly, 83 mins.)†

Diamonds on Wheels (Great Britain, 1973)*½ Peter Firth, Patrick Allen, George Seawell. Disney adventure with a trio of young car fanciers who find a seemingly abandoned sportscar and set about restoring it, unaware that some jewel thieves stashed their loot in it. Typical Disney adventure. (Dir: Jerome Courtland, 87 mins.)

Diane (1956)** Lana Turner, Pedro Armendariz, Roger Moore. King's son about to be married to an Italian princess is enamoured of a glamorous French countess. Overstuffed costume drama. (Dir: David Miller, 102 mins.)

Diary for My Children (Hungary, 1984)***½ Zsuzsa Czinkoczi, Anna Polony, Jan Nowicki, Tamas Toth. Like many films made behind the Iron Curtain, this one says as much by omission and metaphor as by direct statement. It's the story of a teenage girl, taken from Hungary as a baby, who returns to Budapest from the Soviet Union after World War II and clashes with her pro-Communist aunt and the newly forming society around her. (Dir: Marta Meszaros, 106 mins.)

Diary of a Chambermaid (1946)**½ Paulette Goddard, Burgess Meredith. A bewitching chambermaid is hired by a family of eccentrics, where she is involved in amorous byplay and finally murder. Odd, uneven comedy-drama. (Dir: Jean Renoir, 86 mins.)†

Diary of a Chambermaid (France-Italy, 1965)***½ Jeanne Moreau, Michel Piccoli, Georges Geret, Françoise Lugagne. Octave Mirbeau's novel and Jean Renoir's 1946 film are transformed into another one of director Luis Buñuel's lacerating critiques of fascism. Moreau plays a young maid in 1939 France who looks askance at her upper-middle-class employers in this dark, incisive comedy. (79 mins.)†

Diary of a Country Priest (France, 1951)**** Claude Laydu, Jean Riveyre, Marie-Monique Arkell, Nicole Maurey. A quiet, exquisitely wrought expression of faith from filmmaker Robert Bresson about the trials and sacrifices of a young parish priest in rural France. Though one of Bresson's most austere works, the film remains his least enigmatic; the struggle toward grace is perceived by the viewer as a tangible reality, and the tribulations of the soul are dramatized with astonishing clarity. (120 mins.)†

Diary of a Lost Girl (Germany, 1929)***½ Louise Brooks, Fritz Rasp, Sybille Schmitz, Josef Ravensky. Brooks's radiant screen presence illuminates this tragic tale of a wayward girl who suffers various indignities after losing her virtue to a lecherous pharmacist. Memorable, including the brilliantly implied decadence of the sequences set in the "school for wayward girls." (Dir: G. W. Pabst, 104 mins.)†

Diary of a Mad Housewife (1970)**** Richard Benjamin, Carrie Snodgress, Frank Langella. Perceptive drama boasts marvelous performance by Carrie Snodgress as a bored New York housewife-mother, and Frank Langella as a dashing and thoroughly selfish writer with whom she has an affair. (Dir: Frank Perry, 94 mins.)†

Diary of a Madman (1963)**½ Vincent Price, Nancy Kovack. Price plays a French judge who finds he's possessed by a demon, decides life's not worth living. Based on a story by Guy de Maupassant. (Dir: Reginald Le Borg, 96 mins.)†

Diary of Anne Frank, The (1959)*** Joseph Schildkraut, Millie Perkins, Shelley Winters, Ed Wynn, Diane Baker, Richard Beymer, Lou Jacobi. Faithful screen translation of the hit Broadway play about the true, harrowing experiences of the Jewish Frank family and their friends when they are forced to hide from the Nazis in a factory attic in Amsterdam for two long years. Millie Perkins is visually perfect as the young Anne Frank whose spirit gives the group the courage to go on when they lose all hope, but her thesping leaves much to be desired. Winters won a Supporting Oscar. (Dir: George Stevens, 170 mins.)†

Diary of Anne Frank, The (MTV 1980)***½ Melissa Gilbert, Maximilian Schell, Joan Plowright, James Coco, Clive Revill. Remake of the saga of Jews hiding in Nazi-occupied Amsterdam contains more life and emotion than the earlier version. (Dir: Boris Sagal, 104 mins.)

Diary of a Shinjuku Thief (Japan, 1969)***½ Tadanori Yokoo, Rie Yokoyama, Moichi Tanabe, Tetsu Takahashi. Sexual politics highlight tale of a petty thief and his girlfriend caught up in violent Japanese student riots. Director Nagisa Oshima crafts an erotic, intellectually charged parallel to contemporary student unrest in France and the U.S. (94 mins.)

Diary of a Teenage Hitchhiker (MTV 1979)*½ Charlene Tilton, Katherine Helmond, Dick Van Patten. After watching this sensationalized film, teenaged girls will probably think twice before thumbing. (Dir: Ted Post, 104 mins.)†

Diary of Forbidden Dreams—See: **What?** (1973)

Dick Tracy (1945)** Morgan Conway, Anne Jeffreys, Mike Mazurki, Jane Greer. Sleuth tracks down Splitface, a maniacal killer bent on revenge. Acceptable comic-strip heroics. (Dir: William Berke, 62 mins.)†

Dick Tracy (1990)*** Warren Beatty, Madonna, Al Pacino, Glenne Headly, Charlie Korsmo, Dustin Hoffman, Seymour Cassel, Mandy Patinkin, James Keane, William Forsythe, Charles Durning, Paul Sorvino, Dick Van Dyke, James Caan, Michael J. Pollard, Estelle Parsons, R. G. Armstrong, Kathy Bates, Mary Woronov. Terrifically enjoyable cops 'n' robbers movie, more parody than thriller. Pacino steals the movie as the chief villain, but vampy Madonna and lovely Headly are almost as good. Terrific make-up (try to spot the many guest stars in cameos), production design, music—a paper thin script, but you can't have everything. (103 mins.)†

Dick Tracy Meets Gruesome (1947)**½ Ralph Byrd, Boris Karloff, Anne Gwynne, Edward Ashley. Sleuth goes after a quartet of bank robbers, using a new kind of paralyzing gas. Fast-moving comic-strip melodrama, with Karloff giving it added allure. (Dir: John Rawlins, 65 mins.)†

Dick Tracy's Dilemma (1947)** Ralph Byrd, Lyle Latell, Kay Christopher, Ian Keith, will not see Lucifer at a pep rally, you will see several nubile cheerleaders held captive by a coven of devil worshippers. Suspense builds to a fever pitch as the high school's Peeping-Tom janitor betrays the innocent but mature-looking schoolgirls, who must battle with Sheriff B. L. Z. Bub and his overweight wife. Recommended for camp addicts. (Dir: Greydon Clark, 92 mins.)†

Satan's Satellites (1958)* Judd Holdren, Aline Towne, Leonard Nimoy. Invaders from another planet land on Earth to carry out their dirty work. Juvenile sci-fi thriller, cut down from the 1952 serial *Zombies of the Stratosphere.* (Dir: Fred Brannon, 70 mins.)

Satan's School for Girls (MTV 1973)** Pamela Franklin, Roy Thinnes, Kate Jackson, Lloyd Bochner, Jo Van Fleet, Cheryl Jean Stoppelmoor (Ladd). Girl enrolls in a private school to get to the bottom of her younger sister's suicide. Non-frightening horror pic resurrected on videotape due to the presence in the cast of two "Charlie's Angels." (Dir: David Lowell Rich, 74 mins.)†

Satan's Triangle (MTV 1975)**½ Kim Novak, Doug McClure. Melodrama about the infamous "Devil's Triangle," an area where ships, planes, and people just disappear off the face of the Earth. Helicopter rescue pilots come to the aid of a distressed vessel and find find a beautiful woman survivor. The surprise twist at the end is a good one. (Dir: Sutton Rolley, 72 mins.)

Satellite in the Sky (Great Britain, 1956)**½ Kieron Moore, Lois Maxwell. A British made science-fiction tale about an earth satellite. (Dir: Paul Dickson, 84 mins.)

Satin Vengeance—See: **Naked Vengeance**

Satisfaction (1988)* Justine Bateman, Liam Neeson, Trini Alvarado, Debbie Harry. You can't get no enjoyment from this quickie about a female rock band that pulls no stops when it comes to clichés: There are tough street gangs, beach dudes, an overdose, bad cover versions of oldies, a disillusioned songwriter (Neeson), and Justine belting her little heart out, all for naught. (Dir: Joan Freeman, 92 mins.)†

Saturday Night and Sunday Morning (Great Britain, 1961)**** Albert Finney, Shirley Ann Field. A wonderful, robust film, expertly directed by Karel Reisz, detailing the life and loves of a young working-class rascal from the English midlands. Incisive comment on mores of the working class that captures the mood of such a dreary industrial community. Electric, vital performance of Finney deservedly shot him to stardom. An admirable piece of filmmaking in every detail. (98 mins.)

Saturday Night at the Baths (1975)*** Robert Aberdeen, Ellen Sheppard, Don Scotti, Steven Ostrow. Well-made comedy from the era of sexual freedom and disco, set at the Continental Baths. A straight piano player gets a job in the Baths' house band, but has to overcome his homophobia. (Dir: David Buckley, 86 mins.)

Saturday Night at the Palace (South Africa, 1988)**½ John Kani, Paul Slabolepszy, Bill Flynn. Racial violence is the subject of this schematic but powerful drama about a vicious white brutalizer and his roommates (Slabolepszy and Flynn, who co-wrote the script) and their drunken, ultimately tragic encounter with a black restaurant manager (Kani). Some subtlety would have helped. (Dir: Robert Davies, 87 mins.)

Saturday Night Fever (1977)***½ John Travolta, Karen Lynn Gorney, Joseph Cali, Barry Miller, Julie Bovasso, Donna Pescow. Driving, powerful film about the Brooklyn boy whose love of dancing lifts him out of his working-class rut; a huge box-office and critical success. Capitalizes on disco fever with Travolta's riveting dancing sequences. Screenplay by Norman Wexler has some perceptive comments to make on the social and sexual rituals of working-class kids in Brooklyn. (Dir: John Badham, 119 mins.)†

Saturday's Children (1940)**½ John Garfield, Anne Shirley, Claude Rains, Lee Patrick, George Tobias. Somewhat depressing tale of a dreamer who struggles to support his wife, while both of them try to maintain their dignity under trying financial conditions. (Dir: Vincent Sherman, 101 mins.)

Saturday's Hero (1951)*** John Derek, Donna Reed, Sidney Blackmer, Aldo Ray. A handsome youth tries to rise above his immigrant family's background by going to college on a football scholarship. Better than usual performances from the actors involved. (Dir: David Miller, 111 mins.)

Saturday's Heroes (1937)**½ Van Heflin, Marian Marsh, Richard Lane, Alan Bruce, Willie Best, Al St. John. Vigorous college football drama, with a twist: a well-known athlete speaks out against commercialization of sports and special privileges for players. Above average, with a dynamite performance by Heflin. (Dir: Edward Killy, 58 mins.)

Saturday the 14th (1981)½ Richard Benjamin, Paula Prentiss, Severn Darden, Jeffrey Tambor. Inept spoof of haunted house pictures. This combination of *Friday the 13th* and "The Munsters" looks like the work of grade school students. (Dir: Howard R. Cohen, 75 mins.)†

Saturday the 14th Strikes Back (1989)½ Jason Presson, Ray Walston, Avery

Schreiber, Patty McCormack, **Michael** Berryman. How we long for the days when only good movies, or at least popular ones, spawned sequels. No improvement over its predecessor. (Dir: Howard R. Cohen, 78 mins.)†

Saturn 3 (Great Britain, 1980)** Kirk Douglas, Farrah Fawcett, Harvey Keitel. Douglas and Fawcett have made their Malibu in outer space, only to face the intrusion of madman Keitel and his rogue robot, who upset their plastic paradise by insinuating that they could get down to work, with Earth starving and all. Uneven and marred by a weak ending. (Dir: Stanley Donen, 105 mins.)†

Satyricon—See: **Fellini Satyricon**

Savage, The (1952)**½ Charlton Heston, Susan Morrow. Man raised by the Sioux is torn between loyalties when war threatens between the Indians and the whites. (Dir: George Marshall, 95 mins.)

Savage (MTV 1972)**½ Martin Landau, Barbara Bain. Landau and Bain are TV journalists digging into the questionable background of a Supreme Court nominee. (Dir: Steven Spielberg, 78 mins.)†

Savage Beach (1990)** Dona Spier, Hope Marie Carlton, John Aprea, Bruce Penhall, Teri Weigel. Sequel to *Picasso Trigger* finds buxom D.E.A. agents Spier and Carlton on a remote Pacific island where various shady types are trying to locate a cache of gold lost there during WWII. An improvement over writer-director Andy Sidaris's other films in that the tongue-in-cheek humor is mostly intentional. (95 mins.)†

Savage Bees, The (MTV 1976)** Ben Johnson, Michael Parks. Predictable New Orleans-based drama about the influx of African killer bees brought here by a visiting cargo ship. (Dir: Bruce Geller, 106 mins.)†

Savage Dawn (1985)*½ George Kennedy, Richard Lynch, Karen Black, Lance Henricksen, Claudia Udy, Mickey Jones. Ex-Army buddies try to retire peacefully to a desert mining town, but are forced back into action when a gang of bad-tempered bikers roll in. Violent action for the undemanding. (Dir: Simon Nutchern, 102 mins.)†

Savage Drums (1951)** Sabu, Lita Baron, H. B. Warner, Sid Melton. OK exotic melodrama has Sabu helping his people end tribal warfare. Silly, but at least it moves at a pretty fast clip. (Dir: William Berke, 73 mins.)

Savage Eye, The (1961)*** Barbara Baxley. A dramatized documentary about a woman's lonely days following her recent divorce and the series of adventures she forces herself into in order to combat the feeling of desperation. Miss Baxley is excellent and the documentary-flavored

914

technique works beautifully. (Dir: Ben Maddow, 68 mins.)

Savage Guns, The (1962)** Richard Basehart, Don Taylor, Alex Nicol. A loner picked on by a sadistic villain gets bailed out by a gunfighter. Not worth a trip out west. (Dir: Michael Carreras, 63 mins.)

Savage Harvest (1981)½ Tom Skerritt, Michelle Phillips, Shawn Stevens. While the idea of lions munching on bad actors in Africa *sounds* like fun, the idea of their eating a bad writer/director would have been much better. (Dir: Robert Collins, 86 mins.)

Savage Innocents, The (1960)*** Anthony Quinn, Yoko Tani, Peter O'Toole. Unusual drama of Eskimo life, and the struggle of one family to keep alive in the barren wastes. Some spectacular photography, gripping scenes. (Dir: Nicholas Ray, 110 mins.)

Savage Island (U.S.-Italy-Spain, 1984)½ Linda Blair, Ajita Wilson, Christina Lai, Anthony Steffen. What "director" Beardsley has done here is to take a sleazy women's prison camp flick (originally titled *Escape from Hell*), chop out about 35 minutes, tack on a frame story with Blair as an escapee, and rerelease it to an audience that probably can't tell the difference between these things anyway. Featuring the usual busty women in flimsy prison togs that just can't seem to stay on. (Dirs: Edward Muller, Nicholas Beardsley, 79 mins.)†

Savage Is Loose, The (1974)½ George C. Scott, Trish Van Devere, John David Carson. Embarrassing effort. Playing a scientist, Scott is stranded on a desert island with his wife and their young son. The action centers on the boy's growing up without a proper mate upon whom to vent his lust. One wit referred to this as the "Swiss Family Oedipus." (Dir: George C. Scott, 114 mins.)†

Savage Messiah, The (Great Britain, 1972)*** Dorothy Tutin, Scott Antony, Helen Mirren, Lindsay Kemp, Peter Vaughan. Director Ken Russell's flamboyant style is well suited to this fervid retelling of the intense relationship between painter-sculptor Henri Gaudier and a woman twenty years his senior. An exemplary cast conveys the overheated atmosphere Russell relishes. (100 mins.)

Savage Mutiny (1953)** Johnny Weissmuller, Angela Stevens. Holy nuclear paranoia! Jungle Jim's got to clear off an entire island because of impending tests for an atomic bomb. (Dir: Spencer Bennet, 73 mins.)

Savage Pampas (Spain, 1968)* Robert Taylor, Ron Randell. Dull, western set in Argentina during the late 1800s. Taylor portrays an army officer who tries to keep his military unit intact after interference from a band of Argentinian renegades. (Dir: Hugo Fregonese, 100 mins.)

Savage Run—See: **Run, Simon, Run**

Savages (1972)** Sam Waterston, Kathleen Widdoes, Susan Blakely. Misconceived social satire uses a decadent garden party as a metaphor for the decline of Western civilization. (Dir: James Ivory, 108 mins.)†

Savages (MTV 1974)**½ Andy Griffith, Sam Bottoms, Noah Beery. Griffith plays a New York lawyer who goes to a desert area to hunt bighorn sheep with guide Bottoms. After Griffith kills an old prospector and pretends it was an animal, he and Sam begin a cat-and-mouse game of life and death in the desert. Suspenseful in parts. (Dir: Lee H. Katzin, 72 mins.)†

Savage Seven, The (1968)** Robert Walker, Jr., Larry Bishop, Joanna Frank, John Garwood, Adam Roarke, Duane Eddy, John (Bud) Cardos, Beach Dickerson, Gary Littlejohn, Penny Marshall. One of the better AIP motorcycle movies, with bikers pitted against Indians by the corrupt businessmen who control a shanty town. Produced by Dick Clark and photographed by Laszlo Kovacs. (Dir: Richard Rush, 96 mins.)†

Savage Sisters (1973)* Gloria Hendry, Cheri Caffaro, Rosanna Ortiz, John Ashley, Sid Haig, Eddie Garcia. Cruddy action pic about a money-grubber who goes after a cool million in American greenbacks with the help of two guerrilla cuties and a retired whore. Savage silliness. (Dir: Eddie Romero, 89 mins.)

Savage Streets (1984)** Linda Blair, John Vernon, Johnny Venocur. After her deaf-mute sister is raped and a pregnant friend is tossed off a bridge, Blair decides to play Charles Bronson and get even. (Dir: Danny Steinmann, 93 mins.)†

Savage Wilderness—See: **Last Frontier, The**

Savannah Smiles (1983)**½ Mark Miller, Donovan Scott, Chris Robinson, Michael Parks, Bridgette Anderson, Peter Graves. Appealing sentimental yarn. Savannah, a neglected rich moppet, runs away from her mansion, right into the hands of two bungling ex-cons. They hold her for a reward until they grow to love her. (Dir: Pierre De Moro, 105 mins.)†

Save the Tiger (1973)*** Jack Lemmon, Jack Gilford, Patricia Smith, Laurie Heineman. Lemmon gives an Oscar-winning performance as a garment manufacturer at the end of his tether. Remarkable acting by Gilford as Lemmon's partner. (Dir: John G. Avildsen, 99 mins.)†

Saving Grace (1986)* Tom Conti, Giancarlo Giannini, Fernando Rey, Erland Josephson, Edward James Olmos. A mildewed conceit about a fictitious pope who takes a Roman holiday and leaves the Vatican to mingle with his flock. Conti gives a mannered performance; there are no saving graces here. (Dir: Robert Young, 112 mins.)†

Sawdust and Tinsel (Sweden, 1953)*** Harriet Andersson, Ake Groenberg, Hasse Ekman. Writer-director Ingmar Bergman's 18th film is set in the eerie world of a traveling circus caravan. (95 mins.)†

Saxon Charm, The (1948)*** Robert Montgomery, Audrey Totter, Susan Hayward, John Payne. Montgomery is good in this character study of a vicious Broadway producer. Story is at times hard to believe, but sustains interest throughout. (Dir: Claude Binyon, 88 mins.)

Saxophone Colossus (1987)**½ This documentary tribute to jazzman Sonny Rollins consists mostly of music, mixed with little snatches of interviews. Jazz aficionados will be thrilled by the musical segments, but the film fails to develop any personal perspective on the man. (Dir: Robert Mugge, 101 mins.)†

Say Amen, Somebody (1983)**** Thomas Dorsey, Willie Mae Ford, "Mother" Smith, Zella Jackson Price, the Barrett Sisters, the O'Neal Twins. Rousing, joyous documentary on the history and art of gospel music. Don't tap your toes, we dare you. (Dir: George T. Nierenberg, 100 mins.)†

Say Anything... (1989)** John Cusack, Ione Skye, John Mahoney, Joan Cusack. Ordinary high school student John Cusack falls in love with class brain Skye, whose father has higher hopes for her. Do you really *need* to see another teen dating-angst movie? A heartfelt effort, but one containing nothing that hasn't already been done to death. (Dir: Cameron Crowe, 93 mins.)†

Say Goodbye, Maggie Cole (MTV 1972)**½ Susan Hayward, Darren McGavin. Strong performances by Hayward and McGavin give this one about doctors working in a slum area a boost. It's a tearjerker, with Hayward playing a recently widowed doctor who goes back into practice with McGavin, a gruff but dedicated ghetto G. P. (Dir: Jud Taylor, 73 mins.)†

Say Hello to Yesterday (Great Britain, 1970)**½ Leonard Whiting, Jean Simmons, Evelyn Laye. Modest, simply constructed romance of a suburban housewife, Simmons, and a young mod, played with exuberance by Whiting. They meet and part within the space of her ten-hour trip to London. A twist on *Brief Encounter.* (Dir: Alvin Rakoff, 92 mins.)†

Sayonara (1957)** Marlon Brando, Miyoshi Umeki, Red Buttons, James Garner, Ricardo Montalbán. Long, vulgar, obvious soap opera. The story involves two parallel romances in occupation Japan, and none of the tears are earned. From a James Michener novel. (Dir: Joshua Logan, 147 mins.)†

Say One for Me (1959)** Bing Crosby, Debbie Reynolds, Robert Wagner. Bing back in priestly togs again, but this time he's almost defeated by a weak plot about a show business parish, a chorus girl, and a night club manager with designs on her, all culminating in the Big Benefit Show. (Dir: Frank Tashlin, 119 mins.)

Say Yes (1986)* Jonathan Winters, Art Hindle, Logan Ramsey, Lissa Layng. Horrendous comedy about a man who will collect a bundle if he weds within twenty-four hours. Stupid waste of Winters, whose part was reportedly inserted into the film in order to save it. He doesn't. (Dir: Larry Yust, 88 mins.)†

Scalawag (1973)** Kirk Douglas, Mark Lester, Neville Brand, Lesley-Anne Down. Pirate film with all the clichés on board. Douglas directed and stars as a bearded peg-leg pirate. Best appreciated by 10-year-olds who adore comic books. (93 mins.)

Scalawag Bunch, The (Italy, 1975)** Mark Damon, Louis Davila, Silvia Dionisio. Sir Henry of Nottingham bands together a group of forest dwellers, takes the name Robin Hood, and sets about turning the people of the kingdom against usurper Prince John. Cheaply made but entertaining adaptation. (Dir: George Ferron, 103 mins.)†

Scalpel (1976)**½ Robert Lansing, Judith Chapman, Arlen Dean Snyder. Pretty good, involved Georgia-made thriller. Plastic surgeon Lansing makes over the face of go-go dancer Chapman to resemble his missing daughter so that he can get his hands on the latter's inheritance. A twist ending. (Dir: John Grissmer, 95 mins.)†

Scalphunters, The (1968)*** Burt Lancaster, Ossie Davis, Shelley Winters, Telly Savalas. Entertaining western which mixes excitement with an ample amount of comedy. Lancaster is at his athletic and charming best as a fur trapper whose pelts are stolen. Enter Davis as an educated runaway slave and the plot thickens. (Dir: Sydney Pollack, 102 mins.)

Scalplock (MTV 1966)*½ Dale Robertson, Diana Hyland, Robert Random, Sandra Smith, Lloyd Bochner, James Doohan, Herbert Voland. Undistinguished western about a gambler who wins a failing railroad in a poker game and tries to rebuild it. Pilot for the series *Iron Horse*. (Dir: James Goldstone, 100 mins.)

Scandal (Japan, 1950)*** Toshiro Mifune, Yoshiko Yamaguchi, Takashi Shimura. Early Akira Kurosawa film is a stirring and proud drama about personal honor. It tells the story of a young man and

woman, both members of the artistic community, who are libeled by a scandalous magazine article and prepare to sue the offenders. (105 mins.)

Scandal (Great Britain, 1989)*** John Hurt, Joanne Whalley-Kilmer, Bridget Fonda, Ian McKellen, Roland Gift, Jeroen Krabbé. The story of Britain's most infamous scandal, the Profumo Affair, which toppled the government when it was discovered that a cabinet minister shared a lover with a Soviet attaché. A well-written, well-acted drama that may require a little hard attention from Yanks unfamiliar with the story. Released to U.S. theaters in an R-rated 105 min. version; both it and the unrated version are on video. (Dir: Michael Caton-Jones, 114 mins.)†

Scandal at Scourie (1953)**½ Greer Garson, Walter Pidgeon. The stars of this costume drama are more than adequate but the script is steeped in sentiment as it recounts the problems of a Canadian couple in adopting an orphan. (Dir: Jean Negulesco, 89 mins.)

Scandal in a Small Town (MTV 1988)*½ Raquel Welch, Christa Denton, Frances Lee McCain, Ronny Cox. The morals of a local barmaid (Welch), not her charge of anti-Semitism against a local teacher, become the central issue here, right down to the amusing scene where a prosecuting attorney presents a list of various men Raquel has dallied with in high school. (Dir: Anthony Page, 96 mins.)†

Scandal in Paris, A (1946)*** George Sanders, Signe Hasso, Akim Tamiroff. The story of Vidocq, the thief and blackguard who cleverly talks his way into becoming Prefect of Police. Tasty costume melodrama intelligently directed, well written and acted. (Dir: Douglas Sirk, 99 mins.) AKA: **Thieves' Holiday.**

Scandalous (1984)* John Gielgud, Robert Hays, Pamela Stephenson. A reporter trying to solve a murder is blackmailed and then framed for the murder. Gielgud fans may enjoy seeing him don disguises, but there's no disguising the failure of this comedy. (Dir: Rob Cohen, 94 mins.)†

Scandalous Adventures of Buraikan (Japan, 1970)*** Tatsuya Nakadai, Tetsuro Tamba, Shima Iwashita, Suisen Ichikawa, Shoichi Ozawa. Erotic black comedy, stunningly presented, about three people who meet in the red-light district of 1842 Tokyo and compare their dreams and plan challenges to the society and authorities that they feel oppress them. (Dir: Masahiro Shinoda, 104 mins.)

Scandal Sheet (1931)*** George Bancroft, Clive Brook, Kay Francis, Gilbert Emery, Lucien Littlefield, Regis Toomey. Powerful newspaper drama, with a ruthless editor who specializes in discrediting people finding himself involved in a deadly scandal. Rigorous, violent, and very capably done. (Dir: John Cromwell, 77 mins.)

Scandal Sheet (1952)**½ Broderick Crawford, Donna Reed, John Derek. Overdone newspaper yarn about a couple of reporters who crack a murder case which involves their editor-friend. Energetically played. (Dir: Phil Karlson, 82 mins.)

Scandal Sheet (MTV 1985)*** Burt Lancaster, Robert Urich, Lauren Hutton, Pamela Reed. Lancaster stars as an unscrupulous editor of a "gossip rag" called *Inside World*. Reed is the honest reporter sucked into the sleazy publication, while Urich and Hutton play the Hollywood couple with a secret that could ruin them if uncovered. Nicely cynical, and refreshingly free of happy endings. (Dir: David Lowell Rich, 104 mins.)

Scandal Street (1938)**½ Lew Ayres, Louise Campbell, Roscoe Karns, Porter Hall, Virginia Weidler, Cecil Cunningham, Edgar Kennedy. Dissection of the suspicion and malice lurking beneath the surface of small-town America, with a new librarian in town the subject of harmful gossip. Unusual attempt to present a different viewpoint. (Dir: James Hogan, 62 mins.)

Scanners (Canada, 1981)*** Jennifer O'Neill, Stephen Lack, Patrick McGoohan. A small group of social misfits are imbued with telepathic powers. The logic of this isn't sufficiently consistent to push this into classic status, but the film is loaded with good ideas (maybe too many), and the execution is intermittently powerful. Director David Cronenberg's technical faculties aren't always up to the forcefulness of his conceptions. (102 mins.)†

Scapegoat, The (Great Britain, 1959)**½ Alec Guinness, Bette Davis, Nicole Maurey. Uneven comedy-drama about an English schoolteacher whose exact double, a French nobleman, offers him his family and responsibilities. From the novel by Daphne Du Maurier. (Dir: Robert Hamer, 92 mins.)

Scar, The (1948)*** Paul Henreid, Joan Bennett. A gangster gets a new face, and a girl makes a new personality to go along with it, but too late, for he must pay the penalty. Suspenseful melodrama. AKA: **Hollow Triumph**. (Dir: Steve Sekely, 83 mins.)†

Scaramouche (1952)*** Stewart Granger, Eleanor Parker, Janet Leigh, Mel Ferrer. Exciting and colorful adventure drama set in 18th-century France. Granger handsomely fits the role of the swashbuckling and romancing hero. (Dir: George Sidney, 118 mins.)†

Scarecrow (1973)**½ Gene Hackman, Al Pacino, Dorothy Tristan, Ann Wedgeworth. Hackman and Pacino are superb as a pair of drifter-losers who team up to travel from California to Philadelphia, where Hackman plans to open up a car wash. A kind of Seventies version of Steinbeck's *Of Mice and Men*. Marred by a poor climax. (Dir: Jerry Schatzberg, 104 mins.)†

Scarecrow in a Garden of Cucumbers (1972)* Holly Woodlawn, Tally Brown, Suzanne Skillen. Low-low-budget theatrical satire, with songs, about a small-town girl in the Big Apple. The girl is played by transvestite Woodlawn, who's the only reason to sit through this. (Dir: Robert J. Kaplan, 82 mins.)

Scared Stiff (1945)**½ Jack Haley, Barton MacLane, Veda Ann Borg, George E. Stone, Ann Savage, Arthur Aylesworth. Amusing mystery-comedy with nosy reporter Haley, searching for some important chess pieces, trapped in a haunted house. Pleasant enough diversion for a war-weary nation. AKA: **Treasure of Fear**. (Dir: Frank McDonald, 65 mins.)

Scared Stiff (1953)*** Dean Martin, Jerry Lewis, Lizabeth Scott, Dorothy Malone, Carmen Miranda. Singer and his busboy friend flee from a murder charge and land on a mysterious island to help an heiress in distress. Remake of Bob Hope's *The Ghost Breakers* works well with Dean and Jerry, blends laughs and chills expertly. (Dir: George Marshall, 108 mins.)†

Scared Straight! Another Story (MTV 1980)*** Stan Shaw, Don Fullilove, Randy Brooks. Fictional, often frightening follow-up to the award-winning documentary in which troublemaking kids visit a prison to be scared about life behind bars. (Dir: Richard Michaels, 104 mins.)

Scared to Death (1947)** Bela Lugosi, Douglas Fowley, Joyce Compton, George Zucco, Nat Pendleton. A low-budget thriller that benefits from Bela's piercing authority. The pieces of a puzzling murder are revealed to us one at a time in this fright-nighter narrated by a dead woman who may have been . . . "SCARED TO DEATH!" Your only chance to see Lugosi in color, for what it's worth. (Dir: Christy Cabanne, 65 mins.)†

Scarf, The (1951)**½ John Ireland, Mercedes McCambridge, Emlyn Williams. An innocent man, tied to a murder by circumstantial evidence, he must find the real killer in order to clear himself.

917

Tense low-budget thriller. (Dir: E. A. Dupont, 93 mins.)

Scarface (1983)**½** Al Pacino, Michelle Pfeiffer, Steven Bauer, Mary Elizabeth Mastrantonio, Robert Loggia, F. Murray Abraham. As the unscrupulous Cuban immigrant who arrives in the U.S. as boat person but becomes a drug kingpin, Pacino delivers a juicy, almost caricatured performance. Filled with melodramatic excesses, the movie is exciting on a pulp magazine level but still feels dragged out despite all the pumped-up violence. (Dir: Brian DePalma, 170 mins.)†

Scarface Mob, The (1962)**½** Robert Stack, Keenan Wynn, Neville Brand. Eliot Ness and a special force of lawmen band into "The Untouchables," out to get the goods on Al Capone and his mob. Originally the opening installments in the TV series, this crime drama still looks pretty good. (Dir: Phil Karlson, 96 mins.)†

Scarface: The Shame of the Nation (1932)**** Paul Muni, Ann Dvorak, Boris Karloff. Dark, exhilaratingly violent work was almost too potent for its time. It holds up startlingly well in ours. Muni gives his best performance as the simian hood Tony Camonte, whose one redeeming virtue is that he loves his sister a lot. Brilliantly made underworld melodrama. AKA: **The Shame of the Nation.** (Dir: Howard Hawks, 99 mins.)†

Scarlet and the Black, The (MTV 1983)**½** Gregory Peck, Christopher Plummer, John Gielgud, Raf Vallone, Ken Colley. Peck becomes the Scarlet Pimpernel of the Vatican, and outwits Nazis, circa 1943, by harboring refugees from concentration camps. A real-life drama filled with intrigue, disguises, and derring-do. (Dir: Jerry London, 156 mins.)†

Scarlet Angel (1952)**½** Rock Hudson, Yvonne De Carlo, Amanda Blake. Adventure yarn with Rock playing a sea captain who is constantly being used by vixen Yvonne. (Dir: Sidney Salkow, 81 mins.)

Scarlet Claw, The (1944)*** Basil Rathbone, Nigel Bruce, Arthur Hohl. Of the modernized Sherlock Holmes films, this probably is the most satisfyingly authentic. The setting is the Canadian moors and the mood is patriotic. (Dir: Roy William Neill, 74 mins.)†

Scarlet Clue, The (1945)**½** Sidney Toler, Mantan Moreland, Ben Carter. Fairly suspenseful Chan entry about a labyrinthine plot to lift radar plans from the government. (Dir: Phil Rosen, 65 mins.)

Scarlet Coat, The (1955)** Cornel Wilde, Michael Wilding, Anne Francis, George Sanders. Heavy-handed historical costume drama about the American Revolution. (Dir: John Sturges, 101 mins.)

Scarlet Dawn (1932)**½** Douglas Fairbanks, Jr., Nancy Carroll, Lilyan Tashman, Guy Kibbee, Sheila Terry. Stylish but sluggish love story set during the Russian Revolution. An aristocrat in exile falls for a servant girl in this beautifully designed romance. (Dir: William Dieterle, 76 mins.)

Scarlet Empress, The (1934)**** Marlene Dietrich, John Lodge, Sam Jaffe, Louise Dresser. One of director Josef von Sternberg's greatest films, with a rich Dietrich performance as Catherine the Great. Literally overspilling its frame with bric-a-brac and veils, the film avoids political content as it descends into a world of mystery and sensuality. (110 mins.)

Scarlet Hour, The (1956)** Tom Tryon, Jody Lawrence, Carol Ohmart, Elaine Stritch, E. G. Marshall. Waste of a good cast in an uninvolving, poorly written thriller about a man who reaches his breaking point and plots to kill his wife. (Dir: Michael Curtiz, 95 mins.)

Scarlet Letter, The (1926)**** Lillian Gish, Lars Hanson, Henry B. Walthall, Karl Dane. Atmospheric rendering of the Nathaniel Hawthorne classic about Hester Prynne, who wore the mark of the Adulteress rather than reveal the identity of the man who impregnated her. Atmospheric and moving, with exemplary performances and direction making this the best of several versions of this tale. (Dir: Victor Seastrom [Sjostrom], 80 mins.)

Scarlet Letter, The (1934)* Colleen Moore, Hardie Albright, Henry B. Walthall, William Farnum, Alan Hale, Cora Sue Collins. Hopelessly dated, static rendering of Hawthorne's classic tale of repression and adultery in early New England. Comic relief is improbably added. (Dir: Robert G. Vignola, 70 mins.)†

Scarlet Letter, The (West Germany-Spain, 1973)**½** Senta Berger, Hans Christian Blech, Lou Castel. Wim Winders's version of the classic tale is good enough, but his fans will be disappointed to see that it bears little of his distinctive stamp. Photographed by Robby Muller. (94 mins.)†

Scarlet Pimpernel, The (Great Britain, 1934)*** Leslie Howard, Merle Oberon, Joan Gardner, Raymond Massey, Nigel Bruce. Solid swashbuckling entertainment with Howard the impeccably dressed and impossibly noble embodiment of the heroic freedom fighter. The definitive *Pimpernel;* polished entertainment. (Dir: Harold Young, 95 mins.)†

Scarlet Pimpernel, The (MTV 1982)*** Anthony Andrews, Jane Seymour, Ian McKellen. The gallant hero is back to swash his share of buckles in this sumptuous refilming of the tale of derring-do circa the French Revolution. (Dir: Clive Donner, 150 mins.)†

Scarlet Street (1945)***½ Edward G. Robinson, Joan Bennett, Dan Duryea, Margaret Lindsay, Rosalind Ivan. Fritz Lang's darkest American film is a twisted moral tale that benefits from Robinson's fine performance as a company man who is driven to embezzlement as a result of his passion for a scheming vixen (Bennett). Lang's impeccable shadowed visions set this apart from subsequent tales of seduction by a femme fatale. (98 mins.)†

Scarlett O'Hara War, The (MTV 1980)*** Tony Curtis, Sharon Gless, Harold Gould, Bill Macy, Morgan Brittany, George Furth. Taken from the "Moviola" miniseries, this polished production revolves about the legendary search for the actress to play Margaret Mitchell's unsinkable heroine. A juicy melodrama entertainingly crammed with equal parts history, gossip, and star turns. (Dir: John Erman, 105 mins.)

Scarred (1984)** Jennifer Mayo, Jackie Berryman, David Dean. Gritty but unconvincing drama about a teenage prostitute who tries to better her life. AKA: Street Love. (Dir: RoseMarie Turko, 85 mins.)†

Scars of Dracula, The (Great Britain, 1970)* Christopher Lee, Denis Waterman, Jenny Hanley. Dracula horrors pepped up with sex, violence and lots of gore . . . *not* for the kids. (Dir: Roy Ward Baker, 94 mins.)†

Scavenger Hunt (1979)*½ Richard Benjamin, James Coco, Scatman Crothers, Ruth Gordon, Cloris Leachman, Vincent Price, Richard Masur, Cleavon Little, Roddy McDowall, Tony Randall, Willie Aames. The premise—would-be heirs to a fortune are sent out on a scavenger hunt—peters out long before the final scene. (Dir: Michael Schultz, 104 mins.)†

Scavengers (1987)* Kenneth Gilman, Brenda Bakke. Bird-watcher becomes entangled in a KGB-CIA operation. An adventure that doesn't know if it wants to be serious or parody, though it's lousy as either. (Dir: Duncan McLachlan, 94 mins.)†

Scavengers, The (1959)**½ Vince Edwards, Carol Ohmart. In his pre-Ben Casey days, Edwards gets mixed up with shady women and shadier killers in the Orient. (Dir: John Cromwell, 79 mins.)

Scene of the Crime (1949)*** Van Johnson, Gloria De Haven, Tom Drake, Arlene Dahl, Leon Ames, John McIntire. Dynamic, dark film about a cop who quits the force when his partner is killed;

when his replacement is also slain, he returns to seek vengeance. Johnson is excellent in this taut, realistic thriller. (Dir: Roy Rowland, 94 mins.)

Scene of the Crime (France, 1986)**½ Catherine Deneuve, Danielle Darrieux, Wadeck Stanczak, Nicolas Giraudi, Victor Lanoux. Two escaped convicts transform the lives of a mother and son: to the mother (Deneuve), one convict brings a reawakening of her passionate impulses; to the son, a glimpse at his own mortality, when he is saved from an attack by the intercession of the same noble jailbird (Stanczak). Occasional outbursts of stylish flair from director André Téchine are the bright spots of this subdued character study. (90 mins.)†

Scenes From a Mall (1991)** Bette Midler, Woody Allen, Bill Irwin, Daren Firestone, Rebecca Nickels, Paul Mazursky. A middle-aged married couple (Midler and Allen) come clean with each other about their infidelities while spending a day shopping at a mega-mall. Hit-and-miss comedy is a single sketch idea badly stretched to the full-length breaking point. Something's seriously wrong with a movie in which a mime gets most of the laughs and a surfboard gets most of the attention. (Dir: Paul Mazursky, 87 mins.)†

Scenes From a Marriage (Sweden, 1973)**** Liv Ullmann, Erland Josephson, Bibi Andersson. Ingmar Bergman's stunning, telescopic examination of a crumbling marriage, originally made as six 50-minute programs for Swedish TV. This superb restructuring of that footage dissects different events, quarrels, lovemaking, misunderstandings, etc., over more than ten years of marriage, divorce and a new, more mature relationship. Ullmann is, to no one's surprise, astonishing and Josephson is nearly as remarkable. (168 mins.)†

Scenes From a Murder (Italy, 1972)** Telly Savalas, Anne Heywood, Giorgio Piazza, Rossella Falk. Savalas plays a murderer involved in a cat-and-mouse chase after a beautiful actress. (Dir: Alberto DeMartino, 90 mins.)†

Scenes From the Class Struggle in Beverly Hills (1989)*** Jacqueline Bisset, Ray Sharkey, Robert Beltran, Ed Begley, Jr., Mary Woronov, Wallace Shawn. Generally funny sex farce, set in a Beverly Hills mansion filled with hedonistic characters. The plot hinge is a bet between two gardeners as to which of them can be the first to seduce the other's employer. (Dir: Paul Bartel, 102 mins.)†

Scent of a Woman (Italy, 1975)*** Vittorio Gassman, Agostina Belli, Alessandro Momo. Gassman scores a triumph in this Italian comedy-drama of a blind rogue forced to pursue his quarry through his other senses. Bravura acting reigns over sense, since the film's values are questionable. (Dir: Dino Risi, 103 mins.)

Scent of Mystery (1960)** Denholm Elliott, Peter Lorre, Beverly Bentley. Discovering that a young American heiress is about to be murdered, an Englishman and a sour-visaged cab driver set about to save her, sight unseen. Released in theaters with an accompanying track of scents, such as perfume and tobacco odors, which were triggered mechanically to serve as clues to the mystery. (Dir: Jack Cardiff, 125 mins.)

Schatten—See: **Warning Shadows**

Schizo (Great Britain, 1977)* Lynne Frederick, John Leyton, Stephanie Beacham, John Fraser. Is skating star Frederick a split personality who killed her mother years ago? Is someone trying to drive her insane? Are we supposed to care? (Dir: Pete Walker, 109 mins.)†

Schizoid (1980)* Klaus Kinski, Mariana Hill, Craig Wasson, Donna Wilkes. Convoluted psycho-babble thriller about a woman who seeks help after dreaming of a murder that then occurs. (Dir: David Paulsen, 91 mins.)†

Schlock (1973)**½ John Landis, Saul Kahan, Joseph Piantadosi. A missing link runs amok and is responsible for a series of "banana killings." Along the way, parodies of horror films add up to a few genuine laughs. AKA: **The Banana Monster**. (Dir: John Landis, 80 mins.)†

School Daze (1988)*** Larry Fishburne, Giancarlo Esposito, Tisha Campbell, Kyme, Joe Seneca, Ossie Davis, Spike Lee. Filmmaker-actor Lee tries to single-handedly make up for the recent dearth of black cinema with this combination of comedy, music, and a lesson on racial identity. What is lacking in discipline is made up for in energy. The thumbnail plot line concerns the rift between the "wannabees" (blacks who try to lose their blackness) and "jigaboos" (blacks who have a sense of their own identity) at an all-black college. (Dir: Spike Lee, 120 mins.)†

School for Love (France, 1955)*½ Brigitte Bardot, Jean Marais. Two sisters at a conservatory fall for the same music teacher. Trite little love story. (Dir: Yves Allegret, 72 mins.)

School for Scoundrels (Great Britain, 1960)*** Ian Carmichael, Alastair Sim, Terry-Thomas. Innocent young man joins a school with an unusual course in successmanship. Enjoyable comedy has some pointed laughs, a cast of capable performers. (Dir: Robert Hamer, 94 mins.)

School for Sex (Great Britain, 1969)*½

Derek Aylward, Rose Alba, Hugh Latimer, Nosher Powell. Burned in a divorce settlement, Aylward opens an institute to teach young women how to marry for money. More slapstick than satire. (Dir: Pete Walker, 80 mins.)†

School Spirit (1985)½ Tom Nolan, Elizabeth Foxx, Roberta Collins, John Finnegan, Larry Linville. High school student killed in an accident returns to Earth to lose his virginity before going to the Great Beyond. Even hard-core porn is more respectable than this sniggering garbage. (Dir: Alan Holleb, 90 mins.)†

School that Ate My Brain, The—See: **Zombie High**

Scorchy (1976)*½ Connie Stevens, Cesare Danova, William Smith, Joyce Jameson. A honkysploitation movie—all the cheaply produced thrills and nonstop action of a Pam Grier movie, only perky, white-bread Stevens is in the lead—she's in hot pursuit of a drug dealer sneaking heroin around in a statue. (Dir: Howard Avedis, 99 mins.)†

Score (U.S.-Yugoslavia, 1973)**½ Gerald Grant, Claire Wilbur, Calvin Culver, Lynn Lowry. Sex farce for mainstream audiences by director Radley Metzger, the master of glossy soft-core erotica in the '60s, about two couples who get together for group sex only to have the guys and girls opting for same-sex scenarios. (90 mins.)†

Scorned and Swindled (MTV 1984)*** Tuesday Weld, Keith Carradine, Peter Coyote, Sheree North, Fionnula Flanagan. Weld plays a lonely antiques dealer who's suckered into marriage only to find herself without a dime. When another victim (Carradine) joins forces with her, the swindled duo race cross country to hunt down their betrayer. A persuasive slice of seedy Americana that's based on a true incident. (Dir: Paul Wendkos, 104 mins.)

Scorpio (1973)**½ Burt Lancaster, Alain Delon, Paul Scofield, J. D. Cannon, John Colicos. Adequate spy thriller. Lancaster, stoic and stolid, is the agent who is marked for extinction by fellow agent Scorpio (Delon), and the cat-and-mouse chase is on. (Dir: Michael Winner, 114 mins.)

Scorpio Letters, The (MTV 1967)* Alex Cord, Shirley Eaton. Dull, obscure, and listless thriller about two agents hired by the British to uncover a blackmailing ring. (Dir: Richard Thorpe, 98 mins.)

Scorpion (1986)* Tommy Tulleners, Don Murray, Robert Logan, Allen Williams. As a government agent protecting an informant, ex-karate champ Tulleners lacks charisma, and hardly even gets to show off his martial arts skills. (Dir: William Riead, 98 mins.)†

Scorpion Woman, The (Austria, 1990)** Angelica Domrose, Fritz Hammel, Peter Andorai, Heinz Weixelbraun, Michael Schindelbeck. Pleasant, but uninvolving, comedy-melodrama, with a surprise ending that isn't worth waiting for. A woman judge's life turns upside down after she takes a young male lover who turns out to be bisexual. (Dir: Susanne Zanke, 95 mins.)†

Scotland Yard Inspector (Great Britain, 1952)** Cesar Romero, Lois Maxwell, Bernadette O'Farrell. British-made thriller has Romero tracking down his brother's murderer; unexciting low-budget drama. (Dir: Sam Newfield, 73 mins.)

Scotland Yard Investigator (Great Britain, 1945)**½ C. Aubrey Smith, Erich von Stroheim, Stephanie Bachelor, Forrester Harvey. Good low-budget mystery, supported by a strong cast, about the Scotland Yard detective Smith's efforts to recover the Mona Lisa from thief von Stroheim. These two are a show in themselves. (Dir: George Blair, 68 mins.)

Scott Free (MTV 1976)*½ Michael Brandon, Susan St. James, Michael Lerner. The trials of a professional gambler who wins a piece of desert land regarded by Indians as a sacred burial ground. (Dir: William Wiard, 72 mins.)

Scott Joplin (1977)**½ Billy Dee Williams, Art Carney, Clifton Davis. Williams has charisma to spare in this standard bio of legendary ragtime composer Scott Joplin. (Dir: Jeremy Paul Kagan, 96 mins.)

Scott of the Antarctic (Great Britain, 1948)**½ John Mills, Derek Bond, Kenneth More, Christopher Lee. An account of the ill-fated British expedition to the South Pole, with stunning photographic effects, authentic narrative, but as drama it's curiously remote, only occasionally affecting. (Dir: Charles Frend, 110 mins.)†

Scoundrel, The (1935)**½ Noel Coward, Stanley Ridges, Julie Haydon, Martha Sleeper, Eduardo Ciannelli, Alexander Wolcott, Lionel Stander. Strange melodrama that aspires to high sophistication and sometimes succeeds. When a wastrel writer with a penchant for using people dies, his spirit comes back to redeem himself. (Dirs: Ben Hecht, Charles MacArthur, 78 mins.)

Scout's Honor (MTV 1980)**½ Gary Coleman, Katherine Helmond, Pat O'Brien, Wilfred Hyde-White, Harry Morgan. Friendly, entertaining story stars Coleman as an orphan who yearns to be a Cub Scout. The parents of the Scouts are all played by former child TV stars: Jay ("Dennis the Menace") North, Lauren ("Father Knows Best") Chapin, Angela ("Make Room for Daddy") Cartwright, and Paul ("Donna Reed Show") Petersen. (Dir: Henry Levin, 104 mins.)

Scream and Scream Again (Great Britain, 1970)*** Vincent Price, Christopher Lee, Peter Cushing. An above-average, somewhat more sophisticated mad-scientist effort revolving around a series of psychotic murders in England. (Dir: Gordon Hessler, 94 mins.)†

Scream, Baby, Scream—See: **Nightmare House**

Scream, Blacula, Scream (1973)* William Marshall, Pam Grier, Don Mitchell. A laughable sequel to *Blacula*, the horror film about a modern-day vampire who was an actual African prince before a white vampire cursed him in a previous century. (Dir: Bob Kelljan, 95 mins.)†

Scream Dream (1989)* Melissa Moore, Nikki Riggins, Carol Carr, Jesse Raye. Singer Carr, fired from the rock band she was working in, uses her powers of witchcraft to gain revenge. Shot-on-video sleaze, heavy on gore and nudity. (Dir: Donald Farmer, 69 mins.)†

Screamers (Italy-U.S., 1981)½ Barbara Bach, Joseph Cotten, Mel Ferrer, Cameron Mitchell. Producer Roger Corman added twelve minutes of slasher footage to the beginning of an Italian-made adventure. Wayfarers land on an island inhabited by a greedy treasure hunter and a scientist who treats the ocean as his personal fish tank. (Dir: Sergio Martino, 83 mins.)†

Scream for Help (1986)½ David Brooks, Rachael Kelly, Marie Masters. Deliriously funny, overwrought suspense film about an overly imaginative girl who believes her adulterous stepfather is planning to eliminate her mom. (Dir: Michael Winner, 90 mins.)†

Screaming Eagles (1956)** Tom Tryon, Jan Merlin, Martin Milner, Alvy Moore. Typical wartime melodrama about the interconnected lives of several people, leading up to D-Day. There was no excitement left in the formula by this time. (Dir: Charles Haas, 81 mins.)

Screaming Mimi (1958)**½ Anita Ekberg, Phil Carey, Gypsy Rose Lee, Harry Townes, Linda Cherney. Stripper comes under the influence of a possessive psychiatrist after she is attacked by a serial killer. Weird low-budget thriller has a cult following; it's fairly bizarre. (Dir: Gerd Oswald, 79 mins.)

Screaming Skull, The (1958)*½ John Hudson, Peggy Webber, Tom Johnson, Russ Conway. Man tries to drive his wife, recuperating from a nervous breakdown, over the edge by arranging scary happenings in his spooky house. Atmospheric but overly familiar. (Dir: Alex Nicol, 68 mins.)†

Screaming Woman, The (MTV 1972)***

921

Olivia de Havilland, Joseph Cotten, Walter Pidgeon. De Havilland, as a wealthy lady recovering from a nervous breakdown, sees a woman buried alive, but nobody believes her. Based on Ray Bradbury's short story. (Dir: Jack Smight, 73 mins.)

Scream of Fear (Great Britain, 1961)*** Susan Strasberg, Ronald Lewis, Ann Todd. Girl poses as her paralyzed friend to investigate what has happened to her father, nearly loses her life in finding out. Sharply directed thriller. AKA: *Taste of Fear*. (Dir: Seth Holt, 81 mins.)†

Scream of the Wolf (MTV 1972)**½ Peter Graves, Clint Walker, Jo Ann Pflug, Philip Carey, Don Megowan. A retired hunter takes up his weapons once again to pursue a wolf (or is it a wolf-like creature?) responsible for some not-so-clean kills. Script by Richard Matheson. (Dir: Dan Curtis, 72 mins.)

Scream, Pretty Peggy (MTV 1973)**½ Bette Davis, Ted Bessell, Sian Barbara Allen. An innocent college student plays part-time housekeeper for Bette's weird family in their creepy mansion. (Dir: Gordon Hessler, 74 mins.)

Screen Test (1986)* Michael Allan Brown, Monique Gabrielle, Paul Lueken, David Simpatico, Michelle Bauer. Raunch-out comedy about some perpetually tumescent undergrads who pretend to be porn producers in order to get would-be stars to "audition" for them. (Dir: Sam Auster, 84 mins.)†

Screwball Academy (Canada, 1987)* Colleen Camp, Ken Welsh, Christine Cattell. Wan comedy about a peaceful town turned upside down by the arrival of a movie crew. Director "Reuben Rose" is actually director John Blanchard of "SCTV," showing none of that show's style. (90 mins.)†

Screwballs (1983)½ Peter Keleghan, Lynda Speciale, Alan Daveau, Kent Deuters, Linda Shayne, Raven De La Croix. Bottom-of-the-barrel high school sex comedy about some wacky guys scheming to seduce the class virgin, "Purity Busch." The rest of this stupid movie is even less subtle; amazingly, the sequel, *Loose Screws*, is even worse. (Dir: Rafal Zielinski, 80 mins.)†

Scrooge (Great Britain, 1935)*** Seymour Hicks, Donald Calthrop, Robert Cochran, Mary Glynne, Garry Marsh, Maurice Evans. Sturdy version of Dickens's Christmas classic with good special effects. Star Hicks wrote this adaptation himself, after having played the role on stage for many years. (Dir: Henry Edwards, 72 mins.)

Scrooge (Great Britain, 1970)**½ Albert Finney, Alec Guinness, Edith Evans. This musical version of Charles Dickens's timeless yarn is as empty as a neglected Christmas stocking. Albert Finney, as Scrooge, plays the cantankerous, stingy businessman with great flair, and is the main bright spot. Unimaginatively directed by Ronald Neame. (118 mins.)†

Scrooged (1988)*** Bill Murray, Karen Allen, Bobcat Goldthwait, Carol Kane, David Johansen, Robert Mitchum, John Forsythe. Murray is the entire show in this satirical update of "A Christmas Carol" written by "Saturday Night Live" alumni Michael O'Donoghue and Mitch Glazer. The movie is so top-heavy with talent, both in front of and behind the camera, that it can't quite breathe, but the individual pleasures provide plenty of entertainment until the too-sentimental ending. (Dir: Richard Donner, 101 mins.)†

Scrubbers (Great Britain, 1982)** Amanda York, Chrissie Cotterill, Elizabeth Edmunds. Lesbian warfare is the dominating topic in this depressing women's prison film that teeters on the edge of camp. (Dir: Mai Zetterling, 93 mins.)†

Scruples (MTV 1981)** Shelley Smith, Priscilla Barnes, Dirk Benedict, James Darren, Jessica Walter. This glitzy extension of the popular mini-series that starred Lindsay Wagner concerns a woman who inherits a big business and big problems to go with it. The producers have a few scruples loose. (Dir: Robert Day, 104 mins.)

Scudda-Hoo! Scudda-Hay! (1948)** Lon McCallister, June Haver, Walter Brennan, Natalie Wood. Story of a farm boy who gets hold of a pair of mules and then trains them to be the best team around. (Dir: F. Hugh Herbert, 95 mins.)

Scum (Great Britain, 1978)***½ Ray Winstone, Phil Daniels, Julian Firth, Mick Ford. The physical, sexual, and psychological violence of Borstal prison for youthful offenders. Powerful, disturbing, and violent. (Dir: Alan Clarke, 98 mins.)†

Scum of the Earth (1963)* Vickie Miles, Thomas Sweetwood, Sandra Sinclair. This dip into depravity (incredibly tame by today's standards) for a pseudonymous pregore Herschell Gordon Lewis relates how a sweet young thing gets hoodwinked into posing for pornography. Some deliciously funny moments. (Dir: "Lewis H. Gordon," 71 mins.)

Sea Around Us, The (1953)*** An early, influential documentary about the Earth's oceans and sea life, from a book by Rachel Carson. The beautiful underwater photography is still exceptional. Narrated by Don Forbes, produced by Irwin Allen. (61 mins.)†

Sea Chase, The (1955)**½ Lana Turner, John Wayne, Tab Hunter, James Arness. Far-fetched tale of adventure and romance. Wayne skippers a renegade freighter which is bound for Valparaiso. (Dir: John Farrow, 117 mins.)†

Sea Devils (1937)** Victor McLaglen, Preston Foster, Ida Lupino, Donald Woods, Billy Gilbert. Typical vehicle for McLaglen as a brawling Coast Guard seaman who wants his daughter to marry someone above her station, though she prefers tough-guy Foster. Quick-moving adventure, expertly done. (Dir: Ben Stoloff, 85 mins.)

Sea Devils (Great Britain, 1953)**½ Rock Hudson, Yvonne De Carlo. Fisherman turned smuggler gets involved with a beautiful spy during the Napoleonic era. Standard costume melodramatics get a lift from action scenes. (Dir: Raoul Walsh, 91 mins.)†

Sea Fury (Great Britain, 1958)** Stanley Baker, Victor McLaglen, Luciana Paluzzi, Gregoire Aslan, Robert Shaw. Seafaring melodrama, with roughneck captain McLaglen and his sidekick Baker destroying their friendship over a glamorous woman. Baker and McLaglen are excellent, which makes the superficial, patchy script all the more disappointing. (Dir: C. Raker Endfield, 72 mins.)

Sea Gull, The (U.S.-Great Britain, 1968)*** Vanessa Redgrave, Simone Signoret, David Warner, James Mason, Harry Andrews, Kathleen Widdoes. Strong adaptation of Anton Chekhov's play about rural Russia, an enduring, illuminating masterpiece. Static at times, but generally absorbing. (Dir: Sidney Lumet, 141 mins.)

Seagull, The (U.S.S.R., 1971)*** Ludmila Savelyeva, Vladimir Tchetverikov, Alla Demidova, Yuri Yakoviev. Reverential adaptation of Anton Chekov's complex drama fails to fully utilize the possibilities of cinema. Nonetheless, it is still a commanding production with superior acting and staging. (Dir: Yuli Karasik, 98 mins.)

Sea Gypsies, The (1978)**½ Robert Logan, Mikki Jamison-Olson, Cjon Damitri Patterson. A family movie. Logan plays a widower who sets sail with his two daughters and a female photographer (Jamison-Olson) around the world. The photography is excellent, and the plot is based on a true story. (Dir: Stewart Raffill, 101 mins.)†

Sea Hawk, The (1940)**** Errol Flynn, Brenda Marshall, Claude Rains, Donald Crisp, Flora Robson, Una O'Connor, Alan Hale, Gilbert Roland, Henry Daniell. Classic high-seas adventure, a glorious blend of dashing swashbucklers, nefarious pirates, and passionate women. Gorgeous black-and-white photography, stupendous sets, and a magnificent Erich Wolfgang Korngold score. (Dir: Michael Curtiz, 127 mins.)

Sealed Cargo (1951)**** Dana Andrews, Claude Rains. Fishing vessel rescues the captain of a Danish ship, who is really the commander of a mother ship for Nazi subs. Exciting, suspenseful melodrama. (Dir: Alfred L. Werker, 90 mins.)

Sealed Soil, The (Iran, 1978)*** Flora Shabaviz, the villagers of Noo-Asquar. Superb Iranian film about a young village woman who rejects traditional female roles and refuses to get married, leading everyone to treat her as if she were crazy. A warm, gently comic film, made by Mara Nabili, based on her own experiences. (90 mins.)

Sealed Verdict (1948)** Ray Milland, Florence Marly, Broderick Crawford, John Hoyt, John Ridgely. Postwar thriller with prosecutor Milland suspecting that an accused Nazi war criminal is innocent, trying to prove it. Good idea, average handling. (Dir: Lewis Allen, 82 mins.)

Sea Lion, The (1921)**½ Hobart Bosworth, Emory Johnson, Bessie Love, Carol Holloway, Florence Carpenter, Charles Clary. Seafaring melodrama about a brutish South Seas captain who takes some castaways aboard and discovers that they have ties to his own life. Action-packed but unoriginal adventure story. (Dir: Rowland V. Lee, 55 mins.)†

Seance on a Wet Afternoon (Great Britain, 1964)***½ Kim Stanley, Richard Attenborough. Brilliantly acted drama of a professional medium near the brink of insanity, who involves her weak husband in a kidnapping plot. Tremendous performances by Miss Stanley and Attenborough, backed by fine script and direction by Bryan Forbes. (121 mins.)†

Sea of Grass, The (1947)**½ Spencer Tracy, Katharine Hepburn, Robert Walker, Phyllis Thaxter, Melvyn Douglas. The cast fights hard but this western about a man who sees New Mexico turning into a dust bowl and fights to save the grass is disappointing. It never stays with any of its many themes long enough to sustain interest. (Dir: Elia Kazan, 131 mins.)

Sea of Love (1989)*** Al Pacino, Ellen Barkin, John Goodman, Michael Rooker, William Hickey. Investigating a killer whose victims came from personal ads, N.Y. plainclothes cop Pacino puts out an ad himself and has a sizzling affair with the main suspect, the lithe and sensual Barkin. The mystery is a simple "did she or didn't she" scenario that's bound to disappoint. But there's a palpable tension throughout, and Pacino and Barkin bring out the best in each other. (Dir: Harold Becker, 112 mins.)†

Sea of Roses (Brazil, 1977)*** Norma Benguel, Hugo Caruana, Christina Pereua, Otavio Augusto, Miriam Muniz. Manic black comedy about a woman who tries to flee her miserable marriage and deranged family, only to find she can run but she can't hide. Over-the-top in camerawork, performance, and plot. (Dir: Ana Carilina, 90 mins.)

Search, The (1948)*** Montgomery Clift, Aline MacMahon, Wendell Corey, Ivan Jandl. Moving, sensitive story of a war orphan found in the ruins of postwar Europe. (Dir: Fred Zinnemann, 104 mins.)

Searchers, The (1956)**** John Wayne, Jeffrey Hunter, Natalie Wood, Ward Bond, Vera Miles, John Qualen, Harry Carey, Jr. A vigorous, multilayered classic regarded by many as the model western. Embittered by acts of Indian savagery against his family, Ethan (Wayne) single-mindedly tracks down his niece who'd been kidnapped as a child and forced into squawdom by a renegade. Nursing his hatred, Ethan intends to kill not only the Indian buck but also his niece because she's been defiled. A complex film shaded with ambiguities and strikingly directed by John Ford. (119 mins.)†

Searchers of the Voodoo Mountain—See: **Warriors of the Apocalypse**

Search for Bridey Murphy, The (1956)** Louis Hayward, Teresa Wright. Based on the bestseller about a housewife who when under hypnosis recalls a previous life. Quickly made to cash in on the controversy, this drama has only fair entertainment values, except for a good performance by Wright. (Dir: Noel Langley, 84 mins.)

Search for Danger (1949)*½ John Calvert, Albert Dekker, Myrna Dell. It's double-homicide time as the Falcon series fades out on a mystery involving the double-crossing partner of a gambler. (Dir: Jack Bernhard, 62 mins.)

Search for the Gods (MTV 1975)*½ Stephen McHattie, Kurt Russell, Raymond St. Jacques, Ralph Bellamy. Plodding story about three young people who stumble upon a medallion, purported to be more than 50,000 years old, that might have answers to the popular theory about space visitors to Earth two eons ago. (Dir: Jud Taylor, 104 mins.)

Searching Wind, The (1946)*** Robert Young, Sylvia Sidney. Lillian Hellman's story of a career diplomat who has never taken a firm stand on anything is a potentially good drama but never quite makes it. (Dir: William Dieterle, 103 mins.)

Sea Shall Not Have Them, The (Great Britain, 1954)*** Michael Redgrave, Dirk Bogarde. Rescue launch attempts to save a crew of a downed plane, on a rubber raft in the North Sea. Good drama, well acted. (Dir: Lewis Gilbert, 91 mins.)†

Seaside Swingers (Great Britain, 1964)**½ Freddie and the Dreamers, John Leyton, Mike Sarne, Liz Fraser. Zippy little musical about youngsters at a seaside resort and their problems with romance. (Dir: James Hill, 94 mins.)†

Season of Giants, A (MCTV 1991)**½ Mark Frankel, John Glover, F. Murray Abraham, Steven Berkoff, Ornella Muti, Andrea Prodan, Ian Holm, Raf Vallone. The story of Michelangelo is given a sumptuous production, but the script tends to be too talky and the action drawn out. The leading role is played with vigor by British actor Frankel. Despite an earnest attempt to depict the creative atmosphere of the Italian Renaissance, its appeal remains limited. (Dir: Jerry London, 192 mins.)†

Season of Passion (Australia, 1961)*** Ernest Borgnine, John Mills, Anne Baxter, Angela Lansbury. Sugar cane cutters find their annual on-the-town vacation in Sydney has changed, financially and romantically. Offbeat drama, well acted. AKA: **Summer of the Seventeeth Doll**. (Dir: Leslie Norman, 93 mins.)

Season of the Witch (1976)* Jan White, Ray Laine, Anne Muffly, Bill Thunhurst. Pointless and dated sociology from director George Romero. A repressed housewife liberates herself through witchcraft in this tedious thriller devoid of atmosphere, lacking in chills, and riddled with amateurish acting. Originally 130 minutes. AKA: **Hungry Wives** and **Jack's Wife**. (89 mins.)†

Sea Wife (Great Britain, 1957)** Joan Collins, Richard Burton, Basil Sydney. Shipwreck survivors Burton and Collins fall in love, though he never learns that she is a nun. After their rescue, Burton sets off in search of her. The notion of the Welsh Ham and the world's least likely novitiate pitching woo on a desert island sounds campy, but unfortunately it's delivered with an all-too-stiff upper lip. (Dir: Bob McNaught, 82 mins.)†

Sea Wolf, The (1941)***½ Edward G. Robinson, John Garfield, Ida Lupino. Director Michael Curtiz's version of the Jack London novel is brutal and briny, though it has a suffocating visual style. Otherwise, a good Warner Bros. action film, with Robinson the model of a tough tyrant. (90 mins.)†

Sea Wolves (Great Britain-U.S., 1980)**½ Gregory Peck, Roger Moore, David Niven, Trevor Howard. Some commandos come out of retirement long enough to knock a German radio transmitter out of commission. This WWII sea-going adventure is occasionally suspenseful and capably acted. (Dir: Andrew McLaglen, 120 mins.)†

Sebastian (Great Britain, 1968)**½ Dirk Bogarde, Susannah York, Lilli Palmer, Nigel Davenport, Margaret Johnston, John Gielgud. Fast-paced espionage movie with talented cast members running all over the place deciphering codes, dodging double-agents, and falling in love. (Dir: David Greene, 100 mins.)

Sebastiane (Great Britain, 1979)***½ Leonardo Treviglio, Barney James, Richard James, Neil Kennedy. Sincere, respectful story of the martyr is infamous for its plentiful, non-exploitative male nudity and all-Latin dialogue, though it offers an honest detailing of the spirit of Christianity which led to Sebastiane's refusal of Roman orders to kill a young page. (Dirs: Derek Jarman, Paul Humfress, 91 mins.)

Second Awakening of Christa Klages (West Germany, 1977)*** Tina Engel, Sylvia Reize, Katharina Thalbach, Peter Scheider. A progressive child-care center needs money to stay open, so the owner and her boyfriend rob a bank, an act which turns them into fugitives and leads to tragedy. First solo film by director Margarethe von Trotta is rich in plot and potent ideas. (93 mins.)

Second Best Secret Agent, The (1965)* Tom Adams, Veronica Hurst. Adams plays Charles Vine, a British secret agent who tries harder because he's number two. There's a formula which reverses the laws of gravity, but the ingredients for a good film are nowhere in sight. (Dir: Lindsay Shonteff, 96 mins.)

Second Breath (France, 1966)***½ Lino Ventura, Paul Meurisse, Raymond Pellegrin, Christine Fabrega, Marcel Bozzufi. Rousing and philosophical crime film about a gangster who pulls off a daring heist, but may have to turn in his gang, breaking the unwritten code of honor among thieves. (Dir: Jean-Pierre Melville, 150 mins.)

Second Chance (1953)**½ Robert Mitchum, Linda Darnell, Jack Palance, Sandro Giglio. A suspenseful Mitchum vehicle that was originally released in 3-D. Big Bob's an ex-prizefighter in Mexico who becomes romantically involved with a dead mobster's girlfriend (Darnell) pursued by the ever-menacing Palance. (Dir: Rudolph Maté, 81 mins.)

Second Chance (MTV 1972)**½ Brian Keith, Elizabeth Ashley, Juliet Prowse. Loosely woven, fairly pleasant comedy about a stockbroker who acquires a ghost town and fills it with assorted talent in need of another break. The experimental community works until the locals accuse their benefactor of becoming a dictator. (Dir: Peter Tewksbury, 73 mins.)

Second Chance (France, 1976)*** Catherine Deneuve, Anouk Aimee, Charles Denner, Francis Huster, Jean-Jacques Briot. Charming little film directed by the master of fluff, Claude Lelouch, about a woman released from jail and reunited with her eighteen-year-old son, born while she was in prison. (99 mins.)

Second Chorus (1940)**½ Fred Astaire, Paulette Goddard, Burgess Meredith, Charles Butterworth. Cheery B musical. Astaire and Meredith are collegian tooters who aspire to play with Artie Shaw. Goddard is their manager and the love interest. (Dir: H. C. Potter, 83 mins.)†

Second Face, The (1950)**½ Ella Raines, Bruce Bennett, Rita Johnson, John Sutton, Patricia Knight, Jane Darwell. The talented Raines shines in this melodramatic story of a disfigured woman whose life is changed by plastic surgery. Trim B picture, competently made. (Dir: Jack Bernhard, 77 mins.)

Second Fiddle (1939)** Sonja Henie, Tyrone Power, Rudy Vallee, Edna May Oliver. Henie plays an ice-skating teacher who leaves the Midwest for Hollywood and stardom. (Dir: Sidney Lanfield, 86 mins.)

Second Greatest Sex, The (1955)** Jeanne Crain, George Nader, Kitty Kallen, Bert Lahr. *Lysistrata* revamped as a western musical. The women are tired of the men fighting all the time, so they go on a lovestrike. (Dir: George Marshall, 87 mins.)

Second Hand Hearts (1980)* Robert Blake, Barbara Harris, Amber Rose Gold, Bert Remsen, Collin Boone, Shirley Stoler. Secondhand dramatics. Two strangers marry in haste (and viewers get to repent at leisure). (Dir: Hal Ashby, 102 mins.)

Second Honeymoon (1937)**½ Tyrone Power, Loretta Young, Stuart Erwin, Claire Trevor, Marjorie Weaver, Lyle Talbot, J. Edward Bromberg. Sprightly romantic comedy about a divorced couple who fall in love again, though the wife has remarried. Familiar story becomes a charming confection, with both Young and Power ardent and funny, and an energetic supporting cast. (Dir: Walter Lang, 79 mins.)

Seconds (1966)***½ Rock Hudson, Salome Jens, John Randolph, Jeff Corey, Murray Hamilton, Will Geer. A middle-aged businessman discovers he can arrange for a secret organization to give him a "second" chance at life. After submitting to surgery, and psychiatric orientation, he emerges as handsome Rock, with seemingly everything one could ask for. This imaginative story holds your attention. (Dir: John Frankenheimer, 106 mins.)

Second Serve (MTV 1986)**½ Vanessa Redgrave, Richard Venture, Martin Balsam. Transsexual tennis star Renee Richards's story of becoming a woman after years of existing as a man is brilliantly acted by Redgrave. This is fortunate since a lot of dialogue is in the familiar didactic TV vein. (Dir: Anthony Page, 104 mins.)

Second Sight (1989)* John Larroquette, Bronson Pinchot, Bess Armstrong, Stuart Pankin, John Schuck. Mirthless comedy about a detective agency whose only asset is Pinchot, a neurotic psychic. No laughs, a tired, illogical plot—this one's a real stinker. (Dir: Joel Zwick, 84 mins.)†

Second Sight: A Love Story (MTV 1984)**½ Elizabeth Montgomery, Barry Newman. Montgomery convincingly plays a blind lady falling in love with Newman and eventually regaining her sight. (Dir: John Korty, 104 mins.)

Second Thoughts (1983)½ Lucie Arnaz, Craig Wasson, Laurence Luckinbill, Ken Howard. Excruciating film about a woman who remarries only to find her new hubby is twenty years behind the times. (Dir: Lawrence Turman, 98 mins.)

Second Time Around, The (1961)*** Debbie Reynolds, Andy Griffith, Steve Forrest, Juliet Prowse. Sprightly western comedy about a young widow and her children who find themselves stranded in an Arizona town—but she soon livens things up when she becomes sheriff. Good fun. (Dir: Vincent Sherman, 99 mins.)

Second Time Lucky (1985)* Diane Franklin, Roger Wilson, Robert Morley. Franklin and Wilson embarass themselves as reincarnations of Adam and Eve, used as pawns in a game between God and Satan. Hellishly unfunny. (Dir: Michael Anderson, 100 mins.)

Second Woman, The (1951)*** Robert Young, Betsy Drake. The whole community suspects a man of being responsible for the death of his fiancée, but his new love proves them wrong. Good psychological melodrama. (Dir: James V. Kern, 91 mins.)†

Secret, The (France, 1974)*** Jean-Louis Trintignant, Marlene Jobert, Philippe Noiret, Jean-François Adam. An escaped prisoner takes refuge with a couple who live in a remote mountain house. He tells them that he has been a victim of torture and abuse; the man believes him, the woman doesn't. Tense well-acted political thriller is superbly directed by Robert Enrico. (102 mins.)

Secret Admirer (1985)** C. Thomas Howell, Lori Loughlin, Kelly Preston, Dee Wallace Stone, Cliff De Young, Leigh Taylor-Young. The surburbs will never be the same after some love letters (written by teens) end up in the wrong grown-up hands. The film's slapstick treatment of the foibles of the letter-crossed lovers make this film boisterous without being funny. (Dir: David Greenwalt, 90 mins.)†

Secret Agent, The (Great Britain, 1936)*** John Gielgud, Madeleine Carroll, Peter Lorre, Robert Young. Extremely complicated thriller in which a spy accidentally kills an innocent man. The real villain is thus free to hunt down his pursuer and continue his reign of terror. (Dir: Alfred Hitchcock, 93 mins.)†

Secret Agent of Japan (1942)**½ Preston Foster, Lynn Bari, Janis Carter, Victor Sen Yung, Noel Madison. Snappy patriotic thriller of an American posing as a double agent in the Pacific at the beginning of WWII; fast-moving, enjoyable action. (Dir: Irving Pichel, 72 mins.)

Secret Beyond the Door (1948)**½ Joan Bennett, Michael Redgrave. A thriller with Freudian trappings, this is one of those claptrap suspense dramas where the unsuspecting wife starts to wonder if her hubby's going to do her in. The cast is good and the director effectively creates visual approximations of psychological disturbance, but the plot is the same old cat and mouse stuff you've seen a million times. (Dir: Fritz Lang, 98 mins.)†

Secret Bride, The (1935)**½ Barbara Stanwyck, Warren William, Glenda Farrell, Grant Mitchell, Henry O'Neill. Just as a governor's daughter elopes with the state attorney general, her father is impeached for apparently accepting a bribe. They conceal their marriage while he investigates. Fast-moving romantic thriller. (Dir: William Dieterle, 76 mins.)

Secret Ceremony (Great Britain, 1968)*** Elizabeth Taylor, Mia Farrow, Robert Mitchum. Macabre, interesting melodrama. The plot concerns a warped and wealthy Farrow who brings a blowsy Taylor home as a substitute mother, not counting on the sudden appearance of stepfather Mitchum. The TV version is watered down. (Dir: Joseph Losey, 109 mins.)†

Secret Command (1944)*** Pat O'Brien, Carole Landis, Chester Morris, Ruth Warrick. A two-fisted gent puts a stop to sabotage in the California shipyards. Actionful melodrama, well above average. (Dir: A. Edward Sutherland, 82 mins.)

Secret File: Hollywood (1962)½ Robert Clarke, Francine York, Syd Mason, Maralou Gray. After evidence he gathered for a scandal magazine is used to blackmail a famous director, a detective decides to expose the exposé racket. (Dir: Ralph Cushman, 85 mins.)

Secret Fury, The (1950)** Claudette Colbert, Robert Ryan. Bride is claimed to be already married, is sent to an asylum on what looks like a frameup. (Dir: Mel Ferrer, 86 mins.)

Secret Garden, The (1949)*** Margaret O'Brien, Dean Stockwell, Herbert Marshall. An eerie, suspenseful drama about two children, and their discovery of a magical, secret garden. Well acted. (Dir: Fred M. Wilcox, 92 mins.)

Secret Garden, The (MTV 1987)**½ Gennie James, Barret Oliver, Jadrien Steele, Sir Michael Hordern, Billie Whitelaw, Derek Jacobi. A prestige production of the classic children's tale about a spoiled young girl's discovery of a beautiful garden kept locked by a melancholy, hunchbacked widower (Jacobi). A fine retelling of the "kidlit" perennial. (Dir: Alan Grint, 104 mins.)

Secret Heart, The (1946)**½ Claudette Colbert, Walter Pidgeon, June Allyson. Cast helps but there's no spark to this dreary psychological study of a girl who worships her dead father and hates her lovely stepmother. (Dir: Robert Z. Leonard, 97 mins.)

Secret Honor (1984)*** Philip Baker Hall. A bizarre, lacerating blend of fiction, history, and speculation which gives you the dubious privilege of spending ninety minutes with Richard Nixon (Hall). For the millions who believe that Nixon was paranoid towards the end of his presidency, this is a powerful experience, indeed. (Dir: Robert Altman, 90 mins.)†

Secret Invasion, The (1964)**½ Stewart Granger, Raf Vallone, Edd Byrnes, Mickey Rooney. A group of criminals are promised a pardon if they'll participate in a dangerous mission involving the infiltration of Nazi-held territory in Yugoslavia during WWII. (Dir: Roger Corman, 98 mins.)

Secret Life of an American Wife, The (1968)*½ Anne Jackson, Patrick O'Neal, Edy Williams. Misfired comedy about a bored housewife (Jackson) who tries dalliance with a sexy movie star. Director George Axelrod reverses his *The Seven Year Itch* with highly disappointing results. (92 mins.)†

Secret Life of Archie's Wife, The (MTV 1990)**½ Jill Eikenberry, Michael Tucker, Elaine Stritch, Ray Wise. Eikenberry and Tucker make an engaging team in this pleasant, offbeat caper yarn about a discontented married woman whose life takes a turn for the better when she is kidnapped by a bungling bank robber. Mildly amusing antics enhanced by an enthusiastic cast. (Dir: James Frawley, 96 mins.)

Secret Life of Ian Fleming, The (MTV 1990) ** Jason Connery, Kristin Scott Thomas, Joss Ackland, Patricia Hodge, David Warner, Colin Welland, Richard Johnson. Mostly fictional biography of the creator of James Bond. The film falls flat. (Dir: Ferdinand Fairfax, 96 mins.)†

Secret Life of John Chapman, The (MTV 1976)*** Ralph Waite, Susan Anspach, Brad Davis, Pat Hingle. A curiously affecting real-life drama based on the notable book *Blue Collar Journal*. It's a deft adaptation of the chronicle of the president of Pennsylvania's prestigious Haverford College, during his voluntary sojourn doing odd jobs of manual labor. (Dir: David Lowell Rich, 72 mins.)

Secret Life of Kathy McCormick, The (MTV 1988)*½ Barbara Eden, Josh Taylor, Judith-Marie Bergan, Jenny O'Hara. Corny Cinderella tale tailored for Eden who plays a grocery clerk moving up in society. Her biggest problem is keeping the truth from her wealthy suitor. (Dir: Robert Lewis, 96 mins.)

Secret Life of Walter Mitty, The (1947)*** Danny Kaye, Virginia Mayo, Ann Rutherford, Fay Bainter, Boris Karloff. Thurber's story of a man who lived in two worlds—the real one and his own fantasy world—makes an entertaining vehicle for Kaye. Some excellent song sequences and sharp comedy lines make this one above average. (Dir: Norman Z. McLeod, 105 mins.)†

Secret Mission (Great Britain, 1942)**½ James Mason, Stewart Granger, Michael Wilding. British spy drama with excellent actors making the most of the intrigue. (Dir: Harold French, 82 mins.)

Secret Night Caller, The (MTV 1975)** Robert Reed, Hope Lange, Elaine Giftos, Michael Constantine. Offbeat casting works fairly well here, as Robert ("The Brady Bunch") Reed plays a respectable family man with a weakness for making obscene phone calls. (Dir: Jerry Jameson, 72 mins.)

Secret of Convict Lake, The (1951)**½ Glenn Ford, Gene Tierney, Ethel Barrymore, Zachary Scott, Ann Dvorak. Convicts invade a village inhabited only by women; complications arise. Ethel Barrymore, as matriarch of the village, is the only interesting feature. (Dir: Michael Gordon, 83 mins.)

Secret of Dr. Kildare, The (1939)** Lew Ayres, Lionel Barrymore, Laraine Day. Kildare continues his long Hollywood internship, Barrymore is still the barking "heart of gold" Gillespie and Laraine continues as Kildare's pretty combination nurse-sweetheart. (Dir: Harold S. Bucquet, 85 mins.)

Secret of Dr. Mabuse, The—See: **Thousand Eyes of Dr. Mabuse, The**

Secret of Madame Blanche, The (1933)****½** Irene Dunne, Lionel Atwill, Phillips Holmes, Una Merkel, Douglas Watson, Jean Parker. Musical melodrama of a showgirl marrying a rich weakling who commits suicide, leaving her with a baby who is taken from her. Many years later they are reunited under tragic circumstances. Well-produced soap opera. (Dir: Charles Brabin, 67 mins.)

Secret of My Success, The (Great Britain, 1965)***½** Lionel Jeffries, James Booth, Honor Blackman, Stella Stevens, Shirley Jones. Onward and upward in the art of murder, as a constable (Booth) becomes wealthier and wealthier. Tries for comedy in the tradition of *Kind Hearts & Coronets* but "*Secret*" fails in nearly every respect. (Dir: Andrew L. Stone, 112 mins.)

Secret of My Success, The (1987)****** Michael J. Fox, Richard Jordan, Helen Slater, Margaret Whitton. Fox is so engaging a presence that he makes this comedy click part of the time, but the film emerges as more labored than funny. It's sort of a yuppie update of *How to Succeed in Business Without Really Trying*, as an enterprising man from Kansas tries to make it in the Big Apple in record time. (Dir: Herbert Ross, 90 mins.)†

Secret of NIMH, The (1982)******* The voices of John Carradine, Elizabeth Hartman, Dom DeLuise, Derek Jacobi. Entertaining animated feature about a stouthearted lady mouse who stumbles onto a laboratory full of superintelligent rats while trying to get help for her sick child. Director Don Bluth and the team of 16 animators with whom he worked grew disenchanted with the Disney studios and formed their own company; their first product is a welcome return to classically detailed animation and a likeable, easy-to-watch film. (82 mins.)†

Secret of Santa Vittoria, The (1969)****½** Anthony Quinn, Anna Magnani, Hardy Kruger, Virna Lisi. Ponderous direction by Stanley Kramer and a screenplay that savors little of the excellent dialogue found in Robert Crichton's novel dissipate most of the potential inherent in this story of an Italian hill town guarding their wine at the end of WWII. (140 mins.)

Secret of the Blue Room (1933)****½** Lionel Atwill, Gloria Stuart, Paul Lukas, Edward Arnold, Onslow Stevens. First-rate haunted house mystery. A lovely woman of mystery asks her three suitors to spend a night alone in a haunted castle to win her hand. Eerie and suspenseful, with a lively cast of pros. (Dir: Kurt Neumann, 66 mins.)

Secret of the Incas (1954)****½** Charlton Heston, Robert Young, Nicole Maurey, 928

Yma Sumac. Adventurer finds a map holding the location of a priceless gold sunburst, arrives to find an archeological expedition already there. Melodrama with enough intrigue and suspense to hold the action fans. (Dir: Jerry Hopper, 101 mins.)

Secret of the Purple Reef, The (1960)****** Jeff Richards, Peter Falk, Richard Chamberlain. Two brothers arrive to investigate the mysterious sinking of their father's ship. Passable Grade B melodrama. (Dir: William Witney, 80 mins.)

Secret of Treasure Mountain (1956)****** Raymond Burr, Valerie French. A buried Indian treasure is mysteriously guarded by an old man and his attractive daughter. (Dir: Seymour Friedman, 68 mins.)

Secret Partner, The (Great Britain, 1961)****** Stewart Granger, Haya Harareet. Routine meller with Stewart Granger cast as a man who must prove he is innocent of an embezzlement charge and win back his wife in the process. (Dir: Basil Dearden, 91 mins.)

Secret People, The (Great Britain, 1952)****½** Valentina Cortese, Audrey Hepburn, Serge Reggiani. Refugee in London meets her former fiance who persuades her to enter into an espionage plot. Long, leisurely melodrama doesn't have enough spark to lift it much above the ordinary. (Dir: Thorold Dickinson, 87 mins.)

Secret Places (Australia, 1985)****½** Marie-Theres Relin, Tara Macgowran, Cassie Stuart, Jennie Agutter. The film relates the difficult readjustment of a German refugee during WWII as she tries to fit into an English girl's school, where anti-German sentiment runs high. The delicate blossoming of this teenager's friendship with a popular classmate could have made an impactful film if the director had had a firmer grasp on the best way to tell this story. (Dir: Zelda Barron, 96 mins.)†

Secret Policeman's Other Ball, The (Great Britain, 1981)*****½** John Cleese, Graham Chapman, Michael Palin, Terry Jones, Peter Cook, Pamela Stephenson, Pete Townshend, Sting, Eric Clapton, Jeff Beck, Phil Collins. A series of mostly hilarious sketches that will delight Monty Pythonites and other fans of British humor. Poorly filmed; but the content is superior. (Dir: Julien Temple, 91 mins.)†

Secrets (MTV 1977)***** Susan Blakely, Roy Thinnes, Joanne Linville, John Randolph. Pretentious, silly drama about a young married woman with a nice, handsome husband who starts compulsively sleeping around after her possessive mother dies. The camera work is "arty," the script cumbersome. (Dir: Paul Wendkos, 106 mins.)

Secret Six, The (1931)*** Lewis Stone, Wallace Beery, Clark Gable, Jean Harlow, Ralph Bellamy, Johnny Mack Brown, Marjorie Rambeau. A gritty crime drama about two indefatigable reporters on a crusade against bootleggers. Nicely rough-and-tumble. (Dir: George Hill, 83 mins.)

Secrets of a Married Man (MTV 1984)**½ William Shatner, Cybill Shepherd, Michelle Phillips, Glynn Turman. Shatner plays a married man fooling around with hookers and getting vicarious thrills from the street life. Falling hard for one (Shepherd) destroys his marriage and himself. (Dir: William A. Graham, 104 mins.)†

Secrets of a Mother and Daughter (MTV 1983)** Katharine Ross, Michael Nouri, Linda Hamilton, Bibi Besch. Slick women's magazine fare treated seriously as stunning mom and petulant daughter romance the same man. (Dir: Gabrielle Beaumont, 104 mins.)

Secrets of an Actress (1938)**½ Kay Francis, George Brent, Ian Hunter, Gloria Dickson, Isabel Jeans, Penny Singleton. Glamorous actress Francis is loved by architect Hunter, but her heart belongs to married man Brent. Sleek, entertaining soap opera. (Dir: William Keighley, 71 mins.)

Secrets of a Secretary (1931)**½ Claudette Colbert, Herbert Marshall, George Metaxa, Betty Lawford, Mary Boland. An irresponsible heiress loses her fortune and is forced to get a job as a secretary, putting up with social slights from her former equals and getting involved in a murder. OK social drama; Colbert is magnetic. (Dir: George Abbott, 71 mins.)

Secrets of the Lone Wolf (1941)** Warren William, Ruth Ford, Roger Clark. Fair shipboard mystery in which criminals try to coerce Lone Wolf's manservant into stealing the Napoleon gems. Behind the scenes, L.W. lays a trap for the thieves. (Dir: Edward Dmytryk, 67 mins.)

Secrets of the Red Bedroom—See: **Secret Weapons**

Secrets of Three Hungry Wives (MTV 1978)** Jessica Walter, James Franciscus, Eve Plumb, Gretchen Corbett, Heather MacRae. Franciscus is a playboy who preys on suburban housewives and their offspring in this sudsy whodunit. (Dir: Gordon Hessler, 104 mins.)†

Secrets of Women (Sweden, 1952)**½ Anita Bjork, Karl Arne Homsten, Jarl Krulle. Billed as a comedy, "Secrets" is an early Bergman omnibus. Some sisters chew the fat about their past sexual follies as their youngest sibling (perhaps bored by their endless prattle) decides to elope. The funniest and most touching segment involves a long-married couple who find themselves trapped in an elevator. (Dir: Ingmar Bergman, 108 mins.)†

Secret War of Harry Frigg, The (1968)** Paul Newman, Sylva Koscina, Andrew Duggan, Tom Bosley, John Williams. In WWII, a rebellious private is called upon to try and free some captured Allied generals. (Dir: Jack Smight, 110 mins.)†

Secret War of Jackie's Girls, The (MTV 1980)*½ Mariette Hartley, Lee Purcell, Dee Wallace. Hartley leads an all-woman flying squadron in WWII. Ridiculous, contrived story of young beauties, on top secret missions, single-handedly winning the war for the Allies. (Dir: Gordon Hessler, 104 mins.)

Secret Ways, The (1961)**½ Richard Widmark, Sonja Ziemann. Fast-paced but brainless chase thriller behind the Iron Curtain. Widmark tries to smuggle an anti-Communist leader out of Red Hungary. (Dir: Phil Karlson, 112 mins.)

Secret Weapons (MTV 1985)** James Franciscus, Geena Davis, Christopher Atkins, Linda Hamilton, Sally Kellerman. Sex and espionage are the two ingredients in this barely believable drama about gorgeous spies from Russia. Franciscus and Kellerman star as KGB instructors in charge of changing Russian women into Americanized seductresses whose mission is to gather secrets through sex and blackmail. AKA: **Secrets of the Red Bedroom**. (Dir: Don Taylor, 104 mins.)

Secret Witness (MTV 1988)** David Rasche, Paul LeMat, Leaf Phoenix, Kellie Martin. Twelve-year-olds in a summer community innocently play a Peeping Tom game which results in their discovery of a murder. Martin plays a spunky girl who leads her pal (Phoenix) around by the nose. The believable child actors make this worthwhile. (Dir: Eric Laneuville, 96 mins.)

Secret World (France, 1969)**½ Jacqueline Bisset, Jean-François Maurin. Offbeat tale. A young French boy, scarred by his parents' death in a car crash, becomes deeply infatuated with a beautiful English lady visiting his aunt and uncle's château. (Dirs: Robert Freeman, Paul Feyder, 94 mins.)

Security Risk (1954)** John Ireland, Dorothy Malone, Keith Larson, John Craven. Routine Cold War thriller, with vacationing FBI man Ireland uncovering a Communist plot to steal atomic secrets. Malone provides some much-needed electricity for this otherwise damp tale. (Dir: Harold Schuster, 69 mins.)

Seduced (MTV 1985)**½ Gregory Harrison, Cybill Shepherd, José Ferrer, Adrienne Barbeau, Mel Ferrer. Harrison and Shepherd mix murder with seductive bedroom moments. A glossy item to show off the handsome Harrison as a brilliant lawyer whose ascendancy to a corporate presidency is stymied by a murder. (Dir: Jerrold Freedman, 104 mins.)†

Seduced and Abandoned (Italy, 1964)**** Saro Urzi, Stefania Sandrelli. A wonderfully funny film that takes a sardonic, angry view of Sicilian family life and the hypocrisy which plays such an important part in their lives and mores. Pietro Germi, the same wizard responsible for *Divorce, Italian Style*, wrote and directed this witty and bitter view of his countrymen. Story is about what happens in a Sicilian town when a young girl is seduced by the fiancé of her sister. (118 mins.)†

Seduction, The (1982)* Morgan Fairchild, Andrew Stevens, Michael Sarrazin, Vince Edwards, Colleen Camp. Ridiculous film about a TV newsperson who is stalked by a psychotic young photographer. (Dir: David Schmoeller, 104 mins.)†

Seduction of Gina, The (MTV 1984)** Valerie Bertinelli, Michael Brandon, Ed Lauter, Frederick Lehne, Dinah Manoff. Bertinelli plays a medical student's lonely wife who becomes a gambling addict. (Dir: Jerrold Freedman, 104 mins.)

Seduction of Joe Tynan, The (1979)**½ Alan Alda, Meryl Streep, Barbara Harris. A rather facile drama about a charismatic liberal senator (Alda) that has less density than a good Movie of the Week. Alda, who wrote the script, projects a more piquant sense of decency than anyone else in movies, but the dramatic situations are too pat. (Dir: Jerry Schatzberg, 107 mins.)†

Seduction of Mimi, The (Italy, 1974)***½ Giancarlo Giannini, Mariangela Melato, Agostina Belli. Rollicking melange of political humor, Sicilian double standards, and sexual fandangos served up by director Lina Wertmuller. Giannini and Melato strike sparks as a metallurgist and his mistress whose concepts of honor diverge tragically. (89 mins.)

Seduction of Miss Leona, The (MTV 1980)** Lynn Redgrave, Brian Dennehy, Conchata Ferrell, Anthony Zerbe. Sentimental three-hankie drama about a prudish, old-fashioned college professor (Redgrave) who falls in love with a married handyman, skillfully played by Dennehy. (Dir: Joseph Hardy, 104 mins.)

Seduction: The Cruel Woman (West Germany, 1985)**½ Mechthild Grossman, Udo Kier, Shiela McLaughlin. Oddly mundane film about sexual masochism observes a dominatrix and her consorts. The banality of the encounters are the point of this anti-sensationalistic film. Writer-director Monika Treut knows where of she speaks, having written a Ph.D. thesis on Sacher-Masoch. (85 mins.)

930

Seedling of Sarah Burns, The (MTV 1979)**½ Kay Lenz, Martin Balsam, Cliff De Young. Lenz is fine as an introspective young woman who volunteers for an embryo transplant. Once the drama settles into the obvious twist of the young woman becoming too attached to the growing infant in her, the whole thing becomes a soap opera. (Dir: Sandor Stern, 104 mins.)

Seedling, The (India, 1974)*** Anant Nag, Shabana Azmi, Sudhu Meher, Priya Tendulkar. Servant girl, married to a deaf-mute man, is seduced and impregnated by the landlord's son, who also assaults her husband. She vows to avenge the horrors visited upon them in this potent drama attacking the remnants of India's feudal mentality. (Dir: Shyam Benegal, 131 mins.)

Seeds of Evil (1974)½ Katharine Houghton, Rita Gam, Joe Dallesandro, James Congdon. Soporific garden-variety horror flick with Joe as a stud whose sexual prowess turns women literally into clinging vines. (Dir: James H. Kay III, 97 mins.)†

See Here, Private Hargrove (1944)*** Robert Walker, Keenan Wynn, Donna Reed, Robert Benchley. Many an ex-Army man will get plenty of laughs out of this fair adaptation of the famous boot camp best-seller. (Dir: Wesley Ruggles, 101 mins.)

See How She Runs (MTV 1978)***½ Joanne Woodward, John Considine, Lissy Newman. Woodward stars in this extraordinary drama about a divorced teacher who takes up jogging at every moment she can spare, until it becomes central to her existence, a fact to which she insists her family must adjust. Skillful development of the protagonist who develops her running skills enough to enter the Boston Marathon and have her family root for her. (Dir: Richard T. Heffron, 104 mins.)†

See How They Run (MTV 1964)** John Forsythe, Senta Berger, Jane Wyatt, Franchot Tone. Three orphaned children are pursued by their father's murderer when they take incriminating evidence with them to South America. (Dir: David Lowell Rich, 99 mins.)

Seeing Red (1983)**** Pete Seeger, Dorothy Healey, Stretch Johnson, Bill Bailey. A riveting Academy Award-nominated documentary about the American Communist Party, culled from over 400 interview sessions with former and current party members. Directors Julia Reichert and James Klein include archival footage of speeches by Ronald Reagan, Richard Nixon, Hubert Humphrey and Joseph McCarthy. The vision of the party is slightly romanticized, but not uncritical, and the interview subjects are fascinating. (100 mins.)

Seekers, The (1954)—See: **Land of Fury**

Seekers, The (MTV 1979)** Randolph Mantooth, Edie Adams, Neville Brand, Delta Burke, Vic Morrow, Robert Reed, John Carradine, Brian Keith, Ross Martin, Rosey Grier, George Hamilton, Alex Hyde-White, Martin Milner, Ed Harris, Eric Stolz. Custardy-smooth but woefully predictable follow-up to *The Bastard* and *The Rebels*. The Kent clan puts the Revolutionary War behind them to tame the Northwest. Author John Jakes has a bit part. (Dir: Sidney Hayers, 200 mins.)

Seems Like Old Times (1980)*** Chevy Chase, Goldie Hawn, Charles Grodin, Robert Guillaume, George Grizzard. Synthetic farce about marital complications caused by an ex-husband is nevertheless Neil Simon's most efficient original screenplay. It hasn't the richness of the thirties comedies it emulates, but you care about the characters and the situations are mostly funny. (Dir: Jay Sandrich, 102 mins.)†

See My Lawyer (1945)**½ Olsen and Johnson, Grace McDonald, Noah Beery, Jr. The two comics want to squirm out of a movie contract, hire three young lawyers to help them. Amusing musical nonsense. (Dir: Eddie Cline, 67 mins.)

See No Evil (Great Britain, 1971)**½ Mia Farrow, Dorothy Allison, Diane Grayson, Robin Bailey. A suspense thriller which works only part of the way, but the chills are there if you're patient. Farrow plays a blind girl who comes home to her uncle's house after the accident which caused her blindness, and begins living a nightmare. (Dir: Richard Fleischer, 89 mins.)†

See No Evil, Hear No Evil (1989)**½ Gene Wilder, Richard Pryor, Joan Severance, Kevin Spacey. A deaf man and a blind man, both trying to hide their disabilities, are caught up in a murder. Pryor and Wilder mine deft humor from their characters without being cruel or condescending, but the idiot plot defeats them. (Dir: Arthur Hiller, 103 mins.)†

See the Man Run (MTV 1971)**½ Robert Culp, Angie Dickinson, Eddie Albert, June Allyson. Stock kidnapping plot undergoes a far-out twist here. Linked to a kidnapping through a wrong telephone number, an out-of-work actor decides to cut himself in. (Dir: Corey Allen, 73 mins.)

See You in the Morning (1989)**½ Jeff Bridges, Alice Krige, Farrah Fawcett, Drew Barrymore. Uneven comedy-drama about a New York psychiatrist trying to adjust to his role as stepfather to his new wife's kids, while fulfilling his obligations to his own children from his first marriage. A disappointment from writer-director Alan J. Pakula. (119 mins.)†

Seize the Day (1986)*** Robin Williams, Jerry Stiller, Joseph Wiseman, Glenne Headly, William Hickey, Tony Roberts. Involving but downbeat account of an ex-salesman's mid-life crisis: he's lost his job, her personal relationships are ruined, and his possibilities for starting up again in the business world don't seem too hopeful. Based on the novel by Saul Bellow. (Dir: Fielder Cook, 93 mins.)†

Seizure (Canada, 1974)**½ Jonathan Frid, Joe Sirola, Martine Beswick, Hervé Villechaize, Mary Woronov, Troy Donahue. A writer of spooky books finds himself in a spooky situation—trapped in a nightmare as characters from his latest novel stop by to kill off his house guests. Derivative, but the borrowings are from the best sources. (Dir: Oliver Stone, 93 mins.)

Seizure: The Story of Kathy Morris (MTV 1980)**½ Penelope Milford, Leonard Nimoy, Christopher Allport. The real-life crisis of young singer Kathy Morris (excellent acting by Milford). Ms. Morris was struck with a seizure, resulting in an operation which left her in a coma. The film methodically depicts her courageous struggle against adversity, and her eventual victory. (Dir: Gerald Isenberg, 104 mins.)

Sellout, The (1951)**½ Walter Pidgeon, John Hodiak, Audrey Totter, Karl Malden. OK crime yarn. Pidgeon plays a crusading newspaper editor who tries to overthrow the corrupt local law enforcement. (Dir: Gerald Mayer, 83 mins.)

Seminole (1953)**½ Rock Hudson, Barbara Hale, Anthony Quinn, Richard Carlson, Hugh O'Brian. The story of Seminole Indians and their efforts to stay free takes up the bulk of the film and it's interestingly unfolded. (Dir: Budd Boetticher, 87 mins.)

Seminole Uprising (1955)** George Montgomery, Karen Booth, John Pickard. Typical low-budget '50s western, with the cavalry saving the day when Indians revolt. (Dir: Earl Bellamy, 74 mins.)

Semi-Tough (1977)*** Burt Reynolds, Kris Kristofferson, Jill Clayburgh, Robert Preston, Lotte Lenya, Bert Convy, Roger Mosley, Carl Weathers. Generally entertaining, but unfocused, comedy about two football stars both making a fifty-yard dash to the same girl. Amiably, the film wanders all over the place embracing romantic comedy, delivering pigskin satire, and even managing to poke fun at est, but ultimately it dilutes its impact. (Dir: Michael Ritchie, 108 mins.)†

Senator Was Indiscreet, The (1947)*** William Powell, Ella Raines, Peter Lind Hayes. A bird-brained senator lets a hot

931

political diary get out of his hands, and it may spell doom to his machine. Side-splitting farce comedy. Don't miss it. (Dir: George S. Kaufman, 81 mins.)†

Sender, The (Great Britain, 1982)**½ Kathryn Harrold, Zeljko Ivanek, Shirley Knight, Paul Freeman, Sean Hewitt. Ivanek plays a man with psychic powers whose visions infect an entire hospital as his doctor searches for a cure. (Dir: Roger Christian, 91 mins.)†

Send Me No Flowers (1964)*** Doris Day, Rock Hudson, Tony Randall, Clint Walker, Paul Lynde. In this, their least predictable film together, Day is a housewife and Hudson her hypochondriac husband. He mistakenly believes he is dying, and keeps trying to fix her up with other men. (Dir: Norman Jewison, 100 mins.)†

Senilità (Italy, 1961)*** Anthony Franciosa, Claudia Cardinale, Betsy Blair, Philippe Leroy, Raimondo Magni. A repressed man falls in love with a beautiful woman who ends up abusing and humiliating him. A haunting portrait of devastating realism. (Dir: Mauro Bolognini, 110 mins.)

Senior Prom (1959)** Jill Corey, Jimmie Komack, Paul Hampton, Tom Laughlin, Mitch Miller. Harmless little college musical about a young student who makes a hit recording and becomes top man on campus. (Dir: David Lowell Rich, 82 mins.)

Senior Trip (MTV 1981)* Scott Baio, Faye Grant, Rand Brooks, Peter Coffield, Jane Hoffman. Ohio high school graduates visit New York City to sample the theater, museums, and Wall Street board rooms. (Dir: Kenneth Johnson, 104 mins.)†

Senior Year (MTV 1974)* Gary Frank, Glynnis O'Connor, Barry Livingston, Debralee Scott. It's all about the traumas and growing pains of high school seniors in the mid-fifties. (Dir: Richard Donner, 72 mins.)

Sensations (1944)**½ Eleanor Powell, Dennis O'Keefe, W. C. Fields. Dancing star resorts to novel means to obtain publicity. Mild musical; some good moments. (Dir: Andrew L. Stone, 86 mins.)

Sense of Loss, A (U.S.-Switzerland, 1972)*** Enlightening documentary about the fighting, bitterness and religious hatred in Northern Ireland. Interviews bring out the mindless futility of the ongoing violence in that embittered land. (Dir: Marcel Ophuls, 135 mins.)†

Sensitive, Passionate Man, A (MTV 1977)*½ Angie Dickinson, David Janssen, Todd Lookinland, Mariclare Costello. Dreary soap opera about an alcoholic executive of an aerospace company who loses his job, his family, and eventually his life. (Dir: John Newland, 98 mins.)

932

Senso (Italy, 1954)***½ Alida Valli, Farley Granger. Tragic tale of a noblewoman who sacrifices her marriage for a handsome but cowardly soldier. Beautifully photographed and sublimely romantic. AKA: The Wanton Contessa. (Dir: Luchino Visconti, 90 mins.)†

Sentimental Journey (1946)** John Payne, Maureen O'Hara, Cedric Hardwicke, William Bendix. Maudlin, sentimental, sloppy tale of a dying woman who adopts a child to keep her husband company when she dies. (Dir: Walter Lang, 94 mins.)

Sentimental Journey (MTV 1984)** Jaclyn Smith, David Dukes, Jessica Rene Carroll. Smith is a Broadway producer married happily to successful actor Dukes, except that they can't have any children. Enter eight-year-old orphan Libby, whom they adopt, but their problems aren't over . . . not by a long shot! (Dir: James Goldstone, 104 mins.)

Sentinel, The (1977)*½ Chris Sarandon, Cristina Raines, Arthur Kennedy, Ava Gardner. The gates of Hell must be guarded, only no one will apply for the job. Some extremely unpleasant shock scenes, but no real scares. (Dir: Michael Winner, 91 mins.)†

Separate But Equal (MTV 1991)***½ Sidney Poitier, Burt Lancaster, Richard Kiley, Cleavon Little, Gloria Foster, John McMartin. Deeply moving account of the historic effort to desegregate the school system in the South, starting in 1950. The impact of this docudrama is due to both the inherent power of the Supreme Court case in 1954, which found ''separate but equal'' unconstitutional, and to the enormously effective performance of Poitier (his first appearance in a TV drama in 35 years) in the leading role of Thurgood Marshall. Skillfully written and directed drama is absorbing throughout. (Dir: George Stevens, Jr., 192 mins.)

Separate Peace, A (1972)** Parker Stevenson, John Heyl, William Roerick. Two young men at a private school face the transition to manhood in the last years of WWII. The forties ambience is well done, but director Larry Peerce seems as afraid of closeness and commitment as his protagonists. (104 mins.)†

Separate Tables (1958)**** Deborah Kerr, Burt Lancaster, David Niven, Rita Hayworth, Gladys Cooper, Cathleen Nesbitt, Wendy Hiller. Faithful film version of Terence Rattigan's two one-act plays about the guests of a British seaside resort and their individual dramas. Oscar-winning performances by Niven and Hiller. Kerr and Niven come off with top acting honors as a spinster and a charming ex-colonel. Hiller shines as the proprietress of the establishment. (Dir: Delbert Mann, 98 mins.)†

Seppuku—See: **Hara-kiri**

September (1987)** Denholm Elliott, Mia Farrow, Elaine Stritch, Jack Warden, Sam Waterson, Dianne Wiest. Humorless Woody Allen drama about the relationship crisis between an ex-socialite mother (Stritch) and her introverted daughter (Farrow). Another failed attempt by Allen to imitate Ingmar Bergman. (87 mins.)†

September Affair (1950)*** Joan Fontaine, Joseph Cotten, Jessica Tandy. Engineer and concert pianist miss their plane while sightseeing in Naples; when the plane is reported crashed, they find they have a chance to start life anew together. Well made, generally avoids the maudlin. (Dir: William Dieterle, 104 mins.)†

September Gun (MTV 1984)*** Robert Preston, Patty Duke Astin, Sally Kellerman, Christopher Lloyd, Geoffrey Lewis. This offbeat western starts slowly but turns out to be an arresting production. Crusty Preston plays a gunfighter living off past glory who is duped into helping a strong-willed nun care for abandoned Indian children. (Dir: Don Taylor, 104 mins.)†

September Storm (1960)*½ Joanne Dru, Mark Stevens. Model joins adventurers in trying to recover a fortune in Spanish gold from a sunken ship. (Dir: Byron Haskin, 99 mins.)

September 30, 1955—See: **9/30/55**

Sequoia (1934)*** Jean Parker, Samuel S. Hinds, Russell Hardie, Paul Hurst, Willie Fung. Nice little nature film, years before Disney took over the genre, about a deer and a mountain lion raised together as friends striving to avoid hunters in the sequoia forests of the Northwest. (Dir: Chester M. Franklin, 75 mins.)

Serenade (1956)**½ Mario Lanza, Joan Fontaine, Vincent Price, Vincent Edwards. Lanza plays a street singer who is discovered by society playgirl (Fontaine) and concert manager (Price). Overdramatic plot but the opera arias are worthwhile. (Dir: Anthony Mann, 121 mins.)†

Serengeti Shall Not Die (West Germany, 1959)***½ Absorbing Oscar-winning documentary of two zoologists who take a census of wild animals facing extinction on the steppes of Serengeti in Tanganyika. (Dirs: Dr. Bernhard, Michael Grzimek, 84 mins.)

Sergeant, The (France-U.S., 1968)** Rod Steiger, John Phillip Law, Ludmila Mikael. Cut-rate *Reflections in a Golden Eye* set in a dreary Army camp in '52 France where a career sergeant tries to repress his lust for a young private. Under John Flynn's direction and Steiger's

smoldering smoked ham, the film degenerates shrilly. (107 mins.)

Sergeant Deadhead (1965)** Frankie Avalon, Deborah Walley, Cesar Romero, Fred Clark, Buster Keaton. Girl-shy GI (Avalon) turns into a wolf and disrupts a missile base. Silly, harmless antics. (Dir: Norman Taurog, 89 mins.)

Sergeant Madden (1939)*** Wallace Beery, Tom Brown, Alan Curtis, David Gorcey, Fay Holden, Marc Lawrence, Laraine Day. Beery is a sanctimonious cop with two sons—one goes good and one goes bad. Distinguished by a superlative performance by Lawrence and by Josef von Sternberg's haunting direction. (82 mins.)

Sergeant Matlovich vs. the U.S. Air Force (MTV 1978)**½ Brad Dourif, Frank Converse, Stephen Elliott, Marc Singer, William Daniels. As presented here, the character of Sgt. Matlovich, the real-life homosexual who battled with the Air Force to remain in service, is one-dimensional. Dourif does his best to bring the character to life, but little insight is brought to bear on his sexual preference. (Dir: Paul Leaf, 104 mins.)†

Sergeant Murphy (1938)** Ronald Reagan, Mary Maguire, Donald Crisp, Ben Hendricks. Dopey B picture about a U.S. Army cavalryman striving to rehabilitate his horse after it is deemed unfit for service. OK but unexciting. (Dir: B. Reeves Eason, 57 mins.)

Sergeant Rutledge (1960)** Jeffrey Hunter, Constance Towers, Woody Strode. One of director John Ford's lesser westerns. There's rape, racial prejudice and courtroom dramatics thrown together in this muddled sagebrush drama. (118 mins.)

Sergeant Ryker (1968)** Lee Marvin, Bradford Dillman, Vera Miles, Peter Graves, Lloyd Nolan. Lee Marvin as an army sergeant on trial for treason during the Korean conflict. Fleshed out from a 1963 TV show, this is of ordinary interest aside from Marvin's strong performance. (Dir: Buzz Kulik, 85 mins.)†

Sergeants 3 (1962)** Frank Sinatra, Dean Martin, Sammy Davis, Jr., Peter Lawford, Joey Bishop. A supposedly high-camp remake of *Gunga Din* to accommodate Frank Sinatra and his buddies. (Dir: John Sturges, 112 mins.)

Sergeant York (1941)**** Gary Cooper, Walter Brennan, Joan Leslie, George Tobias, Stanley Ridges, Margaret Wycherly, Ward Bond, Noah Beery, Jr., June Lockhart. Story of WWI's greatest hero is told with simplicity and understanding and emerges as a poignant film. Cooper is perfectly cast as the Tennessee hillbilly who captured over a hundred Germans single-handed. (Dir: Howard Hawks, 134 mins.)†

Serial (1980)*** Martin Mull, Tuesday Weld, Bill Macy, Sally Kellerman, Peter Bonerz, Nita Talbot, Christopher Lee, Tom Smothers. For the benefit of those who do not live in California, the screenwriters have changed Cyra McFadden's popular comic novel from a satire of a specific place—Marin County—to a wry look at the American pursuit of the "good life" and inner peace. Mull and Weld star as a relatively sane couple trying to keep a grip on reality while others about them are losing theirs. (Dir: Bill Persky, 92 mins.)†

Serpent, The—See: **Night Flight from Moscow**

Serpent and the Rainbow, The (1988)* Bill Pullman, Cathy Tyson, Zakes Mokae, Paul Winfield. Badly acted, awfully scripted tale of an anthropologist/adventurer who explores the voodoo culture of Haiti searching for a powder that will cause "zombification." A few good nightmarish images and the attractive Tyson can't resurrect this loser. (Dir: Wes Craven, 98 mins.)†

Serpent of the Nile (1953)** Rhonda Fleming, Raymond Burr, William Lundigan. Foolish drama about the Roman Empire in the days of Cleopatra (Fleming) and Mark Antony (Burr) and their eventual suicides. (Dir: William Castle, 81 mins.)

Serpent's Egg, The (West Germany, 1977)** Liv Ullmann, David Carradine, Gert Frobe, Glynn Turman, James Whitmore, Heinz Bennent. It was an exciting idea: director Ingmar Bergman on a big budget doing a horror story about Germany in the early twenties. Well, it's a lousy film, interesting only for its superb art direction and the colossal wrongheadedness of its errors. Ullmann as a seedy cabaret performer fails to be slutty and irresistible. The great director is painfully vulnerable to the lure of his own clichés. (119 mins.)†

Serpico (1973)***½ Al Pacino, John Randolph, Jack Kehoe, Tony Roberts, Cornelia Sharpe. Peter Maas's book about real-life cop Frank Serpico, whose stories about corruption in the New York City police force led to an investigation, is turned into an excellent film by director Sidney Lumet. Pacino is brilliant in the title role of the cop who couldn't keep his mouth shut after witnessing cops on the take. Another plus is the sense of reality conveyed by the use of good New York location footage. (130 mins.)†

Serpico: The Deadly Games (MTV 1976)** David Birney, Allen Garfield, Burt Young, Lane Bradbury, Walter McGinn. A warm-up for an unsuccessful series based on the theatrical film with Al Pacino. Birney seems more like a college professor than a tough N.Y. cop battling

corruption in the force and violence on the streets. (Dir: Robert Collins, 104 mins.)

Servant, The (Great Britain, 1963)***½ Dirk Bogarde, Sarah Miles, James Fox, Wendy Craig. Director Joseph Losey's first collaboration with playwright Harold Pinter explores themes of guilt and power as a manservant (Bogarde) corrupts his employer (Fox). Losey's dark, crowded compositions provide the perfect setting for the class war's Pyrrhic victory. (115 mins.)†

Service De Luxe (1938)**½ Constance Bennett, Vincent Price, Charlie Ruggles, Helen Broderick, Mischa Auer, Halliwell Hobbs. Nifty romantic comedy with chic Bennett as a hard-headed businesswoman running a service bureau that will tackle any job; Price is the customer who eventually warms her heart. Sharp and polished. (Dir: Rowland V. Lee, 85 mins.)

Sesame Street Presents: Follow That Bird (1985)** The Muppets, Dave Thomas, Waylon Jennings, Paul Bartel, Sandra Bernhard. Wobbly translation of the popular children's show has Big Bird venturing across the Midwest to find his friends on Sesame Street after his unsuccessful adoption by the Dodo family. A film that only small kids will enjoy; grown-ups may feel as if they were being forced to inhabit a muppet Internment Camp. (Dir: Ken Kwapis, 88 mins.)†

Sessions (MTV 1983)**½ Veronica Hamel, Jeffrey DeMunn, Jill Eikenberry. Hamel stars as a woman whose controlled life breaks down due to her conflicting identities—as an elegant call girl and as the mother of two young daughters. (Dir: Richard Pearce, 120 mins.)†

Set This Town on Fire (MTV 1972)*** Carl Betz, Chuck Connors, Lynda Day, Nancy Malone, Jeff Corey. Drama about the pressures placed on a respected newspaper publisher sets a slow pace, but the theme is different and fairly interesting. A publisher (Carl Betz) goes along with close friends in having second thoughts over a local hero imprisoned for manslaughter, and then regrets his change of heart. (Dir: David Lowell Rich, 99 mins.)

Settle the Score (MTV 1989)** Jaclyn Smith, Jeffrey DeMunn, Louise Latham, Howard Duff, Amy Wright, Richard Masur. Chicago policewoman Smith returns to her Arkansas home to ferret out the man who raped her twenty years before, discovers three other women have since been similarly attacked— and killed as well. Mystery thriller strains credulity throughout. (Dir: Ed Sherin, 96 mins.)

Set-up, The (1949)*** Robert Ryan, Audrey Totter, Alan Baxter, George Tobias. Tough if pretentious boxing film about a fighter on the skids who refuses to go crooked, helped by the gritty pugnacity of Ryan in the lead. Robert Wise directs rather well, considering limitations of budget and conception. (72 mins.)†

Seven (1979)* William Smith, Barbara Leigh, Christopher Joy, Guich Koock, Art Metrano, Martin Kove, Susan Kiger, Lenny Montana, Terry Kiser. Freelance agent is offered $7 million by the U.S. government to wipe out a gang of Hawaiian mobsters. Suposedly tongue-in-cheek action movie has no laughs, and is so badly photographed that even the impressive Hawaiian scenery and female pulchritude are wasted. (Dir: Andy Sidaris, 100 mins.)†

Seven Alone (1975)**½ Dewey Martin, Aldo Ray, Anne Collins, Stewart Petersen. Adventure film for family viewing. Based on *On to Oregon* by Honore Morrow, it relates the crisis-filled journey of six young brothers and sisters led by a 13-year-old boy across the wild terrain of America during the 1840s. (Dir: Earl Bellamy, 100 mins.)†

Seven Angry Men (1955)*** Raymond Massey, Debra Paget, Jeffrey Hunter, Dennis Weaver. Raymond Massey reprises his John Brown role from *Santa Fe Trail*. Tense climax and fine acting throughout bolster this Civil War western. (Dir: Charles Marquis Warren, 90 mins.)

Seven Beauties (Italy, 1975)***½ Giancarlo Giannini, Shirley Stoler, Fernando Rey, Elena Fiore. A paradoxical black comedy written and directed brilliantly by Lina Wertmuller. "Seven Beauties" is a nickname for a two-bit hoodlum known as the "monster of Naples" before WWII. Giannini's scene in the P.O.W. camp where he tries to save his life by making love to the gross German commandant, superbly played by Stoler, is one of the most searing scenes in modern cinema. (115 mins.)†

Seven Brides for Seven Brothers (1954) **** Jane Powell, Howard Keel, Russ Tamblyn, Tommy Rall. A rare treat—an original Hollywood musical which works in every department. Based loosely on a story by Stephen Vincent Benet, this tune-filled yarn tells of six fur-trapping brothers who come to town to find wives after their eldest brother (Keel) takes lovely Miss Powell as his bride. There's a kidnapping and a great many musical numbers before the happy conclusion. The dances by Michael Kidd are brilliant, and the entire cast is delightful. (Dir: Stanley Donen, 103 mins.)†

Seven Capital Sins (France-Italy, 1962)*** Jean-Louis Trintignant, Marina Vlady, Eddie Constantine, Jean-Pierre Aumont. The sins as depicted by some notable French directors, in an episodic film. (Dirs: Sylvain Dhomme, Eugene Ionesco, Max Douy, Edouard Molinaro, Philippe de Broca, Jacques Demy, Jean-Luc Godard, Roger Vadim, Claude Chabrol, 113 mins.)

Seven Chances (1925)**** Buster Keaton, T. Roy Barnes, Ruth Dwyer. Brilliant comedy built from the premise of a poor man who must marry by sunset or lose a fortune. Subtlety and slapstick mingle in perfect harmony in this most sublimely realized of all Keaton-directed fantasies. (60 mins.)

Seven Cities of Gold (1955)** Anthony Quinn, Richard Egan, Jeffrey Hunter, Michael Rennie, Rita Moreno. Routine costume adventure tale about the Spanish Conquistadors's 18th-century expedition to California in search of the legendary "Seven cities of gold." (Dir: Robert D. Webb, 103 mins.)†

Seven Days in May (1964)***½ Burt Lancaster, Kirk Douglas, Ava Gardner, Fredric March, Edmond O'Brien. An exciting suspense drama concerned with politics and the problems of sanity and survival in a nuclear age. Benefits from taut screenplay by Rod Serling, and the direction of John Frankenheimer, which artfully builds to the finale. (118 mins.)†

Seven Days' Leave (1942)**½ Victor Mature, Lucille Ball. Soldiers on leave discover that one of them will inherit a fortune if he can marry a girl who is already engaged. Mildly amusing musical comedy. (Dir: Tim Whelan, 87 mins.)

Seven Days to Noon (Great Britain, 1950)***½ Barry Jones, Olive Sloane. Tense drama about a deranged atomic scientist who threatens to blow up London if they fail to do his bidding. Excellent thriller; suspense on high throughout. (Dirs: John and Roy Boulting, 93 mins.)

Seven Deadly Sins (France-Italy, 1953)**** Gerard Philipe, Michele Morgan, Françoise Rosay. An episodic yet thoroughly enjoyable film dealing with each of the seven deadly sins. (Dirs: Edouard Molinaro, Jean Dreville, Yves Allegret, Roberto Rossellini, Carlo Rim, Claude Autant-Lara, Georges Lacombe, 120 mins.)

Seven Different Ways—See: **Quick, Let's Get Married**

7 Doors of Death (Italy, 1981)**½ Katherine MacColl, David Warbeck, Sarah Keller, Tony Saint John, Veronica Lazar. Gruesome thriller dealing with evil zombies from the netherworld invading Earth. Originally 90 mins. AKA: **The Beyond**. (Dir: "Louis Fuller" [Lucio Fulci], 80 mins.)†

711 Ocean Drive (1950)**½ Edmond

O'Brien, Joanne Dru, Otto Kruger, Bert Freed. Interesting crime yarn about an ingenious racketeer and the many tricks he employs to outwit the big gambling syndicate. O'Brien is fine in the leading role. (Dir: Joseph M. Newman, 102 mins.)

7 Faces of Dr. Lao (1964)*** Tony Randall, Barbara Eden, Arthur O'Connell. Randall's performance is the best thing about this fantasy set in the last century. He plays Dr. Lao, the mysterious magical Chinese proprietor of a circus that comes to town and generates a wave of good happenings. In addition to playing Dr. Lao, Randall plays six other roles with the aid of elaborate makeup and costumes—all performers in the one-man traveling show—he's great to watch. (Dir: George Pal, 100 mins.)†

Seven Hills of Rome, The (1957)**½ Mario Lanza, Peggie Castle. Mario singing and romancing a la Roma. Lotsa Lanza lungwork. (Dir: Roy Rowland, 104 mins.)

Seven Hours to Judgment (1988)** Beau Bridges, Ron Leibman, Julianne Phillips, Al Freeman, Jr. Driven insane after the muggers who killed his wife escape punishment on a legal technicality, a man kidnaps the judge responsible. (Dir: Beau Bridges, 100 mins.)†

Seven In Darkness (MTV 1969)**½ Milton Berle, Dina Merrill, Sean Garrison, Barry Nelson, Lesley Ann Warren. Highly melodramatic tale. Although its plane-crash-survivor theme is familiar, the fact that all the survivors are blind people on their way to a convention adds an interesting gimmick to the film. (Dir: Michael Caffey, 73 mins.)

Seven Keys to Baldpate (1929)**½ Richard Dix, Miriam Seegar, Margaret Livingston, Joseph Allen, Lucien Littlefield. First talkie version of George M. Cohan's hit play, adapted from Earl Derr Biggers's novel, about a mystery writer at an isolated inn interrupted by a crime and various suspicious characters. Neat comedy-mystery, energetically played. (Dir: Reginald Barker, 72 mins.)†

Seven Keys to Baldpate (1947)*** Philip Terry, Jacqueline White, Eduardo Ciannelli, Margaret Lindsay, Arthur Shields. The oft-filmed George M. Cohan comedy-mystery gets a polished treatment here from a top-flight cast. A mystery writer accepts a bet to spend a night in a notorious spookhouse. (Dir: Lew Landers, 66 mins.)

Seven Little Foys, The (1955)*** Bob Hope, Milly Vitale. Hope is a bit more reserved in this story about the real-life vaudeville family known as the Singing and Dancing Foys. Good production numbers and a guest appearance by James Cagney as George M. Cohan. (Dir: Melville Shavelson, 93 mins.)†

936

Seven Men from Now (1956)*** Randolph Scott, Gail Russell, Lee Marvin, Walter Reed, John Larch. Forceful western, the first of several teaming Scott with director Budd Boetticher. Ex-sheriff Scott searches for the gang that killed his wife during a robbery, and Marvin goes along to try for the loot. Tense and unrelenting, powerfully acted. (77 mins.)

Seven Miles from Alcatraz (1942)*** James Craig, Bonita Granville, Frank Jenks, Cliff Edwards. Interesting, tense B picture with an intriguing plot: two inmates break out of Alcatraz and hole up at a lighthouse, where they find German spies planning sabotage in San Francisco. Very well done, with strong performances. (Dir: Edward Dmytryk, 62 mins.)

Seven Minutes, The (1971)** Wayne Maunder, Marianne McAndrew, Philip Carey, Jay C. Flippen, Edy Williams. Seven minutes is the average time it takes a woman to achieve orgasm in this adaptation of an Irving Wallace novel, and it's also the title of a book on trial for obscenity. (Dir: Russ Meyer, 116 mins.)

Seven Minutes in Heaven (1986)**½ Jennifer Connelly, Maddie Corman, Byron Thames, Alan Boyce, Polly Draper, Marshall Bell. Enjoyable teenage film. Connelly and Corman learn about love and sex, while Thames tries to deal with a bad home situation, in this comedy-drama that boasts effective lead performances, though the awful pseudo-pop score sometimes makes it seem like a TV special. (Dir: Linda Feferman, 90 mins.)†

Seven-Per-Cent Solution, The (1976)***½ Nicol Williamson, Alan Arkin, Robert Duvall, Laurence Olivier, Joel Grey. An enjoyable lark! What would have happened if Sherlock Holmes had met with Sigmund Freud? According to Nicholas Meyer, who adapted his own novel for the screen, Freud could have cured the sleuth of his fondness for cocaine and Holmes could have solved the mystery of one of the psychiatrist's patients. Splendid cast. (Dir: Herbert Ross, 113 mins.)†

Seven Samurai (Japan, 1954)**** Takashi Shimura, Toshio Mifune, Seiji Miyaguchi. The definitive samurai film, and a great deal more. Seven masterless samurai agree to defend a peasant village in sixteenth-century Japan, with a few meals of rice as their only pay. The scope of this epic seems to encompass every aspect of the human condition, while projecting a unique blend of warmth, humor, suspense, and horror. Universally acclaimed, this film was remade as *The Magnificent Seven.* (Dir: Akira Kurosawa, 155 mins.) (Also available in a restored 208 min. version.)†

Seven Seas to Calais (Italy, 1962)** Rod

Taylor, Keith Michell, Irene Worth. Admiral Drake, pirate galleons, and war on the high seas highlight this spaghetti swashbuckler about England's defeat of the Spanish Armada, and her laying claim to the New World, circa 1588. (Dirs: Rudolph Maté, Primo Zeglio, 102 mins.)

Seven Sinners (1940)*** Marlene Dietrich, John Wayne, Albert Dekker, Anna Lee, Broderick Crawford. Honky-tonk singer attracts a handsome lieutenant. Trashy tale atoned for by a fine cast, plenty of rugged action. (Dir: Tay Garnett, 87 mins.)†

Seven Sweethearts (1942)**½ Kathryn Grayson, S. Z. Sakall, Marsha Hunt, Van Heflin. Cute, occasionally entertaining musical about seven lovely girls of Dutch ancestry living in Michigan with their daddy, S. Z. (Cuddles) Sakall. A bit too cute. (Dir: Frank Borzage, 98 mins.)

Seventeen (1940)*** Jackie Cooper, Betty Field, Otto Kruger, Ann Shoemaker. Cooper gives a winsome performance as the turn-of-the-century adolescent in this warmhearted version of Booth Tarkington's classic novel. (Dir: Louis King, 70 mins.)

1776 (1972)*** Ken Howard, William Daniels, Blythe Danner, Howard Da Silva. The hit Broadway musical has been tastefully transferred to the screen. The efforts of our Founding Fathers and the Continental Congress to have the Declaration of Independence ratified may sound like a dry history lesson, but it turns out to be an entertaining, touching film. (Dir: Peter H. Hunt, 150 mins.)†

7th Cavalry, The (1956)*** Randolph Scott, Barbara Hale. Good western about a cavalry unit returning to the scene of Custer's massacre. (Dir: Joseph H. Lewis, 75 mins.)

Seventh Cross, The (1944)***½ Spencer Tracy, Signe Hasso, Hume Cronyn. This is a truly exciting chase melodrama about an anti-Nazi who escapes from a concentration camp in 1936 and attempts to get out of the country. Beautifully acted. (Dir: Fred Zinnemann, 112 mins.)

Seventh Dawn, The (Great Britain, 1964)*½ William Holden, Capucine, Susannah York, Tetsuro Tamba, Michael Goodliffe. A hollow adventure set in Malaya right after WWII. Holden is a wealthy American planter in Malaya who finds himself caught in the web of guerrilla warfare and romantic upheaval. (Dir: Lewis Gilbert, 123 mins.)

Seventh Heaven (1927)*** Janet Gaynor, Charles Farrell, David Butler. Gaynor won the first Best Actress Oscar in this film about love in a garret in Paris. (Dir: Frank Borzage, 119 mins.)

Seventh Heaven (1937)*½ Simone Simon, James Stewart. Corny, inept sound version of the 1927 silent classic. (Dir: Henry King, 102 mins.)

Seven Thieves (1960)*** Edward G. Robinson, Rod Steiger, Joan Collins, Eli Wallach. Tense melodrama about a plot to rob the Monte Carlo gambling vaults. High-gear suspense, fine performances; only drawback is a weak ending. (Dir: Henry Hathaway, 102 mins.)

Seventh Seal, The (Sweden, 1957)**** Max von Sydow, Gunnar Bjornstrand, Bibi Andersson. Director Ingmar Bergman's masterpiece about the philosophical dilemmas of modern man. The setting is 14th-century Sweden. A knight (von Sydow) and his squire return from a crusade to find the black plague spreading death across their land. The knight confronts death incarnate to play a game of chess, with the knight's life at stake. Brilliantly directed and photographed. (105 mins.)†

Seventh Sign, The (1988)** Demi Moore, Michael Biehn, Jürgen Prochnow, Peter Friedman. A young couple awaiting their first child take in a mysterious boarder, and a series of events occur that seem to be connected to the unborn baby. A sometimes admirable attempt at an intelligent supernatural thriller, but the story is handled in too matter-of-fact a way to be very scary or involving. (Dir: Carl Schultz, 97 mins.)†

Seventh Sin, The (1957)** Eleanor Parker, Bill Travers, George Sanders. Wife becomes bored while married to a doctor and begins an affair with a shipping tycoon. Remake of an old Garbo film, *The Painted Veil*, but not an improvement. Mostly soap opera. (Dir: Ronald Neame, 94 mins.)

Seventh Veil, The (Great Britain, 1945) ***½ Ann Todd, James Mason, Albert Lieven, Herbert Lom, Hugh McDermott. Superior psychological gothic romance. A beautiful young pianist (Todd) runs away from her tyrannical guardian (Mason—with a limp, yet) and can't choose between her two boyfriends. A friendly psychiatrist steps in. Beautifully set, fine musical sequences, and Mason's portrayal is archetypical. (Dir: Compton Bennett, 92 mins.)†

Seventh Victim, The (1943)***½ Tom Conway, Kim Hunter, Jean Brooks, Hugh Beaumont, Erford Gage. A supernatural *film noir*, made on a B movie budget, that contains some of the most poetic (yet chilling) moments ever seen in a horror movie. The straightforward story line has Hunter playing a girl who searches Greenwich Village for traces of her missing sister, who's become involved with a group of satanists. The eerie sense of foreboding and despair that underscores her search help to set this picture apart from the rather tame A-budget horror films of the era. (Dir: Mark Robson, 71 mins.)†

Seventh Voyage of Sinbad, The (1958)** Kerwin Mathews, Kathryn Grant, Torin Thatcher. Resolutely dull Ray Harryhausen fantasy film is about Sinbad's search for a roc's egg to restore his girlfriend to her former height (before she met an evil magician). (Dir: Nathan Juran, 87 mins.)†

Seven-Ups, The (1973)** Roy Scheider, Tony LoBianco, Richard Lynch. Producer Philip D'Antoni (*The French Connection, Bullitt*) made a shaky transition to director in this undercover cop story. Scheider leads the team of cops out to stop hoods from kidnapping one another. (103 mins.)†

Seven Ways from Sundown (1960)**½ Audie Murphy, Venetia Stevenson, Barry Sullivan. Well-made western starring Audie Murphy as a ranger with the strange name of Seven-Ways-from-Sundown Jones. (Dir: Harry Keller, 87 mins.)

Seven Women (1965)** Anne Bancroft, Margaret Leighton, Sue Lyon, Flora Robson, Betty Field, Mildred Dunnock, Anna Lee. Absurd China-based western, substituting wily Mongols for the standard complement of Indians. Mission personnel, circa 1935, are trying to protect themselves from a barbaric warlord. (Dir: John Ford, 93 mins.)

Seven Year Itch, The (1955)***½ Marilyn Monroe, Tom Ewell, Evelyn Keyes, Sonny Tufts. Monroe is ideally cast as a sexy model who lives in the same apartment building as a happily married man (Tom Ewell) who finds himself thinking and living like a bachelor when his wife goes on a prolonged summer vacation. Billy Wilder handles both his stars expertly and the result is high style comedy. Great fun. (105 mins.)†

Seven Years Bad Luck (1921)*** Max Linder, Thelma Percy, Alta Allen, Betty Peterson. Charming silent comedy spotlighting the talents of pioneering French clown Linder in his usual character of a debonair man-about-town, here dogged by mishaps after breaking a mirror. Inventive, cosmopolitan humor. (Dir: Max Linder, 85 mins.)†

Severed Head, A (Great Britain, 1971)**½ Lee Remick, Richard Attenborough, Claire Bloom. Talented cast works very hard to be chic in this faithful but awkward adaptation of Iris Murdoch's novel about multiple indiscretions among the British upper crust. (Dir: Dick Clement, 96 mins.)

Sex (1920)**½ Louise Glaum, Peggy Pearce, Irving Cummings, Myrtle Stead-

man. A fascinating curio, one of a rash of sensationalist melodramas popular in the early '20s. A glamorous, amoral actress breaks up a happy marriage for spite, but regrets it when the man she loves deserts her. Most interesting for what it reveals about the era. (Dir: Fred Niblo, 94 mins.)†

Sex (1972)—See: **Women in Revolt**

Sex and the Married Woman (MTV 1977)**½ Joanna Pettet, Barry Newman, Keenan Wynn. Sexual innuendo is all in this comedy about a married lady who writes a book about the sexual experiences of fifty others. (Dir: Jack Arnold, 104 mins.)

Sex and the Single Girl (1964)**½ Tony Curtis, Natalie Wood, Lauren Bacall, Henry Fonda. Helen Gurley Brown's best-seller has been turned into an innocent spoof of the sexual daydreams of Madison Avenue types and their female counterparts. The cast plays it for laughs that aren't always there. (Dir: Richard Quine, 114 mins.)

Sex and the Single Parent (MTV 1979)** Mike Farrell, Susan St. James. Light fare about a pair of divorcees with kids who start going together. (Dir: Jackie Cooper, 104 mins.)

Sexbomb (1989)** Robert Quarry, Linnea (Quigley), Stuart Benton, Delia Sheppard, Stephen Liska. Obnoxious movie producer Quarry is marked for murder by his scheming wife. Spoof of low-budget moviemaking is occasionally funny, especially in scenes on the set of Quarry's latest effort, *I Rip Your Flesh with Pliers*. (Dir: Jeff Broadstreet, 89 mins.)†

Sex Kittens Go to College (1960)* Mamie Van Doren, Tuesday Weld, Louis Nye, Martin Milner. A stripper with a high IQ is picked by a computer to head the science department of a college. Ghastly. (Dir: Albert Zugsmith, 94 mins.)

Sex, Lies, and Videotape (1989)** James Spader, Andie MacDowell, Peter Gallagher, Laura San Giacomo. Vastly overrated independent feature investigates a quartet of irritatingly empty characters. Spader is centerstage as an "artsy" type (he wears black, talks vague, and has no visible means of support) who challenges the belief systems of a neurotic woman, her oily yuppie husband, and her sexpot sister. The impotent Spader's metier of videotaping women as they discuss their sexual desires and frustrations is an outrageous plot device introduced as a way for the characters to grope each other emotionally and utter stoically pretentious dialogue. (Dir: Steven Soderbergh, 100 mins.)†

Sex Madness (1937)½ Completely serious attempt to educate audiences about the evils of sexual promiscuity and the dangers of syphilis. A cult classic. (53 mins.)†

Sex O'Clock News, The (1986)½ Doug Ballard, Lydia Mahan, Wayne Knight, Kate Weiman, Joy Bond. Lame spoof parodying newscasts and TV commercials. (Dir: Roman Vanderbes, 86 mins.)†

Sex Symbol, The (MTV 1974)*½ Connie Stevens, Shelley Winters, Jack Carter, William Castle, Don Murray, James Olson, Nehemiah Persoff, Malachi Throne. Sleazy "fictional" biography of a famous blonde movie queen who dates a senator, an intellectual, and has trouble with the studio heads. (Dir: David Lowell Rich, 72 mins.)

Sextette (1977)½ Mae West, Tony Curtis, Ringo Starr, Dom De Luise, Timothy Dalton, George Hamilton, Alice Cooper. The lady who invented sex on the screen came out of retirement at eighty-plus to make a fool of herself. Mae plays a much-married sex symbol who is being deluged by her ex-husbands on her current honeymoon. (Dir: Ken Hughes, 91 mins.)†

Sgt. Pepper's Lonely Hearts Club Band (1978)*½ Peter Frampton, the Bee Gees, Alice Cooper, George Burns, Billy Preston, Steve Martin, Donald Pleasence. Fairly stupid, badly filmed rip-off of the music of the Beatles by performers who had nothing to do with it. (Dir: Michael Schultz, 111 mins.)†

Shack Out on 101 (1955)*** Terry Moore, Frank Lovejoy, Lee Marvin, Keenan Wynn, Whit Bissell. A shameless but energetic slice of Red paranoia. Waitress Moore has got to juggle her dishes along with the men in her life, while striving to fight the inroads of Communism and to remember what the daily blue plate special is. (Dir: Edward Dein, 80 mins.)†

Shadey (Great Britain, 1987)*½ Antony Sher, Billie Whitelaw, Patrick Macnee. A murky exercise in black humor about a mind-reading man with a gift for putting inner visions and thoughts onto film. (Dir: Philip Saville, 90 mins.)†

Shadow Box, The (MTV 1980)*** Joanne Woodward, Christopher Plummer, James Broderick, Valerie Harper, Sylvia Sidney, Ben Masters, Melinda Dillon. The Pulitzer Prize–winning play by Michael Cristofer works better as a film, thanks to director Paul Newman. (111 mins.)†

Shadow Chasers (MTV 1985)**½ Dennis Dugan, Trevor Eve, Nina Foch, Hermione Baddeley. A dedicated anthropologist and a gangly news reporter chase the same paranormal funny business in California. (Dir: Kenneth Johnson, 104 mins.)

Shadow In the Sky (1951)**½ Ralph Meeker, Nancy Davis, James Whitmore, Jean Hagen. Trouble ensues when a war vet's brother-in-law comes to live with him, after being discharged from a hospital with a psychological disorder. (Dir: Fred M. Wilcox, 78 mins.)

Shadow in the Street (MTV 1975)**½ Tony LoBianco, Sheree North. Tony LoBianco stars as an ex-con struggling to survive as a sympathetic parole agent. (Dir: Richard D. Donner, 74 mins.)

Shadow Man (Great Britain, 1953)**½ Cesar Romero, Kay Kendall. London gambling saloon owner Romero gets involved with murder, romance, and jealousy in this tense thriller. (Dir: Richard Vernon, 75 mins.)

Shadow of a Doubt (1943)**** Teresa Wright, Joseph Cotten, Patricia Collinge, Henry Travers. Gripping suspense film in the grand Hitchcock tradition. A niece suspects her uncle of being the Merry Widow murderer. This thriller, one of Hitchcock's best, beautifully captures the small town atmosphere. Screenplay cowritten by Thornton Wilder. Uniformly good performances. (108 mins.)†

Shadow of a Doubt (MTV 1991)**½ Mark Harmon, Margaret Welsh. Diane Ladd, Tippi Hedren, Shirley Knight. Quite good remake of Alfred Hitchcock's 1943 classic, updated to the '50s. Harmon is Uncle Charlie, a killer whose prey is rich, older women. Only his namesake niece (Welsh) suspects her loving uncle may very well be the Merry Widow murderer. Engrossing, right up to the suspenseful climax. (Dir: Karen Arthur, 96 mins.)

Shadow of China (U.S.-Japan, 1991)** John Lone, Vivian Wu, Sammi Davis, Koichi Sato. Slow-moving drama exploring Chinese-Japanese politics and corruption in Hong Kong ought to have been better. Lone and Wu flee a torn China in 1976 and end up in a demoralized Hong Kong. Mesmerizing cinematography is a plus. (Dir: Mitsuo Yanagimachi, 100 mins.)†

Shadow of Evil (France-Italy, 1964)** Kerwin Mathews, Robert Hossein, Pier Angeli. Flimsy plot concerns mad scientist, plague-contaminated rats in Bangkok. (Dir: André Hunebelle, 92 mins.)

Shadow of Fear (Great Britain, 1956)**½ Mona Freeman, Jean Kent, Maxwell Reed. Melodrama with some suspense but no surprises. (Dir: Albert S. Rogell, 76 mins.)

Shadow of the Cat, The (Great Britain, 1961)** Andre Morell, Barbara Shelley, William Lucas, Freda Jackson. A cat stalks her mistress's murderers. Moderately chilling. (Dir: John Gilling, 79 mins.)

Shadow of the Hawk (Canada, 1976)* Jan-Michael Vincent, Chief Dan George, Marianne Jones, Marilyn Hassett. A medicine man uses his city-bred grandson (Jan-Michael) as a ghostbuster to make troublesome spirits go to the happy hunting ground for cloddish thrillers. (Dir: George McCowan, 92 mins.)

Shadow of the Thin Man (1941)**½ William Powell, Myrna Loy, Barry Nelson, Donna Reed. Nick is solving a racetrack crime and, although it lacks the freshness of the others, it's still entertaining. (Dir: W. S. Van Dyke II, 97 mins.)†

Shadow on the Land (MTV 1968)* Jackie Cooper, John Forsythe, Carol Lynley, Gene Hackman. Uninspiring account of American under totalitarian rule, and the two men who seek to foment revolution. (Dir: Richard Sarafian, 100 mins.)

Shadow on the Wall (1950)** Ann Sothern, Zachary Scott, Gigi Perreau, Nancy Davis. Unconvincing murder meller—a child is sole witness to a murder for which her father has been unjustly convicted. (Dir: Patrick Jackson, 84 mins.)

Shadow on the Window (1957)**½ Phil Carey, Betty Garrett, John Barrymore, Jr., Jerry Mathers. Pretty good poverty-row psychological thriller, about a housewife kidnapped by a mentally disturbed criminal; bare-bones script, but effective direction by William Asher. (73 mins.)

Shadow Over Elveron (MTV 1968)** James Franciscus, Shirley Knight, Leslie Nielsen, Franchot Tone, Don Ameche. Predictable drama about a corrupt law officer in a small town and a dedicated young doctor who faces up to him and the town. (Dir: James Goldstone, 99 mins.)

Shadow Riders, The (MTV 1982)** Tom Selleck, Sam Elliott, Ben Johnson, Geoffrey Lewis, Jeffrey Osterhage. A routine western reuniting the cast of *The Sacketts*. In still another Louis L'Amour yarn, Selleck, Elliott, and Osterhage are brothers again, close-knit Texans who fought on opposite sides of the Civil War. (Dir: Andrew V. McLaglen, 104 mins.)

Shadows (1922)**½ Lon Chaney, Marguerite De La Motte, Harrison Ford, John Sainpolis, Walter Long. Chaney is smashing as a Chinese outcast coming to the aid of his minister friend in this otherwise preposterous melodrama; his great talent makes it worth seeing. (Dir: Tom Forman, 85 mins.)†

Shadows (1959)*** Lelia Goldoni, Ben Carruthers, Hugh Hurd. A seminal work for American independent cinema, director John Cassavetes's first feature parlayed the beat atmosphere of the late fifties into a model for low-budget narrative films bursting with personal expression. Cassavetes examines imperfect relationships—tentative, fervent, and cruel—with skeptical compassion. (87 mins.)

Shadows in the Night (1944)**½ Warner Baxter, Nina Foch, George Zucco. Above-average entry as Crime Doctor plies his sleuthing trade against a haunted-house backdrop. (Dir: Eugene Forde, 67 mins.)

Shadows of Forgotten Ancestors (U.S.S.R., 1964)*** Ivan Nikolaychuk, Larisa Kadochni lova, Tatiana Bestayeva, Spartak Bagashvili. Mystical folk drama, shot with a wildly moving camera, about a man who falls in love with the daughter of the man who caused his father's death, but ends up marrying a woman reputed to be a sorceress. Unusual. (Dir: Sergo Paradjanov, 100 mins.)†

Shadows Over Chinatown (1946)** Sidney Toler, Mantan Moreland, Victor Sen Yung. The mysteries of Chinatown are pretty shadowy, but Charlie Chan throws enough light on them to nab a killer and expose an insurance racket. (Dir: Terry Morse, 61 mins.)

Shadow Warrior, The—See: **Kagemusha**

Shadowzone (1989)** David Beecroft, Louise Fletcher, James Hong, Shawn Weatherly, Lu Leonard. Scientists conducting dream research at an underground Arizona lab unleash a monster from another dimension. Starts out strong but soon abandons plot and logic for the usual monster mayhem. (Dir: J. S. Cardone, 88 mins.)†

Shady Lady (1945)**½ Charles Coburn, Robert Paige, Ginny Simms, Alan Curtis, Martha O'Driscoll. Pleasant B musical, with con artist Coburn deciding to go straight with the aid of niece Simms, finding it tougher than he expected. Coburn acts everyone else off the screen. (Dir: George Waggner, 94 mins.)

Shaft (1971)*** Richard Roundtree, Moses Gunn, Charles Cioffi. Black super-cop takes on the Mafia in Harlem. Action-packed thriller with some nice touches and a nearly perfect last ten minutes. (Dir: Gordon Parks, 106 mins.)†

Shaft in Africa (1973)** Richard Roundtree, Frank Finlay, Vonetta McGee, Cy Grant, Neda Arneric. John Shaft busts up the heinous crime crew running an Africa-to-France slave market. (Dir: John Guillermin, 112 mins.)

Shaft's Big Score (1972)*** Richard Roundtree, Moses Gunn, Drew Bundini Brown, Joseph Madcolo, Kathy Imrie. Maybe the best of the *Shaft* flicks, with lots of brawling brutality and almost nonstop violence. Shaft pits his macho badness against a mobster who's iced his main man. (Dir: Gordon Parks, 104 mins.)

Shaggy D.A., The (1976)**½ Dean Jones, Suzanne Pleshette, Tim Conway. Another slick Disney creation, sequel to *The Shaggy Dog*. Jones is a district attorney who turns into a canine at embarrassing times. (Dir: Robert Stevenson, 91 mins.)†

Shaggy Dog, The (1959)*** Fred Mac-Murray, Jean Hagen, Tommy Kirk, Annette Funicello. Cheerful tale of a boy's transformation into an old English sheep dog by way of a mystical antique ring. (Dir: Charles Barton, 104 mins.)†

Shag: The Movie (1989)**½ Phoebe Cates, Scott Coffey, Bridget Fonda, Annabeth Gish, Page Hannah, Tyrone Power, Jr., Carrie Hamilton. Not just another teen picture, this bright movie features a likable cast and a colorful "retro" look. Set in the summer of 1963, the plot is a variant on *Where the Boys Are*, with four Southern high school girls spending their last carefree summer in Myrtle Beach. (Dir: Zelda Barron, 98 mins.)†

Shakedown (1950)**½ Howard Duff, Peggy Dow, Brian Donlevy, Bruce Bennett, Peggie Castle, Lawrence Tierney. Effective *noir* about a ruthless, corrupt photographer who resorts to blackmail. Cogent, fast-moving B picture. (Dir: Joseph Pevney, 80 mins.)

Shakedown (1988)*** Peter Weller, Sam Elliott, Patricia Charbonneau, Antonio Fargas, Blanche Baker. A hip young lawyer and his grizzled cop friend investigate the corrupt elements of the Manhattan police force in this wonderfully entertaining but logicless action flick. Weller fights his battles in court and beds down with assistant D.A. Charbonneau, while tough guy Elliott handles all the action, whether it's leaping from a Forty-second Street theater marquee or hanging onto the wheel of an ascending plane. (Dir: James Glickenhaus, 105 mins.)†

Shakedown on the Sunset Strip (MTV 1988)*½ Perry King, Season Hubley, Joan Van Ark. An honest cop (King) decides to take on a notorious madam (Van Ark) who has powerful connections in L.A.'s city government. Purportedly based on real incidents, this TV movie has some bright spots, owing to good casting and a colorful script. (Dir: Walter Grauman, 96 mins.)

Shake Hands with the Devil (1959)*** James Cagney, Don Murray, Dana Wynter, Glynis Johns, Michael Redgrave. An excellent cast make up for the shortcomings of the script in this rather grim tale of the Irish rebellion. (Dir: Michael Anderson, 100 mins.)

Shake, Rattle and Rock (1956)*½ Lisa Gaye, Michael Connors, Fats Domino, Joe Turner, Margaret Dumont. A TV performer wants to open a rock-and-roll club for teenagers, but meets with opposition from snooty squares. (Dir: Edward Cahn, 72 mins.)

Shaker Run (New Zealand, 1986)* Cliff Robertson, Leif Garrett, Lisa Harrow. Shaky action pic about Robertson helping a scientist-on-the-run keep a deadly virus from falling into the wrong hands. (Dir: Bruce Morrison, 90 mins.)†

Shakespeare Wallah (India, 1965)*** Geoffrey Kendal, Laura Lidell, Felicity Kendall, Shashi Kapoor. A family of Shakespearean actors tours the land, playing for increasingly indifferent Indian audiences. Finely acted scenes from the Bard's plays are interwoven with personal dramas. (Dir: James Ivory, 115 mins.)†

Shakiest Gun in the West, The (1968)*½ Don Knotts, Barbara Rhoades, Jackie Coogan, Don Barry. In this remake of Bob Hope's *Paleface,* Don plays a cowardly salesman who has to stand up to a band of outlaws when he's mistaken for someone else. (Dir: Alan Rafkin, 101 mins.)†

Shalako (Great Britain, 1968)** Sean Connery, Brigitte Bardot, Honor Blackman, Stephen Boyd, Jack Hawkins. Despite a powerhouse cast, this western (about European big-game hunters in Indian-infested New Mexico, 1880) limps along under the pointless direction of Edward Dmytryk. (114 mins.)†

Shallow Grave (1987)** Tony March, Lisa Stahl, Tom Law. Lukewarm thriller about four college girls who get on the bad side of a Georgia sheriff when they see him commit murder. Talented filmmakers working with a shoddy script. (Dir: Richard Styles, 89 mins.)†

Shall We Dance (1937)*** Fred Astaire, Ginger Rogers. Revue artist and a ballet dancer are forced to pose as married. Fine musical comedy, with great dancing, tuneful Gershwin melodies. (Dir: Mark Sandrich, 120 mins.)†

Shame (1962)***½ William Shatner, Frank Maxwell, Beverly Lunsford. Both Shatner and director Roger Corman should be very proud of this unjustly neglected, low-budget effort. The story, adapted from the blistering novel by "Twilight Zone" writer Charles Beaumont, concerns a young man who comes into a small Southern town bent on stirring up racial hatred. Utilizing actual Missouri locations, the film has an authentic, disturbingly commonplace atmosphere, which reinforces its strong message about the simple-mindedness of bigotry. AKA: **The Intruder** and **I Hate Your Guts.** (84 mins.)

Shame (Sweden, 1968)*** Liv Ullmann, Max von Sydow, Gunnar Bjornstrand. Director Ingmar Bergman focuses on war in modern society, and how it degrades and humiliates us all. Married concert violinists flee to a small island to escape the civil war raging on the mainland. Ullmann is profoundly moving playing von Sydow's wife, trying to hang on to her own dignity while her husband and everyone around her lose theirs. (103 mins.)

Shame (Australia, 1988)* Deborra-Lee Furness, Tony Barry, Simone Buchanan. A thoroughly unpleasant drama which contains the sort of senseless violence common to any grade B potboiler, but which presents it under the guise of a redemptive "message" about persecution and apathy. A female stranger rides her motorcycle into a small Australian town and changes the lives of everyone in it by convincing a young girl to press charges against the gang of boys who raped her; the brutal results are not pleasant to watch. (Dir: Steve Jodrell, 90 mins.)†

Shameless Old Lady, The (France, 1965)**** Sylvie. Delightful, touching film about a 70-year-old widow who makes a late stab at putting a little fun in her life, after living a very quiet and sedate life. French character actress Sylvie gives a luminous and endearing performance. (Dir: Rene Allio, 94 mins.)

Shame of the Nation, The—See: **Scarface: The Shame of the Nation**

Shaming, The—See: **Good Luck, Miss Wyckoff**

Shampoo (1975)*** Warren Beatty, Julie Christie, Lee Grant, Carrie Fisher, Tony Bill, Jack Warden, Goldie Hawn. Insightful, complicated comedy that has something serious to say, often in very acerbic ways, about the morals and manners of our times. Beatty, who co-wrote the screenplay with Robert Towne, gives one of his most engaging performances as a hedonistic stud, a Beverly Hills hairdresser out to bed down with as many of his customers as time and energy permit. (Dir: Hal Ashby, 112 mins.)†

Shamrock and the Rose, The (1927)**½ Mack Swain, Olive Hasbrouck, Edmund Burns, Maurice Costello. Typical interfaith comedy of the '20s, modeled on the wildly popular *Abie's Irish Rose*, about the feud between the Cohens and the Kellys, and their teenage offspring, who fall in love. Exuberant acting enlivens tired material. (Dir: Jack Nelson, 69 mins.)†

Shamus (1973)**½ Burt Reynolds, Dyan Cannon. As a private eye, Reynolds smiles, smacks, kisses, and belts his way through a series of thugs, mugs, broads, and cops while trying to get to the bottom of a large export deal involving government arms. (Dir: Buzz Kulik, 99 mins.)†

Shane (1953)**** Alan Ladd, Jean Arthur, Van Heflin, Brandon de Wilde, Jack Palance. Truly epic western, among the

best ever made. Simple story of a gunfighter coming to the aid of homesteaders has been filmed with amazing skill by George Stevens, with some of the finest scenic values ever put on film. There's action, drama, fine performances. (118 mins.)†

Shanghai (1935)**½ Loretta Young, Charles Boyer, Warner Oland, Fred Keating, Charles Grapewin, Alison Skipworth. Unusual soap opera of an American socialite visiting Shanghai who falls in love with a Eurasian financier. Their love is above racism, but society, even in that exotic locale, won't accept an interracial relationship. Strong drama. (Dir: James Flood, 76 mins.)

Shanghai Express (1932)**** Marlene Dietrich, Clive Brook, Anna May Wong, Warner Oland. The keen eye of Josef von Sternberg crafted this, the ultimate experiment in Hollywood studio exoticism. Its plot concerns Shanghai Lily (Dietrich) and her reunion of sorts with ex-lover Brook on the slow-moving but incident-filled train to Shanghai. When Brook is taken hostage by a scheming rebel leader (Oland), Lily uses her somewhat tarnished virtue as ransom. The cinematography is peerless, the dialogue fine-tuned to camp perfection, and La Dietrich is at her most alluring. (84 mins.)

Shanghai Gesture, The (1941)** Gene Tierney, Walter Huston, Ona Munson, Eric Blore, Victor Mature. A tycoon is drawn into a web of evil in an Oriental gambling den, with his daughter as one of the lures. Arty, slow, far-fetched melodrama, but incredibly lurid for a Hollywood film of the forties. (Dir: Josef von Sternberg, 106 mins.)†

Shanghai Story, The (1954)**½ Ruth Roman, Edmond O'Brien. Americans in Shanghai are imprisoned by the Communists. (Dir: Frank Lloyd, 99 mins.)

Shanghai Surprise (1987)*½ Madonna, Sean Penn, Paul Freeman, Richard Griffiths. Missionary Madonna and ne'erdo-well Penn compete with assorted bad guys in 1930's China for a cache of opium. The story has some interesting twists and turns and the stars are better than their negative publicity, but the movie as a whole waddles along with no strong guiding hand. Executive producer George Harrison contributed the songs and has a cameo appearance as a restaurant bandleader. (Dir: Jim Goddard, 97 mins.)†

Shanks (1974)**½ Marcel Marceau, Philippe Clary, Cindy Eilbacher. A weird tale of a mute puppeteer who inherits an invention that makes dead bodies able to move. Much of this is genuinely creepy (especially if you think mimes are pretty scary to begin with). (Dir: William Castle, 93 mins.)

Shannon's Deal (MTV 1989)*** Jamey Sheridan, Elizabeth Pena, Martin Ferraro, Jenny Lewis, Miguel Ferrer, Claudia Christian, Richard Edson. Pilot for the gritty series about a Philadelphia lawyer, with a weakness for gambling, starting over with a small practice. Unlike most TV lawyers, Shannon aims to get all of his cases settled without having to go to court. Written by John Sayles. (Dir: Lewis Teague, 96 mins.)

Shape of Things to Come, The (Canada, 1979)*½ Jack Palance, Barry Morse, John Ireland, Carol Lynley. A loose but rather hackneyed adaptation of the H. G. Wells classic. (Dir: George McCowan, 95 mins.)

Sharing Richard (MTV 1988)*½ Ed Marinaro, Eileen Davidson, Nancy Frangione, Hillary Bailey Smith, Lisa Jane Persky. Flat farce with a one-joke premise: Three women, all friends, consciously share a boyfriend, divorced plastic surgeon Marinaro. (Dir: Peter Bonerz, 96 mins.)

Shark (1969)* Burt Reynolds, Barry Sullivan, Arthur Kennedy, Silvia Pinal. Burt and the boys look for booty while sharks nip at their heels. Watch this and you'll end up rooting for the sharks. (Dir: Sam Fuller, 92 mins.)†

Sharkfighters, The (1956)** Victor Mature, Karen Steele, James Olson. A naval research team of scientists headed by Victor Mature set out to find a shark repellent. (Dir: Jerry Hopper, 73 mins.)

Shark Kill (MTV 1976)* Richard Yniguez, Phillip Clark, Jennifer Warren. A made-for-TV ripoff of *Jaws*. It features a great white shark dining off divers until a macho marine biologist and an oil company consultant go fishing. (Dir: William A. Graham, 72 mins.)

Shark River (1953)** Steve Cochran, Carole Mathews, Warren Stevens. Brother accompanies a Civil War vet who has killed a man in the Everglades. Good scenery, but otherwise so-so melodrama. (Dir: John Rawlins, 80 mins.)†

Shark's Treasure (1974)*½ Cornel Wilde, Yaphet Kotto. Written, directed, and produced by its star, Cornel Wilde. A fishing-boat captain and crew look for sunken treasure, but not without interference from a band of escaped convicts and sharks. (95 mins.)†

Sharky's Machine (1981)*** Burt Reynolds, Vittorio Gassman, Brian Keith, Rachel Ward, Charles Durning, Bernie Casey, Henry Silva, Earl Holliman. Burt Reynolds is Sharky, the tough cop who leads his pack on the trail of a gangland leader and falls for a beautiful hooker. Good action scenes, and a romantic plot straight out of *Laura*. (Dir: Burt Reynolds, 119 mins.)†

Sharon: Portrait of a Mistress (MTV 1977)**½ Trish Van Devere, Patrick O'Neal, Sam Groom. Van Devere is appealing as a woman trapped in the life-style of a mistress. Everything goes along predictably until an unmarried man (Groom) takes an interest in her. (Dir: Robert Greenwald, 104 mins.)

Shattered Dreams (MTV 1990)** Lindsay Wagner, Michael Nouri, Georgeann Johnson, James Karen, Irene Miracle. Fact-based story about Charlotte Fedders (Wagner), a beautiful yet insecure housewife, married to a notable Washington official (Nouri), who was secretly a victim of battering and assault. Brutal tale lacks impact due to flat, uninteresting direction and a preachy script. (Dir: Robert Iscove, 96 mins.)

Shattered Dreams: Picking Up the Pieces (Great Britain, 1987)*** Hardhitting documentary about the realities of modern-day Israel. Tough-minded film studies the beginnings of the Jewish nation, but stresses contemporary issues including its conflict with Palestinians, the rise of a peace movement, economic stagnation, and other moral and ethical issues. AKA: *Israel's Shattered Dreams*. (Dir: Victor Schonfeld, 173 mins.)

Shattered Innocence (MTV 1988)* Jonna Lee, Melinda Dillon, John Pleshette. Following a PBS "Frontline" documentary on the life and tragic suicide of adult film star Shauna Grant (Colleen Applegate), this shoddy "message picture" was made for television. Her story has been broadly whitewashed so that the girl seems to walk blindly into her cocaine-induced dilemma. (Dir: Sandor Stern, 96 mins.)

Shattered Spirits (MTV 1986)*** Martin Sheen, Melinda Dillon, Matthew Laborteaux, Lukas Haas, Roxana Zal. Martin Sheen plays a father who is hooked on the bottle but refuses to think of it as a problem; this engrossing melodrama focuses on the effect a drinker has on the other members of his family. (Dir: Robert Greenwald, 104 mins.)

Shattered Vows (MTV 1984)**½ Valerie Bertinelli, Patricia Neal, Caroline McWilliams, David Morse. Bertinelli is quite good as a naïve teenager who wants to become a nun. However, once she meets a handsome young priest, her natural feelings and desires toward him threaten her sacred vows. (Dir: Jack Bender, 104 mins.)

She (Great Britain, 1925)*** Betty Blythe, Carlyle Blackwell, Mary Odette. Lavish, stirring version of the epic adventure by Sir H. Rider Haggard, who wrote the scenario and the titles for this production. The semi-mystical tale of explorers, searching for a lost city, who find the domain of an ageless, autocratic queen is still oddly compelling, and Blythe is terrific. (Dir: Leander DeCordova, 98 mins.)

She (1935)**½ Helen Gahagan, Randolph Scott, Helen Mack, Nigel Bruce, Gustav von Seyffertitz. Gahagan incarnates the role of H. Rider Haggard's immortal heroine, who jumps at the chance to retrieve a centuries-old love in the form of a rugged explorer (Scott). The set designs and exotic dance numbers were quite imaginative for the time. (Dirs: Irving Pichel, Lansing Holden, 96 mins.)

She (Great Britain, 1965)** Ursula Andress, John Richardson, Peter Cushing, Christopher Lee. Lesser remake of H. Rider Haggard's exotic romance. (Dir: Robert Day, 92 mins.)

S*H*E (MTV 1980)** Omar Sharif, Cornelia Sharpe, Anita Ekberg. Slick production values, exotic location shooting, and the beautiful Sharpe as a sexy female James Bond-type are the draws here. S*H*E (Securities Hazards Expert) is hot on the trail of international blackmailers who plan to jeopardize the world's oil supply if their demands aren't met. (Dir: Robert Lewis, 96 mins.)†

Sheba Baby (1975)*½ Pam Grier, Austin Stoker, D'Urville Martin. Pam's a private eyeful who challenges the mob when they muscle in on her papa's loan company. (Dir: William Girdler, 90 mins.)

She-Beast, The (Italy-Yugoslavia, 1965)*½ Barbara Steele, Ian Ogilvy, John Karlsen, Jay Riley, Mel Welles. Ancient spirit of an executed witch inhabits a pretty, young bride honeymooning in Transylvania, not the best place for celebrating connubial bliss. Poor. (Dir: Mike Reeves, 74 mins.)†

She Couldn't Say No (1954)*** Robert Mitchum, Jean Simmons. Oil heiress wishes to repay citizens of her home town for childhood kindnesses, disrupts the community in doing so. Pleasant, enjoyable comedy. (Dir: Lloyd Bacon, 89 mins.)

She Couldn't Take It (1935)*** George Raft, Joan Bennett, Walter Connolly, Billie Burke, Lloyd Nolan, Alan Mowbray, Donald Meek. A financier imprisoned for tax evasion takes a liking to a hood who wants to reform; when they get out of jail he hires him to look after his dizzy family. Lively screwball comedy, blithely directed by Tay Garnett. (75 mins.)

She Creature, The (1956)** Chester Morris, Marla English, Tom Conway, Cathy Downs. A two-bit Svengali uses his pretty assistant to summon up a creature that he hopes to use to eliminate his romantic rival. Not scary, but not schlocky either. (Dir: Edward L. Cahn, 76 mins.)

She Cried Murder! (MTV 1973)*½ Telly Savalas, Lynda Day George, Mike Farrell, Kate Reid, Jeff Toner. Widow witnesses a murder and has to face the killer, who turns out to be the inspector conducting the police investigation. Lacks plausibility or suspense. (Dir: Herschell Daugherty, 73 mins.)

She Demons (1958)** Irish McCalla, Victor Sen Yung, Tod Griffin, Rudolph Anders. Ridiculous melodrama of three hapless men trapped on an uncharted island with blonde bombshell McCalla. A favorite of bad-movie buffs. (Dir: Richard E. Cunha, 80 mins.)†

She Devil (1957)* Mari Blanchard, Jack Kelly, Albert Dekker. Unbelievably bad science-fiction tale about a she-monster. (Dir: Kurt Neumann, 77 mins.)

She-Devil (1989)** Meryl Streep, Roseanne Barr, Ed Begley, Jr., Sylvia Miles, A Martinez, Linda Hunt. Drawn in broad grotesque strokes, the humor of this watered-down adaptation of Fay Weldon's darkly comic novel seldom strikes the right chord. Story of an unattractive housewife's revenge on her nebbish husband and the glamorous romance novelist who stole him is underscored by lamentable dramatic overtones that are beyond the minimal range of comedienne Barr, who underplays. Streep, however, does a terrific job of overplaying her one-dimensional role. (Dir: Susan Seidelman, 99 mins.)†

She-Devils on Wheels (1968)½ Betty Connell, Pat Poston, Nancy Lee Noble, Christie Wagner, Ruby Tuesday. The real goods for fans of bad biker movies; gore *auteur* Herschell Gordon Lewis crafted this cheaper-than-cheap, gaudily colored epic depicting the activities of the "Maneaters on Motorbikes," a woman's gang that beats, verbally abuses, or jumps the bones of any male who gets in their way. (83 mins.)†

She Done Him Wrong (1933)**** Mae West, Cary Grant, Gilbert Roland. The best West film. Grant is the Salvation Army officer who meets his match in Mae, who tells him bluntly: "You can be had." Based on West's play *Diamond Lil*. (Dir: Lowell Sherman, 66 mins.)†

Sheena (1984)½ Tanya Roberts, Ted Wass, Donovan Scott, Trevor Thomas, Elizabeth of Toro. The comic strip heroine swings to the screen. Sheena involves herself in the struggle of two brothers for a throne, but the audience would find more drama on a leisurely drive through Lion Country Safari. (Dir: John Guillermin, 117 mins.)†

Sheepman, The (1958)*** Glenn Ford, Shirley MacLaine. Engaging, conventionally heroic western about a sheepman who tries to forge détente in a acting of Robert Morley. Worth seeing for Kerr. (Dir: George Cukor, 112 mins.)

Edward Scissorhands (1990)***½ Johnny Depp, Winona Ryder, Dianne Wiest, Anthony Michael Hall, Kathy Baker, Robert Oliveri, Vincent Price, Alan Arkin, Conchata Ferrell. A benevolent inventor (Price) creates a boy (Depp) with scissors in place of hands, who's taken from his gothic castle by an Avon lady (Wiest) to taste life in a surreal suburb. Wonderful fantasy is a colorful fable about love and acceptance; switching from comic delight to somber reality in a powerful ending that doesn't drop out. (Dir: Tim Burton, 100 mins.)†

Eegah! (1962)½ Arch Hall, Jr., Richard Kiel, Marilyn Manning. Couple of teenagers come upon a prehistoric caveman, who follows them to the city. Ridiculous thriller. (Dir: Arch Hall, Sr., 90 mins.)†

Effect of Gamma Rays on Man-in-the-Moon Marigolds, The (1972)*** Joanne Woodward, Nell Potts, Roberta Wallach, Judith Lowry. Adapted from Paul Zindel's Pulitzer Prize-winning play. Highlight of the film is Miss Woodward's performance, which captures all of the desperate dreams of a widow with two children who has not resigned herself to obscurity. (Dir: Paul Newman, 101 mins.)

Effi Briest (West Germany, 1974)***½ Hanna Schygulla, Wolfgang Schenck, Ulli Lommel, Karl-Heinz Bohm. Seventeen-year-old girl is forced to marry a diplomat much older than her; years later, he discovers that she has had an affair and challenges the lover to a duel. One of Rainer Werner Fassbinder's best films, featuring short, rigidly stylized scenes, intense, monochromatic photography and superb acting. (140 mins.)†

Egg and I, The (1947)*** Claudette Colbert, Fred MacMurray, Marjorie Main, Louise Allbritton, Percy Kilbride. A memorably funny comedy about trials and tribulations on a chicken farm. This picture introduced the characters of Ma and Pa Kettle (Marjorie Main and Percy Kilbride). (Dir: Chester Erskine, 108 mins.)†

Egyptian, The (1954)** Edmund Purdom, Victor Mature, Peter Ustinov, Bella Darvi, Gene Tierney, Michael Wilding. Typical fifties Hollywood biblical spectacular. (Dir: Michael Curtiz, 140 mins.)†

Eiger Sanction, The (1975)**½ Clint Eastwood, George Kennedy, Jack Cassidy. A rambling film based on the best-selling novel by Trevanian. Eastwood plays a college art professor who also happens to be an assassin for a secret U.S. government agency known in this film as CII. (Dir: Clint Eastwood, 128 mins.)†

8½ (Italy, 1963)**** Marcello Mastroianni, Claudia Cardinale, Sandra Milo, Anouk Aimee. A stunningly edited semiautobiographical filmic psychoanalysis by director Federico Fellini as he records the life and fantasies of a noted filmmaker who is having artistic difficulties completing his new project. A complex, stimulating, adventurous masterpiece. (135 mins.)†

18 Again (1988)*½ George Burns, Charlie Schlatter, Tony Roberts, Anita Morris, Miriam Flynn, Red Buttons. An unimpressive entry in the recently overworked genre of body-switching comedies. This time, it's an eighty-one-year-old grandfather (Burns) whose spirit inhabits the body of his eighteen-year-old grandson (Schlatter), a college freshman. What follows is a feature-length Burns impression by young comic actor Schlatter, and not enough of the real thing. (Dir: Paul Flaherty, 100 mins.)†

Eighteen and Anxious (1957)** Martha Scott, Jackie Coogan. A girl has a wild fling despite her mother's overprotective ways and almost winds up dead. Pure soap opera all the way. (Dir: Joe Parker, 93 mins.)

Eight Iron Men (1952)***½ Bonar Colleano, Lee Marvin, Arthur Franz. Absorbing drama of the war in Italy, and a squad of soldiers tied down by heavy enemy fire. Good character sketches, some welcome moments of grim humor. Fine performances. (Dir: Edward Dmytryk, 80 mins.)

Eight Is Enough: A Family Reunion (MTV 1987)** Dick Van Patten, Mary Frann, Adam Rich. Fans of the 1977–81 series about the enormous Bradford clan can play catch-up with this pleasant TV movie. It's Dad's fiftieth birthday and everyone comes home (except Betty Buckley, replaced by Frann) to celebrate it. (Dir: Harry Harris, 96 mins.)

Eight is Enough Wedding, An (MTV 1989)**½ Dick Van Patten, Sandy Faison, Grant Goodeve, Joan Prather, Willie Aames, Adam Rich. Another reunion movie with most of the original cast brought back together for Goodeve's wedding. Van Patten and his chattering Bradford crew are as amiable as ever. (Dir: Stan Lathan, 96 mins.)

Eight Men Out (1988)*** John Cusack, Clifton James, Christopher Lloyd, John Mahoney, Charlie Sheen, David Strathairn, D. B. Sweeney. Entertaining account of the infamous 1919 "Black Sox" scandal. Filmmaker John Sayles perfectly captures the feelings of dissatisfaction an exploited employee feels for his cheap and unscrupulous boss—the film posits this as the chief reason that eight of the Chicago White Sox threw the World Series—as well as the reverence felt for the players by the fans.

Lush period detail (done on Sayles' usual low budget) and a brisk pace. (120 mins.)†

8 Million Ways to Die (1986)*** Jeff Bridges, Rosanna Arquette, Alexandra Paul, Randy Brooks, Andy Garcia, Lisa Sloan. An alcoholic cop on the skids tries to rescue a prostitute-in-distress and finds himself sucked into the L.A. underworld: A brutal, cynical film about a shamus trying to live up to his personal code of honor. (Dir: Hal Ashby, 115 mins.)†

Eight O'Clock Walk (Great Britain, 1954)*** Richard Attenborough, Cathy O'Donnell. An innocent young taxi driver is placed on trial for the murder of an eight-year-old girl. Tense mystery, above average. (Dir: Lance Comfort, 87 mins.)

Eight on the Lam (1967)* Bob Hope, Jonathan Winters, Jill St. John, Phyllis Diller. Bank teller Hope finds a lot of cash, but nobody steals any laughs in this stinker. (Dir: George Marshall, 106 mins.)

84 Charing Cross Road (1987)**½ Anne Bancroft, Anthony Hopkins, Judi Dench. Low-key film version of the stage success. Detailing a transatlantic romance conducted entirely through the mail, the film demonstrates how a business correspondence turns into a friendship; charming performances. (Dir: David Jones, 97 mins.)†

84 Charlie Mopic (1989)*** Jonathan Emerson, Nicholas Cascone, Richard Brooks, Jason Tomlins. Unique Vietnam movie portrays the terrors and rigors of jungle patrol from the point of view of the infantrymen. (Dir: Patrick Duncan, 95 mins.)†

Eighty Steps to Jonah (1969)** Wayne Newton, Jo Van Fleet, Mickey Rooney. A young man on the run from the police comes across a camp for blind children. (Dir: Gerd Oswald, 107 mins.)

80,000 Suspects (Great Britain, 1963)*** Claire Bloom, Richard Johnson. Occasionally gripping drama showing the attempts to track down smallpox carriers when an epidemic hits a town. (Dir: Val Guest, 113 mins.)

83 Hours 'Til Dawn (MTV 1990)*** Peter Strauss, Robert Urich, Paul Winfield, Samantha Mathis. Well-crafted script keeps this thriller plausible. Strauss, a sociopath with a high I.Q. and a low esteem for mankind, kidnaps wealthy businessman Urich's daughter and buries her underground with just enough air for an allotted time. (Dir: Donald Wrye, 96 mins.)

El Amor Brujo (Spain, 1986)**½ Antonio Gades, Cristina Hoyos, Laura Del Sol, Juan Antonio Jimenez, Emma Penella, Gomez de Jereez. The story concerns passionate love affairs among the gyp-

sies. However, the flamenco dancing is more vital and hot-blooded than anything the film's dramatic portions offer. (Dir: Carlos Saura, 100 mins.)†

El Cid (1961)*** Charlton Heston, Sophia Loren, Raf Vallone, Hurd Hatfield. Great battle scenes, superb Spanish settings, magnificent costumes, and the attractive presence of stars Charlton Heston and Sophia Loren. The saga of the hero, El Cid, who became a legend in Spanish history, makes an entertaining screen epic. (Dir: Anthony Mann, 184 mins.)†

El Diablo (MCTV 1990)**½ Anthony Edwards, Louis Gossett, Jr., John Glover, Robert Beltran. The old West with a comic edge—a bespectacled schoolteacher (Edwards) and an old gunslinger (Gossett) attempt to rescue an innocent schoolgirl from desperado El Diablo. Engaging performances and a humorous view of the Wild Western frontier spark this leisurely paced, offbeat yarn. (Dir: Peter Markle, 108 mins.)†

El Diputado—See: Deputy, The

El Dorado (1967)*** John Wayne, Robert Mitchum, Christopher George. Ripsnortin' old-fashioned Howard Hawks-directed western fun. Gunfighter (Wayne) helps a whiskey-sodden sheriff (Mitchum) redeem himself and clean up the baddies. (127 mins.)†

El Dorado (Spain, 1987)***½ Omero Antonutti, Lambert Wilson, Eusebio Poncela. A less surreal but equally powerful version of the story told in *Aguirre, the Wrath of God*, about the 1560 Spanish expedition up the Amazon River in search of the mythical city of gold. Magnificently filmed in widescreen; see it in a theater if you possibly can. (Dir: Carlos Saura, 130 mins.)

Eleanor and Franklin (MTV 1976)**** Jane Alexander, Edward Herrmann, Ed Flanders, Rosemary Murphy. Screenwriter James Costigan has adapted Joseph P. Lash's Pulitzer Prize-winning book illuminating the special relationship between plain Eleanor and her more dynamic, dashing cousin, Franklin Delano Roosevelt. The title roles are brilliantly realized by Jane Alexander and Edward Herrmann. (Dir: Daniel Petrie, 208 mins.)

Eleanor and Franklin: The White House Years (MTV 1977)**** Jane Alexander, Edward Herrmann, Priscilla Pointer. More of the public and personal history of Eleanor and Franklin Roosevelt, dramatizing sections of Joseph Lash's book. The best scenes are those dealing with WWII. Superb acting. (Dir: Daniel Petrie, 144 mins.)

Eleanor and Lou Gehrig Story, The—See: **Love Affair, A: The Eleanor and Lou Gehrig Story**

Eleanor: First Lady of the World (MTV 1982)** Jean Stapleton, E. G. Marshall, Coral Browne. At one point, everybody seemed to be playing Mrs. Roosevelt. If you want to see the worst impersonation of her, tune in for this. The storyline follows the ex-First Lady's progress after FDR's demise, as she dispenses good works and achieves a place in history. (Dir: John Erman, 104 mins.)

Eleanor Roosevelt Story, The (1965)**** Eloquent, truly inspiring documentary biography of Mrs. FDR, graphically portrayed in newsreel and still pictures and especially in the words of Archibald MacLeish's narrative. (Dir: Richard Kaplan, 91 mins.)

Electra (Greece, 1962)*** Irene Papas, Aleka Katselli, Yannis Fertis, Phoebus Rhazis. Fine filmization of classic Euripedes drama about Electra and Orestes' plotting to kill their mother, Clytemnestra, whom they think responsible for the murder of their father. (Dir: Michael Cacoyannis, 113 mins.)

Electra Glide in Blue (1973)*** Robert Blake, Billy Green Bush, Elisha Cook, Jr., Mitchell Ryan. Macho action-pic in which pint-sized Blake overcompensates for his shortness by outsmarting all the criminals he encounters. Fast and violent enough to satisfy the action crowd and full of the trademark Blake bravado. (Dir: James William Guercio, 106 mins.)†

Electric Dreams (1984)** Lenny Von Dohlen, Virginia Madsen, Maxwell Caufield, the voice of Bud Cort. A shy architect who utilizes his computer to court his music-loving neighbor. Playing music which the girl hears through the walls, the computer strikes a responsive chord, but eventually Edgar the computer wants the dream girl for himself. (Dir: Steve Barron, 95 mins.)†

Electric Horseman, The (1979)*** Robert Redford, Jane Fonda, Valerie Perrine, Willie Nelson, John Saxon. A genuinely entertaining film. Redford is a drunken ex-rodeo champ now resigned to endorsing breakfast cereal with a prize-winning race horse. Sonny (Redford) eventually sobers up enough to save the steroid-fed horse from the evil corporate sponsor. Fonda is the gutsy newswoman out to get the scoop, and ends up falling for both Redford and his cause. (Dir: Sydney Pollack, 121 mins.)†

Electronic Monster, The (Great Britain, 1957)** Rod Cameron, Mary Murphy. Interesting science-fiction yarn about a group of experimenting scientists who work with dream-inducing devices. AKA: **Escapement.** (Dir: Montgomery Tully, 72 mins.)†

Elektrela (Hungary, 1974)*** Mari Torocsik, Gyorgy Joszef, Gyorgy Cserhalmi, Joszef Madaras, Lajos Balazsovits. Hungarian interpretation of the Elektra myth marked by stunning tracking shots, long camera takes, dashing horseman, Hungarian folk songs, whips, nudes, and exotic dances. (Dir: Miklos Jancso, 76 mins.)

Element of Crime, The (Denmark, 1985) ***½ Michael Elphick, Esmond Knight, Jerold Wells, Me Me Lei. Visually stunning thriller about a cop who so doggedly pursues his quarry (a psychotic murdering little girls) that he stands in danger of losing his own identity. Far above the standard European policer. (Dir: Lars Von Trier, 104 mins.)†

Elena and Her Men—See: **Paris Does Strange Things**

Elena et Les Hommes—See: **Paris Does Strange Things**

Eleni (1985)** Kate Nelligan, Linda Hunt, John Malkovich, Paul Smith. Nicholas Gage's best-selling tribute to his mother was a searing emotional experience for many readers. Unfortunately, onscreen, this tale of a Greek mother who gives her life to save her children from the Greek communist faction in her village has minimal impact. The intertwined stories of Eleni's personal sacrifice plus the present-day search for her killers by her son, author Nicholas Gage, are clumsily scripted and directed without vitality. (Dir: Peter Yates, 117 mins.)†

Elephant Boy (Great Britain, 1937)*** Sabu, Walter Hudd. Kipling's "Toomai, of the Elephants"; a small native lad claims he knows the congregating place of the elephant hordes. Fine jungle scenes, made on location. Interesting, often poetic story. (Dirs: Robert Flaherty, Zoltan Korda, 100 mins.)†

Elephant God, The (India, 1978)*** Soumitra Chatterjee, Siddartha Chatterjee, Santosh Dutta, Utpal Dutta. A mystery-adventure from director Satyajit Ray finds a private detective and his teenage cousin investigating the theft of a valuable statuette known as "The Elephant God." Pleasant, clever, and rife with wonderful characters. (112 mins.)

Elephant Man, The (1980)**** John Hurt, Anne Bancroft, Anthony Hopkins, Freddie Jones, Wendy Hiller. Director David Lynch's concerns go beyond the hideously deformed Elephant Man and his endless search for love and acceptance. They embrace the Victorian Age itself, a time when, dominated by machines, the upper class came to feel that throwing the proper suit of clothes on a problem eliminated it. The eerie black and white camerawork, with its attention to detail, surfaces, and shadows, and the generally acute acting, create a hypnotic fairy tale. (125 mins.)†

307

Elephant Man, The (MTV 1982)**½ Philip Anglim, Kevin Conway, Penny Fuller, Richard Clarke, Glenn Close. Although adapted from Bernard Pomerance's Tony Award-winning play, this TV production is far outshined by David Lynch's very different 1980 film treatment of the same factual material. There are excellent performances by Anglim as the deformed Merrick and Conway as his sympathetic doctor (both repeating their stage roles), but the drama's abstract treatment of deformity and theatrical stylization just don't work as well on the small screen. (Dir: Jack Hofsiss, 100 mins.)†

Elephant Walk (1954)**½ Elizabeth Taylor, Peter Finch, Dana Andrews. A muddled soap opera. Miss Taylor (who replaced Vivien Leigh) is ravishingly beautiful as the young English bride who comes to her new husband's (Peter Finch) tea plantation in Ceylon and finds the adjustment to a new life difficult. (Dir: William Dieterle, 103 mins.)†

Elevator, The (MTV 1974)** James Farentino, Roddy McDowall, Craig Stevens, Carol Lynley, Myrna Loy. An elevator stalls following a robbery in a high-rise office building, trapping the thief and seven passengers. A stalled drama. (Dir: Jerry Jameson, 78 mins.)

Elevator to the Gallows—See: **Frantic** (1958)

11 Harrowhouse (1974)** Charles Grodin, Candice Bergen, John Gielgud, James Mason. Muddled, contrived robbery caper. Grodin is a diamond salesman enlisted by a mad millionaire (Trevor Howard) to steal millions of dollars' worth of diamonds. AKA: **Anything for Love.** (Dir: Aram Avakian, 95 mins.)†

11th Commandment, The (1988)** Bernie White, Marilyn Hassett, Dick Sargent, Greg Mullavey. Man institutionalized by relatives who want to get their hands on his money escapes to seek murderous revenge (if the family doesn't kill itself off first battling over his estate). Uninspired time waster. AKA: **Body Count.** (Dir: Paul Leder, 93 mins.)†

11th Victim (MTV 1979)**½ Bess Armstrong, Maxwell Gail, Harold Gould, Eric Burdon. Earnest telefeature about a young lady who leaves her job as a TV newswoman in the Midwest and goes to Hollywood, where she teams up with a police investigator to get to the bottom of her younger sister's murder. (Dir: Jonathan Kaplan, 104 mins.)

Eliminator, The—See: **Deadly Games**

Eliminators, The (1986)* Andrew Prine, Denise Crosby, Roy Dotrice, Patrick Reynolds. A man-droid, a jungle guide, a martial artist, and a lady genius all join hands to bring you this nonsensical tripe about dispatching a mad scientist to the fate he deserves. (Dir: Peter Manoogian, 96 mins.)†

308

Elisa, My Life (Spain, 1977)*** Geraldine Chaplin, Fernando Rey, Norman Brisky, Isabel Mestres. Drama about woman, separated from her husband, who visits her author father whom she has not seen in years. Mature theme about memory and love has great performance by Rey as the author. (Dir: Carlos Saura, 125 mins.)

Elizabeth of Ladymead (Great Britain, 1948)*** Anna Neagle, Hugh Williams, Isabel Jeans, Bernard Lee. Sprightly, episodic comedy-drama about the four mistresses of an English manor house in different historical eras; Neagle is less icy than usual, and the whole film is warmly attractive. (Dir: Herbert Wilcox, 97 mins.)

Elizabeth the Queen—See: **Private Lives of Elizabeth and Essex, The**

Ella Cinders (1926)*** Colleen Moore, Lloyd Hughes, Alfred E. Green, Harry Langdon, Russell Hopton. Lively comedy about a downtrodden young lady who relives the Cinderella story when she wins a contest and is sent to Hollywood. There her troubles begin, and she ends up sneaking into a studio and causing general mayhem. Several cameos by important directors and stars. Dir: Alfred E. Green, 75 mins.)†

Ellery Queen series. Although the armchair detective was a big hit on radio and attempted television several times with series and TV movies, the movies never did right by the master detective. Two rarely seen films, *The Spanish Cape Mystery* (1953) and *The Mandarin Mystery* (1936), are deservedly obscure. Following these was a B-movie series with Ralph Bellamy as the mystery writer who used his sophisticated sleuthing whenever his detective dad came up short. William Gargan took over for Bellamy for three lackluster entries, *A Close Call for Ellery Queen, Desperate Chance for Ellery Queen,* and *Enemy Agents Meet Ellery Queen.*

Ellery Queen (MTV 1975)*** Jim Hutton, Ray Milland, Kim Hunter, David Wayne, Monte Markham, John Hillerman. Handsomely mounted and wisely set in the forties, this detective movie launched a short-lived TV series. Hutton uses his boyish persona to give us an Ellery who's a bit of a bumbler, but still canny enough to help his policeman-papa out on a case involving the murder of a man's mistress. Better than many entries in the B-movie series of Queen mysteries. AKA: **Too Many Suspects.** (Dir: David Greene, 78 mins.)

Ellery Queen and the Murder Ring (1941)** Ralph Bellamy, Margaret Lindsay. Why is Stack Memorial Hospital no longer a safe place to convalesce? That's what

Ellery has to discover after the hospital's owner is found strangled. (Dir: James Hogan, 65 mins.)

Ellery Queen and the Perfect Crime (1941) *½ Ralph Bellamy, Margaret Lindsay. Imperfect Queen mystery in which Ellery cracks a case involving stock fraud and bankruptcy leading to a young man's disappearance. (Dir: James Hogan, 68 mins.)

Ellery Queen: Don't Look Behind You (MTV 1971)*** Peter Lawford, Harry Morgan. In this film, Lawford and his American uncle, played by Harry Morgan, team up to crack an ominous multiple-murder case. Mystery fans will enjoy following Queen's clever analysis of the hidden clues. (Dir: Barry Shear, 100 mins.)

Ellery Queen, Master Detective (1940)**½ Ralph Bellamy, Margaret Lindsay. First of the Ellery Queen films that were made at Columbia Studios with suave Bellamy. Here, Ellery investigates a murder at a resort when a wealthy healthnut decides to disinherit his heirs. (Dir: Kurt Neumann, 66 mins.)

Ellery Queen's Penthouse Mystery (1941) **½ Ralph Bellamy, Charley Grapewin. Bellamy exercises his famous detective skills as he becomes entangled in a case involving an Oriental ventriloquist who's murdered after smuggling jewels into America. (Dir: James Hogan, 69 mins.)

Ellie (1984)* Shelley Winters, Edward Albert, Pat Paulsen, George Gobel. Barnyard black comedy played as if the cast of "Hee-Haw" were trying for something a little more sophisticated. The porcine Winters plays a gal who marries old geezers for their fortunes and disposes of them after their wills have been changed in her favor. (Dir: Peter Wittman, 90 mins.)†

Ellis Island (MTV 1984)**½ Richard Burton, Faye Dunaway, Peter Reigert, Greg Martyn, Alice Krige, Ann Jillian, Melba Moore, Milo O'Shea, Emma Samms, Liam Neeson, Stubby Kaye, Kate Burton. Miniseries based on Fred Mustard Stewart's novel about the experiences of different people who immigrated to America at the turn of the twentieth century. More soap opera than history lesson. (Dir: Jerry London, 300 mins.)†

Elmer Gantry (1960)***½ Burt Lancaster, Jean Simmons, Dean Jagger, Arthur Kennedy, Shirley Jones, Patti Page. The ultimate statement about the business side of evangelism. Lancaster is Gantry, a high-spirited con man who transforms the ministry of earnest evangelist Simmons. Lengthy but juicy drama based on the novel by Sinclair Lewis; well-deserved Oscars were won by Burt, director Richard Brooks for his fine screenplay, and Shirley Jones for her tawdry turn as a dark secret from Gantry's past. (Dir: Richard Brooks, 145 mins.)†

Elmer the Great (1933)*** Joe E. Brown, Patricia Ellis, Frank McHugh, Claire Dodd, Preston Foster, Sterling Holloway, J. Carrol Naish. Excellent Brown vehicle, from a play by Ring Lardner and George M. Cohan, about a baseball pitcher who just can't help telling tall tales; he gets involved with gangsters trying to throw the series. Great baseball atmosphere. (Dir: Mervyn LeRoy, 74 mins.)

El Norte (1984)*** Zaide Silva Gutierrez, David Villalpando, Lupe Ontiveros. Two Indian youths from Guatemala flee their country when their parents are murdered by soldiers. Eventually making it to L.A., they almost manage to realize their own version of the American dream. Politically interesting without being polemical, and deeply moving.* (Dir: Gregory Nava, 139 mins.)†

Elopement (1951)** Clifton Webb, Anne Francis, William Lundigan. Crusty individual gets involved with young love. Another sneering Webb portrayal, if you like 'em. (Dir: Henry Koster, 82 mins.)

El Sur (Spain, 1983)*** Omero Antonutti, Iciar Bollan, Sonsoles Aranguren, Aurore Clement. In a small town in northern Spain, a young girl discovers that her father's hermetic, driven behavior masks a long-suppressed secret. A hushed, psychologically acute drama, especially perceptive about the inner lives of children. (Dir: Victor Erice, 94 mins.)

El: This Strange Passion (Mexico, 1952)***½ Delia Garces, Luis Beristan, Arturo DeCordova, Aurora Walker. Biting black comedy from the master of the form, Luis Buñuel, has forty-year-old male virgin marrying a stunningly beautiful woman only to succumb to paranoid jealousy. Buñuel is unrelenting in his satirical swipes at the clergy, at obsessive love, and at a moralizing society. (100 mins.)†

El Topo (Mexico, 1971)*** Alexandro Jodorowsky, Mara Lorenzio, David Silva. An ambitious, fascinating, violence-filled allegorical western about the Old Testament and man's search for meaning in his life that fills the screen with a dazzling panorama of assorted grotesqueries. (Dir: Alexandro Jodorowsky, 123 mins.)

Elusive Corporal, The (France, 1962)***½ Jean-Pierre Cassel, Claude Brasseur. Director Jean Renoir's memorable, bittersweet film about freedom and a Frenchman in a WWII POW camp. In *Corporal*, we learn that men's dreams are often more elusive than grand. (108 mins.)†

Elusive Pimpernel, The (Great Britain, 1950)*** David Niven, Margaret Leighton, Cyril Cusack, Jack Hawkins, Robert Coote. Niven has a high time in the dual role of the dashing Scarlet Pimpernel, who fights for the oppressed, and the hero's cover-identity, a spoiled dandy that no one could suspect of bravery. A resplendent French Revolution swashbuckler. (Dirs: Michael Powell, Emeric Pressburger, 109 mins.)

Elves (1989)** Dan Haggerty, Deanna Lund, Julie Austin, Borah Silver. Department store Santa battles a Nazi plot to revive the Third Reich with the aid of an elf who carries Hitler's genetic code. Pretty peculiar tale at least doesn't take itself seriously. (Dir: Jeff Mandel, 89 mins.)†

Elvira Madigan (Sweden, 1967)**** Pia Degermark, Thommy Berggren. One of the most exquisite, romantic movies ever made. Based on a true story about a young Swedish Army officer around 1900 who runs off with Elvira, a lovely young circus artist. The leads are most attractive, but most of all it is director Bo Widerberg's triumph as he offers some of the most glorious images ever seen. English dubbed. (89 mins.)†

Elvira, Mistress of the Dark (1988)*½ Elvira (Cassandra Peterson), W. Morgan Sheppard, Daniel Greene, Susan Kellermann, Jeff Conaway. Feature vehicle for the popular TV horror hostess only hangs a lot of dumb, off-color jokes (many having to do with Elvira's imposing bust) on a predictable plot involving small-town conservatives and a magic book. (Dir: James Signorelli, 100 mins.)†

Elvis! (MTV 1979)***½ Kurt Russell, Season Hubley, Shelley Winters. Kurt Russell is adept at re-creating Elvis in manner, appearance, speech, and performance. Takes us from Elvis's meager beginnings to the triumphant '71 comeback engagement in Las Vegas. (Dir: John Carpenter, 150 mins.)†

Elvis and Me (MTV 1988)*** Dale Midkiff, Susan Walters, Billy Green Bush, Linda Miller. Melodramatic adaptation of Priscilla Beaulieu Presley's memoir about life with the one, the only Mr. Pres. Although based on real incidents, it plays like pulp fiction, as a teenage Army brat ends up married to the once and future "King." (Dir: Larry Peerce, 192 mins.)†

Elvis and the Beauty Queen (MTV 1981)** Don Johnson, Stephanie Zimbalist. Don Johnson plays Elvis, who is enchanted by Linda Thompson, a Memphis beauty queen. Linda's job during the five-year affair is to keep Elvis from drugs, but mostly it's a losing battle. (Dir: Gus Trikonis, 104 mins.)

Elvis: That's the Way It Is (1970)*** Elvis Presley. Good backstage examination of

Presley preparing his club act and taking it on the road. Not too objective, but useful and informative about the anatomy of showmanship. (Dir: Denis Sanders, 107 mins.)†

Emanon (1986)* Stuart Paul, Cheryl M. Lynn, Jeremy Miller, Patrick Wright, Tallie Cochrane. Mysterious Bowery bum named "Emanon" (try spelling it backwards) helps a crippled rich boy and his mother save their fashion design business. Not nearly as heartwarming as it thinks it is. (Dir: Stuart Paul, 98 mins.)†

Embassy (Great Britain, 1972)** Richard Roundtree, Max von Sydow, Chuck Connors, Ray Milland, Broderick Crawford. Verbose spy-pic. A Russian defector wants to come in out of the cold, but the KGB turns up the heat while the good-guy agents play spy games with the Russians. (Dir: Gordon Hessler, 90 mins.)†

Embassy (MTV 1985)**½ Nick Mancuso, Blanche Baker, Eli Wallach, Sam Wanamaker, Richard Masur. Concerns an American tourist accused of murder and a pair of defectors who may or may not be the real culprits. (Dir: Robert Lewis, 104 mins.)

Embryo (1976)** Rock Hudson, Barbara Carrera, Diane Ladd, Roddy McDowall. An unusual sci-fi premise does not get the inspired treatment it merits. A woman grown artificially outside the womb starts aging at an alarming rate. Carrera is scary as the experiment gone awry. AKA: **Created to Kill.** (Dir: Ralph Nelson, 104 mins.)†

Emerald Forest, The (1985)*** Powers Boothe, Charley Boorman, Dira Pass, Meg Foster. Director John Boorman (*Excalibur*) works his visual magic again in this tale of an engineer in Brazil whose son is kidnapped by the local Indians. When he finds his son ten years later, he discovers that the boy has become a full-fledged member of the tribe. As the father learns about their unique society, the film conveys a sense of respect for the natives as well as portraying the tragedy of the boy caught between two worlds. (113 mins.)†

Emergency (MTV 1972)** Robert Fuller, Kevin Tighe, Bobby Troop, Randolph Mantooth, Julie London. A rescue squad covers a barrage of accidents—auto crashes, a tunnel cave-in, and even a high-wire accident victim. Pilot for the TV series. (Dir: Jack Webb, 100 mins.)

Emergency (MTV 1979)** Randy Mantooth, Kevin Tighe, Deidre Lenihan, Patty McCormack. Gage and DeSoto are reunited. This time they are attending a paramedics' convention in San Francisco and become involved with two female paramedics from the Bay area. (Dir: Georg Fenady, 100 mins.)

Emergency Room (MTV 1983)** Sarah Purcell, LeVar Burton, Gary Frank, Penny Peyser, Paul Stewart, Kenneth Kimmins, Julie Sommars, Gary Lockwood, Conchata Ferrell. Shades of *Medical Center* and *Ben Casey*, this routine visit to a busy hospital E.R. stars the freshly scrubbed (and never quite convincing) Purcell as the caring but firm head doctor. (Dir: Lee H. Katzin, 96 mins.)

Emergency Ward—See: *Carey Treatment, The*

Emergency Wedding (1950)** Larry Parks, Barbara Hale. Silly little comedy about a couple who love each other but don't like each other enough to make a go of their marriage. (Dir: Edward Buzzell, 78 mins.)

Emigrants, The (Sweden, 1971)**** Max von Sydow, Liv Ullmann, Eddie Axberg, Svenolof Bern. Profoundly touching story about the hardships of a Swedish peasant family who came to America's Midwest in the middle of the 19th century. Pace is slow and lyrical. Acting by everyone is subtle and emotional. A stirring reaffirmation of the faith, bravery, and inner strength of human beings. (Dir: Jan Troell, 148 mins.)

Emil and the Detectives (Germany, 1931)***½ Rolf Wenkhaus, Fritz Rasp, Olga Engl, Kaethe Haack, Inge Lundgut. The best adaptation of Erich Kastner's classic children's novel. Young Emil engages the entire child population of Berlin to track down a nefarious thief who robbed him. Gently comic, well paced, filled with action and adventure. Both adults and children will love it. (73 mins.)

Emil and the Detectives (1964)**½ Walter Moseby, Walter Slezak, Bryan Russell. When a young boy is robbed en route to visit his aunt, he decides to catch the crook. Instead of calling the cops, he teams up with kid detectives. (Dir: Peter Tewksbury, 99 mins.)

Eminent Domain (U.S.-Britain-Poland-Canada, 1990)** Donald Sutherland, Anne Archer, Johdi May, Paul Freeman. Disappointing paranoia thriller set in Communist Warsaw in 1979. Sutherland is a secure politburo member until one day all his privileges are stripped away without reason. The dated story takes a backseat to the stately Warsaw locations. (Dir: John Irvin, 102 mins.)†

Emissary, The (South Africa, 1989)** Ted LePlat, Terry Norton, Andre Jacobs, Robert Vaughn. KGB agents attempt to force a U.S. diplomat in Africa to work for them by threatening his wife. Low-key political thriller. (Dir: Jan Scholtz, 94 mins.)†

Emitai (Senegal, 1971)*** Robert Fontaine, Michel Remaudeau, Pierre Blanchard, Ibou Camara, Ousmane Camara. A mystical African tribe is forced to join the ranks of the French army in WWII: The women in the village begin a resistance fight against their colonizers. Director Ousmane Sebene explores the myths, rituals, and history of the Diolas. (101 mins.)

Emma (1932)***½ Marie Dressler, Richard Cromwell, Myrna Loy, Jean Hersholt, John Miljan. Heartwarming melodrama. Dressler was Oscar-nominated here as a devoted nanny whose strength of character eventually attracts the attention of the head of the household. (Dir: Clarence Brown, 73 mins.)

Emma Mae (1976)**½ Jerri Hayes, Ernest Williams II, Charles David Brooks III, Eddie Allen. Black girl from the deep South comes to Los Angeles to attend college and moves in with cousins in a ghetto neighborhood. Culture clashes ensue as this smart girl is led astray. Worth seeing. Misleadingly retitled **Black Sister's Revenge** on video. (Dir: Jamaa Fanaka, 100 mins.)†

Emmanuelle (France, 1974)**½ Sylvia Kristel, Marika Green, Daniel Sarky, Alain Cuny, Jeanne Colletin, Christine Boisson. This is a very lush soft-core film about a nice young woman whose libertine husband urges her to explore all the possibilities of sex. (Dir: Just Jaeckin, 92 mins.)†

Emmanuelle 4 (France, 1984)* Sylvia Kristel, Mia Nygren, Patrick Bauchau. The most ludicrous plot-premise yet: trying to escape her ex-lover, Kristel undergoes extensive surgery, becoming (surprise of surprises!) a different, younger actress. (Dir: Francis Giacobetti, 95 mins.)†

Emmanuelle—The Joys of a Woman (France, 1976)* Sylvia Kristel, Umberto Orsini, Catherine Rivet, Frederic Lagache. Tepid sequel that continues the exploits of the screen's leading sexual adventuress. (Dir: Francis Giacobetti, 92 mins.)†

Emma—Queen of the South Seas (MTV 1988)*½ Barbara Carrera, Steve Bisley, Hal Holbrook. Based on the true story of an important woman in the colonial struggles of nineteenth-century Samoa, this bloated TV movie proves once again that fiction is duller than life. (Dir: John Banas, 200 mins.)

Emperor Jones, The (1933)*** Paul Robeson, Dudley Digges, Frank Wilson. Adaptation of the expressionistic O'Neill play, with the great Robeson. Director Dudley Murphy added a lot of material explaining how hustler Jones got to be an emperor; surprisingly, these additional realistic details of a southern black on the make and on the road are the best parts of the film. (72 mins.)†

Emperor of the North (1973)*½ Lee Marvin, Ernest Borgnine, Keith Carradine. A

311

sadistic, violent film with a pretentious script. The setting is Oregon in 1933. Marvin is a train-riding hobo; Carradine is his would-be protégé; Borgnine is the brutal conductor who threatens to kill any freeloaders who want to hop his freight. (Dir: Robert Aldrich, 120 mins.)

Emperor's Candlesticks, The (1937)**½ William Powell, Luise Rainer, Robert Young, Maureen O'Sullivan, Frank Morgan, Douglas Dumbrille, E. E. Clive. WWI spy romance set in czarist Russia and Vienna, has dashing Powell falling in love with his opposite number Rainer. From a story by Baroness Orczy. (Dir: George Fitzmaurice, 89 mins.)

Emperor Waltz, The (1948)*** Bing Crosby, Joan Fontaine. Pleasing operetta finds Bing as a phonograph salesman trying to sell one to Emperor Franz Joseph of Austria, and wooing a countess on the side. (Dir: Billy Wilder, 106 mins.)

Empire of Passion, The (France-Japan, 1976)*** Tatsuya Fuji, Eiko Matsuda, Aoi Nakajima, Meika Seri. Japan's most compulsive commercial avant-gardist, Director Nagisa Oshima (Boy, The Ceremony), makes a companion piece to his In the Realm of the Senses that is punctiliously traditional. It's a rendition of the Double Indemnity plot told as a Japanese ghost story. (105 mins.)

Empire of the Ants (1977)* Joan Collins, Robert Lansing, John David Carson, Albert Salmi, Robert Pine. Ludicrous Big-Bug flick in which the unstoppable Collins hit another low point of her career. She plays a tough tour guide shepherding tourists around a vacation paradise that turns into hell when ants slurp up radioactive waste and become mankind's masters. (Dir: Bert I. Gordon, 90 mins.)†

Empire of the Sun (1987)**½ Christian Bale, John Malkovich, Miranda Richardson, Nigel Havers. This epic of wartime China opens on a bold note, grandly presenting the turmoil of the Japanese invasion of Shanghai; Bale plays an English boy who is separated from his parents and has to survive in an internment camp, with the aid of morally ambiguous Basie (Malkovich). (Dir: Steven Spielberg, 152 mins.)†

Empire State (Great Britain, 1987)*½ Ray McAnally, Cathryn Harrison, Martin Landau. A dud that follows the lines of several uninteresting characters whose lives intersect at a club called Empire State, where anything can happen, and nothing does, until the concluding brutal fight/shoot-out. (Dir: Ron Peck, 102 mins.)†

Empire Strikes Back, The (1980)*** Mark Hamill, Harrison Ford, Carrie Fisher, Billy Dee Williams, Alec Guinness, Frank Oz, David Prowse, Anthony Daniels. Continuation of the Star Wars saga is engrossing entertainment and almost nonstop action. Princess Leia falls in love with brash Han Solo (Ford), Luke (Hamill) learns how to use the Force, Darth Vader (Prowse) reveals a shocking secret, C-3PO (Daniels) manages to fall apart and be put back together. A masterpiece of special effects as rendered by a team of experts, and almost everything an action fantasy should be. (Dir: Irvin Kershner, 118 mins.)†

Employees Entrance (1933)*** Warren William, Loretta Young, Wallace Ford, Alice White, Allen Jenkins. Sharp, racy comedy-drama of the lives of people working in a big department store. William is terrific as the obsessed store manager, and White is a standout as what can only be described as a bimbo. Frank treatment of sex in this pre-Production Code movie. (Dir: Roy Del Ruth, 75 mins.)

Empress Yang Kwei Fei, The (Japan, 1955)*** Masayuki Mori, Machiko Kyo, So Yamamura, Sakae Ozawa. Beautifully costumed, designed, and photographed tale of Chinese emperor marrying a handmaiden who incurs the scorn and contempt of the courtiers around her. Lavish look at prejudice and snobbery by master director Kenji Mizoguchi. AKA: The Princess Yang Kwei Fei. (125 mins.)

Empty Canvas, The (1964)*½ Bette Davis, Horst Buchholz, Catherine Spaak. Based on an Alberto Moravia novel. Mama Bette tries to keep a tight rein on her son (Buchholz) who's absolutely obsessed with young and spicy Catherine Spaak. There's a great deal of silly dialogue and some graphic sex scenes (for 1964). (Dir: Damiano Damiani, 118 mins.)†

Enchanted April (1935)**½ Ann Harding, Katherine Alexander, Frank Morgan, Reginald Owen, Ralph Forbes. Off-beat romantic comedy-drama of a group of women who rent an Italian villa for a month, intending to get away from men (naturally, they don't succeed!). Unusual and intelligent. (Dir: Harry Beaumont, 66 mins.)

Enchanted Cottage, The (1945)*** Robert Young, Dorothy McGuire. Two people are thrown together and find love in their mutual unhappiness. Sensitive, touching romantic drama. (Dir: John Cromwell, 91 mins.)

Enchanted Desna, The (U.S.S.R., 1964)*** Yevgeni Samoilov, Volodya Gontcharov, Zinaida Kirienkova, V. Orlovsky. On leave from the horrors of WWII, a soldier finds solace in the memories of the Ukraine of his youth, dreaming of its peace and beauty. Excellently directed by Julia Solntseva from detailed screenplays written by her late husband, famed director Alexander Dovzhenko; the last and best of three of his unfilmed works completed by his widow. (81 mins.)

Enchanted Forest (1945)**½ Edmund Lowe, Billy Severn, Harry Davenport, Brenda Joyce. Good children's story about a disaffected youngster who learns about life from an old man who lives with the animals in the forest. (Dir: Lew Landers, 78 mins.)

Enchanted Island (1958)*½ Jane Powell, Dana Andrews, Don Dubbins, Arthur Shields. Herman Melville's *Typee* badly brought to the screen. About two runaway sailors who live among a tribe of cannibals. If one can accept Jane Powell as a blue-eyed native girl, this will suffice. (Dir: Allan Dwan, 94 mins.)†

Enchantment (1948)*** David Niven, Teresa Wright, Evelyn Keyes, Farley Granger. Occasionally interesting story about a doddering old colonel (Niven) who relives his romantic past via the reverie route. The flashbacks are triggered by Niven's grandson's romantic problems. (Dir: Irving Reis, 102 mins.)

Encore (Great Britain, 1952)***½ Glynis Johns, Kay Walsh, Nigel Patrick. Three Somerset Maugham stories—a playboy tries to get money from his brother; a spinster makes things rough on ship passengers; and a high-dive artist has a fear of an accident. Excellent entertainment. (Dir: Pat Jackson, 90 mins.)†

Encounters in the Night—See: **Intimate Encounters**

End, The (1978)**½ Burt Reynolds, Dom DeLuise, Sally Field, Kristy McNichol, Carl Reiner, Norman Fell, Pat O'Brien, David Steinberg, Joanne Woodward. An outrageous comedy about a man dying of cancer, and his attempt to set his life straight before he does himself in. (Dir: Burt Reynolds, 101 mins.)†

Endangered Species (1982)*** Robert Urich, JoBeth Williams, Paul Dooley, Hoyt Axton, Peter Coyote, Marin Kanter, Gailord Sartain. Cattle ranchers in Colorado find cattle killed and mutilated. A retired New York detective arrives on the scene and together with a courageous newspaper publisher and a lady sheriff begins to unravel the mystery that involves secret experiments. Too many plot threads, but offbeat material and good performances. (Dir: Alan Rudolph, 97 mins.)†

Endless Game, The (MTV 1990)** Albert Finney, George Segal, Ian Holm, Anthony Quayle, Kristin Scott Thomas. British secret agent Finney is driven, despite government opposition, to find out the truth behind the murder of his former lover and fellow agent. Obscure Cold War thriller. (Dir: Bryan Forbes, 100 mins.)†

Endless Love (1981)** Brooke Shields, Martin Hewitt, Shirley Knight, Don Murray, Richard Kiley. Brooke Shields is asked to do little more than look beautiful, but newcomer Martin Hewitt has to carry the burden of acting out a boy's obsession for her that turns into madness (he isn't up to it). (Dir: Franco Zeffirelli, 115 mins.)†

Endless Night (Great Britain, 1971)*** Hayley Mills, Hywel Bennett, Britt Ekland, George Sanders, Per Oscarsson, Lois Maxwell, Peter Bowles. A rich American girl marries a chauffeur, but madness and a murder scheme become the couple's unexpected guests in their new dream house in this artful thriller. (Dir: Sidney Gilliat, 99 mins.)†

Endless Summer, The (1966)***½ This lovely feature-length documentary about the joys of surfing around the world is a good one. Director, cinematographer, writer Bruce Brown is largely responsible for the glorious, lyrical footage which captures the exhilaration and the danger of this sport. (Dir: Bruce Brown, 95 mins.)†

End of a Day, The (France, 1939)***½ Louis Jouvet. A moving and sensitive film by the great French director Julien Duvivier. Louis Jouvet stars in the award-winning drama of a group of actors playing out their final scenes in a retirement home. (95 mins.)

End of Innocence, The (1990)***½ Dyan Cannon, John Heard, George Coe, Lola Mason, Rebecca Schaeffer, Steve Meadows. The stages of a woman's life from birth to adult breakdown and recovery are creatively interpreted in star-writer Cannon's powerful feature directorial debut. (Dir: Dyan Cannon, 102 mins.)†

End of St. Petersburg, The (U.S.S.R., 1927)***½ Ivan Chuvelov, Vera Baranovskaya, A. P. Khristiakov, V. Obolednski. In 1917 Russia, an unschooled peasant boy goes to St. Petersburg and witnesses the October Revolution. Film commissioned by the Soviet government puts a human face on the revolution and contains some extraordinary montages. (Dir: Vsevolod Pudovkin, 122 mins.)†

End of Summer, The (Japan, 1961)***½ Ganjiro Nakamura, Setsuko Hara, Yoko Tsukasa, Yumi Shirakawa, Michiyo Aratama. Somber film by Yasujiro Ozu about three daughters objecting to their elderly father's reuniting with his former mistress. Lyrical beginning slowly changes to moody, unsettling study of family relationships. Ozu at the top of his form; Nakamura is a standout as the old man. AKA: **Early Autumn.** (103 mins.)

End of the Affair, The (Great Britain,

313

1955)*** Deborah Kerr, Van Johnson, John Mills. Well-acted although overlong story of a love affair between an American and the wife of a British civil servant. Based on a Graham Greene novel. (Dir: Edward Dmytryk, 106 mins.)

End of the Game (West Germany-Italy, 1976)**½ Jon Voight, Jacqueline Bisset, Robert Shaw, Martin Ritt. Confusing murder melodrama with fine performances. Director Ritt takes a leading role in this film, and he's quite good as a policeman who tries to prove an old friend of his from his youth killed a woman thirty years ago. AKA: **Getting Away with Murder**. (Dir: Maximilian Schell, 103 mins.)

End of the Line (1988)** Wilford Brimley, Levon Helm, Mary Steenburgen, Barbara Barrie, Henderson Forsythe, Bob Balaban, Kevin Bacon, Holly Hunter. This well-intentioned effort has a fine slice-of-life first half hour, but then dies a slow and painful death as it becomes a comedy about the foibles of big business. Brimley and Helm star as two railroad employees who get laid off and subsequently decide to journey from Arkansas to Chicago to discuss the matter with the head of the corporation. (Dir: Jay Russell, 105 mins.)†

End of the Night (1990)*** Eric Mitchell, Audrey Matson, Nathalie Devaux, Darroch Greer, Sam Bress, Mark Mikesell. Director Keith McNally's quirky yet enthralling first feature is a black-and-white vision about a man who, after a bizarre shower accident, finds his life turned upside down during his wife's pregnancy. (Dir: Keith McNally, 98 mins.)

End of the Road (1970)** Stacy Keach, Dorothy Tristan, Harris Yulin, James Earl Jones, Grayson Hall. A confused, symbol-laden, plangent adaptation of John Barth's book about a college faculty member having an illicit affair with a comrade's wife. Superb performances go down the drain. (Dir: Aram Avakian, 110 mins.)†

End of the World in Our Usual Bed in a Night Full of Rain, The (Italy-U.S., 1978)** Giancarlo Giannini, Candice Bergen, Anne Byrne. The first English-language feature by writer-director Lina Wertmuller is an obscure examination of a husband and wife. He's a male chauvinist and a communist journalist, and she's an American feminist and photographer; their attitudes constantly clash as they review their marriage. AKA: **A Night Full of Rain**. (Dir: Lina Wertmuller, 104 mins.)†

Enemies: A Love Story (1989)**** Ron Silver, Anjelica Huston, Lena Olin, Margaret Sophie Stein, Alan King, Judith Malina, Paul Mazursky. Expert adaptation of the tragicomic Issac Bashevis Singer novel set in post-WWII N.Y., detailing the struggles of Polish refugee Silver to accept life and cope with three dissimilar wives. Silver excels in a difficult part, but the film spotlights the three actresses: Stein as the gentile wife, Huston as the old-country wife he thought dead, and Olin as a camp survivor who sublimates her pain in sensual pleasure. (Dir: Paul Mazursky, 118 mins.)†

Enemy, The (Turkey, 1979)***½ Aytac Arman, Gungor Bayrak, Guven Sengli, Kamil Sonmez, Sevket Altug. An unhappy laborer lands work as a poisoner of stray dogs. Grim drama about the everyday life of the wretched of the earth. (Dir: Zeki Okten, 160 mins.)

Enemy Agents Meet Ellery Queen (1942)** William Gargan, Gale Sondergaard. Ellery's caught in the cross fire between Gestapo agents and the U.S. Marine Corps, both trying to nab some jewelry being smuggled in a mummy case. (Dir: James Hogan, 65 mins.)

Enemy Below, The (1957)*** Robert Mitchum, Curt Jurgens. Interesting WWII drama in which an American destroyer and a German U-boat play cat and mouse in the Atlantic ocean. Good photography heightens the action. Superior performances. (Dir: Dick Powell, 98 mins.)†

Enemy from Space (Great Britain, 1957)*** Brian Donlevy, John Longden, Sidney James, Bryan Forbes, Vera Day, Michael Ripper. Another excellent Dr. Quatermass tale from Britain, following up *The Creeping Unknown*. Aliens are taking over human beings in preparation for an invasion, and it's up to the doctor to seek them out. Scary effects and atmosphere. Followed by *Five Million Years to Earth*. AKA: **Quatermass II**. (Dir: Val Guest, 84 mins.)†

Enemy Mine (1985)*½ Louis Gossett, Jr., Dennis Quaid, Brion James, Richard Marcus, Carolyn McCormick, Bumper Robinson. A cosmic *Defiant Ones* tale about an all-American space guy and an alien hermaphroditic lizard who must overcome antipathy in order to survive. (Dir: Wolfgang Petersen, 112 mins.)†

Enemy of the People, An (1976)***½ Steve McQueen, Bibi Andersson. An outstanding adaptation of Henrik Ibsen's classic play about a Norwegian doctor whose townspeople turn against him. Strangely suppressed by the studio that produced it, this fine, if not very commercial, film has never been released theatrically. Don't miss it. (Dir: George Schaefer, 103 mins.)

Enemy Territory (1987)**½ Gary Frank, Ray Parker, Jr., Jan-Michael Vincent. A low-rent thriller about a vicious hoodlum gang of blacks. Getting into the ghetto proves easier than ghettoing out for a rather naïve white insurance salesman, who makes the mistake of irritating a testy gang member whose buddies respond by going on an all-out rampage. (Dir: Peter Manoogian, 89 mins.)†

Enforcer, The (1951)*** Humphrey Bogart, Zero Mostel, Everett Sloane, Ted de Corsia, Bob Steele. Bogart plays a crusading D.A. running down Sloane's mob, which includes hoods de Corsia and Mostel. Director Bretaigne Windust's finest effort, marred only by persistent rumors that Raoul Walsh did the best scenes. (87 mins.)†

Enforcer, The (1976)** Clint Eastwood, Harry Guardino, Bradford Dillman, Tyne Daly. In this "Dirty Harry" outing, Eastwood is joined by a female partner, Miss Daly, ruffling Harry's male-chauvinist mien until.... The mindless violence, here, follows from the mayor's being kidnapped by some homicidal maniacs. (Dir: James Fargo, 96 mins.)†

England Made Me (Great Britain, 1972)*** Peter Finch, Michael York, Hildegard Neil, Michael Hordern. Graham Greene's prescient, ironic first novel, published in 1935, has received an intelligent treatment on the screen. Richly evocative of pre-WWII Berlin, the film focuses on the moral conflict between an innocent British idealist (York) and the decadent Germany he visits in 1935, especially as personified in a corrupt industrialist (Finch). (Dir: Peter Duffell, 100 mins.)

Englishman Abroad, An (Great Britain, MTV 1985)**** Alan Bates, Coral Browne. In 1958, on tour in Moscow with London's Old Vic Theatre Company, the actress Coral Browne met the infamous Guy Burgess, the British spy who defected to the U.S.S.R. She spent a day with him, learning of his nostalgia for British clothes and gossip, as well as his unrepentant attitude toward his treason. Based on this encounter, scriptwriter Alan Bennett has fashioned a superb comic-tragic portrait of a lonely outcast masterfully acted by Alan Bates, with Ms. Browne playing herself. (Dir: John Schlesinger, 60 mins.)

Enigma (Great Britain-France, 1983)**½ Martin Sheen, Brigitte Fossey, Sam Neill, Derek Jacobi, Frank Finlay, Michael Lonsdale. Another spy film that pits a lone agent recruited by the CIA against the vast network of the KGB. The story is a sound one, and Sheen is earnest and capable as the East German refugee turned CIA spy out to get a coded microprocessor. (Dir: Jeannot Szwarc, 101 mins.)†

Enjo (Japan, 1958)**** Raizo Ichikawa, Ganjiro Nakamura, Tatsuya Nakadai. Superb adaptation of Yukio Mishima's *Temple of the Golden Pavilion*, directed with brutal precision by Kon Ichikawa. A high-strung young man destroys the architectural beauty he so passionately admires. AKA: **Conflagration**. (96 mins.)

Enola Gay: The Men, the Mission, the Atomic Bomb (MTV 1980)**½ Patrick Duffy, Billy Crystal, Gary Frank, Gregory Harrison. This carefully documented history lesson depicts the decision to drop the atomic bomb on Hiroshima, the secrecy surrounding the mission, the training of the men, and finally the flight of the *Enola Gay* on August 6, 1945. (Dir: David Lowell Rich, 156 mins.)†

Enormous Changes (1985)*** Ellen Barkin, Kevin Bacon, Maria Tucci, Ron McLarty. Screenwriter John Sayles (*Matewan, The Brother from Another Planet*) adapted a trio of short stories by Grace Paley into this sensitive, beautifully acted anthological drama about three New York women whose lives are at crossroads. The best of the segments stars Barkin as a welfare mom who's almost at the end of her rope. AKA: **Enormous Changes at the Last Minute**. (Dirs: Mirra Bank, Ellen Hovde, 115 mins.)†

Enrapture (1990)** Kevin Thomas, Ona Simms, Harvey Siegel, Deborah Blaisdell, Jane Hamilton. Struggling actor takes a job as chauffeur to a rich man and his hot-to-trot wife, who causes even more trouble dead than she did alive. Mystery thriller with a few interesting twists. (Dir: Chuck Vincent, 86 mins.)†

Ensign Pulver (1964)** Robert Walker, Burl Ives, Millie Perkins. Director Joshua Logan, who guided *Mr. Roberts* to success on stage, hoped to repeat the feat but failed in this sequel. (104 mins.)†

Enter Laughing (1967)*** Shelley Winters, Elaine May, Jose Ferrer, Jack Gilford, Reni Santoni. Carl Reiner's funny Broadway lark about a young Jewish boy from the Bronx who wants to be a star of stage'n screen made a star out of Alan Arkin, but it didn't do the same for Reni Santoni, who has neither the range nor the warmth to do justice to this meaty role. But Reiner's romp is still a funny vehicle and there are a lot of laughs along the way, especially from Elaine May and Jack Gilford. (Dir: Carl Reiner, 112 mins.)†

Enter Madame (1935)**½ Elissa Landi, Cary Grant, Lynne Overman, Sharon Lynne. Opera star Landi marries man-about-town Grant, but he thinks she's more interested in her career than in him. Very nice early Grant appearance with the lovely but forgotten Landi, helmed with a light touch by the underrated Elliott Nugent. (83 mins.)

Entertainer, The (Great Britain, 1960)**** Laurence Olivier, Joan Plowright, Brenda de Banzie. Story about an unpleasant, third-rate British music-hall performer on the skids, photographed against the backdrop of a depressing English sea-

315

side resort. Olivier's bravura performance captures all the shabbiness, banality, pathos, and false hope of the hero. De Banzie (his comforting wife) is outstanding in a fine supporting cast, which includes Albert Finney in a small part. John Osborne wrote the screenplay from his play, which also starred Olivier. (Dir: Tony Richardson, 97 mins.)

Entertainer, The (MTV 1976)**½ Jack Lemmon, Sada Thompson, Ray Bolger. Lemmon gives a moving performance, which is reason enough to see this version. The locale has been foolishly changed from Brighton, England, to Santa Cruz, California; Ray Bolger is effective playing Archie's showbiz dad. (Dir: Donald Wrye, 98 mins.)

Entertaining Mr. Sloane (Great Britain, 1976)*** Beryl Reid, Harry Andrews, Peter McEnery. Fine, literate black comedy based on Joe Orton's play. McEnery plays Mr. Sloane, a young hustler who is boarded by the blowsy, kittenish Kate. But complications arise when Ed, Kate's latently homosexual brother, also lusts for the young boy. (Dir: Douglas Hickox, 94 mins.)†

Enter the Dragon (1973)*** Bruce Lee, John Saxon, Jim Kelly, Ahna Capri. Quite enjoyable, with muscular direction by Robert Clouse. Completed shortly before martial arts expert Lee's death at 32. (Dir: Robert Clouse, 98 mins.)†

Enter the Ninja (1982)**½ Franco Nero, Susan George, Sho Kosugi, Alex Courtney, Will Hare, Zacki Noy, Dale Ishimoto. Plenty of action, superbly mounted, and a straightforward script with Franco Nero, well cast as the Ninjutsu warrior, who takes on a whole scriptful of bad guys including petroleum executives out to control the world's oil fields. (Dir: Menahem Golan, 94 mins.)†

Enthusiasm (U.S.S.R., 1931)***½ Fascinating documentary by seminal filmmaker Dziga Vertov is an examination of the agricultural and industrial workers of the Ukraine's Donets basin. Vertov's first sound film is a commemoration of both labor and filmmaking. Filled with dynamic montages, it is a study of old and new Russia that is every bit original today as it was in the '30s. (96 mins.)

Entity, The (1983)*½ Barbara Hershey, Ron Silver, Jacqueline Brooks. A single mother of three finds her hard-won self-sufficiency is destroyed when an evil supernatural force begins raping her. This *Poltergeist* with a sex drive is merely cheap thrills and things that go bump in the bedroom. Based on an actual case in Los Angeles—where else? (Dir: Sidney Furie, 125 mins.)†

Entre Nous (France, 1983)*** Miou-Miou, Isabelle Huppert, Guy Marchand. French director Diane Kurys has fashioned a melancholy look at two women who try to liberate themselves in the fifties. After barely surviving WWII, they find themselves trapped in stifling, conventional marriages. Leaving their husbands behind, the duo run off to Paris. Based on Kurys's mother's life. AKA: **Coup de Foudre**. (110 mins.)†

Epic That Never Was, The (Great Britain, MTV 1965)**** Charles Laughton, Merle Oberon, Emlyn Williams. A fascinating behind-the-scenes glimpse at a Josef von Sternberg spectacular that was abandoned before completion due to Merle's near-fatal car accident. Long before the BBC's "I, Claudius," von Sternberg had directed this film, footage of which is included, along with interviews with some of the participants in the original movie. Narrated by Dirk Bogarde. (Dir: Bill Duncalf, 60 mins.)†

Equal Justice (MTV 1990)**½ Joe Morton, Sarah Jessica Parker, Jane Kaczmarek, James Wilder, Barry Miller, Cotter Smith, Geroge DiCenzo. Pilot for the series about lawyers at work in the district attorney's office of a large city. Though it covers the same bases as "L.A. Law," the approach is more thoughtful and less soap-operatic. (Dir: Thomas Carter, 96 mins.)

Equinox (1971)*** Edward Connell, Barbara Hewitt, Frank Bonner, Robin Christopher, Jack Woods. A low-budget but highly imaginative sci-fi outing in which a group of overly zealous students lock horns with Satan himself. As they search for their missing professor and explore the various rites of devil-worship, they discover too much for Beelzebub to allow them to live. (Dir: Jack Woods, 80 mins.)†

Equinox Flower (Japan, 1958)*** Shin Saburi, Fujiko Yamamoto, Kinuyo Kanaka, Ineko Arima, Keiji Sada. Director Yasujiro Ozu's first color film is a delicate study of two teenage girls who make a pact to protect each other from any forced marriages their parents may be planning for them. Expressive use of pastel colors and affectionate comedy make this one of Ozu's most popular films. (118 mins.)

Equus (1976)*** Richard Burton, Peter Firth, Colin Blakely, Joan Plowright, Harry Andrews, Eileen Atkins, Jenny Agutter. This is an absorbing adaptation of the stage hit. The basic story involves a young man who has a strange sexual and mystical fixation on horses. The more important plot element is a questioning of the right of the psychiatrist to treat an injured psyche. (Dir: Sidney Lumet, 137 mins.)†

Eraserhead (1977)*** Jack Nance, Charlotte Stewart, Jeanne Bates. An amazing, nightmarish favorite on the midnight movie circuit. A steady stream of horrifying images assaults us during the course of this film, whose plot mainly deals with a man's inability to cope with his mutant child. Primarily for lovers of the bizarre and not, definitely not, for the squeamish or young children. (Dir: David Lynch, 100 mins.)†

Erendira (Spain, 1984)*** Irene Papas, Claudia Ohana. A bizarre R-rated fairy tale, and the first screenplay by Nobel Prize-winner Gabriel Garcia Marquez. Papas plays a gorgon of a grandmother to Ohana's Erendira, an overworked, sweet young thing who accidentally sets fire to grandma's house. (Dir: Ray Guerra, 103 mins.)†

Eric (MTV 1975)*** John Savage, Patricia Neal, Claude Akins, Mark Hamill, Eileen McDonough. Doris Lund's best-selling book about her son Eric's brave struggle with cancer becomes a sound and emotional drama. Miss Neal plays the boy's mother with restraint and dignity, allowing her son to set up his own ground rules in his bout with leukemia. (Dir: James Goldstone, 100 mins.)†

Erik the Viking (Great Britain, 1989)** Tim Robbins, Gary Cady, Antony Sher, Imogen Stubbs, Terry Jones, John Cleese, Tim McInnerny, John Gordon Sinclair, Charles McKeown, Mickey Rooney, Eartha Kitt. A boatload of British character actors are wasted in this disappointing comedy-adventure written and directed by Monty Python's Terry Jones. Seeking the meaning of life and an end to warfare, an inquisitive Viking leads a sea voyage in search of the home of the gods, encountering (among other perils) one of the cheapest-looking sea monsters ever put on film. (103 mins.)†

Ernest Goes to Camp (1987)** Jim Varney, Victoria Racimo, Lyle Alzado. Mild family comedy about a klutzy handyman at a summer camp and the six delinquents that he tries to help in his quest to become a bona fide camp counsellor. (Dir: John Cherry III, 90 mins.)†

Ernest Goes to Jail (1990)**½ Jim Varney, Gailard Sartain, Bill Byrge, Barbara Bush, Randall "Tex" Cobb, Charles Napier. Ernest P. Worrell meets his evil double, a nasty big-time criminal who plans to rob the bank where Ernest works while our hero is mistakenly sent to prison in his place. Some of the gags are stretched beyond endurance, but Varney seems so glad to be playing two characters that he works overtime on his silly noises, funny faces, and spine-snapping pratfalls. (Dir: John Cherry, 81 mins.)†

Ernest Hemingway's The Sun Also Rises— See: **Sun Also Rises, The** (1985)

Ernesto (Italy, 1979)**½ Martin Halm, Virna Lisi, Michele Placido. This affable coming-of-age story is marred by the central character's lack of warmth.

Still, this period romance is notable for lush camerawork and some sexy peripheral characters. Ernesto loses his virginity to a male laborer and then to twin aristocratic girls before finding true love with a teenage boy who shares his love for music. (Dir: Salvatore Samperi, 95 mins.)

Ernest Saves Christmas (1988)**½ Jim Varney, Douglas Seale, Oliver Clark. OK, Ernest P. ("Hey, Vern!") Worrell isn't everyone's cup of tea, but if you don't mind him then you and the kids should enjoy this palatable Christmas comedy that finds Florida cabbie Ernest helping Santa pick his replacement. (Dir: John Cherry, 90 mins.)†

Ernie Kovacs: Between the Laughter (MTV 1984)**½ Jeff Goldblum, Melody Anderson, Cloris Leachman, Edie Adams, Madolyn Smith. The brilliant TV comic Ernie Kovacs suffered a traumatic personal crisis at the time he was building his career, and this TV movie deals with the subject with honesty and understanding. Ernie's first wife ran off with his two daughters, and he went through a nightmare trying to track them down. (Dir: Lamont Johnson, 104 mins.)†

Eroica (Poland, 1957)*** Barbara Polomska, Leon Neiemzyk, Edward Dziewonski, Roman Klosowski. Two tales linked by the theme of war point out man's ability to be heroic when survival is at stake. First part is story of black marketeer who becomes involved with the Polish underground struggle against the Nazis. Second is about keeping morale in a concentration camp high through imaginative illusion. (Dir: Andrzej Munk, 83 mins.)

Errand Boy, The (1961)**½ Jerry Lewis, Howard McNear, Sig Ruman, Fritz Feld. Strictly for fans of Lewis. He's a goofy paper hanger who gets involved in a Hollywood studio management mix-up. (Dir: Jerry Lewis, 92 mins.)†

Escapade (Great Britain, 1955)*** John Mills, Yvonne Mitchell, Jeremy Spenser, Alastair Sim, Peter Asher. Superb British drama about teenage sons of a noted pacifist taking drastic steps to plead for world peace. Thoughtful adaptation of a popular British play, well acted by a good cast. (Dir: Philip Leacock, 87 mins.)

Escapade in Japan (1957)*** Teresa Wright, Cameron Mitchell, Jon Provost. American boy's plane is forced down, so he joins with a Japanese lad to reach his parents. Attention-holding tale which benefits from fascinating Japan locations, good performances. (Dir: Arthur Lubin, 92 mins.)†

Escape (1940)*** Norma Shearer, Robert Taylor. Good exciting melodrama based on a best-selling novel. Story is about an American trying to get his mother out of a concentration camp in prewar Nazi Germany. (Dir: Mervyn LeRoy, 104 mins.)

Escape (Great Britain, 1948)*** Rex Harrison, Peggy Cummins. Fascinating study of a man who is sentenced to jail for what he considers a just act. His defiance of the law, escape, and eventual surrender make this an intriguing film. (Dir: Joseph Mankiewicz, 78 mins.)

Escape (MTV 1980)**½ Timothy Bottoms, Kay Lenz. A fairly suspenseful true prison escape yarn about a young American who intends to be the first man to walk out of Mexico's Lecumberri Prison since Pancho Villa did it in '13. (Dir: Robert Lewis, 104 mins.)

Escape Artist, The (1982)**½ Griffin O'Neal, Raul Julia, Teri Garr, Joan Hackett, Gabriel Dell, Desi Arnaz, Sr. A good movie is trying to escape from this one, which is often appealing, sometimes funny, and features a likable debut by Griffin O'Neal (Ryan's son) as a teenager learning the art of escape to avenge his late escape-artist father. (Dir: Caleb Deschanel, 96 mins.)†

Escape from Alcatraz (1979)*** Clint Eastwood, Patrick McGoohan. One of the better prison films, based on fact and the book by J. Campbell Bruce. It casts Clint as Frank Norris, a prisoner who attempted to escape from the Rock with two other inmates in '62 and was never heard from again. Eastwood is ideal in this type of role, and McGoohan is equally forceful as the tough warden. (Dir: Don Siegel, 112 mins.)†

Escape from Bogen County (MTV 1977)** Jaclyn Smith, Mitchell Ryan, Michael Parks. Familiar yarn about a ruthless small-town politician who makes his wife a virtual prisoner in her own home. (Dir: Steven Stern, 104 mins.)

Escape from East Berlin (U.S.-West Germany, 1962)**½ Don Murray, Christine Kaufmann. Based on a true story, this drama generates a good deal of suspense. Don Murray plays a man who engineers an escape tunnel leading to the western sector of Berlin and safety. (Dir: Robert Siodmak, 94 mins.)

Escape from Fort Bravo (1953)*** Eleanor Parker, William Holden, John Forsythe. Good western film set during the Civil War. The plot concerns the relationship between the Union captain (Holden) and the people in Fort Bravo. There's a very exciting sequence toward the end of the film in which a large group of hostile Indians pin down a party escaping from the fort. (Dir: John Sturges, 98 mins.)

Escape from Iran: The Canadian Caper (MTV 1981)**½ Gordon Pinsent, Chris Wiggins, Diana Barrington, Robert Joy, James Douglas. A middling re-creation of a footnote to history, this telefilm chronicles the swift work done by the Canadian ambassador in Iran that resulted in the escape of six Americans who would otherwise have been claimed as hostages during the long and grueling siege of the U.S. embassy in 1980. (Dir: Lamont Johnson, 96 mins.)

Escape from New York (1981)**½ Kurt Russell, Lee Van Cleef, Ernest Borgnine, Donald Pleasence, Isaac Hayes, Season Hubley, Harry Dean Stanton, Adrienne Barbeau. It's 1997 and New York is a maximum security prison. That's what director John Carpenter envisions in this futuristic adventure yarn that plays like a comic book come to life. Kurt Russell, sporting an eye-patch and a leather shirt-vest, is a master criminal/war vet who has been chosen to get the President of the United States out of New York where he had force-landed by accident. (99 mins.)

Escape from Planet Earth (1967)* Grant Williams, Henry Wilcoxon, Ruta Lee, Mala Powers, Bobby Van, Casey Kasem, Mike Farrell. Coed crew of a spaceship finds the Earth has been destroyed, plans to propagate the species. We don't know which notion is scarier: being on a cramped spaceship with Van, Kasem, and Farrell, or a future race descended entirely from them. AKA: **The Doomsday Machine.** (Dirs: Lee Sholem, Harry Hope, 91 mins.)†

Escape from Safehaven (1988)* Rick Gianasi, John Wittenbauer, Roy Macarthur, William Beckwith. Inept postapocalyptic action (oh, what hath *Mad Max* wrought!) set inside a maximum-security complex designed to protect people from the lawlessness outside. Trouble is, it's even worse inside, as our heroes have to battle the goons who run Safehaven. (Dir: Brian Thomas Jones, 85 mins.)†

Escape from Sobibor (MTV 1987)*** Alan Arkin, Joanna Pacula, Rutger Hauer, Hartmut Becker, Jack Shepherd. Exciting fact-based drama with ample emotional impact. Blessed with an exceptional cast, this WWII drama documents the largest full-scale escape of prisoners from a Nazi concentration camp ever attempted, an escape attempted against almost insurmountable odds. (Dir: Jack Gold, 156 mins.)

Escape from the Planet of the Apes (1971) *** Roddy McDowall, Kim Hunter, Bradford Dillman, Sal Mineo. The third in the simian cycle of films and a fairly good sci-fi story. Hunter and McDowall, in ape makeup, escape from their planet in the very spaceship that brought Charlton Heston to their world two films before . . . but they go back in time to the present, the seventies. Followed by *Conquest of the Planet of the Apes*. (Dir: Don Taylor, 98 mins.)†

Escape from Zahrain (1962)**½ Yul

Brynner, Sal Mineo, Jack Warden, Madlyn Rhue. Rebel leader in an Arab oil state escapes along with some fellow-convicts, and they make a dash for the border. (Dir: Ronald Neame, 93 mins.)

Escape in the Desert (1945)**½ Helmut Dantine, Jean Sullivan, Philip Dorn. A hopped-up version of *The Petrified Forest* which removed the original's depth, added some Nazis for timeliness and came up with a mediocre adventure tale. (Dir: Edward A. Blatt, 81 mins.)

Escape Me Never (1947)**½ Errol Flynn, Ida Lupino, Eleanor Parker, Gig Young, Reginald Denny. Interesting period piece concerns poverty-stricken artists in Italy at the turn of the century. Composer Flynn has to decide between elegant rich girl Parker and faithful Lupino. Flynn is quite good in an atypical role. The music composed by his character was contributed by Erich Wolfgang Korngold. (Dir: Peter Godfrey, 104 mins.)

Escapement—See: **Electronic Monster, The**

Escape to Athena (Great Britain, 1979)** Roger Moore, David Niven, Elliott Gould, Stefanie Powers, Richard Roundtree. This bungled WWII adventure yarn, filmed in Greece, can't decide whether it's comedy or drama. (Dir: George P. Cosmatos, 117 mins.)†

Escape to Burma (1955)*½ Barbara Stanwyck, Robert Ryan. Fugitive finds refuge and romance in an isolated jungle home. Threadbare melodrama, nothing new. (Dir: Allan Dwan, 86 mins.)†

Escape to Glory (1940)*** Constance Bennett, Pat O'Brien, John Halliday, Melville Cooper, Alan Baxter, Edgar Buchanan, Bruce Bennett. Tense wartime drama with an excellent cast has a British ship attacked by German subs at the start of WWII, affecting the various passengers and crew. (Dir: John Brahm, 74 mins.)

Escape to Mindanao (MTV 1968)**½ George Maharis, Willi Koopman, Nehemiah Persoff, James Shigeta. Good adventure. George Maharis stars in a drama about a prisoner-of-war back in 1942, who's perfectly happy to spend the rest of the war simply staying alive in the camp. (Dir: Don McDougall, 95 mins.)

Escape to the Sun (Israel, 1972)* Laurence Harvey, Joseph Chaplin, John Ireland, Jack Hawkins. Poor film about the plight of Russian Jews. Harvey evokes little menace as the villainous Russian intelligence man on the trail of a motley group of dissidents. (Dir: Menahem Golan, 105 mins.)†

Escape to Witch Mountain (1975)*** Eddie Albert, Ray Milland, Kim Richards, Ike Eisenmann, Donald Pleasence. Two kids blessed with unusual powers investigate how they came by their gifts. Intriguing Disney fantasy. (Dir: John Hough, 104 mins.)†

Escape 2000 (Australia, 1981)½ Steve Railsback, Olivia Hussey, Michael Craig, Carmen Duncan. Repulsive Australian S&M spectacle that has political undesirables being led on a *Most Dangerous Game*-like chase by their wardens in the near future. If constant whippings, decapitations, and burnings are your idea of a good time, this one's for you. (Dir: Brian Trenchard-Smith, 80 mins.)†

Escort West (1959)*½ Victor Mature, Rex Ingram, Elaine Stewart, Noah Beery. Dull western has a Confederate soldier (Mature) teaming up with two New England sisters and a black Union soldier in their trek out west. (Dir: Francis D. Lyon, 75 mins.)

Esther and the King (1960)*½ Joan Collins, Richard Egan, Daniella Rocca. When his queen is murdered, a Persian king chooses a Judean maiden to replace her. She intends to influence him in ceasing persecution of the Jews. Long, rambling, Biblical drama. (Dir: Raoul Walsh, 109 mins.)

Esther Waters (Great Britain, 1948)**½ Dirk Bogarde, Kathleen Ryan, Fay Compton, Cyril Cusack, Ivor Barnard. Good drama of the rise of a womanizing scoundrel, with fascinating ambiance and some terrific scenes of 19th-century horseracing events. (Dir: Peter Proud, 108 mins.)

Eternal Evil (Canada, 1985)**½ Winston Rekert, Karen Black, John Novak, Andrew Bednarski, Lois Maxwell. Filmmaker experimenting with astral projection (separating the soul from the body) runs afoul of some nasty souls who move to new bodies when their current ones get old—and their current ones have one foot in the grave and the other on a banana peel. Mildly intriguing mystical thriller, better made than written. (Dir: George Mihalka, 86 mins.)†

Eternal Love (Japan, 1961)*** Hideko Takamine, Yoshi Kato, Keiji Sada, Kiyoshi Nonmura. The pains, losses, and memories of a bitter and shallow marriage are the subject of this compassionate and sentimental look at the life of a woman who weds a man she does not love. (Dir: Keisuke Kinoshita, 107 mins.)

Eternally Yours (1939)** David Niven, Loretta Young, Broderick Crawford. Ladies, if you ever plan to marry a magician, watch what happens to Loretta Young when she falls for trickster David Niven. Good cast wasted on trite material. (Dir: Tay Garnett, 110 mins.)†

Eternal Return, The (France, 1943)*** Jean Marais, Madeleine Sologne, Jean Marat, Yvonne de Bray. Beautiful modernization of the Tristan and Isolde legend, with Marais and Sologne as the lovers kept apart by fate. Atmospheric, stylized film from a script by Jean Cocteau. (Dir: Jean Delannoy, 100 mins.)†

Eternal Sea, The (1955)**½ Sterling Hayden, Alexis Smith, Dean Jagger. True story of a Navy officer who continues to serve, despite an artificial limb. Factual but overlong war drama. (Dir: John H. Auer, 110 mins.)

E.T. The Extra-Terrestrial (1982)**** Dee Wallace, Henry Thomas, Peter Coyote, Robert MacNaughton, Drew Barrymore, K. C. Martel, Sean Frye, Tom Howell. An exceptional fantasy film. Accidentally left behind by his interplanetary scouting party, the creature we come to know as E.T. finds refuge and friendship with a young boy named Elliot. (Dir: Steven Spielberg, 115 mins.)†

Eunice (MTV 1984)**½ Carol Burnett, Ken Berry, Vicki Lawrence, Betty White, Harvey Korman. The family of characters from the "Carol Burnett Show" return for a drama covering 25 years in the lives of the bickering family. (Dirs: Harvey Korman, Roger Beatty, 104 mins.)

Eureka (1981)**½ Gene Hackman, Theresa Russell, Rutger Hauer, Jane Lapotaire, Ed Lauter, Mickey Rourke. The melodramatic plot concerns a prospector (Hackman) who fashions a dynasty of wealth, but then loses his daughter (Russell) to a devil-may-care adventurer (Hauer). (Dir: Nicolas Roeg, 130 mins.)†

Eureka Stockade (Australia, 1949)*** Chips Rafferty, Jane Barrett, Peter Finch. Four gold-seekers in early Australia band together to fight a despotic governor, get public sentiment on their side. Impressive historical drama contains plenty of action. (Dir: Harry Watt, 103 mins.)

Europa 51 (Italy, 1952)*** Ingrid Bergman, Alexander Knox, Giulietta Masina, Ettore Giannini. Director Roberto Rossellini's love for actress Bergman is strongly exhibited in this melodrama; she plays an American society woman who causes the death of her son, and then gives her life over to the poor until she is declared insane. AKA: **The Greatest Love.** (118 mins.)†

Europeans, The (1979)**½ Lee Remick, Robin Ellis, Lisa Eichhorn, Wesley Addy, Tim Woodward, Kristin Griffith. Miserably mounted adaptation of Henry James. There is enough interest in the story, even as bowdlerized as it is, that the film plays itself out without boredom. (Dir: James Ivory, 90 mins.)†

Eu te Amo—See: **I Love You**

Eve Knew Her Apples (1945)**½ Ann Miller, William Wright, Robert Williams. A zippy screwball musical about a girl on the run from her persistent fiancé. Fast-

tappin' Ann is the whole show, and she's a delight. (Dir: Will Jason, 64 mins.)

Evel Knievel (1971)*** George Hamilton, Sue Lyon. Evel Knievel is an American folk hero who's performed some of the most daring death-defying stunts ever executed on a motorcycle. Hamilton evokes the cocksure flamboyance necessary to play the spectacular daredevil who dresses like a rock star and basks in the adoration of his fans. (Dir: Marvin Chomsky, 90 mins.)†

Evelyn Prentice (1934)**½ William Powell, Myrna Loy, Una Merkel, Harvey Stephens, Rosalind Russell, Pat O'Malley, Billy Gilbert. Thoughtful soap opera of a successful lawyer and his dissatisfied wife; well played, but a little too much heavy breathing. (Dir: William K. Howard, 80 mins.)

Even Dwarfs Started Small (West Germany, 1970)***½ Helmut Doring, Gerd Gickel, Gisela Hertwig, Paul Glauer. Unpatronizing tale by writer-director Werner Herzog about imprisoned dwarfs who carry out acts of rebellion when the warden's away. Strange, disturbing, and altogether fascinating. Quintessential Herzog. (96 mins.)

Evening in Byzantium, An (MTV 1978)**½ Glenn Ford, Eddie Albert, Vince Edwards, Shirley Jones, Erin Gray, Patrick Macnee, Gregory Sierra. When terrorists strike the Cannes Film Festival, the celluloid flies. This movie, based on Irwin Shaw's best-selling book, features Ford as a conniving producer mingling with a galaxy of stars. (Dir: Jerry London, 200 mins.)

Evening with the Royal Ballet, An (Great Britain, 1963)***½ Margot Fonteyn, Rudolf Nureyev. The young Nureyev and the ageless Fonteyn perform beautifully together to the music of Ravel, Chopin, and Tchaikovsky. Valuable cinematic record. (Dirs: Anthony Havelock-Allan, Anthony Asquith, 85 mins.)†

Event, An (Yugoslavia, 1969)***½ Pavle Vujisic, Serdjo Mimica. Deeply moving story set in Yugoslavia during WWII, loosely based on a story by Anton Chekov. Directed by Vatroslav Mimica, story concerns an old peasant and his grandson who set out to sell their decrepit horse. (93 mins.)

Eve of Destruction (1991)*½ Gregory Hines, Renee Soutendijk, Michael Greene, Kurt Fuller. Standard robot-goes-amok action film with lots of violence but no surprises. This time the robot's a female, and she's been created in the identical likeness of her inventor, a woman technocrat (Soutendijk in a dual role). Hines is grossly miscast as a military man stalking the creature. (Dir: Duncan Gibbins, 98 min.)†

Eve of St. Mark, The (1944)*** Anne Baxter, Vincent Price, William Eythe. Maxwell Anderson's poetic commentary on war is an often moving, occasionally stilted film. (Dir: John M. Stahl, 96 mins.)

Evergreen (Great Britain, 1934)***½ Jessie Mathews, Sonnie Hale, Betty Balfour. Musical comedy with a score by Rodgers and Hart, gargantuan production numbers. Wildly improbable plot about a young lady who poses as her mother, a former stage star. She then falls in love with the man who is pretending to be her son! (Dir: Victor Saville, 90 mins.)†

Ever In My Heart (1933)**½ Barbara Stanwyck, Otto Kruger, Ralph Bellamy, Ruth Donnelly, Frank Albertson, Donald Meek. Stanwyck marries German Kruger, but the outbreak of WWI ruins their lives. Stanwyck gives it her all in this romantic drama with a downbeat ending. (Dir: Archie Mayo, 70 mins.)

Ever Since Eve (1937)*½ Marion Davies, Robert Montgomery, Patsy Kelly. Marion's last film and a pitiful swan song. A boss's interest is piqued by a pretty girl after office hours, but he doesn't realize that she's really his plain-Jane secretary. (Dir: Lloyd Bacon, 79 mins.)

Eversmile, New Jersey (Argentina-Great Britain, 1989)** Daniel Day-Lewis, Mirjana Jokovic, Gabriela Acher. American dentist travels the back roads of rural Argentina. Occasionally goofy but ultimately unsatisfying satire. (Dir: Carlos Sorin, 94 mins.)

Everybody Does It (1949)***½ Paul Douglas, Linda Darnell, Celeste Holm. A businessman takes up singing, discovers he really has a voice—with Douglas in the role, it's a howl from beginning to end. Sharp dialogue helps, too. (Dir: Edmund Goulding, 98 mins.)

Everybody's All-American (1988)*½ Dennis Quaid, Jessica Lange, Timothy Hutton, John Goodman. Hopelessly corny, underwritten, and overdirected romance follows the 25-year marriage of two shallow characters, a former college football star and his ex-beauty queen wife. Any Harlequin Romance offers more depth. (Dir: Taylor Hackford, 127 mins.)†

Everybody's Baby: The Rescue of Jessica McClure (MTV 1989)*** Beau Bridges, Pat Hingle, Roxana Zal, Will Oldham, Whip Hubley, Walter Olkewicz, Patty Duke. Excellent dramatic re-creation of the 1987 grand scale rescue of the eighteen-month-old baby who was trapped in a narrow well shaft for nearly sixty hours. Without embellishing the facts, this emotional story emphasizes the people who worked diligently to avoid a tragedy. (Dir: Mel Damski, 96 mins.)

Everybody's Fine (Italy, 1990)*** Marcello Mastroianni, Michelle Morgan, Salvatore Cascio, Marino Cenna, Roberto Nobile, Valeria Cavali. Charming bittersweet tale of a retired civil servant (a delightful Mastroianni) journeying from his Sicilian home to the Italian mainland to visit each of his five children, all of whom live in different cities. (Dir: Giuseppe Tornatore, 120 mins.)

Everybody Sing (1938)** Judy Garland, Allan Jones, Fanny Brice, Reginald Owen. Garland is the main reason for viewing this shouting match masquerading as a musical comedy. An eccentric theatrical household puts on a show to get back in the limelight, but you'll be wishing these hams had stayed in obscurity. (Dir: Edwin L. Marin, 80 mins.)

Everybody Wins (Great Britain-U.S., 1990)*½ Debra Winger, Nick Nolte, Will Patton, Judith Ivey, Kathleen Wilhoite, Jack Warden. Hired by Winger to prove a young man innocent of murder, private detective Nolte uncovers a web of corruption in a quiet New England town. Cryptic, artificial, and badly cast. (Dir: Karel Reisz, 97 mins.)†

Every Day's a Holiday (1937)*** Mae West, Edmund Lowe, Charles Butterworth, Walter Catlett, Lloyd Nolan. Even with the movie censors snapping at her heels, Mae's still delightful as a propitious dame who returns to even the score after the police department escorts her out of Manhattan. (Dir: Edward Sutherland, 80 mins.)

Every Girl Should Be Married (1948)**½ Cary Grant, Betsy Drake, Franchot Tone, Diana Lynn. A shopgirl uses her wiles to land a bachelor doctor. Mild, undistinguished comedy. (Dir: Don Hartman, 85 mins.)†

Every Little Crook and Nanny (1972)*½ Victor Mature, Lynn Redgrave, Paul Sand, Maggie Blye, Austin Pendleton, John Astin, Dom DeLuise. A dancing school is taken over by the mob as a bookie joint. Broad playing, especially by Mature as the amiably vulgar mob chieftain, can't save the unfunny script. (Dir: Cy Howard, 92 mins.)

Every Man for Himself (France-Switzerland, 1980)***½ Isabelle Huppert, Jacques Dutronc, Nathalie Baye, Roland Amstutz. A bitterly cynical, coldly amusing contemplation of man's inhumanity to man, as evidenced by the lives of a frustrated wife leaving her lover in order to survive emotionally, a country lass wo becomes a whore in order to survive financially, and the man mixed up with both of them. Through it all, director Jean-Luc Godard's carefully composed camerawork and editing overshadow the

321

script. Wondrous use of slow motion. (87 mins.)

Every Man for Himself and God Against All— See: **Mystery of Kaspar Hauser, The**

Every Man Needs One (MTV 1972)* Ken Berry, Connie Stevens, Gail Fisher, Steve Franken, Henry Gibson, Nancy Walker. Male chauvinist architect hires a feminist assistant. Would-be "hip" comedy from the Aaron Spelling factory was dated before they finished it. (Dir: Jerry Paris, 76 mins.)

Every Night at Eight (1935)*** Alice Faye, Patsy Kelly, George Raft, Frances Langford, Walter Catlett. Tuneful Fox musical primarily for devotees of the talented stars who chirp their melodic way through some classic numbers. The backstage plot is a serviceable trifle about three singing gals acquiring bandstand stardom. (Dir: Raoul Walsh, 81 mins.)

Everything for Sale (Poland, 1968)*** Andrzej Lapicki, Beata Tyszkiewicz, Daniel Olbrychski, Elabieta Czyzewska. Director Andrew Wajda's tribute to his friend and favored star Zbingniew Cybulski. During the making of a film, the leading man is killed doing a stunt (just as Cybulski died in 1967). Fascinating film filled with vigorous images of friendship and movie making. (98 mins.)

Everything Happens at Night (1939)*** Ray Milland, Robert Cummings, Sonja Henie. Thanks to good playing by its leading men, this film about two reporters trying to find a Nobel Prize-winner is good entertainment. (Dir: Irving Cummings, 77 mins.)

Everything I Have Is Yours (1952)**½ Marge & Gower Champion, Dennis O'Keefe. Wedded song and dance team find married life interfering with their stage careers. Aside from the dancing of the Champions, nothing particularly novel about this routine musical. (Dir: Robert Z. Leonard, 92 mins.)

Everything's Ducky (1961)** Mickey Rooney, Buddy Hackett, Jackie Cooper, Joanie Sommers. Two sailors and a talking duck—fill in the rest. Rooney and Hackett try hard for laughs, which aren't there. (Dir: Don Taylor, 81 mins.)

Everything You Always Wanted to Know About Sex, but Were Afraid to Ask (1972)*** Woody Allen, Lou Jacobi, Anthony Quayle, Gene Wilder, Burt Reynolds, Tony Randall. A series of lunatic, hysterical sketches about everyone's favorite indoor sport. The best sketch involves a mild-mannered doctor falling head over heels in love with one of his patients—an Armenian sheep named Daisy. Besides that it's your only chance to see a forty-feet-high female breast, Lynn Redgrave wearing a chastity belt,

and Woody playing a sperm. (Dir: Woody Allen, 87 mins.)†

Every Time We Say Goodbye (1986)*½ Tom Hanks, Cristina Marsillach, Benedict Taylor. Hanks seems mighty uncomfortable portraying a WWII pilot who falls for a Sephardic Jewess in this half-baked romance about star-crossed lovers battling religious prejudice, culture clash, and every Romeo and Juliet cliché known to man. (Dir: Moshe Mizrahi, 97 mins.)†

Every Which Way but Loose (1978)*½ Clint Eastwood, Sondra Locke, Geoffrey Lewis, Beverly D'Angelo, Ruth Gordon. Cloddish comedy followed by *Any Which Way You Can*. Eastwood plays a muscular fool, whose notions of gallantry are moronically out of place in these free-wheeling times. (Dir: James Fargo, 115 mins.)†

Eve Wants to Sleep (Poland, 1957)**½ Barbara Lass, Ludwik Benoit, Stanislaw Mikulski, Zygmut Zintel. Terrific little comedy about a student arriving a day early at her dormitory; while trying to find a place to sleep she becomes involved in a robbery plot being staged by a gang of thieves and the local police. (Dir: Tadeusz Chmielwski, 98 mins.)

Evictors, The (1979)** Michael Parks, Jessica Harper, Vic Morrow, Sue Ane Langdon. Southern period gothic from writer-director Charles B. Pierce. A young couple (Parks and Harper) move into a house that turns out to have a haunted, bloody history. (92 mins.)†

Evil, The (1978)**½ Richard Crenna, Joanna Pettet, Andrew Prine. Crenna stumbles on the devil himself in a crumbling mansion. Surprisingly decent entry, considering its low production budget. (Dir: Gus Trikonis, 89 mins.)†

Evil Altar (1989)*½ William Smith, Pepper Martin, Robert Zdar, Theresa Cooney. Cheapo horror film set in a small town run by evil Smith, who stays in charge as long as he delivers young souls to the devil. (Dirs: Jim Winburn, Ryan Rao, 87 mins.)†

Evil Below, The (South Africa, 1987) *½ Wayne Crawford, June Chadwick, Sheri Able, Ted Le Platt. Divers seeking treasure in a ship that sank three centuries ago set off what appears to be an evil curse. No monsters here, nor anything else that's likely to keep you awake until the end. (Dir: Jean-Claude Dubois, 92 mins.)†

Evil Dead, The (1983)** Bruce Campbell, Ellen Sandweiss, Betsy Baker, Hal Delrich, Sarah York. Clever directorial touches and an imaginative storyline explain the film's cult following, but it's been wildly overpraised. At a remote cabin, some college kids disturb the sleep of the dead, who retaliate by having these cut-ups start cutting each other up. Not-so-grand Guignol and amateurish acting dilute the suspense, except for one astonishing scene in which a girl is stalked through the woods by an unseen evil. (Dir: Sam Raimi, 85 mins.)†

Evil Dead II (1987)*** Bruce Campbell, Sarah Berry, Dan Hicks, Kassie Wesley, Theodore Raimi. Sequel to the cult horror hit finds Campbell still besieged at a mountain cabin by vicious forest spirits, this time joined by the daughter of the professor who unleashed them. Almost plotless film is an excuse for director Sam Raimi to show off his undisciplined but technically precocious style. (84 mins.)†

Evil Eden (France-Mexico, 1956)*** Georges Marchal, Simone Signoret, Michel Piccoli, Michele Girandon. Technically outstanding potboiler about group of French visitors fleeing a revolution in a remote Central American mining town. One of director Luis Buñuel's work-for-hire films made after his exile from Spain, film still displays his sardonic touches and contempt for greed and hypocrisy. (105 mins.)

Evil Eye, The (Italy, 1964)**½ John Saxon, Leticia Roman, Valentina Cortese. Young doctor and a frightened girl uncover a series of unsolved murders when she fears the worst has happened to her aunt. (Dir: Mario Bava, 92 mins.)

Evil In Clear River (MTV 1988)** Lindsay Wagner, Randy Quaid, Thomas Wilson Brown. Overwrought melodrama confronts the problem of anti-Semitism with all the simplicity of Frank Capra, and none of the style. The cliché-ridden plot centers on a mother's concerns that her hockey star son is being taught to hate by the history teacher he reveres. Quaid is quite convincing as the popular, narrow-minded teacher, who's also hockey coach and mayor of his small town. (Dir: Karen Arthur, 96 mins.)

Evil In the Deep—See: **Treasure of Jamaica Reef**

Evil Mind, The—See: **Clairvoyant, The** (1934)

Evil of Frankenstein, The (Great Britain, 1964)** Peter Cushing, Peter Woodthorpe. Baron Frankenstein returns to his castle, finds his homemade creature encased in ice, and starts all over again. This version shown on U.S. TV was re-edited, with pointless new scenes filmed and added. The original 84 min. British version is on video, and rates an extra half star. (Dir: Freddie Francis, 97 mins.)†

Evil Roy Slade (1972)** John Astin, Dom De Luise, Dick Shawn. A crazy, offbeat comedy that might amuse the youngsters. Astin plays the title role of a mean, unremorseful outlaw who has never been loved. While robbing a bank he meets and kisses curvy but pure Pamela Austin, and love hits Evil Roy. (Dir: Jerry Paris, 100 mins.)

Evils of the Night (1985)½ Neville Brand, Aldo Ray, John Carradine, Tina Louise, Julie Newmar. Ridiculous sci-fi horror film has lots of eighties gore and nudity, but sets, costumes, and acting out of the worst fifties Z movie. Aliens land on our planet in search of Earth teenagers—and they can have the brainless bunch that appear in this junk. (Dir: Mardi Rustam, 86 mins.)†

Evil Spawn (1987)½ Bobbie Bresee, John Carradine. Aging actress Bresee partakes of a rejuvenating serum that promises to make her young overnight. It does (or so she claims, though she really doesn't look any different before and after), but it also periodically turns her into a giant murderous insect. Not even bad enough to be campy, just boringly incompetent. (Dir: Kenneth J. Hall, 88 mins.)†

Evilspeak (1982)** Clint Howard, R. G. Armstrong, Claude Earl Jones, Joseph Cortese. Bizarre horror flick about a computer whiz kid who—after being abused by his offensive classmates at a military academy—seeks revenge. (Dir: Eric Weston, 89 mins.)†

Evil That Men Do, The (1984)** Charles Bronson, Theresa Saldana, Rene Enriquez, Joseph Maher, Antoinette Bower. Violent flick about a contract killer (Bronson) who abandons retirement to stop a sadistic doctor who teaches torture techniques to repressive dictatorships. (Dir: J. Lee Thompson, 89 mins.)†

Evil Under the Sun (Great Britain, 1982)**½ Peter Ustinov, Diana Rigg, Maggie Smith, Roddy McDowall, Jane Birkin, Denis Quilley, James Mason, Nicholas Clay, Sylvia Miles, Colin Blakely. Hercule Poirot (Ustinov) pokes about a sunny resort in this film with eye-filling photography and a complicated plot involving trickily timed alibis, but the film's rather torpid, as if the mystery had fallen asleep under the sun. (Dir: Guy Hamilton, 102 mins.)†

Evita Peron (MTV 1981)*** Faye Dunaway, James Farentino, Rita Moreno, Jose Ferrer, Michael Constantine, Katy Jurado, Jeremy Kemp. A flashy accounting of the politics and amours of Argentine dictator Juan Peron and Evita Peron. The film ends up glamorizing these notorious historical figures, but Dunaway's old-movie-style finesse enhances her performance, since Evita always envisioned herself as a star anyway. (Dir: Marvin Chomsky, 200 mins.)

Ewok Adventure, The (MTV 1984)**½ Eric

Walker, Warwick Davis, Fionnula Flanagan, Guy Boyd, Aubree Miller. Producer George Lucas brings his furry Ewok creatures from *Return of the Jedi* to the forefront. Production values are better than the script in this fable about a brother and sister in search of their parents after their spaceship crashes. (Dir: John Korty, 104 mins.)

Ewoks: The Battle for Endor (MTV 1986)** Warwick Davis, Aubree Miller, Sian Phillips, Wilford Brimley, Niki Bothelo. Kids deserve better than this tale of a girl and her Ewok pal who set out with an old codger to rescue an Ewok family held by an evil king. (Dirs: Jim and Ken Wheat, 104 mins.)

Excalibur (1981)*** Nigel Terry, Helen Mirren, Nicol Williamson, Nicholas Clay, Cherie Lunghi, Paul Geoffrey. Visually impressive rendering of the Arthurian legend brilliantly preserves its full mythic force, rendering the allusive aspects of the saga fully credible to a modern audience and illuminating why the tales have survived so vividly in our imaginations. (Dir: John Boorman, 140 mins.)†

Ex-Champ (1939)**½ Victor McLaglen, Constance Moore, Tom Brown. Former champ turned doorman undertakes to train a young boxer. Fairly interesting melodrama. (Dir: Phil Rosen, 64 mins.)

Exclusive (1937)** Fred MacMurray, Frances Farmer, Charles Ruggles, Lloyd Nolan, Ralph Morgan, Fay Holden, Horace McMahon. Hard-hitting but improbable newspaper yarn has a girl reporter (Farmer) joining the newspaper game and trying to outscoop both her boyfriend and her father (Ruggles). (Dir: Alexander Hall, 85 mins.)

Exclusive Story (1936)**½ Franchot Tone, Madge Evans, Stuart Erwin, Robert Barrat, Joseph Calleia, J. Farrell MacDonald, J. Carroll Naish. Reporter Erwin comes to the aid of a storekeeper who's being shaken down by the mob. Average newspaper drama given the glossy MGM treatment. (Dir: George B. Seitz, 75 mins.)

Excuse My Dust (1951)**½ Red Skelton, Macdonald Carey, Sally Forrest. Amusing Skelton comedy about the days of the "Horseless Carriage." Some good gags, pleasant performers. (Dir: Roy Rowland, 82 mins.)

Execution, The (MTV 1985)½ Loretta Swit, Rip Torn, Valerie Harper, Barbara Barrie, Jessica Walter, Sandy Dennis. A group of chic survivors of Nazi concentration camps gets revenge on an ex-Nazi who now runs a California restaurant. (Dir: Paul Wendkos, 104 mins.)

Executioner, The (Great Britain, 1970)**½ George Peppard, Joan Collins, Nigel Patrick. Suave George Peppard is an

American-trained British agent who, along with the necessary quota of sidekicks, must track down the traitor involved in a massacre at a country estate. (Dir: Sam Wanamaker, 107 mins.)†

Executioner, The (1978)½ Duke Mitchell, Lorenzo Dodo, Vic Caesar, Jimmy Williams. Mitchell wrote and directed himself as a sentimental mob hit man in this ludicrous gangster saga. (84 mins.)†

Executioner Part II, The (1980)* Chris Mitchum, Aldo Ray, Antoine John Mottet, Renée Harmon. Cop Mitchum, hunting the vigilante who's been blowing up street gangs, finds the trail leads to a buddy from Vietnam. Really lousy junk that has nothing to do with either of the two films listed above—just what is this supposed to be a sequel to? (Dir: James Bryant, 85 mins.)†

Executioner's Song, The—The Gary Gilmore Story (MTV 1982)**½ Tommy Lee Jones, Rosanna Arquette, Steven Keats, Eli Wallach, Christine Lahti. Norman Mailer's screenplay of his book about the life of the Utah killer who was put to death by a firing squad in 1977 at his own insistence emerges as a relentlessly downbeat portrait of a man responding like a vicious animal whenever rejected or repulsed. (Dir: Lawrence Schiller, 208 mins.)†

Execution of Private Slovik, The (MTV 1974)**** Martin Sheen, Mariclare Costello, Matt Clark, Ned Beatty, Gary Busey. Sheen's performance as WWII soldier Eddie Slovik, the first serviceman to be executed for desertion since the Civil War, is profoundly moving in this hard-hitting TV movie. Slovik's battle experience makes firing a rifle an impossible duty and leads to his desertion and execution. (Dir: Lamont Johnson, 104 mins.)

Execution of Raymond Graham, The (MTV 1985)*** George Dzundza, Kate Reid, Jeff Fahey, Lois Smith, Josef Sommer. This TV film covers actual elapsed time as a convicted killer scheduled to be executed waits for intervention by the governor. Tightly constructed drama. (Dir: Daniel Petrie, 104 mins.)†

Executive Action (1973)*½ Burt Lancaster, Robert Ryan, Will Geer, John Anderson. Reckless thriller purporting to outdo the findings of the Warren Commission with the "real" facts about JFK's assassination. Screenplay by Dalton Trumbo, based on a story by Donald Freed and Mark Lane. (Dir: David Miller, 91 mins.)†

Executive Suite (1954)*** William Holden, June Allyson, Fredric March, Barbara Stanwyck, Shelley Winters, Nina Foch, Paul Douglas, Walter Pidgeon. A big cast effectively brings this best-selling novel about big business to the screen. There are many subplots that tend to get in the way of the main story. (Dir: Robert Wise, 104 mins.)

Exile, The (1947)*** Douglas Fairbanks, Jr., Maria Montez, Henry Daniell, Nigel Bruce. An interesting change of pace for renowned director Max Ophuls, whose specialty was romantic films like *Letter from an Unknown Woman*. This elegant swashbuckler about a king smitten with a commoner shows that Doug really could follow in his father's footsteps. (95 mins.)

Exit Laughing—See: **Are You There?**

Ex-Lady (1933)**½ Bette Davis, Gene Raymond, Frank McHugh. Bette's bad in this one. Turning up her nose at marriage, Ms. Davis flashes her eyes and livens up the proceedings with enough electricity for three movies as the girl who does Gene Raymond wrong. (Dir: Robert Florey, 65 mins.)

Ex-Mrs. Bradford, The (1936)***½ William Powell, Jean Arthur. Amateur sleuth with the aid of his ex-wife solves some racetrack murders. Delightful comedy-mystery, smooth and sophisticated. (Dir: Stephen Roberts, 100 mins.)†

Exodus (1960)*** Paul Newman, Eva Marie Saint, Lee J. Cobb, Sal Mineo. Producer-director Otto Preminger put considerable stress on scope and pictorial splendor in bringing Leon Uris's best-selling novel about the hardships of Jewish refugees in the new Israel to the screen. Episodic but generally exciting, well acted and of considerable historic interest. (213 mins.)†

Exo-Man, The (MTV 1977)** David Ackroyd, Anne Schedeen, Jose Ferrer, Jack Colvin, Kevin McCarthy, Harry Morgan. A physics professor who has been crippled by mobsters strikes back by donning the latest thing in Revenge Wear—a suit that enables him to move about and put his tormentors behind bars. Average action high jinks. (Dir: Richard Irving, 104 mins.)†

Exorcist, The (1973)*** Ellen Burstyn, Max von Sydow, Lee J. Cobb, Kitty Winn, Jason Miller, Linda Blair. The story deals with a twelve-year-old girl in a prosperous home in Georgetown, who becomes possessed by demons and is finally saved when the vile spirits are exorcised and driven from her body. Based on William Peter Blatty's best-selling novel, the film takes itself quite seriously, even though its primary purpose is to scare the hell out of the audience, and it certainly succeeds. (Dir: William Friedkin, 122 mins.)†

Exorcist II: The Heretic (1977)½ Linda Blair, Richard Burton, Louise Fletcher, James Earl Jones. This may be the worst sequel in the history of film. Linda Blair is possessed by an ancient evil spirit, while Burton tries to exorcise his rites. (Dir: John Boorman, 118 mins.)†

Exorcist III, The (1990)**½ George C. Scott, Ed Flanders, Brad Dourif, Jason Miller, Nicol Williamson, Scott Wilson, Viveca Lindfors. Ambitious continuation to the original *The Exorcist*. It is fifteen years later and Scott, as Detective Kinderman (taking over for the late Lee J. Cobb), comes across the wrathful demon conducting its reign of terror from an insane asylum. At times confusing, this occasionally intriguing thriller, directed and written by William Peter Blatty (author of *The Exorcist*), is a horror tale served with a wee dose of intelligence. At the time of this film's release, Linda Blair appeared in her own sequel (of sorts) called *Repossessed*, which spoofs *The Exorcist* and her Oscar-nominated performance. (Dir: William Peter Blatty, 105 mins.)†

Expedition (India, 1962)*** Soumitra Chatterjee, Waheeda Rehman, Robi Ghosh, Ruma Guhn Thakurta. Surprising commercial success by director Satyajit Ray involves a cabbie caught up in a ring of drug smugglers, white slavers, and prostitutes. Ray's innate humor and warmth come across in this effective crime thriller. (150 mins.)

Experience Preferred but Not Essential (Great Britain, 1983)*** Elizabeth Edmunds, Ron Bain. Gentle character comedy. We follow the young, shy student Annie through her summer as a waitress in a seaside resort with a staff of bizarre but charming characters. (Dir: Peter Duffell, 80 mins.)†

Experiment in Terror (1962)*** Glenn Ford, Lee Remick, Stefanie Powers, Ross Martin. High-tension thriller about a girl and her sister terrorized by a criminal with a plan to pull off a robbery, while the FBI frantically tries to prevent a tragedy. Director Blake Edwards uses unusual cinematography and San Francisco backgrounds to full effect. (123 mins.)†

Experiment Perilous (1944)*** Hedy Lamarr, George Brent, Paul Lukas. Doctor investigates the death of a wealthy philanthropist's sister, suspects foul play. Well-done mystery. (Dir: Jacques Tourneur, 91 mins.)†

Experts, The (1989)** John Travolta, Arye Gross, Kelly Preston, Deborah Foreman, James Keach, Charles Martin Smith. New York hipsters Travolta and Gross are tricked into teaching American customs to a town full of Soviet spy trainees in this silly comedy. Made in 1987. (Dir: Dave Thomas, 83 mins.)†

Explorers (1985)** Ethan Hawke, River Phoenix, Jason Presson, Dick Miller,

Amanda Peterson, Dana Ivey, James Cromwell. Three children travel to the stars aboard a spaceship of their own construction in this poorly structured sci-fi comedy. What starts off as an enchanting adventure turns bizarre. (The version on video is 107 mins.) (Dir: Joe Dante, 110 mins.)†

Explosive Generation, The (1961)*** Patty McCormack, William Shatner. When a high school teacher is expelled for teaching sex education, his students rush to his defense. Unusual adult drama. (Dir: Buzz Kulik, 89 mins.)

Exposed (1983)**½ Nastassia Kinski, Rudolf Nureyev, Harvey Keitel. A highly stylized film on the best things in life— modeling, terrorism, and classical music. A midwestern Kinski comes to New York, becomes a high fashion model, and gets involved with classical musician/anti-terrorist Nureyev and terrorist Keitel. (Dir: James Toback, 100 mins.)†

Expresso Bongo (Great Britain, 1960)**** Laurence Harvey, Sylvia Syms, Cliff Richard. Delightful mixture of fantasy and realism, as a small-time agent uses any means to push a teenage singer into the big-time. Great stylish performance by Harvey as the agent; excellent script with witty dialogue. (Dir: Val Guest, 109 mins.)†

Exquisite Corpses (1988)**½ Zoe Tamerlaine Lund, Gary Knox, Daniel Chapman, Ruth Collins. Oklahoma musician comes to New York City hoping to hit the big time, gets involved with a woman looking to murder her husband. Oddball black comedy wanders all over the place, but uses N.Y.C. underbelly effectively. (Dir: Temistocles Lopez, 95 mins.)†

Exterminating Angel, The (Mexico, 1962)**** Silvia Pinal, Enrique Rambal, Jacqueline Andere, Jose Baviera. A black comedy with allegorical overtones that slam the bourgeoisie. Invitees at a posh dinner party cannot bring themselves to leave. Eventually they find temporary respite in a church, where even · God abandons them. A banquet of Buñuelian surrealism. (Dir: Luis Buñuel, 95 mins.)

Exterminator, The (1980)* Christopher George, Samantha Eggar, Robert Ginty, Steve James, Tony Di Benedetto. Vietnam vet seeks revenge on the street gang that has assaulted his friend. The best revenge is not watching this. (Dir: James Glickenhaus, 101 mins.)†

Exterminator II (1984)* Robert Ginty, Mario Van Peebles, Deborah Geffner, Frankie Faison. With help of a black sidekick, a Vietnam vet cleans up a tough neighborhood in an armored garbage truck after his girl friend is beaten, crippled,

326

then killed. (Dir: Mark Buntzman, 89 mins.)†

Extra Day, The (Great Britain, 1956)*** Richard Basehart, Simone Simon. Adventures and aspirations of a bit player in a film studio. Well-acted, different comedy-drama. (Dir: William Fairchild, 83 mins.)

Extra Girl, The (1923)*** Mabel Normand, Ralph Graves, Ramsey Wallace. The wonderful Normand's last picture before scandal destroyed her career. She plays a small-town girl who comes to Hollywood to get a break in the movies; somehow she gets involved with oil swindlers, too! Normand gives a delightfully warm, human performance. (87 mins.)†

Extraordinary Seaman, The (1969)* David Niven, Faye Dunaway, Alan Alda, Mickey Rooney. A supposedly whimsical, nautical tale set in the Pacific of WWII about a captain refusing to give up an abandoned ship. (Dir: John Frankenheimer, 80 mins.)

Extreme Close-Up (MTV 1990)*** Blair Brown, Craig T. Nelson, Morgan Weisser, Samantha Mathis. Gripping emotional drama about a boy mourning his dead mother by digging out all the family home videos. There is a startling twist at the end and the videos have fascinating amateurish touches. First-rate TV movie material. (Dir: Peter Horton, 96 mins.)

Extreme Prejudice (1987)** Nick Nolte, Powers Boothe, Michael Ironside, Maria Conchita Alonso, Rip Torn. Texas Ranger Nolte battles seedy drug trafficker Boothe in this contemporary western that's quite funny. The screenplay shows the evidence of too many cooks (four screenwriters are credited). (Dir: Walter Hill, 104 mins.)†

Extremities (1986)** Farrah Fawcett, James Russo, Alfre Woodard, Diana Scarwid. An action-packed but empty-headed film version of a play that plays around with the complex topic of rape, even as it panders to male fantasies. Fawcett's much ballyhooed emergence as an actress. (Dir: Robert M. Young, 91 mins.)†

Eye Creatures, The (1965)½ John Ashley, Cynthia Hull, Chet Davis, Warren Hammack. An astigmatic thriller about extraterrestrial eyeballs who battle Earthmen. A revamp of the equally horrendous. *Invasion of the Saucer Men*. (Dir: Larry Buchanan, 80 mins.)†

Eye for an Eye, An (1966)*** Robert Lansing, Pat Wayne. An offbeat western yarn. Revenge is the keynote of this tale, which has Lansing teaming up with the blinded Pat Wayne as the two prepare for a shootout with villains. AKA: **Talion**. (Dir: Michael Moore, 92 mins.)

Eye for an Eye (1981)** Chuck Norris, Christopher Lee, Richard Roundtree, Matt Clark, Mako. Chuck Norris, the Caucasian Bruce Lee, stars in this yarn about a San Francisco cop who hunts down the killers of his partner with a group of martial arts experts. Short on acting, long on kicks. (Dir: Steve Carver, 104 mins.)†

Eye of the Cat (1969)*** Eleanor Parker, Michael Sarrazin, Gayle Hunnicutt. A frightening, macabre tale that revolves around wealthy invalid Eleanor Parker (who has numerous cats as pets) and her nephew's (Sarrazin) scheme to get her money. (Dir: David Lowell Rich, 102 mins.)

Eye of the Devil (Great Britain, 1967)*½ Deborah Kerr, David Niven, David Hemmings, Sharon Tate, Edward Mulhare, Emlyn Williams, Donald Pleasence. Many good actors are wasted in the not-so-spooky doings at a French chateau. (Dir: J. Lee Thompson, 92 mins.)

Eye of the Eagle (1987)** Brett Clark, Cec Verrell, William Steis, Ed Crick. Army squad in Vietnam battles the "Lost Command," a renegade band of American AWOLs and MIAs. Germ of an interesting idea receives a pedestrian war-movie treatment. (Dir: Cirio H. Santiago, 84 mins.)†

Eye of the Eagle II: Inside the Enemy (1989)*½ William Field, Ken Jaconson, Ronald William Lawrence, Shirley Tesoro. Private falls in love with a Vietnamese girl, uncovers a drug ring headed by his commanding officer. Lackluster crime tale in a wartime setting has nothing in common with the above except its title. (Dir: Carl Franklin, 79 mins.)†

Eye of the Needle (1981)**** Donald Sutherland, Kate Nelligan, Ian Bannen. An old-fashioned spy yarn with plenty of action, most of which comes in the last third. Sutherland gives another of his quiet, menacing performances as a WWII German spy working in England and he's hypnotic to watch. His playing is matched by Nelligan, as a British housewife living in a remote island, who has a sexual dalliance with the spy when he's washed ashore during a storm. The plans for the D-Day invasion figure importantly and the climactic scenes will keep you riveted. (Dir: Richard Marquand, 112 mins.)†

Eye of the Tiger (1986)** Gary Busey, Yaphet Kotto, Seymour Cassel, Bert Remsen, William Smith, Denise Galik. Bombastic Busey over-emphatically plays an ex-Viet vet/ex-con tangling with a motorcycle gang. Did we mention that the gang murdered his wife? Did we mention that they drove his daughter into a catatonic state? Did we mention that the writer of this film must have spent his formative years watching *Death Wish*? (Dir: Richard Sarafian, 90 mins.)†

Eye on the Sparrow (MTV 1987)**½ Mare Winningham, Keith Carradine, Sandy McPeak, Kaaren Lee, Conchata Ferrell. Winningham and Carradine shine as a blind couple fighting bureaucracy to adopt children. Both actors lend a special sense of dignity to their portrayals of two real-life individuals who fought to overcome discrimination against the handicapped. (Dir: John Korty, 104 mins.)

Eyes Behind the Stars (Italy, 1972)*½ Robert Hoffman, Nathalie Delon, Martin Balsam. Do you believe that the government is covering up evidence of extra-terrestrial visits? The writer-director of this lackluster sci-fi tale about a journalist digging up evidence of such a conspiracy certainly seems to, though he fails to grab the audience's attention. (Dir: Roy Garrett, 95 mins.)†

Eyes in the Night (1942)**½ Edward Arnold, Ann Harding, Donna Reed, Allan Jenkins, Horace (Stephen) McNally, Rosemary DeCamp, Barry Nelson, Mantan Moreland, Marie Windsor. Nifty mystery with Arnold as blind detective Duncan McClain, whose work brings him in between a woman and her stepdaughter feuding over the same beau. (Dir: Fred Zinnemann, 80 mins.)

Eyes of a Stranger (1981)* Lauren Tewes, Jennifer Jason Leigh, John DiSanti. A distasteful, exploitative mad-killer film. The violence is used in particularly unpleasant ways, generally in conjunction with sexual aggression. (Dir: Ken Wiederhorn, 85 mins.)†

Eyes of Charles Sand, The (MTV 1972)**½ Peter Haskell, Sharon Farrell, Barbara Rush, Brad Dillman. Splashy melodrama. Young business success Charles Sand (Haskell) inherits a gift of visionary sight and is soon besieged by a babbling redhead crying for help. (Dir: Reza Badiyi, 75 mins.)

Eyes of Fire (1985)**½ Dennis Lipscomb, Guy Boyd, Rebecca Stanley, Sally Klein, Fran Ryan, Karlene Crockett. Unusual setting for a horror film: the American frontier in the 18th-century, where a group of settlers are tormented by Indian spirits in a remote valley. Interesting visuals and special effects, but the script is too lacking in incident and interest. (Dir: Avery Crounse, 86 mins.)†

Eyes of Hell—See: **Mask, The**

Eyes of Laura Mars, The (1978)** Faye Dunaway, Tommy Lee Jones, Brad Dourif, René Auberjonois, Raul Julia, Frank Adonis, Lisa Taylor. This story of

327

a psychic fashion photographer (Faye Dunaway) and a rugged, expressionless policeman (Tommy Lee Jones) investigating a series of ice pick murders is a visually flashy, but pointless exercise in voyeurism and "punk-chic." (Dir: Irvin Kershner, 104 mins.)†

Eyes of the Mummy, The (Germany, 1918)***½ Pola Negri, Emil Jannings, Harry Liedthe, Max Laurence. Terrific silent horror film directed by Ernst Lubitsch. An artist rescues a young woman being held prisoner in an Egyptian tomb by a mummy, who then follows her to London. Jannings is perfectly creepy as the mummy, and Lubitsch uses his ever-moving camera to express horror. (55 mins.)

Eyes, The Mouth, The (Italy-France, 1982)** Lou Castel, Angela Molina, Emanuele Riva, Mechel Piccoli. Family black sheep, an actor, returns home after suicide of brother to comfort mother and uncle. He then begins affair with brother's pregnant lover, and starts to have mental breakdown. Tough to watch, especially when actor pretends to be a dog or sulks or shouts for no reason. (100 mins.)†

Eyes Without a Face—See: **Horror Chamber of Dr. Faustus, The**

Eye Witness (Great Britain, 1949)*** Robert Montgomery, Patricia Wayne (Patricia Cutts). An American lawyer goes to England to save a friend from a murder charge. Neat melodrama, well played. (Dir: Robert Montgomery, 104 mins.)

Eyewitness (1981)*** William Hurt, Sigourney Weaver, Christopher Plummer, Irene Worth, James Woods, Pamela Reed, Kenneth McMillan. An exciting romantic mystery by the writer (Steve Tesich) and director (Peter Yates) of *Breaking Away*. William Hurt plays a New York City janitor who pretends to have witnessed a murder in order to kindle a relationship with a beautiful, self-assured TV newswoman (Sigourney Weaver). The two quickly find themselves embroiled in a complicated conspiracy—and a tentative, teasingly uncertain romance. (102 mins.)†

Fabulous Baker Boys, The (1989)*** Jeff Bridges, Michelle Pfeiffer, Beau Bridges, Ellie Raab, Jennifer Tilly. Well-played and exceptionally scripted character study of three individuals on the lowest rung of the show business ladder. The Bridges play the Baker Boys, two piano-playing siblings whose nightclub act is a failure until they hire a hardboiled hooker (Pfeiffer) as a vocalist. Beau gives his best performance in some years as the dedicated older brother, while Jeff and the slinky Pfeiffer strike sparks in a series of 1940s-tinged, steamy (but nonexplicit) scenes of seduction. (Dir: Steve Kloves, 113 mins.)†

Fabulous Baron Munchausen, The (1961)— See: **Baron Munchausen**

Fabulous Baron Munchausen, The (Czechoslovakia, 1962)***½ Milos Kopecky, Jana Brejchova. Czech animator/director Karel Zeman applies his considerable talents to set in motion the story of Baron M., that great tale-spinner, as seen through the drawings and conceptions of 19th-century illustrator Gustave Doré. (84 mins.)

Fabulous Dorseys, The (1947)** Tommy and Jimmy Dorsey, Janet Blair. The biography of the famous bandleaders who fought each other as they fought to the top. Mild musical; good tunes, not much on plot. (Dir: Alfred E. Green, 88 mins.)†

Fabulous World of Jules Verne, The (Czechoslovakia, 1961)*** Louis Tock, Ernest NaVara. An enormously stylish animation enterprise, using contemporary engravings and ornate models to tell several of Verne's fantastic stories. AKA: **The Fantastic Invention.** (Dir: Karel Zeman, 83 mins.)

Face at the Window, The (Great Britain, 1939)** Tod Slaughter, Marjorie Taylor, John Warwick, Leonard Henry. Barnstorming British horror king Slaughter is in typical eyeball-rolling form as a criminal terrorizing Paris along with his deformed brother. Not meant to be taken any too seriously. (Dir: George King, 65 mins.)†

Face Behind the Mask, The (1941)*** Peter Lorre, Evelyn Keyes. Often exciting thriller, thanks to Lorre's able performance as a hideously scarred criminal who falls in love with a gentle blind girl (Keyes). (Dir: Robert Florey, 69 mins.)

Face in the Crowd, A (1957)***½ Andy Griffith, Patricia Neal, Anthony Franciosa. An excellent screenplay by Budd Schulberg is well directed by Elia Kazan and gives Andy Griffith the best role of his career, as a backwoods, guitar-playing bum who becomes a national TV personality. Patricia Neal is equally as good as a reporter who discovers and protects and finally destroys the big man. (125 mins.)†

Face in the Rain, A (1963)*** Rory Calhoun, Marina Berti. During WWII an American boy is sheltered from the enemy by the mistress of a German commandant. Suspenseful melodrama. (Dir: Irvin Kershner, 91 mins.)

Face in the Sky (1933)**½ Spencer Tracy, Marion Nixon, Lila Lee. An unusual but consistently enjoyable outing that changes from romance down on the farm to life, love, and music in the big city. (Dir: Harry Lachman, 73 mins.)

Face of a Fugitive (1959)**½ Fred MacMurray, Lin McCarthy. Competently made western. MacMurray, falsely accused of murder, changes his identity when he decides to settle in a town, but trouble follows his trail. (Dir: Paul Wendkos, 81 mins.)

Face of Another (Japan, 1966)*** Tatsuya Nakadai, Machiko Kyo, Kyoko Kishida, Eiji Okada, Mikijiro Hira. A man whose face was burned in an accident is given a new one by a surgeon and learns that every man is who he chooses to be. Existential allegory from the writer (Japanese novelist Kobo Abe) and director of *Woman in the Dunes* isn't quite up to that level, with a solid basis but too much flashy cinema trickery. (Dir: Hiroshi Teshigahara, 124 mins.)†

Face of Fear—See: **Peeping Tom**

Face of Fear (MTV 1971)**½ Ricardo Montalban, Jack Warden, Elizabeth Ashley, Dane Clark. Interesting cat-and-mouse suspense feature. Ashley is a schoolteacher stricken with leukemia who hires a killer to do her in, then discovers her "illness" was misdiagnosed. Good acting and some tense moments highlight this Quinn Martin production. (Dir: George McCowan, 72 mins.)

Face of Fire (1959)**½ Cameron Mitchell, James Whitmore, Bettye Ackerman. Disfigured in a fire, a well-liked local handyman becomes a social outcast. Odd little drama produced in Sweden. (Dir: Albert Band, 83 mins.)

Face of Fu Manchu, The (Great Britain, 1965)*** Christopher Lee, Nigel Green, James Robertson-Justice, Tsai Chin. Horror film fiend Lee debuts as the unstoppable Dr. Fu, out to destroy the world again and stocking up on poison in the mountains of Tibet. First of a popular new Fu Manchu series; followed by *The Brides of Fu Manchu*. (Dir: Don Sharp, 96 mins.)

Face of Rage, The (MTV 1983)***½ Dianne Wiest, George Dzundza, Graham Beckel, Jeffrey DeMunn, Keith Szarabajka, Lorraine Toussaint, Danny Glover, Tom Waites. A change-of-pace entry on the trauma of rape victims and the motivations of their attackers turns out to be an emotional hard-hitting drama. George Dzunda is a sympathetic psychologist who's conducting an experimental encounter group with both rapists and the victims. The film follows one young woman (Dianne Wiest) whose life crumbles after a rape attack and eventually lands in the therapy session. (Dir: Donald Wrye, 104 mins.)

Face of the Enemy (1989)** Rosana DeSoto, George DiCenzo, Cindy Cryer. A man obsessed with the time he spent as a hostage of Iranian terrorists kidnaps a woman he believes to have been one of his captors and holds her prisoner in his basement. Some interesting ideas go undeveloped. (Dir: Hassan Ildari, 92 mins.)

Faces (1968)***½ John Marley, Gena Rowlands, Lynn Carlin, Seymour Cassel. Concerns the disintegration of the marriage, after a fourteen-year period, of a middle-class couple in California. What is unique is not the plotline, which is familiar enough, but the revelatory nature of the experience, watching the actors who suggest an improvisatory quality about their work. A stunning, perceptive study of American manners and morals. (Dir: John Cassavetes, 129 mins.)

Faces Of Women (Ivory Coast, 1985)***½ Eugenie Cisse Roland, Sidiki Bakaba, Kouadid, Brou. Two films in one, shot a decade apart on a shoestring budget, and linked by dances and chants of an all-female chorus. Both tell fables about the status of women in the Ivory Coast. An exhilarating film, filled with comedy and the joy of discovery. (Dir: Desire Ecare, 105 mins.)

Face That Launched a Thousand Ships, The —See: **Loves of Three Queens, The**

Face to Face (1952)**** Robert Preston, James Mason, Marjorie Steele. Package of two stories: "The Secret Sharer" (James Mason), a shipboard drama, and "Bride Comes to Yellow Sky" (Robert Preston, Marjorie Steele), a tale of a sheriff in a small western town. Both tastefully produced, literate, well acted. (Dirs: John Brahm, Bretaigne Windust, 90 mins.)†

Face to Face (Sweden, 1975)**** Liv Ullmann, Erland Josephson. A devastating masterpiece, Bergman's thirty-ninth film, featuring one of the most remarkable acting performances (Ullmann's) in modern cinema. This award-winning drama is about a psychiatrist (Ullmann) who goes through a nervous breakdown. There are very few other contemporary actresses who could be so convincing and convey so many varied emotions and passions. (Dir: Ingmar Bergman, 136 mins.)

Face to Face (MTV 1990)**½ Elizabeth Montgomery, Robert Foxworth, Lou Antonio, Ronald Lacey. Paleontologist Montgomery arrives at a dig site in Kenya only to find it already occupied by Englishman Foxworth, digging for the meerschaum clay used to make pipes. Animosity between them seethes in this well acted but rather predictable comedy-drama with some fine insights into tribal life. (Dir: Lou Antonio, 96 mins.)

Facts of Life, The (1960)*** Lucille Ball, Bob Hope. Two of show business's funniest comics are teamed in this laugh-filled comedy about the many sides of marriage. Many scenes border on slapstick but they're skillfully carried off by the two old pros. (Dir: Melvin Frank, 103 mins.)

Facts of Life Down Under, The (MTV 1987)** Cloris Leachman, Lisa Whelchel, Nancy McKeon, Kim Fields, Mindy Cohn, MacKenzie Astin, Mario Van Peebles. A cultural exchange program enables the girls to flock to Australia for adventure galore in this tame travelogue comedy. Nothing stops these girls; we can't wait for "Facts of Life Goes to a Nursing Home." (Dir: Stuart Margolin, 104 mins.)

Facts of Life Goes to Paris, The (MTV 1982)** Charlotte Rae, Lisa Whelchel, Nancy McKeon, Mindy Cohn, Kim Fields. Series fans will enjoy this little adventure in which the show's stars are transferred to gay Paree, where they enroll in a French cooking school. (Dir: Asaad Kelada, 104 mins.)

Facts of Murder, The (Italy, 1959)*** Claudia Cardinale, Pietro Germi, Franco Fabrizi, Eleanora Rossi-Drago. Absorbing story of a humanistic police inspector investigating an ugly murder case, his reactions to the people he meets during its course. (Dir: Pietro Germi, 110 mins.)

Fade In (1968)** Burt Reynolds, Barbara Loden. Reynolds and Miss Loden appeared in this drama about the movie business and the people involved in an on-location film shooting, but it never was released theatrically in the U.S. Tune in and judge for yourself. (Dir: Jud Taylor, 93 mins.)

Fade to Black (1980)** Dennis Christopher, Linda Kerridge. A young cinephile, obsessed with Marilyn Monroe, murders his enemies in the guise of his movie heros. The plot gimmick allows the film to re-create moments from *Dracula, White Heat, Psycho*, etc., but none of the new scenes are as good as the originals. (Dir: Vernon Zimmerman, 100 mins.)†

Fahrenheit 451 (Great Britain, 1966)***½ Oskar Werner, Julie Christie, Cyril Cusack. One of the best, though perhaps the least appreciated, of director François Truffaut's films. About a future where books are burned and their readers are hunted down. Adapted from a Ray Bradbury story. Superb Bernard Herrmann score. (111 mins.)†

Falling of Raymond, The (MTV 1971)**½ Jane Wyman, Dean Stockwell, Dana Andrews. Wyman playing a schoolteacher who is thinking of retiring when an old student who failed an important test

a few years past shows up with vengeance on his mind. (Dir: Boris Sagal, 73 mins.)

Fall Safe (1964)***½ Henry Fonda, Dan O'Herlihy, Walter Matthau. Nightmarish problem drama of what might happen when, through an error, a SAC plane is ordered to bomb Moscow. This develops into a gripping, suspenseful tale of something that could possibly happen. (Dir: Sidney Lumet, 111 mins.)†

Fair Trade—See: Skeleton Coast

Fair Wind to Java (1953)*** Fred MacMurray, Victor McLaglen, Vera Ralston. Sea captain battles a pirate chief on the high seas. Well-made adventure melodrama contains a lot of action, plenty of excitement. (Dir: Joseph Kane, 92 mins.)

Fairy Tales (1979)** Don Sparks, Irwin Corey, Sy Richardson, Brenda Fogarty, Nai Bonet, Martha Reeves, Linnea Quigley, Angelo Rossitto. The makers of *Cinderella* (1977) return with another bawdy musical that revels in cheapness, bad jokes, and sex. A handsome prince must sire an heir, but has become so jaded by the perpetual attentions of women that he's become impotent, leading to a search for the young lady who can revive him. So cheerful in its dirty-mindedness that you can't really hate it. (Dir: Henry Tampa, 79 mins.)†

Faithful In My Fashion (1946)*** Donna Reed, Tom Drake. Sergeant returns to his shoe-clerking job after the war and falls for a pretty salesgirl. Modest but light, ingratiating comedy, good fun. (Dir: Sidney Salkow, 81 mins.)

Faithless (1932)**½ Tallulah Bankhead, Robert Montgomery, Louise Closser Hale, Hugh Herbert, Sterling Holloway. Glossy depression-era soap opera has Bankhead trying to conceal her scandalous past from new lover Montgomery. Nothing special. (Dir: Harry Beaumont, 76 mins.)

Fakebook—See: American Blue Note

Fake-Out (1982)* Pia Zadora, Telly Savalas, Desi Arnaz, Jr. Synthetic crime film in which precious Pia is induced to spill the beans on her former hoodlum lover. This vanity production is unexceptional except for one scene in which Zadora teaches aerobics to a bevy of hardened penitentiary babes in jail. AKA: **Nevada Heat**. (Dir: Matt Cimber, 96 mins.)†

Falcon, The (Hungary, 1970)***½ Ivan Andonov, Gyorgy Banffy, Judit Meszleri. Director Istvan Gaal gained world recognition with his allegory about a falcon-training center run by a dour martinet who brooks no disobedience from his workers and tames his birds with the same steely determination. A visitor to the center flees in terror, finding himself in unknown territory fearing an attack by the falcons. Tense and daring. (90 mins.)

Falcon series. Michael Arlen's debonair detective character covered a lot of territory, including a TV show (1954) and a radio show in addition to this movie series. Here, George Sanders played Gay Falcon, the uppercrust amateur sleuth; he was later replaced by his real-life sibling brother Tom Conway in the role of brother Tom Falcon. The series eventually petered out with low, low-budget entries with John Calvert like *The Devil's Cargo, Appointment with Murder,* and *Search for Danger.* But fans of the Saint would do better watching these two films in addition to those reviewed below: *The Gay Falcon* and *A Date with the Falcon.*

Falcon and the Co-Eds (1943)*** Tom Conway, Jean Brooks. The Falcon goes to a girls' school to look into the death of an instructress. Above-average mystery, well done. (Dir: William Clemens, 68 mins.)

Falcon and the Snowman, The (1985)*** Timothy Hutton, Sean Penn, Lori Singer, Pat Hingle. Truth is stranger than fiction in this tale about Daulton Lee and Christopher Boyce, two young Americans convicted of selling secrets to the Russians in 1977. Conjecture about why these two All-American boys turned traitor forms the framework of this fascinating film, but the ambiguities of the case aren't satisfactorily resolved here. (Dir: John Schlesinger, 131 mins.)†

Falcon in Danger, The (1943)**½ Tom Conway, Jean Brooks. The Falcon's got a fascinating mystery to solve here as a passenger plane lands at an airport with nobody on board. Above-average entry. (Dir: William Clemens, 69 mins.)

Falcon in Hollywood, The (1944)*** Tom Conway, Barbara Hale, Veda Ann Borg, Sheldon Leonard. Snappy entry. A costume designer's husband is murdered, and the Falcon has to turn the film capital upside down to solve the mystery. (Dir: Gordon Douglas, 67 mins.)

Falcon in Mexico (1944)**½ Tom Conway, Mona Maris. The Falcon trails a killer from New York to Mexico. Pleasant mystery with good backgrounds. (Dir: William Berke, 70 mins.)

Falcon in San Francisco, The (1945)** Tom Conway, Rita Corday, Edward S. Brophy, Sharyn Moffett, Fay Helm, Robert Armstrong. Tepid entry in which the Falcon tries to unravel a silk-smuggling operation in San Francisco. (Dir: Joseph H. Lewis, 65 mins.)

Falcon Out West (1944)**½ Tom Conway, Barbara Hale. A cowboy is murdered in an eastern nightclub, causing the Falcon to head west to find the killer. OK mystery. (Dir: William Clemens, 64 mins.)

Falcon's Adventure, The (1946)** Tom Conway, Madge Meredith, Edward S. Brophy, Robert Warrick, Ian Wolfe, Myrna Dell. After he comes to the rescue of a kidnapped Brazilian beauty (whose father's formula for synthetic diamonds is a hot property), Tom Falcon gets into real trouble when he's blamed for this man's death. (Dir: William Berke, 61 mins.)†

Falcon's Alibi, The (1946)** Tom Conway, Rita Corday, Vince Barnett, Jane Greer, Elisha Cook, Jr., Jason Robards, Sr. In the course of helping a social secretary out of a scrape involving stolen gems, the Falcon ends up getting picked up for homicide. (Dir: Ray McCarey, 62 mins.)

Falcon's Brother, The (1942)**½ George Sanders, Tom Conway, Jane Randolph. The Falcon teams up with his brother (the brother is played by Sanders's real-life sibling, Tom Conway, who took over the series after this). Together they defeat an Axis conspiracy against the U.S.'s good relations with South America. (Dir: Stanley Logan, 63 mins.)

Falcon's Gold (MTV 1982)**½ John Marley, Simon MacCorkindale, Louise Vallance, George Touliatos, Blanco Guerra. Made-for-cable feature that spotlights cliff-hanging adventure and some pretty outlandish fantasy. Marley leads an expedition into the Mexican mountains to search for lost treasures, instead finds a heap of trouble from bad guy Touliatos and crew. Based on a story by Arthur Conan Doyle. (Dir: Bob Schulz, 90 mins.)

Falcon Strikes Back (1943)**½ Tom Conway, Harriet Hilliard. The Falcon avoids a trap set for him by a gang of criminals. Neat mystery with a surprise solution. (Dir: Edward Dmytryk, 66 mins.)

Falcon Takes Over, The (1942)*** George Sanders, Lynn Bari, Ward Bond. This is probably the best of the series featuring Sanders as the detective created by Michael Arlen. The story is an adaptation of Raymond Chandler's *Farewell My Lovely.* Witty script, sophisticated acting. (Dir: Irving Reis, 63 mins.)

Fall Break—See: **Mutilator, The**

Fallen Angel (1945)**½ Alice Faye, Dana Andrews, Linda Darnell. Dana marries Alice for her money, hoping to latch on to Linda after he gets some dough. But, alas, Linda is murdered and he's a suspect. (Dir: Otto Preminger, 97 mins.)

Fallen Angel (MTV 1981)*** Richard Masur, Dana Hill, Melinda Dillon, Ronny Cox. A thirteen-year-old girl with family problems becomes prey to a child molester, a coach of a girls' softball team. This frank, often exploitative and frightening material works due in large part to Richard Masur's performance as the molester posing as a friend, the understanding grownup. (Dir: Robert Lewis, 104 mins.)†

Fallen Idol, The (Great Britain, 1949)**** Ralph Richardson, Michele Morgan, Bobby Henrey. An ambassador's small son idolizes a servant, who has a nagging wife but loves an embassy clerk. When the wife is accidentally killed, the boy innocently points suspicion toward the servant. Superb drama of an adult world seen through the eyes of a child; merits praise in every respect. Written by Graham Greene. (Dir: Carol Reed, 94 mins.)†

Fallen Sparrow (1943)*** John Garfield, Maureen O'Hara. Survivor of a Spanish Brigade returns to America to tangle with Nazi spies. Smooth, excellently produced melodrama. (Dir: Richard Wallace, 94 mins.)†

Fall from Grace (MTV 1990)*½ Bernadette Peters, Kevin Spacey, Richard Herd, Beth Grant, John McLiam, Richard Paul, Jean Kasem. Ridiculous tabloid-style account of the events leading to the downfall of "televangelists" Jim and Tammy Bakker. Script paints Jim as a cardboard cutout, while trying to make Tammy into a tragic heroine. The truth *had* to be more interesting than this. (Dir: Karen Arthur, 96 mins.)†

Falling in Love (1984)**½ Meryl Streep, Robert De Niro, Dianne Wiest, Harvey Keitel. The charisma of Streep and De Niro almost carries this lightweight soap opera. Two railroad commuters, in a Westchester suburb of New York City, meet by accident and then fall in love, which is especially understandable in De Niro's case. (Dir: Ulu Grosbard, 106 mins.)†

Falling in Love Again (1980)*½ Susannah York, Elliott Gould, Stuart Paul, Michelle Pfeiffer, Kaye Ballard. Relentlessly charmless drama about a man (Gould) locked in memories of his idealized past, a time when he pursued a gorgeous shiksa. The cast is trapped by the soggy sentiments. (Dir: Steven Paul, 103 mins.)†

Fall of the House of Usher, The (1960)—See: House of Usher

Fall of the House of Usher, The (MTV 1982)*½ Martin Landau, Robert Hays, Charlene Tilton, Dimitra Arliss, Ray Walston. Adaptation of the Edgar Allan Poe story tries to be literate, ends up simply boring. Made in 1978, not shown until four years later. (Dir: James L. Conway, 101 mins.)†

Fall of the Roman Empire, The (1964)*** Stephen Boyd, Alec Guinness, Christopher Plummer, Sophia Loren, James Mason, Omar Sharif. Story of the decadence of Rome after the death of Marcus Aurelius, a gargantuan spectacle dramatized with brilliant visual discipline. (Dir: Anthony Mann, 188 mins.)†

False Faces (1932)*** Lowell Sherman, Peggy Shannon, Lila Lee, Berton Churchill, David Landau. Weird story of a con artist-doctor who gains fame and fortune as a plastic surgeon, and almost gets away with murder. Witty and intelligent. (Dir: Lowell Sherman, 74 mins.)†

False Witness (MTV 1989)**½ Phylicia Rashad, Philip Michael Thomas, Teri Austin, George Grizzard. Ambitious New Orleans D. A. Rashad and private investigator Thomas are both lovers and partners on a grisly rape-murder case. But when they disagree on methods, their relationship takes a dangerous turn. Involving adaptation of a Dorothy Uhnak novel. (Dir: Arthur Allan Seidelman, 96 mins.)

Falstaff—See: **Chimes at Midnight**

Fame (1980)*** Irene Cara, Eddie Barth, Maureen Teefy, Lee Curreri, Anne Meara. This cross-section of four years at New York's High School for the Performing Arts is exciting in spite of some nasty plot contrivances. Unabashedly dedicated to virtues of toil, talent, and upward mobility. Did these kids suffer this much in grade school? (Dir: Alan Parker, 134 mins.)†

Fame Is the Name of the Game (MTV 1966)** Tony Franciosa, Jill St. John, Jack Klugman, Susan St. James. Involved melodrama about a magazine writer who gets his lumps when he investigates the supposed suicide of a girl. (Dir: Stuart Rosenberg, 100 mins.)

Fame Is the Spur (Great Britain, 1949)***½ Michael Redgrave, Rosamund John. The saga of a liberal English statesman who refuses to sacrifice his ideals. Thoughtful, finely performed and directed drama. (Dirs: John and Roy Boulting, 116 mins.)

Family, The (France-Italy, 1970)** Charles Bronson, Jill Ireland, Michel Constantin, Telly Savalas. Hit man Bronson gets double-crossed and looks for revenge (so what else is new?). Lina Wertmuller is one of the credited scripters. (Dir: Sergio Sollima, 109 mins.)

Family, The (Italy, 1986)**** Vittorio Gassman, Fanny Ardant, Stefania Sandrelli, Philippe Noiret. Director Ettore Scola's impressive study of one Italian family from 1906 through the present day concentrates on small, significant details in such a way that this unnamed family becomes an archetype that's readily identifiable to everyone. The central figure is Carlo (Gassman), a proud academic who preserves a lifelong passion for a beautiful pianist (Ardant). This relationship, fraught with petty squabbles, comes across as wholly realistic, as do all the other interrelationships among family members. (128 mins.)†

Family Affair, A (1937)**½ Lionel Barrymore, Spring Byington, Mickey Rooney. This mild little comedy was the start of the Hardy series. Mr. Barrymore gave way to Lewis Stone in the later editions, however. (Dir: George B. Seitz, 80 mins.)

Family Affair (Great Britain, 1954)** Bebe Daniels, Ben Lyon, Horace Percival. Lukewarm comedy based on a popular British radio series starring the Lyon family (Daniels was Mrs. Lyon) as themselves. (Dir: Val Guest, 81 mins.)

Family Business (France, 1987)*** Fanny Ardant, Johnny Hallyday, Guy Marchand. A lightweight comedy about the home life of a professional safecracker would seem an odd project for director Costa-Gavras, who usually deals with politically weighty subjects, but the results are a pleasant surprise. (98 mins.)

Family Business (1989)***½ Sean Connery, Dustin Hoffman, Matthew Broderick, Rosana DeSoto, Janet Carroll, Victoria Jackson. Love of family and the allure of crime highlight this delightful comedy-drama about three generations of thieves trying for the big score. Vincent Patrick's script (from his novel) is filled with richly drawn characters and resonant dialogue. Director Sidney Lumet makes his beloved New York City and its colorful citizens shine in this vastly underrated film. (115 mins.)†

Family Diary (Italy, 1962)***½ Marcella Mastroianni, Jacques Perrin, Valerie Ciangottini, Salvo Randone. Beautiful, sensitive story of older brother Mastroianni grieving over the untimely death of his younger sibling Perrin. Tale of family love and devotion is heartbreaking, brilliantly designed and acted, and wonderfully photographed by Giuseppe Rotunno. (Dir: Valerio Zurlini, 122 mins.)

Family Enforcer (1977)** Joseph Cotten, Joe Pesci, Lou Criscuolo. Another urban gangster melodrama. Story of a fledgling mafioso learning his trade in the slums of Jersey City has a nice feel for atmosphere and some predictable ironies, but the derivativeness blunts the impact. (Dir: Ralph De Vito, 89 mins.)†

Family Flight (MTV 1972)**½ Rod Taylor, Dina Merrill. Out of the old desert plane-crash plot comes a pretty fair flying show. A strained San Diego, Calif., family develops togetherness and maturity when they work their way out of a tight spot. (Dir: Marvin Chomsky, 73 mins.)

Family for Joe, A (MTV 1990)** Robert Mitchum, Chris Furth, Maia Brewton, Jarrad Paul, David Nelson. Series pilot casts Mitchum as a homeless old man

who is recruited to play the grandfather of four kids trying to stay out of foster homes. Mitchum deserves better, though he does what he can. (Dir: Jeffrey Melman, 96 mins.)

Family Game, The (Japan, 1983)*** Yusaku Matsuda, Juzo Itami, Saori Yuki, Ichirota Miyagawa. New Wave director Yoshimitsu Morita takes a sharp swipe at modern Japanese mores in this madcap, satirical jab at the country's mixed-up culture. The film centers on the interaction between a smart-aleck son of a frantic bourgeois couple and the tutor hired to improve his grades. (107 mins.)

Family Honeymoon (1948)**½ Claudette Colbert, Fred MacMurray, Gigi Perreau. One joke is stretched too far in this thin comedy. A widow with three children takes her brood with her on her second honeymoon. Some funny scenes. (Dir: Claude Binyon, 80 mins.)

Family Jewels, The (1965)** Jerry Lewis, Donna Butterworth. Jerry Lewis produced, directed, co-authored, and plays seven (count 'em) parts. An orphaned heiress has to decide which of her six uncles (all Lewis) she wants to be her guardian. In case you're counting, Lewis also plays the family chauffeur. The results are alternately funny and tedious. (100 mins.)†

Family Kovak, The (MTV 1974)** James Sloyan, Sarah Cunningham, Andrew Robinson, Tammi Bula, Richard Gilliland. Fair domestic drama of a middle class family dealing with a bribery scandal involving their eldest son. (Dir: Ralph Senensky, 72 mins.)

Family Life (Great Britain, 1971)—See: Wednesday's Child

Family Life (Poland, 1971)*** Daniel Olbrychski, Jan Nowicki, Jan Kreczmar. Young engineer returns to his family's dilapidated country mansion, where he must confront drunken father and mentally unbalanced sister. Somber, moody drama examines responsibility to one's relations and confronts human needs and confidence. (Dir: Krzysztof Zanussi, 93 mins.)†

Family Man, The (MTV 1979)*** Ed Asner, Meredith Baxter Birney, Anne Jackson. Asner and Birney are delightful in this adult tale of a middle-aged married man who falls for a younger woman. (Dir: Glenn Jordan, 104 mins.)

Family Next Door, The (1939)*½ Hugh Herbert, Joy Hodges, Eddie Quillan, Ruth Donnelly. Derivative comedy about a bumbling plumber and his supportive family. (Dir: Joseph Santley, 60 mins.)

Family Nobody Wanted, The (MTV 1975)**½ Shirley Jones, James Olson, Katherine Helmond. Heartwarming, sentimental story of a minister and his loving wife, and the brood of kids of different races that they adopt. A true story. (Dir: Ralph Senensky, 72 mins.)

Family of Spies (MTV 1990)*** Powers Boothe, Lesley Ann Warren, John M. Jackson, Graham Beckel, Jeroen Krabbé. True story of John Walker, the U.S. navy officer who sold defense secrets to the Soviet Union for almost two decades, eventually bringing his sons into his operation. Overlong, but Boothe's compelling performance sustains attention. (Dir: Stephen Gyllenhaal, 240 mins.)

Family Plot (1976)*** Karen Black, Bruce Dern, Barbara Harris, Ed Lauter, William Devane. A return to the tongue-in-cheek, prewar director Alfred Hitchcock. Of course, there's plenty of suspense and a whiz of a plot. Kidnapping, robbery, arson, and murder are involved, along with a little petty larceny. (120 mins.)†

Family Reunion (MTV 1981)*½ Bette Davis, David Huddleston, John Shea, J. Ashley Hyman. Ponderous domestic drama about a New England clan squabbling over the disposition of family land. Sl-l-l-l-ow going, with Bette seeming to pause dramatically in between syllables. (Dir: Fielder Cook, 200 mins.)

Family Rico, The (MTV 1972)**½ Ben Gazzara, James Farentino, Jo Van Fleet, Dane Clark, John Marley. Adaptation of a Georges Simenon novel avoids gangland shooting and gore in *The Godfather* style, and focuses on a character study of a crime syndicate chief instead. Remake of the feature *The Brothers Rico* (1957). (Dir: Paul Wendkos, 73 mins.)

Family Secret, The (1951)**½ John Derek, Lee J. Cobb, Jody Lawrence. A young man accidentally kills his best friend and doesn't report it to the police. Strange circumstances keep the suspense mounting until the climax. (Dir: Henry Levin, 85 mins.)

Family Secrets (MTV 1984)**½ Maureen Stapleton, Melissa Gilbert, Stefanie Powers. As mother, daughter, and grandmother, Powers, Gilbert, and Stapleton come out sparring during a family weekend; it's truth time at Granny's house. Powers is cast as the put-upon advertising executive, unable to communicate with her mother or daughter. (Dir: Jack Hofsiss, 104 mins.)†

Family Sins (MTV 1987)**½ James Farentino, Jill Eikenberry, Andrew Bednarski. Sober study of a family in crisis that's more than vaguely reminiscent of *The Great Santini* and *Ordinary People*. Farentino plays a zealous father who demands too much of his younger son; both he and Eikenberry (as the mom-in-the-middle) deliver strong performances. (Dir: Jerrold Freedman, 96 mins.)

Family Ties Vacation (MTV 1985)**½ Meredith Baxter Birney, Michael Gross, Michael J. Fox, Justine Bateman, Tina Yothers, Charles McKeown, James Saxon, John Moulder-Brown. A visit to London with the Keaton family covers all bases. Good for fans; this is part sitcom, part sightseeing tour. (Dir: Will Mackenzie, 104 mins.)

Family Upside Down, A (MTV 1978)*** Fred Astaire, Helen Hayes. Astaire and Hayes make it hard to resist this drama about the problems of growing old. Astaire is a retired house painter, shattered by heart attacks, who ends up in a rest home while his wife (Hayes) frets over their separation. (Dir: David Lowell Rich, 104 mins.)†

Family Way, The (Great Britain, 1967)***½ Hayley Mills, John Mills, Hywel Bennett. Compassionate look at the troubles of young newlyweds (Miss Mills and Bennett). Fine performances by all. John Mills and Marjorie Rhodes are the parents. (Dirs: John and Roy Boulting, 115 mins.)

Fan, The (1949)**½ Jeanne Crain, Madeleine Carroll, George Sanders. Oscar Wilde's comedy of manners, about a lady with a past who uses her daughter to crash society. Attractive production enhances the slightly old-fashioned sentiments of the story. (Dir: Otto Preminger, 89 mins.)

Fan, The (1981)** Lauren Bacall, Maureen Stapleton, James Garner, Michael Biehn. Rather grisly psycho thriller about a fan who takes a proprietary interest in a beloved Broadway musical star. Although the film plays on memories of Bacall's film career, the movie is satisfying neither as a nostalgia-laced shocker nor as a regular slasher film. Based on a bestseller, but the ending's been changed. (Dir: Edward Bianchi, 95 mins.)†

Fancy Pants (1950)*** Bob Hope, Lucille Ball. Bob poses as a gentlemen's gentleman in this hyped-up version of *Ruggles of Red Gap*. Could have been funnier, but the stars help it over the rough spots. (Dir: George Marshall, 92 mins.)†

Fandango (1985)**½ Judd Nelson, Kevin Costner, Sam Robards, Chuck Bush. During the Vietnam crisis in the early seventies, four college buddies have their last fling—to them an epic adventure—one long and prank-filled drive. The dialogue gets a bit heavyhanded at times, but this joyride coasts along smoothly most of the time. (Dir: Kevin Reynolds, 92 mins.)†

Fanfan the Tulip (France, 1951)*** Gerard Philipe, Gina Lollobrigida, Marcel Herrand, Noel Roquevert. International hit comedy-adventure features an army soldier rescuing Louis XV's daughter from highwayman, going off to war, and defeating Austria single-handedly, then returning for the princess's hand. (Dir: Christian-Jacque, 104 mins.)

Fanny (France, 1932)***½ Raimu, Orane Desmazis, Charpin, Pierre Fresnay. The middle panel of the great Marcel Pagnol Marseilles trilogy. In this one, the pregnant Fanny marries the wealthy Panisse and learns to love him despite feelings for her Marius, who has left to go to sea. As usual, it is Raimu's Cesar who dominates the proceedings, with his emotional range and subtlety the rival of Chaplin's. A feast of robust humor. (Dir: Marc Allegret, 120 mins.)†

Fanny (1961)*** Leslie Caron, Horst Buchholz, Maurice Chevalier, Charles Boyer. The enchanting cast makes this love story entertaining. The tale about young lovers parting, a marriage of convenience, and a reunion which almost destroys everyone's life is a bit overlong but works fairly well most of the time. Director Joshua Logan chose to eliminate the songs from this straight film version based on the Broadway musical, but he uses the familiar score as background music. (133 mins.)†

Fanny and Alexander (West Germany, 1983)**** Gunn Wallgren, Allan Edwall, Jarl Kulle, Borje Ahlstedt, Bertil Guva, Jan Malmsjo, Ewa Froling. Set in director Ingmar Bergman's hometown of Uppsala in 1907, this joyous, magical film concentrates on the Ekdahl family and covers a two-year period in which an abundance of events transpire. A complex and intricate story of this wealthy family gradually centers the focus on Fanny and Alexander, the children of one of the Ekdahl sons. Has been shown on cable television and on European television in a seven-hour version. (197 mins.)†

Fanny by Gaslight—See: **Man of Evil**

Fanny Hill (U.S.-West Germany, 1964)* Letitia Roman, Miriam Hopkins, Alex D'Arcy, Ulli Lommel. This lackluster version of the bawdy classic tries to substitute burlesque humor for titillation and falls flat. Fans of director Russ Meyer should note that he made this for another producer, and it contains none of his inimitable frenetic style. (104 mins.)†

Fanny Hill (Great Britain, 1983)** Lisa Raines, Wilfred Hyde-White, Shelley Winters, Oliver Reed, Paddy O'Neil. Unpretentious adaptation of the Victorian classic features an attractive cast and good production values. Raines isn't much of an actress (though she's not really called on to be), so the veteran names in the cast overact in compensation. (Dir: Gerry O'Hara, 92 mins.)†

Fantasia (1940)**** Leopold Stokowksi, Deems Taylor. Extraordinary animated feature marks one of the high points of Walt Disney's achievements in theatrical films. The best of the seven sequences are *Night on Bald Mountain* and *The Sorcerer's Apprentice* (starring Mickey Mouse!), but all of them have achieved a classic reputation. (Story Dirs: Joe Grant, Dick Huemer, 120 mins.)

Fantasies (1973)* Kathleen Collins (Bo Derek), Peter Hooten, Anna Alexiades, Therese Bohlin. Ms. Derek was a teenager when she made this hooter about efforts to turn an empty Greek island into a tourist haven. Directed in dismal amateur-night style by her future husband John Derek. Plays like a wistful greeting card saluting soft porn. AKA: **And Once upon a Love.** (81 mins.)

Fantasies (MTV 1982)** Suzanne Pleshette, Barry Newman, Robert Vaughn, Patrick O'Neal, Lenora May. The cast of a late-night soap opera called "Middletown, U.S.A." is being picked off one at a time. Plot takes all the predictable turns. (Dir: William Wiard, 104 mins.)

Fantastic Invasion of Planet Earth, The—See: **Bubble, The**

Fantastic Invention, The—See: **Fabulous World of Jules Verne, The**

Fantastic Journey, The (MTV 1977)** Ike Eisenmann, Jared Martin, Carl Franklin, Scott Thomas, Susan Howard. A boat-load of Americans disappear in the Bermuda Triangle only to be tossed onto the shores of the lost city of Atlantis. (Dir: Andrew McLaglen, 104 mins.)

Fantastic Planet (France-Czechoslovakia, 1973)*** Voices of Barry Bostwick, Nora Heflin. An animated feature about some giants called "Draags" who fight and then reconcile with a tiny race of creatures. Superb animation. (Dir: Rene Laloux, 71 mins.)†

Fantastic Voyage (1966)*** Stephen Boyd, Arthur Kennedy, Raquel Welch, Donald Pleasence. A team of surgeons and scientists shrink to bacteria size in order to enter the human body to perform a delicate brain operation. The color work and the animation are first-rate, and the kids and adults will enjoy this striking, exciting, futuristic journey. (Dir: Richard Fleischer, 100 mins.)†

Fantastic World of D.C. Collins, The (MTV 1984)** Bernie Casey, Marilyn McCoo, Gary Coleman, Shelley Smith, Fred Dryer. Take Walter Mitty down a few sizes and you've got this collection of daydream sequences featuring Gary Coleman in various guises including General Patton and a James Bond special agent, as he plays a UN diplomat's son prone to fantasies. (Dir: Leslie Martinson, 100 mins.)

Fantasy Island (MTV 1977)**½ Bill Bixby, Sandra Dee, Peter Lawford, Hugh O'Brian, Loretta Swit. A group of adventurous souls come to a private island where they have been promised they can live out their wildest fantasies. Pilot for the hit series. (Dir: Richard Lang, 98 mins.)†

Fantomas (France-Italy, 1964)* Jean Marais, Mylene Demongeot. France's lackluster contribution to the James Bond mania, based on the *Fantomas* novels by Allain and Souvestre about an unrelievedly evil supercriminal. (Dir: Andre Hunebelle, 104 mins.)

Far Country, The (1955)*** James Stewart, Ruth Roman, Corinne Calvet. Lively adventure about cattle rustling, Alaska-style. Stewart pulls out all the stops as a peaceful cowpoke who gets trampled on at every turn until he just explodes. (Dir: Anthony Mann, 97 mins.)†

Farewell (Germany, 1930)*** Aribet Mog, Brigitte Horney, Vladimar Sokoloff, Emilia Unda. Excellent character drama set in an apartment building in Berlin directed by Robert Siodmak, his first solo feature in Germany before Hitler's actions forced him to go to Hollywood. Superbly written; great use of overlapping sound, with lyrical camera movements that overcome the confinement of the single setting. (71 mins.)

Farewell, The (Finland, 1982)*** Sanna Hultman, Pirkko Nurmi, Kerstin Tidelius, Carl-Axel Heiknert, Gunnar Bjornstrand. Woman growing up in Finland of the 1930s and 1940s must battle her mean-spirited father and her vain, sadistic mother for acceptance of her lesbianism. Dark, brooding movie, set primarily in a dreary old mansion, explores familiar Scandinavian theme of overpowering family relationships. (Dir: Tuija-Maija Niskanen, 90 mins.)

Farewell Friend (1968)** Alain Delon, Charles Bronson. Seen-it-all-before saga of former mercenaries who chum up to rob company vaults. AKA: *Honor Among Thieves*. (Dir: Jean Herman, 119 mins.)

Farewell, My Lovely (1975)**½ Robert Mitchum, John Ireland, Charlotte Rampling, Sylvia Miles. This is the third filmization (after *Murder, My Sweet* and *The Falcon Takes Over*) of Raymond Chandler's popular detective yarn set in the forties and it's seen better days. The low-life characters that Phillip Marlowe (Mitchum) encounters in his quest to locate the girlfriend of an ex-con make for interesting individual scenes, but the tale never quite hangs together. Sequel: *The Big Sleep* (1978). (Dir: Dick Richards, 97 mins.)†

Farewell to Arms, A (1932)***½ Helen Hayes, Gary Cooper. Hayes is magnifi-

cent as the English nurse in Hemingway's tragic romance. Film is fairly good, but it's all hers. Parts of the story dealing with war are not as effective as the romance. (Dir: Frank Borzage, 78 mins.)

Farewell to Arms, A (1957)**½ Jennifer Jones, Rock Hudson, Vittorio De Sica. Hemingway's novel of the love affair between a soldier and a nurse in WWI has been given a huge production with spectacular scenery, big-name cast; but the love story threatens to collapse under all the tonnage. (Dir: Charles Vidor, 150 mins.)

Farewell to Manzanar (MTV 1976)***½ Yuki Shimoda, Nobu McCarthy, Akemi Kikumura, Clyde Kusatsu, Mako. A superb TV drama. To prevent any espionage in WWII, all Japanese, American-born or not, were sent to detention camps, families split up, and property confiscated. It's a sorry chapter in American history, and it comes to life as we watch a peaceful fisherman's family being incarcerated in Camp Manzanar. (Dir: John Korty, 98 mins.)

Farewell to the King (1989)*½ Nick Nolte, Nigel Havers, James Fox, Marius Weyers. Confusing, pretentious epic about WWII deserter Nolte, who becomes king of a South Seas island but must save it from both the British and the Japanese at the end of the war. The original novel was probably good, but as adapted by director John Milius it's impossible to follow. Forget the farewell—don't bother saying hello! (114 mins.)†

Far from Home (1988)**½ Matt Frewer, Drew Barrymore, Richard Masur, Karen Austin, Susan Tyrell, Jennifer Tilly, Dick Miller. Black-comic thriller begins when Frewer and daughter Barrymore run out of gas at Nevada trailer park populated by weirdos and beset by a series of killings. Mystery with erotic trappings raises a few sparks; watchable for the cast of character actors hamming it up. (Dir: Meiert Avis, 86 mins.)†

Far from the Madding Crowd (Great Britain, 1967)*** Julie Christie, Alan Bates, Terence Stamp, Peter Finch. Thomas Hardy's novel about a beautiful girl who manages to make a shambles out of three men's lives is not completely successful as brought to the big screen by director John Schlesinger. Julie Christie never finds quite the right beat as the willful farm girl who betters her station in life but can't seem to find love. (169 mins.)†

Far from Vietnam (France, 1967)***½ Politically charged documentary about America's role in the Vietnam War as seen by nine major international directors. Mere existence of film indicates how central that war was to an understanding of the dynamics and counter-culture of the '60s. (Dirs: Jacques Demy, Jean-Luc Godard, Claude Lelouch, Alain Resnais, Joris Ivens, Agnes Varda, Chris Marker, William Klein, Ruy Guerra, 115 mins.)

Far Horizons, The (1955)**½ Charlton Heston, Fred MacMurray, Donna Reed, Barbara Hale, William Demarest, Alan Reed. Hollywood's version of the historical Lewis and Clark Expedition with a stress on the romance between Clark and the Indian guide, Sacajawea. Good photography. (Dir: Rudolph Mate, 108 mins.)

Farm, The—See: **Curse, The**

Farmer, The (1977)* Gary Conway, Angel Tompkins, Michael Dante, George Memmoli. To pay up the mortgage on his land, a WWII vet becomes a hired killer. His outrage against the system expressed by incessant violence becomes the heart of the film. (Dir: David Berlatsky, 97 mins.)

Farmer's Daughter, The (1940)** Martha Raye, Charlie Ruggles, Richard Denning, William Frawley, William Demarest. Farm girl Raye attaches herself to rehearsals of a new play (a vanity production for a millionaire's talentless girlfriend) being held in a local barn. Slapstick comedy, low on laughs but loaded with Martha. (Dir: James Hogan, 60 mins.)

Farmer's Daughter, The (1947)*** Loretta Young, Joseph Cotten, Ethel Barrymore, Charles Bickford. Fiery Swedish servant girl makes a fight for a congressional seat, soon has everyone rooting for her. Fine comedy-drama combines patriotism and good humor in an expert blend. Wonderfully acted. Look for James Arness and Cy Barker in bit parts. (Dir: H. C. Potter, 97 mins.)†

Farmer's Other Daughter, The (1964)** Judy Pennebaker, Bill Michael, William Guhl, Harry Lovejoy, Jean Bennett. Once-risqué comedy of the sort that only played drive-ins below the Mason-Dixon line. The brief nudity has been edited out, leaving a broad farce about a farmer trying to save his land with the help of the government. Video curio features a mini-concert by country group the Kentucky Colonels, who relentlessly plug their record label. AKA: **Farm Girl**. (Dir: John Patrick Hayes, 84 mins.)†

Farmer Takes a Wife, The (1935)*** Janet Gaynor, Henry Fonda, Charles Bickford, Slim Summerville, Andy Devine, Jane Withers, Margaret Hamilton, John Qualen, Dick Foran. Fonda made his film debut in this adaptation of the Broadway hit he starred in, a rural set against the early days of the Erie Canal. Nice performances and an interesting historical setting. Remade in 1953. (Dir: Victor Fleming, 91 mins.)

Farmer Takes a Wife, The (1953)** Betty Grable, Dale Robertson, John Carroll, Eddie Foy, Jr., Thelma Ritter. Average yarn about a young girl shipping up and down the Erie Canal in the 1820s who finds security in the arms of a stolid if sexy farmer. Stylized sets are used to good advantage. The leads are short on character candle-power. (Dir: Henry Levin, 81 mins.)†

Farm Girl—See: **Farmer's Other Daughter, The**

Far North (1988)*** Jessica Lange, Charles Durning, Tess Harper, Donald Moffat, Ann Wedgeworth, Patricia Arquette. Unusual low-key allegory about the demise of the farming lifestyle in the northern part of America, written and directed by Sam Shepard. An ailing father (Durning) gives his willful daughter (Lange) a mission: shoot the horse that nearly killed him in a wagon accident. The message and symbolism may be obscure, but the humorous passages work quite well; Shepard's picturesque visuals seem inspired by the directors he has collaborated with in the past. (90 mins.)†

Far Pavilions, The (MCTV 1984)** Ben Cross, Amy Irving, Omar Sharif, John Gielgud, Christopher Lee, Rossano Brazzi, Saeed Jaffrey. Tale of a nineteenth-century British officer in India torn between his mother country and his Hindu upbringing and in love with a princess promised to another. Costumes and scenery are sumptuous, but the plot is thin and old. Originally a six-hour miniseries. (Dir: Peter Duffell, 108 mins.)†

Farrebique (France, 1947)**** One of the great documentaries tells the story of a peasant farm family living in southwest France. Lyrical camerawork and fluid editing beautifully capture the hardships and relations of their day-to-day lives. Many memorable scenes include bread-baking sequence and the arrival of spring (in thrilling time-lapse photography). (Dir: Georges Rouquier, 85 mins.)

Farrell for the People (MTV 1982)** Valerie Harper, Ed O'Neill, Gregory Sierra, Eugene Roche. Failed pilot for another proposed lawyer series. The storyline rather unconscionably echoes the Norman Mailer-Jack Henry Abbott affair as Harper prosecutes a case involving a celebrity who campaigned for the release of a convict who subsequently committed murder. (Dir: Paul Wendkos, 104 mins.)

Fascist, The (Italy, 1961)*** Ugo Tognazzi, Georges Wilson, Stefania Sandrelli. A hardcore Fascist captures a famous professor who's a thorn in the side of the enemy. But on the way back to Rome the professor turns the tables. Amusing comedy-drama. (Dir: Luciano Salce, 102 mins.)

Fashions of 1934 (1934)*** William Powell, Bette Davis. An inconsequential plot is lifted out of the commonplace by delightful performances by Powell and Davis. Sometimes Warner Brothers threw in everything but the kitchen sink; this film even has a Busby Berkeley production number as Powell and loyal sidekick Davis elbow their way into the world of Parisian haute couture. (Dir: William Dieterle, 78 mins.)

Fast and Furious (1939)*** Franchot Tone, Ann Sothern, Ruth Hussey, Lee Bowman, Allyn Joslyn, Mary Beth Hughes, Granville Bates. Last of three lighthearted MGM mysteries, modeled after the *Thin Man* series, with husband and wife team of Joel and Garda Sloane investigating murder at a seaside beauty pageant. Maybe these characters would have caught on if they hadn't been played by different actors in each film! (The other entries were *Fast Company* and *Fast and Loose* [1939].) (Dir: Busby Berkeley, 70 mins.)

Fast and Loose (1930)**½ Miriam Hopkins, Frank Morgan, Charles Starrett, Ilka Chase, Carole Lombard. Socialite Hopkins falls in love with poor boy Starrett in this social comedy, which leans a little too heavily on the star's charm; look for Lombard in a small part. Co-written by Preston Sturges. (Dir: Fred Newmeyer, 75 mins.)

Fast and Loose (1939)**½ Robert Montgomery, Rosalind Russell, Reginald Owen, Ralph Morgan, Etienne Girardot, Sidney Blackmer. Montgomery and Russell take over as Nick and Nora Charles manqués to Joel and Garda Sloane in this sequel to *Fast Company*. Swift-paced comedy-mystery concerns a country house party and a stolen Shakespeare manuscript; bright and expertly played. Followed by *Fast and Furious*. (Dir: Edwin L. Marin, 80 mins.)

Fast and Loose (Great Britain, 1954)**½ Kay Kendall, Brian Reece. Husband is stranded in the country with a glamour girl; wife becomes suspicious. Pleasant comedy. (Dir: Gordon Parry, 75 mins.)

Fast and Sexy (Italy, 1960)** Gina Lollobrigida, Dale Robertson. A good comedy idea that gets bogged down with sentiment. Gina is a joy to behold but Dale Robertson as an Italian is a little much. (Dir: Vittorio De Sica, 98 mins.)

Fast and the Furious, The (1954)** Dorothy Malone, John Ireland, Bruce Carlisle, Iris Adrian. It's neither. Just a formula action-pic about a man falsely accused, and his close calls avoiding capture by the cops. (Dir: Edward Sampson, 73 mins.)

Fast Break (1979)** Gabe Kaplan, Harold Sylvester, Mike Warren. TV-flavored sitcom antics as the obnoxious Kaplan coaches basketball at a sleepy midwestern college. The twist here is that Gabe enhances his chances by importing his streetwise N.Y. students to play for him. (Dir: Jack Smight, 107 mins.)†

Fast Charlie—the Moonbeam Rider (1979)** David Carradine, Brenda Vaccaro, L. Q. Jones. Inconsequential story of motorcycle racers just after WWI. The personable cast make the most of a slight story about a war veteran who is tempted to fix a race. (Dir: Steve Carver, 99 mins.)

Fast Company (1938)**½ Melvyn Douglas, Florence Rice, Louis Calhern, Claire Dodd, Shepperd Strudwick, Nat Pendleton, Douglass Drumbrille, George Zucco, Dwight Frye. A connoisseur of rare books uses his expertise to solve a crime, with the help of his wife and henchman. Neat, witty comic mystery, the first of three films designed to capitalize on the appeal of the *Thin Man*'s Nick and Nora Charles with another husband and wife team. Followed by *Fast and Loose* (1939). (Dir: Edward Buzzell, 73 mins.)

Fast Company (1953)**½ Howard Keel, Polly Bergen. Trainer has a knack of making a certain horse win, goes into partnership with a pretty owner. Amusing racing comedy. (Dir: John Sturges, 67 mins.)

Faster Pussycat...Kill! Kill! (1966)*** Tura Satana, Haji, Lori Williams, Stuart Lancaster. Independent filmmaker Russ Meyer's cult classic is certainly not for all tastes—it's hard to imagine anyone over the age of thirty enjoying it. Three go-go dancers drive fast, twist even faster, and generally raise hell in the California desert. Once seen, Tura Satana is not easily forgotten. (Dir: Russ Meyer, 84 mins.)†

Fastest Guitar Alive, The (1967)** Roy Orbison, Sammy Jackson, Maggie Pierce. Misadventures of a couple of Confederate operators out to rob a mint. (Dir: Michael Moore, 87 mins.)†

Fastest Gun Alive, The (1956)**½ Glenn Ford, Broderick Crawford, Jeanne Crain. Storekeeper gets a reputation as a fast gun, is challenged by a gunman to a duel. Fairly suspenseful western flamboyantly acted by Ford and Crawford. (Dir: Russell Rouse, 92 mins.)

Fast Food (1989)**½ Clark Brandon, Randal Patrick, Tracy Griffith, Jim Varney, Michael J. Pollard, Traci Lords, Pamela Springsteen. Two young con artists open a burger joint, taking on fast-food magnate Varney in the process. Funny junk-food comedy isn't very nourishing, but it's a guilty pleasure anyway. (Dir: Michael A. Simpson, 92 mins.)†

Fast Forward (1985)* Monique Cintron, John Scott Clough, Noel Conlon, Don Franklin, Tamara Mark. A breakdancing movie with a twist: an integrated group of Ohio schoolkids dream of catching a bus for the "big time," New York, where they will compete in the "annual rock group shoot-out." Dance: 10, Script: 3! (Dir: Sidney Poitier, 110 mins.)†

Fast Friends (MTV 1979)**½ Edie Adams, Dick Shawn, Carrie Snodgress, Mackenzie Phillips. Behind-the-scenes look at a network TV talk show presided over by a not-so-nice host. (Dir: Steven H. Stern, 104 mins.)

Fast Talking (Australia, 1986)*½ Rod Zuanic, Toni Allaylis, Chris Truswell. Steve, a fast-talker, seems to talk his way out of fitting into responsible society. Lacks a point of view. (Dir: Ken Cameron, 93 mins.)†

Fast Times at Ridgemont High (1982)*** Sean Penn, Jennifer Jason Leigh, Judge Reinhold, Robert Rowanus, Brian Backer, Phoebe Cates. Entertaining, music-filled drama of teenage life in a California high school. Corny, but populated by amusing characters and sometimes very sensitive in depicting their growing pains. (Dir: Amy Heckerling, 92 mins.)†

Fast Walking (1982)* James Woods, Kay Lenz, Robert Hooks, M. Emmet Walsh. Rotten prison melodrama. A basically decent white prison guard finds himself caught between white bigots trying to bump off a black leader and the leader's followers who are trying to break him out of jail. Written, directed, and produced abysmally by James B. Harris. (115 mins.)†

Fast Workers (1933)** John Gilbert, Robert Armstrong, Mae Clarke, Sterling Holloway, Virginia Cherrill. Strange, unsuccessful story of two construction workers and their rivalry at work and in love; descends into weighty melodrama. A failed experiment. (Dir: Tod Browning, 68 mins.)

Fatal Attraction (Canada, 1980)** Sally Kellerman, Stephen Lack, John Huston, Lawrence Dane, John Peter Linton. Sometimes funny, generally pretentious story of psychologist Kellerman and teacher Lack whose erotic games, based on children's stories, begin to escalate in intensity. AKA: **Head On.** (Dir: Michael Grant, 98 mins.)†

Fatal Attraction (1987)***½ Michael Douglas, Glenn Close, Anne Archer, Ellen Hamilton Latzen, Stuart Pankin. Happily married Douglas has a weekend fling with Close, little knowing that she is a dangerous obsessive who'll come to threaten him and his family. Slick and often terrifying movie touched a lot of nerves and became a box office smash.

The original ending, changed after preview audiences found it unsatisfying, is now available on a special video version. (Dir: Adrian Lyne, 120 mins.)†

Fatal Beauty (1987)** Whoopi Goldberg, Sam Elliott, Rubén Blades, Harris Yulin. Goldberg plays an undercover cop who's out to bust the backers of an insidious cocaine ring. (Dir: Tom Holland, 103 mins.)†

Fatal Confession: A Father Dowling Mystery (MTV 1987)*½ Tom Bosley, Tracy Nelson, Sada Thompson, Leslie Nielsen, Susan Blakely, Peter Scolari. The supposed suicide of a young, adopted millionaire is investigated by a sleuth with a white collar. (Dir: Chris Hibler, 104 mins.)

Fatal Exposure (MCTV 1990)** Mare Winningham, Nick Mancuso, Christopher McDonald. Standard suspense thriller about a recently divorced mother pitted against a sadistic killer on a rural island off the Pacific Northwest. Leisurely paced tale offers nothing new but profits from a better-than-average performance from the always-reliable Winningham. (Dir: Alan Metzger, 92 mins.)

Fatal Hour, The (1940)*½ Boris Karloff, Marjorie Reynolds, Grant Withers. Mundane Mr. Wong mystery with Boris trying to solve crimes and overcome a script riddled with implausibilities. (Dir: William Nigh, 67 mins.)†

Fatal Vision (MTV 1984)***½ Karl Malden, Gary Cole, Eva Marie Saint, Gary Grubbs, Mitchell Ryan, Andy Griffith. Gripping TV movie. In 1970, the family of Dr. Jeffrey MacDonald was brutally murdered, and he was charged with the slayings. Cole, in his starring debut, is first rate as the All-American former Green Beret who steadfastly maintains his innocence. (Dir: David Greene, 198 mins.)†

Fata Morgana (West Germany, 1971)**** Werner Herzog's brilliant visual ode to man and nature, a stunning, surrealistic interpretation of the world's beginning. Gorgeously photographed in the Sahara desert, with music ranging from Couperin to Johnny Cash and Leonard Cohen. A great, must-see film. (78 mins.)

Fat City (1972)***½ Stacy Keach, Jeff Bridges, Susan Tyrrell. Director John Huston's deeply moving drama about a washed-up 31-year-old boxer (Keach) —benefits from the superb, lean, compassionate screenplay of Leonard Gardner, based on his novel. The protagonist is a boxer but this heartbreaking film is not essentially about boxing—it's about the lonely, empty life of some of the urban poor and their limited expectations. (96 mins.)†

Fate Is the Hunter (1964)*** Glenn Ford, Nancy Kwan, Rod Taylor, Suzanne

Pleshette. A sometimes exciting drama which has Ford playing an airlines investigator who leaves no stone unturned in trying to piece together the whys and wherefores of a fatal crash that took more than fifty lives. The flashback technique works well. (Dir: Ralph Nelson, 106 mins.)

Fat Guy Goes Nutzoid (1986)½ Tibor Feldman, Douglas Stone, Max Alexander, John Mackay. In this one, an overweight young man escapes from a home for the mentally retarded. If that's your idea of a hilarious premise, have fun. (Dir: John Golden, 85 mins.)†

Father (Hungary, 1966)*** Andras Balint, Miklos Gabor, Kati Solyom, Klari Tolnay. Young man searches for understanding about his deceased father, who aided Jews during WWII. The boy has a Jewish girlfriend, and both become involved in the intellectual fallout from the Hungarian Uprising of 1956. Humorous and telling tale about conflict between generations. (Istvan Szabo, 95 mins.)†

Father Brown, Detective—See: Detective, The

Father Damien: The Leper Priest (MTV 1980)** Ken Howard, Mike Farrell, Wilfred Hyde-White. TV series star Ken Howard is miscast as Father Damien, the Roman Catholic priest who gave his life to improve the conditions of a leper colony in Hawaii a century ago, bucking government officials and the church itself in his crusade. AKA: **Damien the Leper Priest.** (Dir: Steven Gethers, 104 mins.)†

Father Figure (MTV 1980)**½ Hal Linden, Timothy Hutton, Martha Scott, Jeremy Licht. Linden is trying to make friends with his two sons, from whom he has been separated for five years. After a rocky start, things warm up in a slow-moving yet well-meaning film. (Dir: Jerry London, 104 mins.)†

Father Goose (1964)**½ Cary Grant, Leslie Caron. Cary Grant foregoes his customary polish and trim wardrobe for the role of a genial, fun-loving drifter named Walter who assists the Australian Navy during WWII by becoming a plane spotter on a remote atoll in the South Seas. Leslie Caron, with a group of children in tow, descends upon the island, and Grant's peaceful mission turns into a free-for-all. (Dir: Ralph Nelson, 115 mins.)†

Father Is a Bachelor (1950)** William Holden, Coleen Gray, Charles Winninger. Lightweight comedy about a roustabout bachelor and his involvement with five orphans, a lovable old medicine showman, and a judge's daughter. (Dir: Norman Foster, 84 mins.)

Father Knows Best Reunion (MTV 1977)**½ Robert Young, Jane Wyatt, Elinor Donahue, Billy Gray, Lauren Chapin. Heartwarming comedy-drama reunion show. Young and Wyatt (both very effective) are about to celebrate their thirty-fifth wedding anniversary, and since she feels lonely, he sends for the kids. (Dir: Marc Daniels, 78 mins.)

Father of Hell Town (MTV 1985)** Robert Blake, Whitman Mayo, Amy Green, Tim Scott, Vonetta McGee. Robert Blake plays a ghetto priest walking the streets of L.A. aiding junkies, prostitutes, and troubled kids. (Dir: Don Medford, 104 mins.)

Father of the Bride (1950)***½ Spencer Tracy, Elizabeth Taylor, Joan Bennett. One of the best comedies ever made about the many important and unimportant things that make a young bride's wedding day a success. Tracy, as the bride's father and/or financial backer, has a field day in the role and there seldom has been a more beautiful bride than Elizabeth. (Dir: Vincente Minnelli, 93 mins.)

Father's Dilemma (Italy, 1952)**** Aldo Fabrizi, Gaby Morlay. A very funny comedy revolving around a communion dress and a father's efforts to find it after he has lost it. (Dir: Alessandro Blasetti, 88 mins.)

Father's Homecoming, A (MTV 1988)**½ Michael McKean, Jonathan Ward, Peter Michael Goetz. Better-than-average family drama about the new headmaster (McKean) at a New England prep school, dealing with the school's new co-ed policy, school-vs.-town conflicts, and his own teenagers. (Dir: Rich Wallace, 96 mins.)

Father's Little Dividend (1951)*** Elizabeth Taylor, Spencer Tracy, Joan Bennett. Refreshing sequel to *Father of the Bride*, all the characters are present and the laughs come fast and furious. What an excellent farceur Tracy was—see this one if you like well-done family comedies. (Dir: Vincente Minnelli, 82 mins.)†

Father's Revenge, A (MTV 1988)*½ Brian Dennehy, Joanna Cassidy, Ron Silver. Hardworking actor Dennehy plays a father who adopts terrorist tactics to retrieve his kidnapped stewardess daughter. Unmemorable teledrama. (Dir: John Herzfeld, 96 mins.)

Father Takes a Wife (1941)*** Adolphe Menjou, Gloria Swanson, John Howard, Desi Arnaz, Helen Broderick. Charming trifle about a glamourpuss who vacates the theater for a steady marriage and then rocks the marital boat by taking on a protegé, an action that makes her husband boil over. (Dir: Jack Hively, 79 mins.)

Father Was a Fullback (1949)** Fred MacMurray, Maureen O'Hara, Thelma Ritter. Football coach's efforts to win the Big Game and solve his family problems simultaneously. Bright comic touches by Thelma Ritter. (Dir: John M. Stahl, 84 mins.)

Fathom (1967)**½ Raquel Welch, Tony Franciosa, Clive Revill. Entertaining, mindless spy spoof with the title role being bikinied rather than acted by the truly ravishing Raquel Welch. The plot is as busy as Miss Welch, involving a stolen figurine and the parade of villains who are after it. (Dir: Leslie H. Martinson, 90 mins.)

Fat Man, The (1951)** J. Scott Smart, Julie London, Rock Hudson. Radio's famed serial reaches the screen and plays like a radio show, heavy on exposition and slow on action. (Dir: William Castle, 77 mins.)

Fat Man and Little Boy (1989)*½ Paul Newman, Dwight Schultz, Bonnie Bedelia, John Cusack, Laura Dern, John C. McGinley, Natasha Richardson, Del Close. Talky, fragmented misfire about creation of the first pair of atomic bombs. Trying to make an epic drama about the Manhattan Project meetings and laboratory sessions is like trying to film a calculus textbook. (Dir: Roland Joffé, 126 mins.)†

Fatso (1980)*½ Dom DeLuise, Anne Bancroft, Ron Carey, Candice Azzara. Given the talent involved, this is a disappointing film about an obese Italian-American's (DeLuise) quest to diet. (Dir: Anne Bancroft, 94 mins.)†

Faust (Germany, 1962)**** Emil Jannings, Gosta Ekman, Camilla Horn, Wilhelm Dieterle. Legendary tale of elderly professor who sells his soul to the devil in order to be young again. Director F. W. Murnau's last German film, a silent classic, features imaginative sets and Carl Hoffman's sublime photography; Jannings, as Mephistopheles, is brilliant. (136 min.)

FBI Story, The (1959)** James Stewart, Vera Miles, Murray Hamilton, Nick Adams. The film trades its soul for Bureau approval. Neither the personal story, nor Stewart as an agent, nor the "factual" material coalesce. Under Mervyn LeRoy's lackluster direction, the film meanders without drama, inspiration, or truth. (149 mins.)†

FBI Story, The: The FBI Versus Alvin Karpis, Public Enemy Number One, The (MTV 1974)**½ Robert Foxworth, Harris Yulin, Eileen Heckart. Submachine gun blasts fill the screen as thirties killer Alvin Karpis and his gang run rampant, kidnapping and robbing banks and trains. Takes pains not to glamorize Karpis, effectively portrayed by Robert Foxworth. (Dir: Marvin Chomsky, 100 mins.)

F.D.R., the Last Year (MTV 1980)***½ Jason Robards, Jr., Eileen Heckart, Edward Binns, Larry Gates, Kim Hunter. Intensely moving account of the last twelve wartime months of the president's life. Robards focuses on Roosevelt's resiliency despite congestive heart failure, presenting him as a buoyant spirit beaten down at times, but never giving up. (Dir: Anthony Page, 153 mins.)

Fear (West Germany, 1955)** Ingrid Bergman, Mathias Wieman, Kurt Kreuger. English-dubbed. An indiscreet woman is blackmailed by her lover's ex-girl, then worries that her husband will find out. AKA: **Angst.** (Dir: Roberto Rossellini, 84 mins.)

Fear (MCTV 1990)*** Ally Sheedy, Lauren Hutton, Michael O'Keefe, Dina Merrill. Frightening suspense thriller about a psychic (Sheedy) who is unwillingly drawn into the mind of a serial killer who murders his victims with their ultimate fear of death. Tense direction and a chilling Henry Mancini score make this a truly riveting tale of terror. (Dir: Rockne S. O'Bannon, 90 mins.)†

Fear, Anxiety and Depression (1989)** Todd Solondz, Max Cantor, Alexandra Gersten, Stanley Tucci. Comedy about pretentiously arty New Yorkers. Writer-director-star Todd Solondz has Woody Allen's fascination with ugly people and slightly surreal point of view. (85 mins.)†

Fear Chamber—See: Chamber of Fear

Fear City (1985)**½ Tom Berenger, Billy Dee Williams, Jack Scalia, Melanie Griffith, Rossano Brazzi. Slick thriller with Berenger and Scalia as strip-club owners whose dancers are being murdered and Williams as a cop trying to catch the killer. Director Abel Ferrara (*Ms. 45*) brings a glossy style to the story that fits the Times Square setting well. (95 mins.)†

Fear in the City (Italy, 1980)* Michel Constantin, Gianni Manera, Fred Williamson. Competing factions of the Sicilian Mafia and a black crime organization battle to wipe each other out. (Dir: Gianni Manera, 102 mins.)†

Fear in the Night (1947)*** Paul Kelly, DeForest Kelley. An innocent dupe is made to think he has murdered by use of hypnosis. Tense mystery, well above average. Remade as *Nightmare*, 1956. (Dir: Maxwell Shane, 72 mins.)†

Fear in the Night (Great Britain, 1972)*** Ralph Bates, Judy Geeson, Peter Cushing, Joan Collins. Tingly psychological thriller from Hammer Films. A neurotic young woman, just married, goes to stay at the lonely boys' school where her husband teaches. Strange things start to happen and she begins to fear for her sanity. (Dir: Jimmy Sangster, 85 mins.)†

Fear Is the Key (Great Britain, 1972)* Barry Newman, Suzy Kendall. Alistair MacLean's heavily plotted novel about a deep-sea treasure-recovery expert and his run-in with an international group of thieves, plays like a cartoon-book adventure. (Dir: Michael Tuchner, 103 mins.)

Fearless Frank (1969)* Jon Voight, Monique Van Vooren, Severn Darden. Ur-

341

ban morality tale casts Voight as a country boy turned mechanized evil-fighter in the big city, counterpointed by his reforming replica, "False Frank." (Dir: Philip Kaufman, 78 mins.)

Fearless Vampire Killers, The: or, Pardon Me, But Your Teeth Are In My Neck (U.S.-Great Britain, 1967)** Roman Polanski, Sharon Tate, Jack MacGowran, Ferdy Mayne. Polanski not only directed this meandering comedy-horror story but also played the assistant to the mad professor who comes to Transylvania to obliterate the local vampires. A 111-minute version is also available on video. (98 mins.)†

Fearmaker, The (Mexico, 1974)** Katy Jurado, Paul Picerni, Sonia Amelio, Fernando Soler. After opera star Jurado inherits her father's fortune, her manager and sister plot to kill her for the money. Plenty of plot twists but slow going. AKA: House of Fear. (Dir: Anthony Carras, 90 mins.)†

Fearmakers, The (1958)** Dana Andrews, Mel Torme, Dick Foran. A mixed-up drama about crime and violence tied in with political intrigue. (Dir: Jacques Tourneur, 83 mins.)

Fear No Evil (MTV 1969)*** Louis Jourdan, Lynda Day, Bradford Dillman. A young lady keeps a nightly rendezvous with her dead fiancé. The absorbing story delves into the macabre world of the occult that worships evil demons, and the finale involving an enchanted full-length mirror may jolt you. (Dir: Paul Wendkos, 98 mins.)

Fear No Evil (1981)** Stefan Arngrim, Elizabeth Hoffman, Kathleen Rowe McAllen, Frank Birney. Three archangels have come to Earth to oppose Satan, who takes the form of a troubled teenager whose powers include the ability to raise the dead. A few chilling moments including a grisly passion play that turns into reality. (Dir: Frank Laloggia, 96 mins.)†

Fear on Trial (MTV 1975)***½ William Devane, George C. Scott. John Henry Faulk's book about the infamous blacklisting in TV in the fifties and how it ruined his most promising radio and TV career finally has been made into a film, and a surprisingly good one at that. Devane plays the homespun radio personality whose name appears on the powerful AWARE bulletin, a publication created by two vicious businessmen who took it upon themselves to "safeguard" the entertainment industry from infiltration by leftwingers in the McCarthy era. A film to be seen. (Dir: Lamont Johnson, 100 mins.)

Fear Strikes Out (1957)***½ Anthony Perkins, Karl Malden, Norma Moore. Don't miss this fine drama with Anthony

342

Perkins giving his best screen performance to date as baseball player Jim Piersall. The film deals mostly with Piersall's personal problems, which contributed to his nervous breakdown. Karl Malden is excellent as Piersall's pushy father. (Dir: Robert Mulligan, 100 mins.)†

Feather and Father (MTV 1977)**½ Stefanie Powers, Harold Gould. Pilot for a TV series. Gould is charming as the ex-con artist who keeps tending to revert; Powers as Feather, the righteous lawyer, is less than adequate. (Dir: Buzz Kulik, 78 mins.)

Feathered Serpent, The (1948)*½ Roland Winters, Keye Luke, Victor Sen Yung, Mantan Moreland, Carol Forman. Charlie Chan the Inscrutable investigates a lost temple in Mexico. (Dir: William Beaudine, 61 mins.)

Fedora (West Germany, 1978)*** William Holden, Marthe Keller, José Ferrer, Hildegard Neff, Michael York, Henry Fonda. It's about time director Billy Wilder, curdled cynic, was recognized for the compassionate romantic he has always been. An aging Hollywood director meets a reclusive retired star and finds her beauty mysteriously unchanged. Here Wilder contemplates celebrity, the vanity of art, and shows us characters in the throes of raging against the dye dying of their light. (113 mins.)

Feds (1988)**½ Rebecca DeMornay, Mary Gross, Ken Marshall. Famil but engaging comedy with ex-Marine DeMornay and lawyer Gross trying to help each other get through basic training at the FBI Academy. Best scene has Gross cutting loose and trying to pick up a drunken sailor. (Dir: Dan Goldberg, 83 mins.)†

Feelin' Up! (1976)½ Malcolm Groome, Kathleen Seward, Rhonda Hansome. This chaotic hash about an uptight young man whose attempt to liberate himself through a freer sexual lifestyle would make even a self-respecting pornographer cringe. (Dir: David Secter, 82 mins.)†

Feel My Pulse (1928)*** Bebe Daniels, Richard Arlen, William Powell, George Irving, Melbourne MacDowell. Lighthearted comedy-thriller of an heiress, brought up to believe her health is delicate, who discovers unexpected stamina when she gets mixed up in a wild adventure involving bootleggers and a charming reporter. Silent screwball comedy much like director Gregory LaCava's later work. (86 mins.)†

Feet First (1930)*** Harold Lloyd, Barbara Kent, Robert McWade, Sleep'n'Eat (Willie Best). Lloyd hadn't yet mastered talkie technique yet, and this is more a remake of his silent comedies than an original creation. Still funny, but the rhythm is off. (Dir: Clyde Bruckman, 83 mins.)

Fellini Satyricon (Italy-France, 1969)*½ Martin Potter, Hiram Keller, Capucine, Donyale Luna, Lucia Bose, Gordon Mitchell, Alain Cuny. Once again, director Federico Fellini dazzles the eye with a series of ghastly, picaresque, beautiful, freaky, ravishing, bestial images as he turns his attention to recreating the world of Petronius Arbiter, Rome circa 50–66 A.D. But movie math finds that in this *Satyricon* the whole adds up to considerably less than the sum of its parts. (120 mins.)†

Fellini's Casanova (Italy, 1976)**½ Donald Sutherland, Tina Aumont, Cicely Browne. An enormously disappointing, overlong narrative about the celebrated 18th-century Venetian rake, Giovanni Jacopo Casanova de Seingat. (Dir: Federico Fellini, 166 mins.)

Fellini's Roma (Italy-France, 1972)** Peter Gonzales, Stefano Majore, Anna Magnani, Gore Vidal. Not one of director Federico Fellini's best, an often self-indulgent grab bag of comedy, drama, fantasy moving from childhood to the present day, intended to be a sardonic commentary on the collapse of Rome and of Western Europe. (113 mins.)

Fellow Traveler (Great Britain-U.S., 1990)***½ Ron Silver, Hart Bochner, Imogen Stubbs, Daniel J. Travanti, Katherine Borowitz. Powerful, original drama of the McCarthy blacklist era, when many in Hollywood were unable to work because of accusations (true or false) that they had once been communist sympathizers. Silver plays a successful scriptwriter who is forced to work in London after his best friend commits suicide and the witchhunters come looking for him. (Dir: Philip Saville, 91 mins.)†

Female Animal, The (1958)** Hedy Lamarr, Jane Powell, Jan Sterling, George Nader. Romantic melodrama. A Hollywood star, Miss Lamarr, is saved from death by a handsome extra, Nader. (Dir: Harry Keller, 83 mins.)

Female Artillery (MTV 1973)**½ Dennis Weaver, Ida Lupino. Average western. A group of unescorted women and children traveling west by wagon train meet up with a stranger on the run, played by Weaver. (Dir: Marvin Chomsky, 73 mins.)

Female Jungle (1956)** Jayne Mansfield, Lawrence Tierney, John Carradine, Kathleen Crowley, Bruno VeSota. Jayne's undulating as a trampy good-time girl is the main attraction. Otherwise, the film is a negligible policer about a cop investigating the demise of an actress. (Dir: Bruno VeSota, 56 mins.)†

Female on the Beach (1955)*** Joan Crawford, Jeff Chandler, Jan Sterling. A socko combination of glossy soap opera and lady-in-distress thriller, as Joan suffers agonies of indecision over whether the handsome hunk she's just wed is a murderous gigolo. It's the kind of movie where Jeff can say things like "A woman's no good to a man unless she's a little scared." (Dir: Joseph Pevney, 97 mins.)

Female Trap, The—See: **The Name of the Game Is Kill!**

Female Trouble (1975)***½ Divine, Edith Massey, Mink Stole, David Lochary, Mary Vivian Pearce. Dawn Davenport (Divine), the heroine of director John Waters's bitterly funny cult comedy, would do anything to become famous, working her way up from waitress to go-go girl to cat burglar to media freak to convicted murderess. For those with a predilection for cruel comedies, this is must-viewing with some of the sickest one-liners in underground film history. (95 mins.)†

Feminine Touch (The (1941)**½ Rosalind Russell, Don Ameche, Van Heflin. Occasionally funny comedy about a professor who brings his wife to New York and discovers the woman in her. (Dir: W. S. Van Dyke, 97 mins.)

Feminist and the Fuzz, The (MTV 1970)*½ Barbara Eden, David Hartman, Farrah Fawcett, Jo Anne Worley, Harry Morgan, Julie Newmar, Penny Marshall. Chauvinist pig meets lady libber. Fuzzy. (Dir: Jerry Paris, 73 mins.)

Femmes de Personne (France, 1986)*** Marthe Keller, Jean-Louis Trintignant, Caroline Cellier, Fanny Cotencon, Philippe Leotard. A moody character study about four women for whom the benefits of successful careers and sexual liberation have not resulted in great personal satisfaction. (Dir: Christopher Frank, 106 mins.)

Femmes Fatales (France, 1978)***½ Jean-Pierre Mareille, Jean Rochefort. Director Bertrand Blier's second feature is a mordant fantasy: a gynecologist (Mareille) and a pimp (Rochefort) decide that they have had it with women and sex and repair to the countryside to get celibate. The revolution spreads, the women strike back in force, the film ends as science fiction, which gives you the general idea. Provocative comedy. (81 mins.)

Fer-de-Lance (MTV 1974)* David Janssen, Hope Lange, Ivan Dixon, Jason Evers. Ridiculous adventure set on a sub trapped undersea and beset with poisonous snakes, demented crewmen, and a diver pinned by falling rocks. AKA: **Death Dive**. (Dir: Russ Mayberry, 100 mins.)

Ferocious Female Freedom Fighters (1982)

**★★½ Eva Arnez, Barry Prima. Whatever this foreign-made thriller was about to begin with, newly overdubbed dialogue by the L.A. Connection comedy troupe has turned it into an occasionally hilarious spoof about a female wrestler whose family is kidnapped by mobsters. No *What's Up Tiger Lily?* but silly fun anyway. (Dir: Jopi Burnama, 74 mins.)†

Ferris Bueller's Day Off (1986)*½ Matthew Broderick, Jeffrey Jones, Alan Ruck, Mia Sara, Cindy Pickett, Jennifer Grey, Edie McClurg, Charlie Sheen. A dispiriting popular success about a teen con artist and alleged free spirit who pulls the wool over the immediate world's eyes and gets away with playing hooky. (Dir: John Hughes, 102 mins.)†

Ferry to Hong Kong (Great Britain, 1960)** Curt Jurgens, Orson Welles, Sylvia Syms. Slow-moving, outdated melodrama about a drifter who winds up aboard a ferryboat and turns hero when the ship is attacked. (Dir: Lewis Gilbert, 103 mins.)†

Feud, The (1989)*** René Auberjonois, Ron McLarty, Joe Grifasi, Scott Allegrucci, Gayle Mayron. Through a series of misunderstandings and unfortunate coincidences, two families in neighboring small towns find themselves in a bitter feud. Satire of Norman Rockwell Americana based on Thomas Berger's novel works by toning down Berger's superciliousness and fleshing out his broad cast of characters. (Dir: Bill D'Elia, 96 mins.)†

Feudin' Fools (1952)** Bowery Boys, Anne Kimbell, Dorothy Ford. The Boys get involved in the hillbilly feudin' of the Smiths and the Joneses. Sach just happens to be the Jones who inherits the family farm. (Dir: William Beaudine, 63 mins.)

Feudin', Fussin' and a-Fightin' (1948)** Donald O'Connor, Marjorie Main, Percy Kilbride, Penny Edwards, Joe Besser, I. Stanford Jolley. Hillbilly musical-comedy made palatable by the ever-lively O'Connor as a traveling salesman shanghaied into a footrace between two feuding towns. (Dir: George Sherman, 70 mins.)

Fever In the Blood, A (1961)**½ Efrem Zimbalist, Jr., Angie Dickinson, Jack Kelly, Don Ameche. A judge, a D.A., and a senator all have their eye on the governor's chair, and a murder trial is used to further their political ambitions. Drama of political maneuvering is salty enough to hold the attention. (Dir: Vincent Sherman, 117 mins.)

Fever Pitch (1985)* Ryan O'Neal, Chad Everett, Catherine Hicks, John Saxon. O'Neal, as a prizewinning sportswriter, investigates the state of gambling in America and becomes a compulsive gambler himself. A must for fans of

bad movies. (Dir: Richard Brooks, 95 mins.)†

Few Days In Weasel Creek, A (MTV 1981)** Mare Winningham, John Hammond, Kevin Geer, Nicholas Pryor, Glenn Morshower, Tracey Gold, Colleen Dewhurst. Genuine talent goes to waste in this rambling yarn about two runaway people who meet and fall in love. (Dir: Dick Lowry, 104 mins.)

Few Days with Me, A (France, 1988)**½ Daniel Auteuil, Sandrine Bonnaire, Danielle Darrieux, Jean-Pierre Marielle. Thin but sporadically amusing comedy about a young man of wealthy family who, after a nervous breakdown, abandons everything to move in with a waitress he has just met. (Dir: Claude Sautet, 127 mins.)

ffolkes (Great Britain, 1980)*** Roger Moore, James Mason, Anthony Perkins, Michael Parks, Jeremy Clyde. Entertaining caper comedy-thriller. Gruff Moore, in a character role as a woman-hating commando, has to stop Perkins and cohorts from blowing up a costly oil platform in the North Sea. AKA: **Assault Force.** (Dir: Andrew V. McLaglen, 92 mins.)†

F for Fake (France, 1973)*** Orson Welles directed this semidocumentary about such liars, fakers, and charlatans as author Clifford Irving of the Howard Hughes book contract scam and art forger Elmyr de Hory. Uneven—some of it spurious, some engaging. (Dir: Orson Welles, 85 mins.)

Flancés, The (Italy, 1963)**½ J. Carlo Cabrini, Anna Canzli. Simple tale of an engaged couple who are separated when he must go north to find work. Director Ermanno Olmi exhibits visual control and solicitude for the feelings of the working classes. (85 mins.)

Fickle Finger of Fate, The (U.S.-Spain, 1967)* Tab Hunter, Luis Prendes, Patty Shepard. Nonsense about an American tourist who helps Spanish authorities track down the thief who stole a religious candlestick known as "The Fickle Finger of Fate." (Dir: Richard Rush, 91 mins.)

Fiddler on the Roof (1971)*** Topol, Molly Picon, Norma Crane, Leonard Frey. The long-running, prize-winning Broadway musical hit based on the stories of Sholem Aleichem survives the transfer to the big screen quite well. It details the story of Tevye, the poor dairy farmer who tries to marry off his three daughters. Set in a small Ukranian village in 1905, *Fiddler* is carried by a splendid score including such rousing songs as "If I Were a Rich Man" and "Tevye's Dream." (Dir: Norman Jewison, 180 mins.)†

Field, The (Ireland, 1990)*** Richard Harris, John Hurt, Tom Berenger, Sean Bean, Francis Tomelty, Brenda Fricker. An Irish tenant farmer faces the loss of the land his family has worked for years when it's put up for auction, and bid on by an American (Berenger). What power the film has comes from Harris's performance as the fiercely tenacious aging patriarch. Although he only rents the land, he battles for his lush green pasture as if he's fighting for his very soul. (Dir: Jim Sheridan, 110 mins.)†

Field of Dreams (1989)*** Kevin Costner, James Earl Jones, Amy Madigan, Burt Lancaster, Ray Liotta, Timothy Busfield. Sentimental fantasy will either charm or annoy you. Farmer Costner hears messages from an invisible voice, leading him to build a baseball diamond in his cornfield. Baseball serves as a metaphor for pre-'60s innocence in this touching but vague New Age fable. (Dir: Phil Alden Robinson, 106 mins.)†

Field of Honor (France, 1988)*** Cris Campion, Pascale Rocard, Eric Wapler. Low-key, timeless 19th-century war drama about a young man who agrees to be drafted in place of a rich merchant's son. The film effectively captures his feelings as well as those of the ones he leaves behind. (Dir: Jean-Pierre Denis, 87 mins.)†

Fiend, The (Great Britain, 1972)** Ann Todd, Patrick Magee, Tony Beckley. Odd, unpleasant shocker about a weird religious sect and the psychotics who belong to it. (Dir: Robert Hartford-Davis, 87 mins.)

Fiendish Plot of Dr. Fu Manchu, The (1980)** Peter Sellers, Helen Mirren, David Tomlinson, Sid Caesar. Sellers's last film, in which he plays several different roles, is a pathetically inept farce. The plot, ironically, has Fu (Sellers) incessantly returning from the brink of death to continue his hunt for the elixir of youth. (Dir: Piers Haggard, 108 mins.)†

Fiend Who Walked the West, The (1958)** Hugh O'Brian, Robert Evans, Dolores Michaels. Ex-cellmate of an escaped killer is freed to help track him down, then finds his life and family's welfare threatened by the "fiend." (Dir: Gordon Douglas, 101 mins.)

Fiend Without a Face (Great Britain, 1958)* Marshall Thompson, Terence Kilburn. Poor science-fiction melodrama in which scientists combat monsters created as a result of experiments by the U.S. Air Force in Canada. (Dir: Arthur Crabtree, 74 mins.)†

Fiercest Heart, The (1961)** Stuart Whitman, Juliet Prowse, Raymond Massey, Geraldine Fitzgerald. Army deserters in South Africa (1837) join some Boers on a trek, protect them from warring Zulus. (Dir: George Sherman, 91 mins.)

Fiesta (1947)** Esther Williams, Ricardo Montalbán, Akim Tamiroff, Mary Astor, Cyd Charisse, John Carroll. Esther Williams plays a lady bullfighter in this piece of MGM Latin-American folderol with lots of colorfully inauthentic dancing. (Dir: Richard Thorpe, 104 mins.)

Fifth Avenue Girl (1939)** Ginger Rogers, Walter Connolly, James Ellison. Millionaire arranges a romance between his son and a plain Jane. Strained, dull comedy. (Dir: Gregory La Cava, 83 mins.)

5th Day of Peace, The (Italy, 1972)** Richard Johnson, Franco Nero. Prisoner-of-war story which starts out interesting but soon falters into obvious plot twists. (Dir: Giuliano Montaldo, 100 mins.)†

Fifth Floor, The (1980)*½ Dianne Hull, Bo Hopkins, Patti D'Arbanville. Horror thriller about a disco waitress. From a story by Howard Avedis, producer and director, and exec producer Marlene Schmidt. (90 mins.)†

Fifth Horseman Is Fear, The (Czechoslovakia, 1965)**** Powerfully presented story of a Jewish doctor (Miroslav Machacek) harboring a fugitive in Nazi-occupied Prague. Grim, strong sequences stay in the memory. An excellent example of the capabilities of the heretofore neglected Czechoslovakian filmmakers. (Dir: Zbynek Brynych, 100 mins.)

Fifth Missile, The (MTV 1986)*½ Robert Conrad, Sam Waterston, David Soul, Richard Roundtree, Yvette Mimieux. Unbelievable nonsense in the guise of a psychological thriller about a nuclear submarine. A sub crew runs amok and its gung ho commander becomes a crazed Captain Queeg when they inhale a coating of toxic paint. (Dir: Larry Peerce, 156 mins.)

Fifth Musketeer, The (Austria-Great Britain, 1979)** Beau Bridges, Sylvia Kristel, Ursula Andress, Cornel Wilde, Rex Harrison. Still another version of Alexandre Dumas's *Man in the Iron Mask*. Bridges, in the dual role of King Louis XIV and his twin brother Philippe, falls short of the antic heroics needed to carry off the title role with style and conviction. (Dir: Ken Annakin, 103 mins.)†

55 Days at Peking (1963)*** Charlton Heston, Ava Gardner, David Niven, Flora Robson, Leo Genn. Nicholas Ray planned and started directing this blockbuster spectacle set during the Boxer Rebellion (Andrew Marton finished it). Good action uncoils within an intelligent political context. (150 mins.)†

Fifty Roads to Town (1937)**½ Don Ameche, Ann Sothern, Jane Darwell, Slim Summerville, John Qualen, Stepin

Fetchit. Comedy-thriller of three fugitives on the lam from various troubles, all stranded by a snowstorm in a country cabin. (Dir: Norman Taurog, 81 mins.)

52 Pickup (1986)*** Roy Scheider, Ann-Margret, Vanity, John Glover, Clarence Williams III. Scheider stars as a hard-boiled, self-made businessman who fights back against a trio of colorful (and slimy) blackmailers in this fast-paced thriller that incorporates an unusual amount of sex-related activities into a familiar "revenge" plotline. Elmore Leonard co-wrote the script from another of his best-selling novels. (Dir: John Frankenheimer, 114 mins.)†

Fighter, The (1951)***½ Richard Conte, Vanessa Brown, Lee J. Cobb. In revolution-torn Mexico of 1910, a young patriot offers his services as a boxer to raise money for the cause. Well-made melodrama. (Dir: Herbert Kline, 78 mins.)

Fighter, The (MTV 1983)* Gregory Harrison, Glynnis O'Connor, Pat Hingle, Steve Inwood. An empty story that gives Gregory Harrison another excuse to take off his clothes. Suddenly finding himself unemployed when his mill closes down, Harrison tries his hand at boxing to pull in a few bucks. (Dir: David Lowell Rich, 104 mins.)

Fighter Attack (1953)**½ Sterling Hayden, Joy Page. Another war yarn with Sterling Hayden cast as a heroic major who leads an important mission before the film runs its course. (Dir: Lesley Selander, 80 mins.)

Fight for Jenny, A (MTV 1986)** Lesley Ann Warren, Philip Michael Thomas, Jaclyn-Rose Lester. Thomas is teamed with Warren as an interracial couple. They fall for each other and then have to face court battles over Lesley Ann's daughter from an earlier marriage. (Dir: Gilbert Moses, 104 mins.)

Fight for Life (MTV 1987)** Jerry Lewis, Patty Duke, Morgan Freeman, Jaclyn Bernstein, Barry Morse, Gerard Parkes. "Disease-of-the-week" drama with Lewis kvetching all over the place as the father of an epileptic girl. Like a short version of one of his telethons, without the music or comedy. (Dir: Elliot Silverstein, 104 mins.)

Fighting Back (MTV 1980)**½ Robert Urich, Bonnie Bedelia, Richard Herd, Howard Cosell. True story of Pittsburgh Steeler Rocky Bleier's miraculous football comeback after he was seriously injured in Vietnam. (Dir: Robert Lieberman, 104 mins.)

Fighting Back (1982)*½ Tom Skerritt, Patti Lupone, Ted Ross, Michael Sarrazin, Yaphet Kotto, David Rasche. A Philadelphia merchant fights back when crime begins running rampant in his community. Unlike other similar films, our hero's not alone; his neighbors band together. AKA: **Death Vengeance**. (Dir: Lewis Teague, 98 mins.)†

Fighting Choice (MTV 1986)** Beau Bridges, Karen Valentine, Patrick Dempsey. A teen sues his parents for the right to determine his own medical treatment—a life-threatening operation for his severe epilepsy. (Dir: Ferdinand Fairfax, 104 mins.)

Fighting Father Dunne (1948)***½ Pat O'Brien, Darryl Hickman. A St. Louis priest establishes a home for orphan newsboys. Sincere, well-made drama, good entertainment. (Dir: Ted Tetzlaff, 93 mins.)†

Fighting Fools (1949)**½ Bowery Boys, Frankie Darro. The Boys get Johnny Higgins (Darro) to kick his drinking habit and train for the boxing ring. (Dir: Reginald LeBorg, 69 mins.)

Fighting Kentuckian, The (1949)**½ John Wayne, Vera Ralston, Oliver Hardy. Frontiersman courting an aristocrat's daughter foils a plot to steal land from French settlers. (Dir: George Waggner, 100 mins.)†

Fighting Lady, The (1945)**½ Color documentary made during WWII. Its picture of shipboard life and naval combat is compelling. (Dir: William Wyler, 61 mins.)

Fighting Lawman, The (1953)** Wayne Morris, Virginia Grey. Routine western fare about a lawman who comes under a wicked woman's influence but everything turns out for the best. (Dir: Thomas Carr, 71 mins.)

Fighting Mad (1976)*** Peter Fonda, Lynn Lowry, Philip Carey. Concentrating on character rather than wallowing in violent excess, the movie's quite a compelling tale about a man who returns home to find his family's homestead is being eyed hungrily by a real estate concern. (Dir: Jonathan Demme, 90 mins.)†

Fighting Prince of Donegal, The (1966)*** Peter McEnery, Susan Hampshire. During the reign of Elizabeth I, an Irish rebel endeavors to band his people together. Flavorful juvenile swashbuckler. (Dir: Michael O'Herlihy, 112 mins.)†

Fighting Seabees, The (1944)***½ John Wayne, Susan Hayward, Dennis O'Keefe. Tough construction foreman and a Navy man organize a work battalion to repair installations close to Japanese lines. Rousing war melodrama, loaded with action. (Dir: Edward Ludwig, 100 mins.)†

Fighting 69th, The (1940)***½ James Cagney, Pat O'Brien. This picture is as corny as they come but is one of the most stirring war pictures you'll ever see. Topflight entertainment. (Dir: William Keighley, 89 mins.)

Fighting Sullivans, The—See: **Sullivans, The**

Fighting Trouble (1956)** Huntz Hall, Stanley Clements, Danny Welton. Sach and Duke attempt to photograph a notorious gangster for a newspaper. With Clements replacing Leo Gorcey, the series ran out of steam. (Dir: George Blair, 61 mins.)

Figures in a Landscape (Great Britain, 1971)*** Robert Shaw, Malcolm McDowell. A commissioned project, directed in Spain by Joseph Losey, that was largely rewritten by star Shaw during production. An overly conscious and allegorical work of art, but saved by the concreteness of its rugged action. (110 mins.)

File of the Golden Goose, The (Great Britain, 1969)** Yul Brynner, Charles Gray, Edward Woodward. American secret agent, played in an obvious manner by Brynner, infiltrates a counterfeiting ring with the help of Scotland Yard. (Dir: Sam Wanamaker, 105 mins.)

File on Thelma Jordon, The (1950)**½ Barbara Stanwyck, Wendell Corey, Paul Kelly, Joan Tetzel. This Robert Siodmak-directed film has a contrived melodramatic plot (a D.A. falls in love with a murder suspect and throws the case to save her), a lot of nice *film noir* touches, and a typically professional portrayal by Stanwyck. (100 mins.)

Fillmore (1972)***½ Last days of the Fillmore West in San Francisco are documented, mainly focusing on the great acts that appeared there and their music. Included are Santana, the Grateful Dead, and the Jefferson Airplane. (Dir: Richard T. Heffron, 105 mins.)

Final Accord (Germany, 1936)*** Willy Birgel, Lil Dagover, Maria Von Tasnady, Theodor Loos. Quality melodrama about woman who returns to Germany after the death of her husband, a criminal, to seek her son, now living with an orchestra conductor. Wonderfully directed by Detlef Sierck, before he moved to Hollywood and changed his name to Douglas Sirk. (100 mins.)

Final Assignment (1980)*½ Genevieve Bujold, Michael York, Colleen Dewhurst, Burgess Meredith. The assignment is to smuggle a Soviet child out of the U.S.S.R. It becomes especially difficult when the woman pulling off the scheme is an outspoken Canadian reporter (Bujold) who is not only involved with a high-ranking Soviet propagandist, but is already being monitored by the KGB. (Dir: Paul Almond, 100 mins.)†

Final Chapter—Walking Tall (1977)* Bo Svenson, Margaret Blye, Forrest Tucker. Saga of real-life Tennessee sheriff Buford Pusser, who died under mysteri-

ous circumstances after crusading against vice and corruption, comes to an end in this third film about his exploits. (Dir: Jack Starrett, 112 mins.)†

Final Combat, The—See: **Le Dernier Combat**

Final Comedown, The (1972)** Billy Dee Williams, D'Urville Martin, Celia Kaye, Raymond St. Jacques, Pamela Jones, R. G. Armstrong. Young black man, frustrated by racism, becomes drawn to the doctrines of a militant group that sees violence as the solution. Cynical but serious film is now mostly an interesting sociological artifact. (Dir: Oscar Williams, 83 mins.)†

Final Conflict, The (Great Britain, 1981)** Sam Neill, Rossano Brazzi, Don Gordon, Lisa Harrow. In the third part of the *Omen* trilogy, the Antichrist, Damien (Neill), has matured into a corrupt politician who—along with his vicious dog—plans to take over the world. Pales in comparison to *The Omen*, yet interesting at times and—like the first two—very bloody and gruesome. (Dir: Graham Baker, 108 mins.)†

Final Countdown, The (1980)*** Kirk Douglas, Martin Sheen, Katharine Ross, James Farentino. Caught in a time warp, the commanders aboard today's carrier U.S.S. *Nimitz* must decide whether to prevent the bombing of Pearl Harbor in '41. The premise, which is surprisingly believable, combines with the photography, special effects, and a surprise ending to make an entertaining film. (Dir: Don Taylor, 103 mins.)†

Final Crash—See: **Steelyard Blues**

Final Days, The (MTV 1989)**** Lane Smith, David Ogden Stiers, Ed Flanders, Theodore Bikel, Graham Bekel, James B. Sikking, Richard Kiley, Amanda Wyss, Gary Sinise. Superb adaptation of the book by Bob Woodward and Carl Bernstein chronicling the personal effects of the Watergate scandal on Richard Nixon. Smith is outstanding as the disgraced president, avoiding caricature and creating an understanding (if not forgiving) portrait of a man facing a self-created downfall. (Dir: Richard Pearce, 144 mins.)

Final Exam (1981)*½ Cecile Bagdadi, Joel S. Rice, Ralph Brown, Deanna Robbins. Below-average escaped-lunapic in which suspense is built by wondering when the interminable scenes will actually end. Menace is obviated by having the stalker stalk without remembering to slash—until the last ten minutes. (Dir: Jimmy Huston, 90 mins.)†

Final Extra, The (1927)*** Marguerite de la Motte, Grant Withers. After a star reporter is gunned down investigating a bootlegging ring run by the mysterious ''Shadow,'' cub reporter Withers gets his big break. Old-fashioned silent mystery in which the villain's secret identity is no secret at all. (Dir: James P. Hogan, 76 mins.)†

Final Jeopardy, The (MTV 1985)*½ Richard Thomas, Mary Crosby. Irresponsible drama that adds to the general public's phobias about inner-city dangers. Thomas plays a businessman who takes his wife with him on what is to be an ordinary business meeting in a seedy section of a big city, and then the terror begins. (Dir: Michael Pressman, 104 mins.)

Final Justice (1985)** Joe Don Baker, Venantino Venantini, Rossano Brazzi, Bill McKinney. A gun-toting sheriff who has his own methods of law enforcement is bounced off the force, but gets a new job escorting a hoodlum to Italy, where his methods fit right in with the violence-drenched terrain. (Dir: Greydon Clark, 90 mins.)†

Final Notice (MTV 1989)**½ Gil Gerard, Melody Anderson, Jackie Burroughs, Kevin Hicks, Louise Fletcher, David Ogden Stiers, Steve Landesberg. Private eye Gerard investigating a Cincinnati killer who has gone from mutilating pictures of women in library books to the real thing. Average detective thriller with a dollop of panache. (Dir: Steven H. Stern, 88 mins.)†

Final Option, The (Great Britain, 1982)* Judy Davis, Lewis Collins, Richard Widmark, Robert Webber. Preposterous adventure film about a radical anti-nuclear group who take over an American embassy and will stop at nothing to end the proliferation of nuclear weapons. The film never reconciles its pretentious political overtones with the spy thriller aspects of its storyline. (Dir: Ian Sharp, 125 mins.)†

Final Programme, The—See: **Last Days of Man on Earth, The**

Final Terror, The (1981)* John Friedrich, Rachel Ward, Daryl Hannah, Adrian Zmed, Mark Metcalf. Some teens, who somehow have never seen *Friday the 13th*, go camping in the woods where they shouldn't. (Dir: Andrew Davis, 82 mins.)†

Final Test, The (Great Britain, 1953)***½ Jack Warner, Robert Morley. Star cricket batsman is dismayed when he finds his son wants to be a poet. Witty, finely written comedy-drama. Recommended. (Dir: Anthony Asquith, 84 mins.)

Finders Keepers (1952)**½ Tom Ewell, Julia Adams. Tom Ewell makes this wacky comedy seem better than it really is. He plays an ex-con who wants to go legit but his two-year-old son's innocent habits almost land him back in stir. (Dir: Frederick de Cordova, 74 mins.)†

Finders Keepers (1984)*** Michael

O'Keefe, Lou Gossett, Jr., David Wayne, Beverly D'Angelo, Pamela Stephenson, Ed Lauter. A screwball surprise from director Richard Lester. On a cross-country train trip, an unsuccessful Roller Derby manager hooks up with a larcenous couple who've just stolen five million bucks which they've stashed in a casket that's supposed to contain a Vietnam veteran. The pursuit of ill-gotten gain has seldom been handled in such an off-the-wall, hilarious manner. (92 mins.)†

Finders Keepers, Lovers Weepers (1968)** Anne Chapman, Paul Lockwood, Gordon Wescourt. There are go-go dancers galore, and simulated violence to boot, in this obscure Russ Meyer outing. The sordid plotline concerns the attempted robbery of a go-go bar and the many lives it touches. (71 mins.)†

Find the Lady (Canada, 1976)* Lawrence Dane, John Candy, Michel Rooney, Alexandra Bastedo, Peter Cook. Don't be fooled by the video packaging which promotes this as a John Candy movie: he only has a supporting role, and not a very good one at that. Dopey comedy about inept cops only made it to the U.S. market to cash in on Candy's later success. (Dir: John Trent, 79 mins.)†

Fine Madness, A (1966)***½ Sean Connery, Joanne Woodward, Jean Seberg. Sean Connery gives a very fine performance as a bold, outspoken, radical poet who gets caught up in his own momentum. Joanne Woodward as his waitress-wife is brash and funny, and the rest of the cast, mostly made up of Broadway actors, adds greatly to the inventive screwball comedy. Unconventional fun. (Dir: Irvin Kershner, 104 mins.)

Fine Mess, A (1986)½ Ted Danson, Howie Mandel, Maria Conchita Alonso, Stuart Margolin, Richard Mulligan, Jennifer Edwards, Paul Sorvino. Loosely inspired by *The Music Box*; Laurel and Hardy should haunt director Blake Edwards from the Great Beyond. Sloppy slapstick about an actor and a carhop on the run from gangsters. (Dir: Blake Edwards, 100 mins.)†

Fine Pair, A (Italy, 1968)* Rock Hudson, Claudia Cardinale, Thomas Milian. Complicated caper as police captain Hudson is tricked by Cardinale into aiding in a heist. (Dir: Francesco Maselli, 89 mins.)

Finest Hours, The (Great Britain, 1964)***½ This prize-winning documentary is stunning on several counts—scenes of Churchill's childhood, his early adventures in India and South Africa, followed by his remarkable career, which thrust him into the heart of most of the great events of this century. (Dir: Peter Baylis, 114 mins.)†

Finger Man (1955)**½ Frank Lovejoy, Forrest Tucker. Criminal is released from prison to get the goods on an underworld boss. Fast-moving crime melodrama. (Dir: Harold Schuster, 82 mins.)†

Finger Points, The (1931)**½ Richard Barthelmess, Fay Wray, Regis Toomey, Clark Gable, Robert Elliott, J. Carroll Naish. Odd, sluggish crime drama based on a true story that was a big scandal at the time: a Chicago reporter on the take from the mob goes too far and is rubbed out. Barthelmess does what he can with an underwritten script, and Gable is certainly a standout as a bowler-hatted gangster, but the movie doesn't jell. Story by W. R. Burnett. (Dir: John Francis Dillon, 88 mins.)

Fingers (1978)**½ Harvey Keitel, Jim Brown, Michael V. Gazzo, Tisa Farrow, Tanya Roberts. Compelling character study of a man whose life suddenly falls apart piece by piece. Keitel gives the performance of his career as a talented concert pianist whose underworld ties threaten to destroy his chances. However, director James Toback's flashy, episodic script combines high-voltage interpersonal drama with failed attempts at sexual violence. (91 mins.)†

Fingers at the Window (1942)*** Lew Ayres, Laraine Day, Basil Rathbone, Miles Mander, Walter Kingsford, Charles D. Brown. Enjoyable little comic-mystery, with a flamboyant young actor (Ayres) solving a crime at an insane asylum with the help of a pretty girl (Day). (Dir: Charles Lederer, 80 mins.)

Finian's Rainbow (1968)**½ Fred Astaire, Petula Clark, Tommy Steele, Al Freeman, Jr., Keenan Wynn. This broke ground when it opened as a Broadway musical in the late forties, but was dated by the time Francis Ford Coppola directed it for the screen. The best feature of this musical, concerned with leprechauns and racism, is Astaire in the leading role; he's funny, and even dances and sings a bit. (145 mins.)†

Finish Line (MTV 1989)** James Brolin, Josh Brolin. The Brolins play a highly competitive track coach and his son, who resorts to steroid use out of fear of not living up to dad's expectations. The family drama is fine, but the story falls prey to the usual antidrug clichés. (Dir: John Nicolella, 96 mins.)†

Finnegan, Begin Again (MCTV 1985)**½ Mary Tyler Moore, Robert Preston, Sam Waterston, Sylvia Sidney, David Huddleston. Preston has a senile wife at home (Sidney) and writes an advice-to-the-lovelorn column. Moore is a schoolteacher having an affair with a married undertaker (Waterston). (Dir: Joan Micklin Silver, 114 mins.)†

Fire!—See: Irwin Allen's Production of Fire!

Fire and Ice (1983)* Voices of James Ostrander, Maggie Roswell, Stephen Mendel, Susan Tyrell. Animator Ralph Bakshi's worst film suffers from the sterility of his rotoscoping technique (which here amounts to little more than tracing live actors) and a simpleminded story of good and evil in a prehistoric kingdom. Bakshi and co-producer Frank Frazetta collaborated on the story and character designs. (81 mins.)†

Fire and Ice (1987)*½ John Eaves, Suzy Chaffee, Willy Bogner. Bravura ski sequences do not a movie make, such as this one-note outing about a dim-witted skier (Eaves) who follows the light of his life (hyper-perky ski champ Chaffee) to Aspen. With narration by John Denver(!). (Dir: Willy Bogner, 83 mins.)†

Fireball, The (1950)** Mickey Rooney, Pat O'Brien, Marilyn Monroe. An orphan kid becomes a hot-shot roller skater, but his ego gets the best of him. (Dir: Tay Garnett, 84 mins.)

Fireball 500 (1966)*½ Frankie Avalon, Annette Funicello, Fabian, Chill Wills, Harvey Lembeck. Fabian and Frankie compete for glory on the racetrack and for Annette off of it. Fans of the trio's campy beach party movies will be disappointed, and who else would even think of watching this in the first place? (Dir: William Asher, 92 mins.)

Fireball Forward (MTV 1972)**½ Ben Gazzara, Eddie Albert, Edward Binns, Ricardo Montalbán. WWII drama, by the *Patton* writing-producing team, actually uses excess battle footage taken while shooting that movie. Story focuses on command problems after a major general takes charge of a division plagued by bad luck and poor morale. (Dir: Marvin Chomsky, 100 mins.)

Fire Birds (1990)* Nicolas Cage, Tommy Lee Jones, Sean Young, Bryan Kestner, Mary Ellen Trainor. Risable *Top Gun* clone may have been intended as a tongue-in-cheek parody, but we doubt it. There's almost no plot conflict as hotshot Army helicopter pilot Cage (both over- and underacting) trains to fly special assault choppers and battle a generic South American drug cartel. This one gets the bird. (Dir: David Green, 85 mins.)†

Firebird 2015 A.D. (1981)** Darren McGavin, Doug McClure, George Toulatos, Mary Beth Rubens. In a future when the world's oil supplies have been almost completely depleted, a government agency has been set up to destroy privately owned automobiles. Fast-paced action movie wears out its welcome with too many chases, too little plot. (Dir: David Robertson, 97 mins.)†

Firecreek (1968)**½ Henry Fonda, James Stewart, Inger Stevens, Gary Lockwood, Dean Jagger. Timid sheriff Stewart vs. gangleader Fonda, whose men are terrorizing the town. Unduly protracted, but some good performances. (Dir: Vincent McEveety, 104 mins.)

Fire Down Below (1957)*** Rita Hayworth, Robert Mitchum, Jack Lemmon. Mitchum and Lemmon are two adventurers who meet and fall for Rita, a shady lady. A ship's explosion traps Lemmon in the debris and Mitchum risks his life to save him. (Dir: Robert Parrish, 110 mins.)†

Firefighter (MTV 1986)** Nancy McKeon, Barry Corbin, Guy Boyd, Vincent Irizarry, Amanda Wyss. Nancy McKeon stars as L.A.'s first firewoman, Cindy Fralick. Can Cindy pass that rigorous physical? Can she endure male chauvinism? (Dir: Robert Lewis, 96 mins.)

Firefly, The (1937)*** Jeanette MacDonald, Allan Jones, Warren William, George Zucco, Billy Gilbert. Outstanding operetta about spies during the Napoleonic war. This lavish production (originally in sepia tone) showcases Ms. MacDonald at her best and is graced by a memorable Rudolf Friml score. (Dir: Robert Z. Leonard, 131 mins.)

Firefox (1982)* Clint Eastwood, Freddie Jones, David Huffman. A sluggish, far-fetched action film; Eastwood plays a U.S. pilot who goes to Russia to steal a supersecret plane that can't be detected by radar. (Dir: Clint Eastwood, 137 mins.)†

Firehead (1991)**½ Christopher Plummer, Chris Lemmon, Martin Landau, Brett Porter, Gretchen Becker. Interesting sci-fi tale about a Soviet defector whom U.S. scientists turn into a telekinetic superman capable of shooting lasers from his eyes. He goes out of control and the chase is on. B-movie fun. (Dir: Peter Yuval, 88 mins.)†

Firehouse (MTV 1972)**½ Richard Roundtree, Vince Edwards. Racism in an all-white fire-engine company. An Archie Bunker–type fireman (Edwards) leads his close-knit company in the hazing of a new black recruit (Roundtree). (Dir: Alex March, 73 mins.)†

Firehouse (1986)*½ Barrett Hopkins, John Anderson. Lukewarm *Police Academy* clone set at a fire-fighting academy, where the first female graduates have to prove that they're up to par. (Dir: J. Christian Ingvorsen, 91 mins.)†

Fire In the Sky, A (MTV 1978)**½ Richard Crenna, Elizabeth Ashley. Pretty fair disaster movie. A comet seems to be headed straight for Phoenix, Arizona, but city officials dally over evacuation plans. When the panic button is pushed the show takes off with good special effects and crowd scenes in Phoenix. (Dir: Jerry Jameson, 156 mins.)

Fire Maidens of Outer Space (Great Britain, 1955) ½ Susan Shaw, Anthony Dexter, Paul Carpenter, Harry Fowler. A kindergarten pageant would probably have a bigger budget than this grade Z sci-fi. He-man astronauts encounter some shapely space-chicks who feel a cosmic mating urge swelling within them. (Dir: Cy Roth, 80 mins.)

Fireman, Save My Child (1932)**½ Joe E. Brown, Evelyn Knapp, Lillian Bond, George Meeker, Guy Kibbee. Brown can't decide between being a firefighter or a ballplayer; nice effort, but not one of his best comedies. (Dir: Lloyd Bacon, 67 mins.)

Fireman, Save My Child (1954)** Spike Jones, Buddy Hackett. A turn-of-the-century slapstick comedy-musical about a group of misfit firemen who are more trouble than a four-alarmer. (Dir: Leslie Goodwins, 80 mins.)

Firemen's Ball, The (Czechoslovakia, 1967)*** Vaclav Stockel, Josef Svet. Funny, touching, and observant study of petty bureaucratic minds and people in a small Czechoslovakian town. Simple story concerns the effort to honor a fire chief who is retiring at the ripe old age of eighty-six. The ceremony is turned into a shambles and the film makes its points about politics, life and art in understated but unerringly accurate terms. (Dir: Milos Forman, 73 mins.)†

Fire on the Mountain (MTV 1981)** Ron Howard, Buddy Ebsen, Julie Carmen, Rossie Harris. Earnest realtor teams up with rancher, who refuses to give up his land for an Army missile base. (Dir: Donald Wrye, 104 mins.)

Fire Over Africa (Great Britain, 1954)** Maureen O'Hara, Macdonald Carey. Undercover agents work against great odds to smash a smuggling ring operating in Tangier. Mild melodrama. (Dir: Richard Sale, 84 mins.)

Fire Over England (Great Britain, 1937)**½ Laurence Olivier, Vivien Leigh, Flora Robson, Raymond Massey. Spectacular tale about the Spanish Armada surrounding the English. Olivier and Leigh make an attractive pair, and the film was an effective morale booster as WWII threatened to break out. (Dir: Willam K. Howard, 89 mins.)†

Firepower (Great Britain, 1979)** Sophia Loren, James Coburn, O. J. Simpson, Eli Wallach, Anthony Franciosa. Involved thriller that makes little sense. The three leads are determined to get at a wealthy man, well guarded in a secluded fortress, for various reasons. (Dir: Michael Winner, 104 mins.)†

Fire Sale (1977)** Alan Arkin, Rob Reiner, Vincent Gardenia, Anjanette Comer, Kay

Medford, Sid Caesar. A black comedy that is utterly hilarious and downright stupid by turns, depending on the viewer's tolerance for high-pitched ethnic hysteria. Arkin and Reiner are brothers who plan on burning down their father's store for the insurance, but poor old Poppa (Gardenia) isn't as dead as they had thought. Script by Robert Klane, author of *Where's Poppa?* (Dir: Alan Arkin, 88 mins.)

Fires on the Plain (Japan, 1959)*** Eiji Funakoshi, Osamu Takizawa, Mickey Curtis. Director Kon Ichikawa's absurdist humor almost salvages this antiwar indictment in which routed Japanese soldiers on Leyte resort to cannibalism in order to survive. The film is harsh, forceful, yet recalcitrantly arty in mostly wrongheaded ways. (105 mins.)†

Firestarter (1984)*** Drew Barrymore, George C. Scott, David Keith, Heather Locklear, Martin Sheen, Louise Fletcher. A tyke with the gift of pyro-kinesis (the ability to start fires) is pursued by government agents hoping to harness her fiery talents for their own purposes. Still another adaptation of a Stephen King novel, but terrific special effects keep the plot fueled, igniting a nice scary blaze throughout most of its running time. (Dir: Mark Lester, 116 mins.)†

Firewalker (1986)* Chuck Norris, Louis Gossett, Jr., Melody Anderson, Will Sampson, Sonny Landham. Adventurers Norris and Gossett run afoul of cheap papier-mâché sets, racially stereotyped villains, a bad guy whose eyepatch keeps switching eyes, and some of the worst editing in movie history, while searching for a hidden cache of gold. (Dir: J. Lee Thompson, 104 mins.)†

Fire with Fire (1986)*½ Virginia Madsen, Craig Sheffer, Jeffrey Jay Cohen. Overly lyrical teen-confession tripe. He's in a minimum security juvenile detention camp; she's a dewy-eyed romantic convent girl. After the two adolescents run off together, the nuns and prison guards literally try to mow them down. (Dir: Duncan Gibbins, 104 mins.)†

Fire Within, The (France, 1963)**** Maurice Ronet, Jeanne Moreau, Lena Skerla. Director Louis Malle's portrait of the last twenty-four hours in the life of a man emerging from an alcoholism cure is a penetrating study of a man at the end of his rope. (110 mins.)

First Affair (MTV 1983)** Loretta Swit, Joel Higgins, Melissa Sue Anderson. Freckled, blue-eyed Sue Anderson plays a naïve Harvard freshman who falls in love with the husband of her English professor. (Dir: Gus Trikonis, 104 mins.)†

First Blood (1982)** Sylvester Stallone,

Richard Crenna, Brian Dennehy. Stallone plays a heroic Vietnam veteran who wages his own war against the sheriff of a small town in which he was unfairly jailed and grossly mistreated. His beefy nonacting doesn't diminish the cheap, violent brand of excitement found here. Sequel: *Rambo: First Blood Part Two.* (Dir: Ted Kotcheff, 94 mins.)†

First Born (1984)**½ Teri Garr, Peter Weller, Christopher Collet, Corey Haim, Sarah Jessica Parker. A divorced mother needs to be saved by her firstborn child from a relationship with an undesirable suitor. The impressive acting doesn't lift this film out of the ordinary, and the potential for a moving exploration of feelings is sadly missed by resorting to excessive melodramatics. (Dir: Michael Apted, 104 mins.)†

First Date (Taiwan-U.S., 1989)*** Chang Shi, Li Xing Wen, Shi Jun, Peter Wang. Slight but charming tale of a boy in 1950s Taiwan experiencing sexual awakenenings and the responsibilities of adulthood for the first time. From the writer-director of *A Great Wall*, Peter Wang, who has a funny supporting part as the boy's drunkenly garrulous father. (90 mins.)

First Deadly Sin, The (1980)** Frank Sinatra, Faye Dunaway, David Dukes. As the aging cop who must nab a deranged murderer while dealing with the slow death of his wife (Dunaway), Sinatra is subdued but convincing. Unfortunately the film is routine and slow-moving. (Dir: Brian Hutton, 112 mins.)†

First Family (1980)** Bob Newhart, Gilda Radner, Madeline Kahn, Harvey Korman, Buck Henry. A well-intentioned comedy misfire about an American president who seeks to improve relations with an African country, and has an eccentric family. (Dir: Joan Darling, 104 mins.)†

First Lady (1937)*** Kay Francis, Anita Louise, Verree Teasdale, Preston Foster, Walter Connolly, Victor Jory. From the play by George S. Kaufman and Katherine Dayton. Sharp, witty political satire about the wife of an honest Secretary of State who wants him to run for President; the cast make the most of Kaufman's dialogue. (Dir: Stanley Logan, 82 mins.)

First Legion, The (1951)***½ Charles Boyer, William Demarest, Barbara Rush. A Jesuit seminary in a small town is the center of attraction when a miracle seemingly occurs, but it is disbelieved by one of the priests. This is a sensitive drama, wonderfully well acted, directed, written. (Dir: Douglas Sirk, 86 mins.)†

First Love (1939)***½ Deanna Durbin, Robert Stack, Eugene Pallette. A Cinderella story complete with the big ball at the end and Prince Charming (none other than Robert Stack). Young Deanna Durbin got her first screen kiss by Stack in this film. (Dir: Henry Koster, 90 mins.)

First Love (Great Britain-France-Switzerland, 1970)**½ John Moulder Brown, Dominique Sanda, Maximilian Schell. Baffling adaptation of Turgenev's 1870 novel about a young man (Brown) who falls in love with his father's mistress (Sanda). The love story is more schmaltzy than genuinely lyrical, and shifts wildly and inappropriately in mood. (Dir: Maximilian Schell, 90 mins.)†

First Love (1977)** William Katt, Susan Dey, John Heard, Beverly D'Angelo. Nice performances can't overcome this hard-boiled look at campus affairs that gets more depressing as the movie goes on. (Dir: Joan Darling, 92 mins.)†

First Man into Space (Great Britain, 1959)** Marshall Thompson, Marla Landi. Dated sci-fi about space travel complete with a space creature. Strictly for the kiddies, and very young kiddies at that. (Dir: Robert Day, 77 mins.)†

First Men in the Moon (Great Britain, 1964)** Lionel Jeffries, Martha Hyer. A mediocre version of the H. G. Wells novel, in which a Victorian eccentric is forced into a moon voyage. The attitude toward the material is appropriately larky, but the film has no distinction. (Dir: Nathan Juran, 103 mins.)†

First Monday in October (1981)**½ Walter Matthau, Jill Clayburgh, Barnard Hughes, Jan Sterling, James Stephens, Joshua Bryant. Matthau bites off more than he can chew in the role of a U.S. Supreme Court justice warring with the first woman appointed to the highest court of the land. Jill Clayburgh is more at home in the role of the precedent-setting first woman justice. (Dir: Ronald Neame, 98 mins.)†

First Name: Carmen (France, 1984)***½ Maruscha Detmers, Jacques Bonaffe, Myriem Roussel, Jean-Luc Godard, Christophe Odent. A wickedly witty and passionate update of Merimee's *Carmen* (this time Beethoven's music replaces Bizet in the background). Although claiming to be an independent filmmaker, Carmen's artistic activities are a cover for bank robbing and kidnapping. In the middle of a stylized bank robbery, a security guard spots the irresistible Carmen and runs off with her. The film is really a summation of Godard's iconoclastic career, and he directs this fable with surprising, innovative twists. (85 mins.)†

First Nudie Musical, The (1976)**½ Cindy Williams, Stephen Nathan, Bruce Kimmel, Diana Canova. Comedy about a failing pornographer who decides to make the first all-singing, all-dancing sex movie is oddly inoffensive once you get past the premise. The humor is of the dopey sort that induces giggling if it gets you in the right mood. (Dirs: Mark Haggard, Bruce Kimmel, 100 mins.)†

First Olympics—Athens 1896, The (MTV 1984)*** Louis Jourdan, Angela Lansbury, Honor Blackman, Bill Travers, David Ogden Stiers. A stirring salute to the men who first engineered the idea of the competitive international games. A sort of scaled-down companion piece to the big-screen hit *Chariots of Fire*. (Dir: Alvin Rakoff, 260 mins.)†

First Power, The (1990)½ Lou Diamond Phillips, Tracy Griffith, Jeff Kober, Mykel T. Williamson, Elizabeth Arlen, Dennis Lipscomb. The first few reels of this tale of a cop whose nemesis is a reincarnated serial killer granted immortality by the Devil has such odd rhythms that you start to think the movie is going for something different. Turns out it looks that way because the filmmakers can't grasp even the most basic principles of film storytelling. One of the most incompetent movies to get a theatrical release from a major studio in recent memory. (Dir: Robert Resnikoff, 98 mins.)†

First Spaceship on Venus (East Germany-Poland, 1960)*½ Guenther Simon, Yoko Tani, Oldrick Lukes, Michal Postnikow. Team of scientists trace the source of a mysterious message to the planet Venus. Atrociously dubbed sci-fi with an antinuke message is hard to judge, as fifty-two minutes were sloppily cut out by the U.S. distributor. Production design is striking, but what's left of the plot (adapted from Stanislaw Lem's novel *The Astronauts*) is hard to follow. (Dir: Kurt Maetzig, 78 mins.)†

First Steps (MTV 1985)*** Judd Hirsch, Amy Steel, Kim Darby, Frances Lee McCain. A true-life story about a young woman who became a paraplegic after an auto accident and fought the hard battle to walk (with the aid of pioneering bio-engineer Dr. Jerrold Petrofsky) to receive her diploma upon graduation from college. Uplifting drama. (Dir: Sheldon Larry, 104 mins.)

First Teacher, The (U.S.S.R., 1965)*** Bolot Beishenaliev, Natalia Arinbasarova, Idris Nogaibayev. First feature by Andrei Mikhalkov-Koncalovsky is dramatic story of a former Red Army officer opening a school in a small village, falling in love with a girl who residents demand he marry. Trouble ensues and violence shatters the rural peace in this fascinating study of a stranger in a strange land. (98 mins.)

First Texan, The (1956)** Joel McCrea, Felicia Farr. Lively western about the days when Texas fought for and gained independence from Mexico. (Dir: Byron Haskin, 82 mins.)

First 36 Hours of Dr. Durant, The (MTV 1975)**½ Scott Hylands, Katherine Helmond, Lawrence Pressman, Peter Donat, Dana Andrews. Stirling Silliphant ("Route 66," "Naked City," "Longstreet") turned out this medical pilot film on hospital life seen through the eyes of a young resident. (Dir: Alexander Singer, 72 mins.)

First Time, The (1952)*** Robert Cummings, Barbara Hale, Jeff Donnely, Mona Barrie. Fast and funny comedy dealing with the financial woes of a newly married couple. Cummings is excellent as the male in the middle. (Dir: Frank Tashlin, 89 mins.)

First Time, The (France, 1978)*** Alain Cohen, Charles Denner, Zorica Lozic. More of writer-director Claude Berri's examination of his early life, with young Cohen as a teenage version of the Claude Langmann he played in *The Two of Us* ('68). Claude is now sixteen and attempting to have his first romantic conquest. Pleasant Gallic humor. (85 mins.)

First Time, The (MTV 1982)**½ Susan Anspach, Peter Barton, Edward Winter, Jennifer Jason Leigh, Harriet Nelson. A teenager follows her boyfriend to San Diego, and the girl's mother sets out to find her. Mother, however, refuses to equate her own sexual desires with her daughter's needs. The parallels are well drawn, but this kind of generational conflict drama is commonplace. (Dir: Noel Nosseck, 104 mins.)

First Time, The (1983)** Tim Choate, Krista Errickson, Marshall Efron, Wallace Shawn. Set in a college where the women outnumber the men, our hero Charlie's inexperience at love is compensated by his expertise at filmmaking. Wickedly sending up the pretentiousness of film schools, *The First Time* isn't much more than a student film itself in conception and execution. (Dir: Charlie Loventhal, 95 mins.)†

First to Fight (1967)*½ Chad Everett, Marilyn Devin, Dean Jagger, Bobby Troup. Grade C drama with Chad Everett cast as a Marine who wins the Congressional Medal of Honor, returns to the States, trains troops, and then returns to combat and freezes under fire. (Dir: Christian Nyby, 97 mins.)

First Traveling Saleslady, The (1956)** Ginger Rogers, Carol Channing, James Arness. Ginger Rogers takes to the west selling corsets during the turn-of-the-century in this light comedy. Some funny situations but most are labored visual jokes. (Dir: Arthur Lubin, 92 mins.)

First Turn-On, The (1984)* Georgia Harrell, Michael Sanville, Googy Gress. Four nerdy campers trapped in a cave reminisce about the first time they "did it." Embarrassing Troma sex comedy features Vincent D'Onofrio in a small role as "Lobotomy": you can bet it's not the star item on his résumé. (Dirs: Michael Herz, Samuel Weil, 84 mins.)

First You Cry (MTV 1978)***½ Mary Tyler Moore, Anthony Perkins, Florence Eldridge, Jennifer Warren, Richard Crenna. TV newswoman Betty Rollin's candid book about her mastectomy and the readjustment period following the operation makes a poignant film with Mary submerging her patented TV personality to honestly convey the anxiety, depression, and torment of the situation, going from stoicism to tears of rage before beginning to build a new life for herself. One of the best made-for-TV films of the decade. (Dir: George Schaefer, 104 mins.)

Fish Called Wanda, A (1988)**** John Cleese, Jamie Lee Curtis, Kevin Kline, Michael Palin. Repressed lawyer Cleese finds his life a little more lively when he becomes involved with a trio of thieves who think that he knows the location of their hidden loot. Oscar-winner Kline is a standout in a manic performance as a sort of id with feet, but everything else works perfectly as well in this hilarious farce co-written by Cleese and director Charles Crichton (*The Lavender Hill Mob*). (105 mins.)†

Fish Hawk (Canada, 1981)** Will Sampson, Charlie Fields, Geoffrey Bowes, Mary Pirie, Don Francks. A gentle story about friendship between an Indian hunter and a young boy. (Dir: Donald Shebib, 95 mins.)†

Fish That Saved Pittsburgh, The (1979)* Julius Erving, Stockard Channing, Jonathan Winters. Comedy about a woebegone pro basketball team that uses astrology to win a championship. Film is woebegone too. (Dir: Gilbert Moses, 102 mins.)†

F.I.S.T. (1978)*** Sylvester Stallone, Rod Steiger, Peter Boyle, Melinda Dillon, Tony Lo Bianco, Kevin Conway. Overlong but engrossing drama about a Jimmy Hoffa–like character who rises to union prominence and power the hard way. (Dir: Norman Jewison, 145 mins.)†

Fistful of Chopsticks, A—See: **They Call Me Bruce?**

Fistful of Dollars, A (Italy-Spain-West Germany, 1964)*** Clint Eastwood, Marianne Koch, Gian Maria Volonte. This was to Italian westerns what *The Great Train Robbery* was to westerns. It also made Eastwood an international star. (Dir: Sergio Leone, 96 mins.)†

Flatful of Dynamite, A (Italy, 1972)*** Rod Steiger, James Coburn, Romolo Valli, Maria Monte. Wide-open, true-to-form Sergio Leone–directed spaghetti western. Coburn talks reluctant petty crook Steiger into joining his side of a revolution. AKA: **Duck, You Sucker.** (139 mins.)†

Fist in His Pocket (Italy, 1966)***½ Lou Castel, Paola Pitagora, Marino Mase. Young director Marco Bellocchio made his first film about a decaying family into a grim, frequently grotesque study of rampant psychopathology. A morbidly fascinating drama, well acted. (105 mins.)

Flats of Blood (Australia, 1988)* Edward John Stazak, John Stanton, Rowena Wallace, Jim Richards. Underwritten sequel to *Day of the Panther* has martial arts superspy Jason Blade out to rescue his kidnapped girlfriend. The two films were made at the same time, an unnecessarily optomistic move. (Dir: Brian Trenchard-Smith, 90 mins.)†

Fists of Fury (China, 1969)*** Bruce Lee, Miao Ker Hsiu, James Tien. Muddy colors, out-of-focus cinematography, stupid plot, amateurish acting made worthwhile by the leaping, kicking, clawing presence of Bruce Lee as the honorable country boy who just happens to be a fighting genius. (Dir: Lo Wei, 103 mins.)†

Fitzcarraldo (West Germany, 1982)***½ Klaus Kinski, Claudia Cardinale, Paul Hittscher, Jose Lewgoy. A dazzling film about a mad Irishman after Sweeney Fitzgerald, known as Fitzcarraldo in turn-of-the-century Peru, whose obsession was to build a great opera house on the Amazon River. Much of this bizarre adventure is absorbed with his incredible attempt to haul a steamship over a hill from one jungle river to another. (Dir: Werner Herzog, 158 mins.)†

Fitzwilly (1967)**½ Dick Van Dyke, Edith Evans, Barbara Feldon, John McGiver, Harry Townes. Van Dyke plays a butler whose stuffy exterior hides a heart of pure larceny, culminating in a try for a heist of Gimbel's department store. Amusing bit of whimsy, helped by a fine cast. (Dir: Delbert Mann, 102 mins.)

Five (1951)* James Anderson, Susan Douglas, Charles Lampkin, William Phipps. Pretentious nonsense about the survivors of a nuclear holocaust. The pieties are deadlier than the fallout. (Dir: Arch Oboler, 93 mins.)

Five Against the House (1955)***½ Kim Novak, Guy Madison, Brian Keith. Engrossing drama about four college students and a glamorous nightclub singer who plan to hold up a large gambling casino in Reno, merely as an experiment. (Dir: Phil Karlson, 84 mins.)

Five and Ten (1931)** Irene Rich, Marion Davies, Leslie Howard, Richard Bennett.

Wealthy Davies rejects Howard, then sets out to wreck his marriage when he weds Rich. Star power helps this potboiler adapted from a Fannie Hurst novel. (Dir: Robert Z. Leonard, 88 mins.)

Five Bloody Graves—See: **Gun Riders**

Five Branded Women (1960)** Silvana Mangano, Van Heflin, Barbara Bel Geddes, Vera Miles. Five girls suffer the wrath of the people when they are found to be friendly to the Nazis, but redeem themselves in the Underground. Clumsy WWII drama set in Yugoslavia. (Dir: Martin Ritt, 106 mins.)

Five Came Back (1939)*** Chester Morris, Wendy Barrie. Plane crashes in the jungle, and is able to take off with only five passengers. Suspenseful melodrama. Remade as *Back from Eternity* (1956). (Dir: John Farrow, 75 mins.)

Five Card Stud (1968)** Dean Martin, Inger Stevens, Roddy McDowall, Robert Mitchum. Somebody's been eliminating the participants in a poker session that ended in violence. (Dir: Henry Hathaway, 103 mins.)

Five Corners (1988)** Jodie Foster, Tim Robbins, Todd Graff, John Turturro. This unusual little period piece about Bronx life in 1964 starts off like *The Lords of Flatbush*, with perceptive details and humorous episodes involving familiar neighborhood characters, and ends up like any Jimmy Cagney hoodlum-holds-off-cops picture. The hoodlum is Turturro, an ex-con psycho who's out to get Foster (trying her best Bronx accent); once the picture turns into his story, it loses the wonderful grasp it had on everyday reality. (Dir: Tony Bill, 92 mins.)†

Five Days from Home (1978)**½ George Peppard, Neville Brand, Sherry Boucher. OK drama, produced and directed by Peppard, casts him as an ex-lawman convicted of manslaughter for killing his wife's lover. With only six days left on his sentence, he breaks out of a Louisiana prison to see his critically injured son. (109 mins.)

Five Days One Summer (1982)** Sean Connery, Betsey Brantley, Lambert Wilson. An unconvincing soap opera on the rocks, set in the thirties, concerning a doctor from Scotland (Sean Connery) who is married but involved in a forbidden affair with a young woman. (Dir: Fred Zinnemann, 121 mins.)†

Five Desperate Women (MTV 1971)* Robert Conrad, Anjanette Comer, Bradford Dillman, Joan Hackett, Stefanie Powers, Denise Nicholas. A ludicrous thriller about five college girls holding a reunion on a remote island where a lunatic is running amok. (Dir: Ted Post, 104 mins.)

Five Easy Pieces (1970)**** Jack Nicholson, Karen Black, Susan Anspach, Fannie Flagg, Billy Green Bush. An impressive, beautifully observed film about a dropout from middle-class America (Nicholson) who picks up work along the way on oil-rigs when his life isn't spent in a squalid succession of bars and motels in northwest America. (Dir: Bob Rafelson, 96 mins.)†

Five Finger Exercise (1962)** Rosalind Russell, Jack Hawkins, Richard Beymer, Maximilian Schell. Another domineering woman role for Russell, in a sluggish drama about a silly demanding wife who nearly wrecks her family's existence. Based on a Broadway play, which was far better, film emerges as talky, unconvincing. (Dir: Daniel Mann, 109 mins.)

Five Fingers (1952)**** James Mason, Danielle Darrieux, Michael Rennie, Richard Loo. A superb film; one of the most daring real-life espionage agents' deeds are shown with an almost documentary reality. Suspenseful and engrossing all the way. (Dir: Joseph L. Mankiewicz, 108 mins.)

Five Gates to Hell (1959)* Neville Brand, Patricia Owens, Dolores Michaels. Ridiculous plot has a band of glamorous Red Cross nurses who go through a series of adventures after being captured by hostile guerrillas in the Far East. (Dir: James Clavell, 98 mins.)

Five Golden Dragons (Great Britain, 1967)** Robert Cummings, Margaret Lee, Maria Perschy, Christopher Lee, Rupert Davies, Klaus Kinski, Brian Donlevy, Dan Duryea, George Raft, Maria Rohm. Playboy Cummings on holiday in Hong Kong gets on the wrong side of the Chinese Mafia in this mediocre adventure. (Dir: Jeremy Summers, 93 mins.)†

Five Golden Hours (Great Britain, 1961)**½ Ernie Kovacs, Cyd Charisse, George Sanders. Professional "mourner" who consoles widows and is not above a bit of crookery, teams with a beautiful baroness in a swindling scheme, which backfires. (Dir: Mario Zampi, 90 mins.)

Five Graves to Cairo (1943)*** Franchot Tone, Anne Baxter, Erich von Stroheim, Akim Tamiroff. A lone Britisher hides out among the French inhabitants of a village in North Africa as Rommel's troops advance. (Dir: Billy Wilder, 96 mins.)

Five Guns West (1955)**½ John Lund, Dorothy Malone, Mike Connors, Jack Ingram. Roger Corman's directorial debut. An efficiently packaged assemblage of sagebrush clichés about five Civil War prisoners drafted into the Confederacy

for a perilous mission involving a stolen gold shipment. (78 mins.)

Five Heartbeats, The (1991)** Robert Townsend, Tico Wells, Diahann Carroll, Harold Nicholas. Show-biz rags-to-riches story about a 1960s black rhythm-and-blues group sputters in the script department and collapses under the weight of innumerable clichés. Spends too much time depicting the quintet's rise; then, when they finally make it big, drugs suddenly appear and their collapse is immediate. Alas, even the film's music is unmemorable. (Dir: Robert Townsend, 121 mins.)†

500-Pound Jerk, The (MTV 1973)** James Franciscus, Alex Karras. A hillbilly is groomed as an Olympic hopeful; picks up steam when the scene shifts to Munich and Olympic action blends into the story. (Dir: William Kronick, 73 mins.)

Five Loose Women—See: **Fugitive Girls**

Five Man Army, The (1970)*½ Peter Graves, James Daly. Predictable adventure tale set in north Mexico in 1914, involving a band of Americans fighting Mexican revolutionaries. (Dir: Don Taylor, 105 mins.)

Five Miles to Midnight (U.S.-France-Italy, 1962)** Sophia Loren, Anthony Perkins, Gig Young. Young scoundrel survives a plane crash and goes into hiding, forcing his wife to carry out his plan to collect from the insurance company. (Dir: Anatole Litvak, 110 mins.)

Five Million Years to Earth (Great Britain, 1967)*** James Donald, Andrew Keir, Barbara Shelley. Are creatures from outer space menacing modern London? The old sci-fi question is suspensefully examined in a good one for the buffs. (Dir: Raymond Baker, 98 mins.)

Five Minutes to Live—See: **Door-to-Door Maniac**

Five of Me, The (MTV 1981)**½ David Birney, Robert L. Gibson, Herb Armstrong, Liam Sullivan, Russ Marin. Involving multiple personality story. Birney plays a Korean War veteran who may turn into a sadistic animal or a child in the blink of an eye. (Dir: Paul Wendkos, 104 mins.)†

Five Pennies, The (1959)*** Danny Kaye, Barbara Bel Geddes, Tuesday Weld. Pleasant biography of jazzman Red Nichols, a good change of pace for Kaye. But the sound track glistens with solos by Nichols himself, Bob Crosby, and notably, Louis Armstrong. (Dir: Melville Shavelson, 117 mins.)

Five Star Final (1931)*** Edward G. Robinson, H. B. Warner, Marion Marsh, Boris Karloff, Ona Munson, Aline MacMahon. A penetrating drama about a newspaper reporter and his power-hungry editor. A powerful story remade as *Two*

Against the World. (Dir: Mervyn LeRoy, 89 mins.)

5,000 Fingers of Dr. T, The (1953)**½ Hans Conried, Tommy Rettig, Mary Healy, Peter Lind Hayes. A curious film fantasy about a boy who hates piano lessons and dreams about the tortures inflicted by his teacher. The whimsically surreal script was co-written by Theodore Geisel (Dr. Seuss). AKA: **Dr. Suess's The 5,000 Fingers of Dr. T.** (Dir: Roy Rowland, 89 mins.)†

$5.20 an Hour Dream, The (MTV 1980)*** Linda Lavin, Richard Jaeckel, Nicholas Pryor. A serious look at a divorced woman who fights the system in order to get a top-paying job usually given to men on an assembly line. Ms. Lavin is both appealing and vulnerable in the lead role. (Dir: Russ Mayberry, 104 mins.)

Five Weeks in a Balloon (1962)** Red Buttons, Fabian, Barbara Eden, Cedric Hardwicke, Peter Lorre. Lightweight adaptation of an early Jules Verne novel; a balloon-propelled gondola is dispatched by the British government to lay claim to some East African territory. (Dir: Irwin Allen, 101 mins.)†

Fixed Bayonets (1951)**½ Richard Basehart, Gene Evans, Richard Hylton. Interesting and often graphic account of a group of American soldiers in Korea during the hard winter of 1951. Many scenes have a documentary flavor and Basehart is very good as a corporal who has a chance to be a hero. (Dir: Samuel Fuller, 92 mins.)

Fixer, The (1968)*** Alan Bates, Dirk Bogarde, Georgia Brown, Elizabeth Hartman, Hugh Griffith. A deeply moving drama about anti-Semitism in tsarist Russia around 1911, based on Bernard Malamud's Pulitzer Prize-winning novel. Based on a true story of a Russian Jewish peasant (Bates) who was wrongly imprisoned for the "ritual murder" of a gentile child in Kiev. Much of the film, detailing the protagonist's life in prison, is unrelenting, but it pays off as we see the peasant-handyman gain in dignity as the efforts to humiliate him and make him confess fail. (Dir: John Frankenheimer, 132 mins.)

Flame, The (1947)*** John Carroll, Vera Ralston, Broderick Crawford. Penniless playboy hits upon an elaborate plan of getting rid of his brother so he will inherit a fortune. Capable melodrama keeps the interest. (Dir: John H. Auer, 97 mins.)

Flame and the Arrow, The (1950)*** Burt Lancaster, Virginia Mayo, Robert Douglas, Aline MacMahon, Nick Cravat. A genuine sleeper—a rousing acrobatic adventure story with a subtle visual style. It seems every bit as satisfying on the matinee level as the

later *Crimson Pirate*. (Dir: Jacques Tourneur, 88 mins.)†

Flame and the Flesh, The (1954)** Lana Turner, Pier Angeli, Carlos Thompson. A corny, overdone tale of an unfortunate woman whose luck has just about run out. (Dir: Richard Brooks, 104 mins.)

Flame Barrier, The (1958)** Arthur Franz, Kathleen Crowley. Scientist disappears in the Yucatan jungles while searching for a lost satellite, so his wife hires two adventurers to locate him. Passable science fiction, some suspenseful moments. (Dir: Paul Landres, 70 mins.)

Flame in My Heart, A (France-Switzerland, 1987)**½ Myriam Mezieres, Aziz Kabouche, Benoit Regent, Biana. Intense study of one woman's complete emotional confusion. Mercedes (Mezieres, who also scripted) is an actress who leaves her obsessed Arab lover only to become obsessed herself with a bland journalist. Shot in black and white on 16mm, this low-budget production has sensuously haunting photography, some surprisingly graphic sex scenes, and, on the minus side, incredibly ridiculous dialogue and plot twists. (Dir: Alain Tanner, 110 mins.)

Flame in the Streets (Great Britain, 1961)** John Mills, Sylvia Syms, Johnny Sekka. Sober drama of racial conflict in Britain. A white girl announces her plans to marry a black West Indian. (Dir: Roy Ward Baker, 93 mins.)

Flame Is Love, The (MTV 1979)**½ Linda Purl, Shane Briant, Timothy Dalton. This film adaptation of the Barbara Cartland novel is about the adventures of a young American heiress who travels to Europe for a trousseau but ends up experiencing more than she bargained for. Won't disappoint her legions of readers. (Dir: Michael O'Herlihy, 104 mins.)†

Flame of Araby (1952)*½ Maureen O'Hara, Jeff Chandler. Rudolph Valentino lives again—well, not quite—as Jeff Chandler dons the trappings of a desert sheik who woos and wins the not-so-fiery princess Maureen O'Hara. (Dir: Charles Lamont, 77 mins.)

Flame of New Orleans, The (1941)*** Marlene Dietrich, Bruce Cabot. Glamorous doll chooses wealthy suitor rather than the adventurous rogue she loves. Not among Dietrich's best but it's still Dietrich. (Dir: Rene Clair, 78 mins.)

Flame of the Barbary Coast (1945)**½ John Wayne, Ann Dvorak, Joseph Schildkraut. Montana cattleman falls for a San Francisco saloon singer and opens his own gambling hall. Standard period melodrama. (Dir: Joseph Kane, 91 mins.)†

Flame of the Islands (1955)**½ Yvonne DeCarlo, Howard Duff, Zachary Scott,

James Arness. Many men fight for the love of a beautiful but dangerous nightclub singer. Overly involved but interesting melodrama; good Bahama locations. (Dir: Edward Ludwig, 90 mins.)†

Flame over India (Great Britain, 1959)*** Kenneth More, Lauren Bacall, Herbert Lom. Exciting adventure melodrama about a soldier assigned to rescue a Hindu prince and his American governess when rebellion breaks out. Practically the entire film is one big, rousing chase aboard a train, with action aplenty. Superior escapist fare. (Dir: J. Lee Thompson, 130 mins.)

Flame to the Phoenix, A (Great Britain, 1983)** Fredrick Treves, Ann Firbank, Malcolm Jamieson. Poland, 1939. With Hitler's forces at the border, undercover British diplomats plot strategy while retired General Treves organizes underground opposition for a long, bloody struggle. British, Polish, German characters all speak with the same British accent, which makes this talky drama a bit difficult for American ears. (Dir: William Brayne, 80 mins.)†

Flamingo Kid, The (1984)*** Matt Dillon, Richard Crenna, Jessica Walter, Hector Elizondo, Janet Jones. Surprise! A wonderful film about a teenager coming of age in 1963; a Brooklyn kid learns about life one summer in a beach club. Dillon's adventures at the club and his heated discussions at home are equally interesting, and the supporting cast, most especially Crenna as a hot-shot club member, is top-notch. (Dir: Garry Marshall, 100 mins.)†

Flamingo Road (1949)*** Joan Crawford, Zachary Scott, David Brian, Sydney Greenstreet, Gertrude Michael, Gladys George. A juicily enjoyable melodrama in which Joan is improbably cast as a carnival dancer. Greenstreet plays a vicious political boss pulling the strings of his puppet candidate, who was once involved with Joan. A cynical look at the world of greased palms and political backstabbing; wait until you hear Joan compare Sydney to a dead elephant. Remade as a TV movie and soap-opera series in 1980. (Dir: Michael Curtiz, 94 mins.)

Flamingo Road (MTV 1980)*½ Morgan Fairchild, Kevin McCarthy, Barbara Rush, Mark Harmon, Howard Duff, Stella Stevens, Woody Brown. In this pilot for a prime-time soap, the formula is down pat—aristocrats act like commoners to get their way in business and romance. Not as memorably sleazy as the original with Joan Crawford. (Dir: Gus Trikonis, 104 mins.)

Flaming Star (1960)*** Elvis Presley, Steve Forrest, Barbara Eden, Dolores Del Rio, John McIntire. Grim, well-done out-

door drama gives Presley a good role, and he makes the most of it. He's a part-Kiowa lad who tries to put a halt to bloodshed between Indians and settlers. (Dir: Don Siegel, 101 mins.)†

Flanagan (1985)** Philip Bosco, Geraldine Page, Linda Thorson, William Hickey, Brian Bloom. This movie might have passed muster as a ''Playhouse 90'' drama in the fifties. It's about a cab driver yearning to stop suffering the slings and arrows of outrageous passengers and become a Shakespearean actor. AKA: **Walls of Glass.** (Dir: Scott Goldstein, 100 mins.)†

Flap(1970)½ Anthony Quinn, Shelley Winters, Tony Bill. A despicable film pretending to deal with the many ways the United States government has cheated the American Indian tribes. Exploitative drivel. (Dir: Carol Reed, 106 mins.)

Flareup (1969)* Raquel Welch, James Stacy. Miss Welch portrays a go-go dancer on the run from a psychopath killer as if she were trying for a self-parody. (Dir: James Nelson, 100 mins.)

Flashback (1990)*** Dennis Hopper, Keifer Sutherland, Carol Kane, Paul Dooley, Cliff De Young, Richard Masur, Michael McKean. Green young FBI agent Sutherland is assigned to escort captured '60s radical Hopper to jail. The comedy works because of the engaging byplay of the two. Kane is wonderful as a sensitive nurturing woman whose heart, mind, and soul are still in the summer of love. Filled with hippie music and memorabilia, and an action-packed train ride. (Dir: Franco Amurri, 108 mins.)†

Flashdance (1983)** Jennifer Beals, Michael Nouri, Marine Jahan (dance double for Beals), Lilia Skala, Sunny Johnson. A mediocre drama which centers around the life of a young aspiring dancer (Alex), who is a welder by day, erotic dancer by night. In the evenings she performs exciting modern dance routines at the local bar, but her dream is to be a part of the Pittsburgh Ballet. Some snazzy choreography compensates for the totally unbelievable script. (Dir: Adrian Lyne, 100 mins.)†

Flash Gordon (1980)*** Sam Jones, Max von Sydow, Melody Anderson, Topol, Ornella Muti, Timothy Dalton, Brian Blessed, Peter Wyngarde. A delightful romp, light-years ahead of the thirties sci-fi serial. Director Mike Hodges and screenwriter Lorenzo Semple, Jr., succeed through a blend of sophistication and unabashedness. (110 mins.)†

Flash of Green, A (1984)*** Ed Harris, Blair Brown, Richard Jordan, George Coe, Joan Goodfellow, Jean De Baer, Helen Stenborg. Writer-director Victor

Nunez's drama adapted from John D. MacDonald's 1962 novel succeeds in capturing the sleepy tempo of a small Florida town and the corruption seething beneath it. By accepting a bribe from a local politician fighting environmentalists over proposed use of the local bay, Jimmy Wing (Harris) mixes up the elements of his personal distress—terminally ill wife, repressed desire for his recently widowed friend—with the sensitive local issue. An uncommonly human look at crime and betrayal. (131 mins.)†

Flashpoint (1984)*½ Kris Kristofferson, Treat Williams, Rip Torn, Kevin Conway, Tess Harper. A limp, unconvincing thriller. Kristofferson and Williams play border patrolmen who discover hidden money that's linked to a greater conspiracy. TV commerical director William Tannen gives the film a flashy look but fails to cover the loopholes in the screenplay. (93 mins.)†

Flask of Fields, A**** W. C. Fields. Three short comedies: The Golf Specialist (1930), The Fatal Glass of Beer (1933), and The Dentist (1933). These outrageous, amazing shorts are among his best works. Censored scenes from *The Dentist*, showing Fields climbing all over a female patient whose tooth just won't budge, are restored; you can certainly see why they were cut out in the first place! (61 mins.)†

Flatbed Annie & Sweetiepie: Lady Truckers (MTV 1979)**½ Annie Potts, Kim Darby, Harry Dean Stanton, Arthur Godfrey. Darby and Potts make an ingratiating pair of big-rig drivers. (Dir: Robert Greenwald, 104 mins.)†

Flatliners (1990)*½ Kiefer Sutherland, Julia Roberts, Kevin Bacon, William Baldwin, Oliver Platt. Quintet of pretentious medical students pontificate about life and death as they experiment with brain cessation tests on each other. Tiresome. (Dir: Joel Schumacher, 111 mins.)†

Flat Top (1952)** Sterling Hayden, Richard Carlson, Bill Phipps, John Bromfield, William Schallert, Phyllis Coates. Actual battle footage highlights this story of pilots on an aircraft carrier run by skipper Hayden, who knows that strict discipline is the best way to save lives. (Dir: Lesley Selander, 83 mins.)†

Flavor of Green Tea over Rice, The (Japan, 1953)***½ Shin Saburi, Michiyo Kogure, Koji Tsuruta, Keiko Tsushima, Kuniko Miyake. An unhappy middle-class marriage is slowly unraveling, until a carefree romantic niece arrives on the scene and compels the drifting couple to reexamine the state of their union. Film evolves as a series of telling domestic moments, directed with grace and subtlety by Yasujiro Ozu. (115 mins.)

Flaxfield, The (Belgium-Holland, 1983)**½ Vic Moeremans, Dora van der Groen, Rene van Sambeek, Gusta Gerritsen. Scenic but uninvolving story, set at the turn-of-the-century, about a stubborn old farmer who quarrels with his son over management of the farm they work together. (Dir: Jan Gruyaert, 90 mins.)

Flea in Her Ear, A (U.S.-France, 1968)** Rex Harrison, Rosemary Harris, Louis Jourdan, Rachel Roberts, John Williams. Flatfooted French farce, with the philandering spouse, the vengeful wife, numerous misunderstandings, much running around. Superb cast wasted. (Dir: Jacques Charon, 94 mins.)

Fleet's In, The (1942)**½ Dorothy Lamour, William Holden, Betty Hutton. Some good specialty numbers and lively direction make this silly film passable entertainment. Story concerns the "lover" of the Navy's attempts to score with a virtuous gal. (Dir: Victor Schertzinger, 93 mins.)

Flesh (1932)*** Wallace Beery, Karen Morley, Ricardo Cortez, Jean Hersholt, Herman Bing, Ward Bond, Nat Pendleton. Remarkably gritty, powerful story of desperate Morley marrying good-natured German wrestler Beery after being deserted by her no-good lover Cortez, who then returns to torment her. Strong stuff, superbly acted and directed. (Dir: John Ford, 95 mins.)

Flesh (1969)** Joe Dallesandro, Geraldine Smith, Barry Brown, Candy Darling, Jackie Curtis. The first film credited to director Paul Morrissey (*Trash, Heat*), this features a lot of wandering about the streets of New York by a desultory male hustler. Funny in a deadpan way. (105 mins.)†

Flesh and Blood (1922)**½ Lon Chaney, Edith Roberts, Noah Beery, De Witt Jennings, Jack Mulhall, Kate Price. After fifteen years of unjust imprisonment, Chaney escapes to seek vengeance disguised as a crippled beggar. He discovers that his daughter, who doesn't recognize him, loves the son of his enemy. Chilling drama is entirely dependent on Chaney's remarkable talents. (Dir: Irving Cummings, 74 mins.)†

Flesh and Blood (MTV 1979)***½ Suzanne Pleshette, Tom Berenger, Mitchell Ryan, Kristin Griffith. Pete Hamill's best-seller about a street-wise punk who rises to become a heavyweight contender, becomes an even better film. Berenger is electrifying as Bobby, the brawling, troubled, yet appealing young man who enters into a short-lived alliance with his still attractive young mother, perfectly realized by Pleshette. (Dir: Jud Taylor, 200 mins.)

Flesh + Blood (1985)**½ Rutger Hauer,

Jennifer Jason Leigh, Tom Burlinson, Jack Thompson, Susan Tyrrell. Often exciting and more than occasionally gruesome adventure, set in the Middle Ages, concerning a virginal damsel who gets kidnapped and abused by a band of brawling outcasts. (Dir: Paul Verhoeven, 126 mins.)†

Flesh and Blood Show, The (Great Britain, 1973)*½ Ray Brooks, Jenny Hanley, Luan Peters, Judy Matheson, Robin Askwith. Actors at an abandoned seaside theater to rehearse a new play are stalked and killed by their backer. (Dir: Pete Walker, 93 mins.)†

Flesh and Fantasy (1943)***½ Charles Boyer, Edward G. Robinson, Betty Field, Barbara Stanwyck. Three exciting and mysterious tales all well acted and gripping. The one starring Robinson as a man told by a fortune teller that his palm says "Murder" is the best, but they're all quite good. (Dir: Julien Duvivier, 93 mins.)

Flesh and Flame—See: Night of the Quarter Moon

Flesh and Fury (1952)**½ Tony Curtis, Jan Sterling, Mona Freeman. Tony Curtis shows the first signs of acting talent in this prize-fighting yarn. He plays a deaf mute who stumbles into the boxing game and winds up a champion. (Dir: Joseph Pevney, 82 mins.)

Flesh and the Devil (1927)**½ Greta Garbo, John Gilbert, Lars Hanson, Barbara Kent, Eugenie Besserer. Slow to start, but extremely steamy when it gets going, this showcase for Garbo's beauty casts her as a married temptress who breaks up the lifelong friendship between cadets Gilbert and Hanson. Superior acting makes the fundamentally hackneyed story compelling; beautiful photography by William Daniels and set design by Cedric Gibbons. (Dir: Clarence Brown, 109 mins.)†

Flesh and the Fiends (Great Britain, 1960)*** Peter Cushing, Donald Pleasence, George Rose. Dastardly grave robbers supply bodies for medical experiments in old Scotland. Horror thriller has some fine performances. AKA: Mania. (Dir: John Gilling, 87 mins.)†

Flesh and the Woman (France-Italy, 1958)** Gina Lollobrigida, Arletty, Jean-Claude Pascal, Peter Van Eyck. Pretty but vapid remake of the 1934 Le Grand Jeu. Spurned by girlfriend Lollobrigida, lawyer Pascal joins the Foreign Legion, where he meets an amnesia victim who is her exact double. (Dir: Robert Siodmak, 102 mins.)

Fleshburn (1984)* Steve Kanaly, Sonny Landham, Karen Carlson, Macon McCalman, Robert Cimento. Barren revenge tale about a Viet vet who deposits the shrinks who had committed him to a

sanitarium smack-dab in the middle of the desert. (Dir: George Gage, 90 mins.)†

Flesh Creatures, The—See: Horror of the Blood Monsters

Flesh Eater—See: Revenge of the Living Zombies

Flesh Eaters, The (1964)*½ Martin Kosleck, Rita Morley. Four individuals get washed up on the shore of a deserted island, inhabited only by a mad German scientist. (Dir: Jack Curtis, 87 mins.)

Flesh-Eating Mothers (1989)* Robert Lee Oliver, Donatella Hecht, Valarie Hubbard. The title is about as funny as it gets in this, yet another horror film parody about cannibalism in suburbia. (Dir: James Aviles Martin, 90 mins.)†

Flesh Feast (1970)½ Veronica Lake, Phil Philbin, Heather Hughes, Martha Mischon, Chris Martel. Miami doctor uses maggots to restore her aging patient's youthful complexions, but draws the line when she discovers her latest client is . . . Adolph Hitler! (Dir: Brad Ginter, 72 mins.)†

Flesh for Frankenstein—See: Andy Warhol's Frankenstein

Flesh Gordon (1974)* Jason Williams, Suzanne Fields, Joseph Hudgins, John Hoyt. Silly soft-core spoof on the popular science fiction serials of the 1930s. Space hero Williams battles evil forces on the planet Porno, which is ruled by the evil Emperor Wang. (Dirs: Howard Ziehm, Michael Benveniste, 78 mins.)†

Fletch (1985)*** Chevy Chase, Tim Matheson, Richard Libertini, Joe Don Baker, Geena Davis, Dana Wheeler-Nicholson. Chase plays an obnoxious newspaper reporter who uncovers a network of police drug dealers and corrupt businessmen when he's hired to murder a tycoon. Constantly amusing and entertaining, thanks to Chase's wry handling of the material. (Dir: Michael Ritchie, 97 mins.)†

Fletch Lives (1989)*** Chevy Chase, Julianne Philips, Hal Holbrook, Cleavon Little, Lee Ermey, Richard Libertini. Newspaperman Fletch inherits a southern mansion, and gets caught up in a murder mystery when he goes to claim it. The plot is so-so, but the character provides a perfect showcase for Chase's brand of smart-aleck humor. (Dir: Michael Ritchie, 95 mins.)†

Flicks (1981)*½ Martin Mull, Pamela Sue Martin, Joan Hackett, Betty Kennedy, Richard Belzer. Generally witless spoof of old-time movies in the form of an evening at the Bijou, with coming attractions, cartoon, and movie parody. (Dir: Peter Winograd, 79 mins.)†

Flight (1929)**½ Jack Holt, Ralph Graves, Lila Lee. "Gentleman Jack" Holt and Graves are buddies who fight and fly in the Marine Air Corps; nice star performances and great aerial footage make this one fun. (Dir: Frank Capra, 116 mins.)†

Flight Command (1940)**½ Robert Taylor, Walter Pidgeon, Paul Kelly, Ruth Hussey, Nat Pendleton, Red Skelton. Patriotic tale of tyro pilot Taylor trying to make good in the Navy Air Corps. (Dir: Frank Borzage, 116 mins.)

Flight for Freedom (1943)**½ Rosalind Russell, Fred MacMurray, Herbert Marshall. Moderately engrossing film of an aviatrix who breaks world flying records and ultimately gets involved in patriotic spy efforts before crashlanding her plane in the Pacific. (Dir: Lothar Mendes, 101 mins.)

Flight from Ashiya (1964)** Yul Brynner, Richard Widmark, George Chakiris, Suzy Parker, Shirley Knight. With the Air Rescue Service, looking for survivors and recalling their pasts. Airborne soap opera. (Dir: Michael Anderson, 100 mins.)

Flight from Destiny (1941)*** Thomas Mitchell, Geraldine Fitzgerald. An offbeat story of a man with only six months to live. Thomas Mitchell's superb acting gives this story a tremendous wallop if you're willing to accept his actions. (Dir: Vincent Sherman, 73 mins.)

Flight from Glory (1937)*** Chester Morris, Whitney Bourne, Onslow Stevens, Van Heflin, Richard Lane, Sally Ward. Superior drama of pilots, unable to work elsewhere, who fly a dangerous, often fatal supply run over mountainous terrain under tyrannical boss Stevens, who keeps them virtual slaves in a company town. (Dir: Lew Landers, 66 mins.)†

Flight from Vienna (1956)*** Theodore Bikel, John Bentley, Adrienne Scott, Carina Helm, Donald Gray. To prove that his intentions are genuine, a defecting Hungarian official is required to return to Hungary and help a scientist defect. (Dir: Denis Kavanagh, 58 mins.)†

Flight 90: Disaster on the Potomac (MTV 1983)**½ Richard Masur, Dinah Manoff, Donnelly Rhodes. Re-creation of the 1982 Washington, D.C. airliner crash in which five survivors were pulled out of icy waters. (Dir: Robert Lewis, 104 mins.)

Flight Nurse (1953)** Joan Leslie, Forrest Tucker. Two pilots both love the same nurse, and if this sounds familiar don't blame us. (Dir: Allan Dwan, 90 mins.)

Flight of Black Angel (MCTV 1990)*** Peter Strauss, William O'Leary, K. Callan, Michele Pawk, Michael Keys Hall. Chilling doomsday thriller about an unstable U.S. Air Force pilot (O'Leary) who threatens to drop a nuclear device over Las Vegas. Grim, relentlessly suspenseful tale will keep viewers transfixed. (Dir: Jonathan Mostow, 104 mins.)†

Flight of the Doves (Great Britain, 1971)*** Ron Moody, Jack Wild, Dorothy McGuire, Stanley Holloway. Moody has a virtuoso role playing a detective of many disguises trying to track down two young orphans. (Dir: Ralph Nelson, 105 mins.)

Flight of the Eagle, The (Sweden, 1982)*** Max von Sydow, Goran Stangertz, Sverre Anker Ousdal. Story of S. A. Andree, the Swedish explorer whose 1897 attempt to fly a balloon over the North Pole with two compatriots forms the basis of this handsome film. Although long, and at times methodical, the film contains well-developed characters and breathtaking photography. (Dir: Jan Troell, 141 mins.)†

Flight of the Intruder (1991)* Danny Glover, Willem Dafoe, Brad Johnson, Rosanna Arquette. Boring misguided Vietnamera war picture set on an aircraft carrier you're hoping would sink. The characters are ridiculous, the acting is atrocious, and the screenplay is Exhibit A in how *not* to construct a story. If you believe that President Nixon ordered the carpet bombing of North Vietnam because a maverick jet fighter crew attacked Hanoi on their own, which is the ludicrous plot of this stinker, then you'll believe anything. Directed—if that's the word—by John Milius. (Dir: John Milius, 113 mins.)†

Flight of the Lost Balloon, The (1960)*½ Marshall Thompson, Mala Powers. A little science fiction—a little jungle adventure—a little plot—and you have it. And you can keep it. (Dir: Bernard Woolner, 91 mins.)

Flight of the Navigator, The (1986)*** Joey Cramer, Howard Hesseman, Veronica Cartwright, Cliff De Young. A fine mix of special effects and Disney drama as a young boy tries to find the link between a flying saucer and his disappearance for eight years (although he hasn't aged one day). (Dir: Randall Kleiser, 88 mins.)†

Flight of the Phoenix, The (1966)***½ James Stewart, Richard Attenborough, Peter Finch, Hardy Kruger. An exciting old-fashioned adventure about a group of plane crash survivors who fight to rebuild their plane and save themselves. Director Robert Aldrich stages a fantastic finale which generates edge-of-the-seat suspense. (147 mins.)†

Flight to Berlin (West Germany-Great Britain, 1983)**½ Tusse Silberg, Paul Freeman, Lisa Kreuzer, Eddie Constantine. Brooding film is less a thriller than an exploration of the conventions of that genre; interesting, but not recommended for casual viewers. (Dir: Christopher Petit, 90 mins.)

Flight to Holocaust (MTV 1977)** Patrick Wayne, Christopher Mitchum, Fawne Harriman, Desi Arnaz, Jr., Sid Caesar, Rory Calhoun, Greg Morris, Lloyd Nolan, Paul Williams. When a jet crashes unexpectedly against the side of a skyscraper, Wayne, Mitchum, and crew (these lads are clearly not their fathers) come to the rescue. Mediocre outing lacks the unsubtle but effective touch of disaster specialist Irwin Allen. (Dir: Bernard L. Kowalski, 96 mins.)

Flight to Mars (1951)** Cameron Mitchell, Marguerite Chapman, Arthur Franz, Virginia Huston, Morris Ankrum. Crew of the first spaceship to land on Mars discovers an underground civilization of women in mini-skirts and inhospitable leaders. Standard '50s sci-fi notable only for being the first (and one of the few) such films photographed in color. (Dir: Lesley Selander, 72 mins.)†

Flim Flam Man, The (1967)**½ George C. Scott, Michael Sarrazin, Sue Lyon, Harry Morgan, Jack Albertson. A robust ingratiating performance by George C. Scott as a rural con artist makes this picture seem better than it really is. Tale about the adventures of a con man and his protégé, a young Army deserter, winningly played by Michael Sarrazin. (Dir: Irvin Kershner, 104 mins.)†

Flipper (1963)**½ Chuck Connors, Luke Halpin, Flipper. Youthful fans of the TV series will get a bang out of this film on which it was based. As everybody knows, Flipper is the remarkable dolphin whose relationship with young Luke blossoms into a real friendship when he saves the wounded dolphin's life. (Dir: James Clark, 90 mins.)

Flipper's New Adventure (1964)**½ Luke Halpin, Flipper, Pamela Franklin. Second *Flipper* feature is again nice kiddie fare, as boy and dolphin head out to sea rather than be separated. (Dir: Leon Benson, 92 mins.)†

Flipper's Odyssey (MTV 1966)**½ Brian Kelly, Luke Halpin, Tommy Norden. In this feature-length episode of the popular television show, everyone's favorite dolphin becomes separated from his adopted human family and must find his way home. Still good family fare, with added nostalgia value. (Dir: Paul Landres, 77 mins.)†

Flirtation Walk (1934)**½ Ruby Keeler, Dick Powell, Pat O'Brien. Dick goes to West Point for this one and it is fair entertainment. A little bit too long, it still comes out an interesting West Point story with some pleasant music for diversion. (Dir: Frank Borzage, 97 mins.)

Flirting with Fate (1938)**½ Joe E. Brown, Beverly Roberts, Wynne Gibson, Leo Carrillo. A theatrical troupe finds itself stranded in South America and beset by thieves. Not one of Brown's best; Carrillo, as a Latino bandido, steals scenes from him with ease. (Dir: Frank McDonald, 69 mins.)

Floating Weeds (Japan, 1959)**** Ganjiro Nakamura, Haruko Sugimura, Machiko Kyo, Ayako Wakao. One of Yasujiro Ozu's best is the tale about an acting troupe that visits the island where the leading player's ex-mistress lives with their son. Problems are caused by the star's jealous current lover. Lightly comic and magnificently photographed in color by the master Kazuo Miyagawa. Remake of Ozu's 1934 silent *A Story of Floating Weeds.* (119 mins.)†

Flood! (MTV 1976)**½ Robert Culp, Richard Basehart, Teresa Wright. TV disaster pic about a collapsing dam that destroys a small town. (Dir: Earl Bellamy, 106 mins.)†

Floods of Fear (Great Britain, 1958)**½ Howard Keel, Anne Heywood. Wrongly convicted of murder, a man escapes during a flood and proves his innocence. Frequently exciting melodrama. (Dir: Charles Crichton, 82 mins.)

Flood Tide (1958)** George Nader, Cornell Borchers. Man tries to convince authorities that a crippled youngster whose testimony has convicted a man of murder is a habitual liar. Undistinguished melodrama. (Dir: Abner Biberman, 82 mins.)

Floradora Girl, The (1930)** Marion Davies, Lawrence Gray, Walter Catlett, Ilka Chase, Jed Prouty, Anita Louise. Unevenly paced but charming period comedy about the famous six original stars of the turn-of-the-century Broadway hit *Floradora;* the story is silly, but Davies is enchanting, and there are several bright musical numbers. (Dir: Harry Beaumont, 80 mins.)

Florence Nightingale (MTV 1985)**½ Jaclyn Smith, Timothy Dalton, Claire Bloom. Attenuated bio-drama on nursing pioneer Florence Nightingale. Fetching Jaclyn Smith stars as the headstrong young woman who, over the objections of her high-society family, chooses to spend her time with the sick and needy. (Dir: Daryl Duke, 104 mins.)

Florentine Dagger (1935)** Margaret Lindsay, Donald Woods, C. Aubrey Smith, Henry O'Neill. Flawed whodunit about the murder of an art dealer; sparked by interesting directorial flourishes. (Dir: Robert Florey, 69 mins.)

Florida Straits (MCTV 1986)** Raul Julia, Fred Ward, Daniel Jenkins, Jaime Sanchez, Victor Argo, Antonio Fargas. In the '30s they probably would have done this with Gable in the Julia role and Wallace Beery in the Ward role. Perhaps they could have put some life into this saga about three treasure-seekers trying to locate a cache of gold hidden in dangerous Cuba. (Dir: Mike Hodges, 96 mins.)†

Flor Sylvestre (Mexico, 1945)*** Dolores Del Rio, Pedro Armendariz, Emilio Fernandez. Handsomely produced melodrama about two families who find themselves on opposite sides of the Mexican revolution. Del Rio actually gets a chance to act after years of mainly decorative parts in American movies, and does quite well. (Dir: Emilio Fernandez, 94 mins.)†

Flower Drum Song (1961)*** Nancy Kwan, James Shigeta, Miyoshi Umeki, Juanita Hall, Benson Fong, Jack Soo. The Rodgers & Hammerstein musical play about a Chinese picture-bride in San Francisco is colorfully decked out on film, with some capable players and good song numbers. (Dir: Henry Koster, 133 mins.)†

Flowers in the Attic (1987)* Victoria Tennant, Kristy Swanson, Jeb Stuart Adams, Louise Fletcher. Adaptation of V. C. Andrews's popular but trashy novel is equally silly and tedious, as four youngsters are imprisoned in the attic of the family mansion by their mother and grandmother. (Dir: Jeffrey Bloom, 95 mins.)†

Flowing Gold (1940)**½ Frances Farmer, John Garfield, Pat O'Brien, Raymond Walburn, Cliff Edwards. Farmer's famous mud scene is the highlight of this formulaic Warner Bros. oil field drama. Garfield and O'Brien fight for her hand as Farmer's father (Walburn) tries to tame her. Both Garfield and Farmer give dynamic performances. (Dir: Alfred E. Green, 82 mins.)

Fluffy (1965)** Tony Randall, Shirley Jones. Professor gets into a lot of trouble when he escorts a tame lion around. Mild comedy on the silly side; the lion gets most of the laughs. (Dir: Earl Bellamy, 92 mins.)

Fly, The (1958)*** Vincent Price, Herbert Marshall. During a scientific experiment, a miscalculation causes a man to turn into a mutation. Superior science-fiction thriller with a literate script for a change, plus good production effects and capable performances. (Dir: Kurt Neumann, 94 mins.)†

Fly, The (1986)***½ Jeff Goldblum, Geena Davis, John Getz. Director David Cronenberg's most polished horror film, a thoughtful rethinking of the 1958 camp classic about a scientist who invents a teleportation machine and accidentally mixes genes with a stowaway fly. The

characters are well rounded and the scientist's tender romance with a reporter provides a human dimension, and a dose of dark humor is added for good measure. (95 mins.)†

Fly II, The (1989)*½ Eric Stoltz, Daphne Zuniga, Lee Richardson. The adventures of Brundlefly Jr. Sequel abandons the central human concerns of the '86 film to concentrate on gruesome special effects. The ending is particularly nasty. (Dir: Chris Walas, 104 mins.)†

Fly Away Home (MTV 1981)*½ Bruce Boxleitner, Tiana Alexander, Michael Beck, Randy Brooks, Teri Copley, Brian Dennehy, Lynne Moody, Keye Luke. Failed pilot for a series set in Vietnam during the war has Boxleitner as a cameraman looking for a story just as the Tet offensive is beginning. Dull and predictable except for a subplot involving Luke as a corrupt Vietnamese. (Dir: Paul Krasny, 96 mins.)

Fly by Night (1942)**½ Nancy Kelly, Richard Carlson, Martin Kosleck. Slick little spy story about an intern who becomes involved in espionage when the inventor he works for is kidnapped. (Dir: Robert Siodmak, 74 mins.)†

Flying Deuces, The (1939)*** Stan Laurel, Oliver Hardy, Reginald Gardiner, Jean Parker. Laurel and Hardy join the Foreign Legion, sing and dance "Shine On, Harvest Moon," and Ollie ends up reincarnated as a mule. (Dir: A. Edward Sutherland, 65 mins.)†

Flying Down to Rio (1933)*** Dolores Del Rio, Fred Astaire, Ginger Rogers. Beautiful girl has to choose between two men down in Rio. Pretty corny, but Astaire-Rogers dancing is still tops. (Dir: Thornton Freeland, 72 mins.)†

Flying High (MTV 1978)* Jim Hutton, Kathryn Witt, Pat Klous, Connie Sellecca. This is the pilot (no pun intended) for a lamentable series about a trio of stewardesses and their exploits in the air and on the ground. (Dir: Peter Hunt, 104 mins.)

Flying Irishman (1939)*** Doug Corrigan, Paul Kelly. Story of "Wrong Way" Corrigan, who made a spectacular flight—in reverse. Entertaining, amusing comedy-drama. (Dir: Leigh Jason, 72 mins.)

Flying Leathernecks (1951)** John Wayne, Robert Ryan. Strict Marine officer is disliked by his squadron, but in wartime all is forgotten. Badly written, slow war drama; some good actual battle scenes. (Dir: Nicholas Ray, 102 mins.)†

Flying Missile, The (1951)** Glenn Ford, Viveca Lindfors. Grim and superficial drama about guided missiles and the men who build and test them. Cliché script prevents actors from doing anything with their roles. (Dir: Henry Levin, 93 mins.)

Flying Saucer (Italy, 1964)** Alberto Sordi, Monica Vitti, Silvana Mangano. An account of what happens when an invasion from Mars is threatened. Science-fiction opus is a field day for Sordi, playing four separate roles; but the fun is relatively sparse. (Dir: Tinto Brass, 95 mins.)

Flying Serpent, The (1946)** George Zucco, Ralph Lewis, Hope Kramer, Milton Kibbee. Silly horror flick about the Aztec god Quetzalcoatl, a flying serpent (quite a bit smaller here than in the 1982 *Q*) harnessed by Zucco to kill his enemies. The supporting cast and special effects are laughable, but Zucco gives it a weirdly believable intensity, and makes it watchable. (Dir: ''Sherman Scott'' [Sam Newfield], 59 mins.)

Flying Tigers (1942)***½ John Wayne, John Carroll, Anna Lee. Squadron leader and his reckless buddy vie for the affections of a pretty nurse while fighting the Japanese. Familiar but lively war melodrama; fine special effects. (Dir: David Miller, 102 mins.)†

Flying Wild (1941)**½ Leo Gorcey, Bobby Jordan. There's comedy, action, and suspense in this *East Side Kids* entry revolving around airplanes and espionage. (Dir: William West, 64 mins.)

FM (1978)** Michael Brandon, Eileen Brennan, Cleavon Little, Cassie Yates, Martin Mull, Alex Karras. Music-oriented film with an FM station as the vehicle for two hours of madness. The motley crew of disc jockeys include a burnt-out but friendly giant, a sex-crazed midnight owl, an acid-tongued cynic, and a California EST graduate. (Dir: John Alonzo, 110 mins.)

Fog, The (1980)**½ Adrienne Barbeau, Hal Holbrook, Janet Leigh, Jamie Lee Curtis, John Houseman. Occasionally scary ghost story about a town menaced by vengeance-seeking spirits, who've bided their time for 100 years. (Dir: John Carpenter, 91 mins.)†

Fog Island (1945)** George Zucco, Lionel Atwill, Jerome Cowan, Sharon Douglas, Veda Ann Borg, Ian Keith. Zucco, ruined by a prison stretch and the murder of his wife, gets out and invites all those responsible to his island estate for a weekend of revenge. Tidy little chiller. (Dir: Terry Morse, 72 mins.)†

Fog over Frisco (1934)*** Bette Davis, Lyle Talbot, Margaret Lindsay, Donald Woods. When the Capone clones bump off a hedonistic heiress (Davis), her noble sister trails them until justice prevails. In a flashy, all-too-brief role, Bette shakes the audience out of its complacency; you can really sense her thrill-seeking character giddily racing toward self-destruction. (Dir: William Dieterle, 68 mins.)

Folies Bergère (1935)**½ Maurice Chevalier, Ann Sothern, Merle Oberon, Eric Blore. The charming, talented Chevalier plays a tycoon who hires a double—a music hall entertainer—to impersonate him, only to find that his wife and his mistress don't quite appreciate the gag. The musical numbers, choreographed by Dave Gould, are spectacular. (Dir: Roy Del Ruth, 84 mins.)

Folks at Red Wolf Inn—See: **Terror at Red Wolf Inn**

Follow a Star (Great Britain, 1959)**½ Norman Wisdom, June Laverick. Cleaning store employee who wants a stage career is duped by a scheming popular singer into using his voice. (Dir: Robert Asher, 93 mins.)

Follow Me, Boys (1966)** Fred MacMurray, Vera Miles, Lillian Gish, Kurt Russell, Charlie Ruggles, Elliot Reid. Disney plucks our heartstrings with steel gloves in this overdone but well-meaning pic about a man who settles in a sleepy community and finds fulfillment in founding a scout troop. (Dir: Norman Tokar, 131 mins.)†

Follow Me Quietly (1949)*** William Lundigan, Dorothy Patrick. Detective traps psychopathic killer. Well-made, exciting melodrama. (Dir: Richard Fleischer, 59 mins.)†

Follow That Camel (Great Britain, 1967)** Phil Silvers, Kenneth Williams, Jim Dale. Fun in the Foreign Legion as Sergeant Phil Silvers is forced to aid a friend in a whacky plan. Vaudeville in the desert. (Dir: Gerald Thomas, 95 mins.)†

Follow That Dream (1962)**½ Elvis Presley, Arthur O'Connell, Joanna Moore. Strictly for Presley fans! He sings, drawls, and gets into plenty of trouble in this comedy about a group of hillbilly homesteaders who settle in a small Florida town which turns into a fairly thriving community. (Dir: Gordon Douglas, 110 mins.)†

Follow the Boys (1944)*** George Raft, Vera Zorina. A hoofer does his bit for the war effort by entertaining with the U.S.O. Slender story is helped by many stars making brief appearances, best of which is a routine by W. C. Fields. (Dir: A. Edward Sutherland, 122 mins.)

Follow the Boys (1963)** Connie Francis, Paula Prentiss, Janis Paige, Russ Tamblyn. American girls at large on the French Riviera. (Dir: Richard Thorpe, 95 mins.)

Follow the Fleet (1936)**** Fred Astaire, Ginger Rogers, Lucille Ball, Randolph Scott, Harriet Hilliard. Song and dance man joins the Navy when his girl turns him down. Fine musical, Astaire and Rogers in top form, as are Berlin tunes. (Dir: Mark Sandrich, 110 mins.)†

Follow the Leader (1944)** Leo Gorcey, Huntz Hall, Dave Durand. In the spirit of wartime patriotism, even the Army shows up when the Bowery Boys pursue some crooks. The usual. (Dir: William Beaudine, 65 mins.)

Follow the Sun (1951)**½ Glenn Ford, Anne Baxter, Dennis O'Keefe. The biography of golfer Ben Hogan, his ups and downs. Golf fans will vote it great—others, the usual sports saga. (Dir: Sidney Lanfield, 93 mins.)

Follow Your Dreams—See: **Independence Day**

Follow Your Heart (MTV 1990)* Patrick Cassidy, Catherine Mary Stewart, Frances Sternhagen, Jane Alexander. Ex-marine drifter Cassidy finds the family he never had when he is stranded in Wyoming. (Dir: Noel Nosseck, 96 mins.)

Folly to Be Wise (Great Britain, 1953)***½ Alastair Sim, Roland Culver. The trials and tribulations of an Army chaplain make a delightfully witty comedy. (Dir: Frank Launder, 91 mins.)

Food of the Gods, The (1976)* Marjoe Gortner, Pamela Franklin, Ida Lupino, Ralph Meeker. Animals grow to outrageous proportions and terrorize a group of hunters and travelers. (Dir: Bert I. Gordon, 88 mins.)†

Food of the Gods II (Canada, 1988)* Paul Coufos, Lis Schrage, Colin Fox, Jackie Burroughs. Ambrosia it's not. In-name-only sequel in which laboratory rats on a college campus grow to giant size and wreak the usual havoc. (Dir: Damian Lee, 91 mins.)†

Fool for Love (1985)** Sam Shepard, Kim Basinger, Randy Quaid, Harry Dean Stanton. Set in the decaying West, with lots of seedy motel signs blinking to denote moral squalor, Basinger and Shepard spar as they try to come to grips with an illicit self-destructive bond they cannot break. From Shepard's play. (Dir: Robert Altman, 105 mins.)†

Foolin' Around (1980)**½ Gary Busey, Annette O'Toole, Cloris Leachman, Eddie Albert, John Calvin, Tony Randall. A throwback to those screwball comedies of the thirties with a patina of the eighties morality. Burly poor guy (Gary Busey) falls for a rich girl (Annette O'Toole) and goes through all the paces to woo and win her. (Dir: Richard T. Heffron, 111 mins.)†

Foolish Wives (1922)*** Erich von Stroheim, Miss Du Pont, Maud George, Mae Busch. Von Stroheim wrote and directed this sophisticated, complex drama of a dashing European nobleman who tries to seduce the wife of an American envoy (along with every other woman who crosses his path). Detailed production is visually elegant. (107 mins.)†

Fool Killer, The (1965)**½ Anthony Perkins, Salome Jens, Dana Elcar, Edward Albert. Runaway boy teams with a tormented Civil War veteran who has lost his memory, and together they are involved in a mysterious murder. (Dir: Servando Gonzalez, 103 mins.)†

Fools (1970)* Jason Robards, Jr., Katharine Ross, Scott Hylands. Trite December-May romance as fifty-year-old horror-film-star Robards falls in love with the anxiety-ridden wife of a millionaire. (Dir: Tom Gries, 93 mins.)†

Fools for Scandal (1938)** Carole Lombard, Fernand Gravet, Ralph Bellamy, Allan Jenkins, Isabel Jeans, Marie Wilson. Foolish concoction about a madcap fling in gay Paree, where Lombard dallies with a down-on-his-luck nobleman. (Dir: Mervyn LeRoy, 81 mins.)

Fools of Fortune (Great Britain, 1990)**½ Mary Elizabeth Mastrantonio, Iain Glen, Julie Christie, Michael Kitchen, Sean McClory. The serenity of a peaceful Irish Protestant family is shattered when they are drawn into the battle between Republican forces and the Black-and-Tan soldiers during the Civil War that wracked the United Kingdom after World War I. (Dir: Pat O'Connor, 109 mins.)

Fools Parade (1971)**½ James Stewart, George Kennedy, Anne Baxter, Strother Martin, Kurt Russell, William Windom. Stewart is very good in this tale about a man who is released from prison after serving forty years and has plans to open a business with the $25,000 he earned while behind bars. However, a guard at the prison has other plans for the money. (Dir: Andrew McLaglen, 98 mins.)

Footlight Glamor (1943)*** Penny Singleton, Arthur Lake, Larry Simms, Ann Savage. Above-average entry in the *Blondie* series; an attractive actress arrives at the Bumstead household and appears to have designs on Dagwood as well as on a stage career. Zingy backstage comedy. (Dir: Frank Strayer, 75 mins.)

Footlight Parade (1933)***½ James Cagney, Joan Blondell, Dick Powell, Ruby Keeler, Guy Kibbee. An immensely entertaining backstage musical whose straight sequences are every bit as entertaining as the musical segments. With his fabulous flying feet, Cagney stars as a producer specializing in creating live stage shows to be featured between films at double features. The numbers include "Shanghai Lil," "By a Waterfall," and "Honeymoon Hotel," all outlandish and captivating in the best Busby Berkeley tradition. (Dir: Lloyd Bacon, 100 mins.)†

Footlight Serenade (1942)** ½ John Payne, Betty Grable, Victor Mature. Routine backstage musical with uninspired score. TV's Phil Silvers is in there to hold up the comedy. (Dir: Gregory Ratoff, 80 mins.)†

Footloose (1984)**½ Kevin Bacon, Lori Singer, John Lithgow, Dianne Wiest. In this *Flashdance*-inspired teen pic, a student transfers into the Bible Belt and brings some big-city influences with him. He can't keep from tapping his feet, even when he's stepping on the adult population's toes. (Dir: Herbert Ross, 106 mins.)†

Footsteps (MTV 1972)**½ Richard Crenna, Joanna Pettet. Better-than-average football yarn with Crenna as the hero-villain, a skillful defense coach who cuts corners to win. (Dir: Paul Wendkos, 73 mins.)

Footsteps in the Dark (1941)**½ Errol Flynn, Brenda Marshall. Occasionally amusing comedy-drama with Errol as a slick detective. One of the amusing scenes is contributed by William Frawley. (Dir: Lloyd Bacon, 96 mins.)

Footsteps in the Fog (Great Britain, 1955)** Stewart Granger, Jean Simmons. Mediocre costume melodrama about an ambitious servant girl and her diabolical employer. Well played by the cast. (Dir: Arthur Lubin, 90 mins.)

Footsteps in the Night (1957)**½ Bill Elliott, Don Haggerty, Douglas Dick. Policeman investigates a motel murder, saves an innocent man. Good low-budget mystery developed logically and interestingly. (Dir: Jean Yarbrough, 62 mins.)

For a Few Dollars More (Italy, 1967)**½ Clint Eastwood, Lee Van Cleef, Klaus Kinski, Jose Egger, Gian Maria Volonté. Resembling its predecessor, *A Fistful of Dollars*, this spaghetti western has Eastwood playing the stranger with no name, and the expected overdose of violence. Eastwood plays a bounty hunter like a zombie, pairing with Van Cleef to hunt Mexican bandits. (Dir: Sergio Leone, 131 mins.)†

For Better, For Worse (1974)*½ Gene Hackman, Liv Ullmann, Susan Tyrrell, Eileen Heckart. A misbegotten western by a talented Swedish director who's definitely not at home on the range. Hackman treats his new bride as mere property until hardship teaches them mutual respect. AKA: *Zandy's Bride*. (Dir: Jan Troell, 116 mins.)

Forbidden (1932)** Barbara Stanwyck, Adolphe Menjou, Ralph Bellamy, Henry Armetta, Dorothy Peterson. Early Frank Capra film about an unmarried schoolteacher who takes a cruise to enliven her dull existence and ends up having an affair with a man unable to wed her. The usual soapsuds, with director Capra bringing nothing to it, but Stanwyck is luminous. (81 mins.)

Forbidden (1954)** Tony Curtis, Joanne Dru. Adventure set in Macao (where else?) where two old flames (Curtis and Dru) rekindle their passion only to have their love and lives threatened by bigtime racketeers. Good actors at the mercy of the gangsters and the script. (Dir: Rudolph Mate, 85 mins.)

Forbidden (MCTV 1985)**½ Jacqueline Bisset, Jurgen Prochnow, Irene Worth, Amanda Cannings. Slow-moving but well-acted account of a forbidden romance between a Jew and a Christian in Berlin during WWII. Bisset is a highborn Christian who meets a Jewish writer (Prochnow) and they fall in love despite the danger to them both. (Dir: Anthony Page, 115 mins.)†

Forbidden Alliance—See: **Barretts of Wimpole Street, The** (1934)

Forbidden Cargo (Great Britain, 1954)*** Nigel Patrick, Elizabeth Sellars. Complaints send a private investigator to a coastal town, where he uncovers a smuggling racket. Well-done melodrama, at once amusing and suspenseful. (Dir: Harold French, 83 mins.)

Forbidden Dance, The (1990)½ Laura Herring, Jeff James, Barbra Brighton, Miranda Garrison, Sid Haig, Richard Lynch. The worst of the rash of lambada movies, and that's saying something. The princess of a Brazilian tribe whose existence is threatened by multinational developers seeks to bring attention to her plight by winning a TV dance contest. It didn't make much sense to us, either. (Dir: Greydon Clark, 97 mins.)†

Forbidden Fruit (France, 1958)**½ Fernandel, Francoise Arnoul. Fernandel is cast in a dramatic role as a middle-aged married man who has an affair with a pretty young girl. (Dir: Henri Verneuil, 97 mins.)

Forbidden Games (France, 1952)**** Brigitte Fossey, Georges Poujouly. Superb, poignant film about a poor family who take in a little girl whose parents are killed in an air raid. The youngest son and the little girl become great friends and learn to rely on one another for understanding. (Dir: René Clement, 87 mins.)†

Forbidden Love (MTV 1982)*½ Yvette Mimieux, Andrew Stevens, Dana Elcar, Lynn Carlin. A young, handsome intern and a rich, elegant lady in her forties have an affair in this poorly developed love story. (Dir: Steven Stern, 104 mins.)†

Forbidden Nights (MTV 1990)** Melissa Gilbert, Robin Shou, Victor K. Wong, Khigh Dhiegh. American teacher Gilbert falls in love with a radical student leader in China circa 1979. Attempt to capitalize on the student uprisings in China without confronting the issues head-on results in little more than a tepid romance in an unusual setting. (Dir: Waris Hussein, 96 mins.)

Forbidden Planet (1956)***½ Walter Pidgeon, Anne Francis, Leslie Nielsen, Earl Holliman. Better-than-average science-fiction pic. The year is 2200 A.D. and the planet is Altair-4. Good use of visual gimmicks and sound effects in this tale derived from *The Tempest*. (Dir: Fred McLeod Wilcox, 98 mins.)†

Forbidden Relations (Hungary, 1983)** Lili Monori, Miklos B. Szekely, Mari Torocsik. An earnest, well-intentioned film, but a failure. Monori plays a bereaved widow who begins an affair with the recently divorced Szekely. Even after they discover they are half-brother and half-sister they continue to live together, shocking their community. (Dir: Zsolt Kezdi Kovacs, 90 mins.)

Forbidden Street, The (1949)** Dana Andrews, Maureen O'Hara. Melodrama set in London slums with soap opera tendencies. Nice performance by Dame Sybil Thorndike as a crusty old witch. (Dir: Jean Negulesco, 91 mins.)

Forbidden Sun (1989)** Lauren Hutton, Cliff De Young, Robert Beltran, Viveka Davis, Renee Estevez. Minor follow-up to *The Wicker Man*, written by that film's director, with a similar framework but none of the suspense or subtle horror. A troubled girl at a school on the island of Crete combines her interest in Greek myths with a misplaced desire for revenge. AKA: **Buildance**. (Dir: Zelda Barron, 88 mins.)†

Forbidden World (1982)*½ Jesse Vint, June Chadwick, Dawn Dunlap, Linden Chiles, Fox Harris. Producer Roger Corman's shot at cashing in on the success of *Alien*, with the crew of a spaceship stalked by a monster they've accidentally let on board. Gets half a star for the gruesomely original ending. Leftover footage from this has been turning up in other Corman flicks ever since. AKA: **Mutant**. (Dir: Allan Holzman, 82 mins.)†

Forbidden Zone (1980)* Herve Villechaize, Susan Tyrrell, Marie-Pascale Elfman, Viva. This campy B&W cult item is worth a look for connoisseurs of weirdness. They may be amused by the antics of a bizarre family who fall into the Forbidden Zone, ruled over by a libidinous midget king and his cuckoo consort played by the modern cinema's biggest ham, Susan Tyrrell. (Dir: Richard Elfman, 76 mins.)†

Forbin Project, The—See: **Colossus: The Forbin Project**

Forced Entry (1984)½ Tanya Roberts, Ron Max, Nancy Allen, Robin Leslie. Originally shot in 1975. A sleazoid action pic about a scumbag rapist-killer who goes after Tanya (didn't he know about her "Charlie's Angels" training?). (Dir: Jim Sotos, 83 mins.)†

Forced March (1989)**½ Chris Sarandon, Renée Soutendijk, John Seitz, Josef Sommer. Thoughtful approach to the subject of Nazi death camps: an actor wrestles with his portrayal of Hungarian poet Miklos Radnoti, who died in a labor camp. By cutting away from the film about Radnoti to the story of the actor who is portraying him, *Forced March* emphasizes that such horrors cannot adequately be conveyed by art. Unfortunately, the approach yields an emotional dead end. (Dir: Rick King, 104 mins.)

Forced Vengeance (1982)**½ Chuck Norris, Mary Louise Weller, David Opatoshu. Making the most of its Hong Kong locales, the film trails after Chuck as he rescues the daughter of his employer, who was rubbed out by the gambling syndicate. (Dir: James Fargo, 90 mins.)†

Force Five (MTV 1975)* Gerald Gordon, Nick Pryor, William Lucking. Predictable TV pilot about a group of ex-cons forming a police undercover unit. (Dir: Walter Grauman, 72 mins.)

Force of Arms (1951)**½ William Holden, Nancy Olson, Frank Lovejoy. An Army officer and a young WAC meet and fall in love in the midst of war (WWII). Very reminiscent of *A Farewell to Arms* but not as effective. Good performances by the stars. (Dir: Michael Curtiz, 100 mins.)

Force of Evil (1949)*** John Garfield, Beatrice Pearson. The "numbers" racket is broken wide open when one of its hirelings refuses to play ball any longer. Competent crime melodrama. (Dir: Abraham Polonsky, 78 mins.)†

Force of One, A (1979)** Jennifer O'Neill, Chuck Norris, Clu Gulager, Ron O'Neal, James Whitmore, Jr. Two world karate champions are pitted against each other as Norris is engaged by a small California town's narcotics squad to teach its members the martial arts in fighting a drug ring. (Dir: Paul Aaron, 96 mins.)†

Force 10 from Navarone (Great Britain, 1978)** Robert Shaw, Edward Fox, Harrison Ford, Franco Nero, Barbara Bach. Sequel-of-sorts to the excellent *The Guns of Navarone*, using a couple of Alistair MacLean characters to poor advantage. Carl Foreman, producer-writer of the first screenplay, did the story of a group of WWII commandos who must destroy a bridge in Yugoslavia that is vital to the Germans. (Dir: Guy Hamilton, 118 mins.)†

Ford: The Man and the Machine (MTV 1987)**½ Cliff Robertson, Hope Lange, Heather Thomas, Michael Ironside. Biography of Henry Ford II, who ran the automobile empire his father built with ruthless efficiency but had more trouble with his family and mistress. Well acted. (Dir: Allan Eastman, 200 mins.)

Foreign Affair, A (1948)*** Marlene Dietrich, Jean Arthur, John Lund. Director Billy Wilder's satire on post–WWII American puritanism vis-à-vis the defeated Germans is deft, and less nasty than its reputation. Stars Arthur as an Iowa congresswoman on a junket to wicked Berlin, Lund as the officer who tries to cope with her moralizing, and Dietrich as an ex-Nazi chanteuse. (116 mins.)

Foreign Body (Great Britain, 1986)**½ Victor Banerjee, Warren Mitchell, Geraldine McEwan, Denis Quilley, Amanda Donohoe, Anna Massey, Trevor Howard. A slight, disarming social comedy about an Indian hotel clerk who accidentally stumbles into a position as doctor to socially prominent people. (Dir: Ronald Neame, 100 mins.)†

Foreign Correspondent (1940)**** Joel McCrea, Laraine Day, Herbert Marshall, George Sanders, Albert Basserman. McCrea is an American reporter in pre–WWII London who gets involved with a Nazi spy ring and the kidnapping of a European political figure (Basserman). (Dir: Alfred Hitchcock, 119 mins.)†

Foreign Exchange (MTV 1970)** Robert Horton, Sebastian Cabot, Jill St. John. One of two made-for-TV features starring Robert Horton as former British agent John Smith, adventurer and fatalist who gets involved in a prisoner-exchange plot that backfires. (Dir: Roy Baker, 72 mins.)

Foreign Intrigue (1956)*** Robert Mitchum, Genevieve Page. Overlong but sometimes exciting melodrama. Press agent finds plenty of surprises when he checks into the past of his deceased employer. Filmed in Europe. (Dir: Sheldon Reynolds, 100 mins.)

Foreman Went to France, The (Great Britain, 1942)*** Tommy Trinder, Clifford Evans, Constance Cummings, Robert Morley. A factory foreman is trapped in France by the onrush of the Nazis, joins with two Tommies and a girl to escape across the Channel. One of the best of its kind, a fast, thrilling "chase" melodrama. (Dir: Charles Frend, 88 mins.)

Forest, The (1983)** Dean Russell, Michael Brody, Elaine Warner, John Batis, Ann Wilkinson. Title setting provides the backdrop for a slasher story

Forest Rangers, The (1942)**½ Fred MacMurray, Susan Hayward, Paulette Goddard. When a forest ranger marries a socialite, his former girl tries to show her up. Mildly pleasant comedy-drama, but the cast is better than the material. (Dir: George Marshall, 87 mins.)

Forever (MTV 1978)** Stephanie Zimbalist, Dean Butler, John Friedrich, Diana Scarwid. Even so worthy a director as John Korty can't avoid the tedium that comes from watching a pair of handsome youngsters kiss and smile, kiss and smile, for what seems like forever. (104 mins.)†

Forever Amber (1947)**½ Linda Darnell, Cornel Wilde, George Sanders, Richard Greene, Jessica Tandy. As entertainment it's flashy, splashy, and silly, if that's enough. Peggy Cummins was fired after shooting began, and Darnell was rushed in to fill the title role of the lively wench who sacrifices love and honor to get ahead at the court of Charles II (Sanders). (Dir: Otto Preminger, 138 mins.)

Forever and a Day (1943)**** Ida Lupino, Charles Laughton, Merle Oberon, Brian Aherne, Ray Milland. The saga of a house in London, and of the generations who lived in it. Each sequence shows care, fine casting, direction, writing. (Dirs: René Clair, Edmund Goulding, Cedric Hardwicke, Frank Lloyd, Victor Saville, Robert Stevenson, Herbert Wilcox, 104 mins.)†

Forever Darling (1956)** Lucille Ball, Desi Arnaz, James Mason. Silliness about a guardian angel who comes to earth to save a marriage, isn't worthy of the talents of the cast. For Lucy addicts primarily. (Dir: Alexander Hall, 96 mins.)

Forever Evil (1986)* Red Mitchell, Tracey Huffman, Kent Johnson, Diane Johnson. Survivors of monstrous attacks by cultists who worship an ancient god band together to keep them from bringing him back to earth. Sub-H. P. Lovecraft horror movie doesn't last forever; it just seems that way. (Dir: Roger Evans, 110 mins.)†

Forever Female (1953)*** Ginger Rogers, William Holden, Paul Douglas, Pat Crowley, James Gleason. Tangy backstage comedy with Rogers keeping her coyness in check for a change. She plays an over-the-hill star who grudgingly concedes that she's a bit long in the tooth to play ingenues. (Dir: Irving Rapper, 93 mins.)

Forever, Lulu (1987)* Hanna Schygulla, Deborah Harry, Annie Golden, Alec Baldwin. Incredibly awful urban comedy that casts Schygulla as a down-on-her-luck novelist who is drawn up in the affairs of a mysterious gangster's moll (Harry). Hanna's talents are wasted in this poor *Desperately Seeking Susan* clone. (Dir: Amos Kollek, 86 mins.)†

Forever Mary (Italy, 1991)*** Michele Placido, Alesandro Di Sanzo, Francesco Benigno, Claudio Amendola. Well-meaning variation of *To Sir, With Love*, Italian style. A dedicated teacher (Placido) takes on the challenge of educating reform school boys. When a transvestite prostitute is admitted into the male domain, the educator uses uncommon methods of getting the outcast accepted. A mature, sensitive drama that successfully works on your emotions. (Dir: Marco Risi, 100 mins.)

Forever My Love (Austria, 1955)** Romy Schneider, Karl Boehm. Three films compressed into one, recounting the life and love of Elizabeth of Bavaria (Schneider) and Franz Josef (Boehm). Like Viennese pastry, nice and sweet, but a lot of it makes you sick. (Dir: Ernst Marischka, 147 mins.)

Forever Young (Great Britain, 1985)*** James Aubrey, Nicholas Gecks, Alec McCowen, Karen Archer, Liam Holt. A moving, contemplative film about awkward passions. An altar boy has a harmless crush on a priest whose friend has seduced the boy's mother. (Dir: David Drury, 84 mins.)†

Forever Young, Forever Free (South Africa, 1976)** Karen Valentine, Jose Ferrer. Filmed on location in Africa; the photography is the chief inducement to watch this sentimental story about a white orphan boy and his African herdboy pal. (Dir: Ashley Lazarus, 78 mins.)

Forgiven Sinner, The (France, 1962)***½ Jean-Paul Belmondo, Emmanuele Riva. Disillusioned, bitter war widow is helped by the understanding of a kindly priest during WWII. Meticulously detailed, well-acted drama, sober and thoughtful. (Dir: Jean-Pierre Melville, 101 mins.)

Forgotten Man, The (MTV 1971)**½ Dennis Weaver, Lois Nettleson, Anne Francis, Andrew Duggan. Weaver's strong, intelligent performance is the main virtue of this rather ordinary TV movie. The plot concerns an American POW who returns from Vietnam to discover that his family and business have irrevocably changed while he was gone. (Dir: Walter Grauman, 72 mins.)

Forgotten Prisoners: The Amnesty Files (MCTV 1990)*** Ron Silver, Hector Elizondo, Roger Daltry. A deeply moving and often harrowing account of how Amnesty International functioned in Turkey, where appalling torture was a normal investigative technique of the police. First-rate cast, including Silver and Elizondo. (Dir: Robert Greenwald, 92 mins.)†

For Heaven's Sake (1926)*** Harold Lloyd, Jobyna Ralston. Charming comedy in which Lloyd falls head over heels for a mission girl. (Dir: Sam Taylor, 62 mins.)

For Heaven's Sake (1950)**½ Clifton Webb, Joan Bennett, Robert Cummings, Joan Blondell, Edmund Gwenn, Gigi Perreau. Whimsical comedy about a couple of aging angels (Webb & Edmund Gwenn) who come to earth to save a marriage. (Dir: George Seaton, 92 mins.)

For Keeps (1988)*½ Molly Ringwald, Randall Batinkoff, Kenneth Mars, Miriam Flynn, Conchata Ferrell. The next phase of the Brat Pack phenomenon: the characters stay the same age but accept adult responsibilities. Molly and her beau experience parenthood in this oft-intolerable comic drama that seems like an overdeveloped after-school special. (Dir: John G. Avildsen, 98 mins.)†

For Ladies Only (MTV 1981)**½ Gregory Harrison, Patricia Davis, Dinah Manoff, Louise Lasser, Lee Grant, Marc Singer. Slickly produced yarn about a recent fad—male strippers. A serious young actor takes up stripping to pay the rent. (Dir: Mel Damski, 104 mins.)†

For Love Alone (Australia, 1985)** Helen Buday, Sam Neil, Hugo Weaving. In '30s Australia, a starry-eyed girl yearns for true love, chasing after Mr. Wrong until his heartlessness opens her eyes to the Mr. Right who's been there all along. (Dir: Stephen Wallace, 101 mins.)†

For Love and Honor (MTV 1983)**½ Cliff Potts, Shelley Smith, Yaphet Kotto, Gary Grubbs. A rough-and-tumble entry about the Army's 88th Airborne Division's guys and gals. (Dir: Gary Nelson, 104 mins.)

For Love of Ivy (1968)**½ Sidney Poitier, Abbey Lincoln, Beau Bridges. Disappointing romance. Story concerns a young domestic who decides to quit being a maid and go to secretarial school. (Dir: Daniel Mann, 102 mins.)†

For Love or Money (1933)—See: **Cash**

For Love or Money (1963)**½ Kirk Douglas, Mitzi Gaynor, Gig Young, Thelma Ritter. Attorney is hired by a wealthy widow to act as matchmaker for her three gorgeous daughters and the men she has selected for their mates. Douglas tries comedy for a change of pace, with questionable success. (Dir: Michael Gordon, 108 mins.)

For Love or Money (MTV 1984)** Suzanne Pleshette, Gil Gerard, Jamie Farr, Ray Walston, Mary Kay Place. Highly uneven backstage TV game show comedy where everyone panders to greed. Despite all the silliness, Pleshette and Gerard surprise with charming moments as contestants who go for the money and are happy to lie in their pursuit of instant wealth. (Dir: Jerry Hughes, 104 mins.)

For Lovers Only (MTV 1982)½ Deborah Raffin, Gary Sandy, Andy Griffith, Katherine Helmond. If the "Love Boat" docked at "Fantasy Island," the passengers would probably be the same ones as those in this predictable time waster about a honeymoon resort known as Bliss's Cove Haven. (Dir: Claudio Guzman, 104 mins.)

For Me and My Gal (1942)*** Judy Garland, Gene Kelly, George Murphy. For his film debut, Kelly is a hoofer who's all heel, even unto injuring himself to escape the draft (rough stuff in '42). Garland teams well with the newcomer; Busby Berkeley's direction is attentive and fluid; and if the script had taken Kelly a bit further the film might have been extraordinary instead of merely good. (104 mins.)†

For Men Only—See: **Tall Lie, The**

Formula, The (1980)**½ Marlon Brando, George C. Scott, Marthe Keller, Sir John Gielgud. Colorful, entertaining performance by Marlon Brando as an international oil cartel big shot highlights this thriller about intrigue, as a lethal fight for a synthetic fuel formula unfolds. But John G. Avildsen's direction is sluggish and the film looks too much like a made-for-TV mystery. (117 mins.)†

For Pete's Sake (1974)**½ Barbra Streisand, Michael Sarrazin, Estelle Parsons, Molly Picon. An uneven attempt at screwball comedy. Streisand is a young Brooklyn matron who gets mixed up with the Mafia, goofs miserably as a call girl, and winds up in the middle of a rampaging herd of rustled cattle in downtown Brooklyn. (Dir: Peter Yates, 90 mins.)†

Forsaking All Others (1934)**½ Joan Crawford, Clark Gable, Robert Montgomery. Lots of MGM starpower in an affable trifle. Joan Crawford finds Clark Gable slightly dull as a companion (plausibility problems right there), and she almost goes off with Robert Montgomery. (Dir: W. S. Van Dyke, 84 mins.)

For Singles Only (1968)* John Saxon, Mary Ann Mobley, Lana Wood. One of those simple-minded comedies about life in a California "swingles" apartment complex inhabited by assorted buxom ladies and beefcake men. (Dir: Arthur Dreifuss, 91 mins.)

Fort Apache (1948)***½ John Wayne, Henry Fonda, Shirley Temple, Pedro Armendariz, Ward Bond. A martinet commander (modeled on General Custer) leads his command to defeat by Indians. Fonda plays the megalomaniac, with Wayne, beginning to mature as an actor,

an effective counterweight as a pragmatic officer. The implication that Fonda dies a hero regardless of his folly is hard to accept. (Dir: John Ford, 127 mins.)†

Fort Apache, The Bronx (1981)*** Paul Newman, Edward Asner, Kathleen Beller, Danny Aiello, Pam Grier, Rachel Ticotin. A notable film that works on several levels. Newman plays a well-intentioned policeman on the beat in the squalid, largely devastated South Bronx of New York City where most of the film was shot. Focuses on the way the police interact and respond to the civilian population and the inevitable process of both parties being brutalized and doing brutalizing things themselves. Grier is mesmerizing in the role of a strung-out prostitute. (Dir: Daniel Petrie, 125 mins.)†

Fort Bowie (1958)**½ Ben Johnson, Jan Harrison, Kent Taylor. U.S. Cavalry fort is threatened by Apaches from without and love intrigues from within. Above-average western. (Dir: Howard W. Koch, 80 mins.)

Fort Defiance (1951)*** Dane Clark, Ben Johnson. Above-average Grade B western with Johnson out for revenge against Clark for deserting during the Civil War. (Dir: John Rawlins, 81 mins.)

Fort Dobbs (1958)** Clint Walker, Virginia Mayo, Brian Keith. An average western epic with the cowboys and Indians fighting it out. (Dir: Gordon Douglas, 90 mins.)

For the First Time (U.S.-West Germany-Italy, 1959)** Mario Lanza, Johanna von Koczian, Zsa Zsa Gabor. Opera star (Lanza) finds romance with a deaf girl (von Koczian). Lanza's last film. (Dir: Rudy Mate, 97 mins.)

For the Love of Benji (1977)**½ Benji, Patsy Garrett, Cynthia Smith, Allen Fiuzat, Ed Nelson. Innocuous but diverting pooch-adventure in which Benji hotfoots it all over Athens as international spies play dogcatcher and try to grab him for the secret formula stamped on his paw. (Dir: Joe Camp, 84 mins.)†

For the Love of It (MTV 1980)**½ Deborah Raffin, Jeff Conaway, Adam West, Don Rickles, Eve Arden. If you like your comedies on the frantic side, you'll enjoy this wacky excursion which finds gorgeous model Raffin on the run after she accidentally acquires some Soviet plans. (Dir: Hal Kanter, 104 mins.)†

For the Love of Mary (1948)**½ Deanna Durbin, Edmond O'Brien, Don Taylor. Deanna Durbin is a switchboard operator at the White House and meets many men not solely involved with politics. Charming little comedy. (Dir: Frederick de Cordova, 90 mins.)

For Those Who Think Young (1964)* Nancy Sinatra, Paul Lynde, James Darren, Pamela Tiffin. About a college where surfing and romance seem to be the major subjects. For those who think stupid! (Dir: Leslie Martinson, 96 mins.)

Fort Massacre (1958)** Joel McCrea, Forrest Tucker, Susan Cabot. Joel McCrea's in the saddle again and trouble's not far behind. Good action scenes with plenty of gun smoke and Indian warfare. (Dir: Joseph Newman, 80 mins.)

Fort Osage (1952)** Rod Cameron, Jane Nigh, Douglas Kennedy, Iron Eyes Cody. Frontier scout leads a wagon train to safety and foils an Indian uprising. (Dir: Lesley Selander, 72 mins.)

Fortress (MCTV 1985)*½ Rachel Ward, Sean Garlick, Rebecca Rigg. Specious rubbish about a schoolmarm who must teach her charges how to survive in the wilderness after they've been kidnapped. (Dir: Arch Nicholson, 120 mins.)†

Fort Ti (1953)** George Montgomery, Joan Vohs. An Indian scout joins with the English forces to capture the French-held Fort Ticonderoga. Routine western. Originally in 3-D. (Dir: William Castle, 73 mins.)

Fortunate Pilgrim (MTV 1988)** Sophia Loren, Edward James Olmos, John Turturro, Anna Strasberg, Yorgo Voyagis. Sophia gets a role she can sink her pearly whites into: a widowed Italian immigrant who encounters countless melodramatic obstacles. With Yugoslavia standing in for New York, this miniseries boasts some very nice period detail, but seems drawn out. (Dir: Stuart Cooper, 192 mins.)

Fortune, The (1975)*** Warren Beatty, Jack Nicholson, Stockard Channing. Director Mike Nichols obviously loved the screwball comedies of the thirties and tried to create a seventies valentine to them. Beatty and Nicholson are con artists who lure an heiress, Channing, from her father's home and plan to wed, bed, and kill her—not necessarily in that order. Deft, witty. (86 mins.)

Fortune and Men's Eyes (Canada-U.S., 1971)*** Wendell Burton, Zooey Hall, Michael Greer. Harrowing, shocking account of homosexuality in prison. (Dir: Harvey Hart, 102 mins.)

Fortune Cookie, The (1966)*** Jack Lemmon, Walter Matthau. Walter Matthau's Academy Award-winning performance as Best Supporting Actor is a joy, and carries this uneven comedy. Jack Lemmon takes a backseat, or more literally a wheelchair, to Matthau's portrayal as his money-hungry brother-in-law, who sees a chance to score big when Lemmon is knocked down by a football player while performing his job as a TV cameraman. (Dir: Billy Wilder, 125 mins.)†

Fortunes of Captain Blood (1950)**½ Louis Hayward, Patricia Medina. The dashing Captain Peter Blood, the Spanish Main's most feared buccaneer, is with us once more, this time in the guise of Louis Hayward. (Dir: Gordon Douglas, 91 mins.)

Fort Utah (1967)* John Ireland, Virginia Mayo, Robert Strauss. Weary tale of reformed gunfighter (Ireland) and Indian agent (Strauss) hot on the trail of an Indian-massacring Army deserter (Scott Brady). The horses look plastic, the rocks papier-mâché, Fort Utah itself appears to have been constructed from popsicle sticks. (Dir: Lesley Selander, 84 mins.)

Forty Carats (1973)**½ Liv Ullmann, Edward Albert, Gene Kelly, Binnie Barnes, Nancy Walker. The Broadway success about an older woman and a young lover plays like glossy soap opera on the screen. Liv Ullmann lacks comic finesse as the 40-year-old divorcée who falls under the spell of a 22-year-old (Albert) while vacationing in Greece. (Dir: Milton Katselas, 110 mins.)†

48-Hour Mile, The (MTV 1970)** Darren McGavin, William Windom, Kathy Brown, Carrie Snodgress. McGavin plays a private eye on an assignment involving two women in love with the same man. (Dir: Gene Levitt, 97 mins.)

48 HRS. (1982)***½ Nick Nolte, Eddie Murphy, Annette O'Toole, Frank McRae, James Remar, David Patrick Kelly. We haven't had an action film with this much charisma generated by a team of leading men in a long time. Nolte plays a tough loner on the San Francisco police force. The minute Murphy comes on screen the pace of the film picks up. He plays a cool, funny con, with plenty of nerve and a tinge of desperation, more about his need for sex than his need for freedom. Sequel: *Another 48 HRS.* (Dir: Walter Hill, 96 mins.)†

Forty Guns (1957)*** Barbara Stanwyck, Barry Sullivan. The Forty Guns of the title must go off forty times each in this literal "shoot 'em up" western, but Sam Fuller's all-the-stops-pulled-out directorial style is quite exciting in this idiosyncratic western about the Tombstone territory of Arizona and the men who tamed it. (80 mins.)

40 Guns to Apache Pass (1967)*½ Audie Murphy, Michael Burns, Kenneth Tobey. Ye olde predictable western: Apaches, a renegade selling guns, an experienced soldier inspiring a tenderfoot volunteer. (Dir: William Witney, 95 mins.)

Forty-Niners, The (1954)**½ Bill Elliott, Virginia Grey, Harry Morgan. Marshal makes friends with a gambler in order to track down some killers. Well-done western. (Dir: Thomas Carr, 71 mins.)

49th Man, The (1953)**½ John Ireland, Suzanne Dalbert. Fast-moving spy film about U.S. Security Investigators' tracking down of an A-bomb parts smuggling outfit. Tense climax. (Dir: Fred F. Sears, 73 mins.)

49th Parallel, The (Great Britain, 1941)***½ Laurence Olivier, Leslie Howard, Raymond Massey, Eric Portman, Glynis Johns. Gripping war drama of a German U-boat sunk off Canada, its survivors trying to reach safety in neutral territory. The manhunt is exciting, picturesque, with actual background shooting. AKA: **The Invaders.** (Dir: Michael Powell, 105 mins.)†

40 Pounds of Trouble (1963)** Tony Curtis, Phil Silvers, Suzanne Pleshette, Claire Wilcox. Limp reworking of Shirley Temple's *Little Miss Marker,* the one about the woman-hating gambler who takes a tyke under his wing and softens up. (Dir: Norman Jewison, 106 mins.)

42nd Street (1933)**** Dick Powell, Ruby Keeler, Ginger Rogers, Warner Baxter, Una Merkel. The archetypal backstage musical, complete with the young understudy going on after the star breaks her leg a few hours before the big opening and, of course, Busby Berkeley extravaganzas. Baxter is the producer who rushes around and moves the plot along. (Beware of the poorly colorized version.) (Dir: Lloyd Bacon, 98 mins.)†

47 Ronin, The (Japan, 1941–42)**½ Chojuro Kawarazaki, Yoshizaburo Arashi, Mantoyo Mimasu, Kenemon Nakamura. Director Kenji Mizoguchi's version of the extremely popular Japanese tale, based on an eighteenth-century incident in which ronin (masterless samurai) pledged to a lord avenged his murder, resulting in their own deaths. Not one of the best versions of the story—Mizoguchi abhorred violence, and adapted the story under duress—but has its fascinations for those willing to spend some time with it. AKA: **The Genroku Chusingara** and **Loyal 47 Ronin.** (222 mins.)†

For Us the Living: The Medgar Evers Story (MTV 1983)***½ Howard Rollins, Jr., Irene Cara, Margaret Avery, Roscoe Lee Browne, Larry Fishburne. Excellent dramatization of a period of civil rights history in the South. Medgar Evers was one of the charismatic leaders of the movement and was assassinated in June 1963. This is not just another civil rights drama. It's the moving story of a flesh-and-blood man with an earnest dedication to an unpopular cause. (Dir: Michael Schultz, 90 mins.)

Forward March—See: Doughboys

For Whom the Bell Tolls (1943)*** Gary Cooper, Ingrid Bergman, Akim Tamiroff. Turgid realization of the Hemingway novel about the Spanish Civil War, but noteworthy for depth in casting and performance. Cooper is again an admirable Hemingway hero; Bergman evokes both the dream and reality in the novel's conception. Most TV prints run 130 mins. (Dir: Sam Wood, 170 mins.)

For Your Eyes Only (1981)*** Roger Moore, Carole Bouquet, Lynn-Holly Johnson, Topol. This James Bond adventure is right on target. Agent 007 must find a nuclear submarine activating device that has been lost in a sea crash; his adventures en route to victory are more plausible than usual for a Bond adventure film. Roger Moore has never been cooler, crisper, or better than he is in this. (Dir: John Glen, 128 mins.)†

Foster and Laurie (MTV 1975)*** Perry King, Dorian Harewood. Excellently produced, well-acted police film based on the true-life slaying of two cops, Gregory Foster and Rocco Laurie, in New York City, 1972. (Dir: John Llewelyn Moxey, 98 mins.)

Foul Play (1978)*** Goldie Hawn, Chevy Chase, Dudley Moore, Burgess Meredith, Marilyn Sokol. Very funny comedy thriller in which bewildered librarian Hawn witnesses murder and mayhem and can't seem to prove what she's seen. Chase gets laughs as the smooth detective who becomes both protector and lover. The plot concerns an assassination attempt on the pope while he is attending a performance of "The Mikado." (Dir: Colin Higgins, 116 mins.)†

Found Money (MTV 1983)** Sid Caesar, Dick Van Dyke. Pleasing fare about outsmarting computers. Van Dyke and Caesar team up as New York nice guys bypassing cold-hearted bankers by handing out unused funds to good samaritans. (Dir: Bill Persky, 104 mins.)

Fountain, The (1934)**½ Ann Harding, Brian Aherne, Paul Lukas, Jean Hersholt, Ralph Forbes, Ian Wolfe. WWI story has Harding torn between husband Lukas, injured in the war, and lover Aherne. Harding's graceful, intelligent performance redeems this soap opera. (Dir: John Cromwell, 83 mins.)

Fountainhead, The (1949)*** Gary Cooper, Patricia Neal, Raymond Massey, Kent Smith, Robert Douglas. Cooper stars as Ayn Rand's archetypal individualist, an architect modeled on Frank Lloyd Wright who is willing to blow up his own work rather than see it perverted by public housing bureaucrats. Elaborate and highly stylized, the film's humanist virtues shine through. (Dir: King Vidor, 114 mins.)†

Four Adventures of Reinette and Mirabelle (France, 1988)***½ Joelle Miquel, Jessica Forde, Marie Riviere, Fabrice

371

Luchini. Spirited and sophisticated comedy about two women, a naive provincial art student and a worldly Parisian scholar, who decide to share an apartment together and have four precise adventures with characters from the streets of Paris. Filled with wisdom, idealism, and beauty. One of director Eric Rohmer's best. (95 mins.)

Four Bags Full (France, 1957)*** Jean Gabin, Bouvril. Award-winning French film combining comedy with a good dramatic plot about two men who take great risks during the Nazi occupation in Paris. Excellent performances. (Dir: Claude Autant-Lara, 84 mins.)

Four Daughters (1938)***½ Claude Rains, John Garfield, Gale Page, Lola Lane, Priscilla Lane, Rosemary Lane. Beautifully acted adaptation of the Fannie Hurst story about four small-town girls and the men in their lives. (Dir: Michael Curtiz, 90 mins.)

Four Days in Dallas—See: **Ruby and Oswald**

Four Days' Leave (Switzerland, 1949)**½ Cornel Wilde, Josette Day, Simone Signoret. A sailor on tour in Switzerland falls for the girl in the watch shop, enters in a skiing contest, wins both. Highly amusing, pleasant comedy with beautiful scenery. (Dir: Leopold Lindtberg, 98 mins.)

Four Days of Naples, The (U.S.-Italy, 1962)***½ Regina Bianchi, Jean Sorel, Lea Massari. Epic reenactment chronicling the spontaneous anti-Nazi uprising in Naples, which liberated the city after WWII. (Dir: Nanni Loy, 116 mins.)

Four Desperate Men (Australia, 1960)*** Aldo Ray, Heather Sears. Cornered criminals hole up on an island off Sydney, Australia, and threaten to blow up the entire town if they're not permitted to escape. Tense drama with the on-scene shooting (both varieties) adding to the suspense. Well acted. (Dir: Harry Watt, 104 mins.)

4D Man (1959)*** Robert Lansing, Lee Meriwether, Patty Duke, Guy Raymond, Robert Strauss, James Congdon. Clever sci-fi thriller about scientist who develops a method of transposing matter, enabling him to pass through walls, windows, water, and women. (Dir: Irvin S. Yeaworth, Jr., 85 mins.)†

Four Feathers, The (1929)**½ Richard Arlen, Fay Wray, Clive Brook, William Powell. A rather effective version of the A. E. W. Mason story with first-rate location work and a good sense of narrative coherence. Arlen is the lad who must prove his bravery to fiancée Wray and friends Brook and Powell. (Dirs: Ernest Schoedsack, Lothar Mendes, 80 mins.)

Four Feathers, The (Great Britain, 1939)***½ Ralph Richardson, John Clements, June Duprez, C. Aubrey Smith. The best of imperialistic epics, directed with verve and precision by Zoltan Korda. A young aristocrat (Clements) isn't cut out for a military career, so when he resigns his commission on the eve of the expedition to the Sudan, he is branded a coward by his friends and sweetheart and must set the disgrace right. Remade as *Storm over the Nile*. (115 mins., originally 140 mins.)†

Four Feathers, The (MTV 1978)*** Beau Bridges, Robert Powell, Harry Andrews, Simon Ward, Jane Seymour, Richard Johnson. TV adaptation of the classic story holds its own in comparison to the numerous filmings, with Bridges good as the British officer wrongly accused of cowardice. (Dir: Don Sharp, 110 mins.)†

Four for Texas (1963)*½ Dean Martin, Frank Sinatra, Anita Ekberg. The laughs are scarce in this western comedy that pits the two stars against each other until they join forces against a third party. (Dir: Robert Aldrich, 124 mins.)

Four Friends (1981)* Craig Wasson, James Leo Herlihy, Jodi Thelen. An unqualified disaster. Purporting to be the first film to honestly evoke the social unrest of the sixties, this pretentious claptrap proceeds without logic or character motivation. (Dir: Arthur Penn, 114 mins.)†

Four Frightened People (1934)*½ Claudette Colbert, Herbert Marshall, Mary Boland, William Gargan, Leo Carrillo. A lame lost-on-a-deserted-isle adventure; one of DeMille's few flops. Thank God for Boland. (78 mins.)

Four Girls in Town (1957)*** Julie Adams, Elsa Martinelli, Sydney Chaplin, George Nader. Hollywood story about four hopeful misses who arrive to make good in the flicks. Offbeat handling of the usual success story makes this one stand out. (Dir: Jack Sher, 85 mins.)

Four Guns to the Border (1954)** Rory Calhoun, Colleen Miller, George Nader. Western fare served with all the necessary ingredients intact. (Dir: Richard Carlson, 82 mins.)

Four Horsemen of the Apocalypse, The (1921)**** Rudolph Valentino, Alice Terry, Alan Hale, Wallace Beery. From the Argentine pampas to the Paris of WWI, the film aspires to saga and achieves it—even the central metaphor of the Four Horsemen is literally, and impressively, rendered. Valentino himself shows sensitivity as an actor. (Dir: Rex Ingram, 120 mins.)

Four Horsemen of the Apocalypse, The (1961)**½ Glenn Ford, Ingrid Thulin, Charles Boyer, Lee J. Cobb, Paul Henreid. Superficial, but sporadically involving drama of an Argentine family and their involvements in WWII, updated but hardly improved from the old silent version. (Dir: Vincente Minnelli, 153 mins.)†

Four Hours to Kill (1935)*** Richard Barthelmess, Helen Mack, Gertrude Michael, Joe Morrison, Dorothy Tree, Ray Milland, John Howard, Henry Travers. Fast, episodic thriller takes place within the confines of a vaudeville theater during one night when a killer escapes and tracks down the man who turned him in. Barthelmess is superb; fine supporting players. Script by Norman Krasna. (Dir: Mitchell Leisen, 71 mins.)

400 Blows, The (France, 1959)**** Jean-Pierre Léaud. Memorable study of an adolescent boy, neglected by his selfish parents, who discovers some unpleasant facts about life. The boy is played with great sensitivity by Jean-Pierre Léaud. The excellent photography and superb editing set the mood for this touching film. (Dir: François Truffaut, 99 mins.)†

Four in a Jeep (Switzerland, 1951)*** Ralph Meeker, Viveca Lindfors. Dramatic story of the international M.P. patrol in Vienna, and of a girl who needs their help. (Dir: Leopold Lindtberg, 97 mins.)

Four Jacks and a Jill (1942)**½ Ray Bolger, Desi Arnaz, June Havoc, Eddie Foy, Jr., Anne Shirley, Jack Durant, Fritz Feld, Henry Daniell. High-powered cast in a backstage musical comedy about girl who's not sure who she wants to marry. (Dir: Jack Hively, 68 mins.)†

Four Jills in a Jeep (1944)** Kay Francis, Carole Landis, Martha Raye, Phil Silvers. A big cast in a boring musical about the experiences of its female stars when they went overseas for the U.S.O. (Dir: William Seiter, 89 mins.)

Four Kinds of Love—See: **Bambole**

Four Men and a Prayer (1938)*** Loretta Young, Richard Greene, George Sanders, David Niven. This sturdy melodrama contains many of John Ford's directorial touches. Four brothers share an intense family bond as they band together to solve their father's murder. (85 mins.)

Four Mothers (1941)** Priscilla Lane, Rosemary Lane, Lola Lane, Gale Page, Claude Rains, Jeffrey Lynn. A reupholstered sequel to *Four Daughters* in which one of the daughters' hubbies suffers financial reverses and the entire clan gets into the act to bail him out. Soap opera, pure and simple. (Dir: William Keighley, 86 mins.)

Four Musketeers, The (1975)*** Raquel Welch, Oliver Reed, Richard Chamberlain, Faye Dunaway, Michael York, Charlton Heston, Simon Ward, Geraldine Chaplin. This sequel/continuation of the 1974 *Three Musketeers* offers more joyous

escapades of rogues, gallant damsels, derring-do and swordplay. Loaded with marvelous sight gags. (Dir: Richard Lester, 107 mins.)†

Four Nights of a Dreamer (France, 1971)***½ Isabelle Weingarten, Guillaume Des Forets, Maurice Monnoyer. Young Parisian artist stops girl from killing herself; they meet on successive nights to discuss life and love. Based on Dostoevsky's *White Nights*. (Dir: Robert Bresson, 87 mins.)

Four Poster, The (1952)*** Rex Harrison, Lilli Palmer. Fine screen treatment of hilarious Broadway comedy about a married couple who go through their lives in scenes played in and around their four-poster bed. Excellent performances by the stars. (Dir: Irving Reis, 103 mins.)

Four Rode Out (1969)*½ Sue Lyon, Pernell Roberts, Leslie Nielsen, Julian Mateos. A young sheriff and a Pinkerton man take a suspected murderer and his girlfriend into custody and trek through the desert. (Dir: John Peyser, 99 mins.)†

Four's a Crowd (1938)**½ Errol Flynn, Olivia de Havilland, Rosalind Russell. A lot of funny situations help this not-so-funny comedy about a wealthy heiress and her beaux. (Dir: Michael Curtiz, 100 mins.)

Four Seasons, The (1981)*** Alan Alda, Carol Burnett, Len Cariou, Sandy Dennis, Jack Weston, Rita Moreno, Bess Armstrong. Perceptive, amusing, and often poignant story about marriage in America. Alda also wrote and directed this observant essay about life and love in the suburbs. (117 mins.)†

Four Skulls of Jonathan Drake, The (1959)** Eduard Franz, Henry Daniell, Valerie French, Grant Richards. Awful sci-fi about a scientist fighting to end a voodoo curse. (Dir: Edward L. Cahn, 70 mins.)

Four Sons (1940)**½ Don Ameche, Eugenie Leontovich. Drama of a Czech family ripped apart by the Nazi invasion is almost a fine film but reaches for more than it is able to give. Still worth seeing as an antiwar story. Remake of a silent classic. (Dir: Archie Mayo, 89 mins.)

14 Going on 30 (MTV 1988)*½ Steve Eckholdt, Daphne Ashbrook, Patrick Duffy, Harry Morgan, Loretta Swit, Alan Thicke. Dippy Disney fare about a lovesick kid who "grows up" with the aid of a friend's invention and has a chance to prevent his favorite teacher from marrying an obnoxious gym instructor. (Dir: Paul Schneider, 96 mins.)

Fourteen Hours (1951)*** Richard Basehart, Barbara Bel Geddes, Paul Douglas, Grace Kelly (debut), Debra Paget. Director Henry Hathaway keeps the suspense sharply in focus in this drama about a mentally disturbed man who stands on a ledge of a Manhattan hotel threatening to jump for a period of fourteen hours. (92 mins.)

Fourth Man, The (Netherlands, 1984)*** Jeroen Krabbe, Rene Soutendijk. Dutch director Paul Verhoeven's audacious black comedy. A quasi-degenerate, quasi-Catholic writer gets bizarre visions of a bloody future, all of which come to pass when he sets up housekeeping with a seductive woman he meets on a lecture tour. (104 mins.)†

Fourth Protocol, The (Great Britain, 1987)**½ Michael Caine, Pierce Brosnan, Joanna Cassidy, Ned Beatty, Betsy Brantley, Matt Frewer. Predictable espionage, adapted by Frederick Forsyth from his novel. Super-spy Caine has to stop the Russians from detonating one of the nuclear bombs America keeps in Britain. (Dir: John Mackenzie, 119 mins.)†

Fourth Story (MCTV 1990)**½ Mark Harmon, Mimi Rodgers, Cliff De Young, Paul Gleason. Quirky, romantic detective thriller features Harmon as a private detective investigating the disappearance of Rodgers' husband. The handsome gumshoe suspects foul play as he predictably falls for his beautiful client. Amiably directed story alternates between comedy and suspense, but the transitions are not always successful. (Dir: Ivan Passer, 90 mins.)†

Fourth War, The (1990)*** Roy Scheider, Jurgen Prochnow, Tim Reid, Lara Harris, Harry Dean Stanton. Near the East German-Czechoslovakian border, a petty grudge between an American and a Soviet colonel threatens to escalate into something completely out of control. The point that professional warriors exist to fight wars, even if they have to invent them, is forcefully made by director John Frankenheimer. (91 mins.)†

Four Wives (1939)**½ Lane Sisters, Eddie Albert, John Garfield, Claude Rains. The *Four Daughters* ride again, this time as wives and mothers. But this time they ran out of breath and came up with a very ordinary movie. (Dir: Michael Curtiz, 110 mins.)

Fox, The (1968)*** Sandy Dennis, Keir Dullea, Anne Heywood. Sensitive dramatization of D. H. Lawrence's novella about a relationship between two young lesbians. The brooding story, filmed largely in rural Canada, benefits greatly from the restrained, moving performances from the three leads. (Dir: Mark Rydell, 110 mins.)

Fox and His Friends (West Germany, 1975)**** Rainer Werner Fassbinder, Peter Chatel, Karlheinz Bohm, Adrian Hoven. A film with an extremely bitter outlook on life, showing that even groups that are themselves discriminated against will cavalierly exploit others. After a poor, struggling homosexual comes into a small fortune, he's adopted as sort of a pet by an upwardly mobile gay man and his entourage, who know a good meal ticket when they see one. Fascinating study of duplicity in relationships. (Dir: Rainer Werner Fassbinder, 123 mins.)†

Fox and the Hound, The (1983)*** Fine animation and a heartwarming story add up to one of Disney's better cartoon features of recent vintage. A fox and hound, though enemies by nature, are reared together and only encounter difficulties when they grow up and must become the hunter and the hunted. (Dir: Art Stevens, 83 mins.)

Foxes (1980)**½ Jodie Foster, Sally Kellerman, Cherie Currie, Randy Quaid, Scott Baio. About four young girls who share an apartment in suburban Los Angeles. The screenplay delivers some facile observations along with some genuinely disquieting, sociological inquiry. (Dir: Adrian Lyne, 106 mins.)†

Foxes of Harrow, The (1947)**½ Rex Harrison, Maureen O'Hara, Richard Haydn. Fans of historical fiction will be disappointed with this dime novel tale, but there's enough excitement to please less discerning viewers. Tells of the rise to fame and fortune of an adventurer in 1820 New Orleans. (Dir: John M. Stahl, 117 mins.)

Foxfire (1955)**½ Jane Russell, Jeff Chandler, Dan Duryea. Anya Seton's novel is brought to the screen as a glossy love story with overtones of adventure. Jeff Chandler is well cast as the dedicated mining engineer who has to learn to understand his new socialite wife. (Dir: Joseph Pevney, 92 mins.)

Foxfire (MTV 1987)*** Jessica Tandy, Hume Cronyn, John Denver, Gary Grubbs, Harriet Hall. The warm, folksy Broadway play, which earned Jessica Tandy a Tony, makes a successful transition to television. Tandy is incandescent as an aging, widowed hill woman who refuses to leave her mountain homeland despite tempting offers from developers; Cronyn makes the most of his scenes as the ghost of Ms. Tandy's not-so-better-half. (Dir: Jud Taylor, 96 mins.)

Foxhole in Cairo (Great Britain, 1961)** Peter Van Eyck, James Robertson Justice, Adrian Hoven. British Intelligence trails a German agent sent to Cairo by Rommel to determine the Allied line of defense. (Dir: John Moxey, 79 mins.)

Foxtrap (Italy-U.S., 1986)* Fred Williamson, Chris Connelly, Arlene Golonka,

374

Donna Owen, Beatrice Palme. Professional tough guy Williamson is sent to Italy to locate a missing girl and bring her home. But when he finds out he's been used to an evil end. . . . Williamson also produced and directed this, as well as contributing the original story; that's one more strike than he needs to be out of the game. (88 mins.)†

Foxtrot (Mexico-Switzerland, 1976)* Peter O'Toole, Charlotte Rampling, Max von Sydow, Jorge Luke. At the outset of WWII, a Rumanian aristrocrat and his wife flee to a deserted island, only to find that they have brought the causes of the war with them. Unnecessary attempt at a *Rules of the Game*-type allegory fails on all counts; O'Toole looks completely lost. (Dir: Arturo Ripstein, 91 mins.)†

Foxy Brown (1974)*½ Pam Grier, Peter Brown, Terry Carter. Grier is foxy indeed, but this is a brutal blaxploitation flick about a nurse nursing a grudge against some drugsters. (Dir: Jack Hill, 94 mins.)†

Fra Diavolo—See: **Devil's Brother, The**

Fragment of Fear (Great Britain, 1970)**½ David Hemmings, Gayle Hunnicutt, Flora Robson, Wilfred Hyde-White. Former drug addict Hemmings goes through a slow emotional breakdown. Strange, unexplainable events lead him to question his own sanity. OK whodunit. (Dir: Richard C. Sarafian, 95 mins.)

Fragrance of Wild Flowers, The (Yugoslavia, 1978)*** Ljuba Tadic, Sonja Divac, Nemanja Zivic, Rastislava Gacic. A famous actor storms out of a rehearsal and flees to the country to escape the pressures and publicity of performing, only to find he is more interesting as a recluse than as a star. Satirical comedy pokes fun at the media, actors, and the notion of privacy in a socialist state. (Dir: Srdjan Karanovic, 92 mins.)

Framed (1947)*** Glenn Ford, Janis Carter, Barry Sullivan. Man is marked for death by two crooks who wish to steal money from a bank. Suspenseful melodrama with a good cast. (Dir: Richard Wallace, 82 mins.)

Framed (1975)** Joe Don Baker, Conny Van Dyke, Gabriel Dell, John Marley, Brock Peters. Tough Nashville gambler Baker, sent to prison on a phony rap, comes back seeking revenge. Violent good-ol'-boy shoot-'em-up from the team who made *Walking Tall*. (Dir: Phil Karlson, 106 mins.)†

Frances (1982)**½ Jessica Lange, Kim Stanley, Sam Shepard, Jeffrey DeMunn. Conventional Hollywood bio-epic of the tragic thirties actress, Frances Farmer. Heavy-handed direction and a fictionalized subplot destroy credibility in this true story of a woman institutionalized for being too honest for her own good. Towering above this standard star-on-the-skids movie is Jessica Lange's magnificent performance. (Dir: Graeme Clifford, 139 mins.)†

Francis (1950)**½ Donald O'Connor, Patricia Medina. This was the first of a series of films featuring the box-office-winning gimmick, Francis, The Talking Mule. Donald O'Connor takes a backseat to the bellowing burro (Chill Wills supplies Francis's voice). (Dir: Arthur Lubin, 91 mins.)

Francis Covers the Big Town (1953)**½ Donald O'Connor, Nancy Guild. Francis, The Talking Mule and sidekick Donald O'Connor go through a series of narrow escapes as they get a scoop for the papers on underworld activities. (Dir: Arthur Lubin, 86 mins.)

Francis Gary Powers: The True Story of the U-2 Spy Incident (MTV 1976)**½ Lee Majors, Nehemiah Persoff, Noah Beery, Jr., Lew Ayres. Moderately interesting account of how Powers (a Lockheed employee working for the CIA) was shot down over Russia in 1960, tried for espionage, and sentenced to a prison term. (Dir: Delbert Mann, 104 mins.)†

Francis Goes to the Races (1951)**½ Donald O'Connor, Piper Laurie. The Talking Mule gets information from his equine relatives and causes his innocent master, O'Connor, a great deal of trouble. (Dir: Arthur Lubin, 88 mins.)

Francis Goes to West Point (1952)**½ Donald O'Connor, Lori Nelson. O'Connor and his talking-mule sidekick end up at West Point after they become heroes in a sabotage plot. (Dir: Arthur Lubin, 81 mins.)

Francis in the Haunted House (1956)** Mickey Rooney, Virginia Welles. When Donald O'Connor screamed ''no'' to any more Francis epics, Universal tried once again with Mickey Rooney as the mule's confidant but without much success. (Dir: Charles Lamont, 80 mins.)

Francis in the Navy (1955)** Donald O'Connor, Martha Hyer, David Janssen, Jim Backus, Clint Eastwood. After a go at West Point and the WACs in previous films, Francis makes some choice comments about the nautical division of our armed services. (Dir: Arthur Lubin, 80 mins.)†

Francis Joins the WACs (1954)**½ Donald O'Connor, Julie Adams. Silly, but Francis's fans will enjoy the hijinks that he and Donald O'Connor go through when a mistake sends Don back into the service—as a WAC recruit! (Dir: Arthur Lubin, 94 mins.)

Francis of Assisi (1961)** Bradford Dillman, Dolores Hart, Stuart Whitman.

Cumbersome, frequently inept narrative of St. Francis and the founding of his order in the 13th century. (Dir: Michael Curtiz, 111 mins.)

Frank and I (France-U.S., 1984)* Jennifer Inch, Christopher Pearson, Sophie Favier, April Hyde. Turgid adaptation of a Victorian erotic novel about a runaway orphan girl, disguised as a boy, taken in by a well-to-do writer. Even the shorter 75 min. version shown on cable TV is too long for such thin material. (Dir: Gerard Kikoine, 105 mins.)†

Frankenhooker (1990)**½ James Loritz, Patty Mullen, Charlotte Helmkamp, Shirley Stoler, Louise Lasser. Robustly absurd horror comedy updates the Frankenstein premise with a sexy female monster, created from the parts of dead prostitutes, wreaking havoc on the denizens of Times Square. Obviously not for the genteel. (Dir: Frank Henenlotter, 90 mins.)†

Frankenstein (1931)**** Boris Karloff, Colin Clive, Mae Clarke, John Boles, Edward Van Sloan, Dwight Frye. In the wake of *Dracula,* Universal unleashed the monster who was to be their longest-lasting perennial, the brainchild of one Henry Frankenstein (Clive), a frustrated scientist with a God complex. Director James Whale's uncanny ability to render eerie atmosphere and the eternally eloquent performance given by a speechless Karloff make this a movie-milestone worth returning to. A restored version is now available. (71 mins.)†

Frankenstein (MTV 1973)**½ Robert Foxworth, Susan Strasberg, Bo Svenson, Heidi Vaughn, Philip Bourneuf, John Karlen, Willie Aames. TV-movie version of the Mary Shelley classic boasts the production values and gothic sensibility of producer Dan Curtis (''Dark Shadows''). Foxworth is a thoughtful mad scientist, while Svenson gives a sympathetic rendering of his creation. (Dir: Glenn Jordan, 130 mins.)†

Frankenstein and the Monster from Hell (Great Britain, 1974)* Peter Cushing, Shane Briant, Madeline Smith, David Prowse. Imagine the Frankenstein monster trying to modify his antisocial behavior at a mental institution run by Baron F. himself? Ridiculous. (Dir: Terence Fisher, 93 mins.)

Frankenstein Conquers the World (U.S.-Japan, 1966)** Nick Adams, Tadao Takashima, Kumi Mizuno. A sealed box containing the living heart of the Frankenstein monster is shipped from Nazi Germany to Japan, only to be caught in the Hiroshima blast. (Dir: Inoshiro Honda, 87 mins.)

Frankenstein Created Woman (1967)* Peter Cushing, Susan Denberg. This one dwells on the baron's attempt to create a gorgeous woman from a deformed creature. Strictly for fans who relish another visit to the baron's laboratory. (Dir: Terence Fisher, 92 mins.)

Frankenstein '88—See: **The Vindicator**

Frankenstein General Hospital (1988)* Mark Blankfield, Leslie Jordan, Kathy Shower, Irwin Keyes. Completely mirthless comedy set in a hospital run by an inept staff, including Dr. Bob Frankenstein building the usual monster in the basement. (Dir: Deborah Roberts, 90 mins.)†

Frankenstein Island (1982)½ John Carradine, Cameron Mitchell, Robert Clarke. Hot-air balloonists crash on an island inhabited by bikini-clad girls and a descendant of everyone's favorite mad scientist. Some once-respectable names should be ashamed for appearing in this junk. (Dir: Jerry Warren, 76 mins.)†

Frankenstein Meets the Space Monster (1965)* James Karen, Nancy Marshall. Man-like robot saves his inventors from outer space creatures bent on invading Earth. Outlandish science-fiction horror. (Dir: Robert Gaffney, 78 mins.)†

Frankenstein Meets the Wolf Man (1943)**½ Bela Lugosi, Lon Chaney, Patric Knowles, Ilona Massey, Lionel Atwill, Maria Ouspenskaya. It's only natural that these two cutups should get to know each other, and when they do meet, the countryside is crowded with corpses. Pretty lively horror film. (Dir: Roy William Neill, 72 mins.)†

Frankenstein Must Be Destroyed (Great Britain, 1969)*½ Peter Cushing, Simon Ward, Veronica Carlson. This time Peter Cushing stars as the insane doctor who is very busy transplanting brains. (Dir: Terence Fisher, 97 mins.)*

Frankenstein 1980 (Italy, 1973)*½ John Richardson, Renato Romano, Xiro Papas, Gordon Mitchell. Obscure European horror movie has the man-made monster literally falling to pieces, murdering people to obtain new body parts as replacements for the transplanted ones his brain is rejecting. Originally 96 mins. (Dir: Mario Mancini, 86 mins.)†

Frankenstein—1970 (1958)** Boris Karloff, Charlotte Austin. The real Baron von Frankenstein would turn in his crypt if he saw what they're doing to his castle in this film—a TV troupe is using it as the locale of a horror show. (Dir: Howard W. Koch, 83 mins.)†

Frankenstein's Daughter (1958)* John Ashley, Sandra Knight, Sally Todd, Donald Murphy, Harold Lloyd, Jr. The title suggests fun for horror-film fans but doesn't deliver. (Dir: Richard Cunha, 85 mins.)†

Frankenstein: The True Story (MTV 1973)

376

*** James Mason, David McCallum, Michael Sarrazin, John Gielgud. The quality of performance is so uniformly high in this faithful version of the Frankenstein tale, based on Mary Shelley's gothic novel, that it holds your interest and casts a tantalizing spell of horror. (Dir: Howard Smight, 200 mins.)

Frankenstein Unbound—See: **Roger Corman's Frankenstein Unbound**

Frankie and Johnny (1966)* Elvis Presley, Donna Douglas. Elvis digs girls and gambling in this shoddy musical based on the folk ballad. (Dir: Frederick de Cordova, 87 mins.)†

Frank Nitti: The Enforcer (MTV 1988)*½ Anthony LaPaglia, Vincent Guastaferro, Trini Alvarado, Michael Moriarty. TV movie follow-up to DePalma's *Untouchables* recounts the actual end of famed gunman Frank Nitti (he committed suicide) and the rise and fall that led up to it. So-so crime drama with some flashes of period style and a mean-looking LaPaglia as Capone's heir apparent. (Dir: Michael Switzer, 96 mins.)

Frantic (France, 1958)*** Jeanne Moreau, Maurice Ronet. A cool, ironic twist-of-fate drama about two lovers planning an ingenious murder scheme, which naturally goes awry. AKA: **Elevator to the Gallows**. (Dir: Louis Malle, 90 mins.)†

Frantic (1988)*** Harrison Ford, Emmanuelle Seigner, Betty Buckley. Ford stars as an American surgeon in Paris who searches for his wife, kidnapped because of a luggage foul-up. A gripping thriller that marks a welcome return from director Roman Polanski (let's forget *Pirates*), who strengthens the otherwise routine material with a curious sense of parody (obviously aimed toward Hitchcock) and his usual sense of eccentric detail. (120 mins.)†

Frasier, the Sensuous Lion (1973)** Michael Callan, Katherine Justice, Frank de Kova, Malachi Throne, Marc Lawrence, Peter Lorre, Jr., Joe E. Ross, John Qualen. Zoologist studying a lion discovers the cat can talk. The two spend most of the film on the run from crooks who want to sell Frasier's glands as an aphrodisiac. Slapstick comedy not quite for kids. Victor Jory supplies Frasier's voice. (Dir: Pat Shields, 97 mins.)†

Fraternity Row (1977)*** Peter Fox, Gregory Harrison, Nancy Morgan, Scott Newman. Engrossing film about a fifties college fraternity hazing that ends tragically. (Dir: Thomas J. Tobin, 104 mins.)

Fraternity Vacation (1985)*½ Stephen Geoffreys, Sheree J. Wilson, Cameron Dye. Two frat brothers bet a rival that they will be the first to bed the foxiest chick in Palm Springs. Another jockular

juvenile sex comedy. (Dir: James Frawley, 95 mins.)†

Fraulein (1958)*½ Dana Wynter, Mel Ferrer. Ridiculous drama that traces a young German girl's hard times during the last days of WWII. (Dir: Henry Koster, 98 mins.)

Fraulein Doktor (Italy-Yugoslavia, 1968)*½ Suzy Kendall, Kenneth More, Capucine. Silly espionage film. Suzy Kendall plays a WWI Mata Hari–type spy, based on the real-life exploits of Anna Maria Lesser, a notorious German spy during WWI. (Dir: Alberto Lattuada, 102 mins.)

Freakmaker, The—See: **Mutations, The**

Freaks (1932)***½ Leila Hyams, Olga Baclanova, Harry Earles, Wallace Ford. A cult classic, this unusual picture is a terrifying vision of life among the inhabitants of the sideshow world. The performers are real freaks, and this film is not for the squeamish. (Dir: Tod Browning, 64 mins.)†

Freaky Friday (1976)*** Jodie Foster, Barbara Harris, John Astin. Surprisingly funny slapstick charmer from Disney. Based on a best-selling children's book, the film exploits the comic disasters that occur when a mother and daughter magically trade places for one day. (Dir: Gary Nelson, 95 mins.)†

Free and Easy (1930)*** Buster Keaton, Anita Page, Robert Montgomery, Trixie Friganza. One of Keaton's best sound vehicles has him as a small-town swain following his contest-winning girlfriend to Hollywood. Takes a while to warm up, but once Keaton hits the studios, hilarious mayhem breaks loose. Page is terrible, but a very young Montgomery has some good scenes with Keaton. Featuring some brilliant comic set pieces, including a breathtaking marionette routine and the mini-musical that contains the title song. Look for cameo appearances by Lionel Barrymore, Cecil B. DeMille, and Jackie Coogan. (Dir: Edward Sedgwick, 92 mins.)

Freebie and the Bean (1974)*** Alan Arkin, James Caan, Loretta Swit, Jack Kruschen, Valerie Harper, Alex Rocco. San Francisco cops Freebie (Caan), who doesn't pay for anything if he can help it, and Bean (Arkin), a Mexican-American, tear up everything in their way to bring in a top gangster. The original buddy-cop movie is loud, racist, and violent—but it sure is funny. Terrific stunt gags include an auto chase that terminates in one of the upper floors of an apartment building. (Dir: Richard Rush, 113 mins.)

Freedom (MTV 1981)**½ Mare Winningham, Jennifer Warren, Tony Bill, Roy Thinnes, Peter Horton. A well-intentioned drama about alienation be-

377

tween a teenager and her mother. Since Mare's character is a self-styled singer in the story line, Janis Ian has supplied a number of songs. (Dir: Joseph Sargent, 104 mins.)

Freedom Fighter (MTV 1988)*½ Tony Danza, Colette Stevenson, Sid Caesar, David McCallum. Danza cuts an unlikely figure as a courageous GI who aids East Germans in their attempts to escape to the West before the construction of the Berlin Wall is completed. (Dir: Desmond Davis, 96 mins.)

Freedom Road (MTV 1979)** Muhammad Ali, Kris Kristofferson, Ron O'Neal. The former heavyweight champ plays an ex-slave who becomes a U.S. senator from South Carolina during Reconstruction in this earnest, slow-paced version of the Howard Fast novel. (Dir: Jan Kadar, 208 mins.)†

Free for All (1949)** Ann Blyth, Robert Cummings. An innocent bit of nonsense about an inventor who comes up with a tablet that supposedly turns water into gasoline. (Dir: Charles Barton, 83 mins.)

Free Ride (1986)* Gary Hershberger, Reed Rudy, Peter DeLuise, Warren Berlinger, Mamie Van Doren. Two preppies raise all kinds of heck at the last school that will take them. If this sounds like a novel plot, you haven't been to the movies much in the last ten years. (Dir: Tom Trbovich, 82 mins.)†

Free Soul, A (1931)*** Norma Shearer, Clark Gable, Lionel Barrymore, Leslie Howard, James Gleason. Well-cast melodrama, a bit dated but played to the hilt by Gable as a mobster dallying with the sexually awakened daughter of a boozing attorney, who has the gangster for a client. This courtroom drama based on the memoirs of Adela Rogers St. John was extremely frank for the thirties. Remade tamely as *The Girl Who Had Everything*. (Dir: Clarence Brown, 91 mins.)

Freeway (1988)** Darlanne Fluegel, James Russo, Billy Drago, Richard Belzer, Michael Callan. A beautiful widow and a hard-edged bounty hunter search for a psychotic gunman who stalks his victims on the freeways of L.A. Too little insight into the characters, but a whole lot of raucous gunplay. (Dir: Francis Delia, 91 mins.)†

Freeway Maniac, The (1989)*½ Loren Winters, James Courtney, Shepard Sanders, Donald Hotton. Boring combination horror movie and horror parody, centering on an escaped murderer who winds up on the set of a low-budget movie. Cartoonist Gahan Wilson gets a co-writing credit, but it's hard to discern any of his uniquely mordant wit here. Songs by ex-Doors guitarist Robby Krieger are equally disappointing. (Dir: Paul Winters, 93 mins.)†
378

Free, White and 21 (1962)**½ Frederick O'Neal, Annalena Lund. Pseudo-documentary about the Texas trial of a black man accused of raping a white civil-rights worker. The realistic approach sometimes lacks drama, but this is refreshingly free of sensationalism. (Dir: Larry Buchanan, 105 mins.)†

Free Woman, A (West Germany, 1972)**½ Margarethe von Trotta, Friedhelm Ptok, Walter Sedlmayer, Martin Luttge. Considered at the time to be the first great film of the women's liberation movement; wife divorces husband and has trouble adjusting to life away from him and her son. Tediously directed by Volker Schlondorff, film is truthful, but its point is made early and often. (100 mins.)

French Can-Can (France, 1955)**** Jean Gabin, Françoise Arnoul, Maria Felix, Dora Doll, Valentine Tessier. Jean Renoir's tribute to the great Parisian dance wonder is a deceptively exhilarating musical that sneaks up on some profound ideas about the nature of theater and of art. It's a standard tale of an impresario (Jean Gabin) down on his luck and trying to get a show mounted despite the financial odds. Renoir makes his simple story a dazzlingly complex meditation and still delivers the goods as straight entertainment. (93 mins.)†

French Connection, The (1971)***½ Gene Hackman, Fernando Rey, Roy Scheider, Eddie Egan, Sonny Grosso. Marvelously exciting yarn about a New York cop (Hackman) busting a huge international narcotics ring smuggling vast quantities of heroin into the U.S. Five Oscars, including Best Picture, Actor, and Director. (Dir: William Friedkin, 104 mins.)†

French Connection II (1975)*** Gene Hackman, Fernando Rey. The sequel to the Academy Award-winning film about New York cop Popeye Doyle and his adventures with the international narcotics ring doesn't pack the punch of the original, but it's still exciting. Gene Hackman is Popeye once again, on the trail of the elusive kingpin of the French narcotics syndicate (Fernando Rey also repeats his role from the original), and the action set in Marseilles adds to the chase drama. (Dir: John Frankenheimer, 118 mins.)†

French Detective, The (France, 1978)*** Lino Ventura, Patrick Dewaere, Victor Lanoux. Melodrama about two dedicated French cops out to stop a ruthless politician. The charismatic Ventura, always worth watching, is the old-school tough-guy type, and Dewaere is his young, cynical assistant. Downbeat entertainment. (Dir: Pierre Graniere-Deferre, 93 mins.)†

Frenchie (1951)** Joel McCrea, Shelley

Winters. Comedy and drama are juggled in this awkward western about a gal who comes back to the town which sent her away to settle a few scores. (Dir: Louis King, 81 mins.)

French Key, The (1946)*** Albert Dekker, Mike Mazurki, Evelyn Ankers, John Eldredge, Joe DeRita. Smart-talking amateur sleuth and his brawny assistant find a corpse in their hotel room. Confusing but entertaining thriller. (Dir: Walter Colmes, 64 mins.)

French Lesson, The (Great Britain, 1986)**½ Jane Snowden, Alexandre Sterling, Diane Blackburn, Oystein Wilk, Raoul Delfosse. Fairly charming comedy of manners about an English lass whose sojourn in France rounds off her education in affairs of the heart. (Dir: Brian Gilbert, 90 mins.)†

French Lieutenant's Woman, The (1981) *** Meryl Streep, Jeremy Irons, Hilton McRae. Adaptation of John Fowles's popular novel, written by Harold Pinter. Interesting attempt to tell the story of an enigmatic, haunting woman in England in the last century, with modern overtones. It's now about a film company shooting a movie, with the stars having an affair at the same time they are portraying the period characters. Stimulating, generally compelling. (Dir: Karel Reisz, 124 mins.)†

French Line, The (1954)** Gilbert Roland, Jane Russell. Multi-millionairess travels to Paris posing as a model, falls in love with a dashing Frenchman. Boring musical. (Dir: Lloyd Bacon, 102 mins.)†

Frenchman's Creek (1944)**½ Joan Fontaine, Basil Rathbone, Arturo de Cordova, Nigel Bruce. Costume film about an unholy alliance between an English lady and a French pirate. Swashbuckling and romantic! (Dir: Mitchell Leisen, 113 mins.)

Frenchman's Farm (Australia, 1987)** Tracy Tainsh, Ray Barrett, Norman Kaye, John Meillon. Law student can't persuade anyone that she has just witnessed a murder—one that happened forty years ago. Mediocre ghost story. (Dir: Ron Way, 88 mins.)†

French Postcards (1979)** Marie-France Pisier, Miles Chapin, Blanche Baker, Debra Winger, Mandy Patinkin. Sometimes pleasant, often plodding comedy about American exchange students in Paris and their introduction to life and love. (Dir: Willard Huyck, 95 mins.)†

French Quarter (1977)** Bruce Davison, Virginia Mayo, Lindsay Bloom, Lance Legault, Ann Michelle. Stories set in modern-day and turn-of-the-century New Orleans are juxtaposed, with the entire cast playing double roles, connected by a reincarnated woman who lived in both

eras. Interesting when it works, which isn't often enough. (Dir: Dennis Kane, 101 mins.)†

French, They Are a Funny Race, The (France, 1957)**½ Martine Carol, Jack Buchanan. Fast and sporadically funny spoof on the French people as seen through the eyes of an English novelist, retired from the British Army and residing in Paris with his glamorous French wife. (Dir: Preston Sturges, 83 mins.)

French Way, The (1952)** Josephine Baker, Micheline Presle, Georges Marchal, Almos, Jean Tissier. Baker, still beautiful though past her prime, is the only reason to see this flimsy comedy about two young lovers who need her help to persuade their feuding parents to let them marry. (Dir: Jacques De Baroncelli, 73 mins.)†

French Without Tears (1940)*½ Ray Milland, Ellen Drew. Title should be "Comedy Without Laughs" in this boring film about an Englishman fighting for the attentions of a French lass. (Dir: Anthony Asquith, 67 mins.)

Frenzy (Great Britain, 1972)*** Jon Finch, Alec McCowen, Vivien Merchant, Barry Foster, Barbara Leigh-Hunt. A marvelous suspense film directed by that master of the genre, Alfred Hitchcock. The wrong man becomes the chief suspect when his ex-wife is murdered—we've seen this plot before, but Hitchcock keeps the pace spinning with humor and invention. (116 mins.)†

Fresh Horses (1988)** Andrew McCarthy, Molly Ringwald, Patti D'Arbanville. College boy McCarthy falls for backwoods bad girl Ringwald, discovering the truth about her too late. Gets a half star for an unconventional, serious approach. (Dir: David Anspaugh, 105 mins.)†

Freshman, The (1925)*** Harold Lloyd, Jobyna Ralston, Brooks Benedict, Hazel Keener, James Anderson. In the biggest-grossing comedy of the silent era, Harold plays a would-be Ivy Leaguer at a university, where he struggles to become a football hero. Lloyd's genius with gags retains its freshness today. (Dir: Sam Taylor, 76 mins.)

Freshman, The (1990)***½ Marlon Brando, Matthew Broderick, Bruno Kirby, Penelope Ann Miller, Frank Whaley, B.D. Wong, Maximilian Schell, Bert Parks, Paul Benedict. Generally sparkling comedy about a film student (Broderick) who delivers exotic animals to a floating restaurant catering to Euro-trash. His boss is a mobster—Brando, who offers a technically brilliant and altogether delicious spoof of his *Godfather* persona. Gloriously well acted. Written and directed by the inventive Andrew Bergman. (Dir: Andrew Bergman, 102 mins.)†

Freud (1962)*** Montgomery Clift, Susannah York, Susan Kohner, David McCallum, Larry Parks. The early struggle for recognition and the general work of Sigmund Freud, the founder of modern psychiatry, are depicted in often interesting fashion. Main storyline involves Freud's treatment of a young patient, well played by Ms. York. (Dir: John Huston, 139 mins.)

Frida (Mexico, 1984)*** Ofelia Medina, Juan Jose Gurrola, Max Kerlow. Biography of Frida Kahlo, considered by many the most important female painter of the 20th-century. Her surrealistic paintings provide background as film recalls a tragic childhood accident and her relationships with artist Diego Rivera and Leon Trotsky. (Dir: Paul Leduc, 108 mins.)

Friday Foster (1975)**½ Pam Grier, Yaphet Kotto, Godfrey Cambridge, Thalmus Rasulala. Intricately plotted conspiracy picture about a model-photographer who witnesses the assassination of a black tycoon. (Dir: Arthur Marks, 90 mins.)

Friday the 13th (1980)** Betsy Palmer, Harry Crosby, Adrienne King, Kevin Bacon. The kids who attempt to reopen a summer camp where grisly murders occurred two decades before are set up to be the victims of an arbitrary scenario. Producer-director Sean S. Cunningham's technique is crude. (91 mins.)†

Friday the 13th, Part 2 (1981)* Amy Steel, John Furey, Adrienne King, Betsy Palmer. Camp Blood earns its nickname, as more camp counselors get slashed and dismembered in loving detail. Pointless and gory. (Dir: Steve Miner, 87 mins.)†

Friday the 13th, Part 3 (1982)* Dana Kimmel, Paul Kratka, Tracie Savage. Jason returns yet again to commit more gory murders at Camp Crystal Lake. Originally filmed in 3D. (Dir: Steve Miner, 96 mins.)†

Friday the 13th, The Final Chapter (1984)½ Crispin Glover, Kimberly Beck, Barbara Howard, Lawrence Monoson. More teens are annihilated by the indefatigable Jason, the "camp" killer. (Dir: Joseph Zito, 91 mins.)†

Friday the 13th, Part V: A New Beginning (1985)** John Shepherd, Corey Feldman, Melanie Kinnaman. Camp humor enlivens another segment of the usual slashings. (Dir: Danny Steinmann, 92 mins.)†

Friday the 13th, Part VI: Jason Lives (1986)** Thom Mathews, Jennifer Cooke, David Kagen, Kerry Noonan, Renee Jones. The usual series of bloody murders, but writer-director Tom McLoughlin shows a sense of humor and a nice eye for detail. (88 mins.)†

Friday the 13th, Part VII—The New Blood (1988)** Lar Park Lincoln, Kevin Blair, Terry Kiser, Kane Hodder. "Carrie" meets Jason as a telekinetic girl takes on the masked murderer after he sharpens his axe on a dozen or so of her contemporaries. A little better than usual. (Dir: John Carl Buechler, 88 mins.)†

Friday the 13th Part VIII: Jason Takes Manhattan (1989)*½ Jensen Daggett, Scott Reeves, Barbara Bingham. Despite the title, the big guy with the hockey mask and lousy disposition only spends a few minutes in the Big Apple at the end. Those scenes are good, but don't make up for the tediousness of the previous 85 minutes, which take place on a cruise ship. (Dir: Rob Hedden, 96 mins.)†

Frieda (Great Britain, 1947)**½ Mai Zetterling, David Farrar, Glynis Johns. RAF officer brings his German war bride to his home town, where she is looked upon with suspicion and hatred. Powerful drama, intelligently handled, excellently acted. (Dir: Basil Dearden, 97 mins.)†

Friendly Fire (MTV 1979)**** Carol Burnett, Ned Beatty, Sam Waterston. Deeply moving, poignant film about an Iowa farm family who turn against the war after their son dies in Vietnam and they learn that he died from "friendly fire"—accidental shelling by American artillery. Burnett turns in her best acting performance to date. (Dir: David Greene, 162 mins.)

Friendly Persuasion (1956)**** Gary Cooper, Dorothy McGuire, Tony Perkins, Marjorie Main. Touching story about a family of Quakers who live in peace and contentment on their land in Indiana until the Civil War breaks out and disrupts their lives. Dorothy McGuire and Gary Cooper are perfectly cast in their roles as the parents. (Dir: William Wyler, 139 mins.)†

Friendly Persuasion (MTV 1975)**½ Richard Kiley, Shirley Knight, Clifton James, Michael O'Keefe, Kevin O'Keefe. A smooth, professional job of retailoring the classic 1956 film for TV, but not in the same league. The storyline concerns a pacifist Quaker family torn apart by opposing ideals during the Civil War. (Dir: Joseph Sargent, 104 mins.)

Friends (1971)* Sean Bury, Anicee Alvina, Pascale Roberts, Sady Rebbot. Sappy tale of fourteen-year-old French orphan and a neglected fifteen-year-old English child who steal off to a beach cottage to play house for a year. Remembered, if at all, only for the Elton John score. Sequel: *Paul and Michelle.* (Dir: Lewis Gilbert, 101 mins.)

Friendships, Secrets, and Lies (MTV 1979)*** Cathryn Damon, Tina Louise, Paula Prentiss, Stella Stevens, Loretta Swit, Shelley Fabares, Sondra Locke.

Sorority sisters become suspects when a baby's skeleton is discovered after being buried for twenty years. A bit bumpy at first, but interest picks up as the characters talk about their fears, their dependence on men, and their romantic naïveté. (Dirs: Ann Zane Shanks, Marlena Laird, 104 mins.)

Friends, Lovers and Lunatics (Canada, 1989)** Daniel Stern, Sheila McCarthy, Elias Koteas, Page Fletcher. Unwilling to take no for an answer, flaky Stern hounds his ex-girlfriend and her new lover while they're trying to enjoy a camping trip. A few laughs, but nothing to stay up late for. AKA: **Crazy Horse.** (Dir: Stephen Withrow, 87 mins.)†

Friends of Eddie Coyle, The (1973)***½ Robert Mitchum, Peter Boyle, Richard Jordan. A tough, unsentimental, first-rate drama about a Boston hoodlum. Mitchum plays Eddie Coyle, a small-time mobster who winds up turning stoolie. (Dir: Peter Yates, 102 mins.)

Fright (1956)*½ Eric Fleming, Nancy Malone. Psychiatrist investigates a young woman who has taken on the personality of the mistress of Crown Prince Rudolph of Austria in 1889, attempts to save her from self-destruction. AKA: **Spell of the Hypnotist.** (Dir: W. Lee Wilder, 80 mins.)†

Fright (Great Britain, 1971)*** Susan George, Ian Bannen, Honor Blackman. Baby-sitter George is terrorized by strange happenings in a deserted house. Not for children. (Dir: Peter Collinson, 87 mins.)

Frightened Bride, The (Great Britain, 1952)**½ Mai Zetterling, Michael Denison. A family tries to escape the past when one of the sons is convicted of murdering a girl, sees it start all over again with the younger son. (Dir: Terence Young, 75 mins.)

Fright House (1987)* Paul Borghese, Al Lewis, Duane Jones, Jennifer Delora, Jackie James. A pair of horror stories, one about a coven of witches who sacrifice college students and the other about a headmistress who stays young by draining the energy of her charges. Cheaply made and technically inept production is not redeemed by the writing, which merely trots out the usual clichés. (Dir: Len Anthony, 110 mins.)†

Frightmare (1974)*** Rupert Davies, Sheila Keith, Deborah Fairfax, Paul Greenwood, Andrew Sachs. Only the British could make a horror movie like this, about a middle-class cannibal wife and her husband, who is trying to get her to kick the habit. Look for Sachs (Manuel from "Fawlty Towers") sans Spanish accent in a small role. Released on video as *Frightmare II* to avoid confusion with the unrelated 1981 film (which just made

it even more confusing). (Dir: Peter Walker, 86 mins.)†

Frightmare (1981)*½ Ferdinand Mayne, Luca Bercovici, Nita Talbot, Leon Askin, Donna McDaniel, Peter Kastner. Horror star dies on the set, but comes back to life to terrorize the teenagers who desecrated his tomb. Nothing you haven't seen done better many times before. (Dir: Norman Thaddeus Vane, 86 mins.)†

Frightmare II—See: **Frightmare** (1974)

Fright Night (1985)**½ Chris Sarandon, William Ragsdale, Amanda Bearse, Stephen Geoffreys, Roddy McDowall, Jonathan Stark. The special effects are top of the line, but the underdeveloped script is end of the line, as a teenager suspects his new neighbor is a vampire. Aided by a creature-feature TV host who's stopped believing in himself (yes, the movie has pathos, too), he hunts down the bloodsucker. (Dir: Tom Holland, 106 mins.)†

Fright Night Part 2 (1988)**½ Roddy McDowall, William Ragsdale, Traci Lin. The vampire hunters have a whole quartet of monsters to destroy in this respectable sequel. Not as good as the first, but a decent mix of thrills and laughs with good special effects. (Dir: Tommy Lee Wallace, 101 mins.)†

Fringe Dwellers, The (Australia, 1987)** Justine Saunders, Kristina Nehm, Bob Maza, Kylie Belling, Denis Walker. Australian director Bruce Beresford returned to his home soil with this account of an aboriginal family's attempts to assimilate into the white mainstream. Good performances by a largely non-professional cast, but overall, this is a disappointment. (98 mins.)†

Frisco Jenny (1933)** Ruth Chatterton, Donald Cook, James Murray, Louis Calhern. San Francisco mob queen Chatterton is brought down by a new D.A. who doesn't know he's her illegitimate son! Far-fetched gangster soaper. (Dir: William A. Wellman, 70 mins.)

Frisco Kid (1935)*** James Cagney, Margaret Lindsay. Typical, fast-moving Cagney melodrama. Plenty of fighting in this tale of revenge on the Barbary Coast. (Dir: Lloyd Bacon, 80 mins.)

Frisco Kid, The (1979)** Gene Wilder, Harrison Ford, Ramon Bieri, Val Bisoglio. The premise of a rabbi making his way across the U.S. to join a congregation in San Francisco is a potentially intriguing one, but the director fails to fit all the pieces together. (Dir: Robert Aldrich, 88 mins.)†

Frisco Lil (1942)*½ Irene Hervey, Kent Taylor, Samuel S. Hinds, Milburn Stone. Hervey takes a job at a casino to prove her father is innocent of murder. (Dir: Erle C. Kenton, 60 mins.)

Frisco Sal (1945)**½ Susanna Foster, Turhan Bey, Alan Curtis. Girl gets a job as a singer in a Barbary Coast saloon while seeking the killers of her brother. Nicely produced costume melodrama with music. (Dir: George Waggner, 63 mins.)

Frissons—See: **They Came from Within**

Fritz the Cat (1972)*** An X-rated animated feature, based on the successful ''underground'' comic strip by social satirist Robert Crumb. Director/designer/writer Ralph Bakshi and his raunchy on-screen characters puncture just about every myth and sacred cow they swing at. (77 mins.)†

Frogmen, The (1951)**½ Richard Widmark, Dana Andrews, Jeffrey Hunter, Robert Wagner. Slow-paced story of the Navy's heroes of the deep and their dangerous exploits during the war. Interesting underwater photography. (Dir: Lloyd Bacon, 96 mins.)

Frogs (1972)**½ Ray Milland, Sam Elliott, Joan Van Ark. Rip-off of *Willard*, using amphibians instead of rodents. There is a nice, swampy atmosphere, and some cheerful, tongue-in-cheek acting. (Dir: George McCowan, 91 mins.)†

From a Far Country: Pope John Paul II (Great Britain-Italy-Poland, 1981)**½ Sam Neill, Christopher Cazenove, Lisa Harrow, Warren Clarke, Cezary Morawski, Maurice Denham. Although this film biography has an ''official'' air about it, having been co-produced in Poland, it's a dull (if picturesque) account of the early life of the first non-Italian pontiff. (Dir: Krzysztof Zanussi, 120 mins.)

From Beyond (1986)*** Jeffrey Combs, Barbara Crampton, Ted Sorel, Ken Foree. Another graphic horror film from the people who made *Re-Animator*, again based on an H. P. Lovecraft story. Sorel plays a scientist whose experiments with a dormant sensory organ in the human brain lead to monstrous beings from another dimension invading ours. Fast-paced, with generous amounts of scares and humor. (Dir: Stuart Gordon, 85 mins.)†

From Beyond the Grave (Great Britain, 1973)*** Peter Cushing, Margaret Leighton, Ian Bannen, Donald Pleasence, David Warner, Diana Dors. One of the more imaginative horror anthologies. When you step into Cushing's curio shop, you may get more than a fun antique to take home. (Dir: Kevin Connor, 97 mins.)†

From Hell It Came (1957)* Tod Andrews, Tina Carver. Science-fiction-horror film with witch doctors and walking dead. To hell with it. (Dir: Dan Milner, 71 mins.)

From Hell to Borneo (1964)** George Montgomery, Torin Thatcher, Julie Gregg. Soldier of fortune fights to keep control of his private island when he's menaced by pirates and a notorious gangster. (Dir: George Montgomery, 96 mins.)†

From Hell to Texas (1958)**½ Don Murray, Diane Varsi. Interesting western drama about a young cowboy who tries to mind his own business and avoid trouble during a time when gunmen ruled the territory. (Dir: Henry Hathaway, 100 mins.)

From Hell to Victory (France-Italy-Spain, 1979)** George Peppard, George Hamilton, Horst Buchholz, Jean-Pierre Cassel, Capucine, Sam Wanamaker, Anny Duperey, Ray Lovelock, Howard Vernon, Lambert Wilson. Six friends of different nationalities are separated by the outbreak of WWII, but vow to reunite at their favorite Paris café. What happens to each afterwards provides enough subplots for three movies, though none are satisfyingly worked out. Check out Hamilton's fake French accent. (Dir: ''Hank Milestone'' [Umberto Lenzi], 100 mins.)†

From Here to Eternity (1953)**** Burt Lancaster, Montgomery Clift, Deborah Kerr, Philip Ober, Frank Sinatra, Ernest Borgnine, Jack Warden, Donna Reed. A tight, tough screenplay, sensitive directing, and superb acting characterize this adaptation of the James Jones novel set on an army base in Hawaii in the months before Pearl Harbor. One of the best American films of the 1950s, well-deserving of its Oscar for Best Film. Sinatra and Reed each won Supporting Oscars as well for their work in roles surprisingly different from their earlier images. (Dir: Fred Zinnemann, 118 mins.)†

From Mao to Mozart: Isaac Stern in China (1980)**** Excellent documentary covering a trip to China by Isaac Stern, one of the world's greatest violinists, to give a series of master classes to China's most promising young violinists. The scenes showing Stern instructing young talented musicians are superb, as are some visually stunning sequences of China and its vibrant people. (Dir: Murray Lerner, 88 mins.)†

From Nashville with Music (1969)**½ Marilyn Maxwell, Leo G. Carroll, Marty Robbins, Merle Haggard, Buck Owens. Jaunty musical comedy, with some great country-western songs, about New York City couple who end up at the Grand Ole Opry by mistake. Worth seeing just for teamwork of Maxwell and Carroll. (Dir: Eddie Crandall, 87 mins.)

From Noon til Three (1976)** Charles Bronson, Jill Ireland. Uneven, offbeat satire directed and written by Frank D. Gilroy, based on his novel. The complex plot deals with the unusual relationship between a drifter-turned-bank robber (Bronson) and a rich widow (Ireland) in a tragicomic exploration of our culture. (104 mins.)

From Russia, with Love (Great Britain, 1964)***½ Sean Connery, Daniela Bianchi, Lotte Lenya, Robert Shaw. High-class, diverting hokum. Perhaps the best of the Sean Connery series of James Bond adventures. Agent 007 is on a tricky mission and he executes more narrow escapes than you can count. Sean Connery is, as always, suave, indestructible, and a wow with the ladies. (Dir: Terence Young, 118 mins.)†

From the Dead of the Night (MTV 1989) *** Lindsay Wagner, Bruce Boxleitner, Robin Thomas, Robert Prosky. Fashion designer Wagner survives a near-death experience, only to find that the six shadowy figures she saw on the "other side" aren't done with her yet. Overlong, but delivers some good scares if you stick with it. (Dir: Paul Wendkos, 192 mins.)

From the Earth to the Moon (1958)**½ Joseph Cotten, George Sanders, Debra Paget. Scientist discovering a new source of energy plans to send a rocket to the moon. Jules Verne sci-fi adventure; predictably, the special effects take top honors. (Dir: Byron Haskin, 100 mins.)†

From the Hip (1987)**½ Judd Nelson, Elizabeth Perkins, John Hurt, Darren McGavin, Ray Walston. Nelson is a yuppie lawyer who uses courtroom theatrics to work his way up in the legal world. His first big case, though, proves to be more difficult than expected—he's set to defend a client whose innocence he's not sure of. Tedious comedy shifts gears midway to become a fairly decent courtroom drama; Hurt is winningly despicable. (Dir: Bob Clark, 111 mins.)†

From the Life of the Marionettes (German, 1980)** Robert Atzorn, Christine Buchegger, Martin Benrath, Rita Russek. Inferior Ingmar Bergman film about a man who sublimates his murderous hatred of his wife by strangling a prostitute. Director Bergman jerks these unappetizing characters about so unconvincingly the film becomes hollow. (104 mins.)†

From the Mixed-up Files of Mrs. Basil E. Frankweiler (1973)** Ingrid Bergman, Sally Prager, George Rose, Johnny Doran, Madeline Kahn. Two suburban youngsters run away to live in New York's Metropolitan Museum for a week. Disappointing. AKA: **The Hideaways**. (Dir: Fielder Cook, 105 mins.)

From the Terrace (1960)*** Paul Newman, Joanne Woodward, Ina Balin, Leon Ames, Myrna Loy. John O'Hara's mammoth novel about big business, social strata, and marriage problems turned into a lengthy but well-acted film drama, helped by steady performances, good production. (Dir: Mark Robson, 144 mins.)†

From This Day Forward (1946)*** Joan Fontaine, Mark Stevens, Rosemary DeCamp, Henry Morgan, Bobby Driscoll. Young couple tries hard to adjust to the postwar world. Well-acted, interesting romantic drama, co-scripted by Garson Kanin. (Dir: John Berry, 95 mins.)

Front, The (1976)*** Woody Allen, Zero Mostel, Andrea Marcovicci, Joshua Shelley, Georgann Johnson. Woody Allen excels in a straight role as a pal fronting for a blacklisted writer. Walter Bernstein's original screenplay doesn't hold up all the way, but it does bring some humor to a nightmare-real situation full of anguish and suffering. (Dir: Martin Ritt, 94 mins.)†

Frontier—See: **Aerograd**

Frontier Gal (1945)*** Yvonne DeCarlo, Rod Cameron, Andy Devine. Yvonne DeCarlo, as a saloon operator, marries Rod Cameron, a fugitive wanted by the law, and the trouble begins. (Dir: Charles Lamont, 84 mins.)

Frontier Uprising (1961)*½ Jim Davis, Nancy Hadley, Ken Mayer. Fearless frontier scout Davis leads a wagon train into Mexican-owned California, unaware that Indians are ready to attack. Nice location photography in this otherwise standard western. (Dir: Edward L. Cahn, 68 mins.)

Front Page, The (1931)***½ Pat O'Brien, Adolphe Menjou, Frank McHugh, Edward Everett Horton, Mary Brian. A film classic. Fast and furious action and dialogue, as reporter O'Brien and editor Menjou battle corruption (and each other). Fascinatingly filmed by director Lewis Milestone, with a cast of stalwarts. (101 mins.)†

Front Page, The (1974)**½ Jack Lemmon, Walter Matthau, Carol Burnett, Susan Sarandon, David Wayne. Third version of the hit play about the Chicago newspaper world and the city-room gang. As a nostalgic romp, this film can be enjoyed on its own level, but much of the humor is awfully dated and everyone punches across their lines with an urgency that seems misplaced. See *His Girl Friday* instead. Remade in an even poorer version as *Switching Channels*. (Dir: Billy Wilder, 105 mins.)

Front Page Story (Great Britain, 1954)*** Jack Hawkins, Elizabeth Allan, Eva Bartok, Derek Farr. A day in the life of a daily newspaper, covering stories of a woman on trial for murder, a mother killed in an accident, etc. Dramatic, absorbing, well acted. (Dir: Gordon Parry, 95 mins.)

Front Page Woman (1935)**½ Bette Davis, George Brent, Roscoe Karns, Winifred Shaw. Reporter Davis tries to prove that a woman can be as good a "newsman" as any male; she solves a murder and scoops her boyfriend in the process. OK comedy-drama from Warner Bros., with a good mystery to keep you guessing. (Dir: Michael Curtiz, 80 mins.)

Frozen Dead, The (Great Britain, 1967)** Dana Andrews. Gruesome experiments involving resuscitation of frozen bodies lead to murder. Routine thriller. (Dir: Herbert J. Leder, 95 mins.)

Frozen Ghost, The (1945)** Lon Chaney, Jr., Evelyn Ankers. A hypnotist, working in a wax museum, uncovers a murder plot. Typical melodramatics, with a harried performance by Chaney. (Dir: Harold Young, 61 mins.)

Fruits of Passion, The (France-Japan, 1981)* Klaus Kinski, Isabelle Illiers, Arielle Dombasie, Peter. Awful sequel to *The Story of O*, adapted from Pauline Reage's novel by Reage and director Shuji Terayama. Sir Stephen puts "O" in an Oriental brothel, only to have his careful control shattered by jealousy. Too serious to be salacious, and too incoherent to watch. (83 mins.)

F. Scott Fitzgerald and "The Last of the Belles" (MTV 1974)**½ Richard Chamberlain, Blythe Danner, Susan Sarandon, David Huffman. Interesting, uneven attempt to dramatize a portion of Fitzgerald's life and his short story, "The Last of the Belles." The action is intercut between two separate dramas, with the short story, about a small-town flirt who keeps a steady flow of WWI Army officers buzzing around her, coming off best. (Dir: George Schaefer, 98 mins.)

F. Scott Fitzgerald in Hollywood (MTV 1976)** Jason Miller, Tuesday Weld, Julia Foster. Another look at the saga of F. Scott Fitzgerald and Zelda, those enduring icons of the Jazz Age. Miller's humorless performance as the writing genius gone sour is strictly one-note, but Tuesday Weld, in an all-too-brief appearance as the moth-like Zelda, teetering on the brink of madness, fares much better. (Dir: Anthony Page, 98 mins.)

Fugitive, The (1947)*** Henry Fonda, Pedro Armendariz, Dolores Del Rio. In Mexico, a priest refuses to support the anticleric government. Gripping but slow-moving drama. (Dir: John Ford, 104 mins.)†

Fugitive Family (MTV 1980)** Richard Crenna, Mel Ferrer, Eli Wallach. A predictable melodrama about an undercover agent and his family beginning a new life in the Napa Valley wine country after testifying against a mobster. (Dir: Paul Krasny, 99 mins.)

Fugitive from the Empire (MTV 1981)*½ Lane Caudell, George Kennedy, Victor Campos, Belinda Bauer, Kabir Bedi. A few entertaining special effects highlight this rather mundane fantasy-adventure with Lane Caudell as Toran of Malveel, out to reclaim control over a land of magic and witchcraft. (Dir: Nick Corea, 104 mins.)

Fugitive Girls (1971)* Jabie Abercrombie, Renee Bond. A bunch of nasty gals escape from a women's prison and head in search of the loot that one of them buried. Noteworthy only to fans of legendary bad moviemaker Edward D. Wood, Jr., who wrote this and has a small role as a gas station attendant. AKA: *Five Loose Women*. (Dir: A. C. Stephen, 90 mins.)†

Fugitive Kind, The (1960)** Anna Magnani, Marlon Brando, Joanne Woodward, Victor Jory. Woeful misfire of Tennessee Williams's *Orpheus Descending*, with a blond Brando as a guitar-playing drifter. Magnani is too earthy and offbeat to mix with Brando's quicksilver irony. Woodward and Jory fare better, but this is essentially hooey. (Dir: Sidney Lumet, 135 mins.)

Fugitive Lovers, The (1934)**½ Robert Montgomery, Madge Evans, Nat Pendleton, Ted Healy. Funny madcap comedy of two runaways who meet on a bus trip, with interesting touches by director Richard Boleslawski. Most notable for an early appearance of The Three Stooges, still Healy's sidekicks, billed here as "The Three Julians"! (84 mins.)

Fulfillment of Mary Gray, The (MTV 1989)** Cheryl Ladd, Ted Levine, Lewis Smith. At the turn of the century, impotent farmer Levine wants wife Ladd to bear him a son with the aid of his younger brother. Self-serious but underdeveloped drama. (Dir: Piers Haggard, 96 mins.)

Full Confession (1939)*** Victor McLaglen, Joseph Calleia, Sally Eilers. A priest hears a murderer's confession, cannot divulge the information. Gripping, well-done drama. (Dir: John Farrow, 73 mins.)

Fuller Brush Girl, The (1950)*** Lucille Ball, Eddie Albert, Lee Patrick. Ball was cast in the Red Skelton part in this sequel to *The Fuller Brush Man*. One of the few starring movie roles where Ball reveals even a particle of her comic talent, largely due to the inspired slapstick inventions of scripter Frank Tashlin. (Dir: Lloyd Bacon, 85 mins.)

Fuller Brush Man, The (1948)*** Red Skelton, Janet Blair. Salesman stumbles into a murder mystery, traps the hoodlums. Wild and woolly slapstick, well-done. (Dir: S. Sylvan Simon, 93 mins.)†

Full Exposure: The Sex Tapes Scandal (MTV 1989)*½ Lisa Hartman, Anthony Dawson, Vanessa Williams, Jennifer O'Neill. Unapologetically sleazy stuff about the investigation into the murder of a prostitute who was using videotapes of her clients for blackmail. (Dir: Noel Nosseck, 96 mins.)

Full Fathom Five (1990)* Michael Moriarty, Maria Rangel, Michael Cavanaugh. Preposterous action flick takes place on a submarine days before the U.S. invasion of Panama in December 1989. A crazed Panamanian takes over a Soviet sub with nuclear missiles, paving the way for a U.S. sub to do away with the vessel before the madman blows up Houston. Boring, low-budget mess. (Dir: Carl Franklin, 78 mins.)†

Full Hearts and Empty Pockets (Italy-West Germany, 1963)** Thomas Fritsch, Alexandra Stewart, Gino Cervi, Senta Berger, Linda Christian, Françoise Rosay. A penniless young German looks for *la dolce vita* in Rome and finds it, becoming a huge financial success and losing everything with equal speed. Pleasant but minor tale. (Dir: Camillo Mastrocinque, 88 mins.)†

Full Metal Jacket (1987)**** Matthew Modine, Dorian Harewood, Adam Baldwin, Vincent D'Onofrio, Kevyn Major Howard, Lee Ermey. Director Stanley Kubrick's long-awaited, disturbing drama about young Marines struggling to survive while fighting in Vietnam at the time of the Tet Offensive. A riveting masterpiece that ranks with the most memorable war films. (120 mins.)†

Full Moon High (1981)*** Adam Arkin, Ed McMahon, Elizabeth Hartman, Roz Kelly, Bill Kirchenbauer, Kenneth Mars, Alan Arkin. This predates *Teen Wolf* and mines the same teen-identity-crisis material with more panache. Enough spirited comedy is on tap for horror-film-parody fans. (Dir: Larry Cohen, 94 mins.)

Full Moon in Blue Water (1988)** Gene Hackman, Teri Garr, Burgess Meredith. Bar owner Hackman refuses to let go of the memory of his dead wife, much to the chagrin of would-be lover Garr. Even a team as attractive as these two need a heartier script than this lightweight comedy piffle. (Dir: Peter Masterson, 95 mins.)†

Full Moon in Paris (France, 1984)** Pascale Ogier, Fabrice Luchini, Tcheky Karyo. This empty-headed ennui concerns a girl who feels stifled by her live-in love affair, so she rents a second apartment. However, she's so self-absorbed and limited, you'll wish that she would get lost. (Dir: Eric Rohmer, 102 mins.)†

Full of Life (1957)*** Judy Holliday, Richard Conte, Salvatore Baccaloni. Charming and heartwarming comedy-drama about newlyweds who move in with the husband's father when the wife announces she's going to have a baby. (Dir: Richard Quine, 91 mins.)

Fun and Games (MTV 1980)**½ Valerie Harper, Max Gail, Cliff De Young. An earnest, if oversimplified, attempt to examine sexual harassment on the job. Harper is thoroughly believable as a divorced factory worker who decides to fight for her rights. (Dir: Alan Smithee, 104 mins.)

Funeral, The (Japan, 1985)***½ Nobuko Miyamoto, Tsutomu Yamazaki. An acerbic social satire about a trendy young Japanese couple who have to familiarize themselves with the complex funeral ritual. Funny and gracefully handled. (Dir: Juzo Itami, 123 mins.)

Funeral Home (Canada, 1982)** Lesleh Donaldson, Kay Hawtrey, Barry Morse. Teenager goes to stay with her grandmother, and a string of mysterious deaths begins. (Dir: William Fruet, 93 mins.)†

Funeral in Berlin (1967)**½ Michael Caine, Oscar Homolka, Eva Renzi, Guy Doleman. Shot on location in Berlin, the authentic footage—showing the Berlin Wall—adds to the suspense of the story about the possible defection of the head of Russian security (Homolka). (Dir: Guy Hamilton, 102 mins.)†

Funhouse, The (1981)** Cooper Huckabee, Largo Woodruff, Sylvia Miles, William Finley, Kevin Conway. Sporadically scary horror flick about a monster terrorizing teens in a fun house. (Dir: Tobe Hooper, 96 mins.)†

Fun in Acapulco (1963)** Elvis Presley, Ursula Andress, Paul Lukas. What distinguishes this one from the myriad of other Presley films is some nifty scenery. Scenic beauty of a different kind is amply provided as the cameras explore the topographies of Ursula Andress and Elsa Cardenas. (Dir: Richard Thorpe, 97 mins.)†

Funland (1987)** David L. Lander, Bruce Mahler, William Windom, Robert Sacchi, Mike McManus, Jan Hooks. Uneven comedy set in the world's tackiest amusement park, centering around the plans of disturbed clown Bruce Burger to seek vengeance on the park's corporate owners. (Dir: Michael Simpson, 86 mins.)†

Funny (1989)*** What's funny (as in ironic) about this slickly assembled documentary is that the professional entertainers come off as flat, while the anecdotes and one-liners told by unknowns are solidly laugh-inducing and worth remembering. (Dir: Bran Ferren, 81 mins.)

Funny About Love (1990)** Gene Wilder, Christine Lahti, Mary Stuart Masterson, Robert Prosky. Duffy and Meg want to have a baby. They try everything and talk you to death in the process. Wilder is Duffy, all shtick and no substance, and Christine Lahti is totally wasted as Meg. (Dir: Leonard Nimoy, 101 mins.)†

Funny Dirty Little War, A (Argentina, 1984)*** Federico Luppi, Hector Bidonde. A cleverly conceived albeit sketchy satire about Juan Peron's shaky attempt to regain power in Argentina with the Left and Right forming an uneasy alliance. (Dir: Hector Olivera, 80 mins.)†

Funny Face (1957)**** Fred Astaire, Audrey Hepburn, Kay Thompson. Astaire at his best, top George Gershwin tunes, colorful Parisian scenics, all combine to make a sprightly musical about a fashion photographer who turns a girl working in a bookstore into a high-fashion model. Top entertainment. (Dir: Stanley Donen, 103 mins.)

Funny Farm (1988)**½ Chevy Chase, Madolyn Smith, Joseph Maher. Two tired New Yorkers buy a secluded country house and have typical misadventures among the bizarre townsfolk. When they decide to sell, they pay the locals to act like a Norman Rockwell picture come to life. A mostly flat, uninvolving comedy with smatterings of hilarity. (Dir: George Roy Hill, 99 mins.)†

Funny Farm, The (Canada, 1982)**½ Eileen Brennan, Peter Aykroyd, Jack Carter, Tracy Bregman, Howie Mandel, Marjorie Gross, Lou Dinos, Miles Chapin. Making it big as a comedian is theme of story about Ohio man going to L.A. to do stand-up in local club run by wonderful Brennan. Mandel is outrageous, but the movie as a whole lacks driving force. Lots of bad jokes clutter what could have been a clever view-from-the-inside film. (Dir: Ron Clark, 95 mins.)†

Funny Girl (1968)***½ Barbra Streisand, Omar Sharif, Walter Pidgeon, Anne Francis, Lee Allen, Kay Medford. The nifty musical in which Barbra plays Broadway star Fanny Brice. Barbra is fabulous, giving one of the most triumphant performances in the long history of musical films. Herb Ross staged the musical numbers with flair. (Dir: William Wyler, 155 mins.)†

Funny Lady (1975)*½ Barbra Streisand, James Caan, Omar Sharif, Roddy McDowall, Ben Vereen, Carole Wells. A major disappointment, this lavish follow-up to *Funny Girl* features Streisand's voice at the height of its beauty

and a few good numbers lost in lumbering overproduction. The screenwriter (Jay Presson Allen) and tunesmiths (Kander and Ebb) of *Cabaret* foolishly try to graft that film's cynicism onto a traditional biopic about Fanny Brice, possibly the warmest, most lovable comedienne in showbiz history. Worse yet, cold and haughty Streisand seems to be giving us not funny Fanny but an approximation of Molly Picon trying to do the Duchess of Windsor. (Dir: Herbert Ross, 137 mins.)†

Funnyman (1971)*** Peter Bonerz. Loosely structured film about a comic in an improvisational troupe and his trials and tribulations with show biz and sex. (Dir: John Korty, 98 mins.)

Funny Thing Happened on the Way to the Forum, A (1966)*** Zero Mostel, Phil Silvers, Jack Gilford, Michael Crawford, Michael Hordern, Buster Keaton. The mad, bawdy Broadway musical set in ancient Rome with the great Mostel playing a sly, eager-to-be-free slave is transferred to the screen with zest and style. It's burlesque at its best, and director Richard Lester keeps the cast working at a breakneck pace for laughs. (99 mins.)†

Fun with Dick and Jane (1977)*** Jane Fonda, George Segal, Ed McMahon. Parts of this comedy about contemporary life are quite funny and zany. The writers and director, however, never seem to have quite made up their minds whether they wanted to produce a satire or an apologia for some of the more repellent values of American middle-class life. Segal plays an unemployed aerospace executive who, quite casually, turns to armed robbery to maintain his luxurious lifestyle. (Dir: Ted Kotcheff, 95 mins.)†

Furies, The (1950)*** Barbara Stanwyck, Judith Anderson, Walter Huston, Wendell Corey. A strikingly violent adult western for its time. This example of Freud on the range is overwrought and never less than compelling. An ambitious daughter (Stanwyck) grapples for power with her iron-willed father (Huston). (Dir: Anthony Mann, 109 mins.)

Further Adventures of Tennessee Buck, The (1988)* David Keith, Kathy Shower, Brant Van Hoffmann. A drunken "great white hunter" who serves as a guide for an air-headed yuppie couple. Indiana Jones he's not, nor are his adventures exciting or humorous or even mildly provocative (though Keith shoots for all three). (90 mins.)†

Further Perils of Laurel and Hardy, The (1967)***½ Expert Robert Youngson's compilation of some hilarious sequences from Stan and Ollie's silent film period. (Dir: Robert Youngson, 99 mins.)

Fury (1936)**** Spencer Tracy, Sylvia Sidney, Bruce Cabot, Walter Abel, Walter Brennan. Director Fritz Lang's first American film is a sharp, terrifying study of mob hysteria as a town tries to lynch an innocent murder suspect. Tracy survives, however, and returns to take revenge. (94 mins.)

Fury, The (1978)** Kirk Douglas, Carrie Snodgress, Amy Irving, Andrew Stevens, John Cassavetes. Director Brian DePalma tries to follow in Hitchcock's footsteps, and trips over his own derivativeness. Two telepathic teens are hounded by a secret organization seeking to use their powers for nefarious deeds. (117 mins.)†

Fury at Furnace Creek (1948)*** Victor Mature, Coleen Gray, Reginald Gardiner, Albert Dekker. This is a standout western with a strong mix of detective-story elements, featuring Mature in a struggle to clear his father, an Army general, of a charge that his bungling led to the Indian massacre of a cavalry troop. (Dir: H. Bruce Humberstone, 88 mins.)

Fury at Gunsight Pass (1956)** Neville Brand, David Brian, Richard Long, Lisa Davis. Bad guys rule the roost in a frontier town, at least for most of the film's running time. (Dir: Fred F. Sears, 68 mins.)

Fury at Showdown (1957)*½ John Derek, John Smith, Nick Adams. Derek plays a former gunfighter who returns to his hometown to face the anger of the townspeople. (Dir: Gerd Oswald, 75 mins.)

Fury at Smugglers' Bay (Great Britain, 1962)** Peter Cushing, Bernard Lee, Michele Mercier. Head of a cutthroat band of shipwreckers holds a community in the grip of terror. (Dir: John Gilling, 92 mins.)

Fury of Hercules, The (Italy, 1960)*½ Brad Harris, Alan Steel. More muscle stuff as ol' Herc leads a rebellion for the good guys. (Dirs: V. Scega, Gianfranco Parolini, 95 mins.)

Fury of the Congo (1951)**½ Johnny Weissmuller, Sherry Moreland, William Henry, Lyle Talbot. An imaginative "Jungle Jim" entry about natives being exploited by a drug ring. (Dir: William Berke, 69 mins.)

Fury of the Pagans (Italy, 1963)** Rossana Podesta, Edmund Purdom, Livio Lorenzon, Carlo Calo. Costume adventure as only the Italians can make them. Clan leader in ancient Rome wins the territory and saves his dream date. As schlocky as they get. (Dir: Guido Malatesta, 86 mins.)

Fury of the Wolfman, The (Spain, 1971)½ Paul Naschy, Perla Cristal, Michel Rivers, Mark Stevens. Naschy's fifth time out as sympathetic werewolf Waldemar Daninsky, still looking for a cure. Naschy's movies are supposed to be pretty good in their original forms, before they've been dubbed and re-edited for U.S. release, but it's hard to tell from what's left. (Dir: José Maria Zabalza, 80 mins.)†

Future Cop (MTV 1976)*½ Ernest Borgnine, Michael Shannon, John Amos. This pilot follows the adventures of two cops on the beat—Borgnine as the old-timer and Shannon as the rookie who's also a robot. (Dir: Jud Taylor, 72 mins.)

Future Cop (1985)—See: Trancers

Future Force (1989)**½ David Carradine, Robert Tessier, Anna Rapagna, Dawn Wildsmith. *Robocop*-like sci-fi set in the near future, where law enforcement has been turned over to private firms. Carradine plays a cynical bounty hunter who becomes the hunted when he asks the wrong questions about his employers. (Dir: David A. Prior, 84 mins.)†

Future Hunters (1986)**½ Robert Patrick, Linda Carol, Ed Crick, Richard Norton. Anthropology student and her boyfriend, visiting the site of an ancient temple, become part of a futuristic struggle that will decide the fate of the Earth. Well-paced adventure in the *Indiana Jones* mode, if not quite on that level. (Dir: Cirio H. Santiago, 100 mins.)†

Future Kill (1984)* Edwin Neal, Marilyn Burns, Gabriel Folse, Alice Villarreal. Unendurably cruel exploitationer about punk anti-nukers who clash violently with frat kids. (Dir: Ronald W. Moore, 83 mins.)†

Futureworld (1976)**½ Blythe Danner, Peter Fonda, Arthur Hill. Amusing technological thriller about a hotel resort staffed by robots. Fonda plays a nononsense reporter hot on the trail of the hotel's owner who's out to rule the world, of course. (Dir: Richard T. Heffron, 104 mins.)†

Futz (1969)*½ Seth Allen, John Bakos, Mari-Claire Charba, Peter Craig, Sally Kirkland. Dated adaptation of an unfilmable off-Broadway hit (for the La Mama troupe) retains avant-garde theatrical techniques that don't work at all on screen. It all has to do with the individual versus the community; what plot there is revolves around a farmer in love with his pig (ridden in one scene by a young, nude Kirkland). A sixties relic that you'd hardly want to watch all the way through. (Dir: Tom O'Horgan, 92 mins.)†

Fuzz (1972)**½ Burt Reynolds, Yul Brynner, Raquel Welch. Uneven and scatterbrained police yarn that relies on the easygoing style of Reynolds as a police detective, and the underplayed

387

villainy of Brynner as a culprit with a penchant for bombings. (Dir: Richard Colla, 92 mins.)†

Fuzzy Pink Nightgown, The (1957)** Jane Russell, Ralph Meeker, Keenan Wynn. Russell, as a movie star with blonde hair, is kidnapped by two clumsy guys and the fun begins. Good for a few chuckles. (Dir: Norman Taurog, 87 mins.)

F/X (1986)*** Bryan Brown, Brian Dennehy, Diane Venora, Cliff De Young, Mason Adams. A movie special-effects man is recruited by a government witness-relocation agency to stage a fake murder of a Mafia boss; at least, it's supposed to be a fake. This is a spiffy thriller that ultimately disappoints because it leaves too many plot threads unsatisfactorily resolved. (Dir: Robert Mandel, 107 mins.)†

FX2—The Deadly Art of Illusion (1991)*½ Bryan Brown, Brian Dennehy, Rachel Ticotin, Joanna Gleason, Philip Bosco, Kevin J. O'Connor. This dismally failed follow-up to the 1986 sleeper hit *FX* features Brown and Dennehy as a movie special effects expert and ex-cop who join forces to combat a serial killer and, in a subplot that strains credulity, retrieve some priceless antique coins stolen from the Vatican. (Dir: Richard Franklin, 107 mins.)†

Gabe Kaplan as Groucho (MTV 1982)*** Gabe Kaplan, Michael Tucci, Connie Danese. Kaplan does a good enough Groucho impression to make this both believable and entertaining. The play was co-written by Marx's son and it provides insights into his character along with a healthy supply of quips and one-liners. Little of the material comes from his movies, so even avid fans will find this fresh. (Dir: John Bowab, 90 mins.)†

Gable and Lombard (1976)*½ Jill Clayburgh, James Brolin, Red Buttons. A really bad picture about the love affair of two great stars. (Dir: Sidney J. Furie, 131 mins.)

Gabriela (Brazil-Italy, 1984)** Sonia Braga, Marcello Mastroianni. A middling screen version of the novel "Gabriella, Clove and Cinnamon" that's fortunately full of Brazilian sunshine and sexual allure. A voluptuous free spirit from the Brazilian backwoods wanders into a provincial village and flirts with respectability. (Dir: Bruno Barreto, 102 mins.)†

Gabriel Over the White House (1933)*** Walter Huston, Karen Morley, Franchot Tone, Jean Parker, Dickie Moore. That ace comedy director, Gregory La Cava (*My Man Godfrey, Stage Door*), makes this feel-good fantasy sparkle. A grafter

becomes president and is transformed into a defender of the little people. (87 mins.)

Gaby (1956)**½ Leslie Caron, John Kerr. A somewhat weak remake of *Waterloo Bridge*. A young soldier falls in love with a ballerina before he's shipped to the front during WWII. (Dir: Curtis Bernhardt, 97 mins.)

Gaby—A True Story (1987)**½ Liv Ullmann, Norma Aleandro, Robert Loggia, Rachel Levin. Painfully well-intentioned, finely acted but inordinately depressing true-life tale of a brave cerebral palsy victim dealing with her lifelong handicap. (Dir: Luis Mandoki, 114 mins.)

Gaijin (Brazil, 1979)*** Kyoko Tsukamoto, Antonio Fagunoes, Jiro Kawarasaki. First film by Tizuka Yamasaki, a Brazilian woman of Japanese descent. Moving story of 800 heroic turn-of-the-century emigrés from Japan to Brazil who arrive in their new country only to find resistance, exploitation, and a shattering clash of cultures. (105 mins.)

Gally, Gally (1969)*** Beau Bridges, Melina Mercouri, Brian Keith, George Kennedy, Margot Kidder. Norman Jewison produced and directed this uneven but generally appealing comedy based on Ben Hecht's reminiscences of his days as a cub reporter on a Chicago paper. The period is 1910, when young bumpkin Ben Harvey comes to the big city and lands at the jolliest bordello in town. (117 mins.)

Galactic Gigolo (1988)*½ Carmine Capobianco, Debi Thibeault, Ruth Collins. Meet our lovable sleaze-ball alien as he wins a trip to Earth on a game show and comes to Prospect, Connecticut, to seduce each and every woman he meets. Look for talking carrots, horny girls, and Hasidic hillbillies. A few good laughs in a galaxy of mediocrity. (Dir: Gorman Bechard, 82 mins.)†

Galaxina (1980)* Dorothy R. Stratten, Stephen Macht, Avery Schreiber. The late Dorothy Stratten is the only reason for watching this science-fiction spoof. Stratten plays an attractive and sexy robot in a police space-cruiser. Nauseatingly silly. (Dir: William Sachs, 95 mins.)†

Galaxy of Terror (1981)*½ Edward Albert, Jr., Erin Moran, Ray Walston, Bernard Behrens, Zalman King. More *Alien*-inspired atrocities as astronauts become fast-food-in-orbit for some nasty space creatures. (Dir: B. D. Clark, 80 mins.)†

Galileo (Great Britain-Canada, 1974)*** Topol, Edward Fox, John Gielgud, Clive Revill. Uneven but often absorbing version of Bertold Brecht's stimulating play as adapted by, and earlier played on the stage by, Charles Laughton. Opens in 1609 in Padua with an impoverished

Galileo seeking funds both to support his family and his scientific research, which scandalized the intellectual and political establishment of the time. Topol playing Galileo is simply not an actor of enough range and power to play such a demanding role. (Dir: Joseph Losey, 145 mins.)

Gallant Hours, The (1960)**½ James Cagney, Dennis Weaver, Richard Jaeckel, Ward Costello. Cagney's restrained performance as Admiral Halsey is the only worthwhile thing about this otherwise routine war film, based on events in the South Pacific campaign during WWII. (Dir: Robert Montgomery, 111 mins.)

Gallant Journey (1946)**½ Glenn Ford, Janet Blair. Biography of the man who contributed to aviation by experimenting with glider planes. Factual but not very exciting drama. (Dir: William Wellman, 85 mins.)

Gallant Lady (1934)*** Ann Harding, Clive Brook, Otto Kruger, Dickie Moore. Predictable but beguiling tale of a purposeful mother who contrives to regain her son born out of wedlock. Sentimental, though less so than was customary then, and stylish. (Dir: Gregory La Cava, 81 mins.)

Gallant Legion, The (1948)*** William Elliott, Adrian Booth, Bruce Cabot. Texas Ranger fights the leader of a powerful group desiring to split Texas into sections. Exciting western, well done. (Dir: Joseph Kane, 88 mins.)

Gallery of Horrors (1967)* John Carradine, Lon Chaney, Jr., Rochelle Hudson, Roger Gentry, Vic McGee. Cheap, lousy anthology of five horror stories about vampires, zombies, and the like. Carradine, Chaney, and Hudson appear in one segment each; the rest of the cast appears to be straight from the high school play. AKA: **Dr. Terror's Gallery of Horrors** and **Return from the Past.** (Dir: David L. Hewitt, 84 mins.)†

Gallipoli (Australia, 1981)**** Mark Lee, Mel Gibson, Robert Grubb, Tim McKenzie, David Argue. Australian director Peter Weir presents the futile WWI Australian campaign against the Turks on the beach of Gallipoli. A powerful, poignant military drama, *Gallipoli* focuses on the friendship of two western Australian youths in order to personalize the historical tragedy. Excellent performances, technically flawless. (110 mins.)†

Galloping Major, The (Great Britain, 1951)*** Basil Radford, Jimmy Hanley. A retired major has his eye on a race horse, but when bidding time comes he buys a broken-down temperamental nag by mistake. This one gets very funny at times. (Dir: Henry Cornelius, 82 mins.)

Gal Who Took the West, The (1949)** Yvonne DeCarlo, Charles Coburn, Scott Brady. Amusing comedy-drama set in the wild and woolly West. Miss DeCarlo plays an entertainer who takes the Arizona frontier by storm. (Dir: Frederick de Cordova, 84 mins.)

Gal Young Un (1979)*** Dana Preu, David Peck, J. Smith. Based on a good short story by Marjorie Kinnan Rawlings, produced on a shoestring, and written, directed, photographed, and edited by Victor Nuñez, the film has impeccable artistic credentials. A middle-aged woman victimized by a fast-talking hustler manages to have the last laugh; Preu carries herself with dignity, but Peck fails to convince as her seducer. (105 mins.)†

Gambit (1966)*** Shirley MacLaine, Michael Caine, Herbert Lom. Shirley MacLaine as a Eurasian lady of intrigue, Michael Caine as an ambitious but not very effective crook, and a jaunty story about a proposed theft of a valuable art treasure add up to fun. With a little more care, this film could have been very good indeed, but it's still entertaining as is. (Dir: Ronald Neame, 108 mins.)†

Gambler, The (1974)*** James Caan, Paul Sorvino, Lauren Hutton. James Caan is very good in this story of a compulsive gambler who eventually gets what he seems to be striving for: humiliation and a brutal beating. Along the way, the educated college professor with the double life cons and uses everyone who cares for him. (Dir: Karel Reisz, 111 mins.)†

Gambler, The (MTV 1980)—See: **Kenny Rogers as the Gambler**

Gambler, The—The Adventure Continues— See: **Kenny Rogers as the Gambler—The Adventure Continues**

Gambler III: The Legend Continues, The (MTV 1987)** Kenny Rogers, Bruce Boxleitner, Linda Gray, Melanie Chartoff, George Durning, Dean Stockwell, Charles Durning. Rogers returns, this time helping to get an equitable settlement for Native Americans about to be shafted by a crafty senator (Durning). An atmosphere of fun prevails, with the cast adopting a let's-dress-up attitude and (wisely) not taking it all too seriously. (Dir: Dick Lowry, 192 mins.)

Gambler from Natchez, The (1954)** Dale Robertson, Debra Paget. Adventurer goes after the varmint who killed his pa. Churns a well-worn path down that old celluloid river. (Dir: Henry Levin, 88 mins.)

Gambling Lady (1934)**½ Barbara Stanwyck, Joel McCrea, Pat O'Brien, Claire Dodd, Sir C. Aubrey Smith, Phillip Reed, Arthur Treacher. The daughter of a professional gambler, a victim of the gambling bug herself, marries the scion of a stuffy upper-class family, which disapproves. Pleasant vehicle for Stanwyck and McCrea, with a strong supporting cast. (Dir: Archie Mayo, 66 mins.)

Game Is Over, The (France, 1966)**½ Jane Fonda, Peter McEnery, Michel Piccoli. A heavy-breathing revamp of Zola's *La Curee*, in which La Fonda marries a wealthy man with a virile young son and prefers performing her connubial duties in sonny boy's bedroom. (Dir: Roger Vadim, 96 mins.)†

Game of Danger—See: **Bang! You're Dead**

Game of Death, A (1945)**½ John Loder, Audrey Long, Edgar Barrier. Big-game hunter is shipwrecked on an island owned by a madman who makes sport of hunting human prey. Exciting version of famous story, *The Most Dangerous Game*; thriller fans should like. (Dir: Robert Wise, 72 mins.)

Game of Death (1979)*½ Bruce Lee, Gig Young, Hugh O'Brian, Colleen Camp, Dean Jagger, Kareem Abdul-Jabbar, Chuck Norris, Kim Tai Jong. Six years after his death, Bruce Lee was seen in the footage he had shot for this last film. Intercut with clips from *Enter the Dragon* (1973) and new footage with Lee look-alike Kim Tai Jong, this infantile script deals with mob attempts to muscle in on kung fu star's success. (Dir: Robert Clouse, 102 mins.)†

Gamera the Invincible (Japan, 1965)** "Aw, we're not afraid of a turtle!" sneers one rock 'n' rolling teenager, not knowing that said turtle is sixty meters long, has giant fangs, breathes fire, and flies like a Frisbee. The version shown on TV features added footage with Brian Donlevy and Albert Dekker. (Dir: Noriaki Yuasa, 79 mins.)†

Gamera vs. Baragon—See: **War of the Monsters**

Gamera vs. Gaos (Japan, 1967)*½ Giant fire-breathing turtle battles giant fire-breathing bat (or maybe it's a fox). Fewer monsters than *Wrestlemania*, but just as funny. AKA: **Return of the Giant Monsters.** (Dir: Noriaki Uyasa, 87 mins.)

Gamera vs. Zigra (Japan, 1971)*½ An added dimension of thrills—Gamera's opponent this time is a giant shark from outer space, so they can fight on land and sea! Just when you thought you'd seen it all! (Dir: Noriaki Yuasa, 91 mins.)

Games (1967)*** Simone Signoret, Katharine Ross, James Caan. Offbeat, macabre drama with novel and ghoulish plot turns along the way. Katharine Ross is convincing playing a young wife, quite rightfully worried about her well-being. You've got to pay close attention

to this intellectual chiller-diller about a warped, rich young couple who indulge in way-out "games" of a kind not condoned by civilized society. (Dir: Curtis Harrington, 100 mins.)

Games, The (Great Britain, 1969)**½ Ryan O'Neal, Michael Crawford, Charles Aznavour. Episodic drama about the grueling preparation of long-distance runners for the Olympic marathon race, enlivened by the great race itself at the end of the film. (Dir: Michael Winner, 96 mins.)

Games Mother Never Taught You (MTV 1982)*** Loretta Swit, Sam Waterston, David Spielberg, Christopher Allport. Deft TV movie, with an excellent performance by Loretta Swit as a secretary climbing the executive corporate ladder. Ms. Swit plays a married woman who suddenly finds herself pitted against opportunistic males who resent her presence in the executive suite. (Dir: Lee Philips, 104 mins.)

Gamma People, The (Great Britain, 1956)** Paul Douglas, Eva Bartok. Moderate drama with science-fiction and political overtones concerning a gamma ray invention by which people are transformed into either geniuses or imbeciles. (Dir: John Gilling, 79 mins.)†

Gandhi (Great Britain-India, 1982)***½ Ben Kingsley, Candice Bergen, Edward Fox, Sir John Gielgud, Martin Sheen, John Mills, Trevor Howard. Epic account of Mahatma Gandhi's lifelong struggle against English imperialism in India. Filmed on a lavish scale, the film works as an intimate cerebral biography and as a stirring adventure tale. Fortunately, Ben Kingsley's insightful performance as Gandhi and the movie's panoramic visual sweep propel the storyline forward. Winner of eight Academy Awards, including Best Picture, Actor, Director, and Screenplay. (Dir: Richard Attenborough, 200 mins.)†

Gang's All Here, The (1943)***½ Alice Faye, Carmen Miranda, Edward Everett Horton, Eugene Pallette, Charlotte Greenwood, Benny Goodman. A dazzling musical treat that is a proud entry in the Camp Hall of Fame. In one movie, we get Charlotte Greenwood kicking up her long legs and Carmen Miranda spinning on her spike heels. The plot concerns a wartime Romeo who's in love with Faye but engaged to another girl; the simple plot is merely an excuse for sumptuous production numbers including one famous sequence in which chorus girls dance with oversized bananas. A wacky and irresistible extravaganza. (Dir: Busby Berkeley, 103 mins.)

Gangster, The (1947)*** Barry Sullivan, Belita, John Ireland. The leader of a mob lets his inner fear and insecurity get the best of him, loses his gang; is finally mowed down by a rival outfit. Interesting psychological study of a hoodlum. (Dir: Gordon Wiles, 84 mins.)

Gangster Story (1960)* Walter Matthau, Carol Grace. Notorious killer-robber tries to break away from a crime syndicate when he falls in love, but it's too late. (Dir: Walter Matthau, 65 mins.)

Gang That Couldn't Shoot Straight, The (1971)*½ Jerry Orbach, Leigh Taylor-Young, Jo Van Fleet, Robert De Niro, Lionel Stander. Ethnic humor at its most offensive. This film version of Jimmy Breslin's book deals with a dimwit mob involved in rubbing out a rival gang boss. (Dir: James Goldstone, 96 mins.)

Gang War (1958)**½ Charles Bronson, Kent Taylor. Teacher's wife is slain by hoodlums, he becomes a one-man vengeance committee. Good performances lift this from the gangster rut. (Dir: Gene Fowler, Jr., 75 mins.)

Garbage Pail Kids Movie, The (1987)** Anthony Newley, Mackenzie Astin, Katie Barberi. Gross-out kiddie picture based on the bad-taste bubble gum cards. Newley runs a curio shop where the "kids" (actually midgets in grotesque costumes) rally to help a local wimp. (Dir: Rod Amateau, 100 mins.)†

Garbo Talks (1984)** Anne Bancroft, Ron Silver, Carrie Fisher, Catherine Hicks, Hermione Gingold, Steven Hill. An uneven mixture of pious sentiment and misfired gags. A terminally ill woman's last request is to meet Greta Garbo. The screenplay has a few nice insights, but the film's fatally crass. (Dir: Sidney Lumet, 103 mins.)†

Garde à Vue (France, 1982)***½ Michel Serrault, Lino Ventura, Romy Schneider, Guy Marchand, Elsa Lunghini. On a rainy New Year's Eve, a prominent attorney (Michel Serrault) becomes the prime suspect in the rape and murder of two little girls. This elegant, low-keyed mystery unfolds deftly with intriguing psychological insights, as a relentless police inspector (Lino Ventura) interrogates his suspect, stripping away layers of defense. (Dir: Claude Miller, 87 mins.)

Garden, The (Great Britain, 1990)*** Kevin Collins, Roger Cook, Jody Graber, Spencer Lee, Pete Lee-Wilson, Tilda Swinton. Electrifying images of Christianity and homosexual persecution are combined with a vibrant and poetical allegory about AIDS and mortality in this tour-de-force example of independent filmmaking. (Dir: Derek Jarman, 91 mins.)

Garden Murder Case, The (1936)** Edmund Lowe, Virginia Bruce, Gene Lockhart, Frieda Inescort, Douglas Walton, Nat Pendleton. Solving a trio of murders is on Philo Vance's agenda in this whodunit with good support lent by Inescort, Lockhart, and Walton as the victims. (Dir: Edwin L. Marin, 62 mins.)

Garden of Allah, The (1936)**½ Marlene Dietrich, Charles Boyer, Basil Rathbone, John Carradine. One of the early Technicolor films, this full flowering of romanticism will be irresistible to fans of Boyer and Dietrich, who look into each other's languorous eyes and resist temptation. In this, their only film together, Hollywood's favorite foreign sex symbols play a holy man and the femme fatale who desires him; the desert has never looked lovelier either. (Dir: Richard Boleslawski, 90 mins.)†

Garden of Earthly Delights, The (Spain, 1970)*** Luchy Sota, Jose Luis Lopez Vasquez. Bizarre black comedy about a crippled magnate who has lost his memory but not his money. His relatives try to shock him into remembering the location of his fortune by staging disturbing scenes from his boyhood. (Dir: Carlos Saura, 99 mins.)†

Garden of Evil (1954)**½ Gary Cooper, Susan Hayward, Hugh Marlowe, Cameron Mitchell, Richard Widmark. Too much scowling and glowering in this interesting but misguided western, in which director Henry Hathaway builds to a simmering anticlimax. Ex-sheriff Cooper and gambler Richard Widmark team up to rescue a woman's husband from a mine, only to be trapped by an Indian attack. (100 mins.)

Garden of the Finzi-Continis, The (Italy-West Germany, 1970)**** Dominique Sanda, Lino Capolicchio, Helmut Berger, Fabio Testi. Director Vittorio De Sica's finest film since the postwar years is a melancholy, slowly paced rendering of an aristocratic Jewish family's downfall in Mussolini's Italy. As patricians living in a walled estate, the family is impervious to the political events that will engulf them. The acting is flawless. (95 mins.)†

Garden of the Moon (1938)**½ Pat O'Brien, Margaret Lindsay, John Payne, Melville Cooper, Isabel Jeans. The negligible plot about a bandleader squabbling with a nightclub owner does no damage to the wonderful musical numbers staged by director Busby Berkeley. (94 mins.)

Gardens of Stone (1987)**½ James Caan, Anjelica Huston, James Earl Jones, D.B. Sweeney, Dean Stockwell, Mary Stuart Masterson. Director Francis Coppola's sentimental exploration of homefront reactions to the Vietnam war centers on a mellowed-but-still-hardbitten sergeant (Caan) and a gung-ho young private who wants to be shipped into combat. Caan's performance is fine, but this personal slice of contemporary history fails to register any coherent viewpoint. (112 mins.)†

Gargoyles (MTV 1972)*** Cornel Wilde, Jennifer Salt, Bernie Casey. Wilde, as a professor researching a book on demonology, unearths a few living gargoyles from the Carlsbad Caverns. There are some genuine scares in this above-average television horror film. (Dir: B. W. L. Norton, 74 mins.)†

Garment Jungle, The (1957)*** Lee J. Cobb, Kerwin Mathews, Gia Scala. Forceful drama about the control by the rackets of the garment industry in a big city. Performances are good, with a standout bit by Robert Loggia as a brave union organizer. (Dir: Vincent Sherman, 88 mins.)

Gaslight (1944)*** Charles Boyer, Ingrid Bergman, Joseph Cotten, Angela Lansbury, Dame May Whitty, Terry Moore. Exciting psychological melodrama about a man who is trying to drive his wife to insanity. Not as good as the Broadway hit "Angel Street" but still good entertainment. (Dir: George Cukor, 114 mins.)†

Gas-s-s....Or It May Become Necessary to Destroy the World in Order to Save It! (1970)**½ Robert Corff, Elaine Giftos, Ben Vereen, Bud Cort, Cindy Williams, Talia Shire. Meandering end-of-the-world youth satire. Storyline about a defense plant in Alaska which springs a gas main leak, and everyone over their twenties perishes. (Dir: Roger Corman, 79 mins.)†

Gate, The (Canada, 1987)**½ Stephen Dorff, Louis Tripp, Christa Denton, Kelly Rowan, Jennifer Irwin. Young boy and his friend and teenage sister accidentally discover and open a gate to Hell in the backyard. Derivative storyline, but the film is sparked by well-drawn characters and excellent effects. (Dir: Tibor Takacs, 86 mins.)†

Gate of Hell (Japan, 1954)***½ Kazuo Hasegawa, Machiko Kyo. Winner of both the Grand Prix at Cannes and the Academy Award. About the bloody consequences of a soldier's lust for a noblewoman, which she does not return but is ill equipped to reject. Director Teinosuke Kinugasa serves up the choreographed battles and delicate, intelligent color that are virtues of Japanese cinema. (89 mins.)†

Gates of Heaven (1978)***½ On the surface, this extraordinary documentary tells the story of how a pet cemetery in California changed hands from a sympathetic, pet-loving old man to a businesslike family of entrepreneurs; on deeper levels, it is one of the most affecting portraits of winning and losing in America that's ever been put on film.

Filmmaker Errol Morris lets the individuals involved sketch their own personalities with revealing monologues that begin on the subject of the cemetery and inevitably end with their own personal concerns. (82 mins.)†

Gates of Hell, The (Italy, 1983)** Christopher George, Katriona MacColl, Janet Agren, Carlo de Mejo. Extremely gory horror flick about a suicidal priest and homicidal zombies. AKA: **Twilight of the Dead**. (Dir: Lucio Fulci, 93 mins.)†

Gates of Paris (France, 1957)***½ Pierre Brasseur, Henri Vidal. Loafer hides a hunted criminal. Beautiful performances and fine direction of René Clair make this comedy-drama a standout import that packs a wallop in its own quiet way. (103 mins.)

Gathering, The (MTV 1977)***½ Edward Asner, Maureen Stapleton, Lawrence Pressman. Powerful performance by Asner in a nice old-fashioned family drama. A successful engineer discovers he's dying; when his estranged wife discovers his secret, she suggests a Christmas reunion of the whole family. (Dir: Randal Kleiser, 104 mins.)†

Gathering, Part II, The (MTV 1979)*** Maureen Stapleton, Rebecca Balding, Jameson Parker, Efrem Zimbalist, Jr. Picks up the action two years after the father's death. Stapleton again plays the strong Kate Thornton, who takes over her husband's business and has to deal with her children's reactions to her new romance at another Christmas family reunion. Well-acted drama. (Dir: Charles S. Dubin, 104 mins.)

Gathering of Eagles, A (1963)**½ Rock Hudson, Mary Peach, Rod Taylor. It's the Strategic Air Command this time, with the stern officer whose devotion to duty causes complications in his home life. Some fine aerial camerawork and good performances, along with a story that suffers from slowness when it's on the ground. (Dir: Delbert Mann, 115 mins.)

Gathering of Old Men, A (MTV 1987)***½ Richard Widmark, Louis Gossett, Jr., Holly Hunter, Will Patton, Joe Seneca, Woody Strode, Tiger Haynes. A canny and insightful drama. After the shooting of a racist Cajun farmer, sheriff Widmark expects a lynch mob, but it doesn't turn out that way. Louis Gossett, Jr. leads a band of prideful old blacks in this adaptation of Ernest Gaines's novel. (Dir: Volker Schlondorff, 104 mins.)

Gator (1976)** Burt Reynolds, Lauren Hutton, Jerry Reed. Burt's fans should tune in for the usual quota of car chases and moonshine. This sequel to *White Lightning* marked Reynolds's debut as a director. (116 mins.)†

Gator Bait (1974)** Claudia Jennings, Sam Gilman, Doug Dirkson, Clyde Ventura, Don Baldwin, Ben Sebastian, Tracy Sebastian. Florida swamp gal Jennings (in outfits that leave a lot exposed to mosquito attacks) gets even with the local rednecks who've been harassing her. Sleazy, extremely violent drive-in favorite. (Dirs: Ferd and Beverly Sebastian, 93 mins.)†

Gator Bait II: Cajun Justice (1988)*½ Jan McKenzie, Tray Loren, Paul Muzzcat, Jerry Armstrong, Ben Sebastian. Almost a remake of its predecessor. Brother of the Claudia Jennings character marries a city girl and brings her to his swamp home, where she is eventually driven to violence in order to protect herself. In worst revenge-movie fashion, the camera dwells on her brutalizations as an excuse for having her turn around and do the same to her tormentors. (Dirs: Ferd and Beverly Sebastian, 94 mins.)†

Gauguin the Savage (MTV 1980)** David Carradine, Lynn Redgrave, Barrie Houghton. Disappointing, handsomely mounted production on the life of painter Paul Gauguin filmed in France and Tahiti. (Dir: Fielder Cook, 125 mins.)

Gauntlet, The (1977)*** Clint Eastwood, Sondra Locke, Pat Hingle. Clint runs the action film gauntlet again. While trying to bring in a witness to a murder, he runs afoul of the mob and his own police force. A stylish, above-average Eastwood film. (Dir: Clint Eastwood, 109 mins.)†

Gay Bride, The (1934)**½ Carole Lombard, Chester Morris, ZaSu Pitts, Nat Pendleton, Leo Carrillo, Joe Twerp. Gold-digger Lombard marries mobster Pendleton, even though she despises him, for his money. Gritty comedy-drama has star chemistry to recommend it. (Dir: Jack Conway, 80 mins.)

Gay Deception, The (1935)*** Francis Lederer, Frances Dee, Benita Hume, Alan Mowbray, Akim Tamiroff, Lionel Stander. A prince ends up a doorman; but passing through his hotel door is true love in the form of a secretary. A fairy-tale romance infused with charm. (Dir: William Wyler, 77 mins.)

Gay Desperado, The (1936)*** Nino Martini, Ida Lupino, Leo Carrillo, Harold Huber, Mischa Auer. A bubbly musical comedy about an heiress and a singer, both held captive by a music-loving band of outlaws. Lots of directorial inventiveness adds luster to this spoof of gangster movies. (Dir: Rouben Mamoulian, 85 mins.)

Gay Divorcee, The (1934)**** Ginger Rogers, Fred Astaire, Edward Everett Horton, Alice Brady. Love sick dancer pursues his light-o'-love until she gives in. Fine

musical. (Dir: Mark Sandrich, 107 mins.)†

Gay Falcon, The (1941)**½ George Sanders, Wendy Barrie, Allen Jenkins, Anne Hunter. The aristocratic amateur detective has to clear his chauffeur, who's accused of killing a woman for her jewels. In the process, the Falcon uncovers an insurance scam. (Dir: Irving Reis, 67 mins.)

Gay Lady (Great Britain, 1949)*** Jean Kent, James Donald. A music hall entertainer makes the grade when she marries a young duke. Pleasant turn-of-the-century romance, well acted. AKA: **Trottie True.** (Dir: Brian Desmond Hurst, 91 mins.)

Gay Purr-ee (1962)**½ Pleasant animated cartoon about a pussycat who goes to Paris, is saved from the villain, etc. Voices of Judy Garland and Robert Goulet and the songs of Harold Arlen are assets. (Dir: Abe Levitow, 86 mins.)†

Gay Sisters, The (1942)** Barbara Stanwyck, George Brent, Geraldine Fitzgerald, Gig Young, Nancy Coleman. Long, dull, tiresome melodrama about one of Hollywood's favorite topics, the bad apple in a fine family. (Dir: Irving Rapper, 108 mins.)

Gazebo, The (1959)*** Glenn Ford, Debbie Reynolds, Carl Reiner, John McGiver. When a TV mystery writer is blackmailed, he decides on murder as the way out, takes a shot at a shadowy figure in his home, later discovers the real blackmailer has been murdered—so who did he kill? Wacky comedy gets the laughs. (Dir: George Marshall, 100 mins.)

Geek Maggot Bingo (1983)*½ Robert Andrews, Brenda Bergman, Richard Hell, Donna Death, Zacherle. Another self-conscious low-budget attempt to create a "cult" movie by padding a hokey monster movie plot with purposely "bad" acting (by performers who probably couldn't do any better if they tried), and endless "in" jokes and cameos. (Dir: Nick Zedd, 73 mins.)†

Geisha, A (Japan, 1953)**** Michiyo Kogure, Ayako Wakao, Seizaburo Kawazy, Cheiko Naniwa. Director Kenji Mizoguchi's masterpiece returns to his favorite theme, the subjugation of women in Japanese society. Here he contrasts the role of a geisha in the pre- and post-WWII eras. Sensitive and austere study of women, history, and a unique aspect of Japanese culture. (87 mins.)

Geisha Boy, The (1958)**½ Jerry Lewis, Marie McDonald, Suzanne Pleshette, Sessue Hayakawa. Jerry as an inept magician who joins a U.S.O. unit touring the Orient works mightily to produce some laughs in this comedy and succeeds to a fair degree. (Dir: Frank Tashlin, 98 mins.)

Gemini Man (MTV 1976)* Ben Murphy, Katherine Crawford, Richard Dysart, Dana Elcar. This boring pilot was NBC's second try at the invisible-man gimmick. Ben Murphy is the special agent for a think-tank outfit, who can disappear at will. (Dir: Alan Levi, 98 mins.)

Gene Krupa Story, The (1960)** Sal Mineo, Susan Kohner, James Darren. Corny account of the rise to fame by drummer Gene Krupa. (Dir: Don Weis, 101 mins.)

General, The (1927)**** Buster Keaton, Marion Mack. With his slapstick genius in full display, Buster plays a comic Confederate in the Civil War South. When his train is stolen by Northern spies, Buster's rebel with a cause infiltrates Union lines to retrieve his locomotive. The photography recalls the work of photographer Matthew Brady and adds depth to a laugh-filled movie. (Dir: Buster Keaton, 74 mins.)†

General Della Rovere (Italy, 1960)**** Sandra Milo, Hannes Messemer, Vittorio De Sica. Roberto Rossellini directs a compelling and moving drama of heroism thrust upon an unlikely hero. De Sica gives the performance of his life as a threadbare con man who is forced into martyrdom when he impersonates an Italian resistance leader. (129 mins.)†

General Died at Dawn, The (1936)**** Gary Cooper, Madeleine Carroll, Akim Tamiroff, Dudley Digges, Porter Hall. Clifford Odets scripted this exotic adventure, well directed by Lewis Milestone, about a mercenary in China (Cooper) falling in love with a spy and clashing with an evil warlord. Novelist John O'Hara has a small role. (100 mins.)†

General Idi Amin Dada (France, 1978)**½ Barbet Schroeder's revealing documentary shows both gentle and cunning sides of the Ugandan dictator. Amin takes part in swimming meets (he never loses) and orders women to manage hotels ("They're better at housekeeping"). Crocodiles appear, aides disappear. Music by Amin. Cinematography by Nestor Almendros. (107 min.)

General Line, The (U.S.S.R., 1929)***½ Marfa Lapkina, Vasya Buznekov, Kostya Vasiliev. Director Sergei Eisenstein's last silent film is a brilliantly edited, comic satire about the conversion of a peasant woman to socialism. Filled with memorable montages, the movie's humor displeased party officials but made it a hit with the public. (90 mins.)†

Generation (1969)** David Janssen, Kim Darby, Carl Reiner. Unsuccessful filming of the moderately entertaining play about the relationship between a rebellious young couple and her establish-

ment father. (Dir: George Schaefer, 104 mins.)†

Generation (MTV 1985)*½ Richard Beymer, Hanna Cutrona, Marta DuBois, Priscilla Pointer, Cristina Raines, Bert Remsen. A pilot for a proposed series. It's New Year's Eve 1999, and the Breed family is suffering from the same problems that most families do, with technological overtones. (Dir: Michael Tuchner, 104 mins.)

Generation, A (Poland, 1954)***½ Tadeusz Lomnicki, Urszula Modrzynska, Roman Polanski, Zbigniew Cybulski. Energetic, visionary first feature by Andrzej Wajda about a young Polish Resistance fighter during WWII who aids escapees from the Warsaw Ghetto, falls in love with a girl who leads a youth group, and discovers new-found qualities of courage, leadership, and maturity. (85 mins.)

Genesis II (MTV 1973)**½ Alex Cord. Fans of Gene Roddenberry's imaginative science-fiction series "Star Trek" might enjoy this science-fiction film. Alex Cord stars as a 20th-century space scientist who is discovered almost two centuries later in a natural catastrophe. Sci-fi hocus-pocus, served up with a straight face as warring tribes seek to pick the scientist's brain. (Dir: John Llewellyn Moxey, 97 mins.)

Genevieve (Great Britain, 1953)**** John Gregson, Kenneth More, Dinah Sheridan, Kay Kendall. A divinely funny romp about two English couples who are old-car buffs and enter their trophies in a cross-country race. (Dir: Henry Cornelius, 86 mins.)†

Genghis Khan (U.S.-Great Britain-West Germany-Yugoslavia, 1965)** Omar Sharif, Stephen Boyd, James Mason, Eli Wallach. Mongol youth grows up to be the mighty Genghis Khan, seeking vengeance upon the rival chieftain who killed his father. Large-scale spectacle has the action, but the story and acting are only average for the genre. (Dir: Henry Levin, 124 mins.)

Genocide (1982)**** Powerful, shattering restatement of the atrocities inflicted upon the Jews under the Nazis. Narrated by Orson Welles and Elizabeth Taylor, with a vivid collection of filmclips, photographs, and letters from the victims. (Dir: Arnold Schwartzman, 90 mins.)

Genroku Chusingura—See: 47 Ronin, The

Gentle Annie (1944)**½ James Craig, Donna Reed, Marjorie Main. Entertaining little western with Miss Main playing the part of a lovable train robber. Based on a MacKinlay Kantor novel, this offers slightly different types of bad men. (Dir: Andrew Marton, 80 mins.)

Gentle Giant (1967)**½ Dennis Weaver, Vera Miles, Ralph Meeker, Clint Howard,

Huntz Hall. Youngsters may go for this uncomplicated tale of a boy and a bear that led to the TV series "Gentle Ben." (Dir: James Neilson, 93 mins.)†

Gentle Gunman, The (Great Britain, 1952)*** John Mills, Dirk Bogarde. A gunman for the Irish rebels believes in more peaceful means for obtaining their goal. Good melodrama. (Dir: Basil Dearden, 86 mins.)

Gentleman After Dark, A (1942)*½ Brian Donlevy, Miriam Hopkins, Preston Foster. A reformed thief struggles to bring up his daughter properly, despite the efforts of his wife. Sentimental drama, hammily acted. (Dir: Edward L. Marin, 77 mins.)

Gentleman at Heart, A (1942)**½ Cesar Romero, Carole Landis, Milton Berle. Fairly amusing comedy about a racketeer who goes into the art business. Berle and Romero are partners in crime and when the material is passable, they'll make you laugh. (Dir: Ray McCarey, 66 mins.)

Gentleman Bandit, The (MTV 1981)**½ Ralph Waite, Julie Bovasso, Jerry Zaks, Estelle Parsons. Waite plays an Italian priest in need of money who is mistakenly picked up as a kindly stick-up artist. Absorbing true-life tale. (Dir: Jonathan Kaplan, 104 mins.)

Gentleman Jim (1942)*** Errol Flynn, Jack Carson, Alexis Smith. Errol plays Jim Corbett in this exciting biography of the suave boxer which also presents an interesting panorama of boxing's early years as an outlawed sport. (Dir: Raoul Walsh, 104 mins.)†

Gentleman's Agreement (1947)*** Gregory Peck, Dorothy McGuire, John Garfield, Anne Revere, Celeste Holm. Based on a best-seller by Laura Z. Hobson, Moss Hart's adaptation shows Peck as a magazine writer who masquerades as a Jew in order to report firsthand on high-society discrimination. It's contrived nonsense, though director Elia Kazan puts his excellent cast through the paces efficiently. Oscars for Best Picture, Director, Supporting Actress (Holm). (118 mins.)

Gentlemen Marry Brunettes (1955)**½ Jane Russell, Jeanne Crain. Beautiful sisters on the loose in Paris is the inviting theme of this dull musical. The girls are fun to look at, but the picture doesn't match their charms. (Dir: Richard Sale, 97 mins.)

Gentlemen Prefer Blondes (1953)*** Marilyn Monroe, Jane Russell, Charles Coburn, Elliot Reid, Tommy Noonan. An elaborate screen version of the popular musical about two show business beauties on the prowl en route to Paris. Miss Monroe is well cast as the blonde bombshell who really believes "diamonds are a girl's best friend." (Dir: Howard Hawks, 91 mins.)†

Gentle Rain, The (U.S.-Brazil, 1966)*½ Christopher George, Lynda Day George, Fay Spain. Two social outcasts, a frigid upper-class girl and a disturbed mute architect, meet in Rio de Janeiro and fall in love. Awkwardly done and mawkish. (Dir: Burt Balaban, 94 mins.)

George McKenna Story, The (MTV 1986)*** Akosua Busia, Denzel Washington, Lynn Whitfield, Richard Masur, Ray Buktenica, Virginia Capers. Solid how-to-do-it movie about a black high school principal who transforms a run-down, gang-infested school into a place of learning and pride. (Dir: Eric Laneuville, 104 mins.)

George Raft Story, The (1961)**½ Ray Danton, Julie London, Barbara Nichols, Neville Brand, Jayne Mansfield. Biography of the screen badman, his rise from hoofer to movie star. Not as bad as might be expected; doesn't stick too close to facts. (Dir: Joseph M. Newman, 106 mins.)

George's Island (Canada, 1989)*** Nathaniel Moreau, Ian Bannen, Sheila McCarthy, Maury Chaykin. An orphan boy fights to stay with his eccentric grandfather, who assures him that a nearby island is the site of a treasure buried by Captain Kidd. Kids will love the ridiculous depictions of grown-up meddlers, while adults will enjoy its unpretentious, non-saccharine style. (Dir: Paul Donovan, 89 mins.)

George Stevens: A Filmmaker's Journey (1985)***½ Superlative documentary tracing the career of one of Hollywood's most acclaimed and ambitious directors. Unlike other similar nonfiction films, this is not a mere star-studded exercise in hero worship; a real sense of the director's personality emerges. A beautiful tribute written and directed by Stevens's son. (Dir: George Stevens, Jr., 113 mins.)†

George Washington Slept Here (1942)*** Jack Benny, Ann Sheridan, Charles Coburn, Hattie McDaniel, Percy Kilbride, Franklin Pangborn. Jack has fun in this screen adaptation of the Broadway hit about a city-dwelling family that buys a Pennsylvania farmhouse. Ending is weary but there's a lot of fun before it. (Dir: William Keighley, 93 mins.)

George Washington: The Forging of a Nation (MTV 1986)** Barry Bostwick, Patty Duke, Penny Fuller, Jeffrey Jones, Richard Bekins, Paul Collins, Guy Paul, Farnham Scott. A continuation of the successful mini-series about our nation's founding father. Unfortunately, the dramatic opportunities from this later period in his life are less juicy. (Dir: William A. Graham, 208 mins.)

George White's Scandals (1934)*** Alice Faye, Rudy Vallee, Jimmy Durante, Adrienne Ames, Gregory Ratoff, Dixie Dunbar, Gertrude Michael, George White. Based on the lavish series of stage presentations, this is a splashy backstage musical, with Faye making her screen debut. (Dirs: George White, Thornton Freeland, Harry Lachman, 80 mins.)

George White's Scandals (1935)**½ Alice Faye, Ned Sparks, James Dunn, Lyda Roberti, Cliff Edwards, Eleanor Powell, Benny Rubin, George White. Not as sparkling as its predecessor, this musical deals with Alice's climb from small-town talent to big-city star, which strains her relationship with her partner-boyfriend. Alice, Lyda, and Eleanor (in her screen debut) give this one pizazz. (Dir: George White, 83 mins.)

George White's Scandals (1946)** Joan Davis, Jack Haley, Phillip Terry, Martha Holliday, Jane Greer. Tired putting-on-a-show musical. Joan and Jack bill and coo, to the consternation of Jack's old maid aunt, but the show must go on anyway. (Dir: Felix E. Feist, 95 mins.)†

Georgia, Georgia (1972)** Diana Sands, Dirk Benedict, Minnie Gentry. Heavy-handed, occasionally effective melodrama about a black American singer (Sands) and her affair with a white photographer (Benedict) she meets in Scandinavia. Convoluted storyline is filled with unresolved racial problems. (Dir: Stig Bjorkman, 91 mins.)†

Georgia Peaches (MTV 1980)* Tanya Tucker, Terri Nunn, Lane Smith, Dirk Benedict. A down-home adventure with car chases and country music, as Tanya, Terri, and Dirk play reluctant undercover agents trying to snare a crook. (Dir: Daniel Haller, 104 mins.)

Georgy Girl (Great Britain, 1966)**** Lynn Redgrave, Alan Bates, James Mason, Charlotte Rampling. A very touching, charming, and thoroughly entertaining comedy-drama with top-notch characterizations played superbly by the cast. Lynn Redgrave, in the title role of the frumpy British lass who's satisfied with living life vicariously through her swinging London roommate, is quite marvelous and deeply moving. (Dir: Silvio Narizzano, 100 mins.)†

German Sisters, The (West Germany, 1981)***½ Jutta Lampe, Barbara Sukowa, Doris Schade, C. Verenice Rudolph. Based on an actual incident, film deals with two sisters, a feminist journalist and a member of a revolutionary group, who discover truths about each other when the latter is jailed and goes on a hunger strike. Director Margarethe von Trotta churns out the polemics in this disturbing and well acted film. (107 mins.)

396

Germany, Pale Mother (West Germany, 1980)***½ Eva Mattes, Ernest Jacobi, Elisabeth Stepanek, Angelika Thomas. Devastating chronicle of young bride whose husband goes to fight in WWII and her struggle to survive in a Germany wracked by war and famine. Mattes is extraordinary in this unusual look at the homefront from the German side. A relentlessly harrowing, uncompromising tale of the madness of war. (Dir: Helma Sanders-Grahms, 123 mins.)

Germany, Year Zero (Italy, 1948)***½ Edmund Moeschka, Franz Kruger, Barbara Hintz, Erich Guhne. Tragic tale of a young boy, trying to feed his family in post-WWII Berlin, who poisons his ailing father in order to ease the burden. Unforgettable film shot by neo-realist director Roberto Rossellini on location; the scenes of Berlin in ruins after the war are incredible. (78 mins.)

Geronimo (1940)** Preston Foster, Ellen Drew. The kids may like this childish dramatization of the white man's scrapes with the Apaches, but it's not particularly good for a top budget western. (Dir: Paul H. Sloane, 89 mins.)

Geronimo (1962)** Chuck Conners, Kamala Devi, Ross Martin, Pat Conway, Adam West, Denver Pyle. Generally good western speaks out against the abuse of native Americans by the U.S. in the 1800s, but ruins it with a phony happy ending. (Dir: Arnold Lavin, 101 mins.)

Gertrud (Denmark, 1964)***½ Nina Pens Rode, Baard Owe, Bendt Rothe, Ebbe Rode. Masterpiece of static camerawork, story of a woman who leaves her husband for a man who can't love her completely. She then rejects other marriage proposals, resigned to the fact that ideal love doesn't exist. Carl Dreyer wrote and shot this work as a series of conversations à deux, with nearly immobile long takes and minimalist performances. Slow pace of film creates its own tempo. Worth a look. (116 mins.)†

Gervaise (France, 1956)*** Maria Schell, François Perier, Suzy Delair, Armand Mestral. A washerwoman is abandoned with only her two children for comfort, later marrying a man who leads them both to alcoholism. Set in 1850s Paris, lavishly produced film is fifth and best screen adaptation of Emile Zola's L'Assommoir. Schell is outstanding as the woman. (Dir: René Clement, 116 mins.)†

Getaway, The (1972)*** Steve McQueen, Ali MacGraw, Ben Johnson, Sally Struthers. Adventurous excitement: McQueen and MacGraw generate electricity together as an ex-con and his wife pursuing money and eluding cops. (Dir: Sam Peckinpah, 122 mins.)†

Get Carter (Great Britain, 1971)*** Michael Caine, Britt Ekland, Ian Hendry. British gangster film set in the north of England; a cheap hood returns home to investigate his brother's death. One of Caine's best performances. Director Michael Hodges captures the dreary quality of life in the industrial towns. (111 mins.)

Get Christie Love! (MTV 1974)** Teresa Graves, Harry Guardino. Even TV films get remade. Here's a reworking of an earlier pilot (*Bait*) about a lady special investigator dedicated to her job. (Dir: William Graham, 100 mins.)†

Get Crazy (1983)*½ Malcolm McDowell, Allen Goorwitz, Daniel Stern, Lou Reed, Franklin Ajaye. This sloppy send-up of the rock music scene deals with a reunion concert of some bizarre performers. For rock music fans only; lots of celebrity cameos. (Dir: Allan Arkush, 92 mins.)†

Get On With It!—See: Carry on TV

Get Out Your Handkerchiefs (France-Belgium, 1978)***½ Gerard Depardieu, Patrick Dewaere, Carole Laure. Ribald comedy about the roles of the sexes in the emotional revolution—a droll work of incisive intellect. Oscar for Best Foreign Film. (Dir: Bertrand Blier, 108 mins.)†

Get Smart, Again! (MTV 1989)**½ Don Adams, Barbara Feldon, Dick Gautier, Bernie Kopell, Kenneth Mars. Adams has fun slipping back into his staccato delivery as CONTROL's most incompetent agent in this nostalgic update of the popular sixties TV show. (Dir: Gary Nelson, 96 mins.)

Getting Away From It All (MTV 1972)** Larry Hagman, Barbara Feldon, Gary Collins, E. J. Peaker. Lighthearted comedy about two New York couples who buy a small island in Maine. (Dir: Lee Philips, 74 mins.)

Getting Away With Murder—See: End of the Game

Getting Even (1986)*½ Edward Albert, Audrey Landers, Joe Don Baker, Rod Piloud, Billy Streater. Weak-kneed minor thriller about an enterprising Texan who pinches a deadly chemical from the Commies in Afghanistan for Uncle Sam. (Dir: Dwight H. Little, 90 mins.)†

Getting Gertie's Garter (1945)**½ The efforts of Dennis O'Keefe to retrieve a garter from Marie McDonald that would get him in trouble with sweetie Sheila Ryan. Comedy has many good chuckles. (Dir: Allan Dwan, 72 mins.)

Getting It Right (Great Britain, 1989)**½ Jesse Birdsall, Helena Bonham-Carter, Peter Cook, Lynn Redgrave, John Gielgud. A virginal hairdresser begins an unusual night when he attends a trendy party. Quirky but realistic characters blend well with satire. (Dir: Randal Kleiser, 102 mins.)†

Getting Married (MTV 1978)**½ Richard Thomas, Bess Armstrong, Mark Harmon, Katherine Helmond, Van Johnson. Predictable romantic comedy about an up-and-coming songwriter's fancy for a pretty TV newscaster, and his no-holds-barred efforts to break up her forthcoming wedding to another guy. (Dir: Steven Hilliard Stern, 104 mins.)

Getting of Wisdom, The (Australia, 1977)*** Susannah Fowle, Hilary Ryan, Alix Longman. A young girl determinedly sets out to prove herself amidst the snobbery of a boarding school in this pleasantly satirical film. In the vein of *My Brilliant Career*, but not as memorable. (Dir: Bruce Beresford, 101 mins.)†

Getting Over (1980)* John Daniels, Gwen Brisco, Mary Hopkins. Owner of the independent "Impossibly Funky" record label does his best to expose his musical acts. Hokey comedy-drama with some very unfunky music. (Dir: Bernie Rollins, 108 mins.)†

Getting Physical (MTV 1984)**½ Sandahl Bergman, David Naughton, Alexandra Paul, John Aprea. A young lady becomes addicted to rebuilding her body after she is accosted by a mugger. Underdeveloped drama! (Dir: Steven Hilliard Stern, 104 mins.)†

Getting Straight (1970)** Elliott Gould, Candice Bergen, Robert F. Lyons. Hippiedom alienation at its shallowest. Gould plays an ex-vet tiptoeing between the administration and the radical students so he can get his master's degree. (Dir: Richard Rush, 124 mins.)

Get to Know Your Rabbit (1972)*** Tom Smothers, Orson Welles. Inventive comedy. Ad exec Smothers learns to be a tap-dancing magician from Welles, acquiring an appropriately seedy trade to drop out on. (Dir: Brian DePalma, 91 mins.)

Get Yourself a College Girl (1964)½ Mary Ann Mobley, Chad Everett, Nancy Sinatra, Stan Getz. Story is periodically interrupted by dubbed-in tunes from the Animals, the Dave Clark Five, and Stan Getz. (Dir: Sidney Miller, 87 mins.)

Ghastly Ones, The (1968)½ Don Williams, Maggie Rogers, Hal Belsoe, Veronica Radburn. Tedious horror movie about murders at a Victorian mansion where a family has gathered for the reading of a will. (Dir: Andy Milligan, 81 mins.)†

Ghettoblaster (1989)**½ Richard Hatch. R. G. Armstrong, Richard Jaeckel, Diane Moser. Ex-army officer returns to the Los Angeles neighborhood where he was raised and, finding it overrun by gangs, uses his training to clean things up. Slightly above-average exploitation with a real feeling for the problems of the inner city. (Dir: Alan A. Stewart, 82 mins.)†

Ghidrah, the Three-Headed Monster (Japan, 1965)** Yosuke Natsuki, Takashi Shimura. Together for the first time, Godzilla, Mothra, and Rodan save Tokyo from the ravages of this parvenu from the provinces. (Dir: Inoshiro Honda, 85 mins.)†

Ghost (1990)*** Patrick Swayze, Demi Moore, Whoopi Goldberg, Tony Goldwyn, Rick Aviles, Gail Boggs, Armelia McQueen, Vincent Schiavelli. Audiences love this romantic thriller set in two worlds, the spiritual and the physical. Swayze and Moore are a blissfully happy downtown Manhattan couple who seem to have it all until he's killed by a street assailant. He remains on earth as a ghost, discovers his friend is in danger, and enlists the help of a medium (richly played by Goldberg, who won the Oscar for Best Supporting Actress), to warn her. The film overcomes its own absurdity and sentimentality because of the chemistry of the players and the directorial touch of Jerry Zucker that's never heavy-handed and never undermines the story's good will and momentum. Nominated for Best Picture, it was top box-office grosser of the year. (Dir: Jerry Zucker, 127 mins.)†

Ghost, The (Italy, 1963)*** Barbara Steele, Peter Baldwin, Leonard Elliott, Harriet White. Steele is haunted by the husband she thought she'd killed. Memorable ending in this perverse thriller. (Dir: "Robert Hampton" [Riccardo Freda], 93 mins.)†

Ghost and Mr. Chicken, The (1966)** Don Knotts, Joan Staley. Typesetter who wants to be a reporter stumbles into a murder case. As a vehicle for Knotts, this comedy should please his fans; for others, it's pretty silly. (Dir: Alan Rafkin, 90 mins.)

Ghost and Mrs. Muir, The (1947)*** Rex Harrison, Gene Tierney. Comedy about a widow's friendship with the ghost of a sea captain has charm and humor, but fails to sustain an entire film. (Dir: Joseph L. Mankiewicz, 104 mins.)†

Ghost Breakers, The (1940)*** Bob Hope, Paulette Goddard, Richard Carlson, Paul Lukas. Good Hope comedy, which combines chills with laughs. Bob goes along to Cuba to help Paulette claim a haunted castle. (Dir: George Marshall, 82 mins.)

Ghostbusters (1984)** Dan Aykroyd, Bill Murray, Sigourney Weaver, Harold Ramis. The Ghostbusters are college scientists who go into the spook-eliminating business for themselves, complete with TV commercials. Murray is the Big Spooker here as Aykroyd and Ramis are relatively subdued. (Dir: Ivan Reitman, 105 mins.)†

Ghostbusters 2 (1989)*** Bill Murray, Dan Aykroyd, Sigourney Weaver, Harold Ramis, Rick Moranis, Ernie Hudson, Peter MacNichol. As sloppy as the original, this sequel is still more engaging and less forced, with all of the cast in fine form. New Yorkers will appreciate the many jokes about the monstrous state of life in the Big Apple. (Dir: Ivan Reitman, 110 mins.)†

Ghost Catchers (1944)**½ Olsen and Johnson, Gloria Jean. Ole and Chic run a night club next door to a house hired by a southern colonel in town to produce a show, and the house is said to be haunted. Entertaining, zany comedy-mystery. (Dir: Edward F. Cline, 67 mins.)

Ghost Chase (1988)* Jason Lively, Jill Whitlow, Tim McDaniel. In need of money to finish their latest movie, two fledgling filmmakers call up the ghost of a dead uncle's butler to help them find the old man's hidden fortune. (Dir: Ronald Emmerich, 89 mins.)†

Ghost Chasers (1951)**½ Bowery Boys, Bernard Gorcey, Robert Coogan, Lloyd Corrigan, Lela Bliss. Sach befriends a ghost named Edgar. Light fluff that's an amusing combination of comedy and fantasy. (Dir: William Beaudine, 69 mins.)

Ghost Dad (1990)** Bill Cosby, Kimberly Russell, Denise Nicholas, Ian Bannen. Pretty poor ghost-spoof does provide some humor and charm in the person of Bill Cosby, as a yuppie dad who learns the hard way that his kids need him too. Special effects are fine, but the constant mugging wears thin. (Dir: Sydney Poitier, 88 mins.)†

Ghost Dancing (MTV 1983)*** Dorothy McGuire, Bruce Davison, Bo Hopkins, Richard Farnsworth, Victoria Racimo. An aging, impoverished farm owner (Dorothy McGuire) blows up a water pipeline in hopes of publicizing the plight of the dying Paiute Valley, which has been drained by the water and power authority of a nearby city. (Dir: David Greene, 100 mins.)

Ghost Fever (U.S.-Mexico, 1987)* Sherman Hemsley, Luis Avalos, Jennifer Rhodes, Joe Frazier. "Alan Smithee," the director credited here, is the phony name used by the Director's Guild when the real director wants his name taken off of a movie. That should tell you everything you need to know. (86 mins.)†

Ghost Goes West, The (Great Britain, 1935)***½ Robert Donat, Jean Parker. The spirit of a Scottish rogue returns to modern times to help a young member of the family. Charming fantasy-comedy, written by Robert E. Sherwood. (Dir: René Clair, 100 mins.)†

Ghost In Monte Carlo, A (MTV 1990)** Sarah Miles, Lysette Anthony, Oliver Reed, Christopher Plummer, Samantha Eggar, Fiona Fullerton, Ron Moody, Joanna Lumley. Typical Barbara Cartland bodice-ripper, handsomely produced by Lew Grade, with an innocent young girl just out of a convent school accompanying her aunt to Monte Carlo, where they find love and intrigue. (Dir: John Hough, 92 mins.)†

Ghost In the Invisible Bikini, The (1966)*½ Tommy Kirk, Deborah Walley, Boris Karloff, Basil Rathbone, Aron Kincaid, Jesse White, Harvey Lembeck, Nancy Sinatra, Francis X. Bushman, George Barrows, Patsy Kelly. Last of seven entries in the *Beach Party* series, and they should have stopped much earlier. Recently deceased Karloff must do a good deed before he can get into heaven, and that's where the partying teens come in. Music by the Bobby Fuller Four; unfortunately, they don't do "I Fought the Law." (Dir: Don Weis, 82 mins.)

Ghost In the Noonday Sun (Great Britain, 1973)* Peter Sellers, Anthony Franciosa, Spike Milligan, Clive Revill, Peter Boyle, Richard Villiers, Bill Kerr. Lamentably unfunny pirate comedy with Sellers as a ship's cook who takes control and guides the crew in search of a hidden treasure. Never released theatrically and supposedly unfinished (with direction rumored to have been completed by Milligan when Sellers and director Peter Medak had a falling out); whatever the reason, it's a mess. (93 mins.)†

Ghost of a Chance (MTV 1987) **½ Dick Van Dyke, Redd Foxx, Geoffrey Holder. A rather sweet reworking of an old plot, in which Heaven goofs, giving a man time to redeem himself on Earth with good works. (Dir: Don Taylor, 104 mins.)

Ghost of Cypress Swamp, The (MTV 1977)**½ Vic Morrow, Jeff East. The Disney camp's first made-for-TV effort. Young Lenny, played by Jeff East, tracks a wounded black panther through the interior of the forbidden Great Cypress Swamp and finds a hermit. (Dir: Vincent McEveety, 106 mins.)

Ghost of Dragstrip Hollow, The (1959)*½ Jody Fair, Nancy Anderson, Martin Braddock, Russ Bender. Silly yarn about "hot rod" groups that tries to mix chills with laughs in a haunted house setting. (Dir: William Hole, Jr., 65 mins.)

Ghost of Flight 401 (MTV 1978)** Ernest Borgnine, Gary Lockwood, Tina Chen, Kim Basinger, Eugene Roche, Beverly Todd. A mezza-mezza TV flick about the spirit of a dead pilot who's not content to rest in his own wreck and, instead, goes hauling its ectoplasm over to other airplanes. Not nightmarish enough. (Dir: Steven Hilliard Stern, 104 mins.)

Ghost of Frankenstein, The (1942)**½ Cedric Hardwicke, Lon Chaney, Jr., Lionel Atwill, Ralph Bellamy, Bela Lugosi, Evelyn Ankers. Fourth of the original Universal Studios series with Chaney failing to fill Boris Karloff's monster boots. The monster's deformed sidekick, Lugosi, proves he's the brains of the operation by sneakily arranging for the transplanting of his brain into the monster's cranium. (Dir: Erle C. Kenton, 68 mins.)

Ghost of Zorro (1959)*½ Clayton Moore, Pamela Blake, Roy Barcroft, George J. Lewis, Eugene Roth. Young surveyor helps a man and his daughter extend telegraph lines against the opposition; the surveyor's granddad was Zorro, so he adopts the old disguise. Feature version of a 1949 serial, with plenty of action, little sense. (Dir: Fred C. Brannon, 69 mins.)

Ghost Ship, The (1943)*** Richard Dix, Russell Wade, Ben Bard, Lawrence Tierney. A long-lost Val Lewton-produced feature (because of a plagiarism suit). One of the first low-budget efforts of director Mark Robson, it has decent pace, no fat, successful eeriness. (69 mins.)

Ghosts of Berkeley Square (Great Britain, 1947)** Robert Morley, Felix Aylmer, Yvonne Arnaud, Robert Beaumont, Martita Hunt, Ernest Thesiger, Wilfrid Hyde-White. Because of their less-than-honorable deaths, British officers Morley and Aylmer are sent back to Earth to haunt a decaying old mansion. Airy British comedy. (Dir: Vernon Sewell, 85 mins.)†

Ghosts on the Loose (1943)** Leo Gorcey, Huntz Hall, Bobby Jordan, Bela Lugosi, Ava Gardner. Misshapen comedy-suspense tale, dominated by the East Side Kids's ruckus. Bela Lugosi, as a below-ground Nazi, and Ava Gardner, making her film debut as a nice girl, are rarely on screen, alas. (Dir: William Beaudine, 64 mins.)†

Ghost Story (1981)* John Houseman, Douglas Fairbanks, Jr., Melvyn Douglas, Fred Astaire, Alice Krige, Craig Wasson. A slow-moving, unscary horror movie. The screenwriters made the serious error of altering Peter Straub's novel, and lost most of the atmosphere in the process. Only the most pedestrian part of the plot remains, about four old friends guarding a frightening secret. (Dir: John Irvin, 110 mins.)†

Ghost Town (1988)**½ Franc Luz, Catherine Hickland, Jimmie F. Skaggs. Western deputy investigating a missing person discovers a ghost town inhabited by undead citizens, victims of a curse. OK mix of two genres provides some straight thrills. (Dir: Richard Governor, 85 mins.)†

Ghostwriter (1989)** Audrey Landers, Judy Landers, Jeff Conaway, Tony Franciosa, David Doyle, Joey Travolta, John Matuszak, Dick Miller. A murdered movie star and a writer team up to expose the former's killer. The Landers sisters are comfortable together, but this wan comedy does little to exploit their possibilities. (Dir: Kenneth J. Hall, 94 mins.)†

Ghoul, The (Great Britain, 1933)** Boris Karloff, Cedric Hardwicke, Ernest Thesiger, Anthony Bushell, Ralph Richardson, Kathleen Harrison. Karloff returned to England to star in this dim horror flick about a mad archaeologist's quest for a mystical gem that will bring him eternal life. Though the cast is impressive, Karloff is really the only good thing about the film. (Dir: T. Hayes Hunter, 73 mins.)†

Ghoulies (1986)*½ Lisa Pelikan, Peter Liapis, Michael Des Barres, Jack Nance, Peter Risch. Ludicrous horror film about a man who dabbles with the occult in his home, thus unleashing a slew of supernatural creatures who have been awaiting such a chance. Shabby. (Dir: Luca Bercovici, 84 mins.)†

Ghoulies II (1988)* Damon Martin, Royal Dano, Phil Fondacaro. Sequel to the *Gremlins* rip-off finds the munchkin monsters wreaking havoc in a carnival. John (*Troll*) Buechler's puppet effects are, as always, on the Punch and Judy level. (Dir: Albert Band, 89 mins.)†

Giant (1956)***½ James Dean, Rock Hudson, Elizabeth Taylor, Carroll Baker, Dennis Hopper, Mercedes McCambridge, Chill Wills, Jane Withers, Sal Mineo, Earl Holliman, Rodney (Rod) Taylor. Sprawling epic about the death of old Texas and the rise of the oil millionaires. George Stevens won a Best Director Oscar for this visually impressive adult western. Dean's last performance. (201 mins.)†

Giant Behemoth, The (Great Britain, 1959)** Gene Evans, Andre Morell. Prehistoric monster rises from the sea and flips its giant lid before it is itself destroyed. (Dir: Eugene Lourie, 80 mins.)

Giant from the Unknown (1958)** Buddy Baer, Sally Fraser. Low-budget shocker with few surprises. Superstitious California villagers think a spirit from the past is seeking revenge and thereby hangs the yarn. (Dir: Richard E. Cunha, 77 mins.)†

Giant Gila Monster, The (1959)*½ Don Sullivan, Lisa Simone. This title should get some kind of truth-in-advertising award—it tells you all you need to know about the picture. (Dir: Ray Kellogg, 74 mins.)†

Giant Leeches, The—See: **Attack of the Giant Leeches**

G.I. Blues (1960)**½ Elvis Presley, Juliet Prowse. Tank sergeant becomes the number-one contender to break down the resistance of an iceberg nightclub dancer. Pleasant Presley musical should satisfy his fans, while others should find some fun along the way. (Dir: Norman Taurog, 104 mins.)†

Gideon of Scotland Yard (Great Britain, 1959)*** Jack Hawkins. Police inspector has a multitude of assorted crimes on his hands, all part of police routine. (Dir: John Ford, 91 mins.)

Gideon's Trumpet (MTV 1980)*** Henry Fonda, Jose Ferrer, John Houseman, Fay Wray. The real-life story of Clarence Earl Gideon (Fonda), a drifter with little education, who was arrested in the early sixties for breaking and entering. The Supreme Court decided he was entitled to a lawyer, although he could not afford to pay for one. (Dir: Robert Collins, 104 mins.)†

Gidget (1959)**½ Sandra Dee, Cliff Robertson, James Darren, Arthur O'Connell, Joby Baker. The original in the "Gidget" films—strictly for the teen set. Miss Dee is pert and Robertson is wasted. (Dir: Paul Wendkos, 95 mins.)†

Gidget Gets Married (MTV 1971)*½ Monie Ellis, Michael Burns, Don Ameche. Gidget is led down the aisle to the waiting arms of her long-time boyfriend. No surprises here. (Dir: James Sheldon, 72 mins.)

Gidget Goes Hawaiian (1961)** Deborah Walley, James Darren, Carl Reiner, Peggy Cass. Walley (succeeding to the role Sandra Dee created two years before) pursues Darren while on vacation with her family. (Dir: Paul Wendkos, 102 mins.)†

Gidget Goes to Rome (1963)** Cindy Carol, James Darren. The teenager does as it says in the title, gets involved in some romantic complications. Comedy mainly for the pre-adult set; others can look at the scenery. (Dir: Paul Wendkos, 101 mins.)†

Gidget Grows Up (MTV 1969)**½ Karen Valentine, Robert Cummings, Edward Mulhare. A made-for-TV feature which shows the all-American teenager grown up, having an innocent affair with an older man (Mulhare). (Dir: James Sheldon, 75 mins.)

Gidget's Summer Reunion (MTV 1985)** Caryn Richman, Dean Butler, Allison

Barron, Don Stroud, Anne Lockhart, Vincent Van Patten. Gidget's now a travel agent and Moondoggie wants to be an architect. But their marriage is in trouble. (Dir: Bruce Bilson, 104 mins.)

Gift, The (MTV 1979)*** Gary Frank, Julie Harris, Allison Argo, Glenn Ford. Adaptation of Pete Hamill's book about a young man coming of age in the '50s. Frank is excellent as a Brooklyn lad who joins the Navy and grows up while on Christmas leave. (Dir: Don Taylor, 99 mins.)

Gift, The (France, 1982)** Clio Goldsmith, Pierre Mondy, Claudia Cardinale. A sex farce about a lower-echelon bank executive who has an affair with a woman who is really a call girl hired for him by his co-workers on the occasion of his retirement. (Dir: Michel Lang, 105 mins.)†

Gifted One, The (MTV 1989)**½ Pete Kowanko, John Rhys-Davies, G. W. Bailey, Gregg Henry. Absorbing tale of a man born with strong telepathic powers but knows little about his origins. After his adoptive parents die, he sets out on an odyssey to find out who and what he is. Good premise for a proposed series that wasn't picked up. (Dir: Stephen Herek, 96 mins.)

Gift of God, The (Upper Volta, 1982)***½ Serge Yanago, Rosine Yanago, Joseph Nikiema, Colette Kabore. Wonderful story of mute boy found wandering in African bush, adopted by young couple who wait for his speech to return so they can learn his identity. First feature by Gaston J. M. Kabore is sensitive and gorgeously photographed, with glorious respect for the innocence of children. (70 mins.)

Gift of Life, The (MTV 1982)*** Susan Dey, Paul LeMat, Edward Herrmann, Cassie Yates. The subject is surrogate motherhood, a popular item in afternoon soaps. Sensitively written entry neatly balances both sides of the complex subject. (Dir: Jerry London, 104 mins.)

Gift of Love, The (1958)** Lauren Bacall, Robert Stack, Evelyn Rudie. A remake of the four-handkerchiefer *Sentimental Journey*. Overly sentimental and sticky plot concerns a childless couple who adopt a strange little girl. (Dir: Jean Negulesco, 105 mins.)

Gift of Love, The (MTV 1978)*½ Marie Osmond, Timothy Bottoms. An indifferently acted, updated version of the O. Henry classic "The Gift of the Magi." (Dir: Don Chaffey, 104 mins.)

Gift of Love: A Christmas Story, The (MTV 1983)** Lee Remick, Angela Lansbury, Polly Holliday, Mark Hulswit, Joseph Warren, Michael Pearlman. Earl Hamner

("The Waltons") comes up with another Yuletide yarn heavy on sentiment. Using a confusing dream framework, the story takes Remick back home in a fantasy to visit her dead parents and aunt. (Dir: Delbert Mann, 104 mins.)

Gift of the Magi (MTV 1978)** Debby Boone, John Rubinstein. Another not very accomplished version of O. Henry's famous tale, with a musical score. (Dir: Marc Daniels, 78 mins.)

Gig, The (1985)**½ Wayne Rogers, Cleavon Little, Andrew Duncan, Jerry Matz, Joe Silver. A modest but mildly enjoyable comedy-drama of the Catskills. A group of amateur musicians break away from their routine existences in order to cut loose at a musical engagement. (Dir: Frank Gilroy, 92 mins.)†

Gigantis the Fire Monster—See: **Godzilla Raids Again**

Gigi (1958)**** Maurice Chevalier, Leslie Caron, Louis Jourdan, Hermione Gingold, Eva Gabor, Isabel Jeans, Jacques Bergerac. This sophisticated musical won nine Academy Awards, including Best Picture. With a lovely score and the director's unfailing eye for visual detail, the film about the lovable gamine who's raised to be a courtesan but settles for true love is like vintage champagne that doesn't lose its sparkle. (Dir: Vincente Minnelli, 116 mins.)†

Gigot (1962)**½ Jackie Gleason, Katherine Kath. A somewhat moving performance by Jackie Gleason as a Chaplinesque mute in Paris who becomes the protector of a French streetwalker and her little daughter is the best feature of this maudlin entry. (Dir: Gene Kelly, 104 mins.)

Gilda (1946)*** Rita Hayworth, Glenn Ford, George Macready, Joseph Calleia, Stephen Geray. One of the steamiest films of the postwar period, due to Hayworth's sultry performance as the seductive title character. Ford plays Johnny, a hard-boiled gambler who has to deal with his feelings for the fiery redhead when she comes back into his life as the wife of his sinister boss (Macready). The strangely twisted bonds that develop among the three leads is a fascinating example of Hollywood's tempering of blatant sexuality. Freudian overtones aside, what most fans remember is Rita's immortal black satin strip to "Put the Blame on Mame." (Dir: Charles Vidor, 110 mins.)†

Gilda Live (1980)**½ Gilda Radner, Don Novello, Paul Shaffer. Faithfully mounted filmization of Radner's rather pallid Broadway showcase. Radner's material is so thin that it demands allegiance from its viewers as a prerequisite to amusement. (Dir: Mike Nichols, 96 mins.)†

Gilded Lily, The (1935)*** Claudette Colbert, Fred MacMurray, Ray Milland. Amusing romantic comedy about a girl who achieves fame and notoriety by turning down a titled suitor. (Dir: Wesley Ruggles, 90 mins.)

Gimme an "F" (1984)* Stephen Shellen, Mark Keyloun, Jennifer C. Cooke, Beth Miller, John Karlen. You got it. This timid comedy about preparations for a cheerleading contest certainly deserves an "F." (Dir: Paul Justman, 100 mins.)†

Gimme Shelter (1970)*** Mick Jagger, Charlie Watts, Melvin Belli. A stunning documentary about the Rolling Stones' concert in December 1969 at Altamont which wound up with an on-camera knife slaying. Disturbing, powerful essay on one aspect of the rock and drug culture at the end of the 1960s. (Dirs: David Maysles, Albert Maysles, Charlotte Zwerin, 91 mins.)†

Ginger (1971)½ Cheri Caffaro, Cindy Barnett, Kerr Kerr, William Grannell. The relentlessly unappealing Caffaro in the first of three action films (all written and directed by her husband) starring her as Ginger, socialite turned man-hating do-gooder. Racist, obnoxious, and incompetent; the video version seems to have lost an entire reel near the end! Sequels: *The Abductors, Girls Are for Loving*. (Dir: Don Schain, 102 mins.)†

Ginger Ale Afternoon (1989)** Dana Anderson, John M. Jackson, Yeardly Smith. One argumentative afternoon in the lives of a young couple who live in a Texas trailer camp. The stars aren't up to carrying this entire film (adapted from a play), but it's a laudable attempt at a character study. (Dir: Rafal Zielinski, 88 mins.)†

Ginger and Fred (Italy, 1985)*** Giulietta Masina, Marcello Mastroianni, Franco Fabrizi, Frederick Ledebur. There's plenty of director Federico Fellini's visual brilliance in this intoxicating spectacle about the once-popular dance team, Ginger and Fred (Masina and Mastroianni), reuniting after thirty years to appear on a Rome TV talent show. Masina is touching as the naive, sentimental Amelia, who's unaware that her dance partner has fallen on hard times. The TV studio, with its circus-like atmosphere, functions as a stylized world of fantasy, complete with one of Fellini's favorite images: the ringmaster (Fabrizi). (127 mins.)†

Ginger In the Morning (1973)*½ Monte Markham, Sissy Spacek, Susan Oliver. After the break-up of his marriage, an advertising executive falls in love with a young hitchhiker. Chaotic melodrama. (Dir: Gordon Wiles, 93 mins.)†

Girl, The (Sweden, 1987)* Franco Nero, Clare Powney, Bernice Stegers, Christopher Lee. A married lawyer (Nero) initiates an affair with a precocious fourteen-year-old schoolgirl (Powney), with violent consequences. An inane, unduly protracted softcore melodrama with a woefully mismatched "international" cast. (Dir: Arne Mattsson, 104 mins.)†

Girl, a Guy and a Gob, A (1941)*** Lucille Ball, Edmond O'Brien, George Murphy. Secretary is in love with her boss, but is engaged to a sailor. Cute comedy produced by Harold Lloyd, has some good laughs. (Dir: Richard Jones, 91 mins.)†

Girl and a Boy, A: The First Time—See: *Young Love, First Love*

Girl Called Hatter Fox, The (MTV 1977)**½ Ronny Cox, Joanelle Romero, Conchata Ferrell. A biting drama. Romero makes a promising screen debut as Hatter, a half-crazed New Mexico Indian girl who's been kicked from pillar to post, an orphan wracked by fear and hate. Cox, as a stubborn low-keyed doctor searching for clues to her animal behavior, gives his best TV performance. (Dir: George Schaefer, 104 mins.)

Girl Can't Help It, The (1956)*** Tom Ewell, Jayne Mansfield, Edmond O'Brien. An amusing, raucous comedy about an average press agent who gets mixed up with a mobster and his moll. Some rock 'n' roll songs help to spark the proceedings, and Ewell's expert clowning adds greatly. (Dir: Frank Tashlin, 99 mins.)†

Girl Crazy (1943)***½ Mickey Rooney, Judy Garland, June Allyson, Nancy Walker. Mickey and Judy have it all to themselves and they make the Gershwin score a pure delight. Story of the rich young Easterner whose dad exiles him to a small school out west never gets in the way of the Rooney-Garland talent. Remade as *When the Boys Meet the Girls*, 1965. (Dir: Norman Taurog, 99 mins.)†

Girl Friends (1978)*** Melanie Mayron, Eli Wallach, Bob Balaban, Anita Skinner, Viveca Lindfors. Perceptive, poignant low-budget entry. Melanie Mayron is a young photographer out to make it on her own in Manhattan, light years past Marjorie Morningstar. Very authentic in locale, detail, and emotion, the film makes squirrelly virtues out of its low-budget purity, but its affection for even the satirized characters overcomes a certain stinginess of ambition. (Dir: Claudia Weil, 86 mins.)†

Girl from Hunan (China, 1988)** Na Renhua, Liu Qing, Deng Xiaotuang. A turn-of-the-century drama, one of the only films made in the People's Republic of China to be seen here, focusing on the social mores surrounding a young girl's arranged marriage and illicit pregnancy. Handsome, but slow and understated to the point of invisibility. (Dirs: Xie Fei, U Lan, 99 mins.)

Girl from Jones Beach, The (1949)**½ Virginia Mayo, Eddie Bracken, Ronald Reagan. Mild comedy about an artist's amusing search for the perfect female model. (Dir: Peter Godfrey, 78 mins.)

Girl from Lorraine, A (France, 1980)*** Nathalie Baye, Bruno Ganz, Angela Winkler, Piérre Vernier. Thirty-year-old woman with high hopes leaves her small town to find work in Paris, only to become mired in a miserable affair and other ills of the big city. Director Claude Goretta paints a too-obvious picture of nasty Paris. (112 mins.)

Girl from Missouri, The (1934)**½ Jean Harlow, Lionel Barrymore, Franchot Tone. Cute, harmless comedy about a young lady from Missouri who by use of her physical assets achieves success in the big city. (Dir: Jack Conway, 80 mins.)

Girl from Petrovka, The (1974)*½ Goldie Hawn, Hal Holbrook, Anthony Hopkins. Hawn makes an unconvincing Russian girl who lives by her wits and falls for American newspaperman Holbrook. Nyet! (Dir: Robert Ellis Miller, 104 mins.)†

Girl from Tenth Avenue, The (1935)** Bette Davis, Ian Hunter, Colin Clive, Alison Skipworth. Bette gets her man; only he belongs to someone else. Trash redeemed by the Duse of the Depression. (Dir: Alfred E. Green, 69 mins.)

Girl-Getters, The (Great Britain, 1964)*** Oliver Reed, Jane Merrow. Girl-chasing photographer has phenomenal success in his conquests, but the tables are turned when he meets a glamor girl one summer. Well-done drama of life and love among the younger set. AKA: **The System.** (Dir: Michael Winner, 79 mins.)

Girl Happy (1965)** Elvis Presley, Shelley Fabares. Typical Presley film for his fans. Elvis is a nightclub entertainer who finds love in Fort Lauderdale during those college Easter vacations. For the record, there are twelve songs delivered by Elvis and cast. (Dir: Boris Sagal, 96 mins.)†

Girl He Left Behind, The (1956)** Tab Hunter, Natalie Wood, Jim Backus. Silly comedy about a young boy who is drafted into the peacetime Army. (Dir: David Butler, 103 mins.)

Girl Hunters, The (Great Britain, 1963)** Mickey Spillane, Shirley Eaton, Lloyd Nolan. Mike Hammer beats his way through assorted mayhem while trying to locate his missing secretary. (Dir: Roy Rowland, 103 mins.)

Girl in Black Stockings, The (1957)**½ Anne Bancroft, Mamie Van Doren, Lex Barker. Some gorgeous suspects in a double murder. Passable whodunit, with nicely filled stockings. (Dir: Howard W. Koch, 73 mins.)

Girl in Blue, The (Canada, 1973)**½ David Selby, Maud Adams. Feeling stifled in his current relationship, a lawyer sets out to find a woman he met briefly on a ferryboat years earlier. Whimsical romance is none too realistic, but appealing supporting characters and Montreal locations boost it a bit. AKA: **U-Turn.** (Dir: George Kaczender, 105 mins.)†

Girl in Distress—See: **Jeannie**

Girl in Every Port, A (1928)*** Victor McLaglen, Robert Armstrong, Louise Brooks, William Demarest. Very recognizably Howard Hawks-directed silent has two merchant seamen fighting at first and then forming a fast friendship, only to have it destroyed by a scheming femme fatale from a carnival, played with cool sensuality by Brooks. Humorous, quick-paced. (62 mins.)

Girl in Every Port, A (1952)** Groucho Marx, William Bendix, Marie Wilson. Navy pals acquire two race horses and try to conceal them on board ship. Tame comedy isn't what one would expect of the talent involved. (Dir: Chester Erskine, 86 mins.)†

Girl in His Pocket (France, 1957)** Jean Marais, Genevieve Page. A wacky French comedy about a handsome scientist whose experiments lead to wild results—he concocts a solution which reduces people to 3″ in size. (Dir: Pierre Kast, 82 mins.)

Girl in the Empty Grave, The (MTV 1977)*½ Andy Griffith, Sharon Spelman, Jonathan Banks, James Cromwell. Yet another pilot with Andy Griffith as a sheriff; this time he's out to nab a murderer. (Dir: Lou Antonio, 104 mins.)

Girl in the Painting, The (Great Britain, 1948)*** Mai Zetterling, Guy Rolfe, Robert Beatty. Army major runs into a spy plot when he tries to help a girl regain her memory. Good melodrama. (Dir: Terence Fisher, 89 mins.)

Girl in the Park, The—See: **Sanctuary of Fear**

Girl in the Picture, The (Great Britain-Scotland, 1986)** John Gordon-Sinclair, Irina Brook, David McCay, Gregor Fisher. A palatable but rather flat romance; a Scottish photographer grapples with his feelings for his girlfriend, whom he wants to leave until he finds out she is leaving him first. (Dir: Cary Parker, 90 mins.)†

Girl in the Red Velvet Swing, The (1955)**½ Ray Milland, Joan Collins, Farley Granger. One of the most sensational murders of the early 1900s was millionaire Harry K. Thaw's killing of famed architect Stanford White over his wife Evelyn Nesbitt Thaw. Their story is brought to the screen in an elaborate production with a good cast who do very nicely despite the soap opera overtones of the script. (Dir: Richard Fleischer, 109 mins.)

Girl in White, The (1952)** June Allyson, Gary Merrill, Arthur Kennedy. A soap opera about one of the first women doctors to invade a man's world. Miss Allyson weeps, smiles, and looks bewildered throughout the "sudsy" drama. (Dir: John Sturges, 93 mins.)

Girl Most Likely, The (1957)*** Jane Powell, Cliff Robertson, Kaye Ballard. Girl has a tough time choosing her dream man; musical version of a successful Ginger Rogers film (*Tom, Dick and Harry*) is helped considerably by ingenious production numbers staged by Gower Champion. (Dir: Mitchell Leisen, 98 mins.)†

Girl Most Likely to…, The (MTV 1973)**½ Stockard Channing, Edward Asner, Joe Flynn, Jim Backus, Chuck McCann. Bizarre comedy about a homely, dumpy college girl who is transformed into a lovely, sexy dish after a car accident and plastic surgery. The twist here is that she goes about seeking revenge in no uncertain terms. Script by Joan Rivers. (Dir: Lee Philips, 74 mins.)

Girl Named Sooner, A (MTV 1975)*** Cloris Leachman, Richard Crenna, Lee Remick, Susan Deer. Cloris Leachman is superb as a mean, shrewd hill-country woman. Concerns her neglected, mistreated eight-year-old granddaughter, but it's Cloris who dominates, with her plan to disown the child in exchange for a government handout. (Dir: Delbert Mann, 98 mins.)

Girl Named Tamiko, A (1962)**½ Laurence Harvey, France Nuyen. Moderately interesting drama which has Harvey playing a Eurasian who is a bitter expatriate from Tokyo eager to gain admission to the United States. (Dir: John Sturges, 110 mins.)

Girl Next Door, The (1953)** Dan Dailey, June Haver, Dennis Day. Nightclub star falls for a cartoonist, whose offspring complicates matters. Nothing to sing or draw about. (Dir: Richard Sale, 92 mins.)

Girl of the Golden West, The (1938)*** Jeanette MacDonald, Nelson Eddy, Leo Carillo, Buddy Ebsen, Walter Pidgeon. Pleasant musical adventure about sweet thing MacDonald and rough tough Eddy falling in love. Bouncy score by Gus Kahn and Sigmund Romberg. (Dir: Robert Z. Leonard, 120 mins.)†

Girl of the Limberlost, A (MCTV 1990)*** Joanna Cassidy, Annette O'Toole, Heather Fairfield. A homey and faithful adaptation of Gene Stratton-Porter's turn-of-the-century story about a wonderful young farm girl growing up in Indiana. Fairfield, in the title role, will win your heart as she faces the taunts of her affluent schoolmates but wins the confidence of the school's music teacher. (Dir: Burt Brinckerhoff, 96 mins.)

Girl of the Night (1960)*½ Anne Francis, Lloyd Nolan, Kay Medford, Julius Monk. Embarrassing study of a prostitute who tries to run away from her profession. (Dir: Joseph Cates, 93 mins.)

Girl on a Motorcycle—See: **Naked under Leather**

Girl on the Bridge (1951)*½ Beverly Michaels, Hugo Haas. Old watchmaker saves a girl from suicide, marries her, is forced into murder when her former lover reappears. On the corny side. (Dir: Hugo Haas, 77 mins.)

Girl on the Late, Late Show, The (MTV 1974)** Don Murray, Lorraine Stephens, Bert Convy, Gloria Grahame, Van Johnson, Ralph Meeker. Murray is a TV talk show exec who plays detective, attempting to find a missing movie actress (Grahame) of the 1950s. (Dir: Gary Nelson, 104 mins.)

Girl Rush (1944)** Alan Carney, Wally Brown, Frances Langford, Vera Vague, Robert Mitchum, Paul Hurst. So-so comedy with team of Carney and Brown as vaudevillians unable to leave San Francisco at the height of the Gold Rush. Langford steals the film, and it's fun seeing young Mitchum. (Dir: Gordon Douglas, 65 mins.)†

Girl Rush, The (1955)** Rosalind Russell, Fernando Lamas, Eddie Albert, Gloria De Haven. Museum employee arrives in Las Vegas to claim partnership in a hotel left by her gambler-father. Tries for musical gaiety that fizzles for the most part. (Dir: Robert Pirosh, 85 mins.)†

Girls, The (Sweden, 1968)*** Bibi Andersson, Harriet Andersson, Gunnel Lindblom, Erland Josephson. Strident feminist plea overwhelms story in this tale of three actresses, currently performing *Lysistrata*, and their utterly miserable private lives. Film's merit comes from brilliant performances of the three leads and director Mai Zetterling's talented way with a camera. (100 mins.)

Girls About Town (1931)*** Kay Francis, Lilyan Tashman, Joel McCrea, Eugene Pallette, Alan Dinehart. Racy early George Cukor effort explores the lives of ladies who use men to get ahead in the big city; good script and fast pace elevate this pre-Code tale. (82 mins.)

Girl Said No, The (1930)*½ William Haines, Leila Hyams, Polly Moran, Marie Dressler, Francis X. Bushman, Clara Blandick. Bank clerk goes to extremes when the girl he cares for constantly refuses him. Antique comedy, but Dressler and Moran are a blessing. (Dir: Sam Wood, 90 mins.)

Girls Are for Loving (1973)½ Cheri Caffaro, Timothy Brown, Jocelyn Peters. The last and worst of the three *Ginger* movies: along with the poor plotting, inept action and general misanthropy, this one has Caffaro singing as well! (Better make that "as badly.") (Dir: Don Schain, 90 mins.)†

Girls' Dormitory (1936)**½ Simone Simon, Herbert Marshall, Ruth Chatterton, Tyrone Power. Simon is outstanding in her first American film. Story of a girl in love with the headmaster of her school isn't too well written. (Dir: Irving Cummings, 66 mins.)

Girls! Girls! Girls! (1962)** Elvis Presley, Stella Stevens, Benson Fong. A trivial comedy. Elvis is trying to choose among a bevy of beauties, and the suspense is nil. (Dir: Norman Taurog, 105 mins.)†

Girl Shy (1924)*** Harold Lloyd, Jobyna Ralston, Richard Daniels. Paralyzingly shy poor boy Lloyd writes a best-seller on romance, and in a wild chase, saves his sweetheart from marrying the wrong man; wonderfully funny silent comedy. (Dir: Fred Newmeyer, 65 mins.)

Girls in Prison (1956)*½ Richard Denning, Joan Taylor, Mae Marsh, Raymond Hatton, Jane Darwell, Adele Jergens. An outrageous script about a basically nice girl who's an accomplice in a bank robbery and later becomes an escaped convict. Convict the director and writer. (Dir: Edward L. Cahn, 87 mins.)

Girls in the Night (1953)*½ Joyce Holden, Glenda Farrell, Harvey Lembeck. Turgid melodrama about slum life in New York and one family's efforts to better their lot. Enough incidents for three such films. (Dir: Jack Arnold, 83 mins.)

Girls in the Office, The (MTV 1979)**½ Susan St. James, Barbara Eden, Tony Roberts, David Wayne. Glossy glimpse of women trying to rise in the hierarchy of a large department store. St. James is effective as an ambitious worker who pays a big price to see her dreams realized. Predictable, but not boring. (Dir: Ted Post, 104 mins.)

Girls Just Want to Have Fun (1985)**½ Sarah Jessica Parker, Lee Montgomery, Morgan Woodward, Jonathan Silverman, Helen Hunt, Holly Gagnier. Better-than-average teensploitation. A shy teenager must circumvent her strict papa's rules as well as the tongue-clucking admonitions of her Catholic school nuns, as she tries to dance her way onto the local dance video show. (Dir: Alan Metter, 87 mins.)†

Girls' Nite Out (1984)* Julie Montgomery, James Carroll, Suzanne Barnes, Rutanya Alda, Hal Holbrook. Low-budget shocker about a psychopath murdering young women during a college scavenger hunt. Bloody and borderline offensive, but many ludicrous touches—including the killer dressing up in a bear suit—make the movie simply laughable. (Dir: Robert Deubel, 92 mins.)†

Girls of Huntington House, The (MTV 1973)**½ Shirley Jones, Mercedes McCambridge, Sissy Spacek, Pamela Sue Martin. Jones proves she can handle a dramatic role as the new teacher in a small school for unwed mothers. (Dir: Alf Kjellin, 73 mins.)†

Girls of Pleasure Island, The (1953)** Leo Genn, Don Taylor, Audrey Dalton. Englishman with three beautiful daughters lives an idyllic island life until a detachment of Marines lands to build an air strip. Mild wartime comedy. (Dir: F. Hugh Herbert, 95 mins.)

Girls of the White Orchid (MTV 1983)** Jennifer Jason Leigh, Ann Jillian, Thomas Byrd. Based on actual cases, this exposé deals with young, innocent entertainers who go to Japan to sing in nightclubs but end up in a notorious prostitution ring run by the Japanese Mafia. A must for sleaze fans. AKA: **Death Ride to Osaka.** (Dir: Jonathan Kaplan, 104 mins.)†

Girls on the Beach (1964)** Lana Wood, The Beach Boys, Noreen Corcoran. "Sally Sorority" (Miss Corcoran) promises her sisters the Beatles at a benefit performance to pay off the mortgage on their boardinghouse. The Beach Boys, the Crickets, and Lesley Gore do nicely. (Dir: William N. Witney, 80 mins.)

Girls' School Screamers (1986)½ Mollie O'Mara, Sharon Christopher, Mari Butler, Beth O'Malley. Derivative scream-a-thon. Six dumb-bunny women and one weird nun take inventory of a haunted mansion's art treasures bequeathed to their school. (Dir: John Finegan, 82 mins.)†

Girls' Town (1959)*½ Mamie Van Doren, Mel Tormé, Paul Anka, Maggie Hayes, Ray Anthony, Cathy Crosby, Gigi Perreau, Jim Mitchum, Gloria Talbott. Sleazy bit of trash about a "girl" (Van Doren) sent to a correctional school unjustly who manages to uncover the real culprit. Distasteful in theme and handling, but Van Doren-ites will enjoy watching Mamie act through her tight bodices. AKA: **Innocent and the Damned.** (Dir: Charles Haas, 92 mins.)

Girl, the Gold Watch and Dynamite, The (MTV 1981)*½ Lee Purcell, Philip MacHale, Burton Gilliam, Jack Elam, Zohra Lampert. Paltry comic sequel to the popular comedy about the yuppie who comes across a watch with time-stopping capabilities. Far from timeless comedy. (Dir: Bill Averback, 104 mins.)

Girl, the Gold Watch and Everything, The (MTV 1980)**½ Robert Hays, Pam Dawber, Jill Ireland, Maurice Evans. Tale revolves around Kirby Winter (Hays), who inherits a magic gold watch from his multimillionaire uncle. Hays is affable and handsome, and comedienne Dawber is pretty and surprisingly talented. (Dir: William Wiard, 104 mins.)

Girl Who Came Between Them, The (MTV 1990)*½ Cheryl Ladd, Anthony John
405

Denison, Melissa Chan, Julia Nickson-Soul, Joe Spano. A couple's happy marriage is strained when the husband brings home a thirteen-year-old Vietnamese girl he believes to be his daughter. Poorly scripted examination of adoption, with both parents unreasonable and unsympathetic. (Dir: Mel Damski, 96 mins.)

Girl Who Came Gift Wrapped, The (MTV 1974)**½ Karen Valentine, Richard Long, Dave Madden, Farrah Fawcett. Harmless comedy casting Miss Valentine as a young lady who is thrust upon a successful man-about-town publisher of a sophisticated girlie magazine. Count the possibilities, and then see how many are trotted out. (Dir: Bruce Bilson, 78 mins.)

Girl Who Had Everything, The (1953)** Elizabeth Taylor, Fernando Lamas, William Powell, Gig Young. Criminal lawyer's daughter becomes infatuated with a suave crook. Old-hat melodrama with very little. Remake of A Free Soul, 1931. (Dir: Richard Thorpe, 69 mins.)

Girl Who Knew Too Much, The (1969)** Nancy Kwan, Adam West, Robert Alda. Adventurer hired by the CIA tracks down the assassin who killed a syndicate boss, only to find that the Communists are trying to take over his mob. Campy. (Dir: Francis D. Lyon, 95 mins.)

Girl Who Spelled Freedom, The (MTV 1986)*** Wayne Rogers, Mary Kay Place, Kieu Chinh, Kathleen Sisk, Jade Chinn, Margot Pinvidic. A true-life tale that tugs at the heartstrings. A young Cambodian refugee becomes a spelling bee champion just a few months after fleeing her country for her new adopted homeland of America. (Dir: Simon Wincer, 104 mins.)†

Girl with a Suitcase (France-Italy, 1961) ***½ Claudia Cardinale, Jacques Perrin. Absorbing and sensitively played Italian language drama about a sixteen-year-old boy and his innocent and brief romance with a beautiful, sensual girl who lives by her wits. (Dir: Valerio Zurlini, 96 mins.)

Girl with Green Eyes, The (Great Britain, 1964)*** Rita Tushingham, Peter Finch, Lynn Redgrave. Edna O'Brien's touching novella, The Lonely Girl, receives a diffuse treatment from director Desmond Davis. The material, about a writer's affair with a country girl, is beautifully acted. (Dir: Desmond Davis, 91 mins.)

Giselle (Cuba, 1964)***½ Dancer Alicia Alonso became an international star with this interpretation of the famed ballet. Alonso is so brilliant here that she simply is the entire movie. (Dir: Enrique Pineda Barnet, 90 mins.)†

Git! (1965)** Jack Chaplain, Heather North. Runaway orphan trains an English setter to become a fine hunting dog.

Harmless little boy-and-dog drama; children will like it best. (Dir: Ellis Kadison, 92 mins.)†

Give a Girl a Break (1953)**½ Marge and Gower Champion, Debbie Reynolds. Three girls compete for a top spot in a new Broadway musical. Tuneful but standardized musical with some engaging routines by the dancing Champions. (Dir: Stanley Donen, 82 mins.)

Give 'Em Hell, Harry (1975)***½ This is basically a photographed stage play, but James Whitmore is so splendid impersonating Harry Truman (without makeup), and Truman's words and personality are so rousing, that this is a joy. (Dir: Peter H. Hunt, 104 mins.)†

Give Me a Sailor (1938)**½ Martha Raye, Bob Hope, Betty Grable. If you consider Martha Raye funny, you'll love her in this slapstick romp about a plain-looking girl winning a "beautiful legs" contest. (Dir: Elliott Nugent, 80 mins.)

Give Me Your Heart (1936)**½ Kay Francis, George Brent, Roland Young, Patric Knowles, Frieda Inescort, Henry Stephenson, Halliwell Hobbes. Typical Francis soap opera, expertly done as usual, has the star giving up her illegitimate baby and hiding her past from nice-guy Brent. Good production values and strong supporting cast (plus Francis's wardrobe!) make this enjoyable. (Dir: Archie Mayo, 87 mins.)

Give My Regards to Broad Street (Great Britain, 1984)** Paul McCartney, Ringo Starr, Bryan Brown, Barbara Bach, Linda McCartney, Ralph Richardson, Tracey Ullman. After a fourteen-year screen absence, McCartney made this musical fantasy piffle about a rock star who loses some valuable recording tapes. This elaborate home movie reunites McCartney with Ringo Starr in both recording studio and production numbers, and offers the last screen appearance of Sir Ralph Richardson. (Dir: Peter Webb, 108 mins.)†

Give My Regards to Broadway (1948)** Dan Dailey, Charles Winninger. A father who is waiting for vaudeville to come back and the romances of his kids make up the ingredients for this film. Some good standard songs, well done by Dailey, are the only redeeming features. (Dir: Lloyd Bacon, 89 mins.)

Given Word, The (Brazil, 1962)***½ Leonardo Vilar, Dionizio Azevedo, Gloria Menezes, Carlos Torres. To give thanks to heaven for curing his donkey, farmer drags an enormous cross to a church—where the priest won't let him enter after he discovers the farmer's voodoo beliefs. Extraordinary look at a clash of wills between two men who both believe in the power of religion. Best Film, Cannes Film Festival 1962. (Dir: Anselmo Duarte, 98 mins.)

Give Out, Sisters (1942)** Peggy Ryan, Andrews Sisters, Dan Dailey, Grace McDonald, Charles Butterworth, Walter Catlett, William Frawley, Donald O'Connor. Telegraph messenger lands a tryout in a nightclub. (Dir: Edward F. Cline, 65 mins.)

Give Us Wings (1940)**½ Billy Halop, Huntz Hall, Wallace Ford. Unscrupulous head of an aerial crop-dusting outfit employs some tough kids to fly for him. Minor but speedy melodrama. (Dir: Charles Lamont, 62 mins.)

Gizmo! (1980)**** Hilarious documentary demonstrating many crazy (some not so bad) inventions and why they never caught on. (Dir: Howard Smith, 79 mins.)†

Gladiator, The (1938)**½ Joe E. Brown, Man Mountain Dean, June Travis, Dickie Moore, Lucien Littlefield. Standard vehicle for Brown as a campus wimp turned into a sports hero by a secret serum whipped up in the science department. Offers plenty of opportunities for Brown to display his acrobatic training. (Dir: Edward Sedgwick, 70 mins.)

Gladiator, The (MTV 1986)**½ Ken Wahl, Nancy Allen, Robert Culp, Rick Dees. Ken Wahl stars as a car mechanic by day and an angry vigilante by night, out to stop drunk and dangerous drivers after his brother is killed by one. Predictable but vigorous action-pic by the talented director of *Ms. 45*. (Dir: Abel Ferrara, 104 mins.)†

Glamour Boy (1941)**½ Jackie Cooper, Susanna Foster, Jackie Searl, Walter Abel, Darryl Hickman, Ann Gillis, William Demarest. Appealing satire of Hollywood features Jackie as a former child star coaching a new film prodigy. (Dir: Ralph Murphy, 79 mins.)

Glass Alibi, The (1946)**½ Paul Kelly, Anne Gwynne, Douglas Fowley. An unscrupulous reporter sees a chance to commit a perfect crime, but fate trips him up. Sturdy crime drama, showing what talented filmmakers can do with a small budget. (Dir: W. Lee Wilder, 70 mins.)

Glass Bottom Boat, The (1966)*½ Doris Day, Rod Taylor, Arthur Godfrey, Paul Lynde. A relentlessly sophomoric and unfunny outing finding Doris up to her pretty blonde hair in an espionage ring. (Dir: Frank Tashlin, 110 mins.)

Glass Cage, The (1963)** John Hoyt, Arline Sax, Robert Kelljan. Detective becomes involved with a strange girl who has a dominating elder sister and a sinister father. (Dir: Antonio Santean, 78 mins.)

Glass House, The (MTV 1972)***½ Vic Morrow, Alan Alda, Clu Gulager. As a deterrent to crime, this Truman Capote–written prison drama is hard to beat—a

shocker to the core, besides being a savage indictment of our penal system. In filming it at Utah State Prison in semidocumentary style, director Tom Gries turns his cameras on a new guard, a college professor up for manslaughter, and a kid doing time on a drug rap. Their initiation into the system, with guards looking the other way as a con boss runs "the glass house," turns into a reign of terror. (73 mins.)†

Glass Key, The (1935)*** Edward Arnold, George Raft, Ray Milland. Good, exciting Dashiell Hammett melodrama about crime, murder, and politics. Characters are superbly drawn and overshadow the routine plot. (Dir: Frank Tuttle, 80 mins.)

Glass Key, The (1942)*** Alan Ladd, Veronica Lake, Brian Donlevy, Robert Preston, William Bendix. Dashiell Hammett novel about a good-natured, crooked politician saved from a murder frame-up by his taciturn henchman. The action, under Stuart Heisler's direction, captures some of the gritty atmosphere. (85 mins.)†

Glass Menagerie, The (1950)**½ Arthur Kennedy, Gertrude Lawrence, Jane Wyman, Kirk Douglas. A Tennessee Williams play, whose fragile poetic nature somehow survives insensitive direction and less-than-inspired casting. Kennedy is good in the easy role, but Lawrence is miscast as the mother. Wyman and Douglas shine. (Dir: Irving Rapper, 107 mins.)

Glass Menagerie, The (MTV 1973)**½ Katharine Hepburn, Sam Waterston, Joanna Miles, Michael Moriarty. Hepburn is woefully miscast as Amanda Wingfield, the fading southern belle desperately trying to instill confidence in her sad crippled daughter while steering her poetry-writing son toward a more remunerative career. Fortunately, the other cast members are convincing. (Dir: Anthony Harvey, 100 mins.)

Glass Menagerie, The (1987)**½ Joanne Woodward, John Malkovich, Karen Allen, James Naughton. Tennessee Williams's timeless, magical masterwork is given a pedestrian treatment by director Paul Newman. However, Malkovich does deliver a tightly brilliant performance as the narrator-brother, and Allen does shine as the beguiling keeper of the menagerie. (130 mins.)†

Glass Mountain, The (Great Britain, 1950)***½ Michael Denison, Dulcie Gray, Valentina Cortese. A composer writes an opera inspired by a beautiful Italian girl, but finds he has lost interest in his wife in doing so. Well-done romantic drama with fine musical score, performances. (Dir: Henry Cass, 94 mins.)

Glass Slipper, The (1955)*** Leslie Caron, Michael Wilding. Caron is perfectly cast as Cinderella in this musical fantasy that works most of the way. Don't look for anything but a fairy tale, exquisitely mounted, and you'll be entertained. (Dir: Charles Walters, 94 mins.)†

Glass Tower, The (West Germany, 1957)** Lilli Palmer, O. E. Hasse, Peter Van Eyck. German-made soap opera about an actress who is virtually kept a prisoner by her wealthy husband in a specially built glass palace. (Dir: Harold Braun, 93 mins.)

Glass Wall, The (1953)*** Vittorio Gassman, Gloria Grahame. Interesting off-beat story about a foreigner who jumps ship in New York after he is refused entry. His exploits lead him to the UN building—the glass wall—where he almost kills himself. (Dir: Maxwell Shane, 80 mins.)

Glass Web, The (1953)**½ Edward G. Robinson, John Forsythe. Strictly for the whodunit fans. A murder mystery involving members of the staff of a weekly TV show titled "Crime-of-the-Week." (Dir: Jack Arnold, 81 mins.)

Gleaming the Cube (1988)** Christian Slater, Steven Bauer, Min Luong. Slater, a rebel on a skateboard, seeks the murderers of his brother. Not as bad as it sounds, if you don't mind watching lots of skateboarding or listening to Slater's nonstop Jack Nicholson imitation. (Dir: Graeme Clifford, 105 mins.)†

Glen and Randa (1971)*** Steven Curry, Shelley Plimpton. An ambitious, seriously flawed, but often provocative apocalyptic vision of two survivors of an atomic holocaust. Third film, but first commercial release for the talented but undisciplined writer-director Jim McBride. (94 mins.)†

Glenn Miller Story, The (1954)*** James Stewart, June Allyson, Charles Drake, George Tobias, Harry Morgan. Highly romanticized biography of the famed band leader who was lost during World War II. The personal charm of Stewart as Glenn Miller, and Allyson, as his loving wife, carry the film's sentimental sequences. Plenty of the big band sound. (Dir: Anthony Mann, 116 mins.)†

Glen or Glenda? (1953)½ Daniel Davis, Dolores Fuller, Bela Lugosi, Lyle Talbot, Timothy Farrell, Charles Crafts, "Tommy" Haynes. Intended as a plea of tolerance for transvestitism by the director (an inveterate cross-dresser himself who used to wear ladies' dainties under his combat fatigues in the service and who appears here using the pseudonym "Daniel Davis"), this camp classic combines stock footage of endless freeways, dream sequeces with a devil dressed in a Woolworth's Halloween disguise, multiple storylines about those men afflicted with a passion for clinging fabrics, and weird, interpolated diatribes from Bela Lugosi warning us about—well, it's never clear, but it's got something to do with snails and puppy dog tails and redefining male sexuality. Some video versions run shorter. AKA: **I Led Two Lives** and **I Changed My Sex**. (Dir: Edward D. Wood, Jr., 67 mins.)†

Glitch (1988)**½ Will Egan, Steve Donmyer, Julia Nickson, Dick Gautier, Ted Lange. Dumb but diverting comedy with two cutups at loose in a mansion with 100 bathing beauties, the stars of an exploitation movie being made there. (Dir: Nico Mastorakis, 90 mins.)†

Glitter Dome, The (MCTV 1985)** James Garner, John Lithgow, Margot Kidder, Colleen Dewhurst, John Marley. Joseph Wambaugh's tough, tawdry, and often lurid novel about the underbelly of Hollywood society has been turned into a sleazy TV film. Garner is a police detective out to crack a porno movie operation. (Dir: Stuart Margolin, 95 mins.)†

Global Affair, A (1964)** Bob Hope, Lilo Pulver, Yvonne DeCarlo. A featherweight comedy not worthy of Hope's talents. He's a United Nations staff member who becomes the temporary guardian of an abandoned baby left at the UN. (Dir: Jack Arnold, 84 mins.)

Gloria (1980)***½ Gena Rowlands, Juan Adames, Buck Henry, Julie Carmen. A former gangster's moll (Rowlands, inimitable) is on the run with a Puerto Rican kid marked for death by the mob; although she doesn't like the kid, she is willing and able to kill to protect him. Director John Cassavetes, in collaboration with cinematographer Fred Schuler, has found a new way of looking at the landscape of New York City, and his rhythms are consistently fresh and illuminating. (121 mins.)†

Glorifying the American Girl (1929)** Mary Eaton, Edward Crandall, Eddie Cantor, Helen Morgan, Rudy Vallee, Florenz Ziegfeld, Texas Guinan. An early talkie revue. Forget the storyline about an aspiring Ziegfeld chorine not ready for a nuptial stranglehold, and enjoy guest spots by Morgan, Cantor, and Vallee. This was the only film personally supervised by the Great Flo himself. (Dirs: Millard Webb, John Harkrider, 87 mins.)†

Glory (1956)*½ Margaret O'Brien, Walter Brennan, Charlotte Greenwood. Another in the endless line of stories about a girl (or boy) and a horse. No glory for anyone involved. (Dir: David Butler, 100 mins.)†

Glory (1989)*** Matthew Broderick, Denzel Washington, Morgan Freeman, Cary Elwes, Jihmi Kennedy, Andre Braugher, Cliff DeYoung. True story of the first regiment of black soldiers raised to fight in the Civil War. Broderick is good in a tricky part as the white colonel chosen to lead the regiment, but top honors go to Oscar-winner Washington. Major drawback is that the film, in giving due credit to these overlooked heroes, tends to glorify war. (Dir: Edward Zwick, 122 mins.)†

Glory Alley (1952)**½ Leslie Caron, Ralph Meeker. An entertaining yarn about a soldier who comes home to New Orleans and tries to pick up where he left off with his girl. A great deal of jazz is played throughout the film by such stars as Louis Armstrong, Jack Teagarden, and others. (Dir: Raoul Walsh, 79 mins.)

Glory at Sea (Great Britain, 1952)*** Trevor Howard, Richard Attenborough, Sonny Tufts. Captain of a lend-lease ship during WWII earns the respect of his crew after committing some errors. Good melodrama has excitement, compactness, fine performances. (Dir: Compton Bennett, 88 mins.)

Glory Brigade, The (1953)*** Victor Mature, Lee Marvin, Richard Egan. Unpretentious but well-made, fast-moving story of Greek UN forces in war-torn Korea. Different sort of war plot, above average. (Dir: Robert D. Webb, 82 mins.)

Glory Days (MTV 1988)**½ Robert Conrad, Shane Conrad, Jennifer O'Neill. Conrad Sr., who directed, is quite good as a middle-aged man who retires from his successful business to realize the one dream he never accomplished—to be a college football star. (96 mins.)

Glory Glory (MCTV 1989)**½ Ellen Greene, Richard Thomas, James Whitmore. Greene's brazen, gutsy turn as a sex-and-drug-abusing rocker who becomes a star as singing evangelist "Sister Ruth" is the high point of this otherwise limp satire of the telereligion industry. (Dir: Lindsay Anderson, 210 mins.)†

Glory Guys, The (1965)** Tom Tryon, Senta Berger, Andrew Duggan, James Caan. Soldier Tom Tryon is forced by an order from his commanding officer to send raw recruits into action against the Sioux. Screenplay by Sam Peckinpah. (Dir: Arnold Laven, 112 mins.)

Glory Stompers, The (1967)*½ Dennis Hopper, Jody McCrea, Chris Noel, Jock Mahoney, Casey Kasem. Biker Hopper (in his pre-*Easy Rider* days) and his gang kidnap the leader of another gang, leading to a climactic battle royale. Average stuff, though sixties fans won't want to miss an authentic movie "love-in" and an appearance by DJ Kasem as the aptly-named "Mouth." (Dir: Anthony M. Lanza, 85 mins.)

Glove, The (1978)**½ John Saxon, Roosevelt Grier, Joanna Cassidy, Aldo Ray, Joan Blondell, Kennan Wynn, Jack Carter. Ex-con seeks revenge on those who did him wrong, inflicting violence with a leather and steel glove. Fun cast features veteran stars in comic bits commenting on the action. (Dir: Ross Hagen, 91 mins.)†

Glump!—See: **Please Don't Eat My Mother**

G-Men (1935)*** James Cagney, Lloyd Nolan. Crime-busting story with Cagney on the side of the law for a change. (Dir: William Keighley, 85 mins.)

Gnome-Mobile, The (1967)**½ Walter Brennan, Ed Wynn. Walt Disney treat for the kids. Brennan plays the dual role of a wealthy businessman and a gnome who must find a wife for his grandson. (Dir: Robert Stevenson, 104 mins.)†

Goalie's Anxiety at the Penalty Kick, The (West Germany-Austria, 1971)** Arthur Brauss, Kai Fisher, Marie Bardischewski, Erika Pluhar. The goalie commits a meaningless murder, only to find that you only get out of murder what you put into it. In case you are in the middle of this picture wondering if something is going to happen, let me perform the act of mercy and tell you: nope. (Dir: Wim Wenders, 101 mins.)†

Go Ask Alice (MTV 1973)*** Jamie Smith Jackson, Andy Griffith, Julie Adams, William Shatner. Provocative fare. The disturbing subject of the indiscriminate use of drugs by high school kids has seldom been portrayed with more validity than in this made-for-TV film. Based on the real-life diary of a young girl caught up in addiction from the age of fifteen. (Dir: John Korty, 73 mins.)

Go-Between, The (Great Britain, 1971)***½ Julie Christie, Alan Bates, Dominic Guard, Michael Redgrave, Margaret Leighton. Harold Pinter adapted the L. P. Hartley novel about a young boy's involvement as a go-between in an illicit Victorian love affair and how it affects the development of his personality. (Dir: Joseph Losey, 116 mins.)

God Bless the Child (MTV 1988)*** Mare Winningham, L. Scott Caldwell, Obba Babatunde, Dorian Harewood. A single parent becomes a victim of harrowing circumstances that place her and her seven-year-old daughter among the homeless. A disturbing drama that thankfully remains realistic and doesn't present any easy outs. (Dir: Larry Elikann, 96 mins.)

God Bless the Children—See: **Psychiatrist, The: God Bless the Children**

Godchild, The (MTV 1974)**½ Jack Palance, Jack Warden, Jose Perez. Rousing remake of the 1948 John Ford-John Wayne film, *Three Godfathers*. Three Civil War prisoners running from the Confederates and Apaches come across

409

a dying woman about to give birth. (Dir: John Badham, 72 mins.)

Goddess, The (1958)***½ Kim Stanley, Lloyd Bridges, Steven Hill. An original screenplay by Paddy Chayefsky about a lonely girl who becomes "a love goddess of the silver screen"; the lady finds phonies and misses happiness. A striking and powerful performance by Kim Stanley. (Dir: John Cromwell, 105 mins.)†

Godfather, The (1972)**** Marlon Brando, Al Pacino, James Caan, Sterling Hayden, Robert Duvall, Diane Keaton, John Cazale, Talia Shire, John Marley, Richard Conte. One of the most riveting American movies of the decade. An absolutely superb performance by Brando as the aging head of a powerful Mafia clan, with fine performances from the supporting cast, especially Al Pacino playing Brando's youngest son. Set in 1945 on Long Island with other sequences shot on location in Sicily. Based on the best-selling novel by Mario Puzo, this is one of the few times where the film is an improvement on the book. (Dir: Francis Ford Coppola, 175 mins.)†

Godfather, Part II, The (1974)**** Al Pacino, Robert De Niro, Robert Duvall, Diane Keaton, Talia Shire, John Cazale, Lee Strasberg, Michael V. Gazzo. Oscar winner for Best Picture is even better in many ways than its predecessor. Michael Corleone (Pacino) has consolidated the power handed to him by his father, as the film flashes back and forth between the early life of the late Don Vito and the ongoing story of his embattled family after his death. (Dir: Francis Ford Coppola, 200 mins.)†

Godfather, Part III, The (1990)***½ Al Pacino, Diane Keaton, Talia Shire, Andy Garcia, Eli Wallach, Joe Mantegna, Bridget Fonda, George Hamilton, Sofia Coppola, Franc D'Ambrosia, Helmut Berger, Donal Donnelly, John Savage, Richard Bright, Raf Vallone, Franco Citti, Don Novello, Vittorio Duse, Al Martino. A fitting coda to director Francis Ford Coppola's epic saga about the Corleone crime family, completing the greatest trilogy in motion picture history. Pacino is exceptional as the aging Don Michael striving to legitimize his family's business by cutting a deal with the Roman Catholic Church. The film is rich with the colors of autumn, and it's filled with memories and regret for tragedies past. There are two extraordinary sequences of violence, one set at a mob casino meeting and the other, towards the end, cross-cut between a Palermo opera house and the Vatican itself. Garcia and Shire, as Michael's nephew and sister, give electrifying performances. Co-written by Coppola and Mario Puzo.

Impact greatly marred, alas, by the truly wretched acting of Sofia Coppola playing Pacino's daughter. She gives what may be the worst performance in a major film within recent memory. (Dir: Francis Ford Coppola, 164 mins.)†

God Forgives, I Don't (Italy-Spain, 1969)** Terence Hill, Bud Spencer, Frank Wolff, Gina Rovere. Commonplace spaghetti western about a gunslinger searching for the loot from a train robbery. (Dir: Giuseppe Colizzi, 101 mins.)

God Is My Co-Pilot (1945)**½ Dennis Morgan, Dane Clark, Raymond Massey. Tribute to the famous Flying Tigers is very trite and only occasionally exciting. (Dir: Robert Florey, 90 mins.)

God Is My Partner (1957)** Walter Brennan, Marion Ross. OK for severe sentimentalists; fine acting and a contrived story. (Dir: William F. Claxton, 80 mins.)

God's Country (1985)*** Louis Malle's warm documentary about the small Minnesota farming town of Glencoe is an affectionate look at people still imbued with the pioneer spirit and desire to attain the American Dream. Malle's sincere portrait never sentimentalizes or mocks, merely recording simple people trying to avoid pitfalls of a complex world. (87 mins.)

Godsend, The (Great Britain, 1979)** Malcolm Stoddard, Cyd Hayman, Angela Pleasence, Patrick Barr. Spawn-of-Satan horror film about sweet little blonde girl left at family's farm; farm folks suddenly become victims of hideous deaths. (Dir: Gabrielle Beaumont, 93 mins.)†

God's Gift to Women (1931)** Frank Fay, Joan Blondell, Laura La Plante, Charles Winninger, Louise Brooks, Margaret Livingston. A rare chance to witness Broadway star Frank Fay on the screen with his highly individual brand of comedy, as he plays a lothario who gives up all for one love. (Dir: Michael Curtiz, 72 mins.)

God's Little Acre (1958)**½ Robert Ryan, Aldo Ray, Tina Louise. Erskine Caldwell's novel reaches the screen with some of the passion diluted. Robert Ryan is most effective as the head of the Walden clan, whose mad obsession that there's gold on his land leads him to near tragedy. (Dir: Anthony Mann, 110 mins.)†

Gods Must Be Crazy, The (South Africa, 1979)*** Marius Weyers, Sandra Prinsloo, Nixau, Jamie Uys. Slapstick, eccentric comedy from South Africa; a pilot drops a Coke bottle while flying over a tribe in Botswana who take it as a gift from the gods. But when the revered object causes fighting among the natives, their chief decides to go to the "end of the world" and return it. (Dir: Jamie Uys, 109 mins.)†

Gods Must Be Crazy II, The (South Africa, 1990)** Nixau, Lena Farugia, Hans Strydom. Disappointing follow-up comes across forced. Occasional slapstick is amusing as the lovable bushman (Nixau) searches for two children accidentally taken into civilization. Story is side-tracked by an irrelevant political sub-plot, but is redeemed by lovable close-ups of mugging wildlife. (Dir: Jamie Uys, 97 mins.)†

Gods of the Plague (West Germany, 1969)***½ Harry Baer, Hanna Schygulla, Margarethe von Trotta, Gunter Kaufmann, Ingrid Craven. Rainer Werner Fassbinder's tribute to American gangster movies; gritty ode to *film noir* is shot in glossy grays and high-contrast lighting. (90 mins.)

Godson, The (France, 1972)***½ Alain Delon, Nathalie Delon. Alain Delon plays a contract killer caught between the police and the syndicate. His isolation is poignantly brought out by the distinguished French director Jean-Pierre Melville. (103 mins.)

Godspell (1973)**½ Victor Garber, David Haskell. The long-running American rock musical, an international hit, comes to the screen as a stimulating if rather long vaudeville turn...based on the Gospel according to St. Matthew. (Dir: David Greene, 103 mins.)

God Told Me To—See: **Demon, The**

Godzilla series. The big green lizard with the radioactive breath first appeared in a serious Japanese film, *Gojira*, in which he pointedly symbolized the destruction wreaked on Japan by the atom bomb. It was only released in this country in a truncated version called *Godzilla, King of the Monsters*, but the original was one of the biggest popular and critical hits of all time in Japan. After a few appearances, Godzilla became a "good" monster, called out to save the Earth from a "bad" monster in a fight that invariably wiped out most of the city of Tokyo. Aside from the films listed below, Godzilla also stomps through *Gigantis, The Fire Monster, King Kong vs. Godzilla, Ghidrah the Three-Headed Monster, Son of Godzilla, Destroy All Monsters*, and *Terror of Mechagodzilla*.

Godzilla, King of the Monsters (Japan, 1954)**½ Raymond Burr, Takashi Shimura, Momoko Kochi. Godzilla's first appearance is so far above the later entries that it hardly seems fair to mention it as part of the same series. A blatant symbol of the atomic bomb, the ancient monster rises from the sea and blindly destroys everything in its path. Unfortunately, the original Japanese version is still not generally available, although it was shown briefly in 1982;

this version, prepared for American audiences, cut 20 minutes and added absurd footage of Raymond Burr as a reporter and commentator. (Dir: Inoshiro Honda, 80 mins.)†

Godzilla 1985 (Japan, 1985)* Raymond Burr, Keiju Kobayashi, Ken Tanaka. This was supposed to be the new, serious Godzilla—no more of that kiddie matinee, guy-in-the-lizard-suit stuff. Burr ought to play Perry Mason and defend poor Godzilla against the damage this script did to his comeback. (Dir: Kohji Hashimoto, 91 mins.)†

Godzilla Raids Again (Japan, 1959)** Hiroshi Koizumi, Setsuko Wakayama. The first of numerous sequels to the original *Godzilla* finds our old scaly friend trashing the city of Osaka after being awakened by atomic testing. Originally released as *Gigantis the Fire Monster*, due to legal difficulties. (Dirs: Motoyoshi Odo, Hugo Grimaldi, 78 mins.)†

Godzilla's Revenge (Japan, 1969)* Kenji Sahara, Tomonori Yazaki. Easily the silliest of the Godzilla movies, and that's saying something. An unhappy young boy dreams about going to Monster Island and taking lessons in self-respect from Minya, the son of Godzilla, who is having similar problems. (Dir: Inoshiro Honda, 92 mins.)

Godzilla vs. Megalon (Japan, 1976)* Katsunikio Sasaki, Hiroyuki Kawase. A lot of junky Japanese monsters gang up on each other, but Godzilla gets the upper claw with a new super-duper robot to help him. (Dir: Jun Fukada, 80 mins.)

Godzilla vs. Monster Zero (Japan, 1966)* Nick Adams, Akira Takarada. An alien planet wants to borrow Godzilla and Rodan to defeat Monster Zero, better known as Ghidrah. Or are the space guys really after total domination of Planet Earth? AKA: **Monster Zero**. (Dir: Inoshiro Honda, 90 mins.)†

Godzilla vs. Mothra—See: **Godzilla vs. the Thing**

Godzilla vs. the Bionic Monster—See **Godzilla vs. the Cosmic Monster**

Godzilla vs. the Cosmic Monster (Japan, 1977)** Masaaki Daimon, Kazuma Aoyama. This time it's a giant mechanical replica of Godzilla, forged by aliens, that takes on the famed monster. He's assisted by a friendly, furry creature and the result is a passable monster mash. (Dir: Jun Fukada, 82 mins.)†

Godzilla vs. the Sea Monster (Japan, 1966)** Akira Takarada, Toru Watanabe. The kids will enjoy this tale of the giant prehistoric monster who goes around doing good. In this one he and the special-effects men wage a battle with an evil giant shrimp. AKA: **Ebirah, Horror of the Deep.** (Dir: Jun Fukuda, 88 mins.)†

Godzilla vs. the Smog Monster (Japan, 1972)** Pollution spawns a monster who spews smog until Godzilla comes to the rescue. Don't inhale! (Dir: Yoshimitsu Banno, 87 mins.)†

Godzilla vs. the Thing (Japan, 1964)*½ Mothra fights the giant reptile Godzilla, and the kiddies might be thrilled by this English-dubbed monstrosity. AKA: **Godzilla vs. Mothra.** (Dir: Inoshiro Honda, 90 mins.)

Go for Broke (1951)*** Van Johnson. The exploits of the 442nd Regimental Combat Team, which was comprised of Nisei (Americans of Japanese ancestry), are graphically portrayed in this above-average drama set in Italy and France during WWII. (Dir: Robert Pirosh, 92 mins.)†

Gog (1954)**½ Richard Egan, Constance Dowling, Herbert Marshall. Scientists working on a prototypical space station discover a mysterious pattern of sabotage, seemingly controlled by a giant computer. Low-budget but very well-done science fiction, shot in 3-D and Technicolor. (Dir: Herbert L. Strock, 85 mins.)

Go! Go! Go! World (Italy, 1964)** One of the better attempts to duplicate *Mondo Cane*, this features the usual sleazy assortment of weird and woolly oddities and horrors of life in the "civilized" world. The snotty, condescending narration is a drawback. (Dirs: Antonio Margheriti, Renato Marvi, 85 mins.)†

Goha (France-Tunisia, 1957)*** Omar Cherif (Sharif), Zina Bouzaiane, Lauro Gazzolo, Garriel Jabbour. Arab folk tale expertly filmed in gorgeous color in exotic locations tells fable of handsome young man who pretends to be stupid in order to steal the bride of the town's wise man. Cherif is terrific, just as he would be years later after changing his name to Sharif and gaining world fame. (Dir: Jacques Baratier, 90 mins.)

Goin' Coconuts (1978)½ Donny Osmond, Marie Osmond, Herb Edelman, Harold Sakata, Kenneth Mars. Rancid chase comedy. Donny and Marie play themselves badly, as Marie's necklace is sought by thieves in Hawaii. The worst thing to happen to Hawaii since Don Ho's tiny bubbles. (Dir: Howard Morris, 93 mins.)

Going Ape (1981)½ Tony Danza, Jessica Walter, Danny DeVito, Art Metrano, Stacey Nelkin. Putrid monkeyshines, with Danza inheriting a fortune if he plays nursemaid to three orangutans. Sometimes it's hard to tell the cast from the monkeys. (Dir: Jeremy J. Kronsberg, 87 mins.)†

Going Berserk (1983)½ John Candy, Joe Flaherty, Eugene Levy. Uninspired lunacy involving three of TV's SCTV vets. This broad comedy, in which Candy plays a chauffeur who saves his politician father-in-law from a quasi-religious cult, is a series of loosely structured gags in search of a movie to give them some body. (Dir: David Steinberg, 85 mins.)†

Going for the Gold: The Bill Johnson Story (MTV 1985)**½ Anthony Edwards, Dennis Weaver, Wayne Northrop. The tale of a hot dog skier, a one-time car thief, who tells the world he's going to win the gold at the Olympic downhill in Sarajevo, and then does it. (Dir: Don Taylor, 104 mins.)†

Going Hollywood (1933)*** Marion Davies, Bing Crosby, Fifi D'Orsay, Stuart Erwin, Ned Sparks, Patsy Kelly. Bubbly parody of thirties movie-making as starry-eyed Davies shucks off her stuffy career and takes off for Tinseltown. (Dir: Raoul Walsh, 80 mins.)

Going Home (1971)** Robert Mitchum, Brenda Vaccaro, Jan-Michael Vincent. Ineffective drama tries to analyze the effect on a boy of seeing his mother die after being stabbed by his father. Performances by Mitchum, Vaccaro, and Vincent help but can't save this entry. (Dir: Herbert Leonard, 97 mins.)

Going in Style (1979)***½ Art Carney, George Burns, Lee Strasberg. A refreshingly low-key comedy-drama in which three old men, who feel life has passed them by, decide to pull off a bank heist. Superbly acted, this is one of the few Gray Power movies that isn't condescending to old people. (Dir: Martin Brest, 97 mins.)†

Going My Way (1944)*** Bing Crosby, Barry Fitzgerald, Gene Lockhart, Rise Stevens, William Frawley, Carl "Alfalfa" Switzer. Although its classic status has slipped a few notches, this remains a lightweight, enjoyable comedy-drama with music. Winning an Oscar, Crosby plays a priest with some new-fangled ideas about revitalizing a New York parish presided over by crusty but lovable Fitzgerald. Sequel: *Bells of St. Mary's.* (Dir: Leo McCarey, 130 mins.)†

Going Places (France, 1974)***½ Jeanne Moreau, Gerard Depardieu, Patrick Dewaere, Miou-Miou, Brigitte Fossey. A compelling, maddening comedy-drama about two Rabelaisian louts who steal, fornicate, and generally act like swine all over France. But somehow director Bertrand Blier has managed to combine many disparate elements into a disturbing, provocative tapestry. (117 mins.)†

Going Steady (1958)**½ Molly Bee, Alan Reed, Jr. High school seniors keep their marriage a secret until the bride becomes pregnant. Cute comedy-drama, nothing sensational but entertaining. (Dir: Fred F. Sears, 79 mins.)†

Going to the Chapel (MTV 1988)*½ Barbara Billingsley, Eileen Brennan, Joel Brooks, Michele Green, Cloris Leachman, Scott Valentine, Max Wright, Dick Van Patten, John Ratzenberger, Mark-Linn Baker. All-star TV cast plays two feuding families with a son and a daughter who want to marry. Only Brennan recognizes dumb comedy for what it is and plays wonderfully around it. (Dir: Paul Lynch, 96 mins.)

Going Undercover (1988)* Chris Lemmon, Jean Simmons, Lea Thompson, Viveca Lindfors, Nancy Cartwright. Would-be private eye Lemmon, hired to chaperone rich bitch Thompson through Europe, has to save her after she is kidnapped. Lousy comedy was made in 1984 but unreleased until '88. It should have stayed undercover. (Dir: James Kenelm Clarke, 88 mins.)†

Goin' South (1978)**½ Jack Nicholson, Mary Steenburgen, Christopher Lloyd, John Belushi. Nicholson directs this often charming romantic western and plays a death-row thief saved from the gallows by a prudish woman (Steenburgen) who is willing to marry him so he can work in a mine she owns. (105 mins.)†

Goin' to Town (1935)*** Mae West, Paul Cavanagh. As the wealthy widow of an oil man, Mae is at her sexy, satirical best as she tries to "bust" into society. This contains the magnificent scene where she throws an operatic evening for her Newport friends, and sings the title role in Massenet's "Samson et Delilah," with fervor and considerable authority. (Dir: Alexander Hall, 74 mins.)

Go Into Your Dance (1935)**½ Al Jolson, Ruby Keeler. A fairly pedestrian musical. Keeler, then Jolson's wife, makes a game effort to dance and is charmingly clumsy. Jolson dominates the vehicle, and the "I'm a Latin from Manhattan" and "About a Quarter to Nine" numbers are memorable. (Dir: Archie Mayo, 89 mins.)

Go, Johnny, Go! (1958)*½ Alan Freed, Jimmy Clanton, Sandy Stewart, Ritchie Valens, Jackie Wilson, Chuck Berry, JoAnn Campbell, The Cadillacs. Orphan boy is aided by a disc jockey on the road to stardom as he becomes a big-time pop singer. (Dir: Paul Landres, 75 mins.)†

Gold (Great Britain, 1974)* Roger Moore, Susannah York, Bradford Dillman, Ray Milland, John Gielgud. A ridiculous thriller. Moore is the hero, dragged unwit-

tingly into a nefarious plot to boost prices on the world gold market. Filmed on location in the mines of South Africa. (Dir: Peter Hunt, 120 mins.)

Goldbergs, The (1950)*** Gertrude Berg, Philip Loeb, Eli Mintz, Betty Walker, Barbara Rush, David Opatoshu. Warm and funny film version of classic radio and television program about Bronx family and its bedrock mother, Molly. Who can ever forget her calling: "Yoohoo, Mrs. Bloom?" Terrific stuff, wonderfully acted. (Dir: Walter Hart, 83 mins.)

Gold Diggers of 1933 (1933)***½ Warren William, Joan Blondell, Aline MacMahon, Ruby Keeler, Dick Powell, Ginger Rogers. The movie for which Busby Berkeley designed some of his best-known mad dance numbers. Berkeley's inspirations include pattern dancing with neon violins and the famous "Remember My Forgotten Man" finale. Blondell and William make a surprisingly steamy team, MacMahon slings the wisecracks, Keeler and Powell are in love, and Ginger Rogers sings "We're in the Money" in pig Latin. (Dir: Mervyn Le Roy, 96 mins.)†

Gold Diggers of 1935 (1935)*** Dick Powell, Ruby Keeler, Adolphe Menjou, Gloria Stuart, Alice Brady, Hugh Herbert, Glenda Farrell, Frank McHugh, Wini Shaw. Directed entirely by Busby Berkeley (his first solo as choreographer and director), this tart musical features some of his best numbers, including the ludicrous but lovely "The Words Are in My Heart" with its waltzing pianos, and Berkeley's masterpiece, "Lullaby of Broadway," a complete story in itself about a day in the life of a Manhattan playgirl. The plot concerns dithery Hugh Herbert as a stooge and Alice Brady as a scrooge, both of whom are ripe for fleecing, with some of the money earmarked to produce the proverbial big musical show. Silly, tuneful, and entertaining. (98 mins.)

Gold Diggers of 1937 (1936)**½ Dick Powell, Joan Blondell, Victor Moore, Jane Wyman, Osgood Perkins. Above-average musical with a fair score and a good assist from Moore as a none-too-healthy millionaire. (Dir: Lloyd Bacon, 101 mins.)

Golden Age of Comedy, The (1957)**** A welcome nostalgic glimpse of some of the screen's funniest scenes featuring the all-time great clowns of Hollywood—Charlie Chaplin, Laurel and Hardy, Keystone Kops, Will Rogers, plus others. (Dir: Robert Youngson, 79 mins.)†

Golden Arrow, The (1936)** Bette Davis, George Brent, Eugene Pallette, Dick Foran. Flimsy but fetching romantic comedy buoyed by Davis, who is knocked down a few pegs by virile reporter Brent. They enter a marriage of convenience that naturally leads to love. (Dir: Alfred E. Green, 68 mins.)

Golden Arrow, The (Italy, 1964)* Tab Hunter, Rossana Podesta. Romantic fantasy with Tab Hunter as the handsome young prince who disguises himself as a beggar to try to gain the hand of a voluptuous princess. (Dir: Antonio Margheriti, 91 mins.)

Golden Blade, The (1953)** Rock Hudson, Piper Laurie. Costume nonsense in old Baghdad with Rock seeking to avenge the death of his father and meeting Princess Piper—all this and a magic sword yet. (Dir: Nathan Juran, 81 mins.)

Golden Boat, The (1990)*** Michael Kirby, Federico Muchnik, Michael Stumm. Hip, off-beat yarn about a mysterious weirdo who, while not killing victims in Lower Manhattan, stalks two young men he claims are his sons. Appearances by directors Jim Jarmusch and Barbet Schroeder. (Dir: Raul Ruiz, 83 mins.)

Golden Boy (1939)*** William Holden, Barbara Stanwyck, Adolphe Menjou, Lee J. Cobb. Clifford Odets' brilliant fight drama has lost some of its wallop in forty years. Still worth seeing for direction and performances, particularly for the supporting cast. Holden's first big break. (Dir: Rouben Mamoulian, 100 mins.)†

Golden Child, The (1986)*½ Eddie Murphy, Charles Dance, Charlotte Lewis, Victor Wong, J. L. Reate, Randall "Tex" Cobb. Lame attempt to cross-breed Murphy's smart comedy flair with an exotic Spielbergian adventure film. He plays Chandler Jarrell, a social worker who specializes in helping missing kids. Apparently Chandler is destined to rescue the Golden Child, a mystical kiddie who can save the world from evil (but not, apparently, from calculated hokum like this). (Dir: Michael Ritchie, 93 mins.)†

Golden Coach, The (Italy, 1952)***½ Anna Magnani, Duncan Lamont, Nada Fiorelli, Odoardo Spandaro. Magnificent story of actress (Magnani) touring Peru with celebrated troupe, wooed by a bullfighter and nobleman. Jean Renoir's film is filled with great characters and grand style. (101 mins.)†

Golden Earrings (1947)**½ Ray Milland, Marlene Dietrich. A British spy is hidden by a gypsy girl in this aimless comedy that was quite successful when it was released. (Dir: Mitchell Leisen, 95 mins.)

Golden Eye, The (1948)*½ Roland Winters, Victor Sen Yung, Tim Ryan. The slippage of quality in the Chan series continued with this programmer set in a tapped-out gold mine in Arizona. Chan mines a solution to a mystery involving an elaborate smuggling operation. (Dir: William Beaudine, 69 mins.)

Golden Gate (MTV 1981)* Perry King, Richard Kiley, Jean Simmons, Mary Crosby, John Saxon. Unsold pilot about a San Francisco publishing clan. Clumsy and poorly acted. (Dir: Paul Wendkos, 104 mins.)

Golden Gate Murders, The (MTV 1979)** David Janssen, Susannah York. The murder mystery aspects of this film are routine, but romance blossoms between a hard-nosed detective (Janssen) and a nun (York). (Dir: Walter Grauman, 104 mins.)

Goldengirl (1979)** Susan Anton, Curt Jurgens, Harry Guardino, James Coburn, Leslie Caron. Anton is adequate in her starring debut focusing on a scientist (Jurgens) who subjects his daughter to dangerous drugs, transforming her into an abnormally tall Olympic track star, but with tragic results. (Dir: Joseph Sargent, 104 mins.)†

Golden Girl (1951)**½ Mitzi Gaynor, Dale Robertson, Dennis Day, James Barton. If you disregard the cornball plot about the ups and downs a dancer named Lotta Crabtree (Miss Gaynor) has during the Civil War and just watch Mitzi dance and listen to Dennis Day sing, this film can be fun. (Dir: Lloyd Bacon, 108 mins.)

Golden Horde, The (1951)** Ann Blyth, David Farrar. Overproduced epic about the barbaric sweep of Genghis Khan out of Asia. Miss Blyth is sorely miscast as a voluptuous princess of Samarkand who falls in love with a visiting crusader named Sir Guy (David Farrar). (Dir: George Sherman, 77 mins.)

Golden Idol, The (1954)*½ Johnny Sheffield, Anne Kimbell, Paul Guilfoyle, Smoki Whitfield. Tired retread in which Bomba has to retrieve a priceless statue stolen from the Watusis. (Dir: Ford Beebe, 71 mins.)

Golden Madonna, The (Great Britain, 1949)**½ Phyllis Calvert, Michael Rennie. Artist and a girl attempt to retrieve a valuable painting that was accidentally sold in Italy. Pleasant romantic comedy-drama. (Dir: Ladislas Vajda, 88 mins.)

Golden Mask, The (Great Britain, 1952)**½ Van Heflin, Wanda Hendrix, Eric Portman. Reporter accompanies an expedition seeking buried treasure in North Africa. Fairly exciting melodrama with fine location backgrounds. (Dir: Jack Lee, 88 mins.)

Golden Mistress, The (1954)**½ John Agar, Rosemarie Bowe. Treasure hunters incur voodoo vengeance when they steal an idol. (Dir: Joel Judge, 83 mins.)

Golden Moment, The: An Olympic Love Story (MTV 1980)*½ Stephanie Zimbalist, David Keith, Richard Lawson, Victor French, Jack Palance. A story of the all-consuming desire to win a gold medal in the 1980 Moscow Olympics plus a predictable romance between a young American decathlon athlete (Keith) and a pretty Russian gymnast (Zimbalist). (Dir: Richard C. Sarafian, 199 mins.)

Golden Needles (1974)* Elizabeth Ashley, Burgess Meredith, Joe Don Baker, Ann Sothern. The "needles" refer to acupuncture, and the opening setting is Hong Kong for this absurd combination of karate and Fu Manchu. (Dir: Robert Clouse, 92 mins.)

Goldenrod (MTV 1977)**½ Tony Lo Bianco, Gloria Carlin. Story about a rodeo star on the Canadian circuit, circa 1950s, whose career experiences ups, downs, and ups. (Dir: Harvey Hart, 106 mins.)†

Golden Salamander, The (Great Britain, 1950)*** Trevor Howard, Anouk Aimée. British archaeologist goes to North Africa to collect valuable antiques, gets mixed up in gun running. Exciting, well-made melodrama. (Dir: Ronald Neame, 96 mins.)

Golden Seal, The (1983)**½ Steve Railsback, Michael Beck, Penelope Milford, Torquil Campbell, Seth Sakai. Heart-tugging adventure tale of a boy's plight to rescue a golden seal from extinction. The boy's relationship with this unique animal is well rendered, and the attempts of mercenary grownups to destroy his animal friend add excitement. (Dir: Frank Zuniga, 94 mins.)†

Golden Voyage of Sinbad, The (1974)** John Phillip Law, Caroline Munro, Tom Baker. Seafaring adventurer sails to find a golden crown. Along the way, he meets a nasty sorcerer and assorted monsters. The special effects are good, but the story and acting are only average. Strictly for kids. (Dir: Gordon Hessler, 105 mins.)†

Goldfinger (Great Britain, 1964)***½ Sean Connery, Honor Blackman, Gert Frobe, Bernard Lee. One of the best of the early James Bond adventures, with Connery in fine form as our hero, more than enough gimmickry and gadgetry to satisfy series fans, and Gert Frobe providing one of Bond's most memorable foes as Auric Goldfinger, whose plans to relieve Fort Knox of its gold can only be stopped by 007. (Dir: Guy Hamilton, 108 mins.)†

Goldie and the Boxer (MTV 1980)** O. J. Simpson, Melissa Michaelsen, Vincent

Gardenia, Gordon Jump. The story, set in the forties, concerns a down-and-out boxer, Joe Gallagher (O. J.), who returns to the ring managed by a cute little girl (Michaelsen). A hokey fairy tale drenched in "you can do it" sentimentality. (Dir: David Miller, 104 mins.)

Goldie and the Boxer Go to Hollywood (MTV 1981)**½ O. J. Simpson, Melissa Michaelsen. The unlikely but loving couple continue their adventures in Tinsel Town while trying to hide from a promoter out to get O. J. and the adoption board. (Dir: David Miller, 104 mins.)

Gold Is Where You Find It (1938)**½ George Brent, Olivia de Havilland, Claude Rains, Margaret Lindsay, John Litel, Barton MacLane. Viewers can glean some good entertainment from this action-tale about feuding miners and farmers, because the cast is pure gold. A standard Warner Brothers adventure, but the actors transform the dross into watchable melodrama. (Dir: Michael Curtiz, 90 mins.)

Gold of Naples, The (Italy, 1955)***½ Sophia Loren, Vittorio De Sica, Toto, Silvana Mangano. Four generally well-done stories about life in Naples. (Dir: Vittorio De Sica, 107 mins.)

Gold of the Amazon Women (MTV 1979)½ Anita Ekberg, Bo Svenson, Donald Pleasence. It's sexpot Anita Ekberg's comeback. In this drivel, she plays the queen of an Amazon tribe in South America who holds the key to a treasure in gold sought by a group of eager adventurers. (Dir: Mark Lester, 104 mins.)†

Gold of the Seven Saints (1961)*½ Clint Walker, Roger Moore, Chill Wills, Leticia Roman. Several bands of outlaws chase a pair of rich trappers over hill and dale. For diehard western chase fans only. (Dir: Gordon Douglas, 88 mins.)

Gold Raiders (1951)** George O'Brien, The Three Stooges (Moe Howard, Larry Fine, Shemp Howard), Sheilah Ryan, Monte Blue, Lyle Talbot. Obscure Stooges comedy with a western setting casts them as sidekicks to an insurance agent trying to protect shipments of gold from outlaws. The Stooges were at their best in shorts; a feature is too long to endure their antics. (Dir: Edward Bernds, 56 mins.)†

Gold Rush, The (1925)**** Charles Chaplin, Mack Swain, Tom Murray. One of the greatest comedies ever. Using the backdrop of the Klondike, Chaplin combines a touching love story with some of the funniest scenes ever filmed. Includes the classic dance where Chaplin uses two bread rolls, and the pantomime sequence where he eats an old shoe. (Dir: Charles Chaplin, 100 mins.)†

Gold Rush Maisie (1940)** Ann Sothern,

Lee Bowman, Virginia Wiedler, John J. Hamilton, Mary Nash, Slim Summerville, Scotty Beckett. Pert Maisie Ravier, show biz's most determined trouper, ends up stranded in a mining camp where she catches gold fever. Her boundless enthusiasm nets her no treasures, but she does manage to find farm work for an indigent family. (Dir: Edward L. Marin, 82 mins.)

Goldstein (1965)**½ Lou Gilbert, Ellen Madison, Philip Kaufman, Nelson Algren, Severn Darden. Off beat entry based on a story by Martin Buber. Symbolic comedy about a bedraggled modern-day prophet who rises out of a lake near Chicago to wander the city streets. Episodic, at times very witty. (Dirs: Benjamin Manaster, Philip Kaufman, 85 mins.)

Goldwyn Follies, The (1938)*** Adolphe Menjou, the Ritz Brothers, Vera Zorina, Kenny Baker, Edgar Bergen, Charlie McCarthy, Bobby Clark. A big musical, without much inspired comedy but with good production numbers. The last score by George Gershwin, featuring many superb songs, including "Love Walked In," "Love Is Here to Stay." Choreography by George Balanchine. (Dir: George Marshall, 115 mins.)†

Golem, The (Germany, 1920)**** Paul Wegener, Albert Steinruck, Ernst Deutsch, Lyda Salmonova. Silent horror masterpiece about 16th-century Polish rabbi who makes a monster out of clay to help his people fight the Emperor's expulsion of Jews from the Prague ghetto. Still-eerie film features stunning Expressionistic sets designed by Hans Poelzig. (Dirs: Carl Boese, Paul Wegener, 75 mins.)†

Golgotha (France, 1935)**½ Robert Le Vigan, Jean Gabin, Charles Granval, Harry Baur, Andre Bacque. Reverent but overproduced account of events leading up to the crucifixion and resurrection of Jesus Christ. Goes for spectacle rather than feeling, though it's certain not to offend anyone. (Dir: Julien Duvivier, 97 mins.)†

Goliath Against the Giants (Italy, 1961)*½ Brad Harris, Gloria Milland. His kingdom is in jeopardy from rascally ministers, so Goliath swings into action. We root for the giants in these films. (Dir: Guido Malatesta, 90 mins.)

Goliath and the Barbarians (Italy, 1960)*½ Steve Reeves, Chelo Alonso, Bruce Cabot. Rebels led by muscleman Reeves battle savage hordes who have been terrorizing the land. Typical spectacle with the usual assortment of battles. (Dir: Carlo Campogalliani, 86 mins.)†

Goliath and the Dragon (Italy, 1960)*½ Mark Forrest, Broderick Crawford, Eleanora Ruffo. Muscleman goes through a variety of supertests to save the land from an evil ruler. Outlandish English-dubbed spectacle—amusing novelty seeing Crawford as corrupt politician in costume. (Dir: Vittorio Cottafavi, 87 mins.)†

Goliath and the Vampires—See: **Vampires, The**

Goliath at the Conquest of Damascus (Italy, 1964)* Rock Stevens, Helga Line. Muscleman leads an army against savage marauders no differently than a thousand other inept English-dubbed spectacles. (Dir: Domenico Paolella, 80 mins.)

Goliath Awaits (MTV 1981)* Mark Harmon, Christopher Lee, Eddie Albert, John Carradine, Robert Forster, Emma Samms, Alex Cord, Frank Gorshin. Unbelievable tale about some people trapped on the ocean's floor for over forty years and how they relate to the explorers who discover them and want to bring them up for air. (Dir: Kevin Connor, 200 mins.)

Goliath, the Rebel Slave (Italy, 1963)*½ Gordon Scott, Massimo Serrato. Once again the musclebender rights wrongs and brings peace in his time. (Dir: Mario Caiano, 80 mins.)

Go, Man, Go (1954)**½ Dane Clark, Sidney Poitier, Pat Breslin. Promoter gets an idea for an all-Negro basketball team, which becomes the Harlem Globetrotters. Sports fans should get a boot out of the fast court scenes; for others, an interesting drama. (Dir: James Wong Howe, 82 mins.)

Gomar the Human Gorilla—See: **Night of the Bloody Apes**

Go Naked In the World (1961)*½ Gina Lollobrigida, Anthony Franciosa, Ernest Borgnine. Histrionics dominate in this tale of a high-class prostitute who comes between (not literally) father and son. Gina is attractive, but all that yelling . . . ! (Dir: Ronald MacDougall, 103 mins.)

Gone Are the Dayes (MCTV 1984)** Harvey Korman, Susan Anspach, Robert Hogan, Bibi Besch. Korman is a police lieutenant who is assigned to protect the Dayes, a family that witnessed a mob killing. However, the Dayes are trying to get away from both the hoods and the police detective. Innocuous chase comedy. (Dir: Gabrielle Beaumont, 90 mins.)†

Gone Are the Days (1963)***½ Ossie Davis, Ruby Dee, Godfrey Cambridge, Alan Alda. Screen version by Ossie Davis of his Broadway hit, *Purlie Victorious;* a brash, satiric swipe at racism and Uncle Tomism in the South by updating Negro folk tales to contemporary struggles. Farcical lampoon, topicality, and energetic acting make for good entertainment. (Dir: Nicholas Webster, 100 mins.)

416

Gone In 60 Seconds (1974)**½ Toby Halicki, Marion Busia, James McIntire, George Cole, Jerry Daugirda, Parnelli Jones, Gary Bettenhausen. Worldwide box office smash treated with scorn in the U.S., but director-star H.B. "Toby" Halicki was doing something right. Standard drama a setup for absolutely wild, forty-minute chase sequence which is as good as they get. (103 mins.)†

Gone to Earth (Great Britain, 1950)*** Jennifer Jones, Cyril Cusack, Sybil Thorndike, David Farrar. A strange Welsh girl (Jones) in the late 19th century, who is dominated by superstition and an attachment to her pet fox, marries a minister but has stirrings for the manly squire (Farrar). It's ripe material—uneven, but worth seeing. AKA: **The Wild Heart**. (Dirs: Michael Powell, Emeric Pressburger, 110 mins.)

Gone with the Wind (1939)**** Clark Gable, Vivien Leigh, Leslie Howard, Olivia de Havilland, Hattie McDaniel, Butterfly McQueen, Thomas Mitchell, Ona Munson, Ann Rutherford, Evelyn Keyes, George Reeves, Laura Hope Crews. This landmark film, based on Margaret Mitchell's mammoth novel, won eight Academy Awards. The siege of Atlanta and the hardships of the South during the Civil War are masterfully unfolded in this terrific spectacle. Leigh's performance is fetching as Scarlett O'Hara, and Gable still makes the ladies' hearts flutter as Rhett Butler. Part spectacle, part history, a dash of biography, and all smashing entertainment. Although Victor Fleming is credited as director, many other cooks worked on this broth, including George Cukor, William Cameron Menzies, Selznick himself, and Sam Wood. (Dir: Victor Fleming, 219 mins.)†

Gong Show Movie, The (1980)* Chuck Barris, Robin Altman, Jaye P. Morgan, Rip Taylor. The string of outrageously bad musical and comedy acts are much more sexually explicit than those seen on the TV series, and are tied to a plot about host Barris's nervous breakdown. Give it the gong! (Dir: Chuck Barris, 89 mins.)†

Gonza the Spearman (Japan, 1986)*** Hiromi Goh, Shima Iwashita, Shohej Hino, Misako Tanaka. Adaptation of a Chikamatsu *bunraku* play tells the story of an ambitious bodyguard who agrees to marry the daughter of an absent lord in order to increase his social standing, even though he had previously promised to marry another. Somewhat complicated, careful tale of love and honor with a shockingly violent climax. (Dir: Masahiro Shinoda, 121 mins.)†

Good Against Evil (MTV 1977)* Dack Rambo, Elyssa Davalos, Dan O'Herlihy.

Exorcist rip-off in which a young lady (Elyssa Davalos) has been selected for the Devil. (Dir: Paul Wendkos, 79 mins.)

Goodbye Again (1961)** Ingrid Bergman, Yves Montand, Anthony Perkins. Ingrid as a "mature" interior decorator who enters into an affair with "young American boy" Perkins. Romantic drama on the tedious side, based on Françoise Sagan's novel. (Dir: Anatole Litvak, 120 mins.)

Goodbye Charlie (1964)* Debbie Reynolds, Tony Curtis, Walter Matthau, Pat Boone. Debbie plays the reincarnation of a woman-chasing Casanova named Charlie in an awful screen transfer of a sleazy Broadway flop. (Dir: Vincente Minnelli, 116 mins.)

Goodbye Columbus (1969)*** Richard Benjamin, Ali MacGraw, Jack Klugman, Nan Martin, Michael Meyers. Successful adaptation of Philip Roth's acclaimed novella about Jewish life in the Bronx in the 1950s. So much of the film is charming, observant, and accurate that one can forgive the lapses from director Larry Peerce. Screen debut for Benjamin, deftly playing a college dropout who meets the stylish Ali at a country club. (105 mins.)†

Goodbye Girl, The (1977)*** Richard Dreyfuss, Marsha Mason, Quinn Cummings. Oscar-winning Dreyfuss and playwright Neil Simon are an unbeatable combination in this enjoyable romantic comedy set in New York. Mason is a Broadway chorine whose lover skipped town and sold his apartment lease to Dreyfuss, a stage actor from Chicago trying to make it in the big city. The trouble is, Mason and her worldly ten-year-old daughter (Cummings) are still in the apartment. (Dir: Herbert Ross, 110 mins.)†

Goodbye, Mr. Chips (Great Britain, 1939)**** Robert Donat, Greer Garson, John Mills, Paul Henreid. Story of the life of an English schoolteacher taken from the James Hilton novel is brilliant screen entertainment. Donat's Oscar-winning portrayal of the lovable Mr. Chips is an acting masterpiece. (Dir: Sam Wood, 114 mins.)†

Goodbye, Mr. Chips (1969)** Peter O'Toole, Petula Clark, Michael Redgrave. Mundane musical remake. O'Toole plays the shy professor who falls in love with a musical-comedy actress, complete with outlandish friends and a racy past. (Dir: Herbert Ross, 151 mins.)

Goodbye, My Fancy (1951)**½ Joan Crawford, Robert Young, Eve Arden. Bright comedy-drama about a lady politician who returns to her alma mater to receive an honorary degree and digs up a lot of old scandals. Based on the Broadway

success. (Dir: Vincent Sherman, 107 mins.)

Goodbye, My Lady (1956)**½ Walter Brennan, Brandon de Wilde, Phil Harris, Sidney Poitier. A family movie about an old man, a young boy, and a dog who live through adventures that would make Huck Finn's mouth water. (Dir: William Wellman, 94 mins.)†

Goodbye, New York (1985)*** Julie Hagerty, Amos Kollek, David Topaz. Multi-talented Kollek produced, wrote, directed, and starred in this low-budget delight. A yuppie American Princess sleeps through her scheduled landing, and lands in hot water in Israel, sans money or baggage. (90 mins.)†

Goodbye, Norma Jean (1975)* Misty Rowe, Terence Locke, Patch Mackenzie, Stuart Lancaster. Depressingly sleazy, and highly fictionalized, biography of Marilyn Monroe in her pre-star days. Ten years later producer-director Larry Buchanan recut it and added thirty minutes of new footage to come up with a "sequel," *Goodnight, Sweet Marilyn*. (95 mins.)†

Goodbye People, The (1986)*** Judd Hirsch, Martin Balsam, Pamela Reed, Ron Silver, Gene Saks. Sentimental neurotic comedy about a hot dog vendor, his insecure daughter, and a banjo-plucking stranger who strums his way into their Coney Island existence. (Dir: Herb Gardner, 105 mins.)†

Good Companions, The (Great Britain, 1933)*** Edmund Gwenn, John Gielgud, Jessie Matthews. The popular J.B. Priestley novel about itinerant players in the English countryside is given a charming mounting. Stiff-upper-lip cinema at its most authentic, with middle-class virtues snug and transcendent. (Dir: Victor Saville, 113 mins.)

Good Companions, The (Great Britain, 1957)**½ Eric Portman, Celia Johnson, Hugh Griffith. A none-too-satisfactory remake. The two young leads lack the charm and charisma of the '33 stars. Colorful and moderately entertaining. (Dir: J. Lee Thompson, 104 mins.)

Good Dame (1934)**½ Fredric March, Sylvia Sidney, Jack LaRue, Russell Hopton, Walter Brennan. Strong carnival atmosphere and fine performances lift this otherwise ordinary tale of a fast-talking carny barker who doesn't appreciate the loyal girl who loves him until it's almost too late. (Dir: Marion Gering, 74 mins.)

Good Day for a Hanging (1959)** Fred MacMurray, Maggie Hayes, Robert Vaughn. Ex-lawman captures a charming killer, but the townspeople refuse to believe him guilty. Offbeat western moves too slowly, but tries to be different. (Dir: Nathan Juran, 85 mins.)

Good Die Young, The (Great Britain, 1954)**½ Richard Basehart, John Ireland, Gloria Grahame, Margaret Leighton, Laurence Harvey. Four men from assorted backgrounds plan a daring robbery. (Dir: Lewis Gilbert, 100 mins.)

Good Earth, The (1937)**** Paul Muni, Luise Rainer. Pearl Buck's great novel of famine, plague and the fight for survival in China is one of the greatest films Hollywood ever made. Both Muni and Rainer give faultless portrayals in this still wonderful film. (Dir: Sidney Franklin, 138 mins.)†

Good Fairy, The (1935)***½ Margaret Sullavan, Herbert Marshall, Frank Morgan, Alan Hale. Sullavan, one of Hollywood's loveliest actresses, shines as a buttinski who tries to help legal whiz Marshall become a successful attorney. The writer, Preston Sturges, did a wonderful job recreating the spirit of Ferenc Molnar's play, and this assignment helped pave the way for his niche as the premier comedy writer-director of the forties. (Dir: William Wyler, 90 mins.)

Good Father, The (Great Britain, 1986)*** Anthony Hopkins, Jim Broadbent, Harriet Walker, Fanny Viner, Simon Callow, Joanne Whalley. A beautifully textured tale of an angry middle-aged man striking out at the world; Hopkins plays an embittered executive, outwardly successful but inwardly seething over his failed marriage. (Dir: Mike Newell, 90 mins.)†

Goodfellas (1990)**** Robert De Niro, Ray Liotta, Joe Pesci. Director Martin Scorsese brilliantly captures the appeal of the obligatory violence and the almost sensual lure of financial riches in one of the most searing and involving Mafia-gangster films in the history of cinema. Based on author Nicholas Pileggi's 1985 book about a real hoodlum named Henry Hill (Liotta), the film is a little too long and too violent, but you'll be fascinated by the despicable array of low-life rats, virtually all of them superbly acted. Pesci won the Oscar for Best Supporting Actor. (Dir: Martin Scorsese, 146 mins.)†

Good Fight, The (1984)**** Bill Bailey, Milt Wolff. An excellent political documentary about more than 3,000 Americans who joined the Abraham Lincoln Brigade to fight in the Spanish Civil War from 1936–1939. Newsreel clips, anecdotes from veterans, and a Hollywood film, *Blockade*, are deftly edited together to produce this valuable, ennobling history lesson. (Dir: Noel Buckner, 98 mins.)

Good Girls Go to Paris (1939)**½ Joan Blondell, Melvyn Douglas. Waitress with a yen to see Paris tries her wiles on the scion of a social family. Amusing comedy. (Dir: Alexander Hall, 80 mins.)

Good Guys and the Bad Guys, The (1969)**½ Robert Mitchum, George Kennedy, David Carradine, Lois Nettleton, Douglas Fowley. Entertaining western fare with Mitchum as an aging sheriff who teams with his old enemy Kennedy to ward off a planned train robbery. (Dir: Burt Kennedy, 90 mins.)

Good Guys Wear Black (1979)** Chuck Norris, Anne Archer, James Franciscus, Lloyd Haynes, Dana Andrews. Norris has to save America from conspirators with his lethal legs. Flabby plotting, but action galore. (Dir: Ted Post, 96 mins.)†

Good Humor Man, The (1950)*** Jack Carson, Lola Albright. Slapstick all the way—but many funny moments as Jack Carson gets involved with murderers and blondes and the police. (Dir: Lloyd Bacon, 79 mins.)

Good Luck, Miss Wyckoff (1979)* Anne Heywood, Donald Pleasence, Robert Vaughn, Earl Holliman, Dorothy Malone, Carolyn Jones. Dreary adaptation of William Inge novel about the tragic rape of a virginal schoolteacher. Talented cast is at a loss with wretched script and uninspired direction. AKA: **The Sin, The Shaming.** (Dir: Marvin J. Chomsky, 105 mins.)†

Good Morning (Japan, 1959)***½ Chishu Ryu, Kuniko Miyake, Yoshiko Kuga, Keiji Sada, Masahiko Shimazu. Delightful comedy about two little boys who beg their father to buy a television; he refuses, telling them to ''shut up!'' The kids then refuse to speak, refuse even to say ''good morning.'' Director Yasujiro Ozu's mastery of color and the quality of the acting gives film that something special. (97 mins.)

Good Morning . . . and Goodbye! (1967)**½ Alaina Capri, Stuart Lancaster, Pat Wright, Haji, Don Johnson. Perfunctory Russ Meyer movie about middle-aged husband Lancaster's failure to satisfy his young new wife, leading her to sleep around, causing problems in turn for his teenage daughter. (78 mins.)†

Good Morning, Babylon (Italy, 1987)*** Vincent Spano, Joaquim De Almeida, Greta Scacchi, Charles Dance, Omero Antonutti, Desiree Becker. A moving glimpse backward at the inception of the American film industry, seen through the eyes of two Italian brothers who are rescued by fate and given the chance to work on D. W. Griffith's *Intolerance* as set designers. Unfortunately, the celebrated Italian filmmakers, the Tavianis, aren't entirely comfortable working in English. (Dirs: Paolo and Vittorio Taviani, 116 mins.)†

Good Morning, Judge (1943)*** Dennis O'Keefe, Mary Beth Hughes, Louise Albritton, Louise Beavers. A fetching little farce. A song publisher finds himself up against a lady lawyer in a plagiarism suit. Breezy complications abound. (Dir: Jean Yarbrough, 66 mins.)

Good Morning, Miss Dove (1955)**½ Jennifer Jones, Robert Stack. A nostalgic film about a dearly beloved middle-aged school teacher and her effect on her former pupils. (Dir: Henry Koster, 107 mins.)

Good Morning, Vietnam (1987)*** Robin Williams, Forest Whitaker, Tung Thanh Tran, Bruno Kirby, James Edson. Role of an Armed Forces Radio deejay in 1965 Saigon allows Williams to give a hilarious series of semi-improvised shticks, and he also shines in the dramatic parts of the film as his character tries to integrate into a people who would rather see the U.S. out of their country. (Dir: Barry Levinson, 121 mins.)†

Good Mother, The (1988)** Diane Keaton, Liam Neeson, Jason Robards, Ralph Bellamy, James Naughton. A provocative issue—how does a single mother balance her sexual needs with the proper upbringing of her child?—gets shallow treatment here. Keaton's ex-husband alleges that her lover has committed improprieties with their daughter and sues for custody. Badly directed by Leonard Nimoy, who supplies golden hues where grit is needed. (103 mins.)†

Good Neighbor Sam (1964)** Jack Lemmon, Romy Schneider, Dorothy Provine. Seemingly endless comedy about an ad man who has to pose as another woman's husband, the consequences therefrom, etc. Lemmon is funny, but he can't do it without help from the writers, which he doesn't receive here. (Dir: David Swift, 130 mins.)†

Good News (1930)** Bessie Love, Cliff Edwards, Mary Lawlor. Like many early sound movies, this is a transcription of a Broadway musical hit with most of the original cast. The scene is Taft College, and the problem is whether the football star will flunk the exam or play in the big game, and whether the guys will get the girls and vice versa. The De Sylva-Brown-Henderson songs are still hummable: ''The Best Things in Life Are Free'' and ''Varsity Drag.'' (Dirs: Nick Grinde, Edgar J. MacGregor, 90 mins.)

Good News (1947)***½ June Allyson, Peter Lawford, Patricia Marshall, Joan McCracken, Mel Tormé. Taken for granted when first released, this blessedly unpretentious musical ranks with the most pleasurable films in the genre. Lawford's the football player in need of coaching when it comes to finding true love, and Allyson's the tutor who's going to educate him. Snappy nostalgic fun, this quintessential campus musical enchants with its De Sylva-Brown-Henderson score and its stunning choreography by Charles Walters, also making his directorial debut. (95 mins.)

Goodnight, My Love (MTV 1972)**½ Richard Boone, Barbara Bain. The nostalgia craze reaches back to the forties and all those thrillers, with Barbara Bain doubling for Lauren Bacall; Richard Boone playing an older and much heavier version of Bogey's gumshoe; and Michael Dunn cast as his wisecracking dwarf sidekick. Everyone goes around spouting tight-lipped jargon, and even the sinister fat man (Victor Buono) is on hand to complete the picture. (Dir: Peter Hyams, 73 mins.)

Goodnight, Sweet Marilyn (1984)* Paula Lane, Misty Rowe, Jeremy Slate, Phyllis Coates, Stuart Lancaster. Supposedly a revelation of the "real" reasons behind Marilyn Monroe's death, this sleazy drama is a thin excuse to reuse over an hour of footage from *Goodbye, Norma Jean*, schlock producer-director Larry Buchanan's earlier effort to cash in on the Monroe cult. (90 mins.)†

Good Sam (1948)** Gary Cooper, Ann Sheridan, Edmund Lowe, Ray Collins, Joan Lorring. Do-gooder always gets into trouble trying to help others. Good cast can't make up for thin, only occasionally amusing story. (Dir: Leo McCarey, 114 mins.)†

Good Sport, A (MTV 1984)** Lee Remick, Ralph Waite, Janie Sell, Sam Gray. An amiable romantic comedy about a lovable slob of a sportswriter (Waite) and an aloof fashion editor (Remick). Their two worlds collide and, after some self-imposed obstacles, they manage to fall in love. (Dir: Lou Antonio, 104 mins.)

Good, the Bad and the Ugly, The (Italy, 1966)*** Clint Eastwood, Eli Wallach, Lee Van Cleef. The third Eastwood spaghetti western racked up huge box-office receipts in the U.S. and Europe. Wallach mugs delightfully, Van Cleef is evil incarnate, and Eastwood is a fine ambiguous hero. (Dir: Sergio Leone, 161 mins.)†

Good Times (1967)*** Sonny and Cher, George Sanders. Sonny and Cher star in a mad romp in which they play themselves. Sonny wants them to become movie stars, and his fantasies about their would-be films are quite funny. (Dir: William Friedkin, 91 mins.)

Good To Go (1986)**½ Art Garfunkel, Robert Doqui, Harris Yulin, Hattie Winston, Richard Brooks. So-so drama about journalist Garfunkel unjustly accused of rape and murder. Strange mix of police plot and Washington D.C.'s homegrown hip-hop music scene. AKA:

Short Fuse. (Dir: Blaine Novak, 87 mins.)†

Good Wife, The (Australia, 1987)**½ Rachel Ward, Bryan Brown, Sam Neill, Steven Vidler, Jennifer Claire. Ward lends her sensual presence to the role of a sexually frustrated wife who trades in small-town complacency for a passionate affair with the town's hotel barman, after tiring of her husband and brother-in-law. (Dir: Ken Cameron, 92 mins.)†

Goonies, The (1985)*½ Sean Astin, Josh Brolin, Jeff Cohen, Corey Feldman, Kerri Green, John Matuszak, Anne Ramsey, Ke Huy Quan, Martha Plimpton. A crude Spielberg-produced adventure tale about youngsters trying to save their homes from land developers by finding a pirate treasure. The child actors articulate so badly (though loudly) you'll think you wandered into a foreign film without subtitles. (Dir: Richard Donner, 111 mins.)†

Gor (1987)* Urbano Barberini, Rebecca Ferratti, Paul Smith, Oliver Reed. Simpleminded sword'n'sorcery stuff about a college professor transported to the barbarian land of Gor, helping a beautiful princess save a mystic relic from an evil despot. You're right, you've seen it before. Sequel: *Outlaw of Gor.* (Dir: Fritz Kiersch, 94 mins.)†

Gorath (Japan, 1962)** Ryo Ikebe, Akihiko Hirata. Average sci-fi about an enormous planetary body hurtling toward the Earth. More "scientific" than most of this genre. (Dir: Inoshiro Honda, 83 mins.)†

Gordon's War (1973)** Paul Winfield, Carl Lee, David Downing, Grace Jones. A black veteran returns home from Vietnam and learns that his wife has died from a drug overdose. Enraged, he declares war on the Harlem drug lords. (Dir: Ossie Davis, 89 mins.)†

Gore Vidal's Billy the Kid (MTV 1989)**½ Val Kilmer, Duncan Regehr, Julie Carmen, Wilford Brimley, Rene Auberjonois, Michael Parks, Albert Salmi. A gritty and serious look at the mythic aspects of the young gunslinger who fired the imagination of many. Kilmer gives too introspective a performance as Billy, who lived and died by the gun. Scriptwriter Vidal has a cameo as a graveside minister. (Dir: William Graham, 96 mins.)†

Gore Vidal's Lincoln (MTV 1988)*** Sam Waterston, Mary Tyler Moore, John Houseman, Richard Mulligan, John McMartin, Ruby Dee, Cleavon Little. A well-crafted, touching, and unsensationalized view of a seemingly mythic figure in U.S. history. Waterston's profoundly realistic portrayal of Lincoln is low-key but magnetic, and Mary manages to bring humanity to an unsympathetic role. Although occasional liberties are taken, this mini-series presents history without cheapening or overplaying it. (Dir: Lamont Johnson, 192 mins.)

Gorgeous Hussy, The (1936)** Joan Crawford, Franchot Tone, Robert Taylor, Melvyn Douglas, James Stewart, Lionel Barrymore, Louis Calhern. Fictionalized biography of Peggy Eaton, the notorious belle of Washington during Jackson's administration. Picture tells little of her notoriety and emerges as a dull, overly long love story. (Dir: Clarence Brown, 102 mins.)

Gorgo (Great Britain, 1961)*** Bill Travers, William Sylvester, Vincent Winter. Sea monster is captured and put on display in London, but its parent comes after it to wreak havoc on the city. If all those terrible horror thrillers haven't taken the edge off, here's a good one—well made and exciting. (Dir: Eugene Lourie, 78 mins.)†

Gorgon, The (Great Britain, 1964)**½ Peter Cushing, Christopher Lee, Barbara Shelly, Richard Pasco. Village terrorized when murders occur, the victims turned to stone. Well-made horror thriller has its share of suspenseful sequences. (Dir: Terence Fisher, 83 mins.)†

Gorilla, The (1939)** The Ritz Brothers, Anita Louise, Patsy Kelly, Lionel Atwill, Bela Lugosi. Loose-limbed haunted-house spoof in which the Ritz Brothers try to nab a killer. Silly gags with those Ritz crackers at half-mast. (Dir: Allan Dwan, 66 mins.)†

Gorilla at Large (1954)** Anne Bancroft, Cameron Mitchell, Lee J. Cobb, Lee Marvin, Raymond Burr. A murder mystery unfolded amidst the gaudy atmosphere of a cheap carnival. (Dir: Harmon Jones, 84 mins.)

Gorillas in the Mist (1988)**** Sigourney Weaver, Bryan Brown, Julie Harris, John Omirah Miluwi. Beautifully photographed, genuinely moving drama based on the career and abbreviated life of the American anthropologist Dian Fossey, who went to remotest Africa to save the embattled mountain gorilla. Weaver is stunning as the increasingly enraged Fossey, and there's a touching romance involving her with a visiting American photographer working for *National Geographic*. Good script by Anna Hamilton Phelan. (Dir: Michael Apted, 125 mins.)†

Gorky Park (1983)** William Hurt, Lee Marvin, Joanna Pacula, Ian Bannen, Brian Dennehy. Vague and unexciting spy thriller based on the best-seller. A Russian police detective determines to solve a triple murder in Moscow's Gorky Park and uncovers corruption in the Kremlin. Missing are the intense characterizations and detailed descriptions of the Soviet political machine that made the novel so gripping. (Dir: Michael Apted, 130 mins.)†

Gorp (1980)* Michael Lembeck, Dennis Quaid, Philip Casnoff, Rosanna Arquette (debut). Silly shenanigans at a Jewish summer camp in the Catskills. Instead of "Meat Balls," you get "Matzoh Balls." Stale ones. (Dir: Joseph Ruben, 90 mins.)†

Gosh!—See: **Alice Goodbody**

Gospel (1982)***½ The Hawkins Family, the Clarke Sisters, the Mighty Clouds of Joy, James Cleveland, Shirley Caesar. The sheer joyous power of gospel music is displayed in this concert film featuring some of the best performers on the circuit. (Dirs: David Levick, Frederick Ritzenberg, 92 mins.)†

Gospel According to St. Matthew, The (Italy-France, 1964)**** Enrique Irazoqui, Margherita Caruso, Susanna Pasolini. Graphic, rough, fiercely realistic filming of the story of Christ, using only the words and scenes described by St. Matthew. Director Pier Paolo Pasolini, an avowed Marxist and atheist, portrays Christ as a determined revolutionary. The cast, composed only of nonprofessionals, including Pasolini's own mother, is persuasive, visually affecting. (136 mins.)†

Gospel According to Vic, The (Great Britain, 1986)*** Tom Conti, Helen Mirren, Brian Pettifer. Unassuming feel-good comedy. Conti, a skeptical teacher, receives notoriety as the recipient of a "miracle" in this genial exploration of the need to believe in miracles, and also in the faith and hard work it takes to make them happen. (Dir: Charles Gormley, 94 mins.)†

Gossip Columnist, The (MTV 1980)** Kim Cattrall, Bobby Vinton, Robert Vaughn, Martha Raye, Dick Sargent, Bobby Sherman. Geared for those who enjoy glossy soap operas about glamorous people. Cattrall is a young syndicated gossip columnist who uncovers some unethical moves by a Hollywood figure (Vaughn) with his eye on a political career. (Dir: James Sheldon, 104 mins.)

Gotcha (1985)*½ Linda Fiorentino, Anthony Edwards, Nick Corri, Marla Adams, Alex Rocco, Christopher Rydell. A feeble attempt to jazz up the overworked "let's-lose-our-virginity" genre for teens. The convoluted storyline concerns an 18-year-old college kid who graduates from playing "Gotcha," a campus espionage game, into real-life intrigue after being initiated into sex by a woman with ties to European spies. (Dir: Jeff Kanew, 97 mins.)†

Go Tell It on the Mountain (MTV 1985)** Paul Winfield, Rosalind Cash, Ruby Dee, James Bond III, Olivia Cole. James Baldwin's early novel about a Harlem

421

family living, loving, and hating in the 1930s makes an interesting but sporadically effective drama with first-rate acting. (Dir: Stan Lathan, 117 mins.)

Go Tell the Spartans (1978)***½ Burt Lancaster, Craig Wasson, Marc Singer. Lean, intelligent movie about the early days of American advisers in Vietnam. Superlative acting by the three leads, and straightforward direction by Ted Post. (114 mins.)†

Gotham (MCTV 1988)*** Tommy Lee Jones, Virginia Madsen, Colin Bruce, Frederic Forrest. One of the most original, and at times perplexing, movie mysteries of recent years. Jones plays a private eye hired to find a client's missing wife—the only problem being that she's already dead. By turns brilliantly cynical and seemingly pointless. (Dir: Lloyd Fonvielle, 100 mins.)†

Gothic (Great Britain, 1987)** Gabriel Byrne, Julian Sands, Natasha Richardson, Miriam Cyr, Timothy Spall. Stylish and overwrought film, in which director Ken Russell depicts the stormy, drug-ridden get-together of Lord Byron, Percy and Mary Shelley, and some others, on a night that would inspire Mary Shelley to write *Frankenstein*. (90 mins.)†

Go West (1940)**½ Marx Brothers, John Carroll, Robert Barrat. There's a funny opening bit in a ticket office and a systematic disassembling of a moving train at the climax, but the film contains much of the Marx Brothers' weakest material. (Dir: Edward Buzzell, 81 mins.)†

Go West, Young Girl (MTV 1978)**½ Karen Valentine, Sandra Will, Stuart Whitman. Valentine and newcomer Will star in this busted comedy pilot set in the Old West. They play a pair of adventurous ladies who set out to find Billy the Kid. (Dir: Alan J. Levi, 78 mins.)

Go West, Young Man (1936)*** Mae West, Warren William, Randolph Scott, Una Merkel, Elizabeth Risdon. Entertaining comedy about what happens when a screen star makes a personal appearance and is forced to mingle with the common folk. (Dir: Henry Hathaway, 90 mins.)

Goyokin (Japan, 1969)*** Tatsuya Nakadai, Tetsuro Tamba, Kunie Tanaka, Yoko Tsukasha. In the 1830s, a period in which the Japanese social system was breaking down, a former samurai stands with the Shogun government against his brother-in-law, who has stolen a shipment of their gold. (Dir: Hideo Gosha, 124 mins.)

Grace Kelly (MTV 1983)**½ Cheryl Ladd, Lloyd Bridges, Diane Ladd, Alejandro Rey, Ian McShane. Matter-of-fact retelling of the true Cinderella tale of the beautiful girl from Philadelphia who grew up to become an Oscar winner, then princess of the almost mythical kingdom of Monaco. (Dir: Anthony Page, 104 mins.)

Grace Quigley (1985)**½ Katharine Hepburn, Nick Nolte, Elizabeth Wilson, Chip Zein, William Duell, Kit Le Fever. A dotty old widow convinces a hit man to kill off her aged friends who don't want to live anymore. An eccentric and sometimes very effective movie. AKA: **The Ultimate Solution of Grace Quigley**. (Dir: Anthony Harvey, 88 mins.)†

Gracie Allen Murder Case (1939)**½ Gracie Allen, Warren William, Ellen Drew, H. B. Warner, William Demerest. Gracie's many fans will have a picnic watching this silly little murder-mystery. Gracie (George Burns isn't in this one) "helps" veteran film sleuth Philo Vance solve a case. (Dir: Alfred E. Green, 74 mins.)

Graduate, The (1967)**** Dustin Hoffman, Anne Bancroft, Katharine Ross, William Daniels, Murray Hamilton, Norman Fell, Buck Henry. A brilliant, funny, and touching film directed by Mike Nichols, who won an Academy Award for this box-office smash. In his first major role Hoffman is both hilarious and deeply moving as young college graduate who returns to his parents' affluent California swimming-pool world, which he despises, and tries to find his own values. Look for Richard Dreyfuss in a bit part. (105 mins.)†

Graduation Day (1981)*½ Christopher George, Patch MacKenzie, E. Danny Murphy, E. J. Peaker, Michael Pataki, Vanna White. Yet another mad-slasher flick, this one revolving around the death of a high school track star. (Dir: Herb Freed, 85 mins.)†

Graffiti Bridge (1990)* Prince, Ingrid Chavez, Morris Day. Prince's sequel to *Purple Rain* is a major mess. He's part-owner of a nightclub and is constantly fighting with his partner (Day) about the type of entertainment they should feature. There's also an angel who sleeps with Prince and lots of MTV musical numbers. Even Prince's die-hard fans will have trouble sitting through this. (Dir: Prince, 95 mins.)†

Grambling's White Tiger (MTV 1981)* Bruce Jenner, Harry Belafonte, LeVar Burton, Ray Vitte, Deborah Pratt. California quarterback Jenner enrolls in Louisiana's all-black college hoping for a pro football career. A true (but poorly acted) story of reverse integration. (Dir: Georg Stanford Brown, 104 mins.)†

Grand Baby, The (1983)** Esther Rolle, Larry Scott, Whitman Mayo, Max Gail. After his mom dies, a withdrawn boy must cope with a move to a hostile Southern neighborhood. However, when his grandmother's in danger of losing her house, he steels his courage and enlists the entire neighborhood's aid in saving it. (Dir: Henry Johnson, 90 mins.)

Grand Central Murder (1942)*** Van Heflin, Patricia Dane, Cecelia Parker. Private eye solves the murder of an actress in Grand Central Station. Good compact mystery. (Dir: S. Sylvan Simon, 73 mins.)

Grand Highway, The (France, 1988)*** Anémone, Richard Bohringer, Antoine Hubert, Vanessa Guedj. A touching reminiscence from director Jean-Loup Hubert, who cast his son Antoine as Louis, a little boy who has to spend the summer with Mama's best friend and her husband while Mama gives birth. During his stay, Louis learns lots of neat tricks with the local tomboy, and about grown-up behavior from the married couple, who persistently argue to cover up grief for their dead son. Hubert successfully blends comic and tender moments. (Dir: Jean-Loup Hubert, 104 mins.)†

Grand Hotel (1932)**** John Barrymore, Greta Garbo, Lionel Barrymore, Wallace Beery, Joan Crawford, Jean Hersholt, Lewis Stone. This typical MGM superstar vehicle makes for classy entertainment, with John Barrymore as a jewel thief romancing a very tired ballerina played by Greta Garbo. Lionel Barrymore has but months to live, but is making the most of it despite the soggy presence of boss Wallace Beery, a gross industrialist, who is out to bed stenographer Joan Crawford. (Dir: Edmund Goulding, 113 mins.)†

Grand Illusion (France, 1937)**** Jean Gabin, Pierre Fresnay, Erich von Stroheim, Marcel Dalio, Julien Carette, Dita Parlo. A classic. Jean Renoir's study of men in war explores the bonds that bind them: be they national, fraternal, or social-class. The conflicts of these bonds are complex and troubling, and Renoir in all his implacable optimism scants none of these ponderables, though his faith was easier held before the second war than after. (111 mins.)†

Grandma's Boy (1922)*** Harold Lloyd, Mildred Davis, Anna Townsend, Charles Stevenson. Delightful silent comedy, one of Lloyd's classics, has the young hero convinced that he's a coward, unworthy of the girl he loves; his grandmother comes to his rescue with a charm that will give him courage. Like all of Lloyd's comedies, it's not just a laugh a minute, but full of warmth, perception, and human feeling. (Dir: Fred Newmeyer, 81 mins.)

Grandmother's House (1989)*** Eric Foster, Kim Valentine, Brinke Stevens, Ida Lee. Two youngsters are sent to live with their grandparents after their father's death leaves them orphaned. But something's not quite right in this house,

as the kids learn when they discover a woman held hostage. Nifty suspenser is full of surprises right up to the end. (Dir: Peter Rader, 89 mins.)†

Grand Prix (1966)**½ James Garner, Eva Marie Saint, Yves Montand, Toshiro Mifune, Brian Bedford. Sappy story about the European auto racing circuit, greatly aided by some magnificent shots of the racing itself, and what it feels like to be traveling well over 100 miles an hour going around sharp turns. The racing scenes are among the best ever to hit the screen. (Dir: John Frankenheimer, 179 mins.)†

Grand Slam (1933)**½ Loretta Young, Paul Lukas, Frank McHugh, Glenda Farrell, Helen Vinson, Ferdinand Gottschalk, Roscoe Karns. Romantic comedy of a couple who parlay their skill at bridge into a big money career; this parody of the then-epidemic bridge craze is still original and amusing. (Dir: William Dieterle, 67 mins.)

Grand Slam (Italy-France-West Germany, 1967)*** Edward G. Robinson, Adolfo Celi, Janet Leigh, Robert Hoffman, Klaus Kinski. A professor and a gangster embark on a split-second scheme to heist some diamonds. Perfect-crime capers demand ingenuity and suspense for success, and this has both. (Dir: Giuliano Montaldo, 120 mins.)

Grand Theft Auto (1977)**½ Ron Howard, Nancy Morgan, Marion Ross, Leo Rossi. Too many car chases and crashes, but this is an amiable enough comedy. Howard is eloping with lovely heiress Morgan and the whole city of Los Angeles seems to be in pursuit of the lovebirds. (Dir: Ron Howard, 89 mins.)†

Grandview, U.S.A. (1984)** Jamie Lee Curtis, Patrick Swayze, C. Thomas Howell, Jennifer Jason Leigh. Small-town Americana about a demolition derby and the pangs of adolescence. Lots of flashy visuals and the usual busy music soundtrack used to fill in the plot holes. (Dir: Randal Kleiser, 98 mins.)†

Grapes of Wrath, The (1940)**** Henry Fonda, Jane Darwell, John Carradine, Charley Grapewin, Dorris Bowden, John Qualen. John Steinbeck's novel of impoverished migratory workers and their struggle to get to California and find work is one of the all-time great films. John Ford's direction and a superb cast make this story of a group of people who were almost destroyed by the Depression a "must." Oscars for Ford and Darwell. (128 mins.)†

Grasshopper, The (1970)***½ Jacqueline Bisset, Jim Brown, Joseph Cotten. Remarkable, neglected film about how a young girl eager to enter show business ends up a marginal entertainer, and then a wasted, common whore. (Dir: Jerry Paris, 95 mins.) †

Grass Is Always Greener over the Septic Tank, The (MTV 1978)**½ Carol Burnett, Charles Grodin, Alex Rocco. From Erma Bombeck's witty best-selling novel, which unfortunately reads better than it plays. Writer-mother-wife-and-chief-bottle-washer Dorothy Benson (Burnett), her ad agency exec husband (Grodin), and their two kids leave New York City for the supposedly good life of the suburbs and encounter one pitfall after another. (Dir: Robert Day, 104 mins.) †

Grass Is Greener, The (1960)*** Cary Grant, Deborah Kerr, Jean Simmons, Robert Mitchum. Martini-dry comedy about an American millionaire who complicates the wedded bliss of an English couple. Overdose of brittle Noël Cowardish dialogue makes the pace slow but the cast is good, the production attractive. (Dir: Stanley Donen, 105 mins.) †

Grass Is Singing, The—See: **Killing Heat, The**

Grave of the Vampire (1973)*** Michael Pataki, William Smith. Nightmarish horror-chiller that can't quite sustain the tension level of its opening sequence in which a vampire-on-the-prowl rapes a girl in a graveyard. After the unfortunate woman gives birth to a demi-vampire, the film becomes bizarre and heart-breaking as she gives her lifeblood to nurse her thirsty infant. A complex, low-budget item that ultimately becomes a revenge melodrama as the son goes after his ruthless vampiric Papa. (Dir: John Hayes, 95 mins.) †

Graveyard of Horror (Spain, 1971)* Bill Curran, Beatriz Lacy, Victor Israel. Badly dubbed, incoherent Spanish horror about a man investigating the death of his wife. (Dir: Miguel Madrid, 88 mins.) †

Graveyard Shift (1987)**½ Silvio Oliviero, Helen Papas, Cliff Stokes, Dorin Ferber, Dan Rose. Interesting, if not always successful, attempt to do something different with a vampire movie. This bloodsucker sucker is a New York cabbie who considers reforming when he falls in love with a dying woman. Bleak and stylish, though occasionally simple for its own sake. (Dir: Gerard Ciccoritti, 87 mins.) †

Graveyard Shift II—See: **The Understudy: Graveyard Shift II.**

Graveyard Shift (1990)*½ David Andrews, Kelly Wolf, Stephen Macht, Brad Dourif, Andrew Divoff. Less-than-satisfactory horror film based on a short story by Stephen King. The reopening of a long-dormant textile mill leads to the discovery of leftovers from a nearby cemetery. All rather redundant. (Dir: Ralph S. Singleton, 95 mins.) †

Gravy Train—See: **Dion Brothers, The**

Grayeagle (1978)** Ben Johnson, Iron Eyes Cody, Lana Wood, Jack Elam, Paul Fix, Alex Cord. Traditional western tale with a strong script, but indifferent direction. A westerner searches for the Indian who kidnapped his daughter years before. (Dir: Charles B. Pierce, 104 mins.)

Gray Lady Down (1978)**½ Charlton Heston, Stacy Keach, David Carradine, Ned Beatty. Technocratic thriller—well mounted, logically paced—about a downed submarine slipping off the continental shelf and the rescue operation attempting against time to raise it. (Dir: David Greene, 111 mins.) †

Grease (1978)** John Travolta, Olivia Newton-John, Stockard Channing, Jeff Conaway, Dinah Manoff, Didi Conn. High-kicking greasers drift through high school, more concerned with romance than studying in a film filled with pleasant pop tunes and lots of sexual innuendo. (Dir: Randal Kleiser, 110 mins.) †

Grease 2 (1982)*½ Maxwell Caulfield, Michelle Pfeiffer, Adrian Zmed, Lorna Luft, Didi Conn. A strained attempt to keep the money rolling in with a sequel. This time it's 1961 at Rydell High, with a new group of students causing mayhem. (Dir: Patricia Birch, 115 mins.) †

Greased Lightning (1977)*** Richard Pryor, Pam Grier, Beau Bridges, Cleavon Little, Richie Havens. Pryor gives an authoritative performance in this respectful biography of Wendell Scott, the first black professional racing-car driver, who started out running moonshine before WWII and battled prejudice for many years before being allowed to race against whites. (Dir: Michael Schultz, 96 mins.) †

Greaser's Palace (1972)** Albert Henderson, Michael Sullivan, Luana Anders, Toni Basil. Robert Downey, gifted director of *Putney Swope*, has become self-indulgent. Allegorical story of Jesus. Full of parody and bright ideas which never conquer or compete with the dreariness of the symbolism. (91 mins.) †

Great Alligator, The (Italy, 1981)*½ Barbara Bach, Mel Ferrer, Richard Johnson. In this predictable horror film, tourists frolic on a picturesque isle while the natives summon up a tribal god. (Dir: Sergio Martino, 80 mins.) †

Great American Beauty Contest, The (MTV 1973)**½ Louis Jourdan, Eleanor Parker, Robert Cummings, Joanna Cameron, Farrah Fawcett. Behind-the-scenes drama about the beauty-contest business complete with proposed hanky-panky between judge and contestant. (Dir: Robert Day, 73 mins.)

Great American Broadcast, The (1941)*** Alice Faye, Jack Oakie, John Payne, Cesar Romero. History of radio is used as a background for a tuneful film, loaded with specialty acts. Jack Oakie is at his best and this one is grand entertainment. (Dir: Archie Mayo, 92 mins.)

Great American Cowboy, The (1974)***½ Larry Mahan, Phil Lyne. Academy Award–winning documentary about the hardships and rewards of the rodeo circuit, follows two stars as they prepare for competition. (Dir: Kieth Merrill, 90 mins.)†

Great American Pastime, The (1956)** Tom Ewell, Anne Francis, Ann Miller, Dean Jones. Moderately entertaining comedy about a suburban lawyer who becomes manager of his son's little-league team. (Dir: Herman Hoffman, 89 mins.)

Great American Traffic Jam, The (MTV 1980)** John Beck, Shelley Fabares, Marcia Wallace, Lisa Hartman, Vic Tayback. A gridlocked melodrama about a traffic controller who puts his marriage on the "off-ramp" while he tries to untangle a monumental traffic jam. AKA: **Gridlock**. (Dir: James Frawley, 104 mins.)†

Great American Tragedy, A (MTV 1972)*** George Kennedy, Vera Miles, William Windom, James Woods. Story about a successful aerospace engineer whose life undergoes a complete reversal when he's fired from the job he has held for twenty years. This modern-day dilemma has been explored in documentaries, but the dramatic treatment it receives here drives the facts home. Above average. (Dir: J. Lee Thompson, 73 mins.)

Great Balloon Adventure, The—See: **Olly Olly Oxen Free**

Great Balls of Fire (1989)**½ Dennis Quaid, Wynona Ryder, John Doe, Stephen Tobolowsky, Trey Wilson, Alec Baldwin, Lisa Blount, Mojo Nixon, Peter Cook, Joe Bob Briggs. Somehow this biography of primal rock'n'roller Jerry Lee Lewis managed to miss 95 percent of the drama in "The Killer"'s dark and troubled life, concentrating only on his fall from grace after he married his thirteen-year-old cousin. The film has energy and style, but Quaid's impersonation of Lewis is distractingly weird. (Dir: Jim McBride, 109 mins.)†

Great Bank Hoax, The (1979)**½ Richard Basehart, Burgess Meredith, Paul Sand, Ned Beatty, Michael Murphy.. A tidy comedy that didn't get much notice in its brief theatrical release. The story concerns the bumbling officers of a small-town Georgia bank, who stage a fake robbery to cover up their embezzlement. (Dir: Joseph Jacoby, 89 mins.)†

Great Bank Robbery, The (1969)** Kim Novak, Clint Walker, Zero Mostel. Although this comedy-western boasts the presence of Mostel as a wily would-be bank robber and a plot that sounds like it can't miss, it peters out long before it gets up a full head of steam. The yarn is about three separate plans to rob a top-security bank in the western town of Friendly, circa 1880. (Dir: Hy Averback, 98 mins.)

Great Battle, The (West Germany-Yugoslavia, 1979)*½ Helmut Berger, Samantha Eggar, Stacy Keach, Henry Fonda, John Huston, Giuliano Gemma, Edwige Fenech. Narrated by Orson Welles. Set during the last North African campaign of WWII, with action centering on the German Panzer Corps in Tunisia. Sloppily assembled international production. AKA: **Battleforce** and **Battle of the Mareth Line**. (Dir: "Humphrey Longan" [Umberto Lenzi], 97 mins.)†

Great British Train Robbery, The (West Germany, 1965)*** Horst Tappert, Hans Cossy, Isa Miranda, Gunther Neutze. Despite the improbable idea of having Germans recreate the famous British train robbery of 1963, the attempt comes off. Crisp, realistic, well-paced—and nonviolent. Originally made for West German TV. (Dirs: John Olden, Clause Peter Witt; 104 mins.)

Great Caruso, The (1951)*** Mario Lanza, Ann Blyth. Screen biography of the noted opera tenor was a fitting vehicle for Lanza and his powerful voice. Music devotees should revel in the many songs, arias presented. Others should find it a well-made, consistently interesting drama. (Dir: Richard Thorpe, 109 mins.)†

Great Cash Giveaway Getaway, The (MTV 1980)*½ George Hamilton, Albert Salmi, James Keach, Elissa Leeds. Teenagers run off with funds from a drug ring and embark on a spending spree. (Dir: Michael O'Herlihy, 104 mins.)

Great Catherine (Great Britain, 1968)**½ Peter O'Toole, Jeanne Moreau, Zero Mostel, Jack Hawkins, Akim Tamiroff. Mostel is marvelously funny in this sporadically entertaining adaptation of George Bernard Shaw's one-act play, *Whom Glory Still Adores*. Moreau, playing Catherine, is overshadowed by the maniacal Mostel. (Dir: Gordon Flemyng, 98 mins.)

Great Chase, The (1962)**½ Compilation of old films stressing the action elements; scenes of Fairbanks, William S. Hart, Lillian Gish, many others. (Compiled by Paul Killiam, 77 mins.)†

Great Dan Patch, The (1949)** Dennis O'Keefe, Gail Russell, Ruth Warrick. The story of the greatest trotting horse of them all, told through the family who owned him. Mild, slow, but of some interest to horse lovers. (Dir: Joseph M. Newman, 94 mins.)

Great Day in the Morning (1956)**½ Virginia Mayo, Robert Stack, Ruth Roman,

Raymond Burr. The loyalties of an assortment of townspeople are tested when the Civil War breaks out. Slightly offbeat western drama with good performances, some above-average touches in the direction. (Dir: Jacques Tourneur, 92 mins.)†

Great Diamond Robbery, The (1953)** Red Skelton, Cara Williams, James Whitmore, Steven Geray, Dorothy Stickney. Diamond cutter falls into the clutches of crooks who try to fleece him of his money. Ordinary comedy is beneath the talents of those involved. (Dir: Robert Z. Leonard, 69 mins.)

Great Dictator, The (1940)**** Charlie Chaplin, Jack Oakie, Paulette Goddard, Reginald Gardiner, Billy Gilbert, Maurice Mosovich, Henry Daniell. Chaplin in his famous dual role: as a poor Jew in a ghetto, and as Adenoid Hynkel, The Great Dictator. There is a mistaken-identity plot, and Jack Oakie is on hand as Napoloni. The picture is like all Chaplin, very funny and very trenchant. (Dir: Charlie Chaplin, 128 mins.)†

Great Escape, The (1963)**** Steve McQueen, James Garner, Charles Bronson, James Coburn, David McCallum, Donald Pleasence, Richard Attenborough. A fine, big blockbuster of a movie about Allied prisoners attempting a daring escape from a POW camp during WWII. The entire cast is top-notch, and the action builds from the very beginning to the exciting climax. Watch for Steve McQueen's mad motorcycle dash for safety, one of the most hair-raising action sequences ever filmed. (Dir: John Sturges, 168 mins.)†

Greatest, The (1977)**½ Muhammad Ali, Ernest Borgnine, John Marley, Lloyd Haynes, Robert Duvall, James Earl Jones, Paul Winfield. Biographical film of the celebrated, outspoken heavyweight champ. Ali plays himself reasonably well. Ponderous screenplay trots out too many fight-yarn clichés. (Dir: Tom Gries, 101 mins.)†

Greatest Gift, The (MTV 1974)*** Glenn Ford, Julie Harris, Lance Kerwin. Don't let the sanctimonious title put you off, this is a lovely made-for-TV movie reminiscent of *To Kill a Mockingbird*. It's all about life in the South back in 1940, as seen through the eyes of a thirteen-year-old boy who thinks his preacher father is the greatest man in the world. (Dir: Boris Sagal, 100 mins.)

Greatest Love, The—See: **Europa 51**

Greatest Show on Earth, The (1952)***½ James Stewart, Charlton Heston, Betty Hutton, Cornel Wilde, Gloria Grahame, Henry Wilcoxon, Lyle Bettger, Lawrence Tierney, Dorothy Lamour.... Or, director Cecil B. DeMille visits the circus, resulting in the Big Top show to end 'em all. Splendiferous production of circus life captures all the thrills and excitement, plus a storyline that holds it all together capably. Entertainment plus. Oscars: Best Picture, Best Story. (153 mins.)†

Greatest Story Ever Told, The (1965)* Max von Sydow, Telly Savalas, Dorothy McGuire, Charlton Heston, Jose Ferrer, Claude Rains, Van Heflin, Robert Loggia, Sidney Poitier, John Wayne, many more. Director George Stevens's folly, in its full, elephantine length. An unnerving roster of cameo appearances tends to undermine the sincerity of the biblical proceedings, which are spectacular and spectacularly dull. Shown on TV at 141 mins.; 196 mins. on video. (225 mins.)†

Greatest Thing That Almost Happened, The (MTV 1977)** Jimmie Walker, James Earl Jones, Deborah Allen. Walker flounders in the serious role of a young basketball player stricken with leukemia; Jones is his widowed dad. (Dir: Gilbert Moses, 104 mins.)

Great Expectations (Great Britain, 1946) **** John Mills, Valerie Hobson, Finlay Currie, Alec Guinness, Bernard Miles, Francis L. Sullivan, Jean Simmons, Martita Hunt. The Dickens classic of the young orphan lad whose path crosses that of an escaped convict who aids him in the world. Faithfully transcribed, painstakingly produced, superlatively directed, acted, photographed. A film great. (Dir: David Lean, 115 mins.)

Great Expectations (U.S.-Great Britain, MTV 1974)**½ Michael York, Sarah Miles, James Mason, Margaret Leighton, Robert Morley, Anthony Quayle, Rachel Roberts. A reasonably good remake of the Dickens classic. (Dir: Joseph Hardy, 103 mins.)

Great Flamarion, The (1945)**½ Erich von Stroheim, Mary Beth Hughes, Dan Duryea. A vaudeville trick-shot artist is tricked by a woman into murdering her husband, while she beats it with another man. Standard melodrama, made palatable by von Stroheim's fine acting. (Dir: Anthony Mann, 78 mins.)

Great Flirtation, The (1934)**½ Elissa Landi, Akim Tamiroff, Adolphe Menjou, David Manners, Lynne Overman, Raymond Walburn. A great Hungarian actor and his actress-wife come to the U.S. When the thespian goes to audition, he finds that he's an unknown. Moderately entertaining. (Dir: Ralph Murphy, 71 mins.)

Great Gabbo, The (1929)*** Erich von Stroheim, Betty Compson, Don Douglas, Betty Bronson, Margie Kane. This is von Stroheim's first talking film, and he gives a fascinating performance as a disgruntled ventriloquist. Based on a story by Ben Hecht. (Dir: James Cruze, 96 mins.)†

Great Gambini, The (1937)** Akim Tamiroff, Marion Marsh, Genevieve Tobin, William Demarest, Reginald Denny, Roland Drew. Mind reader predicts an inevitable murder and then has to solve the crime. Fair Grade B whodunit, but you won't need a crystal ball to figure out whodunit. (Dir: Charles Vidor, 70 mins.)

Great Garrick, The (1937)*** Brian Aherne, Olivia de Havilland, Edward Everett Horton, Lionel Atwill, Marie Wilson, Lana Turner. Ponderous, moderately entertaining biography of famous actor David Garrick. (Dir: James Whale, 91 mins.)

Great Gatsby, The (1949)**½ Alan Ladd, Betty Field, Barry Sullivan, Ruth Hussey, Macdonald Carey, Shelley Winters, Howard Da Silva. Alan Ladd is not half the actor Robert Redford is, but at least casting him as Gatsby in this version displayed sensitivity for what the role is all about. This is an intelligent attempt that fails through lack of ambition. (Dir: Elliott Nugent, 92 mins.)

Great Gatsby, The (1974)*** Robert Redford, Mia Farrow, Karen Black, Sam Waterston, Bruce Dern, Scott Wilson, Howard Da Silva, Edward Herrmann, Patsy Kensit. Classy adaptation of F. Scott Fitzgerald's enduring novel about the Beautiful People of rich WASP society in New York and Long Island of the 1920s. Redford is such a skillful actor that you tend to overlook the fact that he's a mite too genteel and civilized, given Gatsby's modest background and hustling business career with bootlegging connections. There are numerous flaws in the film but director Jack Clayton has caught the look and sometimes the feel of this rich if emotionally impoverished crowd. (144 mins.)†

Great Gilbert and Sullivan, The (Great Britain, 1953)***½ Maurice Evans, Robert Morley, Eileen Herlie, Peter Finch. The biography of the leading exponents of light operetta who established a legion of worshippers. Elaborately produced, finely portrayed, with many scenes of their most famous works well represented. (Dir: Sidney Gilliat, 105 mins.)

Great Gildersleeve, The (1942)** Harold Peary, Jane Darwell, Charles Arnt. Peary re-creates his role as the always-in-a-jam character from radio's "Fibber McGee" show in this comedy that will appeal mostly to those in a nostalgic mood. (Dir: Gordon Douglas, 61 mins.)

Great Gundown, The (1977)*½ Robert Padilla, Malila St. Duval, Richard Rust, Steven Oliver. Extremely violent western with "The Savage" (Padilla) leading a gang of guns-for-hire in search of villainous Rust. Not much plot, but plenty of shooting. (Dir: Paul Hunt, 95 mins.)†

Great Guns (1941)** Stan Laurel, Oliver Hardy, Sheila Ryan, Dick Nelson, Edmund MacDonald. When their employer joins the Texas cavalry, gardener Stan and chauffeur Ollie enlist in order to stay with him. Lesser Laurel and Hardy comedy doesn't have enough good gags for a feature film. Look for Alan Ladd in a bit part. (Dir: Monty Banks, 73 mins.)†

Great Guy (1937)*** James Cagney, Mae Clarke, James Burke, Matty Fain. Cagney is an ex-prizefighter who still enjoys using his fists to clean up graft in high places. He holds the exalted title of Chief Inspector of the Department of Weights and Measures, and the results are as typically and enjoyably Cagney-esque as any of his thirties vehicles. (Dir: John G. Blystone, 75 mins.)

Great Houdinis, The (MTV 1976)**½ Paul Michael Glaser, Sally Struthers, Ruth Gordon, Vivian Vance, Bill Bixby, Adrienne Barbeau, Peter Cushing, Nina Foch. Paul Michael Glaser is well cast as Harry Houdini, the arrogant performer who rose from a third-rate vaudevillian to the rank of internationally famous escape artist. (Dir: Melville Shavelson, 108 mins.)

Great Ice Rip-Off, The (MTV 1974)**½ Lee J. Cobb, Gig Young. A standard caper. Young plays a leader of a small gang of jewel thieves. Cobb is a retired cop. (Dir: Dan Curtis, 72 mins.)

Great Impersonation, The (1935)** Edmund Lowe, Valerie Hobson, Wera Engels, Spring Byington. Fair spy thriller with Lowe in a dual role, playing both a German munitions man and an English nobleman. Plenty of complicated intrigue, but not many thrills. (Dir: Alan Crosland, 67 mins.)

Great Impostor, The (1961)**½ Tony Curtis, Edmond O'Brien, Arthur O'Connell, Karl Malden, Gary Merrill, Joan Blackman, Raymond Massey. Based on the life story of Ferdinand Demara, con artist supreme, who takes on different professions and personalities. Curtis has a field day in this uneven but generally satisfying tale. (Dir: Robert Mulligan, 112 mins.)†

Great Jewel Robber, The (1950)* David Brian, Marjorie Reynolds, Jacqueline de Wit. Tedious account of an inept thief who almost gets caught every time he attempts a robbery. (Dir: Peter Godfrey, 91 mins.)

Great John L., The (1945)*** Greg McClure, Linda Darnell, Barbara Britton. The biography of the great heavyweight champ (John L. Sullivan), as he rises to the top and falls from the heights to drunkenness and disgrace. Nicely done, with exciting, often hilarious ring sequences. (Dir: Frank Tuttle, 96 mins.)

Great Lie, The (1941)**½ Bette Davis, George Brent, Mary Astor, Lucille Watson, Grant Mitchell, Hattie McDaniel. Mary has a child by George, who is Bette's husband, and Bette raises the child as her own, which is the great lie. Very talky, never compelling but soap opera fans may like it. Astor won a Supporting Actress Oscar. (Dir: Edmund Goulding, 107 mins.)†

Great Locomotive Chase, The (1956)** Fess Parker, Jeffrey Hunter, Jeff York, Claude Jarman, Jr. Big Fess Parker cuts an imposing figure playing a Union soldier who leads a dangerous mission behind the Confederate lines in order to destroy strategic railroad bridges. Fair Civil War outing. AKA: **Andrews' Raiders.** (Dir: Francis D. Lyon, 85 mins.)†

Great Lover, The (1949)*** Bob Hope, Rhonda Fleming, Roland Young. Another of Hope's smooth comic performances in this typical funny Hope film filled with intrigue, beautiful women, and enough plot twists to make you dizzy. (Dir: Alexander Hall, 80 mins.)†

Great Man, The (1957)*** Jose Ferrer, Dean Jagger, Julie London. Fairly honest treatment of Al Morgan novel about a ruthless TV personality who was loved by his public and despised by the people who really knew him. Ferrer plays a reporter who sets out to find out about "The Great Man" after his untimely death. (Dir: Jose Ferrer, 92 mins.)

Great Man's Lady, The (1942)**½ Barbara Stanwyck, Joel McCrea, Brian Donlevy, Katherine Stevens. Occasionally entertaining story of a greedy man who struck it rich in silver and the lady who guided him to the straight and narrow. With all the trimming, it's little more than a mediocre western. (Dir: William Wellman, 90 mins.)

Great Man's Whiskers, The (MTV 1973)**½ Dean Jones, Dennis Weaver. Old-fashioned drama about a young girl's letter to President Lincoln suggesting he grow whiskers to hide his look of sadness. The best part—an ingratiating meeting between Lincoln and the youngster—comes in the last act. (Dir: Philip Leacock, 99 mins.)

Great Man Votes, The (1939)**** John Barrymore, Virginia Weidler. Scholar who has turned to drink reforms when the Children's Society threatens to take away his offspring. Superb drama, with moments of high comedy; fine performances, a gem of a movie. (Dir: Garson Kanin, 70 mins.)

Great McGinty, The (1940)***½ Brian Donlevy, Akim Tamiroff, Muriel Angelus, William Demarest, Allyn Joslyn. Fable about the rise of a dumb guy to the governor's mansion is delightful entertainment and Donlevy is superb in the title role. (Dir: Preston Sturges, 81 mins.)†

Great McGonagall, The (Great Britain, 1975)*½ Spike Milligan, Peter Sellers, Julia Foster, John Bluthal, Victor Spinetti. Impenetrably weird comedy from the ever-odd Milligan, here playing an unemployed Scotsman with a new aim in life: to become Britain's poet laureate. Like a single Goon Show or Monty Python sketch that refuses to end; Milligan's indecipherable Scottish accent doesn't help. Sellers plays Queen Victoria, and even that gets tiresome soon. (Dir: Joe McGrath, 95 mins.)

Great Missouri Raid, The (1950)** Macdonald Carey, Ellen Drew, Wendell Corey. Modernized retelling of the story of Frank and Jesse James, fifties style. Attempt at deeper characterization still doesn't lift this above the familiar western rut. (Dir: Gordon Douglas, 83 mins.)

Great Moment, The (1944)**½ Joel McCrea, Betty Field, Harry Carey, Franklin Pangborn, Grady Sutton, William Demarest. Story of the Boston dentist who was first to use ether is well done, but not a particularly outstanding biography. (Dir: Preston Sturges, 83 mins.)†

Great Mouse Detective, The (1986)***½ Voices of Vincent Price, Barrie Ingham, Val Bettin, Alan Young. The new generation of Disney animators have created an entertaining and richly detailed cartoon that successfully mixes the studio's old magic with a humorous modern sensibility. The film follows the thrilling adventures of a miniscule Sherlockian sleuth who attempts to foil a takeover of England's royal rodent family. Well-paced fun that's sure to please everyone. (Dirs: John Musker, Ron Clements, Dave Michener, Burny Mattison, 72 mins.)†

Great Muppet Caper, The (1981)*** The Muppeteers (Jim Henson, Frank Oz, Dave Goelz, Jerry Nelson, Richard Hunt), Diana Rigg, Charles Grodin, John Cleese, Robert Morley, Peter Ustinov, Jack Warden, Peter Falk. Hot on the trail of thieves who've stolen the Fabulous Baseball Diamond, The Muppets make this London-set sequel to *The Muppet Movie* fun for all. The Miss Piggy-Kermit romance is less cloying, the Joe Raposo score is more hummable, and the human actors blend in delightfully. (Dir: Jim Henson, 95 mins.)†

Great Niagara, The (MTV 1974)**½ Richard Boone, Michael Sacks, Randy Quaid. Adventure yarn set in the Depression era of a prideful old man (Richard Boone) and his dominance over his two sons who don't want to follow in their father's footsteps. (Dir: William Hale, 72 mins.)

Great Northfield Minnesota Raid, The (1972)*** Robert Duvall, Cliff Robertson,

Luke Askew, R. G. Armstrong. Writer-director Philip Kaufman has created a quirky anti-western about the last hurrah of the James and Younger gangs, when they launched an ill-fated holdup far north of their usual turf. Kaufman's wit, his interweaving of mood, character, and motif, and the mass of bizarre and hilarious detail help to overcome the bland familiarity of the material. (104 mins.) †

Great Outdoors, The (1988)*½ John Candy, Dan Aykroyd, Stephanie Faracy, Annette Bening, Robert Prosky. Writer-producer John Hughes reprises his National Lampoon *Vacation* movies in this shtick-in-the-mud comedy about two families sharing a cabin in the woods during a summer holiday. Candy is always watchable, but even his fans should detour away from this. (Dir: Howard Deutch, 90 mins.) †

Great Profile, The (1940)** John Barrymore, Mary Beth Hughes, John Payne, Anne Baxter. Sad to see the greatest of them all in a Grade B comedy, supposedly about his own backstage shenanigans. (Dir: Walter Lang, 82 mins.)

Great Race, The (1965)***½ Tony Curtis, Jack Lemmon, Natalie Wood, Peter Falk, Keenan Wynn, Arthur O'Connell, Ross Martin, Vivian Vance, Dorothy Provine. The cast plus an extravagant production are the stars of this farce, which chronicles the first New York-to-Paris car race in the early 1900s. Lemmon and Falk are the show-stealers as the evil (but dumb) villains racing against squeaky-clean Curtis. (Dir: Blake Edwards, 150 mins.) †

Great Rupert, The (1950)**½ Jimmy Durante, Terry Moore. Jimmy and a friendly squirrel combine talents to make happiness. Slim story tied to Durante antics. Amusing. (Dir: Irving Pichel, 86 mins.)

Great Santini, The (1979)***½ Robert Duvall, Blythe Danner, Michael O'Keefe. A powerful, sensitive family drama concerning a professional warrior (Duvall) who finds his only battle plan for dealing with his family during peacetime is evasive action. Duvall's Marine Corps fighter pilot is a vivid, tightly held portrayal of a man who brooks no rebellion at home but is egged on by his own internal contradictions to self-destructive rebellion. (Dir: Lewis John Carlino, 118 mins.) †

Great Scout and Cathouse Thursday, The (1976)½ Lee Marvin, Elizabeth Ashley, Kay Lenz, Oliver Reed, Robert Culp. Vulgar, disjointed western comedy inhabited by such characters as a lesbian madam, a half-breed Indian who's a Harvard graduate, a teenage prostitute, and a money-hungry Indian scout, among others. (Dir: Don Taylor, 102 mins.) †

Great Sinner, The (1949)** Gregory Peck, Ava Gardner, Melvyn Douglas, Walter Huston, Ethel Barrymore, Frank Morgan, Agnes Moorehead. Uncredited adaptation of Dostoevsky's story "The Gambler" casts Peck as the great writer(!), lured into the world of gambling when he tries to rescue his future father-in-law from his own debts. Thin drama with camp appeal for students of Russian literature. (Dir: Robert Siodmak, 110 mins.)

Great Sioux Massacre, The (1965)** Joseph Cotten, Darren McGavin, Philip Carey. A low-budget western that attempts, once again, to tell the story behind Custer's last stand. (Dir: Sidney Salkow, 91 mins.)

Great Sioux Uprising, The (1953)** Jeff Chandler, Faith Domergue. Routine western produced on a big scale with the accent on action. A former Union officer almost single-handedly prevents a "great Sioux uprising." (Dir: Lloyd Bacon, 80 mins.)

Great Skycopter Rescue, The (1982)* Aldo Ray, William Marshall, Terry Micos, Terri Taylor, Russell Johnson. Designers of an experimental aircraft use it to fight off villains trying to take over a small town. Viewers will need rescuing after about ten minutes. (Dir: Lawrence D. Foldes, 96 mins.)

Great Smokey Roadblock, The (1976)** Henry Fonda, Eileen Brennan, Robert Englund, John Byner, Dub Taylor, Susan Sarandon, Melanie Mayron. A down-on-his-luck truck driver burns rubber to make one last haul before the truck company can take his rig away. A middle-aged *Smokey and the Bandit*. AKA: **The Last of the Cowboys.** (Dir: John Leone, 84 mins.) †

Great Spy Mission, The—See: Operation Crossbow

Great St. Louis Bank Robbery, The (1959)** Steve McQueen, David Clarke, Molly McCarthy, Graham Denton. An early McQueen effort—he's a football hero who goes wrong and becomes involved in the plot of the title. Filmed on location, it has a gritty realism, but slack pacing. (Dirs: Charles Guggenheim, John Stix, 86 mins.)

Great St. Trinian's Train Robbery, The (Great Britain, 1966)** Frankie Howerd, Reg Varney, Desmond Walter Ellis, Cyril Chamberlain, Dora Bryan. Last and least of the *St. Trinian's* movies pits the monstrous little schoolgirls against a group of thieves who have stored $7 million in their school. (Dirs: Frank Launder, Sidney Gilliat, 94 mins.) †

Great Train Robbery, The (Great Britain, 1979)***½ Sean Connery, Lesley Anne Down, Donald Sutherland, Alan Webb. Immensely entertaining fluff about the first train robbery, masterminded by rogue

429

Sean Connery in 1855. (Dir: Michael Crichton, 111 mins.)†

Great Train Robbery, The: The Cinema Begins (1895–1922)**** Three historic milestones in the history of filmmaking: **The Great Train Robbery,** directed by Edwin S. Porter; **First Programs,** by Louis and Auguste Lumiere; and **Billy Whiskers.** The first two films on this program are not merely important documents, but also entertaining viewing, with still-amazing special effects by pioneers Porter and the Lumiere brothers; *Billy Whiskers* is more in the nature of comic relief, starring one of the first animal stars—Billy the goat! (42 mins.)†

Great Victor Herbert, The (1939)** Allan Jones, Walter Connolly, Susanna Foster, Mary Martin. Inaccurate film biography of the famous composer, but twenty-eight of his songs well performed compensate. (Dir: Andrew L. Stone, 91 mins.)

Great Waldo Pepper, The (1975)*** Robert Redford, Bo Svenson, Susan Sarandon, Bo Brundin, Margot Kidder. An appealing homage to the barnstorming pilots of the early 1920s. Redford plays Pepper, a daredevil who regrets having missed the opportunity to trade shoot-outs with the great German aces of WWI, and senses that America of the mad twenties doesn't share his passion for aerial acrobatics. (Dir: George Roy Hill, 107 mins.)†

Great Wall, A (U.S.-China, 1986)**½ Peter Wang, Sharon Iwai, Kelvin Han Yee, Li Qinqin. The first American feature made in China, and a moderate success. A study of contrasting lifestyles, this sketchy, unassuming comedy follows the travails of a Chinese-American family who visit their homeland, where their culture clashes with the Chinese in a tamely humorous manner. (Dir: Peter Wang, 100 mins.)†

Great Wallendas, The (MTV 1978)*** Lloyd Bridges, Britt Ekland, Taina Elg, John van Dreelen, Cathy Rigby. This dramatization of the triumphs and tragedies of a unique family of high-wire artists is a rewarding experience. Bridges is superb as the indomitable Karl Wallenda, whose unquenchable spirit breathes life into his clan. (Dir: Larry Elikann, 104 mins.)†

Great Waltz, The (1938)** Luise Rainer, Fernand Gravet, Miliza Korjus, Hugh Herbert, Lionel Atwill, Curt Bois. Lavish but dull screen biography of Johann Strauss. The music, however, is sheer delight. (Dir: Julien Duvivier, 100 mins.)

Great War, The (France-Italy, 1961)***½ Vittorio Gassman, Silvana Mangano, Alberto Sordi, Bernard Blier. Unusual, fascinating mixture of low comedy and high drama, as a couple of stiffs find themselves becoming heroes in WWI.

430

Gassman is particularly good. (Dir: Mario Monicelli, 118 mins.)

Great White Hope, The (1970)***½ James Earl Jones, Jane Alexander, Lou Gilbert, Chester Morris, Hal Holbrook. Film captures much of the passion of the original Broadway play and the dazzling, virtuoso performance of James Earl Jones as Jack Johnson, the first black heavyweight boxing champion. Playwright Howard Sackler and director Martin Ritt show the way Johnson was victimized and humiliated by a racist, white society, and subjected to what must have been the ultimate degradation— being forced to take a dive in a fixed championship fight and lose to a white opponent whom he could easily have beaten. (101 mins.)†

Great Ziegfeld, The (1936)***½ William Powell, Myrna Loy, Luise Rainer, Fanny Brice, Virginia Bruce, Frank Morgan, Ray Bolger, Reginald Owen. This lavish, flamboyant musical salute to Florenz Ziegfeld, the master showman, remains one of the few musicals to capture a Best Picture Oscar, and looks as if MGM spent every penny it had on it, particularly in the spectacular "A Pretty Girl Is Like a Melody" number. Filled with specialty numbers by talents from the actual follies, this bio-musical is vastly entertaining. (Dir: Robert Z. Leonard, 176 mins.)†

Greed (1924)**** Gibson Gowland, Jean Hersholt, ZaSu Pitts. More than a masterpiece. Adaptation of Frank Norris' novel *McTeague* sets out to tell all the truth about man's lust for wealth. Director Erich von Stroheim's original version ran nine hours, and the studio cut it to less than two. What remains is the finest piece of mad realism ever perpetrated. Von Stroheim took his actors to Death Valley so that they could really sweat out those climactic passions, and it shows. Pitts does fine work as a tragedienne. (112 mins.)†

Greed in the Sun (France-Italy, 1964)** Jean-Paul Belmondo, Lino Ventura, Reginald Kernan, Bernard Blier. French truck drivers in Northern Africa. Parched scenery, ancient Moroccan villages form stark backgrounds for disjointed tale. (Dir: Henri Verneuil, 122 mins.)

Greeks Had a Word for Them, The (1932)*** Joan Blondell, Ina Claire, Madge Evans, David Manners, Lowell Sherman, Betty Grable. Fast-paced and funny farce about three gals hunting the marital jungles for rich hubbies. Remade and revamped dozens of times (e.g., *How to Marry a Millionaire*), but this comedy's luster hasn't dimmed. AKA: **3 Broadway Girls.** (Dir: Lowell Sherman, 79 mins.)

Greek Tycoon, The (1978)½ Anthony Quinn,

Jacqueline Bisset, Raf Vallone, Edward Albert, James Franciscus. Deserves its listing as one of the worst films of all time. A thinly veiled peek into the boudoir of that controversial couple, Jackie O. and Aristotle Onassis. (Dir: J. Lee Thompson, 112 mins.)†

Green Berets, The (1968)½ John Wayne, David Janssen, Jim Hutton, Aldo Ray, Raymond St. Jacques, Bruce Cabot, Jack Soo, George Takei, Patrick Wayne, Richard Pryor. Wayne's preposterous attempt to make a WWII-type movie with a Vietnam setting; ends with the sun setting in the east. (Dirs: John Wayne, Ray Kellog, 141 mins.)†

Green Card (1990)*** Gerard Depardieu, Andie MacDowell, Bebe Neuwirth, Gregg Edelman, Robert Prosky. Charming romantic comedy about a rough-hewn Frenchman (Depardieu) who marries a plant-loving American woman in order to remain in the United States. She also needs to wed in order to get a plum Manhattan apartment, but the marriage-of-convenience soon goes awry. Has a running gag about vegetarianism; it may be the first movie with a tofu consciousness. Written, directed, and produced by Peter Weir, it's a refreshing farce that isn't afraid to be bittersweet. (Dir: Peter Weir, 108 mins.)†

Green Dolphin Street (1947)** Lana Turner, Van Heflin, Donna Reed, Frank Morgan. A girl sails to New Zealand to marry her sister's fellow and sets off a feature-length series of clichés and outlandish gimmicks. (Dir: Victor Saville, 141 mins.)†

Greene Murder Case, The (1929)**½ William Powell, Florence Eldridge, Jean Arthur. Philo Vance sets a trap for a crafty killer who has been picking off members of a family one by one. Fine cast, snappy story. (Dir: Frank Tuttle, 69 mins.)

Green-Eyed Blonde, The (1957)* Susan Oliver, Linda Plowman. Trashy film about a young moll who creates havoc when she is put in a correctional institute for wayward girls. (Dir: Bernard Girard, 76 mins.)

Green Eyes (MTV 1977)*** Paul Winfield, Rita Tushingham, Lemi Strong, emotional drama about a black American Vietnam war veteran who returns to Saigon in 1973 to find his son, born to a Vietnamese bar girl. (Dir: John Erman, 96 mins.)†

Green Fingers (Great Britain, 1947)*** Robert Beatty, Nova Pilbeam, Carol Raye. A fisherman who has talent as a bonesetter refuses to study for a degree and goes into practice for society patients. Well-acted drama, with a slightly new plot twist. (Dir: John Harlow, 83 mins.)

Green Fire (1954)**½ Stewart Granger, Grace Kelly, Paul Douglas, John Ericson. Colorful drama about love, adventure, and emerald mining in South America. Princess Grace and Granger have some torrid love scenes in this one. (Dir: Andrew Marton, 100 mins.)

Green for Danger (Great Britain, 1946)***½ Alastair Sim, Trevor Howard, Sally Gray, Leo Genn. Witty, well-written comedy-mystery with impeccable British style and well-controlled daffiness. Sim is a model of comic finesse as the inspector who tries to locate a mad killer who is dispatching patients on the operating table. (Dir: Sidney Gilliat, 93 mins.)

Green Glove, The (1952)**½ Glenn Ford, Geraldine Brooks, Sir Cedric Hardwicke. Minor little chase drama concerning wartime treasures. European backgrounds are more exciting than the film. (Dir: Rudolph Mate, 88 mins.)

Green Goddess, The (1930)**½ George Arliss, H. B. Warner, Alice Joyce, Ralph Forbes. Superb early talkie, with Arliss sublimely wily as a dangerous Rajah. (Dir: Alfred E. Green, 74 mins.)

Green Grass of Wyoming (1948)*** Peggy Cummins, Charles Coburn, Robert Arthur, Lloyd Nolan, Burl Ives. Another pleasant horse story for the youngsters. All about wild stallions, frisky mares and even some trotting races. (Dir: Louis King, 89 mins.)

Green Grow the Rushes (Great Britain, 1952)***½ Richard Burton, Honor Blackman. When the government comes snooping around a small village, the natives are afraid their whiskey-smuggling business is in danger. Extremely pleasant, humorous comedy. (Dir: Derek Twist, 77 mins.)

Green Hell (1940)*** Douglas Fairbanks, Jr., Joan Bennett, George Sanders, Vincent Price, Alan Hale. Jungle expedition searching for Inca treasure is attacked by savages. Fairly standard idea given bite by a fine cast and director. (Dir: James Whale, 97 mins.)

Green Helmet, The (Great Britain, 1961)** Bill Travers, Nancy Walters, Ed Begley, Jack Brabham. Aging race-car driver falls in love with a girl who fears for his life. (Dir: Michael Forlong, 88 mins.)

Green Ice (1981)** Ryan O'Neal, Omar Sharif, Anne Archer, John Larroquette. O'Neal gets involved with the ruthless agent of a corrupt government who controls the emerald industry. A cross between a James Bond movie (without all the fancy gadgets) and *Romancing the Stone* (without all the high spirits). Music by Bill Wyman. (Dir: Ernest Day, 115 mins.)†

Green Light, The (1937)**½ Errol Flynn, Anita Louise, Margaret Lindsay, Sir

Cedric Hardwicke, Henry O'Neill, Spring Byington. From the mystical-philosophical Lloyd C. Douglas novel, this tells of a doctor who discovers the meaning of life and the value of self-sacrifice when he is unjustly blamed for the death of a patient. The story is a bit choppy, but Flynn gives a strong performance. (Dir: Frank Borzage, 85 mins.)

Green Man, The (Great Britain, 1957)*** Alastair Sim, George Cole, Terry Thomas. In the cozy tradition of British little-man comedy, this farce concerns a watchmaker who leads a double life—he's also a paid assassin. With Sim in one of his most characteristic roles, delightful, wicked, and hilarious. (Dir: Robert Day, 80 mins.)

Green Mansions (1959)** Audrey Hepburn, Anthony Perkins, Lee J. Cobb, Sessue Hayakawa, Henry Silva. Young man in the jungles of Venezuela meets a strange girl of the forest, falls in love with her. Based on a novel that would be difficult for anyone to film adequately, this fantasy tries hard, manages some affecting scenes, pretty scenery. (Dir: Mel Ferrer, 101 mins.)

Green Room, The (France, 1978)** François Truffaut, Nathalie Baye. A dour, morbid enterprise full of pompous self-importance. Director Truffaut and Baye play characters obsessed by the honoring of the dead. Based on two stories by Henry James. (Dir: François Truffaut, 94 mins.)†

Green Slime, The (U.S.-Japan, 1969)½ Robert Horton, Richard Jaeckel, Bud Widom, Luciana Paluzzi. The Earth is going to collide with an asteroid gone wild, and Robert Horton is dispatched to blow it up from the space station called Gamma III. The monster itself ranks with *The Creeping Terror* and *Robot Monster* as filmdom's shoddiest lurking fiends. (Dir: Kinji Fukasaku, 88 mins.)

Green Wall, The (Peru, 1969)***½ Julio Aleman, Sandra Riva, Raul Martain. City dwellers struggle to make a home in the Peruvian forests. Simple story about breaking through the so-called green barrier of the lush wilds is breathtaking to look at. First Peruvian film to make an impact in U.S. theaters. (Dir: Armando Robles Godoy, 110 mins.)

Greenwich Village (1944)**½ Carmen Miranda, Don Ameche, William Bendix, Felix Bressart, Vivian Blaine. Likeable Fox musical set in 1922, with the studio's musical stars here in abundance. Ameche plays a long-hair composer adapting his compositions for a Broadway revue. Some sparkle, but the production values aren't up to par. (Dir: Walter Lang, 82 mins.)

Green Years, The (1946)*** Charles Co-

burn, Tom Drake, Beverly Tyler, Hume Cronyn, Dean Stockwell. Occasionally moving and generally interesting adaptation of A. J. Cronin's novel about an Irish lad who goes to live with his grandparents in Scotland. Coburn as the boy's great-grandfather is a treat. (Dir: Victor Saville, 127 mins.)

Greetings (1968)*** Robert De Niro, Jonathan Warden, Gerrit Graham, Allan Garfield. A loosely constructed, episodic film about two young men trying to coach their buddy on how to weird out the Army psychiatrist and thereby flunk the draft physical. There's also a lot of sexual horseplay—all of it directed with zestful, if at times painfully self-indulgent, good humor. Sequel: *Hi, Mom!* (Dir: Brian DePalma, 88 mins.)†

Gregory's Girl (Scotland, 1982)*** Dee Hepburn, Gordon John Sinclair, Claire Grogan. An immensely charming, touchingly funny film about adolescent love, and awkwardness. Stunningly filmed in a suburban town in Scotland, this film is overflowing with superb young performers. (Dir: Bill Forsyth, 99 mins.)†

Gremlins (1984)***½ Hoyt Axton, Phoebe Cates, Zach Galligan, Polly Holliday, Frances Lee McCain, Dick Miller, Judge Reinhold. An inventor obtains a cute, exotic pet for his son; he's warned never to expose the tiny creature to harsh light, never to get it wet, and never to feed it after midnight. When the rules are ignored, the cute creature spawns hordes of vicious gremlins. (Dir: Joe Dante, 105 mins.)†

Gremlins 2: The New Batch (1990)***½ Zach Galligan, Phoebe Cates, John Glover, Christopher Lee, Robert Prosky, Dick Miller, Haviland Morris, voices of Howie Mandel, Tony Randall. You'll have to watch this delightful sequel several times to catch all the jokes and pokes devised by director Joe Dante and writer Charlie Haas, along with lots of cameos and "in" jokes for rabid movie buffs. The mischievous monsters take over a huge Manhattan office building, and the gags start to fly. (105 mins.)†

Grendel Grendel Grendel (Australia, 1982)*** The voices of Peter Ustinov and Keith Michell. Ustinov dubs the behemoth Grendel and Michell his adversary Beowulf in this ingenious animated adaptation of the late John Gardner's novel *Grendel*. (Dir: Alexander Stitt, 88 mins.)†

Grey Fox, The (Canada, 1983)*** Richard Farnsworth, Jackie Burroughs, Wayne Robson, Ken Pogue. After spending thirty-three years in prison, a stage-coach robber is released into a strange new world of nickelodeons and speeding trains. Rather than retire, the veteran thief shifts his modus operandi to holding up locomotives. (Dir: Philip Borsos, 92 mins.)†

Greyfriars Bobby (U.S.-Great Britain, 1961)*** Donald Crisp, Laurence Naismith. Appealing Disney entry for children about a shepherd's faithful Skye terrier who wins the affection of the city of Edinburgh. (Dir: Don Chaffey, 91 mins.)†

Grey Gardens (1975)***½ A special documentary about two very unconventional people—Edith Bouvier Beale and her daughter, Edie. These two ladies are shown living their daily lives—arguing, reminiscing and even singing—with a startling clarity by the Maysles brothers. What results is not so much a study of two famous "crazy ladies," but instead a document of bitter memories, lost dreams, and futile hopes. (Dirs: David and Albert Maysles, Ellen Hovde, Muffie Meyer, 94 mins.)

Greystoke: The Legend of Tarzan, Lord of the Apes (U.S.-Great Britain, 1984)*** Christopher Lambert, Ian Holm, Ralph Richardson, James Fox, Ian Charleson, Andie McDowall. A visually sumptuous, serious retelling of the Tarzan story that attempts to turn the material in Burroughs's escapist novels into the stuff of classical fiction, with mixed results. Director Hugh Hudson painstakingly recreates the jungle atmosphere. Andie McDowall's voice was dubbed by Glenn Close. (129 mins.)†

Gridlock—See: **Great American Traffic Jam, The**

Grievous Bodily Harm (Australia, 1988)*** Colin Friels, John Waters, Bruno Lawrence, Shane Briant. Better-than-average *noir*. A missing femme fatale is hunted by both an amoral journalist looking to boost his sagging reputation and her ex-husband. (Dir: Mark Joffe, 136 mins.)†

Griffin and Phoenix: A Love Story (MTV 1976)**½ Peter Falk, Jill Clayburgh. Falk, estranged from his wife and two boys, discovers he is dying of cancer and splits the scene. Meanwhile, Clayburgh, a young and vital woman, is told she too has a short time to live, and the two doomed individuals meet. The movie runs out of sentimental steam long before the fadeout, but the two stars give it a good try. (Dir: Daryl Duke, 92 mins.)†

Grifters, The (1990)***½ Anjelica Huston, John Cusack, Annette Bening, Pat Hingle. Set in the sunlit, but definitively *noir* Los Angeles underworld, this powerful drama depicts a shadowy landscape that is unmistakably the creation of pulp writer Jim Thompson whose novel is the source for this quirky excursion into scamming, suspicion, sex, and seduction. Director Stephen Frears and screenwriter Donald Westlake have negotiated this malevolent mine field with high style, taut suspense, and black humor. The entire cast is perfect especially Huston, Cusack, and Bening. Produced by Martin Scorsese. (Dir: Stephen Frears, 119 mins.)†

Grim Prairie Tales (1990)*** James Earl Jones, Brad Dourif, William Atherton, Lisa Eichhorn. Lively first feature from director Wayne Coe mixes the western and horror genres with surprisingly startling results. Anthology style supernatural tale plays like *The Twilight Zone* set in the Old West. For viewers seeking the unusual. (Dir: Wayne Coe, 90 mins.)†

Grim Reaper, The (Italy, 1962)*** Francesco Ruiu, Giancarlo DeRosa, Romano Labate, Vincenzo Ciccora. Rome police investigate the murder of a prostitute, and different witnesses to the woman's life give dissimilar stories about her. First feature by twenty-two-year-old director Bernardo Bertolucci, based on treatment by Pier Paolo Pasolini. (100 mins.)†

Grim Reaper, The (Italy, 1981)*½ Tisa Farrow, Saverio Vallone, Vanessa Steiger. Italian gore thriller about some tourists whose sightseeing is interrupted by a killer. AKA: **Anthropophagus.** (Dir: "Joe d'Amato" [Aristide Massaccesi], 81 mins.)†

Gringo (1985)*½ John Spacely. A rather unpleasant, semi-documentary starring a real-life drug addict and his pals. (Dir: Lech Kowalski, 80 mins.)

Grisbi (France, 1953)*** Jean Gabin, Rene Dary, Jeanne Moreau. Fast-paced story of the Paris underworld and the men who take the big risks for big stakes. (Dir: Jacques Becker, 94 mins.)

Grissly's Millions (1945)*** Paul Kelly, Virginia Grey. Murder strikes when a group of relatives gather together waiting for a wealthy old man to die. Above-average mystery, well written. (Dir: John English, 54 mins.)

Grissom Gang, The (1971)***½ Scott Wilson, Tony Musante, Irene Dailey, Kim Darby, Robert Lansing. Robert Aldrich directed this aggressively unpleasant tale of an heiress who is kidnapped and has a love affair with one of her cretinous abductors. Bracingly original. (127 mins.)†

Grizzly (1976)** Christopher George, Andrew Prine, Richard Jaeckel, Joan McCall. A bearable thriller. When a giant bear begins to stalk innocent victims in a national park, the park commission sends in the troops. (Dir: William Girdler, 92 mins.)†

Groom Wore Spurs, The (1951)* Ginger Rogers, Jack Carson, Joan Davis. A pretty woman attorney is hired to keep a high-flying cowboy movie star out of trouble. Dull, badly played, unfunny comedy. (Dir: Richard Whorf, 80 mins.)

Groove Tube, The (1974)***½ Chevy Chase, Ken Shapiro, Richard Belzer, Buzzy Linhart. A wacky, satirical, scatological series of maniacal sketches that started out life in an off-off Broadway showcase where the sketches were seen on TV screens. Television itself is the target of much of the humor, some of it sophomoric, some excruciatingly funny. (Dir: Ken Shapiro, 75 mins.)†

Gross Anatomy (1989)** Matthew Modine, Christine Lahti, Daphne Zuniga, Todd Field, John Scott Clough, Zakes Mokae. Looking for a lucrative career, cynical Modine enters medical school, certain that he can fake his way through his studies just as he has in everything else. (Dir: Thom Eberhardt, 107 mins.)†

Grotesque (1988)*½ Linda Blair, Tab Hunter, Donna Wilkes, Guy Stockwell. Plastic surgeon seeks revenge on the gang of punks who massacred his family. (Dir: Joe Tornatore, 79 mins.)†

Grounds for Marriage (1951)**½ Van Johnson, Kathryn Grayson, Barry Sullivan. Somewhat silly but amusing tale about an opera singer who decides to make a play for her doctor who just so happens to be her ex-husband. (Dir: Robert Z. Leonard, 91 mins.)

Groundstar Conspiracy, The (1972)***½ George Peppard, Michael Sarrazin, Christine Belford, Cliff Potts, James Olson. A topflight thriller. Peppard plays a government agent assigned to uncover a conspiracy which caused the destruction of a vital secret space unit, and left behind a lone survivor (Sarrazin) who's been badly burned. Peppard has him undergo plastic surgery and brainwashing, so he can be set free and trailed. (Dir: Lamont Johnson, 103 mins.)†

Ground Zero (Australia, 1988)**½ Colin Friels, Jack Thompson, Donald Pleasance. A political thriller with an antinuclear message and an interesting film culture subtext. Friels searches for the reasons for his father's murder in the films of the British nuclear tests in the Australian outback in the fifties. (Dirs: Michael Pattinson, Bruce Myles, 100 mins.)†

Group, The (1966)*** Joan Hackett, Jessica Walter, Joanna Pettet, Kathleen Widdoes, Candice Bergen, Shirley Knight, Elizabeth Hartman, Larry Hagman, Hal Holbrook, Richard Mulligan. Mary McCarthy's novel about Vassar grads in the thirties is immeasurably helped by a brilliant ensemble of talented actresses, but the screenplay reduces most of the characterizations to quick, obvious traits and eliminates almost all the social and

political observations. (Dir: Sidney Lumet, 150 mins.)†

Grown-Ups (MCTV 1985)** Charles Grodin, Marilu Henner, Martin Balsam, Jean Stapleton, Kerry Segal. Jules Feiffer play about a writer (Grodin) struggling to deal with his stifling parents (Balsam and Stapleton) and his wife and daughter (Henner and Segal) who compete for his affection. No real revelations; in the end, it's about nothing more than people arguing. (Dir: John Madden, 106 mins.)†

Gruesome Twosome (1967)* Elizabeth Davis, Chris Martel, Rodney Bedell, Gretchen Welles. Wigmaker and her son get their raw materials from less-than-willing college girls in this black comedy from gore specialist Herschell Gordon Lewis. (72 mins.)†

Grumpy (1930)** Cyril Maude, Phillips Holmes, Paul Cavanagh, Paul Lukas. Cantankerous old lawyer straightens out a diamond theft and clears the path for young love. Interesting curio. (Dirs: George Cukor, Cyril Gardner, 74 mins.)

Grunt! The Wrestling Movie (1986)* Jeff Dial, Robert Glaudini, Marilyn Dodds Farr. Professional wrestling is a great subject for a comedy, but this isn't it. The "real" thing is funnier. (Dir: Allan Holzman, 90 mins)†

Guadalcanal Diary (1943)***½ William Bendix, Lloyd Nolan, Preston Foster, Richard Conte, Anthony Quinn, Richard Jaeckel. A worthy tribute to the men who fought on Guadalcanal is this stirring action film. Despite the mock heroics it's still one of the best war films. (Dir: Lewis Seiler, 93 mins.)†

Guardian, The (MCTV 1984)*½ Louis Gossett, Jr., Martin Sheen, Arthur Hill. An outlandish melodrama about a nononsense ex-military man hired to protect tenants after a murder occurs on their premises. A rape, beatings, burglaries, and another killing happen in rapid succession. (Dir: David Greene, 101 mins.)†

Guardian, The (1990)** Jenny Seagrove, Dwier Brown, Carey Lowell, Brad Hall, Miguel Ferrer. Less-than-original terror tale about evil invading a yuppie environment does have a well-developed sense of style, with director William Friedkin maintaining a keen sense of tension for the first half of this story about a British governess with the bad habit of sacrificing her young charges to a Druid tree god. Once she is found out—and becomes a sort of deranged Mary Poppins, flying through the woods—the tension rapidly dissolves. (98 mins.)†

Guardian of Hell (Italy, 1985)½ Sandy Samuel, Frank Garfield. Something like a horror-pic version of *Agnes of God*; a nun is raped by the Devil and gives birth to a demonic child who spreads unclean influences in the convent. (Dir: Stefan Oblowski, 85 mins.)†

Guardsman, The (1931)***½ Alfred Lunt, Lynn Fontanne, Roland Young, ZaSu Pitts. A superior film adaptation of Ferenc Molnar's Broadway hit about the conceited Austrian actor (Lunt) who goes to elaborate lengths to test his wife's (Fontanne's) marital fidelity. (Dir: Sidney Franklin, 83 mins.)

Guendalina (France-Italy, 1957)**½ Jacqueline Sassard, Raffaele Mattioli. Guendalina (Sassard) befriends a young student on the Italian Riviera while her parents are planning a divorce. A gentle, sensitive look at adolescence. (Dir: Alberto Lattuada, 95 mins.)

Guerillas in Pink Lace (1964)** George Montgomery, Joan Shawlee, Valerie Varda. Five showgirls and an adventurer disguised as a priest make an unlikely combination to escape from enemy-held Manila, but they do—only to wind up on an island also held by the enemy. (Dir: George Montgomery, 96 mins.)

Guernica (Italy, 1976)***½ Mariangela Melato. An elaborate phantasm of political scatology directed by Fernando Arrabal from one of his lesser plays. There are arid patches, but the force of the surrealistic anger comes through undiminished. (110 mins.)

Guess Who's Coming for Christmas? (MTV 1990)**½ Richard Mulligan, Barbara Barrie, Paul Dooley, Beau Bridges. An old-timer (Mulligan) in a small town meets a fellow from outer space (Bridges). (Dir: Paul Schneider, 96 mins.)

Guess Who's Coming to Dinner? (1967) *** Spencer Tracy, Katharine Hepburn, Sidney Poitier, Katharine Houghton, Beah Richards, Cecil Kellaway, Isabel Sanford. Sidney comes to woo Kate and Spencer's daughter. Result: one frequently sophomoric sentimental screenplay, buoyed up by a glorious bow-out performance by the deservedly legendary screen team. (Dir: Stanley Kramer, 112 mins.)†

Guess Who's Sleeping in My Bed? (MTV 1973)**½ Dean Jones, Barbara Eden, Ken Mars. Ex-husband Jones barges in on his ex-wife, Miss Eden, with his new wife and infant child, and asks to be put up awhile. (Dir: Theodore J. Flicker, 90 mins.)

Guest, The (Great Britain, 1964)*** Donald Pleasence, Alan Bates, Robert Shaw. About an old derelict (Pleasence) invited to spend the night in a rundown London house, who becomes involved with two neurotic brothers. (Dir: Clive Donner, 105 mins.)

Guest in the House (1944)**½ Anne Baxter, Ralph Bellamy, Ruth Warrick, Marie McDonald. A young girl taken in by an average household sets to poisoning their minds against each other. Psychological melodrama has its moments. (Dir: John Brahm, 121 mins.)†

Guest Wife (1945)*** Claudette Colbert, Don Ameche. Married woman is persuaded to pose as a war correspondent's wife to fool his boss. Amusing romantic comedy. (Dir: Sam Wood, 90 mins.)†

Guide for the Married Man, A (1967)*** Walter Matthau, Robert Morse, Inger Stevens. Walter Matthau's comedic talents are put to good use in this broad comedy about philandering husbands, and the efforts they expend to keep the news from reaching their wives. Featuring cameos by eighteen guest stars. (Dir: Gene Kelly, 89 mins.)†

Guide for the Married Woman, A (MTV 1978)** Cybill Shepherd, Barbara Feldon, George Gobel. Predictable yarn about a bored housewife (Shepherd) who takes the advice of a liberated woman friend (Feldon) and tries to put a little adventure in her life. (Dir: Hy Averback, 104 mins.)

Guilt of Janet Ames, The (1947)*** Rosalind Russell, Melvyn Douglas, Sid Caesar, Nina Foch. Woman embittered by the death of her husband in the war is shown the light by a journalist. Interesting drama. (Dir: Henry Levin, 83 mins.)

Guilty, The (1947)**½ Don Castle, Bonita Granville. Two friends are in love with the same girl, and she has a twin sister. One of them is murdered, and from there it's anybody's guess as to who, what, and why. (Dir: John Reinhardt, 70 mins.)

Guilty Bystander (1950)*** Zachary Scott, Faye Emerson. A private eye down on his luck snaps out of the fog when he finds his little child has been kidnapped. (Dir: Joseph Lerner, 92 mins.)

Guilty by Suspicion (1991)**½ Robert De Niro, Annette Bening, George Wendt, Patricia Wettig, Sam Wanamaker, Martin Scorcese. Disappointing, passionless drama about the anti-Communist witch-hunt in the movie industry in the 1950s takes few chances and offers no surprises. It's like a dull history lesson by a qualified professor; well done but uninteresting. By the time the characters begin to fight back against the immoral hysteria, the movie's nearly over. See Martin Ritt's *The Front* for a more honest account of the horrors of blacklisting in films and TV during the 1950s and early '60s. (Dir: Irwin Winkler, 105 mins.)†

Guilty Conscience (MTV 1985)*** Anthony Hopkins, Blythe Danner, Swoosie Kurtz. Clever mystery yarn with Hopkins playing a philandering criminal lawyer considering ways to murder his wife (Danner). The screenplay is excellent, and the plot has plenty of twists and turns. (Dir: David Greene, 104 mins.)

435

Guilty of Innocence: The Lenell Geter Story
(1987)** Dorian Harewood, Dabney
Coleman, Hoyt Axton, Debbi Morgan,
Victor Love, Dennis Lipscomb, Paul
Winfield. Based on the real-life 1982
Dallas case of an engineer wrongly accused and sentenced to life imprisonment,
this sad commentary on how the due
process of the law misfired has been
made into the expected headline horror-
story. (Dir: Richard T. Heffron, 104 mins.)

**Guilty or Innocent: The Sam Sheppard Murder
Case** (MTV 1975)**½ George Peppard,
Barnard Hughes, Walter McGinn. Lengthy
recreation of the bizarre 1954 Cleveland
murder case where osteopath Sam Sheppard was accused of murdering his wife.
Good performances, especially by Peppard
as Sheppard and Hughes as a defense
attorney, key the drama, and the production gives the right feeling for the tempo
and the thinking in 1954. (Dir: Robert
Michael Lewis, 144 mins.)

Gulag (MCTV 1985)*** David Keith,
Malcolm McDowell, David Suchet, Warren Clarke. A sensitive and provocative
drama. Keith is an American sportscaster
who is set up by the KGB and sentenced to ten years in a labor camp.
Keith and a small group of his fellow
prisoners, including an Englishman
(McDowell), execute an ingenious escape plan, and the suspense during this
sequence is heart-pounding. (Dir: Roger
Young, 130 mins.)†

Gulliver's Travels (1939)**½ The Fleischer
brothers, Disney's only real competition
in the animation field, created this tune-
filled treatment of Swift's great work.
(Dir: Dave Fleischer, 74 mins.)†

Gumball Rally, The (1976)*** Michael Sarrazin, Tim McIntire, Gary Busey, Susan
Flannery, Nicholas Pryor, Raul Julia.
Fairly breezy precursor to those interminable Burt Reynolds cross-country car-
crash spectaculars. The cast is fresher
here, the tone less desperate, the film
better. (Dir: Chuck Bail, 107 mins.)†

Gumshoe (Great Britain, 1971)** Albert
Finney, Billie Whitelaw, Janice Rule.
This is a homage to Dashiell Hammett,
Raymond Chandler, etc., and the screen
image of Humphrey Bogart, but they
can't quite pull off this most American
genre down Liverpool way. Music by
Andrew Lloyd Webber. (Dir: Stephen
Frears, 88 mins.)†

Gumshoe Kid, The (1990)**½ Jay Underwood, Tracy Scoggins, Vince Edwards,
Arlene Golonka. Nice little private-eye
spoof concerning a young would-be
detective tracking down a kidnapper.
Friendly and unpretentious. (Dir: Joseph
Manduke, 98 mins.)†

Gun, The (MTV 1974)*** Stephen Elliott,
Jean Le Bouvier, Wallace Rooney. Am-
436

bitious semi-documentary shows the life
of a gun from the day it comes off the
assembly line through its various owners.
Ironically, the gun is fired only twice . . . at
the factory for testing purposes and at the
very end. (Dir: John Badham, 72 mins.)

Gun and the Pulpit, The (MTV 1974)***
Marjoe Gortner, Estelle Parsons, Slim
Pickens. Marjoe Gortner (who was so
compelling in *Marjoe*) is well suited for
this colorful role of a gunslinger who
finds himself in the garb and guise of a
small-town preacher while running hard
from a posse. The script is full of clever
dialogue. (Dir: Dan Petrie, 78 mins.)

Gun Battle at Monterey (1957)** Sterling Hayden, Pamela Duncan, Ted de Corsia, Lee
Van Cleef. Revenge rides the trails once
more in this action-filled western. A
double-dealing partner gets his comeuppance! (Dir: Carl G. Hittleman, 67 mins.)

Gun Belt (1953)**½ Tab Hunter, George
Montgomery, William Bishop. Fairly entertaining, low-budget western about an
outlaw who wants to go straight and his
old "buddies" who have different plans.
(Dir: Ray Nazarro, 77 mins.)

Gun Crazy (1949)***½ Peggy Cummins,
John Dall, Morris Carnovsky. Ex-carnival
girl persuades her husband to join her in
a series of robberies, and they become
wanted criminals. Excellent lovers-on-the
run saga, replete with *noir* psychoses
and expertly filmed robbery sequences.
(Dir: Joseph Lewis, 86 mins.)†

Gun Duel in Durango—See: Duel in Durango

Gun Fever (1958)*½ Mark Stevens, John
Lupton, Jana Davi, Larry Storch. Revenge drama as a rancher goes after the
killer of his parents. Unknown to the
boy, the criminal is the father of his best
friend. Clichéd plot plays like a western soap opera. (Dir: Mark Stevens, 81
mins.)

Gunfight, A (1971)**½ Kirk Douglas, Johnny Cash, Jane Alexander, Raf Vallone,
Karen Black, Keith Carradine. There's
lots of talk before this offbeat western
justifies its title, but a good part of the
dialogue is crisp. Also, the stars are
interesting as a couple of has-been gunfighters who decide to face each other
in one last duel—staged in a bullring
and attended by a ticket-buying audience. (Dir: Lamont Johnson, 90 mins.)†

Gunfight at Comanche Creek (1964)** Audie
Murphy, Colleen Miller, DeForest Kelley.
Catchpenny western features a National
Detective Agency man, bent on unmasking
a cold-blooded group of outlaws. (Dir:
Frank McDonald, 91 mins.)

Gunfight at Dodge City, The (1959)** Joel
McCrea, Julie Adams, John McIntire.
Bat Masterson is elected sheriff and pro-
ceeds to clean up the town. (Dir: Joseph
M. Newman, 81 mins.)

Gunfight at the OK Corral (1957)*** Burt Lancaster, Kirk Douglas, Rhonda Fleming, Jo Van Fleet, John Ireland, Lee Van Cleef, Frank Faylen, Kenneth Tobey, DeForest Kelley, Earl Holliman. Directed with authority, this tale about the legendary shoot-out involving Doc Holliday, Wyatt Earp, and the Clanton gang saves its big guns for the climax; but the build-up leading to this admittedly slam-bang finish could have benefitted from sharper scripting. Vivid, sprawling action picture. (Dir: John Sturges, 122 mins.)†

Gunfighter, The (1950)***½ Gregory Peck, Jean Parker, Karl Malden, Helen Westcott, Skip Homeier, Richard Jaeckel. One of Peck's best performances as the would-be-retired gunslinger Johnny Ringo. Homeier, determined to grab the ''Fastest Gun'' title for himself, forces Ringo into one more shoot-out. Very off beat western for its time. (Dir: Henry King, 84 mins.)†

Gunfighters (1947)*** Randolph Scott, Barbara Britton, Forrest Tucker. Gunslinger wants to hang up his pistols, but lands in the middle of a range war. Well-made western with some rugged action. (Dir: George Waggner, 87 mins.)

Gunfighters of Abilene (1960)* Buster Crabbe, Barton MacLane, Judith Ames. Totally predictable western adventure. Gunman investigates brother's disappearance. (Dir: Edward L. Cahn, 66 mins.)

Gunfire at Indian Gap (1957)*½ Vera Hruba Ralston, Anthony George, George Macready, Glenn Strange. Dull western about some outlaws trying to rob a payroll from a stagecoach relay station. (Dir: Joseph Kane, 70 mins.)

Gun for a Coward (1957)** Fred MacMurray, Jeffrey Hunter, Dean Stockwell, Janice Rule. Rancher faces trouble trying to raise two younger brothers, one a hothead, the other accused of cowardice. (Dir: Abner Biberman, 73 mins.)

Gun Fury (1953)**½ Rock Hudson, Donna Reed, Phil Carey, Lee Marvin, Neville Brand. Hudson's beautiful fiancée (Reed) is kidnapped by a lustful gunslinger and the search for revenge is on. Slow-paced but interesting western drama. (Dir: Raoul Walsh, 83 mins.)†

Gunga Din (1939)**** Cary Grant, Douglas Fairbanks, Jr., Victor McLaglen, Sam Jaffe, Eduardo Ciannelli, Montagu Love, Robert Coote, Abner Biberman, Joan Fontaine. Three members of Her Majesty's Indian Regiment foil a native uprising with the aid of a loyal water boy. Crammed with spectacle, action, comedy, this is one of the most enjoyable adventure films ever made. (Dir: George Stevens, 117 mins.)†

Gung Ho! (1943)** Randolph Scott, Noah Beery, Jr., Alan Curtis, Robert Mitchum, David Bruce. During WWII the Marines raid Japanese-held Makin Island. War melodrama has plenty of action. (Dir: Ray Enright, 88 mins.)†

Gung Ho (1986)*** Michael Keaton, Gedde Watanabe, George Wendt, Mimi Rogers, John Turturro, Sab Shimono, Clint Howard, Soh Yamamura. An energetic culture-clash comedy with a topical premise. Keaton persuades a Japanese company to pump new life into a closed auto factory, only the Yanks and the Japanese approach their work from wildly different perspectives. Good combination of Americana and cheerful satire. (Dir: Ron Howard, 111 mins.)†

Gun Glory (1957)** Stewart Granger, Rhonda Fleming, Steve Rowland, Chill Wills. Gunfighter returns to his ranch to find he's hated by his grown son. (Dir: Roy Rowland, 88 mins.)

Gun Hawk, The (1963)** Rory Calhoun, Rod Cameron, Ruta Lee, Rod Lauren. Outlaw gunman tracked by the sheriff dissuades a youngster from following the same crooked trail. Formula hoss opera. (Dir: Edward Ludwig, 92 mins.)

Gun in the House, A (MTV 1981)*½ Sally Struthers, David Aykroyd, Dick Anthony Williams, Jeffrey Tambor. Exploitative film about gun control in which overwrought Struthers murders an intruder, and we're treated to a procession of pros and cons about defending yourself in your own home. Defend yourself by not watching. (Dir: Ivan Nagy, 104 mins.)†

Gunman's Walk (1958)*** Van Heflin, Tab Hunter, Kathryn Grant, James Darren. Rancher tries to bring his sons up properly, but the black sheep of the family causes tragedy for all. Superior western, especially in the acting and directing departments. (Dir: Phil Karlson, 97 mins.)

Gun Moll—See: **Jigsaw** (1949)

Gunn (1967)**½ Craig Stevens, Laura Devon, Edward Asner, Sherry Jackson. Private eye Peter Gunn matches wits and fists with gangland and murderers in an actionful mystery feature. Elements are the same, and fans of the TV series should enjoy. (Dir: Blake Edwards, 94 mins.)

Gunpoint (1966)** Audie Murphy, Joan Staley. Local sheriff overcomes all obstacles to capture an outlaw gang. Routine western. (Dir: Earl Bellamy, 86 mins.)

Gun Riders (1969)* Jim Davis, Scott Brady, Robert Dix, John Carradine, Jim Davis, Paula Raymond, Vicki Volante. Cliché-ridden tale of settlers terrorized by gunfighters. The aging stars disport themselves as if they'd just entered the Dodge City Rest Home. AKA: **Five Bloody Graves.** (Dir: Al Adamson, 98 mins.)†

Gunrunner, The (Canada, 1983)** Kevin Costner, Sara Botsford, Gerard Parkes,

Paul Soles. In Montreal of the 1920s, gunrunner Costner takes on the local mob and liquor smugglers. Standard gangster opus that went (deservedly) unseen until it appeared on video to cash in on Costner's later success. (Dir: Nardo Castillo, 92 mins.)†

Gun Runners (1958)**½ Audie Murphy, Eddie Albert, Everett Sloane, Patricia Owens. Interesting adventure about a man who risks his life for a big share of profit for illegal gun-running. Based on Hemingway's *To Have and Have Not*. (Dir: Don Siegel, 83 mins.)

Guns, The (Brazil, 1963)*** Atila Iorio, Nelson Xavier, Maria Gladys, Hugo Carvana. Violent and grim tale of starving peasants following a sacred ox only to become embroiled in gun battle involving soldiers guarding the mayor's private food stock. Director Ruy Guerra stresses government ill-treatment of the poor in this early *Cinema Novo* effort. (110 mins.)

Guns at Batasi (Great Britain, 1964)***½ Richard Attenborough, Jack Hawkins, Flora Robson, Mia Farrow. A provocative drama dealing with the strife-ridden climate prevalent in Africa of the early 1960s. Richard Attenborough, as an old school British sergeant major stationed right in the middle of the upheaval, gives a splendid performance. The conflict builds to a tense climax in which the natives plan violent action against the British subjects and their supporters. (Dir: John Guillermin, 103 mins.)†

Guns for San Sebastian (France-Mexico-Italy, 1967)** Anthony Quinn, Anjanette Comer, Charles Bronson. Plodding adventure yarn set during the 1750s and filmed in a Mexican village. Quinn plays a renegade who is thrust into the unlikely position of impersonating a priest of a poor mission. (Dir: Henri Verneuil, 110 mins.)

Guns, Girls and Gangsters (1959)* Mamie Van Doren, Gerald Mohr, Lee Van Cleef. Poor crime-melodrama, badly acted, although Mamie works her customary mammary magic. (Dir: Edward L. Cahn, 70 mins.)

Gunsight Ridge (1957)** Joel McCrea, Mark Stevens, Joan Weldon. Routine western yarn with McCrea playing top hand of the territory. Stevens is well cast as a ruthless culprit who gets his just desserts. (Dir: Francis D. Lyon, 85 mins.)

Guns in the Heather—See: **Spy Busters**

Gunslinger (1956)*½ Beverly Garland, John Ireland. When her husband is ambushed, his wife takes over as town marshal; a killer is brought in to get her, too. Western goes off in all directions, gets laughably far fetched by the end. (Dir: Roger Corman, 83 mins.)†

Gun Smoke (1931)** Richard Arlen, Mary Brian, William Boyd. Big-city gangsters are licked by cowpokes in a western town. Here's the switch: Arlen is the cowpoke and Bill "Hoppy" Boyd is the city crook. (Dir: Edward Sloman, 64 mins.)

Gunsmoke (1953)** Audie Murphy, Susan Cabot. Not to be confused with the long-running TV series of the same name. Just another Audie Murphy starrer in which he plays the stranger in town who has to prove his worth before he's accepted. (Dir: Nathan Juran, 79 mins.)

Gunsmoke: Return to Dodge (MTV 1987)**½ James Arness, Amanda Blake, Buck Taylor, Fran Ryan. A pleasant reunion with the stars of TV's legendary western hit. Matt Dillon's arch-rival is on the loose, and poor Matt's still ailing from his last battle with an outlaw. Thankfully, Miss Kitty is in attendance as nurse and confidante, and those bad hombres don't stand a chance. (Dir: Vincent McEveety, 96 mins.)

Gunsmoke: The Last Apache (MTV 1990)**½ James Arness, Richard Kiley, Michael Learned, Amy Stock-Poynton, Hugh O'Brian, Geoffrey Lewis. Of the *Gunsmoke* crew, only Matt Dillon is on hand for this TV movie that more closely resembles an update of *The Searchers*. Matt tries to ransom a daughter he never knew he had from the Apaches. Unlike the John Ford classic, this telefilm displays respect and understanding for native Americans. (Dir: Charles Cornell, 96 mins.)

Guns of August, The (1964)***½ Documentary based on Barbara Tuchman's Pulitzer Prize-winning book about the causes and effects of WWI. Old newsreel footage compiled in a capable manner. Good for historians, students, and WWI buffs. Narrator: Fritz Weaver. (Dir: Nathan Kroll, 99 mins.)†

Guns of Darkness (Great Britain, 1962)** David Niven, Leslie Caron, James Robertson Justice, David Opatoshu. Businessman and his wife are caught in the turmoil of a South American revolution, find themselves helping the overthrown president escape. Drama gets itself tangled in deeper meanings, never quite makes itself clear. (Dir: Anthony Asquith, 95 mins.)

Guns of Fort Petticoat (1957)**½ Audie Murphy, Kathryn Grant. This is a good story idea that could have made a better film if more attention had been paid to the script. Murphy is a deserter during the Civil War who doesn't agree with his power-hungry colonel's ideas about pointless attacks on the Indians. (Dir: George Marshall, 82 mins.)

Guns of Navarone, The (1961)**** Gregory

Peck, David Niven, Anthony Quinn, Anthony Quayle, Irene Papas, James Darren, Gia Scala, Stanley Baker, Richard Harris. One of the best WWII adventure films. A great cast bolsters this tense tale involving a group of heterogeneous soldiers and green guerrilla fighters who must destroy one of the most heavily guarded German fortresses in the Aegean. (Dir: J. Lee Thompson, 159 mins.)†

Guns of the Magnificent Seven (1969)*½ George Kennedy, James Whitmore, Monte Markham, Bernie Casey, Joe Don Baker, Fernando Rey. Third *Magnificent Seven* film. Set in Mexico in the 1890s, the group attempts to rescue a Mexican Robin Hood who has been caught by the government. (Dir: Paul Wendkos, 106 mins.)†

Guns of the Timberland (1960)** Alan Ladd, Jeanne Crain, Gilbert Roland, Frankie Avalon. Routine action melodrama about a fight between lumbermen and townspeople who don't want the trees cut down. (Dir: Robert D. Webb, 91 mins.)

Gun That Won the West, The (1955)*½ Dennis Morgan, Paula Raymond, Richard Denning. Cavalry Scouts tangle with the Sioux and Cheyenne Indians. Dated. (Dir: William Castle, 71 mins.)

Gun the Man Down (1956)** James Arness, Angie Dickinson, Emile Meyer, Robert Wilke. When his crime partners ditch him during a robbery, a desperado becomes obsessed with giving them cause for regret. Average six-gun-justice pic. AKA: **Arizona Mission.** (Dir: Andrew McLaglen, 78 mins.)

Guru, The (U.S.-India, 1969)*** Michael York, Utpal Dutt, Rita Tushingham. A strange, generally rewarding and magnificently photographed film made in India. One of the themes of the film is the conflict of Eastern and Western cultures. British pop singer (Michael York) arrives in India to study the sitar with an Indian guru. (Dir: James Ivory, 112 mins.)

Gus (1976)** Tim Conway, Don Knotts, Ed Asner, Gary Grimes. Harmless nonsense from the Disney camp. The stars take a backseat to a mule that kicks field goals. (Dir: Vincent McEveety, 96 mins.)†

Gus Brown and Midnight Brewster (MTV 1985)*½ John Schneider, Ron Glass, Teri Copley, Harvey Vernon. Schneider, (Gus Brown) and Glass (Midnight) are WWII army buddies, and they plan to continue their relationship in a business venture involving a racing dog named Slick. At least the post-WWII setting is new; nothing else is. (Dir: Jim Fargo, 104 mins.)

Guts and Glory: The Rise and Fall of Oliver North (MTV 1989)** David Keith, Annette

O'Toole, Bryan Clark, Terry O'Quinn, Barnard Hughes, Paul Dooley, Amy Stock-Poynton, Peter Boyle, Miguel Ferrer. Somewhat whitewashed and eviscerated account of the Iran-Contra affair from the point of view of North veers away from too many questions and issues to be satisfying from any perspective. Maybe if they'd waited until all of the facts were known before rushing out this TV-movie. . . . (Dir: Mike Robe, 192 mins.)

Guyana, Cult of the Damned (Mexico-Spain-Panama, 1980)½ Stuart Whitman, Gene Barry, Yvonne De Carlo, Joseph Cotten, John Ireland, Bradford Dillman, Jennifer Ashley. Sleazy exploitation of the Jonestown tragedy at Guyana. Whitman impresses as a chilling look-alike for the Rev. Jim Jones (here called Johnson), but the rest of the cast deserves a toast of Kool-Aid. (Dir: Rene Cardona, Jr., 90 mins.)

Guyana Tragedy: The Story of Jim Jones (MTV 1980)***½ Powers Boothe, Ned Beatty, Veronica Cartwright, Randy Quaid, LeVar Burton, Irene Cara, Rosalind Cash, Brad Dourif, Meg Foster, Diane Ladd, James Earl Jones, Colleen Dewhurst, Diana Scarwid. The events that led up to the Guyana tragedy in '78 are dramatized in this absorbing if somewhat oversimplified account of self-styled messiah Jim Jones and his People's Temple. Boothe is excellent as the minister who got sidetracked and drunk with power, aided by drugs and the unquestioning adoration of his flock. (Dir: William A. Graham, 208 mins.)†

Guy Named Joe, A (1943)**½ Spencer Tracy, Irene Dunne, Van Johnson, Ward Bond, James Gleason, Lionel Barrymore, Esther Williams. Spencer comes back from the dead to try and make Van a better Air Corps pilot in this often entertaining but occasionally stupid fantasy. Tracy is excellent but he is often up against too much script trouble. Remade in 1989 as *Always*. (Dir: Victor Fleming, 118 mins.)†

Guys and Dolls (1955)*** Marlon Brando, Jean Simmons, Frank Sinatra, Vivian Blaine, Robert Keith, Stubby Kaye, Veda Ann Borg, Regis Toomey, Sheldon Leonard. The musical success concerning a gambler who meets a Salvation Army girl, a floating crap game, and an assortment of Damon Runyon's colorful characters. The Frank Loesser songs are marvelous, the cast is perfect, and the atmosphere is flashy and captivating. (Dir: Joseph L. Mankiewicz, 138 mins.)†

Guy Who Came Back, The (1951)** Paul Douglas, Linda Darnell, Joan Bennett, Zero Mostel. Soap opera about a former football star who can't seem to make it after his career comes to a standstill due to an injury. (Dir: Joseph M. Newman, 91 mins.)

Gymkata (1985)* Kurt Thomas, Tetchie Agbayani, Richard Norton, Edward Bell, John Barrett. World champion gymnast Kurt Thomas is recruited by the CIA to convince an Asian country to install a "Star Wars" defense system. Using the ludicrous "new" martial art of gymkata, which looks like a combination of kung fu and break dancing, Thomas tries to save the world. (Dir: Robert Clouse, 89 mins.)†

Gypsy (1962)*** Natalie Wood, Rosalind Russell, Karl Malden, Paul Wallace, Ann Jillian, Parley Baer. Not as good as the Broadway original, but an interesting backstage musical all the same. An excellent score by Jule Styne and Stephen Sondheim enhances the film about the stage mother of them all, Rose Hovick, whose daughters grew up to be Gypsy Rose Lee and June Havoc. (Dir: Mervyn LeRoy, 149 mins.)†

Gypsy and the Gentleman (Great Britain, 1958)** Melina Mercouri, Keith Michell, Flora Robson, Patrick McGoohan. Villain tries to cheat his sister out of her inheritance to keep his Gypsy lady friend in a proper manner. Wildly theatrical costume drama, may be fun if not taken seriously. (Dir: Joseph Losey, 89 mins.)

Gypsy Colt (1954)**½ Donna Corcoran, Ward Bond, Frances Dee. Appealing tale for the kids, as wonderful-colt Gypsy proves that she and her small mistress can't be kept apart. Remake of *Lassie Come Home*. (Dir: Andrew Marton, 72 mins.)

Gypsy Girl (Great Britain, 1966)*** Hayley Mills, Ian McShane, Laurence Naismith. A poignant drama that benefits from good English location sites and a sensitive performance by Mills as a retiring young girl who is looked upon by her village as a troublemaker. McShane also registers as a Gypsy lad who saves Hayley from being sent to a home. (Dir: John Mills, 102 mins.)

Gypsy Moths, The (1969)**½ Deborah Kerr, Burt Lancaster, Gene Hackman, Scott Wilson, William Windom, Bonnie Bedelia. The story about a trio of barnstorming free-fall parachutists and the turmoil they cause when they hit a small Kansas town during the 4th of July holiday is wonderful at times, and unendurably slow-moving at others. The flying scenes are marvelous. (Dir: John Frankenheimer, 110 mins.)

Gypsy Warriors, The (1978)** James Whitmore, Jr., Tom Selleck, Joseph Ruskin, Lina Raymonds, Kenneth Tigar. Routine pilot for a Stephen J. Cannell-written WWII series that never took off.

Selleck and Whitmore, Jr. star as a pair of U.S. Army captains working with a band of European gypsies behind enemy lines. (Dir: Lou Antonio, 77 mins.)†

Gypsy Wildcat (1944)** Maria Montez, Jon Hall, Gale Sondergaard, Nigel Bruce. A band of Gypsies gets involved with counts and barons and their treachery. (Dir: Roy William Neill, 75 mins.)

Hadley's Rebellion (1984)** Griffin O'Neal, Charles Durning, William Devane, Adam Baldwin. Teen from the deep South who dreams of becoming a wrestler is transplanted to a prep school in Los Angeles, where he has trouble fitting in. Well-intentioned but superficial examination of teenage growing pains. (Dir: Fred Walton, 96 mins.)†

Hagbard and Signe (Denmark-Sweden-Iceland, 1967)***½ Eva Dahlbeck, Gunnar Bjornstrand, Gitte Haenning, Oleg Vidov. A stark, beautiful color film, shot in Iceland. A Scandinavian Romeo-Juliet story about young love in the Middle Ages, marred only by some excessive violence in its battle scenes. (Dir: Gabriel Axel, 92 mins.)

Hail! Hail! Rock 'n' Roll—See: **Chuck Berry: Hail! Hail! Rock 'n' Roll**

Hail Hero! (1969)**½ Michael Douglas, Arthur Kennedy, Teresa Wright, Peter Strauss. Muddled point of view in this well-meaning drama about a young man who enlists during the Vietnam war even though he believes strongly in antiwar philosophies. (Dir: David Miller, 100 mins.)†

Hail Mafia (France-Italy, 1965)* Eddie Constantine, Jack Klugman, Elsa Martinelli, Henry Silva. A dead-end drama about a man who finds himself trapped when he kills the only man who can revoke a Mafia contract on his life. Bid this a fast Hail and Farewell! (Dir: Raoul J. Levy, 90 mins.)

Hail Mary (Je Vous Salue Marie) (Switzerland-France, 1984)**½ Myriem Roussel, Thierry Rode, Philippe Lacoste, Manon Anderson. Once again Jean-Luc Godard retells a classic story in his distinctive but frustratingly incoherent manner. This time, it's a modern-dress version of the story of the Virgin Mary. (100 mins.)†

Hail the Conquering Hero (1944)**** Eddie Bracken, William Demarest, Ella Raines, Raymond Walburn, Franklin Pangborn. Riotous satire about wartime hero worship, and what happens in a small American town when a young man contrives a Marine-hero history for himself. (Dir: Preston Sturges, 101 mins.)†

Hail to the Chief (1973)**½ Dan Resin, Richard B. Shull, Joseph Sirola, Patricia

Ripley, Gary Sandy, Lee Meredith, Mary Louise Weller. Spotty satire that has a Nixon-like Imperial President (Resin) imprisoning the youth movement in concentration camps. A crew of familiar faces show themselves off to good advantage, but the laughs disappear after a while. (Dir: Fred Levinson, 85 mins.)

Hair (1979)*** Treat Williams, John Savage, Beverly D'Angelo, Annie Golden, Dorsey Wright, Don Dacus, Miles Chapin, Nicholas Ray. Based on the hit musical of the sixties about a young draftee's pre-induction visit to the world of flower-children. Doesn't live up to the exceptional promise of its first fifteen minutes but the musical movement is acutely choreographed by Twyla Tharp. (Dir: Milos Forman, 121 mins.)†

Hairdresser's Husband, The (France, 1990)***½ Jean Rochefort, Ana Galiena, Henri Hocking, Maurice Chevit, Ticky Holgado, Roland Bertin, Philippe Clevenot. Director Patrice Leconte hits all the right notes in this extraordinary study of sexual obsession. Rochefort, as the man who dreams of marrying a hairdresser, and Galiena, as his wife, are magnificent. Engrossing and erotic. (Dir: Patrice Leconte, 91 mins.)

Hairspray (1988)***½ Ricki Lake, Divine, Jerry Stiller, Colleen Fitzpatrick, Debbie Harry, Sonny Bono, Ruth Brown, Mink Stole, Pia Zadora. Filmmaker provocateur John Waters returned to the screen with this high-spirited and (as peculiar as it sounds) suprisingly wholesome slice of early sixties nostalgia. Hefty Tracy Turnblad (Lake) longs to be on a lily-white local TV dance show program, but she also hopes for an end to racial discrimination. Waters gleefully sends up the teen "make out" movies of the fifties and sixties and the message pictures of that era, while also drawing on his own rose-colored recollections of the period. The film's look is wonderfully tacky, and the casting is a series of masterstrokes—Bono and Harry as a colorfully gauche couple, Zadora as a beatnik chick, and the oddest couple of all, Stiller and (in his last, glorious role) Divine. (94 mins.)†

Hairy Ape, The (1944)*** William Bendix, Susan Hayward, John Loder, Dorothy Comingore, Alan Napier. A rough ship's stoker falls for a red-headed wench who uses him as a pawn in her conquest of other men. From the play by Eugene O'Neill, a good production, well acted. (Dir: Alfred Santell, 90 mins.)

Half a Hero (1953)** Red Skelton, Jean Hagen. Writer gets in over his head when he buys a modern home in the country to please the wife. Very mild comedy with a few chuckles. (Dir: Don Weis, 71 mins.)

Half Angel (1951)** Loretta Young, Joseph Cotten, Cecil Kellaway, Jim Backus. For Loretta's fans. The versatile Miss Young plays a nurse who's suffering from split personality and the whole thing's played for comedy. (Dir: Richard Sale, 77 mins.)

Half a Sixpence (Great Britain-U.S., 1967)**½ Tommy Steele, Cyril Ritchard, Julia Foster, Penelope Horner. English star Tommy Steele plays the orphan of Edwardian England who inherits a fortune in this musical adaptation of the 1905 H. G. Wells novel, *Kipps*. Occasionally sprightly, with some diverting musical numbers. (Dir: George Sidney, 148 mins.)†

Half-Human (Japan, 1955)*½ John Carradine, Akira Takarada, Kenji Kasahara. Veteran actor John Carradine is cast as a scientist, in scenes added to the U.S. version of this predictable horror film complete with a prehistoric monster. (Dir: Inoshiro Honda, 70 mins.)†

Half Moon Street (1986)** Sigourney Weaver, Michael Caine, Patrick Kavanagh, Keith Buckley. An American woman living in London turns to working for an escort service to support herself and winds up getting involved in political intrigue. Clumsy adaptation of Paul Theroux's interesting novella. (Dir: Bob Swaim, 90 mins.)†

Half-Naked Truth, The (1932)***½ Lee Tracy, Lupe Velez, Franklin Pangborn. Remarkable comedy based on stories, true or otherwise, about master publicist Harry Reichenbach. Brilliant performances and bright repartee. (Dir: Gregory La Cava, 77 mins.)

Half of Heaven (Spain, 1988)**½ Angela Molina, Margarita Lozano, Fernando Fernán-Gómez. A quirky comedy that treats the earthy and the surreal with straight-faced aplomb. A young woman (Molina) escapes her cruelly oppressive family to search for success as a meat vendor in Madrid, using psychic powers inherited from her grandmother to give herself a boost. Too long and at times impenetrable, but often charming. (Dir: Manuel Gutiérrez Aragón, 127 mins.)†

Half Shot at Sunrise (1930)*** Bert Wheeler, Robert Woolsey, Robert Rutherford, Dorothy Lee, Edna May Oliver. Popular Broadway and vaudeville stars Wheeler and Woolsey's first film cast them as doughboys on the loose in Paris during WWI. Humorous skits, blackouts, and musical numbers galore. (Dir: Paul Sloane, 78 mins.)†

Hallelujah! (1929)***½ Daniel L. Haynes, Nina Mae McKinney. A young man becomes a preacher, but is tempted, goes wrong, and meets tragedy before he can return to his church. One of the first serious films on a black theme, with an all-black cast; a strong, well-acted drama with music. (Dir: King Vidor, 106 mins.)

Hallelujah, I'm a Bum (1933)*** Al Jolson, Madge Evans, Frank Morgan, Harry Langdon, Chester Conklin. The writers and cast went out on a limb for this unusual topical musical. Filmed with rhyming dialogue and beautiful ballads, this classy musical concerns a tramp itching to go respectable when Cupid's arrow strikes. (Dir: Lewis Milestone, 82 mins.)

Hallelujah the Hills (1963)*** Peter H. Beard, Martin Greenbaum, Sheila Finn, Peggy Steffans, Taylor Mead. Inventive comedy about two men in love with the same woman. The woman is played by two actresses (and you thought Buñuel did it first); this neat bit of casting reflects the playful air that permeates this N.Y. underground film. (Dir: Adolfas Mekas, 88 mins.)

Hallelujah Trail, The (1965)*½ Burt Lancaster, Lee Remick, Brian Keith, Jim Hutton, Donald Pleasence, Martin Landau. This clumsy comedy finds Lancaster assigned to protect a valuable liquor shipment, which attracts a band of thirsty Indians and a ladies' temperance league. (Dir: John Sturges, 167 mins.)

Halliday Brand, The (1957)**½ Joseph Cotten, Viveca Lindfors, Betsy Blair, Ward Bond. A talented cast makes most of this western drama bearable but, for the most part, the script defeats them. (Dir: Joseph H. Lewis, 77 mins.)

Halloween (1978)*** Jamie Lee Curtis, Donald Pleasence, Nancy Loomis, P.J. Soles, Nick Castle. Well-done, low-budget horror hit. It's Halloween, and a madman has escaped and is returning to his hometown for a rampage of murders. Director John Carpenter knows how to scare his audience. (90 mins.)†

Halloween II (1981)*½ Jamie Lee Curtis, Donald Pleasence, Charles Cyphers, Pamela Susan Shoop, Lance Guest. Not as chilling as the original, this is a slasher flick in which Michael the Maniac returns to terrorize everyone's favorite scream queen, Jamie Lee Curtis. (Dir: Rick Rosenthal, 92 mins.)†

Halloween III: Season of the Witch (1982)** Tom Atkins, Stacey Nelkin, Dan O'Herlihy, Ralph Strait. This nonsequel concerns a maniacal toy manufacturer who plots the world's most tasteless practical joke—the killing of innocent children on Halloween night. Mediocre and gory. (Dir: Tommy Lee Wallace, 96 mins.)†

Halloween 4: The Return of Michael Myers (1988)* Donald Pleasence, Ellie Cornell, Danielle Harris, George P. Wilbur. More teenagers systematically bite the dust in this sluggish product designed as a sequel to the original *Halloween*. (Dir: Dwight H. Little, 88 mins.)†

Halloween 5 (1990)** Donald Pleasence, Danielle Harris, Wendy Kaplan, Ellie Cornell, Donald L. Shanks. The usual plot, but this entry is an improvement thanks to some sharply directed shock scenes and a strong performance by Harris. (Dir: Dominique Othenin-Girard, 96 mins.)†

Halls of Anger (1969)**½ Calvin Lockhart, Janet MacLachlan, Rob Reiner, Jeff Bridges, Edward Asner. A second helping of *To Sir, With Love*. Handsome Calvin Lockhart plays a black high-school vice-principal, who is the focal point of bussed-in white students. The resulting tensions erupt all over the place in episodic fashion. (Dir: Paul Bogart, 103 mins.)

Halls of Montezuma (1951)**½ Richard Widmark, Jack Palance, Robert Wagner, Karl Malden, Jack Webb, Richard Boone. The Marines are once more displayed by by Hollywood as the roughest, toughest, brawliest, and bravest of all. (Dir: Lewis Milestone, 113 mins.)†

Hallucination Generation (1966)½ George Montgomery, Danny Stone, Reante Kasche, Tom Baker, Marianne Kantner. A group of "heads" led by Montgomery turn on to the good vibes in this acid-washed curiosity that makes for good party viewing. (Dir: Edward A. Mann, 90 mins.)

Hambone and Hillie (1984)** Lillian Gish, Timothy Bottoms, Candy Clark, O. J. Simpson, Robert Walker. Hambone dog story that wastes Gish as an old woman who gets separated from her beloved pooch, which manages the long trek back to her. (Dir: Roy Watts, 89 mins.)†

Hamburger (1986)* Leigh McCloskey, Randi Brooks, Dick Butkus, Jack Blessing, Chuck McCann. If a randy rich boy doesn't get his college degree he loses his inheritance, so he picks the easiest course available—management of a Buster Burger restaurant at a fast-food college. No laughs to go. (Dir: Mike Marvin, 90 mins.)†

Hamburger Hill (1987)** Anthony Barrile, Michael Patrick Boatman, Don Cheadle, Dylan McDermott. A reactionary war saga that offers a bloody, violent account of the struggle by American forces to secure a particular hill in Vietnam. As in any standard forties' war picture, the soldiers can be differentiated by the clichés each represents. (Dir: John Irvin, 109 mins.)†

Hamlet (Great Britain, 1948)**** Laurence Olivier, Jean Simmons, Basil Sydney, Eileen Herlie, Stanley Halloway, Anthony Quayle, Peter Cushing. Shakespeare's tragedy of the Danish prince brought to life by Olivier; film-making at its finest, should be seen by all. The greatest play in all literature superbly directed and performed by the greatest actor of his era—a perfect combination. Oscars for Best Picture, Best Actor. (Dir: Laurence Olivier, 153 mins.)†

Hamlet (Great Britain, 1969)**½ Nicol Williamson, Judy Parfitt, Anthony Hopkins, Marianne Faithfull. A filmed version of Williamson's riveting performance of this classic on the stage. This film, directed by Tony Richardson, has serious flaws—the supporting cast ranges from adequate to terrible, and the text has been unnecessarily trimmed, even diluting most of the famous Hamlet soliloquies. (114 mins.)†

Hamlet (1990)***½ Mel Gibson, Glenn Close, Alan Bates, Ian Holm, Helena Bonham-Carter, Paul Scofield. Gibson, an accomplished screen actor, is surprisingly compelling in this visually ravishing new production of what remains, after four centuries of challenges, the greatest single play ever written. Gibson has little command of the glories of the poetry playing the world's most famous Dane, but he is a physically commanding Hamlet and, occasionally, quite poignant. Close and Gibson are nearly the same age, so the mother-son relationship is never believable, but their near incestuous relationship, more pronounced here than in most other versions of Hamlet, is entirely believable. Scofield, one of the half-dozen greatest living actors, is superb in the tiny role of the ghost of Hamlet's father. Glorious color scenes and costumes filmed on location in Scotland. (Dir: Franco Zeffirelli, 135 mins.)†

Hammer (1972)** Fred Williamson, Vonetta McGee, William Smith, Charles Lampkin, Elizabeth Harding, Mel Stewart. Two-fisted action as Williamson enters the world of boxing through the efforts of a crooked crime kingpin (Lampkin). Fierce fighting with a plotline as old as time. (Dir: Bruce Clark, 92 mins.)

Hammerhead (Great Britain, 1968)* Vince Edwards, Judy Geeson, Peter Vaughn, Diana Dors. Poor spy yarn with Edwards as a secret agent out to crack an international plot involving plans to infiltrate a nuclear defense system (what else!). (Dir: David Miller, 99 mins.)

Hammersmith Is Out (1972)** Richard Burton, Elizabeth Taylor, Peter Ustinov, Beau Bridges, George Raft. Uneven, sometimes funny attempt at making the legend of Faust a timely theme. Burton plays Hammersmith, a lunatic, who promises Bridges he can have anything if he frees him. (Dir: Peter Ustinov, 108 mins.)†

Hammett (1983)*½ Frederic Forrest, Peter Boyle, Marilu Henner, Roy Kinnear, Elisha Cook, Jr., Sylvia Sidney. Dashiell Hammett's years as a Pinkerton man moonlighting as a writer. A confused *film noir*. (Dir: Wim Wenders, 97 mins.)†

Hancocks, The—See: **Dark Side of Innocence, The**

Hand, The (Great Britain, 1961)**½ Derek Bond, Ronald Leigh Hunt, Reed De Rouen, Ray Cooney. London is gripped by a series of murders in which the victims' limbs are amputated. The motive dates back to WWII prison camp in this trim, gruesome little thriller. (Dir: Henry Cass, 60 mins.)†

Hand, The (1981)*½ Michael Caine, Andrea Marcovicci, Viveca Lindfors. A ludicrous horror film; a cartoonist's hand, severed in a car accident, follows him to carry out his murderous thoughts. (Dir: Oliver Stone, 104 mins.)†

Handful of Dust, A (Great Britain, 1988)***½ James Wilby, Kristin Scott Thomas, Rupert Graves, Anjelica Huston, Alec Guinness. A handsomely mounted and quite involving adaptation of the novel by Evelyn Waugh. Wilby and Scott Thomas play an aristocratic couple whose marriage is on the rocks; the inevitable dissolution of their relationship, as a result of the sudden death of their young son, leads to some very unusual circumstances. (Dir: Charles Sturridge, 118 mins.)†

Hand in Hand (Great Britain, 1961)***½ Philip Needs, Loretta Parry, Sybil Thorndike. An eight-year-old Roman Catholic boy and a Jewish girl of the same age meet in school and become chums. They start hitchhiking to London to meet the Queen, but their friendship is soon tested. (Dir: Philip Leacock, 73 mins.)

Handle with Care (1958)** Dean Jones, Joan O'Brien, Thomas Mitchell. Young law student persuades his classmates to investigate unethical practices in a small town. (Dir: David Friedkin, 82 mins.)

Handle with Care (1977)***½ Paul Le Mat, Candy Clark, Ann Wedgeworth, Charles Napier, Marcia Rodd. This sleeper about the CB radio craze never found the large audience it deserved. It's a rarity, a satire that remains affectionate toward its characters without being condescending. Several vignettes are interwoven, including one about a trucker with wives in different cities and one about a young man who initiates a campaign against abuse of the CB airwaves. AKA: **Citizens Band**. (Dir: Jonathan Demme, 98 mins.)†

Handmaid's Tale, The (1990)**½ Natasha Richardson, Faye Dunaway, Aidan Quinn, Elizabeth McGovern, Victoria Tennant, Robert Duvall, Blanche Baker, Traci Lind. Harold Pinter wrote the screenplay for this faithful but insubstantial adaptation of Margaret Atwood's visionary novel set in a future American society where the few remaining fertile women are forced to bear children for members of the military elite. (Dir: Volker Schlondorff, 118 mins.)†

Hand of Death Part 25—See: Unmasked Part 25

Hand of Night, The—See: Beast of Morocco

Hands Across the Table (1935)*** Carole Lombard, Fred MacMurray, Ralph Bellamy. Delightful comedy about the romance of a manicurist and an unemployed charmer. Highly entertaining. (Dir: Mitchell Leisen, 80 mins.)

Hands of a Stranger (MTV 1987)** Blair Brown, Armand Assante, Beverly D'Angelo. A story of cops, rape, and adultery that starts off excitingly, then dissipates in its second half. (Dir: Larry Elikann, 208 mins.)

Hands of a Strangler (1961)*½ Mel Ferrer, Dany Carel, Christopher Lee. Pianist has the hands of a murderer grafted on when he is mutilated in an accident. Mediocre thriller. AKA: **The Hands of Orlac.** (Dir: Edmond T. Greville, 95 mins.)†

Hands of Orlac, The (1961)—See: Hands of a Strangler

Hands of the Ripper (Great Britain, 1971)**½ Eric Porter, Angharad Rees, Jane Merrow. The novel premise features the daughter of Jack the Ripper seeking psychiatric help from Porter (a disciple of Freud) when she claims to inherit her father's murderous tendencies. (Dir: Peter Sasdy, 85 mins.)†

Hands Over the City (Italy, 1963)**½ Rod Steiger, Salvo Randone, Guido Alberti, Angelo D'Alessandro. Corruption and cover-up among politicians is director Francesco Rosi's theme in this tense drama about deaths resulting from the collapse of a building in Naples during an election campaign. (105 mins.)

Hangar 18 (1980)** Darren McGavin, Robert Vaughn, Gary Collins. Close encounters of the silliest kind. A crashed UFO is discovered and the government covers up the fact that it contains the bodies of aliens. A new ending was tacked on for TV. (Dir: James L. Conway, 93 mins.)†

Hanged Man, The (MTV 1964)** Robert Culp, Edmond O'Brien, Vera Miles. Gunman out to avenge the murder of a friend. Remake of *Ride the Pink Horse* has little of its finesse. (Dir: Don Siegel, 87 mins.)

Hanged Man, The (MTV 1974)**½ Steve Forrest, Cameron Mitchell, Sharon Acker. A western-mystical adventure about a gunman who fantastically survives a hanging, and then dedicates himself to truth and justice. (Dir: Michael Caffey, 90 mins.)†

Hang 'Em High (1968)**½ Clint Eastwood, Inger Stevens, Ed Begley, Pat Hingle, Charles McGraw. Steely avenger sets out to take care of those varmints who strung him up and left him for dead. Should please nondiscriminating western buffs. (Dir: Ted Post, 114 mins.)†

444

Hangfire (1991)** Brad Davis, Kim Delaney, Jan-Michael Vincent, George Kennedy, Yaphet Kotto. A gang of escaped convicts who take over a New Mexico village, and battle a National Guard unit that comes to the rescue. Top stunts enhance film's patented adventure elements. (Dir: Peter Maris, 89 mins.)†

Hanging by a Thread (MTV 1979)** Patty Duke Astin, Joyce Bulifant, Bert Convy. Producer Irwin Allen, master of disaster, is at it again! A disabled tramcar high above a gorge is the setting, and flashbacks tell us the secrets of the trapped victims. (Dir: Georg Fenady, 208 mins.)

Hangin' With the Homeboys (1991)***½ Doug E. Doug, Mario Joyner, John Leguizamo, Nestor Serrano, Kimberly Russell, Mary B. Ward. Heartfelt look at the lives of four young men from the South Bronx examines their views of themselves and their dreams for the future as they spend 24 hours together working, talking, dancing, and remembering. Beautifully acted and sharply written by the director. (Dir: Joseph P. Vasquez, 88 mins.)†

Hanging Tree, The (1959)***½ Gary Cooper, Maria Schell, Karl Malden, George C. Scott. An underrated western drama when it was first released. Gary Cooper gives a fine performance as a man torn between law and order and his secret past. The photography helps to sustain the sober mood of the film. (Dir: Delmer Daves, 106 mins.)

Hangman, The (1959)** Robert Taylor, Fess Parker, Tina Louise. Grim U.S. marshal is determined to track down a wanted man but finds himself pitted against an entire town. Draggy western. (Dir: Michael Curtiz, 86 mins.)

Hangman's Knot (1952)*** Randolph Scott, Donna Reed, Lee Marvin. Action-filled western with hero Randolph Scott fighting off vigilantes and winning Donna Reed. (Dir: Roy Huggins, 81 mins.)

Hangmen Also Die (1943)*** Brian Donlevy, Walter Brennan, Dennis O'Keefe, Anna Lee. A doctor assassinates the notorious Nazi Heydrich the Hangman, and as a result a wave of terror sweeps occupied Czechoslovakia. Tense, gripping melodrama. (Dir: Fritz Lang, 131 mins.)

Hangover Square (1945)***½ George Sanders, Laird Cregar, Linda Darnell. Police inspector Sanders tries to discover if a decent, talented composer who suffers from amnesia is a psychotic killer. Fine musical score by Bernard Herrman. (Dir: John Brahm, 77 mins.)

Hangup (1974)*½ William Elliot, Marki Bey, Cliff Potts, Michael Lerner, Wally Taylor, Timothy Blake. Another blaxploitation outing dealing with drug dealing and its eventual consequences. Its one claim to notoriety is the fact that it was the last film that Henry Hathaway directed. (94 mins.)

Hanky Panky (1982)** Gene Wilder, Gilda Radner, Kathleen Quinlan, Richard Widmark. Lightweight homage to Hitchcock's cross-country chase films, with Wilder as the innocent man, Radner as the tagalong mystery woman, and Widmark as the villain. Adequate comedy-thriller. (Dir: Sidney Poitier, 107 mins.)†

Hannah and Her Sisters (1986)*** Woody Allen, Michael Caine, Mia Farrow, Barbara Hershey, Dianne Wiest, Max von Sydow, Maureen O'Sullivan, Lloyd Nolan. Woody Allen's affectionate family portrait of three sisters. The main story is a slim skeleton about an affair between Hannah's husband and her youngest sister, but Allen drapes it with very funny subplots. Oscars for Caine and Wiest. (Dir: Woody Allen, 107 mins.)†

Hanna K (France, 1983)** Jill Clayburgh, Gabriel Byrne, Jean Yanne. Soap opera overtones blur the serious premise that Israel has become a police state. Clayburgh plays an American lawyer in Israel who must defend an Arab accused of terrorism. (Dir: Costa-Gavras, 111 mins.)†

Hanna's War (1988)**½ Maruschka Detmars, Ellen Burstyn, Anthony Andrews, Donald Pleasence, David Warner. Interesting true story of Hanna Senesh, an Israeli martyr who fought for the establishment of Palestine during WWII and was executed in Hungary as a spy. (Dir: Menahem Golan, 158 mins.)†

Hannibal (Italy, 1960)** Victor Mature, Rita Gam, Gabriele Ferzetti, Milly Vitale. Unexceptional sword'n'sandal epic, with Mature looking at home in gladiator togs as the Carthaginian general who led troops and elephants over the Alps to attack Rome. Noted "B" director Edgar G. Ulmer is credited as director, but he probably only supervised the English language version; the rest was handled by Ludovico Bragaglia. (103 mins.)

Hannibal Brooks (Great Britain, 1969)** Oliver Reed, Michael J. Pollard, Wolfgang Preiss, Helmut Lohner. Mildly enjoyable without much inventiveness is its trunk. A soldier has to steal a pachyderm from a German zoo and lead it to safety. (Dir: Michael Winner, 101 mins.)

Hannie Caulder (Great Britain, 1971)** Raquel Welch, Robert Culp, Ernest Borgnine, Strother Martin, Jack Elam, Christopher Lee, Diana Dors. A trio of vermin-ridden villains rape Welch after killing her husband and setting fire to her home. The resilient Raquel bounces back, learns how to shoot a gun like Jesse James and sets out for revenge. (Dir: Burt Kennedy, 85 mins.)

Hanoi Hilton, The (1987)** Michael Moriarty, Jeffrey Jones, Paul LeMat, Stephen Davies, Lawrence Pressman, Aki Aelong, Gloria Carlin, David Soul. A retrogressive effort to dignify Vietnam POWs that ends up doing them a disservice; their many torments are depicted in a one-dimensional style that's painfully reminiscent of bad WWII prison-camp films. (Dir: Lionel Chetwynd, 123 mins.)†

Hanover Street (Great Britain, 1979)*½ Harrison Ford, Lesley-Anne Down, Christopher Plummer, Alec McCowen, Richard Masur, Patsy Kensit, John Ratzenberger. Cloying, romantic WWII yarn with a married woman falling madly for an American bomber pilot, and vice versa, of course. To complicate matters, her lover and husband (Plummer) are sent on a dangerous mission together. (Dir: Peter Hyams, 105 mins.)†

Hans Christian Andersen (1952)*** Danny Kaye, Jeanmaire, Farley Granger. Kaye as the teller of fairy tales, who falls in love with a beautiful ballerina. Ideal children's entertainment with some spectacular fantasy scenes—adults may become impatient with the excessive amount of sweetness and light. (Dir: Charles Vidor, 120 mins.)†

Hanussen (Hungary—West Germany, 1988)*** Klaus Maria Brandauer, Erland Josephson. Director Istvan Szabo's third examination (after *Mephisto* and *Colonel Redl*) into the soul of Germany prior to WWII once again focuses on Brandauer as a man who sets aside his personal ethics to play a public role—a psychic whose predictions win him favor with the Nazis. Less sweeping than the previous films, but Brandauer's subtle performance is excellent. (140 mins.)†

Happening, The (1967)**½ Anthony Quinn, Faye Dunaway, George Maharis, Michael Parks, Milton Berle, Robert Walker, Jr. A group of young beach-type vagrants accidentally kidnap former big-time mafia hood Quinn and the plot takes off. However, the scripters and director Elliot (*Cat Ballou*) Silverstein can't make up their minds between a way-out comedy, or an offbeat comedy-drama. (101 mins.)

Happiest Days of Your Life, The (Great Britain, 1950)*** Alastair Sim, Margaret Rutherford. Merry mixups when a group of schoolgirls are billeted at a boys' school by mistake. Hilarious madcap comedy. (Dir: Frank Launder, 81 mins.)

Happiest Millionaire, The (1967)**½ Fred MacMurray, Tommy Steele, Greer Garson, Geraldine Page, Gladys Cooper, Lesley Ann Warren. A long but cheery musical with the Disney stamp all over it. It deals with the goings-on in the wacky household of a millionaire who has little patience with conventionality. A welcome attempt at an original musical but everyone tries too hard, especially Steele. (Dir: Norman Tokar, 144 mins)†

Happily Ever After (MTV 1978)**½ Suzanne Somers, Bruce Boxleitner, Eric Braeden, John Rubinstein. Lightweight comedy-drama designed as a vehicle for Somers, who can't make more than a cutout of her character, a vulnerable young singer drowning in the opportunistic world of Las Vegas show business. (Dir: Robert Scheerer, 104 mins.)

Happily Ever After (Brazil, 1986)*** Regina Duarte, Paulo Castelli, Patarício Bisso, Flavio Galvao. Sunny, sultry sex comedy. A well-to-do housewife has a madcap fling with a bisexual Lothario, who teaches her how to kick up her heels before her eventual return to hearth and home, none the worse for wear. (Dir: Bruno Barreto, 92 mins.)

Happiness Ahead (1934)*** Dick Powell, Josephine Hutchinson, Frank McHugh, John Halliday, Ruth Donnelly, Dorothy Dare. Stop searching for that musical about the world of window washing. This is it! Charming comedy about a wealthy lass who pretends to be poor and falls for working slob Powell. Some fun songs, especially: "Pop Goes Your Heart." (Dir: Mervyn LeRoy, 86 min.)

Happiness Cage, The (1972)**½ Christopher Walken, Joss Ackland, Ralph Meeker, Ronny Cox. Unusual drama concerning Army pacification experiments. Walken shows early promise as one of the tested; the intriguing subject matter carries us through slow patches. (Dir: Bernard Girard, 94 mins.)

Happiness Is a Warm Clue—See: Charlie Chan (Happiness Is a Warm Clue)

Happy (MTV 1983)*** Dom DeLuise, Henry Silva, Dee Wallace, Tony Burton. Offbeat drama about a clown who becomes a hero when a man barges into a nightclub and opens fire on the patrons. Eventually, the killer begins stalking the clown in this good blend of suspense and comedy. (Dir: Lee Phillips, 104 mins.)

Happy Anniversary (1959)*** David Niven, Mitzi Gaynor, Carl Reiner, Patty Duke. The hit Broadway show about a couple celebrating their thirteenth (for good luck) anniversary makes a perfect screen comedy and David Niven couldn't be better, as the husband. (Dir: David Miller, 81 mins.)

Happy As the Grass Was Green (1978)** Geraldine Page, Pat Hingle, Graham Beckel, Rachel Thomas. Sixties ideals come back into the fore in this tardy drama concerning the spiritual wanderings of a confused young man. His visit to a Mennonite community brings him special enlightenment, and the audience a cure for insomnia. (Dir: Charles Davis, 105 mins.)

Happy Birthday, Gemini (1980)* Robert Viharo, Rita Moreno, Madeline Kahn,

Alan Rosenberg, Sarah Holcomb. Writer-director Richard Benner has adapted Albert Innaurato's hit comedy *Gemini* so that its edges have been softened but not its derisive nature. (107 mins.)

Happy Birthday To Me (Canada, 1981)*½ Glenn Ford, Melissa Sue Anderson, Tracy Bregman, Jack Blum, Matt Craven, Sharon Acker. A convoluted slasher pic. When a little girl's playmates could shoulder her birthday party, she grows up with a grudge. But is she using them as human Pin The Tail on the Donkey targets with an assortment of murder weapons? (Dir: J. Lee Thompson, 108 mins.)†

Happy Birthday, Wanda June (1971)*** Rod Steiger, Susannah York, George Grizzard, Don Murray, William Hickey, Pamelyn Ferdin. Literal rendering of Kurt Vonnegut's maniacal play. Steiger plays a modern Ulysses, back from an eight-year search for diamonds in Africa, returning to a perky car-hop wife who has collected a handful of college degrees in his absence. The ensuing re-education of a devout male chauvinist creates the laughs. (Dir: Mark Robson, 105 mins.)

Happy Ending, The (1969)** Jean Simmons, John Forsythe, Shirley Jones, Bobby Darin, Dick Shawn, Lloyd Bridges. Top cast and writing and direction by Richard Brooks leave this still an empty "woman's picture," reminiscent of forties vehicles for Crawford, Stanwyck, and Davis. Simmons is wonderful as a wife disillusioned after sixteen years of marriage. (Dir: Richard Brooks, 112 mins.)

Happy Endings (MTV 1983)**½ Lee Montgomery, Jill Schoelen, Sarah Nevin. Is an eighteen-year-old songwriter capable of raising his younger brothers and sisters, or should relatives take over the job? Writer Chris Beaumont re-creates his teenage experiences playing parent in an upbeat sentimental fashion. (Dir: Jerry Thorpe, 104 mins.)

Happy Endings (MTV 1983)** John Schneider, Catherine Hicks, Ana Alicia. Schneider and Hicks try light romantic comedy in San Francisco and wear themselves out. The story of friends who become lovers aims for fun and playfulness, but the material is too thin. (Dir: Noel Black, 104 mins.)

Happy Go Lovely (Great Britain, 1951)*** Vera-Ellen, David Niven, Cesar Romero. American producer in Edinburgh tries to produce a big musical show, and a chorus girl and a millionaire are enticed into the plot. Diverting musical comedy. (Dir: H. Bruce Humberstone, 87 mins.)†

Happy Go Lucky (1943)**½ Mary Martin, Dick Powell, Betty Hutton, Eddie Bracken, Rudy Vallee. Pleasant, undistinguished musical about a stenographer who saves her money for a big husband-hunting cruise. (Dir: Curtis Bernhardt, 81 mins.)

Happy Hooker, The (1975)** Lynn Redgrave, Jean-Pierre Aumont, Lovelady Powell, Nicholas Pryor, Tom Poston. Xaviera Hollander's experiences as a madam have been turned into a light comedy that ignores the raunchy specifics of the profession in favor of recounting a businesswoman's rise to success. (Dir: Nicholas Sgarro, 96 mins.)†

Happy Hooker Goes to Hollywood, The (1979)½ Martine Beswicke, Adam West, Phil Silvers, Richard Deacon, Chris Lemmon, Edie Adams, Dick Miller. If you can see through the vaseline-smeared lens, this soft-core comedy may elicit a laugh or two—not as a result of the dim-witted plotline (about the transformation of Ms. Hollander's book into a movie), but from the familiar faces shamelessly going for a quick paycheck. (Dir: Alan Roberts, 85 mins.)†

Happy Hooker Goes to Washington, The (1977)*½ Joey Heatherton, George Hamilton, Ray Walston, Jack Carter. Refusing to believe that business and pleasure don't mix, the Happy Hooker tries to make capital in the Capitol. (Dir: William Levey, 89 mins.)†

Happy Hour (1987)*½ Richard Gilliland, Jamie Farr, Rich Little, Tawny Kitaen, Eddie Deezen. Lame farce about rival breweries battling over an additive that makes beer addictive. As rival private eyes, Farr and Little are about all that's worth watching here. (Dir: John De Bello, 88 mins.)†

Happy Is the Bride (Great Britain, 1959)*** Ian Carmichael, Janette Scott, Cecil Parker, Terry-Thomas. The strain of going through with their wedding almost causes the betrothed couple to call the whole thing off. Amusing little domestic comedy, nicely played. (Dir: Roy Boulting, 84 mins.)

Happy Land (1943)**½ Don Ameche, Frances Dee, Harry Carey, Ann Rutherford, Cara Williams, Richard Crane, Harry Morgan, Dickie Moore. Sentimental slice of WWII patriotic philosophizing in which a father questions the meaning of his son's death in battle. Calculated to make you feel warm all over, and it works. See if you can spot a five-year-old Natalie Wood making her film debut. (Dir: Irving Pichel, 73 mins.)

Happy Landing (1938)**½ Sonja Henie, Don Ameche, Cesar Romero, Jean Hersholt, Ethel Merman, Lon Chaney Jr. Entertaining, though not outstanding, is this little musical about a plane that makes a forced landing in Norway near Henie's home. (Dir: Roy Del Ruth, 102 mins.)

Happy Mother's Day, Love, George—See: **Run, Stranger, Run**

Happy New Year (France, 1973)*** Lino Ventura, Françoise Fabian, Charles Gerard, Andre Falcon. In the sunny French Riviera, an escaped convict (Ventura) plans a major jewel heist and inadvertently falls in love with the beautiful owner of an antique store nearby. Claude (*A Man and a Woman*) Lelouch delivers a fine, visually engaging film full of delightful humor, playful twists, and much suspense involving the robbery. (112 mins.)†

Happy New Year (1987)** Peter Falk, Charles Durning, Wendy Hughes, Tom Courtenay. A pointless but sporadically entertaining Americanization of Claude Lelouch's 1973 film. This time the setting is Palm Beach, Falk is the unregenerate jewel thief, and Hughes is the antique dealer he falls for. Falk's unlikely turns in drag provide a couple of ripe comic moments. (Dir: John Avildsen, 85 mins.)†

Happy Road, The (1957)*** Gene Kelly, Barbara Laage, Bobby Clark, Brigitte Fossey, Michael Redgrave. Engaging escapades of two youngsters who become fugitives in the French countryside when they run away from their Swiss school, and of their respective parents, a U.S. businessman widower and a French divorcée, in pursuit. (Dir: Gene Kelly, 100 mins.)

Happy Thieves, The (1962)** Rita Hayworth, Rex Harrison, Joseph Wiseman, Alida Valli, Brita Ekman (Britt Ekland). The attractiveness of the two stars compensates somewhat for this mediocre comedy about sophisticated art thieves. Filmed in Madrid. (Dir: George Marshall, 88 mins.)

Happy Time, The (1952)***½ Charles Boyer, Louis Jourdan, Marsha Hunt, Linda Christian, Bobby Driscoll. A fine comedy about the ups and downs in the daily lives of an eccentric family headed by Boyer. (Dir: Richard Fleischer, 94 mins.)

Happy Together (1989)** Patrick Dempsey, Helen Slater, Dan Schneider, Kevin Hardesty, Marius Weyers. Sitcom-level comedy about students Dempsey, a shy would-be novelist with nothing to write about, and Slater, an actress who avoids real life, assigned the same dorm room by a computer glitch. The actors could have done better with this concept; as is, the highlight comes with unrelated dance parodies that show off Dempsey's acrobatic abilities. (Dir: Mel Damski, 96 mins.)†

Happy Years, The (1950)*** Dean Stockwell, Darryl Hickman, Leon Ames, Leo G. Carroll. Delightful tale of a mischievous boy and his adventures at a boys' school in the 1890s. Often hilariously funny, with Stockwell giving a superb performance. Fine fare for the entire family. (Dir: William Wellman, 110 mins.)

Hara-Kiri (Japan, 1962)***½ Tatsuya Nakadai, Shima Iwashita, Akira Ishihama, Yoshio Inaba. Honor and the samurai code are at the center of director Masaki Kobayashi's dramatic tale of seventeenth-century shoguns who disperse self-sufficient clans, creating a cadre of rootless, impoverished samurai, men without masters, one of whom, so devastated by this change, plans to commit a final shocking act of ritual suicide. AKA: **Seppuku.** (135 min.)

Harbor of Missing Men (1950)*½ Richard Denning, Barbara Fuller, George Zucco. Fishing boat owner escaping from smugglers is sheltered by a Greek fishing family. Worth missing. (Dir: R. G. Springsteen, 60 mins.)

Hardbodies (1984)½ Grant Cramer, Gary Wood, Michael Rapport, Sorrells Pickard, Teal Roberts, Joyce Jameson. Three horny middle-aged Romeos with the moolah to finance their infantile desires hire a stud to show them the ropes of girl-getting. Softheaded muck. (Dir: Mark Griffiths, 87 mins.)†

Hardbodies: 2 (1986)* Brad Zutaut, Fabiana Udinio, James Karen, Alba Francesca. A young actor falls in love with the waitress that he selects as his costar. He pursues true love while everyone else practices promiscuity and topless sunbathing. (Dir: Mark Griffiths, 95 mins.)†

Hard Boiled Mahoney (1947)**½ Bowery Boys, Dan Seymour, Teala Loring, Bernard Gorcey, Betty Compson. The closest you will get to a Bowery Boys *film noir.* An atypical adventure in which Sach and Slip are mistakenly hired as detectives and risk their lives to find a missing woman. (Dir: William Beaudine, 63 mins.)

Hardcase (MTV 1971)** Clint Walker, Stefanie Powers, Alex Karras. Offbeat western has Walker playing a soldier of fortune who helps Mexican revolutionaries, and finds his wife among them. (Dir: John Llewellyn Moxey, 74 mins.)

Hard Choices (1986)** Margaret Klenck, Gary McCleery, John Seitz, John Sayles, John Snyder. Another love-on-the-run tale about a committed, caring social worker whose ultimate method of aiding her fifteen-year-old client charged with murder is to run away with him. Based on a true story, the film is neither particularly thrilling as an action adventure nor especially impassioned as a love story. (Dir: Rick King, 90 mins.)†

Hard Contract (1969)**½ James Coburn, Lee Remick, Sterling Hayden, Karen Black, Lilli Palmer, Burgess Meredith, 448

Patrick Magee. Interesting but flawed effort to comment on the way in which Americans so readily accept or explain away murder. Coburn portrays an international hit man who has a contract to kill three men. Miss Remick delivers an attractive performance as a jet-set chick who breaks down Coburn's cool and shakes his calm hand as he stalks his triple prey. (Dir: S. Lee Pogostin, 106 mins.)

Hardcore (1979)**½ George C. Scott, Season Hubley, Peter Boyle, Dick Sargent. In exposing the porno world, this feature becomes highly exploitative in itself. A Calvinist, played by Scott, searches for his runaway daughter through a trail of sex films to San Francisco. Writer-director Paul Schrader allowed Scott to be excessively violent in his quest, possibly a comment on how a man with a mission can forget his principles so quickly. (Dir: Paul Schrader, 105 mins.)†

Hard Country (1981)** Jan-Michael Vincent, Kim Basinger, Michael Parks, Tanya Tucker, Daryl Hannah, Richard Moll. Conventional romance with country-and-western trimmings. Urban cowboy concentrates on partying and avoiding marriage. (Dir: David Greene, 104 mins.)†

Hard Day's Night, A (Great Britain, 1964)**** The Beatles, Wilfrid Brambell, Victor Spinetti. During the peak of their popularity the Beatles made their first movie, and to everyone's surprise and delight it turned out to be a stylishly inventive contemporary comedy classic. Director Richard Lester filmed the story about the Beatles on tour in England with a sense of frenzy and unabashed humor, much in the style of the early Marx Brothers' Hollywood comedies, and it works from start to finish. (85 mins.)†

Hard Driver (1973)*** Jeff Bridges, Valerie Perrine, Art Lund, Geraldine Fitzgerald, Ed Lauter, Gary Busey. (Theatrically released as **The Last American Hero.**) Perceptive, involving examination of a real slice of Americana—stock-car racing— in North Carolina. Bridges is marvelous as a young moonshiner, running whiskey past the revenuers, who turns to racing to help his father (Lund) who has been jailed. (Dir: Lamont Johnson, 95 mins.)†

Hard Drivin' (1960)*½ Rory Calhoun, Alan Hale Jr., Connie Hines, John Gentry. Clichéd story of stock racer Calhoun and his attempts to seduce the wife of a young protégé merely serves as an excuse to use footage of the South Carolina "Southern 500." For hard-core race fans only. AKA: **Thunder in Carolina.** (Dir: Paul Helmick, 92 mins.)†

Harder They Come, The (Jamaica, 1973)*** Jimmy Cliff, Carl Bradshaw, Janet Barkley. Cult favorite about a young

Jamaican's attempts to be a pop star, and his eventual demise as an outlaw. His antihero exploits are as involving as those of the spaghetti western heroes he emulates. A vivid but ragged mixture of pop mythology, reggae music, and quick, brutal action, with a wonderful soundtrack keeping it all afloat. (Dir: Perry Henzell, 98 mins.)†

Harder They Fall, The (1956)*** Humphrey Bogart, Jan Sterling, Max Baer, Mike Kane, Rod Steiger. In his last role, Bogart, as a sportswriter dragooned into fronting for a mob-controlled boxer, draws effectively on his weary cynicism. The exposé of the fight racket has a brutal honesty. (Dir: Mark Robson, 109 mins.)†

Hard, Fast and Beautiful (1951)*½ Sally Forrest, Claire Trevor. Girl's mother pushes her into becoming a tennis champ; but the movie never gets over the net. (Dir: Ida Lupino, 79 mins.)

Hardhat and Legs (MTV 1980)**½ Kevin Dobson, Sharon Gless, W. T. Martin, Ray Serra. Cheerful, fun-loving New York tale by old pros Garson Kanin and Ruth Gordon. Gless is the blueblood blonde with great legs, Dobson is the Italian construction worker intent on crossing class lines to win her. (Dir: Lee Philips, 104 mins.)†

Hard Knox (MTV 1984)** Robert Conrad, Joan Sweeny, Red West, Bill Erwin, Dean Hill. Robert Conrad stars as a dedicated Marine Corps pilot who is forced into retirement and ends up running an undisciplined military school. A real overdose of the real macho military ethic plus sentimentality worthy of Michael Landon. (Dir: Peter Werner, 104 mins.)†

Hardly Working (1981)* Jerry Lewis, Susan Oliver. A vulgar, unfunny, dated, slapstick affair which finds Jerry playing an out-of-work clown who tries his hand at various jobs. If you think this is bad, consider that an even longer version played in France! (Dir: Jerry Lewis, 91 mins.)†

Hard Man, The (1957)**½ Guy Madison, Valerie French, Lorne Greene. Madison is a strong-willed cowboy who comes into a town, which is run by one man (indirectly by the man's greedy wife). He gets involved with the woman and almost pays for this mistake with his life. (Dir: George Sherman, 80 mins.)

Hard Rock Zombies (1985)** E. J. Curcio, Sam Mann, Geno Andrews, Mick McMains. Murdered members of a heavy metal band return as zombies in this half-dead horror comedy. A few laughs for rock fans, but mostly pretty stupid, with lousy special effects. (Dir: Krishna Shah, 94 mins.)†

Hard Ticket to Hawaii (1987)½ Dona Speir, Hope Marie Carlton, Ronn Moss, Harold Diamond. If you've ever spent long nights dreaming that Sybil Danning had been on "Charlie's Angels," this is the movie for you. Two blonde drug enforcement agents battle smugglers and a giant, rabid snake on some of Hawaii's more picturesque islands. (Dir: Andy Sidaris, 88 mins.)†

Hard Times (1975)*** Charles Bronson, James Coburn, Jill Ireland, Strother Martin. A tough, lean, remarkably effective fable about a bare-knuckle street fighter slugging his way to a couple of paydays in New Orleans during the Depression era of the 1930s. Bronson energizes this no-nonsense melodrama, and plays well with Coburn portraying an on-the-make small-time hustler and boxing promoter. (Dir: Walter Hill, 97 mins.)†

Hard to Get (1938)** Dick Powell, Olivia de Havilland, Charles Winnenger, Allen Jenkins, Bonita Granville, Melville Cooper, Grady Sutton. Class-conflict comedy misfire; petulant spoiled heiress de Havilland fights with grouchy garage mechanic Powell, and naturally they fall in love. Some rather unpleasant squabbling mars the comedy, though the supporting players are excellent. (Dir: Ray Enright, 80 mins.)

Hard to Handle (1933)**½ James Cagney, Mary Brian, Ruth Donnelly, Allen Jenkins, Claire Dodd, Sterling Holloway. Cagney stars as a fast operator who makes his living promoting various special events and products, including a typical Depression-era dance marathon. Not much of a movie, but a great example of Cagney's boundless charm and energy. (Dir: Mervyn LeRoy, 71 mins.)†

Hard to Hold (1984)*½ Rick Springfield, Janet Eilber, Patti Hansen, Albert Salmi, Bill Mumy. Springfield won't find it hard to hold his fans in his screen debut as a rock singer seeking inspiration while falling for a children's counselor, who doesn't approve of his lifestyle. Most will find this hard to stomach. (Dir: Larry Peerce, 93 mins.)†

Hard to Kill (1990)**½ Steven Seagal, Kelly Le Brock, Bill Sadler, Frederick Coffin, Bonnie Burroughs. Aften seven years in a coma from an attack that left his wife dead, cop Seagal recovers and sets out for revenge on the crooked politician and his cronies who think Seagal is dead. Plenty of violent action, though Seagal and real-life wife Le Brock do less well in the moments without mayhem. (Dir: Bruce Malmuth, 95 mins.)†

Hard Traveling (1986)** J. E. Freeman, Ellen Geer. All the social injustice clichés get aired when drifter Freeman comes to rest in schoolteacher-widow Geer's home in Depression-era California, marries her, and eventually murders a businessman in a desperate effort to support his new family. The film harkens back to the social realism fiction of the 1930s and early 1940s and sacrifices art to ideology just as effectively. (Dir: Dan Bessie, 99 mins.)†

Hardware (1990)** Dylan McDermott, Stacey Travis, Iggy Pop, John Lynch, William Hootkins. Scavengers roam a post-nuclear-war America in familiar plot about high-tech junkies stalking each other. (Dir: Richard Stanley, 92 mins.)†

Hard Way, The (1942)**½ Ida Lupino, Dennis Morgan, Joan Leslie, Jack Carson. It's an old ambitious-girl-stepping-on-everyone-in-her-way plot, but Miss Lupino gives it some dignity. The first half is well done but producer's luck runs out in the final reels. (Dir: Vincent Sherman, 109 mins.)

Hard Way, The (1991)*½ Michael J. Fox, James Woods, Stephen Lang, Annabella Sciorra. Woods is way over the top in this clunky comedy about a hardboiled New York City cop forced to show a spoiled actor (Fox) the ropes of how to portray a policeman. The laughs peter out, the action is flat, and the ending Hitchcock rip-off is hardly an homage. (Dir: John Badham, 115 mins.)†

Hardys Ride High, The (1939)**½ Lewis Stone, Mickey Rooney, Cecilia Parker, Ann Rutherford, Virginia Grey, Marsha Hunt. Spruced-up Hardy entry as America's favorite middle-class family inherits a fortune and tries to avoid getting the bends as they rise rapidly in the social world. (Dir: George B. Seitz, 80 mins.)

Harem (France, 1985)* Nastassia Kinski, Ben Kingsley, Zohra Segal. Lushly filmed yawner about Wall Streeter Kinski kidnapped by sensitive sheik Kingsley to be part of his harem, though he wants her to love him rather than submit out of fear. (Dir: Arthur Joffe, 113 mins.)†

Harem (MTV 1986)** Nancy Travis, Art Malik, Sarah Miles, Yaphet Kotto, Julian Sands, Cheri Lunghi, Omar Sharif, Ava Gardner. Sprawling romantic drama set in the early 1900s; Sharif plays the sultan who buys a kidnapped American beauty. Gardner is the sultan's first wife and therefore a natural enemy of the American interloper, who eventually (but not soon enough) gets rescued from the harem. (Dir: Billy Hale, 208 mins.)

Harem Girl (1952)*½ Joan Davis, Peggie Castle, Arthur Blake. Typically raucous and cheerful Joan Davis comedy set in an Arabian Nights locale. (Dir: Edward Bernds, 70 mins.)

Harlan County U.S.A. (1977)**** An effective documentary about coal miners on strike in Kentucky. What makes this so special is the ability of the filmmaker to capture the lives of these courageous workers without patronizing them or glorifying them. An Oscar for Best Documentary. (Dir: Barbara Kopple, 103 mins.)†

Harlem Globetrotters, The (1951)**½ Thomas Gomez, Dorothy Dandridge. A dull story about one of the members of the famous Negro basketball team. The basketball game scenes are the best things in the film, and they're terrific! Dorothy Dandridge has a small nonsinging part. (Dir: Phil Brown, 80 mins.)

Harlem Globetrotters on Gilligan's Island, The (MTV 1981)½ Bob Denver, Alan Hale, Jr., Russell Johnson, Dawn Wells. Inane gibberish featuring most of the series's original cast along with the famous basketball team. A mad scientist discovers an energy source and plans to rule the world. Chinese water torture would be preferable. (Dir: Peter Baldwin, 104 mins.)

Harlem Nights (1989)** Eddie Murphy, Richard Pryor, Redd Foxx, Danny Aiello, Michael Lerner, Della Reese, Stan Shaw, Jasmine Guy, Arsenio Hall. Nasty and not very funny period piece about Harlem nightlife and gangsters circa 1938. It's really dress-up time for Murphy, who—also billed as writer, director, and executive producer—wisely focuses attention on the film's lush production values and strong supporting cast. (118 mins.)

Harlow (1965)*½ Carol Lynley, Efrem Zimbalist, Jr., Barry Sullivan, Hurd Hatfield, Ginger Rogers, Lloyd Bochner. The worst of the two biopics on Harlow, neither of which captured that sultry comedienne's appeal. Originally shot on videotape. (Dir: Alex Segal, 109 mins.)

Harlow (1965)** Carroll Baker, Mike Connors, Peter Lawford, Martin Balsam, Red Buttons, Angela Lansbury, Rat Vallone, Leslie Nielsen. If you're looking for a definitive biography of the late movie queen of the thirties, skip this one. It's strictly for those who prefer to believe what they read in the movie fan magazines. (Dir: Gordon Douglas, 125 mins.)†

Harness, The (MTV 1971)***½ Lorne Greene, Julie Sommars. A lovely movie version of John Steinbeck's Salinas Valley tale about a withdrawn farmer and his ailing wife. Literate script plus Boris Sagal's careful direction convey the man's torment in trying to find out who he is. (99 mins.)

Harold and Maude (1971)***½ Ruth Gordon, Bud Cort, Vivian Pickles, Ellen Geer. An often wildly funny and original black comedy. Young man of twenty (Cort) has a great flair for inspired sight gags, all relating to death. His companion in love and adventures is a wacky seventy-nine-year-old gloriously played by Gordon. It's a sick comedy all right—but if you go along with the spirit of this farce, it's one of the most inventive

American comedy films in years. (Dir: Hal Ashby, 91 mins.)†

Harold Lloyd's Comedy Classics ***½ Harold Lloyd, Bebe Daniels, Snub Pollard. Four silent short comedies: **The Chef** (1919), **The Cinema Director** (1916), **Two Gun-Gussie** (1918), and **I'm On My Way** (1919). Wonderful shorts made by Lloyd for Keystone, before he discovered his "glasses" character; here he is much more brash and antisocial, and very, very funny. (51 mins.)†

Harper (1966)*** Paul Newman, Arthur Hill, Lauren Bacall, Shelley Winters, Julie Harris, Robert Webber, Robert Wagner, Janet Leigh, Strother Martin. Director Jack Smight's film version of Ross MacDonald's *The Moving Target* casts Newman well as the gum-chewing, wise-guy detective with a penchant for connecting with the tragedy of the mysteries he unravels. The film moves perhaps too slickly for its own good, but it's good genre work. Sequel: *The Drowning Pool*. (121 mins.)†

Harper Valley PTA (1978)**½ Barbara Eden, Nanette Fabray, Ronny Cox, Louis Nye. A surprise box-office hit tied to the Jeannie C. Riley song. Eden is sexy Stella Johnson, who is termed an unfit mother by the puritanical PTA of Harper Valley, Ohio. The comedy of retribution has her getting even by exposing her adversaries' hypocrisies. (Dir: Richard Bennett, 93 mins.)†

Harp of Burma (Japan, 1956)*** Shoji Yasui, Rentara Mikuni, Taniye Kitabayashi. Director Kon Ichikawa has fashioned a poetic antiwar film that has impact. A Japanese Army private takes on a personal crusade to bury all the dead soldiers he finds after the end of WWII. Along his journey's trail, the soldier dons the robes of a Buddhist monk. AKA: **The Burmese Harp**. (Dir: Kon Ichikawa, 116 mins.)†

Harpy (MTV 1971)* Hugh O'Brian, Elizabeth Ashley. Dreary feature about an impossible woman (Miss Ashley) who'll stop at nothing to win and woo her ex-husband, who's about to remarry. There's shouting, rather than acting, and a silly "harpy eagle" figures into the plot, if you're a bird fancier. (Dir: Jerrold Freedman, 99 mins.)

Harrad Experiment, The (1973)*½ James Whitmore, Tippi Hedren, Don Johnson, B. Kirby, Jr., Laurie Walters. Based on the controversial novel, this is a weak, dated attempt to portray a serious look at sexual liberation. Hedren and Whitmore run an experimental college where the students sleep together to lose their sexual hangups. Johnson (of "Miami Vice") is interesting as the immature, sex-starved student. (Dir: Ted Post, 96 mins.)†

Harrad Summer, The (1974)* Richard Doran, Victoria Thompson, Laurie Walters, Robert Reiser, Bill Dana. Inferior sequel to *The Harrad Experiment*. Deserves credit for the not inconsiderable feat of making sex seem boring. (Dir: Steven Hilliard Stern, 103 mins.)†

Harriet Craig (1950)*** Joan Crawford, Wendell Corey, Lucile Watson, Allyn Joslyn. Crawford's star presence eliminates any semblance of character creation in this remake of George Kelly's *Craig's Wife*. Still, it's an effective theatrical piece. Harriet is a grasping middle-class housewife far more devoted to her house and possessions than to her husband and family. (Dir: Vincent Sherman, 94 mins.)

Harry and Son (1984)*½ Paul Newman, Robby Benson, Joanne Woodward, Ellen Barkin, Judith Ivey, Ossie Davis, Wilford Brimley, Morgan Freeman. An out-of-focus examination of the relationship between a hard-headed hard-hat worker and his directionless son. (Dir: Paul Newman, 117 mins.)†

Harry and the Hendersons (1987)** John Lithgow, Melinda Dillon, Don Ameche, David Suchet, Margaret Langrick, Joshua Rudoy, Lanie Kazan. The always-likable Lithgow and excellent creature effects by Rick Baker can't save this pedestrian *E.T.* derivative; a typical Seattle family winds up adopting Bigfoot. (Dir: William Dear, 110 mins.)†

Harry and Tonto (1974)***½ Art Carney, Ellen Burstyn, Larry Hagman, Geraldine Fitzgerald, Josh Mostel, Barbara Rhoades, Arthur Hunnicutt, Melanie Mayron. Art Carney's Academy Award-winning performance, as a New York-based septuagenarian who decides to pack his beloved cat Tonto and head across the United States on his last odyssey. It's a lovely trip, filled with adventures, love, disappointment, people, and death. Director Paul Mazursky doesn't shy away from sentiment. (115 mins.)†

Harry and Walter Go to New York (1976)*½ James Caan, Elliott Gould, Michael Caine, Diane Keaton, Charles Durning, Lesley Ann Warren, Carol Kane. This overplayed farce, circa 1892, dealing with two fumbling, fifth-rate vaudevillians turned reluctant safecrackers, is incredibly boring. (Dir: Mark Rydell, 123 mins.)†

Harry Black and the Tiger (Great Britain, 1958)** Stewart Granger, Barbara Rush. Talky, only occasionally interesting tale about a man who stalks dangerous jungle beasts for profit and thrills. (Dir: Hugo Fregonese, 107 mins.)†

Harry In Your Pocket (1973)**½ James Coburn, Michael Sarrazin, Walter Pidgeon, Trish Van Devere. A slick crime film that explores, at length, the "art" of pickpockets. The Harry of the title is the superdip of them all, and he's played with icy detachment by Coburn. Sarrazin and Miss Van Devere are two new recruits to the world of pickpockets and Walter Pidgeon is a veteran. (Dir: Bruce Geller, 103 mins.)

Harry's Hong Kong (MTV 1987)** David Soul, Mike Preston, Mel Harris, Jan Gan Boyd, Lisa Lu, Russell Wong. Standard oriental intrigue about a soldier of fortune (Soul) who looks into the death of a friend and the disappearance of another man. (Dir: Jerry London, 104 mins.)

Harry's Machine—See: **Hollywood Harry**

Harry's War (1981)**½ Edward Herrmann, Geraldine Page, Karen Grassle, Salome Jens. A nice little throwback to those Frank Capra movies. Herrmann is a guy who thinks he can fight the IRS and win. His adventures with the tax men and his family add up to a pleasant comedy. (Dir: Keith Merrill, 98 mins.)†

Harry Tracy (Canada, 1982)** Bruce Dern, Helen Shaver, Michael C. Gwynne, Gordon Lightfoot. Dern's once again on the wrong side of the law in this fictionalized account of the adventures of Tracy, an outlaw who once rode with Butch Cassidy. Canadian stalwarts Shaver and Lightfoot acquit themselves nicely, but the tone of this mock Western seems all wrong. (Dir: William A. Graham, 111 mins.)†

Hart to Hart (MTV 1979)** Robert Wagner, Stefanie Powers, Roddy McDowall, Jill St. John. A TV series was born of this film about a pair of rich, beautiful sleuths. As hubby and wife, Wagner and Powers aim for the debonair, light touch, skulking around a health spa, but the spark is missing in the mystery. (Dir: Tom Mankiewicz, 104 mins.)

Harum Scarum (1965)* Elvis Presley, Mary Ann Mobley, Fran Jeffries, Michael Ansara. Elvis is a movie star who is kidnapped while he's on a personal appearance tour in the Middle East. (Dir: Gene Nelson, 95 mins.)†

Harvest (France, 1937)**** Gabriel Gabrio, Orane Demazis, Fernandel, Edouard Delmont. A beautiful film telling the simple story of a French peasant family and their struggle for existence, with lovely performances and great depth of feeling. A gem. (Dir: Marcel Pagnol, 105 mins.)†

Harvey (1950)***½ James Stewart, Josephine Hull, Peggy Dow, Jesse White, Cecil Kellaway. Delightful fable of a gentle tippler and the six-foot invisible "rabbit" he has adopted for a friend. Stewart is excellent as the whimsical Elwood P. Dowd, while Oscar-winner Hull is a joy as his straight-laced sister who is continually embarrassed by his

actions. Stewart contributed a six-minute intro to the videocassette version. (Dir: Henry Koster, 104 mins.)†

Harvey Girls, The (1945)***½ Judy Garland, John Hodiak, Ray Bolger, Virginia O'Brien, Angela Lansbury, Marjorie Main, Cyd Charisse. Good score, nice performers, and an ordinary story add up to a fairly good musical. Tale of a group of young ladies who go to the Wild West to become waitresses in a Fred Harvey restaurant is a good background for some nice production numbers. (Dir: George Sidney, 104 mins.)†

Harvey Middleman, Fireman (1965)** Gene Troobnick, Hermione Gingold, Arlene Golonka, Charles Durning. Writer-director Ernest Pintoff is a talented, inventive maker of short animated films such as *The Critic*. But he comes a cropper here with this juvenile, semi-fairy-tale version of a theme dealt with better in Axelrod's *The Seven Year Itch*—the arrested adolescence of many American adult males. (90 mins.)

Has Anybody Seen My Gal (1952)**½ Piper Laurie, Rock Hudson, Charles Coburn. Mildly entertaining package of fads, songs and silly antics of the twenties. The Blaisdells come into a large amount of money and it changes their life drastically. (Dir: Douglas Sirk, 89 mins.)

Hasty Heart, The (Great Britain, 1949)***½ Richard Todd, Patricia Neal, Ronald Reagan. Heartwarming story of a stubborn Scottish soldier who has a short time to live and the friends he makes in an Army hospital. A beautiful performance by Todd as the kilted "Lochy." (Dir: Vincent Sherman, 99 mins.)

Hasty Heart, The (MCTV 1983)*** Gregory Harrison, Cheryl Ladd, Perry King. Remake of the four-hankie weeper set in a WWII army hospital, where a dying Scottish soldier (Harrison) refuses to accept the friendship of his fellow patients. Overlong and overdone—the syrupy music and the fruity accents employed by all three stars are particularly distracting—but effective nonetheless. (Dir: Martin Speer, 135 mins.)†

Hatari! (1962)*** John Wayne, Hardy Kruger, Red Buttons, Elsa Martinelli, Gerard Blain, Bruce Cabot. A well-produced comedy-adventure about a group of he-men who round up African animals for shipment to zoos around the world. The animal sequences, filmed on location in Africa, add immensely to the film's appeal, and Wayne is at home in his role of the top man of the adventure-loving crew. (Dir: Howard Hawks, 159 mins.)†

Hatchet Man, The (1932)*½ Edward G. Robinson, Loretta Young, Dudley Digges. Oriental tong wars and the hatchet of a

Chinese avenger are involved in Robinson's romancing of Young in San Francisco's Chinatown. Early effort by all involved. (Dir: William Wellman, 74 mins.)

Hatchet Murders, The—See: **Deep Red**

Hatfields and the McCoys, The (MTV 1975)*½ Jack Palance, Steve Forrest, John Calvin. The old Hatfield-McCoy feud is trotted out again. Competent cast of strong faces brings a he-man vitality to the tale of feuding Kentucky clans. (Dir: Clyde Ware, 72 mins.)†

Hatful of Rain, A (1957)**** Eva Marie Saint, Anthony Franciosa, Don Murray, Lloyd Nolan. An excellent film version of Michael Gazzo's hard-hitting B'way play about a junkie and the people who love him and therefore suffer with him. (Dir: Fred Zinnemann, 109 mins.)

Hats Off (1937)** Mae Clarke, John Payne, Helen Lynd, Luis Alberni, Skeets Gallagher, Franklyn Pangborn. With appearances by "The Two Stooges" (no relation) and "The Three Radio Rogues," you already know this musical about rival press agents who become romantically entwined is just one more piece of Golden Age schmaltz. Sam Fuller co-wrote the screenplay. (Dir: Boris Patrof, 65 mins.)

Hatter's Castle (Great Britain, 1941)** Robert Newton, Deborah Kerr, Beatrice Varley, James Mason, Emlyn Williams. A Scottish hatter stops at nothing to attain a higher place in society, driving his family mercilessly. Old-fashioned, wheezing costume drama from an A. J. Cronin novel. (Dir: Lance Comfort, 90 mins.)

Hatter's Ghosts, The (France, 1982)***½ Michel Serrault, Charles Aznavour, Monique Chaumette, Aurore Clement. Based on story by George Simeon, Claude Chabrol's delicious mystery is a tale of a town's hatmaker who murders his wife, as well as a number of other women, while still enjoying his nightly get-togethers with the village's men. Perfectly wicked. (129 min.)

Haunted by Her Past (MTV 1987)** Susan Lucci, John James, Finola Hughes, Marcia Strassman. Lucci falls under the spell of a legendary look-alike murderess in this contemporary Gothic. (Dir: Michael Pressman, 96 mins.)

Haunted Honeymoon (Great Britain, 1940)*** Robert Montgomery, Constance Cummings, Robert Newton, Leslie Banks, Googie Withers. Lovers of Dorothy Sayers's aristocratic sleuth Lord Peter Wimsey beware—the main characters are greatly changed in this Hollywoodized version of her classic mystery novel. But the otherwise charming performers really give it their all, and the complex, intriguing plot is intact. (Dir: Arthur B. Woods, 83 mins.)

Haunted Honeymoon (1986)** Gene Wilder, Gilda Radner, Dom DeLuise, Jonathan Pryce, Paul L. Smith. Larry Abbot (Wilder) is a 1930s radio star set to marry his co-star (Radner) at the eerie Abbot mansion, where his aunt (DeLuise in drag) lives in fear of her life. Several amusing moments, but this is rather flimsily conceived. (Dir: Gene Wilder, 88 mins.)†

Haunted Palace, The (1963)**½ Vincent Price, Debra Paget, Lon Chaney, Jr. It's Price sent to chill and thrill. He's a warlock returned from the grave in the person of his descendant, to seek revenge against the villagers who burned him at the stake a century ago. You can't keep a good bogeyman down. (Dir: Roger Corman, 85 mins.)

Haunted Strangler, The (Great Britain, 1958)** Boris Karloff, Anthony Dawson. Farfetched thriller in which Boris is cast as a novelist who does some research on a grisly murder case and becomes so immersed, he starts duplicating some of the violent acts. (Dir: Robert Day, 81 mins.)†

Haunted Summer (1988)**½ Philip Anglim, Laura Dern, Alice Krige, Eric Stoltz. Lord Byron and Percy and Mary Shelley's infamous drug-and-sex filled Swiss summer of 1816 is trotted out again. Not as feverishly hysterical as Ken Russell's *Gothic*, but still aimless. (Dir: Ivan Passer, 106 mins.)†

Haunting, The (1963)***½ Julie Harris, Claire Bloom, Richard Johnson, Russ Tamblyn, Lois Maxwell, Fay Compton. Tingly ghost story about a believer in the supernatural who brings together a group in a supposedly haunted house, where weird things begin to happen. Guaranteed to raise the hackles, definitely should not be seen in a darkened room. Well acted. (Dir: Robert Wise, 112 mins.)†

Haunting of Julia, The (Great Britain-Canada, 1976)**½ Mia Farrow, Keir Dullea, Tom Conti. An unstable woman is plagued by visions of her dead daughter. Farrow's acting enhances this supernatural thriller that transcends an all-too-familiar plotline with graceful camerawork and fine acting. (Dir: Richard Loncraine, 96 mins.)†

Haunting of Morella, The (1990)*½ David McCallum, Nicole Eggert, Christopher Halsted, Lana Clarkson. Roger Corman produced this Edgar Allen Poe adaptation. A witch returns after being burned at the stake to possess the body of her daughter. (Dir: Jim Wynorski, 87 mins.)†

Haunting of Sarah Hardy, The (MCTV 1989)** Sela Ward, Polly Bergen, Morgan Fairchild, Michael Woods, Roscoe Born. Gothic suspense thriller about a beautiful heiress who discovers a plot to kill her for her money. (Dir: Jerry London, 92 mins.)†

Haunting Passion (MTV 1983)**½ Jane Seymour, Gerald McRaney. A sensual ghost story. The idea of a woman with marital problems indulging in sexual fantasies, only to be drawn to a ghost, sounds ridiculous, but director John Korty almost pulls it off. (104 mins.)†

Haunts (1977)* May Britt, Cameron Mitchell, Aldo Ray, William Gray Espy. Slow-moving, unhaunting thriller about a series of unexplained slayings out in the boondocks. Is the local farm girl crazy? Or did her suspicious-looking uncle do it? (Dir: Herb Freed, 98 mins.)†

Haunts of the Very Rich (MTV 1972)**½ Lloyd Bridges, Cloris Leachman, Anne Francis, Moses Gunn. Remember *Outward Bound* and *No Exit*? Here's a variation of their themes, placing a group of strangers together on a plush island, which may or may not be hell. (Dir: Paul Wendkos, 72 mins.)†

Hauser's Memory (MTV 1970)**½ David McCallum, Susan Strasberg, Lilli Palmer. Fairly absorbing drama about the risky business of attempting to use a scientific experiment involving a human memory transplant, before the nature of its result has been tested. (Dir: Boris Sagal, 99 mins.)

Havana (1990)**½ Robert Redford, Lena Olin, Raul Julia, Alan Arkin, Tomas Milian. A genuine disappointment. Director Sydney Pollack's attempt to re-create Cuba in the final days of Batista's rule suffers from wooden acting, unconvincing dramatics. Redford is a card shark who professes no love or hate for Castro's revolution, but he'll forego his neutrality for romance. The problem here is that the romance is right out of *Casablanca*, but the tone is always safely evenhanded, scrubbed clean of much sexual energy. This film isn't even close to capturing the danger and lust, corruption and passion of Cuba in the fifties. (Dir: Sydney Pollack, 140 mins.)†

Have Rocket, Will Travel (1959)*½ The Three Stooges. Strictly for Three Stooges' fans and children under seven years old! All the usual slapstick shenanigans played within an outrageous science fiction plot. Dir: David Lowell Rich, 76 mins.)

Having a Wild Weekend (Great Britain, 1965)**½ Dave Clark Five. The English pop group's first film, and although it doesn't measure up to the Beatles' *A Hard Day's Night*, it has a similar kooky appeal. (Dir: John Boorman, 91 mins.)

Having Babies (MTV 1976)**½ Jessica Walter, Vicki Lawrence, Karen Valentine, Desi Arnaz, Jr. A good cast and fine production values help bolster this story about the personal lives of four

454

expectant mothers who come together while attending classes in natural childbirth. (Dir: Robert Day, 98 mins.)

Having Babies II (MTV 1977)** Tony Bill, Carol Lynley, Lee Meriwether. The second of three movies dealing with the problems and crises of birth, adoption, and love. The vignettes are well paced, but this is basically a soap opera confined to a hospital. (Dir: Robert Day, 104 mins.)

Having Babies III (MTV 1978)** Patty Duke Astin. A group of pregnant women play out their personal dramas predictably—everyone lives happily ever after. Astin's dilemma about a cancer operation during her pregnancy, to be performed by her ex-husband, is most interesting. (Dir: Jackie Cooper, 104 mins.)

Having It All (MTV 1982)** Dyan Cannon, Barry Newman, Hart Bochner, Melanie Chartoff. Dyan is a top fashion designer whose business finds her dividing her time between two husbands in Los Angeles and New York. Some of the script is funny. (Dir: Edward Zwick, 104 mins.)†

Having Wonderful Crime (1945)*** Pat O'Brien, George Murphy, Carole Landis. A lawyer and his two friends turn sleuths to solve the murder of a magician. Fast-paced, breezy comedy-mystery. (Dir: A. Edward Sutherland, 70 mins.)

Having Wonderful Time (1938)**½ Ginger Rogers, Douglas Fairbanks, Jr., Red Skelton, Lucille Ball. City girl goes to the mountains for a vacation and falls in love there. Pretty mild comedy has some good scenes but isn't what it should have been. (Dir: Alfred Santell, 70 mins.)

Hawaii (1966)*** Julie Andrews, Richard Harris, Max von Sydow, Torin Thatcher, Gene Hackman, Carroll O'Connor. This epic film based on James Michener's rambling narrative about the early (1820) settlers of Hawaii amounts to pure escapist adventure fare rather than historical drama, but it's reasonably entertaining. Sit back and share the exploits of the strict missionary (von Sydow), his friendly, outgoing wife (Andrews), and the dashing sea captain (Harris) who loves her. (Dir: George Roy Hill, 190 mins.)†

Hawaiians, The (1970)** Charlton Heston, Geraldine Chaplin, Mako, Tina Chen. Spectacle, Charlton Heston, Hawaiian history (Hollywood-style, of course), and a cast of thousands (or so it seems) still can't make this old-fashioned saga really work. Sequel to *Hawaii*, covering period 1870–1900. (Dir: Tom Gries,134 mins.)

Hawaii Five-O (MTV 1968)*½ Jack Lord, Nancy Kwan, Leslie Nielsen, Lew Ayres. McGarrett's first case (pilot for the TV series) finds him leading his special investigative force on the trail of a deadly weapon that has been killing American secret agents. (Dir: Leonard Freeman, 96 mins.)

Hawkins on Murder (MTV 1973)**½ James Stewart, Bonnie Bedelia, Margaret Markov, Strother Martin. Stewart plays a shrewd lawyer who defends a poor little rich girl—the sensitive, withdrawn type—accused of slaying daddy, stepmother, and stepsister. AKA: **Death and the Maiden.** (Dir: Jud Taylor, 73 mins.)

Hawks (Great Britain, 1988)** Timothy Dalton, Anthony Edwards, Janet McTeer. Maudlin comedy-drama about two terminal cancer patients (Dalton and Edwards) who decide not to spend their remaining time in a hospital ward. Their story might have been interesting, but the script intersects them with a pair of equally ungrounded young women, with the result that no one character is sufficiently developed. (Dir: Robert Ellis Miller, 100 mins.)†

Hawks and the Sparrow, The (Italy, 1966)***½ Toto, Ninetto Davoli, Rossana DiRocco, Renato Capogna. A father and son reject society's trappings and take to the roads of Italy accompanied by an intellectual left-wing talking bird. Comedy and politics mix wildly in director Pier Paolo Pasolini's giddy fable; the bird spouts parables about the Catholic Church and Marxism. (88 min.)†

Hawk, the Slayer (Great Britain, 1980)** Jack Palance, John Terry, Bernard Bresslaw, Roy Kinnear, Ferdy Mayne, Harry Andrews. Low-budget swordplay with the expected derring-do as two brothers, one unbelievably noble and one irredeemably evil, both compete for a magic sword that flies. If the clanking swords don't keep you awake, Palance's noisy histrionics will. (Dir: Terry Marcel, 93 mins.)†

Hawmps (1976)** James Hampton, Christopher Connelly, Jack Elam, Denver Pyle, Slim Pickens. Before the Civil War, the Texas Cavalry Corps experimented with camels rather than horses for desert duty. This historical incident was treated dramatically in *Southwest Passage* (1954) and comically here. Overlong and silly. (Dir: Joe Camp, 126 mins.)†

Haywire (MTV 1980)***½ Lee Remick, Jason Robards, Jr., Deborah Raffin, Dianne Hull, Linda Gray. Brooke Hayward's forthright memoir of her parents, actress Margaret Sullavan and superagent-producer Leland Hayward, is an involving drama with unusually good performances. (Dir: Michael Tuchner, 156 mins.)

Hazard (1948)** Paulette Goddard, Macdonald Carey. Comedy about a girl who falls in love with the detective sent to arrest her. A few laughs. (Dir: George Marshall, 95 mins.)

Hazard of Hearts, A (MTV 1987)** Helena Bonham Carter, Diana Rigg, Edward Fox, Fiona Fullerton, Christopher Plummer, Stewart Granger, Anna Massey, Gareth Hunt. Classically Gothic doings, courtesy of the grand dame of schlock, Barbara Cartland. Bonham Carter plays a young heiress who is won by a handsome lord in a gambling wager (of course). The finale has the wondrous sight of Rigg (the lord's snooty mother) chasing after B.C. ready to run her through with a sword! (Dir: John Hough, 96 mins.)

Hazing, The (1977)*½ Jeff East, Brad David, Charles Martin Smith. A low-budget bomb about the wild life in a college fraternity. The party's over when one of the pledges dies and everyone tries to pass the buck of blame. Watch *Fraternity Row* instead. (Dir: Douglas Curtis, 80 mins.)

H-Bomb (Hong Kong, 1978)* Christopher Mitchum, Olivia Hussey. CIA agent Mitchum is dispatched to Bangkok to retrieve two stolen nuclear warheads from a terrorist who just happens to be the father of his ex-girlfriend. Capped by one of those harmless nuclear explosions that only exist in stupid movies like this one. (Dir: Krung Savrilai, 98 mins.)†

Head (1968)*** The Monkees, Annette Funicello, Timothy Carey, Vito Scotti, Sonny Liston, Frank Zappa, Terry (Teri) Garr (debut). A wildly innovative "trip" movie that has only recently gained recognition, thanks to the fact that its script was written by then-unknown actor Jack Nicholson. The Monkees make fun of their manufactured image ("the money's in, we're made of tin, we're here to give you more") while wandering through a bizarre series of genre-spoofs. Odd, and slightly disconcerting at times, *Head* showed that these four rockers had more talent than they were given credit for, and it also served as an auspicious debut for director Bob Rafelson. (85 mins.)†

Headhunter (1989)*½ Kay Lenz, Wayne Crawford, Steve Kanaly. Miami detectives in the Nigerian section of town investigate murders caused by a demon spirit. A few good special effects are all this one has going for it. (Dir: Francis Schaeffer, 92 mins.)†

Headin' for Broadway (1980)*½ Rex Smith, Terri Treas, Paul Carafotes, Vivian Reed. A lame saga of four aspirants clamoring for the bright lights of Broadway. Headin' for obscurity. (Dir: Joseph Brooks, 89 mins.)

Headless Ghost, The (Great Britain,

1958)**½ Clive Revill, Richard Lyon, David Rose. Unusually good effects enliven this better-than-average comic tale of a haunted castle. Teenage students investigate reports of a headless spirit, and meet more real ghosts than they know what to do with. (Dir: Peter Graham Scott, 63 mins.)

Head Office (1985)** Judge Reinhold, Jane Seymour, Danny De Vito, Eddie Albert, Rick Moranis, Don King, Don Novello. A satirical look at the menacing world of high finance and the insane pressures of office life as an idealistic young businessman is used as a pawn in a South American coup attempt. Some good bits here and there. (Dir: Ken Finkleman, 90 mins.)†

Head On—See: **Fatal Attraction** (1980)

Head over Heels—See: **Chilly Scenes of Winter**

Heads or Tails (France, 1982)*** Philippe Noiret, Michel Serrault. A recently widowed detective becomes friends with the prime suspect in the case of his wife's death. An old-fashioned comedy with strong performances. (Dir: Robert Enrico, 100 mins.)

Healers, The (MTV 1974)**½ John Forsythe, Season Hubley, Pat Harrington. Fairly absorbing pilot film for a proposed series with Forsythe playing the chief of staff of one of those massive medical research complexes where problems abound. (Dir: Tom Gries, 100 mins.)

H.E.A.L.T.H.—See: **Health**

Health (1979)**½ Glenda Jackson, Lauren Bacall, James Garner, Carol Burnett. Robert Altman's sporadically entertaining satire follows the campaigning at a health food convention where Bacall (playing an 83-year-old maiden) and Jackson battle it out for the presidency. Occasionally incisive, *Health* provides a few healthy laughs, mainly thanks to Burnett as a naive presidential advisor on health. AKA: **H.E.A.L.T.H.** (102 mins.)

Hear Me Good (1957)*** Hal March, Joe E. Ross, Merry Anders. Fast-talking promoter finds he has to rig a beauty contest to satisfy a racketeer and his moll. Minor but breezy. Good fun. (Dir: Don McGuire, 80 mins.)

Hear No Evil (MTV 1982)*½ Gil Gerard, Bernie Casey, Wings Hauser, Mimi Rogers. Gerard stars as a stone-deaf gumshoe chasing a motorcycle gang that almost killed him and caused his deafness. Predictable. (Dir: Harry Falk, 104 mins.)

Hearse, The (1980)½ Trish Van Devere, Joseph Cotten, Perry Lang. Excruciatingly boring horror flick about a woman who buys an old house and is subsequently frightened by evil forces. (Dir: George Bowers, 95 mins.)†

Hearst and Davies Affair, The (MTV

1985)**½ Robert Mitchum, Virginia Madsen, Fritz Weaver, Doris Belack. The celebrated love affair between millionaire newspaper tycoon William Randolph Hearst and chorus girl turned movie star Marion Davies becomes an uninspired TV movie. (Dir: David Lowell Rich, 104 mins.)

Heart (1987)* Brad Davis, Jesse Doran, Steve Buscemi. Poverty-row *Rocky* casts Davis as a washed-up ex-slugger attempting a comeback. Shoddily made, and there's not one surprise in the punch-drunk script. (Dir: James Lemmo, 90 mins.)†

Heartaches (1982)*** Annie Potts, Margot Kidder, Winston Rekert, Robert Carradine. A genuinely winning romantic comedy about two women looking for love in Toronto. In this female buddy movie, a pregnant wife runs away from her husband because he's not the father of her baby-to-be and teams up with a streetwise blonde. (Dir: Donald Shebib, 98 mins.)†

Heartbeat (1938)—See: **Le Schpountz**

Heartbeat (1946)*** Ginger Rogers, Jean-Pierre Aumont, Basil Rathbone. Lady pickpocket falls for a dancing diplomat, attains her place in society. Pleasant comedy with a good cast, elaborate production. (Dir: Sam Wood, 102 mins.)

Heart Beat (1979)**½ Nick Nolte, Sissy Spacek, John Heard. Don't expect the real story of the Cassadys and beat novelist Jack Kerouac, for this is a conscious travesty. Nolte and Spacek are remarkably well attuned to writer-director John Byrum's freaked-out vision of rebellion and conformity. (Dir: John Byrum, 109 mins.)†

Heartbeeps (1981)½ Bernadette Peters, Andy Kaufman, Dennis Quaid. If you want to sit through a slow-moving comedy about the love of a pair of robots, here it is. Leaden fantasy. (Dir: Allan Arkush, 88 mins.)†

Heartbreaker (1983)** Fernando Allende, Dawn Dunlap, Peter Gonzales Falcon, Miguel Ferrer, Michael D. Roberts, Rafael Campos. Low-budget feature about members of East L.A. youth gangs seems less interested in the characters than in their lowrider cars. Story of mismatched lovers thankfully lacks gratuitous sex and violence; too bad it's so dull. (Dir: Frank Zuniga, 90 mins.)†

Heartbreakers (1985)*** Nick Mancuso, Peter Coyote, Kathryn Harrold. Exceptional ''buddy'' film about two male friends trying to cope with the trendy L.A. scene. Standout performances by Coyote as a burnt-out artist, and by Mancuso as his sexually troubled confidant. (Dir: Bobby Roth, 98 mins.)†

Heartbreak Hotel (1988)*½ David Keith, Tuesday Weld, Charlie Schlatter. Real-life individuals have often been used in fictional contexts, but never with such silly results as this ridiculous, "heart-warming" tale of a teenager (Schlatter) who kidnaps Elvis Presley (Keith) for his depressed mom (Weld). (Dir: Chris Columbus, 90 mins.)†

Heartbreak House (MTV 1985)*** Rex Harrison, Amy Irving, Rosemary Harris. George Bernard Shaw's play has been shortened and deprived of one character for this production, which improves it. Harrison re-creates his Broadway role as Captain Shotover, who presides with bemusement over the assortment of women (his two daughters and a guest) staying at his house. Like many of Shaw's plays, this is talky but deliciously so. (Dir: Anthony Page, 122 mins.)†

Heartbreak Kid, The (1972)***½ Cybill Shepherd, Charles Grodin, Jeannie Berlin, Eddie Albert. A unique American comedy, directed by Elaine May, that is alternately hilarious, poignant, and irritating. The story is the chronicle of a young New York Jewish couple whose marriage disintegrates on the Florida Turnpike, while they head south, just days after the wedding. (105 mins.)†

Heartbreak Ridge (1986)**½ Clint Eastwood, Marsha Mason, Mario Van Pebbles, Eileen Heckart, Bo Svenson. Clint is in fine form as the Marine trying to build a few good men for the corps and forever losing the battle of the sexes through his intransigence. Although the film allows Eastwood to display star-power, the script insists that he and his recruits prove themselves during the U.S. invasion of Grenada. (Dir: Clint Eastwood, 128 mins.)†

Heartburn (1986)**½ Meryl Streep, Jack Nicholson, Stockard Channing, Maureen Stapleton, Catherine O'Hara, Karen Akers, Jeff Daniels, Richard Masur. Nora Ephron's autobiographical novel about her troubled marriage to Watergate reporter Carl Bernstein is given an acerbic but rather wan treatment. A stab at sophisticated comedy that strives for humorous honesty, but not the knockout comedy anticipated. (Dir: Mike Nichols, 108 mins.)†

Heart Condition (1990)**½ Bob Hoskins, Denzel Washington, Chloe Webb, Ray Baker, Kieran Mulroney, Jeffrey Meek, Roger E. Mosley, Alan Rachins, Ja'net Dubois. Yet another cop-buddy comedy, this one features a gruff, racist cop (Hoskins) and a stylish, savvy lawyer (Washington) who just happens to be a ghost. This unlikely duo set out to capture the drug dealer who killed Washington and is holding their mutual lady love (Webb) hostage. Surprisingly best when it's a comedy, this formulaic out-

ing generally proves to be a waste of time for its three talented leads. (Dir: James D. Parriott, 100 mins.)†

Heart Is a Lonely Hunter, The (1968)**** Alan Arkin, Sondra Locke, Stacy Keach, Cicely Tyson. Carson McCullers's beautiful novel about the life of a deaf-mute in a small southern town is brought to the screen with admirable sensitivity by all those involved. Moving story of loneliness, human boorishness, and cruelty never strikes a false note, and features a remarkable prize-winning performance by Alan Arkin in the role of the deaf-mute. (Dir: Robert Ellis Miller, 125 mins.)†

Heartland (1979)***½ Rip Torn, Conchata Ferrell, Lilia Skala. Excellent, carefully researched low-budget entry about the harsh frontier life in the Rockies circa 1910. Denver widow moves to Wyoming with her young daughter to become the housekeeper for a surly Scottish rancher. (Dir: Richard Pearce, 95 mins.)†

Heart Like a Wheel (1983)***½ Bonnie Bedelia, Hoyt Axton, Beau Bridges, Leo Rossi. Fast-moving, tightly scripted film about a female racing car driver who fought sexism is not a run-of-the-racetrack biopic. The film's background detail captures the historical milieu with painstaking accuracy, and Bedelia plays a demanding part with brilliance and touching sensitivity. (Dir: Jonathan Kaplan, 113 mins.)†

Heart of a Champion: The Ray Mancini Story, The (MTV 1985)**½ Doug McKeon, Robert Blake. Young Doug McKeon might not be the spitting image of lightweight Ray "Boom Boom" Mancini, but he puts energy and life into playing the gutsy fighter. As an added plus, Sylvester Stallone choreographed the ring movements. (Dir: Richard Michaels, 104 mins.)†

Heart of Dixie (1989)** Ally Sheedy, Virginia Madsen, Phoebe Cates, Treat Williams, Don Michael Paul, Kyle Secor, Kurtwood Smith. One more account of the civil rights movement that focuses on the suffering endured by privileged whites who sympathized with the black cause. In this case, it's a Southern college newspaper reporter (Sheedy) who takes a stand after writing about the unjustified beating of a black man at an Elvis concert. Self-righteousness and mint-julep Southern accents reign, with the three female leads and Williams looking forlorn and out of place. (Dir: Martin Davidson, 96 mins.)†

Heart of Glass (West Germany, 1976)***½ Josef Bierbichler, Stefan Guttler, Clemons Scheitz, Sepp Muller. Director Werner Herzog hypnotized his actors while making this strange tale of a small German village that loses the valued secret for making its rare ruby glass. The enraged and frightened villagers turn to magic and murder in a wild effort to get back the ingredient they have lost. One of Herzog's best. (93 mins.)

Heart of Humanity, The (1918)**½ Erich von Stroheim, Dorothy Phillips. A blatant ripoff of Griffith's far superior *Hearts of the World*, this sensationalistic WWI exploitation picture concerns attacks by the beastly Huns on the saintly allies, and includes the famous scenes in which fiendish von Stroheim tears a girl's clothes off with his teeth and throws a baby out the window! Fascinating as a historical document, but ridiculous as drama. (Dir: Allen Holubar, 133 mins.)†

Heart of Midnight (1989)** Jennifer Jason Leigh, Peter Coyote, Frank Stallone, Brenda Vaccaro. Ambitious psychosexual *noir* thriller. Leigh plays a disturbed young woman who makes the mistake of taking over her deceased uncle's business, a "massage parlor," hastening her mental breakdown. (Dir: Matthew Chapman, 93 mins.)†

Heart of Steel (MTV 1983)**½ Peter Strauss, Pamela Reed, Swan, Barry Primus. Timely drama about the plight of unemployed steel workers. The steel mill closes forever, and the anger that wells up in the blue-collar workers soon erupts. (Dir: Donald Wrye, 104 mins.)

Heart of the Matter, The (Great Britain, 1953)***½ Trevor Howard, Elizabeth Allan, Maria Schell, Denholm Elliott. From Graham Greene's novel, about a police commissioner in South Africa who falls in love with an Austrian girl, and is threatened with blackmail. Not always effective drama, but fine performances. (Dir: George More O'Ferrall, 100 mins.)

Heart of the Stag (New Zealand, 1984)*½ Bruno Lawrence, Terence Cooper, Mary Regan, Anne Flannery. Brooding melodrama about a wealthy sheep rancher who becomes unglued when a stranger begins romancing his daughter. (Dir: Michael Firth, 94 mins.)†

Hearts and Minds (1974)***½ A chilling documentary of U.S. involvement in the Vietnam war. The film contains graphic footage, which for all its violence is not nearly so unsettling as the interviews with brutalized American troops. (Dir: Peter Davis, 110 mins.)†

Heart's Desire (Great Britain, 1935)*½ Richard Tauber, Leonora Corbett, Kathleen Kelly, Paul Graetz. Vehicle for Tauber as a Viennese waiter whose dream is to sing at London's Albert Hall. Barebones plot is just an excuse for Tauber to sing selections from popular operettas. (Dir: Paul Stein, 79 mins.)†
458

Hearts Divided (1936)**½ Marion Davies, Dick Powell, Charles Ruggles, Edward Everett Horton, Claude Rains, Arthur Treacher, Henry Stephenson, Hattie McDaniel, Beulah Bondi. Good vehicle for Davies, set in the Napoleonic era; she is an ordinary French girl loved by one of the Emperor's numerous siblings. Elaborate settings and nice songs. (Dir: Frank Borzage, 87 mins.)

Hearts of the West (1975)***½ Jeff Bridges, Alan Arkin, Blythe Danner, Andy Griffith. A charming lark paying homage to the myths of the Old West as seen by an aspiring young writer from Iowa who winds up a star of silent westerns. Deft screenplay is stylishly handled by director Howard Zieff. AKA: **Hollywood Cowboy.** (103 mins.)†

Hearts of the World (1918)***½ Lillian Gish, Robert Harron, Dorothy Gish, Ben Alexander, Erich von Stroheim. Director D. W. Griffith's epic of WWI is episodic but beautifully filmed, with strong performances and some unforgettable scenes (including some authentic war footage, though no one is sure exactly how much). The plot follows the fortunes of one young Frenchman who goes to war and his family's desperation at home in occupied territory. (152 mins.)†

Heartsounds (MTV 1984)*** James Garner, Mary Tyler Moore, Sam Wanamaker, Wendy Crewson. A deeply moving drama based on Martha Lear's best-seller about how she and her physician-husband coped with his series of heart attacks. (Dir: Glenn Jordan, 128 mins.)

Heat (1972)*** Sylvia Miles, Andrea Feldman, Joe Dallesandro, Pat Ast. Campy satire on the Hollywood film community. The short-on-incident, long-on-character plot involves Sally, an aging minor star played convincingly by Miles, who falls madly in love with a young stud (Dallesandro), and who constantly battles with her whacked-out daughter. Intriguing, lively, offbeat. (Dir: Paul Morrissey, 100 mins.)†

Heat (1987)*½ Burt Reynolds, Karen Young, Peter MacNichol, Neill Barry, Howard Hesseman, Diana Scarwid. Burt helps an ex-girlfriend exact revenge on a slimy-gangster rapist. Disorganized and nasty. (Dir: R. M. Richards, 101 mins.)†

Heat and Dust (Great Britain, 1983)*** Julie Christie, Christopher Cazenove, Sashi Kapoor, Greta Scacchi. Shifting back and forth between the twenties and today, the film's parallel stories cover a liberated Englishwoman's research of the history of her long-dead aunt and her unhappy marriage and illicit love affair in India. A literate and graceful fable. (Dir: James Ivory, 130 mins.)†

Heat and Sunlight (1987)*** Rob Nilsson,

Consuelo Faust, Don Bajema. But what would be improvisational self-indulgence in most hands becomes an absorbing film in the hands of talented director-star Rob Nilsson (*Signal 7*). (98 mins.)

Heated Vengeance (1984)* Richard Hatch, Michael J. Pollard, Mills Watson, Ron Max. Vietnam veteran returns to Southeast Asia to find the woman he left there a decade ago, runs afoul of a gang of army deserters turned drug traffickers. Noisy, forgettable shoot-'em-up. (Dir: Edward Murphy, 91 mins.)†

Heathcliff: The Movie (1986)*½ The voice of Mel Blanc as Heathcliff. Cheaply animated cartoon for the big cat's fans only. (Dir: Bruno Bianchi, 75 mins.)†

Heathers (1989)*** Winona Ryder, Christian Slater, Shannen Doherty. A rare black comedy; high school caste systems are viewed through the eyes of two students who hatch a plan to murder some of their school's "best" students. Smart, impressive directorial debut by Michael Lehmann. (102 mins.)†

Heat Line, The (Canada, 1988)*** Gabriel Arcand, Simon Gonzales, Gerard Parkes. French-Canadian road movie finds father and son driving from Florida to Montreal after a death in the family. Not much good happens on the trip, and director Hubert-Yves Rose uses the lonely highway as a metaphor for loss and disorientation. The acting is flawless, and the relationship between the two men grows into something wonderful. (88 mins.)

Heat of Anger (MTV 1972)** Susan Hayward, James Stacy, Lee J. Cobb. Ordinary courtroom drama. Legal eagle Hayward defends contractor Cobb on a murder rap. (Dir: Don Taylor, 74 mins.)

Heat of Desire (France, 1984)**½ Patrick Dewaere, Clio Goldsmith, Jeanne Moreau. In this wry update of *The Blue Angel*, a shy married professor falls into the clutches of a femme fatale. However, rather than cause his ruin, the professor's sexual curriculum vitae achieves a new lease on life. (Dir: Luc Beraud, 89 mins.)†

Heat of the Day, The (MTV 1990)*** Michael Gambon, Patricia Hodge, Michael York, Dame Peggy Ashcroft. Harold Pinter has invested this adaptation of Elizabeth Bowen's novel with an added layer of menace. Patricia Hodge gives a multilayered performance as a woman who learns that her WWII soldier-lover may be an enemy agent. Subtle story, keeping the tension in check. (Dir: Christopher Morahan, 96 mins.)

Heat's On, The (1943)** Mae West, William Gaxton, Victor Moore, Xavier Cugat. West's last movie till '70 was a stinker, though the lady's not to blame. Gaxton,

a hammy Broadway star, overpowers the proceedings. (Dir: Gregory Ratoff, 80 mins.)

Heatwave (Australia, 1983)*** Judy Davis, Chris Haywood, John Gregg. A febrile melodrama with style to burn. A social activist battles the onslaught of urban redevelopment by trying to put the kibosh on plans for a multimillion dollar project. (Dir: Phillip Noyce, 99 mins.)†

Heat Wave (MTV 1974)** Ben Murphy, Bonnie Bedelia, Lew Ayres. Yet another crisis drama that uses the premise of a heat wave hitting an unprepared town. (Dir: Jerry Jameson, 74 mins.)

Heat Wave (MCTV 1990)*** Cicely Tyson, Blair Underwood, James Earl Jones, Sally Kirkland, Margaret Avery. Searing indictment of white Los Angeles in this look back at the Watts riots of 1965 from the point of view of a young black journalist (Underwood). It's not a pretty picture, yet voices of reason are heard on both sides. (Dir: Kevin Hooks, 94 mins.)†

Heaven (1987)*** Diane Keaton's directorial debut, offbeat sensory assault that explores the concept of the afterlife from a number of perspectives. Primarily a collection of statements about heaven made by some of L.A.'s oddest citizens, supplemented by various images of heaven clipped from old movies and edited together in a rock-video manner. (80 mins.)†

Heaven and Earth (Japan, 1990)*** Takaaki Enoki, Masahiko Tsugawa. A historical epic (actually filmed in Canada) about the great battle between feuding warlords that decided the history of modern Japan. Stately, breathtakingly designed, and gorgeously filmed, but sure to lose some of its grandeur on the small screen. (Dir: Haruki Kadowawa, 106 mins.)

Heaven Can Wait (1943)**** Don Ameche, Gene Tierney, Charles Coburn, Marjorie Main, Eugene Pallette, Laird Cregar. This valentine from director Ernst Lubitsch is a remarkably gentle story of a rake's progress and his one true love, in the face of death. The movies have never shown mortality in a sweeter light. (113 mins.)†

Heaven Can Wait (1978)*** Warren Beatty, Julie Christie, James Mason, Jack Warden, Charles Grodin, Dyan Cannon, Buck Henry. A charming remake of *Here Comes Mr. Jordan;* through an error, a football player dies too soon, and he's sent back to Earth only to find that his former body is in no shape to be revived, and that he must continue life in whatever body can be found for him. (Dirs: Warren Beatty, Buck Henry, 100 mins.)†

Heaven Help Us (1985)*** Andrew

459

McCarthy, Kevin Dillon, Mary Stuart Masterson, John Heard, Donald Sutherland, Wallace Shawn, John Cusack, Philip Bosco. Teenage coming-of-age movies are a dime a dozen, but this episodic film set in a Catholic boys' school circa 1963 is a cut above. Nice bits by a large cast. (Dir: Michael Dinner, 104 mins.)†

Heaven Knows, Mr. Allison (1957)*** Deborah Kerr, Robert Mitchum. A somewhat incredible story, which places a rugged U.S. Marine corporal and a gentle Roman Catholic nun on a South Pacific island during WWII, is made palatable by the good performances of its stars. (Dir: John Huston, 107 mins.)

Heavenly Bodies (Canada, 1984)* Cynthia Dale, Richard Rebiere. Disco movies were doing good business. People liked to do aerobic workouts to disco. Therefore, a disco aerobics movie sounds like a good idea, right? Wrong. (Dir: Lawrence Dane, 89 mins.)†

Heavenly Body (1943)** William Powell, Hedy Lamarr. Bedroom farce falls short of its goal. Story of an astronomer's wife who believes a fortune teller and almost runs off with a handsome stranger. (Dir: Alexander Hall, 95 mins.)

Heavenly Kid, The (1985)*½ Lewis Smith, Jason Gedrick, Jane Kaczmarek, Richard Mulligan, Mark Metcalf, Beau Dremann. Far from heavenly fantasy about a greaser who expires in a car crash and returns two decades later to help a troubled teen with girl problems. Illogical scripting runs rampant. (Dir: Cary Medoway, 92 mins.)†

Heaven Only Knows—See: Montana Mike

Heavens Above (Great Britain, 1963)***½ Peter Sellers, Cecil Parker, Isabel Jeans. Sharp, biting satire about a do-gooder clergyman who always manages to make things difficult for his parishioners. (Dirs: John and Roy Boulting, 105 mins.)†

Heaven's Gate (1980)** Kris Kristofferson, Isabelle Huppert, Christopher Walken, John Hurt, Jeff Bridges, Sam Waterston, Brad Dourif, Joseph Cotten, Geoffrey Lewis, Richard Masur, Terry O'Quinn, Micky Rourke. Story is based on a real range war in the 1890s in Johnson County, Wyoming, when the cattle owners declared war on the immigrants who were pouring into the area to establish homesteads on the grazing lands. A wildly overlong, ill-conceived film with a couple of visually stunning sequences. An abridged 150 min. version usually plays on TV. (Dir: Michael Cimino, 220 mins.)†

Heaven with a Barbed Wire Fence (1939)**½ Glenn Ford, Nicholas Conte, Jean Rogers. Two drifters team up with a refugee girl and try to make a living. (Dir: Ricardo Cortez, 62 mins.)

Heaven with a Gun (1969)**½ Glenn Ford,

460

Carolyn Jones. Predictable western yarn. Glenn Ford playing a preacher trying to bring peace (inner and outer) to a small town. (Dir: Lee H. Katzin, 101 mins.)

Heavy Metal (Canada, 1981)**½ Voices of Roger Bumpass, Jackie Burroughs, John Candy, Joe Flaherty, Eugene Levy, Alice Playten, Harold Ramis, Richard Romanos, Zal Yanovsky. Treading on the heels of Ralph Bakshi, this anthology of stories from the popular fantasy magazine centers around a mystical green gem that changes the life of whoever possesses it. Each entry was designed by a different group of international artists, so the film's quality is variable. (Dir: Gerald Potterton, 91 mins.)

Heavy Petting (1989)*** Laurie Anderson, David Byrne, Sandra Bernhard, Allen Ginsberg, William Burroughs, Josh Mostel, Abbie Hoffman, John Oates, Spalding Gray, Ann Magnuson, Zoe Tamerlaine. Comic documentary about America's pre-revolution sexual attitudes. The numerous film clips from movies and "hygiene" documentaries are used for cheap laughs, but they're worth sitting through for the surprisingly frank admissions of the witnesses listed above (wait'll you hear what Spalding Gray used to do with his Davy Crockett cap!) (Dir: Obi Benz, 80 mins.)†

Heavy Traffic (1973)** Joseph Kaufman, Beverly Hope Takinson, Frank DeKova. If you like Ralph Bakshi's modern animation style, this is for you. Others will be offended by the vulgarity permeating every scene. This grimy saga of a New Yorker who escapes the hell of his environment through drawing was X-rated. (Dir: Ralph Bakshi, 77 mins.)

Hedda (Great Britain, 1975)***½ Glenda Jackson, Timothy West, Jennie Linden. Glenda Jackson dominates this powerful film version of a critically acclaimed London stage production, starring Jackson, of Henrik Ibsen's enduring drama about a Nordic femme fatale—a neurotic, controlling, strong-willed woman who is nonetheless alluring to the males in her town. (Dir: Trevor Nunn, 100 mins.)†

Heidi (1937)** Shirley Temple, Jean Hersholt. The youngsters should love this adaptation of Johanna Spyri's juvenile classic. Story of a little Swiss girl's adventures as everybody seems to conspire to take her from her grandfather has warmth and charm. (Dir: Allan Dwan, 88 mins.)†

Heidi (Switzerland, 1953)*** Elsbeth Sigmund, Heinrich Gretler, Thomas Klameth. Excellent film of the children's classic of a little girl living in the Alps with her grandfather, who ends his feud with the village so she can go to school. (Dir: Luigi Comencini, 98 mins.)

Heidi (Austria, 1965)*** Eva-Maria Sing-hammer, Gertraud Mittermayr. Generally well-acted filming of the beloved children's story about a little mountain girl who is taken to the city but cannot survive there. (Dir: Werner Jacobs, 95 mins.)†

Heidi (MTV 1968)*** Maximilian Schell, Jean Simmons, Michael Redgrave, Walter Slezak, Jennifer Edwards. Classy TV adaptation of the Johanna Spyri book. (Dir: Delbert Mann, 104 mins.)†

Heidi and Peter (Switzerland, 1955)** Elsbeth Sigmund, Heinrich Gretler, Thomas Klameth. Sugary sequel to *Heidi* (1953), based on another book by Johanna Spyri, continuing the adventures of the Swiss girl and her family. Once was enough. (Dir: Franz Schnyder, 89 mins.)

Heidi's Song (1982)** Voices of Lorne Greene, Sammy Davis, Jr., Margery Gray. Fairish musical cartoon about the beloved orphan from the Alps. (Dir: Robert Taylor, 94 mins.)†

Heimat (1985)*** Marita Breuer, Michael Lesch, Dieter Schaad, Karin Kienzler. This epic West German mini-series tells the story of the people of Shabbach, a fictional village where "average" rural people reside. Filmmaker Edgar Reitz's 64-year chronicle of these citizens, in particular the Simon family, suffers from being too much of a good thing. (924 mins.)

Heiress, The (1949)***½ Olivia de Havilland, Montgomery Clift, Ralph Richardson, Miriam Hopkins. William Wyler's direction is careful and methodical in this version of the play adapted from Henry James's novella *Washington Square*. De Havilland won a second Oscar for playing the homely girl who falls in love with a dashing fortune hunter Clift, but Richardson dominates the movie with his restrained portrayal of her ramrod father. (115 mins.)†

Heist, The (MTV 1972)** Christopher George. Serviceable action piece about the amateur who must prove his innocence. (Dir: Don McDougall, 73 mins.)

Heist, The (MTV 1989)** Pierce Brosnan, Tom Skerritt, Wendy Hughes, Tom Atkins, Robert Prosky. Muddled revenge drama; Brosnan, fresh out of prison, schemes to get even with the ex-partner who framed him. Makes good use of its racetrack locations, but the intricacies of Brosnan's plot become confusing. (Dir: Stuart Orme, 97 mins.)†

He Knows You're Alone (1981)**½ Don Scardino, Caitlin O'Heaney, Elizabeth Kemp, Tom Hanks, Paul Gleason. A bride-to-be finds her nuptials are a time of terror as other young women are slain—there may be nobody left to see her off on her honeymoon! Fairly chilling slasher film that's a (minor) cut above the rest. (Dir: Armand Mastroianni, 94 mins.)†

Held Hostage: The Sis and Jerry Levin Story (MTV 1991)*** Marlo Thomas, David Dukes, G.W. Bailey. Thomas shines in this real-life drama about Sis Levin, who wouldn't sit back and do nothing when her newsman husband, Jerry Levin (Dukes), was kidnapped in Beirut. Ample servings of intrigue and political maneuvering, filmed on location in Israel. (Dir: Roger Young, 96 mins.)

Helen Keller: The Miracle Continues (MTV 1984)*** Blythe Danner, Mare Winningham, Perry King, Vera Miles, Jack Warden, Peter Cushing, Alexander Knox, Jeff Harding. A cogent continuation of the brilliant film *The Miracle Worker*. Mare Winningham is marvelous as the grown-up Helen Keller embarking on a college career and beginning to feel the alienation of her special place in life. (Dir: Alan Gibson, 104 mins.)

Helen Morgan Story, The (1957)**½ Ann Blyth, Paul Newman, Gene Evans, Cara Williams, Alan King, Richard Carlson. A song-drenched biopic that plays fast and loose with the life story of Helen Morgan. Helen's journey from Schubert Alley to the gutter is far from dull, and Gogi Grant (dubbing Blyth) torches out a number of Morgan's signature tunes memorably on the soundtrack. (Dir: Michael Curtiz, 118 mins.)

Helen of Troy (1955)*** Rossana Podesta, Jacques Sernas, Stanley Baker, Brigitte Bardot, Cedric Hardwicke, Harry Andrews. Epic adventure based on Homer's Iliad tells story of Helen, her abductor Paris, and the legendary war won by the clever Trojan Horse ruse. Lavish and exciting, with great battle scenes and grand pageantry. (Dir: Robert Wise, 118 mins.)

Hell and High Water (1954)**½ Richard Widmark, David Wayne, Bella Darvi. Although the plot is somewhat farfetched, this high adventure tale about the efforts of a hand-picked group of sailors who are assigned the task of breaking up an enemy plan to trigger another major war, has some tense moments and good underwater photographic effects to recommend it. (Dir: Samuel Fuller, 103 mins.)

Hell Below (1933)**½ Robert Montgomery, Walter Huston, Madge Evans, Jimmy Durante, Eugene Pallette, Robert Young, Sterling Holloway. Grim melodrama of the tensions between the officers of a submarine, including the usual conflict over a girl; Huston is excellent as a martinet on the edge of insanity. Some exciting undersea photography, and a chilling climax. (Dir: Jack Conway, 105 mins.)

Hell Below Zero (Great Britain, 1954)**

Alan Ladd, Joan Tetzel. Inept drama of erupting emotions and conflicts aboard an Antarctic ice-breaker. (Dir: Mark Robson, 91 mins.)

Hellbenders, The (Italy-Spain, 1967)** Joseph Cotten, Norma Bengell. The plot involves a Confederate major and his family who steal Union money to rebuild the Confederacy. (Dir: Sergio Corbucci, 92 mins.)†

Hell Bent for Leather (1960)**½ Audie Murphy, Stephen McNally, Felicia Farr. Not a bad western—Murphy is a wandering cowpoke who is framed for a glory-seeking marshal for a crime he didn't commit. (Dir: George Sherman, 82 mins.)

Hellbound: Hellraiser II (1988)*½ Clare Higgins, Ashley Laurence, Ken Cranham, Imogen Boorman. Christy, the young heroine of *Hellraiser*, battles the head of a mental institution where she has been confined and the Cenobites, perverse pleasure seekers from Hell. Even more nasty and disgusting than the original. (Dir: Tony Randel, 96 mins.)†

Hell Canyon Outlaws (1957)**½ Dale Robertson, Brian Keith. Deposed sheriff goes after outlaws who have taken over the town. Above-par western. (Dir: Paul Landres, 72 mins.)

Hellcats, The (1968)*½ Ross Hagen, Dee Duffy, Sharyn Kinzie, Sonny West, Robert F. Slatzer, Eric Lidberg, Gus Trikonis. When a policeman is murdered, his girlfriend and brother infiltrate the female biker gang responsible. Forgettable motorcycle movie doesn't even have any good songs. (Dir: Robert F. Slatzer, 90 mins.)†

Hellcats of the Navy (1957)* Ronald Reagan, Nancy Davis. Positively awful submarine drama that is distinguished only by the presence of a future President and his First Lady (and ooh, what acting!). (Dir: Nathan Juran, 82 mins.)†

Hell Comes to Frogtown (1988)**½ Roddy Piper, Sandahl Bergman, Cec Verrell, Rory Calhoun. After WWIII renders most of the population sterile, the U.S. government sends still-potent Sam Hell (former wrestler "Rowdy" Roddy Piper) on a mission to rescue a group of fertile females from a mutant stronghold. Goofy sci-fi parody is slipshod but lots of fun. (Dir: R. J. Kizer, 86 mins.)†

Hell Divers (1932)**½ Wallace Beery, Clark Gable, Conrad Nagel, Dorothy Jordan, Marjorie Rambeau, Marie Provost, Cliff Edwards, Robert Young. This typical service comedy-adventure concerns two Navy pilots and their mishaps in love and in the air; Beery and Gable make an unusual team. Good of this kind. (Dir: George Hill, 113 mins.)

462

Hell Drivers (Great Britain, 1958)*** Sir Stanley Baker, Patrick McGoohan, Herbert Lom, Wilfrid Lawson. Ex-con goes to work as a truck driver for a haulage company, battles the brutish leader of the drivers. Sturdy drama. (Dir: Cy Endfield, 91 mins.)

Heller in Pink Tights (1960)**½ Sophia Loren, Anthony Quinn. Fairly entertaining western drama about a theatrical troupe touring the untamed frontier in the 1880s. Slightly different plot, some amusing scenes dealing with the backstage life of the era. (Dir: George Cukor, 100 mins.)

Hellfighters (1969)* John Wayne, Katharine Ross, Vera Miles. Typical juvenile Wayne adventure yarn about oil fire fighters. (Dir: Andrew V. McLaglen, 121 mins.)†

Hellfire (1949)**½ William Elliott, Marie Windsor, Forrest Tucker, Jim Davis, H. B. Warner, Paul Fix, Grant Withers, Emory Parnell. Gambler is reformed by a traveling preacher and then promises to build a church in his mentor's memory. (Dir: R. G. Springsteen, 90 mins.)†

Hellgate (1952)**½ Sterling Hayden, Joan Leslie, Ward Bond. An innocent man is convicted of consorting with Civil War guerrillas and sent to suffer the tortures of Hellgate Prison in barren New Mexico. (Dir: Charles Marquis Warren, 87 mins.)

Hellhole (1985)* Ray Sharkey, Marjoe Gortner, Judy Landers, Mary Woronov, Edy Williams. Lurid exploitation filmmaking, only for lovers of the infinitely tacky. After witnessing her mother's murder, Judy loses her memory (but not her sensational figure), and the bad guys send her to a shady sanitarium to keep an eye on her. What with Mary Woronov perfecting instant lobotomies and Edy Williams in a blond wig, sleaze fans will have lots to ponder. (Dir: Pierre DeMoro, 90 mins.)†

Hellinger's Law (MTV 1981)** Telly Savalas, Rod Taylor, Melinda Dillon, Roy Poole. As a Philadelphia attorney out in Houston, to defend an accountant who has infiltrated the Mafia, Savalas has been equipped with a better than average "pilot" script and a minimum of violence. (Dir: Leo Penn, 104 mins.)

Hell in the Pacific (1968)*** Lee Marvin, Toshiro Mifune. Marvin and Mifune are the only characters in this pretentious, visually complex drama about two soldiers marooned on an island during WWII. Despite the insistent allegory, director John Boorman's visual contrasts redeem the UNESCO message, aided by spectacular lensing by Conrad Hall. (Dir: John Boorman, 103 mins.)†

Hellions, The (Great Britain, 1962)** Richard Todd, Anne Aubrey. A western set in South Africa. Five outlaws ride into a frontier town, and the lone lawman is hard put to find help to curtail them. (Dir: Ken Annakin, 87 mins.)

Hell Is for Heroes (1962)*** Steve McQueen, James Coburn, Robert Darin, Bob Newhart. McQueen gives one of his best performances in this nihilistic antiwar film. (Dir: Don Siegel, 90 mins.)†

Hell Night (1981)**½ Linda Blair, Vincent Van Patten, Peter Barton, Jenny Neumann, Kevin Brophy. Some fraternity/sorority pledges are soon sorry they ever tried to get accepted when they have to spend a night in a spooky mansion. The usual schlock, but Linda Blair's many B-movie fans will want to tune in. (Dir: Tom DeSimone, 101 mins.)†

Hello Again (1987)** Shelley Long, Judith Ivey, Gabriel Byrne, Corbin Bernsen, Austin Pendleton. A suburban housewife (Long) gets a second chance at life after being resurrected by her whacked-out hippie sister (Ivey). A meager supernatural comedy; Long's evident charm and vivacity soon wear thin, with only Ivey's character flourishing to perk things up. (Dir: Frank Perry, 96 mins.)†

Hello, Dolly (1969)**½ Barbra Streisand, Walter Matthau, Louis Armstrong. This huge, lavish, ''spectacle'' based on the long-running hit Broadway musical depends almost entirely on Barbra's special magic. However, she is much too young and obviously marriageable for this musical about a meddling matchmaker to make much sense. (Dir: Gene Kelly, 118 mins.)†

Hello Down There (1969)*½ Tony Randall, Janet Leigh, Ken Berry. Witless underwater shenanigans as Randall convinces his family to test an ocean-floor home by living under the sea for a month. (Dir: Jack Arnold, 98 mins.)

Hello, Everybody (1933)* Kate Smith, Randolph Scott, Charley Grapewin, Sally Blane, Julia Swayne Gordon, Jerry Tucker. A girl with a big heart (and a big everything else) saves her farm family by becoming a successful radio singer. Kate's starring role. (Dir: William Seiter, 69 mins.)

Hello, Frisco, Hello (1943)**½ Alice Faye, John Payne, Jack Oakie, Lynn Bari, Laird Cregar, June Havoc. Engaging period musical with Faye as a saloon singer with a lump in her throat for fickle John Payne. Overlong and overstuffed, but the plot doesn't interfere unduly with the succession of evergreen songs, especially the one original tune that became Faye's signature song, ''You'll Never Know.'' (Dir: H. Bruce Humberstone, 98 mins.)

Hello God (U.S.-Italy, 1951)** Errol Flynn, Sherry Jackson, Joe Muzzuca, Armando Formica. Rarely seen antiwar drama with

Flynn as an unnamed soldier who tells us the stories of the four young men killed at Anzio Beach. Flynn made this low-budget film to infuriate the higher-ups at Warner Bros. with whom he was involved in contract disputes. Once matters were settled, he sued to keep it from being shown in the U.S. (Dir: William Marshall, 64 mins.)

Hello Mary Lou: Prom Night II (Canada, 1987)**½ Michael Ironside, Wendy Lyon, Justin Louis, Lisa Schrage. Not a true sequel to *Prom Night*, this horror tale is actually a cross between *Carrie* and *Nightmare on Elm Street* as present-day students are menaced by the spirit of a murdered fifties prom queen (Schrage, whose dark blue eyes compete with the special effects as the film's highlights). (Dir: Bruce Pittman, 96 mins.)†

Hell on Devil's Island (1957)* Helmut Dantine, William Talman, Donna Martell. Contrived, cliché-laden tale of the famous French penal colony. (Dir: Christian Nyby, 74 mins.)

Hell on Frisco Bay (1956)**½ Alan Ladd, Edward G. Robinson, Joanne Dru. Waterfront cop out of prison goes after the gangland big shot who was responsible for framing him. Hard-boiled crime melodrama is reminiscent of the gangster films of the thirties. (Dir: Frank Tuttle, 98 mins.)†

Hello, Sister! (1933)** ZaSu Pitts, Boots Mallory, James Dunn, Terrance Ray, Minna Gombell. Insipid tale of a ''good girl'' who gets ''picked up'' on Broadway and ends up pregnant, notable for being a reshot, reshuffled version of the last film directed by Erich von Stroheim, entitled *Walking Down Broadway*. Some of von Stroheim's explicit touches remain in the dated ribald language and in a rambunctious fight between Gombell and Ray. (55 mins.)

Hello, Sucker (1941)*½ Hugh Herbert, Tom Brown, Peggy Moran. Herbert joins a couple who have purchased a dying vaudeville agency from a swindler: they make it a success. (Dir: Edward Cline, 60 mins.)

Hellraiser (Great Britain, 1987)**½ Andrew Robinson, Clare Higgins, Ashley Laurence, Sean Chapman. Quirky horror film. A decomposed fiend seeks living victims so he can return to human form. (Dir: Clive Barker, 90 mins)†

Hell's Angels (1930)**** Ben Lyon, Jean Harlow, James Hall, John Darrow. The most famous aerial drama of the early thirties still packs a wallop. Story centers on two brothers who join the Royal Flying Corps, cowardly Lyon and noble Hall, and how their actions affect each other, particularly their rivalry over Harlow. (Dir: Howard Hughes, 135 mins.)

Hell's Angels Forever (1983)*** Documentary view of the legendary motorcycle club from the inside. Because the nationwide members trusted the filmmakers, we get some interesting and unusual insights. (Dirs: Richard Chase, Kevin Keating, Leon Grant, 92 mins.)†

Hell's Angels on Wheels (1967)* Jack Nicholson, Adam Roarke, Sonny Barger. Jack Nicholson portrays a gas station pumper named Poet who is taught the joys of motorcycledom by Hell's Angels guru Adam Roarke and then becomes smitten with Roarke's beloved bikette. Holy Harley Davidson! (Dir: Richard Rush, 95 mins.)†

Hell's Belles (1969)*½ Jeremy Slate, Adam Roarke, Jocelyn Lane, Michael Walker, Angelique Pettyjohn. Silly but action-packed revenge melodrama about a motorcyclist who gets even when his bike's pinched. (Dir: Maury Dexter, 98 mins.)

Hell's Crossroads (1957)*½ Stephen McNally, Peggie Castle. Member of the James gang plans to reform. Predictable western. (Dir: Franklin Adreon, 73 mins.)

Hell's Five Hours (1958)*½ Stephen McNally, Coleen Gray, Vic Morrow. An ex-employee of a rocket fuel company is out to blow up the plant, along with his boss's family. (Dir: Jack L. Copeland, 73 mins.)

Hell's Half Acre (1954)**½ Wendell Corey, Evelyn Keyes. Woman goes to Honolulu when she suspects a nightclub owner of being her husband, believed killed at Pearl Harbor. (Dir: John H. Auer, 91 mins.)

Hell's Hinges (1916)***½ William S. Hart, Clara Williams, Louise Glaum, Jack Standing. Hart plays Blaze Tracey, a wrongdoer and roustabout in the wide-open town of Hell's Hinges, whose heart is touched by an innocent minister's sister. Early western portrays the lawlessness and corruption of the frontier town with remarkable clarity, climaxing in the total destruction of every ramshackle structure in an inferno of fire. A landmark film, as astonishing today as it must have been when it was first seen. Co-written and directed by William S. Hart. (65 mins.)†

Hell Ship Mutiny (1957)*½ Jon Hall, John Carradine, Peter Lorre. Ship captain runs into bandits in the South Seas. Waterlogged melodrama. (Dirs: Lee Sholem, Elmo Williams, 66 mins.)

Hell's Island (1955)*** John Payne, Mary Murphy, Francis L. Sullivan. The whereabouts of a stolen ruby sends John Payne on a wild goose chase with murders and plot twists all along the way. (Dir: Phil Karlson, 84 mins.)

Hell's Kitchen (1939)**½ Ronald Reagan,
464

Dead End Kids. Pretty good melodrama with the boys involved in blackmail, torture and straightening out the rather unsavory situation in Hell's Kitchen. (Dirs: Lewis Seiler, E. A. Dupont, 90 mins.)

Hell's Outpost (1954)*½ Rod Cameron, Joan Leslie. A veteran and a banker battle over a mining claim. Routine action melodrama. (Dir: Joseph Kane, 90 mins.)

Hell Squad (1985)* Bainbridge Scott, Glen Hartford, Tina Lederman, Penny Prior, Marvin Miller. Nine Las Vegas showgirls are hired as mercenaries for a special assignment in the Middle East. Silly movie stops just short of being an out-and-out parody. (Dir: Kenneth Hartford, 88 mins.)†

Hellstrom Chronicle, The (1971)***½ Lawrence Pressman. Fascinating documentary film on insects, marred only by inadvertently funny narration by Dr. Hellstrom (Pressman). He tries to make us believe that the creatures will one day conquer the human race. (Dir: Walon Green, 90 mins.)†

Hell to Eternity (1960)*** Jeffrey Hunter, Vic Damone, David Janssen. Effective drama about true-life Marine hero Guy Gabaldon and his wartime (WWII) story. (Dir: Phil Karlson, 132 mins.)†

Hell with Heroes, The (1968)** Rod Taylor, Claudia Cardinale, Harry Guardino. Routine smuggling yarn with a competent cast who can't save it. Taylor runs a small air cargo service and he gets into trouble with the authorities when he accepts a deal to fly some loot for smuggler Guardino. (Dir: Joseph Sargent, 95 mins.)

Hellzapoppin (1941)*** Olsen and Johnson, Mischa Auer, Martha Raye. The two screwballs unfold their own plot when their director tells them they can't make a movie without a story. It depends upon your own taste, but for some this hodge-podge will be screamingly funny; as such, recommended. (Dir: H. C. Potter, 84 mins.)

Help! (1965)*** The Beatles, Leo McKern, Eleanor Bron. Fast and funny silliness. This frenetic farce concerns a cult's trying to nab one of Ringo's rings. (Dir: Richard Lester, 90 mins.)†

Help Wanted: Kids (MTV 1986)**½ Cindy Williams, Bill Hudson, John Dehner, Miriam Flynn, Joel Brooks, Chad Allen, Hillary Wolf. Williams and Hudson star as an unemployed yuppie couple who hire two kids to be their children. (Dir: David Greenwalt, 104 mins.)

Help Wanted: Male (MTV 1982)*** Suzanne Pleshette, Gil Gerard, Bert Convy, Dana Elcar, Harold Gould, Caren Kaye, Ed Nelson. A lightweight comedy that tries to be contemporary but ends up resembling a thirties romance. Magazine editor Pleshette wants a baby but her fiancé is sterile! (Dir: William Wiard, 104 mins.)†

Helsinki Napoli All Night Long (Finland, 1987)**½ Kari Vaananen, Roberta Manfredi, Jean-Pierre Castaldi, Nino Manfredi, Sam Fuller, Eddie Constantine. Talented director Mika Kaurismaki tries to contrive an art house hit with this lighthearted thriller; a Berlin taxi driver and his pals try to make off with a small fortune belonging to drug czar Fuller. Worth a look for movie buffs. (105 mins.)

Helter Skelter (MTV 1976)**** George Di Cenzo, Steve Railsback, Nancy Wolfe, Sondra Blake, Skip Homeier. Terrifying but well-made account of the Manson slayings based on a book by prosecuting attorney Vincent Bugliosi and Curt Gentry, although some of the actual occurrences are necessarily condensed. A chilling docudrama. (Dir: Tom Gries, 175 mins.)†

He Makes Me Feel Like Dancin' (1983)***½ A jubilant documentary about Jacques D'Amboise, a former principal dancer with the N.Y.C. Ballet and his work with underprivileged children, whom he helps to discover the joy of expression through dance. Oscar-winner Best Documentary. (Dir: Emile Ardolino, 90 mins.)

Hemingway's Adventures of a Young Man —See: Adventures of a Young Man

Henderson Monster, The (MTV 1980)**½ Jason Miller, Christine Lahti, Stephen Collins, David Spielberg. Talkative drama looks into the unknown perils of genetics experiments. Miller plays a brilliant Nobel laureate whose safety procedures are questioned by an ambitious, if slightly prejudiced, mayor (Spielberg). (Dir: Waris Hussein, 104 mins.)†

Hennessy (Great Britain, 1975)** Rod Steiger, Lee Remick, Richard Johnson, Trevor Howard, Eric Porter. Moderate suspenser about a retired IRA munitions expert planning to assassinate the Queen as revenge for the deaths of his family. (Dir: Don Sharp, 103 mins.)†

Henry Aldrich series—Henry was the teenager as perpetual bungler. His All-American good-naturedness somehow always managed to save the day.

Henry Aldrich, Boy Scout (1944)**½ Jimmy Lydon, Darryl Hickman. Superior entry in the series; patrol leader Henry must be nice to a new youngster at the request of his father. (Dir: Hugh Bennett, 66 mins.)

Henry Aldrich, Editor (1943)** Jimmy Lydon, Charles Smith. Minor comedy finds reporter Henry covering so many fires he's accused of arson. (Dir: Hugh Bennett, 71 mins.)

Henry Aldrich for President (1941)** Jimmy Lydon, June Preisser. Grade B juvenile tale has Henry running for president of his high school. Mild but pleasant. (Dir: Hugh Bennett, 73 mins.)

Henry Aldrich Gets Glamour (1943)** Jimmy Lydon, Frances Gifford. Cute entry in this juvenile series finds Henry in Hollywood after winning a contest. (Dir: Hugh Bennett, 75 mins.)

Henry Aldrich Haunts a House (1943)** Jimmy Lydon, Charles Smith, John Litel, Olive Blakeney. Standard series entry beefed up by the haunted house shenanigans. (Dir: Hugh Bennett, 73 mins.)

Henry Aldrich Plays Cupid (1944)** Jimmy Lydon, John Litel. Henry decides he'll have a better chance of getting into Princeton if he marries off Mr. Bradley, his high school principal. Obvious but fun. (Dir: Hugh Bennett, 65 mins.)

Henry Aldrich's Little Secret (1944)** Jimmy Lydon, Charles Smith. Henry gets in plenty of hot water when he operates a baby-minding business. Average. (Dir: Hugh Bennett, 75 mins.)

Henry Aldrich Swings It (1943)*½ Jimmy Lydon, Charles Smith. Henry gets a crush on his music teacher and then gets involved in the theft of a Stradivarius violin. Tortuous plot doesn't help the mild comedy. (Dir: Hugh Bennett, 64 mins.)

Henry and Dizzy (1942)** Jimmy Lydon, Charles Smith, Mary Anderson. Henry Aldrich is accused of stealing a motorboat. Mild teenage comedy. (Dir: Hugh Bennett, 71 mins.)

Henry & June (1990)***½ Fred Ward, Maria de Madeiros, Uma Thurman, Richard E. Grant, Kevin Spacey. Thoroughly satisfying drama about writer Henry Miller (Ward in a bravura performance) and his darkly sensual wife June as seen through the eyes of that paragon of narcissism, Anaïs Nin, with whom he had a brief but memorable love affair. Director Philip Kaufman, writing with his wife Rose, has managed to capture the creative energy and demonic wanderlust of Paris in the thirties. This is a movie that isn't afraid of passion, lust, and unbridled sexuality. Superbly acted, it's literate and entertaining, witty and serious. Philippe Rousselot's camera expertly captures the moods of the city and its people. Based on Nin's diaries. The lovemaking scenes, including one lesbian pairing, are genuinely erotic but are not, repeat *not*, pornographic. Also noteworthy for being the first film rated NC-17 by the MPAA. (Dir: Philip Kaufman, 140 mins.)†

Henry VIII and His Six Wives (Great Britain, 1972)*** Keith Michell, Frances Cuka, Charlotte Rampling, Jane Asher, Lynne Frederick. Though based on the famous BBC-TV series, this was designed as a feature film and scripted and directed accordingly. Michell's performance as Henry is first-rate. (Dir: Waris Hussein, 125 mins.)

Henry V (Great Britain, 1944)**** Laurence Olivier, Robert Newton, Leslie Banks, Leo Genn. Olivier's performance is one of the most brilliant ever captured on film, in this, the first film version of Shakespeare's great drama. The entire film is superb in every detail. The battle scenes are brilliantly directed by Olivier, the color photography is breathtaking. (Dir: Laurence Olivier, 137 mins.)†

Henry V (Great Britain, 1989)***½ Kenneth Branagh, Paul Scofield, Derek Jacobi, Ian Holm, Alec McGowen, Judi Dench, Brian Blessed, Emma Thompson, Robbie Coltrane. Energetic, extraordinarily well-acted and perfectly cast version of Shakespeare's drama, adapted and directed by tyro-star Branagh. (135 mins.)†

Henry IV (Italy, 1985)***½ Marcello Mastroianni, Claudia Cardinale, Leopoldo Trieste, Paolo Bonacelli, Luciano Bartoli, Latou Chardons. A masterful adaptation of an exceedingly complex Pirandello play. An aging aristocrat, indulging the delusion that he is a nobleman living in the 11th-century, is visited by relatives who hope to shock him back to sanity. (Dir: Marco Bellocchio, 95 mins.)†

Henry: Portrait of a Serial Killer (1987)**½ Michael Rooker, Tom Towles, Tracy Arnold. Disturbing, fact-based account of a murderer whose life switches gears when he begins to share his "hobby" with his lecherous roommate. Rooker is perfect in the title role, but the acting of his co-stars is flat, the sick humor only occasionally hits the target. (Dir: John McNaughton, 83 mins.)†

Her Adventurous Night (1946)**½ Dennis O'Keefe, Helen Walker, Tom Powers, Fuzzy Knight. Young boy innocently implicates his parents in a robbery and murder. (Dir: John Rawlins, 76 mins.)

Her Alibi (1989)** Tom Selleck, Paulina Porizkova, William Daniels, James Farentino. Mystery novelist, smitten with a beautiful murder suspect, provides a phony alibi for her, and then wonders if he's to be her next victim. Poorly written attempt at screwball comedy is saved only by the charms of its stars. (Dir: Bruce Beresford, 95 mins.)†

He Ran All the Way (1951)*** John Garfield, Shelley Winters. Exciting, contrived melodrama about a killer who holds a decent family at bay and hides out in their home. Excellent performance by Garfield. His last. (Dir: John Berry, 77 mins.)

Herbie Goes Bananas (1980)*½ Charles Martin Smith, Steven W. Burns, John Vernon, Cloris Leachman, Harvey Kor-

man. The Love Bug experiences various "roadblocks" while trying to race in Brazil. Herbie needs spare parts at this point; the fourth *Love Bug* film. (Dir: Vincent McEveety, 100 mins.)†

Herbie Goes to Monte Carlo (1977)** Dean Jones, Julie Sommars, Don Knotts. Third Disney *Love Bug* film has Herbie the Volkswagen entering a road race from Paris to Monte Carlo with his original owner (Jones) as driver. (Dir: Vincent McEveety, 105 mins.)†

Herbie Rides Again (1974)*** Helen Hayes, Ken Berry, Stefanie Powers, Keenan Wynn. Good follow-up to *The Love Bug* finds the lovable Volkswagen in the care of sweet elderly Hayes, whose home is marked for destruction by greedy developer Wynn. (Dir: Robert Stevenson, 88 mins.)†

Her Cardboard Lover (1942)*½ Norma Shearer, Robert Taylor, George Sanders, Frank McHugh, Elizabeth Patterson. Cardboard comedy that was Shearer's last film. A lady hires a suitor to make her slow-to-ignite beau jealous. (Dir: George Cukor, 93 mins.)

Hercules (Italy, 1959)** Steve Reeves. Successful Italian epic, English dubbed, starring muscleman Steve Reeves as Hercules. (Dir: Pietro Francisci, 107 mins.)†

Hercules (1983)* Lou Ferrigno, Sybil Danning, Brad Harris. Lou (Incredible Hulk) Ferrigno sports an impressive physique, and his feats of bravery are amusing on a comic-book level, but inane dialogue and an out-of-place outer space sequence prove too much for even Hercules to overcome. Sequel: *The Adventures of Hercules*. (Dir: Lewis Coates, 99 mins.)†

Hercules Against the Moon Men (Italy, 1965)* Alan Steel. Muscleman comes to the rescue of a country whose inhabitants are forced to undergo a sacrificial ritual imposed on them by invaders from the moon. (Dir: Giacomo Gentilomo, 88 mins.)†

Hercules Against the Sons of the Sun (Italy, 1963)* Mark Forrest, Anna Maria Pace. Muscleman pits himself against the King of the Incas and some sun god worshipers. (Dir: Osvaldo Civirani, 91 mins.)

Hercules and the Captive Women (Italy, 1962)** Reg Park, Fay Spain. The muscleman matches wits with a wicked queen of Atlantis, escapes from the lost city. (Dir: Vittorio Cottafavi, 87 mins.)†

Hercules Goes Bananas (1970)½ Arnold Strong (Schwarzenegger), Arnold Stang, Deborah Loomis, James Karen. Before his current success as a Hollywood hulk, Schwarzenegger followed in the footsteps of muscle builders past by playing the brawny Greek hero in this wickedly bad comedy. Bored in Olympus, Herk visits modern-day N.Y.C., where he loses his powers and finds work as a professional wrestler. AKA: **Hercules in New York** and **Hercules: The Movie**. (Dir: Arthur A. Seidelman, 90 mins.)†

Hercules in New York—See: **Hercules Goes Bananas**

Hercules, Samson and Ulysses (Italy, 1964)* Kirk Morris, Richard L. Lloyd. Mythical superstars team up to defend Greece against the invading Philistines. Musclebound fantasy. (Dir: Pietro Francisci, 92 mins.)

Hercules: The Movie—See: **Hercules Goes Bananas**

Hercules II—See: **Adventures of Hercules, The**

Hercules Unchained (Italy, 1960)** Sequel to *Hercules*—juvenile adventure epic starring muscleman Steve Reeves and an Italian cast. English dubbed. (Dir: Pietro Francisci, 101 mins.)†

Here Comes Mr. Jordan (1941)**** Robert Montgomery, Claude Rains, Evelyn Keyes, Rita Johnson, James Gleason, Edward Everett Horton. Boxer in a plane crash discovers his time isn't up as yet, so the celestial powers have to find him a new body. One of the most unusual, original fantasies ever made; fine entertainment all around. Remade as *Heaven Can Wait*, 1978. (Dir: Alexander Hall, 93 mins.)†

Here Comes the Groom (1951)*** Bing Crosby, Jane Wyman, Franchot Tone, Alexis Smith. Likable Frank Capra comedy with songs about a happy-go-lucky reporter who competes with a real-estate dealer for the hand of a girl. Nice songs, general air of good fun. (Dir: Frank Capra, 113 mins.)†

Here Comes the Navy (1934)**½ James Cagney, Pat O'Brien, Gloria Stuart, Frank McHugh, Dorothy Tree, Robert Barrat, Guinn Williams. Roistering service comedy-adventure with Cagney and O'Brien paired for the first time as enemies who carry on their feud while assigned to the same battleship in the Navy. Energetic, though not their best. (Dir: Lloyd Bacon, 86 mins.)

Here Come the Coeds (1945)**½ Bud Abbott, Lou Costello, Peggy Ryan, Martha O'Driscoll, Lon Chaney, June Vincent. Wacky low comedy with A & C at their silliest. In charge of the maintenance of a girl's school, the daffy duo make a shambles of the place. (Dir: Jean Yarbrough, 87 mins.)

Here Come the Girls (1953)**½ Bob Hope, Tony Martin, Arlene Dahl. Chorus boy is shoved into the limelight as leading man of a show when the star is threatened by a killer. Fairly amusing Hope comedy. (Dir: Claude Binyon, 78 mins.)

Here Come the Marines (1953)** Bowery Boys, Hanley Stafford, Bernard Gorcey, Paul Maxey, Myrna Dell. The boys are drafted into the Marines. Through a series of mishaps, Sach is promoted up the line and is put in charge of the other boys. (Dir: William Beaudine, 66 mins.)

Here Come the Waves (1944)*** Bing Crosby, Betty Hutton. Cute nautical musical about a successful crooner who joins the Navy. (Dir: Mark Sandrich, 99 mins.)

Here Is My Heart (1934)**½ Bing Crosby, Kitty Carlisle, Roland Young, Alison Skipworth, Reginald Owen, William Frawley, Akim Tamiroff. Easygoing Crosby vehicle with the crooner as a radio star falling for a princess and pretending to be a waiter to get close to her. Lots of nice songs and a good supporting cast. (Dir: Frank Tuttle, 77 mins.)

Here's the Knife, Dear: Now Use It—See: **Nightmare** (1963)

Heretic, The—See: **Exorcist II, The Heretic**

Here We Go Round the Mulberry Bush (Great Britain, 1968)*½ Barry Evans, Judy Geeson, Angela Scoular, Denholm Elliott. Stupefyingly awful. Seventeen-year-old student determines to do something about his virginity—i.e., lose it at the first possible opportunity. (Dir: Clive Donner, 96 mins.)

Her First Mate (1933)** Slim Summerville, ZaSu Pitts, Una Merkel, Warren Hymer, Berton Churchill. Early William Wyler-directed comedy about a butcher (Summerville) on a night boat up the Hudson River to Albany who dreams of a life of adventure on the high seas. Instead he meets Pitts and Merkel. (66 mins.)

Her First Romance (1951)** Margaret O'Brien, Allen Martin, Jr. Margaret O'Brien's first teenager film in which she received her first screen kiss. (Dir: Seymour Friedman, 73 mins.)

Her Highness and the Bellboy (1945)** Hedy Lamarr, Robert Walker, June Allyson, Agnes Moorehead. Drab comedy about a bellboy (Walker) who attracts the attention of Princess Hedy while he should be courting sweet June. (Dir: Richard Thorpe, 111 mins.)

Her Husband's Affairs (1948)*½ Franchot Tone, Lucille Ball. In spite of the stars, this is a meaningless farce about a man, his wife, and some crazy invention. (Dir: S. Sylvan Simon, 83 mins.)†

He Rides Tall (1964)** Tony Young, Dan Duryea, Jo Morrow. Marshal finds dirty work on the ranch of his foster-father, instigated by a no-good foreman. Routine western. (Dir: R. G. Springsteen, 84 mins.)

Her Jungle Love (1938)**½ Dorothy

Lamour, Ray Milland, Lynne Overman, J. Carrol Naish, Dorothy Howe, Jonathan Hale, Richard Denning. A silly classic, this campy romance has flier Milland crash on an uncharted island and fall for jungle princess Lamour. (Dir: George Archainbaud, 81 mins.)

Her Life as a Man (MTV 1984)*½ Robyn Douglass, Robert Culp, Marc Singer, Laraine Newman. A poor steal from *Tootsie*, with a twist—a girl reporter disguises herself as a man to land a sports reporter job. (Dir: Robert Miller, 104 mins.)†

Her Majesty Love (1931)** Marilyn Miller, Ben Lyon, W. C. Fields, Ford Sterling, Leon Errol, Chester Conklin. A wealthy family tries to prevent poor wastrel Miller from marrying Lyon, the heir to the family fortune. Soppy musical of interest strictly for Fields's presence as Miller's gauche father; his famous vaudeville juggling act is also captured for the ages. (Dir: William Dieterle, 75 mins.)

Hero, The (Great Britain, 1969)* Richard Harris, Romy Schneider. Forty-year-old Eitan Bloomfield (Harris) is headed for his last game as a soccer superstar. But he won't go without using up every movie cliché he can think of. AKA: **Bloomfield.** (Dir.: Richard Harris, 97 mins.)†

Hero Ain't Nothin' but a Sandwich, A (1978)** Paul Winfield, Cicely Tyson. A well-meaning but inadequately developed domestic drama about a twelve-year-old boy's drug addiction and his attempts at breaking the habit. (Dir: Ralph Nelson, 105 mins.)†

Hero and the Terror (1988)**½ Chuck Norris, Brynn Thayer, Steve James, Jack O'Halloran. Cop Norris tracks down the maniacal killer he accidentally captured years before. (Dir: William Tannen, 96 mins.)†

Hero at Large (1980)***½ John Ritter, Anne Archer, Kevin McCarthy. Ritter is an unemployed actor whose Captain Avenger costume becomes his real-life character, and Archer is the modern girl next door. A pleasant if implausible entertainment. (Dir: Martin Davidson, 98 mins.)†

Heroes (1977)** Henry Winkler, Sally Field. This film about the readjustment process of a Vietnam veteran is like a movie of the week blown up to the big screen. Winkler plays a vet who flees a snake pit and then chases Field across country. (Dir: Jeremy Paul Kagan, 119 mins.)†

Heroes for Sale (1933)***½ Richard Barthelmess, Loretta Young, Aline MacMahon, Gordon Bennett, Robert Barrat, Grant Mitchell, Charlie Grapewin, Margaret Seddon, Douglas Dunbrille, Ward Bond. The life of one American Everyman, brilliantly played by Barthelmess, from

his disastrous service in WWI to the depths of the Depression; it seems that everything that *could* happen to one man happens to Tom Holmes, from war-induced morphine addiction to a conviction for rioting. One of the fastest paced movies you'll ever see, although some scenes that were too political for the studio's taste were cut before its release. A superb, dryly patriotic early work by director William Wellman. (73 mins.)

Heroes of Telemark (Great Britain, 1965)**½ Kirk Douglas, Richard Harris, Ulla Jacobson. A true-life WWII incident is turned into a moderately interesting adventure drama. Kirk Douglas heads a group of brave Norwegians who stop at nothing to destroy a Nazi plant producing essential matter for the development of the atomic bomb. (Dir: Anthony Mann, 131 mins.)

Hero's Island (1962)*½ James Mason, Neville Brand, Rip Torn. A pirate helps a man save his Carolina island from marauders who consider it their own. (Dir: Leslie Stevens, 94 mins.)

Her Panelled Door (Great Britain, 1950)*** Phyllis Calvert, Edward Underdown, Helen Cherry, Richard Burton. A woman found suffering from amnesia tries to retrace her past. Fairly good psychological melodrama; a young Burton adds some interest. (Dirs: George More O'Ferrall, Ladislas Vajda, 84 mins.)

Her Secret Life (MTV 1987)* Kate Capshaw, Jeroen Krabbe, Gregory Sierra, Cliff De Young. Happily married L.A. schoolteacher Capshaw reverts to her previous job as a government agent when they need her to rescue an operative in Cuba. (Dir: Buzz Kulik, 104 mins.)

Hers to Hold (1943)**½ Deanna Durbin, Joseph Cotten, Charles Winninger, Evelyn Ankers, Gus Schilling, Ludwig Stossel, Iris Adrian, Samuel S. Hinds. Mild vehicle for Durbin has her all grown up and in love with soldier Joseph Cotten; luckily, she was a charming actress, and sings some nice numbers, including "Begin the Beguine" and "God Bless America." (Dir: Frank Ryan, 94 mins.)

Her Twelve Men (1954)**½ Greer Garson, Robert Ryan, Barry Sullivan. An attempt to make a humorous "Mr. Chips" out of Greer Garson, as a schoolteacher in a boys' boarding school, just doesn't come off. Greer works hard but the script lets her down. (Dir: Robert Z. Leonard, 91 mins.)

He Said, She Said (1991)*½ Kevin Bacon, Elizabeth Perkins, Nathan Lane, Anthony LaPaglia, Sharon Stone, Phil Leeds, Rita Karin. A failed attempt at a romantic *Rashomon*. A couple of yuppie journalists fall out of love and the film gives us the story from his viewpoint then hers.

He Said is directed by Ken Kwapis; *She Said* by Marisa Silver. Kurosawa they're not. Veteran performers Leeds and Karin act circles around the young cast. (Dirs: Ken Kwapis, Marisa Silver, 115 mins.)†

He's Fired, She's Hired (MTV 1984)** Karen Valentine, Wayne Rogers, Elizabeth Ashley, Howard Rollins. What happens when a middle-aged ad executive is canned, and his wife goes to work in the same business using hubby's ideas? The story is played for laughs, making fun of the ad agency world, and adds up to fair entertainment. (Dir: Marc Daniels, 104 mins.)

He's My Girl (1987)*½ T. K. Carter, David Hallyday, Misha McK, Jennifer Tilly. Yet another cross-dress comedy, with black comedian Carter masquerading as the female escort of aspiring rocker pal Hallyday. (Dir: Gabrielle Beaumont, 104 mins.)†

He's Not Your Son (MTV 1984)** Ken Howard, John James, Ann Dusenberry, Donna Mills. Two couples discover their baby boys have been inadvertently switched when one of the babies requires heart surgery six months later. Abandon this predictable soap opera on someone else's doorstep. (Dir: Don Taylor, 104 mins.)

He Stayed for Breakfast (1940)** Melvyn Douglas, Loretta Young. Communist man learns about life, love and capitalist luxury from a beautiful American girl. Comedy employing *Ninotchka* theme is forced and only occasionally funny. (Dir: Alexander Hall, 89 mins.)

Hester Street (1975)*** Carol Kane, Steven Keats, Doris Roberts, Mel Howard. Writer-director Joan Micklin Silver has come up with a touching and memorable first film about the immigration of a Jewish family to the Lower East Side of New York during the turn of the century. Kane received an Academy Award nomination for her luminous performance as Gitl, the Orthodox Jewish wife who has to shed her old ways and work toward becoming an American. (90 mins.)†

He Walked by Night (1948)***½ Richard Basehart, Scott Brady, Jack Webb. Semi-documentary chase drama showing how the police stalk a killer is an exciting, tense, and absorbing film. Basehart is superb as the killer. (Dir: Alfred L. Werker, 79 mins.)†

He Who Gets Slapped (1924)*** Lon Chaney, Norma Shearer, John Gilbert, Tully Marshall, Ford Sterling, Marc MacDermott. Chaney is a scientist who is cheated of credit for his discovery and deserted by his wife; in despair, he decides to give up everything and disguise himself as a clown. Dark, unrelenting, rather bitter story beautifully made by the great Swedish director Victor Seastrom. (Dir: Victor Seastrom [Sjostrom], 85 mins.)

He Who Must Die (France, 1957)**** Melina Mercouri, Pierre Vaneck, Jean Servais, Gert Frobe. A Greek village, still under Turkish control following WWI, re-enacts the Passion Play for Holy Week, and finds that it still has great meaning for their modern society. (Dir: Jules Dassin, 122 mins.)

He Who Rides a Tiger (Great Britain, 1966)*** Tom Bell, Judi Dench, Paul Rogers, Kay Walsh, Jeremy Spenser. The unlikely love affair between a burglar (Tom Bell) and a young mother (Judi Dench) is compellingly unreeled in this well-directed drama. Good performances. (Dir: Charles Crichton, 103 mins.)

Hex (1973)**½ Tina Herazo (Cristina Raines), Hilarie Thompson, Keith Carradine, Mike Combes, Scott Glenn, Gary Busey, Robert Walker, Jr., Dan Haggerty. Curiosity piece that features a number of then-unknowns acting out an odd little drama that concerns motorbikes, the supernatural, and a post-WWI setting. Raines and Thompson are occult-crazy sisters who introduce a group of bikers to the darker side. (Dir: Leo Garen, 92 mins.)

Hey, Babu Riba (Yugoslavia, 1986)*** Gala Videnovic, Relja Bacic, Nebojsa Bakocevic. Set against the turmoil of postwar Yugoslavia, this tale of four rock 'n' roll-loving friends and the woman they all yearn for works as an Eastern European version of *American Graffiti*, though with more political heft. Well acted and accessible for American audiences. (Dir: Jovan Acin, 109 mins.)†

Hey, Good Lookin' (1982)**½ Voices of Richard Romanus, David Proval, Jesse Wells, Tina Bowman. Those unfamiliar with animator Ralph Bakshi's coarse style may be repulsed by this streetwise portrayal of 1950s Brooklyn street life; but fans accustomed to his downbeat animation might enjoy this crude effort about street gangs, sex, and swearing. (Dir: Ralph Bakshi, 86 mins.)†

Hey, I'm Alive (MTV 1975)**½ Sally Struthers, Edward Asner. In 1963, young Helen Klaban and middle-aged Ralph Flores crashed in the frozen Yukon wilderness and, somehow, managed to survive for forty-nine days. Their harrowing true-life ordeal makes a fairly good film. (Dir: Lawrence Schiller, 72 mins.)†

Hey, Let's Twist (1961)** Joey Dee, Teddy Randazzo, The Starliters, Zohra Lampert, Alan Arbus, The Peppermint Loungers. Fictional account of the dance craze that swept the early sixties, and the club, the Peppermint Lounge, that housed its greatest practitioner (next to Chubby

Checker, of course), Joey Dee. Dated fun. (Dir: Greg Garrison, 80 mins.)

Hey, Rookie (1944)**½ Ann Miller, Larry Parks. Big producer is drafted, stages a big Army show. Pleasant comedy-musical with some above-average material. (Dir: Charles Barton, 77 mins.)

Hey There, It's Yogi Bear (1964)*½ Animated adventures of Yogi Bear. A series of escapades lands him far from Jellystone National Park, in the Chizzling Brothers Circus. For tiny kiddies. (Dirs: William Hanna, Joseph Barbera, 89 mins.)†

Hiawatha (1952)** Vincent Edwards, Keith Larsen, Yvette Dugay. Indian brave tries to prevent a war among tribes perpetrated by a hot-headed warrior. Mildly entertaining adventure based on Longfellow's poem. (Dir: Kurt Neumann, 80 mins.)

Hickey and Boggs (1972)**½ Robert Culp, Bill Cosby. Everyone's chasing $400,000 of stolen bank loot including detectives Al Hickey (Cosby) and Frank Boggs (Culp). (Dir: Robert Culp, 111 mins.)

Hidden Agenda (Great Britain, 1990)***½ Frances McDormand, Brian Cox, Brad Dourif, Mai Zetterling. Hard-hitting superbly crafted political thriller about the investigation into the murder of an American civil liberties activist killed while gathering evidence about atrocities in war-torn Northern Ireland. Entire cast is outstanding. (Dir: Ken Loach, 110 mins.)†

Hidden, The (1987)*** Michael Nouri, Kyle MacLachlan, Ed O'Ross, Clu Gulager, Claudia Christian. Exciting, slickly made sci-fi thriller about an evil alien life form that invades humans and causes them to go on criminal rampages. Nouri is the cop on the case, MacLachlan a good alien in human form who arrives to help. (Dir: Jack Sholder, 98 mins.)†

Hidden Eye, The (1945)*** Edward Arnold, Frances Rafferty. Blind detective uses his powers to save an innocent man and uncover a murder plot. Tightly knit, suspenseful mystery, above average. (Dir: Richard Whorf, 69 mins.)

Hidden Fear (1957)** John Payne, Alexander Knox. Routine crime melodrama set in Copenhagen has American (Payne) arriving on the scene to investigate his young sister's involvement with a group of "intrigue-soaked" characters. (Dir: Andre de Toth, 83 mins.)

Hidden Fortress, The (Japan, 1959)***½ Toshiro Mifune. A gritty fairy tale (said to be the inspiration for *Star Wars*) directed by Akira Kurosawa, about a loyal general (Mifune) and two comic sidekicks who protect a princess fleeing evil forces who seek her destruction. (123 mins.)†

Hidden Room, The (Great Britain, 1949)

Hideaways, The—See: **From the Mixed-Up Files of Mrs. Basil E. Frankweller**

Hide in Plain Sight (1980)***½ James Caan, Jill Eikenberry, Robert Viharo, Danny Aiello, Kenneth McMillan. Caan's directorial debut is simple and direct, telling the story of a workingman whose children are taken from him as part of a government witness relocation program after his ex-wife's second husband rats on the mob. Based on a true story. (98 mins.)†

Hideous Sun Demon (1959)* Robert Clarke, Nan Peterson, Patricia Manning, Patrick Whyte, Fred LaPorta. Science fiction yarn with a scientist once again becoming the victim of his own experimentation. Hideous. (Dir: Robert Clarke, 74 mins.)†

Hide-Out (1934)*** Robert Montgomery, Maureen O'Sullivan, Edward Arnold, Elizabeth Patterson, Mickey Rooney, Whitford Kane, Edward Brophy, Herman Bing. Warm, sprightly comedy-melodrama of a hood hiding out in the country, being reformed by the nice family he's boarding with. (Dir: W. S. Van Dyke, 83 mins.)

Hi Diddle Diddle (1943)**½ Adolphe Menjou, Martha Scott, Pola Negri, Dennis O'Keefe, Billie Burke, June Havoc. Wacky comedy about young lovers who yearn for conventional bliss but are saddled with larcenous parents who enjoy bending the law. (Dir: Andrew L. Stone, 72 mins.)

Hiding Out (1987)** Jon Cryer, Keith Coogan, Annabeth Gish, Oliver Cotton. Occasionally sweet but often labored comedy about a stockbroker hiding from mobsters in his cousin's high school. Some nice moments. (Dir: Bob Giraldi, 98 mins.)†

Hiding Place, The (1975)** Julie Harris, Arthur O'Connell, Eileen Heckart, Jeanette Clift. Based on a true story of two sisters sent to a concentration camp for aiding the Jews. Distinguished cast provides the film with grace. (Dir: James F. Collier, 145 mins.)†

High and Dry (Great Britain, 1953)*** Paul Douglas, Alex Mackenzie, Hubert Gregg. An American businessman runs afoul of a rickety cargo vessel in Scotland in this wryly amusing comedy with the crafty Ealing Studios touch. AKA: **The Maggie**. (Dir: Alexander Mackendrick, 93 mins.)

High and Low (Japan, 1963)**** Toshiro Mifune, Kyoko Kagawa. Gripping crime story from an American novel by Ed McBain. Fascinatingly detailed plot about a kidnapping attempt that turns into a murder case for the hard-working police. (Dir: Akira Kurosawa, 142 mins.)†

High and the Mighty, The (1954)*** John Wayne, Claire Trevor, Robert Stack, Jan Sterling, Laraine Day, David Brian. Passengers on a crippled airplane feel compelled to review their lives and in doing so come to a new awareness. Overlong and episodic but successful in its suspense. (Dir: William Wellman, 147 mins.)

High Anxiety (1977)*** Mel Brooks, Madeline Kahn, Harvey Korman. Affectionate, funny spoof and homage to Alfred Hitchcock and his filmic style. Plot, such as it is, concerns a doctor (Brooks) trying to understand and deal with his own neurosis. Brooks co-wrote the screenplay. (Dir: Mel Brooks, 94 mins.)†

High-Ballin' (Canada, 1978)** Peter Fonda, Jerry Reed, Helen Shaver. Tedious trucker opus, starring Fonda and Reed as old pals who team up with an offbeat lady trucker (Shaver) in taking on the thugs who are out to crush the independent truckers. (Dir: Peter Carter, 100 mins.)†

High Barbaree (1946)*½ Van Johnson, June Allyson, Thomas Mitchell. Two airmen are floating on a raft in the Pacific and while one moans the other bores him to death with the story of his life. (Dir: Jack Conway, 91 mins.)

High Bright Sun, The—See: McGuire Go Home

High Commissioner, The (Great Britain, 1968)**½ Rod Taylor, Christopher Plummer, Lilli Palmer, Franchot Tone, Camilla Sparv, Daliah Lavi, Leo McKern, Clive Revill. Dogged Australian sleuth (Rod Taylor) arrives in London to arrest a political bigwig for murder. (Dir: Ralph Thomas, 93 mins.)

High Cost of Loving, The (1958)*** Jose Ferrer, Gena Rowlands, Jim Backus. Fine, if somewhat thin, satire of a white-collar worker's insecure job. Ferrer directs and plays Jim Fry, who fears he is going to be fired at the same time he learns his wife is pregnant. Entertaining, but the ending is too predictable. (87 mins.)

High Country, The (Canada, 1981)**½ Timothy Bottoms, Linda Purl, George Sims, Jim Lawrence, Bill Berry, Walter Mills. Linda is a handicapped young woman and Timothy is a convict—the two meet and head for the Canadian Rockies. (Dir: Harvey Hart, 101 mins.)†

Higher and Higher (1943)*** Michele Morgan, Jack Haley, Frank Sinatra, Victor Borge. Man unable to pay his servants forms a corporation with them. Entertaining musical comedy. (Dir: Tim Whelan, 90 mins.)†

Higher Ground (MTV 1988)*½ John Denver, Meg Wittner, Richard Masur. Country boy Denver stars in this wholesome, empty telepic as an Alaskan bush pilot who battles drug smugglers, clears his best friend's name, and flies over handsome Alaskan waterways. Masur makes a good counterpart as a nasty villain. (Dir: Robert Day, 96 mins.)

High Flight (Great Britain, 1958)**½ Ray Milland, Kenneth Haigh. Well-acted drama about the training of RAF jet flying cadets. Personal drama revolves around the relationship of instructor Milland and his most brilliant but stubbornly undisciplined pupil. (Dir: John Gilling, 89 mins.)

High Frequency (Italy, 1988)**½ Vincent Spano, Oliver Benny, Isabelle Pasco, Anne Canovos, David Brandon. A few good touches can be found in this tame thriller about satellite relay station workers (Spano and Benny) who witness a murder via a monitor and spend most of the movie trying to alert the woman they think is the killer's next target. Great idea, poorly developed. (Dir: Faliero Rosati, 105 mins.)†

High Heels (France, 1972)*** Jean-Paul Belmondo, Mia Farrow, Laura Antonelli, Daniel Ivernel, Marlene Appelt. Uneven but generally amusing dark comedy about doctor Belmondo, who sings the praises of homely women and marries one (Farrow in ugly-duckling drag) but changes his mind when he meets her sister, Antonelli. AKA: **Doctor Popaul, Scoundrel in White.** (Dir: Claude Chabrol, 95 mins.)†

High Hopes (Great Britain, 1988)*** Philip Davis, Ruth Sheen, Edna Dore, Philip Jackson. Often funny social satire set in modern England, with three couples covering all bases of middle-class life in the Thatcher era. The script is perverse, but the cast is dead on. (Dir: Mike Leigh, 110 mins.)†

High Infidelity (France-Italy, 1964)*** Nino Manfredi, Charles Aznavour, Claire Bloom, Monica Vitti, Jean-Pierre Cassel, Ugo Tognazzi. Four tales of marital "infidelity," minor infractions. Pleasant, often witty quartet, complemented by the performances of some appealing stars. (Directors, in order: Mario Monicelli, Elio Petri, Franco Rossi, Luciano Salce. 129 mins.)

Highlander (1986)**½ Christopher Lambert, Sean Connery, Clancy Brown, Roxanne Hart, Beatie Edney, Sheila Gish. Action-packed fantasy adventure about immortals battling each other through the centuries for supremacy. The myth begins in 1536—the dreamy Scottish Highlands—when MacLeod (Lambert) learns from his charming mentor (Connery) the magic and strength he will need four hundred years later in modern-day New York City to fight the evil Kurgan (Brown) for the "prize." The real stars here are—as in most adventure films nowadays—the technical crew. (Dir: Russell Mulcahy, 111 mins.)†

High Lonesome (1950)*** John Barrymore, Jr., Chill Wills. A mysterious young man wanders into a ranch and sets into motion a series of weird happenings. Expert combination of western and mystery. (Dir: Alan LeMay, 81 mins.)

Highly Dangerous (Great Britain, 1951)*** Margaret Lockwood, Dane Clark. Pretty lady scientist and an American reporter risk their necks obtaining vital information behind the Iron Curtain. (Dir: Roy Baker, 88 mins.)

High Midnight (MTV 1979)**½ Mike Connors, David Birney. Revenge drama about a police cover-up. Connors stars as a by-the-book narcotics officer and Birney is the man whose wife and daughter are killed in a "no-knock" drug raid. (Dir: Daniel Haller, 104 mins.)

High Mountain Rangers (MTV 1987)** Robert Conrad, Christian Conrad, Shane Conrad, Tom Towles, P. A. Christian. Robert Conrad plays a former mountain ranger who pitches in to help round up some prison escapees, one of whom is an old enemy of his. Average action-adventure. (Dir: Robert Conrad, 104 mins.)

High Noon (1952)**** Gary Cooper, Grace Kelly. A western classic; story of a brave lawman who has to face outlaws sworn to kill him on his wedding day. As fine an outdoor drama as one could wish, as witness its numerous awards. Cooper won his second Best Actor Oscar. (Dir: Fred Zinnemann, 85 mins.)†

High Noon, Part Two: The Return of Will Kane (MTV 1980)** Lee Majors, David Carradine, Pernell Roberts. Predictable western yarn. Majors cannot live up to the memory of Oscar-winning Gary Cooper in this watered-down sequel. (Dir: Jerry Jameson, 104 mins.)†

High Plains Drifter (1973)**½ Clint Eastwood, Verna Bloom. You'd swear Sergio Leone directed this ambling, violence-ridden western, but Clint himself called the directorial shots. The stranger (Clint) rides into the town of Lago, killing three varmints, and taking over in anticipation of standing up to three other culprits just released from prison. (105 mins.)†

High Pressure (1932)*** William Powell, Evelyn Brent, Frank McHugh, George Sidney, Guy Kibbee, Ben Alexander. Sharp satire of big business implies that it's 90 percent hype, as hustler Powell builds a fortune in a phony new industry with nothing behind it. Crackling and well played, with one of the last appearances by silent star Brent. (Dir: Mervyn LeRoy, 74 mins.)

High Price of Passion, The (MTV 1986)**½ Richard Crenna, Karen Young, Sean McCann, Terry Tweed, Steven Flynn.

472

Predictable melodrama about a college professor entranced by a hooker. When the prostitute goes her own way, the professor becomes unhinged. Only Crenna's devastating performance as the obsessed academic makes this based-on-fact tale worth seeing. (Dir: Larry Elikann, 104 mins.)

High Risk (MTV 1976)** Victor Buono, Joseph Sirola, Don Stroud. Another pilot for an adventure series. A group of former circus performers exercise their penchant for larceny by executing an elaborate plan to steal a jewel-encrusted mask from a foreign embassy in Washington, D.C. (Dir: Sam O'Steen, 72 mins.)†

High Risk (1981)*½ James Brolin, Bruce Davison, Cleavon Little, Chick Vennera, James Coburn, Anthony Quinn, Lindsay Wagner. Set in the recession years of the seventies, four guys, just tryin' to get a fair shake, buy guns and set off to rob a Colombian cocaine dealer (Coburn) of his millions. (Dir: Stewart Raffill, 74 mins.)

High Road to China (1983)** Bess Armstrong, Tom Selleck. Botched adventure film, which resembles a clumsy spin-off of *Raiders of the Lost Ark*. A rich young woman hires the services of a hard-drinking former WWI pilot to help search for her long-lost father. (Dir: Brian G. Hutton, 105 mins.)†

High Rolling (Australia, 1978)** Joseph Bottoms, Grigor Taylor, Judy Davis, John Clayton, Wendy Hughes. The scenery is better than the story in this Ozzie road movie following the exploits of two pals who turn to crime in order to get by. AKA: **High Rolling in a Hot Corvette.** (Dir: Igor Auzins, 90 mins.)†

High School Caesar (1960)**½ Gary Vinson, John Ashley, Steve Stevens, Judy Nugent, Lowell Brown, Daria Massey. Surprisingly interesting teen flick about rich student with bad attitude (his parents don't give him enough attention) who establishes his own crime syndicate in his high school. Rises above usual efforts of the genre. (Dir: O'Dale Ireland, 72 mins.)†

High School Confidential (1958)** Russ Tamblyn, Mamie Van Doren, Jan Sterling. Made when a teen hero could be a narc. Tamblyn is out to bust the pushers, and Jerry Lee Lewis does the title tune. Lots of jive talk and good dragstrip scenes. (Dir: Jack Arnold, 85 mins.)†

High School Hellcats (1958)** Yvonne Lime, Brett Halsey, Jana Lund, Suzanne Sydney, Heather Ames, Nancy Kilgar. They're tough! They're sizzling! They're high school hellcats! A sadistic gang leader kills the club prez and then goes after a possible witness. A fifties artifact for fans of girl-gang flicks. (Dir: Edward Bernds, 69 mins.)

High School U.S.A. (MTV 1983)* Bob

Denver, Elinor Donahue, Tony Dow, David Nelson, Angela Cartwright. TV child stars from the past endure numbskull material as they portray the grown-ups supervising typical high school students. (Dir: Rod Amateau, 104 mins.)

High Season (Great Britain, 1987)**½ Jacqueline Bisset, James Fox, Irene Papas. Small, likable film about the effects of tourism on a small Greek village. Bisset is typically radiant as an English artist whose quiet way of life is disrupted by a pair of amorous foreigners and the unveiling of a new monument to "the Unknown Tourist." (Dir: Clare Peploe, 104 mins.)†

High Sierra (1941)***½ Humphrey Bogart, Ida Lupino, Arthur Kennedy. Tired old killer-on-the-loose theme receives an exciting rejuvenation from this superb cast aided by an excellent script and production. (Dir: Raoul Walsh, 100 mins.)†

High Society (1955)** Bowery Boys, Gavin Gordon, Bernard Gorcey. Sach is allegedly heir to another fortune (yawn!). It was the only Bowery Boys picture ever to be nominated for an Academy Award (Best Original Story) when Academy members mistook it for the MGM blockbuster of the same title. (Dir: William Beaudine, 61 mins.)

High Society (1956)*** Bing Crosby, Grace Kelly, Frank Sinatra, Celeste Holm, Louis Armstrong. Pleasant musical version of *The Philadelphia Story*, about the efforts of a wealthy man to win back his ex-wife who's about to be remarried, and the reporters who become entangled in the romantic complications. With a stellar cast and a Cole Porter score, it should have been better, but it lacks the sparkle of the original. (Dir: Charles Walters, 107 mins.)†

High Spirits (1988)**½ Peter O'Toole, Steve Guttenberg, Daryl Hannah, Beverly D'Angelo, Liam Neeson, Jennifer Tilly. Ghostly comedy set in an Irish castle where tourist Guttenberg meets and falls in love with long-dead Hannah, trapped there by an ancient curse. Special effects and the large cast are good, but the plot is diffuse and the results are hit-and-miss, the result of excessive post-production studio tampering and re-editing. (Dir: Neil Jordan, 98 mins.)†

High Stakes (Canada, 1986)** David Foley, Roberta Weiss, Winston Rekert, Jackson Davies. Teen who dreams of being a star reporter gets his big break when he stumbles onto a criminal plot to recover a hidden Nazi treasure. Some funny supporting characters and one-liners help compensate for a lot of tiresome slapstick bumbling. (Dir: Larry Kent, 82 mins.)†

High Stakes (1989)*½ Sally Kirkland, Robert LuPone, Richard Lynch. Talky thriller about housewife-turned-hooker Kirkland who decides to get out of the business when she finds a soulmate in stockbroker LuPone. Of course, her pimp has other ideas. Slow going. AKA: **Melanie Rose.** (Dir: Amos Kolleck, 86 mins.)†

High Tide (Australia, 1988)*** Judy Davis, Claudia Karvan, Jan Adele. Superb character study of a woman in transition: Davis hits all the right notes as an aging backup singer (for a cheesy Elvis impersonator) who encounters her past in the form of the daughter she'd left behind many years ago. The characters' motivations seem genuine, thanks to the winning performances of Davis and Karvan. (Dir: Gillian Armstrong, 103 mins.)†

High Time (1960)*** Bing Crosby, Fabian, Tuesday Weld. What happens when a wealthy widower returns to college to complete his education? Episodic comedy starts excellently but wears thin before the conclusion. Generally good fun. (Dir: Blake Edwards, 103 mins.)

High Velocity (1977)*½ Ben Gazzara, Britt Ekland, Paul Winfield, Keenan Wynn, Alejandro Rey, Victoria Racimo. When rich businessman Wynn is kidnapped by terrorists in the Philippines, wife Ekland uses her charms to persuade soldiers-of-fortune Gazzara and Winfield to get him back. Low-flying action with a cast that deserves better scripts. (Dir: Remi Kramer, 106 mins.)†

High Wall (1947)*** Robert Taylor, Audrey Totter, Herbert Marshall. Lady doctor helps a man regain his memory, then proves he didn't kill his wife. Suspenseful, well-acted mystery melodrama. (Dir: Curtis Bernhardt, 99 mins.)

Highway Dragnet (1954)** Joan Bennett, Richard Conte. A routine chase film of an ex-Marine, accused of murdering a girl he has just met. (Dir: Nathan Juran, 71 mins.)

Highwayman, The (MTV 1987)*½ Sam Jones, Jimmy Smits, G. Gordon Liddy. Pilot for the series with Jones as a Fed-on-eighteen-wheels who pursues a crooked businessman, played by everyone's favorite Watergate felon, G. Gordon Liddy. Sam's muscles, G. Gordon's mustache, and various high-speed chases don't add up to two good hours of entertainment. (Dir: Doug Heyes, 96 mins.)

High, Wide and Handsome (1937)*** Irene Dunne, Randolph Scott, Dorothy Lamour. Musical tale of the robust adventure that surrounded the discovery of oil in Pennsylvania around 1860. Music by Jerome Kern and Oscar Hammerstein II. (Dir: Rouben Mamoulian, 110 mins.)

High Wind in Jamaica, A (U.S.-Great Britain, 1965)***½ Anthony Quinn, James Coburn. Good adventure drama with fine acting by the cast headed by Quinn as the captain of a pirate vessel. There's a great deal of action when Quinn's ship encounters another vessel and takes some children and the crew. (Dir: Alexander Mackendrick, 104 mins.)

High Window, The—See: **Brasher Doubloon, The**

Hijack (MTV 1973)** David Janssen and Keenan Wynn are the stars of this suspenseful film about two truck drivers, down on their luck, who take on the job of driving a secret cargo from Los Angeles to Houston. (Dir: Leonard Horn, 90 mins.)

Hijacking of the Achille Lauro, The (MTV 1989)** Karl Malden, Lee Grant, E. G. Marshall, Vera Miles, Barry Otto, Christina Pickles. Thinly scripted depiction of the 1985 hijacking of a cruise ship in which American citizen Leon Klinghoffer was killed by terrorists. Malden and Grant are excellent as Mr. and Mrs. Klinghoffer, but the film gives no insight into the motivations of the hijackers. (Dir: Robert Collins, 96 mins.)

Hilda Crane (1956)**½ Jean Simmons, Guy Madison, Jean-Pierre Aumont, Judith Evelyn, Evelyn Varden. Hilda Crane is, in fifties parlance, "used goods," a divorced woman who's lived with men, and has acquired all those road-to-perdition habits parents feared their daughters would pick up at college. Silly and soapy, but as sinfully satisfying as a pound of chocolate chip cookies. (Dir: Philip Dunne, 87 mins.)

Hill, The (Great Britain, 1965)***½ Sean Connery, Harry Andrews, Ossie Davis. Director Sidney Lumet has etched a chilling study of a British military prison in Africa during WWII. The hitch here is that the inmates are British soldiers. (122 mins.)

Hillbillys in a Haunted House (1967)½ Ferlin Husky, Joi Lansing, Don Bowman, John Carradine, Lon Chaney, Jr., Basil Rathbone, Linda Ho. Country singers on the way from Tennessee to Nashville spend the night at a spooky house, which turns out to be a front for spies. Sequel to *Las Vegas Hillbillys* is even worse. (Dir: Jean Yarbrough, 88 mins.)†

Hill on the Dark Side of the Moon, A (Sweden, 1983)*** Gunilla Nyroos, Thommy Berggren, Lina Pleijel, Bibi Andersson. Set in the Europe of the 1880s and '90s, this engrossing film tells the true story of the doomed love affair between Sonja (Nyroos) and Maxim (Berggren); she's a respected mathematician, he's one of the first radical male feminists. A beautifully photographed film that deals with the paradoxical issues and emotions evoked by the affair. (Dir: Lennart Hjulstrom, 101 mins.)

Hills Have Eyes, The (1977)*** James Whitworth, John Steadman, Janus Blythe,
474

Dee Wallace. An extended family is stranded in the desert when their trailer breaks down, and they are preyed upon by a grisly band of savage genetic mutants, a shocking reverse image of the normal nuclear family. Former literature professor Wes Craven is a director making a serious attempt at social criticism within the horror genre. (90 mins.)†

Hills Have Eyes: Part Two, The (1984)* Tamara Stafford, Robert Houston, Michael Berryman, John Laughlin. Anemic sequel to the cult favorite. Here, teenyboppers en route to a bike race travel the same stretch of desert where the loony mutants from the first film roamed. (Dir: Wes Craven, 86 mins.)†

Hills of Home (1948)*** Lassie, Donald Crisp, Janet Leigh, Edmund Gwenn. Sentimental warm tale of a Scottish doctor and his beloved collie. Certainly the best dog loves man film since *Lassie Come Home*. (Dir: Fred M. Wilcox, 97 mins.)

Hill 24 Doesn't Answer (Israel, 1955)***½ Edward Mulhare, Haya Hayareet. First feature made in Israel. Story of four Israeli volunteers who defended their homeland at the cost of their lives. Grim drama with numerous moving scenes. (Dir: Thorold Dickinson, 100 mins.)

Hi Mom! (1970)*** Robert De Niro, Allen Garfield, Jennifer Salt. Designed as a sequel to *Greetings*, this is an uneven, sometimes frenetic but often lacerating series of vignettes about a Vietnam veteran who decides to make dirty movies. (Dir: Brian DePalma, 87 mins.)

Hindenburg, The (1975)*½ George C. Scott, Anne Bancroft, William Atherton, Burgess Meredith, Charles Durning. Based on the book by Michael M. Mooney about the legendary dirigible disaster of May 6, 1937. The script, however, sabotaged this film, and the best acting is from the exploding dirigible. (Dir: Robert Wise, 125 mins.)†

Hi, Nellie (1934)**½ Paul Muni, Glenda Farrell, Berton Churchill, Donald Meek, Marjorie Gateson. Lightweight Muni vehicle made before Paul took on the fustian mantle of George Arliss at Warner Bros. He's engaging as a troublesome reporter whose boss decides to keep him in line by assigning him an "Advice to the Lovelorn" column. (Dir: Mervyn LeRoy, 75 mins.)

Hips, Hips Hooray (1934)*** Bert Wheeler, Robert Woolsey, Thelma Todd, Dorothy Lee, Ruth Etting. A good vehicle for the boys has cosmetics queen Todd enlisting their aid to shore up her failing business. The usual madcap fun, with a rare film appearance by torch singer Etting. (Dir: Mark Sandrich, 68 mins.)†

Hired Gun, The (1957)** Rory Calhoun, Anne Francis, Vince Edwards, Chuck

Connors. Professional gunfighter is offered a large reward to bring back an escaped murderess. (Dir: Ray Nazarro, 63 mins.)

Hired Hand, The (1971)**½ Peter Fonda, Verna Bloom, Warren Oates. Uneven, but often sensitive drama set in New Mexico in 1880, and directed by Peter Fonda. Verna Bloom takes the acting honors with a moving performance as the patient wife of Fonda, an itinerant cowhand. (93 mins.)†

Hired Wife (1940)*** Rosalind Russell, Brian Aherne. Super-secretary marries her boss for business reasons, finds domesticity more difficult than work. Entertaining comedy. (Dir: William A. Seiter, 93 mins.)

Hireling, The (Great Britain, 1973)*** Sarah Miles, Robert Shaw. Dealing with the absurd rigidities in the British class system of the twenties, this subdued adaptation of an L. P. Hartley novel is ponderous, but Miles does well as the lady who's a bit too friendly to her chauffeur (Shaw), a man desirous of more than friendship. (Dir: Alan Bridges, 108 mins.)

Hiroshima: Out of the Ashes (MTV 1990)**½ Max von Sydow, Judd Nelson, Mako, Tamlyn Tomita. Forty-five years after the atomic bomb was dropped on Hiroshima, Japan, Hollywood attempts to re-create the devastation. Aimed at a generation ignorant of WWII history, the show unfortunately fails. (Dir: Peter Werner, 96 mins.)

Hiroshima, Mon Amour (France, 1959)**** Emmanuele Riva, Eliji Okada. French director Alain Resnais has created a magnificent mood piece in his telling of the unique love story of a French cinema actress and a Japanese architect who meet in Hiroshima years after the war. Emmanuele Riva and Eliji Okada give memorable performances as the lovers. (88 mins.)†

His Brother's Wife (1936)** Barbara Stanwyck, Robert Taylor, John Eldridge, Jean Hersholt, Joseph Calleia, Samuel S. Hinds. Rather dank soap opera has Stanwyck marrying Taylor's brother when he rejects her; eventually they are all thrown together in a malaria research station in South America! (Dir: W. S. Van Dyke, 90 mins.)

His Butler's Sister (1943)*** Deanna Durbin, Franchot Tone, Pat O'Brien. A pleasant romantic comedy that has Durbin's singing to bolster the proceedings. Deanna, as a maid, gets her employer to fall in love with her. (Dir: Frank Borzage, 94 mins.)

His Double Life (1933)**½ Lillian Gish, Roland Young, Montagu Love. Young is a reclusive painter who changes places with his suddenly deceased valet. Gish,

who had been carrying on a romantic correspondence with the servant, meets and marries Young, thinking him to be her beloved. (Dir: Arthur Hopkins, 63 mins.)†

His First Flame (1926)**½ Harry Langdon, Vernon Dent, Ruth Hiatt, Natalie Kingston. Wild story by Frank Capra and Arthur Ripley has Langdon as a firechief's nephew who is fought over by two sisters; one eventually burns a house down to get his attention. Madcap comedy with great sight gags. (Dir: Harry Edwards, 62 mins.)†

His Girl Friday (1940)**** Cary Grant, Rosalind Russell, Ralph Bellamy, Helen Mack, Gene Lockhart. Director Howard Hawks made *Front Page*'s Hildy Johnson into a woman, and that made all the difference. Hawks developed a technique of overlapping the dialogue, with throwaway syllables in front and back, so that the audience could hear every word that counted, and the impression was of even faster delivery. Grant's brilliance as a physical actor has never been so put to the test, and Russell is more than his equal. (92 mins.)†

His Kind of Woman (1951)*** Robert Mitchum, Jane Russell, Vincent Price. Fall guy in a plot to bring an expatriated racketeer back to the U.S. gets wise and rounds up the crooks. Long but lively, entertaining melodrama. (Dir: John Farrow, 120 mins.)

His Majesty O'Keefe (Great Britain, 1954)*** Burt Lancaster, Joan Rice. Action-packed pirate story about the derring-do of a brave adventurer. Fun for the younger set. (Dir: Byron Haskin, 92 mins.)

His Mistress (MTV 1984)** Robert Urich, Julianne Phillips, Cynthia Sikes, Linda Kelsey, Mark Shera, Sachi Parker. Glossy drama starring Urich as a married, wealthy industrialist who falls in love with an attractive and ambitious executive. (Dir: David Lowell Rich, 104 mins.)

History (Italy, 1987)** Claudia Cardinale, Francisco Rabal, Andrea Spada. Tale of a mother and her two sons buffeted about by the fates during the Nazi occupation of Italy strives to emulate the work of the neo-realists, but comes off looking padded and distanced instead. (Dir: Luigi Comencini, 146 mins.)

History Is Made at Night (1937)**½ Charles Boyer, Jean Arthur. The eternal triangle of wife, husband, and other man in a curious mixture of comedy and melodrama. Some bright moments, including a finely portrayed shipwreck sequence. (Dir: Frank Borzage, 110 mins.)†

History Lessons (West Germany, 1973)*** Gottfried Bold, Benedict Zulauf, Johann Unterpertinger. Minimalist master Jean-

Marie Straub directed this revolutionary historical film about four separate witnesses describing Julius Caesar's rise to power in ancient Rome. (85 mins.)

History of Mr. Polly, The (Great Britain, 1949)***½ John Mills, Sally Ann Howes. A young draper carries a dream of adventure replacing his placid life, finally achieves the dream. Witty, tastefully done period comedy-drama. Excellent performances. (Dir: Anthony Pelissier, 96 mins.)

History of the World, Part 1 (1981)* Mel Brooks, Madeline Kahn, Dom DeLuise, Harvey Korman, Gregory Hines, Cloris Leachman. Brooks goes through various periods of history, from the Roman days to the French Revolution with side trips to the Spanish Inquisition, and there are probably only three or four chuckles along the way. (Dir: Mel Brooks, 86 mins.)†

Hit, The (Great Britain, 1984)*** John Hurt, Tim Roth, Laura del Sol, Terence Stamp, Bill Hunter, Fernando Rey. A sardonic, slightly baffling psychological drama about a mob squealer (Stamp), the hit man (Hurt) hired to kill him, an apprentice killer (Roth), and the innocent bystander (del Sol), who accompany him on his final journey. Director Stephen Frears imparts real tension. (97 mins.)†

Hit and Run (1982)**½ Paul Perri, Claudia Cron, Will Lee, Bart Braverman. Teacher Perri, haunted by the death of his wife in a hit-and-run accident, moonlights as a cab driver. When he is framed for a murder, his investigation uncovers clues into his wife's death. Deliberate-paced but engrossing mystery. (Dir: Charles Braverman, 96 mins.)†

Hitched (MTV 1971)* Tim Matheson, Sally Field, Neville Brand. Western-comedy, as a pair of newlyweds overcome mishaps in the early West. (Dir: Boris Sagal, 100 mins.)

Hitcher, The (1986)**½ Rutger Hauer, C. Thomas Howell, Jennifer Jason-Leigh, Jeffrey DeMunn. Brutal but plot-flawed suspenser, brimming over with violent energy, the film creates an odyssey of terror as a teen makes the perilous mistake of picking up a deranged thumber. (Dir: Robert Harmon, 97 mins.)†

Hitchhike (MTV 1974)** Cloris Leachman, Michael Brandon, Sherry Jackson. Miss Leachman picks up a hitchhiker on her way to San Francisco. Her passenger is on the run after murdering his stepmother. (Dir: Gordon Hessler, 74 mins.)

Hitchhiker, The (1953)***½ Frank Lovejoy, Edmond O'Brien, William Talman. Two men on a camping trip are waylaid and held by a desperate fugitive. Excellent, spell-binding melodrama, tense and exciting. (Dir: Ida Lupino, 71 mins.)

Hit Lady (1974)**½ Yvette Mimieux. Yvette Mimieux wrote the screenplay for this predictable but slick gangster drama in which she stars as the beauty playing a cool, collected, and deadly hired assassin. (Dir: Tracy Keenan Wynn, 72 mins.)†

Hitler (1962)** Richard Basehart, Maria Emo. Story of the rise to power of the infamous Nazi dictator. Basehart tries, but misses as Adolf. (Dir: Stuart Heisler, 107 mins.)†

Hitler Gang, The (1944)*** Robert Watson, Martin Kosleck, Victor Varconi, Luis Van Rooten, Sig Ruman, Ludwig Donath. An effective exploration of the rise of Der Führer and his conscienceless cohorts. With a familiar-looking cast of Third Reich faces. (Dir: John Farrow, 101 mins.)

Hitler's Children (1942)*** Tim Holt, Bonita Granville. Two youngsters are caught in the relentless gears of the Nazi war machine. Good drama of wartime Germany. (Dir: Edward Dmytryk, 83 mins.)†

Hitler's Daughter (MCTV 1990)*** Kay Lenz, Melody Anderson, Patrick Cassidy, Veronica Cartwright. Gripping tale of political paranoia revolves around the incredible possibility that Hitler's American-born daughter is secretly alive and planning a resurgence in the nation's capital. There are enough plot twists and good performances to keep the most skeptical viewer involved in this darkly chilling, pessimistic thriller. (Dir: James A. Contner, 96 mins.)

Hitler's Madman (1943)***½ John Carradine, Patricia Morison, Alan Curtis. Douglas Sirk shot his first American film in about a week with incomparable visual style. The narrative of the determined Czech resistance to the barbarities of Reinhard Heydrich is compelling. (84 mins.)

Hitler's SS: Portrait in Evil (MTV 1985)**½ Tony Randall, Jose Ferrer, John Shea, David Warner, Carroll Baker, Bill Nighy, Lucy Gutteridge. The saga of the rise of Adolf Hitler and his Nazi stormtroopers as seen through the eyes of two brothers bent on survival. (Dir: James Goddard, 156 mins.)

Hitler: The Last Ten Days (Great Britain-Italy, 1973)* Alec Guinness, Simon Ward, Diane Cilento, Adolfo Celi. Drivel. The fascination with the Hitler legend seems to be endless, but that still doesn't justify this production, which rehashes facts about Hitler's last days in his bunker fortress and his stormy relationships with Eva Braun and his military henchmen. (Dir: Ennio de Concini, 106 mins.)†

Hit List (1989)**½ Jan-Michael Vincent, Leo Rossi, Lance Henriksen, Charles Napier, Rip Torn, Jere Burns. Better-than-average genre fare with Vincent trying to reclaim his child, accidentally kidnapped by a Mafia assassin. Fast pace and familiar faces cover up the holes in the thin plot. (Dir: William Lustig, 87 mins.)†

Hit Man (1972)**½ Bernie Casey, Pam Grier, Sam Laws. A black remake of the British crime film *Get Carter*, written and directed by George Armitage. Competent melodrama, somewhat hamstrung by budget limitations. (90 mins.)

Hit Parade of 1943—See: **Change of Heart**

Hit the Deck (1955)** Vic Damone, Tony Martin, Jane Powell, Debbie Reynolds, Walter Pidgeon. Failed attempt to make another *On the Town*, this time with three sailors on leave in San Francisco. Good songs include "Sometimes I'm Happy" and "More Than You Know." (Dir: Roy Rowland, 112 mins.)†

Hit the Ice (1943)*** Bud Abbott, Lou Costello, Ginny Simms. Sidewalk photographers are mistaken for bank robbers, catch up with the real crooks in Sun Valley. One of the funnier A & C comedies; plenty of laughs and fast action. (Dir: Charles Lamont, 73 mins.)†

Hit the Road (1941)*½ The Bowery Boys. Four of the Boys are left fatherless after a mob hit and seek shelter with a fifth boy's father on a ranch. (Dir: Joe May, 61 mins.)

Hi-Yo Silver (1940)** Lee Powell, Chief Thunder-Cloud, Herman Brix (Bruce Bennett), Lynn Roberts, Raymond Hatton, Dickie Moore. The masked rider of the plains saddles up once more in this condensation of a 1938 serial. Fair to middling excitement, though Powell's no Clayton Moore. (Dirs: William Whitney, John English, 69 mins.)

H. M. Pulham, Esq. (1941)***½ Hedy Lamarr, Robert Young, Ruth Hussey, Van Heflin. The life of a stuffy Bostonian who is momentarily uprooted from his life by a love affair. Tastefully produced, superbly directed drama, with Young a standout. (Dir: King Vidor, 120 mins.)

Hobbit, The (MTV 1977)***½ Voices of Orson Bean, John Huston, Otto Preminger, Richard Boone, Brother Theodore. Enchanting animated dramatization of J. R. R. Tolkien's popular novel. (Dir: Arthur Rankin, Jr., 78 mins.)†

Hobo's Christmas, A (MTV 1987)*½ Barnard Hughes, Gerald McRaney, Wendy Crewson, William Hickey. Holiday treacle about a hobo who makes a holiday visit back to the son (McRaney) he deserted years before. Old pro Hughes is too genteel to play a hobo, but casting being what it is, he carries it off nicely. (Dir: Will Mackenzie, 96 mins.)†

Hobson's Choice (Great Britain, 1954)***½ Charles Laughton, Brenda de Banzie, John Mills. Delicious working class comedy, with Laughton as a tyrannical bootmaker brought to heel by his plain-spoken daughter and her meek husband. Under David Lean's direction what should have been an innocuous British comedy has style and life. (107 mins.)†

Hobson's Choice (MTV 1983)*** Sharon Gless, Richard Thomas, Jack Warden, Lillian Gish. A nicely astringent remake of the Charles Laughton classic film. In this version, Gless is cast as a woman who turns her mousy husband into a confident, caring man, despite her father's objections. (Dir: Gilbert Cates, 104 mins.)

Hoffman (Great Britain, 1969)**½ Peter Sellers, Sinead Cusack. Certainly not one of Sellers's best entries, but there are some off beat laughs in this story about a lonely middle-aged man who blackmails a young female typist into spending a week in his apartment. (Dir: Alvin Rakoff, 113 mins.)

Holcroft Covenant, The (Great Britain, 1985)*½ Michael Caine, Anthony Andrews, Victoria Tennant, Lilli Palmer. Noel Holcroft discovers his father's bequest is being used to rebuild the Third Reich. Clumsily adapted from the Robert Ludlum book. (Dir: John Frankenheimer, 112 mins.)†

Hold Back the Dawn (1941)***½ Charles Boyer, Olivia de Havilland, Paulette Goddard. Rather exceptional romantic melodrama with a seedy Boyer desperately trying to marry a vulnerable American (de Havilland) in order to enter the United States. Director Mitchell Leisen softened the mordant Billy Wilder–Charles Brackett screenplay. Photographed by Leo Tover. (115 mins.)

Hold Back the Night (1956)**½ John Payne, Mona Freeman. Nothing exceptional but fairly entertaining Korean War story. (Dir: Allan Dwan, 80 mins.)

Hold Back Tomorrow (1956)* Cleo Moore, John Agar. Embarrassingly bad film with inept performances by the stars as a condemned prisoner and a town prostitute who find love just before the death toll. (Dir: Hugo Haas, 75 mins.)

Hold On! (1966)*½ Peter Noone, Shelley Fabares, Herman's Hermits. A juvenile opus geared to spotlight the popular recording group, Herman's Hermits. The plot combines the U.S. Air Space program, a publicity-hungry starlet, a rich girl's romantic attentions, and mobs of screaming female fans. (Dir: Arthur Lubin, 85 mins.)

Hold That Baby! (1949)**½ Bowery Boys, Frankie Darro, Bernard Gorcey, Florence Auer, Gabriel Dell. The Boys operate a laundromat and find a baby between the sheets. The baby is heir to a fortune that his aunts stand to inherit—if they can prevent the Boys from getting him to the reading of the will. Fairly entertaining. (Dir: Reginald Le Borg, 64 mins.)

Hold That Blonde (1945)** Eddie Bracken, Veronica Lake, Frank Fenton, George Zucco, Albert Dekker. Here, Eddie's a klepto, and, when his shrink innocently suggests love as a cure, Eddie falls for a sultry thief. Fitfully amusing. (Dir: George Marshall, 76 mins.)

Hold That Co-ed (1938)***½ John Barrymore, George Murphy, Joan Davis. Barrymore in a hilarious musical comedy about politics and football. The great man appears as a caricature of all political demagogues and he's magnificent. (Dir: George Marshall, 80 mins.)

Hold That Ghost (1941)*** Bud Abbott, Lou Costello, Joan Davis. A & C get involved with a dead gangster in a supposedly haunted house. One of their better comedies. (Dir: Arthur Lubin, 80 mins.)†

Hold That Hypnotist (1957)**½ The Bowery Boys, Stanley Clements, Robert Foulk, Jane Nigh. In a trance, Sach re-experiences a former life in which he was a tax collector who won a treasure map from Blackbeard the Pirate. (Dir: Austen Jewell, 61 mins.)

Hold That Line (1952)**½ Bowery Boys, John Bromfield, Bernard Gorcey, Taylor Holmes, Veda Ann Borg, Bob Nichols, Mona Knox. Two trustees of an Ivy League college send the Boys to college to see the effect of the Boys on their students. Sach develops a vitamin mixture that makes him the star of the football team. (Dir: William Beaudine, 64 mins.)

Hold the Dream (MTV 1986)** Deborah Kerr, Jenny Seagrove, Stephen Collins, James Brolin, Claire Bloom. Although it sports a superb physical production, this sequel to *A Woman of Substance* is just a pale copy of the original. This time Emma Harte's granddaughter struggles to uphold Emma's dream, but boardroom crises and domestic problems pale in comparison with Emma's building an empire. (Dir: Don Sharp, 208 mins.)†

Hold Your Man (1933)***½ Jean Harlow, Clark Gable, Stu Erwin, Elizabeth Patterson, Blanche Frederici. A wonderful star vehicle that still packs lots of zing. Credibility is strained in this serio-comic tale of a hustler and a con girl who stop acting crooked long enough to fall for each other, but the stars are irresistible. (Dir: Sam Wood, 89 mins.)

Hole in the Head, A (1959)***½ Frank Sinatra, Edward G. Robinson, Eleanor Parker, Carolyn Jones, Keenan Wynn,

Thelma Ritter. The last brilliant work of director Frank Capra's career. Sinatra gives a rounded performance as a Miami hotel owner on the verge of financial ruin, scampering everywhere to raise enough capital to stay in business. (120 mins.)

Holiday (1930)*** Ann Harding, Mary Astor, Robert Ames, Edward Everett Horton, Hedda Hopper. The first version of Philip Barry's popular play, remade in 1938, about an up-and-coming but unconventional young man who almost marries the wrong sister. Horton plays the same role in both films. Sparkling dialogue well delivered by a good ensemble. (Dir: Edward H. Griffith, 96 mins.)

Holiday (1938)**** Katharine Hepburn, Cary Grant, Doris Nolan, Lew Ayres, Edward Everett Horton, Binnie Barnes, Ruth Donnelly, Henry Daniell. Incandescent comedy based on Philip Barry's play. Previously filmed in 1930, this is a consummate drawing room comedy. When Cary informs his prospective relatives that he wants to take a "holiday" after making a killing in the stock market, his bride-to-be and money-loving father-in-law are stunned. But Cary has breezed through their Wall Street lives and stirred the emotions of his fiancée's sister (Hepburn), so these two free spirits fly the financial security coop and take their holiday together. (Dir: George Cukor, 93 mins.)†

Holiday Affair (1949)**½ Robert Mitchum, Janet Leigh, Wendell Corey. War widow with a small son must choose between two suitors. Mildly amusing comedy-drama. (Dir: Don Hartman, 87 mins.)†

Holiday Camp (Great Britain, 1947)**½ Flora Robson, Dennis Price, Jack Warner. Typical family has many varied adventures at a vacation resort. Loosely written, uneven comedy-drama. (Dir: Ken Annakin, 97 mins.)

Holiday for Henrietta (France, 1954)***½ Hildegarde Neff, Michel Auclair, Dany Robin. Captivating comedy about the making of a movie, and the participants' inability to distinguish fact from fiction. Remade as *Paris When It Sizzles*. (Dir: Julien Duvivier, 103 mins.)

Holiday for Lovers (1959)** Clifton Webb, Jane Wyman, Carol Lynley, Gary Crosby. Psychiatrist and his wife face the difficulties of keeping their daughters from romance while on a tour of South America. Lightweight romantic comedy has all been done before. (Dir: Henry Levin, 103 mins.)

Holiday for Sinners (1952)*** Gig Young, Janice Rule, Keenan Wynn. The future plans of a young doctor are changed when a broken-down prizefighter commits murder. Offbeat drama taking place in New Orleans during the Mardi Gras. (Dir: Gerald Mayer, 72 mins.)

Holiday in Mexico (1946)*** Walter Pidgeon, Jane Powell, Xavier Cugat. Semi-classical music is spiced with some Latin American melodies in this musical treat. Plot about a widowed ambassador to Mexico and his teenage daughter who tries to run his house doesn't interfere with Miss Powell's singing, Cugat's rhumbas, and Jose Iturbi's piano. (Dir: George Sidney, 127 mins.)

Holiday Inn (1942)**** Bing Crosby, Fred Astaire, Marjorie Reynolds, Virginia Dale, Walter Abel, Louise Beavers. Delightful song-packed showcase for two great stars and a raft of Irving Berlin classics. Bing tires of the rat race and decides to work only on holidays. Meanwhile his ex-partner, Fred, taps out of his life until he discovers his dream partner at Bing's resort. As the girl involved in their romantic tug-of-war, Reynolds's flair and beauty should have ensured her a bigger career, but she'll always be remembered for this musical, which also features some of Astaire's most assured footwork. (Dir: Mark Sandrich, 101 mins.)†

Holiday in Spain—See: Scent of Mystery

Hollow Image (MTV 1979)**½ Robert Hooks, Saundra Sharp, Hattie Winston. Flawed but interesting TV pic about the dilemma of a black woman who is "making it" as a department store fashion buyer, but feels she has lost touch with her black identity. (Dir: Marvin J. Chomsky, 106 mins.)

Hollow Triumph—See: Scar, The

Holly and the Ivy, The (Great Britain, 1953)***½ Ralph Richardson, Celia Johnson, Margaret Leighton, Denholm Elliott. A country parson gathers his family together at Christmas, discovers that because of him they are unhappy. Superlatively acted drama, slowly paced but always absorbing. (Dir: George More O'Ferrall, 80 mins.)

Hollywood Boulevard (1936)** John Halliday, Marsha Hunt, Robert Cummings, Mae Marsh, Esther Dale, Esther Ralston. An actor whose stardom has deserted him tries to recapture his audience by "telling all" to a scandal sheet, despite the effect these tales have on the lives of those close to him. (Dir: Robert Florey, 70 mins.)

Hollywood Boulevard (1976)** Mary Woronov, Candice Rialson, Jonathan Kaplan, Paul Bartel. Many of independent producer Roger Corman's stable of directors appear in this flick on-screen. They're all poking fun at the kind of exploitative films they've specialized in. (Dirs: Joe Dante, Allan Arkush, 83 mins.)†

Hollywood Canteen (1944)**½ Bette Davis, Joan Crawford, Jack Carson, Dane Clark. Davis is the chief hostess and just about everybody—Joan Crawford, John Garfield, Ida Lupino, Peter Lorre, Sydney Greenstreet, Alexis Smith, a very young Eleanor Parker, the Andrews Sisters, Barbara Stanwyck, Jack Carson, Eddie Cantor, and Jack Benny—makes a guest appearance in this piece of WWII propaganda. One of the first directorial efforts of Delmer Daves. (124 mins.)

Hollywood Cavalcade (1939)*** Don Ameche, Alice Faye. Film that traces the history of the motion-picture industry (through 1939) has some wonderful moments. It eventually gets lost in the cliché mill but its earlier scenes are worth catching. (Dir: Irving Cummings, 96 mins.)

Hollywood Chainsaw Hookers (1988)**½ Linnea Quigley, Gunnar Hansen, Jay Richardson, Michelle Bauer. Slickly made sleaze about a group of prostitutes who like to cut through all the nonsense with their customers and get down to worshipping at the altar of their favorite power tool. A private eye stumbles on the cult, led by Hansen (best known as "Leatherface" in *The Texas Chainsaw Massacre*) while searching for a missing girl, played by minor-league cult queen Quigley. Viewers with skewed sensibilities will approve. (Dir: Fred Olen Ray, 76 mins.)†

Hollywood Cop (1987)* David Goss, Susan Schoenhofer, Cameron Mitchell, Troy Donahue, Jim Mitchum, Aldo Ray, Lincoln Kilpatrick. Mother persuades cop Goss to help her retrieve her son, kidnapped by the mobsters who want back the money her husband stole from them. Mixes action, drama, and comedy, all badly. (Dir: Amir Shervan, 101 mins.)†

Hollywood Cowboy—See: Hearts of the West

Hollywood Harry (1986)*** Robert Forster, Kathrine Forster. Engagingly amiable private-eye comedy. Rubber-faced Forster (who also wrote and directed) is perfectly cast as a bored L.A. detective, roused from vegetation by a new case and his adoring niece. AKA: **Harry's Machine.** (99 mins.)†

Hollywood Hotel (1937)***½ Dick Powell, Glenda Farrell, Rosemary and Lola Lane, Frances Langford, Hugh Herbert, Alan Mowbray, Louella Parsons. A genuine sleeper. One of the least known of the finest Hollywood musicals, this Busby Berkeley effort is limber in a way that anticipates the fifties by fifteen years, and shows that Berkeley's style was neither so obvious nor so rigid as the parodists would have us believe. (109 mins.)

Hollywood Knights (1980)** Tony Danza, Fran Drescher, Stuart Pankin, Robert

Wuhl, Michelle Pfeiffer. Highly derivative comedy. 1965-era California high school kids play crude pranks on idiotic teachers and policemen. (Dir: Floyd Mutrux, 91 mins.)†

Hollywood on Trial (1976)***½ Walt Disney, Gary Cooper, Jack Warner, Adolph Menjou, Robert Taylor, Dalton Trumbo, Louis B. Mayer. This fascinating documentary is about the anticommunist witch-hunt conducted against the Hollywood community by the House Committee on Un-American Activities. Director David Helpern, Jr. has culled rare footage and other archival material, including print and radio interviews to present an unslanted look at the celebrity-filled hysteria of the infamous search for Red sympathizers in Lotusland. (Dir: David Helpern, Jr., 105 mins.)†

Hollywood or Bust (1956)*** Dean Martin, Jerry Lewis, Anita Ekberg. A movie nut journeys west to meet his favorite star, picks up a gambler along the way. One of the wackier Martin-Lewis farces has some inventive gags, a fast pace. (Dir: Frank Tashlin, 95 mins.)†

Hollywood Party (1934)** Jimmy Durante, Laurel and Hardy, the Three Stooges, Lupe Velez, Arthur Treacher, Robert Young. Everyone on the MGM lot was in this, and nearly every director there did a piece of it. When they put it all together it didn't gel, so they asked director Allan Dwan to look at it and see what he could do. Dwan concocted a device of having Durante dream the whole mess, so it wouldn't have to seem connected, and for a pretext they had him waiting for his wife to get dressed for the party. Songs by Rodgers and Hart, Gus Kahn, and Arthur Freed. (Dir: Allan Dwan, 68 mins.)

Hollywood Revue of 1929, The (1929)*½ Jack Benny, Conrad Nagel, Joan Crawford, Buster Keaton, John Gilbert, Norma Shearer, Marion Davies, Laurel and Hardy. An all-star revue. (Dir: Charles Reisner, 130 mins.)

Hollywood Shuffle (1987)*** Robert Townsend, Anne-Marie Johnson, Starletta Dupois, Helen Martin, Craigus R. Johnson, Domenick Irrera. A hit-and-miss, appealing satire on Hollywood. Enterprising star-writer-producer-director, Townsend raised his shoestring budget himself, and based this comedy on his own experiences as a black actor in Tinseltown. (82 mins.)†

Hollywood's New Blood (1989)* Bobby Johnson, Francine Lapensee, Joe Balough, Martie Allyne. Wan horror thriller about young actors stalked by the ghosts of a film crew who died in an explosion. The title is about as close as anyone connected with this will ever get to Hollywood. (Dir: James Shyman, 78 mins.)†

Hollywood Story (1951)*** Julie Adams, Richard Conte, Richard Egan, Henry Hull. Intriguing, neatly plotted tale in which a producer begins a film about a real-life unsolved murder mystery in order to unmask the killer. A first-rate B movie. (Dir: William Castle, 77 mins.)

Hollywood Strangler Meets the Skid Row Slasher (1979)½ Pierre Agostino, Carolyn Brandt. Hilarious, almost plotless nonsense with Agostino musing about an ex-lover while he strangles models and makes eyes at magazine store employee Brandt, who gets off by slashing the throats of L.A. bums. There's almost no dialogue, just voice-overs and a stupefying selection of canned background music. Has to be seen to be believed, and even that may not do it. An alternate video version, *The Model Killer*, claims to run 88 mins. but is exactly the same. (Dir: "Wolfgang Schmidt" [Ray Dennis Steckler], 72 mins.)†

Hollywood Vice Squad (1987)* Ronny Cox, Frank Gorshin, Leon Isaac Kennedy, Trish Van Devere, Carrie Fisher, Marvin Kaplan, Joey Travolta. A tacky little cop tale that rode in on the coat-tails of TV's "Miami Vice" and couldn't decide whether it wanted to be a raunchy parody of that show or an original account of "actual cases" encountered on the strip in L.A. The comic moments are unfunny, while the straight dramatic and shoot-'em-up scenes supply the real amusement, including as they do such refugees from television's subcellar as Gorshin, Kaplan, and the redoubtable Joey Travolta. (Dir: Penelope Spheeris, 95 mins.)†

Hollywood Zap (1986)½ Ivan E. Roth, Ben Frank, De Waldron, Annie Gaybis. Tennessee nerd Tucker Downes heads for Los Angeles to find the father he's never met, teaming up with a flatulent video game hustler along the way. Jaw-droppingly awful comedy has to be seen to be believed: if you possibly *can* be offended, this movie will do it. (Dir: David Cohen, 93 mins.)†

Holocaust: 2000 (1978)** Kirk Douglas, Anthony Quayle, Alexander Knox, Virginia McKenna, Simon Ward. A macabre yarn about a father and son who join forces on the building of a nuclear power plant and end up on opposite sides. AKA: **The Chosen** (1978). (Dir: Albert DeMartino, 105 mins.)†

Holy Blood—See: **Santa Sangre**

Holy Innocents, The (Spain, 1985)*** Alfredo Landa, Francisco Rabal, Terele Pavez. A diffuse pastoral family saga that slowly builds into a scathing societal investigation. A series of vignettes reveal the exploitation of a peasant family by their parental, but indifferently brutal, patrons. (Dir: Marcel Camus, 108 mins.)†

Holy Matrimony (1943)***½ Monty Woolley, Gracie Fields. Superbly acted tale of a great artist who poses as his dead valet, gets married and involved in scandal when his wife innocently sells some of his paintings. Wonderful fun. Remake of *His Double Life*, 1933. (Dir: John M. Stahl, 87 mins.)

Holy Mountain, The (U.S.-Mexico, 1973)**½ Alexandro Jodorowsky, Horacio Salinas, Ramona Saunders. Jodorowsky's film about a Jesus-like protagonist who encounters a Zen master/cosmic teacher called the Alchemist (played by the filmmaker). (126 mins.)

Holy Terror—See: **Alice, Sweet Alice**

Homage to Chagall—The Colours of Love (Canada, 1976)***½ A visually stunning, admiring tribute to the great twentieth-century artist Marc Chagall, written, produced, and directed by Canadian documentary filmmaker Harry Rasky. (88 mins.)†

Hombre (1967)***½ Paul Newman, Fredric March, Diane Cilento. Thoughtful, generally absorbing western, starring Paul Newman as a white man raised by Indians. Newman boards a stage on which the rest of the principals are passengers, and there is a final shoot-out between the good guys and the outlaws. The screenplay raises some interesting moral issues and it's all held together by Martin Ritt's taut direction. (111 mins.)†

Home Alone (1990)*** Macaulay Culkin, Joe Pesci, Daniel Stern, John Heard, Catherine O'Hara. You are made of stone if you don't go with the flow of this raucously funny movie about a kid who's left "home alone" by mistake when his family wings to Paris. A pair of bumbling burglars meet their Waterloo when they attempt to rob the kid's home. Eight-year-old Culkin gives the best child's performance seen in a film in a long time. *Home Alone* was a huge box office smash. (Dir: Chris Columbus, 102 mins.)†

Home and the World, The (India, 1985)***½ Soumitra Chatterjee, Victor Banerjee, Swatilekha Chatterjee, Gopa Aich, Jennifer Kapoor. With the sure hand of an experienced master, director Satyajit Ray depicts a passionate domestic drama in the home, which he uses as a window onto the troubled world of Bengal in 1907-8, a province racked by religious strife. A lyrical, moving epic, with camerawork that is austere but graceful. (130 mins.)†

Home at Seven (Great Britain, 1952)*** Ralph Richardson, Margaret Leighton, Jack Hawkins. A bank clerk returns home to discover he has been missing one day, due to amnesia, and that he is a suspect in a murder. Clever mystery melodrama. (Dir: Ralph Richardson, 85 mins.)

Home Before Dark (1958)*** Jean Simmons, Dan O'Herlihy, Rhonda Fleming, Efrem Zimbalist, Jr. Jean Simmons gives a magnificent performance in this drama about a young woman who comes home after being hospitalized for a nervous breakdown. Her struggle to pick up the pieces of her broken life is touchingly portrayed. (Dir: Mervyn LeRoy, 136 mins.)

Homebodies (1974)**½ Frances Fuller, Peter Brocco, Paula Trueman. Six elderly people who are being evicted from a brownstone to make way for a skyscraper take to murder to defend their home. Strange horror comedy for those seeking the offbeat. (Dir: Larry Yust, 96 mins.)†

Homecoming (1948)** Clark Gable, Lana Turner, Anne Baxter, John Hodiak. Clark is married to Anne in this one but through flashbacks he manages to have his torrid box-office dynamite romance with Lana. It has a war background but it's nothing to shout about. (Dir: Mervyn LeRoy, 113 mins.)

Homecoming, The (Great Britain, 1973)**** Cyril Cusack, Ian Holm, Vivien Merchant, Paul Rogers, Michael Jayston. A marvelous adaptation of Harold Pinter's lacerating, fascinating play about the interpersonal relationships of a British working-class family. Paul Rogers, playing Max, a retired butcher who taunts and competes with his three grown sons, is a standout. (Dir: Peter Hall, 116 mins.)

Homecoming: A Christmas Story, The (MTV 1971)*** Patricia Neal, Richard Thomas, Edgar Bergen, Ellen Corby. Pilot for "The Waltons." Earl Hamner, Jr.'s tale about a Virginia mountain clan preparing for Christmas back during the Depression, invests the characters with charm and civility. Neal (the mother) is the guiding light who holds the family together. (Dir: Fielder Cook, 104 mins.)†

Home Fires Burning (MTV, 1989)**½ Sada Thompson, Barnard Hughes, Neil Patrick Harris, Elizabeth Berridge, Bill Pullman, Robert Prosky. Episodic WWII drama set in a small southern town centers around cantankerous Hughes, a newspaperman who makes it difficult for his family to love him. (Dir: Glenn Jordan, 96 mins.)

Home for the Holidays (MTV 1972)** Eleanor Parker, Sally Field, Julie Harris, Walter Brennan. Standard murder melodrama. Unhappy daughter returns for a family get-together, only to become the target of a deranged killer. (Dir: John Llewellyn Moxey, 73 mins.)†

Home from the Hill (1960)***½ Robert Mitchum, Eleanor Parker, George Peppard, George Hamilton. Powerful yarn of a southern town, a roistering landowner, his son, and the youth whose relationship to the family causes tragedy. Fine characterization builds in interest, makes the drama absorbing throughout its length. (Dir: Vincente Minnelli, 150 mins.)†

Home in Indiana (1944)*** Walter Brennan, Lon McCallister, Jeanne Crain, June Haver. The storyline about a blind filly and delightful performances and photography make this film about harness racing a pleasure to see. (Dir: Henry Hathaway, 103 mins.)

Home Is the Hero (Ireland, 1961)*** Arthur Kennedy, Walter Macken. Leisurely, well-acted drama about a violent-tempered man who returns to his household after serving a prison sentence for manslaughter. (Dir: Fielder Cook, 83 mins.)

Home Is Where the Hart Is (1987)* Valri Bromfield, Stephen E. Miller, Deanne Henry, Martin Mull. Brain-dead farce about elderly twin brothers who search for their extra-elderly father (he's 103). (Dir: Rex Bromfield, 94 mins.)†

Home Is Where the Heart Is—See: **Square Dance**

Home Movies (1980)***½ Nancy Allen, Keith Gordon, Kirk Douglas, Gerrit Graham, Vincent Gardenia. This maligned comedy is one of director Brian DePalma's best works. Some of the wacky bits are genuinely inspired. Gordon is the lad who is subjected to "star therapy," calculated to elevate him from being a mere extra in his own life. AKA: **The Maestro.** (Dir: Brian DePalma, 90 mins.)†

Home of the Brave (1949)***½ Lloyd Bridges, Frank Lovejoy, James Edwards. Negro soldier on a dangerous Pacific patrol is made a mental case by the intolerance of his white cohorts. Hard-hitting drama makes its point well, is excellently acted, especially by Edwards. (Dir: Mark Robson, 85 mins.)†

Home of the Brave (1986)*** Laurie Anderson, Joy Askew, Adrian Belew, Richard Laundry. A concert film that features performance artist Laurie Anderson's avant-garde compositions. Enjoyment will depend on how well you respond to her intriguing but complex form of showmanship, commentary, and electronic music. Not for fans of, say, Barbara Mandrell. (Dir: Laurie Anderson, 90 mins.)

Homer and Eddie (1989)**½ James Belushi, Whoopi Goldberg, Karen Black, Nancy Parsons, Tracey Walter, Vincent Schiavelli, Robert Glaudini, Anne Ramsey, Beah Richards, Angelyne, John Waters. Belushi and Goldberg play it straight in this grim road movie as a brain-damaged man and an escaped men-

tal patient subject to fits of violence. The stars are good in non-comic roles. (Dir: Andrei Konchalovsky, 99 mins.)†

Home Remedy (1988)** Seth Barrish, Maxine Albert, Richard Kidney. Quirky but slight satire about a New Jersey man who decides to cave in to boredom. There are some amusing bits, but the movie is essentially pointless. (Dir: Maggie Greenwald, 91 mins.)†

Homestretch, The (1947)** Cornel Wilde, Maureen O'Hara. Some wonderful horse racing shots from Ascot to Churchill Downs but the story makes you wish they had eliminated the actors and just shown the races. Fancy-free horse owner and disapproving wife is the worn frame. (Dir: H. Bruce Humberstone, 96 mins.)

Home Sweet Home (1914)***½ Lillian Gish, Robert Harron, Dorothy Gish, Henry B. Walthall, Mae Marsh, Blanche Sweet. A real extravaganza from director D. W. Griffith, suggested by the life and famous song of John Howard Payne, combining the dissolute life of the composer with amazing fantasy sequences and Payne's eventual arrival in heaven (complete with wings), redeemed by his song! What would have been impossibly corny in any other hands is made to work by Griffith. (76 mins.)†

Home Sweet Homicide (1946)*** Peggy Ann Garner, Randolph Scott. Entertaining hokum about a mystery writer's kids solving a murder. (Dir: Lloyd Bacon, 90 mins.)

Home to Stay (MTV 1978)**½ Henry Fonda, Michael McGuire, Frances Hyland. A grizzled Fonda is excellent as an old farmer recovering from a stroke, who's in jeopardy of being placed in an old folks home by his weary son. (Dir: Delbert Mann, 74 mins.)†

Homicidal (1961)**½ Glenn Corbett, Patricia Breslin, Jean Arless. Shock-master William Castle delivered this, the only truly original twist on the *Psycho* plotline just a year after Janet Leigh stepped in the shower (take that, DePalma). The "homicidal" central character is Emily (Arless), a mysterious girl who takes care of a quivering old Swedish nurse. The final shocking revelation won't surprise attentive viewers, but it still packs quite a wallop. (87 mins.)

Hondo (1953)***½ John Wayne, Geraldine Page, James Arness, Ward Bond. One of Hollywood's best adult westerns. Strong in human relationships with a minimum of violence. Broadway actress Geraldine Page makes her starring film debut in this much underrated western. (Dir: John Farrow, 83 mins.)

Honeyboy (MTV 1982)*½ Erik Estrada, Morgan Fairchild, James McEachin.

Hollywood prizefighting stereotypes on the ropes. The poor man's Arturo de Cordova (Estrada) and the poor man's Lana Turner (Fairchild) act with the urgency of 11½ inch fashion dolls. (Dir: John Berry, 104 mins.)†

Honeychile (1951)** Judy Canova, Eddie Foy, Jr., Walter Catlett, Alan Hale, Jr. Country gal writes a hit song that is attributed to a famous composer by mistake. (Dir: R. G. Springsteen, 90 mins.)

Honey, I Shrunk the Kids (1989)**½ Rick Moranis, Matt Frewer, Marcia Strassman, Kristine Sutherland, Jared Rushton, Thomas Brown, Amy O'Neill. After fiddling with their scientist father's invention, a group of kids are shrunk to the size of gnats and stranded in their backyard. OK Disney comedy-adventure with an inconsistent script and special effects. (Dir: Joe Johnston, 86 mins.)†

Honeymoon (1947)** Shirley Temple, Guy Madison, Franchot Tone. GI has trouble marrying his fiancée, since he only has a three-day pass. Uninspired comedy. (Dir: William Keighley, 74 mins.)

Honeymoon (France, 1986)*½ Nathalie Baye, John Shea, Richard Berry, Peter Donat. Needing to stay in America while her lover is in jail, a Frenchwoman pays an American to marry her. It's supposed to be an in-name-only affair, but the new husband turns out to be a psychotic with other ideas. Overplayed thriller wastes its fine cast. (Dir: Patrick Jamain, 100 mins.)†

Honeymoon Hotel (1964)** Robert Goulet, Nancy Kwan, Robert Morse. When a guy's wedding breaks up at the altar, his wolfish buddy joins him on the honeymoon trip, and they check in at a hotel—for honeymooners only. Flimsy farce. (Dir: Henry Levin, 89 mins.)

Honeymoon in Bali (1939)** Fred Mac-Murray, Madeleine Carroll. Witty romantic comedy about a cold, calculating career girl who is conquered by a man. Silly in spots, but very entertaining. AKA: **My Love for Yours**. (Dir: Edward H. Griffith, 100 mins.)

Honeymoon Killers, The (1970)*** Tony Lo Bianco, Shirley Stoler, Doris Roberts, Mary Jane Higby. Based on the multiple murderers, Martha Beck and Raymond Fernandez, who were executed in 1951. Tony Lo Bianco and Shirley Stoler portray a pair of ruthless killers who pose as a nurse and her brother, and seek out wealthy women who fall prey to their murderous schemes. Written and skillfully directed by Leonard Kastle. (107 mins.)†

Honeymoon Machine, The (1961)*** Steve McQueen, Brigid Bazlen, Jim Hutton, Paula Prentiss. Navy officer gets an idea to use an electronic brain on board his vessel to beat the roulette wheel at the Venice casino. Entertaining comedy, with some youthful players getting the chance to show their stuff. (Dir: Richard Thorpe, 87 mins.)

Honeymoon with a Stranger (MTV 1969)**½ Janet Leigh, Rossano Brazzi. Leigh spends her honeymoon in Spain looking for her husband, who has disappeared, and trying to convince the local police that the man who claims to be her spouse really isn't. (Dir: John Peyser, 73 mins.)

Honey Pot, The (Great Britain-U.S.-Italy, 1967)*** Rex Harrison, Susan Hayward, Cliff Robertson, Capucine, Edie Adams, Maggie Smith. Here Mankiewicz takes his turn at updating Ben Jonson's *Volpone*. Rex Harrison is a wealthy scoundrel who invites three of his former amours to share his last days in his Venetian showplace and the intrigues begin. (Dir: Joseph L. Mankiewicz, 131 mins.)

Honeysuckle Rose (1980)*** Willie Nelson, Dyan Cannon, Amy Irving, Slim Pickens. Not much of interest in the old plotline; director Jerry Schatzberg concentrates his energies on atmosphere, milieu, and music. Nelson is the married, traveling music legend who can't help straying while off the homestead; his easygoing manner is effective. AKA: **On the Road Again**. (119 mins.)†

Hong Kong (1951)** Ronald Reagan, Rhonda Fleming. A WWII veteran and a mission schoolteacher tangle with jewel thieves and murderers in this average adventure story. (Dir: Lewis R. Foster, 92 mins.)

Hong Kong Confidential (1958)**½ Gene Barry, Beverly Tyler. Another in the exposé series of the criminal machines of famous cities. Fast-moving crime drama. (Dir: Edward L. Cahn, 67 mins.)

Honkers, The (1972)** James Coburn, Lois Nettleton, Slim Pickens. "Honkers" refers to wild bulls and available women in this erratic rodeo tale. Coburn tries hard to overcome a plodding script playing a self-centered, second-rate rodeo performer. (Dir: Steve Ihnat, 103 mins.)

Honky (1971)** James Neilson, Brenda Sykes. Neilson plays an All-American boy who falls for the blandishments of a swinging black pusher (Sykes). (Dir: William A. Graham, 89 mins.)†

Honky Tonk (1941)**½ Clark Gable, Lana Turner, Frank Morgan, Claire Trevor. First screen meeting of Gable and Turner. He's a gambler, she's a good girl, and you know all along where they're headed. Enough action and loving, though, to please most of their fans. (Dir: Jack Conway, 105 mins.)

Honky Tonk Freeway (1981)* William Devane, Beverly D'Angelo, Beau Bridges, Jessica Tandy, Hume Cronyn, Geraldine

Page, Teri Garr. Stick this on the off ramp. In this puerile satire on American mores, a tiny town tries to attract national attention and the attendant tourist trade even though there's no access to the main freeway. Loud, mirthless, and desperate. (Dir: John Schlesinger, 107 mins.)†

Honkytonk Man (1983)**½ Clint Eastwood, Kyle Eastwood, John McIntire, Verna Bloom, Alexa Kenin, Matt Clark. Set in the Depression days of the Dust Bowl. Clint, who also produced and directed this, deserves an A for effort, but a C for net result. As the hard-drinking C&W singer, he comes across sympathetically. (122 mins.)†

Honolulu (1939)**½ Eleanor Powell, Robert Young, George Burns, Gracie Allen, Rita Johnson. Before you can say "Aloha Oe" Eleanor has switched places with the owner of a plantation down in Hawaii. Fortunately the grass shack of a plot doesn't get in her way as she taps out some tantalizing numbers, including a technically brilliant hula number. (Dir: Edward Buzzell, 83 mins.)

Honor Among Thieves—See: **Farewell Friend**
Honorary Consul, The—See: **Beyond the Limit**
Honor Thy Father (MTV 1973)*** Joseph Bologna, Raf Vallone. Interesting, well-cast television adaptation of Gay Talese's book about an underworld family. (Dir: Paul Wendkos, 99 mins.)†

Hoodlum Priest, The (1961)***½ Don Murray, Keir Dullea. Murray stars as Father Charles Dismas Clark, the Jesuit priest who befriended young criminal offenders. The film centers on one case in particular, that of a young hotheaded and arrogant ex-con who almost makes it with Father Clark's help and friendship. Murray delivers a fine portrait of a determined man with a mission and Keir Dullea makes a deep impression as the youth he befriends. (Dir: Irvin Kershner, 101 mins.)

Hoodlum Saint, The (1946)**½ William Powell, Esther Williams, Angela Lansbury, James Gleason, Lewis Stone, Rags Ragland, Frank McHugh, Slim Summerville. Pretty good Powell vehicle has a con man getting involved in a fake charity drive and changing his crooked ways, much to the dismay of his gangster colleagues. Lansbury is a standout as a chilly, gold-digging moll. Look for ex-silent comedy star Chester Conklin in a bit role as a policeman. (Dir: Norman Taurog, 91 mins.)

Hook, The (1963)*** Kirk Douglas, Robert Walker, Nick Adams. Korean War drama poses a problem—what does a man do when he's ordered to kill a prisoner of war, even if it will insure his own safety? The development is somewhat sketchily presented, but it's food for

thought. Well acted. (Dir: George Seaton, 98 mins.)

Hook, Line and Sinker (1969)* Jerry Lewis, Pedro Gonzalez, Kathleen Freeman, Peter Lawford, Anne Francis. Lewis plods through this drivel about an insurance salesman who goes on a fishing trip around the world when told he has only two months to live. (Dir: George Marshall, 92 mins.)

Hooligans, The (Spain, 1959)*** Manuel Zarzo, Luis Marin, Oscar Cruz, Juanjo Losado. Terrific debut film by director Carlos Saura has slum boys committing crimes to get money to help one of their number become a bullfighter. Tragedy is highlighted by authentic locales, Saura's sensitivity to his characters' poverty, and expressive camerawork. (90 mins.)

Hooper (1978)***½ Burt Reynolds, Sally Field, Jan-Michael Vincent, Brian Keith. Stuntman-turned-director Hal Needham has fashioned an entertaining yarn about the greatest stuntman in the world, and the hot young challenger to his position. Amiable comedy and earnest feeling are savvily balanced; the elaborate stunt gags are intriguingly staged. (99 mins.)†

Hooray for Love (1935)**½ Ann Sothern, Gene Raymond, Pert Kelton, Lionel Stander, Bill Robinson, Fats Waller. Typical, light backstage musical, mainly interesting for guest appearances by two greats, Robinson and Waller; otherwise, pleasant but not outstanding. (Dir: Walter Lang, 72 mins.)

Hoosiers (1986)*** Gene Hackman, Barbara Hershey, Dennis Hopper, Sheb Wooley, Fern Parsons. Imagine *Rocky* from the point of view of Burgess Meredith's coach character, and you have this engaging sports movie about an underdog Indiana high school basketball team who get to go to the state finals. Hackman is letter-perfect as the authoritative coach who comes from out of nowhere to whip the team into shape. (Dir: David Anspaugh, 114 mins.)†

Hootenanny Hoot (1963)½ Peter Breck, Ruta Lee, Joby Baker, Pam Austin, Johnny Cash, Sheb Wooley, The Brothers Four. Drivel about country music. A bunch of college hootenannyans from Missouri take their down-home act to TV-land. (Dir: Gene Nelson, 91 mins.)

Hopalong Cassidy (1935)**½ William Boyd, Jimmy Ellison, Paula Stone, Robert Warwick, Charles Middleton. The extremely popular western series kicked off its series of sixty-six feature films here with the platinum-haired, black-bedecked Boyd gaining legions of fans as a gallant hero, righting wrongs atop his horse, Topper. (Dir: Howard Bretherton, 62 mins.)

Hope and Glory (Great Britain, 1987)**** Sebastian Rice Edwards, Sarah Miles, Sammi Davis, Ian Bannen, Susan Wooldridge. Filmmaker John Boorman's joyous memoir of what it was like to be an adventurous nine-year-old boy growing up in England during the Blitz, entranced by spectacular visions of enemy planes, friendly soldiers, and destruction and heroism on every corner. With his father off at war (as a typist), young Bill Rohan (Rice Edwards) romps through his days under the not-so-watchful eyes of his distracted mother (Miles) and libidinous older sister (Davis). Funny, touching, splendidly acted, and gorgeously evoked in a rich period production, this is Boorman's least characteristic and possibly finest work. (112 mins.)†

Hoppity Goes to Town (1941)** As in his earlier animated *Gulliver's Travels*, director Dave Fleischer doesn't have enough invention or plot to sustain a feature-length film. Some charm in the all-insect cast and the bug's-eye view of metropolitan life. (77 mins.)†

Hopscotch (1980)*** Walter Matthau, Glenda Jackson, Ned Beatty. Tailored for the pouty charms of Matthau as a renegade CIA man out to expose the dangerous idiocies of the Company. Director Ronald Neame allows the story to poke along, but it's an amiable entertainment. (104 mins.)†

Horizons West (1952)**½ Robert Ryan, Rock Hudson. Familiar story of two brothers returning from the Civil War, one becoming a lawman and the other an outlaw. Better-than-usual cast and direction. (Dir: Budd Boetticher, 81 mins.)

Horizontal Lieutenant, The (1962)**½ Paula Prentiss, Jim Hutton, Jack Carter. A moderately funny service comedy that benefits greatly from the able comedy team of Prentiss and Hutton as a pair of oddballs. (Dir: Richard Thorpe, 90 mins.)

Horn Blows at Midnight, The (1945)** Jack Benny, Alexis Smith, Guy Kibbee. Benny used this film as a running gag for years, claiming in jest that it ruined his movie career. You'll probably agree. (Dir: Raoul Walsh, 78 mins.)

Hornet's Nest (1970)** Rock Hudson, Sylva Koscina. Derring-do during WWII. U.S. Army captain Hudson manages, with the aid of a group of Italian orphans and a sexy German lady doctor, to carry out his sabotage mission against incredible odds. (Dir: Phil Karlson, 109 mins.)

Horrible Dr. Hichcock, The (Italy, 1962)*** Robert Flemyng, Barbara Steele, Teresa Fitzgerald (Maria Teresa Vianello). Compelling period horror film in which a mad doctor refuses to give up the ghost as far as resurrecting his dead bride is concerned. The second wife screams a lot as wife number one continues to show signs of life. (Dir: Robert Hampton, 76 mins.)†

Horrible House on the Hill—See: **Devil Times Five**

Horror at 37,000 Feet, The (MTV 1973)*½ Buddy Ebsen, William Shatner. This is supposed to be a spine-tingling air thriller over the Atlantic, but the ghostly trauma disintegrates at the halfway point and so does the movie. (Dir: David Lowell Rich.)

Horror Chamber of Dr. Faustus, The (France, 1958)***½ Pierre Brasseur, Alida Valli, Edith Scob. An exercise in the macabre directed by French horror artist, Georges Franju. Brasseur is a mad scientist trying to perfect skin grafts for his scarred daughter. Beautifully acted. Franju, despite the crass American release title, managed to evolve a style that was both elegant and expressionistic, pure and magical. AKA: **Eyes Without a Face**. (84 mins.)†

Horror Creatures of the Lost Planet—See: **Horror of the Blood Monsters**

Horror Creatures of the Red Planet—See: **Horror of the Blood Monsters**

Horror Express (Spain, 1972)*** Christopher Lee, Peter Cushing, Telly Savalas, Silvia Tortosa. It's the Trans-Siberian Railroad (with sets left over from *Murder on the Orient Express*). Traveling on board is an excavated primeval fiend who literally sucks the souls out of people. Suspense builds fiercely as the passenger list is decimated. (Dir: Eugenio Martin, 88 mins.)†

Horror Hospital (Great Britain, 1973)**½ Michael Gough, Robin Askwith, Vanessa Shaw. A campy satire of the usual thrillers, some of it funny. It has a mad doctor, a desolate manor, a sarcastic dwarfish assistant, an unseen monster who prowls by night, and so on. (Dir: Antony Balch, 91 mins.)†

Horror Hotel (Great Britain, 1960)**½ Christopher Lee, Betta St. John, Venetia Stevenson. College student doing research in witchcraft stumbles upon a cult in a Massachusetts village. Shuddery little shocker works up some scary moments. (Dir: John Moxey, 76 mins.)†

Horror Hotel Massacre—See: **Eaten Alive**

Horror House (Great Britain, 1969)* Frankie Avalon, Jill Haworth, Dennis Price, George Sewell, Gina Warwick. Frankie (sans Annette) tries the horror genre unsuccessfully, when he visits a supposedly haunted house where visitors are being picked off one by one. Listening to Frankie and Annette sing was scarier. (Dir: Michael Armstrong, 79 mins.)

Horror of Dracula (Great Britain, 1958)*** Peter Cushing, Christopher Lee, Michael Gough. This was a gory, sexy rendering of the Bram Stoker novel for its time, pitting Lee against the Van Helsing of Cushing. Terence Fisher directed, representing the Hammer Studio style at its best. (82 mins.)†

Horror of Frankenstein, The (Great Britain, 1970)½ Ralph Bates, Kate O'Mara, Dennis Price. Lamentable remake finds our old friend the Baron transformed into a horny anti-hero of the mod seventies. (Dir: Jimmy Sangster, 95 mins.)†

Horror of Party Beach, The (1964)½ John Scott, Alice Lyon, Allen Laurel, Marilyn Clarke, Eulabelle Moore, Wayne Tippit. It's a horror movie. It's a fish story! It's a cautionary tale about industrial pollution! It's a musical! It's a love story! It's one of the funniest bad movies of all time. Mankind sows what it reaps when toxic wastes are dumped and then combine with bone, brine, and sludge from the ocean depths to create bloodsucking fish-men who massacre a girl's slumber party, kill visiting tramps from the big city, and scare the wits out of Eulabelle, a stereotyped black maid who undoes decades of work by the NAACP. (Dir: Del Tenney, 72 mins.)†

Horror of the Blood Monsters (1970)½ John Carradine, Robert Dix, Vicki Volante, Joey Benson, Jennifer Bishop. One of the all-time turkeys: schlockmeister Al Adamson got hold of a Filipino horror movie about prehistoric man-monsters and shot some new footage with scientist Carradine leading an expedition to a mysterious planet identified as a source of vampirism. Never mind that the Filipino movie was in black and white—Adamson just tinted those scenes and explained it as the planet's "chromatic radiation." You can spot Adamson as a vampire in the opening sequence, narrated by (Brother) Theodore Gottlieb. Photographed by Vilmos Zsigmond. AKA: **Creatures of the Prehistoric Planet, The Flesh Creatures, Horror Creatures of the Lost Planet, Horror Creatures of the Red Planet, Space Mission of the Lost Planet, Vampire Men of the Lost Planet,** and probably a few other titles as well. (85 mins.)†

Horror on Snape Island (Great Britain, 1972)** Jill Haworth, Bryant Halliday, Anna Palk, Jack Watson, Mark Edwards. Passable thriller about the search for Phoenician treasure on a spooky island that's piling up with corpses. AKA: **Beyond the Fog** and **Tower of Evil.** (Dir: Jim O'Connolly, 85 mins.)

Horror Show, The (1989)** Lance Henrickson, Brion James, Rita Taggert. Shaky sequel to *House 2*, with cop Henrickson's new house haunted by an executed killer (James, whose hammy performance is the one saving grace). (Dir: James Isaac, 95 mins.)†

Horrors of the Black Museum (Great Britain, 1959)**½ Michael Gough, Geoffrey Keen. Gruesome thriller about a famous crime writer with a do-it-yourself technique, providing himself with his own material. (Dir: Arthur Crabtree, 95 mins.)

Horse Feathers (1932)***½ Marx Brothers. Their fans will love this. The gags fly fast and free as Groucho takes over a college. (Dir: Norman McLeod, 80 mins.)†

Horse in the Gray Flannel Suit, The (1968)** Dean Jones, Diane Baker, Fred Clark. Disney comedy about an advertising exec who comes up with a clever scheme to promote his client's upset-stomach remedy and get his young daughter the horse she wants. (Dir: Norman Tokar, 113 mins.)†

Horsemen, The (1971)**½ Jack Palance, Omar Sharif, Leigh Taylor-Young. Action, adventure, and romance on a superficial level but still entertaining. Sharif in still another death-defying desert role—plays the son of an Afghanistan lord's stablemaster. (Dir: John Frankenheimer, 105 mins.)†

Horse Named Comanche, A (1958)** Sal Mineo, Philip Carey, Jerome Courtland. For youngsters. Sal Mineo plays a young Indian, White Bull, who will do almost anything to own a certain wild stallion. (Dir: Lewis R. Foster, 97 mins.)

Horse's Mouth, The (Great Britain, 1958)**** Alec Guinness, Kay Walsh, Ernest Thesiger, Renée Houston, Michael Gough, Robert Coote. Guinness adapted the Joyce Cary novel to star himself as Gulley Jimson, prototypic nonconformist painter. The acting is tremendous, especially Guinness, Walsh as his reluctant cohabitant, and Thesiger as his long-suffering old patron. It's a jaunty, raunchy comedy, in fauvist color, well acted. (Dir: Ronald Neame, 93 mins.)†

Horse Soldiers, The (1959)** John Wayne, William Holden, Constance Towers, Althea Gibson, Hoot Gibson. Sprawling action film set during the Civil War benefits little from its potent casting of Wayne and Holden in the leading roles. They play Union officers who have contrasting viewpoints on war. (Dir: John Ford, 119 mins.)†

Horse Without a Head, The (1963)*** Leo McKern, Jean-Pierre Aumont, Pamela Franklin, Herbert Lom, Vincent Winter. Some children cross paths with larcenous types out to acquire stolen money that had been hidden inside a toy horse. Good family fare. (Dir: Don Chaffey, 89 mins.)†

Hospital, The (1971)***½ George C. Scott, Diana Rigg, Richard Dysart, Barnard Hughes. Funny, if slightly exaggerated, account of the incompetence and slothfulness in a typical American hospital, in this case Metropolitan Hospital in

New York City. Paddy Chayefsky's dialogue and the flamboyant performance of Scott are the two choice ingredients. (Dir: Arthur Hiller, 103 mins.)†

Hospital Massacre (1982)** Barbi Benton, Chip Lucia, Jon Van Ness, Guy Austin. Benton checks into a hospital, unaware that a psycho who's had a grudge against her since childhood works there. She spends the rest of the movie running from him as he slaughters everyone else in sight. OK if you're not already completely burned out on this genre. AKA: **Be My Valentine or Else!, X-Ray,** and **Ward 13.** (Dir: Boaz Davidson, 88 mins.)†

Hostage (MTV 1988)*½ Carol Burnett, Carrie Hamilton, Leon Russom. Carol and daughter Carrie star in this lurid teledrama, with a plot straight out of *Orphans*. Carrie is a young delinquent/escaped convict who develops an intimate rapport with the reserved widow she kidnaps. (Dir: Peter Levin, 96 mins.)

Hostage Flight (MTV 1985)** Ned Beatty, Dee Wallace Stone, Rene Enriquez, Barbara Bosson, Jack Gilford, John Karlen. Overwrought and crassly calculated to work up the audience, this timely drama concerns an airline skyjacked by four armed terrorists. The main thrust of this midair drama is showing the passengers overpower their captors at just the right moment. (Dir: Steven Sterns, 104 mins.)

Hostages (1943)** Luise Rainer, William Bendix, Arturo de Cordova. Fair action film pays tribute to the Czech underground. A group of people are held as hostages after a Nazi is murdered. (Dir: Frank Tuttle, 88 mins.)

Hostage Tower, The (MTV 1980)**½ Keir Dullea, Peter Fonda, Douglas Fairbanks, Jr., Billy Dee Williams, Maude Adams. Debonair crooks steal the Eiffel Tower, taking as hostage the president's mom. (Dir: Claudio Guzman, 104 mins.)

Hostile Guns (1967)** George Montgomery, Yvonne DeCarlo, Brian Donlevy, Richard Arlen. Poor western about a U.S. marshal who has to transport a wagonful of prisoners. (Dir: R. G. Springsteen, 91 mins.)†

Hot Blood (1956)*½ Jane Russell, Cornel Wilde, Luther Adler, Joseph Calleia. A ridiculous tale about a band of gypsies and their fiery adventures. (Dir: Nicholas Ray, 85 mins.)

Hot Car Girl (1958)*½ June Kenney, Richard Bakalyan, John Brinkley, Robert Knapp, Jana Lund, Bruno VeSota, Ed Nelson. Innocent girl makes the mistake of falling for a no-good young hoodlum. (Dir: Bernard L. Kowalski, 71 mins.)

Hot Child in the City (1987)* Leah Ayres, Shari Shattuck. An innocent Kansas girl stalks seedy L.A. nightclubs looking for the murderer of her sister. Crammed with bad music video scenes to kill time. (Dir: John Florea, 85 mins.)†

Hot Dog...The Movie (1984)*½ David Naughton, Patrick Houser, Tracy Smith, Frank Koppola. The usual dumb bunny shenanigans among horny youths pursuing satisfaction on the slopes and dreaming of downhill racing into bedrooms. (Dir: Peter Markle, 96 mins.)†

Hotel (1967)*** Rod Taylor, Catherine Spaak, Karl Malden, Melvyn Douglas, Merle Oberon, Richard Conte, Michael Rennie, Kevin McCarthy, Carmen McRae. Trials and tribulations at a posh New Orleans hotel, mainly the efforts made to keep it from falling into the wrong hands. Many stars, many plots; familiar, but something cooking all the time. (Dir: Richard Quine, 124 mins.)†

Hotel Berlin (1945)*** Faye Emerson, Helmut Dantine. Occasionally interesting adaptation of Vicki Baum's novel centered in a Berlin hotel as Hitler's Germany is collapsing. Most of the characters and situations are contrived but there's some good excitement. (Dir: Peter Godfrey, 98 mins.)

Hotel Colonial (U.S.-Italy, 1987)*½ John Savage, Rachel Ward, Robert Duvall, Massimo Troisi. Improbable international co-production that came from out of nowhere and slid right back. Savage plays an Italian searching for his terrorist brother in the wilds of Colombia. Even the ever-meticulous Duvall can't save it. (Dir: Dinzia T. H. Torrini, 107 mins.)

Hotel Imperial (1939)** Isa Miranda, Ray Milland, Gene Lockhart, Albert Dekker, Reginald Owen. While this revenge melodrama possesses moments of fascination, its main interest is to film buffs who will recall the troubled film was stopped and started several times since it began production as the Marlene Dietrich vehicle *I Loved a Soldier*. It resumed with Margaret Sullavan who broke her arm while being pursued across the set by Stu Erwin. The plot concerns a plucky girl who's searching for the man who caused her sister's death. (Dir: Robert Florey, 67 mins.)

Hotel New Hampshire (1984)½ Jodie Foster, Rob Lowe, Beau Bridges, Nastassia Kinski, Wallace Shawn. Trying to translate John Irving's best-selling hodgepodge of philosophical ideas proved an insurmountable task for the director. Among those characters marching in this parade going nowhere are a lesbian in a bear suit, a girl who becomes enamored of her rapist, and a blind man named Freud. Don't check in. (Dir: Tony Richardson, 110 mins.)†

Hotel Paradiso (Great Britain, 1966)**½ Gina Lollobrigida, Alec Guinness, Robert

Morley. If your tastes lean toward French farce, peppered with British players (Guinness and Morley) and featuring that Italian eyeful Lollobrigida, this amiable and frothy comedy set in Paris during the early 1900s will entertain you. (Dir: Peter Glenville, 96 mins.)

Hotel Reserve (Great Britain, 1944)*** James Mason, Lucie Mannheim, Raymond Lovell, Herbert Lom, Patricia Medina. Offbeat Eric Ambler tale set at a French seaside resort just before the outbreak of WWII, where a mysterious incident leads the inhabitants to believe that one of them is a spy. Unusual setting and atmosphere, fine cast. (Dirs: Lance Comfort, Max Greene, Victor Hanbury, 79 mins.)†

Hotel Sahara (Great Britain, 1951)**½ Yvonne DeCarlo, Peter Ustinov. Amusing satire on the changing attitudes of civilians during a war. Hotel owner DeCarlo is prepared to accept any winner. (Dir: Ken Annakin, 87 mins.)

Hotel Terminus: The Life and Times of Klaus Barbie (France, 1988)**** Director Marcel Ophuls, who made the monumental *The Sorrow and the Pity*, uses Gestapo head Barbie as another tack for his exploration of how people aided in Nazi atrocities, whether purposely or through indifference. The many interviews presented are generally fascinating, though the length is prohibitive. Oscar winner for Best Documentary. (267 mins.)†

Hot Enough for June—See: **Agent 8¾**

Hothead—See: **Coup de Tete**

Hot Ice (Great Britain, 1953)*** Barbara Murray, John Justin. Laughs and thrills evenly divided in one of those spooky mansion-type mysteries. Better than average. (Dir: Kenneth Hume, 65 mins.)

Hot Ice (1973)—See: **Mr. Inside/Mr. Outside**

Hot Lead and Cold Feet (1978)** Jim Dale, Karen Valentine, Darren McGavin, Don Knotts, Jack Elam. Typically silly Disney comedy-western with star Dale playing three parts. (Dir: Robert Butler, 90 mins.)†

Hotline (MTV 1982)** Lynda Carter, Steve Forrest, Granville Van Dusen, Monte Markham, Harry Waters, Jr. Playing an artist-bartender, Lynda becomes involved with a "hotline" service at the crisis center and becomes a potential target of a psychopath. (Dir: Jerry Jameson, 96 mins.)†

Hot Millions (Great Britain, 1968)***½ Peter Ustinov, Maggie Smith, Bob Newhart, Karl Malden, Robert Morley. Amusing comedy about a high-class swindling operation, with some of the action set in London and South America. Ustinov is at his roguish best and there's a delightful performance from Maggie Smith, who seems to have a virtually

488

unlimited acting range. (Dir: Eric Till, 105 mins.)

Hot News (1953)*½ Stanley Clements, Gloria Henry, Ted de Corsia, Veda Ann Borg. Sports columnist matches wits with a vicious crime ring. Old news. (Dir: Edward Bernds, 68 mins.)

Hot Paint (MTV 1988)** Gregory Harrison, John Larroquette, Cyrielle Claire, John Glover. Harrison and Larroquette play a team of unlikely crooks who steal a priceless Renoir and then try to unload it in this occasionally amusing TV movie. (Dir: Sheldon Larry, 96 mins.)

Hot Pepper (1933)**½ Victor McLaglen, Edmund Lowe, Lupe Velez. Another sequel to *What Price Glory?* follows Flagg (McLaglen) and Quirt (Lowe) into civilian life as co-owners of a nightclub who fight over the love of Ms. Velez. (Dir: John G. Blystone, 76 mins.)

Hot Potato (1976)* Jim Kelly, George Memmoli, Geoffrey Binney, Irene Tsu. American special agents are sent to rescue the daughter of a top U.S. senator. (Dir: Oscar Williams, 87 mins.)†

Hot Pursuit (1987)**½ John Cusack, Robert Loggia, Wendy Gazzelle, Jerry Stiller, Monte Markham, Shelley Fabares, Terrence Cooper. A preppie dreams of soaking up the sun with his main squeeze in the tropics. Once there, he faces incarceration, encounters desperate hijackers, and, in general, gets gypped out of the idyllic vacation he had planned. (Dir: Steve Lisberger, 93 mins.)†

Hot Resort (1985)½ Bronson Pinchot, Debra Kelly, Marcy Walker, Frank Gorshin. Oversexed American boys try to score at a posh hotel in the tropics. (Dir: John Robins, 92 mins.)†

Hot Rock, The (1972)*** Robert Redford, George Segal, Ron Liebman, Paul Sand, Zero Mostel. The picture combines comedy and suspense in a delightful mixture, nicely balanced by director Peter Yates. Redford and Segal are hired to steal a diamond. Most of the picture concerns not the robbery but the bungling of the burglars in losing the gem, and trying to get it back. (Dir: Peter Yates, 101 mins.)

Hot Rod (MTV 1979)* Grant Goodeve, Gregg Henry. Time-wasting opus about the National Drag Racing Championships set in a small southern town with more than its share of corrupt politicians. (Dir: George Armitage, 104 mins.)†

Hot Rod Gang (1958)* John Ashley, Gene Vincent, Jody Fair, Steve Drexel. Lousy teensploitation combination of rock 'n' roll and hot roddin'. A socially prominent kid has to conceal his predilection for fast cars and wild music to keep his inheritance. (Dir: Lew Landers, 72 mins.)

Hot Rod Girl (1956)*½ Chuck Connors,

Lori Nelson, John Smith, Frank Gorshin. America International Pictures tripe about Chuck waging a war against reckless hot rodders. (Dir: Leslie Martinson, 75 mins.)

Hot Rod Rumble (1957)*½ Brett Halsey, Leigh Snowden, Richard Hartunian, Joey Forman. Loner joins a hot rod club, is accused of causing another driver's death. (Dir: Leslie Martinson, 79 mins.)

Hot Rods to Hell (1967)** Dana Andrews, Jeanne Crain, Mimsy Farmer. Family on the road terrorized by a teenage gang. (Dir: John Brahm, 92 mins.)

Hot Saturday (1932)**½ Nancy Carroll, Cary Grant, Randolph Scott, Edward Woods, Lillian Bond, Jane Darwell, Jessie Arnold, Grady Sutton. Carroll tries to make her fiancé jealous by pretending to spend the night with notorious rake Grant, but the plan blows up in her face when the town gossips find out about her night of sin. Once-"adult" comedy holds up well; all three leads do fine work. (Dir: William Seiter, 72 mins.)

Hotshot (1987)*½ Jim Youngs, Pele, David Groh. Every sports movie cliché is trotted out for this predictable drama about a would-be soccer player who tracks down soccer star Santos (played by Pele, of course) to learn the True Meaning of Sportsmanship. (Dir: Rich King, 91 mins.)†

Hot Shots (1956)*½ Huntz Hall, Stanley Clements, David Gorcey, Jimmy Murphy, Joi Lansing. The Bowery Boys have a job babysitting a bratty, eight-year-old TV star. (Dir: Jean Yarbrough, 61 mins.)

Hot Spell (1958)*** Shirley Booth, Anthony Quinn, Shirley MacLaine, Earl Holliman. Family drama set in the South with some good acting to recommend it. Booth plays a disillusioned housewife who refuses to face the sad truth that her family has grown away from her. (Dir: Daniel Mann, 85 mins.)

Hot Spot—See: **I Wake Up Screaming**

Hot Spot, The (1990)**½ Don Johnson, Virginia Madsen, Jennifer Connelly, Charles Martin Smith, Jerry Hardin, Bill Sadler, John Hawker. A dusty Texas town is the setting for director Dennis Hopper's lean and lurid look at pulp love and petty thievery. Trashy and unflashy. (Dir: Dennis Hopper, 130 mins.)†

Hot Stuff (1979)** Dom DeLuise, Suzanne Pleshette, Jerry Reed. A law-and-order comedy that may make Dom's fans happy. Miami cops take over a "fence" to entrap burglars. (Dir: Dom DeLuise, 91 mins.)†

Hot Times (1974)* Henry Cory, Gail Lorber, Amy Farber, Bob Lesser. Rambling, pointless sex comedy about horny high schoolers, of interest only as a sidelight in the career of writer-director Jim McBride (*David Holzman's Diary, The Big Easy*). Made for just $5,000, and it looks it. (Dir: Jim McBride, 82 mins.)†

Hot Tomorrows (1977)*** Ken Lerner, Ray Sharkey, Herve Villechaize, Victor Argo, Oingo-Boingo. First film from director Martin Brest (*Midnight Run, Beverly Hills Cop*), who also wrote, edited, and produced this energetic, imaginative black comedy about a young man obsessed with thoughts of death. Narrated by Orson Welles. (73 mins.)

Hot to Trot (1988)*½ Bob Goldthwait, Dabney Coleman, Virginia Madsen, Voice of John Candy. Silly talking-horse comedy which proves that what seemed ridiculous almost forty years ago (*Francis*) is still exactly the same. For what it's worth, the talented and unfortunate cast do their best. (Dir: Michael Dinner, 83 mins.)†

Houdini (1953)*** Tony Curtis, Janet Leigh, Torin Thatcher, Ian Wolfe. Colorful film based on the life and loves of the famous magician. Curtis brings a great deal of energy to the title role and he gets good support from Leigh, as his faithful wife. (Dir: George Marshall, 106 mins.)

Hound Dog Man (1959)**½ Fabian, Carol Lynley, Arthur O'Connell, Stuart Whitman. Not bad backwoods drama about a boy (Fabian) learning something about adult responsibilities. Director Don Siegel does a calculatedly small movie, with its virtues similarly scaled. (87 mins.)

Hound of the Baskervilles, The (1939)***½ Basil Rathbone, Nigel Bruce, Richard Greene, Wendy Barrie, Lionel Atwill, Morton Lowry. Definitive version of Sir Arthur Conan Doyle's classic Sherlock Holmes mystery. A young man, who has inherited an estate from his uncle, suspects foul play and calls on Sherlock Holmes. Good mystery, well produced and suspenseful. (Dir: Sidney Lanfield, 80 mins.)†

Hound of the Baskervilles (Great Britain, 1959)*** Peter Cushing, Christopher Lee. Frightening mystery yarn based on the famous Sherlock Holmes novel reaches the screen in all its macabre fascination with every terror-filled moment intact. (Dir: Terence Fisher, 84 mins.)†

Hound of the Baskervilles, The (Great Britain, 1977)* Dudley Moore, Peter Cook, Denholm Elliott, Spike Mulligan, Joan Greenwood, Jessie Matthews, Roy Kinnear. Witless parody of the Conan Doyle classic. (Dir: Paul Morrissey, 84 mins.)

Hound of the Baskervilles, The (MTV 1972)** Stewart Granger, Bernard Fox. Know-it-all Sherlock Holmes emerges once again, baffling follower Dr. Watson with canny insights as the two investigate Baskerville deaths by the legendary hound. (Dir: Barry Crane, 73 mins.)

Hour Before the Dawn, The (1944)***

Franchot Tone, Veronica Lake, John Sutton, Binnie Barnes, Henry Stephenson, Nils Asther. Odd, interesting wartime melodrama, set in England, has pacifist Tone marrying German governess Lake and eventually discovering that she's a spy; strong performances make it quite compelling. (Dir: Frank Tuttle, 75 mins.)

Hour of Decision (Great Britain, 1957)** Jeff Morrow, Hazel Court. A writer becomes involved in the murder of a gossip columnist. (Dir: Pennington Richards, 74 mins.)†

Hour of Glory—See: **Small Back Room, The**

Hour of the Assassin (1987)* Erik Estrada, Robert Vaughn, Alfredo Alvarez Calderon, Orlando Sacha. Estrada plays a South American who's hired by a group of right-wing generals to return to his native country and wipe out a newly elected democratic leader. Substandard political thriller, with leaden performances by the leads. (Dir: Luis Llosa, 93 mins.)†

Hour of the Furnaces (Argentina, 1968)**** Powerful documentary that explores the oppressive history of Latin American colonization by other countries who exploited the land and its peoples, and calls for a bloody war against such imperialism. A passionate, often enraging piece of cinema that proudly wears its heart and mind—and weapons—on its sleeve. (Dirs: Fernando Solanas, Octavio Getino, 260 mins.)

Hour of the Gun (1967)**½ James Garner, Jason Robards, Robert Ryan. Mediocre western drama with Garner as Wyatt Earp and Robards as "Doc" Holliday. (Dir: John Sturges, 100 mins.)†

Hour of the Star (Brazil, 1987)***½ Marcelia Cartaxo, Jose Dumont, Tamara Taxman. Homely, slow-witted woman leaves her impoverished village to seek work in São Paulo, where she survives by creating a fantasy world for herself. Powerful, resonant film with an uncluttered style merges a sharp sense of irony with genuine compassion for the poor and neglected. (Dir: Suzana Amaral, 96 mins.)†

Hour of the Wolf (Sweden, 1968)*** Max von Sydow, Liv Ullmann, Ingrid Thulin, Erland Josephson. Complex and disturbing Bergman film about a painter (von Sydow) living on an island where, gradually, his dreams and then his daily reality veer toward disintegration of personality and death, all merging in a nightmarish vision. (Dir: Ingmar Bergman, 89 mins.)

Hour of 13, The (1952)**½ Peter Lawford, Dawn Addams. Satisfactory thriller about a gentleman crook who tracks down a mad killer specializing in policemen. (Dir: Harold French, 79 mins.)

House (1986)**½ William Katt, George
490

Wendt, Kay Lenz, Richard Moll, Mary Stavin. Horror author Katt moves into a spooky house to write his Vietnam memoirs, but demons of all sorts begin assailing him almost immediately. This horror film replaces gore with effective funhouse jolts and comedy that works. (Dir: Steve Miner, 92 mins.)†

House 2: The Second Story (1987)**½ Arye Gross, Jonathan Stark, Royal Dano, Bill Maher, John Ratzenberger, Lar Park Lincoln. More funny than scary, the sequel involves a man who moves into a house where his parents were murdered years before and digs up a mischievous 170-year-old corpse. (Dir: Ethan Wiley, 85 mins.)†

House Across the Bay, The (1940)**½ Joan Bennett, George Raft, Walter Pidgeon, Lloyd Nolan. While waiting for her jailbird husband to come out, a singer falls for an aircraft designer; hubby hears of this, seeks revenge. (Dir: Archie Mayo, 72 mins.)†

Houseboat (1958)***½ Sophia Loren, Cary Grant, Martha Hyer, Harry Guardino, Eduardo Ciannelli, Murray Hamilton. Loren and Grant light up the screen with their movie star chemistry. It's a droll romantic comedy about a widowed daddy who acquires a housekeeper with no previous experience. Sophia scores as a surrogate mama and then captures Cary's heart; it's her best Hollywood film. (Dir: Melville Shavelson, 110 mins.)†

House by the Lake, The (Canada, 1976)* Brenda Vaccaro, Don Stroud, Chuck Shamata, Richard Ayres. Extremely violent film about Vaccaro being terrorized during her vacation by a group of sadistic men headed by Stroud. AKA: **Death Weekend**. (Dir: William Fruet, 89 mins.)

House by the River, The (1950)** Louis Hayward, Lee Bowman, Jane Wyatt. Philanderer strangles his maid, implicates his brother in the crime. Well-made but otherwise undistinguished costume thriller. (Dir: Fritz Lang, 88 mins.)

House Calls (1978)*** Walter Matthau, Glenda Jackson, Richard Benjamin, Art Carney. Immensely pleasurable comedy, with Matthau—enjoying the newfound sexual freedom of widowerhood—ultimately courting divorcée Glenda Jackson. The exaggeration of hospital satire could have been flat but for deft performances of the stars. (Dir: Howard Zieff, 96 mins.)†

Householder, The (India, 1963)*** Shashi Kapoor, Leela Naion, Durga Khote, Romesh Thappar, Patsy Dance. Wonderful comedy about newlyweds coming to terms with their arranged marriage. Director James Ivory's first feature and the first collaboration of now-famous team of Ivory, producer Ismail Merchant, and writer Ruth Prawer Jhabvala. (101 mins.)

House Hunting—See: **Make Me an Offer**

House Is Not a Home, A (1964)* Shelley Winters, Robert Taylor, Cesar Romero, Broderick Crawford, Kaye Ballard. Based on the life of Polly Adler—call her "Madam." Whorehouse story unrelieved by finesse. One of Polly's "girls"—Raquel Welch. (Dir: Russell Rouse, 95 mins.)

Housekeeper, The (Great Britain 1987)** Rita Tushingham, Jackie Burroughs, Ross Petty, Tom Kneelbone. Puzzling chiller about a mad dyslexic housekeeper. Bolstered by a gripping performance by Tushingham as a tidy woman who can't read, but sure knows how to kill, the film emerges as neither a creepy scream-a-thon nor a penetrating psychological study. (Dir: Ousami Rawi, 106 mins)†

Housekeeper's Daughter, The (1939)**½ Joan Bennett, Adolphe Menjou, John Hubbard, Victor Mature. A pretty miss helps a mild-mannered man get rid of some racketeers. Mildly amusing comedy with a hilarious finish. Mature's film debut. (Dir: Hal Roach, 80 mins.)

Housekeeping (1987)***½ Christine Lahti, Sara Walker, Andrea Burchill, Anne Pitoniak. Quiet, beautiful story of two teenage sisters whose lives are changed by a charming, vagabond aunt. Under her care, the girls grow in opposite directions, one leaving home to lead a social, "normal" lifestyle, the other oddly drawn to her guardian's eccentric ways. Scottish director Bill Forsyth crafts a wonderfully subtle and touching film that plays directly to the heart of the viewer. Lahti is superlative, giving an honest, winning performance. (117 mins.)†

House of Bamboo (1955)**½ Robert Stack, Robert Ryan, Shirley Yamaguchi. Offbeat drama about a group of Americans in Tokyo who set up a protection racket operation for some easy money. Robert Stack stoically plays the undercover agent assigned to crack the case. (Dir: Samuel Fuller, 102 mins.)

House of Cards (1968)**½ George Peppard, Inger Stevens, Orson Welles. Peppard plays an unlikely tutor in Paris enmeshed in a right-wing operation made up of French aristocrats headed by arch-villain Welles. (Dir: John Guillermin, 105 mins.)

House of Dark Shadows (1970)*** Joan Bennett, Jonathan Frid, Grayson Hall. Fans of the horror-soap "Dark Shadows" will enjoy this theatrical version of the vampire saga. (Dir: Dan Curtis, 98 mins.)

House of Dracula (1945)*½ Lon Chaney, John Carradine, Onslow Stevens, Glenn Strange. Scientist is tricked into helping Count Dracula, also meets up with the Wolf Man and the Frankenstein mon-

ster. Too many ghouls spoil the brew. (Dir: Erle C. Kenton, 67 mins.)

House of Evil (U.S.-Mexico, 1968)*½ Boris Karloff. One of four Mexican horror quickies for which Boris Karloff shot scenes in Los Angeles just before he died. He plays the head of a family whose members are killed by life-sized dolls in his castle. Pretty shabby. AKA: **Dance of Death** and **Macabre Serenade**. (Dir: John Ibanez, 75 mins.)†

House of Exorcism, The (Italy, 1975)* Telly Savalas, Elke Sommer, Sylvia Kosciona, Robert Alda, Alida Valli. After *The Exorcist* hit big, someone got hold of Italian fright specialist Mario Bava's *Lisa and the Devil*, chopped it up, tacked on some stupid new scenes imitating the American film, and released it as this mess. The only favor they did Bava was to credit the direction to the pseudonymous "Mickey Lion." AKA: **Devil in the House of Exorcism**. (93 mins.)†

House of Fear, The (1945)**½ Basil Rathbone, Nigel Bruce, Dennis Hoey. Can Sherlock locate the missing members of the "Good Comrades" club? Better-than-average mystery. (Dir: Roy William Neill, 69 mins.)†

House of Frankenstein (1944)**½ Boris Karloff, Lon Chaney, Jr., John Carradine, J. Carrol Naish, Elena Verdugo. Now Karloff is the scientist, not the monster. Aided by a homicidal maniac, he brings Dracula, the Wolf Man, and the monster back to life. OK for hardened horror fans. (Dir: Erle C. Kenton, 71 mins.)

House of Games (1987)*** Lindsay Crouse, Joe Mantegna, Mike Nussbaum, Lilia Skala. Playwright David Mamet made his directorial debut with this clever, elusive study of the confidence racket and the fascination it exerts over a buttoned-down female psychiatrist. Mantegna is Mike, a suave sharpster who serves as Crouse's guide into the con game; his smooth, brilliant performance registers better than Crouse's intentionally stiff, distanced one. Mike's sugar-coated words form the building blocks of this "house" of deception—Mamet's odd, grammatically precise dialogue comes across as a curious blending of Damon Runyon and Bertolt Brecht. An unusual film, and quite worthwhile. (102 mins.)†

House of Numbers (1957)** Jack Palance, Barbara Lang. Jack Palance plays the dual role of a murderer and his look-alike brother. The story concerns a clever plan for the murderer's escape from prison. (Dir: Russell Rouse, 92 mins.)

House of 1,000 Dolls (West Germany-Britain-Spain, 1967)* George Nader, Vincent Price, Martha Hyer, Ann Smyrner. Calendar art posing as an action thriller.

Two magicians use their tricks to lure young ladies into the world's oldest profession. (Dir: Jeremy Summers, 83 mins.)

House of Rothschild, The (1934)**½ George Arliss, Loretta Young, Robert Young, Boris Karloff. Your basic boring Arliss historical vehicle with the stagy ham being his wily self. This is one of his more colorful films, helped by Loretta Young as his daughter, Robert Young as her suitor, Karloff as the villain, and the Napoleonic wars. (Dir: Albert L. Werker, 86 mins.)

House of Seven Corpses, The (1974)** John Carradine, John Ireland, Faith Domergue. Low-budget horror flick concerning a film crew shooting an occult movie in a real haunted house. The spoof on filmmaking is fun, but the terror elements are not scary. (Dir: Paul Harrison, 90 mins.)

House of Seven Gables, The (1940)*** George Sanders, Margaret Lindsay, Vincent Price. Scheming lawyer falsely accuses his sister's sweetheart of murder, but she waits for him for twenty years to be released from prison. Superbly acted; well-made dramatic version of Hawthorne's classic novel. (Dir: Joe May, 89 mins.)

House of Strangers (1949)***½ Susan Hayward, Edward G. Robinson, Richard Conte. A powerful drama of family conflicts, filled with hatred and revenge. One of the older sons, Richard Conte, has sworn vengeance on his brothers, whom he blames for his father's death. Superb performance by Robinson as the father. (Dir: Joseph L. Mankiewicz, 101 mins.)

House of the Black Death (1965)* Lon Chaney, Jr., John Carradine, Andrea King, Tom Drake, Katherine Victor. Seldom seen until it hit video, this yawner casts Carradine and Chaney (who aren't in any scenes together) as feuding warlock brothers who battle for domination. AKA: *Blood of the Man Devil*, *Blood of the Man Beast* and *Night of the Beast*. (Dirs: Harold Daniels, Reginald Le Borge, 80 mins.)†

House of the Long Shadows (Great Britain, 1982)**½ Peter Cushing, Desi Arnaz, Jr., Vincent Price, Christopher Lee, John Carradine, Sheila Keith. This fourth screen version of *Seven Keys to Baldpate* still manages to eke out a chill or two. An eccentric family tries to survive a long-awaited reunion, but to complicate matters, a writer is in the house to win a wager that he can finish a book in this spookhouse overnight. (Dir: Peter Walker, 96 mins.)†

House of the Seven Hawks, The (Great Britain, 1959)**½ Robert Taylor, Nicole Maurey, Linda Christian. A straightforward espionage adventure yarn. Robert Taylor plays a charter boat captain who gets involved with international thieves and the Dutch police when a mysterious man dies on his vessel. (Dir: Richard Thorpe, 92 mins.)

House of Usher (1960)** Vincent Price, Myrna Fahey, Harry Ellerbe, Mark Damon. Decrepit horror tale about the tainted Ushers and how brother Roderick (Price) executes a plan to end the long line of madness in their family. (Dir: Roger Corman, 79 mins.)

House of Wax (1953)**½ Vincent Price, Phyllis Kirk, Carolyn Jones. Originally made as a 3-D movie, this colorful thriller features sinister Vincent Price lurking in the shadows of a wax museum of horrors. Phyllis Kirk and Carolyn Jones add to the proceedings by screaming and looking terrified. (Dir: Andre de Toth, 88 mins.)†

House of Women (1962)** Shirley Knight, Andrew Duggan, Constance Ford. Innocent expectant mother is convicted of robbery and sent to prison, where she undergoes many trials. Remake of *Caged*. (Dir: Walter Doniger, 85 mins.)

House on Carroll Street, The (1988)*½ Kelly McGillis, Jeff Daniels, Mandy Patinkin, Jessica Tandy. Poor scripting kills the suspense in this thriller about a fifties political activist (McGillis) who stumbles on to a plot to smuggle Nazis into the U.S. Well-mounted period detail doesn't compensate for contrived plotting and unbelievable situations. (Dir: Peter Yates, 100 mins.)†

House on Chelouche Street, The (Israel, 1973)*** Gilda Almagor, Michal Bat-Adam, Shai K. Ophir. Israeli director Moshe Mizrahi's first film is a family drama set in the turbulent period just before partition in Palestine. (120 mins.)

House on Garibaldi Street, The (MTV 1979)***½ Topol, Nick Mancuso, Alfred Burke, Janet Suzman. Re-creates the kidnapping by Israeli agents of Nazi war criminal Adolf Eichmann from Buenos Aires, where he had lived under an assumed identity for many years after WWII. Director Peter Collinson is to be commended for letting the story unfold in almost documentary fashion. (104 mins.)†

House on Green Apple Road, The (MTV 1970)**½ Janet Leigh, Christopher George, Julie Harris, Barry Sullivan. Suspenseful made-for-TV feature that uses flashbacks to fairly good advantage to tell the story of a woman (Miss Leigh) whose extramarital activities lead to murder. The police believe Miss Leigh's been murdered by her distraught husband but they can't come up with a corpse and thereby hangs the mystery. (Dir: Robert Day, 113 mins.)

House on Haunted Hill (1959)*** Vincent Price, Carol Ohmart, Richard Long, Elisha Cook, Jr. A horror film with some laughs if you don't take it too seriously. Host Price rents a haunted house and offers a select group a large reward if they spend the night. (Dir: William Castle, 75 mins.)†

House on 92nd Street (1945)***½ William Eythe, Lloyd Nolan, Signe Hasso. The FBI's battle against the fifth column in a fast-paced, exciting film. This was the first picture to effectively combine documentary techniques with the dramatic, and none of its imitators have topped it. (Dir: Henry Hathaway, 88 mins.)

House on Skull Mountain, The (1974)* Victor French, Janee Michelle, Jean Durand, Mike Evans, Ella Woods. Mysterious killer stalks people gathered at a spooky mansion for the reading of a will. Will anyone survive? Will the viewer be able to stay awake long enough to find out? (Dir: Ron Honthaner, 89 mins.)†

House on Sorority Row, The (1983)**½ Eileen Davidson, Kathryn McNeil, Robin Meloy, Lois Kelso Hunt. Horror film about seven college girls and their psychotic house mother. (Dir: Mark Rosman, 90 mins.)†

House on Telegraph Hill (1951)** Richard Basehart, Valentina Cortese, William Lundigan. Predictable melodrama with a good performance by Basehart as a convincing charmer who marries Cortese, thinking she is someone else. (Dir: Robert Wise, 93 mins.)

House on the Edge of the Park, The (Italy, 1984)* David Hess, Annie Bell, John Morghen, Lorraine De Selle, Cristian Borromeo. Sadistic thriller about punks who invade an isolated country house. (Dir: Ruggero Deodato, 91 mins.)†

House Party (1990)*** Kid'n'Play (Christopher Reid, Christopher Martin), Robin Harris, Full Force, Tisha Campbell, A. J. Johnson. A script with a wonderful ear for the latest teen argot, terrific music, funny performances, and a generally positive atmosphere (marred only by a tasteless anti-gay rap) mark this ingratiating teen comedy that seems to have magically appeared from a better world where films are routinely made for black audiences just as they are for white ones. A minor accomplishment, but a singular one. (Dir: Reginald Hudlin, 100 mins.)†

House That Dripped Blood, The (Great Britain, 1970)*** Peter Cushing, Christopher Lee, Nyree Dawn Porter, Ingrid Pitt. A series of vignettes set in an eerie estate, centering on the line of consecutive owners. The first yarn involves a hack murder-mystery writer who sees his fictional character, a wild strangler, wan-

dering all around the house. In other segments, the house has been turned into a wax museum with a striking statue of Salome; witches roam the place pitted against young innocence; and a film star puts on a genuine Transylvanian cloak for his vampire role. (Dir: Peter Duffell, 101 mins.)†

House That Screamed, The (Spain, 1970)** Lilli Palmer, John Moulder Brown. Mild thriller about a strange reformatory for wayward girls from rich families, located in the south of France and presided over by strict headmistress Palmer. (Dir: Narciso Ibanez Serrador, 94 mins.)

House That Vanished, The (Great Britain, 1973)*½ Andrea Allan, Karl Lanchbury, Maggie Walker, Peter Forbes-Robertson. Overused British horror plot of a young woman tricked into thinking she's insane isn't made any fresher here by the addition of gratuitous nudity and violence. Originally 99 mins.—be thankful there's a shorter version. AKA: **Scream and Die.** (Dir: Joseph Larraz, 84 mins.)†

House That Wouldn't Die, The (MTV 1970)**½ Barbara Stanwyck, Richard Egan, Katharine Winn. Old-fashioned haunted house yarn provides some chills. Miss Stanwyck inherits an old house and goes there with her niece. (Dir: John Llewellyn Moxey, 73 mins.)

House Where Evil Dwells, The (1982)*½ Susan George, Edward Albert, Doug McClure, Amy Barett. A young American couple (George, Albert) move into a haunted house with a history of murder and hara-kiri. Unintentionally funny. (Dir: Kevin Conner, 88 mins.)†

Housewife (1934)** Bette Davis, George Brent, Ann Dvorak, John Halliday, Ruth Donnelly. An ad man picks up where he left off with his former tootsie (Davis) while his wife weeps and moans in long-suffering fashion. (Dir: Alfred Green, 69 mins.)

House Without a Christmas Tree, The (MTV 1972)***½ Jason Robards, Jr., Mildred Natwick, Lisa Lucas. Charming, beautifully played, thoroughly enjoyable family fare. The focus is on a bright little girl of ten named Addie (Lucas); her widowed, undemonstrative father (Robards); and her warm but decisive grandmother (Natwick). Addie's father gives her everything she needs; but he can't seem to understand her urgent desire to have a Christmas tree. (Dir: Paul Bogart, 78 mins.)

Houston Story, The (1956)** Gene Barry, Barbara Hale, Edward Arnold. Predictable gangster plot has Gene Barry striving for a top position in the syndicate centered in Houston, Texas. (Dir: William Castle, 79 mins.)

Houston: The Legend of Texas (MTV

1986)**½ Sam Elliott, Michael Beck, Devon Ericson, James Stephen, G. D. Spradlin. Laconic Elliott plays hero Sam Houston with controlled intensity and some humor, but needs more space to develop Houston's fiery character. As American history lessons go on TV, a slight notch above average. (Dir: Peter Levin, 156 mins.)

Houston, We've Got a Problem (MTV 1974)** Robert Culp, Clu Gulager, Gary Collins, Sandra Dee. Suspense saga based on the near-fatal Apollo 13 mission. In this version, the astronauts dangle in space after a crippling explosion in their spacecraft. (Dir: Lawrence Doheny, 74 mins.)

Howard Beach: Making the Case for Murder (MTV 1989)*** Daniel J. Travanti, Joe Morton, William Daniels, Cliff Gorman, Dan Luria. Powerful, provocative account of the trial of those accused of murder in the infamous racial incident that divided New York City. Prosecutor Joe Hynes (Travanti) demands justice, but defense attorney (Daniels) turns the case around, arguing that it is his clients who are in fact the victims. (Dir: Dick Lowry, 96 mins.)

Howards of Virginia, The (1940)***½ Cary Grant, Martha Scott, Sir Cedric Hardwicke. Spirited backwoodsman is married to an aristocratic Virginia girl at the time of the American Revolution. Their story is a fine example of "flag waving" —with taste. (Dir: Frank Lloyd, 122 mins.)†

Howard the Duck (1986)* Lea Thompson, Jeffrey Jones, Tim Robbins, Miles Chapin. Based on the popular comic book series, the film is a spongy combination of overwrought extra-terrestrial comedy and state-of-the-art special-effects fantasy. Desperation prevails on and off the screen as an alien duck crashes to Earth, falls for a rock 'n' roll singer, and saves our planet from vicious life forms planning an invasion. (Dir: Willard Hyuck, 117 mins.)†

How Awful About Allan (MTV 1970)**½ Anthony Perkins, Julie Harris, Joan Hackett. A run-of-the-mill horror story. Anthony Perkins plays a young man recently returned from a mental institution who is a victim of psychosomatic blindness resulting from a fire that killed his father and scarred his sister (Julie Harris). (Dir: Curtis Harrington, 73 mins.)

How Do I Love Thee (1970)** Jackie Gleason, Maureen O'Hara, Shelley Winters, Rosemary Forsyth, Rick Lenz. This sometimes sentimental, sometimes comic family drama just doesn't work. Gleason is a businessman who has never connected with his son, well played by Lenz. (Dir: Michael Gordon, 98 mins.)

How Funny Can Sex Be? (Italy, 1976)** Giancarlo Giannini, Laura Antonelli, Alberto Lionello, Duilio Del Prete. Not that funny. Eight ribald tales about sex, love, and marriage. Released in U.S. after Giannini and Antonelli became marketable. He is funny, and she is beautiful, but the stories lack depth. (Dir: Dino Risi, 97 mins.)

How Green Was My Valley (1941)**** Walter Pidgeon, Maureen O'Hara, Donald Crisp, Anna Lee, Roddy McDowall, Sara Allgood, Barry Fitzgerald, John Loder, Patrick Knowles. Poignant saga of a coal-mining family in Wales examines the grim, dangerous life down in the mines and the labor dispute that divides a tight-knit family presided over by a loving, but iron-willed patriarch. Hearttugging domestic drama won six Oscars including Best Picture, Best Cinematography, and Best Director. (Dir: John Ford, 118 mins.)†

How I Got Into College (1989)** Anthony Edwards, Corey Parker, Lara Flynn Boyle, Finn Carter, Charles Rocket, Nora Dunn, Phil Hartman, Curtis Armstrong. Comedy about students trying to get into a highly competitive college has some amusing touches from director Savage Steve Holland (*Better Off Dead*), but suffers from a weak script and bland teen stars. (87 mins.)†

How I Spent My Summer Vacation (MTV 1967)** Robert Wagner, Peter Lawford, Jill St. John, Lola Albright, Walter Pidgeon. Cluttered adventure about a ne'er-do-well who thinks he has the goods on a millionaire. (Dir: William Hale, 99 mins.)

How I Won the War (Great Britain, 1967)**½ Michael Crawford, John Lennon, Jack MacGowran, Michael Hordern. Stumbling, sometimes funny attempt to satirize WWII by director Richard Lester, as he tells of a doltish officer who manages to remain alive while his comrades die grisly deaths. (109 mins.)†

Howling, The (1981)** Dee Wallace, Christopher Stone, Patrick Macnee, Dennis Dugan, Belinda Balaski, Kevin McCarthy, Slim Pickens, John Carradine. The premise of human misfits transformed into werewolves when sexually aroused is intriguing, but it is exploited for shock value and cheap laughs. This movie's endless in-jokes may satisfy horror film aficionados but the treatment kills off any possibility for real chills. (Dir: Joe Dante, 90 mins.)†

Howling II, The: Your Sister Is a Werewolf (U.S.-France-Italy, 1984)½ Christopher Lee, Reb Brown, Annie McEnroe, Marsha A. Hunt, Sybil Danning. Farfetched sequel to the tongue-in-cheek werewolf pic. The brother of one of that film's victims tries to rid the world of these hairy devils. With the estimable Sybil Danning baring her fangs and her chest whenever possible. (Dir: Philippe Mora, 91 mins.)†

Howling III, The (Australia, 1987)** Barry Otto, Imogen Annesley, Dasha Blahova, Max Fairchild. Members of two different werewolf tribes—one a marsupial variety that carries its young in pouches—converge down under in this intermittently entertaining movie. (Dir: Philippe Mora, 94 mins.)†

Howling 4, The: The Original Nightmare (1989)*½ Romy Winsor, Michael T. Weiss, Anthony Hamilton, Susanne Severeid. Writer spends a vacation in the country, where she is haunted by wolves. (Dir: John Hough, 94 mins.)†

Howling V, The: The Rebirth (1989)* Philip Davis, Victoria Catlin, Elizabeth She, Ben Cole. Another in-name-only sequel, with a group of European travelers stranded in a spooky castle. The monster doesn't show up until the end, and you can barely see it then. (Dir: Neal Sundstrom, 99 mins.)†

Howling in the Woods, A (MTV 1971)** Barbara Eden, Vera Miles, Larry Hagman, Ruta Lee, John Rubinstein. Pseudo-psychological thriller in which Eden gets horrified whenever she hears the distant wail of wolves—or what sounds like wolves. (Dir: Daniel Petrie, 104 mins.)

How Much Loving Does a Normal Couple Need?—See: Common Law Cabin

How Sweet It Is! (1968)**½ Debbie Reynolds, James Garner, Terry-Thomas, Paul Lynde, Vito Scotti, Elena Verdugo. Mishaps galore dog the steps of a couple on a European vacation. Some genuinely funny sequences. (Dir: Jerry Paris, 99 mins.)†

How Tasty Was My Little Frenchman (Brazil, 1971)***½ Arduino Colassanti, Maria Magalhaes, Ital Natur. Bizarre black comedy about a 16th-century French explorer who is captured and eaten by native Brazilian Indians. One of the strangest films ever made; deeply comic and weirdly shocking. (Dir: Nelson Pereira dos Santos, 80 mins.)

How the West Was Won (1963)*** Gregory Peck, Henry Fonda, James Stewart, Debbie Reynolds, George Peppard. Overlong but well-produced spectacle about the American pioneer spirit. A family of New England farmers heads west in the 1830s. (Dirs: Henry Hathaway, John Ford, George Marshall, 155 mins.)†

How to Beat the High Cost of Living (1980)** Susan Saint James, Jessica Lange, Jane Curtin, Richard Benjamin, Eddie Albert. Another crass comedy from the pen of Robert Kaufman, this time about pampered middle-class housewives who turn to robbery. (Dir: Robert Scheerer, 110 mins.)†

How to Be Very, Very Popular (1955)*** Betty Grable, Sheree North, Robert Cummings. Two chorus kids on the lam find refuge in a college fraternity whose members hide them. (Dir: Nunnally Johnson, 89 mins.)

How to Break Up a Happy Divorce (MTV 1976)* Barbara Eden, Hal Linden, Peter Bonerz, Harold Gould, Marcia Rodd. Dismal comedy. Barbara Eden is too coy for her own good as the energetic ex-wife who campaigns all too vigorously to win her ex back. (Dir: Jerry Paris, 72 mins.)

How to Commit Marriage (1969)* Jackie Gleason, Bob Hope, Jane Wyman. A terrible comedy about the foibles of modern marriage and divorce, wasting top comics Gleason and Hope. (Dir: Norman Panama, 104 mins.)'

How to Get Ahead in Advertising (Great Britain, 1989)*** Richard E. Grant, Rachel Ward, Richard Wilson. Wild comedy-satire written and directed by Bruce Robinson. Cynical ad man sees the error of his ways and attempts to leave the business. But his worst traits are transferred into a boil on his neck which grows into a separate head and takes over his life. (96 mins.)†

How to Make a Monster (1960)*½ Robert H. Harris, Gary Conway. Good idea, bad execution; Hollywood makeup man creates his own monsters. (Dir: Herbert L. Strock, 74 mins.)

How to Make Love to a Negro Without Getting Tired (Canada, 1990)**½ Isaach de Bancole, Maka Kotto, Antoine Durand. Rambling, but occasionally amusing story of a Haitian writer in Montreal who spends most of his time picking up girls. The pretentious script asks many more questions about racism, sexism, and prejudice than it answers. (Dir: Jacques W. Benoit, 97 mins.)

How to Marry a Millionaire (1953)**½ Marilyn Monroe, Lauren Bacall, Betty Grable, William Powell, Cameron Mitchell. The first CinemaScope comedy sends three gold diggers out on the town to catch them each a wealthy husband. Since the three are Monroe, Bacall, and Grable, the results aren't too pallid despite the overfamiliarity of the theme. (Dir: Jean Negulesco, 95 mins.)†

How to Murder a Millionaire (MTV 1990)* Joan Rivers, Alex Rocco, Morgan Fairchild, Telma Hopkins, David Ogden Stiers, Meshach Taylor. Beverly Hills matron Rivers thinks husband Rocco wants to have her killed. Feeble comedy seems to think that assembling a cast of performers who have been funny in other shows is all it needs. (Dir: Paul Schneider, 96 mins.)

495

How to Murder a Rich Uncle (Great Britain, 1958)** Charles Coburn, Nigel Patrick, Wendy Hiller. Coburn is the wealthy relation and the manipulators of the plot include sly and suave Mr. Patrick and his family. (Dir: Nigel Patrick, 80 mins.)

How to Murder Your Wife (1965)*** Jack Lemmon, Virna Lisi, Terry-Thomas. A frantic, often funny farce-comedy; a bachelor wakes up one A.M. to find gorgeous Virna Lisi in his bed with a wedding ring on her left hand. The rest of the action is devoted to Lemmon's frantic efforts to get rid of his Italian spouse, even to the point of contemplating murder. (Dir: Richard Quine, 118 mins.)†

How to Save a Marriage—And Ruin Your Life (1968)**½ Dean Martin, Stella Stevens, Eli Wallach, Anne Jackson, Betty Field, Jack Albertson. A bachelor friend tries to save the marriage of an unfaithful husband, with unexpected results. Strains for laughs at times, but generally amusing. (Dir: Fielder Cook, 108 mins.)

How to Steal a Million (1966)*** Audrey Hepburn, Peter O'Toole, Charles Boyer. The grace and charm of the two stars, and William Wyler's deft direction are displayed in this sophisticated suspense story about the heist of a valuable sculpture from a Paris museum. (127 mins.)

How to Steal an Airplane (MTV 1971)*½ Peter Duel, Clinton Greyn, Sal Mineo, Claudine Longet, Katherine Crawford. An American and a Welshman pose as tourists in Latin America in order to steal a jet from a dictator's son. (Dir: Leslie Martinson, 104 mins.)

How to Stuff a Wild Bikini (1965)*½ Annette Funicello, Dwayne Hickman, Brian Donlevy, Harvey Lembeck, Beverly Adams, Jody McCrea, John Ashley, Frankie Avalon, Buster Keaton, Mickey Rooney. Dreadful teen romp; Avalon hires a witch-doctor to keep Funicello faithful. (Dir: William Asher, 90 mins.)†

How to Succeed in Business Without Really Trying (1967)*** Robert Morse, Michele Lee, Rudy Vallee, Sammy Smith. The whole family will have a lot of fun without really trying to watch this long-running Broadway smash transferred to the big screen. Robert Morse, playing a Protestant what-makes-Sammy-run with a captivating charm, repeats his Broadway triumph. (Dir: David Swift, 119 mins.)†

H2 Worker (1990)*** Compelling and thought-provoking documentary showing the exploitation by the U.S. sugar industry of its migrant Jamaican farmworkers. Director Stephanie Black uses interviews, film clips, and, most effectively, readings from the laborers own letters to and from home to make her point. (Dir: Stephanie Black, 70 mins.)

Huckleberry Finn (1931)**½ Jackie Coogan, Mitzi Green, Junior Durkin, Eugene Pallette, Jackie Searl, Jane Darwell, Clarence Muse. A companion piece to 1930s popular *Tom Sawyer* with some of the same cast reprising their roles. Life on the Mississippi according to Hollywood. (Dir: Norman Taurog, 80 mins.)

Huckleberry Finn (1939)***½ Mickey Rooney, Rex Ingram, Walter Connolly, William Frawley, Victor Kilian. Terrific version of the Mark Twain classic, with Ingram a standout as Huck's companion Jim, the escaped slave, and Rooney excellent in the title role. One of the best. (Dir: Richard Thorpe, 90 mins.)

Huckleberry Finn (1974)** Paul Winfield, Harvey Korman, David Wayne, Jeff East. Twain's durable classic gets a beating in this lumbering "musical adaptation." (Dir: J. Lee Thompson, 113 mins.)†

Huckleberry Finn (MTV 1975)** Ron Howard, Donny Most, Antonio Fargas, Jack Elam, Royal Dano, Merle Haggard. Another look at Samuel Clemens's immortal story, but the sharp edges have been blunted. (Dir: Robert Totten, 104 mins.)†

Hucksters, The (1947)*** Clark Gable, Ava Gardner, Deborah Kerr, Sydney Greenstreet. Adaptation of the novel about advertising that set the style for cheap modern novels is not nearly as pungent as the book. (Dir: Jack Conway, 115 mins.)†

Hud (1963)**** Paul Newman, Patricia Neal, Melvyn Douglas, Brandon de Wilde. A must for movie-drama fans. A superb cast makes this story, about a ruthless young man who tarnishes everything and everyone he touches, ring true from start to finish. Newman is the perfect embodiment of alienated youth, out for kicks with no regard for the consequences. The drama is deepened by the bitter conflict between the callous Hud and his stern and highly principled father (Douglas). (Dir: Martin Ritt, 112 mins.)†

Hudson's Bay (1940)**½ Paul Muni, Gene Tierney. Story of the founding of the Hudson Bay Company is a drawn-out story, lacking action or motivation. (Dir: Irving Pichel, 95 mins.)†

Hue and Cry (Great Britain, 1947)*** Alastair Sim, Valerie White. Enjoyable romp. A meek detective story writer and a group of kids crack a gang of thieves. (Dir: Charles Crichton, 82 mins.)

Huey Long (1985)**** An excellent documentary. Mr. Long was sort of the Will Rogers of demagoguery, a gifted cracker-barrel philosopher who gave the poor what they wanted with one hand and took whatever he could get for himself with the other. (Dir: Ken Burns, 88 mins.)

Huk (1956)*** George Montgomery, Mona Freeman. Huks were marauding guerrillas plundering plantations in Manila. American Montgomery arrives to sell his inherited plantation and stays to fight. Exciting action scenes. (Dir: John Barnwell, 84 mins.)

Hullaballoo over Georgie and Bonnie's Pictures (Great Britain, 1976)*** Peggy Ashcroft, Victor Bannerjee, Jane Booker, Aparna Sen. A relaxed maharaja owns a priceless collection of Indian miniature paintings which his greedy sister wants to sell; and even greedier people want to buy. Ashcroft is fun as one of the treasure seekers in this delightful comedy about possessions and friendship. (Dir: James Ivory, 83 mins.)†

Human Comedy, The (1943)***½ Mickey Rooney, Frank Morgan, Marsha Hunt, Van Johnson. William Saroyan's optimistic philosophy on the human race is beautifully expressed in this story that is almost plotless but deep in characterization and sensitivity. It just tells about a small town in California during WWII, but see it and reaffirm your faith in people. (Dir: Clarence Brown, 118 mins.)†

Human Desire (1954)*** Glenn Ford, Gloria Grahame, Broderick Crawford. A loose adaptation of Emile Zola's *The Human Beast*, about an unfaithful wife (Grahame). Beautifully directed by Fritz Lang. (90 mins.)

Human Duplicators, The (1965)** George Nader, Barbara Nichols, George Macready. Special agent finds superior beings from another world creating a race of robots who will infiltrate key positions paving the way for invasion. Way-out science fiction. (Dir: Hugo Grimaldi, 82 mins.)†

Human Factor, The (1975)½ George Kennedy, John Mills, Raf Vallone, Rita Tushingham, Barry Sullivan. Distasteful rubbish about a computer expert who uses technology to track down his family's killers. (Dir: Edward Dmytryk, 96 mins.)†

Human Factor, The (1979)**½ Richard Attenborough, Derek Jacobi, Robert Morley, Nicol Williamson, Iman. Director Otto Preminger's film of Grahame Greene's novel lacks the richness and depth of Greene's vision. The story concerns a disenchanted veteran secret agent, and the search for a double agent in the ranks. (115 mins.)

Human Feelings (MTV 1978)**½ Nancy Walker, Billy Crystal, Pamela Sue Martin, Jack Carter. In this TV fantasy, God is a woman (Walker) and she wants to wreak vengeance on gaudy, bawdy Las Vegas, and dispatches an emissary, angel Billy Crystal, to handle the job. Cutesy and cloying. (Dir: Ernest Pintoff, 100 mins.)

Human Jungle, The (1954)**½ Gary Merrill, Jan Sterling. Exciting cops-and-robbers yarn with more action than most similar type films. Merrill plays a police captain who comes face to face with some very shady characters of the underworld. (Dir: Joseph M. Newman, 82 mins.)

Human Monster, The—See: **Dark Eyes of London**

Humanoid, The (Italy, 1979)** Richard Kiel, Corinne Clery, Leonard Mann, Barbara Bach, Arthur Kennedy. Kiel, best known for playing "Jaws" in several James Bond films, is the title character in this distaff *Star Wars* rip-off that thankfully doesn't take itself very seriously. Kiel's assignment: stop another one of those mad scientists who are always trying to take over the world. (Dir: George B. Lewis, 100 mins.)

Humanoid Defender (MTV 1985)*½ Terence Knox, Gary Kasper, Aimee Eccles, William Lucking, Gail Edwards, Marie Windsor. Failed pilot about a scientist and his android creation earning a living as do-gooders while they hide out from the nasty government agency that wants to use the 'droid to kill. *J.O.E. and the Colonel* is from the same proposed series. (Dir: Ron Satlof, 94 mins.)†

Humanoids from the Deep (1980)½ Doug McClure, Ann Turkel, Vic Morrow, Cindy Weintraub. Idiotic ecological horror film. Some giant mutant fish decide to mate with women and spawn unintentional laughs. (Dir: Barbara Peeters, 80 mins.)†

Human, Too Human (France, 1972)*** An innovative, exquisitely photographed documentary about life on an assembly line. Director Louis Malle sets out to shatter preconceptions about working on a line, and his caring lyrical story brings the entire process into the category of high art. An interesting and unusual bit of cinema. (77 mins.)

Human Vapor, The (Japan, 1960)*½ Yoshhio Tsuchiya, Kaoru Yachigusa, Tatsuya Mihashi, Keiko Sata. Well-handled Japanese sci-fi about a man who can make himself into vapor at will—a variation on the "Invisible Man" theme. (Dir: Inoshiro Honda, 79 mins.)†

Humongous (1981)*½ David Wallace, Janet Julian, Janit Baldwin. The party is over for a group of rich, oversexed kids when they get shipwrecked on a creepy island inhabited by a half-man half-monster. (Dir: Paul Lynch, 93 mins.)†

Humoresque (1947)*** Joan Crawford, John Garfield, Oscar Levant. Lengthy Fannie Hurst drama of a talented musician from the slums who meets, is sponsored and loved by a wealthy society woman, with the inevitable tragic finale. Spiced up with some Clifford

Odets dialogue, good (classical) music sequences, capable performances. (Dir: Jean Negulesco, 125 mins.) †

Hunchback of Notre Dame, The (1923)***½ Lon Chaney, Patsy Ruth Miller, Ernest Torrence. First major film version of Victor Hugo's novel *Notre Dame de Paris*. But Chaney dominates throughout, and it is well worth seeing because of him. (Dir: Wallace Worsley, 108 mins.) †

Hunchback of Notre Dame, The (1939)**** Charles Laughton, Maureen O'Hara, Edmond O'Brien, Thomas Mitchell, Cedric Hardwicke, George Zucco, Walter Hampden. Based on Hugo's famous novel about the crippled bell ringer and his hopeless love for the beautiful Esmeralda, the film has few equals in recreating an historical period. Laughton's astonishing performance will enthrall you as he shows how this piteous creature achieves a measure of dignity by rescuing the gypsy girl who'd once shown him kindness. Superbly crafted. (Dir: William Dieterle, 115 mins.) †

Hunchback of Notre Dame (France, 1957) **½ Anthony Quinn, Gina Lollobrigida. Acceptable screen version of the classic tale about the deformed bell ringer of Notre Dame and his love for Esmeralda. (Dir: Jean Delannoy, 104 mins.)

Hunchback of Notre Dame, The (MTV 1982)**½ Anthony Hopkins, Lesley-Anne Down, Robert Powell, John Gielgud, Derek Jacobi. A faithful adaptation of Victor Hugo's classic novel, in which a deformed bell ringer falls for a beautiful gypsy. (Dir: Michael Tuchner, 150 mins.) †

Hundra (1985)**½ Laurene Landon, John Ghaffari, Marisa Casel. Exploitation trash, but enjoyable. Taking on the burden of her decimated race, Laurene Landon, her tribe's surviving Amazon, is in a big hurry to conceive before her biological clock winds down. (Dir: Matt Cimber, 109 mins.) †

Hunger, The (1983)**½ Catherine Deneuve, David Bowie, Susan Sarandon, Cliff De Young. Visually dazzling but insipid film. First-time director Tony Scott has given his film a glossy, high-tech veneer, but the plot, a mishmash of horror, romance, science, and sex, is often incoherent. (94 mins.) †

Hungry Hill (Great Britain, 1947)**½ Margaret Lockwood, Dennis Price. Two Irish families feud with each other through the years, bringing despair and poverty. Rambling, drawn out melodrama, has some good moments, some trite ones. (Dir: Brian Desmond Hurst, 92 mins.)

Hungry Pets—See: **Please Don't Eat My Mother**

Hungry Wives—See: **Season of the Witch**

Hunk (1987)** Deborah Shelton, John Allen Nelson, Steve Levitt, Rebeccah Bush, James Coco, Robert Morse, Avery Schreiber. The Faust legend with a Southern California tan. A wimpy computer programmer signs a pact with Satan to be transformed into a handsome hunk. (Dir: Lawrence Bassof, 102 mins.) †

Hunt, The (Spain, 1966)**** Ismael Merlo, Alfredo Mayo. Powerful, brutal, haunting film, superbly directed by young Spaniard Carlos Saura. Three middle-aged men, out on a rabbit-hunting party-picnic, are themselves brutalized by the hunt in this searing drama. (93 mins.)

Hunted Lady, The (MTV 1977)** Donna Mills, Andrew Duggan, Robert Reed. Mills stars as an undercover lady who's being framed. (Dir: Richard Lang, 104 mins.) †

Hunter, The (1980)*½ Steve McQueen, Kathryn Harrold, Eli Wallach, Ben Johnson, LeVar Burton. McQueen gives a sympathetic portrayal as a modern bounty hunter, the real-life Papa Thorson, who chases criminals who've jumped bail and brings them back into the hands of the law. (Dir: Buzz Kulik, 97 mins.) †

Hunters, The (1958)**½ Robert Mitchum, Robert Wagner, May Britt, Lee Philips. Jet pilots in Korea. More melodrama than action, but the pace picks up when "the boys" are aloft, due to some first-rate aerial photography. (Dir: Dick Powell, 108 mins.)

Hunters Are for Killing (MTV 1970)**½ Burt Reynolds, Melvyn Douglas. Burt Reynolds, a man of few words, returns to the wine country aiming to prove his innocence on a murder rap. (Dir: Bernard Kowalski, 99 mins.)

Hunter's Blood (1987)**½ Sam Bottoms, Kim Delaney, Clu Gulager, Ken Swofford, Joey Travolta. Some urbanites go to the woods for rest and relaxation and instead encounter crazed hillbillies who don't cotton to outsiders. (Dir: Robert C. Hughes, 102 mins.) †

Hunt for Red October, The (1990)**½ Sean Connery, Alec Baldwin, Scott Glenn, Sam Neill, James Earl Jones, Joss Ackland, Richard Jordan, Peter Firth, Tim Curry, Jeffrey Jones. Sluggish adaptation of the best-selling Tom Clancy novel about a renegade Soviet submarine captain (Connery, who barely attempts to disguise his Scottish burr) who may or may not be steering his new, top-secret sub to the U.S. for the purpose of defecting. Set in 1984, "shortly before Gorbachev came to power," as the title puts it, the film seems outdated in a post-Cold War era. Even worse, it's way too long and fatally lacking in suspense. (Dir: John McTiernan, 137 mins.) †

Hunting Party, The (Great Britain, 1971)½ Candice Bergen, Oliver Reed, Gene Hackman. Violence-filled western trash, set in Texas in the 1890s. Bergen is married to a sadistic, impotent husband. (Dir: Don Medford, 108 mins.)

Hunt the Man Down (1951)*** Gig Young, Lynne Roberts. Public defender is asked to solve a killing for which an innocent man is charged. Above-average mystery with a good plot. (Dir: George Archainbaud, 68 mins.)

Hunt to Kill—See: **White Buffalo, The**

Hurricane, The (1937)***½ Dorothy Lamour, Jon Hall, Raymond Massey, Mary Astor, C. Aubrey Smith, Thomas Mitchell, John Carradine, Jerome Cowan. The actors take second billing to the special effects in this film. There's a rousing, frightening hurricane sequence that makes the film worth sitting through. Excitingly directed. (Dir: John Ford, 120 mins.)†

Hurricane (MTV 1974)*½ Jessica Walter, Larry Hagman, Frank Sutton, Barry Sullivan. Clichéd disaster pic about a hurricane. (Dir: Jerry Jameson, 72 mins.)†

Hurricane (1979)* Jason Robards, Jr., Mia Farrow, Max von Sydow. Robards plays the U.S. governor of a tropical island, and Farrow plays his daughter, who falls in love with a tribal chieftain. The climactic typhoon is impressive; the rest is a dull remake of *The Hurricane* (1937). (Dir: Jan Troell, 119 mins.)†

Hurry, Sundown (1967)* Michael Caine, Jane Fonda, Robert Hooks, John Phillip Law. A lurid and laughable tale of passions and predicaments of the black and white inhabitants of a Georgia town. Southern movie clichés abound, as bad white guys will stop at nothing to acquire land. (Dir: Otto Preminger, 142 mins.)

Hurry Up or I'll Be 30 (1973)** John Lefkowitz, Linda De Coff, Maureen Byrnes, Danny DeVito, Ronald Anton. Crudely shot, tepid low-budget comedy about meek geek in New York City who vows to make something of himself before his thirtieth birthday, which is approaching fast. (Dir: Joseph Jacoby, 88 mins.)†

Husbands (1970)*** John Cassavetes, Peter Falk, Ben Gazzara. A poignant film about three middle-aged men who go on a drinking binge when a mutual friend dies. The sadness and despair of their lives pour out as they try to escape themselves. (Dir: John Cassavetes, 138 mins.)

Husbands, Wives, Money and Murder (1984)**½ Garrett Morris, Greg Mullavey, Meredith MacRae, Timothy Bottoms. Census taker Morris calls on Mullavey and MacRae, who get pushed over the edge by his incessant questioning. Sporadically amusing black comedy. AKA: **Census Taker, The**. (Dir: Bruce Cook, 95 mins.)†

Hush...Hush Sweet Charlotte (1965)*** Bette Davis, Olivia de Havilland, Joseph Cotten, Cecil Kellaway, Victor Buono, Agnes Moorehead. Suspense horror chiller. Charlotte, a recluse, long notorious for murdering her lover, seems to be slipping further into insanity. Will history repeat itself? You'll be on the edge of your seat trying to figure it out, and Davis is astonishing as Charlotte. (Dir: Robert Aldrich, 133 mins.)†

Hustle (1975)**½ Burt Reynolds, Catherine Deneuve, Paul Winfield, Ben Johnson, Eileen Brennan, Eddie Albert. Involving police drama. Reynolds is well cast as a police detective in love with a high-priced call girl. (Dir: Robert Aldrich, 120 mins.)†

Hustler, The (1961)**** Paul Newman, Piper Laurie, George C. Scott, Jackie Gleason, Myron McCormick, Murray Hamilton, Michael Constantine, Jake LaMotta, Vincent Gardenia. A riveting melodrama about a hotheaded pool shark who has the talent but ultimately may lack the character to be a winner. Writer-director Robert Rossen creates a vivid, seedy world of pool halls, flophouses, cons, and losers, and Newman brings authority to the part of Fast Eddie Felson (a role he reprised in *The Color of Money*). His gripping work is supported by admirable turns from Laurie as his alcoholic lover, Scott as a diabolical promoter, and Gleason as pool legend Minnesota Fats. (135 mins.)†

Hustler of Muscle Beach, The (MTV 1980)* Richard Hatch, Kay Lenz, Jeanette Nolan, Tim Kimber. Exploitation film about bodybuilding contests in Venice, Calif. Paging Arnold Schwarzenegger! (Dir: Jonathan Kaplan, 104 mins.)

Hustling (MTV 1975)*** Lee Remick, Jill Clayburgh, Monte Markham. Effective drama about the streetwalkers of New York. Fay Kanin's gutsy, seamy sad tale, based on Gail Sheehy's book, portrays the prostitutes as victims, pushed around by just about everybody, including their pimps. (Dir: Joseph Sargent, 100 mins.)†

Hypnotic Eye, The (1960)*½ Jacques Bergerac. A silly mystery about a professional hypnotist whose victims are beautiful women whom he instructs to destroy their beauty while under his spell. (Dir: George Blair, 79 mins.)

Hysterical (1983)* The Hudson Brothers, Cindy Pickett, Richard Kiel, Julie Newmar, Bud Cort. The Brothers Hudson cavort on-screen with the subtlety of the Ritz Brothers on amphetamines. Parodies of haunted-house flicks have been done better elsewhere. (Dir: Chris Bearde, 87 mins.)†

Accuse! (Great Britain, 1958)*** Jose Ferrer, Viveca Lindfors, Emlyn Williams, Leo Genn, Anton Walbrook. The famous Capt. Dreyfus trial and conviction is the basis for this drama. Ferrer plays Dreyfus with a commendable restraint. (Dir: Jose Ferrer, 99 mins.)

Aim at the Stars (1960)*** Curt Jurgens, Victoria Shaw. Gripping semi-documentary-styled account of how Werner von Braun, missile expert, came to work for the U.S. after his close association with the Nazis during WWII. (Dir: J. Lee Thompson, 107 mins.)

Am a Camera (Great Britain, 1955)*** Julie Harris, Laurence Harvey, Shelley Winters. The record of a young author and a hard-living, carefree girl in pre-war Berlin. Literate, excellently acted comedy-drama. Forerunner to *Cabaret*. (Dir: Henry Cornelius, 98 mins.)†

Am a Fugitive from a Chain Gang (1932) **** Paul Muni. A scathing indictment of life in a Southern chain gang which has become a film classic. The movie and the book on which it was based caused quite a stir at the time and even led to some investigations. Muni is magnificent in the lead and he's ably assisted by a fine cast. (Dir: Mervyn LeRoy, 100 mins.)†

I, A Man (1967)**½ Tom Baker, Ivy Nicholson, Ingrid Superstar, Cynthia May, Valerie Solanis, Berttina Coffin, Stephanie Graves. Moderately funny Andy Warhol film about Baker obsessed with having sex with as many women as possible. He wants them, he needs them, he gets them. Noteworthy for an appearance by Solanis, who then tried to murder Warhol in June 1968; she's actually quite good as a lesbian here. (99 mins.)

Am a Thief (1935)**½ Mary Astor, Ricardo Cortez, Robert Barrat, Dudley Digges, Irving Pichel. Romantic adventure of jewel thieves set in Europe. Choppy plot, has some interesting moments and good acting. (Dir: Robert Florey, 64 mins.)

Am Curious—Blue (Sweden, 1968)**½ Lena Nyman, Peter Lindgren, Borje Ahlstedt, Vilgot Sjoman. See *I Am Curious—Yellow*. (Dir: Vilgot Sjoman, 103 mins.)†

Am Curious—Yellow (Sweden, 1967)**½ Lena Nyman, Peter Lindgren, Borje Ahlstedt, Magnus Nilsson, Vilgot Sjoman. Historically important film shattered sexual taboos and international box-office records. Story of a woman sociologist conducting a survey about Swedish society is intercut with (among other meanderings) numerous sexual encounters. What was once scandalous now is merely a curiosity piece. Both this and *I Am Curious—Blue* were taken from the same footage, which was too long to release in one film. (By the way, yellow and blue are the colors of the Swedish flag.) (Dir: Vilgot Sjoman, 121 mins.)†

Am My Films: A Portrait Of Werner Herzog (West Germany, 1978)***½ One of the best documentaries ever made about a filmmaker. Baring his strange soul, Herzog talks about his philosophy of the cinema, mythic battles with actor Klaus Kinski on the set of *Aguirre, the Wrath of God*, being bitten by rats while shooting in Africa, and views on everything from the cosmos to psychiatry. Film details events in Herzog's childhood, and searches for the reasons he's so willing to suffer great ordeals to make movies. Bursting with examples of Herzog's unique work. (Dirs: Christian Weisenborn, Erwin Keusch, 96 mins.)

Am the Cheese (1983)**½ Hope Lange, Robert MacNaughton, Don Murray, John Fiedler, Sudie Bond, Robert Wagner. A confusing but well-played yarn about an adolescent who's blocked out a traumatic event. Robert MacNaughton excels as the troubled youth. (Dir: Robert Jiras, 95 mins.)†

Am the Law (1938)*** Edward G. Robinson, Wendy Barrie. Law professor wages a one-man war against protection racketeers. Well-acted, well-done crime melodrama. (Dir: Alexander Hall, 90 mins.)†

Became a Criminal (Great Britain, 1947)*** Trevor Howard, Sally Gray. An ex-pilot framed into prison escapes to square the double-cross. Tense, exciting melodrama; well acted. (Dir: Alberto Cavalcanti, 80 mins.)

Believe in You (Great Britain, 1952)*** Cecil Parker, Celia Johnson, Laurence Harvey, Joan Collins. A wayward young girl and a hoodlum are looked after by a kindly probation officer. (Dir: Basil Dearden, 93 mins.)

Bury the Living (1958)**½ Richard Boone, Theodore Bikel. Each time a manager sticks a black pin on a community cemetery chart, somebody dies. Three-fourths of a good thriller; falls apart at the end, but prior to that has some effective moments. (Dir: Albert Band, 76 mins.)†

Can Get It for You Wholesale (1951)**½ Susan Hayward, Dan Dailey, George Sanders. Story of a heel in the garment industry. Well acted, but somehow unsympathetic, at times rather nasty. AKA: **Only the Best.** (Dir: Michael Gordon, 90 mins.)

Can't Give You Anything But Love, Baby (1940)**½ Broderick Crawford, Johnny Downs. Snappy little musical about a hoodlum who kidnaps a young song-writer to compose a love song for his moll. Some good laughs. (Dir: Albert S. Rogell, 60 mins.)

Ice (1970)*** Gritty, newsreel-style political thriller of '60s unrest gone out of control. In the near future, as war rages in Mexico and Asia, revolutionary groups arm themselves and commit violent acts in the U.S. to protest American involvement. This film offers a unique perspective on a chapter in our history that is for many still an open sore. (Dir: Robert Kramer, 135 mins.)

Ice Castles (1978)**½ Robby Benson, Lynn-Holly Johnson, Colleen Dewhurst. A sentimental film that goes overboard and yet maintains its appeal. Johnson makes her film debut as Alexis, an ice skater with Olympic potential who suddenly goes blind. (Dir: Donald Wrye, 113 mins.)†

Ice Cold in Alex—See: **Desert Attack**

Iced (1988)*½ Debra DeLiso, Doug Stevenson, Ron Kologie, Elizabeth Gorcey. Partiers at a ski resort are stalked and killed by a mysterious psycho who holds them responsible for a death years ago. (Dir: Jeff Kwitney, 85 mins.)†

Ice Follies of 1939 (1939)** Joan Crawford, James Stewart, Lew Ayres, Lewis Stone, Lionel Stander. A real curiosity, with Stewart and Crawford starring on skates. (Dir: Reinhold Schunzel, 90 mins.)

Iceland (1942)**½ Sonja Henie, John Payne. A fair score and Sonja's skating grace this romance of an Iceland girl and a Marine. (Dir: H. B. Humberstone, 79 mins.)

Iceman (Canada, 1984)*** Timothy Hutton, Lindsay Crouse, John Lone. Striking, original entry. In the Arctic, a research team uncovers a frozen man lodged in the ice since prehistoric times. This premise is broadened emotionally by revealing the caveman's inability to cope with his rebirth in modern times. A thought-provoking movie. (Dir: Fred Schepisi, 101 mins.)†

Iceman Cometh, The (1973)***½ Fredric March, Lee Marvin, Robert Ryan, Jeff Bridges, Tom Pedi. March is extraordinary as Harry Hope in the Eugene O'Neill masterpiece. Ryan's valedictory performance as Larry is a highlight of the film version of the play, which is set in a 1912 waterfront combination saloon and flophouse. (Dir: John Frankenheimer, 239 mins.)

Ice Palace (1960)**½ Richard Burton, Robert Ryan, Carolyn Jones. Edna Ferber's sprawling novel about the formation of Alaska as a state makes a long episodic soap opera. (Dir: Vincent Sherman, 143 mins.)†

Ice Pirates (1984)** Robert Urich, Mary Frances Crosby, John Matuszak. A pirate captain leads a rag-tag bunch of adventurers through outer space on a search for precious water. A tired attempt to cross swordplay and space battles. (Dir: Stewart Raffill, 95 mins.)†

Ice Station Zebra (1968)**½ Rock Hudson, Ernest Borgnine, Patrick McGoohan. Sprawling submarine adventure; an elaborate sub is sent to the North Pole on a secret mission involving missile data recorded by a Russian space satellite. (Dir: John Sturges, 148 mins.)†

Ichabod and Mr. Toad—See: **Adventures of Ichabod and Mr. Toad, The**

I Changed My Sex—See: **Glen or Glenda**

Icicle Thief, The (Italy, 1989)**** Maurizio Nichetti, Caterina Sylos Labini, Heidi Komarek, Renato Scarpa. Dazzling comedy filled with narrative-shattering bravado. While objecting to cuts for commercial television in his film (an *hommage* to Vittorio De Sica's *The Bicycle Thief*) a filmmaker suddenly finds himself trapped in the film. Chaos reigns as the film-within-a-film's characters move between real and reel time and the filmmaker tries to restore the cuts from within. (Dir: Maurizio Nichetti, 93 mins.)

I Come in Peace (1990)*½ Dolph Lundgren, Brian Benben, Betsy Brantley. No, it's *not* about Saddam Hussein's entrance into Kuwait! Karate-chopping detective Lundgren (Stallone's opponent in *Rocky IV*) battles an alien from outer space who drains the heroin from his drug-addicted victims, which he then plans to send off to another galaxy. Routine action-adventure flick. (Dir: Craig R. Baxley, 98 mins.)†

I Confess (1953)**½ Montgomery Clift, Anne Baxter, Karl Malden. Even Alfred Hitchcock has to strike out some time and this is one of those times—a priest, well played by Clift, will not violate the sanctity of the confessional even at his own expense. (95 mins.)†

I Could Go On Singing (Great Britain, 1963)*** Judy Garland, Dirk Bogarde, Jack Klugman, Aline MacMahon, Gregory Philips. Dramatically, the film is hackneyed (relating the story of a singer's trip to England to reclaim her illegitimate son), but the musical portions showcase Garland at close to her peak. (Dir: Ronald Neame, 99 mins.)†

I Could Never Have Sex with Any Man Who Has So Little Regard for My Husband (1973)** Carmine Caridi, Andrew Duncan, Cynthia Harris, Lynne Lipton, Dan Greenburg. Two middle-class married couples take a summer cottage at Martha's Vineyard and discuss the sexual possibilities. For what it's worth, this is a rare movie that shows what sex was *really* like in the soporific '70s—all talk and no action. Screenplay from his novel by Dan Greenburg, who has a cameo role. (Dir: Robert McCarty, 86 mins.)

I Cover the Waterfront (1933)**½ Claudette Colbert, Ernest Torrence, Ben Lyon, Wilfrid Lucas. This gritty dockside drama holds up due to Colbert's fine performance as a girl torn between her duty to her daddy, who's a smuggler, and her love for a reporter who's on the verge of exposing her papa. (Dir: James Cruze, 70 mins.)†

I'd Climb the Highest Mountain (1951)*** William Lundigan, Susan Hayward, Gene Lockhart. Sincere, emotionally effective story of a Methodist preacher and his family in the hinterlands of cracker country. (Dir: Henry King, 88 mins.)

Ideal Husband, An (Great Britain, 1948)**½ Paulette Goddard, Michael Wilding, Glynis Johns. Oscar Wilde's comedy of manners and morals in Victorian England. (Dir: Alexander Korda, 96 mins.)

Identification Marks: None (Poland, 1964)***½ Jerzy Skolimowski, Tadeusz Mins, Elzbieta Czyzewska, Jacek Szczek, Andrzej Zarnecki. Skolimowski wore four hats in the creation of his first feature film (art director, writer, actor, director), and his wife, Czyzewska, played multiple parts in this original, witty, superbly detailed story of a young man who spends his last day before being drafted into the army with people who form links to his directionless life. (74 mins.)

Identification of a Woman (Italy, 1982)*** Daniela Silverio, Christine Boisson, Thomas Milian, Sandra Monteleoni. Love, loss, and ennui get a familiar but still enlightening workout in Michelangelo Antonioni's film about a movie director whose life is tied up with women from his past, present, and future. In Antonioni's world, nothing lasts forever, except perhaps his films. (131 mins.)

Identity Unknown (1945)**½ Richard Arlen, Cheryl Walker, Roger Pryor, Bobby Driscoll, Lola Lane, Ian Keith. Intense, moody drama of a shell-shocked veteran with amnesia trying to find his identity. Different and absorbing. (Dir: Walter Colmes, 71 mins.)†

I, Desire (MTV 1982)**½ David Naughton, Dorian Harewood, Brad Dourif, Marilyn Jones, Barbara Stock. A vampirism tale about a law student out to catch a modern-day Ms. Dracula. The sexy vamp mixes business with pleasure by using the men she meets while streetwalking Hollywood Boulevard as her personal blood bank. (Dir: John Llewellyn Moxey, 104 mins.)

I Died a Thousand Times (1955)** Jack Palance, Shelley Winters, Lee Marvin. Fair remake of *High Sierra*. (Dir: Stuart Heisler, 109 mins.)†

Idiot, The (Japan, 1951)***½ Masayuki Mori, Setsuko Hara, Toshiro Mifune, Takashi Shimura. Extraordinary epic version of Dostoyevski's novel, transposed to post-WWII Japan, retains the essence of this tale of madness, love, jealousy, and passion. Director Akira Kurosawa throws his characters into raging blizzards and weirdly lit interiors to establish danger and confusion. (166 mins.)

Idiot's Delight (1939)***½ Clark Gable, Norma Shearer. Robert Sherwood's Pulitzer Prize play loses in the screen version but enough is left to make it worthwhile. Story has enough comedy to keep it going as pure entertainment. (Dir: Clarence Brown, 120 mins.)†

I Dismember Mama (1972)** Zooey Hall, Geri Reischl, Joanne Moore Jordan, Greg Mullavey. A psychotic woman-hater escapes from the asylum to which his mother had him committed. Bleak, depressing movie isn't as bad as its reputation suggests, as long as you're not expecting the gory horror film suggested by the title (it was originally called *Poor Albert and Little Annie*). (Dir: Paul Leder, 87 mins.)†

Idol, The (1966)** Jennifer Jones, Michael Parks, Jennifer Hilary, John Leyton. A trendy, late-sixties potboiler about a perpetually mumbling stud (Parks) and how he carries on with both his best buddy's girlfriend and the buddy's mother. (Dir: Daniel Petrie, 107 mins.)

Idol Dancer, The (1920)**½ Richard Barthelmess, Clarine Seymour, Creighton Hale. Fascinating melodrama from pioneering director D. W. Griffith, concerning a lovely "child of nature" on a tropical island who is loved by a dropout (Barthelmess) and a sickly young missionary (Hale). Some absurd anthropology—all the "natives" are played by white actors in blackface, and nobody seems too sure what race they're supposed to be—but an affecting love story, with splendid performances by the leads. (70 mins.)

Idolmaker, The (1980)*** Ray Sharkey, Peter Gallagher, Paul Land. A rousing, satisfying piece of superslick filmmaking, about a songwriter-promoter (Sharkey) who creates pop idols out of pretty-eyed ethnic kids. (Dir: Taylor Hackford, 119 mins.)†

"I Don't Care" Girl, The (1953)**½ Mitzi Gaynor, David Wayne. George Jessel produced this musical biography of Eva Tanguay and the film is about George Jessel's work in getting the facts about Miss Tanguay. If you disregard the extraneous plot gimmicks, you may enjoy the musical numbers. (Dir: Lloyd Bacon, 78 mins.)

I Don't Want to Be Born—See: **Devil Within Her, The**

I Dood It (1943)**½ Red Skelton, Eleanor Powell. Red's fans may like this slapstick but it's not one of his best. Romance of a pants presser and a movie star is loaded with trite situations and forced humor. (Dir: Vincente Minnelli, 102 mins.)

I'd Rather Be Rich (1964)**½ Sandra Dee, Robert Goulet, Andy Williams, Maurice Chevalier. Millionaire's granddaughter asks a stranger to pose as her fiancé to please the old man, who is ill. Amusing romantic comedy. (Dir: Jack Smight, 96 mins.)

I Dream of Jeannie (1952)** Ray Middleton, Bill Shirley. Story of how Stephen Foster came to write many of his famous tunes. (Dir: Allan Dwan, 90 mins.)

I Dream of Jeannie: 15 Years Later (MTV 1985)** Barbara Eden, Wayne Rogers, Bill Daily, Hayden Rorke. Fans of the enormously popular series "I Dream of Jeannie" will want to see this reunion film that takes a look at the genie and her mortal husband fifteen years after they married. (Dir: Bill Asher, 104 mins.)

I Dream Too Much (1935)** Lily Pons, Henry Fonda. Two music students are happily married until the wife wins success as a singer. Superb vocalizing by Pons is the feature of this pleasant comedy-drama. (Dir: John Cromwell, 110 mins.)†

I Eat Your Skin—See: *Zombies*

I Even Met Happy Gypsies (Yugoslavia, 1967)*** Bekim Fehmiu, Gordana Jovanovic, Olivera Vuco, Mija Aleksic, Bata Zivojinovic. A gypsy trader meets a young girl on one of his travels. Away from his own family, he becomes close to her and learns that her father is an abusive man. A fascinating look at gypsy life with music and beautiful photography. (Dir: Aleksander Petrovic, 90 mins.)

If... (Great Britain, 1969)**** Malcolm McDowell, David Wood, Richard Warwick, Peter Jeffrey, Christine Noonan. A striking, enormously powerful if episodic drama about life in a repressive boys' boarding school in England. (Dir: Lindsay Anderson, 111 mins.)†

If a Man Answers (1962)** Sandra Dee, Bobby Darin, John Lund, Stefanie Powers. Playgirl marries a carefree photographer, resorts to extreme measures to keep him in line after they're married. (Dir: Henry Levin, 102 mins.)

If Ever I See You Again (1978)*½ Joe Brooks, Shelley Hack, George Plimpton. A prominent jingle writer for commercials pursues the girl who turned him down in college. (Dir: Joe Brooks, 105 mins.)†

If I Had a Million (1932)***½ W. C. Fields, George Raft, Gary Cooper, Charles Laughton. Eccentric millionaire decides to will his dough to people picked from the phone book. Enjoyable multi-storied

film, with the Fields and Laughton episodes screamingly funny. (Dirs: Ernst Lubitsch, Norman Taurog, James Cruze, H. Bruce Humberstone, Stephen Roberts, William A. Seiter, 90 mins.)

If I Had My Way (1940)**½ Bing Crosby, Gloria Jean, Charles Winninger, Allyn Joslyn, El Brendel, Claire Dodd, Moroni Olsen. Easygoing vehicle for Crosby as a construction worker (!) trying to help an orphan girl find her uncle in N.Y.C. (Dir: David Butler, 94 mins.)

If It's Tuesday, This Must Be Belgium (1969)*** Suzanne Pleshette, Mildred Natwick, Norman Fell. If you've ever been on a package European tour (and even if you haven't) you'll find plenty of laughs in this saga about a group of travelers who race through seven countries in eighteen days. (Dir: Mel Stuart, 98 mins.)

If It's Tuesday, It Still Must Be Belgium (MTV 1987)** Claude Akins, Lou Liberatore, Courteney Cox, Bruce Weitz. This lame telepic concerns a busload of tourists searching for the driver's missing daughter. (Dir: Bob Sweeney, 96 mins.)

If I Were Free (1933)*** Irene Dunne, Clive Brook, Nils Asther, Vivian Tobin, Henry Stephenson, Laura Hope Crews. Affecting romantic drama of Dunne and Brook trying to extricate themselves from unhappy marriages to others and find happiness together. (Dir: Elliott Nugent, 66 mins.)

If I Were King (1938)*** Ronald Colman, Basil Rathbone, Frances Dee. You'll love Colman as the swashbuckling, romantic François Villon, who, in real life, was a rogue but, in reel life, is a lovable hero. (Dir: Frank Lloyd, 110 mins.)

If I Were Rich—See: *Cash*

If Looks Could Kill (1986)*½ Kim Lambert, Tim Gail, Alan Fisler, Jamie Gillis, Jeanne Marie. Would-be filmmaker takes a job spying on a female bank employee suspected of embezzling. Of course, he immediately falls in love with her in this predictable cut-rate *noir* film. (Dir: Chuck Vincent, 90 mins.)†

If Looks Could Kill (1991)**½ Richard Grieco, Linda Hunt, Roger Rees, Robin Bartlett, Geraldine James, Michael Siberry. Light-hearted comedy-adventure about an American high school student (Grieco) in France with his French class, who's mistaken for a CIA spy and becomes involved in a zany plot to control Europe's monetary system. Hunt, Rees, and Bartlett are all delicious in strong character roles. (Dir: William Dear, 89 mins.)†

I Found Stella Parish (1935)**½ Kay Francis, Ian Hunter, Paul Lukas. Francis's sultry beauty and refined acting style redeemed many a weepie. Here she fears being unmasked after she emigrates to the U.S., hoping to forget her past life. (Dir: Mervyn LeRoy, 84 mins.)

If Things Were Different (MTV 1980)*** Suzanne Pleshette, Don Murray, Tony Roberts, Artie Johnson. Compelling domestic drama with superb acting. Ms. Pleshette is carving out a new life for herself and her two children after her husband (Murray) suffers a nervous breakdown that leaves him catatonic. (Dir: Robert Lewis, 104 mins.)

If Tomorrow Comes (MTV 1971)** Patty Duke, Frank Liu. A tearjerker in which Miss Duke plays a young lady who falls for, and secretly marries, a Japanese-American in southern California a few days before Pearl Harbor. (Dir: George McGowan, 73 mins.)

If Winter Comes (1947)* Walter Pidgeon, Deborah Kerr. Terrible, confused soap opera story that is an insult to its cast. (Dir: Victor Saville, 97 mins.)

If You Could Only Cook (1935)**½ Herbert Marshall, Jean Arthur, Leo Carrillo, Lionel Stander, Gene Morgan. Very funny offbeat comedy, with an unusual teaming of Marshall and Arthur posing as servants of a gangster. (Dir: William A. Seiter, 70 mins.)

If You Could See What I Hear (Canada, 1981)** Marc Singer, R. H. Thomson, Sarah Torgov, Shari Belafonte Harper. Film biography of blind composer Tom Sullivan, marred by a determinedly cheery, insubstantial tone. (Dir: Eric Till, 103 mins.)†

If You Knew Susie (1948)** Eddie Cantor, Joan Davis. Vaudeville team discover a famous ancestor and go to Washington to collect seven billion dollars the government owes them. Mild comedy with music. (Dir: Gordon Douglas, 90 mins.)

Igor and the Lunatics (1985)½ Joseph Eero, Joe Niola, T. J. Michaels. Worthless amateur horror movie about a cult of cannibalistic killers. (Dirs: Billy Parolini, Tom Doran, Brendan Faulkner, 79 mins.)†

I Hate Actors! (France, 1987)*½ Jean Poiret, Michel Blanc, Bernard Blier, Michel Galabru, Pauline Lafont. A 1944 novel about the film business by the great Hollywood screenwriter Ben Hecht becomes a Gallic comic misfire. (Dir: Gerard Krawczyk, 91 mins.)

I Hate Your Guts—See: *Shame* (1962)

I Heard the Owl Call My Name (MTV 1973)*** Tom Courtenay, Dean Jagger, Marianne Jones, Paul Stanley, George Clutesi. A touching, unpretentious drama about an ailing young priest assigned to an Indian fishing village outside of Vancouver, British Columbia. (Dir: Daryl Duke, 74 mins.)

I Hired a Contract Killer (Finland, 1990)***½ Jean-Pierre Léaud, Margi Clarke, Kenneth Colley, Trevor Bowen, Immogen Clare,

Nicky Tesco, Charles Cork. First English language film by director Aki Kaurismaki is a stunning exploration of nihilism about a meek office worker (a brilliant Léaud) who hasn't the courage to kill himself, so he hires his own hit man to do the job. A must see! (Dir: Aki Kaurismaki, 81 mins.)

Ike: The War Years (MTV 1978)*** Robert Duvall, Lee Remick, Dana Andrews, J. D. Cannon, Ian Richardson, Laurence Luckinbill. This wartime tale combines rousing action sequences with a convincingly rendered romance between General Eisenhower and his driver, Kay Summersby. Originally a six-hour miniseries; 291 minutes on video. (Dirs: Melville Shavelson, Boris Sagal, 200 mins.)†

I Killed Einstein, Gentlemen (Czechoslovakia, 1970)*** Jiri Sovak, Jana Brezhova, Lubomir Lipsky, Iva Janzurova. Sci-fi spoof from Oldrich Lipsky, director of hit western satire *Lemonade Joe*. A team of scientists is sent into the past to kill Einstein and alter the course of modern physics. Delightful time-travel comedy. (95 mins.)

Ikiru (Japan, 1952)**** Takashi Shimura, Nabuo Kaneko, Kyoko Seki, Miki Odagiri. Director Akira Kurosawa has fashioned a haunting portrait of a lonely man who has spent his life working as a civil servant, seen his wife die, alienated his son, and discovers he is dying of cancer. Determined to give his last days over to enjoying himself, he finds it is not enough, and pours his energy into getting a playground built on the site of a sewage dump. (143 mins.)†

I Know My First Name Is Steven (MTV 1989)*** Corin Nemec, Cindy Pickett, John Ashton, Arliss Howard, Luke Edwards, Gregg Henry, Ray Walston, Barry Corbin. Gruelling true story of a seven-year-old boy who was kidnapped and held for seven years by a child abuser who told him that his parents had given him away. Second half of the film is equally dramatic in detailing the difficulties the boy had in readjusting to his family when he finally returned. (Dir: Larry Elikann, 192 mins.)

I Know Where I'm Going (Great Britain, 1945)**** Wendy Hiller, Roger Livesey. An enchanting, touching romance about a rich girl on her way to marry an unwanted suitor, who runs away and finds true love on an island in the Scottish Hebrides. Hiller is an irresistible delight. (Dir: Michael Powell, 91 mins.)†

I Know Why the Caged Bird Sings (MTV 1979)*** Diahann Carroll, Ruby Dee, Esther Rolle, Madge Sinclair. Good biopic based on Maya Angelou's poetic reminiscences. Young Maya and her brother

504

are shuttled between their paternal grandmother in Arkansas and their divorced mother in St. Louis. Rolle and Sinclair are memorable. (Dir: Fielder Cook, 104 mins.)†

Il Bidone—See: **Swindle, The**

I Led Two Lives—See: **Glen or Glenda**

Il Grido—See: **Outcry, The**

I Like Money (Great Britain, 1961)** Peter Sellers, Nadia Gray, Herbert Lom. Sellers, as an honest schoolteacher who learns that dishonesty pays off. Sellers makes the mistake of directing himself, resulting in a slow, stiff ironic comedy. (97 mins.)

I Like Your Nerve (1931)** Douglas Fairbanks, Jr., Loretta Young, Edmund Breon, Henry Kolker, Boris Karloff. Light adventure-romance has young Fairbanks falling for Hispanic beauty Young and shaking up South America to get her. Good of this kind, but nothing special. (Dir: William McGann, 69 mins.)

I Live for Love (1935)** Dolores Del Rio, Everett Marshall, Guy Kibbee, Allen Jenkins, Herbert Cavanaugh, Berton Churchill. Mild musical, directed by Busby Berkeley, of Latin American actress Del Rio and street singer Marshall falling in love but separated by the demands of their very different careers. Del Rio comes off better than Marshall in this standard musical that lacks any memorable songs. (64 mins.)

I Live in Fear (Japan, 1955)*** Eiko Miyoshi, Toshiro Mifune, Haruko Togo, Yutaka Sada. Japanese factory owner (Mifune in a typically superb performance) wants to sell everything and move to Brazil. His family, fearful of losing share of his wealth, tries to have him committed. A tragic-comedy of the highest order about old age and greed. (Dir: Akira Kurosawa, 113 mins.)

I Live My Life (1935)** Joan Crawford, Brian Aherne, Frank Morgan, Aline MacMahon, Eric Blore. Dated, cottoncandy star vehicle. Crawford's a society dame; Aherne's a dedicated archaeologist. Naturally, they dig up romance in a plot that might date back to the Etruscans. (Dir: Woody S. Van Dyke, 81 mins.)

I'll Be Home for Christmas (MTV 1988) **½ Hal Holbrook, Eva Marie Saint, Whip Hubley, Courtney Cox, Nancy Travis, Jason Oliver. Heartwarming Christmas tale set in 1944 Maine, where Holbrook and Saint await the return of their children, including two soldier sons. (Dir: Marvin Chomsky, 96 mins.)

I'll Be Seeing You (1944)*** Ginger Rogers, Joseph Cotten, Shirley Temple, Spring Byington, Tom Tully, Chill Wills, John Derek. A wounded vet on furlough meets and falls in love with a convicted killer also out on Christmas furlough. This sort of wartime hokum is emotionally engaging. (Dir: William Dieterle, 85 mins.)

I'll Be Yours (1947)**½ Deanna Durbin, Tom Drake, Adolphe Menjou. Another light and gay Deanna Durbin comedy about a nice girl searching for a niche in the big city. Remake of The Good Fairy, 1935. (Dir: William A. Seiter, 93 mins.)

I'll Cry Tomorrow (1955)***½ Susan Hayward, Richard Conte, Jo Van Fleet, Don Taylor, Eddie Albert. Superb drama based on Lillian Roth's bold and frank story of her days as an alcoholic and her fight to conquer the dreaded disease. Miss Hayward has never been better and she's matched every step of the way by Jo Van Fleet as her bewildered mother. (Dir: Daniel Mann, 117 mins.)†

Illegal (1955)** Edward G. Robinson, Nina Foch. Well-acted but poorly scripted story of the rackets and one couple's involvement. Jayne Mansfield has a brief scene. (Dir: Lewis Allen, 88 mins.)

Illegal Entry (1949)**½ Howard Duff, Marta Toren, George Brent. Fast-paced action drama about the undercover agents who crack open a smuggling operation that deals with illicit border traffic between Mexico and the United States. (Dir: Frederick de Cordova, 84 mins.)

Illegally Yours (1987)* Rob Lowe, Colleen Camp, Kenneth Mars, Harry Carey Jr., Kim Myers. One-time wunderkind director Peter Bogdanovich hits rock bottom with this forced pastiche of screwball comedy clichés. Lowe, miscast as a straight-arrow college dropout, reports for jury duty and finds the defendant is a girl he's had a crush on since the first grade. (102 mins.)†

I'll Get By (1950)**½ June Haver, Gloria De Haven, Dennis Day, William Lundigan. Pleasant musical about a couple of song-pluggers and a singing sister act. Remake of Tin Pan Alley. (Dir: Richard Sale, 83 mins.)

Illicit (1931)**½ Barbara Stanwyck, Ricardo Cortez, James Rennie, Natalie Moorhead, Charles Butterworth, Joan Blondell. Glum romance about the marriage problems of a girl with a past; good cast finds it impossible to strike a spark from dead weight Rennie. Remade, more or less, as Ex-Lady. (Dir: Archie Mayo, 81 mins.)

Illicit Interlude—See: **Summer Interlude**

I'll Never Forget What's 'Is Name (Great Britain, 1967)***½ Oliver Reed, Orson Welles, Carol White. Incisive portrait of a man disillusioned with his shallow life, and the failure of his efforts to change. Alternately witty and uncomfortably real. (Dir: Michael Winner, 99 mins.)

I'll Never Forget You (Great Britain, 1951)**½ Tyrone Power, Ann Blyth, Michael Rennie. Based on the play Berkeley

Square, this charming romantic adventure concerns a scientist who goes back to the 18th-century and relives one of his ancestors' adventures. (Dir: Roy Baker, 90 mins.)

I'll See You in My Dreams (1952)*** Doris Day, Danny Thomas. A romantic biopic on the rise and success of songwriter Gus Kahn. Thomas is quite believable as the songsmith. (Dir: Michael Curtiz, 110 mins.)

I'll Take Romance (1937)**½ Grace Moore, Melvyn Douglas, Helen Westley, Stuart Erwin, Margaret Hamilton. Pretty good comedy-romance with Moore as a diva (naturally) and Douglas as her fast-talking press agent; good music and lovely singing. (Dir: Edward H. Griffith, 85 mins.)

I'll Take Sweden (1965)**½ Bob Hope, Tuesday Weld, Frankie Avalon. For hope fans. Bob is Tuesday Weld's daddy, and he whisks her off to Sweden when her romance with Frankie Avalon reaches the serious stage. However, things get hotter in Sweden when Jeremy Slate pops into Tuesday's life and Dina Merrill becomes interested in Hope. (Dir: Frederick de Cordova, 96 mins.)

Illumination (Poland, 1973)***½ Stanislaw Latallo, Edward Zebrowski, Malgorzata Pritulak, Monika Denisiewicz-Olbrzychska. Young scientist, an ardent supporter of the theory of rational analysis, has his beliefs shattered by the accidental death of his best friend and his own troublesome affair with an older woman. Director Krzysztof Zanussi, a Warsaw University physics and philosophy graduate, has made a difficult but engrossing film about ethics and intellectual thought. (91 mins.)

Illusions (MTV 1983)*½ Karen Valentine, Brian Murray, Ben Masters, Wayne Tippit, Joe Silver, Mark Walker. Mystery piece rambles along, often stumbling in its own web of intrigue. Valentine is a fashion designer traveling around Europe trying to unravel the double life of her recently deceased husband. Most of the scenic locations were actually filmed around Montreal. (Dir: Walter Grauman, 96 mins.)

Illustrated Man, The (1969)***½ Rod Steiger, Claire Bloom, Robert Drivas. Interesting allegorical morality play based on a story by sci-fi writer Ray Bradbury. Scene is a rural camping ground in 1933, where a young man (Drivas) meets a completely tattooed fellow (Steiger). The tattoos each represent a story and as Drivas looks at them, they come to life. (Dir: Jack Smight, 103 mins.)†

Il Mare (Italy, 1962)***½ Umberto Orsini, François Prevost, Dino Mele. Unusual drama about three lonely people whose lives mesh at a house on the bleak Isle of Capri in the dead of winter. An actor
506

meets a confused young alcoholic man, and they in turn become friends with a woman who has arrived to sell the house in which they are staying. Poignant film about physical and emotional isolation, with outstanding acting and magnificent black and white photography. (Dir: Giuseppe Patroni Griffi, 110 mins.)

I Love All of You (France, 1980)**½ Catherine Deneuve, Jean-Louis Trintignant, Gerard Depardieu, Serge Gainsbourg, Alain Souchard. A kaleidoscopic view of one woman's relationships. Deneuve is the lucky lady (or is she?) who relives her three past love affairs—with songwriter Gainsbourg, kindly schnook Trintignant, and rock star Depardieu—as she embarks upon a new one with widower Souchard. (Dir: Claude Berri, 103 mins.)†

I Love a Mystery (1945)** Jim Bannon, Nina Foch, George Macready. The first of a short-lived series of films based on the popular radio series. Has a suitably bizarre plot about a secret society that wants to secure the head of a businessman because he is a dead ringer for their deceased founder. (Dir: Henry Levin, 70 mins.)

I Love a Mystery (MTV 1973)** Ida Lupino, David Hartman, Les Crane, Terry-Thomas, Don Knotts. Three detectives fly to a private island to flush out missing billionaire. (Dir: Leslie Stevens, 99 mins.)

I Love a Soldier (1944)**½ Paulette Goddard, Sonny Tufts, Mary Treen, Walter Sande, Ann Doran, Beulah Bondi, Barry Fitzgerald, Hugh Beaumont. Wartime romance, with young marrieds trying to get to know each other despite separations. Quite an interesting slant on the period. (Dir: Mark Sandrich, 106 mins.)

I Loved a Woman (1933)** Edward G. Robinson, Kay Francis, Genevieve Tobin, J. Farrell MacDonald, Henry Kolker, Robert Barrat. Weird, dark attempt to make an "arty" film, which happened at Warner Bros. every now and then. A businessman is unhinged by his love for a glamorous opera singer; the script doesn't measure up to its ambitions, for worthwhile viewing. (Dir: Alfred E. Green, 91 mins.)

I Love Melvin (1953)**½ Donald O'Connor, Debbie Reynolds. A happy musical with O'Connor cast as a top magazine photographer and Miss Reynolds as a Broadway chorus girl. (Dir: Don Weis, 76 mins.)

I Love My Wife (1970)**½ Elliott Gould, Brenda Vaccaro. Funny but uneven comedy dealing with modern marriage. It's all about what happens to Gould and Vaccaro's matrimonial bliss when hubby starts to roam and rove. (Dir: Mel Stuart, 95 mins.) †

I Love N.Y. (1987)* Scott Baio, Kelly Van Der Velden, Christopher Plummer, Virna Lisi, Jennifer O'Neill, Jerry Orbach. Dumb script and ragged direction derail dismal romantic comedy of Baio, an eager young photographer from N.Y.C.'s Little Italy, in love with the vapid daughter of Broadway superstar. Originally 110 minutes. (Dir: "Alan Smithee" [Gioanni Bozzacchi], 100 mins.) †

I Love Trouble (1948)*** Franchot Tone, Janet Blair. Tough private eye runs into foul play while searching for a missing girl. Smooth, speedy, well-done mystery. (Dir: S. Sylvan Simon, 94 mins.)

I Love You (Brazil, 1981)* Sonia Braga, Paulo Cesar Pereio, Vera Fisher, Tarcisio Meria. One of Brazilian sex goddess Braga's more serious movies; this tale of two recently divorced people taking out their problems in an affair with each other is pretentious and turgid. (Dir: Arnaldo Jabor, 102 mins.) †

I Love You Again (1940)*** Myrna Loy, William Powell. Lots of fun in this silly comedy about a nice, dull husband who, after a bump on the head, recovers from amnesia and becomes his true self, a slick con man. (Dir: W. S. Van Dyke, 99 mins.)

I Love You, Alice B. Toklas (1968)*** Peter Sellers, Leigh Taylor-Young, Jo Van Fleet. A frequently amusing original comedy. Sellers is at his best as a mother-dominated Los Angeles lawyer who leaves his fiancée at the altar not once but twice to seek "the better things in life," as he puts it. (Dir: Hy Averback, 93 mins.) †

I Love You, Goodbye (MTV 1974)**½ Hope Lange, Earl Holliman. Muddled story about a housewife and mother of eighteen years who suddenly craves more meaning in her life and leaves the whole kit and kaboodle to find herself. (Dir: Sam O'Steen, 74 mins.)

I Love You Perfect (MTV 1989)*** Susan Dey, Anthony Jon Dennison, Alley Mills, Tim Scott, Ric Reed. Poignant story about an eccentric woman who seems to have a charmed life until cancer takes over; fine performances. (Dir: Harry Winer, 96 mins.)

I Love You Rosa (Israel, 1971)*** Michal Bat-Adam, Moshe Tal, Avner Heziahou, Gabi Otterman, Yossef Shiloah, Levana Finkelstein. Sentimental comedy-drama about newly widowed woman who, by Jewish law, becomes the property of the brother of her late husband. Unfortunately the brother is an eleven-year-old who is determined to carry out his duties of love and companionship. (Dir: Moshe Mizrahi, 91 mins.)

I Love You to Death (1990)*** Kevin Kline, Tracey Ullman, River Phoenix, Joan Plowright, William Hurt, Keanu Reeves, James Gammon, Victoria Jackson, Miriam Margolyes. Woman discovers her husband has been cheating on her, decides to kill him with the help of her mother and a young coworker. Hilariously broad characterizations and low-key black comedy (the husband proves to be harder to kill than Rasputin). (Dir: Lawrence Kasdan, 96 mins.) †

Il Posto—See: **Sound of Trumpets, The**

I, Madman (1989)*** Jenny Wright, Clayton Rohner. Woman finds an especially scary book in an old bookstore and is compelled to read it, even though the madman she is reading about seems to be haunting her real life. Fun horror movie actually delivers a fair share of shocks along with some spiffy special effects. (Dir: Tibor Takacs, 95 mins.) †

Image, The (MTV 1990)*** Albert Finney, John Mahoney, Kathy Baker, Swoosie Kurtz, Spalding Gray, Wendie Jo Sperber, David Clennon, Marsha Mason. Finney is perfectly cast as the popular star of a "60 Minutes"-type show who in his eagerness to get a story cuts a few corners. When he oversteps his bounds in exposing a savings and loan scam, his confidence begins to ebb. Finney's climactic on-air confession is riveting. (Dir: Peter Werner, 90 mins.) †

Imagemaker, The (1986)** Michael Nouri, Anne Twomey, Jerry Orbach, Jessica Harper, Farley Granger, Richard Bauer. An imaginative but jumbled film about a political media consultant and his strained private life. Marred by a script riddled with credibility problems. (Dir: Hal Weiner, 93 mins.) †

Images (1972)**½ Susannah York, Rene Auberjonois. Peculiar film about a schizophrenic young woman. Director-author Robert Altman tried to create suspense by not identifying the woman's images as rooted in either illusion or fact. Compensations include the camerawork by Vilmos Zsigmond. (101 mins.)

Imagine: John Lennon (1988)**½ Lennon himself probably wouldn't have liked this whitewashed biography that concentrates on the positive aspects of his life while ignoring his dark side, just as it favors his mawkish pop tunes over his more serious music. Still, required viewing for fans due to the extensive home-movie footage of Lennon at work and play. (Dir: Andrew Solt, 103 mins.) †

I'm All Right, Jack (Great Britain, 1960)**** Ian Carmichael, Peter Sellers, Terry-Thomas. Screamingly funny satire on labor-management relations in England, as an inept young man finds himself caught between the two in trying to run a factory. Sellers is priceless as an oafish labor leader, and the entire cast catches the spirit of the fun. Recommended. (Dirs: John and Roy Boulting, 104 mins.)†

I-Man (MTV 1986)** Scott Bakula, Ellen Bry, Joey Cramer, John Bloom, Herschel Bernardi. A superhero pilot that never flew. There are actually three superpowered beings in this Disney telefilm: Bakula, son Cramer, and their pet pooch all are transformed into walking wonders after they take a whiff of magic gas. Like most Disney made-for-TV product, amiable and unnecessary. (Dir: Corey Allen, 96 mins.)

I Married a Centerfold (MTV 1984)**½ Teri Copley, Tim Daly, Diane Ladd, Bert Remsen, Todd Sussman. While this might sound like another insipid TV movie, the story of one man's pursuit of a beautiful "centerfold" is light, breezy entertainment. (Dir: Peter Werner, 104 mins.)†

I Married a Communist—See: **Woman on Pier 13, The**

I Married a Monster from Outer Space (1958)**½ Tom Tryon, Gloria Talbott. The title tells all, as a young bride discovers her husband is really a being from another planet intent on conquering earth. As these sci-fi thrillers go, not bad; has a certain amount of style. (Dir: Gene Fowler, Jr., 78 mins.)†

I Married an Angel (1942)** Jeanette MacDonald, Nelson Eddy, Binnie Barnes, Edward Everett Horton. Rodgers and Hart musical is slaughtered in an inept screen treatment. Banker Eddy dreams about courting an angel (MacDonald) and wakes up to find her a guest in his house. (Dir: W. S. Van Dyke II, 84 mins.)†

I Married a Shadow (France, 1982)**½ Nathalie Baye, Francis Huster, Richard Bohringer, Madeleine Robinson, Guy Trejan. Like the superior 1949 *No Man of Her Own*, this French thriller is based on a Cornell Woolrich tale about two pregnant women, one married and wealthy and one (Baye) poor and abandoned by her lover. When their train crashes, Baye is mistaken for the dead rich woman who was en route to meet her husband's parents for the first time. (Dir: Robin Davis, 110 mins.)†

I Married a Witch (1942)**½ Fredric March, Veronica Lake, Cecil Kellaway, Robert Benchley, Susan Hayward. A luscious witch returns to wreak mischief on the descendants of her persecutors. Whimsical fun. (Dir: René Clair, 76 mins.)†

I Married a Woman (1956)*½ George Gobel, Jessie Royce Landis, Diana Dors. Lonesome George Gobel plays an advertising man perplexed by the problems of coming up with an ad campaign and keeping his wife happy. (Dir: Hal Kanter, 84 mins.)†

I Married Wyatt Earp (MTV 1983)**½ Marie Osmond, Bruce Boxleitner, John Bennett Perry, Ross Martin, Alison Arngrim. One more Osmond vanity production, this one features Marie, who comes off nicely in this often sentimental oater. The plot recounts the real-life travails of the young Jewish woman who married the noted gunslinger and even carried on an affair with his biggest rival. (Dir: Michael O'Herlihy, 96 mins.)

I'm Dancing as Fast as I Can (1982)**½ Jill Clayburgh, Dianne Wiest, Joe Pesci, James Satorius, Ellen Greene, Geraldine Page, Nicol Williamson. Harrowing drama of a successful professional woman who makes television documentaries and who is falling apart when she tries to stop relying on Valium, on which she's been hooked. (Dir: Jack Hofsiss, 106 mins.)†

I'm Dangerous Tonight (MCTV 1990)** Anthony Perkins, Madchën Amick, Dee Wallace Stone, Natalie Schafer, Mary Frann, Daisy Hall. Disappointing supernatural tale by third director Hooper (*Poltergeist*, *Texas Chainsaw Massacre*). A diabolical, ancient cloak altered into a red dress proceeds to sensually possess all who wear it, leading to murder and madness. Good production values and a better-than-average cast enhance this otherwise weak horror offering. (Dir: Tobe Hooper, 96 mins.)†

I Met a Murderer (Great Britain, 1939)*** James Mason, Pamela Kellino. Goaded into murdering his shrewish wife, a farmer flees from the police, is sheltered by a young girl. Brooding, suspenseful melodrama, artistically done. (Dir: Roy Kellino, 78 mins.)

I Met Him in Paris (1937)**½ Claudette Colbert, Melvyn Douglas, Robert Young, Lee Bowman, Mona Barrie, Fritz Feld. Slight but frothy romantic tale of a girl who's got Tom, Dick, and Harry problems in the City of Eternal Light. (Dir: Wesley Ruggles, 86 mins.)

I Met My Love Again (1938)** Joan Bennett, Henry Fonda, Dame May Whitty, Louis Platt. Turgid tale of an impressionable girl running off with a wily seducer. (Dirs: Arthur Ripley, Joshua Logan, 77 mins.)

I'm Going to Be Famous (1982)* Dick Sargent, Meredith MacRae, Vivian Blaine. Utilizing directorial set-ups not glimpsed since the early talkies and dishing out show biz clichés you may have forgotten, this incredible film should only be experienced after one gets a "Backstage Movie" innoculation. The plot concerns show biz stereotypes auditioning for a plum stage role. (Dir: Paul Leder, 96 mins.)

I'm Gonna Git You Sucka (1988)**½ Keenen Ivory Wayans, Bernie Casey, Isaac Hayes,

Jim Brown. Sporadically funny parody of seventies blaxploitation films, with Wayans (who also wrote and directed) assembling an all-star hit patrol to clean up the ghetto. (90 mins.)†

Imitation General (1958)*** Glenn Ford, Red Buttons, Taina Elg. Fast-paced service comedy that treats the subject of war lightly and makes heroes of buffoons. Buttons steals every scene he's in with his very funny portrayal of a corporal who is on a military stratagem that has Master Sergeant Glenn Ford masquerading as a general. (Dir: George Marshall, 88 mins.)

Imitation of Life (1934)*** Claudette Colbert, Warren William, Rochelle Hudson, Louise Beavers, Fredi Washington, Ned Sparks. Far more sentimental than Douglas Sirk's later, icy version of this Fannie Hurst soap opera, John Stahl's film about a working girl (Claudette Colbert) who makes good and about Colbert's black maid (Louise Beavers) and her daughter (Fredi Washington) who passes for white, is believable in the context of thirties melodrama and as rich visually as Stahl's other thirties triumphs over implausibility, *Back Street* and *Magnificent Obsession*. (106 mins.)

Imitation of Life (1959)***½ Lana Turner, John Gavin, Sandra Dee, Dan O'Herlihy, Susan Kohner, Juanita Moore, Troy Donahue, Robert Alda. Epic soap opera, an incredibly lush-looking melodrama drenched in improbable glamour and mood music at every turn. *Imitation* is an elaboration on the more modest 1934 weepie based on Fanny Hurst's novel about two mothers struggling to raise their daughters. (Dir: Douglas Sirk, 124 mins.)†

Immediate Family (1989)* Glenn Close, James Woods, Kevin Dillon, Mary Stuart Masterson, Linda Darlow. Insufferable, predictable comedy-drama about childless yuppie couple (Close and Woods, both surprisingly bad) adopting yet-unborn baby from aimless young folks (Dillon and Masterson) who start to have second thoughts. Film's "you can't be happy without a child" theme is cloyingly overwrought. Lousy script by Barbara Benedek steals shamelessly from *The Big Chill* (which she co-wrote). (Dir: Jonathan Kaplan, 95 mins.)†

Immigrants, The (MTV 1978)** Stephen Macht, Sharon Gless, Aimee Eccles, Richard Anderson, Susan Strasberg, Pernell Roberts, John Saxon. Another Howard Fast novel becomes grist for the TV-movie mill in this overlong, rags-to-riches story about an Italian boy who, not content to put his imprint on the shipping world, yearns for the respectability of San Francisco's high society set. (Dir: Alan J. Levi, 200 mins.)

Immoral Mr. Teas, The (1959)**½ Bill Teas, Ann Peters, Marilyn Wesley. The first of an entire subgenre, the "nudie-cutie" movie (and one of the very few that has remained in circulation) this first feature by filmmaker Russ Meyer is best described as "Jacques Tati turns voyeur." After receiving anesthesia from the dentist, the Hulot-like Mr. Teas has a strange reaction: all the women he sees appear to be naked. Cute and harmless; a one-of-a-kind nostalgia piece. (62 mins.)†

Immortal, The (MTV 1969)**½ Christopher George, Carol Lynley. The fairly original story was the pilot film for a TV series. Christopher George is cast as a younglooking fortyish test-driver-mechanic who discovers he has a unique blood type that slows down his aging process almost to a halt and keeps him from contracting diseases. (Dir: Joseph Sargent, 75 mins.)

Immortal Sergeant, The (1943)*** Henry Fonda, Maureen O'Hara, Thomas Mitchell, Allyn Joslyn, Reginald Gardiner. Solid drama as a corporal finds himself unprepared for the command thrust upon him in Africa. (Dir: John Stahl, 91 mins.)†

Immortal Story, The (France, 1968) *** Orson Welles, Jeanne Moreau, Roger Coggio. Based on the story by Isak Dinesen, this intriguing film has been adapted and directed by Orson Welles, who plays an elderly merchant in the Portuguese colony of Macao on the coast of China during the end of the 19th century. (63 mins.)

I'm No Angel (1933)***½ Mae West, Cary Grant, Edward Arnold, Gertrude Michael, Kent Taylor. Mae West is the lion tamer, but she really wants to tame Cary Grant in this racy hilarious comedy. (Dir: Wesley Ruggles, 87 mins.)

I, Mobster (1959)**½ Steve Cochran, Lita Milan. A criminal tells his story—from a young punk to a big-time mobster. (Dir: Roger Corman, 80 mins.)†

I, Monster (Great Britain, 1971)*** Christopher Lee, Peter Cushing, Mike Raven. Adaptation of Robert Louis Stevenson's *Dr. Jekyll and Mr. Hyde*. Lee gives real depth to the unfortunate creature of the title, and his end is harrowing. (Dir: Stephen Weeks, 75 mins.)

Impact (1949)*** Brian Donlevy, Ella Raines, Helen Walker, Charles Coburn, Anna May Wong, Mae Marsh. Very interesting, twisty thriller, with a disaffected wife planning to kill her husband—but everything goes wrong. Fine performances and an excellent, tight script make this compelling. (Dir: Arthur Lubin, 111 mins.)†

Impasse (1969)***½ Burt Reynolds, Anne Francis. An adventure film of the sort in which fearless heroes deal with both women and danger at about the same emotional level . . . two steps above stoicism. The plot concerns buried WWII treasure in the Philippines. (Dir: Richard Benedict, 96 mins.)

Impatient Heart, The (MTV 1975)**½ Carrie Snodgress, Michael Brandon, Marian Hailey, Michael Constantine, Hector Elizondo. Well-acted but superficially scripted film about a social worker who takes her cases too much to heart but can't untangle her own love affairs. (Dir: John Badham, 104 mins.)

Imperfect Lady, The (1947)**½ Ray Milland, Teresa Wright. In order to aid a gentleman who shielded her, a woman must admit an indiscretion and risk exposing her husband to shame and ruin. (Dir: Lewis Allen, 97 mins.)

Importance of Being Earnest, The (Great Britain, 1952)**** Michael Redgrave, Edith Evans, Dorothy Tutin, Joan Greenwood, Margaret Rutherford. The Oscar Wilde play is unlikely to ever be mounted with a more impeccable array of performers. Wilde's play is probably the most perfect British comedy since the Restoration. (Dir: Anthony Asquith, 95 mins.)†

Impossible Spy, The (MCTV 1987)** John Shea, Eli Wallach, Michal Bat-Adam. Taut drama about Elie Cohen, an Israeli spy who, in the sixties, infiltrated the upper ranks of the Syrian government and helped Israel defeat them in the Six-Day War. (Dir: Jim Goddard, 89 mins.)†

Impossible Years, The (1968)*½ David Niven, Lola Albright, Chad Everett, Christina Ferrare. Stage hit about a psychiatrist who has his problems with his offspring turned into a leering, unattractive film. (Dir: Michael Gordon, 91 mins.)

Imposter, The (1944)**½ Jean Gabin, Richard Whorf, Allyn Joslyn, Ellen Drew, Peter Van Eyck, Ralph Morgan, Eddie Quillan, John Qualen, Milburn Stone. Patriotic WWII drama has a prisoner taking another man's identity to be able to serve in the armed forces; nothing special. (Dir: Julien Duivier, 95 mins.)

Imposter, The (MTV 1984)*½ Anthony Geary, Lorna Patterson, Billy Dee Williams. Con man Geary becomes the principal at a high school where his ex-girlfriend teaches. His motives become purer when he stays on to tackle the school's drug problem. (Dir: Michael Pressman, 96 mins.)†

Impromptu (1990)*** Judy Davis, Hugh Grant, Mandy Patinkin, Bernadette Peters, Julian Sands, Emma Thompson, Anna Massey. Charming comedy-drama about the 19th-century romance between George Sand (Davis) and Frederic Chopin (Grant). Good performances, particularly from Davis as the mannish, assertive author. Impressive directorial debut from acclaimed Broadway director Lapine (*Into the Woods, Sunday in the Park With George*). (Dir: James Lapine, 109 mins.)†

Improper Channels (Canada, 1979)**½ Alan Arkin, Mariette Hartley, Monica Parker, Harry Ditson. Arkin's slightly neurotic brand of humor sparks this uneven, often silly farce about an estranged couple who try various means to recover their daughter after she is mistakenly shanghaied by a meddlesome social worker. (Dir: Eric Till, 91 mins.)†

Improper Conduct (France, 1984)***½ Famed cinematographer Nestor Almendros and director Orlando Jiminez-Leal, both exiles from Fidel Castro's Cuba, collaborated in the making of this powerful documentary. It specifically indicts the Cuban Revolution's brutal suppression of civil rights among homosexuals and other individualists who offend the macho image of the government. An eloquent, provocative film. (110 mins.)

Impulse (1984)** Meg Tilly, Tim Matheson, Hume Cronyn, John Karlen, Amy Stryker, Bill Baxton. *Impulse* begins dynamically as the ordinary inhabitants of a midwestern town revert to primitive behavior. The story line, based on the Defense Department's development of a toxic substance (which gets into the town's milk supply), is still another film reveling in the possibility of a social breakdown. (Dir: Graham Baker, 91 mins.)†

Impulse (1990)*** Theresa Russell, Jeff Fahey, George Dzunda, Alan Rosenberg, Nicholas Mele. The first half of the *noir*ish excursion through the criminal nightlife of L.A. is languid and low-key, but heats up when undercover vice cop Russell, disguised as a prostitute, acts on her long-suppressed desire to take on one of the johns who approaches her. (Dir: Sondra Locke, 108 mins.)†

Impure Thoughts (1985)*½ Brad Dourif, Lane Davies, Terry Beaver. Four friends meet in purgatory and recall their youths in a Catholic school. Comedy-drama is hit or miss until the end, when the symbolism gets too thick. (Dir: Michael A. Simpson, 87 mins.)†

Inadmissible Evidence (Great Britain, 1968)***½ Nicol Williamson, Eleanor Fazan, Jill Bennett, Gillian Hills. John Osborne's searing stage play about a middle-aged English barrister whose emotional disintegration is unsparingly depicted. Williamson's enormous talents keep the viewer absorbed. (Dir: Anthony Page, 96 mins.)

In a Glass Cage (Spain, 1986)**½ Gunter Meisner, David Sust, Marisa Paredes,

Gisela Echevarria. After WWII, a doctor who had tortured young boys for sexual pleasure in a Nazi concentration camp now lives in an isolated Spanish town, confined to an iron lung. He is visited by a young survivor of the camp who relives episodes from the doctor's diary in front of the now-powerless old man. The film is all but impossible to rate: seriously intended, it has been written and directed with a great deal of skill. But its themes of madness and perversity, and the horrifying way in which they are presented, may make the film unwatchable even for serious cineastes. AKA: **Tras el Cristal.** (Dir: Agustin Villaronga, 112 mins.)†

In a Lonely Place (1950)***½ Humphrey Bogart, Gloria Grahame, Frank Lovejoy. Gripping story of a Hollywood writer who is under suspicion of murder and his strange romance with his female alibi. (Dir: Nicholas Ray, 91 mins.)†

In a Shallow Grave (1988)** Michael Biehn, Maureen Mueller, Patrick Dempsey, Michael Beach. Handsome action star Biehn gives a strong performance in the uncharacteristic role of a hideously scarred WWII vet trying to rebuild his life as a farmer and reignite his romance with a local woman. The film, however, is disappointingly undramatic, lacking the passion and feeling of James Purdy's novel. (Dir: Kenneth Bowser, 92 mins.)†

In a Year of 13 Moons (West Germany, 1980)***½ Volker Spengler, Ingrid Craven, Gottfried John, Elisabeth Trissenaar. Fascinating, grotesque tale of a transsexual and her relationship with the man for whom he/she made the change. (Dir: Rainer Werner Fassbinder, 129 mins.)

In Broad Daylight (MTV 1971)** Richard Boone, Suzanne Pleshette, John Marley, Stella Stevens, Whit Bissell. Larry Cohen wrote this farfetched suspense flick with Boone as a recently blinded actor plotting to murder unfaithful wife Stevens and her lover, his best friend. (Dir: Richard Day, 72 mins.)

In Caliente (1935)*** Dolores Del Rio, Pat O'Brien, Glenda Farrell, Wini Shaw, Judy Canova. Hot and spicy Busby Berkeleyana with some of his inimitable choreography. The fizzy little plot concerns itself with a magazine editor becoming smitten with a fiery dancer after panning her terpsichore. (Dir: Lloyd Bacon, 84 mins.)

In Celebration (Great Britain-Canada, 1974)**** Alan Bates, James Bolam, Brian Cox, Bill Owen. The marvelous combination of director Lindsay Anderson and writer David Storey that produced the memorable *This Sporting Life* is reunited in this powerful adaptation of Storey's play about a coal miner's family in a drab town in northern England. (131 mins.)

Incendiary Blonde (1945)*** Betty Hutton, Arturo de Cordova. Entertaining musical framed in a fictitious screen biography of famous speakeasy hostess, Texas Guinan. Good music from the Prohibition era well done by Miss Hutton. (Dir: George Marshall, 113 mins.)

Inchon (U.S.-Korea, 1982)½ Laurence Olivier, Jacqueline Bisset, Ben Gazzara, Toshiro Mifune, Richard Roundtree. A stupendous failed epic about the Battle of Inchon's significance as a turning point in the Korean War. This Mooniemoolah war movie was financed by Unification Church officials who threw money around, although none of it seems to have landed on-screen. (Dir: Terence Young, 104 mins.)

Incident, The (1967)*** Tony Musante, Martin Sheen, Beau Bridges, Jack Gilford, Thelma Ritter, Ed McMahon, Ruby Dee, Brock Peters. Terror on the New York subway, as two hoodlums molest an assorted group of passengers. May seem overdone to non-New Yorkers, but the basic premise—the passivity of people in times of danger—is disturbingly true. (Dir: Larry Peerce, 107 mins.)†

Incident, The (MTV 1990)*** Walter Matthau, Susan Blakely, Robert Carradine, Peter Firth, Barnard Hughes, Harry Morgan, William Schallert, Ariana Ricards. In 1944, a revered old doctor is found dead near a Nazi POW camp in Colorado. One of the prisoners is accused of the murder, and small-town lawyer Matthau is unwillingly assigned to defend him. Provocative, well-made TV movie with a star turn by Matthau. (Dir: Joseph Sargent, 96 mins.)

Incident at Crestridge (MTV 1981)**½ Eileen Brennan, Pernell Roberts, Bruce Davison, Cliff Osmond. Eileen's a lady sheriff in Wyoming, and she's determined to clean up the corruption of a mayor and his crooked cronies. (Dir: Jud Taylor, 104 mins.)

Incident at Phantom Hill (1966)** Robert Fuller, Jocelyn Lane, Dan Duryea. Assorted group engages in a perilous trek to reclaim gold that had been stolen and hidden years before. Undistinguished western. (Dir: Earl Bellamy, 88 mins.)

Incident in San Francisco (MTV 1971)** Christopher Connelly, Richard Kiley. Another slick pilot film for a proposed big city newspaper TV series. Christopher Connelly plays the brash young reporter on the San Francisco *Times* who gets deeply involved in the plight of a man (Richard Kiley) who accidentally causes the death of a young punk while coming to the aid of an old man. (Dir: Don Medford, 98 mins.)

Incident on a Dark Street (MTV 1973)** James Olson, Robert Pine. Fair entry on U.S. attorneys who try court cases on dope peddling and mobsters in the building-contracting business. (Dir: Buzz Kulik, 73 mins.)

In Cold Blood (1967)***½ Robert Blake, Scott Wilson, John Forsythe. Writer-producer-director Richard Brooks's skillful adaptation of Truman Capote's searing novel about two young ex-cons who slaughtered a Kansas farmer and his family in cold blood. Gripping scenes, played in stark documentary style, build up to the actual murders. (134 mins.)†

Incredible Hulk, The (MTV 1977)** Bill Bixby, Susan Sullivan, Jack Colvin, Lou Ferrigno, Charles Siebert. Based on the Marvel comics about that very big, very green superhero, this standard TV action pic led to the series. After radiation exposure, scientist David Banner can turn into muscleman Lou Ferrigno whenever he gets angry. It sure beats spending all those tedious hours at Jack La Lanne. (Dir: Kenneth Johnson, 104 mins.)†

Incredible Hulk Returns, The (MTV 1988)*½ Bill Bixby, Lou Ferrigno, Eric Kramer. The green-skinned goliath returns and meets up with another Marvel Comics staple, the Mighty Thor. It's too bad that scripter-director Nicholas Corea seems never to have read the comics he's adapting; the Hulk's the same old muscular Mr. Hyde, and Thor is a dull hunk of beefcake. (96 mins.)†

Incredible Invasion, The—See: **Sinister Invasion**

Incredible Journey, The (Canada, 1963)*** Emile Genest, John Drainie. Good family picture with all the Disney components. Two dogs and a cat undertake a 250-mile journey through rough Canadian wilderness, encountering a lynx, a mean farm dog, and an inhospitable bear along the way. (Dir: Fletcher Markle, 80 mins.)†

Incredible Journey of Doctor Meg Laurel, The (MTV 1979)**½ Lindsay Wagner, Jane Wyman. A determined young woman doctor returns to her roots in Appalachia to try to help the backwoods inhabitants, who are leery of modern medicine. She locks horns with the local healer, Granny Arrowroot. (Dir: Guy Green, 156 mins.)†

Incredible Melting Man, The (1978)* Alex Rebar, Burr DeBenning, Myron Healey, Michael Aldredge. Lamentable low-budget sci-fi about a man left liquefying after a sojourn in outer space. (Dir: William Sachs, 86 mins.)†

Incredible Mr. Limpet, The (1964)** Don Knotts, Carole Cook, Jack Weston. Mr. Knotts as the man who wished he was a fish—and got his wish, becoming the

512

Navy's secret weapon during WWII. Fantasy may provide some moments of amusement, but the viewer has to be either a Knotts fan or pretty fish-happy. (Dir: Arthur Lubin, 102 mins.)†

Incredible Petrified World, The (1958)*½ John Carradine, Robert Clarke. Scientists attempt to explore the ocean depths and find themselves trapped beneath the sea. Dull sci-fi thriller will petrify audiences. (Dir: Jerry Warren, 78 mins.)†

Incredible Rocky Mountain Race, The (MTV 1978)** Forrest Tucker, Larry Storch. A broad, slapdash frontier comedy about a feud between Mark Twain and Mike Fink that results in an improbable cross-country race from Missouri to California. (Dir: Jim Conway, 104 mins.)†

Incredible Sarah, The (Great Britain, 1976)* Glenda Jackson, Daniel Massey, Douglas Wilmer. An unqualified disaster about the legendary actress Sarah Bernhardt. (Dir: Richard Fleischer, 106 mins.)†

Incredible Shrinking Man, The (1957)***½ Grant Williams, Randy Stuart. Man is exposed to a mysterious fog, begins to grow smaller and smaller. In the better class of sci-fi thrillers—expert trick photography brings much suspense to scenes of a tiny man pitted against nature. Script always makes it seem believable. (Dir: Jack Arnold, 81 mins.)

Incredible Shrinking Woman, The (1981)**½ Lily Tomlin, Charles Grodin, Henry Gibson, Ned Beatty, Mark Blankfield. Pleasant slapstick. Barraged by a combination of household products, a hapless homemaker (Tomlin) starts to shrink. Any feminist or consumer messages are soft-pedaled, but the film's dollhouse environment is not without its charm. (Dir: Joel Schumacher, 88 mins.)†

Incredible Torture Show, The — See; **Bloodsucking Freaks**

Incredible Two-Headed Transplant, The (1971)½ Bruce Dern, Pat Priest, Casey Kasem, Albert Cole, Berry Kroeger, John Bloom. A libidinous escaped convict literally puts his head on the shoulder of a retarded farmer with the help of transplant specialist Dern. A camp classic. (Dir: Anthony M. Lanza, 88 mins.)†

Incredibly Strange Creatures Who Stopped Living and Became Mixed-Up Zombies, The (1963)**½ Cash Flagg (Ray Dennis Steckler), Atlas King, Sharon Walsh. Improvisatory, hallucinatory, shoestring horror film about a gypsy (with a private collection of acid-scarred zombies) who hypnotizes a man into a series of murders at a carnival. Lazlo Kovacs and Vilmos Zsigmond contributed to the arresting color cinematography. AKA: **Teenage Psycho Meets Bloody Mary.** (Dir: Ray Dennis Steckler, 82 mins.)†

In Crowd, The (1988)** Donovan Leitch, Joe Pantoliano, Jennifer Runyon, Page

Hannah. Early-sixties nostalgists may enjoy this drama about Philadelphia teens whose lives revolve around an "American Bandstand"-like dance show. (Dir: Mark Rosenthal, 95 mins.)†

Incubus (1982)* John Cassavetes, John Ireland, Kerrie Keane, Erin Flannery. Bizarre film about an ugly demon whose favorite pastime is raping and killing women. (Dir: John Hough, 90 mins.)†

In Defense of a Married Man (MTV 1990)**½ Jerry Orbach, Judith Light, Michael Ontkean, Pat Corley, Cynthia Sikes. An original premise gives this murder mystery/courtroom drama added appeal. Light is a successful lawyer who finds herself in the unique and difficult position of defending her husband (Ontkean), charged with murder. (Dir: Joel Oliansky, 96 mins.)

In Defense of Kids (MTV 1983)*** Blythe Danner, Sam Waterston, Joyce Van Patten, Georg Stanford Brown, Beth Ehlers, Tony La Torre, Khalif Bobatoon. An ingratiating story about a lady lawyer up to her fetching eyes with troubled youngsters. (Dir: Gene Reynolds, 104 mins.)

Independence (MTV 1987)*** John Bennett Perry, Isabella Hofmann, Anthony Zerbe. A good western revenge drama about a Civil War vet, Sam Hatch (Perry), whose first family is massacred by marauders. When the outlaws return years later to menace Sheriff Hatch's new family, the lawman gets revenge. (Dir: John Patterson, 104 mins.)

Independence Day (1983)**½ Kathleen Quinlan, David Keith, Frances Sternhagen, Cliff DeYoung, Dianne Wiest. OK study of characters living and wanting to escape from a small southwestern town, should have been better given this cast. Wiest is magnificent as a battered wife. AKA: **Follow Your Dreams**. (Dir: Robert Mandel, 110 mins.)†

Indestructible Man, The (1956)* Lon Chaney, Marian Carr. Executed killer is brought back to life, lights up like a Christmas tree. Whole film short-circuits. (Dir: Jack Pollexfen, 70 mins.)†

Indiana Jones and the Last Crusade (1989) **½ Harrison Ford, Sean Connery, Denholm Elliott, Alison Doody, John Rhys-Davies, Julian Glover, River Phoenix. Indy joins his father's lifelong quest for the Holy Grail, battling Nazis who also want the sacred relic. Connery and Elliott have fun with their characters, but director Steven Spielberg fails to recapture the excitement of the previous Indiana Jones movies. (129 mins.)†

Indiana Jones and the Temple of Doom (1984)*** Harrison Ford, Kate Capshaw, Ke Huy Quan, Phillip Stone, Amrish Puri. This box-office smash, the follow-up to **Raiders of the Lost Ark**, actually takes place one year before "Raiders." Only the next breakneck thrill counts in this actioner, in which Indiana must rescue some missing children kidnapped by religious terrorists in the Orient. When not beleaguered by poison or runaway mining cars, Indy, his girl Willie, and a young sidekick are after a stolen sacred jewel. (Dir: Stephen Spielberg, 118 mins.)†

Indianapolis Speedway (1939)**½ Pat O'Brien, Ann Sheridan, John Payne, Gale Page, Frank McHugh, Granville Bates, Regis Toomey. Lively, entertaining version of the tale of rival racing drivers, with the valuable assistance of the Warner Bros. stock company. (Dir: Lloyd Bacon, 82 mins.)

Indian Fighter, The (1955)**½ Kirk Douglas. Douglas is the whole show in this western drama about Sioux uprisings in the Oregon Territory circa 1870. (Dir: Andre de Toth, 88 mins.)

Indian Love Call—See: **Rose Marie**

Indian Paint (1965)** Johnny Crawford, Jay Silverheels. Oft-told story of an Indian boy's love for a wild colt, pleasantly done. (Dir: Norman Foster, 91 mins.)

Indian Scout (1950)** George Montgomery, Ellen Drew, Philip Reed, Noah Beery, Jr. Fair George Montgomery western. Cowboy versus Indians with the usual result. (Dir: Lew Landers, 71 mins.)

India Song (France, 1975)*** Delphine Seyrig, Mathieu Carriere, Michael Lonsdale, Vernon Dobtcheff, Claude Mann. Though set in Calcutta, this story of boredom, depression, extramarital sex, and mental disintegration was shot in a house outside of Paris. Difficult and demanding film isn't for all tastes. (Dir: Marguerite Duras, 120 mins.)

Indict and Convict (MTV 1974)**½ George Grizzard, Eli Wallach, William Shatner, Myrna Loy. A sensational case of a seamy Los Angeles double murder. When the wife of a deputy district attorney and her lover are found shot, the chief suspect, the D.A., claims to have been miles away at the time. (Dir: Boris Sagal, 100 mins.)

Indiscreet (Great Britain, 1958)**** Cary Grant, Ingrid Bergman, Cecil Parker. Delightfully sophisticated comedy about the on-again, off-again romance between a wealthy American diplomat and a ravishing European actress. Grant and Bergman are perfect as the urbane pair of lovers. (Dir: Stanley Donen, 100 mins.)†

Indiscreet (MTV 1988)*½ Robert Wagner, Lesley-Anne Down, Maggie Henderson. Flaccid remake of the above casts Wagner and Down in the leads. Wagner continues to amaze: all these years on screen, and he still relies strictly on charm, and never on talent. (Dir: Richard Michaels, 96 mins.)

Indiscretion of an American Wife (1954)** Jennifer Jones, Montgomery Clift, Gino Cervi, Richard Beymer. Botched attempt to make a neo-realist art film in the American mode, with David Selznick hiring Vittorio de Sica to direct Jennifer Jones and Montgomery Clift as participants in a brief encounter. None of it works very well, yet it's interesting to watch these artistic minds at work in utter futility. The restored 87 min. version, re-titled *Terminal Station*, is slightly better. (63 mins.)†

In Dracula's Castle (MTV 1973)* Johny Whitaker, Scott Kolden, Clu Gulager, Mills Watson. Standard Disney entry, with wholesome youngsters, making their own "Dracula" movie in a spooky castle, fouling up the plans of a gang of jewel thieves. (Dir: Robert Totten, 96 mins.)

In Enemy Country (1968)**½ Tony Franciosa, Anjanette Comer, Paul Hubschmid. Old-fashioned espionage yarn set during WWII. Tony Franciosa is properly stoic as a French agent who leads a mission into Nazi Germany and manages to carry it off. (Dir: Harry Keller, 107 mins.)

I Never Promised You a Rose Garden (1977)*** Kathleen Quinlan, Bibi Andersson, Signe Hasso, Susan Tyrrell. The popular novel about a high school student battling schizophrenia with the aid of a benevolent psychologist is brought to the screen with force and emotional impact. Quinlan's hypnotic acting as the troubled girl is exemplary. (Dir: Anthony Page, 96 mins.)†

I Never Sang for My Father (1970)***½ Melvyn Douglas, Gene Hackman, Estelle Parsons. Deeply moving drama. Hackman as a 40-year-old still trying to play son to Douglas as the father, who is tyrannically obsessed with concepts of strength and pride. (Dir: Gilbert Cates, 90 mins.)†

In Fast Company (1946)*½ Bowery Boys, Bernard Gorcey, Judy Clark, Jane Randolph, Douglas Fowley. Slip (Leo Gorcey) drives a cab for an injured cabbie to help him support his family. The introduction of Louie, Bernard Gorcey's character, is the most significant development in this film for the series and its fans. (Dir: Del Lord, 61 mins.)

Inferno (1953)*** Robert Ryan, Rhonda Fleming, William Lundigan. Suspenseful drama about a pair of ruthless lovers who plot the abandonment of the woman's husband in the Mojave Desert. Robert Ryan plays the abandoned millionaire who manages to survive his plotters' deed. (Dir: Roy Baker, 83 mins.)

Inferno (Italy, 1978)**½ Leigh McCloskey, Irene Miracle, Sacha Pitoeff, Dara Nicolodi. A stylish-looking, but plot-flawed chiller full of creepy atmosphere. Returning from abroad, a young man launches an investigation into his sister's grisly death only to find himself surrounded by evil forces beyond his ken. (Dir: Dario Argento, 107 mins.)†

Infidelity (MTV 1987)** Kirstie Alley, Lee Horsley, Laurie O'Brien, Robert Englund, Lindsay Parker, Courtney Thorne-Smith. Trite soap opera about the perfect couple whose marriage is threatened by miscarriages, two-career dilemmas, and extra-marital affairs. (Dir: David Lowell Rich, 104 mins.)

Informer, The (1935)**** Victor McLaglen, Preston Foster. A brilliant, deeply moving film directed superbly by John Ford, that has, in the four decades since the film was made, become a true cinema classic. Set in Ireland during the time of the Irish rebellion, it concerns a slow-witted traitor who turns in a compatriot and suffers the pangs of conscience. (100 mins.)†

In God We Trust (1980)** Marty Feldman, Peter Boyle, Louise Lasser, Richard Pryor, Andy Kaufman. Feldman directed, co-wrote, and stars in this irreverent but witless slapstick farce about a Trappist monk who meets assorted oddballs in the outside world. (97 mins.)

In Harm's Way (1965)**½ John Wayne, Kirk Douglas, Patricia Neal, Brandon de Wilde. Despite an impressive all-star cast and a fairly interesting WWII setting, this film fails to register a strong impact. There are too many subplots, and the Japanese attack of Pearl Harbor merely serves as a backdrop to love stories of the principals. (Dir: Otto Preminger, 165 mins.)†

Inheritance, The (Great Britain, 1947)*** Jean Simmons, Derrick DeMarney. Girl attempts to foil a wicked uncle's effort to have her put out of the way so he can claim her inheritance. Theatrical Victorian thriller manages to generate considerable suspense. AKA: *Uncle Silas*. (Dir: Charles Frank, 90 mins.)

Inheritance, The (Italy, 1978)*** Anthony Quinn, Dominique Sanda, Fabio Testi. Story of a grasping working-class girl who marries into a wealthy family, only to engage its aging patriarch in a lecherous relationship. Exceptionally titillating trash. (Dir: Mauro Bolognini, 105 mins.)†

Inheritors, The (Austria, 1984)**½ Nikolas Vogel, Roger Schauer. A watchable but rather lunatic exploration of the indoctrination of a German teenager whose family crises lead him into neo-Naziism. At every turn, the director ladles on the horrors of fascism—this is no subtle political seduction like *Lacombe, Lucien*. It's more like *Hitler's Children*, swimming with contemporary teenage sex and violence. (Dir: Walter Bannert, 89 mins.)†

Inherit the Wind (1960)***½ Spencer Tracy, Fredric March, Gene Kelly. The powerful Broadway play dealing with the famous trial in the twenties in which a school-teacher was arrested for teaching Darwin's theory of evolution makes exciting screen entertainment. Tracy and March are excellent as defender and prosecutor, respectively. (Dir: Stanley Kramer, 127 mins.)†

Inherit the Wind (MTV 1988)*** Kirk Douglas, Jason Robards, Darren McGavin, Jean Simmons, Megan Follows. Quality television adaptation of the classic play, with one significant difference: Douglas plays the character of the prosecutor as a fervent religious zealot, reminiscent of the television evangelists of our own era. He and Robards, as the defense attorney, engage in a heated battle, ably supported by a superb supporting ensemble. (Dir: David Greene, 96 mins.)

Initiation, The (1984)*½ Vera Miles, Clu Gulager, James Read, Daphne Zuniga. A girl loses her memory and then almost loses her life as a crazed killer runs around bumping off collegians on her campus. (Dir: Larry Stewart, 97 mins.)†

Initiation of Sarah, The (MTV 1978)** Kay Lenz, Shelley Winters. Lenz stars as a college student who becomes involved in the demonic rituals of an old sorority, and Winters is around to add her brand of histrionic terror. (Dir: Robert Day, 104 mins.)†

In-Laws, The (1979)*** Peter Falk, Alan Arkin, Richard Libertini, Arlene Golonka, Nancy Dussault, Ed Begley, Jr. A standard slapstick premise made fresh by excellent casting. Peter Falk's son is marrying Alan Arkin's daughter, and the new in-laws must thwart the plans of a crazed banana-republic dictator who is trying to destroy the U.S. economy. Falk and Arkin delightfully engage in their particular brands of shtick; they're a perfectly matched odd couple. (Dir: Arthur Hiller, 103 mins.)†

In Like Flint (1967)*** James Coburn, Lee J. Cobb, Jean Hale. Fun and games, spy-spoof style! Sequel to *Our Man Flint* chronicles the outrageous adventures of the "coolest" super-spy of them all, Derek Flint, stylishly played by James Coburn. The plot centers on a diabolical scheme by a group of women to take control of the world. (Dir: Gordon Douglas, 114 mins.)†

In Like Flynn (MTV 1985)** Jenny Sea-

grove, William Gray Espy, Eddie Albert, William Conrad, Robert Webber, Maury Chaykin. Big box-office films invariably breed TV manqués; this unsold pilot, made in Canada, revises the idea behind *Romancing the Stone*, with Seagrove as a novelist assistant and Espy as the adventurous photographer who captures her heart. Derring-do that doesn't. (Dir: Richard Lang, 96 mins.)

In Love with an Older Woman (MTV 1982)**½ John Ritter, Karen Carlson, Jamie Rose, Robert Mandan, Jeff Altman, Robert Townsend. A May-December romance with the genders switched, this comic love story cries out for another lead. Ritter simply struts his usual sitcom persona, though the rest of the cast excel in this story of a young lawyer who falls in love with a woman who has a grown daughter. (Dir: Jack Bender, 96 mins.)

Inmates: A Love Story (MTV 1981)** Kate Jackson, Perry King, Tony Curtis, Shirley Jones, Pamela Reed. A coed prison creates problems in this poignant love story. Jackson plays a tough cookie who's doing time for petty larceny and warms up to former business exec King when he's jailed after being framed by associates. (Dir: Guy Green, 104 mins.)

In Name Only (1939)*** Cary Grant, Carole Lombard, Kay Francis, Charles Coburn. Rich nonconformist Grant and artist Lombard fall in love, but can't marry because his wife (Francis) is holding him to a loveless marriage. The weepy plot is nothing special, but the cast and director John Cromwell give it better than it deserves. (102 mins.)†

In Name Only (MTV 1969)* Michael Callan, Ann Prentiss, Eve Arden. Absurd made-for-TV feature. The warmed-over premise has Callan and Prentiss as marriage consultants discovering three couples whose marriages they arranged are not legally hitched. (Dir: E. W. Swackhamer, 75 mins.)

Innerspace (1987)*** Dennis Quaid, Martin Short, Meg Ryan, Kevin Mc Carthy. Delightful comedy-adventure about a man who's reduced to the size of a molecule for scientific study. Only instead of being inserted into a laboratory rabbit, he winds up inside a rabbity human being; naturally, the man and his tiny visitor are pursued by evil agents. A "fantastic voyage" past the funny bone. (Dir: Joe Dante, 101 mins.)†

Innocence Unprotected (Yugoslavia, 1968)***½ Dragolub Aleksic, Ana Milosavljevic, Bartoljub Gligorijevic, Vera Jovanovic. A circus ironman who made a pro-Serbian movie in 1942 recalls the filming of the picture and its seizure by the Nazis because of its nationalist theme. A blend of newsreel footage, film-within-a-film narrative, and memories of the earlier film's original cast. Director Dusan Makavejev has created a unique fictional work about hanging onto the past and the illusion of fame and power. (78 mins.)

Innocent, The (Italy, 1976)***½ Giancarlo Giannini, Laura Antonelli, Jennifer O'Neill. Director Luchino Visconti's last film is a haunting account of aristocratic chauvinism and sexual double standards in turn-of-the-century Italy. Giannini is excellent as the psychotic husband whose lust cannot be satisfied, Antonelli is sensitive as his tormented wife, and O'Neill is superb as his cunning, possessive mistress. Sumptuous photography, costuming, and setting—elegant villas in Italy—are a plus. (112 mins.)†

Innocent, The (France, 1988)** Sandrine Bonnaire, Simon de la Brosse, Abdel Kechiche, Jean-Claude Brialy. A disappointment from director André Technine, this overtly melodramatic tale of sexual and racial tensions downplays the latter for the former, even though the elements of the tale concerning unease between right-wing factions and Frenchmen of Arab ancestry are clearly more significant. (96 mins.)

Innocent Affair, An (1948)**½ Madeleine Carroll, Fred MacMurray, Buddy Rogers, Rita Johnson, Alan Mowbray. Sprightly comedy of a married couple's misunderstandings; good of this kind. (Dir: Lloyd Bacon, 90 mins.)

Innocent and the Damned—See: **Girls' Town**

Innocent Bystanders (Great Britain, 1973)** Stanley Baker, Geraldine Chaplin, Donald Pleasence, Dana Andrews. Muddled espionage film. Stanley Baker is the aging agent who is sent on his last assignment to bring back a Russian scientist named Kaplan from his exile in Turkey. (Dir: Peter Collinson, 111 mins.)

Innocent Love, An (MTV 1982)** Melissa Sue Anderson, Doug McKeon, Steve Bauer. Doug McKeon gives child prodigies a good name as a fourteen-year-old college math student tutoring and developing a crush on a nineteen-year-old volleyball star. (Dir: Roger Young, 104 mins.)

Innocent Man, An (1989)*½ Tom Selleck, F. Murray Abraham, Laila Robins, David Rasche, Richard Young, Todd Graff. "Wrong man" story creates a tense atmosphere as framed Selleck tries to survive life in prison, but destroys it with an overblown, revenge-filled conclusion. Selleck and Robins as his wife act insufferably noble, and Rasche is laughably atrocious as the dirty cop who set Selleck up. Only Abraham turns in a good performance as Selleck's jailbird mentor. (Dir: Peter Yates, 113 mins.)†

Innocents, The (U.S.-Great Britain, 1961) **** Deborah Kerr, Martin Stephens, Pamela Franklin. Henry James's classic tale dealing with the supernatural, *The Turn of the Screw*, becomes a brilliant suspense film. Deborah Kerr is magnificent as the governess who becomes enmeshed in the eerie household in which the two young children appear to be possessed by ghosts. The entire film is flawless in building to the shattering climax. By all means, don't miss this one, directed by Jack Clayton. (100 mins.)

Innocents in Paris (Great Britain, 1953)**½ Alastair Sim, Margaret Rutherford, Claire Bloom, Laurence Harvey. Londoners take off to see Paris for the first time. Lengthy but amusing film. (Dir: Gordon Parry, 93 mins.)

Innocent Sorcerers (Poland, 1960)*** Zbigniew Cybulski, Tadeusz Lomnicki, Roman Polanski, Jerzy Skolimowski, Krystyna Stypulkowska. A young doctor who enjoys playing in a jazz band tries hard to cope with his mindless girlfriend and the directionless lives of his pals. An unusual and charming foray into the comedy of sex and relationships by director Andrzej Wajda. Future directors Polanski and Skolimowski are wonderful in major roles. (91 mins.)

Inn of the Frightened People—See: **Revenge** (Great Britain, 1971)

Inn of the Sixth Happiness, The (Great Britain, 1958)***½ Ingrid Bergman, Curt Jurgens, Robert Donat. Excellently acted drama of a missionary woman in China and her attempts to lead some children to safety on a perilous trek through enemy territory. Runs to excessive length, but has top work by Bergman and Robert Donat as a mandarin. Donat's last film. (Dir: Mark Robson, 158 mins.)†

In Old California (1942)** John Wayne, Binnie Barnes, Albert Dekker. Young pharmacist sets up shop in Sacramento, bucks the outlaw boss of the town. (Dir: William McGann, 88 mins.)†

In Old Chicago (1938)***½ Tyrone Power, Alice Faye, Don Ameche, Alice Brady. Story of the O'Leary family whose cow is credited with starting the great Chicago fire. Fictional story is interesting and builds neatly into the fire spectacle. Brady won Best Supporting Actress Oscar. (Dir: Henry King, 115 mins.)†

In Old Kentucky (1935)*** Will Rogers, Bill Robinson, Dorothy Wilson, Russell Hardie. Rogers's last film is a simple romance of feuding families in the hills; lovingly done, humorous, and entertaining. (Dir: George Marshall, 86 mins.)

In Our Time (1944)** Ida Lupino, Paul Henreid, Alla Nazimova, Nancy Coleman, Victor Francen, Mary Boland. An earnest but off-target propaganda piece about those familiar "little people" who go after the Nazi fighting forces. The cast tries hard but they always seem like movie stars slumming in Poland as they lead the Resistance. (Dir: Vincent Sherman, 110 mins.)

In Person (1935)*** Ginger Rogers, George Brent, Alan Mowbray, Grant Mitchell, Samuel S. Hinds. Light comedy of movie star Rogers trying to conceal her identity and falling for a guy who doesn't recognize her; charmingly played fun. (Dir: William A. Seiter, 85 mins.)†

In Praise of Older Women (Canada, 1979) **½ Tom Berenger, Karen Black, Susan Strasberg, Helen Shaver. The sexual odyssey of a young man who prefers to bed older, experienced women. Plays on one note, but handsome Berenger has the right touch as the amorous Hungarian swain. (Dir: George Kaczender, 108 mins.)†

Inquisition, The—See: **Garde à Vue**

In Search of America (MTV 1971)*** Carl Betz, Vera Miles, Jeff Bridges. An entertaining tale about a charming family that takes to the road en masse to experience the land and its variety of people. Jeff Bridges is very good as the son who convinces his father (Carl Betz), mother (Vera Miles), and grandmother (Ruth McDevitt) to accompany him on a trek around the country in a reconverted vintage passenger bus. (Dir: Paul Bogart, 72 mins.)

In Search of Gregory (1970)** Julie Christie, Michael Sarrazin, John Hurt. A forgettable adventure. Confused story about a young girl (Christie) living in Rome, who goes to Geneva to find romance at her father's wedding. Julie's disturbed younger brother isn't much help in her quest. (Dir: Peter Wood, 90 mins.)

In Search of Historic Jesus (1979)** John Rubinstein, John Anderson, Nehemiah Persoff, Royal Dano. Less than edifying examination of the question of Jesus' divinity, with the evidence presented ponderously. The reenacted portions are unconvincingly done, with Rubinstein as a hippielike Christ. (Dir: Henning Schellerup, 91 mins.)†

In Search of the Castaways (U.S.-Great Britain, 1962)*** Hayley Mills, Wilfred Hyde-White, Maurice Chevalier, George Sanders. Jules Verne classic adventure yarn, well produced in the Disney manner. Mills plays the daughter of a sea captain who has been abducted. There follows a mind-boggling adventure that pits the cast against earthquakes, floods, and avalanches, which are a tribute to Hollywood special-effects geniuses. (Dir: Robert Stevenson, 104 mins.)†

In Self Defense (MTV 1987)*½ Linda Purl, Terry Lester, Billy Drago, Yaphet Kotto, Gail Edwards, Rick Lenz. Purl testifies against a killer who is freed. When he starts stalking her, Linda goes shopping for a gun and indulges in target practice, with disastrous results. This picture needed better aim, too. (Dir: Bruce Green, 104 mins.)

Inserts (Great Britain, 1975)** Richard Dreyfuss, Veronica Cartwright, Jessica Harper, Bob Hoskins. The writer-director doesn't have a real facility for film technique, but audiences will be intrigued by the storyline nonetheless. A former Hollywood Boy Wonder, now unemployable, becomes a director of porno films back in the 1930s. (Dir: John Byrum, 99 mins.)†

Inside Daisy Clover (1965)**½ Natalie Wood, Christopher Plummer, Robert Redford, Ruth Gordon, Katherine Bard, Roddy McDowall. Glossy gothic melodrama about 1930s Hollywood. Christopher Plummer comes off best as a tyrannical studio head, and Robert Redford is effective in the complex role of a deeply troubled motion-picture matinee idol. Natalie Wood is less successful than her co-stars in the title role, the waif-turned-star-turned-neurotic. (Dir: Robert Mulligan, 128 mins.)

Inside Detroit (1956)** Dennis O'Keefe, Pat O'Brien. The war for control by the rackets of the unions in the automobile industry comes into focus in this overdone drama. (Dir: Fred F. Sears, 82 mins.)

Inside Moves (1980)**½ John Savage, David Morse, Diana Scarwid, Amy Wright, Harold Russell. Director Richard Donner's film about a group of handicapped people who hang out in a local bar. Some authentically observed behavior of the afflicted, but the film often strains for an upbeat tone. (Dir: Richard Donner, 113 mins.)†

Inside Out (1987)**½ Elliott Gould, Howard Hesseman, Jennifer Tilly. Unusual, very downbeat character study of an agoraphobic—a person possessed by the fear of going outside. Gould gives a fine performance as the afflicted gentleman, but this picture conveys a severe sense of claustrophobia. (Dir: Robert Taicher, 87 mins.)

Inside Story, The (1948)** William Lundigan, Marsha Hunt. During a bank holiday in the Depression days of 1933, a thousand dollars is suddenly in circulation, with startling consequences. (Dir: Allan Dwan, 87 mins.)

Inside Straight (1951)** David Brian, Arlene Dahl, Mercedes McCambridge. Ruthless man out to make money lets nothing stand in his way. (Dir: Gerald Mayer, 89 mins.)

Inside the Mafia (1959)** Cameron Mitchell, Elaine Edwards, Robert Strauss. Rival hoods set up a plot to bump off a ganglord arriving for a big power meeting. (Dir: Edward L. Cahn, 72 mins.)

Inside the Third Reich (MTV 1982)**½ Rutger Hauer, Derek Jacobi, Blythe Danner, Sir John Gielgud, Ian Holm, Elke Sommer, Trevor Howard. Fascinating historical docudrama that focuses on Albert Speer, who came from the upper-class German intelligentsia and, after a stint as an architectural student, became Hitler's master builder. A compelling history lesson. (Dir: Marvin Chomsky, 250 mins.)†

Insignificance (Great Britain, 1985)*** Theresa Russell, Michael Emil, Gary Busey, Tony Curtis. Four notable public figures of the 1950s convene in a hotel room to discuss such issues as sex, relativity, and the universe in this original work of art from the director Nicolas Roeg. Working from the satirical script by Terry Johnson, the impressive cast gives juicy and explosive performances. (108 mins.)†

In Society (1944)** Bud Abbott, Lou Costello, Marion Hutton. Dumb plumbers foil an attempted art theft. Usual A&C slap-stick. (Dir: Jean Yarbrough, 75 mins.)

Inspector Calls, An (Great Britain, 1954)*** Alastair Sim, Eileen Moore. A mysterious policeman investigates the family of a girl who has died of poisoning. From J. B. Priestley's mystical drama, this is rather vague, but occasionally interesting. (Dir: Guy Hamilton, 80 mins.)

Inspector Clouseau (Great Britain, 1968)* Alan Arkin, Frank Finlay, Beryl Reid. The talented Alan Arkin fails to erase memories of Peter Sellers in this poor comedy featuring Inspector Clouseau, the detective character from *The Pink Panther*. (Dir: Bud Yorkin, 94 mins.)

Inspector General (1949)***½ Danny Kaye, Walter Slezak. Delightful period farce about an illiterate who's mistaken for a friend of Napoleon's. It's a Danny Kaye romp and one of those rare times when the story comes close to matching his artistry. (Dir: Henry Koster, 102 mins.)†

Inspector Lavardin (France, 1986)***½ Jean Poiret, Bernadette Lafont, Jean-Claude Brialy, Hermine Claire, Jacques Dacmine. Nifty detective thriller features policeman Lavardin, returning from director Claude Chabrol's *Coq Au Vin*, investigating the murder of his former lover's husband. Well-done mystery has lots of surprises and a rash of sexually unique, weirdly comic characters. (103 mins.)

Inspiration (1931)** Greta Garbo, Robert Montgomery, Lewis Stone, Marjorie Rambeau, Beryl Mercer. All that's inspired in this MGM nonsense is Greta herself, although the overproduction almost does her in. Suffering nobly for love, she abandons her beloved because of her shady past. (Dir: Clarence Brown, 74 mins.)

Institute for Revenge (MTV 1979)*½ Sam Groom, Lauren Hutton, Leslie Nielsen. Unsold pilot deals with an organization run by busy computers and adventurous personnel out to help the defenseless. (Dir: Ken Annakin, 104 mins.)

In Tandem (MTV 1974)** Claude Akins, Frank Converse. Truckers side with an orange rancher, pressured to sell his land to an amusement-park group. Pilot for the subsequent series. (Dir: Bernard Kowalski, 78 mins.)

Interiors (1978)*** Diane Keaton, E. G. Marshall, Geraldine Page, Maureen Stapleton, Sam Waterston, Richard Jordan, Mary Beth Hurt, Kristin Griffith. Woody Allen's Bergman-inspired drama is a seriously felt, sly film that encourages the viewer to overlook the howlers in the dialogue. Some of the acting is superlative. Uneven but often moving and involving. (Dir: Woody Allen, 93 mins.)†

Interlude (1957)**½ June Allyson, Rossano Brazzi. Hankies out, ladies...here's a plot about an American librarian in Germany who falls for a married conductor, etc. Soap opera, as such competent. Remake of *When Tomorrow Comes*. (Dir: Douglas Sirk, 90 mins.)

Interlude (Great Britain, 1968)**½ Oskar Werner, Barbara Ferris, Virginia Maskell, Donald Sutherland. The slick tale of an impossible love between a symphony conductor (Oskar Werner) and a newspaperwoman (Barbara Ferris). Some good classical music. Remake of 1957 film. (Dir: Kevin Billington, 113 mins.)

Intermezzo (Sweden, 1936)*** Ingrid Bergman, Gosta Ekman. Effective heart tugger with Bergman a ravishing model of youthful sensuality as a music student in thrall to her teacher (Ekman). Bergman was spotted in this film by producer David O. Selznick, who brought her to Hollywood for a remake. (Dir: Gustav Molander, 70 mins.)†

Intermezzo (1939)*** Leslie Howard, Ingrid Bergman, John Halliday, Edna Best. Story of a married concert violinist (Howard) who has an affair with his beautiful protégée (Bergman). Gregory Ratoff's direction catches their star qualities, but the story is sometimes more wimpy than weepy. (70 mins.)†

Internal Affairs (MTV 1988)**½ Richard Crenna, Kate Capshaw, Cliff Gorman, Lee Richardson, Dennis Boutsikaris, Philip Bosco, Sam Coppola. Overlong but good cop story, a follow-up to

518

Doubletake, with NYPD Lt. Janek (Crenna) and crew investigating another murder whose trail leads to some of New York's finest. Janek returned in *Murder in Black and White*. (Dir: Michael Tuchner, 194 mins.)

Internal Affairs (1990)**½ Richard Gere, Andy Garcia, Laurie Metcalf, Nancy Travis, William Baldwin. Wildly meandering plot about good cops, bad cops, cocaine, and the L.A. art scene is given stylish neo-*noir* gloss by director Mike Figgis, but leaves too many unanswered questions. Gere is terrific as sleazy, horny police officer (four wives, nine kids) under investigation by Garcia and Metcalf. Highly watchable despite its faults. (115 mins.)†

International Airport (MTV 1985)** Gil Gerard, Bill Bixby, Robert Vaughn, Robert Reed, Susan Blakely, Connie Selleca. Pilot film about an international airport. (Dir: Don Chaffey, 104 mins.)

International House (1933)*** W. C. Fields, Burns and Allen, Stuart Erwin. Foolish but occasionally hilarious comedy about an inventor. A fine assortment of characters in this film and, in spite of its age, comedy lovers should enjoy it. (Dir: A. Edward Sutherland, 72 mins.)†

International Lady (1941)** George Brent, Ilona Massey, Basil Rathbone, Gene Lockhart. Derivative espionage thriller, casts Miss Massey as an Axis spy who befuddles FBI man Brent and Scotland Yard ace Rathbone, managing to sing her reports to her waiting cohorts. (Dir: Tim Whelan, 102 mins.)

International Settlement (1938)**½ Dolores Del Rio, George Sanders, June Lang, Dick Baldwin, John Carradine, Keye Luke, Leon Ames. Second-rate thriller has Sanders undercover in the Middle East trying to expose an arms smuggling ring, and falling for lovely Del Rio. Some good twists and turns. (Dir: Eugene Forde, 75 mins.)

International Squadron (1941)**½ Ronald Reagan. Mr. Reagan ends up in the RAF changing from an irresponsible bum to a great hero. Trouble is, the script makes the change unbelievable. (Dir: Lothar Mendes, 87 mins.)

International Velvet (Great Britain, 1978) **½ Tatum O'Neal, Nanette Newman, Christopher Plummer, Anthony Hopkins. Agreeable sequel to *National Velvet* ('44) has the grown Velvet (Newman) coaching her orphaned niece (O'Neal) into becoming a skilled horsewoman who joins the British Olympic riding team and ends up married. (Dir: Bryan Forbes, 126 mins.)†

Internecine Project, The (Great Britain, 1974)** James Coburn, Lee Grant, Harry Andrews. Muddled espionage yarn about a man who will stop at nothing to be appointed to a high-level position in Washington. Coburn and Grant are inadequate. (Dir: Ken Hughes, 89 mins.)†

Interns, The (1962)** Michael Callan, Cliff Robertson, Nick Adams, James MacArthur, Stefanie Powers. A melange of medical clichés about the problems faced by assorted young interns during their year of apprenticeship. (Dir: David Swift, 129 mins.)†

Interns Can't Take Money (1937)*** Joel McCrea, Barbara Stanwyck, Lloyd Nolan. Dr. James Kildare appeared on-screen for the first time in this gritty crime melodrama about an intern battling gangsters. (Dir: Alfred Santell, 77 mins.)

Interrogation (Poland, 1982)***½ Krystyna Janda, Adam Ferency, Janusz Gajos, Anna Romantowska, Agnieszka Holland. An apolitical cabaret singer (Janda in a truly brilliant performance) is subjected to brutal torture by Stalinist Polish authorities demanding she confess to trumped-up antistate charges. Powerful! (Dir: Ryszard Bigajski, 118 mins.)

Interrupted Melody (1955)*½ Eleanor Parker, Glenn Ford, Roger Moore, Cecil Kellaway. The story of Marjorie Lawrence, an Australian opera singer stricken by polio. Eileen Farrell dubbed in as Parker's singing voice. (Dir: Curtis Bernhardt, 106 mins.)

Interval (U.S.-Mexico, 1973)½ Merle Oberon, Robert Wolders. Producer Oberon cast herself as a woman "well over 40" who falls in love with a young American painter. Clumsily written by Gavin Lambert, and directed with a heavy hand indeed by Daniel Mann. (84 mins.)†

Intervista (Italy, 1987)***½ Fascinating self-directed autobiographical documentary by Frederico Fellini about his life in films. A Japanese TV crew interviews Fellini as he reminisces about his first movie studio visit, his movies, his wife and star Giulietta Masina. Music by Nino Rota. (105 mins.)

In the Best Interest of the Child (MTV 1990)*** Meg Tilly, Michael O'Keefe, Ed Begley, Jr., Michele Greene, Marta Woodward. Tilly gives a fine, understated performance as a divorced woman who enlists the aid of an underground railroad to protect her daughter from her sexually abusing ex-husband. Powerful drama depicts an ineffective legal system that views the mother as the criminal. (Dir: David Greene, 96 mins.)

In the Cool of the Day (Great Britain, 1963)**½ Peter Finch, Jane Fonda, Angela Lansbury. The stars form a strange triangle amid the landscape of Greece in this tale about a young, bored wife (Fonda) who falls hopelessly in love with the very married Mr. Finch. (Dir: Robert Stevens, 89 mins.)

In the Custody of Strangers (MTV 1982)**½ Martin Sheen, Jane Alexander, Emilio Estevez, Kenneth McMillan, Ed Lauter, Matt Clark. A serious subject is given a fairly honest treatment. A sixteen-year-old boy goes on a drunken spree, is arrested, and kept overnight in jail when his father won't come and get him. The boy is approached by a homosexual and beats up his attacker, resulting in his being incarcerated for over a month. (Dir: Robert Greenwald, 104 mins.)

In the Devil's Garden—See: **Assault** (1971)

In the French Style (U.S.-France, 1963)*** Jean Seberg, Stanley Baker. Fascinating study of the post-WWII female expatriate, embodied in a young art student who comes to Paris, remains to become involved in a series of passionate, ultimately meaningless love affairs. Incisive Irwin Shaw script. (Dir: Robert Parrish, 105 mins.)

In the Glitter Palace (MTV 1977)**½ Chad Everett, David Wayne, Barbara Hershey, Anthony Zerbe, Howard Duff. Here's a murder mystery that turns out to be better than expected. Chad Everett plays a lawyer digging into a seamy case involving lesbians. The women's side is told with taste and understanding. (Dir: Robert Butler, 106 mins.)

In the Good Old Summertime (1949)*** Judy Garland, Van Johnson, Buster Keaton, Spring Byington, S. Z. Sakall. A must for Judy Garland fans. Warmhearted musical comedy-romance about two clerks in a music shop who have a mutual secret, without knowing it. Based on *The Shop Around the Corner*. (Dir: Robert Z. Leonard, 102 mins.)†

In the Heat of the Night (1967)**** Rod Steiger, Sidney Poitier, Lee Grant, Warren Oates. Exciting, superbly acted and directed film about prejudice, manners, and morals in a small Mississippi town. Poitier portrays a Philadelphia detective who teams with southern sheriff Steiger to solve a murder in a fascinating duel of wits. Academy awards went to Steiger, screenwriter Stirling Silliphant, and the film itself. Later a TV series. (Dir: Norman Jewison, 110 mins.)†

In the Heat of the Night (MTV 1988)** Carroll O'Connor, Howard Rollins, Alan Autry. Pilot for the TV series reviving the characters from the film hit. A high school girl is found murdered, and it's up to Gillespie and Tibbs to find the culprit. (Dir: David Hemmings, 96 mins.)

In the Matter of Karen Ann Quinlan (MTV 1977)*** Brian Keith, Piper Laurie. Keith and Laurie give sensitive, highly emotional performances as Catholic parents Joe and Julie Quinlan who sue for the right to permit their irreparably brain-damaged daughter to die a natural death. A real-life story, handled with compassion and restraint. (Dir: Hal Jordan, 104 mins.)

In the Meantime, Darling (1944)** Jeanne Crain, Eugene Pallette, Mary Nash, Cara Williams, Blake Edwards. A mere bubble of a romantic comedy. The players' charm sustains this forced affair about the pampered rich Miss who's knocked down a peg by her marriage to an ordinary soldier. (Dir: Otto Preminger, 72 mins.)

In the Money (1958)**½ Bowery Boys, Stanley Clements. Sach (Huntz Hall) is hired to babysit a predigreed poodle; and the Boys get mixed up in a diamond smuggling ring on the British side of the Atlantic. This is the final installment in the series. (Dir: William Beaudine, 61 mins.)

In the Mood (1987)** Patrick Dempsey, Talia Balsam, Beverly D'Angelo. The real-life exploits of Sonny Wisecarver, "the Woo-Woo Kid," who married two older, married women, serve as grist for yet another lame teen comedy (this one's a period piece, set in the forties). (Dir: Phil Alden Robinson, 98 mins.)†

In the Name of the Father (Italy, 1971)***½ Renato Scarpa, Yves Beneyton, Lou Caster, Laura Betti, Piero Vida, Aldo Sassi. Rebellious rich kids led by a brooding iconoclast disrupt their Jesuit college by staging a play that subverts the school's rules and attacks the basic principles of Jesuit dogma. Powerful and surreal assault on Italian society. (Dir: Marco Bellocchio, 107 mins.)

In the Navy (1941)**½ Abbott and Costello, Dick Powell. The youngsters should enjoy this crazy film about a radio singer who seeks refuge in the Navy. (Dir: Arthur Lubin, 85 mins.)

In the Realm of the Senses (Japan-France, 1976)***½ Tatsuya Fuji, Eiko Matsuda, Meika Seri, Aoi Nakajima. Married man and his geisha lover escape the harsh realities of life in 1936 Japan by acting out innumerable erotic fantasies, including the "ultimate orgasm" of death. Director Nagisa Oshima's most daring and controversial film is a nonstop depiction of sex with underlying themes of gratification and obsession. (105 mins.)†

In the Secret State (Great Britain, 1985)** Frank Finlay, Matthew Marsh, Natasha Richardson. Disbelieving the explanation that a co-worker's death was a suicide, a British government agent investigates on his own and uncovers a government scandal. OK political thriller, a bit slow moving. (Dir: Christopher Morahan, 107 mins.)†

In the Shadow of Kilimanjaro (Great Britain-

U.S.-Kenya, 1986)* John Rhys-Davies, Timothy Bottoms, Irene Miracle, Michele Carey, Leonard Trolley. Lackluster horror film that tries too hard to scare the pants off us. Driven mad with hunger, 90,000 baboons leave their game reserve to snack on human beings in a story purportedly based on fact. (Dir: Raju Patel, 97 mins.)†

In the Spirit (1990)**½ Elaine May, Marlo Thomas, Jeannie Berlin, Peter Falk, Melanie Griffith, Olympia Dukakis, Michael Emil, Rockets Redglare, Christopher Durang. Confused comedy that starts out as a "New Age" parody, detailing the intersection of three women's lives (May, Thomas, and Berlin, who co-scripted), suddenly transforming into a female buddy movie, with May and Thomas fleeing a murderous crooked cop. Despite its haphazardly assembled plotline, the film does feature sublime comic performances by May and Falk, and some solid one-liners. (Dir: Sandra Seacat, 93 mins.)†

In the Summertime (Italy, 1971)***½ Renato Paracchi, Rosanna Callegari, Gabriele Frontanesi, Mario Cazzaniga. Exceptional romantic comedy-drama about dreams and ideas tells the story of a young man who meets a gentle disillusioned woman and involves her in his fantasies, boosting her spirits and breaking down barriers to friendship. Director Ermanno Olmi also edited, photographed, and co-wrote this wonderful film, considered by many to be his best. (110 mins.)

In the White City (Switzerland, 1983)**½ Bruno Ganz, Teresa Madruga, José Carvalho. A melancholy film that evokes the experience of failing to connect with other people. A ship's engineer disaffectedly wanders around Lisbon, drifts into an affair, and takes soulless home movies that he sends home to his wife. (Dir: Alain Tanner, 108 mins.)

In the Year of the Pig (1969)**** A riveting, informative, and ultimately moving documentary about American involvement in the Vietnam war. Produced and directed by Emile de Antonio, who was responsible for the remarkable '64 documentary *Point of Order. Pig* is a shattering indictment of American policy in Vietnam and Southeast Asia. (101 mins.)†

In the Year 2889 (1968)*½ Paul Petersen, Quinn O'Hara, Charla Doherty, Neil Fletcher, Bill Thurman, Hugh Feagin. Another one of producer-director Larry Buchanan's uncredited rip-offs of Roger Corman movies, this one revamps *The Day the World Ended:* seven survivors of a nuclear war bicker with each other while fighting off mutants. Pretty cheesy,

though better than Buchanan's *Mars Needs Women.* (80 mins.)

In This House of Brede (MTV 1975)*** Diana Rigg, Gwen Watford, Judi Bowker, Denis Quilley, Pamela Brown, Nicholas Clay. Diana Rigg's superb as a successful British businesswoman deciding to exchange her secular life for that of a cloistered Benedictine nun. Far from sentimental religious drama, forceful and rewarding. (Dir: George Schaefer, 100 mins.)

In This Our Life (1942)**½ Bette Davis, Dennis Morgan, Olivia de Havilland, Charles Coburn, George Brent. Flashes of director John Huston's personality are sprinkled throughout this admittedly commissioned work. Davis plays the neurotic with a vengeance, screwing up her sister, her husband, and herself. Howard Koch's adaption of the Ellen Glasgow novel manages to hold her nefarious deeds within a credible dramatic framework. (97 mins.)†

Intimate Agony (MTV 1983)**½ Anthony Geary, Judith Light, Mark Harmon, Arthur Hill, Brian Kerwin, Robert Vaughn. Disaster drama set in a summer resort community. The menace here is herpes. (Dir: Paul Wendkos, 104 mins.)

Intimate Contact (Made for British TV, 1987) *** Claire Bloom, Daniel Massey, David Phelan, Abigail Cruttenden, Mark Kingston, Syliva Syms. An English businessman (Massey) discovers that he has contracted AIDS from a prostitute and has to deal with alienation, fear, and inevitable death. A moving, tightly dramatic portrait of the disease's victims that evokes sympathy without preaching. (Dir: Waris Hussein, 180 mins.)†

Intimate Encounters (MTV 1986)** Donna Mills, James Brolin, Cicely Tyson, Veronica Cartwright. Mills and Brolin are a married couple whose relationship is crumbling due to the wife's descent into sexual fantasies. Typical TV titillation masquerading as psychological drama. (Dir: Ivan Nagy, 104 mins.)

Intimate Lighting (Czechoslovakia, 1966)**** Zdenek Bezusek, Vera Kresadlova, Karel Blazek. Lively social comedy of provincial life in Czechoslovakia. Director and writer Ivan Passer handles the wry, understated humor beautifully. (71 mins.)

Intimate Strangers (MTV 1977)*** Dennis Weaver, Sally Struthers, Tyne Daly, Larry Hagman, Melvyn Douglas. An important subject, wife-beating, is handled with minimum exploitation in this engrossing "social problem" drama. Weaver and Struthers are better than their material, playing a married couple whose marriage falls apart after the man's violent attacks on his wife increase. (Dir: John Llewellyn Moxey, 104 mins.)†

Intimate Strangers (MTV 1985)*½ Teri Garr, Stacy Keach, Cathy Lee Crosby, Priscilla Lopez, Justin Deas, Max Gail, Max Barabas. A disappointing Vietnam POW drama. Teri Garr plays the POW nurse haunted by the past and unable to cope with peacetime life with doctor-husband (Stacy Keach). The plotting is ponderous and predictable and so is the acting. (Dir: Robert Ellis Miller, 104 mins.)

Intolerance (1916)**** Lillian Gish, Robert Harron, Mae Marsh, Constance Talmadge, Bessie Love. Four interconnected stories of injustice in different historical periods are directed with skill (and lavishness) by the great D. W. Griffith. The gigantic palace set in ancient Babylon may be the most elaborate ever built for a film. The performances are strikingly good—especially Marsh and Talmadge. A silent classic. (123 mins.)†

Into the Homeland (MCTV 1987)*½ Powers Boothe, C. Thomas Howell, Paul LeMat, Cindy Pickett, David Caruso. Square-jawed Boothe plays a seasoned ex-cop who infiltrates a white supremacist organization in search of his missing daughter in this made-for-cable quickie that tries to be both a "message picture" and a thriller; it fails both ways. (Dir: Lesli Linka Glatter, 115 mins.)†

Into the Night (1985)*½ Jeff Goldblum, Michele Pfeiffer, David Bowie, Dan Aykroyd, David Farnsworth, Irene Papas, Clu Gulager. A wildly misguided comic thriller about Goldblum getting mixed up with Iranian bad guys after some stolen gems. (Dir: John Landis, 115 mins.)†

Into Thin Air (MTV 1985)*** Ellen Burstyn, Robert Prosky, Sam Robards. A mother battles to find out what happened to her son, ambushed on the road while driving to college. This poignant fact-based drama is depressing but well handled. (Dir: Roger Young, 100 mins.)

Intrigue (MTV 1988)**½ Scott Glenn, Robert Loggia, William Atherton, Eleanor Bron. Good low-key spy featuring Glenn as a cool, contained American undercover agent smuggling a defector (Loggia) from behind the Iron Curtain. The tension seldom lags, leading to a puzzling plot twist at the end. (Dir: David Drury, 96 mins.)

Intruder (1988)**½ Elizabeth Cox, Renée Estevez, Danny Hicks, David Byrnes, Sam Raimi, Alvy Moore. Customers trapped inside a convenience store are stalked and murdered. Slasher movie leavened by some clever directorial touches and a surprise ending. (Dir: Scott Spiegel, 83 mins.)†

Intruder, The (Great Britain, 1953)*** Jack

522

Hawkins, Michael Medwin, George Cole. An Army colonel discovers one of his former regiment rifling his house, decides to contact the old wartime crew to find out what made the lad turn thief. Interesting drama, well done. (Dir: Guy Hamilton, 84 mins.)

Intruder, The (1962)—See: **Shame** (1962)

Intruder in the Dust (1949)**** David Brian, Claude Jarman, Jr., Juano Hernandez. Based on William Faulkner's novel—a lawyer and a lad come to the aid of a black when he's accused of murder. Fine dramatic film for the more discriminating; successful both as a straight whodunit, and as more immediate topical fare. (Dir: Clarence Brown, 87 mins.)

Intruders, The (MTV 1970)**½ Don Murray, Anne Francis, Edmond O'Brien, John Saxon, (Harry) Dean Stanton, Stuart Margolin, Harrison Ford, Gavin McLeod. Moderately absorbing western with Murray as an ex-gunslinger turned marshal and Saxon as a half-breed Indian trying to cope with prejudice. (Dir: William Graham, 95 mins.)

Intruder Within, The (MTV 1981)* Chad Everett, Joseph Bottoms, Jennifer Warren. Dim-witted horror film about a crew on an isolated oil rig. As they dig deeper for oil, they intrude upon the stomping grounds of a mysterious creature that begins to terrorize everyone. (Dir: Peter Carter, 104 mins.)†

Invaders, The—See: **49th Parallel, The**

Invaders from Mars (1953)*** Arthur Franz, Helena Carter, Jimmy Hunt, Leif Erickson, Hillary Brooke, Milburn Stone. This is the perfect Saturday matinee sci-fi film, with production design and direction by William Cameron Menzies, whose work in films includes *Gone with the Wind*. A young boy believes Martians have landed and are taking over his town, beginning with his parents. The townspeople don't believe him, so the intrepid lad sets out to prove it isn't all a bad dream. (78 mins.)†

Invaders from Mars (1986)* Karen Black, Hunter Carson, Laraine Newman, Timothy Bottoms, Louise Fletcher, Bud Cort, James Karen. Ridiculous updated version of the 1950s sci-fi classic. Playing a tyrannical teacher, Louise Fletcher has no problems swallowing a frog, but the audience will have some difficulty swallowing the entire film. (Dir: Tobe Hooper, 100 mins.)†

Invasion Earth: The Aliens are Here (1988)*½ Janice Fabian, Christian Lee, Mel Welles. Story about aliens who take over the audience at a theater where a sci-fi festival is playing is primarily an excuse to revive loads of clips from fifties movies. Only rabid nostalgia fans will care. (Dir: George Maitland, 83 mins.)†

Invasion Earth 2150 A.D. (Great Britain, 1966)**½ Peter Cushing, Bernard Cribbins, Andrew Keir. Fast-paced science fiction pits a small band of freedom fighters against maniacal, super-intelligent robots from outer space, who have been turning humans into programmed slaves. Based on the BBC-TV serial, *Dr. Who*, sequel to *Dr. Who and the Daleks*. AKA: **Daleks—Invasion Earth 2150 A.D.** (Dir: Gordon Flemyng, 84 mins.)

Invasion of Johnson County, The (MTV 1976)**½ Bill Bixby, Bo Hopkins, John Hillerman, Billy Green Bush, Stephen Collins, M. Emmet Walsh, Brion James. Offbeat western adventure yarn. Bixby is a dapper Bostonian Brahmin who finds himself in the Wild West without any funds. He teams up with cowpoke Hopkins, who confesses he has been hired by a private army of men who plan to take the law into their own hands. The plotline's similar to *Heaven's Gate*. (Dir: Jerry Jameson, 98 mins.)

Invasion of the Bee Girls (1973)** Victoria Vetri, William Smith, Anitra Ford, Cliff Osmond, Wright King. A terrific title for an only fitfully amusing spoof, scripted by Nicholas Meyer. The ingenious but underdeveloped plot deals with some demanding creatures who literally love their male dates to death. (Dir: Denis Sanders, 85 mins.)†

Invasion of the Body Snatchers (1956)**** Kevin McCarthy, Dana Wynter, Larry Gates, Carolyn Jones, King Donovan, Virginia Christine. A science-fiction classic. A beautifully controlled work of hysteria, it's the story of invading pod-parasites who take over human beings; the population of a town is replaced by a group of emotionless, soulless aliens. The film can be seen as a hyped-up, outrageous contemplation of McCarthyism, and it has aged extraordinarily well. An uncredited Sam Peckinpah, who also plays a small part, contributed to the screenplay. (Dir: Don Siegel, 80 mins.)†

Invasion of the Body Snatchers (1978)*** Donald Sutherland, Brooke Adams, Leonard Nimoy, Veronica Cartwright, Jeff Goldblum. Well-made remake. Sutherland is a San Francisco health inspector who discovers many friends around him are beginning to act very strangely (in actuality, they've turned into pod people). It's a paranoid's dream come true, with plenty of creeps and chills. Look for Kevin McCarthy and Don Siegel, the star and director of the '56 original, in cameo roles. (Dir: Philip Kaufman, 114 mins.)†

Invasion of the Body Stealers—See: **Thin Air**

Invasion of the Girl Snatchers (1973)½ Elizabeth Rush, Ele Grigsby, David Ros-

ter, Paul Lenzi. Wretched comedy about an amateur detective fighting outer space aliens in the Midwest. Resurrected on video as a "so bad it's good" item, but it's just bad. (Dir: Lee Jones, 90 mins.)†

Invasion of the Saucer Men (1957)** Steve Terrell, Gloria Castillo, Frank Gorshin.. Cool kids spot some invaders from outer space. Enjoyably campy '50s sci-fi relic. (Dir: Edward L. Cahn, 69 mins.)

Invasion of the Star Creatures (1963)* Robert Ball, Frankie Ray, Gloria Victor, Dolores Reed, Mark Ferris. Endearingly stupid sci-fi comedy with lunkheads Ball and Ray, combining the worst of both Abbott & Costello and Martin & Lewis, battling sexy alien amazons and their walking-salad monsters. Written by Jonathan Haze, star of the original *Little Shop of Horrors*. (Dir: Bruno Ve Sota, 81 mins.)

Invasion Quartet (Great Britain, 1961)**½ Bill Travers, Spike Milligan, John Le Mesurier, Maurice Denham, Thorley Walters, Eric Sykes, Gregoire Aslan. Interesting parody of *The Guns of Navarone*, as four Brits infiltrate the Nazis, intent on destroying one of their big guns. (Dir: Jay Lewis, 87 mins.)

Invasion U.S.A. (1985)*** Chuck Norris, Richard Lynch, Melissa Prophet. Rip-roaring, ultra-patriotic fun with macho man Norris performing a number of incredible heroics to save his country from an invasion by Soviet-backed terrorists. (Dir: Joseph Zito, 100 mins.)†

Investigation (France, 1979)*** Victor Lanoux, Jean Carnet, Valerie Mairesse, Michel Robin, Jacques Richard. Intricately plotted French mystery. Keenly probing the psychology of small village life, the film reveals that the hard-working townspeople exhibit more concern for whether the local mill will be closed than they do about the culpability of the mill owner charged with murder. (Dir: Etienne Perier, 116 mins.)†

Investigation of a Citizen Above Suspicion (Italy, 1970)***½ Florinda Bolkan, Gianni Santuccio, Gian Maria Volonte. Complex satirical parable about politics and Fascist ideology. Smug, mentally unbalanced police chief plants evidence against himself to test his underlings, his own status, and his moral and social superiority. Oscar as Best Foreign Film. (Dir: Elio Petri, 112 mins.)

Investigation of Murder, An—See: **Laughing Policeman, The**

Investigation, The: Inside a Terorrist Bombing (MTV 1990)***½ John Hurt, Martin Shaw, Roger Allam, Peter Gowen, Niall Tobin, Donal McCann. Gripping, detailed account of how three British television reporters uncovered evidence indicating that the "Birmingham Six," tried and convicted for an IRA bombing that killed twenty-one people ten years earlier, were in fact innocent victims of a police cover-up. (Dir: Mike Beckham, 138 mins.)†

Invisible Boy, The (1957)**½ Richard Eyer, Philip Abbott. A science-fiction yarn about a young boy and his robot. (The Robot is played by Robbie, the Robot of *Forbidden Planet*.) The kids might enjoy this adventure, which incorporates smuggled cargoes of bombs, rocket ships, spies, scientists, and hokum. (Dir: Herman Hoffman, 85 mins.)

Invisible Creature (Great Britain, 1960)** Sandra Dorne, Tony Wright. Moderate supernatural story about an unfaithful husband with murder on his mind and his wife, who seems to have a protective ghost on her side. (Dir: Montgomery Tully, 70 mins.)

Invisible Kid, The (1988)** Jay Underwood, Wally Ward, Chynna Phillips, Brother Theodore, Karen Black. Dimwitted teen comedy that has the soul of a TV movie, and no brain whatsoever. Underwood continues his late father's experiments, and poof, it's Claude Rains time! (Dir: Avery Crounse, 96 mins.)†

Invisible Man, The (1933)***½ Claude Rains, Henry Travers, Gloria Stuart, Una O'Connor. Despite its age, this horror classic still captures the imagination. Rains turns in a first-rate performance as the hero of H. G. Wells's tale, a demented scientist who has successfully made himself transparent and now wants to rule the world. Philip Wylie co-wrote the dialogue. Look for Walter Brennan, John Carradine, and Dwight Frye in the supporting cast. (Dir: James Whale, 80 mins.)†

Invisible Man, The (MTV 1975)**½ David McCallum, Melinda Fee, Jackie Cooper. A successful pilot film for a short-lived NBC series. David McCallum assumes the title role of the invisible researcher (clad in a blue body-stocking), a man who discovers how to make animals invisible, then plays guinea-pig himself. (Dir: Robert Michael Lewis, 72 mins.)

Invisible Man Returns, The (1940)*** Sir Cedric Hardwicke, Vincent Price, Nan Grey, Cecil Kellaway, Alan Napier. A sequel to *The Invisible Man*. Technical effects are excellent and the dialogue crisp. Concerns a man who uses invisibility to hunt for his brother's murderer. (Dir: Joe May, 81 mins.)

Invisible Man's Revenge, The (1944)**½ Jon Hall, Alan Curtis, Evelyn Ankers, Leon Errol, John Carradine, Gale Sondergaard, Ian Wolfe. Mildly intriguing "Now you see him, now you don't" thriller about a man who disappears long enough to get his hands on an estate—only when he wants to reappear, his doctor has other plans. (Dir: Ford Beebe, 77 mins.)

Invisible Ray, The (1936)** Boris Karloff, Bela Lugosi, Frances Drake, Beulah Bondi. Shudder story about a scientist whose touch is deadly. Karloff and Lugosi keep the yarn perking, but it comes off as familiar stuff for horror fans. (Dir: Lambert Hillyer, 82 mins.)†

Invisible Stripes (1939)**½ George Raft, Jane Bryan, William Holden, Flora Robson, Humphrey Bogart, Paul Kelly, Leo Gorcey. Efficient little melodrama boasting crisp editing, a Warner Bros. specialty, and the staunch Warner stock company lending authority to this tale of a former convict determined to prevent his brother from following in his footsteps. (Dir: Lloyd Bacon, 82 mins).

Invisible Woman, The (1941)*** John Barrymore, Virginia Bruce, Charlie Ruggles, Oscar Homolka, Margaret Hamilton, Edward Brophy, Shemp Howard, Maria Montez. Above-average but little-known sci-fi spoof about a daffy scientist with an invisibility formula. Barrymore headlines a top-drawer cast of character comedians trying to get their hands on a luscious model whom Barrymore has dematerialized. (Dir: Edward Sutherland, 72 mins.)

Invisible Woman, The (MTV 1983)½ Bob Denver, Alexa Hamilton, Harvey Korman, David Doyle, George Gobel, Garrett Morris. Denver is cast adrift as a muddleheaded biochemist whose niece becomes invisible in a lab accident. Shot on video and featuring a laugh track, this plays like the world's longest—and worst—sitcom. (Dir: Alan J. Levi, 104 mins.)

Invitation (1952)*** Dorothy McGuire, Van Johnson, Ruth Roman, Louis Calhern. Dorothy McGuire gives a glowing performance as an invalid who makes a stab for happiness despite the constant presence of death. (Dir: Gottfried Reinhardt, 84 mins.)

Invitation, The (Switzerland-France, 1973)*** Michel Robin, François Simon, Jean-Luc Bideau, Cecille Vassort. Office workers are invited for the afternoon to the home of fellow-worker Remy Placet (Robin), and are surprised to find him ensconced in almost palatial surroundings. By the end of the afternoon, in this subtly crafted film, in-office façades and barriers have come dislodged. (Dir: Claude Goretta, 100 mins.)

Invitation au Voyage (France, 1983)** Laurent Malet, Aurore Clement, Mario Adorf, Nina Scott. A stylish-looking, aberrant film that tries to coast on its sheer perversity. A brother, not wanting to end his incestuous love affair with his recently electrocuted sister, carries her around in a cello case (apparently a good place for corpse preservation) before devising a unique way to keep her spirit alive. (Dir: Peter Del Monte, 93 mins.)†

Invitation to a Gunfighter (1964)** Yul Brynner, Janice Rule, Brad Dexter, George Segal, Pat Hingle, Clifton James, Strother Martin, William Hickey. Western fans should be forewarned that there's more Freud than Zane Grey in this story of renegades and revenge. (Dir: Richard Wilson, 92 mins.)†

Invitation to Happiness (1939)**½ Irene Dunne, Fred MacMurray, Billy Cook, Charlie Ruggles. Well-made but minor little tale of an ambitious fighter who neglects his family while rising to the top. (Dir: Wesley Ruggles, 100 mins.)

Invitation to Hell (MTV 1984)* Susan Lucci, Robert Urich, Joanna Cassidy, Patty McCormack, Soleil Moon Frye, Barret Oliver, Michael Berryman. A woman who's in cahoots with the Devil persuades people to join an "exclusive" country club. (Dir: Wes Craven, 104 mins.)†

Invitation to the Dance (1956)** Gene Kelly, Tamara Toumanova, Carol Haney, Tommy Rall, Igor Youskevitch. Director Gene Kelly's attempt to make an all-dancing musical (no talking, no singing) is a valiant but pretentious stab at a popular art film. A colossally expensive commercial flop. (93 mins.)†

In Which We Serve (Great Britain, 1942)**** Noël Coward, John Mills. Drama of the men of a British destroyer during WWII, from the captain to the crew. Coward wrote, co-directed, composed the music, and plays the leading role, and does a great job in all departments. Stirring, poignant, a great film. (Dirs: Noël Coward, David Lean, 115 mins.)†

I Only Want You to Love Me (West Germany, 1976)***½ Vitus Zeplichal, Alexander Allerson, Elke Aberle, Ernie Mangold, Johanna Hofer, Erika Runge. Young man who spent his entire life trying in vain to please his parents marries a girl and lavishes her with gifts he can't afford. Out of this arrangement comes financial ruin and continuing rejection, leading to tragic violence. Tough, uncompromising, well-acted film based on a true story. (Dir: Rainer Werner Fassbinder, 112 mins.)

I Ought to Be in Pictures (1982)** Walter Matthau, Ann-Margret, Dinah Manoff, Lance Guest, Lewis Smith, Martin Ferrero. Neil Simon's play brought to the screen. Dinah Manoff pulls the stops out as Libby, the daughter of a Hollywood screenwriter, whom she hasn't seen for sixteen years. (Dir: Herbert Ross, 107 mins.)†

I Own the Racecourse (Australia, 1986)**½ Gully Coote, Tony Barry, Norman Kaye, Rodney Burke. A slow-witted boy is tricked into thinking he has purchased a racetrack for $20, but manages to turn the situation to his advantage. Good children's film. (Dir: Stephen Ramsey, 77 mins.)

Ipcress File, The (Great Britain, 1965)***½ Michael Caine, Nigel Green, Guy Doleman, Sue Lloyd, Gordon Jackson. First-rate espionage yarn, based on Len Deighton's best-seller, the tense and complex story follows bespectacled, workaday spy Harry Palmer (Caine) as he investigates the kidnapping of scientists detained behind the Iron Curtain. Followed by *Funeral in Berlin* and *Billion Dollar Brain*. (Dir: Sidney J. Furie, 108 mins.)†

Iphigenia (Greece, 1977)*** Tatiana Papamoskou, Irene Papas, Costa Kazakos. Well acted and anything but dull, but the story of the sacrificial murder of a girl by her father to appease the gods, like all the Greek classics, still awaits the ministrations of a truly epic filmmaker. (Dir: Michael Cacoyannis, 129 mins.)†

I Promise to Pay (1937)**½ Chester Morris, Helen Mack, Leo Carrillo, Thomas Mitchell, Thurston Hall. Interesting social drama about loan sharks preying on ordinary homeowners. Well written and well played. (Dir: D. Ross Lederman, 65 mins.)

I Remember Mama (1948)***½ Irene Dunne, Barbara Bel Geddes, Oscar Homolka, Philip Ober, Ellen Corby, Edgar Bergen, Rudy Vallee. George Stevens directed this intently observed, memorable drama of a mother and her Norwegian immigrant family in San Francisco. Later a long-running TV series. (134 mins.)†

Irene (1940)**½ Anna Neagle, Ray Milland, Roland Young, Alan Marshall, May Robson, Billie Burke, Arthur Treacher. Thin version of the famous musical of the '20s, without many of the songs. A pretty model falls in love with a young upper-cruster, but his family disapproves. (Dir: Herbert Wilcox, 104 mins.)

Irezumi (Japan, 1983)** Tomisaburo Wakayama, Tasayo Utsunomiya, Yusuke Takita, Masaki Kyomoto. A beautifully photographed but bewildering film whose subject matter veers uncomfortably toward the pornographic. A master tattoo artist becomes obsessed with putting his designs on his young mistress. (Dir: Yoichi Takabayashi, 88 mins.)†

Irish Eyes Are Smiling (1944)**½ June Haver, Dick Haymes, Monty Woolley, Anthony Quinn, Maxie Rosenbloom. Routine musical supposedly about the chap who wrote the title song. Some fine Irish melodies but little else. Produced by Damon Runyon. (Dir: Gregory Ratoff, 90 mins.)

Irish in Us, The (1935)**½ James Cagney, Pat O'Brien, Olivia de Havilland, Frank McHugh, Allen Jenkins. A blarney comedy with lots of action and some welcome Warner Bros. faces to make this dated comedy about three brawling Irish brothers palatable. (Dir: Lloyd Bacon, 84 mins.)

Irma La Douce (1963)***½ Jack Lemmon, Shirley MacLaine, Lou Jacobi, Bruce Yarnell, Herschel Bernardi, Joan Shawlee, Tura Satana, Cliff Osmond, Bill Bixby, James Caan (bit). Talented producer-director-writer Billy Wilder took the hit Broadway musical, extracted the musical numbers, and came up with a raucous comedy about Paris prostitutes and their procurers. Lemmon is forced into leading a double life in order to keep his love, streetwalker MacLaine, and his energetic performance is among his best. (147 mins.)†

Ironclads (MCTV 1991)**½ Virginia Madsen, Alex Hyde-White, Reed Edward Diamond, E. G. Marshall, Fritz Weaver. Impressive visual special effects highlight this re-creation of the Civil War's memorable five-hour naval battle between two ironclad ships: the Confederate's *Merrimac* and the Union's *Monitor.* Unfortunately, the exciting adventure tale is bogged down by the customary subplots of love, loyalty, and death in the face of war. (Dir: Delbert Mann, 96 mins.)†

Iron and Silk (1990)*** Mark Salzman, Pan Qingfu, Jeanette Lin Tsui, Vivian Wu, Sun Xudong, Zheng Guo. Film version of actor-writer Salzman's book about his travels in China has a documentary feel and succeeds in presenting a nicely acted and lovingly crafted story about life and culture in that country. (Dir: Shirley Sun, 91 mins.)

Iron Curtain, The (1948)**½ Dana Andrews, Gene Tierney. First major anti-Communist film is based on the Igor Gouzenko incident. He's the Russian who helped round up a Canadian spy ring. Film is confused, episodic, and only has a few exciting scenes. (Dir: William Wellman, 87 mins.)

Iron Eagle (1986)**½ Louis Gossett, Jr., Jason Gedrick, David Suchet, Tim Thomerson. When Uncle Sam proves disinterested in rescuing his captured dad, a teenager gets his pop's flying pal to help him steal a plane to swoop down behind the Iron Curtain to pick up papa. (Dir: Sidney J. Furie, 119 mins.)†

Iron Eagle II (Canada-Israel, 1988)** Louis Gossett, Jr., Mark Humphrey, Stuart Margolin, Alan Scarfe. Gossett is put in charge of a secret camp of U.S. and Soviet pilots training to destroy a nuclear threat in the Middle East. (Dir: Sidney J. Furie, 101 mins.)†

Iron Horse, The (1924)*** George O'Brien, Madge Bellamy, Gladys Hulette, Cyril Chadwick, Fred Kohler, J. Farrell MacDonald, Chief Big Tree, Chief White Spear. Director John Ford's epic adventure of the building of the railroads across North American, following a young surveyor for the Union Pacific company (O'Brien), his love of the boss's daughter, and his battles with his crooked rival. A classic. (119 mins.)

Iron Major, The (1943)*** Pat O'Brien, Robert Ryan, Ruth Warrick, Leon Ames. Life story of Frank Cavanaugh, famous football coach and WWI hero. Well-done biographical drama. (Dir: Ray Enright, 85 mins.)†

Iron Man (1931)*** Lew Ayres, Jean Harlow, Robert Armstrong, John Miljan, Ned Sparks. Taut story of a determined young boxer whose career is threatened by his no-good wife; sharp, gritty pre-Production Code script, strongly acted. (Dir: Tod Browning, 73 mins.)

Iron Man (1951)**½ Jeff Chandler, Evelyn Keyes, Stephen McNally, Jim Backus. A notch or two above the run-of-the-mill boxing yarns. Chandler is good as the peace-loving coal miner turned boxing champ. Look for Rock Hudson and James Arness in small roles. (Dir: Joseph Pevney, 82 mins.)

Iron Mask, The (1929)***½ Douglas Fairbanks, Belle Bennett, Dorothy Revier, Marguerite De La Motte, Leon Barry, Stanley J. Sandford, Gino Corrado, William Bakewell, Nigel De Brulier. Fairbanks's last silent vehicle, from Alexander Dumas's *The Man in the Iron Mask,* a sequel to *The Three Musketeers.* Here, the older but still dashing D'Artagnan is captain of the king's guards, and must prevent a plot to overthrow him. (Dir: Allan Dwan, 87 mins.)†

Iron Mistress, The (1952)**½ Alan Ladd, Virginia Mayo, Joseph Calleia, Phyllis Kirk. Jim Bowie raises a ruckus in New Orleans, taking time out to invent his famous knife, but the film stops short of his final stand at the Alamo. Average swashbuckler. (Dir: Gordon Douglas, 110 mins.)

Iron Petticoat, The (Great Britain, 1956)*½ Bob Hope, Katharine Hepburn, Noelle Middleton, James Robertson Justice, Robert Helpmann, Sidney James. Hope as a pilot acting as bodyguard to frigid Russian Air Force Captain (Hepburn). Both seem understandably embarrassed to be caught in this sub-*Ninotchka* attempt at humor, as was scripter Ben

Hecht, who had his name removed from the credits. (Dir: Ralph Thomas, 87 mins.)

Ironside (MTV 1967)****½** Raymond Burr, Geraldine Brooks, Wally Cox, Kim Darby, Don Galloway, Barbara Anderson, Donald Mitchell, Lilia Skala. Pilot movie for the TV series stars Burr as a gruff, blunt, cantankerous sleuth confined to a wheelchair, crippled by a sniper's bullet. Look for Tiny Tim as a coffeehouse singer. (Dir: James Goldstone, 104 mins.)

Iron Triangle, The (1989)****½** Beau Bridges, Liem Whatley, Haing S. Ngor. Apolitical look at the war in Vietnam as U.S. captain Bridges learns the other side of the story from sympathetic Vietcong Whatley. A minor but noteworthy change of pace in the Vietnam genre. (Dir: Eric Weston, 91 mins.)†

Iron Warrior (Italy, 1987)* Miles O'Keeffe, Savina Gersak, Elizabeth Kaza. Inane sword 'n' sorcery sequel to *Ator the Fighting Eagle* and *Blade Master*. It has something to do with muscle-bound Ator rescuing a deposed medieval princess from a witch who wants to take over the world. (Dir: Al Bradley, 81 mins.)†

Ironweed (1987)*****½** Jack Nicholson, Meryl Streep, Carroll Baker, Michael O'Keefe, Diane Venora, Fred Gwynne, Margaret Whitton, Tom Waits, Joe Grifasi. Nicholson got his first really challenging role in quite some time as a wandering bum who suffers from disquieting flashbacks; Streep is his companion, an ex-radio singer who has her own problems with the past. Together they wander Depression-era Albany, scrounging for work and liquor. Acting at its finest, with both leads at their best. The melancholy screenplay was written by William Kennedy, based on his best-selling novel. (Dir: Hector Babenco, 135 mins.)†

Iroquois Trail (1950)****½** George Montgomery, Brenda Marshall, Glenn Langan, Reginald Denny, Sheldon Leonard, Dan O'Herlihy. Hunter avenging his brother's death uncovers traitors on the frontier. Indifferently adapted from James Fenimore Cooper's *Leatherstocking Tales.* (Dir: Phil Karlson, 85 mins.)

Irreconcilable Differences (1984)****½** Ryan O'Neal, Shelley Long, Drew Barrymore, Sam Wanamaker, Sharon Stone, Allan Garfield. Uneven comedy about Barrymore divorcing her self-centered parents on grounds of emotional abandonment. If only the script had stuck to its sharp satire of self-absorbed Hollywoodians, this might have been first-class. (Dir: Charles Shyer, 117 mins.)†

Irwin Allen's Production of Fire! (MTV 1977)****½** Ernest Borgnine, Vera Miles, Patty Duke Astin, Alex Cord, Donna Mills, Lloyd Nolan, Neville Brand, Ty Hardin, Erik Estrada. Yet another one on devastating forest fires benefits from a better-than-average cast and excellent fire sequences. Sometimes shown at 72 mins. (Dir: Earl Bellamy, 98 mins.)†

Isabel (Canada, 1968)*****½** Genevieve Bujold, Marc Strange, Elton Hayes, Al Waxman. A weird tale of a girl who returns home to find mystery and fear. Atmospheric Canadian coastal backgrounds, and an eerie, other-worldly quality. Interesting and offbeat. (Dir: Paul Almond, 108 mins.)

Isabel's Choice (MTV 1981)****½** Jean Stapleton, Richard Kiley, Peter Coyote, Betsy Palmer, Mildred Dunnock. A tailor-made role for Stapleton, who plays a capable but lonely executive secretary in a large corporation. While her bosses play musical chairs, Jean becomes disenchanted with her work, despite the chance to advance. (Dir: Guy Green, 104 mins.)

Isadora—See: Loves of Isadora

Isadora (1967)******* Vivian Pickles, Peter Bowles, Alex Jawdokimoy. This early entry in a series of telefilm biographies made for the BBC by unconventional filmmaker Ken Russell about dancer Isadora Duncan contains the seeds of his unmistakably wild style: broad characterization, bold camerawork, and impressive images. Structured like a newsreel, it also includes one element he later discarded—historical accuracy. (67 mins.)

I Sailed to Tahiti with an All Girl Crew (1968)* Gardner McKay, Fred Clark, Diane McBain. Young man says he can win a race to Tahiti using an all-girl crew. Male chauvinist antique. (Dir: Richard Bare, 95 mins.)

I Saw What You Did (1965)****** Joan Crawford, John Ireland. Couple of teenage girls play a telephone prank, which upsets a murderer and makes them candidates for his next crime. (Dir: William Castle, 82 mins.)

I Saw What You Did (MTV 1988)****** Shawnee Smith, Tammy Lauren, Candace Cameron, Robert Carradine, David Carradine. For some inexplicable reason, the William Castle shocker was remade into a fairly suspenseful TV movie. Carradine (Robert, that is) plays the murderer who receives a taunting phone call from two mischievous teens. (Dir: Fred Walton, 96 mins.)

I See a Dark Stranger—See: Adventuress, The

I Sent a Letter to My Love (France, 1981)*****½** Simone Signoret, Jean Rochefort, Delphine Seyrig. A reflective, gentle film, *Letter* is the simple story—with a twist—by Moshe (*Madame Rosa*) Mizrahi of a middle-aged invalid and the sister who cares for him. Showcases the talent of Simone Signoret and Jean Rochefort. (Dir: Moshe Mizrahi, 96 mins.)†

Is Everybody Happy? (1943)**½ Ted Lewis, Michael Duane, Larry Parks. Bandleader Ted Lewis, playing himself, guides an unsure soldier to the wedding altar. Forget the soapy plot and enjoy a dozen great tunes, including "It Had to Be You" and "St. Louis Blues." (Dir: Charles Barton, 73 mins.)

Ishi, the Last of His Tribe (MTV 1978)*** Dennis Weaver, Eloy Phil Casados, Devon Ericson, Joaquin Martinez. Sympathetic account of the last wild Indian, hounded by California gold miners, who gave himself up in 1911. Befriended by a Berkeley anthropologist (Weaver), Ishi talks of his past through flashbacks while living in a San Francisco museum. (Dir: Robert Ellis Miller, 104 mins.)

I Shot Jesse James (1949)*** Preston Foster, John Ireland, Barbara Britton. The story of Bob Ford, and the guilty conscience that plagues him after drilling the famous outlaw. (Dir: Samuel Fuller, 81 mins.)

Ishtar (1987)**½ Warren Beatty, Dustin Hoffman, Isabelle Adjani, Charles Grodin, Jack Weston, Tess Harper, Carol Kane. A pleasant (but certainly not modest) little comedy that updates the old Hope-Crosby *Road* pictures, offering us a couple of urban neurotics instead of wisecracking sharpsters. Warren and Dustin play a singing-songwriting duo who become involved in international intrigue when they bring their rancid lounge act to the fictional Saudi city of Ishtar. (Dir: Elaine May, 108 mins.)†

Island, The (Japan, 1962)***½ Nobuko Otowa, Taiji Tonoyama, Shinji Tanaka, Masanori Horimoto. Powerful Japanese film about a family struggling for existence on a remote and barren island. No dialogue, story told through the camera, actions of the principals. Unusual, engrossing drama. (Dir: Kaneto Shindo, 96 mins.)†

Island, The (1980)** Michael Caine, David Warner, Angela Punch McGregor, Zakes Mokae. Big-budget Peter Benchley premise of an inbred band of marauders descended from 17th-century buccaneers. Director Michael Ritchie forgets that action and violence are not interchangeable, with too much of the latter. (113 mins.)†

Island (Australia, 1989)** Eva Sitta, Irene Papas, Anoja Weerasinghe, Chris Haywood, Norman Kaye. Three women—an Australian junkie, a Greek woman trying to forget a tragedy-filled life, and an abandoned Sri Lankan bride—cope with life on a small island off the coast

of Greece. Writer-director Paul Cox's film lacks the bizarre black humor and offbeat charm that marks his best work: this is dead serious and deadly dull. Haywood steals the film in a supporting role as a deaf fisherman. (93 mins.)

Island at the Top of the World, The (1974)** David Hartman, Donald Sinden, Mako, Agneta Eckemyr. Fanciful yarn based on Ian Cameron's novel *The Lost Ones* has aristocrat Sinden leading an airship into the Arctic wastes in 1907 to find his missing son. Special effects overshadow the actors. (Dir: Robert Stevenson, 94 mins.)†

Island Claws—See: **Night of the Claw**

Islander, The (MTV 1978)** Dennis Weaver, Sharon Gless, Peter Mark Richman, Bernadette Peters, Robert Vaughn, Sheldon Leonard. Weaver as a retired lawyer manages to add a trace of sanity to a complicated plot about mobsters, call girls, and a law partner accused of beating a stewardess. (Dir: Paul Krasny, 104 mins.)

Island in the Sky (1953)*** John Wayne, Lloyd Nolan, James Arness, Andy Devine. Wayne exchanges the plains for planes in this adventure film about a dangerous rescue mission in frozen Labrador. Solid script and performances. (Dir: William Wellman, 109 mins.)

Island in the Sun (1957)**½ James Mason, Joan Fontaine, Harry Belafonte, Dorothy Dandridge, Joan Collins, Michael Rennie, John Williams, Stephen Boyd. Alec Waugh's best-seller is watered-down in this screen translation. Revolves around an assorted group of blacks and whites living in the British West Indies, and their political and personal lives. The fact that this film was made in the late fifties limits the portrayal of interracial romances and the film loses some of its intended impact as a result. (Dir: Robert Rossen, 119 mins.)†

Island Monster (Italy, 1953)* Boris Karloff, Renata Vicario, Franco Marzi, Patrizia Remiddi. Obscure Karloff effort isn't a horror movie at all; the "monster" he plays is the leader of a gang of drug smugglers operating from a Mediterranean island. Karloff's voice in the English version was dubbed by another actor, who tries hard to sound like Boris but doesn't succeed. AKA: **Monster of the Island.** (Dir: Roberto Montero, 87 mins.)†

Island of Desire (Great Britain, 1952)** Linda Darnell, Tab Hunter, Donald Grey. Poorly acted film about a woman and a young Marine shipwrecked on an island during WWII. A mature Englishman joins them to complete the triangle. (Dir: Stuart Heisler, 103 mins.)

Island of Doctor Moreau, The (1977)*½ Burt Lancaster, Michael York, Nigel Davenport, Barbara Carrera, Richard Basehart.

Lackluster remake of *Island of Lost Souls*. A man is shipwrecked on an eerie island where a mad scientist's experiments deal with changing animals into men. Effective make-up effects by John Chambers are outweighed by ludicrous scripting. (Dir: Don Taylor, 98 mins.)†

Island of Lost Souls (1933)***½ Charles Laughton, Bela Lugosi, Richard Arlen. It's easy to comprehend why this adaptation of H. G. Wells's *Island of Dr. Moreau* shocked audiences in the thirties; it's still unsettling and disturbing. Raising hamminess to the level of genius, Laughton enacts the maddest of mad scientists, a pudgy vivisectionist obsessed with making men out of animals. Filmed eerily in black and white, the film works on the audience like a shared nightmare in which we experience the shipwrecked souls' growing horror as they become a captive audience for the demented doctor's experiments in altering the animal kingdom. Randolph Scott, Alan Ladd, and Buster Crabbe are among his victims. (Dir: Erle C. Kenton, 70 mins.)

Island of Love (1963)*** Robert Preston, Tony Randall, Georgia Moll, Walter Matthau, Michael Constantine, Titos Vandis. Bright comedy about a fast-talking promoter who cons a gangster into financing a movie stinker, then promotes a Greek island as a paradise spot. (Dir: Morton Da Costa, 101 mins.)

Island of Terror (Great Britain, 1967)*** Peter Cushing, Edward Judd, Carole Gray. Medical experts journey to an island where they discover shell-like creatures that show a penchant for devouring the bones of victims. Well-done science-fiction thriller summons up a good share of shudders. (Dir: Terence Fisher, 90 mins.)†

Island of the Alive (1986)**½ Michael Moriarty, Karen Black, Gerrit Graham, Laurene Landon, James Dixon. Second sequel to *It's Alive* finds the mutated infants being relocated to a deserted island; five years later, one of the fathers (Moriarty) heads an expedition there to see what has become of them. Writer-director Larry Cohen continues his bizarre, horrific satire on parenting and the family here, but the best part of the movie is the frightening first half hour. (94 mins.)†

Island of the Blue Dolphins (1964)**½ Celia Kaye, Larry Domasin, George Kennedy. Youngsters are left alone on an island, and the girl befriends a wild dog who becomes her protector. Pleasant adventure story. (Dir: James B. Clark, 93 mins.)†

Island of the Burning Doomed (Great Britain, 1967)**½ Christopher Lee, Peter Cushing, Patrick Allen, Jane Merrow,

Sarah Lawson. Extra-terrestrials pose the burning question: What would happen to Earth if they caused an intense heat wave in the dead of winter? Intelligently done, without being inspired. AKA: **Night of the Burning Damned** and **Night of the Big Heat**. (Dir: Terence Fisher, 94 mins.)

Island of the Doomed—See: **Maneater of Hydra**

Island of the Snake People—See: **Snake People**

Island Rescue (Great Britain, 1951)**½ David Niven, Glynis Johns, George Coulouris, Kenneth More, Bernard Lee, Anton Diffring. A major is assigned the task of rescuing a prize cow from a British island occupied by the Nazis. Uneven adventure falls midway between comedy and melodrama. (Dir: Ralph Thomas, 87 mins.)

Islands in the Stream (1977)**½ George C. Scott, David Hemmings, Claire Bloom, Gilbert Roland, Susan Tyrrell, Hart Bochner. Film version of Hemingway's posthumously published novel is impressive in spots. A selfish artist (Scott), secure in his self-imposed isolation, finds his peace of mind shattered by the arrival of his three sons. After one boy is killed in war, Scott rejoins the human race and tries to help a family of fleeing refugees. (Dir: Franklin J. Schaffner, 110 mins.)†

Island Sons (MTV 1987)*½ Timothy Bottoms, Joseph Bottoms, Sam Bottoms, Ben Bottoms, Claire Kirkconnell, Richard Narita, Kim Miyori. A plot-heavy Hawaiian adventure with an out-of-the-ordinary casting gimmick: the Faraday brothers, the four sons of a missing business tycoon, are played by the Bottoms brothers. Audiences will have a harder time telling the brothers apart than following the story. (Dir: Alan J. Levi, 104 mins.)

Island Women (1958)* Vince Edwards, Marie Winsor, Marilee Earle. An intergeneration love triangle in seaside Nassau involves two U.S. tourists and an American yachtsman. The calypso setting does nothing to enhance a trite story. (Dir: William Berke, 72 mins.)

Isle of Fury (1936)**½ Humphrey Bogart, Margaret Lindsay, Donald Woods, E. E. Clive. Interesting version of Somerset Maugham's *The Narrow Corner*; an innocent doctor is kidnapped and taken to the West Indies, where his outlook on life changes. (Dir: Frank McDonald, 60 mins.)

Isle of the Dead (1945)*** Boris Karloff, Ellen Drew, Marc Cramer, Alan Napier, Jason Robards, Sr. Greek general on a small island is enmeshed with vampires and witchcraft. Eerie thriller has some good effects. (Dir: Mark Robson, 72 mins.)†

Is My Face Red? (1932)**½ Ricardo Cortez, Helen Twelvetrees, Robert Armstrong, Jill Esmond, Sidney Toler, ZaSu Pitts. Fast-paced, snappy tale of an unscrupulous gossip columnist, superbly played by Cortez, and the trouble he causes. (Dir: William A. Seiter, 66 mins.)

Isn't It Shocking? (MTV 1973)**½ Alan Alda, Louise Lasser, Edmond O'Brien, Will Geer, Lloyd Nolan, Ruth Gordon. Offbeat murder mystery; in the rural New England town of Mount Angel, the elderly are dying, but not from old age. (Dir: John Badham, 90 mins.)

Is Paris Burning? (U.S.-France, 1966)** Jean-Paul Belmondo, Charles Boyer, Leslie Caron, Jean-Pierre Cassel, George Chakiris, Alain Delon, Kirk Douglas, Glenn Ford, Gert Fröbe, E. G. Marshall, Yves Montand, Anthony Perkins, Simone Signoret, Jean-Louis Trintignant, Orson Welles. The best-selling novel about the efforts to save Paris from Hitler's torch is turned into a dull, episodic drama with a series of cameo roles played by an international roster of stars. Script is credited to seven writers, including Gore Vidal and Francis Ford Coppola. (Dir: René Clement, 173 mins.)†

I Spy, You Spy—See: **Bang! Bang! You're Dead!**

Israel's Shattered Dreams—See: **Shattered Dreams**

Istanbul (1957)** Errol Flynn, Cornell Borchers, John Bentley, Torin Thatcher, Leif Thatcher, Nat "King" Cole, Werner Klemperer. Adventurer returns to recover a fortune in diamonds, finds his old flame, presumed dead, alive and an amnesia victim. Shopworn melodrama for Flynn fans. Remake of *Singapore*, 1947. (Dir: Joseph Pevney, 84 mins.)

Istanbul (France, 1985)** Brad Dourif, Dominique Deruddere, Ingrid De Vos, François Beukelaers. Scuzzy American Dourif, on the run from a shady past, meets a penniless student in Belgium and involves him in a kidnapping. (Dir: Marc Didden, 90 mins.)†

Istanbul Express (MTV 1968)**½ Gene Barry, Senta Berger, John Saxon, Mary Ann Mobley. Rather zesty action picture that follows art dealer Barry aboard a train, journeying to Turkey to buy certain valuable papers for the U.S. government at an international auction. (Dir: Richard Irving, 94 mins.)

Is There Sex After Death? (1971)***½ Buck Henry, Alan Abel, Marshall Efron, Holly Woodlawn. A raunchy, outrageous, but often wildly funny satire that mocks all the other films that take themselves seriously and try to capitalize on the "sexual revolution." (Dirs: Alan and Jeanne Abel, 97 mins.)†

It (1927)*** Clara Bow, Antonio Moreno,
530

Priscilla Bonner, William Austin, Jacqueline Gadson. Silly plot can do nothing to dim the luster of Bow, who lights up the screen with warmth and sex appeal every second she's on it. Otherwise, the story concerns a poor shopgirl who loves a rich boy but has to prove to him that she's "not that kind of girl." Breezy and enjoyable. Josef von Sternberg directed some scenes when director Clarence Badger was ill. (72 mins.)†

It (MTV 1990)*** Harry Anderson, Dennis Christopher, Richard Masur, Annette O'Toole, Tim Reid, Richard Thomas, Tim Curry. Stephen King's truly frightening novel becomes a scary TV miniseries. Impressionable young kids should *not* see this show since it is about kids being lured to their deaths by a deadly force that takes on the physical form of a circus clown. Seven childhood friends reunite as adults to fight the evil force. (Dir: Tommy Lee Wallace, 192 mins.)

It Ain't Hay (1943)**½ Bud Abbott, Lou Costello, Grace McDonald, Eugene Pallette, Cecil Kellaway, Shemp Howard, Mike Mazurki. Bud and Lou co-star with a champion racehorse in this amusing, well-cast Damon Runyan adaptation. (Dir: Erle C. Kenton, 72 mins.)

I Take These Men (MTV 1983)* Susan St. James, John Rubinstein, James Murtaugh, Adam West. Susan St. James is the center of attention as a bored housewife toying with the idea of divorce and fantasizing about replacements. (Dir: Larry Peerce, 104 mins.)

I Take This Woman (1940)** Spencer Tracy, Hedy Lamarr. A dedicated doctor thinks his wife, a model, doesn't love him, and so on until you fall asleep. (Dir: W. S. Van Dyke II, 97 mins.)

Italian Connection, The (Italy, 1973)** Henry Silva, Woody Strode, Adolfo Celi, Mario Adorf, Luciana Paluzzi, Sylva Koscina, Cyril Cusack. Action-packed underworld thriller about a New York kingpin sending two hit men to kill some crooks on Italian turf. (Dir: Fernando Di Leo, 92 mins.)†

Italian Job, The (Great Britain, 1969)***½ Michael Caine, Noël Coward, Benny Hill, Raf Vallone, Rossano Brazzi, John Le Mesurier. Caine shines as a criminal who inherits the plans for a gold robbery in Turin, Italy. Fast and entertaining. (Dir: Peter Collinson, 101 mins.)

Italiano Brava Gente—See: **Attack and Retreat**

Italian Straw Hat, The (France, 1927)***½ Olga Tschechowa, Albert Prejean, Marise Maia, Alice Tissot. Brilliantly comic farce about groom who's delayed on the way to his wedding when his horse eats the straw hat of a philandering wife who's making love to a calvary officer by the side of the road. Hilarious silent classic moves along like a finely tuned clock, with terrific sight gags leading to one of the funniest endings in movie history. (Dir: René Clair, 74 mins.)†

It All Came True (1940)**½ Humphrey Bogart, Ann Sheridan, Jeffrey Lynn, ZaSu Pitts, Una O'Connor. Bogie goes soft in this occasionally entertaining story of a gangster whose spirit is captured by some old-time vaudevillians. (Dir: Lewis Seiler, 97 mins.)

It Always Rains on Sunday (Great Britain, 1947)*** Googie Withers, John McCallum, Edward Chapman, Susan Shaw. Story of a family in the slums of London torn apart by crime. Well made, but grim, unpleasant. (Dir: Robert Hamer, 92 mins.)

It Came from Beneath the Sea (1955)** Kenneth Tobey, Donald Curtis, Faith Domergue. A U.S. submarine tangles with a giant octopus that has come from the lower depths of the sea due to the many H-bomb experiments. Ray Harryhausen's special effects are the star here. (Dir: Robert Gordon, 80 mins.)†

It Came from Hollywood (1982)* Dan Aykroyd, Cheech and Chong, John Candy, Gilda Radner. Lame concoction featuring clips from bad movies. Loosely inspired by the books *The Fifty Worst Films of All Time* and *The Golden Turkey Awards*, although those books have not been well served by the inane linking devices starring modern comics who are as unintentionally unfunny as the film clips are unintentionally funny. (Dir: Malcolm Leo, 80 mins.)†

It Came from Outer Space (1953)*** Richard Carlson, Barbara Rush, Russell Johnson, Morey Amsterdam. Good photography and a large budget help to make this first-grade sci-fi entertainment. Carlson, an old hand at fighting visitors from beneath the sea and above the stars, is stalwart once again in the face of faceless creatures. Originally in 3-D. (Dir: Jack Arnold, 81 mins.)†

It Came Upon a Midnight Clear (MTV 1984)* Mickey Rooney, Scott Grimes, Barrie Youngfellow, George Gaynes, Hamilton Camp, Elisha Cook, Annie Potts, Lloyd Nolan. Sappy sentimental tripe about how the angels give a dead grandpa one more Christmas to spend with his adoring grandkid. (Dir: Peter Hunt, 104 mins.)†

It Comes Up Murder—See: **Honey Pot, The**

It Conquered the World (1956)** Peter Graves, Beverly Garland, Lee Van Cleef, Sally Fraser, Charles B. Griffith, Jonathan Haze, Richard (Dick) Miller. Even producer-director Roger Corman himself considered this cheapie about a killer cucumber man from Venus one of his lesser efforts. The cast of Corman regulars make it enjoyable nonsense. (68 mins.)†

It Couldn't Happen Here (Great Britain, 1988)**½ The Pet Shop Boys (Neil Tennant, Chris Lowe), Joss Ackland. Brit techno-pop duo the Pet Shop Boys spend a Felliniesque day fantasizing about various arcane subjects that occasionally appear on the scene in the form of a music video. Certainly well made, but as to what it's supposed to be about, your guess is as good as ours. (Dir: Jack Bond, 90 mins.)

It Couldn't Happen to a Nicer Guy (MTV 1974)**½ Paul Sorvino, Michael Learned, Bob Dishy, Adam Arkin, Roger Bower. Sorvino can't convince anyone that he was forced, at gunpoint, to make love to a very glamorous young lady who picked him up while he was hitchhiking. Smirky comedy, some bright moments. (Dir: Cy Howard, 72 mins.)

It Grows on Trees (1952)**½ Irene Dunne, Dean Jagger, Joan Evans, Richard Crenna. An amusing idea that doesn't quite live up to its expectations. The Baxter family discover two trees in their yard which sprout money (five- and ten-dollar bills) rather than leaves. Naturally, the situation becomes hectic. Dunne's last film. (Dir: Arthur Lubin, 84 mins.)

It Had to Be You (1947)**½ Ginger Rogers, Cornel Wilde, Spring Byington, Ron Randell. Socialite always fails to marry at the last moment, until she meets the right man. Amusing comedy. (Dir: Don Hartman, 98 mins.)

It Had to Be You (1989)*½ Renée Taylor, Joseph Bologna, William Hickey, Eileen Brennan, Tony Randall, Donna Dixon. Would-be actress and playwright lures a director of TV commercials to her apartment, keeping him there until he agrees to read her play. Essentially a two-character drama (padded out with cameos) with the usual jokes, revelations, and tragedies as the unlikely couple become familiar. Poorly filmed, a far cry from Taylor and Bologna's 1971 *Made For Each Other*. (Dirs: Renée Taylor, Joseph Bologna, 105 mins.)

It Had to Happen (1936)**½ George Raft, Rosalind Russell, Leo Carrillo, Alan Dinehart. Unusual political romance has Raft as an immigrant fighting his way to power and falling in love with old-money Russell; interesting background with some sharp observations from director Roy Del Ruth. (79 mins.)

I Thank a Fool (1962)*½ Susan Hayward, Peter Finch. Ridiculous melodrama. Susan Hayward is all stiff upper lip and nobility as an ex-doctor who was charged with euthanasia and served a prison term only to end up as companion-nurse to the wife of the man who prosecuted her (Finch). (Dir: Robert Stevens, 100 mins.)

It Happened at Lakewood Manor (MTV

1977)** Lynda Day George, Robert Foxworth, Myrna Loy, Suzanne Somers, Bernie Casey, Brian Dennehy. A buggy horror film about vacationers being terrorized by insects at a vacation resort. Viewers may itch in discomfort, but there are no big scares. AKA: **Panic at Lakewood Manor** and **Ants**. (Dir: Robert Sheerer, 104 mins.)†

It Happened at the World's Fair (1963)** Elvis Presley, Joan O'Brien, Gary Lockwood, Yvonne Craig. Mix Elvis, the Seattle World's Fair, some romance, and a cute Chinese girl together, and out comes a musical tailored for the fans. (Dir: Norman Taurog, 105 mins.)†

It Happened Here (Great Britain, 1966)***½ Pauline Murray, Sebastian Shaw, Honor Fehrson. Film historian Kevin Brownlow and documentarian Andrew Mollo co-directed this clever, engrossing newsreel-style fable about what might have happened had Britain fallen to the Nazis in World War II. (95 mins.)

It Happened in Athens (1962)* Jayne Mansfield, Trax Colton, Nico Minardos, Bob Mathias. Drab, often distasteful comedy-drama of the 1896 Greek Olympic Games, when a young shepherd wins the marathon, gaining the unwanted hand of an actress (Mansfield). (Dir: Andrew Marton, 92 mins.)

It Happened in Brooklyn (1947)**½ Frank Sinatra, Kathryn Grayson, Peter Lawford, Jimmy Durante, Gloria Grahame. Pleasant, inconsequential musical about ex-sailor Sinatra moving in with Brooklyn janitor Durante and trying to crash the music business. (Dir: Richard Whorf, 105 mins.)†

It Happened One Christmas (MTV 1977)*** Marlo Thomas, Wayne Rogers, Barney Martin, Doris Roberts, Orson Welles, Cloris Leachman, Richard Dysart, Christopher Guest. The ingratiating Thomas in a remake of *It's a Wonderful Life*, taking the part played by James Stewart! Sentimental story about a small town and its concern for one of its caring citizens is OK, but why would you choose this over the original? (Dir: Donald Wrye, 115 mins.)

It Happened One Night (1934)**** Clark Gable, Claudette Colbert, Walter Connolly, Roscoe Karns. Dizzy society girl flees from her father, finds romance with a reporter on a cross-country bus. The granddaddy of all sophisticated comedy romances still packs a lot of entertainment. Great fun. Remade twice as *Eve Knew Her Apples* and *You Can't Run Away From It*. (Dir: Frank Capra, 110 mins.)†

It Happened One Summer—See: **State Fair** (1945)

It Happened on Fifth Avenue (1947)**½ Victor Moore, Ann Harding, Charlie Ruggles,

532

Gale Storm, Don DeFore. A heartwarming family film that gets a lot of air play during Christmastime. A hobo invites some of his pals to live the life of Riley when he comes upon an empty mansion. (Dir: Roy Del Ruth, 115 mins.)

It Happened to Jane (1959)**½ Doris Day, Jack Lemmon, Ernie Kovacs, Steve Forrest. Silly but pleasant comedy about a New England businesswoman dealing in lobsters who manages to throw a wrench into the big-time operations of a railroad. (Dir: Richard Quine, 98 mins.)

It Happened Tomorrow (1944)***½ Dick Powell, Linda Darnell, Jack Oakie, Edgar Kennedy, Sig Rumann. A reporter gets tomorrow's newspaper from a strange little man; then one day he reads his own obituary. Charming fantasy-comedy, with Rene Clair's splendid direction making it a grand show. (84 mins.)†

It Happens Every Spring (1949)*** Ray Milland, Jean Peters, Paul Douglas, Ed Begley, Ted de Corsia, Ray Collins. Funny film about a chemistry professor who discovers a compound that makes baseballs react strangely to bats. His discovery takes him from the lab to the baseball diamond where he becomes a great strike-out pitcher. (Dir: Lloyd Bacon, 80 mins.)

It Happens Every Thursday (1953)**½ Loretta Young, John Forsythe, Frank McHugh, Edgar Buchanan, Jane Darwell, Dennis Weaver. Simple little comedy-drama about a couple of city dwellers who move to a small California community to run the town's weekly newspaper. The comedy stems from Forsythe's outrageous schemes to bolster circulation. (Dir: Joseph Pevney, 80 mins.)

I, the Jury (1953)** Biff Elliot, Preston Foster, Peggie Castle, Elisha Cook, Jr. Film version of the Mickey Spillane novel with Elliot as Mike Hammer, the tough private eye, lacks violence, sex, and especially excitement. (Dir: Harry Essex, 87 mins.)

I, the Jury (1982)*½ Armand Assante, Barbara Carrera, Alan King, Geoffrey Lewis. Assante plays detective Mike Hammer in search of a murderer who killed one of his best buddies. (Dir: Richard T. Heffron, 109 mins.)

It Lives Again (1978)*½ Frederic Forrest, Kathleen Lloyd, Eddie Constantine, John Marley, John P. Ryan, Andrew Duggan. Uninspired sequel to the pediatric chiller, *It's Alive*. A mutant baby on the rampage again. This time, the movie's stillborn. Followed by *Island of the Alive*. (Dir: Larry Cohen, 91 mins.)†

It's a Big Country (1952)**½ Gene Kelly, Janet Leigh, Fredric March. An octet of stories, some better than others, make up the framework of this big valentine to America. One of the best episodes stars Kelly as the son of a Greek immigrant who falls in love with the daughter of a Hungarian farmer. Among the many stars who appear in the various segments are Van Johnson, James Whitmore, Gary Cooper, William Powell, Kennan Wynn, and Ethel Barrymore. (Dirs: Charles Vidor, Richard Thorpe, John Sturges, Don Hartman, Don Weis, Clarence Brown, William Wellman, 89 mins.)

It's a Bikini World (1965)*½ Tommy Kirk, Deborah Walley, Suzie Kaye, Sid Haig. The end of the line for the "beach party" genre, with Kirk and Walley poor replacements for Frankie and Annette. The one saving grace is appearances by The Animals, The Toys, The Gentrys, and especially The Castaways, who sing their garage rock classic "Liar Liar." (Dir: Stephanie Rothman, 86 mins.)

It's a Date (1940)**½ Deanna Durbin, Walter Pidgeon, Kay Francis, Eugene Pallette, S. Z. Sakall, Samuel S. Hinds, Fritz Feld, Charles Lane. Nice vehicle for Durbin has her becoming an unintentional rival of her own mother (Francis) on stage and in love; bubbly and well played, with the usual fine singing by the star. (Dir: William A. Seiter, 103 mins.)

It's a Dog's Life (1955)*** Jeff Richards, Dean Jagger, Edmund Gwenn. The saga of a bull terrier from the Bowery who ultimately is entered in a classy dog show. Charming dog story, thanks to a witty, offbeat screenplay and intelligent direction. (Dir: Herman Hoffman, 87 mins.)

It's a Gift (1934)*** W. C. Fields, Jean Rouverol, Baby LeRoy, Kathleen Howard, Jane Withers. The "Master" is a family man in this one and he gets the usual share of laughs from his bouts with his shrewish wife. Plenty of fun as Fields holds the film together. Remake of Fields's silent *It's the Old Army Game*, 1926. (Dir: Norman McLeod, 70 mins.)†

It's a Great Feeling (1949)*** Dennis Morgan, Jack Carson, Doris Day. A lot of fun in this offbeat satire about what a ham Carson is and how nobody at the studio wants to direct him. Lots of stars come on for comic bits including Errol Flynn, Gary Cooper, Joan Crawford, Sydney Greenstreet, Danny Kaye, Patricia Neal, Eleanor Parker, Ronald Reagan, Edward G. Robinson, and Jane Wyman. (Dir: David Butler, 85 mins.)

It's a Great Life (1943)**½ Penny Singleton, Arthur Lake, Hugh Herbert. Blondie and Dagwood have a horse on their hands, which pleases an eccentric millionaire client of Dagwood's boss. Amusing comedy in the *Blondie* series, with some capable clowning by Herbert. (Dir: Frank Strayer, 75 mins.)

It's Alive! (1968)* Tommy Kirk, Shirley Bonne. Motorists break down in the Ozarks and are imprisoned along with a geologist in the cave of a demented man who wants to feed them to his pet monster. Lacks even the camp value of producer-writer-director Buchanan's usual efforts (e.g., *Zontar, The Thing From Venus*). (Dir: Larry Buchanan, 80 mins.)

It's Alive (1974)**½ John P. Ryan, Sharon Farrell, Andrew Duggan, Guy Stockwell, Michael Ansara. Producer-director-writer Larry Cohen created a grotesque tale of a monstrous baby that goes on a murderous spree and is hunted by the police. An imaginative concept suffers from the low budget and Cohen's inept directing. Sequels: *It Lives Again* and *Island of the Alive*. (90 mins.)†

It's Always Fair Weather (1955)*** Gene Kelly, Dan Dailey, Cyd Charisse, Dolores Gray, Michael Kidd, Jay C. Flippen. Tuneful romp of a musical about three ex-soldiers who meet ten years after VJ-Day in New York City to paint the town the proverbial bright hue. Plenty of songs and some expert group dancing by Kelly, Dailey, and choreographer Michael Kidd. (Dirs: Gene Kelly, Stanley Donen, 102 mins.)†

It's a Mad, Mad, Mad, Mad World (1963)**½ Spencer Tracy, Milton Berle, Edie Adams, Sid Caesar, Dick Shawn, Ethel Merman, Jonathan Winters, Mickey Rooney. Here's director Stanley Kramer's tribute to those screen comedy chases of old. It's a wild, occasionally funny romp about a robbery and the multiple double crosses that follow. (154 mins.)†

It's a Wonderful Life (1946)**** James Stewart, Donna Reed, Lionel Barrymore, Thomas Mitchell, Henry Travers, Beulah Bondi, Gloria Grahame, H. B. Warner, Ward Bond. Frank Capra's drama of a man who thinks his life is worthless but learns otherwise from a friendly angel has become a Christmas perennial. The film is sentimental in the best sense, with a deep, painful strain of melancholy coursing through it. Stewart gives one of his finest performances as George Bailey, whose small-town life of sorrow and sacrifice has led him to the end of his rope. Along comes guardian angel Clarence Oddbody (Travers) to show him what life in Bedford Falls would be like without him. This was Capra's favorite among his own films, and his sensitive direction stands the test of time. (129 mins.)†

It's a Wonderful World (1939)*** James Stewart, Claudette Colbert, Guy Kibbee, Nat Pendleton, Frances Drake, Edgar Kennedy, Hans Conried, Grady Sutton. Screwball comedy version of *The 39 Steps* (without handcuffs). Stewart is the man falsely accused of murder who kidnaps Colbert. The script, which is what makes it go, is by Ben Hecht and Herman J. Mankiewicz; "Swifty Woody" [W. S. Van Dyke II] directed. (86 mins.)

It's Good to Be Alive (MTV 1974)*** Paul Winfield, Ruby Dee, Lou Gossett, Lloyd Gough. Winfield delivers a moving portrait of Brooklyn Dodger catcher Roy Campanella, facing life as a quadraplegic following his tragic 1958 auto accident. Though Winfield bears no resemblance to the squat, boyish "Campy" (who has a cameo appearance), the actor's luminous face carries this venture. (Dir: Michael Landon, 98 mins.)†

It Should Happen to You (1953)***½ Judy Holliday, Jack Lemmon, Peter Lawford, Michael O'Shea. Very funny comedy about a model who rents a billboard overlooking a busy section of New York City and becomes a celebrity sight unseen. Holliday is delightful as Gladys Glover, the enterprising overnight success. (Dir: George Cukor, 81 mins.)†

It's in the Air (1935)**½ Jack Benny, Una Merkel, Nat Pendleton, Mary Carlisle, Ted Healey, Al Shean. Slight gangster comedy has Benny in an unusual role as a con artist with love troubles; Hollywood obviously hadn't discovered his niche. Anyway, pleasant enough, if not the Benny we know. (Dir: Charles Reisner, 80 mins.)

It's in the Bag (1945)*** Fred Allen, Jack Benny, William Bendix, Binnie Barnes, Robert Benchley, Jerry Colonna, John Carradine, Sidney Toler, Don Ameche, Rudy Vallee, Victor Moore. Allen plays host to a plethora of radio comics in this comedy about a search for a chair in which $12 million is hidden. Loosely adapted from the Russian story *The Twelve Chairs*, more faithfully filmed in 1970 under the original title and as *12 + 1*. (Dir: Richard Wallace, 87 mins.)†

It's Love Again (Great Britain, 1936)**½ Jessie Matthews, Robert Young, Sonnie Hale, Sara Allgood. Capable, entertaining Matthews vehicle. Her music hall style is winsome and knowing, and she can dance up a storm; the plot, about an out-of-control rivalry between her and competing journalist Young, is window dressing. (Dir: Victor Saville, 84 mins.)†

It's Love I'm After (1937)*** Bette Davis, Leslie Howard, Olivia de Havilland, Patric Knowles, Bonita Granville, Spring Byington, Eric Blore, E. E. Clive. A daffy screwball comedy that gains added oomph by providing Howard and Davis with a holiday from "serious" acting. Portraying a battling theatrical couple who never quite make it to the altar, the stars act with brio even though the screenplay is deficient of bright one-liners. (Dir: Archie Mayo, 90 mins.)

It's My Turn (1980)*** Jill Clayburgh,
534

Michael Douglas, Charles Grodin, Beverly Garland, Daniel Stern, Jennifer Salt, Dianne Wiest. Attempts to revive the art of sophisticated comedy with newer feminist attitudes, but simply mints newer stereotypes. Clayburgh, a brilliant mathematics professor, is an indecisive klutz who can't handle her feelings or manage her life. (Dir: Claudia Weill, 91 mins.)†

It's Only Money (1962)**½ Jerry Lewis, Zachary Scott, Joan O'Brien, Mae Questel, Jesse White, Jack Weston, Ted de Corsia. Jerry in an amusing role as a TV repairman who becomes heir to a fortune—that is, if an unscrupulous lawyer doesn't put him out of the way permanently. Ex-animator Tashlin was about the only director who knew what to do with Lewis. (Dir: Frank Tashlin, 84 mins.)

It Started in Naples (1960)*** Clark Gable, Sophia Loren, Vittorio De Sica. Lawyer resists the efforts of an Italian waif to take him back to America, until love takes a hand in the shape of the lad's sexy aunt. Good-humored comedy-drama has beautiful Italian scenery, Gable and Loren in good form. (Dir: Melville Shavelson, 100 mins.)†

It Started in Paradise (Great Britain, 1952) *** Martita Hunt, Jane Hylton, Ian Hunter, Kay Kendall. Young dress designer will stop at nothing to achieve success, makes enemies by the score. Elaborately produced, well-acted drama. (Dir: Compton Bennett, 94 mins.)

It Started with a Kiss (1959)**½ Glenn Ford, Debbie Reynolds, Eva Gabor, Fred Clark, Edgar Buchanan, Harry Morgan, Francis Bavier. Flimsy but mildly amusing comedy about an Air Force sergeant, his new bride and a fabulous car, highlighted by splendid scenic backgrounds shot in Spain. (Dir: George Marshall, 104 mins.)

It Started with Eve (1941)***½ Deanna Durbin, Charles Laughton, Robert Cummings, Guy Kibbee. Durbin's best film. Very funny comedy about mistaken identity and its effect on a zany family. Laughton is very good. Remade as *I'd Rather Be Rich*. (Dir: Henry Koster, 90 mins.)

It's Tough to Be Famous (1932)*** Douglas Fairbanks, Jr., Mary Brian, Walter Catlett, Lilian Bond, J. Carroll Naish, Louise Beavers. Sharp, offbeat social comedy-drama of a hero who is used by publicity hounds; snappy dialogue and a perceptive script make this one well worth seeing, and Fairbanks shines. (Dir: Alfred E. Green, 79 mins.)

It Takes a Thief (Great Britain, 1960)*½ Jayne Mansfield, Anthony Quayle. Innocent dupe joins in a bullion robbery, is caught and sent to prison; the old gang terrorizes him when he's released. Stiff British melodrama. (Dir: John Gilling, 90 mins.)

It Takes Two (1988)** George Newbern, Leslie Hope, Kimberly Foster. Sometimes funny but more often confusing comedy about a young man, stranded far from home in Texas and trying to get back in time for his wedding. (Dir: David Beaird, 81 mins.)†

It! The Terror from Beyond Space (1958)* Marshall Thompson, Shawn Smith (Shirley Patterson), Kim Spaulding, Ann Doran. A spaceship returns with an extremely hostile extra-terrestrial. Believe it or not, this was the inspiration for *Alien*, which certainly improved on this shoddy sci-fi. (Dir: Edward L. Cahn, 69 mins.)

Ivan (USSR, 1932)***½ Semyon Shagaida, Pytor Masokha, Stepan Shkurat, D.Golubinsky. Powerful drama with extraordinary images about industrial workers in a young Soviet Union. The three men, each named Ivan, represent various aspects of what is expected of all good Russians. Noteworthy for expressive use of sound, dialogue, and music. Director Alexander Dovzhenko's first sound film. (85 mins.)

Ivanhoe (1953)*** Robert Taylor, Elizabeth Taylor, George Sanders, Joan Fontaine, Finlay Currie, Felix Aylmer, Guy Rolfe, Basil Sydney, Sebastian Cabot. Elaborate production based on Sir Walter Scott's tale of the days of knights and jousts and fair maidens in distress. (Dir: Richard Thorpe, 106 mins.)†

Ivanhoe (MTV 1982)**½ James Mason, Anthony Andrews, Lysette Anthony, Sam Neill, Michael Hordern, Olivia Hussey, Julian Glover, John Rhys-Davies. Sir Walter Scott's durable tale of knights, jousts, maidens in distress, and royal intrigue is played out in a series of predictable action sequences. Despite this, the film provides the right amount of heroics and derring-do. (Dir: Douglas Camfield, 156 mins.)†

Ivan's Childhood (U.S.S.R., 1962)***½ Kolya Burlyaev, Valentin Zubkov, Nikolai Grinko, I. Tarkovskaya. A twelve-year-old boy seeks revenge against the Nazis who killed his entire family, joining Soviet partisans who use him for spying because of his small size. First feature by Andrei Tarkovsky has stunning camera work and a magnificent performance by Burlyaev as the boy. AKA: **My Name is Ivan.** (97 mins.)†

Ivan the Terrible (Russia, 1943)***½ Nikolai Cherkassov, Ludmila Tselikovskaya, Serafina Birman. Russian history on a grand scale as interpreted by the master Russian director, Sergei Eisenstein. The somber, brooding photography is enhanced by gigantic sets, a stirring Prokofiev score, and eloquent performances from an excellent cast. Released in two parts in 1947 and 1959. (186 mins.)†

I've Always Loved You (1946)*** Philip Dorn, Catherine McLeod, William Carter, Maria Ouspenskaya, Felix Bressart, Fritz Feld, Cora Witherspoon. Ultra-romantic film with generous servings of classical music. No one ever directed love stories like Frank Borzage, and his powers of conviction infuse this tale of a pianist who fights against the jealousy he feels toward a gifted student whom he loves. (117 mins.)

I've Lived Before (1956)** Jock Mahoney, Leigh Snowden, Ann Harding, John McIntire, Raymond Bailey, Jerry Paris. Pilot Mahoney discovers he is the reincarnation of a WWI fighter pilot. Interesting idea rather amateurishly handled. (Dir: Richard Bartlett, 82 mins.)

I Vitelloni (Italy, 1953)**** Franco Interlenghi, Franco Fabrizi. Young Lothario won't settle down, even after marriage. Penetrating portrait of youth in a small town in Italy. Well worth seeing. (Dir: Federico Fellini, 103 mins.)†

Ivory Ape, The (MTV 1980)** Jack Palance, Steven Keats, Cindy Pickett, Earle Hyman. An albino gorilla shows up in Africa and is captured by a ruthless (what else) promoter who intends to sell the "ivory ape" to the highest bidder. (Dir: Tom Kotani, 104 mins.)

Ivory Hunter (Great Britain, 1951)*** Anthony Steel, Dinah Sheridan, Harold Warrender. High adventure. A game warden in East Africa tries to preserve wildlife, foils some poachers making away with ivory. (Dir: Harry Watt, 97 mins.)

Ivy (1947)*** Joan Fontaine, Patric Knowles, Herbert Marshall, Richard Ney, Sir Cedric Hardwicke, Lucille Watson, Sara Allgood, Alan Napier. Diabolical drama about a ruthless woman and her evil deeds in her attempt to find personal happiness. (Dir: Sam Wood, 99 mins.)

I Wake Up Screaming (1941)***½ Betty Grable, Victor Mature, Laird Cregar, Carole Landis, William Gargan. Hard, creepy atmosphere bolstered by sharply etched characterizations. When Landis is murdered, her sister (Grable) searches out the killer, with the help of the prime suspect (Mature). AKA: **Hot Spot.** (Dir: H. Bruce Humberstone, 82 mins.)†

I Walk Alone (1947)** Burt Lancaster, Kirk Douglas, Lizabeth Scott. Man returns from prison to find that things have changed in this grim, weak melodrama. (Dir: Byron Haskin, 98 mins.)

I Walked with a Zombie (1943)***½ Frances Dee, Tom Conway. Canadian nurse goes to the West Indies to attend a patient, finds voodooism involved. Suspenseful, well-made thriller. (Dir: Jacques Tourneur, 69 mins.)†

I Walk the Line (1970)*** Gregory Peck,

Tuesday Weld. Interesting drama set in the moonshine country of Tennessee. Miss Weld's performance as a young girl who captivates married Sheriff Peck is the main inducement for watching this. (Dir: John Frankenheimer, 96 mins.)

I **Wanna Hold Your Hand** (1978)*** Nancy Allen, Bobby DiCicco, Mark McClure, Theresa Saldana, Eddie Deezen. A genuine surprise, a delightfully raucous comedy about six New Jersey teenagers trying to crash the Ed Sullivan Show broadcast the night the Beatles appeared. (Dir: Robert Zemeckis, 104 mins.)†

I **Want a Divorce** (1940)**½ Joan Blondell, Dick Powell, Frank Fay, Gloria Dickson, Conrad Nagel, Jessie Ralph, Sidney Blackmer, Louise Beavers, Dorothy Burgess. Trials and tribulations beset young newlyweds Powell and Blondell; light comedy with a good cast to recommend it. (Dir: Ralph Murphy, 75 mins.)

I **Wanted Wings** (1941)**½ Ray Milland, Bill Holden, Wayne Morris, Veronica Lake. Story of three young men taking our prewar Air Cadet training is nothing more than dated propaganda today. (Dir: Mitchell Leisen, 131 mins.)

I **Want Her Dead**—See: **W**

I **Want to Keep My Baby** (MTV 1976)*** Mariel Hemingway, Susan Anspach, Jack Rader. This is a strong, poignant, if lengthy film about a fifteen-year-old girl who becomes pregnant, is abandoned by her teenage lover, decides to have her baby, and is persuaded by various forces to keep the infant and care for it. (Dir: Jerry Thorpe, 106 mins.)

I **Want to Live** (1958)*** Susan Hayward's Academy Award-winning performance is the main attraction in this film based on the sensational and controversial murder trial of vice girl Barbara Graham. The final segment dealing with her execution in the gas chamber packs a real wallop. (Dir: Robert Wise, 120 mins.)†

I **Want to Live** (MTV 1983)** Lindsay Wagner, Martin Balsam, Pamela Reed, Harry Dean Stanton, John Cedar, Robert Ginty, Seymour Cassel. Lindsay fails to follow in Susan Hayward's footsteps in this lackluster TV remake of the life story of Barbara Graham. (Dir: David Lowell Rich, 104 mins.)

I **Want You** (1951)** Dana Andrews, Dorothy McGuire, Farley Granger, Peggy Dow. Samuel Goldwyn's effort to have box office lightning strike twice (*Best Years of Our Lives*) via this slow-moving drama about the effect of the Korean War on a typical American family. (Dir: Mark Robson, 102 mins.)

I **Was a Communist for the F.B.I.** (1951)** Frank Lovejoy, Dorothy Hart. The title tells the whole story. Lovejoy plays Matt Cvetic, a real life FBI agent who posed as a Communist in order to inform on the Reds' activities in the U.S. (Dir: Gordon Douglas, 83 mins.)

I **Was a Mail Order Bride** (MTV 1982)* Valerie Bertinelli, Ted Wass, Kenneth Kimmins, Karen Morrow, Holland Taylor. Tedious romance concerns a Chicago magazine writer (Bertinelli) who dates a lawyer for a feature article on mail order brides. (Dir: Marvin Chomsky, 104 mins.)

I **Was a Male War Bride** (1949)***½ Cary Grant, Ann Sheridan. Cary Grant, as an ex-French Army officer, disguises himself as a WAC in order to accompany his American WAC bride (Ann Sheridan) to the U.S. on a troop ship. The stars and script are hilarious. (Dir: Howard Hawks, 105 mins.)

I **Was an Adventuress** (1940)**½ Vera Zorina, Richard Greene, Erich von Stroheim, Peter Lorre, Sig Ruman, Fritz Feld. Second-rate romantic comedy-adventure has phony countess Zorina marrying Greene and trying to escape her scandalous past, which haunts her in the team of her ex-partners von Stroheim and Lorre, who easily steal the picture. (Dir: Gregory Ratoff, 81 mins.)

I **Was a Teenage Frankenstein** (1957)* Whit Bissell, Gary Conway, Phyllis Coates, Robert Burton. Determined to cash in on the success of *I Was a Teenage Werewolf*, American International Pix made this transplant thriller about a nutty scientist who assembles a monster out of body parts he's gathered from accidents. (Dir: Herbert L. Strock, 72 mins.)

I **Was a Teenage TV Terrorist** (1985)* Julie Hanlon, Adam Nathan, John MacKay, Walt Willey, Saul Alpiner. Bored and hassled in their summer jobs at a cable TV station, two high school students harass the station with a series of pranks, leaving notes that blame an imaginary terrorist group. Pointless comedy looks as if it was written and made by high schoolers as well. AKA: **Amateur Hour.** (Dir: Stanford Singer, 86 mins.)†

I **Was a Teenage Werewolf** (1957)** Michael Landon, Whit Bissell, Yvonne Lime. Evil doctor succeeds in regressing a troubled teenager into a murderous werewolf. (Dir: Gene Fowler, Jr., 76 mins.)†

I **Was a Teenage Zombie** (1987)** Michael Rubin, George Seminara, Steve McCoy, Peter Bush. Yet another spoof of teen-themed horror movies, a little better than average. Prime attraction is a terrific soundtrack featuring the Fleshtones, Dream Syndicate, Violent Femmes, Smithereens, dB's, and more. (Dir: John Elias Michalakias, 92 mins.)†

I **Was Born, But . . .** (Japan, 1932)*** Hideo Sugahara, Tatsuo Saito, Tokkankozo, Takeshi Sakamoto, Mitsuko Yoshikawa. Delightful comedy-drama about two young boys who, seeing their beloved father become more and more subservient to his boss, go on a hunger strike to change the situation. Filled with director Yasujiro Ozu's glorious sense of innocence. (89 mins.)

I Was Monty's Double (Great Britain, 1958)***½ John Mills, Cecil Parker, M. E. Clifton-James. Well-done British war drama about a great plot involving an actor impersonating a general to confuse the Germans in the North African campaign. (Dir: John Guillermin, 100 mins.)

I Will Fight No More Forever (MTV 1975)*** Ned Romero, James Whitmore, Sam Elliott, Sam Ramus, Emilio Delgado. Disturbing historical tale contemplating another incident of governmental persecution of the American Indian. A tribe of Nez Percé Indians gamble on fleeing hardships on a U.S. reservation by moving to Canada. (Dir: Richard T. Heffron, 104 mins.)†

I Will, I Will...For Now (1976)* Elliott Gould, Diane Keaton, Paul Sorvino, Victoria Principal, Robert Alda, Warren Berlinger. Tasteless comedy about a modern married, divorced, and then reunited couple, whose love life leads them to a sex-therapy clinic. (Dir: Norman Panama, 107 mins.)†

I Wonder Who's Kissing Her Now (1947)*** June Haver, Mark Stevens. Highly fictionalized career of songwriter Joe Howard has such a delightful score and so many talented people that we can overlook its childish plot. (Dir: Lloyd Bacon, 104 mins.)

Izzy and Moe (MTV 1985)*½ Jackie Gleason, Art Carney, Cynthia Harris, Zohra Lampert, Dick Latessa, Thelma Lee, Drew Snyder, William Hickey. Gleason and Carney team up once again... only this time they're playing a pair of ex-vaudevillians. Fans won't be able to divorce the "Honeymooners" from their minds as they watch Gleason and Carney get out of scrapes as 1920s bunglers out to bust the booze brigade. Poor version of interesting material. (Dir: Jackie Cooper, 104 mins.)†

Jabberwocky (Great Britain, 1977)*** Michael Palin, Max Wall, Deborah Fallender, John Le Mesurier, Neil Innes, Graham Crowden. Gory, vulgar, wildly uneven, and occasionally maniacally funny Monty Python spin-off. Palin is a medieval peasant who hunts down a dreadful beast that has been terrorizing the countryside. Pythonite Terry Jones appears as the monster's first victim. (Dir: Terry Gilliam, 101 mins.)†

J'Accuse (France, 1919)**** Maryse Dauvry, Romuald Joube, Severin-Mars, Maxime Des Jardins, Angele Guys. Magnificent antiwar film follows two men, one a coarse oaf, the other a poet, in love with the same woman, who fight in WWI. Director Abel Gance makes his pacifist plea for sanity in a world gone mad in the action sequences (featuring actual battle footage). Most electrifying scene has dead soldiers rising from a soldiers' cemetery, contrasted on a split screen with platoons marching through Paris. (150 mins.)†

J'Accuse (France, 1937)***½ Jean Max, Delaitre, Renee Devillers, Victor Francen. Director Abel Gance's sound remake of his 1919 epic about love and war, and the effect the horrors of battle have on one man's spirit. This shorter version still emphasizes the romantic entanglement of the central characters and the friendships altered by war. (95 mins.)

Jackal of Nahueltoro, The (Chile, 1969)***½ Nelson Villagra, Shenda Roman, Hector Noguera, Luis Alarcon, Marcelo Romo. Enthralling recreation of one of Chile's most shocking crimes: the murder of a woman and her five children by a poverty-stricken, illiterate man. While in prison, he's taught reading as well as a moral value system. Directed by Miguel Littin during Chile's creative renaissance under Salvador Allende, the film is a remarkable and powerful document. (89 mins.)

Jack and the Beanstalk (1952)*½ Bud Abbott, Lou Costello, Dorothy Ford, Barbara Brown, Buddy Baer. Costello falls asleep and dreams himself into the fairy tale of Jack and the Beanstalk. For the very young, and A&C fans only. (Dir: Jean Yarbrough, 87 mins.)†

Jackboot Mutiny (West Germany, 1955)*** Carl Ludwig Diehl, Carl Wery, Bernhard Wicki, Kurt Meisel, Erik Frey, Albert Hehn. Eleven years after the event comes this revisionist look at Adolph Hitler and the failed 1944 attempt by German army officers to kill him. In this film, the dictator is portrayed as evil incarnate, a wide-eyed drooling monster with murderous bootlickers for henchmen. Unique look at a dark period in Germany's history was one of the last films directed by G. W. Pabst. (77 mins.)

Jackie Robinson Story, The (1950)*** Jackie Robinson, Ruby Dee, Minor Watson, Louise Beavers, Bernie Hamilton. Interesting biographical film about Jackie's years as the first black man in organized baseball. (Dir: Alfred E. Green, 76 mins.)†

Jack London (1943)*** Michael O'Shea, Susan Hayward, Virginia Mayo, Frank Craven, Ralph Morgan, Louise Beavers, Jonathan Hale. Exciting biographical adventure story of the illustrious career of

Jack London is marred only by O'Shea's lackluster acting. (Dir: Alfred Santell, 94 mins.)†

Jacknife (1989)*** Robert De Niro, Ed Harris, Kathy Baker. Adaptation of an off-Broadway play about three people still suffering traumas caused by the Vietnam war. The script is obviously schematic, but it's still a pleasure to watch what this excellent trio of actors can do with even such mediocre material. (Dir: David Jones, 102 mins.)†

Jack of Diamonds (U.S.-West Germany, 1967)** George Hamilton, Joseph Cotten, Marie Laforet, Maurice Evans, Carroll Baker, Zsa Zsa Gabor. Ordinary adventure about a sophisticated cat burglar and his capers, both at work and at play. (Dir: Don Taylor, 105 mins.)

Jackpot, The (1950)*** James Stewart, Barbara Hale, James Gleason, Fred Clark, Alan Mowbray, Natalie Wood, Lyle Talbot, John Qualen, Fritz Feld. Average man wins a fabulous radio-quiz jackpot and finds his life and wife radically changed. Unjustly neglected comedy is quite funny. (Dir: Walter Lang, 85 mins.)

Jack's Back (1988)*** James Spader, Cynthia Gibb, Rod Loomis. Twists and thrills in the first and last thirds make up for the bloated midsection of this thriller, in which a young man becomes involved in the case of a modern Jack the Ripper. Spader is excellent in a dual role. (Dir: Rowdy Herrington, 96 mins.)†

Jackson County Jail (1976)*** Yvette Mimieux, Tommy Lee Jones, Robert Carradine, Severn Darden, Mary Woronov, Howard Hesseman. Surprisingly good drama from the Roger Corman factory about a woman who stumbles into a nightmare land of hijacking and rape while driving cross-country from California to New York. (Dir: Michael Miller, 84 mins.)†

Jack's Wife—See: **Season of the Witch**

Jack the Ripper (Great Britain, 1959)** Lee Patterson, Eddie Byrne, Betty McDowall, John Le Mesurier. British-made melodrama about notorious killer, with many shock gimmicks—moderately well done. Written by Jimmy Sangster. (Dir: Robert Baker, 88 mins.)†

Jack the Ripper (MTV 1988)*** Michael Caine, Armand Assante, Ray McAnally, Lewis Collins, Ken Bones, Susan George, Jane Seymour. First-rate production with suave Caine as a Scotland Yard inspector on the trail of the elusive Jack the Ripper. (Dir: David Wickes, 192 mins.)

Jacobo Timerman: Prisoner Without a Name, Cell Without a Number (MTV 1983)** Roy Scheider, Liv Ullmann, Terrance O'Quinn, Sam Robards, Zach Galligan, Trini Alvarado. A timid, disappointing glimpse at Argentinian fascism. When Argentinian newspaper publisher Jacobo Timerman printed names of missing citizens during the late 1970s, he was imprisoned and tortured before being released. (Dir: David Greene, 104 mins.)

Jacob's Ladder (1990)**½ Tim Robbins, Elizabeth Peña, Danny Aiello. An intense visual thriller with Robbins giving a sympathetic performance as a Vietnam vet battling what appears to be demons of his past. Intriguing for the first half but by the time you find out what's going on you may no longer care. Jolting visuals but weak script. (Dir: Adrian Lyne, 115 mins.)†

Jacob the Liar (East Germany, 1975)*** Vlastimil Brodsky, Manuela Simon. A haunting drama with some comic touches—about life in a Jewish ghetto in Poland during the Nazi occupation of WWII. A Jewish prisoner invents lies to keep hope alive among his doomed coreligionists. (Dir: Frank Beyer, 95 mins.)

Jacqueline Bouvier Kennedy (MTV 1981)**½ Jaclyn Smith, James Franciscus, Rod Taylor, Stephen Elliott, Donald Moffat, Dolph Sweet. A fan-magazine approach to the life and times of Jackie Kennedy, who rose from society deb to First Lady. (Dir: Stephen Gethers, 156 mins.)†

Jacqueline Susann's Once Is Not Enough—See: **Once Is Not Enough**

Jacques Brel Is Alive and Well and Living in Paris (1975)*½ Elly Stone, Mort Shuman, Joe Masiell, Jacques Brel. Disappointing film version of the world-famous musical revue. Visualizing Brel's idiosyncratic music works against its melancholy grain. Play the album, go to the revue, or see this movie with your eyes closed. (Dir: Denis Heroux, 98 mins.)

Jagged Edge (1985)**½ Glenn Close, Jeff Bridges, Peter Coyote, Robert Loggia, John Dehner, Leigh Taylor-Young, Karen Austin, James Karen. Close plays the defense attorney romanced by her client Bridges, accused of the grisly murder of his wife. Since neither character is ever really fleshed out, what we're left with is a shallow variation of Hitchcock's *Suspicion*. (Dir: Richard Marquand, 108 mins.)†

Jail Bait (1954)½ Dolores Fuller, Lyle Talbot, Tim Farrell, Herbert Rawlinson, Steve Reeves, Clancy Malone. A camp classic, written and directed by Ed (*Plan 9 from Outer Space*) Wood. The torrid plot line concerns a bank robber who seeks plastic surgery from the doctor father of a cohort to avoid getting nabbed for a theater robbery. (Dir: Edward D. Wood, Jr., 70 mins.)

Jailbait Babysitter (1973)½ Theresa Pare, Roscoe Born, Lydia Wagner. "She'll give you anything you want, except legal consent!" claimed the ads for this soft-core comedy about a teen with a knack for getting in trouble with the opposite sex. But her encounters with her hooker mentor, older men, and an understanding boyfriend aren't nearly as sexy or unintentionally funny as that implies. (Dir: John Hayes, 85 mins.)†

Jailbird Rock (1988)* Robin Antin, Valchie Gene Richards, Robin Cleaver, Rhonda Aldrich. The world's first women-in-prison musical—and hopefully the last. Innocent young thing Antin, whose cheerleading career is interrupted when she's slapped in the slammer for shooting her stepfather, helps the other inmates put together a variety show. (Dir: Phillip Schuman, 92 mins.)†

Jail Birds—See: **Pardon Us**

Jail Busters (1955)**½ Bowery Boys, Barton MacLane, Bernard Gorcey, Percy Helton, Lyle Talbot, Fritz Feld, Anthony Caruso. The Boys go undercover in the big house to expose payoffs made to guards so that certain prisoners can lead the easy life while behind bars. (Dir: William Beaudine, 61 mins.)

Jailhouse Rock (1957)*** Elvis Presley, Judy Tyler, Dean Jones, Vaughn Taylor. This may be the best Presley musical, with a great Lieber and Stoller score. Elvis is a con who learns to play in the big house and becomes a rock star. (Dir: Richard Thorpe, 96 mins.)†

Jakarta (1986)**½ Christopher Noth, Sue Francis Pai, Ronald Hunter. Loser Noth, booted out of the CIA after the death of a witness he was supposed to protect, returns to Jakarta and relives past mistakes with shady lady Pai. OK *film noir* update, with good location filming. (Dir: Charles Kaufman, 95 mins.)†

Jake Spanner, Private Eye (MTV 1989)** Robert Mitchum, Ernest Borgnine, John Mitchum, Richard Yniguez, Jim Mitchum, Laurie Latham, Dick Van Patten, Kareem Abdul-Jabbar, Edie Adams, Terry Moore, Sheree North, Clive Revill, Stella Stevens, Nita Talbot, Edy Williams. Retired private eye Mitchum is coaxed back into business by a former enemy, mobster Borgnine, to help retrieve a kidnapped girl. Film is best in brief scenes where the aging characters confront their limitations, but otherwise sinks in uncertainty of tone and too many pointless cameos. (Dir: Lee H. Katzin, 96 mins.)

Jake Speed (1986)*½ Wayne Crawford, Karen Kopins, Dennis Christopher, John Hurt, Leon Ames, Donna Pescow. A fictional character comes to life and wins a damsel's heart by rescuing her sister from loathsome white slavers. Unfunny at any speed. (Dir: Andrew Lane, 104 mins.)†

Jalopy (1953)**½ Bowery Boys, Jane Easton, Bernard Gorcey, Leon Belasco,

Robert Lowery. The Boys develop a fuel that puts a tiger in their old jalopy's tank in order to win races to raise money so that Louie Dumbrowski can pay his bills. (Dir: William Beaudine, 62 mins.)

Jamaica Inn (Great Britain, 1939)*** Charles Laughton, Maureen O'Hara, Robert Newton, Leslie Banks. A country squire is secretly the head of a band of pirates who wreck ships and ransack them. Tense suspense melodrama. Based on the best-selling novel by Daphne du Maurier. (Dir: Alfred Hitchcock, 90 mins.)†

Jamaica Inn (MTV 1985)*** Jane Seymour, Patrick McGoohan, Billie Whitelaw, Peter Vaughan. Check into Jamaica Inn for intrigue and skullduggery in this exciting remake of the Hitchcock film about murderous smugglers. (Dir: Lawrence Gordon Clark, 196 mins.)

Jamaica Run (1953)** Ray Milland, Arlene Dahl, Wendell Corey. Jumbled drama with family skeletons in every closet of a large mansion in Jamaica inhabited by a strange crew including beautiful Arlene Dahl. Ray Milland is a skipper of a schooner who helps things back to normalcy. (Dir: Lewis R. Foster, 92 mins.)

Jamboree (1957)**½ Kay Medford, Robert Pastine, Freda Halloway, Jerry Lee Lewis, Carl Perkins, Fats Domino, Buddy Knox, Slim Whitman, Frankie Avalon, Count Basie, Joe Williams, Jodie Sands, Lewis Lymon and the Teen Chords, Connie Francis, Dick Clark. An insignificant plot about feuding agents is a mere excuse for plenty of extraneous numbers by guest stars. Perkins especially is fabulous, looking amused and not exactly sober. Some great dance numbers and a chance to see a young Slim Whitman make this irresistible to the right audience. (Dir: Roy Lockwood, 85 mins.)

James A. Michener's Dynasty (MTV 1976)**½ Sarah Miles, Stacy Keach, Harris Yulin, Harrison Ford, Amy Irving, Granville Van Dusen, Gerrit Graham. Another opus from the master of overblown epics, this story of a dirt farmer's wife (Miles) who leaves her husband for his brother at least has a sterling cast, and emphasizes characterization instead of its mock historical plotline. (Dir: Lee Phillips, 96 mins.)

James at 15 (MTV 1977)*** Lance Kerwin, Kate Jackson, Melissa Sue Anderson. Novelist Dan Wakefield's finely etched portrait of an Oregon boy who must make new friends when dad takes a teaching post in New England. (Dir: Joseph Hardy, 104 mins.)

James Bond series. Suave and sexy in a supercharged way, Agent 007 had been a popular item in Ian Fleming's books since 1953's *Casino Royale*. The role of ultra-cool secret agent has housed a number of interpreters (and led to dozens of cheap imitations, thus making spy films a cottage industry of the sixties and seventies), but for most people, Sean Connery will always be 007. The series is still going strong with the newest Bond, Timothy Dalton. Fans should catch: *Dr. No, From Russia with Love, Goldfinger, Thunderball, You Only Live Twice, Casino Royale, On Her Majesty's Secret Service, Live and Let Die, The Man with the Golden Gun, The Spy Who Loved Me, Moonraker, For Your Eyes Only, Never Say Never Again, Octopussy,* and *A View to a Kill*.

James Dean (MTV 1976)**½ Stephen McHattie, Michael Brandon, Meg Foster, Candy Clark. Recollection of the 1950s actor's early days by his best friend, Bill Bast (played by Brandon), when the two met at UCLA and struggled together in New York. (Dir: Robert Butler, 98 mins.)†

James Dean Story, The (1957)** Sluggish documentary compilation recounts the life and career of the controversial film star. (Dirs: George W. George, Robert Altman, 82 mins.)†

James Joyce's Women (1985)**½ Fionnula Flanagan. Inspired by Flanagan's acclaimed one-woman show, this exploration of Joyce's genius combines reenactments of the writer's fiction with scenes from Joyce's life. (Dir: Michael Pearce, 88 mins.)†

Jam Session (1944)** Ann Miller, Jess Barker, Charles Brown, Eddie Kane, Louis Armstrong, Nan Wynn. Catchy tunes and some mile-a-minute tap dancing enliven this second-rate musical about a girl who wins a dance contest and then stubbornly refuses to give up her quest for Hollywood stardom. (Dir: Charles Barton, 77 mins.)

Jane and the Lost City (Great Britain, 1987)*½ Sam Jones, Maud Adams, Kirsten Hughes, Jasper Carrott. Tepid cliff-hanger. Jane (Hughes) and "Jungle Jack Buck" (Jones) have to overcome nasty Nazis, led by an adequately campy Adams, in order to reach the "Lost City" and its legendary diamonds. Based on a popular British comic strip. (Dir: Terry Marcel, 93 mins.)†

Jane Austen in Manhattan (1980)** Robert Powell, Anne Baxter, Tim Choate, Katrina Hodiak, Sean Young, Michael Wager, John Guerrasio, Kurt Johnson. Disappointing Merchant-Ivory drama about two rival theater mavens battling for the rights to produce a newly unearthed play by novelist Jane Austen. Lacks expected "behind-the-scenes" appeal; only the acting shines, which it should, considering the heavy hitters involved. (Dir: James Ivory, 108 mins.)†

Jane Doe (MTV 1983)**½ Karen Valentine, William Devane, Eva Marie Saint, David Huffman. Amnesia, that old movie and TV plot device, is trotted out once again in this sometimes interesting murder mystery. Karen Valentine plays a victim of a brutal beating who loses her memory and is somehow connected to a series of savage killings. (Dir: Ivan Nagy, 104 mins.)

Jane Eyre (1934)** Virginia Bruce, Colin Clive, Beryl Mercer, Jameson Thomas, Aileen Pringle. First talkie version of the Charlotte Brontë gothic novel about the young governess who falls in love with her mysterious employer, until she discovers his secret. Stiff, but Clive makes an interesting Mr. Rochester. (Dir: Christy Cabanne, 62 mins.)

Jane Eyre (1944)***½ Orson Welles, Joan Fontaine, Elizabeth Taylor, Margaret O'Brien, Peggy Ann Garner. Effective rendition of the Charlotte Brontë novel, with Welles a brooding, compelling Rochester to Fontaine's governess. Aldous Huxley collaborated on the screenplay, John Houseman produced. (Dir: Robert Stevenson, 96 mins.)

Jane Eyre (MTV 1971)*** George C. Scott, Susannah York, Ian Bannen, Jack Hawkins. Scott's Rochester looms over everything else in this acceptable remake of the Brontë novel. (Dir: Delbert Mann, 110 mins.)

Janis (1975)**½ Concert footage of the late Janis Joplin is spliced together with interviews, but this documentary doesn't provide much insight into the talented rock singer's tormented psyche. (Dirs: Seaton Findlay, Howard Alk, 96 mins.)†

January Man, The (1989)* Kevin Kline, Mary Elizabeth Mastrantonio, Susan Sarandon, Harvey Keitel, Rod Steiger, Danny Aiello. Atrocious comedy-mystery with rogue cop Kline on the trail of a New York serial killer. It's hard to believe that only one year earlier the same screenwriter, John Patrick Shanley, won an Oscar for *Moonstruck*! (Dir: Pat O'Connor, 97 mins.)†

Japanese War Bride (1952)*** Shirley Yamaguchi, Don Taylor, Cameron Mitchell, Marie Windsor, Philip Ahn. Strong, interesting social drama of a serviceman bringing a bride home from occupied Japan, and the effect this has on his community. Well directed by King Vidor. (91 mins.)

Jar, The (1987)* Gary Wallace, Karen Sjoberg. "Arty" horror movie about a young man who accidentally comes into possession of a demon in a bottle. He can't get rid of the thing, and it's slowly driving him crazy with paranoid hallucinations. Plotless and pretentious. (Dir: Bruce Toscano, 90 mins.)

Jarrett (MTV 1973)**½ Glenn Ford, Anthony Quayle, Forrest Tucker, Laraine Stephens, Yvonne Craig, Richard Anderson. Ford stars as an investigator hot on the trail of lost Biblical works in this unsuccessful series plot. In his path are several scheming characters, played to the hilt by Quayle, Tucker, and Craig; routine plotting, but the cast brings it to life. (Dir: Barry Shear, 72 mins.)

Jason and the Argonauts (Great Britain, 1963)**½ Todd Armstrong, Nancy Kovack, Gary Raymond. The tale of Jason and his search for the golden fleece in his endeavors to rescue his land from the rule of a tyrant. Magical special effects should delight the kiddies, and the elders should have a fairly entertaining time of it. (Dir: Don Chaffey, 104 mins.)†

Jassy (Great Britain, 1947)**½ Margaret Lockwood, Dennis Price, Patricia Roc, Basil Sydney, Ernest Thesiger, Torin Thatcher, Maurice Denham. Uninvolving gothic romance with a gypsy girl marrying above her station in nineteenth-century England and battling the aristocracy. Excellent costumes and settings at least make it nice to look at. (Dir: Bernard Knowles, 96 mins.)

Java Head (Great Britain, 1934)**½ John Loder, Anna May Wong, Elizabeth Allan, Edmund Gwenn, Ralph Richardson. Well-done drama, from the novel by Joseph Hergisheimer, of a mixed marriage between a sea captain and a Chinese princess. A serious attempt to deal with unusual subject matter for the time, with a fine cast. (Dir: J. Walter Ruben, 70 mins.)†

Jaws (1975)**** Roy Scheider, Robert Shaw, Richard Dreyfuss, Lorraine Gary, Murray Hamilton. Brilliantly effective as both an adventure film and a horror movie, this adaptation of Peter Benchley's best-seller delivers spine-tingling suspense as a great white shark satisfies his appetite off the coast of Martha's Vineyard. Director Steven Spielberg builds the tension methodically and unerringly, and it pays off with one of the scariest finales ever. Special credit to the special-effects crew (124 mins.)†

Jaws 2 (1978)*½ Roy Scheider, Lorraine Gary, Murray Hamilton. This devalued sequel to *Jaws* is worthwhile only if you have a phobia of teenagers and would enjoy watching them become fish food. (Dir: Jeannot Szwarc, 117 mins.)†

Jaws 3-D (1983)* Bess Armstrong, Dennis Quaid, Louis Gossett, Jr., Lea Thompson (debut). This time, Jaws is a mother whose Baby Jaws dies in captivity. Even so, a fish has to eat, and spectators at

Sea World soon discover they're on the menu. (Dir: Joe Alves, 97 mins.)†

Jaws: The Revenge (1987)* Michael Caine, Lorraine Gary, Lance Guest, Mario Van Peebles, Karen Young, Judith Barsi. A great white shark goes after the late Chief Brody's family. Toothless copy of the original. A different ending was added to the video version, not that it helps any. (Dir: Joseph Sargent, 90 mins.)†

Jayhawkers, The (1959)**½ Jeff Chandler, Fess Parker. Fast-paced western about ruthless men who try to take control of an entire state after the Civil War. (Dir: Melvin Frank, 100 mins.)

Jayne Mansfield Story, The (MTV 1980)**½ Loni Anderson, Arnold Schwarzenegger, Ray Buktenica, Kathleen Lloyd, G. D. Spradlin. The sad Hollywood tale about Jayne Mansfield, the buxom movie star who never quite made it in her career or in her marriage to muscleman Mickey Hargitay. (Dir: Dick Lowry, 104 mins.)†

Jazz Boat (Great Britain, 1960)** Anthony Newley, Anne Aubrey, Lionel Jeffries, David Lodge, James Booth, Leo McKern. Decent kid Newley brags to friends that he's an experienced burglar, and gets roped into participating in a real robbery. Odd melange of crime, comedy, and music works in occasional bits but not as a whole. Nicholas Roeg was one of the cinematographers. (Dir: Ken Hughes, 96 mins.)

Jazzman (U.S.S.R., 1983)*** Igor Sklyar, Alexander Chorny, Pyotr Scherbakov. After a long struggle for acceptance, Russia's first jazz quartet overcame the political antagonism of the late twenties and gradually became a favorite of the Russian people. Based on true events in Russian musical history, the film is brimming with rhythmic jazz and foot-tapping Dixieland music. (Dir: Karen Shakhnazarov, 80 mins.)

Jazz on a Summer's Day (1959)**** Louis Armstrong, Dinah Washington, Thelonious Monk, Gerry Mulligan, Chuck Berry, Big Maybelle, Anita O'Day, and Mahalia Jackson. The Newport Jazz Festival of 1958 is the setting for superbly edited account of the exciting, festive air generated by a host of talents. (Dir: Bert Stern, 85 mins.)†

Jazz Singer, The (1927)**½ Al Jolson, Warner Oland, May McAvoy. The film that brought sound to the movies to stay. Story of a cantor's son who becomes a stage star. Not a very good film, but of historical interest, and Al Jolson's overpowering stage personality does come through. (Dir: Alan Crosland, 90 mins.)†

Jazz Singer, The (1953)*** Danny Thomas, Peggy Lee. This remake did not make history but is nevertheless an entertaining story about a Jewish boy who prefers show business to becoming a cantor like his father before him. Danny Thomas is quite good in the title role. (Dir: Michael Curtiz, 107 mins.)

Jazz Singer, The (1980)* Neil Diamond, Laurence Olivier, Lucie Arnaz, Catlin Adams. Awful remake of Al Jolson's film about the young man whose father wants him to be a Jewish cantor is an expensive vanity production for a pop star (Diamond) out to expand his stardom. (Dir: Richard Fleischer, 115 mins.) †

J.D.'s Revenge (1976)** Glynn Turman, Louis Gossett, Jr., Joan Pringle, David McKnight. Blaxploitation. Glynn Turman plays a student possessed by the spirit of a man who was bumped off in the forties but has waited a long time to come back and satisfy his bloodlust. (Dir: Arthur Marks, 95 mins.) †

Jealousy (MTV 1984)*½ Angie Dickinson, Richard Mulligan, Paul Michael Glaser, Susan Tyrrell, Bo Svenson. Although she plays three diverse personalities—Angie Dickinson is still Angie Dickinson—whether she's a country-western singer dealing with a covetous husband, a woman envious of her teenage daughter's attention to her new husband, or a newlywed jealous of something she can't see. (Dir: Jeffrey Bloom, 100 mins.) †

Jean de Florette (France, 1986)***½ Yves Montand, Gerard Depardieu, Daniel Auteuil. Classically styled adaptation of Marcel Pagnol's novel. This impressively photographed epic about betrayal, idealism, and greed is enhanced by stellar performances by Depardieu as a city-bred hunchback who dreams of devoting himself to the soil and by Montand as his evil neighbor who covets Gerard's land. First of two parts, the second being *Manon of the Spring*. (Dir: Claude Berri, 122 mins.) †

Jeanne Eagels (1957)**½ Kim Novak, Jeff Chandler, Virginia Grey, Agnes Moorehead. A glorified yet watered-down depiction of the rise and fall of actress Jeanne Eagels. (Dir: George Sidney, 109 mins.)

Jeannie (Great Britain, 1941)*** Barbara Mullen, Michael Redgrave, Albert Lieven, Kay Hammond, Wilfred Lawson, Googie Withers, Rachel Kempson. A light comedy with a pretty Scottish girl touring Vienna and being pursued by two men; clever and enjoyable, but not as good as it should have been with these players. AKA: **Girl in Distress**. (Dir: Harold French, 101 mins.)

Jean Renoir, The Boss (France, 1967)*** A reverent tribute to the ''godfather'' of French cinema, concentrating on his masterwork, *The Rules of the Game*. The filmmakers, themselves disciples, extract artistic revelations from the master, proving him to be as amiable an individual as he was a brilliant filmmaker. (Dirs: Jacques Rivette, André S. Labarthe, 60 mins.)

J. Edgar Hoover (MCTV 1987)** Treat Williams, Rip Torn, David Ogden Stiers, Andrew Duggan, Art Hindle, Joe Regalbuto, Louise Fletcher. Superficial account of the life of the director of the FBI through ten presidential administrations, tracing his career as an idealistic young lawyer who at first questions constitutional and political impropriety, but who eventually is corrupted by the power of his office. (Dir: Robert Collins, 120 mins.) †

Jekyll and Hyde (MTV 1990)** Michael Caine, Cheryl Ladd, Joss Ackland, Ronald Pickup, Kim Thomson, Lionel Jeffries. This remake tried to distinguish itself from the myriad other versions of the classic tale by padding the story out with a few new subplots and pseudo-philosophizing. Unfortunately, all of that merely detracts from the main story. Even Caine is below par as the good doctor with an out-of-control evil side. (Dir: David Wickes, 96 mins.)

Jekyll and Hyde...Together Again (1982)* Mark Blankfield, Bess·Armstrong, Krista Errickson, Tim Thomerson. Blankfield is a limber physical comedian, but he can't salvage this slapdash, inane spoof of Jekyll-Hyde movies. (Dir: Jerry Belson, 87 mins.) †

Jennie Gerhardt (1933)** Sylvia Sidney, Donald Cook, Mary Astor, Edward Arnold, Cora Sue Collins, H. B. Warner. An affecting tearjerker, based on a Dreiser novel. Sidney plays a working-class girl who ends up in a Back Street situation. (Dir: Marion Gering, 85 mins.)

Jennifer (1978)** Lisa Pelikan, Bert Convy, Nina Foch. Young girl, awarded a scholarship to an exclusive girls' school, uses her power over snakes to combat her tormentors. Not a bad thriller. (Dir: Brice Mack, 90 mins.) †

Jennifer: A Woman's Story (MTV 1979)** Elizabeth Montgomery, Bradford Dillman, Scott Hylands. Montgomery is a widow battling for control of her husband's boat-building firm. Based on a British TV series. (Dir: Guy Green, 104 mins.)

Jennifer on My Mind (1971)** Michael Brandon, Tippy Walker, Peter Bonerz. Erich Segal wrote the script, a minus entry on the ledger. Society is responsible for the unhappiness of the wealthy young, or didn't you know? Noel Black directs, badly. (90 mins.)

Jenny (France, 1936)*** Françoise Rosay, Charles Vanel, Jean-Louis Barrault, Albert Prejean. Superbly written, strongly structured melodrama about a woman manager of a nightclub where criminals gather, who falls in love with a gangster who is also involved with her daughter. (Dir: Marcel Prevert, 105 mins.)

Jenny (1970)*½ Marlo Thomas, Alan Alda, Vincent Gardenia, Marian Hailey, Elizabeth Wilson. Thomas is an unwed, pregnant girl who leaves her conservative Connecticut home for New York City, where she meets hip young filmmaker Alda, who's looking for a way to beat the draft. Bingo! A "marriage of convenience"! (Dir: George Bloomfield, 86 mins.)†

Jenny's War (MTV 1985)** Dyan Cannon, Christopher Cazenove, Elke Sommer. If you can buy Dyan as a devoted mother who finagles her way into a prisoner of war camp to locate her son and dabble in a bit of spying, then this implausible wartime adventure (based, believe it or not, on a true story) may be for you. (Dir: Steven Gethers, 208 mins.)

Jeopardy (1953)**½ Barbara Stanwyck, Barry Sullivan, Ralph Meeker. Woman trying to find help for her injured husband is captured by an escaped killer. Modest little thriller is well made, but remains a minor drama. (Dir: John Sturges, 69 mins.)

Jeremiah Johnson (1972)*** Robert Redford, Allyn Ann McLerie, Josh Albee, Will Geer, Stefan Gierasch. Offbeat, visually beautiful western about a loner in the mountains of Utah shortly after the Mexican-American War. Redford hunts, lives off the land, and acquires an Indian wife during the course of his picturesque adventures. (Dir: Sydney Pollack, 107 mins.)†

Jeremy (1973)***½ Robby Benson, Glynnis O'Connor, Leonardo Cimino, Pat Wheel. Sensitive portrayal of first love. Robby Benson is enormously appealing as a Jewish would-be cellist, meeting and wooing a Gentile lass who loves to dance. (Dir: Arthur Barron, 90 mins.)

Jericho Mile, The (MTV 1979)***½ Peter Strauss, Richard Lawson, Roger E. Mosley, Miguel Pinero. Strauss is a tense, pent-up lifer at Folsom State Penitentiary, who becomes obsessed with running the fastest mile possible. When the prison officials try to clear the way for Strauss to qualify for the Olympic trials, the story really takes off. Director Michael Mann gives the film a big-budgeted theatrical look. (104 mins.)†

Jerk, The (1979)**½ Steve Martin, Bernadette Peters, Catlin Adams, Jackie Mason. Martin makes his starring debut as the 1980s answer to Jerry Lewis. He plays the white stepchild of black sharecroppers. Some great gags and many misfires. (Dir: Carl Reiner, 93 mins.)†

Jerk, Too, The (MTV 1984)* Mark Blankfield, Stacey Nelkin, Ray Walston, Mabel King, Gwen Verdon. This spastic TV sequel concerns the upcoming nuptials of an heiress and a fortune hunter. (Dir: Michael Schultz, 100 mins.)

Jesse James (1939)*** Tyrone Power, Henry Fonda, Brian Donlevy, Randolph Scott, Nancy Kelly. A superb cast in a highly fictionalized account of the life of America's most famous outlaw. Glorifies him too much but is exciting entertainment. (Dir: Henry King, 106 mins.)†

Jesse James Meets Frankenstein's Daughter (1966)** John Lupton, Cal Bolder, Narda Onyx. Lady scientist, descendant of you-know-who, turns the outlaw's wounded friend into a monster. Monstrous western-horror thriller. (Dir: William Beaudine, 88 mins.)†

Jesse Owens Story, The (MTV 1984)**½ Dorian Harewood, Georg Stanford Brown, Debbi Morgan, Tom Bosley, LeVar Burton. This occasionally stirring tale of the black Olympics champion who peaked early (1936 Olympic Games in Berlin), and then could find little meaningful use for his talents, works best in the inspirational sports footage; the structuring of the flashbacks with Harewood rehashing various injustices is handled poorly and robs the film of vitality. (Dir: Richard Irving, 208 mins.)†

Jessica (U.S.-France-Italy, 1962)** Angie Dickinson, Maurice Chevalier. When a glamorous midwife turns men's heads in a small Italian village, the women of the town pull a "Lysistrata" and go on "strike." (Dir: Jean Negulesco, 112 mins.)

Jesus (Great Britain, 1979)*½ Brian Deacon, Rivka Noiman, Yossef Shiloah, Niko Nitai, David Goldberg. A monotonous dramatization of the Gospel of St. Luke. (Dirs: Peter Sykes, John Kirsh, 117 mins.)

Jesus Christ Superstar (1973)*** Ted Neeley, Carl Anderson, Joshua Mostel, Yvonne Elliman. Substantial film version of the Broadway hit with an emphasis on razzle-dazzle. The songs are superbly integrated into a coherent overall approach. (Dir: Norman Jewison, 107 mins.)†

Jesus of Montreal (Canada, 1989)***½ Lothaire Bluteau, Catherine Wilkening, Johanne-Marie Tremblay, Remy Girard, Robert Lepage. Wickedly funny, provocative, invigorating film about a group of performers who stage a hip version of the Passion Play on a hilltop overlooking Montreal. Some, especially their backers, are scandalized, but many are enthralled by the surprisingly devout but iconoclastic and eclectic production. (Dir: Denys Arcand, 118 mins.)†

Je T'Aime, Je T'Aime (France, 1968)***½ Claude Rich, Anouk Ferjac, Annie Farque, Georges Jamin, Olga Georges-Picot. A young man, rescued from the brink of suicide, agrees to test a time machine. The tests go awry, and events from his life recur in haphazard fashion. A weird journey into fragmented time by director Alain Resnais, the master of dazzling disorienting cinema. (94 mins.)

Jet Benny Show, The (1986)* Steve Norman, Polly McIntyre, Kevin Dees, Ted Luedemann. Stunningly pointless, witless sci-fi parody of the old Jack Benny TV show, with a badly impersonated Benny as a space hero and Rochester his black robot valet. Viewers unfamiliar with the real Benny won't get it; come to think of it, neither did we. (Dir: Roger Evans, 77 mins.)†

Jet over the Atlantic (1959)**½ Guy Madison, Virginia Mayo, George Raft. Fairly interesting drama about a plane which is in danger when a bomb is discovered aboard during the flight from Spain to New York. (Dir: Byron Haskin, 95 mins.)†

Jet Pilot (1957)*½ John Wayne, Janet Leigh, Hans Conried. An odd Josef von Sternberg film that was made under the auspices of Howard Hughes. Leigh plays a Russian spy who's redeemed by love and marriage; Wayne is the hero who converts her to the American way. Film took seven years to make. Viewing time seems somewhat briefer. (112 mins.)

Jetsons: The Movie (1990)*½ Voices of George O'Hanlon, Mel Blanc, Tiffany. Crudely made animated feature based on the popular cartoon series of the sixties. What once had a futuristic appeal now appears dated, with some of the worst animation to be seen in years. (Dirs: William Hanna, Joseph Barbera, 78 mins.)†

Jewel of the Nile, The (1985)** Michael Douglas, Kathleen Turner, Danny De Vito, Spiros Focas, Avner Eisenberg, Paul David Magid. This follow-up to *Romancing the Stone* misses the charm and excitement of the original. Adventurer Jack Colton and novelist Joan Wilder flounder in this tale about a Holy War in the Middle East. (Dir: Lewis Teague, 105 mins.)†

Jewel Robbery (1932)***½ William Powell, Kay Francis, Hardie Albright, Helen Vinson, Alan Mowbray. Completely delightful, stylish comedy-adventure has romance flowering between a dashing jewel thief and his lovely victim; fast, bright, and remarkably sexy, with great chemistry sparking between the stars. (Dir: William Dieterle, 70 mins.)

Jewish Gauchos, The (Argentina, 1976)* Pepe Soriano, Ginamaria Hidalgo, Maria

Rose Gallo, Dora Baret. Unintentionally hilarious melodrama, with songs yet, about Jewish immigrants who settle on the pampas in the early 1900s. Horas on horseback. (Dir: Juan José Jusi, 92 mins.)

Jezebel (1938)***½ Bette Davis, Henry Fonda, Fay Bainter, George Brent, Margaret Lindsay, Richard Cromwell, Donald Crisp, Spring Byington, Henry O'Neill. Immensely entertaining historical drama. Just before the War Between the States, a high-spirited Southern belle flouts convention, drives away the stalwart young man she loves with her unladylike behavior, and later redeems herself by risking her life to nurse him when he contracts yellow fever. Davis makes this Confederate fallen angel one of her most indelible characterizations. Oscars for her as Best Actress and for Bainter in the supporting category. (Dir: William Wyler, 103 mins.)†

Jigsaw (1949)**½ Franchot Tone, Jean Wallace, Myron McCormick, Marc Lawrence. Low-budget *film noir* about an assistant DA tracking down a Klan-like conspiracy; remarkable for its courage in those Red-baiting times, and assisted by cameos from several stars known for their anti-Fascist beliefs, including Marlene Dietrich, Burgess Meredith, John Garfield, and Henry Fonda. AKA: **Gun Moll.** (Dir: Fletcher Markle, 70 mins.)†

Jigsaw (Great Britain, 1962)**½ Jack Warner, Ronald Lewis, Yolande Donlan. Capable whodunit about police investigating a murder, painstakingly putting the clues together. (Dir: Val Guest, 107 mins.)

Jigsaw (1968)**½ Harry Guardino, Hope Lange, Bradford Dillman, Pat Hingle. Fairly engrossing tale about a scientist (Dillman) who thinks he has committed a murder, and hires a private detective to fill in the missing pieces. (Dir: James Goldstone, 97 mins.)

Jigsaw (MTV 1972)**½ James Wainwright, Vera Miles, Richard Kiley. James Wainwright, an offbeat, rugged actor in the Lee Marvin groove, plays the leading role of a police detective in this well-paced pilot for the TV series. AKA: **Man on the Move.** (Dir: William Graham, 99 mins.)†

Jigsaw Man, The (Great Britain, 1984)**½ Michael Caine, Laurence Olivier, Susan George, Robert Powell. A not uninteresting true story about a British double agent (Caine) who had defected to the Soviet Union and returns as a different man (thanks to plastic surgery) in order to uncover a microfilmed list of Soviet spies. (Dir: Terence Young, 96 mins.)†

Jim Buck—See: **Portrait of a Hitman**

Jimi Hendrix (1973)*** Music-filled documentary about the legendary rock guitarist includes insightful interviews with many who knew him and some great renditions of his hits, including classic "Purple Haze" and "Wild Thing." (Dir: Joe Boyd, John Head, Gary Weis, 102 mins.)†

Jimmy and Sally (1933)** Claire Trevor, James Dunn, Lya Lys, Harvey Stephens. Inconsequential Depression romance of a young couple torn apart by the need to make money; relies on the charm of the stars to get by. (Dir: James Tinling, 68 mins.)

Jimmy B. & Andre (MTV 1980)**½ Alex Karras, Madge Sinclair, Curtis Yates. A sentimental true-life story. Greek restauranteur Jimmy Butsicaris becomes the mentor of a young black street-wise kid who hustled to make an honest buck any way he could. (Dir: Guy Green, 104 mins.)

Jimmy Reardon—See: Night in the Life of Jimmy Reardon, A

Jimmy the Gent (1934)**½ James Cagney, Bette Davis, Alice White. This breezy teaming of Cagney and Davis is full of rapid-punch comedy and action. Slightly dishonorable, Jimmy's so determined to woo Bette he's even willing to pretend that he's gone straight. Considering what an attractive team they were, it's a shame the Brothers Warner didn't give them better comedy scripts than this and *The Bride Came C.O.D.* (Dir: Michael Curtiz, 67 mins.)

Jimmy The Kid (1982)*½ Gary Coleman, Paul LeMat, Dee Wallace. Typical vehicle for Coleman, playing a precocious rich kid who's kidnapped by bungling crooks and learns how to better appreciate his childhood because of this experience. (Dir: Gary Nelson, 85 mins.)†

Jim Thorpe, All American (1951)*** Burt Lancaster, Phyllis Thaxter. Burt Lancaster portrays the All-American Indian athlete who rose from an obscure beginning to international fame. Sport fans will enjoy this. (Dir: Michael Curtiz, 107 mins.)

Jinxed (1982)*** Bette Midler, Ken Wahl, Rip Torn. Raunchy vehicle for Midler's off-the-wall comedy. Dealer at blackjack tables (Wahl) is jinxed by small-time gambler (Torn), but figures out a way to get even when he begins an affair with the gambler's mistress (Midler). The couple plot the perfect murder, and what ensues is zany and surprising. (Dir: Don Siegel, 103 mins.)†

Jinx Money (1948)** Bowery Boys, Sheldon Leonard, Wanda McKay, Donald MacBride, John Eldredge. The Boys find a great sum of money won by a now-deceased gangster from gambling. (Dir: William Beaudine, 68 mins.)

Jitterbugs (1943)** Stan Laurel, Oliver Hardy, Robert Bailey, Douglas Fowley, Vivian Blaine. L. and H. do their manly best to prevent gangsters from bothering a pretty singer. Average, but the comic routines add some zing. (Dir: Mal St. Clair, 74 mins.)

Jitters, The (U.S.-Japan, 1989)**½ Sal Viviano, Marilyn Yokuda, James Hong, Frank Dietz. Here's a weird one—the first (and probably last) adaptation of a popular Chinese comedy-fantasy series featuring *jiangshi*, vampire-like zombies that are surprisingly acrobatic (wait 'til you see them bounding around!). More silly than scary, but certainly different. (Dir: John M. Fasano, 79 mins.)†

Jivaro (1954)**½ Fernando Lamas, Rhonda Fleming, Brian Keith. Into the land of head-hunters come the fearless treasure-seeking adventurers with Fernando Lamas at the helm and beautiful Rhonda Fleming not far behind. Action-filled jungle film. (Dir: Edward Ludwig, 91 mins.)

Joanna Francesca (Brazil-France, 1973)**½ Jeanne Moreau, Helber Rangel, Pierre Cardin, Leina Crespi. Lavish drama about evil and decadence at a Brazilian plantation is director Carlos Giegues's critical look at the ruling classes and slavery in his native Brazil. Occasionally goes overboard in depicting the cruelty of the landowners. Moreau's costumes are extraordinary, as they should be, since fashion designer Pierre Cardin is film's co-producer and one of its stars. (114 mins.)

Joan of Arc (1948)**½ Ingrid Bergman, Jose Ferrer, Ward Bond. Mammoth, lavish production based on the life of the French farm girl who led the French armies against England and was later tried as a heretic. Despite the pretensions, the film is top-heavy, and wallows in its own opulence. Originally 145 mins. (Dir: Victor Fleming, 100 mins.)†

Joan of Paris (1942)***½ Michele Morgan, Paul Henreid, Alan Ladd. French girl sacrifices her life so that the English flyers may escape the Gestapo in occupied France. Gripping, suspenseful war drama, excellently acted, well produced. (Dir: Robert Stevenson, 95 mins.)

Jocks (1987)** Scott Strader, Perry Lang, Mariska Hargitay, Richard Roundtree. A tennis team must buck their own school's negativity because the athletic director thinks tennis isn't a manly game. AKA: **Road Trip.** (Dir: Steve Carver, 91 mins.)†

Joe (1970)*** Peter Boyle, Susan Sarandon, Dennis Patrick. Savage, but imperfect film, which benefits greatly from an astonishingly bravura performance by Peter Boyle as a foul-mouthed, reactionary bigot. His monologue in a neighborhood bar, where he meets and befriends an affluent advertising executive who is also a murderer, is one of the most compelling scenes in years. (Dir: John G. Avildsen, 107 mins.)†

Joe and Ethel Turp Call on the President (1939)**½ Ann Sothern, William Gargan, Lewis Stone, Walter Brennan, Marsha Hunt, Al Shean. Amusing Damon Runyan story about a Flatbush postman who, suspended unjustly from his job, pleads his case all the way to the top with the help of his wife and neighbors. (Dir: Robert B. Sinclair, 70 mins.)

J.O.E. and the Colonel (MTV 1985)**½ Gary Kasper, William Lucking, Terence Knox, Gail Edwards, Aimee Eccles. J.O.E. is a human with biologically engineered superpowers considered an ultimate weapon by the government, until he shows he's still too human. He is to be destroyed with the help of a scientist and a colonel, so J.O.E. goes into hiding and continues to do his work, thwarting the enemy. (Dir: Ron Satlof, 104 mins.)

Joe Butterfly (1957)** Audie Murphy, George Nader, Burgess Meredith. GIs in Japan encounter a shrewd native operator who helps them get out the first edition of *Yank*. Disappointing service comedy. (Dir: Jesse Hibbs, 90 mins.)

Joe Dakota (1957)**½ Jock Mahoney, Luana Patten. Stranger rides into town and finds the populace agog with oil fever, uncovers skullduggery behind the drilling. Pleasant little western. (Dir: Richard Bartlett, 79 mins.)

Joe Kidd (1972)**½ Clint Eastwood, John Saxon, Don Stroud, Robert Duvall. Moderately interesting western. The setting is New Mexico at the turn of the century. The plot centers on the Spanish-Americans fighting the land barons for what they believe to be their property. In steps Joe Kidd (Eastwood) to aid the Spaniards and the sparks fly in a flashy, violent finale. (Dir: John Sturges, 88 mins.)†

Joe Louis Story, The (1953)*½ Coley Wallace, Paul Stewart, Hilda Simms, James Edwards, John Marley. Disappointing film biography of the great heavyweight champion; cheaply made, but at least they tried. Ossie Davis has a bit part. (Dir: Robert Gordon, 88 mins.)†

Joe Macbeth (Great Britain, 1955)**½ Paul Douglas, Ruth Roman. Egged on by his grasping wife, a gangster kills his way to the top of the mob. Modernized Shakespeare, a noble experiment that doesn't quite succeed. (Dir: Ken Hughes, 90 mins.)

Joe Palooka—See: **Palooka**

Joe Smith, American (1942)**½ Robert Young, Marsha Hunt, Harvey Stephens,

Darryl Hickman. Fairly effective WWII agitprop about a munitions worker who falls into Nazi hands but keeps his mouth shut for Uncle Sam. (Dir: Richard Thorpe, 63 mins.)

Joe Versus the Volcano (1990)*** Tom Hanks, Meg Ryan, Dan Hedaya, Lloyd Bridges, Ossie Davis, Robert Stack, Abe Vigoda, Carol Kane (cameo). Whimsical fantasy-comedy, straight out of the '30s, about a dreary man who works in the world's most depressing office. (The first twenty minutes are everything that *Brazil* tried to be.) Told he's dying, he accepts a millionaire's offer of a luxurious end if he agrees to offer himself as a sacrifice in a South Seas volcano. Weakest in the middle—Hank fails at projecting dejection and whimsy—but the film succeeds with great character takes and writer-director John Patrick Shanley's flare for the visual. (94 mins.)†

Joey (1986)** Neill Barry, James Quinn, Elisa Heinsohn, Linda Thorson, Rickey Ellis. Unpretentious, compassionate look at a teenager who runs away from home to fulfill himself as a musician. Amateurish but heartfelt, the film attempts to make the generational conflict between Joey and his dad, a retired rock-and-roller, comprehensible. (Dir: Joseph Ellison, 97 mins.)†

John and Mary (1969)**½ Dustin Hoffman, Mia Farrow. Gentle if sometimes tedious study that treads lightly on a resigned affair between two singles who pick each other up at a bar but don't really swing. The action is painfully confined to an apartment interior (with some flashes outdoors) and the acting is constricted by the screenplay, which prefers social commentary to humanism. (Dir: Peter Yates, 92 mins.)

John and Yoko: A Love Story (MTV 1985)*** Mark McGann, Kim Miyori. Cogent biopic about Beatles leader John Lennon and his love, Yoko Ono, during the turbulent times from 1966 to 1980. Romantic scenes between the couple are punctuated by Beatles music, miscarriages, drug busts, deportation charges, child kidnapping, Lennon's womanizing, and his inability to hold a drink. (Dir: Sandor Stern, 132 mins.)†

John F. Kennedy: Years of Lightning, Day of Drums (1964)**** Excellent U.S. government documentary on the Presidential life, and death, of John F. Kennedy, guarantees to stir up all the old emotions. (Dir: Bruce Herschensohn, 88 mins.)

John Goldfarb, Please Come Home (1965)*½ Shirley MacLaine, Peter Ustinov, Richard Crenna. This offbeat comedy set in a mythical Arabian principality doesn't work at all. (Dir: J. Lee Thompson, 96 mins.)

John Loves Mary (1949)**½ Ronald Reagan, Patricia Neal, Jack Carson. Stage comedy about a returning soldier trying to sneak a war bride into this country, while his fiancée wants to get married. Neal's film debut. (Dir: David Butler, 96 mins.)

John Meade's Woman (1937)**½ Edward Arnold, Francine Larrimore, Gail Patrick, George Bancroft, Sidney Blackmer. Pedestrian melodrama of a tycoon in love with the wrong woman; the cast is the only thing that makes it interesting. (Dir: Richard Wallace, 87 mins.)

Johnnie Mae Gibson: FBI (MTV 1986)**½ Lynn Whitfield, Howard E. Rollins, Jr., Richard Lawson, William Allen Young, John Lehne, Marta DuBois, Hugh Gillin. The story of the FBI's first black woman agent, Johnnie Mae Gibson, a determined lady battling everyone, including her husband, to make the grade. (Dir: Bill Duke, 104 mins.)

Johnny Allegro (1949)**½ George Raft, Nina Foch. Raft is once again the shady hoodlum who squares himself with the cops by acting as an undercover agent to expose an international smuggling outfit. Plenty of two-fisted action. (Dir: Ted Tetzlaff, 81 mins.)

Johnny Angel (1945)*** George Raft, Claire Trevor. Merchant Marine officer unravels the murder of his father, smashes a ring of enemy agents. Well-done melodrama. (Dir: Edwin L. Marin, 79 mins.)†

Johnny Apollo (1940)*** Tyrone Power, Dorothy Lamour, Edward Arnold, Lloyd Nolan. Fast-paced gangster melodrama with college grad Power choosing a life of crime out of bitterness over his dad's conviction for fraud. (Dir: Henry Hathaway, 93 mins.)

Johnny Be Good (1988)* Anthony Michael Hall, Robert Downey, Jr., Paul Gleason. Miscasting gangly teen actor Hall as a high school football star is only the first mistake this lame comedy makes. His crisis: whether to accept one of the many outrageous football scholarships he is being offered, or to stay and attend State U. with his girlfriend. Is this really supposed to win our sympathy? (Dir: Bud Smith, 84 mins.)†

Johnny Belinda (1948)***½ Jane Wyman, Lew Ayres, Charles Bickford, Agnes Moorehead. Jane Wyman gives an Oscar-award-winning performance as a deaf-mute in this sensitive and moving story of a person living in a world of silence. (Dir: Jean Negulesco, 103 mins.)†

Johnny Belinda (MTV 1982)*** Richard Thomas, Rosanna Arquette, Dennis Quaid, Fran Ryan, Candy Clark. A sensitive remake of the 1948 movie. This updated version focuses on the loving relationship between a VISTA do-gooder and a mute country girl. (Dir: Anthony Page, 104 mins.)†

Johnny Bull (MTV 1986)**½ Jason Robards, Jr., Colleen Dewhurst, Peter MacNicol, Kathy Bates, Suzanna Hamilton. Here's a throwback to the domestic dramas of early television. Jason Robards and Colleen Dewhurst play the hard-working and long-suffering Papa and Mama in a coal-mining Pennsylvania town post WWII. Their son (Peter MacNicol) brings home a war bride from England (Suzanna Hamilton), and her presence changes all their lives drastically. (Dir: Claudia Weill, 104 mins.)

Johnny Cash: The Man, His World, His Music (1970)*** Johnny Cash, June Carter, Bob Dylan, Don Reed. Quite interesting feature about the famous country-music star. We hear a lot of good Cash tunes, also learn something about Cash himself as we travel with Johnny to his hometown in rural Arkansas where he grew up in poverty. (Dir: Robert Elfstrom, 94 mins.)

Johnny Come Lately (1943)**½ James Cagney, Grace George, Marjorie Lord. A wandering vagabond stops in a small town and helps an old lady run her newspaper. Generally entertaining comedy-drama. (Dir: William K. Howard, 97 mins.)†

Johnny Concho (1956)** Frank Sinatra, Keenan Wynn, Phyllis Kirk, William Conrad. Sinatra as a cowboy is very hard to take! The plot centers around a coward who must face up to a fast gun. (Dir: Don McGuire, 84 mins.)

Johnny Cool (1963)** Henry Silva, Elizabeth Montgomery. Violent, familiar tale of a mafioso (Silva) seeking revenge in gangsterdom. (Dir: William Asher, 101 mins.)

Johnny Dangerously (1984)** Michael Keaton, Joe Piscopo, Peter Boyle, Maureen Stapleton, Griffin Dunne, Marilu Henner. An overextended gangster flick spoof that lights up with a few bright nutty moments. This parody embraces the life of one Johnny Dangerously, who turned to crime to pay his mother's medical bills. (Dir: Amy Heckerling, 90 mins.)†

Johnny Dark (1954)*½ Tony Curtis, Piper Laurie, Don Taylor. Predictable sports car dramatics, hyped a little by a good cast and burning-rubber road shots. (Dir: George Sherman, 85 mins.)

Johnny Doesn't Live Here Anymore—See: **And So They Were Married** (1944)

Johnny Eager (1941)*** Robert Taylor, Lana Turner, Van Heflin. Top-rate gangster melodrama about a good-looking, egotistical hood. Van Heflin's performance as Taylor's confidant and Greek

547

chorus won him an award (a Supporting Actor Oscar) and stardom. (Dir: Mervyn LeRoy, 107 mins.)

Johnny Got His Gun (1971)** Timothy Bottoms, Jason Robards, Jr., Marsha Hunt, Donald Sutherland, Kathy Fields, Diane Varsi. Author Dalton Trumbo directed this earnest, slow-moving adaptation of his own classic antiwar novel about a severely disabled soldier. (111 mins.)†

Johnny Guitar (1954)***½ Joan Crawford, Sterling Hayden, Mercedes McCambridge, Scott Brady. Director Nicholas Ray's unique western drama blends elements of German expressionism, *film noir*, and range-riding shoot-'em-ups to create a heady and intoxicating brew. Joan Crawford plays the mistress of a gambling den on the edge of a frontier settlement, waiting for the railroad to bring her prosperity while fending off the jealous locals who want to run her out of town. A moody, visually striking work that bears Ray's signature of originality throughout, with mesmerizing performances by Crawford and McCambridge. (110 mins.)†

Johnny Handsome (1989)*** Mickey Rourke, Ellen Barkin, Forest Whitaker, Elizabeth McGovern, Lance Henrickson, Morgan Freeman. Punk criminal Rourke, born with hideous facial disfigurement, gets a chance at a new life after a prison doctor reconstructs his face. Once out of prison, though, he returns to the shadowy world on which he depends to get revenge on his betrayers. Unsympathetic, violent film starts fast and never lets up until its final brutal scene. Gorgeously filmed with wonderful performances by the entire cast, especially Rourke and Barkin. (Dir: Walter Hill, 95 mins.)†

Johnny Holiday (1949)***½ William Bendix, Stanley Clements, Hoagy Carmichael, Allen Martin, Jr. Sincere drama. Delinquent boy is reformed at the Indiana Boys' School. (Dir: Willis Goldbeck, 92 mins.)

Johnny in the Clouds (Great Britain, 1945)***½ Douglass Montgomery, John Mills, Michael Redgrave. Story of a flying field in England during WWII, and the various emotional entanglements of the airmen. Stirring war drama with praiseworthy performance, direction. AKA: **The Way to the Stars**. (Dir: Anthony Asquith, 87 mins.)

Johnny Nobody (Great Britain, 1961)*** Nigel Patrick, Aldo Ray, William Bendix, Yvonne Mitchell. When a disliked writer is killed by a mysterious stranger soon known as "Johnny Nobody," the local priest suspects a plot; the villagers are claiming the deed to be a miracle. Offbeat drama. (Dir: Nigel Patrick, 88 mins.)†

Johnny O'Clock (1947)**½ Dick Powell, Evelyn Keyes. Confused, tough tale of an honest gambler who gets accused of murder. Good, rough dialogue but without a purpose. (Dir: Robert Rossen, 95 mins.)

Johnny Shiloh (MTV 1963)**½ Kevin Corcoran, Brian Keith, Eddie Hodges, Darryl Hickman, Regis Toomey. Effective Disney feature (later released to theaters) about Civil War orphan Corcoran who joins the Union army as a drummer boy to help fight "Mr. Lincoln's war," with Keith as the soldier assigned to watch over him. (Dir: James Neilson, 90 mins.)†

Johnny Stool Pigeon (1949)**½ Howard Duff, Shelley Winters, Dan Duryea, Tony Curtis. Routine but well-played crime drama about an ex-con who serves as a "stoolie" for the police in order to uncover a dope ring. (Dir: William Castle, 76 mins.)

Johnny Tiger (1966)**½ Robert Taylor, Geraldine Brooks, Chad Everett, Brenda Scott. Teacher comes to the Seminole Reservation in Florida to instruct the Indian children, finds his task is harder than he bargained for. (Dir: Paul Wendkos, 102 mins.)†

Johnny Tremain (1957)*** Hal Stalmaster, Luana Patten, Sebastian Cabot. America's revolution is the setting for this feature about Johnny Tremain, a silversmith's apprentice in 1773 Boston, who learns the patriotic importance of the colonies' fight against the British. (Dir: Robert Stevenson, 80 mins.)

Johnny Trouble (1957)** Stuart Whitman, Ethel Barrymore, Carolyn Jones. Guy on the road turns over a new leaf when he meets a woman who has never given up hope of her long-lost son's returning. Drama leans toward the maudlin. Barrymore's last. (Dir: John H. Auer, 80 mins.)

Johnny, We Hardly Knew Ye (MTV 1977)*** Paul Rudd, Burgess Meredith, Kevin Conway, William Prince. Solid, absorbing TV drama about John F. Kennedy's years just after WWII, detailing his shift from war hero to politician. (Dir: Gilbert Cates, 104 mins.)

John Paul Jones (1959)**½ Robert Stack, Marisa Pavan, Charles Coburn, Bette Davis. Rambling biography of America's first naval hero, moderately well played by Stack against stacked odds—talky script, static direction. (Dir: John Farrow, 126 mins.)

Johnstown Flood, The (1926)*** George O'Brien, Janet Gaynor, Anders Randolf, Florence Gilbert. Exciting disaster film, with still-unsurpassed special effects and photography by George Schneiderman; the story has an honest engineer warning of the possibility of a great flood, but being ignored by the city fathers for financial reasons. (Dir: Irving Cummings, 70 mins.)†

Jo Jo Dancer, Your Life Is Calling (1986) **½ Richard Pryor, Debbie Allen, Art Evans, Fay Hauser, Barbara Williams, Paula Kelly, Billy Eckstein, Diahnne Abbott. The autobiographical film includes painful details from the Pryor's childhood and from the period of his near-fatal freebasing accident, but the rough edges have been sanded away. (Dir: Richard Pryor, 97 mins.)†

Joke of Destiny Lying in Wait Around the Corner Like a Bandit, A (Italy, 1984)*** Ugo Tognazzi, Piera Degli Esposti, Gastone Moschin. Entertaining political farce about a state official who gets trapped inside his computerized car and suffers through the attempts of his subordinates to free him. Good-natured and laugh-filled. (Dir: Lina Wertmuller, 105 mins.)†

Joker, The (France, 1960)*** Jean-Pierre Cassel, Anouk Aimée, Genevieve Cluny, Pierre Palau. A man enshrines women, all women, as the center of his life, and finally believes he has found the perfect one: she's rich but married, and his dreams are deferred once more. AKA: **Le Farceur.** (Dir: Philippe de Broca, 90 mins.)

Joker Is Wild, The (1957)*** Frank Sinatra, Jeanne Crain, Mitzi Gaynor. The story of nightclub entertainer Joe E. Lewis, who conquered problems with the gang lords of the roaring twenties, and with alcoholism. Played by Sinatra in his standard hipster style, the story has moments of dramatic force, some good nostalgic tunes. (Dir: Charles Vidor, 126 mins.)

Jokers, The (Great Britain, 1967)***½ Michael Crawford, Oliver Reed. An attractive pair of well-to-do brothers, charmingly played by Oliver Reed and Michael Crawford, come up with a wild plot to snatch the Crown Jewels and then give them back. (Dir: Michael Winner, 94 mins.)

Jolly Bad Fellow, A (Great Britain, 1964) *** Leo McKern, Janet Munro, Maxine Audley. Wildly amusing comedy about a scoundrely professor who discovers a poison that will cause painless and untraceable death, and decides to use it. (Dir: Don Chaffey, 94 mins.)

Jolson Sings Again (1949)**½ Larry Parks, Barbara Hale. The rest of the Al Jolson Story. Parks once again mouths the songs that made the "Minstrel of Broadway" famous. (Dir: Henry Levin, 96 mins.)†

Jolson Story, The (1946)***½ Larry Parks, Evelyn Keyes, William Demarest, Bill Goodwin, Ludwig Donath. The film bi-ography of the popular singer from his boyhood to his success on the stage and in talkies. (Dir: Alfred E. Green, 128 mins.)†

Jonah Who Will Be 25 in the Year 2000 (Switzerland, 1976)**** Myriam Boyer, Jean-Luc Bideau, Miou-Miou, Roger Jendly. Director Alain Tanner's affectionate study of a group of sixties radicals trying to make the transition to the seventies. (115 mins.)

Jonathan Livingston Seagull (1973)* Voices of James Franciscus, Juliet Mills, Hal Holbrook, Philip Ahn, Dorothy McGuire, Richard Crenna. Richard Bach's slight parable of a bird convinced there must be something more to life than flying with the flock and eating might have made an acceptable short animated film. (Dir: Hal Bartlett, 101 mins.)†

Jordan Chance, The (MTV 1978)**½ Raymond Burr, Stella Stevens. Burr plays—you guessed it—a criminal lawyer, Frank Jordan, an ex-con who studied law in the pen and only defends those he feels have been given a raw deal by the courts. (Dir: Jules Irving, 104 mins.)

Josepha (France, 1982)** Miou-Miou, Claude Brasseur, Bruno Cremer, Nadine Alari, Anne Laure Meury. Superficial peek into the lives of a bickering theatrical couple who keep acting even when they're not on stage. (Dir: Christopher Frank, 114 mins.)†

Joseph Andrews (Great Britain, 1976)*½ Ann-Margret, Peter Firth, Beryl Reid, Michael Hordern, John Gielgud. Tony Richardson, who directed the joyous *Tom Jones*, takes liberties with another Henry Fielding novel, only with less felicitous results. A charmless farce. (104 mins.)†

Josephine Baker Story, The (MCTV 1991) *** Lynn Whitfield, Rubén Blades, David Dukes, Louis Gossett, Jr., Craig T. Nelson. Whitfield takes the role of Josephine Baker and turns it into a tour de force. The story chronicles the rise of Baker from a childhood of dire poverty to international stardom in the late '20s. Film tries to cram in all of La Baker's life, which dissipates the impact a bit. However, Whitfield's impressive star turn and excellent supporting performances make it worthwhile. (Dir: Brian Gibson, 130 mins.)†

Josette (1938)*** Don Ameche, Simone Simon, Bert Lahr, Joan Davis, Robert Young, William Demarest, Lon Chaney, Jr. Fluffy musical comedy takes advantage of the talents of the performers, and for once the lovely Simon is used to full advantage in a mistaken-identity story. (Dir: Allan Dwan, 73 mins.)

Joshua's Heart (MTV 1990)**½ Melissa Gilbert, Tim Matheson, Matthew Lawrence. A distraught Gilbert emotes over a breakup with her boyfriend and the separation from his son from an earlier marriage. She gives a no-holds-barred performance in this classy tearjerker. (Dir: Michael Pressman, 96 mins.)

Joshua Then and Now (1985)**½ James Woods, Gabrielle Lazure, Alan Arkin, Michael Sarrazin. An astringent comedy about social climbing. A Jewish boy with aspirations meets a Protestant Princess with connections, and the two marry despite divergent backgrounds (which will later tear them apart). (Dir: Ted Kotcheff, 129 mins.)†

Jour de Fete (France, 1948)***½ Jacques Tati, Guy Decomble, Paul Fankeur. Comic craftsman Jacques Tati made his directorial debut with this charming little tale of a town fair in the French provinces. Tati himself plays the bumbling local mailman who gets inspired to jet propel his delivery "à l'Américain." (87 mins.)†

Journey, The (1959)**½ Deborah Kerr, Yul Brynner, Jason Robards, Jr. Brynner parades around as a Russian officer who mixes business (detaining the evacuation of neutral citizens from revolution-torn Hungary circa 1956) and pleasure (putting the make on pale Deborah Kerr). A good cast at the mercy of a mediocre script. (Dir: Anatole Litvak, 125 mins.)

Journey Back to Oz (1974)** Voices of Liza Minnelli, Milton Berle, Margaret Hamilton, Paul Lynde, Ethel Merman, Mickey Rooney. Animated family fare in which Dorothy gets a return trip to the Emerald City. (Not in first class, though; strictly a coach production.) (Dir: Hal Sutherland, 90 mins.)†

Journey for Margaret (1942)*** Robert Young, Laraine Day, Margaret O'Brien. Story of the small, innocent victims of the blitz is splendidly acted, warm melodrama. (Dir: W. S. Van Dyke, 81 mins.)

Journey from Darkness (MTV 1975)**½ Marc Singer, Kay Lenz, Joseph Campanella, William Windom. Marc Singer is effective in this adaptation of a true story about a blind student who doggedly battles his way into medical school. (Dir: James Goldstone, 100 mins.)

Journey Into Autumn (Sweden, 1954)*** Harriet Anderson, Eva Dahlbeck, Ulf Palme, Gunnar Bjornstrand, Inga Landgre, Naima Wifstrand. Two women, both in the fashion industry, travel to another town, where one hopes to rekindle a past romance with a married man. The other spends time teasing a rich man. An unusual drama with touches of wry humor about the dreams of women and the realities of life and the illusion of the camera's lens. (Dir: Ingmar Bergman, 86 mins.)

Journey Into Fear (1942)*** Orson Welles, Joseph Cotten, Dolores Del Rio, Ruth Warrick, Everett Sloane. An effective version of the Eric Ambler thriller (co-written and produced by Orson Welles) set in WWII Turkey as a U.S. armaments expert is sought by Nazi agents. (Dir: Norman Foster, 69 mins.)†

Journey Into Fear (Canada, 1975)** Sam Waterston, Yvette Mimieux, Zero Mostel. This updating of the 1942 espionage yarn set in Turkey and the U.S. of the 1970s dilutes the suspense of the original tale. (Dir: Daniel Mann, 103 mins.)†

Journey Into Light (1951)**½ Sterling Hayden, Viveca Lindfors. A minister loses faith, becomes a derelict, is reformed by a blind girl in a Skid Row mission. (Dir: Stuart Heisler, 87 mins.)

Journey of Hope (Switzerland, 1990)*** Necmettin Cobanoglu, Nur Surer, Emin Sivas, Yaman Okay. Straightforward, earnest story of a Turkish family that emigrates to Switzerland to find a better life, and their dramatic struggles to get there. Well done, rather sentimental, but interesting for its look at an unfamiliar culture. Won the Oscar for Best Foreign Film of 1990. (Dir: Xavier Koller, 110 mins.)

Journey of Natty Gann, The (1985)*** Meredith Salenger, John Cusack, Ray Wise, Lainie Kazan, Scatman Crothers, Barry Miller. A Depression-era youngster travels America's byways in the company of a girl's best friend, a trusty and devoted wolf. With a vibrant performance by newcomer Salenger as the wayfaring adolescent in search of her father, this *Journey* is well worth taking. (Dir: Jeremy Kagan, 101 mins.)†

Journey of Robert F. Kennedy, The (1970) ***½ An engrossing, perceptive and touching portrait of the late Senator Robert F. Kennedy, the man, the politician, the husband and father, and the inspired spokesman for the blacks and the poor. (Dir: Mel Stuart, 75 mins.)

Journey's End (1930)***½ Colin Clive, Ian Maclaren, David Manners. Near-perfect rendering of R. C. Sherriff's classic antiwar play. Clive is unforgettable as the alcoholic captain who cracks under the strain of responsibility. (Dir: James Whale, 120 mins.)

Journey Together (Great Britain, 1946)**½ Richard Attenborough, Jack Watling, Bessie Love, Edward G. Robinson. Patriotic British-American docudrama of U.S. airmen stationed in Britain during WWII, and the struggle for understanding between clashing cultures. Now an antique with good intentions. (Dir: John Boulting, 95 mins.)

Journey to Shiloh (1968)** Michael Sarrazin, Brenda Scott, James Caan, Michael Burns. Action-filled tale about a group of green young men who set out for Virginia to join up and fight for the Confederacy. (Dir: William Hale, 101 mins.)

Journey to the Center of the Earth (1959) ***½ James Mason, Pat Boone, Arlene Dahl, Diane Baker, Thayer David. Juvenile adventure maintaining a credible tone of silliness throughout that understands the continuing appeal of Jules Verne. Mason is the expedition leader whose entourage includes a goose called Gertrude. Has one of Bernard Hermann's most effective scores. (Dir: Henry Levin, 132 mins.)†

Journey to the Center of Time (1967)*½ Scott Brady, Gigi Perreau, Anthony Eisley, Abraham Sofaer. Travelers caught in a time mix-up are forced to battle in prehistoric jungles and the world of the year 5000. (Dir: D. L. Hewitt, 82 mins.)

Journey to the Far Side of the Sun (Great Britain, 1969)*½ Roy Thinnes, Lynn Loring, Herbert Lom, Patrick Wymark. Astronaut Thinnes discovers and explores a planet behind the sun. (Dir: Robert Parrish, 99 mins.)

Journey to the Lost City (West Germany, 1959)*½ Debra Paget, Paul Hubschmid, Walther Reyr, Rene Deltman. A butchered version of two Fritz Lang films that were much better intact (*The Indian Tomb* and *The Tiger of Eschnapur*). Set in mysterious India, this compressed movie deals with an architect who falls head over heels for a dancing girl in a troubled kingdom. (Dir: Fritz Lang, 101 mins.)†

Journey to the 7th Planet (1962)** John Agar, Greta Thyssen. A group of Earthmen comes to grips with beautiful women and strange forces on the planet number 7 in this predictable sci-fi entry. (Dir: Sidney Pink, 83 mins.)

Joy House (France, 1964)**½ Jane Fonda, Alain Delon, Lola Albright. French director Rene Clement is only half successful in making this macabre suspense yarn work—but the half that does is worthwhile. Lola Albright is hiding her lover (a criminal) in a chamber in her Riviera villa, while cousin Jane Fonda is trying to seduce chauffeur Alain Delon. (98 mins.)†

Joy in the Morning (1965)**½ Richard Chamberlain, Yvette Mimieux. The two attractive stars are earnest in this uneven love story about a young couple who face many problems during the early days of their marriage. (Dir: Alex Segal, 103 mins.)

Joyless Street (Germany, 1925)***½ Werner Krauss, Greta Garbo, Asta Nielson, Agnes Esterhazy, Valeska Gert, Jaro Furth. Silent melodrama about the miserable people who live on a single block in post-WWI Vienna, some newly poor and all at the mercy of black marketeers. In one home, inflation has shattered the family's security and a daughter (Garbo in her last European film) considers working in a brothel to help her father. A bittersweet realistic work with lyrical camera movements and excellent performances. Marlene Dietrich can be spotted as an extra. AKA: **The Street of Sorrow**. (Dir: G. W. Pabst, 139 mins.)†

Joy of Living (1937)***½ Irene Dunne, Douglas Fairbanks, Jr. Happy-go-lucky globe trotter romances a career-minded stage star. Delightful romantic comedy, with some good Jerome Kern tunes. (Dir: Tay Garnett, 91 mins.)†

Joy of Sex, The (1984)** Cameron Dye, Michelle Meyrink, Christopher Lloyd, Colleen Camp. Good-natured exploitation that substitutes skin for scatology and swearing, as a sweet young thing desperately tries to do the dirty deed before she "dies." (Dir: Martha Coolidge, 93 mins.)†

Joy Ride (1958)*** Regis Toomey, Ann Doran. Punch-packed little suspense drama about an "average man" who is terrorized by a bunch of young punks then turns the tables on them. (Dir: Edward Bernds, 60 mins.)

Joyride (1977)** Desi Arnaz, Jr., Robert Carradine, Melanie Griffith, Anne Lockhart, Tom Ligon. Confused action pic about two couples who end up turning to crime in Alaska when a labor union official treats the guys shabbily. (Dir: Joseph Ruben, 92 mins.)†

Joysticks (1983)* Joe Don Baker, Leif Green, Jim Greenleaf, Scott McGinnis, Jonathan Gries. Baker tries to convince other parents in his town that there's trouble with their kids—and that's Trouble that starts with T and that rhymes with V and that stands for Video Games! (Dir: Greydon Clark, 88 mins.)†

Juarez (1939)*** Bette Davis, Paul Muni, Brian Aherne, John Garfield, Claude Rains, Donald Crisp, Gale Sondergaard, Joseph Calleia, Gilbert Roland. An engrossing historical drama overstuffed with all the production values Warner Brothers could buy. The legendary revolutionary leader leads the insurgents against the well-intentioned government of Emperor Maximilian, a pawn in a political power struggle waged in Europe and Mexico. This all-star spectacular tries to relate too many storylines at the same time, and it's further diminished by Muni's "momentous" acting: he looks pained and solemn throughout. (Dir: William Dieterle, 132 mins.)†

Jubal (1956)***½ Glenn Ford, Ernest Borgnine, Rod Steiger, Felicia Farr. Superior western. Ford plays a drifter named Jubal Troop who is given a job by a rancher (Borgnine) and immediately starts off a chain reaction of jealousy, hate, and violence. (Dir: Delmer Daves, 101 mins.)†

Jubilee Trail (1953)**½ Vera Ralston, Joan Leslie, Forrest Tucker, Pat O'Brien. Singer helps a young wife overcome skulduggery in old California. (Dir: Joseph Kane, 103 mins.)†

Judex (France-Italy, 1964)**½ Channing Pollock, Francine Berge, Michel Vitold. Slow-moving refilming of a 1916 French silent serial about master-criminal Judex. (Dir: Georges Franju, 96 mins.)†

Judge and Jake Wyler, The (MTV 1972)**½ Bette Davis, Doug McClure. A TV pilot with McClure as an ex-con working for ex-Judge Davis, who runs a detective agency from her fortresslike home. (Dir: David Lowell Rich, 100 mins.)

Judge and the Assassin, The (France, 1975)***½ Philippe Noiret, Michel Galabru, Isabelle Huppert, Jean-Claude Brialy. A superbly directed psychological drama in which a judge has to use his powers of observation to ascertain whether a killer is a madman or merely trying to pull the wool over the law's eyes. (Dir: Bertrand Tavernier, 130 mins.)†

Judge Dee and the Monastery Murders (MTV 1974)* Khigh Dhiegh, Mako, Soon-Teck-Oh, Miiko Taka, Irene Tsu, James Hong, Keye Luke. TV movie tripe about a Chinese detective in the seventh century. (Dir: Jeremy Kagan, 100 mins.)

Judge Hardy and Son (1939)** Mickey Rooney, Lewis Stone, Cecilia Parker. Sentimental Hardy family entry. Mom gets sick, an old couple is being evicted, and other soap opera situations come to a happy, tearful conclusion. (Dir: George B. Seitz, 90 mins.)

Judge Hardy's Children (1938)**½ Mickey Rooney, Lewis Stone. Andy and the judge are in Washington for this one and Andy saves the day for his dad. Good family entertainment. (Dir: George B. Seitz, 80 mins.)

Judge Horton and the Scottsboro Boys (MTV 1976)*** Arthur Hill, Vera Miles, Lewis J. Stadlen, Ken Kercheval, Ellen Barber. In Alabama in 1931, nine poor young black men were arrested and tried for the alleged rape of two promiscuous white women. Despite compelling evidence proving their innocence, they were convicted. This disturbing, absorbing history lesson about racial bigotry in the South focuses on one courageous white judge. (Dir: Fielder Cook, 98 mins.)†

Judge Priest (1934)***½ Will Rogers, Anita Louise, Stepin Fetchit. The Old South is lovingly rendered in this saga of a judge who must battle for re-election. Remade as *The Sun Shines Bright* by the same director. (Dir: John Ford, 71 mins.)†

Judge Steps Out, The (1949)**½ Alexander Knox, Ann Sothern. Probate judge leaves home and finds happiness as a cook in a roadside stand. Occasionally good, generally rather mild comedydrama. (Dir: Boris Ingster, 91 mins.)

Judgment (MCTV 1990)*** Keith Carradine, Blythe Danner, David Strathairn, Jack Warden, Michael Faustino. A carefully handled, provocative true story. Parents in a Louisiana community discover their parish priest has sexually molested a group of young boys. When Catholic church officials attempt to buy off the parents, one couple takes the case to court. None of the scenes are played for sensationalism. (Dir: Tom Topor, 96 mins.)†

Judgement Day (1989)** Kenneth McLeod, David Anthony Smith, Monte Markham, Cesar Romero, Gloria Hayes. Teens backpacking their way through South America pick the wrong day to visit a certain town: it's the one day of the year that Satan rules, claiming the soul of anyone in the vicinity. (Dir: Ferde Grofé, Jr., 93 mins.)†

Judgment at Nuremberg (1961)**** Spencer Tracy, Burt Lancaster, Judy Garland, Richard Widmark, Montgomery Clift, Maximilian Schell, Marlene Dietrich. A searing, thoughtful film from producer Stanley Kramer, based on Abby Mann's memorable TV drama of the same name. Concerns the proceedings at the Nazi War Crimes Trials in Nuremberg and explores, among other things, the degree to which an individual or a nation can be held responsible for carrying out the orders of their leaders. (Dir: Stanley Kramer, 178 mins.)†

Judgment in Berlin (1988)*** Martin Sheen, Sam Wanamaker, Max Gail, Heinz Hoenig, Carl Lumbly, Harris Yulin, Sean Penn. Sheen plays an American judge called in to preside over a trial with international implications: it will decide the fate of two East Germans accused of violently hijacking a Polish airline in order to break through the Iron Curtain to the security of West Berlin. He does an impeccable job (as usual) of interpreting the conflicts left out of the script. (Dir: Leo Penn, 92 mins.)†

Judith (U.S.-Great Britain, 1966)** Sophia Loren, Peter Finch, Jack Hawkins. A mundane melodrama partially filmed in Israel. Judith (Miss Loren) is suffering from the memory of her past, including a tormented stay in a concentration camp, and her travels are motivated by revenge. (Dir: Daniel Mann, 109 mins.)

Judith Krantz's Till We Meet Again—See: Till We Meet Again

Judith of Bethulia (1913)*** Blanche Sweet, Henry B. Walthall, Mae Marsh. Pioneering director D. W. Griffith chose the biblical story of a Jewish woman who single-handedly saves her country from a tyrant for his first feature-length film. Involving drama, sensitively acted, with fine set pieces and battle scenes. (58 mins.)†

Ju Dou (China-Japan, 1989)***½ Gong Li, Li Bao-tian, Li Wei, Zhang Yi, Zhen Ji-an. Beautifully photographed drama of doomed love and dangerous relationships tells the powerful story of a mail-order bride who rebels against the brutality of her husband by entering into an affair with one of his employees. Nominated for an Academy Award. A major work that demands to be seen. (Dir: Zhang Yi-mou, 95 mins.)

Juggernaut (1974)*** Omar Sharif, Richard Harris, David Hemmings. Shirley Knight, Ian Holm. A cumbersome script doesn't help this yarn about a ship that has received threats of being blown up if a million-dollar-plus ransom isn't paid. (Dir: Richard Lester, 110 mins.)†

Juggler, The (1953)*** Kirk Douglas, Milly Vitale. An absorbing drama about the Jewish refugee camps and the fight for rehabilitation; Kirk Douglas gives a powerful performance as a one-time circus juggler. (Dir: Edward Dmytryk, 86 mins.)

Juke Box Rhythm (1959)* Jo Morrow, Brian Donlevy, Jack Jones. Inept musical film. A princess falls in love with a young singer whose father is a Broadway producer. (Dir: Arthur Dreifuss, 81 mins.)

Juke Girl (1942)**½ Ann Sheridan, Ronald Reagan, Faye Emerson, Gene Lockhart. This was supposed to be the sordid tale of conditions among Florida's migratory workers but it emerges as a well-acted, tiresome melodrama. (Dir: Curtis Bernhardt, 90 mins.)

Jules and Jim (France, 1962)**** Oskar Werner, Jeanne Moreau, Henri Serre. The pre-WWI era is evoked by the ménage à trois of Jules (Werner), Jim (Serre), and Catherine (the incomparable Moreau). Catherine is willful, maddening, and entirely herself; she incarnates Jules's and Jim's art and friendship, while remaining an intransigent, perverse, independent individual. (Dir: François Truffaut, 110 mins.)†

Julia (1977)*** Jane Fonda, Vanessa Redgrave, Maximilian Schell, Jason Robards, Meryl Streep. A picture-postcard version of Lillian Hellman's story. Fonda captures the famous authoress's steely strength as she tries to measure up to her two heroes in life, writer Dashiell Hammett and Julia, girlhood friend-turned-political activist (Redgrave). (Dir: Fred Zinnemann, 118 mins.)†

Julia and Julia (Italy, 1988)** Kathleen Turner, Sting, Gabriel Byrne, Gabriele Ferzetti. An ill-conceived, surrealistic journey through one woman's identity crisis as she flits back and forth between two dimensions. (Dir: Peter Del Monte, 97 mins.)†

Julia Has Two Lovers (1991)** Daphna Kastner, David Duchovny, David Charles. Julia receives a second lover when she answers a wrong number, which turns into an intimate, sexual, talkathon fantasy. Clever idea with an improvisational ring to the dialogue, but it ultimately loses momentum. (Dir: Bashar Shbib, 91 mins.)

Julia Misbehaves (1948)**½ Greer Garson, Walter Pidgeon, Elizabeth Taylor. Farce about an ex-chorus girl who is her estranged husband's guest after an eighteen-year separation is ridiculous. (Dir: Jack Conway, 99 mins.)

Julie (1956)** Doris Day, Louis Jourdan, Barry Sullivan. Thoroughly unbelievable melodrama about an airline stewardess terrorized by her insane husband. (Dir: Andrew L. Stone, 99 mins.)

Juliet of the Spirits (Italy, 1965)*** Giulietta Masina, Mario Pisu, Sandra Milo, Valentina Cortese, Sylva Koscina. The wife of an eccentric film director gives vent to all her fantasies, as superb color cinematography and art direction turn the film into a psychological carousel, whirling by us so fast we never quite have time to catch up and figure what the film's about. (Dir: Federico Fellini, 148 mins.)†

Juliette or the Key of Dreams (France, 1951)***½ Gerard Philipe, Yves Robert, Suzanne Cloutier, Jean Caussimon. Gentle fantasy film about young prisoner (Philipe) who dreams of a beautiful woman who leads him on an assortment of fantastic adventures. Expressively shot and designed piece of cinematic whimsy. (Dir: Marcel Carné, 90 mins.)

Julius Caesar (1953)*** John Gielgud, Marlon Brando, James Mason, Deborah Kerr, Greer Garson, Edmond O'Brien, Louis Calhern. Gielgud's multileveled Cassius stands out, and Mason (Brutus) and Brando (Marc Antony) are solid. An elaborate, sturdy, intelligent Hollywood adaptation. (Dir: Joseph L. Mankiewicz, 120 mins.)†

Julius Caesar (Great Britain, 1970)**½ John Gielgud, Jason Robards, Charlton Heston, Richard Chamberlain, Robert Vaughn, Richard Johnson, Diana Rigg. Uneven but generally well-acted version of Shakespeare's classic. (Dir: Stuart Burge, 117 mins.)†

Jumbo—See: Billy Rose's Jumbo

Jumping Jacks (1952)**½ Dean Martin, Jerry Lewis, Mona Freeman. Dean and Jerry play two cabaret entertainers who end up in the paratroop corps, in one of their better early romps. (Dir: Norman Taurog, 96 mins.)

Jumpin' Jack Flash (1986)** Whoopi Goldberg, Stephen Collins, John Wood, Carol Kane. A ragged spy caper held together by Goldberg's assured comic turn as a computer operator who starts to receive messages on her terminal from a British agent trapped behind enemy lines. (Dir: Penny Marshall, 98 mins.)†

June Bride (1948)*** Bette Davis, Robert Montgomery. Not fast and hilarious but enough chuckles to satisfy as Bob plays a magazine writer and Bette his boss. (Dir: Bretaigne Windust, 97 mins.)

June Night (Sweden, 1940)**½ Ingrid Bergman, Marianne Lofgren, Gunnar Sjöberg. Romantic melodrama about a woman who tries to escape her sordid past in a new town. Minor, but a good showcase for the pre-Hollywood Bergman. (Dir: Per Lindberg, 90 mins.)†

Jungle Assault (1989)*½ William Smith, William Zipp. General Smith, retired, makes an unofficial return to active duty when anti-American forces in Central America brainwash his daughter into helping them. Macho right-wing fantasy. (Dir: David A. Prior, 85 mins.)†

Jungle Book, The (1942)** Sabu, Joseph Calleia. Kipling's tale of a boy who grew up with the animals, learned their language, habits. Colorful, occasionally exciting, but sometimes pretty hard to swallow. (Dir: Zoltan Korda, 109 mins.)†

Jungle Book, The (1967)*** The voices of Phil Harris, Louis Prima, Sebastian Cabot, George Sanders, Sterling Holloway. A bright and tuneful Disney animated feature. This update of the Kipling tale pairs some fine comic voices with memorably drawn characters. (Dir: Wolfgang Reitherman and four animation directors, 78 mins.)†

Jungle Cat (1960)**½ Disney documentary on the feline jaguar, its natural life in the Amazon rain forest fully detailed. (Dir: James Algar, 70 mins.)†

Jungle Fever (1991)**** Wesley Snipes, Annabella Sciorra, Spike Lee, John Turturro, Lonette McKee, Anthony Quinn. From its involving opening credits this is an immensely powerful and searing drama about interracial love, racism and the crack subculture. Snipes is superb playing a black architect in a white New York City firm who has a brief and ultimately devastating assignation with his white secretary (Sciorra). Remarkable ensemble performances from everyone, with a notably affecting

portrayal from Turturro as the victimized son of Quinn. (Dir: Spike Lee, 132 mins.)†

Jungle Fighters (Great Britain, 1961)*** Laurence Harvey, Richard Todd, Richard Harris, David McCallum. Rugged war drama about a British patrol in Burma and a dangerous trap set by the Japanese. AKA: **The Long, the Short and the Tall.** (Dir: Leslie Norman, 105 mins.)

Jungle Gents (1954)*½ Bowery Boys, Bernard Gorcey, Laurette Luez, Patrick O'Moore. The Boys go to Africa, where they locate diamonds sniffed out by Sach. (Dir: Edward Bernds, 64 mins.)

Jungle Heat—See: Dance of the Dwarfs

Jungle Jim series. This character (made popular in Alex Raymond's 1920s comic strip and then a 12-chapter movie serial) was embodied in this series by Johnny Weissmuller, a slightly pudgier and more articulate clone of Tarzan who endured poverty-row budgets and outlandish adventures in twelve programs before ending up in a TV series for kids in 1956. Nostalgia buffs who spent their Saturdays watching these films might want to check out the following films in addition to those reviewed below: *The Lost Tribe, Voodoo Tiger, Captive Girl, Pygmy Island, Mark of the Gorilla, Fury of the Congo, Savage Mutiny, Valley of the Headhunters, Cannibal Attack,* and *Devil Goddess.*

Jungle Jim (1948)**½ Johnny Weissmuller, Virginia Grey, George Reeves. Low-budget programmer that kicked off the series with Johnny cast as a bwana hunter. It was a long drop from the major-stardom vine for the former Tarzan. Here, he assists a doctor in attaining a valuable medicine. (Dir: William Berke, 73 mins.)

Jungle Jim in the Forbidden Land (1952)** Johnny Weissmuller, Angela Greene. OK action pic in which Jungle Jim has to crane his neck to look for the land of the giants. (Dir: Lew Landers, 65 mins.)

Jungle Man-Eaters (1954)*½ Johnny Weissmuller, Karin Booth. Dull jungle adventure in which Jungle Jim pools resources with a Scotland Yard inspector to roust a band of diamond smugglers. (Dir: Lee Sholem, 68 mins.)

Jungle Manhunt (1951)** Johnny Weissmuller, Bob Waterfield, Sheila Ryan. Jungle cliffhanger. The plot concerns a female newshound inducing J.J. to help her locate a missing football star. (Dir: Lew Landers, 66 mins.)

Jungle Moon Men (1955)**½ Johnny Weissmuller, Jean Byron. In this imaginative outing, Jungle Jim meets an expert in ancient Egyptian gods. They go to the land of the pygmy moon men. (Dir: Charles S. Gould, 70 mins.)

Jungle Princess, The (1936)** Dorothy

Lamour, Ray Milland, Akim Tamiroff, Lynne Overman. The first in Dottie's long series of native girls clad in silk sarongs. Milland is a pilot downed on an uncharted island, where he discovers her. Pleasant, hokey entertainment. (Dir: William Thiele, 85 mins.)

Junior Bonner (1972)*** Steve McQueen, Robert Preston, Ida Lupino. Junior Bonner (McQueen), onetime rodeo star, returns home to dazzle hometown fans with the skills he no longer has. McQueen is superb in this film, which begins as a reaching for lost frontiers and transforms into a family saga. (Dir: Sam Peckinpah, 100 mins.)†

Junior Miss (1945)*** Peggy Ann Garner, Allyn Joslyn. Cute little teenage comedy that should remind us how youngsters behaved during the 1940s. Based on the hit Broadway play. (Dir: George Seaton, 94 mins.)

Junkman, The (1982)** H. B. Halicki, Christopher Stone, Susan Shaw, Hoyt Axton, Lynda Day George, The Belmonts. Producer-director H. B. "Toby" Halicki wasn't much on plots, which were only a frame for the real subject of his movies—cars, as many as possible crashing into each other as rapidly and loudly as possible. You want it, you got it, more auto wrecks than Burt Reynolds's entire filmography all in one movie. A dubious distinction, to be sure, but it definitely belongs to Halicki. (99 mins.)†

Jupiter's Darling (1955)** Esther Williams, Howard Keel, Marge and Gower Champion, George Sanders. Gay doings in old Rome, as Hannibal Keel captures gorgeous Esther and stops the battle while they romance. Historical spoof doesn't quite make it. (Dir: George Sidney, 96 mins.)

Jupiter's Thigh (France, 1979)** Annie Girardot, Philippe Noiret, Francis Perrin, Catherine Alric. Sequel to *Dear Detective* finds detective Girardot and professor Noiret spending their honeymoon in Greece, where they are caught up in the search for a stolen fragment of an ancient statue. Fans of the original may like this otherwise standard Gallic farce, with the stars coasting their way through. (Dir: Philippe de Broca, 96 mins.)†

Jury Duty: The Comedy (MTV 1990)**½ Bronson Pinchot, Mark Blankfield, Bill Kirchenbauer, Heather Locklear, Lynn Redgrave, Joshua Rifkind, Tracy Scoggins, Alan Thicke, Reginald Veljohnson. Pinchot plays four roles in this silly made-for-television courtroom spoof that seems designed to give extra exposure to the stars of the network's current sitcoms. The embezzlement case presented in court is an excuse to get all of them to mug wildly before the camera. (Dir: Michael Schultz, 96 mins.)

Just a Gigolo (West Germany, 1978)** David Bowie, Kim Novak, Sydne Rome, Marlene Dietrich. A war vet struggles to make the big time in post–WWI Germany, but ends up a pawn in the Berlin underworld. Striving for stylish decadence, it is of primary interest for star watchers, who can catch Bowie's saturnine presence, Novak's timeless beauty, and the legendary Dietrich presence as she growls out the title tune in her inimitable manner. (Dir: Rolf Thiele, 96 mins.)

Just a Little Inconvenience (MTV 1977)**½ Lee Majors, James Stacy, Barbara Hershey. Stacy, who lost an arm and a leg in a motorcycle accident three years before this entry, returns in a story of an embittered war veteran who blames his best friend for his injury. (Dir: Theodore J. Flicker, 104 mins.)

Just an Old Sweet Song (MTV 1976)*** Cicely Tyson, Robert Hooks, Beah Richards, Lincoln Kilpatrick. Touching telefilm with an excellent script by Melvin Van Peebles. The plotline recounts the effect that a two-week vacation in the South has on an urban black family. The performances all have a special resonance, particularly Tyson and Hooks as caring parents. (Dir: Robert Ellis Miller, 72 mins.)

Just Another Secret (MTV 1989)** Beau Bridges, Alan Howard, Kenneth Cranham, Beatie Edney, James Faulkner. Adaptation of a Frederick Forsyth story about a CIA agent investigating the disappearances of five fellow agents in East Germany is just another espionage thriller that falls short on suspense and intrigue. Bridges is unconvincing as the agent who uncovers a plot to assassinate Gorbachev. (Dir: Lawrence Gordon, 92 mins.)†

Just Around the Corner (1938)** Shirley Temple, Joan Davis, Bill Robinson. Shirley dances with "Bojangles" but close your eyes for the rest of this silly film. (Dir: Irving Cummings, 70 mins.)†

Just Before Dawn (1946)** Warner Baxter, Charles D. Brown. Standard crime doctor entry involving the physician-cum-criminologist on the trail of a mad killer. (Dir: William Castle, 65 mins.)

Just Before Dawn (1981)**½ George Kennedy, Mike Kellin, Chris Lemmon. A family camping in the woods is set upon by a pair of murderous mountain men. From the talented director of *Squirm* and *Blue Sunshine*. (Dir: Jeff Lieberman, 90 mins.)

Just Before Nightfall (France, 1971)***½ Michel Bouquet, Stephane Audran, François Perier, Anna Douking, Marina Ninchi. Scandalous film about a man who murders his mistress and then confesses the crime to his wife and the dead woman's husband. They accept his reason for this brutal act, and life goes on as if nothing ever happened, because to all of them the most important aspects of life are appearance and reputation. (Dir: Claude Chabrol, 107 mins.)

Just Between Friends (1986)**½ Mary Tyler Moore, Christine Lahti, Ted Danson, Sam Waterston, Salome Jens. A woman learns that her new best friend was also having a clandestine affair with her husband. Gimmicky, but the attractive cast saves the serious moments and makes the most of the fluffy ones. (Dir: Allan Burns, 120 mins.)†

Just for You (1952)**½ Bing Crosby, Jane Wyman, Ethel Barrymore. Pleasant comedy-drama with songs. Bing plays a successful B'way producer who sets out to win his son and daughter's affection after a long period of concentrating only on his career. (Dir: Elliot Nugent, 104 mins.)

Justice is Done (France, 1950)***½ Michel Auclair, Valentine Tessier, Claude Nollier, Jean Dubucourt. A woman is tried for the crime of euthanasia afrter ending her lover's life. Director André Cayatte, a lawyer by profession, concentrates on the lives, thoughts, and motivations, not of the defendant, but of the jury, in this brilliantly scripted, well-acted, even exciting examination of the way justice is served in France. (105 mins.)

Just Imagine (1930)*** John Garrick, El Brendel, Maureen O'Sullivan. Beguiling bit of antique musical frumpery, about New York City past, present, future—e.g., 1880, 1930, and 1980. Songs by B. G. De Sylva, Lew Brown, and others. (Dir: David Butler, 102 mins.)

Justin Case (MTV 1988)** George Carlin, Molly Hagan, Timothy Stack, Gordon Jump. Comic mystery about an unemployed actress (Hagan) who helps the ghost of a dead detective solve his own murder. Blake Edwards directed this lame exercise, further proof of his recent artistic bankruptcy. (72 mins.)

Justine (1969)**½ Anouk Aimée, Dirk Bogarde, Robert Forster, Anna Karina, Michael York. The mysterious wife of a well-to-do banker in 1930s Alexandria becomes involved in Middle East politics. A large-scale stab at filming part of Lawrence Durrell's *Alexandria Quartet*. Enjoyable performances. (Dirs: George Cukor, Joseph Strick, 116 mins.)†

Just Me and You (MTV 1978)*½ Louise Lasser, Charles Grodin, Julie Bovasso, Paul Fix. A ditsy comedy about two misfits learning a lot of stale homilies about life with a capital L as they travel cross-country. Lasser wrote this and the writing is as unfocused as her performance. (Dir: John Erman, 104 mins.)

Just off Broadway (1942)** Lloyd Nolan, Phil Silvers, Marjorie Weaver. Weak Michael Shayne adventure with the great

detective serving on a murder jury but solving the case on the side. (Dir: Herbert I. Leeds, 66 mins.)

Just One of the Guys (1985)*½ Joyce Hyser, Clayton Rohner, Bill Jacoby, Toni Hudson. A high-school beauty disguises herself as a boy in order to be taken seriously as a writer. She learns that girls who dress as boys can be just as vapid as girls who dress as girls. (Dir: Lisa Gottlieb, 100 mins.)†

Just Suppose (1926)**½ Richard Barthelmess, Lois Moran, Geoffrey Kerr, Bijou Fernandez. Mild romantic comedy vehicle for Barthelmess as a young Ruritanian prince visiting New York and falling in love with an American girl; the story is a flimsy framework for many nice touches, like Barthelmess miming the story of the three bears to a group of schoolchildren, and his first clash with American culture on the dock at New York. (Dir: Kenneth Webb, 62 mins.)†

Just Tell Me What You Want (1980)*** Ali MacGraw, Alan King, Peter Weller, Myrna Loy, Keenan Wynn. Jay Presson Allen's script is a paean to détente between the sexes. King plays a charismatic self-made man, and MacGraw is his mistress of many years who rebels when he liquidates a film production company rather than turn it over to her. There is no coherent comic approach, but the situations are original and fresh and carry you along. (Dir: Sidney Lumet, 112 mins.)†

Just the Way You Are (1984)*½ Kristy McNichol, Michael Ontkean, Kaki Hunter, Robert Carradine, Lance Guest. A crippled flutist (McNichol) falls for a photographer (Ontkean) while vacationing in France. Minor romantic comedy. (Dir: Edouardo Molinaro, 95 mins.)†

Just This Once (1952)**½ Janet Leigh, Peter Lawford. Pleasant comedy about the ins and outs of romance. (Dir: Don Weis, 90 mins.)

Just Tony (1922)*** Tom Mix, Claire Adams, J. P. Lockney, Duke Lee, Tony. Wonderful tribute from the great cowboy star Mix to his famous horse, Tony, adapted from the Max Brand story *Alcatraz*. The story has a cowboy (Mix) saving a wild mustang (Tony) from cruel rustlers; eventually the mustang rescues the cowboy in return. A simple western, very well photographed in the wide-open spaces. (Dir: Lynn F. Reynolds, 58 mins.)†

Just You and Me, Kid (1979)** George Burns, Brooke Shields, Burl Ives, Lorraine Gary, Ray Bolger. What sounded surefire—Burns as an ex-vaudevillian and Shields as a young runaway hiding from a dope pusher—is disappointing indeed. (Dir: Leonard Stern, 93 mins.)†

J. W. Coop (1972)*** Cliff Robertson,

Geraldine Page, Cristina Ferrare, R. G. Armstrong. Robertson co-wrote, produced, directed, and stars in this rodeo story about a released con who tries to climb to the top of the rodeo circuit in the face of the more modernized contenders—specialists who fly to rodeos and compete in several a day. (112 mins.)

Kaddish (1985)*** Steve Brand's powerful documentary about a Jewish survivor of WWII and his activist son is both a telling example of family love and a passionate reminder of the evils of Nazism and its "final solution." The rapport between the two men is genuine and enlightening. Brand spent five years filming the remarkable documentary of history in the past and history in the making: the new doctrine of "never again." (92 mins.)

Kagemusha (Japan, 1980)***½ Tatsuya Nakadai, Tsutomu Yamazaki, Kenichi Hagiwara. Japan's greatest warlord battles to maintain control of the nation. A visually impressive epic from director Akira Kurosawa. The ideas stimulate even as the emotional core remains deliberately obscured. (160 mins.)†

Kaleidoscope (Great Britain, 1966)** Warren Beatty, Susannah York, Clive Revill, Eric Porter. A playboy (Beatty) tries a cleverly crooked way to beat the European gambling casinos in this visually pretty but placid caper. (Dir: Jack Smight, 103 mins.)

Kameradschaft (Germany, 1931)**** Ernst Busch, Alexander Granach, Fritz Kaupers, Gustav Puttjer. Explosion traps workers on the French side of a gigantic underground mine that straddles the borders of France and Germany. When the French rescuers find their task impossible, German counterparts disregard national boundaries in order to join in a common humanitarian effort. Brilliantly staged, riveting film experience. Originally 92 mins. (Dir: G. W. Pabst, 78 mins.)†

Kamikaze '89 (West Germany, 1982)*½ Rainer Werner Fassbinder, Gunther Kaufman, Boy Gobert, Brigitte Meara, Frank Ripploh, Franco Nero. Futuristic spy thriller that has Fassbinder investigating a bomb threat against the "combine," a government/syndicate that runs a high-tech, low-taste Germany. A big disappointment. (Dir: Wolf Gremm, 106 mins.)†

Kanal (Poland, 1957)**** Teresa Izewska. Grim and powerful drama of Polish patriots using the sewers of Warsaw in an attempt to escape from the Nazis during the uprising of 1944. English-dubbed. (Dir: Andrzej Wajda, 91 mins.)†

Kandyland (1988)*½ Kim Evenson, Charles Laulette, Sandahl Bergman. An innocent young thing learns the ropes of working as a stripper from an experienced older dancer. The plot seldom gets in the way of the main attraction, women undressing, which is a virtue or liability depending on your point of view. (Dir: Robert Schnitzer, 93 mins.)†

Kangaroo (1952)** Peter Lawford, Maureen O'Hara. The beautiful on-location photography (Australia) is the best feature of this adventure drama. Lawford is miscast as a sailor who becomes involved in a muddled mistaken identity plot. Miss O'Hara thinks the Australian landscape is the County Cork and plays it accordingly. (Dir: Lewis Milestone, 84 mins.)

Kangaroo (1987)**½ Colin Friels, Judy Davis, John Walton, Hugh Keays-Byrne. Based on the novel by D. H. Lawrence, this wan adaptation has Friels as a controversial British writer who moves to the Australian outback to escape the class problems of his homeland; once there, he is introduced to a right-wing paramilitary organization run by a general nicknamed "Kangaroo." (Dir: Tim Burstall, 105 mins.)†

Kansan, The (1943)**½ Richard Dix, Jane Wyatt, Albert Dekker, Victor Jory, Robert Armstrong, Eugene Pallette. Fast-moving mini-epic western in the *Cimarron* mode, with Dix valiantly cleaning up a corrupt town. Unpretentious, good of this kind. (Dir: George Archainbaud, 79 mins.)†

Kansas (1988)*½ Matt Dillon, Andrew McCarthy, Leslie Hope. Overlong, underplotted drama with hitchhiker McCarthy unwisely hooking up with ex-con Dillon, who involves him in a bank robbery. Dillon is well cast as a psychopath, but the movie concentrates instead on a dull romance between McCarthy and a rich farm girl. (Dir: David Stevens, 115 mins.)†

Kansas City Bomber (1972)*½ Raquel Welch, Helena Kallianiotes, Kevin McCarthy. Raquel barrels her way through this clunky tale of an ambitious roller queen. Only the skating sequences have any vitality. (Dir: Jerrold Freedman, 99 mins.)

Kansas City Confidential (1952)**½ John Payne, Coleen Gray, Preston Foster, Neville Brand. Sharply done crime story of bank robbers. (Dir: Phil Karlson, 98 mins.)†

Kansas City Massacre, The (MTV 1975)**½ Dale Robertson, Bo Hopkins, Lynn Loring, Scott Brady. Robertson is back playing Melvin Purvis, G-man, in this tough gangster saga set during the Depression. Follows the events leading up to the infamous Kansas City massacre at the Union Plaza Railroad Station. (Dir: Dan Curtis, 100 mins.)†

Kansas Raiders (1950)**½ Audie Murphy, Brian Donlevy, Marguerite Chapman. Exciting western adventure about the famous outlaws who joined Quantrill's Raiders and destroyed Lawrence, Kansas. (Dir: Ray Enright, 80 mins.)

Kaos (Italy, 1985)**½ Margarita Lozano, Claudio Bigagli, Massimo Bonetti. Fascinating collection of Italian folktales brimming with humane virtues and directed with a direct, immaculate style. Each typifies different aspects of peasant life, including one about a mother yearning for her sons and another dealing with a man who's driven to transient dementia by the full moon. (Dirs: Paolo and Vittorio Taviani, 188 mins.)

Kapo (France-Italy-Yugoslavia, 1960)**½ Susan Strasberg, Emmanuele Riva. Disguised Jewish girl in Nazi prison camp becomes hardened, murderously intent on her own survival. Movie is effectively graphic about the horrors of the Holocaust and imprisonment, but the melodramatics prove too much for Strasberg, and the film is not worthy of the momentous realities involved. (Dir: Gillo Pontecorvo, 116 mins.)

Karate Kid, The (1984)*** Ralph Macchio, Noriyuki "Pat" Morita, Elisabeth Shue, Martin Kove, Randee Heller. This junior league *Rocky* follows the life of a fatherless kid (Macchio) from New Jersey as he moves to L.A. and runs afoul of some tough valley boys. With the help of a benevolent karate master (Morita), he learns how to defend himself, along with some valuable moral and spiritual lessons. Likable performances make this movie at least a brown belt achievement. (Dir: John Avildsen, 126 mins.)†

Karate Kid, Part II, The (1986)**½ Ralph Macchio, Noriyuki "Pat" Morita, Tamlyn Tomita, Yuji Okumoto. A virtual remake set in the Far East. Daniel journeys with his martial arts mentor to Okinawa to visit Miyagi's ailing father, and encounters some local toughs and a village girl. (Dir: John G. Avildsen, 109 mins.)†

Karate Kid Part III, The (1989)*½ Ralph Macchio, Noriyuki "Pat" Morita, Martin Kove. Disappointing, lifeless sequel merely replays the tired plot without expanding on the characters of Daniel and Mr. Miyagi or the relationship between them. Daniel is tricked by an old enemy into entering a competition in which he will be badly beaten. (Dir: John G. Avildsen, 114 mins.)†

Karen Carpenter Story, The (MTV 1989)**½ Cynthia Gibb, Mitchell Anderson, Peter Michael Goetz. Gibb does quite well as the singer who died of complications from anorexia at the age of 32. But the rest of the story about the Carpenters' rise to stardom is old-hat showbiz. (Dir: Joseph Sargent, 96 mins.)

Kate Bliss and the Ticker Tape Kid (MTV 1978)**½ Suzanne Pleshette, Don Meredith, Harry Morgan, David Huddleston, Tony Randall, Burgess Meredith, Buck Taylor, Harry Carey, Jr., Alvy Moore. Average comedy-western with Pleshette as a turn-of-the-century lady detective who treks west in hot pursuit of a gang of wily bandits led by Meredith. (Dir: Burt Kennedy, 96 mins.)

Kate McShane (MTV 1975)**½ Anne Meara, Christine Belford, Cal Bellini. In this TV pilot, Anne Meara plays a pugnacious Denver, Colorado, lawyer, defending a blueblood in the stabbing of a no-good husband. (Dir: Martin Chomsky, 72 mins.)

Kate's Secret (MTV 1986)* Meredith Baxter Birney, Edward Asner, Shari Belafonte-Harper. Unable to come to grips with her emotional problems, a woman binges on food and purges herself secretly by vomiting. A crude combination of TV-movie clichés, wholly inadequate acting, and stereotyped characters. (Dir: Arthur Allan Seidelman, 104 mins.)

Katherine (MTV 1975)*** Art Carney, Sissy Spacek, Henry Winkler, Jane Wyatt. Well-made film about a girl who forsakes her parents and a life of luxury to become an underground political activist. Spacek is always believable as she goes from idealized liberalism to militant radicalism. (Dir: Jeremy Paul Kagan, 98 mins.)†

Kathleen (1941)*½ Shirley Temple, Herbert Marshall, Laraine Day. Corny hokum about a widower who neglects his daughter then sends for Day to straighten the child out. (Dir: Harold S. Bucquet, 88 mins.)

Kathy O' (1958)*** Patty McCormack, Dan Duryea, Jan Sterling. Publicity man is assigned to a brat of a child movie star, gets involved when she runs away. Plenty of fun in this Hollywood-behind-the-scenes comedy drama. Well played, highly enjoyable. (Dir: Jack Sher, 99 mins.)

Katie Did It (1951)**½ Ann Blyth, Mark Stevens. Moderately entertaining comedy about a small town girl who runs into a New York City slicker who just won't take no for a final answer. (Dir: Frederick de Cordova, 81 mins.)

Katie: Portrait of a Centerfold (MTV 1978)** Kim Basinger, Vivian Blaine, Dorothy Malone. Basinger plays Katie, a Texas lovely whose modeling career turns sour in Hollywood after an assignment as a centerfold piece for a girlie magazine. (Dir: Robert Greenwald, 104 mins.)

Katzelmacher (West Germany, 1969)***½ Hanna Schygulla, Lilith Ungerer, Doris Mattes, Rainer Werner Fassbinder, Elga Sorbas. Fassbinder (who also directed) plays a Greek seeking work in West Germany. Women like him; men assault him. Based on his own play, Fassbinder's second film is a powerful, sensitive study of ignorance and prejudice. (88 mins.)

Keefer (MTV 1978)** William Conrad, Kate Woodville, Cathy Lee Crosby, Michael O'Hara. William Conrad stars as a secret agent during WWII, operating out of a private gambling club in Lisbon. (Dir: Barry Shear, 74 mins.)

Keegans, The (MTV 1976)** Adam Roarke, Spencer Milligan, Heather Menzies, Tom Clancy, Joan Leslie, Priscilla Pointer, Janit Baldwin, Penelope Windust, Judd Hirsch. Run-of-the-mill crime melodrama featuring Roarke as a magazine writer out to prove his football player brother innocent of murder. A few deft touches from director John Badham, but the plot is strictly by-the-numbers. (72 mins.)

Keep, The (1983)*½ Scott Glenn, Alberta Watson, Jurgen Prochnow. Back in WWII some German soldiers are guarding a road next to a medieval edifice. Somehow, Evil Incarnate escapes their vigilance and it runs amok. Although photographed with great stylization, the movie is obvious and portentous. (Dir: Michael Mann, 97 mins.)†

Keep 'Em Flying (1941)**½ Bud Abbott, Lou Costello, Martha Raye. Early A & C comedy with all the slapstick antics that made the pair famous. Martha Raye plays twin sisters. (Dir: Arthur Lubin, 86 mins.)

Keep 'Em Slugging (1943)**½ Dead End Kids, Evelyn Ankers, Shemp Howard, Elyse Knox, Frank Albertson, Don Porter. Leading the kids for a change, Bobby Jordan lands a legit job as shipping clerk, only to be framed for a jewelry theft. Last of the Universal films as the Dead End Kids and probably the best of that lot. (Dir: Christy Cabanne, 60 mins.)

Keeper of the Flame (1942)*** Spencer Tracy, Katharine Hepburn. Good drama, superbly acted by one of our better screen teams. Tracy, writing an article on the death of a great American, discovers that the great man was a fascist. (Dir: George Cukor, 100 mins.)

Keepers, The (France, 1958)*** Pierre Brasseur, Anouk Aimée, Charles Aznavour, Jean-Pierre Mockny, Paul Meurisse. Harrowing drama about a wealthy, creative young man committed to an asylum for the mentally ill by his overbearing father. He flees and attempts to prove his sanity. Shot in an actual asylum, this disturbing film changed French thinking about the regulations and dreadful conditions in such institutions. (Dir: George Franju, 98 mins.)

Keeping Track (Canada, 1987)** Michael Sarrazin, Margot Kidder, Ken Pogue, Alan Scharfe. TV newsman Sarrazin and computer whiz Kidder witness a murder on a train and are soon caught up in an international fight for a scientific discovery. Standard Hitchcock clone made palatable by its stars. (Dir: Robin Spry, 102 mins.)†

Keep Your Powder Dry (1945)**½ Lana Turner, Laraine Day, Susan Peters, Agnes Moorehead, Lee Patrick, Natalie Schafer, June Lockhart. Fairly neat little tale of various young women adapting to wartime service in the WACs and sorting out their social differences. Turner is fine as a bad girl who reforms under the influence of Uncle Sam. (Dir: Edward Buzzell, 93 mins.)

Keetje Tippel—See: **Cathy Tippel**

Kelly (1981)** Robert Logan, Twyla Dawn Vokins, George Clutesi, Elaine Nallee, Doug Lennox. A misfit preadolescent shipped by her fed-up mom in New York to live with her father in Alaska matures remarkably fast into daddy's big strong girl and wilderness maven. (Dir: Christopher Chapman, 95 mins.)

Kelly and Me (1957)**½ Van Johnson, Piper Laurie, Martha Hyer. Song-and-dance man hits the big time when he teams up with a smart police dog. Fairly pleasing show-biz drama. (Dir: Robert Z. Leonard, 86 mins.)

Kelly's Heroes (1970)** Clint Eastwood, Don Rickles, Donald Sutherland. Clumsy copy of *The Dirty Dozen*. Soldiers, turned plunderers under the command of Eastwood, march into German-occupied town to rob the bank during World War II. (Dir: Brian Hutton, 149 mins.)†

Kennel Murder Case, The (1933)*** William Powell, Mary Astor, Eugene Pallette. Philo Vance mystery with the customary sealed-room puzzle. Better mounted than most whodunits of the time. (Dir: Michael Curtiz, 73 mins.)†

Kenner (1969)** Jim Brown, Madlyn Rhue, Robert Coote. Brown is a two-fisted adventurer in this predictable yarn about a man out to avenge his partner's murder amid the teeming background of Bombay, India. (Dir: Steve Sekely, 87 mins.)

Kenny Rogers as the Gambler (MTV 1980)** Kenny Rogers, Christine Belford, Bruce Boxleitner. A Rogers hit song inspired this movie starring the singer in his first dramatic role: a shrewd gambler who befriends a younger chance taker (Boxleitner) and encounters a variety of bad guys. (Dir: Dick Lowry, 104 mins.)†

Kenny Rogers as the Gambler—The Adventure Continues (MTV 1983)**½ Kenny

Rogers, Linda Evans, Bruce Boxleitner, Christine Belford. An engaging sequel to Rogers's successful TV movie finds the grizzly gambler Brady Hawkes, accompanied by sidekick Billy Montana (Boxleitner), chasing varmints who have the audacity to kidnap his son Jeremiah. (Dir: Dick Lowry, 104 mins.)†

Kent State (MTV 1981)*** Jane Fleiss, Charley Lang, Talia Balsam, Keith Gordon, Jeff McCracken. A re-creation of the May 1970 student protest of the Vietnam war and the tragic confrontation with the Ohio National Guard, resulting in the slaying of several students. As the peaceful protesting students face the soldiers' bayonets, tear gas, and, finally, bullets, the breakdown in communication between school officials, state authorities, and police becomes irrevocable and tragic. (Dir: James Goldstone, 156 mins.)†

Kentuckian, The (1955)**½ Burt Lancaster. Lancaster stars as a two-fisted frontiersman in this adventure tale set in the early 1800s. The plot is filled with rugged action, romance, and an ample amount of comedy. (Dir: Burt Lancaster, 104 mins.)†

Kentucky (1938)** Loretta Young, Richard Greene, Walter Brennan. Trite romance set against a horse-breeding background. (Dir: David Butler, 94 mins.)†

Kentucky Fried Movie (1977)*** Evan Kim, Donald Sutherland, George Lazenby, Bill Bixby, Henry Gibson. A sometimes tasteless, often hilarious movie sketch comedy that successfully lampoons TV commercials, soft-core porn flicks, and kung-fu epics. The screenwriters later went on to create *Airplane*. (Dir: John Landis, 78 mins.)†

Kentucky Kernels (1934)*** Bert Wheeler, Robert Woolsey, Noah Beery, Mary Carlisle, Lucille LaVerne, Spanky McFarland, Sleep 'n' Eat (Willie Best), Margaret Dumont. Another good Wheeler and Woolsey vehicle has the boys, as protectors of young McFarland, getting mixed up in a family feud in the Kentucky mountains. Supporting cast is excellent, especially the wildly hammy Beery. Written by Bert Kalmer and Harry Ruby. (Dir: George Stevens, 75 mins.)

Kentucky Moonshine (1938)*** Ritz Brothers. If you don't like the Ritzes, run for the hills because the boys disguised as Kentucky hillbillies have this all to themselves. (Dir: David Butler, 85 mins.)

Kentucky Woman (MTV 1983)*½ Cheryl Ladd, Ned Beatty, Philip Levien, Sandy McPeak, Tess Harper, Lewis Smith, Peter Weller. Cheryl Ladd down in the coal mines with rats and jeering miners. (Dir: Walter Doniger, 104 mins.)

Kerouac (1984)*** Beat novelist Jack
560

Kerouac is the subject of this unusual documentary which includes interviews with his friends, his appearances on television talk shows, and dramatized readings of his work by actor Jack Coultar. Look for Lawrence Ferlinghetti, Allen Ginsberg, William S. Burroughs, Steve Allen, and William F. Buckley. (Dir: John Antonelli, 73 mins.)†

Kettles in the Ozarks, The (1956)** Marjorie Main, Arthur Hunnicutt. Ma Kettle visits Pa's lazy brother and gets in the middle of a heap of trouble with bootleggers and the law. (Dir: Charles Lamont, 81 mins.)

Kettles on Old MacDonald's Farm, The (1957)** Marjorie Main, Parker Fennelly. Last Kettle epic (without Pa Kettle) and the least effective. Some sight gags still work but Pa is sorely missed. (Dir: Virgil Vogel, 80 mins.)

Key, The (Great Britain, 1958)*** Sophia Loren, William Holden, Trevor Howard. A stellar line-up, but this drama doesn't deliver the dramatic impact it sets out to. The premise involves a man (Howard) who gives a duplicate key to his friend (Holden) to Loren's apartment, with the instructions that he must do the same when and if Howard is killed in enemy action during WWII. (Dir: Carol Reed, 125 mins.)†

Key Exchange (1985)*½ Brooke Adams, Ben Masters, Daniel Stern, Danny Aiello, Nancy Mette, Seth Allen, Tony Roberts. A mystery writer with a Casanova complex romances a beautiful talk show producer who wants to exchange apartment keys as a sign of—that dirty word—commitment. Not a believable moment in this overly schematized comedy. (Dir: Barnet Kellman, 90 mins.)†

Keyholes Are for Peeping (1972)½ Samuel Petrillo, Philip Stahl, Lou Silverman, Saul Meth. Outrageously bad sex comedy starring Petrillo, the star of *Bela Lugosi Meets a Brooklyn Gorilla* whose career never recovered after Jerry Lewis sued to make Petrillo stop imitating him. Sammy, desperately in need of a haircut, plays the dual roles of a schlemiel-turned-marriage counselor and his nagging mother, who attempt to give advice to the residents of their apartment building. Softcore sex and borscht belt humor make an unappetizing pair, and producer-director-writer Doris Wishman provides more than our fill of both. (75 mins.)†

Key Largo (1948)*** Humphrey Bogart, Lauren Bacall, Edward G. Robinson, Claire Trevor, Lionel Barrymore. Not a great movie but director John Huston manages to get so much out of his wonderful cast that you're bound to be entertained by this gangster melodrama set in Key West, Florida. Trevor won a

Best Supporting Actress Oscar. (101 mins.)†

Keys of the Kingdom, The (1944)*** Gregory Peck, Thomas Mitchell, Roddy McDowall. Slow, rambling, occasionally moving adaptation of A. J. Cronin's novel about the life of a missionary. Peck's first major film and he does a nice job. (Dir: John M. Stahl, 137 mins.)†

Key to Rebecca, The (MTV 1985)**½ Cliff Robertson, David Soul, Season Hubley, Lina Raymond, Anthony Quayle, David Hemmings, Robert Culp. Suave Nazi agent Soul tries to evade the clutches of heroic British major Robertson. Hot, sandy, and very, very corny. Based on the novel by Ken Follett. (Dir: David Hemmings, 192 mins.)

Key to the City (1950)**½ Clark Gable, Loretta Young. A light comedy romance for indiscriminating film fans, as small town mayors meet and fall in love during a mayors' convention in San Francisco. The action is predictable but fast paced. (Dir: George Sidney, 99 mins.)

Key West (MTV 1973)*½ Stephen Boyd, Ford Rainey, Tiffany Bolling, Sheree North. Predictable yarn. Boyd is a CIA agent floating around in Florida when he becomes the victim of a revenge-seeking maniac. (Dir: Anthony Martin, 72 mins.)

Key West Crossing—See: **Kill Castro**

Key Witness (1960)**½ Jeffrey Hunter, Pat Crowley. Hard-hitting drama about a man who is a witness to a crime and the terror he and his family face because of it. (Dir: Phil Karlson, 82 mins.)

KGOD (1980)*½ Dabney Coleman, Archie Hahn, Nancy Morgan, Charles Haid. Coleman turns a money-losing local TV station into a hot property selling God to the ripe-for-the-fleecing masses of Southern California. AKA: **Pray TV.** (Dir: Rick Friedberg, 84 mins.)

Khartoum (Great Britain, 1966)***½ Charlton Heston, Laurence Olivier. Some well-directed battle scenes and Olivier's splendid performance are two of the best features in this better-than-most spectacle film. Historical fact and Hollywood fiction are combined to tell the tale of confrontation in 1883 between British General Charles Gordon and a militant Arab leader called the Mahdi, who led a bloody *jihad* across Muslim Africa. (Dir: Basil Dearden, 134 mins.)

Kickboxer (1989)**½ Jean-Claude Van Damme, Dennis Chan, Dennis Alexio. To avenge his older brother's death at the hands (feet, actually) of a Thai champion, Van Damme trains to become an expert kickboxer. (Dir: Mark DiSalle, 97 mins.)†

Kickboxer 2: The Road Back (1991)* Sasha Mitchell, Peter Boyle, Dennis Chan.

Lackluster sequel to *Kickboxer*, without popular Jean-Claude Van Damme, finds hunky hard-luck Mitchell (no match in the athletic or acting departments) grunting in the kickboxing ring in order to avenge the burning down of his beloved gym. (Dir: Albert Pyun, 89 mins.)†

Kicks (MTV 1985)*½ Anthony Geary, Shelley Hack, Tom Mason. Geary plays the rich man who encounters an equally eccentric woman (Hack) also into death-defying games. A convoluted affair. (Dir: William Wiard, 104 mins.)

Kid, The (1921)***½ Charles Chaplin, Jackie Coogan, Edna Purviance. One of director Chaplin's most highly regarded features. Coogan (age seven) does a priceless set of Chaplin imitations, as the foundling adopted by the tramp, and together they rule the streets with comic skill and ingenuity. (90 mins.)†

Kid Blue (1973)**½ Dennis Hopper, Warren Oates, Peter Boyle, Ben Johnson, Lee Purcell, Janice Rule. Outlaw whose attempts to follow the straight and narrow are inhibited by a series of routine jobs and way-out acquaintances. Good supporting performances. Shot in 1971. (Dir: Jim Frawley, 108 mins.)

Kid Brother, The (1927)**** Harold Lloyd, Jobyna Ralston, Walter James, Leo Willis, Olin Francis, Eddie Boland, Constantine Romanoff. One of Lloyd's true masterpieces, this is the story of a country boy, the sole runt in the family of the local sheriff, who falls in love with a beautiful carnival girl (Lloyd's first teaming with the delightful Ralston) and ends up saving her and the family honor from a robber. No synopsis can describe the warmth, perception, and charm of the interactions between the characters, not to mentions the endless flow of hysterical sightgags. (Dir: Ted Wilde, 82 mins.)

Kidco (1983)** Scott Schwartz, Clifton James. The ostensibly true story of a group of kids who go into business for themselves. The first half is a witty paean to the entrepreneurial spirit, but the film turns embarrassingly predictable as the government interests step in to spoil the kids' fun. (Dir: Ronald Maxwell, 104 mins.)†

Kid Dynamite (1943)** East Side Kids, Gabriel Dell, Pamela Blake. Contrived competition between two of the Kids when Muggs suspects Danny had him kidnapped so Danny could take his place in a boxing match. (Dir: Wallace Fox, 67 mins.)

Kid for Two Farthings, A (Great Britain, 1955)**** Celia Johnson, Diana Dors, Jonathan Ashmore. Lad in the London slums believes a one-horned goat is a

561

magic unicorn that will bring him luck. Something different; touching, superbly directed comedy-drama, a fine film. (Dir: Carol Reed, 91 mins.)

Kid from Brooklyn, The (1946)*** Danny Kaye, Virginia Mayo, Vera-Ellen. Remake of Harold Lloyd's comedy *The Milky Way* and although not as good, Kaye manages to make it fun. Story concerns a milkman who is turned into a prize fighter. (Dir: Leo McCarey, 113 mins.)†

Kid from Left Field, The (1953)**½ Dan Dailey, Anne Bancroft, Lloyd Bridges. Peanut vendor used his son, operating as batboy, to break a baseball team's slump. Pleasant, but doesn't exactly burn up the league. (Dir: Harmon Jones, 80 mins.)

Kid from Left Field, The (MTV 1979)** Gary Coleman, Robert Guillaume, Ed McMahon. In this sugary remake of a '53 Dan Dailey movie, Coleman plays a batboy for the San Diego Padres who is the son of a former second baseman (Guillaume). (Dir: Adell Aldrich, 104 mins.)†

Kid from Nowhere, The (MTV 1982)**½ Susan Saint James, Beau Bridges, Loretta Swit, Ricky Wittman, Janet MacLachlan, Fred Dryer, René Auberjonois, Nicholas Pryor, Lynn Carlin. Inspirational tale of a boy with Down's syndrome (Wittman, who actually suffers from Down's) and his involvement with the Special Olympics. Good performances directed with great sensitivity by Beau Bridges. (96 mins.)

Kid from Spain, The (1932)**½ Eddie Cantor, Robert Young, Lyda Roberti, Paulette Goddard, Betty Grable (chorines). Given the talents of director Leo McCarey and choreographer Busby Berkeley, this Cantor vehicle should have been more of a romp. Eddie plays his usual simpleton who in this one is mistaken for a bullfighter. (110 mins.)

Kid Galahad (1937)*** Edward G. Robinson, Bette Davis, Humphrey Bogart, Wayne Morris. First-rate boxing melodrama, well acted by an all-star cast. AKA: **The Battling Bellhop.** (Dir: Michael Curtiz, 101 mins.)

Kid Galahad (1962)*** Elvis Presley, Gig Young, Charles Bronson, Lola Albright. Elvis is a fresh-faced boxer who encounters the usual temptations from gangster Bronson, and Young and Albright are the world-weary couple who try to keep him straight. Directed, far better than might be expected, by Phil Karlson. (95 mins.)†

Kid Glove Killer (1942)*** Van Heflin, Marsha Hunt. A superior Grade "B" crime film which uses police labs instead of chases and other contrivances. Many of our modern, adult crime sto-

ries stem from the type of thinking that went into this film. (Dir: Fred Zinnemann, 74 mins.)

Kid Millions (1934)*** Eddie Cantor, Ann Sothern, Ethel Merman, George Murphy. Another of Cantor's extravagant, song-filled comedies made under the Sam Goldwyn banner. Cantor's a millionaire this time. (Dir: Roy Del Ruth, 100 mins.)†

Kidnapped (1938)**½ Freddie Bartholomew, C. Aubrey Smith, Nigel Bruce, Warner Baxter. Robert Louis Stevenson's classic altered for the screen with just the title and character names maintained. Good juvenile adventure tale. (Dir: Alfred Werker, 90 mins.)

Kidnapped (Great Britain, 1960)**½ Peter Finch, James MacArthur. Straightforward Disney production of Robert Louis Stevenson's classic about a young heir whose scheming uncle arranges for his kidnapping, and his adventures at sea with a stalwart Jacobite (anti–King George) Scotsman. Movie lacks vigor, but it's well acted. (Dir: Robert Stevenson, 97 mins.)†

Kidnapped (1948)**½ Roddy McDowall, Dan O'Herlihy, Roland Winters, Sue England, Jeff Corey. Poor, cheaply made version of Robert Louis Stevenson's classic tale of a young Scottish boy pursued for his inheritance; the worst of the three versions, though none is fully satisfactory; not McDowall's fault. (Dir: William Beaudine, 80 mins.)

Kidnapped (Great Britain, 1971)***Michael Caine, Trevor Howard, Jack Hawkins, Donald Pleasence. The fourth cinematization of the famous classic by Robert Louis Stevenson, and a lesser-known sequel, *David Balfour*. The film deals with the fighting between the English and the Scottish during the end of the 18th century. (Dir: Delbert Mann, 100 mins.)†

Kidnapped (1986)* David Naughton, Barbara Crampton, Lance LeGault, Chick Vennera, Kim Evenson. Woman enlists the aid of a California cop to help find her sixteen-year-old sister, who has been kidnapped by a ring of pornographers. Any moral difference between the evil smut peddlers in the story and the makers of this film who use it as an excuse to show naked and beaten women escapes us entirely. (Dir: Howard Avedis, 98 mins.)†

Kidnapping of the President, The (1980)** William Shatner, Hal Holbrook, Van Johnson, Ava Gardner. While on a state visit to Toronto, the president is kidnapped by an international terrorist and held in an armored truck filled with explosives until a huge ransom is paid. Farfetched, unconvincing melodrama. (Dir: George Mendeluk, 113 mins.)†

Kid Rodelo (1966)** Don Murray, Janet Leigh, Broderick Crawford. Dull western made in Spain. Don Murray tries to fight off the greedy crooks after a cache of stolen gold, and keep an eye on fetching Janet Leigh at the same time. (Dir: Richard Carlson, 91 mins.)

Kids Are Alright, The (1979)**½ An uneven but fascinating documentary on The Who. The film covers the entire history of the band, with concert footage of the energetic group on stage and revealing interviews. (Dir: Jeff Stein, 108 mins.)†

Kids Don't Tell (MTV 1985)** Michael Ontkean, JoBeth Williams, Leo Rossi, Ari Meyers. Message movie on child molestation that tells kids to be wary. A documentary filmmaker sees this problem first-hand in this TV movie, which is careful not to sensationalize or exploit. (Dir: Sam O'Steen, 104 mins.)

Kids Like These (MTV 1987)**½ Tyne Daly, Richard Crenna, Martin Balsam, Joey McFarland. Tender message movie about a child with Down's syndrome. Daly hits all the right notes as the boy's caring mom; directed with sensitivity by her husband, Georg Stanford Brown. (96 mins.)

Kid Who Loved Christmas, The (MCTV 1990)**½ Michael Warren, Trent Cameron, Sammy Davis, Jr., Cicely Tyson, Ray Parker, Jr., Della Reese, Esther Rolle, Ben Vereen, Vanessa Williams. Enjoyable family entertainment about a struggling jazz musician wishing to adopt a lovable youngster. Standout jazz numbers. (Dir: Arthur Allan Seidelman, 96 mins.)

Kid with the Broken Halo, The (MTV 1982)**½ Gary Coleman, Robert Guillaume, June Allyson, Ray Walston, Georg Stanford Brown, Mason Adams. Displaying his mischievous charm, Gary is an angel ordered to save souls or face the hot coals. (Dir: Leslie H. Martinson, 104 mins.)†

Kid with the 200 I.Q., The (MTV 1983)** Gary Coleman, Robert Guillaume, Dean Butler, Harriet Nelson. Another Gary Coleman entry where the precocious kid plays a 13-year-old genius entering college. (Dir: Leslie Martinson, 104 mins.)†

Kilimanjaro—See: **In the Shadow of Kilimanjaro**

Kill! (France-West Germany-Italy-Spain, 1972)*½ Jean Seberg, James Mason, Stephen Boyd, Curt Jurgens, Daniel Emilfork, Memphis Slim. Interpol officer Mason deals drugs on the side, vigilante Boyd wants to end the drug trade with the use of his machine gun, and it's hard to tell who we're supposed to sympathize with. AKA: **Kill! Kill! Kill!** (Dir: Romain Gary, 102 mins.)†

Kill and Kill Again (1981)* James Ryan, Anneline Kriel, Ken Gampu, Norman Robinson, Michael Meyer. Ridiculous, violent martial arts flick. James Ryan is the hero out to rescue a kidnapped scientist who has developed a fuel that gets a thousand miles per gallon and a new drug that allows complete mind control. (Dir. Ivan Hall, 100 mins.)†

Killbots—See: **Chopping Mall**

Kill Castro (1980)*½ Stuart Whitman, Robert Vaughn, Caren Kaye, Raymond St. Jacques. Adventurer Whitman is hired by renegade CIA agent Vaughn as part of a plot to unseat Castro. Dull, cheaply made regional movie even wastes the Key West scenery. AKA: **Assignment Kill Castro, Cuba Crossing, Key West Crossing, The Mercenaries,** and **Sweet Dirty Tony.** (Dir: Chuck Workman, 90 mins.)†

Killdozer (MTV 1974)** Clint Walker, Carl Betz, Neville Brand, and James Wainwright all play construction workers on a desolate island, but stunt man Carey Loftin is the real star of this action flick about a bulldozer controlled by an alien creature. (Dir: Jerry London, 74 mins.)

Killer (1990)* Duke Emsberger, Andy Boswell, Jeri Keith Liles, Mark Creter. "Amateurish" is a kind description for this no-budget horror movie about a psycho who turns to killing hitchhikers in revenge for being abused in medical experiments. (Dir: Tony Elwood, 81 mins.)†

Killer, The (Hong Kong, 1989)*** Chow Yun-fatt, Sally Yeh, Danny Lee. All-out action in its purest form with Yun-fatt as a smooth, incurably fair-minded hit man who agrees to one more job in order to pay for an operation to restore the sight of a singer he accidentally blinded. One of the best Hong Kong features ever. (Dir: John Woo, 110 mins.)

Killer Ape, The (1953)** Johnny Weissmuller, Carol Thurston, Max Palmer, Nestor Paiva. Jungle Jim clears himself in a strange criminal case involving a coalition between Watusis and white hunters who perform illegal experiments on jungle animals. (Dir: Spencer Bennet, 68 mins.)

Killer Bat—See: **Devil Bat, The**

Killer Bees (MTV 1974)** Gloria Swanson, Kate Jackson, Edward Albert, Craig Stevens. Old-time movie fans will be curious to see the indomitable Swanson once again in this predictable chiller about a strange family of winegrowers who keep killer bees on the premises. (Dir: Curtis Harrington, 74 mins.)

Killer by Night (MTV 1971)** Robert Wagner, Diane Baker. One of TV's favorite plots—about the highly communicable disease which invades the city, requiring doctors to find the carrier before an epidemic breaks out—gets a new twist. This time the carrier is an armed, dangerous cop killer. (Dir: Bernard McEveety, 100 mins.)

Killer Elite, The (1975)** James Caan, Robert Duvall, Arthur Hill, Bo Hopkins, Gig Young, Helmut Dantine. A confused action picture that centers on the operations of a fictional company specializing in political assassinations. (Dir: Sam Peckinpah, 123 mins.)†

Killer Fish (Great Britain-Brazil, 1979)* Lee Majors, Karen Black, James Franciscus, Margaux Hemingway, Marisa Berenson. Action-horror film in which several parties compete for a treasure "guarded" by man-eating piranhas. (Dir: "Anthony Dawson" [Antonio Margheriti], 101 mins.)†

Killer Force (Switzerland-Ireland, 1975)** Telly Savalas, Peter Fonda, Hugh O'Brian, O. J. Simpson, Maud Adams, Christopher Lee. Savalas investigates robberies at a South African diamond mine, not suspecting that his deputy Fonda is behind them. Crime thriller with a few good sequences. (Dir: Val Guest, 100 mins.)†

Killer Inside Me, The (1976)*** Stacy Keach, Susan Tyrrell, Keenan Wynn, Don Stroud, John Carradine, Charles McGraw. Intriguing drama with exemplary acting by Keach as a lawman who turns psychotic slayer. Violent psychological study based on a novel by Jim Thompson. (Dir: Burt Kennedy, 99 mins.)†

Killer in the Family, A (MTV 1983)**½ Robert Mitchum, James Spader, Lance Kerwin, Salome Jens. Brutal depiction of cold-blooded killers who will do anything to insure their freedom after breaking out of jail. Mitchum plays an irredeemably evil con who talks his three sons into breaking him and a pal out of prison. (Dir: Richard T. Heffron, 104 mins.)

Killer in the Mirror (MTV 1986)** Ann Jillian, Len Cariou, Jessica Walter, Max Gail. Jillian makes the most of an old identical twins ploy in a mistaken identity show. She juggles playing an insecure sister and her conniving, low-life twin; naturally she's in for double trouble by the fade out. (Dir: Frank DeFelitta, 104 mins.)

Killer Is Loose, The (1956)*** Joseph Cotten, Rhonda Fleming, Wendell Corey. Bank robber vows vengeance upon the detective who nabbed him. Suspenseful, exciting drama. (Dir: Budd Boetticher, 73 mins.)

Killer Klowns from Outer Space (1988)**½ Grant Cramer, Suzanne Snyder, John Vernon. Amusing, colorful salute to the fifties B movies about a circus-tent spaceship that lands on Earth and disgorges evil, clownlike aliens. Generally as tacky as the films that inspired it, this is still

564

mindless fun. (Dir: Stephen Chiodo, 86 mins.)†

Killer Leopard (1954)** Johnny Sheffield, Beverly Garland, Barry Bernard, Donald Murphy. Bomba plays jungle boy scout as he helps a beautiful movie star find her missing hubby—only her hubby's not too eager to relinquish his hunt for treasure. (Dir: Ford Beebe, 70 mins.)

Killer McCoy (1947)*** Mickey Rooney, Ann Blyth, Brian Donlevy, Sam Levene, Tom Tully, James Dunn. A gritty prize-fighting drama with Rooney outstanding as a boxer who accidentally kills a pal in the ring. (Dir: Roy Rowland, 104 mins.)

Killer on Board (MTV 1977)** Claude Akins, Beatrice Straight, George Hamilton. The villain is a virus running amok on a panic-stricken cruise ship. (Dir: Philip Leacock, 104 mins.)†

Killer Party (1984) ½ Martin Hewitt, Ralph Seymour, Elaine Wilkes, Paul Bartel. Sophomoric slasher pic about sorority chicks and fraternity brothers holding their April Fool's Day mixer in an abandoned house suffused with an evil presence. Featuring laughably overwrought denouement. (Dir: William Fruet, 92 mins.)†

Killers, The (1946)**** Burt Lancaster, Ava Gardner, Edmond O'Brien, Albert Dekker, Sam Levene. Insurance detective unravels the killing of a washed-up boxer. Suspenseful, excellently produced and directed crime drama, extending Hemingway's taut tale. (Dir: Robert Siodmak, 105 mins.)

Killers, The (1964)***½ Lee Marvin, John Cassavetes, Angie Dickinson, Ronald Reagan, Clu Gulager, Norman Fell, Claude Akins. Terrific crime thriller, loosely based on Hemingway's short story, about a pair of brutal hit men seeking truth about why they were hired to kill their victim. Great armored truck robbery, clever double cross, and brilliant use of flashbacks add to film's well-deserved cult status. Entire cast is wonderful, especially Reagan as a corrupt land developer, giving his finest acting job in his last movie. Directed with style by Don Siegel for TV, but released to theaters instead when networks found it too violent. (95 mins.)†

Killers from Space (1954) ½ Peter Graves, James Seay, Barbara Bestar, Frank Gerstle. Schlocky chiller about a dead man nabbed by space fiends, who bring him back from the Great Beyond to pick his brains for info necessary to control Earth. The monster costumes seem to be odds and ends picked up at Goodwill, and the stock footage is edited in without rhyme or reason. (Dir: W. Lee Wilder, 71 mins.)†

Killer Shrews, The (1959)* James Best,

Ingrid Goude. Monsters (actually some lethargic dogs in shrew costumes) terrorize a remote island in this classic camp monsterpiece. (Dir: Ray Kellogg, 69 mins.)†

Killer's Kiss (1955)*** Jamie Smith, Frank Silvera, Irene Kane. Director Stanley Kubrick's first "official" feature (he disowns *Fear and Desire*) is a show-offy and talented lowlife story of a boxer who finds his girlfriend murdered. Very good for a first try by a nervy kid. (67 mins.)

Killers of Kilimanjaro (Great Britain, 1960)** Robert Taylor, Anthony Newley, Anne Aubrey, Gregoire Aslan, Allan Cuthbertson, Donald Pleasence. Adventure story set in deepest Africa casts Taylor as an engineer surveying the wilds of Kenya for the building of the first African railway. Second-rate *King Solomon's Mine* clone padded out with inferior stock footage. (Dir: Richard Thorpe, 91 mins.)

Killers Three (1969)*½ Robert Walker, Diane Varsi, Dick Clark. Unconvincing saga of a moonshiner who wants to bid adieu to the profession by filching $200,000 from his employer. (Dir: Bruce Kessler, 88 mins.)

Killer That Stalked New York, The (1950)**½ Evelyn Keyes, Charles Korvin. A diamond smuggler enters the U.S. carrying a contagious disease and the fuse is set in a wild search to save the city from death. (Dir: Earl McEvoy, 79 mins.)

Killer Who Wouldn't Die, The (MTV 1976) *½ Mike Connors, Gregoire Aslan, Mariette Hartley. Connors plays a former homicide detective who runs a charter-boat service, but just can't stay away from intrigue and trouble. Before you can reel in a marlin, Connors is hot on the trail of a killer of an undercover agent. (Dir: William Hale, 98 mins.)

Killer Workout (1987)* Marcia Karr, David James Campbell, Fritz Matthews, Ted Prior. Someone's killing the leotarded lovelies at Rhonda's Workout Club. Sooner or later, you just knew that *someone* was going to combine a slasher movie with "20-Minute Workout," and here it is. There's an unexpected ending, but it's not worth struggling through the rest of the movie. AKA: **Aerobicide**. (Dir: David A. Prior, 86 mins.)†

Killing, The (1956)*** Sterling Hayden, Coleen Gray. Crooks plan a daring racetrack robbery. Direction by Stanley Kubrick, a newcomer at that time, is unnecessarily arty but interesting. (Dir: Stanley Kubrick, 83 mins.)†

Killing Affair, A (MTV 1977)** O. J. Simpson, Elizabeth Montgomery, Dean Stockwell. Simpson is paired with Montgomery in this cop show. O. J.'s married detective and Liz's Viki Eaton play a homicide team who slide into an off-hours affair. AKA: **Behind the Badge**. (Dir: Richard C. Sarafian, 104 mins.)

Killing Affair, A (1988)** Peter Weller, Kathy Baker, John Glover. The fine cast tries but can't really make anything of this thin Southern Gothic script set in 1943. Stranger Weller murders a small-town tyrant, then indulges in a talkathon with Baker, the dead man's wife. Made in 1985. (Dir: David Saperstein, 100 mins.)

Killing at Hell's Gate (MTV 1981)** Robert Urich, Deborah Raffin, Lee Purcell, Joel Higgins, George DiCenzo. It's "Deliverance with Dames" time as some whitewater rafters encounter terror in the wilderness. (Dir: Jerry Jameson, 104 mins.)

Killing 'Em Softly (Canada, 1985)*½ George Segal, Irene Cara, Nicholas Campbell. Two appealing performers, Cara and Segal (miscast as an old codger) hit the skids with this lopsided tale of an old man who commits an impetuous murder, and the young pop singer who plays detective so that her boyfriend won't have to take the rap for it. (Dir: Max Fischer, 81 mins.)†

Killing Fields, The (Great Britain, 1984)***½ Sam Waterston, Dr. Haing S. Ngor, John Malkovich, Athol Fugard. A searing, powerful war story focusing on *New York Times* reporter Sydney Schanberg (Waterston) and his Cambodian photographer Dith Pran (Ngor) who together covered Phnom Penh before it fell in 1975. The most lacerating scenes concern Pran's attempt to escape the nightmarish Khmer Rouge "reeducation camps" as Schanberg, back in America, tries to find him. Oscars went to Ngor, the editors, and Chris Menges for his stunning cinematography. (Dir: Roland Joffe, 148 mins.)†

Killing Floor, The (MTV 1985)**½ Damien Leake, Moses Gunn, Clarence Felder, Alfre Woodard, Ernest Rayford, James O'Reilly. Ambitious but flawed docudrama that deals with union discord in the meat-packing industry, plus the Chicago race riots of 1919. (Dir: Bill Duke, 118 mins.)†

Killing Game, The (France, 1967)**½ Jean-Pierre Cassel, Claudine Auger. An often lovely, yet overly tricky film done in an almost pop-art style. A young couple drive a rich young man to distraction. (Dir: Alain Jessua, 94 mins.)

Killing Game, The (1988)* Chad Hayward, Cynthia Killion, Geoffrey Sadwith, Robert Zdar, Julie Noble. Pale stab at *film noir* has Las Vegas killer-for-hire Hayward blackmailed into working for a drug dealer. (Dir: Joseph Mehri, 83 mins.)†

Killing Heat (1984)** Karen Black, John Thaw, John Kani, John Moulder-Brown. This adaptation of Doris Lessing's *The Grass Is Singing* provides some powerful observations about African colonialism, as a nervous city girl marries a farmer and finds her homestead's primitive conditions are unhinging her mind. (Dir: Michael Raeburn, 104 mins.)†

Killing Hour, The—See: **Clairvoyant, The** (1985)

Killing in a Small Town, A (MTV 1990)*** Barbara Hershey, Brian Dennehy, Richard Gilliland, John Terry, Hal Holbrook. True story of a brutal axe murder in a small Texas community. Hershey is a standout. (Dir: Stephen Gyllenhaal, 96 mins.)

Killing Kind, The (1973)** Ann Sothern, John Savage, Ruth Roman, Luana Anders, Cindy Williams, Sue Bernard. After serving a somewhat unfair prison sentence for rape, a now psychotic young man is released and seeks revenge on the women he holds responsible. Worth a look. (Dir: Curtis Harrington, 95 mins.)†

Killing Mind, The (MCTV 1991)**½ Stephanie Zimbalist, Tony Bill, Daniel Roebuck. Entertaining suspense yarn bears a slight resemblance to *Silence of the Lambs*. Zimbalist plays an FBI-trained police sergeant determined to solve the 20-year-old case of *The Ballerina Murder* by tapping into the minds of potential suspects. (Dir: Michael Ray Rhodes, 96 mins.)†

Killing of Randy Webster, The (MTV 1981)**½ Hal Holbrook, Dixie Carter, James Whitmore, Jennifer Jason-Leigh, Sean Penn. Another true-life tale. A teenager steals a van in Houston, giving the cops a wild chase, and winds up with a bullet in his head. (Dir: Sam Wanamaker, 104 mins.)†

Killing of Sister George, The (1968)**½ Beryl Reid, Susannah York, Coral Browne, Ronald Fraser. Black comedy possesses a raw force due to splendid acting. The story concerns an aging actress (Reid) who is in the process of losing both her job on a popular TV soap and her live-in lover (York). (Dir: Robert Aldrich, 138 mins.)†

Killing Stone (MTV 1978)**½ Gil Gerard, Nehemiah Persoff, Corinne Michaels. Michael Landon is the writer-director of this pilot about an ex-convict turned newspaper columnist. (104 mins.)†

Killing Time, The (1987)*½ Beau Bridges, Kiefer Sutherland, Wayne Rogers, Camelia Kath, Joe Don Baker. Lame-duck thriller about an unfaithful wife and sheriff boyfriend who plan to kill the lady's husband and blame it on our pal Kief. (Dir: Rick King, 95 mins.)†

Killjoy (MTV 1981)**½ Kim Basinger, Robert Culp, Stephen Macht, Nancy Marchand, John Rubinstein. A good cast, seamy characters, and the tricky murder story add up to a fairly diverting show. Basinger is the target, the daughter of a womanizing, hotshot surgeon (Macht). (Dir: John Llewellyn Moxey, 104 mins.)†

Kill! Kill! Kill!—See: **Kill!**

Kill Me Again (1989)*** Joanne Whalley-Kilmer, Val Kilmer, Michael Madsen, Pat Mulligan, Bibi Besch. Femme fatale Whalley-Kilmer lucks into a bundle of mob money, then uses her charms to entice sleazy detective Kilmer into a plot to get the mobsters off her back. Double crosses, seductions, and more double crosses, with Whalley-Kilmer attacking her bad-girl role with gusto. (Dir: John Dahl, 94 mins.)†

Kill Me If You Can (MTV 1977)**** Alan Alda, Talia Shire, John Hillerman. Alda is a powerhouse portraying Caryl Chessman's 12-year battle to stay out of San Quentin's gas chamber, winning eight stays of execution through the efforts of his attorney Rosalie Asher (Shire). A powerful polemic against capital punishment. (Dir: Buzz Kulik, 104 mins.)

Kill-Off, The (1989)**½ Loretta Gross, Andrew Lee Barrett, Jackson Sims, Steve Monroe, Cathy Haase. Downbeat study of human nature in a small town where various residents independently decide to kill a malicious gossip before she can ruin any more lives. Adaptation of a Jim Thompson novel. (Dir: Maggie Greenwald, 95 mins.)

Kill Slade (South Africa, 1988)** Patrick Dollaghan, Lisa Brady, Danny Keogh, Anthony Fridjhon. Mercenary is hired to kidnap a female reporter who is threatening to expose a corrupt government. (Dir: D. Bruce McFarlane, 88 mins.)†

Kill the Umpire (1950)**½ William Bendix, Una Merkel. Pretty funny film about an umpire's life—his training, his job, and his love of baseball. (Dir: Lloyd Bacon, 78 mins.)

Kill Zone (1985)* Fritz Matthews, Ted Prior, David James Campbell, William Joseph Zipp. Veteran taking part in war games starts taking them for real, as a result of experimental psychological conditioning. (Dir: David A. Prior, 91 mins.)†

Kim (1950)**½ Errol Flynn, Dean Stockwell, Paul Lukas, Robert Douglas, Thomas Gomez. Rudyard Kipling's best novel rendered in Hollywood schoolboy terms. Nevertheless, a colorful adventure story, with Flynn near the end of his tether and Stockwell as Kim. A trifle stodgily directed by Victor Saville. (113 mins.)†

Kim (MTV 1984)*** Ravi Sheth, Bryan Brown, Peter O'Toole. A spirited, colorful rendition of Rudyard Kipling's engaging tale of Victorian India, seen through the eyes of a half-white street urchin who grows into a British secret service man. (Dir: John Davies, 104 mins.)

Kindergarten Cop (1990)** Arnold Schwarzenegger, Pamela Reed, Linda Hunt, Penelope Anne Miller, Richard Tyson, Carroll Baker. Misguided feature that doesn't seem to know if it's an action thriller, a romantic comedy, or a kid's movie. Schwarzenegger's a cop who goes undercover as a kindergarten teacher in order to solve a crime. The film is a series of set pieces desperately in need of cohesiveness. Hunt, as the principal, is a comic delight. The classroom sequences are cute but predictable. (Dir: Ivan Reitman, 110 mins.)†

Kind Hearts and Coronets (Great Britain, 1949)**** Alec Guinness, Dennis Price, Valerie Hobson, Joan Greenwood. Guinness made a sensation with his portrayal of the eight relatives whom Price must eliminate in order to claim a title in this, director Robert Hamer's (and Ealing Studios') most charming comedy. The satire is biting without being nasty, and the inexorable logic of murder unfolds with a delicious verve. (104 mins.)†

Kind Lady (1935)*** Aline MacMahon, Basil Rathbone. Murdering criminals take over the house of a recluse, intending to rob and kill her. Suspenseful melodrama. (Dir: George B. Seitz, 80 mins.)

Kind Lady (1951)*** Ethel Barrymore, Maurice Evans, Angela Lansbury. A chilling mystery about a sinister retinue of servants who invade an old lady's home and terrorize her. Top-rate performance by the talented cast. (Dir: John Sturges, 78 mins.)

Kind of Loving, A (Great Britain, 1962)***½ Alan Bates, June Ritchie, Thora Hird, Norman Rossiter. Coming near the end of the "kitchen sink" cycle of British realism, this first feature by director John Schlesinger never received due attention. Bates and Ritchie are forced to marry when she becomes pregnant. An old story, but sensitively handled. (112 mins.)†

Kindred, The (1987)** David Allan Brooks, Amanda Pays, Talia Balsam, Kim Hunter, Rod Steiger. A young doctor goes to his recently deceased mother's house to finish her scientific work, only to find that her experiments have had monstrous results. (Dirs: Jeff Obrow, Stephen Carpenter, 92 mins.)†

King: A Filmed Record...Montgomery to Memphis (1970)**** Brilliant, eloquent documentary, recording the remarkable life of Rev. Martin Luther King, Jr. Sequences supervised by directors Joseph L. Mankiewicz and Sidney Lumet. (153 mins.)†

King and Country (Great Britain, 1964)***½ Dirk Bogarde, Tom Courtenay, Leo McKern. Sensitive private is placed on trial for desertion during WWI, is defended by a captain convinced of

his innocence. Brutal study of the injustices of war may prove too strong for the more delicate viewers; but it packs quite a punch, is excellently acted. (Dir: Joseph Losey, 86 mins.)

King and Four Queens, The (1956)** Clark Gable, Eleanor Parker, Jo Van Fleet. King Gable locks horns with four beautiful would-be-widows and their guntoting mother-in-law for a prize of $100,000 in gold. Picture jumps from comedy to drama without much conviction. (Dir: Raoul Walsh, 86 mins.)

King and I, The (1956)**** Yul Brynner, Deborah Kerr, Rita Moreno, Martin Benson. Rogers and Hammerstein's magnificent Broadway musical makes a memorable film, enhanced by sumptuous settings and superb production values. Brynner struts about creating the perfect picture of the absolute monarch as the King of Siam, and Kerr matches him as the spirited British schoolteacher who is hired to tutor the royal offspring. (Dir: Walter Lang, 133 mins.)†

King and the Chorus Girl (1937)***½ Fernand Gravet, Joan Blondell. Excellent comedy about a king who falls in love with a commoner. Very popular subject in 1937. Screenplay by Norman Krasna and Groucho Marx. (Dir: Mervyn LeRoy, 100 mins.)

King Crab (MTV 1980)*** Barry Newman, Julie Bovasso, Jeffrey DeMunn, Joel Fabiani, Gail Strickland, Harold Gould, Anne DeSalvo. Powerful drama charting the feud between brothers Newman and DeMunn, who use the family seafood business as a battleground to compete for their father's favor. Good performances by all; strong direction by telefilm veteran Marvin J. Chomsky. (96 mins.)

King Creole (1958)**½ Elvis Presley, Dolores Hart, Walter Matthau, Carolyn Jones, Dean Jagger. Who but Hal Wallis would have tailored the one halfway decent Harold Robbins novel, *A Stone for Danny Fisher,* as a Presley vehicle? Elvis shows some mettle under Michael Curtiz's competent direction. Young busboy on the verge of delinquency gets his break when he is forced to sing at a New Orleans nightclub and makes a hit. (116 mins.)†

King David (1985)** Richard Gere, Edward Woodward, Alice Krige, Denis Quilley. The film has undeniable grandeur in the first half detailing King Saul's decline. But once the contemporary acting talents of Gere surface, the grandeur degenerates into "great moments from the Bible." (Dir: Bruce Beresford, 114 mins.)†

Kingdom of the Spiders (1977)*** William Shatner, Tiffany Bolling, Woody Strode. Yet another nature-on-the-rampage horror film, but this one is way above average. When pesticides deplete their natural food supply, tarantulas in the Arizona desert begin to turn on humans. (Dir: John "Bud" Cardos, 94 mins.)†

Kingfisher Caper, The (South Africa, 1975)** Hayley Mills, Jon Cypher, David McCallum, Volente Bertotti. Fair actioner about diamond operations off the African coast. Cypher attempts to dredge up enough sparklers to pay off ruthless McCallum, and win David's sister, Jon's sweetheart. (Dir: Dirk De Villiers, 89 mins.)†

King in New York, A (Great Britain, 1957)**½ Charles Chaplin, Dawn Addams, Michael Chaplin. Writer-director Charles Chaplin's last starring film, tinged with his special bittersweet genius. He plays a deposed European monarch who visits America during the McCarthyist hysteria. Hilarious scene as the king is tricked into appearing on live TV by a sultry pitchlady (Addams). Serious statements from the mouth of a young "radical" schoolboy, played by Chaplin's son Michael, who informs on his parents' friends, thereby saving his parents' teaching jobs. An uneven political satire. (105 mins.)†

King Kong (1933)**** Fay Wray, Bruce Cabot, Robert Armstrong, Noble Johnson. The classic monster film, still as much fun as when it came out. It should be noted, however, that audiences of the day weren't any more naive about the Freudian implications of the giant ape on the building than we are. The unedited version (103 mins.) reveals a fouler-tempered Kong. (Dirs: Merian C. Cooper, Ernest B. Schoedsack, 100 mins.)†

King Kong (1976)*** Jeff Bridges, Jessica Lange, Charles Grodin, Ed Lauter. Most critics blasted this overpublicized remake as making a monkey out of the beloved Giant Ape of the thirties. While this version doesn't deliver the thrills and suspense of the original, it remains an oddly effective fable with a romantic sweep and lushness not attempted in the action-oriented classic of 1933. More a bizarre love story than an epic adventure. (Dir: John Guillermin, 134 mins.)†

King Kong Escapes (Japan, 1967)* Rhodes Reason, Mie Hama. Again King Kong's eye for a beautiful woman lands him in trouble. He gets involved in international plots, and comes face-to-face with a mechanical replica of himself. (Dir: Inoshira Honda, 96 mins.)†

King Kong Lives (1986)* Peter Elliot, Brian Kerwin, George Yiasomi, Linda Hamilton, John Ashton, Peter Michael Goetz. But not the movie containing him! This cartoonish simian adventure involves the King's getting a gigantic heart transplant; Lady Kong shows up and helps the Big Ape convalesce. (Dir: John Guillermin, 105 mins.)†

King Kong vs. Godzilla (Japan, 1962)*½ Michael Keith, James Yagi. Typical Japanese sci-fi shenanigans provide a field day for special-effects crews and a day off for script writers. (Dirs: Inoshiro Honda, Thomas Montgomery, 90 mins.)†

King Lear (Great Britain-Denmark, 1970) ***½ Paul Scofield, Irene Worth, Alan Webb, Jack MacGowran, Cyril Cusack. Exciting production of the Shakespeare classic. Two of the greatest theater artists in the world, director Peter Brook and actor Paul Scofield playing Lear, have left their indelible mark on this imaginative version. Major shortcoming of the work is that so many cuts have been made in the text that those who do not know the play extremely well will occasionally be unable to follow the narrative. (Dir: Peter Brook, 137 mins.)

King Lear (U.S.S.R., 1970)*** Yuri Yravet, Galina Volchek, Valentina Shendrikova, Elsa Radzinya, Karl Sebris, Oleg Dal. Visually majestic Soviet version of Shakespeare's drama about the king who must face insanity and sorrow in the wilderness after he confronts his daughters and banishes the youngest from his presence. Script from Boris Pasternak's translation of the original Shakespeare, with music by Dmitri Shostakovich. (Dir: Grigori Kozintsev, 139 mins.)

King Lear (Great Britain, MTV 1983)**** Laurence Olivier, Diana Rigg, John Hurt, Leo McKern, Colin Blakely. A remarkable supporting cast and expensive production mounted by Granada Television marks Olivier's first Shakespearean role created for TV. Despite his physical frailty during this production when he was 75, there are moments—particularly during the "mad scenes"—on the heath—that compare favorably to this acting genius's finest work anywhere in any medium. The luster and magic of his voice is nearly undiminished in this generally estimable full text production shot entirely in a TV studio soundstage. (Dir: Michael Elliot, 170 mins.)†

King Lear (U.S.-Switzerland, 1987)** Burgess Meredith, Peter Sellars, Molly Ringwald, Jean-Luc Godard, Woody Allen. Genius cineaste Godard signed a paper napkin contract with Cannon's Golan and Globus and so inaugurated this enigmatic, confusing, and at times maddening rendition of the Shakespeare perennial. Here, William Shakespeare, Jr., (the fifth) wanders around trying to reconstruct his ancestor's play by focusing on the relationship between a whacked-out gangster (Meredith) and his daughter (Ringwald). There are also humorous cameos by Norman Mailer (who originally scripted this) and Woody Allen, attractive close-ups of Ringwald, and playful work with lighting. End result: an aesthete's lesson in ripping off two wealthy, ambitious Israeli producers. (91 mins.)

King of Alcatraz (1938)*** Lloyd Nolan, Gail Patrick, J. Carrol Naish, Harry Carey, Robert Preston, Anthony Quinn, Richard Stanley (Dennis Morgan), Richard Denning. Exciting caper film has Alcatraz escapees hijacking a passenger ship, being bested by the honest crew; fast-moving, lively, extremely good of this kind. (Dir: Robert Florey, 56 mins.)

King of Burlesque (1936)*** Warner Baxter, Alice Faye, Jack Oakie. A nice score and good performances make this musical entertaining. Story of a burlesque producer who loses his shirt in the arts offers nothing to the film. (Dir: Sidney Lanfield, 83 mins.)†

King of Chinatown (1939)**½ Anna May Wong, Sidney Toler, J. Carrol Naish, Akim Tamiroff, Philip Ahn, Anthony Quinn, Richard Denning. Good melodrama about corruption in Chinatown, with the lovely Wong foiling gang bosses; well done, with an unusual setting. (Dir: Nick Grinde, 60 mins.)

King of Comedy, The (1983)*** Jerry Lewis, Robert De Niro, Sandra Bernhard. A most unusual, sometimes funny, often disturbing drama. De Niro plays a manic autograph hound, Rupert Pupkin, who is convinced that if he can only get a break he'll be the best comedian ever. Lewis is the nation's top television host, Jerry Langford (along the lines of Johnny Carson). The story, scripted by former film critic Paul D. Zimmerman, reflects an acerbic view of the entertainment world, and the crazy way in which fortunes can be made or lost, lives enriched or shattered, or perhaps just wasted. (Dir: Martin Scorsese, 109 mins.)†

King of Hearts (France-Great Britain, 1967)**½ Alan Bates, Genevieve Bujold, Pierre Brasseur. A gentle, sentimental fable from director Philippe de Broca, in which Bates plays an unknown soldier stranded in an insane asylum abandoned by its staff during WWI. (102 mins.)†

King of Jazz, The (1930)**½ Bing Crosby, Paul Whiteman. Musical revue in two-color Technicolor, blackout gags, vaudeville turns, Gershwin's "Rhapsody in Blue," assorted production numbers and—to be sure not to miss anything in this early musical—a brief animated cartoon sequence. Lively musical fun with early thirties flavor. (Dir: John Murray Anderson, 120 mins.)†

King of Kings, The (1927)*** H. B. Warner, Jacqueline Logan, Ernest Torrence, William Boyd, Joseph Schildkraut. Director Cecil B. DeMille's epic of the ministry, crucifixion, and resurrection of Christ. Silent with a music track. (115 mins.)

King of Kings (1961)***½ Jeffrey Hunter, Robert Ryan, Siobhan McKenna, Viveca Lindfors. Excellently produced story of Jesus Christ. Told simply yet with great emotional power, generally well acted. (Dir: Nicholas Ray, 161 mins.)†

King of Love, The (MTV 1987)*½ Nick Mancuso, Rip Torn, Sela Ward, Michael Lerner. Mancuso stars as a Hefner-like "adult" magazine publisher who rises from a troubled background to become a major political figure. The talented cast tries hard, but its efforts are pointless. (Dir: Anthony Wilkinson, 96 mins.)

King of Marvin Gardens, The (1972)***½ Jack Nicholson, Bruce Dern, Ellen Burstyn, Julia Anne Robinson. Nicholson gives a smashing performance as a seedy, philosophical radio personality, and Dern is electrifying as his hyper brother who's always chasing rainbows. Director Bob Rafelson delivers a fully focused and quite incisive dual character study. (104 mins.)

King of New York (U.S.-Italy, 1989)*** Christopher Walken, David Caruso, Larry Fishburne, Victor Argo, Giancarlo Esposito, Wesley Snipes. Star Walken and director Abel Ferrara both live up to the promise they've often displayed in this kinetically violent, nihilistic gangster film. Ambiguously motivated Walken gets out of prison and announces that he will single-handedly take over the entire New York City drug trade, destroying anyone who stands in his way. Both Walken's performance and Ferrara's scary vision of New York City (from a script by Nicholas St. John) rank this film with the work of Scorsese and DePalma. (103 mins.)†

King of the Gypsies (1978)** Eric Roberts, Sterling Hayden, Annette O'Toole, Brooke Shields, Shelley Winters. An unromanticized view of Gypsies as dishonest, repressive, narrowminded anachronisms. The actors are miscast and unconvincing. (Dir: Frank Pierson, 112 mins.)†

King of the Khyber Rifles (1954)** Tyrone Power, Terry Moore, Michael Rennie. Only occasionally interesting adventure epic set in India during a minor revolution. Power is cast as a half-caste (pun intended) British captain in the Khyber patrol. (Dir: Henry King, 109 mins.)†

King of the Mountain (1981)** Harry Hamlin, Joseph Bottoms, Deborah Van Valkenburgh, Dennis Hopper, Richard Cox, Dan Haggerty, Seymour Cassel. A based-on-fact drama about life as a downhill drag race. Some car jocks race their cars down the twists and turns of L.A.'s Mulholland Drive. (Dir: Noel Nosseck, 90 mins.)†

King of the Roaring Twenties (1961)**½

David Janssen, Mickey Rooney. David Janssen carries the cumbersome lead of an uneven script and some glaring miscasting and still comes off rather well in the role of racketeer Arnold Rothstein. The film traces his climb to the top of "gangdom." (Dir: Joseph M. Newman, 106 mins.)

King of the Streets—See: **Alien Warrior**

King of the Underworld (1939)**½ Humphrey Bogart, Kay Francis. Kay Francis is a lady doctor again in this one but she succeeds in outwitting Bogie who is of course the character in the title. (Dir: Lewis Seiler, 80 mins.)

King of the Zombies (1941)½ Mantan Moreland, Dick Purcell, Joan Woodbury. Mind-numbing chiller about a zombie-maker who's raising a manageable group of the living dead so they can fight for the Germans in WWII. (Dir: Jean Yarbrough, 67 mins.)†

King Queen Knave (West Germany-U.S., 1973)*** David Niven, Gina Lollobrigida, John Moulder Brown, Mario Adorf. This adaptation by director Jerzy Skolimowski of a minor Vladimir Nabokov novel captures much of the flavor of the mordant Nabokov wit. A burlesque of Freudian Oedipal struggle, as a doofus of a boy succeeds to fortune despite his dragooned seduction of his aunt and attempted murder of his uncle. (92 mins.)†

King Ralph (1991)** John Goodman, Peter O'Toole, John Hurt, Camille Coduri, Richard Griffiths, Leslie Phillips, Joely Richardson, James Villiers. Fine cast is wasted in this weak comedy about a mediocre Las Vegas lounge singer (Goodman) who, because of a freak accident, becomes King of England. His bumpkin Americanisms quickly grate and his love affair with a stripper is all clichés. Only Griffiths, as a palace aide, and Richardson, as a princess from Finland, score comedic points. (Dir: David S. Ward, 105 mins.)†

King Rat (1965)***½ George Segal, Tom Courtenay, James Fox. An excellent WWII prisoner-of-war story graphically depicts the everyday existence of British and American POWs confined in a Japanese war camp. The interest of the film lies in the character of a thoroughly unscrupulous opportunist, skillfully played by Segal. Well paced and directed by Bryan Forbes. (133 mins.)†

King Richard and the Crusaders (1954)**½ Rex Harrison, Virginia Mayo, Laurence Harvey, George Sanders. Elaborate costume epic based on Sir Walter Scott's tale of the Crusaders, "The Talisman." Many battle scenes keep the action lively. (Dir: David Butler, 114 mins.)

Kings Go Forth (1958)**½ Frank Sinatra, Tony Curtis, Natalie Wood. Implausible

tale mixing war action and racial problems, as a heelish GI romances a beautiful gal with questionable antecedents. (Dir: Delmer Daves, 109 mins.)

Kings of the Road (West Germany, 1976)***½ Rudiger Vogler, Hanns Zischler, Rudolf Schundler, Lisa Kreuzer, Marquard Bohm. Thoroughly enjoyable, albeit long and deliberate, tale of freelance movie projector repairman who joins young man fleeing his oppressive family and travelling along the vast, barren border between East and West Germany. Director Wim Wenders uses American influences on German culture, especially rock music, to create a witty and fascinating fable about what he believes is the decline of his country's once proud film industry. Part of Wenders's "road" trilogy, following *Alice in the Cities* and *The Wrong Move*. (176 mins.)†

Kings of the Sun (1963)**½ Yul Brynner, George Chakiris, Shirley Ann Field. Impressively mounted but empty historical drama about the ancient Mayan civilization. Yul Brynner, wearing little but a loincloth, plays an Indian chief. (Dir: J. Lee Thompson, 108 mins.)

King Solomon's Mines (Great Britain, 1937)*** Paul Robeson, Cedric Hardwicke, Roland Young. Not as scenic as the Technicolor remake, but follows the book more closely. The majestic Robeson, as the mysterious African chieftain Umbopa, fills the screen with a star quality seldom captured by Hollywood. The story of the search for a lost diamond mine is often exciting. From the novel by H. Rider Haggard. (Dir: Robert Stevenson, 80 mins.)†

King Solomon's Mines (1950)***½ Stewart Granger, Deborah Kerr, Richard Carlson, Hugo Haas. Rousing adventure tale of a white hunter guiding a party through darkest Africa in search of a lady's missing husband. Authentic jungle sites filmed magnificently; enough action, suspense for all. Excellent entertainment. (Dirs: Compton Bennett, Andrew Marton, 102 mins.)†

King Solomon's Mines (1985)** Richard Chamberlain, Sharon Stone, Herbert Lom, John Rhys-Davies, Ken Gampu. If you're in the mood for mindless thrills played with tongue-in-cheek attitudes, you may enjoy this. But filmmakers have beaten around this jungle bush once too often. (Dir: J. Lee Thompson, 100 mins.)†

King Solomon's Treasure (Canada-Great Britain, 1977)*½ David McCallum, John Colicos, Patrick Macnee, Britt Ekland, Wilfred Hyde-White. Exotic adventures and cheesy sets thrown into a tale about a treasure hunt. (Dir: Alvin Rakoff, 89 mins.)†

King's Pirate, The (1967)** Doug McClure,

Jill St. John, Guy Stockwell, Mary Ann Mobley. Silly costume comedy-drama about pirates and their adventures, circa eighteenth century. Remake of Flynn's *Against All Flags*, 1952. (Dir: Don Weis, 100 mins.)

King's Rhapsody (Great Britain, 1955)** Anna Neagle, Errol Flynn, Patrice Wymore. Stilted and out-of-date operetta type of story—heir to the throne has to forsake his true love and marry a princess. (Dir: Herbert Wilcox, 93 mins.)

King's Row (1941)**** Robert Cummings, Ronald Reagan, Ann Sheridan, Betty Field, Claude Rains, Judith Anderson, Charles Coburn, Maria Ouspenskaya, Nancy Coleman. Penetrating dissection of a small town's pervasive evil, superbly produced. The idealistic hero's psychiatric training in Vienna doesn't come a moment too soon. (Dir: Sam Wood, 127 mins.)†

King Steps Out, The (1936)**½ Franchot Tone, Grace Moore, Walter Connolly, Elizabeth Risdon, Raymond Walburn, Victor Jory. Enjoyable vehicle for Moore; an attempt to update the traditional operetta form, with princess Moore pretending to be an ordinary girl and falling for the king she's already engaged to. (Dir: Josef von Sternberg, 85 mins.)

King's Thief, The (1955)** Edmund Purdom, Ann Blyth, David Niven. Lively but routine costume thriller, in which a dastardly nobleman tries to steal the Crown Jewels. Purdom foils him. David Niven deserves better. (Dir: Robert Z. Leonard, 78 mins.)

Kingston: The Power Play (MTV1976)**½ Raymond Burr, Bradford Dillman, Dina Merrill. Another Burr pilot, in which he's an editor-publisher-reporter who never lets threats get in the way of his getting the story. (Dir: Robert Day, 104 mins.)

King's Story, A (Great Britain, 1965)*** Overlong but absorbing documentary about the former Edward VIII of Britain, who abdicated his throne in 1936 to marry the woman he loved. Narrated by Orson Welles. (Dir: Harry Booth, 102 mins.)

Kinjite: Forbidden Subjects (1988)½ Charles Bronson, Perry Lopez, Peggy Lipton, Sy Richardson. Reactionary Bronson opus has him battling slimy pimps and perverts in L.A. (Dir: J. Lee Thompson, 97 mins.)†

Kipperbang (Great Britain, 1982)** John Albasiny, Alison Steadman, Garry Cooper, Abigail Cruttenden. An understated glimpse at the rites of adolescence circa 1948. (Dir: Michael Apted, 80 mins.)

Kipps (Great Britain, 1941)***½ Michael Redgrave, Diana Wynyard, Phyllis Calvert. Fine film of H. G. Wells's gentle

satirical comedy about a shopkeeper who inherits a fortune and tries to make his way in high society, neglecting the poor girl who loves him. (Dir: Carol Reed, 112 mins.)†

Kirilan Witness, The (1984)** Nancy Snyder, Ted Leplat, Joel Colodner, Nancy Boykin. A strange shocker about a woman investigating her sister's demise with the unlikely assistance of a plant that witnessed the killing. (Dir: Jonathan Sarno, 88 mins.)†

Kismet (1944)*** Ronald Colman, Marlene Dietrich. If you still care to see this perennial fable of poets and caliphs and poets' daughters this is as good a version as any. (Dir: William Dieterle, 100 mins.)

Kismet (1955)** Ann Blyth, Howard Keel, Vic Damone. Stilted version of Broadway stage success, about the wise beggar and his beautiful daughter in old Baghdad. For those who like songs and razzle-dazzle. (Dir: Vincente Minnelli, 113 mins.)†

Kiss, The (1988)* Joanna Pacula, Meredith Salenger, Nicholas Kilbertus, Mimi Kuzyk, Sabrina Boudot. Overdirected horror; teenager suspects that her aunt is a witch. (Dir: Pen Densham, 96 mins.)†

Kiss and Kill—See: Against All Odds (1968)

Kiss and Tell (1945)*** Shirley Temple, Jerome Courtland. Pleasant, humorous teenage comedy. (Dir: Richard Wallace, 90 mins.)

Kiss Before Dying, A (1956)*** Robert Wagner, Jeffrey Hunter, Virginia Leith, Joanne Woodward. Nicely knit murder story about a young psychopath who cold-bloodedly murders his pregnant girlfriend. Good suspense as the police start to close in on the killer. (Dir: Gerd Oswald, 94 mins.)

Kiss Before Dying, A (1991)* Matt Dillon, Sean Young, Max von Sydow, Diane Ladd, James Russo. Botched drivel, updating of 1956 original, based on the novel by Ira Levin. Dillon is a psychopath who murders his pregnant girlfriend, marries her twin sister (Young in a dual role), and plots his rise in her family's business. Young is terrible, in addition to everything else. (Dir: James Dearden, 96 mins.)†

Kiss Before the Mirror, The (1933)*** Paul Lukas, Nancy Carroll, Frank Morgan, Walter Pidgeon, Jean Dixon, Gloria Stuart, Donald Cook, Walter Brennan. An attorney finds elements of the murder case he is trying reflected in the actions of his family. Stylized, well acted, and fascinating. (Dir: James Whale, 67 mins.)

Kiss Daddy Goodbye (1981)*½ Fabian Forte, Marilyn Burns, Jon Cedar, Marvin Miller. A fairly interesting supernatural premise—the telekinetic children of a murdered man reanimate his body and send it after his killers—is gunned down by flaccid direction, a script lacking in incident, and awful performances. (Dir: Patrick Regan, 92 mins.)†

Kiss Daddy Good Night (1987)*½ Uma Thurman, Paul Richards, Paul Dillon. Would-be "cult" movie tries to blend a *noir* style with the desultory ambience of New York lowlifes. The main characters are the amoral Laura, who wears wigs and rolls drunks, and her older neighbor who has an unquenchable yen for her. Only for the experimentally minded. (Dir: Peter Ily Huemer, 87 mins.)

Kisses for My President (1964)** Fred MacMurray, Polly Bergen, Arlene Dahl. Lightweight, silly comedy about the trials and tribulations of the first lady President of the U.S. (Dir: Curtis Bernhardt, 113 mins.)

Kissin' Cousins (1964)*½ Elvis Presley, Arthur O'Connell, Pam Austin, Jack Albertson, Glenda Farrell. Typical Elvis musical about trying to build a missile site despite resistance from some hicks. (Dir: Gene Nelson, 96 mins.)†

Kissing Bandit, The (1948)** Frank Sinatra, Kathryn Grayson, J. Carrol Naish, Mildred Natwick, Billy Gilbert. Frank Sinatra has had fun all his career putting down this as his most embarrassing vehicle, but it's not that bad. Sinatra played a young businessman who has to live up to the reputation of his bandit father. On second thought, maybe it is that bad. (Dir: Laslo Benedek, 102 mins.)

Kissing Place, The (MCTV 1990)**½ Meredith Baxter-Birney, David Ogden Stiers, Nathaniel Moreau, Victoria Snow. Ten-year-old boy, troubled by uncertain memories of the past, discovers the truth about his parents and why they've moved so frequently. Clinical "problem" drama is not as compelling as it should have been. (Dir: Tony Wharmby, 96 mins.)†

Kiss in the Dark, A (1949)** David Niven, Jane Wyman, Broderick Crawford. Silly nonsense about a stuffed shirt who takes over an apartment house and comes face to face with life. (Dir: Delmer Daves, 87 mins.)

Kiss Me a Killer (1991)** Julie Carmen, Robert Beltran, Guy Boyd. Fast-moving, sensual, low-budget thriller borrows from *The Postman Always Rings Twice*. Set in an East L.A. Hispanic club, the owner's unhappy wife and a club musician plot to bump off the husband (Boyd). (Dir: Marcus Deleon, 92 mins.)†

Kiss Me Deadly (1955)***½ Ralph Meeker, Albert Dekker, Paul Stewart, Wesley Addy, Maxine Cooper, Cloris Leachman. One of *film noir*'s darkest nightmares, this is a grim adaptation of one of Mickey Spillane's

572

"Mike Hammer" thrillers. Meeker is Hammer, a sleazy gumshoe on the trail of "the great whatsit" (actually a box filled with a radioactive substance), who's willing to beat, berate, and otherwise abuse anyone standing in his way. Directed with stunning artistry (and tongue in cheek) by Robert Aldrich, the film has weathered critical distaste to emerge as a cult classic, a brutal and often very funny critique of Spillane's macho sensibility and the nuclear paranoia of fifties America. (105 mins.)†

KISS Meets the Phantom of the Park (MTV 1978)** Anthony Zerbe, KISS (Gene Simmons, Peter Criss, Ace Frehley, Paul Stanley). The rock group KISS are a wild bunch: one spits fire, another triggers rays from his eyes as they outwit an amusement park madman played by old reliable Zerbe. (Dir: Gordon Hessler, 104 mins.)†

Kiss Me Goodbye (1982)* Sally Field, James Caan, Jeff Bridges, Paul Dooley, Claire Trevor. Labored sex comedy about a widow who is about to remarry when the ghost of her dead husband pops up. It's a charmless remake of the Brazilian comedy *Dona Flor and Her Two Husbands*. (Dir: Robert Mulligan, 101 mins.)†

Kiss Me Kate (1953)***½ Kathryn Grayson, Howard Keel, Ann Miller. Cole Porter's delightful Broadway play is turned into a bright entertainment package with songs, dances, and comedy. The score includes the familiar "Wunderbar," "So in Love," and "Always True to You in My Fashion." The stars are perfectly cast with Ann Miller a standout in what may be her best screen role. A truly great score makes this a musical treat. (Dir: George Sidney, 109 mins.)†

Kiss Me Stupid (1964)*** Dean Martin, Ray Walston, Kim Novak, Felicia Farr, Cliff Osmond, Barbara Pepper, Doro Merande, Henry Gibson. Unfairly slammed at the time of its release, this blue comedy has slowly garnered critical favor with the passage of time. Walston is a desperate songwriter whose pitch to a leering performer may have to include lending him his wife. Farcical complications (many of them tasteless) arise. (Dir: Billy Wilder, 124 mins.)

Kiss of Death (1947)*** Victor Mature, Brian Donlevy, Richard Widmark, Mildred Dunnock, Coleen Gray. Widmark made his remarkable debut as a giggling killer. Victor Mature, as a hood who can't stay straight, and Gray, as his girl, really outdo Widmark (it's Mature's best leading performance). Still, how can you compete for attention with a grinning Widmark pushing crippled Dunnock down a flight of stairs so she won't squeal? (Dir: Henry Hathaway, 98 mins.)

Kiss of Evil (Great Britain, 1963)*** Clifford

Evans, Noel Willman. Honeymooning couple are ensnared by the owner of a chateau who turns out to be a vampire. Effective horror thriller. AKA: **Kiss of the Vampire**. (Dir: Don Sharp, 88 mins.)

Kiss of Fire (1955)**½ Jack Palance, Barbara Rush, Martha Hyer. All the ingredients of adventure are present in this fast-paced yarn about Spanish traitors, hostile Indians, rebels, renegades, and a Spanish Robin Hood named El Tigre. (Dir: Joseph Newman, 87 mins.)

Kiss of the Spider Woman (Brazil-U.S., 1985)***½ William Hurt, Raul Julia, Sonia Braga, Jose Lewgoy. A prison cell in a Latin American dictatorship houses two disparate cellmates: Julia as a left-wing journalist and Hurt as a homosexual window dresser. To draw him out, Hurt entertains Julia by re-creating stories from lurid 1940s movies. Given that over two-thirds of the film takes place within the prison cell, the fact that it never once becomes stagy or static is quite impressive. Hurt won the Oscar for Best Actor. (Dir: Hector Babenco, 119 mins.)†

Kiss of the Vampire—See: **Kiss of Evil**

Kiss Shot (MTV 1989)**½ Whoopi Goldberg, Dorian Harewood, Dennis Franz. After losing her office job, single mom Whoopi finds she can make a living as a pool shark in this comedy-drama. The story is predictable, but Whoopi lends a great deal of presence. (Dir: Jerry London, 96 mins.)

Kiss the Blood off My Hands (1948)** Burt Lancaster, Joan Fontaine, Robert Newton. Muddled melodrama about two ill-fated lovers who each commits an accidental murder for the sake of their love. Weak script and fair performances. (Dir: Norman Foster, 79 mins.)

Kiss the Boys Goodbye (1941)**½ Mary Martin, Don Ameche, Oscar Levant, Raymond Walburn, Elizabeth Patterson, Eddie "Rochester" Anderson, Connee Boswell, Virginia Dale. Typical backstage musical of battling sweethearts, an actress and a director; Hollywood didn't know what to do with Martin, and after some more middle-grade material like this, she went back to Broadway. Mildly entertaining, with an unusual chance to see Connee Boswell on her own. (Dir: Victor Schertzinger, 85 mins.)

Kiss the Girls and Make Them Die (Italy, 1966)*½ Mike Connors, Dorothy Provine, Terry-Thomas, Raf Vallone. CIA agent (Connors) after an industrialist (Vallone) with a deadly secret weapon. Tongue-in-cheek secret-agent stuff doesn't come off: a yawn. (Dir: Henry Levin, 106 mins.)

Kiss Them for Me (1957)** Cary Grant,

Jayne Mansfield, Suzy Parker. Even suave Cary Grant can't save this belabored farce about a trio of navy war heroes who arrive in San Francisco for some rest and recreation, with the accent on the latter. (Dir: Stanley Donen, 105 mins.)

Kiss the Other Sheik (Italy-France, 1965)*½ Marcello Mastroianni, Pamela Tiffin, Virna Lisi. Messy comedy composed of the last two segments from the anthology *Paranoia*. The one good plotline has Marcello and Tiffin each attempting to sell their spouse to a wealthy sheik. (Dirs: Luciano Salce, Eduardo De Filippo, 85 mins.)

Kiss Tomorrow Goodbye (1950)**½ James Cagney, Barbara Payton. Cagney is the whole show in a familiar role of an escaped convict who gets his comeuppance in the last scenes of this fast-paced drama. (Dir: Gordon Douglas, 102 mins.)†

Kitchen Toto, The (Great Britain, 1988)*** Edwin Mahinda, Bob Peck, Phyllis Logan. Well-made film set in 1950 Kenya, when British rule was under attack from Mau Mau terrorists. A young black boy finds himself shunned by both the British for whom he works and the Mau Maus who killed his father and want him to join them. Makes its points subtly but forcefully. (Dir: Harry Hook, 96 mins.)†

Kitten with a Whip (1964)** Ann-Margret, John Forsythe, Peter Brown. Juvenile delinquent gal breaks into the home of an aspiring political figure and nearly ruins his career. Sleazy bit of sensationalism. (Dir: Douglas Heyes, 83 mins.)

Kitty (1945)**½ Paulette Goddard, Ray Milland. Costume drama about a girl who rises from poverty to fame, fortune and title (set in England) by indiscreet use of her charms. Moderate entertainment. (Dir: Mitchell Leisen, 104 mins.)

Kitty and the Bagman (Australia, 1982)** Collette Mann, Liddy Clark, David Bradshaw, John Stanton, Val Lehman. A self-conscious spoof of Warner Bros. gangster films that is too long to sustain its obvious satirical flourishes. An English war bride expects her hubby to return a war hero, but instead he is a war deserter and pimp. (Dir: Donald Crombie, 95 mins.)†

Kitty Foyle (1940)** Ginger Rogers, Dennis Morgan, James Craig, Gladys Cooper, Ernest Cossart, Eduardo Ciannelli. Rogers stopped singing and dancing and started acting with a capital A and was rewarded with an Oscar. Working girl Rogers tries to choose between noble doctor Craig and Philadelphia mainliner Morgan. A whitewashed white-collar soap opera. (Dir: Sam Wood, 107 mins.)†

Kitty: Return to Auschwitz (Great Britain,

MTV 1979)**** A lacerating documentary. Focuses on a now middle-aged woman who miraculously survived the horrors of the infamous Nazi concentration camp Auschwitz in 1943 and 1944. She returns with her son to Auschwitz to try to explain what life was like for the Jewish victims and how she and her mother managed to survive. (Producer: Peter Morley, 88 mins.)†

Klansman, The (1974)½ Lee Marvin, Richard Burton, Lola Falana, O. J. Simpson, Luciana Paluzzi, Cameron Mitchell, Linda Evans. A feverish but silly potboiler about racial tensions in the big bad South. Marvin's the sheriff who's got to put a lid on the brewing hostilities after Evans gets raped and the KKK get their sheets in an uproar. AKA: **The Burning Cross.** (Dir: Terence Young, 112 mins.)

Klondike Annie (1936)*** Mae West, Victor McLaglen, Gene Austin. It wasn't often that Mae had a leading man who stood up to her. To fool the police, Mae poses as a Salvation Army lass, and those in need of a hand-out never had it so good. Wait until you hear her sing "I'm an Occidental Woman in an Oriental Mood" and watch her spar with leading man McLaglen. (Dir: Raoul Walsh, 80 mins.)

Klute (1971)**** Jane Fonda, Donald Sutherland, Charles Cioffi, Roy Scheider, Dorothy Tristan. Fonda deservedly won the Academy Award in this psychological thriller. Fonda plays a vulnerable, self-aware, middle-class call girl. Klute (Sutherland), a small-town policeman who comes to New York in search of a missing friend, meets Fonda, and falls in love with her while she's stalked by a psychotic killer. Astutely written and powerfully directed. (Dir: Alan J. Pakula, 114 mins.)†

Knack and How to Get It, The (Great Britain, 1965)***½ Rita Tushingham, Ray Brooks, Donal Donnelly, Michael Crawford. We should be grateful that director Richard Lester has completely reimagined this hit play's action in the mod terms of the time, creating an enduring comedy. Crawford is the chap who'd like to make it with the birds; his roommate Brooks is the man who has the knack. (84 mins.)†

Knickerbocker Holiday (1944)** Nelson Eddy, Charles Coburn. The famous play of Old New York, and of Peter Stuyvesant the governor, and of how love makes a fool out of him. Fine Maxwell Anderson–Kurt Weill songs—including "September Song"—but otherwise, dull, stiffly acted. (Dir: Harry Brown, 85 mins.)†

Knife, The (Netherlands, 1960)*** Ellen Vogel, Paul Bammermans, Reitze Van
574

Der Linden, Marie-Louise Videc, Mia Grossen. Thirteen-year-old boy steals valuable knife from an exhibit only to have it retrieved by his tutor. The fatherless child then steals it again in an attempt to ruin his mother's difficult affair with the tutor. Van Der Linden is superb as the boy in this tense drama told completely from the child's point of view. (Dir: Fons Rademakers, 90 mins.)

Knife in the Head (West Germany, 1978)***½ Bruno Ganz, Angela Winkler, Udo Samel, Hans Honig, Hans Brenner, Carla Egerer. Tense political thriller, with a brilliant performance by Ganz as a man whose memory is destroyed by a police bullet when he calls to pick up his politically active wife at a youth center. Devastating commentary on police-statism engages the audience in an exciting puzzle; is Ganz a terrorist or an innocent victim, and what plot is hatching in his crippled mind? (Dir: Reinhard Hauff, 113 mins.)

Knife in the Water (Poland, 1962)***½ Leon Niemczyk, Jolanta Umecka, Zygmunt Malanowicz. Director Roman Polanski's doctoral dissertation from the Polish Film School is a typical blend of sexual tension and dramatic attenuation. Some masterful confrontations and even better avoidances of confrontation. A minor official and his wife out for a country weekend pick up a hitchhiker, who picks them up. (94 mins.)†

Knightriders (1981)*** Ed Harris, Gary Lahti, Tom Savini, Amy Ingersoll. George A. Romero's grafting of the Arthurian cosmology onto the biker picture is a bold, scintillating inspiration, and in the process, he rethinks the sixties counterculture movie into contemporary terms. (Dir: George A. Romero, 146 mins.)†

Knights and Emeralds (Great Britain, 1986)*** Christopher Wild, Beverly Hills, Warren Mitchell. Winning story of cross-cultural pollination set in a small British town, where a white drummer in a marching band joins a rival black band just before a big competition. Basically an old story, but with many winning touches. (Dir: Ian Emes, 92 mins.)†

Knights of the City (1985)**½ Leon Isaac Kennedy, Nicholas Campbell. Leon plays a gang leader who rocks to the beat of a different drummer and gambles on a music contest as a way out of his violent street life. It's like "Star Search" telecast live from the concrete jungle. (Dir: Dominic Orlando, 81 mins.)†

Knights of the Round Table (1954)**½ Robert Taylor, Ava Gardner, Mel Ferrer, Stanley Baker, Felix Aylmer. MGM's first production in CinemaScope is one of their typical embalmed costumers, featuring King Arthur and the lot. (Dir: Richard Thorpe, 115 mins.)†

Knight Without Armor (Great Britain, 1937)*** Robert Donat, Marlene Dietrich. Suspense tale of couple fleeing from the Russian Revolution. Gripping, well-made Alexander Korda production. (Dir: Jacques Feyder, 107 mins.)†

K-9 (1989)*½ James Belushi, Mel Harris, Kevin Tighe, Ed O'Neill. Dedicated but independent cop Belushi is saddled with a new partner—a police dog—in this formulaic action-comedy. (Dir: Rod Daniel, 102 mins.)†

Knives of the Avenger—See: **Viking Massacre**

Knock on Any Door (1949)**½ Humphrey Bogart, John Derek, Allene Roberts. Willard Motley's frank novel about a young hood in the slums of Chicago makes a powerful motion picture. (Dir: Nicholas Ray, 100 mins.)†

Knock on Wood (1954)*** Danny Kaye, Mai Zetterling. Another treat for Danny Kaye fans. Danny's up to his neck in international adventures as a nightclub puppeteer with a penchant for getting into trouble. (Dir: Norman Panama, 103 mins.)

Knockout (1941)** Arthur Kennedy, Cornel Wilde, Anthony Quinn. Stereotyped fight picture characters combine to knock out good acting and directing. (Dir: William Clemens, 73 mins.)

Knockout, The, and **Dough and Dynamite** (1914)*** Charlie Chaplin, Fatty Arbuckle, Mabel Normand, Syd Chaplin, Mack Sennett, Charlie Chase, Mack Swain. Videocassette features two classic shorts made by Chaplin at Keystone Studios at the time when he was gaining his great fame; *The Knockout* actually stars Arbuckle, with Chaplin in a supporting role as a boxing referee; *Dough and Dynamite* is a knockabout farce directed by Charlie's brother, Syd Chaplin, and has Charlie in charge of a bakery with slapstick results. Not just historically interesting, but riotously funny. (72 mins.)†

Knute Rockne—All American (1940)*** Pat O'Brien, Ronald Reagan, Gale Page, Donald Crisp. Good biography of the Notre Dame football coach, which contains that now immortal movie line, "Go in there and win it for the Gipper." One of the best football films glorifying the old college try. (Dir: Lloyd Bacon, 98 mins.)†

Kojak: The Belarus File (MTV 1985)*** Telly Savalas, Suzanne Pleshette, Max von Sydow, George Savalas. The case involves Nazi war criminals and a series of murders of old Russian immigrants. (Dir: Robert Markowitz, 104 mins.)

Kojak: The Price of Justice (MTV 1987)*** Telly Savalas, Kate Nelligan, Pat Hingle, Brian Murray, Candace Savalas. The story (suggested by a true case and based on the book *The Investigation*, by Dorothy Uhnak), about a woman accused of killing her young sons, is absorbing. (Dir: Alan Metzger, 104 mins.)

Koko—A Talking Gorilla (1978)*** Fascinating documentary about Koko, the female gorilla who had been taught to communicate through sign language. Film explores importance of the discovery and even gives some sense of Koko's own emotions. (Dir: Barbet Schroeder, 85 mins.)

Kona Coast (1968)**½ Joan Blondell, Richard Boone, Vera Miles, Steve Ihnat, Chips Rafferty, Kent Smith. Boone plays a seaman investigating the death of his teenaged daughter. (Dir: Lamont Johnson, 93 mins.)

Konga (Great Britain, 1961)** Michael Gough, Margo Johns. Mad scientist turns a small chimp into a murdering huge gorilla monster. (Dir: John Lemont, 90 mins.)

Kongo (1932)*** Walter Huston, Virginia Bruce, Lupe Velez, Conrad Nagel. Dark, bizarre melodrama with a powerful performance by Huston as the maddened ruler of a remote African outpost seeking revenge on his enemy by kidnapping his daughter (Bruce). Huston lifts it completely out of the ordinary with the depth of his performance. (Dir: William Cowen, 86 mins.)

Kon-Tiki (1951)***½ Excellent documentary of the Thor Heyerdahl expedition, covering 4,300 miles in a raft to the Polynesian Islands. (Dir: Thor Heyerdahl, 73 mins.)

Korczak (Poland, 1991)***½ Wojtek Pszoniak, Ewa Dalkowska, Piotr Kozlowski. Powerful true story, shot in black and white, is a tribute to Janusz Korczak, a Jewish doctor so dedicated to his 200 orphans in the Warsaw ghetto that he chose the Nazis' gas chamber rather than leave the orphans alone to die. Director Wajda incorporates actual Holocaust footage, which adds to the documentary look of the film. Straightforward storytelling will tear at the heart, as a reminder of man's inhumanity to man. (Dir: Andrzej Wajda, 113 mins.)

Koroshi (MTV 1966)** Patrick McGoohan, Yoko Tani. Actually two episodes of the TV series "Secret Agent." Drake, the agent from British Security, is dispatched to Tokyo to get to the bottom of a mystery involving a planned assassination of a UN dignitary. (Dirs: Peter Yates, Michael Truman, 93 mins.)

Kotch (1971)**½ Walter Matthau, Deborah Winters, Felicia Farr. Comedy-drama about an over-70 widower who can't live with his son and daughter-in-law and keep his sanity. He sets out to live his remaining time as a sort of overgrown boy scout, helping out a pregnant teenager. (Dir: Jack Lemmon, 114 mins.)†

Koumiko Mystery, The*** When Chris Marker, noted for unusual documentary views of cities and people, travelled to Tokyo in 1964 to shoot a film about the Olympic Games, he digressed from his game plan and ended up with this unique view of the Japanese people as seen through the eyes of a local girl, a different and mysterious kind of tour guide. (45 mins.)

Koyaanisqatsi (1983)**** Best seen on the big screen, this dazzling documentary journeys across America in search of unusual topography and interesting structures, and films them in a highly personal, avant-garde way. A sort of cinematographic light show of the U.S., given tone by a memorable Philip Glass score. Followed by *Powaqqatsi*. (Dir: Godfrey Reggio, 87 mins.)†

Krakatoa—East of Java (1969)** Maximilian Schell, Diane Baker, Brian Keith, Rossano Brazzi, Sal Mineo, Geoffrey Holder. About the huge volcanic explosion in 1883. They didn't find out that Krakatoa is *west* of Java until the advance publicity was out. Wrong-way script and direction, too. AKA: *Volcano*. (Dir: Bernard Kowalski, 135 mins.)

Kramer vs. Kramer (1979)**** Dustin Hoffman, Jane Alexander, Meryl Streep, Justin Henry. Director Robert Benton has astutely adapted Avery Corman's novel about an advertising man who discovers what child raising means after his wife leaves them. Benton's direction is fluid and he elicits extraordinary performances from the cast. The film has problems resolving the plot, but its char acter truths are persuasive. (105 mins.)

Krays, The (Great Britain, 1990)*** Gary Kemp, Martin Kemp, Billy Whitelaw, Kate Hardie, Gary Love, Susan Fleetwood, Tom Bell, Charlotte Cornwall. Based on the true exploits of twin gangster brothers in the '60s "Swinging London." This richly produced film ably details the maternal obsession, violence, filial devotion, power, and homosexuality of the Krays, who, when asked at the height of their fame if they knew the Beatles, replied: "They know us." Well acted, especially by the Kemp brothers as the Krays, and Whitelaw as their doting mum. (Dir: Peter Medak, 119 mins.)†

Kremlin Letter, The (1970)*** George Sanders, Max von Sydow, Bibi Andersson, Orson Welles, Patrick O'Neal. This picture seemed so despairing when it came out that critics sorely underrated it. The letter of the title is sent by a U.S. official to the U.S.S.R. and proposes the annihilation of China. (Dir: John Huston, 116 mins.)

Kronos (1957)*½ Jeff Morrow, Barbara Lawrence. Poorly made science-fiction thriller featuring the usual interplanetary monster destroyed in time for the kiddies to go to bed and have nightmares. (Dir: Kurt Neumann, 78 mins.)†

Krull (1983)** Ken Marshall, Lysette Anthony, Francesca Annis, Freddie Jones. Another sci-fi, medieval, sword and scorcery mish-mash in which our young hero Prince Colwyn (Marshall) dashes off to save his bride-to-be (Anthony), being held captive by an evil beast on the planet Krull. (Dir: Peter Yates, 126 mins.)†

Krush Groove (1985)* Blair Underwood, Sheila E., The Fat Boys, Kurtis Blow. Fanciers of rap records may enjoy the continuous concert numbers by the cast, but most audience members will be stupefied by the malnourished screenplay about a struggling record company and annoyed by the nonstop, pumped-up energy celebrating the brotherhood of man. A rotten rap-sody. (Dir: Michael Schultz, 95 mins.)†

Kung Fu (MTV 1972)*** David Carradine. The pilot film for the popular western TV series. Carradine stars as a Chinese-American priest trained in discipline, humility, perception, and the art of karate-judo. (Dir: Jerry Thorpe, 75 mins.)†

Kung Fu: The Movie (MTV 1986)**½ David Carradine, Kerrie Keane, Mako. After an eleven-year absence, Carradine, playing a Chinese-American priest with his graceful balletlike martial arts moves, returns to the 1890s for a fight to the death with an Oriental assassin portrayed by Bruce Lee's son Brandon. (Dir: Richard Long, 104 mins.)

Kung Fu Master! (France, 1987)**½ Jane Birkin, Mathieu Demy, Charlotte Gainsbourg, Lou Doillon. A forty-year-old divorcee falls inexplicably in love with a fifteen-year-old friend. Drama is neither exploitative nor a reverse version of *Lolita;* unfortunately, it's not much of anything else, either. Odd title refers to the boy's favorite video game; retitling it *Le Petit Amour* for video should help video store clerks get it in the right aisle. (Dir: Agnes Varda, 80 mins.)†

Kwaidan (Japan, 1964)*** Michiko Aratama, Keiko Kishi, Tasuyai Nakadai. Superb anthology of ghost stories based on Lafcadio Hearn tales. (Dir: Masaki Kobayashi, 164 mins.)†

La Balance (France, 1982)*** Nathalie Baye, Philippe Leotard. Entertaining gangster melodrama with a French twist. When a stoolie is killed, the police find another candidate, a part-time pimp aided by his prostitute-girlfriend, memorably played by Baye. The machinations of the cops and the underworld in gaining the upper hand makes this an atmospheric cops and robbers film. (Dir: Bob Swain, 102 mins.)†

La Bamba (1987)** Lou Diamond Phillips, Esai Morales, Rosana De Soto, Elizabeth Pena. Fans of vintage fifties music will want to catch this biopic about Ritchie Valens, the talented young performer whose lifelong fear of flying foreshadowed his tragic death in a plane crash with Buddy Holly. Unfortunately, the show-biz clichés fly fast and furious. (Dir: Luis Valdez, 106 mins.)†

La Belle Americaine (France, 1961)*** Robert Dhery, Colette Brosset. Enjoyable comedy about an American automobile, and its meaning to an average Frenchman. (Dir: Robert Dhery, 100 mins.)

La Bete Humaine (France, 1938)*** Jean Gabin, Simone Simon. Based on the Zola novel, this Renoir movie was later Americanized and remade as *Human Desire* by Fritz Lang. A train engineer is smitten with the young wife of a stationmaster. When he spots her and her hubby bump off someone, he blackmails them. (Dir: Jean Renoir, 105 mins.)†

La Boum (France, 1981)*** Claude Brasseur, Brigitte Fossey, Sophie Marceau, Denise Grey. Wry, perceptive French comedy about a teenager (Marceau) coming of age while her parents (Brasseur and Fossey) drift apart. A film remarkably sensitive to the points of view of three different generations. (Dir: Claude Pinoteau, 100 mins.)†

L.A. Bounty (1989)*** Sybil Danning, Wings Hauser, Henry Darrow, Lenore Kasdorf, Robert Quarry. "B" movie queen Danning plays a bounty hunter out to avenge the murder of her partner in this surprisingly well-made thriller about drug-smuggling psychos. Hauser's delirious performance as whacked-out killer is unforgettable. (Dir: Worth Keeter, 85 mins.)†

Labyrinth (1986)**½ David Bowie, Jennifer Connelly, Shelley Thompson, Christopher Malcolm. Mildly entertaining, heavy-handed fantasy feature by Muppets creator, Jim Henson. The story concerns a teenage girl, Sarah (Connelly), whose baby brother is kidnapped by goblins and held captive by their king, Jereth (Bowie). The baby is in a castle at the end of a labyrinth, a bewildering maze Sarah must travel through in order to save the child. (Dir: Jim Henson, 101 mins.)†

La Cage Aux Folles (France, 1979)**** Ugo Tognazzi, Michel Serrault. The leads play a happily settled gay couple that is forced to pass as straight when Tognazzi's son, from a previous moment of heterosexual abandon, brings home his prospective in-laws. There are moments that are excruciatingly funny, and one or two others that are genuinely heartbreaking. One of the most successful foreign-language films ever at American box offices. (Dir: Edouard Molinaro, 110 mins.)†

La Cage Aux Folles II (France, 1981)*** Michel Serrault, Ugo Tognazzi, Marcel Bozzuffi, Michel Galabru. The inspired lunacy of the first *La Cage* is turned into a caper film with fairly hilarious results. This time out, the very odd couple gets involved with gangsters, spies, and the police. (Dir: Edouard Molinaro, 101 mins.)†

La Cage Aux Folles III: The Wedding (France, 1986)** Michel Serrault, Ugo Tognazzi, Stéphane Audran, Michel Galabru, Benny Luke. A spirited jab at the funny bone that doesn't manage to surpass its two predecessors. The joy of watching the two leads enlivens this farce about a gay couple who will inherit a fortune if drag queen Albin can marry and produce an heir to validate his claim. (Dir: George Lautner, 87 mins.)†

Lace (MTV 1984)** Bess Armstrong, Phoebe Cates, Brooke Adams, Arielle Dombasle, Angela Lansbury, Anthony Higgins, Herbert Lom, Honor Blackman. Lacey trash about a young sex siren, who approaches her search for her true parentage as an exercise in revenge against whomever abandoned her. The mystery as to which of these women is the girl's mother is feeble to the core, but the entire production, particularly the stylishly dressed Ms. Cates, is pleasing to the eye. (Dir: Billy Hale, 208 mins.)

Lace 2 (MTV 1985)** Phoebe Cates, Brooke Adams, Arielle Dombasle, Anthony Higgins, Deborah Raffin, Christopher Cazenove, James Read. Remember how last time Cates asked "Which one of you bitches is my mother?" Now the world-famous, but parentally deprived miss is looking for a papa. (Dir: Billy Hale, 208 mins.)

Lacemaker, The (France-Switzerland-W. Germany, 1978)***½ Isabelle Huppert, Florence Giorgetti, Yves Beneyton. This touching film illustrates the personality and class differences between a young beautician and a university student she meets on vacation. The inarticulate but affectionate girl and the articulate but neurotic boy represent two very different aspects of French bourgeois life. (Dir: Claude Goretta, 108 mins.)†

La Chevre (France, 1983)*** Pierre Richard, Gerard Depardieu, Corynne Charbit, Michel Robin. Laugh-getting farce about a rich girl's disappearance and the bumbling accountant who's dispatched to bring her back. Joining in the hubbub is a detective who finds, to his chagrin, that clumsiness is contagious. (Dir: Francis Veber, 91 mins.)†

La Chienne (France, 1931)***½ Michel Simon, George Flament, Jean Gehret, Janie Marèze. Melodrama about unassuming clerk, with a dreary job and worse marriage, who gets involved with a heartless prostitute, turning to embezzlement to support her. Director Jean Renoir's early use of direct sound and location filming in the streets of Paris adds to the excellence of the film. Remade as *Scarlet Street*. (100 mins.)†

La Chinoise (France, 1967)**** Anne Wiazemsky, Jean-Pierre Léaud, Francis Jeanson. The brilliant Jean-Luc Godard turns out one of his most stimulating films—one of the times when his genius for movie making meshes perfectly with the ideas he is expressing. This is a film about *ideas*, mostly those of a group of anarchic Maoist students in Paris. (95 mins.)

La Cicada—See: **Cricket, The**

La Collectionneuse (France, 1967)*** Patrick Bauchau, Haydee Politoff, Daniel Pommerulle. The third of Eric Rohmer's *Six Moral Tales* was made before both *My Night at Maud's* and *Claire's Knee*. "La Collectionneuse" is the young Haydee, who sleeps around but never at home with the two intellectual prigs whom she lives with. (Dir: Eric Rohmer, 88 mins.)

Lacombe, Lucien (France, 1974)***½ Pierre Blaise, Aurore Clement, Holger Lowenadler, Therese Giehse. A young peasant is turned down for Resistance activities and falls in with Fascists. A disturbing examination of how easy it may be to be seduced by an ideology. (Dir: Louis Malle, 137 mins.)

L.A. Crackdown (1988)*½ Pamela Dixon, Tricia Parks, Kita Harrison, Jeffrey Olson, Michael Coon. Tough policewoman Dixon tries to save street girls from the horrors of drugs and prostitution. When she loses two to the streets, she seeks revenge on the dealers and pimps she holds responsible. Cheap exploitation pretending to have a social conscience. (Dir: Joseph Merhi, 84 mins.)†

L.A. Crackdown II (1988)*½ Pamela Dixon, Anthony Gates, Joe Vance, Cynthia Miguel, Lisa Anderson, Bo Sabato. Policewoman Dixon has a partner this time, but otherwise its more of the same as they stalk a serial killer who's murdering prostitutes. (Dir: Joseph Merhi, 87 mins.)†

Lacy and the Mississippi Queen (MTV 1978)*½ Debra Feuer, Kathleen Lloyd, Edward Andrews, Jack Elam, Christopher Lloyd, James Keach, Alvy Moore. Two sisters team up to avenge their father's murder in this lame western spoof, an unsold series pilot. (Dir: Robert Butler, 72 mins.)

Lad: A Dog (1962)** Peter Breck, Peggy

McCay, Angela Cartwright. How a collie brings love to a crippled girl, and various other saccharine ingredients. For canine lovers and impressionable youngsters exclusively. (Dirs: Leslie H. Martinson, Aram Avakian, 98 mins.)

L'Addition (France, 1985)** Farid Chopel, Fabrice Eberhard, Victoria Abril, Richard Bohringer, Richard Berry. One of those curiously French exercises in crime chic, with S&M trimmings. An actor becomes involved in a scuffle involving a beautiful mademoiselle, goes to jail, becomes innocently mixed up in a prison break, cripples a prison guard and must then play cat and mouse with this vindictive jailer. AKA: **The Caged Heart** and **The Patsy**. (Dir: Denis Amar, 93 mins.)†

Ladies, The (MTV 1987)**½ Patricia Elliott, Talia Balsam, Robert Webber. A rattled mom, facing divorce, moves in with her independent daughter (Balsam). Light comedy that never takes off, but some moments do hit home. Filmed in 1983. (Dir: Jackie Cooper, 96 mins.)

Ladies and Gentlemen, The Fabulous Stains (1981)** Diane Lane, Ray Winstone, John "Fee" Waybill, Christine Lahti, Laura Dern, Paul Simonon, Paul Cook, Steve Jones. Off-key look at the rock world has Lane and her group "The Stains" becoming an overnight sensation as the result of well-timed publicity maneuvers and a philosophy of not putting out. Directed by ex-record producer Lou Adler. (87 mins.)

Ladies Club, The (1986)*½ Karen Austin, Diana Scarwid, Christine Belford, Bruce Davison, Shera Danese, Arliss Howard. An exploitation melodrama with uncommon brutality and a quasi-feminist twist: A group of rape victims kidnap and castrate various attackers. Carries a certain lurid fascination for revenge fantasists, but that's about it. (Dir: A. K. Allen, 90 mins.)†

Ladies Courageous (1944)**½ Loretta Young, Geraldine Fitzgerald, Evelyn Ankers, Ruth Roman, Anne Gwynne, Diana Barrymore, Frank Jenks, Philip Terry. Young manages to be incredibly chic in uniform in this fairly engrossing story of the WAFs who piloted bombers overseas for delivery to battle areas during WWII; an unusual look at women's essential combat support services during WWII. (Dir: John Rawlins, 88 mins.)

Ladies In Love (1936)**½ Janet Gaynor, Loretta Young, Simone Simon. Overly romantic tale of the affairs of four girls in Budapest. (Dir: Edward H. Griffith, 97 mins.)

Ladies in Retirement (1941)***½ Ida Lupino, Louis Hayward, Evelyn Keyes. Housekeeper kills her employer to save

578

her sisters from being put in an asylum. Gripping suspense drama, excellently acted. (Dir: Charles Vidor, 92 mins.)

Ladies' Man (1931)**½ William Powell, Kay Francis, Carole Lombard, Olive Tell. Interesting, unusual pre-Production Code romantic melodrama of a gigolo trying to reform; another good teaming of Powell and Francis, with Lombard in a secondary role. Sensitively acted. (Dir: Lothar Mendes, 70 mins.)

Ladies' Man, The (1961)**½ Jerry Lewis, Helen Traubel, Pat Stanley. Jerry as a confirmed bachelor who gets a job in a girls' boarding house. This comedy begins like a riot, but soon slows down considerably. (Dir: Jerry Lewis, 106 mins.)†

Ladies of Leisure (1930)**½ Barbara Stanwyck, Ralph Graves, Lowell Sherman, Marie Prevost. In the early thirties, Capra managed to bring out a vulnerable, radiant quality in Stanwyck that was often missing from her later performances. Once again, Stanwyck sparkles as a dame who's trying to salvage her love life after her shady past starts to catch up with her. (Dir: Frank Capra, 98 mins.)

Ladies of the Big House (1931)**½ Sylvia Sidney, Wynne Gibson, Louise Beavers, Jane Darwell, Gene Raymond. Women in prison, '30s style, with Sidney as an innocent girl convicted of a crime she didn't commit. Good supporting players make this better than average. (Dir: Marion Gering, 76 mins.)

Ladies of the Chorus (1949)**½ Adele Jergens, Marilyn Monroe. Former burlesque queen sees her daughter become a star. Marilyn's first big chance. (Dir: Phil Karlson, 61 mins.)

Ladies on the Rocks (Denmark, 1983)*** Annemarie Helger, Helle Ryslinge, Flemming Quist Moller, Hans Henrik Clemmensen, Aksel Erhaedsen, Gyda Hansen. A lightly comic, gently feminist road movie features two average women who tour Denmark performing a bawdy, satirical cabaret act. Filled with telling details about the lonely tackiness of showbiz life on the road. (Dir: Christian Brad Thomsen, 100 mins.)

Ladies Should Listen (1934)** Cary Grant, Frances Drake, Edward Everett Horton. Mild, unsubtle comedy has a telephone operator falling love with a client; Grant is fine, but comedy wasn't Drake's forte. Nothing special. (Dir: Frank Tuttle, 62 mins.)

Ladies They Talk About (1933)**½ Barbara Stanwyck, Preston Foster, Lyle Talbot. Women-behind-bars picture redeemed by Stanwyck and a good supporting cast. A pre-production code comedy-melodrama that was frank enough to attract the watchful eye of the Hays office. (Dir: Howard Bretherton, 68 mins.)

Ladies Who Do (Great Britain, 1963)** Robert Morley, Peggy Mount, Harry H. Corbett. Rather dawdling comedy about a cleaning woman who begins to make her mark on the Stock Exchange, quite by chance. Amusing, thanks to the players, but seldom rises to any great heights. (Dir: C. M. Pennington-Richards, 85 mins.)

La Dolce Vita (Italy, 1960)**** Marcello Mastroianni, Anita Ekberg, Yvonne Furneaux, Anouk Aimee, Lex Barker, Annibale Nincni, Alain Cuny. Federico Fellini's lengthy account of a reporter's encounter with the "sweet life," and the unhappy people who lead it. Takes place over a seven-day period (a decisive one in the reporter's life), offering us an unflinching view of the emptiness brought on by riches and fame. A masterful meditation on a specific era in our history, and the horrific changes that era ushered in. (180 mins.)†

Lady and the Highwayman, The (MTV 1989)**½ Lysette Anthony, Emma Samms, Hugh Grant, Michael York, Oliver Reed, Claire Bloom, John Mills. Handsome costume epic based on a Barbara Cartland novel. A lady falls in love with a lord posing as a highwayman, becoming a pawn in political intrigue. Fun for fans of this type of escapism. (Dir: John Hough, 96 mins.)

Lady and the Mob (1939)*** Ida Lupino, Fay Bainter, Lee Bowman. Wealthy old eccentric takes harsh steps to rid her town of racketeers. Frequently funny comedy. (Dir: Ben Stoloff, 70 mins.)

Lady and the Monster, The (1944)** Vera Ralston, Erich von Stroheim, Richard Arlen, Sidney Blackmer. Another precursor to *Donovan's Brain.* A scientist fiddles with nature and ends up the pawn of a powerful living brain. A bit balmy, but watchable. (Dir: George Sherman, 86 mins.)

Lady and the Outlaw, The (1973)**½ Desi Arnaz, Jr., Gregory Peck. Offbeat western drama casts Arnaz as a half-breed who teams up with a bearded Scotsman (Peck, behind that beard and Scottish brogue) to pull a robbery which ends up in murder. (Dir: Ted Kotcheff, 80 mins.)

Lady and the Tramp (1955)**** Disney goes to the dogs, and the results are delightful. Feeling neglected after a new baby arrives in her master's household, pedigreed Lady runs away and encounters Tramp, a stray who lives by his wits. Against all odds, the star-crossed pooches survive a dogcatcher and a meddling spinster aunt, and save the day by rescuing the baby in this colorful, down-to-earth cartoon with wonderful songs by Peggy Lee and Sonny Burke. (Dirs: Hamilton Luske, Clyde Geronimi, Wildred Jackson, 75 mins.)†

Lady Be Good (1941)*** Eleanor Powell, Robert Young, Red Skelton, Ann Sothern. Gershwin score, a fine cast and a good production add up to better-than-average screen entertainment in this musical about a boy and girl songwriting team. (Dir: Norman Z. McLeod, 111 mins.)

Lady Beware (1987)**½ Diane Lane, Michael Woods, Cotter Smith. Kinky window dresser Lane gets maniacally pursued by psycho-gynecologist Woods in this impeccably fashioned sleaze picture that has pretentions toward being a tale of feminist rage. There are a number of deliciously oddball plot twists, all distinguished by dialogue to howl over. (Dir: Karen Arthur, 108 mins.)†

Lady Blue (MTV 1985)*½ Jamie Rose, Danny Aiello, Tony LoBianco, Bibi Besch, Jim Brown. Jamie Rose plays Katy Mahoney, a savvy police detective who uses her good looks to penetrate assorted criminal nests. This series pilot finds Katy enmeshed in a crusade to erase the allegations attached to a murdered associate. (Dir: Gary Nelson, 104 mins.)

Lady by Choice (1934)**½ Carole Lombard, May Robson, Roger Pryor. Lombard plays a publicity-mad dancer who attempts to convert old sot Robson into a model of motherly respectability. (Dir: David Burton, 78 mins.)

Lady Caroline Lamb (Great Britain-Italy, 1972)*½ Sarah Miles, Jon Finch, Richard Chamberlain, Laurence Olivier. Misguided, melodramatic attempt at portraying the story of Caroline Lamb, who had a brief, two-month affair with the poet Lord Byron. (Dir: Robert Bolt, 123 mins.)†

Lady Chatterley's Lover (Great Britain-France, 1982)**½ Sylvia Kristel, Shane Briant, Nicholas Clay. A detached and subdued adaptation of the D. H. Lawrence novel about a woman whose husband returns from the World War, paralyzed from the waist down and her subsequent search for sexual fulfillment and liberation. (Dir: Just Jaeckin, 101 mins.)†

Lady Consents, The (1936)**½ Ann Harding, Herbert Marshall, Margaret Lindsay, Walter Abel. Neat domestic comedy with good performances about a divorced couple who change their minds; not extraordinary, but fun. (Dir: Stephen Roberts, 75 mins.)

Lady Dances, The—See: **Merry Widow, The** (1934)

Lady Eve, The (1941)**** Barbara Stanwyck, Henry Fonda, Charles Coburn, William Demarest, Eugene Pallette, Eric Blore. Preston Sturges was the best comedy director of the forties and he was equally good at light romance, satire, slapstick, and even a stray serious moment. This is one of the finest of romantic comedies. Fonda is a beer heir
580

who is interested in snakes; Stanwyck is a gold digger who is interested in Fonda. A honey all the way. (97 mins.)†

Lady for a Day (1933)***½ May Robson, Warren William. Poor apple peddler lets her daughter think she is wealthy. Frank Capra's direction gets a lot of mileage out of this old tearjerker. Remade as *Pocketful of Miracles.* (88 mins.)†

Lady for a Night (1941)** John Wayne, Joan Blondell. The lady owner of a Mississippi gambling boat is accused of murdering a wealthy socialite. Slow, corny costume drama. (Dir: Leigh Jason, 87 mins.)†

Lady Frankenstein (Italy, 1971)* Joseph Cotten, Mickey Hargitay, Sarah Bey, Paul Muller. Brain transplantation mixes with kinky sex as the Doc's daughter commits bloody atrocities in her quest for a good time in the sack. (Dir: Mel Welles, 84 mins.)†

Lady from Cheyenne (1941)**½ Loretta Young, Robert Preston, Edward Arnold, Frank Craven, Gladys George. Sturdy vehicle for Young as a feisty schoolmarm making her way in a man's world and not taking any guff from frontier chauvinists. (Dir: Frank Lloyd, 87 mins.)

Lady from Shanghai (1948)*** Rita Hayworth, Orson Welles, Everett Sloane, Glenn Anders. Irish sailor accompanies a beautiful woman and her lawyer husband on a cruise and becomes a pawn in murder. Melodrama is saved by Welles's direction, turning it into a one-of-a-kind thriller. Featuring the famous shoot-out in a room of mirrors. (Dir: Orson Welles, 87 mins.)†

Lady from Texas (1951)**½ Josephine Hull, Howard Duff, Mona Freeman. Miss Hull's special brand of whimsy is wasted on this yarn about an eccentric old lady who turns a whole town upside down, but the film itself is pleasant. Her last film. (Dir: Joseph Pevney, 77 mins.)

Lady from Yesterday, The (MTV 1985)** Wayne Rogers, Bonnie Bedelia, Pat Hingle, Barrie Youngfellow, Tina Chen, Blue Deckert. Tedious domestic drama about post-Vietnam entanglements. A man hears from his wartime Saigon mistress, who wants him to adopt the ten-year-old son he's never seen. Superb performance by Bedelia. (Dir: Robert Day, 104 mins.)

Lady Gambles, The (1949)**½ Barbara Stanwyck, Robert Preston, Stephen McNally. Miss Stanwyck gives a good performance in this melodrama about a woman deeply caught in a compulsive trap of gambling. (Dir: Michael Gordon, 99 mins.)

Lady Godiva (1955)** Maureen O'Hara, George Nader. Normans and Saxons are at each other's throats while history gets a bit of a reshuffling in this familiar tale of adventure. Don't expect too much from Lady Godiva's famous ride. (Dir: Arthur Lubin, 89 mins.)

Lady Godiva Rides Again (Great Britain, 1951)*** Diana Dors, Alastair Sim, George Cole, Dennis Price, Stanley Holloway. Very enjoyable comedy stars the lovely Dors, then a buxom starlet, as a country girl who wins a beauty contest, with terrific supporting players stealing every scene from each other. One of the better British farces of the '50s. (Dir: Frank Launder, 90 mins.)

Lady Has Plans (1942)** Paulette Goddard, Ray Milland. Spy story is comedy-drama and not outstanding in either department. Paulette is mistaken for a tattooed woman spy when she comes to neutral Lisbon and is immediately pursued by all sides. (Dir: Sidney Lanfield, 77 mins.)

Ladyhawke (1985)*** Matthew Broderick, Rutger Hauer, Michelle Pfeiffer. Splendid medieval fantasy about a young thief who meets a knight and his lover afflicted with a strange curse which turns him into a wolf by night, and her into a hawk by day. Things get bogged down in the middle, but the movie is exciting and gorgeously photographed by Vittorio Storaro. (Dir: Richard Donner, 121 mins.)†

Lady in a Cage (1964)** Olivia de Havilland, James Caan, Ann Sothern, Jennifer Billingsley, Jeff Corey. Drama about young toughs who keep a woman (de Havilland) trapped in an elevator while they ransack her apartment. (Dir: Walter Grauman, 97 mins.)†

Lady in a Jam (1942)** Irene Dunne, Ralph Bellamy, Patric Knowles. Daffy comedy about a crazy mixed-up heiress and her love life, especially her love for her psychiatrist. (Dir: Gregory La Cava, 78 mins.)

Lady in Cement (1968)*½ Frank Sinatra, Raquel Welch, Dan Blocker, Richard Conte, Lainie Kazan, Martin Gabel. Frank Sinatra returns as private eye Tony Rome, sleuthing out the mystery of the pretty gal discovered lodged at the bottom of the sea. (Dir: Gordon Douglas, 93 mins.)†

Lady in Distress (Great Britain, 1939)*** Paul Lukas, Michael Redgrave, Sally Gray. Happily married man brings on trouble when he meets a magician's lovely assistant. (Dir: Herbert Mason, 76 mins.)

Lady in Question, The (1940)**½ Brian Aherne, Rita Hayworth, Glenn Ford, Irene Rich, George Coulouris, Lloyd Corrigan, Evelyn Keyes. Son of a Parisian shopkeeper falls in love with the young woman with a secret past whom his father is helping out. Hayworth and Ford's first screen teaming is a remake of the French *Heart of Paris*, with the melodramatic elements softened up. (Dir: Charles Vidor, 81 mins.)†

Lady in Red, The (1979)** Pamela Sue Martin, Robert Conrad, Louise Fletcher, Christopher Lloyd. A sordid biopic about John Dillinger's gun moll. Bloody shootouts follow breathy sex as the very cheap woman of the title discovers the exploitative price of crime. Written by John Sayles. (Dir: Lewis Teague, 93 mins.)

Lady in the Car with Glasses and a Gun, The (U.S.-France, 1970)*** Samantha Eggar, Oliver Reed, John McEnery, Stephane Audran. Better than average suspense as secretary Samantha Eggar takes her boss's car for a holiday in the Mediterranean, oddly retracing a journey she has not taken, and is recognized by people she has not met before. When a body turns up in her trunk, things get serious. (Dir: Anatole Litvak, 105 mins.)

Lady in the Dark (1944)** Ginger Rogers, Ray Milland, Jon Hall, Warner Baxter, Barry Sullivan, Gail Russell, Mischa Auer. Overblown film version of a critically acclaimed but pretentious musical. Relying on grand lady mannerisms, Rogers is a career exec undergoing psychoanalysis as she tries to decide between three men in her life. (Dir: Mitchell Leisen, 100 mins.)

Lady in the Iron Mask (1952)** Louis Hayward, Patricia Medina, John Sutton, Steve Brodie, Alan Hale, Jr. Princess is kept a prisoner locked in an iron mask, so her twin sister will inherit the throne. Usual sort of costume melodrama. (Dir: Ralph Murphy, 78 mins.)

Lady in the Lake (1946)***½ Robert Montgomery, Audrey Trotter, Lloyd Nolan. Just a routine Phillip Marlowe mystery but Montgomery as director experimented by having the audience follow the picture with the hero and the result is good off-beat entertainment. (103 mins.)†

Lady in the Morgue (1938)*** Preston Foster, Frank Jenks. Clever mystery. The body of a beautiful woman disappears from the morgue, and private eye Bill Crane has a heck of a time with gals and gangsters before solving the case. (Dir: Otis Garrett, 80 mins.)

Lady in White (1988)**½ Lukas Haas, Alex Rocco, Len Cariou, Katherine Helmond. Stylish, evocative, but way too long supernatural mystery in which a young boy encounters the ghost of a murdered girl and sets out to solve the crime. Writer-director LaLoggia creates strong atmosphere but goes for nuance and detail at the expense of a compact narrative. (Dir: Frank LaLoggia, 112 mins.)†

Lady Is Willing, The (1942)*** Marlene Dietrich, Fred MacMurray, Aline MacMahon. Broadway star arranges a marriage of convenience with a baby doctor so she can adopt a child. Nicely done drama. (Dir: Mitchell Leisen, 92 mins.)

Lady Jane (Great Britain, 1986)*** Helena Bonham Carter, Cary Elwes, John Wood, Michael Hordern, Jane Laportaire, Sara Kestelman, Patrick Stewart. Expertly produced costume drama that serves up a compelling history lesson about Lady Jane Grey and her husband, who enjoyed a nine-day idealistic reign as King and Queen of England before being beheaded. The film's strong suit is its portrayal of the shifting political fortunes and the infighting on which kingdoms may rise and fall. (Dir: Trevor Nunn, 144 mins.)†

Lady Killer (1933)**½ James Cagney, Margaret Lindsay, Mae Clarke, Leslie Fenton, Henry O'Neill. Fast-paced, racy, pre-Code showbiz/gangster film, with Cagney a hood on the lam who is discovered in Hollywood and becomes a star, only to have his former cronies turn up to blackmail him. Played for laughs rather than melodrama, with plenty of sly movie "in" jokes, and a terrific performance by Clarke as a wisecracking moll. (Dir: Roy Del Ruth, 74 mins.)

Ladykiller of Rome, The (Italy, 1961)*** Marcello Mastroianni, Salvo Randone, Micheline Presle, Andrea Checchi. Director Elio Petri's first film is a thrilling look at faulty police work and corruption as a successful antique dealer is wrongly accused of murder. Mastroianni expertly captures the irony and tragedy of this carefully plotted film. AKA: **The Assassin.** (105 mins.)

Ladykillers, The (Great Britain, 1955)**** Alec Guinness, Cecil Parker, Peter Sellers. Menacingly funny, with a sharp script by William Rose and well-keyed direction by Alexander Mackendrick. Black comedy about a gang of cutthroats undone by the sweet obtuseness of a sly little old lady. (94 mins.)†

Lady L (U.S.-Italy-France, 1965)*** Sophia Loren, Paul Newman, David Niven. Sumptuous settings and Loren and her male co-stars help shore up this lightweight saga of a laundress who works her way up to a title through a series of wacky misadventures. (Dir: Peter Ustinov, 107 mins.)

Lady Liberty (Italy-France, 1971)* Sophia Loren, William Devane, Luigi Proietti. Terrible comedy, would have been even worse in the hands of less capable players. Loren's an Italian bride-to-be who arrives in New York with a mortadella sausage for her bridegroom, but cannot get clearance from customs. (Dir: Mario Monicelli, 95 mins.)

Lady Luck (1946)*** Robert Young, Barbara Hale, Frank Morgan. Nice girl tries to tame a high-rolling gambler by marrying him. Good comedy-drama, well made and satisfying. (Dir: Edwin L. Marin, 97 mins.)

Lady Mobster (MTV 1988)** Susan Lucci, Michael Nader, Roscoe Born, Joseph Wiseman. Predictable, tawdry, silly, and highly watchable. Lucci, daytime's biggest star, goes prime time with this opus about the Mafia and revenge. Susan is taken in by a Mafia boss when her parents are killed. She becomes a high-powered lawyer and reluctantly joins the crime syndicate, seeking revenge against those who killed her loved ones. (Dir: John Llewellyn Moxey, 96 mins.)

Lady of Burlesque (1943)*** Barbara Stanwyck, Michael O'Shea, J. Edward Bromberg, Pinky Lee, Iris Adrian. Strippers are strangled backstage, with one of the cuties eventually figuring out the solution. Entertaining, boisterous mystery based on Gypsy Rose Lee's *The G-String Murders*. Stanwyck is well cast and William Wellman has the right directing style for this kind of racy potboiler. (91 mins.)†

Lady of Secrets (1936)**½ Ruth Chatterton, Otto Kruger, Marian Marsh, Lloyd Nolan, Lionel Atwill. Moody soap opera of a woman whose scandalous past has made her a recluse; strongly emotional drama is compelling. (Dir: Marion Gering, 73 mins.)

Lady of the Camellias, The (France, 1981)***½ Isabelle Huppert, Gian Marie Volonte, Fernando Rey, Bruno Ganz, Yann Babilee, Fabrizio Bentivoglio. Magnificent, lavish version of Dumas *fils* tale about the life and loves of Marguerite Gauthier emphasizes romance over tragedy, with Huppert electric as a hardnosed, ambitious, and heartbreakingly beautiful Camille. Stunning art direction and lyrical cinematography brilliantly captures the lush decadence of the era. (Dir: Mauro Bolognini, 121 mins.)

Lady of the House (MTV 1978)**½ Dyan Cannon, Armand Assante, Zohra Lampert. Cannon shines in this glossy, laundered version of the story of San Francisco's notorious madam, Sally Stanford, who became mayor of the suburb of Sausalito. (Dirs: Ralph Nelson, Vincent Sherman, 104 mins.)

Lady of the Pavement (1929)*** Lupe Velez, William Boyd, Jetta Goudal, Franklin Pangborn, Albert Conti, George Pawcett, Henry Armetta, William Bakewell. The last silent film by the legendary D. W. Griffith is also one of his most poignant, an emotional study of jealousy and revenge, with Goudal as a spurned woman who seeks to get even with her suitor (Boyd) by introducing him to a tawdry cabaret singer (Velez), whom she has instructed in the ways of being a cosmopolitan woman. (93 mins.)

Lady of the Tropics (1939)**½ Robert Taylor, Hedy Lamarr. The ladies may like this torrid romance between the half-native girl and the American millionaire. It's a tragic story which you'll find dated by our standards. (Dir: Jack Conway, 100 mins.)

Lady on a Train (1945)*** Deanna Durbin, Ralph Bellamy, Dan Duryea, Edward Everett Horton, David Bruce. Fairly exciting mystery. A girl sees a man murdered but nobody believes her. Not content to leave well enough alone she follows up what she has seen and becomes involved in an absorbing adventure. (Dir: Charles David, 93 mins.)

Lady on the Bus (Brazil, 1978)** Sonia Braga, Nuno Leal Maia, Jorge Doria, Paulo Cesar Percio. Like *Dona Flor and Her Two Husbands*, this sex comedy is built solely on the earthy sex appeal of Braga and little else. Frigid with her new husband, she finds satisfaction with complete strangers. Lighthearted but forgettable. (Dir: Neville d'Almeida, 102 mins.)†

Lady Pays Off, The (1951)** Linda Darnell, Stephen McNally, Gigi Perreau, Virginia Field. Your payoff is a sweetly forgettable film about a gambling lady who pays off her losses by tutoring the casino owner's little girl. Best for Darnell fans. (Dir: Douglas Sirk, 80 mins.)

Lady Says No, The (1951)** Joan Caulfield, David Niven, James Robertson Justice. Magazine photographer interviews a woman who's written an anti-men book and breaks down her romantic resistance. Ordinary comedy has a good cast that deserves better. (Dir: Frank Ross, 80 mins.)

Lady Scarface (1941)** Dennis O'Keefe, Judith Anderson, Frances Neal, Mildred Coles. Dame Judy plays a murderous mobster queen who breaks the law, bats men around, and leads the cops on a merry chase. Rather than suspense, the film aims for cheap, fast-paced action. (Dir: Frank Woodruff, 69 mins.)

Lady's from Kentucky, The (1939)**½ George Raft, Ellen Drew, ZaSu Pitts, Hugh Herbert, Louise Beavers. Typical horse-racing tale, with Raft as a thoroughbred owner contending with old Kentucky money; nice teaming between Raft and Drew. (Dir: Alexander Hall, 67 mins.)

Lady Sings the Blues (1972)*** Diana Ross, Billy Dee Williams, Richard Pryor. Fictionalized story of singer Billie Holiday employs enough clichés for a dozen films, but comes out a winner solely due to the luminous performance by Ross as Lady Day, which earned her an Academy Award nomination. Not only does Diana re-create the songs of Miss Holiday, duplicating the style without reverting to mimicking, but her dramatic power is surprising and convincing. (Dir: Sidney J. Furie, 144 mins.)

Lady's Morals, A (1930)** Grace Moore, Wallace Beery, Reginald Denny. Moore plays Jenny Lind, the Swedish Nightingale, in this early musical, singing arias and ending up with a blind concert pianist (Denny). Beery plays P. T. Barnum, Lind's impresario in the U.S. (Dir: Sidney Franklin, 75 mins.)

Lady Street Fighter (1981)½ Renee Harmon, Joel D. McCrea, Jr., Liz Renay. Incomprehensible action atrocity about an undercover FBI agent and a vengeance-seeking woman from Amsterdam who team up to fight a drug lord. (No director credited, 73 mins.)†

Lady Takes a Chance, A (1943)*** Jean Arthur, John Wayne, Charles Winninger, Phil Silvers. New York working girl takes a western tour, falls for a brawny cowpoke who doesn't want to be tied down. Fine fun with some hilarious sequences. (Dir: William A. Seiter, 86 mins.)†

Lady Takes a Flyer, The (1958)** Lana Turner, Jeff Chandler. Attractive stars in a very predictable yarn about a beautiful lady who falls for an aviation ace and the trouble they have reconciling their lives. (Dir: Jack Arnold, 94 mins.)

Lady Takes a Sailor, The (1949)*** Jane Wyman, Dennis Morgan, Eve Arden. Slapstick comedy about an efficient girl who always tells the truth has a lot of laughs in its contrived and comic plot. (Dir: Michael Curtiz, 99 mins.)

Lady Vanishes, The (Great Britain, 1938)**** Margaret Lockwood, Paul Lukas, Michael Redgrave, Cecil Parker, Catherine Lacey, Dame May Whitty. Playgirl befriends an old lady on a train, finds she's involved in a spy plot when the lady disappears. Top-notch thriller, directed by Alfred Hitchcock; a classic of its kind. (97 mins.)†

Lady Vanishes, The (Great Britain, 1979)*½ Elliott Gould, Cybill Shepherd, Angela Lansbury, Herbert Lom, Arthur Lowe. Having destroyed musical comedy with *At Long Last Love*, Shepherd goes after suspense films with almost equally disastrous results in this unnecessary remake of the Hitchcock classic. (Dir: Anthony Page, 99 mins.)†

Lady Wants Mink, The (1953)*** Dennis O'Keefe, Ruth Hussey, Eve Arden. Accountant's wife causes trouble when she starts a mink farm. Breezy comedy has some good laughs. (Dir: William A. Seiter, 92 mins.)

Lady Windermere's Fan (1925)*** Ronald Colman, Irene Rich, May McAvoy, Bert Lytell, Edward Martindel. Ernst Lubitsch directed this sparkling version of Oscar Wilde's play, and somehow captured in a silent film the wit and charm of the famous romantic comedy of a lady with a past confronting a highly moral young society matron. A classic. (119 mins.)†

Lady with a Lamp (Great Britain, 1951)*** Anna Neagle, Michael Wilding. Story of courageous nurse Florence Nightingale. Lavishly produced biography, well acted. (Dir: Herbert Wilcox, 112 mins.)

Lady Without Camellias, The (Italy, 1953)*** Lucia Bose, Andrea Cecchi, Alain Cuny. A little-known, impressive early film directed by Michelangelo Antonioni, about a former Milanese shop girl who has a small part in a low-budget quickie movie, and then dreams of becoming a serious, recognized movie star. (105 mins.)

Lady Without Passport, A (1950)**½ Hedy Lamarr, John Hodiak, James Craig. Intrigue and romance in an exotic locale, as Hedy tries to leave Havana. (Dir: Joseph H. Lewis, 72 mins.)

Lady With Red Hair (1940)**½ Miriam Hopkins, Claude Rains, Richard Ainley. Hopkins is at her giddy best in this lighthearted recounting of the life of actress Leslie Carter. The picture dwells on her relationship with impresario David Belasco. (Dir: Curtis Bernhardt, 81 mins.)

Lady With the Dog, The (U.S.S.R., 1960)**** Iya Savvina, Aleksey Batalov. A magnificently acted and directed story based on a Chekhov short story, set in Yalta around 1900. A middle-aged married banker from Moscow meets the unhappy, beautiful young wife of a local petty official. (Dir: Iosif Kheyfits, 86 mins.)

Lafayette (France, 1962)** Michel Le Royer, Howard St. John, Jack Hawkins, Orson Welles, Vittorio De Sica, Edmund Purdom. Muddled, historical drama about the French patriot contributing to the cause of the American Revolutionary War. Maybe if Welles (who plays Ben Franklin!) or De Sica had been behind the camera instead of in front of it. . . .(Dir: Jean Dreville, 110 mins.)

Lafayette Escadrille (1958)*½ Tab Hunter, Etchika Choureau, David Janssen. Corny and melodramatic story about an American boy (Hunter) who runs away to France and joins the Foreign Legion. (Dir: William Wellman, 93 mins.)

La Femme Infidèle (France-Italy, 1969) **** Michel Bouquet, Stéphane Audran, Maurice Ronet. Elegant, intelligent, and sensual: never sordid, frequently funny, and very moving. Director Claude Chabrol's classic of adultery and murder is nearly perfect. (105 mins.)

La Femme Nikita (France, 1991)*** Anne Parillaud, Jean-Hugues Anglade, Tcheky Karyo, Jeanne Moreau. The first half of this film about a vicious woman who lacks love and direction is exceptional; but after she's trained by the police to be a professional assassin, the highly stylized plot drifts into a pale imitation of James Bond. Parillaud, however, is ravishing, and a charismatic screen personality. (Dir: Luc Besson, 117 mins.)†

L'Age D'Or (France, 1930)**** Lya Lys, Gaston Modot, Max Ernst, Pierre Prevert, José Artigas. Hilarious film, made by Luis Buñuel in collaboration with Salvador Dali. A couple in a seacoast town struggle to make love, while everyone (bishops in particular) and everything seems determined to stop them. (60 mins.)†

La Grande Bouffe (France, 1974)***½ Marcello Mastroianni, Ugo Tognazzi, Phillipe Noiret, Michel Piccoli. Four friends decide to eat themselves to death. Black comedy enthusiasts will appreciate watching these stars indulge in the pleasures of the flesh. Very funny, but keep some Alka Seltzer handy. (Dir: Marco Ferreri, 125 mins.)

La Grande Bourgeoise (Italy, 1974)**½ Catherine Deneuve, Giancarlo Giannini, Fernando Rey, Tina Aumont. Gorgeous-looking, albeit slightly sluggish period piece about a man who slays his sister's husband. Based on a true story; a little less stateliness, a little more passion would have helped. (Dir: Mauro Bolognini, 115 mins.)†

La Gran Fiesta (Puerto Rico, 1987)** Daniel Lugo, Luis Prendes, E.G. Marshall, Raul Julia. An abortive effort to layer a critical point in Puerto Rican history with slices of political intrigue and tragic romance. At the last formal ball held at the Casino in Old San Juan, the local gentry must cope with the increased meddling of the U.S. government in their affairs, as well as backstabbing within their own ranks. (Dir: Marcos Zurinaga, 105 mins.)

La Guerre Est Finie (France-Switzerland, 1966)**** Yves Montand, Ingrid Thulin, Genevieve Bujold. A marvelous film about political idealism, superbly directed by Alain Resnais and exquisitely acted by Montand and Thulin. Montand plays, to quiet perfection, the role of an aging revolutionary who fought against Franco in the Spanish Civil War but now knows, and reluctantly understands, that he and his cause will *not* win. (121 mins.)

Laguna Heat (MCTV 1987)** Harry Hamlin, Jason Robards, Rip Torn, Catherine Hicks, Anne Francis. An L.A. cop retreats to his dad's house in Laguna Beach, where he discovers a twenty-year-old cover-up involving corruption and murder. (Dir: Simon Langton, 110 mins.)†

L.A. Heat (1989)*½ Lawrence-Hilton Jacobs, Jim Brown, Kevin Benton. Forgettable cop opera about detective Jacobs stalking a drug kingpin (when he's not busy daydreaming about being a cowboy hero). (Dir: Joseph Mehri, 85 mins.)†

Lair of the White Worm (Great Britain, 1988)*** Amanda Donohoe, Hugh Grant,

Catherine Oxenberg, Sammi Davis, Peter Capaldi, Stratford Johns. No matter what director Ken Russell's recent films seem to be about, they all end up being about sex. This kinky excursion based on a novel by Bram Stoker concerns four people who unwittingly uncover a religion centered around a colossal worm. Russell's visions are as surreal, perverse, and masterful as ever. (93 mins.)†

Laker Girls (MTV 1990)½ Tina Yothers, Paris Vaughan, Shari Sattuck, Paul Johansson, Ken Olandt, Jean Simmons. It may not be true that all cheerleaders are brainless bimbos—but this asinine story of three young women trying to make the exploitative squad of the title does nothing to disprove that stereotype. Garbage. (Dir: Bruce Seth Green, 96 mins.)

L.A. Law (MTV 1986)*** Harry Hamlin, Corbin Bernsen, Jill Eikenberry, Richard Dysart, Michael Tucker, Alfre Woodard. Five Emmys went to this excellent pilot for the popular series about the personal and professional trials of attorneys in a California firm. With most of the regular cast in place, the stories include the death of a senior partner, a glimmer of romance between Stuart and Anne, and the humiliation of a cancer victim (Emmy winner Woodard) at a rape trial. (Dir: Gregory Hoblit, 104 mins.)†

La Lectrice (France, 1988) ***½ Miou-Miou, Christian Ruche, Sylvie Laporte, Maria Casares. Offbeat, affectionate story of young woman who makes a living by reading to people who can't read for themselves. Not as claustrophobic or intellectual as it sounds; film goes off into wonderfully witty passages when the listeners' minds begin to wander and passions for life and for love begin to rise. Miou-Miou is outstanding. (Dir: Michel Deville, 98 mins.)†

La Marseillaise (France, 1938)*** Pierre Renoir, Louis Jouvet, Julien Carette, Gaston Modot. Renoir's stirring film epic parallels the upsurge of the French Revolution with the growing popularity of its rallying anthem, the Marseillaise. (Dir: Jean Renoir, 132 mins.)†

La Maternelle (France, 1933)**** Madeleine Renaud, Mady Berry, Paulette Elambert, Alice Tissot, Henri Debain. Awesomely effective tearjerker. Abandoned by her prostitute mother, a love-starved girl tries desperately to transform a maid at her school into a surrogate mother. Heartbreaking; brilliantly acted. (Dirs: Jean Benoit-Levy, Marie Epstein, 85 mins.)

La Maudite Galette (Canada, 1972) *** Luce Guilbeault, Marcel Sabourin, René Caron. Miser becomes target of robbery plot by his nephew's wife in this crime thriller

that mixes sardonic humor with a real sense of menace. Stark images mark this nifty film about greed and betrayal, with an outstanding turn by Guilbeault. (Dir: Denys Arcand, 105 mins.)

Lambada (1990)* J. Eddie Peck, Melora Hardin, Keene Curtis, Dennis Burkley, Ricky Paull Goldin, Basil Hoffman. Ludicrous attempt to cash in on dance fad has tweedy Beverly Hills math teacher Peck calling himself Blade at night, putting on an earring, and riding his motorcycle to East L.A. so he can dance the lambada with teens while his wife stews at home. But it's all for the best because he's really only doing it to bring math to underprivileged kids. Laughable; even the dance sequences are crude. (Dir: Joel Silburg, 98 mins.)†

Lambada—The Forbidden Dance—See: The Forbidden Dance

L'Americain—See: American, The

L'Ami de Mon Amie—See: Boyfriends and Girlfriends

L'Amour Fou (France, 1968)**½ Jean-Pierre Kalfon, Bulle Ogier, André Labarthe. TV crew films theatre troupe's rehearsal of Racine drama. Director Jacques Rivette delivers his usual intellectual, sensual, personal view of human interaction. Long, demanding film was written and improvised by cast and crew. (256 mins.)

L'Amour Par Terre—See: Love on the Ground

La Muerte Viviente—See: Snake People

Lancelot of the Lake (France, 1974)***½ Luc Simon, Humbert Balsan, Vladimir Antolek-Orsek, Patrick Bernard, Laura Duke Condominas. Director Robert Bresson's masterful retelling of the legends of the knights of the Round Table finds a dispirited group of Knights, having failed to find the Holy Grail, returning to King Arthur at odds with each other and their dreams. Bresson doesn't treat the knights as heroes but as mortals, men whose time has passed as the Age of Chivalry draws to a close. Spectacularly photographed. (83 mins.)

Lancer Spy (1937)**½ George Sanders, Dolores Del Rio, Joseph Schildkraut, Peter Lorre, Virginia Field, Sig Ruman. Colorful, atmospheric spy drama has Sanders as a pre-WWII "mole" in the German army; fast-moving, well-produced suspense. (Dir: Gregory Ratoff, 84 mins.)

Land Before Time, The (1988)*** Voices of Pat Hingle, Helen Shaver, Gabriel Damon, Bill Erwin. Animated feature about baby dinosaurs in search of a legendary green valley is a natural (what kid *doesn't* like dinosaurs?). From the branch of the Spielberg empire that gave us *An American Tale*, this is less strained, though you can still spot the story's efforts at mythological significance. (Dir: Don Bluth, 78 mins.)†

Landlord, The (1970)***½ Beau Bridges, Lee Grant, Pearl Bailey, Diana Sands, Lou Gossett. The entire cast is superb in this story of a young, rich white man who buys a tenement in Brooklyn with dreams of converting it to a showplace home for himself. But he hasn't bargained on the militant black tenants who have no intention of conveniently moving out. The confrontations are very funny, and the satire is devastating. (Dir: Hal Ashby, 114 mins.)

Land of Fury (Great Britain, 1954)**½ Jack Hawkins, Glynis Johns, Noel Purcell. Danger and hardships pioneering in old New Zealand. Well cast, fine outdoor locale, but the plot lacks pace. AKA: The Seekers. (Dir: Ken Annakin, 82 mins.)

Land of No Mercy—See: Ashanti

Land of Silence and Darkness (West Germany, 1971)***½ Werner Herzog's memorable documentary about Fini Straubinger, a 56-year-old deaf and blind woman, is an almost spiritual approach to a way of living that few can appreciate. Straubinger's personality and astonishing ability to overcome her personal challenge make this a fascinating, extraordinarily emotional film. (90 mins.)

Land of the Indians (Brazil, 1979)*** Breathtaking photography highlights factfilled examination of the history, culture, and future of native Brazilian Indians. No-nonsense film explores environmental issues and the effect of encroaching civilization on the indigenous tribes. A thought-provoking, frightening piece of work. (Dir: Zelito Viana, 102 mins.)

Land of the Pharaohs (1955)*** Jack Hawkins, Joan Collins, Dewey Martin. Director Howard Hawks's background as an engineer comes to the fore in this account of the building of the pyramids. The story is a whopper, with Hawkins a visionary pharaoh saddled with an ambitious wife (Collins, purring up a storm). The film doesn't work, but has more than its share of crazy pleasures. (106 mins.)

Land Raiders (1970)** Telly Savalas, George Maharis, Arlene Dahl. Ordinary western about a feud between two brothers, and the woman they both love. (Dir: Nathan Juran, 101 mins.)

Landru (France-Italy, 1962)*** Charles Denner, Michele Morgan, Danielle Darrieux, Hildegard Neff, Stéphane Audran, Jean-Pierre Melville. The macabre tale of Bluebeard, the husband who did away with many wives, is cleverly presented here as a black comedy. AKA: Bluebeard. (Dir: Claude Chabrol, 114 mins.)†

Landscape After Battle (Poland, 1970)***½ Daniel Olbrychski, Tadeusz Janczar,

Stanisława Celinski. Post-WWII limbo is the subject of this disturbing story about two concentration camp survivors who await their future, as both have an affair with a Jewish girl. Director Andrzej Wajda's drama about Poland's tragic past is taken from the writings of Tadeusz Borowski, a child survivor of Auschwitz who committed suicide at age twenty-nine. (110 mins.)

Land That Time Forgot, The (Great Britain, 1974)**½ Doug McClure, Susan Penhaligon, John McEnery. An old-fashioned adventure yarn based on the 1918 novel by Edgar Rice Burroughs. A group from a German sub and the survivors of an Allied ship come together and find themselves in a lost world where prehistoric animals still rule the roost! (Dir: Kevin Connor, 92 mins.)†

Lanigan's Rabbi (MTV 1976)**½ Art Carney, Stuart Margolin, Janis Paige, Janet Margolin. A mildly diverting comedy with Carney as a sympathetic police chief who refuses to believe the town Rabbi (Stuart Margolin) is a real murder suspect. Based on the best-seller *Friday the Rabbi Slept Late*. (Dir: Louis Antonio, 98 mins.)

L'Annee des Meduses (France, 1986)**½ Valerie Kaprisky, Bernard Giraudeau, Caroline Cellier. A travelogue charting sin and seduction under the Riviera sun. Against a background of evenly tanned and perfectly toned bodies, a capricious sex kitten wickedly toys with her victims' affections, including an older man, a married couple, and her mother's lover, who somehow singly manages to remain immune to her charms. (Dir: Christopher Frank, 110 mins.)†

La Notte (Italy-France, 1961)*** Marcello Mastroianni, Jeanne Moreau, Monica Vitti, Bernhard Wicki. Influential film about alienation, Italian style, as Moreau copes with a stifling marriage. Primarily for those who are mesmerized by the director's obsession with non—communicated angst. (Dir: Michelangelo Antonioni, 120 mins.)

La Notte Brava (Italy, 1959)*** Jean-Claude Brialy, Laurent Terzieff, Franco Interlenghi, Elsa Martinelli. A day in the life of three horny Roman studs, petty criminals who aspire to more than their poverty ridden status allows. They have no qualms about selling stolen weapons or enjoying the company of prostitutes, but really just want to be rich and have beautiful girlfriends. The script by Pier Paolo Pasolini makes these low-lives picaresque, honoring their upbringing and condemning Italy's ruling classes. AKA: On Any Street. (Dir: Mauro Bolognini, 93 mins.)

La Nuit de Varennes (France-Italy,

1982)**** Marcello Mastroianni, Harvey Keitel, Hanna Schygulla, Jean-Louis Barrault. The "night" in director Ettore Scola's brilliant film is June 22, 1791, when Louis XVI and Marie Antoinette were arrested after fleeing revolutionary Paris. Witnesses to the fall of the monarchy and the dawning of a new era are an improbable coachful of characters, including Casanova (Mastroianni), Restif de la Bretonne (Barrault), Thomas Paine (Keitel), and the Queen's Lady-in-Waiting (Schygulla). Scola's mix of history and fiction is charming and beautiful. (128 mins.)†

La Parisienne (France-Italy, 1958)***½ Brigitte Bardot, Charles Boyer. Diplomat's daughter goes to great lengths to make her husband pay attention to her. One of Bardot's best films; a sly, sophisticated comedy that is pleasant all the way. (Dir: Michel Boisrond, 85 mins.)

La Passante (France-Germany, 1982)**½ Romy Schneider, Helmut Griem, Michel Piccoli, Mathieu Carriere. Romy Schneider's last film. It concerns a man (Piccoli) who, for no apparent reason, assassinates a Paraguayan ambassador. Although the film juggles flashback sequences awkwardly, it's a moving fade-out for Romy. (Dir: Jacques Rouffio, 106 mins.)†

Larceny (1948)**½ John Payne, Shelley Winters, Dan Duryea, Joan Caulfield. Routine crime-pic with bad guy turning good guy and the gangster's moll who wants to go legit. (Dir: George Sherman, 89 mins.)

Larceny, Inc. (1942)*** Edward G. Robinson, Jane Wyman, Broderick Crawford, Anthony Quinn, Jackie Gleason, Jack Carson. Entertaining story about an ex-con who does his best to go straight. (Dir: Lloyd Bacon, 95 mins.)

La Religieuse—See: The Nun

L'Argent (France-Switzerland, 1983)*** Christian Patey, Sylvie van den Elsen, Michael Briguet. Based on a short story by Tolstoy, this compressed, austere film deals with the falsehoods of the monied class, and how its members casually destroy the life of a worker who tries to play by the same rules used by the scheming rich. (Dir: Robert Bresson, 90 mins.)

La Ronde (France, 1950)**** Anton Walbrook, Simone Signoret, Serge Reggiani, Simone Simon, Daniel Gelin. Director Ophuls's witty, virtuoso version of Arthur Schnitzler's play, showing love as a bitterly comic merry-go-round. Anton Walbrook acts as master of ceremonies and narrator as one love affair overlaps another. (Dir: Max Ophuls, 100 mins.)

Larry (MTV 1974)*** Frederic Forrest, Tyne Daly, Michael McGuire, Robert Walden. This true story, about a man who spent the first twenty-six years of

his life in an institution for the mentally retarded, but who is discovered to possess normal intelligence, is sensitively handled. (Dir: William A. Graham, 104 mins.)

La Salamandre (France, 1972)***½ Bulle Ogier, Jean-Luc Bideau, Jacques Denis. Two Swiss television writers probe into the facts of a story involving a woman accused of attempted murder, but they become too involved with their subject. An amusing, penetrating glimpse into Swiss society, and a sharp exploration of truth and the dangers of untempered idealism. (Dir: Alain Tanner, 125 mins.)

Laserblast (1978)* Keenan Wynn, Roddy McDowall, Cheryl Smith. A teenager wreaks havoc after he picks up a laser gun abandoned by an extraterrestrial. Pitiful. (Dir: Michael Raye, 90 mins.)†

Laserman, The (U.S.-Hong Kong, 1990)**½ Marc Hayashi, Tony Leung, Peter Wang, Joan Copeland, Maryann Urbano, Sally Yeh. An introverted Chinese-American laser expert copes with job problems and family hassles. This hybrid of comedy and intrigue only really clicks when it goes for laughs; blame writer-producer-director Peter Wang. (93 mins.)

La Soufrière (West Germany, 1977)***½ An incredibly daring and unusual documentary by iconoclastic filmmaker Werner Herzog. When he heard that a single resident of the island of Guadaloupe refused to leave his home despite the imminent eruption of a nearby volcano, Herzog put his own life in danger to film his story. A fully realized work of art, as bizarre as it sounds. English narration by Herzog. (30 mins.)

Lassie Come Home (1943)*** Roddy McDowall, Donald Crisp, Lassie. Story of an impoverished family which sells a prize collie is warm, sentimental, and beautifully done. (Dir: Fred M. Wilcox, 88 mins.)

Lassiter (1984)**½ Tom Selleck, Jane Seymour, Lauren Hutton, Bob Hoskins, Ed Lauter. Selleck's a slick, well-dressed cat burglar who is enlisted by a British copper (Hoskins) to steal a fortune in diamonds from the German embassy around the time of Hitler's rise in Europe. (Dir: Roger Young, 100 mins.)†

Last American Hero, The—See: Hard Driver

Last American Virgin, The (1982)*½ Lawrence Monoson, Diane Franklin, Joe Rubbo, Steve Antin. Three friends (the class stud, the class clown, and the class sensitive soul) have nothing on their minds except sex. Smutty and shallow. (Dir: Boaz Davidson, 92 mins.)†

Last Angry Man, The (1959)*** Paul Muni, David Wayne, Betsy Palmer. Paul Muni manages to raise this story of a dedicated general practitioner in Brooklyn above the level of soap opera. The uneven script hampers the talented cast. Muni's last. (Dir: Daniel Mann, 100 mins.)†

Last Angry Man, The (MTV 1974)**½ Pat Hingle, Lynn Carlin. In this version, only the title and the central characters remain . . . the setting is the Brooklyn of 1936 and Hingle brings a dignity and quiet force to the role of Dr. Abelman. (Dir: Jerrold Freedman, 74 mins.)

Last Best Year, The (MTV 1990)*** Mary Tyler Moore, Bernadette Peters, Brian Bedford, Dorothy McGuire, Carmen Mathews, Kate Reid. Even though this TV movie falls into the category of "doomed cancer patient" dramas, it takes a different route in telling the story. Peters is vulnerability personified as the woman whose doctors hand her a death sentence. Moore plays the psychologist who helps Bernadette make the time she has left more than just a waiting game. You will probably shed a tear or two at the end. (Dir: John Erman, 96 mins.)

Last Blitzkrieg, The (1958)** Van Johnson, Kerwin Mathews. Routine war film with some good action shots. The performances are of no help. (Dir: Arthur Dreifuss, 84 mins.)

Last Blood—See: Door-to-Door Maniac.

Last Bridge, The (West Germany, 1954)**** Maria Schell, Bernhard Wicki, Barbara Rutting, Carl Mohner. A tender story about a nurse during the war (WWII) who has loyalties and affections for individuals on both sides—German and Yugoslav. It's one of the most stirring antiwar arguments you'll ever see or hear. Expertly directed on location in Yugoslavia by Helmut Kautner. (90 mins.)

Last Challenge, The (1967)**½ Glenn Ford, Angie Dickinson. Routine but well-played horse opera. Glenn Ford is the former gunslinger turned marshal who has to keep an eager young gun (Chad Everett) from shooting up the town. (Dir: Richard Thorpe, 105 mins.)

Last Child, The (MTV 1971)** Michael Cole, Harry Guardino, Janet Margolin, Van Heflin, Edward Asner, Kent Smith. So-so sci-fi, positing a world where there is a "one-child limit" imposed on every family. Cole and Margolin play a couple who want to break that law. (Dir: John Llewellyn Moxey, 72 mins.)

Last Command, The (1928)**½ Emil Jannings, Evelyn Brent, William Powell. A silent film hailed as a classic more for its stirring plot line than for its actual execution. Jannings (pre-*Blue Angel* but still a ripe victim for humiliation) plays a once-haughty Russian general who ends up in Hollywood after the great revolution and gets cast in a film as . . . a haughty Russian general. (Dir: Josef von Sternberg, 88 mins.)†

Last Command, The (1955)*** Sterling Hayden, Anna Maria Alberghetti, Ernest Borgnine, Richard Carlson. Story of Jim Bowie, and the historic battle of the Alamo. Historical action drama has fine battle scenes, a good cast, and holds the interest. (Dir: Frank Lloyd, 110 mins.)†

Last Cry for Help, A (MTV 1979)*** Linda Purl, Shirley Jones, Tony Lo Bianco. Low-keyed drama about a lonely teenager who tries to be all things to everyone, and ends up trying to take her own life. (Dir: Hal Sitowitz, 104 mins.)†

Last Day, The (MTV 1975)*½ Richard Widmark, Barbara Rush, Robert Conrad, Loretta Swit. The fact that this western is based on the true story about the decline of the Dalton gang doesn't make it any more interesting. (Dir: Vincent McEveety, 100 mins.)

Last Days of Dolwyn, The (Great Britain, 1939)*** Emlyn Williams, Edith Evans, Richard Burton, Hugh Griffith, Anthony James. Strong, compelling drama, written and directed by Williams, of the death of one Welsh valley in the name of progress at the turn of the century. The emphasis is not on social issues, however, but on recording and examining a rural way of life that was vanishing even then. Burton is superb in his first film role as a sensitive village youth. AKA: **Woman of Dolwyn.** (95 mins.)

Last Days of Frank and Jesse James, The (MTV 1986)** Johnny Cash, Kris Kristofferson, Ed Bruce, Gail Youngs, David Allen Coe, Andy Stahl, June Carter Cash, Willie Nelson. Kris Kristofferson and Johnny Cash portray the famous outlaws trying to be like other folks after their personal war against society ends. (Dir: William A. Graham, 104 mins.)†

Last Days of Man on Earth, The (Great Britain, 1973)**½ John Finch, Jenny Runacre, Sterling Hayden, Harry Andrews, Hugh Griffith, Patrick Magee. Overblown science-fiction story about the end of the world. The director's lack of restraint and the actors' scenery-chewing make this fun to watch. AKA: **The Final Programme.** (Dir: Robert Fuest, 89 mins.)†

Last Days of Patton (MTV 1986)**½ George C. Scott, Eva Marie Saint, Richard Dysart, Murray Hamilton, Ed Lauter, Kathryn Leigh Scott. The capably acted teleplay presents the general in peacetime, after the German surrender up until the freak accident that proved fatal. (Dir: Delbert Mann, 104 mins.)†

Last Days of Pompeii (1935)*** Preston Foster, Basil Rathbone, Alan Hale, Dorothy Wilson. Peace-loving blacksmith strives for wealth by becoming a champion gladiator. Average story bolstered by spectacular scenes of the destruction of Pompeii, a technical tour de force. (Dir: Ernest B. Schoedsack, 100 mins.)

Last Days of Pompeii, The (Italy, 1960)**½ Steve Reeves, Christine Kaufman, Barbara Carroll. A watchable, muscle-bound remake of the thirties classic about gladiators, Christianity, and erupting volcanoes. (Dir: Mario Bonnard, 105 mins.)

Last Detail, The (1973)**** Jack Nicholson, Randy Quaid, Otis Young, Carol Kane, Michael Moriarty, Clifton James, Nancy Allen, Gilda Radner. Nicholson gives one of his best, least-mannered performances in this gritty tale of two career Navy officers assigned to escort a young sailor (Quaid) to jail, where he'll serve a harsh sentence on a trumped-up charge. Out of guilt, they try and show the boy a good time along the way. Excellent, if you can see it with its salty language intact. (Dir: Hal Ashby, 103 mins.)†

Last Dinosaur, The (MTV 1977)* Richard Boone, Joan Van Ark, Luther Rackley, Steve Keats. Idiotic yarn starring Richard Boone as a fanatical hunter who is confronted with the biggest prize of all—a dinosaur believed to be extinct. (Dirs: Alex Grasshoff, Tom Kotani, 104 mins.)

Last Dragon, The (1985)**½ Taimak, Vanity, Chris Murney, Julius J. Carry III, Faith Prince, Leo O'Brien. A martial arts cross between *Rocky* and *Raiders of the Lost Ark*. Everything from kung fu to rock videos has been crammed into this silly, but enjoyable tale of a black Bruce Lee enthusiast who must battle the Shogun of Harlem when a mobster's thugs menace a pretty Video Club DJ. (Dir: Michael Schultz, 108 mins.)†

Last Elephant, The (MCTV 1990)** John Lithgow, Isabella Rossellini, James Earl Jones. Low-voltage drama about a band of ivory poachers who threaten not only the endangered elephants but also their human protectors. Weak love story between Lithgow and Rossellini and unsatisfactory plot is redeemed by the on-location African setting. (Dir: Joseph Sargent, 96 mins.)

Last Embrace (1979)*** Roy Scheider, Janet Margolin, Sam Levene, Marcia Rodd, Christopher Walken. Director Jonathan Demme's visual style is remarkably consistent throughout, and it scintillates with imagination and taste. Scheider and Margolin are convincing leads in this thriller about a rattled CIA agent fleeing for his life. (103 mins.)†

Last Emperor, The (Great Britain-Italy-China, 1987)**** John Lone, Joan Chen, Peter O'Toole, Ying Ruocheng, Victor Wong. Stunning epic that traces the life of Pu Yi, China's last emperor, from his sheltered childhood in the Forbidden City to his last days as a humble gardener. Director Bernardo Bertolucci imparts a sense of visual splendor to every image, making full use of the unique resources offered him by the Chinese government (including the right to film in the Forbidden City). Winner of nine Oscars, including Best Picture and Best Director. (166 mins.)†

Last Escape, The (1969)*½ Stuart Whitman, John Collin, Pinkas Braun, Martin Jarvis, Gunther Neutze, Margit Saad. A spy struggles to capture a German rocket scientist from both the Germans and the Russians. Escape it. (Dir: Walter Grauman, 90 mins.)

Last Exit to Brooklyn (West Germany, 1989)**** Stephen Lang, Jennifer Jason Leigh, Burt Young, Peter Dobson, Jerry Orbach, Ricki Lake, Alexis Arquette. Powerful and disturbing adaptation of Hubert Selby's controversial novel. Centered around a massive strike by factory workers, the film expertly interweaves three storylines; the overall effect is rich in atmosphere and superb ensemble acting. The two dramatic plots have to do with characters embarking on tragic sexual odysseys; the comic one, with a family so dumb it lives in blissful ignorance of the crime and depravity that surrounds it. Pointed, unflinching view of the darker alleys of the urban jungle. (Dir: Uli Edel, 110 mins.)†

Last Farewell, The (MTV 1984)**½ Michael Landon, Karen Grassle, Melissa Gilbert. The grand finale of "Little House on the Prairie," before the takeover of Walnut Grove by a sneaky financier. (Dir: Michael Landon, 104 mins.)

Last Flight, The (1931)*** Richard Barthelmess, Helen Chandler, David Manners, Johnny Mack Brown, Elliott Nugent, Walter Byron. After WWI, four veterans find it impossible to go home, and remain on the loose in Paris. Marvelously strange black comedy of the "lost generation," in the style of F. Scott Fitzgerald, with a flip, bitter, exhausted feeling that was deeply characteristic of the period. Impressive performances, including those of Manners and Brown, in their best roles, and Chandler, as a nearsighted beauty who *always* says the wrong thing, right down to the last line. Fine script by John Monk Saunders, who also wrote *The Dawn Patrol*. (Dir: William Dieterle, 90 mins.)

Last Flight of Noah's Ark, The (1980)** Elliott Gould, Genevieve Bujold, Ricky Schroder, Vincent Gardenia. Disney feature operating on the uncomfortable assumption that the lives of human beings are worth risking for the preservation of animals. (Dir: Charles Jarrott, 97 mins.)†

Last Flight Out (MTV 1990)*** Richard Crenna, James Earl Jones, Eric Bogosian, Rosalind Chao, Arliss Howard, Elizabeth Lindsay, Barry Corbin, James Hong, Haing S. Ngor, Stephen Tobolowsky, Soon-Teck Oh. Gripping docudrama set in 1975 Saigon, hours before it fell to the Vietcong, follows the efforts to get Vietnamese civilians who will be branded traitors out of the country on the last commercial air flight to leave Vietnam. (Dir: Larry Elikann, 96 mins.)

Last Fling, The (MTV 1987)** John Ritter, Connie Sellecca, Randee Heller, Paul Sand. Featherweight farce about a bachelor (Ritter) who hears wedding bells when he sees a dream girl (Sellecca), who's already en route to the altar with someone else. (Dir: Corey Allen, 104 mins.)

Last Frontier, The (1956)** Victor Mature, Anne Bancroft, Robert Preston, Guy Madison, James Whitmore. A frontier outpost is almost destroyed due to the arrogant stubbornness of ruthless colonel. Routine western heroics with plenty of battle scenes. AKA: Savage Wilderness. (Dir: Anthony Mann, 98 mins.)

Last Frontier, The (MTV 1986)** Linda Evans, Jack Thompson, Jason Robards, Jr. Evans foregoes her makeup in order to bare the inner depths of her character—a feisty widow overcoming financial hardship and a feud with a neighboring rancher Robards. Evans has minimal acting range, and stripped of her coiffure, gowns, and paint-job, she still seems like a high-fashion doll. (Dir: Simon Wincer, 208 mins.)

Last Gangster, The (1937)*** Edward G. Robinson, James Stewart. Robinson is released after ten years on the rock and finds his world has changed. His futile fight to regain power makes this an interesting, although not superior, film. (Dir: Edward Ludwig, 80 mins.)

Last Gentleman, The (1934)*** George Arliss, Edna May Oliver, Ralph Morgan, Janet Beecher, Charlotte Henry, Donald Meek. Sprightly social comedy has a millionaire trying to protect his fortune from his deadbeat family; wonderful ensemble of actors has a lot of fun with the script. (Dir: Sidney Lanfield, 80 mins.)

Last Giraffe, The (MTV 1979)*** Susan Anspach, Simon Ward, Gordon Jackson. Conservationists and animal lovers will have a field day with this true-life story about the efforts of Ward and Anspach to save the endangered Rothschild giraffe of Kenya. (Dir: Jack Couffer, 104 mins.)

Last Grenade, The (Great Britain, 1969)*½ Stanley Baker, Honor Blackman, Richard Attenborough, Rafer Johnson, Alex Cord. Confused melodrama concerns war and revenge in the Far East intertwined with domestic entanglements, centering on an unbelievable love affair between Baker's gruff soldier and Ms. Blackman's willowy wife of a General. (Dir: Gordon Flemyng, 93 mins.)

Last Hard Men, The (1976)** Charlton Heston, Barbara Hershey, James Coburn,

590

Michael Parks, Chris Mitchum. A sheriff has to track down the escaped convict he had put behind bars after the criminal breaks out and kidnaps his daughter. (Dir: Andrew McLaglen, 98 mins.)

Last Holiday (Great Britain, 1950)**** Alec Guinness, Beatrice Campbell, Kay Walsh, Bernard Lee, Wilfred Hyde-White. Man decides to make it count when he is told he has a short time to live. Excellent comedy-drama with the usual impeccable Guinness performance. Script by J. B. Priestley. (Dir: Henry Cass, 89 mins.)

Last Hours Before Morning (MTV 1975)** Ed Lauter, Rhonda Fleming, Robert Alda, Thalmus Rasulala, George Murdock, Sheila Sullivan. Lauter stars as a 1946 ex-cop, now a private eye working on a hotel murder. (Dir: Joe Hardy, 78 mins.)

Last House on the Left (1972)** David Hess, Lucy Graham, Sandra Cassel, Mark Sheffer. Infamous and still-controversial film retains a punch even in the face of far more violent and gory films that have followed it. A gang of escaped criminals rape and kill two teen-aged girls; a twist of fate brings them to the house of one of the girls' parents, who wreak an equally ugly revenge. The low-budget tawdriness of the production gives it an uncomfortable air of reality; you can't distance yourself from it as you do with a horror movie. Loosely based on Ingmar Bergman's *The Virgin Spring*. There are several versions available on video, neither of them complete—a full print may no longer even exist, which adds to its questionable cult legend. (Dir: Wes Craven, 91 mins.)†

Last House on the Left Part II—See: **Bay of Blood**

Last Hunt, The (1956)*** Stewart Granger, Robert Taylor, Debra Paget. Engrossing action drama about the last of the big buffalo hunters in the Dakotas during the 1880s. (Dir: Richard Brooks, 108 mins.)

Last Hurrah, The (1958)**** Spencer Tracy, Jeffrey Hunter, Pat O'Brien, Dianne Foster, Basil Rathbone, John Carradine, Jane Darwell, Donald Crisp, James Gleason. Version of the Edwin O'Connor novel stars Tracy as Frank Skeffington, last of the old-style political bosses, whose last, losing campaign lets director John Ford explore the tragic fate that awaits men who choose to stand outside the flow of history. Full of good, rich Irish humor, this is ultimately a sad film. (121 mins.)

Last Hurrah, The (MTV 1977)**½ Carroll O'Connor, Dana Andrews, Burgess Meredith, Mariette Hartley, John Anderson. Earnest but ultimately unsuccessful remake of the fine Spencer Tracy movie based on the best-seller. (Dir: Vincent Sherman, 104 mins.)

Last Innocent Man, The (MCTV 1987)*** Ed Harris, Roxanne Hart, David Suchet, Darrell Larson, Rose Gregorio, Clarence Williams III. An ace advocate adept at helping clients beat the rap grows disenchanted with the legal profession, but is lured back by his new lover who wants him to defend her estranged husband on charges of killing a decoy policewoman. A watchable courtroom drama with ethical issues fighting for space with red herrings and torrid love scenes. (Dir: Roger Spottiswoode, 120 mins.)†

Last Laugh, The (Germany, 1924)***½ Emil Jannings, Maly Delschaft. One of the most unusual and interesting of Murnau's films, which shows directorial techniques imitated half a century later by lesser European directors. Jannings plays an elderly hotel doorman forced to retire and surrender his precious uniform, which gave him status in his neighborhood. (Dir: F. W. Murnau, 72 mins.)†

Last Man on Earth, The (U.S.-Italy, 1964)**½ Vincent Price, Franca Bettoia. Scientist finds himself the sole survivor of a plague that has either killed the earth's population or turned them into zombies. Some scary sequences. (Dir: Sidney Salkow, 86 mins.)†

Last Married Couple in America, The (1980)*** George Segal, Natalie Wood, Richard Benjamin, Valerie Harper, Bob Dishy, Dom De Luise. Segal and Wood play a pair who are bewildered by the sexual revolution. Director Gilbert Cates mines quite a bit of laughter from the funny situations that arise, and there is an effort to make a comic statement in favor of fidelity. (103 mins.)†

Last Metro, The (France, 1980)***½ Catherine Deneuve, Gerard Depardieu, Heinz Bennent, Jean Poiret. François Truffaut's entertaining film about a theatrical troupe surviving during the Occupation in Paris boasts smashing performances from Deneuve and Bennent, the latter as a theatrical genius who, because of his Jewish background, is forced into hiding in the theater's basement. (133 mins.)†

Last Mile, The (1932)*** Preston Foster, George E. Stone, Howard Phillips, Alan Roscoe. The classic "big house" drama, based on the hit play by John Wexley, and a model for almost all that would come after; powerful story of a cellblock riot and attempted escape from death row by convicts who have nothing to lose, with vigorous, effective performances. (Dir: Sam Bitschoff, 70 mins.)

Last Mile, The (1958)**½ Mickey Rooney, Frank Conroy. The years have taken some of the bite out of this hard-hitting prison drama. (Dir: Howard W. Koch, 81 mins.)†

Last Movie, The (1971)** Dennis Hopper, Stella Garcia, Sam Fuller, Peter Fonda, Dean Stockwell, Kris Kristofferson. Hopper's ambitious but ultimately jumbled follow-up to *Easy Rider*, explores the fascination that the production of a western holds over a group of Peruvian Indians. The familiar faces listed above all appear briefly on-screen during the "western" opening. (Dir: Dennis Hopper, 110 mins.)

Last Night at the Alamo (1983)*** Sonny Davis, Lou Perry, Tina Hubbard, Steve Matilla, Amanda La Mar, J. Michael Hammond. A quirky little black and white film depicting a run-down Houston saloon about to be razed to make room for a modern skyscraper, and the local denizens taking a stand against the inevitable. (Dir: Eagle Pennell, 80 mins.)†

Last of Mrs. Cheyney, The (1937)**½ Robert Montgomery, William Powell, Nigel Bruce, Joan Crawford, Frank Morgan. Entertaining mix of high society and jewel thieves, from Frederick Lonsdale's play. One of Crawford's most popular vehicles of the thirties. (Dirs: Richard Boleslawski, Dorothy Arzner, 98 mins.)

Last of Mrs. Lincoln, The (MTV 1984) Julie Harris, Michael Cristofer, Robby Benson, Patrick Duffy, Denver Pyle. The underrated Julie Harris gives a magnificent portrayal of Mary Todd Lincoln after the assassination of her husband, as she sinks into penury and insanity. The script is uncertain, but the cast shines. (Dir: George Schaefer, 117 mins.)†

Last of Sheila, The (1973)*** James Coburn, Dyan Cannon, Richard Benjamin, James Mason, Joan Hackett, Raquel Welch, Ian McShane. A nifty, intricate, campy parlor game; producer Coburn invites six friends for a cruise, during which he plans to discover who killed his wife at a party a year ago. (Dir: Herbert Ross, 120 mins.)†

Last of the Badmen (1957)** George Montgomery, Meg Randall, Michael Ansara, James Best. But not the last of the clichés. Chicago detectives of the 1870s chase outlaws who killed one of their fellow agents. (Dir: Paul Landres, 79 mins.)

Last of the Comanches (1953)**½ Broderick Crawford, Barbara Hale. A group of courageous men and women are trekking across a desert to Fort Macklin when Indians attack. Remake of *Sahara*, 1943. (Dir: Andre de Toth, 85 mins.)

Last of the Cowboys, The—See: **Great Smokey Roadblock, The**

Last of the Fast Guns (1958)**½ Jock Mahoney, Gilbert Roland, Linda Cristal. Gunslinger is hired to find a man's missing brother in Mexico, finds danger in the quest. Neat western moves at a speedy clip. (Dir: George Sherman, 82 mins.)

Last of the Good Guys, The (MTV 1978)**½ Robert Culp, Dennis Dugan. Light-spirited cop show which pits an idealistic rebel cop and his buddies against a tough by-the-book sergeant. (Dir: Theodore J. Flicker, 104 mins.)

Last of the Finest, The (1990)** Brian Dennehy, Jeff Fahey, Joe Pantoliano, Bill Paxton. A group of seasoned, no-nonsense cops set out to avenge the death of their buddy by sinking to the level of their drug-dealing adversaries. (Dir: John MacKenzie, 106 mins.)†

Last of the Great Survivors (MTV 1984)*½ Pam Dawber, James Naughton. Haphazard grade-B movie about old folks living in an unsafe building. Most of the time is spent on a romance between Dawber's social worker, who cares for the residents, and Naughton's building inspector. (Dir: Jerry Jameson, 104 mins.)

Last of the Mobile Hot Shots (1970)*½ James Coburn, Lynn Redgrave, Robert Hooks. Muddled interpretation of Tennessee Williams's *Seven Descents of Myrtle*. Jeb (Coburn), the last of the Thoringtons, marries a hooker, Myrtle (Redgrave), so he can return to his decaying plantation and try to sire an heir before cancer kills him. (Dir: Sidney Lumet, 108 mins.)

Last of the Mohicans, The (1936)*** Randolph Scott, Binnie Barnes, Heather Angel. The famous story of the French-Indian wars, and of the noble redmen who helped turn the tide against their brothers. Exciting, elaborately produced western based on James Fenimore Cooper's classic. (Dir: George B. Seitz, 100 mins.)†

Last of the Mohicans, The (MTV 1977)** Steve Forrest, Ned Romero, Andrew Prine, Don Shanks. Forrest stars as the intrepid white hunter who, with his two Indian blood brothers, Chingachgook (Romero) and Uncas (Shanks), helps a British officer escort two young women safely through hostile Indian country. (Dir: James L. Conway, 104 mins.)†

Last of the Red Hot Lovers (1972)**½ Alan Arkin, Sally Kellerman, Paula Prentiss, Renee Taylor. Neil Simon's hit play arrives on the screen with fewer laughs in Simon's own screen treatment of his play about middle-class Barney Fishman's hopes for an extramarital affair. Arkin plays the Don Juan owner of a seafood restaurant who can't remove the smell of fish from his hands as he tries three assignations using his mother's apartment. (Dir: Gene Saks, 98 mins.)†

Last of the Secret Agents? (1966)** Nancy Sinatra, Marty Allen, Steve Rossi. Comedy team of Allen and Rossi play American tourists mixed up in espionage. (Dir: Norman Abbott, 92 mins.)

Last of the Ski Bums (1969)*** A snow skier's version of *The Endless Summer*, except that this world-wide search for perfect powder instead of the perfect wave isn't quite as skillfully done. (Dir: Dick Barrymore, 86 mins.)

Last of the Vikings (Italy-France, 1960)* Cameron Mitchell, Edmund Purdom, Isabelle Corey, Helene Remy. Good-guy Vikings seek vengeance against the Danes. Dubbed and dim-witted. (Dir: Giacomo Gentilomo, 102 mins.)

L.A. Story (1991)*** Steve Martin, Victoria Tennant, Richard E. Grant, Marilu Henner, Sarah Jessica Parker, Susan Forristal, Kevin Pollak, Sam McMurray, Patrick Stuart. This good-natured, funny, and tender comedy about Los Angeles hits all the right satirical buttons (brown air, attitude dining, fitness mania, heavy traffic, youth cult), and so becomes rather more than a wistful ode to love in the Big Orange. Parker steals the film as a nubile sweetheart. (Dir: Mick Jackson, 95 mins.)†

Last Outlaw, The (1936)*** Harry Carey, Hoot Gibson, Henry B. Walthall, Tom Tyler. Co-written by John Ford, this admirable comic western has a notorious outlaw being released from prison after a long stretch, and finding that times have changed. An unsung gem, great fun. (Dir: Christy Cabanne, 72 mins.)

Last Outpost, The (1935)*** Cary Grant, Claude Rains, Gertrude Michael. A defense-of-the-British-Empire melodrama with an amazingly corny plot that is enjoyable anyway. Dashing officer Grant falls in love with the wife of the man (Rains) who saved his life. Exciting series of narrow escapes during the battles between the Kurds and the British in the Sahara Desert. (Dirs: Charles Barton, Louis Gasnier, 88 mins.)

Last Outpost, The (1951)** Ronald Reagan, Rhonda Fleming, Bruce Bennett. Brothers are pitted against each other in this story of the west during the Civil War. Indians add to the confusion. (Dir: Lewis R. Foster, 88 mins.)

Last Picture Show, The (1971)**** Timothy Bottoms, Jeff Bridges, Cybill Shepherd, Ben Johnson, Cloris Leachman, Ellen Burstyn, Eileen Brennan, Clu Gulager, Randy Quaid, Sam Bottoms. A poignant and deeply moving drama about a young boy growing up in a small town (Archer City) in Texas during the early 1950s. Based on the novel by Larry McMurtry, the performances from both established veterans and assorted newcomers like Bottoms are uniformly and unerringly perfect. Both Leachman, playing the vulnerable neglected wife of a high school football coach, and Johnson, a pool-hall owner, won Academy Awards for their performances. (Dir: Peter Bogdanovich, 118 mins.)†

Last Plane Out (1983)**½ Jan-Michael Vincent, Julie Carmen, David Huffman, Mary Crosby, Lloyd Battista, William Windom. Fair adventure flick about an American TV reporter who's trapped in Nicaragua during the last days of Somoza's regime. (Dir: David Nelson, 97 mins.)†

Last Posse, The (1953)*** Broderick Crawford, John Derek, Charles Bickford, Wanda Hendrix. Good western about a ruthless cattle baron who forms a posse to regain $100,000 stolen from him. (Dir: Alfred L. Werker, 73 mins.)

Last Precinct, The (MTV 1986)** Adam West, Keenan Wynn, Yana Nirvana, Lucy Flippen, Wings Hauser. A series pilot about misfit cops. The sight gags never stop and everything goes wrong when these Keystone Kops borrow a drug-sniffing dog to crack a narcotics ring. (Dir: Hy Averback, 104 mins.)

La Strada (Italy, 1954)**** Anthony Quinn, Giulietta Masina, Richard Basehart. An altogether beautiful movie, both touching and amusing, magnificently acted by Masina and Quinn. A brutal, itinerant performer takes in a pathetic slow-witted waif, and her devotion to him is repaid with insults and indifference. Oscar as Best Foreign Film. (Dir: Federico Fellini, 115 mins.)

Last Rebel, The (1971)* Joe Namath, Jack Elam, Victoria George. A Civil War action-pic with Namath saving blacks from lynchings and demonstrating why most athletes are busts as screen stars. (Dir: Denys McCoy, 88 mins.)

Last Remake of Beau Geste, The (1977)**½ Marty Feldman, Ann-Margret, Michael York, Peter Ustinov, Trevor Howard. Breaking away from Mel Brooks, Feldman co-wrote, directed, and starred in a Foreign Legion spoof which is uneven but often enormously funny, and frequently in bad taste—much of it intentional. (84 mins.)†

Last Resort (1986)½ Charles Grodin, Robin Pearson Rose, Ellen Blake. Witless, noisy comedy about a hapless vacationing family whose sunny retreat resembles a war zone. (Dir: Zane Buzby, 86 mins.)†

Last Ride, The (1944)** Richard Travis, Eleanor Parker. Remember the black market in tires? Well, it's the background for this Class B melodrama. (Dir: Ross Lederman, 56 mins.)

Last Ride of the Dalton Gang, The (MTV 1979)** Larry Wilcox, Jack Palance, Randy Quaid. According to this long-winded, scenically attractive western, the Dalton boys were just a bunch of fun-lovin' fellas who stole horses and robbed banks and trains. (Dir: Dan Curtis, 156 mins.)†

Last Rites (1980)—See: **Dracula's Last Rites**

Last Rites (1988)** Tom Berenger, Daphne Zuniga, Chick Vennera, Anne Twomey. Feverish thriller about priest Berenger, son of a high-ranking Mafioso, who becomes involved with murder and Mexican femme fatale Zuniga. (Dir: Donald P. Bellisario, 103 mins.)†

Last Roman, The (West Germany-Rumania, 1968)** Laurence Harvey, Orson Welles, Sylva Koscina, Honor Blackman, Harriet Andersson, Michael Dunn. Lots of action and gore, plus a good international cast. Harvey plays a Roman in 525 A.D. who hopes to turn the Goths and Byzantines against each other and reclaim Rome for Italy. (Dir: Robert Siodmak, 92 mins.)

Last Romantic Lover, The (France, 1978)*½ Dayle Haddon, Gerard Tybat, Fernando Rey. Puerile comedy about a lion tamer who competes in a contest to find the world's most romantic man. Soft-core silliness; Rey provides a few laughs. (Dir: Just Jaeckin, 100 mins.)

Last Run, The (1971)** George C. Scott, Trish Van Devere, Tony Musante. Scott's screen presence is the only decent thing in this chase entry about a retired getaway driver (Scott) who comes back to help a hot-shot hood escape from the police in Spain. John Huston, the original director, was replaced by the plodding Richard Fleischer. (100 mins.)

Last Safari, The (Great Britain, 1967)**½ Gabriella Licudi, Johnny Sekka, Stewart Granger, Kaz Garas. Safari guide Granger antagonized by playboy Garas, with African scenery atoning for the lack of plot and a subpar performance from Garas. (Dir: Henry Hathaway, 110 mins.)

Last Song, The (MTV 1980)*½ Lynda Carter, Ronny Cox, Paul Rudd, Nicholas Pryor, Jenny O'Hara, Dale Robinette. Would-be singer Carter (who performs a few would-be songs here) doesn't know she's carrying tape recordings that incriminate owners of a leaky toxic-waste disposal site. (Dir: Alan J. Levi, 96 mins.)†

Last Stagecoach West (1957)*½ Jim Davis, Mary Castle, Victor Jory, Lee Van Cleef. OK cast does little with boring tale of a stagecoach driver who loses his government mail contracts and is forced out of business. (Dir: Joseph Kane, 67 mins.)

Last Starfighter, The (1984)*** Lance Guest, Dan O'Herlihy, Robert Preston, Barbara Bosson, Catherine Mary Stewart. While proficient at the "Starfighter" video game, Alex is surprised when he's whisked off into space by some extraterrestrials who need his help to save the universe. Not as sharply scripted as it could have been, this is an enjoyable time-killer for video fans who can't get enough action at the local arcade. (Dir: Nick Castle, 100 mins.)†

593

Last Summer (1969)*** Barbara Hershey, Richard Thomas, Bruce Davison, Cathy Burns. Perceptive, beautifully acted drama about the experiences of four teenagers during a summer on Long Island's Fire Island. Restrained screenplay by Eleanor Perry based on the novel by Evan Hunter. The performances are uniformly fine, and Cathy Burns in particular is marvelous. (Dir: Frank Perry, 97 mins.)†

Last Sunset, The (1961)** Kirk Douglas, Rock Hudson, Dorothy Malone, Joseph Cotten, Carol Lynley. Drifter pursued by a lawman arrives at the ranch of an old sweetheart. Combination of *Rawhide* and *Peyton Place*, really gets the emotional relationships a-churning; overwritten, overdirected, overacted. (Dir: Robert Aldrich, 112 mins.)

Last Supper, The (Cuba, 1977)*** Silvanno Rey, Luis Alberto Garcia, Nelsom Villagra, José Antonio Rodriguez. Plantation owner, trying to teach Christianity to his slaves, has them re-enact the Last Supper of Jesus, resulting in a pageant that is wickedly funny and hideously sadistic. A very un-religious and uniquely political film by director Tomas Gutierrez Alea, based on an real incident in Cuban history. (110 mins.)

Last Survivors, The (MTV 1975)** Martin Sheen, Tom Bosley, Diane Baker, Christopher George, Anne Francis, Bethel Leslie, Percy Rodrigues. Gruesome little drama about a lifeboat full of survivors who have to come to a life-or-death decision. (Dir: Lee H. Katzin, 78 mins.)

Last Tango in Paris (Italy-France, 1972)**** Marlon Brando, Maria Schneider, Jean-Pierre Léaud, Catherine Sola. A remarkable film in which Brando, a middle-aged American, meets Schneider, a French girl, while he's apartment-hunting. Without knowing each other, they make love, but their passion soon overwhelms them. Brando gives a moving performance in this controversial film that skyrocketed the reputation of its writer-director. (Dir: Bernardo Bertolucci, 129 mins.)†

Last Temptation of Christ, The (1988)**** Willem Dafoe, Harvey Keitel, Barbara Hershey, Harry Dean Stanton, David Bowie, Verna Bloom, Andre Gregory, Victor Argo. A daring, demanding cinematic experience. Scripter Paul Schrader has skillfully adapted the novel by Nikos Kazantzakis, and Martin Scorsese has brilliantly directed all his players in this haunting retelling of the Passion of Christ. *Temptation* turned out to be one of the most controversial films of the eighties, as numerous fundamentalist groups tried first to buy all rights to the film in order to suppress it, then attempted to pressure theater owners into not showing

594

this challenging masterpiece.(160 mins.)†

Last Time I Saw Archie, The (1961)** Robert Mitchum, Jack Webb, Martha Hyer, France Nuyen. Weak service comedy about a fast-talking "gold brick" and his less confident sidekick. (Dir: Jack Webb, 98 mins.)

Last Time I Saw Paris, The (1954)**½ Elizabeth Taylor, Van Johnson, Donna Reed, Walter Pidgeon. F. Scott Fitzgerald's short story "Babylon Revisited" is expanded and glossed over in this sumptuous but overly dramatic film. Taylor is gorgeous as Johnson's true love and Reed registers strongly in a climactic scene with Johnson. (Dir: Richard Brooks, 116 mins.)†

Last to Go (MTV 1991)*** Tyne Daly, Terry O'Quinn, Annabeth Gish. Daly, in a star turn, gives a gut-wrenching performance as a woman whose seemingly perfect marriage and life changes totally when her husband leaves her for another woman. The actress has never been more appealing than she is in this well-constructed drama. (Dir: John Erman, 96 mins.)

Last Train From Bombay (1952)**½ Jon Hall, Christine Larson, Lisa Ferraday, Douglas R. Kennedy, Michael Fox. An American diplomat gets involved with the intrigues of Bombay when he discovers a friend behind a plot to launch a civil war. Overplotted, but smooth pacing keeps this train on the tracks. (Dir: Fred Sears, 72 mins.)

Last Train From Gun Hill (1959)**½ Kirk Douglas, Anthony Quinn, Earl Holliman, Carolyn Jones. All the action comes at the end of this deliberately paced western drama about a law officer who tries to bring the young killer of his wife to justice. The hitch is the young killer's father and the lawman were the best of friends at one time. (Dir: John Sturges, 94 mins.)†

Last Train From Madrid, The (1937)*** Dorothy Lamour, Lew Ayres, Karen Morley, Gilbert Roland, Lee Bowman, Anthony Quinn, Evelyn Brent, Robert Cummings. The outbreak of the Spanish Civil War drives a diverse group of people on a desperate journey out of the country; taut, intelligent melodrama, with a good gallery of characters. (Dir: James Hogan, 77 mins.)

Last Train Home (MTV 1990)**½ Noam Zylberman, Ron Wite, Timothy Webber, Donna Goodhand, Nick Mancuso, Ned Beatty. Average family adventure story set one hundred years ago in northern Canada, where a young boy sets off in search of his father, on the run after being falsely accused of murdering his employer. (Dir: Randy Bradshaw, 72 mins.)

Last Tycoon, The (1976)*** Robert De Niro, Tony Curtis, Ingrid Boulting, Robert Mitchum, Jeanne Moreau. Rewarding adaptation of F. Scott Fitzgerald's unfinished tragedy about Hollywood and its movie moguls of the late 1920s and 1930s. The character of Monroe Stahr is clearly based on the legendary movie producer Irving Thalberg. De Niro is remarkably effective, capturing Stahr's power and influence in a subtly shaded performance. Faithful, skillful screenplay by Harold Pinter. (Dir: Elia Kazan, 125 mins.)†

Last Unicorn, The (1982)** The voices of Mia Farrow, Alan Arkin, Jeff Bridges, Tammy Grimes. A naïve young unicorn must escape the clutches of the Red Bull and free all the other unicorns from Limbo, but the film remains there. (Dirs: Arthur Rankin, Jr., Jules Bass, 93 mins.)†

Last Valley, The (Great Britain, 1971)** Michael Caine, Omar Sharif, Florinda Bolkan, Nigel Davenport, Arthur O'Connell. Scenery steals the show in this misguided but not altogether uninteresting allegorical adventure epic. The tail end of the Thirty Years War, circa 1641, is the setting for a group of strangers meeting in a hidden valley, where life is tranquil and untouched by the chaos of war. (Dir: James Clavell, 127 mins.)†

Last Voyage, The (1960)**½ Robert Stack, Dorothy Malone, Edmond O'Brien, George Sanders. Suspense drama about a liner ripped by an explosion and the efforts of the passengers and crew to abandon ship. Stretches things a bit too far at times, but the sinking scenes are quite fascinating. (Dir: Andrew L. Stone, 91 mins.)

Last Wagon, The (1956)**½ Richard Widmark, Felicia Farr, Nick Adams. Tough leader brings a wagon train through perilous country. OK western. (Dir: Delmer Daves, 99 mins.)

Last Waltz, The (1978)***½ The Band, Neil Diamond, Bob Dylan, Joni Mitchell, Eric Clapton, Ringo Starr. Director Martin Scorsese, whatever his failings, can never be impersonal, and this elaborate fantasy is anything but a "rockumentary" of the farewell performance of the Band at Winterland in San Francisco. (115 mins.)†

Last Warning, The (1938)*** Preston Foster, Frances Robinson. Above average mystery with amusing dialogue. Private detective is hired to catch a kidnapper who calls himself "The Eye." (Dir: Al Rogell, 70 mins.)

Last Wave, The (Australia, 1977)*** Richard Chamberlain, David Gulpilil, Olivia Hamnett. Director Peter Weir's disquieting mood piece about an Australian lawyer who takes a pro bono assignment defending some aborigines charged with ritual murder. Despite some obscure claptrap, the movie is eerily effective and impeccably controlled. (106 mins.)†

Last Winter, The (Israel, 1983)** Kathleen Quinlan, Yona Elian, Stephen Macht. Soap opera, kibbutz-style, as two war wives both spot a soldier in some news footage and identify him as their husband, a man who's been missing in action since the 1973 Yom Kippur War. One's an Israeli and one's an American woman. (Dir: Riki Shelach Nissimoff, 89 mins.)†

Last Woman, The (France, 1976)**½ Gerard Depardieu, Ornella Muti, Zouzou, Renato Salvatori. Muddled look at contemporary relationships that casts Depardieu as a hulking single father whose sexist attitudes begin to get on budding feminist Muti's nerves. The sex scenes are violently carnal, and the unexpectedly shocking ending will be a definite turnoff for most viewers. (Dir: Marco Ferreri, 111 mins.)

Last Woman on Earth, The (1960)** Antony Carbone, Betsy Jones-Moreland. Moderately entertaining film about the last three people left on earth after fallout does everyone else in. (Dir: Roger Corman, 71 mins.)†

Last Word, The (1979)**½ Richard Harris, Karen Black, Martin Landau, Dennis Christopher, Penelope Milford. A fairly good "little guy vs. the establishment" flick about an inventor who fights to hang onto his apartment in a dilapidated building. That struggle pits him against corrupt politicians who use urban renewal to line their own pockets. (Dir: Roy Boulting, 105 mins.)†

Last Year at Marienbad (France-Italy, 1961)***½ Delphine Seyrig, Giorgio Albertazzi. This is a fascinating, elusive film that was hailed by international critics when it first appeared and has been puzzling and satisfying audiences since that time. Well-photographed symbolic, allegorical drama of a trio at a forlorn spa, and the attempts of a man to lure a mysterious woman away with him. (Dir: Alain Resnais, 93 mins.)†

Las Vegas Hillbillys (1966)* Ferlin Husky, Jayne Mansfield, Mamie Van Doren. Country boy inherits a broken-down saloon, turns it into a success by bringing hillbilly music to Las Vegas. You probably never saw this in the sixties unless you lived in the south. Thin plot padded out with performances by Sonny James, Del Reeves, Bill Anderson, and Husky. Sequel: *Hillbillys in a Haunted House*. (Dir: Arthur C. Pierce, 90 mins.)†

Las Vegas Lady (1976)** Stella Stevens, Stuart Whitman, George DiCenzo. This heist drama in a Nevada amusement park offers no surprises. Miss Stevens hopes to leave her seamy past behind, and Whitman is the casino security guard who might whisk her off to Montana. (Dir: Noel Nosseck, 87 mins.)†

Las Vegas Shakedown (1955)** Dennis O'Keefe, Coleen Gray. Ex-convict swears to kill a gambling house owner who testified against him. (Dir: Sidney Salkow, 79 mins.)

Las Vegas Story, The (1952)**½ Jane Russell, Victor Mature, Vincent Price, Hoagy Carmichael. A murder takes place among the gamblers and hustlers of Las Vegas; pretty good mystery; with excellent performances by the leads. (Dir: Robert Stevenson, 88 mins.)

Las Vegas Strip War, The—See: **Vegas Strip Wars, The**

Las Vegas Weekend (1985)* Barry Hickey, Jace Damon, Macka Foley, Vickie Benson. On its own, this comedy about a computer nerd breaking the bank at Las Vegas and getting all the women he ever wanted is pretty feeble. But it's noteworthy for a very rare appearance by cult figure and Vegas-area resident Ray Dennis Steckler, director of *The Incredibly Strange Creatures Who Stopped Living and Became Mixed-Up Zombies.* (Dir: Dale Trevillion, 82 mins.)†

L'Atalante (France, 1934)**** Jean D'Aste, Michel Simon, Dita Parlo. Jean Vigo's only feature film, an odd, original mixture of poetic lyricism and realistic detail. It's about the fragility of young love, the exponents being a newlywed couple living in a dingy barge on the Seine. From a cursory viewing, the film's tone seems casual, almost arbitrary, but it exerts a mysterious, fatalistic intensity that is difficult to comprehend. (Dir: Jean Vigo, 89 mins.)

Late Autumn (Japan, 1960)***½ Yoko Tsukasa, Setsuko Hara, Chishu Ryu, Mariko Okada. Well-meaning associates of a dead man try to help find a husband for his widow, not understanding that she really wants to find a husband for her daughter. Quietly comic, filled with little treasures of serenity; a perfect example of the simplicity and peace of filmmaker Yasujiro Ozu. (127 mins.)

Late George Apley, The (1947)**½ Ronald Colman, Peggy Cummins. J. P. Marquand's pungent satire on stuffy Boston society emerges on the screen as a pleasing family comedy, milder than *Life with Father* and not as good. (Dir: Joseph L. Mankiewicz, 98 mins.)

Late Show, The (1977)**** Art Carney, Lily Tomlin, Howard Duff, Bill Macy. A sardonic, affectionate paean to the private-eye genre flicks of the 1940s and 1950s. It benefits greatly from a touching, nicely underplayed stint by Art Carney playing a washed-up, aging private eye determined to solve one last tantalizing case. The major credit for the success of the film goes to Robert Benton who not only wrote the wise, knowing original screenplay but directed as well. (94 mins.)†

Late Spring (Japan, 1949)**** Chisu Ryu, Setsuko Hara, Jun Usami, Haruko Sugimura. Director Yasujiro Ozu returns to his beloved theme of marriage and family with this beautiful tale of an elderly widower who lives with his unmarried daughter. Fearing that he is holding her life back, the widower tells her that he's planning to remarry, forcing her to break the bonds and have a life of her own. One of Ozu's great films, rich with gentle humanism and immeasurable happiness. (107 mins.)

Lathe of Heaven, The (MTV 1980)*** Bruce Davison, Kevin Conway. A cerebral sci-fi yarn set in the not-too-distant future. Davison, who is plagued by the fact that his dreams come true, must go to a Voluntary Therapy Clinic, where his therapist (Conway) tries to use the young man's power to build a near-utopian world. Of course, it all backfires. (Dirs: David Loxton, Fred Barzyk, 104 mins.)

Latin Lovers (1953)** Lana Turner, Ricardo Montalbán, John Lund. Lana, a very rich girl, arrives in Brazil for a rest and ends up being chased by a dashing rancher, Ricardo. (Dir: Mervyn LeRoy, 104 mins.)

Latino (1986)** Annette Cardona, Robert Beltran, Tony Plana, Julio Medina, Luis Torrentes, Gavin McFadden. This anti-Contra entry perceives Uncle Sam's gung ho efforts to train the Contras as an exercise in evil. Unfortunately, dramatically, the saintly Sandinistas are no match for the scurrilous but interesting Contras. (Dir: Haskell Wexler, 105 mins.)†

La Tragedie de Carmen (France, 1983)**½ Eva Saurova, Lawrence Dale, Helene Dalanault, Zehava Gal, Howard Hensel. Although this version of Peter Brook's acclaimed stage production of "Carmen" is reworked for the screen, the virtues present in the live presentation—economy and intensity—don't register on screen. The famous opera was streamlined and opera fans may find Brook's abridged "Carmen" disappointing, and the use of three different leads throughout is confusing. (Dir: Peter Brook, 80 mins.)

La Traviata (Italy, 1983)**** Teresa Stratas, Placido Domingo, Cornell MacNeil, Alan Monk, Axelle Gall. Based on Dumas' novel *La Dame aux Camelias*, Verdi's "La Traviata" depicts the 19th-century romantic tragedy. Stratas and Domingo star as the doomed lovers in this powerful, emotionally charged operatic production. Sung in Italian with English subtitles. (Dir: Franco Zeffirelli, 118 mins.)†

La Truite—See: Trout, The

Laughing Policeman, The (1973)**½ Walter Matthau, Lou Gossett, Bruce Dern. Award-winning thriller by Per Wahloo and Maj Sjowall is transplanted from Stockholm to San Francisco in a tense, but diffuse film directed by the unsteady Stuart Rosenberg. Forceful work by Matthau and Gossett, and Dern turns in one of his most accomplished interpretations. (112 mins.)†

Laughing Sinners (1931)** Joan Crawford, Clark Gable, Neil Hamilton, Marjorie Rambeau, Johnny Mack Brown. Heavy, glossy soap opera has society girl Crawford falling for Gable—who's a Salvation Army minister! Any touch of *intentional* humor would have improved this no end. (Dir: Harry Beaumont, 72 mins.)

Laughter (1930)*** Nancy Carroll, Fredric March, Frank Morgan. Dated but lovely comedy-drama about an ex-follies chorine who regrets having married for money, so she takes time out for laughter with the man she truly loves. A sort of screwball drama quite reminiscent of Phillip Barry. (Dir: Harry D'Arrast, 81 mins.)

Laughter in Paradise (Great Britain, 1951)*** Alastair Sim, Joyce Grenfell, Hugh Griffith, Audrey Hepburn. An amusing British comedy, blessed with a delightful Michael Pertwee script, about a prankster who leaves his heirs a fortune if they discharge amiably diabolical tasks. First-rate cast with great depth. (Dir: Mario Zampi, 93 mins.)

Laughter in the Dark (Great Britain, 1969)*½ Nicol Williamson, Anna Karina, Sian Philipps, Peter Bowles, Jean-Claude Drouot. A bitter drama about a prominent art dealer whose demeanor cracks when he becomes obsessed with a scheming vixen who has little regard for fidelity. The subtleties of Vladimir Nabokov's novel leave the filmmakers in the dark. (Dir: Tony Richardson, 101 mins.)

Laura (1944)**** Gene Tierney, Dana Andrews, Clifton Webb, Vincent Price, Judith Anderson, Grant Mitchell, Lane Chandler, Dorothy Adams. One of those happy accidents of compatibility that become Hollywood classics, due to the perfect fusion of cast, director, screenplay, musical score, etc. The original director, Rouben Mamoulian, was replaced by Otto Preminger, who garnished this handsomely mounted thriller with just the right icy, ambiguous sheen. In the course of a homicide investigation, a tough detective finds himself falling for the portrait of the dead woman. Pleasurable as both a suspense film and a love story, the film is blessed with David Raskin's haunting theme music and the ethereally lovely Tierney as Laura, "the face in the misty light." (88 mins.)†

Laura Lansing Slept Here (MTV 1988)* Katharine Hepburn, Karen Austin, Joel Higgins. The great Kate should stop committing mediocre telepics like this forlorn comedy about a celebrity author who has a bet that she can co-exist peacefully with an "average" family for a whole week. (Dir: George Schaefer, 96 mins.)

Lavender Hill Mob, The (Great Britain, 1951)**** Alec Guinness, Stanley Holloway. A mild-mannered bank employee evolves a foolproof plan, he thinks, to make away with an armored car gold shipment. Hilarious comedy, fun all the way, another triumph for Guinness. Audrey Hepburn in a bit. Oscar, Best Story and Screenplay. (Dir: Charles Crichton, 82 mins.)†

La Viaccia—See: Love Makers, The

La Vie Continue (France, 1982)*** Annie Girardot, Jean-Pierre Cassel. A marvelous performance by Girardot enhances this true-to-life story about the adjustments made by a woman with grown children who suddenly finds herself a widow. Remade as *Men Don't Leave*. (Dir: Moshe Mizrahi, 93 mins.)†

L'Avventura (Italy-France, 1960)**** Monica Vitti, Gabriele Ferzetti, Lea Massari. Director Michelangelo Antonioni's studied, perceptive film about empty relationships in an unfeeling world. Story superficially concerns the disappearance of a girl, and the search for her by her lover and her best friend. The slow pace of the film contributes to its overall impact. (145 mins.)†

Law, The (MTV 1974)***½ Judd Hirsch, John Beck. This is not an ordinary cops-and-crooks yarn, but a true-to-life look at a deputy public defender who accidentally latches on to some vital information which could crack a bizarre, unsolved murder case. (Dir: John Badham, 124 mins.)

Law and Disorder (Great Britain, 1958)*** Michael Redgrave, Robert Morley. Two of England's top theatrical and movie names make this comedy worth your attention. Plot concerns a retired crook who can't seem to stay far enough away from trouble. (Dir: Charles Crichton, 76 mins.)

Law and Disorder (1974)**½ Carroll O'Connor, Ernest Borgnine, Karen Black, Allan Arbus. Urban decay blights the neighborhood, so O'Connor, a cabbie, and Borgnine, a chauffeur, pair off as auxiliary cops. The middle-aged duo project outrage at being victimized city dwellers as well. This episodic satire alternates between drama and laughs and fails on both levels, despite some effective scenes. (Dir: Ivan Passer, 99 mins.)†

Law and Jake Wade, The (1958)**½ Robert Taylor, Richard Widmark, Patricia Owens. Good western. Taylor is well cast as a former outlaw turned marshal in a town in New Mexico. His old buddy, played with all the stops pulled by Richard Widmark, pops up and things change. (Dir: John Sturges, 86 mins.)

Law and Order (1932)*** Walter Huston, Harry Carey, Raymond Hatton, Russell Hopton, Ralph Ince, Andy Devine. The Clantons ride the range, and Wyatt Earp and Doc Holliday try to instill in them some much-needed respect for law and order. (Dir: Edward L. Cahn, 70 mins.)

Law and Order (1953)** Ronald Reagan, Dorothy Malone. Customary western story about the retired U.S. marshal who couldn't hang up his holster for any length of time. (Dir: Nathan Juran, 80 mins.)

Law and Order (1969)***½ Documentary essay by Frederick Wiseman about the police force in Kansas City is a compassionate statement about the sometimes dangerous and always delicate task of being a policeman. (81 mins.)

Law and Order (MTV 1976)**½ Darren McGavin, Keir Dullea, Robert Reed, James Olson, Teri Garr. Excessively long TV drama based on Dorothy Uhnak's best-seller about a New York Irish family of cops. (Dir: Marvin J. Chomsky, 144 mins.)

Law and the Lady, The (1951)**½ Greer Garson, Michael Wilding, Fernando Lamas, Marjorie Main, Hayden Rorke, Margalo Gilmore. An adroit look at jewel robbers mingling with the wealthy, the better to steal from them. Polished but unexceptional remake of *The Last of Mrs. Cheyney*. (Dir: Edwin H. Knopf, 104 mins.)

Lawless, The (1950)***½ Macdonald Carey, Gail Russell, John Sands. A hard-hitting and gripping story of bigotry against the Mexican-American fruit pickers in California and a crusading newspaperman's fight against it. Well acted. Tab Hunter's first. (Dir: Joseph Losey, 83 mins.)

Lawless Breed, The (1953)** Rock Hudson, Julia Adams. Ordinary western fare with Hudson playing a marked man who finally stops running and serves a long prison term so that he can end his days a free man. (Dir: Raoul Walsh, 83 mins.)

Lawless Land, The (1988)** Nick Corri, Leon, Xander Berkeley, Amanda Peterson. Average *Mad Max*–type chase movie, set in the near future. Powerful businessman sends his thugs to retrieve his daughter after she elopes with a young man he doesn't approve of. The setting

does nothing more than give an excuse to keep the budget down in this adventure filmed in South America. (Dir: Jon Hess, 80 mins.)†

Lawless Street, A (1955)*** Randolph Scott, Angela Lansbury. Scott as the marshal has a hard job cleaning up the town of Medicine Bend. Gunplay wins the day. (Dir: Joseph H. Lewis, 78 mins.)

Lawman (1971)** Burt Lancaster, Robert Ryan, Lee J. Cobb, Sheree North, Robert Duvall. The lawman is Lancaster riding into town to arrest cowman Cobb and his boys for the accidental shooting of an old man. (Dir: Michael Winner, 99 mins.)

Law of Desire (Spain, 1987)***½ Eusebio Poncela, Carmen Maura, Antonio Banderas, Miguel Molina. Deliciously overwrought homosexual soap opera about a trendy film director yearning to be swept up in an all-consuming passion. When a handsome young man turns up determined to fill the bill, the older man's life goes completely out of control. (Dir: Pedro Almodóvar, 100 mins.)†

Law of the Sea (1932)**½ Ralph Ince, William Farnum, Sally Blane, Priscilla Dean, Rex Bell. Man set adrift at sea by a blackguard who wanted to steal his wife vows to seek revenge, gets it after twenty years. Atmospheric seafaring tale. (Dir: Otto Brower, 60 mins.)†

Law of the Tropics (1941)** Constance Bennett, Jeffrey Lynn, Regis Toomey, Hobart Bosworth. Pretty limp story of a woman trying to conceal her scandalous past from her husband, slightly enlivened by being set in an exotic locale; Bennett is good, as always, but Lynn is a colorless foil for her. (Dir: Ray Enright, 76 mins.)

Lawrence of Arabia (Great Britain, 1962)**** Peter O'Toole, Omar Sharif, Alec Guinness, Anthony Quinn, Jose Ferrer, Jack Hawkins. Director David Lean's marvelous Academy Award–winning spectacle about the legendary British officer and his exploits, military and nonmilitary, in Palestine circa WWI. A remarkable film on many counts: screenwriter Robert Bolt's intelligent screenplay; O'Toole's portrayal of the complex homosexual hero; Lean's directorial work and certainly the cinematography. Lean and his colleagues capture the awesome beauty of the desert as it has never been shown before in a dramatic film. (222 mins.)†

Law vs. Billy the Kid, The (1954)** Scott Brady, Betta St. John. Another version of the notorious career of Billy the Kid and his good friend Pat Garrett. (Dir: William Castle, 73 mins.)

Law West of Tombstone (1938)*** Harry Carey, Tim Holt. Ex-outlaw moves into a new town and establishes law and order. Above-average western has a good cast, better story than usual. (Dir: Glenn Tryon, 80 mins.)

Lawyer, The (1970)*** Barry Newman, Diana Muldaur. A brash, no-holds-barred performance by Newman as a small-town lawyer trying to make it to the top with a local murder case that gets a lot of national attention is the main lure of this film. Loosely based on the true-life murder trial of Dr. Sam Sheppard, the drama focuses more on the attorney than the defendant. (Dir: Sidney J. Furie, 96 mins.)

Lawyer Man (1932)**½ William Powell, Joan Blondell, Claire Dodd, Alan Dinehart. Sharp underworld melodrama has an ambitious attorney getting mixed up with mobsters, despite his girlfriend's objections; the stars really make this one. (Dir: William Dieterle, 72 mins.)

Lazarillo (Spain, 1959)***½ Juan José Menendez, Carlos Casaravilla, Marco Paoletti, Margarita Lozano. A fatherless boy is abandoned by his mother, forcing him to earn his keep from a fascinating assortment of villagers and street people. Both melancholy and comic, this touching film features a grand performance by Paoletti as the boy. (Dir: Cesar Ardavin, 109 mins.)

Lazarus Syndrome, The (MTV 1979)**½ Louis Gossett, Jr., Ronald Hunter, E. G. Marshall. In this pilot, Gossett plays a dedicated, compassionate doctor who joins forces with an ex-newspaperman patient (Hunter) to expose the irresponsibility of a highly respected surgeon-administrator. (Dir: Jerry Thorpe, 78 mins.)†

Lazybones (1925)*** Buck Jones, Madge Bellamy, Jane Novak, ZaSu Pitts, Leslie Fenton, William Norton Bailey. Captivating comedy-drama of small-town life, from the novel by Owen Davis, has Jones (in a non-cowboy role) as an easygoing young man who nearly loses everything by letting others take advantage of him; observant, deeply felt nostalgia directed by Frank Borzage. (79 mins.)

LBJ: The Early Years (MTV 1986)*** Randy Quaid, Patti LuPone, Morgan Brittany, Charles Frank, Pat Hingle, Kevin McCarthy. Quaid's portrayal of Lyndon Baines Johnson is full of vitality in a lively biopic dealing with Johnson's career up to Vietnam. Although it plays fast and loose with the facts about LBJ, it's a good piece of Americana about the making of a politician hell-bent on reaching the top. (Dir: Peter Werner, 156 mins.)

Leadbelly (1976)**½ Roger E. Mosley, James Brodhead, John McDonald, Art Evans. Roger Mosley's performance is extraordinary in this standardized biopic about the famed bluesman; otherwise, the film is superficial. (Dir: Gordon Parks, 121 mins.)

League of Frightened Men (1937)**½ Walter Connolly, Eduardo Cianelli, Irene Hervey, Lionel Stander, Walter Kingsford. Connolly stars as Nero Wolfe in this Rex Stout mystery of college classmates who are being murdered one at a time; well-done, classic suspense. (Dir: Alfred E. Green, 65 mins.)

League of Gentlemen, The (Great Britain, 1960)**** Jack Hawkins, Richard Attenborough, Nigel Patrick. Fine blend of comedy and suspense, as a retired army officer recruits some of his former men to pull off a big robbery. Writing shows much wit, style—performances excellent, direction perceptive. (Dir: Basil Dearden, 114 mins.)†

Lean on Me (1989)**½ Morgan Freeman, Robert Guillaume, Alan North. Sanitized account of New Jersey high school principal Joe Clark, who brought his crime-ridden school under control through disciplinary methods that verged on fascistic. Freeman is terrific as Clark, but John G. Avildsen (*Rocky, The Karate Kid*) directs with a fatal lack of ambiguity, providing a false emotional climax that misses the point of the story. (104 mins.)†

Leap into the Void (Italy 1979)***½ Michel Piccoli, Anouk Aimee, Michele Placido, Gisella Burinato. A beautifully detailed black comedy about a man who cares enough for his emotionally distraught sister to clear the way for her to end it all. Blessed with extraordinary acting, particularly by Placido as the handsome stranger who alters the course of Aimee's life. (Dir: Marco Bellocchio, 120 mins.)

Leap of Faith (MTV 1988)**½ Anne Archer, Sam Neill, Frances Lee McCain, Michael Constantine. Dramatic story about a middle-aged woman who refuses to accept a medical death sentence. A tricky subject, but handled with care and offering hope. (Dir: Stephen Gyllenhaal, 96 mins.)

Learning Tree, The (1969)**½ Kyle Johnson, Alex Clarke. This is the first film directed by famed still photographer Gordon Parks. This autobiographical film about growing up as a black youth in the Kansas of the mid-1920s provides most viewers with a fresh perspective on being black in America. (107 mins.)†

Lease of Life (Great Britain, 1955)***½ Robert Donat, Kay Walsh, Denholm Elliott, Adrienne Corri. Moving drama, superbly acted, as always, by the late Donat. About a dying vicar in a small parish. (Dir: Charles French, 93 mins.)

Leather and Nylon—See: **Action Man**

Leather Boys, The (Great Britain, 1964) *** Rita Tushingham, Dudley Sutton. Moving drama of teenager who marries a serious auto mechanic and then begins to cheat on him. The plot is minor, but the characters are touching. (Dir: Sidney J. Furie, 103 mins.)†

Leatherface: Texas Chainsaw Massacre III (1990)* Kate Hodge, Viggo Mortensen, William Butler, Ken Foree, R. A. Mihailoff. California couple chased by the cannibal clan; most of the gore was cut in order to get this an "R" rating; it may be restored on video, but we doubt it'll make this any better. AKA: **The Texas Chainsaw Massacre III.** (Dir: Jeff Burr, 81 mins.)†

Leather Saint, The (1956)** John Derek, Paul Douglas, Cesar Romero. Young minister becomes a fighter to aid polio victims. Undistinguished boxing drama has all the familiar plot ingredients. (Dir: Alvin Ganzer, 86 mins.)

L'Eau à la Bouche (France, 1966)*** Bernadette Lafont, Françoise Brion, Alexandra Stewart, Michel Gálabru. Stylish sex farce, once quite shocking. Several couples meet for the reading of a will in an isolated chateau where they proceed to change partners. Insubstantial, but handsomely directed. (Dir: Jacques Doniol-Valcroze, 86 mins.)

Leave 'em Laughing (MTV 1981)***½ Mickey Rooney, Anne Jackson, Red Buttons, William Windom. Mickey is devastating as a Chicago clown Jack Thum, a supermarket children's performer who adopts orphans and rejected kids. Whether telling corny stories to sad-faced kids, or getting drunk over the news he has cancer, Rooney has his audience by the throat. (Dir: Jackie Cooper, 104 mins.)†

Leave Her to Heaven (1945)*** Gene Tierney, Cornel Wilde, Jeanne Crain, Vincent Price. Compulsively watchable melodrama about a neurotic bride who goes to tragic ends to hold on to her husband. (Dir: John M. Stahl, 111 mins.)

Leave It to Blondie (1945)**½ Penny Singleton, Arthur Lake, Chick Chandler, Marjorie Weaver. Dagwood finds himself among the finalists in a songwriting contest, although he didn't write it. Entertaining comedy in the *Blondie* series. (Dir: Abby Berlin, 75 mins.)

Leave Yesterday Behind (MTV 1978)**½ John Ritter, Carrie Fisher. Ritter and Fisher are attractive in a romantic drama about a polo player who is permanently crippled during a championship game. (Dir: Richard Michaels, 104 mins.)

Le Bal (France-Italy, 1980)*** Etienne Guichard, Francesca De Rosa. A sumptuous film version of a smash French stage musical that is done without any dialogue. This unique dance-umentary traces French history from the thirties to the present, and comments on France's shifting political climate via dance and body language. (Dir: Ettore Scola, 112 mins.)†

Le Beau Mariage (France, 1982)*** Beatrice Romand, Andre Dussolier, Feodor Atkine, Arielle Dombasle. A young lady is determined to get married and doesn't care whether it's Tom, Dick, or Harry, until she meets a potential husband who's permanently altar-shy. An airy French farce. (Dir: Eric Rohmer, 97 mins.)†

Le Beau Serge (France, 1958)***½ Jean-Claude Brialy, Gerard Blain, Bernadette Lafont. About a young man who goes back from a city to his own village to help a friend. This first feature directed by Claude Chabrol is also the first film of the New Wave. This film is very Catholic in theme and quite controlled in its visual style; it explores the relationships between urban and rural youth in a way that imbues their conflicts with significance beyond the strictures of a situation. (93 mins.)

Le Bonheur (France, 1965)**½ Jean-Claude Drouot, Marie-France Boyer. This unconventional tale of a man whose infidelity causes his wife to kill herself is a bit arty. Pretty to look at, it's not pretty to contemplate since the man happily keeps his mistress once his wife has committed suicide. (Dir: Agnes Varda, 87 mins.)

Le Boucher (France, 1971)**** Stéphane Audran, Jean Yanne, Antonio Passallia. A village schoolteacher politely spurns the advances of a butcher; suddenly, the countryside is beset with unsolved murders. Builds suspense at the same time it develops its characters in greater depth. (Dir: Claude Chabrol, 93 mins.)

Le Cavaleur—See: **Practice Makes Perfect**

Le Caviar Rouge (France-Switzerland, 1987)* Robert Hossein, Candice Patou, Ivan Desny. Leaden spy story in which the KGB tries to trap two of its ex-agents (who are also ex-lovers) into informing on each other. Talky and dull. (Dir: Robert Hossein, 92 mins.)

Le Chagrin et la Pitié—See: **Sorrow and the Pity, The**

Le Crabe Tambour (France, 1977)***½ Jean Rochefort, Claude Rich, Jacques Dufilho. Three seafarers man a supply ship in the North Atlantic and reminisce about a war-loving adventurer. An exciting history lesson even if your knowledge of French colonialism is slight. (Dir: Pierre Schoendoerffer, 120 mins.)†

Le Cri du Hibou (The Cry of the Owl) (France-Italy, 1987)***½ Christophe Malavoy, Mathilda May, Virginie Thevenet. Director Claude Chabrol, the French Hitchcock, lives up to that title with this engrossing psychological mystery. A divorced man casually spies on his pretty neighbor and is slowly drawn into a web of jealousy and murder. So perfectly modulated that even the perverse ending seems appropriate. (102 mins.)

Leda—See: Web of Passion

Le Depart (Belgium, 1967)***½ Jean-Pierre Leaud, Jacqueline Bir, Paul Roland, Catherine Duport. Dreams and fantasies get a surreal interpretation in this sardonic comedy about a hairdresser in love with race cars who wants to drive his boss's Porsche in a road rally. Director Jerzy Skolimowski treats the subject with his wonderful sense of humor and keen eye for detail. (91 mins.)†

Le Dernier Combat (France, 1983)*** Pierre Jolivet, Jean Bouise. An original sci-fi film that's stylish and subtle. The Bomb's gone off, and mankind tries to survive in a world where speech is no longer possible and where food and water are at a premium. (Dir: Luc Besson, 90 mins.)†

Le Distrait—See: Daydreamer, The

Le Doulos (France, 1963)*** Jean-Paul Belmondo, Serge Reggiani, Jean Desailly, Fabienne Dali, Michel Piccoli. Jean-Pierre Melville's downbeat *film noir* about an ex-con (Reggiani) and his compatriot who may or may not be a "doulos" (stoolie) incorporates many familiar Hollywood crime-movie clichés, and rejuvenates them into a careful-but-compelling European style. His clever handling of several plot twists make this a sure bet for the curious crime buff. (110 mins.)†

Leech Woman, The (1960)** Coleen Gray, Grant Williams. Scientist's wife discovers the secret of perpetual youth and begins to bump off unsuspecting males for their hormones. Well, that's one way to get them. (Dir: Edward Dein, 77 mins.)

Le Farceur—See: Joker, The

Left-Handed Gun, The (1958)*** Paul Newman, John Dehner, Hurd Hatfield. Director Arthur Penn's first feature film was based on Gore Vidal's TV play about Billy the Kid, and although it is ragged cinema, it is strikingly original. Newman plays Billy as a mental defective who becomes enmeshed in a myth-making vise that is both his immortality and his destruction. The film has a shaggy sense of harsh absurdism, with unpredictable, unnerving violence. (102 mins.)†

Left-Handed Woman, The (West Germany, 1977)*** Edith Clever, Bruno Ganz, Gerard Depardieu, Michel Lonsdale, Marcu Muehleisen, Bernhard Wicki. Writer-director Peter Handke's one-note first film about a woman who withdraws completely from her family. Daring study of alienation hampered slightly by the woman's descent into total silence; in fact, her noncommunication forces her family, as well as the viewer, to come to grips with how we relate to loved ones. Robby

Muller's cinematography is wonderfully expressive. (119 mins.)

Left Hand of God, The (1955)**½ Humphrey Bogart, Gene Tierney, Lee J. Cobb. Slow-moving adventure yarn made interesting by the performances of the male stars. Bogart is an American who gets caught up in the private wars of a renegade Chinese warlord, played with much bravado by Cobb. (Dir: Edward Dmytryk, 87 mins.)†

Left, Right and Center (Great Britain, 1960)**½ Alastair Sim, Ian Carmichael, Patricia Bredin. Television personality runs for office on the Conservative ticket and is opposed by a pretty young Laborite—love blossoms. Satire on British politics has its moments, but some of the punch may be lost outside the Commonwealth. (Dir: Sidney Gilliat, 100 mins.)

Legacy (1975)** Joan Hotchkis, George McDaniel, Sean Allen, Dixie Lee. A bitter diatribe based on a stage work which hasn't been successfully translated to the screen. But Hotchkis, who wrote the play and screenplay, is mesmerizing as the highly strung rich woman. Her mental breakdown symbolizes the decay of the upper classes, as she chokes on her own dissatisfaction when material possessions don't bring inner peace. (Dir: Karen Arthur, 90 mins.)

Legacy, The (1979)*½ Katharine Ross, Sam Elliott, Roger Daltrey, Charles Gray, John Standing, Margaret Tyzack. Occult rubbish with the standard amount of gory *Omen*-like death scenes. Roger Daltrey is wise enough to check out early with an unsuccessful tracheotomy. Some viewers might want to remove themselves before he does. (Dir: Richard Marquand, 100 mins.)†

Legal Eagles (1986)**½ Robert Redford, Debra Winger, Daryl Hannah, Terence Stamp, Brian Dennehy, John McMartin. Effervescently played by Redford and Winger, this ramshackle comedy-mystery buzzes along pleasantly throughout. A former assistant D.A. and a bleeding-heart lady advocate team up to clear a mysterious performing artist trying to reclaim her late father's paintings, in a case involving arson, murder, forgery, and insurance scams. If only Ivan Reitman hadn't directed this romantic comedy as if it were *Ghostbusters*. The version shown on broadcast TV features the original, completely different, ending. (114 mins.)†

Legend (1985)* Tom Cruise, Tim Curry, Mia Sara, David Bennent. The makeup job of Tim Curry, as Darkness, is the only thing worth watching in this unexciting fairy tale about unicorns, a princess, elves, and Cruise as a Tarzan/Puck mutation. The last part—when the satanic Darkness finally shows his true colors (red)—is definitely not for kids.

A longer European version exists. (Dir: Ridley Scott, 90 mins.)†

Legend of Billie Jean, The (1985)½ Helen Slater, Peter Coyote, Yeardley Smith, Keith Gordon. Inept, bombastic nonsense; when dirt poor but scrupulous Billie Jean is unjustly implicated in a shooting, she goes on the lam with her kid brother and friends. (Dir: Matthew Robbins, 94 mins.)†

Legend of Boggy Creek, The (1973)* Willie E. Smith, John P. Nixon, John W. Gates, Jeff Crabtree. Inept mixture of fiction and documentary styles, allegedly based on the true experiences of the residents of Fouke, Ark., terrorized for years by the hairy monster that lived in the woods. (Dir: Charles B. Pierce, 90 mins.)†

Legend of Hell House, The (Great Britain, 1973)*** Clive Revill, Roddy McDowall, Pamela Franklin, Gayle Hunnicutt. Well-acted, suspenseful psychic tale. It is believed that Hell House holds the key to determining if there is life after death. A psychologist (Revill), a mental and a physical medium (Franklin and McDowall), and others set out to explore the house and its secrets. Written by Richard Matheson. (Dir: John Hough, 93 mins.)†

Legend of Lizzie Borden, The (MTV 1975)***½ Elizabeth Montgomery, Ed Flanders, Fritz Weaver. Carefully handled version of the famous Lizzie Borden murders. Montgomery gives a tour de force performance playing the celebrated ax-murderess, and the sets and background detail are worthy of a theatrical feature. (Dir: Paul Wendkos, 100 mins.)

Legend of Lobo, The (1962)*** Narrated by Rex Allen. One of the better semi-documentaries from the Disney studios about a cunning gray wolf who, time after time, outwits the human race while valiantly keeping his own pack safe and together. (Dir: James Algar, 67 mins.)†

Legend of Lylah Clare, The (1968)**½ Kim Novak, Peter Finch, Ernest Borgnine. Uneven but interesting old-fashioned melodrama about the movies and those by-now-familiar stereotypes who live, eat, and breathe filmmaking. Novak is the sexy starlet who resembles a flamboyant star of the thirties, Lylah Clare (who died mysteriously and tragically on her wedding night) and gets a crack at playing Lylah in a biographical film. Finch is Lylah's real-life director-husband and history repeats itself as he falls for her reincarnation. (Dir: Robert Aldrich, 130 mins.)

Legend of Nigger Charley, The (1972)** Fred Williamson, D'Urville Martin, Don Pedro Colley, Gertrude Jeanette, Marcia McBroom. Hack-work blaxploitation pic with a western locale. A slave flees Virginia after murdering an inhuman slave overseer. Followed by the equally for-

gettable *The Soul of Nigger Charley*. (Dir: Martin Goldman, 98 mins.)

Legend of Sleepy Hollow, The—See: **Adventures of Ichabod and Mr. Toad**

Legend of Sleepy Hollow, The (MTV 1980)** Jeff Goldblum, Dick Butkus, Paul Sand, Meg Foster. Another version—a poor one—of Washington Irving's classic story of Ichabod Crane (Goldblum) and the headless horseman. (Dir: Henning Schellerup, 104 mins.)†

Legend of the Golden Gun (MTV 1979)** Jeff Osterhage, Hal Holbrook, Carl Franklin, Keir Dullea. Fanciful western about a farmer who turns into a deadly shot in order to seek revenge against Quantrill and his raiders. (Dir: Alan J. Levi, 104 mins.)

Legend of the Lone Ranger, The (1981)* Klinton Spillsbury, Michael Horse, Jason Robards, Christopher Lloyd. It lacks conviction and, most crucially, any discernible point. Klinton Spillsbury (the Lone Ranger) was dubbed; one suspects he was as bad as the dubbing was lousy. (Dir: William A. Fraker, 98 mins.)†

Legend of the Lost (1957)**½ John Wayne, Sophia Loren, Rossano Brazzi. A powerhouse trio of stars and some excellent photography are the only plus factors of this sprawling, overproduced adventure. (Dir: Henry Hathaway, 109 mins.)†

Legend of the Werewolf (Great Britain, 1975)**½ Peter Cushing, Ron Moody, Hugh Griffith, Roy Castle, David Rintoul. Standard hair-raiser about a wolfen fellow who works in a zoo and the policeman-lycanthropy expert who tracks him down. (Dir: Freddie Francis, 87 mins.)†

Legend of Valentino, The (MTV 1975)** Franco Nero, Suzanne Pleshette, Judd Hirsch, Yvette Mimieux. Highly romanticized version of the life of Rudolph Valentino, the legendary silent film star. Enjoyable on a fan magazine level. (Dir: Melville Shavelson, 98 mins.)†

Legend of Walks Far Woman, The (MTV 1982)* Raquel Welch, Bradford Dillman, Nick Mancuso. Welch plays an Indian heroine of the 1870s, facing tribal wars in the white man's culture, before the climactic Indian battle at Little Big Horn. An embarrassment riddled with miscasting. (Dir: Mel Damski, 150 mins.)†

Legion of the Damned—See: **Battle of the Commandos**

Legs (MTV 1983)**½ Shanna Reed, Deborah Geffner, Maureen Teefy, Gwen Verdon. A pleasant "backstage story" about three aspirants to the celebrated high-kicking line of Rockettes at Radio City Music Hall. Former Broadway musical star Gwen Verdon plays a choreographer who once upon a time danced in the lineup herself. (Dir: Jerrold Freedman, 104 mins.)†

Le Joli Mai (France, 1962)***½ Exhilarating documentary asks common Parisians what they think about their city, country, news events, politics, other subjects. Director Chris Marker, a master of this type of film, has crafted a long but amusing work filled with wonderful anecdotes of life in contemporary France, with commentary by Yves Montand in French and Simone Signoret in English. (190 mins.)†

Le Jouet (France, 1976)**½ Pierre Richard, Fabrice Greco, Suzy Dyson, Michael Bouquet, Jacques François. Spoiled rich kid buys a human being, one of his father's employees, to be a plaything. Sporadically funny; the concept is better than the script. Remade as *The Toy*. (Dir: Francis Veber, 92 mins.)

Le Jour Se Leve (France, 1939)***½ Jean Gabin, Jacqueline Laurent, Jules Berry, Arletty, Mady Berry. Unremittingly grim and powerfully acted tale of a fugitive holed up in his room and determined to die rather than give himself up. The critics referred to the film's poetic fatalism, which aptly summarizes the quality of this intense film. (Dir: Marcel Carne, 95 mins.)

Le Mans (1971)** Steve McQueen. Racing fans will appreciate this excitingly photographed account of the famous 24-hour Le Mans endurance race and the participants of the annual event. Steve McQueen, who raced in real life, looks right at home in the role of a determined American out to win the big one despite some near-fatal mishaps in his other attempts. (Dir: Lee H. Katzin, 106 mins.)

Le Million (France, 1931)**** Annabella, Rene Lefevre, Vanda Greville. Famed French comedy. Long before *Umbrellas of Cherbourg*, this innovative, insouciant comedy featured actors who sang all their dialogue. The plot concerns Lotto fever, in the French style. (Dir: Rene Clair, 85 mins.)

Lemonade Joe (Czechoslovakia, 1964)*** Karel Fiala, Olga Schoberova. Wild spoof of Yank westerns with the usual pure hero, purer heroine, dirty varmints. (Dir: Oldrich Lipsky, 84 mins.)

Lemon Drop Kid, The (1951)*** Bob Hope, Marilyn Maxwell. A fast talking race track bum has to come up with a bundle he owes the syndicate or else. The laughs are all there. Remake of the 1934 film with Lee Tracy. (Dir: Sidney Lanfield, 91 mins.)†

Lemon Sisters, The (1990)**½ Diane Keaton, Carol Kane, Kathryn Grody, Elliot Gould, Rubén Blades, Aidan Quinn, Estelle Parsons, Richard Libertini. Three women friends (Keaton, Kane, and Grody) recall memories of their childhood and assist each other as adults in this well-intentioned but listless comedy set in a fading Atlantic City. The movie's not all that bad; it just isn't fully developed. (Dir: Joyce Chopra, 93 mins.)†

Lemon Sky (1987)*** Kevin Bacon, Tom Atkins, Lindsay Crouse, Kyra Sedgwick. Fine adaptation of Lanford Wilson's 1970 play about a sensitive teenage boy visiting his domineering father and his new wife in California. The drama's theatrical origins are undisguised in this highly stylized rendition, anchored by Wilson's powerful writing and Bacon's superb performance. (Dir: Jan Egleson, 106 mins.)

Lena: My 100 Children (MTV 1987)** Linda Lavin, Leonore Harris, Cynthia Wilde. Lavin plays the title character, a real-life Jewish heroine who worked off her guilt for posing as a gentile during the war by taking responsibility for the children of Polish holocaust victims. A touching profile of true courage. (Dir: Edwin Sherrin, 104 mins.)

Lenny (1974)**** Dustin Hoffman, Valerie Perrine, Jan Miner. Dustin Hoffman's bravura portrayal of the tortured, self-destructive, brilliantly inventive comic Lenny Bruce is enough of a reason to see this. The film uses material from Bruce's trials which are "performed" by Hoffman as part of his nightclub act. (Dir: Bob Fosse, 111 mins.)†

Lenny Bruce (1967)**** This is an unedited filmed record of a San Francisco nightclub performance in August of 1965. The photography is uneven, as are some of Bruce's routines, but it remains the best record of this tormented soul's inspired, bizarre, irreverent, and sometimes grotesque humor. AKA: **The Lenny Bruce Performance Film.** (Produced by John Magnuson, 68 mins.)†

Lenny Bruce Performance Film, The—See: **Lenny Bruce**

Lenny Bruce Without Tears (1975)*** A valuable documentary about the comedian Lenny Bruce, who died in 1966, written and directed by Fred Baker. It contains clips from kinescopes of old Bruce TV appearances, interviews with Bruce himself, and people like Kenneth Tynan and Mort Sahl talking about Bruce and his influence on American comedy and society. (78 mins.)

Leona Helmsley: The Queen of Mean (MTV 1990)**½ Suzanne Pleshette, Lloyd Bridges, Joe Regalbuto, Bruce Weitz. The real Leona Helmsley is so indelibly etched in TV viewers' minds after her trial for tax evasion that it takes a strong and capable actress like Pleshette to be convincing in this TV biography. The main lure is Pleshette's full-blown performance as Leona, a woman who kept marrying up until she landed Harry Helmsley, multimillionaire real estate tycoon. (Dir: Richard Michaels, 96 mins.)

Leonard, Part 6 (1987)*½ Bill Cosby, Tom Courtenay, Joe Don Baker, Moses Gunn, Gloria Foster. Cosby spent the summer off from his hit TV series to work on this laughless vehicle that casts him as a high-tech spy who must stop an evil genius (Foster) trying to turn timid animals into killers. (Dir: Paul Weiland, 85 mins.)†

Leopard, The (U.S.-Italy, 1963)***½ Burt Lancaster, Claudia Cardinale, Alain Delon, Paolo Stoppa. The Lampedusa novel, sumptuously realized as elegy by director Luchino Visconti. Lancaster limns the aging aristocrat who knows that his days are numbered after the risorgimento; Delon is his son who flirts with revolution. Among the most poised of all historical films, *The Leopard* unspools as a meticulously detailed emotional experience. (205 mins.)

Leopard in the Snow (Canada, 1978)** Keir Dullea, Susan Penhaligon, Kenneth More, Billie Whitelaw, Jeremy Kemp. Slushy love story about an English girl who falls for a handsome hermit afraid of involvement. (Dir: Gerry O'Hara, 90 mins.)†

Leopard Man, The (1943)*** Margo, Dennis O'Keefe, Jean Brooks. Excellent low-budget thriller from the Val Lewton stable, directed with savage poeticism by Jacques Tourneur. About a series of murders attributed to an escaped leopard. (66 mins.)†

Leo the Last (Great Britain, 1970)*½ Marcello Mastroianni, Billie Whitelaw, Calvin Lockhart, Glenna Forster-Jones. Unsatisfying allegory about a reclusive prince deciding to rejoin society and endeavoring to better the lot of the inhabitants of the ghetto in which he now resides. (Dir: John Boorman, 103 mins.)

Le Petit Soldat (France, 1963)***½ Anna Karina, Michel Subor, Laszlo Szabo, Henri-Jacques Huet, Paul Beauvais. Originally banned by the French government, Jean-Luc Godard's second film tells the story of a hired assassin who is used as a pawn by both sides in the French-Algerian War. Beautifully photographed work offended both Right and Left, especially with its uncompromising depiction of brutality and torture. (88 mins.)

Lepke (1974)*½ Tony Curtis, Anjanette Comer, Michael Callan, Warren Berlinger, Milton Berle. Clumsy "kosher" version of *The Godfather*. Mediocre amalgam of gangster clichés assembled to immortalize Jewish gangster Louis "Lepke" Buchalter of the 1920s. (Dir: Menahem Golan, 109 mins.)†

Le Rayon Vert—See: **Summer**

Le Rouge et le Noir—See: **Red and the Black, The**

Le Samourai—See: **Godson, The**

Les Belles de Nuit—See: **Beauties of the Night**

Les Biches (France, 1968)**** Stéphane Audran, Jacqueline Sassard, Jean-Louis Trintignant, Nane Germon. Exquisite, masterly study of sexual domination. A rich

604

lesbian (Audran) meets a pretty young artist (Sassard) painting on a Paris sidewalk, seduces her, then takes her to St. Tropez. Conflict arises when the suave Trintignant shows up and threatens to break up their love affair. AKA: **Bad Girls.** (Dir: Claude Chabrol, 104 mins.)†

Les Camarades (France, 1970)*** Jean-Paul Giquel, Juliet Berto, Dominique Labourier. Sincere and unflinching political film about a young auto worker who joins union struggle after realizing that his job is only as important as the safety and solidarity of the workers. Expressive camerawork and masterful use of sound highlight powerful message. (Dir: Marin Karmitz, 85 mins.)

Les Carabiniers (France-Italy, 1963)***½ Genevieve Galea, Marino Mase. Ironic, difficult allegory on war which is ultimately worth the trouble necessary to understand it. An important work by one of the masters of movies in the period before he gave up films for polemics. (Dir: Jean-Luc Godard, 80 mins.)

Les Compères (France, 1983)*** Pierre Richard, Gerard Depardieu, Anny Duperey. Entertaining Gallo-maniacal comedy about two ex-lovers of a beautiful married woman who are conned into searching for her runaway son on the pretext that the boy is theirs. (Dir: Francis Veber, 92 mins.)†

Les Enfants Terribles (France, 1950)*** Nicole Stephane, Edouard Dermithe, Renee Cosuna, Jacques Bernard. A haunting film version of Cocteau's novel. The story concerns two adolescents, deliberately detaching themselves from the adult world. While isolating themselves from others, they intertwine through a barrage of mystery games that leads to incest and death. (Dir: Jean-Pierre Melville, 100 mins.)

Le Sex Shop (France, 1973)**½ Claude Berri, Juliet Berto, Nathalie Delon. The director stars in a genial rambling farce about a bookshop owner placed behind the economic eight ball. To survive, he shifts his stock to dirty books, and gets more than he bargained for from his clientele. (Dir: Claude Berri, 92 mins.)†

Les Girls (1957)*** Gene Kelly, Kay Kendall, Mitzi Gaynor, Taina Elg. Very entertaining musical with a talented cast plus a sparkling Cole Porter score. Kelly plays an American hoofer in Paris with three beautiful girls in his act. In between musical numbers, he falls in love with his gorgeous co-workers. Kendall steals every scene she's in. (Dir: George Cukor, 114 mins.)

Les Keufs (Lady Cops) (France, 1988)**½ Josiane Balasko, Isaach de Bankole, Ticky Holgado, Jean-Pierre Leaud. Sort of a distaff, Gallic *Beverly Hills Cop* as female inspector Balasko (who also directed and co-wrote the script) battles pimps, temperamental police chief Leaud and fellow cop Bankole, assigned to investigate her unusual methods. Some nice comic bits, but it eventually settles into the standard car chases and shootouts. (100 mins.)

Les Liaisons Dangereuses (France, 1959)** Jeanne Moreau, Gerard Philipe, Annette Vadim, Jean-Louis Trintignant, Jeanne Valerie. Dreary modernized version of the now-famous 18th-century novel set primarily at a ski resort. Good performances from Moreau and Philipe; catch director Roger Vadim's ridiculously oily and unintelligible introduction! Jazz soundtrack includes Thelonius Monk, Barney Wilem's Orchestra, and Art Blakey's Jazz Messengers. Vadim remade the story in 1976 as *Une Femme Fidele*. (106 mins.)†

Les Misérables, (1935)**** Fredric March, Charles Laughton, John Beal, Florence Eldridge, Rochelle Hudson, Cedric Hardwicke, John Carradine. Remarkably exciting and moving. Richard Boleslawski directed, and it's just about his most lively work. The performances are searing, with March as Valjean and Laughton as Javert, and Eldridge as the pathetic Fantine. Best of the innumerable versions, including the many French. (108 mins.)†

Les Misérables (1952)**½ Michael Rennie, Debra Paget, Robert Newton. Victor Hugo's classic story of an escaped convict and the detective who trails him for a lifetime. (Dir: Lewis Milestone, 104 mins.)

Les Misérables (French-German, 1957)*** Jean Gabin, Bernard Blier, Daniele Delorme, Bourvil, Serge Reggiani. Strong version of the Victor Hugo novel, a bit overlong, but the only chance to see the great Jean Gabin in the classic role of Jean Valjean. (Dir: Jean-Paul Le Chanois, 210 mins.)†

Les Misérables (MTV 1978)***½ Richard Jordan, Anthony Perkins, John Gielgud, Celia Robson. It's handsomely mounted, filmed for the most part in France, and boasts a screen treatment by John Gay that permits the characterizations to build in depth. Jordan is superb as Jean Valjean, the impoverished man who is imprisoned for stealing a loaf of bread for his sister's starving family. Perkins is interesting but strained as Inspector Javert, Valjean's nemesis. (Dir: Glenn Jordan, 156 mins.)†

Les Parents Terribles (France, 1948)*** Josette Day, Yvonne DeBray, Jean Marais, Gabrielle Dorziat. Directed by Jean Cocteau (an adaptation of his own play); a mother feverishly in love with her son clashes with the son's girlfriend, who desires him herself. (98 mins.)

Lesson in Love, A (1954, Sweden)*** Eva Dahlbeck, Gunnar Bjornstrand, Harriet Andersson. A romantic comedy about a gynecologist having an affair with one of his patients, prompting his wife to rekindle a relationship with a former lover. A lighthearted change of pace from the usually more serious Ingmar Bergman. (96 mins.)†

Less Than Zero (1987)* Andrew McCarthy, Robert Downey, Jr., Jami Gertz, James Spader. Dreary, flat story of a spoiled L.A. kid who uses too much cocaine while his friends watch in horror. This sanitized version of Bret Easton Ellis's novel is a cautionary antidrug tale, complete with wooden performances and obvious dialogue. The visual style is occasionally compelling, but this exercise in irritation definitely merits a grade way "less than zero." (Dir: Marek Kanievska, 100 mins.)†

Les Visiteurs du Soir (France, 1942)***½ Arletty, Jules Berry, Marie Dea, Alain Cuny, Fernand Ledoux. In the 13th century, the Devil sends his messengers to earth to corrupt and destroy human souls; but one of them is reformed by love. Remarkably, this celebration of integrity, fidelity, and resistance was made under the Nazi occupation of France; apparently, the Germans just didn't get it. Very well made on a small budget, but with a grasp of form and style. (Dir: Marcel Carne, 110 mins.)

Les Yeux sans Visage—See: **Horror Chamber of Dr. Faustus, The**

Let Freedom Ring (1939)*** Nelson Eddy, Virginia Bruce, Edward Arnold, Lionel Barrymore, Victor McLaglen, Guy Kibbee. An idealistic newspaperman is discouraged in his fight against corruption, and gets some moral support from the ghosts of his ancestors. Simplistic but unusual and enjoyable patriotism. (Dir: Jack Conway, 100 mins.)

Lethal Weapon (1987)*** Mel Gibson, Danny Glover, Gary Busey, Mitchell Ryan, Tom Atkins, Darlene Love, Traci Wolfe. A violent action film, more successful as a stylish genre piece than as a character study of contrasting law-enforcement personalities; one a responsible family man (Glover) and the other an unbalanced cop who is more in tune with criminal psychology than he ought to be. Gibson is terrific as the cocky, killing machine who can't let go of Vietnam. Satisfying action workout. (Dir: Richard Donner, 110 mins.)†

Lethal Weapon 2 (1989)**½ Mel Gibson, Danny Glover, Joe Pesci, Joss Ackland, Patsy Kensit. Murtaugh and Riggs return in an adventure played in an even broader comic-book style than the original. Pesci is fun as the mob accountant they have to protect from South African drug smugglers. Entertaining but a bit too silly. (Dir: Richard Donner, 120 mins.)†

Let It Be (Great Britain, 1970)*** John Lennon, Paul McCartney, George Harrison, Ringo Starr. The Beatles pack it in with a sad and wistful record of their attempt to record a back-to-basics, live-in-the-studio album. Michael Lindsay-Hogg directed, admirably away from Richard Lester's exuberance. In the Beatles' third and last appearance in a feature film, the music is what matters. (88 mins.)†

Let It Rock (West Germany, 1981)* Dennis Hopper, David Hess. Manic rock and roll promoter Hopper stages riots and fakes murder plots in order to get attention for his newly signed band. Berlin-set film is complete disaster, especially Hopper's embarrassingly overwrought performance. Roger Corman bought the U.S. rights and inserted out-of-place footage featuring T.S.O.L., a gritty Los Angeles-based punk band, left over from *Suburbia*. AKA: **White Star**. (Dir: Roland Klick, 75 mins.)†

Let Joy Reign Supreme (France, 1977)***½ Philippe Noiret, Jean Rochefort, Jean Pierre Marielle, Christine Pascal. Bertrand Tavernier (*The Clockmaker*) has fashioned a truly sophisticated historical film about the Regency of Philippe, Duke of Orleans (Philippe Noiret). Although the shifts from aristocratic ennui to servile horror are not always too smooth, this film has some excellent performances and a musical score by the regent himself. (120 mins.)

Let No Man Write My Epitaph (1960)** Burl Ives, Shelley Winters, James Darren. Badly done sequel to *Knock on Any Door*. The performances are on the amateurish side, particularly Shelley Winters, who overacts throughout in the role of a junkie. (Dir: Philip Leacock, 106 mins.)

L'Etoile Du Nord (France, 1983)***½ Simone Signoret, Philippe Noiret. Unconventional but absorbing suspense yarn that works best as a character study. A kept man (Noiret) abandoned by his dead lover's family flees Egypt for France. After Noiret moves into a boarding house run by Signoret, an extremely complex study of relationships evolves. A tour de force for two great French stars. (Dir: Pierre Granier-Deferre, 101 mins.)†

Let's Be Happy (1957)**½ Tony Martin, Vera-Ellen. Vera-Ellen inherits some money and travels to Scotland dancing in the heather all the way. Some lovely on the spot photography. (Dir: Henry Levin, 93 mins.)

Let's Dance (1950)** Fred Astaire, Betty Hutton. Ex-actress and her former part-

ner fight her wealthy mother-in-law when she tries to take away her son. Astaire's superlative dancing gets lost in a sugary, dull plot, and Hutton is hardly his best partner. (Dir: Norman Z. McLeod, 112 mins.)

Let's Do It Again (1953)**½ Jane Wyman, Ray Milland, Aldo Ray. Footloose comedy about an almost divorced couple and their escapades to make each other jealous. Wyman is very funny as the wife. Remake of *The Awful Truth*. (Dir: Alexander Hall, 95 mins.)

Let's Do It Again (1975)*** Sidney Poitier, Bill Cosby, Jimmie Walker, Calvin Lockhart, John Amos, Denise Nicholas. Poitier and Cosby were so engaging in the box office hit *Uptown Saturday Night*, they are reteamed in this brash comedy. To raise money for their lodge, they hypnotize weakling Walker into becoming a boxing champion, to the dismay of some mobsters. (Dir: Sidney Poitier, 112 mins.)†

Let's Face It (1943)** Bob Hope, Betty Hutton. Undistinguished, but occasionally amusing, Hope vehicle about soldiers who agree to help middle-aged married women avoid becoming lonesome. (Dir: Sidney Lanfield, 76 mins.)

Let's Get Harry (1986)** Robert Duvall, Michael Schoeffling, Glenn Frey, Gary Busey, Mark Harmon. Standard mercenary adventure. A young man initiates a rescue mission to Colombia where his brother has been abducted by terrorists. Duvall should have skipped this paycheck. Director Stuart Rosenberg had his name removed from the credits. (Dir: Alan Smithee [pseudonym], 107 mins.)†

Let's Get Tough (1942)**½ East Side Kids, Tom Brown, Florence Rice. The Boys encounter Oriental intrigue in this film, which has a strong streak of patriotism and propaganda, as they undermine a Japanese sect out to overthrow the U.S. government. (Dir: Wallace Fox, 62 mins.)

Let's Go Navy (1951)*** Bowery Boys, Allen Jenkins, Bernard Gorcey, Tom Neal, Paul Harvey. The Boys enlist in the Navy in an attempt to find two crooks, who had dressed in naval uniforms and stolen a charity fund that was entrusted to the Boys. (Dir: William Beaudine, 68 mins.)

Let's Kill Uncle (Great Britain, 1966)**½ Nigel Green, Mary Badham, Pat Cardi, Robert Pickering, Linda Lawson, Nestor Paiva. A gimmicky but well-tuned thriller. A precocious twelve-year-old is trying to permanently remove his uncle when he learns that Uncle has designs on his five million dollar inheritance. (Dir: William Castle, 92 mins.)

Let's Live a Little (1948)**½ Hedy Lamarr, Robert Cummings. A harassed ad man falls for a lady psychiatrist, and vice versa. Pleasant romantic comedy. (Dir: Richard Wallace, 85 mins.)

Let's Make It Legal (1951)**½ Claudette Colbert, Macdonald Carey, Marilyn Monroe, Robert Wagner, Zachary Scott. Mildly amusing comedy about a married couple who decide to get a divorce after 20 years of marriage. (Dir: Richard Sale, 77 mins.)

Let's Make Love (1960)**½ Marilyn Monroe, Yves Montand, Tony Randall. The personal appeal of the two stars make up for the shortcomings of this lightweight comedy-romance played against a show-business background. (Dir: George Cukor, 118 mins.)†

Let's Make Music (1940)**½ Bob Crosby, Elisabeth Risdon, Jean Rogers, Joseph Buloff. Very enjoyable B-musical vehicle for the *other* Crosby, Bob, with his popular band, the Bobcats; the story has an elderly music teacher write a tune that becomes a novelty hit, and her life is changed as a result. The other Crosby was quite as charming on screen as his brother Bing. Includes the Bobcats' contemporary smash hit "Big Noise from Winnetka." (Dir: Leslie Goodwins, 85 mins.)

Let's Rock (1958)** Julius La Rosa, Phyllis Newman, Conrad Janis, Paul Anka, Della Reese. Newman is the only worthwhile thing in this second-rate rock 'n' roll musical comedy. (Dir: Harry Foster, 79 mins.)

Let's Scare Jessica to Death (1971)** Zohra Lampert, Kevin O'Connor, Mariclaire Costello. Lampert, an interesting actress, gives this horror yarn whatever allure it has, but alas, it's not enough. She plays Jessica, a former mental patient, who arrives at an old Connecticut house with her husband and their friend, supposedly for a rest. (Dir: John Hancock, 89 mins.)

Let's Spend the Night Together (1982)*½ Old hat concert film featuring highlights from three Rolling Stones' performances. Let's face facts; after *This Is Spinal Tap*, can anyone watch a rockumentary with a straight face? (Dir: Hal Ashby, 94 mins.)†

Let's Talk About Men (Italy, 1965)*** Nino Manfredi, Margaret Lee, Milena Vukotic, Luciana Paluzzi, Patrizia DeClara, Alfredo Baranchini. Four stories are linked to a fifth denouement in this comic, often political film about men and their relationships with women. Manfredi plays the guy in each segment, all directed in typical scatter shot style by Lina Wertmuller (in reaction to Ettore Scola's *Let's Talk About Women*). (93 mins.)

Let's Talk About Women (Italy-France, 1964)**** Vittorio Gassman, Eleonora Rossi-Drago, Heidi Strop, Sylva Koscina.

A series of sometimes excruciatingly funny vignettes, all of which star Gassman and involve his desire to get into or stay out of bed with some comely wench. The opener, about a gun-slinging stranger making a courtesy call to an isolated farmhouse, is hysterical. (Dir: Ettore Scola, 108 mins.)

Letter, The (1940)**** Bette Davis, Herbert Marshall, James Stephenson, Gale Sondergaard. The height of repressed sexuality is achieved through muted tension between Davis and Stephenson in this hothouse drama from W. Somerset Maugham. William Wyler's slick direction, the spellbinding cinematography, and Davis's consummate acting make this a classic. (Dir: William Wyler, 95 mins.)†

Letter, The (MTV 1982)**½ Lee Remick, Jack Thompson, Ronald Pickup, Ian McShane. Version number four of W. Somerset Maugham's durable melodrama on the passions of a rubber planter's wife. Remick is Leslie, a woman who shoots a man and claims she was defending her honor, neglecting to mention they were lovers. (Dir: John Erman, 104 mins.)

Letter for Evie, A (1945)**½ Marsha Hunt, John Carroll, Spring Byington, Hume Cronyn. Fair Grade B film using the familiar plot about the man who sends his handsome friend's picture to the girl he has been courting by mail. Hume Cronyn is excellent as the deceiver. (Dir: Jules Dassin, 89 mins.)

Letter from an Unknown Woman (1948)**** Joan Fontaine, Louis Jourdan. Director Max Ophuls fashions the screen's most beautifully rendered portrait of unrequited love that, in lesser hands, would have become a soap opera with period trimmings. Fontaine allows her adolescent infatuation with a concert pianist (Jourdan) to become a lifelong obsession. Ophuls's special ability to emotionally "charge" objects and locales is in evidence throughout, and his camera movements effectively surround the characters with a classical, romantic atmosphere. (Dir: Max Ophuls, 90 mins.)†

Letter from Siberia (France, 1957)***½ Visual journal of the vast, mysterious region of the Soviet Union is a brilliant example of documentarian Chris Marker's personal style of filmmaking. He uses footage of the people, scenes of great physical beauty, rich verbal explanation, and cartoons. Fascinating, witty, and enlightening. (60 mins.)

Letter of Introduction, A (1938)*** Adolphe Menjou, Andrea Leeds, Edgar Bergen, Charlie McCarthy, George Murphy, Eve Arden, Ann Sheridan. Leeds storms the theatrical barricades, without realizing the ex-matinee idol helping her is her father. Consistently entertaining, even though there's a bit too much of Bergen and McCarthy, funny as they are. (Dir: John Stahl, 104 mins.)†

Letters, The (MTV 1973)**½ Barbara Stanwyck, Jane Powell, Dina Merrill, Ida Lupino, Leslie Nielsen. Three soap-operaish short stories are tied together by an old gimmick—a trio of letters that have been lost in the mail for a year, drastically altering the lives of the recipients when delivered. (Dirs: Gene Nelson, Paul Krasny, 73 mins.)

Letters from a Dead Man (U.S.S.R., 1986)***½ Rolan Bykov, V. Mikhailov, I. Riklin, V. Sabinin, N. Gryakalova. Nuclear war has turned Earth into a smoldering wasteland. A survivor attempts to understand the world's last epic tragedy by writing letters to his missing son as his wife slowly dies of radiation poisoning. A tense, depressing, but enthralling plea for peace, filmed in muted colors and filled with condemnation for man's ignorance and arrogance. (Dir: Konstantin Lopushansky, 87 mins.)

Letters from Frank (MTV 1979)**½ Art Carney, Maureen Stapleton, Mike Farrell, Margaret Hamilton. Always easy to watch, Carney and Stapleton team up for a drama about retirement, with Art chomping at the bit after being replaced by a computer. (Dir: Edward Parone, 104 mins.)

Letters from Three Lovers (MTV 1973)** June Allyson, Ken Berry, Juliet Mills, Martin Sheen, Belinda J. Montgomery, Robert Sterling, Barry Sullivan, Lyle Waggoner, Henry Jones. Follow-up to *The Letters* employs the same familiar theme—three letters arrive to their intended recipients a year late and change their lives. Intended as a series pilot. (Dir: John Erman, 72 mins.)

Letters to an Unknown Lover (Great Britain-France, 1985)**½ Cherie Lunghi, Yves Beneyton, Mathilda May. Escapee from a German POW camp during WWII pretends to be his dead comrade in order to gain a hiding place with a French woman with whom the dead man had been carrying on a mail-only romance. Slow-paced but diverting mystery-drama. (Dir: Peter Duffell, 100 mins.)†

Letter to Brezhnev (Great Britain, 1985)*** Margi Clarke, Alexandra Pigg, Peter Firth, Alfred Molina. Enjoyable, offbeat romantic comedy about two high-spirited girls who team up with two amiable Russian sailors for a night on the town. The town is Liverpool, and the way it's portrayed (so very weary and sleazy), we can't blame one of the girls for wanting to pack up her bags and move to Russia with her newfound love. (Dir: Chris Bernard, 94 mins.)†
608

Letter to Jane (France, 1972)***½ Boldly controversial movie consists primarily of a single photograph of actress Jane Fonda taken during a visit to North Vietnam at the peak of U.S. intervention in Southeast Asia. Direction by Jean-Luc Godard and Jean-Pierre Gorin provides voice-over commentary touching on politics and culture, much of it pedantic, some of it outrageous. A demanding, annoying, daring film. (55 mins.)

Letter to the Next Generation: A Look at Kent State Twenty Years Later (1990)***½ Engrossing and illuminating documentary by James Klein (*Union Maids, Seeing Red*) explores the events of May 4, 1970, when four Kent State students, some going about their normal business, were murdered by National Guardsmen confronting demonstrators. Klein, a college student in 1970, contrasts his classmates with today's Kent students, who are seen as conservative, materialistic, complacent, and even racist. (78 mins.)

Letter to Three Wives, A (1949)**** Ann Sothern, Linda Darnell, Paul Douglas, Kirk Douglas, Jeanne Crain, and the voice of Celeste Holm. Writer-director Joseph L. Mankiewicz won twin Oscars for this well-constructed suburban comedy-satire about three women who are wickedly advised by a fourth that she has run off with one of their husbands. (102 mins.)†

Letter to Three Wives, A (MTV 1985)**½ Loni Anderson, Michele Lee, Stephanie Zimbalist, Ben Gazzara, Charles Frank, Michael Gross. Miscast remake of the 1949 Oscar-winning movie is still watchable because of the solid story about three women receiving a letter announcing a friend has run away with one of their husbands. (Dir: Larry Elikann, 104 mins.)

Letting Go (MTV 1983)*** John Ritter, Joe Cortese, Sharon Gless, Kit McDonough, Peter Dvorsky. Ritter and Gless play contemporary lovers who become involved with each other after suffering major crises in their lives. (Dir: Jack Bender, 104 mins.)†

Letty Lynton (1932)**½ Joan Crawford, Robert Montgomery, Nils Asther, May Robson. A woman is accused of poisoning one of her lovers in this elegantly produced pre-Production Code melodrama. This was one of Crawford's first shop girl love triangle fables and it gave her a customary number of Adrian outfits to model in exotic settings. A must for fans. (Dir: Clarence Brown, 84 mins.)

Let Us Live (1939)**½ Henry Fonda, Maureen O'Sullivan. Fiancée of an innocent man about to be executed fights to save his life. Grim, overdone but well-acted drama. (Dir: John Brahm, 70 mins.)

Leviathan (1989)**½ Peter Weller, Richard Crenna, Amanda Pays, Daniel Stern, Ernie Hudson, Lisa Eilbacher, Meg Foster, Hector Elizondo. The crew of an ocean-floor mining camp fall prey to a genetic monster. Obviously derived from both *Alien* and *The Thing*, and hurt by a cynical ending, but fine for fans of goopy horror thrillers. (Dir: George P. Cosmatos, 98 mins.)†

L'Homme Blessé (France, 1985)*** Jean-Hugues Anglade, Vittorio Mezzogiorno, Claude Berri, Armin Muller-Stahl, Roland Bertin, Lisa Kreuzer. Erotic fantasies mix with real and imagined violence in this daring story about a young man who finds himself drawn to homosexual sex of a furtive and threatening nature. Controversial theme is treated straightforwardly, using explicit sex, witty dialogue, and top-notch performances. (Dir: Patrice Chereau, 89 mins.)†

Lianna (1983)*** Linda Griffiths, Jane Hallaren, Jon Devries, Jo Henderson, Jessica Wight MacDonald. Moving story of a faculty wife and mother of two, who becomes aware of the lovelessness in her marriage and pursues a lesbian relationship with a professor. Griffiths makes Lianna's search for love and self-awareness convincing, and John Sayles skillfully directs this honest film by avoiding sensationalism. (115 mins.)†

Liar's Moon (1982)**½ Matt Dillon, Cindy Fisher, Christopher Connelly, Susan Tyrrell, Maggie Blye. The screen charisma of teen idol Dillon comes into full play in this slight yarn about a pair of young people who fall in love despite their diverse backgrounds. (Dir: David Fisher, 106 mins.)†

Libel (Great Britain, 1959)**½ Olivia de Havilland, Dirk Bogarde, Paul Massie. A wealthy man is accused of being an impostor, sues for libel; some doubt arises in his wife's mind whether or not he's telling the truth. Fairly interesting drama works up good suspense after a slow start. (Dir: Anthony Asquith, 100 mins.)

Libeled Lady (1936)***½ Jean Harlow, William Powell, Myrna Loy, Spencer Tracy. Screen comedy played by the experts is this offering about a paper, being justly sued for libel, which tries to convert the libel to truth. (Dir: Jack Conway, 98 mins.)†

Liberace (MTV 1988)** Andrew Robinson, John Rubinstein, Rue McClanahan. The first of two TV-movie biographies of the outrageous entertainer. Robinson is actually quite good playing the piano virtuoso who found a way to market his talents and create the ostentatious but endearing showman. The story leans heavily on sentiment and only vaguely touches upon the performer's eccentricities. (Dir: Billy Hale, 96 mins.)

Liberace: Behind the Music (MTV 1988)**½ Victor Garber, Saul Rubinek, Maureen Stapleton, Michael Wikes. Garber stays away from mimicry and creates a full-blown characterization of the public showman and the private man; he's also believable in the musical segments. Stapleton is also quite interesting as Liberace's dominant mother. (Dir: David Greene, 96 mins.)

Liberation of Auschwitz, The (1986)*** Harrowing documentary composed of footage shot at the infamous death camp by Soviet military photographers in January and February of 1945. (Dir: Irmgard von zur Muhlen, 60 mins.)

Liberation of L. B. Jones, The (1970)**½ Roscoe Lee Browne, Lola Falana, Anthony Zerbe, Lee J. Cobb, Lee Majors. Tragedy about a black man who divorces his wife for adultery with a white cop. Jesse Hill Ford's novel had real anger, but William Wyler, directing his last feature, wasn't up to such passion. (102 mins.)†

Liberty (MTV 1986)** Carrie Fisher, George Kennedy, Frank Langella, Chris Sarandon, Claire Bloom, LeVar Burton. Well-meaning but interminable movie about the effort of French sculptor Frederic Auguste Bartholdi (Langella) to build the Statue of Liberty. It's a flag-waving show with the statue's story far more interesting than the others. (Dir: Richard Sarafian, 156 mins.)

Licence to Kill (Great Britain, 1989)*** Timothy Dalton, Carey Lowell, Robert Davi, Talisa Soto, Anthony Zerbe, Frank MacRae, Wayne Newton. James Bond defies orders to undertake a personal vendetta against the Colombian drug lord who tried to kill his CIA friend Felix Leiter. Thinly plotted, but Dalton's steely interpretation of 007 and a smashing action finale make this one of the better Bond flicks. (Dir: John Glen, 133 mins.)†

License to Drive (1988)*½ Corey Haim, Corey Feldman, Carol Kane, Richard Masur. Just another boring major-studio teen picture replete with sly, knowing winks to the adolescent viewer for "audience identification." Haim is a baby-faced teen who pretends he has a driver's license when he actually failed the requisite test. (Dir: Greg Beeman, 90 mins.)†

License to Kill (MTV 1984)**½ Don Murray, Millie Perkins, Penny Fuller, James Farentino. After too many martinis, a successful builder weaves home from the country club in his station wagon and kills a lovely teenager headed for a dazzling future. This searing tale of grief and revenge carries a strong message. (Dir: Jud Taylor, 104 mins.)†

Lie, The (Italy, 1984)* Ben Cross, Stefania Sandrelli, Amanda Sandrelli, Leslie Lyon, Claudia Cavalcanti. Nonsensical drama with plenty of sex but no passion about married Italian journalist (Cross with a bad accent), who enjoys the company of many women. Film is rife with bed-hopping, and plenty of mirrors essential to every scene, a pretentious hint at duality and complicity. Dreadful adaptation of an Alberto Moravia story gives voyeurism a bad name. (Dir: Giovanni Soldati, 97 mins.)†

Liebelei (Austria, 1932)*** Magda Schneider, Luise Ullrich, Willy Eichberger, Wolfgang Liebeneiner. Stridently romantic drama about young officer and violinist's daughter who have a passionate affair until he is killed in a duel. Director Max Ophuls paints a fascinating picture of love and danger, emphasizing music, camera movement, and expressionistic sound. Schneider (actress Romy's mother) gives a magnificent performance. (85 mins.)†

Lies (1983)** Ann Dusenberry, Bruce Davison, Clu Gulager, Terence Knox, Gail Strickland, Bert Remsen, Dick Miller. Involved but only sporadically involving thriller about an actress duped into abetting con artists in bilking an heiress out of her fortune. Overly complicated. (Dirs: Ken and Jim Wheat, 100 mins.)†

Lies My Father Told Me (Canada, 1975)***½ Yossi Yadin, Len Birman, Marilyn Lightstone, Jeffrey Lynas, Ted Allan. A charming, sentimental ethnic memoir about growing up in 1924 in a Jewish "ghetto" in Montreal. Focuses on the relationship of a young boy and his aged grandfather, a robust, free-spirited peddler. (Dir: Jan Kadar, 102 mins.)

Lieutenant Schuster's Wife (MTV 1972)** Lee Grant, Nehemiah Persoff, Eartha Kitt, Paul Burke, Don Galloway. Amateur detective, a New York cop's widow, is determined to clear her husband's good name. (Dir: David Lowell Rich, 73 mins.)

Lieutenant Wore Skirts, The (1956)**½ Tom Ewell, Sheree North. TV writer gets jealous when his wife is taken back into service. Funny at times, but never quite jells. (Dir: Frank Tashlin, 99 mins.)

Life and Assassination of the Kingfish, The (MTV 1977)*** Edward Asner, Nicholas Pryor, Diane Kagan, Fred Cook. The political saga of Huey P. Long, who rose from small-town lawyer to governor of Louisiana and U.S. senator, is candidly presented in a well-produced TV drama starring Asner, whose portrayal of the charming rogue who was labeled a demagogue by most of his critics is excellent. (Dir: Robert Collins, 100 mins.)†

Life and Death of Colonel Blimp, The (Great Britain, 1943)**** Roger Livesey, Anton Walbrook, Deborah Kerr. Old-fashioned, pompous British Army officer finds he's out of date when WWII begins. In full-length form, this is a superb portrait of a windbag; a drastically cut version destroys the impact. (Dirs: Michael Powell, Emeric Pressburger, 163 mins.)†

Life and Nothing But (France, 1989)***½ Phillipe Noiret, Sabine Azema, Pascale Vidal, Maurice Barrier. Beautiful tale of devotion to duty follows Major Dellaplane (Noiret in his 100th film), a man obssessed with the deadly toll of WWI, given the impossibly enormous task of supervising the location and burial of as many of 400,000 war dead as he can find. His task becomes entwined with the sorrows of two women searching for the men they loved. Magnificent imagery and brilliant acting highlight this extraordinary film. (Dir: Bertrand Tavernier, 135 mins.)

Life and Times of Grizzly Adams, The (1974)*½ Dan Haggerty, Marjory Harper, Don Shanks, Lisa Jones. Mediocre "nature" tale of a mountain man, wrongly accused of a crime, who leaves civilization and his eight-year-old daughter for the rugged north country. For the kids. (Dir: Richard Friedenberg, 100 mins.)†

Life and Times of Judge Roy Bean, The (1972)** Paul Newman, Anthony Perkins, Ava Gardner, Stacy Keach, Tab Hunter. Director John Huston makes the cardinal error of pontificating over the film's burlesques. The movie huffs and puffs and blows itself down. Paul Newman postures as the self-appointed Texas judge (circa 1880), and the real interest is in the supporting cameos. John Milius penned the screenplay. (124 mins.)†

Life and Times of Rosie the Riveter, The (1980)**** Riveting documentary interviewing five contemporary women relating their experiences as World War II factory workers, and how they endeavored to remain employed after the war ended. Brilliant interpolation of newsreel footage and fascinating interviews with the women. (Dir: Connie Field, 60 mins.)

Life at the Top (Great Britain, 1965)**½ Laurence Harvey, Jean Simmons, Honor Blackman. Sequel to the successful *Room at the Top* but not as well done. Laurence Harvey repeats his characterization of the opportunist who married the boss's daughter and found true unhappiness. It's competently handled, but too familiar. (Dir: Ted Kotcheff, 117 mins.)

Life Begins (1932)*** Loretta Young, Aline MacMahon, Glenda Farrell, Vivienne Osborne, Elisabeth Patterson, Dorothy Tree, Preston Foster, Eric Linden. Unusual, thoughtful film about the workings of a hospital maternity ward and the lives that pass through it. Very capably done and appealing, with an excellent cast. (Dirs: James Flood, Elliott Nugent, 71 mins.)

Life Begins at College (1937)*** Ritz Brothers, Joan Davis, Tony Martin. This zany film will only appeal to the youngsters and fans of the Ritz Brothers. It's a crazy football comedy played strictly for slapstick. (Dir: William A. Seiter, 94 mins.)

Life Begins at Eight-thirty (1942)**½ Monty Woolley, Ida Lupino, Cornel Wilde. Well acted but dreary drama of an alcoholic,-broken-down actor and his daughter who gives up everything to help him. Too morbid in spite of Woolley's frequent attempts at humor. (Dir: Irving Pichel, 85 mins.)

Life Begins at Forty (1935)*** Will Rogers, Rochelle Hudson, Jane Darwell, Richard Cromwell, Slim Summerville. Another fine vehicle for Rogers, here portraying a small-town newspaper editor coming to the aid of a youth who is accused of a crime he didn't commit. Engaging, perceptive comedy with a touch of drama. (Dir: George Marshall, 85 mins.)

Life Begins for Andy Hardy (1941)**½ Lewis Stone, Mickey Rooney, Judy Garland. Andy gives New York a fling and he almost misses out on starting college. Wait'll you see the troubles he gets into in the big city. (Dir: George B. Seitz, 100 mins.)†

Lifeboat (1944)***½ Tallulah Bankhead, Walter Slezak, William Bendix, John Hodiak, Canada Lee. Director Alfred Hitchcock's briny technical exercise is confined to the boat of the title, with the characters thrashing out the ideological conflicts of WWII in a John Steinbeck screenplay. (96 mins.)†

Lifeforce (1985)** Steve Railsback, Peter Firth, Mathilda May, Frank Finlay. An expedition investigating Halley's Comet comes upon a new form of alien—a sort of space-vampire that draws energy from its victims instead of blood. (Dir: Tobe Hooper, 100 mins.)†

Life for Ruth—See: **Walk in the Shadow**

Lifeguard (1976)**½ Sam Elliott, Kathleen Quinlan, Anne Archer, Stephen Young, Parker Stevenson. Occasionally involving movie about a thirty-plus-year-old lifeguard in California who thinks the time may have come for him to settle down and live a real life as a car salesman. (Dir: Daniel Petrie, 96 mins.)†

Life in the Balance, A (1955)** Ricardo Montalbán, Anne Bancroft, Lee Marvin. Despite the good cast, this cheaply made melodrama about a series of murders and the various suspects generates very little excitement. Mexican locations the chief asset. (Dir: Harry Horner, 74 mins.)

Life Is a Bed of Roses (France, 1983)**½ Vittorio Gassman, Ruggero Raimondi, Geraldine Chaplin, Fanny Ardant, Pierre Arditi, Sabine Azema. A WWII aristocrat starts building "The Temple of Happiness"; shifting to the present day, the movie presents assorted lovers trying to sort themselves out in the still unfinished castle. More bizarre than engaging, with some lovely, fanciful moments. (Dir: Alain Resnais, 111 mins.)

Life Is a Long Quiet River (France, 1990)** Benoit Magimel, Helene Vincent, Andre Wilms, Christine Pignet. French farce ought to have been funnier. A spiteful nurse switches two babies from their rightful families to get revenge on her lover (who is the doctor) because he refuses to marry her. The joke is that the wealthy baby is put into a family of lowly gargoyles and vice versa. Moves too slowly. (Dir: Etienne Chatiliez, 95 mins.)

Life of Brian—See: **Monty Python's Life of Brian**

Life of Émile Zola, (1937)**½ Paul Muni, Joseph Schildkraut. Ho-hum posturing by Muni (as Zola) fails to generate any life in this overstuffed biopic, which is no more palatable for the rightness of its ringing homilies. One of Oscar's sadder hours (this won Best Picture). (Dir: William Dieterle, 130 mins.)†

Life of Her Own, A (1950)*** Lana Turner, Ray Milland, Tom Ewell, Louis Calhern, Ann Dvorak. Unadulterated soap opera with a shaky script, but director George Cukor is able to transform it into a drama of some complexity. Turner is surprisingly effective as the farm girl who makes it in the Big Apple as a top model, but Dvorak is the standout in the showy role of an aging model. (108 mins.)

Life of Jimmy Dolan, The (1933)*** Douglas Fairbanks, Jr., Loretta Young, Aline MacMahon, Guy Kibbee, Fifi D'Orsay, Mickey Rooney. Keen, swiftly paced tale of a cocky, ruthless young boxer who finds himself on the lam; he hides out at a home for orphans (one of whom is a very small but lively Rooney), run by a nice girl and her aunt. There he falls in love and discovers the error of his ways; very effective melodrama. If it sounds familiar, that's because it was remade as *They Made Me a Criminal*, with John Garfield. (Dir: Archie Mayo, 89 mins.)

Life of Riley, The (1949)** William Bendix, Richard Long, James Gleason, Rosemary De Camp, Beulah Bondi. Gravel-voiced Bendix repeats his beloved radio and TV role of Chester Riley in this affable domestic comedy. Riley is surprised to learn that his moving up in the world may depend on daughter Babs's nabbing the boss's son. (Dir: Irving Brecher, 87 mins.)

Life of the Party: The Story of Beatrice (MTV 1982)***½ Carol Burnett, Lloyd Bridges, Marian Mercer, Conchata Ferrell, Geoffrey Lewis, Gail Strickland. Realistic picture of a lady drunk who turned to AA, and later formed the country's first halfway house for women alkies in Los Angeles. Carol pumps life into the true story of Beatrice O'Reilly, a chattering Texas drinker who goes down the drain, then becomes a driving force to help others afflicted with alcoholism. (Dir: Lamont Johnson, 104 mins.)

Life of Vergie Winters, The (1934)*** Ann Harding, John Boles, Helen Vinson, Bonita Granville. From Louis Bromfield's novel, this is the story of a free-thinking girl trying to escape the strictures of conventional social rules; Harding is excellent, as always. (Dir: Alfred Santell, 82 mins.)

Life Upside Down (France, 1965)*** Charles Denner, Anna Gaylor. Young Frenchman about to be married causes concern when he suddenly becomes withdrawn, living in another world. Absorbing, excellently enacted and directed. (Dir: Alain Jessua, 93 mins.)

Life with Blondie (1945)**½ Penny Singleton, Arthur Lake, Ernest Truex. When Daisy becomes a pin-up dog, Blondie and Dagwood have to contend with many inconveniences, including some gangsters. Some good laughs. (Dir: Abby Berlin, 75 mins.)

Life with Father (1947)*** William Powell, Irene Dunne, Elizabeth Taylor, Edmund Gwenn, ZaSu Pitts, Martin Milner, Jimmy Lydon. Charming movie adaptation of Clarence Day's autobiographical play. Director Michael Curtiz can handle comedy but domestic bliss seems beyond his range. Powell and Dunne are perfectly cast, but the film doesn't work the way it should. (118 mins.)†

Life with Henry (1941)**½ Jackie Cooper, Eddie Bracken, Hedda Hopper. Good "Henry Aldrich" comedy as Henry tries to win a trip to Alaska and goes into the soap business. Bracken is a delight as Henry's sidekick. (Dir: Ted Reed, 80 mins.)

Lift, The (Netherlands, 1985)**½ Huub Stapep, Willek Van Ammelrooy, Josine Van Dalsum. Moderately scary but rather silly horror film about an elevator with a penchant for killing off its passengers. This concept only serves to leave the suspense stuck in between stops. (Dir: Dick Maas, 90 mins.)†

Light Ahead, The (1939)***½ David Opatoshu, Isadore Cashier, Helen Beverly. This rare treat from cult director Edgar Ulmer is a restored version of an old
612

Yiddish film. Heading a charming cast, Opatoshu plays a crippled peasant in love with a blind girl in a village stricken with a cholera epidemic. Unexpectedly humorous and deftly directed. (94 mins.)

Light at the Edge of the World, The (U.S.-Spain-Lichtenstein, 1971)* Kirk Douglas, Yul Brynner, Samantha Eggar. Loosely based on an adventure story concocted by Jules Verne, about a wayward lighthouse keeper who has witnessed the wrecking of a ship by pirates and therefore must die. (Dir: Kevin Billington, 101 mins.)†

Lighthorsemen, The (Australia, 1988)** Peter Phelps, John Walton, Tim McKenzie, Jon Blake, Bill Kerr, Anthony Andrews. A heavy-handed war epic based on the campaign of Australian horsemen against Turks and Germans in Beersheba during WWI. Bombastic and clichéd, but the reward for those who stick around is a spectacularly mounted final battle. Released at 140 minutes in Australia, for whose residents this carries more nationalistic and historical weight. (Dir: Simon Wincer, 110 mins.)†

Light in the Forest, The (1958)**½ James MacArthur, Fess Parker, Joanne Dru, Carol Lynley. Walt Disney's superficial, but entertaining version of the Conrad Richter novel. Concerns a white boy raised by Indians and how he learns gradually that he must co-exist with the whites. In time he falls in love with a white girl. (Dir: Herschel Daugherty, 93 mins.)†

Light in the Piazza (1962)*** Olivia de Havilland, Rossano Brazzi, Yvette Mimieux, George Hamilton. Woman and her childhood daughter travel to Italy, where the mother has fears when a nice young lad falls in love with the beautiful but retarded girl. Delicate and disturbing love story graced by beautiful Italian scenics, good performances. (Dir: Guy Green, 101 mins.)

Lightning over Water (1980)***½ Nicholas Ray, Wim Wenders, Ronee Blakely. One-of-a-kind film that documents the efforts made by filmmaker Nicholas Ray to deal with his imminent death by cancer. Ray attempts to start a final film project, aided by his friend, German director Wim Wenders. What results is the film we're watching—a half-real, half-scripted account of Ray's final weeks that is a mesmerizing, disturbing, and ultimately touching chronicle of a life that was truly lived on film. (Dirs: Wim Wenders, Nicholas Ray, 116 mins.)†

Lightning Strikes Twice (1951)**½ Ruth Roman, Richard Todd, Mercedes McCambridge. Despite a hackneyed script about a man acquitted of his wife's murder, Richard Todd manages to create an interesting characterization and gets able support from the two ladies in the cast. (Dir: King Vidor, 91 mins.)

Lightning—The White Stallion (1986)*½ Mickey Rooney, Isabel Lorca. Susan George, Billy Wesley. Can young jockey Lorca ride Lightning to victory, winning back Rooney's fortune and earning the money to pay for the operation that will save her failing sight? Produced (and written, under the pseudonym "Peter Welbeck") by veteran sleazemeister Harry Alan Towers, who seems at a loss as to how to develop a story without whips, gore, or naked women. (Dir: William A. Levey, 93 mins.)†

Light of Day (1987)*½ Michael J. Fox, Joan Jett, Gena Rowlands, Michael McKean, Jason Miller. Superficial rock-and-roll drama that pits a raunchy rocker and single mom (Jett) against her religiously reverent mom (Rowlands) with "responsible" brother Fox in the middle. Writer-director Paul Schrader has not only terribly miscast this film (who could believe these three as a family unit?), but he's also written an unconvincing, cliché-ridden script worthy of the *Flashdance/Footloose* school of blue-collar rock. Nice theme song, though, written by Bruce Springsteen. (107 mins.)†

Lightship, The (1985)** Robert Duvall, Klaus Maria Brandauer, Tom Bower, Robert Costanzo, Badja Djola, William Forsythe. Duvall and Brandauer make an incongruous pair in this retrograde sea-yarn full of submerged meanings: Brandauer underplays to the point of obsequiousness as a captain of a coast guard lightship taken over by three colorful criminals. Worth seeing only for Duvall's over-the-top thesping, if you fancy acting in a vacuum. (Dir: Jerzy Skolimowski, 90 mins.)†

Light That Failed, The (1939)*** Ronald Colman, Ida Lupino, Walter Huston. Superb acting carries this sincere screen version of Kipling's first novel. Story of an artist who is losing his sight is romantic, heroic, and often good drama. (Dir: William Wellman, 97 mins.)

Light Touch, The (1951)**½ Stewart Granger, Pier Angeli, George Sanders. Innocent young girl artist unwittingly provides a suave art thief with a copy of a masterpiece with which he plans a swindle. Good cast, pleasant innocuous entertainment. (Dir: Richard Brooks, 110 mins.)

Light up the Skies—See: **Skywatch**

Light Years (France, 1988)** Voices of Glenn Close, Christopher Plummer, Jennifer Grey, John Shea, Penn and Teller, David Johansen, Terrence Mann. Animated melodrama from the director of *Fantastic Planet*, with a screenplay by sci-fi scribe Isaac Asimov about a prince trying to save his planet from invasion.

A parade of strange creatures is strikingly animated, but the story is ponderous and dull. (Dir: Rene Laloux, 79 mins.)†

Light Years Away (France-Switzerland, 1980)***½ Trevor Howard, Mick Ford, Henri Vorlogeux, Bernice Stegers. Director Alain Tanner continues to develop his cinema of ideas in this unique fable about a reclusive wise man who resides in a dilapidated service station and become a mentor to a punk drifter. At times comic, mysterious, and irritating, with the two leads giving superb performances. (105 mins.)

Like Father, Like Son (Italy, 1957)***½ Marcello Mastroianni, Vittorio De Sica, Antonella Lualdi, Marisa Merlini, Franco Interlenghi, Franco Di Trocchio. Grandly funny story of five Italian families linked through love and marriage. The plot is nothing more than an hilarious series of encounters and daily occurrences, but it's all done with delicious style and fine acting, especially by De Sica as a tailor and Mastroianni as a mechanic. (Dir: Mario Monicelli, 104 mins.)

Like Father, Like Son (1987)**½ Dudley Moore, Kirk Cameron, Margaret Colin. Father (Moore) and son (Cameron) have their brains accidentally switched because of a mysterious Indian potion. The strength of this *Freaky Friday* retread is surprisingly credible acting by both leads. (Dir: Rod Daniel, 97 mins.)†

Likely Story, A (1947)***½ Bill Williams, Barbara Hale. Returned vet thinks he has only a short time to live and gets mixed up with racketeers. Surprisingly good little comedy has many laughs, pleasant players. (Dir: H. C. Potter, 88 mins.)

Like Mom, Like Me (MTV 1978)** Linda Lavin, Kristy McNichol, Patrick O'Neal, Max Gail. Occasionally sensitive, slow-moving account of a mother and her teenage daughter, who face life anew after their college professor husband/father runs off with a student. (Dir: Michael Pressman, 104 mins.)

Like Normal People (MTV 1979)*** Shaun Cassidy, Linda Purl, Hope Lange. The poignant, uplifting real-life story of Roger and Virginia Rae Meyers, a determined retarded couple who fell in love and got married, is handled with restraint. (Dir: Harvey Hart, 78 mins.)

Li'l Abner (1940)** Buster Keaton, Granville Owen, Martha O'Driscoll, Edgar Kennedy. Poor attempt to bring Al Capp's comic-strip town of Dogpatch and its inhabitants to life; despite the cast, the extremely cheap budget and lack of script do it in. Too bad. (Dir: Albert S. Rogell, 78 mins.)†

Li'l Abner (1959)**½ Peter Palmer, Leslie Parrish, Stubby Kaye. The Broadway musical based on the famous cartoon characters of Dogpatch makes a mildly entertaining film. The humor seems forced but the musical numbers are fast paced and colorful. (Dir: Melvin Frank, 113 mins.)†

Lili (1953)***½ Leslie Caron, Mel Ferrer, Jean-Pierre Aumont, Zsa Zsa Gabor. A thoroughly captivating film for youngsters and adults alike, beautifully scored, performed, and produced. Caron is captivating in the title role of a French orphan who joins a small traveling carnival, and soon falls for the charms of a sophisticated magician (Jean-Pierre Aumont), very much the ladies' man although he's married. An unforgettable highlight is a charming dream sequence in which Lili dances with life-size replicas of the puppets. (Dir: Charles Walters, 81 mins.)†

Lilies of the Field (1963)***½ Sidney Poitier, Lilia Skala. Heart-warming drama with an Academy Award–winning performance by Poitier as a handyman who encounters some nuns who have fled from East Germany, and winds up building a chapel for them. Originally released with little fanfare, the film became a big hit, deservedly so. In addition to Poitier, there's a splendid job by Miss Skala, understanding direction by Ralph Nelson. (93 mins.)†

Lili Marleen (West Germany, 1982)**½ Hanna Schygulla, Giancarlo Giannini, Mel Ferrer, Karl Heinz von Hassel. The most expensive and elaborate of all of Rainer Werner Fassbinder's films. Schygulla plays a German chanteuse whose wartime warbling of the title song makes her a favorite among German soldiers and Der Fuehrer himself. Despite a few directorial flourishes, Fassbinder's audacious style is seldom in evidence; it's a rather uncommitted piece of work. (120 mins.)

Liliom (1930)*** Charles Farrell, Rose Hobart, Estelle Taylor, Lee Tracy. The Ferenc Molnár play, which later was made into the musical *Carousel*, is congenial material, about a trouble-prone, scalawag hero who dies and is permitted by heaven to return to earth for a single day. Director Frank Borzage unifies the lovers across time and space to add a dimension of visual profundity. (94 mins.)

Lilith (1964)***½ Warren Beatty, Jean Seberg, Peter Fonda, Kim Hunter, Gene Hackman. Director Robert Rossen creates one of the most intelligent, sensitive portraits of madness ever put on film. The tale is of a trainee therapist (Beatty) whose growing love for a beautiful schizophrenic under his care (Seberg) ends tragically in his own madness. Rossen's film captures beautifully the nuances and subtleties of the interior world of the mentally disturbed. (114 mins.)†

Lillian Russell (1940)** Alice Faye, Don Ameche, Henry Fonda. The fabled stage star who reigned late in the 19th century deserved better screen treatment than she receives here. Old songs are good but her highly fictionalized romances are dreary. (Dir: Irving Cummings, 127 mins.)

Lily in Love (1985)**½ Christopher Plummer, Maggie Smith, Adolph Green, Elke Sommer. An intricately plotted, sophisticated comedy about an arrogant actor who's horrified when his long-suffering playwright wife says he's not right for a romantic screenplay she's written. Plummer and Smith are delightful in this uncredited updating of Molnar's *The Guardsman*. (Dir: Karoly Makk, 103 mins.)†

Lily Tomlin (1987)*** Lily Tomlin, Jane Wagner, Peggy Feury, Cheryl Swannack. An appealing but unenlightening documentary tracing the progress of Tomlin's hit show *The Search for Signs of Intelligent Life in the Universe*. Glimpses of Tomlin at work are rewarding for fans, but the film never probes too deeply. (Dirs: Nicholas Broomfield, Joan Churchill, 89 mins.)

Limbo (1972)** Kate Jackson, Kathleen Nolan, Katherine Justice. Meandering antiwar film centers on the reactions of three wives waiting at an air force base in Florida for their missing husbands in Vietnam. (Dir: Mark Robson, 112 mins.)

Limehouse Blues (1934)**½ George Raft, Jean Parker, Anna May Wong, Kent Taylor. Silly but diverting Hollywood chinoiserie, with the customary lady with a past (an unusual role for Parker) trying to start fresh on the docks of London. (Dir: Alexander Hall, 65 mins.)

Limelight (1952)***½ Charles Chaplin, Claire Bloom, Buster Keaton, Sydney Chaplin, Nigel Bruce. Mawkish in places, the film moves us with its story about a music-hall performer who rescues a ballerina from despair. Chaplin's music hall routines are bitterly comic memories of his early career; he and Keaton perform together for the first and only time. Chaplin won an Academy Award for his musical score in 1972 when the film finally had its Los Angeles premiere. (144 mins.)†

Limit, The (1972)** Yaphet Kotto, Ted Cassidy. Kotto directs with some talent and stars as a tough black cop fighting a gang of toughs. Less brutal, more humane than most films of this genre. (90 mins.)

Limit Up (1989)** Nancy Allen, Dean Stockwell, Brad Hall, Danitra Vance, Ray Charles, Rance Howard, Luana Anders. Wall Street worker Allen, looking to move up and be a broker, makes a deal with the Devil to corner the world soybean market. Limp comedy whose

614

most inspired idea is casting Ray Charles as God, and even that doesn't play as funny as it sounds. (Dir: Richard Martini, 88 mins.)†

L'Immortelle (France, 1962)***½ Jacques Doniol-Valcroze, Françoise Brion, Guido Celano, Sezer Sezin, Catherine Carayon. Two foreigners meet in Istanbul; the woman takes the man on an exotic tour of the city and then disappears, only to reappear and leave again. First film as director by avant-garde novelist Alain Robbe-Grillet, writer of *Last Year at Marienbad*, continues his fascination with the mythically erotic and the theme of life as a disorientating maze. Great use of sound, music, and language. (100 mins.)

Lincoln (1988)—See: *Gore Vidal's Lincoln*

Lincoln Conspiracy, The (1977)** John Anderson, Bradford Dillman. A new twist to the Lincoln assassination plot: Lincoln's assassin, actor John Wilkes Booth, was in cahoots with some members of the U.S. Senate in trying to get rid of the Great Emancipator. Historical mishmash. (Dir: James L. Conway, 104 mins.)†

Linda (MTV 1973)** Stella Stevens, Ed Nelson, John Saxon, John McIntire. John D. MacDonald's mystery-yarn was better in book form. It's the old plot about a sexy blonde wife and her lover framing the naive husband. (Dir: Jack Smight, 90 mins.)

Lindbergh Kidnapping Case, The (MTV 1976)*** Cliff De Young, Anthony Hopkins, Joseph Cotten, Walter Pidgeon, Denise Alexander, Sian-Barbara Allen, Martin Balsam, Dean Jagger, Laurence Luckinbill, Tony Roberts, David Spielberg, Keenan Wynn. Well-made drama on the sensational 1932 tragedy involving the kidnapping of Lindbergh's baby son and the subsequent trial of Bruno Richard Hauptmann. (Dir: Buzz Kulik, 144 mins.)†

Line of Fire: The Morris Dees Story (MTV 1991)*** Corbin Bernsen, Jenny Lewis, Sandy Bull. A tribute to the charismatic Morris Dees, a civil rights lawyer who created the Southern Poverty Law Center and warred against the Ku Klux Klan in true heroic fashion. It's an upbeat drama about a scrapper who believed that you could make a difference—and Dees did. (Dir: John Korty, 96 mins.)

Line Up, The (1958)***½ Eli Wallach, Robert Keith, Warner Anderson, Richard Jaeckel. Two gung ho San Francisco cops pursue two hit men in Don Siegel's exploration of fanaticism on both sides of the law. Tense and gritty; one of Siegel's best. (86 mins.)

Linie 1 (West Germany, 1987)**½ Ilona Schultz, Dieter Landuris, Thomas Ahrens. Here's a rarity—a German movie musical, adapted from a huge stage hit. Set in the trains and stations of the Berlin subway, the movie traces a girl and the assorted punks, druggies, and bums she encounters as she searches for her rock star boyfriend. (Dir: Reinhard Hauff, 96 mins.)

Link (1986)** Terence Stamp, Elisabeth Shue. Lackluster thriller probing the ties between man and ape. When his experimental ape runs amok, the doctor and his female cohort find their lives are in danger. (Dir: Richard Franklin, 103 mins.)†

Lion, The (Great Britain, 1962)** William Holden, Trevor Howard, Capucine, Pamela Franklin. An American lawyer comes to Africa to see his remarried wife and their daughter. (Dir: Jack Cardiff, 96 mins.)

Lion Has Seven Heads, The (Congo, 1970)*** Jean-Pierre Léaud, Gabriele Tinti, Rada Rassimov, Giulio Brogli. Bizarre symbolic depiction of Africa's enslavement by Europeans. Film is part circus, part political tract, often outrageous, and occasionally sadistic. (Dir: Glauber Rocha, 97 mins.)

Lion Has Wings, The (Great Britain, 1939)*** Merle Oberon, Ralph Richardson, June Duprez, Anthony Bushell, Derrick de Marney. Excellent patriotic British WWII docudrama, touting the strength of the air force and its readiness for war; extremely well done if a bit dry compared to U.S. films of this type. (Dirs: Michael Powell, Brian Desmond Hurst, Adrian Brunel, 76 mins.)

Lionheart (1987)* Eric Stoltz, Gabriel Byrne, Nicola Cowper, Dexter Fletcher, Deborah Barrymore, Nicholas Clay. Listless medieval adventure of young knight Stoltz, traveling to Paris to join the Crusades, helping a group of children escape would-be slaver Byrne. (Dir: Franklin J. Schaffner, 104 mins.)†

Lionheart (1991)*½ Jean-Claude Van Damme, Harrison Page, Deborah Rennard. A French Foreign Legionnaire (Van Damme) goes AWOL to get to America to avenge his brother's brutal beating. Lots of kickboxing action, a nifty subplot about dissipated Euro-trash, and a genuine sense of the family raises this film above the norms of the genre. Lionheart says to his niece, "Sometimes life is ugly and stupid and mean." Just like this junk. (Dir: Sheldon Lettich, 105 mins.)†

Lion Hunters, The (1951)** Johnny Sheffield, Morris Ankrum, Ann B. Todd, Douglas Kennedy. Another Bomba entry, as two greedy hunters try to pick their prey in an area where the natives regard their animals as sacred. (Dir: Ford Beebe, 75 mins.)

Lion in Winter, The (Great Britain, 1968)***½ Peter O'Toole, Katharine Hepburn, John Castle, Anthony Hopkins,

Jane Merrow. James Goldman's excellent Broadway play is a superb historical drama, marvelously well acted by O'Toole and Hepburn. Hepburn won an Oscar for her portrayal of the great medieval figure Eleanor of Aquitaine. Narrative starts in 1183 during the reign of King Henry II of England. (Dir: Anthony Harvey, 135 mins.)†

Lion Is in the Streets, A (1953)*** James Cagney, Barbara Hale, Anne Francis. The rise of a ruthless Southern politician is vividly portrayed by Cagney. Familiar but still stirring climax as exposed corruption causes the politician's downfall. (Dir: Raoul Walsh, 88 mins.)

Lion of Africa, The (MCTV 1987)** Brooke Adams, Brian Dennehy, Joseph Shiloa. A volunteer doctor deals with dangerous terrain, bandits, and her overly macho guide as she treks across West Africa in search of medicine. Only the performances of Adams and Dennehy set this apart. (Dir: Kevin Connor, 109 mins.)

Lion of the Desert (1981)** Anthony Quinn, Rod Steiger, Oliver Reed, John Gielgud. Mussolini is set to conquer Libya in the thirties, but Quinn leads the local rebels against him. Lacks visual sweep and variety. (Dir: Moustapha Akkad, 163 mins.)†

Lipstick (1976)½ Margaux Hemingway, Chris Sarandon, Anne Bancroft, Mariel Hemingway. A successful model is savagely raped by a sick composer and then humiliated in and out of court. (Dir: Lamont Johnson, 89 mins.)†

Liquidator, The (1966)**½ Rod Taylor, Trevor Howard, Jill St. John. Taylor is being trained by British Intelligence for a secret mission involving assassinations and such, but the plot doesn't really interfere with the two-fisted action and lovemaking. (Dir: Jack Cardiff, 104 mins.)

Liquid Sky (1983)*** Anne Carlisle, Paula Sheppard. A low-budget but expensive-looking film about aliens who invade the Earth to obtain a euphoria-inducing substance produced during earthlings' orgasms. Imaginative and off-the-wall. (Dir: Slava Tsukerman, 112 mins.)†

Lisa (U.S.-Great Britain, 1962)**½ Stephen Boyd, Dolores Hart, Hugh Griffith, Donald Pleasence. Slightly illogical, but exciting suspense tale about a troubled young Jewish refugee's flight across Europe just after WWII, and the aid she gets from a police officer who accidentally teams up with her. (Dir: Philip Dunne, 112 mins.)

Lisa, Bright and Dark (MTV 1973)*** Anne Baxter, John Forsythe, Kay Lenz, Anne Lockhart, Debralee Scott. Three teenage girls try their own style of group therapy after their girlfriend suffers a nervous breakdown. Better than average. (Dir: Jeannot Szwarc, 78 mins.)

Lisbon (1956)*** Ray Milland, Maureen O'Hara, Claude Rains. Adventurer is hired by an international scoundrel to act as go-between in a kidnapping. Melodrama has dash, pleasant players, and picturesque locale. (Dir: Ray Milland, 90 mins.)†

Listen, Darling (1938)**½ Judy Garland, Freddie Bartholomew, Walter Pidgeon, Mary Astor. Cute little tidbit about a couple of youngsters who try to marry off a widow so they can have a mother and father. (Dir: Edwin L. Marin, 80 mins.)

Listen to Me (1989)*½ Kirk Cameron, Jami Gertz, Roy Scheider, Amanda Peterson, Tim Quill, Anthony Zerbe. Comedy-drama about members of a college debating team, aimed at a teen audience. (Dir: Douglas Day Stewart, 107 mins.)†

Listen to Your Heart (MTV 1983)** Kate Jackson, Tim Matheson, Will Nye, George Coe, Cassie Yates. Love blooms in Chicago between a young book editor and his art director. An easy-to-take boy meets girl story. (Dir: Don Taylor, 104 mins.)†

Listen Up: The Lives of Quincy Jones (1990) *** Fast-paced documentary about jazz great Jones creatively mixes his own comments with those of past and present collaborators including Ray Charles, Frank Sinatra, Big Daddy Kane, Miles Davis, Ella Fitzgerald, and Dizzy Gillespie; also includes energetic footage of Jones at work. A must for music lovers. (Dir: Ellen Weissbrod, 114 mins.)†

List of Adrian Messenger, The (1963)*** George C. Scott, Herbert Marshall, Gladys Cooper, Kirk Douglas, Robert Mitchum, Frank Sinatra. Oddball thriller. George C. Scott is the detective seeking a mass murderer who has the knack of bizarre disguises. (Dir: John Huston, 98 mins.)†

Lisztomania (Great Britain, 1975)** Roger Daltrey, Sara Kestelman, John Justin, Fiona Lewis, Ringo Starr. Director Ken Russell views classical composer Franz Liszt as the first mass culture hero, like a rock star of today, but Russell's development renders the idea progressively less profound. (104 mins.)†

Little Accident (1939)**½ Hugh Herbert, Florence Rice, Richard Carlson, Ernest Truex, Edgar Kennedy, Baby Sandy. Amusing vehicle for Herbert has a bachelor columnist landed with an abandoned baby, and trying to take care of it himself. A bit formulaic, but with plenty of opportunity for laughs. (Dir: Charles Lamont, 65 mins.)

Little Annie Rooney (1925)** Mary Pickford, William Haines, Gordon Griffith, Walter James. Not one of Pickford's best pictures, this stars her as the daughter of an Irish policeman whose boyfriend is unjustly accused of murder; she is first-rate, but the plot wobbles between melodrama and social comedy, and doesn't really succeed as either. (Dir: William Beaudine, 97 mins.)†

Little Big Horn (1951)*** John Ireland, Lloyd Bridges, Marie Windsor. Saga of a small band of cavalry sent to warn Custer of impending Indian attack. Grim, gripping, excellently acted. (Dir: Charles Marquis Warren, 86 mins.)

Little Big Man (1970)*** Dustin Hoffman, Faye Dunaway, Richard Mulligan, Chief Dan George. Sprawling, often moving historical film about the development of the West and how the white man treated the Indians. Much of the narrative unfolds in the form of flashbacks seen through the eyes of a 121-year-old white man, the sole white survivor of Custer's last stand. (Dir: Arthur Penn, 147 mins.)†

Little Boy Lost (1953)***½ Bing Crosby, Claude Dauphin, Christian Fourcade. War correspondent returns to France in search of his son, born during World War II, whom he has never seen. Tender, touching drama. (Dir: George Seaton, 95 mins.)†

Little Caesar (1930)***½ Edward G. Robinson, Glenda Farrell, Sidney Blackmer, Douglas Fairbanks, Jr. One of the great gangster movies. Robinson's portrayal of a merciless killer is a masterpiece which has withstood years of mimicry. (Dir: Mervyn LeRoy, 80 mins.)†

Little Cigars (1973)**½ Angel Tompkins, Billy Curtis, Jerry Maren, Frank Delfino. A fairly amusing not-so-tall tale about a gang of midget mobsters who measure up to the big guys. As far as midget films go, much better than *The Terror of Tiny Town*. (Dir: Chris Christenberry, 92 mins.)

Little Colonel, The (1935)**½ Shirley Temple, Lionel Barrymore, Bill Robinson, Evelyn Venable. Corny, contrived Temple vehicle of the old South, made worthwhile by the old "Bojangles" Robinson dancing with Shirley. (Dir: David Butler, 80 mins.)†

Little Darlings (1980)** Kristy McNichol, Tatum O'Neal, Kris Erickson, Armand Assante. Unabsorbing story of two fifteen-year-old girls at summer camp who are in a race to be the first to lose their virginity. McNichol is much better than the material. (Dir: Ronald Maxwell, 95 mins.)

Little Dorrit (Great Britain, 1987)**** Derek Jacobi, Sarah Pickering, Alec Guinness, Cyril Cusack, Joan Greenwood. Exemplary adaptation of Charles Dickens's novel about life in Victorian England, a scathing indictment of middle-class hypocrisy and upper-class indifference. Screenwriter-director Christine Edzard paints a sharp portrait of a society that has lost touch with basic human values—one that remains only too relevant today. The six-hour film consists of two parts, *Little Dorrit* and *Nobody's Fault*. (360 mins.)

Little Drummer Girl (1984)*** Diane Keaton, Yorgo Voyagis, Klaus Kinski, Sami Frey, Michael Cristofer. Film adaptation of John le Carré's brilliant novel portrays a complex tale of Israeli and Palestinian espionage and terrorism. In one of her best performances, Keaton is a pro-Palestinian actress who becomes employed as a double agent. (Dir: George Roy Hill, 131 mins.)†

Little Egypt (1951)**½ Mark Stevens, Rhonda Fleming, Nancy Guild, Charles Drake. An occasionally gyrating drama about the Gay 90s Chicago Fair, which introduced that sensational Queen of the Undulators, Little Egypt. (Dir: Frederick de Cordova, 82 mins.)

Little Fauss and Big Halsy (1970)*½ Robert Redford, Michael Pollard, Lauren Hutton. Halsy is a suspended motorcycle racer and Fauss is a Walter Mitty bike tuner. Together they race around the Southwest. Directionless drama. (Dir: Sidney Furie, 97 mins.)

Little Foxes, The (1941)**** Bette Davis, Herbert Marshall, Teresa Wright, Dan Duryea, Richard Carlson, Charles Dingle, Carl Benton Reid. Superb film based on Lillian Hellman's strong play about the double dealings of a Southern family presided over by a vixen named Regina, a part tailor-made for Davis's exceptional talents. (Dir: William Wyler, 116 mins.)†

Little Fugitive (1953)*** Richie Andrusco, Ricky Brewster, Winifred Cushing. Unusual and rewarding naturalistic drama about a seven-year-old boy who hides out at Coney Island after he mistakenly believes he's killed another boy with his cap gun. Silver Lion winner at the Venice Film Festival. (Dirs: Ray Ashely, Morris Engel, Ruth Orkin, 75 mins.)

Little Game (MTV 1971)*½ Ed Nelson, Diane Baker, Katy Jurado, Howard Duff, Christopher Shea. A paranoid man thinks his eleven-year-old stepson might be a murderer, and hires a private detective to find out if he's the boy's next victim. Intriguing premise indifferently executed. (Dir: Paul Wendkos, 76 mins.)

Little Giant (1933)** Edward G. Robinson, Mary Astor, Helen Vinson, Kenneth Thomson. Beer czar Robinson abandons gangsterism in a pleasant but unmemorable comic caper about a former bootlegger who tries to become a blue blood. (Dir: Roy Del Ruth, 74 mins.)

Little Giant (1946)** Bud Abbott, Lou Costello, Elena Verdugo. Costello plays a salesman who bilks the crooked manager (Abbott) of the firm he works for, and wins a prize for his effort. Plenty of slapstick. (Dir: William A. Seiter, 91 mins.)

Little Girl Lost (MTV 1988)**½ Tess Harper, Frederic Forrest, Patricia Kalember, Marie Martin. A powerful drama based on real events. Harper and Forrest play a couple who have to buck the system in order to regain custody of their foster child (Martin), a victim of sexual abuse by her real father. (Dir: Sharron Miller, 96 mins.)

Little Girl Who Lives Down the Lane, The (U.S.-Canada, 1976)***½ Jodie Foster, Martin Sheen, Alexis Smith, Scott Jacoby, Mort Schuman. Very involving thriller concerning strangely independent adolescent girl threatened by child molester who knows her guilty secret. Well acted all around. (Dir: Nicholas Gessner, 94 mins.)†

Little Gloria...Happy at Last (MTV 1982)***½ Martin Balsam, Bette Davis, Michael Gross, Lucy Gutteridge, Glynis Johns, Angela Lansbury, Maureen Stapleton. Harrowing docudrama about the childhood of designer Gloria Vanderbilt. A saddening saga of the "poor little rich girl" that also captures the flavor of the lush life of the super-rich in the 1920s and 1930s, contrasted with the economic despair of millions of others. (Dir: Waris Hussein, 208 mins.)†

Little House: Bless All the Dear Children (MTV 1984)** Melissa Gilbert, Dean Butler, Victor French, Richard Bull, Alison Arngrim, Pamela Roylance. Only fans of "Little House on the Prairie" will be engrossed by this tale about Laura's baby daughter being abducted by a crazy woman. (Dir: Victor French, 104 mins.)

Little House: Look Back to Yesterday (MTV 1983)**½ Melissa Gilbert, Dean Butler, Victor French, Richard Bull, Michael Landon, Matthew Laborteaux. In this "Little House on the Prairie" TV-movie, Albert (Laborteaux) faces death from an incurable disease, and he goes home to Walnut Grove for one last look. (Dir: Victor French, 104 mins.)

Little House on the Prairie, The (MTV 1974)**½ Michael Landon, Karen Grassle. TV pilot film about a post–Civil War family trekking from Wisconsin to Kansas to open a new life as homesteaders. It's based on the book by Laura Ingalls Wilder, the real-life daughter of the pioneering family. (Dir: Michael Landon, 100 mins.)†

Little House: The Last Farewell—See: Last Farewell, The

Little Hut, The (Great Britain, 1957)*** Ava Gardner, Stewart Granger, David Niven. The French play about a wife,
618

her husband, and his best friend living a "civilized" existence while shipwrecked on an island makes a frothy, sophisticated film. (Dir: Mark Robson, 78 mins.)

Little Kidnappers, The (Great Britain, 1954)**** Adrienne Corri, Duncan MacRae. Two boys kidnap a baby because they can't have a dog. Brilliant, simple, moving and amusing film. That's all there is to it, but it's a gem. Jon Whiteley and Vincent Winter, the boys, won Special Oscars. (Dir: Philip Leacock, 93 mins.)

Little Ladies of the Night (MTV 1977)**½ David Soul, Lou Gossett, Jr., Linda Purl, Clifton Davis, Carolyn Jones, Lana Wood, Dorothy Malone. Purl is quite good playing the role of a very young teenager forced into prostitution by some threatening pimps after running away from home. (Dir: Marvin Chomsky, 100 mins.)†

Little Laura and Big John (1973)**½ Fabian Forte, Karen Black, Ivy Thayer, Ken Miller, Paul Gleason, Cliff Frates. Brash action-pic about outlaw lovers cruising the Everglades. Fabian and Karen make an odd couple of social outcasts, but their flight from the law is rather arresting. (Dirs: Luke Moberly, Bob Woodburn, 82 mins.)†

Little Lord Fauntleroy (1936)***½ Mickey Rooney, Dolores Costello, Freddie Bartholomew, C. Aubrey Smith, Guy Kibbee, Jessie Ralph. Surprisingly uncloying entertainment with Freddie Bartholomew as the long-lost American heir brought under the tutelage of curmudgeonly C. Aubrey Smith, whose hard heart is tamed by the lovable boy. (Dir: John Cromwell, 98 mins.)†

Little Lord Fauntleroy (MTV 1980)*** Ricky Schroder, Alec Guinness, Eric Porter, Colin Blakely, Rachel Kempson. An impeccable production, perfect in all its period details, highlights this remake of the Freddie Bartholomew classic. Guinness is customarily expert in this warhorse about the urchin who becomes a titled lord. Worth seeing on most counts except for the bundle of mechanical charm playing the title role. (Dir: Jack Gold, 104 mins.).†

Little Man, What Now? (1934)**** Margaret Sullavan, Douglass Montgomery, Alan Hale, Alan Mowbray. The chief merit to this early anti-Nazi film lies not in its political content, but in the lyrical quality of its romance which is none the less transcendent for its squalid setting. A major work by Hollywood's master romanticist, Frank Borzage. (90 mins.)

Little Match Girl, The (MTV 1987)* Keshia Knight Pulliam, Rue McClanahan, William Daniels, John Rhys-Davies. A beguiling tyke brings Christmas cheer to a rich family. Lies somewhere between heartwarming and heartburn, with the emphasis on the latter. (Dir: Michael Lindsay-Hogg, 96 mins.)†

Little Men (1940)**½ Kay Francis, Jack Oakie, George Bancroft. Louisa May Alcott's sequel to her classic *Little Women*. Francis is very good as the grown-up Jo March, who marries and runs an unconventional school for boys. (Dir: Norman Z. McLeod, 84 mins.)†

Little Mermaid, The (1989)***½ Voices of Jodi Benson, Samuel E. Wright, Pat Carroll, Kenneth Mars, Buddy Hackett, René Auberjonois. Wonderful Disney animated feature will enchant youngsters and the child in all of us. A mermaid yearns for the chance to become human so she can experience life above the water. Film deservedly won Oscars for Best Original Score and Best Song ("Under the Sea"). Benson and Wright, providing the musical voices of Ariel the Mermaid and Sebastian the Crab, respectively, are responsible for much of the film's success. (Dirs: John Musker, Ron Clemente, 82 mins.)†

Little Minister, The (1934)*** John Beal, Katharine Hepburn, Donald Crisp, Andy Clyde, Dorothy Stickney, Reginald Denny, Beryl Mercer. James M. Barrie's play of the romance of a Scot minister is charming, subdued, and satisfying. (Dir: Richard Wallace, 110 mins.)†

Little Miss Broadway (1938)** Shirley Temple, Jimmy Durante, George Murphy. Routine Shirley Temple film carrying her from orphanage to success in her foster home. (Dir: Irving Cummings, 71 mins.)†

Little Miss Marker (1934)*** Adolphe Menjou, Charles Bickford, Shirley Temple. A little girl is left with gangsters as security for an IOU. Remade also as *Sorrowful Jones* and *40 Pounds of Trouble*. (Dir: Alexander Hall, 80 mins.)

Little Miss Marker (1980)**½ Walter Matthau, Julie Andrews, Tony Curtis, Sara Stimson, Bob Newhart. Fourth version of the Damon Runyon tale; gambler Sorrowful Jones is melted by the warmth of tiny Stimson, left in his keeping as collateral for a bet. Slow moving but reasonably pleasant. (Dir: Walter Bernstein, 103 mins.)†

Little Mo (MTV 1978)**½ Glynnis O'Connor, Michael Learned, Anne Baxter. Story of the tragic death of Maureen Connolly—the women's tennis champ of the early 1950s—a little girl from San Diego who was determined to be the best at something. (Dir: Dan Haller, 156 mins.)

Little Moon and Jud McGraw (1979)½ James Caan, Stefanie Powers, Robert Walker, Jr., Michael Conrad. The shaky plot veers back and forth from a bungled framing story about a reporter investigating the legend of a western outlaw to the brutal flashbacks of the folk hero Jud McGraw's exploits in the old West. (Dir: Bernard Girard, 90 mins.)

Little Mr. Jim (1946)*** Butch Jenkins, James Craig, Frances Gifford. When tragedy strikes his family, a small lad turns to the Chinese cook for companionship. Touching, well-done drama. (Dir: Fred Zinnemann, 92 mins.)

Little Murders (1971)*** Elliott Gould, Marcia Rodd, Vincent Gardenia, Donald Sutherland, Elizabeth Wilson, Alan Arkin. Jules Feiffer's devastating off-Broadway satire has been turned into an impressive movie. An important document of the violence-ridden New York scene, and what turns the average citizen from apathy to militancy. (Dir: Alan Arkin, 108 mins.)

Little Nellie Kelly (1940)**½ Judy Garland, George Murphy. Granddaughter of a stubborn Irish cop tries to patch up a family feud that has lasted for years. Sentimentality reigns supreme in this comedy-drama. (Dir: Norman Taurog, 100 mins.)

Little Night Music, A (1977)* Elizabeth Taylor, Diana Rigg, Len Cariou, Lesley-Anne Down, Hermione Gingold, Lawrence Guittard. Stephen Sondheim's graceful musical drama of three pairs of lovers quarreling and reuniting in turn-of-the-century Vienna becomes a lumbering and grotesquely miscast movie. The show was based on Ingmar Bergman's film, *Smiles of a Summer Night*. (Dir: Harold Prince, 124 mins.)

Little Nikita (1988)*** Sidney Poitier, River Phoenix, Richard Jenkins. Poitier is an FBI agent who forms a bond with a young man (Phoenix) who discovers that his parents are Communist spies. (Dir: Richard Benjamin, 98 mins.)†

Little Noises (1991)*** Crispin Glover, Steven Schub, Tatum O'Neal, Rik Mayall. Nicely acted film about a failed writer (Glover) who steals the work of a mute poet and pawns it off as his own, only to come to terms with his conscience after finding the poet homeless. Lightly comic, with some fine insights into creativity and honor. First film by director Jane Spencer. (Dir: Jane Spencer, 110 mins.)†

Little Nuns, The (Italy, 1965)*** Catherine Spaak, Sylva Koscina. Charming, tender comedy-drama about the adventures of two nuns who go to the city. (Dir: Luciano Salce, 101 mins.)

Little Old New York (1940)**½ Alice Faye, Fred MacMurray, Richard Greene. Don't take this story about Fulton and his steamboat too seriously and you may have some fun. It's long, slightly miscast but occasionally entertaining. (Dir: Henry King, 100 mins.)

Little Prince, The (1974)**½ Richard Kiley, Steven Warner, Gene Wilder, Bob Fosse, Clive Revill, Donna McKechnie. Disappointing musical version of the enduring book by Antoine de Saint-Exupery about an aviator and the little boy from outer space. Musical score by Lerner and Loewe. (Dir: Stanley Donen, 88 mins.)†

Little Princess, The (1939)***½ Shirley Temple, Anita Louise, Ian Hunter, Cesar Romero, Arthur Treacher. Shirley is a rich little girl in Victorian London who is mistreated when her father (and his fortune) is lost in the Boer War. Amazingly effective and enjoyable for all ages—really. (Dir: Walter Lang, 91 mins.)†

Little Richard Story, The (1990)**½ Little Richard. Confusing documentary made without the cooperation of the subject. Director William Klein is more interested in the craziness surrounding the rock icon than the man or his music. However, there are many terrific clips that are well worth seeing. Otherwise, a disappointment. (Dir: William Klein, 90 mins.)

Little Romance, A (U.S.-France, 1979)*** Laurence Olivier, Broderick Crawford, Diane Lane. Delightful romantic comedy about two precocious children who run off to seal their eternal love with a kiss beneath the Bridge of Sighs in Venice at sunset as the bells toll. Deft and delicate throughout. (Dir: George Roy Hill, 108 mins.)†

Little Sex, A (1982)** Tim Matheson, Kate Capshaw, Edward Herrmann, John Glover, Joan Copeland, Susanna Dalton. Failed comedy about infidelity. A young husband finds it extremely difficult to remain loyal. (Dir: Bruce Paltrow, 95 mins.)†

Little Shepherd of Kingdom Come, The (1961)** Jimmie Rodgers, Luana Patten. Kentucky mountain boy is a wanderer until taken in by a loving family; but he takes the side of the North when the Civil War begins. Pleasing rural tale takes a bit too much time to tell its story. (Dir: Andrew V. McLaglen, 108 mins.)

Little Shop of Horrors, The (1960)*** Jonathan Haze, Jackie Joseph, Mel Welles, Dick Miller, Jack Nicholson. The legendary Roger Corman movie made in two days has more laughs than most big-budget films. The tale of a skid row nudnik who raises a blood-lusting talking plant gets better every time you watch it. (70 mins.)†

Little Shop of Horrors (1986)**** Rick Moranis, Ellen Greene, Vincent Gardenia, Steve Martin, John Candy, Bill Murray. Director Frank Oz exhibits a real flair for staging and filming musical numbers. Based on the off-Broadway 620

hit inspired by the black-comedy cult film, this musical concerns nerdish Seymour Krelborn's discovery of a weird-looking plant that craves human blood. (88 mins.)†

Little Sister, The (1985)**½ John Savage, Tracy Pollan, Roxanne Harat, Jack Kehoe. Probation officer Savage spends his extra time trying to save lost souls in Boston's red-light district, concentrating on rich man's daughter Pollan. Atmospheric drama. (Dir: Jan Egleson, 103 mins.)†

Little Spies (MTV 1986)**½ Mickey Rooney, Robert Costanzo, Peter Smith, Candace Cameron, Adam Carl, Sean Hall. Standard Disney fluff about kids rescuing their pooch from dognappers with the help of a hermit-like WWII hero. (Dir: Greg Beeman, 104 mins.).

Littlest Hobo, The (1958)**½ Buddy Hart, Wendy Stuart. Nice story of a dog's adventures, especially for the kiddies. (Dir: Charles Rondeau, 77 mins.)

Littlest Outlaw, The (1955)**½ Pedro Armendariz, Joseph Calleia, Rodolfo Acosta, Pepe Ortiz, Andres Velasquez. When a horse that's been badly abused by his trainer is ordered to be shot, a young, caring boy rescues him and travels throughout Mexico. Pleasant family fare. (Dir: Roberto Gavaldon, 75 mins.)

Littlest Rebel, The (1935)** Shirley Temple, John Boles, Bill Robinson. Shirley is the heroine of the Civil War in this, and your kids will love it. (Dir: David Butler, 70 mins.)†

Little Theater of Jean Renoir, The (France-Italy-West Germany, 1969)***½ A delightful, if slight, collection of short tales and musical episodes wryly hosted by director Jean Renoir, whose bittersweet, darkly comic view of the human condition bursts with dramatic possibilities. (100 mins.)†

Little Thief, The (France, 1988)***½ Charlotte Gainsbourg, Didier Bezace, Simon de la Brosse, Raoul Billery. François Truffaut had long wanted to create a female counterpart to the hero of his *The 400 Blows;* his longtime assistant Claude Miller did just that in this film adapted from a story outline by Truffaut. Gainsbourg plays a smalltown girl, her mother exiled from the country for consorting with German soldiers, with a penchant for petty thievery and a desire to experience life in the world that she only sees in the movies. Miller wisely restrains the impulse to make an overt homage to the late Truffaut in a gentle but realistic film whose only weak point is a vague ending. (109 mins.)†

Little Tough Guy (1938)** Billy Halop, Huntz Hall, Gabe Dell, Bernard Punsley, David Gorcey, Marjorie Main. The Little Tough Guys foolhardily start a crime wave after Johnny's father is sentenced to die for a crime he never committed. (Dir: Harold Young, 83 mins.) †

Little Tough Guys series—See: **Bowery Boys** series

Little Treasure (1985)*½ Burt Lancaster, Ted Danson, Margot Kidder. Nothing to treasure here. A dying man (Lancaster) has been G-stringing his abandoned stripper daughter along with the promise of great wealth. Abetted by a wanderer (Danson) she tries to dig up 20,000 dollars that her Papa buried after a robbery years before. (Dir: Alan Sharp, 95 mins.) †

Little Vera (U.S.S.R., 1988)*** Natalya Negoda, Andrei Sokolov, Yuri Nazarov. A U.S. hit for all the wrong reasons (i.e., plentiful exposure of star Negoda in *Playboy*), this is a surprisingly bleak black comedy about Soviet family life marred by alcoholism, pregnancy, and overcrowding. An intriguing glimpse into a social structure seldom seen by Western eyes. (Dir: Vasily Pichul, 110 mins.) †

Little Women (1933)**** Katharine Hepburn, Joan Bennett, Jean Parker, Spring Byington, Frances Dee, Paul Lukas. One of the best efforts of producer David Selznick and of director George Cukor. The whole piece is finely acted. Tasteful but not dull, an effective piece of Americana. (120 mins.) †

Little Women (1949)**½ June Allyson, Peter Lawford, Margaret O'Brien, Elizabeth Taylor, Janet Leigh, Mary Astor. Remake of the classic about life in Concord at the time of the Civil War. Entertaining when it's light and gay but when they turn on the tears, it's a mess. (Dir: Mervyn LeRoy, 121 mins.) †

Little Women (MTV 1978)*½ Meredith Baxter Birney, Susan Dey, Ann Dusenberry, Eve Plumb, Greer Garson, Dorothy McGuire, Cliff Potts. A TV-ization of Louisa May Alcott's tale of the March girls growing up and leaving the nest at the time of the Civil War. The worst of the versions. (Dir: David Lowell Rich, 200 mins.)

Little World of Don Camillo (France-Italy, 1953)*** Fernandel, Sylvie, Gino Cervi. Priest feuds with the Communist mayor of his town. Enjoyable comedy-drama with good performances. (Dir: Julien Duvivier, 96 mins.)

Live Again, Die Again (MTV 1974)**½ Walter Pidgeon, Donna Mills, Geraldine Page, Vera Miles. A standard sci-fi item about a woman who returns to her family after being cryogenically frozen for 34 years. (Dir: Richard A. Colla, 74 mins.)

Live a Little, Love a Little (1968)** Elvis Presley, Michele Carey, Don Porter, Rudy Vallee, Dick Sargent. Inconsequential but tuneful Presley outing with Swivel Hips as an overworked shutterbug. (Dir: Norman Taurog, 90 mins.) †

Live a Little, Steal a Lot—See: **Murph the Surf**

Live and Let Die (Great Britain, 1973)*** Roger Moore, Yaphet Kotto, Jane Seymour, Geoffrey Holder. Agent 007 tries to unearth a large heroin operation in the Caribbean. Flashy photography, exotic locales keep things popping along at a nice clip. (Dir: Guy Hamilton, 121 mins.) †

Live Fast, Die Young (1958)** Mary Murphy, Michael Connors. Sister searches for a runaway teenager, finds her in time to prevent her from taking part in a robbery. (Dir: Paul Henreid, 82 mins.)

Live for Life (France-Italy, 1967)** Yves Montand, Candice Bergen, Annie Girardot. A TV reporter and his affairs, marital and extramarital, fancied up with pretty photography by director Claude Lelouch. Despite the frills, it never goes anywhere, not even when it tries for relevancy in a Vietnam sequence. (111 mins.)

Live, Love and Learn (1937)** Robert Montgomery, Rosalind Russell, Mickey Rooney. Aristocratic Roz descends to the hoi polloi when she marries a struggling painter who, in typical MGM fashion, settles down to domestic bliss. Blessedly, the stars went on to better scripts after this. (Dir: George Fitzmaurice, 78 mins.)

Lively Set, The (1964)** James Darren, Pamela Tiffin, Doug McClure, Joanie Sommers. Lad shows more interest in racing engines than college, so he quits to devote his time to putt-putts. (Dir: Jack Arnold, 95 mins.)

Lives of a Bengal Lancer, The (1935)**** Gary Cooper, Franchot Tone, Richard Cromwell, Sir Guy Standing, C. Aubrey Smith, Kathleen Burke. Action escapism at its zestiest, this glorified schoolboys' adventure is a spirited salute to stiff-upper-lip heroics, as the British Empire defends its colonial holdings. Pure excitement, as Cooper and Tone, the experienced soldiers, serve as big brothers to a fledgling recruit (Cromwell). (Dir: Henry Hathaway, 109 mins.) †

Lives of Jenny Dolan, The (MTV 1975)** Shirley Jones, Dana Wynter, Lynn Carlin, George Grizzard, Ian McShane. Shirley Jones is starred in this slick murder-mystery drama, playing a retired investigative reporter who comes back to work for a crack at unearthing the sinister plot behind the governor's assassination, and three other deaths which occurred in the same night. (Dir: Jerry Jameson, 98 mins.)

Live Today for Tomorrow—See: **Act of Murder, An**

Live Wires (1946)**½ Bowery Boys, Mike Mazurki, Pamela Blake. The first in the Bowery Boys series. The overly complicated plot concerns Gorcey's job with the D.A.'s office and how he prevents his sister from running off with his former boss, who turns out to be a crook. (Dir: Phil Karlson, 64 mins.)

Living at Risk (1985)*** Documentary explores the reality of life in Nicaragua under the Sandinistas by following the daily lives of five siblings from a middle-class family. By focusing on so-called average citizens (as opposed to the poor or rich), the film gives new insight into events in that troubled country. (Dirs: Alfred Guzzetti, Susan Meiselas, Richard Rogers, 59 mins.)

Living Daylights, The (Great Britain, 1987)***½ Timothy Dalton, Maryam d'Abo, Jeroen Krabbe, Joe Don Baker, John Rhys-Davies, Art Malik. The best Bond film in years. This thrilling yarn involving a KGB defector who's a double agent benefits from Dalton's debut interpretation of Bond as a man who thrives on danger. (Dir: John Glen, 130 mins.)†

Living Desert, The (1953)***½ This Academy Award–winning film, the first of Walt Disney's True-Life Adventures, is a gorgeous study of animal life in all its forms in the American desert. (Dir: James Algar, 72 mins.)

Living Doll (Great Britain, 1990)*½ Mark Jax, Katie Orgill, Gary Martin, Eartha Kitt. Medical student working at a morgue steals the body of a girl he had admired from a distance, takes it home with him, and becomes a slave to the dead girl's will. Cheap, tasteless horror movie. (Dirs: Peter Litten, George Dugdale, 92 mins.)

Living Free (Great Britain, 1972)*** Susan Hampshire, Nigel Davenport. Exotic African scenery and three tiny lion cubs provide pleasant family entertainment in this sequel to *Born Free*. (Dir: Jack Couffer, 91 mins.)†

Living in a Big Way (1947)***½ Gene Kelly, Marie McDonald, Charles Winninger. Director Gregory La Cava's last film mixes too many modes too uncertainly, but there are brilliant passages. Kelly is back from WWII facing the problems of scarce housing and a wealthy wife. Featuring one of Kelly's most brilliant dance numbers on a construction site. (103 mins.)

Living It Up (1954)** Dean Martin, Jerry Lewis, Janet Leigh. Jerry as a railroad attendant whose sinus trouble is mistaken for radiation, becomes a human-interest story with New York at his feet. Martin and Lewis fans will approve, but the shadow of the original *Nothing Sacred* makes this one shrivel in comparison. (Dir: Norman Taurog, 95 mins.)

Living on Tokyo Time (1987)** Minako Ohashi, Ken Nakagawa. A mild ultra-low budget comedy about a young Japanese woman who visits the U.S. for "an American experience" and winds up in a marriage of convenience to an assimilated Japanese-American dullard who cares more for heavy metal than for her. Some wry moments sink under the weight of stultifying acting and passive characters. (Dir: Steven Okazaki, 83 mins.)†

Living on Velvet (1935)**½ Kay Francis, George Brent, Warren William, Samuel S. Hinds. Entertaining romance has Brent falling for mysterious lady Francis, losing track of her, and desperately trying to find her again; intriguing atmosphere from director Frank Borzage. (80 mins.)

Living Proof: The Hank Williams, Jr. Story (MTV 1983)*** Richard Thomas, Clu Gulager, Allyn Ann McLerie, Lenora May, Liane Langland. An absorbing biopic with country-western trimmings. Thomas gives a powerhouse performance as a son seeking his identity in a world where everyone knew and loved his father. (Dir: Dick Lowry, 104 mins.)

Lizards, The (Italy, 1963)**½ Stefano Sattaflores, Sergio Ferrannino, Toni Petruzzi, Luigi Barbieri. In southern Italy a group of young men cruise chicks and hang out in the sun, just like their counterparts in the U.S.A. First feature by Lina Wertmuller is visually tight and full of rollicking good-natured humor. (85 mins.)

Lizzie (1957)** Eleanor Parker, Richard Boone, Joan Blondell. Psychoshenanigans concerning a drab girl who seems to have another self lurking within her. (Dir: Hugo Haas, 81 mins.)

Lloyds of London (1936)***½ Tyrone Power, Madeleine Carroll, Freddie Bartholomew, George Sanders. Engrossing, often exciting story of the famous English insurance and banking firm. This picture tells of its early history and rise to prominence around the time of the battle of Trafalgar. (Dir: Henry King, 101 mins.)

Loan Shark (1952)**½ George Raft, Dorothy Hart, Paul Stewart. An ex-con smashes a vicious loan-shark racket that has been plaguing workers in a tire plant. Fast moving crime melodrama, with Raft at his best. (Dir: Seymour Friedman, 74 mins.)

Lobsterman from Mars (1989)** Deborah Foreman, Anthony Hickox, Tommy Sledge, Patrick Macnee, Billy Barty, Tony Curtis, Bobby Pickett. Lampoon of '50s sci-fi movies in the form of an amateur movie being viewed by studio head Curtis, who needs a guaranteed money-loser for tax purposes. The joke wears off long before the movie is over, but there are a few laughs along the way. Narrated by Dr. Demento. (Dir: Stanley Sheff, 93 mins.)†

Local Boy Makes Good (1931)**½ Joe E. Brown, Dorothy Lee, Ruth Hall, Robert Bennett. Fun early Brown vehicle has our hero a bashful youth who discovers he has unsuspected athletic ability; lots of opportunities for acrobatic displays. (Dir: Mervyn LeRoy, 67 mins.)

Local Hero (1983)**** Peter Riegert, Burt Lancaster, Denis Lawson. Charming, whimsical comedy with a hard edge about Houston oil executive Riegert sent to Scotland to negotiate the purchase of an entire fishing village. Away from the rat race (or so he thinks), he falls under the spell of the local charm. Writer-director Bill Forsyth's special talent is for background detail, and this is his most beguiling work, marred only slightly by an ironic (but still appropriate) ending. (110 mins.)†

Locket, The (1947)** Laraine Day, Brian Aherne, Robert Mitchum. Beautiful but mentally unbalanced girl ruins the lives of the men who love her. Overdone, confused melodrama. (Dir: John Brahm, 86 mins.)

Lock, Stock and Barrel (MTV 1971)**½ Tim Matheson, Belinda Montgomery, Claude Akins. Uneven, well-cast, carefully produced western farce about newlyweds, hustling preachers, and land swindles. (Dir: Jerry Thorpe, 78 mins.)

Locusts (MTV 1974)** Ben Johnson, Ron Howard. A well-meaning but slow-moving account of a young man, washed out of Navy flight school and returned home to Montana farm country in 1943. A demanding father (Johnson) is cutting down his son (Howard), and the boy finally gets a chance to win back his father's respect. (Dir: Richard Heffron, 78 mins.)

Lodger, The (Great Britain, 1926)***½ Ivor Novello, June, Malcolm Keen, Marie Ault, Arthur Chesney. Hitchcock's first major critical success is a masterful silent film dealing with the effect of crime on ordinary people. It tells the story of a lodger (Novello) who befriends a girl (June) whose fiancé—a detective— becomes so jealous he accuses him of being the strangler of women terrorizing London at the time. (Dir: Alfred Hitchcock, 75 mins.)

Lodger, The (1944)*** George Sanders, Merle Oberon, Laird Cregar. Exciting thriller about Jack the Ripper stalking through London knocking off young, beautiful girls. (Dir: John Brahm, 84 mins.)†

Logan's Run (1976)*** Michael York, Richard Jordan, Jenny Agutter, Farrah Fawcett-Majors, Peter Ustinov, Roscoe Lee Browne. A science-fiction film that is less concerned with philosophizing about the future than providing some entertainment with dazzling sets and futuristic

gadgets. Living in a domed-in hedonistic civilization, Logan (York) is a policeman who hunts down "runners" who attempt to escape the society's law that at thirty you must submit to "renewal," which is actually execution. Later a brief TV series. (Dir: Michael Anderson, 120 mins.)†

Log of the Black Pearl, The (MTV 1974)**½ Ralph Bellamy, Keil Martin, Anne Archer, Jack Kruschen, Glenn Corbett, Henry Wilcox. A ripe, old-fashioned sailing melodrama, filmed in Mexican waters. A young stockbroker inherits an old sailing ship from his ailing grandfather and hunts for sunken treasure. (Dir: Andrew McLaglen, 100 mins.)

Lois Gibbs and the Love Canal (MTV 1982)*** Marsha Mason, Robert Gunton, Penny Fuller, Roberta Maxwell, Jeremy Licht. A straightforward compelling account of a woman who stood up to be counted against the government officials trying to smooth over a toxic chemical dumping disaster at New York State's Love Canal. Mason is excellent as a housewife who finds a new voice and courage to buck the authorities and demand relocation for the families involved in the Love Canal area. (Dir: Glenn Jordan, 104 mins.)†

Lola (France, 1960)***½ Anouk Aimée, Marc Michel, Elina Labourdette, Jaques Harden. Wonderful little story about a small-time nightclub singer (gloriously played by Aimée), who has to choose a lover from three men. A delicious French pastry of a movie made international stars of Aimée and director Jacques Demy, openly drawing inspiration from Max Ophul for his first feature. (91 mins.)†

Lola (U.S.-Great Britain, 1971)**½ Susan George, Charles Bronson. An adult drama about a May-September romance between a liberated sixteen-year-old and a fortyish American writer who meet, have a tempestuous affair, and make the mistake of marrying. (Dir: Richard Donner, 95 mins.)

Lola (West Germany, 1982)***½ Barbara Sukowa, Armin Mueller-Stahl, Mario Adorf. An intriguing, searing indictment of moral corruption and hypocrisy. In a small German city ten years after WWII, a new building commissioner, ostensibly calm and uncorruptible, falls under the spell of Lola, a beautiful prostitute. The tale is resolved not tragically but with wit and irony. (Dir: Rainer Werner Fassbinder, 114 mins.)

Lola Montes (France-West Germany, 1955)**** Martine Carol, Peter Ustinov, Oskar Werner, Anton Walbrook. Extravagant masterpiece tells the story of a courtesan (Carol) who lived with (among others) Franz Liszt and the Austrian emperor and who ended up in a circus

623

ring in New Orleans, selling her kisses and her memories to the masses. (Dir: Max Ophuls, 140 mins.)†

Lolita (U.S.-Great Britain, 1962)*** James Mason, Peter Sellers, Shelley Winters, Sue Lyon. Controversial story of a man of the world suddenly if not inexplicably infatuated with a "nymphet." Satiric, many good sequences, but not a complete success. Good performances, especially from Sellers. (Dir: Stanley Kubrick, 152 mins.)†

Lolly-Madonna XXX (1973)*½ Rod Steiger, Robert Ryan, Jeff Bridges. A family feud in Tennessee with little emotional or intellectual interest. Steiger and Ryan are the fathers who let a small squabble over disputed land escalate into a bloody war. (Dir: Richard C. Sarafian, 103 mins.)

Loneliest Runner, The (MTV 1976)*** Michael Landon, Brian Keith, DeAnn Mears. Story of a little boy, unable to control his bed-wetting, who grows up to become an Olympic champion marathon runner. Writer-director Landon appears at the beginning and the end as the grown-up runner making his final Olympic stadium run before a roaring crowd—a daydream come true. (78 mins.)†

Loneliness of the Long Distance Runner, The (Great Britain, 1962)**** Tom Courtenay, Michael Redgrave. Continually absorbing British film about a rebellious schoolboy whose need for recognition prods him into trying out for the track team. Brilliantly directed by Tony Richardson, with near faultless performances from Courtenay and polished veteran Redgrave. (103 mins.)†

Lonely Are the Brave (1962)*** Kirk Douglas, Walter Matthau, Gena Rowlands, George Kennedy, Carroll O'Connor. As the proverbial last cowboy, Douglas finds himself in deep trouble and unable to pilot his horse past the superhighways and into the wilderness as he is hunted down by truck and helicopter. The cast is phenomenally good. (Dir: David Miller, 107 mins.)†

Lonely Guy, The (1984)**½ Steve Martin, Charles Grodin, Judith Ivey, Steve Lawrence. Hidden in this low-key comedy are some insightful jibes at celebrity and loneliness among the not-so-swinging singles set. Martin's wacky persona, however, is at odds with the straightforward character comedy intended here. Intermittently funny. (Dir: Arthur Hiller, 90 mins.)†

Lonelyhearts (1958)**½ Montgomery Clift, Robert Ryan, Myrna Loy, Dolores Hart, Maureen Stapleton. Overlong and brooding story about an "advice to the lovelorn" columnist who gets too involved with his job and ends up questioning himself about values in life and

love. Disappointing adaptation of Nathanael West's superb novel *Miss Lonelyhearts*. (Dir: Vincent J. Donehue, 101 mins.)†

Lonely Hearts (Australia, 1983)*** Wendy Hughes, Norman Kaye, Jon Finlayson, Julia Blake. This prizewinning Australian comedy is concerned with two perennial losers in the game of love—a middle-aged piano tuner (Kaye) and a sexually repressed bank clerk (Hughes). The pair meet through a dating service and fumble their way toward romance. (Dir: Paul Cox, 95 mins.)

Lonely Lady (1983)½ Pia Zadora, Lloyd Bochner, Bibi Besch, Joseph Cali, Anthony Holland, Jared Martin. Feast of Stone Age performances and Neanderthal dialogue as a long-suffering screenwriter (Zadora) fails to maintain her integrity in an industry more interested in seducing her than producing her. (Dir: Peter Sasdy, 92 mins.)†

Lonely Man, The (1957)**½ Jack Palance, Anthony Perkins, Neville Brand. Tried-and-true plot of a gunfighter's attempts to reform against all odds makes for a well-acted if unexceptional western drama. (Dir: Henry Levin, 87 mins.)

Lonely Passion of Judith Hearne, The (Great Britain, 1987)*** Maggie Smith, Bob Hoskins, Wendy Hiller, Marie Kean, Prunella Scales. Poignant, downbeat tale chronicling the life and hard times of a reserved, middle-aged Irish spinster who tries to conceal her secret affection for the bottle. A near-romance with a gruff Irish-American, superbly incarnated by Hoskins, changes her life for better or worse. Smith's performance is flawless. (Dir: Jack Clayton, 110 mins.)†

Lonely Profession, The (MTV 1969)**½ Harry Guardino, Ina Balin, Jack Carter, Dean Jagger, Dina Merrill. Better-than-average private eye film with a very good performance by Harry Guardino as a small time detective who gets involved in a wild case. (Dir: Douglas Heyes, 96 mins.)

Lone Ranger, The (1956)** Clayton Moore, Jay Silverheels, Lyle Bettger, Bonita Granville. The masked man and faithful Tonto uncover dirty work between Indians and whites. Feature version of popular TV show. (Dir: Stuart Heisler, 86 mins.)†

Lone Ranger and the Lost City of Gold, The (1958)** Clayton Moore, Jay Silverheels, Douglas Kennedy, Charles Watts. The Lone Ranger and Tonto battle to preserve the secrecy of an Indian "Lost City of Gold" against greedy white people. Action-packed. (Dir: Lesley Selander, 80 mins.)†

Loners, The (1972)*½ Dean Stockwell, Pat Stich, Scott Brady, Gloria Grahame, Todd Susman. Dreary tale of three teenagers on the run from southwestern police seeking the killer of a highway patrolman. (Dir: Sutton Roley, 79 mins.)†

Lone Runner, The (1987)* Miles O'Keeffe, Savina Gersak, Michael J. Aronin. Spaghetti Eastern with O'Keeffe looking to recover a kidnapped princess. Shoddy action and some moronic glances between beef-and-cheesecake try to suffice for the plot. (Dir: Ruggero Deodato, 85 mins.)†

Lonesome Cowboys (1968)*** Viva, Tom Hompertz, Eric Emerson, Taylor Mead, Joe Dallesandro, Julian Burroughs, Francis Francine, Allen Midgette, Louis Waldron. Director Andy Warhol takes on the Old West in this weirdly comic tale about wealthy ranch owner Viva's problems with Waldron's gang of cowboys. Two highlights: Viva's comic rape scene at the hands of the gay cowboys, and her nude rendition of hymns. Not for everyone, but one of Warhol's best. Filmed on location in Arizona. (110 mins.)

Lonesome Dove (MTV 1989)***½ Robert Duvall, Tommy Lee Jones, Robert Urich, Danny Glover, Diane Lane, D.B. Sweeney, Ricky Schroeder, Anjelica Huston, Glenne Headly, Frederick Forrest. Excellent adaptation of Larry McMurtry's Pulitzer Prize-winning novel about a cattle drive from Texas to Montana. The characters are rich and colorful, capped by Duvall's philosophizing, woman-loving ex-Texas Ranger. (Dir: Simon Wincer, 384 mins.)

Lone Star (1952)**½ Clark Gable, Ava Gardner, Broderick Crawford, Lionel Barrymore. A big western film with the stress on romance, but why complain when the romantic interest is supplied by Ava Gardner? (Dir: Vincent Sherman, 94 mins.)

Lone Wolf series. Michael Lanyard, the former international jewel thief who favored sleuthing over jewel-napping, often placed his expertise at the disposal of the good guys, despite having been on the wrong side of the law. Played by several different actors, the Lone Wolf was featured in two superlative entries, *Lone Wolf Spy Hunt* and *The Lone Wolf Returns*, among many entertaining programmers. Fans should check out the following films in addition to those below: *Secrets of the Lone Wolf, One Dangerous Night, Passport to Suez,* and *Notorious Lone Wolf.*

Lone Wolf and His Lady, The (1949)*½ Ron Randell, June Vincent, Alan Mowbray. Hired to cover the exhibition of a priceless diamond for a newspaper, the Lone Wolf is suspected of being up to his old tricks when the jewel disappears. (Dir: John Hoffman, 60 mins.)

Lone Wolf in London, The (1947)** Gerald Mohr, Nancy Saunders, Eric Blore. Although accused of jewel thievery himself, the Lone Wolf clears his good name by finding the purloined gems. Sometimes less is Mohr. (Dir: Sidney Salkow, 65 mins.)

Lone Wolf in Mexico, The (1947)** Gerald Mohr, Sheila Ryan. Instead of being accused merely of gem-napping, Lone Wolf finds himself implicated in the murder of a Mexican gambling casino worker. (Dir: Ross Lederman, 69 mins.)

Lone Wolf in Paris, The (1938)**½ Francis Lederer, Frances Drake. Here, the tricky thief who utilizes his sticky fingers for good causes is on the trail of some pawned crown jewels that a princess is trying to retrieve. (Dir: Albert S. Rogell, 66 mins.)

Lone Wolf Keeps a Date, The (1941)*½ Warren William, Frances Robinson, Bruce Bennett. En route to bail out a millionaire with ransom money, two thugs nab the courier and it's up to Lone Wolf to rescue her. (Dir: Sidney Salkow, 65 mins.)

Lone Wolf McQuade (1983)** Chuck Norris, David Carradine, Barbara Carrera, Leon Isaac Kennedy, L. Q. Jones, Robert Beltran. Texas Ranger Norris battles gunrunner Carradine, with whom he shares lover Carrera. Not much plotwise, but it features some of Norris's better martial artistry. (Dir: Steve Carver, 105 mins.)†

Lone Wolf Meets a Lady, The (1940)**½ Warren William, Jean Muir, Eric Blore. The slick jewel-nabber becomes involved with a girl whose costly necklace implicates her in robbery and murder. (Dir: Sidney Salkow, 71 mins.)

Lone Wolf Returns, The (1935)*** Melvyn Douglas, Gail Patrick, Tala Birell. The Lone Wolf battles two low-grade, uncouth crooks who're blackmailing him into pooling resources with them. (Dir: Roy William Neill, 69 mins.)

Lone Wolf Spy Hunt, The (1939)***½ Warren William, Ida Lupino, Rita Hayworth. William's first appearance as Lanyard is generally considered the best of the series—a fast, chic piece of efficient moviemaking. (Dir: Peter Godfrey, 67 mins.)

Lone Wolf Strikes, The (1940)***½ Warren William, Joan Perry, Eric Blore. Terrific entry, in which the jewel-loving crook comes out of retirement to appropriate some pearls for a pal. Fast-paced action and snappy dialogue. (Dir: Sidney Salkow, 57 mins.)

Lone Wolf Takes a Chance, The (1941)** Warren William, June Storey. Quick-moving but minor entry in which the Lone Wolf makes the mistake of betting he can keep out of trouble for twenty-four hours, and is soon embroiled in a robbery from the Treasury Dept., murder, and some chase scenes on a train that keep the film in constant motion. (Dir: Sidney Salkow, 76 mins.)

Long Ago Tomorrow (Great Britain, 1971)*** Malcolm McDowell, Nanette Newman, Georgia Brown. Though the story is somewhat clichéd, the direction and the powerful acting overcome the difficulty. McDowell is impressive as a wheelchair victim who is strengthened by a love affair with another cripple, Miss Newman. (Dir: Bryan Forbes, 111 mins.)†

Longarm (MTV 1988)*½ John T. Terlesky, Whitney Kershaw, Rene Auberjonois. Routine horse stuff about a lady-killin', guntotin' marshal. Terlesky ain't the Duke, nor the Coop. (Dir: Virgil Vogel, 96 mins.)

Long Dark Hall, The (Great Britain, 1951)**½ Rex Harrison, Lilli Palmer. A married man is accused of the murder of a showgirl and nearly is executed for the crime he didn't commit. Just average mystery melodrama; some good courtroom scenes. (Dir: Anthony Bushell, 86 mins.)

Long, Dark Night, The—See: **Pack, The**

Long Day's Dying, The (Great Britain, 1968)** David Hemmings, Tom Bell, Tony Beckley, Alan Dobie. Grisly incident involving three privates and their German prisoner in no-man's land. War is hell; so is an overwrought war movie, despite laudable intentions. (Dir: Peter Collinson, 93 mins.)

Long Day's Journey Into Night (1962)**** Katharine Hepburn, Ralph Richardson, Jason Robards, Jr., Dean Stockwell. An unrelenting, shattering film, magnificently directed by Sidney Lumet. Eugene O'Neill's triumphant tragedy, largely autobiographical, of a New England family and their relationships alternately wavering between love and hate, guilt and pride. Brilliant, haunting performances. (136 mins.)†

Long Days of Summer, The (MTV 1980)** Dean Jones, Joan Hackett, Ronnie Scribner. Director Dan Curtis delves into his youth in Bridgeport, Conn., during the 1930s. In this sequel to *When Every Day Was the Fourth of July*, Jones again plays an up-and-coming Jewish attorney who has to fight prejudice at every turn. (78 mins.)†

Long Duel, The (Great Britain, 1967)*** Yul Brynner, Trevor Howard. Brynner and Howard star in this intelligent adventure epic which pits two men of honor against each other. Brynner plays an Indian leader who fights Howard, representing the British in India during the 1920s. (Dir: Ken Annakin, 115 mins.)

Longest Day, The (1962)*** John Wayne, Henry Fonda, Robert Ryan, Red Buttons, Richard Burton, Richard Todd, Mel Ferrer, Alexander Knox, Curt Jurgens. An account of D-day (June 6, 1944), when the Allies landed in Normandy. All cameos and vignettes, each too neatly packaged to capture the sense of the moment. (Dirs: Andrew Marton, Bernhard Wicki, Ken Annakin, 169 mins.)†

Longest Night, The (MTV 1972)*** David Janssen, James Farentino. Good kidnap yarn based on a case that made headlines years ago. Daughter of a wealthy businessman is abducted by a meticulous, clever young man and his girl friend, and is subsequently buried alive in a specially constructed box with a battery-operated air supply for one week. Tension reaches nerve-racking stage. (Dir: Jack Smight, 73 mins.)

Longest Yard, The (1974)*** Burt Reynolds, Eddie Albert, Jim Hampton, Ed Lauter. Clever, fiercely funny film featuring twelve convicts, murderers, and other scalawags forming a football team to oppose a semi-pro group composed of their own guards. Ferocious gridiron action sees the prisoners take revenge for their captors' senseless brutality. (Dir: Robert Aldrich, 123 mins.)†

Long Gone (MCTV 1987)***½ William L. Petersen, Virginia Madsen, Dermot Mulroney, Henry Gibson. Superb comedy-drama about Stud Cantrell, a minor league baseball manager whose big league dreams didn't reach fruition. Life hands him a second chance in the form of some promising rookies and a beauty queen who wants him to set up home plate at the nearst wedding chapel. (Dir: Martin Davidson, 110 mins.)†

Long Goodbye, The (1973)***½ Elliott Gould, Sterling Hayden, Mark Rydell, Henry Gibson, Jim Bouton, Nina van Pallandt. A gloriously entertaining and sophisticated detective yarn based on Raymond Chandler's novel about an indolent flatfoot, Philip Marlowe (Gould). Marlowe is hired to find a missing husband, is threatened by a Jewish hoodlum (hysterically played by Rydell), and journeys to Mexico. (Dir: Robert Altman, 111 mins.)†

Long Good Friday, The (Great Britain, 1980)***½ Bob Hoskins, Helen Mirren, Eddie Constantine. Exciting, effective gangster story set in London. Hoskins is outstanding as a nervy, determined mob leader trying to hold his operation together in the face of mysterious bombings and murders of his men. Skillful performances, good location filming, crisp dialogue, and a good plot. (Dir: John MacKenzie, 105 mins.)†

Long Gray Line, The (1955)*** Tyrone Power, Maureen O'Hara. Tyrone Power gives one of his best performances as the Irish immigrant who finds a home and love at West Point. John Ford directed with his usual skill. (138 mins.)

Long Hot Summer, The (1958)***½ Paul Newman, Joanne Woodward, Anthony Franciosa, Orson Welles, Lee Remick, Angela Lansbury. Easily the best film rendition of William Faulkner's writing, based on several of his works. Newman became a star as the stranger who stirs up the latent tensions in a small southern town, especially within the family dominated by patriarch Welles. Powerful and well acted. (Dir: Martin Ritt, 117 mins.)

Long Hot Summer, The (MTV 1985)*** Don Johnson, Jason Robards, Jr., Judith Ivey, Cybill Shepherd, Ava Gardner. It won't make you forget the original, but the cast acquit themselves nicely in this remake of the William Faulkner adaptation. (Dir: Stuart Cooper, 208 mins.)†

Long John Silver (Australia, 1953)**½ Robert Newton, Kit Taylor, Rod Taylor. The bold buccaneer battles a rival pirate for the spoils of Treasure Island. Entertaining swashbuckling saga, with Newton giving a broadly humorous portrayal. (Dir: Byron Haskin, 109 mins.)

Long Journey Back (MTV 1978)*** Mike Connors, Cloris Leachman, Stephanie Zimbalist, Kathy Kurtzman. Absorbing, uplifting real-life story about a family's struggle to help a high school girl recover from a school-bus accident in which she has lost a leg and suffered brain damage. (Dir: Mel Damski, 104 mins.)†

Long Journey Home, The (MTV 1987)**- Meredith Baxter Birney, David Birney, Ray Baker, James Sutorius, Daphne Maxwell Reid, Kevin McCarthy. A Vietnam MIA (Birney), presumed dead, comes out of the woodwork just as his wife (real-life spouse Meredith) is about to remarry. Occasionally suspenseful thriller. (Dir: Rod Holcomb, 96 mins.)

Long, Long Trailer, The (1954)*** Lucille Ball, Desi Arnaz. Smoothly made, frequently charming comedy about how a trailer played a part in the honeymoon life of a couple of newlyweds and their difficulties in adjusting to the outdoor life. Good fun. (Dir: Vincente Minnelli, 103 mins.)

Long Lost Father (1934)**½ John Barrymore, Helen Chandler, Donald Cook, Alan Mowbray. Interesting chemistry between the stars lifts this story of a father who tries to help his daughter after years of neglect; sensitive, compelling performances make this worth seeing. (Dir: Ernest B. Schoedsack, 63 mins.)

Long Night, The (1947)** Henry Fonda, Barbara Bel Geddes, Vincent Price, Ann Dvorak. The killer of a shady magician hides out in a hotel room, while his girl pleads with him to give himself up. Dreary, ponderous drama; some good moments. (Dir: Anatole Litvak, 101 mins.)

Long Ride Home, The (1967)**½ Glenn Ford, George Hamilton, Inger Stevens, Paul Petersen, Max Baer. Union officer (Ford) on the trail of escaped Confederate soldiers. AKA: **A Time for Killing.** (Dir: Phil Karlson, 88 mins.)

Long Riders, The (1980)*** The clans Carradine, Keach, Quaid, and Guest; Pamela Reed, Amy Stryker. Director Walter Hill lays on irony and ambiguity to the point that the moral positions of the film—variations on the story of the James-Younger gang—are obscure, yet his approach enriches the moribund western genre. (98 mins.)†

Long Road Home (MTV 1991)***½ Mark Harmon, Lee Purcell, Morgan Weisser. Ace director John Korty has sensitively directed a genuinely moving screenplay by Jane Howard Hammerstein, adapted from a novel by Ronald B. Taylor. It's about migrant farm workers circa Steinbeck's *The Grapes of Wrath,* set in the 1930s. A compassionate, poignant piece of agitprop, and one of the finest made-for-television movies in recent years. Harmon is excellent. (Dir: John Korty, 96 mins.)

Long Rope, The (1961)**½ Hugh Marlowe, Alan Hale, Chris Robinson. Circuit judge finds himself against an entire town when he tries a man for murder. Okay western drama. (Dir: William Witney, 61 mins.)

Long Ships, The (Great Britain-Yugoslavia, 1964)** Richard Widmark, Sidney Poitier. Epic about a brave Viking and his search for a golden bell, opposed by villainous Moors. (Dir: Jack Cardiff, 125 mins.)

Longshot, The (1986)* Tim Conway, Harvey Korman, Jack Weston, Ted Wass, Jonathan Winters, Stella Stevens. Tired slapstick comedy about four bozos who borrow five thousand dollars from the mob to bet on a horse. (Dir: Paul Bartel, 89 mins.)†

Longstreet (MTV 1971)*** James Franciscus, Jeanette Nolan. Absorbing drama. Franciscus excels in this pilot film for a proposed series about a top-flight insurance investigator who is blinded in an explosion which kills his wife. (Dir: Joseph Sargent, 93 mins.)

Long Summer of George Adams, The (MTV 1982)*** James Garner, Joan Hackett, Alex Harvey, Juanin Clay. A very satisfying movie steeped in texture, humor, and country characters. As an Oklahoma railroad man about to be replaced and unable to think about making a new start, James Garner moseys along playing for flavor, ignoring the customary trumped-up action plot. (Dir: Stuart Margolin, 104 mins.)

Long, the Short and the Tall, The—See: **Jungle Fighters**

627

Longtime Companion (1990)***½ Bruce Davison, Campbell Scott, Stephen Caffrey, Mark Lamos, Patrick Cassidy, Mary-Louise Parker, Dermot Mulroney, Michael Schoeffling. Absorbing, revealing account detailing the effects of AIDS on the American gay community through the '80s, as seen through the eyes of two friends who watch their social circle dying around them. (Dir: Norman Rene, 96 mins.)†

Long Time Gone (MTV 1986)** Paul LeMat, Ann Dusenberry, Barbara Stock, Ray Girardin, Eddie Zammit. LeMat plays a hard-living, good-time-seeking private eye suddenly given the responsibility of his nine-year-old son (Wil Wheaton). (Dir: Robert Butler, 104 mins.)

Long Voyage Home, The (1940)**** John Wayne, Thomas Mitchell, Barry Fitzgerald, Mildred Natwick. Based on play by Eugene O'Neill. Tale of merchant seamen, their hopes, dreams, close comradeship. Superbly directed by John Ford, a gripping, dramatic, often beautiful film. (105 mins.)†

Long Wait, The (1954)** Anthony Quinn. Dull Mickey Spillane adventure about an amnesia victim falsely accused of murder. (Dir: Victor Saville, 93 mins.)

Long Walk Home, The (1990)***½ Sissy Spacek, Whoopi Goldberg, Dwight Schultz, Ving Rhames, Dylan Baker, Erika Alexander, Lexi Faith Randall, Richard Habersham, Jason Weaver, Crystal Robbins. Powerful drama about the Montgomery, Alabama, boycott in the mid-50s by blacks who refused to sit in the back of the bus. A history lesson becomes an illuminating work of passion. The acting is top-notch (Goldberg is Spacek's maid, who'd rather walk than ride; both are quietly brilliant), and the fifties look of the film is outstanding. (Dir: Richard Pearce, 97 mins.)†

Long Way Home, A (MTV 1981)**½ Timothy Hutton, Brenda Vaccaro, George Dzundza, John Lehne, Rosanna Arquette. A family drama that tugs at the heartstrings. Hutton stars as a young man who can't accept the fact that he and his brother and sister were wrenched apart when they were little and placed in foster homes. (Dir: Robert Markowitz, 104 mins.)†

Lookalike, The (MCTV 1990)** Melissa Gilbert-Brinkman, Diane Ladd, Frances Lee McCain, Thaao Penghlis. Moderately entertaining thriller plays like an extended "Twilight Zone" episode. A young woman (Gilbert-Brinkman) fears for her sanity when she encounters a little girl bearing a striking resemblance to her daughter, who was killed in a car accident. Bizarre twists ought to keep viewers involved in this somewhat slow-

moving vehicle. (Dir: Gary Nelson, 96 mins.)

Look Back in Anger (Great Britain, 1959)***½ Richard Burton, Claire Bloom, Mary Ure. John Osborne's famous and important play emerges as a powerful comment on the mood in England in the mid 1950s. Richard Burton is a glorious actor and has several excellent scenes. (Dir: Tony Richardson, 99 mins.)†

Looker (1981)**½ Albert Finney, James Coburn, Susan Dey, Leigh Taylor-Young, Dorian Harewood, Tim Rossovich, Darryl Hickman. A pretty good mystery yarn that isn't content to stay within its murder framework and gets too ambitious. Models who have had their already great faces made "perfect" by plastic surgeon Finney suddenly start dying—one at a time. (Dir: Michael Crichton, 94 mins.)†

Look for the Silver Lining (1949)**½ June Haver, Charles Ruggles, Rosemary DeCamp, Gordon MacRae, S. Z. Sakall. Haver plays Marilyn Miller in a pleasant minor musical of no special distinction. (Dir: David Butler, 106 mins.)

Look in Any Window (1961)** Paul Anka, Ruth Roman, Alex Nicol. Paul Anka goes dramatic for the first time in this cheap, sensationalized story of parents who set bad examples for their teenage children and then are surprised when they get into trouble. (Dir: William Alland, 87 mins.)

Looking for Danger (1957)**½ Huntz Hall, Stanley Clements. Bowery Boys flick about Sach and Duke's adventures during WWII in search of "The Hawk," a member of a North African underground organization. (Dir: Austen Jewell, 62 mins.)

Looking for Love (1964)*½ Connie Francis, Jim Hutton, Susan Oliver, Barbara Nichols, Danny Thomas, Johnny Carson, George Hamilton, Paula Prentiss. Laughless comedy with Connie Francis spending most of the movie deciding whether to marry Jim Hutton. (Dir: Don Weis, 83 mins.)

Looking for Mr. Goodbar (1977)*** Diane Keaton, Richard Gere, Tuesday Weld, Tom Berenger. Richard Brooks's film has been grievously misunderstood mostly by the puritanical of mind who have assumed that Brooks was passing some moral judgment on promiscuity by allowing the lead character to be murdered. Keaton is heartbreaking, and "Goodbar" builds to a shattering climax. Based on Judith Rossner's best-selling novel. (135 mins.)†

Looking Glass War, The (Great Britain, 1970)**½ Christopher Jones, Pia Degermark, Ralph Richardson, Paul Rogers, Anthony Hopkins. John le Carré's fine espionage novel has been turned into a mildly entertaining film. A Polish defector is sent into East Germany to gain information on a rocket operation. (Dir: Frank R. Pierson, 106 mins.)†

Lookin' Good—See: **Corky**

Looking Up (1977)**½ Marilyn Chris, Dick Shawn, Doris Belack, Harry Goz. Comic group portrait of a family in transition during the lean years of the seventies. Some of the sentiment seems strained, but the sequences featuring shtick about city living, and the harried-yet-dignified performances given by Chris and Shawn as the couple trying to realize their dream of opening a restaurant, make this one a worthwhile, low-budget effort. (Dir: Linda Yellen, 94 mins.)

Lookin' to Get Out (1982)**½ Jon Voight, Ann-Margret, Burt Young. Occasionally bright comedy about two poor souls running from strong-arm gambling debt collectors and winding up lying their way into a suite at the MGM Grand in Las Vegas and trying to get out of a mess of complications. (Dir: Hal Ashby, 105 mins.)†

Look What's Happened to Rosemary's Baby —See: **Rosemary's Baby II**

Look Who's Laughing (1941)**½ Lucille Ball, Bergen and McCarthy, Fibber McGee and Molly. Hectic happenings when the famous ventriloquist is forced down in the village of Wistful Vista. Pleasing comedy. (Dir: Allan Dwan, 78 mins.)

Look Who's Talking (1989)*½ John Travolta, Kirstie Alley, Olympia Dukakis, George Segal, Abe Vigoda. Americans will go to any lengths to look at a cute baby. Alley plays a single mom whose baby boy thinks with the voice of Bruce Willis. A sloppily constructed crowd pleaser, with two car chase scenes thrown in for the hell of it. (Dir: Amy Heckerling, 93 mins.)†

Look Who's Talking Too (1990)* Kirstie Alley, John Travolta, Olympia Dukakis. The voices of Roseanne Barr, Bruce Willis, Damon Wayans. Dreadful follow-up to *Look Who's Talking* suffers from no plot, shoddy production values, haphazard direction, and a made-in-danger-by-fire ending that is borderline child abuse. Only Barr's line reading (not the lines) gets a star. (Dir: Amy Heckerling, 85 mins.)†

Loophole (1954)**½ Barry Sullivan, Dorothy Malone. Bank teller accused of theft clears himself by nabbing the real culprits. Tightly knit crime melodrama. (Dir: Harold Schuster, 80 mins.)

Loophole (Great Britain, 1980)** Albert Finney, Martin Sheen, Susannah York, Colin Blakely. An average heist movie in which an architect is persuaded to lay the foundations for the break-in of a London bank. (Dir: John Quested, 105 mins.)†

Loose Cannons (1989)* Dan Aykroyd, Gene Hackman, Dom De Luise, Ronny Cox, Nancy Travis, Robert Prosky. They don't come much worse than this torturous buddy comedy about a maverick cop and his off-the-wall schizophrenic partner. The plot has our dismal duo searching for a Nazi porn reel that could end the career of a candidate for the chancellorship of West Germany. (Dir: Bob Clark, 94 mins.)†

Loose Connections (Great Britain, 1983) *** Lindsay Duncan, Stephen Rea. Road comedy about two strangers, a dedicated feminist and a man pretending to be gay, driving to Germany. The plot isn't much, but the dialogue sparkles. (Dir: Richard Eyre, 90 mins.)†

Loose in London (1953)**½ Bowery Boys, Walter Kingsford, Angela Greene. Sach's lineage is traced back to a dying British earl by a group of lawyers, who give him a ticket to London. The rest of the film is a slapstick romp that pits the Boys against Sach's pretentious British relatives. (Dir: Edward Bernds, 62 mins.)

Loose Screws (Canada, 1985)½ Brian Genesse, Lance Van Der Kolk, Alan Deveau, Jason Warren. Teens-in-heat sequel to *Screwballs* is even worse, a numbingly stupid heap of "funny" character names and bad jokes set at a school for troublesome students. The only possible audience for this is voyeurs who live in areas where X-rated movies are illegal. (Dir: Rafal Zielinski, 76 mins.)†

Loose Shoes (1980)*½ Bill Murray, Howard Hesseman, Buddy Hackett, Ed Lauter, Susan Tyrell, Jaye P. Morgan, Murphy Dunne. A hopelessly low-grade collection of film trailer parodies. The two best skits are "Three Chairs for Lefty" (with Murray) and "Skateboarders from Hell" in the beginning, then skip it. Made in 1977. AKA: **Coming Attractions**. (Dir: Ira Miller, 84 mins.)†

Loot (Great Britain, 1972)*** Richard Attenborough, Lee Remick, Milo O'Shea. Black, funny farce, based on a play by the late Joe Orton. Its only fault lies in the failure by the director to open it up from a one-set play. The plot concerns money hidden in a coffin resting in a seedy British hotel. (Dir: Silvio Narizzano, 92 mins.)†

Lord Jeff (1938)**½ Freddie Bartholomew, Mickey Rooney, Charles Coburn, Gale Sondergaard, Peter Lawford. Good kids' melodrama of a boy who falls in with bad company; he is sent to a merchant marine academy, where he reforms, but his old cohorts (including a slinky, purring Sondergaard) turn up to take advantage of him. (Dir: Sam Wood, 78 mins.)

Lord Jim (Great Britain, 1965)*** Peter O'Toole, Eli Wallach, James Mason, Daliah Lavi, Curt Jurgens. A lavish, magnificently photographed and unusually well-acted story of a seaman in the Far East based on Joseph Conrad's famous novel written in 1900. You'll probably enjoy this more if you *haven't* read Conrad's rousing tale. (Dir: Richard Brooks, 154 mins.)†

Lord Love a Duck (1966)*** Roddy McDowall, Tuesday Weld. Director George Axelrod's stinging, savagely funny portrait of teenage morals and mores is quite uneven, but there are numerous individual vignettes that have a bite seldom found in Hollywood films. (104 mins.)

Lord of the Dance/Destroyer of Illusion ***½ A fascinating journey into the mystical world of Tibetan culture is this exploration of the life and rituals of the eleventh reincarnation of spiritual leader Trulshig Rinpoche, who lived in the fifteenth century. Director Richard Khon, a Tibetan scholar, has made a superb documentary about the ceremonies wherein monks become gods to battle malevolent forces of our universe. (105 mins.)

Lord of the Flies, The (Great Britain, 1963)**½ James Aubrey, Tom Chapin, Hugh Edwards, Roger Elwin. A flawed, sporadically gripping filmization of Golding's allegorical tale about schoolboys left to their own resources on a deserted island. The famed stage director Peter Brook directs imaginatively, but sinks into the novel's symbolism rather than finding a way of translating it cinematically. (90 mins.)

Lord of the Flies (1990)* Balthazar Getty, Chris Furrh, Danuel Pipoly, Badgett Dale. Uninspired, amateurishly acted, crudely directed remake of William Golding's novel about British schoolboys marooned on a remote ocean island. Captures none of the dark tension of the 1963 film, demeaning the novel by updating and Americanizing it. Only the color cinematography by Martin Fuhrer earns a star. (Dir: Harry Hook, 87 mins.)†

Lord of the Jungle (1955)*½ Johnny Sheffield, Wayne Morris, Smoki Whitfield, Nancy Hale, Paul Picerni. Bomba protects elephants from poachers. (Dir: Ford Beebe, 69 mins.)

Lord of the Rings, The (1978)*** Animated version of the classic J. R. R. Tolkien tale of Hobbits, Middle-earth, and the ring that gives the holder unlimited, morally ambiguous power. Director Ralph Bakshi used the Rotoscope, beginning with live actors and then animating over them, for startling effects. (130 mins.)†

Lords of Discipline, The (1983)***½ David Keith, Robert Prosky, G. D. Spradlin, Barbara Babcock, Michael Biehn, Rick Rossovich. In this military drama based on Pat Conroy's semiautobiographical novel, Keith is dynamite; the film is tough and often shocking. "*Lords*" is a stern condemnation of the twisted values and false ideas of manliness and racism that permeate "respectable" institutions. (Dir: Franc Roddam, 103 mins.)†

Lords of Flatbush, The (1974)** Henry Winkler, Perry King, Sylvester Stallone, Susan Blakely. Trip back in time to a Brooklyn high school and the camaraderie of male adolescents eager but ultimately afraid to assert their emerging manhood. (Dirs: Stephen F. Verona, Martin Davidson, 85 mins.)†

Lords of Magick, The (1990)*½ Jarrett Parker, Mark Gauthier, Brenden Dillon, Jr., David Snow, Ruth Zackarian. A pair of fledgling magicians from 1,000 years ago travel to modern-day Los Angeles to rescue a kidnapped princess. Mix of fantasy genre with culture-clash comedy yields nothing special. (Dir: David Marsh, 99 mins.)†

Lorna (1964)**½ Lorna Maitland, James Rucker, Hal Hopper. The sort of peculiar creation that only a twisted talent like director Russ Meyer could have created; rural housewife Lorna tries to get what her husband won't give her from an escaped convict. (78 mins.)†

Lorna Doone (Great Britain, 1935)*** Margaret Lockwood, John Loder, Roger Livesey, Victoria Hopper, Roy Emerson. Fine version of the Richard Doddridge Blackmore novel of a girl with a secret in her past who is mixed up with a Robin Hood-like band of outlaws, though she loves an honest farmer; outstanding production values and performances. (Dir: Basil Dean, 89 mins.)

Lorna Doone (1951)**½ Barbara Hale, Richard Greene, Carl Benton Reid, William Bishop. A creditable adaptation of Richard D. Blackmore's romantic melodrama, set in 19th-century England. Greene, as John Ridd, leads a peasant rebellion against the ruthless Doone landowners and captures the heart of Hale's Lorna, the putative princess of the clan. (Dir: Phil Karlson, 82 mins.)

Losers, The (1970)*½ William Smith, Bernie Hamilton, Adam Roarke. Ludicrous saga of five Hell's Angels who go to Cambodia complete with their Yamaha choppers. (Dir: Jack Starrett, 96 mins.)†

Loser Takes All (Great Britain, 1956)**½ Rossano Brazzi, Glynis Johns. Well-acted comedy-drama about a young married couple who win at the tables in Monte Carlo but almost lose each other in the process. (Dir: Ken Annakin, 88 mins.)

Losin' It (1982)** Tom Cruise, Jackie Earle Haley, John Stockwell, Shelley Long. Dumb, derivative comedy about four naïve high school kids on a tear in Tijuana in search of the ultimate bordello might well be titled *Porky's Goes to Mexico.* (Dir: Curtis Hanson, 98 mins.)†

Los Olvidados (The Young and the Damned) (Mexico, 1951)**** Alfonso Mejía, Miguel Inclan, Estela Inda. Director Luis Buñuel's semidocumentary about juvenile gangs in Mexico City. A mind-rending indictment of moral and material poverty. (88 mins.)†

Loss of Innocence (Great Britain, 1961)**** Kenneth More, Danielle Darrieux, Susannah York. Exquisite drama of a young girl at a vacation hotel in France who becomes a woman through her involvement with a handsome jewel thief. Tender, touching, fine performances, colorful photography of the French countryside. (Dir: Lewis Gilbert, 99 mins.)

Lost (Great Britain, 1955)*** David Farrar. Exciting and tense drama about a lost child and the clever police work involved in finding him. (Dir: Guy Green, 89 mins.)

Lost! (Canada, 1986)***½ Kenneth Walsh, Helen Shaver, Michael Hogan. Three people struggle to survive on an overturned boat in the Pacific Ocean as one of them, a religious zealot, sabotages the others' efforts to attract help. Fascinating but grim true story is not for kids. (Dir: Peter Rowe, 94 mins.)†

Lost and Found (1979)**½ George Segal, Glenda Jackson, Paul Sorvino, Maureen Stapleton. A marital comedy with a university backdrop. Some nice moments, and Jackson and Segal have a special chemistry together onscreen. (Dir: Melvin Frank, 102 mins.)†

Lost Angel (1943)*** Margaret O'Brien, James Craig, Marsha Hunt, Donald Meek, Keenan Wynn. One of O'Brien's finest hours. In this sweetly sentimental saga, she plays a sheltered egghead whose existence has been monitored by scientists and robbed of spontaneity. Left to her own devices, she meets up with a reporter who enables her to recapture some of her lost childhood. (Dir: Roy Rowland, 91 mins.)

Lost Angels (1989)** Donald Sutherland, Adam Horowitz, Amy Locane, Celia Weston. Trite drama set in a Southern California psychiatric institution where parents dump rebellious (but sane) teens. Young star Horowitz has fire, but director Hugh Hudson seems more intent on exploiting than illuminating. (116 mins.)†

Los Tarantos (Spain, 1964)*** Carmen Amaya, Sara Lezana, Daniel Martin, Antonio Prieto. Dynamic Spanish flamenco musical version of the story of Romeo and Juliet, with the lovers being from rival gypsy families; told mainly in song and dance, with the fabulous flamenco star Amaya dominating the screen as Juliet's mother; stirring viewing. (Dir: Rovira-Beleta, 81 mins.)

Lost Boundaries (1949)***½ Mel Ferrer, Beatrice Pearson. A light-skinned Negro doctor passes for white in a small New England town. Absorbing drama handles a touchy subject with taste, finesse. Based on fact. (Dir: Alfred L. Werker, 99 mins.)

Lost Boys, The (1987)**½ Corey Feldman, Jami Gertz, Corey Haim, Edward Herrmann, Kiefer Sutherland, Dianne Wiest. Intriguing, often funny tale of contemporary teenagers who happen to be vampires. Imaginative, but slightly out of control. (Dir: Joel Schumacher, 90 mins.)†

Lost Capone, The (MCTV 1990)*** Adrian Pasdar, Ally Sheedy, Eric Roberts. Whether or not this account about the Capone clan bears any semblance of truth, it makes for a provocative drama. Pasdar plays Jimmy Capone, who became a law man in Homer, Nebraska, changed his name, and caused his brother's bootlegging business a great deal of trouble. Roberts delivers a strong, impressive performance as Al Capone. (Dir: John Gray, 96 mins.)†

Lost Command (1966)**½ Anthony Quinn, Alain Delon, George Segal, Claudia Cardinale, Michele Morgan. An all-star cast and well-staged war sequences help keep this action film interesting, despite the pretentious handling of the political and human aspects of the French-Algerian conflict. (Dir: Mark Robson, 129 mins.)

Lost Continent, The (1951)*½ Cesar Romero, Hillary Brooke, Chick Chandler, John Hoyt, Acquanetta. Not too exciting fantasy about an Air Force pilot (Romero) searching for an atom-powered rocket that has crashed on a mountainous island. (Dir: Samuel Newfield, 83 mins.)

Lost Continent, The (Great Britain, 1968)** Eric Porter, Hildegarde Knef (Neff), Suzanna Leigh, Tony Beckley. Balderdash about storm survivors landing on an uncharted land where weird things occur. Comic-strip stuff, played with grim determination. (Dirs: Michael Carreras, Leslie Norman, 89 mins.)

Lost Empire, The (1985)* Melanie Vincz, Raven de la Croix, Angela Aames, Paul Coufos, Angus Scrimm, Linda Shayne. A trio of busty and underdressed female adventurers battle an immortal Satan worshipper on an isolated Pacific island. Directorial debut by Jim Wynorski, undoubtedly the most annoying alumnus of Roger Corman U., substitutes smirky "in" jokes for plot and female skin for production values. (83 mins.)†

Lost Flight (MTV 1969)** Lloyd Bridges, Anne Francis, Ralph Meeker, Bobby Van. Plane crashes on a jungle island and the civilized passengers are forced to live by their wits. (Dir: Leonard Horn, 104 mins.)

Lost Honor of Katharina Blum, The (West Germany, 1975)*** Angela Winkler, Dieter Laser, Jurgen Prochnow. A law-abiding woman briefly involved with a man under police surveillance becomes the target for abuse from both the authorities and the media, as her private life becomes public property. Hard-hitting drama, remade for TV as *The Lost Honor of Kathryn Beck*. (Dirs: Volker Schlondorff, Margarethe von Trotta, 97 mins.)†

Lost Honor of Kathryn Beck, The (MTV 1984)***½ Marlo Thomas, Kris Kristofferson, George Dzundza, John DeVries. Provocative and thoughtful drama. Thomas is superb as a divorced woman who meets Kristofferson at a party and takes him home with her. Little does she realize that he's a suspected terrorist under surveillance, and soon she is hounded unmercifully by the police and the press. (Dir: Simon Langton, 104 mins.)

Lost Horizon (1937)**** Ronald Colman, Sam Jaffe, Jane Wyatt, H. B. Warner, Edward Everett Horton, Margo, Thomas Mitchell, Isabel Jewell, John Howard. This is a lovely, moving story of escapees from a revolution, who find refuge of several sorts in a magical valley in which the only law is to "Be kind." Time has taken the elitist edge off of author James Hilton's utopianism, and added romance and nostalgia. The acting is uniformly expert. (Dir: Frank Capra, 132 mins.)†

Lost Horizon (1973)½ Peter Finch, Liv Ullmann, John Gielgud, Olivia Hussey. Musical remake is unintentionally humorous, and instead of discovering Shangri-La we are mired in self-parody. (Dir: Charles Jarrott, 151 mins.)

Lost in a Harem (1944)** Bud Abbott, Lou Costello, Marilyn Maxwell, John Conte. A slice of nothing about a couple of magicians and their adventure in an Oriental land. (Dir: Charles Reisner, 89 mins.)

Lost in Alaska (1952)**½ Bud Abbott, Lou Costello, Tom Ewell. The Klondike inherits the clowning duo in this fast paced comedy about gold, gambling, and gals. Plenty of funny sight gags make this a notch or two above average A and C fare. (Dir: Jean Yarbrough, 76 mins.)

Lost in America (1985)**½ Albert Brooks, Julie Hagerty, Garry Marshall, Art Frankel. A yuppie Pilgrim's Progress. Passed over for a promotion he expected, an upwardly mobile ad exec packs up his wife in a Winnebago and explores America. Brooks fans will be impressed by this comic journey's unexpected warmth; others will be put off by his egomaniacal style. (Dir: Albert Brooks, 91 mins.)†

Lost in London (MTV 1985)*½ Emmanuel Lewis, Lynne Moody, Ben Vereen, Freddie Jones. The title tells it all, as Lewis runs away from his parents in jolly old London. Lewis and Vereen together constitute cruel and inhuman punishment for the audience. (Dir: Robert Lewis, 104 mins.)

Lost in the Stars (1974)*½ Brock Peters, Melba Moore, Raymond St. Jacques, Clifton Davis. A well-intentioned but stiff and ponderous version of the Maxwell Anderson/Kurt Weill operetta of Alan Paton's novel about South African injustice. (Dir: Daniel Mann, 114 mins.)

Lost Man, The (1969)**½ Sidney Poitier, Joanna Shimkus, Al Freeman, Jr. Poitier in the offbeat role of a hunted criminal, some interesting scenes involving the civil rights movement in this country, plus the excitement of a continuous chase, make this shallow story palatable. (Dir: Robert Alan Arthur, 122 mins.)

Lost Missile, The (1958)** Robert Loggia, Ellen Parker. As a runaway missile threatens New York, a young scientist works against time to stop its course of destruction. Fair cheaply made science-fiction thriller. (Dir: Lester Berke, 70 mins.)

Lost Moment, The (1947)*** Robert Cummings, Susan Hayward, Agnes Moorehead. Young American publisher finds that love letters he has been seeking in Venice cause near-tragedy. Absorbing drama, taken from Henry James's novel, *The Aspern Papers*. (Dir: Martin Gabel, 88 mins.)†

Lost One, The (West Germany, 1951)*** Peter Lorre, Karl John, Helmut Rudolph. Peter Lorre gives a fine performance portraying a resident doctor in a refugee camp in Germany shortly after the end of World War II. The only film directed by Lorre, and he turns in a more than creditable job. (98 mins.)

Lost Patrol (1934)***½ Victor McLaglen, Boris Karloff, Wallace Ford, Reginald Denny, Alan Hale. A British patrol is ambushed by hostile Arabs and picked off one by one. Gripping drama directed by John Ford. (80 mins.)†

Lost Platoon, The (1989)*½ William Knight, David Parry, Stephen Quadros, Lew Pipes. Weird, underwritten mix of horror and war genres about a century-old quartet of undead soldiers wandering from country to country. (Dir: Ted Prior, 86 mins.)†

Lost Squadron, The (1932)*** Joel McCrea, Richard Dix, Erich von Stroheim, Mary Astor. Tyrannical film director makes his aerial stunt men do perilous tricks, so they band together to stop him. Unusual melodrama has plenty of suspense. (Dir: George Archainbaud, 90 mins.)†

Lost Tribe, The (1949)** Johnny Weissmuller, Myrna Dell, Elena Verdugo, Joseph Vitale. Jungle Jim's menagerie helps him combat two dastardly crooks trying to walk off with the treasure of the land of Dzamm. Pretty Dzamm ordinary. (Dir: William Berke, 72 mins.)†

Lost Volcano, The (1950)** Johnny Sheffield, Donald Woods, Marjorie Lord, Elena Verdugo, John Ridgely. Routine jungle odyssey about Bomba's rescue of a zoologist's son from two mercenary guides who think the boy can lead them to a treasure. (Dir: Ford Beebe, 67 mins.)

Lost Weekend, The (1945)**** Ray Milland, Jane Wyman, Philip Terry, Howard Da Silva. Billy Wilder's grim drama, one of the first American films to deal with alcoholism, was a milestone in its time; although its treatment of drinking is now too familiar to shock, it endures as a powerful, unsparing character study. Milland is superb as the failed writer who goes on a bender one lonely weekend and watches his life spiral into the gutter. From Charles Jackson's novel. (Dir: Billy Wilder, 101 mins.)†

Lost World, The (1925)*** Bessie Love, Wallace Beery, Lewis Stone, Lloyd Hughes. Still-exciting silent version of Sir Arthur Conan Doyle's story, which features the eccentric paleontologist Professor Challenger, well played by Beery; the plot concerns a scientific expedition to South America, where living prehistoric creatures are discovered. Naturally, the explorers decide to take a brontosaurus back to London with them, where it causes much mayhem. Terrific special effects by Willis O'Brien, who later created *King Kong*. (Dir: Harry O. Hoyt, 71 mins.)†

Lost World, The (1960)**½ Michael Rennie, Fernando Lamas, Jill St. John. Good screen version of Sir Arthur Conan Doyle's science-fiction story about an expedition into the deep regions of the Amazon. Visual tricks, such as prehistoric beasts doing battle with a helicopter, are the film's best features. (Dir: Irwin Allen, 98 mins.)

Lottery Bride, The (1930)**½ Jeanette MacDonald, John Garrick, Joe E. Brown, ZaSu Pitts, Robert Chisholm. Nutty early musical comedy has MacDonald as a Norwegian girl who enters a dance marathon to help out her no-good brother; matters escalate from there, with one unbelievable incident after another, ending up with a dirigible expedition to the Arctic! And there are plenty of songs, too; fun but outlandish. (Dir: Paul L. Stein, 80 mins.)†

Loudest Whisper, The—See: **Children's Hour, The**

Louisa (1950)**½ Ronald Reagan, Piper Laurie, Charles Coburn, Spring Byington in title role, Edmund Gwenn. Moderate-

ly entertaining film about the trials and tribulations of an average family which has to cope with the young daughter's romantic problems as well as Grandma's. (Dir: Alexander Hall, 90 mins.)

Louis Armstrong—Chicago Style (MTV 1976)*** Ben Vereen, Red Buttons, Margaret Avery, Janet MacLachlan. Based on the early career of the great jazz trumpeter, this film zeroes in on Louis's struggle to avoid playing in a Chicago club run by the mob during the early 1930s. Vereen is terrific in the title role. (Dir: Lee Phillips, 72 mins.)

Louisiana (MTV 1984)* Margot Kidder, Ian Charleson, Lloyd Bochner, Len Cariou, Victor Lanoux. Southern belle Kidder tries to get back the family estate by romancing its new owner, even though she really loves his overseer. Then this pesky Civil War starts up.... Condensed video version runs 130 mins. (Dir: Philippe de Broca, 205 mins.)†

Louisiana Purchase (1941)*** Bob Hope, Victor Moore, Vera Zorina. Delightful comedy about an attempt to frame a senator down Louisiana way. Loads of laughs and Bob's filibuster is a classic. (Dir: Irving Cummings, 98 mins.)

Louisiana Story, The (1948)*** A great social documentary, directed by Robert Flaherty, following the life of one young boy living in the bayous of Louisiana. Score by Virgil Thomson. (77 mins.)†

Loulou (France, 1980)***½ Isabelle Huppert, Gerard Depardieu, Humbert Balsan, Guy Marchand, Bernard Tronczyk. A beautiful, cosmopolitan businesswoman leaves her traditional lover for an earthy, leather-jacketed, uneducated oaf. Erotic, romantic, humorous. (Dir: Maurice Pialat, 110 mins.)†

Love (1927)*** Greta Garbo, John Gilbert, George Fawcett, Emily Fitzroy, Brandon Hurst, Phillipe DeLacy. An early version of Tolstoy's *Anna Karenina*, altered by, among other things, a happy ending. (Dir: Edmund Goulding, 100 mins.)

Love (Hungary, 1971)**** Lili Darvas, Mari Torocsik, Ivan Darvas, Erszi Orsolya. A dying elderly woman is visited daily by her daughter-in-law who reads her letters from the son she thinks is a Hollywood director; he's actually a political prisoner. This magnificent example of pure cinema is a powerful and emotional story of tyranny and hope. The acting is sublime. (Dir: Karoly Makk, 92 mins.)†

Love Affair (1932)**½ Dorothy Mackaill, Humphrey Bogart, Astrid Allwyn, Jack Kennedy. An over-indulged heiress falls for a hard-working aviation engineer, leading to conflict; interesting early appearance by Bogart. (Dir: Thornton Freeland, 68 mins.)

Love Affair (1939)**** Charles Boyer, Irene Dunne, Maria Ouspenskaya, Lee Bowman, Astrid Allwyn, Maurice Moscovich. One of the wittiest and most civilized of the romantic films of the 1930s. Couple meet on shipboard, fall in love, but break their engagement and decide to meet again in six months. Touching, wry, and beautifully acted by the two leads; superior direction by Leo McCarey. Remade by McCarey as *An Affair to Remember*. (89 mins.)

Love Affair, A: The Eleanor & Lou Gehrig Story (MTV 1977)*** Edward Herrmann, Blythe Danner. Less a baseball yarn than a love story. Herrmann is miscast as the great Yankee first baseman, but Danner is sensational as Eleanor, and this is her show, playing a woman madly in love with a good, gentle, serious man. (Dir: Fielder Cook, 104 mins.)

Love Affair: Or, the Case of the Missing Switchboard Operator (Yugoslavia, 1967)*** Eva Ras, Slobodan Aligrudic, Miodrag Andric, Ruzica Sokic. Director Dusan Makavejev brings his collage technique to a clever murder mystery involving a young switchboard operator and a Turkish ratcatcher. (70 mins.)†

Love Among the Ruins (MTV 1975)**** Katharine Hepburn, Laurence Olivier, Richard Pearson. One of the finest made-for-TV movies. Olivier and Hepburn star in this romantic comedy, written with style by James Costigan, and they're magical together. Olivier plays a prestigious London barrister—London circa 1911—who is defending his client (Hepburn) from a suit brought by a younger man who claims she has reneged on her promise to marry him. (Dir: George Cukor, 100 mins.)†

Love Among Thieves (MTV 1987)** Audrey Hepburn, Robert Wagner, Jerry Orbach, Patrick Bauchau, Brion James, Samantha Eggar, Christopher Neame. Robert Wagner is an adventurer out to retrieve priceless Fabergé eggs, which Miss Hepburn has stolen to pay ransom for her kidnapped lover. (Dir: Roger Young, 104 mins.)

Love and Anarchy (Italy, 1972)***½ Giancarlo Giannini, Mariangela Melato, Lina Polito. Enormously powerful political drama about Italian fascism during the 1930s, brilliantly written and directed by Lina Wertmuller. The plot concerns an anarchist peasant who comes to Rome to assassinate Mussolini. Acting splendid throughout. (108 mins.)†

Love and Bullets (1979)*½ Charles Bronson, Rod Steiger, Jill Ireland, Strother Martin, Bradford Dillman, Henry Silva, Michael V. Gazzo. Bronson chases a syndicate kingpin to Switzerland in order to bring back his moll to testify before a grand jury. (Dir: Stuart Rosenberg, 101 mins.)†

Love and Death (1975)***½ Woody Allen, Diane Keaton. One of Woody Allen's funniest, most consistent films. Woody plays a bumbling, to put it mildly, Russian, trying to avoid the draft in the Napoleonic War. Keaton is the pretentious cousin he's loved from afar. Allen takes these dippy characters and parodies 19th-century politics, philosophy, and war; and makes it funny. Full of mocking visual references to every film ever made from a Russian novel, from *The Brothers Karamazov* to *The Twelve Chairs*. A treat. (85 mins.)†

Love and Death in Saigon (Hong Kong, 1989)*** Chow Yun-fatt, Anita Mui, Tony Leung. Director Tsui Hark (*Peking Opera Blues*) skillfully blends sentiment and unpredictable action as Yun-fatt, his cousin, and a beautiful but deadly trigger woman all try to escape the clutches of a suave Japanese gangster and the wartorn nightmare that was Saigon in 1974. (100 mins.)

Love and Hate: A Marriage Made in Hell (MTV 1990)*** Kenneth Welsh, Kate Nelligan. The true, headline-making story about wealthy Canadian rancher/politician Colin Thatcher and the murder of his ex-wife Jo Ann. In this mini-series edited from the top-rated Canadian TV drama, Welsh gives a riveting performance as Thatcher, a man with a popular public image and a devastatingly evil private side. His wife (Nelligan) runs away with two of their three children. The custody battles get ugly and eventually lead to a brutal murder and a sensational trial. Solid and penetrating. (Dir: Francis Mankiewicz, 192 mins.)

Love and Kisses (1965)** Rick Nelson, Kristin Nelson, Jack Kelly. A spinoff of the Nelson family situations, this one has father Ozzie directing son Rick and daughter-in-law Kristin in a mild comedy about the problems occurring when a young couple elope. (87 mins.)

Love and Lies (MTV 1990)*** Mare Winningham, Peter Gallagher, Tom O'Brien, G. W. Bailey, Caroline Williams, M. Emmet Walsh. Winningham plays real-life Houston investigator Kim Paris in this TV mystery that works by drawing solid, believable characters. Paris' assignment is to get close to suspect Gallagher to find out if he was involved in the murder of an elderly couple. (Dir: Roger Young, 96 mins.)

Love and Money (1982)*½ Ray Sharkey, Ornella Muti, Klaus Kinski, Armand Assante. Clumsy, inconsistently comedic thriller about a Los Angeles nobody who manages to involve himself in the political and economic affairs of a tiny South American country. The great director King

634

Vidor appears briefly as Walter Klein. (Dir: James Toback, 90 mins.)

Love and Murder (Canada, 1990)*½ Todd Waring, Kathleen Laskey, Ron White, Wayne Robson. Photographer accidentally records a murder, setting himself up as the killer's next victim. Strictly by the numbers. (Dir: Steven Hilliard Stern, 97 mins.)

Love and Pain and the Whole Damned Thing (1972)*** Maggie Smith, Timothy Bottoms, Charles Baxter. An eccentric, humorous love story notable for the glorious performance of Smith as a spinster who is running away from her two aunts in England. Bottoms plays a college student coming to Europe to flee his tyrannical dad. They meet in Spain, and quickly learn their neuroses complement one another. (Dir: Alan J. Pakula, 110 mins.)

Love at First Bite (1979)*** George Hamilton, Susan St. James, Richard Benjamin, Arte Johnson. Very funny spoof about Count Dracula finding himself caught up in today's disco-swingin' social whirl. George Hamilton, complete with ridiculous Bela Lugosi accent, makes a terrific blood-sucking Count, and the screenplay provides one laugh after another. (Dir: Stan Dragoti, 93 mins.)†

Love at First Sight (Canada, 1974)* Mary Ann McDonald, Dan Aykroyd, Barry Morse. The original "Saturday Night Live" specialized in hilarious bad taste. This disagreeable pre-SNL comedy featuring Dan Aykroyd as a pompous young blind man has all of the bad taste but none of the hilarity. (Dir: Rex Bromfield, 90 mins.)†

Love at Large (1990)***½ Tom Berenger, Elizabeth Perkins, Anne Archer, Kate Capshaw, Annette O'Toole, Ted Levine, Ann Magnuson, Kevin J. O'Connor, Barry Miller, Neil Young, Ruby Dee. Another wryly romantic comedy from writer-director Alan Rudolph, of a stylistic piece with his *Choose Me* and *Trouble in Mind*. P. I. Berenger, on the trail of an errant lover, wanders into a few more interesting cases as well as a most interesting lady detective (Perkins). Full of odd but irresistible characters living in a timeless, slightly narcoticized setting, marked by music from Mark Isham and Leonard Cohen. (97 mins.)†

Love at Stake (1988)** Stuart Pankin, Dave Thomas, Bud Cort, Barbara Carrera, David Graf, Andrea Martin, Anne Ramsay. Overheated parody of Puritan New England which asks the burning question: What if the Salem witch hunts were really part of a real-estate scheme? Occasionally amusing, though with few solid laughs. (Dir: John Moffitt, 88 mins.)†

Love at Twenty (France-Italy-Japan-Poland-West Germany, 1962)***½ Jean-Pierre Léaud, Eleonora Rossi-Drago, Barbara Lass. Five vignettes of love among the young from youthful directors of France, Italy, Japan, West Germany, Poland. (Dirs: François Truffaut, Renzo Rossellini, Shintaro Ishihara, Marcel Ophuls, Andrzej Wajda, 113 mins.)

Love Before Breakfast (1936)**½ Carole Lombard, Preston Foster, Cesar Romero, Janet Beecher, Betty Lawford. Featherweight romantic comedy concerns a daffy socialite who is pursued by two ritzy suitors. Lombard makes this trifle sparkle. (Dir: Walter Lang, 70 mins.)

Love Boat, The: A Valentine Voyage (MTV 1990)** Gavin McLeod, Bernie Kopell, Ted Lange, Jill Whelan, Tom Bosley, Julia Duffy, Jerry Lacy, Roddy Piper, Shanna Reed, Joe Regalbuto. Strictly for fans of the series—all others beware of seasickness! A trio of jewel thieves board the vessel where a box of candy containing the gems is stashed. Naturally, this heart-shaped box of sweets keeps getting shifted, baffling the bumbling thieves. The familiar crew is back with a couple of changes in personnel, but the tired format remains the same. (Dir: Frank Satlof, 96 mins.)

Love Bug, The (1968)*** Dean Jones, Michele Lee, David Tomlinson, Buddy Hackett, Joe Flynn. The first and best of the successful Disney series about Herbie, the Volkswagen with a mind of its own. Fine for grown-ups as well as kids. (Dir: Robert Stevenson, 108 mins.)†

Love Child (1982)** Amy Madigan, Beau Bridges, Mackenzie Phillips, Albert Salmi. True story of an unjustly imprisoned girl who becomes an unwed mother thanks to an irresponsible prison guard. (Dir: Larry Peerce, 96 mins.)†

Love Crazy (1941)*** William Powell, Myrna Loy, Gail Patrick, Jack Carson. Myrna finds innocent Bill in a friendly situation with Gail Patrick. She sues for divorce and Bill fights to keep her in this zany comedy. (Dir: Jack Conway, 99 mins.)

Loved One, The (1965)*** Robert Morse, Jonathan Winters, Anjanette Comer, Milton Berle, John Gielgud, Rod Steiger, Liberace. Irreverent, uneven black comedy, based on the novel by Evelyn Waugh, concerns the sudden suicide of a Hollywood star and his nephew's problems in paying the exorbitant funeral bill. Macabre humor is well played by a large star-studded cast. (Dir: Tony Richardson, 116 mins.)†

Love Finds Andy Hardy (1938)*** Mickey Rooney, Judy Garland, Lewis Stone. Mickey is at his best here and so is Judge Lewis Stone as Andy gets involved with a bevy of young lovelies. (Dir: George B. Seitz, 90 mins.)

Love Flower, The (1920)**½ Richard Barthelmess, Carol Dempster, Anders Randolph. One of director D. W. Griffith's potboilers, this adventure story has some unique elements. A fugitive from justice lives with his daughter on a remote tropical island until their safety is threatened by the detective who has tracked him for years. Shot largely in the Bahamas, this is beautifully filmed, with some amazing underwater photography, and strong performance by Dempster. (65 mins.)†

Love for Ransom (MTV 1977)**½ John Davidson, Barry Primus, Richard Lynch, Susan Sullivan. Predictable pilot for a failed series starring Davidson and Primus as a pair of adventurers who travel the globe in search of missing persons and objets d'art. (Dir: Jack Starrett, 104 mins.)

Love for Rent (MTV 1979)**½ Annette O'Toole, Lisa Eilbacher, David Selby, Darren McGavin, Rhonda Fleming. A girl leaves home and finds her way into working for an escort service, which is really a "prostitution ring," with high-class clientele. (Dir: David Miller, 104 mins.)

Love from a Stranger (1947)**½ Sylvia Sidney, John Hodiak. After marriage, a woman suspects her husband to be a mad strangler with herself intended as his next victim. Acceptably exciting suspense melodrama. (Dir: Richard Whorf, 81 mins.)†

Love God?, The (1969)** Don Knotts, Anne Francis, Edmund O'Brien, James Gregory, Maureen Arthur. Flimsy comedy with Knotts as a bird-lover who ends up a national sex-celebrity adored by swooning females. (Dir: Nat Hiken, 101 mins.)

Love Happy (1949)**½ Marx Brothers, Ilona Massey, Vera-Ellen, Marilyn Monroe, Raymond Burr. Harpo befuddles some crooks who are after a precious diamond. The Marxian madness loses some of its magic in this uneven farce. (Dir: David Miller, 91 mins.)†

Love Has Many Faces (1965)** Lana Turner, Cliff Robertson, Hugh O'Brian, Stefanie Powers. A wealthy playgirl fears she is losing her husband to a young girl. It's soap opera, with the suds a dirty gray. (Dir: Alexander Singer, 105 mins.)

Love Hate Love (MTV 1971)*** Ryan O'Neal, Peter Haskell, Lesley Warren. Sadistic rich man Haskell loses pretty Warren to handsome O'Neal and then makes their lives miserable by dogging their every move, even cross-country to California. The suspense builds nicely. (Dir: George McCowan, 73 mins.)

Love in Germany, A (France-West Germany, 1984)***½ Hanna Schygulla, Pyotr Lysak, Elisabeth Trissenaar, Marie-

636

Christine Barrault. Polish director Andrzej Wajda's fiercely passionate approach to filmmaking finds bold expression in this seething drama, set in a small city in wartime Nazi Germany, about the fatal love affair between a young Polish P.O.W. and an older shopkeeper whose husband is away fighting in the Reich's army. Wajda's hand is amazingly sure and Schygulla is flawless as the shopkeeper. (119 mins.)†

Love-Ins, The (1967)* James MacArthur, Susan Oliver, Richard Todd, Mark Goddard, Carol Booth. A college professor lets celebrity go to his head after he becomes a cult hero. Join the tune-outs instead. (Dir: Arthur Dreifuss, 91 mins.)

Love in the Afternoon (1957)***½ Audrey Hepburn, Gary Cooper, Maurice Chevalier. Enchanting, sophisticated comedy about the escapades of a middle-aged American playboy in Europe. Hepburn is winning as a young music student who falls under the playboy's spell, but Cooper is a bit too old to fit the bill as the "champagne and violins" Casanova. Delightful, nonetheless. (Dir: Billy Wilder, 126 mins.)†

Love in the City (Italy, 1953)***½ Livia Venturini, Antonio Cifariello, nonprofessional cast. One of the earliest, and best, romantic compilation films finds six Italian directors weaving true tales of love in Rome. The segments by Fellini, about matrimonial agencies, and Antonioni, about three women who attempted suicide, are outstanding. (Dirs: Federico Fellini, Michelangelo Antonioni, Cesare Zavattini, Dino Risi, Alberto Lattuada, Francesco Maselli, 90 mins.)†

Love is a Ball (1963)** Glenn Ford, Hope Lange, Charles Boyer. Pure escapist fare. Glenn Ford plays a man of the world who gets involved in a scheme initiated by suave matchmaker Charles Boyer. The plot is predictable. (Dir: David Swift, 111 mins.)

Love is a Dog from Hell (Belgium, 1987)**½ Josse De Pauw, Geert Hunaerts, Michael Pas. Another European journey into the weird mind of American poet-novelist Charles Bukowski. This one's an uneven anthology film that follows the life of a sexually curious young man. The most effective section is the second one, detailing how a horrible skin disease affects his graduation from high school. AKA: Crazy Love. (Dir: Dominique Deruddere, 90 mins.)

Love is a Fat Woman (Argentina, 1988)***½ Elio Marchi, Sergio Poves Campos, Carlos Roffe, Theo McNabny. Absurdist portrait of life in Argentina after the ouster of the military dictators follows a young journalist who refuses to stop asking questions in a society where no one wants to talk about anything unpleasant. A perfect double feature with *Apartment Zero;* director Alejandro Agresti's film sometimes sacrifices structure for the sake of detail, but it is an intriguing and entertaining portrait of a country long at war with itself. (80 mins.)

Love Is a Many-Splendored Thing (1955)****½** Jennifer Jones, William Holden. A romantic tale about the love affair between an American war correspondent and a glamorous Eurasian lady doctor. It's a modern "Madame Butterfly." (Dir: Henry King, 102 mins.)†

Love Is a Racket (1932)****½** Douglas Fairbanks, Jr., Lee Tracy, Ann Dvorak, Frances Dee, Lyle Talbot. Vibrant melodrama of a columnist who wields too much power over celebrities he writes about, leading to trouble; acerbic dialogue and good performances. (Dir: William Wellman, 72 mins.)

Love Is Better Than Ever (1952)****½** Elizabeth Taylor, Larry Parks. Silly romantic comedy somewhat enhanced by the attractive stars. Taylor plays a Connecticut dancing teacher who meets a bachelor about town (Parks) and uses every trick in the book to nab him. (Dir: Stanley Donen, 81 mins.)

Love Is Forever (MTV 1983)****½** Michael Landon, Moira Chen (Laura Gemser), Jurgen Prochnow, Edward Woodward, Priscilla Presley. Taking a leading man stance in this adventure-love story, Landon plays journalist John Everingham who maneuvered a daring escape for the Laotian woman he loved. (Dir: Hall Bartlett, 104 mins.)

Love Is Never Silent (MTV 1985)*****½** Mare Winningham, Phyllis Frelich, Ed Waterstreet, Fredric Lehne, Mark Hildreth, Sid Caesar, Cloris Leachman. Poignant drama about a deaf couple's complete dependence on their hearing daughter. Although some of the drama resorts to clichés, there are electrifying performances by Winningham as the daughter in the middle and Phyllis Frelich and Ed Waterstreet (who are deaf in real life) as her demanding parents. (Dir: Joseph Sargent, 104 mins.)

Love Is News (1937)****** Loretta Young, Tyrone Power, Don Ameche. Forced, contrived comedy about an heiress who decides to marry a reporter because she hates newspapers. Remade, with Power, as *That Wonderful Urge,* 1948. (Dir: Tay Garnett, 78 mins.)

Love Is Not Enough (MTV 1978)****½** Bernie Casey, Renee Brown, Stuart K. Robinson. Pilot for the short-lived TV series "Harris and Company." About a fine, upstanding black family run by a strong, caring father. (Dir: Ivan Dixon, 104 mins.)

Love Laughs at Andy Hardy (1946)****** Mickey Rooney, Lewis Stone, Sara Haden. Postwar Hardy film finds Andy getting out of service and going back to his romances with the same juvenile approach. (Dir: Willis Goldbeck, 93 mins.)†

Love Leads the Way (MCTV 1984)******* Timothy Bottoms, Eva Marie Saint, Patricia Neal, Arthur Hill, Susan Dey, Glynnis O'Connor, Gerald Hiken. Dealing with the acceptance of Seeing Eye Dogs in the United States, *Love Leads the Way* is a moving tribute to man's best friend and to the resilience of the human spirit. Bottoms gives a warm, understated performance. (Dir: Delbert Mann, 104 mins.)†

Loveless, The (1981)***½** Willem Dafoe, Tina L'Hostsky. Marin Kanter. A deadpan homage to *The Wild One* which seems aimed at the Midnight Movie crowd. It's self-consciously burnt-out—a movie in love with leather textures and the advertising signs and logos of the fifties. Bikers drift into town, mix with the local chicks, and bring out the worst in the small-town rednecks. (Dirs: Kathryn Bigelow, Monty Montgomery, 84 mins.)†

Love Letters (1945)*****½** Jennifer Jones, Joseph Cotten, Ann Richards. A young woman develops amnesia when she learns that somebody other than her fellow has been sending her love letters. The real chap shows up, woos her, cures her, wins her. Intricately plotted, skillfully made melodrama builds to a powerful climax. (Dir: William Dieterle, 101 mins.)

Love Letters (1984)****** Jamie Lee Curtis, James Keach, Amy Madigan. A well-meaning drama about sexual obsession. A woman falls for a married man after she has leafed through a box of love letters left behind by her mother, who had led a double life. A parallel between mother and daughter is attempted as the girl experiences the same overheated emotions as her mother and then some. (Dir: Amy Jones, 94 mins.)†

Lovelines (1984)½ Greg Bradford, Mary Beth Evans, Don Michael Paul, Michael Winslow. High school battle of the bands turns into a dumb-ass contest of one-upmanship. (Dir: Rod Amateau, 94 mins.)†

Love Lives On (MTV, 1985)****½** Mary Stuart Masterson, Sam Waterston, Christine Lahti, Louise Latham. A true life story about a teenager who kicks a drug habit, discovers she has cancer, but falls in love and becomes pregnant. The young lady's problem is compounded when she decides to stop chemotherapy and try to have her baby. A thoughtful and moving story, beautifully acted. (Dir: Larry Peerce, 104 mins.)

Love Lottery, The (Great Britain, 1954)****½** David Niven, Peggy Cummins, Anne

Vernon, Herbert Lom. Hollywood satire about a movie star (Niven) who comes to regret allowing himself to be raffled off for a week in a publicity gimmick. Dry British humor with a fine supporting cast. (Dir: Charles Crichton, 89 mins.)

Lovely but Deadly (1983)½ Lucinda Dooling, John Randolph, James Herd, Mel Novak, Marie Windsor. Outrageously bad "Miss Vigilante" film about a teen who avenges her brother's death-due-to-drugs. (Dir: David Sheldon, 80 mins.)†

Lovely to Look At (1952)*** Kathryn Grayson, Howard Keel, Red Skelton, Ann Miller, Zsa Zsa Gabor. Entertaining remake of the musical *Roberta*, with many of the lovely Jerome Kern tunes, such as "Smoke Gets in Your Eyes." The songs take precedence over the thin plot, set in the haute-couture fashion world of Paris. (Dir: Mervyn LeRoy, 105 mins.)

Lovely Way to Die, A (1968)** Kirk Douglas, Sylva Koscina, Eli Wallach, Kenneth Haigh, Martyn Green, Sharon Farrell. Detective (Kirk Douglas) guards a woman accused of murder, sets out to prove her innocent. Film debut of Ali MacGraw. (Dir: David Lowell Rich, 103 mins.)

Love Machine, The (1971)* John Phillip Law, Dyan Cannon, Jackie Cooper, David Hemmings. Jacqueline Susann's tacky best-seller has been further vulgarized in this adaptation. (Dir: Jack Haley, Jr., 108 mins.)†

Love Makers, The (Italy, 1962)*** Jean-Paul Belmondo, Claudia Cardinale, Pietro Germi, Romolo Valli. A boy from the sticks adventures to the big city, where he discovers love with a lady of the evening. The stars shine brightly, and their chemistry ignites this romantic tale. AKA: **La Viaccia**. (Dir: Mauro Bolognini, 103 mins.)

Love, Mary (MTV 1985)*½ Kristy McNichol, Matt Clark, Piper Laurie, David Paymer, Rachel Ticotin. Fact-based drama of a young delinquent overcoming dyslexia, a stroke, and reform school to become a young doctor. (Dir: Robert Day, 104 mins.)

Love Me or Leave Me (1955)***½ Doris Day, James Cagney. The highly dramatic and tune-filled career of singer Ruth Etting becomes the basis for a better than average film biography. Day has seldom been shown to better advantage both vocally and dramatically. Cagney, as a racketeer who loves Ruth, steals every scene he is in. (Dir: Charles Vidor, 122 mins.)†

Love Me Tender (1956)*** Elvis Presley, Richard Egan, Debra Paget. This familiar Civil War western about a divided Southern family introduced Presley to film audiences. (Dir: Robert D. Webb, 89 mins.)†

Love Me Tonight (1932)**** Maurice Chevalier, Jeanette MacDonald. A Parisian tailor woos and wins a princess in this tuneful Rodgers and Hart film musical. Innovative in its day and still effervescent. (Dir: Rouben Mamoulian, 100 mins.)

Love Nest (1951)** June Haver, Marilyn Lundigan, Marilyn Monroe, Jack Paar. Moderately funny comedy about an ex-GI and his wife and their adventures when they buy an apartment house. (Dir: Joseph M. Newman, 85 mins.)

Love of Three Queens—See: **Face That Launched a Thousand Ships, The**

Love on a Pillow (France-Italy, 1962)* Brigitte Bardot, Robert Hossein, James Robertson Justice, Jean-Marc Bory. Ever dreamed of watching Brigitte vacuum cleaning in the nude? Her former husband, Roger Vadim, who directed and co-authored this drivel, gives us all the chance. (102 mins.)

Love on the Dole (Great Britain, 1941)*** Deborah Kerr, Clifford Evans. The problems of a London slum family during the Depression of the 1930s. Grim drama, but well made, well acted. (Dir: John Baxter, 89 mins.)

Love on the Ground (France, 1985)**½ Jane Birkin, Geraldine Chaplin, Andre Dussolier, Jean-Pierre Kalton. A cold-fish director invites two fetching actresses to his home to rehearse a new play, and he manipulates them to try out various ideas about how to resolve the piece. (Dir: Jacques Rivette, 126 mins.)

Love on the Run (1936)**½ Clark Gable, Joan Crawford, Franchot Tone. Clark woos Joan from one end of the globe to the other. He and Tone are foreign correspondents so there's a spy plot too in this wild, cliché-heavy, romantic comedy. (Dir: W. S. Van Dyke, 80 mins.)

Love on the Run (France, 1979)*** Jean-Pierre Léaud, Marie-France Pisier, Claude Jade. More adventures of Antoine Doinel, who was introduced in *The 400 Blows* and played through the years by Léaud. Old and new footage blend for instant nostalgia as the performers are seen over a period of twenty years. (Dir: François Truffaut, 93 mins.)†

Love on the Run (MTV 1985)** Stephanie Zimbalist, Alec Baldwin, Howard Duff. A lawyer goes on the lam with her convict client. Poor thriller. (Dir: Gus Trikonis, 104 mins.)†

Love Parade, The (1929)**½ Maurice Chevalier, Lupino Lane, Lillian Roth. Antiquated musical that still delivers effervescence as the stars toy with each other before falling in step with their love parade. Charming Lubitsch touches and wonderful Jeanette before she became joined at the hip with Nelson Eddy. (Dir: Ernst Lubitsch, 110 mins.)

Lover Boy (Great Britain, 1954)**½ Gerard Philipe, Valerie Hobson, Joan Greenwood. Opportunistic Frenchman in London has a talent for romancing the ladies, uses it—and them—to climb to success and wealth. Savagely bitter comedy. (Dir: Rene Clement, 105 mins.)

Loverboy (1989)** Patrick Dempsey, Kate Jackson, Barbara Carrera, Kirstie Alley, Robert Ginty, Carrie Fisher. Routine farce about a delivery boy who becomes a gigolo for neglected Beverly Hills wives. Disappointingly impersonal direction from talented Joan Micklin Silver. (98 mins.)

Lover Come Back (1946)**½ Lucille Ball, George Brent, Vera Zorina. Brent is a war (WWII) correspondent whose traveling keeps him away from his wife (Ball). Trouble comes in the shape of a war photographer (Zorina). Plenty of laughs for Lucy fans. (Dir: William A. Seiter, 90 mins.)

Lover Come Back (1961)*** Doris Day, Rock Hudson, Tony Randall, Edie Adams. Some good laughs in this Day-Hudson battle of the sexes. He's an advertising tycoon, she's a competitor, it's love on the make. Frequent bright dialogue, direction, clever situations, nice supporting performances. (Dir: Delbert Mann, 107 mins.)

Lovers, The (France, 1958)*** Jeanne Moreau, Jean-Marc Bory, Alain Cuny. A sly French tale of adultery that is more famous for the court cases that surrounded its release in the U.S. than for any of its actual content. Moreau stars as a bored wife who has an affair with an uninhibited young man. (Dir: Louis Malle, 90 mins.)†

Lovers and Liars (Italy, 1979)*½ Giancarlo Giannini, Goldie Hawn, Claudine Auger, Laura Betti, Aurore Clement. Starry-eyed Goldie's visiting Europe, and she falls for an Italian whose old-fashioned macho ideas clash with her ingenuousness. Molto stupido. (Dir: Mario Monicelli, 96 mins.)†

Lovers and Other Strangers (1970)***½ Gig Young, Richard Castellano, Anne Meara, Harry Guardino, Bonnie Bedelia, Michael Brandon, Anne Jackson, Marian Hailey, Beatrice Arthur. A riotously funny portrait of two families who come together for a wedding. (Dir: Cy Howard, 104 mins.)†

Lovers and Thieves (French, 1957)***½ Jean Poiret, Michel Serrault. Director Sacha Guitry's last picture concerns a thief and his victim who are coincidentally involved with each other in more than a simple robbery. Impeccable moviemaking. (Dir: Sacha Guitry, 81 mins.)

Lovers of Paris (France, 1957)*** Gerard Philipe, Danielle Darrieux. A Frenchman finds that the easiest way to success entails a short-cut through the proprietress's boudoir. Sexy French comedy-drama, well acted. (Dir: Julien Duvivier, 115 mins.)

Lovers of Teruel, The (France, 1962)***½ Milko Sparemblek, Milenko Banovitch, Ludmilla Tcherina, Antoine Marin. Ballerina star Tcherina is sublime as a dancer whose real life is slowly becoming like the ballet she is presently appearing in. A superb film, gorgeously shot by Claude Renoir. (Dir: Raymond Rouleau, 90 mins.)

Love She Sought, The (MTV 1990)**½ Angela Lansbury, Denholm Elliott, Robert Prosky. In this fine TV movie Ms. Lansbury plays a retiring Catholic school teacher traveling to Ireland to see a pen pal who certainly knows how to woo by mail. Elliott is the Irish nonconformist who hasn't told all in his letters. (Dir: Joseph Sargent, 96 mins.)

Lovesick (1983)*** Dudley Moore, Elizabeth McGovern, Selma Diamond, Alan King, Alec Guinness, John Huston, Gene Saks. Psychiatry comes in for a friendly but pointed trouncing through the humorous marksmanship of writer-director Marshall Brickman. Psychiatrist Moore, bored with listening to his patients ramble, falls in love with a charming new patient (McGovern). (95 mins.)†

Love 65 (Sweden, 1965)*** Keve Hjelm, Thommy Berggren, Ben Carruthers, Anne-Marie Gyllenspetz, Evabritt Strandberg. Director Bo Widerberg's adaptation of Fellini's 8½, but this story of a film director suffering with a bad marriage and a recalcitrant leading man, though well acted and romantically shot, lack's the power of the Italian classic. (95 mins.)

Loves of a Blonde (Czechoslovakia, 1965)**** Hana Brejchova, Vladimir Pucholt. Milos Forman's touching, wry triumph about a shy girl in a small, male-depleted factory town, and her unconquerable romanticism. Uses humor, pathos, desire, and sorrow in an original, touching way. (Dir: Milos Forman, 88 mins.)†

Loves of Carmen, The (1948)**½ Rita Hayworth, Glenn Ford. Familiar opera about the love of a soldier for a gypsy minus the music. Not a very impressive film, but Miss Hayworth should keep the men awake. (Dir: Charles Vidor, 99 mins.)

Loves of Edgar Allan Poe, The (1942)*½ John Shepperd (Shepperd Strudwick), Linda Darnell, Virginia Gilmore. Uninspired film biography of one of our greatest writers. (Dir: Harry Lachman, 67 mins.)

Loves of Hercules, The (Italy-France, 1960)½ Jayne Mansfield, Mickey Hargitay. See Jayne strangled by a mythological tree! Watch Jayne in a dual role as both a good and an evil woman, both pneumatically splendiferous! Hear atrocious dubbing as Jayne's voice seems to be coming from a member of the Royal Shakespearean troupe. The most Herculean labor here is for the audience to sit through it with a straight face. (Dir: Carlo Ludonico Bragaglia, 94 mins.)

Loves of Isadora, The (Great Britain, 1969)***½ Vanessa Redgrave, James Fox, Jason Robards, Jr. The long, rambling story of Isadora Duncan, the celebrated, tormented, passionate, and damned woman whose revolutionary work became the forerunner of modern dance. Flawed in many respects but Redgrave's no-holds-barred performance as Isadora is electrifying. A partially restored 153 min. version of the little-seen original edit is on video. AKA: **Isadora**. (Dir: Karel Reisz, 131 mins.)†

Loves of Ondine, The (1968)*½ Ondine, Viva, Joe Dallesandro, Pepper Davis, Brigid Polk, Ivy Nicholson. Badly reedited version of Andy Warhol's twenty-four-hour epic **** *(Four Stars)*; what's left is a dull, sloppy peek at the verbal meanderings and sexual exploits of the uninteresting Ondine, whose monstrous ego is exceeded only by director-writer-photographer-editor Warhol's. Not one of Warhol's better efforts; only Viva and Dallesandro are worth watching. (86 mins.)

Loves of Three Queens, The (Italy-France, 1954)** Hedy Lamarr, Gerard Oury, Massimo Serato, Robert Beatty, Caesar Danova. Lamarr dreams of being three famous women from history—Helen of Troy, the Empress Josephine, and Genieve de Brabant—in this little-seen vehicle made by her own production company. Despite impressive credentials, a yawner. AKA: **The Face That Launched a Thousand Ships**. (Dirs: Marc Allégret, Edgar G. Ulmer, 90 mins.)†

Love Songs (France, 1986)*½ Catherine Deneuve, Christopher Lambert, Richard Anconina, Jacques Perrin, Nick Mancuso, Dayle Haddon. The sap content runs high in this concoction about a talent agent (Deneuve) with eyes for her sexy, intense, singing discovery (Lambert). Sort of a failed Lelouch opus with lots of pop-music songs demonstrating that Deneuve and Lambert make beautiful Muzak together. (Dir: Elie Chouraqui, 107 mins.)†

Love's Savage Fury (MTV 1979)** Jennifer O'Neill, Perry King, Raymond Burr, Vernee Watson. Another ripoff of *Gone with the Wind*. The gorgeous O'Neill plays a Southern belle fallen on hard times. There's some nonsense about hidden gold and most of the action takes place in a hellhole of a Yankee prison camp. (Dir: Joseph Hardy, 104 mins.)†

Love Story (Great Britain, 1946)**½

Margaret Lockwood, Stewart Granger, Patricia Roc. A concert pianist goes away for a rest, falls for a man who is loved by another girl. Overlong but interesting romance, with excellent piano, orchestral interludes. (Dir: Leslie Arliss, 108 mins.)

Love Story (1970)** Ali MacGraw, Ryan O'Neal, Ray Milland, John Marley, Katherine Balfour. Both a testament to the studio's commercial shrewdness and to the gullibility of viewers prone to crying over their own mortality. A handsome Ivy League jock, estranged from his Boston Brahmin family, falls for a brilliantly gifted child of the middle classes, who conveniently dies of an incurable disease, thus sparing us further exposure to the worst performance given by a female star in the seventies. Dated, but emblematic of its era. Based on the best-seller by Erich Segal. (Dir: Arthur Hiller, 99 mins.)†

Love Streams (1984)*** Gena Rowlands, John Cassavetes, Diahnne Abbott, Seymour Cassel, Margaret Abbott. Unconventional, gripping drama from director-actor Cassavetes playing a self-centered, successful writer. His conflicts over his writing career vs. his need to establish intimacy with his young son are paralleled with his relationship with his sister (Rowlands), a divorcée who wears her heart on her sleeve. (136 mins.)†

Love Test, The (Great Britain, 1935)*** Judy Gunn, Louis Hayward, Dave Hutcheson, Googie Withers. Early Michael Powell film originally thought to have been lost. Fans of the famed director won't want to miss his early directorial origins. Tale is simply a lightweight romantic comedy set within the confines of a laboratory. (Dir: Michael Powell, 63 mins.)

Love That Brute (1950)**½ Paul Douglas, Jean Peters, Cesar Romero. Gangster puts on a tough front but really has a heart of gold. Pleasant enough comedy. (Dir: Alexander Hall, 85 mins.)

Love Thy Neighbor (1940)*** Jack Benny, Fred Allen, Mary Martin. Film designed to cash in on the Benny-Allen gag feud of radio days is moderately entertaining. Mary has some good numbers while Jack and Fred trade insults. (Dir: Mark Sandrich, 82 mins.)

Love Thy Neighbor (MTV 1984)**½ John Ritter, Penny Marshall, Constance McCashin, Bert Convy. Two of TV's most durable comic actors, John Ritter and Penny Marshall, co-star in an agreeable seriocomedy about marriage, infidelity, and commitments. (Dir: Tony Bill, 104 mins.)

Love Trap—See: **Curse of the Black Widow**

Love Under Fire (1937)**½ Loretta Young, Don Ameche, Frances Drake, Sig Ruman, John Carradine. Some bright lines and a few good scenes but this comedy-drama about spies, which is set against the Spanish Civil War, never comes together as a unit. (Dir: George Marshall, 75 mins.)

Love War, The (MTV 1970)** Lloyd Bridges, Angie Dickinson, Harry Basch, Daniel Travanti, Byron Foulger, Judy Jordan. Farfetched science fiction. Two planets fight over who will control Earth. (Dir: George McCowman, 74 mins.)

Love With a Perfect Stranger (MCTV 1986)** Marilu Henner, Daniel Massey, Sky Dumont. Harlequin romance plot concerns a widowed career woman afraid to trust her emotions. Luckily, she encounters a European who is rich, cultured, and madly in love with her. (Dir: Desmond Davis, uncredited, 90 mins.)†

Love With the Proper Stranger (1963)*** Natalie Wood, Steve McQueen, Edie Adams, Herschel Bernardi. Good performances enhance this contemporary love story. McQueen is a musician, very much his own man, until he becomes involved with Wood. (Dir: Robert Mulligan, 100 mins.)†

Lovey: A Circle of Children, Part II (MTV 1978)***½ Jane Alexander, Ronny Cox. This extraordinary work is based on the real-life experiences of Mary McCracken, a dedicated teacher of children with severe learning disabilities. Alexander is remarkably effective portraying the dynamic woman, divorced after a 23-year marriage, who has found solace and inspiration in the challenge of reaching these seemingly unmanageable children. (Dir: Jud Taylor, 104 mins.)

Loving (1970)***½ George Segal, Eva Marie Saint, Sterling Hayden, Keenan Wynn. A quietly intense movie, humorous, human, and insightful, about a New York illustrator whose suburban family, New York mistress and job prospects are veering toward unwanted routine. Movie's final scene is incongruous in its farcical mayhem, but otherwise the film is sensitive, restrained and, grounded in a peculiarly American reality, rings true. (Dir: Irvin Kershner, 90 mins.)

Loving Couples (1980)**½ Shirley MacLaine, James Coburn, Susan Sarandon, Stephen Collins, Sally Kellerman. Moderately entertaining but very thin romantic comedy. Woman doctor whose husband is a famous surgeon finds him boring and unattentive, and begins an affair with a real estate agent. (Dir: Jack Smight, 97 mins.)†

Loving in the Rain (France, 1974)*** Romy Schneider, Nino Castelnuovo, Alain David, Benedicte Boucher, Suzanne Flon. Beautiful cosmopolitan woman goes on vacation with her fifteen-year-old daughter. The mother has a sizzling affair with a mysterious gentleman, while the daughter discovers the wonders of teenage love. Actor Jean-Claude Brialy, a

veteran of these light-as-air romance soufflés, directed this warmly enjoyable little film. (90 mins.)

Loving Walter (Great Britain, 1986)*** Ian McKellen, Sarah Miles, Barbara Jefford, Arthur Whybrow. McKellen's performance in the difficult role of an unloved retarded man, doomed to a bleak life whether institutionalized or not, imbues this stark film with power. Miles handles the role of June, the mentally ill woman who seduces Walter and creates a brief time of respite for him, with a mastery of her own. (Dir: Stephen Frears, 110 mins.)

Loving You (1957)** Elvis Presley, Lizabeth Scott, Wendell Corey, Dolores Hart. Small-town boy becomes an overnight sensation when he's signed by a lady press agent to sing with her ex-husband's country band. (Dir: Hal Kanter, 101 mins.)†

Lovin' Molly (1974)**½ Blythe Danner, Anthony Perkins, Beau Bridges, Susan Sarandon. Blythe Danner's luminous performance as a Texas lass who wouldn't let convention stand in the way of loving two men at the same time, for a period covering four decades, is the best thing about this strange little film. Based on Larry McMurtry's novel, *Leaving Cheyenne*. (Dir: Sidney Lumet, 98 mins.)

Low Blow (1988)* Leo Fong, Cameron Mitchell, Troy Donahue, Diane Stevenett, Akousa Busia. Ex-cop Fong goes up against the religious cult led by Mitchell in this sub-par martial arts feature. Fong also wrote and produced. (Dir: Frank Harris, 85 mins.)†

Lower Depths, The (France, 1936)*** Jean Gabin, Vladimir Sokoloff, Louis Jouvet, Robert Le Vigan, Suzy Prim, Jany Holt. A financially ruined baron meets a thief who teaches him some hard-learned lessons about life, and takes him to live in a shelter for derelicts. Well acted emotional film based on classic drama by Maxim Gorky. (Dir: Jean Renoir, 92 mins.)†

Lower Depths, The (Japan, 1957)*** Toshiro Mifune, Isuzu Yamada, Ganjiro Nakamura, Kyoko Kagawa. Interesting film version of Maxim Gorky's play by Kurosawa, who doesn't quite overcome the piece's inherent talkiness, but still fashions a moving experience out of this examination of existence at the subsistence level. (Dir: Akira Kurosawa, 125 mins.)

Loyal 47 Ronin, The—See: 47 Ronin, The

Loyalties (Canada, 1987)* Susan Woolridge, Tantoo Cardinal, Kenneth Welsh, Vera Martin, Diane Debassige. Cliché-ridden pseudo-feminist drama, set in a small Alberta town, about the growing friendship between a middle-class British housewife and the hell-raising Indian woman she employs as her housekeeper. (Dir: Anne Wheeler, 100 mins.)†

L-Shaped Room, The (Great Britain,

1962)***½ Leslie Caron, Tom Bell, Brock Peters, Cicely Courtneidge, Emlyn Williams. Beautifully done drama of a pregnant girl taking lodgings in a run-down boarding house, and the struggling young writer who meets, helps, loves her. Leslie Caron never better; rest of the cast excellent, with the script and direction by Bryan Forbes superb. (125 mins.)

Lt. Robin Crusoe U.S.N. (1966)* Dick Van Dyke, Nancy Kwan. Cutesy Disney comedy. Van Dyke parachutes out of his disabled Navy plane and finds a lovely maiden (Kwan) whom he promptly dubs Wednesday. (Dir: Byron Paul, 110 mins.)

Lucan (MTV 1977)** Ned Beatty, Kevin Brophy, Stockard Channing. Here's another version of the old story about the boy raised in a forest with wild animals, attempting to understand modern civilization and the wickedness of man. (Dir: David Greene, 79 mins.)

Lucas (1986)*** Corey Haim, Kerri Green, Charlie Sheen, Courtney Thorne-Smith, Winona Ryder. Endearing coming-of-age film about an ultra-bright teen who loses his head and his common sense over an older woman of sixteen. (Dir: David Seltzer, 90 mins.)†

Lucas Tanner (MTV 1974)**½ David Hartman, Rosemary Murphy, Joe Garagiola. In this pilot film for the TV series, David Hartman plays a midwestern high-school English teacher who understands kids, but battles suspicious parents and jealous cohorts. (Dir: Richard Donner, 74 mins.)

Lucia (Cuba, 1969)***½ Eslinda Nunez, Adela Legra, Raquel Revuelta, Adolfo Liaurado, Ramon Brito. Epic about Cuban history, with three eras seen through the eyes of three different women named Lucia. Each woman takes a stand against Latin machismo, with a background of mystery, intrigue, terrorism, and revolution. One of the great works of Latin American cinema, a thrilling film in the tradition of *Intolerance*. (Dir: Humberto Solas, 160 mins.)

Lucifer Complex, The (1978)* Robert Vaughn, Keenan Wynn, Merrie Lynn Ross, Aldo Ray. The intrepid Vaughn infiltrates a prison camp where clones are being created by none other than Adolf Hitler himself. (Dirs: David L. Hewitt, Kenneth Hartford, 91 mins.)†

Luckiest Man in the World, The (1989)*** Philip Bosco, Doris Belack, Joanne Camp, Moses Gunn. A Scroogelike business-man narrowly escapes death and becomes a changed man, attempting to make amends to the family and associates he has always wronged. His new attitude causes massive confusion for everyone concerned. Gentle comedy from independent writer-

director Frank D. Gilroy (*The Gig*) is a charming find. (82 mins.)

Luck of Ginger Coffey, The (U.S.-Canada, 1964)**** Robert Shaw, Mary Ure. Fine drama of a young Irish immigrant in Montreal with his wife and daughter trying to better himself in the world against all odds, including his own attitude. (Dir: Irvin Kershner, 100 mins.)

Luck of the Irish, The (1948)**½ Tyrone Power, Anne Baxter, Cecil Kellaway. While trying to choose between his newspaper boss's daughter and a sweet colleen, Tyrone has the invaluable aid of a leprechaun. (Dir: Henry Koster, 99 mins.)

Lucky Day (MTV 1991)**½ Olympia Dukakis, Amy Madigan, Chloe Webb, Terence Knox. A sentimental drama given extra depth by the charged performance of Madigan as an overprotective sister whose hatred for her mother colors her entire existence. Webb is Madigan's slightly retarded sister who wins two million dollars in a lottery and is wooed by her recovering alcoholic mother (Dukakis), but not for the reason everyone thinks. (Dir: Donald Wrye, 96 mins.)

Lucky Devils (1932)**½ William Boyd, William Gargan, Dorothy Wilson, Bruce Cabot, Lon Chaney, Jr., Julie Haydon. Enjoyable adventure about Hollywood stuntmen, with plenty of behind-the-screen action revealing how movies were made, and amiable performances, including that of the pre-Hoppy Boyd. (Dir: Ralph Ince, 64 mins.)

Lucky Jim (Great Britain, 1957)**½ Ian Carmichael, Terry-Thomas, Hugh Griffith, Sharon Acker. Kingsley Amis's novel, about a young professor from a lower-class background contending with university snobs, is made into a fairly typical Boulting farce. Much of the social criticism and the misogyny of the book are lost. Carmichael is left to carry the comedy with great charm. (Dir: John Boulting, 95 mins.)†

Lucky Jordan (1942)**½ Alan Ladd, Helen Walker. Ladd carries this film about an AWOL soldier who inadvertently becomes a hero by defeating a gang of Nazi agents. (Dir: Frank Tuttle, 84 mins.)

Lucky Lady (1975)* Gene Hackman, Liza Minnelli, Burt Reynolds, Robby Benson, Michael Hordern. An embarrassment. Hopeless script finds boring characters who are rum-runners off the California coast during Prohibition. (Dir: Stanley Donen, 118 mins.)

Lucky Losers (1950)*½ Bowery Boys, Lyle Talbot, Hillary Brooke. Sach and Slip start working at a Wall Street brokerage firm and end up investigating the death of their boss, which has been attributed to suicide. (Dir: William Beaudine, 69 mins.)

Lucky Luciano (Italy-France-U.S., 1973)** Gian Maria Volonte, Rod Steiger, Edmond O'Brien, Vincent Gardenia. Rather clinical look at the life of a crime boss whose career flourished even after deportation to his native Italy. (Dir: Francesco Rossi, 112 mins.)†

Lucky Me (1954)** Doris Day, Bob Cummings, Phil Silvers, Nancy Walker. Disappointing musical comedy about a chorus girl and friends out of jobs in Florida. (Dir: Jack Donohue, 100 mins.)

Lucky Nick Cain (1950)*** George Raft, Coleen Gray. A gambler on vacation on the Riviera is framed for the murder of a T-man, does some sleuthing on his own to break up an international counterfeiting ring. (Dir: Joseph M. Newman, 87 mins.)

Lucky Night (1939)*½ Myrna Loy, Robert Taylor, Joseph Allen. Pitiful, contrived little nothing about an heiress who marries a poor poet. (Dir: Norman Taurog, 82 mins.)

Lucky Partners (1940)**½ Ronald Colman, Ginger Rogers. Artist shares a sweepstakes ticket with a young woman, which proves lucky. Occasionally amusing comedy. (Dir: Lewis Milestone, 102 mins.)

Lucy & Desi: Before the Laughter (MTV 1991)**½ Frances Fisher, Maurice Bernard. Surprisingly entertaining TV film deals with the tempestuous romance and the less-than-idyllic early married years of Lucille Ball and Desi Arnaz. It is very candid about the Cuban-born Desi's womanizing and what it did to Lucy. However, theirs was also a love story, and the movie never loses sight of that fact. The story doesn't deal with Lucy and Desi's split and eventual divorce. Bernard is pretty good as the Latin lover, but it is Fisher who scores in the role of America's beloved redhead. (Dir: Charles Jarrott, 96 mins.)

Lucy Gallant (1955)**½ Jane Wyman, Charlton Heston, Claire Trevor. Charlton Heston strikes oil and Jane Wyman builds the biggest fashion business in Texas but they find that marriage and careers don't mix. (Dir: Robert Parrish, 104 mins.)

Ludwig (Italy, 1972)*½ Helmut Berger, Trevor Howard, Romy Schneider, Gert Frobe, Silvana Mangano. Overlong, poorly scripted historical drama about Ludwig, the Mad King of Bavaria. Vapid and sterile. (Dir: Luchino Visconti, 173 mins.)

Luggage of the Gods (1983)** Mark Stolzenberg, Gabriel Barre, Gwen Ellison, Martin Haber. Members of a prehistoric tribe, living unchanged somewhere in North America, encounter the modern world when a load of luggage is jettisoned from an airplane into their laps. Ultra-low-budget comedy, similar to *The Gods Must Be Crazy*, provides a few obvious but effective laughs. (Dir: David Kendall, 78 mins.)†

Lullaby of Broadway (1951)** Doris Day, Gene Nelson, Gladys George. More backstage nonsense with music and plenty of dancing. Score includes standards by George Gershwin and Cole Porter which help. Broadway was never like this! (Dir: David Butler, 92 mins.)

Lulu Belle (1948)** Dorothy Lamour, George Montgomery, Albert Dekker, Otto Kruger, Glenda Farrell. Lamour can't hide her natural sweetness as she attempts to extend her range by playing an ambitious singer who prefers fame and fortune to a series of men whom she treats like lapdogs. (Dir: Leslie Fenton, 87 mins.)

Lumiere (France, 1976)*** Jeanne Moreau, Francine Racette, Lucia Bose, Keith Carradine. An insightful film about four actresses ... their lives, loves, and desires. Each character balances traditional needs associated with women (like stability and affection) with the need to shine independently in the light (the "lumiere"). Written and directed by Moreau. (95 mins.)

Luna (Italy, 1978)* Jill Clayburgh, Matthew Barry. A preposterous, arty film about an opera singer (Clayburgh) who tries to help her drug-addict son through withdrawal. Her infinite patience in seeing him through this crisis includes going to bed with him. (Dir: Bernardo Bertolucci, 141 mins.)

Lunch Wagon (1981)** Pamela Bryant, Rosanne Katon, Candy Moore, Rick Padell, Rose Marie. Raucous and only moderately amusing comedy about a trio of beauties who run a lunch wagon near a building site. (Dir: Ernest Pintoff, 88 mins.)†

Lured (1947)**½ Lucille Ball, George Sanders, Boris Karloff, Charles Coburn, Cedric Hardwicke. A dance hall girl disappears in London, so friend Lucille Ball sets out to find her, nearly gets herself killed. Fairly good mystery. AKA: **Personal Column.** (Dir: Douglas Sirk, 102 mins.)

Lure of the Wilderness (1952)**½ Jean Peters, Jeffrey Hunter, Walter Brennan. Young man finds an escaped convict and his daughter hiding out in the swamp, helps him prove his innocence. Remake of 1941's *Swamp Water*. (Dir: Jean Negulesco, 92 mins.)

Lurkers (1988)* Christine Moore, Gary Warner, Marina Taylor. Confused and confusing horror turkey about a woman who is pursued by the same grotesque creatures that haunted her childhood dreams. (Dir: Roberta Findlay, 95 mins.)†

Lust for a Vampire (Great Britain, 1970)*** Michael Johnson, Suzanna Leigh, Yutte Stensgaard, Ralph Bates, Barbara Jefford.

Ravishing young vampirette feels pangs of love for a novelist. AKA: **To Love a Vampire.** (Dir: Jimmy Sangster, 95 mins.)†

Lust for Freedom (1988)* Melanie Coll, William J. Kulzer, Judi Trevor. Bad women's prison movie with campy dialogue overdubbed, though it doesn't begin to approach that level of humor. Only for those who enjoy real women's prison movies. (Dir: Eric Louzil, 91 mins.)†

Lust for Gold (1949)***½ Glenn Ford, Ida Lupino, Gig Young. Excellent film showing how greed and evil take over and ruin basically good people. Edge-of-seat suspense and fine performance by all. (Dir: S. Sylvan Simon, 90 mins.)

Lust for Life (1956)**** Kirk Douglas, Anthony Quinn, James Donald, Pamela Brown. Superb film about the turbulent personal life of artist Vincent van Gogh, masterfully played by Kirk Douglas. Anthony Quinn won his second Oscar for his colorful performance as van Gogh's close friend and severest critic, artist Paul Gauguin. (Dir: Vincente Minnelli, 122 mins.)†

Lust in the Dust (1985)** Divine, Tab Hunter, Lainie Kazan, Cesar Romero, Geoffrey Lewis, Henry Silva. A tame, sporadically amusing sagebrush satire in which Hunter (parodying the Man with No Name from spaghetti Westerns) tries to piece together a fortune-hunting puzzle from maps tattooed on the ample buttocks of Kazan and Divine. (Dir: Paul Bartel, 85 mins.)†

Lusty Men, The (1952)*** Susan Hayward, Robert Mitchum, Arthur Kennedy. When a cowpoke becomes a rodeo star and lets it go to his head, his wife suffers. Very good drama with authentic rodeo atmosphere, solid performances and direction. (Dir: Nicholas Ray, 113 mins.)†

Luther (Great Britain, 1974)*** Stacy Keach, Patrick Magee, Alan Badel, Hugh Griffith. John Osborne's stunning play about the famous 16th-century cleric who changed the course of the world has been shortened and its impact reduced in the move to the screen. Stacy Keach is increasingly effective as the film builds. (Dir: Guy Green, 112 mins.)

Luv (1967)**½ Jack Lemmon, Peter Falk, Elaine May, Eddie Mayehoff. Heavy-handed rendering of Murray Schisgal's clever Broadway play about life and loves among a set of middle-class New Yorkers—part of a group much concerned with self-analysis and psychiatric jargon. Although the script and the performances have been cheapened, Elaine May is genuinely funny. (Dir: Clive Donner, 95 mins.)†

Luxury Liner (1948)** George Brent, Jane Powell, Lauritz Melchior. Good voices but nothing else in this musical about a

ship's captain and his meddling teen-age daughter. (Dir: Richard Whorf, 98 mins.)

Lydia (1941)***½ Merle Oberon, Joseph Cotten, Edna May Oliver, George Reeves, Alan Marshal. An elderly lady has a reunion with four of her lost loves, relives the romantic past. Sensitive, poignant romantic drama, skillfully directed, acted. (Dir: Julien Duvivier, 104 mins.)

Lydia Bailey (1952)**½ Dale Robertson, Anne Francis, Juanita Moore, William Marshall. American lawyer goes to Haiti to get a girl's signature on a legal document, and becomes involved in a war with Napoleonic forces. Pleasant costume adventure moves at a good pace. (Dir: Jean Negulesco, 88 mins.)

M (Germany, 1931)**** Peter Lorre (film debut), Gustav Grundgens, Ellen Widman, Inge Landgut. Suspenseful, psychological crime drama, brilliantly directed by Fritz Lang. Lorre plays a pitiable, disturbed child murderer in Berlin, and the film offers an intriguing delineation of the painstaking methods employed by the police and the underworld, both out to trap the killer. (99 mins.)†

M (1951)** David Wayne, Howard da Silva, Luther Adler, Karen Morley, Martin Gabel. A lot goes wrong in this Americanized update of the classic. Robbed of Fritz Lang's Teutonic influence, the story seems neutered. (Dir: Joseph Losey, 88 mins.)

Ma & Pa Kettle series. Cornball folksiness was the foundation of this popular series that got its start with the film version of *The Egg and I*, with Ma and Pa as supporting characters. The matriarch and patriarch of low humor were rewarded with their own movie series, and fans should catch these following films in addition to those reviewed below: *The Kettles in the Ozarks* and *The Kettles on Old MacDonald's Farm* (even though Percy Kilbride, the original Pa, was not in them).

Ma & Pa Kettle (1949)*** Marjorie Main, Percy Kilbride. The first of the "Ma and Pa Kettle" series and one of the funniest. (Dir: Charles Lamont, 75 mins.)

Ma & Pa Kettle at Home (1954)**½ Marjorie Main, Percy Kilbride. "Ma & Pa Kettle" fans will get a kick out of this comedy in which Pa tries to make the dilapidated farm over into an efficient, prosperous operation. (Dir: Charles Lamont, 81 mins.)

Ma & Pa Kettle at the Fair (1952)**½ Marjorie Main, Percy Kilbride. Cornball comedy with Kettles getting into one impossible predicament after another. Pa buys a sick horse, Ma enters him in a race at the county fair by mistake; Rosie, the Kettles' oldest daughter, falls in love. (Dir: Charles Barton, 77 mins.)

Ma & Pa Kettle at Waikiki (1955)**½ Marjorie Main, Percy Kilbride. The Kettles find themselves in Hawaii in this outing. They are invited to that island paradise by another branch of the Kettle clan which has made millions in canned fruit. (Dir: Lee Sholem, 79 mins.)

Ma & Pa Kettle Back on the Farm (1951)**½ Marjorie Main, Percy Kilbride. More fun as the Kettle clan gets involved with false uranium deposits on their property, in-law trouble via their oldest son's wife's parents, and gangsters who think their property is loaded with uranium. (Dir: Edward Sedgwick, 80 mins.)

Ma & Pa Kettle Go to Town (1950)** Marjorie Main, Percy Kilbride. Strictly for the Kettle-clan fans. Ma and Pa win a trip to New York City in a soft-drink-slogan contest and have a series of predictable but amusing adventures. (Dir: Charles Lamont, 80 mins.)

Ma & Pa Kettle on Vacation (1953)**½ Marjorie Main, Percy Kilbride. The "Kettle" fans will have fun with this broad comedy in which "Ma and Pa" go to Paris and get involved with an international espionage operation. (Dir: Charles Lamont, 75 mins.)

Ma Barker's Killer Brood (1960)** Lurene Tuttle, Tris Coffin, Paul Dubov, Nelson Leigh. Passable Depression tale about a mother who resorts to crime with her four sons. (Dir: Bill Karn, 82 mins.)†

Mabel and Fatty (1914–16)*** Mabel Normand, Fatty Arbuckle, Al St. John. Three delightful short comedies made for Mack Sennett's Keystone Studio, starring the popular team of Arbuckle and Normand; **He Did and He Didn't, Mabel and Fatty Viewing the World's Fair at San Francisco,** and **Mabel's Blunder.** The second is particularly unique, with views of the historic 1914 World's Fair as the backdrop for the duo's adventures. (61 mins.)†

Mac—See also: **Mc**

Macabra—See: **Demonoid, Messenger of Death**

Macabre (1958)** William Prince, Jim Backus. This horror film doesn't rely on monsters for its impact—there are all sorts of fiendish things going on, such as burying people alive, for instance. The cast is better than the vehicle but they seem to enjoy playing at being terrorized. (Dir: William Castle, 72 mins.)

Macabre Serenade—See: **House of Evil**

Macahans, The (MTV 1976)**½ James Arness, Eva Marie Saint, Richard Kiley, Bruce Boxleitner. Sprawling western movie based *How the West Was Won.* Arness plays scout Zeb Macahan, leading his

brother's family west from Bull Run, Virginia, in time to avoid the Civil War. (Dir: Bernard McEveety, 120 mins.)

MAC and Me (1988)* Christine Ebersole, Jonathan Ward, Jade Calegory. Completely shameless ripoff of *E.T.,* with a wheelchair-bound young boy befriending a lost alien from outer space. Even more reprehensible are the continual product plugs, especially for McDonald's, given that this is a movie directed at young children. With the real *E.T.* on video, there's absolutely no excuse to bring this one home. (Dir: Stewart Rafill, 99 mins.)†

Macao (1952)*** Robert Mitchum, Jane Russell, William Bendix, Brad Dexter, Gloria Grahame. Adventurer helps the police to capture a gangster wanted in the U.S. (Dirs: Josef von Sternberg, Nicholas Ray, 80 mins.)†

Macaroni (Italy, 1985)** Jack Lemmon, Marcello Mastroianni, Daria Nicolodi, Isa Danieli, Maria Luisa Saniella. Overcooked, gummy serio-comedy about the life-affirming reunion between a former GI and the brother of the Italian girl he had an affair with during WWII. This convoluted crisscross of American ham and Italian cheese adds up to a pretty stale sandwich. (Dir: Ettore Scola, 104 mins.)†

MacArthur (1977)** Gregory Peck, Dan O'Herlihy, Ed Flanders. This was to have been Peck's *Patton,* but the results don't add up. The film doesn't have the necessary visual sweep and larger-than-life style to complement the outsized heroics of the film's hero. (Dir: Joseph Sargent, 130 mins.)†

MacArthur's Children (Japan, 1985)**½ Masako Natsume, Takaya Yamamuchi, Shiori Sakura, Shima Iwashita, Ken Watanabe, Juzo Itami. Ambitious but failed effort to show Japanese citizens dealing with defeat in WWII, as their country is occupied by American soldiers and their new government tries to rewrite recent history, forbidding children to honor their fathers who died in battle. Fascinating theme keeps getting lost in a maze of character studies. (Dir: Masahiro Shinoda, 123 mins.)†

Macbeth (1948)*** Orson Welles, Roddy McDowall, Jeanette Nolan, Dan O'Herlihy, Edgar Barrier. Perhaps director Orson Welles's most problematic film. He attempted to transpose his Shakespearean vision from stage to film by using the economics and logistics of a Republic western: no budget, three-week schedule, papier-mâché sets on the western ranch. Welles's voice is still one of the great theater instruments around, but his Macbeth is inscrutable. Nolan is ludicrously incompetent playing Lady M. This was Welles's last Hollywood film for ten years. (105 mins.)†

Macbeth (MTV 1960)**½ Maurice Evans, Judith Anderson, Michael Hordern, Ian Bannen, Felix Aylmer, Meg Jenkins. Solid but uninspired version of the Shakespeare play. Drenched in the British tradition of quality, the film can at least point with pride to Anderson's definitive interpretation of Lady M. (Dir: George Schaeffer, 107 mins.)

Macbeth (Great Britain, 1971)***½ Jon Finch, Francesca Annis, Martin Shaw, John Stride. In the uproar over the extreme (but not unwarranted) violence and gore in this film, director Roman Polanski's personal life, and the fact that this was Playboy Enterprises' first production (and that Lady Macbeth did her dream speech in the nude), the merits of the film were largely overlooked. It is a grim, valid conception of the bloody drama. Finch and Miss Annis, the two young leads, expertly portray the murderous couple. (140 mins.)†

Machine Gun Kelly (1958)** Charles Bronson, Susan Cabot. Small-time hoodlum becomes a public enemy due to the goading of a dame. Bronson's good, the film's less so. (Dir: Roger Corman, 80 mins.)†

Machine Gun McCain (1970)** Peter Falk, John Cassavetes, Britt Ekland. The stars are more interesting than this routine crime drama about a raid on a Las Vegas casino controlled by the Mafia. (Dir: Giuliano Montaldo, 94 mins.)

Macho Callahan (1970)** David Janssen, Lee J. Cobb, Jean Seberg, David Carradine. It's Civil War time and Janssen's out to get the man who was responsible for putting him in jail. If this seems like an antebellum "The Fugitive," you're not just whistling "Dixie." (Dir: Bernard Kowalski, 99 mins.)†

MacKenna's Gold (1969)*½ Gregory Peck, Omar Sharif, Camilla Sparv. Overblown, over-produced western. Peck is cast as the marshal who knows where a fabulous fortune in gold is hidden, and Sharif is the villain who wants to get his hands on it. (Dir: J. Lee Thompson, 128 mins.)

Mackintosh & T.J. (1975)**½ Roy Rogers, Clay O'Brien, Joan Hackett. Corny oater shot in Texas marks the return of western star Rogers to his first starring role in 22 years. He's a philosophical ranch hand who befriends a tough kid (O'Brien), and has difficulty with younger hands whose views clash with his. (Dir: Marvin J. Chomsky, 96 mins.)

Mackintosh Man, The (Great Britain, 1973)**½ Paul Newman, Dominique Sanda, James Mason. Outdated thriller about cold-war espionage—the kind of plot that was quite popular in the '60s when spies were busy coming in from the cold. (Dir: John Huston, 98 mins.)†

646

Mack Sennett Comedies Vol. 1 (1915–28)*** Four comic shorts from Mack Sennett's Keystone Studio, starring various silent clowns: **The Eyes Have It**, with Ben Turpin, **The Cannon Ball**, with Chester Conklin, **The Desperate Scoundrel**, with the Keystone Kops, and **Pride of Pikeville**, another Turpin starrer. All are extremely funny. (85 mins.)†

Mack Sennett Comedies Vol. 2 (1915–24)*** Four more Keystone Studio comedies. The first three, **Mabel and Fatty Adrift**, **Mabel, Fatty, and the Law**, and **Fatty's Tintype Tangle**, star the popular team of Mabel Normand and Fatty Arbuckle; the last has Will Rogers satirizing Washington, in **Our Congressman**. Classic laughmakers. (84 mins.)†

Mack the Knife (1989)** Raul Julia, Julia Migenes, Richard Harris, Roger Daltry, Julie Walters, Rachel Robertson, Clive Revill. There have been good and bad productions of *The Threepenny Opera*, but this is without a doubt one of the most disappointing. Director-scripter Menahem Golan picked a letter-perfect cast for this adaptation, and then proceeded to give the Brecht-Weill classic a drastic overhaul that makes it look and sound like a pale imitation of *Oliver!*. Inappropriately lush orchestral scores, the most insipid translation of the lyrics ever done, and artificial sets loaded with synchronized dancers all subdue and eventually smother the fine work done by Julia and Migenes. (122 mins.)†

Macomber Affair, The (1947)***½ Gregory Peck, Joan Bennett, Robert Preston. Hemingway's tale of the triangular difficulties of a husband, wife, and guide on an African hunting expedition. Literate, well acted. (Dir: Zoltan Korda, 89 mins.)

Macon County Line (1974)**½ Alan Vint, Jesse Vint, Max Baer, Cheryl Waters. There is a great deal of violence and some effective drama in this supposedly factual story, about a vengeful southern sheriff who is out for blood after his wife is brutally killed by a pair of drifters. (Dir: Richard Compton, 89 mins.)†

Mad About Men (Great Britain, 1954)** Glynis Johns, Donald Sinden, Margaret Rutherford, Dora Bryan. Girl who intends to do good keeps transferring her affections from her husband to her former fiance. Slow-moving comedy needs more sparkle. (Dir: Ralph Thomas, 90 mins.)

Mad About Music (1938)*** Deanna Durbin, Gail Patrick, Herbert Marshall. Girl attending a swanky Swiss school invents a father to impress classmates. Fine Durbin film. (Dir: Norman Taurog, 100 mins.)

Mad Adventures of Rabbi Jacob (France, 1974)*** Louis De Funes, Suzy Delair, Marcel Dalio. Wonderful slapstick farce.

De Funes plays a bigoted Catholic factory owner whose exasperation causes him to be chased by the police as a political assassin, dumped in a vat of green bubble-gum, chased by Arab terrorists, and finally to impersonate an American rabbi making a pilgrimage back to his birthplace. (Dir: Gerard Oury, 96 mins.)

Madame (France, 1963)*½ Sophia Loren, Robert Hossein. One of Loren's worst films—an inaccurate account of France during Napoleon's reign. (Dir: Christian-Jaque, 104 mins.)

Madame Bovary (France, 1934)**½ Valentine Tessier, Fernand Fabre, Pierre Renoir, Daniel Lecourtois. Director Jean Renoir's dramatic retelling of Flaubert's novel of a woman, bored with her marriage, whose life unravels as she has affairs with other men. Film was originally nearly three hours long, but Renoir was forced to cut it to present length, making for a disjointed, ultimately unsatisfying work, though one which still contains moments of power and beauty. (117 mins.)†

Madame Bovary (1949)*** Jennifer Jones, Van Heflin, Louis Jourdan, Gene Lockhart, James Mason. Miss Jones gives a beautiful performance in the title role of Emma Bovary, an incurable romantic whose many loves led to her destruction. Van Heflin plays Emma's respectable husband and James Mason portrays Gustave Flaubert. (Dir: Vincente Minnelli, 115 mins.)†

Madame Butterfly (1932)**½ Sylvia Sidney, Cary Grant, Charlie Ruggles, Irving Pichel, Helen Jerome Eddy. Good dramatic version of Puccini's opera, with a lovely, touching performance by Sidney in the title role as an innocent Japanese girl betrayed by an American officer. Grant is good, but nothing can make Lieutenant Pinkerton anything less than a jerk. (Dir: Marion Gering, 86 mins.)

Madame Curie (1943)*** Greer Garson, Walter Pidgeon, Henry Travers. Occasionally too slow but generally good screen biography of the discoverers of radium. Garson and Pidgeon are ideal in this informative and entertaining film. (Dir: Mervyn LeRoy, 124 mins.)

Madame Racketeer (1932)**½ Alison Skipworth, Richard Bennett, George Raft, Evelyn Knapp, Gertrude Messinger. Enjoyable comedy-drama has a famous con artist changing her ways for the sake of her grown daughters; Skipworth and Bennett are splendid. (Dir: Alexander Hall, 71 mins.)

Madame Rosa (France-Israel, 1977)***½ Simone Signoret, Claude Dauphin, Samy Ben Youb. Signoret is marvelous as a Jewish ex-prostitute who raises the offspring of working streetwalkers and has a particular affection for a fourteen-year-old Arab boy. The film has humor, warmth, poignance, and love. Oscar, Best Foreign Film. (Dir: Moshe Mizrahi, 105 mins.)†

Madame Satan (1930)**½ Kay Johnson, Reginald Denny, Lillian Roth, Roland Young. This extravaganza was one of director Cecil B. DeMille's few talkies to be set in the dazzling world of the rich. Gaudily outrageous, with a splashy, posh masked ball held in a dirigible and a leap from same into the Central Park reservoir. (105 mins.)

Madame Sin (1972)** Bette Davis, Robert Wagner. With silver-blue eyeshadow splashed over her famous lids, Miss Davis plays an oriental villainess in this handsomely mounted film made in England. The plot has Madame Sin kidnapping a U.S. intelligence agent. (Dir: David Greene, 73 mins.)†

Madame Sousatzka (Great Britain, 1988) ***½ Shirley MacLaine, Navin Chowdhry, Shaban Azmi, Peggy Ashcroft, Twiggy. Must-see film, filled with poetic resonance and a special poignance. Buried beneath garish make-up and jewelry, MacLaine plays a lonely, mysterious London piano teacher of Russian descent who takes too intimate an interest in the lives of her students. Dame Ashcroft is memorable as a lovable old landlady. (Dir: John Schlesinger, 102 mins.)†

Madame X (1929)** Ruth Chatterton, Raymond Hackett, Sidney Toler. Early talkie version of the old war-horse that had already been filmed several times as a silent picture. The overly familiar tale concerns a woman whose indiscretion forces her to sacrifice herself to protect her husband and child. AKA: **Absinthe.** (Dir: Lionel Barrymore, 95 mins.)

Madame X (1937)*** Gladys George, John Beal, Warren William. Best of the "Madame" movies, due to Gladys George's superb delineation of the title role, a prominent man's wife who downslides into promiscuity and alcoholism after her mother-in-law arranges her "death" to prevent a scandal. (Dir: Sam Wood, 72 mins.)

Madame X (1966)** Lana Turner, John Forsythe, Ricardo Montalban. The ancient tearjerker about the tragic lady who sacrifices all for love and her son, given an updated but not improved treatment. (Dir: David Lowell Rich, 100 mins.)†

Madame X (MTV 1981)**½ Tuesday Weld, Len Cariou, Eleanor Parker, Robert Hooks, Jerry Stiller, Jeremy Brett. TV reworking of that perennial salute to the lachrymose. This time Madame protects her family from scandal but is defended in court by her daughter, not her son; does that make this a feminist soap opera? (Dir: Robert Ellis Miller, 104 mins.)

Mad at the World (1955)**½ Frank Lovejoy, Keefe Brasselle, Cathy O'Donnell. When a gang of juvenile delinquents seriously injure a young father's baby, he decides to take the matter in his own hands and goes on the hunt for them. Grim drama, well made. (Dir: Harry Essex, 72 mins.)

Mad Bomber, The (1972)*½ Chuck Connors, Vince Edwards, Neville Brand, Hank Brandt. A surly cop shadows a crazed killer who wants to blow up his enemies. Action-wise, this never really detonates. (Dir: Bert I. Gordon, 95 mins.)†

Mad Bull (1977)**½ Alex Karras, Susan Anspach, Elisha Cook, Jr., Nicholas Colasanto. Karras is a big bruiser in the wrestling ring, but just another overgrown little boy looking for love outside it. (Dirs: Walter Doniger, Len Steckler, 104 mins.)†

M.A.D.D. Mothers Against Drunk Drivers (MTV 1983)*** Mariette Hartley, Paula Prentiss, Grace Zabriskie, John Rubinstein. Moving, emotional drama about a grieving, angry California mother whose daughter is killed by a drunk driver. Mariette Hartley is most believable as the angry mother who develops into a political activist to generate a tough California law. (Dir: Ted Post, 100 mins.)†

Mad Doctor, The (1941)*½ Basil Rathbone, Ellen Drew, John Howard, Ralph Morgan. Basil's a Bluebeard and women and their money are soon parted—permanently. (Dir: Tim Whelan, 90 mins.)

Mad Doctor of Market Street, The (1942)** Lionel Atwill, Claire Dodd, Una Merkel, Nat Pendleton. You'll think twice about visiting the South Pacific after seeing this. Looney Lionel just loves to experiment, as some unwilling natives soon find out. (Dir: Joseph Lewis, 61 mins.)

Mad Dog Morgan (Australia, 1976)**½ Dennis Hopper, Jack Thompson, David Gulpilil. Hopper plays the ravaging Australian bandit in a rather weak genre movie. (Dir: Philippe Mora, 102 mins.)

Mad Dogs and Englishmen (1971)*** Joe Cocker, Leon Russell, Rita Coolidge, Chris Stainton, Claudia Linnear. Concert documentary of Joe Cocker's 1970 U.S. tour, featuring a stellar band assembled by Leon Russell that was one of the largest ever for a rock singer. Cocker is at his incoherent, bluesy best and the band wails with sloppy abandon on such classics as "Delta Lady," "The Letter," "Something," and "Feelin' Alright." A must for rock fans. (Dir: Pierre Adidge, 118 mins.)

Made for Each Other (1939)**½ Carole Lombard, James Stewart, Charles Coburn, Lucile Watson, Louise Beavers. The appealing Stewart and Lombard are married, and the vicissitudes of the little people have rarely been given a more thorough wringing. (Dir: John Cromwell, 85 mins.)†

Made for Each Other (1971)**** Renee Taylor, Joseph Bologna, Paul Sorvino. Delightful, joyous comedy about a pair of losers in New York who meet at an emergency group-therapy session. Hilarious and touching at the same time. (Dir: Robert B. Bean, 104 mins.)

Made in Heaven (1987)*** Timothy Hutton, Kelly McGillis, Maureen Stapleton, Ann Wedgeworth, James Gammon, Mare Winningham, Don Murray. Hutton and McGillis are lovers who meet as spirits in heaven, then search for each other in their next lives on Earth. The episodic nature of the second half seems to obscure the dreamy plot line, but the memorable moments more than suffice. Loads of cameos, including Debra Winger (as a male angel) Ellen Barkin, Neil Young, Tom Petty, and Ric Ocasek. (Dir: Alan Rudolph, 102 mins.)†

Made in Italy (Italy-France, 1965)***½ Anna Magnani, Nino Manfredi, Virna Lisi, Sylva Koscina. Thirty-two short vignettes about modern Italian life comprise this funny, often touching film. (Dir: Nanni Loy, 101 mins.)

Made in Paris (1966)*½ Ann-Margret, Louis Jourdan, Richard Crenna, Edie Adams. Labored romantic comedy. Ann-Margret is a fashion buyer in Paris on her first buying spree, and designer Jourdan gives her the big rush. (Dir: Boris Sagal, 101 mins.)

Made in Sweden (Sweden, 1969)***½ Per Myrberg, Lina Granhagen, Karl-Birger Blomdahl, Borje Ahlstedt, Ingvar Kjellson, Max Von Sydow. Journalist investigates report that powerful Swedish company is running guns in Vietnam. Satisfying thriller includes documentary footage showing tragedy of Southeast Asian war. Superbly acted, with believable romantic subplot, and strong condemnation of corruption in high places. Van Sydow terrific in cameo as villainous corporate chief. (Dir: John Bergenstrahle, 86 mins.)

Made in U.S.A. (France, 1966)***½ Jean-Pierre Leaud, Anna Karina, Laszlo Szabo, Yves Alfonso. Quintessential example of the work of Jean-Luc Godard, shot concurrently with *Two or Three Things I Know About Her*. Loosely adapted from a novel by Richard Stark (a pseudonym for Donald E. Westlake), what plot remains features a woman seeking to identify her lover's killer. Filled with quotes, slogans, obscure references to famous people, a song by a Japanese girl, allusions to Kennedy's assassination, and breathtaking color and pop art images.

One of Godard's best, though not for casual viewers. (85 mins.)

Made In USA (1988)**½ Christopher Penn, Lori Singer, Adrian Pasdar. Dark film about disaffected youth starts well, with Penn and Pasdar, disgusted by industrial Pennsylvania, stealing a car and heading west. But Singer sinks it with a bad, actressy performance as the mouthpiece for the script's major point—that the U.S. has become a giant toxic dump. (Dir: Ken Friedman, 88 mins.)†

Madeleine (Great Britain, 1949)*** Ann Todd, Norman Wooland. The story of Madeleine Smith, who was tried for poisoning her lover in Scotland in 1857. Superbly directed and performed, absorbing drama from beginning to end. (Dir: David Lean, 101 mins.)

Mademoiselle Fifi (1944)*** Simone Simon, John Emery, Alan Napier, Kurt Kreuger, Jason Robards, Sr. Some travelers reveal their true colors during a carriage ride at the time of the Franco-Prussian War. In this expertly crafted B movie, produced by Val Lewton, Simon shines as a laundress unafraid of expressing her patriotism and acting courageously. (Dir: Robert Wise, 69 mins.)

Mademoiselle Striptease—See: **Please Mr. Balzac**

Mad Genius, The (1931)** John Barrymore, Marian Marsh, Donald Cook. Barrymore plays a crazed puppeteer who pulls the strings in other people's lives. A misguided attempt to cash in on his earlier *Svengali*; this time, instead of manipulating a girl's voice, he coaches a boy in a career as a great dancer. (Dir: Michael Curtiz, 81 mins.)

Mad Ghoul, The (1943)**½ David Bruce, Evelyn Ankers. Wild thriller, with an excellent performance by Bruce as a doctor kept in a state of living death. Grisly stuff which horror addicts should enjoy. (Dir: James Hogan, 65 mins.)

Madhouse (Great Britain, 1974)*** Vincent Price, Peter Cushing, Robert Quarry, Adrienne Corri. Spoofy British horror flick that casts veteran Price as an actor who's trying for a comeback in his famous role of "Dr. Death," after spending years in an asylum. Full of in-jokes and offbeat characters, this one also has clips from Roger Corman's Poe series entwined in the plot, as grisly murders plague England and the finger of suspicion points at Vincent. (Dir: Jim Clark, 92 mins.)†

Madhouse (1990)*½ John Larroquette, Kirstie Alley, Alison LaPlaca, John Diehl, Robert Ginty. Feeble, overwrought comedy about hapless yuppie couple forced to share home with cloddish guests, whining relatives, and goofy neighbors. Only Alley and LaPlaca rise above film's stereotyping of pregnant women, Arabs, cat lovers, and even New Jersey. (Dir: Tom Ropelewski, 90 mins.)†

Madigan (1968)***½ Richard Widmark, Henry Fonda, Inger Stevens. A brilliant police thriller directed with sharp-edged verve by Don Siegel. Story of a troubled police commissioner (Fonda) and a maverick detective (Widmark), who are out to get the job done no matter how. (101 mins.)†

Madigan's Millions (Spain-Italy, 1967)*½ Dustin Hoffman, Cesar Romero, Elsa Martinelli. Hoffman's first screen performance, as an Internal Revenue Service agent, is a disaster. He goes to Rome to investigate the holdings of a murdered mobster. (Dir: Stanley Prager, 76 mins.)†

Madison Avenue (1962)** Dana Andrews, Eleanor Parker, Jeanne Crain, Eddie Albert. Routine drama supposedly revealing the naked truth about the cutthroat world of big-time advertising. (Dir: H. Bruce Humberstone, 94 mins.)

Mad Little Island (Great Britain, 1958)**½ Jeannie Carson, Donald Sinden. Scottish islanders are horrified to learn their home is to be turned into a rocket base. A sequel to *Tight Little Island*, not nearly as amusing. (Dir: Michael Relph, 87 mins.)

Mad Love (1935)*** Peter Lorre, Frances Drake, Colin Clive. Mad doctor operates on a pianist mutilated in an accident, grafts the hands of a murderer to him. Atmospheric expressionistic thriller. (Dir: Karl Freund, 70 mins.)

Mad Magician, The (1954)** Vincent Price, Eva Gabor. Vincent Price in a routine mystery—the role he performs with relish. This time he is a deranged magician with a bent for murder. (Dir: John Brahm, 72 mins.)

Mad Max (Australia, 1980)*** Mel Gibson, Joanne Samuel, Hugh Keays-Byrne, Tim Burns, Roger Ward. About the ultimate gang of motorcycle bandits. Director George Miller's provocative, stimulating cheapie is an entertaining action exploitation film, with chases and crashes to satisfy the most jaded thrill-seeker. (93 mins.)†

Mad Max 2—See: **Road Warrior, The**

Mad Max: Beyond Thunderdome (1985) *** Mel Gibson, Tina Turner. Mel's back and Tina's got him! Slambang excitement is delivered as our fuel-depleted future becomes the background for Gibson's type of heroics. (Dirs: George Miller and George Ogilvie, 106 mins.)†

Mad Miss Manton, The (1938)*** Barbara Stanwyck, Henry Fonda. Society girl turns sleuth and investigates a murder. Fast, funny comedy-mystery, very good fun. (Dir: Leigh Jason, 80 mins.)

Mad Monster, The (1942)** George Zucco.

Sarah Padden, Glenn Strange, Johnny Downs. Another unintentionally ridiculous horror flick has Zucco (the *only* watchable thing in the movie is his performance) trying, for mysterious reason, to transform men into monsters. (Dir: Sam Newfield, 72 mins.) †

Mad Monster Party, The (1967)**½ Voices of Phyllis Diller, Boris Karloff, Gale Garnett. Cute animated fare for kids. Frankenstein and the whole crew of super-monsters get together for a wild bash in an enjoyable time-killer for Halloween. (Dir: Jules Bass, 94 mins.) †

Mado (France, 1976)*** Michel Piccoli, Romy Schneider, Charles Denner, Ottavia Piccolo. Piccoli has a role to match his skills as an actor, playing a shallow man with deep feelings, a businessman forced to the edge and striking back in kind. (Dir: Claude Sautet, 130 mins.) †

Madonna of the Seven Moons (Great Britain, 1945)*** Phyllis Calvert, Stewart Granger. An early encounter with a gypsy leaves its mark upon a woman for life, endangers the safety of her daughter. Strong melodrama. Well done. (Dir: Arthur Crabtree, 88 mins.)

Madron (1970)**½ Richard Boone, Leslie Caron. Boone and Caron are far better than this routine western story about a nun and a gunman who team up in a dangerous trek across a desert, stalked by Apaches. Filmed in Israel. (Dir: Jerry Hopper, 93 mins.)

Mad Room, The (1969)*** Stella Stevens, Shelley Winters. Pretty good remake of 1941 *Ladies in Retirement*—a thriller full of suspense and plot twists to set you on the wrong track. Stevens is quite good as a wealthy widow's companion who brings her brother and sister to live with her after they are released from an asylum. (Dir: Bernard Girard, 93 mins.)

Mad Wednesday—See: **Sin of Harold Diddlebock, The**

Madwoman of Chaillot (Great Britain, 1969)** Katharine Hepburn, Yul Brynner, Danny Kaye, Edith Evans, Charles Boyer. John Huston left and was replaced by Bryan Forbes after shooting several weeks of this picture, but it was conceptually flawed from the outset. The producers foolishly tried to make a huge, opulent, star-studded spectacle out of Jean Giraudoux's bittersweet, small-scale morality fable. (132 mins.)

Mad Wax: The Surf Movie (1987)*½ Tom Carroll, Bryce Ellis, Mark Sainsbury. Surfin' dudes discover a magical wax that, when applied to their boards, transports them to the world's most radical surfing beaches. Cheap excuse for a travelogue at least doesn't have any Beach Boys songs on the soundtrack. (Dir: Michael Hohensee, 70 mins.) †

Mad Whirl, The (1925)*** May McAvoy, Jack Mulhall, George Fawcett, Alec B. Francis. Dispassionate look at the Jazz Age, from a normal, small-town perspective, that is far more revealing than Cecil B. DeMille's sexy spectacles. The simple story concerns an ordinary girl, beautifully played by McAvoy, who loves a young man given to a dangerously reckless lifestyle, encouraged by his thoughtless parents. Unromanticized scenes of drunken parties and their aftermath speak volumes more than any preaching. Very well worth watching. (Dir: William A. Seiter, 74 mins.)

Maedchen in Uniform (Germany, 1931)***½ Hertha Thiele, Emilia Unda, Dorothea Wieck, Hedwig Schlichter. Stunning story of girl sent to boarding school where she rejects the repressive atmosphere and finds comfort in a tender relationship with one of the teachers. Powerful and mature treatment of lesbian theme, coupled with erotic images and condemnation of authority puts this all-female feature into the ranks of important cinema, presaging as it does the rise of conformity and oppression through Nazism. U.S. and video prints run 91 mins. (Dir: Leontine Sagan, 110 mins.) †

Maedchen in Uniform (West Germany, 1958)*** Romy Schneider, Lili Palmer, Christine Kaufman, Therese Giehse. Lesser remake features actresses of international status, but doesn't fulfill cinematic needs of story about young girl who falls in love with a teacher at an authoritarian girl's boarding school. Still has some power, with superb performances. (Dir: Geza Radvanyi, 91 mins.)

Maestro, The—See: **Home Movies**

Mae West (MTV 1982)** Ann Jillian, Piper Laurie, Lee DeBroux, Roddy McDowall, Blane Savage, James Brolin. This fictionalized account of Mae West's life invents a long-time love (Brolin) and rearranges incidents in her career to come up with a trite backstage saga of a star. (Dir: Lee Philips, 104 mins.) †

Mafia (France-Italy, 1969)** Claudia Cardinale, Franco Nero, Lee J. Cobb, Nehemiah Persoff. Italian police captain Nero learns first hand how pervasive the Sicilian mob is. Mediocre crime drama. (Dir: Damiano Damiani, 98 mins.)

Mafia Princess (MTV 1986)**½ Susan Lucci, Tony Curtis, Kathleen Widdoes. The best-seller by Antoinette Giancana about her life with her father, Mafia chieftain "Sam" Giancana, is turned into a satisfactory exposé. Lucci portrays the woman who tries to find her own identity within the world of violence ruled by her father. (Dir: Robert Collins, 104 mins.) †

Mafu Cage, The (1978)* Lee Grant, Carol

Kane, Will Geer, James Olson. A peculiar little item that shoots for intensity but winds up being unintentionally hilarious. Passionless Grant is a woman with a problem—her younger, slightly demented sister (Kane) keeps killing her pet apes and bathing in their blood. That's not all she's got to worry about, for her amorous sibling eventually finds out that she is romatically involved with a (gulp) man. AKA: **The Cage and My Sister, My Love.** (Dir: Karen Arthur, 104 mins.)†

Maggie, The—See: **High and Dry**

Magic (1978)**½ Anthony Hopkins, Ann-Margret, Burgess Meredith. An old chestnut: the ventriloquist dominated by his dummy. Claptrap, but if you respond to the premise, rather scary. (Dir: Richard Attenborough, 106 mins.)†

Magical Mystery Tour (Great Britain, 1969)** The Beatles. Originally made for TV, this is a trip worth taking only for the faithful Beatles fans. Tuneful, but oh, those dated drug-oriented psychedelic visuals. (Dir: The Beatles, 60 mins.)†

Magic Bow, The (Great Britain, 1947)**½ Stewart Granger, Phyllis Calvert, Jean Kent, Cecil Parker, Dennis Price. Classical music lovers have a treat in store for them, with this biography of famed violinist Paganini. Offscreen violin solos played by concert artist Yehudi Menuhin. (Dir: Bernard Knowles, 105 mins.)

Magic Box, The (Great Britain, 1952)*** Robert Donat, Margaret Johnston, Maria Schell, many others. The engrossing story of William Friese-Greene, the inventor of the motion picture camera, whose life was a tragedy through hardships and lack of recognition. (Dir: John Boulting, 103 mins.)

Magic Carpet, The (1951)** Lucille Ball, Raymond Burr, John Agar. TV's Perry Mason (Burr) and Lucy (Ball) find themselves in the mystical time of Caliphs and Viziers in this corny Arabian Nights farce. (Dir: Lew Landers, 84 mins.)

Magic Carpet (MTV 1972)** Susan St. James, Jim Backus, Abby Dalton, Wally Cox. A substitute tour guide (St. James) leads Americans through Italy. (Dir: William Graham, 99 mins.)

Magic Christian, The (Great Britain, 1969)*** Peter Sellers, Ringo Starr, Isabel Jeans, Wilfrid Hyde-White, Patrick Cargill, Graham Chapman, John Cleese. Loose series of sketches about rich Guy Grand (Sellers) proving that people will do anything—for the right price. Often funny item that oddly never attracted a cult. Lots of cameos, including Christopher Lee, Raquel Welch, Yul Brynner, and Spike Milligan. Music by Badfinger. (Dir: Joseph McGrath, 95 mins.)†

Magic Face, The (1951)**½ Luther Adler, Patricia Knight, William L. Shirer. WWII

suspense has Adler impersonating Hitler; interesting idea marred by cheap production values, but with good performances: (Dir: Frank Tuttle, 89 mins.)

Magic Fire (1956)** Yvonne DeCarlo, Rita Gam, Alan Badel. Tale of the romantic troubles of composer Richard Wagner. Overdone drama is a victim of ham acting and plodding plot. (Dir: William Dieterle, 95 mins.)

Magic Flute, The (Sweden, 1973)**** Ulrik Gold, Josef Kostlinger. An exquisite adaptation by director Ingmar Bergman of Mozart's opera *The Magic Flute*. Most of the time, Bergman simply photographs the action unfolding during a stage production of the Mozart masterwork. Primarily of interest to opera lovers. (134 mins.)†

Magic Garden, The—See: **Pennywhistle Blues**

Magic Garden of Stanley Sweetheart, The (1970)*½ Don Johnson, Linda Gillin, Michael Grèer, Dianne Hull, Holly Near. A dreary film from those late sixties/early seventies days of druggies and dropping out. (Dir: Leonard Horn, 117 mins.)

Magician, The (Sweden, 1958)***½ Max von Sydow, Ingrid Thulin. An early Ingmar Bergman-directed film that will tingle your spine and stimulate your brain. The supernatural, comic, mystical and the human mingle in this imaginative tale of a magician and his troupe who are detained in a small Swedish community when their magical powers are disbelieved. Visually rich, gothic atmosphere. (102 mins.)†

Magician, The (MTV 1973)**½ Bill Bixby, Keene Curtis, Elizabeth Ashley, Joan Caulfield, Kim Hunter, Barry Sullivan. Playing a suave, polished magician who uses magic tricks to outwit crooks, Bill Bixby displays a good deal of charm in this slick action pilot for the series. (Dir: Marvin Chomsky, 104 mins.)

Magician of Lublin, The (West Germany-Israel, 1979)** Alan Arkin, Louise Fletcher, Shelley Winters, Valerie Perrine. Ambitious, partially successful filming of the wonderful Isaac Bashevis Singer novel about a turn-of-the-century illusionist. (Dir: Menahem Golan, 105 mins.)†

Magic Moments (MCTV 1989)**½ Jenny Seagrove, John Shea, Paul Freeman. The stars give this Harlequin Romance adaptation more substance than it deserves. Seagrove plays an assistant TV producer trying to entice a famous magician (Shea) to appear on TV for the first time. Romance, of course, ensues. (Dir: Lawrence Gordon Clark, 105 mins.)

Magic of Lassie, The (1978)**½ James Stewart, Lassie, Mickey Rooney, Alice Faye, Stephanie Zimbalist, Pernell Roberts. Grandpa Jimmy doesn't want to sell his vineyards to a rich meanie, so the latter takes Lassie away. Good family film. (Dir: Don Chaffey, 90 mins.)†

Magic Sword, The (1962)**½ Basil Rathbone, Anne Helm, Gary Lockwood. Young knight slays the evil dragon and bests the wicked sorcerer to win the hand of the fair princess. (Dir: Bert I. Gordon, 80 mins.)†

Magic Town (1947)**½ James Stewart, Jane Wyman, Kent Smith, Donald Meek, Regis Toomey. A pollster publicizes a small town as being statistically accurate in all polls, which only causes trouble for the town's mild way of life. Uneven comedy, misses fire most of the time; just fair. (Dir: William Wellman, 103 mins.)†

Magnet, The (Great Britain, 1950)***½ Stephen Murray, Kay Walsh, William (James) Fox. An imaginative ten-year-old swindles a lad out of a magnet, is convinced the thing is some sort of charm. Delightful comedy, clean and refreshing, sparklingly written. (Dir: Charles Frend, 78 mins.)

Magnetic Monster, The (1953)**½ Richard Carlson, King Donovan, Jean Byron. A magnetic element's the nemesis here. Growing to enormous proportions, this "attractive" monster causes havoc by drawing in energy and releasing radiation. Unusual sci-fi. (Dir: Curt Siodmak, 76 mins.)

Magnificent Ambersons, The (1942)**** Joseph Cotten, Tim Holt, Anne Baxter, Dolores Costello, Ray Collins, Agnes Moorehead, Richard Bennett, Erskine Sanford. This elegiac masterwork about the passing of a graceful way of life, destroyed by the automobile and other technological advances in the name of progress, is a finely honed melodrama about the fall of the prideful Minafer family. We can only view this film in a truncated version, since the studio recut it and reshot additional material. (Dir: Orson Welles, 88 mins.)†

Magnificent Brute, The (1936)**½ Victor McLaglen, Binnie Barnes, Jean Dixon. Good vehicle for McLaglen, as a tough steel worker mixed up with two women and some stolen money; brisk performances, with Barnes especially good. (Dir: John G. Blystone, 80 mins.)

Magnificent Doll, The (1946)** Ginger Rogers, David Niven, Burgess Meredith. The story of Dolly Madison, the President's wife whose relationship with Aaron Burr nearly altered the course of American history. Elaborate but heavy, not too well-acted drama. (Dir: Frank Borzage, 95 mins.)

Magnificent Dope, The (1942)*** Henry Fonda, Don Ameche, Lynn Bari. Amusing comedy which has the country boy (Fonda), as usual, outwitting the city slickers. (Dir: Walter Lang, 83 mins.)†

Magnificent Fraud, The (1939)** Akim Tamiroff, Lloyd Nolan, Patricia Morison. Loud, yet boring tale of an actor in a mythical South American country, who tries to impersonate an assassinated dictator. (Dir: Robert Florey, 80 mins.)

Magnificent Magical Magnet of Santa Mesa (MTV 1977)** Michael Burns, Dick Blasucci, Jane Connell, Tom Poston, Harry Morgan, Loni Anderson. An inventor comes up with a fabulous "energy disk" which could save the world, though his employers are only interested in making a profit from it. Bland family comedy. AKA: **Adventures of Freddie**. (Dir: Hy Averback, 76 mins.)

Magnificent Matador (1955)**½ Anthony Quinn, Maureen O'Hara. Bullfighter runs away on the day of his protégé's entry into the ring. Good bullfight sequences atone somewhat for a hackneyed plot. AKA: **The Brave and the Beautiful**. (Dir: Budd Boetticher, 95 mins.)†

Magnificent Obsession (1935)*** Irene Dunne, Robert Taylor, Betty Furness. Moving soap opera. A womanizing ne'er-do-well (Taylor) accidentally blinds a wealthy widow (Dunne). In struggling to restore the woman's sight, he becomes a doctor and dedicates his life to helping others. (Dir: John Stahl, 90 mins.)

Magnificent Obsession (1954)*** Jane Wyman, Rock Hudson. Classily produced soap opera which leans heavily on sentiment and turns out to be a four-handkerchief film. Lloyd C. Douglas's novel about one man's devotion to a woman whose blindness he caused is beautifully acted. (Dir: Douglas Sirk, 108 mins.)†

Magnificent Roughnecks (1956)** Jack Carson, Mickey Rooney. Couple of oil men have trouble with rival drillers and rival gals. (Dir: Sherman A. Rose, 73 mins.)

Magnificent Seven, The (1960)*** Yul Brynner, Steve McQueen, James Coburn, Charles Bronson, Robert Vaughn. American remake of Akira Kurosawa's film *The Seven Samurai*, set, of course, in the west. Brynner is a gunfighter who recruits six tough guys to defend a group of Mexican peasants from bandits. John Sturges directs well, though often pretentiously. (126 mins.)†

Magnificent Seven Ride!, The (1972)* Lee Van Cleef, Michael Callan, Stefanie Powers. Van Cleef stars as a marshall who, with an unscrupulous journalist (Callan) and assorted convicts, defends a Mexican border town whose women and children are alone after the townsmen have been murdered by a bunch of desperados. (Dir: George McCowan, 100 mins.)

Magnificent Sinner, The (France, 1960)**½ Romy Schneider, Curt Jurgens. Slow-moving love story of a girl and the czar of Russia, who is not free to marry her, ending tragically in assassination. (Dir: Robert Siodmak, 91 mins.)

Magnificent Yankee, The (1950)*** Louis Calhern, Ann Harding. Superbly acted biographical drama, the story of Oliver Wendell Holmes, Supreme Court justice and man of legal astuteness. Perhaps a bit too placid for some tastes, it is nevertheless a film of rare refinement, well worthwhile. (Dir: John Sturges, 80 mins.)

Magnum Force (1973)** Clint Eastwood, Hal Holbrook, David Soul, Tim Matheson. The blood flows freely as Dirty Harry picks up the trail of a death squad of rookie cops, who are rubbing out the scum of the underworld. Off-beat casting of usually sweet Hal Holbrook as the leader of the heavies is the only interesting break with routine, excessive gunplay. (Dir: Ted Post, 124 mins.)†

Magus, The (Great Britain, 1968)* Anthony Quinn, Candice Bergen, Michael Caine, Anna Karina. John Fowles's complex novel, about a young English schoolteacher (Caine) who arrives on a small Greek island, makes a confusing motion picture. (Dir: Guy Green, 116 mins.)

Mahler (Great Britain, 1974)**½ Robert Powell, Georgina Hale, Rosalie Crutchley. Ken Russell does it to Gustav in this exuberant, but supremely vulgar biography of the genius composer. If there's ever a Society for the Preservation of Famous People's Reputations, Russell's in for a lot of trouble. (115 mins.)†

Mahogany (1975)*½ Diana Ross, Anthony Perkins, Billy Dee Williams. Mediocre picture about a fashion designer (Ross) fighting her way to success, only to find it's lonely at the top. (Dir: Berry Gordy, 109 mins.)†

Maid, The (France, 1990)**½ Martin Sheen, Jacqueline Bisset, Jean-Pierre Cassel, Victoria Shalet. Charming, albeit a touch unbelievable, comedy about a Wall Street investment banker who is transferred to Paris, spots a beautiful woman he desires (Bisset), and spends his month-long lull between jobs by becoming her maid. It seems she badly needs one and is nonplussed by his background. Naturally, complications abound. (Dir: Ian Toynton, 91 mins.)†

Maid in America (MTV 1982)*½ Susan Clark, Alex Karras, Fritz Weaver, Mildred Natwick, Barbara Byrne. A frothy, Frank Capra-type comedy about a loony family and its burly male maid. (Dir: Paul Aaron, 104 mins.)

Maid in Paris (France, 1957)**½ Daniel Gelin, Dany Robin. Wacky French comedy about a young girl, whose father is a movie star, and her amours in gay Paree. (Dir: Gaspard-Huit, 84 mins.)

Maid of Salem (1937)*** Claudette Colbert, Fred MacMurray, Louise Dresser, Gale Sondergaard. Exciting period piece that represents a reasonable approximation of colonial times. Depicting the dark side of the early settlements, the film examines how false accusations of witchcraft could proliferate and tear a community apart. (Dir: Frank Lloyd, 86 mins.)

Maids, The (Great Britain, 1975)***½ Glenda Jackson, Susannah York, Vivien Merchant. A searing screen adaptation of a very theatrical play by Jean Genet, who finds black humor in the vitriol that two servants feel for their betters. Playing cruel games to vent their sexual and emotional frustrations, York and Jackson claw at Genet's dialogue and give powerhouse performances that involve us even when this theater piece's meanings seem obscure. (Dir: Christopher Miles, 95 mins.)

Maid's Night Out (1938)**½ Joan Fontaine, Hedda Hopper, Allan Lane, George Irving, Billy Gilbert, Cecil Kellaway. Typical '30s comedy has madcap heiress Fontaine mistaken for her own maid; nothing special, but pleasant. (Dir: Ben Holmes, 64 mins.)†

Maid to Order (1987)** Ally Sheedy, Beverly D'Angelo, Michael Ontkean, Valerie Perrine, Dick Shawn, Tom Skerritt, Merry Clayton. Lighthearted and slight-minded Cinderella comedy has Sheedy as a rich, spoiled brat who's taught a lesson by her fairy godmother (D'Angelo) as she's reduced to lowly maid status in the household of a trendy L.A. couple (Shawn and Perrine). (Dir: Amy Jones, 95 mins.)†

Mail Order Bride (1964)**½ Buddy Ebsen, Keir Dullea, Lois Nettleton, Warren Oates. Agreeable western comedy. Ebsen attempts to get Dullea to settle down by marrying him off to Nettleton. (Dir: Burt Kennedy, 83 mins.)

Main Attraction, The (1962)** Pat Boone, Nancy Kwan, Mai Zetterling. Picked up by an older circus woman, a mixed-up youth starts straying in his attentions, rouses ire and jealousy among the circus crowd. (Dir: Daniel Petrie, 85 mins.)

Main Event, The (1979)** Barbra Streisand, Ryan O'Neal, Paul Sand. Listless comedy that goes to those screwball films of the thirties for inspiration. Barbra is a cosmetics exec down to her last tube of lipstick, and turns to a prizefighter she owns (he's a tax exemption, you see) to bail her out. (Dir: Howard Zieff, 112 mins.)

Main Street after Dark (1944)**½ Edward Arnold, Dan Duryea, Audrey Totter, Hume Cronyn, Selena Royle. Appealing story of a family of petty thieves whose livelihood is threatened by law and order; well acted by an unusual ensemble. (Dir: Edward L. Cahn, 57 mins.)

Main Street to Broadway (1953)** Tom Morton, Mary Murphy. Young playwright refuses to be discouraged in trying to be a success on Broadway. Trite story of theater life. (Dir: Tay Garnett, 102 mins.) †

Maisie series. Based on the novel *Dark Dame*, the film *Maisie* launched a breezy B-movie series immensely brightened by Ann Sothern, who never broke through to the ranks of major stardom at MGM. Although "Maisie" was a radio program (1945-47 and 1952-59), the quick-thinking ex-chorus girl enjoyed her greatest success in these movie programmers about the enterprising lass constantly getting herself in and out of scrapes. Besides the films reviewed below, Maisie's admirers will want to watch her in: *Congo Maisie, Gold Rush Maisie, Ringside Maisie, Swing Shift Maisie* and *Up Goes Maisie*.

Maisie (1939)*** Ann Sothern, Robert Young, Red Skelton. This pleasant B movie kicked off an entire series of films about the enterprising entertainer from Brooklyn. (Dir: Edward L. Marin, 74 mins.) †

Maisie Gets Her Man (1942)**½ Ann Sothern, Red Skelton, Allen Jenkins. Abandoning a choice position as the target in a knife-throwing act, Maisie teams up with another show-biz hopeful, Skelton, whom she has to get out of scrapes. (Dir: Roy Del Ruth, 86 mins.)

Maisie Goes to Reno (1944)**½ Ann Sothern, John Hodiak, Tom Drake. Maisie gets to exercise her swell pipes with a singing gig in Reno, but she's also busy playing matchmaker, with just enough time left over to fall for a casino worker. (Dir: Harry Beaumont, 90 mins.)

Maisie Was a Lady (1941)*** Ann Sothern, Lew Ayres, Maureen O'Sullivan. Maisie goes from being a headless woman at a fair to working as a maid for an upper-crust family. Good entry. (Dir: Edward L. Marin, 79 mins.)

Major and the Minor, The (1942)*** Ginger Rogers, Ray Milland, Diana Lynn. Rogers plays a broke New York career woman who impersonates a twelve-year-old in order to ride half-fare to her home in Iowa. Milland is the officer who tries to take care of Ginger as she falls in love with him. The director Billy Wilder's ironies are present in abundance. Remade as *You're Never Too Young*. (100 mins.)

Major Barbara (Great Britain, 1941)***½ Wendy Hiller, Rex Harrison, Robert Newton, Robert Morley, Deborah Kerr. George Bernard Shaw collaborated with director Gabriel Pascal on this film version of his play. Hiller stars as the Salvation Army worker, daughter of a munitions manufacturer, who moves from innocence to
654

disillusionment to acceptance of the material and social values of her father's world. A bit slow to start, but an enthusiastic and intelligent rendering of the wonderful Shavian wit. (115 mins.) †

Major Dundee (1965)**½ Charlton Heston, Richard Harris, James Coburn, Jim Hutton, Warren Oates, Senta Berger. Although the film was taken from director Sam Peckinpah and mangled, it's still loaded with action and meaning. Heston is persuasive as a tough commander who leads a cavalry mission across the Mexican border in pursuit of Indians. (134 mins.)

Majorettes, The (1988)*½ Kevin Kindlin, Terrie Godfrey, Mark V. Jevicky, Sueanne Seamens. Masked maniac is killing high school cheerleaders. At least this slasherama has something of a plot along with the murders, though that's about all we can say for it. (Dir: Bill Hinzman, 92 mins.) †

Majority of One, A (1961)**½ Rosalind Russell, Alec Guinness, Ray Danton, Madlyn Rhue. A mild, humorous but stagebound comedy of the romance between a Jewish matron from New York and a Japanese businessman. (Dir: Mervyn LeRoy, 156 mins.)

Major League (1989)**½ Tom Berenger, Charlie Sheen, Corbin Bernsen, Margaret Whitton. Amiably goofy sports comedy about the nation's worst baseball team, whose new owner wants them even worse so she can move the franchise to Miami. The movie scores base hits as writer-director David Ward catalogues the players' superstitions and peculiarities, but strikes out during the inevitable "rousing" finale. (89 mins.) †

Make a Wish (1937)*** Basil Rathbone, Bobby Breen, Ralph Forbes, Marion Claire, Donald Meek. Extremely slight musical vehicle for child singer Breen has him meeting a composer at summer camp; depends on Breen's appeal, which is a matter of taste. (Dir: Kurt Neumann, 76 mins.)

Make Haste to Live (1954)*** Dorothy McGuire, Stephen McNally. Husband returns from prison intending to kill his wife, after failing the first time. Suspenseful mystery-melodrama with a good cast. (Dir: William A. Seiter, 90 mins.)

Make Me an Offer (MTV 1980)**½ Susan Blakely, Patrick O'Neal, John Rubinstein. Blakely is effective as a young woman who leaves her cheating husband and gets it together in the glamorous, high-pressure world of Beverly Hills real estate agents. (Dir: Jerry Paris, 104 mins.) †

Make Mine Chartreuse (1987)* Catherine Colvey, Joseph Bottoms. Hearts and flowers drivel for those too lazy to read the latest Harlequin romance. Career woman finds true love with a successful novelist. (Dir: Jim Kaufman, 80 mins.)†

Make Mine Mink (Great Britain, 1960)***½ Terry-Thomas, Athene Seyler, Billie Whitelaw. Dowager and an ex-officer team to commit larceny, the proceeds going to charity. Often screamingly funny. (Dir: Robert Asher, 101 mins.)†

Make Room for Tomorrow (France, 1982)*** Victor Lanoux, Jane Birkin. Already experiencing marital difficulties, commercial director Lanoux has to deal with the presence of his young son, his father, and his grandfather, all brought together by the grandfather's 90th birthday. Gentle comedy-drama about the similarities and differences between generations. (Dir: Peter Kassovitz, 104 mins.)†

Make Way for a Lady (1936)**½ Herbert Marshall, Anne Shirley, Gertrude Michael, Clara Blandick. Middling family comedy, with an interfering teenager trying to get her father to remarry; nothing outstanding. (Dir: David Burton, 65 mins.)

Make Way for Tomorrow (1937)***½ Victor Moore, Beulah Bondi, Thomas Mitchell. Story of aged parents who have become a burden to their children and must resign themselves to separation. Director Leo McCarey combines tenderness and comedy, amplifying small gestures into poignant moments. Magnificently acted by Moore and Bondi, this is an unrecognized classic of American cinema. (92 mins.)

Make Your Own Bed (1944)*½ Jane Wyman, Jack Carson. Silly little comedy about a private eye and his girl who take jobs as butler and maid supposedly in the line of duty. (Dir: Peter Godfrey, 82 mins.)

Making It (1971)** Kristoffer Tabori, Joyce Van Patten, Marlyn Mason. Redolent of the hypocrisy implicit in Hollywood's version of the New Morality. A seventeen-year-old stud-about-town reforms when his mother has an abortion and the doctors force him to watch. (Dir: John Erman, 95 mins.)

Making Love (1982)*** Michael Ontkean, Kate Jackson, Harry Hamlin, Arthur Hill. The fact that this new-fashioned love triangle was roundly criticized for being a wish-fulfillment fantasy for gays seems hypocritical of mainstream critics. A handsome doctor with a reasonably happy marriage to a successful TV executive is led out of the closet by a fickle writer afraid of commitment. (Dir: Arthur Hiller, 113 mins.)†

Making Mr. Right (1987)** John Malkovich, Ann Magnuson, Glenne Headly, Ben Masters, Laurie Metcalf, Polly Bergen, Jeff Hoyt. Lightweight comedy that has public relations expert Magnuson called in to "package" an android astronaut, who, as luck (and familiar plot twists) would have it, falls madly in love with her. (Dir: Susan Seidelman, 100 mins.)†

Making of a Male Model, The (MTV 1983)**½ Joan Collins, Jon-Eric Hexum, Jeff Conaway, Roxie Roker, Arte Johnson. Flash-trash! The late Hexum rose to stardom playing a cowboy who is discovered by the head of a model agency played with chic cool by Collins. (Dir: Irving Moore, 104 mins.)

Making the Grade (1984)*½ Judd Nelson, Joanna Lee, Gordon Jump, Walter Olkewicz, Dana Olsen. In this routine teensploitation saga, a spoiled rich boy hires a Jersey kid on the lam to attend prep school for him and make passing grades so that his father won't cut him off from the family money. (Dir: Dorian Walker, 105 mins.)†

Mako: The Jaws of Death (1976)** Richard Jaeckel, Jenifer Bishop, Harold (Odd Job) Sakata. A low-budget poor man's *Jaws* in reverse. Jaeckel is an overzealous diver who becomes a one-man army to protect sharks from the hunters of the deep. (Dir: William Grefe, 93 mins.)

Malaga (Great Britain, 1960)** Trevor Howard, Dorothy Dandridge, Edmund Purdom. Jewel thief heads for Spain after a partner who double-crossed him. (Dir: Laslo Benedek, 97 mins.)

Malandro (Brazil, 1986)*½ Edson Celulari, Claudia Ohana, Elba Ramalho, Fabia Sabag. A gaudy, unpleasant musical set in the underworld of WWII Rio de Janeiro, where everyone wears white suits and sweats too much. The plot is borrowed from *Threepenny Opera*, and ends up looking like an old-fashioned song-and-dance extravaganza cast with amateurs and shot through a filter of mud. AKA: *Opera do Malandro* (Dir: Ruy Guerra, 105 mins.)†

Malarek (Canada, 1989)**½ Elias Koteas, Kerrie Keane, Kahil Karn, Al Waxman, Michael Sarrazin, Daniel Pilon. True story based on the autobiograpy of Victor Malarek, a Montreal street kid who became a top investigative reporter. Koteas's charismatic performance makes up for a clichéd (if sincere) plot. (Dir: Roger Cardinal, 100 mins.)†

Malaya (1949)**½ Spencer Tracy, James Stewart, Valentina Cortese. Good old-fashioned tale about a pair of adventurers who combine their skills to smuggle raw rubber out of occupied Malaya. (Dir: Richard Thorpe, 98 mins.)

Malcolm (Australia, 1986)** Colin Fields, John Hargreaves, Lindy Davies, Chris Haywood. Its heart is in the right place, but this light comedy doesn't have too many tricks or surprises up its sleeve. A slightly retarded but mechanically inclined young man loses his job and turns bank robber as an outlet for his wizardry with electronics. (Dir: Nadia Tass, 90 mins.)†

Male Animal, The (1942)***½ Henry Fonda, Jack Carson, Olivia de Havilland. Clever, witty comedy about a dull but principled college professor, his wife, and a former football hero friend from their college days who pays them a visit. Remade as *She's Working Her Way Through College.* (Dir: Elliott Nugent, 101 mins.)

Male Hunt (France-Italy, 1964)*** Jean-Paul Belmondo, Jean-Claude Brialy, Catherine Deneuve. Young man is determined to get married despite the efforts of assorted people to dissuade him. Sprightly comedy. (Dir: Edouard Molinaro, 92 mins.)

Malibu (MTV 1983)**½ James Coburn, Susan Dey, Ann Jillian, William Atherton, Valerie Perrine, Richard Mulligan, Jenilee Harrison. Have a roster handy for this California soap opera to keep track of the endless characters, their superficial interplay, their ulterior motives and affairs, all set in the chic California beach community. (Dir: E. W. Swackhamer, 201 mins.)

Malibu Bikini Shop, The (1984)** Michael David Wright, Bruce Greenwood, Barbra Horan. Plot about two mismatched brothers who inherit a beachfront bikini shop is merely an excuse to present a parade of beach bunnies in and out of their swimwear, though as long as you're not expecting Ingmar Bergman it's OK. (Dir: David Wechter, 99 mins.)†

Malibu Express (1986)* Darby Hinton, Sybil Danning, Art Metrano. Sleazeball adventure flick that serves mainly as an excuse for the well-developed stars to show off their attractive torsos. (Dir: Andy Sidaris, 101 mins.)†

Malice In Wonderland (MTV 1985)*** Elizabeth Taylor, Jane Alexander, Richard Dysart, Joyce Van Patten. Once upon a time in Hollywood, there were two women journalists (gossip columnists) who were so feared that they actually ran the town. Even viewers who never heard of these ladies will enjoy the celebrated backbiting feud between the two columnists, Hedda Hopper and Louella Parsons. (Dir: Gus Trikonis, 104 mins.)

Malicious (Italy, 1973)**½ Laura Antonelli, Turi Ferro, Alessandro Momo, Tina Aumont. A hypocritical, lustful, and devious Sicilian widower hires a stunning young housekeeper, the luscious Antonelli, but his fourteen-year-old son, to assert his sexual identity, sets out to prove her a whore. (Dir: Salvatore Samperi, 97 mins.)†

Malone (1987)** Burt Reynolds, Cliff Robertson, Kenneth McMillan, Cynthia Gibb, Lauren Hutton, Philip Anglim,

Tracey Walter. Playing a CIA drop-out, Burt busts heads and keeps his guns blazing after he uncovers a right-wing conspiracy to seize control of the American government. Convictionless escapism. (Dir: Harley Corkliss, 92 mins.)†

Malou (West Germany, 1981)*½ Ingrid Caven, Grischa Huber, Helmut Griem, Ivan Desny. A troubled schoolteacher retraces the life of her dead mother, an expatriate who lived in Argentina. Sincere but dreary, obvious feminist parable; even Michael Ballhaus's photography is uninspired. (Dir: Jeanine Meerapfel, 94 mins.)†

Malta Story, The (Great Britain, 1954)**½ Alec Guinness, Jack Hawkins. British pilot falls in love with a Maltese girl on that bomb-stricken isle during war. (Dir: Brian Desmond Hurst, 98 mins.)†

Maltese Bippy, The (1969)*½ Dan Rowan, Dick Martin, Carol Lynley, Robert Reed. A "yawn-in" from the two stars of "Laugh-In" trying to capitalize on the success of their TV show. (Dir: Norman Panama, 92 mins.)

Maltese Falcon, The (1931)—See: **Dangerous Female**

Maltese Falcon, The (1941)**** Humphrey Bogart, Mary Astor, Peter Lorre, Sydney Greenstreet, Walter Huston, Lee Patrick, Elisha Cook, Jr., Barton MacLane. The stuff that dreams are made of. A new sort of hero, a rough draft for the sixties/seventies antihero, was introduced to the screen in Bogart's Sam Spade. *"Falcon"* also began a new career for screenwriter John Huston as a director. Huston's talent lay not only in his taut, concise scripting and his dark, drama-laden images (which paved the way for the *film noir* style); he also assembled a cast made in Heaven. The film's plot, involving Spade and a cast of shady characters in a search for an elusive, priceless statuette, has been endlessly imitated but never, never duplicated. Avoid the colorized version. (100 mins.)†

Mama, There's a Man In Your Bed (France, 1989)** Daniel Auteuil, Firmine Richard, Pierre Vernier. Contemporary fable about an executive who receives information about his cheating wife and treacherous co-workers from a friendly, but very poor, black cleaning lady; his response is to fall hopelessly in love with her. The courtship is utterly unbelievable, leaving the viewer awash in a wave of sugar-coated circumstance. AKA: **Romauld et Juliette.** (Dir: Coline Serreau, 111 mins.)†

Mame (1974)*½ Lucille Ball, Beatrice Arthur, Robert Preston. The Broadway musical has been diluted in this screen version starring Ball, who doesn't measure up to the sophisticated grandness of

656

the larger-than-life character. Arthur scores in a recreation of her Broadway part of Mame's best friend, Vera Charles, and the production values are first-class, if a bit overambitious. (Dir: Gene Saks, 131 mins.)†

Mammy (1930)*** Al Jolson, Lois Moran, Lowell Sherman, Louise Dresser. Very entertaining Jolson vehicle, which largely takes place behind the scenes of a traveling minstrel show, complete with Mr. Bones and Mr. Interlocutor; in addition, Jolson gives a subdued, appealing performance, does some terrific songs, and is ably supported by Sherman and Moran. A fascinating look at a classic American show business tradition. (Dir: Michael Curtiz, 84 mins.)

Man, The (1972)**½ James Earl Jones, Martin Balsam, Lew Ayres, William Windom. Occasionally interesting drama about the first black president of the United States, and how he attempts to assert his power. (Dir: Joseph Sargent, 93 mins.)

Man About the House, A (Great Britain, 1947)*** Margaret Johnston, Kieron Moore, Dulcie Gray. Spinsters take a villa in Italy; one of them falls for a dashing young man who proves to be up to no good. (Dir: Leslie Arliss, 83 mins.)†

Man About Town (1939)*** Jack Benny, Rochester (Eddie Anderson), Dorothy Lamour. Jack is a great lover in this one (at least he thinks so) and when the routine musical numbers don't interfere, he and Rochester have a ball. (Dir: Mark Sandrich, 90 mins.)

Man About Town (France, 1947)**½ Maurice Chevalier, Françoise Perrier. Chevalier as a movie-maker in the silent days. Leisurely paced, but pleasant comedy dubbed in English. (Dir: René Clair, 89 mins.)

Man Against the Mob (MTV 1988)*½ George Peppard, Kathryn Harrold, Stella Stevens, Max Gail. Flashy but empty crime drama with Peppard as an honest police detective who uncovers a group of corrupt cops. Style isn't everything. (Dir: Steven Hilliard Stern, 96 mins.)

Man Alive (1945)**½ Pat O'Brien, Ellen Drew, Adolphe Menjou, Rudy Vallee. Husband, though dead, returns and plays "ghost" to haunt a suitor away from his wife. Amusing farce. (Dir: Ray Enright, 70 mins.)

Man Alone, A (1955)***½ Ray Milland, Mary Murphy, Raymond Burr, Ward Bond. Gunslinger exposes the leader of an outlaw band who massacred a stagecoach party. (Dir: Ray Milland, 95 mins.)†

Man and a Woman, A (France, 1966)***½ Anouk Aimee, Jean-Louis Trintignant. A visually stunning, superbly acted, and ultimately very moving contemporary love story. Aimee makes this seeming soap opera become art, not artifice, and she is aided by the direction and the inventive camera work of Claude Lelouch. Trintignant is also fine playing a racing-car driver who woos Aimee. (102 mins.)†

Man and a Woman: Twenty Years Later, A (France, 1986)** Anouk Aimee, Jean-Louis Trintignant, Evelyne Bouix, Marie-Sophie Pochat, Richard Berry. Claude Lelouch reunites the cast and crew of his *A Man and a Woman* to bring the love story of the two central characters up to date. However, this sequel, plotted around the making of a movie about the original romance, is a melange of clutter and self-indulgence, not likely to become a classic. (120 mins.)†

Man and Boy (1972)** Bill Cosby, Gloria Foster, Lief Erickson, Henry Silva, George Spell, Yaphet Kotto. Cosby plays it all too straight as a homesteader in the post–Civil War West. When his horses are stolen, he and his son set out in pursuit. Okay family entertainment, but don't expect any humor. (Dir: E. W. Swackhamer, 98 mins.)†

Man, A Woman and a Bank, A (Canada, 1979)**½ Donald Sutherland, Brooke Adams, Paul Mazursky, Leigh Hamilton. A mild but wacky comedy about a pair of friends who plan to rob a bank by computer. (Dir: Noel Black, 100 mins.)†

Man Bait (Great Britain, 1952)*** George Brent, Marguerite Chapman, Diana Dors. An innocent moment off guard with a blonde gets a book dealer into a mess of trouble, including murder. Nicely done melodrama. (Dir: Terence Fisher, 80 mins.)

Man Beast (1955)½ Rock Madison, Virginia Maynor, George Skaff, Lloyd Nelson, Tom Maruzzi. An expedition to find the Abominable Snowman leads explorers to a new strain of Yeti with a hankering to improve his race with human girlies suitable for breeding. The entire film, including the outdoor scenes, seems to have been filmed in a large walk-in closet. (Dir: Jerry Warren, 72 mins.)†

Man Behind the Gun, The (1952)** Randolph Scott, Patrice Wymore. Depending on how you feel about the dubious charms of Los Angeles, you are either sore at Scott or beholden to him. According to this hokey western, he built the joint single-handed. (Dir: Felix E. Feist, 81 mins.)

Man Betrayed, A (1941)**½ John Wayne, Frances Dee, Wallace Ford, Ward Bond, Edward Ellis. Odd vehicle for Wayne has him as an honest lawyer attacking organized crime, in the person of his lady friend's father; he seems more at home in the saddle. Dee is incredibly beautiful, as usual. (Dir: John H. Auer, 83 mins.)†

Man Between, The (Great Britain, 1953)

***½ James Mason, Claire Bloom, Hildegarde Neff. A Berliner who makes a shady living risks his life to save a kidnapped girl from the Communists. Moody, topical melodrama. (Dir: Carol Reed, 100 mins.)

Man Called Adam, A (1966)**½ Sammy Davis, Jr., Peter Lawford, Cicely Tyson, Ossie Davis, Louis Armstrong. Davis is excellent in the difficult role of a jazz musician who is filled with bitterness and self-pity. (Dir: Leo Penn, 102 mins.)†

Man Called Dagger, A (1968)** Paul Mantee, Terry Moore, Jan Murray, Sue Ann Langdon. Spy spoof has ex-Nazi Koffman (Murray) posing as a meat-packing executive as he plans to take over the world; his domain also includes a farm full of beautiful women. (Dir: Richard Rush, 86 mins.)

Man Called Flintstone, The (1966)**½ Voices of Alan Reed, Mel Blanc, Jean Vander Pyl, June Foray. Yes, there were even secret agents in the Stone Age, and Fred Flintstone and Barney Rubble are recruited to track down the doers of evil: Green Goose and Tanya. (Dirs: William Hanna, Joseph Barbera, 87 mins.)†

Man Called Gannon, A (1969)*** Tony Franciosa, Michael Sarrazin, Susan Oliver, Gavin MacLeod. Well-paced western with a good performance by Franciosa as a drifter who takes a young cowpoke (Sarrazin) under his wing and ends up fighting against him in a small range war. (Dir: James Goldstone, 105 mins.)

Man Called Horse, A (1970)*** Richard Harris, Judith Anderson, Corinna Tsopei. An ambitious, serious western. Harris convincingly plays a white man captured by the Sioux in 1825, tortured, and finally converted to their way of life. (Dir: Elliot Silverstein, 114 mins.)†

Man Called Peter, A (1955)*** Richard Todd, Jean Peters. A fine performance by Todd as Peter Marshall, the Scotsman who became a minister in the U.S. and rose to the high position of U.S. Senate chaplain, makes this film. (Dir: Henry Koster, 119 mins.)†

Man Called...Rainbo, A (1989)* A la What's Up, Tiger Lily? some would-be comics took a pre-Rocky Sylvester Stallone movie (Rebel), re-edited it and dubbed in new dialogue. The unfunny result is almost enough to make you feel sorry for Stallone. (99 mins.)†

Manchu Eagle Murder Caper Mystery, The (1973)**½ Gabriel Dell, Will Geer, Joyce Van Patten, Anjanette Comer, Vincent Gardenia, Barbara Harris, Jackie Coogan, Huntz Hall, Dick Gautier. Pleasant, offbeat take-off of The Maltese Falcon with Dell playing a hard-boiled sleuth investigating the murder of milkman Gautier. (Dir: Dean Hargrove, 80 mins.)

Manchurian Candidate, The (1962)**** Frank Sinatra, Laurence Harvey, Janet Leigh, Angela Lansbury. Brilliantly made story of a soldier brainwashed by the Reds so that he becomes their pawn in an evil plot to take over the country. Can be viewed as a horror thriller, satire, or suspense-mystery drama; successful in all respects. Dazzling technique, excellent performances, an unusual film directed by TV graduate John Frankenheimer. (126 mins.)†

Man Could Get Killed, A (1966)**½ James Garner, Melina Mercouri, Sandra Dee, Tony Franciosa. Businessman in Portugal is mistaken for a secret agent, becomes involved with smugglers. Spoof has some captivating scenery and a competent cast to atone for the plot deficiencies. (Dirs: Ronald Neame, Cliff Owen, 100 mins.)

Mandabi (The Money Order) (Senegal, 1969)*** Mamadou Guye, Ynousse N'Diaye. Early feature from Ousmane Sembene of Senegal, novelist and preeminent director of black Africa is a satire about how "been-tos" (Africans who have been to Europe) condescend to their countrymen. (90 mins.)

Mandalay (1934)*** Kay Francis, Lyle Talbot, Warner Oland, Rafaela Ottiano, Ruth Donnelly. Kay Francis is at her sultriest in this tropical melodrama about a lady with a past who fell for a man with no future. When this bad penny turns up and spoils her chances for happiness, she gives him a nightcap laced with poison. (Dir: Michael Curtiz, 65 mins.)

Mandela (MCTV 1987)*** Danny Glover, Alfre Woodard, John Indi, John Matshikiza. An ambitious and worthy dramatization of the life and times of the real-life South African leader of human rights, Nelson Mandela, who has spent twenty-five years in prison for his outspoken opposition to South Africa's apartheid policy. Mandela rightfully chooses to trace the man's public and private life with sensitivity and a deep-rooted sense of the martyr as man, rather than vice versa. (Dir: Philip Saville, 135 mins.)

Mandingo (1975)½ James Mason, Ken Norton, Susan George, Perry King. Setting is a slave-breeding plantation in Louisiana circa 1840, and this is salacious tripe about a hard-lovin', hard-fightin' stud-slave (Norton). (Dir: Richard Fleischer, 127 mins.)†

Mandrake, The (Itlay, 1965)*** Rosanna Schiaffinao, Toto, Jean-Claude Brialy, Philippe Leroy, Romolo Valli. Machiavelli's drama about a wealthy Florentine's desire to make love to the beautiful wife of an important official. He poses as physician to help her cure her infertility. Well made, superbly acted, with just the right touch of ribald comedy. (Dir: Alberto Lattuada, 99 mins.)

Mandrake (MTV 1979)** Anthony Herrera, Robert Reed, Simone Griffeth. From the old comic strip comes the famed Mandrake the Magician, vanquishing wickedness with all his sleight of hand and magic tricks. (Dir: Harry Falk, 104 mins.)

Mandy (Great Britain, 1953)*** Phyllis Calvert, Jack Hawkins, Mandy Miller. Gripping story of a child born deaf and of her efforts to adjust herself. Fine drama, superlatively acted by Miller. AKA: **Crash of Silence.** (Dir: Alexander Mackendrick, 93 mins.)

Maneater (MTV 1973)** Ben Gazzara, Richard Basehart, Sheree North. Gazzara leads a band of vacationers whose mobile home meets with mechanical difficulty, and accepts help from Basehart, who is a wild-animal trainer. (Dir: Vince Edwards, 74 mins.)

Maneater of Hydra (1969)* Cameron Mitchell, Kai Fischer. A weird baron wreaks havoc on a group of unknowing tourists who have come to his island. AKA: **Island of the Doomed.** (Dir: Mel Welles, 85 mins.)

Man-eater of Kumaon (1948)**½ Sabu, Wendell Corey. Hunter wounds a tiger, then trails him when the beast terrorizes the community. (Dir: Byron Haskin, 79 mins.)

Maneaters Are Loose (MTV 1978)*½ Tom Skerritt, Steve Forrest, Harry Morgan. An animal trainer, down on his luck, releases his two tigers in a national forest area. (Dir: Timothy Galfas, 104 mins.)

Man Escaped (France, 1957)***½ François Leterrier, Charles Le Clainche. Taut and exciting film about a daring escape by a French Resistance leader who is captured by the Germans during WWII. (Dir: Robert Bresson, 94 mins.)

Man Facing Southeast (Argentina, 1987)*** Lorenzo Quinteros, Hugo Soto, Ines Vernengo. Enchanting fantasy that works on many different levels. Rantes (Soto), who claims he is an extraterrestrial, signs himself into the mental hospital run by the beleaguered-but caring Dr. Denis (Quinteros), who quickly recognizes his new patient's special abilities and contagiously humanitarian outlook on life. (Dir: Eliseo Subiela, 105 mins.)†

Man for All Seasons, A (Great Britain, 1966)***½ Paul Scofield, Robert Shaw, Wendy Hiller, Orson Welles, Susannah York, Vanessa Redgrave. Robert Bolt's literate and penetrating treatment of the conflict waged between Sir Thomas More and King Henry VIII makes a smooth transition to the screen. Director Fred Zinnemann has mounted the film with an eye for characterization rather than spectacle, and the result is superior drama. (120 mins.)†

Man Friday (Great Britain, 1975)**½ Peter O'Toole, Richard Roundtree. An amusing, occasionally moving update of Defoe's *Robinson Crusoe*, with some insight into the flaws behind the masterservant relationship. (Dir: Jack Gold, 115 mins.)†

Man from Atlantis (MTV 1977)** Patrick Duffy, Belinda Montgomery, Victor Buono. Pilot film is humdrum science fiction about a man with gills instead of lungs, a survivor from the lost continent of Atlantis. (Dir: Lee H. Katzin, 104 mins.)†

Man from Atlantis: The Death Scouts (1977)** Patrick Duffy, Belinda Montgomery. The water-breathing hero returns to encounter some alien beings reputed to be able to survive underwater, and teams up with the lady oceanographer who originally discovered him. (Dir: Marc Daniels, 106 mins.)

Man from Atlantis: The Disappearances (MTV 1977)**½ Patrick Duffy, Belinda Montgomery. Dr. Merrill (Miss Montgomery) is abducted and whisked to a mysterious island off South America, and our hero needs all his special powers to rescue her. (Dir: Charles Dubin, 72 mins.)

Man from Beyond, The (1922)*** Harry Houdini, Jane Connelly, Erwin Connelly, Frank Montgomery, Arthur Maude. Mystical thriller, with a story by Houdini, concerns a man who is found frozen in a block of ice, and who, on awakening, discovers a modern girl who is the reincarnation of his love of one hundred years ago. Weird drama has many magic tricks and escapes, leading up to a battle on the edge of Niagara Falls! Interesting viewing, one of the few film appearances still extant by the great magician. (Dir: Burton King, 83 mins.)†

Man from Bitter Ridge, The (1955)** Lex Barker, Mara Corday, Stephen McNally. Ordinary western drama about cattle barons and those who oppose them. (Dir: Jack Arnold, 80 mins.)

Man from Button Willow, The (1965)** Animated feature about the adventures of the first government agent, Justin Eagle. The plot centers around Eagle's attempt to rescue a kidnapped senator in the old west. (Dir: David Detiege, 82 mins.)†

Man from Colorado (1948)*** William Holden, Glenn Ford, Ellen Drew. Sadist becomes a federal judge and runs things his way. Good western has offbeat portrayal by Ford. (Dir: Henry Levin, 99 mins.)†

Man from Dakota, The (1940)**½ Wallace Beery, Dolores Del Rio, John Howard, Donald Meek, Robert Barrat. This exciting Civil War adventure has Beery and Howard as Union spies behind enemy lines, meeting up with the gorgeous Del Rio; taut story line and fast pace make this a better than usual Beery film. (Dir: Leslie Fenton, 75 mins.)

Man from Del Rio (1956)** Anthony Quinn, Katy Jurado. This western tale starts out well enough but slowly disintegrates into just another horse opera. (Dir: Harry Horner, 82 mins.)

Man from Down Under, The (1943)**½ Charles Laughton, Binnie Barnes, Richard Carlson, Donna Reed. Nice family comedy has reluctant bachelor Laughton adopting two orphans and raising them as his own; warm, charming, and light as fluff. (Dir: Robert Z. Leonard, 103 mins.)

Man from God's Country (1958)** George Montgomery, Randy Stuart. Cattleman gets involved in a land-grabbing scheme for a proposed railroad. Nothing new. (Dir: Paul Landres, 72 mins.)

Man from Laramie, The (1955)*** James Stewart, Arthur Kennedy, Cathy O'Donnell. Above-average western drama about a man who proves he is a tower of strength against the evil forces of a town. (Dir: Anthony Mann, 104 mins.)†

Man from Majorca, The (Sweden, 1984)*** Tomas Von Bromssen, Sven Woliter, Margreth Weivers, Ernst Gunther, Hakan Serner. Detectives on routine stakeout duty are led into a web of deception and police corruption. Fine thriller, highlighted by good acting and strong script, challenges police methods and official complicity in criminal acts. (Dir: Bo Widerberg, 105 mins.)

Man from Planet X, The (1951)** Robert Clarke, Margaret Field, William Schallert. A friendly alien is betrayed and antagonized by human greed. (Dir: Edgar G. Ulmer, 70 mins.)

Man from Snowy River, The (1982)**½ Kirk Douglas, Tom Burlinson, Terence Donovan, Tommy Dysart, Bruce Kerr, Sigrid Thornton. A big, sprawling, old-fashioned western yarn. Based on a legendary figure in Australian folklore, the story centers on a young man coming of age during the turn of the century in the untamed bush frontier, where horses ran free and ranchers were looked upon as spoilers of the land. Sequel: **Return to Snowy River Part II.** (Dir: George Miller, 105 mins.)†

Man from the Alamo, The (1953)**½ Glenn Ford, Julia Adams. Interesting western adventure about the only man to survive the Alamo massacre. (Dir: Budd Boetticher, 79 mins.)†

Man from the Diner's Club, The (1963)**½ Danny Kaye, Cara Williams, Martha Hyer, Telly Savalas, George Kennedy. Mild amusement. Diners' Club employee makes out an application for a gangster trying to leave the country, and the troubles begin. (Dir: Frank Tashlin, 96 mins.)

Man from Yesterday, The (1932)***

Claudette Colbert, Clive Brook, Charles Boyer, Alan Mowbray. Interesting soap opera with Colbert's first husband returning from the dead after she has married again; good cast strengthens the drama. (Dir: Berthold Viertel, 71 mins.)

Mango Tree, The (Australia, 1977)**½ Geraldine Fitzgerald, Christopher Pate, Diana Craig, Gerald Kennedy. Seasoned with fine performances, the film details a young man's coming-of-age at the time of WWI. (Dir: Kevin Dobson, 93 mins.)†

Manhandled (1924)*** Gloria Swanson, Tom Moore, Lilyan Tashman, Ian Keith, Frank Morgan. One of Swanson's best pictures, this has the glamorous star as a department store clerk who becomes a famous model. Full of funny scenes, including the famous ones of Swanson being crushed on her morning subway ride to work, and her party impressions of other famous stars of the period. Amusing fun. (Dir: Allan Dwan, 80 mins.)

Manhandled (1939)** Dorothy Lamour, Dan Duryea, Sterling Hayden, Irene Hervey. Gloomy *film noir* has obsessed crooked detective Duryea framing innocent Lamour for a murder; plot convolutions become too confusing even for the players. Misfires. (Dir: Lewis R. Foster, 97 mins.)

Manhattan (1979)**** Woody Allen, Diane Keaton, Mariel Hemingway, Michael Murphy, Meryl Streep. Enhanced with a lovely score of old favorites and graced with equally loving shots of New York City, the film concerns a group of neurotic people whose affairs entangle each other. (Dir: Woody Allen, 93 mins.)†

Manhattan Baby (Italy, 1982)* Christopher Connelly, Martha Taylor, Birgitta Boccoli, Giovanni Frezza. Incoherent horror movie about an archaeologist who unearths an ancient Egyptian amulet which turns out to be a conduit for evil beings back into this world. Tame non-shocker, except for a mildly gory finale, directed by Italo zombie specialist Lucio Fulci. (89 mins.)†

Manhattan Melodrama (1934)**½ Clark Gable, William Powell, Myrna Loy. Bank robber John Dillinger was watching this MGM film loosely inspired by his character at the Biograph Theatre in Chicago just before he was ambushed by the FBI. Gable and Powell are two pals who grow up to take opposite sides of the law, and Loy is the lovely lady caught in between. (Dir: Woody Van Dyke, 93 mins.)

Manhattan Project, The (1986)** John Lithgow, Christopher Collet, Cynthia Nixon, Jill Eikenberry. To protest the irresponsibility of a government plutonium plant dumping wastes in his community, a precocious teen decides to build his own atomic bomb using the plant's materials. It's tiresome to contemplate the nobility of this adolescent savior, who plans to save humanity by risking Armageddon. (Dir: Marshall Brickman, 120 mins.)†

Man Hunt (1941)***½ Walter Pidgeon, Joan Bennett, George Sanders, Roddy McDowall, John Carradine. Perfectly constructed thriller by director Fritz Lang. Pidgeon is a British big-game hunter stalking Adolf Hitler, purely, he thinks, for the sport of it. (105 mins.)

Manhunt—See: **Italian Connection, The**

Manhunter (1986)*** William L. Petersen, Tommy Noonan, Joan Allen, Kim Griest, Brian Cox, Stephen Lang, Dennis Farina. Glitzy filmmaking from Michael Mann; his style perfectly suits this police thriller about a neurotic FBI agent specializing in serial killers; he puts himself into their twisted frame of mind in order to psychologically pick up their scent. Sleek and scary. (118 mins.)†

Manhunt for Claude Dallas (MTV 1986)** Matt Salinger, Rip Torn, Pat Hingle, Claude Akins, Lois Nettleton. Another drama torn without much care from the newspaper headlines. Torn plays an Idaho sheriff searching for the elusive Claude Dallas, who shot two game officers and later escaped from prison to become a fugitive folk hero. (Dir: Jerry London, 104 mins.)

Mania—See: **Flesh and the Fiends, The**

Maniac (1934)½ Bill Woods, Horace Carpenter, Ted Edwards. So primitive that it makes *Plane Nine from Outer Space* look like a New Wave masterpiece, this film concerns an actor who plays his ultimate role after he kills a mad doctor and takes his place. (Dir: Dwaine Esper, 67 mins.)†

Maniac (Great Britain, 1963)**½ Kerwin Mathews, Nadia Gray. American artist in France has his life placed in danger when the father of his sweetheart's stepdaughter escapes from a mental institution. Interesting thriller. (Dir: Michael Carreras, 86 mins.)†

Maniac (1978)** Oliver Reed, Deborah Raffin, Jim Mitchum, Stuart Whitman. Off-target thriller in which a psychopath demands a ransom for every citizen of a wealthy township or else his onslaught of deadly arrows will hit their marks. AKA: **Ransom** and **Assault on Paradise**. (Dir: Richard Compton, 87 mins.)†

Maniac Cop (1988)** Tom Atkins, Bruce Campbell, Laurene Landon, Richard Roundtree, William Smith. Promising twist on two exploitation genres—the mad slasher terrorizing New York City seems to be a superhuman policeman—runs out of ideas early. (Dir: William Lustig, 85 mins.)†

Manifesto (1988)* Camilla Soeberg, Alfred Molina, Simon Callow, Eric Stoltz. Bawdy farce set in post-WWI Europe, where the characters in a small village awaiting the arrival of the new king divide their time between plotting or preventing assassinations and seductions. The movie has no center, and is often little more than a well-cast bit of Euro soft-core porn. (Dir: Dusan Makavejev, 96 mins.)

Man I Killed, The—See: **Broken Lullaby**

Manila Calling (1942)**½ Lloyd Nolan, Carole Landis, Cornel Wilde, James Gleason, Elisha Cook, Jr. Muscular wartime adventure with a disparate group joining forces to fend off the enemy; good, stirring patriotic melodrama. (Dir: Herbert I. Leeds, 81 mins.)

Man I Love, The (1946)**½ Ida Lupino, Robert Alda. Singer visiting her family catches the eye of a nightclub owner. Good acting offsets a soapy opera. (Dir: Raoul Walsh, 96 mins.)

Man I Married, The (1940)*** Francis Lederer, Joan Bennett, Lloyd Nolan, Anna Sten. Fascinating anti-Nazi film about an American girl married to a German-American. They visit Germany in '38 and she sees her husband fall for Hitler's doctrines. (Dir: Irving Pichel, 77 mins.)

Man in a Cocked Hat (Great Britain, 1960)**½ Terry-Thomaš, Peter Sellers. Inept clerk in the Foreign Office is sent to a small colony where he proceeds to gum up the works. Sporadically amusing comedy. AKA: **Carleton-Browne of the F. O.** (Dirs: Jeffrey Dell, Roy Boulting, 88 mins.)†

Man in Grey, The (Great Britain, 1943)*** James Mason, Stewart Granger, Margaret Lockwood. An evil marquis carries on with a hussy while married in name only to another. Purple-passioned costume melodrama is redeemed by good performances, particularly from Mason. (Dir: Leslie Arliss, 116 mins.)†

Man in Half Moon Street, The (1944)**½ Nils Asther, Helen Walker, Brandon Hurst, Reginald Sheffield. A modest but eerie shocker about a scientist tampering with the aging process. (Dir: Ralph Murphy, 92 mins.)

Man in Love, A (France, 1987)*** Peter Coyote, Greta Scacchi, Peter Riegert, John Berry, Claudia Cardinale, Jamie Lee Curtis. Highly sensual romance with Coyote slightly miscast as a high-voltage American actor who comes to Rome to play a noted Italian writer. However, his relationship with the ravishing Scacchi does strike some sparks. Nice supporting performances by Cardinale and Riegert. (Dir: Diane Kurys, 108 mins.)†

Man Inside, The (Great Britain, 1958)**½

Jack Palance, Anita Ekberg, Nigel Patrick. Fairly good drama about a group of international jewel thieves who hit the jackpot when a very valuable diamond comes into their possession. (Dir: John Gilling, 90 mins.)

Man Inside, The (1990)*** Jürgen Prochnow, Peter Coyote, Nathalie Baye. Snappy cold-war thriller about the real-life adventures of investigative reporter Gunter Wallraff. The fascinating plot involves the almost incredible infiltration of the West German news media by right-wing forces. Amazing story, tautly directed. (Dir: Bobby Roth, 101 mins.)†

Man in the Attic (1953)** Jack Palance, Constance Smith. Mysterious man takes a room in a lodging house when London is terrorized by Jack the Ripper. Remake of *The Lodger*. (Dir: Hugo Fregonese, 82 mins.)

Man in the Brown Suit, The (MTV 1989)*** Stephanie Zimbalist, Edward Woodward, Rue McClanahan, Tony Randall, Ken Howard. Agatha Christie adaptation set in Egypt with tourist Zimbalist tracking a man she saw running from the scene of a crime to a cruise ship. (Dir: Alan Grint, 96 mins.)

Man in the Dark (1953)**½ Edmond O'Brien, Audrey Totter. A somewhat novel approach to an old gangster story. A convict submits to a brain operation which is supposed to free him from his criminal tendencies but just makes him lose his memory instead. Remake of *The Man Who Lived Twice*. (Dir: Lew Landers, 70 mins.)

Man in the Glass Booth, The (1975)**½ Maximilian Schell, Lois Nettleton, Luther Adler, Lawrence Pressman. Sometimes effective film version about the Holocaust and Adolf Eichmann's trial. Schell plays a wealthy Jew who is accused by the Israeli government of being a notorious war criminal. (Dir: Arthur Hiller, 117 mins.)†

Man in the Gray Flannel Suit, The (1956)**½ Gregory Peck, Jennifer Jones, Fredric March, Marisa Pavan. Sloan Wilson's novel is brought to film in typical Hollywood style—glossy and melodramatic. Peck is as wooden as ever as the Madison Ave. husband whose past comes back and makes him search for answers. (Dir: Nunnally Johnson, 153 mins.)†

Man in the Iron Mask, The (1939)*** Louis Hayward, Joan Bennett. The classic tale of intrigue in France, and the twin brother of Louis XIV who was kept in an iron mask so that no one would see his face. Elaborate costume adventure. (Dir: James Whale, 119 mins.)†

Man in the Iron Mask, The (MTV 1977)*** Richard Chamberlain, Patrick McGoohan, Ralph Richardson, Louis Jourdan. Lav-

ish production and the timeless Alexandre Dumas story add up to an entertaining family film. (Dir: Mike Newell, 104 mins.)†

Man in the Middle, The (1964)**½ Robert Mitchum, France Nuyen, Trevor Howard, Keenan Wynn. American lieutenant stationed in India at the end of WWII shoots a British sergeant. The question whether the American soldier is sane or not becomes the crux of the case. (Dir: Guy Hamilton, 94 mins.)

Man in the Moon (Great Britain, 1961)*** Kenneth More, Shirley Anne Field. British comedy with a good idea, satirizing the attempts to make a missile shot to the moon. Idea is superior to the execution; however, much of it is still quite droll. (Dir: Basil Dearden, 98 mins.)

Man in the Net, The (1959)*½ Alan Ladd, Carolyn Jones, Stan Moger, Tom Helmore. Suspense slips through the net in this melodrama with psychological overtones. Ladd is involved in a murder, but can't clear up some of the facts. (Dir: Michael Curtiz, 98 mins.)

Man in the Saddle (1951)**½ Randolph Scott, Joan Leslie, Ellen Drew. Two women are in love with Scott in this better-than-average western. (Dir: André de Toth, 87 mins.)

Man in the Santa Claus Suit, The (MTV 1979)**½ Fred Astaire, Bert Convy, Gary Burghoff, John Byner. Burghoff, Byner, and Convy each rent a Santa Claus suit from costume shop owner Astaire. Their lives are changed, because the suit is endowed with Fred's magical spell. (Dir: Corey Allen, 104 mins.)†

Man in the Shadow (1957)**½ Jeff Chandler, Orson Welles, Ben Alexander. Sheriff engages in a battle with a tyrannical ranch owner who has ordered a Mexican laborer beaten badly enough to die. (Dir: Jack Arnold, 80 mins.)

Man in the Silk Hat, The (1983)*** A fine documentary about the great French silent comedian Max Linder, who was a major star before WWI, and influenced Chaplin, Keaton, and others, with many clips from his films. Written and directed by Linder's daughter, Maud Linder. (96 mins.)†

Man in the White Suit, The (Great Britain, 1951)**** Alec Guinness, Joan Greenwood, Cecil Parker. Furor in a textile plant when a young scientist invents a cloth material that never wears, tears, or becomes dirty. The industry unites to destroy him and his creation. Top-flight fun. (Dir: Alexander Mackendrick, 84 mins.)†

Man in the Wilderness (1971)*** Richard Harris, John Huston, John Bindon. Based on two actual incidents in the Northwest of the 1820s. Harris is an experienced guide who gets mauled by a bear and is left to die by his expedition companions, led by the menacing Huston. (Dir: Richard C. Sarafian, 105 mins.)

Man Is Not a Bird (Yugoslavia, 1966)***½ Janez Vrhovec, Eva Ras, Milena Dravic, Stijan Arandelovic, Boris Dvornik. Director Dusan Makavejev's first feature contains all of the iconoclastic plot and cinematic devices he became noted for. Black humor, eroticism, Beethoven's "Ode to Joy," political repression, and sexual liberation are blended with startling non-narrative energy and excitement. (80 mins.)†

Manitou, The (1978)* Susan Strasberg, Tony Curtis, Lurene Tuttle, Ann Sothern, Michael Ansara, Stella Stevens, Burgess Meredith. Absurd nonsense! Strasberg is the victim who finds her supposed tumor is actually the fetus of a dead Indian medicine man trying to be reborn. (Dir: William Girdler, 105 mins.)†

Man Killer (1933)*** William Powell, Margaret Lindsay, Ruth Donnelly, Arthur Hohl, Arthur Byron. Gritty pre-Production Code drama about an ex-Secret Service man joining a cheap private detective agency and uncovering a blackmail racket, as well as solving a murder; fine, unsentimental underworld atmosphere, with a crisp, wry performance by Powell and an excellently oily Hohl. AKA **Private Detective 62**. (Dir: Michael Curtiz, 67 mins.)

Mankillers (1987)* Edd Byrnes, Gail Fisher, Lynda Aldon, Edy Williams, William Zipp. Distaff rip-off of *The Dirty Dozen*. Ex-FBI agent Aldon rounds up a squad of tough prisoners (but not so tough that they don't look good in torn T-shirts) to battle drug dealer Zipp. Stupid, cheap exploitation feature. (Dir: David A. Prior, 90 mins.)†

Man Like Eva, A (West Germany, 1983)** Eva Mattes, Lisa Kreuzer, Werner Stocker, Charles Regnier. A biopic with a difference: the part of German wunderkind director Rainer Werner Fassbinder (here named "Eva") is played by one of his actresses, Eva Mattes. Though Mattes has the physical mannerisms down pat, this "life-on-a-movie-set" drama is often quite tedious. (Dir: Radu Gabrea, 89 mins.)

Man-Made Monster (1941)** Lon Chaney, Lionel Atwill. After being used in a series of experiments, a young man finds that he's immune to electric shock. Familiar sci-fi yarn with plenty of technical mumbo-jumbo. (Dir: George Waggner, 60 mins.)

Man Named John, A (Italy, 1965)**½ Rod Steiger, Adolfo Celli. Absorbing, but overly cautious, biography of Pope John XXIII is interesting for its few insights into the impact of this uncommonly forthright papal leader. (Dir: Ermanno Olmi, 94 mins.)

Mannequin (1937)*** Joan Crawford, Spencer Tracy, Leo Gorcey, Alan Curtis, Elisabeth Risdon, Ralph Morgan. This MGM soap opera about a pragmatic girl, initially attracted to Spencer's wealth before falling for him, attains sensitivity in Borzage's hands. A compelling, bittersweet romance. (Dir: Frank Borzage, 95 mins.)

Mannequin (1987)*½ Andrew McCarthy, Kim Cattrall, Estelle Getty, James Spader. With the uncharismatic McCarthy and the decidedly down-to-earth Cattrall, this movie about a department store mannequin who becomes human never really comes to life. (Dir: Michael Gottlieb, 90 mins.)†

Man of Aran (Great Britain, 1934)**** Colman (Tiger) King, Maggie Dillane. A classic. Director Robert Flaherty's brilliant documentary chronicling the barren, meager existence of the inhabitants off the Irish coast remains unparalleled for visual imagery. (132 mins.)†

Man of a Thousand Faces (1957)***½ James Cagney, Dorothy Malone, Jane Greer. Cagney is superb in the satisfying film biography of Lon Chaney, Sr., the silent screen star who was a make-up wizard and created a series of memorable screen characterizations. (Dir: Joseph Pevney, 122 mins.)

Man of Conquest (1939)**½ Richard Dix, Joan Fontaine, Gail Patrick. The story of Sam Houston, soldier, statesman, hero of Texas. With fine, large scale battle scenes, good performances. (Dir: George Nicholls, Jr., 99 mins.)

Man of Flowers (Australia, 1984)*** Norman Kaye, Alyson Best, Chris Haywood. A beautiful "small" film. Plot involves a quirky millionaire who cannot reconcile his puritan upbringing—told in flashbacks with Werner Herzog in cameo as the stern disciplinarian father—with his sexual needs as an adult. He hires a young lady to strip to classical music, always leaving before she finishes, and makes frequent trips to a psychiatrist much loonier than he. (Dir: Paul Cox, 91 mins.)†

Man of Iron (Poland, 1982)**** Jerzy Radziwilowicz, Krystyna Janda, Marian Opania. Andrzej Wajda's sequel to his *Man of Marble* is both a powerful, richly romantic drama and a thrilling historical document. Intertwining the stories of an intimidated alcoholic reporter, an outspoken worker, and a dissident filmmaker, Wajda explores the emotion and confusion of a country on the brink of making history with relentless honesty and perception. (140 mins.)

Man of La Mancha (Italy, 1972)*½ Sophia Loren, Peter O'Toole, James Coco. The international hit musical comes to the screen with a thud! You can't help but wish this stellar cast would simply play Cervantes's classic tale of Don Quixote straight. (Dir: Arthur Hiller, 140 mins.)†

Man of Marble (Poland, 1972)**** Krystyna Janda, Jerzy Radziwilowicz. A young filmmaker, for her graduation film project, decides to investigate the life of a worker-hero in the Stalinist '50s, Birkut (Radziwilowicz), who fell from official favor. Polish censors distorted the political meaning of the film by cutting out the shooting of Birkut by the police, and delayed general release till '77. (Dir: Andrzej Wajda, 150 mins.)

Man of Straw (Italy, 1958)***½ Luisa Della Noce, Pietro Germi, Franca Bettoja, Saro Urzi, Edoardo Nevola. Married man falls in love with young girl, with whom he has an affair they both know must not last. Director Pietro Germi casts himself as the man in this realistic and poignant look at adultery and obsession, with an ending that is shocking and tragic. Superb script and acting. (95 mins.)

Man of the West (1958)**½ Gary Cooper, Julie London, Lee J. Cobb. Routine western with the hero, a reformed gunslinger, pitted predictably against his uncle, a notorious outlaw. (Dir: Anthony Mann, 100 mins.)

Man of the World (1931)**½ William Powell, Carole Lombard, Wynne Gibson, Guy Kibbee. Okay romantic drama of a con man reforming for an honest girl; good star chemistry, but unleavened by much humor. (Dir: Richard Wallace, 71 mins.)

Manon (France, 1949)***½ Michel Auclair, Serge Reggiani, Cecile Aubrey, Gabrielle Dorziat. In post-WWII France, a former Resistance fighter saves a woman Nazi collaborator from angry partisans, and flees to Paris where they have a stormy affair as she turns to prostitution and black market thieving. After he kills someone, she must decide to stand by him or turn him in. Strong, tense tragedy captures sleazy atmosphere of Paris after the war. (Dir: Henri-Georges Clouzot, 100 mins.)†

Man on a String (1960)**½ Ernest Borgnine, Kerwin Mathews. Story of Boris Morros, who served as a double agent to expose Communist espionage. Documentary-type drama has some good moments but never quite hits the mark. (Dir: André de Toth, 92 mins.)

Man on a String (MTV 1972)** Christopher George, William Schallert, Joel Grey, Kitty Winn, Jack Warden. A government undercover man infiltrates gangland, setting up wars between rival mobsters. Standard action formula. (Dir: Joseph Sargent, 73 mins.)

Man on a Swing (1974)**½ Joel Grey, Cliff Robertson. Director Frank Perry almost pulls off this offbeat crime melodrama but it falls apart before the finale. Grey, in a dramatic role as a clairvoyant, gives a solid performance, and Robertson is less stoic than usual as the cop trying to solve the slaying of a young woman. (109 mins.)

Man on a Tightrope (1953)**½ Fredric March, Gloria Grahame, Terry Moore, Cameron Mitchell, Adolphe Menjou. Story of a small German traveling circus troupe. March fares better than the other stars as a jealous husband who loves his unfaithful wife. (Dir: Elia Kazan, 105 mins.)

Man on Fire (1957)**½ Bing Crosby, Inger Stevens, Mary Fickett, E. G. Marshall. The crooner plays a man with a custody problem concerning his son and his divorced wife. Melodramatic soap opera. (Dir: Ranald MacDougall, 95 mins.)

Man on Fire (1987)*½ Scott Glenn, Jade Malle, Joe Pesci, Brooke Adams, Paul Shenar, Danny Aiello. Yet another revenge picture, starring Glenn as an ex-CIA agent who's hired to guard a rich kid who ends up being kidnapped by terrorists. Sloppy production with a dull performance by a grim-faced Glenn. (Dir: Elie Chouraqui, 93 mins.)†

Manon of the Spring (France, 1986)**** Yves Montand, Daniel Auteuil, Emmanuelle Beart. A contemporary masterpiece. Conclusion of the story begun in *Jean de Florette* takes place ten years later, as Jean's daughter learns the truth behind her father's death and sets in motion the events that bring the malefactors to light. See both movies together for maximum effect; we defy anyone to remain dry-eyed at Montand's final scenes. (Dir: Claude Berri, 113 mins.)†

Man on the Eiffel Tower, The (1949)**½ Charles Laughton, Franchot Tone, Burgess Meredith. A police inspector craftily breaks down the resistance of a murderer when evidence is lacking. Intelligent, suspenseful melodrama, made in France. (Dir: Burgess Meredith, 97 mins.)†

Man on the Flying Trapeze, The (1935)***½ W. C. Fields, Mary Brian. Fields is in typical form as a cynical, downtrodden husband and father who, however, gets up and fights. Remake of his silent *Running Wild*. (Dir: Clyde Bruckman, 68 mins.)

Man on the Move—See: **Jigsaw** (1972)

Man on the Roof (Sweden, 1977)***½ Gustav Linstedt, Hakan Serner, Sven Wallter. Gripping foreign film about the Swedish police leaving no stone unturned in order to trap a cop-killer. Impressively detailed without ever letting up on the action. A knockout! (Dir: Bo Widerberg, 110 mins.)

Man Outside (1988)*½ Robert Logan, Kathleen Quinlan, Bradford Dillman, Levon Helm. Ex-lawyer, now living a hermit's existence in the backwoods of Arkansas, is coaxed out of his shell by teacher Quinlan, only to be framed for a crime by evil Dillman. Lackluster drama may be of note to music fans for cameo appearances by co-star Helms's former Band-mates Rick Danko, Garth Hudson, and the late Richard Manuel. (Dir: Mark Stouffer, 109 mins.)†

Manpower (1941)*** Marlene Dietrich, Edward G. Robinson, George Raft. Raft and Robinson want Dietrich and the sparks really fly in this rip-roaring adventure about the hazards faced by the men who risk their lives daily repairing high-tension lines. (Dir: Raoul Walsh, 103 mins.)

Man Proof (1937)**½ Myrna Loy, Rosalind Russell, Franchot Tone, Walter Pidgeon. Big cast plus little story equals ordinary film. Myrna loves Walter who marries wealthy Rosalind but would like to keep little Myrna in his closet. (Dir: Richard Thorpe, 80 mins.)

Man's Castle (1933)***½ Spencer Tracy, Loretta Young, Glenda Farrell. Tracy and Young are two lovers who transcend the Depression in a New York shantytown. Few love stories have achieved such emotional intensity. (Dir: Frank Borzage, 75 mins.)

Man's Favorite Sport? (1964)**½ Rock Hudson, Paula Prentiss, Maria Perschy. Outdoorsman-columnist Hudson suddenly finds he has to live up to his reputation in this Howard Hawks-directed comedy that is funnier than it has any right to be. Rock trying to fish (though he has never fished in his life) in order to save his job is quite a sight. (120 mins.)†

Man's Hope (France-Spain, 1939)*** Nicolas Rodriguez, José Lado, Mejuto. Powerful film about Republican fighters in Spanish Civil War who try to keep food and weapons from reaching Franco's army. Only feature directed by noted author André Malraux, from his novel *L'Espoir*. Filled with astonishing images and an engrossing sense of war as tragedy born of madness. (73 mins.)

Manster, The (1962)½ Peter Dyneley, Jane Hylton. Reporter is injected with some serum and turns into a hairy two-headed monster. Made-in-Japan horror thriller disproves theory that two heads are better than one. (Dirs: Kenneth Crane, George Breakston, 80 mins.)†

Man They Could Not Hang, The (1939)**½ Boris Karloff, Lorna Gray, Robert Wilcox, Roger Pryor. You've seen it before and you'll probably see it again. Boris liked playing hanged criminals who get resurrected so they can avenge themselves on their enemies. (Dir: Nick Grinde, 72 mins.)†

Man Under Suspicion (West Germany, 1984)*** Maximilian Schell, Lena Stolze, Wolfgang Kieling, Robert Aldini. A lawyer defends a young terrorist who may or may not have acted on his own. Sharper direction and editing were in order here, but this tale of an advocate growing obsessed with the controversial case makes a thought-provoking cautionary tale. (Dir: Norbert Kuckelmann, 126 mins.)

Man Upstairs, The (Great Britain, 1959)*** Richard Attenborough, Virginia Maskell, Donald Houston, Bernard Lee. Attenborough delivers a strong performance as a shattered human being who attempts to kill himself after a series of depressing events. Well-made melodrama. (Dir: Don Chaffey, 88 mins.)

Man Who Broke 1,000 Chains, The (MCTV 1987)**½ Val Kilmer, Charles Durning, Sonia Braga, Kyra Sedgewick, Elisha Cook. Based on the true story that inspired *I Am a Fugitive from a Chain Gang*, this hard-hitting drama follows Robert Elliot Burns from a false robbery charge to his eventual flight from the law. Predictable, occasionally engrossing. (Dir: Daniel Mann, 114 mins.)†

Man Who Broke the Bank at Monte Carlo, The (1935)*** Ronald Colman, Joan Bennett, Colin Clive, Nigel Bruce, Montagu Love. Delightful antique, based on the 19th-century popular song, tells of a dashing young man who plans to do just what it says. Depends on the light touch of the players, and succeeds admirably. (Dir: Stephen Roberts, 66 mins.)

Man Who Came to Dinner, The (1941)***½ Monty Woolley, Bette Davis, Jimmy Durante, Ann Sheridan. Fast-paced fun with an all-star cast. Woolley re-creates his stage role, Sheridan Whiteside, patterned after venomous theater critic Alexander Woolcott. When this acid-tongued guest lecturer ends up in a wheelchair on the Stanley household's doorstep, he interferes, blackmails, lies, and runs roughshod over everyone there, including his long-suffering secretary (Davis), and a visiting Hollywood bombshell (Ann Sheridan). (Dir: William Keighley, 112 mins.)†

Man Who Cried Wolf, The (1937)**½ Lewis Stone, Tom Brown, Barbara Read, Marjorie Main. Fine, low-budget thriller, with an actor's histrionics masking a clever murder plot; good idea, ably performed. (Dir: Lewis R. Foster, 66 mins.)

Man Who Changed His Mind, The (Great Britain, 1936)*½ Boris Karloff, Anna Lee, John Loder. Boris as a mad scientist once more—this time he thinks he can transpose the human mind from one body to another. Typical mid-thirties thriller, English-style. AKA: **The Man Who Lived Again** and **The Brainsnatchers**. (Dir: Robert Stevenson, 61 mins.)†

Man Who Cheated Himself, The (1950)**½ Lee J. Cobb, Jane Wyatt, John Dall. An honest cop meets a cheating dame and forgets his honesty. Just fair crime melodrama; good cast better than the story. (Dir: Felix E. Feist, 81 mins.)

Man Who Could Cheat Death, The (Great Britain, 1959)**½ Anton Diffring, Hazel Court, Christopher Lee. Man becomes ageless through a gland operation, becomes a murderer when he learns the secret of eternal youth from the doctor. (Dir: Terence Fisher, 83 mins.)

Man Who Could Talk to Kids, The (MTV 1973)**½ Peter Boyle, Scott Jacoby, Robert Reed, Tyne Daly. Jacoby is a young teenager whose deep-rooted problems cause him to retreat into his own world except for occasional outbursts of violence. (Dir: Donald Wrye, 73 mins.)

Man Who Could Work Miracles, The (Great Britain, 1936)*** Roland Young, Joan Gardner, Ralph Richardson. Good rendition of an H. G. Wells short story in which a timid department store clerk finds he can do whatever he wants. Dated in all the best ways. (Dir: Lothar Mendes, 82 mins.)†

Man Who Dared (1933)**½ Preston Foster, Zita Johann, Joan Marsh. Low-key dramatization of the life of Anton Cernak, the Polish mayor of Chicago who was killed in an assassination attempt on FDR. Unemphatically patriotic story, simply told. (Dir: Hamilton McFadden, 75 mins.)

Man Who Died Twice, The (MTV 1970)**½ Stuart Whitman, Brigitte Fossey, Jeremy Slate, Bernard Lee. Artist presumed dead wanders in Spain, and falls in love with a depressed French girl. (Dir: Joseph Sargent, 100 mins.)

Man Who Fell to Earth, The (Great Britain, 1976)*** David Bowie, Buck Henry, Candy Clark, Rip Torn. An extra-terrestrial comes to our planet from a distant galaxy, desperately seeking a water supply for his people. Has suspense, intrigue, romance of a sort, even humor. The sci-fi effects are absolutely beautiful. (Dir: Nicolas Roeg, 140 mins.)†

Man Who Had His Hair Cut Short, The (Belgium, 1966)*** Beata Tyszkiewicz, Senne Rouffaer, Hector Camerlynck. Compulsive man falls in love with a young girl at the school where he teaches. This platonic love stays with him even after the girl graduates. Years later he meets her, now a renowned actress, accelerating his decline into insanity. A disturbing depiction of the fine line between delusion and reality. (Dir: André Delvaux, 95 mins.)

Man Who Haunted Himself, The (Great Britain, 1970)** Roger Moore, Olga Georges-Picot, Hildegard Neil. Venerable sci-fi gambit drama, as Moore plays a businessman who finds that his double has been slowly taking his place in the office, at his club, and at home. (Dir: Basil Dearden, 94 mins.)†

Man Who Knew Too Much, The (Great Britain, 1934)**½ Peter Lorre, Edna Best, Leslie Banks. Not as good as the '56 film also by director Alfred Hitchcock. Does have re-creation of the siege of Sidney Street and a villain, impersonated by Lorre with fine flair. (84 mins.)†

Man Who Knew Too Much, The (1956)***½ James Stewart, Doris Day. Director Alfred Hitchcock at his best with an exciting suspense yarn complete with murder, assassination plots, kidnappings, and a hair-raising climax. The stars do very nicely in their roles of an American couple vacationing in French Morocco who are accidentally drawn into a series of mysterious adventures. Oscar: Best Song, "Que Sera, Sera" (Jay Livingston and Ray Evans). (120 mins.)†

Man Who Left His Will on Film, The (Japan, 1970)***½ Kazuo Goto, Emiko Iwaski, Sugio Fukuoka, Keichi Fukada. Complex political film about a student radical who finds a movie camera of another leftist who has committed suicide. He retraces the dead youth's life through the developed film. Ordinary on the surface, it soon involves him with people and events of an erotic and turbulent nature. Director Nagisa Oshima continues his dynamic fascination with the turmoil of Japanese youth in the '60s. AKA: **Tokyo Senso Sengo Hiwa**. (94 mins.)

Man Who Lived Again, The—See: **Man Who Changed His Mind, The**

Man Who Lived Twice, The (1936)**½ Ralph Bellamy, Marian Marsh, Thurston Hall. Competent thriller about a killer (Bellamy) who can't easily turn over a new leaf, so he turns his back on his criminal past and goes to a brain transplant clinic for an instant change of mind. (Dir: Harry Lachman, 73 mins.)

Man Who Lived at the Ritz, The (MTV 1988)*** Perry King, Joss Ackland, Leslie Caron, David McCallum. Stylish miniseries starring King as an artist indifferent to the politics of WWII until a woman he cares for meets with tragedy at the hands of the Nazis. Beautifully filmed on location in Europe. (Dir: Desmond Davis, 192 mins.)

Man Who Loved Cat Dancing, The (1973)** Burt Reynolds, Sarah Miles, Jack Warden, Lee J. Cobb, George Hamilton. Contrived western about a gruff but inwardly gentle train robber (Reynolds) and the wretchedly unhappy "lady" who learns to love him (Miles). (Dir: Richard Sarafian, 114 mins.)†

Man Who Loved Redheads, The (Great Britain, 1955)***½ Moira Shearer, John Justin, Gladys Cooper, Denholm Elliott. Throughout his long life, a man seeks the redhead of his youthful dream, becoming enamored of many carrot-tops in the process. (Dir: Harold French, 89 mins.)

Man Who Loved Women, The (France, 1977)** Charles Denner, Leslie Caron, Nelly Borgeaud. Denner plays a man who will go to any lengths to chase a well-turned ankle. Director François Truffaut's experiments in narration work well enough but serve to vitiate the emotional strength of the film. (119 mins.)†

Man Who Loved Women, The (1983)* Burt Reynolds, Julie Andrews, Kim Basinger, Marilu Henner. Why remake Truffaut's second-rate *The Man Who Loved Women*? You won't find an answer watching this lifeless comedy. This film about a Lothario on the loose and the repercussions of his obsession avec les femmes is only rarely brightened by director Blake Edwards's slapstick magic. (110 mins.)†

Man Who Never Was, The (1956)**½ Clifton Webb, Gloria Grahame, Stephen Boyd. Account of Operation Mincemeat, which was instrumental in paving the way for the Allied invasion of Europe in WWII. When the film sticks to the facts, it is engrossing. (Dir: Ronald Neame, 103 mins.)

Man Who Played God, The (1932)**½ George Arliss, Bette Davis, Ray Milland. Arliss plays a musician turned deaf who overcomes bitterness by helping young people. Arliss is awesomely good at this sort of tailor-made tripe—better than Liberace in the remake, *Sincerely Yours*. (Dir: John G. Adolfi, 81 mins.)

Man Who Reclaimed His Head, The (1934)*** Claude Rains, Joan Bennett, Lionel Atwill. Effective anti-war picture, despite its improbable title, stars Rains as a brilliant journalist who sells his brains to an unscrupulous politician by ghostwriting for him. Upshot is war, adultery, misery, but Claude finally . . . well, you guessed it. (Dir: Edward Ludwig, 82 mins.)

Man Who Returned to Life, The (1942)**½ John Howard, Ruth Ford. Good B film about a man who leaves a town to get a fresh start and, years later, learns that they're about to try a man for murdering him. (Dir: Lew Landers, 61 mins.)

Man Who Shot Liberty Valance, The (1962)***½ John Wayne, James Stewart, Lee Marvin, Woody Strode, Vera Miles. One of the greatest of director John Ford's memory westerns, a moving bitter meditation of immortality and survival. Stewart is cast as an idealistic

lawyer who has become famous for killing a notorious badman. Wayne incarnates his own myth with subtle melancholy. (122 mins.)†

Man Who Skied Down Everest, The (Japan, 1975)** Yuichiro Miura. Documentary about a crazed Japanese who uses up vast amounts of money and six lives in order to climb Mount Everest and ski—for 2½ minutes—down one of its slopes. Oscar winner for Best Documentary Feature. (Dirs: F. R. Crawley, James Hager, Dale Hartleben, 86 mins.)†

Man Who Talked Too Much, The (1940)**½ George Brent, Virginia Bruce, Richard Barthelmess, Brenda Marshall, William Lundigan. Taut courtroom drama of a D. A. (Brent) whose lawyer brother (Lundigan) gets in trouble defending a vicious gangster (Barthelmess); remake of *The Mouthpiece*, which was based on fact. (Dir: Vincent Sherman, 75 mins.)

Man Who Understood Women, The (1959)*** Henry Fonda, Leslie Caron. Hollywood genius makes an aspiring actress a star, marries her, then finds he has no time for her. Unevenly balanced but with plenty to recommend it. (Dir: Nunnally Johnson, 105 mins.)

Man Who Wagged His Tail, The (Italy-Spain, 1957)**½ Peter Ustinov, Pablito Calvo. Disliked, miserly lawyer is changed by magic into an ugly dog and must find salvation before he can return to human form. (Dir: Ladislao Vajda, 91 mins.)†

Man Who Wanted to Live Forever, The (MTV 1970)**½ Burl Ives, Sandy Dennis, Stuart Whitman. Fairly gripping drama with a good performance by Ives as a multimillionaire who has built a fantastic medical heart-disease research center for his own sinister purpose. (Dir: John Trent, 99 mins.)

Man Who Wasn't There, The (1983)½ Steve Guttenberg, Jeffrey Tambor, Lisa Langlois, Art Hindle. This sci-fi comedy must be seen to be disbelieved! The supposedly hilarious adventures of a government aide, who stumbles onto an invisibility formula, are handled with crassness and incoherent scripting. (Dir: Bruce Malmuth, 111 mins.)†

Man Who Would Be King, The (1975)**** Michael Caine, Sean Connery, Christopher Plummer. Excellent, rousing treatment of Rudyard Kipling's yarn of greed and ambition in India, circa 1880. Caine and Connery are fine as the pals who decide to resign from the army and set themselves up as deities in Kafiristan. Given a grand treatment by director John Huston, who co-authored the screenplay with Gladys Hill. (127 mins.)†

Man Who Wouldn't Die, The (1942)** Lloyd Nolan, Marjorie Weaver, Helen Reynolds, Henry Wilcoxon, Richard Derr, Paul

Harvey. Detective Michael Shayne investigates murder and blackmail at a mansion and seeks a killer capable of suspended animation. (Dir: Herbert L. Leeds, 78 mins.)

Man Who Wouldn't Talk, The (Great Britain, 1957)**½ Anthony Quayle, Anna Neagle, Zsa Zsa Gabor. Man on trial for the murder of a beautiful secret agent refuses to help himself, is defended by a clever lady barrister. (Dir: Herbert Wilcox, 85 mins.)

Man with a Cloak, The (1951)**½ Joseph Cotten, Barbara Stanwyck, Leslie Caron. An interesting costume drama about a mysterious man who enters two women's lives. (Dir: Fletcher Markle, 81 mins.)

Man with a Million (Great Britain, 1954)*** Gregory Peck, Jane Griffith, Ronald Squire, Wilfred Hyde-White, A. E. Matthews. A man who's supposed to be rich becomes famous and powerful proving that money comes to money. Interesting, entertaining film based on a Mark Twain story. (Dir: Ronald Neame, 90 mins.)

Man with a Movie Camera (USSR, 1928) **** Unforgettable documentary by Dziga Vertov offering extraordinary glimpses of a day in the life of Moscow's inhabitants, using a host of techniques (dissolves, slow motion, animation, freeze frame, split screen) in a revolutionary and exhilarating style that is still impressive. An incalculably influential film. (90 mins.)†

Man with Bogart's Face, The (1980)*** Robert Sacchi, Michelle Phillips, Franco Nero. Sacchi's impression of Humphrey Bogart catches the mannerisms without the emotional depth and delicacy. The film's action is coherent and affectionate, invoking the Bogart myth without messing it up too much. (Dir: Robert Day, 106 mins.)†

Man with My Face, The (1951)**½ Barry Nelson, John Harvey, Lynn Ainley. Neat low-budget thriller stars Nelson as an ordinary man who finds that a mysterious stranger who looks just like him is taking over his life; not as well developed as it could have been, but intriguing. (Dir: Edward Montagne, 86 mins.)

Man with One Red Shoe, The (1985)*½ Tom Hanks, Lori Singer, Dabney Coleman, Jim Belushi, Carrie Fisher, Charles Durning. This particularly unfunny American distillation of the French comedy, *The Tall Blond Man with One Black Shoe*, has Hanks as a violinist who gets caught up in the CIA's cloak-and-dagger games. (Dir: Stan Dragoti, 92 mins.)†

Man with Three Coffins, A (South Korea, 1987)***½ Kim Myung-gon, Yang Soon-suk, Lee Bo-hee, Choi Jin-hee. Complex, engrossing film about widower taking his wife's ashes to be scattered

668

in her native village. He encounters a variety of characters on the way, including a nurse who later becomes possessed by demons. Surreal work touches on traditional cultural and political themes important to Korean audiences, especially self-identity, relations with North Korea, family loss, and ghostly specters. Starkly shot primarily in monochromatic sepia. (Dir: Lee Chang-ho, 105 mins.)

Man Without a Country (MTV 1973)*** Cliff Robertson, Robert Ryan. Nice adaptation of the classic story about Philip Nolan, the misguided patriot who sided with Aaron Burr in his plan to join Texas and Mexico to the United States. (Dir: Delbert Mann, 78 mins.)

Man Without a Star (1955)*** Kirk Douglas, Jeanne Crain, Claire Trevor. Two-fisted western with Douglas taking center stage and keeping it. He plays a lovable character who uses his fists and guns only when his charm fails to do the job. (Dir: King Vidor, 89 mins.)†

Man with the Golden Arm, The (1955)*** Frank Sinatra, Eleanor Parker, Kim Novak, Arnold Stang, Darren McGavin. Nelson Algren's novel of heroin addiction receives director Otto Preminger's usual considered treatment in this once-controversial, still potent film. (119 mins.)†

Man with the Golden Gun, The (Great Britain, 1974)**½ Roger Moore, Christopher Lee, Britt Ekland, Hervé Villechaize. 007 has gone slightly stale. Bond is chasing after a solar energy capsule confiscated by a globe-hopping hit man, played with authority and villainy by Lee. (125 mins.)†

Man with the Green Carnation, The—See: **Trials of Oscar Wilde, The**

Man with the Gun (1955)**½ Robert Mitchum, Jan Sterling, Henry Hull. Absorbing but somewhat ponderous western drama. (Dir: Richard Wilson, 83 mins.)

Man with Two Brains, The (1983)*** Steve Martin, Kathleen Turner, David Warner, Paul Benedict, George Furth, Merv Griffin. Filled with clever sight gags and the silliest dialogue this side of the Three Stooges, the film spoofs mad-scientist pics, but that premise is really just a jumping-off point for Martin to strut his stuff as a brain surgeon who's cheating on his sultry but irredeemably evil wife with a beautiful brain in a jar. The construction's rickety, but the cast is in rare form; the laugh quotient is high. Sissy Spacek supplied the voice of the beloved brain. (Dir: Carl Reiner, 93 mins.)†

Man, Woman and Child (1983)**½ Blythe Danner, Martin Sheen, Sebastian Dungan, Arlene McIntire, Craig Nelson. Superb performances from Sheen and Danner highlight this domestic drama about a family circle in crisis. They portray well-to-do Californians whose marriage is jeopardized when the husband's child from a youthful fling unexpectedly arrives. (Dir: Dick Richards, 99 mins.)†

Many Happy Returns (1934)**½ George Burns, Gracie Allen, Joan Marsh, Franklin Pangborn, George Barbier, William Demarest, Ray Milland, Larry Adler, Guy Lombardo. Funny Burns and Allen comedy has a wisp of plot concerning a department store, but is mainly a vehicle for their vaudeville routines and various musical numbers; most enjoyable. (Dir: Norman McLeod, 60 mins.)†

Many Happy Returns (MTV 1986)** George Segal, Ron Liebman, Helen Shaver, Linda Sorenson. Every taxpayer's nightmare—being audited by the IRS—forms the nucleus of this mild comedy, starring George Segal as an average American barely handling his middle-class struggle, when an unexpected tax investigation knocks him for a loop. (Dir: Steven H. Stern, 104 mins.)

Many Rivers to Cross (1955)*** Robert Taylor, Eleanor Parker, James Arness. Frontier girl goes to extreme lengths to land a marriage-shy adventurer. Good fun. (Dir: Roy Rowland, 92 mins.)

Maracaibo (1958)**½ Cornel Wilde, Jean Wallace, Abbe Lane, Michael Landon. Top fire fighter discovers an old flame while attempting to put out an oil-well blaze. Mildly entertaining melodrama. (Dir: Cornel Wilde, 88 mins.)

Mara Maru (1952)** Errol Flynn, Ruth Roman. He-man adventurer Flynn plays both sides against the middle in this rather dull story of sunken treasures. (Dir: Gordon Douglas, 98 mins.)

Marathon (MTV 1980)**½ Bob Newhart, Herb Edelman, Dick Gautier, Anita Gillette, Leigh Taylor-Young. While on a six-mile run in California, middle-aged, married Newhart falls for a pretty jogger (Taylor-Young) and ends up in the New York Marathon just to be with her. (Dir: Jackie Cooper, 104 mins.)†

Marathon Man (1976)*** Dustin Hoffman, Laurence Olivier, Marthe Keller, Roy Scheider. Exciting thriller about double agents and elderly Nazis, but it's too heavily plotted and suffers from gratuitous violence. Hoffman is customarily splendid, and it's always good to glimpse the genius of Olivier, but his Nazi role is really beneath him. (Dir: John Schlesinger, 120 mins.)†

Marat/Sade (Great Britain, 1967)***½ Patrick Magee, Ian Richardson, Glenda Jackson, Clifford Rose. This radical, terrifying play not only debuted Jackson, but also stars Magee as the sadistic marquis who organizes the inmates of an asylum against his one intellectual rival. Violent, profane, and exciting. (Dir: Peter Brook, 115 mins.)

Marcelino—See: Miracle of Marcelino, The

March of the Wooden Soldiers (1934)*** Oliver Hardy, Stan Laurel, Charlotte Henry. Laurel and Hardy are easy to take in this version of Victor Herbert's *Babes in Toyland*. The production values could be better, but this is more melodic and funnier than the rather mechanical Disney version made in the sixties. (Dirs: Gus Meins, Charles R. Rogers, 73 mins.)†

March or Die (1977)*½ Gene Hackman, Candice Bergen, Terence Hill, Max von Sydow, Catherine Deneuve. Watch and Sleep! Old movie traditions die under the half-baked desert sun here as the loyal Legionnaires fend off attack by blood-thirsty, ubiquitous Arabs. (Dir: Dick Richards, 104 mins.)†

Marciano (MTV 1979)**½ Tony Lo Bianco, Belinda Montgomery, Vincent Gardenia. The story of Rocky Marciano's rise from obscurity to heavyweight champion of the world is reminiscent of all those fight movies of the '40s and the '50s complete with wavy close-ups signaling flashbacks. (Dir: Bernard L. Kowalski, 104 mins.)†

Marco Polo (France-Italy, 1962)** Rory Calhoun, Yoko Tani. Tongue-in-cheek costume adventure. Nephew of the great Khan is rebelling against uncle's wicked prime minister—along comes Marco Polo to help him out. (Dirs: Hugo Fregonese, Piero Pierotti, 90 mins.)

Marco, The Magnificent (1966)* Horst Buchholz, Anthony Quinn, Omar Sharif, Orson Welles. Despite a top-notch cast, this epic tale depicting the voyage of young Marco Polo (Buchholz) from Italy to China, is a dismal flop. (Dirs: Denys De La Patelliere, Noel Howard, 100 mins.)

Marcus-Nelson Murders, The (MTV 1973)***½ Telly Savalas, Marjoe Gortner, José Ferrer, Gene Woodbury. Brooklyn detectives coerce a young black man into confessing to the grisly murder of two New York girls. Savalas's detective is the hero, blowing the whistle on fellow cops as he funnels information to the skilled defense attorney. Authentic New York locations and good performances by the cast, particularly Woodbury as the railroaded suspect, give this controversial material a sharp edge. Pilot for TV's "Kojak." (Dir: Joseph Sargent, 148 mins.)

Marcus Welby M.D.: A Holiday Affair (MTV 1988)** Robert Young, Alexis Smith, Craig Stevens. The lovable M.D. fails to recapture his former magic in this TV movie that finds him, retired and a widower, finding romance with widow Smith while on vacation in Paris. (Dir: Steven Gethers, 96 mins.)

Mardi Gras (1958)**½ Pat Boone, Christine Carere, Gary Crosby, Sheree North, Tommy Sands. Pure escapist fare, Boone and company sing, dance, march, and act their way through the Mardi Gras festival in New Orleans. (Dir: Edmund Goulding, 107 mins.)

Margie (1946)***½ Jeanne Crain, Alan Young, Esther Dale, Conrad Janis, Lynn Bari. One of the few period musicals that sustains its charm without compromising its artistry. Crain plays a pretty but painfully shy adolescent in the late '20s in this screenplay based on Ruth McKinney's *My Sister Eileen*. Henry King's direction is at its best. (94 mins.)

Margin for Error (1943)**½ Joan Bennett, Milton Berle, Otto Preminger. Entertaining but dated comedy-drama about intrigues in the New York office of the German consul before the war. (Dir: Otto Preminger, 74 mins.)

Maria (1987)***½ Memories of, and performances by, Callas highlight excellent documentary about the grand opera singer. Callas is fondly remembered in interviews by friends and co-workers in a film that doesn't gloss over her unhappy private life. English subtitles are used for many arias she sings throughout this well-made biography. (Dir: Tony Palmer, 90 mins.)†

Maria Chapdelaine—See: **Naked Heart, The**

Marianne (1929)*** Marion Davies, Lawrence Gray, Cliff Edwards, George Baxter, Benny Rubin. Delightful musical comedy vehicle for Davies, who is perfectly convincing as a bewitching French girl courted by doughboys during WWI; plenty of songs, dances, and imitations by the star. Engaging fluff. (Dir: Robert Z. Leonard, 112 mins.)

Marianne and Juliane (West Germany, 1982)***½ Jutta Lampe, Barbara Sukowa, Rudiger Vogler. A powerful involving story of relationships and politics in West Germany (circa 1982). Based on the personalities and life histories of the real-life Ensslin sisters: Gudrun, imprisoned as a terrorist, and Christiane, an editor for a feminist magazine. (Dir: Margarethe von Trotta, 106 mins.)

Maria's Lovers (1984)** Nastassia Kinski, John Savage, Robert Mitchum, Bud Cort, Vincent Spano, Keith Carradine. A star turn for Kinski as a WWII woman whose soldier boy returns to find she's no longer the simple girl he left behind. (Dir: Andre Konchalovsky, 103 mins.)†

Marie (1985)**½ Sissy Spacek, Jeff Daniels, Morgan Freeman. An earnest, unembroidered biopic based on the Peter Maas book about Marie Ragghianti, a woman whose social conscience drove her to crusade against government corruption in Tennessee. Spacek's strong acting sustains the film, even in the second half, most of which is confined to a courtroom. (Dir: Roger Donaldson, 111 mins.)†

Marie Antoinette (1937)*** Norma Shearer, Tyrone Power, Robert Morley, John Barrymore. Lavish, well-acted spectacle about the woman who said "Let them eat cake" is visually resplendent; however, the narrative line is choppy. (Dir: W. S. Van Dyke, 170 mins.)†

Marilyn (1963)**½ Marilyn Monroe. A movie-magazine-type review of Monroe's life and career narrated by Rock Hudson. (Edited by Pepe Torres, 83 mins.)†

Marilyn: The Untold Story (MTV 1980)*** Catherine Hicks, Jason Miller, Frank Converse, Viveca Lindfors. Hicks' brilliant performance elevates this biopic about Marilyn Monroe. Based on the Norman Mailer biography. (Dirs: John Flynn, Jack Arnold, Lawrence Schiller, 156 mins.)†

Marine Raiders (1944)**½ Pat O'Brien, Robert Ryan, Frank McHugh, Ruth Hussey, Barton MacLane. Burly wartime adventure, with a routine story of marines in basic training, convincingly acted. (Dir: Harold D. Schuster, 91 mins.)

Marines Fly High, The (1940)*** Richard Dix, Chester Morris, Lucille Ball. Marines foil a revolt in Central America. Fast-moving action melodrama. (Dirs: George Nicholls, Jr., Ben Stoloff, 60 mins.)

Marion Rose White (MTV 1982)**½ Nancy Cartwright, Charles Aidman, Ruth Silveira. The true story of a youngster committed to a California institution for the feeble-minded in the '30s. Has all the ingredients for a nightmare drama. (Dir: Robert Day, 104 mins.)

Marius (France, 1931)**** Raimu, Pierre Fresnay, Charpin, Orane Demazis. Marcel Pagnol's great trilogy opens by introducing us to Marius (a lean and sexy Fresnay), who dreams of going to sea; his love, Fanny (Demazis), who understands his dream; Marius's father, César (Raimu), who runs a Marseilles waterfront bar; and César's wealthy friend Panisse (Charpin). (Dir: Alexander Korda, 120 mins.)†

Marjoe (1972)*** A revealing cinema verité-style documentary about Marjoe Gortner, a charismatic former child prodigy on the evangelist revival circuit. Conceived and directed by Sarah Kernochan and Howard Smith. (92 mins.)†

Marjorie Morningstar (1958)**½ Natalie Wood, Gene Kelly, Everett Sloane, Claire Trevor, Ed Wynn, Carolyn Jones. Glossy soap opera. Wood plays a suburban Jewish girl out to realize her career ambitions in the Big Apple, only to end up as a happy housewife. (Dir: Irving Rapper, 123 mins.)

Mark, The (Great Britain, 1961)***½ Stuart Whitman, Rod Steiger, Maria Schell. One of the finest psychological dramas ever filmed, played with extraordinary distinction and excitement. It combines an honest awareness of the uses of psychiatric therapy as well as its limitations, as it follows the path of a highly disturbed parolee into the threatening world of reality. (Dir: Guy Green, 127 mins.)

Marked for Death (1990)* Steven Seagal, Joanna Pacula, Keith David, Basil Wallace. Substandard cop-versus-drug baron fare finds ex-DEA agent returning to his former neighborhood. Dumb and bloody. (Dir: Dwight H. Little, 98 mins.)†

Marked for Murder (1990)** Wings Hauser, Renée Estevez, James Mitchum, Ross Hagen, Ken Abraham. Villainous manager of a television station sends two innocent young aides to retrieve an incriminating videotape; they don't know that the federal government wants the tape as well. Estevez's father, Martin Sheen, has a cameo in this mediocre thriller. (Dir: Rick Sloane, 93 mins.)†

Marked Woman (1937)***½ Bette Davis, Humphrey Bogart, Jane Bryan, Lola Lane. Even after changing the call girls to dance hostesses, this film is a surprisingly cynical crime-drama inspired by some of Lucky Luciano's less savory business practices. When streetwise Bette's guileless younger sister follows in her high-heel steps and winds up dead, Davis starts spilling the beans on the underworld, braving disfigurement and death threats. (Dir: Lloyd Bacon, 99 mins.)

Mark, I Love You (MTV 1980)**½ James Whitmore, Kevin Dobson. Widower father wants his ten-year-old son back as he begins a second marriage, but the parents of his first wife won't let go of their grandson. (Dir: Gunnar Hellstrom, 104 mins.)

Mark of Cain, The (1984)**½ Robin Ward, Wendy Crewson, Cynthia Keneluk, Antony Parr, August Schellenberg. An often chilling fright-night surprise. Somewhat reminiscent of *Sisters*, this screenplay about twins (one of whom is a psychopath fond of crucifixes) plays with the audience; we're meant to wonder which is the insane one, are they both crazy, have they changed places, etc. (Dir: Bruce Pittman, 90 mins.)†

Mark of the Devil (Great Britain-West Germany, 1970)*½ Herbert Lom, Udo Kier, Reggie Nalder. Infamous in the early seventies for advertising daring audiences to see it, this horror movie about an

eighteenth-century witch-hunter is more sadistic than gory, and much tamer than the eighties gore we've all become used to. (Dir: Michael Armstrong, 90 mins.)†

Mark of the Devil Part 2 (West Germany, 1972)* Jean-Pierre Zola, Erica Blanc, Anton Diffring, Reginald Nalder. Witchhunters Diffring and Nalder use their positions to murder a nobleman and accuse his wife of witchery in order to gain their family fortune. Depressing and nauseating. (Dir: Adrian Hoven, 88 mins.)†

Mark of the Gorilla (1950)** Johnny Weissmuller, Trudy Marshall. It's Halloween time in the jungle, as gold thieves get dressed up as gorillas and nab a jungle princess before Jungle Jim can unmask them. (Dir: William Berke, 68 mins.)

Mark of the Hawk (Great Britain, 1958)** Sidney Poitier, Eartha Kitt, John McIntire. Well-intentioned but rambling, wordy topical drama of a young African politician who is swayed by his terrorist brother, but adheres to nonviolence. (Dir: Michael Audley, 83 mins.)

Mark of the Renegade (1951)**½ Ricardo Montalban, Cyd Charisse, Gilbert Roland. Colorful adventure in Southern California during the middle 19th century. Montalban cuts a fine figure as a Spanish renegade and Charisse is ravishing as a Spanish noblewoman. (Dir: Hugo Fregonese, 81 mins.)

Mark of the Vampire (1935)*** Lionel Barrymore, Bela Lugosi, Lionel Atwill, Elizabeth Allan. Director Tod Browning remade his silent Lon Chaney classic and his talent for the macabre is in full flower here. The plot concerns some vampires who are bleeding a remote village dry and a group of vampire hunters who put several lives at stake. Atmospheric and chilling. (61 mins.)†

Mark of the Vampire (1957)** John Beal, Coleen Gray. Doctor takes pills given him by a dying scientist; they turn him into a vampire. Passable horror thriller. (Dir: Paul Landres, 74 mins.)

Mark of the Whistler (1944)**½ Richard Dix, Janis Carter, Paul Cavanagh. Attempted swindle of an unclaimed bank account. Keeps audiences guessing; see separate entry for the "Whistler" series. (Dir: William Castle, 61 mins.)

Mark of Zorro, The (1920)*** Douglas Fairbanks, Sr., Marguerite de la Motte, Noah Berry. One of Fairbanks's best, with enormous sets that give Doug lots of room to swash and buckle in. (Dir: Fred Niblo, 90 mins.)†

Mark of Zorro, The (1940)*** Tyrone Power, Basil Rathbone, J. Edward Bromberg, Linda Darnell, Gale Sondergaard, Eugene Pallette. This splashy version has enough good spirits and desire to please to carry it past defects. Power makes a good Zorro, probably the best yet. The caliber of swordplay is above average, particularly with the skillful Rathbone swashing. (Dir: Rouben Mamoulian, 93 mins.)

Mark of Zorro, The (MTV 1974)**½ Frank Langella, Gilbert Roland, Yvonne DeCarlo, Ricardo Montalban, Louise Sorel. Here's a zesty remake of the romantic adventures of Don Diego, a fop by day and the avenging bandit known as Zorro by night. (Dir: Don McDougall, 74 mins.)

Marla Hanson Story, The (MTV 1991)** Cheryl Pollak, Dale Midkiff, Kirk Baltz. Ugly and somewhat distasteful story about real-life New York model Marla Hanson who survives a razor attack from a rejected admirer's hired henchmen. Pollak portrays the struggling model who is befriended by an obsessed makeup man. A happy ending awaits, if you have the patience. (Dir: John Gray, 96 mins.)

Marlene (West Germany, 1984)**** Screen legend Marlene Dietrich is the subject of this unusual, funny, and finally moving documentary, directed by Maximilian Schell. Dietrich agreed to be interviewed but refused to appear on camera, and along with scenes from her greatest performances, we hear her modern-day assessments of them—cranky and arbitrary, but often very sharp. (96 mins.)†

Marlowe (1969)*** James Garner, Gayle Hunnicutt, Carroll O'Connor. Garner plays Philip Marlowe, Raymond Chandler's legendary detective, caught under a pile of corpses when he's hired by a mysterious blonde. Pace is fast and tough, but it's the bravura acting that carries the movie. (Dir: Paul Bogart, 95 mins.)†

Marnie (1964)***½ Tippi Hedren, Sean Connery, Diane Baker, Louise Latham, Martin Gable, Bruce Dern. Hedren gives a subtle, moving performance as a frigid kleptomaniac who is tortured by her past and then sexually blackmailed by an aggressive widower (Connery), who has fallen in love with her. (Dir: Alfred Hitchcock, 129 mins.)†

Marooned (1969)**½ Gregory Peck, Gene Hackman, James Franciscus, Lee Grant, Mariette Hartley. This adventure story about astronauts marooned in space misfires: personal stories about the astronauts' wives get in the way. (Dir: John Sturges, 134 mins.)†

Marquise of O, The (France-West Germany, 1975)*** Edith Clever, Bruno Ganz, Peter Luhr. An Italian noblewoman discovers she's pregnant but can't quite figure out how that happened. This morality tale is superbly photographed and costumed, subtly acted, and intellectually stimulating. (Dir: Eric Rohmer, 102 mins.)

Marriage Circle, The (1924)*** Florence Vidor, Marie Prevost, Monte Blue, Creighton Hale, Adolphe Menjou, Esther Ralston. Lighter-than-air Viennese farce from director Ernst Lubitsch, whose title tells it all; a professor's wife flirts with her best friend's husband, who in turn flirts with a handsome young doctor. Sophisticated comedy, played with great élan by the actors. Remade with equally charming results as *One Hour with You*.(90 mins.)†

Marriage-Go-Round, The (1960)** Susan Hayward, James Mason, Julie Newmar. Professor finds himself the target of a Swedish student who has selected him as her perfect mate—trouble is, he's married. Comedy tries for sophistication, becomes strained. (Dir: Walter Lang, 98 mins.)

Marriage Is Alive and Well (MTV 1980)*½ Joe Namath, Jack Albertson, Judd Hirsch. Namath plays a wedding photographer philosophizing on the current state of matrimony. Joe's married examples spend most of the time arguing in this lightweight nonsense. (Dir: Russ Mayberry, 104 mins.)†

Marriage Is a Private Affair (1944)** Lana Turner, James Craig, John Hodiak. Hasty war marriage, boy goes to fight, girl gets restless but all comes to a happy ending in this talky bore. (Dir: Robert Z. Leonard, 116 mins.)

Marriage Italian Style (Italy, 1964)***½ Sophia Loren, Marcello Mastroianni. Not as funny as *Divorce Italian Style*, but the stars carry off this comedy in fine style. About a luscious, happy prostitute and her efforts to trick a wealthy businessman into marriage, and then to hold on to him. Film again makes a meaningful comment on Italy's antiquated laws of marriage and divorce. Dubbed in English. (Dir: Vittorio De Sica, 102 mins.)

Marriage of a Young Stockbroker, The (1971)**½ Richard Benjamin, Joanna Shimkus, Elizabeth Ashley. Occasionally amusing but generally heavy-handed comedy about a young, married, bored stockbroker (Benjamin) who tries to improve his morale through voyeurism. (Dir: Lawrence Turman, 95 mins.)

Marriage of Maria Braun, The (West Germany, 1979)**** Hanna Schygulla, Klaus Lowitsch, Ivan Desny, Gottfried John. Director Rainer Werner Fassbinder's brilliant film about a woman's rise to wealth and power takes its metaphoric impetus from the history of postwar Germany. Schygulla plays a girl who loses her husband after one wedded night, and remains devoted to the principle of her marriage through an incredible sequence of events and lovers. (120 mins.)†

Marriage on the Rocks (1965)**½ Frank

Sinatra, Dean Martin, Deborah Kerr. Screwy comedy. Frank and Deborah get a Mexican divorce by mistake, and Miss Kerr marries Frank's best friend (Martin). (Dir: Jack Donohue, 109 mins.)

Marriage: Year One (MTV 1971)**½ Sally Field, Robert Pratt, William Windom. He's a hard-working, relatively square, dedicated student (Pratt), and she's a modern, involved, anti-Establishment type from a wealthy family (Field). Enough touching moments and fine performances to sustain interest. (Dir: William A. Graham, 104 mins.)

Married? (1925)*** Constance Bennett, Owen Moore, Gordon Standing, Antrim Short, Nick Thompson, Frank Walsh, Julia Hurley. Enjoyable silent melodrama; a New York flapper ends up in the Canadian north. Actually contains a thrilling scene of a powerful lumber mill saw ready to carve up panicky victim! Nasty villains, flaming youth, and ukeleles galore. (Dir: George Terwilliger, 75 mins.)

Married Bachelor (1941)**½ Robert Young, Ruth Hussey, Sam Levene. Frothy comedy about a married man who pretends to be a bachelor in order to perpetuate a career as a writer-lecturer. (Dir: Edward Buzzell, 87 mins.)

Married Man, A (Great Britain, MTV 1984)**½ Anthony Hopkins, Ciaran Madden, Lise Hilboldt. A marital-infidelity drama, British-style, with a side order of murder-mystery, that will pique the interest of those who stay with it. (Dir: Charles Jarrott, 200 mins.)†

Married to the Mob (1988)*** Michelle Pfeiffer, Matthew Modine, Dean Stockwell, Mercedes Ruehl. Screwball farce involving Mafia widow Pfeiffer, trying to start a new life with FBI agent Modine, working undercover to capture the mob boss (Stockwell) who killed her husband and now has eyes for her. (Dir: Jonathan Demme, 103 mins.)†

Married Woman, The (France, 1964)***½ Macha Meril, Bernard Noel, Rita Maiden, Roger Leenhardt, Philippe Leroy. Unusually straightforward narrative from director Jean Luc-Godard tells the story of a woman, greatly influenced by advertising and women's magazines, who divides her time between her husband and her lover. Richly designed film honors feminism and sexuality. (98 mins.)†

Marrying Kind, The (1952)*** Judy Holliday, Aldo Ray, Madge Kennedy. An excellent combination of comedy and pathos make this film of marital ups and downs most entertaining. (Dir: George Cukor, 93 mins.)

Marrying Man, The (1991)** Kim Basinger, Alec Baldwin, Robert Loggia, Armand Assante, Elisabeth Shue, Paul Reiser, Fisher Stevens. Poorly scripted, but nicely acted screwball comedy about a guy (Baldwin) who falls in love with a gangster's gal (Basinger) and through a series of sporadically funny incidents is compelled to marry her four times. Neil Simon's screenplay is weak regarding the main plot, but has some charming side jokes. The direction is woefully inadequate. (Dir: Jerry Rees, 105 mins.)†

Marry Me Again (1953)*** Robert Cummings, Marie Wilson. Girl tries to get her fella to marry her, even if she has more money than he. Enjoyable comedy has some clever gags. (Dir: Frank Tashlin, 73 mins.)

Marry Me! Marry Me! (France, 1968)*** Claude Berri, Elizabeth Wiener, Betsy Blair, Regine. Charming romantic comedy, produced, directed, and written by Claude Berri, who also stars as a Jewish encyclopedia salesman in Paris who's inconveniently fallen in love with a pregnant Belgian girl. (96 mins.)

Marseillaise, The (France, 1938)**½ Louis Jouvet, Pierre Renoir, Julien Carette, Lise Delamare, Gaston Modot, Leon Larive. This film, which was close to director Jean Renoir's heart, tells the story of enthusiastic Frenchmen who march from Marseilles to Paris to witness the overthrow of the monarchy in 1789. (135 mins.)

Mars Needs Women (1968)*½ Tommy Kirk, Yvonne Craig, Byron Lord. Kirk plays the martian "Dop" who has come to Earth to kidnap women for the men of his home planet. (Dir: Larry Buchanan, 80 mins.)†

Marsupials, The—See: **Howling III: The Marsupials**

Martha (West Germany, 1974)***½ Karl-Heinz Bohm, Margit Carstensen, Gisela Fackeldey, Adrian Hoven, Barbara Valentin. Vain rich woman marries a man she hardly knows and their relationship turns sadistic; he comes to dominate her completely after she is paralyzed in an accident. Visually stunning film, filled with cinematic references, brilliantly directed by Rainer Werner Fassbinder. (95 mins.)

Martians Go Home (1990)*½ Randy Quaid, Margaret Cohn, Anita Morris. Stupid comedy, with Martians invading Earth and causing everyone's secret thoughts to be revealed. Cast is wasted on poor script and lousy special effects. (Dir: David Odell, 87 mins.)†

Martin (1978)***½ John Amplas, Lincoln Maazel, Christine Forrest. Martin (Amplas) is a teenager who can make love only to women he has sedated, subsequently slashing their wrists to drink

673

their blood. The film alternates between the banal reality that Martin is a young psychotic, and the possibility that he is indeed a hundred-year-old heir to a family tradition of vampirism. (Dir: George Romero, 95 mins.)†

Martin's Day (Canada, 1985)** Richard Harris, Justin Henry, Lindsay Wagner, James Coburn, Karen Black, John Ireland. Mediocre tale about an escaped convict who kidnaps a little boy, with whom he subsequently develops a strong relationship. (Dir: Alan Gibson, 98 mins.)†

Marty (MTV 1953)*** Rod Steiger, Nancy Marchand. The original television version of Paddy Chayevsky's drama about a shy, lonely butcher yearning for companionship holds up well next to the more famous film version. (Dirs: Delbert Mann, Gordon Duff, 53 mins.)†

Marty (1955)***½ Ernest Borgnine, Betsy Blair, Joe Mantell, Jerry Paris. This remains a moving tale. Borgnine, who won the Best Actor Oscar, has never been better than as the homely butcher who forces himself to go out and socialize after he's consigned himself to a life of loneliness. It won other Oscars for Best Picture, Screenplay, and Director. (Dir: Delbert Mann, 91 mins.)†

Marva Collins Story, The (MTV 1981)**½ Cicely Tyson, Morgan Freeman, Rodrick Wimberly, Kelly Crosby. Tyson gives a fine performance as real-life Chicago schoolteacher Marva Collins who, disillusioned with the conventional public schools, quit and started one of her own. (Dir: Peter Levin, 104 mins.)

Marvin and Tige (1983)** John Cassavetes, Gibran Brown, Billy Dee Williams, Denise Nicholas Hill. Tearjerker about daddy-son bonding, as one of life's little people (white) gives his life meaning by adopting a suicidal youth (black) in this sincere plea for racial tolerance. (Dir: Eric Weston, 104 mins.)†

Mary and Joseph: A Story of Faith (MTV 1979)** Blanche Baker, Jeff East, Colleen Dewhurst. Speculative film depicting the courtship and trials of Mary and Joseph before the birth of Jesus. (Dir: Eric Till, 104 mins.)†

Mary Burns, Fugitive (1935)*** Sylvia Sidney, Melvyn Douglas, Alan Baxter, Pert Kelton, Wallace Ford, Brian Donlevy. A strong, emotional drama about a young woman's unjust imprisonment and struggle to redeem herself. (Dir: William K. Howard, 84 mins.)

Maryjane (1968)** Fabian, Diane McBain, Michael Margotta, Kevin Coughlin, Patty McCormack. The *Reefer Madness* of the sixties, just as silly but not as funny (give it a few decades, however). Caring teacher Fabian is framed on a drug rap, as he tries to save his pupils from that demon weed. (Dir: Maury Dexter, 104 mins.)

Mary Jane Harper Cried Last Night (MTV 1977)*** Kevin McCarthy, Susan Dey, Bernie Casey, Tricia O'Neil. First time a full-length TV movie dealt with the issue of battered children. Standout performance by O'Neil as a tough Brooklyn-born doctor with a history of child abuse in her own life. Casey also scores as the concerned social worker who won't quit even though it means treading on some high-society toes. (Dir: Allen Reisner, 104 mins.)

Maryland (1940)**½ Walter Brennan, Fay Bainter, John Payne. Film about a woman who sells all her horses after her husband is killed in an accident is a fairly good horse story. (Dir: Henry King, 92 mins.)

Mary, Mary (1963)**½ Debbie Reynolds, Barry Nelson, Michael Rennie, Diane McBain. A dashing movie star complicates matters when it appears that a book publisher still loves his ex-wife, and vice versa. Stagey film version of long-running Broadway stage success. (Dir: Mervyn LeRoy, 126 mins.)

Mary of Scotland (1936)*** Katharine Hepburn, Fredric March. Story of the Queen of Scots who defies Queen Elizabeth and is sentenced to death. Elaborately produced, excellently acted historical drama. (Dir: John Ford, 140 mins.)†

Mary Poppins (1964)**** Julie Andrews, Dick Van Dyke, David Tomlinson, Glynis Johns, Elsa Lanchester, Ed Wynn. Although a bit long, this justifiably famous Disney film combines brilliant animated sequences with a charming tale about a magical nanny who transforms the lives of the children in her care. The Sherman Brothers' songs are more hummable than usual, and the choreography is on a par with some of the best MGM musicals. Winner of five Oscars including Best Actress. (Dir: Robert Stevenson, 140 mins.)†

Mary, Queen of Scots (Great Britain, 1971)*** Vanessa Redgrave, Glenda Jackson, Nigel Davenport, Trevor Howard. A lame script with plodding direction and not much concern for historical accuracy diffuses the excitement generated by Vanessa Redgrave's performance. The picture really comes alive in the scenes between Jackson and Redgrave. (Dir: Charles Jarrott, 128 mins.)

Mary White (MTV 1977)***½ Kathleen Beller, Ed Flanders, Fionnula Flanagan. A lovely, human drama inspired by Pulitzer Prize-winning newspaper editor William Allen White's poignant editorial written after the accidental death of his beloved sixteen-year-old daughter, who had steadfastly sought her own identity, even to the point of annoying many. (Dir: Jud Taylor, 104 mins.)†

Mascara (U.S.-Belgium-Netherlands-France, 1987)** Charlotte Rampling, Michael Sarrazin, Derek De Lint, Jappe Claes. Police inspector Sarrazin's repressed incestuous feelings for his sister (Rampling) begin to erupt into violence. Well-directed film provides visual counterparts for the thin line between sanity and insanity, but the script is old news. (Dir: Patrick Coprnad, 98 mins.)†

Masculin-Feminin (France, 1966)**** Jean-Pierre Léaud, Chantal Goya, Marlene Jobert, Michel Debord, Catherine-Isabelle Duport. Masterpiece by Jean-Luc Godard about young man (Léaud) fresh from military service who becomes fascinated by, and involved in, left-wing politics, and enjoys relationship with two women (Jobert and Duport) with whom he lives. Wonderfully expressive study of generational conflicts contains now classic line referring to French youth as the "children of Marx and Coca Cola." (104 mins.)†

M*A*S*H (1970)*** Donald Sutherland, Elliott Gould, Sally Kellerman, Robert Duvall, Tom Skerritt, Jo Ann Pflug, René Auberjonois. The two real stars of this funny film about an American army medical unit during the Korean War are screenwriter Ring Lardner, Jr., who deservedly won an Academy Award, and director Robert Altman. (116 mins.)†

Mask, The (Canada, 1961)** Paul Stevens, Claudette Nevins. Mainly worth seeing for the scary 3-D footage (put together by film montage maven Slavko Vorkapich). Otherwise, it's an inconsequential thriller about an ancient mask that causes those who don it to hallucinate and kill people. AKA: **Eyes of Hell.** (Dir: Julian Roffman, 83 mins.)†

Mask (1985)**½ Cher, Eric Stoltz, Sam Elliott. An indefatigable teen suffers from a hideous disease that inflates his head to twice its normal size; he searches for love and attempts to wean his mom (Cher) off drugs. (Dir: Peter Bogdanovich, 120 mins.)†

Mask of Dijon, The (1946)**½ Erich von Stroheim, Jeanne Bates, Edward Van Sloan, Denise Vernac, Villiam Wright. Cheaply made thriller lifted to unexpected heights by von Stroheim, as a maddened hypnotist planning a murder; his performance is so compelling that this becomes quite potent drama. (Dir: Lew Landers, 73 mins.)

Mask of Dimitrios, The (1944)**½ Zachary Scott, Sydney Greenstreet, Faye Emerson, Peter Lorre. Occasionally exciting adaptation of the Eric Ambler novel about a Dutch mystery writer searching for a master crook whose exploits fascinate him. (Dir: Jean Negulesco, 95 mins.)

Mask of Fu Manchu, The (1932)** Boris Karloff, Myrna Loy, Lewis Stone. "Classic" version of the Sax Rohmer story is a stodgy, dull bit of work by director Charles Brabin (Charles Vidor, uncredited, is said to have done some of it). If your idea of fun is Karloff in long fingernails and Loy in oriental trousers, this may be for you. (72 mins.)

Mask of the Avenger (1951)** John Derek, Anthony Quinn, Jody Lawrance. Young Renato Dimorna (Derek) takes the guise of the Count of Monte Cristo to outwit the evil governor (Quinn) and win back his beloved Maria. (Dir: Phil Karlson, 83 mins.)

Masque of the Red Death, The (Great Britain, 1964)*** Vincent Price, Hazel Court, Patrick Magee, Jane Asher. Most critics agree that this is the best of the American International Poe series. A satanic prince, Prospero (Price), kidnaps a village lass. While deadly pestilence rages outside the castle, Price tempts the maiden to join him in his practice of the black arts. (Dir: Roger Corman, 86 mins.)†

Masque of the Red Death (1989)** Adrian Cox, Claire Hoak, Patrick Macnee, Tracy Reiner. Uninspired remake of Roger Corman's 1964 Poe adaptation, considered to be one of his better films. This time Corman only produced, providing tepid results. Evil Prince Prospero rules his castle with black magic while a deadly plague causes death throughout the land. (Dir: Larry Brand, 83 mins.)†

Masques (France, 1987)*** Philippe Noiret, Robin Renucci, Bernadette Lafont, Anne Brochet, Monique Chaumette. Writer searching for his missing sister visits country home of TV game show host who has interesting guest in his house as well as a few secrets of his own. Stylish, clever mystery. Noiret is wonderful in a scenery-chewing role as the host in this Hitchcockian tale of pretense and masks. (Dir: Claude Chabrol, 100 mins.)

Masquerade (Great Britain, 1965)*** Cliff Robertson, Jack Hawkins, Marisa Mell, Michel Piccoli. A delightful spy spoof. Robertson and Hawkins are a pair of Foreign Office emissaries assigned to kidnap a young prince of a country that possesses vast oil deposits. (Dir: Basil Dearden, 101 mins.)

Masquerade (1988)**½ Rob Lowe, Meg Tilly, Doug Savant, Kim Cattrall, John Glover. Tricky little thriller that unfortunately suffers from artificial dialogue and insipid casting. The plot, about an attractive young heiress and the young yachtsman (Lowe) with a questionable past who courts her, harks directly back to the *noir* melodramas of the forties, but the casting of pretty boy Lowe nearly sinks the whole enterprise. (Dir: Bob Swaim, 91 mins.)†

675

Masquerade in Mexico (1945)** Dorothy Lamour, Arturo de Cordova, Patric Knowles. Vapid semi-musical remake of the ineffable *Midnight*. It's gussied up with a Spanish motif, but somehow the ultra-sophisticated banter seems at odds with all these matadors and Mexicans. This script needs French champagne, not tequila. (Dir: Mitchell Leisen, 96 mins.)

Masquerader, The (1933)**½ Ronald Colman, Elissa Landi. Colman plays two parts in the derring-do tale based on a popular novel by Katherine Cecil Thurston. (Dir: Richard Wallace, 78 mins.)

Massacre (1934)***½ Richard Barthelmess, Ann Dvorak, Clarence Muse, Samuel S. Hinds, Dudley Digges, Arthur Wohl, Robert Barrat, Tully Marshall. Outstanding social drama documenting the plight of American Indians during the Depression. Barthelmess is superb as a conceited Sioux rodeo star, Joe Thunderhorse, who, returning to visit his reservation, encounters prejudice and oppression. Framed for a crime, he escapes to present his case to President Roosevelt's reformed Indian Affairs Bureau, in a cross-country chase reminiscent of *I Was a Prisoner on a Chain Gang*. Not just the best, but really the only attempt to deal with the realities of modern Indian life in the '30s. Muse, as Thunderhorse's valet and henchman; Digges, as a slimy, corrupt reservation agent; and Hohl, as a drug-addicted doctor, are also terrific. (Dir: Alan Crosland, 90 mins.)

Massacre (1956)** Dane Clark, James Craig. Just another western about the Indians massacring the good guys on our side by using guns sold to them by the bad guys. Set in Mexico. (Dir: Louis King, 76 mins.)

Massacre at Central High (1976)** Derrel Maury, Andrew Stevens, Kimberly Beck. An independent teen refuses to join a bullying clique of students, which then turns against him. One by one he stalks his tormentors and even makes plans to blow up his high school. This distaff version of *Carrie* is too disjointed, but deserves points for trying to humanize a trite revenge story. (Dir: Renee Daalder, 85 mins.)†

Massacre in Dinosaur Valley (Italy, 1985)* Michael Sopikiw, Susane Carvall, Milton Morris, Martha Anderson. There aren't any dinosaurs in this inert adventure about survivors of a plane crash in the jungle who endure the usual perils, only to fall into the hands of a mine owner who enslaves his laborers. (Dir: Michael E. Lemick, 82 mins.)†

Massacre in Rome (Italy, 1973)**½ Richard Burton, Marcello Mastroianni, Leo McKern, John Steiner, Anthony Steel. Nazi officer (Burton) orders hundreds of Italians to be killed to avenge the deaths

of thirty-three German soldiers. (Dir: George Pan Cosmatos, 103 mins.)†

Mass Appeal (1984)** Jack Lemmon, Zeljko Ivanek, Charles Durning, Louise Latham. Lemmon's acting schtick is on display in this shallow melodrama about an idealistic seminary student (Ivanek) who challenges the preaching methods of a beloved rector (Lemmon). Bill C. Davis has expanded his own Broadway play for the screen, but not enough to make it satisfying drama. (Dir: Glenn Jordan, 99 mins.)†

Mass Is Ended, The (Italy, 1988)** Nanni Moretti, Ferruccio De Ceresa, Enrica Maria Modugno. A young priest (Moretti) deals with a crushing load of problems, including extramarital affairs, unwed motherhood, and death, all within his own family. An uneven comedy-drama with a sweet performance by the star. (Dir: Nanni Moretti, 94 mins.)

Massive Retaliation (1984)* Tom Bower, Karlene Crockett, Peter Donat. Several families head for their combination summer home/survival camp (how chic!), but nuclear war is about to break out; will desperate outsiders crash their survival party? Will family turn against family? Not nuclear, but this is a bomb nonetheless. (Dir: Thomas A. Cohen, 90 mins.)†

Master and Margarita, The (Yugoslavia-Italy, 1972)*** Ugo Tognazzi, Mimsy Farmer, Alain Cluny, Danilo Stojkovic, Zlatko Madunic, Tasko Nacic. Bizarre allegory about playwright fighting censorship over his new play called *Pontius Pilate*. Various characters represent good and evil; one is thought to be the Devil himself. Farmer plays Margarita in one of her best performances. Film about the rights of artists and writers contains special effects and animation, in the best Yugoslavian tradition. (Dir: Aleksander Petrovic, 101 mins.)

Masterblaster (1987)*½ Jeff Moldovan, Donna Rosae, Joe Hess. "Masterblaster" is one of those real-life games in which contestants stalk each other armed with guns that fire paint pellets. But at the championship, someone starts using real bullets. Awfully tedious in the first half, not much better later. (Dir: Glenn R. Wilder, 94 mins.)

Master Gunfighter, The (1975)½ Tom Laughlin, Ron O'Neal. Laughlin stars as a self-styled avenger of poor Indians who are massacred by Mexicans. (Dir: Tom Laughlin, 121 mins.)

Master Minds (1949)** Bowery Boys, Gabriel Dell, Alan Napier. Sach is kidnapped by a mad scientist, who performs an experiment on him that transfers Sach's brain to the body of an ape-man. (Dir: Jean Yarbrough, 64 mins.)

Master of Ballantrae, The (Great Britain, 1953)**½ Errol Flynn, Yvonne

Furneaux. Another swashbuckling role for Flynn as he surmounts danger after danger. Plenty of adventure and romance. (Dir: William Keighley, 89 mins.)

Master of Ballantrae, The (MTV 1984)**½ Richard Thomas, Michael York, Brian Blessed, Finola Hughes, Ian Richardson. Robert Louis Stevenson's tale concerns the destructive hatred between two brothers: James (York), the unscrupulous rightful heir to Ballantrae in Scotland, is presumed dead after fighting for Bonnie Prince Charlie in 1745, and spends the rest of his evil days trying to reclaim his title and fortune from brother Henry (Thomas). (Dir: Douglas Hickox, 104 mins.)

Master of the World (1961)** Vincent Price, Charles Bronson, Mary Webster. Richard Matheson concocted this gloss on several Jules Verne novels, with Price as a megalomaniacal Captain Nemo of the air. (Dir: William Witney, 104 mins.)†

Masterpiece of Murder, A (MTV 1986)** Bob Hope, Don Ameche, Kevin McCarthy, Jayne Meadows, Yvonne DeCarlo, Frank Gorshin, Stella Stevens. Hope plays a private eye being flimflammed by an art collector. Ameche plays a cat burglar not overly fond of Bob's private investigator, and the two must team up to solve a murder. (Dir: Charles S. Dubin, 104 mins.)

Master Race, The (1944)*** George Coulouris, Nancy Gates, Lloyd Bridges, Osa Massen. German officer flees when the Nazi empire starts to collapse. Good war drama. (Dir: Herbert J. Biberman, 96 mins.)†

Masters of the Universe (1987)** Dolph Lundgren, Frank Langella, Meg Foster, Billy Barty. Derivative sci-fi based on the popular toy and cartoon show. He-Man battles Skeletor for cosmic supremacy. (Dir: Gary Goddard, 106 mins.)†

Masterson of Kansas (1954)** George Montgomery, Nancy Gates. Some of the famous names of the west show up in this western: Bat Masterson, Doc Holliday, Wyatt Earp. (Dir: William Castle, 73 mins.)

Matador (Spain, 1986)*** Assumpta Serna, Antonio Banderas, Nacho Martinez, Carmen Maura, Bibi Andersen. Straight-faced black comedy about an ex-bullfighter and a lady lawyer with something in common: each attains ultimate sexual pleasure by killing their partner at the moment of orgasm. Director Pedro Almodovar (*Law of Desire*) doesn't get all that might be expected from this premise, but his inherent outrageousness and a lot of peripheral oddities make it worthwhile for the adventurous. (107 mins.)†

Mata Hari (1931)***½ Greta Garbo, Ramon Navarro, Lionel Barrymore. Story of WWI's famed spy has become a legend and this film, although not produced for modern tastes, is something of a classic. (Dir: George Fitzmaurice, 100 mins.)

Mata Hari (1985)* Sylvia Kristel, Christopher Cazenove, Oliver Tobias, Gaye Brown, Gottfried Brown, William Fox. Golan-Globus garbage about the legendary WWI spy who seems to enjoy her sexual work so much, it's surprising she has time and energy left to pry out any secrets. (Dir: Curtis Harrington, 108 mins.)†

Match Factory Girl, The (Finland, 1989)*** Kati Outinen, Elina Salo, Esko Nikkari, Vesa Vierikko, Reijo Taipole. Sparse dialogue and slight action highlight this riveting minimalist drama about a girl who works in a match factory, lives in a house where no one talks, meets a man who gets her pregnant, and plots her revenge on the world. For acquired tastes. (Dir: Aki Kaurismaki, 71 mins.)

Match King, The (1932)**½ Warren William, Glenda Farrell, Hardie Albright, Lili Damita. Unusual social drama of an ambitious businessman cornering the world's match market! Acute script, based on fact, casts a candid eye at American business. (Dir: Howard Bretherton, 80 mins.)

Matchmaker, The (1958)*** Shirley Booth, Tony Perkins, Shirley MacLaine, Robert Morse, Paul Ford. Well-meaning matchmaker assumes the responsibility of finding a wife for a wealthy skinflint of a merchant. Generally amusing version of Thornton Wilder's stage play, perhaps too restricted in technique to be completely successful. Story later attained Broadway musical success as *Hello, Dolly!* (Dir: Joseph Anthony, 101 mins.)†

Matewan (1987)**** Chris Cooper, Will Oldham, Mary McDonnell, Bob Gunton, James Earl Jones. Splendid film chronicling a dramatic real-life event: a strike staged by the mine workers of West Virginia in 1920. Filmmaker John Sayles's approach to this incident is unflinching and involving; the cast is uniformly excellent, as is the peerless cinematography by Haskell Wexler. (132 mins.)†

Matilda (1978)½ Elliott Gould, Robert Mitchum, Harry Guardino, Clive Revill. Perfectly awful comedy based on the Paul Gallico book about a boxing kangaroo from Australia (a male named Matilda) who takes on a human challenger, Larry Pennell, for the heavyweight championship. (Dir: Daniel Mann, 103 mins.)†

Matinee (Mexico, 1982)*** Hector Bonilla, Manuel Ojeda, Rodolfo Chavez Martinez, Armando Martin Martinez. Clever adventure-fantasy about young boy whose life turns into a movie matinee after he runs away from mother and sister. Kid's escapades find him caught up in a world of crime and passion. (Dir: Jamie Humberto Hermosillo, 90 mins.)

Mating Game, The (1959)*** Tony Randall, Debbie Reynolds, Paul Douglas. Randall steals the picture with his zany performance as an IRS investigator who comes to check on an unpredictable businessman who hasn't paid his taxes and ends up falling in love with the man's pretty daughter (Miss Reynolds). (Dir: George Marshall, 96 mins.)

Mating of Millie, The (1948)**½ Glenn Ford, Evelyn Keyes. Career woman looks for a mate so she can legally adopt an orphan boy. Fairly amusing comedy-drama. (Dir: Henry Levin, 87 mins.)

Mating Season, The (1951)**½ Gene Tierney, John Lund, Thelma Ritter, Miriam Hopkins, Jan Sterling. Plain-spoken mother of a man who has married well poses as a servant without letting on her relationship to her social daughter-in-law. Amusing comedy hinges largely on Ritter's acid portrayal. (Dir: Mitchell Leisen, 101 mins.)

Mating Season, The (MTV 1980)** Lucie Arnaz, Laurence Luckinbill, Swoosie Kurtz, Diane Stilwell, Joel Brooks. One of those antic-romantic comedies with a whimsical musical score that punctuates the actors' every gesture. New York lawyer Arnez and drycleaning proprietor Luckinbill meet in a bird-watching camp. (Dir: John Llewelyn Moxey, 100 mins.)

Matrimaniac, The (1916)*** Douglas Fairbanks, Constance Talmadge. Sight gags galore as dashing young Fairbanks runs off with his girl just as she's about to marry someone else, and is pursued by her father and the detectives he has hired to keep them apart. Breathless chase movie, enlivened by Talmadge's charm and Fairbanks good-natured stunting. (Dir: Paul Powell, 75 mins.)†

Mattei Affair, The (Italy, 1973)***½ Gian Marie Volonte, Luigi Equarzina, Peter Baldwin, Renato Romano, Franco Graziosi. Impressive speculative film in which the director creates a docu-mystery out of factual material. The film probes the mysterious death of Enrico Mattei, the Italian industrialist who took Italy out of the economic dark ages after WWII. (Dir: Francesco Rosi, 118 mins.)

Matter of Degrees, A (1990)**½ Arye Gross, Tom Sizemore, Judith Hoag, Wendell Pierce, John Doe. Uncertain comedy-drama about apathetic college students of the '80s, centering on graduating senior Gross, who is disgusted with his peers' lack of commitment. (Dir: W. T. Morgan, 100 mins.)

Matter of Dignity, A (Greece, 1957)*** Ellie Lambetti, Georges Pappas, Eleni Zafiriou, Minas Christides, Athena Michaelidou, Michel Nikolinakas. To save her family's honor (and its fading bank account) a young woman agrees to marry a very wealthy man whom she loathes. (Dir: Michael Cacoyannis, 104 mins.)

Matter of Heart, A (1986)***½ Insightful documentary about Carl Jung, the eminent psychiatrist and founder of analytical psychology. Interviews with his friends, associates, and neighbors show almost reverential devotion to the man; film also delves into Jung's private life, including a stormy love affair and his conflicting relationship with Sigmund Freud. (Dir: Mark Whitney, 107 mins.)†

Matter of Humanities—See: Marcus Welby, M.D.

Matter of Innocence, A (Great Britain, 1967)** Hayley Mills, Trevor Howard, Shashi Kapoor. A sentimental, clumsily written tale in which Mills has an affair with a dashing Indian gigolo. Based on a Noël Coward short story. (Dir: Guy Green, 102 mins.)

Matter of Life and Death (MTV 1981)**½ Linda Lavin, Tyne Daly, Salome Jens, Gail Strickland. Lavin is wonderful as real-life crusading nurse Joy Ufema who helped set up new methods to treat the terminally ill. (Dir: Russ Mayberry, 104 mins.)†

Matter of Life and Death, A—See: Stairway to Heaven

Matter of Sex, A (MTV 1984)**½ Jean Stapleton, Dinah Manoff, Pamela Putch, Judge Reinhold. This fine true-life film details the courageous battle by eight women employees to earn a living wage from a smalltown Minnesota bank. Expanded from a documentary called *The Willmar 8*. (Dir: Lee Grant, 104 mins.)

Matter of Time, A (1976)½ Liza Minnelli, Ingrid Bergman, Charles Boyer. Dreadful, drastically edited cataclysm. Bergman plays a daft contessa whose memories of better times fill her maid (Liza) with the confidence she needs in order to become a "somebody." Liza's first and only teaming with her director father. (Dir: Vincente Minnelli, 99 mins.)†

Matter of Who, A (Great Britain, 1961)**½ Terry-Thomas, Alex Nicol, Sonja Ziemann, Honor Blackman. When a man becomes ill aboard a plane, a conscientious investigator for the World Health Organization looks into the matter and becomes involved in an oil swindle plot. Curious mixture of comedy and suspenseful drama. (Dir: Don Chaffey, 90 mins.)†

Matter of Wife...and Death, A (MTV 1975)** Rod Taylor, Dick Butkus, Anne Archer, Joe Santos. A remake of *Shamus*, starring Taylor as the rough-and-tumble private eye. (Dir: Marvin Chomsky, 78 mins.)

Matters of the Heart (MCTV 1990)** Jane Seymour, Chris Gartin, James Stacy, Nan Martin. Average love story benefits from Seymour's shining performance. She portrays a terminally ill, alcoholic, world-famous pianist who reluctantly gets into a passionate affair with her 18-year-old prize student. Tearjerker romance is predictable but still manages to entertain. (Dir: Michael Rhodes, 96 mins.)

Maurice (1987)***½ James Wilby, Rupert Graves, Denholm Elliott. Lyrical rendering of E. M. Forster's posthumously published novel. Maurice nurses a crush on a handsome schoolmate who eventually decides to stay in the closet, then finds fulfillment in the arms of a gamekeeper unafraid of his socially unpopular feelings. Sensitively acted, quality filmmaking. (Dir: James Ivory, 135 mins.)

Maurice Ravel—See: **Ravel**

Maurie (1973)** Bernie Casey, Bo Svenson, Janet MacLachlan, Stephanie Edwards. A tearjerker for men. Maurice Stokes, one of Cincinnati's finest basketball players, was mysteriously paralyzed soon after being named Rookie of the Year of the NBA. (Dir: Daniel Mann, 113 mins.)

Mausoleum (1981)** Bobbie Bresee, Marjoe Gortner, Norman Burton, Maurice Sherbanee, LaWanda Page. Family curse catches up with Bresee, who becomes periodically possessed by a murderous demon. A few good scare effects for the strong-stomached. (Dir: Michael Dugan, 96 mins.)†

Maverick Queen, The (1956)**½ Barbara Stanwyck, Barry Sullivan, Scott Brady. Bandit woman falls for a detective working undercover. (Dir: Joseph Kane, 92 mins.)†

Max and Helen (MTV 1990)**½ Treat Williams, Martin Landau, Alice Krige, Jodhi May, Jonathan Phillips. Williams is almost unbearably moving in this true story of a man who survived both Nazi and Stalinist prison camps, surviving both through love for his wife (Krige) and guilt for having escaped the Nazis without her. (Dir: Philip Saville, 94 mins.)†

Max Dugan Returns (1983)*** Marsha Mason, Matthew Broderick, Donald Sutherland, Jason Robards. A pleasant enough entertainment. A teacher who is coping with raising her teenage son when her long-lost father, Dugan, suddenly re-enters her life. (Dir: Herbert Ross, 92 mins.)†

Max Havelaar (The Netherlands-Java, 1976)***½ Peter Faber, Sacha Bulthuis, Elang Mohamad, Adenan Soesilaningrat. Lush, expansive film based on a classic Dutch novel. A naïve civil servant, sent to colonial Indonesia, tries to reform the corrupt local system only to be brutally thwarted by his own government and by mercantile interests. (Dir: Fons Rademakers, 165 mins.)

Maxie (1985)*½ Glenn Close, Mandy Patinkin, Ruth Gordon, Barnard Hughes, Valerie Curtin. A Clara Bowish flapper possesses the body of the retiring wife of Patinkin, who's both captivated and confounded by his newly transformed mate. (Dir: Paul Aaron, 98 mins.)†

Maximum Overdrive (1986)* Emilio Estevez, Pat Hingle, Laura Harrington, Yeardley Smith. King's self-described "moron movie" is precisely that; a brutal hodge-podge of attacks by killer machines. (Dir: Stephen King, 97 mins.)†

Max Mon Amour—See: **Max, My Love**

Max, My Love (France, 1986)***½ Anthony Higgins, Charlotte Rampling, Pierre Etaix, Christopher Hovik, Victoria Abril, Anne-Marie Besse. Brilliant black comedy about British diplomat in France who discovers his wife has a secret lover: a chimpanzee! Genuinely funny, decorous, sensitive, and sincere. AKA: **Max Mon Amour.** (Dir: Nagisa Oshima, 98 mins.)

Maya (1965)**½ Clint Walker, Jay North, Sajid Khan. Two boys team up to deliver a small, sacred white elephant to a jungle temple in India. (Dir: John Berry, 91 mins.)

Maybe Baby (MTV, 1988)**½ Jane Curtin, Dabney Coleman, Florence Stanley, Julia Duffy. Thirty-nine-year-old Curtin, a successful businesswoman, decides that she wants to have a baby before it's too late. Comedy-drama is better acted than written. (Dir: Tom Moore, 96 mins.)

Maybe I'll Come Home in the Spring (MTV 1971)*** Sally Field, Eleanor Parker, Lane Bradbury, Jackie Cooper. A lovely generation gap drama with superb performances. (Dir: Joseph Sargent, 73 mins.)

Mayday at 40,000 Feet (MTV 1976)** David Janssen, Lynda Day George, Christopher George, Don Meredith, Ray Milland. Patented, cliff-hanger set in a disabled airliner with a killer aboard. (Dir: Robert Butler, 106 mins.)

Mayerling (France, 1936)**** Charles Boyer, Danielle Darrieux, Jean Dax, Suzy Prim. Possibly the greatest film about doomed lovers. Based on fact, this shimmering romance tells of the Crown Prince Rudolf of Austria and how his love for a commoner ended in their double suicide. Exquisite performances. (Dir: Anatole Litvak, 91 mins.)†

Mayerling (Great Britain-France, 1968)* Omar Sharif, Catherine Deneuve, James Mason, Ava Gardner. Ponderous "romantic" reading of history, which ascribes the death of Austrian Crown Prince Rudolf and his mistress to a suicide pact on his hunting estate of Mayerling in 1889. (Dir: Terence Young, 140 mins.)

Mayflower Madam (MTV 1987)** Candice Bergen, Chris Sarandon, Chita Rivera, Victoria Loving, Caitlin Clarke. Notorious "deb gone wrong" Sydney Biddle Barrows (who served as associate producer) gets her story, and character, whitewashed in this highly watchable telepic. (Dir: Lou Antonio, 96 mins.)†

Mayflower: The Pilgrims' Adventure (MTV 1979)**½ Anthony Hopkins, Richard Crenna, Jenny Agutter. Story of the Pilgrims' sixty-day crossing of the Atlantic in 1620. Hopkins commands attention as the ship's captain and fetching Agutter provides the love interest as Priscilla Mullens. (Dir: George Schaefer, 97 mins.)

May Fools (France, 1990)**** Michel Piccoli, Miou-Miou, Michel Duchaussoy, Dominique Blanc, Harriet Walter. An insightful, poignant winner. An elderly country gent enjoys the peaceful life while all of France is embroiled in the student demonstrations of 1968. A serenely charming comedy with a magnificent musical score by Stephane Grappelli. (Dir: Louis Malle, 118 mins.)†

Mayor of 44th Street (1942)**½ George Murphy, Anne Shirley, Richard Barthelmess. Reformed gangster becomes an agent for name bands, has trouble with another not-so-reformed hood. Pleasant comedy-drama. (Dir: Alfred E. Green, 86 mins.)

Mayor of Hell, The (1933)*** James Cagney, Madge Evans, Allen Jenkins, Dudley Digges, Frankie Darro. A popular Cagney vehicle that got remade as *Crime School* and *Hell's Kitchen*. It's the durable tale of a crook whose rigged appointment to supervise a reform school makes him see the light and change the reformatory's poor conditions. (Dir: Archie Mayo, 80 mins.)

Maytime (1937)*** Jeanette MacDonald, Nelson Eddy, John Barrymore. Lovely romance, set in Paris, between (conveniently) a prima donna and a baritone will delight movie lovers. (Dir: Robert Z. Leonard, 140 mins.)

May Wine (France-U.S., 1990)**½ Joanna Cassidy, Lara Flynn Boyle, Guy Marchand, Paul Freeman. Breezy romantic comedy about an American mother and daughter vacationing in Paris who both become infatuated with a French doctor. The always likable Ms. Cassidy and fine location shooting enhance this pleasant outing. (Dir: Carol Wiseman, 85 mins.)†

Maze, The (1953)*** Richard Carlson, Veronica Hurst. Originally produced as a 3-D feature, this horror film has more than its share of visual gimmicks. The plot concerns a house where a mysterious mutation (an outsized frog) dominates the inhabitants. (Dir: William Cameron Menzies, 81 mins.)

Mc—See also: Mac

McCabe & Mrs. Miller (1971)**** Warren Beatty, Julie Christie, Shelley Duvall, Keith Carradine. A stunning yarn about

life, whores, and heroism—or the lack of it—in the bleak Northwest around '02. Beatty is affecting as a small-time gambler on the make who amuses himself, and sometimes the townspeople, by pretending that he's a former gunslinging outlaw, while setting up the town's first bordello in what used to be the Presbyterian Church. (Dir: Robert Altman, 107 mins.)†

McCloud: Who Killed Miss U.S.A.? (MTV 1970)** Dennis Weaver, Craig Stevens, Diana Muldaur. Pilot for the TV series. Weaver plays the title role of a New Mexico deputy marshal who finds himself in New York City on a murder case. (Dir: Richard Colla, 99 mins.)

McConnell Story, The (1955)**½ Alan Ladd, June Allyson, James Whitmore. The romanticized story of real-life jet ace McConnell, acted as if he had lockjaw by Ladd. (Dir: Gordon Douglas, 107 mins.)

McCullochs, The (1975)** Forrest Tucker, Julie Adams, Janice Heiden, Don Grady, William Demarest. A tough-as-nails patriarch copes with rebellion on the home front, when he tries to fit his sons into his own macho image. AKA: **The Wild McCullochs.** (Dir: Max Baer, 93 mins.)

McGuffin, The (Great Britain, 1985)* Charles Dance, Ritza Brown, Brian Glover, Francis Matthews, Phyllis Logan, Jerry Stiller. Hopelessly contrived thriller involving murder, blackmail, political intrigue, Italian film festivals, and bull terriers. Numerous references to Hitchcock classics will only make viewers long for the originals. (Dir: Colin Bucksey, 95 mins.)†

McHale's Navy (1964)** Ernest Borgnine, Tim Conway, Joe Flynn. Feature version of a once-popular TV series, this has the nutty PT crew involved in a horse race and some big betting. (Dir: Edward J. Montagne, 93 mins.)

McHale's Navy Joins the Air Force (1965)** Joe Flynn, Tim Conway. TV series expanded to feature form again, this time without Borgnine. Conway receives most of the attention, as he masquerades as an Air Force looney. (Dir: Edward J. Montagne, 90 mins.)

McKenzie Break, The (Great Britain, 1970)***½ Brian Keith, Helmut Griem. Authentic, vivid WWII drama. Keith gives a tremendous performance as an Irish intelligence agent put in charge of a British prison in Scotland to prevent an escape by captured Germans. (Dir: Lamont Johnson, 108 mins.)

McLintock! (1963)**½ John Wayne, Maureen O'Hara, Patrick Wayne, Chill Wills, Stefanie Powers, Bruce Cabot. It's primarily a comedy, amply supplied with slapstick. Wayne is a cattleman who literally pulls no punches in trying to win his wife back. (Dir: Andrew McLaglen, 127 mins.)

McNaughton's Daughter (MTV 1976)** Susan Clark, Vera Miles, Ralph Bellamy. Series pilot. Clark is a deputy district attorney assigned to prosecute a saintly missionary (Miles) accused of murder. (Dir: Jerry London, 98 mins.)

McQ (1974)** John Wayne, Eddie Albert, Diana Muldaur. He quits the force when his buddy is killed in order to ride the vengeance trail, by car this time. (Dir: John Sturges, 111 mins.)†

McVicar (Great Britain, 1980)*** Roger Daltrey, Adam Faith, Cheryl Campbell, Brian Hall, Steven Berkoff, Ian Hendry. Intriguing tale about England's notorious criminal, John McVicar, and how he engineered his escape from prison. The film was written by the real-life McVicar, who adapted his own book about his criminal exploits and eventual rehabilitation. (Dir: Tom Clegg, 111 mins.)†

Meadow, The (Italy, 1979)*** Isabella Rossellini, Michele Placido, Ermanno Taviani, Severio Marconi, Giulio Brogi, Angela Goodwin. Rossellini is luminous as a young woman torn between the energy of a new romance and her loyalty to her old boyfriend. Film explores the lives of three young professionals as they seek to achieve some kind of fulfillment and avoid hurt and disappointment. (Dirs: Paolo and Vittorio Taviani, 120 mins.)

Meal, The—See: **Deadly Encounter**

Me and My Brother (1969)*** Joseph Chaikin, Julius Orlovsky, John Coe, Allen Ginsberg, Peter Orlovsky, Roscoe Lee Brown, Seth Allen, Christopher Walken, Gregory Corso. Bizarre collaboration of Beat Generation icons resulted in this drama about catatonic schizophrenic who gets involved with an obscure avant-garde acting company, with notions of illusion and reality falling by the wayside. Valuable both for its cast, and as an example of countercultural filmmaker Robert Frank's best work. Written by Frank and Sam Shepard. (95 mins.)

Me and My Gal (1932)*** Spencer Tracy, Joan Bennett, George Walsh. Improbable but engaging concoction teams burlesque and gangster genres, hard-nosed detective Tracy with fine-featured (but gum-chewing) cashier Bennett. A period piece, evocative and witty. (Dir: Raoul Walsh, 78 mins.)

Mean Dog Blues (1978)**½ George Kennedy, Gregg Henry, Kay Lenz, Scatman Crothers, Tina Louise, William Windom, Gregory Sierra. Gritty prison drama about a hitchhiker who gets railroaded on a murder rap. (Dir: Mel Stuart, 108 mins.)†

Me and the Colonel (Great Britain, 1958)***½ Danny Kaye, Curt Jurgens, Nicole Maurey. A delightful serious comedy about military capers involved in the safe escape of fleeing refugees. Kaye registers strongly in a change-of-pace role as a Polish Jew pitted against an anti-Semitic colonel during the final days of WWII. (Dir: Peter Glenville, 109 mins.)

Meanest Man in the World, The (1943)**½ Jack Benny, Priscilla Lane, Edmund Gwenn, Rochester (Eddie Anderson). Jack rises above his material and makes something of this little one-hour comedy about an unsuccessful soft-hearted lawyer who gets rich by becoming mean. (Dir: Sidney Lanfield, 57 mins.)

Meanest Men in the West (MTV 1962)** Charles Bronson, Lee Marvin, James Drury, Lee J. Cobb, Charles Grodin, Albert Salmi. Don't be fooled by the cast and credits: this isn't a movie at all, but two unrelated episodes of the TV series "The Virginian" edited together to look like a feature-length film. (Dirs: Samuel Fuller, Charles S. Dubin, 92 mins.)†

Mean Season, The (1985)**½ Kurt Russell, Mariel Hemingway, Richard Jordan, Richard Masur, Richard Bradford. An acceptable suspenser that could have done with fewer red-herring scare scenes. A newspaper reporter receives a phone call from a serial killer and becomes enmeshed in the maniac's murderous spree. (Dir: Philip Borsos, 106 mins.)†

Mean Streets (1973)***½ Robert De Niro, Harvey Keitel, David Proval, Amy Robinson, Richard Romanus. Excellent portrait of the small-time hoods in New York City's Little Italy and their special code of ethics. De Niro is wonderful as a hanger-on who is into a loan shark for a big sum, and tries to get his childhood friend Charlie, a lower-echelon mafioso, to intervene on his behalf. Director Martin Scorsese, who helped write the screenplay based on his own story, grew up in the neighborhood, and he reveals the brutality, competitiveness, and strong family ties of the neighborhood. (110 mins.)†

Meatballs (1979)*** Bill Murray, Kate Lynch, Chris Makepeace. Popular movie about the hijinks at a summer camp. As head counselor at a budget-minded camp, Murray tells jokes, pulls pranks, and befriends a lonely, depressed twelve-year-old (Makepeace) who ends up a hero a la *Rocky.* (Dir: Ivan Reitman, 92 mins.)†

Meatballs 2 (1984)* Archie Hahn, John Mengatti, Tammy Taylor, Paul Reubens, Richard Mulligan, John Larroquette. Fans of the first film won't gobble up this sequel about a street-wise punk who saves his summer camp by proving himself in the boxing ring. (Dir: Ken Wiederhorn, 95 mins.)†

Meatballs III (1987)½ Sally Kellerman, Patrick Dempsey, Al Waxman, Isabelle Mejias, Shannon Tweed. A slop-bucket comedy about a nerdish summer camper whose quest to get laid is aided by a deceased porn star (Kellerman) who's got to do a good deed before entering the great big grind house in the sky. (Dir: George Mendeluk, 94 mins.)†

Meateater, The (1978)½ Peter M. Spitzer, Arch Joboulian, Dianne Davis, Joe Marmo. A family tries to reopen an old movie palace, unaware that it's occupied by a killer with a Jean Harlow fetish. Avoid it unless you're compelled to see everything weird. (Dir: Derek Savage, 85 mins.)†

Mechanic, The (1972)*½ Charles Bronson, Jan-Michael Vincent, Keenan Wynn. Pretentious crime drama about a hired killer (mechanic) who uses complicated methods to annihilate his victims. (Dir: Michael Winner, 100 mins.)†

Medal for Benny, A (1945)***½ Dorothy Lamour, Arturo de Cordova, J. Carrol Naish. When news reaches a small California town that one of its sons has been killed in action, the town fathers see a chance for some publicity. Touching drama from a Steinbeck story. (Dir: Irving Pichel, 77 mins.)

Medea (Italy-West Germany-France, 1970)** Maria Callas, Laurent Tertzieff, Guiseppi Gentile, Massimo Girotti. Lifeless filmization of the tale of the legendary sorceress who kills through the power of love. Director Pier Paolo Pasolini lacks his usual flourishes. (110 mins.)†

Medical Story (MTV 1975)***½ José Ferrer, Beau Bridges, Carl Reiner. Strong, unusual drama about a hot-shot young doctor who discovers negligence, dishonesty, and cover-ups among the staff at a well-known hospital. Based on a real-life story; script by Abby Mann. (Dir: Gary Nelson, 116 mins.)

Medicine Man, The (1930)** Jack Benny, Betty Bronson, Eva Novak, George E. Stone. Odd little comedy-drama stars Benny as a carnival medicine-show barker rescuing downtrodden Bronson from an alcoholic father; interesting attempt, but none-too-well done. (Dir: Scott Pembroke, 66 mins.)†

Medium, The (1951)***½ Anna Maria Alberghetti, Marie Powers. Menotti's strange, brooding opera, well sung. For specialized tastes, but there is a haunting score and Miss Powers's electric portrayal of a medium-spiritualist. (Dir: Gian-Carlo Menotti, 87 mins.)†

Medium Cool (1969)***½ Robert Forster, Verna Bloom, Peter Bonerz, Marianna Hill, Sid McCoy. Bizarre and personal view of the life of a TV cameraman who becomes emotionally detached not only from the events he films, but also from people and situations in his personal life. Filmed during the 1968 riots in Chicago at the Democratic Convention, Wexler crosses the line between factual and fictional filming in a study of the relationship between photographers and the people and events that pass in front of their lenses. (Dir: Haskell Wexler, 111 mins.)†

Medusa Touch, The (Great Britain, 1978)** Richard Burton, Lee Remick, Lino Ventura. Burton uses eyes and voice to suggest telekinesis in a shaggy-dog horror film. Remick is his eminently reasonable psychiatrist, and Ventura costars, less charismatic in English. (Dir: Jack Gold, 110 mins.)†

Meet Boston Blackie (1941)*** Chester Morris, Rochelle Hudson, Richard Lane, Charles Wagenheim. Morris makes a rambunctious Blackie, in his debut in the series. With Lane as the police chief unshakably convinced that Blackie is up to no good, Wagenheim as the faithful sidekick, and Hudson as the love interest. (Dir: Robert Florey, 61 mins.)

Meet Danny Wilson (1952)**½ Frank Sinatra, Shelley Winters, Alex Nicol, Raymond Burr. Not a bad film but the story line about an entertainer and gangsters does get jumbled to say the least. (Dir: Joseph Pevney, 86 mins.)

Meet Dr. Christian (1939)**½ Jean Hersholt, Dorothy Lovett. The modest series about the wise doctor kicked off here. Dr. Christian tries to raise funds for a new hospital. (Dir: Bernard Vorhaus, 68 mins.)†

Meeting at Midnight (1944)** Sidney Toler, Mantan Moreland, Jacqueline de Wit. When number-one daughter attends a seance and a very real murder occurs, Charlie Chan tries to cut through the hocus-pocus to find the killer. (Dir: Phil Rosen, 67 mins.)†

Meetings With Remarkable Men (1979)**½ Dragan Maksimovic, Terence Stamp, Athol Fugard, Bruce Myers. Peter Brook directs this tale of G. I. Gurdjieff, an inspirational teacher—or a cultist charlatan—whose influence persists in spiritual covens today. (107 mins.)

Meet John Doe (1941)***½ Gary Cooper, Barbara Stanwyck, Walter Brennan, Edward Arnold, Spring Byington, James Gleason. Cooper plays a hobo who makes news by threatening to commit suicide to protest world conditions. Inspired by the newspapers, the public sets out to change his mind. The plot mechanism becomes impossible to resolve, so the ending is necessarily unsatisfying. (Dir: Frank Capra, 132 mins.)†

Meet Me After the Show (1951)** Betty Grable, Macdonald Carey, Rory Calhoun. Efforts of a producer to get his ex-wife, an amnesia case, back in his show. Grable's gams are its chief asset. (Dir: Richard Sale, 86 mins.)

Meet Me at the Fair (1953)*** Dan Dailey, Diana Lynn, Chet Allen. Charming film about a traveling medicine man who gets involved with a runaway orphan and the authorities. (Dir: Douglas Sirk, 87 mins.)

Meet Me in Las Vegas (1956)**½ Dan Dailey, Cyd Charisse, Agnes Moorehead. Wispy little story about a gambling rancher and the dancer who brings him luck doesn't mean a thing—the big news here is the terpsichore, including a "Frankie and Johnnie" ballet that's a knockout. (Dir: Roy Rowland, 112 mins.)

Meet Me in St. Louis (1944)**** Judy Garland, Tom Drake, Margaret O'Brien, Lucille Bremer, Mary Astor. The WWII years brought an outpouring of Americana from the Hollywood studios, but none surpassed this enthralling, sentimental musical about the family nine-too-thrilled to move to the big, bad city and miss out on the 1903 World's Fair right in their own backyard. The marvelous score includes "The Trolley Song," "The Boy Next Door," "Have Yourself a Merry Little Christmas," and "You and I" (in which Leon Ames's singing voice is dubbed by the film's producer, Arthur Freed). (Dir: Vincente Minnelli, 113 mins.)

Meet Mr. Lucifer (Great Britain, 1954)*** Stanley Holloway, Peggy Cummins, Kay Kendall. The devil introduces television into three homes to stir up trouble. Neat, amusing fantasy-comedy; some good laughs. (Dir: Anthony Pelissier, 83 mins.)

Meet Nero Wolfe (1936)**½ Edward Arnold, Lionel Stander, Victor Jory, Joan Perry. Rex Stout's popular detective is personified by Arnold, with Stander as his sidekick Archie. Good, intelligent classic mystery. (Dir: Herbert Biberman, 73 mins.)

Meet the Applegates (1991)**½ Ed Begley, Jr., Stockard Channing, Dabney Coleman, Bobby Jacoby, Cami Cooper. This ecological satire has a great idea: A group of bugs disguise themselves as a typical American family in order to infiltrate and blow up a nuclear power plant and make the world safe for insects. The comedy falters when put to the full-length film test, but it's clever, so take a chance. AKA: **The Applegates.** (Dir: Michael Lehmann, 90 mins.)†

Meet the People (1944)**½ Lucille Ball, Dick Powell, Virginia O'Brien, Bert Lahr, June Allyson. An attractive cast sparks this game but resolutely pedestrian musical. A former stage star tries her darnedest to prove she's just one of the proletariat. (Dir: Charles Riesner, 100 mins.)

Meet the Stewarts (1942)*** William Hold-

en, Frances Dee. Heiress marries a white-collar man, tries to get along on a budget. Pleasing comedy. (Dir: Alfred E. Green, 73 mins.)

Megaforce (1982)½ Barry Bostwick, Persis Khambatta, Edward Mulhare, George Furth, Michael Beck, Henry Silva. A megaturkey about a multinational "phantom" army fighting a group of beach-boy mercenaries for control of a tiny country. More like Megafarce. (Dir: Hal Needham, 99 mins.)†

Meher Baba: Avatar of the Age (1988)***½ Enchanting film portrait of Meher Baba, the extraordinary man who lived in India from 1894 until his death in 1969, and is considered by millions around the world to be the God-man of Avatar, who appears throughout recorded history as Zoroaster, Rama, Buddha, Mohammed, Christ, and Krishna. This mystical journey follows Meher Baba to isolated areas of India where he makes contact with advanced saints and souls in a state of illumination. (Dir: Irwin Luck, 78 mins.)

Mein Kampf (Sweden, 1960)***½ Grim documentation of the horrors of the Hitler regime. (Dirs: Erwin Leiser, Ingemar Ejve, Tore Sjoberg, 117 mins.)†

Melanie (Canada, 1982)**½ Glynnis O'Connor, Burton Cummings, Paul Sorvino, Don Johnson. Illiterate southern woman O'Connor travels to L.A. to try and regain custody of her son from her ex-husband. She and faded rock star Cummings help each other overcome their problems. Good performances make the forgettable script bearable. (Dir: Rex Bromfield, 109 mins.)†

Melba (Great Britain, 1953)*** Patrice Munsel, Robert Morley. Phony film biography of Nellie Melba is distinguished by Miss Munsel singing scores of arias. For opera fans only. (Dir: Lewis Milestone, 113 mins.)

Melinda (1972)** Vonetta McGee, Calvin Lockhart. Another violent, predictable black actioner. A disc jockey seeks revenge after his girlfriend gets iced. (Dir: Hugh Robertson, 109 mins.)

Melo (France, 1987)***½ Sabine Azema, Pierre Arditi, Andre Dussollier, Fanny Ardant. Director Alain Resnais's films have always utilized non-linear structures and narratives to explore his favorite theme, that of memory and its hold on the present. Here, he confronts that same theme in a film with a rigid, hyper-realistic structure. This story of a woman and her love for two men is adapted from a once-popular stage melodrama, and has been filmed on sets in long takes with a minimum of camera movement. The performances are all superb (Azema and Arditi won Césars,

Melody (Great Britain, 1972)*** Mark Lester, Jack Wild, Tracy Hyde. Appealing tale of an eleven-year-old boy who wants to marry a twelve-year-old girl. (Dir: Waris Hussein, 103 mins.)†

Melody Cruise (1933)*** Phil Harris, Charlie Ruggles, Helen Mack, Chick Chandler. Top-notch musical comedy noted for its ribald story line, which has Harris wooing Mack in unabashedly comic fashion. Ruggles is scene-stealingly hilarious. (Dir: Mark Sandrich, 76 mins.)†

Melody for Three (1941)*½ Jean Hersholt, Fay Wray, Walter Woolf King, Astrid Allwyn, Irene Ryan. Taking on the role of matchmaker, meddling medic Dr. Christian manages to reunite a renowned conductor with the woman he loved many years before. (Dir: Erle C. Kenton, 67 mins.)†

Melvin & Howard (1980)**** Paul LeMat, Jason Robards, Jr., Mary Steenburgen, Elizabeth Cheshire, Michael J. Pollard, Pamela Reed. Superb movie that views its blue-collar characters affectionately. Melvin Dummar, a hapless soul, gives eccentric Howard Hughes a lift to Las Vegas, and no one believes him when Hughes bequeaths him the bulk of his multi-million-dollar estate. Filled with telling details about the American dream of success, and enlivened with appealing characterizations. (Dir: Jonathan Demme, 95 mins.)†

Melvin Purvis, G-Man (MTV 1974)*** Dale Robertson, Harris Yulin, Margaret Blye. Cat-and-mouse game between the notorious Machine Gun Kelly and colorful G-man Melvin Purvis. (Dir: Dan Curtis, 74 mins.)†

Member of the Wedding, The (1953)***½ Julie Harris, Ethel Waters, Brandon de Wilde. Hit Broadway play by Carson McCullers brought to the screen with great performances by the trio of stars. The subject matter about a confused tomboy caught between childhood and adolescence is beautifully handled. (Dir: Fred Zinnemann, 91 mins.)†

Memed My Hawk (Great Britain-Yugoslavia, 1986)** Peter Ustinov, Herbert Lom, Simon Dutton. Drama about a gutsy young man who rebels against the feudal tyrant running his Turkish village with an iron hand, circa 1923. (Dir: Peter Ustinov, 104 mins.)†

Memorial Day (MTV 1983)*** Mike Farrell, Shelley Fabares, Keith Mitchell, Bonnie Bedelia, Robert Walden, Edward Herrmann. A lawyer encounters some Vietnam veteran pals, and the bad memories come flooding back. (Dir: Joseph Sargent, 104 mins.)

Memories Never Die (MTV 1982)**½ Lindsay Wagner, Gerald McRaney. A mother faces her children and husband after years in a mental clinic. (Dir: Sandor Stern, 104 mins.)

Memories of a Marriage (Denmark, 1990)*** Frits Helmuth, Ghita Norby, Henning Moritzen. Captivating Danish drama was an Oscar nominee for Best Foreign Film. Family and friends get together at a summer home of a long-married couple, where they recall memories of the relationship throughout different parts of their life. Earnest performances and a slice of real life make this a real winner. (Dir: Kaspar Rostrup, 90 mins.)

Memories of Helen (Brazil, 1970)*** Rosa Maria Pena, Arduino Colassanti, Aurea Campos, Humberto Mauro. A study of the thoughts and feelings of one woman as seen through journals, home movies, and the reminiscences of two friends. Helen is a true innocent, fascinated by romance but yearning to be liberated. A complex and impressive work. (Dir: David Neves, 81 mins.)

Memories of Me (1988)*** Billy Crystal, Alan King, JoBeth Williams. A surgeon decides to make peace with his father (King), a professional movie extra whom he hasn't seen in many years. (Dir: Henry Winkler, 105 mins.)†

Memories of Underdevelopment (Cuba, 1968)**** Sergio Corrieri, Daisy Granados, Eslinda Nunez. A remarkable film about Cuban life in 1961, not long after Castro had come to power. (Dir: Tomas Gutierrez Alea, 104 mins.)†

Memory of Eva Ryker, The (MTV 1980)**½ Natalie Wood, Ralph Bellamy, Robert Foxworth. A multimillionaire (Bellamy) starts to salvage a liner on which his beautiful wife perished, and the complicated plot unfolds. (Dir: Walter E. Grauman, 153 mins.)

Memory of Justice, The (West Germany-U.S., 1976)**** Director Marcel Ophuls's intense, demanding documentary starts with the Nuremberg trials of '46 and goes on to Algeria and Vietnam. (278 mins.)†

Memphis Belle (1990)*½ Matthew Modine, Eric Stoltz, D. B. Sweeney, Billy Zane, Sean Astin, John Lithgow, Harry Connick, Jr. A demographically perfect, apple-cheeked WWII bomber crew has survived twenty-four missions over Germany and can go home if they successfully complete the twenty-fifth. The *Memphis Belle* is their plane, clichés drop like bombs, and none of the acting is believable. It's a war movie for teenyboppers. Based on William Wyler's classic 1944 documentary of the same name. (Dir: Michael Caton-Jones, 107 mins.)†

Men (West Germany, 1985)*** Heiner Lauterbach, Uwe Ochsenknecht, Ulrike Kriener. An ad exec tries to win his wife back from her shaggy-haired lover by rooming with the younger man and finding out what makes him tick. (Dir: Doris Dörrie, 99 mins.)†

Men, The (1950)***½ Marlon Brando, Teresa Wright, Everett Sloane, Jack Webb. Paralyzed war vet tries to adjust. Brando's first film, and a superb one. Dramatic, persuasive, with fine work in every department. (Dir: Fred Zinnemann, 85 mins.)†

Menace, The (1932)*½ Bette Davis, H. B. Warner, Walter Byron. A creaky revenge melodrama. (Dir: Roy William Neill, 64 mins.)

Men Against the Sky (1940)**½ Richard Dix, Wendy Barrie, Edmund Lowe, Kent Taylor, Grant Withers. The lives of workers in an aircraft plant, lent interest by the skill and appeal of the players. (Dir: Leslie Goodwins, 75 mins.)

Menage (France, 1986)**** Gerard Depardieu, Michel Blanc, Miou-Miou. A comic free-for-all; an accomplished burglar adopts a starving couple and inveigles them into a world of housebreaking. (Dir: Bertrand Blier, 84 mins.)

Men & Women: Stories of Seduction (MCTV 1990)** James Woods, Melanie Griffith, Beau Bridges, Elizabeth McGovern, Molly Ringwald, Peter Weller. When you consider the roster of talent and star power that went into these three short films, they should have turned out much, much better. The stories from the works of Ernest Hemingway, Mary McCarthy, and Dorothy Parker have been adapted by Frederic Raphael, Joan Didion and John Gregory Dunne, and Valerie Curtin, and directed by Tony Richardson, Ken Russell, and the aforementioned Mr. Raphael. An ambitious effort that misses the mark. (Dirs: Frederic Raphael, Tony Richardson, Ken Russell, 96 mins.)†

Men Are Not Gods (Great Britain, 1937)** Miriam Hopkins, Gertrude Lawrence, Rex Harrison. A romantic triangle brings near-tragedy to three theatrical people. (Dir: Walter Reisch, 82 mins.)

Me, Natalie (1969)*** Patty Duke, James Farentino, Martin Balsam, Elsa Lanchester, Salome Jens, Nancy Marchand, Al Pacino (debut). A lovable ugly duckling tale. A sheltered plain Jane yearns to become a butterfly as she tries her wings out in Greenwich Village. (Dir: Fred Coe, 111 mins.)

Men at Work (1990)* Charlie Sheen, Emilio Estevez, Leslie Hope. Laughless comedy about two southern California garbage men (Sheen and real-life brother Estevez, the film's writer-director) who dream of opening a surfboard shop, but become involved in an incredibly dumb plot about a murdered councilman and illegal chemical dumping. Phew! (Dir: Emilio Estevez, 98 mins.)†

Men Don't Leave (1990)***½ Jessica Lange, Arliss Howard, Joan Cusack, Kathy Bates, Chris O'Connell, Charlie Korsmo. Gentle comedy-drama about recently widowed Lange; she gets a job in a gourmet food shop, enjoys the romantic company of an undemanding avant-garde musician, and goes into a deep depressive funk. (Dir: Paul Brickman, 115 mins.)†

Men In Her Diary (1945)**½ Peggy Ryan, Jon Hall, Louis Albritton. Secretary keeps a diary of imaginary romances; amusing comedy. (Dir: Charles Barton, 73 mins.)

Men In Her Life, The (1941)**½ Loretta Young, Conrad Veidt, Dean Jagger. Intriguing romance of a ballerina thinking back over her love life on the eve of her marriage; good atmosphere, chic Young. (Dir: Gregory Ratoff, 90 mins.)

Men In Love (1990)** Doug Self, Joe Tolbe, Emerald Starr, Kutira Decosterd. Disappointing, independently made feature about a young man who goes to a New Age retreat in Hawaii to recover from his lover's death from AIDS. Film attempts to explore metaphysical issues in terms of healing with the use of crystals and exploring one's inner self. Good intentions and an eager, inexperienced cast. (Dir: Marc Huestis, 90 mins.)

Men In War (1957)*** Robert Ryan, Aldo Ray. Grim, realistic war film about the Korean War. Good performances make the tale palatable. (Dir: Anthony Mann, 104 mins.)†

Men In White (1934)*** Clark Gable, Jean Hersholt, Otto Kruger, Myrna Loy, Elizabeth Allan, Wallace Ford, Henry B. Walthall. Fine filming of Sidney Kingsley's hit play about an idealistic doctor battling professional indifference, corruption, and the temptation of money; superior ensemble acting. (Dir: Richard Boleslawski, 80 mins.)

Men of Boys Town (1941)** Spencer Tracy, Mickey Rooney. Sequel to *Boys Town* is just a sentimental rehash of a lot of B movies. (Dir: Norman Taurog, 106 mins.)

Men of Respect (1990) **½ John Turturro, Katherine Borowitz, Dennis Farina, Peter Boyle, Rod Steiger. Unusual retelling of *Macbeth* as a contemporary gangster story. Skillful adaptation and several powerhouse performances make this a different and often maddening twist on Shakespeare's masterpiece. (Dir: William Reilly, 107 mins.)†

Men of the Dragon (MTV 1974)** Jared Martin, Robert Ito, Katie Saylor. Fairly mild martial arts film, with high-flying karate kicks and low-blow kung-fu thrusts. (Dir: Harry Falk, 74 mins.)

Men of the Fighting Lady (1954)**½ Van

Johnson, Walter Pidgeon. Routine war film about an aircraft carrier and the men assigned to her. (Dir: Andrew Marton, 80 mins.)

Men of Two Worlds (Great Britain, 1945)**½ Eric Portman, Phyllis Calvert, Robert Adams. Educated native returns to his homeland of East Africa, realizes his people live literally in a different world. (Dir: Thorold Dickson, 107 mins.)

Men's Club, The (1986)* Richard Jordan, Frank Langella, Craig Wasson, Treat Williams, Stockard Channing. A group of middle-aged, maladjusted buddies get together to "relate" and wind up at a luxurious whorehouse, where they proceed to bitch about their mates. (Dir: Peter Medak, 100 mins.)†

Men With Wings (1938)*** Fred MacMurray, Ray Milland, Louise Campbell. Story of two air pioneers, one a stunt flier and war hero, the other a man who dreams of aviation's future. Fair entertainment. (Dir: William A. Wellman, 106 mins.)

Mephisto (Hungary, 1981)***½ Klaus Maria Brandauer, Ildiko Bansagi, Krystyna Janda. Vividly theatrical updating of the Faust legend. Valuing expediency over morality, a German actor climbs to the top of his profession with generous boosts from the Nazi party. Brandauer's performance is a bravura piece of scenery-chewing, an unforgettable celebration of a performer who's sold his soul for good reviews and overnight celebrity. Oscar, Best Foreign Film. (Dir: Istvan Szabo, 144 mins.)†

Mephisto Waltz, The (1971)*** Alan Alda, Jacqueline Bisset, Curt Jurgens, Barbara Parkins. World-famous pianist Jurgens is dying of a rare blood disease when he grants journalist Alda a rare interview. Satanic possession is involved. (Dir: Paul Wendkos, 108 mins.)†

Mercenaries, The—See: **Kill Castro**

Mercenary Fighters (1986)*½ Peter Fonda, Reb Brown, Ron O'Neal, Jim Mitchum. U.S mercenaries are hired to drive African tribesmen off their land. (Dir: Riki Shelach, 91 mins.)†

Merchant of Four Seasons (West Germany, 1971)*** Hans Hirschmuller, Irm Hermann, Andrea Schober, Hanna Schygulla. A bitter tale of a pushcart vendor whose life is a series of bad breaks. Rainer Werner Fassbinder's skillfully distanced direction is mesmerizing. (88 mins.)

Mercy or Murder? (MTV 1987)**½ Robert Young, Frances Reid, Michael Learned. A man is accused of murder after helping his wife (suffering from Alzheimer's) to die. (Dir: Steven Gethers, 104 mins.)

Mermaids (1990)*** Cher, Bob Hoskins, Winona Ryder, Michael Schoeffling, Christina Ricci, Caroline McWilliams, Jan Miner. Nicely acted, affectionate

comedy set during JFK's term as president about an ageless woman (Cher) who moves with her daughters to a new town every time she gets too close to a man. She reluctantly falls for a shoe salesman (Hoskins) in a Massachusetts village after her teenage daughter (Ryder) rebels. The feel for the period is on target, and the movie leaves you feeling good. (Dir: Richard Benjamin, 110 mins.)†

Merrill's Marauders (1962)***½ Jeff Chandler, Ty Hardin, Will Hutchins, Claude Akins. Story of the famous outfit of war-hardened veterans who battled the enemy in Burma. (Dir: Sam Fuller, 98 mins.)

Merrily We Go to Hell (1932)*** Sylvia Sidney, Fredric March, Cary Grant. A society girl (Sidney) marries a newspaperman who has great ambitions and a serious drinking problem. (Dir: Dorothy Arzner, 78 mins.)

Merrily We Live (1938)*** Constance Bennett, Brian Aherne, Alan Mowbray, Billie Burke. Engaging second-string screwball comedy with a surface resemblance to *My Man Godfrey*. Dithery Billie Burke hires a chauffeur without knowing that he's a renowned writer and that her wacky family looks like perfect material to him. (Dir: Norman McLeod, 90 mins.)

Merry Andrew (1958)**½ Danny Kaye, Pier Angeli. The setting is a small circus with Danny cast as a schoolteacher who joins the troupe for a brief interval. (Dir: Michael Kidd, 103 mins.)

Merry Christmas, Mr. Lawrence (Great Britain-Japan, 1983)** David Bowie, Tom Conti, Takeshi, Jack Thompson. A bizarrely constructed yet oddly compelling tale about a Japanese prisoner of war camp circa 1942. The complex relationship between Japanese captors and British prisoners is conveyed by the international cast, but the film lacks clarity as it probes the nature of war. (Dir: Nagisa Oshima, 120 mins.)†

Merry Monahans, The (1944)*** Donald O'Connor, Ann Blyth, Jack Oakie. Story of vaudevillians is so well played, including some cute musical numbers, that it rises above its commonplace plot. (Dir: Charles Lamont, 91 mins.)

Merry Widow, The (1925)**** John Gilbert, Mae Murray, Tully Marshall, Roy d'Arcy, Josephine Crowell. Using the Franz Lehár operetta only as a takeoff (the prince must marry the widow of his wealthiest subject in order to keep the money in the kingdom), director Erich von Stroheim creates a delicious portrait of the Hapsburg Empire in final decay. (110 mins.)

Merry Widow, The (1934)***½ Maurice Chevalier, Jeanette MacDonald, Edward Everett Horton, Una Merkel. It's been done so often that it's lost a lot of its appeal but this Ernst Lubitsch version is a delight. AKA: **The Lady Dances.** (100 mins.)†

Merry Widow, The (1952)** Lana Turner, Fernando Lamas, Una Merkel, Richard Haydn. Heavy-handed version of Franz Lehar's operetta; Turner looks lovely and Lamas sings well. (Dir: Curtis Bernhardt, 105 mins.)

Merton of the Movies (1947)** Red Skelton, Gloria Grahame, Virginia O'Brien, Leon Ames, Alan Mowbray. Poor version of the George S. Kaufman-Marc Connolly play about a simple country boy's attempt to make good in Hollywood. (Dir: Robert Alton, 82 mins.)

Mesa of Lost Women, The (1953)½ Jackie Coogan, Richard Travis, Mary Hill. Coogan is a mad scientist who plans to create a race of superbeings. Hilariously awful. (Dirs: Herbert Tevos, Ron Ormond, 70 mins.)†

Mesmerized (Great Britain-New Zealand-Australia, 1985)* John Lithgow, Jodie Foster, Michael Murphy. In the 1800s, a teenager marries a sexually demented trader. After years of torment, she decides to murder her husband through hypnosis. (Dir: Michael Laughin, 90 mins.)†

Mes Petites Amoureuses (France, 1974) ***½ Martin Loeb, Ingrid Caven, Jacqueline Dufranne, Maurice Pialat. Realistically interpreted, unsentimentalized coming-of-age story about a French teenager who is slowly becoming aware of his sexual awakening and the desirability of girls as romantic friends. Directed with tenderness and a meticulous sense of detail by Jean Eustache. (123 mins.)

Message From Space (Japan, 1978)**½ Vic Morrow, Sonny Chiba, Philip Casnoff. Enjoyable sci-fi flick about eight mercenaries hired to protect a small planet. (Dir: Kinji Fukasaku, 105 mins.)†

Message to Garcia (1936)*** Barbara Stanwyck, Wallace Beery, John Boles, Alan Hale, Herbert Mundin. During the Spanish-American War, a spy risks life and limb to contact the General Garcia of the title. A stellar cast of pros delivers this message with clarity and expressiveness. (Dir: George Marshall, 77 mins.)

Message to My Daughter, A (MTV 1973)**½ Kitty Winn, Bonnie Bedelia. Sentimental tale. Winn is a daughter searching for identity against the background of her dead mother's tape-recorded words of wisdom. (Dir: Robert Michael Lewis, 74 mins.)

Messalina vs. the Son of Hercules (Italy-France, 1963)*½ Richard Harrison, Lisa Gastoni. Glaucus, a British slave brought to Rome, fights for the freedom of his countrymen. (Dir: Umberto Lenzi, 94 mins.)

Messenger of Death (1988)** Charles Bronson, Trish van Devere, Laurence Luckinbill, Jeff Corey, John Ireland. Denver reporter Bronson investigates the massacre of a polygamous family involved in a feud between Mormon factions. (Dir: J. Lee Thompson, 92 mins.)†

Messiah of Evil (1972)**½ Anitra Ford, Joy Bang, Marianna Hill. Spooky no-budget effort about a young woman who visits her artist father's seafront house to investigate complaints about a zombie plague in the nearby village. AKA: **Dead People.** (Dir: Willard Huyck, 89 mins.)†

Messidor (Switzerland, 1979)***½ Catherine Retore, Clementine Amouroux. Compelling drama about two women who meet while hitchhiking. They become involved in a terrifying world of crime and a panic-stricken flight from the law. (Dir: Alain Tanner, 120 mins.)

Metalstorm: Destruction of Jared-Syn (1983)* Jeffrey Byron, Tim Thomerson, Kelly Preston, Mike Preston. An inept sci-fi extravaganza; macho hero tracks down baddies out to control his planet. (Dir: Charles Band, 84 mins.)†

Meteor (1979)**½ Natalie Wood, Sean Connery, Brian Keith, Henry Fonda, Karl Malden. An international network of scientists works to save the Earth from a massive meteor intent on crashing. (Dir: Ronald Neame, 107 mins.)†

Metropolis (Germany, 1926)***½ Brigitte Helm, Alfred Abel, Gustav Frohlich, Rudolph Klein-Rogge. Stylistically brilliant tale of a futuristic society in which a mad scientist exacerbates the oppressed workers' rebellion. This silent classic is available in color-tinted prints with a rock score by Giorgio Moroder. (Dir: Fritz Lang, 120 mins.)†

Metropolitan (1935)*** Lawrence Tibbett, Virginia Bruce, Alice Brady, Ruth Donnelly, Cesar Romero, Luis Alberni. Fine vehicle for the great opera star Tibbett, for once; many opportunities for fine singing. (Dir: Richard Boleslawski, 75 mins.)

Metropolitan (1990)***½ Edward Clements, Christopher Eigemen, Taylor Nichols, Carolyn Farina, Allison Rutledge-Parisi, Dylan Hundley. Literate and witty tale of college-age Park Avenue preps and debs (i.e., WASPs, as in White Anglo-Saxon Protestants) who gather during Christmas break and come to terms with their hopes and hormones. The young ensemble cast is wonderful, especially Clements as an outsider who shakes up the group. Impressive first film by writer-director Whit Stillman. (Dir: Whit Stillman, 98 mins.)†

Mexicali Rose (1929)* Barbara Stanwyck, Sam Hardy, William Janney. Barbara is absurdly miscast as a Mexican senorita. (Dir: Erle C. Kenton, 64 mins.)

Mexican Bus Ride (Mexico, 1951)**½ Lilia Prado, Carmelita Gonzalez, Estebun Marquez. A young newlywed has to travel to Mexico City via a rickety old bus and finds temptation en route. Pleasant comedy from Buñuel's Mexican period. (Dir: Luis Buñuel, 85 mins.)

Mexican Hayride (1948)**½ Bud Abbott, Lou Costello, Luba Malina. Madcap antics get involved with phony silver stock and a lady toreador. (Dir: Charles Barton, 77 mins.)

Mexican Spitfire, The (1939)**½ Lupe Velez, Leon Errol. Senora's husband is aided by Uncle Matt in saving a big contract. Amusing comedy. (Dir: Leslie Goodwins, 67 mins.)

Mexican Spitfire at Sea, The (1942)** Lupe Velez, Leon Errol. The spitfire goes after an advertising contract for her husband en route to Honolulu. Mild comedy. (Dir: Leslie Goodwins, 73 mins.)

Mexican Spitfire's Baby, The (1941)**Lupe Velez, Leon Errol. The spitfire adopts a war orphan, who turns out to be a beautiful French girl. Mild comedy. (Dir: Leslie Goodwins, 69 mins.)

Mexican Spitfire's Blessed Event, The (1943)** Lupe Velez, Leon Errol. The success or failure of a big business deal depends upon a nonexistent baby, so the spitfire tries to get one. Mild comedy. (Dir: Leslie Goodwins, 63 mins.)

Mexican Spitfire's Elephant, The (1942)** Lupe Velez, Leon Errol. The spitfire gets tangled with crooks who try to smuggle a diamond through customs in a miniature elephant. Mild comedy. (Dir: Leslie Goodwins, 64 mins.)

Miami Blues (1990)***½ Alec Baldwin, Fred Ward, Jennifer Jason Leigh, Charles Napier, Obba Babatunde, Nora Dunn, Paul Gleason, Shirley Stoler, Martine Beswicke. Blithe psychotic Baldwin, fresh out of a California prison, arrives in Miami and sets up housekeeping with fresh-faced young hooker Leigh while playing nasty mind games with world-weary detective Ward. Quirky, violent, black comic film faithfully adapted from novel by Charles Willeford. All three leads are terrific, but the movie belongs to Baldwin's wonderfully manic killer. (Dir: George Armitage, 97 mins.)†

Miami Exposé (1956)** Lee J. Cobb, Patricia Medina, Edward Arnold. A police lieutenant tracks down and cracks a vice operation in Florida. Fair cops and robbers. This is typical of how Cobb's brilliant acting was wasted by Hollywood film producers. (Dir: Fred F. Sears, 73 mins.)

Miami Horror (Italy, 1985)* David Warbeck, Laura Trotter, Lawrence Loddi, John Ireland. Mobster tries to force a scientist to help him create a superhuman being to use in criminal schemes, while aliens from another dimension try to get them both out of the monster-making business. Dubbed horror nonsense. (Dir: Martin Herbert, 88 mins.)†

Miami Story, The (1954)** Barry Sullivan, Luther Adler, Beverly Garland. Miami's big crime syndicate is cracked by an ex-gangster and his girl. Routine crime film. (Dir: Fred F. Sears, 75 mins.)

Miami Vice (MTV, 1984)*** Don Johnson, Philip Michael Thomas, Saundra Santiago. Crockett and Tubbs hit the vice-filled Miami streets. (Dir: Thomas Carter, 99 mins.)†

Michael Shayne, Private Detective (1940)*** Lloyd Nolan, Marjorie Weaver. In the capable hands of Mr. Nolan, this fast-talking detective comes to life and is a welcome addition to the list of sleuths found in B films. (Dir: Eugene Forde, 77 mins.)

Mickey (1919)*** Mabel Normand, Lew Cody. Delectable comic showcase, from Mack Sennett's studios, for the talents of the lovely Normand, who plays a Cinderella-like girl who lives with her snooty relations and loves handsome Cody. Very entertaining, and it's easy to see why she was such a great star before scandal destroyed her career (Dir: F. Richard Jones, 65 mins.)†

Mickey One (1965)*** Warren Beatty, Alexandra Stewart, Hurd Hatfield. An absorbing, imaginative film. Electric performance from Beatty as a struggling nightclub comic who's in a jam with mobsters and goes on the lam. (Dir: Arthur Penn, 93 mins.)

Mickey Spillane's Margin for Murder (MTV 1981)**½ Kevin Dobson, Charles Hallahan, Cindy Pickett, Donna Dixon. Kevin Dobson plays Mike Hammer, the angry private eye after hoods who murdered his pal. Routine, but well-played and nicely Hammered home. (Dir: Daniel Haller, 100 mins.)

Micki & Maude (1984)**½ Dudley Moore, Amy Irving, Ann Reinking, Richard Mulligan, George Gaynes. Moore is at his farcical best in this uneven comedy that ultimately loses steam. He plays a bigamist betrothed to both career woman Reinking and fetching cellist Irving. (Dir: Blake Edwards, 115 mins.)†

Microwave Massacre (1983)** Jackie Vernon, Loren Schein, Al Troupe, Claire Ginsberg, Lou Ann Webber. Construction worker rebels against his health-nut wife and kills her, only to accidentally microwave her and discover he likes the taste. Rather tasteless and obvious, but sometimes funny. (Dir: Wayne Berwick, 76 mins.)

Midas Run (1969)** Fred Astaire, Anne Heywood, Richard Crenna, Roddy McDowall, Ralph Richardson. A routine caper as Astaire organizes a plot to steal a gold shipment leaving England by air. (Dir: Alf Kjellin, 106 mins.)

Midas Valley (MTV 1985)** Jean Simmons, Robert Stack, Linda Purl, George Grizzard, Catherine Mary Stewart. Smartly produced soap about big business in Silicon Valley. (Dir: Gus Trikonis, 104 mins.)

Middle Age Crazy (Canada, 1980)** Bruce Dern, Ann-Margret, Graham Jarvis, Eric Christmas, Deborah Wakeman. Middlin' movie inspired by a hit song (which, as usual, proves that a song does not a screenplay make). Succumbing to a middle-age itch, Dern leaves wife Ann-Margret behind for a younger woman. (Dir: John Trent, 95 mins.)†

Middle Man, The (India, 1975)*** Pradip Mukherjee, Aparna Sen, Satya Banerjee, Lily Chakravarty, Dipankar Dey. University graduate can't find work in his field in native Calcutta, so he accepts job as go-between with business that fences goods and handles prostitutes. Good film about making the choice between morality and survival. (Dir: Satyajit Ray, 131 mins.)

Middle of the Night (1959)**½ Fredric March, Glenda Farrell, Lee Grant, Kim Novak. A fairly engrossing filmization of Paddy Chayefsky's hit play about a widower who finds a new meaning of life when he falls for a girl young enough to be his daughter. (Dir: Delbert Mann, 118 mins.)

Middle of the World, The (Switzerland, 1974)**** Philipe Leotard, Olimpia Carlisi. Affecting, intelligent story of a couple trying to forge a nonsexist relationship. He (Leotard) is a small businessman running for parliament; she (Carlisi) is an Italian immigrant waitress. (Dir: Alain Tanner, 115 mins.)

Midnight (1934)—see **Call It Murder**

Midnight (1939)**** Claudette Colbert, Don Ameche, John Barrymore, Mary Astor, Francis Lederer. Scintillating comedy directed by Mitchell Leisen from a script by Charles Brackett and Billy Wilder. Colbert is a girl on her uppers in Paris who finds herself enmeshed in the marital tangles of Barrymore and Astor. (94 mins.)

Midnight (1989)** Lynn Redgrave, Tony Curtis, Frank Gorshin, Rita Gam, Wolfman Jack. Disappointing horror yarn wastes the talents of a good cast. Redgrave is an *Elvira*-inspired television hostess who becomes justifiably alarmed when those surrounding her are murdered by a mysterious killer. (Dir: Norman Thaddeus Vane, 86 mins.)†

Midnight (1981)—See: **Backwoods Massacre**

Midnight Cowboy (1969)***½ Dustin Hoffman, Jon Voight, Sylvia Miles. A devastating, lacerating, superbly acted drama which deservedly won the Academy Award for Best Picture, Best Director (John Schlesinger), and Best Screenplay (Waldo Salt). Story of a male hustler (Voight) and his decrepit buddy (Hoffman) who dream of making it big in New York and retiring to Florida. Based on the novel by James Leo Herlihy. (113 mins.)†

Midnight Alibi (1934)***½ Richard Barthelmess, Ann Dvorak, Helen Chandler, Robert Barrat, Helen Connolly, Vincent Sherman. One of Barthelmess's best sound films, from the wonderful Damon Runyon story "The Old Doll's House"; the star plays a double role, as a hoodlum who hides out in the home of a reclusive old lady, and, in a flashback to 1884, as the lover she lost in her youth; Chandler is lovely as the old lady when young. Barthelmess creates both characters so completely that you might as well be seeing two different actors. Greatly enlivened by Runyon's dialogue and atmosphere, really most entertaining. Look for future director Vincent Sherman playing a gunsel. (Dir: Alan Crosland, 90 mins.)

Midnight Cop (West Germany, 1988)*** Armin Mueller-Stahl, Morgan Fairchild, Michael York, Frank Stallone, Julia Kent, Allegra Curtis. He likes the night and manhandling scantily clad Fairchild, but this cop-after-dark also finds himself in a nasty mystery involving murder, drugs, and blackmail. Mueller-Stahl is excellent as the idiosyncratic, boorish, kinky cop in this unique cult favorite. Movie clichés galore (part of the fun) and a standout jazz score. Co-star Curtis is Tony's daughter. (Dir: Peter Patzak, 100 mins.)†

Midnight Crossing (1988)*½ Faye Dunaway, Daniel J. Travanti, Kim Cattrall, John Laughlin, Ned Beatty. On a sailing expedition, two couples attempt double-crosses while searching for treasure that one of the men buried off the Cuban coast years before. Not Dunaway's finest hour. (Dir: Roger Holzberg, 104 mins.)†

Midnight Dancer (Australia, 1987)**½ Deanne Jeffs, Mary Regan, Kaarin Fairfax, Joy Smithers. Aspiring ballerina takes a job as a chorus girl in a seedy nightclub to support her studies. Appealing story about growing up, less sentimental than you might expect. (Dir: Pamela Gibbons, 97 mins.)†

Midnight Express (Great Britain, 1978)*** Brad Davis, John Hurt, Randy Quaid, Bo Hopkins, Mike Kellin, Paul Smith. A powerful exposé of prison life in a Turkish jail. Based on the experiences of a young man named Billy Hayes, it follows his failed efforts to smuggle out some hashish and his placement into an inhuman prison. Hayes's ever-present desire to get on the "Midnight Express" (prison slang for escape) makes this thriller totally engrossing as it reaches an effective climax. (Dir: Alan Parker, 120 mins.)†

Midnight Girl, The (1925)**½ Lila Lee, Gareth Hughes, Bela Lugosi, Dolores Cassinelli, Charlotte Walker. Wacky melodrama of a young Russian opera singer who comes to New York to get a break, but who ends up working in a nightclub run by a great impresario's son, who's a jazz bandleader! Too unreal to be very compelling dramatically, but with an enjoyable everything-but-the-kitchen-sink spirit that is appealing. Photographed by D. W. Griffith's cameraman, Billy Bitzer. (Dir: Wilfred Noy, 84 mins.)†

Midnight Hour, The (MTV 1985)** Shari Belafonte-Harper, Dick Van Patten, LeVar Burton, Kevin McCarthy, Peter DeLuise. Mild chills mixed with laughs rather than gore. An innocent Halloween party turns into a free-for-all when the spirit of an uninvited witch crashes the party. (Dir: Jack Bender, 104 mins.)

Midnight Lace (1960)*** Doris Day, Rex Harrison, John Gavin, Myrna Loy, Roddy McDowall, Herbert Marshall. An overproduced mystery-thriller in which most of the footage finds lovely Day being terrorized by an unknown phone caller. It's up to you to guess and you'll probably find it easy. (Dir: David Miller, 108 mins.)†

Midnight Lace (MTV 1980)* Mary Crosby, Gary Frank, Celeste Holm, Carolyn Jones, Shecky Greene, Susan Tyrrell. Not a patch on the original, which was a combination soap opera, fashion show, and lady-in-distress thriller. (Dir: Ivan Nagy, 104 mins.)

Midnight Madness (1980)½ David Naughton, Debra Clinger, Ed Deezen, Stephen Furst. Scores of game-loving kids run around Los Angeles hunting for clues that will point them to the winning solution. (Dirs: Michael Nankin, David Wechter, 110 mins.)†

Midnight Man, The (1974)** Burt Lancaster, Susan Clark, Cameron Mitchell. Lancaster plays a night watchman-turned-detective at a small southern college. On parole from a murder conviction, Lancaster is doggedly persistent tracking down the killer of a campus co-ed. Plot is confusing, movie too slow. (Dirs: Roland Kibbee, Burt Lancaster, 117 mins.)

Midnight Mary (1933)*** Loretta Young, Ricardo Cortez, Franchot Tone, Una Merkel, Frank Conroy, Andy Devine, Harold Huber. Powerful, uncompromising story of a poor girl's gradual involvement

in the underworld, and her eventual attempt to go straight; fairly bleak, definitely pre-Production Code look at the lives of have-nots, with very intense acting, and a particularly fine job by Cortez as an abusive hood who is tormented by his real love for Young. Some very strong stuff, still not for children. (Dir: William Wellman, 74 mins.)

Midnight Offerings (MTV 1981)*½ Melissa Sue Anderson, Mary McDonough, Patrick Cassidy, Marion Ross. Horror pic about two possessed girls with powers that would make Sissy Spacek's "Carrie" green with envy. (Dir: Rod Holcomb, 104 mins.)

Midnight Run (1988)***½ Robert De Niro, Charles Grodin, John Ashton, Yaphet Kotto, Dennis Farina. Lightweight but vastly enjoyable adventure-comedy with ex-cop De Niro trying to get bail-jumping ex-mob accountant Grodin from New York to L.A. De Niro and the dry, cagey Grodin are a perfect odd couple, trading barbs and trying to outsmart each other as they're hunted and double-crossed by just about everyone. Filled to bursting with satisfying little moments, many improvised by the two stars. Even the expected car chases and shoot-outs are quite lively. (Dir: Martin Brest, 122 mins.)†

Midnight Story, The (1957)** Tony Curtis, Marisa Pavan, Gilbert Roland. Traffic cop investigates on his own when he is outraged by the murder of a parish priest. Strictly routine production graced by a good cast. (Dir: Joseph Pevney, 89 mins.)

Midsummer Night's Dream, A (1935)***½ James Cagney, Dick Powell, Olivia de Havilland, Joe E. Brown, Mickey Rooney. This was one of the first attempts to bring Shakespeare to the screen and it was, by and large, successful. Rooney's Puck is the highlight of the film. (Dirs: Max Reinhardt, William Dieterle, 117 mins.)†

Midsummer Night's Sex Comedy, A (1982)*** Woody Allen, José Ferrer, Mia Farrow, Julie Hagerty, Tony Roberts, Mary Steenburgen. Delightfully droll if uneven film written and directed by Woody Allen, who this time deals with his favorite subjects in a turn-of-the-century period context. Three couples become entwined during an idyllic weekend in the country. (88 mins.)†

Midway (1976)** Charlton Heston, Henry Fonda, Glenn Ford, James Coburn, Hal Holbrook, Toshiro Mifune, Robert Mitchum. The decisive air-sea battle off Midway Island in the Pacific during WWII, which turned the odds in favor of the U.S. over Japan, is painstakingly recreated via newsreel footage and expensively staged battle scenes. (Dir: Jack Smight, 132 mins.)†

Mighty Barnum, The (1934)**½ Wallace Beery, Adolphe Menjou, Virginia Bruce, Rochelle Hudson, Janet Beecher, Herman Bing. A flashy biopic relating the life and times of the legendary showman. (Dir: Walter Lang, 87 mins.)

Mighty Joe Young (1949)*** Robert Armstrong, Terry Moore, Ben Johnson. Cut-rate *King Kong* is served up by the same producers who made the Academy Award original. Good special effects though the ape is too lovable to inspire terror. (Dir: Ernest B. Schoedsack, 94 mins.)†

Mighty McGurk, The (1946)** Wallace Beery, Dean Stockwell, Edward Arnold, Cameron Mitchell. Contrived and confused drama about an ex-fighter who befriends an orphan boy. (Dir: John Waters, 85 mins.)

Mighty Quinn, The (1989)** Denzel Washington, Robert Townsend, James Fox, Mimi Rogers, M. Emmet Walsh. Trying to clear the name of his innocent friend, a Jamaican police chief searches for the murderer of a wealthy white man. Quirky mystery has unusual characters and locations, but no idea of what to do with them. (Dir: Carl Schenkel, 98 mins.)†

Migrants, The (MTV 1974)*** Cloris Leachman, Ron Howard, Sissy Spacek, Cindy Williams. Worth seeing for Leachman's high-caliber portrait of an earth mother who breathes life into her clan even in the face of her own despair. Tennessee Williams's story about the deprivations endured by migratory workers is effectively adapted by Lanford Wilson. (Dir: Tom Gries, 78 mins.)

Mikado, The (Great Britain, 1939)***½ Kenny Baker, Jean Colin, Martyn Green. The Gilbert and Sullivan operetta of shenanigans in the high court of old Japan, with a wand'ring minstrel wooing a noble lady. Colorfully done, excellently sung. (Dir: Victor Schertzinger, 90 mins.)

Mike's Murder (1984)*** Debra Winger, Mark Keyloun, Darrell Larson, Paul Winfield, Brooke Alderson, Dan Shor. Breaking out of her shell, a mousy bank teller falls for a sexy, irresponsible hunk. When he's slain, she uncharacteristically and foolhardily seeks out the facts, even though the truth proves hurtful and quite dangerous. (Dir: James Bridges, 97 mins.)†

Mikey and Nicky (1976)*** Peter Falk, John Cassavetes, Ned Beatty. Experimental feature from director Elaine May ran outrageously overbudget and showcases some of the worst lighting, cutting, and sound imaginable. Yet the film has genuine power and feeling. Falk and Cassavetes star as old buddies caught up in a squeeze from the mob. (119 mins.)†

Milagro Beanfield War, The (1988)***½ Chick Vennera, Carlos Riquelme, John Heard, Rubén Blades, Daniel Stern, Christopher Walken, Richard Bradford, Sonia Braga, Melanie Griffith. A sunny, spirited fable about a group of New Mexican villagers trying to reclaim their water rights when a rapacious development company moves to turn the town into a golf course. Set against a backdrop of stunning Southwestern vistas and brimming with cheer and good intention, this should delight everyone but hard-core cynics. (Dir: Robert Redford, 118 mins.)†

Mildred Pierce (1945)**** Joan Crawford, Zachary Scott, Jack Carson, Eve Arden, Ann Blyth, Bruce Bennett. More than a mere soap opera, this etched-in-acid film chronicles the flaws in the American dream, as Mildred drives her hubby away with financial nagging and then smothers her daughter with all the advantages she never had. The film snaps and crackles with sarcastic dialogue, memorable characterizations, and Crawford herself—an aura of glamour clings to her even when she's slinging hash or nobly taking the rap for a crime she didn't commit. (Dir: Michael Curtiz, 109 mins.)†

Miles From Home (1988)*** Richard Gere, Kevin Anderson, Judith Ivey, Penelope Ann Miller, Brian Dennehy, John Malkovich, Laurie Metcalf. When the bank forecloses on an Iowa farm, the two brothers who owned it lash back in frustration. Their illegal exploits turn them into folk heroes. One of the few farm movies to take the position that the family farm as a way of life is outmoded, this features fine acting from members of Chicago's Steppenwolf Theater Company. (Dir: Gary Sinese, 112 mins.)†

Miles to Go (MTV 1986)*** Jill Clayburgh, Tom Skerritt, Mimi Kuzyk. Unusual story about one woman's approach in dealing with her cancer. Clayburgh takes the practical route by planning to have herself replaced by her friend but the idea isn't a big hit with her husband or kids, not to mention her friend. (Dir: David Greene, 104 mins.)

Miles to Go Before I Sleep (MTV 1975)**½ Martin Balsam, Mackenzie Phillips, Kitty Winn. Can retired people find renewal by helping teenage delinquents? Balsam will charm you as a gentle widower, but fifteen-year-old Phillips steals the show as Robin, the mercurial delinquent he wants to help. (Dir: Fielder Cook, 78 mins.)

Milkman, The (1950)** Jimmy Durante, Donald O'Connor, Piper Laurie. A waste of talented people—this lightweight comedy with songs about a couple of milkmen and their escapades offers a few laughs. (Dir: Charles Barton, 87 mins.)

Milky Way, The (1936)***½ Harold Lloyd, Adolphe Menjou, Helen Mack. The most impressive Lloyd talkie features an array of deft farceurs. Harold is a milkman who happens to knock down the champion in a brawl, and the gags that develop from the situation are impeccably constructed. (Dir: Leo McCarey, 83 mins.)†

Milky Way, The (France-Italy, 1969)**** Paul Frankeur, Laurent Terzieff, Edith Scob. Director Luis Buñuel's taut, funny and bitter, peculiarly devout history of the Roman Catholic Church in Europe, told in terms of its progress through heresies and schisms. The old master's surrealistic vision of religion is perfectly realized in this little gem. (105 mins.)†

Millenium (1989)* Kris Kristofferson, Cheryl Ladd, Daniel Travanti, Robert Joy, Brent Carver. Overly logical and yet still far-fetched sci-fi saga which has Kristofferson discovering that entire plane loads of people are being hijacked to the future—where the earth is in dire need of repopulation, and time-travelling stewardess Ladd (with a Brigitte Nelson 'do) is the best special agent they could come up with. To be correct storywise, an entire section of the film is repeated; an odd move, but anything's possible in a turkey of this dimension. (Dir: Michael Anderson, 108 mins.)†

Miller's Crossing (1990)***½ Gabriel Byrne, Marcia Gay Harden, John Turturro, Jon Polito, J. E. Freeman, Albert Finney. Melancholy Prohibition Era gangster film is more concerned with character, language, and style than it is with plot and action, but it all works beautifully, sometimes to strangely comic heights. The violence is desperate, the thugs cartoonish, and the movie is mesmerizing. Conceived and written by the Coen brothers; Ethan produced, Joel directed. (Dir: Joel Coen, 115 mins.)†

Millerson Case, The (1947)** Warner Baxter, Nancy Saunders, Barbara Pepper, Clem Bevans, Griff Barnett. The Crime Doctor has to probe beneath surface appearances when a country doctor is murdered as a typhoid fever outbreak occurs in the background. (Dir: George Archinbaud, 72 mins.)

Millhouse: A White Comedy (1971)***½ A harsh satire "documentary" about Richard Milhous Nixon released years before he became our first unindicted co-conspirator president. (Dir: Emile de Antonio, 92 mins.)†

Millionaire, The (1931)*** George Arliss, David Manners, Evelyn Knapp, Noah Beery, Florence Arliss. Neat little comedy vehicle for Arliss. He plays a wealthy self-made man who's advised to retire, but who can't bring himself to stay away from work, much to his wife and daughter's dismay. A nice idea, very deftly played with great enjoyment by the hammy star. (Dir: John Adolfi, 80 mins.)

Millionaire, The (MTV 1978)*½ Robert Quarry, Martin Balsam, Edward Albert. This is an updated version of the series "The Millionaire," with Michael Anthony dispensing million-dollar tax-free checks. (Dir: Don Weis, 104 mins.)

Millionaire for Christy, A (1951)** Fred MacMurray, Eleanor Parker. A secretary goes on the make for a millionaire, and lands him. Mild comedy. (Dir: George Marshall, 91 mins.)

Millionairess, The (Great Britain, 1960)**½ Sophia Loren, Peter Sellers, Alastair Sim, Vittorio De Sica, Dennis Price. As a wealthy woman who believes she can buy and sell people, Loren is supremely beautiful but not quite up to Shaw's ironies. As the Indian idealist who doesn't come with a price tag, Sellers concentrates on his accent in lieu of giving a performance. The result: a fitfully amusing version of Shaw's exploration of avarice. (Dir: Anthony Asquith, 90 mins.)†

Million Dollar Baby (1941)** Ronald Reagan, Priscilla Lane, Jeffrey Lynn. If you think girls who are poor and suddenly get a million dollars should give it up so their boy friend will still love them you may actually enjoy this Hollywood nonsense. (Dir: Curtis Bernhardt, 100 mins.)

Million Dollar Dixie Deliverance, The (MTV 1978)**½ Brock Peters, Kip Niven. The Disney family formula works again in this pre-Civil War tale. Peters helps five Yankee school kids who have been kidnapped for ransom cross the battle lines. (Dir: Russ Mayberry, 104 mins.)

Million Dollar Duck—See: **$1,000,000 Duck**

Million Dollar Face (MTV 1981)*½ Tony Curtis, David Huffman, Herschel Bernardi, Gayle Hunnicutt, Lee Grant. If you enjoy Sidney Sheldon's novels, then try this shallow portrait of the cosmetic business. Featuring a top model, a new ad campaign, underhanded tactics, illegitimate sons popping up, love intrigues, and all the other familiar trappings that run rampant in such drivel. (Dir: Michael O'Herlihy, 104 mins.)†

Million Dollar Infield (MTV 1982)** Rob Reiner, Candy Azzara, Gretchen Corbett, Elizabeth Wilson, Philip Sterling. Spotty, occasionally ironic comedy about a group of men in their thirties who would rather play softball than face the realities of being grown-ups. (Dir: Hal Cooper, 104 mins.)

Million Dollar Kid (1944)** East Side Kids, Gabriel Dell. The Boys straighten out a millionaire's son who has chosen a life of crime. (Dir: Wallace Fox, 65 mins.)

Million Dollar Legs (1939)** Betty Grable, Jackie Coogan, Donald O'Connor, Buster Crabbe, Richard Denning. Typical college comedy, with students trying to save their alma mater from bankruptcy by investing in a racehorse; nothing really special here except the young stars-to-be and Grable's famous legs. (Dir: Nick Grinde, 65 mins.)

Million Dollar Legs (1932)**** W. C. Fields, Jack Oakie, Susan Fleming, Lyda Roberti, Ben Turpin, Hugh Herbert, Billy Gilbert. An indescribably wild, anarchic farce from Fields and Co., set in a mythical (thank God) country, where the strongest man gets to be President. See Fields lift weights; see Lyda Roberti, the Polish bombshell, sizzle the scenery as the "hottest thing in all Klopstokia," Mata Machree. Somehow they all end up at the 1932 Los Angeles Olympics. (Dir: Edward Cline, 64 mins.)

Million Dollar Mermaid (1952)**½ Esther Williams, Victor Mature, Walter Pidgeon. A biography of swimmer Annette Kellerman, which is highly fictionalized but good-spirited entertainment. (Dir: Mervyn LeRoy 115 mins.)

Million Dollar Mystery (1987)*½ Eddie Deezen, Wendy Sherman, Rick Overton, Mona Lyden, Tom Bosley, Rich Hall. A stale chase comedy about a search for millions of dollars stashed in different locations. (Dir: Richard Fleischer, 95 mins.)†

Million Dollar Rip-Off, The (MTV 1976)* Freddie Prinze, Allen Garfield, Linda Scruggs Bogart, Christine Belford. Desultory heist movie about an electronics whiz and his four female partners-in-crime who wreak havoc on the Chicago subway system. (Dir: Alexander Singer, 78 mins.)

Millions Like Us (Great Britain, 1943)*** Patricia Roc, Eric Portman, Gordon Jackson, Megs Jenkins, Basil Radford, Naunton Wayne, Brenda Bruce, Irene Handl. Skillful British WWII drama expresses subtle patriotism, examining the lives of several ordinary people working in an essential aircraft plant, who try to put their differences aside and pull together for the war effort. Remarkably well done. (Dirs: Frank Launder, Sidney Gilliat, 103 mins.)

Million to One, A (1938)** "Herman Brix" (Bruce Bennett), Joan Fontaine, Monte Blue, Kenneth Harlan. Olympic athlete (loosely based on Jim Thorpe), stripped of his title, trains his son to win big in the 1932 games. OK sports drama. (Dir: Lynn Shores, 59 mins.)†

Mill on the Floss, The (Great Britain, 1937)*** Geraldine Fitzgerald, Frank Lawton, Fay Compton, Griffith Jones, Victoria Hopper, James Mason. Strong, capably produced version of George Eliot's novel of hatred and injustice passed from one generation to the next in a family feud; still a potent story, with fine acting and a rousing climactic flood scene. (Dir: Tim Whelan, 94 mins.)†

Mimi (Great Britain, 1935)** Douglas Fairbanks, Jr., Gertrude Lawrence, Austin Trevor, Diana Napier. Seriously misconceived version of *La Bohème*, with the sophisticated Lawrence unbelievable as the downtrodden little demi-mondaine of the title; she and Fairbanks were more than friends at the time this was made, but it certainly doesn't show in the tepid on-screen lovemaking. (Dir: Paul Stein, 98 mins.)

Min and Bill (1930)*** Marie Dressler, Wallace Beery. The teamwork of Dressler and Beery is quite appealing in this early talkie that won Dressler an Oscar. They play tough waterfront denizens who try to stop authorities from removing Marie's daughter to a "decent" home. (Dir: George Hill, 70 mins.)

Mind Benders, The (Great Britain, 1963)**½ Dirk Bogarde, Mary Ure, John Clements. Scientist engages in an experiment to test complete isolation from all the normal senses, emerges a psychological wreck. Good performances. (Dir: Basil Dearden, 101 mins.)

Mind Field (Canada, 1990)* Michael Ironside, Lisa Langlois, Christopher Plummer, Stefan Wodoslawsky. Resolutely awful, badly written, crudely directed jumble about secret CIA shock treatment project damaging thought process of Montreal cop. (Dir: Jean-Claude Lord, 117 mins.)†

Mind Killer (1987)** Joe McDonald, Christopher Wade, Shirley Ross, Kevin Hart. Lonely, sexually frustrated librarian discovers a self-help book that really works—but at a price, as he only discovers when he begins to turn into a slimy monster. (Dir: Michael Krueger, 84 mins.)†

Mind of Mr. Soames, The (Great Britain, 1970)**½ Terence Stamp, Robert Vaughn. Interesting situation marred by false characterizations. Mr. Soames (Stamp) is a thirty-year-old man who has been in a coma since birth. He is to be operated on and brought to life by Dr. Bergen (Vaughn). (Dir: Alan Cooke, 95 mins.)

Mind Over Murder (MTV 1979)*½ Deborah Raffin, David Ackroyd, Bruce Davison, Andrew Prine. Raffin plays a model who sees things before they happen. The plot concerns an aircrash and a psychic murderer. (Dir: Ivan Nagy, 104 mins.)

Mindwalk (U.S.-Australia, 1990)*** Liv Ullmann, Sam Waterson, John Heard, Ione Skye, Emmanuel Montes. Beautifully acted drama in which the central characters engage in a series of philosophical debates on subjects ranging from the environment, morality, politics, to ethics and psychology. Set amidst the spectacular scenery of Mont Saint-Michel along the French seashore, with music by Philip Glass. (Dir: Bernt Capra, 112 mins.)†

Mine Own Executioner (Great Britain, 1947)***½ Burgess Meredith, Kieron Moore. A psychiatrist practicing without a medical degree finds trouble in his domestic life as well as with his patients. Well-made drama. (Dir: Anthony Kimmins, 103 mins.)†

Miniskirt Mob, The (1968)** Jeremy Slate, Diane McBain, Patty McCormack, Ross Hagen, Harry Dean Stanton. A violent biker-thon in which a miniskirted mademoiselle masterminds her gang's persecution of a young married couple. (Dir: Maury Dexter, 82 mins.)

Ministry of Fear (1944)*** Ray Milland, Marjorie Reynolds. Exciting, offbeat spy melodrama, set in wartime England and based on a Graham Greene novel. Good direction and an interesting, mysterious story. (Dir: Fritz Lang, 86 mins.)

Miniver Story, The (Great Britain, 1950)** Greer Garson, Walter Pidgeon, John Hodiak. Peace comes to England after WWII, but not to the Miniver family—daughter's in the midst of a romantic attachment, while Mrs. Miniver discovers personal tragedy. Weepy drama, a travesty of the original *Mrs. Miniver* film. (Dir: H. C. Potter, 104 mins.)

Minnie and Moskowitz (1971)*** Gena Rowlands, Seymour Cassel, Val Avery. Moving study of two dissimilar but lonely people whose unlikely romance illuminates the screen, thanks to fine performances by Rowlands and Cassel. Minnie is an art curator with a duplex apartment and a large library; Moskowitz is a parking lot attendant; they meet when Minnie's blind date threatens her in Moskowitz's lot. (Dir: John Cassavetes, 114 mins.)

Minotaur, Wild Beast of Crete (Italy, 1961)** Bob Mathias, Rosanna Schiaffino. Muscleman faces the dangers brought on by a wicked queen. (Dir: Silvio Amadeo, 92 mins.)

Minstrel Man (MTV 1977)*** Glynn Turman, Ted Ross, Stanley Clay, Sandra Sharp, Art Evans. Filmed on location in Mississippi, this compelling teleplay focuses on the efforts of a group of post-Civil War black minstrel performers to form their own troupe and to present material that would be less degrading to blacks. (Dir: William A. Graham, 104 mins.)

Minute to Pray, A Second to Die, A (U.S.-Italy, 1968)*** Arthur Kennedy, Alex Cord, Robert Ryan. One of the better Italian oaters. Cord is an outlaw epileptic sought by other outlaws, bounty hunters, territorial lawmen, and the vermin who prey on cripples. (Dir: Franco Giraldi, 103 mins.)

Miracle, The (1959)**½ Carroll Baker, Roger Moore, Walter Slezak. An ambitious effort to bring Max Reinhardt's epic play about a novice nun and her rebellion against God to the screen. Baker is miscast and the overblown production values can't overcome the empty melodramatics. (Dir: Irving Rapper, 121 mins.)

Miracle in Milan (Italy, 1951)***½ Emma Gramatica, Francesco Golisano, Paolo Stoppa, Brunella Bovo. An enchanting comedy set in bleak surroundings, *"Miracle"* is the story of Toto, an idealistic young man who leads a group of peasants in their fight against a rich landowner. Director Vittorio De Sica and screenwriter Cesare Zavattini skillfully evoke a poverty-stricken landscape and then add elements of fantasy, like Toto's magic dove which can make a poor person's wishes come true. *"Miracle"* renders heartbreakingly real social conditions with a pathos that's worthy of Chaplin at his best. (100 mins.)

Miracle in the Rain (1956)**½ Jane Wyman, Van Johnson. Sentimental picture about a lonely young woman (Wyman) who meets a young soldier (Johnson) and falls in love. Their joy is interrupted when he ships out but Jane holds on to the hope that he'll come back. (Dir: Rudolph Maté, 107 mins.)

Miracle Landing (MTV 1990)*½ Connie Selecca, Wayne Rogers, Ana-Alicia, Nancy Kwan, James Cromwell, Jay Thomas. It'll be a miracle if you last all the way through this formulaic disaster movie. Which of the passengers on board an airplane that loses its roof over the middle of the Pacific Ocean will come through alive? You'll have to endure plenty of flashbacks revealing their personal lives before you find out. (Dir: Dick Lowry, 96 mins.)

Miracle Mile (1988)***½ Anthony Edwards, Mare Winningham, John Agar. Musician Edwards, given seventy minutes notice that WWIII has started, tries to find his new girlfriend Winningham so that they can get out of L.A. before panic and The Bomb hit. Quite well directed and acted, a powerful, unforgettable thriller laced with black humor. (Dir: Steve De Jarnett, 88 mins.)†

Miracle of Kathy Miller, The (MTV 1981)*** Sharon Gless, Frank Converse, Helen Hunt, Bill Beyers, John de Lancie. Moving, engrossing drama on the grit and determination of an Arizona teenager who makes a miraculous recovery after being struck by a car. (Dir: Robert Lewis, 104 mins.)

Miracle of Marcelino, The (France, 1955)**** Pablito Calvo, Rafael Rivelles. A beautiful and heartwarming film about a little orphan boy, who is raised by monks, and is visited by Christ in a miracle. (Dir: Ladislao Vajda, 90 mins.)

Miracle of Morgan's Creek, The (1944)**** Betty Hutton, Eddie Bracken, Diana Lynn, William Demarest. The real miracle here is director Preston Sturges, and the way in which he was able to deal comically with a theme that would not have been allowed by the censors at the time if it had been depicted solemnly. Small-town girl (Hutton) gets drunk and becomes pregnant, thanks to one of a variety of obliging GIs. The problem is that Betty can't remember which soldier is the daddy-to-be. Thanks to a fine script and the director's deft touch, this is one of the most perceptive and enduring American comedies of the 1940s. (99 mins.)†

Miracle of Our Lady of Fatima, The (1952)*** Gilbert Roland, Frank Silvera, Susan Whitney. Compelling tale of three peasant children who witnessed a vision in the small Portuguese village of Fatima in '17. (Dir: John Brahm, 102 mins.)†

Miracle of the Bells, The (1948)*½ Fred MacMurray, Valli, Frank Sinatra. A movie queen dies, and is taken to her home town to be buried, where a miracle takes place. Long, terribly trite, sentimental drama. (Dir: Irving Pichel, 120 mins.)†

Miracle of the Heart: A Boys' Town Story (MTV 1986)*** Art Carney, Jack Bannon, Casey Siemaszko. Heartwarming story of a neglected child who finds a real home at Boys' Town. It lacks the thumping melodramatic fervor of the MGM classic, but manages to lay on the sentiment without a trowel. (Dir: Georg Stanford Brown, 104 mins.)†

Miracle of the White Stallions (1963)*½ Robert Taylor, Lilli Palmer, Curt Jurgens, Eddie Albert, James Franciscus. A disappointing Disney adventure about sneaking the prized Lippizan horses out of Vienna during WWII. Fine acting by the horses. (Dir: Arthur Hiller, 117 mins.)†

Miracle on Ice (MTV 1981)*** Karl Malden, Andrew Stevens, Steve Guttenberg, Jerry Houser. Hollywood attempts to recreate the saga of the 1980 U.S. Olympic Hockey Team—a bunch of kids who upset the mighty Russians and then defeated Finland for the gold medal in Lake Placid. The game footage is marvelous, and the Hollywood stuff isn't too much of a letdown. (Dir: Steven Hilliard Stern, 152 mins.)†

Miracle on Main Street (1939)**½ Margo, Jane Darwell, Walter Abel, Lyle Talbot. Distinctive little low-budget effort of a down-and-out carny performer who finds an abandoned baby at Christmas, and is inspired to care for it. Earnest attempt to do something different, worth seeing. (Dir: Steve Sekely, 68 mins.)

Miracle on 34th Street (1947)***½ Edmund Gwenn, John Payne, Maureen O'Hara, Natalie Wood. Kris Kringle is hired to play Santa Claus at Macy's and that begins a delightful combination of fantasy, whimsy, and humor. For young and old and all who want to believe in Santa. Those responsible for the colorized version deserve a lump of coal in their Christmas stocking. (Dir: George Seaton, 96 mins.)†

Miracle on 34th Street (MTV 1973)**½ Sebastian Cabot, Jane Alexander, David Hartman, Roddy McDowall. Remake is less charming than its predecessor, but remains pleasant entertainment. (Dir: Fielder Cook, 104 mins.)

Miracles (1986)* Tom Conti, Teri Garr, Paul Rodriguez, Christopher Lloyd. A newly divorced couple (Conti and Garr) are accidentally taken hostage by a pair of bumbling revolutionaries (Rodriguez and Lloyd) and dumped in South America. The thin premise—every bad thing that happens to them results in a "miracle" for someone else—is reduced to a series of throwaway jokes. (Dir: Jim Kouf, 85 mins.)†

Miracle Woman, The (1931)*** Barbara Stanwyck, David Manners, Sam Hardy, Beryl Mercer. There are a lot of neglected early talkies, like this one and *Baby Face*, that reveal a much more versatile Stanwyck than her later work suggests. She's superb as a tent-preacher who uses less than miraculous methods to reach the multitudes. (Dir: Frank Capra, 87 mins.)

Miracle Worker, The (1962)**** Anne Bancroft, Patty Duke, Victor Jory, Inga Swenson, Andrew Prine. Flawless film version of the brilliant Broadway play by William Gibson dealing with the training of blind, deaf Helen Keller. Miss Bancroft deserved the Oscar she won for the role of Miss Keller's teacher, Annie Sullivan. Duke (Oscar, Best Supporting Actress) is equally effective in the role of young Miss Keller. Fine direction by Arthur Penn. (107 mins.)†

Miracle Worker, The (MTV 1979)*** Patty Duke Astin, Melissa Gilbert, Charles Siebert. Astin (who as Patty Duke played the first Broadway and movie versions) gives a superb performance as Helen's dedicated teacher, Annie Sullivan. Gilbert gives a respectable performance as Helen in this fine remake. (Dir: Paul Aaron, 104 mins.)†

Mirage (1965)*** Gregory Peck, Diane Baker, Walter Matthau. Man who believes he has amnesia starts to retrace his past, becomes involved in a murder plot. Suspense thriller starts off well. Mystery fans will like it, although it's never quite believable. Good production. (Dir: Edward Dmytryk, 109 mins.)†

Miranda (Great Britain, 1948)**½ Glynis Johns, Griffith Jones, Margaret Rutherford. Physician on a holiday away from his wife snags an amorous mermaid while fishing. Mildly entertaining fantasy-comedy. (Dir: Ken Annakin, 77 mins.)

Mirror Crack'd, The (Great Britain, 1980)*** Angela Lansbury, Elizabeth Taylor, Rock Hudson, Kim Novak, Tony Curtis, Edward Fox, Geraldine Chaplin. Moderately successful Agatha Christie mystery with Lansbury as the dowdy deducer, Miss Marple, who's poking her nose into a complicated mystery. (Dir: Guy Hamilton, 105 mins.)†

Mirror Has Two Faces, The (France, 1958)*** Michele Morgan, Bourvil, Ivan Desny, Gerard Oury, Sandra Milo, Sylvie, Jane Marten. Homely wife of a simple schoolmaster has plastic surgery which turns her into a ravishing beauty. Her husband's feelings about her then change from boredom to complete jealousy. (Dir: André Cayatte, 98 mins.)

Mirror, Mirror (Denmark, 1978)*** Frits Helmuth, Bodil Kjar, Preben Kaas, Bent Reiner. Unusual comedy about a group of Copenhagen drag queens and their circle of friends. Director Edward Fleming paints a sensitive portrait of people who use illusion to get through life. (107 mins.)

Mirror, Mirror (MTV 1979)** Loretta Swit, Lee Meriwether, Janet Leigh. A cosmetic surgery soap opera. Swit's flatchested housewife wants a breast implant; Leigh's cutesy widow goes to a quack for a face-lift; and Meriwether's model agency prexy submits to an eye-lift. (Dir: Joanna Lee, 104 mins.)

Mirrors (MTV 1985)*½ Timothy Daly, Shanna Reed, Anthony Hamilton, Marguerite Hickey. Newcomer Hickey plays a ballet dancer in New York, making the rounds on Broadway and falling in love. (Dir: Harry Winer, 104 mins.)

Misadventures of Merlin Jones, The (1964) *½ Tommy Kirk, Annette Funicello, Leon Ames, Stuart Erwin, Connie Gilchrist. Flaky Disney comedy about a young university egghead's experiments is woefully unfunny. (Dir: Robert Stevenson, 88 mins.)†

Mischief (1985)*½ Doug McKeon, Chris Nash, Catherine Mary Stewart, Kelly Preston. Unevenly paced mid-America adolescent passage comedy; good acting by McKeon as the uninitiated and Nash as his worldly-wise buddy help. (Dir: Mel Damski, 97 mins.)†

Misery (1990)**½ James Caan, Kathy Bates, Richard Farnsworth, Frances Sternhagen, Lauren Bacall, Graham Jarvis. Wonderfully acted horror comedy (Bates won the Oscar for Best Actress) about an author held captive by his self-proclaimed greatest fan, an unattractive, mean-spirited woman. Based on a novel by Stephen King and scripted by William Goldman, the film suffers from pedestrian direction, and a predictable plot that collapses into *Grand Guignol*. (Dir: Rob Reiner, 107 mins.)†

Misfit Brigade, The (1988)** Bruce Davison, David Patrick Kelly, Don W. Moffett, Jay O. Sanders, David Carradine, Oliver Reed. A squadron is recruited from a German prison during WWII by Nazi officers desperate for fighting men. (Dir: Gordon Hessler, 101 mins.)†

Misfits, The (1961)*** Clark Gable, Marilyn Monroe, Eli Wallach, Montgomery Clift. Pretentious as hell, but affecting. Arthur Miller's original screenplay about a group of modern-day cowboys and a frightened divorcee is more a curiosity piece than good film drama. Last film of Gable and Monroe. (Dir: John Huston, 124 mins.)†

Mishima (1985)***½ Ken Ogata, Masayuki Shionoya, Hiroshi Mikami. The film explores three areas—the last day of novelist Yukio Mishima's life (he stormed a general's office and committed the ritual of hara-kiri), his younger years, and scenes from his novels—each section having its own distinct visual style (the fictional sequences are the most stunning), while an overwhelming musical score by Philip Glass appears throughout. Narration by Roy Scheider. (Dir: Paul Schrader, 122 mins.)†

Misplaced (U.S.-Poland, 1991)*** John Cameron Mitchell, Elzbieta Czyzewska, Viveca Lindfors, Drew Snyder, Deidre O'Connell. Director Yansen's semiautobiographical tale about a mother and son leaving Poland to find a better life in America is a quietly powerful drama. What they didn't expect in the land of opportunity was hardship, rejection, and humiliation. Powerful performances from Czyzewska and Lindfors. (Dir: Louis Yansen, 98 mins.)†

Miss All-American Beauty (MTV 1982)*½ David Dukes, Diane Lane, Cloris Leachman, Jayne Meadows. The trials of a Texas beauty pageant winner who finally rebels over her phony, carefully packaged image. (Dir: Gus Trikonis, 104 mins.)†

Miss Annie Rooney (1942)** Shirley Temple, Guy Kibbee, William Gargan, Dickie Moore. Shirley is a poor kid, but her big crush just happens to be the scion of a wealthy family. (Dir: Edwin L. Marin, 84 mins.)†

Miss Firecracker (1989)*** Holly Hunter, Mary Steenburgen, Tim Robbins, Alfre Woodard, Scott Glenn, Ann Wedgeworth, Trey Wilson. Beth Henley play about a small town Mississippi beauty pageant transfers well to film, with a good cast brightly filling out Henley's usual comic collection of oddballs. Look for a cameo appearance by Christine Lahti. (Dir: Thomas Schlamme, 102 mins.)†

Miss Grant Takes Richmond (1949)*** Lucille Ball, William Holden, James Gleason. Clever comedy about a secretarial school that is a front for a bookie syndicate. (Dir: Lloyd Bacon, 87 mins.)

Missile (1988)*** Documentary filmmaker Frederick Wiseman offers a chillingly sober look at the training undergone by the Air Force officers who man our Minuteman ICBM missiles. His unadorned *cinéma vérite* style creates a startling sense of realism, particularly in the sequence where the officers discuss the idea of "only following orders." (115 mins.)

Missiles of October, The (MTV 1974)*** William Devane, Martin Sheen, Ralph Bellamy, Howard da Silva, Andrew Duggan. Recreation of the events of October 1962, when the U.S. stood on the brink of a nuclear war over Russian missile bases in Cuba. Informative and gripping, with Devane outstanding as John F. Kennedy. (Dir: Anthony Page, 155 mins.)†

Missing (1982)***½ Jack Lemmon, Sissy Spacek, John Shea, Melanie Mayron, David Clennon, Janice Rule, Charles Cioffi. Compelling, powerful, and intense drama about the disappearance of a young American journalist, during the Chilean political coup in September of 1973. Director Constantin Costa-Gavras has created another political thriller which brilliantly portrays the day-to-day fear and terror of a military siege. (122 mins.)†

Missing Children: A Mother's Story (MTV 1982)* Mare Winningham, Polly Holliday, John Anderson, Kate Capshaw, Scatman Crothers. Unconvincing melodrama about a child-care center funneling out kids for adoption in the late '40s. (Dir: Dick Lowry, 104 mins.)

Missing in Action (1984)*½ Chuck Norris, M. Emmet Walsh, James Hong. Rightwing gung-ho action yarn! Norris plays a POW in North Vietnam who, after escaping to the U.S., returns to Vietnam to search for American soldiers missing in action. (Dir: Joseph Zito, 101 mins.)†

Missing in Action 2—The Beginning (1985)*½ Chuck Norris, Soon-teck Oh, Steven Williams, Bennett Ohta, Cosie Costa. Prequel to *Missing in Action*. Now we know why Braddock (Norris) hates Commies. Watch it just for Norris strung up by his heels from a tree with a rat in a sack over his head. (Dir: Lance Hool, 96 mins.)†

Missing Pieces (MTV 1983)*½ Elizabeth Montgomery, Ron Karabatsos, John Reilly. Talented Montgomery puts her hair up and becomes a private eye, doggedly unwinding a long-winded and complicated drug case. (Dir: Mike Hodges, 104 mins.)

Mission, The (1984)*** Parviz Sayyad, Mary Apick, Houshang Touzie. Good thriller from a filmmaker who fled Iran is both suspenseful and politically intriguing. An assassin arrives in New York to eliminate an enemy of the Khomeini regime. Instead, he ends up rescuing the man from muggers and falling under the spell of the man's friendship. (Dir: Parviz Sayyad, 107 mins.)

Mission, The (1986)*** Robert De Niro, Jeremy Irons, Ray McAnally, Liam Neeson, Aidan Quinn. Powerful account of the missionary work carried on among the Indians of 18th-century South America, and the manipulative church politics that put an end to it. Irons plays a saintlike priest who espouses faith as the only answer to a papal order demanding that his mission be shut down; De Niro is his explosive counterpart, a slave-trader-turned-Jesuit who is willing to take up arms to prevent the mission's closing. This political parable contains quietly brilliant performances by the leads, hypnotic cinematography, and an evocative score by Ennio Morricone. (Dir: Roland Joffe, 124 mins.)†

Missionary, The (Great Britain, 1982)***½ Michael Palin, Maggie Smith, Trevor Howard, Denholm Elliott, Michael Hordern, Graham Crowden, David Suchet. Classy comedy with Palin as a naïve clergyman assigned to open a mission dedicated to rescuing ladies of the street who provides them with more than shelter. Palin wrote the screenplay with flair, and director Richard Loncraine deftly handles the low-key gags. (93 mins.)†

Mission Batangas (1968)** Dennis Weaver, Vera Miles, Keith Larsen. Grade B adventure set during WWII in the Philippines. An American pilot stumbles upon a plan to commandeer the Philippine government's stock of gold bullion. (Dir: Keith Larsen, 100 mins.)

Mission Kill (1985)**½ Robert Ginty, Olivia d'Abo, Henry Darrow, Sandy Baron, Cameron Mitchell, Merete Van Kamp. Ex-marine Ginty brings more problems to a war-torn Central American country when he goes there to seek revenge for the murder of a friend, who was running arms to the revolutionaries. Plenty of action keeps the pace moving in a movie that's about as subtle as its title. (Dir: David Winters, 97 mins.)†

Mission Mars (1967)*½ Darren McGavin, Nick Adams, Heather Hewitt, George DeVries, Michael DeBeausset. The first manned rocket from Earth lands on Mars and finds some strange and rather uninteresting forces at work. (Dir: Nick Webster, 95 mins.)†

Mission Over Korea (1953)** John Derek, John Hodiak, Audrey Totter, Maureen O'Sullivan. Two officers argue about their jobs in the Korean conflict and later show their true colors to one another. (Dir: Fred F. Sears, 86 mins.)

Mission to Moscow (1943)*** Walter Huston, Eleanor Parker. A fine, well-played movie adaptation from the book by ex-ambassador to Russia Joseph Davies. (Dir: Michael Curtiz, 123 mins.)

Mississippi (1935)*** Bing Crosby, W. C. Fields, Joan Bennett. Pleasant musical about a young man who refuses to fight a duel and takes refuge as a singer on a showboat. A few good Rodgers and Hart tunes, plus Fields's work as the captain add up to nice entertainment. (Dir: A. Edward Sutherland, 64 mins.)

Mississippi Burning (1988)***½ Gene Hackman, Willem Dafoe, Frances McDormand, Brad Dourif, Lee Ermey. Dramatization of the FBI's 1964 investigation into the murders of three civil rights workers in Mississippi is a powerful piece of filmmaking, though occasionally guilty of rewriting history to dubious ends. Hackman's Oscar-nominated performance carries it; a strong supporting cast in unsympathetic roles helps. (Dir: Alan Parker, 127 min.)†

Mississippi Gambler (1953)*** Tyrone Power, Piper Laurie, Julie Adams. Colorful romantic-adventure with Power perfectly cast as a dashing gambler who plays for high stakes in matters of love, honor, and reputation. (Dir: Rudolph Maté, 98 mins.)

Mississippi Mermaid, The (France-Italy, 1969)*** Jean-Paul Belmondo, Catherine Deneuve. This mail-order bride mystery benefits greatly from the star power of Belmondo and Deneuve. It's one of François Truffaut's stylish imitations of Alfred Hitchcock. Although it doesn't deliver Hitchcock's masterly suspense touches, it remains an enjoyable romantic thriller worth viewing. (123 mins.)

Miss Julie (Sweden, 1951)***½ Anita Bjork, Max Von Sydow, Marta Dorff, Ulf Palme, Anders Henrikson. Powerful filmization of August Strindberg's drama about sexual repression and domination features superb use of flashbacks and flashforwards, and an extraordinary performance by Björk in the title role. (Dir: Alf Sjöberg, 87 mins.)†

Miss Mary (Argentina, 1986)**½ Julie Christie, Sofia Viruboff, Donald McIntire. Christie is impressive as the English governess whose cool competence belies a sexually repressed personality, and whose single tryst with the son of her wealthy employers has devastating results in her life and those of the children in her care. (Dir: Maria Luisa Bemberg, 102 mins.)†

Miss . . . or Myth (1985)*** Compelling documentary that contrasts the 1985 Miss California beauty pageant with a feminist alternative event, the Myth California pageant. Both sides air their philosophies. (Dirs: Geoffrey Dunn, Mark Schwartz, 60 mins.)

Missouri Breaks, The (1976)** Marlon Brando, Jack Nicholson, Harry Dean Stanton, Kathleen Lloyd. An enormously disappointing, muddled western set in Montana during the 1880s. Director Arthur Penn reportedly had to cater to Brando's every whim, including making inane alterations in the script. (126 mins.)†

Missouri Traveler, The (1958)**½ Brandon de Wilde, Lee Marvin, Gary Merrill. Exaggerated piece of Americana about a young runaway who provides for himself by training racehorses. (Dir: Jerry Hopper, 103 mins.)

Miss Oyu (Japan, 1951)***½ Kinuyo Tanaka, Yuji Hori, Kiyoko Hirai, Reiko Kongo, Nobuko Otowa. A wealthy bachelor wants to marry a widow whose son will lose his inheritance if she weds again. Stylish film played with great emotion and depth. (Dir: Kenji Mizoguchi, 96 mins.)

Miss Pinkerton (1932)**½ Joan Blondell, George Brent, Ruth Hall. There are scares and laughter in an old dark house in the B movie based on a Mary Roberts Rinehart yarn. (Dir: Lloyd Bacon, 66 mins.)

Miss Robin Hood (Great Britain, 1953)**½ Margaret Rutherford, Richard Hearne. A meek writer of girls' adventure stories aids a battle-ax in repossessing her recipe for whiskey, which was stolen by a distiller. Screwball comedy isn't as funny as it was meant to be. (Dir: John Guillermin, 78 mins.)

Miss Sadie Thompson (1953)**½ Rita Hayworth, José Ferrer, Aldo Ray. The sultry saga of sinful Sadie Thompson is on view in this remake of Somerset Maugham's *Rain*. Rita plays the island sinner this time while Ferrer screams of fire and brimstone. (Dir: Curtis Bernhardt, 91 mins.)†

Miss Susie Slagle's (1945)**½ Veronica Lake, Joan Caulfield, Lillian Gish, Sonny Tufts, Ray Collins, Billy DeWolfe. Lightweight comedy of the denizens of a rooming house for medical students at the turn of the century; nothing special, but with an agreeable spirit. (Dir: John Berry, 88 mins.)

Miss Tatlock's Millions (1949)*** John Lund, Monty Woolley, Robert Stack, Wanda Hendrix. Movie stunt man agrees to pose as the feebleminded heir to a fortune. Plenty of laughs in this sparkling comedy. (Dir: Richard Haydn, 100 mins.)

Mister—See also: **Mr.**

Mister Cory (1957)*** Tony Curtis, Martha

Hyer, Kathryn Grant. Fast, rowdy, fun-filled story of a lad from the Chicago slums who grows up to be a big-time gambler. (Dir: Blake Edwards, 92 mins.)

Mister Drake's Duck (Great Britain, 1951) *** Douglas Fairbanks, Jr., Yolande Donlan. An American couple buy an English farm, where they encounter a duck that lays uranium eggs. Fast-moving, sprightly comedy. (Dir: Val Guest, 76 mins.)

Mister 880 (1950)*** Burt Lancaster, Dorothy McGuire, Edmund Gwenn. Charming real-life story about a T-man and a UN secretary who investigate a lovable old counterfeiter. Gwenn shines as the money-maker. (Dir: Edmund Goulding, 90 mins.)

Mister Frost (France-Great Britain, 1990)** Jeff Goldblum, Alan Bates, Kathy Baker, Roland Giraud, Jean-Pierre Cassel. Is mass-murderer Goldblum really Satan himself, as he claims? That's what psychiatrist Baker tries to find out, but she's more interested in the question than audiences will be. A disappointment, considering the premise and cast. (Dir: Philippe Setbon, 104 mins.)

Mister Jericho (MTV 1970)**½ Patrick Macnee, Connie Stevens, Herbert Lom. Macnee plays ingenious con artist with a flair and he's matched by Lom as an eccentric millionaire. OK time-passer. (Dir: Sidney Hayers, 85 mins.)

Mister Johnson (1990)*** Pierce Brosnan, Edward Woodward, Maynard Eziashi, Denis Quilley. Powerful and sweeping drama about the building of a road linking south and north Nigeria in the twenties. First-time Nigerian actor Eziashi is enthralling as the man who is the link between African and British cultures. From the novel by Joyce Cary. (Dir: Bruce Beresford, 102 mins.)†

Mister Kingstreet's War (Africa, 1970)*** John Saxon, Tippi Hedren, Rossano Brazzi, Brian O'Shaughnessy. Offbeat African story. Set in 1939, it has game warden Saxon and physician wife Hedren opposing the forces of Italian major Brazzi and a British platoon, just as WWII begins. (Dir: Percival Rubens, 92 mins.)

Mister Moses (1965)** Robert Mitchum, Carroll Baker. Mild adventure epic° in which Mitchum is involved in gem-smuggling. (Dir: Ronald Neame, 113 mins.)

Mister Roberts (1955)**** Henry Fonda, Jack Lemmon, William Powell, James Cagney. A superb cast brings the rollicking B'way comedy to the screen. Henry Fonda repeats his solid character-ization in the title role of Lt. Roberts, who is eager to be transferred to the fighting zone rather than serve on a cargo ship. Jack Lemmon won a Best Supporting Actor Oscar as the opportu-nistic Ensign Pulver. (Dirs: John Ford, Mervyn LeRoy, 123 mins.)†

Mister Scoutmaster (1953)** Clifton Webb. Even Webb's aplomb doesn't save this comedy about a reluctant scoutmaster and his misadventures with a pack of future eagle scouts. (Dir: Henry Levin, 87 mins.)

Mistress (MTV 1987)*½ Victoria Princi-pal, Kerri Keane, Joanna Kerns, Don Murray. A showcase for Principal as a kept woman who is suddenly thrust out into the real world when her lover dies. (Dir: Michael Tuchner, 96 mins.)†

Mistress of Paradise (MTV 1981)* Gene-viève Bujold, Chad Everett, Anthony Andrews, Olivia Cole. Claptrap drama about the turbulent love affair between a wealthy Northern heiress and a sophisti-cated Louisiana plantation owner. (Dir: Peter Medak, 104 mins.)

Mistress of the World (Italy-France-West Germany, 1959)** Martha Hyer, Carlos Thompson, Gino Cervi, Sabu. Wild sci-fi tale of a professor whose invention for controlling the world's magnetic fields is imperiled by Chinese agents. (Dir: William Dieterle, 107 mins.)†

Misty (1961)**½ David Ladd, Arthur O'Connell, Pam Smith. Good adventure story for the kids, as two young chil-dren try to tame a wild pony. From the popular children's story by Marguerite Henry. (Dir: James B. Clark, 92 mins.)

Misunderstood (1984)** Gene Hackman, Henry Thomas, Rip Torn, Huckleberry Fox. Set in Tunisia, this restrained do-mestic drama concerns a newly widowed father and his inability to communicate with one of his two young sons. (Dir: Jerry Schatzberg, 91 mins.)†

Mitchell (1975)* Joe Don Baker, Martin Balsam, John Saxon. Baker plays an-other lawman with "unorthodox" meth-ods. This time out he's battling corrup-tion in Los Angeles. (Dir: Andrew V. McLaglen, 95 mins.)

Mitsou (France, 1957)*** Daniele Delorme, Fernand Gravey, Claude Rich, Odette Laure, François Guerin, Gaby Morlay. A beautiful chorus girl in WWI Paris falls in love with a handsome sol-dier, who rejects her because she lacks social graces and education. Her Sugar Daddy offers to help her overcome those obstacles to love. Based on a story by Colette, film is gorgeously photographed with lavish sets and costumes. (Dir: Jacqueline Audry, 95 mins.)

Mixed Blood (1985)*** Marilia Pera, Richard Ulacia, Geraldine Smith, Linda Kerridge. Fast, lurid, funny, and very violent movie from former Andy Warhol protegé Paul Morrissey. Brazilian star

Pera (*Pixote*) stars as the leader of a gang of juvenile heroin dealers in New York's lower east side, battling to maintain control of her empire against various crooked cops and drug kingpins. (98 mins.)†

Mixed Company (1974)* Barbara Harris, Joseph Bologna. Simple-minded treatment of an inportant subject—an American couple with three children of their own adopting a multiracial family. (Dir: Melville Shavelson, 109 mins.)

Mix Me a Person (Great Britain, 1961)**½ Anne Baxter, Adam Faith, Donald Sinden. Teen guitarist is charged with murder when a policeman is killed. Uneven drama has some absorbing scenes. (Dir: Leslie Norman, 108 mins.)

Moana (1926)*** T'avale, Fa'amgase, Tu'ugaita, Moana, Pe'a. Unique anthropological docudrama from the director who founded that form, Robert Flaherty, shows the traditional life of a Samoan family; beautifully filmed, and still fascinating. (85 mins.)†

Mob, The (1951)*** Broderick Crawford, Ernest Borgnine, Richard Kiley. Good gangland film about a policeman who joins the mob in order to get to the big boys. Well acted; snappy dialogue. (Dir: Robert Parrish, 87 mins.)

Mo' Better Blues (1990)** Denzel Washington, Joie Lee, Wesley Snipes, Spike Lee, Cynda Williams, Rubén Blades, John Turturro, Giancarlo Esposito. Actor-writer-director Lee doesn't seem to know if his unfocused cliché-ridden jazz film is about music, sex, hate, romance, or family. Washington is a trumpeter who dates two women at the same time, bullies his band, and fears passion and commitment to everything but his music. The ending's violence comes out of left field and throws the movie out of whack. (Dir: Spike Lee, 129 mins.)†

Mob Town (1941)*½ Dead End Kids, Dick Foran. The kids choose again between a life of crime and going straight. (Dir: William Nigh, 60 mins.)

Moby Dick (1930)** John Barrymore, Joan Bennett, Lloyd Hughes, Walter Long. Unsatisfying treatment of the Melville classic; with an added love interest! (Dir: Lloyd Bacon, 75 mins.)

Moby Dick (1956)*** Gregory Peck, Orson Welles, Harry Andrews, Richard Basehart, James Robertson-Justice. Ray Bradbury's adaptation is only adequate, but director John Huston's grasp of the material is so intense that some sparks flash. The final whaling scenes are extraordinary by any standard. (116 mins.)†

Model and the Marriage Broker, The (1952)*** Jeanne Crain, Thelma Ritter, Scott Brady. The marriage broker is wisecracking Ritter and the model she

matches up is lovely Crain. Director George Cukor is a master at this kind of sophisticated comedy. (103 mins.)

Model Killer, The—See: Hollywood Strangler meets the Skid Row Slasher

Model Massacre—See: Color Me Blood Red

Model Shop (1969)**½ Anouk Aimée, Gary Lockwood, Alexander Hay. French director Jacques Demy's first U.S. film in English; a troubled youth who runs into Aimée while she is working in one of those Los Angeles spots where you can photograph models for a fee. (Dir: Jacques Demy, 95 mins.)

Model Wife (1941)*** Joan Blondell, Dick Powell, Charlie Ruggles. Fast-paced marital farce wittily played by Blondell and Powell as co-workers forced to keep their marriage secret to protect their jobs. (Dir: Leigh Jason, 78 mins.)

Moderato Cantabile (France, 1960)***½ Jeanne Moreau, Jean-Paul Belmondo, Pascale De Boysson, Didier Haudepin, Valerie Dobuzinsky. Stark drama about a lonely married woman who becomes obsessed with a crime. Expressive, atmospheric film, co-scripted by Marguerite Duras from her novel. (Dir: Peter Brook, 95 mins.)

Modern Girls (1986)½ Daphne Zuniga, Virginia Madsen, Cynthia Gibb. Three girls explore the singles scene, have a blast, meet guys, hang out. (Dir: Jerry Krumer, 82 mins.)†

Modern Hero, A (1934)**½ Richard Barthelmess, Jean Muir, Marjorie Rambeau. Director G. W. Pabst's only American film, adapted from a Louis Bromfield novel with Barthelmess as a rising young man who becomes a ruthless industrialist. (71 mins.)

Modern Love (1989)* Robby Benson, Karla DeVito, Burt Reynolds, Rue McClanahan, Frankie Valli, Kaye Ballard, Louise Lasser. Benson miscalculated his actor, writer, producer, and director skills in this embarrassingly awful comedy-drama. A real-life married couple, Benson and DeVito portray young lovers who experience the trials of courtship, marriage, in-laws, parenthood, and the loss of a loved one. (Dir: Robby Benson, 110 mins.)†

Modern Problems (1981)** Chevy Chase, Patti D'Arbanville, Mary Kay Place, Nell Carter, Brian Doyle-Murray, Dabney Coleman, Mitch Kreindel. Disappointing comedy casts Chase as an air-traffic controller endowed with telekinetic powers. (Dir: Ken Shapiro, 91 mins.)†

Modern Romance (1980)**½ Albert Brooks, Kathryn Harrold, Bruno Kirby, James L. Brooks. Albert Brooks confirms the considerable talent he showed in his *Real Life*. Funny comedy, filled with insight. Brooks plays Everyman as compulsive jerk, unable to handle emotional jolts, overcome rabid possessiveness, or resist the blandishments of canny salesmen. (Dir: Albert Brooks, 100 mins.)†

Moderns, The (1988)***½ Keith Carradine, Linda Fiorentino, John Lone, Wallace Shawn, Geneviève Bujold, Geraldine Chaplin. The near-mythic Lost Generation of Americans living in Paris in the twenties provides the focus for this uniquely sumptuous, visually stirring romantic melodrama from filmmaker Alan Rudolph. Carradine is a caricaturist who encounters an old flame (Fiorentino), now married to a wealthy, very macho businessman who dabbles in the arts (Lone). Their affair is played out in the cafés and salons of the Left Bank intellectuals, where they mingle with literary names (Gertrude Stein, Hemingway et al.). Throughout the film, Rudolph's guiding hand transforms the melodrama and historical circumstance into sheer beauty, wryly commenting on the experiences of these expatriates as he glorifies them. (126 mins.)†

Modern Times (1936)**** Charles Chaplin, Paulette Goddard. One of the all-time greats, a sensational one-man show by Chaplin, writing, directing, producing, scoring, and starring in this eternal saga of Everyman in all times. The Tramp moves from factory worker to department-store janitor to singing waiter as modern times knock him cruelly about. (100 mins.)†

Modesty Blaise (Great Britain, 1956)*½ Monica Vitti, Terence Stamp, Dirk Bogarde. A lumbering film of the comic-strip adventures of sexy super-agent Modesty (Vitti). (Dir: Joseph Losey, 119 mins.)

Mogambo (1953)*** Clark Gable, Ava Gardner, Grace Kelly, Donald Sinden, Laurence Naismith. Tangy remake of *Red Dust*. Gable repeats his role of the white hunter whose life is complicated by two beautiful women. Gardner gives one of her best performances, in a colorful role. (Dir: John Ford, 116 mins.)†

Mohammad, Messenger of God (Great Britain, 1976)* Anthony Quinn, Irene Papas, Michael Ansara, Johnny Sekka, Damien Thomas. An epic about the founding of the Islamic religion. A multimillion-dollar production, filmed in Libya, it is as arid as the desert you'll see. (Dir: Moustapha Akkad, 179 mins.)

Mohawk (1956)** Scott Brady, Rita Gam, Neville Brand, Allison Hayes. Rampaging Injuns decide to give scalp treatments to some unwilling settlers. (Dir: Kurt Neumann, 79 mins.)

Mokey (1942)**½ Donna Reed, Dan Dailey, Bobby Blake, Buckwheat Thomas, Cordell Hickman, Etta McDaniel. Well-acted children's story of a youngster who resents his stepmother, and turns towards delinquency. Fairly mundane plot, lifted by young Robert "Bobby" Blake, who is terrific. (Dir: Wells Root, 88 mins.)

Mole People, The (1956)* John Agar, Hugh Beaumont, Alan Napier. After viewing this monstrosity about subterranean fiends, you'll think twice about mowing your lawn. (Dir: Virgil Vogel, 78 mins.)

Molly (1950)**½ Gertrude Berg, Philip Loeb. Life with the Goldbergs, as Molly's former suitor pays the family a visit. Mildly amusing. (Dir: Walter Hart, 83 mins.)

Molly and Me (1945)*** Monty Woolley, Gracie Fields, Roddy McDowall. Well-played warm comedy about a maid who straightens out her employer's life. Not hilarious, but a very pleasant diversion. (Dir: Lewis Seller, 76 mins.)

Molly Maguires, The (1969)**½ Sean Connery, Richard Harris, Samantha Eggar. In the 1870s the Molly Maguires tried to improve Pennsylvania coal miners' conditions through terrorism. James McParlan (Harris) is a Pinkerton detective who manages to infiltrate the Molly Maguires. Well intentioned, but depressing. (Dir: Martin Ritt, 124 mins.)†

Moment by Moment (1978)* John Travolta, Lily Tomlin. Travolta plays a soulful beach bum (but he's deep spiritually) who falls in love with wealthy Beverly Hills matron Tomlin (but she's capable of great passion underneath her shallow surface). Although this sounds like the makings of a comedy sketch, it instead forms the basis for this unbearably pretentious drama. (Dir: Jane Wagner, 94 mins.)

Moment of Truth (Italy-Spain, 1964)***½ Miguel Mateo Miguelin, Linda Christian, Pedro Basauri, José Gomez, Sevillano. Considered by most to be the greatest bullfighting movie, this international success follows a peasant boy who travels to Barcelona to find fame and fortune in the ring. Director Francesco Rosi uses extraordinary camerawork to detail the unrelenting brutality of man against animal. (110 mins.)

Moment to Moment (1966)**½ Jean Seberg, Sean Garrison, Honor Blackman. Glossy soap opera with suspenseful underpinnings. Wanting to end an illicit affair, a young wife accidentally shoots her paramour, then frantically tries to hide the body—which disappears. (Dir: Mervyn LeRoy, 108 mins.)

Mommie Dearest (1981)*** Faye Dunaway, Diana Scarwid, Steve Forrest, Mara Hobel, Rutanya Alda, Howard da Silva, Harry Goz. Never have the sublime and the ridiculous been so inextricably linked in one film. Based on Christina Crawford's shocking memoirs about life with

Mother the Movie Star, this film contains trenchant sequences about the eternal war between parent and child. Unfortunately, these painful observations co-exist with lurid segments that have already passed into the annals of camp. Dunaway's over-the-top portrayal of the ultimate control-freak goes beyond the hatchet job of Tina's biography. (Dir: Frank Perry, 129 mins.)†

Mom, The Wolfman, And Me (MTV 1980)*** Patty Duke Astin, David Birney, Keenan Wynn, Danielle Brisebois, Viveca Lindfors. A charmingly acted romantic comedy about a divorced fashion photographer and her eleven-year-old daughter. The mother is being pursued by an advertising executive, as well as a schoolteacher who owns an Irish wolfhound (named Wolfman). (Dir: Edmund Levy, 104 mins.)

Mona Lisa (Great Britain, 1986)*** Bob Hoskins, Cathy Tyson, Michael Caine, Robbie Coltrane, Clarke Peters. Director Neil Jordan (Company of Wolves) continues his fascination with myths in this gritty modern-day fairy tale about a two-bit hood who functions as a sawed-off fairy godfather to an exotic-looking call girl searching desperately for a young drug-addicted pal. Bringing these lost souls to life is a superb cast, including Hoskins who, after a prison stretch, returns to criminal activities only to discover there's no longer any honor among thieves. (104 mins.)†

Mondo Cane (Italy, 1963)** More schlocking than shocking documentary about unusual occurrences and bizarre customs around the world. (Producer: Gualtiero Jacopetti, 105 mins.)†

Mondo New York (1988)**½ Shannah Laumeister, Phoebe Legere, Joey Arias, Karen Finley, Dean Johnson. A potpourri of celebrated performers and oddities from Manhattan's Lower East Side. It goes from irritating (Finley) to repugnant (a human explosive who bites the heads off of mice) to refreshingly entertaining (new wavers Arias, John Sex, and Johnson). (Dir: Harvey Keith, 83 mins.)†

Mondo Trasho (1970)½ Divine, Mary Vivian Pearce, Mink Stole, David Lochary. Filmmaker John Waters's first feature-length effort is a mixed bag that never hits a bull's-eye. The first reason for this is the loose, episodic structure, following Pearce and hit-and-run driver Divine; the second, the absence of the stinging dialogue Waters fans are accustomed to. The soundtrack, unfortunately, is composed almost entirely of old pop hits which are tiresome after a while. (Dir: John Waters, 94 mins.)†

Money from Home (1953)** Dean Martin, Jerry Lewis, Pat Crowley. Dean and Jerry are on the spot when Dino's IOUs start showing up and a mobster tells him to pay up or else help throw a horse race. Strained comedy based on a Damon Runyon story is below par. (Dir: George Marshall, 99 mins.)

Money Movers (Australia, 1978)*** Terence Donovan, Ed Devereaux, Tony Bonner. Interesting Australian based-on-fact thriller about the $20 million robbery of a counting house by members of a security company. (Dir: Bruce Beresford, 91 mins.)

Money on the Side (MTV 1982)**½ Linda Purl, Karen Valentine, Jamie Lee Curtis, Richard Masur. Offbeat and interesting. Three married women become prostitutes to help pay the bills. (Dir: Robert Collins, 104 mins.)

Money Pit, The (1986)*½ Tom Hanks, Shelley Long, Alexander Godunov, Maureen Stapleton, Joe Mantegna, Philip Bosco. Gerry-built comedy loosely based on Mr. Blandings Builds His Dream House. After eviction, a yuppie couple locates a dream house which turns into a nightmare. Despite some winning lines and slapstick, this comedy is pretty much the pits. (Dir: Richard Benjamin, 91 mins.)†

Money to Burn (MTV 1973)**½ E. G. Marshall, Mildred Natwick, Alejandro Rey, Cleavon Little. Fun. A sympathetic cast portrays a counterfeiting group. The pace, the people, the plot, and the dialogue all have a sense of humorous larceny. (Dir: Robert Michael Lewis, 72 mins.)†

Money Trap, The (1965)** Glenn Ford, Elke Sommer, Rita Hayworth, Joseph Cotten, Ricardo Montalban. Familiar fare about an honest cop driven to dishonest deeds by his sexy, money-hungry wife. Hayworth comes off best, in a supporting role as an embittered woman who has turned to alcohol for solace. (Dir: Burt Kennedy, 92 mins.)

Mongo's Back In Town (MTV 1971)*** Joe Don Baker, Sally Field. Unvarnished script by convict E. Richard Johnson. Tough, rough, arresting Christmas yarn about a San Pedro killer who returns to help his brother out of a jam over counterfeit plates. (Dir: Marvin Chomsky, 73 mins.)

Monika (Sweden, 1952)*** Harriet Andersson, Lars Ekborg. This early Ingmar Bergman film tells the story of a pair of young lovers who run off to an island for a holiday. She later rejects her baby, and the young man is left with responsibility for the child. Depressing, but sensitively told. AKA: **Summer with Monika**. (96 mins.)†

Monitors, The (1969)*½ Guy Stockwell, Keenan Wynn, Ed Begley, Susan Oliver, Avery Schreiber, Larry Storch. Confused tale about intelligent creatures from outer space who come to Earth to impose a rule of peace. Intelligent idea becomes muddled by an ineffectual point of view that switches between farce, satire, and seriousness. (Dir: Jack Shea, 90 mins.)

Monk, The (MTV 1969)*** George Maharis, Janet Leigh, Carl Betz. Typical private-eye crime tale in which the hero spouts glib dialogue, the plot is incredible, and the writers come up with a plot gimmick every twenty minutes or so. (Dir: George McCowan, 73 mins.)

Monkey Business (1931)*** Marx Brothers. Great comedy is never dated and even Groucho's Depression puns will still make you laugh. The boys are stowaways on a ship and causing their usual amount of trouble. (Dir: Norman McLeod, 77 mins.)†

Monkey Business (1952)*** Cary Grant, Ginger Rogers, Marilyn Monroe. Zany and often hilarious comedy about a scientist (Grant) who discovers a rejuvenation tonic and tries it out himself with surprising results. Monroe has a small but funny part as a foil for Grant's comic shenanigans. (Dir: Howard Hawks, 97 mins.)†

Monkey Grip (Australia, 1983)*½ Noni Hazlehurst, Colin Friels. Long on style and short on substance, this Australian sudser relates the tale of a single mother in love with a drug-addicted musician. (Dir: Ken Cameron, 101 mins.)†

Monkey Hustle, The (1976)** Yaphet Kotto, Rosalind Cash, Rudy Ray Moore, Kirk Calloway. Fair blaxploitation comedy about con artists in the ghetto and how they react when they learn an expressway may wipe out their humble home. (Dir: Larthim Marks, 90 mins.)†

Monkey In Winter, A (France, 1962)*** Jean Gabin, Jean-Paul Belmondo. Two great male stars of French cinema discover they are kindred spirits in this mild, unembellished, anecdotal tale of an old and a young man who postpone reality for a day of drinking and dreams. (Dir: Henri Verneuil, 104 mins.)

Monkey Mission, The (MTV 1981)** Robert Blake, Keenan Wynn. A second TV movie for Robert Blake's pugnacious private eye Joe Dancer. Blake soft pedals the hard-nose approach while trying to swipe a museum vase for a client. (Dir: Russ Mayberry, 104 mins.)

Monkey on My Back (1957)*** Cameron Mitchell, Dianne Foster. Often interesting dramatized biography of boxer Barney Ross, his early rise to fame in the ring, his high-spending days as a gambler, his heroic career in the Marines during WWII, and his narcotics addiction and struggle to kick the habit. (Dir: André de Toth, 93 mins.)

Monkeys, Go Home (1967)* Dean Jones, Maurice Chevalier, Yvette Mimieux.

Bland Disney concoction for the kids. Dean Jones inherits an olive farm in France and hires some chimpanzees to help him pick the crop. (Dir: Andrew McLaglen, 101 mins.)†

Monkey Shines (1988)** Jason Beghe, John Pankow, Kate McNeil, Joyce Van Patten. A law student, paralyzed from the neck down in an accident, is given a trained monkey to do chores and help him cope. But because the monkey's brain has been altered by lab experiments, she begins to carry out her master's darker impulses. Director George Romero abandons the gory black comedy of his zombie films to shoot for raw suspense. But there are too many unexplained elements in his screenplay, and the final sequence contains as many unintentional laughs as shivers. Nice try, but a failed one. (113 mins.)†

Monkey's Uncle, The (1965)*½ Tommy Kirk, Annette Funicello, Leon Ames, Frank Faylen, Arthur O'Connell. A sequel (unasked for) to *The Misadventures of Merlin Jones;* more scientific monkeyshines with monkeys and flying machines. (Dir: Robert Stevenson, 87 mins.)†

Monolith Monsters, The (1957)** Grant Williams, Lola Albright, William Schallert. Strange deaths occur after a meteor shatters in the California desert. A geologist discovers why, at the risk of his life. Standard sci-fi thriller. (Dir: John Sherwood, 77 mins.)

Mon Oncle—See: **My Uncle**

Mon Oncle d'Amerique (France, 1980)***½ Gerard Depardieu, Nicole Garcia, Roger Pierre, Marie Dubois. Unusual movie in which director Alain Resnais returns to his favorite themes of memory and loss. Among the characters under scrutiny is Depardieu, as a textile-plant manager who has an affair with the wife of a country gentleman. In this metaphysical maze, the stars are put through their paces in a film which is simultaneously witty and melancholy. (123 mins.)†

Monsieur Beaucaire (1946)*** Bob Hope, Joan Caulfield, Marjorie Reynolds. One of Bob's most inspired romps, as a barber impersonating a dandy in the court of Louis XV. Directed by old-hand George Marshall in his best period. From the novel by Booth Tarkington. (93 mins.)

Monsieur Hire (France, 1989)***½ Michel Blanc, Sandrine Bonnaire, Luc Thuillier, André Wilms. Brilliantly executed *noir* character study of meek tailor who develops a fixation for the young woman who lives across the way from him. Her eventual discovery of his daily voyeuristic observances of her bind the two together in a relationship that's bound to end in tragedy. In a mere eighty-one minutes, director Patrice Leconte and two sublime leads (Blanc and Bonnaire) fashion a bittersweet tale that is both touching and truly suspenseful. Based on a novel by Georges Simenon. (81 mins.)†

Monsieur Hulot's Holiday (France, 1953)**** Jacques Tati, Michele Rolla, Valentine Camax, Nathalie Pascaud. First film to feature director Tati's friendly, bumbling Hulot. This wonderfully comic, plotless movie about his vacation trip to the seashore features hilarious situations, gleaming camerawork, brilliant sound, and a performance by Tati that is simple, pure, and gloriously cinematic. Though there is almost no dialogue, an English-dubbed print exists, with most of the voices provided by Christopher Lee! Originally 114 mins. (91 mins.)†

Monsieur Verdoux (1947)**** Charlie Chaplin, Martha Raye, Marilyn Nash. Chaplin's sardonic "comedy of murders" is a masterpiece. Chaplin (who directed) plays a bank clerk turned Bluebeard, murdering lonely women for their money after marrying them, all in order to support his lovely storybook family complete with crippled wife. Chaplin gets chilling humor out of his efforts to kill a victim and still get to the bank before it closes, or in his repeated attempts to sink the unsinkable Raye in a grotesque parody of *An American Tragedy*. (123 mins.)†

Monsignor (1983)*½ Christopher Reeve, Geneviève Bujold, Jason Miller, Robert Prosky, Fernando Rey, Adolfo Celi. In striving for high office, a holy man saves the Catholic Church in Rome with some sneaky black marketeering in WWII. This preposterous drama is surprisingly dull for a film about sex and politics in high places. (Dir: Frank Perry, 121 mins.)†

Monster, The (1925)*** Lon Chaney, Gertrude Olsted, Edward McWade, Hallam Cooley, Johnny Arthur. Facetious thriller, from the play by Crane Wilbur, has Chaney having a wonderful time hamming it up as a mad doctor who conducts bizarre, nameless experiments on randomly kidnapped subjects; absurd plot with tongue-in-cheek performances. (Dir: Roland West, 86 mins.)

Monster a Go-Go (1965)½ Phil Morton, June Travis, Henry Hite. Unwatchable. Director Herschell Gordon Lewis bought an unfinished feature film about an astronaut who returns to Earth as a mutated giant. He added a little linking footage and released it with joking publicity as the second feature to one of his own movies. Released on video as a "Le Bad Cinema" presentation, it's not so-bad-it's-good, just a rip-off. (Dirs: Bill Rebane, "Sheldon Seymour"[Lewis], 70 mins.)†

Monster and the Girl, The (1941)**½ Ellen Drew, Robert Paige, Paul Lukas, Joseph Calleia, George Zucco. Boy, does Ellen Drew's family have problems—first, mobsters force her into prostitution, then her dead brother's brain ends up in the body of a gorilla. (Dir: Stuart Heisler, 65 mins.)

Monster Club, The (Great Britain, 1981)** Vincent Price, John Carradine, Simon Ward, Donald Pleasence, Britt Ekland, Stuart Whitman, Patrick Magee. Horror anthology with three scary tales linked by the gimmick of a private club for monsters where vampire Price chats with writer Carradine. Pretty dull, though musical performances by UB40 and the Pretty Things are worthwhile. (Dir: Roy Ward Baker, 97 mins.)†

Monster from Green Hell (1957)*½ Jim Davis, Barbara Turner. Dull horror-filled science-fiction story about huge monsters discovered in the jungles of Africa. (Dir: Kenneth Crane, 71 mins.)†

Monster from the Ocean Floor (1954)* Anne Kimbell, Stuart Wade, Dick Pinner, Jack Hayes, Wyott Ordung. Title says it all: nosy divers investigate rumors of a beastie off the coast of Mexico. You don't see the laughable monster until the end of this, the first film produced by Roger Corman, the budget for which was all of $12,000. Director-co-star Ordung wrote the cult fave *Robot Monster*. (64 mins.)

Monster High (1988)* Dean Iandoli, Diana Frank, David Marriott, Robert M. Lind. More like monster low. Another dumb dumb horror comedy, this one with goofy aliens from the planet Polyester terrorizing students and threatening to blow up the Earth with a basketball-shaped bomb. (Dir: Rudiger Poe, 83 mins.)†

Monster in the Closet (1986)**½ Donald Grant, Denise DuBarry, Claude Akins, Howard Duff, Henry Gibson, Stella Stevens. Shot in 1983, this spoof of grade B monster movies of the fifties concerns a monster who stalks his victim exclusively in their closets. Humor for the desperate. (Dir: Bob Dahlin, 87 mins.)†

Monster of Piedras Blancas, The (1961)*½ Les Tremayne, Jeanne Carmen. Lighthouse keeper is convinced a legendary monster lives in a cave near him. (Dir: Irvin Berwick, 71 mins.)

Monster on the Campus (1958)**½ Arthur Franz, Joanna Moore, Troy Donahue. Scientist injects himself with blood of an ancient fish, turns into a monster. Shocker that delivers the goods. (Dir: Jack Arnold, 76 mins.)

Monster Squad, The (1987)**½ Andre Gower, Robby Kiger, Duncan Regehr, Stephen Macht, Tom Noonan. Engaging horror comedy. Dracula (the deliciously nasty Regehr) brings his monster pals to a small town, and only a group of creature-crazy kids can stop them. (Dir: Fred Dekker, 82 mins.)†

Monster That Challenged the World, The (1957)**½ Tim Holt, Audrey Dalton. Atomic experiments uncover sea beasts who begin their reign of terror. Standard science-fiction horror thriller—better than some, should please the fans. (Dir: Arnold Laven, 83 mins.)

Monster Walks, The (1932)**½ Rex Lease, Vera Reynolds, Mischa Auer, Willie Best. Inconsequential little "old dark house" thriller, with an heiress threatened by her uncle's pet giant killer ape. The comedy relief, Auer and Best, fare best. (Dir: Frank Strayer, 63 mins.)†

Monster Zero—See: **Godzilla vs. Monster Zero**

Montana (1950)** Errol Flynn, Alexis Smith. Cowboys help to make the state of Montana; based on a novel by Ernest Haycox. Smith was almost as pretty as Errol in those days. (Dir: Ray Enright, 76 mins.)

Montana (MTV 1990)*** Gena Rowlands, Richard Crenna, Lea Thompson, Justin Deas, Elizabeth Berridge, Darren Dalton. Modern-day Western, written by Larry McMurtry, is an old-fashioned drama with Rowlands and Crenna as an estranged couple who have always struggled to keep their sprawling ranch (inherited from her father) out of the hands of creditors. When a big money offer comes their way from a power company, Crenna is elated but Rowlands won't have any of it, drawing the lines for a battle of wills. Strong characterizations provide a potent lure for viewers. (Dir: William A. Graham, 120 mins.)†

Montana Belle (1952)** Jane Russell, George Brent, Scott Brady. Belle Starr throws in with the Dalton gang, but is persuaded to reform and turn against the outlaws. (Dir: Allan Dwan, 81 mins.)

Montana Mike (1947)**½ Robert Cummings, Brian Donlevy, Marjorie Reynolds. An angel comes to earth to help reform a western badman. Different kind of western story, pleasant. (Dir: Albert S. Rogell, 95 mins.)

Montana Moon (1930)** Joan Crawford, Johnny Mack Brown, Ricardo Cortez, Dorothy Sebastian, Cliff Edwards. Ludicrous early talkie Crawford vehicle has a spoiled society girl marrying a cowboy against her father's wishes and finding it difficult to adjust to his way of life. Everyone is terrible, and Crawford looks like she can only muster up any enthusiasm for her frequent costume changes. Really a dog, of historical interest only. (Dir: Malcolm St. Clair, 89 mins.)

Monte Carlo (1930)**½ Jeanette MacDonald, Jack Buchanan, ZaSu Pitts. An inventive early talkie musical about a count who poses as a hairdresser to win the heart of a beautiful woman. (Dir: Ernst Lubitsch, 85 mins.)

Monte Carlo (MTV 1986)*½ Joan Collins, George Hamilton, Gene Carradine, Lisa Eilbacher, Lauren Hutton. A shallow wallow in international soapsuds. Impervious to all sense of logic or credibility, the script spotlights Joan as a famed Russian chanteuse with a sideline—spying for the Allies during WWII. (Dir: Anthony Page, 208 mins.)†

Monte Carlo Baby (France, 1952)*½ Audrey Hepburn, Cara Williams, Jules Munshin. Through a mistake, band drummer thinks he is grandfather to a baby, takes the tyke with him on tour. Comedy that mostly misfires. (Dirs: Jean Boyer, Jean Jerrold, 70 mins.)

Monte Carlo Story, The (Italy, 1957)** Marlene Dietrich, Vittorio De Sica, Arthur O'Connell. A fortune hunter and huntress meet in Monte Carlo and foolishly choose love in lieu of wealth. Glamorous settings, including Marlene, are the sole assets of this Riviera trifle. (Dir: Samuel Taylor, 100 mins.)

Montenegro (Sweden-Great Britain, 1981) **½ Susan Anspach, Erland Josephson, Per Oscarsson. Amusing film dealing with sexual repression and immigrant workers in Sweden. A bored American housewife (Anspach) married to a wealthy Swedish businessman is slowly going mad, until she falls in with an assorted group of Balkan immigrants at a sleazy bar. (Dir: Dusan Makavejev, 98 mins.)†

Monterey Pop (1969)***½ The first and one of the best of the rock concert films. The acts include Janis Joplin, the Mamas and the Papas, Jefferson Airplane, Otis Redding (backed by Booker T. and the MGs), Jimi Hendrix, the Who, Country Joe and the Fish, and a finale by Ravi Shankar. (Dir: D. A. Pennebaker, 79 mins.)†

Monte Walsh (1970)* Lee Marvin, Jeanne Moreau, Jack Palance. Boring western! Marvin's cowboy, Monte Walsh, can't get used to the fact the west is changing and his breed is becoming extinct. (Dir: William A. Fraker, 108 mins.)†

Month in the Country, A (Great Britain, 1987)** Colin Firth, Kenneth Branagh, Natasha Richardson, Patrick Malahide. A shell-shocked WWI veteran (Firth) finds solace and unexpected challenge in working to restore a mural in a village church. Gorgeously mounted but dramatically musty, and only sporadically illuminating about the traumas its characters endure. (Dir: Pat O'Connor, 96 mins.)†

Monty Python and the Holy Grail (Great Britain, 1975)*** John Cleese, Graham Chapman, Terry Gilliam, Eric Idle, Terry Jones. Very uneven satiric sketches filmed among the castles, lochs, and moors of Scotland. King Arthur and the Knights of the Round Table have never looked so absurd. (Dirs: Terry Gilliam, Terry Jones, 89 mins.)†

Monty Python's Life of Brian (Great Britain, 1979)***½ Graham Chapman, Terry Gilliam, John Cleese, Terry Jones, Michael Palin, Eric Idle. Nothing's sacred in this irreligious epic from the creative minds of the Monty Python troupe. It follows Brian (Chapman), who happens to be born on the same night as Jesus. Poor Brian gets mistaken for the Messiah and gets in all sorts of trouble with the Romans. Totally hilarious and highly original. (Dir: Terry Jones, 91 mins.)†

Monty Python's The Meaning of Life (Great Britain, 1983)**½ Graham Chapman, John Cleese, Terry Gilliam, Eric Idle, Terry Jones, Michael Palin. The latest import of brazen comedy from the Monty Python madcap satirists is surely the group's most outrageous and uneven film, ranging from a witty spoof guaranteed to offend the devout, to one so gross it will leave you cringing. (Dir: Terry Jones, 101 mins.)†

Moon and Sixpence, The (1942)***½ George Sanders, Herbert Marshall, Eric Blore. Somerset Maugham's dramatic story of a man with the urge to paint, and how he discards his conventional life to follow his calling. Thoughtfully done, tastefully performed. (Dir: Albert Lewin, 89 mins.)

Moonfleet (1955)** Stewart Granger, Viveca Lindfors, Joan Greenwood, George Sanders. A tale of smugglers and blackguards in eighteenth-century England. Granger plays the dashing adventurer Jeremy Fox, who's always flirting with danger. Despite the good cast, the film is disappointing but it should appeal to adventure fans. (Dir: Fritz Lang, 89 mins.)

Moon in Scorpio (1987)** Britt Ekland, John Philip Law, William Smith, Louis Van Bergen, April Wayne, Robert Quarry. Three couples set out on a yachting trip to Acapulco but never arrive—someone on board is killing them. Some nice touches put this a half-star above the usual low-budget stalk-and-slash stuff. (Dir: Gary Graver, 90 mins.)†

Moon in the Gutter, The (France-Italy, 1983) * Nastassia Kinski, Gerard Depardieu. Haunted by the suicide of his sister after she's raped, a stevedore pursues the sister of the man accused of attacking her. The film is awash with pretentiousness. (Dir: Jean Jacques Beneix, 125 mins.)†

Moon Is Blue, The (1953)** William Holden, Maggie McNamara, David Niven. When this comedy about a "virgin" and her determined gentlemen pursuers was first released, it was considered daring for its spicy dialogue and frank depiction of the sexual chase, but by
706

now it's just a mild fizzle. (Dir: Otto Preminger, 95 mins.)†

Moon Is Down, The (1943)***½ Cedric Hardwicke, Lee J. Cobb, Peter Van Eyck, Dorris Bowden. Dated but powerful version of the Steinbeck story of the Nazi occupation of Norway. (Dir: Irving Pichel, 90 mins.)

Moonlighter, The (1953)* Barbara Stanwyck, Fred MacMurray. Dreary western, stars MacMurray as a reprehensible cattle rustler willing to be reformed by self-possessed Miss Stanwyck. (Dir: Roy Rowland, 77 mins.)

Moonlighting (Great Britain, 1982)***½ Jeremy Irons, Eugene Lipinski. Powerful allegorical film with Irons as the only English-speaking member of a Polish work crew on a temporary (and illegal) construction project in London. When martial law is declared in Poland, Irons keeps his workers ignorant of the news, working them mercilessly to finish their job before funds run out. (Dir: Jerzy Skolimowski, 97 mins.)†

Moonlighting (MTV 1985)*** Cybill Shepherd, Bruce Willis, Allyce Beasley. The sprightly pilot film that launched the successful romantic detective series. Former model Cybill acquires a run-down detective agency and decides to give gumshoeing a whirl. (Dir: Robert Butler, 93 mins.)†

Moonlight Sonata (Great Britain, 1938)**½ Charles Farrell, Marie Tempest, Eric Portman, Barbara Greene, Ignace Paderewski. Boring society melodrama, set in Sweden, of all places, of a girl marrying into an aristocratic family; the story only serves as an excuse for performances by the great pianist. Otherwise, it's of little interest. (Dir: Lothar Mendes, 80 mins.)

Moon of the Wolf (MTV 1972)**½ David Janssen, Barbara Rush, Bradford Dillman, John Beradino. Modern-day werewolf tale. After the badly torn body of a young lady is discovered, Sheriff Janssen has his work cut out for him. (Dir: Daniel Petrie, 73 mins.)†

Moon Over Miami (1941)**½ Don Ameche, Betty Grable, Jack Haley, Charlotte Greenwood, Carole Landis, Robert Cummings. Dumbly enjoyable musical about two sisters hunting millionaires in Miami. (Dir: Walter Lang, 91 mins.)†

Moon Over Parador (1988)**½ Richard Dreyfuss, Raul Julia, Sonia Braga, Jonathan Winters, Fernando Rey, Sammy Davis Jr., Polly Holliday, Charo. Amusing tale of an unbelievably hammy actor (Dreyfuss) who is called upon to impersonate the dead dictator of a small Caribbean nation. The schtick flies thick and fast, with Dreyfuss diving headfirst into his role(s), emerging as both irritating and endearing. The fine cast and vibrant direction by Paul Mazursky keep this uneven satire afloat. (105 mins.)†

Moon Pilot (1962)*** Edmund O'Brien, Tom Tryon, Brian Keith. One of Disney's fun spoofs, centering around a not-so-ambitious astronaut who is tricked into orbit by a prankster chimp who will do anything for a laugh. (Dir: James Neilson, 98 mins.)†

Moonraker, The (Great Britain, 1957)** George Baker, Sylvia Syms, Marius Goring. High adventure and court intrigues set in seventeenth-century England. (Dir: David MacDonald, 82 mins.)†

Moonraker (Great Britain, 1979)*** Roger Moore, Lois Chiles, Richard Kiel. With the help of luscious CIA agent Holly Goodhead (Chiles), Bond must stop a madman from destroying the human race and starting over with his own eugenic breed. The action-packed film opens with a free-fall fight where Bond and Jaws (Kiel) battle for one parachute, and ends with a massed laser-gun battle aboard a space station. (Dir: Lewis Gilbert, 126 mins.)†

Moonrise (1948)*** Dane Clark, Lloyd Bridges, Ethel Barrymore. A man becomes a murderer during a brawl, flees, and his girl tries to persuade him to give himself up. Grim, moody drama of the backwoods country. (Dir: Frank Borzage, 90 mins.)†

Moonrunners, The (1975)** James Mitchum, Waylon Jennings, Joan Blackman. Sour-mash action-comedy about a band of bootleggers, based on the real-life exploits of Jerry Rushing, a North Carolina celebrity. Basis for the popular TV series "The Dukes of Hazzard." (Dir: Gy Waldron, 102 mins.)

Moonshine County Express (1977)** William Conrad, Susan Howard. Moonshiners—three sexy sisters—try to outrun the law and a big moonshiner, all pursuing a valuable cache of prime drinking "likker." (Dir: Gus Trikonis, 95 mins.)†

Moonshine War, The (1970)** Alan Alda, Patrick McGoohan, Richard Widmark, Melodie Johnson. Incoherent action pic. The repeal of Prohibition is only a few months away, so revenue agent McGoohan is interested in getting the 150 bottles of aged moonshine hidden on Alda's property. (Dir: Richard Quine, 100 mins.)

Moon's Our Home, The (1936)** Henry Fonda, Margaret Sullavan, Charles Butterworth, Beulah Bondi, Walter Brennan. This lighter-than-air confection about a bickering couple who love each other even though they're mismatched (he's a novelist; she's a movie star) is of principal interest now because Fonda and Sullavan had already been married and divorced when this film was made. (Dir: William Seiter, 76 mins.)†

Moon-Spinners, The (U.S.-Great Britain, 1964)*** Hayley Mills, Joan Greenwood, Eli Wallach. This enjoyable Disney mystery about jewel thieves involves a young girl's misadventures in Crete. Keep an eye out for silent-screen star Pola Negri, appearing as Madame Habib, a shady buyer of stolen goods. (Dir: James Neilson, 118 mins.)†

Moonstruck (1987)***½ Cher, Nicolas Cage, Vincent Gardenia, Olympia Dukakis, Danny Aiello. Cher proved herself to be an able comedienne, and won a Best Actress Oscar for this warm, funny romance. She plays an Italian-American woman who falls in love with her fiancé's brother (Cage); meanwhile, other members of her family are having romantic complications, and it all seems influenced by the full moon. Dukakis won the Oscar for Best Supporting Actress for her wonderful turn as Cher's weary mom. (Dir: Norman Jewison, 104 mins.)†

Moontide (1942)**½ Jean Gabin, Ida Lupino, Thomas Mitchell. Beautifully acted but generally boring mood drama. A dock worker in a California fishing village prevents a waitress from committing suicide and then falls in love with her. (Dir: Archie Mayo, 94 mins.)

Moon Zero Two (Great Britain, 1969)** James Olson, Catherina Von Schell. The Moon is now a colonized community and spaceman Olson is transporting a mammoth sapphire to the Moon, but the bad guys have other plans. (Dir: Roy Ward Baker, 96 mins.)

More (Luxembourg, 1969)***½ Mimsy Farmer, Klaus Grunberg, Louise Wenk, Henry Wolf, Gorges Montant. Perhaps *the* movie that best typifies the heady energy and excitment of the late '60s, capturing the searching, existential spirit of youth influenced by politics, the arts, and sex, drugs, and rock and roll. Uncompromising work touches all the cult bases: German student travels to Paris to seek some meaning to his life, meets Farmer (the actress who best symbolized the era), and finds himself obsessively in love, lost in a drug haze, and chasing dreams on the sun-drenched shores of Ibiza. Great Pink Floyd soundtrack. History and sociology don't get any better than this. (Dir: Barbet Schroeder, 110 mins.)

More American Graffiti (1979)** Candy Clark, Ron Howard, Cindy Williams, Bo Hopkins, Charles Martin Smith. This follow-up to *American Graffiti* links four separate stories together, but never recaptures the spirit of the earlier popular film. (Dir: B. W. L. Norton, 111 mins.)

More Dead Than Alive (1968)*½ Clint Walker, Vincent Price, Anne Francis, Paul Hampton. Walker's a gunslinger who lets his gun talk for him. After he gets out of prison and wants to go straight, he gets a job in Vincent Price's sideshow, but his past won't leave him alone. More dull than exciting. (Dir: Robert Sparr, 101 mins.)

More Than a Miracle (France-Italy, 1967)*** Sophia Loren, Omar Sharif, Dolores del Rio. Sumptuous fairy tale. Sophia is a gorgeous peasant girl who goes to any lengths to land her handsome prince. (Dir: Francesco Rosi, 105 mins.)

More Than a Secretary (1936)*** Jean Arthur, George Brent. Girl takes a job as secretary to the publisher of a health magazine, falls for him. Breezy, entertaining comedy. (Dir: Alfred E. Green, 77 mins.)

More Than Friends (MTV 1978)*** Rob Reiner, Penny Marshall. Breezy, partly autobiographical, romantic comedy based on Reiner's real-life wooing of Marshall. (Dir: Jim Burrows, 104 mins.)

More Than Murder (MTV 1984)**½ Stacy Keach, Lindsay Bloom, Don Stroud. The TV movie that kicked off the series, as Mike Hammer busts hoods and mingles with the pretty girls as he clears his police captain buddy (Stroud) of a bum rap. (Dir: Gary Nelson, 104 mins.)

More the Merrier, The (1943)**** Jean Arthur, Joel McCrea, Charles Coburn. Director George Stevens concocted some brilliant set pieces in this classic comedy in housing-short WWII Washington. The courting scene on the stoop between McCrea and Arthur is justly famous, but the film is stolen by Coburn as the matchmaking Mr. Dingle, and it is a tribute to that fine actor that what might have been insufferable is irresistible. (104 mins.)†

More Wild Wild West (MTV 1980)**½ Robert Conrad, Ross Martin, Jonathan Winters. Winters plays the crazy professor vs. those TV WWW intelligence agents from the late '60s. Conrad and Martin return to their famous roles in a wild, slapstick adventure. (Dir: Burt Kennedy, 104 mins.)†

Morgan (Great Britain, 1966)*** Vanessa Redgrave, David Warner, Robert Stephens. A daffy, dazzling bit of English black comedy with a stunning debut in a major role by Warner, who plays a delightfully mad painter trying to win back the affections of his ex-wife (the gorgeous Vanessa) in decidedly novel fashion. He doesn't succeed, but director Karel Reisz succeeds in keeping the laughs flowing, delivering pathos and truth along the way. (97 mins.)†

Morgan Stewart's Coming Home (1987)*½ Jon Cryer, Lynn Redgrave, Paul Gleason, Viveka Davis. Cryer is whisked away from his boarding school because his

politician papa needs him. Shot in 1985 as *Home Front* with director Paul Aaron taking over for Terry Winsor. (Dir: Alan Smithee [pseudonym], 96 mins.)†

Morgan the Pirate (France-Italy, 1960)** Steve Reeves, with his clothes on plus a beard, plays the legendary buccaneer. (Dirs: Primo Zeglio, André de Toth, 95 mins.)†

Morituri (1965)**½ Marlon Brando, Yul Brynner. Tangled tale of espionage in WWII aboard a German freighter bringing rubber from the Orient to Germany. Brando is a German pacifist working for the British and Brynner is the freighter's captain. (Dir: Bernhard Wicki, 123 mins.)†

Morning After, The (MTV 1974)*** Dick Van Dyke, Lynn Carlin. Van Dyke may surprise you with his fine performance as a successful public relations writer who plunges ever deeper into the world of alcoholism at the expense of his wife, kids, and job. (Dir: Richard T. Heffron, 74 mins.)

Morning After, The (1986)*½ Jane Fonda, Raul Julia, Jeff Bridges, Diane Salinger. Jane Fonda's scrupulously detailed performance as an actress-on-the-skids is the sole redeeming feature of this tediously directed and ineptly written suspense-thriller. The film is structured abysmally; the villain is easily guessable. (Dir: Sidney Lumet, 103 mins.)†

Morning Glory (1933)*** Katharine Hepburn, Douglas Fairbanks, Jr., Adolphe Menjou. Hepburn won her first Oscar for this portrayal of a young girl trying to make it as an actress in the big town. She's arrogant, unmanageable, and ruthless; naturally, no one can resist her. Astringency is the main ingredient of the film's charm. (Dir: Lowell Sherman, 80 mins.)†

Moro Affair, The (Italy, 1986)***½ Gian Maria Volonte, Margarita Lozano, Mattia Sbragia, Daniele Dublino. Resolute dissection of the kidnapping and execution by terrorists of Italian president-elect Aldo Moro in 1978, a case that is still highly controversial. Film asks many unanswered questions—Was Moro abandoned by his own party? Why was the police investigation so inept?—that have never been answered. Volonte is memorable as Moro, the only leader in four decades to unify all of Italy's squabbling political parties. (Dir: Giuseppe Ferrara, 110 mins.)

Morocco (1930)***½ Marlene Dietrich, Gary Cooper, Adolphe Menjou, Francis McDonald, Eve Southern. A truly romantic film in which Josef von Sternberg, obsessed with visual beauty, creates a universe in which passion is the governing principle. Dietrich made her Hollywood bow as the café chanteuse Amy Jolly, who drops the patronage of an older gentleman of means so she can become a camp follower to a Foreign Legionnaire. The sexual tension generated by Cooper and Dietrich makes today's steamy love stories look impoverished; the brazenly outrageous ending still provides an astonishing climax. (92 mins.)†

Morons from Outer Space (Great Britain, 1985)*½ Dinsdale Landen, Mel Smith, Griff Rhys Jones. Four lame-brains from the planet Blob stumble around like the Four Extraterrestrial Stooges. (Dir: Mike Hodges, 105 mins.)†

Mortal Storm, The (1939)***½ Margaret Sullavan, James Stewart, Robert Young, Frank Morgan, Robert Stack, Maria Ouspenskaya. After their families are split between Nazis and anti-Nazis after Hitler's takeover in '33, Stewart and Sullavan try to escape from Germany. (Dir: Frank Borzage, 99 mins.)

Mortal Thoughts (1991)**½ Demi Moore, Glenne Headly, Bruce Willis, John Pankow, Harvey Keitel. Atmospheric mystery about two women unhappy with their marriages and the murder that links and liberates them from their misery. Told entirely in flashback until the red herring-filled ending. The acting is top-notch, especially Keitel as the interrogating detective. (Dir: Alan Rudolph, 104 mins.)†

Mortuary (1983)** Christopher George, Lynda Day George, Mary McDonough, David Wallace. Occasionally scary low-budget horror flick. When a girl's father is found dead, she claims it's murder. (Dir: Howard Avedis, 91 mins.)†

Mosby's Marauders (MTV 1966)*** Kurt Russell, Jack Ging, James MacArthur, Nick Adams. A very young Russell stars as a Confederate soldier who meets and maintains a friendship with Union soldier MacArthur. (Dir: Michael O'Herlihy, 79 mins.)†

Moscow Does Not Believe In Tears (U.S.S.R., 1980)**½ Vera Alentova. Old fashioned, sentimental soap opera demonstrates that the Soviets are every bit as capable of indulging in emotional fraudulence as was heyday Hollywood. Shallow, but enjoyable. (Dir: Vladimir Menshov, 152 mins.)†

Moscow on the Hudson (1984)*** Robin Williams, Maria Conchita Alonso, Cleavant Derricks. A relaxed serio-comedy about a Russian defector who pursues life, liberty, and the pursuit of happiness in the United States, but must also deal with language barriers and low-paying jobs. Williams is superb. (Dir: Paul Mazursky, 115 mins.)†

Moses (Great Britain-Italy, 1975)*** Burt Lancaster, Anthony Quayle, Ingrid Thulin, Irene Papas. The script by Anthony Burgess provides a good mixture of epic spectacle and intimate narrative. Lancaster lends his usual steely presence to the role of the lawgiver. (Dir: Gianfranco De Bosio, 141 mins.)†

Moses and Aaron (Austria, 1975)***½ Louis Devos, Guenther Reich, Eva Csapo, Werner Mann, Richard Salter, Roger Lucas. Musically electrifying version of Arnold Schoenberg's opera about Biblical tale of Moses in the desert. Completely faithful to the libretto and score, with flawless sound, grand performances, and expert use of a Roman ampitheatre in Italy as a set. (Dir: Jean-Marie Straub, 105 mins.)

Mosquito Coast, The (1986)**½ Harrison Ford, Helen Mirren, River Phoenix, Conrad Roberts, Andre Gregory. Based on the Paul Theroux novel. An individualistic inventor quits civilization and brings his family down to the primitive jungles of Central America to "start over." A perceptive look at the psychoses hiding inside the American pioneering spirit. (Dir: Peter Weir, 118 mins.)†

Moss Rose (1947)*** Ethel Barrymore, Peggy Cummins, Victor Mature, Vincent Price. Slow-moving but well-played Victorian mystery drama of a blackmailing chorus girl and an aristocratic family involved in murder. (Dir: Gregory Ratoff, 82 mins.)

Most Beautiful Woman in the World, The —See: Beautiful But Dangerous

Most Dangerous Game, The (1932)*** Joel McCrea, Leslie Banks, Fay Wray. Smashing yarn about a mad big-game hunter who lures men to his island where he can match wits with them as hunter and prey. Crude, but powerful. (Dirs: Ernest B. Schoedsack, Irving Pichel, 63 mins.)†

Most Precious Thing in Life (1934)*** Richard Cromwell, Jean Arthur, Donald Cook, Anita Louise, Jane Darwell, Ward Bond, Paul Stanton, Mary Forbes, John Wray, Ben Alexander. Extraordinary cast tackles unusual story about a mother literally ejected by her snobbish family. Well-made weeper; script by Ethel Hill and Dore Schary. (Dir: Lambert Hillyer, 70 mins.)

Most Wanted (MTV 1976)** Robert Stack, Shelly Novack, Leslie Charleson, Kitty Winn, Sheree North, Tom Selleck. Routine police yarn that was gleaned from the short-lived TV series starring Robert Stack as a police captain of a special unit. (Dir: Walter Grauman, 78 mins.)†

Motel Hell (1980)** Rory Calhoun, Nancy Parsons, Nina Axelrod. Gross-out black comedy. Calhoun is a kindly old farmer whose secret recipe for dried pork fritters includes cured human flesh. (Dir: Kevin Connor, 102 mins.)†

Mother (U.S.S.R., 1926)***½ Nikolai Batalov, Vera Baranovskaya, Anna

Zemtsova, Ivan Koval-Samborski, Vsevolod Oudovkin. In 1905 Russia, mother accidentally turns her son over to the police for his role in a failed strike. Anguished by her act, she accepts communism as the answer to her and Mother Russia's problems. A great silent film, with extraordinary use of montage and stunning visual density. Based on the novel by Maxim Gorky. (Dir: Vsevolod Pudovkin, 90 mins.)†

Mother and Daughter—the Loving War (MTV 1980)**½ Tuesday Weld, Frances Sternhagen, Kathleen Beller. Weld is the whole show in this soap opera that takes a middle-class American woman from her high-school pregnancy to the time she becomes a grandmother. (Dir: Burt Brinckerhoff, 104 mins.)†

Mother and the Whore, The (France, 1973) ***½ Jean-Pierre Leaud, Bernadette Lafont, Françoise Lebrun. This emotionally draining but rewarding marathon was written and directed by Jean Eustache. A narcissistic young man is involved with a nurse and an older woman with whom he shares an apartment. The three wind up sharing the same bed in this maddening film which has an improvisatory quality. (215 mins.)

Mother Carey's Chickens (1938)**½ Fay Bainter, Anne Shirley, Ruby Keeler, James Ellison, Virginia Weidler, Ralph Morgan. Sentimental melodrama from Kate Douglas Wiggins's ever-popular novel about a mother who sacrifices for her children; corny, but well acted, and good of this kind. (Dir: Rowland V. Lee, 82 mins.)

Mother Didn't Tell Me (1950)**½ Dorothy McGuire, William Lundigan. This fast-paced comedy gives McGuire the opportunity to really cut loose in the role of a young bachelorette with a psychosomatic cough. Naturally the doctor turns out to be an eligible, handsome bachelor. (Dir: Claude Binyon, 88 mins.)

Mother Goose a Go-Go—See: **Unkissed Bride, The**

Mother Is a Freshman (1949)** Loretta Young, Van Johnson, Rudy Vallee. Young widow joins daughter on campus and falls in love with English professor. Lightweight comedy, stretching one joke too far. (Dir: Lloyd Bacon, 81 mins.)

Mother, Jugs and Speed (1976)*½ Raquel Welch, Bill Cosby, Harvey Keitel, Allen Garfield, Dick Butkus. The easy camaraderie among three ambulance drivers is not enough to sustain this forced blend of black farce and contrived melodrama. (Dir: Peter Yates, 98 mins.)†

Mother Kusters Goes to Heaven (West Germany, 1976)*** Brigitte Meara, Margit Carstensen, Karl Bohm. Biting social satire about a widow whose husband becomes a symbolic figure after killing one of his bosses and committing suicide. Fassbinder's attack on the German "New Left," here depicted as smiling, affluent back-stabbers, showcases Meara in the title role. (Dir: Rainer Werner Fassbinder, 104 mins.)

Mother Lode (1982)*½ Charlton Heston, Nick Mancuso, Kim Basinger, John Marley. A gold-hunt adventure that's tapped out. Heston plays twins—one bad and one good; the bad one checks out the prospects in a Canadian mine. Written and produced by Heston's son. (Dir: Charlton Heston, 101 mins.)†

Mother's Day (1980)½ Nancy Hendrickson, Deborah Luce, Tiana Pierce, Holden McGuire, Rose Ross. Horrid thriller of a female trio who run up against a crazed crone and her two nutso boys. The three women are tortured, but two survive and return to get even in an equally vicious manner. (Dir: Charles Kaufman, 93 mins.)†

Mother's Day on Walton's Mountain (MTV 1982)*½ Ralph Waite, Michael Learned, Jon Walmsley, Judy Norton-Taylor. Only die-hard Waltons fans will be able to stomach this excessively sentimental tale of the famed TV family. Mary Ellen gets in a car accident on her honeymoon, and she may not be able to have children. (Dir: Gwen Arner, 104 mins.)

Mother Teresa (1986)*** A straightforward, uncluttered documentary about the twentieth century's living saint. (Dirs: Ann and Jeanette Petrie, 81 mins.)†

Mother Wore Tights (1947)**½ Betty Grable, Dan Dailey, Connie Marshall. Gentle account of the life of a vaudeville team has some charm, if you haven't seen too many Fox '40s musicals lately. (Dir: Walter Lang, 107 mins.)

Mothra (Japan, 1961)** Franky Sakai. Giant monster threatens the earth. First-class trick work in this otherwise naive thriller. (Dirs: Inoshiro Honda, Lee Kresel, 99 mins.)†

Motion and Emotion (Great Britain, 1989) *** Paul Joyce's insightful documentary about noted German filmmaker Wim Wenders examines his obsession with American pop culture and his style of directing. Includes an interview with Wenders himself as well as talks with Robby Muller, Ry Cooder, Harry Dean Stanton, Peter Falk, Dennis Hopper, and Samuel Fuller. (Dir: Paul Joyce, 91 mins.)

Motor Psycho (1965)** Haji, Alex Rocco, Stephen Oliver, Coleman Francis. Obscure Russ Meyer movie, made as a second feature to run with *Faster, Pussycat . . . Kill! Kill!*, is a conventional (by Meyer's standards, anyway) tale of revenge, as Haji and Rocco get even with murderous bikers. (73 mins.)†

Mouchette (France, 1966)**** Nadine Nortier, Marie Cardinal, Paul Hebert.

At times unbearably moving story of the last twenty-four hours in the life of a fourteen-year-old peasant girl, based on a novel by Georges Bernanos. Nonprofessional cast. (Dir: Robert Bresson, 80 mins.)

Moulin Rouge (Great Britain, 1952)***½ José Ferrer, Colette Marchand, Zsa Zsa Gabor, Eric Pohlman, Suzanne Flon, Christopher Lee. Biography of painter Henri Toulouse-Lautrec, whose physical deformity caused his despair in love, and who frequented the more notorious quarters of Paris. Colorful drama with flash, dash, and excellent performances. (Dir: John Huston, 119 mins.)†

Mountain, The (1956)**½ Spencer Tracy, Robert Wagner, Claire Trevor, E. G. Marshall, Anna Kashfi. Two brothers climb an Alpine peak to reach the wreckage of a crashed airliner. Tracy is always good to watch. (Dir: Edward Dmytryk, 105 mins.)†

Mountain Family Robinson (1979)** Robert F. Logan, Susan Damante Shaw. Lovely scenery, more fun with wild animals, and little to distinguish itself from its predecessors in the Wilderness Family series. (Dir: John Cotter, 100 mins.)†

Mountain Man (1977)**½ Denver Pyle, Ken Berry, Cheryl Miller. Family film about a man who moves to the Yosemite Valley in the 1860s and wages an almost single-handed battle of conservation against the lumber czars. (Dir: David O'Malley, 104 mins.)†

Mountain Men, The (1980)*** Charlton Heston, Brian Keith, Victoria Racimo. A wild and woolly mountain adventure about two aging trappers battling the wilderness. When one marries an Indian maiden, his struggle to survive is further tested by a tribe with many grievances against the white man. (Dir: Richard Lang, 102 mins.)†

Mountain Road, The (1960)** James Stewart, Glenn Corbett, Lisa Lu. Drab war drama of personal problems and stopping the enemy in China. (Dir: Daniel Mann, 102 mins.)

Mountains of the Moon (1990)***½ Patrick Bergin, Iain Glen, Richard E. Grant, Bernard Hill, Fiona Shaw, Paul Onsongo. Epic about Victorian explorers Burton and Speke and their 1857 expedition to discover the source of the Nile River. Artfully shot by cinematographer Roger Deakins, film captures the beauty and danger of Africa. Both leads are superb. (Dir: Bob Rafelson, 135 mins.)†

Mountaintop Motel Massacre (1986)½ Bill Thurman, Anna Chappell, Will Mitchell. One of the least frightening killers in screen history butchers guests at her isolated motel. (Dir: Jim McCullough, 96 mins.)†

Mourning Becomes Electra (1947)*** Rosalind Russell, Michael Redgrave, Katina Paxinou, Leo Genn, Raymond Massey, Kirk Douglas. Eugene O'Neill's tale of hatred and conflict in a New England family in Civil War days. Long, powerful drama. (Dir: Dudley Nichols, 173 mins.)

Mouse on the Moon, The (Great Britain, 1963)**½ Margaret Rutherford, Ron Moody, David Kossoff. Sequel to the hilarious *The Mouse That Roared* spoofs the race to space but falls short of the rapid-fire satire of the first film. Rutherford is amusing as the graceless yet grand duchess. (Dir: Richard Lester, 85 mins.)

Mousey (MTV 1974)** Kirk Douglas, Jean Seberg, John Vernon. Douglas is a timid biology teacher in Canada who is driven to thoughts of murder by his callous wife (Seberg). It's complicated and not very interesting. (Dir: Daniel Petrie, 74 mins.)

Mouse That Roared, The (Great Britain, 1958)***½ Peter Sellers, Jean Seberg. Here's a comedy delight—an infinitesimal kingdom declares war on the U.S. —and wins! Loads of satiric fun, with Sellers doing a swell job in several assorted roles. (Dir: Jack Arnold, 83 mins.)†

Mouthpiece, The (1932)***½ Warren William, Aline MacMahon, Sidney Fox, Mae Madison, John Wray. Dynamic crime drama of a high-powered mob attorney who finally outsmarts himself; swiftly paced story and forceful acting make great entertainment. (Dirs: Elliott Nugent, James Flood, 90 mins.)

Move (1970)* Elliott Gould, Paula Prentiss, Genevieve Waite, John Larch, Joe Silver. A sour comedy about a man experiencing self-doubts as he changes his place of residence. (Dir: Stuart Rosenberg, 90 mins.)

Move Over, Darling (1963)** Doris Day, James Garner, Polly Bergen, Chuck Connors. Returning from an airplane crash five years before, a wife discovers her husband about to remarry. Remake of *My Favorite Wife*; plodding, strained comedy. (Dir: Michael Gordon, 103 mins.)

Movers and Shakers (1985)*½ Charles Grodin, Walter Matthau, Vincent Gardenia, Tyne Daly, Bill Macy, Gilda Radner, Steve Martin. An unsatisfying, weakly constructed comedy. As a satire of the film biz, this Grodin script tells a piecemeal tale about a studio which buys a best-selling sex technique book for its title, *Sex in Love*, and then can't come up with a decent screenplay. (Dir: William Asher, 80 mins.)†

Movie Crazy (1932)**** Harold Lloyd, Constance Cummings, Kenneth Thomson, Sydney Jarvis, Eddie Fetherstone. An absolute masterpiece, this is one of the most unfailingly hilarious films ever made, from the first moment to the last. Lloyd is a mistakenly self-confident young man who goes to Hollywood to make it in pictures, and wins the love of movie star Cummings. Warm, distinctive human touches make this a joy to watch; keep an eye out for the many gags concerning ducks, including the very first one, which is a pip. Wonderful. (Dir: Clyde Bruckman, 84 mins.)

Movie Maker, The (MTV 1967)**½ Rod Steiger, Robert Culp, Sally Kellerman. Battle for control of a film studio; Steiger, the last of the big-time film moguls, takes on Culp, a young company man. Good acting highlights the Rod Serling script. (Dir: Josef Leytes, 91 mins.)

Movie, Movie (1978)***½ George C. Scott, Barry Bostwick, Trish Van Devere, Red Buttons, Harry Hamlin, Ann Reinking. A two-part movie parody. The first is a spoof of boxing films; the second, a tongue-in-cheek musical. Superb comic performances throughout make this movie-movie a treat-treat. (Dir: Stanley Donen, 106 mins.)†

Movie Murderer, The (MTV 1970)**½ Arthur Kennedy, Warren Oates, Tom Selleck. Kennedy is very good as an aging insurance company investigator who goes out on a limb to prove that a series of fires involving the destruction of movie films are related. (Dir: Boris Sagal, 99 mins.)

Moving (1988)* Richard Pryor, Beverly Todd, Stacey Dash, Randy Quaid. An amiable effort that squeezes every last joke out of the experience of moving. Richard is reduced to being a straight man for oddballs like Quaid, Dana Carvey, and (in an unbilled cameo) Rodney Dangerfield. (Dir: Alan Metter, 89 mins.)†

Moving Target (MTV 1988)*½ Jason Bateman, Tom Skerritt, Jack Wagner. A boy leaves music camp only to find his family missing and his house cleaned out. A lot of movement, no suspense. (Dir: Chris Thomson, 96 mins.)

Moving Targets (Australia, 1987)**½ Carmen Duncan, Michael Atkins, Shane Briant, Redmond Symons. Woman's past as a terrorist comes back to haunt her when an ex-lover, on the run from his own murderous companions, comes to her for help. Tense action drama. (Dir: Chris Langman, 95 mins.)†

Moving Violation (1976)** Stephen McHattie, Kay Lenz, Eddie Albert, Lonny Chapman, Will Geer, Jack Murdock. Standard terror-on-wheels action as a beleaguered couple is pursued by a Southern sheriff. (Dir: Charles S. Dubin, 91 mins.)†

Moving Violations (1985)½ James Keach,

John Murray, Jennifer Tilly, Sally Kellerman. This sophomoric spoof about some misbegotten souls mistreated by police at a traffic school is derivative and needlessly cruel. (Dir: Neal Israel, 90 mins.)†

Mozart Brothers, The (Sweden, 1987)***½ Etienne Glaser, Philip Zanden, Henry Bronett. An original comedy about the clashes that ensue when an avant-garde director tries to put on a new production of Mozart's opera "Don Giovanni" with a tradition-bound opera company. You don't have to be an opera afficionado to appreciate the goings-on. (Dir: Suzanne Osten, 111 mins.)

Mr.—See also: **Mister**

Mr. Ace (1946)** George Raft, Sylvia Sidney, Stanley Ridges, Sara Haden, Jerome Cowan. Sylvia's a lady on the way up and she'll use anybody, even George Raft, to get what she wants. Routine item saved by Raft's flashy presence and Sylvia's acting. (Dir: Edwin L. Marin, 84 mins.)

Mr. and Mrs. Bo Jo Jones (MTV 1971)** Desi Arnaz, Jr., Christopher Norris, Dan Dailey, Dina Merrill, Tom Bosley. Fifties period piece about a high-school kid who marries his pregnant schoolmate. True love follows eventually. (Dir: Robert Day, 73 mins.)

Mr. and Mrs. Bridge (1990)**** Paul Newman, Joanne Woodward, Blythe Danner, Simon Callow, Kyra Sedgwick, Robert Dean Leonard, Austin Pendleton, Margaret Welsh, Saundra McClain. Entertaining, deeply moving, and magnificently acted film drawn from Evan S. Connell's novels *Mr. Bridge* and *Mrs. Bridge* about a '40s-era Kansas City family; provincial good citizens all. The movie is less a straightforward story than a series of delightful vignettes about business, devotion, love, the war, and family. Woodward is particularly wonderful, and richly deserved her Academy Award nomination. Produced by Ismail Merchant; scripted by Ruth Prawer Jhabvala. (Dir: James Ivory, 124 mins.)†

Mr. and Mrs. Smith (1941)*** Carole Lombard, Robert Montgomery, Gene Raymond. Director Alfred Hitchcock's screwball comedy about a marriage that develops a legal hitch contains many a Hitchcockian theme and stylistic tic. Adequate farce with good acting. (95 mins.)†

Mr. Arkadin (Great Britain, 1955)*** Orson Welles, Michael Redgrave, Katina Paxinou, Akim Tamiroff, Mischa Auer. Director Orson Welles again reviews a rich man's past through the memories of those who loved and hated him. A bit confusing, due to budget stringencies forced on Welles. AKA: **Confidential Report**. (99 mins.)

Mr. Belvedere Goes to College (1949)** Clifton Webb, Shirley Temple, Alan Young. Eccentric genius enrolls at a college to get a degree, finds life has its complications. Sequel to Webb's successful *Sitting Pretty*. (Dir: Elliott Nugent, 83 mins.)

Mr. Belvedere Rings the Bell (1951)*** Clifton Webb, Joanne Dru, Hugh Marlowe. Screen adaptation of a Broadway play about life in an old folks' home. When Webb decides to bring some merriment to the home, the fun begins and hardly lets up throughout the film. (Dir: Henry Koster, 87 mins.)

Mr. Billion (1977)**½ Jackie Gleason, Terence Hill, Valerie Perrine, Slim Pickens. Lighthearted film about a young man from Italy (Hill) who inherits a business empire when his uncle in America dies. To claim his fortune, he must reach San Francisco in twenty days. (Dir: Jonathan Kaplan, 93 mins.)†

Mr. Blandings Builds His Dream House (1947)*** Cary Grant, Myrna Loy, Melvyn Douglas. Tired of city life, a married couple buys a run-down country home. Some hilarious moments in this smoothly produced comedy. (Dir: H. C. Potter, 94 mins.)†

Mr. Buddwing (1966)** James Garner, Jean Simmons, Angela Lansbury, Katharine Ross, Suzanne Pleshette. Garner is an amnesiac running all over New York City trying to find out who he is. (Dir: Delbert Mann, 100 mins.)

Mr. Bug Goes to Town—See: **Hoppity Goes to Town**

Mr. Deeds Goes to Town (1936)**** Gary Cooper, Jean Arthur, Lionel Stander, George Bancroft. Comedy masterpiece about a millionaire and some New York con artists defies the years. Traveling to the Big City to settle his uncle's estate, country boy Longfellow Deeds manages to outwit the greedy relatives and lawyers who are disputing his sanity. A "pixilated" screwball classic. (Dir: Frank Capra, 120 mins.)†

Mr. Denning Drives North (Great Britain, 1951)*** John Mills, Phyllis Calvert. An aircraft manufacturer kills a blackmailer, suffers the consequences of conscience until an American lawyer-friend comes to his aid. Suspenseful melodrama, well acted. (Dir: Anthony Kimmins, 93 mins.)

Mr. Destiny (1990)* Michael Caine, James Belushi, Linda Hamilton, Hart Bochner, Jon Lovitz. A mysterious stranger (could he be an angel?) appears to an average guy and offers him the chance to atone for his worst mistake and change his life. Humorless and ludicrous. (Dir: James Orr, 112 mins.)†

Mr. Dynamite (1941)**½ Lloyd Nolan, J. Carrol Naish, Irene Hervey. Baseball star visiting a carnival matches wits with a gang of enemy agents. (Dir: John Rawlins, 63 mins.)

Mr. Forbush and the Penguins—See **Cry of the Penguins**

Mr. Halpern and Mr. Johnson (MCTV 1983)** Jackie Gleason, Laurence Olivier. This teaming of two show-biz giants delivers pint-sized results. Gleason, a dignified CPA, meets Olivier, a self-made man, during the funeral of Olivier's wife. It seems Gleason had a life-long friendship with the dead woman without Olivier's knowledge. (Dir: Alvin Rakoff, 104 mins.)†

Mr. Hex (1946)**½ Bowery Boys, Gabriel Dell. Sach is entered in prize fights after a magician's trance empowers him with superhuman strength. (Dir: William Beaudine, 63 mins.)

Mr. Hobbs Takes a Vacation (1962)**½ James Stewart, Maureen O'Hara, Fabian, Marie Wilson, John Saxon, Reginald Gardiner. Family encounters plenty of trouble when they try to take a vacation in a run-down beach house. Typical father-against-the-world domestic comedy, which Stewart can play in his sleep. (Dir: Henry Koster, 116 mins.)†

Mr. Hoover and I (1989)*½ Sadly, this last work from documentary filmmaker Emile DeAntonio is a self-indulgent waste of time. Supposedly about DeAntonio's runins with FBI director J. Edgar Hoover, most of the film consists of DeAntonio getting his hair cut by a young girlfriend, chatting with friend John Cage as he bakes bread, and rambling to the camera about anything that comes to his mind. (85 mins.)

Mr. Horn (MTV 1979)** David Carradine, Richard Widmark, Karen Black. William Goldman penned this laconic western about the legendary Scott Tom Horn, the man who captured the famous Apache warrior Geronimo. (Dir: Jack Starrett, 208 mins.)†

Mr. Hulot's Holiday—See: **Monsieur Hulot's Holiday**

Mr. Imperium (1951)** Lana Turner, Ezio Pinza. An improbable pair try to prove that May-December romances can work in this light romantic comedy. (Dir: Don Hartman, 87 mins.)

Mr. Inside/Mr. Outside (MTV 1973)**½ Hal Linden, Tony Lo Bianco. Well-acted thriller which takes place inside a foreign embassy—off limits to the local police force because of diplomatic immunity. AKA: **Hot Ice.** (Dir: William Graham, 73 mins.)

Mr. Klein (France-Italy, 1976)***½ Alain Delon, Jeanne Moreau, Michael Lonsdale, Suzanne Flon. Intricately plotted, beautifully directed account of a ruinous identity complex, set against the backdrop of

Jewish persecution in 1942 France. Delon stars (he also produced) as an unscrupulous art merchant who goes on a search for a possible alter ego, another Jewish "Mr. Klein" who's been using his name and reputation to divert suspicion. (Dir: Joseph Losey, 122 mins.)†

Mr. Lord Says No (Great Britain, 1952)*** Stanley Holloway, Kathleen Harrison. Mr. Lord defies the British government when they want him to demolish his home to make way for a new highway. Highly amusing comedy. (Dir: Muriel Box, 76 mins.)

Mr. Love (Great Britain, 1986)**½ Barry Jackson, Maurice Denham. Mild-mannered comedy about a middle-aged gardener whose interest in the fairer sex becomes so all-consuming that the ladies start to respond to his late-blooming lust. (Dir: Roy Battersby, 92 mins.)†

Mr. Lucky (1943)*** Cary Grant, Laraine Day, Charles Bickford. Grant is a gambler redeemed by Day on behalf of the war effort. Directed by H. C. Potter in his finest hour. (100 mins.)†

Mr. Magoo's Christmas Carol (MTV 1962) **** Voices: Jim Backus, Jack Cassidy, Morey Amsterdam, Royal Dano, Paul Frees. Delightful animated version of the Dickens family classic, with a lovely score by Jule Styne and Bob Merrill. A holiday classic. (Dir: Abe Levitow, 53 mins.)†

Mr. Majestyk (1974)* Charles Bronson, Al Lettieri, Linda Cristal. Strictly for Bronson fans. He plays a simple dirt farmer who won't bow to the syndicate. Call this "Dirt Wish." (Dir: Richard Fleischer, 103 mins.)†

Mr. Mike's Mondo Video (1979)*** Michael O'Donoghue, Dan Aykroyd, Sid Vicious, Root Boy Sims. Imaginative, innovative, and far too weird for network television, this bizarre parody of the Italian "mondo" films displayed "Saturday Night Live" writer O'Donoghue's comic sensibility at its ripest, combining "real" oddity footage with subversive rock and surreal fantasies. Viewing this today, one gets the sense of cosmic revolution in full swing, a revolution that was to end when the original "SNL" cast (most of whom make brief appearances here) went on to star in feeble movie projects. (Dir: Michael O'Donoghue, 70 mins.)†

Mr. Mom (1983)**½ Michael Keaton, Teri Garr, Jeffrey Tambor, Ann Jillian. When husband and wife switch Keaton and Garr switch roles, the audience is served an amiable but predictable domestic comedy. The comic possibilities inherent in the role reversal are only dealt with on the surface, but Keaton is a definite plus,

displaying a strong screen presence. (Dir: Stan Dragoti, 108 mins.)†

Mr. Moto series. Sort of a distant relative of the immortal Charlie Chan, Mr. Moto (played by Peter Lorre) was just as inscrutable, but could resort to using body English like jujitsu in place of spouting aphorisms. Fans of the wily half-pint should catch his act in the following films in addition to those reviewed below: *Think Fast, Mr. Moto, Thank You Mr. Moto, Mysterious Mr. Moto,* but try to avoid the comeback flick *Return of Mr. Moto* (1965).

Mr. Moto in Danger Island (1939)**½ Peter Lorre, Jean Hersholt, Amanda Duff. Down in Puerto Rico, Moto tries to break up a diamond-smuggling ring. Life-threatening dangers proliferate as Moto closes in on the deadly swamp where the crooks hide out. (Dir: Herbert Leeds, 63 mins.)

Mr. Moto's Gamble (1938)** Peter Lorre, Keye Luke. The savvy Oriental detective makes life difficult for some syndicate members, as Moto gambles with his life to solve three murders. (Dir: James Tinling, 71 mins.)

Mr. Moto's Last Warning (1939)*** Peter Lorre, Ricardo Cortez, Virginia Field, John Carradine, George Sanders, Robert Coote. As the corpses pile up, Moto races to prevent a scheme to blow up the French fleet at the Suez Canal. Exciting entry with a nifty cast of guest suspects. (Dir: Norman Foster, 71 mins.)†

Mr. Moto Takes a Chance (1938)** Peter Lorre, Rochelle Hudson. That almost-too-clever Japanese sleuth up against intrigue in Indochina. (Dir: Norman Foster, 70 mins.)

Mr. Moto Takes a Vacation (1939)**½ Peter Lorre, Lionel Atwill. Poor Mr. Moto can't even take a vacation without running into crooks in this trim little B movie about Mr. M foiling some jewel thieves after a gem-laden crown. (Dir: Norman Foster, 61 mins.)

Mr. Muggs Rides Again (1945)** East Side Kids, Nancy Brinckman. Muggs is barred from horse racing, based on false evidence from some gamblers. (Dir: Wallace Fox, 62 mins.)

Mr. Muggs Steps Out (1943)**½ Leo Gorcey, Huntz Hall, Billy Benedict. When Muggs is hired as a servant, the rest of the gang ends up working, too. (Dir: William Beaudine, 63 mins.)

Mr. Music (1950)**½ Bing Crosby, Nancy Olson, Charles Coburn. Bing as a composer who would rather golf and loaf than work, and the attempts to get him into action. Mild story, below-par tunes, but Crosby carries the load well. (Dir: Richard Haydn, 113 mins.)

Mr. North (1988)*** Anthony Edwards,

Robert Mitchum, Harry Dean Stanton, Mary Stuart Masterson, Tammy Grimes, Anjelica Huston, Lauren Bacall. A rock-solid cast illuminates this adaptation of Thorton Wilder's *Theophilus North,* scripted and exec-produced by John Huston (the director's father) just prior to his death. Mr. North (Edwards) is a private tutor who gradually gets a reputation as a miracle healer. The atmosphere is apple pie Americana at its most beguiling; Mitchum, Stanton, Masterson, and Bacall all stand out as individuals whose lives are touched by Edwards. (Dir: Danny Huston, 90 mins.)†

Mr. Peabody and the Mermaid (1948)**½ William Powell, Ann Blyth, Irene Hervey, Andrea King. A middle-aged gent has his life changed completely when he comes upon an amorous mermaid. Mildly amusing fantasy. (Dir: Irving Pichel, 89 mins.)†

Mr. Perrin and Mr. Traill (Great Britain, 1948)***½ David Farrar, Marius Goring. Bitterness develops between an old schoolmaster and a younger teacher when the latter makes a better impression with his winning ways. Excellent melodrama. (Dir: Lawrence Huntington, 92 mins.)

Mr. Potts Goes to Moscow—See: **Top Secret**

Mr. Quilp (Great Britain, 1975)** Anthony Newley, David Hemmings, David Warner, Jill Bennett, Michael Hordern. The owner of a curio shop and his daughter are preyed upon by the villainous title character in this forgettable musical based on Dickens's *The Old Curiosity Shop.* AKA: **The Old Curiosity Shop** (Dir: Michael Tuchner, 118 mins.)†

Mr. Ricco (1975)*½ Dean Martin, Eugene Roche, Thalmus Rasulala, Geraldine Brooks, Denise Nicholas. A potentially interesting mystery about a white attorney who backs unpopular causes is diminished by Dean Martin's comatose acting style. (Dir: Paul Bogart, 98 mins.)

Mr. Robinson Crusoe (1932)*** Douglas Fairbanks, Sr., Maria Alba. Doug bets he can live on a deserted island for a year, and his athletic prowess overcomes all odds. Lively adventure is good fun. (Dir: A. Edward Sutherland, 80 mins.)†

Mr. Rock and Roll (1957)** Alan Freed, Little Richard, Frankie Lymon and the Teenagers, Chuck Berry, Lionel Hampton, Clyde McPhatter. All about how rock and roll began, with Alan Freed getting the lion's share of the credit. Better him than Dick Clark. Watch it for the footage of fifties rockers in their prime.(Dir: Charles Dubin, 86 mins.)

Mr. Sardonicus (1961)**½ Guy Rolfe, Oscar Homolka, Ronald Lewis, Audrey Dalton. Doctor is called by his former love to a castle to treat her husband, whose face is paralyzed. Thriller brings off the shudders in efficient fashion. (Dir: William Castle, 89 mins.)

Mrs. Brown, You've Got a Lovely Daughter (Great Britain, 1968)** Stanley Holloway, Mona Washbourne. Herman's Hermits inherit a dog and try to make a racer of him. Inoffensive and mild. (Dir: Saul Swimmer, 95 mins.)†

Mrs. Columbo (MTV 1979)**½ Kate Mulgrew. Sans Peter Falk, Mulgrew plays Mrs. Columbo, a chic housewife, a mom, and a newspaper stringer, who is on the move at a fast clip after she overhears people planning a neighborhood murder. (Dir: Boris Sagal, 104 mins.)

Mrs. Delafield Wants to Marry (MTV 1986)** Katharine Hepburn, Harold Gould, Bibi Besch, Denholm Elliott, David Ogden Stiers. A predictable Golden Oldies romance about Kate finding love lovelier the second time around with a Jewish gent, much to the disgruntlement of her veddy proper family. (Dir: George Schaefer, 104 mins.)

Mr. Skeffington (1944)*** Bette Davis, Claude Rains, Richard Waring. An impeccably designed, overlong soap opera about a flighty social butterfly who marries for money, uses her hubby badly, and then finds that only her true-blue husband will stick by her after her beauty has deserted her. (Luckily for both of them, he's gone blind.) As the spoiled belle of this melodramatic marathon, Davis gives a powerhouse performance. (Dir: Vincent Sherman, 145 mins.)†

Mr. Skitch (1933)*** Will Rogers, ZaSu Pitts, Rochelle Hudson, Eugene Pallette, Charles Starrett. Yet another good Rogers picture, with the beloved comedian cast as the long-suffering father of a typical family who drive across the country to California; engaging homespun comedy. (Dir: James Cruze, 70 mins.)

Mrs. Mike (1949)*** Dick Powell, Evelyn Keyes. Girl undergoes the hardships of rough living when she marries a Mountie. Entertaining drama. (Dir: Louis King, 99 mins.)

Mrs. Miniver (1942)***½ Greer Garson, Walter Pidgeon, Richard Ney, Dame May Whitty, Teresa Wright, Helmut Dantine. Winner of seven Oscars, this dramatic yet simple story of the courage of the British people facing WWII at home is dated, but engrossing entertainment. (Dir: William Wyler, 134 mins.)†

Mr. Smith Goes to Washington (1939)**** James Stewart, Jean Arthur, Claude Rains, Guy Kibbee, Eugene Pallette, Beulah Bondi, Harry Carey, H.B. Warner, Charles Lane, Porter Hall. A naïve young man is elected to the U.S. Senate, but he doesn't conform to the pattern set for him by his manipulative backers, who expected a malleable figurehead, not an

715

honest politician determined to shake things up. Frank Capra's populist idealism was never as palatable as it is here, particularly in the scene where Jimmy carries on a one-man filibuster to thwart the conscienceless power brokers frying to control the Senate. A timeless comedy-drama. (130 mins.)†

Mr. Soft Touch (1949)**½ Glenn Ford, Evelyn Keyes, John Ireland. A sentimental, corny comedy-drama about a gambler who gets involved with a social worker of a local settlement house. (Dirs: Henry Levin, Gordon Douglas, 93 mins.)

Mrs. O'Malley and Mr. Malone (1950)**½ Marjorie Main, James Whitmore. Main, famous for her Ma Kettle characterization, plays a modified version of Ma in this comic murder mystery. (Dir: Norman Taurog, 69 mins.)

Mrs. Parkington (1944)*** Greer Garson, Walter Pidgeon, Edward Arnold, Peter Lawford, Gladys Cooper, Agnes Moorehead. Fictitious story of the lives of a multimillionaire and the poor girl he wed is well told although episodic and occasionally corny. (Dir: Tay Garnett, 124 mins.)

Mrs. Pollifax—Spy (1971)* Rosalind Russell, Darren McGavin. Rosalind Russell tries unsuccessfully to instill zany life into this brainless espionage comedy, in which she plays a middle-aged matron who volunteers her services to the CIA. (Dir: Leslie Martinson, 110 mins.)

Mrs. R: Death Among Friends—See: **Death Among Friends**

Mrs. R's Daughter (MTV 1979)** Cloris Leachman, Season Hubley. A determined mother battles to bring her daughter's rapist to trial in this version of a real-life story. (Dir: Dan Curtis, 104 mins.)†

Mrs. Soffel (1984)**½ Diane Keaton, Mel Gibson, Matthew Modine, Edward Herrmann. The wife of a Pittsburgh prison warden falls for a criminal and helps him to escape from her husband's jail in this beautifully filmed but ineffective melodrama. The physical reproduction of the time is impressive. Unfortunately, the pictorial composition is so dark and severe that it makes the emotional drama remote and unengaging. (Dir: Gillian Armstrong, 110 mins.)†

Mrs. Sundance (MTV 1974)**½ Elizabeth Montgomery, Robert Foxworth, L. Q. Jones. The Sundance Kid's widow (Montgomery) has returned to the U.S. from South America, living a quiet life as a small-town teacher until word gets out that Sundance may be alive and waiting at his old hideout. (Dir: Marvin Chomsky, 78 mins.)

Mr. Superinvisible (Italy-Spain-West Germany, 1974)* Dean Jones, Gastone Moschin, Ingeborg Schoener, Peter Carsten. Bumbling scientist Jones, looking for a cold cure, invents a virus with some bizarre properties. He and his trusty sheepdog battle to keep it out of the hands of enemy agents. Badly plotted Disney-type comedy is too complicated for youngsters, too dumb for adults. (Dir: "Anthony Dawson" [Antonio Margheriti], 91 mins.)†

Mrs. Wiggs of the Cabbage Patch (1934)** W. C. Fields, Pauline Lord, ZaSu Pitts. Depression-era fantasy about a never-say-die woman who raises her poor family while waiting for her wandering hubby to return, as she bravely battles poverty, eviction threats, and other wolves at her door. (Dir: Norman Taurog, 80 mins.)†

Mrs. Wiggs of the Cabbage Patch (1942)**½ Fay Bainter, Hugh Herbert, Vera Vague, Barbara Britton, Carolyn Lee, Carl Switzer. This optimistic fable is well-mounted, but the story worked better in 1934. (Dir: Ralph Murphy, 80 mins.)

Mr. Sycamore (1974)* Jason Robards, Sandy Dennis, Jean Simmons. Lame fantasy. A mailman dreams of planting himself in the ground and becoming a tree. (Dir: Pancho Kohner, 88 mins.)†

Mr. Winkle Goes to War (1944)*** Edward G. Robinson, Ruth Warrick. Thirty-eight-year-old bank clerk is drafted, surprises everybody by becoming a hero. Entertaining, novel war melodrama. (Dir: Alfred E. Green, 80 mins.)†

Mr. Wise Guy (1942)*½ East Side Kids, Douglas Fowley. The Kids break out of reform school to save a pal's brother from the chair. (Dir: William Nigh, 70 mins.)

Mr. Wong, Detective (1938)** Boris Karloff, Grant Withers, Polis, William Gould. Boris is all wong for the role of this Chinese detective; he's no Moto, let alone a Chan. First of several forgettable Wong-turns, this one's about a poison-gas killer. (Dir: William Nigh, 70 mins.)†

Mr. Wong in Chinatown (1939)** Grant Withers, Boris Karloff, Marjorie Reynolds. A Chinese princess is prevented from spending a fortune on planes for her war-torn country. Murdering her in Mr. Wong's apartment wasn't the smartest thing the bad guys could have done. (Dir: William Nigh, 70 mins.)

Ms. 45 (1981)*** Zoe Tamerlis, Steve Singer, Jack Thibeau. Razor-sharp direction accounts for this violent thriller's cult reputation. There's no dearth of films about female vigilantes getting even with the men who violated them, but this lean, imaginative shocker is exploitation filmmaking at its finest. After being raped twice, a mute girl not only kills potential attackers, she actively seeks out men, like a gun-toting Lorelei, and then pumps them full of lead. Nonstop excitement and a gloriously whacked-out finale with our man-hating heroine decked out as a nun, though she's no sister of mercy. (Dir: Abel Ferrara, 84 mins.)†

Mud—See: **Stick-Up, The**

Muddy River (Japan, 1981)***½ Nobutaka Osahara, Minorin Fujita. The best film about the friendship of children since *Forbidden Games* (1951). A youngster delights in his blossoming friendship with another child until he finds out a secret about his pal's family. (Dir: Kohei Oguri, 105 mins.)

Mudhoney (1965)* Hal Hopper, Antoinette Christian, John Furlong, Stu Lancaster, Lorna Maitland. Demented backwoods drama about a jealous husband who's concerned his wife's been fooling around with the hired hand. (Dir: Russ Meyer, 82 mins.)†

Mudlark, The (Great Britain, 1950)*** Irene Dunne, Alec Guinness, Andrew Ray, Finlay Currie, Anthony Steel, Wilfrid Hyde-White. Interesting and charming story about a young orphan who manages to smuggle himself into Windsor Castle to meet Queen Victoria. Dunne, with a good makeup job, is quite good as the queen and Ray is perfect as the boy. (Dir: Jean Negulesco, 99 mins.)†

Muggable Mary: Street Cop (MTV 1982)**½ Karen Valentine, John Getz, Vincent Gardenia, Joe Bell. Women can be darn good cops is the gist of this streets-of-Manhattan movie. Valentine plays a likable, plucky divorcee who takes a pounding before she earns her badge and then moves on to heroism. (Dir: Sandor Stern, 104 mins.)

Mugsy's Girls (1985)* Ruth Gordon, Laura Branigan, Joanna Dierek, Eddie Deezen. God only knows why talented pop star Branigan got involved with this addlepated comedy (released on video years after it was made) about a sextet of sorority sisters who go to Las Vegas to compete in a mud-wrestling championship. Not even recommended for fans of this messy pastime, although you haven't seen anything till you've seen Gordon's stunt double wallow in the ooze. AKA: **Delta Pi.** (Dir: Kevin Brodie, 87 mins.)†

Mug Town (1943)**½ Dead End Kids, Grace McDonald. Trucking racketeers share the spotlight when they try to blame one of the Kids for their crooked schemes—they don't prevail. (Dir: Ray Taylor, 60 mins.)

Mulligan's Stew (MTV 1977)**½ Lawrence Pressman, Elinor Donahue, Johnny Whitaker, Alex Karras. Warm tale of a high-school coach and his wife and three kids who take on four more kids when the coach's sister and brother-in-law die in a plane crash. (Dir: Noel Black, 72 mins.)

Multiple Maniacs (1971)**½ Divine, David Lochary, Edith Massey, Mink Stole. Those with tender sensibilities will be positively revolted by this shocking comedy from filmmaker John Waters. Others, who share Waters's impeccably sleazy sense of humor, will be amazed and amused by the adventures of "Lady Divine" and her traveling carnival of perversions. Includes what must be the most blasphemous sequence in screen history, and a surprise sexual attack by an enormous crustacean. (90 mins.)†

Mummy, The (1932)***½ Boris Karloff, Zita Johann, David Manners, Bramwell Fletcher. In this romance of the ages, the title character—a reawakened Egyptian high priest—actually appears only briefly on the screen at the beginning, and then reappears in the guise of Ardath Bey, an Egyptologist intent on slaying a young Englishwoman possessed by the soul of his dead princess lover. Noted for their peculiarly eerie atmosphere, the Egyptian flashback sequences were reused in later *Mummy* outings. The film was directed by Karl Freund, who served as photographer on *Metropolis* and the Lugosi *Dracula*, and ended his career pioneering the multiple camera set-ups on the "I Love Lucy" series. (72 mins.)†

Mummy, The (Great Britain, 1959)** Christopher Lee, Peter Cushing. Lukewarm remake. Plot concerns an archaeological dig where a mummy comes back to life to deal with the scientists disturbing its rest. (Dir: Terence Fisher, 86 mins.)†

Mummy's Curse, The (1944)** Lon Chaney, Jr., Peter Coe. Pity the mummy who finds himself bucking not only the weather conditions of a Louisiana swamp but also this script. (Dir: Leslie Goodwins, 60 mins.)

Mummy's Ghost, The (1944)** Lon Chaney, John Carradine. The gauze-wrapped mummy of Prince Kharis is in America, searching for the reincarnation of his ancient love. (Dir: Reginald Le Borg, 60 mins.)

Mummy's Hand, The (1940)** Dick Foran, Peggy Moran, Wallace Ford, Cecil Kellaway, Tom Tyler. Two archaeologists excavating Egyptian tombs inadvertently trigger a mummy rampage: unwittingly funny, with a script that unravels faster than the mummy. (Dir: Christy Cabanne, 67 mins.)

Mummy's Shroud, The (Great Britain, 1967)** Andre Morell, John Phillips, David Buck, Elizabeth Sellars, Maggie Kimberley. In 1920, an archaeological exploring group discovers a pharaoh's tomb and gets a curse put on them. No treasures here. (Dir: John Gilling, 90 mins.)

Mummy's Tomb, The (1942)*½ Lon Chaney,

Dick Foran, Turhan Bey. An Egyptian fanatic brings a mummy back to life, and sends it out to do his dirty work. (Dir: Harold Young, 61 mins.)

Munchausen—See: **Adventures of Baron Munchausen, The** (1943)

Munchies (1987)* Harvey Korman, Charles Stratton, Nadine Van Der Velde. Ultra-cheap rip-off of *Gremlins,* directed by that film's editor, in which the most grotesquely unconvincing group of little monsters you'll ever see ravages the countryside in search of snack food. (Dir: Bettina Hirsch, 83 mins.)†

Munster, Go Home (1966)** Fred Gwynne, Yvonne DeCarlo, Al Lewis, Terry-Thomas. Herman Munster inherits a title, and the family goes to England, where they're involved in plenty of creepy doings. (Dir: Earl Bellamy, 96 mins.)

Munsters' Revenge, The (MTV 1981)*½ Fred Gwynne, Yvonne DeCarlo, Al Lewis, Sid Caesar. Duplicate robots of Herman and Grandpa Munster are implicated in a big art theft. (Dir: Don Weis, 104 mins.)†

Muppet Movie, The (1979)*** Jim Henson, Frank Oz, Charles Durning, Austin Pendleton. The celebrated TV puppets with many famous guest stars. Kermit the Frog, most appealing musical-comedy leading man since Bing Crosby, heads for Hollywood and what he believes is stardom, meeting Miss Piggy along the way. A delight, and a triumph for wizard Muppeteer Jim Henson. (Dir: James Frawley, 98 mins.)†

Muppets Take Manhattan, The (1984)*** The Muppets, Dabney Coleman, Joan Rivers, Art Carney, Linda Lavin. After knocking 'em dead with the annual College Revels, the Muppets decide to conquer Broadway. (Dir: Frank Oz, 92 mins.)†

Murder (Great Britain, 1930)*** Herbert Marshall, Norah Baring. Early Hitchcock whodunit that's a must for the Master of Mayhem's followers. An actor sets out to prove a girl's innocence; but which other member of the troupe is the guilty party? (Dir: Alfred Hitchcock, 92 mins.)†

Murder Ahoy (Great Britain, 1964)*** Margaret Rutherford, Lionel Jeffries. Once again Miss Rutherford is magnificent as Agatha Christie's Miss Marple, the geriatric set's counterpart to James Bond. This time she's cast adrift with an unknown murderer on a British naval cadet training ship. (Dir: George Pollock, 93 mins.)†

Murder a la Mod (1968)**½ Jared Martin, Margo Norton, Jennifer Salt. A young filmmaker becomes involved in a brutal murder. DePalma creates some inventive sequences in this low-budget entry. (Dir: Brian DePalma, 80 mins.)

Murder at the Gallop (Great Britain, 1963)*** Margaret Rutherford, Robert Morley. Marvelous Miss Marple is at it again. She manages to solve a double murder and turn down a proposal of marriage in the bargain. (Dir: George Pollock, 81 mins.)†

Murder at the Mardi Gras (MTV 1978)** David Groh, Didi Conn, Barbi Benton, Harry Morgan. A young woman thinks she has witnessed a killing during the Mardi Gras festivities. (Dir: Ken Annakin, 104 mins.)

Murder at the Vanities (1934)*** Carl Brisson, Kitty Carlisle, Jack Oakie. A racy pre-Production Code comedy musical mystery. Lots of songs and plenty of suspects as a gruff inspector is called in to investigate two murders backstage. Featuring "Cocktails for Two" (later massacred by Spike Jones) and the notorious paean to pot, "Sweet Marijuana." Sparkling direction by the underrated Mitchell Leisen. (89 mins.)†

Murder at the World Series (MTV 1977)** Bruce Boxleitner, Hugh O'Brian, Michael Parks, Lynda Day George, Janet Leigh. Standard action fare. A young man, bent on revenge for not making the team in the tryouts, kidnaps a top player's wife—but he gets the wrong girl. (Dir: Andrew McLaglen, 106 mins.)

Murder by Contract (1958)**½ Vince Edwards, Philip Pine, Herschel Bernardi. Good low-budget film about a hired killer who painstakingly sets up his victim, a beautiful woman who is a government witness. (Dir: Irving Lerner, 81 mins.)

Murder by Death (1976)***½ Alec Guinness, Peter Falk, Peter Sellers, James Coco, David Niven, Maggie Smith, Nancy Walker. Entertaining parody of murder mysteries by master comedymarksman Neil Simon. Five of the world's most legendary detectives (modeled on Sam Spade, Miss Marple, etc.) are invited to a weekend at an isolated country house to solve a murder at midnight. (Dir: Robert Moore, 95 mins.)†

Murder by Decree (Canada-Great Britain, 1979)*** Christopher Plummer, James Mason, Donald Sutherland, Geneviève Bujold, David Hemmings, John Gielgud. Sherlock Holmes mystery with Plummer as the supersleuth and Mason as Dr. Watson. A superbly crafted mystery about Jack the Ripper. Not a dull moment, although it does get gory. (Dir: Bob Clark, 120 mins.)†

Murder by Natural Causes (MTV 1979) *** Hal Holbrook, Katharine Ross, Barry Bostwick. Stylish mystery yarn. Holbrook brings a wonderful restraint to the film as a successful mentalist whose coolheaded wife Allison (Ross) is intricately plotting his death. Bostwick is all emotion as a young actor used by Ross to bolster her plan. Now you can tune in and watch them triple-cross one another. (Dir: Robert Day, 104 mins.)†

Murder by Numbers (1990)* Shari Belafonte, Sam Behrens, Ronee Blakley, Dick Sargent, Jayne Meadows, Cleavon Little, Stanley Kamel, Debra Sandlund. Dreadful mystery about murder and betrayal in the contemporary art world tries too hard to be hip. First, and hopefully only, film to use AIDS as a red herring. (Dir: Paul Leder, 90 mins.)†

Murder by Reason of Insanity (MTV 1985) ***½ Candice Bergen, Jurgen Prochnow, Hector Elizondo, Eli Wallach, Alison La Placa. Superb true-life tale. Bergen gives the performance of her career as a woman whose decision to divorce drives her rigid-thinking mate into dangerously violent behavior. Chilling as suspense drama; effective as a psychological study; unimpeachably well-acted. (Dir: Anthony Page, 104 mins.)

Murder by Television (1935)*½ Bela Lugosi, June Collyer, Huntley Gordon. Dated thriller that predicted television could kill people. A scientist is bumped off by a killer who wants to control his TV invention. (Dir: Clifford Sandforth, 60 mins.)

Murder by the Book (MTV 1987)** Robert Hays, Catherine Mary Stewart, Christopher Murney, Fred Gwynne, Celeste Holm, Lewis J. Stadlen. Life imitates art as an unassuming author of detective fiction discovers he can't shake his private-eye alter ego, a he-man private investigator who has become real to him. Caper-comedy by the book. (Dir: Mel Damski, 104 mins.)

Murder Can Hurt You (MTV 1980)*½ Victor Buono, John Byner, Tony Danza, Jamie Farr, Gavin MacLeod, Connie Stevens, Jimmie Walker, Burt Young. A potentially amusing idea has familiar TV personalities spoofing famous TV detectives such as Studsky and Hatch, Nojack, Lt. Palumbo. The novelty wears out quickly. (Dir: Roger Duchowny, 99 mins.)

Murderers Among Us (West Germany, 1946)*** Ernst Borchert, Arno Paulsen, Hidegard Knef, Erna Sellmer. One year after the end of WWII, German filmmakers were exploring the Nazi years, and one of the best and earliest efforts is this drama about a doctor who saw firsthand the horrors of the death camps, and is now ridden with guilt. He must decide whether to testify against his former commander. Coming when it did, this film broke through the fear of Germans discussing their responsibilities for savage acts committed during WWII. (Dir: Wolfgang Staudte, 87 mins.)

Murderers Among Us: The Simon Wiesenthal Story (MTV 1989)*** Ben Kingsley, Renée Soutendijk, Craig T. Nelson, Louisa Haig, Paul Freeman, Anton Lesser. Kingsley gives a strong, moving performance as the WWII concentration camp survivor who dedicated his life to hunting down war criminals. The scenes inside the death camps are not for the squeamish. (Dir: Brian Gibson, 176 mins.)

Murderers' Row (1966)*½ Dean Martin, Ann-Margret, Camilla Sparv, Karl Malden. Martin as Matt Helm just doesn't cut it in the superagent class. Ann-Margret is miscast again—this time she's a kidnapped scientist's daughter—and only villainous Malden comes through with an interesting performance. (Dir: Henry Levin, 108 mins.)†

Murder, He Says (1945)*** Fred MacMurray, Helen Walker, Marjorie Main. Silly, but often hilarious mystery-comedy about a public opinion analyst who stumbles upon an insane family. (Dir: George Marshall, 93 mins.)

Murder in Black and White (MTV 1990)*** Richard Crenna, Diahann Carroll, Cliff Gorman, Philip Bosco, Sam Coppola, Keith David, Fred Gwynne. Crenna's third appearance as NYPD Lt. Frank Janek (after *Doubletake* and *Internal Affairs*), investigating the murder of the new police commissioner. Tighter than the previous entries, with an improbable but satisfying mystery. (Dir: Robert Iscove, 96 mins.)

Murder, Inc. (1960)*** Stuart Whitman, Mai Britt, Henry Morgan, Peter Falk. Relatively factual, unpleasant but fascinating story of a big crime syndicate, and how a young couple is caught in its web. Distinguished by a smashing portrayal by Falk as Abe Reles. (Dirs: Burt Balaban, Stuart Rosenberg, 103 mins.)

Murder in Coweta County (MTV 1983)** Andy Griffith, Johnny Cash, June Carter Cash. Johnny Cash is the dogged, godhonest sheriff. Andy Griffith is the influential businessman who commits murder. Based upon a real case in '40s Georgia. (Dir: Gary Nelson, 104 mins.)†

Murder in Greenwich Village (1937)**½ Richard Arlen, Fay Wray, Raymond Walburn, Thurston Hall. Cute comedy-mystery, with a madcap heiress involving a news photographer in a murder; fast and fluffy. (Dir: Albert S. Rogell, 68 mins.)

Murder in Mississippi (MTV 1990)*** Tom Hulce, Blair Underwood, Jennifer Grey, Josh Charles, C. C. H. Pounder, André Braugher. Stirring, emotional version of events leading up to the 1964 murders of civil right workers Schwerner, Goodman, and Chaney. Unlike *Mississippi Burning*, drama also delves into the causes of the local whites' blind hatred. David Wolper production makes it clear that blacks bore the brunt of the civil rights battle with some courageous whites sharing, not leading, the way. (Dir: Roger Young, 96 mins.)

Murder in Music City (MTV 1979)*½ Sonny Bono, Lee Purcell, Claude Akins, Soggy TV-detective pilot about a snoopy songwriter who drags his mate into a whodunit in Country Music Land. (Dir: Leo Penn, 104 mins.)

Murder in Paradise (MTV 1990)** Kevin Kilner, Barbara Carrera, Mako, Maggie Han, Yuji Okumoto. Burned-out N.Y. cop, trying to rest in Hawaii, comes across a pattern of killings similar to a case he solved long ago. Kilner has that tired look down perfectly playing the hard-drinking lawman. Carrera brightens this austere TV film as (what else) a mystery woman; veteran actor Mako is wasted. (Dir: Fred Walton, 96 mins.)

Murder in Peyton Place (MTV 1977)* Ed Nelson, Dorothy Malone, Christopher Connelly, Tim O'Connor. Stars from the original soap opera cast are on hand as the murders of show heroes Allison MacKenzie and Rodney Harrington are investigated. (Dir: Bruce Keller, 104 mins.)

Murder in Space (MCTV 1987)*½ Wilford Brimley, Arthur Hill, Martin Balsam, Michael Ironside. On a space flight from Mars, several murders occur and viewers get to guess whodunit. (Dir: Steven Hilliard Stern, 89 mins.)†

Murder in Texas (MTV 1981)***½ Katharine Ross, Sam Elliott, Farrah Fawcett, Andy Griffith. A terrifying, true story of a modern-day Bluebeard, an egomaniacal plastic surgeon who thinks disposing of wives permanently is preferable to divorce. This film grips you by the throat as it slowly dawns on the doctor's wife no. 2 that wife no. 1 may have been helped by her hubby to an early grave. (Dir: Bill Hale, 200 mins.)†

Murder in the Blue Room (1944)*½ Anne Gwynne, Donald Cook, Grace McDonald, Confused mystery tale features a haunted house, some jittery girl singers a la the Andrews Sisters, little else. (Dir: Leslie Goodwins, 61 mins.)

Murder in Three Acts (MTV 1986)** Peter Ustinov, Tony Curtis, Emma Samms, Jonathan Cecil, Fernando Allende, Pedro Armendariz, Jr., Frances Lee McCain, Marian Mercer, Nicolas Pryor, Diana Muldaur. Dogged Ustinov faces a tough case as detective Hercule Poirot must solve a pair of poison murders among the privileged. Curtis leads a boring group of actors; pace remains a problem until the final act. (Dir: Gary Nelson, 104 mins.)

Murder is Easy (MTV 1982)**½ Bill Bixby, Lesley-Anne Down, Olivia de Havilland,

Helen Hayes. An Agatha Christie yarn generally translates into a viable mystery, but this TV version is only moderately successful. The plot concerns a sleepy English town rocked by a series of murders. (Dir: Claude Whatham, 104 mins.)

Murder Lust (1986)* Eli Rich, Rochelle Taylor, Dennis Gannon, Bonnie Schneider. Security guard who relieves his sexual frustrations by murdering prostitutes tries to get a job at a home for troubled teens, where he'll be able to find lots of new victims. (Dir: Donald Jones, 90 mins.)†

Murder Man, The (1935)*** Spencer Tracy, Virginia Bruce, Lionel Atwill, Robert Barrat, James Stewart. Forceful story of an alcoholic crime reporter and his disastrous involvement in a murder too close to home; fine acting by Tracy makes this compelling, and Bruce is also excellent in a less glamorous role than usual as his supportive ladyfriend. (Dir: Tim Whelan, 70 mins.)

Murder Me, Murder You (MTV 1983)*** Stacy Keach, Don Stroud, Tanya Roberts, Delta Burke. Crisp mystery movie that was good enough to launch a series. Here Mike Hammer shows a softer side as he seeks his long-lost daughter. (Dir: Gary Nelson, 104 mins.)

Murder Most Foul (Great Britain, 1964)*** Margaret Rutherford, Ron Moody. The sight of Agatha Christie's engaging grande dame of detectives, Miss Marple, as played by Miss Rutherford, is cause for rejoicing. (Dir: George Pollock, 90 mins.)†

Murder My Sweet (1944)**½ Dick Powell, Claire Trevor, Anne Shirley, Otto Kruger, Mike Mazurki. Powell, the sappiest of '30s tenors, became the most moth-eaten tough guy of the '40s. Dick Powell hasn't Bogart's irony or force, but as Raymond Chandler's Philip Marlowe, he's droll and thus gets across the literary conception. (Dir: Edward Dmytryk, 95 mins.)†

Murder of Fred Hampton, The (1971)***½ When Black Panther leader Fred Hampton was murdered during a raid by law enforcement officers in Chicago, filmmakers Michael Gray and Howard Alk were in the middle of shooting their study of the philosophy of the one of the black community's most viable organizations during the turbulent '60s. The brutal and wrenching loss of their subject forced the documentarians to examine the unresolved questions surrounding Hampton's death. The result is a probing and important film. (88 mins.)

Murder of Mary Phagan, The (MTV 1988)*** Jack Lemmon, Peter Gallagher, Rebecca Miller, Robert Prosky, Charles Dutton, Kevin Spacey. A gripping, emotional miniseries that has a good first half and an even better second. The story line, inspired entirely by real events, concerns the 1913 murder of a Georgia factory girl, and the ensuing investigation and trial in which a Jewish factory manager (her boss) was accused of the crime. Once Lemmon steps in, as Georgia Governor John Slaton, the drama is heightened considerably. A genuine American tragedy, sensitively depicted. (Dir: Billy Hale, 216 mins.)

Murder Once Removed (MTV 1971)** John Forsythe, Richard Kiley, Barbara Bain, Joseph Campanella. Bain is the wealthy patient of handsome Dr. Forsythe, who falls for her and considers murdering her husband as a last resort. (Dir: Charles Dubin, 78 mins.)

Murder One (1988)**½ Henry Thomas, James Wilder, Stephen Shellen. Based on a true story, this low-key low-budgeter follows two half-brothers who escape from a Maryland prison and lead their innocent but bored younger brother on a spree of senseless killings. Ironically, the atmosphere of unfocused nihilism which the filmmakers have evoked keeps the movie from becoming anything more than a clinical study. (Dir: Graeme Campbell, 90 mins.)

Murder One, Dancer 0 (MTV 1983)** Robert Blake, Kenneth McMillan, William Prince. Another of Blake's ''Joe Dancer'' films. Here, the detective character is framed for manslaughter while working on a particularly scandalous case in Lotus Land. (Dir: Reza Badiyi, 104 mins.)

Murder on Flight 502 (MTV 1975)**½ Robert Stack, Hugh O'Brian, Fernando Lamas, Walter Pidgeon, Polly Bergen. A 747 from New York to London has reached the ''point of no return'' when a letter is discovered that indicates a potential murderer is aboard. (Dir: George McCowan, 98 mins.)†

Murder on the Moon (MTV 1989)*½ Brigitte Nielsen, Julian Sands, Gerald McRaney, Jane Lapotaire. Preposterous sci-fi whodunit with awful thesps Nielson and Sands awfully miscast—she as an all-American girl, he as a KGB official stationed on the lunar surface. These two feuding (but mutually attracted) investigators are as surprised as we are when they find their quarry is actually a transsexual! (Dir: Michael Lindsay-Hogg, 96 mins.)

Murder on the Orient Express (Great Britain, 1974)***½ Albert Finney, Lauren Bacall, Martin Balsam, Ingrid Bergman, Jacqueline Bisset, Sean Connery, John Gielgud, Wendy Hiller, Anthony Perkins, Vanessa Redgrave, Richard Widmark, Michael York. A terrific mystery for everyone, especially Agatha Christie fans. Set in '34, the complex plot involves a train full of exotic people traveling from Istanbul to Calais. While they are snowbound, one of the passengers is murdered. Fortunately, Hercule Poirot (Finney) is on the train. (Dir: Sidney Lumet, 127 mins.)†

Murder Ordained (MTV 1987)*** Keith Carradine, JoBeth Williams, Terry Kinney. Based on a real-life double murder case involving a small-town housewife and a clergyman. A highway patrolman doggedly pursues the truth about the lovers' predilection for murder. (Dir: Mike Robe, 208 mins.)

Murder or Mercy (MTV 1974)**½ Melvyn Douglas, Bradford Dillman, Denver Pyle. Douglas is excellent as a doctor accused of administering a lethal dose of morphine to his wife, who is dying of cancer. Good courtroom drama. (Dir: Harvey Hart, 74 mins.)†

Murderous Vision (MCTV 1991)*½ Bruce Boxleitner, Laura Johnson, Robert Culp. Grisly thriller pairs a missing persons detective with an attractive psychic, both searching for a fiendish killer who skins the faces of his victims. Sadistic, nonsensical time waster, redeemed slightly by Boxleitner's laid-back performance. (Dir: Gary Sherman, 96 mins.)

Murder Over New York (1940)** Sidney Toler, Marjorie Weaver, Robert Lowery. Chan's on the prowl for an enemy agent who's throwing monkey wrenches into the works of aircraft factories. (Dir: Harry Lachman, 65 mins.)†

Murder, She Said (Great Britain, 1961)*** Margaret Rutherford, James Robertson-Justice, Arthur Kennedy. Miss Jane Marple, as adroit and appealing as ever, poses as a housemaid in an estate full of nefarious goings-on. (Dir: George Pollock, 87 mins.)†

Murders in the Rue Morgue (1932)**½ Bela Lugosi, Sidney Fox. Mad scientist Lugosi, trying to create an ape-woman, kidnaps a toothsome girl for his experiments. The title was taken from Edgar Allan Poe and John Huston wrote some of the dialogue—but the result is still Grade 'B' shock stuff. (Dir: Robert Florey, 62 mins.)

Murders in the Rue Morgue (1971)*** Jason Robards, Jr., Herbert Lom, Michael Dunn. Fourth film version transfers Poe's classic tale of murders to a Paris theater at the turn of the century. The only clue is that all the victims were business associates of the theater owner (Robards). (Dir: Gordon Hessler, 86 mins.)†

Murders in the Rue Morgue (MTV 1986)** George C. Scott, Rebecca De Mornay, Ian McShane, Neil Dickson, Val Kilmer. Even George C. Scott faces a losing battle with this creaky Edgar Allan Poe mystery. A murder without motive brings

Scott's retired, self-pitying French detective back into action, but a sluggish pace handcuffs the no-nonsense Mr. Scott. (Dir: Jeannot Szwarc, 104 mins.)

Murders in the Zoo (1933)*** Lionel Atwill, Kathleen Burke, Randolph Scott, Gail Patrick, Charlie Ruggles. Interesting, streamlined horror film with an abundance of chills as well as palatable comic relief from Ruggles. A madman who traps animals for zoos, also hunts down the men he suspects of dallying with his wife. (Dir: A. Edward Sutherland, 64 mins.)

Murder That Wouldn't Die, The (MTV 1980)* William Conrad, Marj Dusay, Robin Mattson. Conrad is back sleuthing again as Bill Battles, retired L.A. cop digging into his brother's murder in Hawaii while doubling as a special-team football coach. (Dir: Ron Satlof, 104 mins.)

Murder Weapon (1989)* Linnea Quigley, Karen Russell, Lyle Waggoner, Stephen Steward, Michael Jacobs Jr. Even fans of scream queen Quigley, whose films average well below the 'B' level, will be contemptuous of this brainless, thrilless (and apparently scriptless) junk about two escapees from a mental institution who go on a killing spree. The kind of garbage that gives video a bad name. (Dir: Ellen Cabot, 81 mins.)†

Murder Will Out (Great Britain, 1952)*** Valerie Hobson, James Robertson-Justice, Edward Underdown. The aftereffects of the murder of a beautiful secretary involve an acid-tongued author, his wife, and a weak radio personality. Suspenseful mystery, intricately plotted, nicely done. (Dir: John Gilling, 83 mins.)

Murder with Mirrors (MTV 1985)**½ Helen Hayes, Leo McKern, Bette Davis, John Mills, Dorothy Tutin. Made-in-England mystery with Hayes back as sleuth Jane Marple. She's surrounded by good English actors, principally McKern as the canny inspector investigating a case at Davis's mansion. (Dir: Dick Lowry, 104 mins.)

Murdock's Gang (MTV 1973)** Alex Dreier, Janet Leigh. Premise is better than its realization. Revolves around a disbarred criminal attorney who decides to employ ex-cons to solve crimes. (Dir: Charles Dubin, 73 mins.)

Muriel (France, 1963)***½ Delphine Seyrig, Jean-Pierre Kerien, Nita Klein, Martine Vatel, Laurence Badie, Jean-Baptiste Thierrée. Woman haunted by a past relationship asks the man and his niece to join her and her stepson in the country. Memories and realities of life maintain an eerie dominance over them all in this gorgeously photographed, rigidly stylized Alain Resnais film, one of his masterworks. Intense use of sound and music. (115 mins.)

Murieta (Spain, 1965)** Jeffrey Hunter, Arthur Kennedy, Diane Lorys. Foreign-made western about the outlaw Joaquin Murieta, who robbed from the rich during the California Gold Rush of 1849. (Dir: George Sherman, 108 mins.)

Murmur of the Heart (France, 1971)**** Lea Massari, Daniel Gelin, Benoit Fereux. A suspense film: Will the young hero sleep with his mother or not? Delicate comedy of manners about growing up in the France of Dien Bien Phu days. The lifestyle of the upper-middle class is both satirized and loved. (Dir: Louis Malle, 118 mins.)†

Murph the Surf (1975)*** Robert Conrad, Donna Mills, Robyn Millan, Don Stroud, Burt Young, Luther Adler, Paul Stewart. Compact caper film based on the real-life crimes of two Florida ne'er-do-wells who figured a way to steal the "Star of India" gem from New York's American Museum of Natural History. AKA: **Live a Little, Steal a Lot** (Dir: Marvin Chomsky, 101 mins.)†

Murphy's Law (1986)*½ Charles Bronson, Kathleen Wilhoite, Carrie Snodgress, Robert F. Lyons, Richard Romanus, Angel Tompkins. Bronson must pursue a psychopathic murderess out to destroy him and those who assist him; the catch is that Bronson gets manacled to a foul-mouthed teen. Believability vanishes, but obscenities and pumped-up thrills fill in the gaps. (Dir: J. Lee Thompson, 97 mins.)†

Murphy's Romance (1985)*** Sally Field, James Garner, Brian Kerwin. Enchanting May-December romance, with Field as a single woman starting a new life with her son in the Southwest, and then running into the crustily likeable Garner and her devious ex-husband. Director Martin Ritt develops things at his usual leisurely pace, getting nice unassuming performances out of his stars along the way. (107 mins.)†

Murphy's War (Great Britain, 1971)*** Peter O'Toole, Sian Phillips, Philippe Noiret. Complex ideological effort about a WWII Irishman who, after the massacre of the crew of his ship by a German U-boat, seeks revenge at all costs. O'Toole, as the sole survivor of the attack, packs a ferocious wallop into his performance. (Dir: Peter Yates, 106 mins.)†

Murrow (MCTV 1986)**½ Daniel J. Travanti, Dabney Coleman, Edward Herrmann, John McMartin, David Suchet. Provocative but disappointing biopic about the charismatic newscaster who broadened the horizon of network journalism and whose liberal ideals made history, particularly with his challenge of McCarthyism, on-air. Travanti's overly restrained performance sets the production's tone of general blandness. (Dir: Jack Gold, 101 mins.)†

Murs Murs (1981)***½ Murals on buildings, murals on highways, murals everywhere in Los Angeles, are the subject of vibrant, likeable, almost giddy, look at the artists who paint murals as well as the building owners who allow their properties to be used. French director Agnes Varda fell in love with life and art of L.A. while living there. (85 mins.)

Muscle Beach Party (1964)** Frankie Avalon, Annette Funicello, Buddy Hackett. Strictly for beach-party fans. The plot is incidental. (Dir: William Asher, 94 mins.)†

Music Box, The (1989)*** Jessica Lange, Armin Mueller-Stahl, Frederic Forrest, Donald Moffat, Lukas Haas, Cheryl Lynn Bruce, Mari Torocsik, Michael Rooker. An intense courtroom drama that concentrates not so much on the issues it raises as the emotions behind them. The plot proposes the unlikely scenerio of lawyer Lange serving as the defense attorney for her father, accused of vicious Nazi war crimes. (Dir: Costa-Gravas, 126 mins.)†

Music for Millions (1944)**½ Margaret O'Brien, José Iturbi, June Allyson, Jimmy Durante. Lovers of sentimental corn will adore this tearjerker but others are warned to steer clear. Girl cellist who worries about fighting hubby, with June and Margaret the sob sisters working on your emotions. (Dir: Henry Koster, 117 mins.)

Music in My Heart (1940)*** Tony Martin, Rita Hayworth. Singer about to be deported falls for a girl soon to enter into an unhappy marriage with a millionaire. Entertaining comedy with music. (Dir: Joseph Santley, 70 mins.)

Music in the Air (1934)*** Gloria Swanson, John Boles, Douglass Montgomery, June Lang, Reginald Owen. Sprightly backstage musical, with a score by Jerome Kern and Oscar Hammerstein, has Swanson and Boles as a theatrical couple battling and making up during a Broadway production; Swanson is funny, looks lovely, and sings well. (Dir: Joe May, 85 mins.)

Music Lovers, The (Great Britain, 1971)** Richard Chamberlain, Glenda Jackson, Max Adrian. Flamboyant director Ken Russell mixes glorious visual images with nonsense, paying little attention to the historical facts about Russian composer Peter Ilyich Tchaikovsky. (122 mins.)

Music Man, The (1962)***½ Robert Preston, Shirley Jones, Buddy Hackett, Pert Kelton, Ronny Howard, Paul Ford, Hermione Gingold. The saga of Harold Hill, who arrives in River City, Iowa, to organize a boys' band and falls for Marian, the librarian. The Meredith Willson musical hit, filmed with most of its gaiety intact, including Preston's smashing performance and memorable tunes. (Dir: Morton Da Costa, 151 mins.)†

Music Room, The (India, 1958)***½ Chabi Biswas, Tulsi Lahin, Padma Devi, Kali Sarkar, Pinaki Sen Gupta. A wealthy man who has frittered away his fortune chooses to spend his remaining money on a concert of great Indian music. A beautiful, heartfelt tribute to the joy of music by director Satyajit Ray, a composer himself, who also wrote the score for this memorable film. (100 mins.)

Music Teacher, The (Belgium, 1988)** Jose Van Dam, Anne Roussel, Philippe Volter, Patrick Bauchau. Very dull story of a voice teacher planning to use his two students to settle an old rivalry is notable only for the fine music. (Dir: Gerard Corbiau, 95 mins.)†

Mussolini & I (MCTV 1985)**½ Bob Hoskins, Susan Sarandon, Anthony Hopkins, Annie Giradot. Biopic that succeeds as a result of Hoskins' fine turn as Il Duce, and Sarandon's performance as his adult daughter, who serves as our narrator. (Dir: Alberto Negrin, 194 mins.)†

Mustang Country (1976)** Joel McCrea, Patrick Wayne, Nika Mina. Unexceptional western. Joel McCrea portrays a rancher who tries to capture a wild stallion with the assistance of an Indian boy. (Dir: John Champion, 79 mins.)

Mutant—See: **Forbidden World**

Mutant—See: **Night Shadows**

Mutant Hunt (1987)* Rick Gianasi, Mary Fahey, Ron Reynaldi, Bill Peterson, Stormy Spill. Actually, they're not mutants but cyborgs, some of whom go berserk and start killing New Yorkers. Enter macho Gianasi to stop them and find out why they're acting up. (Dir: Tim Kincaid, 77 mins.)†

Mutations, The (Great Britain, 1973)½ Donald Pleasence, Tom Baker. Take one part *Frankenstein,* one part *Freaks,* and one part soap opera, and you have this mutant of a movie. Pleasence is cast as the mad professor who has the stamina to teach biochemistry by day and wreak havoc on human subjects in bizarre experiments by night. (Dir: Jack Cardiff, 92 mins.)

Mutilator, The (1983)½ Matt Mitler, Jack Chatham, Bill Hitchcock. Boring, gory tale of a man who goes bonkers after his young son accidentally kills his own mother. AKA: **Fall Break.** (Dir: Buddy Cooper, 86 mins.)†

Mutineers, The—See: **Pirate Ship**

Mutiny (1952)*** Mark Stevens, Angela Lansbury. Patriots attempt to run the British blockade and get gold bullion from France during the War of 1812.

Speedy maritime adventure. (Dir: Edward Dmytryk, 77 mins.)

Mutiny in Outer Space (1964)** William Leslie, Dolores Faith, Pamela Curran, Richard Garland, Harold Lloyd, Jr., Glenn Langan. Two astronauts on a lunar space station struggle to convince their commander that they must not return to earth because the ship is carrying a deadly virus. Dated sci-fi adventure. AKA: **Space Station X-14.** (Dir: Hugo Grimaldi, 81 mins.)

Mutiny on the Bounty (1935)**** Clark Gable, Charles Laughton, Franchot Tone. One of the great adventure movies of all time. Laughton's award-winning performance as the infamous Captain Bligh is worth canceling all plans, and staying home to watch. Oscar for Best Picture. (Dir: Frank Lloyd, 135 mins.)†

Mutiny on the Bounty (1962)** Marlon Brando, Trevor Howard, Richard Harris. If sheer length and opulence justifies the term "blockbuster," this remake of the famous Gable-Laughton epic qualifies. However, those who fondly recall its predecessor will find the comparisons unfavorable. Brando's curiously erratic portrayal throws the film off-balance. (Dirs: Lewis Milestone, Carol Reed, 179 mins.)†

My American Cousin (Canada, 1986)**½ Margaret Langrick, John Wildman, Richard Donat. Affecting story about a young Canadian girl's sexual awakening and emotional maturing during the summer her male cousin from the States makes an extended visit. Though the characters are underwritten, the movie does evoke the late 1950s and the more innocent tensions of adolescent life in that period. Sequel: *American Boyfriends*. (Dir: Sandy Wilson, 95 mins.)†

My Beautiful Laundrette (Great Britain, 1985)***½ Daniel Day-Lewis, Gordon Warnecke, Saeed Jaffrey, Roshan Seth, Shirley Anne Field. Superb, sensitive comedy-drama about a young Pakistani man living in London and the colorful laundromat he manages with the help of his left-wing, punk lover. Not only does this tender film offer deep insights into the confusions of modern-day Britain, Thatcherian capitalism, and racism, but it also depicts the racially mixed, gay love affair between the two young men positively. (Dir: Stephen Frears, 94 mins.)†

My Best Friend is a Vampire (1988)*½ Robert Sean Leonard, Evan Mirand, Cheryl Pollak, René Auberjonois, Cecilia Peck, Fannie Flagg, David Warner. Dim-witted farce about delivery boy Leonard bitten by sexy vampire Pollak, instructed in vampire etiquette by Auberjonois, and hunted down by Van Helsing manque Warner. Leave it for the kids. (Dir: Jimmy Huston, 90 mins.)†

My Best Friend's Girl (France, 1984)**½

Isabelle Huppert, Coluche, Thierry Lhermitte. A slight, whimsical tale about a man who works days, who asks his friend who works nights to look after his flirtatious girlfriend. Reasonably diverting. (Dir: Bernard Blier, 99 mins.)†

My Bill (1938)**½ Kay Francis, Bonita Granville, Anita Louise, Bobby Jordan, Dickie Moore. A less chic than usual role for Francis; here she is a hardworking widow trying to raise her children alone. Good emotional drama, given a candid, less soapy feel by director John Farrow. (64 mins.)

My Blood Runs Cold (1965)*½ Troy Donahue, Joey Heatherton. Dull melodrama with Donahue playing a psychopath who makes Heatherton's life a nightmare. (Dir: William Conrad, 104 mins.)

My Bloody Valentine (Canada, 1981)**½ Paul Kelman, Lori Hallier, Neil Afleck, Keith Knight. On the eve of the annual Valentine's Day dance, a masked man in a miner's outfit picks on townspeople, who get the axe one by one. (Dir: George Mihalka, 91 mins.)†

My Blue Heaven (1950)**½ Betty Grable, Dan Dailey, David Wayne. Fast-moving musical with Grable and Dailey tapping and singing their way through. The silly plot, which serves as stage waits between numbers, concerns a show-business team and their efforts to adopt a family. (Dir: Henry Koster, 95 mins.)

My Blue Heaven (1990)**½ Steve Martin, Rick Moranis, Joan Cusack, Melanie Mayron. Light comedy about a former mobster relocated to suburbia by the witness protection program. Once there he cheerfully revitalizes the boring new neighborhood. Script fumbles, but the charming performances make it work. Contains the joke, "What's the difference between a light bulb and a pregnant woman?" "You can unscrew the light bulb." (Dir: Herbert Ross, 96 mins.)†

My Bodyguard (1980)**½ Chris Makepeace, Matt Dillon, Adam Baldwin, Martin Mull, Ruth Gordon. This film about a kid bullied so much in school that he has to hire a bodyguard is manipulative, but anyone who has been pushed around by the school bully will appreciate it. You'll cheer when this underdog has his day. (Dir: Tony Bill, 96 mins.)†

My Body, My Child (MTV 1982)*** Vanessa Redgrave, Jack Albertson, Joseph Campanella, James Naughton, Stephen Elliott. Redgrave memorably plays Leenie Cabrezi, a woman whose pregnancy is misdiagnosed at first and who is given various medications. By the time her pregnancy is discovered, she may have done much harm to the unborn child. (Dir: Marvin Chomsky, 104 mins.)

My Boys Are Good Boys (1978)**½ Ralph Meeker, Ida Lupino, Lloyd Nolan, David

Doyle. A hard look at parental responsibility and juvenile delinquency. First half involves a quartet of kids involved in an improbable robbery. The more serious latter half deals with the aftermath of the theft. (Dir: Bethel Buckalew, 90 mins.)†

My Breakfast with Blassie (1983)*** Andy Kaufman, Freddie Blassie, Bob Zmuda. Hysterical send-up of *My Dinner With André* finds media-manipulator Kaufman meeting "King of Men" wrestling manager Blassie for breakfast at Sambo's in Hollywood. The two set out to share their personal philosophies, but wind up interacting with their fellow customers; the sicker the happenings, the funnier it gets. (Dirs: Linda Lautrec, Johnny Legend, 56 mins.)†

My Brilliant Career (Australia, 1979)***½ Judy Davis, Sam Neill, Wendy Hughes. Autobiographical novel (circa 1900) has been transformed into a charming, perceptive, poignant tale about what it was like then for a young woman either growing up in rural Australia. Davis is enormously accomplished and touching in the leading role. (Dir: Gillian Armstrong, 100 mins.)†

My Brother's Keeper (Great Britain, 1948) *** Jack Warner, George Cole. Two convicts escape from prison, and the elder shows the young lad that it pays to go straight. Well-done melodrama. (Dirs: Alfred Roome, Roy Rich, 96 mins.)

My Brother Talks to Horses (1946)**½ Butch Jenkins, Peter Lawford, Edward Arnold. Jenkins is adorable as the little chap who asks racehorses if they're going to win, but the charm of the film's basic theme is left at the post. (Dir: Fred Zinnemann, 93 mins.)

My Chauffeur (1986)*½ Deborah Foreman, Sam Jones, E. G. Marshall, Sean McClory, Penn & Teller, Howard Hesseman. This inane comedy about a young female driver hired by a stuffy all-male company combines screwball farce with gratuitous nudity. (Dir: David Beaird, 97 mins.)†

My Cousin Rachel (1952)***½ Olivia de Havilland, Richard Burton, John Sutton, Ronald Squire. The stars are perfect in this fascinating suspense tale based on Daphne du Maurier's novel about a young man who sets out to prove that his cousin is a treacherous woman and ends up hopelessly in love with her. Low-key photography heightens the mood of this mysterious yarn set in nineteenth-century England. (Dir: Henry Koster, 98 mins.)

My Darling Clementine (1946)***½ Henry Fonda, Linda Darnell, Victor Mature. A super western about Wyatt Earp, and the doings in Tombstone, Ariz. Directed by John Ford who, along with a fine cast, makes up for an almost routine script. (97 mins.)†

My Darling Daughters' Anniversary (MTV 1973)**½ Robert Young, Ruth Hussey, Raymond Massey. Sequel to *All My Darling Daughters*. (Dir: Joseph Pevney, 73 mins.)

My Dearest Señorita (Spain, 1972)*** Jose Luis, Lopez Vazquez. Worthwhile black comedy. Lopez Vazquez, a magnificent actor, plays a middle-aged spinster who suddenly discovers she is really a man, only to learn that being raised as a woman ill-equips a person to function in a man's world. (Dir: Jaime de Arminan, 80 mins.)

My Dear Secretary (1948)*** Laraine Day, Kirk Douglas, Keenan Wynn, Helen Walker, Rudy Vallee. A wolfish author meets a secretary who writes a bestseller. Cute comedy, with Wynn especially amusing. (Dir: Charles Martin, 94 mins.)†

My Demon Lover (1987)**½ Scott Valentine, Michelle Little, Robert Trebor. Panhandler Valentine becomes a monster (literally) whenever sexually aroused, posing problems when he falls for a girl who always goes for the "wrong guys." Uneven script is energetically directed. (Dir: Charlie Loventhal, 86 mins.)†

My Dinner with Andre (1982)*** Andre Gregory, Wallace Shawn. Fascinating filmed account of a dinner conversation between two friends, playwright-actor Shawn and theater director Gregory, discussing everything under the sun. (Dir: Louis Malle, 110 mins.)†

My Dream Is Yours (1949)*** Doris Day, Jack Carson, Lee Bowman, Adolphe Menjou, Eve Arden, Bugs Bunny. Underrated Warner Bros. musical cribs elements from Day's own career story. Director Michael Curtiz adds lots of ambience to the radio-themed rise-to-stardom saga. (101 mins.)

My Fair Lady (1964)***½ Rex Harrison, Audrey Hepburn, Stanley Holloway, Wilfrid Hyde-White, Gladys Cooper, Jeremy Brett, Theodore Bikel. The fabulous Broadway musical makes an entertaining film with most of its charm intact. Harrison deserved the Oscar he won as Prof. Henry Higgins, the British gentleman who turns the cockney flower seller, Eliza Doolittle, into a gracious lady. Miss Hepburn shines in the second half. The lyrics of Alan Jay Lerner and the music of Frederick Loewe make it an unforgettable experience. (Dir: George Cukor, 170 mins.)†

My Father, My Son (MTV 1988)*** Keith Carradine, Karl Malden, Margaret Klenck. Poignant true story about the special relationship between an admiral (Malden) who okayed the use of the defoliant Agent Orange for war use, and his son (Carradine) who served in Viet-

. nam and came down with two forms of cancer due to exposure to the defoliant. Beautifully played by the two leads. (Dir: Jeff Bleckner, 96 mins.)

My Father's House (MTV 1975)** Cliff Robertson, Robert Preston. Muddled attempt at serious drama, bolstered by good performances. Robertson plays the forty-one-year-old successful businessman-husband-father who suffers a heart attack and does some heavy thinking. (Dir: Alex Segal, 96 mins.)†

My Favorite Blonde (1942)*** Bob Hope, Madeleine Carroll, Gale Sondergaard, George Zucco. Luscious British spy Madeleine is forced to enlist the aid of frightened Bob in carrying out her mission and the result is a barrel of laughs. (Dir: Sidney Lanfield, 78 mins.)

My Favorite Brunette (1947)*** Bob Hope, Dorothy Lamour, Peter Lorre. Photographer Bob turns detective to help Dotty out of a jam, and there you have all the ingredients for another romp for Hope fans. (Dir: Elliott Nugent, 87 mins.)†

My Favorite Spy (1942)**½ Kay Kyser, Ellen Drew, Jane Wyman. Bandleader as a flop as a soldier, but is pressed into espionage duty. Pleasant comedy with music. (Dir: Tay Garnett, 86 mins.)

My Favorite Spy (1951)*** Bob Hope, Hedy Lamarr, Francis L. Sullivan. Bob's a small-time burlesque performer who's a double for a spy, with the usual crossed identities. Typical Hope comedy, the sort of thing he does well; fast-paced, generally satisfying. (Dir: Norman Z. McLeod, 93 mins.)

My Favorite Wife (1940)*** Cary Grant, Irene Dunne, Randolph Scott. Wife believed dead returns after years on a desert island when the husband is about to rewed. Excellent comedy, a laugh a minute. (Dir: Garson Kanin, 88 mins.)†

My Favorite Year (1982)*** Peter O'Toole, Bill Macy, Jessica Harper, Lainie Kazan, Lou Jacobi, Mark Linn-Baker, Joseph Bologna. A delightful reminder of the glorious days of live television, and more specifically a zany recollection of the kind of daffy comedy we enjoyed on what is here a thinly disguised "Your Show of Shows." O'Toole is a particular joy as the swashbuckling movie star guest-starring on the program if he can stay sober long enough. (Dir: Richard Benjamin, 92 mins.)†

My First Love (MTV 1988)**½ Beatrice Arthur, Richard Kiley, Joan Van Ark, Anne Francis, Barbara Barrie. Recently widowed Arthur gets in touch with Kiley, her high-school sweetheart, and their romance begins to revive, over the objections of his younger lover Van Ark. The stars add stature to the "romance novel" story. (Dir: Gilbert Cates, 96 mins.)

726

My First Wife (Australia, 1984)***½ John Hargreaves, Wendy Hughes, David Cameron, Anna Jemison, Lucy Angwin. Director Paul Cox's searing portrait, based on his own shattered marriage, of a man mentally falling apart after his wife admits to having an affair and leaves him. Raw, brutal, uncomfortably real. (95 mins.)†

My Foolish Heart (1949)*** Susan Hayward, Dana Andrews, Kent Smith. In this tale of a wartime romance between a lonely girl and a pilot, Hayward's performance has an emotional directness and frank sensuality that redeems the novelettish plot elements. (Dir: Mark Robson, 98 mins.)

My Forbidden Past (1951)** Robert Mitchum, Ava Gardner, Melvyn Douglas. Girl from the wrong part of town inherits a fortune and plans to break up the marriage of the man she loves. Uneven costume melodrama. (Dir: Robert Stevenson, 81 mins.)†

My Friend Flicka (1943)*** Roddy McDowall, Preston Foster, Rita Johnson. Devoid of hokum, this story of a boy's love for an outlaw horse is no *Lassie* or *The Yearling* but it's still a beautiful story and among the better animal films. (Dir: Harold Schuster, 89 mins.)

My Friend Irma (1949)** Marie Wilson, Diana Lynn, Dean Martin, Jerry Lewis, John Lund. This comedy concerns a girl dimwit whose boyfriend discovers a potential singing talent at an orange-juice stand. First film for Martin and Lewis. The gags are obvious. (Dir: George Marshall, 103 mins.)

My Friend Irma Goes West (1950)** Marie Wilson, John Lund, Dean Martin, Jerry Lewis, Diana Lynn. Irma and company follow Dean and Jerry when they go to Hollywood to make their fortune. (Dir: Hal Walker, 90 mins.)

My Gal Sal (1942)*** Rita Hayworth, Victor Mature, Carole Landis. Gay '90s musical about a songwriter's love for a singing star is a harmless frame for some entertaining oldtime music and production numbers. (Dir: Irving Cummings, 103 mins.)

My Geisha (1962)** Shirley MacLaine, Yves Montand, Edward G. Robinson, Bob Cummings. Lengthy comedy about an actress who is so adept at posing as a geisha girl that her husband, not recognizing her, signs her to play the role of "Madame Butterfly." (Dir: Jack Cardiff, 120 mins.)

My Girlfriend's Boyfriend—See: **Boyfriends and Girlfriends**

My Girl Tisa (1948)**½ Lilli Palmer, Sam Wanamaker. Immigrant girl works to bring her father to New York, and to help her boyfriend become a lawyer.

Pleasant but leisurely costume comedy-drama. (Dir: Elliott Nugent, 95 mins.)†

My Heroes Have Always Been Cowboys (1991)**½ Scott Glenn, Kate Capshaw, Ben Johnson, Balthazar Getty, Tess Harper, Gary Busey, Clarence Williams III, Mickey Rooney, Dub Taylor. A professional rodeo rider (a laconic, muscular Glenn) returns to his roots to help his aging father (Johnson) and atone for his past romantic failings. Outstanding rodeo scenes are linked with all-around fine acting in this lovingly crafted, if predictable tale, about men and women in the New West. (Dir: Stuart Rosenberg, 106 mins.)†

My Husband Is Missing (MTV 1978)** Sally Struthers, Tony Musante. A woman journeys to North Vietnam to find her missing husband. (Dir: Richard Michaels, 104 mins.)

My Kidnapper, My Love (MTV 1980)**½ James Stacy, Mickey Rooney, Glynnis O'Connor. Lively tale. Stacy plays a New Orleans news vendor befriending a young, disturbed runaway (O'Connor). (Dir: Sam Wanamaker, 104 mins.)

My Left Foot (Ireland, 1989)**** Daniel Day-Lewis, Brenda Fricker, Ray McAnally, Hugh O'Conor, Fiona Shaw. A magnificent film based on the wondrous accomplishments of Christy Brown, the Irishman who painted and wrote with the toes on his left foot. Day-Lewis deservedly won an Oscar for portraying Brown, who was a victim of cerebral palsy and thought to be retarded until the love and devotion of his caring mother and family encouraged him to reach his artistic potential. Fricker, also an Oscar winner, is equally luminous as his courageous mother. There are scenes of such power in this film that they will remain with you forever. (Dir: Jim Sheridan, 103 mins.)†

My Life as a Dog (Sweden, 1985)*** Anton Glanzelius, Tomas von Bromssen. An off-beat, whimsical comedy that refreshingly captures some bittersweet remembrances of childhood. Because of his mother's illness, a young boy is sent to live with his aunt and uncle. (Dir: Lasse Hallstrom, 101 mins.)†

My Life to Live (France, 1962)*** Anna Karina, Saddy Rebbot, André Labartre. Director Jean-Luc Godard's examination of the life of a prostitute is also his exploration into the mysteries of his then-wife, Karina. Once considered radical and maddening, the film now seems almost quaint. (85 mins.)†

My Life with Caroline (1941)** Ronald Colman, Anna Lee, Reginald Gardiner, Charles Winninger, Gilbert Roland. Silly story of a man married to a flighty younger woman who thinks she *must* have a boyfriend. (Dir: Lewis Milestone, 81 mins.)

My Little Chickadee (1940)*** Mae West, W. C. Fields, Joseph Calleia, Margaret Hamilton. Fields and West's only appearance together in a film delivers ample laughs. West and Fields wrote their own dialogue, which helps. (Dir: Edward Cline, 83 mins.)†

My Little Girl (1986)**½ Mary Stuart Masterson, James Earl Jones, Geraldine Page, Peter Michael Goetz, Pamela Payton-Wright. High school girl, stifled in her rich parents' house, spends the summer working at a home for troubled teenagers. (Dir: Connie Kaiserman, 117 mins.)†

My Little Pony (1986)** Voices of Danny DeVito, Madeline Kahn, Cloris Leachman, Tony Randall, Alice Playten. Young tots fond of the pastel ponies may delight in the heroic horsies defeating the forces of evil. Fair as animation, but a masterpiece of merchandising. (Dir: Michael Joens, 87 mins.)†

My Love Came Back (1940)*** Olivia de Havilland, Jeffrey Lynn, Jane Wyman. A lot of good music decorates this minor tale of a girl violinist who wants a husband, but if you like good music you should be able to tolerate the inoffensive plot. (Dir: Curtis Bernhardt, 85 mins.)

My Love For Yours—See: **Honeymoon in Bali**

My Love Has Been Burning (Japan, 1949)***½ Kinuyo Tanaka, Kuniko Miyabe, Mitsuko Mito, Ichiro Sugai, Koreya Senda. Politically charged, prophetic film about women's rights tells the story of a 19th-century feminist educator whose school is shut down because of her views. (Dir: Kenji Mizoguchi, 84 mins.)

My Lucky Star (1938)*** Sonja Henie, Richard Greene, Cesar Romero. Typical Henie vehicle finds her in college, ice skating in a department store, and just about everything else but it's good fun. (Dir: Roy Del Ruth, 84 mins.)

My Man Adam (1985)* Raphael Sbarge, Page Hannah, Veronica Cartwright, Dave Thomas, Charlie Barnett. High schooler Adam is a Walter Mittyish sort, ignored by his yuppie parents, who stumbles across an evil plot. From there, you're on your own. (Dir: Roger L. Simon, 84 mins.)†

My Man and I (1952)**½ Shelley Winters, Ricardo Montalban, Claire Trevor, Wendell Corey. Mexican boy, a new citizen, has trouble with a stingy rancher and his wife. Uneven drama. (Dir: William Wellman, 99 mins.)

My Man Godfrey (1936)**** Carole Lombard, William Powell, Eugene Pallette, Mischa Auer, Gail Patrick, Alan Mowbray, Alice Brady. Lombard's most unforgettable screwball performance as the

727

madcap heiress who finds gentleman-bum Powell on a garbage heap while on a scavenger hunt. He becomes her family's butler and brings a touch of the common man to the filthy rich. Marvelously funny, and the actors are uniformly excellent. (Dir: Gregory La Cava, 90 mins.)†

My Man Godfrey (1957)**½ June Allyson, David Niven. Disappointing remake of the sophisticated '30s comedy about a butler who competes for his mistress's romantic attentions. (Dir: Henry Koster, 92 mins.)

My Mother's Secret Life (MTV 1984)** Loni Anderson, Paul Sorvino, Amanda Wyss, Douglas Dirkson. Anderson gives a patented performance as a hooker who is reunited with her teenaged daughter and tries for respectability. Tawdry and trite. (Dir: Robert Markowitz, 104 mins.)

My Name Is Bill W. (MTV 1989)***James Woods, JoBeth Williams, Gary Sinese, George Coe, Fritz Weaver, James Garner. A no-holds-barred biography of the man who started Alcoholics Anonymous, Bill Wilson. Woods gives a devastating performance as Wilson, who starts out as a young and ambitious man on the rise but soon finds his entire world reduced to obtaining the next drink. There's no overt preaching; the story speaks for itself. (Dir: Daniel Petrie, 96 mins.)

My Name Is Ivan—See: **Youngest Spy, The**

My Name Is Julia Ross (1945)***½ Nina Foch, Dame May Whitty, George Macready. Engrossing, fascinating and well-played mystery. A girl reports for a job, is drugged and forced into a new identity. (Dir: Joseph H. Lewis, 65 mins.)

My Name Is Nobody (Italy-France-West Germany, 1974)*** Henry Fonda, Terence Hill, Jean Martin. Interesting study of an aging gunfighter (Fonda) and the young, up-and-coming cowboy (Hill) he teams with for one last shoot-'em-up before retiring. Based on an idea by Sergio Leone. (Dir: Tonino Valerii, 115 mins.)†

My New Partner (France, 1985)*** Philippe Noiret, Thierry L'hermitte, Regine. Sassy comedy about a veteran cop who bends the law and his new partner, whose by-the-book attitude yields to his experienced partner's outlook on life. Not distinguished, but the farcical odds and ends are delivered with zest. (Dir: Claude Zidi, 107 mins.)†

My Night at Maud's (France, 1969)***½ Jean-Louis Trintignant, Françoise Fabian, Antoine Vitez, Christine Barrault. Marvelously witty and civilized comedy of manners. Maud, a divorced Protestant exquisitely acted by Fabian, invites a visiting Catholic engineer (Trintignant) to spend the night in her nonexistent spare room. Faultlessly written and directed by Eric Rohmer. (109 mins.)†

My Old Man (MTV 1979)***½ Kristy McNichol, Warren Oates, Eileen Brennan. Expanded version of Ernest Hemingway's short story "My Old Man" becomes a grand, sentimental backstretch yarn about a seedy trainer (Oates) and his watchful, horse-loving daughter (McNichol). Remake of *Under My Skin*. (Dir: John Erman, 104 mins.)†

My Other Husband (France, 1985)** Miou-Miou, Roger Hanin, Eddy Mitchell, Dominique Lavanant. With a pilot in Paris and a sailor tucked away in Normandy, Miou-Miou learns the secret of contented married life is to know how to juggle your husbands. (Dir: Georges Lautner, 110 mins.)†

My Outlaw Brother (1951)** Mickey Rooney, Robert Preston, Robert Stack, Wanda Hendrix. An eastern kid comes west and finds his brother-to-be the mysterious leader of an outlaw band. (Dir: Elliott Nugent, 78 mins.)

My Pal Gus (1952)*** Richard Widmark, Joanne Dru, George Winslow. Fay and Michael Kanin have fashioned a warmhearted comedy-drama about a little boy from a divorced home. Dru plays the proprietress of a school to which Gus is sent and it's with her help that everything turns out for the best. (Dir: Robert Parrish, 83 mins.)

My Palikari (MTV 1982)*** Telly Savalas, Keith Gordon, Michael Constantine. Savalas plays a Greek immigrant who came to America to find his fortune in the restaurant business. As the film opens, it's 1953, and widower Peter Pankos (Savalas) returns with his teenaged son for a visit to the "old country." Unfortunately, their experiences in Greece don't match their expectations. (Dir: Dezso Magyar, 104 mins.)

Myra Breckinridge (1970)½ Mae West, Raquel Welch, John Huston, Rex Reed, Farrah Fawcett, Tom Selleck. A macabre freak show about sexual perversity becomes not erotic or titillating—just numbingly bad in this odious screen version of Gore Vidal's novel. The only witty idea was to cast "critic" Rex Reed in the role of a confused transsexual. (Dir: Michael Sarne, 94 mins.)†

My Reputation (1946)**½ Barbara Stanwyck, George Brent, Lucile Watson, Eve Arden. Soap-opera fans may like this story of a young widow who, in all innocence, dates an army officer and is victimized by gossip and almost loses her sons' love. (Dir: Curtis Bernhardt, 95 mins.)

My Science Project (1985)*½ John Stockwell, Fisher Stevens, Ann Wedgeworth, Dennis Hopper. A teenager brings an abandoned alien time-warp generator into school as his science project, and resultingly stocks the place with gladiators, mutants, and dinosaurs. A bloated youth comedy that seeks to cross the genre's crass jokes with special effects. This project gets a D+. (Dir: Jonathan Betuel, 95 mins.)†

My Side of the Mountain (U.S.-Canada, 1969)*** Ted Eccles, Theodore Bikel. Nice film for children about a Canadian boy who leaves his family to live in the mountains alone. He meets a retired folksinger, played by Bikel, who helps him get adjusted and saves him when he is trapped during the winter. (Dir: James B. Clark, 100 mins.)†

My Sister Eileen (1942)***½ Rosalind Russell, Janet Blair, Brian Aherne. Two small-town sisters arrive in New York to pursue their careers, take a dingy Greenwich Village apartment. Sparkling comedy has many laughs. (Dir: Alexander Hall, 96 mins.)

My Sister Eileen (1955)*** Janet Leigh, Jack Lemmon, Betty Garrett. Musical version of the famed Rosalind Russell movie of the same title (not to be confused with Rosalind Russell's Broadway musical "Wonderful Town" which was based on the same movie). Confused? Despite its origin, this film has songs, dances, and Jack Lemmon to recommend it. (Dir: Richard Quine, 108 mins.)

My Sister, My Love—See: **Mafu Cage, The**

My Six Convicts (1952)*** Millard Mitchell, Gilbert Roland, Marshall Thompson. Very funny film about prison life, unlike most such films. (Dir: Hugo Fregonese, 104 mins.)

My Six Loves (1963)*½ Debbie Reynolds, Cliff Robertson, David Janssen. Broadway star finds six abandoned kids living at her country home, decides to adopt them. Comedy-drama overloaded with sugary sentiment. (Dir: Gower Champion, 100 mins.)

My Son John (1952)* Helen Hayes, Robert Walker, Van Heflin, Dean Jagger. Badly misguided drama of a mother's reactions when she learns her son is a Communist. (Dir: Leo McCarey, 122 mins.)

My Son, My Son (1940)*** Brian Aherne, Louis Hayward, Madeleine Carroll, Laraine Day. Good vintage drama of a young wastrel who proves his father's faith in him by dying a hero. (Dir: Charles Vidor, 117 mins.)

My Stepmother Is an Alien (1988)**½ Dan Aykroyd, Kim Basinger, Jon Lovitz. Underwritten comedy with Basinger sent from another planet to get the secret of a space ray from nerdy scientist Aykroyd. Good special effects but very few laughs. (Dir: Richard Benjamin, 108 mins.)†

Mysterians, The (Japan, 1959)**½ English-dubbed science fiction stuff about a race of intellects from outer space attempting to take over Earth when their planet is destroyed. Elaborate production, often quite imaginative. (Dir: Inoshiro Honda, 85 mins.)†

Mysterious Castles of Clay (1978)***½ This Oscar-nominated documentary presents a vivid view of insects living in and around a termite mound on an African prairie. Narrated by Orson Welles. (90 mins.)

Mysterious Island, The (Great Britain, 1961)***½ Michael Craig, Michael Callan, Herbert Lom, Gary Merrill, Joan Greenwood. There's little of Jules Verne left in this lively adventure, where Craig and Merrill are Yankee escapees from a Confederate prison who sail in a balloon to the eponymous island where they fight some superb Ray Harryhausen creations with the assistance of Lom's Captain Nemo. Perhaps the best of the juvenile fantasies of its period. (Dir: Cy Endfield, 101 mins.)†

Mysterious Island of Beautiful Women (MTV 1979)½ Steven Keats, Clint Walker, Jamie Lynn Bauer, Jayne Kennedy, Kathryn Davis. Numbskull TV-movie about male adventurers encountering an island of belligerent buxom beauties. A cross between *The Admirable Crichton* and a Jantzen swimwear commercial. (Dir: Joseph Pevney, 104 mins.)†

Mysterious Lady, The (1928)**½ Greta Garbo, Conrad Nagel. Garbo is a Russian spy in Berlin, 1915, where she uses and then falls for an Austrian army officer. (Dir: Fred Niblo, 96 mins.)

Mysterious Mr. Moto (1938)*** Peter Lorre, Henry Wilcoxon. An action-packed entry for the series, as the quick-thinking private eye has to break up a band of professional assassins whose next assignment is a man in possession of an important steel formula needed for the war effort. (Dir: Norman Foster, 62 mins.)

Mysterious Two (MTV 1982)*½ John Forsythe, James Stephens, Priscilla Pointer. Two aliens come to Earth in hopes of bringing earthlings back to their galaxy. (Dir: Gary Sherman, 104 mins.)

Mystery in Mexico (1948)**½ William Lundigan, Jacqueline White, Ricardo Cortez, Tony Barrett, Walter Reed. American insurance investigators, searching for a colleague missing in Mexico City, uncover a jewel robbery and hijacking. Well-made melodrama, shot on location. (Dir: Robert Wise, 66 mins.)

Mystery Man (1944)*** William Boyd, Andy Clyde, Jimmy Rodgers. Top-notch Hopalong Cassidy western; fast-paced, fun, and full of action. (Dir: George Archainbaud, 58 mins.)

Mystery of Alexina, The (France, 1985)*** Vuillemin, Valerie Stroh, Veronique Silver, Bernard Freyd. Haunting, bizarre psychological drama based on the memoirs of French hermaphrodite Hercule Barbin in the 1850s. (Dir: Rene Feret, 86 mins.)†

Mystery of Edwin Drood, The (1935)*** Claude Rains, Heather Angel, Valerie Hobson. This is an adaptation of Charles Dickens's final—and uncompleted—novel. Concerns a choirmaster who leads a double life, giving choir lessons by day, smoking opium by night. Nicely played by Rains, and moderately interesting. (Dir: Stuart Walker, 87 mins.)

Mystery of Kaspar Hauser, The (West Germany, 1976)***½ Bruno S., Walter Ladengast, Brigitte Mira. Werner Herzog's mystical tale of a man who has grown up without ever leaving a tiny room. Based on the true story of a young boy who suddenly appeared in a village from out of nowhere in the 1820s. A demanding, but rewarding film. (Dir: Werner Herzog, 110 mins.)

Mystery of Marie Roget, The (1942)**½ Maria Montez, Patric Knowles, John Litel. Crisp detective thriller, from the short story by Edgar Allan Poe. Medical examiner Paul Dupin tries to find out why a famous actress disappeared from home. (Dir: Phil Rosen, 60 mins.)

Mystery of Mr. Wong (1939)** Boris Karloff, Grant Withers. Average Wong whodunit about an altered will and the greedy grappling for a priceless gem smuggled out of the Orient. (Dir: William Nigh, 67 mins.)

Mystery of Picasso, The (France, 1956)**** Marvellously expressive film that probes the creative process. Thanks to the magical properties of cinema, five paintings by Picasso are brought to fruition before our eyes as the famous modern artist creates them onscreen. A dazzling documentary probing the creative impulse. (Dir: Henri-Georges Clouzot, 85 mins.)

Mystery of the Leaping Fish (1916) and **Chess Fever** (1925)*** Douglas Fairbanks, Bessie Love, Alma Rubens. Two classic short comedies; the first, directed by John Emerson, stars Fairbanks as the world's greatest detective, on the trail of miscreants threatening Love; the second, directed by V. I. Pudovkin, is a rare Russian silent social comedy about a chess tournament and its effects on a small town. Both fascinating documents. (64 mins.)†

Mystery of the Wax Museum (1933)*** Lionel Atwill, Fay Wray, Glenda Farrell. Historic color-talkie suspense tale about a mad wax sculptor, whose London museum burns down leaving his fingers crippled, which prompts him to find an alternative sculpting method in New York. (Dir: Michael Curtiz, 77 mins.)†

Mystery of the White Room (1939)*** Bruce Cabot, Helen Mack, Constance Worth. Fine medical thriller, with murder taking place in an operating room; deftly done and unpretentious, from a classic Crime Club mystery. (Dir: Otis Garrett, 58 mins.)

730

Mystery Street (1950)*** Ricardo Montalban, Sally Forrest, Jan Sterling. Neat mystery about police procedure in tracking down a killer in Boston. Emphasis on police lab work, absorbingly done, flavorsome location scenes, good acting. (Dir: John Sturges, 93 mins.)

Mystery Train (1989)*** Youki Kudoh, Masatoshi Nagase, Nicoletta Braschi, Joe Strummer, Screamin' Jay Hawkins, Steve Buscemi, Rick Aviles, Elizabeth Bracco, Cinque Lee. Highly stylized, minimalist anthology film features three tales centered around a flea-bag hotel in Memphis, Tennessee and the people who check in. (Dir: Jim Jarmusch, 110 mins.)†

Mystic Pizza (1988)*½ Julia Roberts, Annabeth Gish, Vincent D'Onofrio. Clichéd, mawkish drama about the romantic problems of three teenage girls in a small Connecticut fishing village. A step above a Barbie Doll cartoon, but only a small one. (Dir: Donald Petrie, 101 mins.)†

Mystic Warrior, The (MTV 1984)** Richard Beltran, Devon Ericson, Rion Hunter. This beautifully appointed production about a young Indian's rise to chiefdom is rife with mysticism not easily dramatized, and softens its impact in order not to offend. (Dir: Richard T. Heffron, 260 mins.)

Mystique—See: **Circle of Power**

My Sweet Charlie (MTV 1970)***½ Patty Duke, Al Freeman, Jr. In a remote Louisiana resort area, a young pregnant southern girl, thrown out by her father, takes refuge in a cottage. Her solitary wait for the arrival of her child is broken when a young black lawyer, also on the run, decides to hide out in the same house. Superbly played by Freeman and Duke. (Dir: Lamont Johnson, 97 mins.)†

My Sweet Little Village (Czechoslovakia, 1986)** Janos Ban, Marian Labuda, Rudolf Brisinski. Quaint pastoral types parade before us to exemplify sleepy village life—e.g., a doctor who spouts poetry, a semi-retarded trucker's assistant who plays Laurel to his partner's put-upon Hardy, and an adulteress wife tired of her jealous hubby. Not one of these vignettes is substantial, or particularly moving, but the lighter comedy moments just about save the film. (Dir: Jiri Menzel, 100 mins.)

My Tutor (1982)**½ Matt Lattanzi, Caren Kaye, Kevin McCarthy, Arlene Golonka. Not as bad as it sounds. A Southern California rich boy is failing French, and his domineering father gets him a twenty-nine-year-old tutor (Kaye) who happens to be a sensitive and willing tutor in more than French. (Dir: George Bowers, 97 mins.)†

My Twentieth Century (Hungary, 1989)*** Dorothy Segda, Oleg Jankowski, Peter Andorai, Gabor Mate. Whimsical fantasy about life at the turn of the century, when anything seemed possible, seen through the eyes and imaginations of twin sisters—one, a con artist, the other, a political idealist. (Dir: Ildiko Enyedi, 104 mins.)

My Two Loves (MTV 1986)**½ Mariette Hartley, Lynn Redgrave, Barry Newman, Sada Thompson. Well-intentioned drama about a homosexual affair between a recently widowed woman and a lesbian. Hartley is excellent as the widow with a teenage daughter who is dating her late husband's partner (Newman) but is attracted to a woman exec (Redgrave) she meets in her new job. (Dir: Noel Black, 120 mins.)

My Uncle (France, 1958)**** Jacques Tati. In a memorable French comedy, Tati the inimitable runs afoul of the modern mechanized world in some inspired pantomime reminiscent of the silent comedy days. Lots of fun. AKA: **Mon Oncle.** (Dir: Jacques Tati, 110 mins.)†

My Uncle Antoine (Canada, 1971)**½ Jean Duceppe, Olivette Thibault, Claude Jutra, Jacques Gagnon. Heartfelt coming-of-age tale about a teenager reaching maturity in 1940s Canada. The French-Canadian local color enriches this revealing saga of adolescent angst. (Dir: Claude Jutra, 110 mins.)

My Uncle from America—See: **Mon Oncle d'Amerique**

My Way Home (Hungary, 1964)***½ Andras Kozak, Sergei Nikonenko. The cruelty of war overshadows the tale of young Hungarian man trying to get home across Russian-occupied territory near the end of WWII. Captured by Soviet soldiers, he becomes close friends with one soldier whose life he tries to save. Powerful imagery and sensitive acting add to the film's majesty. (Dir: Miklos Jancso, 109 mins.)†

My Wicked, Wicked Ways...the Legend of Errol Flynn (MTV 1985)** Duncan Regehr, Barbara Hershey, Hal Linden. Errol Flynn was all the things colorful movie stars are accused of being—controversial, brawling, hard-drinking, womanizing, and terrific copy for gossip columns. Regehr tries to create the Flynn mystique, but the script defeats him at every sensationalized turn. (Dir: Don Taylor, 143 mins.)†

My Wife's Best Friend (1952)**½ Anne Baxter, Macdonald Carey. Wife gets an inadvertent confession of philandering from her husband, and the upsets begin. Unimportant but cute romantic comedy. (Dir: Richard Sale, 87 mins.)

My Wild Irish Rose (1947)** Dennis Morgan, Arlene Dahl, George O'Brien. Standard musical supposedly based on the life of composer Chauncey Olcott. (Dir: David Butler, 101 mins.)

Nabonga (1944)* Buster Crabbe, Julie London, Fifi D'Orsay, Barton MacLane. Buster feels a primal urge to mate with jungle beauty London, but his rival is an overly possessive gorilla. Hilariously awful, with one of the worst gorilla costumes in history. (Dir: Sam Newfield, 75 mins.)†

Nada (France, 1974)*** Fabio Testi, Michel Aumont, Maurice Garrel, Viviane Romance, Michel Duchaussoy, Lou Castel. Violent drama about terrorists who plot to kidnap American ambassador to France during his regular weekly visit to a Parisian brothel. Film is both a cynical study in anarchist politics and an intriguing thriller involving expert police work. Clash between kidnappers and cops is unrelentingly brutal. A tense work with touches of rich black humor. (Dir: Claude Chabrol, 134 mins.)

Nadia (MTV 1984)** Talia Balsam, Jonathan Banks, Johann Carlo. Back flips and somersaults do not a movie make. The film was designed to cash in on the Nadia Comaneci craze after America went gaga over the 1976 Olympic gold medalist from Rumania. (Dir: Alan Cooke, 104 mins.)†

Nadine (1987)*** Jeff Bridges, Kim Basinger, Gwen Verdon, Rip Torn, Glenne Headley, Jerry Stiller. Juicy combination of screwball laughs and thrills as a saloon owner (Bridges) tries to bail his headstrong wife (Basinger) out of hot water involving a photographer's murder. (Dir: Robert Benton, 83 mins.)†

Nail Gun Massacre (1987)*½ Rocky Patterson, Michelle Meyer, Ron Queen, Beau Leland. After a gang of construction workers rape an innocent girl, they start falling victim to a masked killer armed with—well, at least it's not a chainsaw. A few imaginative murders, for slasher fans. (Dir: Terry Lofton, 84 mins.)†

Nairobi Affair (MTV 1984)**½ Charlton Heston, John Savage, Maud Adams. Against the handsome background of Kenya's wildlife park, stoic Heston and Savage engage in father-son rivalry. (Dir: Marvin Chomsky, 104 mins.)†

Naked Alibi (1954)** Sterling Hayden, Gloria Grahame. Fast-moving routine crime melodrama. Sterling Hayden plays an ex-cop who doggedly tracks down a murder suspect. (Dir: Jerry Hopper, 86 mins.)

Naked and the Dead, The (1958)** Aldo Ray, Cliff Robertson, Raymond Massey, Joey Bishop, Lili St. Cyr. Story of combat in the Pacific, and the war of resentment between officers and men, taken from Norman Mailer's best-selling novel. A botched job, unsteadily written and directed, not too well acted, it often becomes a parody of all war dramas. (Dir: Raoul Walsh, 131 mins.)†

Naked Ape, The (1973)*½ Johnny Crawford, Victoria Principal, Dennis Oliveri, Diana Darrin. The Desmond Morris bestseller didn't exactly lend itself to filmization. Sexual innuendo, routine animation and the kitchen sink are thrown in to jazz up the anthropological lessons on tap. (Dir: Donald Driver, 85 mins.)

Naked Cage, The (1986)*½ Shari Shattuck, Angel Tompkins, Lucinda Crosby. Excessively brutal women's prison picture. This time around, the plot concerns an innocent country girl, inordinately fond of horseback riding, who gets a different form of exercise behind bars. (Dir: Paul Nicholas, 97 mins.)

Naked City (1948)*** Barry Fitzgerald, Dorothy Hart, Don Taylor, Howard Duff. New York police investigate a girl's violent death. The "city" is the real star here; fine New York scenes in a conventional plot. Inspiration for the TV series of the same name. (Dir: Jules Dassin, 96 mins.)

Naked Dawn, The (1955)*** Arthur Kennedy, Betta St. John, Roy Engel. A tangled relationship develops between a bandit and the young couple who become his accomplices in a series of capers. Edgar G. Ulmer's knowing, precise direction triumphs over an often faltering screenplay. (82 mins.)

Naked Edge, The (Great Britain, 1961)**½ Gary Cooper, Deborah Kerr, Eric Portman, Diane Cilento, Michael Wilding, Hermione Gingold. Absorbing if not altogether successful film adaptation of the suspense novel *First Train to Babylon* by Max Ehrlich. Cooper, in his last film, plays a middle-aged businessman whose wife begins to suspect him of murder after the arrival of a strange letter. (Dir: Michael Anderson, 100 mins.)

Naked Face, The (1984)*½ Roger Moore, Anne Archer, Art Carney, Elliott Gould, Rod Steiger, David Hedison. Moore plays a wimpy psychiatrist who runs afoul of mobsters when he tries to find out why his former patients are dropping dead. Rod Steiger's overacting as a suspicious police detective provides this unbearably bland film with its only lively moments. (Dir: Bryan Forbes, 103 mins.)†

Naked Gun, The: From the Files of Police Squad! (1988)*** Leslie Nielsen, Priscilla Presley, Ricardo Montalban, George Kennedy. The creators of *Airplane!* are back in form with this gagfest about tough

but dumb cop Nielsen investigating a plot to murder the Queen of England when she visits L.A. As many bad jokes as good ones, but they come flying so fast you'll scarcely notice. (Dir: David Zucker, 89 mins.)†

Naked Heart, The (Great Britain-France, 1950)*½ Michele Morgan, Kieron Moore, Françoise Rosay, Jack Watling. Dreary story of a convent-educated young woman returning home to look for a husband, trying to select from three suitors. Co-written by Roger Vadim. AKA: **Maria Chapdelaine.** (Dir: Marc Allegret, 96 mins.)†

Naked Hills, The (1956)** David Wayne, Marcia Henderson, James Barton, Keenan Wynn, Jim Backus, Denver Pyle, Fuzzy Knight. Uneven story about gold-mad Wayne, who spends forty years searching for gold in 19th-century California, at great expense to his wife and family. (Dir: Josef Shaftel, 73 mins.)

Naked in the Sun (1957)** James Craig, Lita Milan, Barton MacLane, Robert Wark, Jim Boles, Tony Hunter. Average action in this true story of two Indian tribes uniting to fight a slave trader. (Dir: R. John Hugh, 79 mins.)†

Naked Jungle, The (1954)*** Charlton Heston, Eleanor Parker, William Conrad, Abraham Sofaer. Heston and wife Parker are besieged on their South American plantation by an invading army of red ants. Director Byron Haskin has managed enough plausibility and humor to make this into model nonsense. (95 mins.)†

Naked Kiss, The (1964)***½ Constance Towers, Anthony Eisley, Virginia Grey. This brilliant pulp exercise directed by Samuel Fuller opens with a bald prostitute beating a man unconscious with a telephone. But when she tries to go straight, she only finds that respectable society will not forgive her past. (93 mins.)†

Naked Lie (MTV 1989)**½ Victoria Principal, James Farentino, Glenn Withrow, William Lucking. If you can buy Principal as a high powered D.A., you might enjoy this convoluted courtroom drama. She's trying a case in which the judge (Farentino) is not only her long-time lover, but also (unbeknownst to her) the real killer in the case! (Dir: Richard A. Colla, 96 mins.)

Naked Maja, The (1959)** Ava Gardner, Anthony Franciosa. Elaborately mounted but dull drama about the romance between Goya, the painter, and the Duchess of Alba. (Dir: Henry Koster, 111 mins.)

Naked Prey, The (1966)*** Cornel Wilde. A striking adventure film which has some brutal scenes. Wilde plays an African safari guide who watches his party of three hunters brutally killed by a tribe who decide to give him a chance for survival. The jungle code allows Wilde, stripped of his clothing, weapons, and food, to be hunted like a lion by the tribe's best hunters. (Dir: Cornel Wilde, 94 mins.)†

Naked Runner, The (Great Britain, 1967)* Frank Sinatra, Peter Vaughan, Derren Nesbitt, Nadia Gray. Sinatra is conned into a dangerous mission behind the Iron Curtain. (Dir: Sidney J. Furie, 104 mins.)

Naked Spur, The (1953)*** James Stewart, Janet Leigh, Robert Ryan, Ralph Meeker. Good adventure bolstered by a star cast. Filmed on location in the Rockies, the rugged tale follows a group of bounty hunters in pursuit of a killer with a price on his head. (Dir: Anthony Mann, 91 mins.)†

Naked Street (1955)**½ Farley Granger, Anthony Quinn, Anne Bancroft. Underworld leader gets a cheap hoodlum free from a murder rap so the hood can marry his sister. Satisfactory crime drama, well acted. (Dir: Maxwell Shane, 84 mins.)

Naked Truth, The—See: **Your Past Is Showing**

Naked Under Leather (France-Great Britain, 1968)**½ Alain Delon, Marianne Faithfull, Roger Mutton, Marius Goring. Not half bad, but especially memorable for the opening sequence in which Faithfull, clad in a skintight leather jump suit (zipper in front), rides over the verdant countryside for minutes, only to leap into the bedroom of a luxurious ranch house and utter the immortal opening line: "Skin me."AKA: **Girl on a Motorcycle.** (Dir: Jack Cardiff, 91 mins.)

Naked Vengeance (1986)½ Deborah Tranelli, Kaz Garas, Bill McLaughlin, Ed Crick, Henry Strzalkowski. Despicable story of a woman taking violent, cold-blooded revenge on the slobbering rednecks who raped her and killed her family. Humorless and competently made, which only makes it all the more unwatchable. AKA: **Satin Vengeance.** (Dir: Cirio H. Santiago, 97 mins.)†

Naked Youth (1960)—See: **Cruel Story of Youth**

Nakia (MTV 1974)** Robert Forster, Arthur Kennedy, Linda Evans. Forster strikes a heroic pose as an Indian deputy sheriff in this pilot film for the TV series. (Dir: Leonard Horn, 74 mins.)

Name for Evil, A (1970)* Robert Culp, Samantha Eggar, Sheila Sullivan, Mike Lane. Architect Culp, disenchanted with middle-class life, moves his wife to an old mansion in Canada. Pretentious supernatural drama was barely released. (Dir: Bernard Girard, 74 mins.)†

Name of the Game Is Kill, The (1968)* Jack Lord, Susan Strasberg, Collin Wilcox. A violent horror movie, with pretensions of being a way-out parody-drama. About an innocent passerby waylaid by a rather odd and dangerous family. AKA: **The Female Trap.** (Dir: Gunnar Hellstrom, 88 mins.)

Name of the Rose, The (Italy-West Germany-France, 1986)*½ Sean Connery, F. Murray Abraham, William Hickey. Turgid screen version of Umberto Eco's surprise best-seller about some killings in a 14th-century abbey. This prestige film recreates life among these monks and religious hysterics in the most squalid manner possible. (Dir: Jean Jacques-Annaud, 128 mins.)†

Namu, the Killer Whale (1966)** Robert Lansing, Lee Meriwether. When a naturalist befriends a whale, the fishermen in the vicinity object and cause trouble for both Namu and his master. (Dir: Laslo Benedek, 89 mins.)

Nana (France, 1926)***½ Werner Krauss, Jean Angelo, Catherine Hessling, Pierre Champagne, Pierre Philippe. Emile Zola's masterful novel about mediocre actress-prostitute who finds brief love before suffering an ugly death is brought to silent screen in a version rich in character and full of spectacular theatricality. (Dir: Jean Renoir, 98 mins.)

Nana (1934)*** Anna Sten, Lionel Atwill, Phillips Holmes. Producer Samuel Goldwyn made a big play to launch Russian actress Sten as the new Garbo in the title role from Emile Zola's novel. Tale of a high-living whore's downfall is generally lucid and intelligent, if uninvolving. (Dir: Dorothy Arzner, 89 mins.)

Nana (Italy, 1983)** Katya Berger, Jean-Pierre Aumont, Mandy Rice-Davies. Emile Zola's classic yarn about a streetwalker who rises to the highest pinnacle of Parisian society during the late 1880s is given a new soft-core look in this latest screen version. (Dir: Don Walman, 92 mins.)

Nancy Drew and the Hidden Staircase (1939)**½ Bonita Granville, Frankie Thomas, John Litel, Frank Orth, Vera Lewis. The teenage detective foils con artists preying on innocent old ladies; good version of the well-known young people's series, with Granville exactly right as Nancy. (Dir: William Clement, 60 mins.)

Nancy Drew, Detective (1938)**½ Bonita Granville, John Litel, Frankie Thomas. The appealing kickoff for a minor series based on Carolyn Keene's Nancy Drew books. Here, Granville puts the coppers to shame as she ferrets out some kidnappers. (Dir: William Clemens, 60 mins.)

Nancy Drew, Reporter (1939)**½ Bonita Granville, John Litel. In this one Nancy is putting in a month on a paper covering minor assignments but she manages to get her pretty nose on a murder and we're off again. (Dir: William Clemens, 70 mins.)

Nancy Drew—Trouble Shooter (1939)** Bonita Granville, John Litel, Frankie Thomas. Typical entry in the series featuring Granville as the ingenue sleuth. (Dir: William Clemens, 69 mins.)

Nancy Goes to Rio (1950)**½ Jane Powell, Ann Sothern, Barry Sullivan. The plot gets in the way of this otherwise charmingly played musical. Jane Powell and Ann Sothern play daughter and mother performers, respectively. (Dir: Robert Z. Leonard, 99 mins.)

Nancy Steel Is Missing (1937)**½ Victor McLaglen, Walter Connolly, Peter Lorre, June Lang, Jane Darwell, John Carradine. Interesting caper story has crook McLaglen passing off his adopted daughter as a long-lost heiress; a good mystery, with plot twists that will keep you in suspense. (Dir: George Marshall, 85 mins.)

Nanny, The (Great Britain, 1965)*** Bette Davis, William Dix, Jill Bennett, Pamela Franklin. Davis is cast as an English nanny whose sense of reality is clouded due to some deep dark secret in her past. Her charge, a very disturbed young lad fresh out of a junior asylum, is wise to her, but he has trouble making anyone else believe him. Despite the built-in melodrama, Davis's performance is quite restrained. (Dir: Seth Holt, 93 mins.)

Nanook of the North (1922)**** The great documentary of the life and daily hardships of an Eskimo family is still a superb piece of filmmaking and a landmark of film history. The silent version was modernized in 1939 with a music score and narration by Berry Kroeger. (Dir: Robert Flaherty, 65 mins.)

➤ **Nanou** (Great Britain-France, 1986)*** Imogen Stubbs, Jean-Philippe Ecoffey, Daniel Day-Lewis. Very low-key character study of a young British woman who carries on a bumpy love affair with a French anarchist. (Dir: Conny Templeman, 110 mins.)

Napoleon (France, 1927)**** Albert Dieudonne, Antonin Artaud, Abel Gance. This towering masterpiece is one of the greatest films ever made, and has been superbly reconstructed. The fact that Abel Gance directed this epochal and visually stunning biography in 1925-1927 makes the film all the more remarkable. Starts with Napoleon as a young child at a boarding school, and follows his early

734

career until his triumphal entry into Italy. (240 mins.)†

Napoleon (France, 1955)** Raymond Pellegrin, Jean-Pierre Aumont, Orson Welles, Erich von Stroheim, Yves Montand, Jean Gabin, Sacha Guitry. Lavish, star-studded depiction of the life of Napoleon sticks mostly to the emperor's personal life, which may be why it never seems to go anywhere. Most prints run shorter than the original length. (Dir: Sacha Guitry, 190 mins.)†

Napoleon and Samantha (1972)**½ Michael Douglas, Will Geer, Jodie Foster, Johnny Whitaker, Ellen Corby. Two kids want to keep a pet lion. They start out on an adventurous trek across the Oregon terrain to find their good friend Douglas. (Dir: Bernard McEveety, 91 mins.)†

Narrow Corner, The (1933)**½ Douglas Fairbanks, Jr., Ralph Bellamy, Patricia Ellis, Dudley Digges, Sidney Toler. From a story by W. Somerset Maugham, this tells of an honest doctor who is kidnapped by gangsters to prevent him from identifying them and taken to the tropics, where the languid lifestyle changes his outlook on life; interesting concept, capably done. (Dir: Alfred E. Green, 71mins.)

Narrow Margin, The (1952)*** Charles McGraw, Marie Windsor. Detective guards an important grand jury witness aboard a train. Suspenseful crime melodrama. (Dir: Richard Fleischer, 70 mins.)

Narrow Margin (1990)** Gene Hackman, Anne Archer, James B. Sikking, J. T. Walsh, M. Emmet Walsh, Harris Yulin. Pedestrian remake of a better 1952 thriller finds deputy D.A. bringing a reluctant Archer back to L.A. to testify in a mob trial. Most of the film takes place aboard a train, but writer-director Peter Hyams hasn't the style, vision, or wit to carry off what Hitchcock did so well. (Dir: Peter Hyams, 99 mins.)†

Narrow Trail, The (1917)**** William S. Hart, Sylvia Bremer, Milton Ross. Hart stars as "Ice" Harding, a wild, lawless westerner who longs to go straight when he falls in love; but unknown to him, the girl he cares for has a past, too. This forceful, unpretentious story takes the naïve cowboy to San Francisco's raucous Barbary Coast in search of his girl, and the scenes of waterfront low life are remarkably candid; the lovers forgive each other, and win a grubstake to start their new life together in an exciting horse race, featuring Hart's famous steed Fritz. Hart wrote and directed this exceptional film. (56 mins.)†

Nashville (1975)**** Lily Tomlin, Shelley Duvall, Henry Gibson, Ronee Blakley, Karen Black, Barbara Harris, Allen Garfield, Barbara Baxley, Geraldine Chaplin, Keenan Wynn, Keith Carradine. A stunning, bold work of art commenting on the American dream, while focusing on Nashville, the dream center and cultural capital of country music. A work of audacity by director Robert Altman. Chosen as the best picture of the year by the New York Film Critics and the National Society of Film Critics. Won the Academy Award for Best Original Song, "I'm Easy," by Keith Carradine. (159 mins.)†

Nashville Grab (MTV 1981)* Jeff Conaway, Cristina Raines, Gary Sandy, Slim Pickens, Henry Gibson, Dianne Kay. Silly chase yarn about a young singer who is used by two female prisoners to break out of a Nashville jail. (Dir: James L. Conway, 104 mins.)

Nasty Girl, The (Germany, 1990)***½ Lena Stolze, Monika Baumgartner, Michael Gahr, Fred Stillkrauth, Elizabeth Bertram, Robert Giggenbach. Delicious black comedy about a modern German schoolgirl whose essay, "My Town During the Third Reich," stirs up memories of Nazi deeds long forgotten or ignored, causing her to be ostracized and threatened. Stolze is outstanding as both Sonja the young girl and Sonja the mother of two. Based on the true experience of Anja Rosmus. An important film that devilishly pricks the balloon of hypocrisy. (Dir: Michael Verhoeven, 95 mins.)†

Nasty Habits (Great Britain-U.S., 1976)**½ Glenda Jackson, Anne Meara, Anne Jackson, Geraldine Page. The novel *The Abbess of Crewe* by Muriel Spark was an acerbic satire on Watergate set in a convent. This film is played for broader laughs, but the cast wrings those laughs religiously. (Dir: Michael Lindsay-Hogg, 91 mins.)†

Nasty Hero (1987)*½ Scott Feraco, Robert Sedgwick, Carlos Palomino, Mike Starr, Rosanna DaVon. Feraco is framed for car theft, returns to Miami to get even with the real thieves. (Dir: Nick Barwood, 79 mins.)†

Nasty Rabbit, The—See: **Spies-A-Go-Go**

Nate and Hayes (1983)** Tommy Lee Jones, Michael O'Keefe, Max Phipps, Jenny Seagrove. Swashbuckler about an anti-hero who helps a young missionary recapture his fianceé from an evil slave trader. Far-fetched but sporadically entertaining. (Dir: Ferdinand Fairfax, 100 mins.)†

National Lampoon's Animal House (1978)**½ John Belushi, Tim Matheson, John Vernon, Thomas Hulce, Peter Riegert, Stephen Furst, Donald Sutherland, Karen Allen. Belushi is the head slob of the Delta fraternity, which occupies a rundown shanty. These dregs of Faber College indulge in wild toga parties, pranks, and confrontations with the dean and the neighboring Omega house. Taste-

less, but crudely funny. (Dir: John Landis, 109 mins.)†

National Lampoon's Christmas Vacation (1989)** Chevy Chase, Beverly D'Angelo, Juliette Lewis, Johnny Galecki, John Randolph, Diane Ladd, E. G. Marshall, Doris Roberts, Randy Quaid, William Hickey, Mae Questel. This time the Griswald family decides to stay home for the holidays and celebrate with their colorful, irritating relatives. Predictable all the way, with some occasionally amusing bits. (Dir: Jeremiah Chechik, 97 mins.)†

National Lampoon's Class Reunion (1982)*½ Gerrit Graham, Michael Lerner, Stephen Furst, Zane Buzby. Vulgar horror spoof. (Dir: Michael Miller, 84 mins.)†

National Lampoon's European Vacation (1985)* Chevy Chase, Beverly D'Angelo, Dana Hill, Eric Idle, Jason Lively. Distinctly awful follow-up to the first Lampoon *Vacation*. (Dir: Amy Heckerling, 94 mins.)†

National Lampoon's Movie Madness (1982)* Peter Riegert, Diane Lane, Ann Dusenberry, Robert Culp, Robby Benson, Richard Widmark, Christopher Lloyd. This dreadful comedy spoof of movie genres features Benson as a naïve cop reduced to alcoholism and pratfalls. (Dirs: Bob Giraldi, Henry Jaglom, 89 mins.)†

National Lampoon's Vacation (1983)**½ Chevy Chase, Beverly D'Angelo, Christie Brinkley, Imogene Coca. Amusing farce with Chase, who plans a cross-country trip to the famed "Wally World" with his family, only to be involved in one disaster after another. Written by John Hughes. (Dir: Harold Ramis, 98 mins.)†

National Velvet (1944)***½ Mickey Rooney, Elizabeth Taylor, Donald Crisp, Ann Revere, Angela Lansbury, Reginald Owen. The whole family will love this enchanting story of a butcher's daughter and a bum kid who train a horse to win the Grand National. (Dir: Clarence Brown, 123 mins.)†

Native Son (1950)**½ Richard Wright, Jean Wallace, Gloria Madison, Nicholas Joy. Unfortunately, this is a rather poor version of Richard Wright's famous novel, with the author starring as his own creation, the unpremeditated murderer Bigger Thomas. The unprofessional direction and extremely low budget do it in. (Dir: Pierre Chenal, 91 mins.)†

Native Son (1986)*** Carroll Baker, Akosua Busia, Matt Dillon, Victor Love, John Karlen, Elizabeth McGovern, Geraldine Page, David Rasche, Lane Smith, Oprah Winfrey. A competent adaptation of Richard Wright's beloved novel. Good acting ignites this tale of the unfortunate Bigger Thomas, who gets the death sentence after accidentally murdering a white girl. (Dir: Jerrold Freedman, 112 mins.)†

Nativity, The (MTV 1978)**½ Madeline Stowe, John Shea, Jane Wyatt. The story of the Nativity, told from the vantage point of the courtship of Joseph (Shea) betrothed to Mary (Stowe), and the reaction he has to Mary's pregnancy. (Dir: Bernard Kowalski, 104 mins.)

Natural, The (1984)** Robert Redford, Robert Duvall, Glenn Close, Richard Farnsworth, Wilford Brimley, Barbara Hershey, Kim Basinger, Darren McGavin. Bernard Malamud's darkly comic baseball fable comes to the screen with a glossy production and a team of all-stars, but the story's irony and intelligence have been excised. (Dir: Barry Levinson, 134 mins.)†

Natural Enemies (1979)* Hal Holbrook, Louise Fletcher, José Ferrer, Viveca Lindfors. Depressing, pretentious story about a successful publisher who decides to kill his alienated wife and children and himself. (Dir: Jeff Kanew, 100 mins.)†

Naughty but Nice (1939)**½ Ann Sheridan, Dick Powell, Ronald Reagan. Pleasant, diverting little musical which lampoons the popular music business and its relationship to the classics. (Dir: Ray Enright, 90 mins.)

Naughty Marietta (1934)***½ Jeanette MacDonald, Nelson Eddy, Frank Morgan, Elsa Lanchester. Eddy first partnered with MacDonald in this Victor Herbert operetta, and the result was a new team that delighted audiences for many years. (Dir: W. S. Van Dyke, 110 mins.)†

Naughty Nineties, The (1945)** Bud Abbott, Lou Costello, Rita Johnson. Bud and Lou invade the old Southern world of showboats and card sharks on the Mississippi. (Dir: Jean Yarbrough, 76 mins.)†

Navajo Joe (Italy-Spain, 1967)* Burt Reynolds, Aldo Sanbrell. It seems a fierce band of outlaws led by an Indian-hating half-breed has been slaughtering Navajos; Burt goes after the desperados. (Dir: Sergio Corbucci, 89 mins.)

Navigator, The (1924)**** Buster Keaton, Kathryn McGuire. A wondrous gem from the slapstick master. A wealthy two-some find themselves cut adrift from their spoiled lifestyle as they float on an ocean liner heading for sea. Alone together, without a crew, they gradually gain in wisdom while coping with a profusion of sight gags. Touching, funny, and remarkably fresh. (Dirs: Buster Keaton, Donald Crisp, 62 mins.)

Navigator, The (New Zealand, 1988)**½ Bruce Lyons, Hamish McFarlane, Marshall Napier. In an attempt to avoid the Black Plague, villagers from a small British village enter a tunnel which they think will lead to the other side of the earth and wind up in 20th-century New Zealand. Beautifully photographed and filled with portentous visuals, but what it means evaded us completely. (Dir: Vincent Ward, 92 mins.)†

Navy Blue and Gold (1937)*** Robert Young, James Stewart, Lionel Barrymore. The old Annapolis story in the hands of a fine cast turns into an entertaining film. (Dir: Sam Wood, 94 mins.)

Navy Blues (1941)*** Ann Sheridan, Martha Raye, Jack Oakie, Jack Haley, Jackie Gleason. A lot of talented people, plenty of noise, and a few good songs make this zany musical entertaining. (Dir: Lloyd Bacon, 108 mins.)

Navy Comes Through, The (1942)*** Pat O'Brien, George Murphy, Jane Wyatt. The merchant marine keeps the sea lanes open during WWII. Exciting melodrama. (Dir: A. Edward Sutherland, 82 mins.)

Navy SEALS (1990)*½ Charlie Sheen, Michael Biehn, Joanne Whalley-Kilmer, Rick Rossovich, Cyril O'Reilly, Bill Paxton, Dennis Haysbert, Paul Sanchez. The high-tech weaponry outperforms the cast in this hard-to-fathom action-adventure film about elite U.S. Navy commandos who battle Middle Eastern terrorists. (Dir: Lewis Teague, 113 mins.)†

Navy vs. the Night Monsters, The (1966)* Mamie Van Doren, Bobby Van, Anthony Eisley. It seems Antarctica is filled with man-eating plants. . . . (Dir: Michael A. Hoey, 90 mins.)†

Navy Wife (1956)*½ Joan Bennett, Gary Merrill, Shirley Yamaguchi, Maurice Manson. Trivial drama about docile Japanese women revolting against tradition. (Dir: Edward Bernds, 83 mins.)

Nazarin (Mexico, 1959)**** Francisco Rabal, Marga Lopez, Rita Macedo, Ignacio Tarso, Jesus Fernandez. A priest defrocks himself to wander among the poor, living on alms in penitent imitation of Christ. With followers that include a prostitute and a jilted woman, he creates havoc on the surreal Mexican landscape through which he travels before learning to love selflessly: in many ways a recapitulation of Buñuel's cinematic career. (Dir: Luis Buñuel, 95 mins.)†

Nazi Agent (1942)**½ Conrad Veidt, Dorothy Tree, Anne Ayars, Sidney Blackmer, Martin Kosleck, William Tannen. Good WWII suspense, with Veidt in two roles as twins, one a Nazi officer and one an Allied agent who impersonates his brother; fairly low budget, but effectively acted and well directed by Jules Dassin. (83 mins.)

Nazi Hunter: The Beate Klarsfeld Story (MTV 1986)*½ Farrah Fawcett, Tom Conti, Geraldine Page. Fawcett's quest to prove that she is an actress with a capital "A" is beginning to wear thin. Now she's Beate Klarsfeld, a German hausfrau who brings Nazi criminals to justice. The TV-movie is based on real-life incidents but is extremely dull, and Farrah's attempt at a German accent is of the "Hogan's Heroes" variety. (Dir: Michael Lindsay-Hogg, 104 mins.)

Nea (A Young Emmanuelle) (France-West Germany, 1976)***½ Samy Frey, Ann Zacharias, Nelly Kaplan, Micheline Presle. The best sex comedy of its year. Zacharias plays an adolescent girl who writes a best-selling pornographic novel. (Dir: Nelly Kaplan, 103 mins.)†

Neanderthal Man, The (1953)** Robert Shayne, Richard Crane, Robert Long. For some reason, this ridiculous horror flick is weirdly enjoyable, with a scientist going overboard on his experiments with the coelacanth, a surviving prehistoric fish, and accidentally transforming himself into a Neanderthal man. Oops! (Dir: E. A. Dupont, 78 mins.)

Near Dark (1987)*** Adrian Pasdar, Jenny Wright, Lance Henriksen, Bill Paxton, Jenette Goldstein,. The Western meets the vampire genre, as a young man's desire for a beautiful girl leads him to run afoul of her vicious, bloodsucking "family." Distancing at first, this spare, eerie thriller becomes more engrossing (and violent) as it goes along, with an especially nerve-racking middle third. (Dir: Kathryn Bigelow, 95 mins.)†

Neat and Tidy (MTV 1986)½ Skyler Cole, Jill Whitlow, Elke Sommer, Edie Adams, John Astin, Stella Stevens, Larry Storch. One sits through this lame adventure-comedy as if it were all a nightmare; surely no one could have committed something this awful to celluloid. A man on the lam from the law and a girl running away from her mobster chieftain papa rush from Italy to Arabia to the wild west (even though all three areas look suspiciously alike), while they encounter a number of character actors looking understandably embarrassed, and Elvis Presley tunes play on the soundtrack like an anthem of desperation. AKA: **Adventures Beyond Belief.** (Dir: Marcus Thompson, 104 mins.)†

'Neath Brooklyn Bridge (1942)** East Side Kids, Danny (Bobby Jordan) gets cleared of a murder rap by a mute witness who blinks the killer's identity in Morse Code. (Dir: Wallace Fox, 61 mins.)

Nebraskan, The (1953)** Phil Carey, Roberta Haynes. Routine western about having Army Scout winning the trust of Indian War Chief of the Sioux tribe. (Dir: Fred F. Sears, 68 mins.)

Necessity (MTV 1988)*½ Loni Anderson, John Heard, James Naughton. Ridiculous suspense thriller that not only lacks invention, but credibility as well. Loni leaves her drug kingpin husband (Naughton) and then plans to rescue her baby from his clutches with the aid of pilot Heard. AKA: **Blown Away.** (Dir: Michael Miller, 96 mins.)

Necromancy (1972)* Orson Welles, Pamela Franklin. Silly occult thriller. Saga of a strange town whose major business is a factory turning out occult items. Pamela Franklin is a young lady being groomed by a coven of witches as a sacrifice. (Dir: Bert I. Gordon, 82 mins.)

Necropolis (1987)* LeeAnn Baker, Jacquie Fitz, Michael Conte, William K. Reed, Paul Ruben. A 300-year-old witch, looking pretty good for her age, is resurrected in N.Y.C. so that she can provide eternal life for her followers. Sole point of interest: the witch's six breasts (special effects, of course), beating the previous record of four in *The Warrior and the Sorceress*, though we hope this isn't an escalating trend! (Dir: Bruce Hickey, 76 mins.)†

Ned Kelly (Great Britain, 1970)** Mick Jagger, Tony Richardson, Clarissa Kaye. As the Australian cowboy-turned-bandit, Jagger is only a snarl more convincing than Frank Sinatra's cowpoke in *Johnny Concho*. (Dir: Tony Richardson, 100 mins.)

Negatives (Great Britain, 1968)*** Diane Cilento, Peter McEnery, Glenda Jackson. Macabre offbeat drama about a couple who thrive on charades for sexual stimulation (they usually play a famous wife murderer and his victim). Enter a glamorous photographer (Diane Cilento) with an equally warped sense of bedroom play and the film goes off in mad, but interesting tangents. Promising directorial debut by Peter Medak. (90 mins.)†

Neighborhood, The (MTV 1982)**½ Christine Belford, Ron Masak, Ben Masters, Howard Rollins, Jr. When a predominantly white neighborhood starts changing with the arrival of black families, bigotry leads to violent confrontations. Well-meaning drama that gets bogged down in grandstanding. (Dir: Lee H. Katzin, 78 mins.)

Neighbors (1981)**½ John Belushi, Dan Aykroyd, Cathy Moriarty, Kathryn Walker. Belushi is a quiet man living with his wife in suburbia when a crazy man and his sexpot wife move in next door and make their lives a living hell. The one-joke premise wears thin before too long and the performances start to grate. (Dir: John G. Avildsen, 91 mins.)†

Nelson Affair, The (1973)**½ Glenda Jackson, Peter Finch, Michael Jayston, Anthony Quayle, Margaret Leighton, Dominic Guard. The performances of the two leads almost make up for the shortcomings of the pedestrian script about the scandalous love affair between Admiral Lord Nelson and Lady Hamilton. (Dir: James Cellan Jones, 115 mins.)

Neon Ceiling, The (MTV 1971)**½ Gig Young, Lee Grant, Denise Nickerson. Moving drama. There are enough dramatic ingredients here to keep viewers interested—an adolescent awakening to the ways of the world; a philosophical, beer-drinking loner; and a neurotic woman running away from an unsatisfactory marriage. Lee Grant won an Emmy for her performance. (Dir: Frank R. Pierson, 97 mins.)

Neon Maniacs (1986)** Allan Hayes, Leilani Sarelle, Donna Locke, Victor Elliot Brandt, David Muir. A group of various psychos emerge from under the Golden Gate Bridge at night to wreak havoc. (Dir: Joseph Mangine, 91 mins.)†

Neptune Factor, The (1973)*½ Ben Gazzara, Yvette Mimieux, Walter Pidgeon, Ernest Borgnine. A group of adventurers try to rescue three scientists caught in an undersea earthquake, and wind up in what appears to be a very large pet shop aquarium. AKA: **The Neptune Disaster** (Dir: Daniel Petrie, 98 mins.)†

Neptune's Daughter (1949)**½ Esther Williams, Ricardo Montalban, Red Skelton, Betty Garrett. Light and tuneful romantic comedy with Esther's swimming and Red Skelton's funny-man antics. Oscar-winning song (by Frank Loesser), "Baby, It's Cold Outside," is from this film. (Dir: Edward Buzzell, 93 mins.)†

Nero Wolfe (MTV 1979)*** Thayer David, Anne Baxter, Brooke Adams, Tom Mason. David is perfectly cast as Rex Stout's stout, sophisticated sleuth, who manages to mix gourmet cooking with expert detective work. (Dir: Frank D. Gilroy, 104 mins.)

Nest, The (Spain, 1980)***½ Ana Torrent, Luis Politti, Hector Alterio, Patricia Adriani. Rich, elderly widower falls in love with a 13-year-old girl over the objections and warnings of friends and associates. Tragic drama about the innocence of both the young and the old. (Dir: Jaime De Arminan, 97 mins.)†

Nest, The (1988)**½ Robert Lansing, Lisa Langlois, Franc Luz. A low-budget exploitation film, done with more intelligence and humor than most, about a mutant strain of cockroaches. (Dir: Terence H. Winkless, 88 mins.)†

Nesting, The (1981)½ Robin Groves, Christopher Loomis, Michael David Lally, Gloria Grahame, John Carradine. Interminable horror tale about a writer menaced by both the living and the dead. (Dir: Armand Weston, 104 mins.)†

Network (1976)***½ Faye Dunaway, William Holden, Peter Finch, Robert Duvall, Beatrice Straight, Ned Beatty. Paddy Chayefsky's searing, perceptive satire of television network news, about a network TV anchorman who's gone bananas, and the avaricious bastards in the executive suites who capitalize on his madness after initially firing him. Oscars for Straight, Dunaway, and Finch. (Dir: Sidney Lumet, 121 mins.)†

738

Nevada (1944)**½ Robert Mitchum, Anne Jeffreys. Cowpoke stops crooks after mining claims. Fast-moving, well-made western. (Dir: Edward Killy, 62 mins.)

Nevada Heat—See: **Fake-Out**

Nevadan, The (1950)** Randolph Scott, Dorothy Malone, George Macready, Forrest Tucker. Not one of Scott's truly classic '50s westerns, this has him as a marshal pursuing outlaws Macready and Tucker. Okay, but not special. (Dir: Gordon Douglas, 81 mins.)

Nevada Smith (1966)**½ Steve McQueen, Karl Malden, Suzanne Pleshette, Brian Keith, Arthur Kennedy. In this episodic but well-acted film, a half-breed killer tracks down his parents' killers. (Dir: Henry Hathaway, 120 mins.)†

Never a Dull Moment (1950)**½ Irene Dunne, Fred MacMurray. New York songwriter marries a rancher, tries to get used to open-air life. Mildly amusing comedy. (Dir: George Marshall, 89 mins.)

Never a Dull Moment (1968)**½ Dick Van Dyke, Edward G. Robinson, Slim Pickens, Dorothy Provine. Enjoyable, often funny. A mobster kingpin has hired a professional killer when along comes Van Dyke, an actor who is mistaken for the hit man. (Dir: Jerry Paris, 100 mins.)†

Never Con a Killer (MTV 1976)*½ Stefanie Powers, Harold Gould, John Forsythe, Marc Singer. Stefanie Powers plays a brainy lawyer who enlists the help of her con-man father Gould to nail a crooked horse breeder. (Dir: Buzz Kulik, 80 mins.)

Never Cry Wolf (1983)***½ Charles Martin Smith, Brian Dennehy. Superb nature drama has a scientist dropped off in the Arctic wilderness to study the habits of wolves. (Dir: Carroll Ballard, 105 mins.)†

Neverending Story, The (West Germany, 1984)** Noah Hathaway, Barret Oliver, Tami Stronach, Moses Gunn. We thought it was more like the neverending movie. A little boy retreats from reality and finds himself drawn inside the book he's reading, *The Neverending Story* (about the Land of Fantasia, which another little boy must save from an insidious disease which makes people forget their hopes and dreams). (Dir: Wolfgang Peterson, 94 mins.)†

Neverending Story II, The: The Next Chapter (Australia-U.S., 1991)*** Jonathan Brandis, Alexandra Johnes, Kenny Morrison, Clarissa Burt. Excellent special effects and wonderfully bizarre creatures highlight this sequel to the original; will appeal to children and some parents. The Land of Fantasia is under attack and young Bastian Balthazar Bux is called upon to help good triumph over evil. (Dir: George Miller, 89 mins.)†

Never Forget (MCTV 1991)*** Leonard Nimoy, Dabney Coleman, Blythe Danner, Paul Hampton. True story of Mel Mermelstein, a survivor of the Auschwitz-Birkenau concentration camp, who took up the challenge put forth by a revisionist group called IHR (Institute for Historical Review) to prove the Holocaust actually happened. The IHR claims the Holocaust was a hoax conceived by the Jewish people to further their own political and territorial needs. Nimoy makes an earnest Mermelstein and Coleman shines as his offbeat lawyer. Preachy at times, but important nevertheless. (Dir: Joseph Sargent, 96 mins.) †

Never Give an Inch (1971)*** Paul Newman, Michael Sarrazin, Henry Fonda, Lee Remick, Richard Jaeckel. Based on a Ken Kesey novel, this saga about a logging family in Oregon has good acting and glorious scenery going for it. AKA: *Sometimes a Great Notion.* (Dir: Paul Newman, 108 mins.) †

Never Give a Sucker an Even Break (1941)***½ W. C. Fields, Gloria Jean, Margaret Dumont, Leon Errol. A Fields nightmare, as he relates a strange tale of romantic adventures in a mythical country to a skeptical movie producer. No use in describing it—plotless farce has some moments of Fields at his best. (Dir: Edward Cline, 71 mins.) †

Never Let Go (Great Britain, 1960)** Peter Sellers, Richard Todd, Carol White, Elizabeth Sellars. Unpleasant melodrama about car thieves and their bout with the police. Sellers plays it straight and it's a bad job—one of his few film misadventures. (Dir: John Guillermin, 91 mins.) †

Never Let Me Go (1953)**½ Clark Gable, Gene Tierney. Gable plays an American newspaper correspondent who takes tremendous risks to smuggle his wife out of Russia. Some exciting scenes involving the actual escape toward the end of the film. (Dir: Delmer Daves, 94 mins.)

Never Love a Stranger (1958)** John Drew Barrymore, Lita Milan, Steve McQueen. Barrymore portrays a young man who chooses the "fast buck-fast women" path to destruction in this drama based on Harold Robbins's best seller. (Dir: Robert Stevens, 91 mins.) †

Never on Sunday (1960)***½ Melina Mercouri, Jules Dassin. Miss Mercouri delighted the movie audiences of the world with her inimitable performance of a carefree *fille de joie* in this film. A tourist named Homer tries to "reform" her, but his attempt to play Pygmalion has its setbacks. Wonderful Greek musical score. (Dir: Jules Dassin, 91 mins.) †

Never Say Die (1939)**½ Bob Hope, Martha Raye. Bob tries but this is little more than juvenile slapstick about a hypochondriac millionaire who marries a Texas gal because he thinks he has but two weeks to live. (Dir: Elliott Nugent, 82 mins.)

Never Say Goodbye (1946)**½ Errol Flynn, Eleanor Parker, S.Z. Sakall, Lucile Watson. A few laughs in this familiar farce about a man trying to win back his ex-wife but too much of it is contrived and silly. (Dir: James V. Kern, 97 mins.)

Never Say Goodbye (1956)**½ Rock Hudson, Cornell Borchers, George Sanders. Satisfactory remake of a 1945 film, *This Love of Ours.* Story concerns a woman whose husband left her many years ago taking her only daughter with him and how they meet years later and try to pick up the pieces of their torn lives. (Dir: Jerry Hopper, 96 mins.)

Never Say Never Again (1983)**½ Sean Connery, Klaus Maria Brandauer, Max von Sydow, Barbara Carrera, Kim Basinger. Acceptable update of *Thunderball* returns Connery to the role of James Bond. Once again, Bond tries to thwart the plans of that evil group known as SPECTRE after the theft of two nuclear warheads. Connery is in great form as an aging Bond. (Dir: Irvin Kershner, 137 mins.) †

Never So Few (1959)**½ Frank Sinatra, Gina Lollobrigida, Peter Lawford, Steve McQueen. Despite an all-star cast, this turns out to be just another WWII adventure with heavy romantic overtones. (Dir: John Sturges, 124 mins.) †

Never Steal Anything Small (1959)**½ James Cagney, Shirley Jones, Roger Smith, Cara Williams. Cagney as a crooked labor leader who will stop at nothing to become boss of the waterfront. Unlikely blend of satire, song, slapstick never gels, although the cast works hard. (Dir: Charles Lederer, 94 mins.) †

Never Take No for an Answer (Great Britain-Italy, 1951)*** Vittorio Manunta, Denis O'Dea. Small boy tries to take his sick donkey to the crypt of St. Francis, where he is sure the animal will recover. Charming Italian story has plenty of good touches, human interest. (Dirs: Maurice Cloche, Ralph Smart, 82 mins.)

Never to Love (1940)**½ Maureen O'Hara, Adolphe Menjou, Fay Bainter, Herbert Marshall. Restrained remake of *A Bill of Divorcement.* Ms. O'Hara is less forceful than her predecessor (Katharine Hepburn) as the young woman who calls off the marriage engagement after she learns that insanity may run in the family. (Dir: John Farrow, 74 mins.)

Never Too Late (1965)*** Paul Ford, Maureen O'Sullivan, Connie Stevens, Jim Hutton. Broadway comedy hit about a middle-aged couple with a grown, married daughter who discover they are to become parents. Transferred to the screen with all the funny situations intact. (Dir: Bud Yorkin, 104 mins.)

Never Too Young to Die (1986)* John Stamos, Vanity, Gene Simmons, Peter Kwong. If James Bond had matriculated at a U.S. college, he might have roomed with budding secret agent Stamos. The teen hunk plays a fledgling spy so upset over his papa's demise that he's willing to tangle with a hermaphrodite threatening to toxicize Los Angeles's water supply. (Dir: Gil Bettman, 92 mins.)†

Never Wave at a WAC (1952)**½ Rosalind Russell, Paul Douglas, Marie Wilson. Society hostess doesn't realize what she's in for when she joins the Women's Army Corps. Mildly amusing comedy, with a cast of seasoned laugh-getters helping it along. (Dir: Norman Z. McLeod, 87 mins.)

New Adventures of Heidi, The (MTV 1978)** Katy Kurtzman, Burl Ives, John Gavin. Musical based on Johanna Spyri's Heidi books. A spoiled rich runaway, whose mother is dead and whose father is too busy, manages to find a companion in Heidi. (Dir: Ralph Senensky, 104 mins.)

New Adventures of Pippi Longstocking, The (1988)*½ Tami Erin, Eileen Brennan, Dennis Dugan, Dick Van Patten, John Schuck. Pretty much the same as the old adventures, only this time with an American cast. The pig-tailed Ms. Longstocking, heroine of a popular series of children's books, is super-strong and super-obnoxious; kids may like it, but adults will want to be in another room altogether. (Dir: Ken Annakin, 100 mins.)†

New Avengers: The Eagle's Nest (MTV 1976)**½ Patrick Macnee, Joanna Lumley, Gareth Hunt. Can John Steed's new cohorts, lovely Lumley and sturdy Hunt, ever replace Diana Rigg? They're up to their necks in intrigue as a murder investigation takes them to a barren island which houses a retreat for monks. (Dir: Desmond Davis, 104 mins.)

New Centurions, The (1972)**½ George C. Scott, Stacy Keach, Jane Alexander, Scott Wilson, Erik Estrada. Uneven police story, based on the novel by Sgt. Joseph Wambaugh, that falters despite a good acting turn by Scott as a veteran cop who winds up his years of duty and retires. Keach is the hot-shot new cop with new ideas and he gets involved in a series of plot developments that play like separate TV cop shows. (Dir: Richard Fleischer, 103 mins.)†

New Daughters of Joshua Cabe, The (MTV 1976)* John McIntire, Jack Elam, Liberty Williams, Renne Jarrett, Lezlie Dalton. A trio of city girls out in Wyoming do their darndest to release their so-called Dad, Josh Cabe, from a mur-

der rap! (Dir: Bruce Bilson, 72 mins.)

New Faces (1954)*** Ronny Graham, Eartha Kitt, Alice Ghostley, Paul Lynde, Carol Lawrence, Robert Clary. A sprightly Broadway revue, starring talented newcomers; no plot, just a string of songs and skits. (Dir: Harry Horner, 99 mins.)†

New Gladiators, The (Italy, 1983)*½ Jared Martin, Fred Williamson, Claudio Cassinelli, Howard Ross. In the 21st century, the top-rated TV shows feature live gladiatorial contests in which less-than-willing contestants battle to the death. Not really a rip-off of *The Running Man* (1987), which it predates by four years, but a poorly dubbed cheapo anyway. (Dir: Lucio Fulci, 90 mins.)†

New Interns, The (1964)**½ Michael Callan, Barbara Eden, George Segal, Inger Stevens. Fairly interesting drama about hospitals and doctors. There are at least three major plots and as many subplots. (Dir: John Rich, 123 mins.)

New Jack City (1991)*½ Wesley Snipes, Ice-T, Chris Rock, Judd Nelson, Mario Van Peebles, Allen Payne, Russell Wong. Thoroughly unoriginal cops versus drug dealer film is filled with dumb violence, rude sexism, and grotesque stereotypes. Standard storyline features simplistic dialogue and overwrought acting. (Dir: Mario Van Peebles, 97 mins.)†

New Kids, The (1985)* Shannon Presby, Lori Loughlin, James Spader. A tiresome "get-even" drama about two orphans who move to Florida, only to be picked on beyond belief by sadistic bullies. (Dir: Sean Cunningham, 90 mins.)†

New Kind of Love, A (1963)**½ Paul Newman, Joanne Woodward, Thelma Ritter, Eva Gabor, Maurice Chevalier. Mildly enjoyable fluff about how reporter Paul Newman meets and chases fashion designer Joanne Woodward. (Dir: Melville Shavelson, 110 mins.)

New Land, The (Sweden, 1973)**** Liv Ullmann, Max von Sydow, Eddie Axberg. Superb sequel to *The Emigrants;* they were originally intended to be shown together as one film. The saga of the Oskar family documents their hardships in carving a new life in the growing U.S. A remarkable filmed essay on foreign emigration to America. (Dir: Jan Troell, 161 mins.)

New Leaf, A (1971)*** Walter Matthau, Elaine May, James Coco, Jack Weston. Credit is due Miss May, the writer-actor-director whose inventiveness keeps you smiling throughout. Matthau plays a sly snob who's bankrupt and looking for a rich woman to marry within six weeks. He finds May, a rich botanist and one of the world's clumsiest ladies. (102 mins.)†

New Life, A (1988)*** Alan Alda, Ann-

Margret, Hal Linden, Veronica Hamel, John Shea, Mary Kay Place. A thoroughly conventional romantic comedy with appealing performances and writing. As an obnoxious stockbroker, Alda sheds his nice guy persona, but the message of the movie is still that understanding and openness win out in the end. Alda and his wife (A-M) divorce, and each finds new love in yuppie New York. (Dir: Alan Alda, 104 mins.)†

Newlydeads, The (1988)*½ Jim Williams, Jean Levine, Jay Richardson, Roxanna Michaels, Rebecca Barrington. Standard vengeful-zombie flick has at least one novel twist: the wronged corpse is a transvestite killed by a would-be Romeo who found out his date was a he. That aside, it's business as usual when the cross-dressing corpse stalks the honeymooning guests at his killer's sleazy hotel. (Dir: Joseph Mehri, 77 mins.)†

Newman's Law (1974)*½ George Peppard, Roger Robinson, Abe Vigoda. Peppard plays a righteous cop accused of corruption and then suspended, who decides to pursue his case privately. (Dir: Richard Heffron, 98 mins.)†

New Mexico (1951)**½ Lew Ayres, Marilyn Maxwell, Robert Hutton, Andy Devine, Raymond Burr. Rather trim little Western *noir*, with an odd, usually urban cast, of the U.S. cavalry holding off a hostile Indian attack; not a masterpiece, but capable, with an individual slant. (Dir: Irving Reis, 76 mins.)

New Moon (1940)**½ Jeanette MacDonald, Nelson Eddy, Mary Boland. The Sigmund Romberg-Oscar Hammerstein score, as sung by Eddy and MacDonald, and laboring under the heavy touch of director Robert Z. Leonard. (105 mins.)†

New Orleans (1947)**½ Arturo de Cordova, Dorothy Patrick, Billie Holiday, Louis Armstrong, Woody Herman. As a film record of great jazz and blues musicians at their peak, this is indispensable. Forget the plot about the history of jazz, which surfaces intrusively, and concentrate on Billie, Louis, and all the others blasting the roof off and reminding us how much we missed due to Hollywood's neglect of them. (Dir: Arthur Lubin, 89 mins.)

News at Eleven (MTV 1986)**½ Martin Sheen, Peter Riegert, Barbara Babcock, Sheree J. Wilson, Sydney Penny. An attempt to infuse a TV-movie with serious social commentary. Sheen is a TV anchorman who is forced by news director Riegert to punch up a story about sexual harassment. (Dir: Mike Robe, 104 mins.)

New School Teacher, The (1923)**½ Chic Sale, Doris Kenyon, Mickey Bennett,

Russell Griffen. Classic vaudeville routines really make up the body of this comedy starring the then-famous humorist Chic Sale as a new teacher who is the butt of his rowdy students' pranks. Based on a story by Irwin S. Cobb, happily entitled *Young Nuts of America*. Early screwball farce directed by Gregory La Cava. (75 mins.)†

Newsfront (Australia, 1978)***½ Bill Hunter, Wendy Hughes, Gerard Kennedy, Angela Punch. Intercuts history on film with personal history in a slick film about an Australian newsreel cameraman from '48 to '56. Part B&W, part color. (Dir: Phillip Noyce, 110 mins.)†

News Hounds (1947)** Bowery Boys, Gabriel Dell. Slip and Sach are a reporting team cracking a story about gangsters putting the fix on sporting events. (Dir: William Beaudine, 68 mins.)

New Year's Day (1989)*** Henry Jaglom, Gwen Welles, Maggie Jakobson, Melanie Winter, Milos Forman, Michael Emil. Though its narrative is introspective and confined in the style of a one-act play, this is a loose, rambling work by filmmaker Henry Jaglom that contains some extended psychotherapy-like conversations in addition to winning moments of humor and sentiment. The film depicts the interaction between a man moving into an apartment and the three women who are moving out. Some of the characters are underdeveloped (including the one played by Jaglom), but the youngest of the women (Jakobson) emerges as a fully realized, beautifully drawn character. (89 mins.)†

New York Confidential (1955)**½ Broderick Crawford, Anne Bancroft, Richard Conte. Tense and exciting expose of the big crime syndicate working out of New York. Supposedly based on facts. (Dir: Russell Rouse, 87 mins.)

New York, New York (1977)**½ Liza Minnelli, Robert De Niro, Lionel Stander, Barry Primus, Mary Kay Place. A deliberately depressing musical. De Niro is an uninvolved, feckless jazz musician with little appeal, except in the eyes of up-and-coming star, Liza. A sadly arrogant failure, awash with brilliance and feeling and no sense of responsibility toward the audience. Restored version runs 164 mins. (Dir: Martin Scorsese, 153 mins.)†

New York Nights (1983)*½ Corrine Alphen, George Auyer, Bobbi Burns, Marcia McBroom, Peter Matthey. Sleazy Manhattan-based "adult" rip-off of *La Ronde* duplicates its circular plotting: one individual sleeps with second, second sleeps with third, etc., all the way back to the first. Willem Dafoe has a small part. Filmed in 1981. (Dir: Simon Nuchtern, 104 mins.)†

New York's Finest (1988)* Jennifer Delora, Ruth Collins, Heide Paine, Scott Baker, Jane Hamilton. Title refers not to cops but to three hookers who, tired of being treated like bimbos because of their working-class Queens accents and manners, go the *Pygmalion* route in hopes of attracting rich husbands. An "adult" comedy that's anything but. (Dir: Chuck Vincent, 86 mins.)†

New York Stories (1989)*** Nick Nolte, Rosanna Arquette; Heather McComb, Talia Shire, Giancarlo Giannini, Don Novello; Woody Allen, Mia Farrow, Mae Questel, Julie Kavner. Three great directors each contribute a Manhattan-based story to this omnibus film. Martin Scorsese's "Life Lessons," about a painter's obsession with his young protégé, is among his best work ever. Ditto Woody Allen's hilarious "Oedipus Wrecks," the ultimate Jewish mother story. Francis Coppola's pretty but fatuous children's story "Life Without Zoe" is the only clunker. (130 mins.)†

New York Town (1941)**½ Fred MacMurray, Mary Martin, Robert Preston. Occasionally amusing comedy about a sidewalk photographer who befriends a homeless lass. (Dir: Charles Vidor, 94 mins.)

Next Man, The (1976)½ Sean Connery, Cornelia Sharpe, Albert Paulsen. Failed political thriller about Saudi Arabian diplomats, and the effort to kill "The Next Man." (Dir: Richard Sarafian, 108 mins.)

Next of Kin (Great Britain, 1942)***½ Nova Pilbeam, Mervyn Johns, Jack Hawkins. Showing the effects of loose information, how it can lead to enemy ears. Excellent wartime drama. (Dir: Thorold Dickinson, 85 mins.)

Next One, The (U.S.-Greece, 1982)*½ Keir Dullea, Adrienne Barbeau, Jeremy Licht, Peter Hobbs. Inflated parable about a stranger who mysteriously appears on a Greek island and seems to perform miracles, causing discussion as to whether he is the second coming of Christ. Writer-director Nico Mastorakis's ambition exceeds his grasp here. (105 mins.)†

Next Stop, Greenwich Village (1976)***½ Lenny Baker, Shelley Winters, Ellen Greene, Mike Kellin, Christopher Walken. Affectionate, engaging, autobiographical Valentine directed and written by Paul Mazursky about his own growing up in New York's Greenwich Village circa 1953. Two unusually winning performances by newcomers Baker and Greene combine to make this film alternately farcical, rueful, and wistful. (109 mins.)

Next Summer (France, 1986)*** Fanny Ardant, Jean-Louis Trintignant, Claudia Cardinale, Philippe Noiret. Created from an openly feminist perspective, this is a finely crafted and acted study of the way women relate to each other, to their families, to men, and to themselves. The performers create fully realized characters, each offering insight into the mix of dependency and independence of human interaction. (Dir: Nadine Trintignant, 100 mins.)†

Next Time We Love (1936)**½ James Stewart, Margaret Sullavan, Ray Milland. Wife gives up her singing job to accompany her husband on a foreign assignment. Fairly good romantic drama. (Dir: Edward H. Griffith, 87 mins.)

Next to No Time (Great Britain, 1958)**½ Kenneth More, Betsy Drake, Bessie Love, Roland Culver. Pleasant British comedy has shy More going wild on a cruise liner; charmingly acted spoof of Anglo-American differences. (Dir: Henry Cornelius, 93 mins.)

Next Victim, The (Great Britain, 1974)*½ Carrol Baker, T. P. McKenna, Maurice Kaufman, Ronald Lacey, Ian Gelder. Wheelchair-bound woman, the only person in her apartment building during a holiday weekend, is menaced by a killer. Premise has been done better in many other films than in this cheapie. (Dir: James Ormerod, 80 mins.)†

Next Voice You Hear, The (1950)*** James Whitmore, Nancy Davis, Gary Gray. Over-sentimentalized, but nevertheless engrossing drama about a group of people who hear the voice of God on the radio and the effect it has on their lives. (Dir: William Wellman, 82 mins.)

Niagara (1953)*** Marilyn Monroe, Joseph Cotten, Jean Peters. This film boasts two scenic marvels, Niagara Falls and M. M. in various states of undress. Steamy tale of a faithless wife (Monroe) who wants to do away with her jealous hubby. Highlight: Monroe singing "Kiss." (Dir: Henry Hathaway, 89 mins.)†

Nicaragua, No Pasaran (Australia, 1984)***½ Superior documentary by David Bradbury explores the Nicaraguan revolution and the effects of U.S. economic and military pressure on that nation's political, social, and economic life. Bradbury pulls no punches by also pointing out the failings of the ruling Sandinistas. "No pasaran" means "They will not enter." (74 mins.)

Nice Girl? (1941)**½ Deanna Durbin, Franchot Tone, Robert Stack, Walter Brennan, Robert Benchley. Enjoyable vehicle for grown-up Durbin, who is pursued by Tone and Stack; plenty of songs, and engaging Durbin. (Dir: William A. Seiter, 95 mins.)

Nice Girls Don't Explode (1987)**½ Barbara Harris, Michelle Meyrink, Wallace Shawn. Not as dim-witted as its title indicates. Harris plays a mom who has convinced her daughter that she will ignite (literally) if she mingles with the opposite sex. Though the plot clearly has its limits, the cast is particularly charming. (Dir: Chuck Martinez, 92 mins.) †

Nice Little Bank That Should Be Robbed, A (1958)** Tom Ewell, Mickey Rooney, Dina Merrill. Two amateur crooks bungle an elaborately planned bank robbery. Comedy with a clever idea that doesn't live up to its promise. (Dir: Henry Levin, 87 mins.)

Nicholas and Alexandra (Great Britain, 1971)*** Michael Jayston, Janet Suzman, Laurence Olivier, Jack Hawkins, Tom Baker, Alexander Knox, John Wood. Huge, sprawling, uneven, but often interesting historical film about the fourteen-year period leading up to the Russian Revolution. Film focuses on the royal couple, and there's some particularly good acting by Miss Suzman, whose performance earned her an Academy Award nomination. (Dir: Franklin J. Schaffner, 183 mins.) †

Nicholas Nickleby (Great Britain, 1947)*** Derek Bond, Cedric Hardwicke. The Dickens classic tale of a lad who strives to save himself and his family from an evil, miserly uncle. Interesting, well-acted costume melodrama. (Dir: Alberto Cavalcanti, 95 mins.) †

Nick Carter in Prague—See: **Dinner for Adele**

Nick Carter—Master Detective (1939)** Walter Pidgeon, Rita Johnson, Henry Hull. First American feature of Jacques Tourneur. Typical MGM B movie with Pidgeon as the title hero tracking down an industrial spy. (60 mins.)

Nickel Mountain (1984)**½ Patrick Cassidy, Michael Cole, Grace Zabriskie, Heather Langenkamp, Brian Kerwin, Ed Lauter. An appealing if inconsequential May-December love story about two social outcasts—an expectant mother and an overweight man with a heart condition. (Dir: Drew Denbaum, 88 mins.) †

Nickelodeon (1976)*** Ryan O'Neal, Burt Reynolds, Tatum O'Neal, Brian Keith, Stella Stevens, John Ritter, Jane Hitchcock. The freewheeling adventures of early filmmaking are chronicled here. The closing sequence has genuine grandeur, and one can see the nobility of the slapstick conception even when it is not realized. (Dir: Peter Bogdanovich, 121 mins.)

Nickel Ride, The (1975)**½ Jason Miller, Bo Hopkins. Director Robert Mulligan's low-key style is a pleasure to watch for its appreciation of Old Movie narrative virtues. This saga of a crook with a conscience was drastically re-edited by the studio and was unfairly ignored by most critics. (99 mins.)

Nicky's World (MTV 1974)**½ Charles Cioffi, George Voskovec, Olympia Dukakis, Mark Shera. Often touching story about a New York Greek family determined to hang on to their storefront bakery despite pressures from a supermarket chain and the local banks to evict them. (Dir: Paul Stanley, 78 mins.)

Night After Night (1932)** George Raft, Constance Cummings, Mae West. Speakeasy owner gets mixed up with high society. Relic of Prohibition still has some interest, largely due to Mae in her film debut. (Dir: Archie Mayo, 75 mins.)

Night Ambush (Great Britain, 1957)*** Dirk Bogarde, Marius Goring. British soldiers sneak into occupied Crete, capture a German general, and make it to safety with him. Uneven but different war story has some moments. (Dir: Michael Powell, 93 mins.)

Night and Day (1946)**½ Cary Grant, Alexis Smith, Monty Woolley, Jane Wyman, Eve Arden. A life of Cole Porter, told without truth or wit. There are, however, a lot of songs, including Mary Martin singing "My Heart Belongs to Daddy." Grant also sings, with considerable talent. Directed way off the beam by Michael Curtiz. (128 mins.) †

Night and Fog (France, 1955)**** Brilliant, devastating documentary about the horrors of Auschwitz concentration camp, shot in color and intercut with shocking black and white archival footage of the hideously barbaric results of the brutality and madness of the Nazis. One of the greatest short films ever made. Narrated by Michel Bouquet with hauntingly gently music score by Hanna Eisler, a perfect counterpoint to the harsh realitites which occurred. AKA: **Nuit et Brouillard** (Dir: Alain Resnais, 31 mins.) †

Night and Fog in Japan (Japan, 1960)***½ Miyuki Kuwano, Fumio Watanabe, Masahiko Tsugawa, Hiroshi Akutagawa. Student radicals, all veterans of demonstrations against the 1960 U.S.-Japan security pact, come together for a wedding of two of their own. The ceremony is interrupted by arguments about politics and the importance of the demonstrations in which they took part. Director Nagisa Oshima fragments the action with flashbacks, dazzling tracking shots, and theatrical style backouts in this, his most political and adventurous film. (107 mins.)

Night and the City (Great Britain, 1950)***½ Richard Widmark, Gene Tierney, Hugh Marlowe, Googie Withers, Herbert Lom. Director Jules Dassin's gem of an expressionist thriller, filmed in a London artfully relit to resemble New York's lower east side. Widmark gives one of his most underrated performances, nervous and taut, as American low-life on the lam. (95 mins.)

Night at the Opera, A (1935)*** The Marx

Brothers, Kitty Carlisle, Allan Jones, Margaret Dumont. One of the Brothers' funniest. The stateroom scene is one of the greatest continuous laugh inducers ever. The love interest by Jones and Carlisle bores many, but Irving Thalberg knew they would help the picture make money. (Dir: Sam Wood, 90 mins.)†

Night Before, The (1988)* Keanu Reeves, Lori Laughlin, Theresa Saldana, Trinidad Silva. Unfunny comedy about class nerd Reeves, who gets to take teen queen Laughlin to the prom (not knowing that she lost a bet) but undergoes all sorts of misadventures when they take a detour into the wrong part of town. The continual flashbacks are confusing. (Dir: Thom Eberhardt, 85 mins.)†

Nightbreaker (MCTV 1989)***½ Martin Sheen, Emilio Estevez, Lea Thompson, Joe Pantoliano. Memorable drama based on true incidents in which the U.S. Army used soldiers as unwitting guinea pigs, subjecting them to high doses of radiation at nuclear test sites. Sheen and Estevez are excellent playing the same character, a research neurologist observing the experiments, at different ages. Screenplay by T. S. Cook *(The China Syndrome)*. (Dir: Peter Markle, 96 mins.)†

Nightbreed (1990)**½ Craig Sheffer, Anne Bobby, David Cronenberg, Charles Haid, Doug Bradley. Horror novelist Clive Barker's second effort as a director is an improvement over *Hellraiser*, but still disappointing. Tale about a young man and a psychologist obsessed with an ancient but nearly extinct race of shape-shifting monsters was filmed with lots of elaborately ugly beasties, but many were cut during post-production tampering (co-star Suzi Quatro was omitted entirely!) (99 mins.)†

Night Caller from Outer Space (Great Britain, 1965)** John Saxon, Maurice Denham, Patricia Haines, Alfred Burke, Jack Carson, Warren Mitchell. Visitor from one of the moons of Jupiter comes to Earth to find breeding stock to take home with him. Not to sound xenophobic, but this is the type of premise that needs American hands—the British are just too reserved. AKA: **Blood Beast from Outer Space.** (Dir: John Gilling, 84 mins.)†

Night Chase (MTV 1970)**½ David Janssen, Yaphet Kotto. David Janssen is on the run again. He's a world-weary gent taking an all-night cab ride along the California coast after shooting his wife's lover. (Dir: Jack Starrett, 99 mins.)

Night Children*½ David Carradine, Nancy Kwan, Griffin O'Neal, Kamala Lopez. Los Angeles cop Carradine and parole officer Kwan try to save street kids from the influence of nasty gang leader O'Neal. Better they'd saved viewers the time

wasted watching this snoozer. (Dir: Norbert Meisel, 91 mins.)†

Night Club Scandal (1937)**½ John Barrymore, Lynne Overman, Charles Bickford, Louise Campbell. Well-acted, entertaining little mystery. Not a whodunit but interesting as you know who's guilty and watch the police make the mistakes. (Dir: Ralph Murphy, 74 mins.)

Nightcomers, The (Great Britain, 1971)** Marlon Brando, Stephanie Beacham, Harry Andrews, Thora Hird, Verna Harvey. A depraved, filthy lout seduces a proper Victorian lady who turns ravenous in the bedroom. A nasty, perfunctory turn of the screw. Based on characters from Henry James. (Dir: Michael Winner, 96 mins.)†

Night Court (1932)*** Phillips Holmes, Walter Huston, Lewis Stone, Anita Page, Mary Carlisle, Jean Hersholt. Solid, somber crime drama has Huston as a ruthless crooked judge who abuses his power until he's stopped by crusader Stone; big-city corruption is displayed without glamour. An authoritative job by Huston, with good support from the supporting players. (Dir: W. S. Van Dyke, 90 mins.)

Night Creature (1978)** Donald Pleasence, Nancy Kwan, Ross Hagen. Made in Thailand, with Pleasence as a Hemingwayesque writer, living on an island compound in southeast Asia, who becomes obsessed with a man-eating black leopard. (Dir: Lee Madden, 83 mins.)†

Night Creatures (1962)**½ Peter Cushing, Yvonne Romain, Oliver Reed. Village vicar is in reality the head of a notorious smuggling ring. Lively, suspenseful costume thriller. (Dir: Peter Graham Scott, 81 mins.)

Night Cries (MTV 1978)** Susan St. James, William Conrad, Michael Parks. St. James stars in this familiar melodrama about a woman who has lost her child at birth but keeps dreaming he's alive somewhere. A dream therapist (Conrad) tries to convince her she's wrong, and her probing leads to a startling denouement. (Dir: Richard Lang, 104 mins.)†

Night Crossing (1981)** John Hurt, Jane Alexander, Doug McKeon, Keith McKeon, Beau Bridges. Based on the actual adventure of the Strelzyk and Wetzel families, who escaped to the other Germany by hot air balloon in the fall of 1979, this film appears made for very young audiences. (Dir: Delbert Mann, 106 mins.)†

Night Digger, The (Great Britain 1971)**½ Patricia Neal, Pamela Brown, Nicholas Clay. Pseudo-psychopathic horror film that emerges as an understated character study with sexual overtones. English spinster Neal is dominated by her frightening, blind mother (Brown), who adopted her. Into this tense relationship pops Clay, a young man who is accepted by the mother as a housekeeper. (Dir: Alistair Reid, 100 mins.)

Night Editor (1946)*** William Gargan, Janis Carter. Crooked cop gets involved with luscious but mean dame. Well-scripted, well-acted B melodrama. (Dir: Henry Levin, 68 mins.)

Night Evelyn Came Out of the Grave, The (Italy, 1971)* Anthony Steffen, Marina Malfatti, Rod Murdock, Umberto Raho. A blue blood nutcase believes his never-say-die wife won't stay put in her grave, so he keeps killing every woman who reminds him of his departed spouse. (Dir: Emilio Miraglia, 90 mins.)

Night Eyes (1990)**½ Andrew Stevens, Tanya Roberts, Warwick Sims, Karen Elise Baldwin, Cooper Huckabee, Chick Vennera. *Body Heat* clone, with Stevens, hired to spy on cheating wife Roberts, succumbing to her fatal charms himself. A must-see for fans of Roberts, who gives her all in steamy sex scenes. (Dir: Jag Mundhra, 98 mins.)†

Nightfall (1957)***½ Aldo Ray, Brian Keith, Anne Bancroft, Jocelyn Brando, James Gregory, Frank Albertson, Rudy Bond. Excellent *film noir*, adapted from a David Goodis *(Shoot the Piano Player)* novel by Stirling Silliphant and given the right fatalistic touchs by director Jacques Tourneur. Like most Goodis stories, it's about an artist on the skids trying to evade murderous thugs; in this case, innocent Ray is implicated in a murder and chased by the real killers, who think he has their loot. (78 mins.)

Nightfall (1988)*½ David Birney, Sarah Douglas, Alexis Kanner. Isaac Asimov's story about a distant planet with three suns, whose residents are preparing for an unknown disaster that only strikes them once every 1,000 years—night. Audiences unfamiliar with the story will have trouble following it; others will merely be disappointed. (Dir: Paul Mayersberg, 82 mins.)†

Night Fighters (1960)**½ Robert Mitchum, Anne Heywood, Dan O'Herlihy, Richard Harris. The Irish rebellion is the setting of this adventure yarn which has a fine cast of players headed by Robert Mitchum. (Dir: Tay Garnett, 85 mins.)

Night Flight from Moscow (France-Italy-West Germany, 1973)** Yul Brynner, Henry Fonda, Dirk Bogarde, Virna Lisi, Philippe Noiret. An international cast of capable actors gets bogged down in a plot-heavy espionage tale about double agents and their intricate operations in Western Europe. (Dir: Henri Verneuil, 121 mins.)†

Nightflyers (1987)** Catherine Mary Stewart, Michael Praed, John Standing, Lisa Blount. A starship crew (with a captain who appears to them only as a hologram) finds itself under attack by a malevolent force. Initially interesting (and technically slick throughout), this sci-fi thriller ultimately goes nowhere slowly. (Dir: "T. C. Blake" [Robert Collector], 96 mins.)†

Nightforce (1987)½ Linda Blair, James Van Patten, Richard Lynch, Chad McQueen, Claudia Udy, Cameron Mitchell. Blair and four college buddies storm down to Central America where, with the help of ex-CIA agent Lynch, they plan to free a friend being held hostage by terrorists. The blitheness with which vacant American teens are shown blowing away darker-skinned Hispanics in this and lots of similar films may explain why Latin America dislikes us so much. (Dir: Lawrence D. Foldes, 82 mins.)†

Night Freight (1955)**½ Forrest Tucker, Barbara Britton. Railroad operator battles ruthless trucking outfit. (Dir: Jean Yarbrough, 79 mins.)

Night Friend (Canada, 1987)* Heather Kjollesdal, Art Carney, Chuck Shamata, Daniel MacIvor, Real Andrews, Jayne Eastwood. Priest Carney tries to save young teen Kjollesdal from a life of prostitution. Exploitation drama that warns of the dangers of living on the streets but shows them for sensationalistic effect. (Dir: Peter Gerretsen, 94 mins.)†

Night Full of Rain, A—See: **End of the World in Our Usual Bed in a Night Full of Rain, The**

Night Gallery (MTV 1969)**½ Joan Crawford, Richard Kiley, Roddy McDowall, Barry Sullivan, Ossie Davis. This feature is divided into three well-done mystery tales. (Dirs: Boris Sagal, Steven Spielberg [debut], Barry Shear, 98 mins.)†

Night Game (1989)*½ Roy Scheider, Karen Young, Paul Gleason, Carlin Glynn. A maniac is on the rampage once again as a baffled detective attempts to solve the case. Good cast tries hard, but are ultimately defeated by shoddy material. (Dir: Peter Masterson, 95 mins.)†

Night Games (Sweden, 1966)***½ Keve Hjelm, Ingrid Thulin, Lena Brundin, Naima Wifstrand, Jorgen Lindstrom. Wonderfully decadent and erotic film about socially repressed man who, unable to deal with adulthood or sex, rethinks his life's events, especially the total domination of his childhood by his mother. Directed by Mai Zetterling, based on her own novel, powerful film is acerbically funny and maturely sensuous. (105 mins.)

Night Games (MTV 1974)** Barry Newman, Susan Howard, Albert Salmi, Stefanie Powers. Newman is Petrocelli, a lawyer defending a young socialite (Powers) accused of murdering her husband. Nothing special, but the TV series "Petrocelli" soon followed. (Dir: Don Taylor, 104 mins.)

Night Hair Child—See: **What the Peeper Saw**

Night Has a Thousand Eyes, The (1948)****½** Edward G. Robinson, Gail Russell, John Lund, William Demarest, Virginia Bruce. Somewhat portentous rendition of a Cornell Woolrich novelette, with Robinson bug-eyed as a vaudeville mentalist who gradually discovers he has real psychic powers. (Dir: John Farrow, 80 mins.)

Night Has Eyes, The (Great Britain, 1942)****½** Joyce Howard, James Mason, Mary Clare, Wilfred Lawson. Moody romantic melodrama, as a young woman spends her vacation searching for a friend who has disappeared, and meets up with a attractive but troubled recluse. Strong atmosphere and some genuinely intriguing moments raise it above the rather trite plot, and Mason registers effectively in an early role. AKA: **Terror House**. (Dir: Leslie Arliss, 79 mins.)†

Nighthawks (Great Britain, 1979)****½** Ken Robertson, Tony Westrope, Rachel Nicholas James, Maureen Dolan. A sober film about a homosexual teacher who hides his preference by day and searches out lovers by night. Mostly nonprofessional cast is directed with kitchen-sink realism by Ron Peck and Paul Hallam. (113 mins.)

Nighthawks (1981)******* Sylvester Stallone, Rutger Hauer, Billy Dee Williams, Persis Khambatta. This anti-terrorist thriller tries hard to be a "French Connection" for the eighties. Sylvester Stallone plays a New York City cop who is pitted against an international terrorist out to rehabilitate himself with the fraternity by proving his value at garnering publicity in a spectacular manner. As played by Rutger Hauer, making an impressive American debut, the man is a formidable adversary, which keeps the suspense mechanism tightly coiled. (Dir: Bruce Malmuth, 100 mins.)†

Night Heaven Fell, The (France, 1958)***½** Brigitte Bardot, Stephen Boyd, Alida Valli. Steamy passions rise as a countess and her niece both have designs on a handsome neighbor. (Dir: Roger Vadim, 90 mins.)

Night Holds Terror, The (1955)******* Jack Kelly, Vince Edwards, John Cassavetes, Hildy Parks. Creditable low-budget suspense film. Kelly is a factory worker who is kidnapped at gunpoint by three thugs. (Dir: Andrew L. Stone, 86 mins.)

Night in Casablanca, A (1946)****½** The Marx Brothers. The boys are involved in North African intrigue, but they get off enough humor to please their most ardent followers. (Dir: Archie Mayo, 84 mins.)†

Nightingales (MTV 1988)***½** Mimi Kuzyk,

Susan Walters, Britta Phillips. Feeble pap about eight student nurses. The emphasis is on the personality quirks of the young women and not on nursing; for that matter, these "nightingales" could be stewardesses. (Dir: Mimi Feder, 96 mins.)

Nightingale Sang in Berkeley Square, A (1979)****½** Gloria Grahame, Richard Jordan, David Niven, Oliver Tobias, Elke Sommer, Hugh Griffith. A terrific cast breathes life into a rather ordinary tale of an ex-con forced to participate in a bank holdup in England. (Dir: Ralph Thomas, 102 mins.)

Night in Heaven, A (1983)****** Lesley Ann Warren, Christopher Atkins, Carrie Snodgress. Atkins plays a male stripper who's working his way through college. Warren portrays the teacher who fails him in speech class but gives him an "A" in body language. Lurid and surprisingly unexciting. (Dir: John Avildsen, 83 mins.)†

Night in My Future (Sweden, 1948)******* Birger Malmsten, Mai Zetterling, Naima Wifstrand, Gunnar Bjornstrand, Bengt Eklund. Interesting melodrama about young man who is blinded and reassesses his life, learning to play the piano and falling in love with his housekeeper, to whom he becomes a mentor. Early Ingmar Bergman film is expressively shot with a clear-eyed view of life turned upside down, although the *Pygmalion*-esque subplot tosses the film into clichéd territory. (87 mins.)†

Night in Paradise, A (1946)****½** Merle Oberon, Turhan Bey. In old Greece, dashing Aesop, disguised as an old man, falls for a beautiful princess. Romantic costume spectacle doesn't take itself seriously, which is all for the best. (Dir: Arthur Lubin, 84 mins.)

Night in the Life of Jimmy Reardon, A (1988)****½** River Phoenix, Ann Magnuson, Meredith Salenger, Ione Skye, Louanne, Matthew L. Perry. A "quality" teen pic about a promiscuous young man who plans to ditch college for a trip to Hawaii with his rich girlfriend. Filmmaker Richert *(Winter Kills)* is capable of better things than this R-rated feature with a PG mind-set; all the sexuality and character motivations are hinted at rather than explored— in some cases, explicitness (of any kind) helps. (Dir: William Richert, 93 mins.)†

Night into Morning (1951)****½** Ray Milland, John Hodiak, Nancy Davis. Milland is a college professor whose wife and son are killed in an explosion, thereby triggering his battle with the bottle. Not in the same league as *The Lost Weekend*. (Dir: Fletcher Markle, 86 mins.)

Night Is My Future (Sweden, 1947)****** Mai Zetterling, Birger Malmsten. Blinded young man meets a girl who tries to bring him happiness. Plodding drama. (Dir: Ingmar Bergman, 87 mins.)†

Night Key (1937)**½ Boris Karloff, Warren Hull, Jean Rogers. Low-budget thriller has a mild-mannered inventor compelled to aid gangsters; Karloff makes it involving. (Dir: Lloyd Corrigan, 67 mins.)

Nightkill (1980)**½ Jaclyn Smith, James Franciscus, Robert Mitchum, Fritz Weaver, Sybil Danning. A brutal suspense-thriller about a woman whose reluctant involvement in securing an "instant divorce" results in dual games of musical corpses and cat and mouse with an unknown persecutor, who has set a complicated trap for her. (Dir: Ted Post, 97 mins.)†

Nightmare (1942)**½ Brian Donlevy, Diana Barrymore. Fairly exciting suspense tale. An American gambler stumbles into murder, and finds himself hot on the trail of foreign agents. (Dir: Tim Whelan, 81 mins.)

Nightmare (1956)**½ Edward G. Robinson, Kevin McCarthy, Connie Russell, Virginia Christine. Fine mystery, with McCarthy a jazz musician in New Orleans who can't remember if he committed a murder or not; the end twist is a real surprise. Well produced on a low budget. (Dir: Maxwell Shane, 89 mins.)

Nightmare Alley (1947)***½ Tyrone Power, Joan Blondell, Coleen Gray, Helen Walker, Mike Mazurki. A pungent film, this story of a carnival hustler making it as a spiritualist in society circles only to end up a degraded geek is an anomaly in the career of Power. Scriptwriter Jules Furthman rescues much of the nastiness of William Lindsay Gresham's original novel. (Dir: Edmund Goulding, 111 mins.)

Nightmare at Bitter Creek (MTV 1988)** Lindsay Wagner, Tom Skerritt, Constance McCashin, Joanna Cassidy, Janne Mortil. Campers, beware: this violent TV movie, a female take on *Deliverance*, won't encourage any excursions into the wilderness. It follows the exploits of four women who, along with their alcoholic guide, fall prey to the leaders of a peculiar far right-wing group. (Dir: Tim Burstall, 96 mins.)†

Nightmare at Noon (1987)** Wings Hauser, Bo Hopkins, George Kennedy, Brion James, Kimberly Ross, Kimberly Beck. Vacationers Hauser and Beck pass through a most unfriendly little town, where the locals are shooting each other in the streets. It's all the fault of mad scientist James (looking odd in albino drag) in this watered-down thriller. (Dir: Nico Mastorakis, 96 mins.)†

Nightmare at Shadow Woods—See: **Blood Rage**

Nightmare Castle (Italy, 1965)*½ Barbara Steele, Paul Miller, Hega Line, Giorgio Ardisson. Mad doctor kills his wife and her lover, then uses their bodies as experimental subjects; his wife's mentally unbalanced sister, the sole beneficiary of her will, comes to take over the castle. Music by Ennio Morricone. Originally 105 mins. (Dir: "Allen Grunewald" [Mario Caiano], 90 mins.)†

Nightmare Honeymoon (1973)*½ Dack Rambo, Rebecca Dianna Smith, Pat Hingle. A tawdry, scare-pic about a honeymooning couple who are beseiged with rapists, murderers, and other assorted backwoods types that were not mentioned on any of their travel brochures. (Dir: Elliot Silverstein, 115 mins.)

Nightmare Hotel (Spain, 1970)**½ Judy Geeson, Aurora Bautista, Esperanza Roy, Victor Lacazar. Rather nightmarish chiller about a woman who secretly searches for the whereabouts of a missing relative. Despite the irritations of the dubbing and some weak acting, Geeson's danger-ridden search is often edge-of-the-seat stuff; the two crazy innkeepers are the most menacing hoteliers since Norman Bates started checking in guests. (Dir: Eugenio Martin, 95 mins.)

Nightmare House (1969)* Ross Harris, Eugenie Wingate, Chris Martell, Suzanne Stuart, Larry Swanson. An artist who specializes in grotesque portraits uses a surgeon's new reconstructive technique to create living models for his warped works. AKA: **Scream, Baby, Scream.** (Dir: Joseph Adler, 83 mins.)†

Nightmare in Badham County (MTV 1976)** Deborah Raffin, Lynne Moody, Chuck Connors, Ralph Bellamy, Tina Louise, Robert Reed, Della Reese. Two innocent college coeds live a nightmare when a lecherous sheriff throws them into prison after they refuse his advances. Standard "babes-behind-bars" entry wastes a good cast in stock roles. (Dir: John Llewellyn Moxey, 100 mins.)†

Nightmare in Chicago (MTV 1964)**½ Philip Abbott, Robert Ridgely, Ted Knight, Charles McGraw, John Alonzo. Police manhunt for a psychotic killer terrorizing Chicago highways benefits from on-location shooting and good control of horror atmosphere. (Dir: Robert Altman, 80 mins.)

Nightmare in the Sun (1964)*½ Ursula Andress, John Derek, Arthur O'Connell, Aldo Ray. No-good wife of a rancher who's been playing around with the sheriff is the cause of an innocent hitchhiker's involvement in murder and terror. (Dir: Marc Lawrence, 80 mins.)

Nightmare in Wax (1969)*½ Cameron Mitchell, Anne Helm, Scott Brady. A terrible horror film about still another demented soul with his very own wax

747

museum in which to exact revenge on the dummies in his life. (Dir: Bud Townsend, 91 mins.)†

Night of Bloody Horror (1969)* Gerald McRaney, Gaye Yellen, Herbert Nelson, Evelyn Hendricks. A recently released mental patient comes under suspicion when a series of gruesome murders occurs. Low-budget New Orleans-lensed horror with plenty of cheap gore effects. (Dir: Joy N. Houck, Jr., 89 mins.)†

Nightmare on Elm Street, A (1984)**½ John Saxon, Ronee Blakley, Heather Langenkamp, Robert Englund, Amanda Wyss, Nick Corri, Johnny Depp. An interesting premise about the power of fear might have become a dream of a horror movie, but flounders in the director's hands. Some adolescents begin having the same dream as a dead maniac tries to dispose of them from beyond the grave. While the film often approximates the terrifying pull of a nightmare, the director plays it safe. Rather than truly disturb or haunt us, he's only concerned with visualizing this concept in terms of a conventional slasher film. (Dir: Wes Craven, 92 mins.)†

Nightmare on Elm Street 2, A: Freddy's Revenge (1986)** Robert Englund, Kim Myers, Robert Rusler, Mark Patton, Hope Lange, Clu Gulager, Melinda O'Fee. This sequel is in many ways a send-up, wildly imaginative, but out of control. With his knives for fingernails and his slouch hat, Freddy is becoming a camp figure; maybe he should get a job demonstrating ginsu blades with his hands, instead of slashing through the dream states of still more helpless suburban teens (particularly a wimpy boy whose family just moved into Freddy's favorite dream house). (Dir: Jack Sholder, 85 mins.)†

Nightmare on Elm Street 3, A: Dream Warriors (1987)**½ Heather Langenkamp, Patricia Arquette, Larry Fishburne, Priscilla Pointer, Craig Wasson, Brooke Bundy. Freddy, the slashing killer with the ultra-julienne fingernails, gets to dig them into a few more victims here. Langenkamp, the nightmare-spooked heroine of the first film, is now working with distraught patients who discover that Freddy is the man of their dreams. The script is riddled with the usual loopholes and inconsistencies, though it's stylishly directed. (Dir: Chuck Russell, 97 mins.)†

Nightmare on Elm Street 4, A: The Dream Master, (1988)**½ Robert Englund, Lisa Wilcox, Danny Hassel. Dream murderer Freddy kills off the survivors from part three, and then goes after a girl who knows a thing or two about dream warfare. The underdeveloped script nonetheless allows for scary and spectacular special effects nightmares, inventively and stylishly directed. (Dir: Renny Harlin, 91 mins.)†

Nightmare on the 13th Floor (MCTV 1990)**½ Michele Greene, James Brolin, Louise Fletcher, John Karlen, Terri Treas. Guests have a mysterious way of not checking out of the grand Wessex Hotel in this chilling tale of murder and mayhem. A travel writer (Greene) arrives at the stately Victorian hotel to write a promotional piece, only to become distracted when she witnesses a grisly ax murder. Thrills mount at an escalating pace as hotel employees Brolin (back working at a "Hotel") and Fletcher seem to know more about the decapitations then they are willing to admit in this supernatural tale of horror. (Dir: Walter Grauman, 96 mins.)

Nightmares (1983)*½ Cristina Raines, Emilio Estevez, Moon Zappa, Veronica Cartwright. A below-average horror omnibus. The film's four episodes deal with a smokeaholic risking her life for her next puff, a video arcade freak who literally gets into the game, a priest pursued by an evil car, and a giant rat with maternal instincts. (Dir: Joseph Sargent, 99 mins.)†

Night Monster (1942)**½ Nils Asther, Ralph Morgan, Irene Hervey, Leif Erickson, Lionel Atwill, Bela Lugosi. Quite a good creeper; the twisty plot concerns a reclusive invalid (Morgan) whose physicians are being mysteriously murdered, one after another. With this cast, you definitely can't tell the victims from the killer, and the ending is a surprise. (Dir: Ford Beebe, 80 mins.)

'Night, Mother (1986)**½ Sissy Spacek, Anne Bancroft, Ed Berke, Carol Robbins. The gimmicky Pulitzer Prize-winning drama uses suicide for shock value; on stage, it had undeniable impact. On screen, the shallowness of this contrivance shows too obviously despite two dynamic performances. Bancroft plays the mother, the voice of reason trying to dissuade her daughter from giving in to despair. (Dir: Tom Moore, 96 mins.)†

Night Moves (1975)**½ Gene Hackman, Susan Clark, Jennifer Warren. A disappointing, though sharply observed melodrama shot on location in California and Florida about a private eye (Hackman) who goes to Florida to find a runaway girl-drifter; never quite jells. (Dir: Arthur Penn, 100 mins.)†

Night Must Fall (1937)*** Robert Montgomery, Rosalind Russell, May Whitty. Montgomery, previously cast as a debonair leading man, plays a psychotic killer in the popular Emlyn Williams thriller. Chilling melodrama. (Dir: Richard Thorpe, 117 mins.)

Night Must Fall (Great Britain, 1964)** Albert Finney, Mona Washbourne, Susan Hampshire. Inadequate, overwrought remake of the 1937 classic film thriller. The suspense falters before night falls. (Dir: Karel Reisz, 105 mins.)

Night My Number Came Up, The (Great Britain, 1955)***½ Michael Redgrave, Alexander Knox. Well-acted British drama of an Air Force officer's troubled dreams and their effect on his work. (Dir: Leslie Norman, 94 mins.)

Night Nurse (1931)*** Barbara Stanwyck, Ben Lyon, Joan Blondell, Clark Gable, Charlotte Merriam. Terse, gripping thriller of a nurse who discovers a grim plot to murder two small children for their inheritance in the household she works for; crackling dialogue and vivid acting, with Gable a standout as a particularly nasty hood. More strong stuff from director William Wellman. (72 mins.)

Night of Courage (MTV 1987)*½ Barnard Hughes, Daniel Hugh Kelly, Geraldine Fitzgerald. When a Hispanic teenager is murdered by a vicious white gang, the youth's teacher tries to uncover the truth. (Dir: Elliot Silverstein, 104 mins.)

Night of Dark Shadows, The (1971)**½ Kate Jackson, David Selby, Lara Parker, Grayson Hall. Lesser of the two "Dark Shadows" films; this one features an enchanting Parker as the witch who puts a spell on Selby. (Dir: Dan Curtis, 96 mins.)

Night of January 16th (1941)** Robert Preston, Ellen Drew. Fair little mystery about a sailor who is left a huge legacy but must solve a few mysteries before he can touch the dough. (Dir: William Clemens, 79 mins.)

Night of Mystery (1937)* Grant Richards, Roscoe Karns, Helen Burgess. Poor revamp of *The Greene Murder Case*. (Dir: E. A. Dupont, 71 mins.)

Night of Nights, The (1939)** Pat O'Brien, Olympe Bradna, Roland Young. A broken-down playwright makes a comeback after being reunited with his long-lost daughter. Corny, sentimental trash which is well acted. (Dir: Lewis Milestone, 86 mins.)

Night of 1,000 Cats—See: **Blood Feast** (1972)

Night of Terror (MTV 1972)** Donna Mills, Catherine Burns, Martin Balsam. Seeking a vital piece of information, a killer stalks two young women (Miss Mills and Catherine Burns) who share an apartment. (Dir: Jeannot Szwarc, 73 mins.)

Night of Terror (1986)½ Renée Harmon, Frank Neuhaus, Lauren Brent, Henry Lewis. Awful murder mystery about a woman out for vengeance after her doctorlover has her committed to a sanitarium. Shot on video, with music dubbed in so ineptly that it drowns out the dialogue! (Dir: Felix Gerard, 105 mins.)†

Night of the Beast—See: **House of the Black Death**

Night of the Big Heat—See: **Island of the Burning Doomed**

Night of the Blood Beast (1958)* Michael Emmet, Angela Greene, John Baer, Ed Nelson. A man returns from outer space with an alien embryo growing inside him. Good idea—sloppy execution. AKA: **Creature from Galaxy 27.** (Dir: Bernard Kowalski, 65 mins.)†

Night of the Blood Monster (Great Britain, 1972)*½ Christopher Lee, Maria Schell, Maria Rohm, Margaret Lee. Bloody awful stomach-churner about political chicanery in 17th-century England. (Dir: Jess Franco, 84 mins.)

Night of the Bloody Apes (Mexico, 1968)½ Jose Elias Moreno, Carlos Lopez Moctezuma, Armando Silvestre, Norma Lazareno. Doctor saves the life of his son by transplanting a gorilla's heart into his body. The drawback—junior becomes a hairy, violent murderer. This being a Mexican horror movie, the day is saved by a lady wrestler. We can only hope that the doctors performing the actual open-heart surgery seen here were more competent than the filmmakers who clumsily inserted it in this dreadful movie. AKA: **Gomar the Human Gorilla.** (Dir: René Cardona, Sr., 82 mins.)†

Night of the Burning Damned—See: **Island of the Burning Doomed**

Night of the Claw (1982)½ Barry Nelson, Nita Talbot, Robert Lansing. Unintentionally funny monster film; a coastal town finds itself beseiged by a huge man-eating crab. Only for horror fans and seafood lovers. AKA: **Island Claws.** (Dir: Herman Cardenas, 80 mins.)†

Night of the Comet (1984)**½ Catherine Mary Stewart, Kelli Maroney, Robert Beltran, Mary Woronov, Geoffrey Lewis. Interesting last-people-on-earth saga involving two California teenagers who encounter bloodthirsty zombies after a comet hits earth, destroying the population. This low-budget sci-fi quickie has its share of off-beat moments and laughs. (Dir: Thom Eberhardt, 100 mins.)†

Night of the Counting Years, The (Egypt, 1969)***½ Zouzou El Hakim, Ahmed Marie, Nadia Loutfy, Ahmad Hegazi, Gaby Karraz. Visual masterpiece about illegal trade in ancient Egyptian artifacts as it relates to the "discovery" of a mummy-filled tomb in Thebes in 1881. Engrossing, beautifully photographed film provides great insight into Egyptian history and culture. (Dir: Shadi Abdelsalm, 100 mins.)

Night of the Creeps (1986)*** Jason Lively, Jill Whitlow, Steve Marshall, Tom Atkins, Wally Taylor. Writer-director Fred Dekker's first film is a wild amalgam of every

B-horror archetype, convention, and dialogue cliché in movie history, yet is also an effective horror-comedy in its own right. The plot concerns college students who battle alien-possessed zombie axe-murderers, assisted by a cop who had fought them years before. (86 mins.)†

Night of the Death Cult (Spain, 1975)**½ Victor Petit, Maria Kosti, Maria Kosti, Sandra Mozarowsky. New doctor in a Spanish village discovers that people are committing human sacrifices to appease a band of undead priests. Fourth and last entry in a popular Spanish series, offers legitimate chills, anticlimactic ending. AKA: **Night of the Seagulls**. (Dir: Amando de Ossorio, 85 mins.)†

Night of the Demon (1979)* Michael J. Cutt, Joy Allen, Bob Collins, Jodi Lazarus. A group of students head to the woods in search of Bigfoot. Differs from innumerable other dull movie depictions of the legendary creature only by being excessively gory. (Dir: James C. Wasson, 97 mins.)†

Night of the Demons (1988)*** Lance Fenton, Cathy Podewell, Alvin Alexis, Linnea Quigley. Teens spending the night in a haunted funeral parlor read a demonic spell as a joke. This being a horror movie, the spell works, and they spend the rest of the night battling bloodthirsty demons. Good of its type, with a socko ending. (Dir: Kevin S. Tenney, 98 mins.)†

Night of the Following Day, The (1969)**½ Marlon Brando, Richard Boone, Rita Moreno. Complex, contrived, generally muddled melodrama. Marlon is an accomplice in a kidnapping in France, but the only real quality in the film is found in a few scenes where Brando displays his unique magnetism and acting brilliance. (Dir: Hubert Cornfield, 93 mins.)

Night of the Fox (MCTV 1990)** George Peppard, Deborah Raffin, Michael York, David Birney, John Mills, Andrea Ferreol, Juliet Mills. Soldier-of-fortune (Peppard) is ordered to capture a colonel (Birney) who knows the secret of the impending invasion of Normandy. Large cast and on-location shooting add considerably to this ambitious, but ultimately disappointing production. (Dir: Charles Jarrot, 192 mins.)

Night of the Howling Beast (Spain, 1975)* Paul Naschy, Grace Mills, Castillo Escalona, Silvia Solar. Spanish horror star Naschy's eighth film as werewolf Waldemar Daninsky, this time joining an expedition to search for the Abominable Snowman. AKA: **The Werewolf and the Yeti**. (Dir: Miguel Iglesias Bonns, 87 mins.)†

Night of the Generals, The (France-Great Britain, 1967)** Peter O'Toole, Omar Sharif, Tom Courtenay, Donald Pleasence, Philippe Noiret. A compelling premise—a Nazi intelligence officer trails a general who murders prostitutes—and a cast to dream about. However, Hans Helmut Kirst's novel becomes interminable under director Anatole Litvak's ponderous hand. Filmed in Warsaw and Paris. (148 mins.)†

Night of the Ghouls (1960)½ Duke Moore, Kenne Duncan, Paul Marco, Tor Johnson, Criswell. Deliriously funny camp classic as a phony spiritualist finds he's more talented at resurrecting the dead than he realized. With a bloodcurdling climax in which Criswell, the world's most fallible clairvoyant, leads a pack of ghouls attired like door-to-door salesmen. AKA: **Revenge of the Dead**. (Dir: Edward Wood, Jr., 69 mins.)†

Night of the Grizzly (1966)**½ Clint Walker, Martha Hyer. Predictable adventure about a former lawman who goes to Wyoming with his family to start a new life. He encounters a bear who threatens his existence, and he pursues it with a vengeance. (Dir: Joseph Pevney, 102 mins.)†

Night of the Hunter (1955)**** Robert Mitchum, Lillian Gish, Shelley Winters, Peter Graves, James Gleason. A masterpiece, the only directorial effort by actor Charles Laughton. Nightmarishly haunting parable of children on the run from their evil preacher-stepfather. Mitchum gives his greatest performance as the avaricious false preacher who spellbinds adults and scares children. Scripted by James Agee from the novel by Davis Grubb. (93 mins.)†

Night of the Iguana, The (1964)***½ Richard Burton, Ava Gardner, Deborah Kerr, Sue Lyon. Thanks to John Huston's expert direction, Tennessee Williams's searing drama about genteel losers down on their luck in Mexico becomes a satisfying, moving film. Burton is perfect as a defrocked clergyman bent on destruction; Kerr is superb playing an anguished spinster; and Gardner, in one of the best performances of her career, plays the proprietress of a seedy resort hotel with a remarkable sensuality. (125 mins.)†

Night of the Juggler (1980)** James Brolin, Cliff Gorman, Richard Castellano, Julie Carmen. Brolin plays an ex-cop who chases a maniac all over New York City in a desperate effort to retrieve his kidnapped daughter. Overplotted thriller starts out decently but collapses quickly. (Dir: Robert Collins, 101 mins.)†

Night of the Lepus (1972)½ Stuart Whitman, Janet Leigh, Rory Calhoun. When an Arizona ranch is overrun with enormous rabbits reproducing at an alarming rate, a serum is sought to curtail the birth boom. Only for dumb bunnies. (Dir: William Claxton, 99 mins.)

Night of the Living Babes (1987)*½ Michelle McClennan, Connie Woods, Andrew Nichols. Foolish horror-movie parody about two suburban guys who spend a night at "Madame's Mondo's Fantasy Palace," where they become potential victims of her sex-change ray. Not as outrageous as its creators would like to think. (Dir: Jon Valentin, 60 mins.)†

Night of the Living Dead (1968)***½ Judith O'Dea, Russell Streiner, Duane Jones. Director George A. Romero's gruesome low-budget horror film is still extremely unsettling although its many imitators have eroded its shock value. Shot in Pittsburgh, the film—tawdry, threadbare, and terrifying—features zombies who devour the entrails of the living. The colorized version makes the living dead look like candidates for the Emmett Kelly School of Zombiedom. (90 mins.)†

Night of the Living Dead (1990)**½ Tony Wood, Patricia Tallman, Tom Towles. Unnecessary, but well-made remake of George Romero's 1968 black-and-white cult horror classic. Chilling tale about a group of people taking refuge in a rural Pennsylvania house as the recently dead come back to life still packs a wallop. Updated version, directed by Romero's longtime makeup collaborator (Savini), will most likely appeal to the curious and younger generation of filmgoers. (Dir: Tom Savini, 89 mins.)†

Night of the Quarter Moon (1959)* Julie London, John Drew Barrymore, Nat Cole. Social family backs a man who discovers his wife has Negro blood. Trashy drama handles a serious problem luridly. AKA: **Flesh and Flame**. (Dir: Hugo Haas, 96 mins.)

Night of the Seagulls—See: **Night of the Death Cult**

Night of the Shooting Stars, The (Italy, 1982)**** Omero Antonutti. A magnificent and deeply moving drama, co-directed by Paolo and Vittorio Taviani, about the final days of World War II in a small farming community in Tuscany. Some of the townspeople still follow orders of the Germans and their Italian collaborators, others sneak out of the doomed village at night in search of the approaching American forces. In the final sequence a local "civil war" erupts as neighbors kill each other. Set in a golden wheat field, this sequence of mindless slaughter is one of the most haunting episodes in any film within recent memory. (106 mins.)†

Night of the Zombies (Italy-Spain, 1983)½ Margit Evelyn Newton, Frank Garfield, Selan Karay, Robert O'Neil. Another European rip-off of George Romero's *Living Dead* horror films, with some particularly hilarious dubbing and lots of interminable jungle stock footage added to pad out the running time. The zombies here are accidentally created by scientists working on a method of population control. (Dir: Vincent Dawn, 99 mins.)†

Night Partners (MTV 1983)**½ Diana Canova, Yvette Mimieux, Arlen Dean Snyder, M. Emmet Walsh. A well-meaning drama about two housewives, fed up with crime and the lack of sympathy for its victims, who team up nightly to patrol the streets of Bakersfield, California. (Dir: Noel Nosseck, 104 mins.)†

Night Passage (1957)**½ James Stewart, Audie Murphy, Dan Duryea, Dianne Foster, Brandon de Wilde. Fairly interesting western about a railroad trouble shooter trying to recover a stolen payroll. Things get sticky when his brother turns up on the side of the outlaws. (Dir: James Neilson, 90 mins.)

Night Patrol (1985)* Linda Blair, Pat Paulsen, Jaye P. Morgan, Jack Riley, Murray Langston, Billy Barty, Pat Morita. Low-budget rip-off of *Police Academy*. Langston (previously seen with a paper bag over his head as "The Unknown Comic") comes out of hiding as the wimpy cop who hides from his midget captain (Barty) and makes out with the busty police dispatcher (Blair). (Dir: Jackie Kong, 104 mins.)†

Night People (1954)**½ Gregory Peck, Broderick Crawford, Rita Gam. Interesting cloak and dagger yarn set in Berlin concerning the efforts of the U.S. Army Intelligence Corps to get a young American soldier, who has been kidnapped, out of the Russian sector. (Dir: Nunnally Johnson, 93 mins.)

Night Plane from Chungking (1943)**½ Robert Preston, Ellen Drew. Well done, contrived little B action film about a plane downed in China containing one traitor on its passenger list. (Dir: Ralph Murphy, 69 mins.)

Night Porter, The (Italy-U.S., 1974)** Dirk Bogarde, Charlotte Rampling, Isa Miranda. Sexploitation masquerading as Art. Years after the fall of Nazism, an ex-concentration camp bigwig encounters one of his former victims. They renew their twisted relationship, complete with S&M trimmings. (Dir: Liliana Cavani, 115 mins.)†

Night Prowler, The (Australia, 1978)** Kerry Walker, John Frawley, Ruth Cracknell. Odd mixture of psychology and satire has obese, neurotic Walker, a young woman in Sydney of the late '60s, pretending to have been raped by a night prowler so that she can become one herself. (Dir: Jim Sharman, 90 mins.)

Night Rider, The (MTV 1979)** David Selby, Percy Rodrigues, Pernell Roberts. Selby is a mild-mannered lawyer who turns into an avenging Zorro-like character when the sun goes down. (Dir: Hy Averback, 90 mins.)

Night Runner, The (1957)** Ray Danton, Merry Anders. Parolee from a mental hospital goes berserk, turns into a killer. (Dir: Abner Biberman, 79 mins.)

Night School (1981)* Leonard Mann, Rachel Ward, Drew Snyder, Joseph R. Sicari, Nicholas Cairis. A leather-clad killer decapitates women attending classes at a Boston college. Typical slasher stuff. (Dir: Kenneth Hughes, 88 mins.)†

Night Shadows (1984)** Wings Hauser, Bo Hopkins, Lee Montgomery, Jody Medford, Jennifer Warren. Toxic waste turns townspeople into zombie-like creatures. AKA: *Mutant* (Dir: John "Bud" Cardos, 99 mins.)

Night Shift (1982)*** Henry Winkler, Michael Keaton, Shelley Long. This lovable low-minded comedy about two morgue employees who go into business as "love brokers" for a bunch of friendly neighborhood prostitutes transcends its offensive premise with sharp writing, acting, and direction. Keaton makes an astoundingly self-assured screen debut as fast-talking, slow-thinking, con artist Billy Blazejowski. (Dir: Ron Howard, 105 mins.)†

Nightside (MTV 1980)** Doug McClure, Michael Cornelison, John DeLancie. McClure and Cornelison star as a pair of Los Angeles cops whose shift is the wee small hours of the morning when anything and everything happens. (Dir: Bernard Kowalski, 78 mins.)

Night Slaves (MTV 1970)** James Franciscus, Lee Grant, Leslie Nielsen. A muddled sci-fi yarn which generates some suspense during the first few scenes but deteriorates into a somewhat silly plot, involving inhabitants from outer space and their takeover of a small town. (Dir: Ted Post, 73 mins.)

Nights of Cabiria (Italy, 1957)**** Giulietta Masina, Francois Perier, Amedeo Nazzari. A simple-minded prostitute is taken in by every man she meets. Finely acted and well directed by Federico Fellini. Basis for the musical *Sweet Charity*. Very moving thanks to Masina's sensitive acting. (110 mins.)†

Night Song (1947)**½ Dana Andrews, Merle Oberon, Ethel Barrymore, Hoagy Carmichael. Oddly compelling soap opera of a blind composer who spurns the love of an heiress out of pride, but she finds a way to help him anyway. Romantic mood is enhanced by a sweeping score. (Dir: John Cromwell, 101 mins.)

Night Stalker, The (MTV 1972)*** Darren McGavin, Carol Lynley, Claude Akins. Exciting piece of foolishness involving a breezy reporter and a fanged vampire in

Las Vegas, a perfect setting for the entertainment. In the old tradition of wisecracking newsmen, McGavin shines as a nosy reporter sparring with the Vegas establishment over vampire killings. (Dir: John Llewellyn Moxey, 73 mins.)†

Night Stalker, The (1987)*½ Charles Napier, Michelle Reese, Katherine Kelly Lang. Standard tough-cop picture with the expected number of harried car chases, violent gunplay, brutal fisticuffs, and a psychotic "stalker" preying on women. (Dir: Max Kleven, 89 mins.)†

Nightstick (1987)** Bruce Fairbairn, Kerrie Keane, John Vernon, Robert Vaughn, Isaac Hayes, Leslie Nielsen. Lone-wolf cop Fairbairn, the kind who gets results by bending the rules, fights extortionists who will blow up Manhattan unless banker Vernon coughs up $5 million. Routine suspense drama with the uncharismatic Fairbairn the weak link. (Dir: Joseph L. Scanlan, 94 mins.)†

Night Strangler, The (MTV 1973)**½ Darren McGavin, Jo Ann Pflug, Margaret Hamilton. Sequel to the thriller *The Night Stalker*. McGavin repeats his newspaper reporter role tracking down a story to Seattle, Wash., where a nocturnal strangler is on the prowl. (Dir: Dan Curtis, 73 mins.)

Night Terror (MTV 1977)*½ Valerie Harper, Richard Romanus, Michael Tolan. Predictable melodrama which uses a time-worn device of having someone witness a killing and then have to flee for his life. (Dir: E. W. Swackhamer, 76 mins.)

Night That Panicked America, The (MTV 1975)** Paul Shenar, Cliff DeYoung, Vic Morrow, Eileen Brennan. On October 30th, 1938, the now-famous Orson Welles radio broadcast of H. G. Wells's "War of the Worlds" struck a chord of panic in the hearts of millions of listeners, who mistook the dramatization about an invasion from Mars for the real thing. Film recreates the radio show in authentic detail, and speculates about what radio listeners did, in well-constructed fictional vignettes, brought to life by a hand-picked cast. (Dir: Joseph Sargent, 98 mins.)

Night the Bridge Fell Down, The (MTV 1983)* James MacArthur, Desi Arnaz, Jr., Leslie Nielsen, Barbara Rush, Eve Plumb. A boring three-hour Irwin Allen disaster film about people trapped on a collapsing bridge. (Dir: Georg Fenady, 156 mins.)

Night the Lights Went Out in Georgia, The (1981)**½ Kristy McNichol, Dennis Quaid, Mark Hamill, Don Stroud. The only reason to see this loud, brawling film is Kristy McNichol, as a sister tagging after her country singing brother as they try to crack the recording business in Nashville. (Dir: Ronald F. Maxwell, 110 mins.)†

Night the World Exploded, The (1957)** Kathryn Grant, William Leslie. Pretentious science fiction melodrama dealing with the end of the world by destructive forces found deep in the Earth's crust. (Dir: Fred F. Sears, 64 mins.)

Night They Raided Minsky's, The (1968) ***½ Jason Robards, Bert Lahr, Britt Ekland, Norman Wisdom, Elliott Gould. Forget the story line about a pert, innocent Amish girl from the sticks of Pennsylvania (Ekland) who storms Broadway and ends up stripping—in burlesque. Just enjoy the many engaging things in the film, including some nostalgic scenes which capture the attractive, sleazy quality of old-time burlesque, and the comedians whose "racy" material filled out the stage waits between the strippers. Lahr's last film; he died during production and a double was used in some scenes. (Dir: William Friedkin, 99 mins.)

Night They Saved Christmas, The (MTV 1984)** Jaclyn Smith, Paul LeMat, Art Carney, Paul Williams, June Lockhart. The kids might enjoy this fluff fantasy film about an oil-drilling expedition that is working dangerously close to Santa's toy factory and may destroy Christmas. (Dir: Jackie Cooper, 104 mins.)†

Night They Took Miss Beautiful (MTV 1977)*½ Phil Silvers, Stella Stevens, Sheree North, Chuck Connors. Terrorists take over a flight to the Bahamas with beauty contestants and a government courier carrying a deadly germ packet on board. (Dir: Robert Michael Lewis, 104 mins.)

Night Tide (1961)*** Dennis Hopper, Linda Lawson, Luana Anders. A low-budget drama with plenty of innovative touches. A young sailor meets a young carnival girl who believes she's really a mermaid transformed into an earthling and she fears her evil streak. (Dir: Curtis Harrington, 84 mins.)†

Night to Dismember, A (1981)½ Samantha Fox, Dee Cummins, Diane Cummins, Bill Szarka, Saul Meth. A narrator relates, over mostly silent footage, this incomprehensible tale of a girl released from a home for the criminally insane who may be responsible for a new set of murders. (Dir: Doris Wishman, 70 mins.)†

Night to Remember, A (1942)***½ Brian Aherne, Loretta Young, Gale Sondergaard, Sidney Toler, Blanche Yurka. Mystery writer and wife turn detectives when they find a body in their Greenwich Village apartment. Bright comedy-mystery has some hilarious lines, smart performances. (Dir: Richard Wallace, 91 mins.)†

Night to Remember, A (Great Britain, 1958)**** Kenneth More, Honor Blackman, David McCallum. Impressive achievement—documentary-like retelling of the ill-fated maiden voyage of the *Titanic*, magnificently detailed, authentic, stirring saga of heroism of "grace under pressure." Superb Eric Ambler script, Roy Baker direction, performances by the huge cast. (123 mins.)†

Night Train (Great Britain, 1940)***½ Rex Harrison, Margaret Lockwood, Paul Henreid. With the help of the secret service, a scientist's daughter saves a valuable formula from the Nazis. Excellent suspense thriller, one of the best of its kind. AKA: **Night Train to Munich**. (Dir: Carol Reed, 93 mins.)

Night Train to Terror (1985)½ John Phillip Law, Cameron Mitchell, Marc Lawrence, Charles Moll, Meredith Haze. A must for bad-movie buffs, this features segments condensed from three other obscure horror movies and connects them with a meaningless frame featuring God and Satan arguing on a train. Hilariously inept. (Dirs: John Carr, Jay Schlossberg-Cohen, Philip Marshak, Tom McGowan, Gregg Tallas, 93 mins.)†

Night Unto Night (1949)* Ronald Reagan, Broderick Crawford, Viveca Lindfors. Boring, tiresome melodrama about the romance of two characters who'd be better off dead. (Dir: Don Siegel, 92 mins.)

NightVision (1987)* Stacy Carson, Shirley Ross, Tony Carpenter, Ellie Martins. Video store employee is possessed by a satanic videocassette. This takes forever to get to the monster stuff, which isn't even that original—at least four other recent movies have featured evil videotapes. (Dir: Michael Krueger, 100 mins.)†

Night Visions (MTV 1990)** Loryn Locklin, James Remar, Jon Tenney. Another fright tale from scare specialist Wes Craven (director of *Nightmare on Elm Street*). Locklin goes overboard but is effective as a telepathic grad student who changes personalities while working with the police on a serial killer case. Melodramatic at every turn. (Dir: Wes Craven, 96 mins.)

Night Visitor, The (Great Britain, 1971)*** Max von Sydow, Liv Ullmann, Trevor Howard. A neat little thriller, which draws its strength from three fine performances and a fast, intricate plot. An ax-murderer is imprisoned, but another crime with the same *modus operandi* is committed—could he have done it? One hint: Keep your eye on the bird. (Dir: Laslo Benedek, 106 mins.)†

Night Walker, The (1964)**½ Barbara Stanwyck, Robert Taylor. Woman is terrorized by nightmares, which seem to be instigated by her husband who supposedly was killed in a fire. Suspense drama with some spooky moments. (Dir: William Castle, 86 mins.)

Night Warning (1982)** Susan Tyrrell, Jimmy McNichol, Marcia Lewis, Julia Duffy, Bo Svenson. A slasher-rama worth seeing for Tyrrell's full-throttle performance as a madwoman with obsessive tendencies towards her young ward. To their regret, a number of outsiders try to help him lead a normal life, but Auntie Susan has one hand on her apron strings and the other on a knife. (Dir: William Asher, 96 mins.)†

Nightwars (1988)** Brian O'Connor, Dan Haggerty, Cameron Smith, Steve Horton. Apparently having run out of variations on their standard war movie scenarios, the people at Action International ripped off Freddy Krueger this time for a story about two guilt-ridden Vietnam vets who relive the horrors of war in their dreams—but wake up with real wounds. (Dir: David A. Prior, 88 mins.)†

Night Watch (Great Britain, 1973)* Elizabeth Taylor, Laurence Harvey, Billie Whitelaw, Robert Lang. Is Taylor's husband really trying to do her in? The poor man's *Gaslight*. (Dir: Brian Hutton, 98 mins.)†

Nightwing (1979)*** Nick Mancuso, David Warner, Kathryn Harrold. An interesting thriller. A plague of infected vampire bats strikes a Hopi-Navajo reservation in the Southwest. The locale is interesting, the plotting tense, and the special effects spectacular. (Dir: Arthur Hiller, 103 mins.)†

Night Without Sleep (1952)**½ Linda Darnell, Gary Merrill, Hildegarde Neff. Mentally disturbed man is driven to murder. Minor but well-acted little psychothriller. (Dir: Roy Baker, 77 mins.)

Night Without Stars (Great Britain, 1951)**½ David Farrar, Nadia Gray. Blinded man in France becomes involved with black marketeers and murder, returns to England to have his sight restored, so he can solve the mystery. (Dir: Anthony Pelissier, 86 mins.)

Night World (1932)** Lew Ayres, Mae Clarke, Boris Karloff, Dorothy Revier, Clarence Muse, Hedda Hopper, George Raft. Extraordinary, sensationalistic melodrama, most definitely pre-Code, of one night in the varied lives of the denizens of an underworld-connected nightclub. Sizzling and very entertaining, with floor show choreography by Busby Berkeley. (Dir: Hobart Henley, 56 mins.)

Night Zoo, The (Canada, 1988)**½ Gilles Maheu, Roger Le Bel, Corrado Mastropasqua. A French-Canadian import that can't make up its mind what it is. It starts out as a brutal crime story and ends up focusing on a man's relationship with his dying father. The sentimental portion is clearly superior, but it

can't wash away the lingering traces of the earlier vicious, senseless violence. (Dir: Jean-Claude Lauzon, 115 mins.)†

Nijinsky (Great Britain, 1980)**½ Alan Bates, George de la Pena, Leslie Browne. Director Herbert Ross's life of the great dancer who went mad is handsomely mounted, though the drama is shallow. Bates is superbly convincing as impresario Sergei Diaghilev. (129 mins.)

Nikki, Wild Dog of the North (U.S.-Canada, 1961)*** Jean Coutu, Emile Genest, Uriel Luft, Robert Rivard. A wolf dog, separated from his beloved master, strikes up a friendship with a bear cub and is later unwillingly trained as a fight-dog. Above-average Walt Disney nature adventure. (Dirs: Jack Couffer, Don Haldane, 74 mins.)†

9½ Weeks (1986)* Mickey Rourke, Kim Basinger, Margaret Whitton. Reports of the controversy surrounding the film's excised sex scenes were vastly more juicy than anything you'll see on screen in this commercial for swinging singles down S&M way. Far from creating a turn-on, the allegedly torrid affair of a horny Wall Street exec and a hot-to-trot art gallery entrepreneur gives promiscuity a bad name. (Dir: Adrian Lyne, 113 mins.)†

9 Deaths of the Ninja (1985)*½ Sho Kosugi, Brent Huff, Emilia Lesniak, Blackie Dammett. Ninja-trained U.S. agent Kosugi and his two sidekicks battle a drug lord who is holding a busload of citizens hostage. Attempts to add some levity to the kicking and chopping only make the story seem dumber than it already is. (Dir: Emmett Alston, 94 mins.)†

Nine Girls (1944)*** Evelyn Keyes, Jinx Falkenburg, Ann Harding, Nina Foch. Hated sorority girl is murdered, and one of the girls turns sleuth to find the killer. Well written, nicely acted and directed mystery. (Dir: Leigh Jason, 78 mins.)

Nine Hours to Rama (U.S.-Great Britain, 1963)***½ Horst Buchholz, José Ferrer, Diane Baker. Absorbing political drama about the nine hours leading up to the assassination of India's Mahatma Gandhi. Buchholz plays the rebellious Indian youth who is assigned to kill Gandhi, and though his romantic entanglements slow the action, the pace picks up before the shattering climax. (Dir: Mark Robson, 125 mins.)

Nine Lives Are Not Enough (1941)**½ Ronald Reagan, Faye Emerson, Joan Perry, James Gleason, Howard da Silva. Lively low-budget mystery has a newspaperman getting involved in a murder case when the police are baffled; typical, good-natured second feature. (Dir: A. Edward Sutherland, 63 mins.)

Nine Lives of Fritz the Cat, The (1974)**

Voices of Skip Hinnant, Reva Rose, Bob Holt, Pat Harrington, Jr. Neither R. Crumb nor Ralph Bakshi had anything to do with this sequel to the original adult cartoon *Fritz the Cat* that finds the now-tamer tabby fantasizing about his earlier, more anarchic life while being scolded by his wife. Better than ''The Flintstones,'' but not much. (Dir: Robert Taylor, 77 mins.)†

Nine Months (Hungary, 1977)*** Jan Nowicki, Lili Monori, Djoko Rodic. A woman iron worker has a torrid affair with an actor who becomes insanely jealous when he discovers she has a child by a married university professor. Powerful drama with a central female character who refuses to bow to conventional concepts of womanhood. The photography by Janos Kende exquisitely contrasts the dark somber factories with snowy landscapes. (Dir: Marta Meszaros, 93 mins.)

9/30/55 (1977)*** Richard Thomas, Susan Tyrrell, Thomas Hulce. It's the date James Dean was killed in an auto accident. Thomas has seldom been better as a young high-school senior who affectionately apes his hero and shares his own adoration with a girlfriend. Offbeat, uneven, affecting. (Dir: James Bridges, 101 mins.)

9 to 5 (1980)**½ Jane Fonda, Lily Tomlin, Dolly Parton, Dabney Coleman, Sterling Hayden, Henry Jones, Marian Mercer. Secretaries gang up on a piggish boss thereby consigning the whole story to easy stereotypes and meaningless satire. The three main players, Fonda, Parton, and Tomlin, are intelligent and appealing, but the film can't escape its own calculated origins. (Dir: Colin Higgins, 111 mins.)†

1918 (1985)**½ Matthew Broderick, William Converse-Roberts, Hallie Foote. Small town Americana about the effects of WWI and a raging flu epidemic that changes life in a small Texas town irrevocably. Obviously a labor of love by writer Horton Foote, this restrained character study of the residents of Harrison, Texas, circa 1918 is subdued to a fault, but nonetheless superlatively acted and handsomely produced. (Dir: Ken Harrison, 91 mins.)†

1984 (Great Britain, 1955)*** Edmond O'Brien, Michael Redgrave, Jan Sterling, Donald Pleasence. Orwell's image of what our world will be like in '84 has been converted to an interesting if somewhat confused film. (Dir: Michael Anderson, 91 mins.)

1984 (Great Britain, 1984)**½ John Hurt, Richard Burton. A bleak look at a totalitarian future that's visually faithful to the famous book, but maybe oppres-

sively so. Unfortunately, the experience of the book isn't really captured here; only the externals in this good, but misguided try. (Dir: Michael Radford, 123 mins.)†

1941 (1979)** Dan Aykroyd, Ned Beatty, John Belushi, Lorraine Gary, Treat Williams, Nancy Allen, Robert Stack, Christopher Lee, Toshiro Mifune, Warren Oates, Slim Pickens, Eddie Deezen, Sam Fuller, Mickey Rourke. A raucous film that spent $28 million for a few laughs and much destruction. Farce based on a real incident in which a Japanese sub was spotted off the coast of southern California six days after the attack on Pearl Harbor. TV showings include 25 mins. of footage deleted from the theatrical release. (Dir: Steven Spielberg, 118 mins.)†

1900 (Italy-France-West Germany-U.S., 1977)** Robert De Niro, Gerard Depardieu, Donald Sutherland, Dominique Sanda, Burt Lancaster. This failed epic attempts to tell the Italian workers' struggle, with two families facing political upheaval in Italy at the turn of the century. A ''director's cut'' 311 minute version was released in 1991.(Dir: Bernardo Bertolucci, 243 mins.)†

1919 (Great Britain, 1986)**½ Maria Schell, Paul Scofield, Frank Finlay, Diana Quick, Colin Firth. Vague psychological drama. Schell and Scofield brilliantly play two insular souls scarred by history and by emotional defeats who, in addition to their loneliness, share the distinction of being the only living patients of Freud. As they reminisce and reach out to each other, the film achieves flashes of power without successfully resolving the issues stirred up. (Dir: Hugh Brody, 99 mins.)

1990: The Bronx Warriors (Italy, 1983)* Vic Morrow, Christopher Connelly, Fred Williamson. Another post-apocalyptic rip-off as fearsome thugs mix it up with evil government officials in the ruins of a futuristic Bronx, which looks a whole lot like it did in 1983. (Dir: Enzo G. Castellari, 84 mins.)†

1969 (1988)** Robert Downey Jr., Kiefer Sutherland, Winona Ryder, Bruce Dern, Joanna Cassidy. Playwright Ernest Thompson (*On Golden Pond*) makes his directorial debut in this none-too-accurate bit of nostalgia that looks more like it was *made* in 1969. College buddies Downey and Sutherland try to stay out of the army and live free while their parents are forced to the realization that the times, they are a-changin'. (90 mins.)†

90 Days (Canada, 1986)**½ Stefan Wodoslawsky, Christine Pak, Sam Grana. In one of the parallel plots of this slight, charming comedy, a young man and his potential mail-order bride from Korea get to know each other. In the other story, the man's friend adjusts to the prospect of being a sperm donor. (Dir: Giles Walker, 99 mins.)†

90 Degrees in the Shade (Czechoslovakia-Great Britain, 1965)***½ Anne Heywood, James Booth, Ann Todd, Donald Wolfit. Married food-store manager has an affair with a stock girl and has been stealing from the liquor supply; it spells tragedy. Superior dramatic fare. (Dir: Jiri Weiss, 86 mins.)

99 44/100% Dead (1974)* Richard Harris, Bradford Dillman, Edmond O'Brien, Ann Turkel, Chuck Connors. Camped-up gangster flick; professional killer is caught in a squeeze between two mobsters muscling each other for control. (Dir: John Frankenheimer, 98 mins.)†

99 River Street (1953)***½ John Payne, Evelyn Keyes, Peggie Castle, Ian Wolfe, Frank Faylen. Taxi driver is aided by an ambitious actress. Sharp melodrama. (Dir: Phil Karlson, 83 mins.)

99 Women (Italy-Spain-West Germany, 1969)* Maria Schell, Luciana Paluzzi, Mercedes McCambridge, Herbert Lom, Maria Rohm. Sleazy women's prison stuff, minus the camp elements that made more recent variations of this genre popular. (Dir: Jess Franco, 90 mins.)†

92 in the Shade (1975)*** Peter Fonda, Warren Oates, Elizabeth Ashley, Margot Kidder. With considerable flair, Thomas McGuane directed and adapted his own novel about a rival Florida fishing-boat captains. The original tragic ending was toned down in the later release. (93 mins.)†

Ninja 3: The Domination (1985)* Lucinda Dickey, Sho Kosugi, Jordan Bennett. A telephone company employee becomes haunted by the ghost of a nasty ninja. (Dir: Sam Firstenberg, 93 mins.)†

Ninotchka (1939)***½ Greta Garbo, Melvyn Douglas, Bela Lugosi, Ina Claire. Delightful comedy about a Soviet female comrade who learns the meaning of life and love from an American in Paris. (Dir: Ernst Lubitsch, 120 mins.)†

Ninth Configuration, The—See: **Twinkle, Twinkle, Killer Kane**

Nitwits, The (1935)**½ Bert Wheeler, Robert Woolsey, Betty Grable, Evelyn Brent, Erik Rhodes, Hale Hamilton. Riotous Wheeler and Woolsey comedy has the boys running an office and fighting among themselves; builds up to a truly lunatic final chase. (Dir: George Stevens, 81 mins.)

Noah's Ark (1929)*** Dolores Costello, George O'Brien, Noah Beery, Louise Fazenda, Nigel De Brulier, Anders Randolph, Guinn Williams, Myrna Loy. Wild intermingling of the story of Noah's ark with a modern one has seven people

caught in a train wreck flash back to their counterparts in biblical times; full of orgies, sacrifices, pagan rites, falling temples, lightning bolts, and, of course, the final flood. Exciting special effects, even today. (Dir: Michael Curtiz, 75 mins)†

Nob Hill (1945)** George Raft, Joan Bennett, Vivian Blaine, Peggy Ann Garner. Saloon owner in the brawling San Francisco days breaks down the resistance of a blue-blooded socialite. Pleasant but unimportant drama with music. (Dir: Henry Hathaway, 95 mins.)

Nobi—See: **Fires on the Plain**

Nobody Lives Forever (1946)**½ John Garfield, Geraldine Fitzgerald, Walter Brennan, Faye Emerson, George Tobias. A hustler comes back from the war and tries to swindle an innocent girl; of course he falls for her. (Dir: Jean Negulesco, 100 mins.)

Nobody's Child (MTV 1986)***½ Marlo Thomas, Ray Baker, Caroline Kava. Harrowing drama based on the true story of Marie Balter, a woman confined to a mental institution for twenty years. Eventually released, she went on to graduate from Harvard. (Dir: Lee Grant, 104 mins.)

Nobody's Fool (1986)*½ Rosanna Arquette, Eric Roberts, Louise Fletcher, Jim Youngs, Mare Winningham, Gwen Welles. A town kook, suffering from low self-esteem after being impregnated and abandoned, reevaluates her existence when a visiting Shakespeare company plays her backward burg; through the makeshift magic of the traveling theatrical troupe, she comes to life again. (Dir: Evelyn Purcell, 107 mins.)†

Nobody's Perfect (1968)** Doug McClure, Nancy Kwan, James Whitmore, David Hartman. The plot of this service comedy revolves around a missing Buddha statue, some crazy sailors, and a jinxed village. (Dir: Alan Rafkin, 103 mins.)

Nobody's Perfect (1990)*½ Chad Lowe, Gail O'Grady, Patrick Breen, Todd Schaefer, Robert Vaughn. Silly teen-oriented male-in-drag comedy with a dash of *Tootsie* and *Some Like It Hot* thrown in. Bashful Lowe puts on make-up and a skirt, and joins the women's college tennis team to get closer to the beautiful blonde of his dreams. (Dir: Robert Kaylor, 89 mins.)

Nobody's Perfekt (1981)* Gabe Kaplan, Alex Karras, Robert Klein, Susan Clark, Paul Stewart, Alex Rocco, Peter Bonerz. Wretched farce about three losers who fight back after their car is wrecked and the city doesn't play fair about compensation. (Dir: Peter Bonerz, 95 mins.)†

Nobody Waved Goodbye (Canada, 1964)***½ Peter Kastner, Julie Biggs, Claude

Rae. Made on a small budget, this film beautifully documents the plight of a young eighteen-year-old who steals a car and runs away with his girl friend. (Writer-Dir: Don Owen, 80 mins.)

Nocturna (1979)*½ Nai Bonet, John Carradine, Yvonne DeCarlo, Brother Theodore, Tony Hamilton. Bonet, the granddaughter of elderly Count Dracula, is given to disco dancing and stripping at the least provocation. (Dir: "Harry Tampa" [Harry Hurwitz], 83 mins.)†

Nocturne (1946)*** George Raft, Lynn Bari. Detective refuses to believe the death of a woman-chasing songwriter was suicide. Smooth mystery, interesting and suspenseful. (Dir: Edwin L. Marin, 88 mins.)

Nocturne (1990)** T. Ryder Smith, Gabriel Amor, Mark Woodcock, Lisa Allyn Worth. Sincere exploration of the problems of finding a gay relationship in New York City is filmed without the usual stereotypes and with a focus on love, respect, strength, and responsibility. The black-and-white cinematography beautifully captures Manhattan's vibrance. (Dir: Mark T. Harris, 100 mins.)

No Dead Heroes (1987)*½ Max Thayer, John Dresden, Toni Nero. American war hero is captured by the Soviets, who plant a microchip in his brain that makes him do their bidding. The plot's been done before, generally better than here. (Dir: J. C. Miller, 90 mins.)†

No Deposit, No Return (1976)** David Niven, Darren McGavin, Kim Richards, Brad Savage, Barbara Feldon. Lackluster Disney comedy in which two rich kids connive to spend an Easter holiday with their busy widowed mom (Feldon). They induce two inept crooks to offer them for ransom to their wealthy grandfather (Niven), who's glad to be rid of the kids for a while. (Dir: Norman Tokar, 112 mins.)†

No Down Payment (1957)**½ Joanne Woodward, Tony Randall, Jeffrey Hunter, Barbara Rush, Cameron Mitchell. Problems of four married couples living in a postwar housing project. Sort of a pre-fab *Peyton Place*, with as much underhand plotting going on. (Dir: Martin Ritt, 105 mins.)

No Drums, No Bugles (1971)** Martin Sheen. Based on a true story, this features Sheen in a virtually one-man show as a Virginia farmer who chose to live for three years in a cave in the Blue Ridge Mountains during the Civil War rather than fight in the army. Sheen is good, but the film is amateurishly made, and the surrealistic ending is frustrating. (Dir: Clyde Ware, 85 mins.)†

No End (1984)*** Maria Pakulnis, Aleksander Bardini, Grazyna Szapolwska, Jerzy Radziwillowicz. A young libertarian lawyer dies suddenly, leaving an unresolved case as well as a grieving wife and son. They try to get along without him, but there is "no end" to his power as his ghost watches over them and his unfinished case. Set in Poland under martial law in the early '80s, film's allegory is a bit too obvious, but it's still an unusual and interesting work. (Dir: Krzysztof Kielowski, 108 mins.)

No Escape—See: **City on a Hunt**

No Exit (France, 1955)*** Arletty, Gaby Sylvia, Frank Villard, Nicole Courcel, Daniele Delorme, Yves Deniaud. Jean-Paul Sartre's existential drama about three strangers, each with current problems and past secrets, trapped in a hotel room. Well-crafted film was opened up with addition of more characters, but tense roundelay of central figures still remains story's fascinating main focus. (Dir: Jacqueline Audry, 99 mins.)

No Highway in the Sky (Great Britain, 1951)*** James Stewart, Marlene Dietrich, Glynis Johns, Jack Hawkins. Absent-minded professor insists a new commercial airline is not safe. Very good mixture of suspense and gentle comedy, excellently played by Stewart and Dietrich. (Dir: Henry Koster, 98 mins.)

No Holds Barred (1952)** Bowery Boys, Hombre Montana. Sach gets a strange power which enables him to become a phenomenal wrestler. (Dir: William Beaudine, 65 mins.)†

No Holds Barred (1989)** Hulk Hogan, Joan Severance, Kurt Fuller, Tiny Lister. Cheap starring vehicle for wrestling superstar Hogan plays like a cross between *Rocky III* and *The Garbage Pail Kids Movie*, though it has a few funny bits and camp appeal. (Dir: Thomas J. Wright, 92 mins.)

No Leave, No Love (1946)** Van Johnson, Keenan Wynn. Van's fans may be able to endure this long, forced comedy about a couple of Marines loose in the big city with plenty of money, thanks to a radio appearance. (Dir: Charles Martin, 119 mins.)

No Love for Johnnie (Great Britain, 1961)*** Peter Finch, Stanley Holloway, Mary Peach, Billie Whitelaw. Brilliantly acted drama about a member of parliament whose political and domestic affairs are both failures, and of his love for a young model. (Dir: Ralph Thomas, 96 mins.)†

Nomads (1986)** Pierce Bronsan, Lesley-Anne Down, Anna-Marie Montecelli, Adam Ant. Some good ideas and visual style, but this fantasy doesn't quite come off. Anthropologist Brosnan has bad experiences with a strange group of punks; after he dies in hospital, a doctor (Down) begins reliving his days of terror. Margaret Mead never had such problems. (Dir: John McTiernan, 93 mins.)†

No Man Is an Island (1962)**½ Jeffrey Hunter, Marshall Thompson. Story based on fact about a navy radioman who is trapped by the outbreak of WWII, becomes a guerrilla in the hills of Guam. Done in a straightforward manner, with a good performance by Hunter. (Dir: John Monks, Jr., 114 mins.)

No Man of Her Own (1932)**½ Clark Gable, Carole Lombard, Dorothy Mackaill, Grant Mitchell, Elizabeth Patterson. A card shark is reformed by love. Not as potent as it used to be; Gable and Lombard's only co-starring film. (Dir: Wesley Ruggles, 85 mins.)†

No Man of Her Own (1949)***½ Barbara Stanwyck, John Lund, Jane Cowl, Lyle Bettger, Phyllis Thaxter, Richard Denning. What could have been an ordinary, if improbable, sudser turns out (through fine acting and, apparently, sheer concentration) to be astonishingly involving. The plot, from a story by Cornell Woolrich, involves a down-and-out woman who changes identities with a wealthy war widow when the latter is killed in a train wreck. (Dir: Mitchell Leisen, 98 mins.)

No Man's Land (MTV 1984)** Stella Stevens, Sam Jones, Donna Dixon, Melissa Michaelsen. Silly western farce starring Stevens as a sheriff, who, along with her three beautiful daughters, nabs various desperados. (Dir: Philip Leacock, 104 mins.)

No Man's Land (Switzerland, 1985)**½ Hughes Quester, Jean-Philippe Ecoffey, Betty Berr, Myriam Mezieres, Marie-Luce Felber. The French-Swiss border is the setting for this existential, *noir*ish crime caper film about small-time smugglers getting in over their heads with a major money swindle. Director Alain Tanner's detached intellectualism makes for a coolly fascinating drama. (110 mins.)

No Man's Land (1987)** Charlie Sheen, D. B. Sweeney, Randy Quaid. Sweeney gets an undercover mission to investigate playboy/car thief Sheen and becomes hopelessly infatuated with his life-style. All glitz and no heart; some nice sports cars, though. (Dir: Peter Werner, 106 mins.)†

No Man's Woman (1955)*½ Marie Windsor, John Archer, Patric Knowles, Nancy Gates, Percy Helton, Morris Ankrum. Poverty Row mystery about the search for the murderer of a coldhearted, double-crossing woman. (Dir: Franklin Adreon, 70 mins.)

No Maps on My Taps (1978)*** Sandman

Sims, Chuck Green, Bunny Briggs. Three great hoofers speak with their feet in this delightful documentary on tap dancing as an expression of black heritage and culture. (Dir: George T. Nierenberg, 60 mins.)

No Mercy (1986)**½ Richard Gere, Kim Basinger, Jeroen Krabbe, William Atherton, Bruce McGill, George Dzundza. No great shakes, but one of Gere's better recent roles as a Chicago detective who goes to New Orleans to investigate the murder of his partner, and ends up protecting a beautiful woman (Basinger) from the vicious kingpin who "owns" her. Well-caught atmosphere and some solid suspense. (Dir: Richard Pearce, 109 mins.)†

No Minor Vices (1948)**½ Dana Andrews, Lili Palmer, Louis Jourdan, Jane Wyatt. Pretty good domestic comedy of a young couple whose happiness is imposed on by the charming but shiftless Jourdan; nothing extra special, but deftly played. (Dir: Lewis Milestone, 96 mins.)

No More es (1935)**½ Joan Crawford, Robert Montgomery, Franchot Tone. Lighter-than-air romantic nonsense about Crawford using Tone to rein in her playboy husband. Stylishly played fluff. (Dir: Edward H. Griffith, 81 mins.)

No, My Darling Daughter (Great Britain, 1961)**½ Michael Redgrave, Juliet Mills, Michael Craig, Roger Livesey. Tycoon realizes his daughter is at that grown-up age, entrusts her to a friend while on a business trip—and the trouble really begins. (Dir: Betty Box, 97 mins.)

No Name on the Bullet (1959)*** Audie Murphy, Joan Evans, Charles Drake, Virginia Grey, Warren Stevens. Offbeat, grim little western. A hired gunman comes into a small town to kill an unnamed person; everyone has something to hide and the respectable citizens begin to turn on one another. (Dir: Jack Arnold, 77 mins.)

None But the Brave (1965)** Frank Sinatra, Clint Walker, Tommy Sands, Tony Bill. Routine World War II action drama set in the Pacific, notable only because Sinatra also tried his hand at directing for the first time. Sinatra's platoon of Marines (he's the company medic) crash on an island occupied by a small band of Japanese soldiers. (105 mins.)†

None But the Lonely Heart (1944)*** Cary Grant, Ethel Barrymore, June Duprez, Barry Fitzgerald, Jane Wyatt, Dan Duryea, George Coulouris. A Cockney layabout comes to self-discovery when he learns his mother is dying. Clifford Odets wrote and directed, with shaky technique but basic earnestness. (113 mins.)†

None Shall Escape (1944)***½ Alexander Knox, Marsha Hunt. A Nazi officer is put on trial, and his crimes are reviewed. Gripping drama packs a punch. Set in the future: made during WWII, but taking place *after* the war. (Dir: André de Toth, 85 mins.)

Non-Stop New York (Great Britain, 1937)** John Loder, Anna Lee, Francis L. Sullivan. Fairly intriguing but ultimately disappointing semi-science fiction mystery set aboard the first nonstop transatlantic flight. (Dir: Robert Stevenson, 70 mins.)

No Nukes (1980)***½ Jane Fonda, Ralph Nader, Jackson Browne, Bruce Springsteen, Carly Simon, Bonnie Raitt, James Taylor, the Doobie Brothers, Crosby, Stills and Nash, and other rock acts in a filmed concert to benefit the antinuclear power forces. (Dirs: Julian Schlossberg, Danny Goldberg, Anthony Potenza, 103 mins.)†

No One Cries Forever (South Africa, (1985)** Howard Carpendale, Elke Sommer, Zoli Marki. High-class call girl meets and fall in love with a game warden on leave from his African preserve, tries to escape the madam who controls her life. Top-billed Sommer has only a small role in this dull mélange of romance and action. (Dir: Jans Rautenback, 94 mins.(†

Noose Hangs High, The (1948)** Bud Abbott, Lou Costello, Leon Errol, Cathy Downs. Typical Abbott and Costello film this time involving $50,000 stolen from the boys by some bad men. (Dir: Charles Barton, 77 mins.)

No Other Love (MTV 1979)**½ Richard Thomas, Julie Kavner, Elizabeth Allen. Two slightly retarded young adults, while living at a hostel run by a caring couple, fall in love and hope to get married. (Dir: Richard Pearce, 104 mins.)

No Place Like Homicide (Great Britain, 1961)** Kenneth Connor, Sidney James, Shirley Eaton, Donald Pleasence. The one about all the relatives gathered in a spooky mansion to hear the reading of the will, done for laughs—only it might have been better played straight. Remake of Karloff's *The Ghoul*. (Dir: Pat Jackson, 87 mins.)

No Place to Hide (1956)*½ David Brian, Marsha Hunt, Keenan Wynn. The search is on for two boys who have innocently acquired pellets of deadly germs. Slow moving treatment robs this drama made in the Philippines of practically all its suspense. (Dir: Josef Shaftel, 71 mins.)

No Place to Hide (MTV 1981)*½ Mariette Hartley, Kathleen Beller, Keir Dullea. Another predictable thriller in which a young girl is marked for death by a stranger who never leaves any clues. (Dir: John Llewellyn Moxey, 104 mins.)

No Place to Run (MTV 1972)**½ Herschel Bernardi, Scott Jacoby. Touching oldman—youngboy drama, helped by the casting of Bernardi and Jacoby. Bernardi plays an aging man forced to flee with his adopted son from authorities. (Dir: Delbert Mann, 73 mins.)†

Nora (West Germany, 1973)*** Margit Carstensen. A quickie, shot on videotape by director Rainer Werner Fassbinder. Hothouse rendition of Ibsen's *A Doll's House*. (100 mins.)

Nora Prentiss (1947)** Ann Sheridan, Kent Smith, Robert Alda. Meaningless, hackneyed melodrama about a doctor who almost loses everything just because he meets and falls for Miss Sheridan. (Dir: Vincent Sherman, 111 mins.)

No Regrets for Our Youth (Japan, 1946) ***½ Denjiro Okochi, Eiko Miyoshi, Setsuko Hara. Director Akira Kurosawa's first major work is a meaty drama of the young left faced with the political realities of the fascist Japanese military state of the '30s. (111 mins.)

No Resting Place (Great Britain, 1951)**½ Michael Gough, Eithne Dunne. A drama of Irish vagrants, one of whom becomes a fugitive with his family when he accidentally kills a gamekeeper. Grim, beautifully photographed. (Dir: Paul Rotha, 77 mins.)

No Retreat, No Surrender (1986)* Kurt McKinney, Jean-Claude Van Damme. Derivative claptrap that laughably mixes up the plots of *Rocky IV* and *The Karate Kid*. A youngster who manages to communicate with the ghost of Bruce Lee is inspired to battle local thugs as well as knock out a Russian lummox in a big karate match. (Dir: Corey Yuen, 90 mins.)†

No Retreat, No Surrender II (1989)* Loren Avedon, Max Thayer, Cynthia Rothrock. Anglo Bruce Lee manqué and buddies thwart a Soviet attempt to take over Southeast Asia. Only for fervid fans of flying feet. (Dir: Corey Yuen, 92 mins.)†

Norliss Tapes, The (MTV 1973)** Roy Thinnes, Angie Dickinson, Claude Akins. A serious Thinnes plays an investigator of the occult involved in tracking down the mystery of a deceased sculptor who appears to be very much alive. (Dir: Dan Curtis, 74 mins.)

Norman, Is That You? (1976)* Redd Foxx, Pearl Bailey, Dennis Dugan, Michael Warren. A one-joke affair about parents discovering their strapping, handsome young son is sharing his digs with his gay lover. (Dir: George Schlatter, 92 mins.)

Norman Loves Rose (Australia, 1983)* Carol Kane, Tony Owen, Warren Mitchell, Myra De Groot. An awful Australian sex-comedy. Kane plays a housewife who finds carnal fulfillment with a twelve-year-old. (Dir: Henri Safran, 98 mins.)†

Norma Rae (1979)*** Sally Field, Ron Leibman, Beau Bridges, Pat Hingle. Field surprised critics and captured an Oscar for her full-textured, gutsy portrayal of a union organizer who comes up from the ranks. Working to instill the spirit of a common cause at her plant does not endear her to management. Director Ritt elicits fine performances from the entire cast, and has created a rousing liberal drama which is heartfelt and stirring. (Dir: Martin Ritt, 113 mins.)†

No Room for the Groom (1952)** Tony Curtis, Piper Laurie. Silly comedy about newlyweds who never get to enjoy a honeymoon has Tony Curtis mugging throughout and Piper Laurie looking perplexed. Obvious plot gimmicks often backfire. (Dir: Douglas Sirk, 82 mins.)

Norseman, The (1978)** Lee Majors, Mel Ferrer, Cornel Wilde. Low-grade actioner set in 1006, as Viking prince Majors comes to North America in search of his father, King Ferrer. (Dir: Charles B. Pierce, 90 mins.)†

North Avenue Irregulars, The (1979)** Edward Herrmann, Susan Clark, Cloris Leachman, Barbara Harris, Karen Valentine. Pleasant Disney comedy based on a true story. The ladies of the parish of newly arrived minister Herrmann help him in combating a local bookie operation. (Dir: Bruce Bilson, 99 mins.)†

North Beach and Rawhide (MTV 1985)** William Shatner, Tate Donovan, James Olson, Ron O'Neal. William Shatner stars as an ex-con who runs a correctional ranch for juvenile delinquents. (Dir: Harry Falk, 104 mins.)

North by Northwest (1959)**** Cary Grant, Eva Marie Saint, James Mason, Martin Landau, Leo G. Carroll. Master of suspense Alfred Hitchcock apparently had lots of fun directing this tongue-in-cheek spy thriller, and you'll have fun watching it. Grant accidentally becomes entangled in one of those typically sinister Hitchcockian plots which never make much sense. (136 mins.)†

North Dallas Forty (1979)***½ Nick Nolte, Mac Davis, Dayle Haddon, Bo Svenson, John Matuszak, Steve Forrest, Dabney Coleman. Witty and wise comedy about the battered lives of pro footballers. Nolte's considerable talent is almost matched by Mac Davis, a singer who makes an impressive debut—and for that matter, by pro player John Matuszak, who acts better than many professionals. (Dir: Ted Kotcheff, 120 mins.)†

Northern Lights (1978)*** Susan Lynch, Robert Behling. Gritty independent feature, set in North Dakota in 1915, depicts the struggle of Norwegian and Swedish immigrants to live off the stark prairie land. (Dirs: Rob Nilsson, John Hanson, 90 mins.)†

Northern Pursuit (1943)**½ Errol Flynn,

Julie Bishop, Helmut Dantine, Gene Lockhart. Errol, still winning the war single-handed, is a Canadian Mountie in this one pursuing a Nazi aviator who's dashing through Canada bent on sabotage. (Dir: Raoul Walsh, 94 mins.)†

North Shore (1987)*½ Matt Adler, Gregory Harrison, Nia Peeples. Surf's up for a "hot dog" (Adler) who goes from Arizona to where the boards are—Hawaii's North Shore. There he makes a friend ("soul surfer" Harrison), has a romance, and enters a big-time surf-off. (Dir: William Phelps, 92 mins.)†

North Star, The (1943)**½ Anne Baxter, Dana Andrews, Walter Huston. Russian propaganda from Hollywood (thanks to our WWII alliance with the U.S.S.R.). Lillian Hellman wrote the screenplay; plenty of "For every one that falls, ten will rise to take his place" and "You cannot keel the spirit of a free peepul." An excellent cast is stranded. AKA: **Armored Attack.** (Dir: Lewis Milestone, 105 mins.)†

Northstar (MTV 1986)** Greg Evigan, Deborah Wakeham, Mitchell Ryan. An astronaut returns from outer space with his five senses intensified. (Dir: Peter Levin, 78 mins.)

North to Alaska (1960)*** John Wayne, Stewart Granger, Ernie Kovacs, Capucine, Fabian. Big, brawling, lusty adventure about a couple of prospectors who have woman trouble in addition to their other problems. (Dir: Henry Hathaway, 122 mins.)†

Northville Cemetery Massacre, The (1976)* David Hyry, Carson Jackson, J. Craig Collicut, Jan Sisk. Head south. Misleadingly titled movie pits a grungy but non-troublemaking biker gang against the people of a small town when the local sheriff tries to pin a rape rap on them. (Dir: William Dear, 81 mins.)†

Northwest Mounted Police (1940)*** Gary Cooper, Madeleine Carroll, Paulette Goddard, Robert Preston, Preston Foster. DeMille's tribute to the Mounties is a typical lavish, colorful, action-packed and shallow story, but if you like action-packed sagas, here it is. (Dir: Cecil B. DeMille, 125 mins.)

Northwest Outpost (1947)*½ Nelson Eddy, Ilona Massey. Historical melodrama of California's early days, when White Russian settlers populated the territory. Mostly dull, stiffly acted. (Dir: Allan Dwan, 91 mins.)

Northwest Passage (1939)***½ Spencer Tracy, Robert Young, Walter Brennan. The kids will love it and so will most historical adventure fans as Spencer Tracy fights the Indians in his search for the Northwest Passage. (Dir: King Vidor, 125 mins.)†

Norwood (1970)* Glen Campbell, Kim

Darby, Joe Namath. Insipid saga of a country boy, fresh from Vietnam, who sets out from Texas to New York to become a TV singer. (Dir: Jack Haley, Jr., 95 mins.)

No Sad Songs for Me (1950)** Margaret Sullavan, Wendell Corey, Viveca Lindfors, Natalie Wood. Well-acted, but messy soap opera about a woman who starts setting her affairs straight, which includes promoting a love affair for her husband and her friend, when she finds she is dying of cancer. Good performances but limiting script. Sullavan's last film. (Dir: Rudolph Maté, 89 mins.)

Nosferatu (Germany, 1922)***½ Max Schreck, Alexander Granach, Greta Schroeder. Director F. W. Murnau's is the best directed version of the Dracula story. Superbly atmospheric. (63 mins.)†

Nosferatu in Venice (Italy, 1988)*½ Klaus Kinski, Barbara De Rossi, Yorgo Voyagis, Donald Pleasence, Christopher Plummer, Maria Cumani Quasimodo. Sequel to Werner Herzog's 1979 remake of *Nosferatu* was made without Herzog's participation, and that makes all the difference. Kinski returns as the vampire, looking to become human again and end his bloodsucking days. (Dir: Augusto Caminito, 96 mins.)

Nosferatu the Vampyre (West Germany, 1979)***½ Klaus Kinski, Isabelle Adjani, Bruno Ganz, Roland Topor. Mesmerizing color remake of Murnau's classic. This vampire is no sexy count but a loathsome, disease-spreading creature; the film is fascinating as it evokes the wretched details of the pestilence, and quite haunting. (Dir: Werner Herzog, 105 mins.)

No Small Affair (1985)**½ Jon Cryer, Demi Moore, George Wendt, Ann Wedgeworth, Jeffrey Tambor. Amiable romantic comedy about a sixteen-year-old (Cryer) with an obsession for both photography and a sexy twenty-two-year-old singer (Moore). Despite his innocence and nerdy appearance, Cryer's devotion to her pays off. (Dir: Jerry Schatzberg, 103 mins.)†

Nostalghia (U.S.S.R.-Italy, 1983)*** Oleg Yankovsky, Dominziana Giordano, Erland Josephson, Patrizia Terreno. Russian filmmaker Andrei Tarkovsky's first film made outside the Soviet Union is a very personal meditation on expatriate artists that has Yankovsky playing Tarkovsky's surrogate, a Russian poet who travels to Italy to research the life of an eighteenth century Russian composer. Tarkovsky's images are exquisitely composed, but they comprise so much of the film's length that their mesmerizing quality soon dissolves and what we're left with is a *very* slow-moving picture. (130 mins.)

No Surrender (Great Britain, 1986)** Michael Angelis, Avis Bunnage, James Ellis, Tom Georgeson, Elvis Costello. Impenetrable political satire. The story concerns a dingy nightclub in Ireland during New Year's Eve, where opposing political sides are accidentally gathered for the riotous festivities. (Dir: Peter Smith, 100 mins.)†

Not a Love Story (Canada, 1981)*** An illuminating and deeply disturbing documentary about pornography produced by women filmmakers at the National Film Board of Canada. (Dir: Bonnie Sherr Klein, 75 mins.)

Not a Penny More, Not a Penny Less (MTV 1990)** Edward Asner, Ed Begley, Jr., Brian Protheroe, Nicholas Jones, Maryam D'Abo, Jenny Agutter. After a scheme set up by con man Asner leaves them broke, four British professional men scheme to use their talents to return the favor and retrieve their money. Lighthearted caper lacks sufficient plausibility to sustain its length. (Dir: Clive Donner, 186 mins.).

Not as a Stranger (1955)**½ Robert Mitchum, Frank Sinatra, Olivia de Havilland, Gloria Grahame. This is a somewhat watered down version of Morton Thompson's best-selling novel about doctors and their degrees of dedication to their chosen profession. (Dir: Stanley Kramer, 136 mins.)

Notebook From China (Denmark, 1987)***½ Beautiful documentary of a 6,000 mile journey through China, including remote and agricultural regions rarely seen by Westerners. The film follows stories of a number of people and takes a detailed look at the Beijing Opera's version of *The Marriage of Figaro*. An amazing adventure in one of the world's most mysterious lands. (Dir: Jorgen Leth, 80 mins.)

Not for Publication (1984)**½ Nancy Allen, David Naughton, Laurence Luckinbill. Silly but likable farce about a girl who moonlights as a political aide while digging up dirt for a *National Enquirer*-type publication. Abetted by a shy photographer and her trusty midget, she uncovers political corruption in N.Y.C. and regains control of her father's once-admirable newspaper. (Dir: Paul Bartel, 87 mins.)†

Nothing But a Man (1964)**** Ivan Dixon, Abbey Lincoln. Moving, hard-hitting film about a Negro couple who strive for dignity in an Alabama town. Ivan Dixon and Abbey Lincoln are excellent as the newlyweds who meet with more than their share of opposition as they try to make a life for themselves. (Dir: Michael Roemer, 92 mins.)

Nothing But the Best (Great Britain, 1964) ***½ Alan Bates, Denholm Elliott, Harry Andrews, Millicent Martin. A vastly underrated comedy gem, with a superb performance by Bates as a British working-class stiff who wants to better his lot and uses his wiles, charm, and wit to reach the "top." Along the way, he encounters obstacles which he disposes of with alacrity and aplomb until he possibly has to resort to murder. Does he or doesn't he? Tune in and find out, and have a good time along the way. (Dir: Clive Donner, 99 mins.)

Nothing But the Night (Great Britain, 1972)** Christopher Lee, Peter Cushing, Diana Dors. Odd British shocker starts out as a mystery but strays into mass murder, insanity, illicit experiments, and the search for eternal life. (Dir: Peter Sasdy, 90 mins.)

Nothing But the Truth (1941)*** Bob Hope, Paulette Goddard. Bob is good, but much of the story is old hat in this tale of a man who bets that he can tell only the truth for twenty-four hours. Some laughs, of course, but not Bob's best. (Dir: Elliott Nugent, 90 mins.)

Nothing But Trouble (1991)½ Dan Aykroyd, Chevy Chase, Demi Moore, John Candy. Unmitigated disaster about America's weirdest speed trap; motorists are tormented, then killed. A woeful waste of comedic talent. Aykroyd plays two roles, scripted, and makes his inept directorial debut. (Dir: Dan Aykroyd, 85 mins.)†

Nothing in Common (1986)*** Tom Hanks, Jackie Gleason, Hector Elizondo, Eva Marie Saint, Bess Armstrong. Polished serio-comedy, stronger in the comedy department. Playing a self-centered advertising whiz kid, Hanks is forced to mature and care for his parents after they divorce and his dad refuses to seek help for his diabetes. Hilarious jibes at the ad-agency racket keep the soap suds at low tide. (Dir: Garry Marshall, 118 mins.)†

Nothing Personal (1980)* Donald Sutherland, Suzanne Somers, Dabney Coleman, Lawrence Dane, Roscoe Lee Browne. A puerile comedy with Sutherland and Somers fighting the establishment to save endangered seals. (Dir: George Bloomfield, 98 mins.)†

Nothing Sacred (1937)*** Carole Lombard, Fredric March, Walter Connolly, Charles Winninger, Sig Ruman, John Qualen, Maxie Rosenbloom, Hattie McDaniel. A girl thought to be dying is turned into the "Sweetheart of New York City" as a newspaper publicity stunt. The pace is crackling, the dialogue hilarious, and the actors electrifying, especially March and Lombard as the wiseacre lovebirds. (Dir: William Wellman, 77 mins.)†

No Time for Breakfast (France, 1976)*** Annie Girardot, François Perier, Jean-Pierre Cassel, Isabelle Huppert. Girardot

plays a head of surgery who has to juggle the demands of her profession, her teenage children, her diplomat husband, her lovers, and the news that she may have cancer. Her emotional facility is overwhelming. (Dir: Jean-Louis Bertucelli, 100 mins.)

No Time for Comedy (1940)*** James Stewart, Rosalind Russell, Genevieve Tobin, Charles Ruggles, Allyn Joslyn. Loose adaptation of the S. N. Behrman hit benefits from the cast but loses its satiric bite. As it now stands it's the story of a country boy who becomes a successful writer and must face the accompanying consequences. Stewart and Russell are at their best. (Dir: William Keighley, 93 mins.)

No Time for Flowers (1952)**½ Paul Christian, Viveca Lindfors. An actor is hired by the Communists to test the fidelity of an embassy clerk, but they both foil the Reds. Fairly amusing comedy filmed in Austria; no *Ninotchka*, but pleasant enough. (Dir: Don Siegel, 83 mins.)

No Time for Love (1943)*** Claudette Colbert, Fred MacMurray, Richard Haydn, Ilka Chase, June Havoc. Amusing comedy about a lady photographer who falls for a sand-hog. Routine tale is superbly told and delightful viewing. (Dir: Mitchell Leisen, 83 mins.)

No Time for Sergeants (1958)*** Andy Griffith, Myron McCormick, Nick Adams. Andy Griffith is the whole show as the Georgia farm boy who gets drafted into the Army and creates mayhem among his superiors and colleagues. It's a virtuoso comedy performance. The supporting cast is fine. (Dir: Mervyn LeRoy, 111 mins.)†

No Time to Be Young (1957)** Robert Vaughn, Roger Smith, Merry Anders. Slight drama about a trio of young men who find their backs are up against the wall and therefore plan a robbery. (Dir: David Lowell Rich, 82 mins.)

Not in Front of the Children (MTV 1982)**½ Linda Gray, John Getz, John Lithgow. Earnest but ultimately disappointing film based upon a true life case. Linda Gray plays a divorced woman with children and a live-in lover whom the children adore. But her ex-husband takes her to court on the grounds that her living arrangement could affect the children's moral values. (Dir: Joseph Hardy, 104 mins.)

Not Just Another Affair (MTV 1982)** Victoria Principal, Gil Gerard. An unlikely but still pleasant love story about a soon-to-be married lady who insists upon remaining celibate until her wedding night. (Dir: Steven H. Stern, 104 mins.)

Not My Kid (MTV 1985)*** George Segal, Stockard Channing, Viveka Davis. Hard-hitting emotional drama detailing the reaction of a surgeon's family to fifteen-year-old Susan, who's clever at hiding her supplies and habit, and is dangerously close to oblivion. (Dir: Michael Tuchner, 104 mins.)†

Not of This Earth (1957)½ Paul Birch, Beverly Garland. This film about a blood-thirsty alien checking out the Earth as a potential plasma-bank is so low budget, one of its chase scenes is repeated verbatim! The film's title could serve as its review. (Dir: Roger Corman, 67 mins.)

Not of This Earth (1988)**½ Traci Lords, Arthur Roberts, Lenny Juliano, Ace Mask. Aptly campy remake of the above updates the original storyline, relying on snappy dialogue. (Dir: Jim Wynorski, 82 mins.)†

Not of This World (MTV 1991)** Lisa Hartman, A Martinez, Pat Hingle, Luke Edwards. A sci-fi thriller short on special effects but long on dialogue. A meteor shower deposits an alien in a small midwestern town; the alien heads for a power plant. Hartman leads the climactic battle in this moderately entertaining fantasy reminiscent of those 1950s double-bill monster-on-the-loose yarns. (Dir: Jon Daniel Hess, 96 mins.)

Notorious (1946)**** Ingrid Bergman, Cary Grant, Claude Rains, Louis Calhern, Leopoldine Konstantin. Alfred Hitchcock's brooding, romantic spy thriller is dark and complex. Ingrid Bergman plays a war criminal's daughter pressured by a government agent (Cary Grant) into working as a counterspy in Brazil. As passion begins to smolder between them, she's forced into marriage with the very enemy they're pursuing. (Dir: Alfred Hitchcock, 102 mins.)†

Notorious Gentleman, The (Great Britain, 1945)***½ Rex Harrison, Lilli Palmer. The story of a charming but scoundrelly wastrel who goes through life without purpose until love redeems him. Absorbing ironic comedy-drama, with a fine performance from Harrison. (Dir: Frank Launder, 108 mins.)

Notorious Landlady, The (1962)*** Kim Novak, Jack Lemmon, Fred Astaire. Young American in London rents an apartment from a beautiful but mysterious girl whom the police suspect of having murdered her husband, and promptly gets involved. Generally entertaining comedy, thanks to Lemmon. (Dir: Richard Quine, 123 mins.)

Notorious Lone Wolf, The (1946)** Gerald Mohr, Janis Carter. The Lone Wolf and his butler must clean up a museum theft in this standard mystery set at the end of WWII. (Dir: Ross Lederman, 64 mins.)

Notorious Sophie Lang (1934)**½ Gertrude Michael, Paul Cavanagh, Arthur

Hoyt, Alison Skipworth. Taut thriller of a girl who gets involved with gangsters and who aids the police in an undercover operation; offbeat and clever. (Dir: Ralph Murphy, 64 mins.)

Not Quite Human (MCTV 1987)*½ Alan Thicke, Jay Underwood, Robyn Lively, Joseph Bologna. A teenage android is brought to life and sent to high school by a kind scientist in this instantly forgettable comedy adventure. (Dir: Steven Stern, 104 mins.)

Not Quite Paradise (1986)*½ Joanna Pacula, Sam Robards, Ewan Stewart, Selina Cadell. A straightlaced American Jewish boy goes overboard for kibbutz life when he falls for a native Israeli. Not quite viewable. (Dir: Lewis Gilbert, 105 mins.)†

Not Reconciled (West Germany, 1965)**½ Martha Stander, Heinrich Hargesheimer, Carlheinz Hargesheimer, Daniele Huillet Straub, Henning Harmssen, Ulrich Hopmann. Epic Heinrich Böll novel about three generations of Germans all affected by the rise of Nazism. Its theme is that Nazism was not an aberration but an ongoing undercurrent of German culture. (Dir: Jean-Marie Straub, 53 mins.)

No Trees in the Street (Great Britain, 1959)**½ Stanley Holloway, Sylvia Syms, Herbert Lom, Ronald Howard. Director J. Lee Thompson makes a good attempt at showing the slum living conditions of pre-war London and the various personalities caught in them. (99 mins.)

Not With My Wife, You Don't (1966)**½ Tony Curtis, Virna Lisi, George C. Scott, Carroll O'Connor. Occasionally diverting marital comedy featuring Tony Curtis as a jealous husband-Air Force officer, and Virna Lisi, as his beautiful Italian wife. (Dir: Norman Panama, 118 mins.)

Not Without My Daughter (1991)** Sally Field, Alfred Molina, Sheila Rosenthal, Roshan Seth. Partially true story of an American woman married to an Iranian-born doctor who takes her and their daughter to his homeland, embraces Islam, and tells his wife that she can leave, but the child must stay. Tense drama is given jingoistic treatment that undercuts its potency. The Iranians are crude caricatures of human beings and the film ends up being another prison escape picture. (Dir: Brian Gilbert, 117 mins.)†

Novel Affair, A (Great Britain, 1957)*** Margaret Leighton, Ralph Richardson, Rossano Brazzi. Witty, sophisticated comedy about a respectably married authoress of a sexy novel and her over-amorous chauffeur. (Dir: Muriel Box, 83 mins.)

Now and Forever (1934)**½ Gary Cooper, Carole Lombard, Shirley Temple.

Thief Gary sees the light thanks to adorable Shirley. Not a bad film. (Dir: Henry Hathaway, 82 mins.)

Now and Forever (Australia, 1983)*½ Cheryl Ladd, Robert Coleby, Carmen Duncan. Ladd suffers nobly as an impeccably dressed heroine whose hubby is falsely accused of rape. (Dir: Adrian Carr, 93 mins.)†

No Way Out (1950)***½ Richard Widmark, Linda Darnell, Sidney Poitier (feature debut). Biting drama about a Negro-hating, cop-hating hoodlum who incites a big race riot and almost ruins a Negro intern's chances of becoming a doctor. Director Joseph L. Mankiewicz gets top performances from his cast. (106 mins.)

No Way Out (1987)**½ Kevin Costner, Gene Hackman, Sean Young, Will Patton. Sporadically effective thriller about a naval officer investigating a murder he knows his boss committed, although he himself becomes the chief suspect. Inspired by *The Big Clock*. (Dir: Roger Donaldson, 114 mins.)†

No Way to Treat a Lady (1968)*** Rod Steiger, Lee Remick, George Segal. A black comedy suspense yarn which affords Rod Steiger a tour-de-force as a psychotic killer who uses ingenious disguises to trick his victims. George Segal does very well as a harassed police detective who gets brief phone calls from the killer and builds a strange alliance as a result. (Dir: Jack Smight, 108 mins.)

Nowhere to Go (Great Britain, 1958)**½ George Nader, Bernard Lee, Maggie Smith, Bessie Love, Geoffrey Keen, Andree Melly. Intelligent but contrived suspense story about a very unlucky criminal. (Dir: Seth Holt, 87 mins.)

Nowhere to Hide (MTV 1977)** Lee Van Cleef, Tony Musante, Edward Anhalt. Some suspense in this Edward Anhalt yarn about the problems of protecting a witness, a former hit man, against a syndicate boss who assures the law he will get the witness before the trial. (Dir: Jack Starrett, 79 mins.)†

Nowhere to Hide (1987)* Amy Madigan, Daniel Hugh Kelly, Robin MacEachern, Michael Ironside. Talented Ms. Madigan deserves better than this inane action film about a Marine widow pursued by baddies who are after a faulty helicopter part (got that?) her son is hiding in his toy. (Dir: Mario Azzopardi, 90 mins.)†

Nowhere to Run (MTV 1978)**½ David Janssen, Stefanie Powers. Janssen brings his world-weary presence to a Las Vegas gambling tale. He's worked out a nifty blackjack system with a special goal in mind—to be freed of his unfaithful wife (Powers). (Dir: Richard Lang, 104 mins.)

Now Voyager (1942)**** Bette Davis, Claude Rains, Paul Henreid, Gladys Cooper, Bonita Granville. Davis is superb as the over-protected Charlotte, who bravely sails forth on a therapeutic cruise, meets a married continental charmer, consummates a never-to-be rekindled night of passion and later plays surrogate mother to his troubled child. Beautifully scored by Max Steiner. (Dir: Irving Rapper, 117 mins.)†

Now You See Him, Now You Don't (1972)** Kurt Russell, Joe Flynn, Jim Backus, Cesar Romero, William Windom. Sequel to the 1970 *The Computer Wore Tennis Shoes*. A Disney entry (using the old gimmick of invisibility) that's strictly for the kids. The stars all participate in a bit of hectic activity to save a nearly bankrupt college. (Dir: Robert Butler, 88 mins.)†

Now You See It, Now You Don't (MTV 1968)*½ Jonathan Winters, Luciana Paluzzi. Inept comedy about a proposed theft of a Rembrandt which is thwarted by an art expert insurance man who performs above the call of duty. (Dir: Don Weis, 100 mins.)

Nude Bomb, The (1980)** Don Adams, Sylvia Kristel, Vittorio Gassman, Rhonda Fleming. Generally disappointing comeback for Adams as Maxwell Smart, Agent 86, from the old "Get Smart" TV series. AKA: **The Return of Maxwell Smart.** (Dir: Clive Donner, 94 mins.)†

Nude Restaurant (1967)*** Viva, Taylor Mead, Louis Waldron, Julian Burroughs. Story about a woman, who, when she isn't having sex with every man she wants, rants (while nearly nude) about the condition of women in America. (Dir: Andy Warhol, 100 mins.)

Nudity Required (1988)* Julie Newmar, Troy Donahue, Brad Zutaut, Billy Frank, Edy Williams. Silly comedy with loads of gratuitous nudity (including Ms. Newmar). Two pals pretend they are Hollywood producers so they can pick up girls. Nothing funny here. (Dir: John Bowen, 87 mins.)†

Nudo di Donna (Italy, 1982)*** Nino Manfredi, Eleonora Giorgi, Jean-Pierre Cassel. Frequently droll comedy. Bored with his sexy wife, a Venetian bookseller wanders into the palazzo of a fashion photographer and sees a life-sized nude portrait of a woman who looks like his spouse (but supposedly isn't), his curiosity is aroused and he begins hot pursuit! (Dir: Nino Manfredi, 112 mins.)

Nuit et Brouillard—See: **Night and Fog**

Number One (1969)* Charlton Heston, Jessica Walter, Diana Muldaur, Al Hirt. "Number One" delivers zero! A pretentious screenplay about the insecurity of an aging forty-year-old quarterback. (Dir: Tom Gries, 105 mins.)

Number 17 (Great Britain, 1932)***½ John Stuart, Anne Casson, Donald Calthrop. Directed by the master, Alfred Hitchcock, before he started to work on bigger-budgeted films like *The 39 Steps*. A classy entry throughout, with—of course—a splendid chase finale sequence. (83 mins.)†

Numéro Deux (France, 1975)*** Pierre Oudry, Alexandre Rignault, Sandrine Battistella, Rachel Stefanopol. Simple story, with a difference, about weary husband, unable to perform sexually, his tense wife, their kids, and their in-laws, who go about their daily lives. Difference is that the director is Jean-Luc Godard; as usual he's ahead of the pack. (90 mins.)

Nun, The (France, 1965)**** Anna Karina, Liselotte Pulver, Micheline Presle. Masterful, subdued, intensely dramatic adaptation of French author Diderot's *La Religieuse*. Set in a convent, it chronicles the anguish of a young and beautiful sister (Miss Karina) who refuses to take her vows, or Christ, quite seriously enough. First-rate direction from Jacques Rivette, who also co-authored the screenplay. AKA: **La Religieuse**. (140 mins.)

Nuns on the Run (Great Britain, 1990)*** Eric Idle, Robbie Coltrane, Camille Coduri, Janet Suzman, Doris Hare, Lila Kaye. If *Some Like It Hot* were remade with the "Carry On" cast, it would probably look like this broad farce about two inept crooks forced to hide out in a nunnery. The slim premise offers a suprising amount of good-natured laughs, with Idle and Coltrane endearing as our habit-ed heros, and Coduri as Idle's sweet, nearsighted girlfriend. Supremely lively music by the German band Yello. (Dir: Jonathan Lynn, 90 mins.)†

Nun's Story, The (1959)**** Audrey Hepburn, Peter Finch, Edith Evans, Peggy Ashcroft, Dean Jagger, Colleen Dewhurst. The best-selling novel is brought to the screen with taste and skill by a talented cast headed by Audrey Hepburn. The story follows a young girl through her early convent days, her taking of the vows and her work in Africa. Peter Finch gives a fine account of himself as a non-religious doctor working in the Congo. (Dir: Fred Zinnemann, 149 mins.)†

Nunzio (1978)*** David Proval, James Andronica, Tovah Feldshuh, Morgana King, Vincent Russo. Very appealing and moving story of a young retarded man and his struggles with life and love in Brooklyn. (Dir: Paul Williams, 87 mins.)

Nurse (MTV 1980)**½ Michael Learned, Robert Reed, Tom Aldredge. Medical drama adapted from Peggy Anderson's best-seller. Learned winningly portrays a doctor's widow who resumes her nursing career, running things in a New York City hospital. (Dir: David Lowell Rich, 98 mins.)†

Nurse Edith Cavell (1939)**½ Anna Neagle, George Sanders. Story of the brave nurse who served the allies so gallantly during WWI. Impressive drama, well acted. (Dir: Herbert Wilcox, 98 mins.)†

Nutcracker—See: **Nutcracker Sweet**

Nutcracker, The (1986)**½ The Pacific Northwest Ballet Company. An ambitious, not wholly successful attempt to create an original dance film out of both the famous Tchaikovsky ballet and the original source material, a fairy tale called "The Nutcracker and the Monkey King." (Dir: Carroll Ballard, 85 mins.)†

Nutcracker Prince, The (U.S.-Canada, 1990)** Voices of Keifer Sutherland, Megan Follows, Peter O'Toole, Phyllis Diller, Mike MacDonald. Disappointing animated feature might please youngsters in another rendition of the famed children's classic. A little girl is magically shrunk into a land where her toys and nutcrackers come to life. (Dir: Paul Schibli, 73 mins.)†

Nutcracker Sweet (Great Britain, 1982)* Joan Collins, Finola Hughes, William Franklyn, Paul Nicholas, Carol White. In this ludicrous drama of the dance, Collins plays a social butterfly who rules a ballet company with an iron hand. Call this "Turning Pointless." AKA: **Nutcracker**. (Dir: Anwar Kawadri, 101 mins.)†

Nuts (1987)*** Barbra Streisand, Richard Dreyfuss, Maureen Stapleton, Karl Malden, Eli Wallach, Robert Webber, James Whitmore. A high-class hooker is charged with manslaughter. The solid performances given by the seasoned supporting cast lend extra weight to this dramatically confined exploration of the hooker's supposed "insanity." *Nuts* successfully transcends the potentially stagy aspect of its material through a skillful use of flashbacks and close-ups. (Dir: Martin Ritt, 116 mins.)†

Nutty, Naughty Chateau (France-Italy, 1963)**½ Monica Vitti, Curt Jurgens, Jean-Claude Brialy, Jean-Louis Trintignant. Excellent cast of stars in a slight comedy concerning a young man who takes refuge in a strange chateau where everyone is dressed in seventeenth century garb. Based on a Françoise Sagan play. (Dir: Roger Vadim, 102 mins.)

Nutty Professor, The (1963)*** Jerry Lewis, Stella Stevens, Del Moore, Kathleen Freeman, Howard Morris. Perhaps Lewis's finest film. Employing a twist on the Jekyll-Hyde tale, Jerry plays a goofy college professor who turns into a campus swinger with the aid of a concoction he devised in his lab. (Dir: Jerry Lewis, 107 mins.)†

Objective Burma (1945)***½ Errol Flynn, William Prince. Another superb war movie. This one is about paratroopers dropped in Burma with their objective being a Japanese radar station. It's exciting entertainment. (Dir: Raoul Walsh, 142 mins.)

Object of Beauty, The (1991)*** John Malkovich, Andie MacDowall, Lolita Davidovich, Rudi Davies, Joss Ackland. Quirky, enjoyable little comedy of manners about a flat-broke yuppie couple who reluctantly decide to sell their one valuable possession, a small sculpture by Henry Moore, only to find it has been stolen. Their experience with complete desperation eventually teaches them to love and trust each other. Excellent performances all around, especially from Malkovich who gives a daring and dazzling "romantic" performance. (Dir: Michael Lindsay-Hogg, 101 mins.)†

Obliging Young Lady (1941)***½ Joan Carroll, Edmond O'Brien, Ruth Warrick, Eve Arden. Young girl involved in a court fight is sent to a mountain resort where complications arise over her parentage. Delightful comedy, many laughs. (Dir: Richard Wallace, 80 mins.)

Oblomov (U.S.S.R., 1981)*** Oleg Tabakov, Yuri Bogatryev, Elena Soloyei, Andrei Popov. This film version of the celebrated Russian novel of 1859 about a man who would like to spend his life sleeping is filled with ironic observations, and sharply etched characters. (Dir: Nikita Mikhalkov, 146 mins.)

Oblong Box, The (U.S.-Great Britain, 1969)** Vincent Price, Christopher Lee. Price is a nineteenth century Englishman who does his brother dirt, and lives to regret it. All the expected touches, including coffins, not-dead corpses, mutilations, etc., are present for fans of this genre. (Dir: Gordon Hessler, 91 mins.)†

Obsessed (Canada, 1988)*** Kerrie Keane, Daniel Pilon, Saul Rubinek, Alan Thicke, Colleen Dewhurst. Realistic treatment of a woman's consuming desire for vengeance as she searches for the driver who killed her son. (Dir: Robin Spry, 103 mins.)†

Obsessed with a Married Woman (MTV 1985)** Jane Seymour, Tim Matheson. Beautiful Seymour is married, successful, and open to an affair. Matheson is a writer assigned by Seymour to do an in-depth piece on mistresses. Glossy nonsense. (Dir: Richard Lang, 104 mins.)

Obsession (1976)*½ Geneviève Bujold, Cliff Robertson, John Lithgow. A rich businessman (Robertson) suffers from guilt because his wife was killed during a kidnapping scheme. Fifteen years later he discovers her double, and the past is dredged up disastrously. (Dir: Brian De-Palma, 98 mins.)†

Obsessive Love (MTV 1984)**½ Yvette

Mimieux, Simon MacCorkindale. Mimieux is a mentally troubled typist transformed into a sleek Hollywood beauty to woo her soap opera hero (MacCorkindale). (Dir: Steven H. Stern, 104 mins.)

O. C. and Stiggs (1984)*½ Daniel H. Jenkins, Neill Barry, Paul Dooley, Tina Louise, Martin Mull, Jane Curtin, Ray Walston, Louis Nye, King Sunny Adé, Dennis Hopper. One of director Robert Altman's worst, a feeble comedy about two smug teens who torment their neighbor, a materialistic businessman. (109 mins.)†

Ocean's Eleven (1960)**½ Frank Sinatra, Dean Martin, Sammy Davis, Jr., Joey Bishop, Peter Lawford, Angie Dickinson. Ill-assorted group decides to pull a daring Las Vegas robbery, and it nearly comes off. (Dir: Lewis Milestone, 127 mins.)†

Oceans of Fire (MTV 1986)** Gregory Harrison, Billy Dee Williams, Lyle Alzado, Ken Norton, David Carradine, Ray "Boom Boom" Mancini, Cynthia Sikes. The action-filled world of offshore oil rigs and the men who risk their lives to bring in a gusher. (Dir: Steven Carver, 104 mins.)

Octagon, The (1980)** Chuck Norris, Karen Carlson, Lee Van Cleef, Art Hindle, Jack Carter. Norris is hired to protect a lady from fierce ninja warriors. Superb footwork from Mr. Kung fu, and enough body-slamming violence for action fans. (Dir: Eric Karson, 103 mins.)†

Octaman (1971)½ Kerwin Mathews, Pier Angeli, Jeff Morrow, Jerry Guardino, Norman Fields. Laughable sci-fi thriller. Directed by the writer of *Creature from the Black Lagoon*, of which this is a complete rip-off. (Dir: Harry Essex, 83 mins.)†

October—See: **Ten Days That Shook the World**

October Man, The (Great Britain, 1947)*** John Mills, Joan Greenwood. Man suffering from a head injury is suspected of murdering a model, proves his innocence. Good mystery has plenty of suspense. (Dir: Roy Baker, 86 mins.)

Octopussy (1983)*** Roger Moore, Louis Jourdan, Maud Adams. James Bond foils a subversive communist plot to launch a nuclear strike against the American military in West Germany. Witty dialogue, cleverly staged action sequences, and cartoon gadgetry make a fast-moving and spirited "popcorn" movie. (Dir: John Glen, 122 mins.)†

Odd Angry Shot, The (Australia, 1979)*** Graham Kennedy, John Hargreaves, Bryan Brown. An elite group of Australian soldiers sent to help out in Vietnam find that a real war is nothing like the athletic competition they'd been anticipating. Well-made war film from a different perspective. (Dir: Tom Jeffrey, 90 mins.)†

Odd Balls (Canada, 1984)*½ Foster Brooks, Mike MacDonald, Konnie Krome, Milan Cheylon. A personable turn by Brooks, who for once isn't doing his patented drunk routine, is the only saving grace of this umpteenth imitation of *Meatballs*. (Dir: Miklos Lente, 92 mins.)†

Odd Couple, The (1968)***½ Jack Lemmon, Walter Matthau, Herb Edelman, Carole Shelley. Neil Simon's hit play about two grumpy ex-marrieds (Lemmon and Matthau) who take up housekeeping together in New York. It's one of the few times in Hollywood history where the film version has improved on the Broadway original, and much of the credit for this happy state of affairs goes to director Gene Saks, even though he does have a nearly foolproof screenplay and cast to work with. Later a TV series. (105 mins.)†

Odd Job, The (Great Britain, 1978)** Graham Chapman, David Jason, Diana Quick, Bill Paterson, Michael Elphick. Comedy with Monty Python's Chapman as a depressed insurance salesman who hires a hit man to kill him, then changes his mind. Chapman wrote this as a vehicle for himself and pal Keith Moon, but he lost interest when Moon couldn't be used. The lack of interest is contagious. (Dir: Peter Medak, 86 mins.)†

Odd Jobs (1984)* Paul Reiser, Robert Townsend, Scott McGinnis, Paul Provenza. Sloppy, forced slapstick about how four college buddies spend their summer vacation, gainlessly employed for the most part. (Dir: Mark Story, 88 mins.)†

Odd Man Out (Great Britain, 1947)**** James Mason, Kathleen Ryan, Robert Newton. Gripping story of the last hours of a wounded fugitive from a holdup during the Irish rebellion. Remade as *The Lost Man*. (Dir: Carol Reed, 113 mins.)†

Odd Obsession (Japan, 1959)*** Ganjiro Nakamura, Machiko Kyo, Tatsuya Nakadai, Junko Kano. An aging man, obsessed with the loss of his sexual potency, instigates an affair between his young wife and his daughter's fiancé in the hope that jealousy will restore his sex drive. A perverse, bleak black comedy, masterfully directed by Kon Ichikawa. (96 mins.)†

Odds Against Tomorrow (1959)***½ Harry Belafonte, Robert Ryan, Shelley Winters, Ed Begley, Gloria Grahame. A brilliant, somber caper film that concentrates on its characters rather than the "job." Ryan is a bigoted crook who accepts a shot at a big score, then balks when he finds that his proposed partner

is black—classy jazzman Belafonte, who's in debt up to his ears. The subdued intensity with which director Robert Wise explores these characters and their surroundings helps to make their problems (including the central one of race) seem more vivid, while also offering the sterling cast a number of chances to shine. (96 mins.)

Odessa File, The (Great Britain-West Germany, 1974)**½ Jon Voight, Maximilian Schell, Mary Tamm, Maria Schell. Frederick Forsyth's novel about an earnest German journalist who stumbles upon the whereabouts of a Nazi war criminal and risks his life to get him, is only moderately successful in transition to the screen. Voight's wonderful performance and the excellent confrontation scene between him and Maximilian Schell's evil SS officer, compensate for several lesser scenes. (Dir: Ronald Neame, 128 mins.)†

Ode to Billy Joe (1976)*½ Robby Benson, Glynnis O'Connor. You get to find out why Billy Joe jumped off the Tallahatchee Bridge in this adolescent romance about youngsters coming of age in the South. This trend of turning pop song hits into films should be discouraged at all costs. (Dir: Max Baer, 100 mins.)†

Odette (Great Britain, 1950)***½ Anna Neagle, Trevor Howard. The true story of an heroic Frenchwoman who worked underground for the duration of the war fighting the Nazis. Excellent drama, all the more inspiring because it actually happened. (Dir: Herbert Wilcox, 106 mins.)

Odongo (Great Britain, 1956)** Rhonda Fleming, Macdonald Carey. Passion, if little else, is set loose in the jungles of Africa when a Kenya white hunter and a woman doctor find themselves on the same safari. (Dir: John Gilling, 85 mins.)

Oedipus Rex (Italy, 1967)***½ Franco Citti, Julian Beck, Silvano Mangano, Carmelo Bene, Pier Paolo Pasolini, Alida Valli. Masterful retelling of Sophocles play about Oedipus unwittingly killing his father and marrying his mother despite warning. Using beautiful desertscapes and Moorish architecture as backdrops, actor-director Pasolini (he plays the High Priest) frames drama around opening and closing scenes set in the present. Grand mix of music includes Roman songs, ancient Japanese melodies, Mozart, and works by Pasolini himself. Filmed in Morocco. (110 mins.)†

Oedipus the King (Great Britain, 1967)*** Christopher Plummer, Orson Welles, Lilli Palmer, Richard Johnson, Donald Sutherland. If you approach this all-star version of the classic play in terms of a stimulating history-drama class, you'll find it well worth your time. (Dir: Philip Saville, 97 mins.)

Off Beat (1986)** Judge Reinhold, Meg Tilly, Cleavant Derricks, Joe Mantegna. A likeable but inconsequential romantic comedy about mistaken identity. Posing as a policeman, our hero falls for a lady cop who has vowed never to wed one of the boys in blue. (Dir: Michael Dinner, 92 mins.)†

Offence, The (Great Britain, 1973)*** Sean Connery, Trevor Howard, Vivien Merchant, Ian Bannen. Connery is extremely moving as a cop who kills a child molester during an interrogation, because the criminal has forced the detective to face himself. (Dir: Sidney Lumet, 118 mins.)

Officer and a Gentleman, An (1982)*** Richard Gere, Debra Winger, Louis Gossett, Jr., David Keith, Robert Loggia, Lisa Blount, Lisa Eilbacher. The story of a rootless young man who survives the rigors of an officer's training program to become a better human being. Old-fashioned type of film, but with more modern attitudes expressed through gritty language, and the characters' sexual freedom. Charismatic performances by the entire cast. (Dir: Taylor Hackford, 126 mins.)†

Officer and the Lady, The (1941)**½ Bruce Bennett, Rochelle Hudson, Roger Pryor. Cop exposes two crooks who have pulled a robbery, even though his girl may be implicated. Fast moving crime melodrama. (Dir: Sam White, 60 mins.)

Official Story, The (Argentina, 1985)**** Hector Alterio, Norma Aleandro, Chela Ruiz. This story deals with one sheltered woman's growing realization that the child her husband adopted is the orphan of a couple slain by the military, a power structure that her husand had cooperated with in his quest for success. The film's interpretation of her dawning political education and her incipient awareness of her spouse's callousness is devastating. (Dir: Luis Puenzo, 110 mins.)†

Off Limits (1953)**½ Bob Hope, Mickey Rooney, Marilyn Maxwell. A fight manager is drafted and manages to break all the regulations when he tries to develop a new fighter. Mildly amusing Hope comedy with Rooney lending capable support. (Dir: George Marshall, 89 mins.)

Off-Limits (1988)* Willem Dafoe, Gregory Hines, Fred Ward, Amanda Pays, Scott Glenn. Disappointing and obvious thriller. Dafoe and Hines star as a pair of hip plainclothes detectives who walk their beat in 1968 Saigon. Their race to find a vicious serial killer is loaded with pointlessly obscene dialogue, the requisite shoot-outs, and a skillfully avoided

affair between Dafoe and a cute French nun (Pays). (Dir: Christopher Crowe, 101 mins.)†

Off-Sides (MTV 1984)**½ Tony Randall, Eugene Roche. A group of hippies cook up a game between them and a small town police force, with surprising results. Fairly entertaining. AKA: **Pigs vs. Freaks.** (Dir: John Lowry, 104 mins.)

Offspring, The (1987)*½ Vincent Price, Clu Gulager, Terry Kiser, Harry Caesar, Cameron Mitchell. Price, as the historian of a small town called Oldfield, relates four tales of evil that occurred there in the past. He also gives this shocker its only touch of class; the stories themselves range from underdeveloped to downright disgusting. (Dir: Jeff Burr, 96 mins.)

Off the Minnesota Strip (MTV 1980)*** Mare Winningham, Michael Learned, Hal Holbrook. Newcomer Winningham is splendid as Michele, a confused teenager who runs away to New York and becomes a prostitute. She returns to her midwestern home to find her parents and school friends unable to provide the compassion and understanding she so desperately needs. (Dir: Lamont Johnson, 104 mins.)

Off the Wall (1983)*½ Paul Sorvino, Rosanna Arquette, Patrick Cassidy, Billy Hufsey, Monte Markham, Mickey Gilley, Gary Goodrow, Stu Gilliam, Lewis Arquette. Ms. Arquette isn't in this film much, and she's the only reason you could ever have for watching this lamebrained comedy about two goofballs who get thrown into a Southern jail on a bum rap. (Dir: Rick Friedberg, 85 mins.)†

Of Human Bondage (1934)*** Leslie Howard, Bette Davis, Frances Dee. Filmmakers tried three times to adapt Somerset Maugham's long novel about a sensitive doctor who falls blindly in love with a self-serving waitress. This first version, which treats only a small part of the book, is more worthy of attention than the others. Bette Davis's performance as the slatternly waitress Mildred helped usher in a new modernity to screen acting; despite a faltering Cockney accent, her portrayal is startingly fresh and vivid, and she summons up a scary, ravaged anger in her scenes of decline. (Dir: John Cromwell, 83 mins.)†

Of Human Bondage (1946)**½ Paul Henried, Eleanor Parker. Somerset Maugham's novel about a cripple with a brilliant mind who's destroyed by his love for a wench actually falls apart in this disappointing screen treatment. (Dir: Edmund Goulding, 105 mins.)

Of Human Bondage (Great Britain, 1964)** Kim Novak, Laurence Harvey. The classic Somerset Maugham novel remade with only flashes of power. Harvey gives a superficial performance, but Novak is surprisingly good. (Dir: Ken Hughes, 98 mins.)†

Of Human Hearts (1938)***½ Walter Huston, James Stewart, Beulah Bondi. You'll like this sensitive, dramatic tale of a backwoods family in Ohio. Story tells of a young physician who is sent for by Lincoln during the Civil War because he has neglected writing to his mother. (Dir: Clarence Brown, 103 mins.)

Of Life and Love (Italy, 1958)*** Anna Magnani. Several romantic plots, including Magnani as a famous screen actress. Skimpy tales but Magnani is customarily convincing. (Dirs: Giorgio Pastina, M. Soldati, Luchino Visconti, Aldo Fabrizi, 103 mins.)

Of Love and Desire (1963)½ Merle Oberon, Steve Cochran, Curt Jurgens. Oberon plays the embarrassing, unfulfilling role of a promiscuous Latin socialite drawn to Steve Cochran's macho good-guy. (Dir: Richard Rush, 97 mins.)

Of Mice and Men (1939)**** Burgess Meredith, Lon Chaney, Betty Field. Steinbeck's classic tale of a feebleminded soul and his protector, set on the migratory farms of the Salinas Valley. A film masterpiece! Excellent all around. (Dir: Lewis Milestone, 107 mins.)

Of Mice and Men (MTV 1981)**½ Robert Blake, Randy Quaid, Lew Ayres, Pat Hingle. Fine performances highlight this remake of the 1939 classic about a farmhand who befriends a simpleton. (Dir: Reza Badiyi, 125 mins.)†

Of Pure Blood (MTV 1986)*** Patrick McGoohan, Lee Remick, Richard Munch. Intricate mystery which gets a plus for its originality. Lee Remick portrays a successful businesswoman who travels to Germany to learn the truth about her son's tragic death, but she discovers a surprising link between her son's demise and a well-kept secret dating back to the Nazis. (Dir: Joseph Sargent, 104 mins.)†

Of Unknown Origin (1984)**½ Peter Weller, Jennifer Dale. If you've been looking for a horror film about a rampaging rodent terrorizing a household—this is it. (Dir: George Cosmatos, 102 mins.)†

Oh, Alfie! (Great Britain, 1975)*½ Alan Price, Jill Townsend, Joan Collins, Paul Copley, Sheila White, Rula Lenska. In-name-only sequel to *Alfie* pairs the relentless ladykiller with an equally amoral female counterpart. The songs by star Price (former singer for the Animals) aren't bad, but most everything else is. AKA: *Alfie, Darling*. (Dir: Ken Hughes, 99 mins.)†

O'Hara's Wife (MTV 1982)*½ Ed Asner, Mariette Hartley, Jodie Foster, Tom Bosley. Inane fantasy film about a widower whose dead wife returns as a ghost and acts as his loving advisor in family and business matters. (Dir: William Bartman, 87 mins.)†

O'Hara, United States Treasury (MTV 1971)** David Janssen, Lana Wood. Vintage Webb drama, with clipped speech and a no-nonsense air. Customs agent Janssen chases narcotics smugglers around the country. (Dir: Jack Webb, 99 mins.)

Oh! Calcutta! (1972)*½ Raina Barrett, Mark Dempsey, Samantha Harper, Patricia Hawkins, Bill Macy, Mitchell McGuire. Hard to believe that this series of sketches caused so much fuss in the late '60s: you'd think no one had ever seen a naked person before. Indifferently videotaped in live performance, this lacks any visual interest. What's left are some sub-par skits written by John Lennon, Jules Feiffer, Dan Greenburg, Robert Benton, Sam Shepard, and Kenneth Tynan, all of whom will thankfully be remembered for better things. (Dir: Gillaume Martin Aucion, 108 mins.)†

Oh Dad, Poor Dad, Mamma's Hung You in the Closet and I'm Feelin' So Sad (1967)* Rosalind Russell, Robert Morse, Jonathan Winters, Barbara Harris. Arthur Kopit's Broadway play was a fragile but funny satire that possessed a certain nightmarish quality—the ruinous cinema version ruins what quality the original had. A black comedy about a mother (R.R.) who scoots around with an emotionally smothered son and her late husband's corpse. Some parts directed by Alexander Mackendrick, which he'd no doubt be pleased to forget. (Dir: Richard Quine, 86 mins.)

O. Henry's Full House (1952)*** Charles Laughton, David Wayne, Marilyn Monroe, Anne Baxter, Jeanne Crain, Jean Peters, Gregory Ratoff, Farley Granger, Fred Allen, Oscar Levant, Richard Widmark, Dale Robertson. An all-star cast enacts a quintet of O. Henry's short stories, best of which is "The Last Leaf." (Dirs: Henry Hathaway, Howard Hawks, Henry King, Henry Koster, Jean Negulesco, 117 mins.)

Oh God (1977)**½ George Burns, Teri Garr, Paul Sorvino, John Denver. God's attempts to save the world from itself are amusing, but a little more irreverence and a lot less of Denver's platitudinizing would have made this first rate. (Dir: Carl Reiner, 110 mins.)†

Oh God! Book II (1980)** George Burns, David Birney, Suzanne Pleshette. George Burns is back to give God a bad name in this sequel. Unable to leave well enough alone, Burns returns to single out a nine-year-old to help him get a better image on earth. (Dir: Gilbert Cates, 94 mins.)†

Oh God, You Devil (1984)** George Burns, Ted Wass, Roxanne Hart, Robert Desiderio, Eugene Roche, Ron Silver. Middling star vehicle for Burns, scoring both as God and Satan. The mischievous devil switches a famous rock star with a struggling musician ready to sell his soul. (Dir: Paul Bogart, 96 mins.)†

Oh, Heavenly Dog! (1980)*½ Chevy Chase, Benji, Jane Seymour, Omar Sharif, Donnelly Rhodes, Robert Morley. Chevy is reincarnated as a dog in order to solve his own murder. (He should have been reincarnated as an appealing actor, but that would take us into the realm of wishful biography.) The result is unsatisfying for kids and grown-ups too. (Dir: Joe Camp, 103 mins.)†

Oh Men! Oh Women! (1957)*** David Niven, Tony Randall (debut), Ginger Rogers, Dan Dailey, Barbara Rush. Tony Randall steals the film in the role of a zany patient of psychoanalyst David Niven. As it turns out, they're both in love with the same woman, Barbara Rush. Based on the hit B'way play. Lots of laughs if you like gags about analysts. (Dir: Nunnally Johnson, 90 mins.)

Ohms (MTV 1980)** Ralph Waite, David Birney, Talia Balsam. Farmers are the good guys, the power company and its lawyers are the bad guys, in this acceptable tale about eminent domain. (Dir: Dick Lowry, 104 mins.)

Oh, What a Lovely War (Great Britain, 1969)***½ Laurence Olivier, Ralph Richardson, John Mills, Vanessa Redgrave, Maggie Smith, John Gielgud, Dirk Bogarde, Jack Hawkins, Michael Redgrave, Susannah York. Oh what a lovely film actor-producer-director Richard Attenborough has made from a series of inspired sketches about man's continuing folly. Using real songs popular in Britain before and during WWI, Attenborough has skillfully given a cohesive form and narrative to this material, and employed in the process just about every great name in the British theater. (139 mins.)

Oh, You Beautiful Doll (1949)** June Haver, S. Z. Sakall, Charlotte Greenwood. This Fox musical biopic of Fred Fisher is little more than skeletal entertainment. Some charm, from the turn-of-the-century tunes and Haver's presence. (93 mins.)

Oil for the Lamps of China (1935)*** Pat O'Brien, Josephine Hutchinson, Jean Muir, Lyle Talbot. Sterling melodrama about an American building a life for himself in China despite numerous setbacks. The exotic background lifts this out of the ordinary; the relationships depicted are surprisingly adult and the screenplay is devoid of oversimplification. (Dir: Mervyn LeRoy, 110 mins.)

770

Okefenokee (1960)* Peter Coe, Henry Brandon, Peggy Maley, Serena Sande. Ludicrous drama of Florida drug smugglers aided by Seminole Indians. When one of their women is raped, however, the Seminoles seek revenge. (Dir: Roul Haig, 78 mins.)

Okinawa (1952)** Pat O'Brien, Cameron Mitchell. Action-packed war drama about the heroic crew of the destroyer U.S.S. Blake and their part in the invasion of Okinawa (WWII). (Dir: George Brooks, 67 mins.)

Oklahoma! (1955)** Gordon MacRae, Shirley Jones, Rod Steiger, Gloria Grahame, Gene Nelson. Director Fred Zinnemann's literalism couldn't be more inappropriate for this sophisticated hokum that revolutionized the American theater. Nelson's dancing is good, though the inspiration of Agnes De Mille's choreography is dissipated onscreen. Still a great Rodgers and Hammerstein score. (145 mins.)†

Oklahoma City Dolls, The (MTV 1982)**½ Susan Blakely, Ronee Blakley. Predictable, well-acted drama stars Susan Blakely as a woman tired of working overtime at her company compensating for the absent men who are out playing football. Demanding equal rights, Blakely organizes an all-girl football team. (Dir: E. W. Swackhamer, 104 mins.)

Oklahoma Crude (1973)** George C. Scott, Faye Dunaway, John Mills. The plot concerns wildcatters who battle the greedy oil concerns trying to gobble them up. Scott and Dunaway dig into their earthy roles with gusto, but the script and direction are unexceptional. Result: No gusher. (Dir: Stanley Kramer, 108 mins.)

Oklahoma Kid, The (1939)*** James Cagney, Humphrey Bogart. Hard-hitting western with the acting, mainly Cagney as a cowboy avenging his dad's lynching, holding up a weak script. (Dir: Lloyd Bacon, 90 mins.)†

Oklahoman, The (1957)** Joel McCrea, Barbara Hale. A quiet western with McCrea as a widower who settles in a small town. (Dir: Francis D. Lyon, 73 mins.)†

Old Acquaintance (1943)*** Bette Davis, Miriam Hopkins, Gig Young. Davis writes serious fiction while Hopkins makes a mint with pulp romances. The girls vie for the same men, bitching it up in high style. Directed rather well by Vincent Sherman. Remade as *Rich and Famous*. (110 mins.)

Old Boyfriends (1979)*** Talia Shire, Keith Carradine, Richard Jordan, John Belushi. Methodical plotting and characterization infuse this screenplay by the brothers Schrader. There is everywhere evidence of intelligence and care; Shire plays a depressive psychologist who takes to the road to seek out and rectify her past. (Dir: Joan Tewkesbury, 103 mins.)†

Old Curiosity Shop—See: **Mr. Quilp**

Old Dark House, The (1932)***½ Charles Laughton, Raymond Massey, Boris Karloff, Melvyn Douglas, Ernest Thesiger, Gloria Stuart. Highly enjoyable gothic thriller about a group of travelers stranded in a lonely mountain home during a storm. A fantastic cast, impeccably directed by James Whale; literate, scary, funny, and above all, bizarre. (Dir: James Whale, 75 mins.)

Old Dark House, The (Great Britain, 1963)**½ Tom Poston, Robert Morley, Janette Scott. American salesman spends the night in a creepy mansion, where the heirs are bumped off one by one. Fairly effective thriller, with a welcome note of lightness. (Dir: William Castle, 86 mins.)

Old Dracula (Great Britain, 1976)* David Niven, Teresa Graves, Peter Bayliss. Senile farce. Niven plays an aged bloodsucker casually perusing *Playboy* for edible victims. What next? "On Golden Crypt"? (Dir: Clive Donner, 89 mins.)

Old Enough (1984)** Sarah Boyd, Rainbow Harvest, Susan Kingsley, Danny Aiello. A pleasant, innocuous film about two teenage girlfriends from opposite sides of the social scale. Unfortunately, some scenes appear forced, and the adult characters are stereotyped. (Dir: Marisa Silver, 91 mins.)†

Oldest Profession, The (France-West Germany-Italy, 1967)**½ Jeanne Moreau, Jean-Claude Brialy, Raquel Welch, Jacques Charrier, Anna Karina. The prostitute traced from prehistory to future times, in six chronological chapters. (Dirs: Franco Indovina, Mauro Bolognini, Philippe de Broca, Michael Pfleghar, Claude Autant-Lara, Jean-Luc Godard, 97 mins.)†

Old Fashioned Way, The (1934)***½ W. C. Fields, Judith Allen, Baby LeRoy. A "must" for students of comedy as are all of Fields' starring films. Here he's the head of an acting troupe that appropriately performs "The Drunkard." A one-man show. (Dir: William Beaudine, 74 mins.)

Old Gringo (1988)**½ Jane Fonda, Gregory Peck, Jimmy Smits, Pedro Armendariz, Jr., Jenny Gago. Torpid drama badly miscasts Fonda as a spinster who journeys to Mexico and gets caught up in Pancho Villa's revolutionary movement while discovering her own sexual yearnings. Film has moments of raw power and sheer beauty, but airy script by Aida Bornik and director Luis Puenzo (based on a Carlos Fuentes novel) lacks cohesion and historical accuracy. Peck,

as writer Ambrose Bierce, and Smits, as an officer in Villa's army, are both excellent. (119 mins.)†

Old Gun, The (France, 1976)*** Philippe Noiret, Romy Schneider. Expertly directed revenge melodrama about a doctor whose family is slaughtered by Nazis. Skillfully interweaving flashbacks of the family's idyllic past with the physician's inconsolable present state, the film offers a spellbinding character study of a man who can only purge himself of guilt and grief by systematically eliminating those who destroyed his wife and child. (Dir: Robert Enrico, 141 mins.)†

Old Hutch (1936)**½ Wallace Beery, Eric Linden, Cecilia Parker, Elizabeth Patterson. One of Beery's better vehicles, as a tramp who finds a large sum of money and can't decide what to do with it. (Dir: Walter Ruben, 80 mins.)

Old Ironsides (1926)*** Charles Farrell, Wallace Beery, Esther Ralston, George Bancroft, Johnnie Walker. Satisfying historical adventure has a youth (Farrell) shanghaied onto the famous naval vessel, and learning his craft on the way to fight the notorious Barbary pirates of the early 19th-century; nice, simple romance, combined with rousing action and humorous touches. A fine characterization by Beery. (Dir: James Cruze, 111 mins.)†

Old Los Angeles (1948)*** William Elliott, John Carroll, Catherine McLeod, Joseph Schildkraut, Andy Devine. Man finds that gold miners are being cheated and his brother was murdered, tries to find the guilty one. Good western, moves at a fast pace. (Dir: Joe Kane, 87 mins.)

Old Maid, The (1939)*** Bette Davis, Miriam Hopkins, Jane Bryan. Davis must give up her baby to be raised by her married sister (Hopkins) when her suitor is killed in the Civil War. The late Casey Robinson adapted Zoë Akins's adaptation for the stage of the Edith Wharton novel. What remains is soap opera, but still an awesomely effective tear machine. (Dir: Edmund Goulding, 100 mins.)†

Old Man and the Sea, The (1958)*** Spencer Tracy. Ernest Hemingway's story about a determined Cuban fisherman is not sure-fire screen material, however Tracy is excellent in the leading role. Fine camerawork (two of the cinematographers were James Wong Howe and Floyd Crosby) adds to the mood of the film. (Dir: John Sturges, 86 mins.)

Old Man and the Sea, The (MTV 1990)** Anthony Quinn, Gary Cole, Patricia Clarkson, Valentina Quinn, Francesco Quinn, Alexis Cruz. Fans of Ernest Hemingway will especially dislike this diluted adaptation of the short novel.

The simple story of a fisherman's battle with the sea has been inanely padded out with extra plots involving a Hemingway-type writer and other fatuous characters. (Dir: Jud Taylor, 96 mins.)

Old Man Rhythm (1935)**½ George Barbier, Buddy Rogers, Barbara Kent, Betty Grable, Eric Blore. Yet another version of the story that has a father going back to college to keep an eye on his ladies' man of a son; fluffy comedy, nothing special. (Dir: Edward Ludwig, 75 mins.)

Old Man Who Cried Wolf, The (MTV 1970)*** Edward G. Robinson, Martin Balsam, Diane Baker. Skillful performance by Edward G. Robinson as an old man who witnesses the murder of an old friend but can't convince anyone of it. (Dir: Walter Grauman, 73 mins.)

Old Yeller (1957)*** Dorothy McGuire, Fess Parker, Tommy Kirk, Kevin Corcoran, Chuck Connors. A Disney classic. The title character is a terrific mongrel dog, redeemed from his bad ways by the love of a Texas ranch family. McGuire and Parker head the adoptive family, and Kirk and Corcoran are the two kids who get into and out of innumerable scrapes with the help of the faithful "Old Yeller." (Dir: Robert Stevenson, 83 mins.)†

Oliver (Great Britain, 1968)**** Ron Moody, Mark Lester, Shani Wallis, Oliver Reed, Jack Wild, Hugh Griffith. This superlative musical directed by Carol Reed won five Academy Awards including those for Best Picture and Direction. With an assist from Charles Dickens and captivating songs by Lionel Bart, taken from his smash hit theatrical musical, Reed has given new life to the classic tale about the luckless orphan Oliver Twist. (153 mins.)†

Oliver and Company (1988)**½ Voices of Bette Midler, Billy Joel, Cheech Marin, Dom DeLuise, Richard Mulligan, Roscoe Lee Browne, Robert Loggia. Animated version of *Oliver Twist*, recast with animal heroes in modern-day Manhattan, is an all-round family pleaser in best Disney style, reminiscent of *101 Dalmatians*. (Dir: George Scribner, 72 mins.)

Oliver's Story (1978)*½ Ryan O'Neal, Candice Bergen, Nicola Pagett, Edward Binns, Ray Milland. O'Neal returns to little success in this sequel to *Love Story*. As the young widower pursues a Bonwit Teller heiress, the theme is money rather than love. (Dir: John Korty, 92 mins.)†

Oliver Twist (1922)*** Jackie Coogan, Lon Chaney, Gladys Brockwell, George Seigmann, Edouard Trebaol, Esther Ralston, Gertrude Claire. A commendable silent version of Charles Dickens'

classic novel, with a good performance by Coogan as the unfortunate orphan, and a striking one by Chaney as Fagin the pickpocket master. (Dir: Frank Lloyd, 77 mins.)†

Oliver Twist (1933)** Dickie Moore, Irving Pichel, Doris Lloyd, William "Stage" Boyd, Barbara Kent. Nonclassic version of a classic book in which a lot of Hollywood actors have a Dickens of a time with doing right by the book. (Dir: William Cowen, 77 mins.)†

Oliver Twist (Great Britain, 1948)**** Alec Guinness, John Howard Davies. The Dickens classic of an orphan boy and lower depths London, superbly done, reverently produced, fine performances. Guinness brings a touch of humor to his portrayal of mean old Fagin and his performance is a joy. (Dir: David Lean, 105 mins.)†

Oliver Twist (MTV 1982)***½ George C. Scott, Tim Curry, Michael Hordern, Richard Charles. An exceptional TV-ization of the story of the loveable urchin who falls in with pickpockets before being rescued by a wealthy benefactor. Benefits from Scott's brilliant performance as Fagin and an unfailing sense of period detail. (Dir: Clive Donner, 104 mins.)†

Olive Trees of Justice, The (France, 1962)*** Pierre Prothon, Jean Pelegri. An Algerian-born Frenchman returns to Algeria where his father lies dying, and comes to grips with the Arab-French hostilities. It's a moving, lyrical, incisive document about war and humanitarian concerns. (Dir: James Blue, 90 mins.)

Olivia (France, 1950)*** Edwige Feuillere, Simone Simon, Yvonne De Bray, Suzanne Dehelly, Lesly Meynard, Rita Roanda. An English girl attends a French boarding school in the 1880s. Initially enchanted by the fun and learning at the school, she soon discovers that students are divided into groups favoring one or the other of the owners, with sexual exploration through lesbianism creating dramatic tension. Directed with taste and conviction by Jacqueline Audry. (Dir: Jacqueline Audry, 96 mins.)

Ollie Hopnoodle's Haven of Bliss (MCTV 1988)*** Dorothy Lyman, James B. Sikking, Jerry O'Connell, Jean Shepherd. Another charming story from the pen of homespun humorist Jean Shepherd (*A Christmas Story*). This time around we view Shepherd's perennial surrogate Ralphie as he and his family go on a frantic summer vacation. (Dir: Dick Bartlett, 90 mins.)

Olly Olly Oxen Free (1978)**½ Katharine Hepburn, Kevin McKenzie, Dennis Dimster. Hepburn plays an eccentric lady who runs a junkyard and helps two small boys in their quest to launch a huge hot-air balloon. (Dir: Richard A. Colla, 89 mins.)

O Lucky Man! (Great Britain, 1973)**** Malcolm McDowell, Ralph Richardson, Rachel Roberts. Provocative, complicated epic drama, brilliantly directed by Lindsay (*If . . .*) Anderson with a superb cast. About a hustling young man making his way in the neo-fascist world of modern England, where individuals, institutions, businesses, and governments are murderous and corrupt. (180 mins.)†

Olympia (Olympische Spiele) (Germany, 1936)**** Talented Nazi director Leni Riefenstahl edited the 1936 Olympics in Munich to make a great film. She was inhibited by the propaganda requirements of the Third Reich and by the four gold medals won by American Negro Jesse Owens, so she opted for the grace and poetry of bodies in motion. A bit long, but lovely. (225 mins.)†

Olympic Visions—See: **Visions of Eight**

Omar Khayyam (1957)** Cornel Wilde, Debra Paget, Raymond Massey, Michael Rennie, John Derek. Adventurer and poet battles a gang of assassins who intend to take over Persia. Opulent production. (Dir: William Dieterle, 101 mins.)

Omega Man, The (1971)*½ Charlton Heston, Rosalind Cash, Anthony Zerbe. Tacky reworking of the novel, *I Am Legend;* Heston battles a group of robed zombies as he plays the lone human survivor of an atomic war. (Dir: Boris Sagal, 98 mins.)†

Omega Syndrome (1987)** Ken Wahl, George DiCenzo, Nicole Eggert, Doug McClure. Boozy journalist Wahl enlists the aid of scene-stealing buddy DiCenzo to help him free his daughter, held hostage by right-wing terrorists. If you must watch stuff like this, this one isn't as offensive as the average vigilante flick. (Dir: Joseph Manduke, 88 mins.)†

Omen, The (1976)*** Gregory Peck, Lee Remick, David Warner, Billie Whitelaw. The devil returns in the form of a five-year-old boy sired by the devil himself, and inadvertently adopted by a wealthy American couple. Earnest acting, especially by Whitelaw as a maid sent by the devil to care for the boy. Sequels: *Damien* and *The Final Conflict.* (Dir: Richard Donner, 110 mins.)†

On a Clear Day You Can See Forever (1970)*** Barbra Streisand, Yves Montand, Jack Nicholson. The combination of Streisand and a melodic score by Alan Jay Lerner and Burton Lane adds up to pleasant fare. Barbra's a young woman who discovers acute ESP powers which send her to psychiatrist Montand. He puts her under hypnosis and off she goes to reenact her past lives.

(Dir: Vincente Minnelli, 129 mins.)†

On an Island with You (1948)**½ Esther Williams, Peter Lawford, Jimmy Durante, Ricardo Montalban, Cyd Charisse. A lot of Esther in bathing suits is what this romance of a naval flyer and an actress offers. (Dir: Richard Thorpe, 107 mins.)

On Any Street—See: **La Notte Brava**

On Any Sunday (1971)**½ Interesting documentary about motorcycle racing from the creator of *Endless Summer.* Primarily for bike enthusiasts. (Dir: Bruce Brown, 91 mins.)†

On Approval (Great Britain, 1944)***½ Beatrice Lillie, Googie Withers, Clive Brook, Roland Culver. Droll deadpan farce, featuring a superbly arch quartet of players and a once-shocking "trial marriage." (Dir: Clive Brook, 80 mins.)†

Onassis: The Richest Man in the World—See: **Richest Man in the World: The Story of Aristotle Onassis**

On Borrowed Time (1939)***½ Lionel Barrymore, Cedric Hardwicke, Beulah Bondi. Warm, sentimental fantasy about an old man who isn't ready to die so he chases "Death" up a tree. Good adaptation of the stage success. (Dir: Harold S. Bucquet, 98 mins.)

Once Around (1991)***½ Richard Dreyfuss, Holly Hunter, Danny Aiello, Laura San Giacomo, Gena Rowlands, Roxanne Hart, Danton Stone. Often a very affecting comedy about an eccentric Boston Italian family whose eldest daughter (Hunter) marries an aggressive Lithuanian man (Dreyfuss) who seems too good to be true. But surprise—he really is rich, nice, and happy. The ensemble cast is wonderful in this feel-good movie about discovery, friendship, and acceptance. (Dir: Lasse Hallstrom, 115 mins.)†

Once a Thief (1950)**½ June Havoc, Cesar Romero, Marie McDonald, Lon Chaney, Jr., Iris Adrian. Low-budget melodrama of a shoplifter trying to reform but being drawn deeper into crime by a no-good guy; OK attempt to do something different. (Dir: W. Lee Wilder, 88 mins.)

Once a Thief (1965)*** Ann-Margret, Alain Delon, Jack Palance, Van Heflin. Absorbing crime yarn which benefits from Alain Delon's restrained performance as an ex-con who tries to go straight but has little luck. (Dir: Ralph Nelson, 107 mins.)

Once Before I Die (1966)*½ John Derek, Ursula Andress, Ron Ely, Richard Jaeckel. John Derek produced and directed this routine opus, taking place in the Philippines in WWII, on a shoestring and it shows. (97 mins.)

Once Bitten (1985)* Lauren Hutton, Jim Carrey, Karen Kopins, Cleavon Little. A cute title but a bloody bad movie about a seductive vamp of a vampire who's eager to neck with a virgin adolescent, quite a scarce commodity in the 1980s. (Dir: Howard Storm, 93 mins.)†

Once in a Lifetime (1933)*** Jack Oakie, Sidney Fox, Aline McMahon, ZaSu Pitts. The famous George S. Kaufman-Moss Hart play about the havoc wreaked by the coming of sound movies is given a lively if stage-bound rendition. (Dir: Russell Mack, 80 mins.)

Once in Paris... (1978)*** Wayne Rogers, Jack Lenoir, Gayle Hunnicutt. This bittersweet story of a transient affair is little more than a series of anecdotes, some charming, some dramatic. Rogers is a screenwriter called to Paris to doctor a script; under the tutelage of his shady chauffeur (Lenoir), he comes to a more European attitude about love and friendship. (Dir: Frank Gilroy, 100 mins.)†

Once Is Not Enough (1975)**½ Deborah Raffin, Kirk Douglas, Alexis Smith, David Janssen, Brenda Vaccaro, George Hamilton. Jacqueline Susann's highly readable novel about the beautiful people and their sexual exploits reaches the screen with many changes but sit back and enjoy the trashiness. (Dir: Guy Green, 121 mins.)†

Once More, My Darling (1949)**½ Robert Montgomery, Ann Blyth. Nicely played comedy about a young lady who sets her cap for a somewhat older film matinee idol who is recalled to active duty in the Army. (Dir: Robert Montgomery, 94 mins.)

Once More, with Feeling (1960)*** Yul Brynner, Kay Kendall. A bit of sophisticated fluff that relies on the charm of its two stars—and they are very winning. Brynner plays an egotistical symphony conductor who discovers he doesn't want his beautiful wife to divorce him after all. Kendall, as always in her regrettably short career, is a comedic joy. (Dir: Stanley Donen, 92 mins.)

Once Upon a Dead Man (MTV 1971)**½ Rock Hudson, Susan St. James, Jack Albertson, Rene Auberjonois, John Schuck. Pilot for "McMillan & Wife." You'll like Rock as the rich big-city police commissioner and Susan as his very loving wife. (Dir: Leonard Stern, 104 mins.)

Once Upon a Family (MTV 1980)***½ Barry Bostwick, Lee Chamberlain, Nancy Marchand, Elizabeth Wilson. TV's answer to *Kramer vs. Kramer.* Bostwick is excellent as a man who suddenly finds himself in the role of father-mother and chief dishwasher when his frustrated wife walks out to seek a life of her own. (Dir: Richard Michaels, 94 mins.)

Once Upon a Honeymoon (1942)**½ Ginger Rogers, Cary Grant, Walter Slezak. Director Leo McCarey's ambitious film is brilliantly conceived and erratically executed. Grant, an American radio correspondent covering the early years of
774

WWII, falls for Rogers, an ex-burlesque queen married to a top Nazi functionary (Slezak). (116 mins.)†

Once Upon a Horse (1958)** Dan Rowan, Dick Martin, Martha Hyer. Couple of dumb cowboys steal cattle and rob the bank of the beautiful owner of the town, but eventually wish they hadn't. (Dir: Hal Kanter, 85 mins.)

Once Upon a Scoundrel (1973)**½ Zero Mostel, Katy Jurado, Tito Vandis. Mostel's last film, released only after years of litigation, is a fable about the warming up of a Scrooge-like figure. Occasionally amusing comedy set in Mexico about a land baron who loves a young wench. (Dir: George Schaefer, 90 mins.)†

Once Upon a Spy (MTV 1980)** Eleanor Parker, Ted Danson, Christopher Lee. Predictable comedy-adventure pilot. Tall, handsome Danson plays a computer expert who becomes a reluctant spy when the villainous Lee manages to steal NASA's ultimate computer, which weighs in excess of 3000 tons. (Dir: Ivan Nagy, 104 mins.)

Once Upon a Starry Night (MTV 1978)** Dan Haggerty, Denver Pyle, Jack Kruschen, Ken Curtis. Haggerty's Grizzly Adams and his crazy old mountain man, Pyle's Mad Jack, are back with corn pone for the kids. A winter avalanche forces a pair of youngsters and their uncle to take shelter in Grizzly's cabin while Adams goes off to hunt for their parents. (Dir: Jack B. Hively, 78 mins.)

Once Upon a Texas Train (MTV 1988)** Willie Nelson, Richard Widmark, Shaun Cassidy, Chuck Connors, Jack Elam, Kevin McCarthy, Dub Taylor, Stuart Whitman, Angie Dickinson. Or "the over-the-hill gang" strikes again. Nelson is a grizzled old bandit; Widmark his old Texas Ranger arch rival. The plot, like the actors, needs geriatric care. (Dir: Burt Kennedy, 96 mins.)

Once Upon a Time (1944)**½ Cary Grant, Janet Blair, Ted Donaldson. Theatrical producer forms a "partnership" with a boy who has a dancing caterpillar. Mild comedy never quite hits the mark intended. (Dir: Alexander Hall, 89 mins.)

Once Upon a Time in America (1984)**** Robert De Niro, James Woods, Elizabeth McGovern, Treat Williams, Tuesday Weld, Burt Young, Joe Pesci, Danny Aiello, Bill Forsythe, Darlanne Fleugel, James Russo, Jennifer Connolly. Director Sergio Leone's last film, which he spent over a decade getting made, is a masterpiece, a hypnotic essay on the unshakable hold of memory and regret. De Niro and Woods, as friends who rise from poverty in New York's Jewish ghetto to criminal power in the thirties, are the central characters in a story that moves effortlessly between decades. Avoid the hacked-up 143 min. version that played U.S. theaters (and is available on video); the complete version is also on video. Network TV runs a middle version comprising elements of both; stick with the long one. (227 mins.)†

Once Upon a Time in the West (Italy-U.S., 1969)***½ Jason Robards, Jr., Henry Fonda, Claudia Cardinale, Charles Bronson. This iconoclastic western fable is spaghetti western wizard Sergio Leone's best film. The extremely complicated plot involves a mysterious man whom an evil gunslinger sends desperados to track down. Harmonica music, scenic vistas, and lots of shoot-'em-up scenes highlight this stylized homicide on the range. Written by (how's this for a team) Leone, Bernardo Bertolucci and Dario Argento! Shorn of 25 mins. for years, but recently restored to full length on home video.(165 mins.)†

Once You Kiss a Stranger (1969)** Carol Lynley, Paul Burke. Glossy but empty melodrama about the country-club set and their intrigues. Remake of *Strangers on a Train*. (Dir: Robert Sparr, 106 mins.)

On Company Business (1980)***½ Important epic documentary history of the U.S. Central Intelligence Agency includes rare footage, incredible interviews with agents and victims, and a straightforward overview of the power and politics of the CIA and its role in America and the world. The viewer never feels the film's length. (Dir: Allan Francovich, 180 mins.)

On Dangerous Ground (1951)*** Robert Ryan, Ida Lupino, Ward Bond, Ed Begley. Unusual psychological drama directed by Nicholas Ray, delineating the moral profile of a burnt-out cop (Ryan), who hates humanity because of what he's seen on the street. The resolution (involving a hackneyed city-country opposition and a redemptive blind girl played by Lupino) is disappointing. (82 mins.)†

On Dress Parade (1939)** The Dead End Kids. The Kids are cleaned up for a plot that revolves around Slip's getting his act together at military school. (Dirs: William Clemens, Noel Smith [uncredited], 62 mins.)

One and Only, The (1978)** Henry Winkler, Kim Darby, Hervé Villechaize. Winkler tries to breathe life into this heavy-handed comedy about the actor who turned into Gorgeous George, the wrestler. (Dir: Carl Reiner, 98 mins.)†

One and Only, Genuine, Original Family Band, The (1968)**½ Walter Brennan, Janet Blair, Lesley Ann Warren, John Davidson. Nostalgia, homespun humor and a hummable score make this Disney family musical a treat. The Bowers are a family band that may be harmonious when performing, but their politics strike a discordant note. (Dir: Michael O'Herlihy, 110 mins.)†

One Body Too Many (1944)** Bela Lugosi, Jack Haley, Jean Parker, Blanche Yurka, Lyle Talbot, Douglas Fowley. Haley arrives to sell insurance, but the prospective client has already expired; Jack has to crack a mystery case when the corpse starts disappearing. (Dir: Frank McDonald, 75 mins.)†

One Cooks, the Other Doesn't (MTV 1983)** Joe Bologna, Suzanne Pleshette, Rosanna Arquette. Bologna works his quizzical look overtime as a man sharing living quarters with a young bride, an ex-wife, and his teenage son for economic reasons. Agreeable comedy. (Dir: Richard Michaels, 104 mins.)†

One Crazy Summer (1986)* John Cusack, Demi Moore, Bobcat Goldthwait, Joel Murray, Curtis Armstrong. Lame writing and limp direction are the hallmarks of this lunatic comedy about two teens rescuing an adolescent damsel in distress from land developers who want to seize her family's property. (Dir: Savage Steve Holland, 95 mins.)†

One Cup of Coffee (1991)*** William Russ, Glenn Plummer, Noble Willingham. Yet another take on the minor league baseball story in this remarkably effective tale of a white over-the-hill pitcher who teaches a black rookie everything he knows. Film goes for sentiment (amidst the reality of broken team buses and sparse fan turnouts) and succeeds. (Dir: Robin A. Armstrong, 98 mins.)

One Dangerous Night (1943)*½ Warren William, Marguerite Chapman. Weak Lone Wolf entry involving a blackmailing thug who gets bumped off. (Dir: Michael Gordon, 77 mins.)

One Dark Night (1982)*½ Robin Evans, Melissa Newman, Meg Tilly, Adam West. Nifty (but poorly executed) premise involves a man with the gift of robbing teenage girls of their bioenergy. (Dir: Thomas McLoughlin, 89 mins.)†

One Day in the Life of Ivan Denisovich (Great Britain-Norway-U.S., 1971)**** Tom Courtenay, Alfred Burke. A remarkably moving, heartbreaking account, in straightforward cinematic fashion, of the indignities and horrors of the Russian prison labor camps. The time is 1950, the setting the Siberian wilderness. Ivan (Courtenay) is in the eighth year of a ten-year sentence. Based on the much-celebrated Alexander Solzhenitsyn's novel. (Dir: Casper Wrede, 100 mins.)†

One Deadly Summer (France, 1984)*** Isabelle Adjani, Suzanne Flon, Alain Suchon. Set in a small French village, this psychological drama about a dis-

775

turbed woman's search for three men (her father included) who beat up and raped her mother years ago, is told from multiple viewpoints. Adjani gives a sublimely steamy performance. (Dir: Jean Becker, 130 mins.)†

One Desire (1955)**½ Rock Hudson, Anne Baxter, Natalie Wood. A costume soap opera about a gal from the wrong side of the tracks who tries to cross over into the local social register. (Dir: Jerry Hopper, 94 mins.)

One-Eyed Jacks (1961)***½ Marlon Brando, Karl Malden, Katy Jurado. Outlaw out of prison goes hunting for the friend who betrayed him. Eccentric, majestic western close to the vest of Brando's temperament, so good one wishes he would direct again. (Stanley Kubrick began as director, only to be fired by the producer-star.) (Dir: Marlon Brando, 141 mins.)†

One Fine Day (Italy, 1969)***½ Brunetto Del Vita, Vitaliano Damioli, Lidia Fuortes, Maria Crosignani. Advertising executive runs down a laborer on the day he is offered the directorship of the company. On trial for reckless driving, he reexamines his life. A beautiful, humanistic look at people caught up in tragic and complex situations. (105 mins.)

One Flew Over the Cuckoo's Nest (1975)**** Jack Nicholson, Louise Fletcher, Brad Dourif, William Redfield, Will Sampson. A stunning adaptation of Ken Kesey's novel that deservedly won Academy Awards for Best Actor (Nicholson), Best Picture, Best Director (Forman), and Best Actress (Fletcher). Nicholson is really breathtaking: there's not a false note in his remarkable portrait. Fletcher, playing Nurse Ratched, subtly manages to be almost always unpleasant, often insensitive, but never resorting to caricature. (Dir: Milos Forman, 129 mins.)†

One Foot in Heaven (1941)***½ Fredric March, Martha Scott, Beulah Bondi, Gene Lockhart. This story of a minister's life is funny, sad, moving, and interesting. Superbly acted by Mr. March as the minister and Martha Scott as his devoted wife. (Dir: Irving Rapper, 108 mins.)

One Foot in Hell (1960)**½ Alan Ladd, Don Murray, Dolores Michaels. Revenge-obsessed man takes job as deputy, intending to get even with townspeople responsible for the death of his wife. (Dir: James B. Clark, 90 mins.)

One Frightened Night (1935)*** Wallace Ford, Regis Toomey, Charley Grapewin, Raffaela Ottiano, Hedda Hopper, Fred Kelsey. A surprisingly good programmer about a mansion full of greedy relatives and the murder of an ersatz heiress. (Dir: Christy Cabanne, 67 mins.)

One From the Heart (1982)*** Frederic Forrest, Teri Garr, Raul Julia, Nastassia Kinski, Lainie Kazan, Harry Dean Stanton. Francis Ford Coppola's risky romantic confection sparkles with technical brilliance highlighted by impressionistic studio settings as a stand-in for Las Vegas. The talented cast act out the story of a bickering couple (Forrest and Garr) who meet their "dream mates" (Julia and Kinski). (101 mins.)†

One Girl's Confession (1953)** Cleo Moore, Hugo Haas, Glenn Langan. Tiresome melodrama about a young girl's predicament caused by her stealing $25,000 from her evil employer. (Dir: Hugo Haas, 74 mins.)

One Good Cop (1991)** Michael Keaton, Rene Russo, Anthony La Paglia, Kevin Conway, Rachel Ticotin. Schizoid comedy-action yarn that unevenly and clumsily alternates between outbursts of violence and bubbling sentimentality. Good cop (Keaton) adopts three endearing little girls when his partner (La Paglia) is killed. Keaton spends the rest of the film searching for a drug lord killer, when he's not at home with the girls playing *Mr. Mom*. (Dir: Heywood Gould, 107 mins.)†

One Heavenly Night (1931)** Evelyn Laye, John Boles, Leon Errol. Operetta about a humble flower seller capturing a count's heart. (Dir: George Fitzmaurice, 80 mins.)

One Hour with Max Linder (1907-12)*** Short comedies directed by and starring the great French silent clown, including **Max Learns to Skate** and **Troubles of a Grass Widower**. A most entertaining look at Linder's influential *boulevardier* character, the man in the silk hat. (60 mins.)†

One Hour with You (1932)***½ Maurice Chevalier, Jeanette MacDonald, Roland Young, Charles Ruggles, Genevieve Tobin. Oscar Stevens's music, Lubitsch's famous touch, and a good cast add up to a delightful operetta about a marital tiff. (Dirs: Ernst Lubitsch, George Cukor, 84 mins.)

101 Dalmatians (1961)***½ This Disney feature cartoon was one of his best in decades. Parent dogs fight rousingly to rescue their pups from extermination. (Dirs: Wolfgang Reitherman, Hamilton S. Luske, Clyde Geronimi, 80 mins.)†

100 Men and a Girl (1937)*** Deanna Durbin, Leopold Stokowski, Adolphe Menjou. Light comedy drama about a poor violinist's daughter who sings at a great concert with maestro Leopold Stokowski conducting. (Dir: Henry Koster, 90 mins.)

100 Rifles (1969)* Jim Brown, Raquel Welch, Burt Reynolds. Nonsensical adventure which follows an American sheriff (Brown) as he joins an Indian revolt against the Mexican oppressors. (Dir: Tom Gries, 110 mins.)†

One in a Million (1936)*** Sonja Henie, Don Ameche, Ritz Brothers, Adolphe Menjou. Sonja's first American film and her skating is a treat to watch. Plot concerns a Swiss girl whose father is training her for the Olympics. (Dir: Sidney Lanfield, 94 mins.)

One in a Million: The Ron LeFlore Story (MTV 1978)**½ LeVar Burton, Madge Sinclair, Paul Benjamin, Billy Martin. Burton is appealing in this drama, which dutifully chronicles the struggle of the young black, desperately poor teenager to escape from the horrors of the ghetto in Detroit. (Dir: William A. Graham, 104 mins.)

One Is a Lonely Number (1972)**½ Trish Van Devere, Janet Leigh, Monte Markham, Melvyn Douglas. Van Devere is a young woman who is thrust back into the world of men on the make after her husband leaves her. (Dir: Mel Stuart, 97 mins.)

One Little Indian (1973)** James Garner, Vera Miles, Clay O'Brien, Pat Hingle, Andrew Prine. Corporal Garner plays a deserter stuck in the desert with one little Indian and a camel as he makes his escape across the burning sands. Disappointing Disney. (Dir: Bernard McEveety, 90 mins.)†

One Magic Christmas (1985)*½ Mary Steenburgen, Harry Dean Stanton, Elisabeth Harnois, Arthur Hill, Robbie Magwood, Gary Basarba. Nothing works in this yuletide schlag, with Steenburgen playing a Mother Scrooge whose family wants her to regain her Christmas glow despite the family's financial straits. (Dir: Philip Borsos, 100 mins.)†

One Man Jury (1978)*½ Jack Palance, Chris Mitchum, Pamela Shoop, Angel Tompkins. The verdict is guilty as far as this film's overuse of violence goes. A trigger-happy cop executes vicious criminals. (Dir: Charles Martin, 104 mins.)†

One Man Out (1989)** Stephen McHattie, Deborah Van Valkenburgh, Aharon Ipale. An unstable ex-CIA agent, now working as a one-man death squad in a South American country ruled by a military dictatorship, has a change of heart when he falls in love with a beautiful American journalist. (Dir: Michael Kennedy, 95 mins.)†

One Man's China (Great Britain, 1972) ***½ A fascinating pictorial essay directed by veteran journalist-filmmaker Felix Greene that presents the most comprehensive and up-to-date documentary on mainland China that was then available. (189 mins.)

One Man's War (France, 1981)*** Stirring documentary takes French newreels made during the German occupation (1940-44), some of which depict illusionary views of the benevolence of the Third Reich, and links them with readings from the diaries of German officer and writer Ernst Junger, who was often critical of Nazism. (Dir: Edgardo Cozarinsky, 105 mins.)

One Man's War (MCTV 1991)***½ Anthony Hopkins, Norma Aleandro, Rubén Blades, Fernanda Torres, Leonardo Garcia. Gripping and disturbing drama about real-life Paraguayan doctor and artist Joel Filartiga and his family's struggle against the dictatorship that ruled the South American country in 1976. Hopkins is an outspoken critic of the government, which leads to the persecution of his family, and the murder of his son. A marvelous cast brings this horrific drama to throbbing life. (Dir: Sergio Toledo, 95 mins.)†

One Man's Way (1964)**½ Don Murray, Diana Hyland. Those who read Norman Vincent Peale's bestselling book *The Power of Positive Thinking* will want to tune in for this Hollywood version of the famed clergyman's life, despite its episodic treatment. (Dir: Denis Sanders, 105 mins.)

One Man Too Many (France, 1967)*** Bruno Cremer, Jean-Claude Brialy, Jacques Perrin, Pierre Clementi, Michel Piccoli, Claude Brasseur. A group of French resistance fighters free some fellow countrymen from the Germans, only to discover that one of them is a Nazi spy, whom they then must decide whether to kill. (Dir: Costa-Gavras, 110 mins.)

One Million B.C. (1940)** Carole Landis, Victor Mature, Lon Chaney, Jr. Story of the struggle of the cave men for survival in prehistoric times. Often rather ridiculous, sometimes fascinating; at least, it's different. Some footage by D.W. Griffith. (Dirs: Hal Roach, Hal Roach, Jr., 80 mins.)†

$1,000,000 Duck (1971)**½ Dean Jones, Sandy Duncan, Joe Flynn, Tony Roberts, James Gregory. A fairly funny fantasy about a duck who lays golden eggs. (Dir: Vincent McEveety, 91 mins.)

One Million Years B.C. (Great Britain, 1966)*½ Raquel Welch, John Richardson, Percy Herbert, Martine Beswick. This is a remake of a 1940s opus called *One Million B.C.*, and serves as a showcase for Raquel's physical charms. (Dir: Don Chaffey, 100 mins.)

One Minute to Zero (1952)** Robert Mitchum, Ann Blyth. Colonel carries on a romance before leaving for the perils of Korea. Unconvincing war melodrama. (Dir: Tay Garnett, 105 mins.)†

One More River (1934)*** Colin Clive, Diana Wynyard, C. Aubrey Smith.

Adapted from the John Galsworthy novel by R. C. Sheriff. A wife runs away with her lover and her husband has them pursued by detectives. (Dir: James Whale, 88 mins.)

One More Saturday Night (1986)½ Tom Davis, Al Franken, Moira Harris. It takes place during one weekend in a tiny Minnesota town, but the laughs are so infrequent this plays like Eternity reset in the Midwest. (Dir: Dennis Klein, 95 mins.) †

One More Time (British, 1969)* Peter Lawford, Sammy Davis, Jr., Esther Anderson. Lousy sequel to Salt and Pepper. The duo play London bistro owners who go to the castle of Lawford's brother when he dies. (Dir: Jerry Lewis, 93 mins.)

One More Tomorrow (1946)** Ann Sheridan, Dennis Morgan, Jane Wyman, Alexis Smith. They're trying to say something about war profiteering but it's poorly presented and emerges as a foolish twisting of Philip Barry's play The Animal Kingdom. (Dir: Peter Godfrey, 88 mins.)

One More Train to Rob (1971)** George Peppard, Diana Muldaur. A western tale of vengeance set in California of the 1880s. After Peppard is framed for a train robbery and is released from prison, he seeks out his former double-crossing partners, now leading respectable lives. (Dir: Andrew McLaglen, 104 mins.)

One Mysterious Night (1944)**½ Chester Morris, Janis Carter, Richard Lane, William Wright, George E. Stone, Dorothy Malone. The police swallow their pride once more as they enlist Boston Blackie's aid, this time in locating the fabulous Blue Star of the Nile diamond. (Dir: Oscar "Bud" Boetticher, 61 mins.)

One Night in Lisbon (1941)**½ Madeleine Carroll, Fred MacMurray, Billie Burke. Romantic comedy about an American pilot and an aristocratic English girl in wartime Britain has a few scattered laughs. (Dir: Edward H. Griffith, 97 mins.)

One Night in the Tropics (1940)*** Allan Jones, Nancy Kelly, Robert Cummings, Bud Abbott, Lou Costello. In this movie, Abbott and Costello began as a team, playing second fiddles in the story of overly cautious Cummings who takes out love insurance on his wedding to Kelly, then finds he has a rival in broker Jones. Amusing musical with songs by Jerome Kern, Oscar Hammerstein II, and Dorothy Fields. (Dir: A. Edward Sutherland, 82 mins.)

One Night of Love (1934)*** Grace Moore, Lyle Talbot, Tullio Carminati. Tuneful musical about an American girl who goes to Italy to become an opera star and promptly falls under the spell of her maestro. (Dir: Victor Schertzinger, 80 mins.) †

One Night Stand (1977)½ Chapelle Jaffe, Brent Carver. Incomprehensible adaptation for Canadian TV of what looks not to have been a very good play in the first place. A Toronto woman wants to break loose for a night, so she picks up a man in a bar and brings him home. Instead of having sex, they talk, endlessly and boringly. (Dir: Allan Winton King, 93 mins.) †

One Night Stand (Australia, 1984)*** Tyler Coppin, Cassandra Delaney, Jay Hackett, Saskia Post. Ironic, quirky movie about four young people trapped in the Sydney Opera House when nuclear war starts. Not really a horror film (though the implications are of course horrifying), with a script that treats the Bomb as the ultimate tasteless joke on humanity. Featuring an appearance by Midnight Oil. (Dir: John Duigan, 94 mins.) †

One of My Wives Is Missing (MTV 1976)**½ Jack Klugman, Elizabeth Ashley, James Franciscus. Klugman plays a resort-area police detective called by Franciscus to investigate the disappearance of his wife. (Dir: Glenn Jordan, 98 mins.)

One of Our Aircraft Is Missing (Great Britain, 1941)***½ Godfrey Tearle, Eric Portman, Hugh Williams. The crew of a downed bomber tries to get back to England from its landing place in Holland. Excellent war melodrama, suspenseful, well acted. (Dirs: Michael Powell, Emeric Pressburger, 106 mins.) †

One of Our Dinosaurs Is Missing (Great Britain, 1975)*** Helen Hayes, Peter Ustinov, Clive Revill. Entertaining Disney lark concerning a secret formula which is hidden in a dinosaur skeleton in London's History Museum. (Dir: Robert Stevenson, 97 mins.)

One of Our Own (MTV 1975)**½ George Peppard, Zohra Lampert, William Daniels. Peppard is into the surgery game as chief of services in a major hospital. (Dir: Richard Sarafian, 100 mins.)

One on One (1977)**½ Robby Benson, Annette O'Toole. Underscripted college basketball saga is strictly sub-Rocky. (Dir: Lamont Johnson, 99 mins.) †

One Plus One—See: Sympathy for the Devil

One Police Plaza (MTV 1986)**½ Robert Conrad, George Dzundza, James Olson, Jamey Sheridan, Larry Riley, Lisa Barnes, Joe Grifasi. This time out Conrad's a tough New York police lieutenant who goes against all authority to get to the bottom of a young woman's murder. (Dir: Jerry Jameson, 104 mins.)

One Potato, Two Potato (1964)***½ Barbara Barrie, Bernie Hamilton, Richard Mulligan. Vivid sensitive drama about an interracial courtship and marriage between a hesitant white divorcee and a strong, but mild-mannered black man.

The climax is a shattering courtroom custody battle for the woman's daughter between Miss Barrie and her ex-husband. (Dir: Larry Peerce, 92 mins.)

One Rainy Afternoon (1936)** Francis Lederer, Ida Lupino, Roland Young, Hugh Herbert, Mischa Auer. Flimsy romance about a man-about-town who pursues a beautiful girl he meets in a movie theater. (Dir: Rowland V. Lee, 79 mins.)†

One Russian Summer (Italy-Great Britain, 1973)*½ Oliver Reed, John McEnery, Carol Andre, Claudia Cardinale. A melodrama (based on Lermontov's *Vadim*) about a cripple who tries to turn the tables on a spiteful landowner in czarist Russia. Overacted to the nth degree. (Dir: Antonio Calenda, 112 mins.)

One Shoe Makes It Murder (MTV 1982)** Robert Mitchum, Angie Dickinson, Mel Ferrer, John Harkins, Howard Hesseman. In his TV movie debut, Mitchum plays a detective who gets in over his head with some shifty types, particularly a venal rich man keeping tabs on his unfaithful wife. One big star doesn't make it any good. (Dir: William Hale, 104 mins.)†

One Sings, The Other Doesn't (France-Belgium, Curaçao, 1976)**½ Valerie Mairesse, Theres Liotard. Insightful, but dated, feminist film. Two women, a free spirit who shuns convention, and a tradition-minded widow who misses her dear departed are enriched by their friendship. (Dir: Agnes Varda, 120 mins.)†

One Spy Too Many (MTV 1968)** Robert Vaughn, David McCallum, Rip Torn. Culled from *The Man from UNCLE* series. Illya and Napoleon Solo employ their super-secret agent tactics to hunt down a mad scientist bent on brainwashing the world via a "will gas." (Dir: Joseph Sargent, 100 mins.)

One Step to Hell (U.S.-Italy-Spain, 1968)*½ Ty Hardin, Pier Angeli, Rossano Brazzi, George Sanders, Dale Cummings, Helga Line. In 1905 South Africa, three escaped convicts kidnap the wife of a prospector, forcing her to take them to his secret gold mine. Hardin is the cop on their trail in this forgettable adventure, filmed on location in Spain and Africa. (Dir: Sandy Howard, 94 mins.)†

One Summer Love—See: Dragonfly

One Sunday Afternoon (1933)**½ Gary Cooper, Frances Fuller, Fay Wray. The earliest version of *The Strawberry Blonde*. No songs this time, but enough gossamer charm to make this fading antique worthwhile. Cooper plays a dentist who's better at pulling teeth than at picking the right girl. (Dir: Stephen Roberts, 93 mins.)

One Sunday Afternoon (1948)**½ Dennis Morgan, Janis Paige, Don DeFore, Dorothy Malone. James Cagney carried this nostalgic gay '90s tale when it was called *The Strawberry Blonde* but he's not around to support this musical version. (Dir: Raoul Walsh, 90 mins.)

One Terrific Guy (MTV 1986)*½ Mariette Hartley, Wayne Rogers, Laurence Luckinbill. A midwestern high school coach (Wayne Rogers) is conducting sex research that he shouldn't be; and mother Mariette Hartley and daughter Susan Rinell are on to his ploy. (Dir: Lou Antonio, 120 mins.)

One That Got Away, The (Great Britain, 1957)**** Hardy Kruger, Colin Gordon. Cocky captured German pilot insists on trying to escape. Based on fact, this is a crack suspense drama, finely made and brilliantly acted by Kruger. (Dir: Roy Baker, 106 mins.)†

One Third of a Nation (1939)**½ Sylvia Sidney, Leif Erickson, Myron McCormick, Sidney Lumet, Iris Adrian. Strong social criticism condemning slum landlords, showing the effects of demeaning, inferior housing on one girl (Sidney) and her delinquent brother (young Sidney Lumet). Effective and well done. (Dir: Dudley Murphy, 79 mins.)†

1000 Convicts and a Woman (1972)½ Alexandra Hay, Sandor Eles, Harry Baird. 1000 clichés and a bad cast. A teenybopper temptress gets sent home to the family manse, which is now an experimental prison filled to the brim with male convicts! (Dir: Ray Austin, 92 mins.)

1001 Arabian Nights (1960)**½ Color cartoon feature, with Mr. Magoo, the voice of Jim Backus, back in old Bagdad. The nearsighted one is a lamp dealer whose nephew, Aladdin, gets the lamp with the genie, etc. (Dir: Jack Kinney, 76 mins.)

One Touch of Venus (1948)**½ Ava Gardner, Robert Walker, Dick Haymes, Eve Arden, Tom Conway. A Greek statue of Venus comes to life in a department store, causes romance and misunderstandings. Appealing musical comedy. (Dir: William A. Seiter, 81 mins.)†

One Trick Pony (1980)*½ Paul Simon, Blair Brown, Rip Torn. Simon plays an aging musician who can no longer make sense of his marriage or his career. Unfortunately, his emoting leaves almost as big a hole in the screen as another singing actor, Neil Diamond. (Dir: Robert Young, 98 mins.)†

One, Two, Three (1961)***½ James Cagney, Horst Buchholz, Pamela Tiffin, Arlene Francis. Director Billy Wilder comes up with another of his glib sophisticated comedy romps which gives James Cagney the opportunity to overplay expertly in the role of a Coca-Cola executive in West Germany. The amusing plot examines the Cold War, East German beatniks, the internationality of Coca-Cola, and various other subjects. (108 mins.)†

One Way or Another (Cuba, 1974)*** Mario Balmaseda, Mario Limonta, Yolanda Cuellar, Guillermo. Clever mix of documentary footage and fiction tells a story of two lovers, a factory worker and an educated schoolteacher, who examine each other's diverse backgrounds as they prepare to accept Castro's revolution. Director Sara Gomez Yera, the first woman in Cuba to direct a feature, died during production. (78 mins.)

One Way Passage (1932)***½ William Powell, Kay Francis, Aline MacMahon. Moving drama about the romance of an escaping convict and a girl dying of heart trouble, avoids being corny and emerges as an affecting melodrama. Remade as *Till We Meet Again*. (Dir: Tay Garnett, 69 mins.)

One Way Street (1950)**½ James Mason, Marta Toren, Dan Duryea, William Conrad, Jack Elam. The charm of the stars make up for the inadequacies of the script in this chase melodrama about thieves, lovers, and intrigue. (Dir: Hugo Fregonese, 79 mins.)

One Way to Love (1945)**½ Chester Morris, Janis Carter, Marguerite Chapman. Bright comedy-romance of a battling couple on a cross-country train journey trying to write a radio show together; nice chemistry between the B-level stars. (Dir: Ray Enright, 83 mins.)

One Way Wahine (1965)*½ Anthony Eisley, Joy Harmon, Edgar Bergen. Silly story about gangsters hiding out in Hawaii with $100,000. (Dir: William O. Brown, 80 mins.)

One Woman or Two (France, 1987)** Gerard Depardieu, Sigourney Weaver, Ruth Westheimer, Michel Aumont, Zabou. This contemporary French reworking of the screwball classic *Bringing Up Baby* has Depardieu as an archeologist who's unearthed the bones of "the first French woman," and Weaver as an American who dupes him by using his "find" in an ad for a new perfume. Some pleasant moments, but this one's too screwy even for a screwball comedy. (Dir: Daniel Vigne, 97 mins.)†

One Woman's Story (Great Britain, 1949) ***½ Ann Todd, Trevor Howard, Claude Rains. Woman married to rich broker meets her former lover in Switzerland, and the affair begins once more. Poignant, sparklingly acted romantic drama. AKA: **The Passionate Friends**. (Dir: David Lean, 86 mins.)

On Fire (MTV 1987)** John Forsythe, Carroll Baker, Gordon Jump. "Dynasty"'s John Forsythe plays a sixty-year-old arson inspector whose life begins to crumble when he's forced into retirement, in this slow, shallow look at the problems of age discrimination. (Dir: Robert Greenwald, 104 mins.)

On Golden Pond (1981)*** Henry Fonda, Katharine Hepburn, Jane Fonda, Doug McKeon, Dabney Coleman, William Lanteau. A dream casting coup. Henry Fonda as an aging retired professor whose life is ebbing, Katharine Hepburn as his wife, and Jane Fonda as their daughter who has had a tense, estranged relationship with her father. Directed with sensitivity by Mark Rydell and smoothly, if sentimentally scripted by Ernest Thompson from his play. Henry Fonda won the Oscar for best actor while on his deathbed. (Dir: Mark Rydell, 109 mins.)†

On Her Majesty's Secret Service (Great Britain, 1969)*** George Lazenby, Diana Rigg, Telly Savalas. As Agent 007, Lazenby is about as animated as Westminster Abbey, but there are enough exciting scenes in this hokum to keep most Bond fans entertained. The plot concerns the bad guys' plan to conquer the world using a virus. (Dir: Peter Hunt, 140 mins.)†

Onibaba (Japan, 1964)*** Nobuko Otawa, Jitsuko Yoshimura, Kel Sato, Jukichi Uno. Creepy tale of two women in medieval Japan, a young widow and her mother-in-law, who live on an isolated plain and lure warriors to their deaths, selling their armor and throwing the bodies into a deep hole in the ground. When the daughter-in-law falls in love with a potential victim, the older woman schemes to keep them apart. (Dir: Kaneto Shindo, 103 mins.)†

Onion Field, The (1979)**½ John Savage, James Woods, Franklyn Seales, Ted Danson, Ronny Cox. This true story of a cop killing is an object lesson in the limitations of undiluted naturalism. There is little in this literal adaptation of Wambaugh's nonfiction piece beyond the straight facts, and those facts go largely undramatized. Though James Woods's portrait of a psychopath garnered the critical raves, it is the stooge portrayed by Franklyn Seales that is the genuinely complex creation. (Dir: Harold Becker, 126 mins.)†

Onionhead (1958)**½ Andy Griffith, Felicia Farr, Walter Matthau, Joey Bishop. Not as funny as Griffith's army tour in *No Time for Sergeants* but this Coast Guard comedy has its moments. This time, Griffith is the ship's cook aboard a buoy tender. (Dir: Norman Taurog, 110 mins.)

Only Angels Have Wings (1939)**** Cary Grant, Jean Arthur, Richard Barthelmess, Thomas Mitchell, Sig Ruman, John Carroll, Rita Hayworth. Director Howard Hawks' masterpiece examines the lives and loves of the pilots of a small commercial airline in Latin America. Spare, brittle screenplay by Jules Furthman.

Exemplary acting from the large cast. (121 mins.)†

Only Game in Town, The (1970)*½ Elizabeth Taylor, Warren Beatty, Charles Braswell. Taylor is absurdly cast as a Las Vegas dancer who tangles romantically with a piano player (Beatty). (Dir: George Stevens, 113 mins.)

Only the French Can—See: **French Can Can**

Only the Lonely (1991)** John Candy, Maureen O'Hara, Ally Sheedy, Anthony Quinn, James Belushi. Maudlin melodrama about a lonely 38-year-old cop (Candy) who falls in love with a funeral home cosmetician (Sheedy), much to the chagrin of his feisty mother (beautifully played by O'Hara) with whom he lives. Rehashed soap opera material is written by the director and produced by John Hughes. (Dir: Chris Columbus, 105 mins.)†

Only the Valiant (1951)** Gregory Peck, Barbara Payton, Gig Young, Ward Bond. Peck stars as the misunderstood cavalry officer who must win back his men's respect. Action galore. (Dir: Gordon Douglas, 105 mins.)†

Only Thing You Know, The (Canada, 1972)***½ Anne Knox, Allan Royal, John Denos, Linda Huffman. Eighteen-year-old girl leaves home and finds that freedom isn't all she thought it would be. Touching film avoids clichés and makes a big statement. (Dir: Clark Mackey, 81 mins.)

Only Two Can Play (Great Britain, 1962)*** Peter Sellers, Mai Zetterling, Richard Attenborough. A comedy delight. Sellers is a frustrated Don Juan who tries some extramarital maneuvering, with disastrous results. Witty performance by Zetterling as the object of his desires. (Dir: Sidney Gilliat, 106 mins.)†

Only When I Larf (Great Britain, 1968)** Richard Attenborough, David Hemmings, Alexandra Stewart. An innocuous caper about a trio of British con artists who try to fleece some African diplomats. (Dir: Basil Dearden, 104 mins.)

Only When I Laugh (1981)*** Marsha Mason, Kristy McNichol, Joan Hackett, James Coco. Playing an alcoholic actress, Mason delivers the goods in this Neil Simon reworking of his Broadway flop *The Gingerbread Lady*. Simon wisely doesn't go for the wisecrack every time in this thoughtful script. (Dir: Glenn Jordan, 120 mins.)†

Only With Married Men (MTV 1974)*½ David Birney, Michele Lee, Dom De-Luise, Judy Carne, Gavin MacLeod. Ms. Lee doesn't want to go through the hassle involved in dating single guys, so she goes out "only with married men." (Dir: Jerry Paris, 72 mins.)†

Only Yesterday (1933)*** Margaret Sul-

lavan, John Boles, Billie Burke, Reginald Denny. Strong, pre-code drama about an unwed mother; Sullavan's shimmering debut. (Dir: John Stahl, 105 mins.)

On Moonlight Bay (1951)*** Doris Day, Gordon MacRae, Leon Ames, Billy Gray, Mary Wickes, Rosemary DeCamp. Booth Tarkington's Penrod stories make charming material for this romantic Day musical. (Dir: Roy Del Ruth, 95 mins.)

On Our Merry Way (1948)** Paulette Goddard, Burgess Meredith, Dorothy Lamour, James Stewart, Henry Fonda, Fred MacMurray. Questions asked by an inquiring reporter lead to a series of humorous stories. A good idea that doesn't come off; due to inept scripting. (Dirs: King Vidor, Leslie Fenton, 99 mins.)

On the Avenue (1937)*** Madeleine Carroll, Dick Powell, Alice Faye, the Ritz Brothers. Lively musical with excellent songs by Irving Berlin. Carroll is an heiress outraged by a revue satirizing her foibles, but she falls in love with its easygoing star (Powell). Later revamped as *Let's Make Love*. (Dir: Del Ruth, 89 mins.)

On the Beach (1959)***½ Gregory Peck, Ava Gardner, Fred Astaire, Anthony Perkins. Nevil Shute's searing novel about the last people on earth, who face death from radioactivity after WWIII. The film remains a powerful comment against war. (Dir: Stanley Kramer, 134 mins.)†

On the Beat (Great Britain, 1962)*** Norman Wisdom, Jennifer Jayne. Stumbling car cleaner at Scotland Yard wants to be a policeman, gets his chance when he poses as a crook to trap jewel robbers. Amusing. (Dir: Robert Asher, 105 mins.)

On the Double (1961)**½ Danny Kaye, Dana Wynter, Margaret Rutherford, Wilfrid Hyde-White. Danny's a GI whose imper sonations land him in hot water during WWII. The talented Mr. Kaye doesn't get much help from the scriptwriters, but there are some nice moments. (Dir: Melville Shavelson, 92 mins.)

On the Edge (1986)*** Bruce Dern, John Marley, Billy Bailey, Jim Haynie. A runner returns home after a long absence to compete in a race he was disqualified from 20 years earlier. At the same time, he hopes to reestablish ties with his father. Released to theaters at 91 mins., two video versions run 86 mins. and 95 mins. (latter with a complete extra subplot about Dern's interracial romance). (Dir: Rob Nilsson, 91 mins.)†

On the Fiddle—See: **Operation Snafu**

On the Line (Spain, 1984)** David Carradine, Jeff Delger, Scott Wilson, Victoria Abril, Jesse Vint, Sam Jaffe. Guard working the U.S.-Mexico border falls in love with a Mexican prostitute and risks his job to bring her across. (Dir: José Luis Boaru, 103 mins.)†

On the Nickel (1979)** Donald Moffat, Penelope Allen, James Gammon, Ralph Waite. Woebegone independent feature about life on skid row in LA indulges in every sentimentality at a snail's pace. Waite wrote, produced, and directed, and plays the flashiest part. (96 mins.)†

On the Right Track (1981)**½ Gary Coleman, Maureen Stapleton, Michael Lembeck, Norman Fell, Lisa Eilbacher. Coleman fans will enjoy this sentimental comedy about an orphan living by his wits in a railway station, and the people who unofficially adopt him. (Dir: Lee Philips, 98 mins.)†

On the Riviera (1951)*** Danny Kaye, Gene Tierney, Corinne Calvet. Fast and funny comedy about the international set and their gay escapades on the Riviera, the playground of the rich. Kaye sings, dances, clowns, and makes love to Gene Tierney. Watch for Gwen Verdon in a can-can number. (Dir: Walter Lang, 90 mins.)

On the Road Again—See: **Honeysuckle Rose**

On the Threshold of Space (1956)**½ Guy Madison, Virginia Leith, John Hodiak, Dean Jagger. Early adventure of astronauts in training, quite interesting today as a reflection of the values and technical expertise of the times. (Dir: Robert D. Webb, 98 mins.)

On the Town (1950)**** Gene Kelly, Frank Sinatra, Betty Garrett, Ann Miller, Vera Ellen, Jules Munchin. The successful Broadway show by Leonard Bernstein, Betty Comden, and Adolph Green receives the Hollywood treatment. The result is an entertaining, tuneful, brilliantly choreographed and directed musical about three sailors on liberty in N.Y.C. (Dirs: Gene Kelly, Stanley Donen, 98 mins.)†

On the Waterfront (1954)**** Marlon Brando, Eva Marie Saint, Karl Malden, Lee J. Cobb, Rod Steiger. Forceful, super-charged melodrama about the docks of New Jersey—the workers, the bosses, the criminals, and their families. Brilliantly acted by all with Brando a superb standout. Winner of many Oscars including Best Film. Brando's shattering performance is among the finest ever recorded on film, and Steiger got his start to stardom here. The scene between them in an auto is superbly played and directed. Brando and Saint won Oscars (she for Best Supporting Actress). (Dir: Elia Kazan, 108 mins.)†

On the Yard (1979)*** John Heard, Thomas Waites, Mike Kellin. A plausible prison picture about stormy relationships in the Big House. Based on a novel by Malcolm Braly, who served time at San Quentin; he also scripted. (Dir: Raphael D. Silver, 102 mins.)†

On Thin Ice: The Tai Babilonia Story (MTV 1990)**½ Rachael Crawford, Charlie Stratton, William Daniels, Denise Nicholas. The story of a focused kid who bypasses her teens to become a champion figure skater. Unfortunately, Tai Babilonia's life takes a downward spin into depression, drink, and even a suicide attempt before she sees the light. Skating sequences by Babilonia and Gardner make it worth sitting through the depressing story. (Dir: Zale Dalen, 96 mins.)

On Valentine's Day (1986)**½ William Converse-Roberts, Hallie Foote, Steven Hill, Rochelle Oliver, Matthew Broderick. Part of Horton Foote's nine-play cycle, the film takes place in Harrison, Texas, where Horace and Elizabeth Robedaux are moving up in the world in 1917. (Dir: Ken Harrison, 106 mins.)†

On Wings of Eagles (MTV 1986)*** Richard Crenna, Burt Lancaster, Esai Morales, Paul LeMat. Exciting adventure based on a true-life story. A businessman decides to bypass diplomacy and the excuses of his government in order to set free two of his employees captured by the Iranians. The commando raid itself is a dazzling set piece. (Dir: Andrew McLaglen, 260 mins.)

On Your Toes (1939)** Vera Zorina, Eddie Albert. Screen treatment of the Rodgers and Hart musical which first introduced the ballet "Slaughter on Tenth Avenue." (Dir: Ray Enright, 94 mins.)

Open Admissions (MTV 1988)**½ Jane Alexander, Dennis Farina, Estelle Parsons, Michael Beach. This adaptation of a Broadway play about a system where college students are merely passed on, rather than educated, benefits from a good performance from Alexander as a caring teacher almost beaten by the system. Beach is also effective as a pupil from the ghetto whose frustration leads to a confrontation with his equally frustrated teacher. (Dir: Gus Trikonis, 96 mins.)

Open City (Italy, 1946)**** Aldo Fabrizi, Anna Magnani. Roberto Rossellini's picture of Rome during the occupation, as a priest aids the underground in routing the Nazis. Powerful, gripping, among the first of the superb postwar Italian films. Italian dialogue. English sub-titles. (Dir: Roberto Rossellini, 105 mins.)†

Open Doors (Italy, 1989)***½ Gian Maria Volonte, Ennio Fantastichini, Renzo Giovampietro, Renato Carpentieri. Volonte is superb as a judge in fascist Italy who fights to save a murderer from the death penalty because he believes the man was driven to violence and that the death penalty is wrong. An emotional and powerful film that is never strident. (Dir: Gianni Amelio, 109 mins.)

Open House (1987)* Joseph Bottoms, Adrienne Barbeau, Rudy Ramos, Mary Stavin, Scott Thompson Baker, Tiffany Bolling. Radio psychologist Bottoms and real estate broker Barbeau search for a madman who is murdering L.A. real estate agents and their clients. The murder scenes are more sadistic than scary in this snail's-paced mystery-thriller. (Dir: Jag Mundhra, 95 mins.)†

Opening Night (1978)*** Gena Rowlands, Joan Blondell, Ben Gazzara, Zohra Lampert. Directed with all the Cassavetes trademarks and incandescently acted by Rowlands and Blondell. The plot concerns an actress who is devastated when one of her biggest fans dies on the very night she opens in a new play. (Dir: John Cassavetes, 144 mins.)

Open the Door and See All the People (1964)** Maybelle Nash, Alec Wilder. Conflict of two households run by elderly sisters, one a crab, the other open and generous. (Dir: Jerome Hill, 82 mins.)

Opera (Italy, 1987)** Cristina Marsillach, Urbano Barbarini, Daria Nicolodi, Ian Charleson. Mysterious, brutal murders haunt the La Scala opera house where a radical director is rehearsing an avant-garde performance of *Macbeth*. Stylish Italian terror specialist Dario Argento's film follows his usual pattern, but his devotion to design and mechanics at the expense of plot and characterization make this play uncomfortably like self-parody. And we're talking about the uncut version; who knows what shape it'll be in when the American distributors get done with it. AKA: **Terror at the Opera**. (90 mins.)

Opera Do Malandro—See: **Malandro**

Opera Prima (Spain, 1980)***½ Oscar Ladoire, Paula Molina, Antonio Resines, Marisa Paredes. Love, sex, and modern music are a weird triangle in this wonderfully offbeat romantic comedy about a male journalist's wild affair with his breathtakingly beautiful female cousin. A superb example of freer post-Franco Spanish cinema, filled with energy, youth, witty dialogue, and an interesting view of incest. (Dir: Fernando Trueba, 94 mins.)

Operation, The (MTV 1990)*** Joe Penny, Kathleen Quinlan, Lisa Hartman, Jason Beghe, John Santucci, Googy Gress. Well scripted mystery with some surprising twists as OB-GYN Penny fights two battles: a divorce from wife Quinlan, who co-owns his clinic; and a malpractice suit from patient Hartman, who claims he performed an unnecessary hysterectomy on her. (Dir: Thomas J. Wright, 192 mins.)

Operation Amsterdam (Great Britain, 1959)** Alexander Knox, Peter Finch, Eva Bartok. Exciting true-life incident emerges as routine suspense outing about a frantic attempt, in 1940, to smuggle out of Holland a fortune in industrial diamonds before the Nazis arrive. (Dir: Michael McCarthy, 105 mins.)†

Operation Bikini (1963)** Tab Hunter, Frankie Avalon, Scott Brady, Gary Crosby, Eva Six. Demolition squad seeks out an American sub held by the Japanese to destroy new radar equipment on it. (Dir: Anthony Carras, 83 mins.)

Operation C.I.A. (1965)*½ Burt Reynolds, Danielle Aubry. Brave undercover agent foils an assassination plot in Saigon. (Dir: Christian Nyby, 90 mins.)†

Operation Conspiracy (Great Britain, 1956)** Philip Friend, Mary Mackenzie. Undercover operator combats foreign agents after nuclear information, meets an old flame and murder along the way. Routine thriller. (Dir: Joseph Stirling, 69 mins.)

Operation Crossbow (1965)*** George Peppard, Tom Courtenay, Sophia Loren, Lilli Palmer, Trevor Howard, Jeremy Kemp. Rip-roaring WWII espionage adventure crammed with as much action as possible. Peppard, Courtenay, and Kemp play a trio of agents assigned to destroy a heavily guarded Nazi munitions installation who keep things buzzing. Exciting finale. (Dir: Michael Anderson, 116 mins.)

Operation Cross Eagles (U.S.-Yugoslavia, 1969)** Richard Conte, Rory Calhoun. Routine WWII thriller about a commando group behind German lines assigned to capture a German commandant and exchange him for an American captain. (Dir: Richard Conte, 90 mins.)†

Operation Daybreak (Great Britain, 1976)*** Timothy Bottoms, Anthony Andrews, Anton Diffring. Suspenseful drama based on the assassination of brutal Nazi Reinhard Heydrich (Diffring) in WWII. Czech patriots, trained as commandos in England, succeed in killing Heydrich, but one by one, they are tracked down by the Germans and captured or shot. (Dir: Lewis Gilbert, 118 mins.)

Operation Diplomat (Great Britain 1953)**½ Guy Rolfe, Lisa Daniely. A doctor called in to perform an emergency operation at a deserted country house suspects his patient may be an important missing diplomat. (Dir: John Guillermin, 70 mins.)

Operation Disaster (Great Britain, 1950)***½ John Mills, Nigel Patrick. A submarine on a routine cruise hits an old mine, and sinks to the bottom with twelve men still surviving. Tense, finely written and played story of rescue operations. (Dir: Roy Baker, 102 mins.)

Operation Eichmann (1961)** Werner Klemperer, Ruta Lee. Sensationalized account of the reign of terror in the German concentration camps presided over by Adolf Eichmann. (Dir: R. G. Springsteen, 93 mins.)

Operation Kid Brother (Italy, 1967)*½ Neil Connery, Daniela Bianchi, Anthony Dawson, Bernard Lee, Adolfo Celi. The producers of this low-budget quickie tried to capitalize on Sean Connery's success in the Bond films and cast his real-life brother, Neil Connery, in the role of a cosmetic surgeon thrust into the world of espionage. (Dir: Alberto De Martino, 104 mins.)

Operation Mad Ball (1957)*** Jack Lemmon, Ernie Kovacs, Mickey Rooney, Arthur O'Connell, Kathryn Grant. Delightful wacky Army comedy about an operator who upsets all rules and regulations in his search for fun for himself and his buddies. Kovacs is great as a bewildered officer and his scenes with Lemmon are gems. (Dir: Richard Quine, 105 mins.)

Operation Manhunt (1954)**½ Harry Townes, Jacques Aubuchon. The story of Igor Gouzenko, Russian code clerk who forsook the Communists and defected to the West. Gouzenko appears briefly. (Dir: Jack Alexander, 77 mins.)

Operation Mermaid (Great Britain, 1963) *** Mai Zetterling, Keenan Wynn, Ronald Howard. America gathers together a crew of ex-commandos to search for hidden Nazi treasure. Well-knit melodrama with a good cast, suspense. (Dir: John Ainsworth, 86 mins.)

Operation Pacific (1951)*½ John Wayne, Patricia Neal. Overlong and tedious story of a cautious and efficient skipper of a submarine. (Dir: George Waggner, 111 mins.)

Operation Petticoat (1959)***½ Cary Grant, Tony Curtis, Dina Merrill. A big, big hit comedy highlighting Cary Grant's ageless appeal and Tony Curtis's energetic performing, about a sub and its mad, mad crew and their unbelievable exploits in the South Pacific. Fun for all. Later a TV series. (Dir: Blake Edwards, 124 mins.)†

Operation Secret (1952)*** Cornel Wilde, Phyllis Thaxter, Steve Cochran, Karl Malden. Good espionage thriller about the dangerous activities of the French underground, known as "The Maquis," during WWII. (Dir: Lewis Seiler, 108 mins.)

Operation Snafu (Great Britain, 1961)** Alfred Lynch, Sean Connery, Stanley Holloway, Wilfrid Hyde-White. Lynch and Connery as a pair of cronies in the RAF, out to swindle fellow soldiers during WW II. (Dir: Cyril Frankel, 97 mins.)

Operation Snatch (Great Britain, 1962)**½ Terry-Thomas, George Sanders. A bungling officer is sent to Gibraltar during WWII to make sure the Barbary apes stay there—legend has it that as long as they do, Gibraltar will remain in the British Empire. Occasionally funny. (Dir: Robert Day, 83 mins.)

Operation St. Peter's (Italy, 1968)* Edward G. Robinson, Lando Buzzanca, Jean-Claude Brialy. An aging hood (Robinson) hits the comeback trail with a scheme to rob the Pieta from the Vatican. A botched operation. (Dir: Lucio Fulci, 100 mins.)

Operation Thunderbolt (Israel, 1977)**½ Klaus Kinski, Assaf Dayan, Gila Almagor. Wanly efficient depiction of the Entebbe hostage rescue raid, containing some logistical details not available to the American filmmakers who did versions. (Dir: Menahem Golan, 120 mins.)†

Operation Warhead—See: **Operation Snafu**

Operator 13 (1933)** Marion Davies, Gary Cooper, Jean Parker, Katherine Alexander. Davies plays an actress who becomes a Union spy during the Civil War and finds herself involved with Confederate he-man Cooper. Based on a real-life story. (Dir: Richard Boleslawski, 86 mins.)

Opportunity Knocks (1990)* Dana Carvey, Robert Loggia, Todd Graff, Julia Campbell, Milo O'Shea, James Tolken, Doris Belack. Woefully weak comedy with Carvey as a petty con artist who dupes a pleasant family into thinking he's a creative business genius. He's too weak a presence to carry a feature-length film; what works in "Saturday Night Live" sketches doesn't pass muster on the big screen. (Dir: Donald Petrie, 105 mins.)†

Opposing Force (1987)*** Lisa Eichhorn, Tom Skerritt, Anthony Zerbe, Richard Roundtree, Robert Wightman, John Considine, Michael James. Air Force officer Eichhorn volunteers to be the first woman to take a tough training program on an isolated tropical island. But after she parachutes in, she finds it's rougher than she'd expected: the commander has upped the "training" to include psychological torture and rape. An intelligently made thriller, worth looking for. (Dir: Eric Karson, 97 mins.)†

Opposite Sex, The (1956)*** June Allyson, Joan Collins, Dolores Gray, Ann Sheridan, Ann Miller, Joan Blondell. Slickly produced, updated remake of *The Women*. The supporting cast is very good, particularly Collins. (Dir: David Miller, 117 mins.)

Optimists, The (Great Britain, 1974)*** Peter Sellers, Donna Mullane, John Chaffey. Sentimental story of London slum kids befriended by old busker Sellers. (Dir: Anthony Simmons, 110 mins.)

Options (1989)** Matt Salinger, Joanna

Pacula, John Kani. A nerdy Hollywood dealmaker goes to Africa to get the story of a Belgian princess working in the jungle, only to get involved in her kidnapping. (Dir: Camilo Vila, 92 mins.)†

Oracle, The (1984)** Caroline Capers Powers, Roger Neil, Pam LaTesta, Victoria Dryden. *Poltergeist* for apartment dwellers. The spirit of a murdered man tries to force the woman who has moved into his apartment to take revenge on his killers. Atmospheric, but ruined by clumsy editing. (Dir: Roberta Findlay, 95 mins.)†

Oranges Are Not the Only Fruit (Great Britain, MTV 1989)**½ Geraldine McEwan, Charlotte Coleman, Kenneth Cranham. An offbeat British production about a young adopted girl who is whipped into religious frenzy by her evangelist stepmother. The young lady accepts it all until she finds that she has sexual yearnings for a female member of her flock. Downbeat and uncompromising in its truth. The drama is a bit overlong but well acted. (Dir: Beeban Kidron, 144 mins.)

Orca (1977)*½ Richard Harris, Charlotte Rampling, Will Sampson, Bo Derek, Keenan Wynn, Robert Carradine, Scott Walker. In this aquatic disaster, Harris fights to the death with a whale whose mate and child he has killed. (Dir: Michael Anderson, 92 mins.)†

Orchestra Conductor (Poland, 1980)***½ John Gielgud, Andrzej Seweryn, Krystyana Janda, Jan Ciercierski. Emotion-packed drama with Gielgud as an emigré Polish orchestra conductor who triumphantly returns to his native land after fifty years away. His visit is marred by his own embarrassment over political pressures that accompany his return. Director Andrzej Wajda's most personal view of an artist's integrity and commitment, a searing study of exiles and the conflicts they face. (101 mins.)

Orchestra Rehearsal (Italy-Monaco, 1978) *½ Balduin Baas, Clara Colosimo, Elisabeth Labi. Director Federico Fellini's film lacks resonance, consistency, and bite. An extended soliloquy by a hapless German conductor confronted by rebellious instrumentalists speaks directly to a core of human feeling. Nino Rota's last score. (72 mins.)

Orchestra Wives (1942)*** Glenn Miller, Ann Rutherford, George Montgomery, Cesar Romero. Silly story about girls married to musicians serves to give the Miller crew a chance to fill the screen with some wonderful arrangements. (Dir: Archie Mayo, 98 mins.)†

Ordeal (MTV 1973)**½ Arthur Hill, Diana Muldaur, James Stacy. Hill is cast in the role of a man who is badly injured and left to fend for himself in the desert by a hateful wife and her lover, in this predictable man-versus-nature drama. (Dir: Lee H. Katzin, 73 mins.)

Ordeal by Innocence (Great Britain, 1984)** Donald Sutherland, Faye Dunaway, Christopher Plummer, Sarah Miles. Agatha Christie story but instead of Poirot or Marple, we get a dour Donald S. reopening a murder investigation on his own because he might have proved the accused man's innocence. AKA: **Agatha Christie's Ordeal by Innocence** (Dir: Desmond Davis, 91 mins.)†

Ordeal of Bill Carney, The (MTV 1981)**½ Richard Crenna, Betty Buckley, Jeremy Licht, Martin Mull, Ray Sharkey. After an accident in which he became a quadriplegic, Carney lost the custody of his two sons and began a legal battle to win them back. (Dir: Jerry London, 104 mins.)†

Ordeal of Dr. Mudd, The (MTV 1980)*** Dennis Weaver, Richard Dysart, Nigel Davenport, Arthur Hill. An infamous episode in American history—the railroading of Dr. Samuel Mudd, sent to prison for setting the broken leg of John Wilkes Booth, President Lincoln's assassin—becomes a portrait of dogged courage as Dr. Mudd endures the horrors of prison. (Dir: Paul Wendkos, 104 mins.)†

Ordeal of Patty Hearst, The (MTV 1979)*** Dennis Weaver, Lisa Eilbacher. Good dramatization of the kidnapping in '74 of the heiress who later turned radical, and her eventual arrest by FBI agents. Eilbacher is well cast as Patty in a script that doesn't build undue sympathy for her. (Dir: Paul Wendkos, 156 mins.)

Order of the Black Eagle (1985)*½ Ian Hunter, Charles K. Bibby, William Hicks, Anna Rapagna. Unasked-for sequel to *Unmasking the Idol* finds secret agent Duncan Jax and his sidekick Typhoon the Baboon confronted with that perennial Z-movie threat, a plot to revive Hitler's frozen corpse. (Dir: Worth Keeter, 93 mins.)†

Orders Are Orders (Great Britain, 1954)**½ Brian Reece, Margot Grahame, Peter Sellers. British farce about a movie company descending on an army camp to shoot a film on location. (Dir: David Paltenghi, 78 mins.)

Orders to Kill (Great Britain, 1958)***½ Eddie Albert, Paul Massie, Lillian Gish, Irene Worth. Engrossing spy thriller concerning an American intelligence agent's mission to kill a supposedly French Nazi collaborator. Tight and tense. Acting is very good. (Dir: Anthony Asquith, 93 mins.)

Ordet (Denmark, 1955)***½ Emil Hass Christensen, Preben Lerdorff Rye, Caj

Kristiansen, Henrik Malberg. Stern and demanding farmer refuses to allow one of his sons to marry daughter of man with whom he disagrees on religious philosophy. Powerful study of love and faith. Based on noted Kai Munk drama. (Dir: Carl Dreyer, 125 mins.)†

Ordinary Heroes (1985)** Richard Dean Anderson, Valerie Bertinelli, Richard Baxter, Liz Torres. Two attractive stars breathe life into this all-too-familiar drama about a Vietnam veteran (in this case, he's been blinded) and his bumpy adjustment to civilian life. (Dir: Peter H. Cooper, 104 mins.)†

Ordinary People (1980)**** Mary Tyler Moore, Donald Sutherland, Timothy Hutton, Judd Hirsch, Elizabeth McGovern. Judith Guest's probing novel about an upper-middle-class family and the interior problems which tear them apart is brought to the screen with care and excellence. Director Robert Redford and a choice cast create an understated drama of enormous impact. (123 mins.)†

Oregon Trail, The (1959)*½ Fred MacMurray, Gloria Talbott. Top star doesn't necessarily mean a top western. MacMurray is lost on the prairie. (Dir: Gene Fowler, Jr., 86 mins.)

Oregon Trail, The (MTV 1976)*½ Rod Taylor, Douglas V. Fowley, Blair Brown, Andrew Stevens. Western tale with the weatherbeaten Taylor heading a pioneer family en route to Oregon. (Dir: Boris Sagal, 98 mins.)

Organization, The (1971)*** Sidney Poitier, Barbara McNair, Ron O'Neal. Poitier repeats his characterization of Virgil Tibbs. Tibbs reluctantly joins forces with a well-organized vigilante group determined to smash the drug traffic in their area. (Dir: Don Medford, 106 mins.)†

Organizer, The (Italy, 1964)**** Marcello Mastroianni, Renato Salvatori, Annie Girardot. Absorbing drama of textile workers involved in a factory strike years ago. Tremendous performances by Mastroianni as a professor who leads them to fight for their rights. (Dir: Mario Monicelli, 126 mins.)

Orgy of the Dead (1965)½ Criswell, Fawn Silver, Pat Barringer. Awesomely idiotic item in which two car-crash victims discover a mysterious version of purgatory where Criswell and a Vampira lookalike force them to watch a series of topless go-go dancers! (Dir: A.C. Stephen, 90 mins.)†

Oriental Dream—See: **Kismet** (1944)

Orphans (1987)*** Albert Finney, Matthew Modine, Kevin Anderson. Finney plays a street-smart crook who ends up functioning as a father figure to a young kidnapper and his troubled brother. Contrived, but compelling. (Dir: Alan J. Pakula, 120 mins.)†

786

Orphans of the Storm (1922)**** Lillian Gish, Dorothy Gish, Joseph Schildkraut. A remarkable spectacle directed by D.W. Griffith, based on a play called *Two Orphans* set during the French Revolution. Griffith uses and improves upon the standard melodramatic tricks of his time so that Lillian Gish—searching for and finally finding an adopted blind sister—achieves a moving moment even in today's cinema. A memorable landmark of the silent era. (120 mins.)†

Orphan Train (MTV 1979)*** Jill Eikenberry, Kevin Dobson, Linda Manz. A warm, entertaining story set in the late 1850s that recounts the troubled journey of a group of New York City orphans to the Midwest, where, they hope, they will be adopted by farm families. (Dir: William A. Graham, 156 mins.)†

Orpheus (France, 1949)**** Jean Marais, Maria Casares, François Perier, Juliette Greco with the Maenads on motorcycles. Director Jean Cocteau creates his own mythology for his own purposes. Marais is a poet, besieged by admirers, who hears voices from other worlds over the radio and meets Death, black-gloved, when she comes through the mirror. Defies comparison with anything else in cinema. A magical work. (95 mins.)†

Orpheus Descending (MCTV 1990)***½ Vanessa Redgrave, Kevin Anderson. Tennessee Williams's lyrical play successfully revived by Redgrave and company in London and New York and transferred to film with admirable results. Redgrave is luminous as Lady Torrance, an Italian immigrant who is married to an older man dying of cancer. Enter Anderson as Val Xavier, a sexy young man traveling the byways and highways looking for salvation. (Dir: Peter Hall, 117 mins.)†

Oscar (1991)*½ Sylvester Stallone, Peter Riegert, Chazz Palminteri. Crummy and clumsy farce. Stallone, giving a rotten performance, is a reformed gangster lost in a maze of greedy bankers, rival gangsters, the police, and rebellious daughters. Cameos galore, but they don't help. (Dir: John Landis, 109 mins.)†

Oscar, The (1966)** Stephen Boyd, Elke Sommer, Eleanor Parker, Ernest Borgnine, Milton Berle, Tony Bennett, Jill St. John. A big, splashy, sexy soap opera about an unscrupulous actor who uses everyone to further his career. (Dir: Russell Rouse, 119 mins.)†

Oscar Wilde (Great Britain, 1960)*** Robert Morley, John Neville, Ralph Richardson. One of two British films, made in 1960, about the tragic libel trial of the famed playwright in the 1890s, when he was accused of sodomy and sexual perversion. (Peter Finch starred in *The Trial of Oscar Wilde*.) This filming is the harsher. Morley, physically close to the real Wilde, gustily exudes the wit and decay of the man. (Dir: Gregory Ratoff, 96 mins.)

O'Shaughnessy's Boy (1935)**½ Wallace Beery, Jackie Cooper, Spanky McFarland, Henry Stephenson, Sara Haden. Good Beery-Cooper teaming has a father separated from his son and searching faithfully for him; corny but effective. (Dir: Richard Boleslawski, 88 mins.)

O.S.S. (1946)*** Alan Ladd, Geraldine Fitzgerald. Fairly exciting drama about a mission by America's cloak and dagger heroes. A bit obvious, but interesting story. (Dir: Irving Pichel, 107 mins.)

Ossessione (Italy, 1942)**** Massimo Girotti, Clare Calamai, Elio Marcuzzo. The first great Italian neo-realist film was unseen in the U.S. for more than thirty years because it was based on James M. Cain's novel *The Postman Always Rings Twice*, only it was wartime and they didn't get the rights. A remarkable debut film for director Luchino Visconti. (135 mins.)

Osterman Weekend, The (1983)*½ John Hurt, Rutger Hauer, Burt Lancaster, Craig T. Nelson, Dennis Hopper. Based on Robert Ludlum's best-seller, the plot is too contrived for the slapdash direction it receives. Hurt plays a CIA agent who convinces a journalist that three of his friends are Soviet spies. (Dir: Sam Peckinpah, 102 mins.)†

Otello (Italy, 1986)*** Placido Domingo, Katia Ricciarelli, Justino Diaz. *Otello* benefits from on-location filming and Zeffirelli's swirling camera movements. One can quibble with the director's pruning and his musical and textural transpositions, but this particular filmed opera should have wide audience appeal. (Dir: Franco Zeffirelli, 124 mins.)†

Othan (West Germany-Italy, 1970)*** Adriano Apra, Ennio Lauricella, Olimpia Carlisi, Anne Brumagne, Anthony Pensabene, Jubarithe Semaran. 17th-century play about the 69 A.D. murder of Servius Sulpicus Galba by Marcus Salvius Otho is brought to minimalist life in contemporary Rome by directors Jean-Marie Straub and his wife Daniele Huillet. A fascinating, gloriously shot, beautifully dressed movie that is outrageously, maddeningly slow, often nothing more than a filmed series of tableaux. Co-star Semaran is actually Straub, wonderful as a villain; Apra, starring as Otho, is a noted Italian film critic. (84 mins.)

Othello (France-U.S., 1951)**** Orson Welles, Michael MacLiammoir, Fay Compton, Robert Cook, Suzanne Cloutier. Director Orson Welles's first foreign film was shot in snatches over the years. *Othello* is compromised by his limitations as an actor; as usual, he makes

virtues of his faults. A muscular film, bounding rather than smoldering with jealous energy. Exultantly theatrical and filmic. (91 mins.)

Othello (Great Britain, 1965)***½ Laurence Olivier, Frank Finlay, Maggie Smith. The fourth filmed version of Shakespeare's masterpiece, and it's a towering achievement, largely due to the genius of Olivier. He is arguably the greatest actor of the century, and he does full justice to the demanding role of the crazed Moor, Othello. (Dir: Stuart Burge, 166 mins.)

Other, The (1972)**½ Uta Hagen, Diana Muldaur, Chris Connelly. Unpleasant thriller based on Thomas Tryon's horrific novel about twin boys who keep changing identities. (Dir: Robert Mulligan, 100 mins.)†

Other Francisco, The (Cuba, 1975)*** Miquel Benavides, Ramon Veloz, Alena Sanches, Margarita Balboa. Hardhitting drama, based on noted 19th-century antislavery novel, about the roots of black rebellion in Cuba. Slaves were inhumanely treated, some like animals, and this tough-minded film follows one couple who are treated so harshly that they can't even maintain a relationship because their emotional repression is as hideous as their societal enslavement. (Dir: Santiago Llapur, 97 mins.)

Other Hell, The (Italy, 1980)*½ Franca Stoppi, Carlo de Mejo. A priest arrives at a convent to investigate the grisly murders of several nuns. The killer's identity never becomes clear in this gory Italian thriller with seemingly endless scenes of victims walking through dark corridors, punctuated with loud pounding music by Goblin. More gross than scary; looks like it was edited for U.S. release. (Dir: Stefan Oblowsky, 88 mins.)†

Other Love, The (1947)**½ Barbara Stanwyck, David Niven, Richard Conte, Gilbert Roland. A beautiful concert pianist finds she is ill, throws her life away before realizing a doctor is in love with her. (Dir: André de Toth, 95 mins.)

Other Lover, The (MTV 1985)*½ Lindsay Wagner, Jack Scalia, Max Gail, Millie Perkins. Bland love story with writer Scalia falling in love with a married Wagner. Watch the Other Channel instead. (Dir: Robert Ellis Miller, 104 mins.)

Other Man, The (MTV 1970)** Roy Thinnes, Joan Hackett, Arthur Hill, Tammy Grimes. Hackett's quite good as the rich married lady who falls hopelessly in love with a notorious playboy (Roy Thinnes). (Dir: Richard Colla, 99 mins.)

Other Men's Women (1931)*** Mary Astor, Grant Withers, Regis Toomey, Joan Blondell, James Cagney. Stirring melodrama, with great human feeling, of two railroad worker pals; when one is permanently injured in the line of duty, the other is troubled to find himself attracted to his buddy's wife. Perceptive performances by the three leads; Withers in particular was never so good again. Blondell and Cagney have sharply etched secondary parts. Another uncompromising winner from director William Wellman. (70 mins.)

Other Side of Hell, The (MTV 1978)***½ Alan Arkin, Roger E. Mosley, Morgan Woodward. Nightmare about life in a hospital for the criminally insane. Arkin is superb as Frank Dole, a highly disturbed, intelligent inmate, who is determined to survive. (Dir: Jan Kadar, 156 mins.)

Other Side of Midnight, The (1977)½ Marie France Pisier, John Beck, Susan Sarandon. Dreary melodrama based on the best-selling novel by Sidney Sheldon. The story involves a French movie star and a Washington socialite vying for the affections of a World War II hero. (Dir: Charles Jarrott, 165 mins.)†

Other Side of the Mountain, The (1975)** Marilyn Hassett, Beau Bridges. True-life story of Jill Kilmont, a skier who might have made it to the 1956 Olympics if it hadn't been for an accident which left her paralyzed. Heavy-handed tearjerker. (Dir: Larry Peerce, 103 mins.)†

Other Side of the Mountain Part II, The (1977)** Marilyn Hassett, Timothy Bottoms, Belinda Montgomery. Sudsy account of a paralyzed Olympic hopeful, skier Jill Kilmont, and her experience with true love in the person of a truck driver. (Dir: Larry Peerce, 100 mins.)†

Other Victim, The (MTV 1981)**½ William Devane, Jennifer O'Neill, Todd Sussman. Another wrenching rape drama, this one shedding light on the anger, guilt, and frustration felt by the victim's husband. (Dir: Noel Black, 104 mins.)

Other Woman, The (1954)** Cleo Moore, Hugo Haas. Girl trying to make good in Hollywood plans to blackmail a director. (Dir: Hugo Haas, 81 mins.)

Other Woman, The (MTV 1983)*** Hal Linden, Anne Meara, Madolyn Smith. A middle-aged publisher ditches his young wife to find pleasure with a 48-year-old grandmother. The script is spiced with some light digs at fashionable, trendy youths. (Dir: Melville Shavelson, 104 mins.)

Otley (Great Britain, 1969)*** Tom Courtenay, Romy Schneider, Fiona Lewis, Alan Badel. Engaging secret-agent spoof. Courtenay plays an affable drifter who picks up women and various animate objects that don't belong to him. (Dir: Dick Clement, 90 mins.)

Our Betters (1933)** Constance Bennett, Gilbert Roland. Director George Cukor

does his damnedest to energize Somerset Maugham's drawing-room comedy. The result is a pleasant but talky romance about a titled nobleman's marriage to a rich American commoner. (78 mins.)

Our Blushing Brides (1930)**½ Joan Crawford, Anita Page, Dorothy Sebastian, Robert Montgomery, John Miljan, Edward Brophy. Another slant on *Three On a Match*, with three big city roommates meeting different fates. Crawford looks fabulous wearing a platinum wig in an astounding fashion show; this is truly a shopgirl's dream, with the emphasis on sets, clothes, and romance rather than common sense. A lot of fun if approached in the right spirit. (Dir: Harry Beaumont, 74 mins.)

Our Daily Bread (1934)*** Tom Keene, Karen Morley, Barbara Pepper, John Qualen. American classic of, and about, the depression, directed, financed, and co-authored by a master, King Vidor, as a personal statement of his faith in America. A young couple join a commune where each person ideally contributes an individual skill to help everyone. (74 mins.)†

Our Dancing Daughters (1928)*** Joan Crawford, Dorothy Sebastian, Anita Page, Johnny Mack Brown. This well-made jazz baby film epitomizes what the '20s thought they were all about. Crawford incarnates the ultimate flapper in the role that made her a genuine star. (Dir: Harry Beaumont, 86 mins.)

Our Family Business (MTV 1981)*½ Ted Danson, Sam Wanamaker, Deborah Carney. The family business of the title is crime, and this junior and vastly inferior *Godfather* saga follows a familiar pattern known to fans of the genre. Sam Wanamaker is the patriarch who is just out of jail. (Dir: Robert Collins, 156 mins.)†

Our Hearts Were Growing Up (1946)**½ Diana Lynn, Gail Russell. Silly story about two young girls on a weekend at Princeton University during the 1920s who get mixed up with bootleggers. A few laughs, but mostly forced comedy. (Dir: William D. Russell, 83 mins.)

Our Hearts Were Young and Gay (1944)*** Diana Lynn, Gail Patrick. Delightful little comedy about a trip abroad during the gay year of 1932 by two young, attractive girls. (Dir: Lewis Allen, 81 mins.)

Our Hitler, a Film from Germany (West Germany, 1980)**** Heinz Schubert, Peter Kern, Hellmut Lange, Rainer Von Artenfels, Martin Sperr. Extraordinary seven hour film examining through the blend of realism and poetic expression, with the use of puppets and live actors, the Hitler period and our present relationship with it. (Dir: Hans-Jurgen Syberberg, 420 mins.)

Our Hospitality (1923)**** Buster Keaton, Natalie Talmadge, Joe Keaton, Joe Roberts. Fabulous comedy, one of Keaton's best films; the story is of the hapless son of a Kentucky family who innocently returns to the old homestead only to find himself in the midst of a feud with his lady love's family. Richly packed with humor, not just gags, but real human observation; beautifully conceived, beautifully performed, and beautifully photographed. The acrobatic climax still elicits gasps from any audience. It is generally conceded that although he eschewed screen credit, Keaton actually directed most of his films. (Dirs: Jack Blystone, Buster Keaton, 74 mins.)

Our Little Girl (1935)**½ Shirley Temple, Joel McCrea, Rosemary Ames. Shirley patches up her parents' troubled marriage by drastic means. Sentimental melodrama; fine if you love Shirley. (Dir: John Robertson, 63 mins.)†

Our Man Flint (1966)*** James Coburn, Lee J. Cobb, Gila Golan. This super-gimmicked, high-style spoof of the James Bond films benefits from the suave presence of Coburn, as Flint. The plot, if you care, concerns an organization which plans to take over the world with their secret weapon—controlling the weather. (Dir: Daniel Mann, 107 mins.)†

Our Man Flint: Dead on Target (MTV 1976)** Ray Danton, Sharon Acker. Ray Danton takes over where James Coburn left off in this update of the old, flashy secret-agent spoofs. (Dir: Joseph Scanlon, 72 mins.)

Our Man In Havana (Great Britain, 1960)*** Alec Guinness, Burl Ives, Maureen O'Hara, Noël Coward, Ernie Kovacs. This uneven film version of Graham Greene's novel fluctuates between out and out comedy and stark drama. The plot concerns a vacuum cleaner salesman who is recruited to become a spy but never receives any instructions about his duties as a spy. (Dir: Carol Reed, 107 mins.)

Our Miss Brooks (1956)**½ Eve Arden, Gale Gordon, Richard Crenna. The popular radio and TV series is on the screen. Nothing new but if you were a fan of "Miss Brooks," you'll enjoy this visit with the old crew at Madison High. (Dir: Al Lewis, 85 mins.)

Our Mother's House (Great Britain, 1967)*** Dirk Bogarde, Pamela Franklin, Mark Lester. Entertaining British entry concerns a group of children, the oldest being thirteen, who conceal their invalid mother's death and carry on as a family unit. Enter wandering no-good dad (Bogarde) and the plot takes on shadings of the unexpected. (Dir: Jack Clayton, 105 mins.)

Our Relations (1936)*** Stan Laurel, Oliver Hardy, Sidney Toler. The old *Comedy of Errors* plot line works well for L and H. In this double-trouble laugh riot, Stan and Ollie encounter their twin siblings, whom they haven't seen in years; the resulting confusion will have fans roaring with laughter. (Dir: Harry Lachman, 74 mins.)†

Our Story (France, 1984)*** Alain Delon, Nathalie Baye, Gerard Darmon, Genevieve Fontanel, Michel Galabru. A handsome man meets a beautiful woman on a train. She tells him a story about anonymous one-time sex which they reenact, leaving him obsessed with her afterward. Often humorous film succeeds with excellent performances from Delon and Baye, expertly switching from comedy to drama and back. (Dir: Bertrand Blier, 111 mins.)

Our Time—See: **Death of Her Innocence**

Our Town (1940)*** Frank Craven, William Holden, Martha Scott, Thomas Mitchell, Fay Bainter. Thornton Wilder play loses much of its impact in its screen adaptation. Still folksy and sweet; buoyed by wise performances. (Dir: Sam Wood, 90 mins.)†

Our Very Own (1950)** Ann Blyth, Farley Granger, Joan Evans, Donald Cook, Jane Wyatt, Natalie Wood. Melodramatic yarn about a young girl who accidentally discovers she has been adopted. (Dir: David Miller, 93 mins.)

Our Vines Have Tender Grapes (1945)*** Edward G. Robinson, Margaret O'Brien, Agnes Moorehead. Warm, moving, well-played story about the love people have for each other in a small community. Touching theme delivered with a minimum of corn. (Dir: Roy Rowland, 105 mins.)

Our Wife (1941)**½ Melvyn Douglas, Ruth Hussey. Trumpet player wants to marry a socialite, but his divorce isn't final. Lengthy comedy is too drawn out, but is nicely made. (Dir: John M. Stahl, 95 mins.)

Our Winning Season (1978)** Scott Jacoby, Deborah Benson, Dennis Blank, Randy Herman, Jan Smithers, P. J. Soles. Derivative coming-of-age tale of a high school track star competing for a scholarship. (Dir: Joseph Ruben, 92 mins.)

Out (1982)*½ Peter Coyote, O-Lan Shepard, Jim Haynie, Grandfather Semu Haute, Danny Glover. Adaptation of a book by experimental novelist Ronald Sukenik is better to watch than it is to read, but still annoyingly artsy. Coyote hitchhikes across America, encountering the usual odd denizens (all played by the same few actors). (Dir: Eli Hollander, 82 mins.)†

Outback (Australia, 1971)*** Gary Bond, Chips Rafferty, Donald Pleasence. Offbeat adventure. A young schoolteacher (Bond) in Australia's barren outback is scheduled to fly to Sydney during vacation. To get the plane, he goes to Yago, a small boomtown, where the influence of the roughneck locals nearly destroys him. (Dir: Ted Kotcheff, 99 mins.)

Outback Bound (MTV 1988)** Donna Mills, Andrew Clarke, Nina Foch, John Schneider. Mills plays a fashion-plate down on her luck who travels Down Under to unload an opal mine. The Australian actors in the cast provide the color but Ms. Mills just doesn't cut it. (Dir: John Llewelyn Moxey, 96 mins.)

Outcast, The (1954)*** John Derek, Joan Evans, Jim Davis. Young man returns to Colorado intending to obtain a ranch from his uncle which he thinks is rightfully his. Fast, exciting western. (Dir: William Witney, 90 mins.)†

Outcast, The (1961)—See: **Sin, The**

Outcast of the Islands (Great Britain, 1952)**** Ralph Richardson, Trevor Howard, Robert Morley, Wendy Hiller. A clerk in the South Seas enters into a smuggling plot with the natives, betrays his employer, eventually becomes a broken man. Fine study of moral corruption of man's character, based on Joseph Conrad's story. Directed by Carol Reed with finesse; superbly acted, photographed. (93 mins.)

Outcasts of Poker Flat, The (1952)**½ Anne Baxter, Dale Robertson, Cameron Mitchell, Miriam Hopkins. Four shady characters are run out of a mining town and marooned in a cabin during a snowstorm. Competent Western drama. (Dir: Joseph M. Newman, 81 mins.)

Out Cold (1988)*½ John Lithgow, Teri Garr, Randy Quaid, Bruce McGill, Lisa Blount. Black comic farce about a butcher, who thinks he's responsible for his partner's death, and how he and the dead man's wife try to dispose of the corpse. Waste of a good cast. (Dir: Malcolm Mowbray, 95 mins.)†

Outcry, The (Italy, 1957)*** Steve Cochran, Alida Valli, Betsy Blair, Dorian Gray, Lynn Shaw, Gabriella Pallott. Director Michelangelo Antonioni was prepping for greatness with this drama, made just before his masterpiece *L'Avventura*, about a simple worker who wanders about Italy with his young daughter after his wife abandons them both. A sensitive study of loss, loneliness, and despair. AKA: **Il Grido**. (115 mins.)

Outer Reach—See: **Spaced Out**

Outfit, The (1973)* Robert Duvall, Karen Black, Sheree North, Robert Ryan, Joe Don Baker. Tacky, violent melodrama about criminals trying to outsmart each other. (Dir: John Flynn, 102 mins.)

Out for Justice (1991)* Steven Seagal,

William Forsythe, Jerry Orbach, Jo Champa. Violent rubbish. Seagal's a Brooklyn cop who spends the entire film tracking down a neighborhood bully, played to scenery-chewing perfection by Forsythe. Obscenities abound, limbs break, and blood flows. (Dir: John Flynn, 92 mins.)†

Outing, The (1987)*½ Deborah Winters, James Huston. Repetitive supernatural schlock. A group of teenagers sneaks into a museum with intentions of staying overnight, little knowing that one of them has released an evil genie (or "jinn") from an ancient lamp on display. (Dir: Tom Daley, 85 mins.)

Outland (1981)**½ Sean Connery, Frances Sternhagen, Peter Boyle. Western-style action story transplanted into outer space, as a stubborn, brave marshall arrives on a moon of Jupiter and tries to wipe out bad guys. Connery is charismatic as the marshall, Sternhagen is entertaining as the hard-boiled local doctor. (Dir: Peter Hyams, 109 mins.)†

Outlaw, The (1943)*½ Walter Huston, Thomas Mitchell, Jane Russell, Jack Beutel. The notorious sexy western about Billy the Kid, Doc Holliday (his mentor), and the dame with the bulging blouse who loves him. Subtract all the publicity received by Jane's bosom, and you have a bad western with some good work by Huston and Mitchell, who went along with the joke. (Dir: Howard Hughes, 123 mins.)

Outlaw Blues (1977)**½ Peter Fonda, Susan St. James, James Callahan. A lightweight chase film chronicling the saga of one Bobby Ogden, country singer and composer recently out of jail, out for revenge on the guy who stole his tune and parlayed it into a big hit on the charts. (Dir: Richard T. Heffron, 99 mins.)†

Outlaw Force (1988)½ David Heavener, Paul Smith, Frank Stallone, Robert Bjorkland, Stephanie Cicero, Warren Berlinger. Star Heavener is also credited as director, writer, co-producer, and songwriter (guess who sings them?), so it's not hard to tell who to blame for this hellish revenge drama about a mild-mannered Vietnam veteran pushed to violence by scum who rape and kill his wife and sell his daughter into prostitution. (95 mins.)†

Outlaw Josey Wales, The (1976)**½ Clint Eastwood, Chief Dan George, Sondra Locke. Tough rancher Josey Wales is provided with a powerful motive for revenge in this action-packed western drama. After a renegade massacre of his family, Josey sets off on his mission, meeting vulnerable people one after the other and knocking off enough foes to populate a small town. (Dir: Clint Eastwood, 130 mins.)†

Outlaws, The (MTV 1984)** Charles Rocket, Christopher Lemmon, Charles Napier. A feeble attempt at comedy about a pair of innocent bystanders sent to prison for a jewel heist. (Dir: James Frawley, 104 mins.)

Outlaws (MTV 1986)**½ Rod Taylor, William Lucking, Richard Roundtree, Charles Napier, Richard Roundtree, Charles Napier. A series pilot. Some rootin' tootin' cowboys (four bandits and one reformed galoot) find themselves transported from the old wild West into modern-day Texas, where they must contend with newfangled contraptions, contemporary urban codes of behavior, and some truly evil contemporary felons. (Dir: Peter Werner, 104 mins.)

Outlaws Is Coming, The (1965)** The Three Stooges, Adam West, Nancy Kovack. Moe, Larry and Curley Joe journey west, where Annie Oakley (Kovack) helps them expose a villainous outlaw boss. (Dir: Norman Maurer, 89 mins.)

Outlaw Women (1951)*½ Marie Windsor, Richard Rober, Carla Bolenda. Female gamblers control a border town. Juiceless western. (Dirs: Sam Newfield, Ron Ormond, 76 mins.)†

Out of Africa (1985)*** Meryl Streep, Robert Redford, Klaus Maria Brandauer, Michael Gough. *Africa* is based on Isak Dinesen's adventures of a Danish expatriate (Streep) and her relationships with a lusty plantation owner (Brandauer) and a Great White Hunter (Redford) in the wilds of the dark continent. The film goes for sun-drenched romanticism at every opportunity, though there's hardly enough story to fill the time. (Dir: Sydney Pollack, 155 mins.)†

Out of Bounds (1986)** Anthony Michael Hall, Jenny Wright, Jeff Kober, Meat Loaf. Hall has a right to look confused in this violent film about an Iowa kid who inadvertently acquires a psycho's heroin in L.A. and instantly becomes the city's most wanted criminal. Director Richard Tuggle jettisons all logic to ladle on the red herrings, but achieves little suspense in this infantile thriller. (93 mins.)†

Out of Control (1985)* Martin Hewitt, Betsy Russell, Claudia Udy, Andrew J. Lederer, Sherilyn Fenn. Rich brats are stranded by a plane crash on a remote island populated only by nasty smugglers. With stars like Hewitt and Russell, it's easy to find yourself rooting for the bad guys. (Dir: Allan Holzman, 78 mins.)†

Out of Order (West Germany, 1985)**½ Renée Soutendijk, Gotz George, Wolfgang Kieling, Hannes Jaenicke. Four people, the last to leave an office building on Friday evening, are trapped in a broken elevator. The characters and dialogue are a bit too acerbic for an audience to want to spend ninety minutes with them, though director Carl Schenkel does an admirable job of keeping the enclosed space from becoming visually boring. (88 mins.)†

Out of Season (Great Britain, 1975)** Vanessa Redgrave, Cliff Robertson, Susan George. Atmospheric but unfocused love story about a man who returns to a lover of twenty years ago. She now has an attractive daughter, who may be their love child. (Dir: Alan Bridges, 90 mins.)†

Out of the Blue (1947)**½ George Brent, Virginia Mayo, Ann Dvorak, Turhan Bey, Carole Landis. A husband is in all sorts of hot water when a shady lady passes out in his apartment. Cute romantic comedy. (Dir: Leigh Jason, 84 mins.)†

Out of the Blue (1983)***½ Linda Manz, Dennis Hopper, Sharon Farrell, Don Gordon, Raymond Burr. Harsh, engrossing drama about the miserable lives of a deadbeat trucker and his spaced-out daughter. Its improvisational tone is strengthened by the intense performances of Manz and Hopper. (Dir: Dennis Hopper, 89 mins.)†

Out of the Darkness (MTV 1985)*** Martin Sheen, Hector Elizondo, Matt Clark, Jennifer Salt, Eddie Egan. A competently acted and tightly scripted teleplay about the "Son of Sam" murder cases, with Martin Sheen as the determined New York detective Ed Zigo. (Dir: Jud Taylor, 104 mins.)†

Out of the Fog (1941)*** Ida Lupino, John Garfield, Thomas Mitchell, Eddie Albert. Movie version of Irwin Shaw's *The Gentle People* benefits from wonderful acting by a top drawer cast and Anatole Litvak's skillful direction. Story of a gangster's preying on innocent people wavers between greatness and mediocrity. (86 mins.)

Out of the Past (1947)***½ Robert Mitchum, Jane Greer, Kirk Douglas, Rhonda Fleming. Gas station owner with a past meets a desperate woman and winds up in murder. The ultimate Robert Mitchum movie. Director Jacques Tourneur has created something close to a masterpiece in this adaptation of a novel by Geoffrey Homes. Remade as *Against All Odds*. (97 mins.)†

Out of the Shadows (MCTV 1988)** Charles Dance, Alexandra Paul, Michael J. Shannon. A routine smuggling adventure yarn which hits all the familiar notes but is slightly enhanced by location photography in the scenic Greek Islands. The excitement comes in spurts, and the love story never seems to ignite. (Dir: Willi Patterson, 105 mins.)

Out of This World (1945)**½ Eddie Bracken, Diana Lynn, Veronica Lake. Story of a crooner who makes the girls swoon has some funny moments, but is generally forced comedy. Bracken is the crooner, and he borrows a familiar voice (Bing Crosby's) for the occasion. (Dir: Hal Walker, 96 mins.)

Out of Time (MTV 1988)*½ Bruce Abbott, Bill Maher, Adam Ant. Shopworn sci-fi that incorporates some clumsy humor into its derivative story line. Abbott is a private eye from the future who works with his computer wiz great-grandfather to capture a time-traveling criminal (Ant). (Dir: Robert Butler, 96 mins.)

Out of Towners, The (1970)*** Jack Lemmon, Sandy Dennis, Anthony Holland, Sandy Baron. The ''Out-of-Towners'' are non-New Yorkers in Neil Simon's uneven but frequently funny and sardonic notion of the perils that await the unwary who choose to visit the demilitarized zone of peacetime New York. Lemmon plays an obnoxious, dyspeptic executive from Ohio visiting ''Fun City'' for a job audition. (Dir: Arthur Hiller, 97 mins.)†

Out on a Limb (MTV 1987)**½ Shirley MacLaine, Charles Dance, John Heard, Anne Jackson, Jerry Orbach. MacLaine's beliefs about reincarnation and the powers of meditation are featured in this film in which she plays herself. Playing yourself is never easy but Shirley manages to be her infectious self while educating us on this mystical journey, played out amid the soap-opera aspects of her love life, beginning ten years ago. (Dir: Robert Butler, 260 mins.)

Outpost in Malaya (Great Britain, 1952)** Claudette Colbert, Jack Hawkins. Adventure and intrigue on a rubber plantation form the background for this mediocre film. (Dir: Ken Annakin, 88 mins.)

Outrage (1950)*** Mala Powers, Tod Andrews, Robert Clarke, Raymond Bond, Jerry Paris. A surprisingly daring, and unjustly forgotten, drama about a rape and its aftereffects. Powers (in her film debut) plays a young woman who feeling ''dirty'' after being violated, tries to run away to a new life. Corny toward the end, but Ida Lupino's direction betrays a keen sense of expressionist style throughout. (75 mins.)

Outrage (1964)*** Paul Newman, Claire Bloom, Laurence Harvey, Edward G. Robinson, William Shatner. Conflicting stories are heard in the aftermath of a crime, as a bandit kidnaps a married couple, molests the wife, murders the husband. Story is taken from Japanese film *Rashomon* and set in the West. Intellectually interesting tale of the elusive nature of ''truth'' and how it changes

in the eyes of the beholder. (Dir: Martin Ritt, 97 mins.)

Outrage (MTV 1973)**½ Robert Culp, Thomas Leopold, Marilyn Mason. Disturbing, thought-provoking story about a group of teenage boys who menace a new family in an upper-middle-class neighborhood of a small California community. (Dir: Richard T. Heffron, 74 mins.)

Outrage (MTV 1986)*** Robert Preston, Beau Bridges, Burgess Meredith, Linda Purl, Anthony Newley. A good cast in a meaty courtroom-drama over a legal loophole that allows a blatant miscarriage of justice. But Bridges holds the spotlight as the defense attorney warring with Burgess Meredith's trusty old judge over the concept of putting the court on trial, not the self-confessed defendant. (Dir: Walter Grauman, 104 mins.)

Outrageous! (Canada, 1977)*** Craig Russell, Hollis McLaren, Richert Easley. Female impersonator shacks up chastely with escaped schizophrenic. Clever comedy-drama and Russell is even better out of drag. (Dir: Richard Benner, 100 mins.)†

Outrageous Fortune (1987)*** Bette Midler, Shelley Long, Peter Coyote, Robert Prosky, John Schuck, George Carlin, Anthony Heald. A boisterous variant on the male buddy-buddy movie made irresistible by the wacky teamwork of Long and Midler. Long's an ultraladylike, reserved thespian who gets mixed up with a brash, outspoken actress (Midler) when the two share an acting class and also discover they've shared the same lover. Thanks to this two-timing Romeo, the women get involved in secret agent shenanigans. (Dir: Arthur Hiller, 92 mins.)†

Outriders, The (1950)*** Joel McCrea, Arlene Dahl, Barry Sullivan. Rousing action-filled western about the trek of a wagon train across treacherous Indian territory, and a better than usual script. (Dir: Roy Rowland, 93 mins.)

Outside Chance (MTV 1978)** Yvette Mimieux, Royce Applegate, Dick Armstrong, Susan Batson. A TV rehash of *Jackson County Jail* (with the same star and director); lurid tale of the living hell female prisoners undergo in big bad redneck jails. (Dir: Michael Miller, 100 mins.)

Outside Man, The (France-U.S., 1973)** Jean-Louis Trintignant, Ann-Margret, Roy Scheider, Angie Dickinson. Despite the star-studded cast, this crime melodrama suffers from a lack of cohesive continuity. Trintignant is a hired killer who is earmarked for assassination by American hit-man Scheider. (Dir: Jacques Deray, 104 mins.)

Outsider, The (1961)***½ Tony Curtis, James Franciscus. An absorbing film which bogs down a bit in the last third but it doesn't detract from the overall impact of the true story of American-Indian Ira Hayes who was one of the Marines who helped hoist the flag on Iwo Jima. (Dir: Delbert Mann, 108 mins.)

Outsider, The (MTV 1967)*½ Darren McGavin, Anna Hagan, Edmond O'Brien. McGavin is fine as an ex-con who's hired as a private eye to learn if a young girl has been embezzling funds. (Dir: William Graham, 98 mins.)

Outsider, The (1979)*** Craig Wasson, Sterling Hayden, Patricia Quinn. An idealistic American joins the IRA after a tour in Vietnam, only to discover that he is being used as a sacrificial lamb for propaganda purposes. (Dir: Tony Luraschi, 128 mins.)

Outsiders, The (1983)** Ralph Macchio, C. Thomas Howell, Matt Dillon, Rob Lowe, Patrick Swayze, Diane Lane, Emilio Estevez, Tom Cruise, Leif Garrett, Tom Waits. Rich kids vs. the poor thugs in 1966 Tulsa, Oklahoma. Based on the S. E. Hinton novel, Francis Ford Coppola's adaptation is filmed like an epic, but scripted, acted, and directed like a teen flick. (95 mins.)†

Outside the Law (1921)**½ Lon Chaney, Priscilla Dean, Ralph Lewis, E. A. Warren. Curious Chaney vehicle promotes racial harmony, as a kindly Chinese rescues a gangster and his daughter from a frameup; Chaney, however, is in his element playing a ruthless, power-hungry outlaw. Effective melodrama, and the star's intensity is impressive. (Dir: Tod Browning, 77 mins.)†

Outside the Wall (1950)** Richard Basehart, Marilyn Maxwell, Signe Hasso. Basehart's performance is the only recommendable feature of this tiresome tale of an ex-con who finds a job as a laboratory assistant at a sanitarium and encounters all sorts of evil people. (Dir: Crane Wilbur, 80 mins.)

Outtakes (1985)* Forrest Tucker, Bobbi Wexler, Joleen Lutz, Curt Colbert. Collection of skits satirizing television shows and commercials wants to be another *Groove Tube;* it has the vulgarity but none of the wit. (Dir: Jack M. Sell, 71 mins.)†

Outward Bound (1930)**½ Leslie Howard, Douglas Fairbanks, Jr., Helen Chandler, Beryl Mercer, Alison Skipworth, Alec B. Francis. The classic Sutton Vane play about the shipboard passengers who discover they're on a one-way trip to nowhere. The plot line's been revamped dozens of times, and the film was remade as *Between Two Worlds.* (Dir: Robert Milton, 84 mins.)

Out West with the Hardys (1938)**½ Mickey Rooney, Lewis Stone. Homespun humor. Just as many warm, human problems confront them out west as in their other films. (Dir: George B. Seitz, 84 mins.)

Overboard (MTV 1978)** Cliff Robertson, Angie Dickinson. Cliff and wife Angie embark on a dream vacation, sailing around the world, but tragedy intervenes. (Dir: John Newland, 104 mins.)

Overboard (1987)*** Goldie Hawn, Kurt Russell, Edward Herrman, Katherine Helmond. Seeking revenge (and a cheap housekeeper), carpenter Russell convinces amnesiac rich bitch Hawn that she's really the mother of his brood of undisciplined children. Better than average Goldie vehicle. (Dir: Garry Marshall, 112 mins.)†

Overcoat, The (U.S.S.R., 1959)***½ Roland Bykov, Y. Tolubeyev. Faithful, intelligent adaptation of the classic by Nikolai Gogol, a tragicomic and purely Russian tale of a lowly civil clerk in imperial Russia who dreams only of possessing a new overcoat that will not only warm him, but bolster his dignity and pride. (Dir: Aleksei Batalov, 93 mins.)†

Over-Exposed (1956)*½ Cleo Moore, Richard Crenna, Isobel Elsom, Raymond Greenleaf, Jack Albertson. More like underdeveloped. Trite film about fledgling newspaper photographer Moore working her way to the top. (Dir: Lewis Seiler, 80 mins.)

Overkill (1986)* Steve Rally, John Nishio, Laura Burkett, Allen Wisch, Michelle Bauer. A hardheaded L.A. detective and an equally stubborn Japanese cop team up to battle the Yakuza, Japanese gangsters. (Dir: Ulli Lommel, 82 mins.)†

Overlanders, The (Australia, 1946)***½ Chips Rafferty, Daphne Campbell. When the Japanese threaten invasion of Australia, brave men undertake a great trek across the continent with precious cattle. Engrossing true-life story has the ingredients of a western, war story, and documentary; an unusual film worth seeing. (Dir: Harry Watt, 91 mins.)

Overland Pacific (1954)**½ Jock Mahoney, Peggie Castle. Undercover agent investigates Indian attacks on the railroad, discovers white men behind it all. (Dir: Fred F. Sears, 73 mins.)

Over My Dead Body (1942)** Milton Berle, Mary Beth Hughes, Reginald Denny, Frank Orth, Wonderful Smith, J. Patrick O'Malley. Berle as a would-be writer who can never finish his mystery stories (they get too complicated for him to figure out) provides a fair amount of laughs in this cleverly plotted comedy-mystery. (Dir: Malcolm St. Clair, 68 mins.)

Over the Brooklyn Bridge (1984)* Elliott Gould, Margaux Hemingway, Sid Caesar,

Carol Kane, Burt Young. A heavy-handed romantic comedy about a Brooklyn luncheonette owner who plans to crash the Big Apple big time. (Dir: Menahem Golan, 108 mins.)†

Over the Edge (1979)**½ Michael Kramer, Pamela Ludwig, Matt Dillon. Troubled teens reject the values of their parents, who are so obsessed with their model community they fail to see the breaks in their own family circles. While the film may score points with the anarchy-minded adolescents, the climax of the film, where teens run amok and destroy property, seems deliberately sensationalized. (Dir: Jonathan Kaplan, 95 mins.)†

Over the Hill Gang, The (MTV 1969)*½ Edgar Buchanan, Andy Devine, Rick Nelson, Pat O'Brien. Old Texas Rangers put themselves back into circulation to curtail the crime wave in their town. (Dir: Jean Yarbrough, 72 mins.)

Over the Hill Gang Rides Again, The (MTV 1970)**½ Walter Brennan, Fred Astaire, Chill Wills, Edgar Buchanan. In this outing, Fred Astaire joins the group as a drunken, grizzled ex-lawman who finds his way back thanks to aid from his old cronies. (Dir: George McCowan, 73 mins.)

Over the Top (1987)** Sylvester Stallone, Susan Blakely, David Mendenhall, Robert Loggia. This beefcake fairy tale involves an arm wrestler who wants to regain his son's love after his ex-wife goes the terminal-illness route. (Dir: Menahem Golan, 92 mins.)†

Over There: 1914–1918 (1983)***½ Director Jean Aurel culled rarely seen combat footage, much of it in pristine condition, for this fascinating accout of World War I, "the war to end all wars." Documentary stresses the strategies of the powers in battle and provides relentlessly graphic scenes of the horrors of the struggle. (90 mins.)

Over 21 (1945)**½ Irene Dunne, Charles Coburn, Alexander Knox. Wartime comedy about a wife who stands by her "aging" hubby through the rigors of officers' candidate school. (Dir: Charles Vidor, 102 mins.)

Owen Marshall, Counsellor at Law (MTV 1971)* Arthur Hill, Vera Miles, Joseph Campanella, Dana Wynter. Hippie is charged with the murder of a rich socialite. Pilot for former TV series. (Dir: Buzz Kulik, 100 mins.)

Owl and the Pussycat, The (1970)*** Barbra Streisand, George Segal, Robert Klein. Call girl (Streisand) hooks up with intellectual (Segal) in a raunchy, boisterous, funny outing. The Streisand and Segal duet keeps you happily involved. (Dir: Herbert Ross, 95 mins.)†

Ox-Bow Incident, The (1943)***½ Henry
Fonda, Harry Morgan, Dana Andrews, Jane Darwell, William Eythe, Anthony Quinn. A powerful, relentless anti-lynching drama, with strong performances, especially from Fonda as a cowboy with a conscience. From the novel by Walter Van Tilburg Clark. (Dir: William Wellman, 75 mins.)†

Oxford Blues (1984)*½ Rob Lowe, Ally Sheedy, Amanda Pays, Gail Strickland. *A Yank at Oxford* refurbished with color, rock music, and a teenage cast. Lowe plays the cocky American student who wangles his way into Oxford University to be near the woman he loves. (Dir: Robert Boris, 93 mins.)†

Pacific Destiny (Great Britain, 1956)** Denholm Elliott, Michael Hordern, Gordon Jackson, Susan Stephen. Stiff-upper-lip colonialism is promoted in this true story of the governor of the British Pacific territories in the early 1900s. Nothing special, despite a good cast. (Dir: Wolf Rilla, 97 mins.)

Pacific Heights (1990)** Melanie Griffith, Matthew Modine, Michael Keaton, Laurie Metcalf. The world's worst tenant, a *bona fide whacko*, rents a San Francisco apartment (without a credit check or lease) from an eager yuppie couple and turns their lives into a nightmare: They can't evict him. If this had been shot as a comedy about California's landlord-tenant laws it might have been fun to watch, but much of it is ridiculous and very little works. (Dir: John Schlesinger, 103 mins.)†

Pacific Liner (1939)*** Victor McLaglen, Chester Morris, Wendy Barrie. Ship's doctor tries to stem the spread of cholera aboard an ocean liner, but is hampered by the engineer. Suspenseful melodrama. (Dir: Lew Landers, 76 mins.)

Pack, The (1977)*** Joe Don Baker, Bibi Besch, Richard B. Shull, R. G. Armstrong, Hope Alexander-Willis. Compact chiller about abandoned dogs who turn killer and begin chewing on the populace of a resort town. AKA: **The Long Dark Night**. (Dir: Robert Clouse, 99 mins.)†

Package, The (1989)*** Gene Hackman, Joanna Cassidy, Tommy Lee Jones, Pam Grier, John Heard, Dennis Franz. Fine suspense thriller with military attaché Hackman delivering a soldier for court-martial, caught up in an assassination plot after he disappears. Nifty surprises and violent plot twists add excitement. (Dir: Andrew Davis, 108 mins.)†

Package Tour (Hungary, 1984)***½ Disturbing and provocative documentary follows concentration camp survivors as they take a bus tour of Auschwitz, the notorious prison where thousands of Poles were exterminated. Filled with sorrow but also with humanity and hope. (Dir: Gyula Gazdag, 75 mins.)

Packin' It In (MTV 1983)*½ Paula Prentiss, Richard Benjamin, Tony Roberts, Andrea Marcovicci, Molly Ringwald. Forced comedy about a harassed city family who takes root in the country, and learns under duress how to survive. (Dir: Jud Taylor, 104 mins.)†

Pack of Lies (MTV 1987)***½ Ellen Burstyn, Teri Garr, Alan Bates. A superbly acted TV adaptation of Hugh Whitemore's stage play; the play's flaws are minimized on the small screen. Set in a London suburb in 1961, the story concerns a couple who is persuaded by the British counterintelligence agency to spy on their best friends, who are suspected of espionage. (Dir: Anthony Page, 104 mins.)

Pack Up Your Troubles (1932)**½ Stan Laurel, Oliver Hardy, Mary Carr, James Finlayson, Charles Middleton, Grady Sutton. L and H find themselves drafted into comical complications when they're in Uncle Sam's service during WWI. When not destroying any semblance of order in the armed forces, they're looking after the interests of the daughter of a dead buddy. (Dirs: George Marshall, Ray McCarey, 68 mins.)

Pack Up Your Troubles (1939)** Ritz Brothers, Jane Withers. The Ritzes provide a few laughs in a WWI plot about spies at the front. (Dir: H. Bruce Humberstone, 68 mins.)

Pad (and How to Use It), The (1966)**½ Brian Bedford, Julie Sommars, James Farentino. Comedy about a swinging bachelor and a shy one who team up to woo an unsuspecting young miss. (Dir: Brian Hutton, 86 mins.)

Paddy, the Next Best Thing (1933)**½ Janet Gaynor, Warner Baxter, Walter Connolly, Harvey Stephens. Tomboy Gaynor saves the day when her father wants her older sister to marry a rich man in order to help the family out of financial difficulties. Delightful romantic romp. (Dir: Harry Lachman, 76 mins.)

Padre Nuestro (Spain, 1986)***½ Fernando Rey, Francisco Rabal, Victoria Abril. A dying Vatican cardinal returns to his Spanish home to set his family affairs in order. These include the family winery, much treasured by the Vatican, and the question of who will inherit it: the Cardinal's atheist brother, or his illegitimate daughter, a prostitute. Splendidly acted, beautifully photographed film works both as a straight drama about a man facing death and as a satire. (Dir: Francisco Regueiro, 90 mins.)†

Padre Padrone (Italy, 1977)***½ Omero Antonutti, Saverio Marioni, Marcella

Michelangeli, Fabrizio Forte. Adapted from one of Italy's all-time best-sellers, it's about the struggle of an ignorant shepherd boy to escape his domineering peasant father who hates reading and civilization. This slow-paced epic follows the author from childhood to college and personal reconciliation with his difficult father. A straightforward, moving film. (Dirs: Vittorio, Paolo Taviani, 114 mins.)†

Pagan Love Song (1950)** Esther Williams, Howard Keel. Strictly for escapists—a tuneful and eye-filling musical with the customary swimming sequences. (Dir: Robert Alton, 76 mins.)

Pagans, The—See: **Barbarians, The**

Page Miss Glory (1935)*** Marion Davies, Pat O'Brien, Dick Powell, Mary Astor, Frank McHugh, Lyle Talbot, Patsy Kelly. Clever takeoff on all those Hollywood publicity campaigns and the imaginative hucksters who'll do anything to promote their clients. (Dir: Mervyn LeRoy, 90 mins.)

Page of Madness, A (Japan, 1926)***½ Masao Inoue, Yoshie Nakagawa, Hiroshi Nemoto, Eiko Minami. The years have not altered the power of this brilliant example of pure cinema, with no title cards or subtitles used to tell the story of an old man who does odd jobs at a mental institution in an effort to free his wife who is confined there. (Dir: Teinosuke Kinugasa, 65 mins.)

Paid (1931)**½ Joan Crawford, Kent Douglass (Douglass Montgomery), Marie Prevost. A guiltless gal gets sent up the river and learns prison protocol in a hurry. Despite the penitentiary hardships she undergoes, Crawford loses hope but she never loses her glamour. (Dir: Sam Wood, 80 mins.)

Paid in Full (1950)*** Robert Cummings, Lizabeth Scott, Diana Lynn, Eve Arden. A fashion designer accidentally kills her sister's child in this austere, skillfully made melodrama. (Dir: William Dieterle, 105 mins.)

Paid to Kill (Great Britain, 1954)**½ Dane Clark, Thea Gregory, Paul Carpenter. Good low-budget British thriller. A desperate man hires a hit man to kill him, then changes his mind. (Dir: Montgomery Tully, 70 mins.)

Pain in the A—, A (France-Italy, 1974)*** Lino Ventura, Jacques Brel, Caroline Cellier, Nino Castelnuovo. The French stage hit about the hit man whose attempts to do a thorough job are interrupted by his encounter with an inept would-be suicide. Remade (badly) as *Buddy, Buddy*. (Dir: Edouard Molinaro, 90 mins.)†

Painted Desert, The (1931)*** William Boyd, Helen Twelvetrees, William Farnum, J. Farrell MacDonald, Clark Gable. Atmospheric western starring a pre-"Hopalong Cassidy" Boyd as a mining engineer returning to his desert home to settle a family feud and win his girl away from no-good Gable. Beautifully filmed, with a climactic mine explosion. (Dir: Howard Higgins, 79 mins.)†

Painted Hills, The (1951)**½ Lassie, Paul Kelly, Gary Gray. Typical Lassie adventure. The kids will enjoy the villain who is outsmarted by the crafty canine and her young master. (Dir: Howard F. Kress, 65 mins.)

Painted Veil, The (1934)*** Greta Garbo, Herbert Marshall, George Brent, Warner Oland. Garbo pictures are always a treat and this overly dramatic story of a beautiful woman who is neglected by her husband while in Hong Kong is passable entertainment. Remade as *The Seventh Sin*. (Dir: Richard Boleslawski, 86 mins.)†

Painting the Clouds with Sunshine (1951)** Dennis Morgan, Virginia Mayo, Gene Nelson, Tom Conway, Wallace Ford, Lucille Norman. Three girls head for Las Vegas to find rich husbands. Good songs, including "With a Song in My Heart," "Tip-Toe Through the Tulips," "Birth of the Blues," and the title tune, are about all this has to recommend it. (Dir: David Butler, 87 mins.)

Paint It Black (1989)*** Rick Rossovich, Doug Savant, Julie Carmen, Jason Bernard, Martin Landau, Peter Frechette, Sally Kirkland. Stylish mystery thriller about a mixed-up young man, born to the finer things in life, who becomes obsessed with a sculptor. Cleverly written. (Dir: Tim Hunter, 97 mins.)†

Paint Your Wagon (1969)*½ Lee Marvin, Jean Seberg, Clint Eastwood, Harve Presnell. A dated Broadway musical of the late '40s has been turned into an expensive, stupefying musical. About life and romance in the California boom towns during the gold rush in the 1800s. Yes, Clint and Lee sing. (Dir: Joshua Logan, 164 mins.)†

Pair of Aces (MTV 1990)**½ Willie Nelson, Kris Kristofferson, Helen Shaver, Jane Cameron, Rip Torn, Sonny Carl Davis, Lash LaRue. Low-key western whose main appeal is its star teaming. Texas ranger Kristofferson searches for a serial killer while saddled with Nelson, a safecracker awaiting trial. (Dir: Aaron Lipstadt, 96 mins.)

Paisan (Italy, 1946)**** Carmela Sazio, Garmoore, Robert van Loon, Maria Michi, Bill Tubbs. Director Roberto Rossellini's episodic account of the Allied invasion of Italy during WWII is neo-realist: precise, zealous in pursuit of truth, doggedly historical in viewpoint. (90 mins.)†

Pajama Game, The (1957)***½ Doris Day,

John Raitt, Carol Haney. A lively, infectious musical, about a strike at a pajama factory. The players are engaging, the choreography snappy and original, with dancer Haney a standout in "Steam Heat." From the Broadway hit. (Dirs: George Abbott, Stanley Donen, 101 mins.)†

Pajama Party (1964)** Tommy Kirk, Annette Funicello, Harvey Lembeck, Buster Keaton, Dorothy Lamour, Elsa Lanchester. This one is sillier than most beach-party films because it has a science-fiction bent. Would you believe Kirk as a Martian? (Dir: Don Weis, 85 mins.)

Paleface, The (1948)*** Bob Hope, Jane Russell, Robert Armstrong, Iris Adrian. Dentist becomes western hero because Calamity Jane is doing the shooting for him in this cute spoof of western films. (Dir: Norman Z. McLeod, 91 mins.)†

Pale Rider (1985)*** Clint Eastwood, Michael Moriarty, Carrie Snodgress, Richard Dysart, Christopher Penn. Eastwood's first western since *The Outlaw Josey Wales* is a classically structured, visually spectacular return to form. He plays a drifter who spearheads a group of gold prospectors in their fight against a corporate land baron. The acting is solid, and Eastwood's direction is attentive to the vast and symbolic terrain of the western film. (113 mins.)†

Pal Joey (1957)*** Rita Hayworth, Frank Sinatra, Kim Novak, Barbara Nichols, Elizabeth Patterson. A splashy version of the landmark musical, it scraps most of the brilliant Rodgers and Hart score for the team's better-known tunes. Frank's convincing as the amorous heel whose one goal in life is to own his own nightclub. With the still-luscious Hayworth as the woman who buys his companionship and Novak as the dancer who files down Joey's horns. (Dir: George Sidney, 111 mins.)†

Palm Beach Story (1942)**** Claudette Colbert, Joel McCrea, Mary Astor, Rudy Vallee. Everything works as it should in this hilarious Preston Sturges-directed comedy. Colbert is the young wife fleeing her husband (McCrea), and winding up in Palm Beach surrounded by dizzy millionaires (including the delightful team of Astor and Vallee). (90 mins.)†

Palm Springs Weekend (1963)** Connie Stevens, Ty Hardin, Troy Donahue, Robert Conrad, Stefanie Powers. Strictly for the teenage audience, about the annual Easter Week invasion of Palm Springs by hordes of college kids out to have a good time. (Dir: Norman Taurog, 100 mins.)†

Palmy Days (1931)**½ Eddie Cantor, George Raft, Charlotte Greenwood. Frantically paced comedy set in a health resort overrun by bathing beauties, circa 1930, and gangsters. (Dir: A. Edward Sutherland, 77 mins.)

Palomino, The (1950)** Jerome Courtland, Beverly Tyler. A prize palomino breeding stallion is stolen and as a result the heroine's ranch goes to pot. (Dir: Ray Nazarro, 73 mins.)

Palooka—See: **Joe Palooka**

Pals (MTV 1987)** Don Ameche, George C. Scott, James Greene, Sylvia Sidney. Two retired pals come across 3.6 million bucks by accident and take it on the lam when a mobster, who wants his moolah back, pursues them. (Dir: Lou Antonio, 104 mins.)

Panache (MTV 1976)*½ René Auberjonois, David Healy, Charles Frank, Joseph Ruskin. Devil-may-care royal guards outwit France's wily Cardinal Richelieu; the pratfalls and comedy touches between the fencing scenes fail to amuse. (Dir: Gary Nelson, 72 mins.)

Panama Hattie (1943)**½ Red Skelton, Ann Sothern, Marsha Hunt. Another Broadway musical hit is slaughtered in the screen transition. A fine cast does their best with the plot about blowing up the Canal but the film has no spark. Lena Horne makes her Hollywood debut in this. (Dir: Norman Z. McLeod, 79 mins.)

Pan-Americana (1945)**½ Philip Terry, Eve Arden, Audrey Long, Robert Benchley. One of numerous Hollywood efforts made during WWII to help promote friendship with Latin America. Authentic musical acts make this worth seeing. (Dir: John H. Auer, 84 mins.)

Pandemonium (1982)**½ Tom Smothers, Debralee Scott, Candy Azzara, David L. Lander, Pat Ast, Paul Reubens, Eve Arden, Kaye Ballard, Tab Hunter, Donald O'Connor, Carol Kane, Judge Reinhold. Goofy low-budget parody of slasher movies with a cast overloaded with familiar faces. Smothers holds it together as a Canadian Mountie investigating the murders at It Had to Be U. Enjoyable if you don't mind dropping your brow a little. (Dir: Alfred Sole, 82 mins.)†

Pandora and the Flying Dutchman (Great Britain, 1951)*** James Mason, Ava Gardner. A beautiful playgirl is the replica of the girl for whom the legendary Flying Dutchman was condemned to sail the seas forever; off the coast of Spain, she is visited by a mysterious stranger. Fanciful drama, not always successful, but extremely interesting. (Dir: Albert Lewin, 123 mins.)

Pandora's Box (Germany, 1928)***½ Louise Brooks, Franz (Francis) Lederer, Fritz Kortner. A silent screen classic about a girl with loose morals who drifts from promiscuity to whoredom. One night she makes the fatal mistake of catching the eye of Jack the Ripper. In recent years, Brooks has been deservedly rediscovered. She certainly lights up this expressionistic slice of fatalism with incandescent star power. (Dir: G. W. Pabst, 110 mins.)†

Panhandle (1948)*** Rod Cameron, Cathy Downs. Brawny Cameron mops up a few western varmints, one a young gun played by Blake Edwards, who's now a movie director. (Dir: Lesley Selander, 84 mins.)

Panic (Italy-Great Britain, 1976)* David Warbeck, Janet Agren. A scientist working for the military becomes a monster due to his experiments and terrorizes a town; eventually the military decides to bomb the town to cover up the accident. Gruesome and silly. (Dir: "Anthony Richmond" [Tonino Ricci], 89 mins.)†

Panic at Lakewood Manor—See: **It Happened at Lakewood Manor**

Panic at Malibu Pier—See: **Baywatch: Panic at Malibu Pier**

Panic Button (1963)** Maurice Chevalier, Michael Connors, Jayne Mansfield, Eleanor Parker. Gangster's son goes to Italy to make a pilot for a TV film, which must be a bad one so that the syndicate can take a tax loss. (Dir: George Sherman, 90 mins.)

Panic in Echo Park (MTV 1977)**½ Dorian Harewood, Robin Gannel, Catlin Adams. Good acting bolsters this routine pilot film about a dedicated black doctor who jeopardizes his career when he delves into a possible epidemic that has broken out in a ghetto community. (Dir: John Llewellyn Moxey, 72 mins.)†

Panic in Needle Park, The (1971)*** Al Pacino, Kitty Winn, Alan Vint. Pacino in his first starring role is very effective as a heroin addict who drags a young girl down into his world of hookers, pimps, thieves, and other low-life inhabitants of New York City's "Needle Park." A harrowing film. (Dir: Jerry Schatzberg, 110 mins.)

Panic in the City (1968)*½ Howard Duff, Nehemiah Persoff, Linda Cristal, Anne Jeffreys, Stephen McNally, Dennis Hopper, George Barrows, Stanley Clements, Mike Farrell. Federal agent investigates a Communist plot to nuke L.A. Cheap Red-scare flick, made about ten years too late for anyone to take seriously. (Dir: Eddie Davis, 97 mins.)

Panic in the Parlour (Great Britain, 1957)** Peggy Mount, Cyril Smith, Shirley Eaton, Gordon Jackson. Innocuous comedy of a domineering mother taking over her daughter's wedding, to the groom's resentment. Broadly played and sporadically funny. AKA: **Sailor Beware!** (Dir: Gordon Parry, 81 mins.)

Panic in the Streets (1950)***½ Richard Widmark, Jack Palance, Paul Douglas, Barbara Bel Geddes, Zero Mostel. A dead body in New Orleans is found to be carrying bubonic plague. A courageous doctor and the police track down the source, leading to an exciting climax. Directed by Elia Kazan with on-the-spot location realism, and a good performance from Mostel. (96 mins.)

Panic in Year Zero (1962)*** Ray Milland, Jean Hagen, Frankie Avalon. Forceful drama about a man trying to survive along with his family when the country is devastated by an atomic attack. (Dir: Ray Milland, 95 mins.)†

Panic on the 5:22 (MTV 1974)** James Sloyan, Ina Balin, Lynda Day George. A private railroad club car is taken over by three thugs out to rob and perhaps kill. (Dir: Harvey Hart, 78 mins.)

Papa's Delicate Condition (1963)*** Jackie Gleason, Glynis Johns, Charles Ruggles, Elisha Cook, Jr. Slight, entertaining comedy of manners, morals, and proprieties in a small American town at the turn of the century. The "condition" referred to is drunkenness, and Papa's serious-minded wife is not amused. (Dir: George Marshall, 98 mins.)

Paper Chase, The (1973)*** Timothy Bottoms, John Houseman, Lindsay Wagner, Graham Beckel, Edward Herrmann. Biting comedy-drama about nose-to-the-grindstone law students tyrannized by an icy classroom martinet, Houseman. (Dir: James Bridges, 111 mins.)†

Paper Dolls (MTV 1982)**½ Joan Collins, Joan Hackett, Daryl Hannah, Marc Singer, Alexandra Paul, Jennifer Warren, Craig T. Nelson. This glitzy movie is an insider's look at the marketing of teenage fashion models by ambitious mothers and high-powered agents. (Dir: Edward Zwick, 120 mins.)

Paperhouse (Great Britain, 1988)*** Charlotte Burke, Elliott Spiers, Glenne Headley. Intriguing psychological fantasy about a young girl obsessed with dreams set in a house she has drawn. She finds that, by altering the drawing, she can control the dreams—until the dreams begin to control her waking life. (Dir: Bernard Rose, 94 mins.)†

Paper Lion (1968)*** Alan Alda. Engaging, observant dramatization of George Plimpton's best-seller about his experiences in the world of pro football. (Dir: Alex March, 107 mins.)

Paper Man (MTV 1971)*** Dean Stockwell, Stefanie Powers, James Stacy. Intriguing, imaginative drama. Group of bright college students, using the university computer, create a fictitious human and go off on a buying spree with the character's credit card. Soon the

798

paper man displays puzzling independent behavior which includes murder. (Dir: Walter Grauman, 73 mins.)

Paper Moon (1973)*** Ryan O'Neal, Tatum O'Neal, Madeline Kahn. Finely engraved story of a depression-era Kansas con man selling Bibles to women just turned widows, with the aid of an innocent nine-year-old determined to be corrupted. The interplay between the con man and his tiny sidekick (a real-life father and daughter) is irresistibly sentimental. (Dir: Peter Bogdanovich, 101 mins.)†

Paper Tiger (Great Britain, 1974)*½ David Niven, Toshiro Mifune, Ando, Hardy Kruger. Niven plays a tutor to the son of a Japanese ambassador to a fictious Asian country. Claiming great war feats, the teacher is really a coward at heart, but proves his courage when his pupil is captured by terrorists. (Dir: Ken Annakin, 99 mins.)

Papillon (1973)*** Steve McQueen, Dustin Hoffman, Victor Jory, William Smithers. A generally exciting film based on the best-selling novel about Henri "Papillon" Charriere's real-life escape from the brutal French penal colony of Devil's Island, off the eastern coast of South America. McQueen's escape on a raft is rousing escapist fare. (Dir: Franklin J. Schaffner, 153 mins.)†

Parachute Battalion (1941)** Robert Preston, Nancy Kelly, Edmond O'Brien, Harry Carey, Paul Kelly, Buddy Ebsen. Gungho WWII patriotism from a disparate group of soldiers training as paratroopers. Terrific aerial photography adds excitement. (Dir: Leslie Goodwins, 75 mins.)

Parachute Jumper (1933)** Bette Davis, Douglas Fairbanks, Jr., Leo Carrillo, Frank McHugh, Claire Dodd. A former air ace is tricked into hauling narcotics by a gangster boss. Throwaway programmer. (Dir: Alfred E. Green, 65 mins.)

Parade (France-Sweden, 1974)***½ Jacques Tati, Pia Colombo, Karl Kossmayer, Bertilo. Director-star Tati's last movie (shot on video) is an unusual celebration of circuses, especially of the clown that Tati felt was in all of us. In front of a circus audience, Tati presents magicians, acrobats, and his beloved clowns, and expressively mimes a variety of characters. A sweet, melancholy work. (95 mins.)

Parade, The (MTV 1984)** Rosanna Arquette, Frederic Forrest, Michael Learned, Geraldine Page. Earnest family drama about life in a small Kansas town. The daughter wants to run off with a so-called hoodlum. Dad comes home from prison and can't get a job, and poor Mom can't change anyone's life for the better. (Dir: Peter Hunt, 104 mins.)

Paradine Case, The (1948)*** Gregory

Peck, Alida Valli, Ethel Barrymore, Charles Coburn, Ann Todd, Louis Jourdan, Leo G. Carroll, John Williams. A verbose, but compelling drama about a highly respected attorney whose objectivity falls by the wayside when he defends a coolly beautiful woman on a murder charge. The film disappoints because it's not the kind of nail-biting suspense thriller we've come to expect from Hitchcock; instead this courtroom drama subtly keeps us on tenterhooks about how far the smitten advocate will go in jeopardizing his career and marriage for his destructive obsession. (Dir: Alfred Hitchcock, 125 mins.)†

Paradise (1982)* Willie Aames, Phoebe Cates, Tuvia Tavi. Two beautiful youths in their first bloom of maturity discover sex while stranded in a lush tropical hideaway circa 1823. Even worse than *The Blue Lagoon*. (Dir: Stuart Gillard, 100 mins.)†

Paradise Alley (1961)**½ Hugo Haas, Marie Windsor, Billy Gilbert, Carol Morris, Chester Conklin, Margaret Hamilton. In order to promulgate community sentiment among his neighbors, a veteran movie director claims he's filming a documentary of daily life in his neighborhood. Haas's final film is a welcome break from his usual seduced-by-a-blonde efforts. (Dir: Hugo Haas, 85 mins.)

Paradise Alley (1978)** Sylvester Stallone, Armand Assante, Lee Canalito. Stallone is the writer, star, and naïve, appallingly fearless debut director of this upbeat film about three brothers in the '40s looking to move out of the slums and onto Easy Street. He figures the best plan is to turn one huge brother (Canalito) into a champion wrestler. (107 mins.)†

Paradise Connection, The (MTV 1979)** Buddy Ebsen, Bonnie Ebsen, Marj Dusay. Buddy Ebsen is a Chicago lawyer searching for an estranged son mixed up in drug smuggling. (Dir: Michael Preece, 104 mins.)

Paradise for Three (1938)*** Frank Morgan, Robert Young, Mary Astor, Edna May Oliver, Reginald Owen. Romantic comedy of Astor chasing industrialist Morgan to the German Alps, where they mix with the populace on the eve of WWII. Humor with thoughtful undertones. (Dir: Edward Buzzell, 75 mins.)

Paradise, Hawaiian Style (1966)** Elvis Presley, James Shigeta, Suzanna Leigh. Typical Presley musical for his fans. This time out, Presley is an airline pilot who returns to Hawaii to interest his buddy in setting up a shuttle-plane business. (Dir: Michael Moore, 91 mins.)†

Paradise Lagoon (Great Britain, 1957)*** Kenneth More, Sally Ann Howes, Diane Cilento. A funny comedy based on *The Admirable Crichton*. The plot concerns a group of shipwrecked British families who come to rely on the resourcefulness of a butler. The young lady of a respectable family falls for the servant as does a flighty upstairs maid. (Dir: Lewis Gilbert, 94 mins.)

Paradise Motel (1985)*½ Gary Hershberger, Robert Krantz, Jonna Leigh Stack, Bob Basso. High school student discovers he can make friends with his father's new business—a motel where he lets the class lothario bring an endless parade of girls. Exploitation comedy with a few bright faces. (Dir: Cary Medoway, 87 mins.)†

Parallax View, The (1974)**** Warren Beatty, William Daniels, Hume Cronyn, Paula Prentiss. Fascinating, disturbing story about a political assassination of a senator, not unlike the Kennedys, and one reporter's efforts to get to the bottom of the mystery surrounding this killing. Suddenly witnesses to the assassination start dying off, and one of them goes to reporter Beatty who investigates. (Dir: Alan Pakula, 102 mins.)†

Paramedics (1988)** George Newbern, Christopher McDonald, Lawrence-Hilton Jacobs, John P. Ryan. Another *Police Academy* clone, this one following the exploits of incompetent hospital workers in a slum neighborhood. Some good gags, nothing special. (Dir: Stuart Margolin, 91 mins.)†

Paramount on Parade (1930)**½ Jean Arthur, Clara Bow, Maurice Chevalier, Gary Cooper, Stuart Erwin, Kay Francis, Fredric March, Helen Kane, Jack Oakie, William Powell. One of those musical potpourris that all the big studios cranked out to take advantage of the coming of sound. Our favorite numbers are Helen Kane's classroom ditty, Nancy Carroll's soleful stepping to "Dancing to Save Your Sole," and "Sweeping in the Clouds Away," the spectacular finale featuring Chevalier and some chorines with their heads in the clouds. (Dirs: Dorothy Arzner, Edmund Goulding, Victor Heerman, Edwin Knopf, Rowland V. Lee, Ernst Lubitsch, Lothar Mendes, Victor Schertzinger, A. Edward Sutherland, Frank Tuttle, 102 mins.)

Paranoia (Italy-France, 1968)½ Carroll Baker, Lou Castel, Collette Descombes, Tino Carraro. Bereaved widow is drawn into sexual perversion. Sadistic rubbish. (Dir: Umberto Lenzi, 90 mins.)†

Paranoiac (Great Britain, 1963)*** Janette Scott, Alexander Davion, Oliver Reed. Elaborate, entertaining murder tale; plentiful gore, fanciful props, chilling atmosphere. (Dir: Freddie Francis, 80 mins.)

Parasite (1982)½ Robert Glaudini, Demi Moore, Luca Bercovici, Cherie Currie, Vivian Blaine, Al Fann. Horrific chiller

799

about a parasite that not only grows inside its victims but leaps out to attack more unsuspecting slobs. David Cronenberg–ish idea mishandled by hacks. (Dir: Charles Band, 85 mins.) †

Paratrooper (Great Britain, 1953)** Alan Ladd, Leo Genn, Susan Stephen. A Canadian joins the paratroopers under an assumed name because he has a fear of responsibility due to an earlier service experience. (Dir: Terence Hill, 87 mins.)

Pardners (1956)** Dean Martin, Jerry Lewis, Agnes Moorehead. Eccentric playboy and a ranch foreman head west with a prize bull, foil varmints bent on taking over the ranch. Occasionally snappy comedy. (Dir: Norman Taurog, 88 mins.)

Pardon Mon Affaire (France, 1977)*** Jean Rochefort, Anny Duperey. A French Milquetoast in pursuit of a model imagines himself to be a Lothario. This French sex farce about a man going through the seven-year itch is mildly frothy and pleasant. (Dir: Yves Robert, 105 mins.) †

Pardon My French (U.S.-France, 1951)** Merle Oberon, Paul Henreid. A Boston schoolteacher acquires a French chateau, finds it inhabited by miscellaneous squatters, including a dashing composer and five fatherless children. (Dir: Bernard Vorhaus, 81 mins.)

Pardon My Past (1945)*** Fred MacMurray, Marguerite Chapman. Ex-soldier is mistaken for a wealthy playboy who owes money to some gamblers. Delightful comedy-drama, smoothly done and entertaining. (Dir: Leslie Fenton, 88 mins.)

Pardon My Rhythm (1944)** Gloria Jean, Patric Knowles, Marjorie Weaver. Amiable musical vehicle for Jean as a high school girl trying to get ahead in show business, with the aid of a *very* young Mel Torme and Bob Crosby's band. (Dir: Felix E. Feist, 62 mins.)

Pardon My Sarong (1942)*** Bud Abbott, Lou Costello, Virginia Bruce, the Ink Spots. Two bus drivers on a playboy's yacht land on a tropic isle, where they thwart villains trying to steal the temple jewels. (Dir: Erle C. Kenton, 84 mins.)

Pardon My Trunk (Italy, 1953)** Vittorio De Sica, Sabu. De Sica plays a schoolteacher who receives a real live elephant as a gift from an Indian Prince whom he has befriended. Sounds hilarious but isn't. (Dir: Gianni Franciolini, 78 mins.)

Pardon Us (1931)**½ Stan Laurel, Oliver Hardy, Walter Long, James Finlayson, June Marlowe, Wilfred Lucas. Laurel and Hardy's first feature film is a takeoff on the prison drama *The Big House*. Poorly directed, but it still contains some great comedy routines and a memorable musical interlude from Ollie. AKA: **Jail Birds.** (Dir: James Parrott, 55 mins.) †

Parenthood (1989)**½ Steve Martin, Mary Steenburgen, Dianne Wiest, Jason Robards, Rick Moranis, Tom Hulce, Martha Plimpton, Keanu Reeves, Harley Kozak, Leaf Phoenix. Comedy-drama about the title subject, as viewed in every possible permutation by each member of an extended middle-class family. Many nice moments. (Dir: Ron Howard, 124 mins.) †

Parents (1988)** Randy Quaid, Mary Beth Hurt, Sandy Dennis. Peculiar horror satire set in fifties suburbia. Upwardly mobile parents Quaid and Hurt move with their son into a new house, but the boy has violent nightmares and trouble adapting. The ending doesn't really fit the rest of the movie, and the whole thing is far too self-consciously "arty." (Dir: Bob Balaban, 85 mins.) †

Parent Trap, The (1961)*** Hayley Mills, Maureen O'Hara, Brian Keith, Leo G. Carroll, Charlie Ruggles, Una Merkel, Joanna Barnes. Hayley Mills is wonderful playing twins in this family comedy-drama produced by the Walt Disney studio. (Dir: David Swift, 124 mins.) †

Parent Trap: Two, The (MCTV 1986)** Hayley Mills, Tom Skerritt, Carrie Kei Heim, Bridgette Anderson. A disappointing follow-up to the classic Disney comedy of errors about twins. This time, the dual Hayleys have trouble with their own mischievous offspring. (Dir: Robert F. Maxwell, 95 mins.)

Paris after Dark (1943)**½ George Sanders, Philip Dorn, Brenda Marshall, Madeleine LeBeau. Taut anti-Nazi film, with Sanders as a society doctor who's really the head of the French Underground. Suspenseful atmosphere. (Dir: Leonide Moguy, 85 mins.)

Paris Belongs to Us (France, 1960)***½ Betty Schneider, Gianni Esposito, Daniel Crohem, Jean-Claude Brialy, Claude Chabrol, Jean-Luc Godard, Jacques Demy. Stark tale of illusion and reality centered on an amateur production of *Pericles*. Moodily atmospheric film. (Dir: Jacques Rivette, 140 mins.)

Paris Blues (1961)*** Paul Newman, Joanne Woodward, Sidney Poitier, Diahann Carroll, Louis Armstrong. Two pairs of lovers meet in the City of Lights. Newman and Poitier play jazz musicians and there's a lot of good music thrown in as a bonus. (Dir: Martin Ritt, 98 mins.)

Paris by Night (Great Britain, 1990)**½ Charlotte Rampling, Michael Gambon, Robert Hardy, Niamh Cusack, Jane Asher. Interesting but constricted melodrama about a British woman, a member of the European Parliament, who must take stock of her rising career and failing marriage after she meets a fascinating man. (Dir: David Hare, 100 mins.) †

Paris Calling (1941)**½ Elisabeth Bergner,

Basil Rathbone, Randolph Scott, Lee J. Cobb, Gale Sondergaard, Eduardo Ciannelli. Propaganda-plus, but a solidly crafted melodrama. While those Nazis are goose-stepping all over Paris, a woman learns that her husband may be playing footsie with the bad guys. (Dir: Edward L. Marin, 95 mins.)

Paris Does Strange Things (France, 1957)**½ Ingrid Bergman, Mel Ferrer, Jean Marais, Juliette Greco. A flirtatious Polish princess who's down on her luck attracts a wealth of admirers. Disappointing, but not without its pleasures. Rereleased in 1986 in its original length (98 mins.) as *Elena et Les Hommes*. (Dir: Jean Renoir, 86 mins.)†

Paris Express (Great Britain, 1952)**½ Claude Rains, Marta Toren, Herbert Lom. Femme fatale plunges a bookkeeper into a web of murder and robbery. Well-acted but complicated melodrama. (Dir: Harold French, 83 mins.)†

Paris Holiday (1958)**½ Bob Hope, Fernandel, Anita Ekberg, Martha Hyer, Preston Sturges. Typical Bob Hope comedy with Bob sharing the clowning honors with France's Fernandel. (Dir: Gerd Oswald, 100 mins.)†

Paris Honeymoon (1939)**½ Bing Crosby, Shirley Ross, Franciska Gaal. Pleasant, inconsequential Crosby film about the romance of an American with a French peasant girl. (Dir: Frank Tuttle, 85 mins.)

Paris Is Burning (1991)***½ A poignant, illuminating award-winning documentary about drag balls in New York's Harlem, and the rarefied art of voguing. Young, white, female director Jennie Livingston sometimes simply puts her camera in front of the various transvestites and other participants. These black and Hispanic gay men have some heartbreaking things to say about their own life, culture, and insecurities. An impressive directorial debut indeed. (Dir: Jennie Livingston, 78 mins.)

Paris Model (1953)** Marilyn Maxwell, Paulette Goddard, Eva Gabor. Thin comedy about four women who purchase copies of the same "original" dress. (Dir: Alfred E. Green, 81 mins.)

Paris Playboys (1954)*½ Bowery Boys, Bernard Gorcey, Fritz Feld, Veola Vonn, Steve Geray. Sach's resemblance to a Professor Le Beau is exploited in an effort to lure the French scientist out of his hiding in Paris. Unfunny and forced. (Dir: William Beaudine, 65 mins.)

Paris, Texas (1984)*** Harry Dean Stanton, Nastassia Kinski, Dean Stockwell, Hunter Carson, Aurora Clement, Bernhard Wicki. A man is reunited with his brother's family, who've been raising the son he abandoned when his wife ran off. The film's most touching when it relates how the careworn man re-establishes a relationship with his son. (Dir: Wim Wenders, 150 mins.)†

Paris Trout (MCTV 1991)***½ Dennis Hopper, Barbara Hershey, Ed Harris. Peter Dexter's award-winning book has been brought to the screen with love and care. Set in a small Georgia town in the '50s, the drama plays like a William Faulkner yarn. Hopper is a twisted businessman named Paris Trout, who is not above brutalizing his beautiful wife (Hershey) or shooting a poor black mother and her young daughter because he is owed $800. Harris plays his attorney, who knows Paris should pay for his crime, but defends him in court. The shocking finale will stay with you long after the movie ends. (Dir: Stephen Gyllenhaal, 99 mins.)†

Paris Underground (1945)*** Constance Bennett, Gracie Fields. American and her English companion are caught by the Nazi invasion of France, work for the underground throughout the war. Interesting melodrama, based on fact. (Dir: Gregory Ratoff, 97 mins.)

Paris Vu Par...—See: **Six in Paris**

Paris When It Sizzles (1964)* William Holden, Audrey Hepburn, Noël Coward. This is a leaden romance about a screenwriter and his girl Friday fantasizing situations for a film script. (Dir: Richard Quine, 110 mins.)†

Park Is Mine, The (MCTV 1985)* Tommy Lee Jones, Helen Shaver, Yaphet Kotto. A Viet vet goes off his peacetime trolley after his bugged-out friend commits suicide. Skip it. (Dir: Steven Hilliard Stern, 102 mins.)†

Park Row (1952)*** Gene Evans, Mary Welch. The story of a crusading editor in old New York who tried to publish his paper despite opposition from a larger journal. Hard-hitting, well-acted melodrama. (Dir: Samuel Fuller, 83 mins.)

Parlor, Bedroom and Bath (1931)**½ Buster Keaton, Charlotte Greenwood, Reginald Denny, Cliff Edwards. Creaky but funny farce, with Keaton taken home by the driver who ran into him and causing romantic havoc among the ladies of the household. (Dir: Edward Sedgwick, 69 mins.)

Parnell (1937)** Clark Gable, Myrna Loy, Edmund Gwenn, Donald Crisp. One of Gable's worst pre-war films. Story of the great Irish patriot is poorly written and terribly miscast. (Dir: John M. Stahl, 118 mins.)

Parole (MTV 1982)*** James Naughton, Lori Cardille, Mark Soper, Ted Ross. This carefully wrought drama about our parole system invokes anguish and sympathy. After three years of sexual abuse behind bars, a parolee (Soper) emerges angry and confused, but finds help with a savvy parole officer. (Dir: Michael Tuchner, 104 mins.)

Parole, Inc. (1949)**½ Michael O'Shea, Turhan Bey, Evelyn Ankers, Lyle Talbot. OK poverty-row melodrama about an investigator going undercover to nab corruption in the parole board. (Dir: Alfred Zeisler, 71 mins.)

Parrish (1961)*** Claudette Colbert, Karl Malden, Troy Donahue, Connie Stevens. An entertaining soaper. The plot drags when it centers on the sappy title character (Donahue), but the unlikely romance between his widowed mother (Colbert) and a flashy tycoon (Malden) is interesting and portrayed with conviction by the two experts. (Dir: Delmer Daves, 140 mins.)

Parsifal (West Germany, 1982)***½ Michael Kutter, Karin Krick, Edith Clever, Armin Jordan, voices of Reiner Goldberg, Yvonne Minton, Wolfgang Schone. Richard Wagner's opera is magnificently adapted by visionary director Hans-Jurgen Syberberg. Epic production features Syberberg's stylistic use of puppets, living tableaus, and rear projection. (255 mins.)

Parson and the Outlaw (1957)** Anthony Dexter, Buddy Rogers, Sonny Tufts, Marie Windsor. Billy the Kid tries to reform, but is forced to pick up his gun again when a clergyman friend is killed. (Dir: Oliver Drake, 71 mins.)

Parson of Panamint, The (1941)*** Charlie Ruggles, Ellen Drew. Offbeat western about a wild town that grew up with a gold strike and its young, hard-hitting, yet gentle parson, who is almost executed as a murderer. (Dir: William McGann, 84 mins.)

Parting Glances (1986)***½ Richard Ganoung, John Bolger, Steve Buscemi. The plot concerns a young writer whose present lover is leaving him for a foreign-based job, while his ex-lover is dying of AIDS. Entertaining, perceptive independent filmmaking. (Dir: Bill Sherwood, 90 mins.)†

Partisans of Vilna (1986)*** Through a series of interviews, newsreel footage, and music, this film pays tribute to a group of heroes, the Jewish resistance fighters of Vilna, Lithuania, who battled the Nazis and survived the Holocaust. (Dir: Josh Waletzky, 130 mins.)†

Partner (Italy, 1968)***½ Pierre Clementi, Stefania Sandrelli, Sergio Tofano, Tina Aumont. A painfully shy young man invents a second identity as a stronger, more secure individual. (Dir: Bernardo Bertolucci, 105 mins.)

Partners (1982)** Ryan O'Neal, John Hurt, Kenneth McMillan, Robyn Douglass, Jay

Robinson. One-joke comedy about two cops—one homosexual, the other one straight—posing as lovers in order to crack a murder case in Los Angeles's homosexual community. (Dir: James Burrows, 98 mins.)†

Partners in Crime (MTV 1973)** Lee Grant, Harry Guardino, Bob Cummings. Grant plays a judge who resigns to become a detective with an ex-con for her partner. (Dir: Jack Smight, 78 mins.)

Parts: The Clonus Horror—See: Clonus Horror, The

Part Two: Walking Tall—See: Walking Tall: Part 2

Party, The (1968)*** Peter Sellers, Claudine Longet, Marge Champion, Denny Miller, Gavin MacLeod. Director Blake Edwards's effortless celebration of the sight gag. Clumsy Indian bit player Sellers, who has just destroyed a remake of *Gunga Din*, finds himself at a posh party at his producer's Hollywood home. (99 mins.)†

Party Camp (1987)* Andrew Ross, Kerry Brennan, Billy Jacoby, Jewel Shepard. Another *Meatballs* rip-off, with the new counselor at Camp Chipmunk fighting for his right to party against the preps and jocks. (Dir: Gary Graver, 96 mins.)†

Party Crashers, The (1958)** Mark Damon, Bobby Driscoll, Connie Stevens, Frances Farmer. Teenage gang members get into trouble when they intrude on a party at a roadhouse. (Dir: Bernard Girard, 78 mins.)

Party Girl (1958)***½ Robert Taylor, Cyd Charisse, Lee J. Cobb, John Ireland. Taylor is a crippled mouthpiece for the mob who meets his match in cynical vulnerability in Charisse. Directed with flair and vigor. (Dir: Nicholas Ray, 98 mins.)

Party Line (1988)*½ Leif Garrett, Greta Blackburn, Richard Hatch, Shawn Weatherly, Richard Roundtree. One of about half a dozen late '80s films about slashers who find their victims from phone sex services. (Dir: William Webb, 91 mins.)†

Pascali's Island (Great Britain, 1988)*** Ben Kingsley, Charles Dance, Helen Mirren. Kingsley's strong interpretation of the title character, a Turkish spy who falls in league with a dapper con man (Dance), enlivens this picturesque tale of admiration and betrayal. (Dir: James Dearden, 104 mins.)†

Passage, The (Great Britain, 1979)* Anthony Quinn, James Mason, Patricia Neal, Malcolm McDowell, Kay Lenz, Christopher Lee. World War II is the background and the Pyrenees serve as backdrop for the brutal tale of a chemist and family who are escaping from the Nazis with the aid of shepherd Quinn. (Dir: J. Lee Thompson, 99 mins.)

Passage To India, A (Great Britain,

1984)**** Peggy Ashcroft, Judy Davis, Victor Banerjee, Alec Guinness. Marvelously acted, visually spectacular pageant of the clash of English and Indian cultures in the 1920s. Story focuses around a young Englishwoman (Davis) who accuses an Indian doctor of sexual improprieties, leading to a memorable court trial. One of Lean's many accomplishments is that he makes the huge crowd scenes and panoramas no less involving than intimate personal scenes. Based on E. M. Forster's novel. (Dir: David Lean, 163 mins.)

Passage to Marseille (1944)*** Humphrey Bogart, Claude Rains, Sydney Greenstreet, Peter Lorre, Michele Morgan. Confused but often exciting story of convicts who escape from Devil's Island to join forces with the free French. (Dir: Michael Curtiz, 110 mins.)†

Passage West (1951)**½ John Payne, Dennis O'Keefe, Arleen Whelan, Frank Faylen, Mary Anderson, Dooley Wilson, Mary Beth Hughes. Gritty western with an unusual premise. A gang of prison escapees hide out in a wagon train taking a religious community to California. (Dir: Lewis R. Foster, 80 mins.)

Passenger, The (Italy, 1975)**** Jack Nicholson, Maria Schneider, Ian Hendry, Jenny Runacre. A TV reporter exchanges identities with a man who dies at his hotel in Africa. Meanwhile, the reporter's wife is planning a film tribute to her "late" husband's work, which causes more complications. This haunting film is not so much a conventional mystery as a mood piece and a riveting philosophical journey, as the man's new life doesn't provide him with the escape he desperately wants. (Dir: Michelangelo Antonioni, 123 mins.)†

Passe Ton Bac D'Abord (France, 1979)***½ Sabine Haudepin, Philippe Marland, Annick Alane, Michel Caron. Authentic, well-written character drama about France's "blank generation," drifting young people who see little reason to continue studying when they face low-paying jobs or no work at all. A fresh young cast and beautiful vistas of the French coast add to this finely directed film. (Dir: Maurice Pialat, 85 mins.)

Passing of the Third Floor Back, The (Great Britain, 1935)*** Conrad Veidt, Anna Lee, René Ray. Odd filming of the whimsical book by the Victorian novelist Jerome K. Jerome. Episodic story about the effect a stranger has on the lives of some discontented inhabitants of a boardinghouse. Excellent cast, fine production. (Dir: Berthold Viertel, 90 mins.)

Passion (Germany, 1919)*** Pola Negri, Emil Jannings, Harry Liedtke. Spectacular version of the life of Louis XV's notorious mistress, Madame du Barry. Elegant, emotive, and intriguing, this huge hit helped establish the international reputation of the German film industry. (Dir: Ernst Lubitsch, 70 mins.)†

Passion (1954)**½ Cornel Wilde, Yvonne De Carlo, Raymond Burr, Lon Chaney, Jr., Rodolfo Acosta, John Qualen. Mexican-American Wilde takes the law into his own hands to revenge his family in this modest but colorful historical adventure. (Dir: Allan Dwan, 84 mins.)†

Passion (Japan, 1964)*** Ayako Wakao, Yusuke Kawazu, Kyoko Kishida, Eiji Funakoshi. Well-directed, black comedy about a married woman who falls in love with another woman, which her husband tolerates because he too is having an affair, with another man. (Dir: Yasuzo Masumura, 90 mins.)

Passion (France-Switzerland, 1982)** Isabelle Huppert, Hanna Schygulla. An alienated and inaccessible Godard film that may displease even avant-garde film buffs. It's nearly impossible to detail the plot in which Godard combines a film within a film and tableaux vivants of famous paintings in what seems an arbitrary fashion. (Dir: Jean-Luc Godard, 87 mins.)

Passion and Paradise (MTV 1989)** Armand Assante, Catherine Mary Stewart, Mariette Hartley, Wayne Rogers, Rod Steiger. Fact-based story set in the Bahamas in 1943, where the son-in-law of a murdered tycoon fights accusations that he is the killer. Trashy, but with a good performance by Assante. (Dir: Harvey Hart, 192 mins.)

Passionate Friends, The—See: One Woman's Story

Passionate Plumber, The (1932)**½ Buster Keaton, Jimmy Durante, Irene Purcell, Polly Moran, Gilbert Roland, Mona Maris. Frederick Lonsdale's play, Her Cardboard Lover, retooled as a stagebound vehicle for Keaton and Durante, who made a pretty good team. Uncoordinated and unevenly paced, but with some funny moments. (Dir: Edward Sedgwick, 73 mins.)

Passionate Sentry, The (Great Britain, 1953)*** Nigel Patrick, Peggy Cummins. The romantic story of a palace guard and the girls who chase him. Pleasant comedy. (Dir: Anthony Kimmins, 84 mins.)

Passionate Summer (Great Britain, 1958)** Virginia McKenna, Bill Travers. Tropic schoolmaster's love-starved wife makes a play for a young teacher. (Dir: Rudolph Cartier, 103 mins.)

Passionate Thief, The (Italy, 1962)**½ Anna Magnani, Ben Gazzara. Uneven comedy about a small-time bit player who inadvertently keeps thwarting the attempts of a pickpocket on New Year's Eve. (Dir: Mario Monicelli, 105 mins.)†

Passione D'Amore (Italy, 1982)***½ Bernard Giraudeau, Valeria D'Obici. Ettore Scola has reversed the dynamics of the traditional fairy tale in which a fair damsel falls in love with an ugly man with a beautiful soul. A handsome young cavalry captain becomes emotionally entwined in the fate of an ugly spinster. Filmed in soft pastels with an emphasis on its late nineteenth-century decor, the story is a curious blend of romantic precepts, Freudian insights, and Italian realism. (Dir: Ettore Scola, 117 mins.)†

Passion Flower (MTV 1986)** Bruce Boxleitner, Barbara Hershey, Nicol Williamson. Boxleitner is a bland bank official and Hershey a scheming heiress in a romantic drama that is not as steamy and sexy as the title suggests. With a subplot about smuggling and securities shuffling and with Singapore as the stomping ground, all the components are there for serious intrigue, but something is missing (like passion) and the story falls flat. (Dir: Joseph Sargent, 104 mins.)

Passion of Anna, The (Sweden, 1969)***½ Max von Sydow, Liv Ullmann, Bibi Andersson, Erland Josephson. Marvelous complex psychological drama about four people on an island in desolation and despair. Von Sydow is Andreas Winkelman, who has taken refuge in a hermit's existence. His actions are the catalyst for uncovering the others' self-deception. (Dir: Ingmar Bergman, 99 mins.)

Passion of Beatrice—See: **Beatrice**

Passion of Joan of Arc, The (France, 1928)**** Renée Falconetti, Eugene Sylvain, Andre Berley, Michel Simon. Director Carl Dreyer concentrated his forceful biographical film on the last days of St. Joan's life—her trial, including numerous interrogations by church counsels and her martyrdom at the stake. Using the actual trial transcripts for a script, Dreyer was able to focus on Joan's suffering and devotion to her belief by extensively using close-ups. This jarringly intimate film style helps underscore the brilliance of Mlle. Falconetti's performance (she was reputed to have had a breakdown under Dreyer's strict direction); the divine intensity she radiates as Joan eventually seems to possess the film itself. (85 mins.)

Passions (MTV 1984)**½ Joanne Woodward, Lindsay Wagner, Richard Crenna, Mason Adams, John Considine, Viveca Lindfors. Woodward is a widow vowing to get even with her late husband's mistress, Wagner. A far from impassioned film. (Dir: Sandor Stern, 104 mins.)

Passport to Adventure—See: **Passport to Destiny**

Passport to China (Great Britain, 1961)** Richard Basehart, Lisa Gastoni. Adventurer attempts a rescue of an American secret agent and a Formosan pilot missing in Red China. (Dir: Michael Carreras, 75 mins.)

Passport to Destiny (1944)**½ Elsa Lanchester, Gordon Oliver, Lenore Aubert, Lionel Royce, Fritz Feld, Gavin Muir. Unusual thriller has a woman posing as a cleaning lady in an effort to kill Hitler; carried by Lanchester's spirited performance. AKA: **Passport to Adventure**. (Dir: Ray McCarey, 65 mins.)

Passport to Pimlico (Great Britain, 1949)*** Stanley Holloway, Hermione Baddeley, Margaret Rutherford. When an old charter is discovered in a small section of London claiming the land still belongs to the Duke of Burgundy, the inhabitants decide to secede from England. Hilarious comedy, highly original, witty. (Dir: Henry Cornelius, 72 mins.)†

Passport to Suez (1943)** Warren William, Ann Savage, Eric Blore, Sheldon Leonard, Lloyd Bridges. Those swinish Germans try to persuade Lone Wolf to steal documents from the English embassy, and in the background spies, double agents, and various international schnooks complicate matters. (Dir: André De Toth, 71 mins.)

Passport to Treason (Great Britain, 1955)** Rod Cameron, Lois Maxwell. Private detective called to help a friend finds him murdered, starts investigating. (Dir: Robert S. Baker, 70 mins.)

Pass the Ammo (1988)*** Bill Paxton, Linda Kozlowski, Tim Curry, Annie Potts, Anthony Geary. TV evangelists are an easy target for satire, but this engaging comedy about a couple who decide to get back the $50,000 that a preacher swindled them out of eschews cheap shots and succeeds with well-drawn characters and situations. (Dir: David Beaird, 91 mins.)†

Password Is Courage, The (Great Britain, 1962)**½ Dirk Bogarde, Maria Perschy. Reasonably interesting account of the WWII exploits of Charles Coward, a real-life hero who made many daring escapes from Nazi prison camps. (Dir: Andrew L. Stone, 116 mins.)

Pat and Mike (1952)*** Spencer Tracy, Katharine Hepburn, Jim Backus, William Ching, Aldo Ray. Funny comedy with the irresistible Tracy-Hepburn combination. Hepburn plays a golf pro and Tracy is a big-time sports promoter and their business merger eventually turns to romance. (Dir: George Cukor, 95 mins.)†

Patch of Blue, A (1965)** Sidney Poitier, Elizabeth Hartman, Shelley Winters, Wallace Ford, Ivan Dixon. A moving, well-acted film about a sensitive relationship which develops between a blind white girl and a black man. Poitier and Hartman bring a touching credibility to their roles. (Dir: Guy Green, 105 mins.)

Patchwork Girl of Oz, The (1914)*** Violet MacMillan, Frank Moore, Fred Woodward, Pierre Couderc. Early silent feature combines several plotlines into one concerning a scientist trying to rescue the inhabitants of Oz who have been turned to stone. Imaginative and entertaining. (Dir: J. Farrell Macdonald, 60 mins.)†

Patent Leather Kid, The (1927)***½ Richard Barthelmess, Molly O'Day, Matthew Betz, Arthur Stone. Comedy-drama of cocky boxer who puts his career above patriotism when WWI breaks out and refuses to enlist. Strong characterizations make this an enduring treat. (Dir: Alfred Santell, 90 mins.)

Paternity (1982)** Burt Reynolds, Lauren Hutton, Beverly D'Angelo. Burt Reynolds once again fails to register as a light comedian. Despite the contemporary story line about Reynolds hiring a surrogate mother, this romantic comedy is old-fashioned and derivative. (Dir: David Steinberg, 94 mins.)†

Pat Garrett and Billy the Kid (1973)*½ James Coburn, Kris Kristofferson, Katy Jurado, Jason Robards, Rita Coolidge, Harry Dean Stanton, Bob Dylan. Has some interest, mainly due to Coburn's performance as the gunman-turned-sheriff who sets out to catch his one-time friend, Billy the Kid. (Dir: Sam Peckinpah, 106 mins.)†

Pather Panchali (India, 1956)**** Subir Banerji. First film in a mighty trilogy by Indian director Satyajit Ray. Beautifully done story of a poverty stricken family in a Bengali village. Superb performances. (112 mins.)

Pathfinder (Norway, 1988)***½ Mikkel Gaup, Nils Utsi, Svein Scharffenberg, Helgi Skulason. Powerfully mesmerizing adventure based on a legendary Lapland tale. A young boy (Gaup—not related to the director) witnesses the savage slaying of his family by a hostile tribe. Captured, he is turned into a "pathfinder," leading the aggressors to his people, while secretly plotting to outwit the evil warriors. Mystical yarn was a much-deserved Academy Award Nominee for Best Foreign Film. (Dir: Nils Gaup, 88 mins.)†

Pathfinder, The (1952)**½ George Montgomery, Helena Carter, Jay Silverheels, Walter Kingsford, Elena Verdugo. Brawny, low-budget version of Cooper novel, set during the French and Indian War, with British scout infiltrating unexplored territory behind enemy lines. (Dir: Sidney Salkow, 78 mins.)

Paths of Glory (1957)**** Kirk Douglas, Ralph Meeker, Adolphe Menjou, Wayne Morris, George Macready. A masterpiece about a French Army division fighting in Verdun during WWI. Kirk Douglas is excellent as an officer who believes in treating his men as human beings. The plot concerns scapegoats who're sacrificed to cover a general's mistake. (Dir: Stanley Kubrick, 86 mins.)

Patricia Neal Story, The (MTV 1981)***½ Glenda Jackson, Dirk Bogarde, Ken Kercheval, Jane Merrow. A story of indomitable courage sharpened by superb acting. This is the gripping, thoughtful account of actress Patricia Neal's astonishing recovery from three strokes. (Dirs: Anthony Harvey, Anthony Page, 104 mins.)

Patrick (Australia, 1978)*** Susan Penhaligon, Robert Helpmann, Julia Blake. A worthy horror entry. Comatose in a thirdrate private hospital bed, Patrick passes his time with psychokinetic mischief. (Dir: Richard Franklin, 90 mins.)†

Patriot, The (West Germany, 1979)*** Hannelore Hoger, Dieter Mainka, Alfred Edel, Beate Holle. A Frankfurt history teacher attempts to create new ways of narrating Germany's past history to present-day students. Intriguing but difficult film uses unusual film techniques. (Dir: Alexander Kluge, 120 mins.)

Patriot, The (1986)* Gregg Henry, Simone Griffeth, Michael J. Pollard, Jeff Conaway, Leslie Nielsen, Stack Pierce. The Navy SEAL Unit has to retrieve an atom bomb appropriated by three dimwits unconcerned about detonating the nuke. Below sea level and below average. (Dir: Frank Harris, 88 mins.)†

Patriot Game, The (France, 1978)***½ Illuminating documentary on the struggle to wrest northern Ireland from England and unify it with southern Ireland. Told largely from the point of view of the provisional wing of the IRA. (Dir: Arthur MacCaig, 97 mins.)

Patsy, The (1964)** Jerry Lewis, Ina Balin, Keenan Wynn, Peter Lorre. This particular story line concerns a Hollywood bellboy tapped for movie stardom. The pace is frantic, the slapstick routines everpresent. (Dir: Jerry Lewis, 101 mins.)†

Patsy, The (1985)—See: L'Addition

Patterns (1956)*** Van Heflin, Everett Sloane, Beatrice Straight, Ed Begley. Compelling Rod Serling drama. Executive becomes involved in power squeeze in large corporation. (Dir: Fielder Cook, 83 mins.)

Patti Rocks (1988)*½ Chris Mulkey, John Jenkins, Karen Landry. Two guys talk filthy on a ride to visit the girl, "Patti Rocks" whom one of them made pregnant. A low-budget relationship picture of the worst kind. (Dir: David Burton Morris, 86 mins.)

Patton (1970)**** George C. Scott, Karl Malden, Stephen Young, Michael Strong. Scott's magnificent performance as General George S. Patton earned him an Oscar, and the film was selected as the best of 1970 by the Academy Award members. It's a gutsy, tough, comparatively honest and fascinating portrait of the WWII general whose military bravado and love of war made him a hero, and also caused him to be relieved of his command in Sicily. In addition to Scott's monumental performance, the film boasts a series of brilliantly staged battle sequences, tracing Patton's career in the North African, Sicilian, and European campaigns. (Dir: Franklin Schaffner, 170 mins.)†

Patty Hearst (1988)*** Natasha Richardson, William Forsythe, Ving Rhames, Francis Fisher. A provocative, artfully realized depiction of the infamous kidnapping of heiress Patty Hearst, and her subsequent indoctrination into the SLA, a shabby but determined terrorist organization. The opening section, dealing with Hearst's imprisonment by the group, skillfully communicates a nightmarish sense of claustrophobia. The film's only difficulties lie in the fact that director Paul Schrader and scripter Nicholas Kazan set the story entirely within Hearst's perspective, which ends up obscuring certain motivations and actions. Throughout, Natasha Richardson does an admirable job as Hearst, filling in some of the plot's deficits with a passionate, three-dimensional performance. (108 mins.)†

Paula (1952)*** Loretta Young, Kent Smith, Tommy Rettig. Paula (Loretta Young) takes a young boy, who is a mute as a result of a "hit and run" accident, into her home. Strange events come into focus as a result. (Dir: Rudolph Maté, 80 mins.)

Paul and Michelle (France-Great Britain, 1974)*½ Anicee Alvina, Sean Bury, Keir Dullea, Ronald Lewis, Catherine Allegret. Sequel to *Friends* with the teens of that film a little older, but still struggling with the demands of family and the real world as he tries to finish school while she cares for their baby. (Dir: Lewis Gilbert, 103 mins.)

Pauline at the Beach (France, 1983)*** Arielle Dombasle, Pascal Greggory, Amanda Langlet, Feodor Atkine. A light erotic romance, a game of musical beds played by some attractive French vacationers in Normandy. Comically exploring its characters' romantic delusions, the film's ironic tone may prove to be too refined for some American audiences. (Dir: Eric Rohmer, 94 mins.)†

Pawnbroker, The (1965)***½ Rod Steiger, Geraldine Fitzgerald, Brock Peters, Thelma Oliver, Jaime Sanchez. One of the most shattering, powerful and honest films made in America in the sixties. Superbly directed by Sidney Lumet in New York's Harlem. Story concerns a Jewish pawnbroker, victim of Nazi persecution, who loses all faith in his fellow man until he realizes no man is an island. Uniformly fine performances. (Dir: Sidney Lumet, 116 mins.)†

Pawnee (1957)** George Montgomery, Bill Williams, Lola Albright, Raymond Hatton. Cliché-ridden western of a white raised by Indians who becomes a wagon train scout and ends up fighting his own tribe. (Dir: George Waggner, 80 mins.)

Payback (1988)*½ Roger Rodd, Denise Dougherty, Jeannie Daly, Deron McBee. Uninvolving made-for-video yarn pits ex-CIA agent Rodd against neo-fascists trying to take over the U. S. with the aid of a secret new assault weapon. (Dir: Addison Randall, 85 mins.)†

Payday (1972)***½ Rip Torn, Elayne Heilveil, Ahna Capri. Observant and deeply moving film about a second-rate country and western singer (Torn) whose road to Mecca—in this case, Nashville, Tenn.—is littered with men and women used and abandoned when he no longer needs them. Honest, knowing screenplay by Don Carpenter; superbly directed by Daryl Duke. (103 mins.)†

Payment Deferred (1932)**½ Charles Laughton, Maureen O'Hara, Dorothy Peterson, Verree Teasdale, Ray Milland. Stagey but effective melodrama about a mousey little man driven to murder his rich relative to get out of a financial scrape. (Dir: Lothar Mendes, 80 mins.)

Payment on Demand (1951)**½ Bette Davis, Barry Sullivan, Jane Cowl. Miss Davis's marriage to Barry Sullivan is on the rocks and headed toward divorce— but first, we have a series of flashbacks depicting the past, and Bette really pours it on. (Dir: Curtis Bernhardt, 88 mins.)

Pay or Die (1966)*** Ernest Borgnine, Zohra Lampert. Well-acted and realistically brutal account of the Mafia's activities in New York City during the years preceding WWI, based on fact. (Dir: Richard Wilson, 111 mins.)†

Payroll (Great Britain, 1961)**½ Michael Craig, Françoise Provost, Billie Whitelaw. Wife of a murdered armored-car guard works with the police in trapping a gang of robbers. Tough, fast-paced crime melodrama, well acted. (Dir: Sidney Hayers, 94 mins.)

Peach Thief, The (Bulgaria, 1964)*** Nevena Kokanova, Rade Markovic, Mikhail Mikhailov, Vasil Vachev. Near the end of WWI, a woman spends her empty days sitting in her garden's peach orchard while her husband runs the local military and POW camps. A war prisoner flees and ends up in her garden to steal some peaches. They meet and fall in love in this sensitive and touching drama. (Dir: Vulo Radev, 84 mins.)

Peacock Fan, The (1929)*** Lotus Long, Wong Foo, Fujii Kishii, Lucien Prival. Good mystery of a legendary Chinese fan that brings bad luck to its owners. (Dir: Phil Rosen, 65 mins.)†

Peanut Butter Solution, The (Canada, 1985)*** Matthew Maillot, Patricia Thompson, Alison Podbrey. Clever family-oriented mystery-comedy about a boy who enters an eerie dilapidated building and is so frightened that his hair falls out. A silly professor and some peanut butter solve the puzzle to this charming tale. (Dir: Michael Rubbo, 93 mins.)†

Pearl, The (1947)***½ Pedro Armendariz, Maria Elena Marques. An excellent film about a poor fisherman who finds a luscious pearl which changes his life. Pedro Armendariz is superb as the bewildered fisherman who can't believe what is happening to him and his wife. Based on a John Steinbeck story. (Dir: Emilio Fernandez, 77 mins.)†

Pearl of Death, The (1944)*** Basil Rathbone, Nigel Bruce, Evelyn Ankers, Rondo Hatton. Sherlock Holmes dispenses his usual deductive pearls of wisdom as he tries to thwart a criminal after a precious pearl. Straight-lined mystery with no frills. (Dir: Roy William Neill, 69 mins.)†

Pearl of the South Pacific (1955)** Virginia Mayo, Dennis Morgan, David Farrar, Mervyn Vye. Silly South Seas melodrama has a beautiful girl stranded on an island, endangered by thieves who are after the natives' store of black pearls. Good for a laugh; hard to believe it was ever intended to be serious. (Dir: Allan Dwan, 86 mins.)†

Pearls of the Crown, The (France, 1937)*** Sacha Guitry, Renée Saint-Cyr, Arletty, Raimu, Claude Dauphin, Jean-Louis Barrault. Pleasant, wittily scripted fantasy about seven pearls given to noted persons over the years (including Napoleon, Josephine, Henry VIII, and Mary, Queen of Scots), and the search for them in modern times. (Dirs: Sacha Guitry, Christian-Jacque, 120 mins.)

Peau D'Ane—See: Donkey Skin

Pedestrian, The (Germany, 1974)*** Maximilian Schell, Gustav Rudolf Sellner, Peter Hall. A stimulating mystery drama that asks questions about the guilt and responsibility of Germans regarding crimes against humanity. A wealthy industrial leader is discovered to have been a Nazi officer who wiped out an entire Greek village during WWII. Newshounds won't let go of their "hot" story, and

we witness the repercussions in the man's life. (Dir: Maximilian Schell, 97 mins.)†

Peck's Bad Boy (1921)*** Jackie Coogan, Wheeler Oakman, Doris May, James Corrigan, Raymond Hatton. Entertaining version of the stories of George Wilbur Peck about a small-town boy who continually finds himself in hot water. Coogan is charming and natural. Titles by humorist Irwin S. Cobb. (Dir: Sam Wood, 51 mins.)†

Peck's Bad Boy (1934)*** Jackie Cooper, Thomas Meighan, Dorothy Peterson, Jackie Searl, O. P. Heggie. Another good version of the classic childrens' stories, with Cooper fine in the title role and good supporting players. The soap-opera subplot was a mistake, but overall this is enjoyable viewing. (Dir: Edward F. Cline, 70 mins.)†

Peck's Bad Boy with the Circus (1938)** Tommy Kelly, Ann Gills, Edgar Kennedy, Benita Hume, Spanky MacFarland, Billy Gilbert. OK but unspectacular circus story grafted onto the well-known George W. Peck stories about a mischievous boy; supporting cast carries it. (Dir: Edward F. Cline, 78 mins.)†

Peeper (1976)** Michael Caine, Natalie Wood, Kitty Winn, Thayer David. Silly, occasionally engaging spoof of private-eye films, with Caine as a British eye in L.A. in '47. (Dir: Peter Hyams, 87 mins.)

Peeping Tom (Great Britain, 1960)**** Carl Boehm, Moira Shearer, Anna Massey, Maxine Audley, Esmond Knight. A stunning thriller that is as potent a statement on the nature of filmmaking-as-voyeurism as it is a brilliantly executed study of psychotic fixation. Boehm plays Mark, a camera fanatic who works at a British film studio by day and stalks beautiful women with his camera-weapon by night. His unnatural obsession with fear leads him to film his victims' reactions to their impending deaths and watch them afterward in his own screening room. Gifted director Michael Powell's treatment of this highly original tale is nightmarishly disturbing, equal to the best work of Hitchcock. (109 mins.)†

Pee-wee's Big Adventure (1985)**** Pee-wee Herman, Jan Hooks, Elizabeth Daily, Mark Holton, Diane Salinger, Cassandra Peterson. Pee-wee's picaresque adventures as he searches for his beloved stolen bicycle last seen en route to Texas. The film's set decoration and camera work look as if the contents of a colorful toy box had been spilled onto the screen. Wonderful! (Dir: Tim Burton, 90 mins.)†

Peg o' My Heart (1922)*** Laurette Taylor, Mahlon Hamilton, Russell Simpson. Sentimental comedy, starring the stage actress Taylor in a charming performance as an orphaned Irish girl who is brought to live with her mother's snobbish English relatives. Timeworn story uplifted by Taylor's star performance. (Dir: King Vidor, 70 mins.)

Peg o' My Heart (1933)*** Marion Davies, Onslow Stevens, J. Farrell MacDonald, Juliette Compton, Alan Mowbray. Remake tailored as a vehicle for Davies, who is charming. The songs specially written for her are quite effective. (Dir: Robert Z. Leonard, 86 mins.)

Peggy (1950)** Diana Lynn, Rock Hudson, Charles Coburn. Silly, unpretentious little comedy about college life, football heroes and the girls who scream over them, and the big Rose Bowl Tournament. (Dir: Frederick de Cordova, 77 mins.)

Peggy Sue Got Married (1986)*** Kathleen Turner, Nicolas Cage, Barry Miller, Catherine Hicks, Joan Allen, Kevin J. O'Connor, Jim Carrey, Don Murray, Barbara Harris, Leon Ames, Maureen O'Sullivan. A feel-good fantasy about a woman who magically returns to her 1950s high school days and brings her 1980s sensibility and attitudes with her. Francis Coppola's crisp direction and Turner's powerhouse personality make up for the flaws in the slightly garbled screenplay, which never sufficiently capitalizes on the conflicts. (104 mins.)†

Peking Express (1951)** Joseph Cotten, Corinne Calvet, Edmund Gwenn. Romance and adventure aboard a speeding train, with a doctor and a wandering lady in the midst of it. Remake of a Dietrich film, *Shanghai Express*, and as usual the original was better. (Dir: William Dieterle, 95 mins.)

Peking Opera Blues (Hong Kong, 1986)*** Cherie Chung, Lin Ching Hsia, Sally Yeh, Mark Cheng. Entertaining concoction that is both a full-fledged farce and an all-out action saga. Set in 1913, the film follows the efforts of three dissimilar girls and their efforts to topple an evil general. Tsui Hark directs with verve, an occasional dash of menace, and tongue firmly in cheek. (100 mins.)

Pelle the Conqueror (Denmark, 1988)**** Max von Sydow, Pelle Hvenegaard. Oscar-winning epic (Best Foreign Film) set in 19th-century Denmark, with immigrant widower von Sydow and son Pelle trying to make a new life as farm laborers. Von Sydow's Oscar-nominated portrayal of a flawed, beaten character is superb. (Dir: Bille August, 140 mins.)†

Penalty, The (1941)** Edward Arnold, Lionel Barrymore, Marsha Hunt, Robert Sterling, Veda Ann Borg, Gloria DeHaven. A gangster's son reforms and helps the authorities capture his own father. Gritty and uncompromising, but

808

hampered by low-budget production. (Dir: Harold S. Bucquet, 79 mins.)

Penalty Phase (MTV 1986)**½ Peter Strauss, Melissa Gilbert, Jonelle Allen. Strauss has a juicy role as the judge who will probably be destroyed if he makes a legally correct decision that would increase the community. Plot lines about prisoners' rights, election politics, and political corruption are all bandied about, but the script gets its message across intelligently. (Dir: Tony Richardson, 104 mins.)

Pendulum (1969)*** George Peppard, Jean Seberg, Richard Kiley. Interesting action drama with George Peppard well cast as a Washington, D.C., police captain who becomes a chief suspect when his wife and her lover are murdered. (Dir: George Schaefer, 106 mins.)†

Penelope (1966)** Natalie Wood, Ian Bannen, Dick Shawn, Peter Falk. Silly, occasionally entertaining comedy in which Wood plays a zany young woman who befuddles even her psychiatrist when she holds up her husband's bank. (Dir: Arthur Hiller, 97 mins.)

Penguin Pool Murder, The (1932)*** Edna May Oliver, James Gleason, Mae Clarke, Robert Armstrong, Donald Cook, Edgar Kennedy. The first of several delightful "Hildegarde Withers" mysteries, starring Oliver as an astringent schoolteacher turned amateur detective. (Dir: George Archainbaud, 70 mins.)

Penitent, The (1988)** Raul Julia, Armand Assante, Rona Freed. Peculiar tale about a farmer (Julia) who channels his doubts and sexual frustrations into the activities of a sect that reenacts the Crucifixion every year. The religious metaphors really start to fly when his wild childhood friend (Assante) comes to visit. A change of pace, but hard to recommend. (Dir: Cliff Osmond, 94 mins.)†

Penitentiary (1979)** Leon Isaac Kennedy, Thommy Pollard, Hazel Spears, Badja Djola, Wilbur "Hi-Fi" White. Kennedy, a man unjustly imprisoned, makes his mark in jail with his fast fists. (Dir: Jamaa Fanaka, 99 mins.)

Penitentiary 2 (1982)* Leon Isaac Kennedy, Mr. T. Kennedy's fast fists fly in this disappointing sequel. This time the unjustly imprisoned ex-con is out to settle a score with the no-good no-account who murdered his girlfriend. A sort of "Rocky with a Record." (Dir: Jamaa Fanaka, 109 mins.)†

Penitentiary 3 (1987)* Leon Isaac Kennedy, Anthony Geary, Ric Mancini, The Haiti Kid, Jim Bailey. Boxer Too Sweet is back in prison (on a phony charge, of course), trying to keep clear of the corrupt officials and inmates who want him to fight for their profit. So many outrageously bad bits, it's hard to name the worst, but Geary's performance gets the nod. (Dir: Jamaa Fanaka, 91 mins.)†

Penn and Teller Get Killed (1989)** Penn Jillette, Teller, Caitlin Clarke, David Patrick Kelly, Leonard Cimino. The comic duo find their lives threatened when one of their practical jokes is taken too seriously. The movie is designed as a practical joke on the audience, and the punch line is great, but the rest of the movie flounders while marking time. (Dir: Arthur Penn, 91 mins.)†

Pennies from Heaven (1936)*** Bing Crosby, Madge Evans, Edith Fellows, Louis Armstrong. Wandering drifter befriends a homeless waif, soon has a pretty truant officer on their trail. Outdated but still amusing musical. (Dir: Norman Z. McLeod, 81 mins.)

Pennies from Heaven (1981)***½ Steve Martin, Bernadette Peters, Jessica Harper, Vernel Bagneris, Christopher Walken, John McMartin. A clever blend of entertainment and social comment about the gap between the happy songs of the Depression, and the grim realities of those caught in the web of fate. Elegantly designed and photographed, and thoroughly unusual. Scripted by Dennis Potter. (Dir: Herbert Ross, 107 mins.)†

Penn of Pennsylvania—See: **Courageous Mr. Penn**

Penny Princess (Great Britain, 1951)*** Yolande Donlon, Dirk Bogarde, Edwin Styles, Laurence Naismith. Slender but captivating comedy of an American shopgirl who turns out to be the ruler of a small European country, applying her marketing expertise to its economic problems. (Dir: Val Guest, 91 mins.)

Penny Serenade (1941)*** Cary Grant, Irene Dunne, Beulah Bondi. An honorable tearjerker, expertly directed by George Stevens. Grant and Dunne try to hold their marriage together by adopting a child. (120 mins.)†

Pennywhistle Blues (South Africa, 1952)***½ Something different—comedy about a thief who loses his stolen loot, as it passes from hand to hand. Utterly delightful, charming, funny. AKA: **Magicagic Garden**. (Dir: Donald Swanson, 63 mins.)†

Penrod and His Twin Brother (1938)**½ Billy Mauch, Bobby Mauch, Spring Byington, Frank Craven. A vehicle for the Mauch twins based on the Booth Tarkington "Penrod" series. Good Americana. (Dir: William McGann, 63 mins.)

Penrod and Sam (1937)**½ Billy Mauch, Spring Byington, Frank Craven, Craig Reynolds. Booth Tarkington's youthful midwestern hero Penrod foils some bank robbers in this entry; low-budget, but well done. (Dir: William McGann, 64 mins.)

Penrod's Double Trouble (1938)** Billy Mauch, Bobby Mauch, Dick Purcell, Kathleen Lockhart, Gene Lockhart. OK children's story, based on Tarkington's characters, about a double taking Penrod's place. (Dir: Lewis Seiler, 61 mins.)

Pension Mimosas (France, 1935)*** Françoise Rosay, Paul Bernard, Alerme, Lise Delamare. Opulent comedy-drama, rich in well-written characters, about a woman who runs a boarding house catering to high-rollers from the local casinos. (Dir: Jacques Feyder, 110 mins.)

Penthouse (1933)*** Warner Baxter, Myrna Loy, Charles Butterworth, Mae Clarke. Sparkling crime melodrama with comic overtones. Baxter's a mouthpiece who's been dumped by the Mob, and Myrna's a lady of the night who can help clear him of trumped-up murder charges. Star chemistry at its most bewitching and, happily, in the service of a clever screenplay. (Dir: W. S. Van Dyke, 90 mins.)

Penthouse, The (Great Britain, 1967)** Suzy Kendall, Terence Morgan. Excessively brutal drama about a day of sadism and terror when two intruders invade a penthouse shared by a married man and his young mistress. (Dir: Peter Collinson, 97 mins.)

Penthouse, The (MTV 1989)**½ Robin Givens, David Hewlett, Robert Guillaume, Donnelly Rhodes. Millionaire's daughter is held captive in her penthouse suite by a mad young man whom she knew as a child. (Dir: David Greene, 96 mins.)

People, The (MTV 1972)*** Kim Darby, William Shatner, Diane Varsi, Dan O'Herlihy. Adapted from Zenna Henderson's science-fiction novel, the soft, gentle tale takes its time as a new schoolteacher puzzles over an isolated community of stoic parents and students who don't laugh, sing, or play games. Her quiet probing into the community's past results in an unusual revelation, and the climactic scenes contain a Thoreau-like message. (Dir: John Korty, 73 mins.)†

People Across the Lake, The (MTV 1988)** Valerie Harper, Gerald McRaney, Barry Corbin, Tammy Lauren. Mild horror outing, with Harper and McRaney as city folks who move to the country for peace and quiet, only to discover murder and madness in their lakeside community. Nothing really new here. (Dir: Arthur Allen Seidelman, 96 mins.)

People Against O'Hara, The (1951)*** Spencer Tracy, Diana Lynn, John Hodiak, Pat O'Brien, James Arness. Good film about lawyers—not merely their performance of duty but their personal involvements. (Dir: John Sturges, 102 mins.)

People Like Us (MTV 1990)*** Connie Sellecca, Ben Gazzara, Eva Marie Saint,

Jean Simmons, Dennis Farina. Highly entertaining dramatization of Dominick Dunne's wonderful best-selling tome about New York's idle rich who keep track of each other through the society columns. Among the many subplots, the most touching involves the gay son of one of the leading families who ultimately dies of AIDS. Saint will chill you to the bone as the young man's mother who throws away the silverware and breaks the dishes he has used. (Dir: Billy Hale, 192 mins.)

People on Sunday (Germany, 1929)*** Brigitte Borchert, Christl Ehlers, Annie Schreyer. Brash and energetic cinema verité-style silent film follows twenty-four hours in the lives of four Berliners. First screen credits for co-directors Robert Siodmak and Edgar Ulmer, and co-writers Billy Wilder and Curt Siodmak. The cinematographer's assistant was Fred Zinnemann. (72 mins.)

People Next Door, The (1970)** Eli Wallach, Julie Harris, Hal Holbrook, Cloris Leachman. One of many films dealing with suburbia and teenage drugs. (Dir: David Greene, 93 mins.)

People That Time Forgot, The (Great Britain, 1977)** Patrick Wayne, Doug McClure. Forgettable lost-civilization movie with prehistoric monsters, raging volcanoes, and primitive cavemen. Based on a yarn by Edgar Rice Burroughs. (Dir: Kevin Conner, 90 mins.)†

People Toys—See: **Devil Times Five**

People vs. Dr. Kildare, The (1941)**½ Lew Ayres, Lionel Barrymore, Laraine Day, Bonita Granville, Red Skelton, Alma Kruger. Series entry beefed up by a change of locale as Kildare's sued for an emergency operation that leaves a skating star paralyzed. (Dir: Harold S. Bucquet, 78 mins.)

People vs. Jean Harris, The (MTV 1981)** Ellen Burstyn, Martin Balsam, Richard Dysart, Peter Coyote, Priscilla Morrill. Murder trial drama was obviously rushed into production to capitalize on the sensational Diet Doctor case. (Dir: George Schaefer, 150 mins.)†

People Will Talk (1935)**½ Charlie Ruggles, Mary Boland, Leila Hyams, Dean Jagger. Marital comedy of a couple who set out to show their errant daughter the error of her ways by pretending to fight. Deft farceurs Ruggles and Boland make this entertaining. (Dir: Alfred Santell, 67 mins.)

People Will Talk (1951)***½ Cary Grant, Jeanne Crain, Sidney Blackmer, Walter Slezak, Hume Cronyn, Finlay Currie. Remarkably funny, stringent social comedy from producer-director Joseph L. Mankiewicz. Dr. Pretorius, the hero, falls in love with a young lady who is
810

expecting another man's child, and marries her anyway. (110 mins.)

Pepe (1960)** Cantinflas, Shirley Jones, Dan Dailey. Shaky plot doesn't do right by Mexico's great comedian in his Hollywood showcase as he plays a ranch foreman who goes to the cinema city to try and get back his pet horse. Originally 195 mins. (Dir: George Sidney, 157 mins.)

Pepe Le Moko (France, 1936)*** Jean Gabin, Mirielle Balin, Gabriel Gabrio. A gangster hiding from the police in Africa finds that his attraction for a femme fatale may prove fatal. Most intriguing. (Dir: Julien Duvivier, 90 mins.)†

Peppermint Frappe (Spain, 1968)***½ Jose Luis Lopez Vasquez, Geraldine Chaplin, Alfredo Mayo. Strong drama about a doctor who is so in love with his brother's wife that he decides to turn his plain nurse into a clone of her, a plan that goes frighteningly awry. Chaplin is magnificent in a dual role as the women. Dedicated to Luis Buñuel. (Dir: Carlos Saura, 94 mins.)

Peppermint Soda (France, 1979)***½ Odile Michel, Eleanore Klarwein, Anouk Ferjac. About sisters growing up in the early '60s, discovering men, sex, and lipstick. Kurys's eye is so sure and her direction so precise that the film bursts open with truth and fresh insight. (Dir: Diane Kurys, 97 mins.)

Perceval (France, 1978)**½ Fabrice Luchini, Marc Eyraud, Arielle Dombasie, Andre Dussollier, Marie-Christine Barrault. Tediously long tale of the young knight's quest, inspired by a vision, for the Holy Grail. Based on an unfinished 12th-century poem, the entire film is shot on pastel-colored sets, and spoken in the original verse form. Tough going, but fans of director Eric Rohmer may like it. (Dir: Eric Rohmer, 140 mins.)

Perfect (1985)** John Travolta, Jamie Lee Curtis, Anne De Salvo, Laraine Newman, Marilu Henner. Travolta struggles with this ill-conceived journalism pic which mainly details his pursuit of an aerobics instructor played by Jamie Lee Curtis. (Dir: James Bridges, 120 mins.)†

Perfect Clown, The (1925)*** Larry Semon, Kate Price, Dorothy Dwan, G. Howe Black, Otis Harlan, Joan Meredith. Fine example of the comic talents of Semon, a popular '20s performer. Here he's a bungling clerk instructed to deliver a large sum of cash to the bank. Typical slapstick, broad and very funny at times. (Dir: Fred Newmeyer, 65 mins.)†

Perfect Couple, A (1979)** Paul Dooley, Marta Heflin, Titos Vandis, Henry Gibson. Director Robert Altman's sour temperament ill equips him for romantic comedy. (110 mins.)†

Perfect Friday (Great Britain, 1970)***½ Stanley Baker, Ursula Andress, David

Warner. Deft comedy thriller. Baker plays a British banker who, when faced with customer Andress, realizes he can steal a million dollars. Warner plays an aristocratic loafer also involved in the caper. (Dir: Peter Hall, 94 mins.)

Perfect Furlough, The (1959)*** Tony Curtis, Janet Leigh, Keenan Wynn, Elaine Stritch, Linda Cristal. Service comedy which borders on slapstick most of the way. Curtis works hard as a khaki-clad Lothario who gets into one insane predicament after another. Cristal gets some of the film's best lines as a movie queen involved in a big publicity stunt that backfires. (Dir: Blake Edwards, 93 mins.)

Perfect Gentlemen (MTV 1978)*** Lauren Bacall, Ruth Gordon, Lisa Pelikan, Sandy Dennis. A sprightly comedy caper film. The stars' husbands are all serving time in a country club prison, and these ladies decide to try a little larceny on their own. (Dir: Jackie Cooper, 104 mins.)

Perfectly Normal (Canada, 1991)**½ Robbie Coltrane, Michael Riley, Deborah Duchene, Patricia Gage. Quietly observed comedy about the growing friendship between two lonely men provides a few gentle laughs. Coltrane is a down-on-his-luck restaurateur who takes up with an introverted cabdriver (Riley). Offbeat tale doesn't always work, but still deserves a look. (Dir: Yves Simoneau, 104 mins.)†

Perfect Marriage, The (1947)** Loretta Young, David Niven. Comedy about the problems of a couple who, after ten years of marriage, find they can't stand each other makes a labored, tedious film. (Dir: Lewis Allen, 87 mins.)

Perfect Match, A (MTV 1980)**½ Linda Kelsey, Michael Brandon, Colleen Dewhurst, Charles Durning, Lisa Lucas. A thirty-two-year-old mother can only be saved by a bone marrow transplant from the teenaged daughter she gave up for adoption. (Dir: Mel Damski, 104 mins.)

Perfect Match, The (1988)*½ Marc McClure, Jennifer Edwards. Only extreme romance addicts should bother with this heavy-handed account of two lonely people who meet through a personals column and lie about their jobs and accomplishments to impress each other. (Dir: Mark Deimel, 93 mins.)†

Perfect People (MTV 1988)*½ Lauren Hutton, Perry King, Priscilla Barnes. Yeah, sure—with a little bit of exercise and plastic surgery, you, too, can look like stars Hutton and King. Here, they play two overweight, overage specimens who decide to "change" for the better. But, hey, attractive people have problems too (enviable ones). (Dir: Bruce Seth Green, 96 mins.)

Perfect Specimen, The (1937)** Errol Flynn, Joan Blondell, Hugh Herbert, Edward Everett Horton. Slow-moving whimsy about a sheltered, wealthy young man (Flynn) whose applecart is upset when a girl unexpectedly lands on his doorstep. (Dir: Michael Curtiz, 90 mins.)

Perfect Strangers (1950)*½ Ginger Rogers, Dennis Morgan, Thelma Ritter. Pure corn and soap opera. A couple of jurors at a murder trial meet and fall in love amid the court proceedings. (Dir: Alexander Korda, 111 mins.)

Perfect Strangers (1985)**½ Anne Carlisle, Brad Rijn, John Woehrle. A hard-edged thriller about a professional hit man's quandary of whether to kill a two-year-old who witnessed his assassination of a drug dealer, complicated by his romance with the boy's mother and growing affection for the child. Interesting thriller offers a cogent analysis of contemporary social tensions. (Dir: Larry Cohen, 90 mins.)†

Perfect Weapon, The (1991)*½ Jeffrey Speakman, John Dye, Mako, James Hong. The new kid on the karate block, Speakman, looks good and kicks well, but this formulaic adventure about drug dealers offers nothing new. In fact it's even a bit racist in its depiction of Koreans who need a white martial arts master to save them. (Dir: Mark DiSalle, 90 mins.)†

Perfect Witness (MTV 1989)**½ Aidan Quinn, Brian Dennehy, Stockard Channing, Laura Harrington, Joe Grifasi, Ken Pogue. Quinn accidentally witnesses a mob killing, then sees his life destroyed as he and his family become pawns in a battle between the gangsters and prosecutor Dennehy. Believable script profits from good acting and New York location photography. (Dir: Robert Mandel, 103 mins.)†

Perfect Woman (Great Britain, 1949)**½ Patricia Roc, Stanley Holloway, Nigel Patrick, Miles Malleson, Irene Handl. Clever comedy about a scientist who creates a robot that behaves like the "perfect" woman, much to the annoyance of his real daughter. (Dir: Bernard Knowles, 89 mins.)

Performance (Great Britain, 1970)*** Mick Jagger, James Fox, Anita Pallenberg. Jagger presides over a decadent household where gangster-on-the-lam Fox seeks refuge. This film was ahead of its time: audiences didn't know how to respond to its sex, violence, and a complicated visual style. Novelist Donald Cammell and cinematographer Nicolas Roeg directed. Repellent but fascinating. (106 mins.)†

Peril (France, 1985)** Christophe Malavoy, Nicole Garcia, Michel Picoli, Richard Bohringer. Convoluted French suspense; a handsome drifter causes havoc in a middle-class community. (Dir: Michel Deville, 100 mins.)†

Perilous Holiday (1946)*** Pat O'Brien, Ruth Warrick, Alan Hale, Edgar

Buchanan. Adventurer in Mexico City stumbles upon a counterfeiting ring that doesn't stop at murder. (Dir: Edward H. Griffith, 89 mins.)

Perilous Journey, A (1953)**½ Vera Ralston, David Brian, Scott Brady, Charles Winninger, Hope Emerson, Leif Erickson. In the mid-19th century, a group of women band together to sail to California in search of husbands. Typically vigorous adventure from director R. G. Springsteen. (90 mins.)

Perilous Voyage (MTV 1969)* Michael Parks, William Shatner, Michael Tolan, Louise Sorel, Lee Grant. Latin-American bandit holds a boat and its passengers hostage. (Dir: William Graham, 104 mins.)

Perils of Gwendoline, The (France, 1985)* Tawny Kitaen, Brent Huff, Zabou, Bernadette Lafont. Mon dieu! A French rip-off of *Raiders of the Lost Ark* all sexed up and vulgarized. Based on a comic strip, this film deals with our heroine's search for her missing father and plays like the Sadomasochistic Sunday Funnies. (Dir: Just Jaeckin, 88 mins.)†

Perils of Pauline, The (1947)*** Betty Hutton, John Lund, Billy de Wolfe. Fabricated biography of Pearl White, the queen of silent-movie serials. Frantic, but many good scenes of life on the Hollywood sets. (Dir: George Marshall, 96 mins.)†

Perils of Pauline, The (1967)** Pat Boone, Pamela Austin, Terry-Thomas. Austin is all blonde innocence in this pilot about a put-upon orphan who goes through a series of incredible adventures that would make Alice's wonderland excursion seem predictable. (Dirs: Herbert B. Leonard, Joshua Shelley, 99 mins.)

Period of Adjustment (1962)*** Tony Franciosa, Jane Fonda, Jim Hutton, Lois Nettleton, Jack Albertson. A rarity, a Tennessee Williams comedy—not his best work, but as transferred to the screen quite pleasant, refreshing entertainment, well played by a young cast. It's all about the problems of a young married couple in adjusting to the rigors of domestic life, and it has many amusing scenes. (Dir: George Roy Hill, 112 mins.)

Permanent Record (1988)*** Keanu Reeves, Alan Boyce, Jennifer Rubin, Michelle Meyrink, Pamela Gidley. A high school student's suicide devastates his classmates, particularly one close friend (Reeves, who gives a fine performance) as he tries to come to terms with the tragedy. An insightful, well-handled youth drama that only slips into theatricality at the very end. (Dir: Marisa Silver, 91 mins.)†

Perri (1957)**½ Generally enjoyable Disney documentary about a year in the life of a forest squirrel. Based on a Felix Salten book. (Dirs: Paul Kenworthy, Jr., Ralph Wright, 75 mins.)

Perry Mason series. Having been indifferently served by Warner Bros. with their early series with Warren William, Erle Stanley Gardner's hard-to-beat attorney hung up his shingle successfully on TV with Raymond Burr achieving small-screen stardom. TV nostalgia buffs gave in to Perry-mania in the eighties when Perry, Della Street, and Paul Drake's son turned up in some highly rated TV films, starting with *Perry Mason Returns*. Besides the films reviewed below, die-hard fans may want to check out the earlier Perry Mason series; the Warner Bros. entries are *The Case of the Black Cat, The Case of the Curious Bride, The Case of the Howling Dog, The Case of the Lucky Legs*, and *The Case of the Stuttering Bishop*.

Perry Mason Returns (MTV 1985)**½ Raymond Burr, Barbara Hale, William Katt, Al Freeman, Jr. Fans of the long-running Perry Mason series will enjoy this reunion, with Burr back on active courtroom duty when his trusty secretary Della Street (Hale) is charged with the murder of her current employer. Also on tap is Paul Drake, Jr., played by Hale's real-life son, William Katt. (Dir: Ron Satlof, 104 mins.)†

Perry Mason: The Case of the Avenging Angel (MTV 1988)*½ Raymond Burr, Barbara Hale, William Katt, Erin Gray, Larry Wilcox, Don Galloway. Perry defends a military man (Wilcox) who's been framed. Average. (Dir: Christian I. Nyby, II, 96 mins.)

Perry Mason: The Case of the Lady in the Lake (MTV 1988)*½ Raymond Burr, Barbara Hale, William Katt, David Ogden Stiers, David Hasselhoff, John Beck. The mammoth barrister takes on the defense of a man accused of murdering his wealthy young wife. Routine courtroom whodunit. (Dir: Ron Satlof, 96 mins.)

Perry Mason: The Case of the Lethal Lesson (MTV 1989)*½ Raymond Burr, Barbara Hale, Alexandra Paul, Brian Keith. Below-average case has Mason investigating the death of a student at a college where he is guest lecturing. (Dir: Christian Y. Nyby II, 96 mins.)

Perry Mason: The Case of the Lost Love (MTV 1987)**½ Raymond Burr, Jean Simmons, Gene Barry, Robert Walden, Gordon Jump, Robert Mandan, Barbara Hale, William Katt, David Ogden Stiers. Simmons plays Perry's old flame, whose husband (Barry) is accused of murder. Political greed is the theme, and it's a creaky one, but Mason fans won't mind. (Dir: Ron Satlof, 104 mins.)

Perry Mason: The Case of the Murdered Madam (MTV 1987)** Raymond Burr, Barbara Hale, William Katt, David Ogden Stiers, Ann Jillian. This time out, the victim is a former-madam-turned-press-relations-specialist (Jillian) who was somehow involved in a banking fraud. Old-fashioned hokum, for P.M. fans only. (Dir: Ron Satlof, 96 mins.)

Perry Mason: The Case of the Notorious Nun (MTV 1986)*** Raymond Burr, Barbara Hale, William Katt, Timothy Bottoms. The intrepid attorney is back for a second, more racy case about a nun accused of murdering a priest. Again William Katt does the legwork, steadfast Barbara Hale gives encouragement, and Burr lumbers in a staid, respectable manner. (Dir: Ron Satlof, 104 mins.)

Perry Mason: The Case of the Scandalous Scoundrel (MTV 1987)** Raymond Burr, Barbara Hale, William Katt, David Ogden Stiers, Robert Guillaume. A sleazy tabloid publisher is murdered, and once again it's up to Perry to weed out the culprit. (Dir: Christian Nyby, 96 mins.)

Perry Mason: The Case of the Shooting Star (MTV 1986)**½ Raymond Burr, Barbara Hale, William Katt, Joe Penny. Burr returns a third time as TV's favorite lawyer. Joe Penny plays a well-known director who apparently shoots a talk show host on the air. (Dir: Ron Satlof, 104 mins.)

Perry Mason: The Case of the Sinister Spirit (MTV 1987)**½ Raymond Burr, Barbara Hale, William Katt, David Ogden Stiers, Robert Stack. Perry faces unexplained mysteries, ghosts, and several tricky suspects in this haunted hotel mystery that will intrigue fans of the series. (Dir: Richard Lang, 104 mins.)

Persecution (Great Britain, 1974)* Lana Turner, Ralph Bates, Trevor Howard. Tawdry, gothic terror as Lana plays a very sick woman who does away with her husband. (Dir: Don Chaffey, 96 mins.)†

Persecution and Assassination of Jean-Paul Marat as Performed by the Inmates of the Asylum of Charenton Under the Direction of the Marquis de Sade, The—See: **Marat/Sade**

Persona (Sweden, 1966)**** Liv Ullmann, Bibi Andersson, Gunner Bjornstrand. Director Ingmar Bergman's masterpiece is less enigmatic today, seeming emotionally direct and thematically accessible. Ullmann is an actress who has decided to remain mute; her babbling nurse is played by Andersson as a surrogate for our decent impulses and petulant disappointments. There is no more moving expression of spiritual anguish in cinema. (81 mins.)†

Personal Affair (Great Britain, 1953)**½ Gene Tierney, Leo Genn, Glynis Johns, Pamela Brown. Teacher is implicated when a romantic schoolgirl suddenly disappears. Well-made but conventional drama. (Dir: Anthony Pelissier, 82 mins.)

Personal Best (1982)*** Mariel Hemingway, Patrice Donnelly, Scott Glenn, Kenny Moore. Women athletes compete for places on the Olympic team, and also fall in love. Interesting for its exploration of the lesbian relationship, and some stunning visuals. (Dir: Robert Towne, 122 mins.)†

Personal Choice (1989)—See: **Beyond the Stars**

Personal Column—See: **Lured**

Personal Property (1937)** Jean Harlow, Robert Taylor, Reginald Owen, Una O'Connor. Bob does everything to win Jean in this one. He poses as a butler and a sheriff's deputy but before the first reel is over you know he'll win her. (Dir: W. S. Van Dyke, 84 mins.)

Personals, The (1982)**½ Bill Schoppert, Karen Landry, Michael Laskin, Paul Eiding. Perceptive examination of the singles scene, in which a divorced man, attractive and outgoing, seeks true love. Not fleshed-out enough, but the film lives up to its modest slice-of-life intentions. (Dir: Peter Markle, 92 mins.)†

Personals (MTV 1990)**½ Stephanie Zimbalist, Jennifer O'Neill, Robin Thomas. Widow Zimbalist stalks her husband's killer, sexy psychopath O'Neill, who gets his victims from personal ads. The direction and first-rate performances by both actresses make the run-of-the-mill movie worth your while. (Dir: Steven H. Stern, 93 mins.)†

Personal Services (Great Britain, 1987)*** Julie Walters, Alec McCowen, Shirley Stelfox. A naughty but nice comedy about a madam who caters to peculiar tastes. In typically restrained British fashion, the film recounts this sexual entrepreneur's encounters with her mildly kinky clients. Based on the life of Cynthia Paine. (Dir: Terry Jones, 103 mins.)†

Pete Kelly's Blues (1955)**½ Jack Webb, Janet Leigh, Peggy Lee, Edmond O'Brien, Lee Marvin. Fairly successful reenactment of the people and sounds in the jazz world of the '20s. Webb gives his usual wooden performance in the lead. Lee went dramatic in this one and surprisingly did very well. (Dir: Jack Webb, 95 mins.)†

Pete 'n' Tillie (1972)**½ Walter Matthau, Carol Burnett, Geraldine Page, René Auberjonois. Burnett and Matthau are a pair of middle-aged realists who meet, have an affair, marry, have a child, and have to deal with the fact that the boy is dying. With less talented stars this could have been soap opera junk, but they keep it afloat in a sea of pathos. Page's bitchy comic relief earned an Oscar nomination. (Dir: Martin Ritt, 100 mins.)†

Peter Gunn (MTV 1989)*** Peter Strauss, Pearl Bailey, Barbara Williams, Charles Cioffi, Jennifer Edwards, David Rappaport. Sequel to the ultra-cool TV series is still set in the '60s, with Gunn (Strauss) hired by a Mafia boss to prove he didn't rub out a rival mobster. Action, atmosphere, nostalgia, and a good performance by Strauss add up to a highly watchable TV movie. (Dir: Blake Edwards, 96 mins.)

Peter Ibbetson (1935)*** Gary Cooper, Ann Harding, John Halliday, Ida Lupino. Weirdly affecting though dated supernatural romance. Though Peter is in jail for life, he and his childhood sweetheart continue to meet in their dreams. (Dir: Henry Hathaway, 88 mins.)†

Peter Lundy and the Medicine Hat Stallion (MTV 1977)*** Leif Garrett, Mitchell Ryan. A charming movie, aided by author Marguerite Henry's storytelling skills about frontier life. Her hero is a sixteen-year-old boy riding for the Pony Express. (Dir: Michael O'Herlihy, 104 mins.)

Peter Pan (1924)***½ Betty Bronson, Ernest Torrence, Cyril Chadwick, Anna May Wong. Wonderful silent version of classic tale captures spirit of James M. Barrie's fantasy. Clever effects and grand characterizations add to film's appeal. (Dir: Herbert Brenon, 101 mins.)

Peter Pan (1953)**½ Voices of Bobby Driscoll, Hans Conried, Kathryn Beaumont, Heather Angel. Walt Disney's animated version of James M. Barrie's play. Conried's Captain Hook is movie's highlight (he also did Mr. Darling), but drab songs and patronizing depictions of Indians keep film from being a classic. (Dirs: Hamilton Luske, Clyde Geronimi, Wilfred Jackson, 76 mins.)†

Pete's Dragon (1977)*** Helen Reddy, Jim Dale, Mickey Rooney, Red Buttons, Shelley Winters, Sean Marshall. Even weighed down with Reddy, this is sprightly Disney fare about a friendless kid who's befriended by a klutzy dragon. Deft combination of live action with animation. (Dir: Don Chaffey, 134 mins.)†

Petit Con (France, 1984)*** Bernard Brieux, Guy Marchand. Eager to distance himself from his rich and successful dear old dad, our eighteen-year-old hero deliberately pursues the lower classes in search of higher enlightenment, only to be disappointed by everyone he meets and trusts. Funny, biting satire. (Dir: Gerard Lauzier, 90 mins.)†

Petrified Forest, The (1936)*** Bette Davis, Leslie Howard, Humphrey Bogart, Dick Foran. In the godforsaken, dried-up middle of nowhere, a disillusioned drifter sacrifices himself to provide an escape route for a starry-eyed girl trapped there. Certainly, Robert Sherwood's play's conceits about individuality seem a bit threadbare, but the film's ability to view life through its characters' poetry-colored glasses remains gripping. (Dir: Archie Mayo, 83 mins.)†

814

Pet Sematary (1989)*** Dale Midkiff, Fred Gwynne, Denise Crosby, Brad Greenquist. Certainly the darkest, most visceral adaptation of a Stephen King novel. Similar to the classic story *The Monkey's Paw*, this story's real horror is in watching the disintegration of a family after their desire to have their dead child back comes true. After every male horror director in the book failed at adapting King, it took a woman, Mary Lambert (*Siesta*) to do it right. (102 mins.)†

Petticoat Fever (1936)**½ Robert Montgomery, Myrna Loy, Reginald Owen. Perennial summer stock favorite fails to ring the bell as good movie comedy. Bob is all alone in Labrador when Myrna arrives, thanks to a plane crash, with her fiancé. (Dir: George Fitzmaurice, 81 mins.)

Petty Girl, The (1950)*** Robert Cummings, Joan Caulfield, Elsa Lanchester, Melville Cooper, Mary Wickes. Cummings plays an artist who specializes in glamour girls. His unlikely model is prim school teacher Caulfield. (Dir: Henry Levin, 87 mins.)

Petulia (1968)**** George C. Scott, Julie Christie, Richard Chamberlain, Joseph Cotten, Shirley Knight. A modern masterpiece. Scott is the surgeon with identity problems and Christie is the unhappily married girl who offers him the possibility of some meaning. Finely supported by Knight and Chamberlain. (Dir: Richard Lester, 105 mins.)†

Peyton Place (1957)*** Lana Turner, Diane Varsi, Hope Lange, Arthur Kennedy, Lloyd Nolan, Betty Field, Russ Tamblyn, Mildred Dunnock. Here's the original film which served as the basis for the popular TV soap opera. It's actually much better than you may expect. Lana Turner and a fine supporting cast bring to life all the shady secrets of the New England town which made Grace Metalious's book a best-seller. Sequel: *Return to Peyton Place*. (Dir: Mark Robson, 157 mins.)†

Peyton Place: The Next Generation (MTV 1985)** Dorothy Malone, Barbara Parkins, Tim O'Connor, Pat Morrow. The granddaddy of prime-time soaps returns for a one-night stand. The new generation behave as wildly as their predecessors, while the oldtimers now muddle around as if by rote. (Dir: Larry Elikann, 104 mins.)

Phaedra (U.S.-Greece-France, 1962)**½ Melina Mercouri, Anthony Perkins, Raf Vallone. Lots of heavy breathing in this supercharged updating of a Greek classic. Among the neo-Greek tragedians is Mercouri, who frequents the arms of her stepson instead of her lusty Greek tycoon husband. (Dir: Jules Dassin, 115 mins.)

Phantasm (1979)***½ Michael Baldwin,

Bill Thornbury, Reggie Bannister, Angus Scrimm. A truly original horror movie, written, directed, co-produced, photographed, and edited by twenty-one-year-old Don Coscarelli. Two teenagers break into a mausoleum to investigate some odd happenings and find a bizarre world, presided over by "the Tall Man" (Scrimm, a memorable-looking fellow). It's full of unforgettable images, including a sinister hearse and a deadly, flying silver ball. (90 mins). †

Phantasm II (1988)** James Le Gros, Reggie Bannister, Angus Scrimm, Paula Irvine. Disappointing sequel. The survivors of the first film set out in search of the Tall Man, who is raiding small towns of their dead. Where *Phantasm* was an original, this shows that writer-director Don Coscarelli has been adversely influenced by all of his imitators. The result is a textbook of modern horror movie clichés: you could cut the movie into random chunks, reassemble it, and have pretty much the same thing. (90 mins.) †

Phantom Baron, The (France, 1943)*** Jany Holt, Odette Joyeux, Alain Cuny, Jean Cocteau. Fantasy about a countess, her daughter, and her uncle the baron, a sleepwalker who disappears one night for ten years. Fascinating film rich in horror and romance has superb dialogue (written by co-star Cocteau) and a terrific surprise ending. (Dir: Serge De Poligny, 100 mins.)

Phantom Express, The (1932)** William Collier, Jr., Sally Blane, J. Farrell MacDonald, Hobart Bosworth. Adventure with a clever premise: outlaws fake a "phantom" train, making engineers think they're about to have a head-on crash and slam on the brakes. Unfortunately, the histrionics don't live up to the idea, and the script is weak. (Dir: Emory Johnson, 66 mins.) †

Phantom from Space (1953)½ Ted Cooper, Steve Acton, Burt Wenland, Lela Nelson, Tom Daly, Noreen Nash, Dick Sands. Low, low-budget howler about an invisible man from outer space and how he's misunderstood by earthlings lacking in hospitality. (Dir: W. Lee Wilder, 73 mins.) †

Phantom India (France, 1969)**** Director Louis Malle's brilliant six-hour essay on India, an unending succession of dazzling imagery and cultural shock. There are religious festivals in Madras, a malnourished village giving daily offerings of precious grain to feed rats, and scenes of urban life in Bombay and others. (360 mins.)

Phantom Lady (1944)***½ Franchot Tone, Ella Raines, Thomas Gomez, Elisha Cook, Jr., Regis Toomey. A very intriguing mystery film. A man is convicted of murdering his wife and a few people who believe him innocent try to clear him. (Dir: Robert Siodmak, 87 mins.)

Phantom of Chinatown (1940)** Keye Luke, Lotus Long, Grant Withers, Paul McVey, Charles Miller. Luke replaced Boris Karloff as Hugh Wiley's clever Oriental sleuth, Mr. Wong, in this final entry to the series, a dull effort about an archaeologist who is murdered for an ancient scroll. (Dir. Phil Rosen, 62 mins.) †

Phantom of Crestwood, The (1932)*** Karen Morley, Ricardo Cortez, H. B. Warner, Pauline Frederick, Anita Louise. This stylish adaptation of a radio drama stars Cortez as a detective investigating the murder of an adventuress involved in blackmail. (Dir: J. Walter Ruben, 77 mins.)

Phantom of Death (Italy, 1988)*½ Michael York, Donald Pleasence, Edwige Fenech. Musician York, victim of a rare disease that is making him age rapidly, goes on a spree of murder. Italian horror movie lacks the usual gore, leaving only York's dependable acting to distinguish it. (Dir: Ruggerio Deodato, 91 mins.) †

Phantom of Hollywood, The (MTV 1974)** Jack Cassidy, Broderick Crawford, Skye Aubrey, Jackie Coogan. High melodrama on the hokey side. A disfigured actor goes amok when the movie studio back lot (the actor's secret home for thirty years) is torn down. (Dir: Gene Levitt, 74 mins.)

Phantom of Liberty, The (France, 1974)**** Jean-Claude Brialy, Monica Vitti, Adolfo Celi, Michel Piccoli. The phrase *Phantom of Liberty* is from Karl Marx; the genius on screen is director Luis Buñuel. The first episode is set in Spain in the early 19th century and there are dazzling visual images throughout. (104 mins.) †

Phantom of Paris, The (1931)*** John Gilbert, Leila Hyams, Lewis Stone, Jean Hersholt, Ian Keith, C. Aubrey Smith. Atmospheric thriller with Gilbert excellent as a famous magician unjustly accused of murder, using his talents to find the real killer. From a Gaston Leroux novel. (Dir: John S. Robertson, 72 mins.)

Phantom of the Jungle (1955)* Jon Hall, Ray Montgomery, Anne Gwynne. Weak melodrama of an American doctor who saves scientists from the wrath of African natives in a dispute over sacred tablets. (Dir: Spencer Bennet, 75 mins.)

Phantom of the Opera, The (1925)**½ Lon Chaney, Mary Philbin, Norman Kerry. An over-long silent film that does, however, still have its effective moments, especially the celebrated unmasking scene. The oft-repeated plot concerns the disfigured, corpselike figure who skulks underneath the Paris Opera House and waits to revenge himself on those who stole his music. (Dir: Rupert Julian, 94 mins.)†

Phantom of the Opera (1943)*** Nelson Eddy, Susanna Foster, Claude Rains. This rendition provides almost as much opera as phantom, with Eddy and Foster warbling away, oblivious to the crazed antics of Rains, who makes a good monster. The film looks superb under the color lighting of Hal Mohr, who was awarded a cinematography Oscar. (Dir: Arthur Lubin, 92 mins.)†

Phantom of the Opera, The (Great Britain, 1962)**½ Herbert Lom, Heather Sears, Edward DeSouza. Another version of the old Lon Chaney thriller about a hideously scarred creature terrorizing an opera house. (Dir: Terence Fisher, 84 mins.)

Phantom of the Opera, The (MTV 1983)*** Maximilian Schell, Jane Seymour, Michael York, Jeremy Kemp, Diana Quick. The classic thriller with overtones of "Beauty and the Beast" and *Faust* is reworked with a remarkable cast and fine direction by Robert Markowitz. (104 mins.)

Phantom of the Opera, The (1989)* Robert Englund, Jill Schoelen, Alex Hyde-White, Bill Nighy. Pointlessly relocated to London, this Phantom is an unsympathetic killer instead of the tragic madman usually seen. (Dir: Dwight H. Little, 90 mins.)†

Phantom of the Opera, The (MTV 1990)**½ Burt Lancaster, Charles Dance, Teri Polo, Ian Richardson, Andrea Ferreol, Jean-Pierre Cassel. Lavish adaptation by playwright Arthur Kopit has neither songs nor scares, sticking to straight romantic melodrama. Handsome production was filmed in France in authentic locations. (Dir: Tony Richardson, 192 mins.)

Phantom of the Paradise (1974)*** Paul Williams, Jessica Harper, William Finley. A rock musical version of the popular *Phantom of the Opera* theme. Updating the plot to the world of the modern music business, the film creates a wildly funny portrait of the record industry's venality and the dangers of quick celebrity. (Dir: Brian De Palma, 92 mins.)†

Phantom of the Rue Morgue (1954)*** Karl Malden, Patricia Medina, Steve Forrest, Merv Griffin, Erin O'Brien-Moore. Eerie horror film about an insane murderer in Paris and his many coldblooded murders. Remake of *Murders in the Rue Morgue*. (Dir: Roy Del Ruth, 84 mins.)

Phantom Planet (1961)** Dean Fredericks, Richard Kiel, Colleen Fredericks, Tony Dexter, Francis X. Bushman. A miniscule movie about the miniscule inhabitants of the planet Rheton. (Dir: William Marshall, 82 mins.)†

Phantom President, The (1932)** George M. Cohan, Claudette Colbert, Jimmy Durante, Sidney Toler. Skimpy musical comedy notable for the dual-role appearance of Cohan as a presidential hopeful mixed up with a performer who resembles him. Phantom laughs, too. (Dir: Norman Taurog, 80 mins.)

Phantom Stagecoach, The (1957)** William Bishop, Kathleen Cowley, Frank Ferguson, Richard Webb, Percy Helton. Subpar western about stagecoach companies vying for trade and tourist routes. Some exciting action sequences make it palatable. (Dir: Ray Nazarro, 69 mins.)

Phantom Thief, The (1946)** Chester Morris, Jeff Donnell, Richard Lane. Boston Blackie's got to locate a killer despite a smoke screen consisting of assorted ersatz-supernatural occurrences. (Dir: D. Ross Lederman, 65 mins.)

Phantom Tollbooth, The (1970)*** Butch Patrick. A bit of live action and lots of animation are used to bring the Norton Juster novel to the screen. It's charming for young children, as bored Butch takes a trip through the mysterious tollbooth with the Kingdom of Wisdom as a goal. (Dirs: Chuck Jones, Abe Levitow, David Monahan, 90 mins.)†

Pharaoh (Poland, 1965)*** George Zelnik, Barbara Bryl, Krystyna Mikolajewska, Piotr Pawlowski. Visually stunning historical epic about ancient Egypt stresses realism over pageantry, but includes some stupendous battle scenes. The plot centers around young Prince Rameses's love for a Jewish girl, which incurs the wrath of a high priest. (Dir: Jerzy Kawalerowicz, 183 mins.)

Pharaoh's Curse (1957)** Mark Dana, Ziva Rodann. Archeological expedition encounters a monster from thousands of years ago in Egypt. (Dir: Lee Sholem, 66 mins.)

Phar Lap (Australia, 1984)*** Tom Burlinson, Ron Leibman, Martin Vaughn, Judy Morris. A true story of the champion Australian racehorse of the twenties and thirties. Although the horse's American owner all but despaired at first, a trainer and stable boy sensed something special about the horse and became determined to push their four-legged friend onto the right track. Inspirational and touching. (Dir: Simon Wincer, 106 mins.)†

Phase IV (Great Britain, 1973)** Nigel Davenport, Lynne Frederick, Michael Murphy. Chilling images of destruction are wasted in this derivative script concerning the takeover of the earth by an ant population that has begun organizing itself for a coup against mankind. (Dir: Saul Bass, 93 mins.)†

Phenix City Story, The (1955)*** Richard Kiley, John McIntire, Edward Andrews. Hard-hitting drama dealing with the expose of one of the most corrupt "Sin-

Cities'' in the United States: Phenix City, Alabama. Kiley and Andrews are standouts in a fine cast in this film based on actual news data. (Dir: Phil Karlson, 100 mins.)

Phffft! (1954)***½ Judy Holliday, Jack Lemmon, Kim Novak, Jack Carson. Judy Holliday and Jack Lemmon make the most hilarious movie team since the days of Jean Arthur and James Stewart in this fast-paced, sometimes funny story of a marriage that almost goes phffft! (Dir: Mark Robson, 91 mins.)

Philadelphia Experiment, The (1984)**½ Michael Paré, Nancy Allen, Bobby Di Cicco, Eric Christmas, Kene Holliday. When tests are conducted during the WWII years to make U.S. battleships invisible to radar, one of the experimental boats disappears completely and two sailors find themselves stranded in 1984. The film's resourcefulness lies in combining the humor of the seemen's reactions to modern times with the suspense of their attempts to return to the past. (Dir: Stewart Raffill, 102 mins.)†

Philadelphia, Here I Come (1975)*** Donal McCann, Siobhan McKenna, Des Cave, Eamon Kelly, Fidelma Murphy, Liam Redmond. Well-acted adaptation of the hit play about a young man trying to decide whether to leave Ireland and move to Philadelphia to live with his aunt. Lovely comedic touches highlight a unique perspective on the allure of the U.S.A. (Dir: John Quested, 95 mins.)

Philadelphia Story, The (1940)***½ Katharine Hepburn, Cary Grant, James Stewart, Ruth Hussey, John Howard, Roland Young. First-rate cast sparks this brittle adaptation of Philip Barry's play about a socialite preparing for her second marriage, but still in love with her first spouse. Much of the dialogue is witty, and the stars are at their best. (Dir: George Cukor, 112 mins.)†

Philo Vance series. S. S. Van Dine's gentleman's gentleman detective was limned by many actors, but William Powell probably made the greatest impact. No matter which actor interpreted him, Philo always brought a touch of class to the world of crime-solving in the films reviewed below, as well as plying his investigative trade in these following cases: *The Canary Murder Case, The Greene Murder Case, The Bishop Murder Case, The Benson Murder Case, The Kennel Murder Case, The Dragon Murder Case, The Casino Murder Case, The Garden Murder Case, Night of Mystery, The Gracie Allen Murder Case,* and *Calling Philo Vance.*

Philo Vance's Gamble (1947)*½ Alan Curtis, Terry Austin. Vance tackles the Mob and investigates three murders. (Dir: Basil Wrangell, 62 mins.)

Philo Vance's Return (1947)*½ William Wright, Terry Austin. Philo's determined to crack a case involving the slaying of a playboy and several of his boudoir-mates. (Dir: William Beaudine, 64 mins.)

Philo Vance's Secret Mission (1947)*½ Alan Curtis, Sheila Ryan. Low-grade Vance entry involving the murder of the owner of a detective magazine. (Dir: Reginald Le Borg, 58 mins.)

Phobia (Canada, 1980)* Paul Michael Glaser, Susan Hogan, John Colicos. An embarrassing thriller starring Glaser as a psychiatrist treating patients with various phobias who are giving one by one under mysterious circumstances. (Dir: John Huston, 90 mins.)†

Phoenix, The (MTV 1981)* Judson Scott, Shelley Smith, E. G. Marshall, Fernando Allende. Story centers around an ancient God-like being who's brought back to life after being discovered in a 2,000-year-old tomb. The "Phoenix" is amazingly tan and coiffured after 2,000 years. (Dir: Douglas Hickox, 78 mins.)

Phone Call, The (Canada, 1991)**½ Michael Sarrazin, Linda Smith, Ron Lea, Vlasta Vrana. Intriguing variation of *Fatal Attraction.* Married Sarrazin misdials a phone sex service and gets a male line by mistake, which provokes a psychopathic caller into threatening his life and family. Story cops out with gay overtones but is compelling nonetheless. (Dir: Allan A. Goldstein, 91 mins.)†

Phone Call from a Stranger (1952)*** Shelley Winters, Gary Merrill, Michael Rennie, Bette Davis, Keenan Wynn. Merrill stars in this good episodic drama as the lone survivor of a plane crash who takes it upon himself to contact some of his traveling companions' relatives. Most of the action unfolds via flashbacks. (Dir: Jean Negulesco, 96 mins.)†

Phony American, The (West Germany, 1962)*** William Bendix, Michael Hinz, Christine Kaufmann, Ron Randell. Spirited German WWII orphan is fascinated by things American and wants to become a citizen and join the U.S. Air Force, much to the amazement of those around him. Decidely different, and entertaining, twist on the "coming to America" theme. (Dir: Akos Rathony, 73 mins.)

Physical Evidence (1988)*½ Theresa Russell, Burt Reynolds, Ned Beatty. Lawyer Russell defends violent cop Reynolds, accused of the murder of a mobster. Reynolds is good, but there's too little of him and too much of Russell, who is miscast and very bad. Written as a sequel to *Jagged Edge,* this paint-by-numbers mystery will keep no one in suspense. (Dir: Michael Crichton, 99 mins.)†

Piano for Mrs. Cimino, A (MTV 1982)*** Bette Davis, Keenan Wynn, Alexa Kenin. Miss Davis is a seventy-three-year-old woman labeled senile, and placed in a nursing home. The first half, involving the old woman's depression is well plotted and more interesting than the second half, when she fights back. (Dir: George Schaefer, 104 mins.)†

Picasso Summer, The (1969)**½ Albert Finney, Yvette Mimieux. Offbeat romantic tale just misses. It's a strange mixture of surrealism and reality, with Finney and Mimieux playing a couple who adore Picasso and form an alliance based on their mutual love for the great artist's work. (Dir: Serge Bourguignon, 96 mins.)

Picasso Trigger, The (1988)* Steve Bond, Dona Speir, Hope Marie Carlton, Roberta Vasquez, Guich Koock. Sequel to *Hard Ticket to Hawaii* follows the same format as all of writer-director Andy Sidaris's movies: tongue-in-cheek action set in Hawaii and starring a cast of ex-''Playboy'' centerfolds. At its worst when it's trying to be funny; the rest isn't much better. Followed by *Savage Beach*. (98 mins.)†

Piccadilly Incident (Great Britain, 1946)*** Anna Neagle, Michael Wilding, Reginald Owen, Frances Mercer. In wartime England, a man thinks his wife has been killed, but she returns after he has married again. (Dir: Herbert Wilcox, 88 mins.)

Piccadilly Jim (1936)*** Robert Montgomery, Madge Evans, Billie Burke, Frank Morgan, Robert Benchley. P. G. Wodehouse's story of a cartoonist and his bumbling father is turned into a delightful comedy. (Dir: Robert Z. Leonard, 97 mins.)

Picking Up the Pieces (MTV 1985)*** Margot Kidder, David Ackroyd, Barbara Rhoades, Ari Meyers, James Farentino, Joyce Van Patten. An interesting study of the process of divorce with a marvelous performance by Kidder as a wife who never realized what being on her own would mean. (Dir: Paul Wendkos, 104 mins.)

Pickpocket (France, 1959)***½ Martin LaSalle, Marika Green, Jean Pelegri. An austere meditation written and directed by Robert Bresson, about an educated thief who believes that the road to heaven is paved with bad intentions and that somehow God wants him to steal. (75 mins.)

Pick-Up (1933)**½ Sylvia Sidney, George Raft, William Harrigan, Lilian Bond, Clarence Wilson. Surprisingly direct pre-Code romantic melodrama with Sidney as a conwoman who reforms when she falls for honest cabbie Raft, even though she's married to an imprisoned gangster. Minor but capably done. (Dir: Marion Gering, 76 mins.)

818

Pickup (1951)**½ Beverly Michaels, Hugo Haas. Occasionally effective drama about an old man who marries a cheap girl he picks up and the complications that arise when a handsome younger man enters the picture. (Dir: Hugo Haas, 78 mins.)

Pickup Alley (Great Britain, 1957)** Victor Mature, Anita Ekberg, Trevor Howard. Routine crime matter, Mature is a narcotics agent whose sleuthing takes him to London, Lisbon, Athens, Rome, etc. (Dir: John Gilling, 92 mins.)

Pick-Up Artist, The (1987)* Molly Ringwald, Robert Downey, Jr., Dennis Hopper, Danny Aiello, Harvey Keitel. There's not laugh one to be had while watching the title operator (Downey) put the make on a sullen and sarcastic museum tour guide (Ringwald). Downey is mercilessly irritating as the "artist" who looks as though he couldn't pick up his own laundry. Terribly written and directed by James Toback. (90 mins.)†

Pickup on 101 (1972)** Lesley Ann Warren, Martin Sheen, Jack Albertson, Michael Ontkean. Ambling anti-establishment road movie about the adventures of a college drop-out, a hobo, and a musician on the open road. (Dir: John Florea, 93 mins.)

Pickup on South Street (1953)**½ Richard Widmark, Jean Peters, Richard Kiley, Thelma Ritter. Pickpocket unwittingly lifts a message destined for enemy agents and becomes a target for a Communist spy ring. Brutal melodrama, but very well done. (Dir: Samuel Fuller, 80 mins.)†

Pick-Up Summer (Canada, 1981)**½ Michael Zelniker, Carl Marotte, Helen Udy, Karen Stephen. Amusing teen picture, from the Canadian point of view, about kids having a good time getting ready for a summer full of pinball games and beauty pageants, with some motorcycle gang thugs thrown in for tension. Just like the good old U.S. of A. AKA: **Pinball Summer, Pinball Pick-Up.** (Dir: George Mihalka, 92 mins.)†

Pickwick Papers, The (Great Britain, 1953)**** James Hayter, Nigel Patrick, James Donald, Joyce Grenfell, Kathleen Harrison, Hermione Gingold. In the picturesque 1830s, goodhearted Mr. Pickwick and his friends travel about England in search of adventure. Touching and hilarious. From the stories by Charles Dickens. (Dir: Noel Langley, 109 mins.)†

Picnic (1956)**** Kim Novak, William Holden, Rosalind Russell, Susan Strasberg, Arthur O'Connell, Cliff Robertson. Superb screen version of William Inge's Pulitzer Prize-winner. Holden plays a down-at-the-heels drifter who looks up an old college friend and then falls for his girlfriend. Strutting through the town, Holden's sexuality affects the women of the town in different ways by stirring up romantic longings. (Dir: Joshua Logan, 113 mins.)†

Picnic at Hanging Rock (Australia, 1976)***½ Rachel Roberts, Dominic Guard, Anne Lambert, Helen Morse. Mystical, dreamlike horror film which poses no easy answers to what really happened to a group of Australian schoolgirls who disappeared on Valentine's Day. Based on the novel by Joan Lindsay, the film is a rewarding entry for those who like their thrillers done with a subtle hand. (Dir: Peter Weir, 110 mins.)†

Picnic on the Grass (France, 1959)*** Paul Meurisse, Catherine Rouvel, Fernand Sardou, J. P. Grandval, Micheline Gary. This is the film that most clearly seems a tribute to Jean Renoir's famous painter father, August. Photographed in a style evocative of Impressionism, this eye-filling but somewhat vague film dramatizes the process by which a scientist dedicated to artificial insemination and controlling mankind's future scientifically is somehow transformed and humanized by the love of a country girl. (Dir: Jean Renoir, 95 mins.)

Picture Mommy Dead (1966)**½ Don Ameche, Martha Hyer, Zsa Zsa Gabor. A complicated mystery which sustains its interest despite the hokey aspects of the script involving a young girl who loses her memory after the tragic death of her mother. (Dir: Bert I. Gordon, 88 mins.)†

Picture of Dorian Gray, The (1945)*** George Sanders, Hurd Hatfield, Donna Reed, Angela Lansbury, Peter Lawford. Oscar Wilde's novel receives as perceptive a treatment as could be expected from producer-writer-director Albert Lewin. Impeccably epigrammatic deliveries from Hatfield as Dorian and Sanders as an evil cad, plus the irresistible pathos of Lansbury's innocent songstress. (110 mins.)†

Picture of Dorian Gray, The (MTV 1973)*½ Shane Briant, Charles Aidman, Nigel Davenport, Fionnula Flanagan, Linda Kelsey. Far less compelling than the original version with Hurd Hatfield. (Dir: Glenn Jordan, 180 mins.)†

Picture Show Man, The (Australia, 1977)***½ Rod Taylor, John Meillon. Delightful, sentimental comedy about the start of the movie business in Australia centers around the showmen who first brought films into the outback and bush. A must for movie lovers. (Dir: John Power, 99 mins.)

Picture Snatcher (1933)**½ James Cagney, Patricia Ellis, Alice White, Ralph Bellamy. Snazzy crime drama with Cagney vivid as a hood who finds he has a talent for photography and becomes a top tabloid cameraman. Filled with action and street-smart dialogue; good support from White as a sexy party-girl,

and Bellamy as a tough newspaper editor. (Dir: Lloyd Bacon, 76 mins.)

Piece of the Action, A (1977)** Sidney Poitier, Bill Cosby, James Earl Jones, Denise Nicholas. Two con guys help troubled kids in this admirable attempt to blend comedy with social commentary. (Dir: Sidney Poitier, 135 mins.)†

Pieces (U.S.-Italy-Spain, 1983)½ Christopher George, Frank Brana, Paul Smith, Edmund Purdom, Lynda Day George. A madman with a chainsaw decapitates, eviscerates, and otherwise incapacitates students at a big city college. (Dir: Juan Piquer Simon, 92 mins.)†

Pied Piper, The (1942)***½ Monty Woolley, Anne Baxter, Otto Preminger, Roddy McDowall. Wartime story of an Englishman who hates kids and finds himself stuck with a pack of them and trying to escape the Nazis. Warm, amusing, and powerful film. (Dir: Irving Pichel, 86 mins.)

Pied Piper of Hamelin, The (MTV 1957)** Van Johnson, Claude Rains, Kay Starr. Musical version of the fairy tale about the piper who rids the town of rats. (Dir: Bretaigne Windust, 92 mins.)†

Pie in the Sky—See: Terror in the City

Pierrot le Fou (France, 1965)***½ Jean-Paul Belmondo, Anna Karina, Graziella Galvani, Dirk Sanders, Raymond Devos, Samuel Fuller. Godard's most entertaining take-off on the Hollywood adventure film. Belmondo, a disillusioned intellectual, runs away with his kid's babysitter (Karina), only to find that once they've reached paradise (a secluded island hideaway), their romance has fallen apart. Godard's mastery of the possibilities of the wide screen and of technicolor, and his ingenious ability to create images that activate the mind as much as they delight the eye, complements the "lovers-on-the-run" story line. (Dir: Jean-Luc Godard, 112 mins.)

Pier 13 (1940)** Lynn Bari, Lloyd Nolan, Joan Valerie, Douglas Fowley, Chick Chandler. Low-budget mystery has Nolan as a waterfront cop who finds that his waitress girlfriend's sister is involved in shady dealings. (Dir: Eugene Forde, 66 mins.)

Pigeon, The (MTV 1969)** Sammy Davis, Jr., Pat Boone, Dorothy Malone, Ricardo Montalban. Although Sammy works very hard as a private detective, this clichéd feature falls short. Malone is the widow of a former syndicate bigwig who kept a diary and the Mafia wants the little black book. (Dir: Earl Bellamy, 74 mins.)

Pigeon That Took Rome, The (1962)**½ Charlton Heston, Elsa Martinelli, Harry Guardino, Brian Donlevy. Tough infantry officer is sent behind Nazi lines into occupied Rome to see what's cooking, sends pigeons back with messages, finds time for some romance. (Dir: Melville Shavelson, 101 mins.)

Pigs—See: **Daddy's Deadly Darling**

Pigs and Battleships (Japan, 1961)*** Hiroyuki Nagato, Tetsuro Tamba, Yitsuko Yoshimura. Allegorical satire about the owner of a brothel frequented by American naval personnel; forced out of business, he establishes a pig farm. Weird but bright crime story includes a pig stampede, filmed like a cattle stampede in a Hollywood western. (Dir: Shohei Imamura, 108 mins.)

Pigskin Parade (1936)**½ Stuart Erwin, Betty Grable, Judy Garland, Jack Haley, Patsy Kelly. The talented cast of this bright but negligible musical about a hayseed turned football hero all went on to better things. Socking this musical over the goal post are Grable's exuberance and young Judy's singing, as well as some expert clowning. (Dir: David Butler, 95 mins.)

Pig Sty (Italy, 1969)***½ Pierre Clementi, Jean-Pierre Leaud, Anne Wiaszemsky, Ugo Tognazzi. Powerful parable about how the middle class will sacrifice individuals to maintain their comfortable status. Writer-director Pier Paolo Pasolini meshes two grotesque tales in brilliant fashion, presenting images of beauty and horror. (90 mins.)

Pigs vs. Freaks—See: **Off-Sides**

Pilgrimage (1933)*** Henrietta Crosman, Heather Angel, Norman Foster, Marian Nixon, Hedda Hopper. Touching, delicately wrought tale of an iron-willed woman living with an uneasy conscience after she sends her son off to war in order to prevent a marriage she doesn't approve of. (Dir: John Ford, 95 mins.)

Pillars of the Sky (1956)**½ Jeff Chandler, Dorothy Malone, Ward Bond, Lee Marvin. Western fans will buy this tale of a no-account, hard-drinking, woman-chasin' Sgt. who finally sees the error of his ways after a series of action-packed scenes. (Dir: George Marshall, 95 mins.)

Pillow of Death (1945)** Lon Chaney, Jr., Brenda Joyce, Edward Bromberg, Rosiland Ivan, Clara Blandick. Low-budget mystery in the *Inner Sanctum* series stars Chaney in a conventional tale of an ordinary attorney apparently going on a murder spree. (Dir: Wallace Fox, 66 mins.)

Pillow Talk (1959)***½ Doris Day, Rock Hudson, Tony Randall, Thelma Ritter, Nick Adams. Deft comedy with Day managing to keep her virginity and her suitors. Randall is very funny; Hudson is surprisingly skillful. Frothy dialogue makes this a fine film of its kind. (Dir: Michael Gordon, 105 mins.)†

Pillow to Post (1945)** Ida Lupino, Sydney Greenstreet, William Prince, Stuart Erwin, Ruth Donnelly. Forgettable comedy; an enterprising young woman pretends to be married to a soldier to get a room. (Dir: Vincent Sherman, 92 mins.)

Pilot, The (1980)** Cliff Robertson, Diane Baker, Frank Converse, Dana Andrews, Milo O'Shea, Ed Binns. Robertson stars in a routine, depressing drama as a frustrated airline pilot unhappy with his job and marriage. (Dir: Cliff Robertson, 99 mins.)†

Pilot No. 5 (1943)*½ Van Johnson, Franchot Tone, Marsha Hunt, Gene Kelly, Alan Baxter. The pilot named in the title wants to go on a dangerous mission and numerous flashbacks convey why. (Dir: George Sidney, 70 mins.)

Pimpernel Smith (Great Britain, 1941)***½ Leslie Howard, Francis Sullivan, Mary Morris. A mild-mannered professor becomes an undercover leader against the Nazis. Delightfully witty, exciting melodrama, very good. (Dir: Leslie Howard, 122 mins.)

Pin (Canada, 1988)*** David Hewlett, Cindy Preston, John Ferguson. Effective suspense thriller about a boy who becomes intrigued with a doll used by his doctor father to calm young patients. After his parents' death, he adopts the doll as a friend, believing it is real and willing to do anything to stay together with it and his sister. (Dir: Sandor Stern, 102 mins.)

Pinball Pick-Up—See: **Pick-Up Summer**

Pinball Summer—See: **Pick-Up Summer**

Pine Canyon Is Burning (MTV 1977)**½ Kent McCord, Diana Muldaur. Modest tale about a widowed fireman trying to raise two kids while working out of a lonely fire station. (Dir: Chris Nyby III, 79 mins.)

Pink Cadillac (1989)**½ Clint Eastwood, Bernadette Peters, Michael Des Barres, Timothy Carhart, Geoffrey Lewis. One of Eastwood's redneck comedies. He plays a skip tracer who, against his better judgment, comes to the aid of housewife Peters, on the run from both the law and a neo-Nazi group. (Dir: Buddy Van Horn, 122 mins.)†

Pink Chiquitas, The (Canada, 1986)*½ Frank Stallone, Claudia Udy, Bruce Pirrie. Unsexy, unfunny attempt at an "SCTV"-style parody. A pink meteor changes the women of a small town into sex-hungry amazons. (Dir: Anthony Currie, 85 mins.)†

Pink Flamingos (1973)**½ Divine, Mary Vivian Pearce, Mink Stole, David Lochary, Edie Massey. John Waters' notorious bad-taste cult classic tells the delightfully disgusting story of Divine, "the filthiest person alive," and her torrid rivalry with the Marbles (Stole and Lochary), a married couple who sell babies and send very nasty things through the mails. By all means not for children or anyone capable of being offended! (Dir: John Waters, 92 mins.)

Pink Floyd: The Wall (Great Britain, 1982) *** Bob Geldof, Christine Hargreaves, Bob Hoskins, James Laurenson. This is *not* a concert film, but rather an almost wordless, largely metaphorical adaptation of the best-selling rock album. Director Alan Parker and writer-musician Roger Waters have fashioned this film as the story of Pink, a boy who goes through the dehumanizing British school system and grows up to be an alienated, unstable rock star. AKA: **The Wall.** (95 mins.)†

Pink Jungle, The (1968)** James Garner, Eva Renzi, George Kennedy. Dull action drama set in a banana republic in South America. (Dir: Delbert Mann, 104 mins.)

Pink Motel (1983)* Phyllis Diller, Slim Pickens, Brad Cowgill, Terri Berland, Cathryn Hartt, Andrea Howard, Tony Longo. Goofy couple Diller and Pickens run a motel noted for its cheap rates, shabby rooms, colorful visitors, and non-stop sex. (Dir: Mike MacFarland, 88 mins.)†

Pink Nights (1985)* Shaun Allen, Kevin Anderson, Larry King, Jonathan Jancovic Michaels. The punk milieu gets worked over in this pointless comedy about a guy who's a flop with the gals until he shares a flat with three members of the opposite sex. Unimaginatively familiar. (Dir: Philip Koch, 85 mins.)†

Pink Panther series. Fans of Blake Edwards comedies know that the Pink Panther is both a fabulous gem and a cartoon character who first found favor after appearing in the credits of the first film in this series. The other immortal comic creation from these films is the bungling Inspector Clouseau who destroys both evidence and suspects in his crime-solving zeal. Besides the films reviewed below, fans of this generally enjoyable series can catch the klutzy private eye in: *A Shot in the Dark,* and *Return of the Pink Panther,* as well as *Revenge of the Pink Panther, Trail of the Pink Panther, Curse of the Pink Panther* and *Inspector Clouseau.*

Pink Panther, The (1964)***½ Peter Sellers, David Niven, Capucine, Claudia Cardinale, Robert Wagner. The high-voltage names of the cast is enough for fans to tune in, and Peter Sellers's bumbling French inspector is a comic gem. Sellers is after a clever jewel thief known as the Phantom, and the Phantom is after a priceless gem. Inventive direction by Blake Edwards. (113 mins.)†

Pink Panther Strikes Again, The (Great Britain, 1976)***½ Peter Sellers, Herbert Lom, Lesley-Anne Down. Fourth farce about addle-brained Inspector Clouseau is tops. This time Sellers is pitted against his former chief, the villainous Dreyfus (Lom), a rascal in control of a device that threatens to destroy the world.

Expertly directed by Blake Edwards. (103 mins.)†

Pink String and Sealing Wax (Great Britain, 1945)**½ Googie Withers, Gordon Jackson. Tavernkeeper's dissatisfied wife uses a chemist's son in her plan to murder her husband. (Dir: Robert Hamer, 89 mins.)

Pink Ulysses (Netherlands, 1990)*** Jose Teunissen, Jos Ijland, Dolf Wilkens, Eric de Bruyn. Homer meets John Waters in this bizarre, thoroughly original interpretation of the Odyssey, which features muscular men and beautiful women, sitcom dialogue and fashion hints, dating tips and classical music, homoeroticism and recipes, heterosexual daydreams and rug-making. Achingly funny and totally over the top. (Dir: Eric de Kuyper, 98 mins.)

Pinky (1949)*** Jeanne Crain, William Lundigan, Ethel Barrymore, Ethel Waters. Strong racial drama dealing with light-skinned Negro girl who comes home to the South. Director Elia Kazan gets excellent performances all around. (102 mins.)†

Pinocchio (1940)**** Voices of Dickie Jones, Evelyn Venable, Cliff Edwards. From Carlo Collodi's story about the puppet boy who becomes human. The Disney version is a marvel: the animation is dazzling and the songs are catchy and clever. Oscars for Best Original Score and Best Original Song. (Supervising Dirs: Ben Sharpsteen, Hamilton Luske, 88 mins.)†

Pinocchio and the Emperor of the Night (1987)*½ Voices of Edward Asner, Tom Bosley, Linda Gray, Jonathan Harris, James Earl Jones, Rickie Lee Jones, Don Knotts. Even your toddler will be able to tell the difference between this leaden (or should that be wooden?) sequel and the Disney classic. Flat animation and forgettable ditties reign as Pinocchio embarks once again on the road to temptation with a carnival run by the "emperor of the night" ("Darth" Earl Jones). (Dir: Hal Sutherland, 95 mins.)

Pin-Up Girl (1944)** Betty Grable, John Harvey, Martha Raye, Joe E. Brown, Eugene Pallette, Mantan Moreland, J. Farrell MacDonald. Silly Grable vehicle casts her as a prim secretary masquerading as a musical comedy star in a wispy plot that's merely an excuse to tie a lot of mediocre musical and comedy routines together. Brown and Raye come off best. (Dir: Bruce Humberstone, 83 mins.)†

Pioneers of the French Cinema Vols. 1-2 (1895-1925)**** Two collections of the works of trailblazing French filmmakers, including short pieces by the Lumière brothers and George Melies. Vol. 1 includes *A Trip to the Moon* and *The Conquest of the Pole.* Vol. 2 contains Ferdinand Zecca's *D'Ou Vient Il?* and

Cheval Emballe, plus *Le Pecheur de Perles* and *Le Reve de L'Astronome*. Fascinating viewing. (60 mins. each)†

Pioneer Woman (MTV 1973)**½ William Shatner, Joanna Pettet. Old-fashioned western adventure. A family uproots itself and sets out for the promised farmland in Nebraska, only to meet with hostility from the squatters and a seemingly endless line of personal defeats. (Dir: Buzz Kulik, 78 mins.)†

Pipe Dreams (1976)** Gladys Knight, Barry Hankerson, Bruce French, Sherry Bain. Meandering tale of a woman who trails after her footloose hubby and tries to stake her claim to happiness during the construction of the oil pipeline in Alaska. Half-baked (Dir: Stephen Verona, 89 mins.)†

Piranha (1978)*** Bradford Dillman, Heather Menzies, Keenan Wynn, Kevin McCarthy, Barbara Steele. Amusing and scary low-budget riff on the *Jaws* theme. In trying to locate two missing teens, our hero (Dillman) and heroine (Menzies) accidentally unleash a breed of experimental piranha capable of spawning in fresh water. The government has been experimenting with them for military use in Vietnam; instead the fish declare war on everyone in their path. (Dir: Joe Dante, 92 mins.)†

Piranha II: The Spawning (U.S.-Italy, 1983)*½ Tricia O'Neil, Steve Marachuk, Lance Henriksen. Piranhas that fly attack a tropical resort. The premise is ridiculous, but the direction's lively and the movie is notable as the feature debut of James Cameron, who went on to do *The Terminator* and *Aliens*. Only for horror film die-hards. (95 mins.)†

Pirate, The (1948)**** Judy Garland, Gene Kelly, Walter Slezak, Gladys Cooper, George Zucco, the Nicholas Brothers. A rollicking, tongue-in-cheek musical about a girl infatuated with a famed pirate. The audacious, vain, ragged actor who loves her decides to impersonate the buccaneer to impress her. Kelly and Garland are in fine form; Cole Porter's lovely score includes "Love of My Life" and "Be A Clown"; Kelly does some dynamite specialty numbers with the Nicholas Brothers. (Dir: Vincente Minnelli, 102 mins.)†

Pirate, The (MTV 1978)** Franco Nero, Eli Wallach, Anne Archer, Christopher Lee. Harold Robbins's best-selling novel makes an ordinary film about an Arab prince brought up in the west and his second marriage to an American sexpot. (Dir: Kenneth Annakin, 208 mins.)

Pirate and the Slave Girl (Italy, 1961)½ Lex Barker, Massimo Serato, Michele Malaspina, Chelo Alonso, Enzo Maggio. Laughable swashbuckler about pirate Barker joining the fight against the evil

ruling classes. Ragged costumes, ragged sets, and ragged script sink this sea-bitten junk in the Mediterranean. Strictly for the beef-and-cheesecake crowd. (Dir: Piero Pierotti, 87 mins.)

Pirate Movie, The (1982)*½ Kristy Mc—Nichol, Christopher Atkins. Seeking to capitalize on the successes of the irreverent Broadway version of *The Pirates of Penzance*, this is a ghastly update of the Gilbert and Sullivan operetta. (Dir: Kenneth Annakin, 105 mins.)†

Pirates (1986)**½ Walter Matthau, Cris Campion, Charlotte Lewis, Damien Thomas. Matthau epitomizes the scalawags of yore as Captain Red, a scoundrel who spends much of the film's running time double-crossing his comrades and slaying Spaniards as he tries to steal a priceless Aztec throne. Director Polanski has an eye for both atmosphere and scope, but the rampant vulgarity and grossness won't be universally welcomed by all viewers. (Dir: Roman Polanski, 124 mins.)†

Pirate Ship (1949)* Jon Hall, Adele Jergens, Noel Cravat, George Reeves. Shopworn plot about angry pirates staging a mutiny while Hall tries hard to keep things calm. Cheaply made, and it shows. AKA: **The Mutineers**. (Dir: Jean Yarbrough, 62 mins.)

Pirates of Blood River, The (Great Britain, 1962)**½ Kerwin Mathews, Peter Arne, Glenn Corbett, Oliver Reed, Christopher Lee, Andrew Keir. Nifty cast in fun adventure of war between French Huguenots and pirates. Terrific swordplay boosts this historical drama. (Dir: John Gilling, 87 mins.)

Pirates of Capri, The (1949)** Binnie Barnes, Louis Hayward, Alan Curtis, Rudolph (Massimo) Serato. Action predominates this underwritten tale of Italian folks fighting a despot. Crisp direction by cult fave Ulmer and a score by Nino Rota are the reasons to view this swashbuckler. AKA: **Capt. Sirocco**. (Dir: Edgar G. Ulmer, 94 mins.)

Pirates of Monterey (1947)** Maria Montez, Rod Cameron, Mikhail Rasumny, Gilbert Roland, Gale Sondergaard. Traveling to California to marry a soldier, Maria's heart is tempted by a brigand. In the background, battles rage over Mexican supremacy in 1800s California. (Dir: Alfred L. Werker, 77 mins.)

Pirates of Penzance (1983)** Kevin Kline, Linda Ronstadt, Angela Lansbury, George Rose, Rex Smith. This stagy movie version of the Gilbert and Sullivan operetta—about pirates and "the very model of a modern major general" and his covey of daughters—was much better on stage. (Dir: Wilford Leach, 112 mins.)†

Pit and the Pendulum, The (1961)**½ Vincent Price, John Kerr, Barbara Steele.

This thriller has all the stock ingredients inherent to horror yarns including the castle on the hill, a fantastic torture chamber, walled-up coffins and screams in the night. Kerr plays the young innocent who comes to Price's Spanish castle to investigate his sister's mysterious death and falls prey to the spooky goings-on. (Dir: Roger Corman, 80 mins.)†

Pitfall (1948)***½ Dick Powell, Jane Wyatt, Lizabeth Scott. A momentary philandering with a glamorous charmer brings tragedy to a happily married man. Strong drama, tense, well acted. (Dir: Andre de Toth, 84 mins.)

Pit Stop (1969)* Brian Donlevy, Dick Davalos, Sid Haig, Ellen McRae (Burstyn). You'll need a few pit stops to get through this dull flick about poor sports in the sport of car racing. (Dir: Jack Hill, 92 mins.)

Pittsburgh (1942)** John Wayne, Marlene Dietrich, Randolph Scott. Miner's drive for power costs him his friends and the woman he loves. Sluggish melodrama. (Dir: Lewis Seiler, 91 mins.)

Pixote (Brazil, 1980)**** A shattering drama about a ten-year-old orphan street kid trying to survive in the corrupt violence-ridden world of impoverished São Paulo. Devastating performances from both professional actors and amateurs. (Dir: Hector Babenco, 127 mins.)†

Pizza Triangle, The—See: **Drama of Jealousy, A**

P.J. (1968)*** George Peppard, Gayle Hunnicutt, Raymond Burr, Brock Peters, Wilfrid Hyde-White, Susan St. James. Intricate hard-hitting detective yarn. Tale involves Peppard as a small-time private eye hired by wealthy tycoon Burr to watch over Burr's beautiful mistress Hunnicutt. (Dir: John Guillermin, 109 mins.)

P.K. and the Kid (1982)**½ Molly Ringwald, Paul LeMat, Alex Rocco. Odd item that received recognition only after Ringwald achieved carrot-topped stardom. She plays a girl who flees her slimy, lecherous stepfather (Rocco) and ends up traveling with a champion wristwrestler (LeMat). Light and disarming, except for the points where the evil Rocco vents his frustration. (Dir: Lou Lombardo, 90 mins.)†

Place Called Today, A (1972)½ J. Herbert Kerr, Jr., Lana Wood, Cheri Caffaro, Richard Smedley. Against the backdrop of a mayoral election in a racially troubled city, the four lead characters scream their political philosophies into one another's faces for the duration of the movie. Unbearably smug and self-righteous. (Dir: Don Schain, 103 mins.)†

Place for Lovers, A (Italy-France, 1968)* Faye Dunaway, Marcello Mastroianni.

Trashy soap opera with the stars playing sophisticated lovers amid the sumptuous setting of a Venetian villa. (Dir: Vittorio De Sica, 88 mins.)

Place in the Sun, A (1951)***½ Montgomery Clift, Elizabeth Taylor, Shelley Winters, Keefe Brasselle, Anne Revere, Raymond Burr. Although this brooding romantic drama has little in common with its source, Dreiser's *An American Tragedy*, it exerts a melancholy, foreboding power all its own. Clift plays the poor relation of a wealthy manufacturer who falls in love with a beautiful socialite (Taylor) while having an affair with a factory girl (Winters) who becomes pregnant. Clift gives a stunningly sensitive performance as a man who knows his social class has doomed him, and Taylor is perceptive as his dream girl. Unfortunately, Winters's whiny, mannered work as the victim of ambition fails to elicit sympathy, and throws the film off balance. (Dir: George Stevens, 122 mins.)†

Place of One's Own, A (Great Britain, 1945)*** Margaret Lockwood, James Mason. Elderly couple buy an old house, take in a girl as companion, and find she is influenced by spirits. Entertaining drama, well acted. (Dir: Bernard Knowles, 91 mins.)

Place of Weeping, A (South Africa, 1986)**½ James Whyle, Geina Mhlope, Charles Comyn. Earnest anti-apartheid film, clumsily made but powerful nonetheless. A vile South African farmer rules his employee's lives like a prison warden; in one case he beats a black worker to death. (Dir: Darrell Roody, 88 mins.)†

Places in the Heart (1984)*** Sally Field, Lindsay Crouse, Ed Harris, Amy Madigan, John Malkovich, Danny Glover. Poignant, beautifully acted drama. This Depression-era tale concerns the efforts of a recently widowed woman (Field) to hold onto her home and two children by farming cotton. A tornado, Ku Klux Klan threats, and an extramarital affair subplot are thrown into the narrative, but the best scenes are those involving the determined mother just trying to survive. Winner Academy Award for Best Actress (Field) and for Best Original Screenplay (Benton). (Dir: Robert Benton, 110 mins.)†

Place to Call Home, A (MTV 1987)** Linda Lavin, Lane Smith, Lori Loughlin, Paul Cronin. Linda Lavin plays a naïve American carving a new life in rugged Australia. You can figure the plot out quickly—the forlorn sheep ranch, the inevitable drought, the homesick kids and the shearing handyman, and brave Linda stuck there amongst the koalas and kiwis. (Dir: Russ Mayberry, 104 mins.)

Plague (Canada, 1978)** Celene Lomez, Daniel Pilon, Kate Reid. Deadly bacteria are created in a genetic research laboratory, spreading a plague that threatens the world. (Dir: Ed Hunt, 90 mins.)

Plague Dogs, The (Great Britain, 1984)***½ Voices of John Hurt, James Bolan, Christopher Benjamin. Expressive animated adaptation of Richard Adams's novel about a group of dogs who escape from the scientists who have been experimenting on them, searching the English lake district for a safe home. Delightful and enlightening film. (Dir: Martin Rosen, 86 mins.)†

Plague of the Zombies, The (Great Britain, 1966)**½ Andre Morell, Diane Clare, Brook Williams, Jacqueline Pearce. This horror thriller shows how Haitian voodoo is put to profitable use in a Cornish town. Polished but occasionally draggy. (Dir: John Gilling, 90 mins.)

Plain Clothes (1988)**½ Arliss Howard, Suzy Amis, George Wendt, Diane Ladd, Seymour Cassel. Offbeat teen comedy about a young cop who goes undercover in high school to clear his younger brother of a murder charge. The amusing cast sparks the haphazard mystery plot. (Dir: Martha Coolidge, 98 mins.)†

Plainsman, The (1936)*** Gary Cooper, Jean Arthur, Charles Bickford, Porter Hall, Anthony Quinn, James Ellison. Rootin', shootin' western, loaded with action. A DeMille spectacle about Wild Bill Hickock, Calamity Jane and Buffalo Bill, among others. (Dir: C. B. DeMille, 113 mins.)†

Plainsman, The (1966)** Don Murray, Guy Stockwell, Bradford Dillman, Abby Dalton. Wild Bill Hickok, Buffalo Bill, and Calamity Jane foiling Indians and gun runners. (Dir: David Lowell Rich, 92 mins.)†

Plainsman and the Lady, The (1946)**½ William Elliott, Vera Hruba Ralston, Gail Patrick, Andy Clyde, Joseph Schildkraut. Unique cast highlights this agreeable pony express western complete with dangers on the trail, wise-crackin' saloon dames, and nasty gunfights. (Dir: Joseph Kane, 88 mins.)

Planes, Trains and Automobiles (1987)**½ Steve Martin, John Candy, William Windom, Edie McClurg. Director John Hughes's uneven slapstick comedy pairs an uptight exec (Martin) trying to get to Chicago for Thanksgiving with a pushy chatterbox (Candy) who's his unwanted but unavoidable companion. As their trip becomes a nightmare of missed connections and far-flung detours, the two develop a tentative friendship. Both stars are fine, but the gags are hit-and-miss and the mawkish ending is a miscalculation. (93 mins.)†

Planet Earth (MTV 1974)*** John Saxon, Janet Margolin, Ted Cassidy, Diana Muldaur. Saxon and company come out of suspended animation to encounter a civilization run by women. Good sci-fi with a solid cast from Gene Roddenberry. (Dir: Marc Daniels, 75 mins.)

Planet of Blood (1966)** Basil Rathbone, John Saxon, Judi Meredith, Dennis Hopper. Spaceship is sent to Mars to investigate a mysterious missile; therein is found a survivor from another world with a passion for human blood. (Dir: Curtis Harrington, 80 mins.)†

Planet of the Apes (1968)***½ Charlton Heston, Kim Hunter, Maurice Evans, James Daly, Roddy McDowall. Exciting science-fiction film based on Pierre Boulle's book *Monkey Planet*. This sci-fi thriller even has some political and sociological comments on our troubled times. Four astronauts crash on a distant planet ruled by simians. The makeup men who devised the fantastic ape masks rate a special bow. Followed by four sequels (beginning with *Beneath the Planet of the Apes*) and a TV series. (Dir: Franklin J. Schaffner, 112 mins.)†

Planet of the Vampires—See: **Demon Planet, The**

Planets Against Us (Italy-France, 1961)** Michel Lemoine, Maria Pia Luzi, Marco Guglielmi, Jany Clair, Otello Toso. Alien robot, escaped from its home planet, lands on Earth, where its touch is deadly. Mediocre sci-fi with a few good special effects. (Dir: Romano Ferara, 85 mins.)†

Plan Nine from Outer Space (1959)½ Gregory Walcott, Mona McKinnon, Vampira, Tor Johnson, Bela Lugosi, Dudley Manlove, Criswell. The most popular of the "so bad it's good" movies, and certainly the most famous. It gets funnier every time you see it. The plot, some incomprehensible nonsense about aliens seeking to destroy mankind before we annihilate the universe, is irrelevant. Watch it for the rock-bottom production values, priceless bad dialogue, and awful acting. "Star" Lugosi is seen in only a few brief scenes, repeated ad infinitum, shot just before he died. He's replaced by a double who looks nothing like him and is at least a foot taller. (Dir: Edward D. Wood, Jr., 79 mins.)†

Platinum Blonde (1931)*** Jean Harlow, Loretta Young, Robert Williams. Early screwball comedy, with refreshing dialogue crisply paced, yet compromised by lack of visual verve or style. (Dir: Frank Capra, 90 mins.)

Platinum High School (1960)* Mickey Rooney, Terry Moore, Dan Duryea. Father visits an exclusive military school investigating the death of his son, finds it was no accident. AKA: **Trouble at 16**. (Dir: Charles Haas, 93 mins.)

Platoon (1986)**** Tom Berenger, Willem Dafoe, Charlie Sheen, Francesco Quinn, Johnny Depp, Keith David, Kevin Dillon. A devastating masterpiece about the Vietnam War, which won the Oscar for Best Picture and Best Direction in 1987. Based on writer-director Oliver Stone's own experiences while fighting in Vietnam, *Platoon* focuses on one young soldier (Sheen) fighting on the Cambodian border, and the film alternates intimate scenes with unforgettable action sequences. In sharp contrast to the Vietnam revenge fantasies of the early and mid-eighties, *Platoon* is truthful and illuminating, with standout performances from the entire cast. (120 mins.)

Platoon Leader (1988)** Michael Dudikoff, Robert F. Lyons, Michael De Lorenzo, Rich Fitts, William Smith. Vietnam serves as the basis for a straight war film with no political subtext (even though that in itself is a political subtext), with Dudikoff the new lieutenant at a U.S. firebase in Vietnam. Not bad, if a jungle shoot-'em-up is all you're looking for. (Dir: Aaron Norris, 100 mins.)†

Playboy of the Western World, The (Ireland, 1962)**** Siobhan McKenna, Gary Raymond. Beautiful, lyrical, and long-overdue film of the classic Irish play of J. M. Synge. The actual plot about a young stranger who becomes the idol of a small village is less important than the soaring, poetic language of the play and the lovely performance of McKenna. (Dir: Brian Desmond Hurst, 100 mins.)

Play Dirty (Great Britain, 1969)*½ Michael Caine, Harry Andrews, Nigel Davenport. Another World War II adventure which borrows the "Dirty Dozen" plotting. Caine is the officer in charge of a group of mercenaries and misfits who set out to blow up that ever-present important enemy fuel depot. (Dir: Andre de Toth, 117 mins.)

Players (1979)*½ Ali McGraw, Dean-Paul Martin, Maximilian Schell. In this soap opera, McGraw is the "older woman," kept by tycoon Schell while she falls in love with young tennis pro Martin. (Dir: Anthony Harvey, 120 mins.)†

Play Girl (1940)**½ Kay Francis, James Ellison, Mildred Coles, Nigel Bruce, Margaret Hamilton, Katharine Alexander. Low-budget vehicle for Francis as a shrewd call girl who teaches an ambitious young lady the ropes. Candid, well-played melodrama. (Dir: Frank Woodruff, 75 mins.)

Playgirl (1954)**½ Shelley Winters, Barry Sullivan. Moderately interesting drama about a woman's concern for her young sister's reputation. (Dir: Joseph Pevney, 85 mins.)

Playgirl Killer (Canada, 1966)½ William Kerwin, Jean Christopher, Andree Champagne, Neil Sedaka. Insane artist murders his beautiful models in order to get them to stay still. Relentlessly padded horror movie with plenty of unintentional laughs. "Guest star" Sedaka is featured in a subplot that has nothing to do with the rest of the movie. AKA: **Decoy for Terror**. (Dir: Erick Santamaria, 86 mins.)†

Playing Away (Great Britain, 1987)**½ Norman Beaton, Robert Urquhart, Helen Lindsay. Cultures and classes clash in this gentle, occasionally pointed comedy about the residents of a stuffy English village whose lives are disrupted with the arrival of a cricket team from the West Indies. Familiar, but deftly handled by Trinidadian director Horace Ové. (100 mins.)†

Playing for Keeps (1986)*½ Daniel Jordano, Matthew Penn, Leon W. Grant, Mary B. Ward, Harold Gould. Another variant on those Mickey Rooney-Judy Garland flicks where the enterprising kids get together to put on a show—here the adolescents convert a country hotel into a teen resort dedicated to rock 'n roll. (Dirs: Harvey and Bob Weinstein, 105 mins.)†

Playing for Time (MTV 1980)**** Vanessa Redgrave, Shirley Knight, Maud Adams, Jane Alexander. Shattering drama about life in the Auschwitz death camp, one of the Nazis' most murderous camps for European Jewry. Based on a book by Fania Fenelon, herself a survivor of the camps, and adapted by Arthur Miller. Luminous, bravura performance by Redgrave playing Fenelon. (Dir: Daniel Mann, 150 mins.)†

Playing With Fire (MTV 1985)*½ Gary Coleman, Cicely Tyson, Ron O'Neal, Yaphet Kotto, Salome Jens. Corny drama with Coleman as a teenage firebug. (Dir: Ivan Nagy, 104 mins.)

Play It Again, Sam (1972)*** Woody Allen, Susan Anspach, Diane Keaton, Tony Roberts. Woody is a compulsive Bogart fantasizer and it drives his wife (Anspach) out of his life, which drives him into the arms of his best friend's wife, Keaton. Lacy, in an uncanny Bogart imitation, pops up every now and then as Bogart's spirit, and keeps things bubbling. Allen fans will love it. (Dir: Herbert Ross, 84 mins.)†

Play It As It Lays (1972)*** Tuesday Weld, Anthony Perkins, Adam Roarke, Tammy Grimes. Joan Didion adapted her disturbing novel, and the result is a film that captures the meaningless void of Hollywood existence in a terse, unsentimental style. Weld gives an extraordinary performance as Maria Wyeth, the actress who undergoes a breakdown. (Dir: Frank Perry, 101 mins.)

Playmates (1941)**½ Kay Kayser, May Robson, Lupe Velez, John Barrymore, Patsy Kelly, Peter Lind Hayes. Sprightly musical-comedy about classically trained actor joining forces with big band leader in silly scheme to pay back taxes. Barrymore (in his final film) and Kelly are fun to watch, but where do they get these plots? (Dir: David Butler, 94 mins.)†

Playmates (MTV 1972)*** Alan Alda, Doug McClure, Connie Stevens, Barbara Feldon. Alda and McClure play divorced men who form a bond and decide to keep tabs on their ex-wives. Clever and original. (Dir: Theodore J. Flicker, 74 mins.)†

Play Misty for Me (1971)*** Clint Eastwood, Jessica Walter, Donna Mills. Eastwood made a promising directorial debut with this mystery about a sexy disc jockey on a California radio station, and his involvement with a psychotic. Walter is first-rate playing the dangerous listener who takes charge of Eastwood's life when he makes the mistake of entering into what he thinks is a casual affair. (Dir: Clint Eastwood, 102 mins.)†

Playtime (France, 1968)**** Jacques Tati. A wonderful Tati triumph. He again plays the lovable Mr. Hulot, this time in an ultra-modern Paris, all skyscrapers, glass, and computers. (Dir: Jacques Tati, 108 mins.)†

Plaza Suite (1971)*** Walter Matthau, Maureen Stapleton, Barbara Harris, Lee Grant. Matthau is supplied with three juicy comic roles (a businessman rekindling his love for his wife, a Hollywood producer saddled with a gossip freak, and the papa of a very reluctant bride) by playwright Neil Simon in this film version of the hit play—and he's good in all of them. (Dir: Arthur Hiller, 114 mins.)†

Please Believe Me (1950)**½ Deborah Kerr, Robert Walker, Peter Lawford, Mark Stevens. A wacky comedy about a trio of bachelors who give a new heiress the rush. (Dir: Norman Taurog, 87 mins.)

Please Don't Eat My Mother! (1972)** Buck Kartalian, René Bond, Alicia Friedland, Lyn Lundgren. Suitably cheesy low-budget remake of *The Little Shop of Horrors:* goofy middle-aged Peeping Tom Kartalian finds an odd plant in a flower shop that thrives on human blood. AKA: **Hungry Pets** and **Glump.** (Dir: Jack Beckett, 98 mins.)

Please Don't Eat the Daisies (1960)*** Doris Day, David Niven, Janis Paige. Friendly comedy about a drama critic, his wife and four children—the critic has problems with his work, the wife has problems with renovating an old house in the country, and things become quite hectic in general. (Dir: Charles Walters, 111 mins.)

Please Mr. Balzac (France, 1956)** Brigitte Bardot, Daniel Gelin. Routine comedy whose only asset is Bardot as a girl who writes a scandalous novel, and lams out for Paris when her prudish family objects. AKA: **Mademoiselle Striptease.** (Dir: Marc Allegret, 99 mins.)†

Please Murder Me (1955)** Raymond Burr, Angela Lansbury, Lamont Johnson. A brilliant attorney sacrifices his career and scruples to defend a murderess with whom he is in love. Muddled melodrama. (Dir: Peter Godfrey, 78 mins.)

Please Turn Over (Great Britain, 1959)** Ted Ray, Jean Kent. Silly comedy. The actors are far better than their material. Plot concerns a girl who writes a sexy novel and causes a commotion. (Dir: Gerald Thomas, 86 mins.)

Pleasure Cove (MTV 1979)** Tom Jones, Constance Forslund, Joan Hackett, Harry Guardino. Singer Jones plays a handsome crook in this opus about life at a swanky island resort. (Dir: Bruce Bilson, 104 mins.)

Pleasure Cruise (1933)**½ Roland Young, Genevieve Tobin, Ralph Forbes, Una O'Connor. Matrimonial comedy of a bored wife going on a cruise without her husband, finding out she likes him best after all. Airy and expertly done. (Dir: Frank Tuttle, 70 mins.)

Pleasure of His Company, The (1961)**½ Fred Astaire, Debbie Reynolds, Lilli Palmer, Tab Hunter. Debonair charmer returns home for his daughter's wedding but tries to break up the couple when he finds her to be attractive. Good cast takes advantage of some witty lines to give this comedy a fair amount of fun. (Dir: George Seaton, 115 mins.)

Pleasure Palace (MTV 1980)** Omar Sharif, Hope Lange, José Ferrer, Victoria Principal, Gerald S. O'Loughlin. Sharif plays a gentlemanly high roller, invited to Las Vegas to save casino owner Lange from a crude Texan and his associates. No dice! (Dir: Walter Grauman, 104 mins.)†

Pleasures (MTV 1986)** Joanna Cassidy, Linda Purl, Barry Bostwick, Tracy Nelson. Glossy sex opera. Joanna Cassidy is the recently abandoned wife picking up with a former lover, Purl is her lovesick sister swept away by a rock star, and her daughter Nelson seeks adventure with one of the locals while on a South American tour. (Dir: Sharron Miller, 104 mins.)

Pleasure Seekers, The (1964)**½ Ann-Margret, Carol Lynley, Pamela Tiffin, Anthony Franciosa, Brian Keith, Gene Tierney. A well-produced remake of *Three Coins in the Fountain* with the locale shifted from Rome to Spain. Three young girls looking for romance find it amid the Spanish architecture. (Dir: Jean Negulesco, 107 mins.)

Plenty (1985)** Meryl Streep, Charles Dance, John Gielgud, Tracey Ullman, Sam Neill, Ian McKellan, Sting. Adapted by David Hare from his play, the film concerns an enigmatic young woman whose memories of her work for the Resistance during the Nazi occupation of France during WWII outshine the trying age in which she now lives. (Dir: Fred Schepisi, 124 mins.)†

Plot Against Harry, The (1968)***½ Martin Priest, Ben Lang, Maxine Woods, Henry Nemo. Superb deadpan comedy of a Jewish gangster who exits prison only to confront a series of family and business problems. Everyone in the no-name cast plays their role to a "T" in this gem that went unreleased until 1989 because it was deemed uncommercial. (Dir: Michael Roemer, 81 mins.)†

Plot Thickens, The (1936)**½ James Gleason, ZaSu Pitts, Owen Davis, Jr., Louise Latimer. Pitts replaced Edna May Oliver as schoolmarm-sleuth Hildegarde Withers, but the magic didn't take in this mediocre mystery. (Dir: Ben Holmes, 67 mins.)

Plot to Assassinate Hitler, The (Germany, 1955)**½ Maximilian Schell. Story of the German officers' plan to eliminate the hated Nazi leader unfolds in documentary fashion, is frequently gripping despite the familiarity of the narrative. (Dir: Falck Harnack, 90 mins.)

Plough and the Stars, The (1936)** Barbara Stanwyck, Preston Foster, Barry Fitzgerald, Una O'Connor, J. M. Kerrigan. Disappointing version of Sean O'Casey's wonderful play about the months leading up to the Easter Week uprising in Dublin in '16. (Dir: John Ford, 73 mins.)

Ploughman's Lunch, The (Great Britain, 1984)*** Jonathan Pryce, Tim Curry, Charlie Dore, Rosemary Harris, Frank Finlay, Simon Stokes. An unscrupulous journalist practices political expediency to rise to the top in Tory England. The political observations are a bit too pat, but this remains brittle and engrossing. (Dir: Richard Eyre, 107 mins.)†

Plumber, The (Australia, 1980)*** Judy Morris, Ivar Kants, Robert Coleby. An off-kilter black comedy in which everyone's worst dreams about the local plumber come true. Weir's ability to instill mundane settings and situations with tension serves him well here, as a demented handyman demolishes the home of a hapless couple, and then threatens to become a permanent fixture in their house. (Dir: Peter Weir, 76 mins.)†

Plunderers, The (1948)**½ Rod Cameron, Ilona Massey, Forrest Tucker, Adrian Booth. Cliché-ridden western has bandits and the U.S. Cavalry joining forces to fend off an Indian attack. (Dir: Joseph Kane, 87 mins.)

Plunderers, The (1960)**½ Jeff Chandler, John Saxon, Dolores Hart. Sprawling western drama about a group of outlaws and their effect on a town. (Dir: Joseph Pevney, 94 mins.)

Plunder in the Sun (1953)** Glenn Ford, Diana Lynn, Patricia Medina. An Aztec fortune is the prize in this involved modern day treasure hunt. (Dir: John Farrow, 81 mins.)

Plunder Road (1957)***½ Gene Raymond, Wayne Morris. Make a thousand grade B crime tales and you're bound to turn out one gem . . . this is it! Superior melodrama about an attempted $10 million theft. (Dir: Hubert Cornfield, 76 mins.)

Plutonium Incident, The (MTV 1980)**½ Janet Margolin, Powers Boothe, Bo Hopkins, Joseph Campanella, Bibi Besch, Nicholas Pryor. Occasionally involving yarn about a plutonium-processing plant, whose management tries to crush a worker's attempt to unionize in order to press for better safety conditions. (Dir: Richard Michaels, 104 mins.)

Plymouth Adventure (1952)*** Spencer Tracy, Gene Tierney, Van Johnson. Good adventure epic about the Pilgrims' voyage on the Mayflower and the hardships they encounter when they land at Plymouth, Mass. (Dir: Clarence Brown, 105 mins.)

Poacher's Daughter, The (Ireland, 1958)**½ Julie Harris, Harry Brogan, Tim Seely. Irresponsible son with an eye on motor bikes and flashy ladies is finally straightened out by a sincere girl. Mildly amusing comedy. (Dir: George Pollack, 74 mins.)

Pocketful of Miracles (1961)*** Glenn Ford, Bette Davis, Hope Lange, Ann-Margret, Peter Falk, Thomas Mitchell, Edward Everett Horton, Jack Elam. Veteran director Frank Capra brings this Damon Runyon yarn to the screen with a liberal mixture of corn, sentiment, and broad performances. The plot revolves around a street vendor called Apple Annie (Davis) and the lengths she and her friends go to help her masquerade as a society matron when her daughter pays a surprise visit. Remake of *Lady for a Day*. (136 mins.)†

Pocket Money (1972)*** Paul Newman, Lee Marvin, Strother Martin, Christine Belford, Wayne Rogers, Kelly Jean Peters. Naïve Newman and his alcoholic sidekick Marvin go searching through Mexico to buy a herd of cattle for civil boss Martin. The duo are suckers for every swindler with a bum steer, but their charming presence redeems the screenplay, which is chock full of character development and short on plot. (Dir: Stuart Rosenberg, 102 mins.)†

Poetry in Motion (1982)***½ Wonderful documentary features twenty-four modern poets (including Charles Bukowski, Robert Creeley, Allen Ginsberg, Ntozake Shange, William Burroughs, Jim Carroll, and Amiri Baraka) reading from their own work, along with exhilarating interviews. (Dir: Ron Mann, 90 mins.)†

Point, The (MTV 1971)***½ Charming animated feature musical fantasy. It tells the story of Oblio, a little boy who is born without a point on his head in a kingdom where everything and everyone has a literal point. The images are superb, and the musical score by Harry Nilsson creates the appropriate mood. Original narration by Ringo Starr has recently been replaced in TV showings by Alan Thicke. (Dir: Fred Wolff, 73 mins.)†

Point Blank (1967)***½ Lee Marvin, Angie Dickinson, Keenan Wynn, John Vernon, Lloyd Bochner, Carroll O'Connor. A flashy, ultra-violent revenge melodrama. Marvin becomes an agent for the destruction of his enemies in the L.A. underworld, but they die by their own hands. (Dir: John Boorman, 92 mins.)†

Point of Order (1964)**** Brilliant, deeply disturbing documentary about the Army-McCarthy hearings in the spring of 1954. (Dir: Emile de Antonio, 97 mins.)

Pointsman, The (Holland, 1988)* Jim Van der Woude, Stephane Escoffier. Pointless. A curious item about a very ugly man who switches trains, and the beautiful, lost stranger who ends up living with him. Obscure symbolism is the order of the day; watching this is like slow water torture. (Dir: Jos Stelling, 95 mins.)†

Poison (1991)***½ Buck Smith, Edith Meeks, Larry Maxwell, Susan Norman, Scott Renderer, James Lyons, John R. Lombardi, Millie White, Anne Giotta, Al Quagliata, Michelle Sullivan. One of the most audacious and original American films in years. This powerful, demanding, and disturbing work, influenced by the writings of Jean Genet, is comprised of three segments that explore patricide committed by a young boy, the influence of horror films on American society, and sexuality in a men's prison. Often outrageously comic, this is mature and intelligent movie-making at its best. (Dir: Todd Haynes, 85 mins.)

Poison Ivy (MTV 1985)**½ Robert Klein, Michael J. Fox, Caren Kaye, Nancy McKeon. Enjoyable summer camp comedy stocked with familiar TV faces. Pranks and love affairs are the main activities. (Dir: Larry Elikann, 104 mins.)†

Poker Alice (MTV 1987)**½ Elizabeth

Taylor, George Hamilton, Tom Skerritt, Richard Mulligan, David Wayne, Susan Tyrrell. Taylor goes west, winning every poker hand before riding off into the sunset with bounty hunter Skerritt. (Dir: Arthur Allan Seidelman, 104 mins.)†

Police (France, 1986)**½ Gerard Depardieu, Sophie Marceau, Richard Anconina, Pascale Rocard, Sandrine Bonnaire. A moderately exciting crime drama with a good, brutal performance by Depardieu as a tough cop on the trail of a group of drug runners. Director Maurice Pialat pays very close attention to the gritty daily details of police work, and the result is sometimes tedious but often compelling. (Dir: Maurice Pialat, 114 mins.)

Police Academy (1984)*** Steve Guttenberg, Kim Cattrall, Michael Winslow, George Gaynes, Bubba Smith. This raucous comedy aimed at the college crowd and teen market tries to do for the police force what *Airplane* did for the airlines. While it's not consistently funny, the movie has a fair amount of funny sight gags as the police academy lowers its standards drastically and allows some unlikely recruits to join. (Dir: Hugh Wilson, 101 mins.)†

Police Academy 2 (1985)**½ Steve Guttenberg, Howard Hesseman, George Gaynes, Michael Winslow, Colleen Camp, David Graf, Bobcat Goldthwait, Art Metrano, Bubba Smith. More predictable lunacy from the boys in blue who are trying to rid the precinct of punk hoodlums. (Dir: Jerry Paris, 97 mins.)†

Police Academy 3: Back in Training (1986)** Steve Guttenberg, Bubba Smith, David Graf, Michael Winslow, Marion Ramsey, Art Metrano, Tim Kazurinsky, Bobcat Goldthwait, George Gaynes. This time, the law and order goofballs help their school win a competition against a rival academy. Silly fun worth a look. (Dir: Jerry Paris, 82 mins.)†

Police Academy 4: Citizen's Patrol (1987)*½ Steve Guttenberg, Bubba Smith, Michael Winslow, David Graf, Tim Kazurinsky, Sharon Stone, Bobcat Goldthwait, Colleen Camp, George Gaynes, G. W. Bailey. More slapstick shenanigans from the Keystone Kops of contemporary times. This time, the bumbling law enforcers enlist the aid of the local citizenry in their care. (Dir: Jim Drake, 89 mins.)†

Police Academy 5: Assignment Miami Beach (1988)*½ Bubba Smith, Michael Winslow, Janet Jones, George Gaynes, René Auberjonois. This go-around, the high jinks center on a stolen cache of diamonds. (Dir: Alan Myerson, 90 mins.)†

Police Academy 6: City Under Siege (1989)*½ Bubba Smith, David Graf, Michael Winslow, G.W. Bailey, George Gaynes, Kenneth Mars, Gerrit Graham. If you liked the others, you'll like this one, too. The inept cops tackle a criminal gang whose "mysterious" leader will be spotted immediately by anyone over the age of six. (Dir: Peter Bonerz, 84 mins.)†

Police Force (1985)*** Jackie Chan, Brigette Lin, Maggie Cheung. Some intricately choreographed set pieces highlight this hilarious, action-packed thriller, capped by a shopping-mall climax that has to be seen to be believed. (Dir: Jackie Chan, 85 mins.)†

Police Story (MTV 1973)**½ Vic Morrow, Ed Asner, Chuck Connors, Sandy Baron, Harry Guardino. Gutsy, realistic police drama based on material written by Los Angeles lawman Joseph Wambaugh, who portrays police as human beings—this was a pilot for the TV series. (Dir: William Graham, 74 mins.)

Police Story: The Freeway Killings (MTV 1987)**½ Angie Dickinson, Richard Crenna, Ben Gazzara, Don Meredith, Tony LoBianco, James B. Sikking. This uneven drama retains the old "Police Story" style, and stays up-to-date with a serial killer loose on the freeways. (Dir: William Graham, 156 mins.)

Police Woman Centerfold (MTV 1983)** Melody Anderson, Ed Marinaro, Donna Pescow, Bert Remsen. A pretty, naïve, small-town lady cop decides it's OK to pose for a girlie magazine and wonders why she becomes a pariah when the photos are published. (Dir: Reza Badiyi, 104 mins.)†

Pollyanna (1960)***½ Hayley Mills, Jane Wyman, Agnes Moorehead, Donald Crisp, Nancy Olson, Richard Egan, Adolphe Menjou. Enjoyable family fare about a young girl who changes the life of almost everyone she comes in contact with, due to her optimistic outlook on life. 13-year-old Mills is perfect as Pollyanna, a role which lets her use her cute mannerisms naturally, and the supporting cast is absolutely right. (Dir: David Swift, 134 mins.)†

Polly Comin' Home (MTV 1990)**½ Keshia Knight Pulliam, Phylicia Rashad, Anthony Newley, Celeste Holm, Dorian Harewood. Enjoyable family musical. Determined to match up straight-laced Aunt Polly with the handsome minister, little Polly must face a sour Englishman hired by her Aunt to run the local orphanage. It's a thin story, but director Allen has everyone bursting out into song; Anthony Newley comes off best in that department. (Dir: Debbie Allen, 96 mins.)

Polly of the Circus (1932)*½ Marion Davies, Clark Gable, C. Aubrey Smith. Upright young minister Gable jeopardizes his position in the church by marrying Davies, the "flyer" in a circus trapeze act. (Dir: Alfred Santell, 69 mins.)

Polo Joe (1936)** Joe E. Brown, Carol Hughes, Skeets Gallagher, Joseph King, Fay Holden, George E. Stone. Poorly scripted Brown vehicle casts him as a guy whose girlfriend only goes for polo players. (Dir: William McGann, 65 mins.)

Poltergeist (1982)***½ JoBeth Williams, Craig T. Nelson, Beatrice Straight, Zelda Rubinstein, Dominique Dunne, Oliver Robins, Heather O'Rourke. A haunted house yarn bursting with special effects. A family in a suburban development is faced with menacing phenomena—a child who disappears, furniture that moves by itself, and weird powers gusting through the house and menacing everyone. Producer Steven Spielberg is rumored to have directed some scenes. (Dir: Tobe Hooper, 114 mins.)†

Poltergeist II (1986)*½ JoBeth Williams, Craig T. Nelson, Heather O'Rourke, Julian Beck, Zelda Rubinstein, Oliver Robins, Will Sampson. They're back to kidnap little Carol Anne (O'Rourke) and torment and frighten the rest of the Freeling family. (Dir: Brian Gibson, 91 mins.)†

Poltergeist III (1988)*½ Tom Skerritt, Nancy Allen, Heather O'Rourke, Zelda Rubinstein. The special effects aren't that good, and the story is a weak replay of the previous two films. (Dir: Gary Sherman, 97 mins.)†

Polyester (1981)***½ Divine, Tab Hunter, Edith Massey, Stiv Bators, Mary Garlington, Ken King, Mink Stole. Filmed in Odorama, director John *(Pink Flamingos)* Waters's bid for mainstream commercial success lacks the harsh edges of his earlier work, but manifests a surprising amount of satiric bite. Our heroine, Francine Fishpaw, suffers the degradations of dealing with a promiscuous go-go girl of a daughter, a son who's the Baltimore Foot Stomper, and a porn king husband who drives her to alcoholism. (86 mins.)†

Pom-Pom Girls, The (1976)* Jennifer Ashley, Lisa Reeves, Robert Carradine. Exploitation material about teen studs and stud-ettes frolicking about, trading off innuendos and wreaking havoc all in the name of a good time. (Dir: Joseph Ruben, 90 mins.)†

Pony Express (1953)**½ Charlton Heston, Rhonda Fleming, Jan Sterling, Forrest Tucker. Buffalo Bill and Wild Bill Hickok team up to see that the mail goes through. (Dir: Jerry Hopper, 101 mins.)

Pony Soldier (1952)**½ Tyrone Power, Cameron Mitchell, Robert Horton. Mountie tries to stop a tribe of rebellious Indians from going on the warpath. Lively action melodrama goes through its familiar paces with speed and dispatch. (Dir: Joseph M. Newman, 82 mins.)

Poor Albert and Little Annie—See: **I Dismember Mama**

Poor Cow (Great Britain, 1967)**½ Carol White, Terence Stamp. Life in the lower depths, as a girl seeks happiness for her baby and contends with a husband in jail. White is particularly impressive in this saga of the sexual mores of the English low-income worker. (Dir: Kenneth Loach, 104 mins.)

Poor Devil (MTV 1973)**½ Sammy Davis, Jr., Jack Klugman, Adam West, Christopher Lee. Pilot film in which Davis plays the devil's bumbling disciple. (Dir: Robert Scheerer, 78 mins.)

Poor Little Rich Girl, The (1936)*** Shirley Temple, Alice Faye, Jack Haley. Shirley isn't an orphan in this one so she runs away from home and gets picked up by a vaudeville team. Typical Temple vehicle but more pleasant than most. (Dir: Irving Cummings, 79 mins.)†

Poor Little Rich Girl (1917)**** Mary Pickford, Madeline Traverse, Charles Wellesley, Gladys Fairbanks. Beautiful film of eleven-year-old heiress Pickford longing to escape her overprotected world and live like other children. Wonderfully acted, with the diminutive star made to seem smaller with cleverly designed sets and camera angles. (Dir: Maurice Tourneur, 70 mins.)†

Poor Little Rich Girl (MTV 1987)*** Farrah Fawcett, Bruce Davison, Kevin McCarthy, Burl Ives, Stéphane Audran, James Read. Soapy biography of the woman who made millions from the five-and-ten, Barbara Hutton, the Woolworth heiress. Fawcett as Hutton marries and marries (seven husbands in all) before she falls into patterns of self-destructive alcoholism and drug addiction. (Dir: Charles Jarrott, 240 mins.)

Poor Pretty Eddie—See: **Red Neck Country**

Poor White Trash (1957)½ Douglas Fowley, Bill Hays, Peter Graves, Lita Milan, Tim Carey. Mostly poor white junk about a Cajun girl romanced by a northern pretty boy to the jealous outrage of a local he-man. But daring enough at the time to drive the censor boards crazy and to make this a drive-in classic. AKA: **Bayou.** (Dir: Harold Daniels, 84 mins.)†

Pop Always Pays (1940)** Leon Errol, Dennis O'Keefe, Adele Pearce, Walter Catlett, Marjorie Gateson. Mild comedy has father Errol letting his daughter marry only on the condition that her suitor raise $1,000. (Dir: Leslie Goodwins, 66 mins.)†

Popcorn (U.S.-Jamaica, 1991)**½ Jill Schoelen, Tom Villard, Dee Wallace Stone, Derek Rydall, Malcolm Danare, Ray Walston, Tony Roberts. A university film professor stages a horror movie marathon to raise money for his department, and a maniac is loose in the theater. Simpleminded fun includes some clever fright

films-within-the-film and lots of silly terror. (Dir: Mark Herrier, 91 mins.)†

Pope John Paul II (MTV 1984)*** Albert Finney, Alfred Burke, John McEnery. Finney, in his TV movie debut, singlehandedly lifts this drama up a notch with a sensational performance as the Vatican's current pontiff, Karol Wojtyla. Flashbacks provide revealing insights into Wojtyla's early days, including his yearning to be an actor and the harsh, ambition-dampening realities of the Nazi takeover of Poland in WWII. (Dir: Herbert Wise, 104 mins.)†

Pope of Greenwich Village, The (1984)* Mickey Rourke, Eric Roberts, Daryl Hannah, Geraldine Page, Kenneth McMillan. A slice of pseudo–Italian-Americana that strains credibility throughout. Two cousins make the mistake of committing a burglary that misfires and causes an undercover cop's death. (Dir: Stuart Rosenberg, 122 mins.)†

Popeye (1980)*½ Robin Williams, Shelley Duvall, Paul L. Smith, Paul Dooley, Wesley Ivan Hurt. Jules Feiffer's screenplay misses the spirit of the Segar strip and the Fleischer cartoons, and despite director Robert Altman's efforts to impart an ensemble theatricality to the goings-on, the project just rambles around. Cute songs composed by Harry Nilsson. (114 mins.)†

Popeye Doyle (MTV 1986)**½ Ed O'Neill, Matthew Laurence, Audrey Landers, James Handy, Candy Clark. TV-ized follow-up to *The French Connection* saga is a standard action pic sparked by O'Neill's authoritative portrayal of Popeye Doyle, who's involved here in a drug-homicide case that's linked to terrorism and the balance of power in the Middle East. (Dir: Peter Levin, 104 mins.)

Popi (1969)*** Alan Arkin, Miguel Alejandro, Rita Moreno. Arkin's luminous performance as the New York Puerto Rican widower who wants a better life for his two sons is the film's main attraction. He will win your heart as he comes up with an outrageous plan to set his boys adrift in a boat off the Florida coast in hopes of their finding a better home with some wealthy people after being rescued. (Dir: Arthur Hiller, 115 mins.)

Poppy (1936)*** W. C. Fields, Rochelle Hudson, Richard Cromwell, Lynne Overman. When W. C. is on screen, this is a delight. Story of a carnival bum who tries to pass his daughter off as a missing heiress. (Dir: A. Edward Sutherland, 74 mins.)

Poppy Is Also a Flower, The (1966)*½ Trevor Howard, E. G. Marshall. A cast of all-stars (Yul Brynner, Omar Sharif, Marcello Mastroianni, Rita Hayworth, Angie Dickinson, and more) fill cameo roles in this dope-smuggling tale, and they weigh it down. (Dir: Terence Young, 100 mins. Video version, 85 mins.)†

Porgy and Bess (1959)*** Sidney Poitier, Dorothy Dandridge, Sammy Davis, Jr., Pearl Bailey, Diahann Carroll. George Gershwin's opera about the inhabitants of Catfish Row, and a crippled beggar who cares for a beautiful but reckless girl. Lavishly produced by Samuel Goldwyn, with the superb score brilliantly sung. However, the show is staged unimaginatively—some of the performances are not on a par with the musical end. (Dir: Otto Preminger, 116 mins.)

Pork Chop Hill (1959)*** Gregory Peck, Rip Torn, George Peppard, Harry Guardino. Stark, hard-hitting war drama about the last hours of the Korean War. (Dir: Lewis Milestone, 97 mins.)†

Porky's (1982)*½ Kim Cattrall, Scott Colomby, Kaki Hunter, Nancy Parsons, Susan Clark, Alex Karras, Dan Monahan. A raucously blue descendant of "beach-blanket-bingo" movies, this film revolves around the sexual mores of the déclassé of 1954. (Dir: Bob Clark, 94 mins.)†

Porky's II: The Next Day (1983)½ Dan Monahan, Kaki Hunter, Wyatt Knight, Bill Wiley. This sequel to 1982's surprise sex-comedy hit *Porky's* is not an improvement over the original. (Dir: Bob Clark, 97 mins.)†

Porky's Revenge (1985)½ Dan Monahan, Wyatt Knight, Tony Ganios, Mark Herrier, Kaki Hunter, Scott Colomby, Nancy Parsons. Last and worst installment about the high-spirited high schoolers who tangle with Porky, the piggish owner of an illegal casino. (Dir: James Komack, 94 mins.)†

Pornographers, The (Japan, 1966)***½ Shoichi Ozawa, Massaomi Kondo, Sumiko Sakamoto, Keiko Sagawa. Weird black comedy involves a salesman and part-time filmmaker who cares for and lusts after the daughter of the widow with whom he lives. Demanding but worthwhile film about the layers of people's sexual emotions, a very different kind of cinema from director Shohei Imamura. (128 mins.)†

Port Afrique (Great Britain, 1956)** Pier Angeli, Phil Carey, Anthony Newley. French Morocco is the setting for this dull story of revenge and murder. Lovely Pier Angeli plays a nightclub singer involved in the shady goings-on. (Dir: Rudolph Maté, 92 mins.)

Portnoy's Complaint (1972)* Richard Benjamin, Karen Black, Lee Grant. Roth's best-selling novel, about the sexual hangups and fantasies of a Jewish boy growing up in New Jersey, is unrecognizable in this celluloid massacre. (Dir: Ernest Lehman, 101 mins.)†

Port of Call (Sweden, 1948)**½ Bengt Eklund, Ivine-Christine Jonsson. Early Ingmar Bergman film about a promiscuous girl who's redeemed by the love of a sailor. A must-see for the director's fans, who'll want to see his favorite themes in their earliest expression. Dubbed. (100 mins.)†

Port of New York (1949)*** Scott Brady, Yul Brynner, K. T. Stevens. When a government agent is killed working on a narcotics case, his buddy crashes through to get the goods on the gang. Competent crime melodrama, made in New York. Brynner's film debut, with his own hair. (Dir: Laslo Benedek, 79 mins.)

Port of Seven Seas (1938)** Wallace Beery, Maureen O'Sullivan, John Beal. An earlier version of *Fanny*, as the Marseilles girl loves a lad who goes to sea; when babytime is near, her father and an elderly suitor come to the rescue. (Dir: James Whale, 81 mins.)

Portrait in Black (1960)**½ Lana Turner, Anthony Quinn, Sandra Dee, John Saxon, Richard Basehart, Lloyd Nolan, Anna May Wong. Typical example of slick Hollywood mystery-romance. Ingredients: bedridden tycoon, dissatisfied wife, weak-willed doctor in love with wife; mix well with murder, conscience pangs, and revenge. It's all nicely garnished, but still hash. (Dir: Michael Gordon, 112 mins.)

Portrait of a Hitman (1977)* Jack Palance, Richard Roundtree, Bo Svenson, Ann Turkel, Rod Steiger. Confused, contrived crime thriller about a hit man hired to kill a friend, with whom he's already competing for the love of the same woman. Shoddy production values, wasted cast, and overly complicated plot make this one a misfire. (Dir: Allan A. Buckhantz, 87 mins.)†

Portrait of a Life (India, 1988)***½ Soumitra Chatterjee, Madhavi Chakrabarty, Avory Dutta. Graceful, poignant, and inspiring drama about a simple teacher in an impoverished rural school in 1930s India who begins a lifelong effort to write the first dictionary devoted to Bengali words. Chatterjee is brilliant in this glorious film. (Dir: Raja Mitra, 130 mins.)

Portrait of a Mobster (1961)**½ Vic Morrow, Leslie Parrish. Strictly for fans of gangster movies. Morrow gives a tight-lipped performance as Dutch Schultz, the notorious hood of the Prohibition era. (Dir: Joseph Pevney, 108 mins.)

Portrait of an Escort (MTV 1980)*½ Susan Anspach, Tony Bill, Edie Adams, Mary Frann, Cyd Charisse, Kevin McCarthy. A divorcée's neighbors think she's "fast" after she takes a job with an escort service as a professional date. (Dir: Steven Hilliard Stern, 104 mins.)

Portrait of a Rebel: Margaret Sanger (MTV 1980)** Bonnie Franklin, David Dukes, Richard Johnson. Time is the early years of the century when Margaret Sanger took on the medical profession, the courts, the Senate, and the Catholic Church in her battle to give women birth control information. (Dir: Virgil Vogel, 104 mins.)

Portrait of a Showgirl (MTV 1982)** Lesley Ann Warren, Rita Moreno, Diane Kay, Tony Curtis. Warren is a Las Vegas showgirl trying to carve a niche for herself after running away from New York and from an unhappy relationship. (Dir: Steven Hilliard Stern, 104 mins.)†

Portrait of a Sinner (Great Britain, 1959)** Nadja Tiller, Tony Britton, William Bendix. Temptress keeps a young man and her elderly boss on a string, but really craves the man who did her dirt years before. (Dir: Robert Siodmak, 96 mins.)

Portrait of a Stripper (MTV 1979)**½ Lesley Ann Warren, Edward Herrmann, Vic Tayback. Warren gives a finely etched performance as a young widow with a son, who begins work in a strip joint to meet her expenses. (Dir: John Alonzo, 104 mins.)†

Portrait of a White Marriage (MCTV 1988) *** Martin Mull, Fred Willard, Mary Kay Place, Harry Shearer, Robin Williams (cameo). A feature-length outgrowth of Martin Mull's clever and amusing cable series "The History of White People in America." This time around, Mull takes an active part in the storyline as a seedy daytime talk show host who visits the small town where bickering white couple Hal and Joyce Harrison (Willard, Place) live. (Dir: Harry Shearer, 100 mins.)†

Portrait of Clare (Great Britain, 1951)** Margaret Johnston, Richard Todd, Robin Bailey, Ronald Howard, Jeremy Spenser. British drama tells the life story of one "ordinary" woman, told in flashbacks as she thinks over her life. Warm, unpretentious, and very well done. (Dir: Lance Comfort, 100 mins.)

Portrait of Jason (1967)***½ Shirley Clarke's groundbreaking documentary about Jason, a black junkie and homosexual prostitute. Clarke filmed her subject in a liquor- and marijuana-fueled twelve-hour marathon during which she asks probing questions and shouts insults at him. A seminal work of the '60s new American cinema. (105 mins.)†

Portrait of Jennie (1949)***½ Jennifer Jones, Joseph Cotten, Ethel Barrymore, David Wayne. An artist encounters a strange, beautiful girl in Central Park, paints her, and then falls in love with her, although he suspects she is the spirit of a dead girl. A haunting fantasy that's suffused with a real romantic glow. Jones's ethereal loveliness has never been

seen to better advantage. (Dir: William Dieterle, 86 mins.)†

Portrait of Teresa (Cuba, 1979)***½ Daisy Granados, Raul Pomares, Adolfo Llaurado, Alina Sanchez. Powerful exploration of the role of *machismo* in post-revolutionary Cuba focuses on a married homemaker who incurs the wrath of her husband when she becomes involved in cultural and political causes. Popular cinema verité style film was inspired by Fidel Castro's mandate to make women and men equal in Cuban society. (Dir: Pastor Vega, 115 mins.)†

Portrait of the Artist as a Young Man, A (Great Britain, 1977)**½ Bosco Hogan, T. P. McKenna, John Gielgud, Rosaleen Linehan, Maureen Potter. Director Joseph Strick attacks another classic novel, with predictable results. However, with Gielgud delivering the hellfire sermon and actors like McKenna and Hogan, there are moments of eloquence and power. Shot on location in Dublin. (92 mins.)†

Posed for Murder (1989)* Charlotte J. Helmkamp, Carl Fury, Rick Gianasi, Michael Merrins. Model is stalked by a murderer in this forgettable non-thriller. (Dir: Brian Thomas Jones, 90 mins.)†

Poseidon Adventure, The (1972)*** Gene Hackman, Ernest Borgnine, Shelley Winters, Stella Stevens, Jack Albertson, Carol Lynley, Red Buttons, Roddy McDowall, Leslie Nielsen, Pamela Sue Martin. It's New Year's Eve on the "Poseidon" when a 90-foot tidal wave turns the huge ocean liner upside-down and the stage is set for the survival of the fittest among the all-star passenger list. Sequel: *Beyond the Poseidon Adventure*. (Dir: Ronald Neame, 117 mins.)†

Positive (1990)***½ Larry Kramer, Phil Zwickler, Michael Callen. Audacious documentary from Rosa Von Praunheim (*A Virus Knows No Morals, Silence Equals Death*) attacks the medical and political communities and their alleged slow response to the AIDS crisis. Much of the film's boldness comes from emphasizing the gay aspects of an issue which some see as both a health and a civil rights issue. (90 mins.)

Positive I.D. (1987)*** Stephanie Rascoe, John Davies, Steve Fromholz, Laura Lane. Effective low-budget psychological thriller about a rape victim who assumes a second, nighttime identity as a bar-hopping seductress. Complicated goings-on, but the kicker at the end makes the buildup worthwhile. (Dir: Andy Anderson, 105 mins.)†

Posse (1975)***½ Kirk Douglas, Bruce Dern. Offbeat, interesting western, part allegory, part morality story. Douglas directing as well as playing the leading role, an affable Texas marshall, circa 1890. (94 mins.)†

Posse from Hell (1961)** Audie Murphy, John Saxon, Zohra Lampert, Vic Morrow. No surprises, but action fans will probably stick with it, as a gunslinger goes after four escaped killers. (Dir: Herbert Coleman, 89 mins.)

Possessed (1931)*** Clark Gable, Joan Crawford, Wallace Ford, Skeets Gallagher. Gable and Crawford were always a hot item together, and their chemistry elevates this sharp Depression romance of a factory worker who puts her man's well-being ahead of her own. (Dir: Clarence Brown, 72 mins.)

Possessed (1947)***½ Joan Crawford, Van Heflin, Geraldine Brooks, Raymond Massey, Stanley Ridges. A hard-edged, absorbing study of schizophrenia, with some audacious directorial touches and Crawford's most complex performance. This portrayal of mental illness is subtly effective as Crawford becomes unable to trust her perception of reality as her unrequited passion for a handsome womanizer leads to madness and murder. (Dir: Curtis Bernhardt, 108 mins.)

Possessed, The (MTV 1977)** James Farentino, Joan Hackett, Claudette Nevins, Diana Scarwid. Farentino plays a defrocked priest who appears at a girls' school to do battle against evil. (Dir: Jerry Thorpe, 78 mins.)

Possession (France-West Germany, 1981)* Isabelle Adjani, Sam Neill, Heinz Bennent. Self-described as an intellectual horror film, this film is pointlessly gory and overwrought from the word go. Adjani has a field day as a neurotic gal who gives birth to an evil manifestation of her own hysteria! Originally ran 127 mins. (Dir: Andrzej Zulawski, 97 mins.)†

Possession of Joel Delaney, The (1972)** Shirley MacLaine, Perry King. Oddball thriller. New York divorcee MacLaine chases after her kid brother Joel (King) who becomes possessed by the spirit of a deceased Puerto Rican friend who used to chop off girls' heads! Some scenes shake you up, but the terror is in slow motion. (Dir: Waris Hussein, 105 mins.)

Possessors, The (France, 1958)**½ Jean Gabin, Pierre Brasseur. Story of a family and their involvement with the stock exchange. Literate French drama, slow-moving but well acted. (Dir: Denys De La Patelliere, 94 mins.)

Postcards From the Edge (1990)***½ Meryl Streep, Shirley MacLaine, Gene Hackman, Dennis Quaid, Richard Dreyfuss, Annette Bening, Rob Reiner, Dana Ivey. Hip, exquisitely acted, and thoroughly entertaining comedy, based on Carrie Fisher's novel, about the love-hate relationship between a show biz superstar mother (MacLaine) and her actress daughter (Streep). Streep got an Oscar nomination for her immensely moving portrait. Lots of cameos by Hollywood notables and a crackling script by Fisher add to the enjoyment. (Dir: Mike Nichols, 101 mins.)†

Postman Always Rings Twice, The (1946)***½ Lana Turner, John Garfield, Cecil Kellaway, Hume Cronyn, Leon Ames, Audrey Totter. This version of James M. Cain's novel soft-pedaled the brutal sexuality of the book in favor of smoldering looks and dialogue riddled with double entendres. Turner's shallow beauty was perfectly suited to the role of the amoral wife who plots to murder her husband, but even luscious Lana is overshadowed by Garfield's street-smart bravado as the drifter who becomes her co-conspirator and lover. There is something intriguing about Hollywood's notion of hinted sexuality. (Dir: Tay Garnett, 113 mins.)†

Postman Always Rings Twice, The (1981)**½ Jack Nicholson, Jessica Lange, John Colicos, Anjelica Huston, Michael Lerner. The film looks handsome, but it just lies there. Rafelson cuts out of scenes before their payoff, leaving audiences unfamiliar with the tale stranded. Nicholson inhabits the period convincingly, and Lange manages to transform Cora from a fantasy projection into a real character. (Dir: Bob Rafelson, 97 mins.)†

Potemkin (U.S.S.R., 1925)**** Alexander Antonov, Vladimir Barski, Grigori Alexandrov, Mikhail Gomorov. It's impossible to overstate the importance of this landmark film as both a technical achievement and an emotionally stirring recreation of history. The story of the 1905 mutiny on the battleship *Potemkin*, followed by a government massacre of civilian supporters as well as the ship's crew, is audaciously filmed by director Sergei Eisenstein. The Odessa Steps sequence is only one of the unforgettable scenes. (Dir: 65 mins.)†

Poto and Cabengo (1979)*** Engrossing documentary about six-year-old twins who created their own private language in order to communicate with each other to the exclusion of the people around them. Fascinating film touches on the hopes of an entreprenurial American society channeled through the twins. (Dir: Jean-Pierre Gorin, 77 mins.)

Pot o' Gold (1941)** James Stewart, Paulette Goddard. The gal's rich pop hates dance bands, but nevertheless she lands Horace Heidt's orchestra on pop's program. Pleasant musical comedy. (Dir: George Marshall, 86 mins.)†

Pound (1970)*** Lawrence Wolf, Elsie Downey, Marshall Efron. Director Robert Downey's erratically insane satire of impounded dogs (played by humans) awaiting an owner or the big sleep—the latter can only come when Con Edison fixes the gas lines. (92 mins.)

Pound Puppies and the Legend of Big Paw (1988)* Voices of George Rose, B. J. Ward, Ruth Buzzi, Brennan Howard. This extended cartoon commercial for a line of doggy dolls is no worse than the bulk of Saturday morning television programs, but isn't that bad enough? (Dir: Pierre DeCelles, 76 mins.)†

Pourquoi Pas?—See: **Why Not?**

Pouvoir Intime—See: **Blind Trust**

P.O.W., The Escape (1986)* David Carradine, Charles R. Floyd, Mako. Set in the closing days of the war in Vietnam, this mundane action film details the escape attempts of some prisoners. Short on action, logic, suspense. (Dir: Gideon Amir, 90 mins.)

Powaqqatsi (1988)*** Godfrey Reggio's follow-up to *Koyaanisqatsi*, again with a spellbinding Philip Glass score, explores the third world, comparing the traditional harmony of the underdeveloped areas with the squalor of cities. Not as kinetically exciting as its predecessor (there are no high-speed sequences here), but nonetheless an absorbing experience, best seen on a big screen. (89 mins.)

Powder Keg (MTV 1971)** Rod Taylor, Dennis Cole. Railroad blowups, dirty bandits, rape, and a Stutz Bearcat roadster, circa 1914, keep the action barreling along in this film. Troubleshooters Taylor and Cole are hired to handle Mexican hijackers. (Dir: Doug Heyes, 93 mins.)†

Powder River (1953)** Rory Calhoun, Corinne Calvet, Cameron Mitchell. Routine western about a gunman turned marshall and the collection of stock characters with whom he matches wits and/or guns. (Dir: Louis King, 78 mins.)

Power (MTV 1980)*** Joe Don Baker, Karen Black, Ralph Bellamy, Brian Keith. Script by Ernest Tidyman on the rise to power of a tough labor leader, patterned after Jimmy Hoffa. Baker is splendid as '30s Chicago meat dock worker Tommy Vanda, who moves up the labor ranks with help from the mob and eventually becomes arrogant and totally corrupt. (Dir: Barry Shear, 200 mins.)

Power (1986)** Richard Gere, Julie Christie, Gene Hackman, Kate Capshaw, Denzel Washington, E. G. Marshall, Beatrice Straight, Fritz Weaver. Tepid drama about a media consultant who finds himself disgusted with his politician clients. Gere plays the slick manipulator with a lack of conviction that is

834

echoed by the hollow script: (Dir: Sidney Lumet, 111 mins.)†

Power, The (1968)** George Hamilton, Suzanne Pleshette, Michael Rennie, Yvonne De Carlo. Reasonably interesting, sci-fi yarn about a mind which has fantastic power to do almost anything as long as it's evil! Hamilton tries to oppose this "power" since he too possesses a "powerful" mind. (Dir: Byron Haskin, 109 mins.)

Power, The (1984)** Susan Stokey, Warren Lincoln, Lisa Erickson. Middling horror thriller about an ancient idol that kills or possesses its owners. (Dirs: Jeffrey Obrow, Stephen Carpenter, 95 mins.)†

Power and the Glory, The (1933)**½ Spencer Tracy, Colleen Moore, Ralph Morgan, Helen Vinson. Tracy is a tycoon risen from the working classes, with elaborate flashbacks demonstrating how he used everyone on his way to the top. Director William K. Howard, however, is not up to realizing the screenplay's complexities. Script by Preston Sturges. (76 mins.)

Power and the Prize, The (1956)**½ Robert Taylor, Elisabeth Mueller, Burl Ives. Taylor plays the ambitious executive who finds he fought too hard for things he really didn't want after he falls in love with an attractive refugee. (Dir: Henry Koster, 98 mins.)

Power of the Whistler (1945)**½ Richard Dix, Janis Carter, Jeff Donnell, Loren Tindall. Murderer Dix, suffering from amnesia, becomes involved with innocent Carter, who may become his next victim if she doesn't discover his identity before he does. Good entry in the "Whistler" series, efficiently directed by Lew Landers. (66 mins.)

Powers Girl, The (1942)** George Murphy, Anne Shirley, Carole Landis, Dennis Day, Benny Goodman. A fast-talking agent makes a Powers model out of a dainty dish, but falls for her sister. Tolerable comedy. (Dir: Norman Z. McLeod, 93 mins.)

Power Within, The (MTV 1979)*½ Art Hindle, Edward Binns, Eric Braeden, Susan Sullivan, David Hedison. Lightning doesn't strike in this dull adventure tale of a man who's turned into a superhero after being struck by lightning. (Dir: John Llewellyn Moxey, 78 mins.)

Powwow Highway (1988)*** A Martinez, Gary Farmer, Amanda Wyss. An activist Indian and his passive buddy leave their Cheyenne reservation to visit his sister and encounter racial hatred on the road. (Dir: Jonathan Wacks, 91 mins.)

Practically Yours (1945)** Fred MacMurray, Claudette Colbert, Robert Benchley, Cecil Kellaway, Rosemary DeCamp. A pilot accidentally sends a message of love to a girl before he crashes into the Pacific. (Dir: Mitchell Leisen, 89 mins.)

Practice Makes Perfect (France, 1979)**½ Jean Rochefort, Nicole Garcia, Annie Girardot, Danielle Darrieux, Lila Kedrova. Another fluff piece from director Philippe de Broca, starring Rochefort as a celebrated concert pianist who tries to juggle his wife, life, career, daughters, ex-wife, and mistress. AKA: Le Cavaleur. (104 mins.)

Prancer (1989)**½ Sam Elliott, Rebecca Harrell, Cloris Leachman, Rutanya Alda, Abe Vigoda, Michael Constantine. Farm girl whose widowed father is fighting a losing battle to save the family farm convinces herself that an injured reindeer belongs to Santa Claus, and sets about nursing it back to health. Family story has its charms when it's not aping E. T. (Dir: John Hancock, 103 mins.)†

Prayer for the Dying, A (U.S.-Great Britain, 1987)**½ Mickey Rourke, Bob Hoskins, Alan Bates, Sammi Davis. Both Rourke and director Mike Hodges were dissatisfied with this competent thriller about a disillusioned IRA hit man who wants out, but there are assorted virtues. In addition to several cliff-hanging turns in the plot, there is also a campy performance by Bates as a mob boss who doubles as a mortician. (104 mins.)†

Pray for Death (1986)* James Booth, Robert Ito, Sho Kosugi, Michael Constantine. Brutal martial arts flick about a ninja warrior who steps on the toes of the underworld. (Dir: Gordon Hessler, 93 mins.)†

Pray for the Wildcats (MTV 1974)*** Andy Griffith, William Shatner, Robert Reed, Marjoe Gortner, Angie Dickinson. An offbeat tale. Griffith plays an unscrupulous tycoon who gleefully manipulates three ad agency execs beyond the point of endurance. (Dir: Robert Michael Lewis, 100 mins.)†

Pray TV (1980)—See: KGOD

Pray TV (MTV 1982)**½ John Ritter, Ned Beatty, Madolyn Smith, Louise Latham. Beatty is all evangelical slickness and huckster charm as Reverend Freddy Stone, who spreads God's Word over the Divinity Broadcasting Company. Enter young, dewy-eyed, newly ordained Ritter, who works for Stone during the summer and finds that antennas have replaced missionaries. (Dir: Robert Markowitz, 104 mins.)

Predator (1987)** Arnold Schwarzenegger, Carl Weathers, Sonny Landham, Elpidia Carrillo, Jesse Ventura. Fine special effects combined with extreme violence. Arnold heads a guerilla mission, but his squad has more than Contras to contend with; there's a chameleonlike visitor from outer space, and he's dropped into Latin America to hunt for humans. (Dir: John McTiernan, 106 mins.)†

Predator 2 *½ Danny Glover, Maria Conchita Alonso, Gary Busey, Rubén Blades. Los Angeles in 1937 is attacked by the invisible creature from another planet in this silly sequel to Predator, which squanders special effects, acting, talent, and celluloid. (Dir: Stephen Hopkins, 102 mins.)†

Prehistoric Women (1950)½ Laurette Luez, Allan Nixon, Joan Shawlee, Judy Landon. It's back to the caves in this "story of romance when the world was young," more cheesecake in loincloths made for "adults only" theaters of the '50s. That aspect has lost its appeal (these cave women wear lengthy loincloths), but there are savage beasts, tribal dances, and, of course, prehistoric lust. (Dir: Gregory G. Tallas, 74 mins.)†

Prehistoric Women (Great Britain, 1967)* Martine Beswick, Edina Ronay, Michael Latimer, Carol White. Dark-haired Amazons make life miserable for male slaves and push the beautiful blonde babes around. Apparently, it wasn't always true that blondes have more fun. (Dir: Michael Carreras, 91 mins.)

Prelude to Fame (Great Britain, 1950)*** Guy Rolfe, Kathleen Byron, Jeremy Spenser. A boy is found to have musical talent, becomes a child prodigy conductor, but finds fame has its sadness too. Drama, well written and directed, finely acted. (Dir: Fergus McDonnell, 78 mins.)

Premature Burial, The (1962)** Ray Milland, Hazel Court, Heather Angel. Edgar Allan Poe's intricate and engrossing suspense tale about a man who fears he will be buried alive is impoverished by this screen treatment, so packed with contrivances, clichés, and gloomy decors as to be absurd. (Dir: Roger Corman, 81 mins.)†

Premonition, The (1976)*½ Sharon Farrell, Richard Lynch, Jeff Corey, Ellen Barber. If you get a premonition not to watch this murky thriller, follow it. Some psychics try to locate a missing girl. (Dir: Robert Allen Schnitzer, 94 mins.)†

Preppie Murder, The (MTV 1989)** Danny Aiello, William Baldwin, Joanna Kerns, Lara Flynn Boyle, William Devane, J. C. Quinn. Typically exploitative telefilm about Robert Chambers, the prep school grad convicted of murdering a girl during a "rough sex" encounter in New York's Central Park. Baldwin is sorely miscast as the "irresistible bad boy" Chambers. (Dir: John Herzfeld, 96 mins.)

Preppies (1984)** Dennis Drake, Steven Holt, Peter Brady Reardon, Cindy Manion. Soft-core sex teaser with mild laughs. Three Ivy Leaguers are studying the law, but they spend more time chasing skirts, and it may cost one of them an inheritance. (Dir: Chuck Vincent, 93 mins.)†

Prescription: Murder (MTV 1968)**½ Peter Falk, Gene Barry. Entertaining, engrossing mystery fare. Falk plays Columbo, the cigar-smoking, trench coat-carrying, detective who just can't buy successful Hollywood psychiatrist Barry's airtight alibi. (Dir: Richard Irving, 99 mins.)†

Presenting Lily Mars (1943)*** Van Heflin, Judy Garland, Fay Bainter, Richard Carlson, Spring Byington, Marilyn Maxwell. Slight, well-done little tale of a stage-struck girl and her loving, eccentric family. Heflin is good as the exasperated producer continually hounded by the aspiring actress. (Dir: Norman Taurog, 104 mins.)†

President's Analyst, The (1967)***½ James Coburn, Godfrey Cambridge. Wacky, rewarding satire. The premise is tremendously original, and although it falters towards the end, the story offers some wild chases and amusing sequences with analyst Coburn becoming more and more paranoid, thanks to his delicate assignment as secret headshrinker to the President. (Dir: Theodore J. Flicker, 104 mins.)†

President's Lady, The (1953)**½ Susan Hayward, Charlton Heston, Fay Bainter, Carl Betz, John McIntire. Heston's effective performance as Andrew Jackson makes this costume drama, based on Irving Stone's best-seller about the romance between the young Jackson and a married woman, worthwhile. (Dir: Henry Levin, 96 mins.)

President's Mistress, The (MTV 1978)** Beau Bridges, Karen Grassle, Larry Hagman, Susan Blanchard. High-style hokum about a beautiful blonde who is having an affair with the President; word flashes out that the lady is a Russian spy. (Dir: John Llewellyn Moxey, 104 mins.)†

President's Plane Is Missing, The (MTV 1971)**½ Buddy Ebsen, Peter Graves, Rip Torn, Raymond Massey, Arthur Kennedy. The premise—the threat of a nuclear attack by Red China—was devised before relations improved. A fictional President boards Air Force One, which crashes soon thereafter. (Dir: Daryl Duke, 100 mins.)†

Presidio, The (1988)**½ Sean Connery, Mark Harmon, Meg Ryan, Jack Warden, Mark Blum. Connery and Harmon, who first locked horns in the army, renew their battle in San Francisco, where Connery is the CO of the titular military base and Harmon is a cop. Ryan ups the ante as Connery's daughter, who falls in love with Harmon. There's a good cast, flashy direction, and plenty of action here, 836

but no script to give any of it a foundation. (Dir: Peter Hyams, 97 mins.)†

Pressure Point (1962)*** Sidney Poitier, Bobby Darin, Peter Falk. A black psychiatrist (Poitier) is treating a prison inmate (Darin) who is a racist and a member of the Nazi party. Compelling drama photographed in razor-like B&W by Ernest Haller. (Dir: Hubert Cornfield, 91 mins.)

Prestige (1932)** Ann Harding, Melvyn Douglas, Adolphe Menjou, Clarence Muse. Exotic melodrama of a French colonial outpost in Indochina is marred by repulsive racism and a ridiculously cliché-ridden script. An unusually humorless production from director Tay Garnett. (73 mins.)

Presumed Innocent (1990)*** Harrison Ford, Bonnie Bedelia, Raul Julia, Brian Dennehy, Greta Scacchi, Paul Winfield. Crackerjack whodunit about a married lawyer accused of murdering a woman who turns out to be his mistress. Lots of red herrings, legal strategies, and sexual fireworks that truly add to the suspense. A beautiful Scacchi is especially good as the mistress. (Dir: Alan Pakula, 127 mins.)†

Pretender, The (1947)*** Albert Dekker, Catherine Craig. Businessman marries for money, hires a gangster to eliminate his rival; through an error, he finds himself the intended victim. Tight, suspenseful melodrama. (Dir: W. Lee Wilder, 69 mins.)

Pretty Baby (1950)**½ Dennis Morgan, Betsy Drake, Edmund Gwenn, Zachary Scott. Funny comedy about a resourceful working girl who uses gimmicks to get to the top in her career. (Dir: Bretaigne Windust, 92 mins.)

Pretty Baby (1978)**½ Keith Carradine, Brooke Shields, Susan Sarandon, Antonio Fargas. Too careful and tasteful, but an effective inquiry into the passion of a photographer for an 11-year-old prostitute in Storyville, New Orleans. Carradine's physical inarticulateness is immensely effective, and Shields does well with the caprices of the preadolescent whore. (Dir: Louis Malle, 109 mins.)†

Pretty Boy Floyd (1960)** John Ericson, Joan Harvey, Barry Newman. Fictionalized account of one of the nation's big-time killers. (Dir: Herbert J. Leder, 96 mins.)

Pretty Boy Floyd (1974)—See: **Story of Pretty Boy Floyd, The**

Pretty in Pink (1986)*½ Molly Ringwald, Harry Dean Stanton, Jon Cryer, Andrew McCarthy, Annie Potts. Written and produced by John Hughes, who seems to farm his worst scripts out to other directors. The plot is older than D. W. Griffith—poor girl falls in love with rich boy—and not at all disguised by the eighties mufti in which it's dressed up. Technically slick, but it has no feeling for the lives and cares of real teenagers. And it's hard to feel too sorry for a financially underprivileged teenager who has her own car and answering machine! (Dir: Howard Deutch, 96 mins.)†

Prettykill (1987)½ David Birney, Season Hubley, Yaphet Kotto, Susannah York. An inane attempt at a thriller about a schizophrenic prostitute. (Dir: George Kaczender, 95 mins.)†

Pretty Maids All in a Row (1971)**½ Rock Hudson, Angie Dickinson, Telly Savalas, John David Carson, Roddy McDowall, James Doohan. Vadim tries to do an Americanized version of his once naughty French salutes to male lust with a black comedy about a guidance counselor who murders his female students rather than advising them. Offbeat and sporadically effective. (Dir: Roger Vadim, 92 mins.)

Pretty Poison (1968)***½ Anthony Perkins, Tuesday Weld, John Randolph, Beverly Garland. Absorbing, low-budget psychological drama about a paranoid young man (Perkins) and his girlfriend (Weld), *"Poison"* boasts first-rate performances, a notably adroit screenplay by Lorenzo Semple, Jr., and a promising debut from young director Noel Black. (89 mins.)

Pretty Smart (1987)½ Tricia Leigh Fisher, Lisa Lorient, Dennis Cole, Patricia Arquette. Smug, stupid sexploitation film about girls at a posh school in the Mediterranean. (Dir: Dimitri Logothetis, 84 mins.)†

Pretty Woman (1990)*** Richard Gere, Julia Roberts, Ralph Bellamy, Jason Alexander, Laura San Giacomo, Hector Elizondo, Alex Hyde-White, Larry Miller. Hooker Roberts is hired by Donald Trump-type businessman Gere to be his escort for a week while he wheels and deals in Beverly Hills. Overlong *Pygmalion* clone plays like it was made by computers that had been fed every feel-good romantic comedy of the past three decades. (Dir: Garry Marshall, 117 mins.)†

Prey, The (1983)* Debbie Thureson, Steve Bond, Lori Lethin, Robert Wald, Jackie Coogan. A group of teenagers hike into the woods to an isolated campsite, and are killed one by one by a deformed killer. (Dir: Edwin Scott Brown, 80 mins.)†

Price of Fear, The (1956)** Merle Oberon, Lex Barker. Muddled melodrama about a woman who is responsible for a hit and run accident and goes to extremes to keep it a secret. (Dir: Abner Biberman, 79 mins.)

Prick Up Your Ears (Great Britain, 1987) *** Gary Oldman, Alfred Molina, Vanessa Redgrave, Wallace Shawn, Julie Walters. This screen biography of playwright Joe Orton excels at presenting the unsavory details of his personal life, but stints on providing real insight into the creative process. This powerfully acted film traces Orton's stormy relationship with his lover Kenneth Halliwell from their college days to the stressful time of Orton's first success; that success tears their damaged relationship to shreds and drives Halliwell to kill Orton and commit suicide. (Dir: Stephen Frears, 108 mins.)†

Pride and Extreme Prejudice (MTV 1990) **½ Brian Dennehy, Alan Howard, Lisa Eichhorn, Leonie Hellinger, Simon Cadell. Good Frederick Forsyth espionage yarn showing the inner workings of an international group of spies. Dennehy is the American dispatched to East Germany to collect important data about the Russians. (Dir: Ian Sharp, 93 mins.)†

Pride and Prejudice (1940)**** Greer Garson, Laurence Olivier, Edmund Gwenn, Mary Boland, Edna Mae Oliver, Maureen O'Sullivan. This Jane Austen adaptation is lively, gracious, and entertaining. Olivier and Garson are well matched. Robert Z. Leonard's direction, for once, is exemplary. Aldous Huxley worked on the script with Jane Murfin. (116 mins.)†

Pride and the Passion, The (1957)**½ Cary Grant, Sophia Loren, Frank Sinatra. Over-produced spectacle set during the Spanish Revolution against Napoleon. The real star of the overlong epic is an enormous cannon which is abandoned by the Spanish Army, and retrieved by the band of guerrillas with the aid of a British naval officer. (Dir: Stanley Kramer, 132 mins.)†

Pride of Jesse Hallam, The (MTV 1981)**½ Johnny Cash, Ben Marley, Brenda Vaccaro, Eli Wallach, Guy Boyd. Cash is surprisingly effective as an unschooled man who can't cope with big city pressures when he has to bring his daughter to a metropolitan hospital. (Dir: Gary Nelson, 104 mins.)†

Pride of St. Louis, The (1952)**½ Dan Dailey, Joanne Dru, Richard Crenna. Sentimentalized biography of Dizzy Dean, baseball pitcher extraordinary, character de luxe. (Dir: Harmon Jones, 93 mins.)†

Pride of the Blue Grass (1954)** Lloyd Bridges, Vera Miles. Routine racetrack story with some action on the turf for racing fans. (Dir: William Beaudine, 71 mins.)

Pride of the Bowery (1941)*½ East Side Kids, Mary Ainslee. Very little plot and character motivation in this tale of a would-be boxer at odds with the straight-arrow guys at the camp where he's sent for training. (Dir: Joseph H. Lewis, 61 mins.)†

Pride of the Marines (1945)***½ John Garfield, Eleanor Parker, Dane Clark, Rosemary DeCamp, John Ridgely. Moving, human story of Al Schmid, the marine who was blinded by a grenade after killing two hundred Japanese. It's an account of his adjustment to blindness and it's told with simplicity and taste. (Dir: Delmer Daves, 119 mins.)

Pride of the Yankees, The (1942)***½ Gary Cooper, Teresa Wright, Walter Brennan, Babe Ruth, Dan Duryea. A solid biopic of baseball legend Lou Gehrig. The role of the courtly baseball hero fit Cooper like a baseball glove; his rendition of Gehrig's farewell speech at Yankee Stadium is a classic movie scene. (Dir: Sam Wood, 127 mins.)†

Priest Killer, The (MTV 1971)*½ George Kennedy, Raymond Burr, Don Galloway. Kennedy introduces his TV role of Sarge, the former cop-turned-priest, as he teams with Burr's Chief Ironside in this familiar hunt for a priest killer. (Dir: Richard Colla, 100 mins.)

Priest of Love (Great Britain, 1981)*** Ian McKellen, Janet Suzman, Ava Gardner, Penelope Keith, John Gielgud. Sensitive, always interesting drama about D. H. Lawrence, his stormy but devoted relationship with his wife, Frieda, his struggles to create, and his battles with censors. (Dir: Christopher Miles, 125 mins.)†

Priest's Wife, The (Italy-France, 1970)** Marcello Mastroianni, Sophia Loren. Frothy nonsense about an earthy singer who falls in love with a man of the cloth. (Dir: Dino Risi, 106 mins.)

Primal Scream (1988)* Kenneth J. McGregor, Sharon Mason, Julie Miller, Jon Maurice, Joseph White, Mickey Shaughnessy. Great title for a horror movie; unfortunately, this is a sci-fi thriller that seems to have nothing to do with the title. Futuristic private eye investigates murders tied into the development of a new "energy catalyst." (Dir: William Murray, 92 mins.)†

Prime Cut (1972)**½ Lee Marvin, Gene Hackman, Angel Tompkins, Sissy Spacek. Uneven gangland tale with the old breed (Marvin), from Chicago, trying to collect from the Kansas City young turk (Hackman). (Dir: Michael Ritchie, 91 mins.)†

Prime Minister, The (Great Britain, 1941)** John Gielgud, Diana Wynyard, Fay Compton. Despite the remarkable sets and costumes, and three fine performances, this Disraeli biopic is an elaborate, reverent bore. (Dir: Thorold Dickinson, 94 mins.)

Prime of Miss Jean Brodie, The (Great Britain, 1969)***½ Maggie Smith, Robert Stephens, Pamela Franklin, Celia Johnson. Don't miss Smith's Academy Award-winning performance as the irrepressible, irresistible, and thoroughly mad teacher at an exclusive girls' school. She mesmerizes you at every turn, as her wide-eyed charges raptly listen to her speak of her affairs, her misguided allegiances to Mussolini and Franco, and her dedication to love, art, and truth. (Dir: Ronald Neame, 116 mins.)†

Prime Risk (1985)** Keenan Wynn, Toni Hudson, Lee Montgomery, Sam Bottoms. Scruffy adventure tale with a tricky premise that pays off fitfully. Two people decide to take revenge on their banks by ripping off their computers but stumble across an international terrorist scheme to destroy the U.S. monetary system. (Dir: W. Farkas, 98 mins.)†

Prime Suspect (MTV 1982)*** Mike Farrell, Teri Garr, Veronica Cartwright, Lane Smith. Powerful exposé of media irresponsibility. Farrell is cast as a law-abiding citizen suddenly accused of sex murders and is practically convicted by TV coverage. (Dir: Noel Black, 104 mins.)†

Prime Target (MTV 1989)** Angie Dickinson, Joseph Bologna, David Soul, Yaphet Kotto, Joe Regelabuto, Charles Durning. Dickinson's back in uniform, this time as a tough New York police sergeant looking into the mysterious deaths of two other female officers. Farfetched plot, for Angie fans only. (Dir: Robert Collins, 96 mins.)

Primrose Path, The (1940)*** Ginger Rogers, Joel McCrea, Marjorie Rambeau, Miles Mander, Harry Travers. Strange little comedy-drama about a girl from the wrong side of the tracks who falls in love with an exceptionally honest young working man. (Dir: Gregory La Cava, 93 mins.)†

Prince and the Pauper, The (1937)***½ Errol Flynn, Claude Rains, Mauch Twins, Alan Hale, Henry Stephenson, Barton MacLane. Exciting, skillful adaptation of Mark Twain's story about a beggar who changes places with a prince. (Dir: William Keighley, 118 mins.)†

Prince and the Pauper, The (1978)—See: **Crossed Swords**

Prince and the Showgirl, The (Great Britain, 1957)*** Laurence Olivier, Marilyn Monroe, Sybil Thorndike, Jeremy Spencer, Richard Wattis. Romantic story of a Balkan prince and an American chorus girl in London at the time of the Coronation of King George V (1912). The plot is slight but the dialogue sprightly, the period setting interesting. (Dir: Laurence Olivier, 117 mins.)†

Prince of Bel Air, The (MTV 1986)** Mark Harmon, Kirstie Alley, Robert Vaughn, Patrick Laborteaux, Deborah Harmon. This attempt at a contemporary love story set in the swinging world of Bel Air, Calif., relies too heavily on the undeniable charm of its stars. Glib and superficial. The "R"-rated version on video contains a few extra scenes. (Dir: Charles Braverman, 96 mins.)†

Prince of Central Park, The (MTV 1977)*** T. J. Hargrave, Ruth Gordon, Lisa Richard, Marc Vahanian. A charming story about a 12-year-old boy and his younger sister, who run away from their foster home and take refuge in a tree house in Central Park. (Dir: Harvey Hart, 74 mins.)†

Prince of Darkness (1987)**½ Donald Pleasence, Jameson Parker, Victor Wong, Lisa Blount, Dennis Dun. John Carpenter's typically stylish direction brings a number of chills to the thin script he wrote under the pseudonym Martin Quartermass (a reference to the classic British sci-fi series). Pleasence plays a priest who calls in a physics professor friend and several of his graduate students to help stop the return of Satan via a canister of foul liquid. (100 mins.)†

Prince of Foxes (1949)*** Tyrone Power, Orson Welles, Wanda Hendrix, Everett Sloane. Atmospheric historical drama of a social-climbing artist who throws his lot in with Cesare Borgia, a Renaissance tyrant. (Dir: Henry King, 107 mins.)

Prince of Pennsylvania, The (1988)*½ Keanu Reeves, Fred Ward, Amy Madigan, Bonnie Bedelia, Demetria Mellot. Annoying comedy-drama about a self-infatuated teen scheming to straighten out hypocritical adults. (Dir: Ron Nyswaner, 93 mins.)†

Prince of Pirates (1953)** John Derek, Barbara Rush. Derek, Prince Roland of Hagen takes to the high seas of adventure to destroy the Spanish Armada. (Dir: Sidney Salkow, 80 mins.)

Prince of Players (1955)*** Richard Burton, Maggie McNamara, Raymond Massey, John Derek. An excellent performance by Burton in the role of famous Shakespearean actor Edwin Booth makes this uneven biography worthwhile. (Dir: Philip Dunne, 102 mins.)

Prince of the City (1981)*** Treat Williams, Jerry Orbach, Don Billett, Kenny Marino. Riveting true story about a narcotics cop who decides to reveal corruption. "*Prince*" is a detailed look at the process by which a man who starts out to redeem himself by revealing some truths, is drawn step-by-step into giving information about his police pals. (Dir: Sidney Lumet, 167 mins.)†

Princes in Exile (Canada, 1990)*** Zachary Ansley, Nicholas Shields, Stacie Mistysyn, Andrea Roth, Alexander Chapman, Chuck Shamanta. Sensitive and insightful drama, which isn't afraid to be witty, about a group of teens who attend a summer camp for children with cancer. Light years ahead of the typical "disease" movie. Filled with great performances and a love of life. (Dir: Giles Walker, 104 mins.)†

Princess Academy, The (1987)* Eva Gabor, Lu Leonard, Richard Paul, Carole Davis. Feeble teensploitation about schoolgirls playing pranks on one another in a posh finishing school in Switzerland. (Dir: Bruce Block, 90 mins.)†

Princess and the Cabbie, The (MTV 1981)** Valerie Bertinelli, Robert Desiderio, Cynthia Harris, Peter Donat, Shelley Long. Sincere, slow-moving tale revolves around a concerned, well-read cabbie who convinces a shy Ms. Bertinelli that she can become a "normal" person despite her dyslexia. (Dir: Glenn Jordan, 104 mins.)

Princess and the Pirate, The (1944)*** Bob Hope, Virginia Mayo, Walter Brennan, Victor McLaglen. Typical Bob Hope film which should please his legions of fans. This time out, he's caught up in the sinister machinations of the scourge of the seas—buccaneers! (Dir: David Butler, 94 mins.)†

Princess Bride, The (1987)*** Cary Elwes, Mandy Patinkin, Chris Sarandon, Christopher Guest, Wallace Shawn, André the Giant, Peter Falk, Carol Kane, Billy Crystal. An engaging fairy tale comedy which mixes romance, magic, and swashbuckling action. A young boy becomes enthralled with a fantasy story told to him by his grandfather, and he spends an entire day listening to the adventures of a hilarious group of heroes attempting to save a beautiful girl. (Dir: Rob Reiner, 100 mins.)†

Princess Comes Across, The (1936)*** Carole Lombard, Fred MacMurray, William Frawley. Adventures of a bogus princess as she travels aboard a luxury liner and gets involved in some amusing incidents with a few zany characters. (Dir: William K. Howard, 76 mins.)

Princess Daisy (MTV 1983)** Lindsay Wagner, Merete Van Kamp, Paul Michael Glaser, Robert Urich, Claudia Cardinale, Rupert Everett. This wallow in purple passions involves an indomitable heroine who survives her half brother's lust and the constraints of great wealth to rise to great heights that she discovers are meaningless without true love. (Dir: Waris Hussein, 200 mins.; 188 mins. on tape.)†

Princess of the Nile (1954)**½ Debra Paget, Jeffrey Hunter, Michael Rennie, Lee Van Cleef, Jack Elam. Campy melodrama about an Egyptian princess torn between several suitors, none of whom are remotely convincing as ancient Egyptians.

Only interesting for its unintentional humor. (Dir: Harmon Jones, 71 mins.)

Princess O'Rourke (1943)***½ Robert Cummings, Olivia de Havilland, Jane Wyman. A pleasant, diverting comedy about a guy who discovers his fianceé is a queen. (Dir: Norman Krasna, 94 mins.)

Princess Tam-Tam (France, 1935)*** Josephine Baker, Viviane Romance, Albert Prejean, Germaine Aussey. Charming musical, with extravagant production values, about an exotic maiden posing as an Indian princess who takes Paris by storm. A rare chance to see the bewitching Baker. (Dir: Edmond T. Greville, 77 mins.)†

Princess Yang Kwei Fei, The—See: **The Empress Yang Kwei Fei**

Prince Valiant (1954)*½ James Mason, Janet Leigh, Robert Wagner, Debra Paget, Sterling Hayden. It's colorful enough, with adequate period mounting, but the attempt to render a live-action comic strip is stilted. (Dir: Henry Hathaway, 100 mins.)

Prince Who Was a Thief, The (1951)** Tony Curtis, Piper Laurie. Typical Hollywood film about the plush pageantry of the Arabian Nights. (Dir: Rudolph Maté, 88 mins.)

Principal, The (1987)*½ Jim Belushi, Louis Gossett, Jr., Rae Dawn Chong, Michael Wright, Esai Morales. Overly familiar tale of a man who is dumped into the hell of an inner-city educational system where he thinks he can make a difference. Trite and violent. (Dir: Christopher Cain, 109 mins.)†

Prison (1988)**½ Lane Smith, Viggo Mortensen, Chelsea Field. The spirit of a wrongfully executed man causes mayhem at the prison where he died. Creepy atmosphere and genuine scares help hide the fact that the movie could use some trimming. (Dir: Renny Harlin, 102 mins.)†

Prisoner, The (Great Britain, 1955)***½ Alec Guinness, Jack Hawkins. A cardinal is imprisoned and relentlessly questioned by the police of a Communist state. An actor's show; Guinness and Hawkins display superb performances in this gripping topical drama. (Dir: Peter Glenville, 91 mins.)†

Prisoner of Second Avenue, The (1975)*½ Jack Lemmon, Anne Bancroft. Frantic serio-comedy about a man (Lemmon) who loses his job in an ad agency after twenty-two years. The Neil Simon play self-destructs on screen. (Dir: Melvin Frank, 99 mins.)†

Prisoner of Shark Island, The (1936)*** Warner Baxter, Gloria Stuart, John Carradine, Harry Carey. True story of the doctor who innocently set Booth's injured leg after the Lincoln assassination. The doctor was given a prejudiced trial and sent to Shark Island. Interesting film directed by John Ford. (94 mins.)

Prisoner of War (1954)** Ronald Reagan, Steve Forrest. Volunteering to get information on how American prisoners are being treated, an undercover agent suffers in a Korean P.O.W. camp. (Dir: Andrew Marton, 81 mins.)†

Prisoner of Zenda, The (1937)***½ Ronald Colman, Madeleine Carroll, Douglas Fairbanks, Jr., David Niven, C. Aubrey Smith, Mary Astor, Raymond Massey. The durable old melodrama of the king's double, who's called in to do an impersonation when the royal one is kidnapped. A swashbuckler to the core, done with great style, lavish production. Superior fun. (Dir: John Cromwell, 120 mins.)

Prisoner of Zenda, The (1952)*** Stewart Granger, James Mason, Deborah Kerr, Robert Coote. Remake of the Anthony Hope chestnut follows the '37 version scene by scene but lacks the panache of the earlier film. (Dir: Richard Thorpe, 100 mins.)†

Prisoner of Zenda, The (1979)**½ Peter Sellers, Lynne Frederick, Lionel Jeffries, Elke Sommer, Gregory Sierra. Remake #4 for this royal masquerade. Sellers's antics rise far above the material as he plays a number of different characters. (Dir: Richard Quine, 108 mins.)†

Prisoners of the Casbah (1953)**½ Gloria Grahame, Turhan Bey, Cesar Romero. Second-rate exotic melodrama about a princess escaping persecution with her gallant admirer. Colorful but trashy. (Dir: Richard Bare, 78 mins.)

Prisoners of the Lost Universe (MCTV 1983)*½ John Saxon, Richard Hatch, Kay Lenz. This *Star Wars* rip-off finds a Southern California TV personality and her comrade/adversary accidentally entering "another dimension." (Dir: Terry Marcel, 104 mins.)†

Prison for Children (MTV 1987)*** Betty Thomas, John Ritter, Raphael Sbarge, Kenny Ransom, Josh Brolin. An above-average crime statistics horror tale, TV-style, as an orphaned teen is sent to a real hellhole of a correctional facility. (Dir: Larry Peerce, 104 mins.)

Prison Ship—See: **Star Slammer: The Escape**

Prison Stories: Women on the Inside (MCTV 1990)*** Rachel Ticotin, Lolita Davidovich, Rae Dawn Chong, Annabella Sciorra. A truly memorable trio of hard-hitting stories set in women's prisons and a distinct departure from the generally campy approach to this genre. There's a great deal of profanity and the gritty situations smack of harsh realism. The first, "Esperanza," focuses on a young mother whose son changes from a loving kid to a streetwise punk. "Parole Board" features Davidovich as a woman serving a prison term for killing her abusive husband. "New Chicks" probably comes closest to depicting the claustrophobic existence and the social caste system that exists in prison. Sciorra and Chong are superb as new girls in the cell block. (Dirs: Donna Deitch, Joan Micklin Silver, Penelope Spheeris, 96 mins.)†

Prison Train (1938)**½ Fred Keating, Linda Winters, Clarence Muse, Faith Bacon, Alexander Leftwich. Taut chase thriller about a gangster being taken across country by train to Alcatraz. Savvy and fast paced. (Dir: Gordon Wiles, 66 mins.)

Private Affairs of Bel Ami, The (1947)*** George Sanders, Angela Lansbury, Ann Dvorak, Frances Dee, John Carradine. Witty, stringent telling of the Guy de Maupassant story of a charming, ruthless schemer and his victims. (Dir: Albert Lewin, 112 mins.)

Private Angelo (Great Britain, 1949)*** Peter Ustinov, Maria Denis. A cowardly private in the Italian army manages to pass himself off as a hero to his townspeople. Frequently delightful comedy, good fun. (Dirs: Peter Ustinov, Michael Anderson, 102 mins.)

Private Battle, A (MTV 1980)**½ Jack Warden, Anne Jackson, David Stockton. Real-life story of author Cornelius Ryan's four-year bout with cancer. (Dir: Robert Lewis, 104 mins.)

Private Benjamin (1980)**½ Goldie Hawn, Eileen Brennan, Armand Assante, Mary Kay Place. Hawn is engaging as a Jewish princess who ends up enlisting in the army, but the story rambles off. (Dir: Howard Zieff, 110 mins.)†

Private Buckaroo (1942)*½ Andrews Sisters, Harry James, Joe E. Lewis. Bigtime band is drafted, and everyone gets together to put on a camp show. (Dir: Edward Cline, 68 mins.)†

Private Conversations: On the Set of Death of a Salesman (1986)***½ Behind the scenes glimpse at the acclaimed production of Arthur Miller's classic play, starring Dustin Hoffman. (Dir: Christian Blackwood, 82 mins.)†

Private Eyes (1953)*** Bowery Boys, Rudy Lee. The Boys open the Eagle Eye Detective Agency after an accident gives Sach mind-reading ability. (Dir: Edward Bernds, 64 mins.)

Private Eyes, The (1980)** Don Knotts, Tim Conway, Bernard Fox. A silly detective spoof. After Lord and Lady Morley are killed in a suspicious accident, will their beautiful daughter be joining them? (Dir: Lang Elliott, 91 mins.)†

Private Files of J. Edgar Hoover, The (1978)**½ Broderick Crawford, José Ferrer, Michael Parks, Rip Torn, Ronee Blakley. Sensationalized look behind the scenes at Hoover, the FBI, and recent American history. Directed, produced, and written by Larry Cohen. (112 mins.)†

Private Function, A (Great Britain, 1985) ***½ Michael Palin, Maggie Smith, Denholm Elliott, Richard Griffiths. Laughfilled farce that suggests the best English comedies of the fifties. Palin and Smith star as a foot doctor and his social-climbing wife who kidnap a pig earmarked for the nuptials of Princess Elizabeth and Prince Philip in post-WWII England. (Dir: Malcolm Mowbray, 93 mins.)†

Private Hell 36 (1954)*** Ida Lupino, Howard Duff, Steve Cochran. Two detectives recover missing loot, turn greedy when they do. Suspenseful crime melodrama with some bright dialogue. (Dir: Don Siegel, 81 mins.)†

Private History of a Campaign That Failed, The (MTV 1981)*** Pat Hingle, Edward Herrmann, Harry Crosby. A successful dramatization of a Mark Twain essay that portrays the ignorance of war. A self-organized militia of teenage boys are provoked into killing an innocent man by a war-hungry veteran. The ghost of the victim returns years later to offer a soul-shattering "prayer" about the horrors of war. (Dir: Peter Hunt, 90 mins.)

Private Lessons (1981)**½ Sylvia Kristel, Eric Brown, Howard Hesseman, Pamela Bryant. A European housekeeper teaches teen Eric Brown about lovemaking. (Dir: Alan Myerson, 87 mins.)†

Private Life of Don Juan, The (Great Britain, 1935)** The last film made by Douglas Fairbanks, Sr., as he portrays the romantic rogue of legendary fame. Merle Oberon is featured. Slow, dull costume melodrama. (Dir: Alexander Korda, 100 mins.)†

Private Life of Henry VIII, The (Great Britain, 1933)***½ Charles Laughton, Wendy Barrie, Miles Mander. Laughton's impersonation of the great monarch is an immortal slice of ham, and director Alexander Korda's lush production showcases the star well. It's British "tradition of quality" near its apex. (97 mins.)†

Private Life of Sherlock Holmes, The (1970)*** Robert Stephens, Colin Blakely, Genevieve Page, Stanley Holloway, Clive Revill. A great deal of wit and polish went into this offbeat yarn about the famous detective, and the mystery takes a second place to the eccentricities of the principals involved. (Dir: Billy Wilder, 125 mins.)†

Private Lives (1931)***½ Norma Shearer, Robert Montgomery, Reginald Denny, Una Merkel. Americanizing Noël Coward's comedy works surprisingly well. Shearer is up to the repartee and works well with Montgomery. Deft direction from the normally plodding Sidney Franklin compounds the surprises. (84 mins.)

Private Lives of Adam and Eve, The (1960)* Mickey Rooney, Mamie Van Doren, Mel Tormé. Silly, tasteless film combining dream sequences set in Eden and present day melodrama. The cast is a strange assortment of singers turned actors, actors turned comics and comics turned actors, etc. (Dir: Albert Zugsmith, 87 mins.)

Private Lives of Elizabeth and Essex, The (1939)*** Bette Davis, Errol Flynn, Donald Crisp, Olivia de Havilland, Vincent Price. Davis turns in a shaded, detailed performance as Elizabeth I, and Flynn, though mismatched and miscast, keeps his aplomb as a dashing Essex. Michael Curtiz directs with considerable technical skill but not much sympathy for the material. (120 mins.)†

Private Navy of Sergeant O'Farrell, The (1968)* Bob Hope, Phyllis Diller, Jeffrey Hunter, Gina Lollobrigida. Bob bungling his way through World War II in the Pacific. (Dir: Frank Tashlin, 92 mins.)

Private Number (1936)**½ Robert Taylor, Loretta Young, Basil Rathbone. Corny story of a secret marriage between a housemaid and her boss's son. (Dir: Roy Del Ruth, 80 mins.)

Private Parts (1972)*** Ayn Ruymen, Lucille Benson, Laurie Main. Teenage girl runs away from home and goes to live with her neurotic aunt. There are some genuinely surprising twists and scares. (Dir: Paul Bartel, 87 mins.)

Private Potter (Great Britain, 1962)**½ Tom Courtenay, Mogens Wieth, James Maxwell. Young soldier (Courtenay) defends himself from the charge of cowardice by claiming he saw a vision of God while on patrol. A bizarre thriller. (Dir: Caspar Wrede, 90 mins.)

Private Practices (1986)*** An enlightening documentary about a sex surrogate, a woman who helps men overcome their sexual inadequacies. (Dir: Kirby Dick, 75 mins.)†

Private Property (1960)** Corey Allen, Warren Oates, Kate Manx. Two drifters step into the life of a beautiful, neglected housewife; slow-paced sex and seduction, which explode in a violent finale. (Dir: Leslie Stevens, 79 mins.)

Private Resort (1985)½ Johnny Depp, Karyn O'Bryan, Rob Morrow, Emily Longstreth. On their Miami vacation at a luxury hotel, two randy guys pursue every woman in sight when not being undermined by a hotel thief and a house detective. (Dir: George Bowers, 83 mins.)†

Private's Affair, A (1959)** Sal Mineo, Christine Carere, Barbara Eden, Gary Crosby, Terry Moore, Jim Backus. Four draftees and their girlfriends are tapped for a big army show, but complications interfere. (Dir: Raoul Walsh, 92 mins.)

Private School (1983)* Phoebe Cates, Betsy Russell, Kathleen Wilhoite, Matthew Modine, Ray Walston, Sylvia Kristel. Pretty much rock-bottom; boys from a private school try to break into the neighboring girls' school. (Dir: Noel Black, 97 mins.)†

Private Sessions (MTV 1985)**½ Mike Farrell, Maureen Stapleton, Kelly McGillis, Tom Bosley, Greg Evigan. Farrell stars as a psychotherapist in New York who believes in a more personal approach to solving his patients' problems. Intriguing low-key drama. (Dir: Michael Pressman, 104 mins.)

Privates on Parade (Great Britain, 1984)*** John Cleese, Denis Quilley, Nicola Pagett. British stage smash, about a troupe of vaudevillians performing for soldiers fighting Communists in post-WWII Singapore, comes to the screen in fine form. A clever black comedy with music. (Dir: Michael Blakemore, 95 mins.)†

Private's Progress (Great Britain, 1956)***½ Dennis Price, Ian Carmichael, Terry-Thomas, Richard Attenborough. An earnest but stumbling young man is called into the army, where he makes a mess of things. Often hilariously funny. (Dir: John Boulting, 97 mins.)

Private War of Major Benson, The (1955)*** Charlton Heston, Julie Adams, Tim Hovey, Sal Mineo. Hard-bitten army officer is forced to accept a transfer to a military school as commanding officer. Enjoyable if a bit prolonged comedy is a welcome change of pace for Heston; good share of chuckles. (Dir: Jerry Hopper, 105 mins.)

Private Worlds (1935)**½ Claudette Colbert, Charles Boyer, Joel McCrea, Joan Bennett. Story of intrigue in a mental hospital is antiquated but might interest those who like modern psychiatric stories. (Dir: Gregory La Cava, 84 mins.)

Privilege (Great Britain, 1967)**½ Paul Jones, Jean Shrimpton. Vintage hysteria about how media packaging of rock stars turns them into near-religious figures with substantial potential for political influence. (Dir: Peter Watkins, 101 mins.)

Privilege (1990)** Alice Spivak, Novella Nelson, Blaire Baron. Arty, socially conscious, semidocumentary about women's experience of menopause. Good idea unfortunately marred by trendy preachiness. (Dir: Yvonne Rainer, 103 mins.)

Prize, The (1963)**½ Paul Newman, Elke Sommer, Edward G. Robinson. Writer in Stockholm to accept the Nobel Prize becomes involved in a spy plot to kidnap a scientist. Overlong thriller tries for the Hitchcock touch, only occasionally succeeds. (Dir: Mark Robson, 136 mins.)

Prize Fighter, The (1979)** Tim Conway, Don Knotts, David Wayne. Dopey, broad comedy about boxing business hokum in the '30s. (Dir: Michael Preece, 99 mins.)†

Prizefighter and the Lady, The (1933)**½ Max Baer, Myrna Loy, Jack Dempsey, Walter Huston. This picture was made to cash in on Baer's popularity after he floored Max Schmeling. Surprise was that Baer could act, and the film is reasonably entertaining. (Dir: W. S. Van Dyke, 103 mins.)

Prize of Arms, A (Great Britain, 1962)*** Stanley Baker, Tom Bell, Helmut Schmid. A band of men attempt to rob an army payroll in a seemingly perfect crime that goes astray. Suspenseful, well acted. (Dir: Cliff Owen, 105 mins.)

Prize of Gold, A (Great Britain, 1955)*** Richard Widmark, Mai Zetterling. An exciting drama set in occupied Berlin concerning a fabulous scheme to steal a shipment of gold bullion from the Berlin airlift. (Dir: Mark Robson, 98 mins.)

Prizzi's Honor (1985)**** Jack Nicholson, Kathleen Turner, Anjelica Huston, William Hickey, John Randolph, Lee Richardson, Robert Loggia. If you turned the *Godfather* films upside down and turned a Tracy-Hepburn comedy inside out and then cross-pollinated them, you might end up with something as original and inspired as this tale of a hit man who falls hard for a cool beauty whose talents include ripping off casinos and four contract killings a year. Among those putting the Prizzi family's mafia honor at stake are Nicholson and Turner as the murderous lovers, Hickey as an emaciated paisan of Brando's Don Corleone and the magnificent Huston as a lady scorned who stalks the mob turf looking deceptively like a Madonna envisioned by Modigliani. The entire cast is perfection. (Dir: John Huston, 129 mins.)†

Probe (MTV 1971)*½ Hugh O'Brian, Elke Sommer, Burgess Meredith, John Gielgud. Pilot for the defunct series has O'Brian playing a private eye backed by many modernistic devices. (Dir: Russell Mayberry, 100 mins.)

Probe (MTV 1988)*½ Parker Stevenson, Ashley Crow, Jon Cypher. Dull pilot for the series about a scientific whiz kid and his perky secretary. Here they're pitted against a megacomputer that's fouling up various city utilities. (Dir: Sandor Stern, 96 mins.)

Problem Child (1990)*½ John Ritter, Amy Yasbeck, Jack Warden, Michael Oliver, Michael Richards, Gilbert Gottfried. An obnoxious brat, the quintessential child from hell (even orphanages don't want him) is adopted by a yuppie couple. The comedy is tasteless and cruel. You wouldn't let your own kid torture the cat; why watch this one do it? (Dir: Dennis Dugan, 81 mins.)†

Prodigal, The (1955)*½ Lana Turner, Edmund Purdom. Draggy epic—it's 70 B.C. folks, and that wicked high priestess Lana is making it rough all over. (Dir: Richard Thorpe, 114 mins.)

Producers, The (1968)***½ Zero Mostel, Gene Wilder, Dick Shawn, Estelle Winwood. A preposterous, often wildly funny tale about an impoverished Broadway theater producer who stages a ghastly play in the hopes of making his fortune by selling more than 100% of the show to investors. Conceived, written, and directed by Mel Brooks. The show within a show is called *Springtime for Hitler*. Wilder's flawless performance as Mostel's nervous henchman earned him an Academy Award nomination. Shawn playing Hitler is very funny too, once you accept the premise of this lunacy, which earned Brooks an Academy Award for his screenplay. (88 mins.)†

Professionals, The (1966)***½ Burt Lancaster, Lee Marvin, Claudia Cardinale, Jack Palance, Robert Ryan, Ralph Bellamy. Splendid, rip-snorting, old-fashioned adventure yarn, circa 1917. The plot has Bellamy hiring our he-men to fetch his allegedly kidnapped wife back from Mexico where she has been taken by bandito Palance. (Dir: Richard Brooks, 117 mins.)†

Professional Soldier (1936)**½ Victor McLaglen, Freddie Bartholomew. Tale of a retired colonel who is paid to kidnap the youthful king of a mythical European country had a lot of potential, but it didn't come off. (Dir: Tay Garnett, 78 mins.)

Professional Sweetheart (1933)** Ginger Rogers, ZaSu Pitts, Norman Foster, Frank McHugh, Edgar Kennedy, Betty Furness, Gregory Ratoff, Franklin Pangborn, Sterling Holloway. Amateurish spoof of radio shows and the stunts used to promote them. (Dir: William A. Seiter, 68 mins.)

Professor Beware (1938)**½ Harold Lloyd, Phyllis Welch, Lionel Stander. It's all Mr. Lloyd and very little script in this silly comedy about a professor trying to unravel a 3000-year-old love story that meets its modern counterpart. (Dir: Elliott Nugent, 93 mins.)

Programmed to Kill (1986)**½ Sandahl Bergman, Robert Ginty, Louise Caire Clark, Peter Bromilow. U.S. scientists resurrect fatally injured terrorist Bergman as a cyborg, but the experiment soon goes bad and she turns on her creators. Slow going at first, picks up steam when the rampaging Bergman becomes a Tina Terminator. (Dirs: Allan Holzman, Robert Short, 91 mins.)†

Projectionist, The (1971)**** Chuck McCann, Ina Balin, Rodney Dangerfield. Wacky, appealing, low-budget winner written, directed, produced, and edited by Harry Hurwitz. McCann plays Captain Flash, with impersonations along the way of Bogart, Beery, and Oliver Hardy. The projectionist works in a movie house and has difficulty separating the real world from the movie world. (88 mins.)†

Project: Kill (1977)*½ Leslie Nielsen, Gary Lockwood. A government man in a CIA-like agency makes a mysterious exit and is hunted down by his ex-partner. (Dir: William Girdler, 104 mins.)†

Project Moonbase (1953)½ Ross Ford, Hayden Rorke, Barbara Morrison, Larry Johns, Donna Martell. Laughable relic about space travel that's riddled with anti-Communist sentiment and chauvinistic attitudes about women. (Dir: Richard Talmadge, 63 mins.)

Project M-7 (Great Britain, 1953)*** Phyllis Calvert, James Donald, Herbert Lom. At a secret research station, an inventor is designing a plane that will fly at fantastic speeds. One of his colleagues is a spy. (Dir: Anthony Asquith, 79 mins.)

Project X (1987)*** Matthew Broderick, Helen Hunt, Bill Sadler, Johnny Ray McGhee, Jonathan Stark, Robin Gammell. A solid, commercial suspense film about an Air Force pilot involved in top secret military training and enmeshed in a surprising adventure involving a chimpanzee who can communicate in sign language. (Dir: Jonathan Kaplan, 107 mins.)†

Promise (MTV 1986)***½ James Garner, James Woods, Piper Laurie, Peter Michael Goetz. Probing drama about familial responsibility. Garner portrays a happy-go-lucky bachelor who has to change his lifestyle when he takes on the responsibility of his younger schizophrenic brother after the death of their mother. Garner is superb as the man forced to mature when his life is disrupted; Woods is mesmerizing as the disturbed brother who is helpless but never pathetic. (Dir: Glenn Jordan, 104 mins.)

Promise, A (Japan, 1986)*** Rentaro Mikuni, Sachiko Murase, Choichiro Kawarazaki. Meditative study of euthanasia as seen through the eyes of a Japanese family whose aged mother has been mercy-killed by an unidentified member of the household, an act which rips the clan apart. A stirring and emotional film which examines human dignity and tough choices. (Dir: Yoshishige Yoshida, 123 mins.)

Promise, The (1978)** Kathleen Quinlan, Stephen Collins, Beatrice Straight. Clumsy, old-fashioned soap opera. Young Collins and Quinlan are in love, but his tough-minded mother, Straight, objects.

A convenient auto accident gives Straight the chance to tell her son that Quinlan is dead. They meet again, but he doesn't recognize her, since she's had plastic surgery. (Dir: Gilbert Cates, 97 mins.)

Promise at Dawn (U.S.-France, 1970)**½ Melina Mercouri, Assaf Dayan, Francois Raffoul, Despo. Entertaining melodrama, based on Romain Gary's remembrances of life with Mother. Mama was a larger-than-life actress who provides young Romain with a globe-trotting upbringing. If only Mercouri didn't ham it up until you want to put her in restraints. (Dir: Jules Dassin, 101 mins.)

Promised a Miracle (MTV 1988)*** Rosanna Arquette, Judge Reinhold, Tom Bower, Vonni Ribisi. Arquette and Reinhold effectively shed their lighthearted comic personas with this disturbing teledrama about two misguided parents who listened to their friends and neighbors and stopped giving their diabetic son insulin, believing he had been divinely healed. Based on real events, this serves as a shocking argument against blind faith, particularly in the sequence where the couple believe their dead child will become a modern-day Lazarus. (Dir: Stephen Gyllenhaal, 96 mins.)

Promised Land (1988)**½ Jason Gedrick, Kiefer Sutherland, Meg Ryan, Tracy Pollan. Downbeat teen drama follows a small-town misfit whose return home two years after high school graduation sparks problems and revelations. (Dir: Michael Hoffman, 101 mins.)

Promise Her Anything (1966)**½ Warren Beatty, Lionel Stander, Robert Cummings, Hermione Gingold, Keenan Wynn, Leslie Caron. Pleasant romantic comedy. Beatty plays a destitute young filmmaker who sets out to woo and win a young widow (Caron). (Dir: Arthur Hiller, 98 mins.)

Promise Him Anything (MTV 1975)* Frederic Forrest, Meg Foster, Eddie Albert, Tom Ewell. Inane story about computer dating. The twist here is that the man sues the woman in small-claims court for breach of contract when she refuses to deliver the "anything goes" promised on her computer application card. (Dir: Edward Parone, 72 mins.)

Promise of Love, The (MTV 1980)*½ Valerie Bertinelli. Bertinelli plays a frightened 28-year-old Vietnam War widow, untrained for much of anything. Earnest, and tedious. (Dir: Don Taylor, 104 mins.)

Promises In the Dark (1979)**½ Kathleen Beller, Marsha Mason, Ned Beatty. A young girl (Beller) is helped to confront her dying of cancer by an understanding doctor (Mason). Good intentions almost carry it through. (Dir: Jerome Hellman, 115 mins.)†

Promises, Promises (1963)* Jayne Mansfield, Marie McDonald, Mickey Hargitay, Tommy Noonan, Fritz Feld, T. C. Jones. Tedious shipboard comedy; the hackneyed plotline involves two couples who can't figure out who impregnated whom. (Dir: King Donovan, 75 mins.)†

Promises to Keep (MTV 1985)*½ Robert Mitchum, Christopher Mitchum, Bentley Mitchum, Tess Harper, Claire Bloom. Three generations of Mitchums star together in a story about a father-son-grandson relationship. A turgid melodrama about a man coming to terms with leaving his wife and kid thirty years ago. (Dir: Noel Black, 104 mins.)

Promise to Keep, A (MTV 1990)**½ Dana Delany, William Russ. If you think you've got trouble as a harassed parent, watch Delany and Russ play a couple with three children who become saddled with four more boys after death strikes relatives. The drama is about parents giving until it hurts. (Dir: Rod Holcomb, 96 mins.)

Prom Night (1980)**½ Jamie Lee Curtis, Leslie Nielsen, Casey Stevens, Antoinette Bower, Eddie Benton, Michael Tough. This entry in the cut-and-slash genre about a mad killer (what else?) stalking the students of Hamilton High is no *Carrie*, but it's better than most of its kind. (Dir: Paul Lynch, 91 mins.)†

Prom Night II—See: **Hello Mary Lou: Prom Night II**

Prom Night III: The Last Kiss (Canada, 1990)* Tim Conlon, Cyndy Preston, Courtney Taylor, David Stratton. Routine horror sequel; murdered prom queen Mary Lou Mahoney returns. (Dirs: Ron Oliver, Peter Simpson, 95 mins.)†

Promoter, The (Great Britain, 1952)***½ Alec Guinness, Valerie Hobson, Glynis Johns, Petula Clark. Guinness romps his way through the tale of a lad from the slums who pushes his way to success. Witty, always intelligent, always entertaining. (Dir: Ronald Neame, 88 mins.)

Prophecy (1979)*½ Talia Shire, Robert Foxworth, Armand Assante. Industrial pollution has somehow created a mutant monster, and visiting scientists discover that there are some things that man was not meant to tamper with. (Dir: John Frankenheimer, 100 mins.)†

Protector, The (1985)** Jackie Chan, Danny Aiello, Kim Bass, Roy Chiao. Two coppers, one dumpy and flat-footed, one wiry and fleet-footed, run afoul of a drug syndicate and fight back. For Chan fans (Jackie, not Charlie). (Dir: James Glickenhaus, 94 mins.)†

Protocol (1984)**½ Goldie Hawn, Chris Sarandon, Richard Romanus, Gail Strickland, Andre Gregory, Cliff De Young. Semi-sunny entertainment from Goldie as a cocktail waitress who gets involved in international politics. After saving the life of a Mideast potentate, Hawn proves useful in helping Uncle Sam set up a military base, but ends up giving cold-hearted U.S. officials a democracy lesson. (Dir: Herbert Ross, 96 mins.)†

Prototype (MTV 1983)*** Christopher Plummer, David Morse. Better than average sci-fi film about a distrustful scientist who won't hand over his robot to the Pentagon. An offbeat, often entertaining yarn about scientists who worry about government use of their discoveries. (Dir: David Greene, 104 mins.)†

Proud and the Beautiful, The (France, 1957)***½ Gérard Philipe, Michele Morgan. While her husband is a victim of the plague in Mexico, a woman falls for and revitalizes a drunken doctor. (Dir: Yves Allegret, 94 mins.)

Proud and the Profane, The (1956)*** William Holden, Deborah Kerr, Thelma Ritter. War and soap opera, but well mixed to form a reasonably entertaining film. It's the story of a war widow who meets and falls for a tough Marine colonel while serving in the Pacific during WWII. (Dir: George Seaton, 111 mins.)

Proud Men (MTV 1987)*½ Charlton Heston, Peter Strauss, Nan Martin. Old granite-jaw Heston stars in this predictable generation gap story as a dying, conservative rancher who's reunited with his son (Strauss) who went AWOL in Vietnam. (Dir: William Graham, 96 mins.)

Proud Ones, The (1956)*** Robert Ryan, Virginia Mayo, Jeffrey Hunter. Good western centers around a gun-toting marshal and the men who tried to break the law. (Dir: Robert D. Webb, 94 mins.)

Proud Ones, The (France, 1980)*** Jacques Dufilho, Bernadette Lesache, François Cluzet, Ronan Hubert, Arnel Hubert. Director Claude Chabrol moved away from his usual thrillers with this dramatic study of a village in the Breton region of France, and the effect the time and tide of 20th-century history have on its people. AKA: **The Horse of Pride**. (118 mins.)†

Proud Rebel, The (1958)*** Alan Ladd, Olivia de Havilland, David Ladd (debut), Dean Jagger. Touching story of a Civil War veteran and his mute son who go to work for a farm woman as the father hopes to find a doctor who can cure the boy's affliction. Superior family entertainment. (Dir: Michael Curtiz, 103 mins.)†

Proud Valley, The (Great Britain, 1940)*** Paul Robeson, Edward Chapman, Simon Lack, Rachel Thomas, Clifford Evans. One of Robeson's best vehicles; he is a roving merchant seaman who settles down in a Welsh coal-mining village. Robeson sings Handel's "Elijah" and the spiritual "Deep River," backed by a Welsh choir. (Dir: Pen Tennyson, 72 mins.)

Providence (France-Great Britain-Switzerland, 1977)** Dirk Bogarde, John Gielgud, Ellen Burstyn, David Warner, Elaine Stritch. On his deathbed, a crusty old writer composes his final novel in his head. Tossing and turning at night, he visualizes his masterpiece using characters based on his family members. The complicated structure doesn't help matters, because the international cast all act in different styles. (Dir: Alain Resnais, 104 mins.)†

Provincial Actors (Poland, 1979)*** Halina Labonarska, Tadeusz Huk, Iwona Biernacka. Freewheeling story about the backstage problems of a theatrical troupe. The artifices of the theater are deftly transferred to the screen in this engaging, intelligent, often witty film. (Dir: Agnieszka Holland, 121 mins.)

Provoked (1989)** Cindy Maranne, McKeiver Jones 3rd, Sharon Blair, Bob Fall, Phyllis Durant, Ona Sims. Excons take over a building, threatening to kill its occupants unless the city meets their demands. Ex-TV wrestling star Maranne blows away the bad guys in this acceptable action feature. (Dir: Rick Pamplin, 88 mins.)†

Prowler, The (1951)*** Van Heflin, Evelyn Keyes. Patrolman investigating a prowler falls for a disc jockey's wife, plans to do away with him. Strong, gripping melodrama, excellently acted. (Dir: Joseph Losey, 92 mins.)

Prowler, The (1981)* Farley Granger, Vicki Dawson, Christopher Goutman, Cindy Weintraub. A creepy, unappetizing horror film in which a WWII veteran may be on the prowl for more murder thirty-five years after his original crime. Excessively gory. (Dir: Joseph Zito, 88 mins.)†

Prudence and the Pill (1968)* David Niven, Deborah Kerr, Keith Michell. Sleazy, witless comedy about birth control which fizzles long before the fadeout. (Dirs: Fielder Cook, Ronald Neame, 98 mins.)

Psyche 59 (Great Britain, 1964)** Patricia Neal, Curt Jurgens, Samantha Eggar. Blind wife suspects there's something fishy between her husband and her sexy younger sister, and by golly, she's right. Lumbering drama seldom gets out of low gear. (Dir: Alexander Singer, 94 mins.)

Psychiatrist: God Bless the Children, The (MTV 1970)**½ Roy Thinnes, Pete Duel, Barry Brown, Luther Adler. Thinnes stars as a psychiatrist who really cares about his patients. (Dir: Daryl Duke, 98 mins.)

Psychic, The (1968)½ Dick Genola, Robin Guest, Bobbi Spencer. Unintentionally funny tale of an ad exec who gains psychic powers after he falls off a ladder.

AKA: **Copenhagen's Psychic Loves.** (Dir: James F. Hurley, 90 mins.)†

Psychic Killer (1975)* Jim Hutton, Paul Burke, Julie Adams, Nehemiah Persoff, Neville Brand, Aldo Ray, Della Reese. Hutton has the power to kill his enemies over long distances in this *Psycho* rip-off that you'll want to keep a distance from. (Dir: Raymond Danton, 90 mins.)†

Psycho (1960)**** Anthony Perkins, Janet Leigh, Simon Oakland, John Anderson, Vera Miles, Martin Balsam, John Gavin, John McIntire. Alfred Hitchcock's macabre masterpiece broke all of the existing rules for horror films and filmmakers, set the standard for a generation of new ones, and kept uncounted masses out of their showers. Today, it remains unexcelled in its brilliant manipulation of audience expectations. Leigh plays a young secretary who embezzles money from her firm and heads west, only to find an unexpected brand of justice meted out at the lonely Bates Motel. Score by Bernard Herrmann. (109 mins.)†

Psycho II (1983)**½ Anthony Perkins, Vera Miles, Meg Tilly, Dennis Franz, Robert Loggia. A well-acted successor to Alfred Hitchcock's 1960 classic. Perkins and Miles reprise their original roles in this ingeniously plotted but not especially scary thriller. (Dir: Richard Franklin, 113 mins.)†

Psycho III (1986)**½ Anthony Perkins, Diana Scarwid, Jeff Fahey, Roberta Maxwell. This time, Perkins directs as well as playing Norman Bates. This sequel, in which Bates falls in love with a runaway nun (Scarwid), is aided immeasurably by self-conscious black humor, though the explicit gore (added by the studio) is gratuitous. (94 mins.)†

Psycho IV: The Beginning (MCTV 1990)** Anthony Perkins, Olivia Hussey, Henry Thomas, C.C.H. Pounder. Promising but ultimately disappointing prequel to *Psycho*. A late night radio talk show host (Pounder) delving into the topic of matricide throws Norman Bates (Perkins) off the deep end once again. Through flashbacks we get to see how a young Norman (Thomas) became psychologically twisted by his sexually dominating mother (Hussey). There are clever sparks of ingenuity as writer Joseph Stefano, who penned the original screenplay, fleshes out characters and situations only touched upon in 1960. However, the gimmick of using Bernard Herrmann's classic score backfires since it reminds viewers that they might be better off watching Hitchcock's terrifying masterpiece instead. (Dir: Mick Garris, 96 mins.)†

Psycho-Circus—See: **Circus of Fear**

Psycho Girls (1986)**½ John Haslett Cuff, Darlene Mignacco. Die-hard horror fans will enjoy this none-too-serious tale of a writer whose party goes awry when an uninvited guest takes over and introduces some unpleasant games. (Dir: Gerard Ciccoritti, 89 mins.)†

Psychomania (1963)*½ Lee Philips, Shepperd Strudwick, Dick Van Patten, Sylvia Miles, James Farentino. Contrived murder-mystery that tries to be both arty and commercial, achieving neither. (Dir: Richard Hilliard, 90 mins.)†

Psychomania (Great Britain, 1971)** George Sanders, Nicky Henson, Mary Larkin, Beryl Reid. A horror pic about a Hell's Angel type who comes back from the dead, invincible. Never a dull or comprehensible minute in this Faust-on-wheels. (Dir: Don Sharp, 95 mins.)†

Psychopath, The (Great Britain, 1966)** Patrick Wymark, Margaret Johnston. Competent British cast goes through the paces in this tale about multiple murder and a strange German household. (Dir: Freddie Francis, 83 mins.)

Psychos in Love (1987)* Carmine Capobianco, Debi Thibeault, Frank Stewart. Infuriatingly smirky gore-film parody about two psychotic murderers who fall in love and move in together. Cheaplooking and full of unfunny "in" jokes (Dir: Gorman Bechard, 87 mins.)†

Psych-Out (1968)**½ Susan Strasberg, Jack Nicholson, Adam Roarke, Dean Stockwell, Bruce Dern, Henry Jaglom. A deaf runaway searches for her brother and runs into low-lifes in San Francisco. Fairly interesting glimpse of the drug culture of the period. (Dir: Richard Rush, 82 mins.)

PT 109 (1963)**½ Cliff Robertson, Ty Hardin, Robert Culp. The story of John F. Kennedy, naval hero of WWII, and his exploits in the Pacific. (Dir: Leslie Martinson, 140 mins.)†

Puberty Blues (Australia, 1983)** Nell Scofield, Jad Capelja, Geoff Rhoe, Tony Hughes. Teenagers will be teenagers, even in Australia. In portraying the universality of teenage sexuality, the director ignores specifics which might make his characters seem more affecting. (Dir: Bruce Beresford, 87 mins.)†

Public Affair, A (1962)*** Myron McCormick, Edward Binns, Judson Pratt, Jacqueline Loughery, Paul Birch, Harry Carey, Jr. Unusual drama of a California state senator working within the system to clean up crooked collection agency practices. (Dir: Bernard Girard, 75 mins.)

Public Enemy (1931)***½ James Cagney, Jean Harlow, Joan Blondell, Beryl Mercer, Mae Clarke. A classic with Cagney exploding onscreen with his kinetic Irish gangster portrayal. A dynamite opus —and catch that famous "grapefruit" scene. (Dir: William A. Wellman, 84 mins.)†

Public Enemy's Wife (1936)*** Pat O'Brien,

Margaret Lindsay, Robert Armstrong, Cesar Romero, Dick Foran. An insanely jealous killer breaks out of prison to make sure his wife is faithful; the FBI enlists her help in catching him. Gritty thriller. (Dir: Nick Grinde, 65 mins.)

Public Eye, The (Great Britain, 1972)*½ Mia Farrow, Topol, Michael Jayston. Thinly plotted yarn about a stuffy English aristocrat who hires a Greek private detective to see if his wife is having an affair. (Dir: Carol Reed, 95 mins.)

Public Hero No. 1 (1935)*** Lionel Barrymore, Jean Arthur, Chester Morris. Exciting, occasionally amusing drama of the destruction of a gang of outlaws by the then movie favorites, the G-men. (Dir: J. Walter Rubin, 91 mins.)

Public Pigeon No. 1 (1956)** Red Skelton, Vivian Blaine, Janet Blair. Mild comedy. Lunchroom counter man is taken in by a gang of crooks, but he turns the tables on them. (Dir: Norman Z. McLeod, 79 mins.)

Pueblo (MTV 1973)***½ Hal Holbrook. Absorbing dramatization of the seizure in 1968 by the North Koreans of the U.S.S. *Pueblo*, an American naval vessel equipped with electronic devices used in spying missions. (Dir: Anthony Page, 108 mins.)

Pulp (Great Britain, 1972)**½ Michael Caine, Mickey Rooney, Lionel Stander. Occasionally amusing satire; a writer of cheap detective thrillers is caught up in the reality of one of his fantasies. (Dir: Mike Hodges, 92 mins.)†

Pulse (1988)*** Cliff De Young, Roxanne Hart, Joey Lawrence. Intriguing thriller that plays to modern paranoia, about an L.A. couple whose household appliances seem to be taking on minds of their own. Writer-director Paul Golding builds the premise plausibly, leading up to an exciting finale. (91 mins.)†

Pumping Iron (1977)*** Arnold Schwarzenegger, Louis Ferrigno, Mike Katz, Franco Colombu. A fascinating documentary about world-champion bodybuilders. One of the many strengths is that the directors, George Butler and Robert Fiore, have avoided the considerable temptation of making bodybuilding and those dedicated to it seem altogether grotesque. (85 mins.)†

Pumping Iron 2 (1985)** Lori Bowen, Varla Dunlap, Bev Francis, Rachel McLish. The unusual world of female bodybuilders could have been approached from several viewpoints, but this film never shakes off the aura of a freak show that permeates throughout. (Dir: George Butler, 107 mins.)†

Pumpkin Eater, The (Great Britain, 1964) ***½ Anne Bancroft, Peter Finch, James Mason. Absorbing, brilliantly acted story of a woman's personal insecurity and her crumbling marriage. Screenplay by Harold Pinter, from the novel by Penelope Mortimer. (Dir: Jack Clayton, 110 mins.)

Pumpkinhead (1987)**½ Lance Henriksen, John DiAquino, Kerry Remsen. Backwoods father conjures up an ancient monster to avenge the murder of his son by a motorcycle gang. (Dir: Stan Winston, 86 mins.)†

Pump Up the Volume (1990)**½ Christian Slater, Scott Paulin, Ellen Greene, Samantha Mathis, Chris Jacobs, Annie Ross, Mimi Kennedy, Cheryl Pollak, Seth Green, Ahment Zappa, Billy Morrissette, Lala. One of the better teen angst movies. Well acted if uneven story of a high school student who starts his own pirate radio station to help his friends make it through the night with forbidden music and sage advice on growing up. (Dir: Allan Moyle, 105 mins.)†

Punch and Jody (MTV 1974)** Glenn Ford, Ruth Roman, Pam Griffin. Glenn Ford is a self-made, small-time circus boss who is suddenly made the guardian of a teenaged daughter he didn't know existed. (Dir: Barry Shear, 74 mins.)

Punchline (1988)** Sally Field, Tom Hanks, John Goodman, Mark Rydell, Kim Greist, Paul Mazursky, Taylor Negron. Lengthy and very grating exploration of the complicated lives led by stand-up comedians. Field plays a housewife with strong comic aspirations; Hanks is her abrasive mentor and would-be lover. (Dir: David Seltzer, 123 mins.)†

Punishment Park (1971)*** Paul Alelyanes, Carmen Argenziano, Stan Armsted. Surreal, frightening film takes the form of a futuristic television show in which war protestors participate in a grueling, deadly game. From the director of *The War Game*. (Dir: Peter Watkins, 88 mins.)

Punk Vacation (1987)*½ Sandra Bogan, Stephen Falchi, Roxanne Rogers, Don Martin. Mohawked motorcycle mamas terrorize a small town. (Dir: Stanley Lewis, 88 mins.)†

Puppet Master (1989)**½ Paul Le Mat, Irene Miracle, Matt Roe, William Hickey, Barbara Crampton. Horror tale of a group of psychics brought to a spooky old hotel; atmospheric if farfetched. (Dir: David Schmoeller, 90 mins.)†

Puppet Master II (1990)**½ Elizabeth MacClellan, Collin Bernsen, Charlie Spradling, Steve Welles, Nita Talbot. Clever sequel sports excellent David Allen stop-motion special effects. Allen also directs this time out as a group of psychic researchers are once again picked off by the feisty, fiendish puppets in a deserted hotel. (Dir: David Allen, 88 mins.)†

Puppet on a Chain (Great Britain, 1970)** Sven-Bertil Taube, Barbara Parkins, Alexander Knox. Routine international smuggling entry, about an American narcotics agent tracking down his prey in Amsterdam. (Dir: Geoffrey Reeve, 97 mins.)†

Purchase Price, The (1931)*** Barbara Stanwyck, George Brent, Leila Bennett, Lyle Talbot, Hardie Albright, Anne Shirley. Humorous drama of a bootlegger's moll who becomes the mail-order bride of a midwestern farmer. Director William Wellman is characteristically candid about life in the fast lane *and* life in the country. (70 mins.)

Pure Hell of St. Trinian's, The (Great Britain, 1960)**½ Joyce Grenfell, Cecil Parker, George Cole. Girls' school full of mischievous lovelies receives a visit from an Eastern potentate with an eye out for harem wives. (Dir: Frank Launder, 94 mins.)

Purgatory (1988)½ Tanya Roberts, Julie Pop, Hal Orlandini. Sleazier than usual women's prison movie, set in an unnamed African country. (Dir: Ami Artzi, 93 mins.)†

Purlie Victorious—See: **Gone Are the Days**

Purple Gang, The (1959)** Barry Sullivan, Robert Blake. Barry Sullivan represents the law and a group, known as the Purples, make his job a tough one. Blake is very effective as a young hood with a taste for killing. (Dir: Frank McDonald, 85 mins.)

Purple Haze (1983)*½ Peter Nelson, Chuck McQuary. The 1960s are recreated in painstaking detail, but this shaggy-hippie story about two college dropouts is rather er déjà-vu material. (Dir: David Burton Morris, 97 mins.)

Purple Heart, The (1944)*** Dana Andrews, Richard Conte, Farley Granger, Sam Levene, Richard Loo. Powerful, brutal story of the trial of an American crew shot down by the Japanese during the Tokyo Raid. (Dir: Lewis Milestone, 99 mins.)†

Purple Hearts (1984)** Cheryl Ladd, Ken Wahl, Stephen Lee. A Harlequin romance about a handsome doctor and wistful nurse falling in love during the Vietnam War. (Dir: Sidney Furie, 116 mins.)†

Purple Hills, The (1961)** Gene Nelson, Kent Taylor, Joanna Barnes. Arizona cowboy kills an outlaw, but a gambler also puts in a claim for the reward; both are menaced by Indians friendly to the outlaw. (Dir: Maury Dexter, 60 mins.)

Purple Mask, The (1955)**½ Tony Curtis, Coleen Miller, Gene Barry, Angela Lansbury. A count puts on "the Purple Mask" and performs acts of derring-do which have Napoleon baffled. High adventure with some fun. (Dir: H. Bruce Humberstone, 82 mins.)

Purple Noon (France, 1960)*** Alain Delon, Maurice Ronet, Marie Laforet. Director René Clement has fashioned a tightly paced mystery with an excellent performance by Delon as a fun-loving loafer who gets into an almost unbelievable situation involving a forgery, murder and impersonations. (115 mins.)

Purple People Eater, The (1988)** Ned Beatty, Neil Patrick Harris, Shelley Winters, Peggy Lipton. Kids' movie based on the popular fifties novelty song, with the "one-eyed, one-horned flying purple people eater" (well, it doesn't really eat anyone) forming a rock'n'roll band with a California teen. Dopey but cute. Look for cameos by Little Richard and Chubby Checker. (Dir: Linda Shayne, 92 mins.)†

Purple Plain, The (Great Britain, 1954)*** Gregory Peck, Brenda De Banzie, Bernard Lee. A flier crashes in the jungle, fights his way back to civilization. Good suspense story. (Dir: Robert Parrish, 100 mins.)

Purple Rain (1984)**½ Prince, Appolonia Kotero, Clarence Williams III, Olga Karlatos, Morris Day. Prince makes a smashing film debut. The plot (with some autobiographical elements tossed in) concerns still another hard-rockin' warbler struggling to rise from the ashes of his past—in this case his relationship with his alcoholic father. (Dir: Albert Magnoli, 111 mins.)†

Purple Rose of Cairo, The (1985)*** Mia Farrow, Jeff Daniels, Danny Aiello, Dianne Wiest, Edward Herrmann. Farrow plays a Depression-era waitress suffering the slings of the hash house and the arrows of outrageous fortune. When she escapes to the movies she is surprised to find her cinema "Prince Charming" walk out of the film and into her life. Despite all the cleverness, the film is a downer, with director Woody Allen denying the audience a happy ending. Brilliant re-creation of the thirties, but a cold-hearted achievement. (84 mins.)†

Purple Taxi, The (France-Italy-Ireland, 1977)** Charlotte Rampling, Fred Astaire, Peter Ustinov, Edward Albert, Philippe Noiret. A group of attractive expatriates living in Ireland spend their time falling in love with, and hurting, each other, for no apparent reason. (Dir: Yves Boisset, 107 mins.)†

Pursued (1947)*** Robert Mitchum, Teresa Wright, Judith Anderson, Dean Jagger. Spanish-American War vet seeks the man who killed his father years ago in a family feud. Offbeat western. (Dir: Raoul Walsh, 101 mins.)†

Pursuit (MTV 1972)*** Ben Gazzara, E. G. Marshall, Martin Sheen. Suspenseful thriller based on a novel by Michael Crichton. The plot concerns a wealthy leader of an extremist group who plans to destroy a large number of people in a major city (San Diego) via lethal nerve gas. (Dir: Michael Crichton, 73 mins.)†

Pursuit of D. B. Cooper, The (1981)*** Robert Duvall, Treat Williams, Kathryn Harrold, Ed Flanders. Amusing caper and chase film. Dogged insurance investigator pursues a former Green Beret soldier who has pulled a daring heist on an airliner and parachuted to safety. (Dir: Roger Spottiswoode, 100 mins.)†

Pursuit of Happiness, The (1971)**½ Michael Sarrazin, Barbara Hershey, Arthur Hill, E. G. Marshall, Ruth White. Decent tale of a young man who accidentally runs over a jaywalker and, because of his rebellious attitude, faces long imprisonment. (Dir: Robert Mulligan, 93 mins.)†

Pursuit of the Graf Spee (Great Britain, 1956) *** John Gregson, Anthony Quayle, Peter Finch. True story of the German ship, and its scuttling off South America. Excellently produced war tale, good factual material. (Dirs: Michael Powell, Emeric Pressburger, 106 mins.)†

Pursuit to Algiers (1945)** Basil Rathbone, Nigel Bruce, Marjorie Riordan. A novel setting has Sherlock Holmes at sea as he tries to crack a case involving a songbird mixed up with jewel thieves. (Dir: Roy William Neill, 65 mins.)†

Pushover (1954)*** Kim Novak, Fred MacMurray, Dorothy Malone, E. G. Marshall. Pretty good drama about a cop who is seduced into neglecting his duty by a blonde man-trap. Kim Novak registered in this, her first major film assignment. (Dir: Richard Quine, 88 mins.)

Putney Swope (1969)**½ Allen Garfield, Alan Abel, Mel Brooks. A satire of various American sacred cows in the form of a fable about the rise of a black Madison Ave. advertising agency called Truth and Soul. Dated. (Dir: Robert Downey, 84 mins.)†

Puttin' on the Ritz (1930)**½ Harry Richman, Joan Bennett, James Gleason, Aileen Pringle, Lilyan Tashman. Creaky vehicle for nightclub star Richman does contain some first-class songs, including the title tune, and "I'll Get By," "I'll Travel Along," and "With You." (Dir: Edward H. Sloman, 88 mins.)

Puzzle of a Downfall Child (1971)*** Faye Dunaway, Barry Primus, Viveca Lindfors, Barry Morse, Roy Scheider. Brilliant and unsettling character study of a former fashion model who retires to her beach house to write the memoirs of her emotional breakdown. (Dir: Jerry Schatzberg, 104 mins.)

Pygmalion (Great Britain, 1938)**** Leslie Howard, Wendy Hiller, Scott Sunderland,

Wilfrid Lawson. This adaptation of the George Bernard Shaw play represents classical British cinema at its best! Sterling performances by Howard (Henry Higgins), Hiller (Eliza), and Lawson (Doolittle). Shaw liked the movie, even with the altered ending. (Dirs: Anthony Asquith, Leslie Howard, 96 mins.)†

Pygmy Island (1950)** Johnny Weissmuller, Ann Savage, David Bruce. Low-grade, likeable programmer. Jungle Jim battles jungle dangers to find a fiber plant for Uncle Sam. (Dir: William Berke, 69 mins.)

Pyro (1963)** Barry Sullivan, Martha Hyer. Badly burned engineer vows vengeance upon the woman who jealously started the blaze in which his family perished. Grim melodrama. (Dir: Julio Coll, 93 mins.)

Python Wolf—See: **CAT Squad: Python Wolf**

Pyx, The (Canada, 1973)**½ Christopher Plummer, Karen Black, Donald Pilon, Lee Broker. Murky but entrancing thriller about a policeman who delves into darker areas than he ever dreamed of when he investigates a prostitute's murder. (Dir: Harvey Hart, 111 mins.)†

Q (1982)**½ Michael Moriarty, Candy Clark, Richard Roundtree, David Carradine. That's short for Quetzlcoatl, a successor to all those giant, prehistoric feathered friends from fifties horror films. In this quirky black comic thriller, a foolish gangster invades Q's home, which is the top of New York's Chrysler Building. (Dir: Larry Cohen, 92 mins.)†

Q & A (1990)**½ Nick Nolte, Timothy Hutton, Armand Assante, Patrick O'Neal, Lee Richardson, Jenny Lumet, Paul Calderon, Fyvush Finkel. Corrupt cop Nolte is investigated by police attorney Hutton for the shooting death of a street punk. Director Sidney Lumet's examination of police pressures and corruption loses its focus. (134 mins.)†

Q Planes (Great Britain, 1939)***½ Laurence Olivier, Ralph Richardson, Valerie Hobson. Spies are lurking around Britain's aircraft, but they are foiled by a young test pilot and a crafty Scotland Yard man. Good thriller, with Richardson's policeman's role being delightfully acted. AKA: **Clouds Over Europe**. (Dir: Tim Whelan, 78 mins.)

Quackser Fortune Has a Cousin in the Bronx (Ireland, 1970)**½ Gene Wilder, Margot Kidder. A comedy-drama of easygoing charm, personified in the central character of a free spirit named Quackser Fortune who prefers being a dung collector to joining the sweating masses. (Dir: Waris Hussein, 90 mins.)†

Quadrophenia (Great Britain, 1979)*** Phil Daniels, Mark Wigett, Leslie Ash, Sting.
850

Feeling alienated from just about everyone, a British teen joins up with the "mod" movement, gaining a temporary feeling of belonging to something important. The Who's booming soundtrack articulates the character's concerns perfectly. (Dir: Franc Roddam, 115 mins.)†

Quality Street (1937)*** Katharine Hepburn, Franchot Tone, Fay Bainter. Costume romance showcases Hepburn; Tone, her sweetheart, goes off to the Napoleonic wars and fails to recognize her upon his return, so she masquerades as her niece to win him back. (Dir: George Stevens, 84 mins.)

Quantez (1957)** Fred MacMurray, Dorothy Malone, Sydney Chaplin, John Gavin. Four men and a woman escape a posse after a bank robbery, hole up in a deserted Mexican town, where their emotions get the better of them. (Dir: Harry Keller, 80 mins.)

Quarantined (MTV 1970)**½ John Dehner, Gary Collins, Sharon Farrell. Pilot for a proposed medical series. A family of doctors run a modern clinic atop a hill near the sea. (Dir: Leo Penn, 73 mins.)

Quantrill's Raiders (1958)**½ Steve Cochran, Diane Brewster, Gale Robbins, Leo Gordon. William Clark Civil War biopic details raid by murderous Confederate guerrilla fighter Quantrill on an arsenal to deprive Union soldiers of weapons and send them to the Rebels. (Dir: Edward Bernds, 69 mins.)

Quare Fellow, The (Great Britain-Ireland, 1962)*** Patrick McGoohan, Sylvia Syms, Walter Macken. A biting, intense prison drama, also packed with the Irish humor which characterized Brendan Behan's original play. Written and directed by Arthur Dreifuss. (85 mins.)

Quarterback Princess (MTV 1983)*** Helen Hunt, Don Murray, Barbara Babcock, Dana Elcar, John Stockwell. Can a girl quarterback on a high school football team become homecoming queen and walk off with the best-looking boy at school? (Dir: Noel Black, 104 mins.)†

Quartermass Experiment, The—See: **Creeping Unknown, The**

Quatermass II—See: **Enemy From Space**

Quartet (Great Britain, 1948)**** Dirk Bogarde, Françoise Rosay, Honor Blackman, Cecil Parker, Mai Zetterling. The most satisfying of the Somerset Maugham anthologies. (Dirs: Ken Annakin, Ralph Smart, Harold French, Arthur Crabtree, 120 mins.)†

Quartet (Great Britain-France, 1981)*** Maggie Smith, Alan Bates, Isabelle Adjani, Anthony Higgins. Based on a work by Jean Rhys, this drama set in 1920s Paris is rich in atmosphere, and has an excellent cast to spin the old story of a young, vulnerable French woman who is sheltered by a complicated couple (Dir: James Ivory, 101 mins.)†

Quebec (1951)** Corinne Calvert, Patric Knowles, John Barrymore, Jr., Barbara Rush. When the Canadians rebel against England, fighting for freedom is the wife of the British forces' commander. (Dir: George Templeton, 85 mins.)

Queen, The (1968)**** Harlow, Jack Doroshow, Andy Warhol, Terry Southern. A remarkable and tasteful documentary about one aspect of the subculture of American male homosexuals. The title refers to the winner of a beauty pageant for transvestites. (Dir: Frank Simon, 68 mins.)

Queen Bee (1955)*** Joan Crawford, Barry Sullivan, John Ireland, Fay Wray, Betsy Palmer. A Southern socialite's determination to dominate and rule everyone around her leads to destruction. (Dir: Ranald MacDougall, 95 mins.)

Queen Christina (1933)***½ Greta Garbo, John Gilbert, Lewis Stone. Garbo is at her best in this portrait of the inner conflicts of a Swedish queen of the 17th century. It is a romantic story, beautifully told. (Dir: Rouben Mamoulian, 110 mins.)†

Queen Elizabeth—See: **Salome** (1923)

Queen for a Day (1951)*** Phyllis Avery, Adam Williams, Edith Meiser, Darren McGavin. Stories of the contestants of the radio show are presented, some comic, some dramatic. Generally well-done episodic film. (Dir: Arthur Lubin, 107 mins.)

Queenie (MTV 1987)** Mia Sara, Kirk Douglas, Martin Balsam, Joel Grey, Claire Bloom, Sarah Miles, Topol. In his roman à clef, Michael Korda chose to tell the thinly veiled story of his aunt by marriage, the glamorous movie star Merle Oberon. The fictional "Queenie" rises from her half-caste, outcast status in Calcutta to the heights of Hollywood. (Dir: Larry Peerce, 260 mins.)†

Queen Kelly (1928)***½ Gloria Swanson, Walter Byron, Seena Owen. This reconstructed version of director Erich von Stroheim's uncompleted epic melodrama was first released in 1985. The first half of the film, showing Swanson as the orphan who has an affair with the fiancé of the queen, is intact; the second portion, showing Swanson's rise to become "queen" of her own bordello, is presented with the aid of production stills and never-before-seen footage. Von Stroheim's majestic decadence is apparent throughout this fragmented classic. The older, unfinished (but longer) version is on video. (96 mins.)†

Queen of Blood—See: **Planet of Blood**

Queen of Burlesque (1946)** Evelyn Ankers, Marion Martin, Carleton G. Young, Alice Fleming, Rose LaRose, Craig Reynolds. Tired suspense film set in a burlesque theater. Backstage hijinks and nastiness don't overcome woeful script and stiff acting. (Dir: Sam Newfield, 70 mins.)

Queen of Diamonds (1990)** Tinka Menkes. Stark, minimalist independent feature, shot on the tawdry streets of Las Vegas, displaying the desolate life of a female blackjack dealer. Depressing, competent, and overlong. (Dir: Nina Menkes, 77 mins.)

Queen of Hearts (Great Britain, 1990)***½ Vittorio Duse, Joseph Long, Anita Zagaria, Eileen Way. Sweet, funny film about an Anglo-Italian family's lives, loves, and the myths they create about themselves; witty, nostalgic, and full of feeling. Masterful direction by Amiel and uniformly fine acting make this a joy throughout. (Dir: Jon Amiel, 103 mins.)†

Queen of Outer Space (1958)* Zsa Zsa Gabor, Eric Fleming, Laurie Mitchell, Paul Birch. Camp classic about some especially macho astronauts who crashland on Venus, where queen Mitchell has banned all men. It somewhat spoils the fun to realize that the story (by Ben Hecht, of all people) was intended as a parody. (Dir: Edward Bernds, 80 mins.)

Queen of Spades, The (Great Britain, 1948)*** Anton Walbrook, Edith Evans, Ronald Howard. Bizarrely overmounted adaptation of the Pushkin story about a Russian officer who is obsessed with learning the secret of winning at cards. (Dir: Thorold Dickinson, 96 mins.)

Queen of the Nile (Italy, 1962)** Jeanne Crain, Edmund Purdom, Vincent Price. Nefertiti's daughter is loved by a young sculptor who escapes execution and fights for her. (Dir: Fernando Cerchio, 85 mins.)

Queen of the Pirates (Italy, 1960)*½ Gianna Maria Canale, Scilla Gable, Paul Muller, Massimo Serato. Eye-popping sets and costumes are wasted in this swashbuckler about a pirate queen battling a duke with treachery on his mind. Sequel: *Tiger of the Seven Seas*. (Dir: Mario Costa, 79 mins.)

Queen of the Stardust Ballroom (MTV 1975)***½ Maureen Stapleton, Charles Durning, Michael Brandon, Michael Strong. Stapleton's lonely widow with grown-up kids, meeting and falling in love with Durning's shy postman, evokes moments of warmth and sympathy. The over-the-hill couple have much to offer, and their moments together, dancing old '30s steps in a ballroom jammed with lively peers, simply lift one's spirits. (Dir: Sam O'Steen, 100 mins.)

Queen's Guards, The (Great Britain, 1960)**½ Daniel Massey, Raymond Massey, Robert Stephens, Jack Watson, Ian Hunter. Sedate story of a young officer in the

Royal Regiment. Script is hackneyed, but the behind-the-scenes look at regimental life is fascinating. (Dir: Michael Powell, 110 mins.)

Queens Logic (1991) **½ Kevin Bacon, Linda Fiorentino, John Malkovich, Joe Mantegna, Ken Olin, Tony Spiridakis, Tom Waits, Chloe Webb, Jamie Lee Curtis. A group of friends from Queens, N.Y., separated by change and distance, reunite and discover that their neighborhood roots are hard to shake. Screenwriter Spiridakis occasionally captures the comic poignancy of reminiscence. (Dir: Steve Rash, 113 mins.)†

Queens of Babylon (Italy, 1956)* Rhonda Fleming, Ricardo Montalban, Carlo Nichi, Roldano Lupi. Overblown costume epic, about events in the Hanging Gardens of Babylon and neighboring venues, gives history a bad name. (Dir: Carlo Bragaglia, 98 mins.)

Quelmada—See: **Burn!**

Quentin Durward (Great Britain, 1955)*** Robert Taylor, Kay Kendall, Robert Morley. Fine costume drama, well acted and better written than most. Exciting action scenes. From the novel by Sir Walter Scott. (Dir: Richard Thorpe, 101 mins.)

Querelle (West Germany, 1983)**½ Brad Davis, Franco Nero, Jeanne Moreau. A surreal, gaudy adaptation of Jean Genet's novel about a murderous homosexual sailor on leave in a seedy seaport, the film is overflowing with knowing glances, but makes very little narrative sense. The production design, creating a town of dark alleyways and low-life bars, is a triumph of theatrical stylization, and the best reason to see the film. (Dir: Rainer Werner Fassbinder, 107 mins.)†

Quest, The (MTV 1976)**½ Tim Matheson, Kurt Russell, Brian Keith, Keenan Wynn. Enjoyable western of brothers separated after an Indian raid—one a city boy training to be a doctor, and the other raised by Indians. (Dir: Lee H. Katzin, 98 mins.)

Quest, The (Australia, 1986)** Henry Thomas, Tony Barry, Tamsin West, Rachel Friend. Somewhere in an aboriginal burial ground dwells a monster who may or not be friendly; kids venture there to contact the creature. (Dir: Brian Trenchard-Smith, 93 mins.)†

Quest for Fire (France-Canada, 1982)***½ Everett McGill, Rae Dawn Chong, Ron Perlman, Nameer El-Kadi. Imaginative, expertly realized adventure fantasy looking at prehistoric man's attempts to survive in the Ice Age. Director Jean-Jacques Annaud and Screenwriter Gerard Brach look back 80,000 years ago in the manner that science fiction fantasizes about the future. A special language has been

created by Anthony Burgess, and a body language was devised by Desmond Morris. (Dir: Jean-Jacques Annaud, 97 mins.)†

Quest for Love (Great Britain, 1971)*** Tom Bell, Joan Collins, Denholm Elliott. Not a love story but a strange, gentle science-fiction flick, from a short story by John Wyndham. A physicist, after an accident at his lab, finds himself in a parallel world. (Dir: Ralph Thomas, 91 mins.)†

Question of Adultery, A—See: **Case of Mrs. Loring, The**

Question of Guilt, A (MTV 1978)*½ Tuesday Weld, Ron Liebman, Alex Rocco. Depressing character assassination drama about a murder case that's rigged by the police: witnesses are pressured to lie because the suspect is a loose woman. (Dir: Robert Butler, 104 mins.)†

Question of Honor, A (Italy, 1965)*** Ugo Tognazzi, Nicoletta Machiavelli, Tecla Scarano, Bernard Blier. Bizarre comedy-drama about salt-mine worker Tognazzi faced with the prospect of killing his own wife to salvage his *and* her honor. (Dir: Luigi Zampa, 110 mins.)

Question of Honor, A (MTV 1982)*** Ben Gazzara, Paul Sorvino, Robert Vaughn, Tony Roberts, Danny Aiello. Budd Schulberg adapts Sonny Grosso's 1978 thriller on police power games, and Gazzara plays the honest cop set up by federal agents. It's a true story, a sad and depressing one, as Gazzara's narcotics detective attempts to maneuver an Italian drug smuggler, who happens to be a federal stool pigeon! (Dir: Jud Taylor, 156 mins.)†

Question of Love, A (MTV 1978)*** Gena Rowlands, Jane Alexander, Ned Beatty. Thoughtful, sensitive drama based on a real-life child custody trial opposing a lesbian mother to her ex-husband. (Dir: Jerry Thorpe, 104 mins.)†

Question of Silence, A (Holland, 1984)** Cox Habbema, Edda Barends, Nelly Frijda, Henriette Tol. A female psychiatrist is appointed to examine three women, on trial for the seemingly senseless, brutal murder of a shopkeeper. (Dir: Marleen Gorris, 92 mins.)†

Question 7 (U.S.-West Germany, 1961)** Michael Gwynn, Margarete Jahnen, Christian de Bresson. Heavy-handed anti-Communist tract about an East German schoolboy, the son of a minister, who can win a scholarship only if he denies his religious views. (Dir: Stuart Rosenberg, 107 mins.)†

Questor Tapes, The (MTV 1974)***½ Robert Foxworth, Mike Farrell, Dana Wynter, Lew Ayres, John Vernon. While engaged on a massive project to build an android (a robot with human characteristics), a famous scientist disappears.

The creature soon goes after him. Taut script, fine performances, especially Foxworth as the robot. (Dir: Richard A. Colla, 100 mins.)

Que Viva Mexico (U.S.S.R., 1932)**½ Though unfinished, the footage shot for director Sergei Eisenstin's Mexican documentary project was assembled in 1979 by his assistant Grigori Alexandrov (working from Eisenstein's notes) into this approximation of what it might have been. The result is visually stunning and heavily didactic. (90 mins.)

Quick and the Dead, The (MCTV 1987)*** Tom Conti, Kate Capshaw, Sam Elliott, Kenny Morrison. Based on the Louis L'Amour best-seller, the film follows the friendship of a tenderfoot family traveling across the wilderness and a life-saving gunslinger who defends them against attack. (Dir: Robert Day, 91 mins.)†

Quick, Before It Melts (1965)** Robert Morse, George Maharis, Anjanette Comer, Norman Fell. Silly comedy. Morse and Maharis are a writer and photographer, respectively, who invade a military installation, Little America, and almost cause an international scandal. (Dir: Delbert Mann, 98 mins.)

Quick Change (1990)** Bill Murray, Geena Davis, Randy Quaid, Jason Robards, Bob Elliot, Phillip Bosco, Tony Shalhoub. Meandering, scattershot comedy about a gang of errant bank robbers who have more problems with the pitfalls of living in New York City than with the police. Some gags work; most don't. (Dirs: Howard Franklin, Bill Murray, 89 mins.)†

Quick Gun, The (1964)* Audie Murphy, Merry Anders, James Best, Ted de Corsia, Frank Ferguson. A man redeems himself when he fights a gang of outlaws and saves a town from being overrun. (Dir: Sidney Salkow, 87 mins.)

Quick, Let's Get Married (1964)½ Ginger Rogers, Ray Milland, Michael Ansara, Barbara Eden, Walter Abel, Elliott Gould. Hopeless trash about brothel owner Rogers and conman Milland trying to scam naïve prostitute Eden. Not released until 1971. Film debut of Gould, poor fellow. AKA: **Seven Different Ways**. (Dir: William Dieterle, 96 mins.)

Quick Millions (1931)*** Spencer Tracy, Marguerite Churchill, Sally Eilers, Robert Burns, George Raft, Edgar Kennedy, Leon Ames. Powerful melodrama telling the story of one man's rise and fall in the trucking racket, with an insightful script and a vigorous performance by Tracy. (Dir: Rowland Brown, 72 mins.)

Quicksand (1950)**½ Mickey Rooney, Jeanne Cagney, Peter Lorre. A young man "borrows" twenty bucks from a cash register, intending to pay it back,

but circumstances pile up to the point where his life is at stake. Neat little melodrama has suspense, a subdued Rooney. (Dir: Irving Pichel, 79 mins.)

Quicksilver (1986)*½ Kevin Bacon, Paul Rodriguez, Larry Fishburne, Whitney Kershaw, Jami Gertz. A former businessman trades in peddling commodities for pedaling a ten-speed. The film has ten speeds, too. All of them in low gear. (Dir: Tom Donnelly, 106 mins.)†

Quiet American, The (1958)*** Audie Murphy, Michael Redgrave, Claude Dauphin, Gloria Moll. Graham Greene's angry novel comes to the screen a bit watered down in its approach towards Americans. Murphy is miscast as the hero but a good supporting cast makes up for it. (Dir: Joseph L. Mankiewicz, 120 mins.)

Quiet Cool (1986)** James Remar, Adam Coleman, Jared Martin, Nick Cassavetes, Daphne Ashbrook, Fran Ryan. Violence erupts in a sylvan setting when a cop with a teen in tow battles vicious marijuana farmers. The teen seeks revenge, the cop seeks justice in this brutal, stunt-dominated adventure for fans who seek fast-paced action. (Dir: Cay Borris, 100 mins.)†

Quiet Earth, The (New Zealand, 1985)*** Bruno Lawrence, Alison Routledge, Peter Smith. Amusing, sometimes tense science-fiction fantasy about a scientist (Lawrence) who wakes up one morning to find himself the only one left after everyone has mysteriously vanished. The plot turns predictable when other survivors appear. (Dir: Geoff Murphy, 91 mins.)†

Quiet Man, The (1952)**** John Wayne, Maureen O'Hara, Barry Fitzgerald, Victor McLaglen, Mildred Natwick. Director John Ford's Oscar-winner is a tribute to an Ireland that exists in the imagination of songwriters and poets. Wayne is a boxer who returns to his native village to claim the family homestead and win the heart and hand of the local beauty (O'Hara). First, however, he must win over her hard-drinking, protective brother. Superior filmmaking. (129 mins.)†

Quiet Place in the Country, A (Italy, 1969) ***½ Franco Nero, Vanessa Redgrave, Madeleine Damien. Haunting gothic tale of an overworked artist obsessed by the ghost of a summer house's former occupant. Tense mystery is highlighted by exquisite cinematography and powerful Ennio Morricone score. (Dir: Elio Petri, 106 mins.)

Quiet Please, Murder (1942)**½ George Sanders, Gail Patrick, Richard Denning, Lynne Roberts, Sidney Blackmer. Nifty thriller about a murderous thief who steals valuable volumes from libraries and copies them for sale to private collectors. Modest but intriguing. (Dir: John Larkin, 70 mins.)

Quigley Down Under (U.S.-Australia, 1990)*** Tom Selleck, Laura San Giacomo, Alan Rickman, Chris Haywood. Rousing western set in the outback of Australia will entertain even nonlovers of the Western genre. Selleck has the screen presence to be cast as a stoic American defending aborigines (substituting Indians) against an evil landowner (Rickman). Good score, splendid photography, and powerhouse performances from Giacomo and Rickman enhance this lively adventure. (Dir: Simon Wincer, 120 mins.)

Quiller Memorandum, The (U.S.-Great Britain, 1966)**½ George Segal, Alec Guinness, Max von Sydow, Senta Berger. Uneven spy-drama. Segal is an American agent in Berlin looking for the head of a neo-Nazi party that is gaining momentum in present-day Germany. (Dir: Michael Anderson, 105 mins.)†

Quilombo (Brazil, 1984)*** Antonio Pompeo, Zeze Motta, Toni Tornado, Antonio Pitanga, Vera Fischer, Mauricio Do Valle. Dynamic, musically rich saga about a 17th-century jungle community founded by runaway black slaves. (Dir: Carlos Diegues, 120 mins.)

Quincannon, Frontier Scout (1956)** Tony Martin, Peggie Castle, John Bromfield. Martin as a cowboy. He seems very uncomfortable not being in a tux in front of a nightclub audience singing Neapolitan songs. (Dir: Lesley Selander, 83 mins.)

Quinns, The (MTV 1977)**½ Barry Bostwick, Susan Browning, Geraldine Fitzgerald. Pilot film about four generations of an Irish clan who work for the New York City Fire Department. (Dir: Daniel Petrie, 78 mins.)

Quintet (1979)*½ Paul Newman, Bibi Anderson, Fernando Rey, Vittorio Gassman, Brigitte Fosey, Nina Van Pallandt. A wintry-looking puzzle piece with a coldhearted intellectual approach toward portraying the aftermath of nuclear war. A handful of survivors sit around playing a game which should have been called "Pin the Tail on Ingmar Bergman." (Dir: Robert Altman, 110 mins.)†

Quo Vadis (1951)***½ Robert Taylor, Deborah Kerr, Leo Genn, Peter Ustinov. A really big one—the Christians are persecuted, Rome burns, Taylor loves Kerr, and just about everything else happens in this splashy spectacle. Some weak moments, but some fine ones too, notably from Ustinov. Lavish throughout. (Dir: Mervyn LeRoy, 171 mins.)†

Rabbit, Run (1970)* James Caan, Jack Albertson, Arthur Hill, Carrie Snodgress, Anjanette Comer. John Updike's novel rather badly brought to the screen. The story concerns a couple whose marriage in Reading, Pa., begins to disintegrate the moment the wedding ceremony is over. The film falls apart too. (Dir: Jack Smight, 94 mins.)

Rabbit Test (1978)½ Billy Crystal, Joan Prather, Alex Rocco, Imogene Coca, Norman Fell, Fannie Flagg, Alice Ghostley, George Gobel, Rosie Grier, Paul Lynde, Roddy McDowall, Sheree North, Tom Poston, Charlotte Rae, Joan Rivers, Jimmie Walker. Rivers co-wrote and directed this abysmal comedy about the world's first pregnant man. There's not much plot, just a ceaseless string of tasteless—not funny, just tasteless—jokes about homosexuals, Poles, etc. (84 mins.)†

Rabbit Trap, The (1959)** Ernest Borgnine, Bethel Leslie, David Brian. Draftsman dominated by his job and boss is called back from a vacation, which proves to change his life. (Dir: Philip Leacock, 72 mins.)

Rabid (Canada, 1977)**½ Marilyn Chambers, Frank Moore, Joe Silver. A weird horror flick that helped firm up director David (*Dead Zone, Scanners*) Cronenberg's reputation as a maverick terrifier. A woman awakens from a skin graft operation with unexpected complications. She contracts rabies, and a monstrous growth attached to her body starts attacking everyone within reach. (91 mins.)†

Rabid Grannies (Belgium, 1989)**½ Catherine Aymerie, Caroline Brackman, Danielle Daven, Raymond Lescot, Anne Marie Fox. Wild horror movie about a family gathered for the joint birthday party of two elderly sisters, who become vicious monsters due to a "gift" from their black-sheep nephew, a demon worshipper. Despite the title, not a spoof; gore galore, and they mean it. (Dir: Emmanuel Kervyn, 83 mins.)†

Race for Glory (1989)** Alex McArthur, Peter Berg, Pamela Ludwig, Ray Wise, Bert Kwouk, Lane Smith. A pair of small-town friends are separated when one pursues his dream of becoming an international motorcycle racer. Hokey sports melodrama with feel-good ending. (Dir: Rocky Lang, 96 mins.)†

Race for Life (Great Britain, 1954)**½ Richard Conte, Mari Aldon, Peter Illing, Meredith Edwards, George Coulouris. Terrific race car footage enhances passable drama about driver Conte touring Europe's main speed tracks while coming to terms with his fractious marriage. (Dir: Terence Fisher, 70 mins.)

Race for the Double Helix, The—See: **Double Helix, The**

Race for Your Life, Charlie Brown (1977)** Better production values than in the specials made for TV. The "Peanuts" gang are away at summer camp. (Dir: Bill Melendez, 75 mins.)†

Racers, The (1955)** Kirk Douglas, Gilbert Roland, Bella Darvi, Cesar Romero, Lee J. Cobb. The drama is contrived and woven out of the conflicts, both professional and personal, among the denizens of the European sports car racing world. (Dir: Henry Hathaway, 112 mins.)

Race Street (1948)**½ George Raft, William Bendix, Marilyn Maxwell, Harry Morgan, Frank Faylen. Ex-crook trying to go straight infiltrates a protection racket gang in this poverty-row thriller. Meager production values, but tense and very well acted. (Dir: Edwin L. Marin, 79 mins.)

Race to the Yankee Zephyr (Australia-New Zealand, 1981)** Ken Wahl, Lesley Ann Warren, Donald Pleasence, George Peppard, Grant Tilly. An action tale that doesn't exactly race along. Several adventurers are at odds over who should retrieve a treasure lost at sea during WWII. (Dir: David Hemmings, 108 mins.)

Race With the Devil (1975)**½ Peter Fonda, Loretta Swit, Warren Oates, Lara Parker. Thinly plotted but suspenseful yarn about two vacationing couples who encounter a cult of Satan worshippers engaging in a ritualistic sacrifice and have to flee for their lives. (Dir: Jack Starrett, 89 mins.)†

Rachel and the Stranger (1948)*** Loretta Young, William Holden, Robert Mitchum. Frontier wanderer stops at the cabin of a backwoodsman and wife and settles their problems. Entertaining comedy-drama. (Dir: Norman Foster, 93 mins.)†

Rachel, Rachel (1968)**** Joanne Woodward, James Olson, Estelle Parsons, Geraldine Fitzgerald. A beautiful, deeply moving story of a young spinster, thanks largely to a superb screenplay by Stewart Stern. Woodward gives a restrained, poignant portrayal of the lonely, sexually inhibited schoolteacher living in a small town in Connecticut. (Dir: Paul Newman, 101 mins.)†

Rachel River (1989)**½ Craig T. Nelson, Pamela Reed, Zeljko Ivanek, James Olson, Viveca Lindfors, Alan North. Rambling story of repressed, lonely characters in a small Minnesota town. Worth seeing as a workout for a group of underrated actors. (Dir: Sandy Smolan, 90 mins.)

Racing Blood (1954)** Bill Williams, Jean Porter, Jimmy Boyd (debut). Colt born with a split hoof is supposed to be destroyed, but a stable boy and his uncle make him a winner. (Dir: Wesley Barry, 76 mins.)

Racing With the Moon (1984)*** Sean Penn, Elizabeth McGovern, Nicolas Cage, John Karlen. An engaging WWII love story blessed by ex-actor Richard Benjamin's direction, which makes the most of a conventional screenplay. The story traces two relationships through disasters and eventual triumphs. Very well acted. (108 mins.)†

Rack, The (1956)*** Paul Newman, Wendell Corey, Edmond O'Brien, Anne Francis, Walter Pidgeon. A war hero returns from a Korean prison camp and faces trial for treason. Well-acted courtroom drama grips the attention throughout. (Dir: Arnold Laven, 100 mins.)

Racket, The (1951)*** Robert Mitchum, Lizabeth Scott, Robert Ryan. Police captain opposes a big racketeer who stops at nothing. Nicely produced, exciting crime melodrama. (Dir: John Cromwell, 88 mins.)†

Racket Busters (1938)** George Brent, Humphrey Bogart, Penny Singleton. Bogart moves in on the trucking industry, meets opposition from Brent. (Dir: Lloyd Bacon, 71 mins.)

Racket Man, The (1944)**½ Tom Neal, Larry Parks, Hugh Beaumont. Racketeer reformed by the Army becomes an undercover agent after black marketeers. Lively, well-done action melodrama. (Di: D. Ross Lederman, 65 mins.)

Racquet (1979)* Bert Convy, Edie Adams, Phil Silvers, Lynda Day George, Susan Tyrrell, Bruce Kimmel, Bjorn Borg, Bobby Riggs. Unbelievable tripe about tennis pro Convy flaunting his sex appeal. (Dir: David Winters, 89 mins.)

Rad (1986)*½ Bill Allen, Lori Loughlin, Talia Shire, Ray Walston, Jack Weston. A local boy wheels against the jaundiced racing establishment and wins the big race. It's a dramatic commercial for BMX bikes. Predictable. (Dir: Hal Needham, 91 mins.)†

Radioactive Dreams (1986)* John Stockwell, Michael Dudikoff, Lisa Blount, Michele Little, Don Murray, George Kennedy. This is a post-apocalypse teen comedy (that may be a first, but it's still not any good). In 2010, fifteen years after Armaged don, two bozos raised only on 1940s detective fiction try to adjust to life after the Big Bomb. Comedy fallout that could kill. (Dir: Albert F. Pyun, 95 mins.)†

Radio Days (1987)*** Mia Farrow, Seth Green, Julie Kavner, Diane Keaton, Tony Roberts, Danny Aiello, Jeff Daniels, Josh Mostel, Dianne Wiest. Writer-director Woody Allen's warm tribute to the medium that time forgot spotlights both the people whose lives revolved around their favorite radio programs (a Jewish family living in Rockaway Beach) and the people who created those aural fantasies (exemplified by Farrow, a cigarette girl trying to hit the big time). (85 mins.)†

Radio On (Great Britain, 1979)*** David Beames, Sting, Lisa Kreuzer. Thoughtful "road" movie, co-produced by Wim Wenders, about a disc jockey who travels around the British Isles hoping to unravel the mystery of his brother's death. Contemplative drama offers some powerfully stark images and great music by Devo, Kraftwerk, David Bowie, and Lena Lovich. (Dir: Chris Petit, 101 mins.)

Radium City (1987)***½ Fascinating documentary about factory workers of the 1920s who painted radium numbers on clock faces and were poisoned by the deadly substance. A gripping, alarming film about shattered lives that shocks and saddens. (Dir: Carole Langer, 110 mins.)

Ra Expeditions, The (1974)***½ Engrossing documentary record of anthropologist Thor Heyerdahl's two ocean voyages aboard a small papyrus boat to prove that pre-Columbians were capable of crossing the Atlantic. (Dir: Lennart Ehrenborg, 93 mins.)

Rafferty and the Gold Dust Twins—See: **Rafferty and the Highway Hustlers**

Rafferty and the Highway Hustlers (1975)**½ Sally Kellerman, Mackenzie Phillips, Alan Arkin. Slight tale about a couple of footloose and fancy-free (and larcenous) females who get men to give them rides at gunpoint. Their victim is Arkin, playing a not-too-bright driving test inspector. AKA: **Rafferty and the Gold Dust Twins**. (Dir: Dick Richards, 91 mins.)†

Raffles (1930)*** Ronald Colman, Kay Francis, Bramwell Fletcher, David Torrence, Alison Skipworth. Adept early talkie version of the popular story of a British ex-officer who's so bored with civilian life that he takes to jewel thievery for sport. Sprightly script and sparkling performances. (Dirs: George Fitzmaurice, Harry D'Arrast, 72 mins.)

Raffles (1939)** Olivia de Havilland, David Niven. Weakly done film about the adventures of an amateur cracksman thief. (Dir: Sam Wood, 72 mins.)

Rage (1966)* Glenn Ford, Stella Stevens. Outrageous melodrama with heavy breathing substituting for acting. Ford plays a disillusioned drunken doctor in a Mexican village who gets a second lease on life with the help of world-weary Stevens. (Dir: Gilberto Gazcon, 103 mins.)

Rage (1972)*½ George C. Scott, Richard Basehart. Army helicopter accidentally sprays a rancher and his son with poison gas. Scott plays the rancher, and this marked his directorial debut. (105 mins.)†

Rage (MTV 1980)*** David Soul, James Whitmore, Yaphet Kotto, Caroline McWilliams. A dramatic look at the

856

effect of group therapy on rapists. The film details the transformation of a sullen sex offender into a more open human being after understanding and releasing his own rage over his own childhood sexual abuse. (Dir: Bill Graham, 104 mins.)†

Rage at Dawn (1955)**½ Randolph Scott, Forrest Tucker, J. Carrol Naish, Mala Powers, Edgar Buchanan. Gritty, forceful western, with Scott tracking the gang of bandits who killed his wife in the course of a robbery. (Dir: Tim Whelan, 87 mins.)†

Rage in Harlem, A (1991)** Forest Whitaker, Gregory Hines, Robin Givens, Zakes Mokae, Danny Glover. Flawed crime-caper-comedy set in 1956 features the appealing Givens (the ex-Mrs. Mike Tyson) as a gangster's girl on the run with stolen gold who hides out in Harlem. But the plot is too absurd. Whitaker, as a nerdish accountant who takes in the sexy moll, and Mokae, portraying a transvestite madam (Big Kathy), are just a few of the engaging performers to grace this agreeable, lighthearted entertainment. Surprisingly, Givens gives a droll, sexy performance. (Dir: Bill Duke, 115 mins.)†

Rage in Heaven (1941)**½ George Sanders, Robert Montgomery, Ingrid Bergman, Lucile Watson, Oscar Homolka, Philip Merivale. Strange, grim mystery about the final dissolution of a psychotic and its effect on his unsuspecting family. Complex, unusual plot, remarkable performance by Montgomery. (Dir: W. S. Van Dyke, 83 mins.)

Rage of Angels (MTV 1983)*½ Jaclyn Smith, Ken Howard, Kevin Conway, Ronald Hunter. Smith is Sidney Sheldon's heroine, a lady lawyer clever enough to outwit Manhattan's legal biggies, but still a dummy where men are concerned. (Dir: Buzz Kulik, 208 mins.)†

Rage of Angels: The Story Continues (MTV 1986)*½ Jaclyn Smith, Ken Howard, Angela Lansbury, Susan Sullivan, Michael Nouri, Mason Adams, Brad Dourif. It's about the troubled relationship of a boringly pretty attorney and her illegitimate son's father who's now the Vice-President of the United States. Glossy soap opera about sin in high places. (Dir: Paul Wendkos, 208 mins.)

Rage of Honor (1987)* Sho Kosugi, Lewis Van Bergen, Robin Evans. Kosugi plays a narcotics investigator who's rarin' to kick the hell out of the scummy thugs who tortured and murdered his assistant. (Dir: Gordon Hessler, 91 mins.)†

Rage of Paris, The (1938)**½ Danielle Darrieux, Douglas Fairbanks, Jr., Louis Hayward. Frothy comedy about a sensible Parisian girl who campaigns vigorously to snare a wealthy husband but succumbs to true love. Dated but well played. (Dir: Henry Koster, 78 mins.)†

Rage of the Buccaneers—See: **Black Pirate, The**

Rage to Kill (1988)* James Ryan, Oliver Reed, Cameron Mitchell, Maxine John. Sort of a *Rambo*-ized account of the invasion of Grenada, as race driver Ryan teams up with CIA agent Mitchell to overthrow dictator Reed. (Dir: David Winters, 92 mins.)†

Rage to Live, A (1965)*½ Suzanne Pleshette, Bradford Dillman, Ben Gazzara, Bethel Leslie. John O'Hara's novel of the life and loves of a near-nymphomaniac (Pleshette), vulgarized by Hollywood hacks. (Dir: Walter Grauman, 101 mins.)

Raggedy Anne and Andy (1977)*** Voices of Didi Conn, Mark Baker, Joe Silver, Fred Stuthman. Animated musical version of the classic children's book contains some superb sequences. Supervised and directed by English animation wizard Richard Williams. (84 mins.)†

Raggedy Man (1981)*** Sissy Spacek, Eric Roberts, William Sanderson, Tracey Walter, Sam Shepard. An exquisitely photographed and meticulously designed vision of homefront World War II, seen through the eyes of a working mother. Spacek's heartfelt portrayal brings this low-key film to life. (Dir: Jack Fisk, 94 mins.)†

Raggedy Rawney, The (Great Britain, 1988)**** Dexter Fletcher, Zoe Nathenson, Bob Hoskins, Zoe Wanamaker, Ian Dury. Anti-war fable about a shell-shocked young soldier who falls in with a group of gypsies. In this assured directorial debut, actor Hoskins (who also co-wrote the script) fills the screen with raw humor and strong characters. (102 mins.)

Raging Bull (1980)**** Robert De Niro, Cathy Moriarty, Joe Pesci, Frank Vincent, Nicholas Colasanto. Film biography of middleweight champion Jake La Motta concentrates on his personal battles. De Niro won the Oscar for Best Actor. Exquisite. B&W. (Dir: Martin Scorsese, 128 mins.)†

Raging Tide, The (1951)** Richard Conte, Shelley Winters, Stephen McNally, Charles Bickford, Alex Nicol. Predictable crime melodrama. Conte plays a murderer on the run who learns too late the value of honesty. (Dir: George Sherman, 93 mins.)

Rags to Riches (MTV 1987)** Joseph Bologna, Douglas Seale, Kimiko Gelman. A kickoff for a series featuring a millionaire (Bologna), his butler, and six exuberant orphans frolicking about the tycoon's estate. (Dir: Bruce Seth Green, 104 mins.)†

Ragtime (1981)*** James Cagney, Brad Dourif, Moses Gunn, Elizabeth McGovern, Kenneth McMillan, Howard E. Rollins, Jr., Mary Steenburgen, Mandy Patinkin, Pat O'Brien, Donald O'Connor, Norman Mailer. The atmosphere of the time is used mainly as a wraparound, with most stress on the battle of a black musician against the racism inflicted upon him. (Dir: Milos Forman, 155 mins.)†

Raid, The (1954)**½ Van Heflin, Anne Bancroft, Richard Boone. Interesting and well-made western set after the Civil War. A group of Confederate soldiers escape from a Union prison and plan the burning and sacking of a small Vermont town. (Dir: Hugo Fregonese, 83 mins.)†

Raiders, The (1952)**½ Richard Conte, Viveca Lindfors, Barbara Britton, Hugh O'Brian. Strong western about a settler seeking revenge against the crooked businessmen who stole his land. Better script than usual. AKA: **Riders of Vengeance**. (Dir: Lesley Selander, 80 mins.)

Raiders of the Living Dead (1985)* Robert Deveau, Donna Asali, Scott Schwartz, Zita Johann. Reporter discovers an island where a mad doctor is busily creating zombies. (Dirs: Brett Piper, Samuel M. Sherman, 83 mins.)

Raiders of the Lost Ark (1981)*** Harrison Ford, Karen Allen, Denholm Elliott, Ronald Lacey, Wolf Kahler, John Rhys-Davies. An archeologist is trying to track down the long missing Ark of the Covenant before the dastardly Nazis unearth it. Energetic and exciting. Sequels: *Indiana Jones and the Temple of Doom* and *Indiana Jones and the Last Crusade*. (Dir: Steven Spielberg, 115 mins.)†

Raiders of the Seven Seas (1953)**½ John Payne, Donna Reed. Bold pirate captures a countess, saves her from the rascal she is to marry. Lively costume adventure. (Dir: Sidney Salkow, 88 mins.)

Raid on Entebbe (MTV 1976)***½ Peter Finch, Martin Balsam, Horst Bucholz, Jack Warden, Yaphet Kotto, Charles Bronson. A dramatization of the heroic rescue of hijacked airline passengers by Israeli commandos at Entebbe. (Dir: Irvin Kershner, 118 mins.)†

Raid on Rommel (1971)*½ Richard Burton, John Colicos. Quickie filmed in Mexico, documenting the superhuman infiltration of the Germans in North Africa. Led by Burton, the commando group weaves through enemy lines with the ease of Rommel himself. (Dir: Henry Hathaway, 99 mins.)†

Railroaded (1947)*** John Ireland, Hugh Beaumont, Sheila Ryan. The law gets a desperate criminal who has involved an innocent youth. Tight, suspenseful crime opus, well above average. (Dir: Anthony Mann, 72 mins.)†

Railroad Man, The (Italy, 1956)***½ Pietro Germi, Luisa Della Noce, Sylva Koscina, Saro Urzi. Brilliantly acted all around, this late neo-realist film from director-star Germi tells, in precise and enthralling form, about an Italian railroad worker and his family coping with life's travails during a difficult period in their simple lives. (110 mins.)

Rails into Laramie (1954)** John Payne, Mari Blanchard, Dan Duryea. Another passable western about the pioneering group of he-men who tamed the lawless frontier in order to bring the rails into Laramie. (Dir: Jesse Hibbs, 81 mins.)

Railway Children, The (Great Britain, 1970)*** Dinah Sheridan, Jenny Agutter, Sally Thomsett, Gary Warren. Family entertainment. An engaging and entertaining film version of the Edwardian children's classic story about three children who are relocated with their mother to a Yorkshire village on a railroad line. (Dir: Lionel Jeffries, 108 mins.)†

Rain (1932) Joan Crawford, Walter Huston, William Gargan, Guy Kibbee, Walter Catlett, Beulah Bondi. With this adaptation of the Maugham chestnut, Crawford, surprisingly vibrant and vulgar, gave the performance of her then-young career as Sadie Thompson, the good-time girl of the tropics, engaged in a battle for her soul with a hypocritical man of the cloth (Huston). Despite the theatrical source material, this early talkie suffers none of the staginess of its contemporaries; Director Lewis Milestone delivers some exquisite visual interludes, displaying the tropical atmosphere inhabited by Sadie and company. (Dir: Lewis Milestone, 93 mins.)†

Rainbow (MTV 1978)*** Andrea McArdle, Michael Parks, Piper Laurie, Martin Balsam, Jack Carter. Nostalgic film about the young Judy Garland is a corny, sentimental treat packaged in the old Hollywood style. McArdle sings better than she acts. (Dir: Jackie Cooper, 104 mins.)†

Rainbow, The (1989)*** Sammi Davis, Paul McGann, Amanda Donohoe, David Hemmings, Glenda Jackson. D. H. Lawrence's novel about the sexual and emotional maturation of a Victorian girl, a predecessor to *Women in Love*, is well-filmed by Ken Russell (who adapted the later novel in 1970). With respect to Lawrence, Russell eschews his usual theatrics and delivers a literate adult film. (112 mins.)†

Rainbow Brite and the Star Stealer (1985)** Rainbow Brite must keep the bright lights burning in the universe when a villainess threatens to shift the world into permanent darkness. Saccharine, indifferently animated cartoon. (Dirs: Bernard Deyries, Kimio Yabuki, 85 mins.)†

Rainbow Drive (MCTV 1990)**½ Peter Weller, Sela Ward, Kathryn Harrold. On the night of a multiple murder, tough homicide cop (Weller) just happens to be at the home of the married woman with whom he is having an affair. Weller makes the gruesome discovery of five dead bodies but smells a cover-up when the cops say there are only four bodies and he's warned to stay off the case. This somewhat intriguing drama keeps you guessing in the beginning but then, unfortunately, falls flat. (Dir: Peter Roth, 96 mins.)†

Rainbow Island (1944)** Dorothy Lamour, Eddie Bracken, Gil Lamb, Barry Sullivan. A rather colorless musical comedy about merchant marines trying to get their hands on the local beauties on a deserted island. (Dir: Ralph Murphy, 97 mins.)

Rainbow Jacket, The (Great Britain, 1954)*** Robert Morley, Kay Walsh, Honor Blackman, Wilfrid Hyde-White. Disbarred jockey takes a lad in hand and teaches him the tricks of the trade. Familiar but well constructed racing melodrama. (Dir: Basil Dearden, 99 mins.)

Rainbow 'Round My Shoulder (1952)**½ Frankie Laine, Charlotte Austin, Billy Daniels. Lively musical about a Hollywood studio messenger who gets a screen test and winds up in the movies. (Dir: Richard Quine, 78 mins.)

Rainbow Serpent, The (France, 1983)***½ Serge Avedikian, Illios Sikinos. Satire of romantic musicals and detective movies tells the story of a cop who investigates a bodybuilder and falls in love with him. (Dir: Phillippe Vallois, 91 mins.)

Rainbow Trail, The (1925)*** Tom Mix, Anne Cornwall, George Bancroft, Lucien Littlefield. Wonderful Zane Grey western with Mix as a cowpoke, on the way to rescue his uncle from outlaws, who joins a wagon train. Vigorous action, beautifully photographed on location. (Dir: Lynn Reynolds, 58 mins.)†

Rainmaker, The (1956)*** Katharine Hepburn, Burt Lancaster, Wendell Corey, Lloyd Bridges, Wallace Ford, Earl Holliman. N. Richard Nash's hit play about a frightened spinster who's transformed into a woman ready for love by a visiting con man relies mainly on Hepburn's personal magnetism. Lancaster blusters and bellows as Starbuck, the rainmaker who has a drought-ridden town in the palm of his hand. (Dir: Joseph Anthony, 121 mins.)†

Rain Man (1988)***½ Dustin Hoffman, Tom Cruise, Valeria Golina. Highly enjoyable, poignant comedy-drama with hustler Cruise discovering that he has an older brother (Hoffman), an autistic savant, and "kidnapping" him in an attempt to get money from their late father's estate. A bit overlong and aimless as the two drive cross-country, but worth the time. Oscar winner for Best Picture, Director, Actor (Hoffman) and Original Screenplay. (Dir: Barry Levinson, 135 mins.)†

Rain or Shine (1930)**½ Joe Cook, Louise Fazenda, William Collier, Jr., Joan Peers. Circus manager tries everything to make a success of a failing show owned by the girl he loves. Mainly a showcase for Cook, a famed, much-admired stage comedian who rarely appeared on screen. (Dir: Frank Capra, 92 mins.)

Rain People, The (1969)***½ James Caan, Shirley Knight, Robert Duvall. A thoughtful, quiet film. Knight is the married, pregnant housewife who feels trapped in her Long Island home and therefore hops into her car one day and flees. Along the way, she picks up loser James Caan, a retarded ex-college football star. Original screenplay and direction by Francis Ford Coppola. (102 mins.)†

Rains Came, The (1939)** Tyrone Power, Myrna Loy, George Brent. Well-edited special effects of flood and earthquake enliven an otherwise dolorous film. Power is absurdly cast as a noble Indian physician. Remade as *The Rains of Ranchipur*. (Dir: Clarence Brown, 104 mins.)

Rains of Ranchipur, The (1955)**½ Lana Turner, Richard Burton, Fred MacMurray, Michael Rennie, Joan Caulfield. Elaborately produced remake of *The Rains Came*, about the forbidden romance between the wife of an English nobleman (Turner) and a progressive Hindu doctor (Burton). (Dir: Jean Negulesco, 104 mins.)

Raintree County (1957)**½ Montgomery Clift, Elizabeth Taylor, Eva Marie Saint, Lee Marvin, Nigel Patrick, Rod Taylor, Agnes Moorehead. Lots of gussied-up production trappings and a lush musical score enhance this somewhat thin saga. Monty ponders metaphysics, Eva Marie waits for him to come to his senses, and Liz, a cracked Southern belle, unleashes a few miscegenational skeletons from her closet and slowly goes mad. (Dir: Edward Dmytryk, 168 mins.)†

Rainy Day Friends (1986)*½ Esai Morales, Chuck Bail, Carrie Snodgress, Janice Rule, Lelia Goldoni, John Phillip Law. A drenched-in-bathos soap opera with homilies in place of a script. A street-smart teen grapples with cancer. (Dir: Gary Kent, 105 mins.)

Raise the Titanic (1980)* Jason Robards, Jr., Richard Jordan, Anne Archer. Tedious screen version of the best-seller about recovering the sunken *Titanic*. A disaster to rank with the original sinking! (Dir: Jerry Jameson, 112 mins.)†

Raising Arizona (1987)*** Nicolas Cage,

Holly Hunter, Trey Wilson, John Goodman, William Forsythe, Sam McMurray, Frances McDormand, Randall ''Tex'' Cobb. When two mismatched lovebirds—a petty thief and his favorite female cop—find no other way to have a child, they steal one. High-energy comedy, the sort that switches into high gear each time a small slump occurs. (Dir: Joel Coen, 94 mins.)†

Raisin in the Sun, A (1961)***½ Sidney Poitier, Ruby Dee, Claudia McNeil, Diana Sands. Lorraine Hansberry's Broadway play about a Negro family attempting to break away from their crowded Chicago apartment by moving into an all-white neighborhood. It's practically a photographed stage play, but the dialogue is pungent and direct, the performances excellent. (Dir: Daniel Petrie, 128 mins.)†

Rally Round the Flag, Boys! (1958)** Paul Newman, Joanne Woodward, Joan Collins, Jack Carson, Tuesday Weld. Max Shulman's funny novel about the citizens of Putnam's Landing and their reactions to an army missile base in their backyard gets the overdone Hollywood treatment. (Dir: Leo McCarey, 106 mins.)

Rambo: First Blood Part II (1985)** Sylvester Stallone, Richard Crenna, Martin Kove, Charles Napier, Julia Nickson. Rambo returns to the jungles of Nam to locate American MIAs in this implausible box office smash sequel to *First Blood*. It's an updated WWII flick with the Vietnamese equalling the Japanese and the Nazis now transposed into Russians. Implausible, but a box office smash. (Dir: George P. Cosmatos, 98 mins.)†

Rambo III (1988)*½ Sylvester Stallone, Richard Crenna, Marc de Jonge, Kurtwood Smith. Rambo has retired to the seclun of a temple where he works with monks until his old buddy Trautman gets captured by the Commies while working with Afghani rebels. Flagrantly reactionary, incredibly boring. (Dir: Peter Macdonald, 104 mins.)†

Ramona (1936)**½ Loretta Young, Don Ameche, Kent Taylor, Pauline Frederick. Romantic drama set in old California about the trials of the Indian peons, and their Spanish overlords. (Dir: Henry King, 90 mins.)

Rampage (1963)** Robert Mitchum, Elsa Martinelli, Jack Hawkins, Sabu. Mitchum's a big game hunter who's got to bring back some rare examples of jungle cats from the Malayan wilds. (Dir: Phil Karlson, 98 mins.)

Ramparts of Clay (France-Tunisia-Algeria, 1970)***½ Leila Schenna, villagers of Tehouda. Authentic fiction film about the coming of age of a young Tunisian girl just after her country's independence from France. Heartbreaking story is so crisply photographed you can feel the heat of the region. (Dir: Jean-Louis Bertucelli, 85 mins.)†

Ramrod (1947)*½ Veronica Lake, Joel McCrea, Arleen Whelan, Don DeFore. Veronica tries to be Barbara Stanwyck in this western drivel about a lady rancher who drives her men and her cattle with equal cruelty. (Dir: André de Toth, 94 mins.)†

Ran (Japan-France, 1985)***½ Tasuya Nakadai, Satoshi Terao, Jinpachi Nezu, Daisuke Ryu. A complex epic of majestic scope. An aging warlord splits his kingdom among his three sons, rashly banishes the one loving son who objects to this decision, finds himself thrown out into the wilderness by his other two ruthless offspring, and then teeters over the brink of madness as his kingdom topples around him. A visually extraordinary weaving of plot strands from *King Lear* with a Japanese folk legend, *Ran* (translated as "Chaos") paints scenes of domestic intrigue on a broad canvas of warring clans in a stormy universe. (Dir: Akira Kurosawa, 160 mins.)†

Rancho Deluxe (1975)***½ Jeff Bridges, Elizabeth Ashley, Sam Waterston, Clifton James, Slim Pickens. Thanks largely to a quirky, wry, picaresque screenplay by talented novelist Thomas McGuane, this western spoof works quite well most of the time. Bridges and Waterston play two nonchalant cattle rustlers who finally do wind up in the pokey, but they and you will have some droll fun before the final fadeout. (Dir: Frank Perry, 93 mins.)

Rancho Notorious (1952)***½ Marlene Dietrich, Arthur Kennedy, Jack Elam, Mel Ferrer. Cowboy seeking the killer of his fiancée runs across a gambler and dance hall queen who may hold the key. Western with a punch—excellently acted and directed, keeps the interest on high throughout. (Dir: Fritz Lang, 89 mins.)†

Random Harvest (1942)*** Ronald Colman, Greer Garson, Susan Peters, Philip Dorn. Colman has amnesia so he must learn to love Garson over again. Lots of sentiment; Mervyn LeRoy directed with technical competence and without finer sensibility. From the novel by James Hilton. (124 mins.)†

Ranger, The (MTV 1974)** James G. Richardson, Colby Chester, Jim B. Smith, Michael Conrad. Executive producer Jack Webb hoped with his "Sierra" series that he could do for park rangers what he had done for paramedics and cops in patrol cars. No such luck. (Dir: Christian I. Nyby II, 72 mins.)

Rangers of Fortune (1940)**½ Fred MacMurray, Albert Dekker, Gilbert Roland. Offbeat western. Story of three renegades who help an old man and a young girl. (Dir: Sam Wood, 82 mins.)

860

Ransom! (1956)**½ Glenn Ford, Donna Reed, Leslie Nielsen. Somewhat hysterical drama of an industrialist who debates whether to pay the ransom when his son is kidnapped. (Dir: Alex Segal, 109 mins.)

Ransom (1978)—See: **Maniac** (1978)

Ransom for a Dead Man (MTV 1971)**½ Peter Falk, Lee Grant. Grant plays a brilliant lawyer who coolly murders her husband, then watches lawmen puzzle over her adroit kidnap-ransom, cover-up scheme. Columbo slowly zeroes in on the true picture. (Dir: Richard Irving, 100 mins.)

Ransom for Alice (MTV 1977)*½ Yvette Mimieux, Gil Gerard, Barnard Hughes, Gene Barry, Charles Napier. Mimieux and Gerard play 1880s deputy marshalls covering the Seattle waterfront in this hokey pilot film for a series. (Dir: David Lowell Rich, 79 mins.)

Rape and Marriage—The Rideout Case (MTV 1980)**½ Mickey Rourke, Linda Hamilton, Rip Torn, Eugene Roche, Conchata Ferrell, Gail Strickland, Gerald McRaney. Disturbing film explores the 1978 rape suit brought by an Oregon wife against her husband. The issues surrounding the case are brought into sharp focus, and the cast articulates the character's feelings exceptionally well. (Dir: Peter Levin, 96 mins.)

Rape of Love (France, 1977)** Nathalie Nell, Alain Foures, Michele Simonnet, Pierre Arditi. Fairly absorbing account of a woman's painful decision to prosecute the men who raped her. (Dir: Yannick Bellon, 117 mins.)†

Rape of Richard Beck, The (MTV 1985)** Richard Crenna, Meredith Baxter Birney, Pat Hingle, George Dzundza, Frances Lee McCain, Cotter Smith. Crenna is a tough police sergeant who treats criminals with disdain and their victims with little compassion. The macho detective becomes a changed man after he himself is attacked and raped by two sadistic hoodlums. (Dir: Karen Arthur, 104 mins.)

Rape Squad—See: **Act of Vengeance** (1974)

Rapid Fire (1989)** Ron Waldron, Michael Wayne, Dawn Tanner, Joe Spinell, Del Zamora. U.S. agent hunts down escaped terrorists armed with a deadly new rapid-fire machine gun. Low-budget shoot-'em-up, made for video. (Dir: David A. Prior, 83 mins.)†

Rappin' (1985)* Mario Van Peebles, Tasia Valenza. This one has a hero named Rappin' John Hood fighting some evil landlords with a mouth that won't stop. (Dir: Joel Silberg, 92 mins.)†

Rapture (U.S.-France, 1965)** Melvyn Douglas, Patricia Gozzi, Dean Stockwell. A romantic drama with pretensions toward art. Douglas plays a retired judge who keeps his beautiful daughter (Gozzi) isolated from the world; enter Stockwell as a handsome, intelligent fugitive. (Dir: John Guillermin, 98 mins.)

Rare-Book Murder, The—See: Fast Company (1938)

Rare Breed, The (1966)** James Stewart, Maureen O'Hara, Brian Keith. Cowhand is entrusted to deliver a prize bull, paving the way for romance with its original owner. Pleasant, slow-moving western. (Dir: Andrew V. McLaglen, 97 mins.)†

Rascals and Robbers—The Secret Adventures of Tom Sawyer and Huck Finn (MTV 1982)**½ Patrick Creadon, Anthony Michael Hall, Anthony Zerbe, Allyn Ann McLerie, Anthony James. This time the adventures of Tom and Huck are completely new (not adapted from Twain's story), and kids just might be the best audience. (Dir: Dick Lowry, 104 mins.)†

Rashomon (Japan, 1951)**** Toshiro Mifune, Machiko Kyo. Superb film about a quartet of people involved in a rape-murder which takes place in the forest. Japan's leading filmmaker Akira Kurosawa combines pictorial beauty and poetic cinema techniques to achieve an exciting and memorable screen experience. (90 mins.)†

Rasped (U.S.-Ukraine, 1990)***½ Sergei Shakurov, Tatiana Kochemasova, Stanislav Stankevich, Georgii Drozd, Alexii Cerebriakov, Marina Mogilevskaya. Unique and enthralling drama with powerful performances, which fictionalizes and humanizes the tragic disaster after the nuclear power plant at Chernobyl exploded and burned. Postproduction was completed at George Lucas's state-of-the-art technical facilities in California. AKA: Decay. (Dir: Mikhail Belikov, 103 mins.)

Raspberry Ripple (Great Britain, 1987)**½ John Gordon Sinclair, Faye Dunaway, Nabil Shaban, Rosie Kerslake. Pale imitation of a Dennis Potter (*Pennies From Heaven*) script with Sinclair as a crippled young Scot residing in an institution and fantasizing about a life of crime à la '30s gangsters films. Dunaway is impressive as always in a dual role as the matron of the institution and a rival criminal. (Dir: Nigel Finch, 85 mins.)

Rasputin (U.S.S.R., 1985)**½ Alexei Petrenko, Anatoly Romashin, Velta Linne. Bizarre accounting of the Svengali-like hold that the mad Rasputin had on the Russian Court. (Dir: Elem Klimov, 104 mins.)

Rasputin and the Empress (1932)*** John, Ethel, and Lionel Barrymore, Diana Wynyard, Ralph Morgan. The only film with all three Barrymores; a remarkable look at a romanticized White Russia before the Revolution. (Dir: Richard Boleslawski, 130 mins.)

Rasputin—The Mad Monk (Great Britain, 1966)**½ Christopher Lee, Barbara Shelley, Richard Pasco, Francis Matthews. Putting historical inaccuracy aside, this is an effective, colorful shocker about Rasputin's insinuation of himself into the last of Russia's royal households, thanks to his uncanny hypnotic powers and sexuality. (Dir: Don Sharp, 92 mins.)

Ratboy (1986)*** Sondra Locke, S. L. Baird, Robert Townsend, Christopher Hewett, Gerrit Graham. Offbeat fable about a strange creature who's discovered and exploited by various high pressure Los Angelenos out for a buck. About midway through, it falls apart. (Dir: Sondra Locke, 105 mins.)†

Rate It "X" (1986)**½ A narrow-minded documentary exploration of sexism in America that's composed entirely of interviews with men. (Dirs: Lucy Winer, Paula de Koenigsberg, 95 mins.)

Ratings Game, The (MCTV 1984)**½ Danny DeVito, Rhea Perlman, Gerrit Graham, Ronnie Graham. DeVito stars in and directs this opus which tells the story of a streetwise, self-made trucking millionaire who wants to be a Hollywood producer. The gimmick involves a rating service and the names of 100 families who could make a hit of any TV show if they tuned in. Sporadically funny. (102 mins.)†

Rationing (1944)**½ Wallace Beery, Marjorie Main, Donald Meek, Connie Gilchrist, Henry O'Neil. WWII homefront comedy with Beery as a meatpacker hassled by townspeople who want him to ignore rationing regulations. (Dir: Willis Goldbeck, 93 mins.)

Raton Pass (1951)**½ Dennis Morgan, Patricia Neal, Steve Cochran. Exciting western. Husband and wife fight tooth and nail for a cattle empire. (Dir: Edwin L. Marin, 84 mins.)

Rat Pfink a Boo Boo (1966)½ Vin Saxon, Carolyn Brandt, Titus Moede, Kogar the Swinging Ape. When evil threatens, rock star Lonnie Lord and his gardener Titus Twimbley rush into a closet and become caped crimefighters Rat Pfink and Boo Boo. Mostly improvised movie starts out as a serious thriller, then halfway through becomes a parody of "Batman." Whether or not it was intended to be, it's pretty funny all the same. The title was supposed to be *Rat Pfink and Boo Boo*, but the titlemaker screwed up and filmmaker Ray Dennis Steckler couldn't afford to have it fixed! (72 mins.)†

Rat Race, The (1960)*** Tony Curtis, Debbie Reynolds, Jack Oakie, Kay Medford, Don Rickles. Tough-tender story of the Big City, of a love affair developing between a naïve aspiring mu-

861

sician and a brittle-minded dancer. Nice N.Y. atmosphere, some good lines, insight into character. (Dir: Robert Mulligan, 105 mins.)

Rats, The (West Germany, 1955)*** Maria Schell, Heidemarie Hatheyer, Curt Jurgens, Gustav Knuth. The bleakness of post-WWII Berlin is expertly captured in this taut drama about a pregnant woman, abandoned by her lover, who decides to give the newborn baby to a woman who has always wanted a child, an act which leads to conflict later on. (Dir: Robert Siodmak, 91 mins.)

Rattle of a Simple Man (Great Britain, 1964)**½ Harry H. Corbett, Diane Cilento, Thora Hird. Diverting sex comedy features Corbett as a shy bachelor who has to spend a night with entertainer Cilento to win a bet. Knowing of the wager, the girl graciously helps him. (Dir: Muriel Box, 96 mins.)†

Ravagers (1979)* Richard Harris, Ann Turkel, Ernest Borgnine, Art Carney, Anthony James, Woody Strode, Alana Hamilton. An Armageddon drama, set in the 1990s. Harris is a man bent on revenge against a gang of lawless killers who have murdered his wife. He teams up with Carney, Turkel, and Borgnine —they're about as menacing as a gang of accountants. (Dir: Richard Compton, 91 mins.)

Ravel (Canada, 1988)*** Larry Weinstein's film biography of the French composer does what every musical biography should do: lets the music itself explain its creator's greatness. Brief narrated segments and interviews with the composer's friends and colleagues alternate with lengthy excerpts from a broad spectrum of Ravel's works. AKA: **Maurice Ravel.** (Dir: Larry Weinstein, 105 mins.)

Raven, The (1935)*** Boris Karloff, Bela Lugosi. Lurid thriller about a plastic surgeon who adores the works of Edgar Allan Poe. Karloff is effective as a gangster who needs a face-lift, and Bela is sinister as a deranged doctor. (Dir: "Lew Landers" [Louis Friedlander], 61 mins.)†

Raven, The (France, 1943)***½ Pierre Fresnay, Pierre Larquey, Ginette Leclerc, Helene Manson, Micheline Francey. Superbly directed drama about residents of a small French village who are receiving hate mail written by someone who knows the most intimate details of their lives. This exceptional mystery was remade in 1951 as *The Thirteenth Letter.* AKA: **Le Corbeau.** (Dir: Henri-Georges Clouzot, 92 mins.)†

Raven, The (1963)*** Vincent Price, Peter Lorre, Boris Karloff, Hazel Court, Olive Sturgess, Jack Nicholson. Three horror greats were teamed in this pop Gothic spoof of the popular Corman-Poe films. Good-guy sorcerer Price is cajoled by friend Lorre (who's been transformed into the title bird) to visit the castle of conjurer emeritus Karloff; Price and Karloff end up in a black magic duel that's low-budgeted but high-spirited. (Dir: Roger Corman, 85 mins.)†

Raven's Dance (Finland, 1980)***½ Pertti Kalinainen, Paavo Katajsaari, Hilka Matikainen, Eero Kemila. Three residents of northern Finland live in peace and harmony until plans for a highway force them to confront the despoilers of their land. With brilliant acting and a stunning thirty-minute silent opening sequence glorifying nature. (Dir: Markku Lehmuskallio, 80 mins.)

Raven's End (Sweden, 1963)***½ Thommy Berggren, Emy Storm, Keve Hjelm, Ingvar Hirdwall. Fresh autobiographical tale of struggling young writer who lives with his alcoholic father and self-defeated mother in a dreary apartment during the Depression. (Dir: Bo Widerberg, 100 mins.)

Raw—See: **Eddie Murphy Raw**

Raw Deal (1948)*** Dennis O'Keefe, Claire Trevor, Marsha Hunt, Raymond Burr. Framed into prison by the mob, a gangster escapes and goes seeking vengeance. Excellent melodrama with fine direction, photography (by John Alton), good performances. (Dir: Anthony Mann, 79 mins.)

Raw Deal (1986)**½ Arnold Schwarzenegger, Darren McGavin, Sam Wanamaker, Paul Shenar, Blanche Baker, Kathryn Harrold. A rather campy shoot-'em-up flick in which Arnold butts heads with low-lifes while administering multiple contusions to the English language. Unfairly booted out of the FBI, Arnold must single-handedly pulverize a sizable chupk of the Mafia in a violent cartoon that's energetically directed and spiffily acted, (Dir: John Irvin, 97 mins.)†

Raw Edge (1956)** Rory Calhoun, Yvonne De Carlo. Routine western with rancher Calhoun's hired hands plotting to kill him. (Dir: John Sherwood, 76 mins.)

Rawhead Rex (Great Britain-Ireland, 1987)* David Dukes, Kelly Piper, Hugh O'Connor. A mythic monster runs amok in a little Irish town. Horror outing with a totally artificial-looking creature at its center; notable only for being the scripting debut of bloody bard Clive Barker. (Dir: George Pavlou, 89 mins.)†

Rawhide—See: **Desperate Siege**

Rawhide Years, The (1956)*** Tony Curtis, Colleen Miller, Arthur Kennedy. Fast, funny western yarn about double crosses and false accusations which cause Tony to become a hunted fugitive bent on clearing his name. (Dir: Rudolph Maté, 85 mins.)

Raw Meat (Great Britain, 1973)**½ Donald

Pleasence, David Ladd, Sharon Gurney, Christopher Lee, Clive Swift, Norman Rossington. Flamboyant horror film with enough shock value to coast over its defects. A subterranean race of cannibals is alive and thriving under the London underground. AKA: **Death Line.** (Dir: Gary Sherman, 87 mins.)

Raw Wind in Eden (1958)**½ Esther Williams, Jeff Chandler, Rossana Podesta. A mildly entertaining adventure yarn with an island setting and two-fisted men fighting over statuesque Miss Williams. (Dir: Richard Wilson, 89 mins.)

Raymie (1960)**½ David Ladd, Julie Adams, Richard Arlen, John Agar. The charm of this film can be attributed to Ladd's completely believable performance as a boy who loves animals and fish, especially barracuda. Good family film fare. (Dir: Frank McDonald, 72 mins.)

Ray of Sunshine, A (Austria, 1933)***½ Annabella, Gustav Frolich, Paul Otto, Hans Marr. Masterful early Austrian sound film, a brilliant evocation of urban romance, about a young couple struggling to survive in Vienna during the Great Depression. Enchanting film was directed by Paul Fejos, who would also make films in Hollywood. (85 mins.)

Razorback (Australia, 1984)*** Gregory Harrison, Bill Kerr, Arkie Whitely. Due to the muscular visual style from a director trained in rock videos and to the atmospheric art direction, this horror film develops razor-sharp tension as a monstrous porker runs hog-wild and disposes of several unfortunate Aussies. (Dir: Russell Mulcahy, 94 mins.)†

Razor's Edge, The (1946)**½ Tyrone Power, Gene Tierney, Clifton Webb, John Payne, Anne Baxter, Herbert Marshall. Story of a man's search for faith, adapted from Somerset Maugham's novel, is a rambling, charismatically performed film which has some high spots but fails to hold up. An "A" for effort but the book was too difficult to adapt. (Dir: Edmund Goulding, 146 mins.)†

Razor's Edge, The (1984)* Bill Murray, Catherine Hicks, James Keach, Theresa Russell, Denholm Elliott, Brian Doyle-Murray. This remake of Maugham's story about a man's search for the meaning of life after experiencing the horrors of war is stuffed with anachronistic dialogue and attitudes, jam-packed with inept scene transitions and filled with unfortunate performances. As the lead character, Murray falls back on his wise guy personality and is unappealing. (Dir: John Byrum, 120 mins.)†

Reach for the Sky (Great Britain, 1956)***½ Kenneth More, Muriel Pavlow, Alexander Knox, Nigel Green.

Amazing true story of Douglas Bader, an ebullient character who became a WWII flying ace and squadron commander despite having lost both legs in an accident several years earlier. (Dir: Lewis Gilbert, 108 mins.)

Reaching for the Moon (1917)*** Douglas Fairbanks, Eileen Percy, Richard Cummings. Rapid-fire, frantic comedy with Fairbanks as a young clerk who dreams he is the long-lost heir to the throne of a Ruritanian kingdom. Story by Anita Loos. (Dir: John Emerson, 60 mins.)†

Reaching for the Moon (1931)*½ Douglas Fairbanks, Jr., Bebe Daniels, Edward Everett Horton, Jack Mulhall, Bing Crosby. A dated, flat comedy about a clock-watching businessman who's led around by the nose by a snooty hedonistic heiress. Daniels's behavior toward the lovestruck Fairbanks is intended to be charming but comes across as cruel and callous. (Dir: Edmund Goulding, 62 mins.)†

Reaching for the Sun (1941)**½ Joel McCrea, Ellen Drew, Eddie Bracken, Albert Dekker, Billy Gilbert. Original, realistic romance of a country boy and a city girl trying to make a life together, despite their differences. Flawed script, but a worthy try. (Dir: William Wellman, 90 mins.)

Reader, The—See: **La Lectrice**

Ready, Willing and Able (1937)** Ruby Keeler, Lee Dixon, Allen Jenkins, Louise Fazenda, Carol Hughes. Get ready for a willing and able cast in this minor musical about two songwriters searching for a star for their new show. Famous for the dance number on the typewriter to "Too Marvelous for Words." (Dir: Ray Enright, 95 mins.)

Real American Hero, A (MTV 1978)** Brian Dennehy, Forrest Tucker, Ken Howard. Pilot film based on the real-life Tennessee sheriff Buford Pusser, best known from the *Walking Tall* films. (Dir: Lou Antonio, 104 mins.)

Real Genius (1985)*** Val Kilmer, Gabe Jarret, Michelle Meyrink, William Atherton, Patti D'Arbanville, Jonathan Gries. An undisciplined but sometimes hilarious youth comedy about smart kids who are more obsessed with science than sex. The characters in question are college students who are unknowingly constructing a secret weapon for their creepy teacher. When the prodigies discover how they've been used, all sorts of technological hell breaks loose. (Dir: Martha Coolidge, 104 mins.)†

Real Glory, The (1939)*** Gary Cooper, David Niven, Andrea Leeds. Rousing action film about three soldiers who aid in trying to squelch the terrorist uprising in the Philippines. (Dir: Henry Hathaway, 100 mins.)

Real Life (1979)*** Albert Brooks, Charles Grodin, Frances Lee McCain, J. A. Preston. Brooks's feature debut is self-indulgent and overblown, which is just right for this hilarious examination of cinematic excessiveness. Brooks mockingly uses his own name as a pompous director who tries to turn the daily activities of a "normal" American family into a documentary on a par with *Citizen Kane*. (Dir: Albert Brooks, 99 mins.)†

Real Men (1987)*½ James Belushi, John Ritter, Barbara Barrie. Superspy Belushi has to dupe meek civilian Ritter, the double of a dead agent, into helping him on a CIA mission to save the world. Spoof deserves some credit for its deadpan approach to bizarre material; unfortunately, that tactic kills the laughs in what should have been a surefire comedy. (Dir: Dennis Feldman, 86 mins.)†

Re-Animator (1985)*** Jeffrey Combs, Bruce Abbott, Barbara Crampton, David Gale. Based on several stories by H. P. Lovecraft, the story begins with a young doctor who has discovered a "re-animating" serum, one that restores the dead to life—sort of. This movie is *so* gross that it crosses the line (quite intentionally) into humor, although never at the expense of the story. What the bad guy, who is reduced to carrying his own head around, almost does to the heroine at the end is not to be missed, and the entire final sequence is Grand Guignol unequalled even by Romero. (Dir: Stuart Gordon, 86 mins.)†

Reap the Wild Wind (1942)*** Ray Milland, John Wayne, Paulette Goddard, Susan Hayward, Robert Preston, Lynne Overman, Raymond Massey, Hedda Hopper. Lavish Cecil B. DeMille adventure tale of an 1840 love triangle off the Florida Keys where the most profitable thing a man could do was wreck ships. Oscar: Best Special Effects. (124 mins.)†

Rearview Mirror (MTV 1984)**½ Michael Beck, Tony Musante, Lee Remick. Nightmare movie with one aim—to frighten. Beck is properly scary as the deranged convict who commandeers a pretty woman (Remick) to drive through the wild, swampy Carolina countryside. (Dir: Lou Antonio, 104 mins.)

Rear Window (1954)**** James Stewart, Grace Kelly, Raymond Burr, Wendell Corey, Thelma Ritter. Alfred Hitchcock-directed suspense treat—photographer is laid up in his apartment, takes to examining his neighbors through binoculars, and becomes convinced his neighbor (Burr) has killed his wife. Nail-biting tension laced with some scenes of sharp sophisticated comedy, a delight from beginning to end. (112 mins.)†

Reason to Live, A (MTV 1985)*½ Deidre

Hall, Peter Fonda, Carrie Snodgress, Ricky Schroder. Can a kid talk his hardluck dad out of suicide? Cute Schroder can't get through to his father (Fonda) after Mom walks out. (Dir: Peter Levin, 104 mins.)

Reason to Live, a Reason to Die, A—See: **Massacre at Fort Holmes**

Rebecca (1940)**** Laurence Olivier, Joan Fontaine, Judith Anderson, George Sanders, Gladys Cooper, Nigel Bruce, Reginald Denny, Leo G. Carroll. An impeccably crafted Gothic love story, this adaptation of Daphne Du Maurier's best-seller was Alfred Hitchcock's first American film. The mystery of Rebecca's death and the heartbreaking attempts of the new bride to emulate her sophisticated predecessor are interwoven by Hitchcock into an eerie triangle between husband, new bride, and the first Mrs. de Winter. Unsurpassed as a mystery-romance, this atmospheric classic is Alfred's only film to win a Best Picture Oscar. (130 mins.)†

Rebecca of Sunnybrook Farm (1938)**½ Shirley Temple, Randolph Scott, Jack Haley, Bill "Bojangles" Robinson. If you like Shirley you'll love her in this, but if you want your kids to see a faithful screen adaptation of the famous children's book, this is not it. (Dir: Allan Dwan, 74 mins.)†

Rebel (Australia, 1986)** Matt Dillon, Debbie Byrne, Bryan Brown. Dillon is Rebel, an American deserter from WWII who falls for a nightclub songbird in wartime Australia. Unconvincing drama. (Dir: Michael Jenkins, 93 mins.)†

Rebel in Town (1956)*** John Payne, Ruth Roman, J. Carrol Naish, Ben Cooper. Potent, thoughtful western about ex-Rebel renegades on their way to California after the Civil War. When one of them accidentally shoots a boy, rage builds up among the townspeople until a lynching is threatened. (Dir: Alfred L. Werker, 78 mins.)

Rebellion (Japan, 1967)*** Toshiro Mifune, Takeshi Kata, Michikoi Otsuka, Yoko Tsukasa, Tatsuya Nakadai. Intense drama about a feudal 18th-century lord whose authority over all things, especially romance, is challenged by a young man who refuses to part with his wife because of a traditional ritual which affects their lives. Filled with stylized swordplay. (Dir: Masaki Kobayashi, 121 mins.)

Rebel Rousers (1967)**½ Cameron Mitchell, Bruce Dern, Diane Ladd, Jack Nicholson, Harry Dean Stanton. Rousing sixties melodrama only for camp lovers and sociologists. A "shocker" about Dern offering his pregnant girlfriend as the prize in a drag race. Check out Nicholson's striped pants! (Dir: Martin B. Cohen, 78 mins.)†

Rebels, The (MTV 1979)**½ Andrew Stevens, Don Johnson, Doug McClure, Jim Backus, Joan Blondell, Tom Bosley, Rory Calhoun. John Jakes rides again in another TV installment of one of his books. This sequel to *The Bastard* deals with Philip Kent's activities during the Revolutionary War. (Dir: Russ Mayberry, 200 mins.)

Rebel Storm (1990)**½ Zach Gilligan, Rod McCary, Wayne Crawford, June Chadwick, John Rhys-Davies, Elizabeth Kiefer. Spirited, tongue-in-cheek sci-fi adventure set in 2099 A.D., when the U.S. is a vast wasteland controlled by fascists via television while hordes of displaced people travel the country in outsized armed vehicles. AKA: *Rising Storm*. (Dir: Francis Shaeffer, 85 mins.)†

Rebel Without a Cause (1955)***½ James Dean, Natalie Wood, Sal Mineo, Jim Backus, Ann Doran, Dennis Hopper, Nick Adams. Sensitively acted story of a teenager who is not satisfied with a world he never made. Dean's performance is touching and exciting; Wood and Mineo are first-rate. (Dir: Nicholas Ray, 111 mins.)†

Reckless (1934)** Jean Harlow, William Powell, Franchot Tone. Some good performers are wasted in this trashy chronicle of a chorus girl and her effect on people's lives. (Dir: Victor Fleming, 96 mins.)

Reckless (1984)*½ Aidan Quinn, Daryl Hannah, Kenneth McMillan, Lois Smith. Mix equal parts *All the Right Moves, The Wild One, The Loveless . . .* No, stop! You've seen this before. A young motorcycle-riding punk becomes enamored of a pretty young thing who wants to redeem him. Stylish direction, thin plot. (Dir: James Foley, 90 mins.)†

Reckless Disregard (MCTV 1985)**½ Tess Harper, Ronny Cox, Leslie Nielsen, Kate Lynch. Controversial, timely movie about a TV show which may or may not have been guilty of "reckless disregard" in making accusations against a clinic. (Dir: Harvey Hart, 104 mins.)†

Reckless Moment, The (1949)***½ James Mason, Joan Bennett, Geraldine Brooks, Henry O'Neill. A woman who has killed a scoundrel to protect her family finds herself in the clutches of a blackmailer. Well acted and directed, this is a good melodrama. (Dir: Max Ophuls, 82 mins.)

Reckoning, The (Great Britain, 1969)*** Nicol Williamson, Rachel Roberts. Williamson stars as a ruthless businessman who has made a success in southern England but is forced to return to his home in the north to visit his dying father. (Dir: Jack Gold, 109 mins.)

Record, The (West Germany-Switzerland, 1984)*** Uwe Ochsenknecht, Laszlo I. Kisch, Catarina Raacke. Satiric parable about a TV addict who tries to cash in by setting the world's record for nonstop television watching. The measure of the movie's success is that, after watching it, you'll want to take an ax to your own TV. (Dir: Daniel Helfer, 92 mins.)

Recreation, The (France, 1961)**½ Jean Seberg, Christian Marquand. Interesting weaving of suspense and first love as Seberg plays a teenager infatuated with a sculptor involved in a murder. Based on a Françoise Sagan story. (Dir: Françoise Moreuil, 87 mins.)

Recruits (1986)** Alan Deveau, Annie McAuley, Lolita David. A goofy combination of sex and silliness runs rampant throughout this tale of fledgling coppers enduring the horrors of recruiting camp as well as the strain of on-the-job slapstick. (Dir: Rafal Zielinski, 82 mins.)†

Red Alert (MTV 1977)*** William Devane, Ralph Waite, Michael Brandon, Adrienne Barbeau. Gripping suspense drama about troubles within a nuclear power plant. Provokes many questions about nuclear power-plant safety, and our growing dependence upon computer control. (Dir: William Hale, 106 mins.)†

Red and the Black, The (France, 1957)***½ Gerard Philipe, Danielle Darrieux, Antonella Lualdi. Stendhal's great work is given a sensitive and successful treatment on film, but don't expect all the novel's subtleties. A young man from provincial nineteenth-century France aspires to greatness, chooses first the Church, then gentleman's employment, and gentlewoman's seduction, to accomplish his ends. (Dir: Claude Autant-Lara, 145 mins.)

Red and the White, The (Hungary, 1967)***½ Tatyana Konyukova, Krystyna Mikolajewska, Mikhail Kasakov. Powerful and spectacular film tells the bitter and tragic story of Hungarian nationals fighting with the Red Army against White Russian troops in 1918. Told with minimal dialogue and sweeping imagery. (Dir: Miklos Jancso, 90 mins.)†

Red Badge of Courage, The (1951)**½ Audie Murphy, Bill Mauldin, Arthur Hunnicutt, John Dierkes, Royal Dano, Andy Devine. From Stephen Crane's novel of the Civil War. Terribly mangled by the studio, John Huston's film about a reluctant hero is still a remarkably powerful discussion of war. (69 mins.)†

Red Badge of Courage, The (MTV 1974)*** Richard Thomas, Warren Berlinger, Wendell Burton, Charles Aidman. This faithful adaptation of Stephen Crane's classic Civil War novel about fear under fire stars Thomas as Henry Fleming, the youth who questions his courage in battle, runs away, and then fights again in a fit of madness with his tattered company of greenhorns. (Dir: Lee Philips, 74 mins.)

Red Ball Express (1952)** Jeff Chandler, Alex Nicol, Sidney Poitier, Hugh O'Brian, Jack Kelly. Routine WWII drama. Chandler plays a tough but human leader of the truck division known as the Red Ball Express. (Dir: Budd Boetticher, 83 mins.)

Red Balloon, The (France, 1955)**** A small boy finds a balloon which follows him everywhere and fills his need for friendship. When the balloon ultimately lifts the child to the sky, it's a lovely liberating expression of the freedom of childhood. Imaginative and superbly photographed. (Dir: Pascal Lamorisse, 34 mins.)†

Red Beard (Japan, 1965)***½ Toshiro Mifune, Yuzo Kayama, Yoshio Tsuchiya. Superb period piece about the clash between a rash young doctor and his superior in a medical clinic struggling for survival. The re-creation of nineteenth-century Japan is evocative, and the story is powerfully acted. AKA: **Akahige**. (Dir: Akira Kurosawa, 185 mins.)†

Red Danube, The (1949)**½ Walter Pidgeon, Janet Leigh, Peter Lawford, Ethel Barrymore, Angela Lansbury. Interesting but overdramatic story of political intrigue and romance in Europe. A handsome British officer and a lovely ballerina are plagued by the Communists. (Dir: George Sidney, 119 mins.)

Red Dawn (1984)*½ Patrick Swayze, C. Thomas Howell, Ron O'Neal, Powers Boothe, Harry Dean Stanton, Lea Thompson. Contemptible fable from right-wing idealogue John Milius. Rather than wage nuclear war, the Russian-Cuban forces invade the United States after America is abandoned by her Allies. When their town is taken by Communist troops in this conventional war, some teenagers head for the hills and build their own resistance movement against the invaders. (114 mins.)†

Red Desert (Italy-France, 1964)***½ Monica Vitti, Richard Harris. Considered by some to be Michelangelo Antonioni's finest achievement, this story of a woman trying to cope with her neurosis in the face of a modernized, mechanistic society is a meditation on the beauty of a man-made world. His use of color to express emotional states was commendably audacious, and Vitti is superb. (120 mins.)

Red Dragon (1945)** Sidney Toler, Fortunio Bonanova, Benson Fong. Slow-paced Charlie Chan outing about a plot to steal a scientist's plans for an atomic bomb. (Dir: Phil Rosen, 64 mins.)

Red-Dragon (Italy-West Germany, 1967)* Stewart Granger, Rosanna Schiaffino,
866

Horst Frank, Suzanne Roquette. FBI agents Granger and Schiaffino pursue a smuggling gang through Hong Kong. (Dir: Ernest Hofbauer, 89 mins.)

Red Dust (1932)***½ Clark Gable, Jean Harlow, Mary Astor, Gene Raymond. Sexy hothouse comedy-drama, with Gable and Harlow at their easiest together. The film is frank, funny, and not sunk by the dramatics of Astor having an affair with Gable while husband Raymond is out scouting rubber. Remade with Gable as *Mogambo*. (Dir: Victor Fleming, 83 mins.)†

Red Earth, White Earth (MTV, 1988)** Genevieve Bujold, Timothy Daly, Ralph Waite, Richard Farnsworth. Farm opera with prodigal son Daly returning home to find the family farm under claim by Indians and his family beset by personal turmoil. Complicated story suffers from unsympathetic characters. (Dir: David Greene, 96 mins.)

Red Flag: The Ultimate Game (MTV, 1981)*½ Barry Bostwick, Joan Van Ark, William Devane. Melodramatic account of highly motivated pilots involved in dangerous war games and the women who wait for them. (Dir: Don Taylor, 104 mins.)†

Red Garters (1954)**½ Rosemary Clooney, Jack Carson, Gene Barry, Guy Mitchell. Satire of westerns uses all the standard plot ramifications: man seeks revenge for brother's death, falls for the purty town girl, etc. All done with stylized sets, costumes. It doesn't work but represents a try for something different. (Dir: George Marshall, 91 mins.)

Redhead and the Cowboy, The (1950)** Glenn Ford, Rhonda Fleming, Edmond O'Brien. At the close of the Civil War a cowhand is mistaken for a Confederate spy by a beautiful courier, gets himself tangled in espionage. (Dir: Leslie Fenton, 82 mins.)

Red-Headed Stranger (1986)*½ Willie Nelson, Morgan Fairchild, Katharine Ross, Royal Dano. A tepid Willie Nelson vehicle about a parson who travels with his bride to a new church in Montana, where he ends up divorcing his wife with his six-guns and also tangling with some varmints over the town's water rights. (Dir: William Witliff, 105 mins.)†

Red-Headed Woman (1932)*** Jean Harlow, Chester Morris, Charles Boyer, Lewis Stone. Harlow's shopgirl doesn't care what it takes to crash society, and she marries her boss, whose friends don't accept her. Brash fun. Harlow at her funniest and Boyer in a small role as a chauffeur. (Dir: Jack Conway, 74 mins.)†

Redhead from Manhattan (1943)** Lupe Velez, Michael Duane. Theatrical star agrees to impersonate her cousin until the cousin has her baby, which causes romantic mix-ups. (Dir: Lew Landers, 63 mins.)

Redhead from Wyoming, The (1952)**½ Maureen O'Hara, Alexander Scourby, Alex Nicol, Jack Kelly, Dennis Weaver. Snappy sagebrush adventure about a fiery-tempered redhead with interests on both sides of the law. (Dir: Lee Sholem, 80 mins.)

Red Heat (U.S.-West Germany, 1985)*½ Linda Blair, Sylvia Kristel, Sue Kiel. Linda's back in a women's prison. This time it's in East Germany, after being unlucky enough to get too close to a defecting scientist. In the role of the bitch prisoner who runs everything, Kristel provides a few outrageous moments, but otherwise this is straight formula. (Dir: Robert Collector, 104 mins.)†

Red Heat (1988)**½ Arnold Schwarzenegger, James Belushi, Peter Boyle, Ed O'Ross, Larry Fishburne. Russian cop Schwarzenegger teams up with Chicago police detective Belushi. Director Walter Hill borrows too much from his own *48 HRS.*, though his handling of the perfunctory chase and shoot-out sequences makes this a must-see for fans of high-wired violence. (103 mins.)†

Red, Hot and Blue (1949)**½ Betty Hutton, Victor Mature, June Havoc, William Demarest. Girl ambitious to get ahead in the theater is helped by a director and a publicist but runs afoul of gangsters. Pleasant comedy is mainly a showcase for Hutton's brassy talents. (Dir: John Farrow, 84 mins.)

Red House, The (1947)*** Edward G. Robinson, Lon McCallister, Judith Anderson, Rory Calhoun, Julie London. A farmer holds a terrifying secret concerning a sinister house in the woods. Good suspense thriller. (Dir: Delmer Daves, 100 mins.)†

Red Inn, The (France, 1954)***½ Fernandel, Françoise Rosay, Julien Carette, Marie-Claire Olivia. Hugely enjoyable comedy-mystery, set in the early 1800s, about a disparate party stranded at a mysterious inn where murders are occurring. Fernandel, as a wise, seasoned monk, turns detective to clear up the puzzle. Fascinating and delightful. (Dir: Claude Autant-Lara, 100 mins.)†

Red Kimona, The (1925)**½ Priscilla Bonner, Theodore von Eltz, Tyrone Power. Tale of a young woman's descent into prostitution and murder, to be finally redeemed by an honest young man's love. Ridiculous story is a fascinating social document of the '20s nevertheless. (Dir: Walter Lang, 60 mins.)†

Red King, White Knight (MTV 1989)*** Tom Skerritt, Max von Sydow, Helen Mirren, Tom Bell, Neil Dugeon, Gavan O'Herlihy, Barry Corbin, Clarke Peters, Shane Rimmer. Ex-CIA agent Skerritt is called back into duty to stop the assassination of Mikhail Gorbachev by KGB officials who aren't too happy with Glasnost. Politically hip script is the basis for this above-average spy thriller. (Dir: Geoff Murphy, 104 mins.)†

Red Light (1949)** George Raft, Virginia Mayo, Raymond Burr. Another "innocent-man-sent-to-prison" mystery drama, with Raft playing his usual Great Stone Face. (Dir: Roy Del Ruth, 83 mins.)

Red Light Sting, The (MTV 1984)** Farrah Fawcett, Beau Bridges, Harold Gould. Easy-to-take yarn about cops running a San Francisco brothel to nail suave mobsters. (Dir: Rod Holcomb, 104 mins.)†

Red Line 7000 (1965)**½ James Caan, Laura Devon, Charlene Holt. Race car drivers are driven to succeed in a standard racetrack drama fueled by the energy of the attractive cast. Howard Hawks fans regard this film highly, but others may find it's just another stock, stock-car drama. (Dir: Howard Hawks, 110 mins.)

Red Mountain (1951)**½ Alan Ladd, Lizabeth Scott, John Ireland, Arthur Kennedy. Confederate officer assigned to raider Quantrill discovers the leader is out for himself alone, goes on the hunt for him. Well-made moves at a fast clip. (Dir: William Dieterle, 84 mins.)

Redneck (Italy-Great Britain, 1972)*½ Franco Nero, Telly Savalas, Mark Lester. A grade "Z" low-budget crime chase thriller. (Dir: Silvio Narizzano, 87 mins.)†

Red Neck County (1975)* Leslie Uggams, Shelley Winters, Michael Christian, Ted Cassidy, Dub Taylor, Slim Pickens. They don't cotton to wealthy Yankee ladies, especially black ones, way down South. But they pick the wrong rich, black, northern chick to pick on when they mess with Leslie. AKA: **Poor Pretty Eddie.** (Dir: Richard Robinson, 86 mins.)

Redneck Zombies (1988)½ Lisa DeHaven, William E. Benson, P. Floyd Piranha, Zoofoot. This exploitation flick, shot on video, is a tasteless, abysmal attempt at a cult film. Made by gore fans who can sling plenty of blood but have no idea what makes a good horror film. (Dir: Pericles Lewnes, 90 mins.)†

Red Planet Mars (1952)** Peter Graves, Andrea King, Marvin Miller, Herbert Berghof. The first born-again sci-fi movie. The Ruskies and the Americans put aside their cold war difficulties when it's discovered that the Voice of Radio Free Mars belongs to God. A movie only the Moral Majority could love; so, in a way, this imbecilic religion-in-space film was ahead of its time. (Dir: Harry Horner, 87 mins.)

Red Pony, The (1949)*** Robert Mitchum, Myrna Loy, Peter Miles. Ranch boy is gifted with a colt, grows to love him but the colt escapes. John Steinbeck story receives a good production, but moves rather leisurely. (Dir: Lewis Milestone, 89 mins.)†

Red Pony, The (1973)*** Henry Fonda, Maureen O'Hara, Ben Johnson, Jack Elam, Clint Howard, Richard Jaeckel. Expert TV adaptation of Steinbeck's book about a boy's troubled relationship with his dad and his attachment to a pet pony who helps him escape his problems with his family. (Dir: Robert Totten, 104 mins.)

Red Psalm (Hungary, 1971)***½ Lajos Balazsovits, Andras Balint, Gyongyi Buros. Magnificent in its use of color, this emotional allegory tells the story about a strike by farm workers on an estate owned by a strident count who calls in the militia. Everything stops when the farmers break into a grand ethnic dance, putting off the inevitable clash with the army. (Dir: Miklos Jancso, 88 mins.)

Red River (1948)**** John Wayne, Montgomery Clift, Walter Brennan, Joanne Dru, John Ireland, Noah Beery, Jr., Coleen Gray, Paul Fix, Harry Carey, Sr., Harry Carey, Jr. Sprawling, lusty western blessed with extraordinary direction and the surprisingly forceful teaming of the screen's foremost macho man with the screen's most sensitive introvert. In this exemplary western, Wayne and Clift play a cattle baron and his son at odds over the way John runs his empire. The film climaxes in a memorable knock-down-drag-out confrontation between the two during a cattle drive over the Chisholm Trail. A restored "director cut" is available on video. (Dir: Howard Hawks, 133 mins.)†

Red River (MTV 1988)*½ James Arness, Bruce Boxleitner, Gregory Harrison, Ray Walston. Pallid, unnecessary remake of the Hawks classic about a two-fisted rancher (Arness) and his young charge. (Dir: Richard Michaels, 96 mins.)

Reds (1981)***½ Warren Beatty, Diane Keaton, Edward Herrmann, Jack Nicholson, Paul Sorvino, Maureen Stapleton, Jerzy Kosinski. Courageous, monumental movie biography of radical journalist John Reed, his wife, Louise Bryant, and their involvement in the American radical movement and the Russian Revolution. A brilliant mix of personal stories, the sweep of history, and the passion to change the world. (Dir: Warren Beatty, 199 mins.)†

Red Salute (1935)** Barbara Stanwyck, Robert Young, Hardie Albright, Cliff Edwards, Ruth Donnelly. What would Joe McCarthy have made of this screwball comedy? He'd have seen red as Stanwyck falls for a soldier boy while her first boyfriend spreads Communist doctrine to the masses. (Dir: Sidney Lanfield, 78 mins.)

Red Scorpion (1989)* Dolph Lundgren, M. Emmet Walsh, Al White, Brion James. Sent to assassinate an African rebel leader, a Russian agent instead teams up with the natives to drive out the Communists. Lundgren has an imposing presence but no acting ability, and the movie is a yawner. (Dir: Joseph Zito, 102 mins.)†

Red Shoes, The (Great Britain, 1948)**** Moira Shearer, Anton Walbrook. An impresario persuades a ballerina to give up her romance with a composer and sacrifice all for art. Beautiful design and superb dancing, but an overdone dramatic plot. Still, this is practically everyone's favorite ballet film. (Dirs: Michael Powell, Emeric Pressburger, 133 mins.)†

Red Skies of Montana (1952)** Richard Widmark, Jeffrey Hunter, Richard Boone. Adventure yarn about the brave band of forest fire fighters. Hunter's efforts to gain revenge for his father's accidental death in a mission led by Widmark merely serves as a stage wait between holocausts. (Dir: Joseph M. Newman, 89 mins.)

Red Sky at Morning (1971)**½ Richard Thomas, Claire Bloom, Desi Arnaz, Jr., Richard Crenna. Despite some flaws, this nostalgic excursion about a teenage boy coming into his own in New Mexico in 1944 works fairly well, thanks largely to Thomas's performance in the leading role. (Dir: James Goldstone, 113 mins.)

Red Sonja (1985)*½ Arnold Schwarzenegger, Brigitte Nielsen, Sandahl Bergman, Paul Smith, Ronald Lacey. Pumped-up sword and sorcery actioner in which beefcake boy Schwarzenegger joins in the heroics with the title character, thus making the world safe for people with beautiful bodies. (Dir: Richard Fleischer, 88 mins.)†

Red Sorghum (China, 1987)***½ Gong Li, Jiang Wen, Liu Ji. Absorbing story of the lives of two strong-willed rural Chinese in the 1920s and '30s. The story is rich in incident, and the photography of the Chinese countryside, seldom seen by American audiences, is breathtaking. (Dir: Zhang Yimou, 91 mins.)

Red Spider, The (MTV 1988)*½ James Farentino, Amy Steel, Jennifer O'Neill. The characters from *One Police Plaza* return in this by-the-numbers murder mystery. Farentino plays a N.Y.C. police lieutenant who investigates a series of Chinatown murders distinguished by spider markings. (Dir: Jerry Jameson, 96 mins.)

Red Sun (France-Italy-Spain, 1971)* Charles Bronson, Ursula Andress, Alain

Delon, Toshiro Mifune, Capucine. International cast in a dull western about a falling-out between a pair of crooks. Only interesting point is the absurdity of a Japanese samurai in full dress in the middle of the 1860s West. (Dir: Terence Young, 112 mins.)

Red Sundown (1956)** Rory Calhoun, Martha Hyer, Dean Jagger. Usual western tale about the lawless renegade turned lawful deputy and the trouble he encounters before and after the transition. (Dir: Jack Arnold, 81 mins.)

Red Tent, The (Italy-U.S.S.R., 1971)**½ Peter Finch, Sean Connery, Hardy Kruger, Claudia Cardinale. Well-acted adventure film about the '28 rescue of the crew of the dirigible *Italia*, commanded by General Umberto Nobile (Finch), which crashed during a North Pole flight. (Dir: Mikhail K. Kalatozov, 121 mins.)†

Red Tomahawk (1967)* Howard Keel, Joan Caulfield, Broderick Crawford. After Custer's defeat at Little Bighorn, the U.S. Cavalry takes on the Sioux and gamblers from the town of Deadwood. (Dir: R. G. Springsteen, 82 mins.)

Reefer Madness (1936)½ Dave O'Brien, Warren McCollum, Dorothy Short, Kenneth Craig, Lillian Miles. An unflinching look at "the new drug menace, the real public enemy #1—Marihuana!" Average Joes and Janes turn loco, becoming psycho killers and brazen hussies, all because of a little toke. (Dir: Louis Gasnier, 67 mins.)†

Reflecting Skin, The (Great Britain, 1990)*** Viggo Mortensen, Lindsay Duncan, Jeremy Cooper, Sheila Moore, Duncan Fraser. Beautifully photographed psychological thriller about the strange events that haunt a seven-year-old boy who lives in the middle of the Idaho prairie in '50s America. The film's tense exploration of the power of nightmares and suggestion is particularly effective. (Dir: Philip Ridley, 93 mins.)

Reflection of Fear, A (1973)** Robert Shaw, Sally Kellerman, Mary Ure, Sondra Locke. Thin *Psycho*-type mystery as a young girl's alter ego goes on a murderous rampage. (Dir: William A. Fraker, 90 mins.)†

Reflections in a Golden Eye (1967)*** Elizabeth Taylor, Marlon Brando, Brian Keith, Julie Harris, Robert Forster. A spirited slice of Southern Gothic. For sensation seekers, the film offers whippings, adultery, fetishism, and nude horseback riding. Brando (replacing the late Montgomery Clift) plays an ineffectual Major who plays soldier with his men, and house with his lusty wife, while sublimating his fierce love for a taciturn private. (Dir: John Huston, 108 mins.)†

Reflections of Murder (MTV 1974)*** Sam Waterston, Tuesday Weld, Joan Hackett.

A competent remake of *Diabolique*, the classic French thriller. A schoolmaster is murdered by his wife and his former mistress. They put his body in the private school's unused swimming pool, but when they drain the pool some days later, the body is gone and the suspense builds to the fascinating close. (Dir: John Badham, 100 mins.)†

Reformer and the Redhead, The (1950)** June Allyson, Dick Powell, David Wayne. Zany comedy bordering on the ridiculous with Allyson as an unpredictable redhead with a nose for trouble and Powell as the patient reformer. (Dir: Norman Panama, 90 mins.)

Reform School Girl (1957)*½ Gloria Castillo, Ross Ford, Ed "Kookie" Byrnes, Jack Kruschen, Sally Kellerman, Yvette Vickers. A young innocent has a rough time of it, what with attempted rape by her uncle and being sent to a reformatory because she rode in a hit-and-run vehicle. (Dir: Edward Bernds, 71 mins.)

Reform School Girls (1986)**½ Sybil Danning, Wendy O. Williams, Pat Ast. Parody of the "women's prison" genre that reworks the standard plot clichés, this-time for *intentional* high camp. As the trashy trio who run the "school," Ast, Williams, and Danning possess just the right mixture of sadistic ingenuity and twisted fashion sense. (Dir: Thomas DeSimone, 98 mins.)†

Reggae Sunsplash (Jamaica-West Germany, 1980)*** Documentary filmed at the Sunsplash II Festival in Montego Bay, Jamaica, includes a brilliant concert performance from Bob Marley, as well as other reggae highlights from Peter Tosh, Burning Spear, and Third World. (Dir: Stefan Paul, 107 mins.)†

Rehearsal for a Crime—See: **Criminal Life of Archibaldo de la Cruze, The**

Rehearsal for Murder (MTV 1982)*** Robert Preston, Lynn Redgrave, Patrick Macnee, Lawrence Pressman. A cerebral whodunit with an ending guaranteed to fool everyone. Preston is the Broadway playwright constructing a play within a play to reveal the murderer of his fiancée and leading lady. An intricate puzzle performed with style by a good cast. (Dir: David Greene, 104 mins.)†

Reign of Terror—See: **Black Book** (1949)

Reincarnation of Peter Proud, The (1975)** Michael Sarrazin, Margot Kidder, Jennifer O'Neill. Clunky yarn: university professor has a recurring dream and suddenly discovers, via a TV documentary, his relation to a man killed decades before. (Dir: J. Lee Thompson, 104 mins.)†

Reivers, The (1969)***½ Steve McQueen, Sharon Farrell, Mitch Vogel, Rupert Crosse. Not all of William Faulkner's novels have survived the transfer to film very well, but this charming tale about the adventures of a 12-year-old boy with some of his older buddies is a notable exception. The journey follows a northward route up to Memphis, and McQueen, giving one of his most winning performances to date, is a big help. (Dir: Mark Rydell, 107 mins.)†

Rejuvenator, The (1988)**½ Vivian Lanko, John MacKay, James Hogue. Horror fans will enjoy this tale of an aging actress who discovers a serum that makes her young again. Of course, there are these unfortunate side effects.... Yes, it's an old, old plot, but it's redone here with a bit of panache. AKA: **Rejuvenatrix**. (Dir: Brian Thomas Jones, 86 mins.)†

Rejuvenatrix—See: **Rejuvenator, The**

Relentless (1948)*** Robert Young, Marguerite Chapman, Akim Tamiroff. A cowboy is accused of murder and, after escaping, sets out to clear himself. Well-made western. Color. (Dir: George Sherman, 89 mins.)

Relentless (MTV 1977)**½ Will Sampson, Monte Markham, John Hillerman. A drama about Arizona state troopers' pursuit of a band of bank robbers, led by a former major. (Dir: Lee H. Katzin, 78 mins.)

Relentless (1989)**½ Judd Nelson, Robert Loggia, Meg Foster, Patrick O'Bryan, Leo Rossi, Mindy Seger. Psychotic killer Nelson, abused as a child, randomly selects his victims from the telephone book. Film's descent into clichés finally reduces its power, but this nifty little thriller is well acted all around. (Dir: William Lustig, 92 mins.)†

Reluctant Astronaut, The (1967)*½ Don Knotts, Arthur O'Connell, Leslie Nielsen, Joan Freeman, Jesse White. Juvenile tale about a silly, nervous nut who "reluctantly" becomes an astronaut. (Dir: Edward Montagne, 101 mins.)

Reluctant Debutante, The (1958)**½ Rex Harrison, Kay Kendall, Sandra Dee, Angela Lansbury, John Saxon. Lightweight comedy fluff sparked considerably by the charm and attractiveness of its leading players—Harrison and Kendall. The story revolves around a zany British couple who choose to have their American-as-apple-pie daughter make her debut in England. (Dir: Vincente Minnelli, 94 mins.)

Reluctant Dragon, The (1941)*** Robert Benchley, Ducky Nash, Florence Gill. One of Disney's first experiments mixing live action and animation, with humorist Benchley touring the studios and watching artists working on the cartoon short of the title, a delightful tale of a dragon who will do practically anything for a quiet life. (Dir: Alfred L. Werker, 72 mins.)†

Reluctant Heroes, The (MTV 1971)** Ken Berry, Jim Hutton. Berry is exceptionally adroit playing the role of Lt. Murphy, a war lieutenant who finds himself heading a dangerous mission against the enemy. (Dir: Robert Day, 73 mins.)

Remains to Be Seen (1953)**½ June Allyson, Van Johnson, Angela Lansbury, Dorothy Dandridge. Band vocalist and an apartment house manager who wants to be a drummer get tangled in a murder case. Mildly entertaining mystery-comedy, helped by a good supporting cast. (Dir: Don Weis, 89 mins.)

Remarkable Andrew, The (1942)**½ William Holden, Brian Donlevy. Ghosts of our founding fathers come to the aid of a timid young man fighting graft. Interesting, well-played hokum. (Dir: Stuart Heisler, 81 mins.)

Remarkable Mr. Pennypacker, The (1959)** Clifton Webb, Dorothy McGuire, Charles Coburn, Jill St. John, David Nelson. Scalawag specializes in large families and small talk—not much of it very amusing either. (Dir: Henry Levin, 87 mins.)

Rembrandt (Great Britain, 1936)*** Charles Laughton, Gertrude Lawrence, Elsa Lanchester. The most intelligent of director Alexander Korda's historical spectacles, but not for art lovers. A lusty, yet emotionally affecting performance by Laughton. (84 mins.)

Remedy for Riches (1940)** Jean Hersholt, Dorothy Lovett, Jed Prouty, Edgar Kennedy. Dr. Christian is the voice of reason here as he guesses the truth about a phony oil scheme and protects his fellow citizens from being exploited. (Dir: Erle C. Kenton, 60 mins.)†

Remember? (1939)** Robert Taylor, Greer Garson, Lew Ayres. Silly little comedy about a guy who elopes with his friend's fiancée, and then the friend, instead of shooting his pal, uses the couple for some nonsensical experiment. (Dir: Norman Z. McLeod, 83 mins.)

Remember Last Night? (1935)**½ Edward Arnold, Constance Cummings, Robert Young, Robert Armstrong, Sally Eilers, Reginald Denny. Terrific ensemble acting and a clever script make up for the structural defects of this thriller about a group of socialites who witnessed a murder while out on a spree—but were all too drunk to remember what they've seen. (Dir: James Whale, 81 mins.)

Remember My Name (1978)*** Anthony Perkins, Geraldine Chaplin, Berry Berenson, Moses Gunn, Jeff Goldblum. Involving, moody drama about psychotic Chaplin and her desire for revenge on ex-husband Perkins and his second wife. She's just out of jail after a long stretch for the killing of Perkins's mistress. (Dir: Alan Rudolph, 94 mins.)

Remember the Day (1941)*** Claudette Colbert, John Payne, Douglas Croft, Ann B. Todd. Sentimental story of a teacher's life, her guidance of one pupil and her unhappy romance. (Dir: Henry King, 85 mins.)

Remember the Night (1940)*** Fred MacMurray, Barbara Stanwyck, Beulah Bondi. Warm, moving story of a DA who takes a shoplifter home with him when court recesses for the Xmas holidays. (Dir: Mitchell Leisen, 86 mins.)

Remember When? (MTV 1974)** Jack Warden, William Schallert, Jamie Smith Jackson. Writer Herman Raucher, who struck gold with the film *Summer of '42*, is still on the '40s nostalgia trail. Here he wrote a pilot for a proposed TV series about the home front during WWII. (Dir: Buzz Kulik, 96 mins.)

Remembrance of Love (MTV 1982)**½ Kirk Douglas, Eric Douglas, Pam Dawber, Robert Clary. Father (Douglas) and daughter (Dawber) show up in Tel Aviv for the 1981 World Gathering of Holocaust Survivors. The excellent premise limps along as Dawber meets a handsome security officer and her recently widowed and depressed Dad comes alive after being reunited with his long lost love from World War II. (Dir: Jack Smight, 104 mins.)

Remington Steele—The Steele That Wouldn't Die (MTV, 1987)** Pierce Bronson, Stephanie Zimbalist, Doris Roberts, Jack Scalia. Newlyweds Steele and Laura run afoul of immigration officials, bogus archaeologists, menacing revolutionaries, and a murderer or two. For fans of the series only. (Dir: Chris Hibler, 104 mins.)

Remote Control (1988)** Kevin Dillon, Deborah Goodrich, Jennifer Tilly. The energetic young cast is the best thing in this nonsense about videotapes programmed by fiendish aliens to turn viewers into murderous maniacs. Tilly is fun as the hero's punk girlfriend. (Dir: Jeff Lieberman, 88 mins.)†

Remo Williams: The Adventure Continues (1985)**½ Fred Ward, Joel Grey, Wilford Brimley, George Coe, Kate Mulgrew. A slipshod but diverting action flick based on the old *Destroyer* books. While one appreciates the attempt to design a down-to-earth hero, this brown-bag James Bond only comes to life intermittently. (Dir: Guy Hamilton, 121 mins.)†

Renaldo and Clara (1978)* Bob Dylan, Sara Dylan, Joan Baez, Ronee Blakley, Ronnie Hawkins. Long, repetitious, self-indulgent film written and directed by and with Dylan in which his personality and his relationships are dissected, discussed, and acted out as many musicians (Arlo Guthrie, Roberta Flack, and others) perform with his Rolling Thunder Revue. (232 mins.)

Rendezvous (France, 1985)**½ Juliette Binoche, Lambert Wilson, Wadeck Stanczak, Jean-Louis Trintignant. Unusual sensual drama. An attractive provincial (Binoche) arrives in Paris to become a stage actress and becomes involved, romantically and otherwise, with three driven individuals: the wimpish Stanczak, the menacing Wilson (who dies and then haunts her), and theater director Trintignant, who transforms her into a reluctant "Juliet." (Dir: André Téchiné, 82 mins.)†

Rendezvous at Midnight (1935)*½ Ralph Bellamy, Valerie Hobson, Irene Ware. Ponderous opening and lack of a supporting cast hinder Bellamy as he plays a police commissioner tracking a killer. (Dir: Christy Cabanne, 60 mins.)

Rendezvous Hotel (MTV 1979)** Bill Daily, Jeff J. Redford, Teddy Wilson. Daily becomes a manager of a Santa Barbara, Calif., hotel in this madcap comedy. (Dir: Peter Hunt, 104 mins.)

Rendezvous with Annie (1946)**½ Eddie Albert, Faye Marlowe, Gail Patrick. Army pilot flies home secretly to spend a few hours with his wife, but this leads to complications. Many amusing moments. (Dir: Allan Dwan, 89 mins.)

Renegades (1930)** Warner Baxter, Myrna Loy, Noah Beery, Bela Lugosi. French Foreign Legion officer Baxter becomes fatally attracted to an alluring German spy. Antique adventure. (Dir: Victor Fleming, 84 mins.)

Renegades (1946)** Evelyn Keyes, Willard Parker, Larry Parks, Edgar Buchanan. A young ingenue spurns the love of a doctor to run away with an evil outlaw. (Dir: George Sherman, 88 mins.)†

Renegades, The (MTV 1982)** Philip Casnoff, Patrick Swayze, Randy Brooks, Kurtwood Smith. Tedious pilot for a series about a bunch of tough-talking youths used by the police as special operatives. Here they take on some mean gunrunners. (Dir: Roger Spottiswode, 96 mins.)

Renegades (1989)**½ Kiefer Sutherland, Lou Diamond Phillips, Rob Knepper, Jami Gertz. Philadelphia cop Sutherland and Lakota Indian Phillips team up to track a gang of thieves and settle some family scores. Jack Sholder (*The Hidden*) directs the nonstop action scenes with panache, but has only the thinnest of plots to peg them on. (106 mins.)

Rent-a-Cop (1988)** Burt Reynolds, Liza Minnelli, James Remar, Richard Masur, Dionne Warwick. Burt goes into business as "rent-a-cop" and becomes involved with a psychotic killer (Remar) and a wise-cracking hooker (Liza). (Dir: Jerry London, 96 mins.)†

Rented Lips (1988)**½ Martin Mull, Dick Shawn, Jennifer Tilly, Edy Williams, Robert Downey, Jr., June Lockhart, Kenneth Mars, Shelley Berman. Oddball farce about two anxious filmmakers who get a job shooting a cheesy porn flick. (Dir: Robert Downey, 82 mins.)†

Repeat Performance (1947)*** Joan Leslie, Louis Hayward, Benay Venuta, Tom Conway, Richard Basehart. Classy B movie. A woman gets a new lease on life when she is able to relive events from the passing year up to the moment of a fatal mistake. (Dir: Alfred Werker, 93 mins.)

Repentance (U.S.S.R., 1987)** Avtandil Makharadze, Zeinab Botsvadze, Edisher Giorgobiani. *Repentance* has some imaginative surrealistic dream sequences and a very funny opening where a politician's corpse, fresh from interment, keeps popping up all over town. Slowly paced. (Dir: Tengiz Abuladze, 145 mins.)†

Repo Man (1984)**** Emilio Estevez, Harry Dean Stanton, Tracey Walter, Olivia Barash, Dick Rude. Alienated youth Estevez is a sort of Candide wandering through an L.A. of punk rockers, government agents, junkyard mystics, dead aliens, and Repo Men. A bizarre, outrageously funny movie. (Dir: Alex Cox, 92 mins.)†

Report on the Party and the Guests, A (Czechoslovakia, 1966)***½ Ivan Vyskocil, Jan Klusak, Zdenka Skvorecka. Brilliant comic allegory about guests at a party who persecute the one guest who refuses to pretend that he's having a good time. Condemned by the Czech National Assembly, the film was finally shown in 1968. (Dir: Jan Nemec, 71 mins.)†

Report to the Commissioner (1975)*** Michael Moriarty, Yaphet Kotto, Hector Elizondo, Susan Blakely. Highly charged cop story. A puddin'-headed rookie cop is used as a scapegoat by his superiors when he accidentally kills a sexy young lady who is actually an undercover cop. (Dir: Milton Katselas, 112 mins.)†

Repossessed (1990)** Linda Blair, Leslie Nielsen, Ned Beatty, Jake Steinfeld, Jack LaLanne. Silly, sophomoric comedy modeled after *Airplane* and *The Naked Gun*, providing lame results. Blair, now married with two children, becomes repossessed by the devil while watching TV. Plenty of green bile and a wacky performance from Nielsen provides occasional laughts. (Dir: Bob Logan, 78 mins.)†

Reprisal (1956)**½ Guy Madison, Felicia Farr, Kathryn Grant. Good film with a novel approach to westerns—the plot concerns the racial issue. (Dir: George Sherman, 74 mins.)

Reptile, The (Great Britain, 1966)**½ Noel

Willman, Jennifer Daniels, Ray Barrett, Jacqueline Pearce. Slithery thriller about a woman who can change into a snake and the various people who get under her skin. (Dir: John Gilling, 90 mins.)

Reptilicus (1962)*½ Carl Ottosen, Ann Smyrner. Prehistoric beast is dug up and sent to a Copenhagen laboratory, where it thaws out and escapes. (Dir: Sidney Pink, 81 mins.)

Repulsion (Great Britain, 1965)***½ Catherine Deneuve, Ian Hendry, Yvonne Furneaux. A chilling horror tale about the mental deterioration of a disturbed girl. Painfully shy of men, Deneuve becomes terrified at the thought of her sister leaving her alone for the weekend. A modern horror classic. (Dir: Roman Polanski, 105 mins.)†

Requiem for a Gunfighter (1965)*½ Rod Cameron, Stephen McNally, Tim McCoy. Gunslinger is mistaken for a judge, decides to play along with the impersonation and rids the town of the baddies. (Dir: Spencer G. Bennet, 91 mins.)

Requiem for a Heavyweight (1962)***½ Anthony Quinn, Julie Harris, Jackie Gleason, Mickey Rooney. This drama of a washed-up pug and the employment counselor who tries to help him land a job is based on the highly successful TV presentation. Cast contributes excellent performances. (Dir: Ralph Nelson, 95 mins.)

Requiem for Dominic (Germany-Romania, 1991)*** Felix Mitterer, Viktoria Schubert, August Schmolzer, Angelica Schutz. Unnerving political thriller (set in Timisoara, Romania in 1989) blends fiction and truth. California-based director Dornhelm, who is a Romanian refugee, returned to find out the truth about his boyhood friend, Dominic Paraschiv, who was framed by the communist regime as an executioner of anti-Communists killed from torture. Unsettling use of graphic footage taken from the film's vivid, hypnotic power. (Dir: Robert Dornhelm, 88 mins.)

Rescue, The (1988)*½ Kevin Dillon, Christina Harnos, Marc Price, Edward Albert. When their fathers are captured by North Korea, five Army kids take it upon themselves to rescue them. (Dir: Ferdinand Fairfax, 98 mins.)†

Rescue from Gilligan's Island (MTV 1978)* Bob Denver, Alan Hale, Jim Backus. Everyone's favorite shipwreck victims return for more misadventures. (Dir: Leslie Martinson, 104 mins.)

Rescuers Down Under, The (1990)*** Voices of Bob Newhart, Eva Gabor, John Candy, George C. Scott. Bernhard and Miss Bianca, heroic mice created by novelist Margery Sharp, are called to Australia to save a little boy and the local fauna from a ruthless villain. Highlighted by brilliant animation and Candy as the voice of Wilber the albatross. (Dirs: Hendel Butoy, Mike Gabriel, 109 mins.)†

Resident Alien (1990)*** Thoroughly delightful quasi-documentary about the writer Quentin Crisp, the doyen of homosexual pop culture. Crisp is filmed on his jaunts around Manhattan, which include enjoyable chats with his singing, acting, and writing friends such as Sting, John Hurt, Holly Woodlawn, the late Emil de Antonio, and Sally Jesse Raphael. (Dir: Jonathan Nossiter, 85 mins.)

Resting Place (MTV 1986)*** John Lithgow, Richard Bradford, Morgan Freeman, C. C. H. Pounder, G. D. Spradlin, Frances Sternhagen. Sensitive drama about a deceased black Vietnam War hero whose family is barred from burying his body in an all-white cemetery in the South. It turns out the dead hero's squadron is harboring a secret that could be damaging to all concerned. (Dir: John Korty, 104 mins.)

Restless (Greece, 1971)* Raquel Welch, Richard Johnson, Dame Flora Robson. From Raquel you'd expect a little sex appeal; from the director of *Rambo* you'd hope for a little action. What you get instead is an interminable affair between a restless Greek housewife and her childhood friend. (Dir: Jorgo Pan [George P.] Cosmatos, 75 mins.)†

Restless Breed, The (1957)** Scott Brady, Anne Bancroft. Routine western drama about a man bent on revenge for his father's murder. (Dir: Allan Dwan, 81 mins.)

Restless Natives (Great Britain, 1986)**½ Joe Mullaney, Vincent Friell, Teri Lally. Droll, good-natured comedy that lacks the spark and inventiveness to be first class. Two Scottish lads begin robbing tour buses out on the countryside and become something of a tourist attraction. (Dir: Michael Hoffman, 90 mins.)

Restless Years, The (1958)** John Saxon, Sandra Dee, Margaret Lindsay, Teresa Wright. Small-town dressmaker tries to keep her daughter's illegitimacy a secret, but the secret's out. (Dir: Helmut Kautner, 86 mins.)

Resurrection (1980)*** Ellen Burstyn, Sam Shepard, Roberts Blossom, Clifford David. A superb performance by Burstyn as a woman who discovers she has the power to heal the sick dominates this fascinating drama that strains credibility but is intriguing because it is so unusual. (Dir: Daniel Petrie, 103 mins.)†

Resurrection of Zachary Wheeler, The (1971)**½ Angie Dickinson, Bradford Dilman, James Daly, Leslie Nielsen, Jack Carter. Rather absorbing sci-fi about a U.S. senator shipped to a strange clinic after an auto accident. (Dir: Bob Wynn, 100 mins.)†

Retaliator, The—See: **Programmed to Kill**

Retik, the Moon Menace (1952)* George Wallace, Aline Towne. Feature version of serial *Radar Men from the Moon.* Moon men seek to enslave earth but are foiled by Commando Cody. (Dir: Fred C. Brannon, 100 mins.)

Retreat, Hell! (1952)** Frank Lovejoy, Richard Carlson, Anita Louise. Undistinguished Korean War drama. (Dir: Joseph H. Lewis, 95 mins.)†

Retribution (1988)*** Dennis Lipscomb, Leslie Wing, Suzanne Snyder, Jeff Pomerantz, Hoyt Axton. A depressed artist attempts suicide, only to mysteriously return to life, whereupon he becomes a psychic murderer. This supernatural mystery has an unusual amount of mood and style for a low-budget shocker, and it features an excellent lead performance by Lipscomb. (Dir: Guy Magar, 108 mins.)†

Return, The (1981)** Jan-Michael Vincent, Cybill Shepherd, Martin Landau, Raymond Burr, Neville Brand. Minor sci-fi drama, with Vincent and Shepherd being revisited by aliens who first appeared to them when they were kids. AKA: **The Alien's Return.** (Dir: Greydon Clark, 91 mins.)†

Return, The (1985)** Karlene Crockett, John Walcutt, Lisa Richards, Frederic Forrest, Anne (Lloyd) Francis. The premise is intriguing—a girl falls in love with a guy who is the reincarnation of her dead grandfather, but the direction is unremarkable, and the plot development's indifferently handled. (Dir: Andrew Silver, 78 mins.)†

Return Engagement (1983)*** Offbeat, often hilarious film records the meeting of two polar opposites, '60s LSD guru Timothy Leary and convicted Watergate criminal G. Gordon Liddy, on a lecture tour of college campuses as they discuss whatever strikes their fancy. (Dir: Alan Rudolph, 89 mins.)†

Return from the Ashes (Great Britain, 1965)*** Maximilian Schell, Ingrid Thulin, Samantha Eggar. The cast plus some interesting plot twists make this weird suspense film worthwhile. After years in a Nazi concentration camp which left her scarred, Miss Thulin undergoes plastic surgery and returns to Paris eager to pick up her life. In the interim, her husband and stepdaughter have become lovers, and a strange twist of fate unites the trio in a diabolical game of wits. (Dir: J. Lee Thompson, 108 mins.)

Return from the Past—See: **Gallery of Horrors**

Return from the Sea (1954)*** Jan Sterling, Neville Brand, John Doucette, Paul Langton. Sensitive, realistic romance of an idealistic sailor who's finally found the girl he's been looking for in a jaded but honest waitress; they plan to marry but must endure waiting and scrimping. Well-acted, especially by Sterling. (Dir: Lesley Selander, 80 mins.)

Return from Witch Mountain (1978)** Bette Davis, Christopher Lee, Kim Richards, Ike Eisenmann. Sequel to Disney's *Escape to Witch Mountain* has those two kids from outer space being used as pawns for the schemes of mad scientist Lee. (Dir: John Hough, 93 mins.)†

Returning Home (MTV 1975)**½ Dabney Coleman, Tom Selleck, James R. Miller, Whitney Blake. Remake is not as good as award-winning 1946 film *The Best Years of Our Lives*. (Dir: Daniel Petrie, 72 mins.)

Return of a Man Called Horse, The (1976)*** Richard Harris, Gale Sondergaard, Geoffrey Lewis. English aristocrat (Harris) returns to counter what the whites have been doing to the Indians. Sequel to *A Man Called Horse.* Superior in every way to its predecessor, the film does also tend to revel in gratuitous sadism. (Dir: Irvin Kershner, 125 mins.)†

Return of Ben Casey (MTV 1988)*½ Vince Edwards, Al Waxman, Gwynyth Walsh. Still the same old sourpuss with a heart of gold as he helps out two troubled young people. (Dir: Joseph L. Scanlan, 96 mins.)

Return of Charlie Chan, The—See: **Charlie Chan (Happiness Is a Warm Clue)**

Return of Count Yorga (1971)*** Robert Quarry, Mariette Hartley, Roger Perry. Superior sequel to *Count Yorga,* who this time snatches his prospective soulmate after disposing of her family. Terrifying moments abound as the girl's strong-willed boyfriend tries to stake his claim and get her back. (Dir: Bob Kelljan, 97 mins.)

Return of Desperado, The (MTV 1988)*½ Alex McArthur, Robert Foxworth, Billy Dee Williams. Who asked for it? This tired horse opera has the desperado joining with a female reporter to take on a greedy land baron to swindle black homesteaders. (Dir: E. W. Swackhamer, 96 mins.)

Return of Doctor X, The (1939)** Humphrey Bogart, Wayne Morris, Rosemary Lane, Dennis Morgan, Lya Lys, Huntz Hall. The whole show here is an offbeat performance by Bogart as a zombie, being pursued by the usual spoilsports. (Dir: Vincent Sherman, 62 mins.)

Return of Don Camillo, The (France, 1953)***½ Fernandel, Gino Cervi. Fernandel once more delights all as the hilariously unconventional priest Don Camillo. A small village is turned inside out and vastly changed by the pixie

874

padre's arrival. Inventive writing and acting. (Dir: Julien Duvivier, 115 mins.)

Return of Dracula, The—See: **Curse of Dracula, The**

Return of Draw Egan, The (1916)**** William S. Hart, Louise Glaum, Margery Wilson, Robert McKim. One of Hart's best westerns, about a notorious, rough-and-ready outlaw who changes his ways for the sake of an honest woman. Hart's picture of the West is, as always, frank, unaffectedly loving, and scenic. (Dir: William S. Hart, 55 mins.)†

Return of Frank Cannon, The (MTV 1980)**½ William Conrad, Allison Argo, Burr DeBenning, Diana Muldaur, Joanna Pettit, James Hong. So-so whodunit. It seems Cannon's old Army Intelligence buddy is dead, and he's not so sure it's the suicide everyone makes it out to be.... (Dir: Corey Allen, 96 mins.)

Return of Frank James, The (1940)***½ Henry Fonda, Gene Tierney, John Carradine, Jackie Cooper, Henry Hull. Tautly directed sequel to *Jesse James,* which follows Frank as he sets out to find the man who shot his brother in the back, Bob Ford. Humorous, direct, fast-paced, perhaps better than the original. (Dir: Fritz Lang, 92 mins.)†

Return of Jack Slade (1955)**½ John Ericson, Marie Blanchard, Neville Brand, Angie Dickinson. OK low-budget western about the son of a notorious outlaw who becomes a lawman to make up for his father's wrongs. (Dir: Harold Schuster, 79 mins.)

Return of Jesse James, The (1950)**½ John Ireland, Ann Dvorak, Hugh O'Brian. Small-time outlaw is a dead ringer for the late Jesse; he becomes a big-timer by cashing in on the James name. (Dir: Arthur Hilton, 75 mins.)

Return of Joe Forrester, The (MTV 1975)**½ Lloyd Bridges, Pat Crowley, Jim Backus. Bridges stars in this pilot film as Forrester, who returns to his old job as a cop on the beat, where his presence always spelled security to the neighborhood shopkeepers and tenants. (Dir: Virgil W. Vogel, 78 mins.)

Return of Marcus Welby, M.D., The (MTV 1984)** Robert Young, Darren McGavin, Morgan Stevens, Jessica Walter. The venerable Dr. Welby discovers he may be headed for forced retirement. (Dir: Alexander Singer, 104 mins.)

Return of Martin Guerre, The (France, 1983)***½ Gerard Depardieu, Nathalie Baye. Scintillating, thought-provoking historical tale of a medieval peasant who disappears not long after his marriage. Years later he returns to reclaim his place. A superb blend of period re-creation and romantic fable. (Dir: Daniel Vigne, 111 mins.)†

Return of Maxwell Smart, The—See: **Nude Bomb, The**

Return of Mickey Spillane's Mike Hammer, The (MTV 1986)**½ Stacy Keach, Lauren Hutton, Vince Edwards, Stephen Macht. Hammer works both coasts as he tries to help an actress and her young daughter in a kidnapping case. (Dir: Ray Danton, 104 mins.)

Return of Monte Cristo, The (1946)**½ Louis Hayward, Barbara Britton, George Macready. Nephew to Edmund Dantes is framed to Devil's Island by enemies who wish to prevent him from claiming the Monte Cristo inheritance. OK costume melodrama. (Dir: Henry Levin, 91 mins.)

Return of Mr. Moto, The (Great Britain, 1965)* Henry Silva, Terence Longdon. Dreary attempt to resurrect the B movie sleuth. Silva seems too much like a heavy for the role. (Dir: Ernest Morris, 71 mins.)

Return of October, The (1948)**½ Glenn Ford, Terry Moore, James Gleason. Girl buys a racehorse because it reminds her of a dead uncle. In spite of corny Kentucky Derby finale, this has some laughs. (Dir: Joseph H. Lewis, 89 mins.)

Return of Peter Grimm, The (1935)*** Lionel Barrymore, Helen Mack, Edward Ellis, Donald Meek. Man who dominated his household before death returns from the Beyond to find things changed. Interesting, well-acted drama. (Dir: George Nicholls, Jr., 82 mins.)†

Return of Rubén Blades, The (1985)*** Blades is the king of Latin salsa, a Panamanian in New York who has electrified popular music with his unique rhythms. This entertaining documentary takes in his graduation from Harvard Law School, a return visit to his parents in Central America, and a recording session with Linda Ronstadt. (Dir: Robert Mugge, 90 mins.)†

Return of Sabata, The (Italy-Spain, 1981)* Lee Van Cleef, Reiner Schone, Annabelle Incontrera, Jacqueline Alexandre. Van Cleef, who made a reputation following in Clint Eastwood's spaghetti western boots, made his own series of films playing an ex-Confederate officer. (Dir: "Frank Kramer" [Gianfranco Parolini], 106 mins.)

Return of Sam McCloud, The (MTV 1989)**½ Dennis Weaver, J. D. Cannon, Terry Carter, Diana Muldaur, Patrick Macnee, Kerrie Keane, Roger Rees, David McCallum. McCloud, now a U.S. senator, investigates the death of his niece after she learned too much about the chemical manufacturer she was working for. (Dir: Alan J. Levi, 96 mins.)

Return of Sherlock Holmes, The (MTV 1987)**½ Margaret Colin, Michael Pennington, Lila Kaye, Barry Morse, Nicholas Guest, Connie Booth, Paul Maxwell. Boston private-eye Colin, a descendant of Dr. Watson, inherits an English manor and discovers the body of Sherlock Holmes in suspended animation. (Dir: Kevin Connor, 104 mins.)

Return of Superfly, The (1990)* Nathan Purdee, Margaret Avery, Sam Jackson. Poor sequel to 1973's far superior urban action tale. This time drug-dealer Priest has reformed and moved to Paris, but he returns to New York City for one more dreary round of pro-forma violence. (Dir: Sig Shore, 97 mins.)†

Return of Swamp Thing, The (1989)*½ Louis Jourdan, Heather Locklear, Dick Durock, Sarah Douglas. Knock-off sequel to *Swamp Thing*. Some of the special effects are good, especially the Swamp Thing costume, but director Jim Wynorski treats everything as a low-camp joke. (90 mins.)†

Return of the Ape Man (1944)** Bela Lugosi, John Carradine, George Zucco, Judith Gibson. A mad scientist experiments with brain transplants in his search for the missing link. Ripe hamminess of the cast, with plenty of competition, provides the fun in this one. (Dir: Philip Rosen, 60 mins.)

Return of the Beverly Hillbillies (MTV 1981)* Buddy Ebsen, Donna Douglas, Nancy Kulp. This follow-up's paper-thin plot revolves around the President's request to solve the energy crisis with Granny's moonshine. (Dir: Robert Leeds, 104 mins.)

Return of the Dragon (Hong Kong, 1973)*** Bruce Lee, Chuck Norris, Nora Miao. A martial arts treat with the dream team of Norris and Lee. Wisp of a plot about Lee aiding his restaurant-owning relatives from mobster muscling in. (Dir: Bruce Lee, 91 mins.)†

Return of the Evil Dead—See: **Night of the Seagulls**

Return of the Fly (1959)** Vincent Price, Brett Halsey. Sequel to the successful box-office thriller *The Fly* doesn't live up to its predecessor's chilly sequences. (Dir: Edward L. Bernds, 80 mins.)†

Return of the Giant Monsters—See: **Gamera vs. Gaos**

Return of the Gunfighter (MTV 1966)**½ Robert Taylor, Chad Everett, Ana Martin. Lively western about a gunslinger who goes looking for the murderers of an old friend. (Dir: James Neilson, 98 mins.)

Return of the Incredible Hulk, The (MTV 1977)** Bill Bixby, Lou Ferrigno, Jack Colvin. Bixby again plays mild-mannered scientist David Banner, who is transformed, whenever he gets angry, into a seven-foot, green, raging creature. (Dir: Alan Levi, 104 mins.)

Return of the Jedi (1983)*** Mark Hamill, Carrie Fisher, Harrison Ford, Alec Guinness, Billy Dee Williams, Denis Lawson. A dazzling and generally triumphant sci-fi charmer, but an air of complacency renders this conclusion the least dynamic of the *Star Wars* trilogy. Among the highlights are Luke battling Darth Vader, Princess Leia saving her virtue from Jabba the Hutt, and the spectacle of adorable Ewoks running rampant. (Dir: Richard Marquand, 133 mins.)†

Return of the Killer Tomatoes (1988)**½ Anthony Starke, George Clooney, Karen Mistal, John Astin. Silly sci-fi spoof with mad scientist Astin trying to take over the world with the vicious vegeta bles (or is that ferocious fruits?) that terrorized the world in *Attack of the Killer Tomatoes*. You'll enjoy it if you're in a goofy mood to begin with. (Dir: John DeBello, 98 mins.)†

Return of the Living Dead, The (1985)***½ Clu Gulager, James Karen, Don Calfa, Thom Mathews, Linnea Quigley. Half remake, half parody of *Night of the Living Dead*, this is that rare horror movie that is both funny and frightening, often at the same time. The cast— especially Karen and Gulager—is every bit as good as the excellent, outrageously disgusting special effects. A must-see for those with strong stomachs. (Dir: Dan O'Bannon, 90 mins.)†

Return of the Living Dead Part II (1988)* James Karen, Thom Mathews, Michael Kenworthy. Witless sequel apes the style of its predecessor without understanding what made it work. The result is gory and dumb. (Dir: Ken Wiederhorn, 89 mins.)†

Return of the Man from U.N.C.L.E. (MTV 1983)**½ Robert Vaughn, David McCallum, Patrick Macnee, Gayle Hunnicutt, Geoffrey Lewis, Anthony Zerbe, Tom Mason. A new rendition of the glittery, computerized, mid-'60s super-agent hit. (Dir: Ray Austin, 104 mins.)

Return of the Mod Squad, The (MTV 1979)**½ Clarence Williams III, Peggy Lipton, Michael Cole, Sugar Ray Robinson. Sequel to the old TV series, about three young undercover police officers. (Dir: George McCowan, 104 mins.)

Return of the Pink Panther, The (Great Britain, 1974)*** Peter Sellers, Christopher Plummer, Herbert Lom. Imagine Sellers, as the immortal Inspector Clouseau, let loose with a vacuum cleaner, a steam bath, an organ grinder and his monkey, and a waxed dance floor, all in the same very funny film. Once again, the fabled Pink Panther diamond is stolen, and the klutzy inspector takes the case. (Dir: Blake Edwards, 113 mins.)†

Return of the Rebels (MTV 1981)½ Barbara Eden, Don Murray, Robert Mandan, Christopher Connelly, Michael Baseleon, Patrick Swayze. A clumsy tale of an old motorcycle gang reuniting after twenty years to rid Eden's campground area of young hoodlums. (Dir: Noel Nosseck, 104 mins.)

Return of the Scarlet Pimpernel (Great Britain, 1938)**½ Barrie K. Barnes, Sophie

Stewart, Margaretta Scott, James Mason, Anthony Bushell. Pretty good se quel. Barnes is fine as Sir Percy Blakeney, who must rescue his beloved French wife from kidnappers in this adventure. From a novel by Baroness Orczy. (Dir: Hans Schwartz, 88 mins.)

Return of the Secaucus Seven, The (1980) ***½ Director John Sayles, making a feature-length debut in 16-mm for $60,000, presents a reunion of aging '60s types coping with disillusion. More originality and depth than *The Big Chill*. Literate, funny, and engrossing. (106 mins.)†

Return of the Seven (1966)* Yul Brynner, Robert Fuller, Jordan Christopher. Disappointing sequel to the 1960 John Sturges film *The Magnificent Seven*. (Dir: Burt Kennedy, 96 mins.)†

Return of the Six Million Dollar Man and the Bionic Woman, The (MTV 1987)** Lee Majors, Lindsay Wagner, Richard Anderson, Martin Anderson, Gary Lockwood, Martin Landau, Lee Majors II. The Six Million Dollar Man and the Bionic Woman rekindle their romance and wipe out dastardly reactionaries when not comforting the Bionic Boy. (Dir: Ray Austin, 104 mins.)

Return of the Soldier, The (Great Britain, 1983)***½ Alan Bates, Julie Christie, Ann-Margret, Glenda Jackson, Ian Holm, Frank Finlay. A finely meshed ensemble of actors bring this love story to life. A soldier (Bates) suffering selective amnesia returns home without remembering his marriage to a beautiful, haughty woman (Christie), as two other women, a spinster suffering years of unrequited love for him (Ann-Margret) and his plain childhood sweetheart (Jackson), yearn for further involvement with him. (Dir: Alan Bridges, 101 mins.)†

Return of the Tall Blond Man with One Black Shoe, The (France, 1974)*** Pierre Richard, Mireille Darc, Jean Rochefort. Frequently funny sequel finds Richard again playing a naïve classical musician caught up in the world of espionage. (Dir: Yves Robert, 89 mins.)†

Return of the Texan (1952)** Dale Robertson, Joanne Dru, Walter Brennan, Richard Boone. Talky drama about the obstacles faced by a handsome widower who comes back to the homestead where he grew up. (Dir: Delmer Daves, 88 mins.)

Return of the Vampire (1944)** Bela Lugosi, Nina Foch, Frieda Inescort, Roland Varno. Routine horror film with the vampire foiled when his monster assistant gets religious. (Dirs: Lew Landers, Kurt Neumann, 69 mins.)†

Return of the Whistler, The (1948)** Michael Duane, Lenore Aubert, Ann Shoemaker. Plot concerns the disappearance of a man's fiancée, whose whereabouts prove as hard to trace as her mysterious path. (Dir: Ross Lederman, 63 mins.)

Return of the World's Greatest Detective, The (MTV 1976)*½ Larry Hagman, Jenny O'Hara, Nicholas Colasanto, Woodrow Parfey. Based on the George C. Scott–Joanne Woodward movie *They Might Be Giants*. Here, the adept Hagman plays a bumbling police officer who suffers a concussion only to believe he's Sherlock Holmes. (Dir: Dean Hargrove, 72 mins.)

Return to Boggy Creek (1977)** Dawn Wells, Dana Plato, Louis Belaire, John Hofeus. Taking off from Charles B. Pierce's semidocumentary *The Legend of Boggy Creek*, this is a totally fictional kids' film in which a bigfoot-like Boggy Creek creature ends up saving a group of children from a violent storm. Unrelated to Pierce's own *Boggy Creek II*. (Dir: Tom Moore, 85 mins.)

Return to Dodge—See: **Gunsmoke: Return to Dodge**

Return to Earth (MTV 1976)**½ Cliff Robertson, Shirley Knight, Ralph Bellamy, Stefanie Powers. Edwin "Buzz" Aldrin, the second man to walk on the moon, is the subject of this moderately engrossing movie. (Dir: Jud Taylor, 72 mins.)†

Return to Eden (Australia, 1983)**½ Rebecca Gilling, James Reyne, Wendy Hughes. Aussie mini-series hauls out all the clichés in this tale of a wealthy ugly duckling who survives a murder attempt by her husband, alters her appearance, and comes back for revenge. Satisfying for soap opera buffs. (Dir: Karen Arthur, 259 mins.)†

Return to Fantasy Island (MTV 1978)**½ Ricardo Montalban, Adrienne Barbeau, Horst Bucholz, Joseph Campanella, George Chakiris, Joseph Cotten, George Maharis, Cameron Mitchell, France Nuyen, Karen Valentine, Herve Villechaize. Second visit to that land of dreams gone awry, presided over by Mr. Roarke (Montalban), the deity with the Mexican accent, and Tattoo (Villechaize), that cheap little device for exposition. Before the series took its niche, the fantasies were quite cruel, indeed. (Dir: George McCowan, 96 mins.)

Return to Green Acres (MTV 1990)** Eddie Albert, Eva Gabor, Tom Lester, Alvy Moore, Pat Buttram, Henry Gibson, John Scott Clough, Mary Tanner. Disappointing reunion of most of the original cast of the cult comedy series, with Oliver and Lisa Douglas (Albert, Gabor) temporarily returning to New York but coming back to save Hooterville from land developer Gibson. The dementedly surrealistic edge is missing, leaving only some tired, once-wacky characters. (Dir: William Asher, 96 mins.)

Return to Haifa (Palestine, 1982)*** Paul Mattar, Hanan Al Haj Ali, Jamal Solei-

man. Provocative, intelligent drama about a Palestinian couple's return to Haifa twenty years after they were forced to leave in 1948. (Dir: Kassem Hawal, 84 mins.)

Return to Horror High (1987)* Brendan Hughes, Lori Lethin, Alex Rocco, Vince Edwards, Philip McKeon. A low-budget film crew goes to a deserted high school that was the site of a mass murder, only to find history repeating itself. Unusual narrative structure for a slasher flick and a number of humorous moments are completely undone by paceless direction. (Dir: Bill Froehlich, 95 mins.)†

Return to Macon County (1975)**½ Nick Nolte, Don Johnson. Nolte and Johnson, as a pair of itinerant drag-racing bums, are much better than their material as they again get in trouble with the law. A sequel of sorts to *Macon County Line*. (Dir: Richard Compton, 104 mins.)†

Return to Mayberry (MTV 1986)*** Andy Griffith, Ron Howard, Don Knotts, Jim Nabors, George Lindsey, Hal Smith, Jack Dodson, Howard Morris. The familiar characters from the long-running "The Andy Griffith Show" reassemble as the latest election for sheriff pits Andy Taylor (Griffith) vs. his former deputy, Barney Fife (Knotts). A worthwhile reprise. (Dir: Bob Sweeney, 104 mins.)†

Return to Oz (1985)** Fairuza Balk, Nicol Williamson, Piper Laurie, Jean Marsh. A strange foray into fantasy that takes little Dorothy on adventures that more closely resemble those in Frank Baum's classic children's books. An atmospheric but depressing children's tale that was reportedly worked on by George Lucas and Steven Spielberg, who gave pointers to the director when he ran into problems. (Dir: Walter Murch, 118 mins.)†

Return to Paradise (1953)**½ Gary Cooper, Roberta Haynes. Slow-moving story of the romance of a bum and a native girl in the South Seas. (Dir: Mark Robson, 100 mins.)

Return to Peyton Place (1961)** Carol Lynley, Eleanor Parker, Jeff Chandler, Mary Astor, Robert Sterling, Tuesday Weld, Brett Halsey, Luciana Paluzzi. Souped-up trash. Lynley plays a budding author who bares all of Peyton Place's sins and attains best-sellerdom but not true happiness with a married man (Chandler). Astor is excellent as the town's leading bigot, and the film's highpoint of idiocy occurs when Paluzzi tries to induce a miscarriage on skis. (Dir: José Ferrer, 122 mins.)†

Return to Salem's Lot, A (1987)*** Michael Moriarty, Samuel Fuller, Andrew Duggan, Ricky Addison Reed, Evelyn Keyes. Sequel to Stephen King's story finds anthropologist Moriarty and his young son encountering vampires in a small Northeastern town. Scary scenes are balanced by amusing depiction of modern vampires and Fuller's funny performance as a Nazi hunter turned destroyer of bloodsuckers. (Dir: Larry Cohen, 100 mins.)†

Return to Snowy River Part II: The Legend Continues (Australia, 1988)** Tom Burlinson, Sigrid Thornton, Brian Dennehy, Nicholas Eadie. Sequel to the 1982 Aussie western *The Man from Snowy River*; lush photography and some exciting horse wrangling don't compensate for the slow, stiff-jointed storytelling. (Dir: Geoff Burrowes, 97 mins.)†

Return to Waterloo (Great Britain, 1985)***½ Ken Colley, Valerie Holliman, Dominique Barnes. On his daily train ride into work from the London suburbs, a middle-aged man ponders his disappointments and fantasies. Written and directed by Ray Davies, of the long-lived rock band the Kinks. Quite interesting. (60 mins.)†

Reuben, Reuben (1983)*** Tom Conti, Kelly McGillis, E. Katherine Kerr. A sophisticated screen adaptation of Peter DeVries's novel about a womanizing poet. Conti has an actor's field day as the oversexed man of letters who uses the English language not to hone his craft but to impress American ladies. (Dir: Robert Ellis Miller, 101 mins.)†

Reunion (MTV 1980)** Kevin Dobson, Joanna Cassidy, Linda Hamilton, Lew Ayres. Glossy soap opera about a twenty-year high school reunion. Dobson is quite good as the former basketball hero who rekindles a romance with his high school sweetheart. (Dir: Russ Mayberry, 104 mins.)

Reunion (France-German-Britain-U.S., 1991)*** Jason Robards, Christien Anholt, Samuel West. Leisurely paced memory piece, written by Harold Pinter, serves as a reminder of the anti-Semitism that existed in Hitler's Germany. Robards is a businessman journeying back to his native Germany, which triggers recollections of two schoolmates (one Jewish) in 1933. How the flashbacks tie into Robards' voyage is the film's subtle mystery. (Dir: Jerry Schatzberg, 120 mins.)

Reunion at Fairborough (MCTV 1985)**½ Robert Mitchum, Deborah Kerr, Judi Trott, Red Buttons, Barry Morse. The yarn concerns a reunion at an air base in England of a group of WWII flyers as Mitchum rekindles his affair with a woman he left forty years before. (Dir: Herbert Wise, 100 mins.)

Reunion in France (1942)**½ Joan Crawford, John Wayne. Joan saves France with Wayne's assistance as an American flyer. Entertaining propaganda. (Dir: Jules Dassin, 104 mins.)†

Reunion in Reno (1951)**½ Mark Stevens, Peggy Dow. Lightweight comedy-drama about a little girl who turns a Reno divorce lawyer's life into a merry-go-round when she decides to investigate the possibility of divorcing her parents. (Dir: Kurt Neumann, 79 mins.)

Reunion in Vienna (1933)**½ John Barrymore, Diana Wynyard, Frank Morgan, May Robson, Una Merkel. Top-notch cast. Barrymore's nobleman is eager to relive his romantic past with Wynyard in this charming antique. (Dir: Sidney Franklin, 100 mins.)

Reveille with Beverly (1943)** Ann Miller, William Wright, Dick Purcell. Miller is a dynamo as a disc jockey who puts on a big show with Frank Sinatra, Duke Ellington, Count Basie, Bob Crosby, and the Mills Brothers. (Dir: Charles Barton, 78 mins.)

Revenge (MTV 1971)**½ Shelley Winters, Stuart Whitman, Bradford Dillman. Shelley Winters in an over-the-top performance as a distraught mother who imprisons the man she believes had raped her daughter. (Dir: Jud Taylor, 78 mins.)

Revenge (Great Britain, 1971)* Joan Collins, James Booth, Sinead Cusack, Ray Barrett, Kenneth Griffith. An unpleasant melodrama. A pub owner's little girl is murdered, and the outraged father and his crony kidnap the recluse they suspect of the crime. AKA: **Inn of the Frightened People, Terror from Under the House** and **Behind the Cellar Door.** (Dir: Sidney Hayers, 89 mins.)†

Revenge (1990)*½ Kevin Costner, Anthony Quinn, Madeleine Stowe, Miguel Ferrer, Sally Kirkland, Joe Santos. Ludicrous tale of U.S. Air Force pilot in Mexico to visit his friend, corrupt millionaire Quinn. Costner beds Quinn's young wife, beginning an ordeal of ugly betrayal and brutal revenge. (Dir: Tony Scott, 124 mins.)†

Revenge for a Rape (MTV 1976)½ Mike Connors, Robert Reed, Deanna Lund, Tracy Brooks Swope, Larry Watson. Contrived story about a nice-guy geologist who becomes a marauding killer when his young, pregnant wife is brutally raped by three drunken hunters. (Dir: Timothy Galfas, 100 mins.)

Revenge of Al Capone, The (MTV 1989)**½ Keith Carradine, Ray Sharkey, Scott Paulin. As the famous underworld figure, Sharkey gives a lively performance, though there's little else to recommend this. (Dir: Michael Pressman, 96 mins.)

Revenge of Frankenstein, The (Great Britain, 1958)*** Peter Cushing, Francis Matthews, Eunice Gayson, Michael Gwynn, Lionel Jeffries, Michael Ripper. This sequel to *The Curse of Frankenstein* has Cushing continuing his well-intended but obsessive experiments while running a charity hospital. Both thought-provoking and gruesome—qualities you don't find in too many horror movies. Followed by the inferior *Evil of Frankenstein*. (Dir: Terence Fisher, 91 mins.)†

Revenge of the Cheerleaders (1976)* Jeril Woods, Rainbeaux Smith, Helen Lang, Patrice Rohmer, Carl Ballantine. More brainless high school sexcapades, a bit better than *The Cheerleaders*. (Dir: Richard Lerner, 88 mins.)†

Revenge of the Conquered (Italy, 1964)* Burt Nelson, Wandisa Guida. Gypsy lad loves a princess, but she's turned against him by a swine who wants her for himself. Poor costume adventure dubbed in English. (Dir: Luigi Capuano, 91 mins.)

Revenge of the Creature (1955)** John Agar, Lori Nelson. Sequel to *The Creature from the Black Lagoon* has the gill man captured and taken to a Florida oceanographic institute. Look for Clint Eastwood in his movie debut as a lab worker. Followed by *The Creature Walks Among Us*. (Dir: Jack Arnold, 82 mins.)

Revenge of the Dead—See: **Night of the Ghouls**

Revenge of the Living Zombies (1988)* Bill Hinzman, John Mowood, Leslie Ann Wick, Kevin Kindlin. Thin, boring rip-off of *Night of the Living Dead*. AKA: **Flesh Eater**. (Dir: Bill Hinzman, 84 mins.)†

Revenge of the Nerds (1984)** Robert Carradine, Anthony Edwards, Tim Busfield, Andrew Cassese. This nerd version of *Animal House* lets the little guys get revenge on the campus jocks and beauties who have put them down. (Dir: Jeff Kanew, 90 mins.)†

Revenge of the Nerds II: Nerds in Paradise (1987)*½ Robert Carradine, Curtis Armstrong, Larry B. Scott. Predictable, slapped-together sequel finds the misfit fraternity running up against the jocks again at an all-college conference in Fort Lauderdale. (Dir: Joe Roth, 85 mins.)†

Revenge of the Ninja (1983)** Sho Kosugi, Keith Vitali, Virgil Frye, Arthur Roberts. Kosugi's martial arts displays and choreography are the true stars of this standard story, in which a closet ninja has to drag out the black pajamas when he runs afoul of drug smugglers. (Dir: Sam Firstenberg, 88 mins.)†

Revenge of the Pink Panther (Great Britain, 1978)** Peter Sellers, Dyan Cannon, Herbert Lom. In number six of the series Sellers gives an unconscionably sloppy performance (sadly, his last) as Inspector Clouseau, redeemed only in his scenes with a goofy Cannon. The sequel, *Trail of the Pink Panther*, featured outtakes of Sellers. (Dir: Blake Edwards, 99 mins.)†

Revenge of the Pirates (Italy, 1951)*½ Maria Montez, Jean-Pierre Aumont, Milly Vitale. Swashbuckling skullduggery in old Maracaibo, as the beautiful marquesa is saved from a fate worse than etc. (Dir: Primo Zeglio, 95 mins.)

Revenge of the Stepford Wives (MTV 1980)*½ Sharon Gless, Julie Kavner, Audra Lindley, Don Johnson. In this unnecessary sequel to *The Stepford Wives*, reporter Gless investigates the strange apathy of those Stepford women. Followed by *The Stepford Children*. (Dir: Robert Fuest, 100 mins.)†

Revenge of the Teenage Vixens From Outer Space (1985)**½ Lisa Schwedop, Howard Scott, Amy Crumpacker, Sterling Ramberg. Some cosmic vixens come looking for a "hot time" on Earth. Mindless fun. (Dir: Jeff Farrell, 84 mins.)†

Revenge of the Zombies (1943)*½ John Carradine, Gale Storm, Robert Lowery, Veda Ann Borg, Mantan Moreland. Cheap thrills. Carradine overenunciates as if he were reciting Shakespeare's "Seven Ages of Man" restaged in a mad scientist lab. He tinkers with unfortunates who cross his path, but every zombie will have his day. (Dir: Steve Sekely, 61 mins.)

Revengers, The (1972)** William Holden, Susan Hayward, Ernest Borgnine. Western riddled with clichés. Holden is bent on revenge and enlists a motley crew of killers. (Dir: Daniel Mann, 110 mins.)

Reversal of Fortune (1990)***½ Jeremy Irons, Glenn Close, Ron Silver, Christine Baranski, Stephen Mailer, Uta Hagen, Annabelle Sciorra, Fisher Stevens, Julie Hagerty. Well-crafted docudrama, which works as both a witty satire of the old-moneyed rich and as an entertaining mystery, about Claus von Bulow's appeal of his conviction for his wife's attempted murder. The movie gets too cute when depicting the antics of attorney Alan Dershowitz's team of gung-ho law students, but the story's so fascinating that this can be overlooked. Irons won the Oscar for Best Actor, and Close, as the comatose Sunny (her part is all flashback) is magnificent. Scripted by Nicholas Kazin from Dershowitz's book. Co-produced by Oliver Stone and Edward R. Pressman. (Dir: Barbet Schroeder, 110 mins.)†

Revolt at Fort Laramie (1957)**½ John Dehner, Frances Helm. Army fort is split upon the outbreak of the Civil War, with the commander torn between loyalty to the South and duty as an officer. (Dir: Lesley Selander, 73 mins.)

Revolt in the Big House (1958)**½ Gene Evans, Robert Blake. Cons plan a daring escape. (Dir: R. G. Springsteen, 79 mins.)

Revolt of Job, The (Hungary, 1984)*** Ferenc Zenthe, Hedi Temessy, Gabor Feher. A Jewish couple, fearful that Nazis will wipe out their traditions, adopt a young Christian boy and try to instill in him their values and heritage. A touching film about how the Holocaust touched the lives of a Hungarian family in 1943. (Dir: Imre Gyongyossy, 98 mins.)

Revolt of Mamie Stover, The (1956)**½ Jane Russell, Richard Egan, Joan Leslie, Agnes Moorehead. Above-average melodrama of a beautiful young girl, forced to leave town, who goes to Hawaii and earns a small fortune as a dance hall hostess during WWII. Based on a novel by William Bradford Huie. (Dir: Raoul Walsh, 93 mins.)

Revolt of the Zombies (1936)* Dean Jagger, Dorothy Stone, Robert Noland, George Cleveland. The plot concerns a man who raises the dead during World War I to create his own army of the living dead in Cambodia. (Dir: Victor Halperin, 65 mins.)†

Revolution (1985)* Al Pacino, Nastassia Kinski, Donald Sutherland, Joan Plowright, Annie Lennox, Dave King. Bland, big-budget epic about a father and son's experiences during the American Revolution. What could have been a mediocre miniseries instead becomes a live-action Disney film, complete with overdrawn bad guys (the British), simplified good guys (the colonists) and friendly natives (the Indians). Pacino's accent suggests that he grew up in a Brooklyn suburb of Great Britain. (Dir: Hugh Hudson, 123 mins.)†

Revolutionary, The (1970)**½ Jon Voight, Seymour Cassel, Robert Duvall, Jennifer Salt. Unusual drama, set in a fictional locale, which casts Voight as a student-turned-revolutionary who leaves his friends to join up with union activists led by Duvall and, later, anarchists. A minor entry in both stars' careers; Cassel steals the picture as a hip, fast-talking militant. (Dir: Paul Williams, 100 mins.)

Reward, The (1965)* Max von Sydow, Yvette Mimieux, Efrem Zimbalist, Jr., Gilbert Roland. Good cast, caught in a clichéd western, about the greed that overcomes a five-man posse who begin eliminating one another. Little suspense. (Dir: Serge Bourguignon, 92 mins.)

Reward (MTV 1980)** Michael Parks, Annie McEnroe, Richard Jaeckel. Parks, cast as an ex-cop bent on vindicating his dead partner, is amiable, but you've seen this story before. (Dir: E. W. Swackhamer, 78 mins.)

Rhapsody (1954)** Elizabeth Taylor, Vittorio Gassman, John Ericson, Louis Calhern. Taylor plays a wealthy woman involved with a pianist and a violinist in this long and turgid romance, which isn't redeemed by sequences of classical music dubbed in by Claudio Arrau and Michael Rabin. (Dir: Charles Vidor, 115 mins.)

Rhapsody in Blue (1945)**½ Robert Alda, Oscar Levant, Charles Coburn, Alexis Smith. This is a trite, pedestrian film biography of the great George Gershwin but it's simply loaded with his magnificent music. (Dir: Irving Rapper, 139 mins.)

Rhinestone (1984)*½ Dolly Parton, Sylvester Stallone, Richard Farnsworth, Ron Leibman, Tim Thomerson. Top-heavy star vehicle that will only please the die-hard fans of the two leads. Parton plays a C&W singer who bets she can turn a tone-deaf cabbie into a successful singer. Rather than upstage each other, the two well-endowed stars up-chest each other. (Dir: Bob Clark, 111 mins.)†

Rhino (1964)**½ Robert Culp, Shirley Eaton, Harry Guardino. An exciting show for the younger set. About a zoologist who goes after a rare white rhino. (Dir: Ivan Tors, 91 mins.)

Rhinoceros (1974)** Gene Wilder, Zero Mostel, Karen Black. Considering the fine cast and the at least semi-classic nature of Ionesco's play, this picture is a disappointment. Largely at fault are the senselessly updated screenplay and the trendy direction of Tom O'Horgan. (101 mins.)

Rhubarb (1951)*** Ray Milland, Jan Sterling, Gene Lockhart. When a millionaire who owns a baseball club passes on, a cat inherits the team; as a mascot the feline leads the club toward a pennant. Zany comedy. (Dir: Arthur Lubin, 95 mins.)

Rhythm on the Range (1936)** Bing Crosby, Martha Raye, Bob Burns, Frances Farmer. Cowboy Bing romances an heiress and a prize cow in this forced comic offering. (Dir: Norman Taurog, 88 mins.)

Rhythm on the River (1940)*** Bing Crosby, Mary Martin, Oscar Levant, Basil Rathbone. A couple of successful ghost song writers try and click on their own, but only succeed in falling in love. Pleasant musical. (Dir: Victor Schertzinger, 94 mins.)

Rhythm Romance—See: **Some Like It Hot** (1939)

Rice Girl (Italy, 1959)** Elsa Martinelli, Michel Auclair. Lust and love in the rice fields, as a girl finds promise of happiness after a hard past. (Dir: Raffaello Matarazzo, 90 mins.)

Rich and Famous (1981)** Candice Bergen, Jacqueline Bisset, David Selby, Hart Bochner, Michael Brandon. Unfocused melodrama about the complex subjects of female friendship, success, and sexuality. Bergen is boisterous as a housewife who finds success and loses her husband as a result of writing pulp fiction, while Bisset is sullen as the "serious" novelist who lurches from one empty affair to the next. (Dir: George Cukor, 117 mins.)†

Rich and Strange (Great Britain, 1931)*** Joan Barry, Henry Kendall, Betty Amann. A strange, semi-humorous early Hitchcock where the title really tells it all. A discontented young couple suddenly come into a large sum of money, and decide to take a trip around the world. (Dir: Alfred Hitchcock, 91 mins.)

Richard Pryor—Here and Now (1983)*** Less contemplative than his other concert films, *Here and Now* should please Pryor fans. (Dir: Richard Pryor, 94 mins.)†

Richard Pryor Is Back Live in Concert (1979) ***½ Practically the same concert Pryor gave one day earlier in the same auditorium in *Richard Pryor Live in Concert*. (Dir: Jeff Margolis, 78 mins.)

Richard Pryor Live in Concert (1979)***½ Captures Pryor in all his glory, unfettered by mass media restraints. A remarkable document of a brilliant, maniacally funny act. (Dir: Jeff Margolis, 78 mins.)†

Richard Pryor Live on the Sunset Strip (1982)***½ Even funnier than Pryor's previous film based on his nightclub appearances. Hilarious routines, tinged with social satire and underlying rage. (Dir: Joe Layton, 82 mins.)†

Richard's Things (Great Britain, 1981)*½ Liv Ullmann, Amanda Redman, Tim Pigott-Smith. Slow-moving, talky drama about a woman (Ullmann) who finds out her husband—after he's killed in an accident—was having an affair with another woman (Redman). Both women share their grief, fight, and eventually end up falling in love with each other. Written by Frederic Raphael (*Darling*), and it weighs a ton. (Dir: Anthony Harvey, 104 mins.)†

Richard III (Great Britain, 1955)**** Laurence Olivier, Claire Bloom, Ralph Richardson, John Gielgud. Olivier is wickedly funny, reveling in the evil ambition of Shakespeare's totally villainous king. Marvelous film of the humpbacked king and his conquests on the battlefield and in the boudoir. (Dir: Laurence Olivier, 158 mins.)†

Rich Are Always With Us, The (1932)**½ Ruth Chatterton, George Brent, Adrienne Dore, Bette Davis. Charming, dated trifle about noble Chatterton forgiving her hubby again and again. A vehicle about the upper crust that gives the stars a chance to exercise their perfect diction and demonstrate their flair for being clotheshorses. (Dir: Alfred E. Green, 73 mins.)

Richest Cat in the World (MTV 1986)**½ Ramon Bieri, Steve Kampmann, Caroline McWilliams, Stephen Vinovich. Silly Disney comedy about a cat who inherits a large sum of money and is held for ransom by the disgruntled relatives of the deceased. The starring feline steals the spotlight, but the script still holds a few suprises. (Dir: Gregg Beeman, 96 mins.)

Richest Girl in the World, The (1934)*** Miriam Hopkins, Joel McCrea, Fay Wray, Reginald Denny, Henry Stephenson. Charming but dated champagne-class comedy about an heiress who wants to make sure her Mr. Right wants her heart, not her bankroll. (Dir: William A. Seiter, 76 mins.)

Richest Man in the World, The: The Story of Aristotle Onassis (MTV 1988)*½ Raul Julia, Jane Seymour, Francesca Annis, Anthony Quinn. This glossy, overromanticized biography of Onassis plays up not only his remarkable business savvy but also his highly publicized romantic liaisons. The details of his difficult early life may surprise you, but his three love affairs are presented in a cheap, torrid fashion. (Dir: Waris Hussein, 192 mins.)

Richie Brockleman, Private Eye (MTV 1976)** Dennis Dugan, Suzanne Pleshette, Norman Fell. Husky-voiced Pleshette is good as an amnesiac who hires a young would-be Sam Spade to find out who she is. (Dir: Hy Averback, 78 mins.)

Rich Kids (1979)**½ Trini Alvarado, John Lithgow, Paul Dooley, Kathryn Walker, Irene Worth. Intelligent and pleasant but shallow film about children of divorce. (Dir: Robert M. Young, 96 mins.)†

Rich Men, Single Women (MTV 1990)* Suzanne Somers, Heather Locklear, Deborah Adair, Larry Wilcox, John Allen Nelson, Joel Higgins. Mindless rip-off of *How to Marry a Millionaire* has Somers, Adair, and Locklear pretending to own a Malibu mansion in order to snare rich husbands. (Dir: Elliot Silverstein, 96 mins.)

Rich, Young and Pretty (1951)**½ Jane Powell, Vic Damone, Fernando Lamas, Wendell Corey, Danielle Darrieux. A typical MGM musical built around Jane Powell's soprano talents. She's a Texan's daughter who finds her long-lost mom in gay Paree. (Dir: Norman Taurog, 95 mins.)

Ricochet Romance (1954)** Marjorie Main, Chill Wills, Rudy Vallee. Main is back playing her "Ma Kettle" characterization in everything but name. Some funny moments. (Dir: Charles Lamont, 80 mins.)

Riddle of the Sands (Great Britain, 1978) **½ Michael York, Jenny Agutter, Simon MacCorkindale. A man agrees to accompany his former school chum on a pleasure jaunt. The two men are soon involved in stopping a German plot to invade England in this perfectly civilized and satisfying low-key adventure film. (Dir: Tony Maylam, 98 mins.)†

Ride a Crooked Mile (1938)** Akim Tamiroff, Frances Farmer. Corny, overdone drama about a boy who decides to help his growling thief of a father break out of Leavenworth. (Dir: Alfred E. Green, 78 mins.)

Ride a Crooked Trail (1958)**½ Audie Murphy, Gia Scala, Walter Matthau, Henry Silva. An outlaw cons a town into believing he's a U.S. marshall. Decent wild west action. (Dir: Jesse Hibbs, 87 mins.)

Ride a Wild Pony (Australia, 1975)** Michael Craig, John Meillon, Robert Bettles, Eva Griffith. Two Aussie kids fight over a pony back in the Edwardian period. Fair children's film. (Dir: Don Chaffey, 104 mins.)

Ride Back, The (1957)*** Anthony Quinn, Lita Milan, William Conrad. The plot, about a U.S. law officer tracking a wanted murderer in Mexico, unfolds slowly but the actors give honest characterizations. (Dir: Allen H. Miner, 79 mins.)

Ride Beyond Vengeance (1966)** Chuck Connors, Michael Rennie, Gloria Grahame, Joan Blondell, James MacArthur. Familiar western drama told in flashback by a saloon keeper. Connors returns to his home after getting a stake and is robbed and branded by a band of outlaws. (Dir: Bernard McEveety, 101 mins.)

Ride 'em Cowboy (1942)*** Bud Abbott, Lou Costello, Dick Foran, Anne Gwynne. One of the better Abbott and Costello vehicles has them out west on a dude ranch. Songs by the Merry Macs and Ella Fitzgerald are a restful break. (Dir: Arthur Lubin, 82 mins.)

Ride in the Whirlwind (1966)*** Cameron Mitchell, Jack Nicholson, Tom Filer, Millie Perkins. Downbeat, European-style western about three drifters who become the prey of an angry posse. Nicholson's existential, enigmatic screenplay makes this seem just like Kafka on horseback. (Dir: Monte Hellman, 82 mins.)†

Ride Lonesome (1959)*** Randolph Scott, Karen Steele, Pernell Roberts. Good Scott western epic which should appeal to his fans. He plays a former sheriff who captures a young renegade and brings him to justice. (Dir: Budd Boetticher, 73 mins.)

Ride Out for Revenge (1957)**½ Rory Calhoun, Gloria Grahame, Lloyd Bridges. Calhoun upholds the law and meets with a great deal of opposition from the bad guys. (Dir: Bernard Girard, 79 mins.)

Rider on the Rain (France-Italy, 1969)*** Charles Bronson, Marlene Jobert, Jill Ireland. Satisfying thriller that suspends credulity but keeps you guessing through neat psychological twists. Mellie (Jobert) has been raped in her home but has dropped her attacker with a shotgun blast. Arrogant investigator Dobbs (Bronson) appears on the trail of an escaped inmate. (Dir: René Clement, 119 mins.)†

Riders of the Purple Sage (1925)*** Tom

Mix, Beatrice Burnham, Arthur Morrison, Warner Oland, Fred Kohler, Marion Nixon. Terrific silent western, from the novel by Zane Grey, about a Texas Ranger who devotes his life to finding his kidnapped sister and niece. Breathless action, beautifully filmed on location. (Dir: Lynn Reynolds, 60 mins.)

Riders of the Storm (Great Britain, 1986)**½ Dennis Hopper, Michael J. Pollard, Eugene Lipinski, Nigel Pegram. Offkilter comic fantasy about a planeload of Vietnam vets who decide to sabotage the presidential campaign of a conservative female politician. Despite certain flagrantly ludicrous angles to the plot—from our first view, we realize the candidate is a man in drag (Pegram)—this throwback to the anarchic comedy of the sixties remains watchable for Hopper's portrayal of the plane's whacked-out captain. AKA: **The American Way**. (Dir: Maurice Phillips, 92 mins.)†

Riders of Vengeance—See: **Raiders, The**

Riders to the Stars (1954)**½ William Lundigan, Herbert Marshall, Richard Carlson, Martha Hyer, Dawn Addams. Fair science-fiction thriller about three men sent into outer space to investigate certain meteor behavior. (Dir: Richard Carlson, 81 mins.)

Ride the High Country (1962)**** Joel McCrea, Randolph Scott, Mariette Hartley (debut). An absolutely first-rate western, which gives Scott and McCrea the best roles of their lives, and they make the most of it. Directed by Sam Peckinpah in a controlled way—unlike many of his later violence-laden films. Two old-time lawmen sign on to escort gold from the goldfields to the bank, meeting trouble along the way. (94 mins.)†

Ride the Man Down (1952)*** Rod Cameron, Brian Donlevy, Ella Raines. Ranch foreman keeps it from land grabbers while awaiting the new owners. Fast-paced, exciting western with a good cast. (Dir: Joseph Kane, 90 mins.)†

Ride the Pink Horse (1947)*** Robert Montgomery, Wanda Hendrix, Thomas Gomez, Andrea King, Fred Clark, Iris Flores. Suspenseful tale of a hoodlum helped by a Mexican girl when he is crossed by his employers. Out-of-the-ordinary crime drama with superb direction by Montgomery. Remade as **The Hanged Man**. (101 mins.)

Ride the Wild Surf (1964)** Tab Hunter, Fabian, Barbara Eden. A group of young bronzed surfers engage in romantic interludes in between their riding the big waves. (Dir: Don Taylor, 101 mins.)

Ride to Hangman's Tree, The (1967)** Jack Lord, James Farentino, Melodie Johnson. A remake, for no discernible reason, of **Black Bart**. Three partners in crime decide to try and go straight. (Dir: Al Rafkin, 90 mins.)

Ride Vaquero (1953)** Robert Taylor, Ava Gardner, Howard Keel, Anthony Quinn. Sluggish western concerns a smoldering beauty who causes the downfall of some notorious outlaws. (Dir: John Farrow, 90 mins.)

Riding High (1943)*** Dorothy Lamour, Victor Moore, Dick Powell. Big-budgeted musical with little entertainment value. Something about a silver mine, a young man who wants to save it, and some musical nothings. (Dir: George Marshall, 89 mins.)

Riding High (1950)**½ Bing Crosby, William Demarest, Coleen Gray, Charles Bickford. Mark Hellinger's story about a businessman who'd rather spend his time at the racetrack is turned into a pleasant comedy with songs. Remake of *Broadway Bill*. (Dir: Frank Capra, 112 mins.)

Riding Shotgun (1954)** Randolph Scott, Wayne Morris. Scott is riding and shooting in his usual manner. (Dir: André de Toth, 74 mins.)

Riding Tall (1972)** Andrew Prine, Gilmer McCormick. A rodeo rider stops wandering long enough to fall for a pretty college dropout. (Dir: Patrick J. Murphy, 92 mins.)

Riding the Edge (1989)*½ Raphael Sbarge, Catherine Mary Stewart, Peter Haskell, Lyman Ward, Michael Sarne. Teen Sbarge and his motorbike invade the Middle East to rescue his dad, a scientist held captive by terrorists. As familiar as it sounds. (Dir: James Fargo, 95 mins.)†

Riding with Death (MTV 1976)* Ben Murphy, Katherine Crawford, Jim Stafford, Richard Dysart. Pilot for a forgotten TV series about a government agent who gains the power of invisibility after exposure to nuclear radiation. (Dirs: Alan J. Levi, Don McDougall, 97 mins.)†

Riffraff (1935)** Jean Harlow, Spencer Tracy, Mickey Rooney. Cliché-filled, melodramatic story of the tuna fishing industry in California. (Dir: J. Walter Ruben, 96 mins.)

Riffraff (1947)*** Pat O'Brien, Anne Jeffreys. Crooks are after an oil field survey in Panama, but are foiled by the local jack-of-all-trades. Well-done melodrama holds the interest. (Dir: Ted Tetzlaff, 80 mins.)†

Rififi (France, 1954)**** Jean Servais, Carl Mohner, Jules Dassin. There's a classic robbery scene in this exciting story about some crooks whose mutual distrust traps them all. A superior caper film. (Dir: Jules Dassin, 115 mins.)†

Right Cross (1950)**½ Dick Powell, June Allyson, Ricardo Montalban, Lionel Barrymore, Marilyn Monroe. Good prizefighting story about a Mexican box-er who desperately wants to become a champion. (Dir: John Sturges, 90 mins.)

Right Hand Man, The (Australia, 1987)* Rupert Everett, Hugo Weaving, Arthur Dignam. Everett plays a wealthy, one-armed diabetic who has his carriage driver/companion impregnate the woman he loves to produce an heir for his (Everett's) domineering mother. (Dir: Di Drew, 101 mins.)

Right of the People, The (MTV 1986)*½ Michael Ontkean, Jane Kaczmarek, Billy Dee Williams, John Randolph, M. Emmet Walsh. An incredibly manipulative piece of rabble-rousing with Ontkean as a district attorney whose wife and children are killed during a robbery, which precipitates his becoming a crusader for a law that allows everyone to carry guns. (Dir: Jeffrey Bloom, 104 mins.)

Right of Way (MCTV 1984)** Bette Davis, Jimmy Stewart, Melinda Dillon, Priscilla Morrill. This meandering tale focuses on the old couple, who decide to die together when Davis is diagnosed as terminally ill. (Dir: George Schaefer, 103 mins.)†

Right Stuff, The (1983)***½ Sam Shepard, Scott Glenn, Fred Ward, Ed Harris, Dennis Quaid, Veronica Cartwright, Barbara Hershey, Pamela Reed, Levon Helm, Jeff Goldblum. Long, rambling but often exhilarating essay on the original American space program. A detailed contemplation of the male mystique and the astronauts' obsession with qualifying for the pioneering space flights. Writer-director Philip Kaufman has chosen to tell two different stories—the first about the test pilot Chuck Yeager (Shepard), the first man to break the sound barrier, and the second about the public's myths and illusions about astronauts and the whole space program. A unique aviation epic despite its shortcomings, with some spectacular aerial photography. (191 mins.)†

Right to Die (MTV 1987)** Raquel Welch, Michael Gross, Bonnie Bartlett. Welch tries admirably to go dramatic in this fact-based TV movie about a wife and mother suffering from Lou Gehrig's disease. Her thespian talents can't cut it, however, and the teleplay is remarkably reminiscent of countless other "illness" TV movies. (Dir: Paul Wendkos, 96 mins.)

Right to Kill? (MTV 1985)***½ Frederic Forrest, Christopher Collet, Justine Bateman, Karmin Murcelo, Ann Wedgeworth. Excellent dramatization of a true story. Richard Jahnke, Jr. killed his father and was arrested. This hard-hitting film examines the motives for that murder and presents a gripping story about an abused family dominated by a sadistic father. (Dir: John Erman, 104 mins.)

Rikky and Pete (Australia, 1988)**½ Stephen Kearney, Nina Landis, Tetchie Agbayani. Pleasant but slight comedy about a female geologist who moonlights as a country singer (Landis) and her mechanical wizard brother. The two venture to a remote section of Australia, looking for a new life, and encounter a colorful assortment of oddballs. (Dir: Nadia Tass, 107 mins.)

Rikyu (Japan, 1990)*** Rentaro Mikuni, Tsutomu Yamazaki, Yoshiko Mita. Elegant, beautifully photographed Japanese historical drama about a remarkable 16th-century warlord, Hiyedoshi Toyotomi, who was enigmatic, measured, and demanding. (Dir: Hiroshi Teshigahara, 116 mins.)

Ring, The (1952)**½ Gerald Mohr, Lalo Rios, Rita Moreno. Mexican lad from the Los Angeles slums is turned into a boxing prospect, gets too cocky as a result. Smoothly made drama of fighting and racial discrimination, nicely acted. (Dir: Kurt Neumann, 79 mins.)

Ringer, The (1952)**½ Herbert Lom, Mai Zetterling, Donald Wolfit, William Hartnell. Low-budget Edgar Wallace mystery about a master criminal taking the side of the law in revenge for his sister's murder. Snappy plotting and a superior cast. (Dir: Guy Hamilton, 78 mins.)

Ring of Bright Water (Great Britain, 1969)*** Bill Travers, Virginia McKenna, Peter Jeffrey. This family picture features the couple of *Born Free* fame, Travers and McKenna. In this outing, the pair offer the same compassionate treatment to Mijbil, the otter, that they gave to Elsa, the lioness. (Dir: Jack Couffer, 107 mins.)†

Ring of Fear (1954)** Mickey Spillane, Pat O'Brien, Clyde Beatty. Cops and robbers in a circus tent performed mostly by nonactors—Beatty, Spillane, and tamed animals. (Dir: James Grant, 93 mins.)

Ring of Fire (1961)** David Janssen, Joyce Taylor, Frank Gorshin. A try for suspense as some hoodlums capture a lawman and hold him hostage in their flight for freedom. (Dir: Andrew L. Stone, 91 mins.)

Ring of Passion (MTV 1978)***½ Bernie Casey, Stephen Macht, Britt Ekland. A first-rate boxing movie, with Casey as the great heavyweight champion Joe Louis and Macht as a sympathetic Max Schmeling who wanted nothing to do with Hitler's racist madness but was afraid to speak out. (Dir: Robert Michael Lewis, 104 mins.)

Ring of Treason (Great Britain, 1964)*** Bernard Lee, William Sylvester, Margaret Tyzack. Staccato suspense in this story of a Russian spy ring in London. Lee is an ex-navy man taken to drink and mixing in with vile people. Based on Britain's Portland spy case. (Dir: Robert Tronson, 90 mins.)

Ringside Maisie (1941)** Ann Sothern, George Murphy, Robert Sterling, Maxie Rosenbloom, Virgina O'Brien. Maisie almost ends up on the ropes when she can't choose between a boxing manager and a promising pugilist who (wouldn't you know it) gets temporarily blinded. (Dir: Edward L. Marin, 96 mins.)

Rings on Her Fingers (1942)**½ Henry Fonda, Gene Tierney, Laird Cregar. Well played but overdone tale of a girl who is conned into fronting for swindlers and falls for her first victim. (Dir: Rouben Mamoulian, 85 mins.)

Rio Bravo (1959)***½ John Wayne, Dean Martin, Ricky Nelson, Walter Brennan, Angie Dickinson. Regarded as a minor classic, this Howard Hawks western mixes humor and horse opera with masterful results. Sheriff John Wayne enlists the aid of some misfits to prevent a jail escape. (141 mins.)†

Rio Conchos (1964)** Richard Boone, Stuart Whitman, Tony Franciosa. Action-packed western about a group who set out to recover some stolen rifles which are earmarked for sale to the Apaches. (Dir: Gordon Douglas, 107 mins.)†

Rio Grande (1950)*** John Wayne, Maureen O'Hara, Victor McLaglen, Claude Jarman, Jr., Ben Johnson, Harry Carey, Jr. Tough cavalry commander (Wayne) awaits orders to cross a river so he can clean up marauding Indians. John Ford epic western has beautiful scenery, good action, and plenty of drama as the commander also comes to grips with his feelings for his son, who's one of his newest enlistees. (Dir: John Ford, 105 mins.)†

Rio Lobo (1970)** John Wayne, Jorge Rivero, Jennifer O'Neill, Jack Elam. Director Howard Hawks and star Wayne just aren't up to their old high standards in this Civil War-era western. (114 mins.)†

Rio Rita (1929)**½ Bebe Daniels, John Boles, Bert Wheeler, Robert Woolsey. Early talkie, a sagebrush operetta adapted from the Ziegfeld stage hit, is not too bad. (Dir: Luther Reed, 135 mins.)

Rio Rita (1942)*** Kathryn Grayson, Bud Abbott, Lou Costello. A and C fans and even a few others will enjoy this musical about a ranch which is infested with Nazi spies. (Dir: S. Sylvan Simon, 91 mins.)

Riot (1969)**½ Gene Hackman, Jim Brown, Mike Kellin. This typical prison drama concerns a group of cons who take over a section of the prison, hold some guards as hostages, and the fireworks begin. (Dir: Buzz Kulik, 97 mins.)

Riot in Cell Block 11 (1954)***½ Neville Brand, Leo Gordon, Emile Meyer. Grim, violent, but thoughtful prison drama based on the experiences of producer Walter Wanger (who was incarcerated for shooting Jennings Lang). (Dir: Don Siegel, 80 mins.)†

Riot on Sunset Strip (1967)* Aldo Ray, Mimsy Farmer, Michael Evans, Laurie Mock, Tim Rooney. Ray is a concerned cop and father whose violent outburst helps usher in the tumultuous "riot" of the title. (Dir: Arthur Dreifuss, 85 mins.)

Rip-Off (Canada, 1971)*** Don Scardino, Ralph Endersby, Mike Kukulewich, Peter Gross. Affectionate comedy about four young men who try to join the hippie counterculture. Their attempts at alternate lifestyles end humorously, but provide lessons about themselves and life. (Dir: Donald Shebib, 94 mins.)

Riptide (1934)**½ Norma Shearer, Herbert Marshall, Robert Montgomery, Lilyan Tashman. Glossy nonsense about Shearer's ability to throw her head back and strike grand movie star poses. Norma marries a cold-blooded Brit but gets involved in a hot affair with Montgomery. (Dir: Edmund Goulding, 90 mins.)

Rise and Fall of Legs Diamond, The (1960)*** Ray Danton, Elaine Stewart, Karen Steele, Jesse White, Simon Oakland. Fast-moving and impressive account of the career of a hoodlum who rose to national infamy. (Dir: Budd Boetticher, 101 mins.)†

Rise and Shine (1941)*** Jack Oakie, Linda Darnell, Milton Berle, George Murphy, Walter Brennan, Sheldon Leonard. Occasionally hilarious comedy about a dumb football hero's adventures. (Dir: Allan Dwan, 93 mins.)

Rise of Catherine the Great, The—See: **Catherine the Great**

Rise of Louis XIV, The (France, 1966)**** Jean-Marie Patte, Raymond Jourdan, Silvagni, Pierre Barrat. One of a series of brilliant historical films directed by Roberto Rossellini for Italian TV. Begins with the last days and death of Mazarin, includes the building of Versailles, and ends as Louis XIV forces his court to watch him devour a 14-course meal. (100 mins.)

Rising of the Moon (Ireland, 1957)*** Frank Lawton, Denis O'Dea, Cyril Cusack. Trio of Irish tales directed by John Ford. Full of the old blarney but still charming. (81 mins.)

Rising Son (MCTV 1990)*** Brian Dennehy, Piper Laurie, Matt Damon. Top-notch drama about a family crisis set against the backdrop of the devastating 1981 economic setbacks of the Reagan administration. Story focuses on a pre-med student (Damon) who returns to his auto factory town in Pennsylvania to tell his proud father (Dennehy) he's decided to drop out of school. Meanwhile his father receives another severe blow when a corporate takeover shuts down the plant where he's been employed since WWII. Superb acting by Dennehy and Laurie, and an impressive performance by newcomer Damon. Credit also goes to director John Coles for his sensitive depiction of the gradual unveiling of an American tragedy. (Dir: John Coles, 96 mins.)†

Rising Storm—See: **Rebel Force**

Risk, The (Great Britain, 1960)*** Peter Cushing, Tony Britton, Virginia Maskell, Donald Pleasence. When a cure for plague is discovered, then withheld, resentment causes a scientist to become prey for foreign agents after the formula. (Dirs: Roy and John Boulting, 81 mins.)

Risky Business (1983)*** Tom Cruise, Bronson Pinchot, Nicholas Pryor, Rebecca DeMornay, Richard Masur. A genuine sleeper about an upper-class suburban teenager, who, upon meeting a beautiful call girl, ends up turning his vacationing parents' home into a brothel. First-time director Paul Brickman has taken a worn-out genre, the teenage sex comedy, and fashioned an artful, slick, and funny fable about coming of age. (98 mins.)†

Rita Hayworth: The Love Goddess (MTV 1983)* Lynda Carter, Michael Lerner, John Considine. Short shrift is given to Rita's meteoric career in favor of covering her failed marriages to Orson Welles and Aly Kahn. (Dir: James Goldstone, 104 mins.)†

Rita, Sue and Bob Too (Great Britain, 1987)*** Siobhan Finneran, Michelle Holmes, George Costigan. A scabrous sex comedy in which two Northern England girls are deflowered by the man for whom they baby-sit, and they all form a merry trio—until his wife finds out. Rarely has sex been more hilariously deglamorized than it is for the film's two coltish, ill-tempered heroines, who see their affair with Bob as something between an entertainment, a nuisance, and a good reason to cut gym class. (Dir: Alan Clarke, 95 mins.)†

Rite, The (Sweden, 1969)***½ Ingrid Thulin, Anders Ek, Erik Hell, Gunnar Bjornstrand. Intricate and disturbing drama from director Ingmar Bergman about a famed acting troupe whose members must bare their personal lives after one of their performances is charged with obscenity. Thulin, as one of the actresses, is dazzling in this somber and devastatingly personal film. (74 mins.)

Ritual of Evil (MTV 1969)**½ Louis Jourdan, Anne Baxter, Diana Hyland. Entertaining feature starring Jourdan as a psychiatrist interested in the bizarre world of the occult. A young heiress's death brings about Jourdan's investigation of the events leading to the tragedy. (Dir: Robert Day, 98 mins.)

Rituals (Canada, 1978)* Hal Holbrook, Lawrence Dane, Robin Gammell, Gary Reineke. Deliver us from this *Deliverance*-styled suspenser. A thriller about some doctors stalked during their vacation. AKA: **The Creeper**. (Dir: Peter Carter, 100 mins.)

Ritz, The (Great Britain, 1976)*** Jack Weston, Rita Moreno, Kaye Ballard, F. Murray Abraham, Treat Williams, Bessie Love, Jerry Stiller. A manic, fast-paced farce, set in a sleazy Manhattan homosexual bathhouse. Adapted by Terence McNally from his Broadway play. Director Richard Lester keeps things going along at a frantic pace. Moreno, playing a hopelessly untalented but very determined pop singer, is hilarious. (91 mins.)†

Rivals (1972)** Joan Hackett, Robert Klein, Scott Jacoby. Intense, occasionally pretentious study of the relationship between a young boy (Jacoby) and his mother (Hackett), and the jealousy that erupts when Mom starts going out with a hip tour guide (Klein). AKA: **Deadly Rivals**. (Dir: Krishna Shah, 101 mins.)†

River, The (India, 1951)**** Nora Swinburne, Esmond Knight. Story of an English family living in India, and of the hardships and difficulties involved in their maturity. Off the beaten path; a pictorially beautiful, fascinating drama, directed by Jean Renoir. (99 mins.)†

River, The (1984)*** Mel Gibson, Sissy Spacek, Scott Glenn, Shane Bailey, Becky Jo Lynch. A family battles flood waters that threaten to destroy their farm, but the drama gets lost in the deluge. (Dir: Mark Rydell, 122 mins.)†

River Gang (1945)**½ Gloria Jean, Keefe Brasselle, John Qualen. Waterfront girl who lives in a land of fantasy becomes involved in murder and a crime ring. (Dir: Charles David, 60 mins.)

River Lady (1948)*½ Yvonne De Carlo, Rod Cameron, Dan Duryea. Riverboat gambling queen falls for a logger, builds a big logging syndicate. (Dir: George Sherman, 78 mins.)

River of Death (1989)* Michael Dudikoff, Robert Vaughn, Donald Pleasence, Herbert Lom, L. Q. Jones, Cynthia Erland. Inept adaptation of a lesser Alistair MacLean novel about an expedition into the Amazon jungle. Shot in South Africa. (Dir: Steve Carver, 100 mins.)

River of Gold (MTV 1971)*½ Roger Davis, Suzanne Pleshette, Dack Rambo, Ray Milland, Melissa Newman. Two freewheeling buddies (Rambo and Davis) get involved with a group of mysterious people—a rich man looking for hidden treasure (Milland); a poet's widow (Ple-

shette) and the poet's mistress (Newman). (Dir: David Friedkin, 72 mins.)

River of Mystery (MTV 1971)**½ Vic Morrow, Claude Akins, Niall MacGinnis, Louise Sorel, Edmond O'Brien. Adventure tale about a hunt for diamonds in Brazil by a group of seedy characters. (Dir: Paul Stanley, 104 mins.)

River of No Return (1954)**½ Marilyn Monroe, Robert Mitchum, Rory Calhoun, Tommy Rettig. Action-packed backwoods adventure yarn; Monroe plays a saloon singer who enlists widower Mitchum's aid when her shiftless gambler husband deserts her. (Dir: Otto Preminger, 91 mins.)†

River Rat (1984)** Tommy Lee Jones, Martha Plimpton, Brian Dennehy. Fair drama about an ex-convict (Jones) who returns to his Mississippi River home only to encounter difficulty with his plucky daughter (Plimpton) and to receive threats from his underhanded parole officer (Dennehy). (Dir: Tom Rickman, 93 mins.)†

River's Edge, The (1957)*** Anthony Quinn, Ray Milland, Debra Paget. Better than average crime melodrama about a killer who menaces his old girlfriend and her husband's life in an attempt to smuggle a stolen fortune into Mexico. (Dir: Allan Dwan, 87 mins.)

River's Edge (1987)***½ Crispin Glover, Keanu Reeves, Ione Skye Leitch, Dennis Hopper. A disturbing drama about ignorance and apathy. Based on an actual incident which took place in the northwest, a brutish high school boy strangles his girlfriend on the river's edge and then displays no remorse or guilt. What is far more chilling is that most of his peers go along with the attempted cover-up. Hopper all but steals the film as a burnt-out biker. (Dir: Tim Hunter, 99 mins.)†

Riviera (MTV 1987)*½ Ben Masters, Elyssa Davalos, Richard Hamilton, Jon Finch. A former government agent finds himself in mortal danger when he journeys to Europe to investigate his late father's business. (Dir: "Alan Smithee" [John Frankenheimer], 104 mins.)

Road Back, The (1937)** John King, Richard Cromwell, Slim Summerville, Andy Devine, Barbara Read, Louise Fazenda, Noah Beery, Jr. What happens when the boys return from war? That's the question this sequel to Erich Maria Remarque's *All Quiet on the Western Front* asks. Unfortunately, at least in this adaptation, the answer is, not enough. (Dir: James Whale, 105 mins.)

Roadblock (1951)**½ Charles McGraw, Joan Dixon, Milburn Stone. Insurance investigator turns crook to get enough money for his girlfriend. Well-acted, suspenseful crime melodrama. (Dir: Harold Daniels, 73 mins.)

Road Games (Australia, 1981)**½ Stacy Keach, Jamie Lee Curtis, Marion Edward, Grant Page, Bill Stacey. Trucker Keach encounters eccentrics, a runaway heiress (Curtis), and a mad slasher while driving across the Australian outback. Enjoyable suspenser with Hitchcockian trappings. (Dir: Richard Franklin, 100 mins.)†

Road House (1948)*** Ida Lupino, Richard Widmark, Cornel Wilde, Celeste Holm. A good cast lifts this routine melodrama out of the ranks of mediocrity. Widmark plays a sadistic road house owner who has his enemy paroled in his custody so he can torture him. (Dir: Jean Negulesco, 95 mins.)

Road House (1989)** Patrick Swayze, Ben Gazzara, Kelly Lynch, Sam Elliott. Expert bouncer Swayze is hired to make a rowdy bar safe for patrons and musicians. Violent, high-spirited fun for a while, but this modern-dress western soon wears thin. (Dir: Rowdy Harrington, 115 mins.)†

Roadhouse 66 (1985)* Judge Reinhold, Willem Dafoe, Karen Lee, Kate Vernon. Inane highway hijinks by way of Route 66 as a snotty rich kid and a tough loner mix it up with the local rednecks and two women lookin' for some lovin'. (Dir: John Mark Robinson, 90 mins.)†

Roadie (1980)** Meat Loaf, Art Carney, Blondie, Alice Cooper, Hank Williams, Jr., Roy Orbison. A meretricious movie. Luckily, the ungainly Meat Loaf, as the Texas boy who can fix anything, carries the movie with genuine charisma, and he can act too. (Dir: Alan Rudolph, 105 mins.)†

Roadkill (Canada, 1989)*** Valerie Buhagiar, Don McKeller, Gary Quigley, Mark Tarantino. Highly original road movie about a woman sent to find a missing rock band lost in sparsely populated northern Ontario. Black and white film perfectly captures the flavor of traveling on the road and tantalizes the audience with a rash of interesting characters. (Dir: Bruce McDonald, 80 mins.)

Road Raiders, The (MTV 1989)*½ Bruce Boxleitner, Susan Diol, Reed McCants, Noble Willingham, Mark Blankfield. American saloon owner in 1942 Manila puts together a misfit bunch to help fight WWII in this overly familiar pilot full of anachronisms and lifts from "The 'A' Team" and The Dirty Dozen. (Dir: Richard Lang, 96 mins.)

Road Show (1941)**½ Adolphe Menjou, Carole Landis, Patsy Kelly. A playboy and his screwy friend from an insane asylum join a traveling carnival. Completely mad, amusing farce. (Dirs: Hal Roach, Hal Roach, Jr., Gordon Douglas, 87 mins.)

Road to Bali (1952)**½ Bob Hope, Bing Crosby, Dorothy Lamour. Later Hope-Crosby teaming, back in the South Seas with the spirits flagging and the color unflattering, but series fans will still be amused. Watch for Carolyn Jones in her film debut. (Dir: Hal Walker, 90 mins.)†

Road to Corinth, The (France, 1967)*** Jean Seberg, Maurice Ronet, Christian Marquand, Michel Bouquet, Claude Chabrol. Well-acted spy thriller in the tradition of Alfred Hitchcock and Ian Fleming satisfies with a stylistic tongue-in-cheek production from director-co-star Chabrol about the widow of a murdered NATO security officer who must prove she didn't kill her husband. (90 mins.)

Road to Denver, The (1955)**½ John Payne, Mona Freeman, Lee J. Cobb, Skip Homeier, Lee Van Cleef. Cowhand tries to keep his hot-headed brother out of trouble when the kid joins up with the outlaws. Pretty fair western. (Dir: Joseph Kane, 90 mins.)

Road to Glory, The (1936)***½ Fredric March, Warner Baxter, Lionel Barrymore. William Faulkner co-wrote the script with Joel Sayre. Remarkably strong WWI story of a French regiment at the front, and the strains, stresses, and misunderstandings between commanders and men. (Dir: Howard Hawks, 95 mins.)

Road to Hong Kong (1962)**½ Bing Crosby, Bob Hope, Joan Collins, Dorothy Lamour. The last of the Road pictures, with only a brief appearance by Lamour. The plot centers around a couple of hustlers who find themselves up to their necks in international intrigue and interplanetary hokum. (Dir: Norman Panama, 91 mins.)

Road to Morocco (1942)*** Bob Hope, Bing Crosby, Dorothy Lamour, Anthony Quinn. Zany Hope-Crosby comedy is a bit too silly, but gets its share of laughs. A few good songs help. (Dir: David Butler, 83 mins.)

Road to Rio (1947)*** Bob Hope, Bing Crosby, Dorothy Lamour, the Andrews Sisters, Gale Sondergaard. Crazy, delightful antics in Rio de Janeiro expertly handled by experts. Good fun. (Dir: Norman Z. McLeod, 100 mins.)†

Road to Ruin, The (1928)** Helen Foster, Grant Withers, Florence Turner, Charles Miller. Sensationalistic melodrama of a girl who goes wrong after smoking and drinking sap her moral strength, leading her into prostitution. Ludicrously overblown but fascinating period piece. (Dir: Norton S. Parker, 65 mins.)†

Road to Salina, The (France-Italy, 1971)**½ Robert Walker, Rita Hayworth, Ed Begley, Mimsy Farmer. Hayworth's earthy performance is the best reason to see this twisted tale of a prodigal son who returns home for a fling with a girl who may be his sister. (Dir: George Lautner, 96 mins.)†

Road to Singapore (1940)*** Bob Hope, Bing Crosby, Dorothy Lamour, Anthony Quinn, Charles Coburn. First of the *Road* films and not much to offer except for Bob and Bing's presence as two playboys who go to Singapore to forget women. (Dir: Victor Schertzinger, 92 mins.)

Road to Utopia (1945)***½ Bing Crosby, Bob Hope, Dorothy Lamour, Hillary Brooke. Vaudeville team involved in search for Alaskan gold mine but—forget the plot— this one is funny. (Dir: Hal Walker, 90 mins.)†

Road to Yesterday, The (1925)*** Joseph Schildkraut, Jetta Goudal, Vera Reynolds, William Boyd, Iron Eyes Cody. Modern story of two troubled couples is paralleled by an elaborate fantasy of the 17th century, which takes place *during* a train wreck! Typically nutty extravaganza from director Cecil B. DeMille, not to be taken seriously, but great fun all the same. (136 mins.)†

Road to Zanzibar (1941)***½ Bob Hope, Bing Crosby, Dorothy Lamour, Una Merkel, Eric Blore. Satire on all jungle pictures is one of the funnier entries in the *Road* series. Bing and Bob tour Africa as a couple of carnival hustlers. (Dir: Victor Schertzinger, 92 mins.)

Road Trip—See: **Jocks**

Road Warrior, The (Australia, 1982)***½ Mel Gibson, Emile Minty, Virginia Hay, Bruce Spence. Gibson reprises his title role from the cult film *Mad Max* in this vastly superior sequel. Max is a post-apocalyptic Shane, reluctantly rescuing a band of settlers menaced in their oil-refinery-cum-homestead by marauding bikers. Director George Miller's camera goes everywhere, fluidly and kinetically recording the action, of which there is plenty. (94 mins.)†

Roald Dahl's Danny, the Champion of the World—See: **Danny, the Champion of the World**

Roaring Twenties, The (1939)**** James Cagney, Priscilla Lane, Gladys George, Humphrey Bogart, Jeffrey Lynn, Frank McHugh. Bootleggers in New York, in one of the best Hollywood gangster films ever. Cagney gives a light, sure performance, and the pace is crisp. Director Raoul Walsh emerged with this film as the Hollywood action man with a lot extra. (106 mins.)†

Robber's Roost (1955)**½ George Montgomery, Richard Boone, Sylvia Findley, Bruce Bennett, Peter Graves. Low-budget Zane Grey western with crippled rancher Bennett hiring rival gangs to guard his stock. Burly, colorful, and well acted. (Dir: Sidney Salkow, 83 mins.)

Robbery (Great Britain, 1967)**½ Stanley Baker, Joanna Pettet, James Booth, Frank Finlay, Barry Foster. This tense melodrama based on the hijacking of the London night mail train is only partially successful. The plans for the robbery and its actual execution are well handled, but the characterizations are overdrawn and get in the way. (Dir: Peter Yates, 114 mins.)†

Robbery Under Arms (Great Britain, 1957)**½ Peter Finch, Ronald Lewis, David McCallum, Jill Ireland. Two brothers join an outlaw on a cattle-stealing venture in Australia. (Dir: Jack Lee, 83 mins.)

Robe, The (1953)**½ Richard Burton, Jean Simmons, Victor Mature, Michael Rennie, Richard Boone. The first film made in the CinemaScope process— which means nothing for TV viewers. The Lloyd C. Douglas novel about a Roman tribune ordered to crucify the Messiah, and his conversion to Christianity when he dons the robe of Jesus, is reverent, stately, impressively produced. (Dir: Henry Koster, 135 mins.)†

Roberta (1935)*** Irene Dunne, Randolph Scott, Fred Astaire, Ginger Rogers. Charming, leisurely paced musical about a group of American entertainers who find themselves running a Parisian dress shop. Consistently entertaining, but the film really soars whenever Fred and Ginger hit the dance floor. (Dir: William A. Seiter, 105 mins.)†

Robert et Robert (France, 1979)*** Charles Denner, Jacques Villeret, Jean-Claude Brialy, Regine, Germaine Montero. Winningly comical. Both Roberts are lonely men who live with their mothers. They meet in the waiting room of a matrimonial service and become fast friends, each encouraging the other to come out of his shell. (Dir: Claude Lelouch, 105 mins.)†

Robin and Marian (Great Britain, 1976)**½ Audrey Hepburn, Sean Connery, Robert Shaw, Richard Harris, Nicol Williamson, Denholm Elliott, Ian Holm. A revisionist view of medieval history and our friends from Sherwood Forest. Thanks largely to the two stars, this tale of Robin Hood, twenty years after he left Sherwood Forest to join Richard the Lionhearted on the Crusades, is occasionally affecting, although the film's tone is deliberately downbeat. (Dir: Richard Lester, 106 mins.)†

Robin and the Seven Hoods (1964)*** Frank Sinatra, Dean Martin, Bing Crosby, Sammy Davis, Jr., Barbara Rush, Peter Falk. Entertaining musical spoof of the Prohibition days in Chicago. Sinatra and his cronies are well suited to their roles of small-time hoods who fleece the rich and give to the less affluent. The original musical score is very good, including "My Kind of Town" and "Style." (Dir: Gordon Douglas, 103 mins.)†

Robin Hood (1922)**** Douglas Fairbanks, Wallace Beery, Enid Bennett, Alan Hale. Superb, lavish production with an energetic Fairbanks as the famous outlaw. Fabulous sets, costumes, and pageantry, with humor, excitement, and thrills. One of the great silent pictures. (Dir: Allan Dwan, 120 mins.)†

Robin Hood (1973)*** Voices of Brian Bedford, Phil Harris, Monica Evans, Peter Ustinov, Terry-Thomas, Andy Devine, Pat Buttram, Roger Miller, Carole Shelley, George Lindsey. Engaging Disney cartoon, not in a league with their finest achievements, but a respectable entry among their latter-day work. Recasting the "Robin Hood" legend with animals works beautifully. (Dir: Wolfgang Reitherman, 83 mins.)†

Robin Hood: Prince of Thieves (1991)*** Kevin Costner, Mary Elizabeth Mastrantonio, Morgan Freeman, Alan Rickman. After a sluggish start, and though burdened by Costner's stolid performance as Robin with a ludicrous American accent, this revisionist account of derring-do in Sherwood Forest and environs come gloriously alive. Overlooking some of the inanities of the script, old and young will enjoy the spectacle and the costumes. (Dir: Kevin Reynolds, 141 mins.)†

Robin Hood of El Dorado, The (1936)*** Warner Baxter, Ann Loring, Bruce Cabot, Margo, J. Carrol Naish, Edgar Kennedy. Historical drama of a Mexican-American who becomes an outlaw wreaking revenge for injustices to his people. Stirring and colorful, with director William Wellman's characteristically uncompromising view. (86 mins.)

Robinson Crusoe (MTV 1974)*** Stanley Baker, Ram John Holder. Baker is the shipwrecked, resourceful hero of the Daniel Defoe novel. The wrenching aches of solitude are evoked, as are the methodical feats of labor Crusoe devised to keep himself occupied in body and mind. (Dir: James MacTaggart, 104 mins.)†

Robinson Crusoe on Mars (1964)*** Adam West, Vic Lundin, Paul Mantee. Despite its ridiculous title this is an imaginative and intelligent sci-fi film about an American spaceman marooned on Mars. (Dir: Byron Haskin, 109 mins.)†

Robocop (1987)***½ Peter Weller, Nancy Allen, Ronny Cox, Kurtwood Smith, Dan O'Herlihy. Smashing, graphically violent thriller set in the future, in which a murdered policeman is transformed into a robotic crimefighter. Great action scenes, solid acting, and abundant humor and futuristic detail make this a winner. (Dir: Paul Verhoeven, 103 mins.)†

Robocop 2 (1990)*** Peter Weller, Nancy Allen, Daniel O'Herlihy, Tom Noonan, Belinda Bauer, Gabriel Damon, Patricia Charbonneau, John Glover. This high-voltage sequel finds the armored crime fighter battling both an outbreak of a lethal, addictive drug and a titanic cyborg, cleverly named "Robocop 2." (Dir: Irvin Kershner, 117 mins.)†

Roboman—See: Who?

Robot Holocaust (1987)** Norris Culf, Nadine Hart. Passable sci-fi about a bleak future where rebels battle the Dark One for control of the environment after robots with a serious shortage of breathable air. (Dir: Tim Kincaid, 79 mins.)†

Robot Jox (1990) ** Gary Graham, Anne-Marie Johnson, Paul Koslo, Hilary Mason. Routine sci-fi tale is set in a nuclear-devastated future where superpowers battle it out with gigantic piloted robots. Expert special effects are the main highlight. (Dir: Stuart Gordon, 84 mins.)†

Robot Monster (1953)½ George Nader, Selena Royle, George Moffett, Claudia Barrett. After spacemen blast Earth, a handful of plucky survivors battle Ro-Man, a gorilla monster wearing a deep-sea diver's helmet; this attire sets the ludicrous tone for the entire film. (Dir: Phil Tucker, 63 mins.)†

Robot vs. the Aztec Mummy, The (Mexico, 1960)½ Ramon Gay, Rosita Arenas. Laughably bad sci-fi in which a mummy who's been jealously guarding a treasure for centuries gets into a brouhaha with some tomb robbers, who later decide to fix the mummy's wagon by creating an indestructible robot. (Dir: Rafael Portillo, 64 mins.)†

Rob Roy, the Highland Rogue (1954)** Richard Todd, Glynis Johns, James Robertson Justice, Michael Gough. Best western with kilts, starring Todd as leader of the 18th-century clan Mac Gregor who leads his men against the new English King George. (Dir: Harold French, 81 mins.)†

Rocco and His Brothers (France-Italy, 1960)***½ Alain Delon, Renato Salvatori, Annie Girardot, Katina Paxinou, Claudia Cardinale. Drama of a woman and her sons who come to Milan to find livelihoods. Many subplots meticulously woven together to make a broad canvas of contemporary Italy. Absorbing despite the length. (Dir: Luchino Visconti, 152 mins.)†

Rockabye (1932)** Constance Bennett, Joel McCrea, Paul Lukas, Walter Pidgeon. Sentimental melodrama; an actress makes it to the top, only to find herself unfulfilled until she opts for motherhood and sacrifices her career for her husband. (Dir: George Cukor, 70 mins.)

Rockabye (MTV 1986)*** Valerie Bertinelli, Rachel Ticotin, Jason Alexander. Exceptional drama about a mother's determined search for her 3-year-old son who was kidnapped from her in broad daylight for eventual sale on the black market. (Dir: Richard Michaels, 120 mins.)

Rock-A-Bye Baby (1958)** Jerry Lewis, Marilyn Maxwell, Connie Stevens. Uneven farce with Jerry Lewis playing bachelor father to a Hollywood starlet's baby. (Dir: Frank Tashlin, 103 mins.)

Rock All Night (1957)** Dick Miller, Russell Johnson, Abby Dalton, The Platters, Robin Morse. Low-budget thriller about two thugs holding a barful of patrons hostage. (Dir: Roger Corman, 63 mins.)

Rock Around the Clock (1956)** Bill Haley and His Comets, Johnny Johnston. Quickie musical produced to capitalize on the popularity of Haley. Johnston is around to further the plot—which is fairly nonexistent. (Dir: Fred F. Sears, 77 mins.)†

Rock Around the World (Great Britain, 1957)** Tommy Steele, Patrick Westwood, Hilda Fenemore. Mild biography of teen-idol Steele. Several popular British teen acts appear and make it quite clear why they never made it in the U.S. AKA: **The Tommy Steele Story.** (Dir: Gerard Bryant, 71 mins.)

Rock Baby, Rock It (1957)* Johnny Carroll, Johnny Dobbs, Don Coats. One of the worst teen exploitation pictures of the '50s, which is really saying something. To save a building from gangsters, teens hold a benefit concert with one lousy act after another. (Dir: Murray Douglas Sporup, 84 mins.)†

Rockers (Jamaica, 1978)*** Gregory Isaacs, Leroy "Horsemouth" Wallace, Winston Rodney, Robbie Shakespeare. Musical drama about a drummer who enlists the aid of his Rasta "brothers" to retrieve his stolen motorbike. Unusual look at Rastafarian culture in a high-spirited film filled with reggae music. (Dir: Theodoros Bafaloukos, 99 mins.)†

Rocket Gibraltar (1988)** Burt Lancaster, Suzy Amis, Patricia Clarkson, John Glover, Bill Pullman, Kevin Spacey. Trite drama about a family reunion held at the Long Island summer home of a retired writer (Lancaster). A talented cast of adults gets little to do as the story focuses on the grandchildren's efforts to fulfill Lancaster's peculiar last wish—to be given a flaming Viking burial. (Dir: Daniel Petrie, 100 mins.)†

Rocket Man, The (1954)*½ Charles Coburn, Anne Francis, George Winslow. Adopted boy helps the town get rid of crooks by means of a mysterious gun. Childish fantasy; scripted by Lenny Bruce, but you'd never know it. (Dir: Oscar Rudolph, 79 mins.)

Rocketship X-M (1950)** Lloyd Bridges, Hugh O'Brian, Osa Massen, John Emery. Heading for the Moon, some astronauts land on Mars instead, where they find the ruins of an ancient civilization. The version on videocassette has tinted sequences and some additional footage. (Dir: Kurt Neumann, 77 mins.)†

Rocket to the Moon (MTV 1986)**½ Judy Davis, John Malkovich, Eli Wallach, Connie Booth, William Hootkins. Well-acted production of a routine Clifford Odets play, set in 1938, about a timid dentist whose life and values are changed when a lively young woman comes to work in his office. Davis and Malkovich are exceptional, bringing life to clichéd parts. Shot on videotape. (Dir: John Jacobs, 110 mins.)†

Rockford Files, The (MTV 1974)** James Garner, Lindsay Wagner. Pilot film for the TV series starring Garner as a private eye who insists on a $200-a-day fee from his pretty client (Miss Wagner) for fingering the murderer of her wino father. Garner uses his easygoing dry wit to advantage. (Dir: Richard T. Heffron, 74 mins.)

Rock Hudson (MTV 1990)**½ Thomas Ian Griffith, Daphne Ashbrook, Andrew Robinson, Diane Ladd. Story of the actor's rise to movie stardom while hiding his homosexuality and his eventual death from AIDS plays like a typical Hollywood saga. Griffith's likable performance keeps this a notch above the fan magazine level. (Dir: John Nicolella, 96 mins.)

Rocking Horse Winner, The (Great Britain, 1949)***½ Valerie Hobson, John Mills, John Howard Davies. D. H. Lawrence's superb short story becomes a heart-breaking movie. A boy discovers he can keep his parents together by the money he wins predicting winners at the track. (Dir: Anthony Pelissier, 91 mins.)

Rockin' the Blues (1955)**½ Manatan Moreland, F. E. Miller, Connie Carroll, The Harptones, The Wanderers, Linda Hopkins. Low-budget concert film with great music, in an all rhythm-and-blues line-up. (Dir: Arthur Rosenblum, 66 mins.)†

Rock 'n' Roll High School (1979)*** P. J. Soles, Vincent Van Patten, Mary Woronov, Clint Howard, Paul Bartel, The Ramones. This low-budget rock 'n' roller is a likable, energetic treat. Even if The Ramones's music isn't music to your ears, you'll get a kick out of these rhythm-crazy rebels who are tired of wasting time getting a good education. (Dir: Alan Arkush, 94 mins.)†

Rock 'n' Roll Mom (MTV 1988)*½ Dyan Cannon, Michael Brandon, Telma Hopkins. Cannon looks quite sexy in the trendy teenybopper outfits she wears as the title character in this Disney telefilm, but the plot—about a mother who hides her commonplace identity when she hits the big time in the music biz—is threadbare. (Dir: Michael Schultz, 96 mins.)

Rock 'n' Roll Nightmare (Canada, 1987)** Jon-Mikl Thor, Paula Francescatto, Rusty Hamilton. Dumb horror movie about a heavy metal band fighting demons in their rehearsal retreat. (Dir: John Fasano, 89 mins.)†

Rock 'n' Rule (1983)**½ The voices of Don Francks, Catherine O'Hara, Paul LeMat. Expert animation highlights this futuristic rock film that shortchanges us in the story department but makes up for it in the music track (which features Debbie Harry, Earth, Wind and Fire, and Lou Reed, among others). (Dir: Clive A. Smith, 85 mins.)†

Rock, Pretty Baby (1957)** John Saxon, Luana Patten, Sal Mineo, Fay Wray. Slight plot about a high school band leader out to win the big contest tied to vast amount of rock-and-roll numbers. Teenagers should appreciate. (Dir: Richard Bartlett, 89 mins.)

Rock, Rock, Rock (1956)**½ Tuesday Weld, Alan Freed, Frankie Lymon and the Teenagers, Chuck Berry, The Moonglows, The Flamingos, LaVern Baker. Lots of fantastic vintage fifties music. In her screen debut, Weld is an ambitious teen who's just got to get a strapless evening gown for her prom. (Dir: Will Price, 83 mins.)†

Rocktober Blood (1986)*½ Tray Loren, Donna Scoggins, Cana Cockrell. A rock star executed for a killing spree may have come back from the dead with vengeance on his mind. Typical vegematic slasher picture. (Dir: Beverly Sebastian, 88 mins.)†

Rocky (1976)*** Sylvester Stallone, Talia Shire, Burgess Meredith, Burt Young, Carl Weathers. The Academy Award-winner about a loutish lug who wants to become a boxing champ. Stallone makes you care for him in the screenplay written by him, and Shire, playing his painfully shy girlfriend, is splendid. Uses the slums of Philadelphia to good advantage for much of the on-location scenes. (Dir: John G. Avildsen, 119 mins.)†

Rocky II (1979)**½ Sylvester Stallone, Talia Shire, Burt Young, Burgess Meredith, Carl Weathers. Rocky is down on his luck and struggling for another shot at the title. Shameless manipulation conjures up emotional responses from the earlier film. (Dir: Sylvester Stallone, 119 mins.)†

Rocky III (1982)*** Sylvester Stallone, Mr. T., Burgess Meredith, Talia Shire, Burt Young, Carl Weathers. This time Rocky learns a lesson because he has let fame and fortune go to his head. A carefully worked out repeat of the ritual that casts Rocky as the underdog and allows the audience to do what they came for—cheer him to victory. (Dir: Sylvester Stallone, 99 mins.)†

Rocky IV (1985)** Sylvester Stallone, Talia Shire, Burt Young, Carl Weathers, Brigitte Nielsen, Dolph Lundgren. As in *Rocky III*, Rocky is prompted by the death of a comrade to fight an unbeatable monster. The hulk is now a Russian, built up with modern machinery and (gasp!) steroids. (Dir: Sylvester Stallone, 90 mins.)†

Rocky V (1990)**½ Sylvester Stallone, Talia Shire, Burt Young, Sage Stallone, Tommy Morrison, Burgess Meredith. Another of the interminable *Rocky* sequels sends Rocky Balboa back to his roots after a crooked accountant leaves him penniless. He opens a gym in South Philadelphia, trains a hot new boxer, and rediscovers the joys of marriage and fatherhood. This is a somewhat kinder and gentler take on the legend. (Dir: John G. Avildsen, 103 mins.)†

Rocky Horror Picture Show, The (Great Britain, 1975)*** Tim Curry, Susan Sarandon, Barry Bostwick, Meat Loaf. The midnight show phenomenon is based on a British rock musical which flopped on the U.S. stage. Primarily a spoof of old monster movies, but to update the proceedings the chief weirdo at the castle is a bisexual named Frank N. Furter who wears lipstick and sings. (Dir: Jim Sharman, 100 mins.)†

Rocky Mountain (1950)** Errol Flynn, Patrice Wymore. Opposing forces unite to fight a common enemy, the attacking Indians. (Dir: William Keighley, 83 mins.)

Rodan (Japan, 1957)** Kenji Sawara. Japanese-made science fiction film about a huge flying monster. (Dir: Inoshiro Honda, 72 mins.)†

Rodeo (1952)**½ John Archer, Jane Nigh. Girl takes over a rodeo when the promoter skips with the loot, makes it a success. (Dir: William Beaudine, 70 mins.)

Rodeo Girl (MTV 1980)** Katharine Ross, Bo Hopkins, Candy Clark. Tired of being a housewife, Ross hits the rodeo circuit with Clark, going against the wishes of husband Hopkins. Little action, much boredom. (Dir: Jackie Cooper, 104 mins.)†

Roe vs. Wade (MTV 1989)*** Holly Hunter, Amy Madigan, Kathy Bates, James Gammon, Chris Mulkey, Terry O'Quinn. The emotional, despairing story behind the 1973 Supreme Court decision which legalized abortion. Denied an abortion in Texas, a pregnant woman (Hunter) allows a novice lawyer (Madigan) to argue her case, and to take it clear to the Supreme Court. (Dir: Gregory Hoblit, 93 mins.)†

Roger and Henry: The Mitera Target (MTV 1977)*½ John Davidson, Barry Primus, Carole Mallory, Anne Randall Stewart. Forgotten pilot film about two unctuous men-for-hire who make a living finding lost objects and individuals. (Dir: Jack Stewart, 72 mins.)

Roger and Me (1989)**** Neophyte filmmaker and ex-muckraking journalist Michael Moore's movie about the death blow dealt to Flint, Michigan when General Motors decided to close most of its operations there is a devastating funeral oration for the American Dream. The ironic humor in this startlingly funny movie comes from the mind-bogglingly stupid reactions of public leaders, who wasted millions of dollars in foolhardy attempts to revive the city's economy. Moore was criticized for altering the chronology of some events for dramatic impact, a complaint that misses the point: this film is an admittedly one-sided howl of outrage at a blithely indifferent American economic system that can destroy the lives of workers and brag about it to stockholders. A must-see. (90 mins.)†

Roger Corman's Frankenstein Unbound (1990)** John Hurt, Raul Julia, Bridgit Fonda, Jason Patric. A strange atmospheric occurrence enables a scientist in 2031 to return to 1817 and chat with the poets Byron and Shelley, Mary Godwin (before she was married and wrote *Frankenstein*), and a living Dr. Frankenstein who has actually created a monster. Talky and uneventful. Based on a novel by Brian W. Aldiss. AKA: **Frankenstein Unbound.** (Dir: Roger Corman, 86 mins.)†

Roger Touhy, Gangster (1944)**½ Preston Foster, Victor McLaglen. Fairly good crime film loosely based on Touhy's career. (Dir: Robert Florey, 65 mins.)

RoGoPaG (Italy, 1962)*** Rosanna Schiaffino, Bruce Balabin, Alexandra Stewart, Jean-Marc Bory, Orson Welles, Ugo Tognazzi, Renato Salvatori, Lisa Gastoni. Insightful, serio-comic omnibus film about the problems of modern life: an oversexed American pesters a flight attendant; a couple faces very annoying sales techniques; a couple has a post-nuke love affair; an actor in a Passion play dies on the cross. (Dirs: Roberto Rossellini, Ugo Gregoretti, Jean-Luc Godard, Pier Paolo Pasolini, 125 mins.)

Rogue Cop (1954)*** Robert Taylor, Janet Leigh, George Raft, Anna Francis, Steve Forrest. Better than usual cops and robbers yarn. Raft is a standout as a syndicate czar who is more than a bit sadistic. Taylor is effective as a detective

who's on the take. (Dir: Roy Rowland, 92 mins.)

Rogue Male (Great Britain, MTV 1976)*** Peter O'Toole, John Standing, Alastair Sim, Cyd Hayman, Harold Pinter. A classily produced remake of the Fritz Lang classic, *Man Hunt*, that is interesting although it lacks the immediacy and the memorable direction of the 1941 original. A member of the British gentry embarks on a mission to assassinate Hitler and in turn gets tracked down by the Führer's henchmen. (Dir: Clive Donner, 100 mins.)

Rogue River (1950)*** Rory Calhoun, Peter Graves. A state policeman and his ne'er-do-well cousin become involved in a bank robbery. Exceptionally well-written, lively melodrama, well above average. (Dir: John Rawlins, 81 mins.)

Rogue's Gallery (1968)** Roger Smith, Dennis Morgan, Brian Donlevy, Jackie Coogan, Edgar Bergen. Private eye yarn that started out as a TV pilot; Smith is John Rogue (that's the title, folks) and he goes through a tussle trying to keep his client from killing himself. (Dir: Leonard Horn, 88 mins.)

Rogue's March (1953)** Peter Lawford, Richard Greene, Janice Rule. Average costume drama about a British regiment stationed in India. (Dir: Allan Davis, 84 mins.)

Rogues of Sherwood Forest (1950)** John Derek, Diana Lynn, George Macready, Alan Hale. A Saturday matinee adventure pic for kids. The son of Robin Hood robs from the rich, battles the villainous, changes history, etc. (Dir: Gordon Douglas, 80 mins.)

Rogue Song, The (1930)**½ Lawrence Tibbet, Catherine Dale Owen, Laurel and Hardy. Tibbett does a fine acting turn, highlighted by his operatic baritone in the role of a Robin Hood of Russia hunted by Cossacks. (Dir: Lionel Barrymore, 108 mins.)

Rogue's Regiment (1948)*½ Dick Powell, Marta Toren, Vincent Price. Intelligence officer joins the Foreign Legion in search of an escaped Nazi bigwig. Dull melodrama. (Dir: Robert Florey, 86 mins.)

Role, The (India, 1977)*** Smita Patil, Anant Nag, Amrish Puri, Naseeruddin Shah. An actor gets his mistress's daughter into movies as a singer. After a series of romantic upheavals, they marry, only to have her become the breadwinner of the family. Well-acted drama. (Dir: Shyam Benegal, 142 mins.)

Rollerball (1975)*½ James Caan, Ralph Richardson, John Houseman. A repellent allegory which purports to be criticizing the violence of professional sports, but winds up glorifying the sport of rollerball—a futuristic combination of rugby, roller skating and gladiator-fight-to-the-death spectacles. (Dir: Norman Jewison, 123 mins.)†

Roller Blade (1986)*½ Suzanne Solari, Jeff Hutchinson, Shaun Michelle. Derivative action pic set in the decaying future. Some roller derby amazons bravely go on a spin to help save the helpless from enslavement. (Dir: Donald Jackson, 88 mins.)†

Roller Boogie (1979)** Linda Blair, Jim Bray, Beverly Garland. Talented director Mark L. Lester fails to energize this pallid disco teenpic. Blair fakes her way through. (103 mins.)†

Rollercoaster (1977)**½ George Segal, Henry Fonda, Timothy Bottoms, Richard Widmark. This suspenser has its ups and downs, but drums up thrills along the way. Pursued by a determined detective, a mad bomber travels the country and blackmails the owners of amusement parks. (Dir: James Goldstone, 119 mins.)†

Roll, Freddy, Roll (MTV 1974)** Tim Conway, Jan Murray, Ruta Lee. A man who accidentally finds himself a short-term celebrity as he tries to break a Guinness world record for staying on roller skates for more than a week. (Dir: Billy Persky, 72 mins.)

Rolling Man (MTV 1972)**½ Dennis Weaver, Agnes Moorehead, Don Stroud, Sheree North, Jimmy Dean. A born loser wanders about the country after serving a prison term, looking for his son and dreaming of becoming a successful racecar driver. Uneven, but has a sense of reality. (Dir: Peter Hyams, 73 mins.)

Rolling Thunder (1977)** William Devane, Tommy Lee Jones, Linda Haynes. A Viet vet returns from war, but he's only a shell of his former self. When his wife and son are murdered, his energy is recharged and he sets out to wreak havoc for revenge. Unconvincing. (Dir: John Flynn, 99 mins.)†

Rolling Vengeance (1987)** Don Michael Paul, Lawrence Dane, Ned Beatty. The only two memorable things about this movie are both very nasty: (1) Beatty's sneering performance as the man responsible for the slaughter of our hero's family, and (2) the truck our hero uses as his weapon of vengeance—a mean mother outfitted with numerous sharp and explosive objects. (Dir: Steven H. Stern, 90 mins.)†

Rollover (1981)*** Jane Fonda, Kris Kristofferson, Hume Cronyn, Josef Sommer. Engrossing, extremely complex thriller involving murder and intrigue in the world of high finance and exploring what might happen should Arab oil money be suddenly withdrawn from American banks instead of redeposited ("rolled over") as expected. (Dir: Alan J. Pakula, 118 mins.)†

Romance (1930)*** Greta Garbo, Gavin Gordon, Lewis Stone, Elliott Nugent. Early talkie vehicle for Garbo is a delicate, faded antique. An elderly bishop tells his nephew of the beautiful Italian diva he once loved and lost. Garbo is convincing as the lonely opera singer who longs for her native sun. Altogether charming. (Dir: Clarence Brown, 76 mins.)

Romance in the Dark (1938)** John Boles, Gladys Swarthout, John Barrymore, Claire Dodd, Fritz Feld. Trite musical has Boles trying to turn Barrymore's attentions away from the girl he wants by distracting him with innocent Swarthout. Only one good number, "The Nearness of You." (Dir: H. C. Potter, 80 mins.)

Romance of a Horsethief (U.S.-Yugoslavia, 1971)*** Yul Brynner, Eli Wallach, Jane Birkin, David Opatoshu. Director Abraham Polonsky's farce of Jewish ghetto life in a Russian village at the turn of the century is more complex than *Fiddler on the Roof*. Funny and charming, the film nonetheless builds toward a revolutionary view of a people and of history. (100 mins.)

Romance of Rosy Ridge, The (1947)*** Van Johnson, Thomas Mitchell, Janet Leigh (debut). With tensions high after the Civil War, a mysterious stranger is looked upon with suspicion by a southern-sympathizing Missouri farmer. Well-made, charming drama. (Dir: Roy Rowland, 106 mins.)

Romance on the High Seas (1948)*** Doris Day, Jack Carson, Janis Paige, Oscar Levant. This was Doris's first film. Light little romantic comedy with a cruise background doesn't interfere too much with a delightful score. (Dir: Michael Curtiz, 99 mins.)

Romance on the Orient Express (MTV 1985)**½ Cheryl Ladd, Stuart Wilson, Sir John Gielgud. A mundane but scenic love story with Ladd playing a magazine editor who encounters a handsome Englishman while traveling on the Orient Express (Wilson). For armchair travelers and die-hard romantics. (Dir: Laurence Gordon Clark, 104 mins.)

Romancing the Stone (1984)*** Kathleen Turner, Michael Douglas, Danny DeVito. A timid romance novelist finds herself enmeshed in an intrigue involving a special map which leads to a giant emerald. Accompanied by a free-spirited fortune hunter (Douglas), she finds love and adventure in a wild chase through the jungles of Colombia. (Dir: Robert Zemeckis, 101 mins.)†

Roman Holiday (1953)**** Gregory Peck, Audrey Hepburn, Eddie Albert. Comedy delight about a newspaperman in Rome who meets and falls for a lonely princess traveling incognito. Oscar-winning performance by Hepburn, smart William Wyler direction, a production with great charm, completely captivating. (119 mins.)†

Roman Holiday (MTV 1987)** Tom Conti, Catherine Oxenberg, Ed Begley, Jr., Eileen Atkins. The kind of TV movie that provides a group of actors with a free trip to a glamorous locale. Conti is a talented actor and Oxenberg has the looks, but this remake of the Wyler classic holds nothing new. (Dir: Noel Nosseck, 96 mins.)

Romanoff and Juliet (1961)*** Peter Ustinov, Sandra Dee, John Gavin, Akim Tamiroff, John Phillips. Peter Ustinov wrote, directed, and stars in this sprightly comedy spoof set in a mythical country in which the daughter of the American ambassador falls in love with the Russian ambassador's son. (103 mins.)

Roman Scandals (1933)*** Eddie Cantor, Ruth Etting, David Manners, Edward Arnold, Gloria Stuart, Alan Mowbray. Bright musical comedy sends Cantor back to ancient Rome. Chipper songs and grand production numbers by Busby Berkeley. Lucille Ball has a bit part. (Dir: Frank Tuttle, 92 mins.)†

Roman Spring of Mrs. Stone, The (Great Britain, 1961)*** Vivien Leigh, Warren Beatty, Jill St. John, Lotte Lenya, Coral Browne. Based on Tennessee Williams's novella. All the decadence of the takers and the taken along the Via Veneto in Rome is bared in this tale about an aging actress who succumbs to taking a young paid-for lover. Beatty and Leigh are good, but Lenya as a ruthless procurer gives the best performance. (Dir: José Quintero, 104 mins.)†

Romantic Comedy (1984)**½ Dudley Moore, Mary Steenburgen, Francis Sternhagen, Ron Leibman. Disappointing transfer of a so-so Broadway hit by Bernard Slade. The main attraction is the star chemistry between Moore and Steenburgen as successful writing partners whose romantic teamwork never quite clicks. (Dir: Arthur Hiller, 103 mins.)†

Romantic Englishwoman, The (Great Britain-France, 1975)***½ Glenda Jackson, Helmut Berger, Michael Caine. A paperback novelist stymied by writer's block, matches up his wife with a gigolo and waits to see what will happen. His writing starts flowing again but so does his jealousy as his plotting gets out of hand. Literate, brittle, with Caine and Jackson making amusing sparring partners spouting Tom Stoppard and Thomas Wiseman's witty dialogue. (Dir: Joseph Losey, 115 mins.)†
894

Rome Adventure (1962)** Troy Donahue, Suzanne Pleshette, Angie Dickinson, Rossano Brazzi. The usual travelogue romance. Librarian out to have some fun and a young architectural student meet and romance in Italy. (Dir: Delmer Daves, 119 mins.)†

Romeo and Juliet (1936)**½ Norma Shearer, Leslie Howard, John Barrymore, Basil Rathbone, Edna May Oliver, C. Aubrey Smith, Violet Kemble Cooper, Ralph Forbes, Andy Devine. Irving Thalberg's production stars his wife (Shearer) as a Juliet a bit long in the tooth, and Howard as a poetical Romeo with his sexuality in his throat. George Cukor's direction is intelligent but too much aware of doing a classic. There are points of interest in Barrymore's eccentric Mercutio and Rathbone's fiery Tybalt. (140 mins.)

Romeo and Juliet (Great Britain, 1954) *** Laurence Harvey, Susan Shentall, Flora Robson, Mervyn Johns, Bill Travers. Shakespeare's tragedy of star-crossed lovers, beautifully filmed (in color) in Italy. Pictorially splendid, but the performances leave something to be desired. (Dir: Renato Castellani, 140 mins.)†

Romeo and Juliet (Great Britain, 1966)**** Margot Fonteyn, Rudolf Nureyev, David Blair. Excellent filming of the British Royal Ballet's interpretation of Prokofiev's ballet. (Dir: Paul Czinner, 126 mins.)†

Romeo and Juliet (Great Britain-Italy, 1968)*** Leonard Whiting, Olivia Hussey, Milo O'Shea, Michael York. Director Franco Zeffirelli's visually ravishing version of Shakespeare's tragic romance of tender young love. Romeo (17-year-old Whiting) and Juliet (15-year-old Hussey) are appealing in their youthfulness but not compelling enough performers. The feel for fifteenth-century Verona is right and the Mercutio-Tybalt duel is sensational. (152 mins.)†

Romero (1989)*** Raul Julia, Richard Jordan, Ana Alicia, Tony Plana, Harold Gould. Julia gives an intelligent, moving performance as Oscar Romero, the archbishop of El Salvador, who was assassinated by the military government in 1980 for speaking out against the country's injustices to its own people. (Dir: John Duigan, 94 mins.)†

Rome Express (Great Britain, 1932)***½ Esther Ralston, Conrad Veidt, Cedric Hardwicke. Exciting mystery-adventure set aboard speeding European train finds fun group of passengers battling thieves. Often imitated, remade as *Sleeping Car to Trieste*. (Dir: Walter Forde, 94 mins.)

Romuald et Juliette—See: **Mamma, There's a Man in Your Bed**

Rona Jaffe's Mazes and Monsters (MTV 1982)**½ Tom Hanks, Wendy Crewson, David Wallace, Chris Makepeace. Based on Jaffe's book, the film concerns four students whose involvement with "Dungeons and Dragons" leads to disaster for one of them. (Dir: Steven Hilliard Stern, 104 mins.)†

Ronja, Robber's Daughter (Sweden, 1986)** Hanna Zetterberg, Dan Hafstrom, Borje Ahistedt. Children's story, set in the picturesque Great Forest of medieval times, about the daughter of the leader of a band of rovers. (Dir: Tage Danielsson, 124 mins.)

Roof, The (Italy, 1957)*** Gabriella Pallotti, Giorgio Listuzzi. Poverty-stricken young couple overcome red tape in finding a new home and happiness. Gentle drama directed by Vittorio De Sica. (91 mins.)

Rooftops (1989)**½ Jason Gedrick, Troy Beyer, Eddie Velez. This well-made urban dance film wastes its grit and talent on a stock story about teen delinquents. (Dir: Robert Wise, 95 mins.)†

Rookie, The (1990)**½ Clint Eastwood, Charlie Sheen, Raul Julia, Sonia Braga. Eastwood's a tough cop who finds himself in bondage having sex with the seductive Braga, who runs a car theft ring with Julia in this typical cops and robbers effort from the current master of the form. The requisite auto chases and crashes, lots of blood, and a rookie officer along for the ride (Sheen) show some laziness in Eastwood's direction. Harmless action done with style. (Dir: Clint Eastwood, 121 mins.)†

Rookies, The (MTV 1972)** Darren McGavin, Paul Burke, Cameron Mitchell, Robert F. Lyons, Georg Stanford Brown, Sam Melville, Michael Ontkean, Jennifer Billingsley, Logan Ramsey. Pilot for the TV series about a new breed of questioning, caring, college-trained police recruits. (Dir: Jud Taylor, 72 mins.)

Room at the Top (Great Britain, 1959)**** Laurence Harvey, Simone Signoret, Heather Sears, Hermione Baddeley, Donald Wolfit. Powerful drama of an opportunist who stops at nothing to make a position for himself in life. Searing in its intensity, superbly acted—Oscar-winning performance by Signoret. (Dir: Jack Clayton, 115 mins.)†

Room for One More (1952)*** Cary Grant, Betsy Drake, Lurene Tuttle. Modest fare performed with consummate professionalism by Grant and his then-wife, Drake, as a couple who cannot resist adopting forsaken children. (Dir: Norman Taurog, 98 mins.)

Room Service (1938)**½ The Marx Brothers, Ann Miller, Lucille Ball. Broke producer and his aides stall from being kicked out of their hotel room. Amusing comedy, but not the Marxes at their best. Remade as *Step Lively*. (Dir: William A. Seiter, 78 mins.)†

Room Upstairs, The (MTV 1987)** Stockard Channing, Sam Waterston, Linda Hunt, Sarah Jessica Parker, Renee Estevez. Channing is a teacher of disabled children who has as much difficulty with her students as she does with the boarders in her family home. (Dir: Stuart Margolin, 104 mins.)

Room With a View, A (Great Britain, 1985)***½ Helena Bonham-Carter, Maggie Smith, Denholm Elliott, Julian Sands. This adaptation of E. M. Forster's satirical novel is filled with moments of visual transcendence. Everything has an impressionistic glow as young Lucy Honeychurch ventures from Venice back to England, awakening her social and sexual consciousness in the process. All the performances are witty and on the mark. (Dir: James Ivory, 115 mins.)†

Rooney (1958)*** Barry Fitzgerald, John Gregson. Dublin dustman aids a bedridden man henpecked by his grasping relatives. Delightful little Irish comedy, good fun. (Dir: George Pollack, 88 mins.)

Rooster (MTV 1982)**½ Paul Williams, Pat McCormick, J. D. Cannon, Ed Lauter, Jill St. John, Delta Burke, Charlie Callas, Henry Darrow, Pamela Hensley, Lara Parker, William Daniels, John Saxon, Eddie Albert, Marie Osmond, Severn Darden. Williams and McCormick make a delightful duo in this silly but enjoyable mystery-comedy. The many familiar faces in the cast are used to good effect. (Dir: Russ Mayberry, 96 mins.)

Rooster Cogburn (1975)**½ John Wayne, Katharine Hepburn, Anthony Zerbe, Strother Martin. Concerns the murder of spinster Eula Goodnight's minister father (shades of *The African Queen*), and the theft by desperadoes of some nitroglycerin. Marshall Rooster Cogburn (from *True Grit*) rides off to catch the miscreants. The star chemistry is the only thing of interest here. (Dir: Stuart Millar, 107 mins.)†

Roots of Heaven, The (1958)*** Errol Flynn, Juliette Greco, Trevor Howard, Eddie Albert, Orson Welles. Interesting ambitious film based on Romain Gary's prize-winning novel about a group comprised of adventurers, opportunists, and one idealist who join forces in an effort to protect the African elephant (threatened with destruction and eventual extinction by ivory hunters). (Dir: John Huston, 131 mins.)

Roots: The Gift (MTV 1988)*** Louis Gossett, Jr., LeVar Burton, Kate Mulgrew, Avery Brooks, Shaun Cassidy, Michael Learned. Gossett and Burton reprise their roles as Fiddler and Kunta Kinte, yearning for freedom at Christmastime, 1775. A worthy sequel to the original miniseries. (Dir: Kevin Hooks, 96 mins.)

Rope (1948)***½ James Stewart, John Dall, Farley Granger, Cedric Hardwicke. With a story related to the Leopold-Loeb case, this truly frightening classic concerns two college boys who kill for thrills. Full of suspense and ingenious camera work from director Alfred Hitchcock, his first film in color. (80 mins.)†

Rope of Sand (1949)**½ Burt Lancaster, Corinne Calvet, Claude Rains, Peter Lorre, Sam Jaffe, Paul Henreid. Adventurer returns to claim a hidden fortune in diamonds, fights off the machinations of a police chief and a diamond company executive after the cache. Hard-boiled melodrama heavy on the rough stuff; action fans should like it. (Dir: William Dieterle, 104 mins.)

Rorret (Italy, 1987)*** Lou Castel, Anna Galiena, Enrica Rosso. Remarkable film about a strange man, superbly played by Castel, who owns (and lives behind the screen of) the Peeping Tom Cinema. He shows horror movies and enjoys watching the fear of the female members of the audience through the curtain, later stalking them to complete his voyeuristic pleasures. (Dir: Fulvio Wetzl, 105 mins.)

Rosalie (1937)*** Eleanor Powell, Nelson Eddy, Frank Morgan, Ilona Massey, Ray Bolger. Outrageous MGM musical about a college football hero (Eddy) romancing an incognito Balkan princess (Powell). (Dir: W. S. Van Dyke, 122 mins.)†

Rosalie Goes Shopping (1990)*** Marianne Sagebrecht, Brad Davis, Judge Reinhold, Alex Winter. Consumerism is the target of this sporadically brilliant comedy about an emigré German woman who interprets the American dream as nonstop buying. The storyline seems to head in different directions with each new scene, but there is a consistently high level of screwball acting from Sagebrecht, Davis, and Reinhold. (Dir: Percy Adlon, 94 mins.)†

Rosa Luxemburg (West Germany-Poland, 1987) **½ Barbara Sukowa, Daniel Olbrychski, Otto Sander. Sukowa's incandescent portrayal of the famed radical leader whose pacifist views netted her many enemies distinguishes this intelligent but rather sketchy biography. (Dir: Margarethe von Trotta, 122 mins.) –

Rosary Murders, The (1987)** Donald Sutherland, Charles Durning, Josef Sommer, Belinda Bauer. Someone's offing priests and nuns, and it's up to Fr. Koesler (Sutherland) to find out who. Messy whodunit, with some occasionally effective moments of suspense, and

896

an unsatisfying denouement. Screenplay cowritten by tough-guy novelist Elmore Leonard. (Dir: Fred Walton, 101 mins.)†

Rose, The (1979)*** Bette Midler, Alan Bates, Frederic Forrest. Midler's first major movie is a dramatic account of the life of a Janis Joplin-type singer, with a lot of the Midler personality mixed in. She does good work dramatically, and the Bill Kerby–Bo Goldman screenplay is excellent. (Dir: Mark Rydell, 134 mins.)†

Rose and the Jackal, The (MTV 1990)*½ Christopher Reeve, Madolyn Smith Osborne, Carrie Snodgress, Kevin McCarthy. Intriguing historical drama set during the Civil War about the efforts of Allan Pinkerton, founder of the famous detective agency, to dissuade a wealthy Southern widow from spying for the Confederate cause. (Dir: Jack Gold, 96 mins.)†

Roseanna McCoy (1949)** Farley Granger, Joan Evans (debut), Raymond Massey, Richard Basehart. Trite melodrama depicting the legendary feudin' hill families of the Hatfields and the McCoys. (Dir: Irving Reis, 89 mins.)

Rose Bowl Story (1952)** Vera Miles, Marshall Thompson, Natalie Wood. Usual sort of football story, OK for those who love quarterbacks. (Dir: William Beaudine, 73 mins.)

Rosebud (1974)½ Peter O'Toole, Richard Attenborough, Cliff Gorman, John V. Lindsay. Heavily plotted nonsense about politics, espionage, the C.I.A., the Israel-Arab war and dozens of other subjects. (Dir: Otto Preminger, 126 mins.)

Rosebud Beach Hotel (1984)* Peter Scolari, Colleen Camp, Eddie Deezen, Hamilton Camp, Christopher Lee. Insufferable soft-porn comedy about a milquetoast-type who has to prove himself to his fiancée's father at a seedy resort hotel. (Dir: Harry Hurwitz, 90 mins.)†

Roseland (1977)*** Lou Jacobi, Teresa Wright, Christopher Walken, Geraldine Chaplin. Director James Ivory's three-fold story, set around the tattered dance palace near New York's Times Square; uneven, but buoyed by many character vignettes. (103 mins.)†

Rose Marie (1935)*** Jeanette MacDonald, Nelson Eddy, James Stewart. Loose adaptation of the original operetta of love and adventure with the Mounted Police is still good entertainment, thanks to the delightful score and top voices. (Dir: W. S. Van Dyke, 113 mins.)†

Rose Marie (1954)**½ Ann Blyth, Howard Keel, Fernando Lamas, Bert Lahr, Marjorie Main. Here, the heroine is a French-Canadian trapper's daughter, instead of an opera star on the lam. Well-sung version of the Friml operetta. (Dir: Mervyn LeRoy, 105 mins.)

Rosemary (West Germany, 1958)***½ Nadja Tiller, Peter Van Eyck. Devastating German satire on its own middle-class morality. Based on the real-life story of a call girl whose social ambitions become a menace to her admirers, it keeps you glued to the screen from sophisticated beginning to cynical end. (Dir: Rolf Thiele, 99 mins.)

Rosemary's Baby (1968)**** Mia Farrow, Ruth Gordon, John Cassavetes, Charles Grodin, Maurice Evans, Ralph Bellamy, Sidney Blackmer. Roman Polanski adapted Ira Levin's best-seller about witchcraft as practiced on New York's Central Park West, and also directed this exciting horror film. Farrow is bewitching as the innocent wife sold by her ambitious husband to a cult of devil-worshippers. Oscar: Gordon, Best Supporting Actress. (136 mins.)†

Rosemary's Baby II (MTV 1976)**½ Ruth Gordon, Patty Duke Astin, Ray Milland. Rosemary's Baby, Adrian/Andrew, finds himself torn between his human and inhuman sides. (Dir: Sam O'Steen, 104 mins.)

Rosenbergs Must Not Die, The (France, 1981)*** Marie-Jose Nat, Giles Segal. During the Red Scare of McCarthyism in the '50s, a time of fear and paranoia, two American scientists were indicted and tried for stealing atomic secrets for the Russians. French director Stellio Lorenti has put together a fascinating film in the Rosenberg's behalf. (123 mins.)

Rosencrantz and Guildenstern Are Dead (Great Britain-U.S., 1990)*** Gary Oldman, Tim Roth, Richard Dreyfuss. Playwright Tom Stoppard has scripted and directed this film version of his own highly successful stage comedy about two minor characters in Shakespeare's *Hamlet*. What worked in the theater doesn't click quite as well on screen, although there are a few comic moments and the acting is a pleasure to watch. (Dir: Tom Stoppard, 118 mins.)†

Rose of Washington Square (1939)** Al Jolson, Alice Faye, Tyrone Power. Alice and Al sing some of the most memorable songs of the twenties and it is, of course, the highlight of this rip-off of Fanny Brice's life. (Dir: Gregory Ratoff, 86 mins.)†

Roses Are for the Rich (MTV 1987)** Lisa Hartman, Morgan Stevens, Bruce Dern, Joe Penny, Howard Duff, Richard Masur, Kate Mulgrew, Jim Youngs, Betty Buckley. A standard revenge melodrama about an Appalachian girl who vows to settle a score with the man she accuses of killing her husband and destroying her family. (Dir: Michael Miller, 208 mins.)

Rose Tattoo, The (1955)***½ Anna Magnani, Burt Lancaster, Marisa Pavan, Ben Cooper, Virginia Grey, Jo Van Fleet. Tennessee Williams play about an earthy dressmaker with a fond memory of her deceased husband finding love anew with a burly truck driver. Beautifully played by Magnani, who copped the Academy Award. Sensitively written, directed. (Dir: Daniel Mann, 117 mins.)†

Rosetti and Ryan: Men Who Love Women (MTV 1977)** Tony Roberts, Squire Fridell, Patty Duke Astin, Bill Dana, Susan Anspach. The pilot film for the subsequent series. Two cocky lawyers defend a lady accused of doing in hubby on the family yacht. (Dir: John Astin, 106 mins.)

Rosie (1967)*½ Rosalind Russell, Sandra Dee, Brian Aherne, Vanessa Brown. A tasteless comedy-drama about a madcap rich woman whose ungrateful daughters hope to prove she's crazy. (Dir: David Lowell Rich, 98 mins.)

Rosie: The Rosemary Clooney Story (MTV 1982)**½ Sondra Locke, Tony Orlando, Penelope Milford, John Karlen, Cheryl Anderson. Another "rise and fall of a star" story. The bumpy road from band singing to recording contracts to the drug-ridden bad years is chronicled in predictable, but credible, fashion. (Dir: Jackie Cooper, 104 mins.)†

Rotten to the Core (Great Britain, 1965)**½ Charlotte Rampling, Ian Bannen, Anton Rogers, Eric Sykes. Sly comedy of a bumbling bunch of crooks who nearly make off with several million pounds. (Dir: John Boulting, 87 mins.)

Rouge Baiser (France, 1986)*** Charlotte Valandrey, Lambert Wilson, Marthe Keller, Gunther Lamprecht. A tasty French romance about a radical girl whose political fancy for Stalin ends up on the back burner when she falls for the enemy—a cynical bourgeois photographer. (Dir: Vera Belmont, 110 mins.)

Rough Cut (1980)** Burt Reynolds, Lesley-Anne Down, David Niven, Patrick Magee, Timothy West. The tired old plot about a jewel thief's yen for a "sophisticated" lady. (Dir: Don Siegel, 112 mins.)†

Roughly Speaking (1945)*** Jack Carson, Rosalind Russell, Robert Hutton, Alan Hale. Ambitious wife struggles to aid her ne'er-do-well husband in his business schemes, while raising a large family. Long but deftly acted, pleasantly done comedy drama. (Dir: Michael Curtiz, 117 mins.)

Roughnecks (MTV 1980)** Ana Alicia, Wilford Brimley, Cathy Lee Crosby, Steve Forrest, Kevin Geer, A Martinez, Stephen McHattie, Vera Miles, Harry Morgan. Two old hands at oil drilling and their headstrong colleague aid a friend whose ranch has seen better years. An updated western, with all the attendant clichés. (Dir: Bernard McEveety, 192 mins.)

Rough Night in Jericho (1967)* Dean Martin, George Peppard, Jean Simmons. Violent, unnecessary brutality with Dean Martin as a sober heavy. Peppard is the hero this time out, and the lady struggling to keep her stagecoach line out of crooked Martin's grasp is Simmons. (Dir: Arnold Laven, 104 mins.)

Rough Riders—See: *Angels' Wild Women*

Roughshod (1949)*** Robert Sterling, Gloria Grahame, Claude Jarman, Jr., John Ireland, Martha Hyer, Jeff Corey. Intense B western about a group of travellers pursued by a deranged rancher who thinks they're out to kill him. Unusual idea, perceptively done. (Dir: Mark Robson, 88 mins.)

Rounders, The (1965)*** Glenn Ford, Henry Fonda, Sue Ane Langdon, Denver Pyle, Edgar Buchanan, Chill Wills. Ford and Fonda are a very ingratiating pair of modern-day horse wranglers who share some comical adventures in this engaging tale, written and directed by Burt Kennedy. The two have their hands full when they attempt to break a stubborn horse and this becomes the film's funniest running gag. (Dir: Burt Kennedy, 85 mins.)

Round Midnight (U.S.-France, 1986)*** Dexter Gordon, François Cluzet, Gabrielle Haker, Lonette McKee, Sandra Reaves-Phillips, Christine Pascal, Herbie Hancock, Martin Scorsese. Inspired by the events in the life of Bud Powell, an expatriate musician in Paris, the film spins a touching tale about a burned-out jazz musician who seeks approval abroad and embraces a friendship with a French fan who devotes his life to saving the self-destructive musician from himself. One wishes the overall impact were less subdued, but this is a bittersweet mood piece, gracefully directed and a must for jazz buffs. (Dir: Bertrand Tavernier, 130 mins.)†

Round-Up, The (Hungary, 1965)***½ Janos Gorbe, Tibor Molnar, Andras Kozak, Gabor Agardy. Masterpiece from director Miklos Jancso about a group of 19th-century peasants who are suspected of taking part in revolutionary acts against the state and rounded up by Austro-Hungarian troops who brutally torture and kill them. (94 mins.)

Roustabout (1964)**½ Elvis Presley, Barbara Stanwyck. Barbara runs a carnival, and Elvis is a vagabond youth who joins the show and sings in a honky-tonk on the midway. (Dir: John Rich, 101 mins.)†

Roxanne (1987)***½ Steve Martin, Daryl Hannah, Rick Rossovich, Shelley Duvall, Michael J. Pollard, Matt Lattanzi. A wonderful, romantic comedy quite brilliantly performed by Martin, who also wrote the deft screenplay based on the classic Rostand play of 1897, *Cyrano de Bergerac*. The update finds Cyrano changed from a dueling cavalier into a fire chief in a small ski resort in the northwest. The ravishing Daryl Hannah is Roxanne, but this is Martin's triumph throughout, with superb assistance from director Fred Schepisi. (106 mins.)

Roxanne: The Prize Pulitzer (MTV 1989)* Perry King, Chynna Phillips, Courteney Cox, Caitlin Brown, Betsy Russell. High-gloss TV trash version of the bitter divorce between wealthy Herbert Pulitzer and his young wife, Roxanne. Hard to care much about any of these people, especially as portrayed in this vapid junk. (Dir: Richard Colla, 96 mins.)

Roxie Hart (1942)*** Ginger Rogers, Adolphe Menjou, George Montgomery, Nigel Bruce, Lynne Overman, Spring Byington, Phil Silvers. This version of Maurine Watkins's *Chicago* is mostly a raucous success, despite lapses in tone. Rogers murders her two-timing boyfriend and gets sprung through the efforts of mouthpiece Menjou. (Dir: William Wellman, 75 mins.)

Royal African Rifles, The (1953)** Louis Hayward, Veronica Hurst, Michael Pate, Angela Greene. Lackluster adventure of a British Army officer delivering guns to besieged troops. We were rooting for the natives. (Dir: Lesley Selander, 75 mins.)

Royal Bed, The (1930)**½ Lowell Sherman, Nance O'Neil, Mary Astor, Anthony Bushell, Robert Warwick. Sprightly satire of the henpecked king of a small country letting himself go when his wife is away. (Dir: Lowell Sherman, 75 mins.)†

Royal Family of Broadway, The (1930)*** Fredric March, Ina Claire, Mary Brian. A broad, hilarious spoof of the Barrymore clan. This one really shows its age but the spiffy cast milks the script for all its worth. (Dirs: Cyril Gardner, George Cukor, 82 mins.)

Royal Flash (Great Britain, 1975)*** Malcolm McDowell, Florinda Bolkan, Alan Bates, Oliver Reed. In between stealing the hearts of ladies fair, an English captain swashbuckles and engages in less honorable pursuits. Pretty good slapstick moments punctuate this flashy film with an attractive cast supplying the derring-do. (Dir: Richard Lester, 98 mins.)†

Royal Hunt of the Sun, The (Great Britain, 1969)** Robert Shaw, Christopher Plummer, Nigel Davenport. Peter Shaffer's play was effective onstage, but opened up to spectacle proportions, its verbal posturings become silly. Shaw is no more than stolid as Pizarro, but Plummer is in high-camp heaven as the Inca emperor

Atahualpa, with sinuous body movements and bird language. An expensive flop. (Dir: Irving Lerner, 110 mins.)

Royal Romance of Charles and Diana, The (MTV 1982)* Catherine Oxenberg, Christopher Baines, Ray Milland, Dana Wynter, Stewart Granger, Olivia de Havilland. Insipid version of the royal courtship. (Dir: Peter Levin, 100 mins.)

Royal Scandal, A (1945)**½ Tallulah Bankhead, William Eythe, Charles Coburn, Anne Baxter. Rollicking farce about the libidinous Empress Catherine the Great of Russia and her amorous intrigues. Tallulah's brittle comic stylishness makes this a royal treat for all. (Dirs: Otto Preminger, Ernst Lubitsch, 94 mins.)

Royal Wedding (1951)*** Fred Astaire, Jane Powell, Peter Lawford. Merry musical romance with lovely dances by Astaire and good chirping by Powell. A brother and sister act (Jane & Fred) are in London during the time of Queen Elizabeth's wedding. (Dir: Stanley Donen, 93 mins.)†

R.P.M. (Revolutions per Minute) (1970)*½ Anthony Quinn, Ann-Margret, Gary Lockwood. What starts out as an interesting film about college unrest in the late '60s turns into simple-minded drama before long. (Dir: Stanley Kramer, 92 mins.)†

Rubber Gun, The (Canada, 1977)*** Steve Lack, Peter Brawley, Pam Holmes, Pierre Robert. Tense crime caper film about quiet young man Lack who rejects his past and becomes a drug dealer. Film examines the members of a commune and their relations with each other, as well as their devotion to Lack, who leads them into a dazzling underworld adventure. (Dir: Allan Moyle, 86 mins.)

Ruby (1977)** Piper Laurie, Stuart Whitman, Janit Baldwin. Piper Laurie plays the one-time mistress of a gangster, who had her lover killed in the thirties. Many years later, her lover's spirit invades the daughter's body to seek revenge on all of those who did him dirt. A muddled mixture of *The Exorcist* and *Carrie*. (Dir: Curtis Harrington, 85 mins.)†

Ruby and Oswald (MTV 1978)** Michael Lerner, Frederic Forrest. Manipulative, "docudrama" based on *some* of the known facts about the murder of Lee Harvey Oswald by Jack Ruby. The audience is shown the real footage of Kennedy's arrival in Dallas and his funeral, interspersed with fictional scenes performed by actors. (Dir: Mel Stuart, 156 mins.)

Ruby Gentry (1952)*** Jennifer Jones, Charlton Heston, Karl Malden, Josephine Hutchison. A supercharged drama about a sexy wench who seeks revenge on an elaborate scale when her true love decides to marry a more respected female in the community. (Dir: King Vidor, 82 mins.)†

Ruckus (1981)** Dirk Benedict, Linda Blair, Ben Johnson. Benedict plays a moody drifter who meets up with a young widow (Blair) whose husband was killed in Vietnam. When the two begin to develop a relationship, the local rednecks try to run him out of town. Lots of plotholes. (Dir: Max Kleven, 104 mins.)†

Rude Awakening (1989)** Richard "Cheech" Marin, Eric Roberts, Robert Carradine, Julie Hagerty, Buck Henry, Cindy Williams, Louise Lasser, Andrea Martin, Cliff DeYoung. Well-intentioned but low-on-laughs culture shock comedy about hippies Marin and Roberts emerging from twenty years in a South American jungle to find that former comrades Carradine and Hagerty have turned into heartless, ambitious yuppies. (Dirs: Aaron Russo, David Greenwalt, 100 mins.)†

Rude Boy (Great Britain, 1980)**½ The Clash, Ray Gange, John Green. A rebellious teen gets a job as a road manager for the rock group The Clash, and goes on tour. Clash fans will be overjoyed, but not the uninitiated. (Dirs: Jack Hazan, David Mingay, 133 mins.)†

Ruggles of Red Gap (1935)**** Charles Laughton, Charles Ruggles, Mary Boland. Hilarious tale of the English butler who suddenly finds himself in the American West, when he is won by an American in a poker game. Laughton, at his best, and a superb cast make this one of the all-time great comedies. (Dir: Leo McCarey, 100 mins.)†

Rulers of the Sea (1939)*** Margaret Lockwood, Douglas Fairbanks, Jr., Will Fyffe. Interesting drama of the first steam crossing of the Atlantic which led to the beginning of the luxury liner. (Dir: Frank Lloyd, 97 mins.)

Rules of Marriage, The (MTV 1982)***½ Elizabeth Montgomery, Elliott Gould, Michael Murphy. Veteran writer Reginald Rose has come up with an incisive, frank look at a contemporary marriage in which the double standard is shattered once and for all. Montgomery gives one of her best performances, and Gould matches her as the philandering husband who reacts with wounded pride when he discovers he is cuckolded by his wife and best friend. (Dir: Milton Katselas, 208 mins.)

Rules of the Game, The (France, 1939)**** Marcel Dalio, Nora Gregor, Roland Toutain, Gaston Modet, Julien Carette, Jean Renoir. Loosely based on *Les Caprices de Marianne* by Alfred de Musset, this masterwork was damaged during WWII after its controversial premiere and was finally restored to the director's original cut in 1961. Jean Renoir's directorial control is astonishing in this haunting film touching on the love affairs of the jaded aristocracy and the serving class during one weekend in the country. The film's richness is dazzling. (110 mins.)†

Ruling Class, The (Great Britain, 1971)**** Peter O'Toole, Alastair Sim, Harry Andrews, Arthur Lowe, Coral Browne. Biting satire, madcap farce about the English upper classes. O'Toole plays the mad fourteenth Earl of Gurney, who has inherited his father's huge estate. He thinks he's Jesus Christ and when his family tries to cure him, he becomes Jack the Ripper. (Dir: Peter Medak, 155 mins.)†

Ruling Voice, The (1931)*** Walter Huston, Loretta Young, Doris Kenyon, David Manners, John Halliday, Dudley Digges. Vigorous gangster melodrama, with ruthless mobster Huston softened up by his idealistic daughter. Huston's dynamic acting makes it. (Dir: Rowland V. Lee, 76 mins.)

Rumba (1935)** George Raft, Carole Lombard, Margo, Lynne Overman, Gail Patrick, Akim Tamiroff. A hot-to-trot sequel to *Bolero*. George and Carole glide through a stormy romance as the script stumbles about unconvincingly. (Dir: Marion Gering, 77 mins.)

Rumble Fish (1983)***½ Matt Dillon, Mickey Rourke, Diane Lane, Dennis Hopper, Diana Scarwid, Vincent Spano, Nicolas Cage, Christopher Penn, Larry Fishburne, Tom Waits. Not just another teen picture, director Francis Ford Coppola's visionary adaptation of S. E. Hinton's popular novel has two things those other films don't: a brain and a look. The simple story line—about a young punk (Dillon) and the adoration he has for his older brother, "The Motorcycle Boy" (played by the tragically hip Rourke)—is given added resonance by Coppola's visual and aural experimentation, which includes shooting in b&w to reflect the color blindness of a key character. (94 mins.)†

Rumor of War, A (MTV 1980)***½ Brad Davis, Keith Carradine, Michael O'Keefe, Richard Bradford, Brian Dennehy, Steve Forrest. This superlative drama adapted from a bestseller views the Vietnam experience through the eyes of one soldier. Trenchantly, the teleplay traces the downward spiral of the central character's life as he is transformed from an unquestioning, wide-eyed recruit to a nerve-wracked veteran charged with a war crime. (Dir: Richard T. Heffron, 200 mins.)†

Rumpelstiltskin (1987)** Amy Irving,

Robert Symonds, Billy Barty, Priscilla Pointer. A competently directed but rather unimaginative retelling of the Grimm fairy tale about the mischievous midget who may have been the first black market baby buyer. A family affair for Irving who was directed by her brother David Irving and co-starred with her mom, Pointer. (84 mins.)†

Run (1991)* Patrick Dempsey, Kelly Preston, Ken Pogue, Alan C. Peterson. A Harvard law student (an unceasingly mugging Dempsey), hired to drive a car to Atlantic City, accidently kills a gangster's son and is forced to run for his life. Loud and violent Hitchcock rip-off adds nothing to the genre. (Dir: Geoff Burrowes, 89 mins.)†

Run a Crooked Mile (MTV 1969)**½ Louis Jourdan, Mary Tyler Moore. Jourdan plays a school teacher who becomes an amnesia victim and lives the life of a wealthy playboy for a two-year period, marrying Moore in the interim. (Dir: Gene Levitt, 100 mins.)

Run, Angel, Run! (1969)** William Smith, Valerie Starrett, Margaret Markov. Smith is a former member of the Devil's Advocates motorcycle gang and has exposed them in a magazine article. He and Starrett have to avoid them at all costs. (Dir: Jack Starrett, 95 mins.)†

Runaround, The (1946)*** Broderick Crawford, Ella Raines, Rod Cameron. Fast-moving comedy about two guys who are hired to trail a runaway heiress who is about to marry a deckhand. (Dir: Charles Lamont, 86 mins.)

Runaway (MTV 1973)** Ben Johnson, Ed Nelson, Vera Miles, Martin Milner, Ben Murphy. A ski train roars down a mountainside when the brakes freeze in this story which mixes scares with character bits. (Dir: David Lowell Rich, 73 mins.)

Runaway (1984)* Tom Selleck, Cynthia Rhodes, Gene Simmons, Kirstie Alley. The special effects star in a tedious futuristic yarn about a society served by robots. (Dir: Michael Crichton, 99 mins.)†

Runaway Barge, The (MTV 1975)*½ Tim Matheson, Bo Hopkins, Jim Davis, Nick Nolte. Modern-day boatmen get involved in a kidnapping and a hijacking. (Dir: Boris Sagal, 78 mins.)†

Runaway Bus, The (Great Britain, 1954)** Frankie Howerd, Margaret Rutherford, Petula Clark. A bus lost in a London fog commandeered by a screwy driver has an international thief aboard. Very mild comedy, misfires often. (Dir: Val Guest, 75 mins.)†

Runaway Nightmare (1982)½ Michael Cartel, Al Valletta, Cindy Donlan. Two worm ranchers are kidnapped by a group of beautiful women, who enlist them in an attempt to steal plutonium from the Mafia. (Dir: Michael Cartel, 105 mins.)†

Runaways, The (MTV 1975)** Josh Albee, Dorothy McGuire, Van Williams, John Randolph, Neva Patterson. TV film about a young boy's friendship with a runaway leopard. (Dir: Harry Harris, 72 mins.)†

Runaway Train (1985)*** Jon Voight, Eric Roberts, Rebecca DeMornay, Kyle Heffner, John Ryan, T. K. Carter, Kenneth McMillan. The hurtling locomotive of the title carries desperate passengers, including escaped convicts Voight and Roberts who are fleeing untenable prison conditions. Exciting adventure adapted from an unused script by Akira Kurosawa. (Dir: Andrei Konchalovsky, 107 mins.)†

Run for Cover (1955)*** James Cagney, Viveca Lindfors, John Derek, Ernest Borgnine, Jean Hersholt. Taut western story about a duo of bandits and their reformation. (Dir: Nicholas Ray, 93 mins.)

Run for the Sun (Great Britain, 1956)** Richard Widmark, Jane Greer, Trevor Howard. Author and lady reporter crash in the jungle, come upon an English traitor and a wounded Nazi, who hunt them. (Dir: Roy Boulting, 99 mins.)

Run for Your Money, A (Great Britain, 1949)***½ Donald Houston, Alec Guinness, Meredith Edwards, Moira Lister, Hugh Griffith, Joyce Grenfell. Two Welsh coal miners have various misadventures when they visit London. Delightful comedy, raising many chuckles. Excellently acted. (Dir: Charles Frend, 83 mins.)

Runner Stumbles, The (1979)** Dick Van Dyke, Kathleen Quinlan, Maureen Stapleton, Beau Bridges. Muddled melodrama. Van Dyke is a priest who falls in love with a spirited nun. Based on a play by Milan Stitt. (Dir: Stanley Kramer, 99 mins.)†

Running (Canada, 1979)*½ Michael Douglas, Susan Anspach, Lawrence Dane, Eugene Levy. A pseudo-*Rocky* with Douglas as a middle-class dud who gives up hearth and home to run and run and run. (Dir: Steven Hilliard Stern, 103 mins.)

Running Against Time (MCTV 1990)*** Robert Hays, Catherine Hicks, Sam Wanamaker. Good performances and an intriguing premise highlight this immensely entertaining tale of time travel. Hays stumbles upon the secret invention of a time transporter. He arrives in Dallas on November 22, 1963 hoping to stop President Kennedy's assassination. Well-conceived fantasy has original plot twists to make the subject seem fresh. (Dir: Bruce Seth Green, 96 mins.)

Running Brave (Canada, 1983)** Robby Benson, Pat Hingle. Benson tries to submerge his cloying personality in the part of a half-Sioux star who scored an unexpected triumph at the 1964 Olympics. Unfortunately, his puppy dog mannerisms wear thin quickly. (Dir: D. S. Everett, 106 mins.)†

Running Man, The (Great Britain, 1963)*** Laurence Harvey, Lee Remick, Alan Bates. Scoundrel fakes his death in a glider crash, joins with his wife in a plan to defraud the insurance company. Fairly ordinary story polished by fine performances, Carol Reed's suspenseful direction. (103 mins.)

Running Man, The (1987)**½ Arnold Schwarzenegger, Maria Conchita Alonso, Richard Dawson, Yaphet Kotto, Jesse "the Body" Ventura. Tough-edged sci-fi, courtesy of Stephen King (here pseudonymously Richard Bachman), about a police state of the future where the most popular game show features supposed criminals getting destroyed in gimmicky, bloody ways by costumed muscle men. Awesome Arnie plays the good guy who gets forced into playing. (Dir: Paul Michael Glaser, 100 mins.)

Running on Empty (1988)** Christine Lahti, River Phoenix, Judd Hirsch, Jonas Abry, Martha Plimpton. Misconceived tale of two fugitive sixties radicals (Lahti, Hirsch) who live out of a suitcase with their two sons. The film chooses not to concentrate on the radicals themselves, but instead unfortunately focuses on their teenage son (Phoenix), who longs for a tomboy (Plimpton), and has a promising future as a pianist. (Dir: Sidney Lumet, 115 mins.)†

Running Out (MTV 1983)**½ Deborah Raffin, Tony Bill, Toni Kalem. Touching drama of a runaway mother who returns to heal the breach with her family after a 12-year absence. (Dir: Robert Day, 104 mins.)

Running Scared (1986)*** Gregory Hines, Billy Crystal, Steven Bauer, Dan Hedaya. Hines and Crystal are the funniest crime busters this side of Nolte and Murphy in this action-comedy that lacks the brisk pace and constant one-liners of *48 HRS.*, but seems a lot more natural and spontaneous. Hines and Crystal are shooting off either their mouths or their guns as they portray two Chicago policemen trying to survive the mean streets long enough to retire and open up a bar in Key West. (Dir: Peter Hyams, 107 mins.)†

Running Target (1956)*** Arthur Franz, Doris Dowling. Different sort of outdoor drama, about a sheriff leading a posse after four escaped convicts. Exceptionally good photography, performances. (Dir: Marvin Weinstein, 83 mins.)

Running Wild (1955)**½ Mamie Van Doren, William Campbell, KeenanWynn, Walter Coy. Sleazy grade B movie with more zest than most. Some car thieves run up against a determined policeman. (Dir: Abner Biberman, 81 mins.)

Running Wild (1927)***½ W. C. Fields, Mary Brian, Claude Buchanan, Marie Shotwell. Hilarious silent feature is a must for Fields fans. Fields is his usual nasty self when his shy personality is altered after an encounter with a hypnotist. Believing he is a lion, Fields makes life unbearable for his dominating wife and boss. (Dir: Gregory La Cava, 68 mins.)†

Runnin' Kind, The (1987)* David Packer, Brie Howard, Pleasant Gehman, Susan Strasberg, Kenneth Tigar. Ohio teen spends the summer after graduation in L.A. looking for the drummer of an all-female band. Completely uninteresting, with boring situations and worse characters. (Dir: Max Tash, 101 mins.)†

Run of the Arrow (1956)**½ Rod Steiger, Sarita Montiel, Brian Keith. Bitter ex-Confederate private joins the Sioux Indian nation in their fight against the country, then realizes where his heart really lies. (Dir: Samuel Fuller, 86 mins.)†

Run Silent, Run Deep (1958)*** Clark Gable, Burt Lancaster, Don Rickles. An interesting war drama about submarine warfare and the bitter conflict of the sub commander (Gable) and his lieutenant (Lancaster). Exciting photography adds to the suspense. (Dir: Robert Wise, 93 mins.)†

Run, Simon, Run (MTV 1970)*** Burt Reynolds, Inger Stevens. Reynolds gives a strong performance as an American Indian who returns to the reservation after serving a long prison term for a murder he didn't commit. AKA: **Savage Run.** (Dir: George McCowan, 73 mins.)

Run, Stranger, Run (1973)** Patricia Neal, Cloris Leachman, Bobby Darin, Ron Howard. Gothic horror set in Nova Scotia. Everyone has a skeleton in the closet. (Dir: Darren McGavin, 90 mins.)†

Run Till You Fall (MTV 1988)*½ Jamie Farr, Fred Savage, Shelley Fabares, C.C.H. Pounder, Clyde Kusatsu, Beatrice Straight. Overly sentimental father-son drama reuniting "M*A*S*H" colleagues Farr and Mike Farrell as star and director, respectively. Farr is a bumbling private eye raising money for his son's operation. (96 mins.)

Run Wild, Run Free (Great Britain, 1969)** John Mills, Mark Lester, Gordon Jackson, Sylvia Syms. Lester plays a mute whose salvation comes through his love for a wild pony. (Dir: Richard C. Sarafian, 100 mins.)

Rush to Judgement (1967)**½ A documentary film about the assassination of President John F. Kennedy, conceived by producer Mark Lane as a "brief for the defense" of Lee Harvey Os-

wald. (Dir: Emile de Antonio, 122 mins.)

Russia House, The (1990)*** Sean Connery, Michelle Pfeiffer, Roy Scheider, James Fox, John Mahoney, J. T. Walsh, Klaus Maria Brandauer, Ken Russell, Michael Kitchen. Dense, involving spy thriller about an offbeat saxophone-playing English publisher who is given a manuscript that contains Soviet state secrets. The story predates *glasnost,* so it loses in the dramatic tension department. Tom Stoppard adapted John le Carré's novel for the screen. Rarely seen views of Moscow and Leningrad help make it all compelling. (Dir: Fred Schepisi, 120 mins.)†

Russian Roulette (Canada, 1975)*½ George Segal, Cristina Raines, Denholm Elliott, Louise Fletcher. Muddled spy thriller about an attempted assassination of Soviet Premier Kosygin in Vancouver, Canada by the KGB (Dir: Lou Lombardo, 104 mins.)†

Russians Are Coming, the Russians Are Coming, The (1966)*** Alan Arkin, Paul Ford, Carl Reiner, Theodore Bikel, Eva Marie Saint, John Phillip Law, Brian Keith, Jonathan Winters. Wacky, amusing comedy about a Soviet submarine which runs aground off the shore of Nantucket. Boasts a delightful performance by Arkin as a Russian sailor. (Dir: Norman Jewison, 120 mins.)†

Russkies (1987)** Leaf Phoenix, Whip Hubley, Peter Billingsley, Susan Walters. Three kids make friends with a stranded Russian sailor in this *glasnost*-era comedy that's nearly as mindless as the title suggests. (Dir: Rick Rosenthal, 98 mins.)†

Rustler's Rhapsody (1985)** Tom Berenger, Andy Griffith, Fernando Rey, Marilu Henner, Sela Ward. A tumbleweed spoof about singing cowboy movies, home on the range, where the laughs are few and far between. (Dir: Hugh Wilson, 88 mins.)†

Rust Never Sleeps (1979)*** Neil Young in concert (backed by the band Crazy Horse) during one of his strongest phases covers a broad range of his earlier work as well as his heavier, punk-inspired material. The music is terrific, but the impenetrable Devo-inspired presentation is merely distracting. (Dir: "Bernard Shakey" [Young], 111 mins.)†

Ruthless (1948)***½ Zachary Scott, Diana Lynn, Sydney Greenstreet. Scott excels as a ruthless, ambitious man who ruins lives left and right. The director was the prodigious Poverty Row director Edgar Ulmer, and he gets the most out of his high-powered cast. (104 mins.)

Ruthless People (1986)***½ Danny DeVito, Judge Reinhold, Helen Slater, Bette Midler, Anita Morris. Hilarious black comedy, in which DeVito plans to kill his harridan wife (Midler) only to be overjoyed when she is kidnapped. And that's just the beginning of Dale Launer's variation on O.Henry's "The Ransom of Red Chief" played for maximum laugh-power by a perfect cast. (Dirs: Jim Abrahams, David Zucker, Jerry Zucker, 93 mins.)†

Rutles, The—All You Need Is Cash (MTV 1978)***½ Eric Idle, Neil Innes, Rikki Fataar, John Halsey. This terrific parody of the Beatles will appeal most to those Beatlemaniacs who will get the endless "in" jokes, but it's just as funny for all. The songs by Innes are masterful pastiches of old Beatles tunes—you'll swear you've heard them before, and you'll be humming them afterward. With guest appearances by Mick Jagger, Paul Simon, George Harrison, John Belushi, and others. (Dirs: Eric Idle, Gary Weiss, 70 mins.)†

Ryan's Daughter (Great Britain, 1970)*** Robert Mitchum, Trevor Howard, Sarah Miles, John Mills, Christopher Jones. A wildly cinematic experience, featuring Oscar-winning camerawork roving over Ireland. Unabashedly sentimental tale about a pampered, indulged, married woman (Miles) and her desire for a British soldier (Jones). Mitchum plays her schoolteacher husband with feeling that highlights the film, and Mills won an Oscar for his portrayal of a crippled mute. (Dir: David Lean, 192 mins.)†

Ryan White Story, The (MTV 1989)*** Lukas Haas, Judith Light, George C. Scott, Sarah Jessica Parker. True story of a 13-year-old hemophiliac who contracted AIDS from a blood transfusion and had to fight his fear-stricken neighbors for his right to remain in school. (Dir: John Herzfeld, 96 mins.)

Saadia (1953)*½ Cornel Wilde, Mel Ferrer, Rita Gam. Muddled costume epic set in Morocco where a young girl who believes she is a sorceress, a dashing leader of the Berber tribes, and a doctor engage in a war against plague and belief in black magic. (Dir: Albert Lewin, 82 mins.)

Sabaka (1955)** Boris Karloff, Reginald Denny, Victor Jory, Lisa Howard, Jay Novello. Silly, exotic melodrama, with the British Army trying to stamp out a cult of fanatical murderers in colonial India. (Dir: Frank Ferrin, 81 mins.)

Sabata (Italy, 1970)** Lee Van Cleef, William Berger, Linda Veras. In his first appearance, gambler Sabata is hired to pull off a robbery by a trio of crooked businessmen. (Dir: "Frank Kramer" [Gianfranco Parolini], 107 mins.)

Sabotage (Great Britain, 1936)*** Sylvia Sidney, Oscar Homolka, John Loder, Desmond Tester. Exciting thriller, from Joseph Conrad's novel *The Secret Agent*, about a girl unwittingly married to a traitor. Strikingly filmed by Alfred Hitchcock. (76 mins.)†

Saboteur (1942)*** Robert Cummings, Priscilla Lane, Otto Kruger. The master of suspense, Alfred Hitchcock, uses all of the gimmicks in this WWII spy story set in Nevada and New York. Exciting climax in the Statue of Liberty. (108 mins.)†

Sabre Jet (1953)**½ Robert Stack, Coleen Gray, Richard Arlen, Julie Bishop, Amanda Blake. Wives wait for their husbands to return from Korean missions. (Dir: Louis King, 96 mins.)

Sabrina (1954)***½ Humphrey Bogart, Audrey Hepburn, William Holden, John Williams. When rich playboy Holden falls in love with the chauffeur's daughter (Hepburn), stodgy older brother Bogart is coerced into easing her away from him. Bogie is memorable in an atypical role in this sparkling romantic comedy. (Dir: Billy Wilder, 113 mins.)†

Sacco and Vanzetti (Italy, 1971)*** Gian Maria Volonte, Riccardo Cucciolla, Cyril Cusack. This documents the case of two Italian immigrants, admitted anarchists accused of robbery, but (in this film's view) innocent of the crimes they are being prosecuted for. Based on the world-famous 1920s Massachusetts court case. Powerful indictment of American political hysteria. (Dir: Giuliano Montaldo, 120 mins.)†

Sacred Ground (1985)** Tim McIntire, Jack Elam, L. Q. Jones. Struggle between a tribe of Indians and a fur trapper over a half-breed child born on sacred burial grounds. (Dir: Charles B. Pierce, 100 mins.)†

Sacrifice, The (Sweden, 1986)**½ Erland Josephson, Susan Fleetwood, Valerie Mairesse, Allan Edwall, Sven Wollter. A difficult film to assess, *The Sacrifice* is about a man's private spiritual quest in the face of nuclear Armageddon and how he tries to strike a bargain with God at his own expense. The camerawork by Sven Nykvist is masterful. (Dir: Andrei Tarkovsky, 145 mins.)†

Sacrilege (France, 1988)** Myriem Roussel, Alessandro Gassman, Renato De Carmine. *Hail Mary* star Roussel plays a young Renaissance nun who is seduced by a nobleman with the aid of a cynical priest. The religious aspect is a smoke screen for an otherwise standard, exploitative period melodrama. (Dir: Luciano Odorisio, 104 mins.)†

Sadat (MTV 1983)*** Louis Gossett, Jr., Madolyn Smith, John Rhys-Davies, Jeffrey Tambor. A deeply moving and poignant film of a sad and, in some ways, ennobling history lesson. Gossett, playing the visionary Nobel Prize-winning statesman Anwar el-Sadat, gives a great performance. (Dir: Richard Michaels, 200 mins.)

Saddle the Wind (1958)**½ Robert Taylor, Julie London, John Cassavetes. Gunman turns in his weapons and becomes a rancher but is forced to return to them to face a showdown with his reckless younger brother. (Dir: Robert Parrish, 84 mins.)

Saddle Tramp (1950)*** Joel McCrea, Wanda Hendrix, Ed Begley, Jeanette Nolan, John McIntire. McCrea plays a lovable "saddle tramp" who doesn't want any trouble but ends up right in the middle of a big-scale range war. Entertaining. (Dir: Hugo Fregonese, 77 mins.)

Sad Horse, The (1959)**½ David Ladd, Chill Wills, Patrice Wymore, Rex Reason. Good children's story of a misunderstood boy developing a friendship with a throroughbred horse; unpretentious family entertainment. (Dir: James B. Clark, 78 mins.)

Sadie and Son (MTV 1987)* Debbie Reynolds, Brian McNamara, Sam Wanamaker. Reynolds should be put out to pasture after this brainless outing as an aging N.Y.C. cop who ends up walking the beat with her son, a frustrated comedian who puts on police blues only to please Mama. (Dir: John Llewellyn Moxey, 96 mins.)

Sadie McKee (1934)*** Joan Crawford, Gene Raymond, Franchot Tone, Esther Ralston, Edward Arnold. One of Crawford's best three-hankie soapers; she stars as a poor-but-honest housemaid who marries alcoholic millionaire Arnold even though she really loves dashing but irresponsible musician Raymond. Elegantly produced, chicly costumed, well played. (Dir: Clarence Brown, 90 mins.)

Sadie Thompson (1928)***½ Gloria Swanson, Lionel Barrymore, Raoul Walsh, Charles Lane. Strong silent version of W. Somerset Maugham's story about a fun-loving tart who falls in love with a burly Marine and is taken advantage of by an obsessed religious fanatic; powerful drama, extremely well acted and directed. Swanson is marvelous. (Dir: Raoul Walsh, 97 mins.)†

Sad Sack, The (1957)*** Jerry Lewis, David Wayne, Phyllis Kirk, Peter Lorre. Jerry in the army again, as inept as ever, getting mixed up with spies and Arabian intrigue. (Dir: George Marshall, 98 mins.)†

Safari (1940)**½ Douglas Fairbanks, Jr., Madeleine Carroll, Tullio Carminati, Billy Gilbert. Vigorous jungle adventure, with effete nobleman Carminati hiring dashing Fairbanks to guide him and his snooty fiancée into the forest; naturally a romantic triangle develops. (Dir: Edward H. Griffith, 80 mins.)

Safari (Great Britain, 1956)**½ Janet Leigh, Victor Mature, John Justin. Brave white hunter heads a safari that meets with the savage tribes of the Mau Mau. (Dir: Terence Young, 91 mins.)

Safari Drums (1953)** Johnny Sheffield, Douglas Kennedy. The junior jungle man fights yet another murderous jungle guide. Average series entry. (Dir: Ford Beebe, 71 mins.)

Safecracker, The (Great Britain, 1958)** Ray Milland, Barry Jones. Milland plays a safe expert who turns thief and is imprisoned. During WWII his knowledge is put to use on a dangerous mission. (Dir: Ray Milland, 96 mins.)

Safe in Hell (1933)*** Sally Eilers, Donald Cook, Ralf Harolde, Morgan Wallace. Superb, uncompromising drama about a prostitute accused of murder who escapes to a Pacific island with no extradition treaties, inhabited by the dregs of society, where she must wait until her fiancé can clear her. The seedy, degenerate parody of normal life the outlaws have created for themselves is displayed by director William Wellman with unflinching candor. Still strong stuff. (65 mins.)

Safe Place, A (1971)*** Tuesday Weld, Orson Welles, Philip Proctor, Jack Nicholson. A very special, rarely seen film about a person who, like the protagonist of *Slaughterhouse Five*, has become "unstuck in time." Weld plays the character, a young woman who flashes back to past experiences, including visits with a resplendent father-figure magician (Welles), while she goes through relationships with an insecure young man (Proctor) and a cocky ex-lover (Nicholson). The dreamlike structure may confuse at first, but underlying the convoluted story line is a wealth of emotional insight, and some brilliantly natural acting by the perfect lead performers. (Dir: Henry Jaglom, 92 mins.)

Safety Last (1923)***½ Harold Lloyd, Mildred Davis. Comedy comes first here. The laughter builds relentlessly as Harold's Horatio Alger-type character tries to tame the big, bad city. The film's climax is the classic scene with Lloyd hanging suspended from a skyscraper and clutching the hands of a giant clock—it's the perfect combination of thrills and laughter. (Dirs: Fred Newmeyer, Sam Taylor, 71 mins.)

Saga of Hemp Brown, The (1958)** Rory Calhoun, Beverly Garland, John Larch. Army lieutenant is dismissed from the service when he's framed for a payroll robbery; with the aid of a traveling show he goes after the true culprit. (Dir: Richard Carlson, 79 mins.)

Sahara (1943)*** Humphrey Bogart, Dan Duryea, Lloyd Bridges, J. Carrol Naish, Rex Ingram, Bruce Bennett. American tank with an assorted crew outwits the Nazis in the desert. Frequently exciting war drama, well done. Remade as *Last of the Comanches*. (Dir: Zoltan Korda, 97 mins.)†

Sahara (1983)* Brooke Shields, Horst Buchholz, John Mills, Steve Forrest. A ludicrous romance, set in 1927, in which heiress Shields disguises herself as a man to enter a car race across the Sahara. (Dir: Andrew V. McLaglen, 104 mins.)†

Saigon (1948)** Alan Ladd, Veronica Lake, Luther Adler, Morris Carnovsky. Routine adventure story set in Indochina involving a black marketeer and half a million dollars. (Dir: Leslie Fenton, 94 mins.)†

Saigon Commandos (1987)** Richard Young, P. J. Soles, John Allen Nelson, Joonee Gamboa. Military policeman stationed in Vietnam uncovers a plot by a South Vietnamese politician to start an anti-U.S. rebellion. OK blend of tough-cop and war genres. (Dir: Clark Henderson, 91 mins.)†

Sail a Crooked Ship (1962)** Robert Wagner, Dolores Hart, Ernie Kovacs, Carolyn Jones, Frankie Avalon. Young man gets tangled with a gang of crooks who intend to use an old Liberty ship to pull a bank robbery in Boston. (Dir: Irving S. Brecher, 88 mins.)

Sailing Along (Great Britain, 1938)** Jessie Matthews, Jack Whiting, Roland Young, Alastair Sim, Athene Seyler. Mediocre vehicle for the usually sprightly Matthews. She plays a would-be star who relinquishes life on a river barge for tripping the light fantastic. (Dir: Sonnie Hale, 94 mins.)

Sail Into Danger (Great Britain, 1957)** Dennis O'Keefe, Kathleen Ryan, James Hayter, Pedro de Cordova. OK thriller about a American getting involved with smugglers on a trip to Spain. Simplistic script lacks tension. (Dir: Kenneth Hume, 72 mins.)

Sailor Beware!—See: **Panic In the Parlor**

Sailor Beware (1951)**½ Dean Martin, Jerry Lewis, Corinne Calvet, Robert Strauss, Marion Marshall. Martin and Lewis in the Navy, with Jerry getting a reputation as a lady-killer. Pleasant enough. (Dir: Hal Walker, 108 mins.)

Sailor of the King (Great Britain, 1953)**½ Jeffrey Hunter, Michael Rennie, Wendy Hiller. Another WWII drama. It's the British Navy against the Nazi U-boats in this one. Rennie plays the British commander with commendable restraint.

Hunter portrays the novice who finally gets the chance to show the stuff of which heroes are made. (Dir: Roy Boulting, 83 mins.)

Sailor's Luck (1933)*½ James Dunn, Sally Eilers, Victor Jory. Routine comedy romance. This naval misfire is short on plot, acting, and direction. (Dir: Raoul Walsh, 78 mins.)

Sailor Takes a Wife, The (1945)** Robert Walker, June Allyson, Hume Cronyn, Audrey Totter, Eddie Anderson, Reginald Owen. Mild and uninvolving romance between sailor Walker and starry-eyed Allyson. (Dir: Richard Thorpe, 91 mins.)

Sailor Who Fell from Grace with the Sea, The (Great Britain, 1976)**½ Kris Kristofferson, Sarah Miles, Jonathan Kahn. When sailor Kristofferson begins an affair with lonely widow Miles in a secluded coastal town, her young son who looks up to him feels that it is an intrusion on the order of the natural world and sets about righting it. The adaptation of a Yukio Mishima novel doesn't quite work in this Westernized version, though it's striking in many ways. (Dir: Lewis John Carlino, 104 mins.)†

Saint—See also **St.**

Sainted Sisters, The (1948)**½ Joan Caulfield, Barry Fitzgerald, Veronica Lake. Barry reforms a couple of con girls for him in this film which completely depends on him for its appeal. (Dir: William Russell, 89 mins.)

Saint In London, The (Great Britain, 1939)**½ George Sanders, Sally Gray. The Saint picks up a wounded man on a road and is plunged into crooked doings. Entertaining mystery. (Dir: John Paddy Carstairs, 72 mins.)

Saint In New York, The (1938)*** Kay Sutton, Louis Hayward, Sig Ruman. The first *"Saint"* film. He helps a civic committee clean up a gang of racketeers. Good melodrama, well made, and exciting. (Dir: Ben Holmes, 71 mins.)

Saint In Palm Springs (1941)**½ George Sanders, Wendy Barrie. The Saint is entrusted to deliver three valuable stamps to a girl for her inheritance. Entertaining mystery. (Dir: Jack Hively, 65 mins.)

Saint Jack (1979)*** Ben Gazzara, Denholm Elliott, James Villiers. An American in Singapore, a pimp with a heart of gold, is played by Gazzara as a thoughtful, sweet character. He tries to survive xenophobia and competition, services servicemen on R and R, and makes a few low-keyed friendships along the way. (Dir: Peter Bogdanovich, 112 mins.)†

Saint Joan (1957)*½ Richard Widmark, Richard Todd, John Gielgud, Kenneth Haigh, Jean Seberg. A poor filmization of Shaw's play marred by stodgy direction. (Dir: Otto Preminger, 110 mins.)†

Saint Meets the Tiger (Great Britain, 1942)

**½ Hugh Sinclair, Jean Gillie. The Saint gets on the trail of a gang that has stolen a fortune in gold. Lively detective story. (Dir: Paul Stein, 70 mins.)

Saint's Double Trouble, The (1940)** George Sanders, Helene Whitney, Bela Lugosi. The Saint traps a look-alike who has been engaging in diamond smuggling. Fair mystery. (Dir: Jack Hively, 68 mins.)

Saint's Girl Friday, The (Great Britain, 1953) ** Louis Hayward, Naomi Chance, Diana Dors. The Saint investigates the murder of a socialite friend. Fair mystery. (Dir: Seymour Friedman, 68 mins.)

Saint Strikes Back (1939)*** George Sanders, Wendy Barrie, Barry Fitzgerald. The Saint helps a girl trap thieves who have framed her father. Good detective story, well made. (Dir: John Farrow, 64 mins.)†

Saint's Vacation, The (Great Britain, 1940)** Hugh Sinclair, Sally Gray, Arthur MacRae, Cecil Parker, Leueen McGrath. On a sojourn in Switzerland, the Saint gets involved in wartime espionage as the Allies and the Germans try to fight over a music box whose tune contains a secret code. (Dir: Leslie Fenton, 60 mins.)

Saint Takes Over, The (1940)*** George Sanders, Wendy Barrie. The Saint arrives back in America to save a friend from a murder charge. Above average entry. (Dir: Jack Hively, 69 mins.)

Sakharov (MCTV 1984)***½ Jason Robards, Jr., Glenda Jackson, Frank Finlay, Michael Bryant, Anna Massey. A moving, timely drama about the courageous Russian scientist and Nobel Peace Prize winner Andrei Sakharov. Chronicles Sakharov's decision to champion the free speech movement in Russia, which led to house arrest, forced hospitalization, and exile from his Moscow home. A powerful drama thanks in part to a superb performance by Robards. (Dir: Jack Gold, 119 mins.)†

Salaam Bombay! (India, 1988)***½ Shafiq Syed, Sarfuddin Qurrassi, Raju Barnad. Semidocumentary about homeless children living in squalid, overcrowded Bombay. Director Mira Nair used real street urchins and locations, and the result is a lyrical and illuminating work about the nature of brutalizing poverty. (113 mins.)†

Salamander, The (1983)** Franco Nero, Anthony Quinn, Martin Balsam, Eli Wallach, Christopher Lee, Claudia Cardinale. Picture postcard settings and an all-star cast can't save this obvious melodrama about a neo-fascist plot to take over the government of Italy. (Dir: Peter Zinner, 107 mins.)†

Salem's Lot (MTV 1979)*** David Soul, James Mason, Bonnie Bedelia, Lance Kerwin, Geoffrey Lewis, Lew Ayres,

Ed Flanders, Marie Windsor. Stephen King's novel about vampires is turned into a truly scary horror film about a novelist (Soul) returning to his hometown, which is enveloped in deadly terror involving a vampire and his ruthless consort (Mason). There are three different versions—the original 200 mins. TV movie, an abridged version of 150 mins., and the video version, 112 mins. but with added scenes only shown in Europe. (Dir: Tobe Hooper, 200 mins.)†

Salesman (1969)**** Innovative, revealing; altogether shattering documentary, cinema-verité style, about the lives of several Bible salesmen in the South. Produced, directed, and photographed by the gifted brother team of Albert and David Maysles, this is one of the most extraordinarily honest glimpses of contemporary American life ever captured on film. (90 mins.)

Sallah (Israel, 1964)*** Hayam Topol, Geula Noni, Gila Almagor, Shraga Friedman. Charming tale of an Oriental Jew who moves to Israel with his wife and seven kids, and the trials and tribulations they incur while settling into their new life. Folksy and sweetly sentimental. (Dir: Ephraim Kishon, 105 mins.)

Sally and Saint Anne (1952)**½ Ann Blyth, Edmund Gwenn, Gregg Palmer, Hugh O'Brian. Corny but heartwarming story of a zany family and one member in particular, namely Sally (Blyth), who really believes that Saint Anne is their patron saint. (Dir: Rudolph Maté, 90 mins.)

Sally, Irene and Mary (1938)*** Alice Faye, Joan Davis, Marjorie Weaver, Tony Martin, Fred Allen, Jimmy Durante, Gregory Ratoff, Gypsy Rose Lee. Trio of struggling singers turn a barge into a modern-day showboat. Good fun, with several musical numbers by Martin, Faye, and Durante. (Dir: William A. Seiter, 86 mins.)

Sally of the Sawdust (1925)*** Carol Dempster, W. C. Fields, Alfred Lunt, Erville Anderson. First version of the play *Poppy*, about a girl raised by her juggler father who falls in love with an upper-class boy. Charmingly done, and the extensive footage of Fields's amazing juggling routines is enthralling. (Dir: D. W. Griffith, 91 mins.)†

Salome (1953)**½ Rita Hayworth, Stewart Granger, Charles Laughton, Judith Anderson. Overproduced and overlong story of Salome and the events leading up to her famous dance of the seven veils. Rita sheds the veils while Laughton leers and Anderson flares her talented nostrils. (Dir: William Dieterle, 103 mins.)†

Salome (1923) and **Queen Elizabeth** (1912) *** Two extraordinary examples of early filmmaking make up this compilation tape. Alla Nazimova stars in her own production of *Salome,* based upon Oscar Wilde's scandalous play; the drama is stilted, but the amazing decor is a show in itself. Sarah Bernhardt's *Queen Elizabeth* is badly filmed, but offers glimpses of what made her "the Divine Sarah." (91 mins.)†

Salome's Last Dance (1988)**½ Glenda Jackson, Stratford Johns, Nicholas Grace, Imogen Millais-Scott. A night in the life of Oscar Wilde, as interpreted by the master of stylish decadence, Ken Russell. Wilde is invited by a suitably sleazy upper-crust chum to view a distinctly unconventional production of his banned play *Salome*. The resulting night's entertainment has that keen sense of warped sexuality so dear to Russell's work. (90 mins.)†

Salome, Where She Danced (1945)** Yvonne De Carlo, Rod Cameron, Albert Dekker. This passed for intentional camp even when it was made. De Carlo plays a kootch dancer in Austria who is suspected of spying. She flees to the American west. (Dir: Charles Lamont, 90 mins.)†

Salo, or the 120 Days of Sodom (Italy, 1975)***½ Paolo Bonacelli, Caterina Boratto, Giorgio Cataldi, Elsa De Giorgi. Powerful, brutal film set during WWII about gang of privileged Fascists who subject a group of young people to sadomasochistic abuses culminating in murder. Director Pier Paolo Pasolini's last film before his own murder is an unrelenting attack against fascism and the exploitation of humans by other humans. Definitely not for all viewers; this is strong stuff. (117 mins.)†

Salsa (1976)*** Ray Barretto, Willie Colon, Larry Harlow, Mongo Santamaria. Documentary covering two all-star Latin music festivals held in 1973. A good introduction to this danceable, lively music, marred only by Geraldo Rivera's narration. (Dir: Jerry Masucci, 80 mins.)

Salsa (1988)* Robby Rosa, Rodney Harvey, Magali Alvarado, Miranda Garrison, Tito Puente, Celia Cruz. This Latin-flavored *Saturday Night Fever* retread features former Menudo star Rosa as a grease monkey who dreams of dancing his way to fame as a salsa sensation. The insipid plot is merely an excuse for some distinctive choreography by Kenny Ortega (*Dirty Dancing*). (Dir: Boaz Davidson, 97 mins.)†

Salt and Pepper (Great Britain, 1968)** Peter Lawford, Sammy Davis, Jr., Michael Bates, Ilona Rodgers. Couple of carefree London club owners unwittingly and unwillingly become involved in international intrigue. Hipster comedy strains for fun. Sequel: *One More Time*. (Dir: Richard Donner, 101 mins.)

Salt of the Earth (1954)*** Will Geer, Mervin Williams. An interesting, seldom exhibited film about labor-management relations and the exploitation of the working class in America. A worthwhile, more radical examination of some of the themes dealt with in *The Grapes of Wrath*. (Dir: Herbert Biberman, 94 mins.)†

Salty O'Rourke (1945)*** Alan Ladd, Gail Russell, Stanley Clements. Gambler hires a crooked jockey to ride for him. Racetrack story gets a good production, neat script. (Dir: Raoul Walsh, 97 mins.)

Salute to the Marines (1943)**½ Wallace Beery, Fay Bainter, Reginald Owen, Keye Luke, Noah Beery. First-rate WWII Beery vehicle of a retired Marine in the Phillipines who organizes the civilians for resistance when the Japanese attack. Fast-moving and exciting, stronger dramatically than usual. (Dir: S. Sylvan Simon, 101 mins.)

Salut l'Artiste (France-Italy, 1973)***½ Marcello Mastroianni, Françoise Fabian, Jean Rochefort. Mastroianni is marvelous in this charming, affectionate look at the struggles of an unsuccessful bit player. Nicholas has one thing going for him: he believes in the elusive "glamour" of his profession, no matter how humiliating the acting role. Appealing, sardonic humor. (Dir: Yves Robert, 96 mins.)

Salvador (1986)*** James Woods, Jim Belushi, John Savage, Michael Murphy. Director Oliver Stone's scathing look at the social injustice in El Salvador. Stone's humanistic attitude is seen through the lenses of photographer Richard Boyle (Woods), a sleazy news hound who goes through his rites of revolutionization when he's confronted with the government's fascist brutalization of the country's populace. (122 mins.)†

Salvage (MTV 1979)** Andy Griffith, Trish Stewart, Richard Jaeckel. Dull pilot film. Griffith plays an enterprising junkman who goes all the way to the moon for his salvage. (Dir: Lee Philips, 104 mins.)

Salvation! (1987)** Stephen McHattie, Dominique Davalos, Viggo Mortensen, Rockets Redglare, Exene Cervenka. A sloppily constructed, but occasionally funny glimpse at religious show biz. A TV minister is blackmailed by an opportunist whose wife wants to be an evangelical singing star on the tube. (Dir: Beth B., 80 mins.)†

Salvatore Giuliano (Italy, 1961)***½ Salvo Randone, Federico Zardi, Frank Wolff, Fernando Cicero. Gripping and exciting true-life drama about the rise to power of a Mafia chieftain, told in probing semidocumentary style by director Fran-

907

cesco Rosi. The cast includes amateur and professional actors. The story was also the basis for Michael Cimino's *The Sicilian*. (125 mins.)

Salzburg Connection, The (1972)** Barry Newman, Anna Karina, Karen Jensen. Inept treatment of Helen MacInnes's spy thriller in which every country in the world has an agent out to steal a box of incriminating Nazi war documents. (Dir: Lee H. Katzin, 93 mins.)†

Samar (1962)*** George Montgomery, Gilbert Roland, Joan O'Brien, Ziva Rodann. Commandant of a penal colony refuses to bow to his strict superiors, breaks with the administration and leads his people through the jungles to freedom. Highly interesting, unusual story well done; rugged adventure fare. (Dir: George Montgomery, 89 mins.)†

Samaritan: The Mitch Snyder Story (MTV 1986)*** Martin Sheen, Roxanne Hart, Joe Seneca, Stan Shaw, Cicely Tyson. Earnest often affecting real-life drama about Mitch Snyder, who was instrumental in getting the homeless of Washington, D.C. sanctuary. Sheen is the right combination of humanitarian and firebrand, but the film is less successful in realistically conveying the conditions of the street people. (Dir: Richard T. Heffron, 104 mins.)

Samblzanga (Angola, 1972)*** Domingos Oliviera, Elisa Andrade, Dino Abelino, Jean M'Vondo. A young woman is forced to undergo a grueling search for her jailed husband in a country ruled by oppressive forces and on the threshold of revolution. Powerful political film depicts both the tragedy of losing a loved one and the ugliness of a government ruling with brutality and bias. (Dir: Sarah Maldoror, 102 mins.)

Same Time Next Year (1978)*** Alan Alda, Ellen Burstyn. Thanks largely to the performances of Alda and Burstyn, the long-running Broadway play by Bernard Slade was turned into one of the gentler, more touching love stories of the late seventies. A couple, not married to each other, have a secret tryst once a year, for two decades. (Dir: Robert Mulligan, 117 mins.)†

Sam Hill—Who Killed the Mysterious Mr. Foster? (MTV 1971)**½ Ernest Borgnine, Judy Geeson, Bruce Dern, Will Geer, Stephen Hudis. TV pilot about a deputy sheriff who teams up with a little towheaded thief (Hudis) to find out who poisoned the local minister. (Dir: Fielder Cook, 99 mins.)

Sam Marlow, Private Eye—See: **Man with Bogart's Face, The**

Sammy and Rosie Get Laid (Great Britain, 1987)*** Ayub Khan Din, Shashi Kapoor, Frances Barber, Claire Bloom. Another

witty, provocative slice of life in Thatcher's England from the makers of *My Beautiful Laundrette*. Pakistani Sammy and native British Rosie, liberal trendies living in an open marriage, find their lives disrupted when his father, part of a fascist political regime, visits after a long absence and discovers that his beloved England is now swirling with race riots, class wars, and even a wandering ghost. Too many characters serve as props for the film's political agenda, but the writing bristles with intelligence and the acting is first-rate. (Dir: Stephen Frears, 100 mins.)†

Samson (Italy, 1960)* Brad Harris, Brigitte Corey. Muscleman aids his king and restores law and order to the land. Another English-dubbed spectacle mishmash. (Dir: Gianfranco Parolini, 99 mins.)

Samson and Delilah (1949)*** Victor Mature, Hedy Lamarr, George Sanders, Angela Lansbury. Biblical tale of the mighty Samson, whose power was curtailed by the scheming Delilah, given the high-powered DeMille treatment. Some truly spectacular effects, action scenes—also the expected naiveté, hokey sequences. (Dir: Cecil B. DeMille, 128 mins.)†

Samson and Delilah (MTV 1984)** Antony Hamilton, Belinda Bauer, Victor Mature, Daniel Stern, José Ferrer, Maria Schell. A remake of the Cecil B. DeMille opus about the treacherous Delilah, who shears superstrong Samson's locks. Needs cutting! (Dir: Lee Philips, 104 mins.)†

Samson and the Seven Miracles of the World (Italy-France, 1961)* Gordon Scott, Yoko Tani. While battling the Tartars in ancient China, Samson creates earthshattering havoc after being bonked by the Great Gong of Freedom. Ridiculous. (Dir: Riccardo Freda, 80 mins.)

Sam's Son (1984)**½ Eli Wallach, Anne Jackson, Timothy Patrick Murphy, Michael Landon. Heavily autobiographical film based on Landon's becoming a champion javelin thrower and then a movie star with the aid of his father. A fairly good piece of narcissistic entertainment. (Dir: Michael Landon, 104 mins.)

Sam's Song (1971)* Robert De Niro, Jennifer Warren, Jered Mickey, Terrayne Crawford, Viva. Early De Niro film casts him as a New York film editor working on a documentary about Nixon and spending a weekend with rich friends Warren and Mickey. Crawford enters their lives and proceeds to disrupt everyone. Arty and pretentious. An oddly re-edited version called **The Swap** is available on video. (Dir: Jordan Leondopoulos, 92 mins.)†

Samurai (Japan, 1954–1955)***½ Toshiro

Mifune, Rentaro Mikuni, Karuo Yashi-gusa, Sachio Sakai, Koji Tsurata, Akihiko Hirata. Director Hiroshi Inagaki remakes his 1941 black-and-white trilogy into a masterful and enthralling epic about one of Japan's most ancient and mysterious traditions. Mifune is outstanding as Takezo, the young man who becomes the most famous and accomplished samurai. Originally released and available on video as three separate films, subtitled *Musashi Miyamoto*, *Duel at Ichijoji*, and *Duel at Ganryu*. (Part One: 92 mins.; Part Two: 104 mins.; Part Three: 105 mins.)†

Samurai, The (France, 1967)***½ Alain Delon, François Perier, Nathalie Delon, Cathy Rosier, Jacques Le Roy. Heady atmospheric thriller, considered by many to be director Jean-Pierre Melville's magnum opus, tells, with sparse dialogue and somber visuals, the story of a hired killer (a wonderfully laconic Delon) in love with a woman who jeopardizes his life when she lets his secret slip. (95 mins.)

Samurai (MTV 1979)** Joe Penny, James Shigeta, Beulah Quo. Penny as a young District Attorney who often reverts to his martial arts skills to solve his cases. (Dir: Lee Katzin, 90 mins.)

Sam Whiskey (1969)** Burt Reynolds, Clint Walker, Ossie Davis, Angie Dickinson. Predictable western adventure yarn bolstered a bit by the tongue-in-cheek performance of Reynolds as a carefree guy who teams up with seductive Dickinson to retrieve a sunken treasure in gold bars. (Dir: Arnold Laven, 96 mins.)

San Antone (1953)** Rod Cameron, Arleen Whelan, Forrest Tucker, Katy Jurado, Rodolfo Acosta. Civil War-era western, with Texas ranchers torn between the two sides of the conflict. Colorful and brawny, if unintellectual. (Dir: Joseph Kane, 90 mins.)

San Antonio (1945)*** Errol Flynn, Alexis Smith, S. Z. Sakall. Conventional grade A western from Warner Bros., handsome but for aficionados of the genre only. (Dirs: David Butler, Raoul Walsh, 111 mins.)†

Sanctuary (1961)** Lee Remick, Yves Montand, Odetta, Bradford Dillman. Governor's daughter is seduced by a Cajun, who returns after she's married to cause her further trouble. Faulkner's seamy tale of the South in the 1920s given a distorted, choppy treatment. (Dir: Tony Richardson, 90 mins.)

Sanctuary of Fear (MTV 1979)*** Barnard Hughes, Kay Lenz. Hughes's performance as G. K. Chesterton's Father Brown, detective, is a treat. But the script takes us on a repetitive trip through a young girl's nightmarish experience of unexplained murders and disappearances. (Dir: John Llewellyn Moxey, 104 mins.)†

Sand (1949)** Mark Stevens, Coleen Gray, Rory Calhoun. The trials and tribulations of a show horse named Jubilee. (Dir: Louis King, 78 mins.)

Sandakan 8 (Japan, 1975)***½ Kinuyo Tanaka, Yoko Takakashi, Komaki Kurihara, Eitaro Ozawa. An elderly woman tells a young journalist the story of her life, including the sad times spent working in a brothel. Demanding and moving political drama examines the treatment of women in Japanese society and the pressures put on them to "perform" for men as wife, lover, or whore. (Dir: Kei Kumai, 121 mins.)†

Sand and Blood (France, 1987)*** Sami Frey, Andre Dussolier, Patrick Catalifo, Maria Casares. Absorbing, lyrical story of a self-defeated matador and a Spanish doctor who hates bullfighting for what it represents about his homeland. The two become friends and a gradual change occurs in their ideas and opinions. (Dir: Jeanne Labrune, 101 mins.)

Sand Castle, The (1961)***½ Barry Cardwell, Alec Wilder. A diverting try for something away from the usual run, showing an afternoon in a boy's life at the seashore. (Dir: Jerome Hill, 67 mins.)

Sandcastles (MTV 1972)** Jan-Michael Vincent, Bonnie Bedelia, Mariette Hartley. Vincent and Bedelia try to bring off this love story about a man who dies in an auto crash, and returns to make amends for a previous act of thievery. (Dir: Ted Post, 73 mins.)

Sanders (Great Britain, 1964)**½ Richard Todd, Marianne Koch, Albert Lieven. Young woman doctor arrives at a remote African outpost and finds a dedicated doctor involved in smuggling diamonds, with a policeman on his trail. (Dir: Lawrence Huntington, 83 mins.)

Sanders of the River (Great Britain, 1935)*** Paul Robeson, Leslie Banks, Nina Mae McKinney. Robeson lends dignity to an apology for British imperialism in Africa. AKA: **Coast of Skeletons.** (Dir: Zoltan Korda, 98 mins.)†

San Diego, I Love You (1944)*** Jon Hall, Louise Allbritton, Edward Everett Horton, Eric Blore, Buster Keaton. This funny screwball comedy revolves around the sale of a collapsible life raft and Allbritton's antics with her younger brothers, the butler who came with her house, and the third richest man in the U.S.A. (Dir: Reginald Le Borg, 81 mins.)

Sandokan the Great (Italy, 1965)*½ Steve Reeves, Genevieve Grad. Strongman Reeves plays a sultan's son who turns jungle guerrilla to free his father. (Dir: Umberto Lenzi, 105 mins.)

Sand Pebbles, The (1966)**½ Steve McQueen, Richard Attenborough, Candice Bergen, Richard Crenna, Mako,

Simon Oakland. A sprawling, overlong adventure drama set in China during the 1920s. McQueen gives a commanding low-key performance as an independent sailor-engineer who clashes with his superiors after he becomes politically aware of the situation around him. (Dir: Robert Wise, 195 mins.)†

Sandpiper, The (1965)** Elizabeth Taylor, Richard Burton, Eva Marie Saint, Charles Bronson. The presence of Taylor and Burton and the grandeur of the great Big Sur location shots don't really make up for this limp and saccharine love story between a liberated artist and a dedicated, married and confused minister. (Dir: Vincente Minnelli, 116 mins.)†

Sands of Beersheba (U.S.-Israel, 1965)**½ Diane Baker, David Opatoshu, Tom Bell. American girl in Israel meets the friend of her fiancé who was killed in the 1948 fighting, soon finds herself caught between love and war. (Dir: Alexander Ramati, 89 mins.)

Sands of Iwo Jima (1949)***½ John Wayne, John Agar, Forrest Tucker. Officer's son has no liking for the traditions of the Marine Corps, but a tough sergeant makes him see otherwise under stress of battle. Some of the best war scenes ever staged are here, together with a splendid performance by Wayne. (Dir: Allan Dwan, 109 mins.)†

Sands of the Kalahari (Great Britain, 1965)*** Stuart Whitman, Stanley Baker, Susannah York, Harry Andrews, Theodore Bikel, Nigel Davenport. A strange he-man adventure involving the survivors of a plane crash in Africa's dangerous Kalahari Desert. Whitman plays an arrogant professional hunter whose desire to prove his strength leads to destruction. There's a fantastic finale in which Whitman pits his prowess against a tribe of wild baboons. (Dir: Cy Endfield, 119 mins.)

Sandy Gets Her Man (1940)** Baby Sandy, Stuart Erwin, Una Merkel, Edgar Kennedy, William Frawley. Slight but fairly funny comic vehicle for the forgotten child star Baby Sandy, here busy finding her mother a new husband. (Dirs: Otis Garrett, Paul Smith, 74 mins.)

Sandy Is a Lady (1940)** Baby Sandy, Nan Grey, Tom Brown, Eugene Pallette, Mischa Auer, Edgar Kennedy. Another appearance by Baby Sandy; this time, the infant comes to the aid of her struggling family. (Dir: Charles Lamont, 65 mins.)

San Francisco (1936)***½ Clark Gable, Spencer Tracy, Jeanette MacDonald. Entertaining, well played drama of love and adventure as the notorious Barbary Coast comes to grips with snobbish Nob Hill. The famous earthquake is a perfect climax. (Dir: W. S. Van Dyke, 120 mins.)

San Francisco International (MTV 1970)**½ Pernell Roberts, Clu Gulager, Van Johnson. If you liked *Airport*, you'll like this film. The main plot—a big heist of a cargo plane carrying three million in cash— is well done, and a subplot climaxed by a 14-year-old boy taking a plane up on his own should delight air-minded small fry. (Dir: John Llewellyn Moxey, 96 mins.)

San Francisco Story (1952)** Joel McCrea, Yvonne De Carlo. Miner is persuaded by a newspaper editor to help him fight vice in the city. (Dir: Robert Parrish, 80 mins.)

Sangaree (1953)** Fernando Lamas, Arlene Dahl, Francis L. Sullivan, Patricia Medina. Sangaree, a Georgia plantation, is the scene of this turbulent drama about pirates and family jealousies. (Dir: Edward Ludwig, 94 mins.)

Sanity Clause (Canada, 1990)**½ Louis Del Grande, Martha Gibson, Kenner Ames, George Sperdakos. Pointed comedy about a quartet of mental patients accidentally released from a halfway house trying to regain the rights to an invention stolen from one of them. (Dirs: David Barlow, George McCowan, 96 mins.)

Sanjuro (Japan, 1962)*** Toshiro Mifune, Tatsuya Nakadai, Takashi Shimura. Lighthearted sequel to *Yojimbo* has samurai Mifune aiding a band of young, untried warriors against a corrupt politician. Lots of fun; not as deadly serious as director Akira Kurosawa's other samurai films. (96 mins.)†

San Pedro Bums, The (MTV 1977)**½ Darryl McCullough, John Mark Robinson, Stuart Pankin. Five youngsters live a carefree existence on their run-down tuna boat. When their good friend, lovingly known as Pop, falls victim to a robbery by some local bullies, they attempt to right the wrong. (Dir: Barry Shear, 79 mins.)

San Quentin (1937)** Pat O'Brien, Humphrey Bogart, Ann Sheridan, Barton MacLane. There have been better prison pictures than this tripe. In this one Bogart's sister (Sheridan) falls in love with the warden (O'Brien). MacLane plays a sadistic guard. (Dir: Lloyd Bacon, 70 mins.)

San Quentin (1946)**½ Lawrence Tierney, Barton MacLane, Marian Carr, Harry Shannon. An organized group of ex-inmates are outraged when one of their number turns back to crime, and they hunt him down themselves. Strong B picture with an unusual, worthy theme. (Dir: Gordon M. Douglas, 66 mins.)

Sanshiro Sugata (Japan, 1943)*** Susumu Fujita, Dunjiro Okochi, Yukiko Todoroki, Ranko Hanai. Director Akira Kurosawa cut his teeth on hand-to-hand combat in this, his first feature film. The title character is a spirited young judo student who knows how to brawl, but learns the discipline essential to martial arts from a wise judo master. The showdown between Sugata and the dandified villain on a windswept mountainside is the first pure example of Kurosawa's lyrical brand of violence. (82 mins.)†

Sansho the Bailiff (Japan, 1954)**** Kinuyo Tanaka, Kyoko Kagawa, Yoshiaki Hanayagi, Masao Shimizu. Son and daughter of a noble family are kidnapped and sold as slaves. Years later the son escapes to search for his mother. Director Kenji Mizoguchi weaves the story of a monstrous act and its repercussions in humanistic and lyrical terms. A classic of Japanese cinema. (125 mins.)†

Sans Soleil (France, 1982)***½ Poetic documentary, inimitably directed by Chris Marker, in which he waxes philosophical via the camera about the cultural disorientation he feels when visiting Iceland, Japan, and West Africa. Filled with recurring and diverse images, breathtaking scenes, and diary entries, Marker's surreal film even includes special effects and fascinating use of videotape technology. (100 mins.)

Santa Claus Conquers the Martians (1964) ½ Pia Zadora, John Call, Leonard Hicks, Donna Conforti, Vincent Beck. A cheesy-looking fantasy filmed in an airplane hangar on Long Island, New York. Martian parents grow perplexed when their kids turn green with envy over the Earthling Christmas celebrations they've glimpsed on TV. Cosmic tragedy strikes when the Martians kidnap two nosy Earth kids and Saint Nick himself, before realizing they can transform one of their own jolly buffoons into a facsimile of the beloved toymaker. It stars Pia Zadora in her child-star phase as a Martian moppet. (Dir: Nicholas Webster, 80 mins.)†

Santa Claus: The Movie (1985)*½ Dudley Moore, John Lithgow, David Huddleston, Burgess Meredith, Judy Cornwell, Jeffrey Kramer. Ho-Ho-Hum nonsense about how Santa first came to be and how a Scrooge-like toymaker objects to the bearded one's largesse. One of those desperate, family events inflicted on us to make the season jolly. (Dir: Jeannot Szwarc, 112 mins.)†

Santa Fe (1951)**½ Randolph Scott, Janis Carter, Jerome Courtland, Jock Mahoney, Irving Pichel, Chief Thundercloud. Defeated Confederate soldier Scott gets a job with the Santa Fe railroad, tangling with robbers, who turn out to include his own brothers. Good, fast moving actioner. (Dir: Irving Pichel, 89 mins.)

Santa Fe Passage (1955)*** John Payne, Faith Domergue, Rod Cameron. Indian-hating scout takes a job with a wagon train. Actionful western, above average. (Dir: William Witney, 90 mins.)

Santa Fe Trail (1940)**½ Errol Flynn, Olivia de Havilland, Van Heflin, Ronald Reagan, Raymond Massey. A lot of action, plus an elaborate production make up for the shaky history-lesson plot involving Custer and John Brown among others. (Dir: Michael Curtiz, 110 mins.)†

Santa Sangre (Italy, 1989)*** Axel Jodorowsky, Blanca Guerra, Guy Stockwell, Sabrina Dennison. Wildly excessive film from director Alexandro Jodorowsky, his first since *Holy Mountain* in 1973, uses bizarre but unforgettable imagery to tell the story of two circus performers, an armless woman and her insane son who acts as his mother's hands, even to strangling his lovers at jealous mama's demand. This film may delight or appall you, but you won't forget it. (118 mins.)†

Santee (1972)*½ Glenn Ford, Michael Burns, Dana Wynter. Uneven western. Ford is a mean bounty hunter out for revenge who softens enough to take the homeless son of one of his victims under his wing. (Dir: Gary Nelson, 91 mins.)†

Santiago (1956)*** Alan Ladd, Lloyd Nolan, Rossana Podesta, Chill Wills, Paul Fix. Ladd and Nolan are unwilling partners running guns to Cuban revolutionaries, during the island's fight for independence from Spain. This would be a routine actioner, were it not for mordant and, in spots, extremely risqué script. (Dir: Gordon Douglas, 93 mins.)

São Bernardo (Brazil, 1972)*** Othon Bastos, Isabel Ribeiro, Nildo Parente, Vande Lacerda, Mario Lago. A wealthy aged man sits alone in his seedy mansion recalling the events of his life, including his good fortune (he began poor), and his sorrows (the death of his wife). Intensely personal human drama about dreams, joys, loneliness, and longings. (Dir: Leon Hirszman, 110 mins.)

Sapphire (Great Britain, 1959)***½ Nigel Patrick, Yvonne Mitchell. The murder of a good-time girl leads police to racial problems in untangling the mystery. A good whodunit enhanced by some perceptive comments on current social problems; hits the mark either way. First-rate screenplay and excellent performances. (Dir: Basil Dearden, 92 mins.)

Saps at Sea (1940)**½ Stan Laurel, Oliver Hardy, Ben Turpin. Middle-level Laurel and Hardy in a small boat. (Dir: Gordon Douglas, 57 mins.)†

Saraband (Great Britain, 1948)*** Stewart Granger, Joan Greenwood. An unhappy girl married to a man in line for the English throne falls in love with an adventurer, but the affair ends tragically. Costume romance has a stylish presentation, especially in the direction.

(Dirs: Michael Relph, Basil Dearden, 96 mins.)

Saracen Blade, The (1954)** Ricardo Montalban, Betta St. John. Not many clichés are omitted in this costume adventure about the Crusades and the days of knights and their valiant deeds. (Dir: William Castle, 76 mins.)

Saracens, The (Italy, 1960)*½ Richard Harrison, Ana Mori Obaldi. Adventurer returns to find pirates in possession of his castle, forms a guerrilla band to rout them. (Dir: Roberto Mauri, 89 mins.)

Saragossa Manuscript, The (Poland, 1964) *** Zbigniew Cybulski, Joanna Jedryka, Iga Cembrzynska, Slawomir Linder. Enjoyable epic fantasy about a Belgian Army officer's encounter with two attractive princesses as he travels to Madrid. Based on Jan Potocki's 1813 Polish novel. (Dir: Wojciech Has, 175 mins.)

Sarah and Son (1930)**½ Ruth Chatterton, Fredric March, Fuller Mellish, Jr., Gilbert Emery. A poverty-stricken mother's child is adopted against her will; years later, now wealthy, she tries to get him back. Potent, expertly made soap opera, well acted by Chatterton and March. (Dir: Dorothy Arzner, 86 mins.)

Sarah, Plain and Tall (MTV 1991)*** Glenn Close, Christopher Walken, Lexi Randall, Margaret Sophie Stein, Jon De Vries, Christopher Bell. Beautifully produced story about a Maine spinster (Close) who answers an ad placed by a Kansas widower with two children. A slow-but-steady love blossoms between the two adults. Excellently acted by the entire cast. (Dir: Glenn Jordan, 96 mins.)

Sarah T.—Portrait of a Teenage Alcoholic (MTV 1975)*** Linda Blair, Verna Bloom, William Daniels, Larry Hagman. Linda Blair is quite convincing as a mixed-up fifteen-year-old hooked on secret drinking. (Dir: Richard Donner, 100 mins.)

Saratoga (1937)**½ Clark Gable, Jean Harlow, Walter Pidgeon, Lionel Barrymore, Frank Morgan. Gable is a bookie and Harlow is a racing man's daughter in this romantic comedy of the racing world. Miss Harlow died before completing this film. (Dir: Jack Conway, 92 mins.)

Saratoga Trunk (1945)**½ Gary Cooper, Ingrid Bergman, Flora Robson, Jerry Austin, Florence Bates. Elaborate version of Edna Ferber's novel, with the social commentary left out. In an odd bit of casting, Ingrid is a Creole beauty from the wrong side of the tracks, bent on achieving a fortune; Cooper is a rough-edged Texas millionaire. Star chemistry compensates for the watered-down script. (Dir: Sam Wood, 135 mins.)

Sarge—the Badge or the Cross (MTV 1971)*** George Kennedy, Ricardo Montalban. This drama about a cop who turns priest after his wife is killed in a car bombing tragedy manages to avoid the clichés such a plot might trigger and holds your interest throughout. (Dir: Richard Colla, 99 mins.)

Sarraounia (Burkino Faso, 1986)***½ Ai Keita, Jean-Roger Milo, Feodor Atkine, Jean Edmond, Roger Mirmont. Visual masterpiece about tribal conflict and the struggle against colonialism in Africa. Keita is sublime in the title role of warrior-healer Queen Sarraounia in this illuminating, lyrical drama. (Dir: Med Hondo, 121 mins.)

Saskatchewan (1954)**½ Alan Ladd, Shelley Winters, J. Carrol Naish, Hugh O'Brian. Mountie needs all the help he can muster to drive the Sioux Indians back across the border. Fast-moving if familiar. (Dir: Raoul Walsh, 87 mins.)

Satan Bug, The (1965)*** George Maharis, Richard Basehart, Anne Francis, Dana Andrews. Intriguing suspense tale with Basehart playing a diabolical doctor bent on destroying mankind. (Dir: John Sturges, 114 mins.)

Satanic Rites of Dracula, The (Great Britain, 1973)* Christopher Lee, Peter Cushing, Michael Coles, Freddie Jones, Joanna Lumley. Dracula threatens humanity with a virus. Last of the Hammer Studios Dracula series. AKA: **Count Dracula and His Vampire Bride** and **Dracula Is Dead and Well and Living in London.** (Dir: Alan Gibson, 84 mins.)†

Satan Met a Lady (1936)**½ Warren William, Bette Davis, Alison Skipworth, Arthur Treacher. Second film version of Dashiell Hammett's *The Maltese Falcon* is played tongue in cheek. William is a sublimely seedy detective, unheroic and just half a brain ahead of being a derelict. (Dir: William Dieterle, 75 mins.)†

Satan Never Sleeps (1962)*½ William Holden, Clifton Webb, France Nuyen. Tasteless and banal drama about two priests who perilously oppose the Chinese Reds when they take over their mission. Poorly developed. (Dir: Leo McCarey, 126 mins.)

Satan's Brew (West Germany, 1976)*** Kurt Raab, Margit Carstensen, Volker Spengler, Ingrid Caven, Helen Vita. Poet Raab murders his female lover and plagiarizes from the writings (while absorbing the homosexual lifestyle) of Nietzschean poet Stefan George. Director Rainer Werner Fassbinder's evilly amusing film compiles styles and ideas from German expressionism, sexual politics, and screwball comedy. (100 mins.)

Satan's Cheerleaders (1977)*½ Kerry Sherman, John Ireland, Yvonne De Carlo, Jacqueline Cole, Jack Kruschen, John Carradine, Sydney Chaplin. While you will not see Lucifer at a pep rally, you will see several nubile cheerleaders held captive by a coven of devil worshippers. Suspense builds to a fever pitch as the high school's Peeping-Tom janitor betrays the innocent but mature-looking schoolgirls, who must battle with Sheriff B. L. Z. Bub and his overweight wife. Recommended for camp addicts. (Dir: Greydon Clark, 92 mins.)†

Satan's Satellites (1958)* Judd Holdren, Aline Towne, Leonard Nimoy. Invaders from another planet land on Earth to carry out their dirty work. Juvenile sci-fi thriller, cut down from the 1952 serial *Zombies of the Stratosphere.* (Dir: Fred Brannon, 70 mins.)

Satan's School for Girls (MTV 1973)** Pamela Franklin, Roy Thinnes, Kate Jackson, Lloyd Bochner, Jo Van Fleet, Cheryl Jean Stoppelmoor (Ladd). Girl enrolls in a private school to get to the bottom of her younger sister's suicide. Non-frightening horror pic resurrected on videotape due to the presence in the cast of two "Charlie's Angels." (Dir: David Lowell Rich, 74 mins.)†

Satan's Triangle (MTV 1975)**½ Kim Novak, Doug McClure. Melodrama about the infamous "Devil's Triangle," an area where ships, planes, and people just disappear off the face of the Earth. Helicopter rescue pilots come to the aid of a distressed vessel and find a beautiful woman survivor. The surprise twist at the end is a good one. (Dir: Sutton Rolley, 72 mins.)

Satellite in the Sky (Great Britain, 1956)**½ Kieron Moore, Lois Maxwell. A British made science-fiction tale about an earth satellite. (Dir: Paul Dickson, 84 mins.)

Satin Vengeance—See: **Naked Vengeance**

Satisfaction (1988)* Justine Bateman, Liam Neeson, Trini Alvarado, Debbie Harry. You can't get no enjoyment from this quickie about a female rock band that pulls no stops when it comes to clichés: There are tough street gangs, beach dudes, an overdose, bad cover versions of oldies, a disillusioned songwriter (Neeson), and Justine belting her little heart out, all for naught. (Dir: Joan Freeman, 92 mins.)†

Saturday Night and Sunday Morning (Great Britain, 1961)**** Albert Finney, Shirley Ann Field. A wonderful, robust film, expertly directed by Karel Reisz, detailing the life and loves of a young working-class rascal from the English midlands. Incisive comment on mores of the working class that captures the mood of such a dreary industrial community. Electric, vital performance of Finney deservedly shot him to stardom. An admirable piece of filmmaking in every detail. (98 mins.)

Saturday Night at the Baths (1975)*** Robert

Aberdeen, Ellen Sheppard, Don Scotti, Steven Ostrow. Well-made comedy from the era of sexual freedom and disco, set at the Continental Baths. A straight piano player gets a job in the Baths' house band, but has to overcome his homophobia. (Dir: David Buckley, 86 mins.)

Saturday Night at the Palace (South Africa, 1988)**½ John Kani, Paul Slabolepszy, Bill Flynn. Racial violence is the subject of this schematic but powerful drama about a vicious white brutalizer and his roommates (Slabolepszy and Flynn, who co-wrote the script) and their drunken, ultimately tragic encounter with a black restaurant manager (Kani). Some subtlety would have helped. (Dir: Robert Davies, 87 mins.)

Saturday Night Fever (1977)***½ John Travolta, Karen Lynn Gorney, Joseph Cali, Barry Miller, Julie Bovasso, Donna Pescow. Driving, powerful film about the Brooklyn boy whose love of dancing lifts him out of his working-class rut; a huge box-office and critical success. Capitalizes on disco fever with Travolta's riveting dancing sequences. Screenplay by Norman Wexler has some perceptive comments to make on the social and sexual rituals of working-class kids in Brooklyn. (Dir: John Badham, 119 mins.)†

Saturday's Children (1940)**½ John Garfield, Anne Shirley, Claude Rains, Lee Patrick, George Tobias. Somewhat depressing tale of a dreamer who struggles to support his wife, while both of them try to maintain their dignity under trying financial conditions. (Dir: Vincent Sherman, 101 mins.)

Saturday's Hero (1951)*** John Derek, Donna Reed, Sidney Blackmer, Aldo Ray. A handsome youth tries to rise above his immigrant family's background by going to college on a football scholarship. Better than usual performances from the actors involved. (Dir: David Miller, 111 mins.)

Saturday's Heroes (1937)**½ Van Heflin, Marian Marsh, Richard Lane, Alan Bruce, Willie Best, Al St. John. Vigorous college football drama, with a twist: a well-known athlete speaks out against commercialization of sports and special privileges for players. Above average, with a dynamite performance by Heflin. (Dir: Edward Killy, 58 mins.)

Saturday the 14th (1981)½ Richard Benjamin, Paula Prentiss, Severn Darden, Jeffrey Tambor. Inept spoof of haunted house pictures. This combination of *Friday the 13th* and "The Munsters" looks like the work of grade school students. (Dir: Howard R. Cohen, 75 mins.)†

Saturday the 14th Strikes Back (1989)½ Jason Presson, Ray Walston, Avery

Schreiber, Patty McCormack, **Michael** Berryman. How we long for the days when only good movies, or at least popular ones, spawned sequels. No improvement over its predecessor. (Dir: Howard R. Cohen, 78 mins.)†

Saturn 3 (Great Britain, 1980)** Kirk Douglas, Farrah Fawcett, Harvey Keitel. Douglas and Fawcett have made their Malibu in outer space, only to face the intrusion of madman Keitel and his rogue robot, who upset their plastic paradise by insinuating that they could get down to work, with Earth starving and all. Uneven and marred by a weak ending. (Dir: Stanley Donen, 105 mins.)†

Satyricon—See: **Fellini Satyricon**

Savage, The (1952)**½ Charlton Heston, Susan Morrow. Man raised by the Sioux is torn between loyalties when war threatens between the Indians and the whites. (Dir: George Marshall, 95 mins.)

Savage (MTV 1972)**½ Martin Landau, Barbara Bain. Landau and Bain are TV journalists digging into the questionable background of a Supreme Court nominee. (Dir: Steven Spielberg, 78 mins.)†

Savage Beach (1990)** Dona Spier, Hope Marie Carlton, John Aprea, Bruce Penhall, Teri Weigel. Sequel to *Picasso Trigger* finds buxom D.E.A. agents Spier and Carlton on a remote Pacific island where various shady types are trying to locate a cache of gold lost there during WWII. An improvement over writer-director Andy Sidaris's other films in that the tongue-in-cheek humor is mostly intentional. (95 mins.)†

Savage Bees, The (MTV 1976)** Ben Johnson, Michael Parks. Predictable New Orleans-based drama about the influx of African killer bees brought here by a visiting cargo ship. (Dir: Bruce Geller, 106 mins.)†

Savage Dawn (1985)*½ George Kennedy, Richard Lynch, Karen Black, Lance Henricksen, Claudia Udy, Mickey Jones. Ex-Army buddies try to retire peacefully to a desert mining town, but are forced back into action when a gang of bad-tempered bikers roll in. Violent action for the undemanding. (Dir: Simon Nutchern, 102 mins.)†

Savage Drums (1951)** Sabu, Lita Baron, H. B. Warner, Sid Melton. OK exotic melodrama has Sabu helping his people end tribal warfare. Silly, but at least it moves at a pretty fast clip. (Dir: William Berke, 73 mins.)

Savage Eye, The (1961)*** Barbara Baxley. A dramatized documentary about a woman's lonely days following her recent divorce and the series of adventures she forces herself into in order to combat the feeling of desperation. Miss Baxley is excellent and the documentary-flavored
914

technique works beautifully. (Dir: Ben Maddow, 68 mins.)

Savage Guns, The (1962)** Richard Basehart, Don Taylor, Alex Nicol. A loner picked on by a sadistic villain gets bailed out by a gunfighter. Not worth a trip out west. (Dir: Michael Carreras, 63 mins.)

Savage Harvest (1981)½ Tom Skerritt, Michelle Phillips, Shawn Stevens. While the idea of lions munching on bad actors in Africa *sounds* like fun, the idea of their eating a bad writer/director would have been much better. (Dir: Robert Collins, 86 mins.)

Savage Innocents, The (1960)*** Anthony Quinn, Yoko Tani, Peter O'Toole. Unusual drama of Eskimo life, and the struggle of one family to keep alive in the barren wastes. Some spectacular photography, gripping scenes. (Dir: Nicholas Ray, 110 mins.)

Savage Island (U.S.-Italy-Spain, 1984)½ Linda Blair, Ajita Wilson, Christina Lai, Anthony Steffen. What "director" Beardsley has done here is to take a sleazy women's prison camp flick (originally titled *Escape from Hell*), chop out about 35 minutes, tack on a frame story with Blair as an escapee, and rerelease it to an audience that probably can't tell the difference between these things anyway. Featuring the usual busty women in flimsy prison togs that just can't seem to stay on. (Dirs: Edward Muller, Nicholas Beardsley, 79 mins.)†

Savage Is Loose, The (1974)½ George C. Scott, Trish Van Devere, John David Carson. Embarrassing effort. Playing a scientist, Scott is stranded on a desert island with his wife and their young son. The action centers on the boy's growing up without a proper mate over whom to vent his lust. One wit referred to this as the "Swiss Family Oedipus." (Dir: George C. Scott, 114 mins.)†

Savage Messiah, The (Great Britain, 1972)*** Dorothy Tutin, Scott Antony, Helen Mirren, Lindsay Kemp, Peter Vaughan. Director Ken Russell's flamboyant style is well suited to this fervid retelling of the intense relationship between painter-sculptor Henri Gaudier and a woman twenty years his senior. An exemplary cast conveys the overheated atmosphere Russell relishes. (100 mins.)

Savage Mutiny (1953)* Johnny Weissmuller, Angela Stevens. Holy nuclear paranoia! Jungle Jim's got to clear off an entire island because of impending tests for an atomic bomb. (Dir: Spencer Bennet, 73 mins.)

Savage Pampas (Spain, 1968)* Robert Taylor, Ron Randell. Dull, western set in Argentina during the late 1800s. Taylor portrays an army officer who tries to keep his military unit intact after interference from a band of Argentinian renegades. (Dir: Hugo Fregonese, 100 mins.)

Savage Run—See: **Run, Simon, Run**

Savages (1972)** Sam Waterston, Kathleen Widdoes, Susan Blakely. Misconceived social satire uses a decadent garden party as a metaphor for the decline of Western civilization. (Dir: James Ivory, 108 mins.)†

Savages (MTV 1974)**½ Andy Griffith, Sam Bottoms, Noah Beery. Griffith plays a New York lawyer who goes to a desert area to hunt bighorn sheep with guide Bottoms. After Griffith kills an old prospector and pretends it was an animal, he and Sam begin a cat-and-mouse game of life and death in the desert. Suspenseful in parts. (Dir: Lee H. Katzin, 72 mins.)†

Savage Seven, The (1968)** Robert Walker, Jr., Larry Bishop, Joanna Frank, John Garwood, Adam Roarke, Duane Eddy, John (Bud) Cardos, Beach Dickerson, Gary Littlejohn, Penny Marshall. One of the better AIP motorcycle movies, with bikers pitted against Indians by the corrupt businessmen who control a shanty town. Produced by Dick Clark and photographed by Laszlo Kovacs. (Dir: Richard Rush, 96 mins.)†

Savage Sisters (1973)* Gloria Hendry, Cheri Caffaro, Rosanna Ortiz, John Ashley, Sid Haig, Eddie Garcia. Cruddy action pic about a money-grubber who goes after a cool million in American greenbacks with the help of two guerrilla cuties and a retired whore. Savage silliness. (Dir: Eddie Romero, 89 mins.)

Savage Streets (1984)** Linda Blair, John Vernon, Johnny Venocur. After her deaf-mute sister is raped and a pregnant friend is tossed off a bridge, Blair decides to play Charles Bronson and get even. (Dir: Danny Steinmann, 93 mins.)†

Savage Wilderness—See: **Last Frontier, The**

Savannah Smiles (1983)**½ Mark Miller, Donovan Scott, Chris Robinson, Michael Parks, Bridgette Anderson, Peter Graves. Appealing sentimental yarn. Savannah, a neglected rich moppet, runs away from her mansion, right into the hands of two bungling ex-cons. They hold her for a reward until they grow to love her. (Dir: Pierre De Moro, 105 mins.)†

Save the Tiger (1973)*** Jack Lemmon, Jack Gilford, Patricia Smith, Laurie Heineman. Lemmon gives an Oscar-winning performance as a garment manufacturer at the end of his tether. Remarkable acting by Gilford as Lemmon's partner. (Dir: John G. Avildsen, 99 mins.)†

Saving Grace (1986)* Tom Conti, Giancarlo Giannini, Fernando Rey, Erland Josephson, Edward James Olmos. A mildewed conceit about a fictitious pope who takes a Roman holiday and leaves the Vatican to mingle with his flock. Conti gives a mannered performance; there are no saving graces here. (Dir: Robert Young, 112 mins.)†

Sawdust and Tinsel (Sweden, 1953)*** Harriet Andersson, Ake Groenberg, Hasse Ekman. Writer-director Ingmar Bergman's 18th film is set in the eerie world of a traveling circus caravan. (95 mins.)†

Saxon Charm, The (1948)*** Robert Montgomery, Audrey Totter, Susan Hayward, John Payne. Montgomery is good in this character study of a vicious Broadway producer. Story is at times hard to believe, but sustains interest throughout. (Dir: Claude Binyon, 88 mins.)

Saxophone Colossus (1987)**½ This documentary tribute to jazzman Sonny Rollins consists mostly of music, mixed with little snatches of interviews. Jazz aficionados will be thrilled by the musical segments, but the film fails to develop any personal perspective on the man. (Dir: Robert Mugge, 101 mins.)†

Say Amen, Somebody (1983)**** Thomas Dorsey, Willie Mae Ford, "Mother" Smith, Zella Jackson Price, the Barrett Sisters, the O'Neal Twins. Rousing, joyous documentary on the history and art of gospel music. Don't tap your toes, we dare you. (Dir: George T. Nierenberg, 100 mins.)†

Say Anything... (1989)** John Cusack, Ione Skye, John Mahoney, Joan Cusack. Ordinary high school student John Cusack falls in love with class brain Skye, whose father has higher hopes for her. Do you really *need* to see another teen dating-angst movie? A heartfelt effort, but one containing nothing that hasn't already been done to death. (Dir: Cameron Crowe, 93 mins.)†

Say Goodbye, Maggie Cole (MTV 1972)**½ Susan Hayward, Darren McGavin. Strong performances by Hayward and McGavin give this one about doctors working in a slum area a boost. It's a tearjerker, with Hayward playing a recently widowed doctor who goes back into practice with McGavin, a gruff but dedicated ghetto G. P. (Dir: Jud Taylor, 73 mins.)†

Say Hello to Yesterday (Great Britain, 1970)**½ Leonard Whiting, Jean Simmons, Evelyn Laye. Modest, simply constructed romance of a suburban housewife, Simmons, and a young mod, played with exuberance by Whiting. They meet and part within the space of her ten-hour trip to London. A twist on *Brief Encounter.* (Dir: Alvin Rakoff, 92 mins.)†

Sayonara (1957)** Marlon Brando, Miyoshi Umeki, Red Buttons, James Garner, Ricardo Montalbán. Long, vulgar, obvious soap opera. The story involves two parallel romances in occupation Japan, and none of the tears are

915

earned. From a James Michener novel. (Dir: Joshua Logan, 147 mins.)†

Say One for Me (1959)** Bing Crosby, Debbie Reynolds, Robert Wagner. Bing back in priestly togs again, but this time he's almost defeated by a weak plot about a show business parish, a chorus girl, and a night club manager with designs on her, all culminating in the Big Benefit Show. (Dir: Frank Tashlin, 119 mins.)

Say Yes (1986)* Jonathan Winters, Art Hindle, Logan Ramsey, Lissa Layng. Horrendous comedy about a man who will collect a bundle if he weds within twenty-four hours. Stupid waste of Winters, whose part was reportedly inserted into the film in order to save it. He doesn't. (Dir: Larry Yust, 88 mins.)†

Scalawag (1973)** Kirk Douglas, Mark Lester, Neville Brand, Lesley-Anne Down. Pirate film with all the clichés on board. Douglas directed and stars as a bearded peg-leg pirate. Best appreciated by 10-year-olds who adore comic books. (93 mins.)

Scalawag Bunch, The (Italy, 1975)** Mark Damon, Louis Davila, Silvia Dionisio. Sir Henry of Nottingham bands together a group of forest dwellers, takes the name Robin Hood, and sets about turning the people of the kingdom against usurper Prince John. Cheaply made but entertaining adaptation. (Dir: George Ferron, 103 mins.)

Scalpel (1976)**½ Robert Lansing, Judith Chapman, Arlen Dean Snyder. Pretty good, involved Georgia-made thriller. Plastic surgeon Lansing makes over the face of go-go dancer Chapman to resemble his missing daughter so that he can get his hands on the latter's inheritance. A twist ending. (Dir: John Grissmer, 95 mins.)†

Scalphunters, The (1968)*** Burt Lancaster, Ossie Davis, Shelley Winters, Telly Savalas. Entertaining western which mixes excitement with an ample amount of comedy. Lancaster is at his athletic and charming best as a fur trapper whose pelts are stolen. Enter Davis as an educated runaway slave and the plot thickens. (Dir: Sydney Pollack, 102 mins.)

Scalplock (MTV 1966)*½ Dale Robertson, Diana Hyland, Robert Random, Sandra Smith, Lloyd Bochner, James Doohan, Herbert Voland. Undistinguished western about a gambler who wins a failing railroad in a poker game and tries to rebuild it. Pilot for the series *Iron Horse*. (Dir: James Goldstone, 100 mins.)

Scandal (Japan, 1950)*** Toshiro Mifune, Yoshiko Yamaguchi, Takashi Shimura. Early Akira Kurosawa film is a stirring and proud drama about personal honor. It tells the story of a young man and

916

woman, both members of the artistic community, who are libeled by a scandalous magazine article and prepare to sue the offenders. (105 mins.)

Scandal (Great Britain, 1989)*** John Hurt, Joanne Whalley-Kilmer, Bridget Fonda, Ian McKellen, Roland Gift, Jeroen Krabbé. The story of Britain's most infamous scandal, the Profumo Affair, which toppled the government when it was discovered that a cabinet minister shared a lover with a Soviet attaché. A well-written, well-acted drama that may require a little hard attention from Yanks unfamiliar with the story. Released to U.S. theaters in an R-rated 105 min. version; both it and the unrated version are on video. (Dir: Michael Caton-Jones, 114 mins.)†

Scandal at Scourie (1953)**½ Greer Garson, Walter Pidgeon. The stars of this costume drama are more than adequate but the script is steeped in sentiment as it recounts the problems of a Canadian couple in adopting an orphan. (Dir: Jean Negulesco, 89 mins.)

Scandal in a Small Town (MTV 1988)*½ Raquel Welch, Christa Denton, Frances Lee McCain, Ronny Cox. The morals of a local barmaid (Welch), not her charge of anti-Semitism against a local teacher, become the central issue here, right down to the amusing scene where a prosecuting attorney presents a list of various men Raquel has dallied with in high school. (Dir: Anthony Page, 96 mins.)†

Scandal in Paris, A (1946)*** George Sanders, Signe Hasso, Akim Tamiroff. The story of Vidocq, the thief and blackguard who cleverly talks his way into becoming Prefect of Police. Tasty costume melodrama intelligently directed, well written and acted. (Dir: Douglas Sirk, 99 mins.) AKA: **Thieves' Holiday.**

Scandalous (1984)* John Gielgud, Robert Hays, Pamela Stephenson. A reporter trying to solve a murder is blackmailed and then framed for the murder. Gielgud fans may enjoy seeing him don disguises, but there's no disguising the failure of this comedy. (Dir: Rob Cohen, 94 mins.)†

Scandalous Adventures of Buraikan (Japan, 1970)*** Tatsuya Nakadai, Tetsuro Tamba, Shima Iwashita, Suisen Ichikawa, Shoichi Ozawa. Erotic black comedy, stunningly presented, about three people who meet in the red-light district of 1842 Tokyo and compare their dreams and plan challenges to the society and authorities that they feel oppress them. (Dir: Masahiro Shinoda, 104 mins.)

Scandal Sheet (1931)*** George Bancroft, Clive Brook, Kay Francis, Gilbert Emery, Lucien Littlefield, Regis Toomey. Powerful newspaper drama, with a ruthless editor who specializes in discrediting people finding himself involved in a deadly scandal. Rigorous, violent, and very capably done. (Dir: John Cromwell, 77 mins.)

Scandal Sheet (1952)**½ Broderick Crawford, Donna Reed, John Derek. Overdone newspaper yarn about a couple of reporters who crack a murder case which involves their editor-friend. Energetically played. (Dir: Phil Karlson, 82 mins.)

Scandal Sheet (MTV 1985)*** Burt Lancaster, Robert Urich, Lauren Hutton, Pamela Reed. Lancaster stars as an unscrupulous editor of a "gossip rag" called *Inside World*. Reed is the honest reporter sucked into the sleazy publication, while Urich and Hutton play the Hollywood couple with a secret that could ruin them if uncovered. Nicely cynical, and refreshingly free of happy endings. (Dir: David Lowell Rich, 104 mins.)

Scandal Street (1938)**½ Lew Ayres, Louise Campbell, Roscoe Karns, Porter Hall, Virginia Weidler, Cecil Cunningham, Edgar Kennedy. Dissection of the suspicion and malice lurking beneath the surface of small-town America, with a new librarian in town the subject of harmful gossip. Unusual attempt to present a different viewpoint. (Dir: James Hogan, 62 mins.)

Scanners (Canada, 1981)*** Jennifer O'Neill, Stephen Lack, Patrick McGoohan. A small group of social misfits are imbued with telepathic powers. The logic of this isn't sufficiently consistent to push this into classic status, but the film is loaded with good ideas (maybe too many), and the execution is intermittently powerful. Director David Cronenberg's technical faculties aren't always up to the forcefulness of his conceptions. (102 mins.)†

Scapegoat, The (Great Britain, 1959)**½ Alec Guinness, Bette Davis, Nicole Maurey. Uneven comedy-drama about an English schoolteacher whose exact double, a French nobleman, offers him his family and responsibilities. From the novel by Daphne Du Maurier. (Dir: Robert Hamer, 92 mins.)

Scar, The (1948)*** Paul Henreid, Joan Bennett. A gangster gets a new face, and a girl makes a new personality to go along with it, but too late, for he must pay the penalty. Suspenseful melodrama. AKA: **Hollow Triumph**. (Dir: Steve Sekely, 83 mins.)†

Scaramouche (1952)*** Stewart Granger, Eleanor Parker, Janet Leigh, Mel Ferrer. Exciting and colorful adventure drama set in 18th-century France. Granger handsomely fits the role of the swashbuckling and romancing hero. (Dir: George Sidney, 118 mins.)†

Scarecrow (1973)**½ Gene Hackman, Al Pacino, Dorothy Tristan, Ann Wedgeworth. Hackman and Pacino are superb as a pair of drifter-losers who team up to travel from California to Philadelphia, where Hackman plans to open up a car wash. A kind of Seventies version of Steinbeck's *Of Mice and Men*. Marred by a poor climax. (Dir: Jerry Schatzberg, 104 mins.)†

Scarecrow in a Garden of Cucumbers (1972)* Holly Woodlawn, Tally Brown, Suzanne Skillen. Low-low-budget theatrical satire, with songs, about a small-town girl in the Big Apple. The girl is played by transvestite Woodlawn, who's the only reason to sit through this. (Dir: Robert J. Kaplan, 82 mins.)

Scared Stiff (1945)**½ Jack Haley, Barton MacLane, Veda Ann Borg, George E. Stone, Ann Savage, Arthur Aylesworth. Amusing mystery-comedy with nosy reporter Haley, searching for some important chess pieces, trapped in a haunted house. Pleasant enough diversion for a war-weary nation. AKA: **Treasure of Fear**. (Dir: Frank McDonald, 65 mins.)

Scared Stiff (1953)*** Dean Martin, Jerry Lewis, Lizabeth Scott, Dorothy Malone, Carmen Miranda. Singer and his busboy friend flee from a murder charge and land on a mysterious island to help an heiress in distress. Remake of Bob Hope's *The Ghost Breakers* works well with Dean and Jerry, blends laughs and chills expertly. (Dir: George Marshall, 108 mins.)†

Scared Straight! Another Story (MTV 1980)*** Stan Shaw, Don Fullilove, Randy Brooks. Fictional, often frightening follow-up to the award-winning documentary in which troublemaking kids visit a prison to be scared about life behind bars. (Dir: Richard Michaels, 104 mins.)

Scared to Death (1947)** Bela Lugosi, Douglas Fowley, Joyce Compton, George Zucco, Nat Pendleton. A low-budget thriller that benefits from Bela's piercing authority. The pieces of a puzzling murder are revealed to us one at a time in this fright-nighter narrated by a dead woman who may have been . . . "SCARED TO DEATH!" Your only chance to see Lugosi in color, for what it's worth. (Dir: Christy Cabanne, 65 mins.)†

Scarf, The (1951)**½ John Ireland, Mercedes McCambridge, Emlyn Williams. An innocent man, tied to a murder by circumstantial evidence, he must find the real killer in order to clear himself.

Tense low-budget thriller. (Dir: E. A. Dupont, 93 mins.)

Scarface (1983)** Al Pacino, Michelle Pfeiffer, Steven Bauer, Mary Elizabeth Mastrantonio, Robert Loggia, F. Murray Abraham. As the unscrupulous Cuban immigrant who arrives in the U.S. as boat person but becomes a drug kingpin, Pacino delivers a juicy, almost caricatured performance. Filled with melodramatic excesses, the movie is exciting on a pulp magazine level but still feels dragged out despite all the pumped-up violence. (Dir: Brian DePalma, 170 mins.)†

Scarface Mob, The (1962)**½ Robert Stack, Keenan Wynn, Neville Brand. Eliot Ness and a special force of lawmen band into "The Untouchables," out to get the goods on Al Capone and his mob. Originally the opening installments in the TV series, this crime drama still looks pretty good. (Dir: Phil Karlson, 96 mins.)†

Scarface: The Shame of the Nation (1932) **** Paul Muni, Ann Dvorak, Boris Karloff. Dark, exhilaratingly violent work was almost too potent for its time. It holds up startlingly well in ours. Muni gives his best performance as the simian hood Tony Camonte, whose one redeeming virtue is that he loves his sister a lot. Brilliantly made underworld melodrama. AKA: **The Shame of the Nation.** (Dir: Howard Hawks, 99 mins.)†

Scarlet and the Black, The (MTV 1983)**½ Gregory Peck, Christopher Plummer, John Gielgud, Raf Vallone, Ken Colley. Peck becomes the Scarlet Pimpernel of the Vatican, and outwits Nazis, circa 1943, by harboring refugees from concentration camps. A real-life drama filled with intrigue, disguises, and derring-do. (Dir: Jerry London, 156 mins.)†

Scarlet Angel (1952)**½ Rock Hudson, Yvonne De Carlo, Amanda Blake. Adventure yarn with Rock playing a sea captain who is constantly being used by vixen Yvonne. (Dir: Sidney Salkow, 81 mins.)

Scarlet Claw, The (1944)*** Basil Rathbone, Nigel Bruce, Arthur Hohl. Of the modernized Sherlock Holmes films, this probably is the most satisfyingly authentic. The setting is the Canadian moors and the mood is patriotic. (Dir: Roy William Neill, 74 mins.)†

Scarlet Clue, The (1945)**½ Sidney Toler, Mantan Moreland, Ben Carter. Fairly suspenseful Chan entry about a labyrinthine plot to lift radar plans from the government. (Dir: Phil Rosen, 65 mins.)

Scarlet Coat, The (1955)** Cornel Wilde, Michael Wilding, Anne Francis, George Sanders. Heavy-handed historical costume drama about the American Revolution. (Dir: John Sturges, 101 mins.)

Scarlet Dawn (1932)**½ Douglas Fairbanks, Jr., Nancy Carroll, Lilyan Tashman, Guy Kibbee, Sheila Terry. Stylish but sluggish love story set during the Russian Revolution. An aristocrat in exile falls for a servant girl in this beautifully designed romance. (Dir: William Dieterle, 76 mins.)

Scarlet Empress, The (1934)**** Marlene Dietrich, John Lodge, Sam Jaffe, Louise Dresser. One of director Josef von Sternberg's greatest films, with a rich Dietrich performance as Catherine the Great. Literally overspilling its frame with bric-a-brac and veils, the film avoids political content as it descends into a world of mystery and sensuality. (110 mins.)

Scarlet Hour, The (1956)** Tom Tryon, Jody Lawrence, Carol Ohmart, Elaine Stritch, E. G. Marshall. Waste of a good cast in an uninvolving, poorly written thriller about a man who reaches his breaking point and plots to kill his wife. (Dir: Michael Curtiz, 95 mins.)

Scarlet Letter, The (1926)**** Lillian Gish, Lars Hanson, Henry B. Walthall, Karl Dane. Atmospheric rendering of the Nathaniel Hawthorne classic about Hester Prynne, who wore the mark of the Adulteress rather than reveal the identity of the man who impregnated her. Atmospheric and moving, with exemplary performances and direction making this the best of several versions of this tale. (Dir: Victor Seastrom [Sjostrom], 80 mins.)

Scarlet Letter, The (1934)* Colleen Moore, Hardie Albright, Henry B. Walthall, William Farnum, Alan Hale, Cora Sue Collins. Hopelessly dated, static rendering of Hawthorne's classic tale of repression and adultery in early New England. Comic relief is improbably added. (Dir: Robert G. Vignola, 70 mins.)†

Scarlet Letter, The (West Germany-Spain, 1973)**½ Senta Berger, Hans Christian Blech, Lou Castel. Wim Winders's version of the classic tale is good enough, but his fans will be disappointed to see that it bears little of his distinctive stamp. Photographed by Robby Muller. (94 mins.)†

Scarlet Pimpernel, The (Great Britain, 1934)*** Leslie Howard, Merle Oberon, Joan Gardner, Raymond Massey, Nigel Bruce. Solid swashbuckling entertainment with Howard the impeccably dressed and impossibly noble embodiment of the heroic freedom fighter. The definitive *Pimpernel;* polished entertainment. (Dir: Harold Young, 95 mins.)†

Scarlet Pimpernel, The (MTV 1982)*** Anthony Andrews, Jane Seymour, Ian McKellen. The gallant hero is back to swash his share of buckles in this sumptuous refilming of the tale of derring-do circa the French Revolution. (Dir: Clive Donner, 150 mins.)†

Scarlet Street (1945)***½ Edward G. Robinson, Joan Bennett, Dan Duryea, Margaret Lindsay, Rosalind Ivan. Fritz Lang's darkest American film is a twisted moral tale that benefits from Robinson's fine performance as a company man who is driven to embezzlement as a result of his passion for a scheming vixen (Bennett). Lang's impeccable shadowed visions set this apart from subsequent tales of seduction by a femme fatale. (98 mins.)†

Scarlett O'Hara War, The (MTV 1980)*** Tony Curtis, Sharon Gless, Harold Gould, Bill Macy, Morgan Brittany, George Furth. Taken from the "Moviola" miniseries, this polished production revolves about the legendary search for the actress to play Margaret Mitchell's unsinkable heroine. A juicy melodrama, entertainingly crammed with equal parts history, gossip, and star turns. (Dir: John Erman, 105 mins.)

Scarred (1984)** Jennifer Mayo, Jackie Berryman, David Dean. Gritty but unconvincing drama about a teenage prostitute who tries to better her life. AKA: Street Love. (Dir: RoseMarie Turko, 85 mins.)†

Scars of Dracula, The (Great Britain, 1970)* Christopher Lee, Denis Waterman, Jenny Hanley. Dracula horrors pepped up with sex, violence and lots of gore . . . *not* for the kids. (Dir: Roy Ward Baker, 94 mins.)†

Scavenger Hunt (1979)*½ Richard Benjamin, James Coco, Scatman Crothers, Ruth Gordon, Cloris Leachman, Vincent Price, Richard Masur, Cleavon Little, Roddy McDowall, Tony Randall, Willie Aames. The premise—would-be heirs to a fortune are sent out on a scavenger hunt—peters out long before the final scene. (Dir: Michael Schultz, 104 mins.)†

Scavengers (1987)* Kenneth Gilman, Brenda Bakke. Bird-watcher becomes entangled in a KGB-CIA operation. An adventure that doesn't know if it wants to be serious or parody, though it's lousy as either. (Dir: Duncan McLachlan, 94 mins.)†

Scavengers, The (1959)**½ Vince Edwards, Carol Ohmart. In his pre-Ben Casey days, Edwards gets mixed up with shady women and shadier killers in the Orient. (Dir: John Cromwell, 79 mins.)

Scene of the Crime (1949)*** Van Johnson, Gloria De Haven, Tom Drake, Arlene Dahl, Leon Ames, John McIntire. Dynamic, dark film about a cop who quits the force when his partner is killed; when his replacement is also slain, he returns to seek vengeance. Johnson is excellent in this taut, realistic thriller. (Dir: Roy Rowland, 94 mins.)

Scene of the Crime (France, 1986)**½ Catherine Deneuve, Danielle Darrieux, Wadeck Stanczak, Nicolas Giraudi, Victor Lanoux. Two escaped convicts transform the lives of a mother and son: to the mother (Deneuve), one convict brings a reawakening of her passionate impulses; to the son, a glimpse at his own mortality, when he is saved from an attack by the intercession of the same noble jailbird (Stanczak). Occasional outbursts of stylish flair from director André Téchine are the bright spots of this subdued character study. (90 mins.)†

Scenes From a Mall (1991)** Bette Midler, Woody Allen, Bill Irwin, Daren Firestone, Rebecca Nickels, Paul Mazursky. A middle-aged married couple (Midler and Allen) come clean with each other about their infidelities while spending a day shopping at a mega-mall. Hit-and-miss comedy is a single sketch idea badly stretched to the full-length breaking point. Something's seriously wrong with a movie in which a mime gets most of the laughs and a surfboard gets most of the attention. (Dir: Paul Mazursky, 87 mins.)†

Scenes From a Marriage (Sweden, 1973)**** Liv Ullmann, Erland Josephson, Bibi Andersson. Ingmar Bergman's stunning, telescopic examination of a crumbling marriage, originally made as six 50-minute programs for Swedish TV. This superb restructuring of that footage dissects different events, quarrels, lovemaking, misunderstandings, etc., over more than ten years of marriage, divorce and a new, more mature relationship. Ullmann is, to no one's surprise, astonishing and Josephson is nearly as remarkable. (168 mins.)†

Scenes From a Murder (Italy, 1972)** Telly Savalas, Anne Heywood, Giorgio Piazza, Rossella Falk. Savalas plays a murderer involved in a cat-and-mouse chase after a beautiful actress. (Dir: Alberto DeMartino, 90 mins.)†

Scenes From the Class Struggle In Beverly Hills (1989)*** Jacqueline Bisset, Ray Sharkey, Robert Beltran, Ed Begley, Jr., Mary Woronov, Wallace Shawn. Generally funny sex farce, set in a Beverly Hills mansion filled with hedonistic characters. The plot hinge is a bet between two gardeners as to which of them can be the first to seduce the other's employer. (Dir: Paul Bartel, 102 mins.)†

Scent of a Woman (Italy, 1975)*** Vittorio Gassman, Agostina Belli, Alessandro Momo. Gassman scores a triumph in this Italian comedy-drama of a blind rogue forced to pursue his quarry through his other senses. Bravura acting reigns over sense, since the film's values are questionable. (Dir: Dino Risi, 103 mins.)

Scent of Mystery (1960)** Denholm Elliott, Peter Lorre, Beverly Bentley. Discovering that a young American heiress is about to be murdered, an Englishman and a sour-visaged cab driver set about to save her, sight unseen. Released in theaters with an accompanying track of scents, such as perfume and tobacco odors, which were triggered mechanically to serve as clues to the mystery. (Dir: Jack Cardiff, 125 mins.)

Schatten—See: **Warning Shadows**

Schizo (Great Britain, 1977)* Lynne Frederick, John Leyton, Stephanie Beacham, John Fraser. Is skating star Frederick a split personality who killed her mother years ago? Is someone trying to drive her insane? Are we supposed to care? (Dir: Pete Walker, 109 mins.)†

Schizoid (1980)* Klaus Kinski, Mariana Hill, Craig Wasson, Donna Wilkes. Convoluted psycho-babble thriller about a woman who seeks help after dreaming of a murder that then occurs. (Dir: David Paulsen, 91 mins.)†

Schlock (1973)**½ John Landis, Saul Kahan, Joseph Piantadosi. A missing link runs amok and is responsible for a series of "banana killings." Along the way, parodies of horror films add up to a few genuine laughs. AKA: **The Banana Monster**. (Dir: John Landis, 80 mins.)†

School Daze (1988)*** Larry Fishburne, Giancarlo Esposito, Tisha Campbell, Kyme, Joe Seneca, Ossie Davis, Spike Lee. Filmmaker-actor Lee tries to single-handedly make up for the recent dearth of black cinema with this combination of comedy, music, and a lesson on racial identity. What is lacking in discipline is made up for in energy. The thumbnail plot line concerns the rift between the "wannabees" (blacks who try to lose their blackness) and "jigaboos" (blacks who have a sense of their own identity) at an all-black college. (Dir: Spike Lee, 120 mins.)†

School for Love (France, 1955)*½ Brigitte Bardot, Jean Marais. Two sisters at a conservatory fall for the same music teacher. Trite little love story. (Dir: Yves Allegret, 72 mins.)

School for Scoundrels (Great Britain, 1960)*** Ian Carmichael, Alastair Sim, Terry-Thomas. Innocent young man joins a school with an unusual course in successmanship. Enjoyable comedy has some pointed laughs, a cast of capable performers. (Dir: Robert Hamer, 94 mins.)

School for Sex (Great Britain, 1969)*½ Derek Aylward, Rose Alba, Hugh Latimer, Nosher Powell. Burned in a divorce settlement, Aylward opens an institute to teach young women how to marry for money. More slapstick than satire. (Dir: Pete Walker, 80 mins.)†

School Spirit (1985)½ Tom Nolan, Elizabeth Foxx, Roberta Collins, John Finnegan, Larry Linville. High school student killed in an accident returns to Earth to lose his virginity before going to the Great Beyond. Even hard-core porn is more respectable than this sniggering garbage. (Dir: Alan Holleb, 90 mins.)†

School that Ate My Brain, The—See: **Zombie High**

Scorchy (1976)*½ Connie Stevens, Cesare Danova, William Smith, Joyce Jameson. A honkysploitation movie—all the cheaply produced thrills and nonstop action of a Pam Grier movie, only perky, white-bread Stevens is in the lead—she's in hot pursuit of a drug dealer sneaking heroin around in a statue. (Dir: Howard Avedis, 99 mins.)†

Score (U.S.-Yugoslavia, 1973)**½ Gerald Grant, Claire Wilbur, Calvin Culver, Lynn Lowry. Sex farce for mainstream audiences by director Radley Metzger, the master of glossy soft-core erotica in the '60s, about two couples who get together for group sex only to have the guys and girls opting for same-sex scenarios. (90 mins.)†

Scorned and Swindled (MTV 1984)*** Tuesday Weld, Keith Carradine, Peter Coyote, Sheree North, Fionnula Flanagan. Weld plays a lonely antiques dealer who's suckered into marriage only to find herself without a dime. When another victim (Carradine) joins forces with her, the swindled duo race cross country to hunt down their betrayer. A persuasive slice of seedy Americana that's based on a true incident. (Dir: Paul Wendkos, 104 mins.)

Scorpio (1973)**½ Burt Lancaster, Alain Delon, Paul Scofield, J. D. Cannon, John Colicos. Adequate spy thriller. Lancaster, stoic and stolid, is the agent who is marked for extinction by fellow agent Scorpio (Delon), and the cat-and-mouse chase is on. (Dir: Michael Winner, 114 mins.)

Scorpio Letters, The (MTV 1967)* Alex Cord, Shirley Eaton. Dull, obscure, and listless thriller about two agents hired by the British to uncover a blackmailing ring. (Dir: Richard Thorpe, 98 mins.)

Scorpion (1986)* Tommy Tulleners, Don Murray, Robert Logan, Allen Williams. As a government agent protecting an informant, ex-karate champ Tulleners lacks charisma, and hardly even gets to show off his martial arts skills. (Dir: William Riead, 98 mins.)†

Scorpion Woman, The (Austria, 1990)** Angelica Domrose, Fritz Hammel, Peter Andorai, Heinz Weixelbraun, Michael Schindelbeck. Pleasant, but uninvolving, comedy-melodrama, with a surprise ending that isn't worth waiting for. A woman judge's life turns upside down after she takes a young male lover who turns out to be bisexual. (Dir: Susanne Zanke, 95 mins.)†

Scotland Yard Inspector (Great Britain, 1952)** Cesar Romero, Lois Maxwell, Bernadette O'Farrell. British-made thriller has Romero tracking down his brother's murderer; unexciting low-budget drama. (Dir: Sam Newfield, 73 mins.)

Scotland Yard Investigator (Great Britain, 1945)**½ C. Aubrey Smith, Erich von Stroheim, Stephanie Bachelor, Forrester Harvey. Good low-budget mystery, supported by a strong cast, about the Scotland Yard detective Smith's efforts to recover the Mona Lisa from thief von Stroheim. These two are a show in themselves. (Dir: George Blair, 68 mins.)

Scott Free (MTV 1976)*½ Michael Brandon, Susan St. James, Michael Lerner. The trials of a professional gambler who wins a piece of desert land regarded by Indians as a sacred burial ground. (Dir: William Wiard, 72 mins.)

Scott Joplin (1977)**½ Billy Dee Williams, Art Carney, Clifton Davis. Williams has charisma to spare in this standard bio of legendary ragtime composer Scott Joplin. (Dir: Jeremy Paul Kagan, 96 mins.)

Scott of the Antarctic (Great Britain, 1948)**½ John Mills, Derek Bond, Kenneth More, Christopher Lee. An account of the ill-fated British expedition to the South Pole, with stunning photographic effects, authentic narrative, but as drama it's curiously remote, only occasionally affecting. (Dir: Charles Frend, 110 mins.)†

Scoundrel, The (1935)**½ Noel Coward, Stanley Ridges, Julie Haydon, Martha Sleeper, Eduardo Ciannelli, Alexander Wolcott, Lionel Stander. Strange melodrama that aspires to high sophistication and sometimes succeeds. When a wastrel writer with a penchant for using people dies, his spirit comes back to redeem himself. (Dirs: Ben Hecht, Charles MacArthur, 78 mins.)

Scout's Honor (MTV 1980)**½ Gary Coleman, Katherine Helmond, Pat O'Brien, Wilfred Hyde-White, Harry Morgan. Friendly, entertaining story stars Coleman as an orphan who yearns to be a Cub Scout. The parents of the Scouts are all played by former child TV stars: Jay ("Dennis the Menace") North, Lauren ("Father Knows Best") Chapin, Angela ("Make Room for Daddy")

Cartwright, and Paul ("Donna Reed Show") Petersen. (Dir: Henry Levin, 104 mins.)

Scream and Scream Again (Great Britain, 1970)*** Vincent Price, Christopher Lee, Peter Cushing. An above-average, somewhat more sophisticated mad-scientist effort revolving around a series of psychotic murders in England. (Dir: Gordon Hessler, 94 mins.)†

Scream, Baby, Scream—See: **Nightmare House**

Scream, Blacula, Scream (1973)* William Marshall, Pam Grier, Don Mitchell. A laughable sequel to *Blacula*, the horror film about a modern-day vampire who was an actual African prince before a white vampire cursed him in a previous century. (Dir: Bob Kelljan, 95 mins.)†

Scream Dream (1989)* Melissa Moore, Nikki Riggins, Carol Carr, Jesse Raye. Singer Carr, fired from the rock band she was working in, uses her powers of witchcraft to gain revenge. Shot-on-video sleaze, heavy on gore and nudity. (Dir: Donald Farmer, 69 mins.)†

Screamers (Italy-U.S., 1981)½ Barbara Bach, Joseph Cotten, Mel Ferrer, Cameron Mitchell. Producer Roger Corman added twelve minutes of slasher footage to the beginning of an Italian-made adventure. Wayfarers land on an island inhabited by a greedy treasure hunter and a scientist who treats the ocean as his personal fish tank. (Dir: Sergio Martino, 83 mins.)†

Scream for Help (1986)½ David Brooks, Rachael Kelly, Marie Masters. Deliriously funny, overwrought suspense film about an overly imaginative girl who believes her adulterous stepfather is planning to eliminate her mom. (Dir: Michael Winner, 90 mins.)†

Screaming Eagles (1956)** Tom Tryon, Jan Merlin, Martin Milner, Alvy Moore. Typical wartime melodrama about the interconnected lives of several people, leading up to D-Day. There was no excitement left in the formula by this time. (Dir: Charles Haas, 81 mins.)

Screaming Mimi (1958)**½ Anita Ekberg, Phil Carey, Gypsy Rose Lee, Harry Townes, Linda Cherney. Stripper comes under the influence of a possessive psychiatrist after she is attacked by a serial killer. Weird low-budget thriller has a cult following; it's fairly bizarre. (Dir: Gerd Oswald, 79 mins.)

Screaming Skull, The (1958)*½ John Hudson, Peggy Webber, Tom Johnson, Russ Conway. Man tries to drive his wife, recuperating from a nervous breakdown, over the edge by arranging scary happenings in his spooky house. Atmospheric but overly familiar. (Dir: Alex Nicol, 68 mins.)†

Screaming Woman, The (MTV 1972)***

921

Olivia de Havilland, Joseph Cotten, Walter Pidgeon. De Havilland, as a wealthy lady recovering from a nervous breakdown, sees a woman buried alive, but nobody believes her. Based on Ray Bradbury's short story. (Dir: Jack Smight, 73 mins.)

Scream of Fear (Great Britain, 1961)*** Susan Strasberg, Ronald Lewis, Ann Todd. Girl poses as her paralyzed friend to investigate what has happened to her father, nearly loses her life in finding out. Sharply directed thriller. AKA: *Taste of Fear.* (Dir: Seth Holt, 81 mins.)†

Scream of the Wolf (MTV 1972)**½ Peter Graves, Clint Walker, Jo Ann Pflug, Philip Carey, Don Megowan. A retired hunter takes up his weapons once again to pursue a wolf (or is it a wolf-like creature?) responsible for some not-so-clean kills. Script by Richard Matheson. (Dir: Dan Curtis, 72 mins.)

Scream, Pretty Peggy (MTV 1973)**½ Bette Davis, Ted Bessell, Sian Barbara Allen. An innocent college student plays part-time housekeeper for Bette's weird family in their creepy mansion. (Dir: Gordon Hessler, 74 mins.)

Screen Test (1986)* Michael Allan Brown, Monique Gabrielle, Paul Lueken, David Simpatico, Michelle Bauer. Raunch-out comedy about some perpetually tumescent undergrads who pretend to be porn producers in order to get would-be stars to "audition" for them. (Dir: Sam Auster, 84 mins.)†

Screwball Academy (Canada, 1987)* Colleen Camp, Ken Welsh, Christine Cattell. Wan comedy about a peaceful town turned upside down by the arrival of a movie crew. Director "Reuben Rose" is actually director John Blanchard of "SCTV," showing none of that show's style. (90 mins.)†

Screwballs (1983)½ Peter Keleghan, Lynda Speciale, Alan Daveau, Kent Deuters, Linda Shayne, Raven De La Croix. Bottom-of-the-barrel high school sex comedy about some wacky guys scheming to seduce the class virgin, "Purity Busch." The rest of this stupid movie is even less subtle; amazingly, the sequel, *Loose Screws,* is even worse. (Dir: Rafal Zielinski, 80 mins.)†

Scrooge (Great Britain, 1935)*** Seymour Hicks, Donald Calthrop, Robert Cochran, Mary Glynne, Garry Marsh, Maurice Evans. Sturdy version of Dickens's Christmas classic with good special effects. Star Hicks wrote this adaptation himself, after having played the role on stage for many years. (Dir: Henry Edwards, 72 mins.)

Scrooge (Great Britain, 1970)**½ Albert Finney, Alec Guinness, Edith Evans. This musical version of Charles Dickens's timeless yarn is as empty as a neglected Christmas stocking. Albert Finney, as Scrooge, plays the cantankerous, stingy businessman with great flair, and is the main bright spot. Unimaginatively directed by Ronald Neame. (118 mins.)†

Scrooged (1988)*** Bill Murray, Karen Allen, Bobcat Goldthwait, Carol Kane, David Johansen, Robert Mitchum, John Forsythe. Murray is the entire show in this satirical update of "A Christmas Carol" written by "Saturday Night Live" alumni Michael O'Donoghue and Mitch Glazer. The movie is so top-heavy with talent, both in front of and behind the camera, that it can't quite breathe, but the individual pleasures provide plenty of entertainment until the too-sentimental ending. (Dir: Richard Donner, 101 mins.)†

Scrubbers (Great Britain, 1982)** Amanda York, Chrissie Cotterill, Elizabeth Edmunds. Lesbian warfare is the dominating topic in this depressing women's prison film that teeters on the edge of camp. (Dir: Mai Zetterling, 93 mins.)†

Scruples (MTV 1981)** Shelley Smith, Priscilla Barnes, Dirk Benedict, James Darren, Jessica Walter. This glitzy extension of the popular mini-series that starred Lindsay Wagner concerns a woman who inherits a big business and big problems to go with it. The producers have a few scruples loose. (Dir: Robert Day, 104 mins.)

Scudda-Hoo! Scudda-Hay! (1948)** Lon McCallister, June Haver, Walter Brennan, Natalie Wood. Story of a farm boy who gets hold of a pair of mules and then trains them to be the best team around. (Dir: F. Hugh Herbert, 95 mins.)

Scum (Great Britain, 1978)***½ Ray Winstone, Phil Daniels, Julian Firth, Mick Ford. The physical, sexual, and psychological violence of Borstal prison for youthful offenders. Powerful, disturbing, and violent. (Dir: Alan Clarke, 98 mins.)†

Scum of the Earth (1963)* Vickie Miles, Thomas Sweetwood, Sandra Sinclair. This dip into depravity (incredibly tame by today's standards) for a pseudonymous pregore Herschell Gordon Lewis relates how a sweet young thing gets hoodwinked into posing for pornography. Some deliciously funny moments. (Dir: "Lewis H. Gordon," 71 mins.)

Sea Around Us, The (1953)*** An early, influential documentary about the Earth's oceans and sea life, from a book by Rachel Carson. The beautiful underwater photography is still exceptional. Narrated by Don Forbes, produced by Irwin Allen. (61 mins.)†

Sea Chase, The (1955)**½ Lana Turner, John Wayne, Tab Hunter, James Arness. Far-fetched tale of adventure and romance. Wayne skippers a renegade freighter which is bound for Valparaiso. (Dir: John Farrow, 117 mins.)†

Sea Devils (1937)** Victor McLaglen, Preston Foster, Ida Lupino, Donald Woods, Billy Gilbert. Typical vehicle for McLaglen as a brawling Coast Guard seaman who wants his daughter to marry someone above her station, though she prefers tough-guy Foster. Quick-moving adventure, expertly done. (Dir: Ben Stoloff, 85 mins.)

Sea Devils (Great Britain, 1953)**½ Rock Hudson, Yvonne De Carlo. Fisherman turned smuggler gets involved with a beautiful spy during the Napoleonic era. Standard costume melodramatics get a lift from action scenes. (Dir: Raoul Walsh, 91 mins.)†

Sea Fury (Great Britain, 1958)** Stanley Baker, Victor McLaglen, Luciana Paluzzi, Gregoíre Aslan, Robert Shaw. Seafaring melodrama, with roughneck captain McLaglen and his sidekick Baker destroying their friendship over a glamorous woman. Baker and McLaglen are excellent, which makes the superficial, patchy script all the more disappointing. (Dir: C. Raker Endfield, 72 mins.)

Sea Gull, The (U.S.-Great Britain, 1968)*** Vanessa Redgrave, Simone Signoret, David Warner, James Mason, Harry Andrews, Kathleen Widdoes. Strong adaptation of Anton Chekhov's play about rural Russia, an enduring, illuminating masterpiece. Static at times, but generally absorbing. (Dir: Sidney Lumet, 141 mins.)

Seagull, The (U.S.S.R., 1971)*** Ludmila Savelyeva, Vladimir Tchetverikov, Alla Demidova, Yuri Yakoviev. Reverential adaptation of Anton Chekov's complex drama fails to fully utilize the possibilities of cinema. Nonetheless, it is still a commanding production with superior acting and staging. (Dir: Yuli Karasik, 98 mins.)

Sea Gypsies, The (1978)**½ Robert Logan, Mikki Jamison-Olson, Cjon Damitri Patterson. A family movie. Logan plays a widower who sets sail with his two daughters and a female photographer (Jamison-Olson) around the world. The photography is excellent, and the plot is based on a true story. (Dir: Stewart Raffill, 101 mins.)†

Sea Hawk, The (1940)**** Errol Flynn, Brenda Marshall, Claude Rains, Donald Crisp, Flora Robson, Una O'Connor, Alan Hale, Gilbert Roland, Henry Daniell. Classic high-seas adventure, a glorious blend of dashing swashbucklers, nefarious pirates, and passionate women. Gorgeous black-and-white photography, stupendous sets, and a magnificent Erich Wolfgang Korngold score. (Dir: Michael Curtiz, 127 mins.)

Sealed Cargo (1951)**** Dana Andrews, Claude Rains. Fishing vessel rescues the captain of a Danish ship, who is really the commander of a mother ship for Nazi subs. Exciting, suspenseful melodrama. (Dir: Alfred L. Werker, 90 mins.)

Sealed Soil, The (Iran, 1978)*** Flora Shabaviz, the villagers of Noo-Asquar. Superb Iranian film about a young village woman who rejects traditional female roles and refuses to get married, leading everyone to treat her as if she were crazy. A warm, gently comic film, made by Mara Nabili, based on her own experiences. (90 mins.)

Sealed Verdict (1948)** Ray Milland, Florence Marly, Broderick Crawford, John Hoyt, John Ridgely. Postwar thriller with prosecutor Milland suspecting that an accused Nazi war criminal is innocent, trying to prove it. Good idea, average handling. (Dir: Lewis Allen, 82 mins.)

Sea Lion, The (1921)**½ Hobart Bosworth, Emory Johnson, Bessie Love, Carol Holloway, Florence Carpenter, Charles Clary. Seafaring melodrama about a brutish South Seas captain who takes some castaways aboard and discovers that they have ties to his own life. Action-packed but unoriginal adventure story. (Dir: Rowland V. Lee, 55 mins.)†

Seance on a Wet Afternoon (Great Britain, 1964)***½ Kim Stanley, Richard Attenborough. Brilliantly acted drama of a professional medium near the brink of insanity, who involves her weak husband in a kidnapping plot. Tremendous performances by Miss Stanley and Attenborough, backed by fine script and direction by Bryan Forbes. (121 mins.)†

Sea of Grass, The (1947)**½ Spencer Tracy, Katharine Hepburn, Robert Walker, Phyllis Thaxter, Melvyn Douglas. The cast fights hard but this western about a man who sees New Mexico turning into a dust bowl and fights–to save the grass is disappointing. It never stays with any of its many themes long enough to sustain interest. (Dir: Elia Kazan, 131 mins.)

Sea of Love (1989)*** Al Pacino, Ellen Barkin, John Goodman, Michael Rooker, William Hickey. Investigating a killer whose victims came from personal ads, N.Y. plainclothes cop Pacino puts out an ad himself and has a sizzling affair with the main suspect, the lithe and sensual Barkin. The mystery is a simple "did she or didn't she" scenario that's bound to disappoint. But there's a palpable tension throughout, and Pacino and Barkin bring out the best in each other. (Dir: Harold Becker, 112 mins.)†

923

Sea of Roses (Brazil, 1977)*** Norma Benguel, Hugo Caruana, Christina Pereua, Otavio Augusto, Miriam Muniz. Manic black comedy about a woman who tries to flee her miserable marriage and deranged family, only to find she can run but she can't hide. Over-the-top in camerawork, performance, and plot. (Dir: Ana Carilina, 90 mins.)

Search, The (1948)*** Montgomery Clift, Aline MacMahon, Wendell Corey, Ivan Jandl. Moving, sensitive story of a war orphan found in the ruins of postwar Europe. (Dir: Fred Zinnemann, 104 mins.)

Searchers, The (1956)**** John Wayne, Jeffrey Hunter, Natalie Wood, Ward Bond, Vera Miles, John Qualen, Harry Carey, Jr. A vigorous, multilayered classic regarded by many as the model western. Embittered by acts of Indian savagery against his family, Ethan (Wayne) single-mindedly tracks down his niece who'd been kidnapped as a child and forced into squawdom by a renegade. Nursing his hatred, Ethan intends to kill not only the Indian buck but also his niece because she's been defiled. A complex film shaded with ambiguities and strikingly directed by John Ford. (119 mins.)†

Searchers of the Voodoo Mountain—See: **Warriors of the Apocalypse**

Search for Bridey Murphy, The (1956)** Louis Hayward, Teresa Wright. Based on the bestseller about a housewife who when under hypnosis recalls a previous life. Quickly made to cash in on the controversy, this drama has only fair entertainment values, except for a good performance by Wright. (Dir: Noel Langley, 84 mins.)

Search for Danger (1949)*½ John Calvert, Albert Dekker, Myrna Dell. It's double-homicide time as the Falcon series fades out on a mystery involving the double-crossing partner of a gambler. (Dir: Jack Bernhard, 62 mins.)

Search for the Gods (MTV 1975)*½ Stephen McHattie, Kurt Russell, Raymond St. Jacques, Ralph Bellamy. Plodding story about three young people who stumble upon a medallion, purported to be more than 50,000 years old, that might have answers to the popular theory about space visitors to Earth two eons ago. (Dir: Jud Taylor, 104 mins.)

Searching Wind, The (1946)*** Robert Young, Sylvia Sidney. Lillian Hellman's story of a career diplomat who has never taken a firm stand on anything is potentially good drama but never quite makes it. (Dir: William Dieterle, 103 mins.)

Sea Shall Not Have Them, The (Great Britain, 1954)*** Michael Redgrave, Dirk Bogarde. Rescue launch attempts to save a crew of a downed plane, on a rubber raft in the North Sea. Good drama, well acted. (Dir: Lewis Gilbert, 91 mins.)†

Seaside Swingers (Great Britain, 1964)**½ Freddie and the Dreamers, John Leyton, Mike Sarne, Liz Fraser. Zippy little musical about youngsters at a seaside resort and their problems with romance. (Dir: James Hill, 94 mins.)†

Season of Giants, A (MCTV 1991)**½ Mark Frankel, John Glover, F. Murray Abraham, Steven Berkoff, Ornella Muti, Andrea Prodan, Ian Holm, Raf Vallone. The story of Michelangelo is given a sumptuous production, but the script tends to be too talky and the action drawn out. The leading role is played with vigor by British actor Frankel. Despite an earnest attempt to depict the creative atmosphere of the Italian Renaissance, its appeal remains limited. (Dir: Jerry London, 192 mins.)†

Season of Passion (Australia, 1961)*** Ernest Borgnine, John Mills, Anne Baxter, Angela Lansbury. Sugar cane cutters find their annual on-the-town vacation in Sydney has changed, financially and romantically. Offbeat drama, well acted. AKA: **Summer of the Seventeeth Doll**. (Dir: Leslie Norman, 93 mins.)

Season of the Witch (1976)* Jan White, Ray Laine, Anne Muffly, Bill Thunhurst. Pointless and dated sociology from director George Romero. A repressed housewife liberates herself through witchcraft in this tedious thriller devoid of atmosphere, lacking in chills, and riddled with amateurish acting. Originally 130 minutes. AKA: **Hungry Wives** and **Jack's Wife**. (89 mins.)†

Sea Wife (Great Britain, 1957)** Joan Collins, Richard Burton, Basil Sydney. Shipwreck survivors Burton and Collins fall in love, though he never learns that she is a nun. After their rescue, Burton sets off in search of her. The notion of the Welsh Ham and the world's least likely novitiate pitching woo on a desert island sounds campy, but unfortunately it's delivered with an all-too-stiff upper lip. (Dir: Bob McNaught, 82 mins.)†

Sea Wolf, The (1941)***½ Edward G. Robinson, John Garfield, Ida Lupino. Director Michael Curtiz's version of the Jack London novel is brutal and briny, though it has a suffocating visual style. Otherwise, a good Warner Bros. action film, with Robinson the model of a tough tyrant. (90 mins.)†

Sea Wolves (Great Britain-U.S., 1980)**½ Gregory Peck, Roger Moore, David Niven, Trevor Howard. Some commandos come out of retirement long enough to knock a German radio transmitter out of commission. This WWII sea-going adventure is occasionally suspenseful and capably acted. (Dir: Andrew McLaglen, 120 mins.)†

Sebastian (Great Britain, 1968)**½ Dirk Bogarde, Susannah York, Lilli Palmer, Nigel Davenport, Margaret Johnston, John Gielgud. Fast-paced espionage movie with talented cast members running all over the place deciphering codes, dodging double-agents, and falling in love. (Dir: David Greene, 100 mins.)

Sebastiane (Great Britain, 1979)***½ Leonardo Treviglio, Barney James, Richard James, Neil Kennedy. Sincere, respectful story of the martyr is infamous for its plentiful, non-exploitative male nudity and all-Latin dialogue, though it offers an honest detailing of the spirit of Christianity which led to Sebastiane's refusal of Roman orders to kill a young page. (Dirs: Derek Jarman, Paul Humfress, 91 mins.)

Second Awakening of Christa Klages (West Germany, 1977)*** Tina Engel, Sylvia Reize, Katharina Thalbach, Peter Scheider. A progressive child-care center needs money to stay open, so the owner and her boyfriend rob a bank, an act which turns them into fugitives and leads to tragedy. First solo film by director Margarethe von Trotta is rich in plot and potent ideas. (93 mins.)

Second Best Secret Agent, The (1965)* Tom Adams, Veronica Hurst. Adams plays Charles Vine, a British secret agent who tries harder because he's number two. There's a formula which reverses the laws of gravity, but the ingredients for a good film are nowhere in sight. (Dir: Lindsay Shonteff, 96 mins.)

Second Breath (France, 1966)***½ Lino Ventura, Paul Meurisse, Raymond Pellegrin, Christine Fabrega, Marcel Bozzufi. Rousing and philosophical crime film about a gangster who pulls off a daring heist, but may have to turn in his gang, breaking the unwritten code of honor among thieves. (Dir: Jean-Pierre Melville, 150 mins.)

Second Chance (1953)**½ Robert Mitchum, Linda Darnell, Jack Palance, Sandro Giglio. A suspenseful Mitchum vehicle that was originally released in 3-D. Big Bob's an ex-prizefighter in Mexico who becomes romantically involved with a dead mobster's girlfriend (Darnell) pursued by the ever-menacing Palance. (Dir: Rudolph Maté, 81 mins.)

Second Chance (MTV 1972)**½ Brian Keith, Elizabeth Ashley, Juliet Prowse. Loosely woven, fairly pleasant comedy about a stockbroker who acquires a ghost town and fills it with assorted talent in need of another break. The experimental community works until the locals

accuse their benefactor of becoming a dictator. (Dir: Peter Tewksbury, 73 mins.)

Second Chance (France, 1976)*** Catherine Deneuve, Anouk Aimee, Charles Denner, Francis Huster, Jean-Jacques Briot. Charming little film directed by the master of fluff, Claude Lelouch, about a woman released from jail and reunited with her eighteen-year-old son, born while she was in prison. (99 mins.)

Second Chorus (1940)**½ Fred Astaire, Paulette Goddard, Burgess Meredith, Charles Butterworth. Cheery B musical. Astaire and Meredith are collegian tooters who aspire to play with Artie Shaw. Goddard is their manager and the love interest. (Dir: H. C. Potter, 83 mins.)†

Second Face, The (1950)**½ Ella Raines, Bruce Bennett, Rita Johnson, John Sutton, Patricia Knight, Jane Darwell. The talented Raines shines in this melodramatic story of a disfigured woman whose life is changed by plastic surgery. Trim B picture, competently made. (Dir: Jack Bernhard, 77 mins.)

Second Fiddle (1939)** Sonja Henie, Tyrone Power, Rudy Vallee, Edna May Oliver. Henie plays an ice-skating teacher who leaves the Midwest for Hollywood and stardom. (Dir: Sidney Lanfield, 86 mins.)

Second Greatest Sex, The (1955)** Jeanne Crain, George Nader, Kitty Kallen, Bert Lahr. *Lysistrata* revamped as a western musical. The women are tired of the men fighting all the time, so they go on a lovestrike. (Dir: George Marshall, 87 mins.)

Second Hand Hearts (1980)* Robert Blake, Barbara Harris, Amber Rose Gold, Bert Remsen, Collin Boone, Shirley Stoler. Secondhand dramatics. Two strangers marry in haste (and viewers get to repent at leisure). (Dir: Hal Ashby, 102 mins.)

Second Honeymoon (1937)**½ Tyrone Power, Loretta Young, Stuart Erwin, Claire Trevor, Marjorie Weaver, Lyle Talbot, J. Edward Bromberg. Sprightly romantic comedy about a divorced couple who fall in love again, though the wife has remarried. Familiar story becomes a charming confection, with both Young and Power ardent and funny, and an energetic supporting cast. (Dir: Walter Lang, 79 mins.)

Seconds (1966)***½ Rock Hudson, Salome Jens, John Randolph, Jeff Corey, Murray Hamilton, Will Geer. A middle-aged businessman discovers he can arrange for a secret organization to give him a "second" chance at life. After submitting to surgery, and psychiatric orientation, he emerges as handsome Rock, with seemingly everything one could ask for. This imaginative story holds your attention. (Dir: John Frankenheimer, 106 mins.)

Second Serve (MTV 1986)**½ Vanessa Redgrave, Richard Venture, Martin Balsam. Transsexual tennis star Renee Richards's story of becoming a woman after years of existing as a man is brilliantly acted by Redgrave. This is fortunate since a lot of dialogue is in the familiar didactic TV vein. (Dir: Anthony Page, 104 mins.)

Second Sight (1989)* John Larroquette, Bronson Pinchot, Bess Armstrong, Stuart Pankin, John Schuck. Mirthless comedy about a detective agency whose only asset is Pinchot, a neurotic psychic. No laughs, a tired, illogical plot—this one's a real stinker. (Dir: Joel Zwick, 84 mins.)†

Second Sight: A Love Story (MTV 1984)**½ Elizabeth Montgomery, Barry Newman. Montgomery convincingly plays a blind lady falling in love with Newman and eventually regaining her sight. (Dir: John Korty, 104 mins.)

Second Thoughts (1983)½ Lucie Arnaz, Craig Wasson, Laurence Luckinbill, Ken Howard. Excruciating film about a woman who remarries only to find her new hubby is twenty years behind the times. (Dir: Lawrence Turman, 98 mins.)

Second Time Around, The (1961)*** Debbie Reynolds, Andy Griffith, Steve Forrest, Juliet Prowse. Sprightly western comedy about a young widow and her children who find themselves stranded in an Arizona town—but she soon livens things up when she becomes sheriff. Good fun. (Dir: Vincent Sherman, 99 mins.)

Second Time Lucky (1985)* Diane Franklin, Roger Wilson, Robert Morley. Franklin and Wilson embarass themselves as reincarnations of Adam and Eve, used as pawns in a game between God and Satan. Hellishly unfunny. (Dir: Michael Anderson, 100 mins.)

Second Woman, The (1951)*** Robert Young, Betsy Drake. The whole community suspects a man of being responsible for the death of his fiancée, but his new love proves them wrong. Good psychological melodrama. (Dir: James V. Kern, 91 mins.)†

Secret, The (France, 1974)*** Jean-Louis Trintignant, Marlene Jobert, Philippe Noiret, Jean-François Adam. An escaped prisoner takes refuge with a couple who live in a remote mountain house. He tells them that he has been a victim of torture and abuse; the man believes him, the woman doesn't. Tense well-acted political thriller is superbly directed by Robert Enrico. (102 mins.)

Secret Admirer (1985)** C. Thomas Howell, Lori Loughlin, Kelly Preston, Dee Wallace Stone, Cliff De Young, Leigh Taylor-Young. The suburbs will never be the same after some love letters (written by teens) end up in the wrong grown-up hands. The film's slapstick treatment of the foibles of the letter-crossed lovers make this film boisterous without being funny. (Dir: David Greenwalt, 90 mins.)†

Secret Agent, The (Great Britain, 1936)*** John Gielgud, Madeleine Carroll, Peter Lorre, Robert Young. Extremely complicated thriller in which a spy accidentally kills an innocent man. The real villain is thus free to hunt down his pursuer and continue his reign of terror. (Dir: Alfred Hitchcock, 93 mins.)†

Secret Agent of Japan (1942)**½ Preston Foster, Lynn Bari, Janis Carter, Victor Sen Yung, Noel Madison. Snappy patriotic thriller of an American posing as a double agent in the Pacific at the beginning of WWII; fast-moving, enjoyable action. (Dir: Irving Pichel, 72 mins.)

Secret Beyond the Door (1948)**½ Joan Bennett, Michael Redgrave. A thriller with Freudian trappings, this is one of those claptrap suspense dramas where the unsuspecting wife starts to wonder if her hubby's going to do her in. The cast is good and the director effectively creates visual approximations of psychological disturbance, but the plot is the same old cat and mouse stuff you've seen a million times. (Dir: Fritz Lang, 98 mins.)†

Secret Bride, The (1935)**½ Barbara Stanwyck, Warren William, Glenda Farrell, Grant Mitchell, Henry O'Neill. Just as a governor's daughter elopes with the state attorney general, her father is impeached for apparently accepting a bribe. They conceal their marriage while he investigates. Fast-moving romantic thriller. (Dir: William Dieterle, 76 mins.)

Secret Ceremony (Great Britain, 1968)*** Elizabeth Taylor, Mia Farrow, Robert Mitchum. Macabre, interesting melodrama. The plot concerns a warped and wealthy Farrow who brings a blowsy Taylor home as a substitute mother, not counting on the sudden appearance of stepfather Mitchum. The TV version is watered down. (Dir: Joseph Losey, 109 mins.)†

Secret Command (1944)*** Pat O'Brien, Carole Landis, Chester Morris, Ruth Warrick. A two-fisted gent puts a stop to sabotage in the California shipyards. Actionful melodrama, well above average. (Dir: A. Edward Sutherland, 82 mins.)

Secret File: Hollywood (1962)½ Robert Clarke, Francine York, Syd Mason, Maralou Gray. After evidence he gathered for a scandal magazine is used to blackmail a famous director, a detective decides to expose the exposé racket. (Dir: Ralph Cushman, 85 mins.)

Secret Fury, The (1950)** Claudette Colbert, Robert Ryan. Bride is claimed to be already married, is sent to an asylum on what looks like a frameup. (Dir: Mel Ferrer, 86 mins.)

Secret Garden, The (1949)*** Margaret O'Brien, Dean Stockwell, Herbert Marshall. An eerie, suspenseful drama about two children, and their discovery of a magical, secret garden. Well acted. (Dir: Fred M. Wilcox, 92 mins.)

Secret Garden, The (MTV 1987)**½ Gennie James, Barret Oliver, Jadrien Steele, Sir Michael Hordern, Billie Whitelaw, Derek Jacobi. A prestige production of the classic children's tale about a spoiled young girl's discovery of a beautiful garden kept locked by a melancholy, hunchbacked widower (Jacobi). A fine retelling of the "kidlit" perennial. (Dir: Alan Grint, 104 mins.)

Secret Heart, The (1946)**½ Claudette Colbert, Walter Pidgeon, June Allyson. Cast helps but there's no spark to this dreary psychological study of a girl who worships her dead father and hates her lovely stepmother. (Dir: Robert Z. Leonard, 97 mins.)

Secret Honor (1984)*** Philip Baker Hall. A bizarre, lacerating blend of fiction, history, and speculation which gives you the dubious privilege of spending ninety minutes with Richard Nixon (Hall). For the millions who believe that Nixon was paranoid towards the end of his presidency, this is a powerful experience, indeed. (Dir: Robert Altman, 90 mins.)†

Secret Invasion, The (1964)**½ Stewart Granger, Raf Vallone, Edd Byrnes, Mickey Rooney. A group of criminals are promised a pardon if they'll participate in a dangerous mission involving the infiltration of Nazi-held territory in Yugoslavia during WWII. (Dir: Roger Corman, 98 mins.)

Secret Life of an American Wife, The (1968)*½ Anne Jackson, Patrick O'Neal, Edy Williams. Misfired comedy about a bored housewife (Jackson) who tries dalliance with a sexy movie star. Director George Axelrod reverses his *The Seven Year Itch* with highly disappointing results. (92 mins.)†

Secret Life of Archie's Wife, The (MTV 1990)**½ Jill Eikenberry, Michael Tucker, Elaine Stritch, Ray Wise. Eikenberry and Tucker make an engaging team in this pleasant, offbeat caper yarn about a discontented married woman whose life takes a turn for the better when she is kidnapped by a bungling bank robber. Mildly amusing antics enhanced by an enthusiastic cast. (Dir: James Frawley, 96 mins.)

Secret Life of Ian Fleming, The (MTV 1990) ** Jason Conery, Kristin Scott Thomas, Joss Ackland, Patricia Hodge, David Warner, Colin Welland, Richard Johnson. Mostly fictional biography of the creator of James Bond. The film falls flat. (Dir: Ferdinand Fairfax, 96 mins.)†

Secret Life of John Chapman, The (MTV 1976)*** Ralph Waite, Susan Anspach, Brad Davis, Pat Hingle. A curiously affecting real-life drama based on the notable book *Blue Collar Journal*. It's a deft adaptation of the chronicle of the president of Pennsylvania's prestigious Haverford College, during his voluntary sojourn doing odd jobs of manual labor. (Dir: David Lowell Rich, 72 mins.)

Secret Life of Kathy McCormick, The (MTV 1988)*½ Barbara Eden, Josh Taylor, Judith-Marie Bergan, Jenny O'Hara. Corny Cinderella tale tailored for Eden who plays a grocery clerk moving up in society. Her biggest problem is keeping the truth from her wealthy suitor. (Dir: Robert Lewis, 96 mins.)

Secret Life of Walter Mitty, The (1947)*** Danny Kaye, Virginia Mayo, Ann Rutherford, Fay Bainter, Boris Karloff. Thurber's story of a man who lived in two worlds—the real one and his own fantasy world—makes an entertaining vehicle for Kaye. Some excellent song sequences and sharp comedy lines make this one above average. (Dir: Norman Z. McLeod, 105 mins.)†

Secret Mission (Great Britain, 1942)**½ James Mason, Stewart Granger, Michael Wilding. British spy drama with excellent actors making the most of the intrigue. (Dir: Harold French, 82 mins.)

Secret Night Caller, The (MTV 1975)** Robert Reed, Hope Lange, Elaine Giftos, Michael Constantine. Offbeat casting works fairly well here, as Robert ("The Brady Bunch") Reed plays a respectable family man with a weakness for making obscene phone calls. (Dir: Jerry Jameson, 72 mins.)

Secret of Convict Lake, The (1951)**½ Glenn Ford, Gene Tierney, Ethel Barrymore, Zachary Scott, Ann Dvorak. Convicts invade a village inhabited only by women; complications arise. Ethel Barrymore, as matriarch of the village, is the only interesting feature. (Dir: Michael Gordon, 83 mins.)

Secret of Dr. Kildare, The (1939)** Lew Ayres, Lionel Barrymore, Laraine Day. Kildare continues his long Hollywood internship, Barrymore is still the barking "heart of gold" Gillespie and Laraine continues as Kildare's pretty combination nurse-sweetheart. (Dir: Harold S. Bucquet, 85 mins.)

Secret of Dr. Mabuse, The—See: **Thousand Eyes of Dr. Mabuse, The**

Secret of Madame Blanche, The (1933)**½ Irene Dunne, Lionel Atwill, Phillips Holmes, Una Merkel, Douglas Watson, Jean Parker. Musical melodrama of a showgirl marrying a rich weakling who commits suicide, leaving her with a baby who is taken from her. Many years later they are reunited under tragic circumstances. Well-produced soap opera. (Dir: Charles Brabin, 67 mins.)

Secret of My Success, The (Great Britain, 1965)*½ Lionel Jeffries, James Booth, Honor Blackman, Stella Stevens, Shirley Jones. Onward and upward in the art of murder, as a constable (Booth) becomes wealthier and wealthier. Tries for comedy in the tradition of *Kind Hearts & Coronets* but "*Secret*" fails in nearly every respect. (Dir: Andrew L. Stone, 112 mins.)

Secret of My Success, The (1987)** Michael J. Fox, Richard Jordan, Helen Slater, Margaret Whitton. Fox is so engaging a presence that he makes this comedy click part of the time, but the film emerges as more labored than funny. It's sort of a yuppie update of *How to Succeed in Business Without Really Trying*, as an enterprising man from Kansas tries to make it in the Big Apple in record time. (Dir: Herbert Ross, 90 mins.)†

Secret of NIMH, The (1982)*** The voices of John Carradine, Elizabeth Hartman, Dom DeLuise, Derek Jacobi. Entertaining animated feature about a stouthearted lady mouse who stumbles onto a laboratory full of superintelligent rats while trying to get help for her sick child. Director Don Bluth and the team of 16 animators with whom he worked grew disenchanted with the Disney studios and formed their own company; their first product is a welcome return to classically detailed animation and a likeable, easy-to-watch film. (82 mins.)†

Secret of Santa Vittoria, The (1969)**½ Anthony Quinn, Anna Magnani, Hardy Kruger, Virna Lisi. Ponderous direction by Stanley Kramer and a screenplay that savors little of the excellent dialogue found in Robert Crichton's novel dissipate most of the potential inherent in this story of an Italian hill town guarding their wine at the end of WWII. (140 mins.)

Secret of the Blue Room (1933)**½ Lionel Atwill, Gloria Stuart, Paul Lukas, Edward Arnold, Onslow Stevens. First-rate haunted house mystery. A lovely woman of mystery asks her three suitors to spend a night alone in a haunted castle to win her hand. Eerie and suspenseful, with a lively cast of pros. (Dir: Kurt Neumann, 66 mins.)

Secret of the Incas (1954)**½ Charlton Heston, Robert Young, Nicole Maurey,
928

Yma Sumac. Adventurer finds a map holding the location of a priceless gold sunburst, arrives to find an archeological expedition already there. Melodrama with enough intrigue and suspense to hold the action fans. (Dir: Jerry Hopper, 101 mins.)

Secret of the Purple Reef, The (1960)** Jeff Richards, Peter Falk, Richard Chamberlain. Two brothers arrive to investigate the mysterious sinking of their father's ship. Passable Grade B melodrama. (Dir: William Witney, 80 mins.)

Secret of Treasure Mountain (1956)** Raymond Burr, Valerie French. A buried Indian treasure is mysteriously guarded by an old man and his attractive daughter. (Dir: Seymour Friedman, 68 mins.)

Secret Partner, The (Great Britain, 1961)** Stewart Granger, Haya Harareet. Routine meller with Stewart Granger cast as a man who must prove he is innocent of an embezzlement charge and win back his wife in the process. (Dir: Basil Dearden, 91 mins.)

Secret People, The (Great Britain, 1952)**½ Valentina Cortese, Audrey Hepburn, Serge Reggiani. Refugee in London meets her former fiance who persuades her to enter into an espionage plot. Long, leisurely melodrama doesn't have enough spark to lift it much above the ordinary. (Dir: Thorold Dickinson, 87 mins.)

Secret Places (Australia, 1985)**½ Marie-Theres Relin, Tara Macgowran, Cassie Stuart, Jennie Agutter. The film relates the difficult readjustment of a German refugee during WWII as she tries to fit into an English girl's school, where anti-German sentiment runs high. The delicate blossoming of this teenager's friendship with a popular classmate could have made an impactful film if the director had had a firmer grasp on the best way to tell this story. (Dir: Zelda Barron, 96 mins.)†

Secret Policeman's Other Ball, The (Great Britain, 1981)***½ John Cleese, Graham Chapman, Michael Palin, Terry Jones, Peter Cook, Pamela Stephenson, Pete Townshend, Sting, Eric Clapton, Jeff Beck, Phil Collins. A series of mostly hilarious sketches that will delight Monty Pythonites and other fans of British humor. Poorly filmed; but the content is superior. (Dir: Julien Temple, 91 mins.)†

Secrets (MTV 1977)* Susan Blakely, Roy Thinnes, Joanne Linville, John Randolph. Pretentious, silly drama about a young married woman with a nice, handsome husband who starts compulsively sleeping around after her possessive mother dies. The camera work is "arty," the script cumbersome. (Dir: Paul Wendkos, 106 mins.)

Secret Six, The (1931)*** Lewis Stone, Wallace Beery, Clark Gable, Jean Harlow, Ralph Bellamy, Johnny Mack Brown, Marjorie Rambeau. A gritty crime drama about two indefatigable reporters on a crusade against bootleggers. Nicely rough-and-tumble. (Dir: George Hill, 83 mins.)

Secrets of a Married Man (MTV 1984)**½ William Shatner, Cybill Shepherd, Michelle Phillips, Glynn Turman. Shatner plays a married man fooling around with hookers and getting vicarious thrills from the street life. Falling hard for one (Shepherd) destroys his marriage and himself. (Dir: William A. Graham, 104 mins.)†

Secrets of a Mother and Daughter (MTV 1983)** Katharine Ross, Michael Nouri, Linda Hamilton, Bibi Besch. Slick women's magazine fare treated seriously as stunning mom and petulant daughter romance the same man. (Dir: Gabrielle Beaumont, 104 mins.)

Secrets of an Actress (1938)**½ Kay Francis, George Brent, Ian Hunter, Gloria Dickson, Isabel Jeans, Penny Singleton. Glamorous actress Francis is loved by architect Hunter, but her heart belongs to married man Brent. Sleek, entertaining soap opera. (Dir: William Keighley, 71 mins.)

Secrets of a Secretary (1931)**½ Claudette Colbert, Herbert Marshall, George Metaxa, Betty Lawford, Mary Boland. An irresponsible heiress loses her fortune and is forced to get a job as a secretary, putting up with social slights from her former equals and getting involved in a murder. OK social drama; Colbert is magnetic. (Dir: George Abbott, 71 mins.)

Secrets of the Lone Wolf (1941)** Warren William, Ruth Ford, Roger Clark. Fair shipboard mystery in which criminals try to coerce Lone Wolf's manservant into stealing the Napoleon gems. Behind the scenes, L.W. lays a trap for the thieves. (Dir: Edward Dmytryk, 67 mins.)

Secrets of the Red Bedroom—See: **Secret Weapons**

Secrets of Three Hungry Wives (MTV 1978)** Jessica Walter, James Franciscus, Eve Plumb, Gretchen Corbett, Heather MacRae. Franciscus is a playboy who preys on suburban housewives and their offspring in this soapy whodunit. (Dir: Gordon Hessler, 104 mins.)†

Secrets of Women (Sweden, 1952)**½ Anita Bjork, Karl Arne Homsten, Jarl Krulle. Billed as a comedy, *"Secrets"* is an early Bergman omnibus. Some sisters chew the fat about their past sexual follies as their youngest sibling (perhaps bored by their endless prattle) decides to elope. The funniest and most touching segment involves a long-married couple who find themselves trapped in an elevator. (Dir: Ingmar Bergman, 108 mins.)†

Secret War of Harry Frigg, The (1968)** Paul Newman, Sylva Koscina, Andrew Duggan, Tom Bosley, John Williams. In WWII, a rebellious private is called upon to try and free some captured Allied generals. (Dir: Jack Smight, 110 mins.)†

Secret War of Jackie's Girls, The (MTV 1980)*½ Mariette Hartley, Lee Purcell, Dee Wallace. Hartley leads an all-woman flying squadron in WWII. Ridiculous, contrived story of young beauties, on top secret missions, single-handedly winning the war for the Allies. (Dir: Gordon Hessler, 104 mins.)

Secret Ways, The (1961)**½ Richard Widmark, Sonja Ziemann. Fast-paced but brainless chase thriller behind the Iron Curtain. Widmark tries to smuggle an anti-Communist leader out of Red Hungary. (Dir: Phil Karlson, 112 mins.)

Secret Weapons (MTV 1985)** James Franciscus, Geena Davis, Christopher Atkins, Linda Hamilton, Sally Kellerman. Sex and espionage are the two ingredients in this barely believable drama about gorgeous spies from Russia. Franciscus and Kellerman star as KGB instructors in charge of changing Russian women into Americanized seductresses whose mission is to gather secrets through sex and blackmail. AKA: **Secrets of the Red Bedroom**. (Dir: Don Taylor, 104 mins.)

Secret Witness (MTV 1988)** David Rasche, Paul LeMat, Leaf Phoenix, Kellie Martin. Twelve-year-olds in a summer community innocently play a Peeping Tom game which results in their discovery of a murder. Martin plays a spunky girl who leads her pal (Phoenix) around by the nose. The believable child actors make this worthwhile. (Dir: Eric Laneuville, 96 mins.)

Secret World (France, 1969)**½ Jacqueline Bisset, Jean-François Maurin. Offbeat tale. A young French boy, scarred by his parents' death in a car crash, becomes deeply infatuated with a beautiful English lady visiting her aunt and uncle's château. (Dirs: Robert Freeman, Paul Feyder, 94 mins.)

Security Risk (1954)** John Ireland, Dorothy Malone, Keith Larson, John Craven. Routine Cold War thriller, with vacationing FBI man Ireland uncovering a Communist plot to steal atomic secrets. Malone provides some much-needed electricity for this otherwise damp tale. (Dir: Harold Schuster, 69 mins.)

Seduced (MTV 1985)**½ Gregory Harrison, Cybill Shepherd, José Ferrer, Adrienne Barbeau, Mel Ferrer. Harrison and Shepherd mix murder with seductive bedroom moments. A glossy item to show off the handsome Harrison as a brilliant lawyer whose ascendancy to a corporate presidency is stymied by a murder. (Dir: Jerrold Freedman, 104 mins.)†

Seduced and Abandoned (Italy, 1964)**** Saro Urzi, Stefania Sandrelli. A wonder fully funny film that takes a sardonic, angry view of Sicilian family life and the hypocrisy which plays such an important part in their lives and mores. Pietro Germi, the same wizard responsible for *Divorce, Italian Style,* wrote and directed this witty and bitter view of his countrymen. Story is about what happens in a Sicilian town when a young girl is seduced by the fiancé of her sister. (118 mins.)†

Seduction, The (1982)* Morgan Fairchild, Andrew Stevens, Michael Sarrazin, Vince Edwards, Colleen Camp. Ridiculous film about a TV newsperson who is stalked by a psychotic young photographer. (Dir: David Schmoeller, 104 mins.)†

Seduction of Gina, The (MTV 1984)** Valerie Bertinelli, Michael Brandon, Ed Lauter, Frederick Lehne, Dinah Manoff. Bertinelli plays a medical student's lonely wife who becomes a gambling addict. (Dir: Jerrold Freedman, 104 mins.)

Seduction of Joe Tynan, The (1979)**½ Alan Alda, Meryl Streep, Barbara Harris. A rather facile drama about a charismatic liberal senator (Alda) that has less density than a good Movie of the Week. Alda, who wrote the script, projects a more piquant sense of decency than anyone else in movies, but the dramatic situations are too pat. (Dir: Jerry Schatzberg, 107 mins.)†

Seduction of Mimi, The (Italy, 1974)***½ Giancarlo Giannini, Mariangela Melato, Agostina Belli. Rollicking melange of political humor, Sicilian double standards, and sexual fandangos served up by director Lina Wertmuller. Giannini and Melato strike sparks as a metallurgist and his mistress whose concepts of honor diverge tragically. (89 mins.)

Seduction of Miss Leona, The (MTV 1980)** Lynn Redgrave, Brian Dennehy, Conchata Ferrell, Anthony Zerbe. Sentimental three-hankie drama about a prudish, old-fashioned college professor (Redgrave) who falls in love with a married handyman, skillfully played by Dennehy. (Dir: Joseph Hardy, 104 mins.)

Seduction: The Cruel Woman (West Germany, 1985)**½ Mechthild Grossman, Udo Kier, Shiela McLaughlin. Oddly mundane film about sexual masochism observes a dominatrix and her consorts. The banality of the encounters are the point of this anti-sensationalistic film. Writer-director Monika Treut knows whereof she speaks, having written a Ph.D. thesis on Sacher-Masoch. (85 mins.)

930

Seeding of Sarah Burns, The (MTV 1979)**½ Kay Lenz, Martin Balsam, Cliff De Young. Lenz is fine as an introspective young woman who volunteers for an embryo transplant. Once the drama settles into the obvious twist of the young woman becoming too attached to the growing infant in her, the whole thing becomes a soap opera. (Dir: Sandor Stern, 104 mins.)

Seedling, The (India, 1974)*** Anant Nag, Shabana Azmi, Sudhu Meher, Priya Tendulkar. Servant girl, married to a deaf-mute man, is seduced and impregnated by the landlord's son, who also assaults her husband. She vows to avenge the horrors visited upon them in this potent drama attacking the remnants of India's feudal mentality. (Dir: Shyamam Benegal, 131 mins.)

Seeds of Evil (1974)½ Katharine Houghton, Rita Gam, Joe Dallesandro, James Congdon. Soporific garden-variety horror flick with Joe as a stud whose sexual prowess turns women literally into clinging vines. (Dir: James H. Kay III, 97 mins.)†

See Here, Private Hargrove (1944)*** Robert Walker, Keenan Wynn, Donna Reed, Robert Benchley. Many an ex-Army man will get plenty of laughs out of this fair adaptation of the famous boot camp best-seller. (Dir: Wesley Ruggles, 101 mins.)

See How She Runs (MTV 1978)***½ Joanne Woodward, John Considine, Lissy Newman. Woodward stars in this extraordinary drama about a divorced teacher who takes up jogging at every moment she can spare, until it becomes central to her existence, a fact to which she insists her family must adjust. Skillful development of the protagonist who develops her running skills enough to enter the Boston Marathon and have her family root for her. (Dir: Richard T. Heffron, 104 mins.)†

See How They Run (MTV 1964)** John Forsythe, Senta Berger, Jane Wyatt, Franchot Tone. Three orphaned children are pursued by their father's murderer when they take incriminating evidence with them to South America. (Dir: David Lowell Rich, 99 mins.)

Seeing Red (1983)**** Pete Seeger, Dorothy Healey, Stretch Johnson, Bill Bailey. A riveting Academy Award-nominated documentary about the American Communist Party, culled from over 400 interview sessions with former and current party members. Directors Julia Reichert and James Klein include archival footage of speeches by Ronald Reagan, Richard Nixon, Hubert Humphrey and Joseph McCarthy. The vision of the party is slightly romanticized, but not uncritical, and the interview subjects are fascinating. (100 mins.)

Seekers, The (1954)—See: **Land of Fury**

Seekers, The (MTV 1979)** Randolph Mantooth, Edie Adams, Neville Brand, Delta Burke, Vic Morrow, Robert Reed, John Carradine, Brian Keith, Ross Martin, Rosey Grier, George Hamilton, Alex Hyde-White, Martin Milner, Ed Harris, Eric Stolz. Custardy-smooth but woefully predictable follow-up to *The Bastard* and *The Rebels*. The Kent clan puts the Revolutionary War behind them to tame the Northwest. Author John Jakes has a bit part. (Dir: Sidney Hayers, 200 mins.)

Seems Like Old Times (1980)*** Chevy Chase, Goldie Hawn, Charles Grodin, Robert Guillaume, George Grizzard. Synthetic farce about marital complications caused by an ex-husband is nevertheless Neil Simon's most efficient original screenplay. It hasn't the richness of the thirties comedies it emulates, but you care about the characters and the situations are mostly funny. (Dir: Jay Sandrich, 102 mins.)†

See My Lawyer (1945)**½ Olsen and Johnson, Grace McDonald, Noah Beery, Jr. The two comics want to squirm out of a movie contract, hire three young lawyers to help them. Amusing musical nonsense. (Dir: Eddie Cline, 67 mins.)

See No Evil (Great Britain, 1971)**½ Mia Farrow, Dorothy Allison, Diane Grayson, Robin Bailey. A suspense thriller which works only part of the way, but the chills are there if you're patient. Farrow plays a blind girl who comes home to her uncle's house after the accident which caused her blindness, and begins living a nightmare. (Dir: Richard Fleischer, 89 mins.)†

See No Evil, Hear No Evil (1989)**½ Gene Wilder, Richard Pryor, Joan Severance, Kevin Spacey. A deaf man and a blind man, both trying to hide their disabilities, are caught up in a murder. Pryor and Wilder mine deft humor from their characters without being cruel or condescending, but the idiot plot defeats them. (Dir: Arthur Hiller, 103 mins.)†

See the Man Run (MTV 1971)**½ Robert Culp, Angie Dickinson, Eddie Albert, June Allyson. Stock kidnapping plot undergoes a far-out twist here. Linked to a kidnapping through a wrong telephone number, an out-of-work actor decides to cut himself in. (Dir: Corey Allen, 73 mins.)

See You In the Morning (1989)**½ Jeff Bridges, Alice Krige, Farrah Fawcett, Drew Barrymore. Uneven comedy-drama about a New York psychiatrist trying to adjust to his role as stepfather to his new wife's kids, while fulfilling his obligations to his own children from his first

marriage. A disappointment from writer-director Alan J. Pakula. (119 mins.)†

Seize the Day (1986)*** Robin Williams, Jerry Stiller, Joseph Wiseman, Glenne Headly, William Hickey, Tony Roberts. Involving but downbeat account of an ex-salesman's mid-life crisis: he's lost his job, her personal relationships are ruined, and his possibilities for starting up again in the business world don't seem too hopeful. Based on the novel by Saul Bellow. (Dir: Fielder Cook, 93 mins.)†

Seizure (Canada, 1974)**½ Jonathan Frid, Joe Sirola, Martine Beswick, Hervé Villechaize, Mary Woronov, Troy Donahue. A writer of spooky books finds himself in a spooky situation—trapped in a nightmare as characters from his latest novel stop by to kill off his house guests. Derivative, but the borrowings are from the best sources. (Dir: Oliver Stone, 93 mins.)

Seizure: The Story of Kathy Morris (MTV 1980)**½ Penelope Milford, Leonard Nimoy, Christopher Allport. The real-life crisis of young singer Kathy Morris (excellent acting by Milford). Ms. Morris was struck with a seizure, resulting in an operation which left her in a coma. The film methodically depicts her courageous struggle against adversity, and her eventual victory. (Dir: Gerald Isenberg, 104 mins.)

Sellout, The (1951)**½ Walter Pidgeon, John Hodiak, Audrey Totter, Karl Malden. OK crime yarn. Pidgeon plays a crusading newspaper editor who tries to overthrow the corrupt local law enforcement. (Dir: Gerald Mayer, 83 mins.)

Seminole (1953)**½ Rock Hudson, Barbara Hale, Anthony Quinn, Richard Carlson, Hugh O'Brian. The story of Seminole Indians and their efforts to stay free takes up the bulk of the film and it's interestingly unfolded. (Dir: Budd Boetticher, 87 mins.)

Seminole Uprising (1955)** George Montgomery, Karen Booth, John Pickard. Typical low-budget '50s western, with the cavalry saving the day when Indians revolt. (Dir: Earl Bellamy, 74 mins.)

Semi-Tough (1977)*** Burt Reynolds, Kris Kristofferson, Jill Clayburgh, Robert Preston, Lotte Lenya, Bert Convy, Roger Mosley, Carl Weathers. Generally entertaining, but unfocused, comedy about two football stars both making a fifty-yard dash to the same girl. Amiably, the film wanders all over the place embracing romantic comedy, delivering pigskin satire, and even managing to poke fun at est, but ultimately it dilutes its impact. (Dir: Michael Ritchie, 108 mins.)†

Senator Was Indiscreet, The (1947)*** William Powell, Ella Raines, Peter Lind Hayes. A bird-brained senator lets a hot political diary get out of his hands, and it may spell doom to his machine. Side-splitting farce comedy. Don't miss it. (Dir: George S. Kaufman, 81 mins.)†

Sender, The (Great Britain, 1982)**½ Kathryn Harrold, Zeljko Ivanek, Shirley Knight, Paul Freeman, Sean Hewitt. Ivanek plays a man with psychic powers whose visions infect an entire hospital as his doctor searches for a cure. (Dir: Roger Christian, 91 mins.)†

Send Me No Flowers (1964)*** Doris Day, Rock Hudson, Tony Randall, Clint Walker, Paul Lynde. In this, their least predictable film together, Day is a housewife and Hudson her hypochondriac husband. He mistakenly believes he is dying, and keeps trying to fix her up with other men. (Dir: Norman Jewison, 100 mins.)†

Senilità (Italy, 1961)*** Anthony Franciosa, Claudia Cardinale, Betsy Blair, Philippe Leroy, Raimondo Magni. A repressed man falls in love with a beautiful woman who ends up abusing and humiliating him. A haunting portrait of devastating realism. (Dir: Mauro Bolognini, 110 mins.)

Senior Prom (1959)** Jill Corey, Jimmie Komack, Paul Hampton, Tom Laughlin, Mitch Miller. Harmless little college musical about a young student who makes a hit recording and becomes top man on campus. (Dir: David Lowell Rich, 82 mins.)

Senior Trip (MTV 1981)* Scott Baio, Faye Grant, Rand Brooks, Peter Coffield, Jane Hoffman. Ohio high school graduates visit New York City to sample the theater, museums, and Wall Street board rooms. (Dir: Kenneth Johnson, 104 mins.)†

Senior Year (MTV 1974)* Gary Frank, Glynnis O'Connor, Barry Livingston, Debralee Scott. It's all about the traumas and growing pains of high school seniors in the mid-fifties. (Dir: Richard Donner, 72 mins.)

Sensations (1944)**½ Eleanor Powell, Dennis O'Keefe, W. C. Fields. Dancing star resorts to novel means to obtain publicity. Mild musical; some good moments. (Dir: Andrew L. Stone, 86 mins.)

Sense of Loss, A (U.S.-Switzerland, 1972)*** Enlightening documentary about the fighting, bitterness and religious hatred in Northern Ireland. Interviews bring out the mindless futility of the ongoing violence in that embittered land. (Dir: Marcel Ophuls, 135 mins.)†

Sensitive, Passionate Man, A (MTV 1977)*½ Angie Dickinson, David Janssen, Todd Lookinland, Mariclare Costello. Dreary soap opera about an alcoholic executive of an aerospace company who loses his job, his family, and eventually his life. (Dir: John Newland, 98 mins.)

Senso (Italy, 1954)***½ Alida Valli, Farley Granger. Tragic tale of a noblewoman who sacrifices her marriage for a handsome but cowardly soldier. Beautifully photographed and sublimely romantic. AKA: **The Wanton Contessa**. (Dir: Luchino Visconti, 90 mins.)†

Sentimental Journey (1946)** John Payne, Maureen O'Hara, Cedric Hardwicke, William Bendix. Maudlin, sentimental, sloppy tale of a dying woman who adopts a child to keep her husband company when she dies. (Dir: Walter Lang, 94 mins.)

Sentimental Journey (MTV 1984)** Jaclyn Smith, David Dukes, Jessica Rene Carroll. Smith is a Broadway producer married happily to successful actor Dukes, except that they can't have any children. Enter eight-year-old orphan Libby, whom they adopt, but their problems aren't over . . . not by a long shot! (Dir: James Goldstone, 104 mins.)

Sentinel, The (1977)*½ Chris Sarandon, Cristina Raines, Arthur Kennedy, Ava Gardner. The gates of Hell must be guarded, only no one will apply for the job. Some extremely unpleasant shock scenes, but no real scares. (Dir: Michael Winner, 91 mins.)

Separate But Equal (MTV 1991)***½ Sidney Poitier, Burt Lancaster, Richard Kiley, Cleavon Little, Gloria Foster, John McMartin. Deeply moving account of the historic effort to desegregate the school system in the South, starting in 1950. The impact of this docudrama is due to both the inherent power of the Supreme Court case in 1954, which found "separate but equal" to be unconstitutional, and to the enormously effective performance of Poitier (his first appearance in a TV drama in 35 years) in the leading role of Thurgood Marshall. Skillfully written and directed drama is absorbing throughout. (Dir: George Stevens, Jr., 192 mins.)

Separate Peace, A (1972)** Parker Stevenson, John Heyl, William Roerick. Two young men at a private school face the transition to manhood in the last years of WWII. The forties ambience is well done, but director Larry Peerce seems to be afraid of closeness and commitment as his protagonists. (104 mins.)†

Separate Tables (1958)**** Deborah Kerr, Burt Lancaster, David Niven, Rita Hayworth, Gladys Cooper, Cathleen Nesbitt, Wendy Hiller. Faithful film version of Terence Rattigan's two one-act plays about the guests of a British seaside resort and their individual dramas. Oscar-winning performances by Niven and Hiller. Kerr and Niven come off with top acting honors as a spinster and a charming ex-colonel. Hiller shines as the proprietress of the establishment. (Dir: Delbert Mann, 98 mins.)†

Seppuku—See: **Hara-kiri**

September (1987)** Denholm Elliott, Mia Farrow, Elaine Stritch, Jack Warden, Sam Waterson, Dianne Wiest. Humorless Woody Allen drama about the relationship crisis between an ex-socialite mother (Stritch) and her introverted daughter (Farrow). Another failed attempt by Allen to imitate Ingmar Bergman. (87 mins.)†

September Affair (1950)*** Joan Fontaine, Joseph Cotten, Jessica Tandy. Engineer and concert pianist miss their plane while sightseeing in Naples; when the plane is reported crashed, they find they have a chance to start life anew together. Well made, generally avoids the maudlin. (Dir: William Dieterle, 104 mins.)†

September Gun (MTV 1984)*** Robert Preston, Patty Duke Astin, Sally Kellerman, Christopher Lloyd, Geoffrey Lewis. This offbeat western starts slowly but turns out to be an arresting production. Crusty Preston plays a gunfighter living off past glory who is duped into helping a strong-willed nun care for abandoned Indian children. (Dir: Don Taylor, 104 mins.)†

September Storm (1960)*½ Joanne Dru, Mark Stevens. Model joins adventurers in trying to recover a fortune in Spanish gold from a sunken ship. (Dir: Byron Haskin, 99 mins.)

September 30, 1955—See: **9/30/55**

Sequoia (1934)** Jean Parker, Samuel S. Hinds, Russell Hardie, Paul Hurst, Willie Fung. Nice little nature film, years before Disney took over the genre, about a deer and a mountain lion raised together as friends striving to avoid hunters in the sequoia forests of the Northwest. (Dir: Chester M. Franklin, 75 mins.)

Serenade (1956)**½ Mario Lanza, Joan Fontaine, Vincent Price, Vincent Edwards. Lanza plays a street singer who is discovered by society playgirl (Fontaine) and concert manager (Price). Overdramatic plot but the opera arias are worthwhile. (Dir: Anthony Mann, 121 mins.)†

Serengeti Shall Not Die (West Germany, 1959)***½ Absorbing Oscar-winning documentary of two zoologists who take a census of wild animals facing extinction on the steppes of Serengeti in Tanganyika. (Dirs: Dr. Bernhard, Michael Grzimek, 84 mins.)

Sergeant, The (France-U.S., 1968)** Rod Steiger, John Phillip Law, Ludmila Mikael. Cut-rate *Reflections in a Golden Eye* set in a dreary Army camp in '52 France where a career sergeant tries to repress his lust for a young private. Under John Flynn's direction and Steiger's

smoldering smoked ham, the film degenerates shrilly. (107 mins.)

Sergeant Deadhead (1965)** Frankie Avalon, Deborah Walley, Cesar Romero, Fred Clark, Buster Keaton. Girl-shy GI (Avalon) turns into a wolf and disrupts a missile base. Silly, harmless antics. (Dir: Norman Taurog, 89 mins.)

Sergeant Madden (1939)*** Wallace Beery, Tom Brown, Alan Curtis, David Gorcey, Fay Holden, Marc Lawrence, Laraine Day. Beery is a sanctimonious cop with two sons—one goes good and one goes bad. Distinguished by a superlative performance by Lawrence and by Josef von Sternberg's haunting direction. (82 mins.)

Sergeant Matlovich vs. the U.S. Air Force (MTV 1978)**½ Brad Dourif, Frank Converse, Stephen Elliott, Marc Singer, William Daniels. As presented here, the character of Sgt. Matlovich, the real-life homosexual who battled with the Air Force to remain in service, is one-dimensional. Dourif does his best to bring the character to life, but little insight is brought to bear on his sexual preference. (Dir: Paul Leaf, 104 mins.)†

Sergeant Murphy (1938)** Ronald Reagan, Mary Maguire, Donald Crisp, Ben Hendricks. Dopey B picture about a U.S. Army cavalryman striving to rehabilitate his horse after it is deemed unfit for service. OK but unexciting. (Dir: B. Reeves Eason, 57 mins.)

Sergeant Rutledge (1960)** Jeffrey Hunter, Constance Towers, Woody Strode. One of director John Ford's lesser westerns. There's rape, racial prejudice and courtroom dramatics thrown together in this muddled sagebrush drama. (118 mins.)

Sergeant Ryker (1968)** Lee Marvin, Bradford Dillman, Vera Miles, Peter Graves, Lloyd Nolan. Lee Marvin as an army sergeant on trial for treason during the Korean conflict. Fleshed out from a 1963 TV show, this is of ordinary interest aside from Marvin's strong performance. (Dir: Buzz Kulik, 85 mins.)†

Sergeants 3 (1962)** Frank Sinatra, Dean Martin, Sammy Davis, Jr., Peter Lawford, Joey Bishop. A supposedly high-camp remake of *Gunga Din* to accommodate Frank Sinatra and his buddies. (Dir: John Sturges, 112 mins.)

Sergeant York (1941)**** Gary Cooper, Walter Brennan, Joan Leslie, George Tobias, Stanley Ridges, Margaret Wycherly, Ward Bond, Noah Beery, Jr., June Lockhart. Story of WWI's greatest hero is told with simplicity and understanding and emerges as a poignant film. Cooper is perfectly cast as the Tennessee hillbilly who captured over a hundred Germans single-handed. (Dir: Howard Hawks, 134 mins.)†

Serial (1980)*** Martin Mull, Tuesday Weld, Bill Macy, Sally Kellerman, Peter Bonerz, Nita Talbot, Christopher Lee, Tom Smothers. For the benefit of those who do not live in California, the screenwriters have changed Cyra McFadden's popular comic novel from a satire of a specific place—Marin County—to a wry look at the American pursuit of the "good life" and inner peace. Mull and Weld star as a relatively sane couple trying to keep a grip on reality while others about them are losing theirs. (Dir: Bill Persky, 92 mins.)†

Serpent, The—See: **Night Flight from Moscow**

Serpent and the Rainbow, The (1988)* Bill Pullman, Cathy Tyson, Zakes Mokae, Paul Winfield. Badly acted, awfully scripted tale of an anthropologist/adventurer who explores the voodoo culture of Haiti searching for a powder that will cause "zombification." A few good nightmarish images and the attractive Tyson can't resurrect this loser. (Dir: Wes Craven, 98 mins.)†

Serpent of the Nile (1953)** Rhonda Fleming, Raymond Burr, William Lundigan. Foolish drama about the Roman Empire in the days of Cleopatra (Fleming) and Mark Antony (Burr) and their eventual suicides. (Dir: William Castle, 81 mins.)

Serpent's Egg, The (West Germany, 1977)** Liv Ullmann, David Carradine, Gert Frobe, Glynn Turman, James Whitmore, Heinz Bennent. It was an exciting idea: director Ingmar Bergman on a big budget doing a horror story about Germany in the early twenties. Well, it's a lousy film, interesting only for its superb art direction and the colossal wrongheadedness of its errors. Ullmann as a seedy cabaret performer fails to be slutty and irresistible. The great director is painfully vulnerable to the lure of his own clichés. (119 mins.)†

Serpico (1973)***½ Al Pacino, John Randolph, Jack Kehoe, Tony Roberts, Cornelia Sharpe. Peter Maas's book about real-life cop Frank Serpico, whose stories about corruption in the New York City police force led to an investigation, is turned into an excellent film by director Sidney Lumet. Pacino is brilliant in the title role of the cop who couldn't keep his mouth shut after witnessing cops on the take. Another plus is the sense of reality conveyed by the use of good New York location footage. (130 mins.)†

Serpico: The Deadly Games (MTV 1976)** David Birney, Allen Garfield, Burt Young, Lane Bradbury, Walter McGinn. A warm-up for an unsuccessful series based on the theatrical film with Al Pacino. Birney seems more like a college professor than a tough N.Y. cop battling corruption in the force and violence on the streets. (Dir: Robert Collins, 104 mins.)

Servant, The (Great Britain, 1963)***½ Dirk Bogarde, Sarah Miles, James Fox, Wendy Craig. Director Joseph Losey's first collaboration with playwright Harold Pinter explores themes of guilt and power as a manservant (Bogarde) corrupts his employer (Fox). Losey's dark, crowded compositions provide the perfect setting for the class war's Pyrrhic victory. (115 mins.)†

Service De Luxe (1938)**½ Constance Bennett, Vincent Price, Charlie Ruggles, Helen Broderick, Mischa Auer, Halliwell Hobbs. Nifty romantic comedy with chic Bennett as a hard-headed businesswoman running a service bureau that will tackle any job; Price is the customer who eventually warms her heart. Sharp and polished. (Dir: Rowland V. Lee, 85 mins.)

Sesame Street Presents: Follow That Bird (1985)** The Muppets, Dave Thomas, Waylon Jennings, Paul Bartel, Sandra Bernhard. Wobbly translation of the popular children's show has Big Bird venturing across the Midwest to find his friends on Sesame Street after his unsuccessful adoption by the Dodo family. A film that only small kids will enjoy; grown-ups may feel as if they were being forced to inhabit a muppet Internment Camp. (Dir: Ken Kwapis, 88 mins.)†

Sessions (MTV 1983)**½ Veronica Hamel, Jeffrey DeMunn, Jill Eikenberry. Hamel stars as a woman whose controlled life breaks down due to her conflicting identities—as an elegant call girl and as the mother of two young daughters. (Dir: Richard Pearce, 120 mins.)†

Set This Town on Fire (MTV 1972)*** Carl Betz, Chuck Connors, Lynda Day, Nancy Malone, Jeff Corey. Drama about the pressures placed on a respected newspaper publisher sets a slow pace, but the theme is different and fairly interesting. A publisher (Carl Betz) goes along with close friends in having second thoughts over a local hero imprisoned for manslaughter, and then regrets his change of heart. (Dir: David Lowell Rich, 99 mins.)

Settle the Score (MTV 1989)** Jaclyn Smith, Jeffrey DeMunn, Louise Latham, Howard Duff, Amy Wright, Richard Masur. Chicago policewoman Smith returns to her Arkansas home to ferret out the man who raped her twenty years before, discovers three other women have since been similarly attacked— and killed as well. Mystery thriller strains credulity throughout. (Dir: Ed Sherin, 96 mins.)

934

Set-up, The (1949)*** Robert Ryan, Audrey Totter, Alan Baxter, George Tobias. Tough if pretentious boxing film about a fighter on the skids who refuses to go crooked, helped by the gritty pugnacity of Ryan in the lead. Robert Wise directs rather well, considering limitations of budget and conception. (72 mins.)†

Seven (1979)* William Smith, Barbara Leigh, Christopher Joy, Guich Koock, Art Metrano, Martin Kove, Susan Kiger, Lenny Montana, Terry Kiser. Freelance agent is offered $7 million by the U.S. government to wipe out a gang of Hawaiian mobsters. Suposedly tongue-in-cheek action movie has no laughs, and is so badly photographed that even the impressive Hawaiian scenery and female pulchritude are wasted. (Dir: Andy Sidaris, 100 mins.)†

Seven Alone (1975)**½ Dewey Martin, Aldo Ray, Anne Collins, Stewart Petersen. Adventure film for family viewing. Based on *On to Oregon* by Honore Morrow, it relates the crisis-filled journey of six young brothers and sisters led by a 13-year-old boy across the wild terrain of America during the 1840s. (Dir: Earl Bellamy, 100 mins.)†

Seven Angry Men (1955)*** Raymond Massey, Debra Paget, Jeffrey Hunter, Dennis Weaver. Raymond Massey reprises his John Brown role from *Santa Fe Trail*. Tense climax and fine acting throughout bolster this Civil War western. (Dir: Charles Marquis Warren, 90 mins.)

Seven Beauties (Italy, 1975)***½ Giancarlo Giannini, Shirley Stoler, Fernando Rey, Elena Fiore. A paradoxical black comedy written and directed brilliantly by Lina Wertmuller. "Seven Beauties" is a nickname for a two-bit hoodlum known as the "monster of Naples" before WWII. Giannini's scene in the P.O.W. camp where he tries to save his life by making love to the gross German commandant, superbly played by Stoler, is one of the most searing scenes in modern cinema. (115 mins.)†

Seven Brides for Seven Brothers (1954) **** Jane Powell, Howard Keel, Russ Tamblyn, Tommy Rall. A rare treat—an original Hollywood musical which works in every department. Based loosely on a story by Stephen Vincent Benet, this tune-filled yarn tells of six fur-trapping brothers who come to town to find wives after their eldest brother (Keel) takes lovely Miss Powell as his bride. There's a kidnapping and a great many musical numbers before the happy conclusion. The dances by Michael Kidd are brilliant, and the entire cast is delightful. (Dir: Stanley Donen, 103 mins.)†

Seven Capital Sins (France-Italy, 1962)*** Jean-Louis Trintignant, Marina Vlady, Eddie Constantine, Jean-Pierre Aumont. The sins as depicted by some notable French directors, in an episodic film. (Dirs: Sylvain Dhomme, Eugene Ionesco, Max Douy, Edouard Molinaro, Philippe de Broca, Jacques Demy, Jean-Luc Godard, Roger Vadim, Claude Chabrol, 113 mins.)

Seven Chances (1925)**** Buster Keaton, T. Roy Barnes, Ruth Dwyer. Brilliant comedy built from the premise of a poor man who must marry by sunset or lose a fortune. Subtlety and slapstick mingle in perfect harmony in this most sublimely realized of all Keaton-directed fantasies. (60 mins.)

Seven Cities of Gold (1955)** Anthony Quinn, Richard Egan, Jeffrey Hunter, Michael Rennie, Rita Moreno. Routine costume adventure tale about the Spanish Conquistadors's 18th-century expedition to California in search of the legendary "Seven cities of gold." (Dir: Robert D. Webb, 103 mins.)†

Seven Days in May (1964)***½ Burt Lancaster, Kirk Douglas, Ava Gardner, Fredric March, Edmond O'Brien. An exciting suspense drama concerned with politics and the problems of sanity and survival in a nuclear age. Benefits from taut screenplay by Rod Serling, and the direction of John Frankenheimer, which artfully builds to the finale. (118 mins.)†

Seven Days' Leave (1942)**½ Victor Mature, Lucille Ball. Soldiers on leave discover that one of them will inherit a fortune if he can marry a girl who is already engaged. Mildly amusing musical comedy. (Dir: Tim Whelan, 87 mins.)

Seven Days to Noon (Great Britain, 1950)***½ Barry Jones, Olive Sloane. Tense drama about a deranged atomic scientist who threatens to blow up London if they fail to do his bidding. Excellent thriller; suspense on high throughout. (Dirs: John and Roy Boulting, 93 mins.)

Seven Deadly Sins (France-Italy, 1953)**** Gerard Philipe, Michele Morgan, Françoise Rosay. An episodic yet thoroughly enjoyable film dealing with each of the seven deadly sins. (Dirs: Edouard Molinaro, Jean Dreville, Yves Allegret, Roberto Rossellini, Carlo Rim, Claude Autant-Lara, Georges Lacombe, 120 mins.)

Seven Different Ways—See: **Quick, Let's Get Married**

7 Doors of Death (Italy, 1981)**½ Katherine MacColl, David Warbeck, Sarah Keller, Tony Saint John, Veronica Lazar. Gruesome thriller dealing with evil zombies from the netherworld invading Earth. Originally 90 mins. AKA: **The Beyond**. (Dir: "Louis Fuller" [Lucio Fulci], 80 mins.)†

711 Ocean Drive (1950)**½ Edmond

O'Brien, Joanne Dru, Otto Kruger, Bert Freed. Interesting crime yarn about an ingenious racketeer and the many tricks he employs to outwit the big gambling syndicate. O'Brien is fine in the leading role. (Dir: Joseph M. Newman, 102 mins.)

7 Faces of Dr. Lao (1964)*** Tony Randall, Barbara Eden, Arthur O'Connell. Randall's performance is the best thing about this fantasy set in the last century. He plays Dr. Lao, the mysterious magical Chinese proprietor of a circus that comes to town and generates a wave of good happenings. In addition to playing Dr. Lao, Randall plays six other roles with the aid of elaborate makeup and costumes—all performers in the one-man traveling show—he's great to watch. (Dir: George Pal, 100 mins.)†

Seven Hills of Rome, The (1957)**½ Mario Lanza, Peggie Castle. Mario singing and romancing a la Roma. Lotsa Lanza lungwork. (Dir: Roy Rowland, 104 mins.)

Seven Hours to Judgment (1988)** Beau Bridges, Ron Leibman, Julianne Phillips, Al Freeman, Jr. Driven insane after the muggers who killed his wife escape punishment on a legal technicality, a man kidnaps the judge responsible. (Dir: Beau Bridges, 100 mins.)†

Seven in Darkness (MTV 1969)**½ Milton Berle, Dina Merrill, Sean Garrison, Barry Nelson, Lesley Ann Warren. Highly melodramatic tale. Although its plane-crash-survivor theme is familiar, the fact that all the survivors are blind people on their way to a convention adds an interesting gimmick to the film. (Dir: Michael Caffey, 73 mins.)

Seven Keys to Baldpate (1929)**½ Richard Dix, Miriam Seegar, Margaret Livingston, Joseph Allen, Lucien Littlefield. First talkie version of George M. Cohan's hit play, adapted from Earl Derr Biggers's novel, about a mystery writer at an isolated inn interrupted by a crime and various suspicious characters. Neat comedy-mystery, energetically played. (Dir: Reginald Barker, 72 mins.)†

Seven Keys to Baldpate (1947)*** Philip Terry, Jacqueline White, Eduardo Ciannelli, Margaret Lindsay, Arthur Shields. The oft-filmed George M. Cohan comedy-mystery gets a polished treatment here from a top-flight cast. A mystery writer accepts a bet to spend a night in a notorious spookhouse. (Dir: Lew Landers, 66 mins.)

Seven Little Foys, The (1955)*** Bob Hope, Milly Vitale. Hope is a bit more reserved in this story about the real-life vaudeville family known as the Singing and Dancing Foys. Good production numbers and a guest appearance by James Cagney as George M. Cohan. (Dir: Melville Shavelson, 93 mins.)†

936

Seven Men from Now (1956)*** Randolph Scott, Gail Russell, Lee Marvin, Walter Reed, John Larch. Forceful western, the first of several teaming Scott with director Budd Boetticher. Ex-sheriff Scott searches for the gang that killed his wife during a robbery, and Marvin goes along to try for the loot. Tense and unrelenting, powerfully acted. (77 mins.)

Seven Miles from Alcatraz (1942)*** James Craig, Bonita Granville, Frank Jenks, Cliff Edwards. Interesting, tense B picture with an intriguing plot: two inmates break out of Alcatraz and hole up at a lighthouse, where they find German spies planning sabotage in San Francisco. Very well done, with strong performances. (Dir: Edward Dmytryk, 62 mins.)

Seven Minutes, The (1971)** Wayne Maunder, Marianne McAndrew, Philip Carey, Jay C. Flippen, Edy Williams. Seven minutes is the average time it takes a woman to achieve orgasm in this adaptation of an Irving Wallace novel, and it's also the title of a book on trial for obscenity. (Dir: Russ Meyer, 116 mins.)

Seven Minutes in Heaven (1986)**½ Jennifer Connelly, Maddie Corman, Byron Thames, Alan Boyce, Polly Draper, Marshall Bell. Enjoyable teenage film. Connelly and Corman learn about love and sex, while Thames tries to deal with a bad home situation, in this comedy-drama that boasts effective lead performances, though the awful pseudo-pop score sometimes makes it seem like a TV special. (Dir: Linda Feferman, 90 mins.)†

Seven-Per-Cent Solution, The (1976)***½ Nicol Williamson, Alan Arkin, Robert Duvall, Laurence Olivier, Joel Grey. An enjoyable lark! What would have happened if Sherlock Holmes had met with Sigmund Freud? According to Nicholas Meyer, who adapted his own novel for the screen, Freud could have cured the sleuth of his fondness for cocaine and Holmes could have solved the mystery of one of the psychiatrist's patients. Splendid cast. (Dir: Herbert Ross, 113 mins.)†

Seven Samurai (Japan, 1954)**** Takashi Shimura, Toshio Mifune, Seiji Miyaguchi. The definitive samurai film, and a great deal more. Seven masterless samurai agree to defend a peasant village in sixteenth-century Japan, with a few meals of rice as their only pay. The scope of this epic seems to encompass every aspect of the human condition, while projecting a unique blend of warmth, humor, suspense, and horror. Universally acclaimed, this film was remade as *The Magnificent Seven.* (Dir: Akira Kurosawa, 155 mins.) (Also available in a restored 208 min. version.)†

Seven Seas to Calais (Italy, 1962)** Rod

Taylor, Keith Michell, Irene Worth. Admiral Drake, pirate galleons, and war on the high seas highlight this spaghetti swashbuckler about England's defeat of the Spanish Armada, and her laying claim to the New World, circa 1588. (Dirs: Rudolph Maté, Primo Zeglio, 102 mins.)

Seven Sinners (1940)*** Marlene Dietrich, John Wayne, Albert Dekker, Anna Lee, Broderick Crawford. Honky-tonk singer attracts a handsome lieutenant. Trashy tale atoned for by a fine cast, plenty of rugged action. (Dir: Tay Garnett, 87 mins.)†

Seven Sweethearts (1942)**½ Kathryn Grayson, S. Z. Sakall, Marsha Hunt, Van Heflin. Cute, occasionally entertaining musical about seven lovely girls of Dutch ancestry living in Michigan with their daddy, S. Z. (Cuddles) Sakall. A bit too cute. (Dir: Frank Borzage, 98 mins.)

Seventeen (1940)*** Jackie Cooper, Betty Field, Otto Kruger, Ann Shoemaker. Cooper gives a winsome performance as the turn-of-the-century adolescent in this warmhearted version of Booth Tarkington's classic novel. (Dir: Louis King, 70 mins.)

1776 (1972)*** Ken Howard, William Daniels, Blythe Danner, Howard Da Silva. The hit Broadway musical has been tastefully transferred to the screen. The efforts of our Founding Fathers and the Continental Congress to have the Declaration of Independence ratified may sound like a dry history lesson, but it turns out to be an entertaining, touching film. (Dir: Peter H. Hunt, 150 mins.)†

7th Cavalry, The (1956)*** Randolph Scott, Barbara Hale. Good western about a cavalry unit returning to the scene of Custer's massacre. (Dir: Joseph H. Lewis, 75 mins.)

Seventh Cross, The (1944)***½ Spencer Tracy, Signe Hasso, Hume Cronyn. This is a truly exciting chase melodrama about an anti-Nazi who escapes from a concentration camp in 1936 and attempts to get out of the country. Beautifully acted. (Dir: Fred Zinnemann, 112 mins.)

Seventh Dawn, The (Great Britain, 1964)*½ William Holden, Capucine, Susannah York, Tetsuro Tamba, Michael Goodliffe. A hollow adventure set in Malaya right after WWII. Holden is a wealthy American planter in Malaya who finds himself caught in the web of guerrilla warfare and romantic upheaval. (Dir: Lewis Gilbert, 123 mins.)

Seventh Heaven (1927)*** Janet Gaynor, Charles Farrell, David Butler. Gaynor won the first Best Actress Oscar in this film about love in a garret in Paris. (Dir: Frank Borzage, 119 mins.)

Seventh Heaven (1937)*½ Simone Simon, James Stewart. Corny, inept sound version of the 1927 silent classic. (Dir: Henry King, 102 mins.)

Seven Thieves (1960)*** Edward G. Robinson, Rod Steiger, Joan Collins, Eli Wallach. Tense melodrama about a plot to rob the Monte Carlo gambling vaults. High-gear suspense, fine performances; only drawback is a weak ending. (Dir: Henry Hathaway, 102 mins.)

Seventh Seal, The (Sweden, 1957)**** Max von Sydow, Gunnar Bjornstrand, Bibi Andersson. Director Ingmar Bergman's masterpiece about the philosophical dilemmas of modern man. The setting is 14th-century Sweden. A knight (von Sydow) and his squire return from a crusade to find the black plague spreading death across their land. The knight confronts death incarnate to play a game of chess, with the knight's life at stake. Brilliantly directed and photographed. (105 mins.)†

Seventh Sign, The (1988)** Demi Moore, Michael Biehn, Jürgen Prochnow, Peter Friedman. A young couple awaiting their first child take in a mysterious boarder, and a series of events occur that seem to be connected to the unborn baby. A sometimes admirable attempt at an intelligent supernatural thriller, but the story is handled in too matter-of-fact a way to be very scary or involving. (Dir: Carl Schultz, 97 mins.)†

Seventh Sin, The (1957)** Eleanor Parker, Bill Travers, George Sanders. Wife becomes bored while married to a doctor and begins an affair with a shipping tycoon. Remake of an old Garbo film, *The Painted Veil,* but not an improvement. Mostly soap opera. (Dir: Ronald Neame, 94 mins.)

Seventh Veil, The (Great Britain, 1945)***½ Ann Todd, James Mason, Albert Lieven, Herbert Lom, Hugh McDermott. Superior psychological gothic romance. A beautiful young pianist (Todd) runs away from her tyrannical guardian (Mason—with a limp, yet) and can't choose between her two boyfriends. A friendly psychiatrist steps in. Beautifully set, fine musical sequences, and Mason's portrayal is archetypical. (Dir: Compton Bennett, 92 mins.)†

Seventh Victim, The (1943)***½ Tom Conway, Kim Hunter, Jean Brooks, Hugh Beaumont, Erford Gage. A supernatural *film noir,* made on a B movie budget, that contains some of the most poetic (yet chilling) moments ever seen in a horror movie. The straightforward story line has Hunter playing a girl who searches Greenwich Village for traces of her missing sister, who's become involved with a group of satanists. The eerie sense of foreboding and despair that underscores her search help to set this picture apart from the rather tame A-budget horror films of the era. (Dir: Mark Robson, 71 mins.)†

Seventh Voyage of Sinbad, The (1958)** Kerwin Mathews, Kathryn Grant, Torin Thatcher. Resolutely dull Ray Harryhausen fantasy film is about Sinbad's search for a roc's egg to restore his girlfriend to her former height (before she met an evil magician). (Dir: Nathan Juran, 87 mins.)†

Seven-Ups, The (1973)** Roy Scheider, Tony LoBianco, Richard Lynch. Producer Philip D'Antoni (*The French Connection, Bullitt*) made a shaky transition to director in this undercover cop story. Scheider leads the team of cops out to stop hoods from kidnapping one another. (103 mins.)†

Seven Ways from Sundown (1960)**½ Audie Murphy, Venetia Stevenson, Barry Sullivan. Well-made western starring Audie Murphy as a ranger with the strange name of Seven-Ways-from-Sundown Jones. (Dir: Harry Keller, 87 mins.)

Seven Women (1965)** Anne Bancroft, Margaret Leighton, Sue Lyon, Flora Robson, Betty Field, Mildred Dunnock, Anna Lee. Absurd China-based western, substituting wily Mongols for the standard complement of Indians. Mission personnel, circa 1935, are trying to protect themselves from a barbaric warlord. (Dir: John Ford, 93 mins.)

Seven Year Itch, The (1955)***½ Marilyn Monroe, Tom Ewell, Evelyn Keyes, Sonny Tufts. Monroe is ideally cast as a sexy model who lives in the same apartment building as a happily married man (Tom Ewell) who finds himself thinking and living like a bachelor when his wife goes on a prolonged summer vacation. Billy Wilder handles both his stars expertly and the result is high style comedy. Great fun. (105 mins.)†

Seven Years Bad Luck (1921)*** Max Linder, Thelma Percy, Alta Allen, Betty Peterson. Charming silent comedy spotlighting the talents of pioneering French clown Linder in his usual character of a debonair man-about-town, here dogged by mishaps after breaking a mirror. Inventive, cosmopolitan humor. (Dir: Max Linder, 85 mins.)†

Severed Head, A (Great Britain, 1971)**½ Lee Remick, Richard Attenborough, Claire Bloom. Talented cast works very hard to be chic in this faithful but awkward adaptation of Iris Murdoch's novel about multiple indiscretions among the British upper crust. (Dir: Dick Clement, 96 mins.)

Sex (1920)**½ Louise Glaum, Peggy Pearce, Irving Cummings, Myrtle Stead-

man. A fascinating curio, one of a rash of sensationalist melodramas popular in the early '20s. A glamorous, amoral actress breaks up a happy marriage for spite, but regrets it when the man she loves deserts her. Most interesting for what it reveals about the era. (Dir: Fred Niblo, 94 mins.)†

Sex (1972)—See: **Women in Revolt**

Sex and the Married Woman (MTV 1977)**½ Joanna Pettet, Barry Newman, Keenan Wynn. Sexual innuendo is all in this comedy about a married lady who writes a book about the sexual experiences of fifty others. (Dir: Jack Arnold, 104 mins.)

Sex and the Single Girl (1964)**½ Tony Curtis, Natalie Wood, Lauren Bacall, Henry Fonda. Helen Gurley Brown's best-seller has been turned into an innocent spoof of the sexual daydreams of Madison Avenue types and their female counterparts. The cast plays it for laughs that aren't always there. (Dir: Richard Quine, 114 mins.)

Sex and the Single Parent (MTV 1979)** Mike Farrell, Susan St. James. Light fare about a pair of divorcees with kids who start going together. (Dir: Jackie Cooper, 104 mins.)

Sexbomb (1989)** Robert Quarry, Linnea (Quigley), Stuart Benton, Delia Sheppard, Stephen Liska. Obnoxious movie producer Quarry is marked for murder by his scheming wife. Spoof of low-budget moviemaking is occasionally funny, especially in scenes on the set of Quarry's latest effort, *I Rip Your Flesh with Pliers*. (Dir: Jeff Broadstreet, 89 mins.)†

Sex Kittens Go to College (1960)* Mamie Van Doren, Tuesday Weld, Louis Nye, Martin Milner. A stripper with a high IQ is picked by a computer to head the science department of a college. Ghastly. (Dir: Albert Zugsmith, 94 mins.)

Sex, Lies, and Videotape (1989)** James Spader, Andie MacDowell, Peter Gallagher, Laura San Giacomo. Vastly overrated independent feature investigates a quartet of irritatingly empty characters. Spader is centerstage as an "artsy" type (he wears black, talks vague, and has no visible means of support) who challenges the belief systems of a neurotic woman, her oily yuppie husband, and her sexpot sister. The impotent Spader's metier of videotaping women as they discuss their sexual desires and frustrations is an outrageous plot device introduced as a way for the characters to grope each other emotionally and utter stoically pretentious dialogue. (Dir: Steven Soderbergh, 100 mins.)†

Sex Madness (1937)½ Completely serious attempt to educate audiences about the evils of sexual promiscuity and the dangers of syphilis. A cult classic. (53 mins.)†

Sex O'Clock News, The (1986)½ Doug Ballard, Lydia Mahan, Wayne Knight, Kate Weiman, Joy Bond. Lame spoof parodying newscasts and TV commercials. (Dir: Roman Vanderbes, 86 mins.)†

Sex Symbol, The (MTV 1974)*½ Connie Stevens, Shelley Winters, Jack Carter, William Castle, Don Murray, James Olson, Nehemiah Persoff, Malachi Throne. Sleazy "fictional" biography of a famous blonde movie queen who dates a senator, an intellectual, and has trouble with the studio heads. (Dir: David Lowell Rich, 72 mins.)

Sextette (1977)½ Mae West, Tony Curtis, Ringo Starr, Dom De Luise, Timothy Dalton, George Hamilton, Alice Cooper. The lady who invented sex on the screen came out of retirement at eighty-plus to make a fool of herself. Mae plays a much-married sex symbol who is being deluged by her ex-husbands on her current honeymoon. (Dir: Ken Hughes, 91 mins.)†

Sgt. Pepper's Lonely Hearts Club Band (1978)*½ Peter Frampton, the Bee Gees, Alice Cooper, George Burns, Billy Preston, Steve Martin, Donald Pleasence. Fairly stupid, badly filmed rip-off of the music of the Beatles by performers who had nothing to do with it. (Dir: Michael Schultz, 111 mins.)†

Shack Out on 101 (1955)*** Terry Moore, Frank Lovejoy, Lee Marvin, Keenan Wynn, Whit Bissell. A shameless but energetic slice of Red paranoia. Waitress Moore has got to juggle her dishes along with the men in her life, while striving to fight the inroads of Communism and to remember what the daily blue plate special is. (Dir: Edward Dein, 80 mins.)†

Shadey (Great Britain, 1987)*½ Antony Sher, Billie Whitelaw, Patrick Macnee. A murky exercise in black humor about a mind-reading man with a gift for putting inner visions and thoughts onto film. (Dir: Philip Saville, 90 mins.)†

Shadow Box, The (MTV 1980)*** Joanne Woodward, Christopher Plummer, James Broderick, Valerie Harper, Sylvia Sidney, Ben Masters, Melinda Dillon. The Pulitzer Prize–winning play by Michael Cristofer works better as a film, thanks to director Paul Newman. (111 mins.)†

Shadow Chasers (MTV 1985)**½ Dennis Dugan, Trevor Eve, Nina Foch, Hermione Baddeley. A dedicated anthropologist and a gangly news reporter chase the same paranormal funny business in California. (Dir: Kenneth Johnson, 104 mins.)

Shadow in the Sky (1951)**½ Ralph Meeker, Nancy Davis, James Whitmore, Jean Hagen. Trouble ensues when a war vet's brother-in-law comes to live with

him, after being discharged from a hospital with a psychological disorder. (Dir: Fred M. Wilcox, 78 mins.)

Shadow in the Street (MTV 1975)**½ Tony LoBianco, Sheree North. Tony LoBianco stars as an ex-con struggling to survive as a sympathetic parole agent. (Dir: Richard D. Donner, 74 mins.)

Shadow Man (Great Britain, 1953)**½ Cesar Romero, Kay Kendall. London gambling saloon owner Romero gets involved with murder, romance, and jealousy in this tense thriller. (Dir: Richard Vernon, 75 mins.)

Shadow of a Doubt (1943)**** Teresa Wright, Joseph Cotten, Patricia Collinge, Henry Travers. Gripping suspense film in the grand Hitchcock tradition. A niece suspects her uncle of being the Merry Widow murderer. This thriller, one of Hitchcock's best, beautifully captures the small town atmosphere. Screenplay cowritten by Thornton Wilder. Uniformly good performances. (108 mins.)†

Shadow of a Doubt (MTV 1991)**½ Mark Harmon, Margaret Welsh, Diane Ladd, Tippi Hedren, Shirley Knight. Quite good remake of Alfred Hitchcock's 1943 classic, updated to the '50s. Harmon is Uncle Charlie, a killer whose prey is rich, older women. Only his namesake niece (Welsh) suspects her loving uncle may very well be the Merry Widow murderer. Engrossing, right up to the suspenseful climax. (Dir: Karen Arthur, 96 mins.)

Shadow of China (U.S.-Japan, 1991)** John Lone, Vivian Wu, Sammi Davis, Koichi Sato. Slow-moving drama exploring Chinese-Japanese politics and corruption in Hong Kong ought to have been better. Lone and Wu flee a torn China in 1976 and end up in a demoralized Hong Kong. Mesmerizing cinematography is a plus. (Dir: Mitsuo Yanagimachi, 100 mins.)†

Shadow of Evil (France-Italy, 1964)** Kerwin Mathews, Robert Hossein, Pier Angeli. Flimsy plot concerns mad scientist, plague-contaminated rats in Bangkok. (Dir: André Hunebelle, 92 mins.)

Shadow of Fear (Great Britain, 1956)**½ Mona Freeman, Jean Kent, Maxwell Reed. Melodrama with some suspense but no surprises. (Dir: Albert S. Rogell, 76 mins.)

Shadow of the Cat, The (Great Britain, 1961)** Andre Morell, Barbara Shelley, William Lucas, Freda Jackson. A cat stalks her mistress's murderers. Moderately chilling. (Dir: John Gilling, 79 mins.)

Shadow of the Hawk (Canada, 1976)* Jan-Michael Vincent, Chief Dan George, Marianne Jones, Marilyn Hassett. A medicine man uses his city-bred grandson (Jan-Michael) as a ghostbuster to make troublesome spirits go to the happy hunting ground for cloddish thrillers. (Dir: George McCowan, 92 mins.)

Shadow of the Thin Man (1941)**½ William Powell, Myrna Loy, Barry Nelson, Donna Reed. Nick is solving a racetrack crime and, although it lacks the freshness of the others, it's still entertaining. (Dir: W. S. Van Dyke II, 97 mins.)†

Shadow on the Land (MTV 1968)* Jackie Cooper, John Forsythe, Carol Lynley, Gene Hackman. Uninspiring account of American under totalitarian rule, and the two men who seek to foment revolution. (Dir: Richard Sarafian, 100 mins.)

Shadow on the Wall (1950)** Ann Sothern, Zachary Scott, Gigi Perreau, Nancy Davis. Unconvincing murder meller—a child is sole witness to a murder for which her father has been unjustly convicted. (Dir: Patrick Jackson, 84 mins.)

Shadow on the Window (1957)**½ Phil Carey, Betty Garrett, John Barrymore, Jr., Jerry Mathers. Pretty good poverty-row psychological thriller, about a housewife kidnapped by a mentally disturbed criminal; bare-bones script, but effective direction by William Asher. (73 mins.)

Shadow Over Elveron (MTV 1968)** James Franciscus, Shirley Knight, Leslie Nielsen, Franchot Tone, Don Ameche. Predictable drama about a corrupt law officer in a small town and a dedicated young doctor who faces up to him and the town. (Dir: James Goldstone, 99 mins.)

Shadow Riders, The (MTV 1982)** Tom Selleck, Sam Elliott, Ben Johnson, Geoffrey Lewis, Jeffrey Osterhage. A routine western reuniting the cast of *The Sacketts*. In still another Louis L'Amour yarn, Selleck, Elliott, and Osterhage are brothers again, close-knit Texans who fought on opposite sides of the Civil War. (Dir: Andrew V. McLaglen, 104 mins.)

Shadows (1922)**½ Lon Chaney, Marguerite De La Motte, Harrison Ford, John Sainpolis, Walter Long. Chaney is smashing as a Chinese outcast coming to the aid of his minister friend in this otherwise preposterous melodrama; his great talent makes it worth seeing. (Dir: Tom Forman, 85 mins.)†

Shadows (1959)*** Lelia Goldoni, Ben Carruthers, Hugh Hurd. A seminal work for American independent cinema, director John Cassavetes's first feature parlayed the beat atmosphere of the late fifties into a model for low-budget narrative films bursting with personal expression. Cassavetes examines imperfect relationships—tentative, fervent, and cruel—with skeptical compassion. (87 mins.)

940

Shadows in the Night (1944)**½ Warner Baxter, Nina Foch, George Zucco. Above-average entry as Crime Doctor plies his sleuthing trade against a haunted-house backdrop. (Dir: Eugene Forde, 67 mins.)

Shadows of Forgotten Ancestors (U.S.S.R., 1964)*** Ivan Nikolaychuk, Larisa Kadochni Iova, Tatiana Bestayeva, Spartak Bagashvili. Mystical folk drama, shot with a wildly moving camera, about a man who falls in love with the daughter of the man who caused his father's death, but ends up marrying a woman reputed to be a sorceress. Unusual. (Dir: Sergo Paradjanov, 100 mins.)†

Shadows Over Chinatown (1946)** Sidney Toler, Mantan Moreland, Victor Sen Yung. The mysteries of Chinatown are pretty shadowy, but Charlie Chan throws enough light on them to nab a killer and expose an insurance racket. (Dir: Terry Morse, 61 mins.)

Shadow Warrior, The—See: **Kagemusha**

Shadowzone (1989)** David Beecroft, Louise Fletcher, James Hong, Shawn Weatherly, Lu Leonard. Scientists conducting dream research at an underground Arizona lab unleash a monster from another dimension. Starts out strong but soon abandons plot and logic for the usual monster mayhem. (Dir: J. S. Cardone, 88 mins.)†

Shady Lady (1945)**½ Charles Coburn, Robert Paige, Ginny Simms, Alan Curtis, Martha O'Driscoll. Pleasant B musical, with con artist Coburn deciding to go straight with the aid of niece Simms, finding it tougher than he expected. Coburn acts everyone else off the screen. (Dir: George Waggner, 94 mins.)

Shaft (1971)*** Richard Roundtree, Moses Gunn, Charles Cioffi. Black super-cop takes on the Mafia in Harlem. Action-packed thriller with some nice touches and a nearly perfect last ten minutes. (Dir: Gordon Parks, 106 mins.)†

Shaft In Africa (1973)** Richard Roundtree, Frank Finlay, Vonetta McGee, Cy Grant, Neda Arneric. John Shaft busts up the heinous crime crew running an Africa-to-France slave market. (Dir: John Guillermin, 112 mins.)

Shaft's Big Score (1972)*** Richard Roundtree, Moses Gunn, Drew Bundini Brown, Joseph Madcolo, Kathy Imrie. Maybe the best of the *Shaft* flicks, with lots of brawling brutality and almost nonstop violence. Shaft pits his macho badness against a mobster who's iced his main man. (Dir: Gordon Parks, 104 mins.)

Shaggy D.A., The (1976)**½ Dean Jones, Suzanne Pleshette, Tim Conway. Another slick Disney creation, sequel to *The Shaggy Dog*. Jones is a district attorney who turns into a canine at embarrassing times. (Dir: Robert Stevenson, 91 mins.)†

Shaggy Dog, The (1959)*** Fred MacMurray, Jean Hagen, Tommy Kirk, Annette Funicello. Cheerful tale of a boy's transformation into an old English sheep dog by way of a mystical antique ring. (Dir: Charles Barton, 104 mins.)†

Shag: The Movie (1989)**½ Phoebe Cates, Scott Coffey, Bridget Fonda, Annabeth Gish, Page Hannah, Tyrone Power, Jr., Carrie Hamilton. Not just another teen picture, this bright movie features a likable cast and a colorful "retro" look. Set in the summer of 1963, the plot is a variant on *Where the Boys Are*, with four Southern high school girls spending their last carefree summer in Myrtle Beach. (Dir: Zelda Barron, 98 mins.)†

Shakedown (1950)**½ Howard Duff, Peggy Dow, Brian Donlevy, Bruce Bennett, Peggie Castle, Lawrence Tierney. Effective *noir* about a ruthless, corrupt photographer who resorts to blackmail. Cogent, fast-moving B picture. (Dir: Joseph Pevney, 80 mins.)

Shakedown (1988)*** Peter Weller, Sam Elliott, Patricia Charbonneau, Antonio Fargas, Blanche Baker. A hip young lawyer and his grizzled cop friend investigate the corrupt elements of the Manhattan police force in this wonderfully entertaining but logicless action flick. Weller fights his battles in court and beds down with assistant D.A. Charbonneau, while tough guy Elliott handles all the action, whether it's leaping from a Forty-second Street theater marquee or hanging onto the wheel of an ascending plane. (Dir: James Glickenhaus, 105 mins.)†

Shakedown on the Sunset Strip (MTV 1988)*½ Perry King, Season Hubley, Joan Van Ark. An honest cop (King) decides to take on a notorious madam (Van Ark) who has powerful connections in L.A.'s city government. Purportedly based on real incidents, this TV movie has some bright spots, owing to good casting and a colorful script. (Dir: Walter Grauman, 96 mins.)

Shake Hands with the Devil (1959)*** James Cagney, Don Murray, Dana Wynter, Glynis Johns, Michael Redgrave. An excellent cast make up for the shortcomings of the script in this rather grim tale of the Irish rebellion. (Dir: Michael Anderson, 100 mins.)

Shake, Rattle and Rock (1956)*½ Lisa Gaye, Michael Connors, Fats Domino, Joe Turner, Margaret Dumont. A TV performer wants to open a rock-and-roll club for teenagers, but meets with opposition from snooty squares. (Dir: Edward Cahn, 72 mins.)

Shaker Run (New Zealand, 1986)* Cliff Robertson, Leif Garrett, Lisa Harrow. Shaky action pic about Robertson helping a scientist-on-the-run keep a deadly virus from falling into the wrong hands. (Dir: Bruce Morrison, 90 mins.)†

Shakespeare Wallah (India, 1965)*** Geoffrey Kendal, Laura Lidell, Felicity Kendall, Shashi Kapoor. A family of Shakespearean actors tours the land, playing for increasingly indifferent Indian audiences. Finely acted scenes from the Bard's plays are interwoven with personal dramas. (Dir: James Ivory, 115 mins.)†

Shakiest Gun in the West, The (1968)*½ Don Knotts, Barbara Rhoades, Jackie Coogan, Don Barry. In this remake of Bob Hope's *Paleface*, Don plays a cowardly salesman who has to stand up to a band of outlaws when he's mistaken for someone else. (Dir: Alan Rafkin, 101 mins.)†

Shalako (Great Britain, 1968)** Sean Connery, Brigitte Bardot, Honor Blackman, Stephen Boyd, Jack Hawkins. Despite a powerhouse cast, this western (about European big-game hunters in Indian-infested New Mexico, 1880) limps along under the pointless direction of Edward Dmytryk. (114 mins.)†

Shallow Grave (1987)** Tony March, Lisa Stahl, Tom Law. Lukewarm thriller about four college girls who get on the bad side of a Georgia sheriff when they see him commit murder. Talented filmmakers working with a shoddy script. (Dir: Richard Styles, 89 mins.)†

Shall We Dance (1937)*** Fred Astaire, Ginger Rogers. Revue artist and a ballet dancer are forced to pose as married. Fine musical comedy, with great dancing, tuneful Gershwin melodies. (Dir: Mark Sandrich, 109 mins.)†

Shame (1962)***½ William Shatner, Frank Maxwell, Beverly Lunsford. Both Shatner and director Roger Corman should be very proud of this unjustly neglected, low-budget effort. The story, adapted from the blistering novel by "Twilight Zone" writer Charles Beaumont, concerns a young man who comes into a small Southern town bent on stirring up racial hatred. Utilizing actual Missouri locations, the film has an authentic, disturbingly commonplace atmosphere, which reinforces its strong message about the simple-mindedness of bigotry. AKA: **The Intruder** and **I Hate Your Guts.** (84 mins.)

Shame (Sweden, 1968)**** Liv Ullmann, Max von Sydow, Gunnar Bjornstrand. Director Ingmar Bergman focuses on war in modern society, and how it degrades and humiliates us all. Married concert violinists flee to a small island to escape the civil war raging on the mainland. Ullmann is profoundly moving playing von Sydow's wife, trying to hang on to her own dignity while her husband and everyone around her lose theirs. (103 mins.)

Shame (Australia, 1988)* Deborra-Lee Furness, Tony Barry, Simone Buchanan. A thoroughly unpleasant drama which contains the sort of senseless violence common to any grade B potboiler, but which presents it under the guise of a redemptive "message" about persecution and apathy. A female stranger rides her motorcycle into a small Australian town and changes the lives of everyone in it by convincing a young girl to press charges against the gang of boys who raped her; the brutal results are not pleasant to watch. (Dir: Steve Jodrell, 90 mins.)†

Shameless Old Lady, The (France, 1965)**** Sylvie. Delightful, touching film about a 70-year-old widow who makes a late stab at putting a little fun in her life, after living a very quiet and sedate life. French character actress Sylvie gives a luminous and endearing performance. (Dir: Rene Allio, 94 mins.)

Shame of the Nation, The—See: **Scarface: The Shame of the Nation**

Shaming, The—See: **Good Luck, Miss Wyckoff**

Shampoo (1975)*** Warren Beatty, Julie Christie, Lee Grant, Carrie Fisher, Tony Bill, Jack Warden, Goldie Hawn. Insightful, complicated comedy that has something serious to say, often in very acerbic ways, about the morals and manners of our times. Beatty, who co-wrote the screenplay with Robert Towne, gives one of his most engaging performances as a hedonistic stud, a Beverly Hills hairdresser out to bed down with as many of his customers as time and energy permit. (Dir: Hal Ashby, 112 mins.)†

Shamrock and the Rose, The (1927)**½ Mack Swain, Olive Hasbrouck, Edmund Burns, Maurice Costello. Typical interfaith comedy of the '20s, modeled on the wildly popular *Abie's Irish Rose*, about the feud between the Cohens and the Kellys, and their teenage offspring, who fall in love. Exuberant acting enlivens tired material. (Dir: Jack Nelson, 69 mins.)†

Shamus (1973)**½ Burt Reynolds, Dyan Cannon. As a private eye, Reynolds smiles, smacks, kisses, and belts his way through a series of thugs, mugs, broads, and cops while trying to get to the bottom of a large export deal involving government arms. (Dir: Buzz Kulik, 99 mins.)†

Shane (1953)**** Alan Ladd, Jean Arthur, Van Heflin, Brandon de Wilde, Jack Palance. Truly epic western, among the

best ever made. Simple story of a gunfighter coming to the aid of homesteaders has been filmed with amazing skill by George Stevens, with some of the finest scenic values ever put on film. There's action, drama, fine performances. (118 mins.)†

Shanghai (1935)**½ Loretta Young, Charles Boyer, Warner Oland, Fred Keating, Charles Grapewin, Alison Skipworth. Unusual soap opera of an American socialite visiting Shanghai who falls in love with a Eurasian financier. Their love is above racism, but society, even in that exotic locale, won't accept an interracial relationship. Strong drama. (Dir: James Flood, 76 mins.)

Shanghai Express (1932)**** Marlene Dietrich, Clive Brook, Anna May Wong, Warner Oland. The keen eye of Josef von Sternberg crafted this, the ultimate experiment in Hollywood studio exoticism. Its plot concerns Shanghai Lily (Dietrich) and her reunion of sorts with ex-lover Brook on the slow-moving but incident-filled train to Shanghai. When Brook is taken hostage by a scheming rebel leader (Oland), Lily uses her somewhat tarnished virtue as ransom. The cinematography is peerless, the dialogue fine-tuned to camp perfection, and La Dietrich is at her most alluring. (84 mins.)

Shanghai Gesture, The (1941)** Gene Tierney, Walter Huston, Ona Munson, Eric Blore, Victor Mature. A tycoon is drawn into a web of evil in an Oriental gambling den, with his daughter as one of the lures. Arty, slow, far-fetched melodrama, but incredibly lurid for a Hollywood film of the forties. (Dir: Josef von Sternberg, 106 mins.)†

Shanghai Story, The (1954)**½ Ruth Roman, Edmond O'Brien. Americans in Shanghai are imprisoned by the Communists. (Dir: Frank Lloyd, 99 mins.)

Shanghai Surprise (1987)*½ Madonna, Sean Penn, Paul Freeman, Richard Griffiths. Missionary Madonna and ne'er-do-well Penn compete with assorted bad guys in 1930's China for a cache of opium. The story has some interesting twists and turns and the stars are better than their negative publicity, but the movie as a whole waddles along with no strong guiding hand. Executive producer George Harrison contributed the songs and has a cameo appearance as a restaurant bandleader. (Dir: Jim Goddard, 97 mins.)†

Shanks (1974)**½ Marcel Marceau, Philippe Clary, Cindy Eilbacher. A weird tale of a mute puppeteer who inherits an invention that makes dead bodies able to move. Much of this is genuinely creepy (especially if you think mimes are pretty scary to begin with). (Dir: William Castle, 93 mins.)

Shannon's Deal (MTV 1989)*** Jamey Sheridan, Elizabeth Pena, Martin Ferraro, Jenny Lewis, Miguel Ferrer, Claudia Christian, Richard Edson. Pilot for the gritty series about a Philadelphia lawyer, with a weakness for gambling, starting over with a small practice. Unlike most TV lawyers, Shannon aims to get all of his cases settled without having to go to court. Written by John Sayles. (Dir: Lewis Teague, 96 mins.)

Shape of Things to Come, The (Canada, 1979)*½ Jack Palance, Barry Morse, John Ireland, Carol Lynley. A loose but rather hackneyed adaptation of the H. G. Wells classic. (Dir: George McCowan, 95 mins.)

Sharing Richard (MTV 1988)*½ Ed Marinaro, Eileen Davidson, Nancy Frangione, Hillary Bailey Smith, Lisa Jane Persky. Flat farce with a one-joke premise: Three women, all friends, consciously share a boyfriend, divorced plastic surgeon Marinaro. (Dir: Peter Bonerz, 96 mins.)

Shark (1969)* Burt Reynolds, Barry Sullivan, Arthur Kennedy, Silvia Pinal. Burt and the boys look for booty while sharks nip at their heels. Watch this and you'll end up rooting for the sharks. (Dir: Sam Fuller, 92 mins.)†

Sharkfighters, The (1956)** Victor Mature, Karen Steele, James Olson. A naval research team of scientists headed by Victor Mature set out to find a shark repellent. (Dir: Jerry Hopper, 73 mins.)

Shark Kill (MTV 1976)* Richard Yniguez, Phillip Clark, Jennifer Warren. A made-for-TV ripoff of *Jaws*. It features a great white shark dining off divers until a macho marine biologist and an oil company consultant go fishing. (Dir: William A. Graham, 72 mins.)

Shark River (1953)** Steve Cochran, Carole Mathews, Warren Stevens. Brother accompanies a Civil War vet who has killed a man in the Everglades. Good scenery, but otherwise so-so melodrama. (Dir: John Rawlins, 80 mins.)†

Shark's Treasure (1974)*½ Cornel Wilde, Yaphet Kotto. Written, directed, and produced by its star, Cornel Wilde. A fishing-boat captain and crew look for sunken treasure, but not without interference from a band of escaped convicts and sharks. (95 mins.)†

Sharky's Machine (1981)*** Burt Reynolds, Vittorio Gassman, Brian Keith, Rachel Ward, Charles Durning, Bernie Casey, Henry Silva, Earl Holliman. Burt Reynolds is Sharky, the tough cop who leads his pack on the trail of a gangland leader and falls for a beautiful hooker. Good action scenes, and a romantic plot straight out of *Laura*. (Dir: Burt Reynolds, 119 mins.)†

Sharon: Portrait of a Mistress (MTV 1977)**½ Trish Van Devere, Patrick O'Neal, Sam Groom. Van Devere is appealing as a woman trapped in the life-style of a mistress. Everything goes along predictably until an unmarried man (Groom) takes an interest in her. (Dir: Robert Greenwald, 104 mins.)

Shattered Dreams (MTV 1990)** Lindsay Wagner, Michael Nouri, Georgeann Johnson, James Karen, Irene Miracle. Fact-based story about Charlotte Fedders (Wagner), a beautiful yet insecure housewife, married to a notable Washington official (Nouri), who was secretly a victim of battering and assault. Brutal tale lacks impact due to flat, uninteresting direction and a preachy script. (Dir: Robert Iscove, 96 mins.)

Shattered Dreams: Picking Up the Pieces (Great Britain, 1987)*** Hardhitting documentary about the realities of modern-day Israel. Tough-minded film studies the beginnings of the Jewish nation, but stresses contemporary issues including its conflict with Palestinians, the rise of a peace movement, economic stagnation, and other moral and ethical issues. AKA: **Israel's Shattered Dreams**. (Dir: Victor Schonfeld, 173 mins.)

Shattered Innocence (MTV 1988)* Jonna Lee, Melinda Dillon, John Pleshette. Following a PBS "Frontline" documentary on the life and tragic suicide of adult film star Shauna Grant (Colleen Applegate), this shoddy "message picture" was made for television. Her story has been broadly whitewashed so that the girl seems to walk blindly into her cocaine-induced dilemma. (Dir: Sandor Stern, 96 mins.)

Shattered Spirits (MTV 1986)*** Martin Sheen, Melinda Dillon, Matthew Laborteaux, Lukas Haas, Roxana Zal. Martin Sheen plays a father who is hooked on the bottle but refuses to think of it as a problem; this engrossing melodrama focuses on the effect a drinker has on the other members of his family. (Dir: Robert Greenwald, 104 mins.)

Shattered Vows (MTV 1984)**½ Valerie Bertinelli, Patricia Neal, Caroline McWilliams, David Morse. Bertinelli is quite good as a naïve teenager who wants to become a nun. However, once she meets a handsome young priest, her natural feelings and desires toward him threaten her sacred vows. (Dir: Jack Bender, 104 mins.)

She (Great Britain, 1925)*** Betty Blythe, Carlyle Blackwell, Mary Odette. Lavish, stirring version of the epic adventure by Sir H. Rider Haggard, who wrote the scenario and the titles for this production. The semi-mystical tale of explorers, searching for a lost city, who find the domain of an ageless, autocratic queen is still oddly compelling, and Blythe is terrific. (Dir: Leander DeCordova, 98 mins.)

She (1935)**½ Helen Gahagan, Randolph Scott, Helen Mack, Nigel Bruce, Gustav von Seyffertitz. Gahagan incarnates the role of H. Rider Haggard's immortal heroine, who jumps at the chance to retrieve a centuries-old love in the form of a rugged explorer (Scott). The set designs and exotic dance numbers were quite imaginative for the time. (Dirs: Irving Pichel, Lansing Holden, 96 mins.)

She (Great Britain, 1965)** Ursula Andress, John Richardson, Peter Cushing, Christopher Lee. Lesser remake of H. Rider Haggard's exotic romance. (Dir: Robert Day, 92 mins.)

S*H*E (MTV 1980)** Omar Sharif, Cornelia Sharpe, Anita Ekberg. Slick production values, exotic location shooting, and the beautiful Sharpe as a sexy female James Bond-type are the draws here. S*H*E (Securities Hazards Expert) is hot on the trail of international blackmailers who plan to jeopardize the world's oil supply if their demands aren't met. (Dir: Robert Lewis, 96 mins.)†

Sheba Baby (1975)*½ Pam Grier, Austin Stoker, D'Urville Martin. Pam's a private eyeful who challenges the mob when they muscle in on her papa's loan company. (Dir: William Girdler, 90 mins.)

She-Beast, The (Italy-Yugoslavia, 1965)*½ Barbara Steele, Ian Ogilvy, John Karlsen, Jay Riley, Mel Welles. Ancient spirit of an executed witch inhabits a pretty, young bride honeymooning in Transylvania, not the best place for celebrating connubial bliss. Poor. (Dir: Mike Reeves, 74 mins.)†

She Couldn't Say No (1954)*** Robert Mitchum, Jean Simmons. Oil heiress wishes to repay citizens of her home town for childhood kindnesses, disrupts the community in doing so. Pleasant, enjoyable comedy. (Dir: Lloyd Bacon, 89 mins.)

She Couldn't Take It (1935)*** George Raft, Joan Bennett, Walter Connolly, Billie Burke, Lloyd Nolan, Alan Mowbray, Donald Meek. A financier imprisoned for tax evasion takes a liking to a hood who wants to reform; when they get out of jail he hires him to look after his dizzy family. Lively screwball comedy, blithely directed by Tay Garnett. (75 mins.)

She Creature, The (1956)** Chester Morris, Marla English, Tom Conway, Cathy Downs. A two-bit Svengali uses his pretty assistant to summon up a creature that he hopes to use to eliminate his romantic rival. Not scary, but not schlocky either. (Dir: Edward L. Cahn, 76 mins.)

944

She Cried Murder! (MTV 1973)*½ Telly Savalas, Lynda Day George, Mike Farrell, Kate Reid, Jeff Toner. Widow witnesses a murder and has to face the killer, who turns out to be the inspector conducting the police investigation. Lacks plausibility or suspense. (Dir: Herschell Daugherty, 73 mins.)

She Demons (1958)** Irish McCalla, Victor Sen Yung, Tod Griffin, Rudolph Anders. Ridiculous melodrama of three hapless men trapped on an uncharted island with blonde bombshell McCalla. A favorite of bad-movie buffs. (Dir: Richard E. Cunha, 80 mins.)†

She Devil (1957)* Mari Blanchard, Jack Kelly, Albert Dekker. Unbelievably bad science-fiction tale about a she-monster. (Dir: Kurt Neumann, 77 mins.)

She-Devil (1989)** Meryl Streep, Roseanne Barr, Ed Begley, Jr., Sylvia Miles, A Martinez, Linda Hunt. Drawn in broad grotesque strokes, the humor of this watered-down adaptation of Fay Weldon's darkly comic novel seldom strikes the right chord. Story of an unattractive housewife's revenge on her nebbish husband and the glamorous romance novelist who stole him is underscored with lamentable dramatic overtones that are beyond the minimal range of comedienne Barr, who underplays. Streep, however, does a terrific job of overplaying her one-dimensional role. (Dir: Susan Seidelman, 99 mins.)†

She-Devils on Wheels (1968)½ Betty Connell, Pat Poston, Nancy Lee Noble, Christie Wagner, Ruby Tuesday. The real goods for fans of bad biker movies; gore *auteur* Herschell Gordon Lewis crafted this cheaper-than-cheap, gaudily colored epic depicting the activities of the "Maneaters on Motorbikes," a woman's gang that beats, verbally abuses, or jumps the bones of any male who gets in their way. (83 mins.)†

She Done Him Wrong (1933)**** Mae West, Cary Grant, Gilbert Roland. The best West film. Grant is the Salvation Army officer who meets his match in Mae, who tells him bluntly: "You can be had." Based on West's play *Diamond Lil*. (Dir: Lowell Sherman, 66 mins.)†

Sheena (1984)½ Tanya Roberts, Ted Wass, Donovan Scott, Trevor Thomas, Elizabeth of Toro. The comic strip heroine swings to the screen. Sheena involves herself in the struggle of two brothers for a throne, but the audience would find more drama on a leisurely drive through Lion Country Safari. (Dir: John Guillermin, 117 mins.)†

Sheepman, The (1958)*** Glenn Ford, Shirley MacLaine. Engaging, conventionally heroic western about a sheepman who tries to forge détente in a cattle town. (Dir: George Marshall, 85 mins.)

Sheer Madness (Germany-France, 1985) ***½ Hanna Schygulla, Angela Winkler, Peter Striebeck, Agnes Fink, Franz Buchrieser. A spellbinding, graceful film about two women whose powerful bond becomes both liberating and life-threatening. The conclusion is extraordinary in that it both ties together the film's preceding action yet creates new ambiguity. (Dir: Margarethe von Trotta, 105 mins.)†

She Gets Her Man (1945)**½ Joan Davis, Leon Errol, William Gargan, Milburn Stone, Vivian Austin. Robustly funny vehicle for Davis as the inept daughter of a famous female sleuth expected to carry on in her mother's footsteps. Davis and Errol made a very droll team. (Dir: Erle C. Kenton, 74 mins.)

Sheik, The (1921)**½ Rudolph Valentino, Agnes Ayres, Adolphe Menjou, Walter Long, Lucien Littlefield, George Waggner. Throbbing hearts and purple passions under the desert sun. Playing an oversexed desert royal who carries an English girl off to his tent, Rudy popped his eyes and women the world over swooned. (Dir: George Melford, 73 mins.)

Sheila Levine Is Dead and Living in New York (1975)*½ Jeannie Berlin, Roy Scheider, Rebecca Dianna Smith. Disappointing adaptation of Gail Parent's book of the familiar story of a spoiled Jewish girl from the suburbs who comes to New York in search of a husband and self-identity. (Dir: Sidney J. Furie, 112 mins.)

She Knows Too Much (MTV 1989)**½ Meredith Baxter Birney, Robert Urich, Erik Estrada. Birney and Urich make an amusing comic team as a paroled jewel thief and a bumbling fed who discover a political cover-up. (Dir: Paul Lynch, 96 mins.)

She Learned About Sailors (1934)**½ Lew Ayres, Alice Faye, William Green, Frank Mitchell, Jack Durant. The troubled romance of sailor Ayres and nightclub chanteuse Faye is assisted by rowdy seamen Mitchell and Durant. Fairly ordinary musical, with some good songs. (Dir: George Marshall, 78 mins.)

She Lives! (MTV 1973)*** Desi Arnaz, Jr., Season Hubley, Anthony Zerbe. An excellent performance by Hubley makes this a fine film. It's a *Love Story* clone about a young couple who discover the girl is dying, but unlike Ali MacGraw, Miss Hubley rages against that good night, refusing to go gently. (Dir: Stuart Hagmann, 73 mins.)

She'll Be Wearing Pink Pajamas (Great Britain, 1985)**½ Julie Walters, Anthony Higgins, Jane Evers, Janet Henfrey, Paula Jacobs. A coltish comedy about several women changing their lives through an outdoor survival session. Spirited acting ensemble enhances the script. (Dir: John Godschmidt, 90 mins.)†

Shell Seekers, The (MTV 1989)***½ Angela Lansbury, Patricia Hodge, Anna Carteret, Christopher Brown, Irene Worth, Sam Wanamaker, Sophie Ward, Michael Gough. While recovering from a heart attack, a widow ponders her life and tries to come to terms with the lives of her less-than-happy children. Effective drama adapted from the novel by Rosamunde Pilcher. (Dir: Waris Hussein, 96 mins.)

She Loves Me Not (1934)*** Bing Crosby, Miriam Hopkins, Kitty Carlisle, Lynne Overman. Tuneful Crosby vehicle spiced by Hopkins's effervescent playing of a performer on the lam. Leaving the scene of a murder, Miriam seeks refuge in Bing's college dormitory. (Dir: Elliott Nugent, 83 mins.)

Sheltering Sky, The (1990)*** Debra Winger, John Malkovich, Campbell Scott, Jill Bennett, Timothy Spall, Eric Vu-An, Paul Bowles. The cinematography by Vittorio Storaro is breathtakingly beautiful, the music by Ryuichi Sakamoto is hauntingly provocative. Bowles narrates this film (from his novel), about three lost souls, sex-starved intellectuals who think it's a lark to visit North Africa after WWII. They whine and wander and wound each other with their witty words. It's often tiresome but the good moments outshine the bad. Try to see this visual stunner in a movie house. (Dir: Bernardo Bertolucci, 137 mins.)†

She Married Her Boss (1935)***½ Claudette Colbert, Melvyn Douglas, Jean Dixon, Raymond Walburn. Unjustly neglected classic comedy with stars Colbert and Douglas at their impeccable best. (Dir: Gregory LaCava, 90 mins.)

She Must Be Seeing Things (1987)*** Sheila Dabney, Lois Weaver, Kyle DeCamp. While her lover is on the road, a lesbian finds and reads her diary. Jealous, she disguises herself as a man and follows her friend, hoping to unlock the puzzle of what she has read. Bold and elegiac film paints a searing picture of voyeurism and obsession. (Dir: Sheila McLaughlin, 95 mins.)

Shenandoah (1965)**½ James Stewart, Glenn Corbett, Doug McClure, Katharine Ross. Family entertainment with James Stewart playing the' head of a household torn apart by the Civil War, and giving one of his best performances. (Dir: Andrew McLaglen, 105 mins.)†

Shepherd of the Hills, The (1941)** John Wayne, Betty Field, Harry Carey. Good cast bogged down by sentimentality in the Harold Bell Wright tale of a man who returns to the Ozarks to face his son's hatred. Nice color photography by Charles Lang. (Dir: Henry Hathaway, 98 mins.)

She Played with Fire (Great Britain, 1958)**½ Jack Hawkins, Arlene Dahl. Melodrama about a beautiful woman who has a bad influence on men. (Dir: Sidney Gilliat, 95 mins.)

Sheriff, The (MTV 1971)**½ Ossie Davis, Ruby Dee, Ross Martin, Moses Gunn. Stars Ossie Davis as an elected black sheriff in a California town. Explosive situation develops when a black girl is raped and a white man is the chief suspect. (Dir: David Lowell Rich, 73 mins.)

Sheriff of Fractured Jaw, The (Great Britain, 1958)*** Kenneth More, Jayne Mansfield, Robert Morley, Henry Hull. Amusing western comedy. A British gentleman tries to establish his gunsmith business in the wild and woolly west of frontier days, and ends up sheriff of a lawless town. (Dir: Raoul Walsh, 102 mins.)

Sherlock Holmes series. Movie fans followed the adventures of the Baker Street detective, his sidekick Doctor Watson, and his perpetual nemesis Moriarty in many films, most memorably those with Basil Rathbone, starting with two period pieces, *The Hound of the Baskervilles* (1939) and *The Adventures of Sherlock Holmes* (1939). After these, Sherlock was updated to WWII as a combination secret agent and detective. In addition to the films reviewed below, fans will want to see Rathbone's other exercises in deductive reasoning: *The Scarlet Claw, The Pearl of Death, The House of Fear, The Woman in Green, Pursuit to Algiers, Terror by Night* and *Dressed to Kill* (1946). Other Holmes-related adventures include: *The Hound of the Baskervilles* (1959, 1972 and 1977), *A Study in Scarlet, The Seven Per Cent Solution, Murder by Decree, The Private Life of Sherlock Holmes, A Study in Terror, They Might be Giants, The Triumphs of Sherlock Holmes, Sign of Four, The Return of the World's Greatest Detective, Young Sherlock Holmes,* and *The Return of Sherlock Holmes.*

Sherlock Holmes (1932)*** Clive Brook, Reginald Owen, Ernest Torrence. Handsomely mounted early Holmes adaptation; Torrence is especially appealing playing Moriarty. (Dir: William K. Howard, 68 mins.)

Sherlock Holmes and the Deadly Necklace (Great Britain-West Germany, 1964)**½ Christopher Lee, Senta Berger, Thorley Walters. Holmes and Dr. Watson once again combat the evil Moriarty, who's after a valuable necklace. (Dir: Terence Fisher, 85 mins.)

Sherlock Holmes and the Secret Weapon (1942)*** Basil Rathbone, Nigel Bruce, Lionel Atwill. Imaginative Holmesian exercise beefed up by the intense competition between Holmes and archrival Moriarty. Sherlock's aiding the war effort by trying to stop vital information from falling into the Gestapo's hands. (Dir: Roy William Neill, 68 mins.)†

Sherlock Holmes and the Spider Woman (1944)*** Basil Rathbone, Nigel Bruce, Gale Sondergaard, Dennis Hoey. Sondergaard proves to be a more than equal adversary for the great Holmes in this, one of the best of the Rathbone-Bruce series. She plays a scheming villainess who is behind a series of unexplained "suicides" of men holding large insurance policies. (Dir: Roy William Neill, 62 mins.)†

Sherlock Holmes and the Voice of Terror (1942)*** Basil Rathbone, Nigel Bruce, Evelyn Ankers, Reginald Denny, Thomas Gomez. Persuasive programmer in which the British government enlists Holmes's aid in taking a Nazi radio broadcast off the airwaves. (Dir: John Rawlins, 65 mins.)†

Sherlock Holmes Faces Death (1943)*** Basil Rathbone, Nigel Bruce, Hillary Brooke. Dr. Watson seeks Sherlock's help in unraveling the mystery of Musgrave's mansion, where the homicides are piling up. Enjoy the film's high point, as Sherlock puts the suspects on the mansion's checkered floor and moves them about like chess pieces. (Dir: Roy William Neill, 68 mins.)†

Sherlock Holmes in New York (MTV 1976)*** Roger Moore, John Huston, Patrick Macnee, Gig Young, Charlotte Rampling. Moore as Holmes matches wits with Huston's wily Professor Moriarty over a scheme to steal gold from the major companies. (Dir: Boris Sagal, 104 mins.)

Sherlock Holmes in Washington (1943)*** Basil Rathbone, Nigel Bruce, Henry Daniell, George Zucco. One of the better entries. Holmes goes to the nation's capital in pursuit of a nest of Nazi spies and some highly critical microfilm. (Dir: Roy William Neill, 70 mins.)†

Sherlock Jr. (1924)**** Buster Keaton, Kathryn McGuire. Keaton may have made funnier films, or even more profound ones, but nothing touches this, the definitive silent-comedy meditation on the meaning of cinema. Fast-moving and surreal, it hasn't dated a whit. Wildly hilarious masterpiece. (Dir: Buster Keaton, 57 mins.)

Sherman's March (1986)**½ Ross McElwee. A generally enjoyable but amorphous docu-comedy. McElwee set out to make an impassioned documentary about Sherman's march to the sea during the Civil War, but instead ended up filming his failed romantic encounters in a contemporary battle of the sexes. (Dir: Ross McElwee, 155 mins.)

She Said No (MTV 1990)**½ Veronica Hamel, Judd Hirsch, Lee Grant, Ray Baker, Mariclare Costello. Engrossing, well-acted courtroom drama about a smooth establishment lawyer (Hirsch) who rapes, then attacks his victim (Hamel) in court when he sues her for slander. (Dir: John Patterson, 96 mins.)

She's a Soldier Too (1944)**½ Beulah Bondi, Nina Foch, Jess Barker, Lloyd Bridges, Percy Kilbride, Shelley Winters. Patriotic B picture about a lady cabdriver helping a soldier find his long-lost son. Worth watching. (Dir: William Castle, 67 mins.)

She's a Sweetheart (1944)** Larry Parks, Jane Frazee, Jane Darwell, Nina Foch. Middling little wartime musical, with a backstage romance between Parks and Frazee providing plenty of opportunities for singing and dancing. OK of this type. (Dir: Del Lord, 69 mins.)

She's Back (1989)** Carrie Fisher, Robert Joy, Matthew Cowles, Joel Sweto. Sporadically funny comedy of murdered Fisher haunting husband Joy, nagging him to get revenge on the burglars who killed her. Starts out well, but runs out of steam. (Dir: Tim Kincaid, 90 mins.)†

She's Back on Broadway (1953)*** Virginia Mayo, Steve Cochran, Gene Nelson, Frank Lovejoy, Patrice Wymore. Neat little backstage melodrama of a movie star returning to the stage and her ex-lover, now a famous director on the skids. Well done. (Dir: Gordon Douglas, 95 mins.)

She's Been Away (Great Britain, 1990)***½ Peggy Ashcroft, Geraldine James, James Fox, Jackson Kyle, Hugh Lloyd. Superb drama that deserves to be seen. Ashcroft has been locked away in a mental institution for 60 years. Now that it's being torn down she must move in with her nephew's troubled family, which demands readjustment on both parties behalf. Assured direction and flawless performances make this a winner. First film in 15 years by brilliant theater director Hall. (Dir: Peter Hall, 107 mins.)†

She's Dressed to Kill (MTV 1979)** Eleanor Parker, John Rubinstein, Jessica Walter, Clive Revill, Corinne Calvet. Parker is the haute couture designer who plans a big comeback to be staged at her sumptuous mountain home. Naturally, the top beautiful people are invited and the murderer strikes. AKA: **Someone's Killing the World's Greatest Models.** (Dir: Gus Trikonis, 104 mins.)†

She's Gotta Have It (1986)*** Tracy Camila Johns, Tommy Redmond Hicks, John Canada Terrell, Spike Lee, Raye Dowell. A bright, perceptive comedy about a sexy Brooklynite and the three men and one woman vying for her affection, shot in black and white on a shoestring budget. (Dir: Spike Lee, 84 mins.)†

She's Having a Baby (1988)* Kevin Bacon, Elizabeth McGovern, Alec Baldwin, William Windom, Cathryn Damon. Pretentious, sexist comedy about two young marrieds who struggle with his career, her parents, and the possibility of producing offspring. Director-scripter John Hughes needs to be forced to watch the films of Mazursky and Rohmer to learn how an adult relationship comedy can be handled successfully. (106 mins.)†

She's In the Army Now (MTV 1981)** Kathleen Quinlan, Jamie Lee Curtis, Susan Blanchard, Julie Carmen, Melanie Griffith, Janet MacLachlan. A cross between *Private Benjamin* and *An Officer and a Gentleman*, but not as good as either. (Dir: Hy Averback, 104 mins.)†

She's Out of Control (1989)** Tony Danza, Catherine Hicks, Ami Dolenz, Wallace Shawn. Sitcom shenanigans, with Danza unable to cope with his fifteen-year-old daughter's overnight transformation into a heartbreaker beauty via grooming tips from Dad's girlfriend (Hicks). (Dir: Stan Dragoti, 95 mins.)

She's Working Her Way Through College (1952)** Virginia Mayo, Steve Cochran, Gene Nelson, Ronald Reagan. A burlesque queen goes to college. Remake of *The Male Animal*. (Dir: H. Bruce Humberstone, 101 mins.)

She Waits (MTV 1972)** Patty Duke, David McCallum, Dorothy McGuire, Lew Ayres. Ghost-story enthusiasts get still another tale full of curtains rustling, and a mother-in-law warning that evil spirits are lurking about the family mansion. (Dir: Delbert Mann, 73 mins.)†

She Went to the Races (1945)**½ James Craig, Frances Gifford, Ava Gardner, Edmund Gwenn, Reginald Owen. Cute low-budget comedy about a serious-minded girl who invented a successful system for betting on horseraces, falling for a happy-go-lucky gambler. (Dir: Willis Goldbeck, 86 mins.)

She-Wolf of London (1946)** June Lockhart, Don Porter. Routine lady werewolf thriller. After watching Lockhart in this, you'll be examining re-runs of "Lassie" with a suspicious eye. (Dir: Jean Yarbrough, 61 mins.)

She Wore a Yellow Ribbon (1949)**** John Wayne, Joanne Dru, John Agar. Most elegiac of all westerns, beautiful and subtle in detailing an aging officer's reluctance to quit when the Indians threaten. Like its retiring cavalry officer, the film ages well. (Dir: John Ford, 103 mins.)†

She Wouldn't Say Yes (1945)** Rosalind Russell, Lee Bowman, Adele Jergens. Roz shouldn't have said yes to this script. With her customary aplomb, Roz plays a lady shrink involved with one of her patients. (Dir: Alexander Hall, 87 mins.)

She Wrote the Book (1946)**½ Joan Davis, Jack Oakie, Mischa Auer, Kirby Grant, Gloria Stuart. Comedy vehicle for Davis as a prissy teacher who's written a torrid bestseller. Good supporting cast helps a lot. (Dir: Charles Lamont, 72 mins.)

Shield for Murder (1954)*** Edmond O'Brien, Marla English, John Agar, Carolyn Jones. Crooked cop kills a bookmaker and hides twenty-five grand. Brutal crime melodrama is well made, nicely acted. (Dirs: Howard Koch, Edmond O'Brien, 80 mins.)

Shifting Sands (1918)**½ Gloria Swanson, Joe King, Lillian Langdon. An early vehicle for a young but already glamorous Swanson as a poor-but-honest slum girl trying to support her invalid sister and make it as an artist. Swanson's star quality shines. (60 mins.)†

Shinbone Alley (1971)*** Voices of Eddie Bracken, Carol Channing, John Carradine. Feature-length cleverly animated cartoon based on the characters, archy the cockroach and mehitabel the cat. (Dir: John D. Wilson, 84 mins.)†

Shine on Harvest Moon (1944)**½ Ann Sheridan, Dennis Morgan, Jack Carson, Marie Wilson. Some good old songs but not much more in this ridiculously fictionalized biography of entertainers Nora Bayes and Jack Norworth. (Dir: David Butler, 112 mins.)†

Shining, The (1980)**½ Jack Nicholson, Shelley Duvall, Danny Lloyd, Scatman Crothers, Barry Nelson, Anne Jackson, Joe Turkel. Eerie atmosphere and arresting images of violence abound, but we're never wrapped up in this ironic Stephen King tale of a failed writer who trundles his wife and psychically gifted son off to a caretaker job. (Dir: Stanley Kubrick, 142 mins.)†

Shining Hour, The (1938)*** Joan Crawford, Margaret Sullavan, Robert Young, Melvyn Douglas. A compelling melodrama about family dissension. A farmer is determined to stop his brother from wedding a worldly woman, but he finds himself attracted to her himself. (Dir: Frank Borzage, 80 mins.)

Shining Season, A (MTV 1979)*** Timothy Bottoms, Allyn Ann McLerie, Rip Torn. This real-life tale of an Olympic-class miler cut down by cancer is a heart wringer. Bottoms plays Albuquerque's John Baker, always on the move, bursting with life until cancer takes over. (Dir: Stuart Margolin, 104 mins.)

Shining Star—See: That's the Way of the World

Shining Victory (1941)***½ James Stephenson, Geraldine Fitzgerald, Donald Crisp. A selfless psychiatric researcher is loved by his devoted assistant, and tragedy strikes. This simple, straightforward plot is turned into a magically moving picture, due to fine production values and deeply romantic performances. (Dir: Irving Rapper, 80 mins.)

Ship Ahoy (1942)**½ Eleanor Powell, Red Skelton, Bert Lahr, Frank Sinatra. Entertaining but trite little musical about a girl who is unwittingly helping enemy agents. (Dir: Edward Buzzell, 95 mins.)

Shipmates Forever (1935)**½ Dick Powell, Ruby Keeler. Musical about Annapolis has a nice score and a tired story. Interesting Annapolis setting and the music make it attractive entertainment. (Dir: Frank Borzage, 108 mins.)

Ship of Fools (1965)**½ Simone Signoret, Oskar Werner, Lee Marvin, Vivien Leigh, Michael Dunn, George Segal, Elizabeth Ashley, José Ferrer, Lilia Skala, Kaaren Verne. Director Stanley Kramer's adaptation of the Katherine Anne Porter novel reduces her ironies to bromides on the moral dangers of social appeasement. Still, some star turns recommend the film. (149 mins.)†

Ships With Wings (Great Britain, 1941)*** John Clements, Michael Wilding, Michael Rennie, Ann Todd. A pilot cashiered from the service becomes a hero aboard an aircraft carrier when WWII breaks out. (Dir: Sergei Nolbandov, 89 mins.)

Ship That Died of Shame, The (Great Britain, 1955)*** Richard Attenborough, Virginia McKenna. Drama about the conversion of a one-time heroic war ship into a smuggling vessel. Top performances. (Dirs: Michael Relph, Basil Dearden, 91 mins.)

Shipwrecked (U.S.-Norway, 1991)*** Stian Smestad, Gabriel Byrne, Bjorn Sundquist, Eva Von Hanno. Thoroughly enjoyable family adventure, which weakens a bit in the middle, but recovers. An engrossing tale about a young lad who signs on as a cabin boy on a seagoing ship in order to save the family farm and comes face-to-face with dangerous pirates, being marooned, and the struggle to survive. (Dir: Nils Gaup, 93 mins.)†

Shiralee, The (Great Britain, 1957)*** Peter Finch, Elizabeth Sellars, Dana Wilson, Rosemary Harris, Tessie O'Shea, Sidney James, George Rose. Depression-era story of a roving Australian workman who takes his five-year-old daughter with him when he finds her mother unfit. (Dir: Leslie Norman, 99 mins.)

Shirley Valentine (1989)***½ Pauline Collins, Tom Conti, Julia McKenzie, Alison Steadman, Joanna Lumley, Sylvia Syms, Bernard Hill. Delightful adaptation of the one-woman play that won a Tony Award for Collins as a Liverpool housewife who sees an escape from her humdrum routine when her best friend invites her on a trip to Greece. Playwright Willy Russell's dialogue is choice, and Collins gives it her all. (Dir: Lewis Gilbert, 108 mins.)†

Shirts/Skins (MTV 1973)*** Bill Bixby, Doug McClure, McLean Stevenson, Leonard Frey. Fascinating, forthright story about a group of moderately successful men who turn a weekly basketball match into a hide-and-seek, win-or-lose contest which escalates into near disaster. (Dir: William Graham, 73 mins.)

Shivers (1975)—See: **They Came From Within**

Shivers (1981)—See: **Dreszcze**

Shoah (France, 1985)**** Shoah means annihilation in Hebrew. In this remarkable documentary, director Claude Lanzmann, through indefatigable research, and superb interviewing builds a cumulative impact throughout this searing, invaluable "Witness" to the virtual extinction, by the Nazis of the Jewish community in Europe during WWII. *Shoah* consists mostly of interviews with those few Jews who survived being at the death camps and the SS officers, talking, with great detachment, about exactly how the death factories worked. The most powerful film ever made about the Holocaust. (570 min.)†

Shock, The (1923)**½ Lon Chaney, Virginia Valli, Jack Mower, William Welsh, Henry Barrows. Strange, disjointed melodrama of crippled criminal Chaney induced to reform by a woman's love and the San Francisco earthquake. The special effects are cheap, but Chaney's complex, deeply felt performance is thoroughly engrossing. (Dir: Lambert Hillyer, 96 mins.)†

Shock (1946)** Vincent Price, Lynn Bari. Price plays a murdering psychiatrist whose newest patient has witnessed his recent spouse-icide. The old B movie cat-and-mouse game, with the skulking shrink trying to prolong the victim's selective amnesia indefinitely. (Dir: Alfred Werker, 70 mins.)†

Shock Corridor (1963)*** Peter Breck, Constance Towers, Gene Evans, James Best, Hari Rhodes. Maverick filmmaker Sam Fuller will take any chance and revitalize any cliché in order to make his point, and this cult classic about a reporter's exploration of the daily life of a mental institution proves that once and for all. Breck plays a Pulitzer-hungry journalist who decides to have himself committed to an asylum so he can investigate an unsolved murder that occurred there. The bizarre inmates he encounters, his nightmares about his stripper girlfriend, and the super-8 home movie footage (Sam's own) used to represent the inmates' traumas all have the manic stamp of Fuller's imagination. (101 mins.)†

Shocker (1989)** Michael Murphy, Peter Berg, Mitch Pileggi, Cami Cooper, Theodore Raimi. An obvious attempt by writer-director Wes Craven to create another profitable *Nightmare on Elm Street*-type horror series, with an executed mass murderer living on in electrical systems and television sets, continuing to terrorize the family of his last victim. Some clever moments. (110 mins.)†

Shocking Miss Pilgrim, The (1947)** Betty Grable, Dick Haymes. Tedious musical about women's suffrage and the first lady secretary set in 1874 Boston. (Dir: George Seaton, 85 mins.)

Shockproof (1949)*** Cornel Wilde, Patricia Knight. Female ex-con falls for her parole officer while trying to go straight. Well-made melodrama with a slightly different slant. Leads were married at the time. (Dir: Douglas Sirk, 79 mins.)

Shock to the System, A (1990)***½ Michael Caine, Swoosie Kurtz, Elizabeth McGovern, John McMartin, Peter Riegert, Will Patton, Jenny Wright. Delicious adaptation of Simon Brett novel tells disturbing but wickedly funny story of business executive Caine, who uses murder as a corporate tool. Entire cast is outstanding in perversely elegant film. (Dir: Jan Egleson, 89 mins.)†

Shock Treatment (1964)*½ Lauren Bacall, Stuart Whitman, Roddy McDowall, Carol Lynley. Objectionable film about an actor who is paid to be committed to an asylum, where he is to obtain information concerning the whereabouts of stolen money from a psychotic patient. (Dir: Denis Sanders, 94 mins.)

Shock Treatment (Great Britain, 1981)*** Jessica Harper, Cliff De Young, Richard O'Brien, Charles Gray. Imaginative and colorful sequel to *The Rocky Horror Picture Show*. Here "Denton, U.S.A." is a giant labyrinthian TV station where the breakup of Brad and Janet's ideal marriage is played out on several vapid TV programs. Aside from the broad lampooning of video mediocrity and several catchy tunes, the film stands as a terrific vehicle for the talented Ms. Harper (who solos every five minutes) and a chance to see the delightful "*Rocky*" cast at work again. (Dir: Jim Sharman, 95 mins.)†

Shock Waves (1977)*** Peter Cushing, Brooke Adams, John Carradine, Luke Halprin. This bizarre horror flick is imaginative throughout and, on occasion, quite chilling. An abandoned island is the dumping ground of a Nazi experiment in creating a Master Race Army, a batallion of storm troopers that can stay alive under water. AKA: **Death Waves.** (Dir: Ken Wiederhorn, 86 mins.)†

Shoeshine (Italy, 1946)**** Rinaldo Smerdoni, Franco Interlenghi. Director Vittorio De Sica's best film is a heart tugger of substantial dimensions. Our emotions are constantly aroused in this story of two street kids who want to save up to buy a horse, but overpowering emotion builds to such a climax that all is forgiven. (93 mins.)

Shoes of the Fisherman, The (1968)** Anthony Quinn, Laurence Olivier, John Gielgud, Barbara Jefford, Oskar Werner. A simple-minded Pope opera based upon Morris West's thoughtful novel. Concerns a Russian Pope and his influence on world peace. (Dir: Michael Anderson, 157 mins.)†

Shogun (MTV 1980)***½ Richard Chamberlain, Toshiro Mifune, Yoko Shimada, Damien Thomas, Alan Badel. James Clavell's massive novel about feudal Japan became one of TV's most successful mini-series. Chamberlain's English hero, Blackthorne, faces shipwrecks, Japanese samurai and beautiful ladies in this superb production, which was drastically re-edited to this shorter running time. (Dir: Jerry London, 125 mins.)†

Shoot (Canada, 1976)½ Cliff Robertson, Ernest Borgnine, Henry Silva, James Blendick, Helen Shaver, Kate Reid. Violent, unbelievable tale of a hunting accident that turns the woods into a war zone. (Dir: Harvey Hart, 98 mins.)†

Shooter (MTV 1988)*½ Jeffrey Nordling, Alan Ruck, Noble Willingham, Jeffrey Alan Chandler, Helen Hunt. Combat photographers on the loose in Vietnam. It's "click, click, click" all the way, as the photojournalists capture action at the front and in the streets of Saigon. However, all of the characters are cardboard figures. (Dir: Gary Nelson, 96 mins.)

Shooters, The (1990)*½ Benjamin Schick, Robin Sims, Aldo Ray, Ray Essler, Randy Hogen. Mildly diverting comedy about a misfit squad of soldiers who have to prove their worth by doing well in a war games competition. (Dir: Peter Yuval, 87 mins.)†

Shoot First (Great Britain, 1953)*** Joel McCrea, Evelyn Keyes. American officer thinks he has killed a man while hunting, but becomes involved in a spy plot while clearing himself. Well-knit thriller enlivened by good comedy sequences. (Dir: Robert Parrish, 88 mins.)

Shoot First: A Cop's Vengeance (MTV 1991)**½ Dale Midkiff, Alex McArthur, G. D. Spradlin, Terry O'Quinn. Slightly-above-average true-life cop drama. Midkiff is a Texas officer watching his partner (McArthur) take the law into his own hands. It's the old vigilante tale in modern dress. (Dir: Mel Damski, 96 mins.)

Shooting, The (1967)**½ Millie Perkins, Will Hutchins, Jack Nicholson, Warren Oates. Offbeat western. Miss Perkins, bent on revenge, gets two young cowpokes to help her in her deeds. (Dir: Monte Hellman, 82 mins.)†

Shooting Party, The (Great Britain, 1985)*** James Mason, John Gielgud, Dorothy Tutin, Edward Fox. A gathering of upper crust elitists enjoy the civilized pleasures of pheasant hunting until unexpected violence destroys the game. The actors, particularly Mason in this superb and final performance of his distinguished career, comprise an impeccable ensemble. (Dir: Alan Bridges, 108 mins.)†

Shooting Stars (MTV 1983)* Billy Dee Williams, Parker Stevenson, Efrem Zimbalist, Jr., Frank McRae, Dick Bakalyan. Williams and Stevenson are two actors in a TV show about private eyes. Their jealous co-star starts a smear campaign that costs the actors their jobs, so they become real-life private eyes. (Dir: Richard Lang, 104 mins.)†

Shootist, The (1976)*** John Wayne, Ron Howard, James Stewart, Lauren Bacall. Western drama about an old gunman dying of cancer who decides to "exit" with all guns a-blazin' and take a few mean varmints with him. (Dir: Don Siegel, 100 mins.)†

Shoot Loud, Louder, I Don't Understand (Italy, 1966)**½ Marcello Mastroianni, Raquel Welch. A zany, if not hilarious, comedy about the wild goings-on in a strange household inhabited by Marcello Mastroianni and his eccentric uncle. (Dir: Eduardo de Filippo, 100 mins.)†

Shoot Out (1971)** Gregory Peck, Dawn Lyn, Pat Quinn. A tired western, undistinguished but not bad. Based on Will James's novel *The Lone Cowboy*. (Dir: Henry Hathaway, 95 mins.)

Shoot-Out at Medicine Bend (1957)*½ Randolph Scott, James Craig, Angie Dickinson, James Garner. Typical Scott oater in which good predictably triumphs over evil. (Dir: Richard L. Bare, 87 mins.)

Shootout in a One Dog Town (MTV 1973)**½ Richard Crenna, Stefanie Powers, Jack Elam, Arthur O'Connell. Slick western yarn with a twist ending. Crenna is a small-town banker entrusted with a

$200,000 deposit and must use all his resources to keep it from being stolen by a gang of desperadoes. (Dir: Burt Kennedy, 74 mins.)

Shoot the Moon (1982)*** Albert Finney, Diane Keaton, Karen Allen, Peter Weller, Dana Hill, Viveka Davis, Tina Yothers. Powerful drama of a marriage that breaks up, its effect on the children, the husband's relationship with his mistress, the wife's liaison with her newfound lover, and the inability of the couple to make a clean break. Depressing but compelling. (Dir: Alan Parker, 123 mins.)†

Shoot the Piano Player (France, 1960)**** Charles Aznavour, Marie Dubois, Nicole Berger, Michele Mercier, Albert Remy. Director François Truffaut calls this "a pastiche of the Hollywood B film." Ironic story of a timid pianist (magnificently played by Aznavour) who has retreated from the concert stage to play in a second-rate café. Pictorially stunning, with canny use of the scope frame. (92 mins.)†

Shoot the Sun Down (1981)*½ Margot Kidder, Geoffrey Lewis, Christopher Walker. Aimless western using the *Stagecoach* gimmick of throwing disparate types together; some Way-Out-West wayfarers are locked in a search for gold. (Dir: David Leed, 93 mins.)†

Shoot to Kill (1947)**½ Edmund MacDonald, Russell Wade, Vince Barnett, Susan Walters. Effective, moody thriller about an ambitious prosecutor willing to bend the law to his own ends who tangles with a dangerous escaped prisoner. Gritty, tense atmosphere, forceful performances. (Dir: William Berke, 64 mins.)

Shoot to Kill (1988)*** Sidney Poitier, Tom Berenger, Kirstie Alley, Clancy Brown, Richard Masur. Poitier, in fine form after a ten-year absence from acting, plays an FBI agent who teams with hiking guide Berenger to pursue a vicious killer who has fled into the mountains. Familiar black cop/ white cop dynamics ensue, but the stars and some crisp action scenes carry the film. (Dir: Roger Spottiswoode, 110 mins.)†

Shop Angel (1932)** Marion Shilling, Holmes Herbert, Anthony Bushell, Walter Byron. Low-budget romance of a department store dress designer who gets involved with a scheme to blackmail her boss, falling in love with his daughter's fiancé. Ordinary story well acted and well produced. (Dir: E. Mason Hopper, 71 mins.)†

Shop Around the Corner, The (1940)**** Margaret Sullavan, James Stewart, Frank Morgan, Joseph Schildkraut. Lovely romantic comedy, set in Prague, about two shop assistants who fall in love by mail. Stewart and Miss Sullavan are

charming together. (Dir: Ernst Lubitsch, 97 mins.)

Shop on High Street, The—See: **Shop on Main Street, The**

Shop on Main Street, The (Czechoslovakia, 1965)**** Ida Kaminska, Josef Kroner. One of the most heartrending and moving films ever. A Slovak (Kroner) befriends and protects an elderly Jewess (Kaminska) until he receives a deportation order. Kaminska is altogether extraordinary and richly deserved the critical acclaim she received. Exquisitely directed by Jan Kadar and Elmar Klos. Oscar: Best Foreign Film. AKA: **The Shop on High Street**. (128 mins.)†

Shopworn (1932)** Barbara Stanwyck, Regis Toomey, ZaSu Pitts, Lucien Littlefield. Silly soap opera about a waitress railroaded into prison by her lover's snobbish mother. When she gets out, she becomes a singing star. Stanwyck does her best with dumb material. (Dir: Nick Grinde, 72 mins.)

Shopworn Angel, The (1938)*** Margaret Sullavan, James Stewart, Sam Levene, Walter Pidgeon. Sentimental romance with a 1917 setting is beautifully acted and quiet-ly touching. (Dir: H. C. Potter, 85 mins.)

Shore Leave (1925)*** Richard Barthelmess, Dorothy Mackaill, Ted McNamara, Nick Long. Delightful comedy about a tough sailor who meets a lonely seamstress while on leave; he forgets all about her, but she sets to work readying a derilict ship she owns for his return. Two-character romantic comedy, deliciously played. (Dir: John S. Robertson, 68 mins.)†

Short Circuit (1986)**½ Ally Sheedy, Steve Guttenberg, Fisher Stevens, G. W. Pendleton. Struck by lightning, an adorable state-of-the-art robot/soldier escapes to become a pop-culture spouting peacenik. Sheedy and Guttenberg set out to save him from the nasty folks over in the Defense Dept. (Dir: John Badham, 99 mins.)†

Short Circuit 2 (1988)*½ Fisher Stevens, Michael McKean, Cynthia Gibb, Jack Weston. That eager-to-learn robot heads for the big city in this silly sequel. Young kids will still enjoy it, but Stevens's ludicrous portrayal of a malapropism-spouting Indian scientist makes it hard going for anyone over the age of ten. (Dir: Kenneth Johnson, 112 mins.)†

Short Cut (Czechoslovakia, 1981)*** Jiri Schmitzer, Magda Vasaryova, Rudolf Hrusinsky, Haromir Hanzlik. Nostalgic, gently comic film about the inhabitants of a small Czech village prior to WWI, living in a world unfazed by outside events until the coming of radio pushes them into the present. (Dir: Jiri Menzel, 98 mins.)

Short Cut to Hell (1957)**½ Robert Ivers, Georgann Johnson. Professional killer is double-crossed after committing murder, seeks his revenge. Interesting for two reasons: it's a remake of *This Gun for Hire*, and it was directed by James Cagney, who handles his task nicely. (87 mins.)

Shortest Day, The (Italy, 1963)**½ Franco Franchi, Ciccio Ingrassia. Two zany soldiers accidentally destroy Germany's secret weapon during WWII. A rather cheerful burlesque of *The Longest Day*. (Dir: Sergio Corbucci, 82 mins.)

Short Eyes—See: **Slammer**

Short Film about Killing, A (Poland, 1988)***½ Miroslaw Baka, Krzysztof Globisz, Jan Tesarz. A young man without goals or hope murders a belligerent cabdriver. When he is sentenced to death, a public outcry results. Powerful film, designed to illustrate the commandment "Thou shalt not kill," depicts both killings with brutal images meant to disturb audiences. (Dir: Krzysztof Kieslowski, 84 mins.)

Short Films of D. W. Griffith, The (1911–12)**** Videocassette collection of three influential early films of groundbreaking director D. W. Griffith. *The Battle*, with Charles West and Blanche Sweet, is an elaborately produced, exciting Civil War adventure. *The Female of the Species* is a remarkable western starring Mary Pickford, Claire McDowell, and Dorothy Bernard as pioneer women lost in the western desert who struggle with interpersonal rivalries as well as starvation and thirst. *The New York Hat* is one of Griffith's most famous productions, a comedy (written by 14-year-old Anita Loos) starring Mary Pickford as a smalltown girl who becomes the victim of unjustified gossip when she accepts the gift of a stylish hat. All were directed with amazing skill, and remain vastly entertaining. (59 mins.)†

Short Fuse—See: **Good to Go**

Short Time (1990)**½ Dabney Coleman, Matt Frewer, Teri Garr, Barry Corbin, Joe Pantoliano. Pleasant, fast-moving action comedy about veteran police detective, only days away from retirement, who is mistakenly told he has a terminal disease. So that he can leave his family a hefty insurance payment, he tries to get himself killed in the line of duty. Not believable for a second, but it works thanks to brisk direction by Gregg Champion and three likable leads. (97 mins.)†

Short Walk to Daylight (MTV 1972)** James Brolin, Abbey Lincoln. Suspense adventure tale about seven passengers on a New York subway train who try to find their way to safety after an earthquake destroys a good part of the city. (Dir: Barry Shear, 73 mins.)

Shotgun (1955)**½ Sterling Hayden, Yvonne De Carlo, Zachary Scott. Interesting western, hero out to avenge a brutal murder. (Dir: Lesley Selander, 81 mins.)

Shot in the Dark, A (1964)***½ Peter Sellers, Elke Sommer, Herbert Lom, George Sanders, Tracy Reed, Graham Stark, Burt Kwouk. Best of the Pink Panther films has bumbling Inspector Clouseau convinced maid Sommer is innocent of murder, despite mountains of evidence to the contrary. Energetic farce is full of classic scenes, wonderful music by Henry Mancini. Alan Arkin took over the role in the sequel, *Inspector Clouseau;* Sellers next played Clouseau in *The Return of the Pink Panther*. (Dir: Blake Edwards, 101 mins.)†

Shout, The (Great Britain, 1979)***½ Alan Bates, Susannah York, John Hurt. Implications of menace and sexual aggression are forcefully conveyed by Bates as a scruffy madman, Hurt as a highstrung composer, and York as the wife who comes under a spell cast by the sinister Bates. (Dir: Jerzy Skolimowski, 87 mins.)†

Shout at the Devil (Great Britain, 1986)* Lee Marvin, Roger Moore, Barbara Parkins, Sam Holm, Jean Kent. I don't know about the devil, but this film shouts at the audience with plane crashes, explosions, etc. Marvin, who seems weighed down by the bags under his eyes, and Moore, who looks as if tanning rigor mortis were stiffening his performance, play WWI adventurers in this petrified action pic. (Dir: Peter Hunt, 147 mins.)†

Showboat (1929)*** Laura LaPlante, Alma Rubens, Elsie Barlett, Joseph Schildkraut. Original version of Kern-Hammerstein musical, once feared lost, filmed as a silent with music added after shooting. Prologue features the cast of the Broadway production, including the legendary Helen Morgan. (Dir: Harry Pollard, 130 mins.)

Show Boat (1936)**** Irene Dunne, Allan Jones, Helen Morgan, Paul Robeson, Charles Winninger, Hattie McDaniel. A magnificent movie musical. Somehow, the director better known for reviving the horror genre with *Frankenstein* also managed to breathe new life into the musical comedy form with this definitive version of the landmark musical. Director James Whale's expressionistic style enhances the plot of this melodramatic tale about two contrasting love affairs on a Mississippi riverboat. A powerhouse musical with an evergreen score and a beautiful song written especially for the film, "I Have the Room Above Her." (113 mins.)†

Show Boat (1951)*** Kathryn Grayson, Howard Keel, Ava Gardner, Marge and Gower Champion, Joe E. Brown, Agnes Moorehead. The unforgettable Jerome Kern score is still a big asset to this colorful version of the noted musical drama of love aboard a Mississippi show boat. Otherwise, the cast is highly capable, the song numbers put over with zest. (Dir: George Sidney, 107 mins.)†

Show Business (1944)*** Eddie Cantor, Joan Davis, George Murphy, Constance Moore. Fans of Banjo Eyes and the Queen of Slapstick will be in their glory as Cantor and Davis deliver comedy routines and songs in a socko vaudevillian style. The plot has Cantor's talent take him from the Bowery to the Follies. (Dir: Edwin L. Marin, 92 mins.)†

Showdown, The (1950)*** William Elliott, Walter Brennan, Marie Windsor, Jim Davis, Harry Morgan. Former state trooper looking for his brother's killer finds suspects in a gambling house. (Dirs: Dorrell, Stuart McGowan, 86 mins.)

Showdown (1963)** Audie Murphy, Kathleen Crowley, Charles Drake. Two drifters are imprisoned with some outlaws, who force them to hand over some stolen bonds. (Dir: R. G. Springsteen, 79 mins.)

Showdown (1972)**½ Rock Hudson, Dean Martin, Susan Clark. Above-average western. Good-guy Rock is a sheriff who has to track down his old childhood buddy who has chosen the crooked path. (Dir: George Seaton, 99 mins.)

Showdown at Boot Hill (1958)**½ Charles Bronson, Robert Hutton, John Carradine, Fintan Meyler, Carole Mathews. A bounty hunter kills a criminal but can't collect his money when the townspeople, who liked the dead fellow, refuse to identify his body. (Dir: Gene Fowler, Jr., 73 mins.)†

Show of Force, A (1990)** Amy Irving, Lou Diamond Phillips, Kevin Spacey, Erik Estrada, Robert Duvall, Andy Garcia. Brazilian director Bruno Barreto's first U.S. movie is little more than a vanity piece for his girlfriend Irving, cast as a TV news reporter investigating government complicity in the deaths of two Puerto Rican terrorists. Loosely based on a true 1978 incident, film fails to impress as an indictment of U.S. covert actions. Prominently billed Duvall and Garcia appear only briefly. (93 mins.)†

Show People (1928)*** Marion Davies, William Haines, Dell Henderson, Paul Ralli. Charming comedy of country girl Davies (modeled on Gloria Swanson) determined to make it big in Hollywood, but becoming a slapstick star rather than a glamour queen. Wonderful backstage fun with lots of star cameos. (Dir: King Vidor, 82 mins.)†

Show Them No Mercy (1935)*** Rochelle Hudson, Cesar Romero, Bruce Cabot, Edward Norris, Edward Brophy, Warren Hymer. An innocent young couple and their baby unwittingly become involved with a vicious gang of kidnappers. Tense, intelligent thriller remade in western form as *Rawhide*. (Dir: George Marshall, 76 mins.)†

Shriek in the Night, A (1933)** Ginger Rogers, Lyle Talbot, Arthur Hoyt, Purnell Pratt. Dated programmer with Ginger and Lyle both trying to get the goods on a murderer. (Dir: Albert Ray, 66 mins.)†

Shriek of the Mutilated (1974)½ Tawn Ellis, Alan Brock, Jennifer Stock, Darcy Brown, Michael Harris. Viewers are likely to shriek too. A mutilated monster mash about some students trying to get the goods on bigfoot. Instead, they run into abominable snowmen and then discover that the yetis are ersatz. (Dir: Michael Findlay, 92 mins.)

Shrike, The (1955)*** José Ferrer, June Allyson, Ed Platt, Joy Page, Mary Bell. The impressive B'way play by Joseph Kramm is brought to the screen and weakened by miscasting of Allyson in the role of the domineering wife who nearly destroys her husband by her love turned to jealousy and a watered-down script which reverts to a happy ending. Ferrer repeats his B'way role as the husband and is very effective. (Dir: José Ferrer, 88 mins.)

Shut My Big Mouth (1942)**½ Joe E. Brown, Adele Mara, Victor Jory, Fritz Feld, Pedro de Cordoba, Lloyd Bridges, Forrest Tucker, Noble Johnson, Chief Thundercloud. One of Brown's best later vehicles has him as a tenderfoot out West becoming sheriff by accident, and tangling with outlaw Jory. Sprightly comedy. (Dir: Charles Barton, 71 mins.)

Shuttered Room, The (Great Britain, 1967)*½ Carol Lynley, Gig Young, Oliver Reed. Contrived mystery yarn. Lynley comes back to her New England home town with her husband, Gig Young, and learns some shocking things about her family tree. (Dir: David Greene, 99 mins.)

Shy People (1987)**½ Barbara Hershey, Jill Clayburgh, Martha Plimpton, Merritt Butrick, Mare Winningham. Emigré Russian director Andrei Konchalovsky, in his fourth American film, has concocted a movie that is equally full of beautiful, resonant images and laughable plot elements and characterizations. The story concerns a New York journalist (Clayburgh) who takes her spoiled teenage daughter to visit a cousin (Hershey) who lives with her four wild sons deep in the Louisiana bayou. Worth watching for many reasons, but it's far from a great film—it's difficult even to tell just what the movie's purpose is. (118 mins.)†

Siberian Lady Macbeth (Yugoslavia, 1962) *** Olivera Markovic, Ljuba Tadic, Miodrag Lazarvic, Bojan Stupica. Bizarrely melodramatic tale about the idle wife of a merchant who, when her husband is away, takes a lover, a wanton drifter with whom she commits murder. Based on a 1865 story by Nikolai Leskow. (Dir: Andrzej Wajda, 95 mins.)

Sibling Rivalry (1990)*** Kirstie Alley, Jami Gertz, Bill Pullman, Carrie Fisher, Scott Bakula, Ed O'Neill, Sam Elliott. An unhappy homemaker takes the advice of her free-spirited sister and has an affair in a hotel room. The lover dies in her arms, which leads to wonderfully comic plot twists about a lost brother, new drapes, and marital honesty. A well-acted, finely written American farce. (Dir: Carl Reiner, 88 mins.)†

Sicilian, The (1987)* Christopher Lambert, Barbara Sukowa, Terence Stamp, John Turturro. Muddled melodrama about a Sicilian outlaw who steals from the rich Mafia to buy land for the poor farmers which fails to convey any grandeur or excitement. Haphazard combination of soap opera, revenge drama, and epic hero worship. The "director's cut" released on video runs 146 mins. (Dir: Michael Cimino, 115 mins.)†

Sicilian Clan, The (France, 1969)*** Jean Gabin, Alain Delon, Lino Ventura. Heist caper with style and restrained acting. Gabin heads a family that occasionally indulges in a spectacular crime. They spring an old friend, Delon, and embark on their biggest job yet—stealing a cache of diamonds from a DC-8. (Dir: Henry Verneuil, 116 mins.)

Sid and Nancy (1986)***½ Gary Oldman, Chloe Webb, Drew Scofield, David Hayman. A harrowing, offbeat account of the tortured lives and love affair of Sex Pistols star Sid Vicious and his groupie-manager, Nancy Spungen. One doesn't have to like punk rock music or feel sympathy for these rebellious drug-addicted losers to be carried away by the film's ability to mine humor out of the most anguished circumstances. (Dir: Alex Cox, 111 mins.)†

Siddhartha (1972)**½ Shashi Kapoor, Simi Garewal, Pinchoo Kapoor, Romesh Shama. Despite Sven Nykvist's imaginative cinematography and the director's good intention, this philosophical head trip will be rough going for those not in synch with Hesse's college crowd pleaser novel. (Dir: Conrad Rooks, 95 mins.)

Siddharta and the City—See: **Adversary, The**

Side by Side (MTV 1982)*½ Marie Osmond, Joseph Bottoms. Sugary saga of the Osmond family and how Mom, Pop, and the children started in show biz. (Dir: Russ Mayberry, 104 mins.)

Side by Side (MTV 1988)** Milton Berle, Sid Caesar, Danny Thomas, Morey Amsterdam, Marjorie Lord. A trio of elderly gents who decide to fight against their mandatory retirement by starting their own clothing firm. (Dir: Jack Bender, 96 mins.)

Sidecar Racers (1974)*½ Ben Murphy, Wendy Hughes, John Clayton, Peter Graves. Dangerous sport of two-man motorcycle racing finds Murphy, a visiting American, teaming with an Australian for the big race. Noisy! (Dir: Earl Bellamy, 100 mins.)

Sidekicks (MTV 1974)**½ Larry Hagman, Lou Gossett. Amiable feature stars Hagman as the white western hustler who keeps selling his black buddy Gossett as a slave. (Dir: Burt Kennedy, 72 mins.)

Side Out (1990)*½ C. Thomas Howell, Peter Horton, Courtney Thorne Smith, Harley Jane Kozak, Terry Kiser. Midwesterner Howell moves to L.A. and persuades dissolute former volleyball champ Horton to clean up his act and get back into the game. Fourth-rate jock opera. (Dir: Peter Israelson, 100 mins.)†

Side Show (MTV 1981)** Lance Kerwin, Connie Stevens, Tony Franciosa, William Windom, Calvin Levels, Red Buttons. Contrived drama about a teenager who joins the circus and grows up quickly. (Dir: William Conrad, 104 mins.)†

Side Street (1949)**½ Farley Granger, Cathy O'Donnell, James Craig, Paul Kelly, Jean Hagen. Although the plot of this low-budget gangster drama is old hat, the performances of Granger and Miss O'Donnell as a pair of newlyweds down on their luck give it added dimension. (Dir: Anthony Mann, 83 mins.)

Sidewalks of London (Great Britain, 1938)**½ Charles Laughton, Vivien Leigh, Rex Harrison. A London street entertainer picks up a waif and sees her go to stardom, sacrificing his love for her to do so. Well acted, but brittle, unconvincing drama with music. AKA: **St. Martin's Lane.** (Dir: Tim Whelan, 84 mins.)†

Sidewalks of New York (1931)*** Buster Keaton, Anita Page, Cliff Edwards. Buster plays a slumlord who falls in love with a lady of the tenements (Page). The comedy is mostly uninspired; you can see that Keaton had no significant creative control of the film. But some flashes of brilliance, worth watching for. (Dirs: Jules White, Zion Myers, 70 mins.)

Sidewalk Stories (1989)*** Charles Lane, Nicole Alysia, Sandye Wilson, Darnell Williams. Writer-director-star Lane's debut feature film is a black-and-white silent comedy about New York's homeless, focusing on a young street artist trying to find the mother of a baby whose father he has seen murdered. An auspicious debut by Charles Lane. (97 mins.)†

Sidney Shorr: A Girl's Best Friend (MTV 1981)*** Tony Randall, Lorna Patterson, Kaleena Kiff, David Huffman, John Lupton. Charming and delightful movie, with Randall as the lonely New Yorker who shares his apartment with a young actress, Patterson. Randall is marvelous as Sidney, the homosexual, beginning a platonic relationship that turns into love and fatherhood. (Dir: Russ Mayberry, 104 mins.)

Siege (MTV 1978)***½ Martin Balsam, Sylvia Sidney, Dorian Harewood, James Sutorius. A gripping story right out of the newspaper headlines about inner city gangs who repeatedly prey on the aged. (Dir: Richard Pearce, 104 mins.)

Siege at Red River, The (1954)**½ Van Johnson, Joanne Dru, Richard Boone. Interesting western with action and history combined to tell the story about the forerunner of the machine gun, the Gatling gun, and how it served to revolutionize warfare. (Dir: Rudolph Maté, 81 mins.)

Siege of Firebase Gloria, The (Australia, 1988)*½ Wings Hauser, R. Lee Emery, Albert Popwell, Gary Hershberger. Clichéd story of a sadistic U.S. Marine serving in Vietnam during the 1968 Tet offensive. (Dir: Brian Trenchard Smith, 95 mins.)†

Siege of Sidney Street, The (Great Britain, 1960)*** Donald Sinden, Nicole Berger, Kieron Moore. Anarchist gang is trapped by police, which develops into one of the bloodiest battles in the annals of British crime. Historical melodrama should interest most viewers. (Dirs: Robert Baker, Monty Berman, 94 mins.)

Sierra (1950)**½ Audie Murphy, Wanda Hendrix, Burl Ives, Dean Jagger, Richard Rober, Tony Curtis, James Arness. Good, low-key western of a father and son on the run from a posse after the father is unjustly accused of murder. (Dir: Alfred E. Green, 83 mins.)

Sierra Baron (1958)**½ Brian Keith, Rick Jason, Mala Powers, Rita Gam. Colorful, burly western, shot on location near the Mexican border, about settlers trying to defend their land against crooks. None too original, but capably done. (Dir: James B. Clark, 80 mins.)

Siesta (U.S.-Great Britain, 1987)** Ellen Barkin, Gabriel Byrne, Julian Sands, Isabella Rossellini, Martin Sheen, Alexi Sayle, Jodie Foster, Grace Jones. A consciously "arty," ultimately preten-tious study of a stunt woman (Barkin) and her fall from grace. She goes to Spain, visits her ex-lover (Byrne), meets some British decadents (Sands and Foster), and kills someone—or did she? Score by jazz legend Miles Davis. (Dir: Mary Lambert, 97 mins.)†

Sigma III (1966)* Jack Taylor, Silvia Solar, Diana Martin. Lumbering CIA agent chases stolen laser-beam device. You need a laser beam to spot any talent in this junk. (Dir: Albert W. Whiteman, 90 mins.)

Signal 7 (1983)*** Bill Ackridge, Dan Leegant, John Tidwell, Bob Elross, Herb Mills, Don Bajema. This uncompromising journey into the fears of two outwardly cocky macho cabbies (both would-be actors) with little hope of ever leaving their fareboxes behind, is hard to shake off. (Dir: Rob Nilsson, 92 mins.)†

Sign of Four (Great Britain, 1983)*** Ian Richardson, David Healey, Trevor Howard. Wonderful Sherlock Holmes yarn with Richardson whose performance echoes the forties' movie incarnation of Holmes as played by Basil Rathbone. (Dir: Desmond Davis, 97 mins.)

Sign of Leo (France, 1959)*** Michele Giradon, Stéphane Audran, Jean Le Poulain, Jess Hahn. Strong debut feature by Eric Rohmer moodily captures a muggy Paris in August, when locals go to the country; an unwelcome setting for an American who lives in the city and has fallen on bad times. Forced to beg, he must come to terms with his life and make changes. (90 mins.)

Sign of the Cross, The (1932)***½ Fredric March, Claudette Colbert, Elissa Landi, Charles Laughton. Not DeMille's best but a fine spectacle of decay in the Rome of Nero during the early days of Christianity. (Dir: Cecil B. DeMille, 140 mins.)

Sign of the Gladiator, The (Italy, 1959)*½ Anita Ekberg, Georges Marchal, Chelo Alonso, Jacques Sernas. A pulchritudinous Palmyran queen heaves her chest in disdain and shuns Roman domination while falling for a Roman general. (Dir: Vittorio Musy Glori, 84 mins.)

Sign of the Pagan (1954)** Jeff Chandler, Jack Palance, Rita Gam. Chandler plays a Roman centurion who is captured by Attila's barbaric army and escapes to prepare for the large scale battle between the Christians and the Huns. (Dir: Douglas Sirk, 92 mins.)

Sign of the Ram (1948)**½ Susan Peters, Alexander Knox. Invalid wife rules her family with an iron hand, not wishing it to elude her grasp. Well acted but generally average drama. (Dir: John Sturges, 84 mins.)

Sign of Zorro, The (1960)** Guy Williams,

Henry Calvin, Gene Sheldon, Britt Lomond, Lisa Gaye. Traveling to California, Zorro, the friend of the friendless, helps his aristocratic papa out of scrapes and pries loose the iron grip of an oppressive commandant. (Dirs: Norman Foster, Lewis R. Foster, 91 mins.)†

Sign o' the Times (1987)**½ Prince, Sheila E., Sheena Easton, Dr. Fink. Love him or hate him, Prince is a charismatic, energetic stage performer, and this slickly produced concert film shows him off to good advantage. (Dir: Prince, 85 mins.)†

Signpost to Murder (1964)**½ Joanne Woodward, Stuart Whitman, Edward Mulhare. The cast is far better than the material in this obvious thriller about an escaped criminal who has been certified insane and his involvement with a lady he meets. (Dir: George Englund, 74 mins.)

Signs of Life (West Germany, 1968)***½ Peter Brogle, Wolfgang Reichmann, Wolfgang von Ungern-Sternberg, Athina Zachropoulou. Remarkable first film by director Werner Herzog about an injured German soldier sent to a Mediterranean island outpost to recuperate. Benumbed by tedium he stages a personal revolt against his condition. (90 mins.)

Silas Marner (Great Britain, 1985)***½ Ben Kingsley, Jenny Agutter. Expert adaptation of the George Eliot novel about a man falsely accused of stealing and robbed of his life savings before a kinder fate sends him a foundling. (Dir: Giles Foster, 92 mins.)†

Silence (Sweden, 1963)*** Gunnel Lindblom, Ingrid Thulin, Jorgen Lindstrom. Two sisters traveling through northern Europe take out their frustrations on each other in this grim, despairing drama. Directed by Ingmar Bergman as part of the trilogy including *Winter Light* and *Through a Glass Darkly*. (95 mins.)†

Silence, The (MTV 1975)*** Richard Thomas, Cliff Gorman. Thomas is most convincing as the real-life West Point cadet who was ostracized by the "silent treatment" by all the other cadets for two years, because of an alleged violation of the academy's honor code. (Dir: Joseph Hardy, 72 mins.)

Silence and the Cry (Hungary, 1968)***½ Zoltan Latinovits, Mari Torocsik, A. Kozak, Andrea Drahota. Harrowing film about events after the first Hungarian Communist regime fell in 1919, when many fled repression. Story follows one man hidden by peasant farmers who are shocked by the barbarity of their new leaders. (Dir: Miklos Jancso, 79 mins.)

Silence at Bethany (1989)**½ Mark Moses, Susan Wilder, Tom Dahlgren, Richard Fancy, Dakin Matthews. A well-meaning, sometimes poignant if ponderous drama depicting the life of Mennonite farmers in 1939. Moses makes a convincing preacher. (Dir: Joel Oliansky, 90 mins.)†

Silence Equals Death (1990)***½ David Wojnarowicz, Allen Ginsberg, Keith Haring. Commanding documentary examines the AIDS crisis through the voices and visions of artists and writers. Much of this bitterly funny film is devoted to performance pieces or watching artists in the process of creating works which relate to the virus's effect on humanity. (Dir: Rosa von Praunheim, 65 mins.)

Silence of the Heart (MTV 1984)*** Mariette Hartley, Dana Hill, Charlie Sheen, Howard Hesseman, Chad Lowe. Strong, contemporary drama about a teenager's suicide and the devasting after shock on his baffled family. (Dir: Richard Michaels, 104 mins.)

Silence of the Lambs, The (1991)**** Jodie Foster, Anthony Hopkins, Scott Glenn, Ted Levine, Anthony Heald, Brooke Smith, Diane Baker. Extraordinarily intense and disturbing thriller about a determined young female FBI agent tracking down a gruesome serial killer by enlisting the professional expertise of a jailed murderer, a former psychiatrist now known as "Hannibal the Cannibal." Although the entire cast is excellent, this is essentially a two-character story, and both Foster and Hopkins are brilliantly effective. She must somehow connect with this frighteningly intelligent psychopath, in order to get him to help her before her quarry kills again, and yet resist being swayed by his taunts and manipulation. Vividly suspenseful, and certainly gory by implication, the film does not actually contain much explicit violence—it's scary enough as it is. (Dir: Jonathan Demme, 120 mins.)†

Silence of the North (Canada, 1981)** Ellen Burstyn, Tom Skerritt, Gordon Pinsent. A mother and children attempt to sur vive in the wilderness. The scenery's beautiful, but the film leaves a lot to be desired. (Dir: Allan Winton King, 94 mins.)†

Silencers, The (1966)**½ Dean Martin, Stella Stevens, Victor Buono, Daliah Lavi. A dedicated attempt to capture the style and the box-office grosses of the socko 007 James Bond spy-spoofs. This was the first of Dean's appearances as suave cocksman Matt Helm. (Dir: Phil Karlson, 102 mins.)

Silent Assassins (1988)** Sam J. Jones, Linda Blair, Jun Chong. L.A. cop Jones tracks down an evil ex-CIA agent who killed his partner and now wants to take over the world. Blair fans should note that she has little to do here. (Dir: Lee Dooyong, 92 mins.)†

Silent Call, The (1961)**½ Gail Russell, David McLean, Roger Mobley. Wispy little drama of a boy's dog, left behind when the family moves from Nevada to Los Angeles, who breaks away and follows the trail. (Dir: John Bushelman, 63 mins.)

Silent Enemy, The (1930)*** Chief Yellow Robe, Chief Long Lance, Chief Akawanush, Spotted Elk, Cheeka. Remarkable docudrama made by an expedition from the Museum of Natural History, in cooperation with Canadian Indian tribes, tells of the Indians' struggle for survival against hunger and disease. A fascinating, one-of-a-kind document. (Dir: H. P. Carver, 84 mins.)†

Silent Enemy, The (Great Britain, 1958)*** Laurence Harvey, Dawn Addams, John Clements. The story of Lionel Crabb, British frogman of WWII fame, whose underwater exploits in stopping the Italian fleet are recounted. Good suspense, absorbing detail, capably performed. (Dir: William Fairchild, 92 mins.)

Silent Gun, The (MTV 1969)** Lloyd Bridges, John Beck, Ed Begley, Pernell Roberts. Routine pilot about still another reformed gunman (Bridges) who helps to rid a small town of the bad guys. (Dir: Michael Caffey, 74 mins.)

Silent Laugh Makers Vols. 1–3 (1917–25)***
Vol. 1 includes four two-reel comedies: *Looking for Sally,* with Charlie Chase as a French immigrant looking for his childhood sweetheart; *Lucky Dog,* an early appearance of Laurel and Hardy; *A Night Out,* with Charlie Chaplin and Ben Turpin out on a tear; and *Hard Knocks,* featuring Charlie Chase as a bank teller clearing himself of embezzling charges. First-class hilarity. (94 mins.)†

Vol. 2 includes three shorts, *Bromo and Juliet,* starring Charlie Chase and Oliver Hardy, the title of which pretty much speaks for itself; *Long Fliv the King,* again starring Chase and Hardy, where a screwball king of a mythical nation battles continuously with the aristocracy; and *Coney Island,* one of Roscoe "Fatty" Arbuckle's most delightful shorts, where he and a very young Buster Keaton contend for the favor of a pretty girl. (107 mins.)†

Vol. 3 includes four shorts: *Picking Peaches,* starring Harry Langdon, with gags by Frank Capra; *All Tied Up,* with "Fat" Karr, "Kewpie" Ross, and "Fatty" Alexander; *Don't Shove,* with Harold Lloyd and Bebe Daniels fighting in a roller rink; and *Some Baby,* starring Snub Pollard, with a scenario by Hal Roach. All of these are fast, furious, and funny. (82 mins.)†

Silent Madness (1984)*½ Belinda Montgomery, Viveca Lindfors, David Greenan, Sydney Lassick. Laughable horror film. Mental hospital doctor Montgomery sets out to recapture a homicidal patient who was accidentally released, while hospital officials send two orderlies out to kill her so they can cover up their mistake. Originally shot in 3-D. (Dir: Simon Nuchtern, 91 mins.)†

Silent Movie (1976)*** Mel Brooks, Marty Feldman, Dom DeLuise, Bernadette Peters, Sid Caesar, Harry Ritz. Director Mel Brooks's movie about a director trying to make a comeback in '76 with a silent movie. Wacky, inventive madness. The gags are written out in the form of subtitles. (88 mins.)†

Silent Night, Bloody Night (1973)**½ Patrick O'Neal, Astrid Heeren, John Carradine, Candy Darling. A pretty scary horror movie set in an old mansion in Massachusetts. Director Ted Gershuny keeps the audience right on the edge of its seat with the suspense, and adds some class in his deft handling of some flashback sequences. (90 mins.)†

Silent Night, Deadly Night (1984)*½ Lilyan Chauvin, Robert Brian Wilson, Britt Leach, Toni Nero, Linnea Quigley. A seasonal slasher pic in which a man dressed as Santa delivers a Christmas sleigh full of murder and mayhem. A field day for Scrooges! (Dir: Charles E. Sellier, 79 mins.)†

Silent Night, Deadly Night Part II (1987)½ Eric Freeman, James L. Newman, Jean Miller, Elizabeth Clayton. Bizarre sequel opens with over a half-hour of "flashback" footage of the original before following the brother of the first film's killer on a rampage of his own. Overacting and unbelievable situations make this one a must for fans of silly cinema. (Dir: Lee Harry, 88 mins.)†

Silent Night, Deadly Night III: Better Watch Out! (1989)*½ Richard Beymer, Bill Moseley, Samantha Scully, Robert Culp. Not quite killed last time, the "Santa Slasher" comes out of a six-year coma with a psychic connection to a young girl. Not as incompetent as its predecessors, but whatever is Monte Hellman (*Two-Lane Blacktop*) doing directing stuff like this? (91 mins.)†

Silent Night, Evil Night—See: **Black Christmas**

Silent Night, Lonely Night (MTV 1969)**½ Lloyd Bridges, Shirley Jones, Cloris Leachman. Well-acted tale about a brief interlude shared by two lonely people during the Christmas holidays in a New England college town. (Dir: Daniel Petrie, 98 mins.)†

Silent Partner, The (Canada, 1978)*** Elliott Gould, Susannah York, Christopher Plummer, Celine Lomez, Michael Kirby.

Curtis Hanson has fashioned an effective script for a well-performed tense thriller. The twisty plot concerns a larcenous bank clerk who foolishly crosses a psychotic robber. (Dir: Daryl Duke, 103 mins.)†

Silent Rage (1983)**½ Chuck Norris, Ron Silver, Steven Keats, Toni Kalem, William Finley, Stephen Furst. There's something irresistible about watching super hero Norris (wooden everywhere but his legs) battle a superhuman zombie returned from the dead and with no intention of returning there. (Dir: Michael Miller, 105 mins.)

Silent Running (1972)*** Bruce Dern, Cliff Potts. Spectacular space effects highlight this skillful science-fiction speculation on the state of ecology in the year 2008. Dern plays the head of a rocket crew who have been sent to orbit Saturn with man's only remaining samples of vegetation. (Dir: Douglas Trumbull, 90 mins.)†

Silent Scream (1980)**½ Rebecca Balding, Cameron Mitchell, Yvonne De Carlo, Barbara Steele. Unexceptional horror film, that demands attention for its stylistic conviction. Worn old plot involves an old house with a murderous secret inhabitant. (Dir: Denny Harris, 87 mins.)†

Silent Sentence (1974)** Jack Elam, Ruth Roman, Diana Ewing. The prostitutes of a small mining town are being brutally murdered. A young detective gets to the bottom of the slaughters and unleashes skeletons in the townsfolk's closets. (Dir: Larry G. Spangler, 80 mins.)

Silent Victory: The Kitty O'Neil Story (MTV 1979)*** Stockard Channing, James Farentino, Colleen Dewhurst. Impressive real-life drama on deaf Kitty O'Neil, the Hollywood stuntwoman who holds the women's world land speed record. Channing is first-rate as Kitty, driven by a determined mom to act like people with normal hearing. (Dir: Lou Antonio, 104 mins.)†

Silent Witness (1932)*** Lionel Atwill, Greta Nissen, Weldon Heybrun, Helen Mack, Alan Mowbray. Repeating the stage role that brought him to Hollywood's attention, Atwill gives an authoritative, rigorous performance in this fine courtroom thriller as an actor who covers up his son's complicity in a crime, and undergoes a demanding trial. (Dirs: Marcel Varnel, R. L. Hough, 73 mins.)

Silent Witness (MTV 1985)* Valerie Bertinelli, John Savage, Chris Nash, Melissa Leo. Bertinelli witnesses a rape by her brother-in-law and her in-laws pressure her to remain silent. A seamy rip-off of the famous barroom rape case in Massachusetts. (Dir: Michael Miller, 104 mins.)†

Silent World, The (France, 1956)**** Wonderful Oscar-winning documentary, Cousteau's exploration of the ocean's depths. Ideal in color. (Dirs: Jacques-Yves Cousteau, Louis Malle, 86 mins.)

Silhouette (MCTV 1990)*** Faye Dunaway, David Rasche, John Terry, Talisa Soto. Better-than-average suspense tale boosted by a good performance from Dunaway. An unidentified killer stalks Dunaway after she witnesses a brutal murder while stranded in a small town. Thrills mount at an escalating pace in this often tense drama. (Dir: Carl Schenkel, 96 mins.)

Silken Affair, The (Great Britain, 1956)**½ David Niven, Genevieve Page, Beatrice Straight. Funny comedy that has Niven playing a somewhat sheepish accountant who decides to take a fling. (Dir: Roy Kellino, 96 mins.)

Silk Stockings (1957)***½ Fred Astaire, Cyd Charisse, Janis Paige, Peter Lorre. Excellently mounted musical based on the Cole Porter Broadway success which was based on *Ninotchka*. Plot has Astaire, as a Hollywood producer, involved with a beautiful Russian agent (Charisse) in Paris. (Dir: Rouben Mamoulian, 117 mins.)†

Silkwood (1983)*** Meryl Streep, Cher, Kurt Russell, Craig T. Nelson, Diana Scarwid, Henderson Forsythe, Fred Ward. Silkwood was a frustrated factory worker in an Oklahoma plutonium plant who grew aware of the dangers of exposure to plant workers. Her awareness may have cost her her life; her death in a car accident left many unanswered questions. Superlative performances from the large cast. (Dir: Mike Nichols, 131 mins.)†

Silverado (1985)***½ Scott Glenn, Kevin Kline, Kevin Costner, Danny Glover, John Cleese, Rosanna Arquette, Jeff Goldblum, Linda Hunt. The western revived in a rousing, well-plotted tale of four outcast heroes trying to free a town from the clutches of corruption. Director Lawrence Kasdan makes no bones about who's good and who's evil. (132 mins.)†

Silver Bears (Great Britain, 1978)**½ Michael Caine, Cybill Shepherd, Louis Jourdan, Stephane Audran, Tom Smothers, Martin Balsam. Complicated comedy about a Las Vegas syndicate boss (Balsam) who sends Caine to Switzerland to buy a bank in order to launder illegal profits. (Dir: Ivan Passer, 113 mins.)†

Silver Bullet—See: **Stephen King's Silver Bullet**

Silver Chalice, The (1954)** Paul Newman, Pier Angeli, Jack Palance, Virginia Mayo, Natalie Wood. This is the story of a Greek youth who makes the

"Silver Chalice" of the Last Supper. Newman's inauspicious film debut. (Dir: Victor Saville, 137 mins.)†

Silver City (1951)**½ Yvonne De Carlo, Edmond O'Brien, Barry Fitzgerald. Assayer trying to escape his past arrives in Silver City to help a girl and her father mine a rich vein, opposed by the owner of the land. Actionful western. (Dir: Byron Haskin, 90 mins.)

Silver City (Australia, 1985)**½ Gosia Dobrowolska, Ivar Kants, Anna Jemison, Debra Lawrence. Polished but plodding drama about a point in Australian history when large-scale immigration was encouraged (the late 1940s). The film delves into the displacement felt by the Polish émigrés by concentrating on the tale of a fiercely independent Polish woman who engages in an affair with a married man. (Dir: Sophie Turkiewicz, 102 mins.)†

Silver Cord, The (1933)**½ Irene Dunne, Laura Hope Crews, Joel McCrea, Eric Linden, Frances Dee. Beautifully acted, somewhat static, adaptation of the Sidney Howard play that betrays its theatrical origins, but is often gripping drama. A grasping mother controls her sons' lives until her new daughter-in-law, Dunne, stands up to her. (Dir: John Cromwell, 74 mins.)

Silver Dollar (1932)** Edward G. Robinson, Bebe Daniels, Aline MacMahon, Robert Warrick. Biopic about the man (H.A.W. Tabor) who helped change a mining town into a major city, Denver, Colorado. (Dir: Alfred E. Green, 84 mins.)

Silver Dream Racer (Great Britain, 1980)* David Essex, Beau Bridges, Cristina Raines, Clarke Peters. Dull story about motorcycle racing in England. Essex plays a mechanic with aspirations to win, while Bridges is the ugly American competing. (Dir: David Wickes, 111 mins.)†

Silver River (1948)**½ Errol Flynn, Ann Sheridan, Thomas Mitchell. Run-of-the-mill western which leans on its name actors for support. Errol is a no-good power-hungry louse in this one but the ladies will still like him. (Dir: Raoul Walsh, 110 mins.)

Silver Streak (1976)*** Gene Wilder, Jill Clayburgh, Richard Pryor, Patrick McGoohan, Ned Beatty. Entertaining adventure-comedy that established Wilder and Pryor as a formidable team. Hoping to relax and recuperate, Wilder's exhausted businessman boards a train from L.A. to Chicago. Instead he finds mystery and mayhem. (Dir: Arthur Hiller, 128 mins.)†

Silver Streak, The (1934)**½ Hardie Albright, Sally Blane, Charles Starrett, William Farnum, Irving Pichel. Persua-sive early "disaster" picture, with a high-speed train carrying medical equipment to a disease-stricken area; good cheapie. (Dir: Thomas Atkins, 72 mins.)†

Silver Whip, The (1953)*** Dale Robertson, Robert Wagner, Rory Calhoun, Kathleen Crowley. Wagner plays an enthusiastic western youth who wants to ape his two best friends, Sheriff Calhoun and stage guard Robertson, and ends up in trouble. (Dir: Harmon Jones, 73 mins.)

Simba (Great Britain, 1955)***½ Dirk Bogarde, Virginia McKenna. Excellent drama dealing with a man's revenge for his brother's death against the hostile Mau Mau tribes of Kenya. (Dir: Brian Desmond Hurst, 99 mins.)

Simon (1980)** Alan Arkin, Austin Pendleton, Judy Graubart, Fred Gwynne. Unsatisfactory, smug satire about a college professor who thinks he's an alien. (Dir: Marshall Brickman, 97 mins.)†

Simon and Laura (Great Britain, 1955) ***½ Kay Kendall, Peter Finch. Amusing British satirical comedy about the "private lives" of a TV husband and wife team. Kendall and Finch are excellent foils as the TV "ideal couple." (Dir: Muriel Box, 91 mins.)

Simon, King of the Witches (1971)*** Andrew Prine, Brenda Scott. Simon is a modern-day magician who lives in a storm drain and supports himself by casting the odd spell. Until the story falls apart in the last half hour, this is an exceptional little movie, with a serious tone seldom seen in movies of this genre. (Dir: Bruce Kessler, 90 mins.)†

Simon of the Desert (Mexico, 1965)**** Claudio Brook, Silvia Pinal, Hortensia Santoveña. Director Luis Buñuel's anarchic humor was never more pungent, his visual style more subtly formal, his gibes at holiness and purity more telling. Simon has been standing on a pillar in the wilderness for 20 years, avoiding temptation; the devil (Pinal) glides over to him in a self-propelling casket. (45 mins.)†

Simple Justice (1989)*½ Cesar Romero, Doris Roberts, Matthew Galle, Cady McLain. Gory revenge melodrama set in motion when a young couple are brutally beaten by robbers. The beastly bad guys are let off scot-free by the liberal courts, and you can pretty much write it yourself from there. (Dir: Deborah Del Prete, 97 mins.)

Simple Story, A (France, 1978)*** Romy Schneider, Bruno Cremer, Claude Brasseur, Arlette Bonnard. A simple story, beautifully told, and boosted by Romy's incandescence in the role of a woman undergoing a mid-life crisis after an abortion. (Dir: Claude Sautet, 110 mins.)†

Sin, The (Japan, 1961)***½ Raizo Ichikawa, Hiroyuki Nagato, Rentaro

Mikune, Ganjiro Nakamura, Eiji Fujimura. Teacher fights against the social prejudices of 19th-century Japanese society. Potent film is a beautiful and sensitive example of the masterful work of director Kon Ichikawa. AKA: **The Outcast** and **The Broken Commandment**. (119 mins.)

Sin, The (1979)—See: **Good Luck, Miss Wyckoff**

Sinbad and the Eye of the Tiger (Great Britain, 1977)** Patrick Wayne, Taryn Power, Jane Seymour. Weak scenario. Sinbad searches for a prince who's been transformed into a tiger by a sorceress's evil spell. (Dir: Sam Wanamaker, 113 mins.)†

Sinbad the Sailor (1947)*** Douglas Fairbanks, Jr., Maureen O'Hara, Walter Slezak, George Tobias, Anthony Quinn. The seafaring storyteller has adventurous experiences with a secret amulet and a beautiful princess. Ridiculous, but enjoyable swashbuckling costume entertainment. (Dir: Richard Wallace, 117 mins.)†

Sinbad of the Seven Seas (Italy, 1986)* Lou Ferrigno, John Steiner, Leo Gullotta, Teagan Clive. Ferrigno as Sinbad is no better (nor very different, for that matter) from Ferrigno as Hercules in this typically dopey dubbed adventure. (Dir: Enzo Girolami Castellari, 93 mins.)†

Sincerely Charlotte (France, 1986)** Isabelle Huppert, Niels Arestrup, Christine Pascal. Offbeat French love story, with a *soupçon* of murder-mystery intrigue. On the run from the police, Charlotte shows up at the home of an old lover, and jolts him out of a settled existence with his new fiancée. (Dir: Caroline Huppert, 92 mins.)†

Sincerely Yours (1955)*½ Liberace, Joanne Dru, Dorothy Malone. It's that man with the candelabra in a heart-tugger full of corn and concerts. Remake of *The Man Who Played God*. (Dir: Gordon Douglas, 115 mins.)†

Since You Went Away (1944)**** Claudette Colbert, Jennifer Jones, Joseph Cotten, Robert Walker, Lionel Barrymore, Shirley Temple, Hattie McDaniel. David O. Selznick's paean to the American homefront during WWII is strong in emotional truth as it chronicles the daily life of one family waging war against anguish, loneliness, and the practical inconveniences of wartime. (Dir: John Cromwell, 172 mins.)†

Sinful Davey (Great Britain, 1969)**½ John Hurt, Pamela Franklin, Nigel Davenport, Ronald Fraser, Robert Morley. Not earth-shattering cinema, but an amiable romp for Huston about a Scottish brigand who finds time for romance in between robbing travelers. (Dir: John Huston, 95 mins.)

Sinful Life, A (1989)* Anita Morris, Rick Overton, Dennis Christopher, Blair Tefkin. Unwatchable comedy about boozing mother Morris and daughter Tefkin (a grating performance by a grown woman as a pre-teen girl) who have to contemplate cleaning up their act when a nosy teacher threatens to have the daughter taken away. The numerous weird characters are obnoxious rather than funny, and the movie as a whole is like 90 minutes of ragged fingernails dragged across a blackboard. (Dir: William Schreiner, 90 mins.)†

Sing (1989)** Lorraine Bracco, Peter Dobson, Jessica Steen, Louise Lasser, Patti LaBelle. The author of *Fame* and *Footloose* extends his range with a movie that doesn't begin with an ''F,'' but earns one anyway. Plot about a talent contest at a Brooklyn high school is a thin excuse for endless musical numbers, none believable in the supposedly realistic context. (Dir: Richard Baskin, 98 mins.)†

Singapore (1947)** Fred MacMurray, Ava Gardner. Adventurer returns to Singapore to find his beloved a victim of amnesia, and married. (Dir: John Brahm, 79 mins.)

Singapore Woman (1941)** Brenda Marshall, David Bruce, Virginia Field, Jerome Cowan, Rose Hobart, Heather Angel. Exotic but dawdling remake of *Dangerous*. A rubber planter wants to extricate a troubled beauty from an oriental jinx. (Dir: Jean Negulesco, 64 mins.)

Sing, Baby, Sing (1936)**½ Alice Faye, Adolphe Menjou, Gregory Ratoff, Ted Healy, Patsy Kelly, the Ritz Brothers. Aspiring singer Faye is discovered by on-the-skids Shakespearean actor Menjou in this fast, funny musical comedy, with several good songs for Faye and some hilarious material by the Ritz Brothers, in their movie debut. (Dir: Sidney Lanfield, 90 mins.)

Sing, Boy, Sing (1958)** Tommy Sands, Lili Gentle, Edmond O'Brien, Nick Adams. Rock'n roll idol's religious training and the pressures of being a star cause him to break under the strain. (Dir: Henry Ephron, 91 mins.)

Singer Not the Song, The (Great Britain, 1961)** John Mills, Dirk Bogarde. Long, glum drama of a priest and a bandit in Mexico, as one tries to reform the other to no avail. Miscast, overwritten, underdirected. (Dir: Roy Baker, 129 mins.)

Singer of Seville—See: **Call of the Flesh, The**

Singing Detective, The (Great Britain, 1986) **** Michael Gambon, Janet Suzman, Patrick Malahide, Alison Steadman, Joanna Whalley. An imaginative, touching, comic, and utterly brilliant piece of work. Mystery writer Philip Marlow (excuse the obvious) sits in a hospital bed and lets his mind float between the events from one of his novels, his own past, and his circumscribed present environment. This teleclassic sprang from the rich and fertile mind of scripter Dennis Potter ("Pennies from Heaven"). (Dir: Jon Amiel, 395 mins.)

Singing Kid, The (1936)** Al Jolson, Sybil Jason, Edward Everett Horton, Lyle Talbot, Allen Jenkins. Not Al's finest hour. A mediocre musical about a singing star who finds true love while giving his vocal chords a rest in the country. (Dir: William Keighley, 85 mins.)

Singing Nun, The (1966)** Debbie Reynolds, Greer Garson, Ricardo Montalban, Chad Everett, Agnes Moorehead. A fictionalized, mawkish account of the story behind the real-life nun who became an international celebrity when her recording of the song "Dominique" was released. (Dir: Henry Koster, 98 mins.)

Singing the Blues in Red (Great Britain, 1988)**½ Gerulf Pannach, Fabienne Babe, Cristine Rose. An East German musician escapes to the West and finds that defection isn't all it's cracked up to be—democracy carries its own disappointments. Despairing social commentary, with a moving performance by Pannach. (Dir: Ken Loach, 110 mins.)†

Singin' in the Rain (1952)**** Gene Kelly, Debbie Reynolds, Donald O'Connor, Jean Hagen, Cyd Charisse. One of the best musicals Hollywood has ever produced. The story line deals with the transition period from silents to talkies in Hollywood films. Kelly and O'Connor are a great dancing team, and Hagen is a standout in the role of a silent film star with a speech problem. (Dirs: Gene Kelly, Stanley Donen, 103 mins.)†

Single Bars, Single Women (MTV 1984)*** Shelley Hack, Christine Lahti, Paul Michael Glaser, Tony Danza, Mare Winningham. Despite some dramatic shorthand and a weak plotline this is a commendable "relationship" comedy-drama about the singles scene. Sharply written and impeccably played story. (Dir: Harry Winer, 104 mins.)†

Single Room Furnished (1968)* Jayne Mansfield, Dorothy Keller, Fabian Dean, Billy M. Greene, Terri Messina. Mansfield tried to demonstrate her versatility in this low-budget chest-heaver about a blushing babe who becomes a prostitute. Sadly exploitative; but for her fans, this is a must, since she was killed before filming was completed. (Dir: "Matteo Ottaviano" [Matt Cimber], 93 mins.)†

Single Standard (1929)**½ Greta Garbo, Nils Asther, Johnny Mack Brown, Dorothy Sebastian. Dumb soap opera vehicle for Garbo as a socialite involved in a series of affairs lacks any motivation to make it compelling. MGM spared

no expense on sets or costumes. Worth seeing just for Garbo. (Dir: John S. Robertson, 73 mins.)

Single Women, Married Men (MTV 1989)* Michelle Lee, Lee Horsley, Julie Harris, Alan Rachins, Carrie Hamilton, Mary Frann, Margaret Avery. After Lee's husband leaves her, she devotes her psychotherapy practice to the problems of women who are having affairs with married men. The usual predictable TV nonsense. (Dir: Nick Havinga, 96 mins.)

Sing Your Worries Away (1942)**½ Bert Lahr, June Havoc, Buddy Ebsen. Entertainers get mixed up with some gangsters trying to pull a swindle. Amusing musical comedy. (Dir: A. Edward Sutherland, 71 mins.)†

Sing You Sinners (1938)*** Bing Crosby, Fred MacMurray, Donald O'Connor, Ellen Drew. Solid entertainment with Bing as a wastrel who strikes it rich at the track. (Dir: Wesley Ruggles, 90 mins.)

Sinister Invasion (U.S.-Mexico, 1986)½ Boris Karloff, Enrique Guzman, Christa Linder. One of four Mexican horror/sci-fi films that the ailing Karloff shot footage for just before his death. Outer space aliens possessing the body of a sex killer in order to steal Karloff's invention. Unwatchable and embarrassing. AKA: **Alien Terror** and **Incredible Invasion**. (Dirs: Juan Ibanez, Jack Hill, 90 mins.)†

Sinister Urge, The (1961)½ Kenne Duncan, Duke Moore, Carl Anthony, Jean Willardson. Edward (*Plan Nine From Outer Space*) Wood, Jr. is at it again with grave warnings about pornography. Two cops try to smash the dirty picture biz years before the Moral Majority started crucifying convenience stores. You were ahead of your time, Ed. AKA: **The Young and the Immoral**. (75 mins.)†

Sink the Bismarck! (Great Britain, 1960)*** Kenneth More, Dana Wynter. A maritime battle of wits as the British forces strive to conquer the pride of Hitler's Navy during WWII. Excellent special effects heighten this well-done semidocumentary-style war story. (Dir: Lewis Gilbert, 97 mins.)†

Sinner's Holiday (1930)*** Grant Withers, Evalyn Knapp, James Cagney, Lucille La Verne, Warren Hymer, Joan Blondell. Cagney steals the picture, as a gutless punk who commits a murder and gets his adoring mother to cover up for him, implicating nice-guy bootlegger Withers. Coney Island's brassy, seedy atmosphere is well conveyed. (Dir: John G. Adolfi, 60 mins.)

Sinner's Holiday (1947)*½ George Raft, George Brent, Randolph Scott, Joan Blondell, Virginia Field. Three relatives answer the call of an aged lady to appear for Christmas dinner. (Formerly

Christmas Eve.) (Dir: Robert Siodmak, 92 mins.)

Sinners in Paradise (1938)** Madge Evans, John Boles, Bruce Cabot, Gene Lockhart, Milburn Stone. Variation on the basic plot of diverse characters trapped in the jungle by a plane crash, this effective low-budget entry has some good acting and stylish direction, if few surprises. (Dir: James Whale, 64 mins.)

Sinners in the Sun (1932)**½ Carole Lombard, Chester Morris, Adrienne Ames, Alison Skipworth, Cary Grant. Glossy but predictable romance, with Lombard and Morris a young working couple who can't afford to marry; they break up and each has a fling with a troubled socialite. (Dir: Alexander Hall, 70 mins.)

Sin of Harold Diddlebock, The (1947)**½ Harold Lloyd, Frances Ramsden, Rudy Vallee. Preston Sturges persuaded silent-screen comic Harold Lloyd to make this rambling farce about a perennial bumbler waiting for Lady Luck. The comic invention is evident everywhere but the timing is sadly off. AKA: **Mad Wednesday.** (Dir: Preston Sturges, 90 mins.)†

Sin of Innocence (MTV 1986)**½ Bill Bixby, Dee Wallace Stone, Megan Follows. Divorced parents remarry and combine families. The kids take out their hostilities on each other until the fighting turns to physical attraction. (Dir: Arthur Allan Seidelman, 104 mins.)

Sin of Madelon Claudet, The (1931)***½ Helen Hayes, Neil Hamilton, Lewis Stone, Robert Young, Cliff Edwards, Jean Hersholt, Marie Prevost, Alan Hale. Strong soap opera, with a script by Charles MacArthur, stars Hayes as a single mother struggling to survive by any means necessary. Hayes's vibrant acting makes this a persuasive drama. (Dir: Edgar Selwyn, 74 mins.)†

Sin Ship, The (1931)**½ Mary Astor, Louis Wolheim, Ian Keith, Hugh Herbert. A rough, amoral sea captain takes aboard a missionary and his wife desperate to reach their destination; he pursues the prudish wife, not realizing that she and her husband are concealing a singular secret. (Dir: Louis Wolheim, 65 mins.)

Sins of Dorian Gray, The (MTV 1983)* Belinda Bauer, Anthony Perkins, Joseph Bottoms, Michael Ironside. In this TV remake, the debauched Dorian (now a girl) is forever young while her screen test ages. (Dir: Tony Maylam, 104 mins.)†

Sins of Rachel Cade, The (1961)**½ Angie Dickinson, Peter Finch, Roger Moore. Although this film lapses into corny preaching, it has Angie Dickinson delivering a creditable acting job as an American nurse doing missionary work in the Belgian Congo. (Dir: Gordon Douglas, 124 mins.)

Sins of the Father (MTV 1985)** James Coburn, Ted Wass, Glynnis O'Connor. Melodrama about a young lady lawyer who's in love with the hot-shot president of the firm as well as his unassuming son. (Dir: Peter Werner, 104 mins.)

Sins of the Mother (MTV 1991)*** Elizabeth Montgomery, Dale Midkiff, Talia Balsam, Heather Fairfield. Compelling psychological drama based on a true story. Montgomery is outstanding as a prominent matriarch who manipulates her son (Midkiff), who is secretly a serial rapist, with alternating mood swings of unnatural possessive love and outbursts of unrelenting cruelty. Unusual subject matter benefits from knockout performances and a mesmerizing, sordid storyline. (Dir: John Patterson, 96 mins.)

Sins of the Past (MTV 1984)** Kim Cattrall, Tracy Reed, Anthony Geary, Kristin Meadows, Debby Boone. Predictable drama about a vengeful father who may be murdering ex-prostitutes he believes are responsible for corrupting his daughter, who was killed by a customer. (Dir: Peter Hunt, 104 mins.)

Sin Town (1942)**½ Constance Bennett, Broderick Crawford, Anne Gwynne, Patric Knowles, Andy Devine, Leo Carrillo, Ward Bond. Fast-moving western adventure about a crusading newspaper editor battling two opportunistic gamblers. Sharply written and directed. (Dir: Ray Enright, 75 mins.)

Siren of Atlantis (1948)* Maria Montez, Jean-Pierre Aumont, Dennis O'Keefe, Henry Daniell, Morris Karnovsky. Even camp aficionados will be hard-pressed to summon up enthusiasm for Maria's preening and posing as Queen of the Lost Continent in this soporific adventure. (Dir: Greg Tallas, 75 mins.)

Siren of Bagdad (1953)**½ Paul Henreid, Patricia Medina, Hans Conried. An Arabian Nights tale done with a flair for comedy—same old story but Hans Conried keeps things going at a bouncy pace. (Dir: Richard Quine, 72 mins.)

Sirocco (1952)** Humphrey Bogart, Marta Toren, Lee J. Cobb, Zero Mostel. Slow-moving melodrama about sinister characters and their shady dealings. (Dir: Curtis Bernhardt, 98 mins.)†

Sis Hopkins (1941)**½ Judy Canova, Susan Hayward, Bob Crosby. Country girl wins out over snooty cats at a girls' school. Amusing comedy. (Dir: Joseph Santley, 98 mins.)

Sisterhood, The (1988)** Rebecca Holden, Chuck Wagner, Lynn-Holly Johnson, Barbara Hooper. Pseudo-feminist sci-fi set in a *Mad Max*-ish future, as female rebels with magical powers break into the "Forbidden Zone" in search of their fellow fighters, exiled by the male government. Aside from the femme fillip, the usual nonsense. (Dir: Cirio H. Santiago, 76 mins.)†

Sister Kenny (1946)***½ Rosalind Russell, Alexander Knox, Philip Merivale, Dean Jagger. Story of the famous nurse and her fight against infantile paralysis. Frequently stirring drama, excellently acted. (Dir: Dudley Nichols, 116 mins.)†

Sister Margaret and the Saturday Night Ladies (MTV 1986)* Bonnie Franklin, Jeanetta Arnette, Trazana Beverly, Jon Chardiet, Rosemary Clooney. Clichéd melodrama starring Franklin as a determined nun out to rehabilitate women leaving prison on parole. With corny dialogue and Franklin's self-righteous performance, this movie needs more rehabilitation than any parolee. (Dir: Paul Wendkos, 104 mins.)

Sisters, The (1938)*** Bette Davis, Errol Flynn, Anita Louise, Jane Bryan, Ian Hunter. Director Anatole Litvak isn't up to the scope and sweep of this tale of three sisters and their marriages at the turn of the century, but the cast is. Davis plays very well against Flynn; Bryan and Louise manage more subtlety in less flashy roles. (120 mins.)

Sisters (1973)*** Margot Kidder, William Finley, Charles Durning, Barnard Hughes, Jennifer Salt. Brian DePalma's scary thriller about Siamese twins (one good, one evil) is tied together with a *Rear Window* tale of a girl reporter who spots one of them committing a murder. It has several edge-of-your-seat sequences. (92 mins.)†

Sister, Sister (MTV 1982)*** Diahann Carroll, Rosalind Cash, Irene Cara, Dick Anthony Williams, Paul Winfield, Robert Hooks. Maya Angelou's beautifully wrought black family drama may be a tad slow, but her work seethes with anger and friction when three sisters open old wounds. An uncompromising dissection of the black middle class. (Dir: John Berry, 104 mins.)

Sister, Sister (1987)**½ Jennifer Jason Leigh, Eric Stoltz, Judith Ivey, Dennis Lipscomb. Gothic psychodrama set in a decaying Southern mansion, where a visiting young man comes between the two sisters. Enjoyably creaky, though the ending is one surprise too many. (Dir: Bill Condon, 91 mins.)†

Sisters, or the Balance of Happiness (West Germany, 1981)***½ Jutta Lampe, Gudrun Gabriel, Rainer Delventhal, Agnes Fink. Two sisters of opposite style and personality share an apartment in this strong drama of self-discovery, brilliantly written and directed by Magarethe von Trotta. (95 mins.)

Sitting Bull (1954)**½ Dale Robertson, Mary Murphy, J. Carrol Naish. Ridiculous, inaccurate tale of Sitting Bull and Custer is loaded with phony action. (Dir: Sidney Salkow, 105 mins.)

Sitting Ducks (1980)**½ Zack Norman, Michael Emil, Patrice Townsend, Richard Romanus. Norman and Emil play two neurotic crooks who embezzle mob collection money and run off to Miami. Largely improvised dialogue makes this a matter of taste, though it has its fans. (Dir: Henry Jaglom, 90 mins.)

Sitting Pretty (1933)**½ Ginger Rogers, Jack Oakie, Jack Haley, Thelma Todd, Gregory Ratoff. Two tunesmiths (Oakie and Haley) take Hollywood by storm while romancing a wholesome Ginger and a seductive Thelma. Lively antique musical, with a dandy score. (Dir: Harry Joe Brown, 85 mins.)

Sitting Pretty (1948)**½ Clifton Webb, Robert Young, Maureen O'Hara. Webb became a popular comic lead with his fussy creation of Mr. Belvedere, the unflappable babysitter with a firm hand for the brats. His memorable scene of pouring oatmeal over a baby's head charmed millions, causing them to neglect the essential smugness of this overextended material. (Dir: Walter Lang, 84 mins.)

Sitting Target (Great Britain, 1972)*½ Oliver Reed, Jill St. John, Ian McShane. A brutal British melodrama that verges on hysteria, starring Reed, who escapes from prison to take care of his unfaithful wife (St. John). (Dir: Douglas Hickox, 99 mins.)

Situation Hopeless—But Not Serious (1965)**½ Robert Redford, Alec Guinness, Michael Connors. An excellent idea that works only part of the way. A lonely German air raid warden captures two American airmen (Redford and Connors) near the end of WWII, and keeps them prisoner in his cellar long after the war is over. (Dir: Gottfried Reinhardt, 97 mins.)

Six Against the Rock (MTV 1987)*** David Carradine, Howard Hesseman, David Morse, Charles Haid, Jan-Michael Vincent, Richard Dysart. Some familiar faces acquit themselves rather well as Alcatraz convicts making that wild and nightmarish escape from the rock back in 1946. The breakout plan and the unexpected obstacles facing the desperate cons will hold your interest. (Dir: Paul Wendkos, 104 mins.)

Six Black Horses (1962)** Audie Murphy, Dan Duryea, Joan O'Brien. A cowboy, a girl, and a killer are set upon by Indians in the desert. Ordinary western. (Dir: Harry Keller, 80 mins.)

Six Bridges to Cross (1955)*** Tony Curtis, George Nader, Julie Adams, Sal Mineo. Well-made gangster film about a loser

963

who keeps getting deeper and deeper into a life of crime until he masterminds a really big caper. Loosely based on the Boston Brink's robbery. (Dir: Joseph Pevney, 96 mins.)

Six-Day Bike Rider (1934)**½ Joe E. Brown, Maxine Doyle, Frank McHugh, Gordon Westcott. Unpretentious comedy vehicle for Brown as a young man who enters a bicycle marathon to impress his girlfriend. Artless and pleasant. (Dir: Lloyd Bacon, 69 mins.)

Six Hours to Live (1932)**½ Warner Baxter, Miriam Jordan, John Boles, Halliwell Hobbes. Original, intriguing drama about an assassinated diplomat at an international peace conference, miraculously brought back to life for six hours, in which time he has to straighten out the futures of his country and his fiancé. Stodgy direction mars this still-interesting film. (Dir: William Dieterle, 80 mins.)

Six in Paris (France, 1965)*** Nadine Ballot, Barbet Schroeder, Johanna Shimkus, Philippe Hiquily, Stéphane Audran, Claude Chabrol. Entertaining anthology. The focus of this one, helmed by some big names of the French "New Wave," is the City of Lights and the romantic foibles of its inhabitants. (Dirs: Claude Chabrol, Jean Douchet, Jean-Luc Godard, Jean-Daniel Pollet, Eric Rohmer, Jean Rouch, 93 mins.)

Six Million Dollar Man, The (MTV 1973)*½ Lee Majors, Martin Balsam, Darren McGavin, Barbara Anderson. Majors stars as a bionic superhero specializing in government missions. Pilot for subsequent TV series. (Dir: Richard Irving, 73 mins.)

Six of a Kind (1934)**** W. C. Fields, George Burns, Gracie Allen. A cross-country motor trip becomes a laugh riot in the hands of the leads. Don't miss Fields's great pool-shooting routine. (Dir: Leo McCarey, 65 mins.)

Six Pack (1982)** Kenny Rogers, Diane Lane, Erin Gray, Barry Corbin. Unabashedly corny story. A family of six, looked after by the teenaged sister, is forced by a crooked sheriff to strip cars. They strip one belonging to a racing driver, played by singer Rogers, who becomes their father figure. (Dir: Dan Petrie, 110 mins.)†

Six-Pack Annie (1975)**½ Lindsay Bloom, Jana Bellan, Ray Danton, Stubby Kaye, Louisa Moritz, Bruce Boxleitner. A good cast in a pleasant minor comedy about a woman who decides to turn tricks in order to turn her mom's diner into a success. (Dir: Graydon David, 88 mins.)

Sixteen Candles (1984)*** Molly Ringwald, Anthony Michael Hall, Paul Dooley, Michael Schoeffling, Gedde Watanabe, Edward Andrews, John Cusack. Molly celebrates her sixteenth birthday by herself, dreaming about a dreamy senior, avoiding the unwanted attentions of a freshman geek, and being ignored by her family, who have forgotten her in their hysteria over her sister's wedding. Writer-director John Hughes's least ambitious and best film, in which he vents both of his tendencies toward teen angst and lowbrow humor, with the result that each tempers the other. (93 mins.)†

16 Days of Glory (1986)***½ An authoritative documentary on the 1984 summer Olympics. Viewers can vicariously feel the thrill of competition, particularly in the decathlon duel between Britain's Daley Thompson and West Germany's Jurgen Hingsen. (Dir: Bud Greenspan, 145 mins.)†

Sixty Glorious Years (Great Britain, 1938)*** Anna Neagle, Anton Walbrook, C. Aubrey Smith, Felix Aylmer. Lavish British biography of Queen Victoria is rather slow, but extremely well produced. Neagle is off-puttingly grand as the young queen, but Walbrook is exceptionally persuasive as her intelligent, loving husband. (Dir: Herbert Wilcox, 90 mins.)

633 Squadron (U.S.-Great Britain, 1964) *** George Chakiris, Cliff Robertson. A good action film. Chakiris and Robertson are assigned to destroy a very important Nazi stronghold in Norway, but complications set in, and an act of heroism above and beyond the call of duty gets the job done. (Dir: Walter Grauman, 94 mins.)

Six Weeks (1982)**½ Dudley Moore, Mary Tyler Moore, Katherine Healey, Shannon Wilcox, Joe Regalabuto. The two Moores are such appealing performers that they can get away with plot devices that would sink lesser stars. Mr. Moore plays a politician running for Congress; Ms. Moore is a rich cosmetics executive who has a terrible ordeal to face—her daughter is dying of leukemia. (Dir: Tony Bill, 107 mins.)†

Sizzle (MTV 1981)**½ Loni Anderson, John Forsythe, Leslie Uggams. An elaborate drama set in Prohibition era Chicago. Forsythe plays a cold-hearted gangster who succumbs to the innocent charms and curvaceous body of small-town girl Anderson, who's arrived in the Windy City to get married. (Dir: Don Medford, 104 mins.)†

Sizzle Beach (1974)* Terry Congie, Leslie Brandner, Roselyn Royce. Three young women head for Malibu and the good life. Aimless comedy-drama would still be rotting in a can somewhere but for a brief appearance by a nineteen-year-old Kevin Costner, on the strength of whose name this was released to video. (Dir: Richard Brandner, 93 mins.)†

Skag (MTV 1980)*** Karl Malden, Piper Laurie, Craig Wasson, Kathryn Holcomb. Fine drama. Malden plays middle-aged steel mill foreman Pete Skagska, who suffers a stroke at the mill. Returning home to recuperate, Skag uncovers family problems alongside worries about his own health and the possibility of impotence. He becomes a hard-hitting, realistic blue-collar dad—a hero. (Dir: Frank Perry, 152 mins.)†

Skateboard (1978)½ Leif Garrett, Allen Garfield, Kathleen Lloyd. Skateboards are a menace and so is this dim-witted film. (Dir: George Gage, 93 mins.)†

Skatetown, USA (1979)* Scott Baio, Flip Wilson, Ruth Buzzi, Ron Palillo. A skimpily plotted saga about a roller disco. (Dir: William Levey, 98 mins.)

Skeezer (1982)*** Karen Valentine, Leighton Greer, Mariclare Costello, Dee Wallace, Tom Atkins, Jeremy Licht. Skeezer is a caring sheepdog who seems to be able to lend a paw to help emotionally troubled kids overcome their problems. Although this sounds too cute to be remotely believable, this true-life tale is perceptive and touching. (Dir: Peter H. Hunt, 120 mins.)†

Skeleton Coast (1988)**½ Ernest Borgnine, Robert Vaughn, Oliver Reed, Leon Isaac Kennedy, Herbert Lom. Army vet Borgnine leads a group of mercenaries into Angola to save his son, a CIA agent being held captive in a border war. For once these stars, who usually sleepwalk their way through these programmers, look lively, making this adventure a cut above average. AKA: **Fair Trade.** (Dir: John "Bud" Cardos, 98 mins.)†

Sketches of a Strangler (1978)*½ Allan Goorwitz (Garfield), Meredith MacRae. Psycho with a fixation on his dead mother uses Hollywood prostitutes as models, then kills them. The killer has more personality than the usual faceless automaton. But suspense and thrills are nil. (Dir: Paul Leder, 91 mins.)†

Ski Bum, The (1971)½ Zalman King, Charlotte Rampling, Dimitra Arliss, Anna Karen. A bummer about a downhill racer who goes downhill in the business world. (Dir: Bruce Clark, 136 mins.)†

Skidoo (1969)½ Jackie Gleason, Carol Channing, Frankie Avalon, John Phillip Law, Burgess Meredith, George Raft, Mickey Rooney, Harry Nilsson, Groucho Marx. A clunker comedy about mobsters with an unfortunate 1960s "with it" tone permeating the film. (Dir: Otto Preminger, 98 mins.)

Ski Fever (U.S.-Austria-Czechoslovakia, 1967)½ Martin Milner, Claudia Martin, Vivi Bach, Toni Sailor. Sleazy tale of an American ski instructor who falls in love with a pupil while the continental instructors teach the other ski bunnies how to slalom in bed. (Dir: Curt Siodmak, 98 mins.)

Ski Lift to Death (MTV 1978)** Deborah Raffin, Charles Frank, Suzy Chaffee. There's a little of everything in this snow smorgasbord—expert skiing sequences, tempting wenches, a scary gondola accident, and a gun-toting killer out on the slopes. (Dir: William Wiard, 104 mins.)

Skin Deep (1989)*½ John Ritter, Vincent Gardenia, Alyson Reed, Julianne Phillips. Whiney, indulgent Blake Edwards movie about how tough it is to be a rich, famous, sex-obsessed, near-alcoholic California writer. No plot to speak of, just Ritter (who looks far too young for the part) alternately bemoaning his midlife crisis and attempting to seduce every attractive woman he meets. A few funny slapstick scenes are all that make this bearable. (101 mins.)†

Skin Game (1971)*** James Garner, Louis Gossett, Susan Clark, Edward Asner. Garner's relaxed charm is put to fine use in this surprisingly agile comedy set in pre-Civil War days. Garner, a con artist, and his sidekick, runaway slave Gossett—also excellent—combine for some funny incidents including the unlikely subject of racism. (Dir: Paul Bogart, 102 mins.)†

Skipalong Rosenbloom—See: **Square Shooter, The**

Ski Party (1965)** Frankie Avalon, Dwayne Hickman, Deborah Walley. A very poor man's *Some Like It Hot*. Avalon and Hickman get into girls' costumes and go on a "ski party" to find out all about the opposite sex and the types of men they adore. (Dir: Alan Rafkin, 90 mins.)

Ski Patrol (1990)**½ Roger Rose, Corby Timbrook, T. K. Carter, Leslie Jordan, George Lopez, Martin Mull, Ray Walston. The wacky crew at a ski lodge fight off the efforts of developer Mull to have their license revoked so that he can take the place over. *Police Academy* that, given its extreme lack of ambition, is better than it has any right to be. (Dir: Richard Correll, 91 mins.)†

Skipper Surprised His Wife, The (1950)**½ Robert Walker, Joan Leslie, Edward Arnold, Spring Byington, Leon Ames. Mild domestic comedy of a naval captain trying to run his home efficiently when his wife is laid up with a broken leg. Good premise isn't satisfyingly developed. (Dir: Elliott Nugent, 85 mins.)

Skippy (1931)***½ Jackie Cooper, Robert Coogan, Mitzie Green, Jackie Searl. Excellent children's film, based on a popular comic strip. Simple plot concerns several children trying to raise money for a dog license. Joseph L. Mankiewicz

965

was one of the scriptwriters. (Dir: Norman Taurog, 85 mins.)

Skirts Ahoy (1952)**½ Esther Williams, Vivian Blaine, Joan Evans, Barry Sullivan, Keefe Brasselle. Typical musical about three sailors and their romances—only this time the sailors are Waves. (Dir: Sidney Lanfield, 109 mins.)

Skokie (MTV 1981)***½ Danny Kaye, John Rubenstein, Ed Flanders, Eli Wallach. This stunning drama is a re-creation of the dilemma faced by Jewish citizens of Skokie, Ill., when neo-Nazis attempted to march. The potent story builds with moving intensity as the locals wrestle with free speech and First Amendment rights. (Dir: Herbert Wise, 150 mins.)

Skull, The (Great Britain, 1965)** Peter Cushing, Christopher Lee, Jill Bennett, Patrick Wymark. An improbable saga about the murderous powers of the notorious Marquis de Sade's skull. (Dir: Freddie Francis, 83 mins.)

Skullduggery (1970)* Burt Reynolds, Chips Rafferty, Edward Fox. Claptrap about an anthropological expedition in New Guinea which stumbles upon a band of blond apelike creatures who may be the missing link in evolution. (Dir: Gordon Douglas, 103 mins.)

Sky Above, the Mud Below, The (France-Belgium-The Netherlands, 1961)**** Absorbing, frequently harrowing documentary exploration of primitive peoples. Oscar: Best Documentary Feature. (Dir: Pierre-Dominique Gaisseau, 90 mins.)†

Sky Bandits (1986)*½ Scott McGinnis, Jeff Osterhage, Miles Anderson. Poorly paced comedy adventure about two fun-loving bank bandits who are coerced into helping the Allies during WWI. (Dir: Zoran Perisic, 90 mins.)

Sky Devils (1932)**½ Spencer Tracy, William Boyd, George Cooper, Ann Dvorak, Billy Bevan. Dopey service comedy of Tracy and Boyd trying to evade action in WWI, becoming heroes anyway. Good performances, especially from Tracy and Dvorak, but weak script. (Dir: Edward Sutherland, 90 mins.)

Sky Dragon (1949)**½ Roland Winters, Keye Luke, Mantan Moreland, Tim Ryan, Milburn Stone, Noel B. Neill, Iris Adrian, Elena Verdugo. Absorbing Charlie Chan feature about solving a complicated theft and murder that takes place in the air. (Dir: Lesley Selander, 64 mins.)

Sky Full of Moon (1952)**½ Carleton Carpenter, Jan Sterling, Keenan Wynn, Robert Burton, Elaine Stewart, Douglas Dumbrille. Low-key romance of a naive cowboy who comes to Las Vegas for a rodeo and falls for a tough casino worker. They fall in love, but she decides he'd be better off back on the ranch. Affecting and unpretentious. (Dir: Norman Foster, 73 mins.)

Sky Hei$t (MTV 1975)*½ Don Meredith, Frank Gorshin, Stefanie Powers. A pilot for a series on choppers. Crooks (Gorshin and Powers) plan to kidnap flying lawmen, led by Meredith, during a gold bullion theft. (Dir: Lee H. Katzin, 100 mins.)

Sky High (1922)***½ Tom Mix, J. Farrell MacDonald, Eva Novak, Sid Jordan, Adele Warner. Exciting non-western Mix adventure about an immigration officer pursuing a ruthless gang of smugglers. Thrills and action galore, beautifully filmed at the Grand Canyon. (Dir: Lynn Reynolds, 51 mins.)†

Skyjacked—See: **Sky Terror**

Skylark (1941)*** Claudette Colbert, Ray Milland, Brian Aherne. Amusing little comedy about a wife who gets the "seven-year itch" and has a brief and enlightening interlude with another man. (Dir: Mark Sandrich, 94 mins.)

Skyline (Spain, 1983)*** Antonio Resines, Beatriz Perez-Porro, Jamie Nos, Roy Hoffman. A droll, unassuming film about a Spanish photographer's adventures in New York. Instead of tilting at windmills, he tries his damnedest to fit into the Manhattan mainstream. (Dir: Fernando Colomo, 83 mins.)

Sky Murder (1940)**½ Walter Pidgeon, Donald Meek, Karen Verne, Edward Ashley, Joyce Compton, Tom Conway, Chill Wills. Good low-budget Nick Carter adventure starring Pidgeon as the famous detective, rescuing a beautiful European refugee from spies. (Dir: George B. Seitz, 71 mins.)

Sky Riders (1976)**½ James Coburn, Susannah York, Robert Culp. Well above the level of most mediocre melodramas, thanks to some exciting, well-photographed scenes of the sport of hang-gliding. The plot you've seen before—American industrialist (Culp) has his wife and children kidnapped by a terrorist group. Coburn and his derring-do glider gang ease down for the rescue. (Dir: Douglas Hickox, 90 mins.)

Skyscraper Souls (1932)*** Warren William, Maureen O'Sullivan, Gregory Ratoff, Anita Page, Jean Hersholt, Wallace Ford, Hedda Hopper. Fascinating drama, with comic touches, of a businessman who sacrifices everyone and everything to build the world's tallest skyscraper. William is terrific in a story obviously inspired by the recent completion of the Empire State Building. (Dir: Edgar Selwyn, 80 mins.)

Sky's No Limit, The (MTV 1984)*** Sharon Gless, Dee Wallace, Anne Archer, David Ackroyd, Barnard Hughes. Gless, Wallace and Archer portray competent, aggressive women openly competing to be the first U.S. woman astronaut in space, circa 1980. An absorbing, well-developed story. (Dir: David Lowell Rich, 104 mins.)

966

Sky's the Limit (1943)*** Fred Astaire, Joan Leslie, Robert Ryan, Robert Benchley. War hero spends his leave in New York and falls in love with a girl. Pleasing musical with great Astaire dancing. (Dir: Edward H. Griffith, 89 mins.)†

Sky Terror (1972)**½ Charlton Heston, Jeanne Crain, Yvette Mimieux. Straightforward, unpretentious tale about a bomb threat aboard an airplane flown by Heston, who is loved by stewardess Mimieux. AKA: **Skyjacked**. (Dir: John Guillermin, 100 mins.)

Sky Trap, The (MTV 1979)**½ Marc McClure, Kitty Ruth, Jim Hutton. Disney adventure yarn. Sailplane pilot (McClure) gets involved in a dope-smuggling caper against his will. (Dir: Jerome Courtland, 104 mins.)

Skyward (MTV 1980)** Bette Davis, Suzy Gilstrap, Howard Hesseman. Sentimental "you can do anything" drama about a 14-year-old paraplegic girl who dreams of flying. (Dir: Ron Howard, 104 mins.)

Skywatch (Great Britain, 1960)**½ Ian Carmichael, Tommy Steele, Benny Hill, Sydney Tafler. Episodic WWII comedy-drama about the assortment of odd characters who man a British searchlight unit. Dramatic moments work better than you might expect. AKA: **Light Up the Sky**. (Dir: Lewis Gilbert, 90 mins.)

Skyway to Death (MTV 1974)** Ross Martin, Stefanie Powers, Bobby Sherman, Tige Andrews, John Astin, Nancy Malone, Joseph Campanella, Severn Darden. Crisis drama about passengers in an aerial tramway between mountain peaks held hostage by a terrorist. (Dir: Gordon Hessler, 73 mins.)

Slacker (1990)*** Richard Linklater, R. Basquez, J. Caggeine, J. Hockey, S. Hockey, M. James, S. Dietert, B. Boyd. Highly original, independent feature offers a series of vignettes about always quirky, often hilarious people in and around Austin, Texas. The film includes tales from conspiracy addicts, auto fanatics, street bums, two-bit philosophers, idle musicians, eccentric women, and petty criminals. (Dir: Richard Linklater, 97 mins.)

Slamdance (1987)* Tom Hulce, Mary Elizabeth Mastrontonio, Virginia Madsen, Harry Dean Stanton, Adam Ant. Dull attempt at *film noir* with Hulce as a cartoonist whose past romantic involvement with a recently murdered blonde lands him in hot water with corrupt cops. (Dir: Wayne Wang, 90 mins.)

Slammer (1977)*** Bruce Davison, Jose Perez, Joseph Carberry. Miguel Pinero's brilliant play *Short Eyes*, about an accused child molester thrown in the tank with hardened types is given conscientious treatment by director Robert M. Young. Powerhouse performances, especially by Davison and Carberry. AKA: **Short Eyes**. (104 mins.)†

Slammer Girls (1986)* Devon Jenkin, Jeff Eagle. Parody of women's-prison movies isn't nearly as funny as the real thing. Features a cast of porno stars moonlighting under pseudonyms. (Dir: Chuck Vincent, 78 mins.)†

Slander (1956)*** Van Johnson, Ann Blyth, Steve Cochran, Marjorie Rambeau, Harold J. Stone, Lurene Tuttle. Forceful social drama of the effects an irresponsible scandal sheet's revelations have on the victims. (Dir: Roy Rowland, 81 mins.)

Slap Shot (1977)*** Paul Newman, Strother Martin, Jennifer Warren, Michael Ontkean, Lindsay Crouse, Melinda Dillon. Foulmouthed, funny, marvelously acted movie about a minor league hockey team. Newman plays an aging player-coach who's a losing coach until he directs his simpleminded charges to act like crazed hoodlums on the ice. (Dir: George Roy Hill, 122 mins.)†

Slapstick of Another Kind (1983)½ Jerry Lewis, Madeline Kahn, Marty Feldman, John Abbott, Jim Backus. This feeble comedy concerns grotesque twins whose parents hide them away without realizing that these freakish kiddies are really messengers from outer space. (Dir: Steven Paul, 87 mins.)†

Slash (1987)* Ron Kristoff, Michael Monty, Gwen Hung. When Cambodian rebels capture secret CIA files, *Soldier of Fortune* pinup Slash is sent to retrieve them. Much killing and gunfire ensue. (Dir: John Gale, 90 mins.)†

Slash Dance (1989)* Cindy Maranne, James Carrol Jordan, Jay Richardson, Joel von Ornsteiner. Another psycho killer stalking dancers, this time against the backdrop of auditions for a new Broadway show. Even the dancing stinks in this one. (Dir: James Shyman, 83 mins.)†

Slattery's Hurricane (1949)**½ Richard Widmark, Linda Darnell, Veronica Lake. Personal drama amid a weather station's reporting of a hurricane. (Dir: André de Toth, 83 mins.)

Slaughter (1972)*½ Jim Brown, Stella Stevens, Rip Torn, Cameron Mitchell, Don Gordon. Poor blaxploitation pic about an ex-Green Beret stalking the Syndicate cretins who bumped off his mom and dad. (Dir: Jack Starrett, 92 mins.)†

Slaughter High (Great Britain, 1986)* Caroline Munro, Simon Scuddamore, Carmine Iannoccone. A former student preys upon alums at a reunion. You've seen it all before. (Dirs: George Dugdale, Mark Ezra, Peter Litten, 89 mins.)†

Slaughterhouse (1987)*½ Sherry Bendorf, Don Barrett, Joe Barton. A slaughterhouse owner and his retarded son kill off their enemies and some incidental nubile teenagers. (Dir: Rick Roessler, 85 mins.)†

Slaughterhouse-Five (1972)*** Michael Sacks, Ron Liebman, Sharon Gans, Valerie Perrine. Ambitious film adaptation of Kurt Vonnegut's complex novel, a parable about Billy Pilgrim, an American Everyman. WWII experiences and mental illness are mixed with other striking images in this demanding if flawed work. (Dir: George Roy Hill, 104 mins.)†

Slaughterhouse Rock (1988)*½ Nicholas Celozzi, Tom Reilly, Donna Denton, Toni Basil. Gore-fest about a rock singer being possessed by the cannibalistic spirit of a dead cavalry commandant. Overreaches its limited budget. Music by Devo. (Dir: Dimitri Logothetis, 90 mins.)†

Slaughter on Tenth Avenue (1957)*** Richard Egan, Jan Sterling, Dan Duryea, Walter Matthau. Assistant DA runs into obstacles when he tries to get the goods on waterfront hoodlums. Compact and informative crime drama, well done. (Dir: Arnold Laven, 103 mins.)

Slaughter's Big Rip-Off (1973)*½ Jim Brown, Ed MacMahon, Brock Peters, Don Stroud, Gloria Hendry. The screen turns into a slaughter house as the self-made vigilante once again butts his head against the mob. (Dir: Gordon Douglas, 93 mins.)†

Slaughter Trail (1951)** Brian Donlevy, Gig Young, Virginia Grey, Andy Devine, Robert Hutton. Good western, interesting story of a cavalry officer trying to trap the culprit who murdered two defenseless Indians. (Dir: Irving Allen, 78 mins.)

Slave Girl (1947)*** George Brent, Yvonne De Carlo. Playboy is sent to Tripoli to rescue imprisoned American seamen. Often quite funny satire on adventure films; some good laughs. (Dir: Charles Lamont, 80 mins.)

Slave Girls From Beyond Infinity (1987)** Elizabeth Cayton, Cindy Beal, Brinke Stevens. Amusingly deadpan homage/spoof of fifties B flicks, in which the title beauties become involved in a *Most Dangerous Game* hunt on a distant planet. (Dir: Ken Dixon, 73 mins.)†

Slave of Love, A (U.S.S.R., 1976)***½ Elena Solovei, Rodion Nakhapetov, Alexander Kalyagin. Delightful bittersweet romance about a penny dreadful film company shooting in the Crimea as the postrevolutionary civil war echoes in the distance. Recommended. (Dir: Nikita Mikhalkov, 94 mins.)†

Slave of the Cannibal God (Italy, 1978)*½ Ursula Andress, Stacy Keach, Claudio Cassinelli, Antonio Marsina. Stacy's got

to rescue luscious Ursula, who's been captured by ill-intentioned natives. (Dir: Sergio Martino, 86 mins.)†

Slaves (1969)* Stephen Boyd, Ossie Davis, Barbara Ann Teer, Gale Sondergaard. A serving of lust and villainy on the old plantation as a sensitive slave (Davis) fights for freedom against the dastardly overseer (Boyd). (Dir: Herbert J. Biberman, 110 mins.)

Slave Ship (1937)*** Warner Baxter, Wallace Beery, Elizabeth Allan, Mickey Rooney, George Sanders. Atmospheric adventure of a slave-ship captain who resolves to quit the trade, only to face a mutiny by his greedy crew. William Faulkner was one of the screenwriters. (Dir: Tay Garnett, 90 mins.)

Slaves of Babylon (1953)** Richard Conte, Linda Christian, Maurice Schwartz. Biblical history suffers another setback with this romanticized nonsense relating how Nebuchadnezzar was defeated by an Israeli shepherd and his army. (Dir: William Castle, 82 mins.)

Slaves of New York (1989)** Bernadette Peters, Adam Coleman Howard, Chris Sarandon, Mary Beth Hurt, Mercedes Ruehl. Episodic adaptation of Tama Janowitz's book about terminally hip New York artists, tied together by Peters as an outsider trying to get "in." (Dir: James Ivory, 115 mins.)†

Slayground (Great Britain, 1984)* Peter Coyote, Mel Smith, Billie Whitelaw. An armed robber's excesses on the job lead to the death of a little girl, whose father hires a hit man to track him down. (Dir: Terry Bedford, 89 mins.)†

Sleazy Uncle, The (Italian, 1989)**½ Vittorio Gassman, Giancarlo Giannini, Andrea Ferreol, Stefania Sandrelli. Engaging sentimental comedy about a colorfully irresponsible uncle (Gassman) who creates havoc for his trusting, long-lost nephew (Giannini). The always wonderful Gassman makes this uneven farce worth a look. (Dir: Franco Brusati, 105 mins.)

Sleepaway Camp (1983)*½ Jonathan Tierston, Felissa Rose, Christopher Collet, Karen Fields, Mike Kellin. The plot concerns a series of murders at—surprise—a summer camp. (Dir: Robert Hiltzik, 89 mins.)†

Sleeper (1973)*** Woody Allen, Diane Keaton, John Beck, Don Keefer. It's Woody's inspired, nutty vision of the future. After undergoing an operation the Woody is frozen and awakens in 2173 to find himself in a police state, where the government has perfected its torture techniques to the point where hapless victims are forced to watch reruns of Howard Cosell on TV. (Dir: Woody Allen, 88 mins.)†

Sleeping Beauty (1959)***½ Voices of Mary Costa, Bill Shirley, Vera Vague. The most impressive post-WWII Disney animated feature. The look of the fairy tale based on 15th-century French manuscripts, with a medieval flattened sense of perspective and harsh, angular lines. (Dirs: Clyde Geronimi, Eric Larson, Wolfgang Reitherman, Les Clark, 75 mins.)†

Sleeping Car, The (1990)**½ David Naughton, Judie Aronson, Kevin McCarthy, Jeff Conaway. Witty horror flick about a passenger train sleeping car, the scene of a gruesome murder a decade earlier, now haunted by ghosts who disturb the passengers. (Dir: Douglas Curtis, 87 mins.)†

Sleeping Car Murders, The (France, 1965)***½ Yves Montand, Simone Signoret, Jean-Louis Trintignant, Jacques Perrin. An intriguing murder mystery mounted with class and taste by Costa-Gavras (Z). The cast are all perfect in this complex tale involving a multiple murderer. (95 mins.)

Sleeping Car to Trieste (Great Britain, 1948)*** Jean Kent, Albert Lieven. Some spies steal a valuable political diary and take off on the Trieste express, aboard which a famous detective outwits them. Neat spy thriller with some good comedy touches. Remake of *Rome Express*. (Dir: John Paddy Carstairs, 95 mins.)

Sleeping City, The (1950)**½ Richard Conte, Coleen Gray, Peggy Dow, Alex Nicol. Convincing drama about a detective who impersonates an intern in a hospital in order to crack a narcotics ring. (Dir: George Sherman, 85 mins.)

Sleeping Dogs (New Zealand, 1977)*** Sam Neill, Ian Mune, Melissa Donaldson, Warren Oates. Ambitious production depicts a modern, English-speaking country undergoing the twin torments of police state repression and an armed resistance movement as seen through the eyes of an innocent bystander. (Dir: Roger Donaldson, 106 mins.)

Sleeping Tiger (Great Britain, 1954)*** Alexis Smith, Dirk Bogarde, Alexander Knox. Psychiatrist brings a criminal to his home for study, but the doctor's wife falls for him. Excellently acted, suspenseful drama. (Dir: Joseph Losey, 89 mins.)

Sleeping With the Enemy (1991)** Julia Roberts, Patrick Bergin, Kevin Anderson, Elizabeth Lawrence, Kyle Secor. Predictable suspense exercise about an abused woman who flees her psychotic husband and takes up with a college drama professor, only to have her obsessive spouse turn up to deliver more torment. Much of the film is a calculated series of dreary melodramatic setups for a final revenge catharsis that's more of a relief to the moviegoer than it is surprising or frightening. (Dir: Joseph Ruben, 99 mins.)†

Sleep, My Love (1947)*** Claudette Colbert, Don Ameche, Robert Cummings. A husband who wants his wife out of the way tries to drive her insane. Familiar suspense melodrama; well done, but nothing new. (Dir: Douglas Sirk, 97 mins.)

Sleepwalk (1986)*½ Suzanne Fletcher, Ann Magnuson. Very slow-moving "art" film about a New York typesetter hired to translate a mysterious Chinese document and becoming involved in murder—or is she just imagining it? (Dir: Sara Driver, 72 mins.)†

Sleepytime Gal (1942)**½ Judy Canova, Jerry Lester. A cake decorator in Miami enters a singing competition, gets mixed up with gangsters. Amusing musical comedy. (Dir: Albert S. Rogell, 84 mins.)

Slender Thread, The (1965)*** Sidney Poitier, Anne Bancroft, Telly Savalas. Sidney Poitier plays a college student who volunteers his services at the "Crisis Clinic" and he has to keep would-be suicide Anne Bancroft on the phone while police attempt to find her whereabouts. (Dir: Sydney Pollack, 98 mins.)

Sleuth (1972)***½ Laurence Olivier, Michael Caine. Marvelous inventive mystery based on the play by Anthony Shaffer. It's a joy to see the great Olivier hamming it up, acting out his own special "games." Caine is equally skillful playing the butt of one of the "games," but it turns out that . . . well, we're *not* going to tell you the plot of this stylish thriller briskly directed by Joseph L. Mankiewicz. Just see and enjoy. (137 mins.)†

Slight Case of Larceny, A (1953)*** Mickey Rooney, Elaine Stewart, Eddie Bracken. Rooney and Bracken make a good team as they play a couple of ex-GIs in trouble over a get-rich-quick scheme. (Dir: Don Weis, 71 mins.)

Slight Case of Murder, A (1938)***½ Edward G. Robinson, Allen Jenkins, John Litel, Ruth Donnelly, Jane Bryan. In this screamingly funny satire of gangster films, (Robinson) is a bootlegger who decides to go straight, confounding friends and enemies alike. (Dir: Lloyd Bacon, 90 mins.)

Slightly Dangerous (1943)**½ Lana Turner, Robert Young, Walter Brennan, Dame May Whitty. Pleasant fluff with Turner in a rare comedy role as a waitress with amnesia. (Dir: Wesley Ruggles, 94 mins.)

Slightly French (1949)*** Dorothy Lamour, Don Ameche. Film director hires a carnival girl to pose as a new French import. Diverting comedy with good musical numbers, smooth direction. Remake of *Let's Fall in Love*. (Dir: Douglas Sirk, 81 mins.)

Slightly Honorable (1939)*** Pat O'Brien, Broderick Crawford, Ruth Terry, Eve Arden, Edward Arnold, Evelyn Keyes. A fast and wacky murder mystery, as a lawyer tangles with crooked politics and sinister killings. Rapid-paced, with bright dialogue and a great cast. (Dir: Tay Garnett, 83 mins.)

Slightly Scarlet (1956)*** John Payne, Arlene Dahl, Rhonda Fleming. Crook intends to turn the tables on his crime syndicate boss and muscle in himself. Unpleasant but well-made, well-acted melodrama. (Dir: Allan Dwan, 99 mins.)†

Slim (1937)*** Pat O'Brien, Henry Fonda, Margaret Lindsay, Stuart Erwin. High-voltage wire and the linesmen who string it are the subject of this movie. A sure-fire blend of romance, action, and comedy. (Dir: Ray Enright, 80 mins.)

Slim Carter (1957)*** Jock Mahoney, Julie Adams, Tim Hovey. Café entertainer becomes a western star and the idol of millions, but it all goes to his head—until an orphan boy takes a hand. Pleasant, slightly different behind-the-scenes comedy-drama. (Dir: Richard Bartlett, 82 mins.)

Slime City (1988)*½ Robert C. Sobin, Mary Hunter, T.J. Merrick. Ultra low-budgeter about a haunted apartment building that turns a new tenant into a slime-dripping killer. Campy humor (some of it intentional) makes this a bit more entertaining than others of its ilk. (Dir: Gregory Lamberson, 85 mins.)

Slime People, The (1963)* Robert Hutton, Susan Hart. As ridiculous as its title—horror film about slimy things trying to take over. (Dir: Robert Hutton, 76 mins.)†

Slipper and the Rose, The (Great Britain, 1976)** Richard Chamberlain, Gemma Craven, Edith Evans. Director Bryan Forbes's tired musical version of the Cinderella story. An air of desperation prevails throughout. (146 mins.)

Slipping Into Darkness (1988)** Michelle Johnson, John DiAquino, Cristen Kauffman. A trio of arrogant, rich college girls are blamed for the death of a retarded town boy, whose brother and friends seek revenge. Valid attempt to portray young class hatred in Middle America sinks under a melodramatic plot. (Dir: Eleanor Gaver, 87 mins.)†

Slither (1973)***½ James Caan, Sally Kellerman, Peter Boyle, Louise Lasser. Very diverting first movie by director Howard Zieff. It's a wild and woolly chase in trailers and campers for a stash of loot, with lots of stops along the way for extravagantly detailed comic vignettes. (97 mins.)

Slithis—See: **Spawn of the Slithis**

Slow Burn (MCTV 1986)*** Eric Roberts, Beverly D'Angelo, Dennis Lipscomb. If you get enthusiastic about voice-over narration and stylized photography, *Slow Burn* is the sort of mystery movie you'll enjoy. It might take a bit of figuring before who did what and why becomes clear, but your patience will be rewarded. (Dir: Matthew Chapman, 93 mins.)†

Slow Dancing in the Big City (1978)**½ Paul Sorvino, Anne Ditchburn, Nicolas Coster. Macho film about ballet is too manipulative to wring out eye moisture. Sorvino is a lovable lug of a columnist who falls in love with Ditchburn. (Dir: John G. Avildsen, 101 mins.)

Slugger's Wife, The (1985)** Michael O'Keefe, Rebecca DeMornay, Martin Ritt, Randy Quaid. Disappointing romantic comedy from the pen of Neil Simon. O'Keefe stars as a smitten baseball player whose hitting depends on how well his love life is going with nightclub singer DeMornay. Routine, with sparse laughs. (Dir: Hal Ashby, 105 mins.)†

Slugs (Spain, 1988)**½ Michael Garfield, Santiago Alvarez, Philip Machale. It sounds pretty dumb—a small town is attacked by carnivorous slugs, mutated by toxic wastes—but this is a solidly made horror thriller that manages to keep a straight face in spite of its premise. (Dir: Juan Piquer Simon, 92 mins.)†

Slumber Party Massacre, The (1982)**½ Michele Michaels, Michael Villela, Andre Honore, Debra Deliso, Robin Stille. A seriocomic slasher film that neither massacres the viewer's sensibilities nor puts them to sleep. Written by Rita Mae Brown and filmed by an all-woman crew. (Dir: Amy Jones, 78 mins.)†

Small Back Room, The (Great Britain, 1949)***½ David Farrar, Kathleen Byron, Jack Hawkins, Anthony Bushell, Michael Gough, Robert Morley. Outstanding wartime drama of a crippled bomb-disposal expert, his love affair with a co-worker, and his struggles with daily peril. Atmospheric, adult drama. AKA: **Hour of Glory**. (Dirs: Michael Powell, Emeric Pressburger, 106 mins.)†

Small Change (France, 1976)**** Eva Truffaut, Tania Torrens, Jean-François Stevenin. A wise, beautiful, poetic comedy about children and a mistreated boy that also happens to be very funny. One of François Truffaut's tenderest, most observant works. (104 mins.)†

Small Circle of Friends, A (1980)*** Brad Davis, Karen Allen, Jameson Parker, John Friedrich, Shelley Long, Gary Springer. Romantic drama about three friends who attend college together during the turbulent late '60s. They share ideas, memories, and each other in this witty little film, which features some nice insights into the era as well as an unabashedly daring ménage à trois. (Dir: Rob Cohen, 112 mins.)†

Smallest Show on Earth, The (Great Britain, 1957)*** Peter Sellers, Margaret Rutherford, Bill Travers, Virginia McKenna. Amusing comedy about a young married couple who inherit a tacky movie theater along with its most improbable staff. (Dir: Basil Dearden, 81 mins.)

Small Killing (MTV 1981)** Edward Asner, Jean Simmons, Andrew Prine, J. Pat O'Malley, Mary Jackson, Sylvia Sidney. Sometimes flawed and far-fetched telefeature has Asner and Simmons teaming up in a mystery-romance about bag ladies acting as messengers for drug dealers. (Dir: Steven Hilliard Stern, 104 mins.)†

Small Sacrifices (MTV 1989)*** Farrah Fawcett, John Shea, Gordon Clapp, Ryan O'Neal, Emily Perkins, Garry Chalk. True story of the shooting of three Oregon children and their mother, who the local DA suspects may have committed the crime herself. Fawcett gives a tight performance as the antisocial, narcissistic mother in this compelling drama. The video version runs 159 mins. (Dir: David Greene, 200 mins.)†

Small Town Girl (1936)*** Janet Gaynor, Robert Taylor, Binnie Barnes, James Stewart, Lewis Stone, Andy Devine. Noteworthy social comedy-drama of village girl Gaynor and socialite intern Taylor, who meet and get married during a drinking spree. Director William Wellman gave the story a realistic treatment, detailing the differences in expectations and assumptions between rich and poor, and the difficult struggle to overcome them. (90 mins.)

Small Town Girl (1953)** Jane Powell, Farley Granger, Ann Miller, Billie Burke, Nat King Cole. A crafty girl tricks a stranger into marriage when he's drunk and then sets out to win his heart. A few good production numbers like Miller's "I've Got That Beat," staged by Busby Berkeley. (Dir: Leslie Kardos, 93 mins.)†

Small Town in Texas, A (1976)** Timothy Bottoms, Susan George, Bo Hopkins, Art Hindle, John Karlen, Buck Fowler. Just released from prison, Bottoms looks up his girlfriend, only to find her now involved with the crooked cop who set him up on a phony charge. Drive-in fare, rather light on violence. (Dir: Jack Starrett, 95 mins.)†

Small World of Sammy Lee, The (Great Britain, 1963)*** Anthony Newley, Julia Foster, Robert Stephens. Sammy (Newley) is a minor Soho personality who must raise some money or face gang brutality; his reactions are a mixture of terror and nonchalance. Neatly crafted suspense, set in the unglamorous, tawdry locales of Soho. (Dir: Ken Hughes, 105 mins.)

Smart Alecks (1941)*½ East Side Kids, Gale Storm, Gabriel Dell, Walter Woolf King. A throwback to earlier East Side Kid plots—in order to get money for baseball uniforms, the kids are lured into illegal dealings. (Dir: Wallace Fox, 63 mins.)

Smart Money (1931)**½ Edward G. Robinson, James Cagney, Margaret Livingstone, Evalyn Knapp, Noel Francis. A smart movie that was the only screen teaming of Cagney and Robinson. The stars turn in adroit performances in this action-packed pic about a barber who goes from cutting hair to cutting in on the gambling racket. (Dir: Alfred E. Green, 90 mins.)

Smart Woman (1948)*** Constance Bennett, Brian Aherne. A lady lawyer has a special prosecutor fall for her. Good melodrama. (Dir: Edward A. Blatt, 93 mins.)

Smashing Time (Great Britain, 1967)*** Rita Tushingham, Lynn Redgrave, Michael York, Anna Quayle, Ian Carmichael. Comic misadventures of two country girls (Redgrave, Tushingham) in the mod world of London. Often harkens back to the old slapstick days; good-humored, enjoyable, knock-about farce. (Dir: Desmond Davis, 96 mins.)

Smash Palace (New Zealand, 1981)*** Bruno Lawrence, Anna Jemison, Greer Robson. A disturbing, insightful import from New Zealand which successfully juggles the provocative elements of family upheaval, junkyards, and the New Zealand wilderness. The film is surprisingly fresh and handles a conventional situation with intelligent performances. (Dir: Roger Donaldson, 100 mins.)†

Smash-Up Alley (MTV 1973)** Darren McGavin, Richard Petty, Noah Beery, Jr. For fans of stock-car racing, the "true" story of the king of the hill, Richard Petty, who plays himself, and his father, Lee, played by McGavin. (Dir: Edward J. Kakso, 72 mins.)

Smash-Up on Interstate 5 (MTV 1976)**½ David Groh, Vera Miles, Harriet Nelson. Another disaster film. This time thirty-nine cars are involved, in which fourteen people die and sixty-two are injured (sound like entertainment to you?) In between, flashbacks take viewers back forty-three hours earlier and introduce all the characters. (Dir: John Llewellyn Moxey, 106 mins.)

Smash-up: The Story of a Woman (1947) **½ Susan Hayward, Lee Bowman, Eddie Albert, Marsha Hunt. Hayward gives a showy portrayal of an alcoholic, but the film's sensationalism is dated. (Dir: Stuart Heisler, 103 mins.)†

Smile (1975)*** Barbara Feldon, Bruce Dern, Michael Kidd, Geoffrey Lewis, Nicholas Pryor, Annette O'Toole. Droll spoof on the biggest goof of all time, the American Beauty Pageant. This one is called the Young American Miss Pageant, and all the expected participants are on hand for the event held in sunny California. There's the sponsor, Dern's used car salesman; the den mother, well played by Feldon; Kidd's sarcastic and bitter Hollywood choreographer down on his luck; and the parade of contestants who give the picture its center. Biting screenplay by Jerry Belson. (Dir: Michael Ritchie, 113 mins.)†

Smile, Jenny, You're Dead (MTV 1974)*** David Janssen, Zalman King, Howard da Silva, Jodie Foster. Janssen plays private eye Harry O (for Orwell), a part created in a similar pilot film. His case involves a model who is being trailed, unbeknownst to anyone, by a psychotic photographer. (Dir: Jerry Thorpe, 90 mins.)

Smiles of a Summer Night (Sweden, 1955)**** Ulla Jacobsson, Eva Dahlbeck, Harriet Anderson, Margit Carlquist, Jarl Kulle. One of director Ingmar Bergman's more accessible works. Some mismatched couples struggle to sort themselves out in this romantic tale, which becomes a very humorous contemplation on the inevitable sadness of human relations. (108 mins.)†

Smilin' Through (1932)*** Norma Shearer, Fredric March, Leslie Howard. Weepy story with Shearer playing an orphan who falls in love with a killer's son. (Dir: Sidney Franklin, 97 mins.)

Smilin' Through (1941)** Jeanette MacDonald, Gene Raymond, Brian Aherne. This remake is not very good. The only screen pairing of real-life husband and wife MacDonald and Raymond. (Dir: Frank Borzage, 100 mins.)†

Smith (1969)*** Glenn Ford, Nancy Olson, Dean Jagger, Keenan Wynn, Warren Oates, Chief Dan George. Ford excels as a nonconformist farmer who champions his persecuted Indian neighbors, even when his community is itching to indict one of the tribe as a murderer. (Dir: Michael O'Herlihy, 112 mins.)†

Smithereens (1983)**½ Susan Berman, Brad Rinn, Richard Hill, Roger Jett. Wren, a 19-year-old sensitive yet tough punk rocker, escapes from the boring, polluted clutches of New Jersey to what she thinks is paradise. The Lower East Side of New York City and New Wave rock 'n' roll are Wren's heaven, and most of her time is spent between the beds of her two fellow music enthusiasts Eric and Paul. (Dir: Susan Seidelman, 93 mins.)†

Smoke (MTV 1970)*** Ronny Howard, 972

Earl Holliman, Andy Devine. Sensitive Disney production deals with a boy who distrusts his new stepfather and extends his love to a stray German shepherd dog. (Dir: Vincent McEveety, 98 mins.)†

Smoke Signal (1955)**½ Dana Andrews, Piper Laurie, Rex Reason, William Talman, Milburn Stone, William Schallert. Colorful western, filmed in Colorado, about a cavalry officer courtmartialed for objecting to a massacre of Indians. Capably done. (Dir: Jerry Hopper, 88 mins.)

Smokey and the Bandit (1977)*** Burt Reynolds, Sally Field, Jerry Reed, Jackie Gleason, Paul Williams, Pat McCormick. Two oddly matched Texas millionaires commission ace driver Smokey to race from Georgia to Texas with a load of illegal beer. The acting is tongue-in-cheek and breezy, the action naturally fast. (Dir: Hal Needham, 97 mins.)†

Smokey and the Bandit II (1980)*½ Burt Reynolds, Jackie Gleason, Sally Field, Dom DeLuise, Paul Williams. Lazy pedestrian sequel to the popular down-home hit. (Dir: Hal Needham, 101 mins.)†

Smokey and the Bandit 3 (1983)* Jackie Gleason, Jerry Reed, Colleen Camp, Pat McCormick, Burt Reynolds. The weakest of the *Smokey and the Bandit* movies stars Gleason reprising his role as the sheriff spreading Southern discomfort along the highways. (Dir: Dick Lowry, 88 mins.)†

Smoky (1934)**½ Victor Jory, Irene Bentley, Frank Campeau, Hank Mann, LeRoy Mason, Leonid Snegoff. The first of several adaptations of the Will James horse opera. Good family entertainment about a horse who goes through a life of hard labor on a junk wagon and faces the slaughterhouse before he's reunited with his beloved master. (Dir: Eugene Forbes, 66 mins.)

Smoky (1946)*** Fred MacMurray, Anne Baxter, Burl Ives. Story of a man's love for his horse is wonderful film fare for the youngsters and those who like sentimental outdoor drama. (Dir: Louis King, 87 mins.)

Smoky (1966)**½ Fess Parker, Diana Hyland. This is the third remake of the famous Will James sentimental story about a horse named Smoky and the events, both good and bad, which befall the animal. (Dir: George Sherman, 103 mins.)

Smoky Mountain Christmas, A (MTV 1986)**½ Dolly Parton, Lee Majors, Dan Hedaya, Anita Morris, Bo Hopkins, René Auberjonois. Parton's special combination of homespun humor and glitzy glamour suits this reworking of the Snow White legend with Dolly as a big movie star returning to her Smoky Mountain origins for the holidays. (Dir: Henry Winkler, 104 mins.)

Smooth as Silk (1946)*** Kent Taylor, Virginia Grey. Attorney murders in a jealous rage, then schemes to cover his crime. Well-knit plot, good direction and performances put this *B* into the *A* class. (Dir: Charles Barton, 65 mins.)

Smooth Talk (1986)***½ Laura Dern, Mary Kay Place, Treat Williams, Levon Helm. Laura Dern flawlessly plays a rebellious 15-year-old who hangs out with her girlfriends, acquires a taste for casual flirting as a sort of rite of passage, and then encounters and is terrorized by a smooth-talking, possibly psychotic lecher (Williams). (Dir: Joyce Chopra, 92 mins.)†

Smorgasbord—See: **Cracking Up**

Smouldering Fires (1925)*** Pauline Frederick, Laura La Plante, Malcolm McGregor, Tully Marshall. Remarkably sophisticated silent drama of a woman executive who falls in love for the first time with a man younger than herself, facing competition when her younger sister returns home from school. Soap-opera material is played with intelligence, sensitivity, and restraint. (Dir: Clarence Brown, 70 mins.)†

Smugglers, The (Great Britain, 1947)**½ Michael Redgrave, Richard Attenborough, Jean Kent, Joan Greenwood, Francis L. Sullivan. A young lad is instrumental in rounding up a gang of smugglers, of which his guardian is the boss. Costume melodrama moves too slowly. (Dir: Bernard Knowles, 90 mins.)

Smugglers, The (MTV 1968)** Shirley Booth, Carol Lynley, Kurt Kasznar, David Opatoshu. Predictable drama. About two American tourists in Europe (Booth and Lynley) who are used as decoys by an international smuggling operation. (Dir: Alfred Hayes, 97 mins.)

Smugglers' Cove (1948)*** Bowery Boys, Amelia Ward, Paul Harvey. The boys go to a Long Island mansion to collect Slip's inheritance and uncover a smuggling operation in the process. (Dir: William Beaudine, 66 mins.)

Smuggler's Island (1951)**½ Jeff Chandler, Evelyn Keyes, Philip Friend, Marvin Miller, Jay Novello. Colorful adventure of deep-sea diver Chandler falling for glamorous Keyes, and tangling with smugglers. Nothing extraordinary, but Keyes and Chandler were a more intelligent than usual pairing. (Dir: Edward Ludwig, 75 mins.)

Smurfs and the Magic Flute, The (1984)*½ This unexcitingly animated feature demonstrates why parents hate taking little kids to G movies and why these tots spend most of their time there at the candy counter. When played, this magic flute, no relation to Mozart's, causes characters named Pee Wee, Johan, and Oily Creep (the bad guy, surprised?) to

dance uncontrollably. The Smurfs don't even appear until the second half. (Dirs: Jose Dutillieu, American version by John Rust, 74 mins.)†

Snafu (1945)**½ Robert Benchley, Conrad Janis. Family is upset when ''their boy'' comes home a hardened teenage soldier. Amusing comedy. (Dir: Jack Moss, 82 mins.)

Snake Eater (Canada, 1989)** Lorenzo Lamas, Josie Bell, Ronnie Hawkins, Cheryl Jeans, Larry Csonka, Ron Palillo. Ex-Marine Lamas puts his special unit training to work when he has to search a swamp for the psycho who kidnapped his sister and murdered the rest of his family. Routine action fare. (Dir: George Erschbamer, 89 mins.)†

Snake People (Mexico-U.S., 1968)* Jack Hill, Boris Karloff, Julissa, Charles East. This scenic island's tourist attractions include voodoo, LSD experimentation, and snake worshippers. A police captain, there on assignment, is confused; you will be too, but you have the option to slither away. AKA: **Cult of the Dead** and **La Muerte Viviente**. (Dir: Enrique Vergara, 90 mins.)†

Snake Pit, The (1948)**½ Olivia de Havilland, Leo Genn, Mark Stevens, Celeste Holm, Beulah Bondi. Social problem drama about the treatment of the mentally ill makes a plea for shock therapy that seems shocking itself today. De Havilland is superb as the young woman who is committed. An important film in its day, it now seems dated and sensational. (Dir: Anatole Litvak, 108 mins.)

Snatched (MTV 1973)**½ Howard Duff, Barbara Parkins, Leslie Nielsen, Sheree North, John Saxon, Robert Reed, Tisha Sterling. Fairly effective kidnapping film. A mastermind kidnaps the wives of three wealthy men and asks for a cool million for each. (Dir: Sutton Roley, 73 mins.)†

Sniper, The (1952)*** Arthur Franz, Adolphe Menjou, Marie Windsor, Richard Kiley. Adult drama about a deranged sniper who baffles police on his trail. Exciting climax. (Dir: Edward Dmytryk, 87 mins.)

Sniper's Ridge (1961)**½ Jack Ging, Stanley Clements. Captain orders a last raid before the Korean peace-talks in an effort to grab glory for himself. (Dir: John Bushelman, 61 mins.)

Snoop Sisters, The (MTV 1972)**½ Helen Hayes, Mildred Natwick, Craig Stevens, Jill Clayburgh. Thanks to the professional elan of its stars, Misses Hayes and Natwick, this comedy-murder mystery holds your interest. The Snoop Sisters, who collaborate on writing mystery novels, get involved in solving the murder of a one-time movie star, played in a brief appearance by real-life, one-time movie star Paulette Goddard. (Dir: Leonard B. Stern, 99 mins.)

Snoopy, Come Home (1972)***½ Don't confuse this "Peanuts" theatrical release with the TV specials, even if they are similar. Story is endearing, dealing with Snoopy's odyssey to find a place where there are no signs bearing the unwelcome greeting "No Dogs Allowed." (Dir: Bill Melendez, 80 mins.)†

Snorkel, The (Great Britain, 1958)*** Peter Van Eyck, Betta St. John, Mandy Miller. Clever murder mystery film with good acting by the principals about a "perfect crime" attempt that nearly succeeds. (Dir: Guy Green, 92 mins.)

Snowball (Great Britain, 1960)**½ Gordon Jackson, Zena Walker, Kenneth Griffith, Daphne Anderson. Capable British social drama of the effects of hurtful gossip on the lives of villagers; low budget, but with an expert cast of familiar faces. (Dir: Pat Jackson, 69 mins.)

Snowball Express (1972)** Dean Jones, Nancy Olson, Harry Morgan, Keenan Wynn, Johnny Whittaker. A slow-lane comedy about the Baxters, who chuck life in the big, bustling City for a new life, but discover they don't have the cash needed to make a go of their proposed ski resort. (Dir: Norman Tokar, 93 mins.)†

Snowbeast (1977)*½ Bo Svenson, Yvette Mimieux, Clint Walker. Scare film for the kiddies about a half-human who goes on a tear, frightening the wits out of vacationers at a ski resort. (Dir: Herb Wallerstein, 106 mins.)†

Snowbound (Great Britain, 1948)*** Robert Newton, Dennis Price, Herbert Lom, Stanley Holloway. A movie director undertakes a dangerous mission to recover some gold bullion in the Italian Alps. (Dir: David Macdonald, 85 mins.)

Snowfire (1958)**½ Molly McGowan, Don Megowan, Claire Kelly. Family film about a little girl who befriends a wild stallion that is considered dangerous by ranchers. (Dirs: Dorrell and Stuart McGowan, 73 mins.)

Snow Job (1972)* Jean-Claude Killy, Daniele Gaubert, Vittorio De Sica. Killy's acting, and that of most others, is as wooden as the Olympic ski champion's skis. Killy dreams up a scheme to rob a local resort and make off with the loot on skis. (Dir: George Englund, 90 mins.)

Snow Kill (MCTV 1990)*½ Terence Knox, Patti D'Arbanville, David Dukes, John Cypher, Joey Travolta. Murder and mayhem on a snowbound, isolated mountaintop. Corporate executives on a survivalist hiking expedition are being killed off one by one by a sadistic escaped convict. Few surprises are in store in this violent and, ultimately, pedestrian

974

thriller. (Dir: Thomas J. Wright, 96 mins.)

Snows of Kilimanjaro, The (1952)**½ Gregory Peck, Susan Hayward, Ava Gardner, Hildegarde Neff. Ernest Hemingway's rambling novel (about a writer seeking meaning and purpose) is brought to the screen with a powerhouse lineup of stars. The result, however, is a disappointment. (Dir: Henry King, 117 mins.)†

Snow White and the Seven Dwarfs (1937)**** Disney's first full-length animated movie is one of the most enchanting films in movie history. Memorable score includes "Someday My Prince Will Come" and "Whistle While You Work." (Just to settle any arguments, the names of the dwarfs are Doc, Happy, Sleepy, Sneezy, Grumpy, Bashful, and Dopey.) (Dir: David Hand, 80 mins.)

Snow White and the Three Stooges (1961)**½ Carol Heiss, Three Stooges, Patricia Medina. The Snow White fairy tale, with the heroine on ice skates and the team of Moe, Curly Joe, and Larry substituting for the Seven Dwarfs. (Dir: Walter Lang, 107 mins.)†

Snub Pollard . . . A Short But Funny Man (1919-23)*** Three of the mustached comedian's best short comedies: *It's a Gift, Looking for Trouble*, and *Mitt the Prince*. Very funny slapstick. (60 mins.)†

Soak the Rich (1936)**½ Walter Connolly, Mary Taylor, John Howard, Lionel Stander. A wealthy businessman's daughter returns from school abroad full of radical ideas, and becomes involved with leftist campus politics. Produced, written, and directed by Ben Hecht and Charles MacArthur, it got its makers in big trouble during the McCarthy witch-hunts. (86 mins.)

S.O.B. (1981)*** Julie Andrews, William Holden, Richard Mulligan, Robert Vaughn, Robert Webber, Robert Preston, Rosanna Arquette, Larry Hagman. An acerbic, often hilarious, largely autobiographical comedy about the Hollywood scene. The plot centers around a filmmaker with a bomb on his hands and the lengths he will go to in order to salvage the film. (Dir: Blake Edwards, 121 mins.)†

So Big (1932)** Barbara Stanwyck, George Brent, Dickie Moore, Bette Davis, Guy Kibbee, Alan Hale. Stanwyck stars as the woman who sacrifices and scrimps to raise her son as an artist, only to see him opt for the rewards of Wall Street instead. Good performances, too much plot. (Dir: William A. Wellman, 90 mins.)

So Big (1953)*** Jane Wyman, Sterling Hayden. Edna Ferber's sentimental novel, complete with every tearful scene and every sacrifice on the part of Miss Wyman's character. A good family picture. Remake of '32 film. (Dir: Robert Wise, 101 mins.)

So Dark the Night (1946)***½ Steven Geray, Micheline Cheirel, Eugene Borden, Theodore Gottlieb. One of the best B films ever made. Geray plays a French detective on leave from his Parisian post, solving a murder in the provincial countryside. (Dir: Joseph Lewis, 71 mins.)

So Dear to My Heart (1948)**½ Burl Ives, Beulah Bondi, Bobby Driscoll. Disney nostalgia, laid on heavily, about life on a country farm in 1903. The animated sequences elevate this sentimental film. (Dir: Harold Schuster, 84 mins.)†

Sodom and Gomorrah (U.S.-France-Italy, 1961)**½ Stewart Granger, Pier Angeli, Stanley Baker, Anouk Aimee, Rossana Podesta. The story of Lot, who leads his people to Sodom, where a cruel queen reigns over a city of sin. Passable biblical spectacle. (Dir: Robert Aldrich, 154 mins.)†

So Ends Our Night (1941)***½ Fredric March, Margaret Sullavan, Glenn Ford, Frances Dee, Erich von Stroheim. Gripping drama of refugees from the Nazis traveling from country to country without passport. Excellent performances. (Dir: John Cromwell, 117 mins.)

So Evil My Love (1948)**½ Ray Milland, Ann Todd, Geraldine Fitzgerald. Well done, but strangely uninteresting drama of love, murder and blackmail in Victorian England. (Dir: Lewis Allen, 109 mins.)

Sofia (1948)** Gene Raymond, Sigrid Gurie, Patricia Morison, Mischa Auer. The title refers not to a lady but to a city; nuclear scientists desperately attempt to escape an onslaught by ruthless Russians in Turkey. OK cold-war thriller. (Dir: John Reinhardt, 82 mins.)

So Fine (1981)** Ryan O'Neal, Jack Warden, Mariangela Melato, David Rounds, Richard Kiel. Threadbare comedy about the antics of America's designer jean industry is filled with holes. Jack Warden really shines as the gruff and lovable desperate dad to Ryan O'Neal's son. (Dir: Andrew Bergman, 89 mins.)†

Soft Beds, Hard Battles—See: **Undercovers Hero**

Soft Boiled (1923)*** Tom Mix, Joseph Girard, Billie Dove, L. C. Shumway. Engaging western comedy, with young cowpoke Mix betting his wealthy uncle he can hold his temper for thirty days. Time-honored premise enlivened by action sequences and entertaining hijinks with Mix and his horse Tony. (Dir: J. G. Blystone, 70 mins.)†

Soft Skin, The (France, 1964)*** Jean Dessailly, Françoise Dorleac. Franeois Truffaut drew a mixed response from the critics on this one. Dessailly por-

trays a Truffaut hero; part married man, part little boy, who enters into an adulterous liaison with an airline stewardess. (120 mins.)†

So Goes My Love (1946)**½ Myrna Loy, Don Ameche, Rhys Williams, Bobby Driscoll. Charming period comedy-drama of Boston socialite Loy married to eccentric inventor Ameche. Warmly acted and directed. (Dir: Frank Ryan, 88 mins.)

Soil—See: **Earth**

Solarbabies (1986) ½ Richard Jordan, Charles Durning, Jami Gertz, Jason Patric, Lukas Haas, Sarah Douglas. Another futuristic space adventure about roller skating orphans trying to moisten their parched universe. This one rips off everything from *Mad Max* to *Oliver* to *Dune* to *Rollerball* to *The Warriors* and still comes up dry. (Dir: Alan Johnson, 94 mins.)†

Solaris (U.S.S.R., 1972)*** Natalya Bondarchuk, Yuri Jarvet. As science fiction, this film hovers somewhere between the satisfying and the pretentious. In outer space, a scientific team encounters flesh and blood counterparts from their past world. (Dir: Andrei Tarkovsky, 165 mins.)

Soldier, The (1982)½ Ken Wahl, Alberta Watson, William Prince, Klaus Kinski. Disgustingly violent tale of a CIA agent who's fighting to smash a plot to destroy half the world's oil supply. (Dir: James Glickenhaus, 88 mins.)†

Soldier Blue (1970)*** Candice Bergen, Peter Strauss, Donald Pleasence. Offbeat, violent, ultimately rewarding "western" about the U.S. Army's unhuman treatment of American Indians, based on the real Sand Creek Massacre of Cheyenne warriors and their families, including children. (Dir: Ralph Nelson, 112 mins.)†

Soldier Girls (1982)**** Nicholas Broomfield and Joan Churchill's award-winning documentary about the *rite de passage* of women, in general, and three female soldiers in particular, in this man's army. It takes us through basic training in Fort Gordon, Ga. The film is less about women in the Army than the adaptability of the Army mentality to either sex. (87 mins.)

Soldier In Skirts—See: **Triple Echo**

Soldier in the Rain (1963)*** Steve McQueen, Jackie Gleason, Tuesday Weld, Tony Bill, Tom Poston. Uneven comedy-drama about the bond of friendship between a worldly-wise master sergeant and his naïve worshipper. Always seems on the verge of something great without actually accomplishing it. However, there's a good share of laughs, some heart-tugs, fine performance by Gleason. (Dir: Ralph Nelson, 88 mins.)†

Soldier of Fortune (1955)**½ Clark Gable, Susan Hayward, Gene Barry. Just another routine adventure story set in Hong Kong. Handsome production and major stars can't disguise the commonplace plot. (Dir: Edward Dmytryk, 96 mins.)

Soldier of Orange (The Netherlands, 1978)***½ Rutger Hauer, Jeroen Krabbé. An intelligent, sensitive war-adventure movie. Hauer plays a charismatic, disengaged, callow student who grows into heroism during the Nazi occupation of the Netherlands. His classmates reach destinies as diverse as their well-delineated characters. (Dir: Paul Verhoeven, 165 mins.)†

Soldier's Story, A (1984)***½ Howard E. Rollins, Jr., Adolph Caesar, Denzel Washington, Larry Riley, Art Evans. During WWII, in a redneck Louisiana town in 1944, the Negro manager of a crackerjack black Army baseball team was found murdered. Whodunit? A black Army captain, a lawyer, is sent from Washington to find out. Superb and well acted, the film transcends stereotypes. (Dir: Norman Jewison, 102 mins.)†

Soldiers Three (1951)** Stewart Granger, David Niven, Robert Newton, Walter Pidgeon. With the boys in India, 1890—a trio of army privates get into one mess after another. Try for a *Gunga Din*-type of adventure misfires. (Dir: Tay Garnett, 87 mins.)

Soleil O (Mauritania, 1970)***½ Robert Liensol, Theo Legitimus, Bernard Fresson, Yane Barry, Ambroise M'Bla. Multilayered story of black Africans who are baptized by a French priest, given new names and encouraged to go to France to work in degrading, low-paying jobs. Highly original. (Dir: Med Hondo, 105 mins.)

Sole Survivor (MTV 1970)**½ Vince Edwards, Richard Basehart, William Shatner. A glossy production, excellent location photography and a good cast enhance this feature about a WWII bomber discovered in the Libyan desert 17 years after it has crashed, with the ghosts of the crew hovering over it. (Dir: Paul Stanley, 100 mins.)

Solid Gold Cadillac, The (1956)*** Judy Holliday, Paul Douglas, Fred Clark. George S. Kaufman-Howard Teichmann satirical play on big business. Holliday, a small stockholder, creates havoc at a board meeting over corrupt corporate practices, and she garners laughs in this streamlined star vehicle. Narrated by George Burns. (Dir: Richard Quine, 99 mins.)†

Solitary Man, The (MTV 1979)**½ Earl Holliman, Carrie Snodgress. Contemporary family drama loses steam before the end. Holliman is better than the script as the man whose wife of 18 years announces that she wants a divorce. (Dir: John Llewellyn Moxey, 104 mins.)

Sol Madrid (1968)** Paul Lukas, Stella Stevens, Telly Savalas, Ricardo Montalbán. Narcotics agent (David McCallum) battles the Mafia in Mexico. (Dir: Brian G. Hutton, 90 mins.)

Solomon and Sheba (1959)** Yul Brynner, Gina Lollobrigida, George Sanders, Marisa Pavan. Yul Brynner plays the wise Solomon. English-fracturing Lollobrigida fares better as the upstart queen who throws Sol's court into an uproar with her pagan ways. Hog-tied by a mundane script, King Vidor compensates with an impressive visual style. (139 mins.)†

So Long at the Fair (Great Britain, 1950)*** Jean Simmons, Dirk Bogarde, Honor Blackman. In Paris with her brother for the Exposition, a young girl is thrown into a panic when he disappears, and everyone who has seen him denies his existence. Interesting melodrama keeps the attention. (Dirs: Terence Fisher, Anthony Darnborough, 86 mins.)

Sombrero (1953)** Ricardo Montalban, Pier Angeli, Vittorio Gassman, Yvonne De Carlo, Cyd Charisse. Story of three bachelors in a small Mexican village and their adventures in love. Wandering plot. (Dir: Norman Foster, 103 mins.)

Some Blondes Are Dangerous (1937)*½ Noah Beery, Jr., William Gargan, Dorothea Kent, Nan Grey. Inferior remake of *Iron Man*, with Beery as the boxer who abandons his manager and girlfriend when he becomes champion, only to regret it later. (Dir: Milton Carruth, 65 mins.)

Somebody Has to Shoot the Picture (MCTV 1990)*** Roy Scheider, Bonnie Bedelia, Robert Carradine, Andre Braugher, Arliss Howard. An original drama that captures your attention right from the start and doesn't let go until the devastating finale. Scheider is a burned-out, prize-winning photographer who is given a bizarre assignment to photograph the electrocution of a prisoner, and accidentally uncovers new evidence regarding his subject. (Dir: Frank Pierson, 105 mins.)†

Somebody Killed Her Husband (1978)* Farrah Fawcett, Jeff Bridges, Tammy Grimes, John Wood, John Glover. A failed mystery-romance in which the greatest mystery is how Farrah became a star. (Dir: Lamont Johnson, 96 mins.)

Somebody Loves Me (1952)** Betty Hutton, Ralph Meeker. Biography of song spinners Blossom Seeley and Benny Fields, their ups and downs in show biz. Thoroughly routine musical primarily for the nostalgically minded. (Dir: Irving Brecher, 97 mins.)

Somebody Up There Likes Me (1956)***½

Paul Newman, Pier Angeli, Everett Sloane, Sal Mineo. The true story of Rocky Graziano's rise from a small time hood to the middle-weight champ of the world. Newman is superb as the original Rocky, and he gets top support from Angeli as his wife, Buloff as a candy store philosopher, Heckart as his mother and Sloane as a fight promoter. (Dir: Robert Wise, 113 mins.)†

Some Came Running (1958)**½ Frank Sinatra, Shirley MacLaine, Dean Martin, Martha Hyer, Arthur Kennedy. An all-star cast brings James Jones's novel about life in a small midwestern town after WWII to the screen. Most of the plot falls into the soap opera groove but the performances, especially MacLaine as a good-time gal, should keep your interest. (Dir: Vincente Minnelli, 127 mins.)†

Some Girls (1988)*** Patrick Dempsey, Jennifer Connelly, Lila Kedrova. Unusual black comedy set in Quebec, where American student Dempsey goes to visit his girlfriend and becomes the object of sexual games with her female relatives. Not a complete success, but original and inventive. (Dir: Michael Hoffman, 94 mins.)†

Some Girls Do (Great Britain, 1969)**½ Richard Johnson, Daliah Lavi, Beba Loncar, Robert Morley. Bulldog Drummond steps once more into the breach, when an archvillain tries putting the kibosh on Britain's plans for a supersonic airplane. (Dir: Ralph Thomas, 93 mins.)

Some Kind of a Nut (1969)* Dick Van Dyke, Angie Dickinson, Zohra Lampert. Hackneyed, unfunny, tale about Manhattan bank teller Van Dyke who upsets everyone around him when he grows a beard. (Dir: Garson Kanin, 89 mins.)

Some Kind of Hero (1982)*½ Richard Pryor, Margot Kidder, Ray Sharkey, Ronny Cox. Eddie Keller (Pryor) is a Vietnam POW who returns to the States to find his money gone, his wife in love with another man, and his mother a stroke victim. Some kind of a major disappointment! (Dir: Michael Pressman, 98 mins.)†

Some Kind of Miracle (MTV 1979)*** Andrea Marcovicci, David Dukes. Wrenching wheelchair drama about a Californian who injures his spine in a body-surfing accident. Dukes is convincing as the quadraplegic making a rare recovery, but Marcovicci steals the show as his distraught fiancée. (Dir: Jerrold Freeman, 104 mins.)

Some Kind of Wonderful (1987)** Eric Stoltz, Mary Stuart Masterson, Lea Thompson, Craig Sheffer, John Ashton, Elias Koteas. John Hughes's script for this comic teen romance is some kinda familiar; this time he pulls a gender switch on his *Pretty in Pink* plot and has

an uncomfortable adolescent *male* ignoring his misfit tomboy friend in favor of his "dream date," an attractive drip who hangs out with the rich kids. By the film's end, everything turns out exactly as you thought it would. (Dir: Howard Deutch, 95 mins.)†

Some Like It Cool (Germany-Italy-France, 1977)* Tony Curtis, Britt Ekland, Sylvia Koscina, Hugh Griffith, Marisa Berenson, Marisa Mell. When Casanova can no longer get it up, Tony subs for the great lover and keeps the libertine's reputation alive. Some of us like it funnier. AKA: **Casanova and Co.** (Dir: "Francois Legrand" [Franz Antel], 87 mins.)

Some Like It Hot (1939)** Bob Hope, Shirley Ross, Una Merkel, Gene Krupa, Richard Denning. Those who like their musical comedies lightweight might enjoy this comedy about a sideshow barker trying to raise funds to stay afloat, but it's pretty forgettable except for the title tune and the song "The Lady's in Love with You." AKA: **Rhythm Romance.** (Dir: George Archainbaud, 64 mins.)

Some Like It Hot (1959)**** Tony Curtis, Marilyn Monroe, Jack Lemmon, Joe E. Brown, George Raft, Joan Shawlee, Mike Mazurki, Pat O'Brien. Director Billy Wilder puts a flawless cast through improbable, riotous capers. Curtis and Lemmon play two musicians on the lam from Chicago mobsters after witnessing a gangland rubout. Monroe is wonderful as scrumptious Sugar Kane; Brown delivers the last line which is a classic topper. (122 mins.)†

Some of My Best Friends Are... (1971)**½ Carleton Carpenter, Sylvia Syms, Gil Gerard. This film, set in a Manhattan gay bar on Christmas Eve, is a little artificial, but worthy of a researching glance. (Dir: Mervyn Nelson, 109 mins.)

Someone Behind the Door (France, 1971)* Charles Bronson, Anthony Perkins, Jill Ireland. Unbalanced brain surgeon (Perkins) uses an amnesia victim (Bronson) to kill his wife's lover. (Dir: Nicholas Gessner, 97 mins.)†

Someone Is Watching Me (MTV 1978)** Lauren Hutton, David Birney, Adrienne Barbeau. Terror show isn't as scary as it should be. The weak spot is top fashion model Hutton, who plays a TV news director being bugged by phone calls, notes, and presents from a nut who keeps track of her every move. (Writer-Dir: John Carpenter, 104 mins.)

Someone I Touched (MTV 1975)**½ Cloris Leachman, James Olson, Glynnis O'Connor, Kenneth Mars. Leachman stars as an over-30 wife who finally becomes pregnant, only to discover that both her husband and a pretty young girl he has had a brief fling with have venereal disease. (Dir: Sam O'Steen, 72 mins.)†

Someone's Killing the World's Greatest Models—See: *She's Dressed To Kill*

Someone to Love (1987)*** Henry Jaglom, Orson Welles, Andrea Marcovicci, Sally Kellerman, Oja Kodar, Michael Emil, Ronee Blakley, Dave Frishberg, Monte Hellman, Kathryn Harrold, Jeremy Kagan, Stephen Bishop, Miles Kreuger. Director Jaglom's follow-up to *Always*, another semidocumentary about obsessive romanticism in which he films a group of friends answering the question, "Why are you alone?" Jaglom makes a genial host, and the results are generally interesting and amusing. Jaglom's friend Orson Welles makes an edifyingly sage appearance at the end. (109 mins.)†

Someone to Remember (1943)*** Mabel Paige, John Craven. Old woman whose son has disappeared years ago becomes a foster mother to some college boys. Touching, well-acted drama, recommended. (Dir: John H. Auer, 80 mins.)

Someone to Watch Over Me (1987)**½ Tom Berenger Mimi Rogers, Lorraine Bracco, Jerry Orbach, John Rubinstein. Visually dazzling but sometimes troubled tale of a cop who falls in love with a rich witness (Rogers) he's assigned to guard. The sequences that work best are the ones that place Berenger in his working-class Queens household; every time he encounters Rogers, all actions are viewed through a smoky haze of "wealth." Fortunately, Berenger's strong lead performance carries the film through the rough spots where Scott's brilliant visual talent flares and the plot sags. (Dir: Ridley Scott, 106 mins.)

Something About Amelia (MTV 1984)*** Ted Danson, Glenn Close, Roxana Zal, Jane Kaczmarek. Startling, provocative drama about incest. Danson plays a middle-class husband-father who has sexual relations with his 13-year-old daughter. (Dir: Randa Haines, 104 mins.)

Something About Love (Canada, 1988)*** Stefan Wodoslawsky, Jan Rubes, Jennifer Dale, Lenore Zann. After years in L.A., a man returns to his family home in a small Canada town when his gruff father begins to show signs of incompetence. The story is nothing special, but the acting makes it worthwile. (Dir: Tom Berry, 93 mins.)

Something Big (1971)* Dean Martin, Brian Keith, Carol White, Honor Blackman. Cartoon characters romp around a western town circa 1870 as Martin plays a naughty criminal. (Dir: Andrew V. McLaglen, 108 mins.)

Something Evil (MTV 1972)*** Sandy Dennis, Darren McGavin, Ralph Bellamy. Steven Spielberg turns to the devil here, and has a ball with scary visual effects.

The devil occupies a Pennsylvania farmhouse, eager to assert his powers on new tenants. (73 mins.)

Something for a Lonely Man (MTV 1968)*** Dan Blocker, Susan Clark, Warren Oates. A very pleasant film. Blocker convinces some settlers to locate in a spot he thinks the railroad will go through. When the train route turns out to be some 20 miles away, he becomes a subject of ridicule. (Dir: Don Taylor, 99 mins.)

Something for Everyone (1970)*** Angela Lansbury, Michael York, Anthony Corlan. Bizarre black comedy with a dash of sophistication and wit. It's Noël Coward cross-pollinated with Edgar Allan Poe, and most of the time it works. Michael York is a sexy opportunist in lederhosen who descends upon the castle of the Countess Von Ornstein, which has seen better days, and proceeds to infiltrate everyone's bedroom. (Dir: Harold Prince, 110 mins.)†

Something for Joey (MTV 1977)*** Geraldine Page, Marc Singer, Jeff Lynas. Heartwarming true-life story about Heisman Trophy winner John Cappelletti and his special relationship with his young brother, Joey, a victim of leukemia. Singer as the college football star Cappelletti gives a sensitive performance, and he's matched by Lynas as Joey. (Dir: Lou Antonio, 108 mins.)

Something for the Birds (1952)**½ Victor Mature, Patricia Neal, Edmund Gwenn. Genial comedy about Washington society. Edmund Gwenn plays an aging engraver in a Washington printing plant who crashes many Washington social functions. The love story revolves around a lobbyist (Victor Mature) and a representative of an ornithology society (Patricia Neal). (Dir: Robert Wise, 81 mins.)

Something for the Boys (1944)**½ Vivian Blaine, Perry Como, Phil Silvers, Carmen Miranda. Tuneful, loud musical loaded with feminine pulchritude and set in a home for war wives. Phil is at his best in this one. (Dir: Lewis Seiler, 85 mins.)

Something in Common (MTV 1986)*** Ellen Burstyn, Tuesday Weld, Patrick Cassidy, Eli Wallach, Don Murray. A sparkling comedy. Burstyn, a widowed career woman, flies into a tizzy when her son falls for a fortyish beauty who's his mom's contemporary. Our sympathies for the characters are never sacrificed on the altar of facile one-liners. (Dir: Glenn Jordan, 104 mins.)†

Something in the Wind (1947)**½ Deanna Durbin, Donald O'Connor, John Dall. Girl disc jockey is mistaken for the amour of a late multimillionaire. Slight comedy has Durbin's fine singing to help it. (Dir: Irving Pichel, 89 mins.)

Something Is Out There (MTV 1988)*½

978

Joe Cortese, Maryam D'Abo, Robert Webber, George Dzundza, Kim Delaney. Nonsensical sci-fi that takes a lead from *The Hidden*, with its plot concerning a hard-bitten cop who isn't getting anywhere investigating a series of murders until he receives aid from a helpful spacewoman who's familiar with the killer, as it comes from her own planet. Basis for the series. (Dir: Richard Colla, 192 mins.)

Something of Value (1957)*** Rock Hudson, Dana Wynter, Sydney Poitier, Wendy Hiller. Compelling fictional story of the Mau Mau uprising. The major conflict of the story centers around Hudson and Poitier, childhood friends who find themselves on opposite sides of the law. Poitier gives an intense performance as the leader of a Mau Mau band, and Hudson is shown to good advantage, too. (Dir: Richard Brooks, 113 mins.)†

Something Short of Paradise (1979)½ Susan Sarandon, David Steinberg, Jean-Pierre Aumont. A lame romantic comedy in which Steinberg acts like Woody Allen (which certainly beats his acting like David Steinberg). Something close to purgatory. (Dir: David Helpern, Jr., 91 mins.)†

Something So Right (MTV 1982)**½ Patty Duke Astin, James Farentino, Ricky Schroder. A warm, sentimental yarn about a troubled kid, his worried, divorced mother, and a hapless Big Brother whose heart is as good as gold. (Dir: Lou Antonio, 104 mins.)

Something Special (1986)** Pamela Segall, Eric Gurry, Mary Tanner, Patty Duke, John Glover. Adolescent confusion at its worst: a young girl is transformed into a boy as a result of a magic spell. A weird, unfocused teen film originally released under the title, *Willy/Milly*. (Dir: Paul Schneider, 90 mins.)†

Something to Live For (1952)*** Ray Milland, Joan Fontaine, Teresa Wright. Deft direction by George Stevens gives added luster to this dramatic story of an alcoholic actress saved by an A.A. member who falls in love with her although he's married. (89 mins.)

Something to Shout About (1943)** Don Ameche, Janet Blair, William Gaxton. Trite backstage plot receives a little support from some Cole Porter music. Best tune: "You'd Be So Nice to Come Home To." (Dir: Gregory Ratoff, 93 mins.)

Something to Sing About (1937)**½ James Cagney, Evelyn Daw, William Frawley, Mona Barrie. One in a slew of backstage-in-Hollywood musicals, this frothy little comedy takes satiric potshots at the film industry. Cagney stars as a New York bandleader who goes to Hollywood, becomes a star, but refuses to get ground up in the star-making machinery of Hollywood. AKA: **The Battling Hoofer.** (Dir: Victor Schertzinger, 93 mins.)†

Something Wicked This Way Comes (1983)**½ Jason Robards, Jonathan Pryce, Pam Grier, Shawn Carson, Vidal Peterson. Leisurely, literal adaptation of Ray Bradbury's fantasy classic. Bradbury himself wrote the script, which tells of a sinister carnival's visit to a small, nondescript American town. (Dir: Jack Clayton, 94 mins.)†

Something Wild (1961)**½ Carroll Baker, Ralph Meeker, Mildred Dunnock, Jean Stapleton. A strange film that weaves a hypnotic spell at the start but soon sinks into predictable melodrama. Baker plays an emotionally disturbed young girl who is saved from doing away with herself by a man who turns the incident to his advantage. (Dir: Jack Garfein, 112 mins.)

Something Wild (1986)*** Jeff Daniels, Melanie Griffith, Ray Liotta, Margaret Colin. Offbeat farce about a repressed businessman who tastes freedom after he's picked up by a mysterious stranger named Lulu. On their freewheeling road trip from N.Y. to Virginia and back, hidden secrets from both their pasts pop up to threaten the fun. Their journey runs the gamut from comedy to suspense with some fine details of East Coast Americana and plenty of hip music and cameos thrown in for good measure. (Dir: Jonathan Demme, 116 mins.)†

Sometimes a Great Notion—See: **Never Give an Inch**

Somewhere I'll Find You (1942)*** Clark Gable, Lana Turner. Clark and Lana burn up the screen in a mediocre adventure story which finds them as correspondents running all over the war-torn world. (Dir: Wesley Ruggles, 108 mins.)

Somewhere in the Night (1946)*** John Hodiak, Lloyd Nolan, Richard Conte, Josephine Hutchinson, Nancy Guild. Vintage *film noir* about an amnesia victim who searches for clues to his past. A top-notch lineup of Hollywood criminal types lend strong support to this suspenseful effort. (Dir: Joseph L. Mankiewicz, 100 mins.)

Somewhere in Time (1980)** Christopher Reeve, Jane Seymour, Teresa Wright. Reeve's playwright becomes enamored of an antique portrait of an actress (Seymour) and wills himself back in time to win her love. Hollywood used to conjure up entertainment out of equally improbable plots, but they had the Star Power to pull it off. (Dir: Jeannot Szwarc, 103 mins.)†

Somewhere Tomorrow (1983)*** Sarah Jessica Parker, Tom Shea, Nancy Addison, Paul Bates, Rick Weber, James Congdon. Odd little gem about a fatherless teenage girl (Parker) who sees the ghost of a young man killed in a plane crash. Pleasing performances and an affectionate script enhance this touching story. (Dir: Robert Wiemer, 87 mins.)†

Son-Daughter, The (1932)*** Helen Hayes, Ramon Novarro, Lewis Stone, Warner Oland, Ralph Morgan, H. B. Warner. Neglected piece of romantic *chinoiserie* about star-crossed lovers whose happiness is shattered when the girl's family arranges a marriage for her. Cast is fine, especially Novarro. (Dir: Clarence Brown, 79 mins.)

Song and the Silence, The (1969)*** Harry Rubin, Annita Koutsouveli, Nana Austin. An unusual, surprisingly effective low-budget film about a group of Hasidic Jews in Poland in 1939, filmed by amateur actors in the Catskill Mountains of New York. An offbeat, often rewarding American entry. (Dir: Nathan Cohen, 80 mins.)

Song Is Born, A (1948)**½ Danny Kaye, Virginia Mayo, Steve Cochran, Benny Goodman, Tommy Dorsey. Remake of *Ball of Fire*, with music added for good measure. Not up to the original although Kaye tries very hard to rise above the material. (Dir: Howard Hawks, 113 mins.)

Song of Bernadette, The (1943)*** Jennifer Jones, Charles Bickford, Gladys Cooper, Lee J. Cobb, Vincent Price, Anne Revere, William Eythe. Adapted from Franz Werfel's book about Bernadette's visions of the Virgin Mary at Lourdes. Despite its colossal length, the film tends to remain tasteful and reasonably effective. Jones won an Oscar. (Dir: Henry King, 156 mins.)†

Song of Freedom (Great Britain, 1937)*** Paul Robeson, Elizabeth Welch, George Mozart, Esme Percy. Good vehicle for Robeson as a singer who finds he is an African prince, returning to his family's homeland to bring the benefits of civilization to his people. The story is secondary to Robeson's singing, which is magnificent. (Dir: J. Elder Wills, 66 mins.)

Song of India (1949)**½ Sabu, Gail Russell, Turhan Bey, Anthony Caruso. Enjoyable jungle hokum, with nature-boy Sabu braving a rajah's wrath by freeing his menagerie of tigers and monkeys. (Dir: Albert S. Rogell, 77 mins.)

Song of Love (1947)** Katharine Hepburn, Paul Henreid, Robert Walker, Henry Daniell, Leo G. Carroll. Turgid musical biopic focusing on the romance between Robert and Clara Schumann and their relationship with the young Johannes Brahms. (Dir: Clarence Brown, 119 mins.)

Song of New Life—See: **Earth**

Song of Norway (1970)* Florence Henderson, Toralv Maurstad, Christina Schollin, Edward G. Robinson, Robert Morley. Poorly made musical biography of composer Edvard Grieg. (Dir: Andrew L. Stone, 142 mins.)†

Song of Russia (1943)**½ Robert Taylor, Susan Peters, John Hodiak. Believe it or not, Robert Taylor is a symphony conductor touring the U.S.S.R. where he meets and weds a Russian girl. This well-meaning, vapid tale was initiated by the U.S. Govt. as propaganda for our former allies in WWII. However, during the Red Witch Hunt of the Fifties, some of this film's participants were rewarded with blacklisting. (Dir: Gregory Ratoff, 107 mins.)

Song of Scheherazade (1947)** Yvonne De Carlo, Jean-Pierre Aumont, Brian Donlevy, Eve Arden. Farfétched story of Rimsky-Korsakoff and his love for a dance girl named Cara. (Dir: Walter Reisch, 106 mins.)

Song of Songs, The (1933)**½ Marlene Dietrich, Brian Aherne, Lionel Atwill. Ultra romantic melodrama fueled by Dietrich's magical presence. A woman loves an artist but is forced to marry his patron. (Dir: Rouben Mamoulian, 90 mins.)

Song of Surrender (1949)**½ Wanda Hendrix, Claude Rains, MacDonald Carey, Andrea King, Henry Hull. Strange historical melodrama about the wife of a museum keeper who falls in love with a young man who moves in next door. Slow-moving plot seems to want to say something, but it's hard to tell what. (Dir: Mitchell Leisen, 93 mins.)

Song of the Exile (Taiwan, 1990)*** Shwu-Fen Chang, Maggie Cheung, Chi-Hung Lee. Sensitive account of a young Chinese woman coming to terms with her stern Japanese mother. The cross-cultural dilemma, detailed through the use of flashbacks, may not be crystal clear to Western viewers, but the emotions depicted are plain, simple, and genuine. (Dir: Ann Hui, 100 mins.)

Song of the Islands (1942)*½ Victor Mature, Betty Grable. If you'd like to see Mature put his muscles into an assortment of sweaters and bathing suits or Grable in a grass skirt, watch this film. If you want entertainment, keep away. (Dir: Walter Lang, 75 mins.)†

Song of the Loon (1970)*** John Iverson, Morgan Royce, Lancer Ward, Jon Evans. Unusual drama set in 1870s California about a young gay man who visits an old mountaineer, thought to be a sage, for answers to questions about his homosexuality. A philosophical treatise on sexual identity, with out a hint of eroticism. (Dir: Andrew Herbert, 79 mins.)

Song of the Open Road (1944)**½ Jane Powell, Edgar Bergen, Bonita Granville, W. C. Fields. Juvenile movie star runs away and joins youngsters who are saving farm crops. Fairly pleasant musical. (Dir: S. Sylvan Simon, 93 mins.)

Song of the Thin Man (1947)*** William Powell, Myrna Loy. Nick and Nora move in jazz circles as they glibly track down a murderer in this one. Good dialogue and atmosphere. Last in the series. (Dir: Edward Buzzell, 86 mins.)†

Song Remains the Same, The (1976)*** Entertaining but *long* concert film starring heavy metal pioneers Led Zeppelin (Robert Plant, Jimmy Page, John Paul Jones, John Bonham) is so rooted in the '70s it becomes a period piece. Concert footage and backstage milieu are mixed with off-beat fantasy sequences. (Dirs: Peter Clifton, Joe Massot, 136 mins.)†

Song to Remember, A (1945)** Paul Muni, Cornel Wilde, Merle Oberon. Story of composer Chopin, and of his tragic love for George Sand. Good piano selections help this lackluster biographical drama. (Dir: Charles Vidor, 113 mins.)†

Song Without End (1960)**½ Dirk Bogarde, Genevieve Page, Capucine. Schmaltzy film biography of Franz Liszt. Decisively superior to *A Song to Remember*, and that's very, very faint praise. Director Charles Vidor died during production and was replaced by George Cukor. (141 mins.)

Songwriter (1984)**½ Willie Nelson, Kris Kristofferson, Lesley Ann Warren. Nelson, as a popular country singer, stars with Kristofferson as an appealing rebel. Both characters are seen as they live their separate lives, joined by their remembrance of their stint as a performing duo years before. Plenty of music. (Dir: Alan Rudolph, 94 mins.)†

Son of Ali Baba (1952)** Tony Curtis, Piper Laurie, Hugh O'Brian. Typical Arabian nights adventure with Curtis cast as the son of Ali Baba and Princess Azura. (Dir: Kurt Neumann, 75 mins.)

Son of a Sailor (1933)**½ Joe E. Brown, Thelma Todd, Jean Muir, Johnny Mack Brown, Samuel S. Hinds. Above-average vehicle for Brown as a sailor afraid of warfare who nevertheless rescues important plans from spies. Funny, spirited comedy, ably supported by Todd and Muir. (Dir: Lloyd Bacon, 70 mins.)

Son of Blob—See: **Beware the Blob**

Son of Captain Blood, The (U.S.-Italy-Spain, 1962)** Sean Flynn, Alessandra Panaro, Ann Todd. Errol Flynn's son, Sean, makes his screen debut, embroiled with his Pa's pirate friends in further sea adventures. (Dir: Tulio Demicheli, 88 mins.)†

Son of Dracula (1943)**½ Lon Chaney, Louise Albritton. A strange fellow known as Count Alucard (that's Dracula spelled backwards) comes to stay at an American manse. Unbelievable horror yarn, but fun anyway. (Dir: Robert Siodmak, 78 mins.)†

Son of Dr. Jekyll (1951)** Louis Hayward, Jody Lawrance. Hollywood never lets a commercial gimmick die—so here's still another in the rash of "son of" films. Not so "horrific" as its predecessor, nor as well done. (Dir: Seymour Friedman, 77 mins.)

Son of Flubber (1963)**½ Fred MacMurray, Nancy Olson, Tommy Kirk. MacMurray's absentminded professor innocently causes trouble again with his invention known as "flubber," an antigravity substance everyone wants. Much visual slapstick. (Dir: Robert Stevenson, 100 mins.)†

Son of Frankenstein (1939)*** Boris Karloff, Basil Rathbone, Bela Lugosi, Lionel Atwill. The new Baron Von Frankenstein learns that his father's monster is running loose, and tries to catch up with the fiend. Lavishly produced, plenty of spine-tingling thrills. (Dir: Rowland V. Lee, 99 mins.)†

Son of Fury (1942)*** Tyrone Power, George Sanders, Gene Tierney. No message in this 18th-century drama but an abundance of action and romance. Ty, who's wronged by Uncle George, leaves England, goes to a Pacific island, finds Gene and a bucket of pearls. He goes back for his revenge. (Dir: John Cromwell, 98 mins.)

Son of Godzilla (Japan, 1967)* Tadao Takashima, Akihiko Hirata. Paper-thin disjointed trash—Godzilla mashes all obstacles on behalf of baby Godzilla. (Dir: Jun Fukuda, 86 mins.)†

Son of India (1932)**½ Ramon Novarro, Madge Evans, Conrad Nagel, Marjorie Rambeau. Exotic romantic melodrama, elaborately produced, with Novarro excellent as a wealthy, educated Indian merchant whose romance with Evans is destroyed by racism. (Dir: Jacques Feyder, 75 mins.)

Son of Kong (1933)*** Robert Armstrong, Helen Mack. Adventurer returns to the island where the mighty King Kong used to dwell, finds another huge gorilla there. Fantastic adventure is good fun. (Dir: Ernest B. Schoedsack, 69 mins.)†

Son of Lassie (1945)** Peter Lawford, June Lockhart, Donald Crisp. Unlike its magnificent predecessor (*Lassie Come Home*) this is little more than a juvenile adventure which will, of course, also appeal to dog lovers. Collie and her master are shot down over Germany during the war and so on to the fadeout. (Dir: S. Sylvan Simon, 102 mins.)

Son of Monte Cristo (1940)*** Louis Hayward, George Sanders, Joan Bennett. The offspring of Dumas's stalwart hero is portrayed by Hayward, as he foils the dastardly plans of dictator Sanders and wins the hand of Bennett, whilst dueling all over the place. Entertaining swashbuckling melodrama. (Dir: Rowland V. Lee, 102 mins.)†

Son of Paleface (1952)*** Bob Hope, Jane Russell, Roy Rogers. Enjoyable western story with Hope playing a mild-mannered Easterner who shows up in the wild and woolly West to collect his inheritance, left by his father who was a famous Indian fighter (Dir: Frank Tashlin, 95 mins.)†

Son of Robin Hood, The (Great Britain, 1959)** David Hedison, June Laverick, David Farrar, Marius Goring. A costume adventure strictly for the kids. When a nasty duke stirs up trouble anew, the son of Robin Hood is sent for—only the son turns out to be a girl. (Dir: George Sherman, 77 mins.)

Son of Sinbad (1954)*½ Dale Robertson, Sally Forrest, Vincent Price. Sinbad is captured by a wicked caliph, must perform arduous tasks to win his freedom. Dull fantasy. (Dir: Ted Tetzlaff, 88 mins.)†

Son of the Gods (1930)**½ Richard Barthelmess, Constance Bennett, Dorothy Mathews, Barbara Leonard, Dickie Moore. Effective drama of social hardships wrought on a white woman and her Oriental boyfriend. In typical fashion of the era, he is revealed to be Caucasian after all, but the film does attempt a realistic portrayal of modern racism. (Dir: Frank Lloyd, 92 mins.)

Son of the Morning Star (MTV 1991)*** Gary Cole, Rosanna Arquette, Stanley Anderson, Terry O'Quinn, David Strathairn, Dean Stockwell. Sprawling epic about George Armstrong Custer's military rise and fall, told against a background of the American Indians' battle against the white man. Cole employs the right combination of arrogance and military pride in the role of Custer. A bit talky, but the actual battle sequences are exciting. (Dir: Mike Robe, 192 mins.)

Son of the Sheik (1926)***½ Rudolph Valentino, Vilma Banky. A rousing sequel to *The Sheik*, full of sandy fights, romance, chases, and escapes. Valentino, in his last film, plays the dual role of father and son. (Dir: George Fitzmaurice, 72 mins.)†

Son Rise: A Miracle of Love (MTV 1979)**½ James Farentino, Kathryn Harrold. Based on the real-life experience of a couple with an autistic son. (Dir: Glenn Jordan, 104 mins.)

Sons and Lovers (U.S.-Great Britain, 1960)**** Trevor Howard, Dean Stockwell, Mary Ure, Wendy Hiller. Absorbing, successful dramatization of D. H. Lawrence's autobiographical novel. Howard is splendid as the gruff coal-mining father of the sensitive, young, would-be artist (Stockwell). Hiller, as the dominant mother, turns in a beautifully controlled performance, and Stockwell keeps up with this high-powered cast. Extremely well directed by Jack Cardiff. (103 mins.)

Sons of Katie Elder, The (1965)**½ John Wayne, Dean Martin, Martha Hyer, Earl Holliman, Michael Anderson Jr. Standard western yarn with entertaining moments. The sons of the title all show up at their ma's funeral determined to make the name of Elder respectable once again. Some of the town bullies have other plans and this sets the stage for brawls-a-plenty. (Dir: Henry Hathaway, 122 mins.)†

Sons of the Desert (1933)***½ Stan Laurel, Oliver Hardy, Charley Chase, Mae Busch. The funniest L & H feature. The title refers to a fraternal order that provides the boys their only escape from noisy, henpecked married life. To go to the national convention, they concoct an incredible tale about a rare tropical malady Stan has, and hilarious complications ensue. (Dir: William A. Seiter, 68 mins.)†

Sons o' Guns (1936)** Joe E. Brown, Joan Blondell, Beverly Roberts, Eric Blore. Undeveloped script hampers the comedy in this light Brown vehicle. A song-and-dance man unwittingly sent to wartime France with a regiment of soldiers becomes a hero anyway, with Blondell's help. (Dir: Lloyd Bacon, 82 mins.)

Sooky (1931)** Jackie Cooper, Robert Coogan. Amiable but inconsequential Cooper repeats his *Skippy* role with these future adventures of the impish character, who began life as a comic strip. (Dir: Norman Taurog, 85 mins.)

Sooner or Later (MTV 1979)**½ Barbara Feldon, Judd Hirsch, Denise Miller, Rex Smith, Lynn Redgrave. A young girl enters her teens and yearns to be just a little older so that she can share a romance with a boy who's 17. (Dir: Bruce Hart, 104 mins.)†

Sophia Loren: Her Own Story (MTV 1980)** Sophia Loren, John Gavin, Rip Torn, Armand Assante, Theresa Saldana, Edmund Purdom. Following Sophia's rise to riches from her poverty-stricken girlhood to her movie stardom. Maybe someone else should have enacted her story. (Dir: Mel Stuart, 150 mins.)†

Sophie's Choice (1982)*** Meryl Streep, Kevin Kline, Peter MacNicol, Rita Karin. In the role of Polish concentration camp survivor Sophie Zawistowska, the enigmatic, haunting woman in William Styron's novel, Streep delivers an Oscar-winning performance. Kline is the right combination of charm, intellect and madness as Sophie's violent lover. Fine performances make this overly studied, fussy film worth seeing. (Dir: Alan J. Pakula, 151 mins.)†

Sophie's Place—See: **Crooks and Coronets**

Sophisticated Gents, The (MTV 1981)***½ Bernie Casey, Rosie Grier, Robert Hooks, Thalmus Rasulala, Melvin Van Peebles, Raymond St. Jacques. This dazzling, multifaceted drama deals with what transpires during the reunion of a black athletic club. More bite and insight than the similarly-themed *That Championship Season*. (Dir: Harry Falk, 200 mins.)

So Proudly We Hail (1943)**½ Claudette Colbert, Paulette Goddard, Veronica Lake, Sonny Tufts. Picture dedicated to our brave Army nurses on Bataan has some effective scenes, but is generally routine drama. (Dir: Mark Sandrich, 126 mins.)†

So Proudly We Hail (MTV 1990)** David Soul, Edward Herrmann, Chad Lowe, Raphael Sbarge, Gloria Carlin, Peter Dobson, Harley Jane Kozak. Professor Herrmann's theories on cultural differences are exploited by white supremacist Soul. Not terribly intriguing, despite the interesting subject. (Dir: Lionel Chetwynd, 96 mins.)

Sorcerer (1977)**½ Roy Scheider, Francisco Rabal. This remake of the French classic, *Wages of Fear* makes interesting viewing, mainly because the basic story of four desperate men who drive a truck filled with nitroglycerine across a South American jungle is so spellbinding. (Dir: William Friedkin, 122 mins.)

Sorcerers, The (Great Britain 1967)*** Boris Karloff, Catherine Lacey, Ian Ogilvy, Elizabeth Ercy, Susan George. First-rate idea about an infirm old couple who invent a machine that lets them impose their will on the young and healthy. Lots of vicarious thrills here. (Dir: Michael Reeves, 87 mins.)

Sorceress (France, 1988)**½ Tcheky Karyo, Christine Boisson, Jean Carmet. Meticulous and very atmospheric account of piety and heresy in thirteenth-century France. Karyo plays Etienne de Bourbon, a monk who condemns a mysterious "woman of the woods" as a heretic, and later regrets his decision. (Dir: Suzanne Schiffman, 90 mins.)

Sorceress, The (France, 1956)*** Marina Vlady, Maurice Ronet. The strange offbeat story of a girl who is believed to be a witch and her struggle to find happiness through love. (Dir: André Michel, 97 mins.)

So Red the Rose (1935)** Margaret Sullavan, Robert Cummings, Randolph Scott, Dickie Moore. Based on the Stark Young novel, this is a well-intentioned but slow-moving look at the Southern side of the Civil War. Only if you're in the mood for history-in-hoopskirts; otherwise wait for *GWTW*. (Dir: King Vidor, 82 mins.)

Sorekara (Japan, 1986)*** Yusaku Matsuda, Miwako Fujitani, Chisu Ryu, Kaoru Kobayashi. In turn-of-the-century Japan, as the nation enters a period of modernization, a wealthy young man with nothing but time on his hands develops an obsessive (but unfulfilled) love for his best friend's wife. Enchanting drama rich with breathtaking visual lyricism. (Dir: Yoshimitsu Morita, 130 mins.)

Sorority Babes in the Slimeball Bowl-o-rama (1988)*½ Linnea Quigley, Andras Jones, Robin Rochelle. Two sorority pledges and three Peeping Toms are forced by their sadistic sorority sisters to steal a trophy from the local bowling alley. On the way, this film suffers from a plot that oscillates from humor to horror, only doing well with the latter. (Dir: David Decoteau, 78 mins.)†

Sorority Girl (1958)*½ Susan Cabot, Dick Miller. Young hussy makes sorority life hell for the innocent, and doesn't do much for the viewing audience either. (Dir: Roger Corman, 60 mins.)

Sorority House Massacre (1986)*½ Angela O'Neill, Wendy Martel, John C. Russell. A psycho killer escapes from a mental hospital to finish the job he started fifteen years ago when he took a pickax to his family. Nothing new here. (Dir: Carol Frank, 74 mins.)†

Sorrow and the Pity, The (Le Chagrin et la Pitié) (France-Switzerland-West Germany, 1970)**** Pierre Mendès-France, Louis Grave, Albert Speer, Anthony Eden. Stunning documentary about anti-Semitism and the division of France between Nazi occupation and the collaborationist Vichy regime during WWII. Many respectable Frenchmen succumbed to the virus of racial and religious bigotry, as director Marcel Ophuls makes devastatingly clear in dozens of interviews. (260 mins.)†

Sorrowful Jones (1949)**½ Bob Hope, Lucille Ball. Bookie Hope gets involved with racketeers and fixed races in this Damon Runyon story. A fairly funny remake of *Little Miss Marker*. (Dir: Sidney Lanfield, 88 mins.)†

Sorry Wrong Number (1948)*** Barbara Stanwyck, Burt Lancaster, Wendell Corey. Overheated, gimmicky radio play made into an overheated, gimmicky film. Stanwyck invests her harridan in distress with human dimension; Lancaster plays her murderous husband. Effective melodrama. (Dir: Anatole Litvak, 89 mins.)†

Sorry, Wrong Number (MTV 1989)** Loni Anderson, Carl Weintraub, Hal Holbrook, Patrick Macnee. Anderson is miscast and inappropriately too fetching in a filmy negligee as the neurotic, bedridden wife who overhears about a plot to kill her on her phone. (Dir: Tony Wharmby, 91 mins.)†

S.O.S. Pacific (Great Britain, 1959)**½ Eddie Constantine, Pier Angeli, Richard Attenborough. Plane crash strands passengers on Pacific isle, and the usual personal tensions result, but with a twist—an atomic bomb is set to go off on a nearby island. Unadulterated melodrama, but still interesting. (Dir: Guy Green, 92 mins.)

S.O.S. Titanic (MTV 1979)*** David Janssen, Cloris Leachman, Susan St. James. The sinking of the luxury liner by an iceberg during its maiden voyage in 1912 is vividly recreated. Story begins with the rescue of the survivors and proceeds through flashbacks. (Dir: Billy Hale, 160 mins.)†

So This Is Love (1953)*** Kathryn Grayson, Merv Griffin. Contrived but entertaining biography of opera singer Grace Moore. (Dir: Gordon Douglas, 101 mins.)

So This Is New York (1948)*** Henry Morgan, Rudy Vallee, Hugh Herbert, Donna Drake. Small-town family comes to the big city to find a man for sister, manages to turn the city on its ear. Extremely clever, funny comedy based on the Ring Lardner novel *The Big Town*. (Dir: Richard A. Fleischer, 79 mins.)

So This Is Paris (1954)*** Tony Curtis, Gloria De Haven, Gene Nelson, Corinne Calvert. Entertaining musical comedy about three sailors on leave in Paris and their encounters with girls, orphans, Paris society, and the gendarmes. (Dir: Richard Quine, 96 mins.)

Sotto Sotto (Italy, 1984)** Enrico Montesano, Veronica Lario, Luisa de Santis. A drawn-out romantic rondelay about a chauvinist male who goes off the deep end when he discovers that his wife is fantasizing about another woman. Some charming bits here and there amid Lina Wertmuller's customary bombast, and a nice spearing of sexual stereotyping. (105 mins.)†

Soul-Fire (1925)***½ Richard Barthelmess, Bessie Love, Carlotta Monterey, Helen Ware. Engrossing drama about the struggles of young composer Barthelmess, told in three parts paralleling the movements of a concerto. Beautifully done. (Dir: John S. Robertson, 70 mins.)†

Soul Kiss, The—See: **Lady's Morals, A**

Soul Man (1986)*** C. Thomas Howell, Arye Gross, Rae Dawn Chong, James Earl Jones. Denied the funds he expected for his Harvard tuition, a crafty white kid turns himself black with supertanning pills so that he can obtain a scholarship slated for the underprivileged. This white-bread comedy is snappy without ever being surprising, but the engaging cast proves that comedy can be amusing even when it is only skin deep. (Dir: Steve Miner, 101 mins.)†

984

Souls at Sea (1937)*** Gary Cooper, George Raft, Frances Dee, Olympe Bradna, Henry Wilcoxon, Robert Cummings, Joseph Schildkraut, Harry Carey, George Zucco. Jam-packed with action, this sea saga is spurred on by Raft's and Cooper's virile screen presences. An exciting tale about an officer (Cooper) who saves his own skin during a shipwreck because he's on a secret antislavery mission, and then must suffer in silence throughout his court martial. (Dir: Henry Hathaway, 92 mins.)

Souls for Sale—See: **Confessions of an Opium Eater**

Soul Soldier (1970)*½ Rafer Johnson, Cesar Romero, Janee Michelle. Worthless western tale concerning loyal but dangerous black soldier guarding the Mexican border in post-Civil War America. (Dir: John Cardos, 84 mins.)

Soul to Soul (1971)*** This captivating musical documentary effectively captures the sights and sounds of a 1971 all-night concert by visiting black American soul and gospel artists, along with African musicians as part of the 14th annual Independence Celebration of Ghana, the first black African nation. Stirring performances by Wilson Pickett, Ike and Tina Turner, Roberta Flack, and Les McCann. (Dir: Denis Sanders, 96 mins.)†

Sound and the Fury, The (1959)**½ Yul Brynner, Joanne Woodward, Stuart Whitman, Ethel Waters. This uneven version of William Faulkner's novel of the decadent South is the story of a young girl trying to find a life of her own away from the tyrannical rule of her uncle. Some fine moments, too often confused, static. (Dir: Martin Ritt, 117 mins.)

Sounder (1972)**** Cicely Tyson, Paul Winfield, Kevin Hooks, Carmen Mathews. One of the most moving and compassionate films in many years. The plot concerns a family of sharecroppers in rural Louisiana during the Depression. The father is imprisoned for stealing a ham, and injured at the prison work farm before he returns home. Tyson is marvelous, a combination of warmth, strength, and tenderness as she carries her family through various crises. (Dir: Martin Ritt, 105 mins.)†

Sound of Anger, The (MTV 1968)** Burl Ives, James Farentino, Guy Stockwell, Dorothy Provine. Pilot for a TV series about two lawyer brothers and their partner. Courtroom case involves a pair of young lovers accused of doing away with the girl's wealthy papa. (Dir: Michael Ritchie, 100 mins.)

Sound Off (1952)**½ Mickey Rooney, Anne James. A mild and often amusing comedy with music about a recruit who falls in love with a WAC officer. (Dir: Richard Quine, 83 mins.)

Sound of Fury, The (1951)**½ Frank Lovejoy, Kathleen Ryan, Richard Carlson, Lloyd Bridges, Adele Jergens. Taut thriller with ordinary guy Lovejoy drawn into a life of petty crime with conscienceless partner Bridges. Compelling, intelligent drama, suspenseful and capably made. (Dir: Cy Enfield, 85 mins.)

Sound of Music, The (1965)***½ Julie Andrews, Christopher Plummer, Eleanor Parker, Richard Haydn, Peggy Wood, Charmian Carr, Nicholas Hammond, Angela Cartwright, Heather Menzies, Marni Nixon, Anna Lee. One of Rodgers and Hammerstein's weaker Broadway shows becomes one of the best film versions of their work, even though the critical elite did not appreciate it. But most of the rest of the world did, and made this one of the most popular films in the history of cinema. Julie plays Maria Von Trapp escaping from Austria and the Nazis with her young children into the haven of Switzerland. Oscars: Best Picture, Best Director, Best Scoring, Best Editing, Best Sound. (Dir: Robert Wise, 174 mins.)†

Sound of Trumpets, The (Italy, 1961)**** Loredana Detto, Sandro Panzeri, Tullio Kezich. Exhilarating drama about a quiet young man from a working-class family who gets his first job at a corporate office in Milan. Simple story is filled with insights into the world of office workers, the humanity of close friends, and the dreams of the poor. One of the most important films of the Italian New Wave. AKA: **Il Posto.** (Dir: Ermanno Olmi, 90 mins.)

Soup for One (1982)** Saul Rubinek, Marcia Strassman, Gerrit Graham, Andrea Martin. Sporadically amusing comedy about a bachelor's indefatigable pursuit of his dream girl. The poor man's *Annie Hall.* (Dir: Jonathan Kaufer, 84 mins.)†

Soursweet (Great Britain, 1988)*** Danny Dun, Sylvia Chang, Jodi Long, Soon-Teck Oh. The title aptly describes the tone of this drama about Chinese emigrants from Hong Kong trying to adapt to life in London. Director Mike Newell (*The Good Father*) counterpoints the struggles of a young family that has opened a restaurant in a blighted neighborhood with a group of drug-running Chinese gangsters. (110 mins.)

Southern Comfort (1981)*** Keith Carradine, Powers Boothe, Fred Ward, T. K. Carter. Atmospheric thriller in the *Deliverance* tradition is still another Vietnam allegory, with the U.S. (nine National Guardsmen) fighting the Vietcong (Louisiana Cajuns) in swampy bayou territory. (Dir: Walter Hill, 106 mins.)†

Southerner, The (1945)***½ Zachary Scott, Betty Field, J. Carrol Naish. A tenant farmer struggles to support his family, in spite of opposition from both man and nature. Directed by Jean Renoir, this is a beautifully detailed, heartfelt film. (91 mins.)†

Southern Star, The (Great Britain-France, 1969)**½ George Segal, Ursula Andress, Orson Welles. A mixed bag of tricks but an entertaining adventure based on a Jules Verne story about the ups and downs of jewel thieves in the wilds of Africa, circa 1900. (Dir: Sidney Hayers, 102 mins.)

Southern Yankee, A (1948)*** Red Skelton, Arlene Dahl, Brian Donlevy. Red's fighting the Civil War in this one and his fans will eat it up. he crawls between the lines carrying a two-sided flag for protection in a really hysterical scene. (Dir: Edward Sedgwick, 90 mins.)

South of Pago Pago (1940)** Victor McLaglen, Jon Hall, Frances Farmer. Sea pirates try to steal the pearls of a tropic isle, but the natives revolt. Dated melodrama. (Dir: Alfred E. Green, 98 mins.)†

South of Reno (1988)**½ Jeffrey Osterhage, Lisa Blount, Joe Phelan, Bert Remsen. Story of a bored, restless young couple living in a small Nevada town, looking for ways to escape their surroundings (and maybe each other) may be worth a look to viewers who don't demand a lot of plot. (Dir: Mark Rezyka, 98 mins.)†

South of St. Louis (1949)**½ Joel McCrea, Alexis Smith, Zachary Scott, Dorothy Malone. Three ranch partners face post-Civil War troubles, become involved in gun running. (Dir: Ray Enright, 88 mins.)

South Pacific (1958)**½ Mitzi Gaynor, Rossano Brazzi, France Nuyen, Ray Walston, John Kerr. Rodgers and Hammerstein's celebrated 1949 Broadway musical about the love story between a U.S. Navy nurse and a suave French planter in the South Pacific during WWII is given a big, lavish production. Gaynor is energetic in the leading role. (Dir: Joshua Logan, 167 mins.)†

South Sea Sinner (1950)** Shelley Winters, Macdonald Carey, Liberace, Frank Lovejoy. This is so bad that, in a macabre way, it's fun to sit through. Winters, complete with feather boa and bleached blonde hair, plays a small time Sadie Thompson on an island inhabited by various shady characters. Liberace is ''Maestro'' the piano playing philosopher who accompanies Winters in her nightclub scenes. (Dir: H. Bruce Humberstone, 88 mins.)

South Sea Woman (1953)*** Burt Lancaster, Virginia Mayo, Chuck Connors. Rollicking, free for all comedy with Lancaster and Connors playing a pair of brawling Marines who end up fighting a large part of the Pacific War single-handedly. (Dir: Arthur Lubin, 99 mins.)

Southwest Passage (1954)**½ John Ireland, Joanne Dru, Rod Cameron. Bank robber joins a caravan testing the value of camels in the desert. Fast-moving western with some new plot angles. (Dir: Ray Nazarro, 82 mins.)

Souvenir (1988)** Christopher Plummer, Catherine Hicks, Christopher Cazenove, Michael Lonsdale. Overly schmaltzy melodrama that tries to impart a message, but winds up being just as profound as a prime-time soap opera. Plummer is an ex-German soldier who returns to France to search for traces of the French provincial girl he loved during WWII. The morally correct screenplay and picturesque locations are undercut by the warmed-over performances of the leads. (Dir: Geoffrey Reeve, 93 mins.)†

So Well Remembered (Great Britain, 1947)**½ John Mills, Martha Scott, Patricia Roc, Trevor Howard, Richard Carlson, Juliet Mills. James Hilton's soap-opera-ish account of a small town in pre-WWII England, narrated by the author. Mills's character is such a goody, and Scott's such a baddie, that it's hard to get involved, though there are some unusual touches. (Dir: Edward Dmytryk, 114 mins.)

Soylent Green (1973)* Charlton Heston, Joseph Cotten, Edward G. Robinson. Insipid sci-fi about New York in the year 2022, teeming with people (over 40 million). Enter Heston as a detective investigating the murder of executive Cotten, and the pace almost comes to a halt. (Dir: Richard Fleischer, 97 mins.)†

So Young, So Bad (1950)**½ Paul Henreid, Catherine McLeod, Anne Francis, Rita Moreno, Anne Jackson. A doctor assigned to a girls' correctional school discovers inhuman conditions prevailing there, fights them. Fairly good melodrama. (Dir: Bernard Vorhaus, 91 mins.)

So You Won't Talk (1940)**½ Joe E. Brown, Frances Robinson, Vivienne Osborne, Bernard Nedell, Tom Dugan. Mild-mannered Brown is mistaken for a notorious gangster in this pleasant comedy. (Dir: Edward Sedgwick, 69 mins.)

Spaceballs (1987)**½ Mel Brooks, Bill Pullman, John Candy, Rick Moranis, Daphne Zuniga. Brooks's amiable spoof of the *Star Wars* craze is filled with inventive gags (like a character named Pizza the Hutt), but it somehow seems too tame. In this drawn-out send-up, some solid laughs are clocked in, though, particularly by Candy as a space canine. (Dir: Mel Brooks, 96 mins.)†

SpaceCamp (1986)**½ Kate Capshaw, Lea Thompson, Leaf Phoenix, Larry B. Scott,

Kate Donovan, Tom Skerritt. Intermittently entertaining space odyssey about some neophyte kid astronauts who go to a training camp for would-be space explorers. The film probes how the children cope when they're accidentally launched into orbit. (Dir: Harry Winer, 107 mins.)†

Space Children (1958)**½ Adam Williams, Peggy Webber, Michel Ray, John Crawford, Jackie Coogan. Interesting low-budget sci-fi thriller with a message, as a superbrain from outer space influences the children of nuclear scientists to try and stop them from sending missiles into space. Cheaply made, but very entertaining. (Dir: Jack Arnold, 69 mins.)

Spaced Invaders (1990)** Douglas Barr, Royal Dano, Ariana Richards, J. J. Anderson. Cute but mischievous Martians raise heck in a quiet midwestern town. Sci-fi slapstick, for kids only. (Dir: Patrick Read Johnson, 100 mins.)†

Spaced Out (Great Britain, 1981)* Tony Maiden, Glory Annen, Barry Stokes, Lynne Ross. Gorgeous female visitors from another planet seize humans for study and maybe a little hanky-panky. Dumb comedy filled with stupid sex jokes, shoddy production values, and bad acting. AKA: **Outer Reach**. (Dir: Norman J. Warren, 85 mins.)†

Space Hunter: Adventures in the Forbidden Zone (1983)* Peter Strauss, Molly Ringwald. Inane tale is a derivative mixture of *Star Wars, Outland,* and dozens of other outer space films. A world-weary bounty hunter rescues three women from a mysterious planet and also gets saddled with an intransigent orphan. (Dir: Lamont Johnson, 90 mins.)†

Space Mission of the Lost Planet—See: Horror of the Blood Monsters

Space Mutiny (South Africa, 1988)* Reb Brown, James Ryan, John Philip Law, Cameron Mitchell. Dreadful hunks-in-space film about starship en route to a new world attacked by space pirates and plagued by mutiny. With outer space footage borrowed from ''Battlestar Galactica''; a bad trip all the way. (Dir: David Winters, 94 mins.)†

Space Rage (1986)*½ Richard Farnsworth, Michael Paré, John Laughlin, William Windom. Sci-fi action set on a prison planet with retired cop Farnsworth hunting down escaped maniac Paré. The futuristic trappings fail to enliven this tired shoot-'em-up. (Dir: Conrad E. Palmisano, 78 mins.)†

Space Raiders (1984)** Vince Edwards, Luca Bercovich, David Mendenhall, Patsy Pease, Drew Snyder. Rag-tag space adventurers are pursued by a formidable foe throughout the universe with a child stowaway on board. Pseudo-*Star Wars,* with high spirits and low budget. (Dir: Howard Cohen, 85 mins.)†

Spaceship (1981)**½ Cindy Williams, Bruce Kimmel, Leslie Nielsen, Gerrit Graham, Patrick Macnee. Low-budget but funny spoof of *Alien*-type sci-fi movies from writer-director-star Kimmel, who was also responsible for *The First Nudie Musical*. AKA: **The Creature Wasn't Nice.** (88 mins.)†

Space Station X-14—See: **Mutiny in Outer Space**

Space Vampires—See: **Astro-Zombies**

Space Zombies—See: **Astro-Zombies**

Spanish Affair, The (1958)**½ Richard Kiley, Carmen Sevilla. Practically nonexistent plot about an American architect falling for a secretary in Spain used as an excuse to show off breathtaking scenery, places of historical interest in Spain. (Dir: Don Siegel, 92 mins.)

Spanish Gardener (Great Britain, 1956)*** Dirk Bogarde, Jon Whiteley. Diplomat's boy makes friends with a gardener, who changes his outlook and way of living. Well acted, interesting drama. (Dir: Philip Leacock, 94 mins.)

Spanish Main, The (1945)**½ Maureen O'Hara, Paul Henreid, Walter Slezak. Dashing adventurer rescues the girl he loves from the clutches of a villainous nobleman. Colorful pirate melodrama has plenty of action. (Dir: Frank Borzage, 101 mins.)†

Sparkle (1976)*** Irene Cara, Lonette McKee, Dwan Smith, Philip M. (Michael) Thomas, Mary Alice, Dorian Harewood. Terrific Curtis Mayfield music enhances this glitzy biography of singing trio (modeled on the Supremes). McKee's stunning performance helps overcome the standard show-biz cliches in this superbly crafted movie. (Dir: Sam O'Steen, 100 mins.)†

Sparkling Cyanide (MTV 1983)*** David Huffman, Deborah Raffin, Anthony Andrews, Nancy Marchand. Agatha Christie puzzler involving a promiscuous wife who is poisoned during her wedding anniversary celebration. You'll have a wonderful time trying to figure out whodunit. (Dir: Robert Lewis, 104 mins.)

Sparks: The Price of Passion (MTV 1990)** Victoria Principal, Ted Wass, Hector Elizondo, William Lucking, Elaine Stritch, Ralph Waite. Principal plays the newly elected mayor of Albuquerque, New Mexico in this formula drama, up to her luxuriant tresses in problems including blackmail and a serial killer. (Dir: Richard Colla, 96 mins.)

Sparrow, The (Egypt, 1973)***½ Mahmoud El Miligui, Mohsena Tewfik, Habiba, Salah Kabil. Imaginative, audacious political drama set after the 1967 Arab-Israeli war centers on Arabs perplexed by their defeat, stage defiant acts in the streets of Cairo and blame corrupt ruling classes and Arab disunity for the debacle. Controversial film was banned for many years in some Middle Eastern nations. (Dir: Youssef Chahine, 120 mins.)

Sparrows (1926)**** Mary Pickford, Gustav von Seffertitz, Roy Stewart, Mary Louise Miller. Outstanding melodrama about a group of abandoned children living on a squalid farm and exploited as slave labor, trying to escape through a quicksand-filled swamp. Beautifully designed and photographed, with Pickford unforgettable as the kids' leader. (Dir: William Beaudine, 84 mins.)

Spartacus (1960)**** Kirk Douglas, Jean Simmons, Laurence Olivier, Tony Curtis, Charles Laughton, Peter Ustinov, John Gavin, Nina Foch. Star-studded, lavishly mounted epic about a slave revolt against the Romans. Director Stanley Kubrick handles the mammoth story without losing sight of the personal drama involved. Douglas is convincing as Spartacus, the slave whose thirst for freedom makes him a natural choice to lead the oppressed out of bondage. An uncut, 197 minute version was released in 1991. (161 mins.)†

Spasms (1983)* Oliver Reed, Peter Fonda, Al Waxman, Marilyn Lightstone. Reed bulges his eyes and sweats a lot as he tries to out-act an equally grotesque killer snake, Waxman's face explodes, Fonda wonders what he's doing here, and the rest of the cast runs away from the berserk cameraman who's supposed to represent the reptile's point of view. (Dir: William Fruet, 87 mins.)†

Spawn of the North (1938)*** Henry Fonda, Dorothy Lamour, George Raft, John Barrymore. Good, rousing adventure tale about the days when Russian pirates tried to take over our salmon industry. Well played and loaded with action. (Dir: Henry Hathaway, 110 mins.)

Spawn of the Slithis (1979)½ Judy Motulsky, Adam Blanchard, Win Condict. One step above a home movie. A leak in an atomic power plant causes underwater mutations who come ashore to eat pets and then the pet owners. AKA: **Slithis.** (Dir: Stephen Traxler, 86 mins.)†

Speak Easily (1932)*** Buster Keaton, Jimmy Durante, Thelma Todd, Ruth Selwyn, Hedda Hopper, Sidney Toler. One of Keaton's best sound vehicles; he plays a stuffy professor who helps a theatrical troupe put on a Broadway show. With a superb movie involving an enormous, out-of-control cyclorama. (Dir: Edgar Sedgwick, 80 mins.)

Special Agent (1935)**½ Bette Davis, George Brent, Ricardo Cortez, Joseph Sawyer, Joseph Crehan, Henry O'Neill, Irving Pichel, J. Carroll Naish. Crusading newspaperman Brent induces bookkeeper Davis to get the lowdown on her sleek gangster boss Cortez. Headline-conscious crime thriller. (Dir: William Keighley, 78 mins.)

Special Bulletin (MTV 1983)***½ Ed Flanders, Kathryn Walker, David Clennon, David Rasche, Christopher Allport. Exciting, award-winning drama about a TV news team held hostage in Charleston, S.C., by nuclear fanatics. Much of the story centers around the TV coverage of the event and how the local news anchors negotiate with the protesters on the one hand and calm their viewing audience on the other. Cleverly conceived thriller. (Dir: Ed Zwick, 104 mins.)†

Special Day, A (Italy, 1977)***½ Sophia Loren, Marcello Mastroianni, John Vernon, Francoise Berd. Weaving personal relationships and political overtones, this absorbing film concerns the historic occasion when Adolf Hitler arrived in Rome for a series of propaganda meetings and parades with Il Duce. The day is also special because an oppressed housewife (Loren) and a homosexual radio announcer (Mastroianni) find themselves drawn together despite their contrasting views on Mussolini. (Dir: Ettore Scola, 110 mins.)†

Special Delivery (West Germany, 1955)**½ Joseph Cotten, Eva Bartok, Joerg Becker, Niall MacGinnis, Gert Froebe. Cold-War comedy, with Cotten an ambassador to an iron curtain country who finds a baby on the doorstep. Slight but enjoyable. (Dir: John Brahm, 86 mins.)

Special Delivery (1976)** Cybill Shepherd, Bo Svenson, Sorrell Booke, Gerrit Graham, Jeff Goldblum, Vic Tayback. Illogical, overly plotted caper about a bank heist by four Vietnam veterans. (Dir: Paul Wendkos, 99 mins.)†

Special Effects (1984)** Eric Bogosian, Brad Rijn, Zoe Tamerlis. Writer-director Larry Cohen's suspense thriller has an offbeat, very original premise, but as usual his execution doesn't live up to his ideas. Bogosian plays a maniacal film director who brutally murders a young actress, then casts her hayseed husband in a *Star 80* type movie about her life and death. A number of witty points about Hollywood megalomania are lost in the hyperventilating plot. (100 mins.)†

Special Friendship, A (MTV 1987)**½ Tracy Pollan, Akosua Busia, LeVar Burton, Josef Sommer. Often touching Civil War drama about a bond between a Virginia plantation owner's daughter and her intellectual slave. (Dir: Fielder Cook, 104 mins.)

Specialists, The (MTV 1975)* Robert York (Urich), Jack Hogan, Maureen Reagan.

Epidemiologists deal with an unknown rash, venereal disease, typhoid, and accidents in a soap factory. (Dir: Richard Quine, 72 mins.)

Special Kind of Love, A—See: **Special Olympics**

Special Olympics (MTV 1978)*** Charles Durning, Irene Tedrow, Herb Edelman, George Parry. A retarded youngster who can't do anything right finds an outlet in running and jumping, learns, grows, toughens, and finally enters the Special Olympics for the handicapped. Touching family film. AKA: **A Special Kind of Love**. (Dir: Lee Philips, 104 mins.)†

Special People (MTV 1984)**½ Brooke Adams, Susan Roman, Sandra Ciccone. Ingratiating TV movie about Canada's Famous People Players, mentally handicapped people who became skillful puppeteers. (Dir: Marc Daniels, 104 mins.)

Special Section (France, 1975)*** Michel Lonsdale, Ivo Garrani, Jacques François. Costa-Gavras directs this scathing, flawed, but involving study of the spineless French Vichy government which collaborated with the Nazis during WWII. About Vichy's fear of reprisals from the German government after a Nazi officer is killed by terrorist underground forces. (Dir: Costa-Gavras, 110 mins.)†

Special Treatment (Yugoslavia, 1980)*** Ljuba Tadic, Milena Dravic, Petar Kralj, Dusica Zegarac. Sharp-witted allegory about an alcohol treatment center run by a progressive physician who uses unorthodox methods to cure his patients. Anti-socialist plot is propelled by the hilarious escapades of an assortment of colorful characters. (Dir: Goran Paskaljevic, 90 mins.)

Speckled Band, The (1931)*** Raymond Massey, Athole Stewart, Lyn Harding, Angela Baddeley, Nancy Price. Massey makes a cold, cerebral Sherlock Holmes in this very stylized detective story, full of elaborate lighting effects and camera angles. A different, intriguing view of the great detective. (Dir: Jack Raymond, 66 mins.)†

Specter of the Rose (1946)*** Judith Anderson, Ivan Kirov, Lionel Stander. Strange tale of a young ballet dancer who is slowly losing his mind, and of the girl who loves him. Written and directed by Ben Hecht, this is a theatrical, but often fascinating, offbeat drama. (90 mins.)

Spectre (MTV 1977)**½ Robert Culp, Gig Young. This slick film by "Star Trek's" Gene Roddenberry deals with a modern Sherlock Holmes and his medical associate confronted by murders at every turn as they delve into power plays by an English financier. (Dir: Clive Donner, 106 mins.)

Spectre of Edgar Allan Poe, The (1974)* Robert Walker, Jr., Cesar Romero, Carol Ohmart. A sloppy effort that uses the real-life demons that haunted Poe as the basis for a horror film. The plot details Edgar's attempts to forestall the mental deterioration of his beloved Lenore, who was driven mad by her accidental near-burial. (Dir: Mohy Quandour, 87 mins.)†

Speed (1936)**½ James Stewart, Wendy Barrie, Ted Healy, Una Merkel, Frank Morgan. Action-packed racing drama, with Stewart romancing the boss's daughter, but finding time to perfect a new motor in time for the Indianapolis 500. An interesting view of a "super-modern" auto plant, circa 1936. (Dir: Edwin L. Marin, 65 mins.)

Speed to Spare (1948)** Richard Arlen, Jean Rogers, Richard Travis, Pat Phelan. Fairly entertaining B picture about an ex-racing car driver, now a trucker, taking on a gang of hijackers. Unpretentious and fast-moving. (Dir: William Berke, 57 mins.)

Speedtrap (1978)** Tyne Daly, Joe Don Baker. Routine crime drama about a pair of investigators (well played) who are hot on the trail of a car-theft organization. (Dir: Earl Bellamy, 104 mins.)†

Speedway (1968)** Elvis Presley, Nancy Sinatra, Bill Bixby, Gale Gordon. A race car driver (Elvis) courts an income tax collector (Nancy) in this routine but colorful Presley vehicle. (Dir: Norman Taurog, 94 mins.)†

Speedy (1928)***½ Harold Lloyd, Ann Christy, Bert Woodruff, Brooks Benedict. Wonderful Lloyd comedy, shot on location in New York City, about a baseball-mad youth who rallies a neighborhood to save the horse-drawn trolley route of his girl's grandfather. Terrific flow of action and gags, with a cameo appearance by Babe Ruth to top it off. (Dir: Ted Wilde, 75 mins.)

Speed Zone (Canada, 1989)* John Candy, Peter Boyle, Donna Dixon, Joe Flaherty, Matt Frewer, Mimi Kuzyk, Eugene Levy, Tim Matheson, Jamie Farr, Melody Anderson, Shari Belafonte, The Smothers Brothers, Brooke Shields, Lee Van Cleef. *Cannonball Run* sequel is so awful that even Burt Reynolds didn't participate. How could so many funny people make such an unfunny movie? (Dir: Jim Drake, 95 mins.)†

Spell, The (MTV 1977)** Lee Grant, James Olson, Susan Myers. Deals with an unhappy high school girl who starts willing bad things to happen to her enemies. In asking audiences to sympathize with the effects of her vengeful concentration, the show inevitably runs into difficulties. (Dir: Lee Philips, 76 mins.)†

Spellbinder (1988)*½ Timothy Daly, Kelly Preston, Rick Rossovich. A twist ending is the only interesting element in this otherwise humdrum tale of an L.A. lawyer who saves a young woman from an attacker and falls in love with her, only to discover that she is a witch. (Dir: Janet Greek, 99 mins.)†

Spellbound (1945)*** Gregory Peck, Ingrid Bergman, Michael Chekhov, Leo G. Carroll, Wallace Ford, John Emery, Rhonda Fleming, Regis Toomey. A Hitchcock thriller where the audience is more concerned with Ingrid getting Gregory onto her analyst's couch than they are with the unlocking of Peck's childhood trauma and the unmasking of a clever killer. Unabashedly romantic, this suspense tale is famous for its eerie Miklos Rosza score and the celebrated dream sequence by Salvador Dali. (111 mins.)†

Spell of the Hypnotist—See: **Fright** (1956)

Spencer's Mountain (1963)** Henry Fonda, Maureen O'Hara, James MacArthur. A pastoral attempt about a land-loving valley dweller who keeps promising to build another home for his wife and family. Too much sweetness and light. The basis for TV's "The Waltons." (Dir: Delmer Daves, 119 mins.)

Spetters (Belgium, 1980)*** Rutger Hauer, Hans van Tongeren, Toon Agerberg, Renee Soutendijk. This outré vision of contemporary Belgium features Hauer as a motorcycle champ and Soutendijk as a saucy concession-stand worker. Imaginative, and teeming with sexuality. (Dir: Paul Verhoeven, 115 mins.)†

Sphinx, The (1933)** Lionel Atwill, Sheila Terry, Theodore Newton, Paul Hurst. Effective, moody poverty-row thriller about a murderer using his mute twin as a perfect alibi. Atwill is excellent. (Dir: Phil Rosen, 64 mins.)

Sphinx (1981) ½ Lesley-Anne Down, Frank Langella, John Gielgud. Egyptologist finds herself in the thick of an intrigue involving stolen riches from ancient tombs. Endless perils, mindless script. (Dir: Franklin Schaffner, 119 mins.)†

Spider, The (1958)** Ed Kemmer, Gene Persson. A big one terrorizes a community. Special effects give this one a passing chill. AKA: **Earth vs. the Spider.** (Dir: Bert I. Gordon, 72 mins.)

Spider and the Fly, The (Great Britain, 1949)*** Guy Rolfe, Eric Portman, Nadia Gray. During WWI, the French espionage service enlists the aid of a safecracker in obtaining important documents from the enemy. Suspenseful spy melodrama. (Dir: Robert Hamer, 87 mins.)

Spider Baby (1964)**½ Lon Chaney, Jr., Beverly Washburn, Mantan Moreland, Carol Ohmart, Jill Banner, Sid Haig. Primitive in the Grant Wood rather than the Ed Wood sense, this is slow in patches, but it is nonetheless a true original, filled with disturbing images and a flair for the grotesque. The Merrye family, suffering from a unique disease caused by inbreeding wipe out meddle-some interlopers, an unlucky mailman, and anyone else who falls into their eccentric web. (Dir: Jack Hill, 80 mins.)†

Spider-Man (MTV 1977)** Nicholas Hammond, David White, Michael Pataki. Pilot film about the comic book hero who's endowed with superpowers after being bitten by a radioactive spider. (Dir: E. W. Swackhamer, 78 mins.)†

Spider's Stratagem, The (Italy, 1969)***½ Alida Valli, Giulio Brogi. Enormously interesting film made by Bernardo Bertolucci for Italian television, based on a short story, by Jorge Luis Borges. A stylish, demanding political whodunit, set in the Po Valley of Italy during the middle 1930s, a time of Mussolini and Italian Fascism. (97 mins.)

Spider Woman Strikes Back, The (1946)**½ Gale Sondergaard, Brenda Joyce, Kirby Grant, Rondo Hatton, Milburn Stone. Low-budget chiller with Sondergaard as the glamorously wicked Spider Woman, a mad scientist with a passion for arachnids. Higher production values than usual for this kind of picture, proficiently directed by Arthur Lubin. (59 mins.)

Spies (Germany, 1928)*** Rudolph Klein-Rogge, Gerda Maurus, Willy Fritsch. This vintage spy thriller made by master director Fritz Lang opens with a pair of hands stealing top secret documents from an Embassy safe, and the intrigue never stops. The cast of characters includes: the master head of the spy ring, Haghi, who has many more identities; Sonia, the sultry lady agent who is assigned to trap the hero but loses her heart to him; and Agent 326, a suave, efficient superagent. (90 mins.)†

Spies-A-Go-Go (1963)* Arch Hall, Jr., Mischa Terr. Inane farce about Russian spies disguised as cowboys landing with an infected rabbit to be let loose to destroy the country. AKA: **The Nasty Rabbit**. (Dir: James Landis, 85 mins.)

Spies Like Us (1985)**½ Chevy Chase, Dan Aykroyd, Steve Forrest. Director John Landis's update of those Bob Hope-Bing Crosby *Road* movies captures their sloppy, casual aura, though only a fraction of the laughs. As a pair of bumbling foreign Service agents sent to Asia as unwitting decoys, Chase and Aykroyd won't win any new fans but should please their old ones. If you get bored, you can watch for the endless cameos, including about a dozen other noted directors. (104 mins.)†

Spike of Bensonhurst (1988)**½ Sasha Mitchell, Ernest Borgnine, Anne DeSal-

vo, Sylvia Miles, Antonia Rey. The first Paul Morrissey (*Andy Warhol's Franken-stein, Mixed Blood*) movie that you could take your grandmother to, as long as she doesn't mind a lot of energetic Brooklyn profanity. Young boxer Spike (Mitchell) tries to use his Mafia connections to get ahead, but gets on the bad side of local capo Borgnine by romancing his daughter. Overlong, but the wonderful cast sparks this tale of mundane mob life. (101 mins.)†

Spiker (1986)** Patrick Houser, Michael Parks, Kristi Ferrell, Christopher Allport. Lackluster account of a U.S. soccer team and all the heartache and hard work that goes into striving for that Olympic gold. (Dir: Roger Tilton, 104 mins.)

Spikes Gang, The (1974)** Lee Marvin, Ron Howard, Gary Grimes, Charlie Martin Smith. Mediocre western filmed in Spain stars Marvin as an elderly outlaw who takes three runaway farm boys under his wing. (Dir: Richard Fleischer, 96 mins.)

Spin a Dark Web (1956)*½ Faith Domergue, Lee Patterson. Ex-GI gets involved with a bad crowd in London and when he tries to break loose they kidnap his girl friend. (Dir: Vernon Sewell, 76 mins.)

Spinout (1966)* Elvis Presley, Shelley Fabares. Strictly for Elvis's fans. This time he's the leader of a musical troupe, with four pretty young things after him. (Dir: Norman Taurog, 90 mins.)†

Spiral Road, The (1962)*** Rock Hudson, Burl Ives, Gena Rowlands. Lengthy but interesting, well-acted drama of a doctor in the remote jungles of Batavia and his discovery of both medical progress and faith. (Dir: Robert Mulligan, 145 mins.)

Spiral Staircase, The (1946)***½ Dorothy McGuire, George Brent, Elsa Lanchester, Ethel Barrymore, Rhonda Fleming. Mute servant girl in a gloomy household is endangered by a mysterious killer. Breathlessly suspenseful mystery, superbly directed, a real thriller. (Dir: Robert Siodmak, 83 mins.)†

Spiral Staircase, The (Great Britain, 1975)*½ Jacqueline Bisset, Christopher Plummer, Gayle Hunnicutt, Sam Wanamaker. Inadequate remake of the scare classic. Bisset does not begin to erase memories of McGuire's performance as the mute servant stalked by a killer who despises women with physical imperfections. (Dir: Peter Collinson, 89 mins.)†

Spirit, The (MTV 1987)*** Sam Jones, Nana Visitor, McKinley Robinson. A tongue-in-cheek, pop hero pilot film based on Wil Eisner's comic book crimefighter. (Dir: Michael Schultz, 104 mins.)

Spirit Is Willing, The (1967)** Sid Caesar, Vera Miles, Barry Gordon, John McGiver, Cass Daley. A couple rent a New England house by the sea, and summer vacation soon turns into a ghosthunt. Mild farce. (Dir: William Castle, 100 mins.)

Spirit of Saint Louis, The (1957)**½ James Stewart, Murray Hamilton, Patricia Smith. Stewart stars as Charles Lindbergh in this sometimes absorbing, sometimes tedious account of his early life and his historic trans-Atlantic solo flight. (Dir: Billy Wilder, 138 mins.)†

Spirit of the Beehive (Spain, 1973)***½ Fernando Fernan Gomez, Teresa Gimpera, Ana Torrent. Time—1940 in a remote Castilian village in post-Civil War Spain. Two children watch a traveling film show of *Frankenstein* and are traumatized by it, with alarming results for one of the children. A fascinating, underplayed drama which builds interest and tension. (Dir: Victor Erice, 98 mins.)†

Spirit of the Dead—See: **Asphyx, The**

Spirit of Youth (1937)** Joe Louis, Clarence Muse, Edna Mae Harris, Mae Turner, Mantan Moreland. Commonplace boxing story with an all-black cast purports to tell the story of Joe Louis, who plays himself (and certainly made a better boxer than actor.) (Dir: Harry Fraser, 65 mins.)†

Spirits of the Dead (France-Italy, 1969)*** Jane Fonda, Peter Fonda, Alain Delon, Brigitte Bardot, Terence Stamp. Based on three tales by Edgar Allan Poe. Fellini's segment is by far the best. (Dirs: Roger Vadim, Federico Fellini, Louis Malle, 117 mins.)

Spiritualist, The—See: **Amazing Mr. X., The**

Spitfire (1934)*** Katharine Hepburn, Robert Young, Ralph Bellamy. Mountain girl falls in love with a married engineer. Fine performances dominate this interesting drama. (Dir: John Cromwell, 88 mins.)

Spitfire (Great Britain, 1942)*** Leslie Howard, David Niven. The story of the inventor of the plane that served so well during WWII. Fine biographical drama. (Dir: Leslie Howard, 90 mins.)†

Splash (1984)*** Tom Hanks, Daryl Hannah, John Candy, Eugene Levy. A gently appealing love story. Our hero (Hanks) hasn't made much of a splash with women, but he didn't reckon on hooking a real live mermaid. Some funny complications arise as their romance is subverted by an overly zealous scientist and the military, who both want to catch the mermaid for their own purposes. (Dir: Ron Howard, 111 mins.)†

Splash, Too (MTV 1988)*½ Todd Waring, Amy Yasbeck, Donovan Scott. This waterlogged sequel follows the further adventures of Allen (Waring) and his mermaid wife, Madison (Yasbeck). Madison goes off on a mission to save her dolphin friend; she, like this movie, is all wet. (Dir: Greg Antonacci, 96 mins.)

Splatter University (1984)½ Francine Forbes, Ric Randig, Cathy Lacommare. Micro-budget slasher flick, with a psychopath (whose identity is obvious from the moment he appears on-screen) bumping off coeds. (Dir: Richard Haines, 77 mins.)†

Splendor (1935)**½ Miriam Hopkins, Joel McCrea, David Niven. Dated romantic epic which seems a bit corny today but there's some good acting especially by Miriam Hopkins. (Dir: Elliott Nugent, 77 mins.)

Splendor in the Grass (1961)***½ Natalie Wood, Warren Beatty, Pat Hingle, Zohra Lampert, Sandy Dennis, Phyllis Diller. Wood and Beatty co-star as two young people making the painful and beautiful discovery of love in a small Kansas town prior to the depression of the thirties. Their sensitive performances make this a must for drama fans who're not above shedding a tear or two. The ending is unsatisfactory, but it doesn't ruin the movie. (Dir: Elia Kazan, 124 mins.)†

Splendor in the Grass (MTV 1981)**½ Melissa Gilbert, Cyril O'Reilly, Eva Marie Saint, Ned Beatty, Michelle Pfeiffer. Unnecessary remake of far superior 1961 film about a pair of high school seniors coming of sexual age in 1928 Kansas. (Dir: Richard C. Sarafian, 104 mins.)

Split, The (1968)*½ Jim Brown, Julie Harris, Diahann Carroll. Double-crosses abound, in a plan to rob the Los Angeles Coliseum of football receipts. Fumbling yarn. (Dir: Gordon Fleming, 91 mins.)

Split Decisions (1988)**½ Craig Sheffer, Jeff Fahey, Gene Hackman, Jennifer Beals. What starts out well as a drama about three generations of Irish immigrants who seek fame in the boxing ring winds up in sub-*Rocky* histrionics as Sheffer fights a grudge match to avenge his brother's death at the hands of the Mob. (Dir: David Drury, 95 mins.)†

Split Image (1982)**½ Michael O'Keefe, Karen Allen, James Woods, Elizabeth Ashley, Brian Dennehy, Peter Fonda. Melodramatic dramatization involving a college athlete who is lured into a cult and is brainwashed. His parents hire a professional deprogrammer to wrest him from the group, and the action turns nasty and violent, but still holds your attention. (Dir: Ted Kotcheff, 111 mins.)†

Split Second (1953)***½ Stephen McNally, Alexis Smith, Jan Sterling. Escaped prisoners hold hostages in a Nevada atom bomb testing area. Terrifically suspenseful. (Dir: Dick Powell, 85 mins.)

Split Seconds to an Epitaph (MTV 1968) **½ Raymond Burr, Don Galloway, Barbara Anderson, Don Mitchell, Joseph Cotten, Lilia Skala, Andrew Prine, Margaret O'Brien, Don Stroud. This two-hour dose of "Ironside" takes on select cinematic qualities (straight out of old melodramatic thrillers) when the wheelchair-bound detective is the key witness to murder, *and* just might be cured of his spinal paralysis. (Dir: Leonard J. Horn, 96 mins.)

Spoiled Children (France, 1973)***½ Michel Piccoli, Christine Pascal, Gerard Jugnot, Michel Aumont. Piccoli rents an apartment in a Paris high-rise so he can work on his new screenplay without any interruptions from his boisterous family, only to land in the middle of a bitter tenant-landlord dispute and fall in love with a woman half his age. Refreshing black comedy about romance and the changing face of Paris. (Dir: Bertrand Tavernier, 113 mins.)

Spoilers, The (1942)*** Marlene Dietrich, John Wayne, Randolph Scott, Margaret Lindsay, Richard Barthelmess. John is out to protect his gold mine and his woman in this one. Loaded with action and a great hand-to-hand fight by Wayne and Scott. (Dir: Ray Enright, 87 mins.)†

Spoilers, The (1955)**½ Anne Baxter, Jeff Chandler, Rory Calhoun, Barbara Britton, Ray Danton. Rex Beach's classic action yarn about the "spoilers" who turned the Yukon into a claim-jumper's paradise, remade with all the flair and flavor intact. (Dir: Jesse Hibbs, 84 mins.)

Spontaneous Combustion (1990)*½ Brad Dourif, Cynthia Bain, Jon Cypher, William Prince, Melinda Dillon, John Landis. Dourif, whose parents were subjected to atomic radiation during experiments in the '50s, has the power to become a human flamethrower in this ludicrous horror movie, another nail in the coffin of director Tobe Hooper's critical reputation. (108 mins.)†

Spook Busters (1946)*½ The Bowery Boys, Douglas Dumbrille, Gabriel Dell. Who you gonna call? Slip and Sach, that's who. The Boys are ghost exterminators in this standard but slightly amusing haunted house comedy. (Dir: William Beaudine, 61 mins.)

Spook Chasers (1957)**½ Huntz Hall, Stanley Clements, Percy Helton. A fairly funny spook spoof about the Bowery Boys inheriting a farmhouse where they find a stash of cash and some night visitors who may or may not be from the spirit world. (Dir: George Blair, 62 mins.)

Spookies (1988)* Flex Ward, Dan Scott, Marcia Pechuka. Straight-to-video schlock that juggles vastly different elements because it's actually parts of two different films edited into one. The predominant one involves some dim-witted teens, an evil magician, and the young woman he preserves through sorcery. (Dirs: Eugenie

Joseph, Thomas Doran, Brendan Faulkner, 90 mins.)†

Spooks Run Wild (1941)*** East Side Kids, Bela Lugosi, David O'Brien, Dorothy Short. One of the best they made and the reason is Bela. It's a slapstick comedy-horror film in which Bela gets a chance to rib the genre he made great. (Dir: Phil Rosen, 69 mins.)†

Sporting Blood (1931)*** Clark Gable, Ernest Torrence, Madge Evans, Lew Cody, Marie Prevost, Harry Holman. Punchy horse-racing drama, with Gable a gambler who wins a thoroughbred and has him readied for the Kentucky Derby, though gangsters try to get him to throw the race. Well photographed and directed, with blood-tingling racing footage. (Dir: Charles Brabin, 82 mins.)

Sporting Club, The (1971)* Robert Fields, Maggie Blye, Nicholas Coster, Jack Warden. Some men come together for a reunion—and at the climax there is an orgy of sorts. In between, a great deal of violence transpires that may have something to do metaphorically with Vietnam or the decline of the American upper class. (Dir: Larry Peerce, 107 mins.)†

Spot—See: **Dogpound Shuffle**

Spot Marks the X (MTV 1986)** Mike the Dog, Barret Oliver, Natalie Gregory, Richard B. Shull, Geoffrey Lewis, David Huddleston. Silly treacle featuring the canine co-star of *Down and Out in Beverly Hills* as a criminal mutt retrained for the straight and narrow by a kid who adopts him. As slim as any Rin-Tin-Tin programmer, and about as funny. (Dir: Mark Rosman, 90 mins.)

Spraggue (MTV 1984)* Michael Nouri, Glynis Johns, James Cromwell, Mark Herrier. Lackluster TV pilot for a series about a Boston professor dabbling in detective work. (Dir: Larry Elikann, 77 mins.)†

Spring Break (1983)*½ David Knell, Perry Lang, Paul Land. The college crowd goes to Fort Lauderdale for wine, women, and surf with predictable results. (Dir: Sean Cunningham, 100 mins.)†

Springfield Rifle (1952)*** Gary Cooper, Phyllis Thaxter, Paul Kelly. Bitter Civil War western about spies and schemers, with Cooper as a good traitor and Kelly as a failed Machiavelli. (Dir: André de Toth, 93 mins.)

Spring in Park Lane (Great Britain, 1948)*** Anna Neagle, Michael Wilding. Delightful comedy concerning romantic complications and mistaken identity. Witty, fun. (Dir: Herbert Wilcox, 90 mins.)

Spring Madness (1938)**½ Maureen O'Sullivan, Lew Ayres, Ruth Hussey, Burgess Meredith, Joyce Compton, Sterling Holloway. Light, engaging college humor, based on a Philip Barry play.

Two free-thinking college students plan to roam Europe after they graduate, until one falls in love. Meredith and Hussey steal every scene they're in. (Dir: S. Sylvan Simon, 80 mins.)

Spring Parade (1940)*** Deanna Durbin, Robert Cummings, Mischa Auer, Henry Stephenson, S. Z. Sakall, Walter Catlett, Reginald Denny. Charming period piece set in Austria, with village girl Durbin helping composer Cummings get his waltzes performed before the emperor. (Dir: Henry Koster, 89 mins.)

Spring Reunion (1957)** Betty Hutton, Dana Andrews, Jean Hagen. Hutton goes dramatic as the spinster who attends her high school class reunion and finds true love at long last. Unbelievable script hampered by awkward acting of Hutton. (Dir: Robert Pirosh, 79 mins.)

Spring Symphony (West Germany 1984)**½ Nastassia Kinski, Herbert Gronemeyer, Edda Sieppel, Rolf Hoppe. Certainly there are fewer sour notes struck in this melody-drenched biopic than in that previous glimpse at Clara Schuman, *Song of Love*. Concentrating on Clara's struggle to defy her tyrannical papa, this film, with Kinski an admirable heroine, is more accurate historically. (Dir: Peter Schamoni, 102 mins.)†

Springtime in the Rockies (1942)**½ Betty Grable, John Payne, Cesar Romero, Jackie Gleason, Charlotte Greenwood. A typical wartime Grable musical. Betty shows her famous gams in the dance numbers, which are the best part of this flimsy storyline about bickering stage partners and their on-again, off-again romance. (Dir: Irving Cummings, 91 mins.)†

Spy Busters (1969)**½ Kurt Russell, Patrick Dawson, Glenn Corbett. An espionage yarn about an American student at an Irish university. After he is entrusted with a message by a dying agent, the plot takes off with kidnappings, chases, and a beautifully photographed glider finale. (Dir: Robert Butler, 90 mins.)

Spy Chasers (1955)*** Bowery Boys, Veola Vonn, Bernard Gorcey, Sig Rumann. Intrigue involving the exiled King and Princess of Truania. Vintage Bowery Boys fare. (Dir: Edward Bernds, 61 mins.)

Spy in Black, The (Great Britain, 1939)*** Conrad Veidt, Valerie Hobson, June Duprez, Marius Goring, Sebastian Shaw. Exciting spy thriller about double crosses engineered by both the Germans and the British during WWI. Adding depth to this espionage plotting is the electricity passing between Veidt, the clever German spy, and Hobson, the equally tricky British agent who fall for each other despite their best efforts to be cold-bloodedly patriotic. (Dir: Michael Powell, 82 mins.)†

Spy in Your Eye (Italy, 1965)* Brett Halsey, Pier Angeli, Dana Andrews. U.S.-Soviet tussle over a "death ray" is deadly dull. (Dir: Vittorio Sala, 88 mins.)

Spy Killer, The (MTV 1969)** Robert Horton, Sebastian Cabot, Jill St. John. Horton is an ex-agent who now earns his living as a shady private eye. His old employer, British Security, enlists his aid for another assignment. (Dir: Roy Baker, 73 mins.)

Spylarks (Great Britain, 1965)** Eric Morecambe, Ernie Wise, William Franklyn. The comedy team of Morecambe and Wise pull their antics all over the place as a pair of inept spies out to crack a sabotage scheme. (Dir: Robert Asher, 104 mins.)

Spy of Napoleon (Great Britain, 1936)**½ Richard Barthelmess, Dolly Haas, Frank Vosper, Francis L. Sullivan. Engrossing historical drama, from a novel by Baroness Orczy. Elaborately mounted, flawed mainly by the writers' expecting the audience to know more about French history than they probably do. (Dir: Maurice Elvey, 98 mins.)†

S*P*Y*S (Great Britain, 1974)** Elliott Gould, Donald Sutherland, Zou Zou, Joss Ackland. Failed attempt to pair that marvelous team from *M*A*S*H* together again for more comedy. Gould and Sutherland are CIA agents whom their boss has decided are expendable. They are. (Dir: Irvin Kershner, 87 mins.)

Spy Smasher Returns (1942)** Kane Richmond, Marguerite Chapman. Feature version of serial *Spy Smasher*. Comic-strip hero and his twin brother go after a master enemy agent, amid fistfights galore, some wild flamboyant action. (Dir: William Witney, 100 mins.)†

Spy Who Came in from the Cold, The (Great Britain, 1965)***½ Richard Burton, Claire Bloom, Oskar Werner. The best-selling novel about hypocrisy and betrayal in the world of espionage is brought to the screen with all its grim realities intact. Burton is effective as a disenchanted agent on his supposedly last assignment, and Oskar Werner is a standout as a member of German Intelligence. (Dir: Martin Ritt, 112 mins.)†

Spy Who Loved Me, The (Great Britain, 1977)***½ Roger Moore, Barbara Bach, Curt Jurgens, Richard Kiel. Bond lovers may rank this with their all-time favorites because of the superb production values. 007 teams up with a luscious Russian agent in this tenth Bond adventure. Can they stop an insane shipping tycoon from destroying the world? Giant Kiel leaves an impression as a toothy villain nicknamed "Jaws." (Dir: Lewis Gilbert, 125 mins.)†

Spy with a Cold Nose (Great Britain,

1966)**½ Laurence Harvey, Daliah Lavi. Funny, if uneven, spy spoof. Title refers to a dog equipped with a microphone-transmitter, which is given to the Russian prime minister by British intelligence. (Dir: Daniel Petrie, 93 mins.)†

Spy With My Face, The (1966)*½ Robert Vaughn, Senta Berger, David McCallum. A theatrical release of an (expanded) episode from the 1964 *Man From U.N.C.L.E.* THRUSH agents kidnap Napoleon Solo (Vaughn) and replace him with a double. The intrigue mounts (mildly). (Dir: John Newland, 86 mins.)

Square Dance (1987)**½ Jane Alexander, Jason Robards, Jr., Winona Ryder, Rob Lowe, Guich Koock. A conventional, subdued coming-of-age film. Luckily, exemplary acting (particularly by Alexander in the atypical role of bed-hopping, neglectful mother) freshens up the standard domestic dramatics on display. Not fitting in anywhere, an ugly duckling blossoms into womanhood without the support of her irresponsible mother and manages to retain her purity of spirit despite the tawdriness of her surroundings. AKA: **Home Is Where the Heart Is.** (Dir: Daniel Petrie, 112 mins.)†

Square Jungle, The (1955)** Tony Curtis, Pat Crowley, Ernest Borgnine, Paul Kelly, David Janssen. Corny prizefight yarn with all the clichés. Tony plays a kid from the wrong side of the tracks who turns to boxing and becomes a champion. (Dir: Jerry Hopper, 86 mins.)

Square of Violence (U.S.–Yugoslavia, 1961)**½ Broderick Crawford, Branko Plesa, Valentina Cortese, Bibi Andersson. When Yugoslav partisans in WWII kill Nazi officers, 300 innocent men are taken hostage by the Germans. Crawford is the partisan responsible for the bombing, torn between his loyalty to the cause and his concern for the 300. A tense, little-known picture, director Leonardo Bercovici's first. (98 mins.)

Square Shooter, The (1951)**½ Maxie Rosenbloom, Max Baer. Two-gun "Skipalong" Rosenbloom tames feared outlaw "Butcher" Baer in this western burlesque. Crude slapstick, but funny at times. AKA: **Skipalong Rosenbloom.** (Dir: Sam Newfield, 72 mins.)

Squaw Man, The (1931)*** Warner Baxter, Lupe Velez, Eleanor Boardman, Charles Bickford, Roland Young. Director Cecil B. De Mille's third film version of the popular melodrama about an exiled British nobleman who marries an Indian maiden. Filmed with restraint and real feeling. (106 mins.)

Squeaker, The (Great Britain, 1937)*** Edmund Lowe, Sebastian Shaw, Ann Todd, Robert Newton, Alastair Sim. Atmospheric Edgar Wallace thriller about a broken-down ex-Scotland Yard inspector trying to redeem himself by catching a notorious criminal, "The Squeaker." Effectively done, acted with verve. (Dir: William K. Howard, 77 mins.)

Squeeze (New Zealand, 1980)*** Robert Shannon, Paul Eady, Donna Akersten, Peter Heperi. Man about to be married discovers his preferences lean more toward men in this sharp-witted comedy-drama about the gay scene in Auckland, N. Z. Occasional clichés slow the pace, but film delivers tale of a man finding his true self in a nonpreachy manner. (Dir: Richard Turner, 82 mins.)

Squeeze, The (1987)*½ Michael Keaton, Rae Dawn Chong, John Davidson, Meat Loaf. Overblown action comedy with too many chases and too few laughs as conceptual artist Keaton and detective Chong uncover an elaborate plot to rig a multimillion-dollar lottery. (Dir: Roger Young, 101 mins.)†

Squeeze Play (1980)* Jim Harris, Jenni Hetrick, Rick Gitlin. Comedy about a battle of the sexes played out on a softball field is a thin excuse for female nudity and smutty jokes. Which would be okay if the jokes were at least funny.... (Dir: Samuel Weil, 92 mins.)†

Squirm (1976)*** Don Scardino, Patricia Pearcy. A downed power line turns the juice on and jolts an underground community of worms into action. Shocked by the electricity, the crawling creatures grow in size and animosity toward human beings. May have you squirming in your seat. (Dir: Jeff Liberman, 92 mins.)†

Squizzy Taylor (Australia, 1984)*½ David Atkins, Jacki Weaver, Alan Cassell, Michael Long, Robert Hughes. Did someone leave something out of this twenties ganster movie set in Australia? Whether Squizzy was a big gangland boss or just a petty punk is never made clear. (Dir: Kevin Dobson, 89 mins.)†

Sssssss (1973)*½ Strother Martin, Heather Menzies. A doltish horror yarn about a demented snake expert who decides to turn young, healthy men into cobras. (Dir: Bernard L. Kowalski, 90 mins.)

SST—Death Flight (MTV 1977)** Lorne Greene, Susan Strasberg, Burgess Meredith. The maiden trip of the first supersonic plane—and the guest list includes celebrities, contest winners, and a scientist carrying a deadly virus. Guess what happens! AKA: **SST—Disaster in the Sky.** (Dir: David Lowell Rich, 106 mins.)

SST—Disaster in the Sky—See: **SST—Death Flight**

St.—See also: **Saint**

Stablemates (1938)**½ Mickey Rooney, Wallace Beery, Arthur Hohl, Margaret Hamilton, Minor Watson. Low-key drama of alcoholic veterinarian Beery redeemed by his relationship with Rooney and his aged horse. Formulaic but expertly made. (Dir: Sam Wood, 89 mins.)

Stacking (1988)*** Christine Lahti, Frederic Forrest, Megan Follows, Jason Gedrick, Peter Coyote. The unusual title of this subdued film about farming in 1954 Montana refers to one young girl's attempts to build a machine that stacks hay with the aid of a boozy friend of her parents (Forrest). Unlike other rural (and urban) sagas about "growing up," this is a mature work that presents three-dimensional characters and three exceptional lead performances. (Dir: Martin Rosen, 97 mins.)†

Stacy's Knights (1983)** Andra Millian, Kevin Costner, Eve Lilith, Mike Reynolds. Passable B movie about a gambling lady who's obsessed with the gambling tables. When her pal is bumped off, she declares war against the casino owners. (Dir: Jim Wilson, 95 mins.)†

Stagecoach (1939)**** Claire Trevor, John Wayne, Thomas Mitchell, Louise Platt, Andy Devine, John Carradine. The classic about a group of assorted passengers on a stage going into Indian country, their reactions under stress. A fine, exciting film, one of the most influential westerns ever made. (Dir: John Ford, 100 mins.)†

Stagecoach (1966)**½ Ann-Margret, Alex Cord, Bing Crosby, Red Buttons. An all-star remake of the classic western. Doesn't live up to its predecessor, but OK on its own terms. (Dir: Gordon Douglas, 114 mins.)

Stagecoach (MTV 1986)*½ Willie Nelson, Kris Kristofferson, Waylon Jennings, Johnny Cash, John Schneider, Mary Crosby, Anthony Franciosa, Anthony Newley. A bevy of country music stars, along with a few wasted Hollywood faces, pile into a stagecoach in the old West to make a trip across Arizona. (Dir: Ted Post, 104 mins.)†

Stage Door (1937)**** Katharine Hepburn, Ginger Rogers, Adolphe Menjou, Ann Miller, Eve Arden, Lucille Ball, Franklin Pangborn. Director Gregory La Cava seamlessly meshes the different styles and personalities of this dream cast in this example of Hollywood filmmaking at its best. Set in an all-girl hotel for struggling artists, the film blends comedy with pathos as it unfolds the lives of the aspiring actresses. (92 mins.)†

Stage Door Canteen (1943)** William Terry, Cheryl Walker. Romantic drama of a soldier boy and a canteen hostess, backgrounded by the famous servicemen's center of WWII. Sticky-sweet plot, with brief glimpses of many "guest stars" helping some. (Dir: Frank Borzage, 132 mins.)†

Stage Fright (Great Britain, 1950)*** Marlene Dietrich, Jane Wyman, Michael Wilding, Richard Todd, Alastair Sim. Alfred Hitchcock, back in an English setting for the first time in over a decade, directs an uneven story about a young man (Todd) suspected of murdering an actress's husband. Dietrich is effective in a music hall role (singing "The Laziest Gal in Town"). (110 mins.)†

Stage Mother (1933)*** Maureen O'Sullivan, Alice Brady, Franchot Tone, Phillips Holmes, Ted Healy. Gritty story of a relentless stage mother manipulating her daughter's career and life. Brady and O'Sullivan are both terrific, though Holmes and Tone do less well as the men in their lives. (Dir: Charles R. Brabin, 85 mins.)

Stage Struck (1936)** Dick Powell, Joan Blondell, Warren William, Jean Madden, Frank McHugh, Carol Hughes, Hobart Cavanaugh, Spring Byington. Powell and Blondell battle over the production of a stage show in this lifeless Warner Bros. musical. Some good bits, and the usual wild Busby Berkeley choreography, but comparatively tame. (Dir: Busby Berkeley, 86 mins.)

Stage Struck (1957)**½ Henry Fonda, Susan Strasberg, Joan Greenwood, Christopher Plummer, Herbert Marshall. Remake of *Morning Glory*, relating the tale of a young girl whose ambitions spur her on to become a great actress. Strasberg doesn't live up to the role, which hurts the film; otherwise, some good New York atmosphere, performances. (Dir: Sidney Lumet, 95 mins.)†

Stage to Thunder Rock (1964)** Barry Sullivan, Marilyn Maxwell, Scott Brady, Lon Chaney, Jr., Keenan Wynn. Standard western about gunslinger and his prisoner. (Dir: William F. Claxton, 82 mins.)

Stage to Tucson (1950)**½ Rod Cameron, Wayne Morris, Sally Eilers. Two Civil War buddies are sent to Tucson to investigate stage coach hijackings and find more trouble than they bargained for. Action-crammed western. (Dir: Ralph Murphy, 82 mins.)

Staircase (Great Britain, 1969)*** Rex Harrison, Richard Burton, Cathleen Nesbitt. Director Stanley Donen brings a plaintive note of desperation to this story of two aging, bickering homosexuals who share a London flat. Harrison manages only surfaces, but Burton turns in one of his best performances as the more vulnerably domestic of the two. (96 mins.)

Stairway to Heaven (Great Britain, 1946)***½ David Niven, Roger Livesey, Kim Hunter, Raymond Massey. Outrageous fantasy-drama, in which Niven plays a flier whose brain is damaged when he bails out of his plane; he has visions that he has actually been to heaven. Very good film. AKA: **A Matter of Life and Death.** (Dirs: Michael Powell, Emeric Pressburger, 104 mins.)

Stakeout (1987)*** Richard Dreyfuss, Emilio Estevez, Aidan Quinn, Madeline Stowe. The palpable chemistry between Dreyfuss and Estevez transforms ordinary material here, thus making this escapism about two cops on a surveillance assignment involving a beautiful woman genuinely enjoyable. (Dir: John Badham, 101 mins.)†

Stakeout on Dope Street (1958)** Abby Dalton, Yale Wexler, Jonathan Haze, Morris Miller, Herschel Bernardi. Three misguided youths come upon some heroin and believe that they can pave the way to Easy Street with it. OK drama. (Dir: Irvin Kershner, 83 mins.)

Stalag 17 (1953)**** William Holden, Don Taylor, Otto Preminger, Robert Strauss, Harvey Lembeck, Peter Graves. Tale of a POW camp is laced with director Billy Wilder's special brand of comedy and cynicism. Holden (Academy Award) plays a sergeant suspected of being a spy. (120 mins.)†

Stalker (U.S.S.R.-West Germany, 1979) ***½ Aleksandr Kaidanovsky, Nikolai Grinko, Anatoly Solonitsin. Extraordinary sci-fi film about a expedition into "the zone," an eerie no-man's-land created by a meteor strike and depicted as a warped version of normality, in search of a strange room that can grant wishes. Demanding, dizzingly hallucinogenic film is boldly photographed and relentless in its depiction of a world gone mystically awry. (Dir: Andrei Tarkovsky, 161 mins.)

Stalking Moon, The (1968)**½ Gregory Peck, Eva Marie Saint, Robert Forster. Peck and Miss Saint do well in this western drama which requires some initial patience before getting into the story. Saint is released after being a prisoner of the Apaches for a number of years, with her nine-year-old half-breed son, but the boy's Indian father stalks them. (Dir: Robert Mulligan, 109 mins.)

Stalk the Wild Child (MTV 1976)**½ David Janssen, Trish Van Devere, Joseph Bottoms. A boy found running with a pack of wild dogs is brought to a university medical center for observation and rehabilitation. (Dir: William Hale, 78 mins.)†

Stallion Road (1947)** Ronald Reagan, Alexis Smith, Zachary Scott. Ron is a veterinarian and Alexis a lovely rancher in this dull romantic drama which offers nothing more than some good looking horses. (Dir: James V. Kern, 97 mins.)

Stamboul Quest (1934)*** Myrna Loy, George Brent, Lionel Atwill, C. Henry Gordon. Herman Mankiewicz's adaptation of the true story of Germany's top WWI spy, Fraulein Doktor, is stylish and exciting. (Dir: Sam Wood, 85 mins.)

Stand Alone (1985)** Charles Durning, Willard Pugh, Pam Grier, Bert Remsen. An old man renowned for his WWII bravery finds his mettle put to the test when he's wounded in a drug-related shoot-out and the law and the media make his life into a public circus. (Dir: Alan Beattie, 90 mins.)†

Stand and Deliver (1988)*** Edward James Olmos, Lou Diamond Phillips, Rosana de Soto, Andy Garcia. Olmos gives a vivid and energetic performance as an educator who truly cares—a real-life high school teacher who instills a love for learning, and a sense of self-worth, into his Hispanic pupils. (Dir: Ramon Mendez, 102 mins.)†

Stand at Apache River (1953)**½ Stephen McNally, Julia Adams, Hugh Marlowe, Hugh O'Brian, Jack Kelly. Familiar western yarn about a group of strangers stranded in a secluded trading post inn waiting for an Apache attack. Some suspense. (Dir: Lee Sholem, 77 mins.)

Stand by for Action (1942)**½ Robert Taylor, Brian Donlevy, Walter Brennan, Charles Laughton, Marilyn Maxwell. The plot about a snooty wartime Naval officer in conflict with the regular Navy man, the sinking of a Japanese ship, and some salty humor create an occasionally entertaining but generally tiresome film. (Dir: Robert Z. Leonard, 109 mins.)

Stand By Me (1986)**½ Wil Wheaton, River Phoenix, Corey Feldman, Jerry O'Connell, Kiefer Sutherland. Sentimental but overrated story of four misfit boys, circa the late fifties, who take an overnight hike into the woods to view a dead body. Director Rob Reiner, working from an autobiographical Stephen King story, ladles on the schmaltz from beginning to end; he gets sincere performances from his young cast, but as written they resemble participants in a sensitivity training workshop more than adolescent boys. (87 mins.)†

Stand by Your Man (MTV 1981)**½ Annette O'Toole, Tim McIntire, Cooper Huckabee, Helen Page Camp, James Hampton. O'Toole shines as Tammy Wynette, the Memphis beauty parlor student who sings her way into the hearts of country music fans despite electric shock treatment, young'uns, and stormy marriages. (Dir: Jerry Jameson, 104 mins.)

Stand-In (1937)**½ Joan Blondell, Leslie Howard, Humphrey Bogart, Alan Mowbray, Jack Carson. Rollicking screwball farce about a timid but efficient accountant sent to reorganize a bankrupt Hollywood studio. He decides to find out how the place works from the bottom up, and learns the ropes from a sexy but under employed "stand-in." (Dir: Tay Garnett, 90 mins.)†

Standing Room Only (1944)**½ Fred MacMurray, Paulette Goddard, Edward Arnold. A secretary books herself and boss on as servants in a Washington home to avoid the hotel room shortage. Funny when it was topical but only mildly amusing today. (Dir: Sidney Lanfield, 83 mins.)

Standing Tall (MTV 1978)** Robert Forster, Linda Evans, Will Sampson, L.Q. Jones, Chuck Connors, Robert Donner. A get-even western set in Depression times. Forster is quite commanding as a half-breed who has trouble surviving due to the interference of an unscrupulous cattle king. (Dir: Harvey Hart, 104 mins.)†

Stand Up and Be Counted (1972)**½ Jacqueline Bisset, Stella Stevens, Steve Lawrence, Gary Lockwood, Loretta Swit. Hollywood discovers women's lib, but insists on adding the usual bunch of stereotypes. Bisset plays a fashion magazine journalist who covers the women's lib scene in Denver. (Dir: Jackie Cooper, 99 mins.)

Stand Up and Cheer (1934)**½ Warner Baxter, Madge Evans, James Dunn, Shirley Temple. Crazy depression musical has the president creating a cabinet post for secretary of amusement in the hope of laughing gloom away. Occasionally amusing but very dated. Will Rogers worked on the screenplay. (Dir: Hamilton MacFadden, 80 mins.)†

Stand Up and Fight (1939)** Wallace Beery, Robert Taylor, Florence Rice, Charles Bickford. It's the stagecoach vs. the encroaching railroad in this standard western about transportation civilizing the Old West. (Dir: W. S. Van Dyke, 105 mins.)

Stanley (1972)** Chris Robinson, Alex Rocco, Susan Carroll, Mark Harris. Another tale of a disturbed Vietnam veteran. This guy (Robinson) relates only to snakes, ignoring all humans except to sic his serpentine sidekicks on them. (Dir: William Grefe, 106 mins.)†

Stanley and Iris (1990)*** Jane Fonda, Robert De Niro, Swoosie Kurtz, Feodor Chaliapin, Martha Plimpton, Harley Cross. Quiet, sensitive movie about illiteracy and isolation. Widow Fonda begins a wary friendship with co-worker De Niro. These two proud but insular people open up to each other as she teaches him to read and he breaks down her loneliness. Directed with feeling and dignity by Martin Ritt. (102 mins.)†

Stanley and Livingstone (1939)*** Spencer Tracy, Cedric Hardwicke, Nancy Kelly, Richard Greene, Walter Brennan.

Reasonably intelligent and moderately entertaining historical epic. Tracy gives his usual professional reading of the intrepid journalist Henry M. Stanley who goes searching for missionary-explorer David Livingstone. (Dir: Henry King, 101 mins.)

Star (1968)** Julie Andrews, Daniel Massey, Robert Reed, Michael Craig, Richard Crenna. Disappointing musical based on the life and career of the legendary Broadway star, English-born actress Gertrude Lawrence. (Dir: Robert Wise, 194 mins.)†

Star, The (1953)*** Bette Davis, Sterling Hayden, Natalie Wood. A fading movie queen finds love and marries, and still desires a comeback. Well-fashioned look at Hollywood backstage. Good performances. (Dir: Stuart Heisler, 89 mins.)

Star Chamber, The (1983)**½ Michael Douglas, Hal Holbrook, Yaphet Kotto, Sharon Gless. A gripping, if plot-flawed, thriller about a judge (Douglas) who, after setting some dangerous criminals free, joins a group of vigilante judges who hire a hit man to do their dirty work. (Dir: Peter Hyams, 109 mins.)†

Starchaser: The Legend of Orin (1985)**½ Can the brave but untested Orin find a way to help spiritual Princess Aviana? This animated galactic adventure uses 3-D better than many live-action films. (Dir: Steven Hahn, 96 mins.)†

Star Crash (Italy, 1979)** Marjoe Gortner, Christopher Plummer, Caroline Munro. Galactic adventure is uneven, occasionally appealing. (Dir: Lewis Coates, 91 mins.)†

Starcrossed (MTV 1985)** Belinda Bauer, James Spader, Clark Johnson, Peter Kowanko. A TV rip-off of the movie *Starman*. Bauer is an alien escaping from evil forces, and she encounters a garage mechanic (Spader) who helps her in her flight. (Dir: Jeffrey Bloom, 104 mins.)

Stardumb (1990)**½ Clete Keith, Doris Anne Spyka, Craig Fleming, Joseph Scott, James Austin. First-time filmmaker finds a backer who will put up the budget for his movie on one condition—his dim-witted son is cast as the star. Sporadically amusing spoof of low-budget moviemaking. (Dir: Harrison Ellenshaw, 103 mins.)

Star Dust (1940)**½ Linda Darnell, John Payne, Roland Young, Charlotte Greenwood. Story of young hopefuls trying to break through in Hollywood is mildly entertaining. (Dir: Walter Lang, 85 mins.)

Stardust (Great Britain, 1974)*** David Essex, Adam Faith, Larry Hagman. Surprisingly good look at the selling of a pop star. The film masterfully captures the atmosphere of the recording business, and this dissection of the rise of a celebrity is compelling and provocative. (Dir: Michael Apted, 107 mins.)

Stardust Memories (1980)**½ Woody Allen, Charlotte Rampling, Jessica Harper, Marie-Christine Barrault, Tony Roberts, Daniel Stern. Woody Allen's most obviously autobiographical movie, in which he plays a director of comedies who wants to make serious films but can't get his audience to accept anything different from him. Most critics felt that Allen's Felliniesque treatment here of his fans as an assortment of grotesque idiots was a slap in the face to his public, but Allen treats himself almost as badly; the character he presents is self-absorbed and emotionally unable to deal with any of his relationships with women. (88 mins.)†

Star 80 (1983)** Mariel Hemingway, Roger Rees, Eric Roberts, Cliff Robertson. Depressing and lurid biopic. Playboy centerfold Dorothy Stratten was groomed for stardom by her possessive husband, and later murdered by him when fame began to pull her from his grasp. As Stratten's two-bit Svengali, Roberts's performance is the only reason to see this sordid film. (Dir: Bob Fosse, 102 mins.)†

Starflight: The Plane That Couldn't Land (MTV 1983)** Lee Majors, Terry Kiser, Hal Linden, Lauren Hutton, Carolyn Coates. An overlong disaster-in-the-sky film. A plane, which is touted as the fastest ever, hits a snag and is thrust into outer space. (Dir: Jerry Jameson, 154 mins.)†

Star Is Born, A (1937)***½ Fredric March, Janet Gaynor, Andy Devine, Adolphe Menjou, Lionel Stander. Here's the original version of the poignant, dramatic story about a famous Hollywood star whose popularity declines as his young actress-wife reaches super stardom. March and Gaynor are perfectly cast and keep the story from slipping into cheap sentimentality. (Dir: William Wellman, 110 mins.)†

Star Is Born, A (1954)**** Judy Garland, James Mason, Charles Bickford, Jack Carson. The clichéd Hollywood story of a husband forced into second place by his wife's career has been often told but it almost doesn't matter thanks to Judy's musical genius and a fine cast. Available in a "restored" version at 170 mins. (Dir: George Cukor, 154 mins.)†

Star Is Born, A (1976)*½ Barbra Streisand, Kris Kristofferson, Gary Busey. The third and worst film version of this tale of Hollywood heartache. Transposing the story line from the Hollywood movie world to the seventies rock world was a fundamental mistake, and the film nev-

er recovers. (Dir: Frank Pierson, 140 mins.)†

Stark (MTV 1985)*** Marilu Henner, Nicolas Surovy, Pat Corley, Seth Jaffe, Dennis Hopper. A crime drama about the rough side of Las Vegas. Surovy is a Kansas detective in Vegas trying to find out what happened to his missing sister. (Dir: Rod Holcomb, 104 mins.)†

Stark: Mirror Image (MTV 1986)** Nicolas Surovy, Michelle Phillips, Kirstie Alley, Pat Corley, Ben Murphy, Dennis Hopper. This familiar detective yarn takes the honest but tough Kansas detective back to Vegas once again. At the trial of the murderer of his ex-partner, Stark discovers his partner may have trafficked in cocaine. (Dir: Noel Nosseck, 104 mins.)

Starlift (1951)** Doris Day, Gordon MacRae, Virginia Mayo, Gene Nelson, Janice Rule, Ruth Roman. All the Warner Brothers stars get together in this one to entertain the troops. Thin plot line serves merely as a wait between acts—and the acts are hardly worth it. (Dir: Roy Del Ruth, 103 mins.)

Starlight Hotel (New Zealand, 1987)*** Peter Phelps, Greer Robson, Alice Fraser, Patrick Smyth. Moody, atmospheric drama about a man unjustly accused of a crime who hooks up with a teenage girl searching for her father in depression-era New Zealand. Breathtaking scenery and great use of trains enhance tale of kindred souls who find friendship under trying conditions. Dreadful musical score, however, almost derails the film. (Dir: Sam Pillsbury, 94 mins.)†

Starlight Slaughters—See: **Eaten Alive**

Starlost: The Beginning—See: **Beginning, The**

Star Maker, The (1939)*** Bing Crosby, Linda Ware, Louise Campbell, Ned Sparks, Laura Hope Crews, Billy Gilbert. None-too-accurate musical biography with Crosby as vaudeville producer Gus Edwards, who discovered Eddie Cantor, Sally Rand, Ray Bolger, George Jessel, and many others. Some good songs, including several by Edwards himself. (Dir: Roy del Ruth, 85 mins.)

Star Maker, The (MTV 1981)** Rock Hudson, Suzanne Pleshette, Melanie Griffith, Teri Copley, April Clough, Cathie Shirriff. Rock plays a director with a great talent for turning promising young sex symbols into stars. (Dir: Lou Antonio, 200 mins.)

Starman (1984)***½ Jeff Bridges, Karen Allen, Charles Martin Smith, Richard Jaeckel, Robert Thalen. A witty, emotionally resonant extraterrestrial fantasy, in which an alien accepts a satellite invitation to visit Planet Earth. Assuming the form of a lovely young widow's late husband, Starman forces her to drive him toward an upcoming rendezvous. Along the way, the two fall in love, as he discovers what it's like to be an "earth person." (Dir: John Carpenter, 115 mins.)†

Star of Midnight (1935)*** William Powell, Ginger Rogers, Paul Kelly, Gene Lockhart, Ralph Morgan, J. Farrell MacDonald. Entertaining comic mystery, with attorney Powell investigating the disappearance of a Broadway star, aided by flirtatious, wise-cracking fiancée Rogers. Clever, fast script and classy production, despite a fairly low budget, make this a winner. (Dir: Stephen Roberts, 90 mins.)

Stars and Bars (1988)**½ Daniel Day-Lewis, Harry Dean Stanton, Kent Broadhurst, Joan Cusack, Spalding Gray, Glenne Headly, Laurie Metcalf, Deirdre O'Connell. Mildly amusing farce about a granted English art appraiser (Lewis) who is sent to purchase a long-lost Renoir from a family of ramshackle southern eccentrics. The numerous cartoonlike "types" that are introduced prove to be little more than loose ends; it's the friendly characters (Cusack, Stanton, and O'Connell) who give the harried Mr. Lewis his best support. (Dir: Pat O'Connor, 94 mins.)†

Stars and Stripes Forever (1952)**½ Clifton Webb, Debra Paget, Robert Wagner, Ruth Hussey, Finlay Currie. Enjoyable musical having practically nothing to do with the life of John Philip Sousa. A friendly little fictional family drama is substituted for biography, but the music is authentic, rousing, and constantly well-performed. (Dir: Henry Koster, 89 mins.)

Stars Are Singing, The (1953)** Rosemary Clooney, Anna Maria Alberghetti, Lauritz Melchior. Singer shelters an escaped immigrant girl, finds she has a fine voice. (Dir: Norman Taurog, 99 mins.)

Starship (Great Britain, 1987)* John Tarrant, Donogh Rees, Deep Roy, Ralph Cotterill, Cassandra Webb. Aside from semi-parodies like the "Doctor Who" TV show, the British have no talent for sci-fi, as demonstrated by this wan *Star Wars* clone about human slaves on a mining planet who revolt against their robot guards. (Dir: Roger Christian, 98 mins.)†

Starship Invasions (Canada, 1978)** Robert Vaughn, Christopher Lee, Helen Shaver. The cast do their best with the subpar script about a UFO expert who befriends a peaceful group of aliens to stop a villainous alien captain from taking over the Earth. (Dir: Ed Hunt, 89 mins.)

Stars In My Crown (1950)**½ Joel McCrea, Ellen Drew, Dean Stockwell. Soap opera about a self-made parson and his effect on a small Southern town. (Dir: Jacques Tourneur, 89 mins.)

Starsky and Hutch (MTV 1975)**½ Paul Michael Glaser, David Soul, Antonio Fargas, Michael Lerner. Pilot for the Seventies hit series about undercover cops who face syndicate hit men. Starsky and Hutch are better rounded cop characters than usual. (Dir: Barry Shear, 72 mins.)

Star Slammer: The Escape (1986)** Ross Hagen, Sandy Brooke, Aldo Ray, John Carradine (of course). Outer space woman's prison comedy. Spotty fun, but it's hard to decide which is better: the meager special FX, the bad jokes piped in over the spaceship's PA, the warden's bust, or the mutated face of Aldo. AKA: **Prison Ship.** (Dir: Fred Olen Ray, 88 mins.)†

Stars Look Down, The (Great Britain, 1939)**** Margaret Lockwood, Michael Redgrave. Dramatic tale of the life of Welsh coal miners, the ensuing tragedy. Grimly realistic, finely directed by Carol Reed, well acted. (110 mins.)†

Star Spangled Girl (1971)*½ Sandy Duncan, Tony Roberts, Todd Susman. Disappointing film version of Neil Simon's stage comedy. A nice girl of the silent majority befriends two male editors of a radical underground newspaper in this situation non-comedy. (Dir: Jerry Paris, 92 mins.)

Star-Spangled Rhythm (1942)*** Bing Crosby, Bob Hope, Veronica Lake, Dorothy Lamour, Alan Ladd and all-star cast. Gigantic variety show is loaded with talent, but most of their ammunition is blank. (Dir: George Marshall, 99 mins.)

Starstruck (Australia, 1982)* Jo Kennedy, Ross O'Donavan, Margo Lee, Max Cullen. Engaging rock-and-roll comedy about a teenage boy who wants to make his singing cousin a superstar and bends a few rules to do it. Lighthearted film takes a few satirical jabs at the media and the tradition of Hollywood musicals. Tuneful, extremely watchable. (Dir: Gillian Armstrong, 95 mins.)†

Start Cheering (1938)**½ Jimmy Durante, Walter Connolly, Joan Perry, Charles Starrett, Broderick Crawford. Peppy college musical has a movie star returning to the campus to complete his education. Worthy for a string of enjoyable musical numbers and guest appearances, including the Three Stooges and Louis Prima. Harmless, light-minded fun. (Dir: Albert S. Rogell, 78 mins.)

Starting Over (1979)*** Burt Reynolds, Candice Bergen, Jill Clayburgh, Austin Pendleton. Engaging comedy of modern manners. Basically a love triangle, with writer Burt trying to choose between teacher Clayburgh and ex-wife Bergen, a writer of hideous pop songs. (Dir: Alan J. Pakula, 106 mins.)†

Star Trek—the Motion Picture (1979)* William Shatner, Leonard Nimoy, DeForest Kelley, James Doohan, Walter Koenig, Nichelle Nichols, George Takei, Stephen Collins, Persis Khambatta. A poor return. The expensive special effects look shoddy and the movie is far too long for the thin script. Robert Wise directs dully and mechanically. (132 mins.)†

Star Trek II: The Wrath of Khan (1982)**** William Shatner, Leonard Nimoy, DeForest Kelley, James Doohan, Walter Koenig, Nichelle Nichols, George Takei, Ricardo Montalban, Bibi Besch, Kirstie Alley, Merritt Butrick, Paul Winfield. Nicholas Meyer directs with the right blend of humor and emotion. The bare-chested Montalban makes a splendid, powerful villain, and no Trekkie will have a dry eye when Mr. Spock makes the ultimate sacrifice. (113 mins.)†

Star Trek III: The Search For Spock (1984)** William Shatner, Leonard Nimoy, DeForest Kelley, James Doohan, Walter Koenig, Nichelle Nichols, George Takei, Christopher Lloyd, Robin Curtis, Merritt Butrick, Judith Anderson, James B. Sikking, John Larroquette. Leonard Nimoy directs with Vulcan seriousness. Kirk reassembles the disbanded crew of the *Enterprise* to search the planet where Spock's body was sent. (103 mins.)†

Star Trek IV: The Voyage Home (1986)**1/2 William Shatner, Leonard Nimoy, DeForest Kelley, James Doohan, Walter Koenig, Nichelle Nichols, George Takei, Catherine Hicks, Jane Wyatt, Mark Lenard, John Schuck, Michael Berryman, Jane Weidlin. Director Leonard Nimoy goes to the opposite extreme from the self-serious *Star Trek III* with this comic adventure that finds the crew of the *Enterprise* in 1986 San Francisco, on a mission to Save the Whales! Entertaining, but too silly. (119 mins.)

Star Trek V: The Final Frontier (1989)*** William Shatner, Leonard Nimoy, DeForest Kelley, James Doohan, Walter Koenig, Nichelle Nichols, George Takei, Laurence Luckinbill, David Warner. It's Captain Kirk's turn to direct and William Shatner surprisingly turns in one of the strongest entries in the series. The *Enterprise* is taken over by Spock's half-brother, who does indeed lead them to "the Final Frontier." A splendid adventure. (108 mins.)†

Start the Revolution Without Me (1970)**1/2 Donald Sutherland, Gene Wilder, Hugh Griffith, Orson Welles. Sutherland and Wilder ham it up to the nth degree as a pair of twins who are separated at birth (one from each set), with two of the lads growing up in French aristocracy while the other pair are reared as peasants. A classic yarn of mistaken

1000

identity. (Dir: Bud Yorkin, 90 mins.)†

Star Wars (1977)***1/2 Mark Hamill, Harrison Ford, Alec Guinness, Carrie Fisher, Peter Cushing, Anthony Daniels, David Prowse, voice of James Earl Jones as Darth Vader. Zowie! A technically dazzling and enjoyable science fiction film for children of all ages. The plot is the bad guys (the galactic empire) vs. the good guys (the rebels). You'll root for the princess (Fisher) to be rescued by two Prince Charmings (Hamill and Ford). (Dir: George Lucas, 121 mins.)†

Star Witness (1931)*** Walter Huston, Chic Sale, Frances Starr, Grant Mitchell, Edward J. Nugent. Powerful crime drama of ordinary family terrorized by gangsters to keep them from testifying about a crime they witnessed. Director William Wellman manages to inject an element of humor, but it is still strong viewing. (68 mins.)

State Fair (1933)*** Will Rogers, Janet Gaynor, Lew Ayres, Sally Eilers, Norman Foster. This basis for the better-known Rodgers and Hammerstein musical version is a folksy and heartwarming study of farm folk. A family's bucolic existence is enlivened by the upcoming state fair. (Dir: Henry King, 80 mins.)

State Fair (1945)*** Jeanne Crain, Dana Andrews, Dick Haymes, Vivian Blaine, Charles Winninger, Fay Bainter, Donald Meek. A picture-perfect slice of small-town Americana. This farmland frolic boasts attractive players and Rodgers and Hammerstein's memorable score including the Oscar-winning "It Might as Well Be Spring." (Dir: Walter Lang, 100 mins.)

State Fair (1962)** Pat Boone, Ann-Margaret, Bobby Darin, Alice Faye, Tom Ewell. Third time around for this musical tale of a family attending the Iowa State Fair, and the various romantic mix-ups. Lacks sparkle. (Dir: José Ferrer, 118 mins.)

State of Grace (1990)** Sean Penn, Ed Harris, Gary Oldman, Robin Wright, John Turturro. Meandering crime film about a gang of small-time Irish-American hoodlums in Manhattan's Hell's Kitchen who can't accept the lessening of their importance and the changes being made in their neighborhood. The acting is wildly over the top, and the plot takes a wrongheaded twist a third of the way through the movie. It ends with a slow-motion tavern shoot-out that would have embarrassed Sam Peckinpah. (Dir: Phil Joanou, 134 mins.)†

State of Siege (France, 1973)*** Yves Montand, Renato Salvatori, O. E. Hasse. Piquant political drama about the kidnapping and assassination of an American "technical expert" on police methods in Uruguay; a strong indictment of American clandestine support for anti-guerrilla fascist activities in Latin America. (Dir: Costa-Gavras, 120 mins.)†

State of the Union (1948)*** Spencer Tracy, Katharine Hepburn, Angela Lansbury, Van Johnson, Adolphe Menjou. An honest businessman is persuaded to run for public office, finds his ideals in danger. Some good satire on the logistics of politics, but this wobbles between comedy and drama. Expert players keep it rolling along, though. (Dir: Frank Capra, 124 mins.)†

State of Things, The (West Germany, 1982)*** Patrick Bachau, Allen Goorwitz, Viva Auder, Paul Getty III, Roger Corman, Sam Fuller. Comically bitter look at filmmaking that was the result of director Wim Wenders's experiences making *Hammett*. Bauchau is Wenders's alter ego, a German director who has to search for his reclusive producer once his Portuguese-based science-fiction film runs out of money. The languid humor of the first half gives way to sharp comic suspense in the second half as Bauchau encounters producer Goorwitz, who's hiding from loansharks in a mobile home. (120 mins.)†

State's Attorney (1932)**** John Barrymore, Helen Twelvetrees, William Boyd, Jill Esmond. Exciting courtroom melodrama about a prominent attorney defending an old pal from the slums, now a powerful gangster, forced to change sides when he becomes district attorney. (Dir: George Archainbaud, 73 mins.)

State Secret (Great Britain, 1950)***½ Douglas Fairbanks, Jr., Glynis Johns, Jack Hawkins, Herbert Lom. Noted surgeon is tricked into aiding the head of a European police state, flees with the secret police not far behind. Excellent suspense thriller played lightly; laughs, thrills and fun. (Dir: Sidney Gilliat, 97 mins.)

Static (1986)*½ Keith Gordon, Amanda Plummer, Bob Gunton. A vacuous satirical odyssey about a man who's invented a machine that transmits pictures from Heaven. (Dir: Mark Romanek, 93 mins.)†

Stationmaster's Wife, The (West Germany, 1977)*** Kurt Raab, Elizabeth Trissenaar, Bernard Helfrich. Originally made for German television, this drama had nearly forty percent of its footage cut for American release. Set in a tiny railway-stop village in prewar Germany, the film presents a masochistic cuckold-hero, his domineering wife, and her various lovers in an atmosphere that reeks of moral decay, and a style that treats everyone with equal contempt. (Dir: Rainer Werner Fassbinder, 111 mins.)

Station Six Sahara (Great Britain-West Germany, 1963)*** Carroll Baker, Peter Van Eyck, Ian Bannen. Into a small group of men running an oil station in the Sahara comes a beautiful blonde who starts the emotions soaring. Lusty melodrama. (Dir: Seth Holt, 99 mins.)

Station West (1948)*** Dick Powell, Jane Greer, Burl Ives, Agnes Moorehead. Army officer goes undercover to trap a gang of hijackers and murderers. Good western. (Dir: Sidney Lanfield, 92 mins.)†

Statue, The (1971)** David Niven, Virna Lisi, Robert Vaughn. Prudish comedy as Miss Lisi carves a nude 18-foot statue of her Nobel Peace Prize–winning husband Niven. The catch—Niven is mad because the bottom half does not resemble him. (Dir: Ron Amateau, 88 mins.)†

Statue of Liberty, The (1986)*** A scrupulously researched documentary in which facts and figures mingle informatively with heartfelt interviews by some famous immigrants. (Dir: Ken Burns, 60 mins.)†

Stavisky (France-Italy, 1974)***½ Jean-Paul Belmondo, Charles Boyer, Anny Duperey. Director Alain Resnais's absorbing drama about corruption in France in the Thirties. Focuses on the famous Stavisky case, a financial swindle conceived by a flamboyant conman (Belmondo) and involving government officials. Production, thanks partly to costumes by Yves St. Laurent, captures the look of rich, decadent France of that time. (117 mins.)

Stay As You Are (France, 1978)** Marcello Mastroianni, Nastassia Kinski, Franciso Rabal. Marcello is an architect who picks up a nubile hitchhiker (Kinski) and begins a May-December romance. The hitch is Nastassia may be Marcello's daughter from a liaison of twenty years earlier. (Dir: Alberto Lattuada, 95 mins.)†

Stay Awake, The (South Africa, 1989)* Shirley Jane Harris, Tanya Gordon, Jayne Hutton, Heath Potter. Despite the title, you'll be dozing halfway through the first reel of this spooker about girls at a slumber party terrorized by a monstrous demon. (Dir: John Bernard, 88 mins.)†

Stay Away, Joe (1968)*½ Elvis Presley, Joan Blondell, Burgess Meredith, Katy Jurado. Stay away, audience. There's trouble afoot for brave injun brave Elvis in this clichéd treatment of our native Americans. (Dir: Peter Tewksbury, 102 mins.)†

Stay Hungry (1976)**½ Jeff Bridges, Sally Field, Arnold Schwarzenegger, R. G. Armstrong, Robert Englund. Eccentric, unfocused comedy-drama about a rich young southerner (Bridges) who takes up with the assorted crazies at a local gym. Writer/director Bob Rafelson (*Five Easy Pieces*) raises more themes than he can develop in the space of one film, but it's amusing nonetheless. (103 mins.)†

Staying Alive (1983)** John Travolta, Cynthia Rhodes, Finola Hughes, Steve Inwood, Julie Bovasso. Disappointing sequel to *Saturday Night Fever*. It's six years later and our determined Tony has moved from Brooklyn to Manhattan to conquer Broadway. John's "travoltage" is intact, but slightly diminished by director Sylvester Stallone's need to film dance as if it were a contact sport. (96 mins.)†

Staying Together (1989)*½ Tim Quill, Dermot Mulroney, Sean Astin, Melinda Dillon, Daphne Zuniga, Stockard Channing, Levon Helm, Dinah Manoff. Generally well acted but uninvolving and unbelievable look at three young brothers in a small town faced with critical changes in their lives. Some of the dialogue is howlingly bad, and the clumsy amputation of several prominent subplots prior to release leaves numerous dangling threads. (Dir: Lee Grant, 91 mins.)†

St. Benny the Dip (1951)*** Dick Haymes, Nina Foch, Roland Young, Freddie Bartholomew. Three con men hide from the police in a mission, where they are duly reformed. Rather pleasant comedy-drama, nice entertainment. (Dir: Edgar G. Ulmer, 81 mins.)†

Steagle, The (1971)**½ Richard Benjamin, Cloris Leachman, Chill Wills, Susan Tyrrell. Liberal college professor Benjamin is so entangled with politics that news of the Cuban missile crisis sends him daydreaming. He acts out those daydreams until the Russians withdraw. Confused and unwieldy. (Dir: Paul Sylbert, 90 mins.)†

Stealing Heaven (Great Britain, 1988)*** Derek de Lint, Kim Thomson, Denholm Elliott. The story of Abelard and Heloise, the 12th-century lovers whose romance was doomed by influence of church and commerce, is strikingly rendered in this handsome, intelligent production filmed in Yugoslavia. A 115-minute "director's cut" is available on video. (Dir: Clive Donner, 108 mins.)†

Stealing Home (1988)* Mark Harmon, William McNamara, Jodie Foster, Blair Brown, John Shea, Harold Ramis. This feeble attempt at a "coming of age" period piece (à la *Summer of '42*) has got what has to be the most confused screenplay in recent memory. Harmon is an ex-baseball player who reminisces about the baby-sitter (Foster) who changed his life. (Dirs: Steven Kampmann, Will Aldis, 98 mins.)†

Steal the Sky (MCTV 1988)**½ Mariel Hemingway, Ben Cross, Sasson Gabai, Nicholas Surovy. Predictable espionage story about an American spy working for the Israelis (Hemingway) and a married Iraqi pilot (Cross). Hemingway is

miscast, and Cross tries too hard, but the scenery is quite picturesque. (Dir: John Hancock, 120 mins.)

Steamboat Bill Jr. (1928)**** Buster Keaton, Ernest Torrence, Marion Byron. Keaton, a recent Yale graduate, comes home after many years to find his father, an irascible Mississippi riverboat captain, in deep trouble with a competing big company. Buster saves the day, though he must brave jail and a great hurricane to do it. One of the best comedies ever made. (Dir: Charles F. Reisner, 70 mins.)†

Steamboat 'Round the Bend (1935)** Will Rogers, Anne Shirley, Irvin S. Cobb. Will Rogers's last film reflects little of his celebrated humor. His nephew stands trial for murder while Rogers searches for that key witness to clear his relative. (Dir: John Ford, 90 mins.)

Steaming (Great Britain, 1985)** Vanessa Redgrave, Sarah Miles, Diana Dors, Patti Love, Brenda Bruce. Fine performances can't disguise the sterility of this stage piece that was a lot steamier onstage. On-screen, the ladies bare their souls as they lower their bath towels, but the film lacks both shock value and dramatic crescendo. (Dir: Joseph Losey, 95 mins.)†

Steel (1979)*½ Lee Majors, Jennifer O'Neill, Art Carney, George Kennedy, Harris Yulin. Labor and management clash on a construction site in this action-packed yarn full of macho heroics and spectacular explosions. (Dir: Steven Carver, 101 mins.)†

Steel Claw, The (1961)**½ George Montgomery, Charito Luna. Marine about to be discharged because of the loss of a hand organizes guerrillas when the Japanese invade the Philippines. (Dir: George Montgomery, 96 mins.)†

Steel Cowboy (MTV 1978)** James Brolin, Rip Torn, Strother Martin, Jennifer Warren. A trucker about to go broke hauls stolen cattle for a black market bigwig, and manages to outsmart the opposition. (Dir: Harvey Laidman, 104 mins.)†

Steel Dawn (1987)* Patrick Swayze, Lisa Niemi, Christopher Neame, Anthony Zerbe. *The Road Warrior* without high-speed chases. Swayze plays a futuristic warrior who journeys to a camp run by Niemi to protect it against a man who murdered his *sensei*. (Dir: Lance Hool, 102 mins.)

Steele Justice (1987)** Martin Kove, Sela Ward, Robert Kim, Soon-Teck Oh. Overwrought flick about Viet vet with problems readjusting to civilian life. He has no problems however waging a one-man war against the Vietnam mafia. (Dir: Robert Boris, 95 mins.)†

Steel Fist, The (1952)** Roddy McDowall, Kristine Miller. Good try at serious drama about a U.S. student trapped in an Iron Curtain country but it doesn't come off. (Dir: Wesley Barry, 73 mins.)

Steel Helmet, The (1951)***½ Gene Evans, Robert Hutton. It's nip-and-tuck with the Reds for a U.N. platoon in the early days of Korea. Packs quite a punch; one of the better films of its type. (Dir: Samuel Fuller, 84 mins.)

Steel Magnolias (1989)*½ Sally Field, Shirley MacLaine, Julia Roberts, Dolly Parton, Darryl Hannah, Olympia Dukakis, Tom Skerrit, Sam Shepard, Kevin J. O'Connor, Dylan McDermott, Bill McCutcheon. Clichéd group of squabbling Southern women are brought together by the angel of death. Overwrought, overacted film captures none of the charm or wit of the original, popular play. (Dir: Herbert Ross, 118 mins.)†

Steel Town (1952)** Ann Sheridan, John Lund, Howard Duff, William Harrigan, Chick Chandler, Nancy Kulp. Usual drama about two guys vying for the same girl and a top spot in a large steel mill. (Dir: George Sherman, 85 mins.)

Steel Trap, The (1952)*** Joseph Cotten, Teresa Wright. A banker steals five hundred thousand dollars on a Friday afternoon, and frantically tries to return it by Monday. Suspenseful melodrama. (Dir: Andrew L. Stone, 85 mins.)

Steelyard Blues (1973)** Jane Fonda, Donald Sutherland, Peter Boyle. Three nonconformists band together to steal an electrical circuit which will enable them to fly away. Tolerance for prank-sterism is required. (Dir: Alan Myerson, 93 mins.)†

Stella (1950)*** Ann Sheridan, Victor Mature, David Wayne, Frank Fontaine. An underrated black comedy with the delicious Sheridan leading an expert troupe through a frantic farce involving a corpse that won't stay put. (Dir: Claude Binyon, 83 mins.)

Stella (1990)*½ Bette Midler, John Goodman, Trini Alvardo, Stephen Collins, Marsha Mason, Eileen Brennan, Ben Stiller. Third, and worst, version of Olive Higgins Prouty's classic sob story about a poor mother who gives up her daughter so she can enjoy the good things in life. Nothing works in this insipid remake. (Dir: John Erman, 106 mins.)†

Stella Dallas (1925)**½ Belle Bennett, Ronald Colman, Alice Joyce, Jean Hersholt, Douglas Fairbanks, Jr. Bennett plays the vulgar woman who gives up her daughter so the kid can have the advantages of an upbringing by a wealthy family. (Dir: Henry King, 112 mins.)

Stella Dallas (1937)**** Barbara Stanwyck, John Boles, Ann Shirley, Barbara O'Neil, Alan Hale, Tim Holt, Marjorie Main. The ultimate Mother-Love weepie in which coarse-grained but selfless Stella vanishes from her daughter Laurel's life to ensure the girl's happiness and upward mobility. Stanwyck's portrayal is a stunning mixture of vulgarity and sensitivity; her climactic scene as she watches her daughter's wedding from out on a rain-soaked sidewalk is a transcendent piece of screen acting. Remade in 1990 as *Stella*. (Dir: King Vidor, 106 mins.)†

Stella Maris (1918)**** Mary Pickford, Conway Tearle, Camille Ankewich, Herbert Standing. One of Pickford's greatest films; she plays two roles: a wealthy, sheltered invalid, and the wizened, plain little maid who adores her and takes drastic steps to protect her. A true classic. (Dir: Marshall Neilan, 65 mins.)†

St. Elmo's Fire (1985)* Emilio Estevez, Rob Lowe, Ally Sheedy, Judd Nelson, Andrew McCarthy, Demi Moore, Mare Winningham. A young adults' *Big Chill* with a group of friends who have just graduated college figuring out what to do with the rest of their lives. Abrasive tripe, with a lot of fine actors wasted. (Dir: Joel Schumacher, 110 mins.)†

Step Across the Border (Germany-Switzerland, 1990)***½ Extraordinary documentary examining the contemporary avant-garde composer Fred Frith. Shot in cities in the U.S., Europe, and Japan while Frith was touring, the film includes appearances by Robert Frank, Jolia Judge, John Zorn, Ted Milton, and Jonas Mekas. The music and black-and-white cinematography are mesmerizing. (Dirs: Nicolas Humbert, Werner Penzel, 91 mins.)

Step Down to Terror (1959)** Colleen Miller, Charles Drake, Rod Taylor, Jocelyn Brando. So-so remake of *Shadow of a Doubt*—son returns home to his family, is eventually found to be a psychotic killer. Just fair suspense melodrama. (Dir: Harry Keller, 76 mins.)

Stepfather, The (1987)***½ Terry O'Quinn, Jill Schoelen, Shelley Hack. Solid, scary horror-suspense thriller, written by Donald Westlake, about a man who moves into new towns, marries into fatherless families, and tries to set up the ideal household with them . . . only to go crazy and brutally kill them later on. In his lead debut, character actor O'Quinn is chilling and heads a fine cast. (Dir: Joseph Ruben, 89 mins.)†

Stepfather II, The: Make Room for Daddy (1989)* Terry O'Quinn, Meg Foster, Caroline Williams, Jonathan Brandis, Mitchell Laurance. Unnecessary sequel. Without original director or writer, O'Quinn is saddled with stupid "campy" dialogue. (Dir: Jeff Burr, 86 mins.)†

Stepford Children, The (MTV 1987)**½

1003

Barbara Eden, Don Murray, Randall Batinkoff, Tammy Lauren, Richard Anderson, Dick Butkus, James Coco, Ken Swofford. Lacking the mystery of what's happening to the Stepfordians, there's no reason to watch this sequel to *Revenge of the Stepford Wives*. (Dir: Alan Levi, 104 mins.)

Stepford Wives, The (1975)**½ Katharine Ross, Paula Prentiss, Tina Louise, Patrick O'Neal, Nanette Newman. Ira Levin's novel about a Connecticut suburb in which the housewife brigade consists of women who love to do housework, satisfy their husbands in every way, and are absolute models of domesticity, comes to the screen with a reasonable amount of chills and an added dollop of satire. Sequel: *Revenge of The Stepford Wives*. (Dir: Bryan Forbes, 115 mins.)†

Stephen King's Silver Bullet (1985)**½ Gary Busey, Everett McGill, Corey Haim, Megan Follows. A commendable attempt to bring some depth to a conventional werewolf flick by making the movie a chiller as well as a valentine to the small, idyllic town terrified. The attention paid to characterizations and local color is commendable, but the debits are numerous. AKA: **Silver Bullet**. (Dir: Daniel Attias, 95 mins.)†

Step Lively (1944)*** Frank Sinatra, George Murphy, Gloria DeHaven. Fast-thinking theatrical producer gets his show on despite financial problems. Lively, enjoyable musical. Remake of *Room Service*. (Dir: Tim Whelan, 88 mins.)

Step Out of Line, A (MTV 1971)*** Peter Falk, Peter Lawford, Vic Morrow, Jo Ann Pflug. Amateurs carry out the robbery of a San Francisco money exchange company in exciting fashion, goofing at crucial moments. (Dir: Bernard McEveety, 100 mins.)

Steppenwolf (U.S.-Switzerland, 1974)** Max von Sydow, Dominique Sanda, Pierre Clementi, Carla Romanelli. Herman Hesse's novel was not an easy subject for filming. The director never finds an appropriate visual equivalent for Hesse's theme of the irrational vs. the rational spirit of mankind. (Dir: Fred Haines, 105 mins.)†

Stereo (Canada, 1969)**½ Ron Mlodzik, Jack Messinger, Iain Ewing, Clara Mayer. Director David Cronenberg's first film, made when he was a student on a budget of $3,500, is a sci-fi piece set at the ''Canadian Institute of Erotic Inquiry'' where subjects' brains are fitted with telepathic devices. Extremely dry, emotionless, technocratic film will be of interest to Cronenberg completists only. (63 mins.)

Sterile Cuckoo, The (1969)***½ Liza Minnelli, Wendell Burton. Touching romance

of Pookie Adams (Minnelli), a kook who insists upon calling all those who won't participate in her world ''weirdos,'' and the innocent straight (Burton) she captivates. Minnelli is quite remarkable in her heartbreaking portrayal of a neurotic college girl creating obvious games to shut out the world. (Dir: Alan J. Pakula, 107 mins.)

Stevie (1978)***½ Glenda Jackson, Trevor Howard, Mona Washbourne. With sensitivity and compassion, Jackson incarnates Stevie Smith, a British poet who wrote profound poetry while living a perfectly ordinary suburban life. Composed almost entirely of monologues delivered by Jackson, the film conveys a natural intimacy that other films try too hard to achieve. An unforgettable tour-de-force by a gifted actress. (Dir: Robert Enders, 102 mins.)

Stewardess School (1986)* Brett Cullen, Mary Cadorette, Sandahl Bergman, Donald Most, Judy Landers, Sherman Hemsley. Yet another *Policy Academy* rip-off, this time set at a training school for stewardesses. The attempts at crude humor are too limp to be outrageous. (Dir: Ken Blancato, 84 mins.)†

St. Helens (1981)** Art Carney, David Huffman, Cassie Yates, Ron O'Neal, Bill McKinney, Albert Salmi. With volcano Mt. St. Helens about to erupt, an old man disregards pleas to desert his threatened home. (Dir: Ernest Pintoff, 90 mins.)†

Stick (1985)*½ Burt Reynolds, George Segal, Candice Bergen, Charles Durning, Castulo Guerra. Burt has taken Elmore Leonard's novel and broken its back by trying to bend it into a star vehicle. After his pal is rubbed out, Burt, playing an ex-con, rubs a crime boss the wrong way and initiates a one-man war against the mob. (Dir: Burt Reynolds, 109 mins.)†

Stick-Up, The (Great Britain, 1977)*½ David Soul, Pamela McMyler, Johnny Wade, Michael Balfour. In depression-era England, an American (Soul) traveling to the site of a robbery picks up a hitchhiking waitress, who lands him in all sort of trouble. Lackluster comic adventure. AKA: **Mud**. (Dir: Jeffrey Bloom, 100 mins.)†

Sticky Fingers (1988)* Helen Slater, Melanie Mayron, Danitra Vance, Eileen Brennan, Carol Kane. Dismal screwball comedy that places an assortment of appealing performers in predictable situations. Slater and Mayron play down-and-out musicians who are asked to mind a bag filled with money; the resulting spending spree, and the petty squabbles transform this into quite a downer. (Dir: Catlin Adams, 97 mins.)†

Stigma (1972)* Philip M. Thomas, Harlan Poe, Josie Johnson. A twenty-three-year-old Philip Michael Thomas is not sufficient reason to suffer through this potboiler about a syphilis epidemic, though his mediocre performance as a doctor is easily the best thing about it. Close-up photos of advanced syphilis sufferers are not for the squeamish. (Dir: David E. Durston, 93 mins.)†

Stiletto (1969)** Alex Cord, Britt Ekland, Barbara McNair. A disjointed pop movie based on the Harold Robbins novel. Cord is a jet-setter with a posh yacht, beautiful women at his side (Ekland and McNair), and killers out to get him. (Dir: Bernard Kowalski, 108 mins.)†

Still Crazy Like a Fox (MTV 1987)**½ Jack Warden, John Rubinstein, Penny Peyser, Robbie Kiger, Graham Chapman. Enjoyable follow-up to the comedy-action series about the nonconformist detective who drags his straight-laced lawyer-son into his cases. (Dir: Paul Krasny, 104 mins.)

Still of the Night (1982)**½ Roy Scheider, Meryl Streep, Jessica Tandy, Sara Botsford. A psychiatrist encounters a beautiful, elusive blonde who may have murdered one of his patients in this entertaining but resolutely formulaic homage to Hitchcock. Director Robert Benton has come up with a few new twists for a very familiar genre, but the film feels cramped and mechanical, right down to its predictable denouement. (91 mins.)†

Still the Beaver (MTV 1983)** Jerry Mathers, Barbara Billingsley, Ken Osmond, Richard Deacon, Tony Dow. If you were weaned on Beaver Cleaver and his family and friends, tune in this update of the Cleaver clan in Mayfield. It's twenty years later and Beaver is beginning to look a little jowly, as he deals with two sons and a wife who wants a divorce. (Dir: Steven Hilliard Stern, 104 mins.)

Stillwatch (MTV 1987)*½ Lynda Carter, Angie Dickinson, Don Murray, Louise Latham, Stuart Whitman. Pure hokum. TV reporter Carter delves into the life of Senator Dickinson. If you buy that, you'll buy anything—such as some ghostly nonsense in Lynda's house, and the warnings from a next-door psychic. (Dir: Rod Holcomb, 104 mins.)

Sting, The (1973)***½ Paul Newman, Robert Redford, Robert Shaw. A marvelously entertaining caper about two deft con men (Newman and Redford) operating in Chicago circa '36. Director George Roy Hill gives the film a fast pace and a glittering visual style. Great wrap-up scene as Newman and Redford swindle Shaw out of a big bundle in one of the most inventive schemes ever depicted on screen. Winner of seven Academy Awards. (129 mins.)†

Sting II, The (1983)** Jackie Gleason, Mac Davis, Teri Garr, Oliver Reed. Gleason and Davis generate zero electricity together as two con men who become the target of a revenge scheme. For self-protection they devise a con in which Davis poses as a heavyweight contender. (Dir: Jeremy Paul Kagan, 102 mins.)†

Stingray (1978)** Christopher Mitchum, Sherry Jackson, Les Lannom. Weird comedy with lots of action and death, as Mitchum and Lannom are pursued by a murderous gang trying to grab the cache of heroin hidden in their car. (Dir: Richard Taylor, 99 mins.)†

Stingray (MTV 1986)** Nick Mancuso, Susan Blakely, Robyn Douglass, Gregory Sierra, Michael Fairman. Pilot film about a stranger who appears during times of trouble in his Corvette Stingray. In this story, he helps a woman involved with the prosecution of mobsters. (Dir: Richard Colla, 104 mins.)

Stir Crazy (1980)** Richard Pryor, Gene Wilder, Georg Stanford Brown, JoBeth Williams, Craig T. Nelson. Uneven comedy of two inept thieves sent to the Big House. The writing and direction are not inspired, but the comic teamwork of Pryor and Wilder is. (Dir: Sidney Poitier, 111 mins.)†

St. Ives (1976)** Charles Bronson, Jacqueline Bisset, Maximilian Schell, John Houseman. Bronson is drawn into a murder by scheming Houseman and Bisset. (Dir: J. Lee Thompson, 98 mins.)†

St. Louis Blues (1939)**½ Dorothy Lamour, Lloyd Nolan, Tito Guizar, Jerome Cowan, Jessie Ralph, William Frawley. Light musical vehicle for sarong-clad Lamour is little more than a framework for lots of agreeable numbers, including the title tune by W. C. Handy and several songs by Frank Loesser and Burton Lane. (Dir: Raoul Walsh, 92 mins.)

St. Louis Blues (1958)**½ Nat Cole, Eartha Kitt, Pearl Bailey, Cab Calloway, Mahalia Jackson, Ruby Dee. The music's everything in this life story of composer W. C. Handy. Story line never really gets going, but the innumerable tunes are superbly performed by Cole, Kitt, and others. (Dir: Allen Reisner, 94 mins.)

St. Louis Kid (1934)*** James Cagney, Patricia Ellis, Allen Jenkins, Robert Barrat, Hobart Cavanaugh. Tough, topical melodrama about a truck driver tangling with strikers and strike-breakers, falsely accused of murdering a labor activist. Slam-bang action, a sharp script, and a vital performance by Cagney. (Dir: Ray Enright, 67 mins.)

St. Martin's Lane—See: Sidewalks of London

Stolen Face, A (Great Britain, 1952)**½ Paul Henreid, Lizabeth Scott, Andre

Morell. Unlikely tale of plastic surgeon Henried altering the face of a prisoner to make her just like the woman who spurned him. Intriguing but rather creepy. (Dir: Terence Fisher, 72 mins.)

Stolen Heaven (1938)**½ Gene Raymond, Olympe Bradna, Glenda Farrell, Lewis Stone. Engaging musical about a pair of jewel thieves who masquerade as fans of a retired musician and hide out in his home, returning his hospitality by helping him make a comeback. (Dir: Andrew L. Stone, 88 mins.)

Stolen Hours (Great Britain, 1963)** Susan Hayward, Michael Craig, Diane Baker. Poor remake of Bette Davis's *Dark Victory* has Hayward as the darling of the international set until she takes ill. (Dir: Daniel Petrie, 97 mins.)

Stolen Kisses (France, 1968)*** Jean-Pierre Léaud, Delphine Seyrig, Michel Lonsdale, Claude Jade. The third film in the Antoine Doinel story is a charming comedy-drama. In this one, our hapless hero is discharged from the army and rebuffed by his girlfriend but manages to score with the boss's wife. (Dir: François Truffaut, 90 mins.)†

Stolen Life, A (1946)*** Bette Davis, Glenn Ford, Dane Clark, Walter Brennan, Charles Ruggles, Bruce Bennett. Bette has a fine time playing twins who are in love with the same man. Then one is killed in an accident and the other takes her place. Farfetched, but fun to watch. (Dir: Curtis Bernhardt, 107 mins.)†

Stolen: One Husband (MTV 1990)** Valerie Harper, Elliott Gould, Brenda Bakke, Brenda Vaccaro, Bruce Davison, Valentina Quinn. Ordinary marital comedy. Gould gets the seven-year-itch eighteen years late, on his and Harper's twenty-fifth wedding anniversary. (Dir: Catlin Adams, 96 mins.)

Stone (MTV 1979)**½ Dennis Weaver, Vic Morrow, Roy Thinnes. Pilot film stars Weaver as Stone, a homicide detective turned famous author. He must track down a mad killer who's following the murder scheme laid out in his book. (Dir: Corey Allen, 104 mins.)

Stone Boy, The (1984)** Robert Duvall, Glenn Close, Frederic Forrest, Jason Presson, Cindy Fisher, Wilford Brimley. A teenage boy is shot accidentally by his younger brother who adored him. Stunned, the young boy is unable to demonstrate his grief; his family mistakenly perceives this as a lack of feeling. (Dir: Chris Cain, 93 mins.)†

Stone Cold (1991)*½ Brian Bosworth, Lance Henriksen, William Forsythe, Arabella Holzbog, Sam McMurray, Richard Gant. Formulaic action film with newcomer Bosworth playing a cop who infiltrates a motorcycle gang. Clichés about bikers contrast with a great per-

formance by Henriksen as the villain, and some exceptional shoot-outs. The Boz doesn't embarrass himself. (Dir: Craig R. Baxley, 91 mins.)†

Stone Cold Dead (Canada, 1980)* Richard Crenna, Paul Williams, Linda Sorenson. A dull crime thriller with detective Crenna battling crime lord Williams. Guaranteed to leave you stone cold. (Dir: George Mendeluk, 97 mins.)

Stone Fox (MTV 1987)**½ Buddy Ebsen, Joey Cramer, Belinda Montgomery. An orphan enters a dog-sled race to save his ailing Granddaddy's farm, and the boy is up against an Indian—Stone Fox—who never loses. Predictable ending. (Dir: Harvey Hart, 104 mins.)

Stone Killer, The (1973)**½ Charles Bronson, Martin Balsam, Ralph Waite, Norman Fell. Violent crime film. Bronson plays a police officer, who stops at nothing to track down the plans of a crazed underworld figure out for revenge for the gangland assassinations of his cronies in 1931. (Dir: Michael Winner, 97 mins.)†

Stone Pillow (MTV 1985)*½ Lucille Ball, Daphne Zuniga, William Converse-Roberts. Lucille divests herself of her carrot-orange hair, in this lambrain tale of a feisty bag lady who shows a namby-pamby social worker how to survive on the streets. (Dir: George Shaefer, 104 mins.)

Stones for Ibarra (MTV 1988)**½ Glenn Close, Keith Carradine, Alfonso Arau. Touching tale about a married couple who move to Mexico to reopen an inherited copper mine, a dream shattered by the discovery that the husband has leukemia. Above average television fare. (Dir: Jack Gold, 96 mins.)

Stonestreet (MTV 1977)* Barbara Eden, Joan Hackett, Richard Basehart. As sleuth Lt. Stonestreet, Eden is miscast digging for clues, leading to a cheap hoodlum. Eden should have kept this pilot in her "I Dream of Jeannie" bottle. (Dir: Russ Mayberry, 78 mins.)

Stoning in Fulham County, A (MTV 1988)**½ Ken Olin, Jill Eikenberry, Ron Perlman. Predictable drama about prejudice works due to the earnestness of the cast. The story centers around the difficult ties in an Amish community when local teen bullies harass an Amish family and accidentally kill a baby. (Dir: Larry Elikann, 96 mins.)

Stooge, The (1952)** Dean Martin, Jerry Lewis, Polly Bergen. Singer uses a song plugger in his act, treats him badly—then flops when the stooge leaves him. No great shakes. (Dir: Norman Taurog, 100 mins.)

Stoogemania (1985)* Josh Mostel, Melanie Chartoff, Sid Caesar, Victoria Jackson. Mostel is so obsessed with the Three

Stooges that he envisions them everywhere in the form of old Stooges clips. Even rabid Stooge fans, the only conceivable audience for this, will be disappointed. (Dir: Chuck Workman, 83 mins.) †

Stoolie, The (1974)**½ Jackie Mason, Dan Frazer, Marcia Jean Kurtz. Genial, sentimental treatment of a police informer who runs off to Miami Beach with $7,500 lent by the police department of N.Y. A touching love story, but laughable underworld tale. (Dir: John Avildsen, 90 mins.)

Stop at Nothing (MCTV 1991)*** Veronica Hamel, Lindsay Frost, David Ackroyd, Annabella Price. Briskly paced, gripping drama about child abuse and the unjust legalities found in the system. Hamel plays a dedicated and driven woman, working with an underground railroad system to protect a little girl from the sexual molestations of her father. (Dir: Chris Thomson, 96 mins.) †

Stop! Look! and Laugh! (1960)** The Three Stooges, Paul Winchell. Half old footage of The Three Stooges comedies and half new stuff featuring Paul Winchell and his dummy Jerry Mahoney. (Dir: Jules White, 78 mins.)

Stop Making Sense (1984)***½ The Talking Heads. Riveting rock concert film that eschews the traditional approach to this sort of material (laser shows, shots of screaming fans, etc.) by focusing on the Talking Heads's eccentric and entertaining stage work, led by David Byrne. Video version contains two extra performances. (Dir: Jonathan Demme, 88 mins.) †

Stop Me Before I Kill (Great Britain, 1961)**½ Claude Dauphin, Diane Cilento, Ronald Lewis. After a crash an auto racer recovers physically but finds himself trying to murder his wife. Fairly entertaining melodrama. (Dir: Val Guest, 108 mins.)

Stopover Tokyo (1957)** Robert Wagner, Joan Collins, Edmond O'Brien. The heroes of this spy thriller manage to survive against extreme odds; show how brave they are; and have beautiful women wish they would give up being Intelligence Agents and settle down. (Dir: Richard L. Breen, 100 mins.) †

Stop the World, I Want to Get Off (Great Britain, 1966)**½ Tony Tanner, Millicent Martin. This literal screen version of the successful Broadway and London musical hit becomes boring, although there are some standout songs including "What Kind of Fool Am I?". (Dir: Philip Saville, 98 mins.)

Stop Train 349 (France-Italy-West Germany, 1964)** Sean Flynn, José Ferrer, Nicole Courcel, Jess Hahn. Young U.S. lieutenant causes an international incident when he refuses to hand over a defector who has sneaked aboard a train headed from East Germany to Frankfurt. Sluggish pacing. (Dir: Rolf Haedrich, 95 mins.)

Stop, You're Killing Me (1952)** Broderick Crawford, Claire Trevor, Virginia Gibson, Bill Hayes. This remake of *A Slight Case of Murder*, about a big time beer baron and his cronies, just doesn't come off. (Dir: Roy Del Ruth, 86 mins.)

Stork Club, The (1945)**½ Barry Fitzgerald, Betty Hutton. Hatcheck girl befriends penniless bum who is, naturally, a billionaire. Silly fable is saved by some nice performances. (Dir: Hal Walker, 98 mins.)

Storm, The (1938)**½ Charles Bickford, Barton MacLane, Preston Foster, Tom Brown, Nan Grey, Andy Devine. A rough, hard-living seaman tries to keep his young brother from following in his footsteps, while battling with his autocratic captain. Action-packed adventure, strongly acted. (Dir: Harold Young, 75 mins.)

Storm (Canada, 1988)*** David Palfy, Stan Kane, Lawrence Elion. College students playing a survival game in the woods find themselves in the real thing when an elderly trio who killed a man there 40 years earlier return for the loot they buried. Terrific finale. (Dir: David Winning, 110 mins.)

Storm and Sorrow (MCTV 1991)*** Lori Singer, Todd Allen, Steven Anderson, Agnes Banfalvy, Marcia Cross. Engrossing true-life story of rock climber Molly Higgins (Singer) who joined an international mountain-climbing expedition in the U.S.S.R. in 1974, which ended in tragedy. She wasn't prepared for the earthquakes, avalanches, and a blizzard of unmerciful fury that took the lives of members of both the U.S. and U.S.S.R. teams. (Dir: Richard Colla, 96 mins.) †

Storm at Daybreak (1933)**½ Kay Francis, Nils Asther, Walter Huston, Phillips Holmes, Eugene Pallette, Jean Parker. Glamorous soap opera set in Serbia at the start of WWI, with Francis as the wife of mayor Huston, falling in love with Hungarian officer Asther. Unusual location adds interest to this otherwise underwritten tale. (Dir: Richard Boleslavsky, 68 mins.)

Storm Center (1956)**½ Bette Davis, Brian Keith, Kim Hunter. Small-town librarian is fired when she refuses to remove a book accused of Communist tendencies from the shelves. Made at the height of popular reaction to McCarthy hysteria, the film trades on liberal impulses in lieu of competent filmmaking. (Dir: Daniel Taradash, 85 mins.)

Storm Fear (1955)**½ Cornel Wilde, Jean Wallace, Dan Duryea. Wounded bank rob ber shows up at his brother's house to seek shelter. Interesting drama, moves a bit too slowly but is well acted. (Dir: Cornel Wilde, 88 mins.)

Storm in a Teacup (Great Britain, 1937)*** Vivien Leigh, Rex Harrison. Candidate for election in a Scottish town is hurt by an accident with a dog, that is played upon by a young reporter into a national incident. Clever, amusing comedy. (Dirs: Victor Saville, Ian Dalrymple, 86 mins.)†

Stormin' Home (MTV 1985)*½ Gil Gerard, Lisa Blount, Emily Moultrie, John Pleshette. A 36-year-old motorcross racer is forced to grow up, but not before he has one more chance to win the big race. (Dir: Jerry Jameson, 95 mins.)

Storm over Lisbon (1944)**½ Vera Hruba Ralston, Richard Arlen, Erich von Stroheim, Robert Livingston, Otto Kruger, Eduardo Cianelli. Conventional thriller, with von Stroheim stealing everything that's not nailed down as the owner of a Portugese nightclub who's really selling secrets to the Nazis. (Dir: George Sherman, 86 mins.)

Storm Over the Nile (Great Britain, 1955)**½ Anthony Steel, Laurence Harvey, James Robertson Justice, Mary Ure. Remake of *Four Feathers* is reasonably exciting. Englishman who resigns his Army commission goes to the Sudan to prove he is not a coward. (Dirs: Terence Young, Zoltan Korda, 107 mins.)

Storm Warning (1951)**½ Ginger Rogers, Ronald Reagan, Doris Day, Steve Cochran. A wildly improbable tale of a model who visits her mousy sister in the Deep South and ends up in deep trouble when she witnesses a KKK slaying involving her cretinous brother-in-law. If you forget its attempt at message drama, this is an enjoyable sleazy melodrama, with Reagan as the Voice of Reason. (Dir: Stuart Heisler, 93 mins.)

Storm Within, The (France, 1948)***½ Jean Marais, Yvonne De Bray, Marcel André, Gabrielle Dorziat. A mother won't accept that her handsome son is growing up, especially when he reveals his love for a beautiful young woman—with whom the boy's father is having an affair. Director Jean Cocteau's expressive use of close-ups and the gorgeous black-and-white images add dimension to this powerful film. AKA: **Les Parents Terribles.** (98 mins.)

Stormy Monday (Great Britain, 1988)*** Melanie Griffith, Tommy Lee Jones, Sting, Sean Bean. A slick mixture of crime and romance set during "America week" in the British town of Newcastle. Griffith and Bean are lovers who both aspire to something better than their present lot; Jones and Sting are their wealthy and influential employers. Solid performances by the four leads. (Dir: Mike Figgis, 93 mins.)†

Stormy Weather (1943)*** Lena Horne, 1008

Bill Robinson, Katherine Dunham, Fats Waller, Dooley Wilson, the Nicholas Brothers, Cab Calloway. Wonderful musical numbers overcome silliness of backstage plot in this tuneful all-black production. Horne is mesmerizing singing the title song, and Waller's "Ain't Misbehavin'" is a show-stopper. (Dir: Andrew L. Stone, 77 mins.)†

Story of Adele H., The (France, 1975)**** Isabelle Adjani, Bruce Robinson, Sylvia Marriott. Mesmerizing film that captures the essential irony of romantic obsession. Displaced from her father's affection by the memory of her drowned sister, Adele, the daughter of Victor Hugo, develops an overriding passion for a British lieutenant who has rejected her. That rejection, or her essentially selfish passion, mentally unbalances Adele, who lives out her years within the confines of her delusion. Oscar-nominated Adjani is unforgettable. (Dir: Francois Truffaut, 97 mins.)†

Story of Alexander Graham Bell, The (1939)***½ Don Ameche, Loretta Young, Henry Fonda. Warm, moving story of the man who gave us the telephone. The ending is a bit ridiculous but most of the film, which traces Bell's early disappointments and failures, is top entertainment. (Dir: Irving Pichel, 97 mins.)†

Story of a Love Affair (Italy, 1950)*** Lucia Rose, Massimo Girotti, Gino Rossi, Ferdinando Sarmi, Marika Rowsy. A cheating wife and her lover contemplate killing her husband, but he dies first, condemning them to live with the guilt of their intended act. Director Michaelangelo Antonioni's first feature reveals his detached style and talent for camera movement. (96 mins.)

Story of a Marriage, The (1987)**½ William Converse-Roberts, Hallie Foote, Matthew Broderick, Steven Hill. Two films based on plays by Horton Foote—*1918* and *On Valentine's Day*—are adapted into a single unified story which also employs about an hour of new footage shot for television. See separate entries for **1918 and On Valentine's Day.** (Dir: Ken Harrison, 240 mins.)

Story of a Three Day Pass, The (France, 1968)***½ Harry Baird, Nicole Berger, Pierre Doris. Low-budget, independently made entry concerns a bittersweet romance of a black GI in peacetime Paris and a Parisian girl (Berger). (Dir: Melvin Van Peebles, 87 mins.)

Story of a Woman (U.S.-Italy, 1969)** Robert Stack, Bibi Andersson, Annie Girardot, James Farentino. Swedish actress Bibi Andersson fluctuates between her American diplomat husband (Robert Stack) and her former flame (James

Farentino). (Dir: Leonardo Bercovici, 101 mins.)

Story of Boys and Girls, The (Italy, 1990)***½ Felice Andreasi, Angiola Baggi, Davide Bechini, Lina Bernardi, Anna Bonaiuto. Charming comedy-drama about an extended Italian family that meets for a celebratory engagement feast in 1936, and eats, and eats, and eats. This is a movie as much about food as it is about friendship and change. The two families involved in the upcoming marriage are from different walks of life, which causes some complications, most of which are assuaged by the 20-course meal. (Dir: Pupi Avati, 93 mins.)

Story of David, A (Great Britain, 1960)**½ Jeff Chandler, Basil Sydney, Barbara Shelley, Donald Pleasence. David is unjustly accused of seeking the throne of Israel. Better-than-usual biblical drama. (Dir: Bob McNaught, 99 mins.)

Story of David, The (MTV 1976)*** Timothy Bottoms, Anthony Quayle, Keith Michell, Jane Seymour, Susan Hampshire. Expertly scripted Bible tale that traces the legend of David from his giant-slaying days to his dalliance with Bathsheba. (Dir: Alex Segal, 250 mins.)

Story of Dr. Wassell, The (1944)** Gary Cooper, Laraine Day, Signe Hasso. True story of an old doctor who rescued some men from the Japanese in Java has been turned into a pulp fiction tale with few facts and little interest. (Dir: Cecil B. De Mille, 136 mins.)

Story of Esther Costello, The (Great Britain, 1957)** Joan Crawford, Rossano Brazzi, Heather Sears. Silly melodrama about a group of greedy promoters who exploit a mute girl as a front for a swindle. The script is cliched and reverts to outrageous melodramatics, but Crawford's fans won't mind. (Dir: David Miller, 103 mins.)

Story of G.I. Joe, The (1945)***½ Burgess Meredith, Robert Mitchum. Incidents in the life of famed war correspondent Ernie Pyle, during the bloody Italian campaign. Fine performance, good drama. (Dir: William Wellman, 109 mins.)

Story of Jacob and Joseph, The (MTV 1974)***½ Keith Michell, Tony Lo-Bianco, Colleen Dewhurst, Herschel Bernardi, Harry Andrews. First-rate Bible stories detailing the rivalry of Jacob and Esau, and the hard times of Joseph, who was betrayed by his brothers. (Dir: Michael Cacoyannis, 104 mins.)

Story of Louis Pasteur, The (1936)**** Paul Muni, Anita Louise, Donald Woods. A wonderful tribute to the French scientist. Muni is superb in this informative, moving film. (Dir: William Dieterle, 87 mins.)†

Story of Mankind, The (1957)*½ Ronald Colman, Hedy Lamarr, Groucho Marx, Virginia Mayo, Peter Lorre, Agnes Moorehead, and others. A poor mixture of comedy and drama as a heavenly tribunal reviews the history and accomplishments of man. (Dir: Irwin Allen, 100 mins.)

Story of O, The (France, 1975)** Corinne Clery, Udo Kier, Anthony Steel, Jean Gaven. Lush, soft-core adaptation of the French novel about a woman's submission to bondage. A sadomasochistic perfume commercial aimed at a "couples" audience. Sequel: *Fruits of Passion*. (Dir: Just Jaeckin, 97 mins.)†

Story of Pretty Boy Floyd, The (MTV 1974)*** Martin Sheen, Kim Darby, Michael Parks, Ellen Corby. Sheen portrays the legendary criminal Pretty Boy Floyd, in this low-key tale set in the Twenties and early Thirties. Good period detail. (Dir: Clyde Ware, 72 mins.)

Story of Robin Hood, The (1952)** Richard Todd, Joan Rice, Peter Finch, James Hayter, Martita Hunt. This version, shot on location in England for Walt Disney, is not quite as thrilling as Errol Flynn's, but it still tells the story adequately. (Dir: Ken Annakin, 84 mins.)

Story of Ruth, The (1960)**½ Elana Eden, Stuart Whitman, Tom Tryon, Viveca Lindfors. Biblical tale of a girl who renounces the worship of pagan gods when she finds the true religion. Stately, interesting drama, despite some dull stretches. (Dir: Henry Koster, 132 mins.)†

Story of Seabiscuit (1949)**½ Lon McCallister, Shirley Temple, Barry Fitzgerald. Biography of famous horse is just an excuse for a run-of-the-mill racing picture. Fitzgerald is good as the trainer and there are a few fine racing scenes. (Dir: David Butler, 93 mins.)

Story of the Beach Boys: Summer Dreams (MTV 1990)**½ Bruce Greenwood, Greg Kean, Arlen Dean Snyder, Casey Sander. Biography of the sun'n'surf band concentrates on drummer Dennis Wilson, slighting the far more interesting story of the group's genius, Brian. Even so, well presented and believable. (Dir: Michael Switzer, 96 mins.)

Story of the Count of Monte Cristo, The (France-Italy, 1961)** Louis Jourdan, Yvonne Furneaux, Pierre Mondy, Bernard Dheran. Third film version of Dumas's novel is faithful to the text, but Jourdan is unexciting as the Count. (Dir: Claude Autant-Lara, 90 mins.)

Story of Three Loves, The (1953)*** Kirk Douglas, Leslie Caron, Pier Angeli, James Mason. Entertaining film for romantics. The stories of three love affairs are unfolded via flashback by three passengers on an ocean liner. (Dirs: Vincente Minnelli, Gottfried Reinhardt, 122 mins.)

Story of Vernon and Irene Castle, The

(1939)*** Fred Astaire, Ginger Rogers, Edna May Oliver, Walter Brennan. The life and successes of the famous dance team early in the century. Not up to Astaire-Rogers standard, but still entertaining biographical musical. (Dir: H. C. Potter, 93 mins.)†

Story of Will Rogers, The (1952)**½ Will Rogers, Jr., Jane Wyman, Eddie Cantor. Slow moving but well done biopic of the great humorist Will Rogers. His son looks a great deal like his father, but he inherited none of his dad's charm, talent or wit. (Dir: Michael Curtiz, 109 mins.)†

Story of Women, The (France, 1988)**½ Isabelle Huppert, François Cluzet, Marie Trintignant. True story of a woman executed in occupied France during the forties for performing abortions. As always, Huppert excels at portraying an unsympathetic character believably. (Dir: Claude Chabrol, 110 mins.)†

Story on Page One, The (1959)*** Rita Hayworth, Anthony Franciosa, Hugh Griffith, Mildred Dunnock, Gig Young. Lawyer agrees to defend two adulterers accused of murdering the lady's husband. Frequently gripping courtroom drama written and directed by Clifford Odets. (123 mins.)

Storyteller, The (MTV 1977)**** Martin Balsam, Patty Duke Astin, Doris Roberts, James Daly. Balsam plays a Hollywood writer whose TV movie about an arsonist may have resulted in tragedy. A disturbed twelve-year-old boy sets fire to his school and dies in the blaze. Balsam is splendid as the agonized writer. (Dir: Robert Markowitz, 104 mins.)

Stowaway (1936)*** Shirley Temple, Alice Faye, Robert Young. One of Shirley's best is this tale of a slain Chinese missionary's daughter who stows away on a playboy's yacht and succeeds in solving all problems. (Dir: William A. Seiter, 86 mins.)†

Stowaway to the Moon (MTV 1975)*** Lloyd Bridges, Michael Link, Jeremy Slate, John Carradine. A boy who's crazy over rockets stows away on board a rocket that's approaching lift-off. Suspenseful and absorbing, this fills the bill for family entertainment. (Dir: Andrew McLaglen, 104 mins.)

Straight for the Heart (Canada-Switzerland, 1991)*** Matthias Habich, Johanne-Marie Trembly, Michael Voita, Jean Francois Pichette. A steely photojournalist returns from Nicaragua to his Montreal home to discover his happy home life with his male and female lovers (they live together in a lusty ménage à trois) has been turned upside down, causing him to suffer a midlife crisis. Well made and mature. (Dir: Lea Pool, 92 mins.)

Straight on Till Morning (Great Britain, 1972)**½ Rita Tushingham, Shane Briant, Tom Bell. More style than substance. Liverpool lass comes to London looking for someone to father a child for her, and meets psycho Briant. (Dir: Peter Collinson, 96 mins.)

Straight Out of Brooklyn (1991)** George T. Odom, Ann D. Sanders, Lawrence Gilliard, Jr., Barbara Sanon, Reana Drummond. Hyper-realistic but clumsy drama about the plight of the residents of Brooklyn's Red Hook housing project is noted for two things: It never flinches in revealing the despair of these Americans, and its writer/producer/director was 19 years old when it was made. (Dir: Matty Rich, 91 mins.)

Straight Through the Heart (West Germany, 1983)*** Beate Jensen, Sepp Bierbichler, Gabriele Litty, Jens Mueller-Rastede. First feature from director Doris Dorrie (Men) is a more serious look at relations between the sexes. An ungrounded young woman agrees to live with a lonely older man. (91 mins.)

Straight Time (1978)*** Dustin Hoffman, Theresa Russell, Harry Dean Stanton, Gary Busey, M. Emmet Walsh. Interesting but garbled attempt to elucidate the mentality of a hardcore criminal. Hoffman makes courageous choices in the role, eschewing charm, but he is not convincing. (Dir: Ulu Grosbard, 114 mins.)†

Straight to Hell (1987)** Sy Richardson, Joe Strummer, Dick Rude, Courtney Love, Zander Schloss, Elvis Costello. Wildly anarchic spoof of Sergio Leone's spaghetti westerns. The take-off has an improvisatory air which unfortunately burns out midway through the picture. Some funny camp dialogue compensates. (Dir: Alex Cox, 86 mins.)†

Strait-Jacket (1964)**½ Joan Crawford, Diane Baker, George Kennedy. Released from a mental hospital years after having committed axe murders, a woman goes to live with her daughter and brother—then axe murders begin again. (Dir: William Castle, 89 mins.)†

Stranded (1935)**½ Kay Francis, George Brent, Patricia Ellis, Donald Woods, Barton MacLane. Romance centered around the construction of the Golden Gate Bridge. Welfare worker Francis and engineer Brent fall in love, but are too busy to get together. Interesting, socially conscious human drama. (Dir: Frank Borzage, 76 mins.)

Stranded (MTV 1986)*** Loni Anderson, Perry King, William Hickey, Elaine Stritch, Joel Brooks, Eugene Roche, Edward Winter. An amusing romantic comedy with two competing ad execs (and ex-lovers) who find themselves adrift in a hot air balloon and then stranded on a deserted island. (Dir: Rod Daniel, 104 mins.)

Stranded (1988)** Ione Skye, Joe Morton,

Susan Barnes, Maureen O'Sullivan. A group of colorful aliens land on Earth and are sheltered from harm by an independent old lady (O'Sullivan) and her granddaughter. (Dir: Tex Fuller, 80 mins.)

Strand—Under the Dark Cloth (Canada, 1989)***½ Insightful documentary about influential photographer Paul Strand touches on his life and art, including his photographs of turn-of-the-century Manhattan. (Dir: John Walker, 81 mins.)

Strange Affair, The (Great Britain, 1968)*½ Michael York, Susan George, Jeremy Kemp. Naïve London copper is really taken in by a wild teenage girl. Vacillating mixture of melodrama and satire. (Dir: David Greene, 106 mins.)

Strange Affection (Great Britain, 1957)**½ Richard Attenborough, Colin Peterson. Boy is accused of murdering his father. Fairly good drama, nice performance by Peterson. (Dir: Wolf Rilla, 84 mins.)

Strange Alibi—See: **Strange Triangle**

Strange and Deadly Occurrence, A (MTV 1974)** Robert Stack, Vera Miles, L. Q. Jones, Herb Edelman. Homeowners, who think they have headaches, will shudder at the events which throw a family into a tailspin when they move into their new home. (Dir: John L. Moxey, 72 mins.)†

Strange Awakening (Great Britain, 1957)* Lex Barker, Carole Mathews. Very contrived melodrama about an amnesia victim who is used in a swindling plot. (Dir: Montgomery Tully, 75 mins.)†

Strange Bargain (1949)*** Martha Scott, Jeffrey Lynn, Harry Morgan, Katherine Emery, Henry O'Neill, Richard Gaines. A suspenseful thriller about a financially strapped bookkeeper who is paid to make his boss's suicide look like a murder. (Dir: Will Price, 68 mins.)

Strange Bedfellows (1964)**½ Rock Hudson, Gina Lollobrigida, Gig Young, Terry-Thomas. Wandering business executive tries to reconcile with his wife in order to improve his corporate image. Fairly entertaining comedy. (Dir: Melvin Frank, 98 mins.)

Strange Behavior (New Zealand, 1981)** Michael Murphy, Dan Shor, Fiona Lewis, Louise Fletcher, Arthur Dingham, Scott Brady. Strange film about a mad scientist who experiments on high school kids. Eerie atmosphere, but poor script. AKA: **Dead Kids.** (Dir: Michael Laughlin, 98 mins.)

Strange Brew (1983)** Dave Thomas, Rick Moranis, Max von Sydow, Paul Dooley, Lynn Griffin. Popular "SCTV" characters, beer-drinking hosers Bob and Doug McKenzie, are brought to the big screen. The highlight is the opening, in which Bob and Doug premiere their homemade sci-fi movie, but after that it's downhill as they battle a brewer intent on controll-

ing the world with drugged beer. (Dirs: Dave Thomas, Rick Moranis, 90 mins.)†

Strange Cargo (1940)***½ Clark Gable, Joan Crawford, Peter Lorre, Ian Hunter, Albert Dekker, Paul Lukas, Eduardo Ciannelli. Stylized allegory of escapees from Devil's Island. One is remarkably, even mysteriously good (Hunter), one is wholly evil (Lukas). The other characters have to choose between them. Director Frank Borzage's style blends the story's gritty, sweaty realism with semi-fantasy. (105 mins.)†

Strange Case of Dr. Rx, The (1942)** Lionel Atwill, Patric Knowles, Anne Gwynne, Samuel S. Hinds, Shemp Howard, Mantan Moreland. Poverty-row thriller starring Atwill, in another convincing performance, as a murderer obsessed with killing people who have been acquitted of murder. Good of this kind. (Dir: William Nigh, 66 mins.)

Strange Case of Madeleine—See: **Madeleine**

Strange Case of Uncle Harry, The—See: **Uncle Harry**

Strange Confession—See: **Imposter, The** (1944)

Strange Death of Adolf Hitler, The (1943)** Ludwig Donath, George Dolenz, Gale Sondergaard. Facial double for Hitler is forced by the Gestapo to pose as Der Führer. Doesn't mean much now, but still intriguing. (Dir: James Hogan, 72 mins.)

Strange Door, The (1952)*½ Charles Laughton, Boris Karloff, Sally Forrest. A horror tale that is intended to be chilling but is often laughable instead. Laughton and Karloff overact outrageously. Based on a Robert Louis Stevenson story. (Dir: Joseph Pevney, 81 mins.)

Strange Homecoming (MTV 1974)** Robert Culp, Barbara Anderson, Glen Campbell. Culp plays a murderer who pops up after a long absence and receives a hero's welcome from his sheriff-brother's family. An unofficial rip-off of *Shadow of a Doubt.* (Dir: Lee H. Katzin, 72 mins.)

Strange Illusion (1945)** James Lydon, Sally Eilers, Warren William, Regis Toomey. *Film noir* curio that retells the story of Hamlet in forties dress. Lydon is particularly bad as the adolescent who believes that the sharpster seducing his mother is the same person who disposed of his dad. Boldly expressionist images by director Edgar G. Ulmer. (80 mins.)

Strange Impersonation (1946)**½ Brenda Marshall, William Gargan, Hillary Brooke, George Chandler, H. B. Warner, Lyle Talbot. Low-budget thriller, lent class by Anthony Mann's stylish direction, concerns a chemist who injects herself with an experimental drug and finds her life falling to pieces. Cheap but inventive. (68 mins.)

Strange Interlude (1932)*** Norma Shearer, Clark Gable, Robert Young. Interesting screen version of Eugene O'Neill's odd play, in which the characters' thoughts are revealed to the audience through voice-overs. The somber plot concerns a young wife who discovers that insanity runs in her husband's family, and decides to have a child by another man. A bit slow-moving and talky, but the acting is excellent. (Dir: Robert Z. Leonard, 110 mins.)

Strange Intruder (1956)**½ Ida Lupino, Edmund Purdom, Ann Harding, Jacques Bergerac, Gloria Talbot. Grim, suspenseful story of a demented ex-soldier who promised his dead buddy he would kill his children rather than let his wife raise them. Tense, capably done, but an ugly concept. (Dir: Irving Rapper, 82 mins.)

Strange Invaders (1983)*** Diana Scarwid, Nancy Allen, Louise Fletcher, Paul Le Mat. Off-the-wall sci-fi film that spoofs space invader flicks. A UFO lands in a remote region of the midwest in the 1950s and deposits aliens who obliterate the town's residents before assuming their human form. (Dir: Michael Laughlin, 99 mins.)†

Strange Lady in Town (1955)**½ Greer Garson, Dana Andrews, Cameron Mitchell, Lois Smith. Greer Garson seems out of place in this western. She plays a determined woman who disturbs Santa Fe's top figures upon her arrival. (Dir: Mervyn LeRoy, 112 mins.)

Strange Love of Martha Ivers, The (1946)*** Barbara Stanwyck, Van Heflin, Kirk Douglas, Lizabeth Scott, Judith Anderson. In this hard-edged melodrama a woman is haunted by memories of a murder long past. Stanwyck gives a bravura performance as the wealthy neurotic; equally fine is Douglas as her bitter, weak husband. (Dir: Lewis Milestone, 117 mins.)†

Strange Love of Molly Louvain, The (1932)** Ann Dvorak, Richard Cromwell, Lee Tracy, Leslie Fenton, Guy Kibbee. Typical unwed mother saga. Dvorak shines as the fallen lady who still has a steady stream of beaux ready to make an honest woman of her. (Dir: Michael Curtiz, 74 mins.)

Strange Mr. Gregory, The (1946)** Edmund Lowe, Jean Rogers, Don Douglas, Frank Reicher, Jonathan Hale. Entertaining thriller of an oddball magician trying to frame his rival for his own murder. Fast-paced and lively, with a sparkling performance by Lowe. (Dir: Phil Rosen, 63 mins.)

Strange New World (MTV 1975)*½ John

Saxon, Kathleen Miller, Keene Curtis. Made-for-TV buffs will recognize this as a further attempt to come up with a satisfactory pilot for a series based on the previous TV film, *Planet Earth*. Saxon stars again, as one of a trio of survivors from an earlier time, brought back to earth. Strange, maybe—but not worth seeing. (Dir: Robert Butler, 100 mins.)

Strange One, The (1957)*** Ben Gazzara, Mark Richman, George Peppard, Pat Hingle, Julie Wilson. Exciting screen version of Calder Willingham's play *End As A Man* about life in a Southern military academy as presided over by a sadistic upper classman. Superb performances by all, with Ben Gazzara a standout in his screen debut. (Dir: Jack Garfein, 97 mins.)

Strange Possession of Mrs. Oliver, The (MTV 1977)**½ Karen Black, George Hamilton. Black has a field day as a housewife who suddenly takes on the personality of a woman who died five years earlier. (Dir: Gordon Hessler, 76 mins.)

Stranger, The (1946)***½ Edward G. Robinson, Orson Welles, Loretta Young. A well-observed thriller. Robinson stalks a Nazi war criminal to a sleepy college town. His man is Welles, married to Loretta Young. Director Welles is especially good at suggesting the menace of connubial domination. (95 mins.)†

Stranger, The (Algeria-France-Italy, 1967)***½ Marcello Mastroianni, Anna Karina, Georges Wilson. Muted, brilliantly photographed film of Albert Camus's sparely written classic novel about alienation. Mastroianni is excellent as the embodiment of Camus's existential philosophy, a man who commits an unmotivated murder under the pitiless heat of the Algerian sun. (Dir: Luchino Visconti, 104 mins.)

Stranger, The (MTV 1973)**½ Glenn Corbett, Lew Ayres, Cameron Mitchell. Old fugitive plot neatly wrapped up in semi-science-fiction trimmings. Astronaut Corbett crashes on an Earth-like planet known as Terra, and must keep on the run. (Dir: Lee H. Katzin, 98 mins.)

Stranger and the Gunfighter, The (Italy-Spain-Hong Kong, 1976)* Lee Van Cleef, Lo Lieh. Gunfighter and martial arts master piece together clues (tatooed on women's bottoms) in search of a treasure. Asinine western. (Dirs: Anthony Dawson, Antonio Margheriti, 106 mins.)†

Stranger at Jefferson High, The (MTV 1981)**½ Stewart Petersen, Dana Kimmell, Philip Brown. Petersen plays the new kid at Jefferson High who holds down a job to help his poor widowed mother with the expenses and has to prove himself to the bullies at Jefferson. Familiar but earnest. (Dir: Lyman Dayton, 104 mins.)

Stranger at My Door (1956)*** Macdonald Carey, Patricia Medina, Skip Homeier. Notorious outlaw takes refuge at the home of a preacher, who tries to reform him. Offbeat western is well done. (Dir: William Witney, 85 mins.)

Stranger From Venus (Great Britain, 1954)**½ Helmut Dantine, Patricia Neal. Remake of *The Day the Earth Stood Still*. Dantine replaces Michael Rennie as the alien from space who brings a message to mankind of peace and brotherhood—or else. Neal repeats her role from the '51 film. AKA: The Venusian. (Dir: Burt Balaban, 76 mins.)†

Stranger In Between, The (Great Britain, 1952)*** Dirk Bogarde, Jon Whiteley, Elizabeth Sellars. Runaway finds a body and is taken captive by the murderer. Suspenseful, well-acted melodrama. (Dir: Charles Crichton, 84 mins.)

Stranger In My Arms, A (1959)** June Allyson, Jeff Chandler, Sandra Dee, Mary Astor. Widow defies her mother-in-law when she meets a man she wants to marry. Good production values, otherwise reminiscent of daytime serials. (Dir: Helmut Kautner, 88 mins.)

Stranger In My Bed (MTV 1986)** Lindsay Wagner, Armand Assante, Doug Sheehan. An overly familiar story of a woman suffering from amnesia. In steps a handsome stranger who offers her a chance to start over again. Only an amnesiac could find this material fresh. (Dir: Larry Elikann, 104 mins.)

Stranger in Our House (MTV 1978)*** Linda Blair, Lee Purcell, Jeremy Slate, Carol Lawrence, Jeff East, Macdonald Carey. *The Exorcist*'s Blair deals with possession once again as her cousin takes over her family, and only Linda can save them. Surprisingly scary. AKA: Summer of Fear. (Dir: Wes Craven, 104 mins.)

Stranger in the House—See: **Black Christmas**

Stranger Is Watching, A (1982)** Rip Torn, Kate Mulgrew, James Naughton, Shawn von Schreiber. Part suspense film, part slasher-rama. A vicious killer kidnaps a girl and a TV correspondent and stashes them away under Grand Central Station. Lots of jolts, but unnecessarily sadistic. (Dir: Sean Cunningham, 92 mins.)†

Stranger Knocks, A (Denmark, 1965)***½ Brigitte Federspiel, Preben Rye. A simple, honest, and moving Danish film that was the subject of a Supreme Court decision in the U.S. In this intense character study, the identity of a passing stranger is revealed to a young war widow as her enemy in a final love scene that is both appropriate and explicit. (Dir: Johan Jacobsen, 81 mins.)

Stranger on Horseback (1955)*** Joel McCrea, Miroslava, Kevin McCarthy. Fightin' judge cleans up a territory run by one man. Colorful western. (Dir: Jacques Tourneur, 66 mins.)

Stranger on My Land (MTV 1988)*½ Tommy Lee Jones, Dee Wallace Stone, Terry O'Quinn, Pat Hingle. Tommy Lee's fightin' mad and won't let the goernment take his land to enlarge a missile base. This overwrought drama is like "The Waltons Meet Rambo." (Dir: Larry Elikann, 96 mins.)

Stranger on the Prowl (Italy, 1953)**½ Paul Muni, Joan Lorring. Fugitive from murder is joined by a small boy in his flight from the police. Grim drama, occasionally interesting. (Dir: Joseph Losey, 82 mins.)

Stranger on the Run (MTV 1968)**½ Henry Fonda, Anne Baxter, Michael Parks, Dan Duryea, Sal Mineo. Well-cast western drama. Fonda is being chased by a band of renegades who've been given badges by a railroad and a free hand to keep things going smoothly in the railroad's town. (Dir: Don Siegel, 97 mins.)

Stranger on the Third Floor (1940)*** Peter Lorre, John McGuire, Margaret Tallichet. Reporter is convinced a condemned man is innocent of murder, especially when the same pattern of crime reoccurs. Carefully produced, suspenseful thriller. (Dir: Boris Ingster, 64 mins.)

Strangers, The (Italy, 1954)**½ Ingrid Bergman, George Sanders. An English couple in Italy, rapidly approaching the point of divorce, experiences a miracle that brings them closer together. Despite the presence of the two stars and Roberto Rossellini's direction, this drama remains vague, rather cold. (97 mins.)

Stranger's Hand, The (Italy-Great Britain, 1954)***½ Trevor Howard, Richard Basehart, Alida Valli. An exciting and tense adventure drama of intrigue acted by an excellent cast. (Dir: Mario Soldati, 86 mins.)

Strangers in Good Company—See: **Company of Strangers, The**

Strangers in Love (1932)**½ Kay Francis, Fredric March, Stuart Erwin, Juliette Compton, George Barbier, Sidney Toler. March enjoys himself mightily playing a good twin and a bad twin; the bad twin disinherits his brother, who still gets the last laugh. (Dir: Lothar Mendes, 76 mins.)

Strangers in 7A, The (MTV 1972)** Andy Griffith, Ida Lupino, Susanne Hildur, Michael Brandon. One of those bank-robbery tales in which the young hoods show their muscle by slapping bystanders around. Griffith and Lupino play the victims who resist the robbers. (Dir: Paul Wendkos, 73 mins.)

Strangers In the City (1962)**½ Robert Gentile, Camilo Delgado, Kenny Delmar, Creta Margos. Uneven tale about a Puerto Rican family trying to adjust to their new lives and American customs when they move to New York City. Explosive material is often gripping. (Dir: Nick Carrier, 80 mins.)†

Stranger's Kiss (1984)**½ Peter Coyote, Victoria Tennant, Richard Romanus, Linda Kerridge. Elaborate and uneven. A crooked entrepreneur finances a film to satisfy his girlfriend but becomes jealous when the love scenes look too convincing. (Dir: Matthew Chapman, 94 mins.)†

Strangers May Kiss (1931)*** Norma Shearer, Robert Montgomery, Neil Hamilton, Marjorie Rambeau, Irene Rich. Glossy soap opera about a foreign correspondent who neglects the woman who loves him until she almost marries another man. Corny, but Shearer is wonderful. (Dir: George Fitzmaurice, 85 mins.)

Strangers on a Train (1951)**** Robert Walker, Ruth Roman, Farley Granger, Marion Lorne. Taut, suspenseful psychological drama directed by the master of suspense, Alfred Hitchcock. Walker and Granger meet on a train and begin an unholy pact involving murder. Effective performance by Walker. (101 mins.)†

Stranger's Return, The (1933)*** Miriam Hopkins, Lionel Barrymore, Franchot Tone, Stuart Erwin, Beulah Bondi, Grant Mitchell. Engaging romantic drama of a girl who leaves her husband and returns to the farm where she grew up. She learns how to live with the natural world all over again, and decides to stay on when her grandfather dies. A forgotten gem. (Dir: King Vidor, 88 mins.)

Strangers: The Story of a Mother and Daughter (MTV 1979)*** Bette Davis, Gena Rowlands. Deliberately paced study of the strained relationship between a rigid mother and the daughter who left home 21 years ago to seek her independence. The daughter returns to her widowed mother's home hoping to bridge the chasm in their lives. Magnificent performances. (Dir: Milton Katselas, 104 mins)†

Strangers When We Meet (1960)*** Kirk Douglas, Kim Novak, Ernie Kovacs, Barbara Rush, Walter Matthau. A lush forbidden romance. Adapted from an Evan Hunter novel, the film concerns two suburban ships passing in the night; and since they don't want to hurt their spouses, they steal their moments of happiness. (Dir: Richard Quine, 117 mins.)

Stranger Than Paradise (1984)**** John Lurie, Eszter Balint, Richard Edson. Deadpan comedy about a couple of deadbeats in New York and their odyssey to Cleveland and Florida with a visiting girl cousin from Hungary. A low-budget cult film, visually striking in its simplicity. (Dir: Jim Jarmusch, 90 mins.)†

Stranger Waits, A (MTV 1987)**½ Suzanne Pleshette, Justin Deas, Tom Atkins, Ann Wedgeworth. Pleshette falls for a handsome-but-mysterious stranger, who seems to have made it a point to insinuate himself into her life. Fairly tasty trash. (Dir: Robert Lewis, 104 mins.)

Stranger Who Looks Like Me, The (MTV 1974)**½ Meredith Baxter, Beau Bridges, Whitney Blake. Thoughtful drama about a pair of adopted young people who set out to find their real parents. Whitney Blake, who is Miss Baxter's real-life mother, plays the girl's mother. (Dir: Larry Peerce, 74 mins.)

Stranger Within, The (MTV 1974)**½ Barbara Eden, George Grizzard. Eden is effective as a normal-appearing woman who finds herself pregnant, though husband Grizzard has been certified impotent. Thus begins the nightmarish story leading to a suspenseful climax. (Dir: Lee Philips, 72 mins.)†

Stranger Within, The (MTV 1990)**½ Kate Jackson, Rick Schroder, Chris Sarandon, Clark Sandford. Good performances punch up this melodrama. Kate is a Korean War widow whose three-year-old son is kidnapped. The action then jumps ahead 16 years when Schroder shows up, announcing that he's her long-lost son. Strains credibility, but eerie turns will keep you involved. (Dir: Tom Holland, 96 mins.)

Stranger Wore a Gun, The (1953)**½ Randolph Scott, Claire Trevor, Joan Weldon, George Macready, Alfonso Bedoya, Lee Marvin, Ernest Borgnine. Gritty western about an embittered Civil War vet who gets involved in a life of crime in Arizona. He decides to go straight and faces his former partner in a climatic shootout. Burly, fast-moving actioner, filmed in 3-D. (Dir: Andre de Toth, 83 mins.)

Strange Shadows in an Empty Room (Canada, 1977)** Stuart Whitman, John Saxon, Tisa Farrow, Gayle Hunnicutt, Martin Landau, Carole Laure. Brutal thriller. The more a cop digs into investigating his sister's death, the more false leads he finds and the more unedifying facts he learns about his sister. (Dir: "Martin Herbert" [Alberto De Martino], 99 mins.)†

Strange Skirts—See: **When Ladies Meet** (1941)

Strange Triangle (1946)**½ Preston Foster, Signe Hasso, Shepperd Strudwick. Well-made poverty-row thriller about a glamorous, money-hungry woman goading the man who loves her into a robbery. AKA: **Strange Alibi**. (Dir: Ray McCarey, 65 mins.)

1014

Strange Voices (MTV 1987)*½ Valerie Harper, Nancy McKeon, Stephen Macht. Schizophrenic histrionics with McKeon as a young girl afflicted with the dread disease and Harper as her caring mom. See *I Never Promised You a Rose Garden* instead. (Dir: Arthur Allan Seidelman, 96 mins.)

Strange Woman, The (1946)*½ Hedy Lamarr, George Sanders, Louis Hayward, Gene Lockhart. A zombiesque period piece about a femme fatale. Director Edgar G. Ulmer's stylish camera work battles Hedy's languid, enervating presence and loses. (100 mins.)

Stranglehold (Great Britain, 1962)**½ Macdonald Carey, Barbara Shelley, Philip Friend. Temperamental movie actor nears the edge of madness when his gangster roles threaten to invade his private life. Well-acted suspense drama. (Dir: Lawrence Huntington, 82 mins.)

Strangler, The (1964)**½ Victor Buono, David McLean, Ellen Corby. City is in terror and police work frantically to nab a psychotic strangler of women. Grim drama lent some distinction by Buono's fine performance. (Dir: Burt Topper, 89 mins.)†

Strapless (Great Britain, 1989)*** Blair Brown, Bruno Ganz, Bridget Fonda, Alan Howard, Michael Gough. American doctor Brown, who has recently ended a long relationship and is having budget problems at the public clinic where she works, is swept off her feet (almost) by enigmatic foreign businessman Ganz. Moody, sometimes opaque but always intriguing adult romance with wonderful characterizations, written and directed by playwright David Hare. (97 mins.)†

Strategic Air Command (1955)**½ James Stewart, June Allyson, Frank Lovejoy, Barry Sullivan. Somewhat interesting drama about the workings of the Strategic Air Command: the atom bomb-carrying planes and the men who are involved. (Dir: Anthony Mann, 114 mins.)†

Stratton Story, The (1949)*** James Stewart, June Allyson, Frank Morgan, Bill Williams. Successful film biography based on the true story of baseball pitcher Monty Stratton who lost his leg in a hunting accident. The combination of Allyson and Stewart is used to good advantage in this sentimental comedy drama. (Dir: Sam Wood, 106 mins.)

Strawberry Blonde (1941)*** Rita Hayworth, James Cagney, Olivia de Havilland. Cagney supports this little comedy about New York in the Gay Nineties. Jim's all over the picture so, in spite of a frail story, you may enjoy yourself. (Dir: Raoul Walsh, 97 mins.)†

Strawberry Statement, The (1970)** Kim Darby, Bruce Davison, Bob Balaban, Bud Cort. This drama about the college upheavals of the sixties doesn't pack a punch. Darby pushes too hard as the strong-willed girl who turns Davison from a mildly concerned college boy into a radical of sorts. (Dir: Stuart Hagmann, 103 mins.)†

Straw Dogs (Great Britain, 1972)*** Dustin Hoffman, Susan George, David Warner. Controversial film because of a half-hour finale of gruesome violence. Hoffman plays a young mathematician who has bought a house on the coast of England in the town where his wife grew up. She is eventually assaulted, and a local citizen is pursued by an angry mob, forcing Hoffman to act. Much of this premise is unbelievable, but the most interesting and effective sequence remains the charged ending where Hoffman gradually begins to enjoy the violence. (Dir: Sam Peckinpah, 113 mins.)†

Streamers (1983)***½ Matthew Modine, David Alan Grier, Mitchell Lichtenstein, Michael Wright, George Dzundza, Guy Boyd. Robert Altman's excellent screen version of the play by David Rabe is a perfect example of the way the arts of theater and film can be merged. The approach is simple: Altman simply presents the play—which is about the interaction between four soldiers stuck in a dingy barracks on the eve of being shipped out to Vietnam—while also exploring the action with smoothly gliding camera work and rapid editing. The cast, performing like a well-oiled machine, deserved the ensemble acting award they received at the Venice Film Festival. (118 mins.)†

Street Angel (1928)*** Janet Gaynor, Charles Farrell, Alberto Rabagliati, Gino Conti. Engrossing, tender romance, with Gaynor an Italian waif on the run from the police who takes refuge with a circus and falls in love with an idealistic painter. Beautifully filmed, sensitively acted drama. (Dir: Frank Borzage, 102 mins.)

Street Asylum (1990)* Wings Hauser, G. Gordon Liddy, Alex Cord, Sy Richardson, Brion James. Dopey, violent tale of cops implanted with device which compels them to kill street scum. Major embarrassment is the performance of Watergate burglar Liddy as goofball mastermind of dumb scheme to clear streets of human detritus. (Dir: Gregory Brown, 94 mins.)†

Streetcar Named Desire, A (1951)**** Marlon Brando, Vivien Leigh, Karl Malden, Kim Hunter. At the time of its release, Elia Kazan's adaptation of Tennessee Williams's Pulitzer Prize-winning play was hailed for ushering in a new era in frank treatment of adult material. Countless films since have been more explicit, but very few have been more subtle, powerful or brilliantly acted. Brando's brooding, brutal Stanley Kowalski made him a star. Matching him all the way is Leigh's Blanche DuBois, in a portrayal that unlayers every nuance of her fragility and desperation. Kazan's direction doesn't attempt to disguise the film's stage origins, but its power is in the dazzling combination of theater and cinema. Oscars went to Leigh, Malden and Hunter. (Dir: Elia Kazan, 125 mins.)†

Streetcar Named Desire, A (MTV 1984)** Ann-Margret, Treat Williams, Randy Quaid, Beverly D'Angelo. The 1950 movie version of Tennessee Williams's play was as close to perfection as you are likely to get. Here, Ann-Margret is Blanche and barely manages to portray the desperation of a woman whose "youth has gone up the waterspout." (Dir: John Erman, 124 mins.)

Streetfight—See: **Coonskin**

Street Killing (MTV 1976)*½ Andy Griffith, Bradford Dillman, Harry Guardino. Andy's a crusading legal eagle who's out to pin an apparent robbery-murder on the mob. (Dir: Harvey Hart, 78 mins.)

Street Love—See: **Scarred**

Street of Chance (1930)**½ William Powell, Kay Francis, Regis Toomey, Jean Arthur. Powell plays a de-ethnicized character based on Arnold Rothstein, a gambler who falls afoul of the mob when he takes his kid brother to the gaming tables to teach him a lesson. Sonny cleans out the pros, and the fat is in the fire. (Dir: John Cromwell, 77 mins.)

Street of Chance (1942)*** Burgess Meredith, Claire Trevor. Amnesia victim regains his memory to find he is wanted for murder. Compact mystery melodrama boasts an excellent cast, good script. (Dir: Jack Hively, 74 mins.)

Street of Dreams (MTV 1988)** Ben Masters, Morgan Fairchild, Diane Salinger, John Hillerman. A seamy Hollywood yarn about a lost beauty (Fairchild) and the amiable detective (Masters) on the case: A tired plot that might have worked with a different cast. (Dir: William A. Graham, 96 mins.)

Street of No Return (France-Portugal, 1989)* Keith Carradine, Valentina Vargas, Bill Duke, Andrea Ferreol. Even the most rabid fans of iconoclastic director Sam Fuller will have trouble standing up for this muddled adaptation of a David Goodis novel about a once-popular singer, now a bum, drawn back into a meeting with the people who caused his downfall. It occasionally looks as though it's supposed to be campy, but mostly it looks howlingly inept. Goodis fans will also be disappointed that Fuller has inserted a happy ending! (90 mins.)

Street of Shame (Japan, 1956)***½ Machiko Kyo, Michiyo Kogure, Ayako

Wakao. Director Kenji Mizoguchi's last work was influential in bringing about the outlawing of prostitution in Japan. Kogure is the standout among the actresses playing prostitutes, whose stories are told. (96 mins.)†

Street of Sorrow, The—See: **Joyless Street, The**

Street of Women (1930)**½ Kay Francis, Alan Dinehart, Marjorie Gateson, Roland Young, Gloria Stuart, Louise Beavers. Enjoyable soap opera, with fashion designer Francis in love with a married architect, but reluctant to alienate him from his daughter. (Dir: Shepard Traube, 70 mins.)

Street People (Italy, 1976)*½ Roger Moore, Stacy Keach, Ivo Garrani, Fausto Tozzi. Action-filled but flavorless Mafioso adventure in which Moore and buddy Keach endeavor to discover which gangland kingpin made off with a million bucks worth of heroin. (Dir: Maurice Lucidi, 92 mins.)†

Streets (1990)**½ Christina Applegate, David Mendenhall, Eb Lottimer, Patrick Richwood. Standard exploitation tale of L.A. street kids is better than it ought to be thanks to strong direction, good performances, and a script that attempts to build sympathy and understanding for these lost lives in between the requisite acts of violence provided by the usual psycho killer. (Dir: Katt Shea Ruben, 83 mins.)†

Street Scene (1931)***½ Sylvia Sidney, William Collier, Jr., David Landau, Beulah Bondi. Elmer Rice's picture of life in the tenement district, adapted by King Vidor from the famous Broadway play, with Sylvia Sidney. Still a powerful, finely made drama. (Dir: King Vidor, 90 mins.)†

Street Smart (1987)*** Christopher Reeve, Kathy Baker, Morgan Freeman, Mimi Rogers, Jay Patterson, Andre Gregory, Anna Maria Horsford. A compelling crime thriller about a journalist (Reeve) who fabricates a sensational story, not realizing it resembles that of a real pimp being prosecuted for murder. Sensing a possible alibi, the procurer links up with the journalist and provides him with some nonfictional, harrowing source material. An interesting study of journalistic corruption with a remarkable performance by Morgan Freeman as the opportunistic pimp. (Dir: Jerry Schatzberg, 96 mins.)†

Streets of Fire (1984)***½ Michael Paré, Diane Lane, Rick Moranis, Amy Madigan, Willem Dafoe, Deborah Van Valkenburgh, Bill Paxton, Lee Ving, Robert Townsend. A uniquely original musical fantasy that combines rock 'n' roll, a proto-western story line, and terrific comic book violence. Paré is the hero, a guy who cruises the streets of a city where no one is over thirty-five and everyone is a hardened rocker, looking for his old flame (Lane), a rock singer who's been abducted by a nasty biker chieftan (Dafoe). Director Walter Hill creates a vivid neon-lit milieu, with strong musical backing from songwriter Jim Steinman, roots musician Ry Cooder, and the Blasters. (93 mins.)†

Streets of Gold (1986)**½ Klaus Maria Brandauer, Adrian Pasdar, Wesley Snipes. A restrained, sentimental tale about the emotional revitalization of a former Russian boxer, bounced from that sport in the U.S.S.R because of his Judaism. In America, he seizes the opportunity to train two streetwise teens to compete against a visiting Russian team. (Dir: Joe Roth, 95 mins.)†

Streets of L.A., The (MTV 1979)*** Joanne Woodward, Fernando Allende. Woodward shines as a harried Los Angeles realtor, a plucky middle-aged divorcee worn down by life's slaps in the face. When her tires are slashed by Chicanos, she invades the Barrio to demand repayment. (Dir: Jerrold Freedman, 102 mins.)†

Streets of Laredo (1949)*** William Holden, Macdonald Carey, William Bendix, Mona Freeman. Two outlaws who have gone straight meet up with their former partner after many years, who is still on the wrong side of the law. Good western with more plot than usual. (Dir: Leslie Fenton, 92 mins.)

Streets of New York (1939)**½ Jackie Cooper, Martin Spellman, Sidney Miller, Buddy Pepper, Bobby Stone. Low-budget drama about an idealistic law student from Hell's Kitchen who unites his neighborhood pals against a gang. Good urban atmosphere and fine performances from the teenage cast. (Dir: William Nigh, 73 mins.)

Streets of San Francisco, The (MTV 1972)**½ Karl Malden, Robert Wagner, Michael Douglas, Kim Darby, Lawrence Dobkin. Pilot film for the police series. Through flashbacks we learn all about a dead girl named Holly (Darby), and mull over the clues along with Malden and Douglas as they work at solving her murder. (Dir: Walter Grauman, 104 mins.)

Street Trash (1987)*½ Mike Lackey, Vic Noto, Bill Chepil. Gross-out shocker set in a Brooklyn junkyard, involving murder, rape, and a strange wine that makes its drinkers melt. Technically slick and fairly well directed, the incoherent script turns it into just another freak show. (Dir: Jim Muro, 91 mins.)

Streetwalkin' (1985)** Julie Newmar, Melissa Leo. A tawdry, violent tale of a brother and sister who head for the Big Apple but end up with the worms in

Times Square, where she has to turn tricks to survive. (Dir: Joan Freeman, 84 mins.)†

Street Warriors (Spain, 1971)½ Christa Leem, Nadia Windell, Victor Petit, Frank Brana. Amoral Spanish teenagers commit every crime in the book, knowing that the courts can do little to punish them because of their youth. Supposedly serious study of juvenile delinquency is just an excuse for the usual exploitation trash. (Dir: José Antonio de la Loma, 105 mins.)†

Street Warriors 2 (Spain, 1974)½ Angel Fernandez Franco, Teresa Giminez, Veronica Miriel, Raul Ramirez. More of the same, even worse in three particularly graphic rape sequences, and moronically dubbed to boot. (Dir: José Antonio de la Loma, 105 mins.)†

Streetwise (1985)**** A powerful documentary about street children living in Seattle, Washington. Based on a *Life* magazine article, the movie looks at how these kids survive on the streets by prostitution, panhandling, and robbery. (Dir: Martin Bell, 92 mins.)†

Street with No Name, The (1948)*** Mark Stevens, Richard Widmark, Lloyd Nolan. Another of those exciting semi-documentary films dealing with the FBI. Nothing unusual about the plot of an agent infiltrating the gang but beautifully done. (Dir: William Keighley, 91 mins.)†

Strictly Dishonorable (1951)** Ezio Pinza, Janet Leigh. Noted opera singer takes steps to combat a newspaper's ire, finds himself in a compromising situation. (Dirs: Melvin Frank, Norman Panama, 94 mins.)

Strike (Russia, 1924)**** I. Kluvkin, Alexander Antonov, Grigori Alexandrov. One of the great achievements of the Russian directorial genius Sergei M. Eisenstein. Story concerns a strike in tsarist Russia, spurred by the suicide of one of the workers after he is fired. (82 mins.)

Strike Force (MTV 1975)* Cliff Gorman, Donald Blakely, Richard Gere. Pilot film about an anti-crime unit consisting of a New York City cop, a state trooper, and a federal agent, hampered by a vague plot and funereal pacing. (Dir: Barry Shear, 72 mins.)†

Strike Force (MTV 1981)** Robert Stack, Dorian Harewood, Richard Romanus, Herb Edelman. Standard cop show. Based in Los Angeles, Stack and company go undercover to nab a psychopathic murderer who kills only on Tuesdays. (Dir: Richard Lang, 78 mins.)†

Strike It Rich (Great Britain-U.S., 1989)*½ Robert Lindsay, Molly Ringwald, John Gielgud, Max Wall, Simon de la Brosse, Michel Blanc, Marius Goring. Accountant Lindsay and his new wife Ringwald spend their honeymoon in Monte Carlo, where he devises a system to win at the roulette wheel. Pale comedy adapted from a minor Graham Greene story. (Dir: James Scott, 84 mins.)†

Strike Me Pink (1936)*½ Eddie Cantor, Ethel Merman, Sally Eilers, William Frawley, Brian Donlevy, Parkyakarkus. For Cantor fans only. His frenetic comedy style is rather grating in this unappetizing musical comedy pitting him against mobsters trying to take over his amusement park. (Dir: Norman Taurog, 100 mins.)

Strike Up the Band (1940)**½ Mickey Rooney, Judy Garland, June Preisser, William Tracy, Paul Whiteman and his orchestra. Big-budget MGM musical is full of energy but never takes off beyond the level of self-conscious trouping. (Dir: Busby Berkeley, 120 mins.)†

Strip, The (1951)**½ Mickey Rooney, Sally Forrest, Vic Damone. Occasionally absorbing drama about an ex-soldier who tries to resume his career as a drummer but is sidetracked by racketeers. Good musical numbers by many guest artists, including Vic Damone, Kay Brown, Louis Armstrong, Jack Teagarden, and Monica Lewis. (Dir: Leslie Kardos, 85 mins.)

Stripes (1981)**½ Bill Murray, Harold Ramis, Warren Oates, John Candy, John Larroquette, P. J. Soles, Sean Young, John Diehl, Judge Reinhold, Dave Thomas, Joe Flaherty. Misfits Murray and Ramis enlist, stupidly believing that the modern-day army is the equivalent of Club Med. Lame comedy is carried entirely by Murray's goofy charm and brief bits from the supporting comics; otherwise, it's one of the worst written and directed money-making comedies of the decade. (Dir: Ivan Reitman, 106 mins.)†

Stripped to Kill (1987)** Kay Lenz, Greg Evigan, Norman Fell. Detective Lenz goes uncovered—er, *under*cover at a glitzy *Flashdance*-type strip bar in order to track down the psycho who has been killing dancers. Pretty tame, though a surprise ending helps. (Dir: Katt Shea Ruben, 87 mins.)†

Stripper, The (1963)**½ Joanne Woodward, Richard Beymer, Claire Trevor, Carol Lynley, Gypsy Rose Lee. Apart from a valiant try by the miscast Woodward, this film is pure soap opera. She plays a girl working in a run-down road show, who decides to try for a new life and ends up falling for a young lad. (Dir: Franklin Schaffner, 95 mins.)†

Stripper (1986)*** Janette Boyd, Sara Costa, Kimberly Holcomb, Loree Menton, Lisa Suarez. A surprisingly good semidocumentary about the take-it-all-off world of the modern-day ecdysiast. The performers are generally well served

by the presentation. (Dir: Jerome Gary, 90 mins.)†

Stroker Ace (1983)½ Burt Reynolds, Loni Anderson, Parker Stevenson, Jim Nabors, Ned Beatty, John Byner. Racecars, chicken suits, fat sheriffs and lame virgin jokes are the main ingredients in another of Reynolds's "good-ol'-boy" comedies. (Dir: Hal Needham, 96 mins.)†

Stromboli (Italy, 1949)*** Ingrid Bergman, Mario Vitale. Poorly received at the time because of the scandal over Bergman's private life, the film now seems remarkably modern. A woman escapes an internment camp by marrying a poor fisherman, only to find herself trapped on his island, a spiritual sort of prison. (Dir: Roberto Rossellini, 107 mins.)†

Strongest Man in the World, The (1975)** Kurt Russell, Eve Arden, Phil Silvers, Joe Flynn, Cesar Romero. Russell engagingly plays a college student who comes up with a vitamin formula that gives him superhuman strength in this Disney comedy. (Dir: Vincent McEveety, 92 mins.)

Stroszek (West Germany, 1977)**** Bruno S., Eva Mattes, Clemens Scheitz. A bizarre, poignant, seriocomic odyssey through America. Possibly Werner Herzog's most accessible film, it views the U.S.A. from a fresh perspective as three German misfits pursue life, liberty, and happiness in America's heartland. Quirky, moving, idiosyncratic; a film to keep you on your toes. (108 mins.)

Structure of Crystals, The (Poland, 1969)***½ Barbara Wrzesinska, Andrzej Wladyslaw Jarema, Jan Myslowicz, Daniel Olbrychski. Intensely philosophical and erotic drama about a scientist who flees the big city with his wife for a remote outpost. Allegorical film examines a subject rarely discussed in movies: the true relationship of science to people. A stunning directorial debut by Krzysztof Zanussi. (137 mins.)

Stuckey's Last Stand (1980)* Whit Reichert, Tom Murray. Lame-brain comedy about an embattled camp counselor and the monstrous kiddies in his care. (Dir: Lawrence Goldfarb, 95 mins.)†

Stuck with Each Other (MTV 1989)**½ Richard Crenna, Tyne Daly, Roscoe Lee Browne, Eileen Heckart, Michael J. Pollard. Bumbling salesman Crenna and secretary Daly swipe a million dollars they found in the safe of their dead boss, then spend the rest of the movie on the run from his crooked partners. Some laughs but ultimately a silly vehicle for two stars who deserve better. (Dir: Georg Sanford Brown, 96 mins.)

Stud, The (Great Britain, 1978)* Joan Collins, Oliver Tobias, Sue Lloyd. Sex and gambling in swinging London are the plot elements of this film version of a novel by Joan's sister Jackie. The stud is the virile manager of a London nitery whose obligations include service in the boudoir. (Dir: Quentin Masters, 90 mins.)

Student Bodies (1981)* Kristen Riter, Matthew Goldsby, Richard Brando, Joe Floyd. This teen comedy commits one crime after another, foremost being its attempt to make splatter films seem funny. The film's troubled production history shows on-screen; watch this spoof manqué and see if you'd want your name listed on the credits. (Dir: Mickey Rose, 86 mins.)†

Student Confidential (1987)* Eric Douglas, Marlon Jackson, Susan Scott, Richard Horian, Ronee Blakley. Director/star Horian also wrote, produced, edited, and scored this unintentionally hilarious update of the old "teens in trouble" melodramas. He plays a wealthy guidance counselor who has problems of his own. Starring celeb siblings Eric (Michael's brother) and Marlon (Michael's brother). (94 mins.)†

Student of Prague, The (Germany, 1912)*** Paul Wegener. Fascinating first film version of a classic German story by Hanns Heinz Ewers, based on the legend of Faust, of a poor student who falls in love with a wealthy woman and sells his soul to the devil to win her. An expressionist classic. (Dir: Stellen Rye, 56 mins.)†

Student of Prague, The (Germany, 1927)**** Conrad Veidt, Werner Kraus, Agnes Esterhazy. Brilliantly stylized version of the famous German tale about a student who sells his soul, in the form of his reflection in a mirror, to a mysterious Lucifer-like figure, only to find that the reflection has escaped and taken over his life. Veidt is superb. (Dir: Henrik Galeen, 60 mins.)

Student Prince, The (1954)** Ann Blyth, Edmund Purdom. Stuffy prince is sent to Heidelberg U. to learn how to unwind, and he does, falling for a winsome waitress. Corny Romberg operetta, with the voice of Mario Lanza on the soundtrack. (Dir: Richard Thorpe, 107 mins.)

Student Prince in Old Heidelberg, The (1927)***½ Ramon Novarro, Norma Shearer, Jean Hersholt, Gustav Von Seyffertiz. Silent comedy-romance about young prince Novarro leaving the palace for the first time to attend a university, learning about the "common people" and falling in love with barmaid Shearer. Stylish, charming, movie. (Dir: Ernst Lubitsch, 105 mins.)

Student Teachers, The (1973)*½ Susan Damante, Brooke Mills, John Cramer, Dick Miller, Bob Harris, Don Steele, Charles Dierkop. One of producer Roger Corman's sillier high school movies, with teachers trying out new techniques on Valley teens. Sophomoric double entendres and heavy breathing abound. Followed by *Summer School Teachers*. (Dir: Jonathan Kaplan, 80 mins.)†

Stud Farm, The (Hungary, 1971)*** Joszef Madras, Ferenc Fabian, Sandor Howath, Karoly Sinka. Bitter look at the madness, cabals, and brutality of Stalinism, seen through the eyes of an inexperienced official caught up in a web of duplicity and vengeance. A vivid look at the Soviet repression of Hungary. Based on a book by Istvan Gaal. (Dir: Andras Kovacs, 100 mins.)

Studs Lonigan (1960)** Christopher Knight, Frank Gorshin, Venetia Stevenson, Jack Nicholson. Rambling tale about the life and loves of a young drifter on Chicago's South Side in the twenties, suffers from Knight's stiff acting in the lead role and a trite ending. Visually excellent, evocative of the era. (Dir: Irving Lerner, 103 mins.)†

Study in Scarlet, A (1933)*½ Reginald Owen, June Clyde, Alan Dinehart, Anna May Wong, Alan Mowbray. Interesting artifact in that Owen had played Doctor Watson in *Sherlock Holmes* (1932). Here, he demonstrates he's not ideally suited for the role of supersleuth Sherlock. (Dir: Edwin L. Marin, 70 mins.)

Study in Terror, A (Great Britain-West Germany, 1965)*** John Neville, Donald Houston, Anthony Quayle. Great detective Sherlock Holmes faces the villainous Jack the Ripper in this entertaining suspense tale buoyed by a flawless British cast. (Dir: James Hill, 94 mins.)†

Stuff, The (1985)* Michael Moriarty, Andrea Marcovicci, Garrett Morris, Paul Sorvino. Stuff and nonsense. Another great concept from writer-director-producer Larry Cohen, who, as director, deserves a better writer and, as producer, should know better than to hire himself to direct. The forced laughs and meager satire on consumerism are impossible to overlook. Killer Tofutti destroys dessert fanciers who learn too late that the habit-forming "Stuff" causes zombiedom. (93 mins.)†

Stuff Stephanie in the Incinerator (1989)* Catherine Dee, William Dane, M. R. Murphy, Dennis Cunningham. Gratuitously retitled dud about a bored rich couple who participate in a role-playing game involving fake kidnappings, murder plots, etc. The only twist is that there *is* no twist—the game ends, and so does the movie. (Dir: Don Nardo, 98 mins.)†

Stuntman (Italy, 1968)** Gina Lollobrigida, Robert Viharo, Marisa Mell. Movie stunt man enticed to rob Indian statue by a pair of lovelies. (Dir: Marcello Baldi, 95 mins.)

Stunt Man, The (1980)**** Peter O'Toole, Steve Railsback, Chuck Bail, Allen Goorwitz, Barbara Hershey. Ambitious, demanding, and remarkably rewarding drama about a fugitive who stumbles into a movie production, is drafted as a stunt man, and begins to lose his grip on reality. O'Toole as an obsessed, dictatorial director gives one of the bravura performances of the decade, and there's good support all along the line. Director-producer Richard Rush worked on the project for nine years and had to wait two years after the film was completed in 1978 to get it released. (129 mins.)†

Stunts (1977)*** Robert Forster, Fiona Lewis, Joanna Cassidy. Excellent whodunit about a maniac who systematically kills off stunt persons while a spectacular action film is being shot near San Luis Obispo. AKA: Who Is Killing the Stuntmen? (Dir: Mark Lester, 89 mins.)†

Stunt Seven (MTV 1979)** Christopher Connelly, Christopher Lloyd, Bob Seagren. Seven Hollywood stunt men form a vigilante group to rescue a kidnapped movie queen. Comic book heroics all the way. (Dir: John Peyser, 104 mins.)

Stunts Unlimited (MTV 1980)* Glenn Corbett, Susanna Dalton, Sam Jones, Chip Mayer. Limited action pic about Hollywood's stunt experts lending their talents to a top secret mission for Uncle Sam. (Dir: Hal Needham, 78 mins.)

St. Valentine's Day Massacre (1967)** Jason Robards, George Segal, Jean Hale. A warmed-over look at the Chicago gangland of the late twenties. The famous "massacre" is the highlight of the film, and the cast is appropriately stern-faced and threatening. (Dir: Roger Corman, 100 mins.)†

Sub-a-Dub-Dub—See: Hello Down There

Subida al Cielo—See: Mexican Bus Ride

Subject Was Roses, The (1968)***½ Patricia Neal, Jack Albertson, Martin Sheen. Compelling film version of Frank D. Gilroy's Pulitzer prize-winning play. It is the story of a young man who returns home from his Army duty after WWII, only to find his quarreling parents still engaged in battle. (Dir: Ulu Grosbard, 107 mins.)

Submarine Alert (1943)** Richard Arlen, Wendy Barrie, Nils Asther, Abner Biberman, Dwight Frye. Low-budget actioner about an FBI man infiltrating a gang of Axis spies who are jamming critical radio frequencies. OK, but not special. (Dir: Frank Mcdonald, 67 mins.)

Submarine Command (1951)**½ William Holden, Nancy Olson, William Bendix. Moderately entertaining war drama with good performances by the principals.

Holden plays a sub commander who is plagued with self-doubt about his part in a past incident which cost some men their lives. (Dir: John Farrow, 87 mins.)

Submarine D-1 (1937)** Pat O'Brien, George Brent, Wayne Morris, Doris Weston, Frank McHugh. Patriotic adventure, made with the Navy's assistance, about the working life of a submarine crew. (Dir: Lloyd Bacon, 100 mins.)

Submarine Patrol (1938)***½ Richard Greene, Nancy Kelly, Preston Foster. Exciting tale of a WWI tub of a subchaser is good fare thanks to John Ford's direction. (Dir: John Ford, 95 mins.)

Submarine Raider (1942)**½ John Howard, Marguerite Chapman, Larry Parks. Exciting, above average B movie, supposedly dramatizing some of the events that took place in the Pacific, December 6 and 7, 1941. (Dir: Lew Landers, 64 mins.)

Submarine X-1 (Great Britain, 1968)** James Caan, Rupert Davies. Scenic shenanigans as naval commander Caan trains three crews to man midget submarines and go against a huge German destroyer during WWII. (Dir: William Graham, 89 mins.)

Subterfuge (U.S.-Great Britain, 1968)** Gene Barry, Joan Collins, Richard Todd, Suzanna Leigh, Michael Rennie. Barry plays an American agent forced to assist British intelligence in a manhunt for a defector. Slight suspense, OK acting. (Dir: Peter Graham Scott, 92 mins.)†

Subterraneans, The (1960)* Leslie Caron, George Peppard, Janice Rule, Nanette Fabray. Trashy, watered-down version of Jack Kerouac's novel about beats, bores, bemused beauties and pre-hippie types in San Francisco. (Dir: Ranald MacDougall, 89 mins.)

Suburbia (1984)** Chris Pederson, Bill Coyne, Jennifer Clay, Don Allen. A low-budget punk modernization of a standard 1950s delinquent vs. authority plotline. Teens flee from their unloving suburban parents and build their own punk community. AKA: The Wild Side. (Dir: Penelope Spheeris, 99 min.)†

Subway (France, 1985)*** Christopher Lambert, Isabelle Adjani, Richard Bohringer. Stylish mixture of MTV and *Diva* has an interesting premise—a group of misfits and thieves live in the nether regions of the Paris subway system—but concentrates instead on gaudy visuals and mediocre pseudo-New Wave music. (Dir: Luc Besson, 108 mins.)†

Subway in the Sky (Great Britain, 1959)** Van Johnson, Hildegarde Neff. Muddled adventure about an American doctor in postwar Berlin who gets involved with murder, the black market and a glamorous nightclub entertainer. (Dir: Muriel Box, 85 mins.)

Subway to the Stars (Brazil, 1988)*** Guilherme Fontes, Taumaturgo Ferreira, Zé Trindade. An Orpheus story set against the colorful backdrop of modern Rio. Vinicius (Fontes), a young musician, loses his girlfriend and mounts a search for her through the underworld. Bold and evocative, if at times obscure. (Dir: Carlos Diegues, 103 mins.)†

Success (1979)—See: **American Success Story, The**

Success, The (Italy-France, 1963)***½ Vittorio Gassman, Anouk Aimee, Jean-Louis Trintignant. Real-estate man consumed with the desire for success despite the ordinary comforts sacrifices his happiness in his quest. Well-acted drama tells its story with the moral sharply outlined. (Dir: Dino Risi, 103 mins.)

Success at Any Price (1934)*** Douglas Fairbanks, Jr., Genevieve Tobin, Frank Morgan, Colleen Moore, Edward Everett Horton. Scalding social drama of a ruthless financier who tramples everyone who gets in his way; stringent, uncompromising script, extremely well done. (Dir: J. Walter Ruben, 75 mins.)

Successful Calamity, A (1932)**½ George Arliss, Mary Astor, Evalyn Knapp, Grant Mitchell, Hardie Albright. Engaging comedy about a millionaire who, fed up with being ignored by his wife and children, tells them he's lost all his money. Deftly played. (Dir: John G. Adolfi, 72 mins.)

Succubus—See: **Devil's Nightmare, The**

Such a Gorgeous Kid Like Me (France, 1972)***½ Bernadette Lafont, Charles Denner, Philippe Leotard. Underrated black comedy from director Francois Truffaut about a milquetoast sociologist who studies, and then becomes enamored of, a very hedonistic mademoiselle. (100 mins.)

Such Good Friends (1971)** Dyan Cannon, James Coco, Jennifer O'Neill, Ken Howard. A sexually frustrated wife (Cannon) discovers that her ailing husband has been philandering with most of their female friends, and sets out to make up for lost time by popping into bed with any willing male. Some scenes are sardonic and funny, some witless and vulgar. (Dir: Otto Preminger, 101 mins.)

Suden (1945)** Maria Montez, Jon Hall, Turhan Bey, Andy Devine, George Zucco. Maria, the high priestess of Universal Studios camp, is in full flower here in a tale about avenging her father's death and avoiding the machinations of the fruity villain, Zucco. It's a toss-up as to whose clothes are wilder, Maria's or Zucco's. (Dir: John Rawlins, 76 mins.)

Sudden Danger (1955)*** Bill Elliott, Tom Drake, Beverly Garland. Detective helps a blind man, whose sight is restored after an operation, to track down his mother's murderer. Rates well above the usual grade B run—exceptionally good direction, logical script, good performances. (Dir: Hubert Cornfield, 85 mins.)

Sudden Death (1985)*½ Denise Coward, Frank Runyeon, Jamie Tirelli. The vigilante killer in this film is nicknamed the "Dum-Dum" killer, and this is a dumb-dumb movie about a female exec who goes on the prowl for rapists after she's brutally attacked. (Dir: Sig Shore, 95 mins.)†

Sudden Fear (1952)*** Joan Crawford, Jack Palance, Gloria Grahame, Michael Connors. Wealthy playwright marries a worthless actor who plans to murder her. Well acted, smoothly produced suspense thriller. (Dir: David Miller, 110 mins.)

Sudden Fortune of the Poor People of Kombach, The (West Germany, 1971)***½ Reinhard Hauff, Georg Lehn, Wolfgang Bachler, Margarethe Von Trotta, Rainer Werner Fassbinder. 19th-century peasants steal money from a tax collector, which leads to their desolation. Strong examination of the tragic dimensions of greed and its cruel consequences. (Dir: Volker Schlondorff, 94 mins.)

Sudden Impact (1983)** Clint Eastwood, Pat Hingle, Sondra Locke, Audrie Neenan. Dirty Harry is back. This time he's tracking a killer with whom he has a lot in common. Unfortunately, Eastwood settles for a slam-bang directorial style that conjures up excitement but doesn't enhance the vigilante storyline, about a woman methodically killing the men who gang-raped her and her sister years before. (117 mins.)†

Suddenly (1954)** Frank Sinatra, Sterling Hayden, Nancy Gates, James Gleason. Dated thriller. Sinatra is impressive as the leader of a pack of hired assassins who plan to murder the President during his stopover in a sleepy little town. Due to uncomfortable echoes of the Kennedy assassination, the film was out of circulation for many years, but it has not reemerged as a long-lost treasure; it is riddled with fifties stereotypes and mouthpiece characters. (Dir: Lewis Allen, 77 mins.)†

Suddenly It's Spring (1947)*½ Fred MacMurray, Paulette Goddard. Forced, contrived comedy about a lawyer who wants to divorce his wife. She doesn't want to divorce him, and away we go. (Dir: Mitchell Leisen, 87 mins.)

Suddenly, Last Summer (1959)*** Elizabeth Taylor, Katharine Hepburn, Montgomery Clift. One of Tennessee Williams's macabre one-act plays has been transferred to the screen in an uneven, but nevertheless effective, presentation. Taylor is having a breakdown because of the events of last summer, when she accompanied her homosexual cousin on his vacation and witnessed his death. Dr. Clift is hired to commit Taylor to an asylum, but he wants to get to the bottom of the mystery. (Dir: Joseph L. Mankiewicz, 114 mins.)†

Suddenly, Love (MTV 1978)** Cindy Williams, Paul Shenar, Joan Bennett. Williams doesn't have the star power to pull off Ross Hunter's glossy, sudsy love story. She plays a Brooklyn girl, influenced by John F. Kennedy, who's determined to rise out of the gutter to become an architect. (Dir: Stuart Margolin, 104 mins.)

Suddenly Single (MTV 1971)**½ Hal Holbrook, Barbara Rush, Margot Kidder, Michael Constantine, Cloris Leachman. Holbrook's abundant charm and talent are put to good use in this modern story about an over-35 druggist who finds himself on his own after ten years of marriage. (Dir: Jud Taylor, 78 mins.)

Sudden Terror (Great Britain, 1971)**½ Lionel Jeffries, Susan George, Mark Lester. A well-done suspense thriller in the accepted vein. Lester is prone to telling tall tales. So you can't really blame his sister and grandfather when they reject his story about witnessing the assassination of a visiting African president on the island of Malta. (Dir: John Hough, 95 mins.)†

Suez (1938)*** Tyrone Power, Loretta Young, Annabella, Joseph Schildkraut, Sidney Blackmer. Well-photographed and lavish film which is supposed to tell the true story of how the Suez Canal was built. If it had done that, it might have been a great film instead of another colorful epic. (Dir: Allan Dwan, 104 mins.)

Suffering Bastards (1990)*** John C. McGinley, David Warshofsky, Pam LaTesta, Rene Rivera, Eric Bogosian. Two dim-witted brothers try to regain their mother's tacky Atlantic City nightclub after she loses it to a con man. Low-budget comedy makes up in bizarre inventiveness what it lacks in production values. (Dir: Bernard McWilliams, 89 mins.)

Sugarbaby (West Germany, 1985)** Marianne Sagebrecht. Eisi Gulp, Toni Berger, Will Spendler, Manuela Denz. A sweetly sexy, loudly stylized, but incredibly overrated film about a portly mortician who sinks into her own flesh until life throws her a life preserver—a handsome hunk of a subway conductor, whom the *zoftig* babe decides to snare. Despite the unsteady tone, some will fancy this erotic tale of a tubby Cinderella who didn't have to crash diet to get her prince. Remade as *Babycakes*. (Dir: Percy Adlon, 86 mins.)†

Sugar Cane Alley (France, 1984)*** Gerry

Cadenat, Darling Legitimus. A poignant look backward at the plight of black workers in 1930s Martinique. The film's sole ray of optimism shines on Jose, an intelligent boy who wins a scholarship which may lift him out of the poverty of his forebears. (Dir: Euzhan Palcy, 103 mins.)†

Sugarfoot (1951)**½ Randolph Scott, Adele Jergens, Raymond Massey, S. Z. Sakall. Sturdy western adventure with Scott an ex-Confederate moving to Arizona after the Civil War, encountering an old enemy who has become a powerful land baron. Fast-moving and colorful. AKA: Swirl of Glory. (Dir: Edwin L. Marin, 80 mins.)

Sugar Hill (1974)**½ Marki Bey, Robert Quarry, Don Pedro Colley, Richard Lawson, Betty Ann Rees. When a black nightclub entrepreneur is murdered, his girlfriend calls upon a high priestess to summon up zombies to carry out her revenge scheme. Far-out and entertaining, although the different elements of action pic and horror film never coalesce. AKA: The Zombies of Sugar Hill. (Dir: Paul Maslansky, 91 mins.)

Sugarland Express, The (1974)***½ Goldie Hawn, William Atherton, Michael Sacks, Ben Johnson. Rewarding comedy-drama. Based on a real-life story of a Texas couple running from the law, trying to regain custody of their baby, who has been farmed out to a foster family while they were in prison for some petty thefts. Fine screenplay by Hal Barwood, Mathew Robbins. (Dir: Steven Spielberg, 108 mins.)†

Suicide Club, The (1988)* Mariel Hemingway, Robert Joy, Lenny Henry, Michael O'Donoghue. Slow-moving tale of an alienated young woman who falls in with a group of well-to-do people who play mysterious games. It seems as if the only point to this incredibly dull bit of decadence was to show Mariel (who also produced) looking dazzling in a variety of fashions. (Dir: James Bruce, 90 mins.)†

Suicide Run—See: Too Late the Hero

Suicide's Wife, The (MTV 1977)½ Angie Dickinson, Gordon Pinsent, Todd Lookinland. The title says it all very clearly—forget this gloomy bore. Angie Dickinson is the numb widow, who doesn't know why her professor husband killed himself. (Dir: John Newland, 104 mins.)

Sullivans, The (1944)**** Anne Baxter, Selena Royle, Ward Bond, Thomas Mitchell. The story of the five heroic brothers who died gallantly in naval service during WWII. Well-made drama pulls the heartstrings. (Dir: Lloyd Bacon, 111 mins.)

Sullivan's Empire (1967)* Martin Milner, Clu Gulager, Karen Jensen, Linden

Chiles, Don Quine. Three sons are reunited when they hear that their plantation-owner father has been kidnapped. The film is full of headhunters, man-eating fish, and a total lack of credibility. (Dirs: Harvey Hart, Thomas Carr, 85 mins.)

Sullivan's Travels (1942)***½ Joel McCrea, William Demarest, Eric Blore, Veronica Lake. Story of a movie director, a specialist in comedy, who wants to make a dramatic film so he sets out to learn about life. Preston Sturges makes this adventure an original, offbeat screen entertainment. (91 mins.)†

Summer (France, 1986)***½ Marie Riviere, Vincent Gauthier, Lisa Heredia. A lonely romantic tries to make something of a summer holiday on her own. Though her dourness puts off both old and new friends, she persists with her own dreamy vision of companionship and love. A bittersweet picaresque fable that culminates in a surprisingly moving epiphany; a must for Rohmer fans and for anyone who's ever expected life to deliver more than it does. AKA: **Le Rayon Vert**. (Dir: Eric Rohmer, 98 mins.)†

Summer and Smoke (1961)** Geraldine Page, Laurence Harvey, Una Merkel, John McIntire, Pamela Tiffin, Rita Moreno. Tennessee Williams's mood piece about a frustrated spinster grappling with the extremes of carnal and romantic love is given a vulgar and obvious screen treatment by Peter Glenville. The director turns a fragile poem about desire into a crude limmerick. Page renders a potent facsimile of her acclaimed stage performance of Alma, a repressed woman who burns inside with love for her high-spirited neighbor (Harvey), but the actress has a lot to compensate for. (118 mins.)†

Summer Camp Nightmare (1986)** Charles Stratton, Chuck Connors, Adam Carl. Misleadingly titled antifascist parable similar to *Lord of the Flies*. A camp counselor sets up a revolution among the other kids, who ignore his megalomania as long as they get what they want (junk food, parties, and sex). Ambitious but unsatisfying, with an anticlimactic ending. AKA: **The Butterfly Revolution**. (Dir: Bert L. Dragin, 88 mins.)†

Summer Fantasy (MTV 1984)** Ted Shackelford, Julianne Phillips, Michael Gross. TV flick about a young lady who fights convention in order to become the first woman lifeguard at a California beach. (Dir: Noel Nosseck, 104 mins.)†

Summer Girl (MTV 1983)**½ Barry Bostwick, Kim Darby, Martha Scott, Murray Hamilton. Drama about a babysitter who menaces an entire household. (Dir: Robert Lewis, 104 mins.)

Summer Heat (1987)**½ Lori Singer, Anthony Edwards, Bruce Abbott, Clu Gulager. Steaming, sluggish tale of a frustrated young housewife's torrid affair with a handsome drifter who takes a dangerously possessive interest in her. (Dir: Michie Gleason, 90 mins.)†

Summer Holiday (1948)**½ Mickey Rooney, Gloria De Haven, Walter Huston, Frank Morgan, Marilyn Maxwell. Musical version of O'Neill's *Ah, Wilderness!* is much admired in some critical circles and uses color brilliantly, but receives no aid from a commonplace score. (Dir: Rouben Mamoulian, 92 mins.)

Summer Holiday (Great Britain, 1963)**½ Cliff Richards, Lauri Peters, Ron Moody. A pleasant old-fashioned-plot musical. A group of young men travel across Europe in a bus, and before too long they meet pretty young girls who join them. (Dir: Peter Yates, 107 mins.)

Summer Interlude (Sweden, 1950)***½ Maj-Britt Nilsson, Birger Malmsten, Alf Kjellin, Georg Funkquist, Stig Olin. Tender Ingmar Bergman drama about a ballerina haunted by a tragic love affair she had in her youth with a boy who was killed. An emotional cripple, she meets a journalist who falls in love with her, and tries to break the spell of her melancholia. A beautiful and lyrical film. AKA: **Illicit Interlude**. (95 mins.)†

Summer Job (1989)½ Amy Baxter, Sherrie Rose, Cari Mayor, George O., Renee Shugart. If we had a lower rating, this movie would get it; in fact, we're tempted to invent one for this alleged comedy about brain-dead college students working at a Miami resort. The people responsible for this must really think that their audiences are morons—no one could make a movie this bad otherwise. (Dir: Paul Madden, 90 mins.)†

Summer Lighting (West Germany, 1972)*** Margarethe Von Trotta, Martin Luttge, Walter Sedimayer, Friedhelm Ptok. A woman gains a sense of independence after a bitter divorce from her domineering husband, which fades when she has difficulty finding a job in a male-dominated world. Effective drama with a great performance by Von Trotta, who co-wrote the script with her husband, director Volker Schlondorff. (100 mins.)

Summer Love (1958)**½ John Saxon, Molly Bee, Jill St. John, Judi Meredith, Rod McKuen. Nearly thirty years before *Dirty Dancing*, there was this rock'n'roll musical about teens hired to entertain at a summer resort. Irresistibly energetic young cast raises cute film above the ordinary. Sequel to *Rock, Pretty Baby* with some of the same faces returning. (Dir: Charles Haas, 85 mins.)

Summer Lovers (1982)**½ Peter Gallagher,

Daryl Hannah, Valerie Quennessen. Gallagher and Hannah are lovers vacationing in Greece, and they encounter a French archaeologist named Lina. They enter into a series of tableaux (scantily clad) on various beaches. (Dir: Randal Kleiser, 98 mins.)†

Summer Magic (1963)**½ Hayley Mills, Dorothy McGuire, Burl Ives, Deborah Walley. An airy trifle from Disney that serves as an attractive showcase for Hayley Mills. She's part of a family that's being raised by widow Dorothy McGuire, who's got to pinch pennies and sort out her kids' problems. (Dir: James Neilson, 100 mins.)†

Summer My Father Grew Up, The (MTV 1991)*** John Ritter, Margaret Whitton, Karen Young, Matthew Lawrence, Joe Spano. Ritter is a divorced father in this interesting, well-written drama by Sandra Jennings. He's an emergency room doctor unaware of the wounds inflicted on his 11-year-old son when the family splits up. (Dir: Michael Tuchner, 96 mins.)

Summer Night—See: **Summer Night With Greek Profile, Almond Eyes, and Scent of Basil**

Summer Night With Greek Profile, Almond Eyes, and Scent of Basil (Italy, 1987)**½ Mariangela Melato, Michele Placido. Wealthy capitalist pig Melato kidnaps ruthless terrorist Placido to teach him a lesson, only to fall in love with him. Hardly *Swept Away*, but still enjoyably sexy. AKA: **Summer Night**. (Dir: Lina Wertmuller, 94 mins.)†

Summer of Fear—See: **Stranger In Our House**

Summer of '42 (1971)*** Jennifer O'Neill, Gary Grimes, Jerry Houser, Oliver Connant. A nostalgic film about a fifteen-year-old boy's coming of sexual age in an island vacation community off New England. Some could label this simple tale about Grimes's adolescent crush on the beautiful twenty-two-year-old war bride (O'Neill) sentimental . . . but it works beautifully. (Dir: Robert Mulligan, 102 mins.)†

Summer of My German Soldier, The (MTV 1978)***½ Kristy McNichol, Michael Constantine, Bruce Davison, Esther Rolle. There's a sweetness and a sensitivity about this story of the relationship between a Jewish teenager, luminously played by McNichol, and an escaping anti-Nazi German POW, acted with tender restraint by Davison. (Dir: Michael Tuchner, 104 mins.)†

Summer of the Seventeenth Doll—See: **Season of Passion**

Summer Place, A (1959)**½ Richard Egan, Dorothy McGuire, Sandra Dee, Constance Ford, Troy Donahue. Sugar-coated tale of a businessman who returns to his

summer home, meets an old flame; love is rekindled, plus an affair begins between his daughter and her son. (Dir: Delmer Daves, 130 mins.)†

Summer Rental (1985)** John Candy, Karen Austin, Richard Crenna, Rip Torn, John Larroquette. Candy is the whole show in this featherweight comedy about a hard-working slob trying to get some rest and relaxation in Florida. (Dir: Carl Reiner, 88 mins.)†

Summer School (1987)*** Mark Harmon, Kirstie Alley, Robin Thomas. California high school gym teacher Harmon is forced to cancel his summer plans and take over a remedial English class featuring the usual assortment of student goofballs. Thin material engagingly played. (Dir: Carl Reiner, 98 mins.)†

Summer School Teachers (1975)** Candice Rialson, Pat Anderson, Rhonda Leigh-Hopkins, Dick Miller. Tired comedy about young teachers sharing romantic adventures while educating the unwilling. Well-paced, but that's about all. (Dir: Barbara Peeters, 87 mins.)†

Summer Solstice (MTV 1981)***½ Henry Fonda, Myrna Loy, Stephen Collins, Lindsay Crouse, Patricia Elliot. As a companion piece to his Oscar-winning performance in *On Golden Pond*, Fonda plays a similar character, an old man living out his twilight years with his true love, his wife of fifty years. Fonda is superb as the artist who always marched to his own drummer. (Dir: Ralph Rosenblum, 56 mins.)

Summer Stock (1950)*** Judy Garland, Gene Kelly. Tuneful musical tailored for the talents of the stars. The plot concerns a farm, run by Judy, which is invaded by a group of show people who want to turn the barn into a summer theater. This sets the stage for many songs and dances including Judy's big number "Get Happy." (Dir: Charles Walters, 100 mins.)†

Summer Storm (1944)***½ George Sanders, Linda Darnell, Anna Lee, Edward Everett Horton. This engrossing adaptation of Anton Chekhov's *The Shooting Party* stars Sanders as a dissipated aristocrat undone by his infatuation for a memorably perverse Darnell. (Dir: Douglas Sirk, 106 mins.)

Summer Story, A (Great Britain, 1988)**½ Imogen Stubbs, James Wilby, Susannah York. Picturesque period romance with a limp, upper-crust hero and a ravishing lower-class heroine. Their difference in class informs this often hollow love story with bittersweet overtones. (Dir: Piers Haggard, 95 mins.)

Summertime (1955)***½ Katharine Hepburn, Rossano Brazzi. Romantic story, set in Venice, about an American schoolmarm and an Italian merchant. You'll seldom see as perceptive or touching a rendition of a spinster tentatively searching for affection as Hepburn delivers here. (Dir: David Lean, 99 mins.)†

Summertime Killer, The (France-Italy, 1972)** Karl Malden, Christopher Mitchum, Raf Vallone. Confusing revenge tale. Young man plans to punish the men who executed his father several years before. Ex-cop (Malden) goes after him, providing several good chases, the picture's main asset. (Dir: Antonio Isasi, 109 mins.)

Summer to Remember, A (MTV 1985)**½ James Farentino, Louise Fletcher, Sean Gerlis, Tess Harper. A sweet family movie about a deaf boy and an orangutan who can communicate with him. The orangutan is susceptible to cruel humans, including a circus hustler, only to be saved by our young hero in a satisfying finale. (Dir: Robert Lewis, 104 mins.)†

Summertree (1971)** Michael Douglas, Barbara Bel Geddes, Jack Warden, Brenda Vaccaro. A sensitive play by Ron Cowen gets mangled in its transfer to film. Douglas plays the young man torn by his parents' beliefs and his own convictions about the Vietnam War and his life in general. (Dir: Anthony Newley, 88 mins.)

Summer Wishes, Winter Dreams (1973) *** Joanne Woodward, Martin Balsam, Sylvia Sidney. Poignant, often perceptive story about a middle-aged New York couple (Woodward and Balsam) who take a trip to rekindle their flagging marriage, going to Bastogne and other sites of his WWII duty. (Dir: Gilbert Cates, 87 mins.)†

Summer with Monika—See: **Monika**

Summer Without Boys, A (MTV 1973)*** Barbara Bain, Kay Lenz, Michael Moriarty. Nostalgia runs high in this tale set on the home front during WWII about an attractive woman and her teenaged daughter and the romantic confrontations they face during a summer stay at a resort. (Dir: Jeannot Szwarc, 73 mins.)

Sun Also Rises, The (1957)**½ Errol Flynn, Ava Gardner, Tyrone Power. Hemingway's sprawling novel about the drifters and dreamers known as the lost generation during the twenties is uneven in its transference to the screen, but contains some good on-location photography and a colorful performance by Flynn as a drunken bon vivant. (Dir: Henry King, 129 mins.)

Sun Also Rises, The (MTV 1985)*½ Jane Seymour, Hart Bochner, Elisabeth Borgnine, Robert Carradine, Zeljko Ivanek, Leonard Nimoy, Stephane Audran, Andrea Occhipinti. Hemingway's famous novel about American expatriates drifting through Europe in the twenties was not turned into a brilliant film in 1957, but that version at least had star power. In this plasticized TV revamp, Hemingway's themes are dwarfed. (Dir: James Goldstone, 208 mins.)

Sunburn (1979)½ Farrah Fawcett, Art Carney, Charles Grodin, Joan Collins, Eleanor Parker. Farrah is a model who's hired by an insurance adjuster (Grodin) to investigate a questionable $5 million claim in Acapulco. (Dir: Richard C. Sarafian, 100 mins.)†

Sun Comes Up, The (1949)** Jeanette MacDonald, Lloyd Nolan, Claude Jarman, Jr. MacDonald's last film was an entry in the Lassie series; she plays a bitter widow warmed by the love of Jarman for his collie. (Dir: Richard Thorpe, 93 mins.)

Sunday Bloody Sunday (Great Britain, 1971)**** Glenda Jackson, Peter Finch, Murray Head, Peggy Ashcroft. A remarkably moving film about the impossibility of love, involving a bisexual triangle of Head-Jackson and Head-Finch. As the callow young sculptor, Head loves both his partners, but not as much as he loves himself and his own ambitions. The overall effect is understated, accentuating the power and poignancy of the movie. Intelligent screenplay by Penelope Gilliatt; brilliantly directed by John Schlesinger. (110 mins.)†

Sunday Dinner for a Soldier (1944)*** Anne Baxter, John Hodiak, Charles Winninger, Connie Marshall, Billy Cummings, Bobby Driscoll. This patriotic heart-tugger may seem a little dated now, but the wholesome plot elements remain in effect. Baxter stars as the oldest sister of four orphans who scrounge up the money to invite a GI over for dinner. (Dir: Lloyd Bacon, 86 mins.)

Sunday Drive (MTV 1986)** Tony Randall, Carrie Fisher, Audra Lindley, Hillary Wolf, Raffi DiBlasio, Ted Wass. The kind of disposable Disney entertainment that you used to have to pay to see in theaters done up for television, with Randall, Lindley, Fisher, et al. in auto hijinks arising from confusion over two look-alike cars. (Dir: Mark Cullingham, 96 mins.)

Sunday in New York (1964)*** Jane Fonda, Rod Taylor, Cliff Robertson, Robert Culp. A girl still pure meets a dashing young man and quite innocently has her brother thinking the wrong things. Comedy that can be called "cute," but pleasantly so—performances are refreshing, pace is smooth. (Dir: Peter Tewksbury, 105 mins.)

Sunday in the Country, A (France, 1984)**½ Louis Decreux, Sabine Azema, Michel Aumont. A widowed impressionist painter is visited by his children and grandchildren one Sunday afternoon. That's about it for the plot in this gorgeous-looking but dull story in which every shot of rural France is photographed in the impressionistic style of the old man's paintings. You'd do better to spend the day at an art museum. (Dir: Bertrand Tavernier, 94 mins.)†

Sunday Lovers (Great Britain-U.S.-Italy-France, 1980)* Gene Wilder, Lino Ventura, Roger Moore, Ugo Tognazzi, Robert Webber, Kathleen Quinlan. A stalled omnibus of four romantic fables with the Italian segment getting the only laughs. (Dirs: Bryan Forbes, Edouard Molinaro, Dino Risi, Gene Wilder, 127 mins.)

Sundays and Cybele (France, 1962)***½ Hardy Kruger, Patricia Gozzi, Nicole Courcel. Touching, beautifully realized story about a troubled young man, an amnesiac, who befriends an orphan girl, pretending to be her father and taking her on Sunday excursions in the park. The man's psychotic tendencies are slowly revealed as the story builds to a terrifying climax. The actors are superb throughout. Oscar: Best Foreign Film. (Dir: Serge Bourguignon, 110 mins.)†

Sundown (1941)**½ Gene Tierney, Bruce Cabot, George Sanders. The British in Africa receive the aid of a jungle girl in defeating the attempts of the Nazis to take over. Second-rate melodrama. (Dir: Henry Hathaway, 91 mins.)†

Sundowners, The (1950)***½ Robert Preston, John Barrymore, Jr., Robert Sterling. A renegade gunman rides in to cause trouble for a boy and his father. Topnotch western, well written, acted. (Dir: George Templeton, 83 mins.)

Sundowners, The (1960)**** Robert Mitchum, Deborah Kerr, Peter Ustinov, Glynis Johns. A heartfelt movie, with director Fred Zinnemann lavishing attentive care on pictorial detail at the same time he relates all his characters to their environment. Mitchum and Kerr are sheepherders in Australia in the twenties; Johns and Ustinov provide some sauce to liven up the show with humor. (113 mins.)†

Sundown: The Vampire in Retreat (1990)*½ David Carradine, Jim Meltzer, Morgan Brittany, Maxwell Caulfield, M. Emmet Walsh, Deborah Foreman, Bruce Campbell, John Ireland. Most peculiar comedy set in Utah, where a colony of vampires who want to break their bloodsucking habits has built a factory to produce artificial blood. The soap-opera tribulations of this group fail to eke anything of interest from the unusual premise. (Dir: Anthony Hickox, 104 mins.)†

Sunflower (Italy, 1970)*** Sophia Loren, Marcello Mastroianni, Ludmilla Savelieva. Fifteen years after her soldier husband had been lost on the Stalingrad front, Loren treks to Moscow to find him. However, in traditional soap opera fashion, he has a new wife. This lyrical tearjerker is beautifully acted and photographed, and Loren's earth-mother presence grounds the plot's more incredible aspects in believability. (Dir: Vittorio De Sica, 105 mins.)

Sun Never Sets, The (1939)** Douglas Fairbanks, Jr., Basil Rathbone, Barabara O'Neil, Lionel Atwill, Virginia Field. Ho-hum procolonialism propaganda, about two brothers in the British foreign service trying to stop a madman from instigating revolution in Africa. The only pluses are the professional jobs turned in by the leads, Rathbone in particular. (Dir: Rowland V. Lee, 98 mins.)

Sunny (1941)**½ Anna Neagle, Ray Bolger, John Carroll, Edward Everett Horton. Lumpy version of the hit Broadway musical about a circus lass who meets and falls for a wealthy young man from New Orleans, though his family disapproves; tired plot, but a classic score by Jerome Kern and Oscar Hammerstein II, and a rare chance to hear Carroll's fine singing voice. (Dir: Herbert Wilcox, 98 mins.)

Sunnyside (1919)—See: **Woman of Paris**

Sunnyside (1979)* Joey Travolta, Andrew Rubin, John Lansing, Talia Balsam. A dismal effort by Joey, John's older brother, to suck stardom out of pseudo-*Saturday Night Fever* material. He inadequately portrays the role of a gang leader wanting to leave the local turf wars behind him in Queens, New York. (Dir: Timothy Galfos, 100 mins.)†

Sunny Side Up (1929)*** Janet Gaynor, Charles Farrell, El Brendel, Marjorie White, Jackie Cooper. Wonderful DeSylva-Brown-Henderson tunes vitalize this time capsule musical. A sweet and sunny tale of an impoverished lass encountering a rich Mr. Right. (Dir: David Butler, 115 mins.)

Sunrise (1927)**** George O'Brien, Janet Gaynor, Bodil Rosing, Margaret Livingstone. Graced with glistening photography that bestows a magical quality, this masterpiece spins a bittersweet fable about temptation and redemption, as a farmer strays from his true love when a big-city vamp eggs him on to dispose of his wife. Winner of several Oscars. (Dir: F. W. Murnau, 110 mins.)

Sunrise at Campobello (1960)*** Ralph Bellamy, Greer Garson. Inspiring story of young FDR, his conquering of the crippling disease of polio enabling him to walk to the rostrum to nominate Al Smith at the Democratic Convention. Based on the stage play, with Bellamy repeating his fine performance as Roosevelt. Greer Garson is surprisingly effective as his wife. Heartwarming drama. (Dir: Vincent J. Donehue, 143 mins.)†

Sun's Burial, The (Japan, 1960)***½ Kayoko Honoo, Koji Nakahara, Masahiko Tsugawa, Fumio Watanabe. Violent drama set in Osaka's worst slum, a hopeless hell where gangs, hookers, and thieves battle for control of an illegal bloodselling business. Director Nagisa Oshima, who has tackled the theme of juvenile delinquency in so many of his films, presents his most desperate characters in a stylized urban nightmare. (87 mins.)

Sunset (1988)** Bruce Willis, James Garner, Malcolm McDowell, Mariel Hemingway, Kathleen Quinlan, Jennifer Edwards, Patricia Hodge. In this meandering light adventure set in 1929 Hollywood, screen cowboy Tom Mix (Willis) and legendary lawman Wyatt Earp (Garner) join forces to solve a murder involving an exclusive bordello and a sinister studio head. Blake Edwards's arthritic script and direction utterly fail to capitalize on the premise, but the film is handsomely mounted and amiably performed by Garner and the miscast Willis. (105 mins.)†

Sunset Beat (MTV 1990)**½ George Clooney, Michael DeLuise, Markus Flanagan, Erik King, Anthony Geary, Ami Dolenz. The creator of "21 Jump Street" offers another group of young, socially conscious crime fighters, members of a special unit who battle psycho extortionist Geary and deal with family problems. (Dir: Sam Weisman, 96 mins.)

Sunset Boulevard (1950)**** Gloria Swanson, William Holden, Erich von Stroheim, Nancy Olson, Jack Webb, Cecil B. DeMille, Hedda Hopper, Buster Keaton, Fred Clark. Director Billy Wilder's darkly humorous, ultimately tragic glimpse at a parade that's gone by. Joe Gillis, a burned-out screenwriter is about to leave Tinseltown when fate lands him in the driveway of legendary Norma Desmond. The once-great, still-proud living legend offers him a writing job on her comeback vehicle along with a comfortable sideline as her live-in lover. Caught in Norma's velvet trap, Joe struggles to regain his soul against the backdrop of Wilder's cynical reflections on the unrelenting cruelty of a business that glorifies the young. With brilliant dialogue ("I'm still big. It's the pictures that got small!") and Swanson's towering portrayal of a high priestess of Hollywood Babylon. (110 mins.)†

Sunset Limousine (MTV 1983)**½ John Ritter, Susan Dey, Martin Short. Mildly amusing comedy bolstered by Ritter as a stand-up comic moonlighting as a chauffeur for a Hollywood limousine service. (Dir: Terry Hughes, 104 mins.)†

Sunshine (MTV 1973)*** Cristina Raines, Cliff De Young, Brenda Vaccaro, Meg Foster, Billy Mumy. An extraordinary tale about a free-spirited young woman, destined to die of bone cancer at the age of twenty. Based on the true-life diary, it can't help but emotionally involve you. (Dir: Joseph Sargent, 121 mins.)

Sunshine Boys, The (1975)***½ George Burns, Walter Matthau, Richard Benjamin. Neil Simon's funny, touching play about two veteran vaudevillians who have shared a hate-love relationship for decades, works even better on the screen, thanks to Matthau and Burns's superb timing as the pair of disgruntled show business codgers. Burns won an Academy Award and he's wonderful. (Dir: Herbert Ross, 111 mins.)†

Sunshine Christmas (MTV 1977)**½ Cliff De Young, Pat Hingle, Eileen Heckart. De Young plays a footloose musician, Sam Hayden, bringing daughter Jill back to his folks in Texas. Sam's homecoming is full of surprises. Sequel to *Sunshine*. (Dir: Glenn Jordan, 104 mins.)

Sunshine Patriot, The (MTV 1968)***½ Cliff Robertson, Dina Merrill, Luther Adler. Good spy story. The familiar plot has an experienced spy, trapped behind the Iron Curtain, cleverly framing an American businessman and switching identities with him. (Dir: Joseph Sargent, 98 mins.)

Sun Shines Bright, The (1953)***½ Charles Winninger, Arleen Whelan, John Russell. Small-town judge has a hard time running for re-election. Superb piece of Americana directed by John Ford—one of his best films. (92 mins.)†

Sun Valley Serenade (1941)*** Sonja Henie, Lynn Bari, Joan Davis, John Payne. Pleasant, entertaining musical set in the fabulous Idaho resort. You'll see and hear the late great Glenn Miller's band; its manager in the film is Milton Berle. (Dir: H. Bruce Humberstone, 86 mins.)

Super Cops (1974)**½ Ron Leibman, David Selby. A saga of two real-life New York cops (Greenberg and Hantz) who earned the nicknames of Batman and Robin because of their unorthodox methods in dealing with criminals. The twist here is that the two rookie cops actually work in the traffic division, but they wage their war on drug traffic during their own off-duty hours. (Dir: Gordon Parks, Jr., 93 mins.)

Superdad (1974)* Bob Crane, Barbara Rush, Kathleen Cody, Kurt Russell, Joe Flynn. Ludicrous tale. Crane is a father trying to get close to his teenaged daughter (Cody) by joining in on all her activities. (Dir: Vincent McEveety, 95 mins.)†

Superdome (MTV 1978)** David Janssen, Donna Mills, Edie Adams. The excitement surrounding a fictional Super Bowl game, particularly the heavy betting, leads to multiple murders in this padded mystery story. (Dir: Jerry Jameson, 104 mins.)

Super Fight, The (1969)** Rocky Marciano, Muhammad Ali. All-time heavyweight boxing greats Marciano and Ali, champions from two eras, meet in this computerized "dream fight," supposedly to determine who was the best of all time. (Dir: Murry Voroner, 70 mins.)

Super Fly (1972)** Ron O'Neal, Carl Lee, Sheila Frazier. O'Neal street-hustles heroin, and he's looking to make that one big score. Thoroughly disreputable exploitation piece with some good acting and direction. (Dir: Gordon Parks, Jr., 97 mins.)†

Super Fly T.N.T. (1973)* Ron O'Neal, Roscoe Lee Browne, Jacques Sernas, Sheila Frazier, Robert Guillaume. Definitely a non-super sequel to *Super Fly* as the badass drug dealer antihero dips into the illegal weapons sale business. "T.N.T." stands for "taint nothin to't," and that pretty much describes this film as well. (Dir: Ron O'Neal, 87 mins.)

Super Fuzz (Italy-U.S., 1981)** Terence Hill, Ernest Borgnine, Joanne Dru, Mark Lawrence. There isn't much plot to this "spaghetti" police comedy, but some episodes are rather amusing. The gags center on a cop's newfound superpowers. (Dir: Sergio Corbucci, 97 mins.)†

Supergirl (1984)**½ Faye Dunaway, Peter O'Toole, Helen Slater, Brenda Vaccaro, Hart Bochner, Peter Cook. A juvenile fantasy about Superman's comic-book cousin, who must zip down to Earth to retrieve the precious omegahedron needed for her planet's survival. Slater is a bit nondescript in the lead, but the film flies high whenever ultracamp villainess Dunaway is on-screen dispensing nastiness. (Dir: Jeannot Szwarc, 105 mins.)†

Supergrass, The (Great Britain, 1985)* Adrian Edmondson, Jennifer Saunders, Alexei Sayle. This feature from members of Britain's popular Comic Strip proves that people who are funny on television should stay there. The plot about a twit who invents an imaginary drug-running operation holds together a lot of unfunny gags. Mow this one down. (Dir: Peter Richardson, 93 mins.)†

Superman (1978)*** Christopher Reeve, Marlon Brando, Valerie Perrine, Ned Beatty, Glenn Ford, Gene Hackman, Margot Kidder, Marc McClure, Phyllis Thaxter, Jackie Cooper. The first installment in the big-budget series detailing the exploits of the Man of Steel spends too much time dwelling on his origin, and too little showing him in battle against the forces of evil. Still, it does have a stellar supporting cast—with Hackman's tongue-in-cheek performance as criminal mastermind Lex Luthor the standout—and Reeve manages to acquit himself nicely with his charmingly awkward portrayal of Krypton's favorite son. An extended 192-minute version has been shown on network television. (Dir: Richard Donner, 142 mins.)†

Superman II (1981)***½ Christopher Reeve, Gene Hackman, Margot Kidder, Jackie Cooper, Valerie Perrine, Susannah York. One of the very few movie sequels that is better than the original, thanks to the droll touches supplied by director Richard Lester. The big difference this time around is that the bad guys are meanies from outer space armed with Kryptonite. (127 mins.)†

Superman III (1983)*½ Christopher Reeve, Richard Pryor, Robert Vaughn, Annette O'Toole, Annie Ross, Margot Kidder. *Superman III* shifts awkwardly from Superman's fling with Lana Lang (Annette O'Toole) to arch-villains zapping his power with a super computer. Another sequel like this and the Man of Steel's enemies won't need Kryptonite to finish him off. Shown on network TV at 142 mins. (Dir: Richard Lester, 124 mins.)†

Superman IV: The Quest For Peace (1987)* Christopher Reeve, Gene Hackman, Margot Kidder, Jon Cryer, Mariel Hemingway. Superman rids the world of atomic weapons, only to have evil Lex Luthor bring them back as part of an international arms deal. Easily the worst (and hopefully the last) of the series; whole chunks of the plot seem to have been cut prior to release, and the special effects are cheap-looking. (Dir: Sidney J. Furie, 89 mins.)†

Superman and the Mole Men (1951)*** George Reeves, Phyllis Coates, Jeff Corey. Interesting action flick. Superman protects Mole Men who surface in a bigoted town where the locals want to destroy the tiny visitors. (Dir: Lee Sholem, 67 mins.)†

Supernatural (1933)**½ Carole Lombard, Randolph Scott, Vivienne Osborne, H. B. Warner, Beryl Mercer, William Farnum. The lovely Lombard's not in her usual element in this eerie tale of a girl who's controlled by a dead murderess's will. (Dir: Victor Halperin, 60 mins.)

Supernaturals, The (1986)* Maxwell Caulfield, Nichelle Nichols, Talia Balsam, Bradford Bancroft, LeVar Burton, Bobby DiCicco. An anti-antebellum horror pic. Haunting a modern day bivouac, the ghosts of Confederate soldiers come back to avenge themselves on visiting Yankees in order to settle a century-old score. (Dir: Armand Mastroianni, 80 mins.)†

Super Sleuth (1937)*** Jack Oakie, Ann Sothern, Edgar Kennedy, Eduardo Ciannelli. Snappy comedy workout for Oakie as a know-it-all detective movie star who tosses his script aside and tries sleuthing for real. (Dir: Ben Stoloff, 70 mins.)

Superstar: The Life and Times of Andy Warhol (1990)***½ Stylish, well-made documentary about painter Warhol, traces his life from Pittsburgh schoolboy to pop art legend, from advertising copy illustrator to chronicler of the *haut monde* of New York City. Crammed with comments from Warhol himself as well as many others, including Lou Reed, Dennis Hopper, Viva, David Hockney, Leo Castelli, Shelley Winters, Roy Lichtenstein, and Liza with a Z. (Dir: Chuck Workman, 87 mins.)

Superstition (1985)** James Houghton, Albert Salmi, Larry Pennell, Lynn Carlin. A young reverend moves into a big old house, and the expected horrors begin when it turns out that a witch, burned at the stake there, left a curse on the place. (Dir: James W. Robertson, 85 mins.)†

Supervixens (1975)* Shari Eubank, Charles Napier, Uschi Digard, Charles Pitts, Stuart Lancaster. Adult filmmaker Russ Meyer may be the most innovative director working in the field of exploitation, but he can't write a coherent script by himself. There is none of the frenetic pacing of Meyer's earlier efforts in this tasteless tale of a gas pump jockey who works at "Martin Borman's Super Service," his bosomy wife, the innocent who resembles her, and a leering, sadistic cop (Napier). (Dir: Russ Meyer, 107 mins.)†

Support Your Local Gunfighter (1971)**½ James Garner, Suzanne Pleshette, Jack Elam, Joan Blondell, Harry Morgan. James Garner casually plays a gambler who runs away from a madam with marriage on her mind, and is mistaken for a gunfighter in the troubled town of Purgatory. (Dir: Burt Kennedy, 92 mins.)

Support Your Local Sheriff (1969)***½ James Garner, Joan Hackett, Walter Brennan, Harry Morgan, Jack Elam, Bruce Dern. Droll western spoof with a funny turn by Garner as an adventurer who stumbles into a town which is feeling the bonanza of a gold rush and becomes its sheriff. (Dir: Burt Kennedy, 93 mins.)†

Suppose They Gave a War and Nobody Came (1970)** Brian Keith, Tony Curtis, Ernest Borgnine, Ivan Dixon, Suzanne Pleshette, Tom Ewell. A mediocre service comedy about three oldtime Army tankmen who have been stationed in a noncombatant base, and their war with the southern town in which it is located. AKA: **War Games.** (Dir: Hy Averback, 113 mins.)†

Sure Fire (1990)*** Tom Blair, Kristi Hager, Robert Ernst, Kate Dezina, Phillip R. Brown, Dennis R. Brown. Top-notch example of American minimalist cinema tells the story of an entrepreneur in barren south-central Utah who wants to turn all the region's dreary small towns into backwater resorts and retirement areas for rich Californians. The dazzling cinematography and the extraordinary music add to the film's offbeat power. Written, edited, and photographed by the director. (Dir: Jon Jost, 83 mins.)

Sure Thing, The (1985)*** John Cusack, Daphne Zuniga, Anthony Edwards, Viveca Lindfors. An appealing tale of opposites attracting. The two leads go on a quest to meet up with her fiancé and his California dream girl, only to find that together they are "the sure thing." (Dir: Rob Reiner, 94 mins.)†

Surf Nazis Must Die (1987)½ Barry Brenner, Gail Neely, Michael Sonye, Dawn Wildsmith. A great title pinned down to a schlocky stab at instant cult status. Set in the near future, the plot concerns Neo-Nazi surfers fighting for beach control. (Dir: Peter George, 80 mins.)†

Surf Party (1964)* Bobby Vinton, Patricia Morrow. Youth will be surfed, and this time it's young love on the beach at Malibu! Vapid kids shaking their bottoms and jumping in and out of bed and onto surfboards. (Dir: Maury Dexter, 68 mins.)

Surf 2 (1984)* Eddie Deezen, Eric Stoltz, Linda Kerridge, Cleavon Little. The height of this beach bomb's wretched "in" joke humor is that *Surf 1* didn't exist. A mad scientist turns the local sex-starved and stoned surfers into zombies with his spiked soft drink. (Dir: Randall Badat, 91 mins.)†

Surprise Package (Great Britain, 1960)** Yul Brynner, Mitzi Gaynor, Noel Coward. Funny idea on paper, perhaps, but it doesn't transfer to the screen. Brynner plays a big-time gambler who is deported to his native Greece, where he becomes involved with a phony King and some hot jewel dealings. (Dir: Stanley Donen, 100 mins.)

Surrender (1950)**½ Vera Ralston, John Carroll, Walter Brennan, Francis Lederer, Jane Darwell. A glamorous fugitive from justice stirs up trouble between two friends in a Mexican border town in this well-made, tense melodrama; stylish B picture. (Dir: Allan Dwan, 90 mins.)

Surrender (1987)** Michael Caine, Sally Field, Steve Guttenberg, Peter Boyle. Michael Caine plays a wealthy novelist trying to hide his riches from an impoverished painter (Field) in the hope she won't take him for all he's got. The charm of the three leads surrenders quickly to jumbled scripting. (Dir: Jerry Belson, 96 mins.)†

Surrender—Hell! (1959)*½ Keith Andes,

Susan Cabot. Jumbled film about an American colonel who forms a band of Filipino guerrillas to fight the Japanese during WWII. (Dir: John Barnwell, 85 mins.)

Survival of Dana, The (MTV 1979)**½ Melissa Sue Anderson, Robert Carradine, Talia Balsam. A drama attempting to explain why kids from affluent families turn to mindless destruction. (Dir: Jack Starrett, 104 mins.)

Survival Quest (1986)** Lance Henriksen, Mark Rolston, Steve Antin, Michael Allen Ryder, Traci Lin, Dermot Mulroney. It's brains versus brawn in this duel between two groups of survivalists. The first is concerned with learning outdoors skills; the second is out for blood. Negligible thrills. (Dir: Don Coscarelli, 96 mins.)†

Survival Run (1979)** Peter Graves, Ray Milland, Vince Van Patten, Pedro Armendariz, Jr. California teenagers are in a van in Mexico. The van breaks down, bad guys step out from behind the cactus.... (Dir: Larry Spiegel, 90 mins.)†

Survive! (Mexico, 1976)* Hugo Stiglitz, Norma Lazaren. Exploitative film based on the real-life incident about a group of air crash victims in 1972 in the Andes who resorted to cannibalism, feeding on the flesh of the dead passengers in order to survive. (Dir: Rene Cardona, 86 mins.)

Surviving (MTV 1985)*** Ellen Burstyn, Paul Sorvino, Marsha Mason, Len Cariou, Zack Galligan, Molly Ringwald. Heartbreaking drama. A seemingly model upper-middle-class high-school student commits suicide with his troubled girlfriend. After the tragedy, the drama finds its focus, tracing the long and difficult adjustment facing the surviving families. (Dir: Waris Hussein, 106 mins.)

Survivors, The (1983)** Robin Williams, Walter Matthau, Jerry Reed. A promising premise is not sustained in this black comedy about the unemployment blues. The teaming of hyperactive Williams with slow-burner Matthau strikes occasional comic sparks, but *Survivors* sinks as the comic material is stretched far too thin. (Dir: Michael Ritchie, 102 mins.)†

Susana (Mexico 1951)**½ Rosita Quintana, Fernando Soler. After one of the briefest and silliest prison breakout scenes in history, Susana finds shelter with a family of naive, strapping ranchers. She seduces every man in sight, only to meet her comeuppance at the hand of an angry mamasita with a whip. (Dir: Luis Buñuel, 82 mins.)†

Susan and God (1940)*** Fredric March, Joan Crawford, Ruth Hussey, John Carroll, Rita Hayworth, Nigel Bruce, Gloria DeHaven. Crawford at her best as a selfish socialite who forces a crisis in her unhappy family when she takes up trendy religious revivalism. (Dir: George Cukor, 115 mins.)

Susan Lennox: Her Fall and Rise (1931)**½ Greta Garbo, Clark Gable, Jean Hersholt. There are only two reasons to see the picture: Garbo and Gable. Gable brings out the sex appeal in Garbo as no other leading man did. (Dir: Robert Z. Leonard, 76 mins.)

Susannah of the Mounties (1939)**½ Shirley Temple, Randolph Scott, Margaret Lockwood, Martin Good Rider, J. Farrell MacDonald, Victor Jory. A nice Canadian adventure for Temple, as an orphan adopted by Mountie Scott and endangered by renegade Indians; fresh and engaging. (Dir: William A. Seiter, 77 mins.)

Susan Slade (1961)** Troy Donahue, Connie Stevens, Dorothy McGuire, Lloyd Nolan, Brian Aherne. Inexperienced girl is seduced, the guy gets himself killed, she finds she's pregnant, Pop has a heart attack, but all's well as long as faithful stableboy Troy is around. (Dir: Delmer Daves, 116 mins.)

Susan Slept Here (1954)*** Debbie Reynolds, Dick Powell, Anne Francis. Amusing comedy with Dick Powell, as a Hollywood writer, given custody of Debbie for a holiday period. Powell is good and Debbie sparkles as usual. (Dir: Frank Tashlin, 98 mins.)

Suspect, The (1944)***½ Charles Laughton, Ella Raines, Henry Daniell. Excellent, velvety thriller directed by Robert Siodmak. Laughton gives a consummate performance as a man who falls in love with an ingenue (Raines) and murders his shrewish wife, making a sympathetic figure out of a weak man. Based on the famous Dr. Crippen murder. (85 mins.)

Suspect (1987)*** Cher, Dennis Quaid, John Mahoney, Philip Bosco, Liam Neeson. Farfetched but engrossing courtroom drama with Cher as a hardworking public defender who works to free a hostile, homeless vet (Neeson) with the aid of a helpful, and amorous, juror (Quaid). *Suspect* moves along at a good clip with nice neo-Hitchcock touches. (Dir: Peter Yates, 122 mins.)†

Suspense (1946)*** Belita, Barry Sullivan, Albert Dekker, Bonita Granville. Small-time sharpie is hired by an ice palace, gets big ideas, and plans to kill the owner to get his dough and his wife. Strong melodrama, a good job in all departments. (Dir: Frank Tuttle, 101 mins.)

Suspicion (1941)*** Cary Grant, Joan Fontaine, Cedric Hardwicke, Isabel Jeans, Leo G. Carroll, Nigel Bruce, Heather Angel. Alfred Hitchcock's intriguing work about emotional vulnerability. Fontaine is the mousey wife who thinks her mysterious, irresponsible husband (Grant) is trying to murder her. The conflict is not as boldly painted as in later Hitchcock films; the emotions are slightly bloodless and distant, but the two stars shine brightly. (99 mins.)†

Suspicion (MTV 1988)** Anthony Andrews, Betsy Blair, Jane Curtin, Sir Michael Hordern. A remake of the Hitchcock classic that doesn't quite make the grade. Andrews fills the bill as the husband suspected of villainy, but Curtin (her hubby produced) is hopelessly miscast as his apprehensive spouse. (Dir: Andrew Grieve, 97 mins.)†

Suspiria (Italy, 1977)*** Joan Bennett, Jessica Harper, Alida Valli. A sweet young thing arrives at a sinister boarding school and discovers some of the students are disappearing. Could an evil coven of witches be behind it? Featuring one of the scariest opening scenes in horror history, *Suspiria* can't sustain that high pitch of terror, but does provide some shocking moments along the way. (Dir: Dario Argento, 97 mins.)†

Sutter's Gold (1936)**½ Edward Arnold, Lee Tracy, Binnie Barnes, Katherine Alexander. Expensive production enhances this otherwise ponderous fictionalized biography of John Sutter, a Swiss immigrant who discovered gold on his California land grant in 1849, launching the famous Gold Rush. (Dir: James Cruze, 69 mins.)

Suzy (1936)** Jean Harlow, Cary Grant, Franchot Tone. There are hugely satisfying bits in this ill-structured melange of comedy, romance, action, and sheer star power. Harlow and Grant pair well, and the screenplay (by Dorothy Parker among others) provides some bright repartee. (Dir: George Fitzmaurice, 99 mins.)

Svengali (1931)*** John Barrymore, Marian Marsh. A classic version of George Du Maurier's *Trilby*, thanks to Barrymore in the title role. (Dir: Archie Mayo, 81 mins.)†

Svengali (Great Britain, 1955)** Hildegarde Neff, Donald Wolfit. The romantic and compelling drama of Trilby and Svengali is once more on the screen, this time not so successfully due to uneven performances and a mediocre script. (Dir: Noel Langley, 82 mins.)†

Svengali (MTV 1983)*½ Peter O'Toole, Jodie Foster, Elizabeth Ashley. An overblown bore. O'Toole shamefully overacts as a flamboyant music teacher who gives pop singer Foster the impetus and training to become a star. (Dir: Anthony Harvey, 104 mins.)†

Swamp Diamonds—See: **Cruel Swamp**

Swamp Fire (1946)** Johnny Weissmuller, Buster Crabbe, Carol Thurston, Virginia Grey, Marcelle Corday. Lackluster drama

about a former Navy man who battles a bayou bigwig for the love of a girl. (Dir: William Pine, 69 mins.)

Swamp Thing (1982)**½ Ray Wise, Adrienne Barbeau, Louis Jourdan. Ludicrous, but somewhat disarming, sci-fi action picture about a scientist who turns into a strong, kindly monster who is half human, half plant when he discovers a secret formula. (Dir: Wes Craven, 92 mins.)†

Swamp Water (1941)**½ Walter Brennan, Walter Huston. Well-acted drama of a fugitive hiding out in Georgia's Okefenokee Swamp. Acting does not make up for the confused script. (Dir: Jean Renoir, 90 mins.)

Swamp Women—See: **Cruel Swamp**

Swan, The (1956)*** Grace Kelly, Alec Guinness, Louis Jourdan. A trio of attractive stars help to make this costume romance entertaining. The plot revolves around Hungary's Crown Prince Albert's required selection of a wife and the intrigues surrounding his reluctant search. Princess Grace's last film (Dir: Charles Vidor, 112 mins.)

Swanee River (1939)**½ Don Ameche, Al Jolson, Andrea Leeds. Ameche as Stephen Foster in a silly musical biopic enlivened by Jolson's savvy showmanship as E. P. Christy (of the Christy Minstrels). (Dir: Sidney Lanfield, 84 mins.)

Swann in Love (France-West Germany, 1984)*** Jeremy Irons, Ornella Muti, Alain Delon, Fanny Ardant, Marie-Christine Barrault. The best-known section of Marcel Proust's massive *Remembrance of Things Past*, is brought to the screen with exquisite taste but little fire. Irons is good as Swann, whose intense love for a social-climbing minx, Odette (Muti), becomes psychological self-torture. Swann's romantic pursuit is detailed against a backdrop of sophisticated Parisian society, which is rendered here with eye-filling sumptuousness. (Dir: Volker Schlondorff, 110 mins.)†

Swan Song (MTV 1980)**½ David Soul, Slim Pickens, Murray Hamilton, Jill Eikenberry. Intense study of a first-rank skier who disqualified himself at the Olympics three years earlier and is back for one last grab at the brass ring. (Dir: Jerry London, 104 mins.)

Swap, The—See: **Sam's Song**

Swarm, The (1978)* Michael Caine, Katharine Ross, Richard Widmark, Richard Chamberlain. Absurd disaster film in which the Army and leading scientists can't prevent a takeover by a swarm of killer bees trekking up from South America. (Dir: Irwin Allen, 111 mins.)†

Swashbuckler (1976)* Robert Shaw, James Earl Jones, Peter Boyle, Genevieve Bujold, Beau Bridges, Geoffrey Holder. A paste-up pirate film, circa 1718 in Jamaica. Shaw flashes his teeth, Boyle hams it up as the villain, and Bujold is wasted. Dir: James Goldstone, 101 mins.)†

Swedenhielms (Sweden, 1935)** Hakan Westergren, Gosta Ekman, Karin Swanstrom. Twenty-year-old Ingrid Bergman has a supporting role in this light comedy about the family of a famous scientist whose plans go awry when he fails to receive the Nobel Prize. (Dir: Gustaf Molander, 88 mins.)†

Sweeney Todd, the Demon Barber of Fleet Street—See: **Demon Barber of Fleet Street, The**

Sweepings (1933)*** Lionel Barrymore, Alan Dinehart, Eric Linden, William Gargan, Gloria Stuart. Effective, powerful story of a man who works all his life to build a department store empire he hopes his children will take over, but finds that they have been spoiled by riches. Fine acting, stylish direction by John Cromwell. (80 mins.)

Sweet Adeline (1935)** Irene Dunne, Donald Woods, Hugh Herbert, Ned Sparks. The Kern-Hammerstein songs are the main attraction here in this soggy Gay Nineties operetta about the sweetheart of a beer garden. (Dir: Mervyn LeRoy, 87 mins.)

Sweet and Low Down (1944)*½ Benny Goodman, Lynn Bari, Jack Oakie. When the Goodman band plays this Grade B film is OK but, unfortunately, there are many moments when they don't play. (Dir: Archie Mayo, 75 mins.)

Sweet Bird of Youth (1962)*** Paul Newman, Geraldine Page, Ed Begley, Shirley Knight, Rip Torn, Mildred Dunnock. No-goodnik causes more trouble when he returns to his home town accompanied by a neurotic actress. Some fine performances, including the one by Oscar-winner Begley, keep things interesting. In this film version of Tennessee Williams's play, Page is fabulous, a truly virtuoso turn. (Dir: Richard Brooks, 120 mins.)†

Sweet Bird of Youth (MTV 1989)**½ Elizabeth Taylor, Mark Harmon, Valerie Perrine, Kevin Geer, Seymour Cassel, Rip Torn. Tennessee Williams's play adapted for television, and not for the better. Taylor fails to project the monumentally wounded ego of the fading movie star she's playing; Harmon fares better as the handsome gigolo using her for his own means. Williams's passion for despairing souls remains touching. (Dir: Nicolas Roeg, 96 mins.)

Sweet Charity (1969)*** Shirley MacLaine, Ricardo Montalban, Chita Rivera, Paula Kelly, John McMartin, Stubby Kaye, Sammy Davis, Jr. Based on Fellini's *Nights of Cabiria*, this splashy adaptation of the Broadway hit suffers from over-production, though many charming sequences stand

out, such as "If My Friends Could See Me Now." MacLaine acquits herself admirably as the taxi dancer with a dance card full of Mr. Wrongs, but she is clearly outclassed in the dance department by co-stars Rivera and Kelly. (Dir: Bob Fosse, 148 mins.)†

Sweet Country (1987)½ Jane Alexander, John Cullum, Jean-Pierre Aumont, Irene Papas, Carole Laure, Joanna Pettet, Randy Quaid. This ambitious political tract about the upheaval of Chile following the assassination of Salvador Allende is an unmitigated disaster, written by the director as if he's somehow grafted the grandeur of Greek Tragedy onto a cartoon on revolutionary politics by Gary Trudeau. Wait until you see Quaid as a priapic Chilean military policeman! (Dir: Michael Cacoyannis, 150 mins.)†

Sweet Dirty Tony—See: **Kill Castro**

Sweet Dreams (1985)**½ Jessica Lange, Ed Harris, Ann Wedgeworth, Dave Clennon. Pleasant, if unextraordinary biography of country singer Patsy Cline. Lange is appealing as the singer whose rise to the top was cut short by untimely death. (Dir: Karel Reisz, 115 mins.)†

Sweethearts (1938)**½ Nelson Eddy, Jeanette MacDonald, Frank Morgan, Ray Bolger. Eddy-MacDonald musical is for fans only. They play a married couple appearing in a Victor Herbert operetta who are manipulated into a spat by their publicity-hungry producer (Morgan). (Dir: W. S. Van Dyke, 120 mins.)†

Sweet Hearts Dance (1988)**½ Don Johnson, Susan Sarandon, Jeff Daniels, Elizabeth Perkins, Kate Reid, Justin Henry. Entertaining comedy about relationships set in a sleepy town in Maine. Contractor Johnson and wife Saradon find themselves growing weary of marriage at the same time that Johnson's best friend, schoolteacher Daniels, is beginning an affair with Perkins. (Dir: Robert Greenwald, 101 mins.)†

Sweet Hostage (MTV 1975)**½ Martin Sheen, Linda Blair. A fine, colorful performance by Sheen as an escaped mental patient lifts this familiar kidnap yarn above the ordinary. He's an eccentric lunatic who spouts poetry, thinks fast on his feet and corrects the poor grammar of his uneducated teenage hostage, well played by Blair. (Dir: Lee Philips, 72 mins.)

Sweet Hours (Spain, 1982)***½ Assumpta Serna, Inaki Aierra, Luisa Rodrigo, Jacques Lalande. Erotic, darkly humorous love story about a playwright who is obsessed with memories of his past, especially his relationship with his mother, which raises the specter of incest in this beautifully structured, magnificently acted film. (Dir: Carlos Saura, 105 mins.)

Sweetie (Australia 1989)**** Genevieve

Lemon, Karen Colston, Tom Lycos, Dorothy Barry, Jon Darling. Original film that is at once both surreal and sentimental, providing a darkly comic view of the "favored child" dilemma. The problems of a romantically confused young woman are aggravated by a visit from her difficult sister Sweetie. Director Jane Campion and co-scripter Gerard Lee stake out new territory in this apparently brutal yet innately tender satire of strained family relations. (97 mins.)†

Sweet Kill—See: **Arousers, The**

Sweet Liberty (1986)**½ Alan Alda, Michael Caine, Michelle Pfeiffer, Lillian Gish, Lois Chiles, Lise Hilboldt, Bob Hoskins. A lighthearted comedy about a history professor (Alda) whose book about the American Revolution is being converted into a commercial movie. He finds his world turned topsy-turvy when the film company decides to shoot the movie in the town he lives in. A nice entertainment but without any real surprise or bite. (Dir: Alan Alda, 106 mins.)†

Sweet Lies (1986)**½ Treat Williams, Joanna Pacula, Julianne Phillips, Laura Manszky. Romantic comedy about a bet among three Parisian women as to who can be the first to lure American insurance investigator Williams into bed. Minor but pleasant timewaster was never released theatrically. (Dir: Nathalie Delon, 96 mins.)†

Sweet Lorraine (1987)*** Maureen Stapleton, Lee Richardson, Trini Alvarado, John Bedford Lloyd. Gentle, affecting comedy-drama about the owner of a Catskills resort (Stapleton) facing up to the fact that she's going to have to sell the beloved place, and her granddaughter's (Alvarado) experiences when she works there for the summer. (Dir: Steve Gomer, 91 mins.)†

Sweet Love, Bitter (1967)** Dick Gregory, Don Murray, Diane Varsi. Interracial friendships are unconvincingly explored in this tale about the downfall of a black jazz musician, partly based on the life of Charlie Parker. (Dir: Herbert Danska, 92 mins.)

Sweet Music (1935)**½ Rudy Vallee, Ann Dvorak, Ned Sparks, Helen Morgan, Robert Armstrong, Allen Jenkins. Ordinary backstage romance, liberally spiced with pleasant songs. Vallee plays a singer trying to sign Dvorak up with his band. Supporting cast adds zest. (Dir: Alfred E. Green, 90 mins.)

Sweet November (1968)*** Sandy Dennis, Anthony Newley, Theodore Bikel, Sandy Baron. A frequently touching, but maddening bittersweet comedy with a twist— the heroine (Dennis) just wants to pop into bed with her various boyfriends without regret or apology, but one of them

wants to get married. (Dir: Robert Ellis Miller, 114 mins.)

Sweet Revenge (1977)*½ Stockard Channing, Sam Waterston, Franklin Ajaye. Sam's a lawyer for the poor folks and Stockard has a bad habit of driving away in cars that don't belong to her. Sam has to defend his lady love, but who's gonna be around to defend this dreary romance? AKA: **Dandy, the All-American Girl**. (Dir: Jerry Schatzberg, 90 mins.)

Sweet Revenge (MTV 1984)*** Kevin Dobson, Wings Hauser, Alec Baldwin, Merritt Butrick, Kelly McGillis. This revenge tale holds your attention with its clever plot twists. Dobson plays a rogue who covers up his tracks neatly until a woman who neither forgets nor forgives finally gets even. (Dir: David Greene, 104 mins.)

Sweet Revenge (1986)** Nancy Allen, Ted Shackelford, Martin Landau. Newswoman Allen falls into the hands of white slavers, escapes, and returns for revenge. Neither sleazy enough to work as trashy fun nor well made enough to transcend the clichés. (Dir: Mark Sobel, 99 mins.)†

Sweet Revenge (MCTV 1990)**½ Rosanna Arquette, Carrie Fisher, John Sessions, Francois-Eric Gendron. Charming romantic-comedy set in Paris. An ambitious corporate lawyer (Fisher) finds herself hit with alimony by her ex-husband. She hires an eccentric, unemployed actress (Arquette) to masquerade as his perfect woman in hopes of a quick marriage. The enjoyable cast has fun in this delightful tale, which harks back to the Hollywood comedies of the '40s. (Dir: Charlotte Brandstrom, 88 mins.)†

Sweet Ride, The (1968)** Jacqueline Bisset, Tony Franciosa, Michael Sarrazin, Bob Denver, Michael Wilding. The loves of a mod girl who hangs around with too many surfers and tennis bums for her own good. Sleazy tale made worth watching by Bisset. (Dir: Harvey Hart, 110 mins.)

Sweet Rosie O'Grady (1943)*** Betty Grable, Robert Young, Adolphe Menjou. One of our WWII pin-up queens proves why in this foolish 1890s musical designed to show off Betty's legs—which it does. (Dir: Irving Cummings, 74 mins.)

Sweet Savior (1971)* Troy Donahue, Renay Granville. Distasteful exploitation of the Charles Manson killings. Donahue plays the leader of a "family" that takes over an orgy given by a pregnant actress in suburban New York. (Dir: Bob Roberts, 90 mins.)

Sweet 16 (1983)** Bo Hopkins, Susan Strasberg, Don Stroud. Low-budget horror effort in which the boys who date newcomer Shirley wind up knifed to death. (Dir: Jim Sotos, 90 mins.)†

Sweet Smell of Success (1957)**** Burt Lancaster, Tony Curtis, Susan Harrison, Martin Milner, Sam Levene, Barbara Nichols. New York after dark provides the backdrop for this sour, stinging portrait of a vengeful newspaper columnist (Lancaster) and a venal press agent (Curtis) who briefly forgo their mutual antipathy in order to destroy a young man's career. The characters' greed-driven negotiations are carried out in smoky nightclubs, jazz joints, and rain-soaked streets. Lancaster plays the vicious power broker with chilling menace, and Curtis is superb. (Dir: Alexander Mackendrick, 96 mins.)†

Sweet Sweetback's Baadasssss Song (1971) *** Melvin Van Peebles, Simon Chuckster, Hubert Scales. A bitter black fairy tale, where all the blacks are potent studs and fine folks, and the whites are as evil as they are ignorant. Van Peebles plays a black, sexually inexhaustible lady-killer on the lam from the police. Written, directed, and musical score by Van Peebles. (97 mins.)†

Sweet, Sweet Rachel (MTV 1971)** Stefanie Powers, Pat Hingle, Alex Dreier, Brenda Scott, Louise Latham, John Hillerman. A hyperactive thriller about an ESP whiz who's battling a killer with extrasensory methods for dispatching his lovely victims. The pilot for the TV series "The Sixth Sense." (Dir: Sutton Roley, 73 mins.)

Sweet William (Great Britain, 1982)***½ Sam Waterston, Jenny Agutter, Anna Massey. A masterful movie about a raffish playwright who becomes involved with a woman who refuses to accept his compulsive philandering. (Dir: Claude Whatham, 90 mins.)†

Swept Away by an Unusual Destiny in the Blue Sea of August (Italy, 1975)*** Giancarlo Giannini, Mariangela Melato. A politicized update of the old "stranded on a desert island" motif. This popular foreign film is a well-played battle of the sexes, in which a working-class Communist hero tries to put a snooty member of the leisure class in (what he thinks is) her place. The sexual tension between the stars is palpable. (Dir: Lina Wertmuller, 116 mins.)†

Swimmer, The (1968)*** Burt Lancaster, Janice Rule, Janet Landgard, Diana Muldaur, Kim Hunter. Absorbing story about a loser (wonderfully played by Lancaster) gradually flipping out of WASP society because he loathes the lifestyle and mores of affluent executives. He swims his way down various pools in Westport, Conn., and viewers who want something different will follow stroke by stroke. (Dirs: Frank Perry, Sydney Pollack, 94 mins.)†

Swimming Pool, The (France 1969)*** Alain

Delon, Romy Schneider, Jane Birkin. St. Tropez-based melodrama. The affair between a writer and his lover is cooled by the arrival of her former boyfriend and his sexy young daughter. Sensual tale of a romantic bond sealed with a crime of passion. (Dir: Jacques Deray, 85 mins.)†

Swimming to Cambodia (1987)***½ Spalding Gray. A brilliant, quirky screen translation of a fascinating stage work by Spalding Gray; it's based on his experiences during the filming of The Killing Fields, in which he had a supporting role. A resourcefully directed and engagingly performed one-man show; Jonathan Demme deserves special acclaim for his imaginative handling of this intellectually stimulating material. (87 mins.)†

Swimsuit (MTV 1989)*½ William Katt, Catherine Oxenberg, Nia Peeples, Tom Villard. This comedy about a "talent hunt" for a swimsuit line is a thin excuse to show plenty of babes in bikinis. (Dir: Chris Thomson, 96 mins.)

Swindle, The (Italy, 1955)**½ Broderick Crawford, Richard Basehart, Giulietta Masina. Drama of three swindlers who con the poor people of Rome out of their money. Directed by Federico Fellini, one of his less successful efforts. AKA: Il Bidone (84 mins.)†

Swing, The (West Germany, 1983)***½ Anja Jaenicke, Lena Stolze, Rolf Illig, Suzanne Herlet, Christine Kaufmann. Offbeat, fun-loving family in 1880s Bavaria lives life to the fullest, entertaining the crown prince, selling antiques, gardening, and enjoying music and art. Weirdly antic, amiable film is rich in period flavor, but gives a contemporary gloss to its picaresque characters, whom the director, Percy Adlon, clearly loves. (133 mins.)

Swinger, The (1966)* Ann-Margret, Tony Franciosa, Robert Coote. Author writes a steaming sex novel and proceeds to live out her heroine's adventures. Leering farce with Ann-Margret looking and acting incapable of reading, much less writing a book. (Dir: George Sidney, 81 mins.)

Swinger's Paradise (1965)* Cliff Richards, Walter Slezak, Susan Hampshire. Supersenseless plot about boy, working as a stunt man in a movie, who simultaneously makes another movie because the leading girl isn't being used right. (Dir: Sidney Furie, 85 mins.)

Swing Fever (1944)** Kay Kyser, Marilyn Maxwell, William Gargan, Nat Pendleton, Maxie Rosenbloom, Ish Kabibble, Lena Horne. Ridiculous musical vehicle for Kyser as a songwriter who dabbles in hypnosis. Pendleton and Rosenbloom lend funny support, and among the OK songs is one fine number by Lena Horne. (Dir: Tim Whelan, 80 mins.)

Swing High, Swing Low (1937)*** Carole Lombard, Fred MacMurray, Dorothy Lamour, Jean Dixon, Charles Butterworth. MacMurray plays a man whose talent with a trumpet can't mask his problems with drinking and gambling. Lombard falls for him, gives his career a boost, and stands by him. Adroit direction and sparkling performances. (Dir: Mitchell Leisen, 95 mins.)†

Swingin' Along (1962)*½ Tommy Noonan, Peter L. Marshall, Barbara Eden, Connie Gilcrist, Alan Carney, Mike Mazurki, Ted Knight. Farce about a scatterbrained delivery boy with artistic ambitions who may get his big break in a songwriting contest—if he can just finish writing one. AKA: **Double Trouble**. (Dir: Charles Barton, 74 mins.)

Swingin' Summer, A (1965)*½ James Stacy, Raquel Welch, the Righteous Brothers, Gary Lewis and the Playboys. Romance, jealousy, and singing among a group of teens who've been left out in the sun too long. (Dir: Robert Sparr, 82 mins.)†

Swing Shift (1984)*** Goldie Hawn, Kurt Russell, Christine Lahti, Ed Harris, Fred Willard. This WWII homefront comedy-drama benefits from meticulous attention to period atmosphere. Hawn excels as the homespun wife who joins an aircraft plant when her husband is called to war. (Dir: Jonathan Demme, 112 mins.)†

Swing Shift Maisie (1943)**½ Ann Sothern, James Craig, Jean Rogers, Connie Gilchrist, Kay Medford. Enjoyable series entry with Maisie ditching show biz temporarily to work in an airplane factory. (Dir: Norman Z. MacLeod, 87 mins.)

Swing Time (1936)**** Fred Astaire, Ginger Rogers, Victor Moore, Eric Blore, Helen Broderick, Betty Furness. In this all-time musical great, Astaire plays a dancer with a yen for gambling who falls for Rogers. This magical romance features the duo's most dazzling footwork as a team. With a phenomenal score including the Oscar-winning "The Way You Look Tonight." (Dir: George Stevens, 103 mins.)†

Swingtime Johnny (1943)**½ Andrews Sisters, Harriet Hilliard, Peter Cookson. Sister act quits show biz and goes to work in a defense plant during WWII. Sprightly musical. (Dir: Edward F. Cline, 61 mins.)

Swing Your Lady (1938)*½ Humphrey Bogart, Nat Pendleton, Penny Singleton, Frank McHugh, Louise Fazenda, Allen Jenkins. Silly musical about a wrestling promoter who discovers a lady wrestler. (Dir: Ray Enright, 72 mins.)

Swirl of Glory—See: **Sugarfoot**

Swiss Family Robinson (1940)*** Thomas Mitchell, Freddie Bartholomew, Tim Holt. The classic of a family marooned on an uninhabited island who find a peaceful existence away from the troubles of the civilized world. Tastefully produced, well acted. (Dir: Edward Ludwig, 93 mins.)

Swiss Family Robinson (1960)*** John Mills, Dorothy McGuire, James MacArthur, Sessue Hayakawa. Living in a tree house with all the conveniences of home—that's the shipwrecked and stranded Robinson family. (Dir: Ken Annakin, 126 mins.)†

Swiss Family Robinson, The (MTV 1975)**½ Martin Milner, Pat Delany, Eric Olson, Michael-James Wixted, Cameron Mitchell. Irwin Allen (the disaster film emperor) turned out this handsomely mounted version of the classic yarn. (Dir: Harry Harris, 74 mins.)

Swiss Miss (1938)** Stan Laurel, Oliver Hardy, Della Lind. The boys are mousetrap salesmen in the Alps. They become foils for an actress who tries to make her composer husband jealous. Too much plot, but the comics manage to get a few laughs. (Dir: John G. Blystone, 73 mins.)†

Switch (MTV 1975)** Robert Wagner, Eddie Albert, Charles Durning. Wagner and Albert team up as private eyes in this pilot, playing the old con game to catch their mark. (Dir: Robert Day, 72 mins.)

Switch (1991)**½ Ellen Barkin, Jimmy Smits, JoBeth Williams, Lorraine Bracco, Tony Roberts, Perry King. Director Edwards attempts another gender "switch" farce that is not up to the caliber of *Victor/Victoria*. Womanizing King is reincarnated in the form of sexy Barkin—the catch is that he/she still has his former male mind. The humorous slapstick flows from Barkin's predicament of a man trapped in a woman's body. Barkin is great in a demanding role, but last minute editing left the film ultimately unsatisfying. (Dir: Blake Edwards, 103 mins.)†

Switching Channels (1988)* Burt Reynolds, Kathleen Turner, Christopher Reeve, Ned Beatty, Henry Gibson. Remake of the classic *His Girl Friday* goes wrong in almost every way. With the setting updated to a CNN type of cable news network, reporter Turner tries to shake the attentions of her boss and ex-husband Reynolds so she can marry fatuous yuppie Reeve. (Dir: Ted Kotcheff, 97 mins.)†

Sword and the Rose, The (1953)*** Richard Todd, Glynis Johns, James Robertson Justice, Michael Gough. Exciting historical romance about Mary Tudor, the headstrong sister of Henry VIII, and her love for a dashing commoner against her brother's wishes. Johns is delightful as the vibrant, willful princess. (Dir: Ken Annakin, 91 mins.)

Sword and the Sorcerer, The (1982)** Richard Lynch, Kathleen Beller, Lee Horsley, George Maharis, Simon MacCorkindale,

Nina Van Pallandt, Anthony Delongis. This combination horror film and barbarian epic has many unintentional laughs. (Dir: Albert Pyun, 100 mins.)†

Sword In the Desert (1949)**½ Dana Andrews, Marta Toren, Stephen McNally, Jeff Chandler. Moderately effective drama about the underground movement for smuggled refugees out of Europe to the Palestine coast. (Dir: George Sherman, 100 mins.)

Sword In the Stone, The (1963)** Indifferently animated Disney film about the King Arthur legend. A plunky youngster proves his kingliness by removing the sword Excalibur from the stone. (Dir: Wolfgang Reitherman, 80 mins.)†

Sword of Gideon, The (MCTV 1986)*** Steve Bauer, Michael York, Rod Steiger, Colleen Dewhurst. Exciting adventure story about a trained commando group hired to avenge the deaths of athletes massacred at the Munich Olympics in 1972. (Dir: Michael Anderson, 150 mins.)

Sword of Lancelot (Great Britain, 1963)*** Cornel Wilde, Jean Wallace, Brian Aherne. The compelling love story of Lancelot, Guinevere, and King Arthur, without the *Camelot* music but with an abundance of action, scope, and fidelity to the old English legend. (Dir: Cornel Wilde, 116 mins.)†

Sword of Sherwood Forest (Great Britain, 1961)**½ Richard Greene, Peter Cushing. Once again Robin Hood outwits the evil Sheriff of Nottingham. Lively swashbuckler. (Dir: Terence Fisher, 80 mins.)†

Sword of the Conqueror (Italy, 1962)*½ Jack Palance, Eleonora Rossi-Drago. Leader of warlike empire covets a beauty of the opposition. (Dir: Carlo Campogalliani, 85 mins.)

Sword of the Valiant (1984)** Sean Connery, Trevor Howard, Miles O'Keeffe. A standard Arthurian adventure. The Green Knight pits his mystical powers against Sir Gawain, one of the King's braver knights. Connery's authoritativeness elevates this second-rate effort. (Dir: Stephen Weeks, 102 mins.)†

Swordsman, The (1947)**½ Larry Parks, Ellen Drew, George Macready. Warring clans stand in the way of a Scotsman who wants to wed his true love, so he tries to make peace. Diverting action pic. (Dir: Joseph H. Lewis, 80 mins.)

Swordsman, The, (Hong Kong, 1990)*½ Samuel Hui, Ceceilia Yip, Pennie Tuen, Cheung Mun. During the Ming Dynasty, a sacred scroll is stolen from the Forbidden City. The action is nonstop, with a confusing storyline. (Try to follow the trails of corrupt eunuchs or three dangerous women, among a score of others.) (Dir: King Hu, 110 mins.)

Swordsman of Siena (France-Italy, 1962)*½

Stewart Granger, Sylva Koscina, Christine Kaufman, Tullio Carminati, Gabriele Ferzetti. Swashbuckler of a mercenary adventurer in the 16th century who finds his sense of moral duty while at the side of a princess, midway through the fighting. (Dir: Etienne Perier, 97 mins.)

Sworn to Silence (MTV 1987)**½ Peter Coyote, Dabney Coleman, Caroline McWilliams, Liam Neeson. Competent issue-oriented drama about two attorneys willing to risk the wrath of their community, which is riddled with a lynch-mob mentality. (Dir: Peter Levin, 104 mins.)

Sybil (MTV 1976)**** Joanne Woodward, Sally Field, Brad Davis, Martine Bartlett. Devastating drama about an artistic, troubled young woman who is unable to handle fears originating from a cruel, mentally ill mother. Field is Sybil, a youngster who develops split personalities to cope with the world, finally undergoing treatment from psychiatrist Woodward. Field's amazing performance in this first-rate production won her an Emmy. (Dir: Daniel Petrie, 208 mins.)†

Sylvester (1985)*½ Richard Farnsworth, Melissa Gilbert, Michael Schoeffling. Horse opera about a feisty Miss who trains a stallion for the big race against (of course) insurmountable odds. (Dir: Tim Hunter, 103 mins.)†

Sylvia (1965)**½ Carroll Baker, George Maharis, Peter Lawford, Edmond O'Brien, Joanne Dru. An old-fashioned melodrama about a young lady who tries to better her poor lot but takes all the wrong steps. (Dir: Gordon Douglas, 115 mins.)

Sylvia (New Zealand, 1985)*** Eleanor David, Tom Wilkinson, Nigel Terry, Mary Regan. Factual tale of teacher Sylvia Ashton-Warner (David) who works with aboriginal children in New Zealand, and redefines educational theories after her experiences. (Dir: Michael Firth, 98 mins.)†

Sylvia Scarlett (1935)*** Katharine Hepburn, Cary Grant, Brian Aherne, Edmund Gwenn. A gently weird pastoral comedy in which Hepburn plays most of the picture in drag and Grant comes into his own as an actor. When the characters get tired of their lives as thieves, they decide to become strolling players—it's that kind of film. Rich with marginal creativity. (Dir: George Cukor, 97 mins.)†

Sympathy for the Devil (Great Britain, 1969)*** Mick Jagger and the Rolling Stones. The Stones can't get it going at a recording session, and director Jean-Luc Godard intercuts these scenes of frustrated creation in a hostile environment with long sequences of revolutionary rhetoric. Maddening for Stones enthusiasts, and pretty rough going for lovers of Godard's earlier humanistic work, but a most interesting oddity nonetheless. AKA: **One Plus One.** (99 mins.)†

Symphony for a Massacre (France-Italy, 1963)**½ Claude Dauphin, Michael Auclair, Jean Rochefort. Excellent acting adds luster to a fairly interesting crime tale, as a member of a gang decides to go independent with his friends' money. (Dir: Jacques Deray, 110 mins.)

Symphony of Six Million (1932)*** Irene Dunne, Ricardo Cortez, Gregory Ratoff. Director Gregory La Cava's masterful melodrama is probably the best of the immigrant success sagas. Cortez is the slum boy who becomes a Park Avenue physician, only to be plagued by a social conscience. (94 mins.)

Synanon (1965)**½ Chuck Connors, Alex Cord, Stella Stevens, Eartha Kitt, Richard Conte. A bit of truth about drug addicts combined with Hollywood melodrama. This downbeat multiplotted story is set in Synanon, a rehabilitation community for drug addicts in California. (Dir: Richard Quine, 107 mins.)

Syncopation (1942)** Adolphe Menjou, Bonita Granville, Jackie Cooper, Benny Goodman, Harry James. Story of the beginnings of jazz, and of a young trumpeter who wanted to make good. (Dir: William Dieterle, 88 mins.)

System, The (1953)** Frank Lovejoy, Joan Weldon, Bob Arthur. A young man discovers that his father is behind a big city's gambling combine. Overacted and clumsily written. (Dir: Lewis Seiler, 90 mins.)

System, The (1966)—See: **Girl–Getters, The**

Table for Five (1982)**½ Jon Voight, Marie-Christine Barrault, Richard Crenna, Millie Perkins. Screenwriter David Seltzer has taken the subject of estranged fathers and personalized it into a drama about a woman who has been remarried to a man who makes a kindly and loving stepfather. As the father, Jon Voight brings a sincerity and suggestion of complexity to the part. (Dir: Robert Lieberman, 122 mins.)†

Tabu (1931)**** Anna Chevalier, Matahi, Hitu. Enthralling drama, starring nonprofessional Tahitian actors, made by the unlikely team of documentarian Robert Flaherty and German expressionist F. W. Murnau. The simple story concerns a native maiden who attempts to break a taboo when she falls in love, but the real beauty of the film lies in its lyrical photography and polished editing. (Dir: F. W. Murnau, 82 mins.)†

Taffin (Great Britain, 1987)* Pierce Brosnan, Ray McAnally, Alison Doody. Small-town Irish lad Taffin (Brosnan) fights the big developers who want to raze the local athletic field to put up a chemical plant. Pretty dull for the man who was almost the new James Bond! (Dir: Francis Megahy, 96 mins.)†

Taggart (1964)**½ Tony Young, Dan Duryea, Peter Duryea, David Carradine. The accent's on action in this sagebrush saga about a man on a personal vendetta while bandits are in hot pursuit. Above par. (Dir: R. G. Springsteen, 85 mins.)

Tagget (MCTV 1991)** Daniel J. Travanti, William Sadler, Roxanne Hart, Lyman Ward. A somber, low-key yarn about a Vietnam veteran. When his nightmares reveal secrets from his war years he must run for his life. Slow-moving tale of paranoia and conspiracy. (Dir: Richard T. Heffron, 96 mins.)

T.A.G., The Assassination Bureau (1982)*½ Robert Carradine, Linda Hamilton, Perry Lang, Kristine De Bell. College kids play a game (like Dungeons and Dragons) all over campus, in which assassins stalk each other. Predictably, the game gets out of control, and one of the players begins killing people to score points. (Dir: Nick Castle, 92 mins.)†

Tail Gunner Joe (MTV 1977)*** Peter Boyle, John Forsythe, Heather Menzies, Burgess Meredith, Patricia Neal, Jean Stapleton. Devastating examination of the rise and fall of Sen. Joseph McCarthy, the demagogue who climbed the road to power in the early fifties with the cry of Communist infiltration. Meredith won an Emmy for his performance. (Dir: Jud Taylor, 144 mins.)

Tail Spin (1939)** Alice Faye, Constance Bennett, Nancy Kelly, Joan Davis, Charles Farrell, Jane Wyman. A slapped-together vehicle for the personable female stars. (Dir: Roy Del Ruth, 84 mins.)

Tailspin: Behind the Korean Airline Tragedy (MTV 1989)*** Chris Sarandon, Michael Murphy, Michael Moriarty, Harris Yulen, Jay Patterson. Dramatization of the 1983 incident in which a Korean passenger plane was shot down by the Soviets exposes the inside story of the U.S. government's reaction to the incident. Moriarty delivers a fine performance as an officer who determines the incident was an error all the way around. (Dir: David Darlow, 82 mins.)†

Tainted (1984)** Shari Shattuck, Park Overall, Gene Tootle, Magilla Schaus. Dark drama of a small-town woman forced to cover up the deaths of her husband and of the man who raped her. *Noir*-ish elements provide visual interest, but the film is hampered by poor writing. (Dir: Orestes Matacena, 93 mins.)†

Tai-Pan (1986)*½ Bryan Brown, Joan Chen, John Stanton, Tim Guinee. Glossy, campy, expensive project. In mid-nineteenth

1037

century China, Brown—a lusty aggressive trader—sets up shop in the Orient, establishes a dynasty, and survives contrived domestic disturbances. (Dir: Daryl Duke, 127 mins.)†

Take, The (1974)*½ Eddie Albert, Billy Dee Williams, Vic Morrow, Frankie Avalon, Albert Salmi. Tiresome actionpic involves a semi-crooked black cop who accepts bribes but won't take any guff from the syndicate kingpin ruling the local ghetto. (Dir: Robert Hartford-Davis, 93 mins.)

Take, The (MTV 1990)** Ray Sharkey, R. Lee Ermey, Larry Manetti, Joe Lala, Lisa Hartman, Orestes Matacena. Ex-cop Sharkey, just out of jail, tries to go straight but gets caught up in the dealings of a Cuban drug cartel. Poorly written and directed crime story slightly salvaged by good characterizations. (Dir: Leon Ichaso, 96 mins.)†

Take a Chance (1933)** James Dunn, Cliff Edwards, June Knight, Lillian Roth, Buddy Rogers. Directionless version of a popular Broadway play about a carny couple trying to hit the big time. (Dirs: Lawrence Schwab, Monte Brice, 80 mins.)

Take a Giant Step (1959)*** Estelle Hemsley, Ruby Dee, Frederick O'Neal, Ellen Holly, Johnny Nash. Beautifully acted drama. A black youth (Nash) enters adolescence, and discovers racial prejudice. (Dir: Philip Leacock, 100 mins.)

Take a Girl Like You (Great Britain, 1970)**½ Hayley Mills, Oliver Reed, Noel Harrison, John Bird, Sheila Hancock. Self-styled ladies' man Reed has his eye on innocent schoolteacher Mills in this slightly sluggish, but suitably swinging, tale of bed hopping in the London suburbs. Based on a novel by Kingsley Amis. (Dir: Jonathan Miller, 101 mins.)

Take a Hard Ride (1975)** Jim Brown, Lee Van Cleef, Fred Williamson, Barry Sullivan, Catherine Spaak, Dana Andrews, Jim Kelly, Harry Carey, Jr. Transporting money to Mexico, Brown is chased by an assortment of colorful characters and an unstoppable band of clichés. (Dir: "Anthony Dawson" [Antonio Margheriti], 103 mins.)†

Take a Letter, Darling (1942)**½ Rosalind Russell, Fred MacMurray. Russell makes something out of nothing in this frail comedy about a lady executive who hires a male secretary-escort and, of course, they fall in love. (Dir: Mitchell Leisen, 93 mins.)

Take Care of My Little Girl (1951)** Jeanne Crain, Jean Peters, Mitzi Gaynor, Jeffrey Hunter. Earnest but unexciting exposé of sorority shenanigans. The bright cast of

20th Century Fox contract players helps. (Dir: Jean Negulesco, 93 mins.)

Take Down (1979)** Edward Herrmann, Kathleen Lloyd, Lorenzo Lamas. Comedy-drama of high school wrestling is worth a look, mainly to see Herrmann's charm as a high school English teacher unwittingly cast as a coach. (Dir: Keith Merrill, 107 mins.)†

Take Her, She's Mine (1962)** James Stewart, Sandra Dee, Audrey Meadows, Robert Morley, Bob Denver. Daddy's efforts to prevent his daughter from leading a beatnik life put him in the soup himself. (Dir: Henry Koster, 98 mins.)

Take It Big (1944)** Jack Haley, Harriet Hilliard, Mary Beth Hughes, Fritz Feld, Fuzzy Knight. B-budget musical, with Haley trying to save his ramshackle ranch by (you guessed it) putting on a show. (Dir: Frank McDonald, 76 mins.)

Take It or Leave It (1944)** Phil Baker, Phil Silvers, Edward Ryan, Marjorie Massow, B. S. Pully. Amiable farce about broke husband Ryan who goes on a game show to win money he owes to his expectant wife's doctor. (Dir: Benjamin Stoloff, 70 mins.)

Take Me High (Great Britain, 1973)**½ Cliff Richard, Debbie Watling, Hugh Griffith, George Cole, Anthony Andrews. Lightweight comic fare spotlighting perennial British pop star Richard. The nonsensical plot, about a troubled hamburger joint, is simply a contrivance to give him maximum tune time. (Dir: David Askey, 90 mins.)

Take Me Out to the Ball Game (1948)**½ Frank Sinatra, Esther Williams, Gene Kelly, Betty Garrett. Promising musical, about the early days of baseball, falters because of forced comedy and a weak script. Of course Miss Williams finds a pool where she can do a water ballet. (Dir: Busby Berkeley, 93 mins.)†

Take Me to Town (1953)*** Ann Sheridan, Sterling Hayden. Good fun with Ann Sheridan at the peak of her comedy finesse as a dance hall girl by the name of Vermilion O'Toole (shades of Scarlett O'Hara). (Dir: Douglas Sirk, 81 mins.)

Take My Life (Great Britain, 1947)** Hugh Williams, Greta Gynt. Opera star's husband is arrested for the murder of a former sweetheart; she sets out to prove his innocence. Well-made murder mystery. (Dir: David Lean, 79 mins.)

Take One False Step (1949)**½ William Powell, Shelley Winters, James Gleason, Marsha Hunt. Moderately absorbing drama about a college professor who becomes entangled with the police after a blonde from his past runs into him on a business trip. (Dir: Chester Erskine, 94 mins.)

Take the High Ground (1953)*** Richard Widmark, Karl Malden, Elaine Stewart.

Colorful and believable story about the tough sergeants who train raw recruits for the U.S. Infantry. (Dir: Richard Brooks, 101 mins.)

Take the Money and Run (1969)***½ Woody Allen, Janet Margolin, Lonny Chapman, Mark Gordon. Woody directed, starred in, and co-authored this lunatic, gloriously funny farce where he plays a timid fumbling gangster who acquires more jail time than jewels. The plot doesn't matter—what does matter is that this is a fast-paced potpourri of frequently inspired sight gags and one-liners. (85 mins.)†

Take This Job and Shove It (1981)**½ Robert Hays, Art Carney, Barbara Hershey, Martin Mull, David Keith, Tim Thomerson, Eddie Albert, Penelope Milford, James Karen. Assembly-line comedy. Robert Hays takes up the gauntlet against big business when a conglomerate moves in to close down a brewery. Look for country singers Johnny Paycheck, David Allen Coe, Charlie Rich, and Lacy J. Dalton in small roles. (Dir: Gus Trikonis, 100 mins.)†

Take Your Best Shot (MTV 1982)** Robert Urich, Meredith Baxter Birney, Jeffrey Tambor. A sympathetic view of the Hollywood actor who battles rejection from all sides as his schoolteacher wife files for divorce when she can no longer bolster her husband's erratic career. (Dir: David Greene, 104 mins.)†

Taking Care of Business (1990)* James Belushi, Charles Grodin, Anne DeSalvo, Loryn Locklin, Stephen Elliott, Hector Elizondo, Veronica Hamel, Mako. A badly acted, one-note comedy. A petty criminal, out on parole, finds the daily planner/wallet of an executive and decides to become the fellow by using his credit cards, etc. (Dir: Arthur Hiller, 108 mins.)†

Taking Off (1971)***½ Lynn Carlin, Buck Henry, Linnea Heacock. Director Milos Forman's first comedy-in-exile about runaway children and their parents is a shrewd adaptation of Czech methods to an American subject. A virtuoso serious comedy. (93 mins.)

Taking of Flight 847, The: The Uli Derickson Story (MTV 1988)**½ Lindsay Wagner, Eli Danker, Sandy McPeak. Wagner portrays real-life heroine Derickson, a German stewardess who served as the go-between for the passengers of a flight taken hostage by Middle Eastern terrorists. There's palpable tension throughout this fact-based teledrama. (Dir: Paul Wendkos, 96 mins.)

Taking of Pelham One Two Three, The (1974)*** Walter Matthau, Robert Shaw, Martin Balsam, Hector Elizondo. A good, solid suspense yarn. Four men get on a New York subway, pull guns, and hold a car full of passengers as hostages, de-manding a million-dollar ransom from the mayor's office. The cast is excellent, including Matthau as a transit detective and Shaw as the cold-blooded leader of the heist. (Dir: Joseph Sargent, 102 mins.)†

Takin' It All Off (1988)* Kitten Natividad, Jean Poremba, Sharona Bonner, Gail Thackeray. Sequel to *Takin' It Off*. When the members of a school for strippers are threatened with eviction, they do what anyone who's ever seen a Judy Garland–Mickey Rooney movie would do—put on a show! The students' performances and a lot of baggy-pants humor make this a less sophisticated equivalent of a burlesque show. (Dir: Ed Hansen, 91 mins.)†

Talent for Loving, A (1969)**½ Richard Widmark, Genevieve Page, Topol, Cesar Romero. A lightweight comedy about the Old West. Widmark is the man who comes to Mexico to claim his land and finds that Romero has a claim on the same land. (Dir: Richard Quine, 101 mins.)

Tale of the Cock (1967)** Don Murray, Linda Evans, David Brian, Angelique Pettyjohn, Don Joslyn, Gary Clarke, Logan Ramsey. Star Murray produced and wrote this gritty drama based on the true story of boxer Tom Harris, an anti-hero if ever there was one—he fights dirty, commits rape, and sidelines as a mob enforcer before cleaning up his act. AKA: **Childish Things** and **The Confessions of Tom Harris**. (Dir: John Derek, 93 mins.)†

Tale of Two Cities, A (1911) and **In the Switch Tower** (1915)*** A compilation of two early silent classics, both big hits in their day. The first, *A Tale of Two Cities*, stars matinee idol Maurice Costello, father of talkie stars Dolores and Helene Costello, as Sydney Carton, the self-sacrificing hero of Dickens' novel. This is a fine production, although only a shortened version survives. Second is *In the Switch Tower*, which stars future director Frank Borzage in an action-packed railroad melodrama. Both are fascinating viewing. (70 mins.)†

Tale of Two Cities, A (1917)***½ William Farnum, Jewel Carmen, Charles Clary, Herschel Mayall. An excellent silent version of the Dickens novel, with a bravura performance by stage actor Farnum as both Sydney Carton and his look-alike Charles Darnay. The trick photography is amazingly well handled. (Dir: Frank Lloyd, 65 mins.)

Tale of Two Cities, A (1935)*** Ronald Colman, Elizabeth Allan, Basil Rathbone, Edna May Oliver. Rousing MGM version of the Dickens novel, redeemed by brilliant casting. The film's most memorable sequence is the storming of the Bastille. Colman is the dissipated lawyer Sydney Carton; Blanche Yurka is Madame Defarge, knitting at the guillotine, the rest of the cast is a sturdily etched gallery of types. Jack Conway's direction is strictly of the *Classics Illustrated* school. (128 mins.) †

Tale of Two Cities, A (Great Britain, 1958)**½ Dirk Bogarde, Cecil Parker. Remake is good, but a step down from the '35 version. (Dir: Ralph Thomas, 117 mins.) †

Tale of Two Cities, A (MTV 1980)**½ Chris Sarandon, Peter Cushing, Kenneth More, Barry Morse, Dame Flora Robson. Acceptable version of Charles Dickens's passionate and noble tale played against the turbulent backdrop of the French Revolution. (Dir: Jim Goddard, 156 mins.)

Tales From the Crypt (Great Britain, 1972)*** Ralph Richardson, Joan Collins, Richard Greene. Five horror tales, attractively mounted and effectively executed. The peg is that five people lost in catacombs encounter an evil monk who shows them their future. (Dir: Freddie Francis, 92 mins.) †

Tales From the Darkside: The Movie (1990)*** Deborah Harry, Christian Slater, David Johansen, William Hickey, James Remar, Rae Dawn Chong, Robert Klein, Steve Buscemi, Matthew Lawrence. Solid stories, a professional cast, and more gore than you can show on TV make this horror anthology worthwhile. Best segment is last, of course, but all three are good. (Dirs: John Harrison, 93 mins.) †

Tales of Hoffmann, The (Great Britain, 1951)*** Robert Rounseville, Moira Shearer. The Offenbach opera is presented in its entirety; the story of the student who has strange adventures. Brilliant production, but yet a highly stylized affair that is not for every taste. (Dirs: Michael Powell, Emeric Pressburger, 138 mins.)

Tales of Manhattan (1942)*** Charles Boyer, Ginger Rogers, Rita Hayworth, Henry Fonda, Cesar Romero, Charles Laughton, Paul Robeson, Edward G. Robinson. Omnibus episode film has a pun in its premise—we follow a suit of formal evening clothes from owner to owner. Some of the anecdotes are quite good, notably Robinson's. (Dir: Julien Duvivier, 118 mins.)

Tales of Ordinary Madness (Italy-France, 1981)*** Ben Gazzara, Susan Tyrrell, Ornella Muti. Arresting tragicomedy based (as was *Barfly*) on the work of Bowery poet Charles Bukowski, with Gazzara as the booze-soaked L.A. writer. (Dir: Marco Ferreri, 108 mins.) †

Tales of Terror (1962)*** Vincent Price, Basil Rathbone, Peter Lorre, Debra Paget. Good, stylish horror: three tales by Edgar Allan Poe retold by director Roger Corman in his inimitable way. (90 mins.) †

Tales of the Third Dimension (1985)** Robert Bloodworth, Kate Hunter, William Hicks, Helene Tryon. Trio of none-too-serious horror tales, involving a vampire cou-
1040

ple, ambitious gravediggers, and a murderous granny. The worst that you can say about any of them is that they're short. (Dirs: Thom McIntyre, Worth Keeter, Todd Durham, 90 mins.) †

Tales That Witness Madness (1973)** Jack Hawkins, Donald Pleasence, Kim Novak. Another horror anthology. An uneven collection at best; the mad tales involve a murderous plant, a not-so-mythical beast, a bike that time-travels, and cannibalism. (Dir: Freddie Francis, 90 mins.)

Talion—See: **Eye for an Eye, An** (1966)

Talk About a Stranger (1952)** George Murphy, Billy Gray, Nancy Davis, Lewis Stone, Kurt Kasznar. Low-budget family drama with overtones of mystery, as a boy suspects an odd new neighbor of poisoning his dog. Unambitious, but fairly competent. (Dir: David Bradley, 65 mins.)

Talk of the Town (1942)**½ Cary Grant, Ronald Colman, Jean Arthur. Director George Stevens has taken some serious material for a light comedy, leavened it, and stretched it out to the point of pointlessness. Anarchist Leopold Dilg (Grant) is on the lam and hiding out in the home of a U.S. Supreme Court nominee (Colman). Luckily, the cast is perfect. (118 mins.) †

Talk Radio (1988)***½ Eric Bogosian, Ellen Greene, Leslie Hope, Alec Baldwin. Adaptation of Bogosian's lacerating play about an abrasive DJ has been diluted somewhat by melding it to the true story of Alan Berg, a DJ who was assassinated by white supremacists. But it's a stunning vehicle for Bogosian, well adapted by director Oliver Stone. (100 mins.) †

Tall Blond Man With One Black Shoe, The (France, 1972)*** Pierre Richard, Bernard Blier, Jean Rochefort, Mirielle Darc, Jean Carmet. Nimble spy spoof energized by some spry slapstick by Richard. Rival secret agents play tug-of-war with the tall blond man, who's been mistaken for a spy. Badly remade as *The Man With One Red Shoe*. Sequel: *Return of the Tall Blond Man With One Black Shoe, The* (Dir: Yves Robert, 90 mins.) †

Tall, Dark and Handsome (1941)*** Cesar Romero, Virginia Gilmore, Milton Berle. Highly amusing comedy about a softhearted gangster, the orphaned son of a deceased mobster and an assortment of crazy characters. Good fun. Remade as *Love That Brute*. (Dir: H. Bruce Humberstone, 78 mins.)

Tall Guy, The (Great Britain, 1989)*** Jeff Goldblum, Emma Thompson, Rowen Atkinson, Emil Wolk. Goldblum is an insecure American actor in London whose career finally takes off when he lands the leading role in a musical version of *The Elephant Man*. Spotty but affable British comedy features a memorably unique sex scene and a hilarious parody of Andrew Lloyd Webber. (Dir: Mel Smith, 92 mins.)†

Tall in the Saddle (1944)*** John Wayne, Ella Raines, George "Gabby" Hayes, Ward Bond. Woman-hating cowboy takes over as ranch foreman only to find the new owners are a spinster and her young niece. Entertaining, fast-paced western. (Dir: Edwin L. Marin, 87 mins.)†

Tall Lie, The (1952)*** Paul Henreid, Kathleen Hughes, Margaret Field. College professor exposes brutal hazing incidents in a fraternity. (Dir: Paul Henreid, 93 mins.)

Tall Man Riding (1955)** Randolph Scott, Dorothy Malone, Peggie Castle. All the ingredients for a predictable western—a crooked gambler, a pretty girl, two or three hired guns, another pretty girl, and Randolph Scott. (Dir: Lesley Selander, 83 mins.)

Tall Men, The (1955)** Jane Russell, Clark Gable, Robert Ryan. Routine western fare. Gable plays the granite-fisted cattle driver, and Miss Russell decorates the wagon train. (Dir: Raoul Walsh, 122 mins.)†

Tall Shadows of the Wind (Iran, 1978)*** Faramaz Gharibian, Nadia Khalilpur, Salid Nikpour. Allegorical tale of a bus driver who, after seeing a scarecrow, decides to mimic it. Bizarre events occur and the superstitious villagers condemn the driver. Radiant cinematography and a vivid musical score enhance this unique and interesting denunciation of superstition and authority. (Dir: Bahman Farmanara, 110 mins.)

Tall Story (1960)*** Anthony Perkins, Jane Fonda (film debut), Tom Laughlin, Anne Jackson, Ray Walston. Charming film features Perkins as a basketball star and Jane's determination to win in a degree and a husband. (Dir: Joshua Logan, 91 mins.)

Tall Stranger (1957)*** Joel McCrea, Virginia Mayo. Good western, well made. Joel joins a wagon train of settlers, helps them fight the bad guys. (Dir: Thomas Carr, 81 mins.)

Tall T, The (1957)**½ Randolph Scott, Richard Boone, Maureen O'Sullivan. Better-than-average Randolph Scott western tale. A good supporting cast keeps the action believable, as Randy battles Boone and his band of killers. (Dir: Budd Boetticher, 78 mins.)

Tall Target, The (1951)*** Dick Powell, Paula Raymond, Adolphe Menjou. Tense suspense yarn about a detective's efforts to thwart a plot to kill President Abraham Lincoln when he stops in Baltimore for a whistle-stop speech. Gripping suspense. (Dir: Anthony Mann, 78 mins.)

Tall Texan, The (1953)*** Lloyd Bridges, Marie Windsor, Lee J. Cobb, Luther Adler. A group of assorted people band together on the desert to seek hidden gold which is cached in an Indian burial ground.

Suspenseful western, off the beaten track. (Dir: Elmo Williams, 81 mins.)

Tamahine (Great Britain, 1963)** Nancy Kwan, John Fraser, Dennis Price. Rather foolish, fast-paced froth about lovely Polynesian girl who disrupts routine of a British boys' school. Naïve, painless. (Dir: Philip Leacock, 85 mins.)

Tamango (France, 1958)** Curt Jurgens, Dorothy Dandridge. Slaves revolt on a ship commanded by a brutal captain. Confused, unpleasant drama, not helped by dubbing of minor roles into English. (Dir: John Berry, 98 mins.)

Tamarind Seed, The (Great Britain, 1974)** Julie Andrews, Omar Sharif, Anthony Quayle. A lush bore. Confused, outdated story of a Cold War Romeo and Juliet. Andrews and Sharif are unconvincing as star-crossed lovers kept apart by international intrigue. (Dir: Blake Edwards, 123 mins.)†

Taming of the Shrew, The (1929)**½ Mary Pickford, Douglas Fairbanks, Edwin Maxwell, Joseph Cawthorn. The movies' most famous couple made their only official appearance together in this early talkie version of Shakespeare's comedy, with a simplified plot and an emphasis on broad humor. An interesting curio, at least. (Dir: Samuel Taylor, 66 mins.)†

Taming of the Shrew, The (U.S.-Italy, 1967)**** Elizabeth Taylor, Richard Burton, Cyril Cusack, Michael Hordern, Natasha Pyne, Victor Spinetti, Michael York. One of the rare occasions when Shakespeare really works on the screen. Credit director Franco Zeffirelli's exquisite mounting, and the spirited, thoughtful playing by stars Taylor and Burton. Burton seems to have been born to play the wily opportunist Petruchio who comes to Padua to woo and wed the man-hating Kate. Taylor is a rare combination of beauty, fire, and luminous femininity as Kate. (126 mins.)†

T.A.M.I. Show, The (1964)*** The Rolling Stones, Chuck Berry, Marvin Gaye, Jan and Dean, The Supremes, Smokey Robinson and The Miracles, Leslie Gore, and many others. Check out all the great sixties talent taking part in the Teenage Awards Music International Show. Released on video with *The Big T.N.T. Show* as **That Was Rock.** (Dir: Steve Binder, 100 mins.)†

Tam Lin (Great Britain, 1971)* Ava Gardner, Ian McShane, Cyril Cusack, Stephanie Beacham. Wretched jet set tale of aging woman who surrounds herself with "beautiful people" in an attempt to stay young. AKA: **The Devil's Widow.** (Dir: Roddy McDowall, 104 mins.)

Tammy and the Bachelor (1957)**½ Debbie Reynolds, Walter Brennan, Leslie Nielsen, Fay Wray. Entertaining combination of corn and hokum. Debbie Reynolds's energetic performance as a backwoods teenager who seems to have a knack for setting things straight is the bright spot of the film. (Dir: Joseph Pevney, 89 mins.)†

Tammy and the Doctor (1963)** Sandra Dee, Peter Fonda (film debut), Macdonald Carey. Backwoods girl becomes a nurse's aide, finds romance with a young doctor. Sticky-sweet stuff for the femme-teen set. (Dir: Harry Keller, 88 mins.)†

Tammy and the Millionaire (1967)* Debbie Watson, Frank McGrath, Denver Pyle. Fourth *Tammy* film is a composite made from four episodes of the '65–'66 TV series. Tammy gets ahead, with support from her backwoodsy relatives, despite uppity neighbors. (Dirs: Sidney Miller, Ezra Stone, Leslie Goodwins, 87 mins.)

Tammy Tell Me True (1961)**½ Sandra Dee, John Gavin, Beulah Bondi. The country girl decides it's time she got an education and packs off to college. Naïve romantic comedy isn't really as bad as it could have been. (Dir: Harry Keller, 97 mins.)

Tampico (1944)** Edward G. Robinson, Victor McLaglen, Lynn Bari. Routine war drama about espionage in the merchant marine. (Dir: Lothar Mendes, 75 mins.)

Tampopo (Japan 1987)*** Tsutomu Yamazaki, Nobuko Miyamoto, Koji Yakusho, Ken Watanabe. Tasty comedy about a young widow and her obsession to create the perfect noodle and become a noodle queen. Eccentric satire al dente. (Dir: Juzo Itami, 117 mins.)†

Tanganyika (1954)** Van Heflin, Ruth Roman, Howard Duff. This jungle drama set in the early 1900s has all the plot ingredients usually found in similar adventure tales—natives, madmen, love, pestilence, and massacre. Strictly for adventure fans. (Dir: André de Toth, 81 mins.)

Tangier (1946)** Maria Montez, Robert Paige, Sabu, Preston Foster, Louise Allbritton. Montez plays a dancer looking for the Nazi who killed her father; Paige portrays a newsman looking for the story that will make his career. (Dir: George Waggner, 74 mins.)†

Tango and Cash (1989)*½ Sylvester Stallone, Kurt Russell, Jack Palance, Brion James, Robert Zdar. Formulaic buddy-cop movie teams rival L.A. cops Stallone and Russell, forced to work together to nab nasty bad guy Palance. Purposely juvenile film is one long homoerotic wink, with the stars' flexed pecs doing a lot of the blinking. Mostly directed by Andrei Konchalovsky, completed by Albert Magnoli after Konchalovsky reputedly left in a dispute over the film's ending. (98 mins.)†

Tango Bar (Argentina/Puerto Rico, 1988)**½ Raul Julia, Valeria Lynch. This film's purpose—a history of the tango, a dance and musical form of tremendous cultural importance in Latin America—is poorly served by its format, a fictionalized framework into which Hollywood film clips and new productions of tangos are inserted. Still, worth seeing for some insight into Latino culture. (Dir: Marcos Zurinaga, 90 mins.)†

Tangos, the Exile of Gardel (Argentina-France, 1985)***½ Marie Laforet, Philippe Léotard, Marina Vlady. Gloriously photographed, poignant comedy-drama about a group of Argentine exiles in Paris who soothe their homesickness by staging an elaborate and electrifying tango ballet drawn from the music of the legendary dancer Carlos Gardel. Touching story with mesmerizing dance sequences. (Dir: Fernando E. Solanas, 125 mins.)

Tank (1984)** James Garner, Shirley Jones, C. Thomas Howell, G. D. Spradlin. A soldier tries to mow down small-town corruption with a Sherman tank after his son is framed for a crime and unjustly imprisoned. OK comedy-drama. (Dir: Marvin Chomsky, 113 mins.)†

Tank Force (Great Britain, 1958)** Victor Mature, Luciana Paluzzi, Leo Genn. Average war tale with Victor Mature playing a troubled American soldier who serves with the British in the African campaign. (Dir: Terence Young, 81 mins.)

Tap (1989)*** Gregory Hines, Suzanne Douglas, Sammy Davis, Jr., Savion Glover. The dancing, by Hines and a bevy of veteran tap dancers, is wonderful, but there's far too little of it. Instead, our time is wasted with a predictable plot about ex-con Hines's involvement with his old criminal companions. Recommended for the dancing; fast-forward through the rest. (Dir: Nick Castle, 110 mins.)†

Tapeheads (1988)*½ John Cusack, Tim Robbins, Doug McClure, Connie Stevens, Clu Gulager, Mary Crosby, Lyle Alzado, Susan Tyrrell. Brash but forgettable comedy with Cusack and Robbins as two young creators of rock videos. The only incentive to see this are the numerous (very brief) celebrity cameos, and a busy, eclectic soundtrack. (Dir: Bill Fishman, 97 mins.)†

Tap Roots (1948)**½ Susan Hayward, Van Heflin, Boris Karloff, Ward Bond, Julie London. The advent of the Civil War destroys plans for two people to marry, and enables the girl to find her true love. Lavish historical drama has some good moments, but generally the plot never seems to resolve itself. (Dir: George Marshall, 109 mins.)

Taps (1981)**½ George C. Scott, Timothy Hutton, Ronny Cox, Sean Penn, Tom Cruise, Brendan Ward. A military academy is to be closed and replaced by a condominium, but the boys are fired with a sense of honor, duty, and love for the military. The National Guard moves to take the grounds by force; a bloodbath ensues. Not very believable, with sometimes pompous dialogue, but makes a strong point against carrying honor and tradition too far. Fine performances. (Dir: Harold Becker, 122 mins.)†

Tarantula (1955)**½ John Agar, Mara Corday, Leo G. Carroll, Clint Eastwood (bit). Giant spider escapes from the lab and begins terrorizing the territory. Well-done technically, this horror thriller carries its share of tense situations. Better than usual. (Dir: Jack Arnold, 80 mins.)

Tarantulas: The Deadly Cargo (MTV 1977)** Claude Akins, Pat Hingle. Also features 300 tarantulas. After a plane crashes in the Southwest, the cargo of hairy spiders are free to feed on the local orange crop and the inhabitants. Foolish stuff. (Dir: Stuart Hagmann, 104 mins.)†

Taras Bulba (1962)**½ Yul Brynner, Tony Curtis, Christine Kaufmann. A comic-book version of the 16th-century Polish revolution. Brynner has the title role of the famed Cossack and Curtis plays one of his sons, bent on revenge against the Poles. (Dir: J. Lee Thompson, 122 mins.)†

Tarawa Beachhead (1958)** Kerwin Mathews, Julie Adams, Ray Danton, Karen Sharpe, Onslow Stevens. Plodding attempt to spice up WWII beach assault action, with a subplot about soldiers' emotional problems. (Dir: Paul Wendkos, 77 mins.)

Target (1952)** Tim Holt, Linda Douglas, Walter Reed, Harry Harvey, Richard Martin. Holt and Martin put themselves at the service of a lady law officer (Douglas) in this routine western. The villain is Reed, trying to oust a group of respectable ranchers so he can claim their land. (Dir: Stuart Gilmore, 60 mins.)

Target (1985)** Gene Hackman, Matt Dillon, Gayle Hunnicutt, Victoria Fyodorova. A peremptory spy-thriller by one of America's best directors, working here at less than full throttle. When his mother is kidnapped, Dillon learns that his seemingly typical father Hackman is an ex-CIA agent. (Dir: Arthur Penn, 117 mins.)†

Target Earth (1954)*½ Richard Denning, Virginia Grey, Kathleen Crowley. Unfrightening sci-fi about people harassed by importunate robots in a deserted city. (Dir: Sherman Rose, 75 mins.)

Target for Killing, A (West Germany, 1966)** Stewart Granger, Curt Jurgens, Mollie Peters, Adolfo Celi, Klaus Kinski, Rupert Davies. Agent Granger is assigned the task of protecting heiress Peters from a Lebanese syndicate that's out to kill her. Humdrum spy stuff with some familiar faces to hold your attention. (Dir: Manfred Kohler, 93 mins.)

Target: Harry (1980)** Vic Morrow, Suzanne Pleshette, Victor Buono, Cesar Romero, Stanley Holloway, Charlotte Rampling. Spy-thriller made for TV in 1968, but eventually shown (over a decade later) in theaters. Morrow is out to retrieve two printing plates stolen from the British Mint, as are villainous Buono and seductive Pleshette. (Dirs: Henry Neill, Roger Corman, 81 mins.)

Target Risk (MTV 1975)** Bo Svenson, Meredith Baxter, Keenan Wynn, John P. Ryan, Robert Coote. Unsold pilot for an action series about a bonded courier hero coerced into participating in a diamond robbery by thieves who've kidnapped his girlfriend. Average. (Dir: Robert Scheerer, 72 mins.)

Targets (1968)***½ Tim O'Kelly, Boris Karloff. Offbeat, occasionally terrifying tale of a psychotic sniper (O'Kelly) and an aging horror-movie star (Karloff) whose paths cross during the most deadly play of all. Low-budget direction by Peter Bogdanovich shows an apt command of the film medium. (92 mins.)†

Target Unknown (1951)**½ Mark Stevens, Alex Nicol, Gig Young, Don Taylor, James Best, Joyce Holden. Interesting wartime drama. When flyers crash land in occupied France, the Nazi swine play on the men's fears and their longings for their sweethearts. (Dir: George Sherman, 90 mins.)

Target Zero (1955)** Richard Conte, Peggie Castle, Charles Bronson, Richard Stapley, L. Q. Jones, Chuck Connors, Strother Martin, Aaron Spelling. The usual grimy exploits in a Korean War setting, with a patrol of Americans and a few British citizens stranded in enemy territory. Solid casting provides the only interest. (Dir: Harmon Jones, 92 mins.)

Tarnished Angels, The (1958)***½ Rock Hudson, Dorothy Malone, Robert Stack, Robert Middleton, Jack Carson. The best film ever made from a William Faulkner novel (*Pylon*). Tawdry tale of stunt flyers during the Depression, and of the southern reporter who is fascinated by them. (Dir: Douglas Sirk, 91 mins.)

Tarnished Lady (1931)**½ Tallulah Bankhead, Clive Brook, Phoebe Foster, Osgood Perkins, Elizabeth Patterson. Suffering in the grand 1930s manner, Tallulah has a cash register for a heart until she sees the light. When she finally falls in love with her wealthy husband, she wonders whether he'll be able to forgive her. (Dir: George Cukor, 83 mins.)

Tars and Spars (1946)**½ Sid Caesar, Alfred Drake, Janet Blair. In spite of Caesar and Drake, this is a bore. However, you will see one of Sid's funniest routines, and it almost makes the film worth sitting through. (Dir: Alfred E. Green, 88 mins.)

Tartars, The (Italy, 1960)* Victor Mature,

Orson Welles. Vikings battle Tartars on the Asian steppes. Result is unrelenting gore, sadistic retaliations. (Dir: Richard Thorpe, 83 mins.)

Tartu—See: Adventures of Tartu

Tarzan series. It's hard to keep track of all the actors who've swung on the famous vine belonging to Edgar Rice Burroughs's Lord of the Jungle. In silent films, Elmo Lincoln ruled the roost (although four other actors tried the role, too); there was also a radio series co-starring Burroughs's daughter in 1932, a comic strip, and much later, a 1966 TV series with Ron Ely. Excluding serials, the Tarzans of the talkies include: Buster Crabbe, Bruce Bennett, Glenn Morris, Lex Barker, Gordon Scott, Denny Miller, Jock Mahoney, Mike Henry, and Ron Ely, but for most fans (if not for Burroughs purists) Johnny Weissmuller *was* Tarzan, even when his budgets contracted and his waistline expanded. Enthusiasts can pick their own favorites from those listed below, and they'll also want to see *Greystoke: Legend of Tarzan, Lord of the Apes.*

Tarzan and His Mate (1934)*** Johnny Weissmuller, Maureen O'Sullivan. Second Tarzan film with Weissmuller has a decent production and some adult situations. Jane is attempting to make a new home for the couple in the jungle. (Dirs: Cedric Gibbons, Jack Conway, 105 mins.)

Tarzan and the Amazons (1945)**½ Johnny Weissmuller, Brenda Joyce, Johnny Sheffield, Henry Stephenson, Barton MacLane, Maria Ouspenskaya. Tarzan fights European traders and rescues Boy from Amazon women. Fairly exciting Tarzan yarn. (Dir: Kurt Neumann, 76 mins.)

Tarzan and the Great River (1967)** Mike Henry, Rafer Johnson. Tarzan is up to his loincloth in trouble as he goes deep into the Amazon region. (Dir: Robert Day, 99 mins.)

Tarzan and the Green Goddess (1938)* Herman Brix, Bruce Bennett, Ula Holt, Frank Baker. Tarzan is caught between two rival factions while trying to recover a secret formula. A minor entry in the series utilizing footage from the serial *The New Adventures of Tarzan* (1935). (Dir: Edward Kull, 72 mins.)

Tarzan and the Huntress (1947)** Johnny Weissmuller, Brenda Joyce, Johnny Sheffield, Barton MacLane, Patricia Morison. Tarzan thwarts a zoological expedition sent into the jungle to bring back exhibits. Good pace, but the same old stuff. (Dir: Kurt Neumann, 72 mins.)

Tarzan and the Jungle Boy (U.S.-Switzerland, 1968)** Mike Henry, Rafer Johnson, Alizia Gur. Tarzan, played by Mike Henry for the third time, goes into the jungle in search of a missing boy. (Dir: Robert Day, 99 mins.)

Tarzan and the Leopard Woman (1946)** Johnny Weissmuller, Brenda Joyce, Johnny Sheffield, Acquanetta, Edgar Barrier. Tarzan matches wits with the high priestess of the Leopard People. A Tarzan flick with cardboard exoticness. (Dir: Kurt Neumann, 75 mins.)

Tarzan and the Lost Safari (Great Britain, 1957)** Gordon Scott, Betta St. John, Yolande Donlan. The jungle man has his work cut out for him when he tries to lead the party of a playboy crashed in the jungle to safety. (Dir: H. Bruce Humberstone, 84 mins.)

Tarzan and the Mermaids (1948)**½ Johnny Weissmuller, Brenda Joyce, Linda Christian, George Zucco, John Laurenz. Pearl thieves have been playing God in order to subjugate the natives. Tarzan to the rescue! Good camera work and a lively story. (Dir: Robert Florey, 68 mins.)

Tarzan and the She-Devil (1953)*½ Lex Barker, Joyce Mackenzie, Raymond Burr, Monique Van Vooren, Tom Conway. Tarzan, accompanied by a herd of wild elephants, makes evil ivory hunters sorry they ever tried to kidnap Jane. This one has little juice, despite the elephants and Monique. (Dir: Kurt Neumann, 75 mins.)

Tarzan and the Slave Girl (1950)** Lex Barker, Vanessa Brown, Denise Darcel, Hurd Hatfield. Temptation comes to Tarzan when busty Darcel comes on like a jungle hut-wrecker; she causes lots of problems when Tarzan doesn't flip his loincloth for her. (Dir: Lee Sholem, 74 mins.)

Tarzan and the Trappers (1958)*½ Gordon Scott, Eve Brent, Ricky Sorensen. The jungle man frees the animals from some villainous trappers, who are also after the riches in a lost city. (Dir: H. Bruce Humberstone, 74 mins.)†

Tarzan and the Valley of Gold (1966)* Mike Henry, David Opatoshu, Manuel Padilla, Jr. Puerile adventure in which Tarzan comes back to the jungle but fights with a gun instead of his fists and powerful yodel. (Dir: Robert Day, 90 mins.)

Tarzan Escapes (1936)**½ Johnny Weissmuller, Maureen O'Sullivan, John Buckler, Benita Hume. More jungle escapism as Tarzan fights off bad guys, wild animals— everyone but Jane. (Dir: Richard Thorpe, 95 mins.)

Tarzan Finds a Son (1939)*** Johnny Weissmuller, Maureen O'Sullivan, Johnny Sheffield, Ian Hunter. Jane and Tarzan adopt an abandoned child (whom they cleverly name Boy) and bring some new life into the series. (Dir: Richard Thorpe, 90 mins.)

Tarzan Goes to India (U.S.-Great Britain-Switzerland, 1962)**½ Jock Mahoney, Mark Dana, Jai. Tarzan does his best to create a sanctuary in India for elephants and other wild animals, whose existence is threatened by the construction of a dam. (Dir: John Guillermin, 88 mins.)

Tarzan in Manhattan (MTV 1989)**½ Joe Lara, Joel Carlson, Kim Crosby, Tony Curtis, Jan-Michael Vincent, Joe Seneca. The vine-swinger is off to N.Y.C. to retrieve Cheetah after the ape is kidnapped by evil big-game hunter Vincent. He's aided by a cabbie named Jane (Crosby) and her dad (Curtis). Modern touches freshen Tarz up a bit, but this is still for fans only. (Dir: Michael Schultz, 96 mins.)

Tarzan of the Apes (1918)*** Elmo Lincoln, Enid Markey, Gordon Griffith, True Boardman, Kathleen Kirkham, George B. French, Rex Ingram. The first Tarzan film, very effectively done, with strongman Lincoln convincing as the English nobleman raised by great apes. The scenario follows the book more closely than most other versions. (Dir: Scott Sidney, 55 mins.)†

Tarzan's Deadly Silence (1970)** Ron Ely, Jock Mahoney, Woody Strode, Gregorio Acosta, Nichelle Nichols. What happens when an actor gets too old to play the eternally youthful Ape Man? In Mahoney's case, he simply sheds his loincloth (taken up by ex-footballer Ely) for a villain's sneer, playing a crazy colonel with a private army in this weak feature composed of two episodes from the '66–'68 TV series. (Dirs: Robert L. Friend, Lawrence Dobkin, 88 mins.)

Tarzan's Desert Mystery (1943)** Johnny Weissmuller, Nancy Kelly, Johnny Sheffield, Otto Kruger, Joseph Sawyer, Lloyd Corrigan. The ultimate claustrophobic studio adventure film as Big T. battles Nazis and studio-bound settings. (Dir: William Thiele, 70 mins.)

Tarzan's Fight for Life (1958)** Gordon Scott, Eve Brent. The jungle man incurs the wrath of a tribal witch doctor when he becomes friendly with a doctor running a hospital in the jungle. (Dir: H. Bruce Humberstone, 86 mins.)

Tarzan's Greatest Adventure (Great Britain, 1959)*** Gordon Scott, Anthony Quayle, Sean Connery, Sara Shane. Tarzan on the trail of four men, including an old enemy, who don't stop at murder in seeking a diamond mine. One of the better jungle adventures—Tarzan speaks whole sentences, the African locations are beautiful, and the story's loaded with action, some of the more spectacular variety. Good fun. (Dir: John Guillermin, 88 mins.)

Tarzan's Hidden Jungle (1955)** Gordon Scott, Vera Miles, Peter Van Eyck, Jack Elam, Rex Ingram. Nothing new in this entry, not even an exploitative gimmick. Tarzan defeats two white hunters sent to slaughter wildlife for profit. Gordon Scott's first go-round as the ape man. (Dir: Harold Schuster, 72 mins.)

Tarzan's Jungle Rebellion (1970)*½ Ron Ely, Manuel Padilla, Jr., Ulla Stromstedt,

Sam Jaffe, William Marshall, Harry Lauter, Lloyd Haynes. Everyone's favorite vine-swinger returns again in this badly assembled compilation of two episodes from the TV show. Ely makes for an incredibly cardboard Tarzan, but the old pros on hand keep this "rebellion" at a tense pitch. (Dir: William Witney, 92 mins.)

Tarzan's Magic Fountain (1949)**½ Lex Barker, Brenda Joyce, Albert Dekker, Evelyn Ankers, Charles Drake, Alan Napier. First and best of Barker's vehicles. The ape man protects a jungle version of Shangri-La from inquisitive visitors. (Dir: Lee Sholem, 73 mins.)

Tarzan's New York Adventure (1942)*** Johnny Weissmuller, Maureen O'Sullivan, Charles Bickford. Circus men kidnap Tarzan's boy, and the jungle man follows them to the big city. Lively entrant in the series, with the change of locale amusing, exciting. (Dir: Richard Thorpe, 71 mins.)

Tarzan's Peril (1951)** Lex Barker, Virginia Huston, George Macready, Dorothy Dandridge, Douglas Fowley. Tarzan intervenes between two warring tribes, one of which has been supplied forbidden weapons by the white man. Good action, but nothing outstanding. (Dir: Byron Haskin, 79 mins.)

Tarzan's Revenge (1938)* Glenn Morris, Eleanor Holm, George Barbier, C. Henry Gordon, Hedda Hopper. Morris won the 1938 Olympic decathlon, but he won no all-round plaudits in any acting competitions. Swimming star Holm is even more inept; this tame jungle adventure packs the excitement of two six-year-olds playing Tarzan in the backyard. (Dir: Ross Lederman, 70 mins.)†

Tarzan's Savage Fury (1952)*½ Lex Barker, Dorothy Hart, Patric Knowles, Charles Korvin. Tarzan leads an expedition in search of diamonds. Inferior jungle drama. (Dir: Cyril Endfield, 81 mins.)

Tarzan's Secret Treasure (1941)**½ Johnny Weissmuller, Maureen O'Sullivan, Johnny Sheffield, Reginald Owen, Barry Fitzgerald, Tom Conway. The ape man repels another band of explorers, this one in search of gold. Efficient Tarzan caper. (Dir: Richard Thorpe, 82 mins.)

Tarzan's Three Challenges (1963)*½ Jock Mahoney, Woody Strode. Tarzan is summoned to Southeast Asia on a special mission involving an heir to a kingdom whose throne and life are threatened. (Dir: Robert Day, 92 mins.)

Tarzan, the Ape Man (1932)*** Johnny Weissmuller, Maureen O'Sullivan, C. Aubrey Smith. This was the daddy of all Tarzan pictures and, as such, is worth your attention. (Dir: W. S. Van Dyke, 100 mins.)†

Tarzan, the Ape Man (1959)*½ Denny Miller, Joanna Barnes. Remake of the first

Weissmuller Tarzan tale, or how Tarzan meets Jane. Also involves a search for the lost graveyard of the elephants. (Dir: Joseph M. Newman, 82 mins.)

Tarzan, the Ape Man (1981)* Bo Derek, Richard Harris, Miles O'Keeffe. Addlepated adventure serves as an excuse for Bo to divest herself of her clothes. The purists will be outraged, and everyone else will be bored. (Dir: John Derek, 112 mins.)†

Tarzan, the Fearless (1933)* Buster Crabbe, Jacqueline Wells (Julie Bishop), E. Alyn Warren. A cheapjack adventure about a pagan cult and a girl's search for her father. This film is actually composed of scenes from the serial *Tarzan, the Fearless*; Buster plays the hero as a mumbling mental deficient. (Dir: Robert Hill, 85 mins.)†

Tarzan the Magnificent (Great Britain, 1960)*** Gordon Scott, Betta St. John, Jock Mahoney, John Carradine. Tarzan captures the murderer of a policeman, but the criminal's family sets out to free him. Good entry in the Tarzan series; doesn't let up the fast pace for a moment. (Dir: Robert Day, 88 mins.)

Tarzan Triumphs (1943)*½ Johnny Weissmuller, Johnny Sheffield, Frances Gifford, Stanley Ridges, Sig Ruman. Nazi paratroopers try to take over a hidden jungle city. Pretty unbelievable, even by Tarzan standards. (Dir: William Thiele, 76 mins.)

Tasio (Spain, 1984)*** Patxi Bisquert, Isidro José Solano, Amaia Lasa. In the mountainous region of Navarre resides a villager named Tasio, a man of such simple beliefs and proud demeanor that he refuses to accept money for his hard work. Fascinating and beautifully shot story is directed in an honest and refreshingly unadorned style. (Dir: Montxo Armendariz, 96 mins.)

Task Force (1949)*** Gary Cooper, Walter Brennan, Jane Wyatt. Story of development of naval aviation and aircraft carriers is too long but contains some interesting scenes and good acting. (Dir: Delmer Daves, 116 mins.)

Taste of Blood, A (1967)* Bill Rogers, Elizabeth Wilkinson, Thomas Wood [William Kerwin], Otto Schlesinger, Eleanor Vaill. Innocent American discovers he's a relation to the Dracula family and picks up their bad habits. Director Herschell Gordon Lewis, going for a more mainstream movie, kept the gore to a minimum here, and the result is simply long and boring. (120 mins.)†

Taste of Evil, A (MTV 1971)** Barbara Stanwyck, Barbara Parkins, Roddy McDowall. Old-fashioned melodrama. Lovely Parkins returns home, cured after years in a sanitarium, only to find herself being terrorized. (Dir: John Llewellyn Moxey, 78 mins.)

1046

Taste of Fear—See: **Scream of Fear**

Taste of Honey, A (Great Britain, 1962)***½ Rita Tushingham, Murray Melvin, Dora Bryan, Robert Stephens. Warmly human drama of an unlovely girl, her sudden entrance into womanhood. Miss Tushingham's performance in this, her first film effort, is remarkable and deeply moving. Based on the fine British play which also was a hit on Broadway. (Dir: Tony Richardson, 100 mins.)†

Taste the Blood of Dracula (1970)*½ Christopher Lee, Geoffrey Keen, Peter Sallis. Big D. sics the children of three families against their daddies. Gore galore, little style, and even less Dracula; Lee's not in it nearly enough. (Dir: Peter Sasdy, 95 mins.)

Tatie Danielle (France, 1991)**½ Tsilla Chelton, Catherine Jacob, Isabelle Nanty, Eric Prat, Laurence Fevrier, Neige Dolsky. Offbeat comedy about a curmudgeonly old woman who is nasty to everyone around her. Film has some wry insights into the care of aging, and the performances are superb, especially Chelton's as the ornery senior citizen. (Dir: Etienne Chatiliez, 106 mins.)

Tattered Dress, The (1957)**½ Jeff Chandler, Jeanne Crain, Jack Carson, Gail Russell. Somewhat muddled but moderately interesting murder drama with a large cast of stars who appear in brief roles. (Dir: Jack Arnold, 93 mins.)

Tattered Web, A (MTV 1971)**½ Lloyd Bridges, Frank Converse, Sallie Shockley, Broderick Crawford. A detective finds his son-in-law is cheating on his daughter, confronts the other woman and accidentally kills her. Guess who is assigned to the case? (Dir: Paul Wendkos, 78 mins.)†

Tattoo (1981)*½ Bruce Dern, Maud Adams, Leonard Frey. What starts out as a fairly plausible and interesting drama soon disintegrates into sensationalism. Dern plays another psycho—this time he's an artist with a penchant for tattooing ladies' bodies. The object of his desire is model Adams, whom he pursues with a determination that borders on the ludicrous. (Dir: Bob Brooks, 103 mins.)†

Tawny Pipit (Great Britain, 1944)*** Bernard Miles, Rosamund John, Niall MacGinnis, Jean Gillie. A charming English comedy, about the effect that the discovery of a nest of very rare birds has on the life of a community. (Dirs: Bernard Miles, Charles Saunders, 81 mins.)

Taxi (1932)*** James Cagney, Loretta Young, George E. Stone. Fast-paced, rowdy flick about rivalry between cab companies. Cagney's worth flagging down in a tailor-made part. (Dir: Roy Del Ruth, 70 mins.)

Taxi (1953)**½ Dan Dailey, Constance Smith, Geraldine Page (film debut). Cab driver helps an Irish immigrant girl with a baby to find her husband. Modest little comedy-drama manages to be quite entertaining; good performances by the leads, New York atmosphere. (Dir: Gregory Ratoff, 77 mins.)

Taxi Blues (U.S.S.R.-France, 1990)***½ Piotr Mamonov, Piotr Zaitchenko, Vladimir Kachpour, Natalia Koliakanova, Hal Singer, Elena Saphonova. Extraordinary film about a brutish cab driver who holds hostage the saxophone belonging to a fare-jumping musician. The two develop a love-hate friendship as each tries to teach the other about his ways of approaching life in this powerful allegory about the old and new Soviet Union. Scripted by, and the first film of, the director. (Dir: Pavel Lounguine, 110 mins.)

Taxi Driver (1976)**** Robert De Niro, Cybill Shepherd, Jodie Foster, Peter Boyle, Albert Brooks, Leonard Harris. A profoundly disturbing story about urban alienation and madness. Robert De Niro's embittered, lonely Vietnam marine veteran who drives a taxi at night while turning into an urban guerrilla is one of the most chilling, repellent characters in modern films. There are other splendid performances, including Foster playing Iris, a twelve-year-old prostitute. Superb musical score—his last—by Bernard Herrmann. (Dir: Martin Scorsese, 112 mins.)

Taxi for Tobruk (France-Spain-Germany, 1961)**½ Lino Ventura, Hardy Kruger, Charles Aznavour. Group of French soldiers stranded in the North African desert capture a German captain and some supplies, make their way toward safety. WWII drama with an ironic twist. (Dir: Denys De La Patelliere, 93 mins.)

Taxing Woman, A (Japan, 1988)***½ Nobuko Miyamoto, Tsutomu Yamazaki, Masahiko Tsugawa. Sharp, engaging satire about a young woman working for the Japanese IRS who persistently seeks to expose a hotel owner who's been cheating on his taxes. (Dir: Juzo Itami, 127 mins.)†

Taxing Woman's Return, A (Japan, 1988) ***½ Nobuko Miyamoto, Rentaro Mikuni, Ryu Chishu. The capable heroine of *A Taxing Woman* returns in this biting satire about corporate greed and materialism in contemporary Japan. Full of breathless action and rife with scathing humor. (Dir: Juzo Itami, 127 mins.)

Taxi Zum Klo (West Germany, 1981)*** Frank Ripploh, Gitte Lederer, Bernd Broaderup, Hans Gerd Mertens. An odyssey into the nighttime world of gay bars, cruising, and romance on the run. Now, with the AIDS crisis, the film seems like a period piece. (Dir: Frank Ripploh, 92 mins.)†

Tax Season (1990)**½ Fritz Bronner, James Hong, Arte Johnson, Jana Grant, Professor Toru Tanaka. Funny spoof of accountants with Cleveland CPA Bronner buying a failing L.A. tax office and accidentally getting the books of cocaine smugglers. (Dir: Thomas Law, 90 mins.)†

Taza, Son of Cochise (1954)** Rock Hudson, Barbara Rush. Standard adventure; the plot concerns the Indians' battle against the invading white man. (Dir: Douglas Sirk, 79 mins.)

Tchaikovsky (U.S.S.R., 1970)*** Innokenti Smoktunovsky, Antonina Shuranova, Evgeni Leonov. Executive-produced by Dimitri Tiomkin, this is a lavish, musically rich, theatrical biography with Smoktunovsky in a superb interpretation of the famed composer. English narration by Laurence Harvey. (Dir: Igor Talankin, 191 mins.)

Tchao Pantin (France, 1985)**½ Coluche, Agnes Soral, Richard Anconia. An unusual foray into cop psychology, this detached thriller eschews excitement but never really fires the audience's imagination. Soured on life, a benumbed ex-cop temporarily rejoins the human race after experiencing a father-son relationship with a young thief. (Dir: Claude Berri, 100 mins.)†

Tea and Sympathy (1956)*** Deborah Kerr, John Kerr, Leif Erickson. The successful Broadway play about an older woman helping a confused young man reach maturity is expanded and toned down somewhat in this film version and thereby loses some of its bite. Miss and Mr. Kerr (no relation) successfully repeat their Broadway roles and manage to evoke the sympathy mentioned in the title. (Dir: Vincente Minnelli, 122 mins.)

Teacher, The (Cuba, 1977)***½ Salvador Wood, Luis Rielo, Louis Alberto Ramirez, Patricio Wood, Rene de la Cruz, El Brigadista. Gentle, elegiac film about a fifteen-year-old volunteer in Cuba's Literacy Brigade. Director Octavio Cortazar captures the essences of the joy of reading, the thrill of self-discovery, and the pleasure of helping others. (113 mins.)

Teachers (1984)** Nick Nolte, JoBeth Williams, Judd Hirsch, Lee Grant, Laura Dern, Ralph Macchio, Allen Garfield. Very disappointing comedy-drama; subplots include the efforts of a former student to sue his high school for graduating him prematurely. Thoroughly synthetic. (Dir: Arthur Hill, 104 mins.)†

Teacher's Pet (1958)*** Clark Gable, Doris Day, Mamie Van Doren, Gig Young. Rollicking comedy with Gable and Day at their respective best. He plays a hardboiled city editor who becomes her star pupil in a journalism class. (Dir: George Stevens, 120 mins.)

Tea for Two (1950)**½ Doris Day, Gordon MacRae, Eve Arden. Mildly diverting musical comedy made long before

Doris went dramatic. Based on the twenties play *No, No, Nanette*. (Dir: David Butler, 98 mins.)

Teahouse of the August Moon (1956)*** Marlon Brando, Glenn Ford, Machiko Kyo, Eddie Albert. John Patrick's successful Broadway comedy about the rehabilitation of an Okinawan village by the U.S. Army is brought to the screen with most of the fun intact. (Dir: Daniel Mann, 123 mins.)†

Tea in the Harem (France, 1986)** Kader Boukhanef, Remi Martin. Realistic study of a teenager of Algerian descent surviving in a sleazy Paris ghetto. Director Mehdi Charef succeeds in exposing depressing characters in an ugly world, and that's the trouble with this film: it's just too bleak, and its characters are all too unsympathetic. (110 mins.)

Teckman Mystery, The (Great Britain, 1954)*** Margaret Leighton, John Justin. Author writing a biography of an airman who crashed is convinced there is something mysterious about the death. Good mystery holds the attention. (Dir: Wendy Toye, 89 mins.)

Teddy at the Throttle (1917) and **Speeding Along** (1927)*** A duo of silent comedies. Gloria Swanson and Teddy, the Sennett dog, co-star in *Teddy at the Throttle*, a classic parody of chase melodramas; the noble hound ends up rescuing Swanson from a speeding train. Next is *Speeding Along*, a title-less slapstick auto racing farce, which has speeding vehicles on the loose in farming country. Both are highly entertaining. (63 mins.)†

Ted Kennedy, Jr. Story, The (MTV 1986)*** Craig T. Nelson, Susan Blakely, Kimber Shoop, Michael J. Shannon. This TV drama deals with Ted Kennedy, Jr. as a twelve-year-old boy who lost a leg to cancer and then bounced back from this trauma to lead a productive life. An adolescent profile in courage that's recommended viewing. (Dir: Delbert Mann, 104 mins.)

Teenage Bad Girl (Great Britain, 1956)*** Anna Neagle, Sylvia Syms, Kenneth Haigh, Wilfrid Hyde-White. Despite its bad title, this British movie about youth and their wild times is well acted and rewarding. (Dir: Herbert Wilcox, 100 mins.)

Teenage Caveman (1958)*½ Robert Vaughn, Darrah Marshall, Leslie Bradley, Frank De Kova. Low-budget prehistoric picture; a rebel with a loincloth itches to find out what secrets are held by the "monster" across the river. (Dir: Roger Corman, 65 mins.)

Teenage Devil Dolls (1955)*½ Barbara Marks, Bramlet L. Price, Jr., Robert A. Sherry, Robert Norman. Antidrug pseudo-documentary charts the downward slide of an aimless high school graduate

after she gets in with bad companions and experiments with drugs. AKA: **One Way Ticket to Hell**. (70 mins.)†

Teenage Doll (1957)*** June Kenney, Fay Spain, John Brinkley. Entertaining teen film produced and directed by Roger Corman when he did these things best; mood and pace are excellent. Kenney is a gang girl who fears for life after knifing a member of a rival gang. (68 mins.)

Teenage Hitchhiker—See: **Diary of a Teenage Hitchhiker**

Teenage Millionaire (1961)*½ Jimmy Clanton, Rocky Graziano, ZaSu Pitts. Teenager left a fortune becomes a recording star. One rock' n' roll number follows another in deadly procession. (Dir: Lawrence Doheny, 84 mins.)

Teenage Monster (1958)* Anne Gwynne, Gloria Castillo, Stuart Wade, Gilbert Perkins, Charles Courtney. Years after exposure to a meteor, a teenager is transformed into a hirsute cretin who goes on a rampage of killing. (Dir: Jacques Marquette, 65 mins.)

Teenage Mutant Ninja Turtles (1990)** Judith Hoag, Elias Koteas, Joch Pais, Michelan Sisti, Leif Tilden, David Forman. Standard adventure yarn about fast-moving, crime-fighting giant turtles who live in the sewers of New York City, eat pizza, and talk in nonstop surfer lingo. Vastly uneven film, great turtle costumes. (Dir: Steve Barron, 93 mins.)†

Teenage Mutant Ninja Turtles II: The Secret of the Ooze (1991)** Paige Turco, David Warner, Michelan Sisti, Leif Tilden, Kenn Troum, Mark Caso, Kevin Clash, François Chau. The oversize, pizza-loving, sewer-dwelling turtles battle more crime in this cheesy, slapdash sequel to the popular original. The secret is nothing more than a ponderous story about how the turtles became huge (radioactive sludge). Kids will probably love it; but if they don't see it, they won't be missing much. (Dir: Michael Pressman, 88 mins.)†

Teenage Psycho Meets Bloody Mary—See: **Incredibly Strange Creatures Who Stopped Living and Became Mixed-Up Zombies, The**

Teenage Rebel (1956)*½ Ginger Rogers, Michael Rennie, Betty Lou Keim. Glamorous mother has trouble with her daughter. Glug. (Dir: Edmund Goulding, 94 mins.)

Teenagers From Outer Space (1959)* David Love, Dawn Anderson. The title tells the story. Not the worst film of its kind but it will do until another one comes along. (Dir: Tom Graeff, 86 mins.)†

Teenage Wolfpack (West Germany, 1958)* Henry Bookholt [Horst Buchholz], Karen Baal, Christian Doermer. German juvenile delinquents can be just as boring as their American counterparts—even more so, as this mysteriously imported item proves. (Did someone feel there was a shortage of homegrown J.D. movies in '58?) (Dir: Georg Tressier, 90 mins.)

Teenage Zombies (1960)½ Don Sullivan, Katherine Victor, Steve Conte. Group of youngsters discovers dirty work on an island inhabited by an evil woman doctor and some monsters. Nonsensical horror thriller; poor. (Dir: Jerry Warren, 73 mins.)†

Teen Vamp (1989)* Beau Bishop, Clu Gulager, Karen Carlson, Angie Brown. Nerdy teen becomes a hip bloodsucker after being bitten by a vampire hooker. Stupid comedy makes *I Was a Teenage Frankenstein* look like Kurosawa by comparison. (Dir: Samuel Bradford, 89 mins.)†

Teen Wolf (1985)**½ Michael J. Fox, Scott Paulin, Jay Tarses, James Hampton. A depressed youth finds out that he can transform into a werewolf at will. Though the movie isn't as clever or inventive as it wants to be; its good-hearted "be yourself" message and the earnest performance by Fox elevate the production above the average teen comedy strata. (Dir: Rod Daniel, 91 mins.)†

Teen Wolf Too (1987)* Jason Bateman, Kim Darby, John Astin, Paul Sand, James Hampton. The star is different, but otherwise this pathetic, half-baked sequel is completely derivative. (Dir: Christopher Leitch, 95 mins.)†

Telefon (1977)*** Charles Bronson, Lee Remick, Tyne Daly. Fairly arresting spy story about a Russian KGB agent (Bronson) on assignment in America teamed with a double agent (Remick). Mission: prevent a psychotic Stalinist from completing a truly deadly series of phone calls aimed at sabotaging U.S. installations all over the land. (Dir: Don Siegel, 100 mins.)†

Telephone, The (1988)½ Whoopi Goldberg, Severn Darden, Amy Wright, Elliott Gould, John Heard. Whoopi's run of luck with mediocre vehicles disconnected with this exercise in agony about a shrill, unemployed actress who conducts her life over the phone. The whole affair seems a poorly filmed version of a bad one-act play; this is unfortunate, considering the talent behind the camera— Harry Nilsson and Terry Southern wrote the screenplay, and Rip Torn makes his directorial debut. (82 mins.)†

Telethon (MTV 1977)*½ Polly Bergen, Lloyd Bridges, Red Buttons, Edd Byrnes, Dick Clark, Janet Leigh, Kent McCord, David Selby, Jimmie Walker. A tell-all exposé about a fund-raising telethon in Vegas and all the participants, who are at cross-purposes. (Dir: David Lowell Rich, 104 mins.)

Tell It to a Star (1945)** Ruth Terry, Robert Livingston, Alan Mowbray, Franklin Pangborn. Cordial but completely unmemorable musical vehicle for Terry as a cigarette girl who achieves her dream of singing with a big band through the help of her uncle, con man Mowbray. Sammy Cahn and Jules Styne wrote the doleful ballads. (Dir: Frank McDonald, 67 mins.)

Tell It to the Judge (1949)**½ Rosalind Russell, Robert Cummings, Gig Young. The stars save this one from total disaster. Corny plot has Roz as a lady lawyer running away from her blonde-chasing husband for most of the film. (Dir: Norman Foster, 87 mins.)

Tell Me a Riddle (1980)*** Melvyn Douglas, Lila Kedrova, Brooke Adams, Dolores Dorn, Bob Elross, Joan Harris, Zalman King. A luminous performance by Lila Kedrova as a dying woman trying to make a connection with her family before the finale. Some may find the talky sequences too long, but Ms. Kedrova's special relationship with daughter Brooke Adams adds up to a touching movie. (Dir: Lee Grant, 90 mins.)†

Tell Me Lies (Great Britain, 1968)*** Glenda Jackson, Peggy Ashcroft, Mark Jones, Robert Lloyd. Produced, directed, and conceived by Peter Brook. A mocking, and frequently lacerating attack on the U.S. war policy in Indochina. Original footage, utilizing members of the Royal Shakespeare Company, is mixed with documentary footage of war violence and destruction in Vietnam. (118 mins.)

Tell Me My Name (MTV 1977)*** Arthur Hill, Barbara Barrie, Bernard Hughes. Flawed but sensitive drama. Barrie gives a wonderful performance as a woman who, when she was eighteen, gave up an illegitimate daughter for adoption. Now, nineteen years later, the young lady arrives to see who her real mother is. (Dir: Delbert Mann, 104 mins.)

Tell Me Sam (France, 1989)**½ Fans of maverick filmmaker Sam Fuller will want to search out this documentary with the director. Interviewed in different locations in Europe, where he's lived for years, the ex-newspaper reporter and infantryman talks about his varied career and the difficulties of getting his films made. (Dir: Emil Weiss, 76 mins.)

Tell Me That You Love Me, Junie Moon (1970)** Liza Minnelli, Ken Howard, Robert Moore. Director Otto Preminger has cheapened Marjorie Kellogg's sensitive novel about three misfits (a physically scarred young girl, an epileptic, and a paraplegic homosexual) who meet in a hospital and decide to live together, commune-style. Minnelli, miscast, gives a shrill performance; Moore overplays shamelessly, but Howard is touching as the young epileptic. (113 mins.)

Tell Me Where It Hurts (MTV 1974)*** Maureen Stapleton, Rose Gregorio, Paul Sorvino, Louise Latham, Doris Dowling, John Randolph. An excellent performance by Stapleton makes this honest drama a must. She plays a housewife who finds that her marriage is going stale, and she joins a neighborhood discussion group which proves instrumental in changing her life. (Dir: Paul Bogart, 104 mins.)

Tell No Tales (1938)**½ Melvyn Douglas, Louise Platt, Gene Lockhart, Douglas Dumbrille, Florence George, Halliwell Hobbes, Everett Brown, Mantan Moreland. Zesty B picture of a young editor trying to save his newspaper. Unusually realistic atmosphere for an MGM picture. (Dir: Leslie Fenton, 68 mins.)

Tell Them Willie Boy Is Here (1969)***½ Robert Redford, Robert Blake, Katharine Ross, Susan Clark, Barry Sullivan. Thanks to the thoughtful screenplay and excellent direction by Abraham Polonsky, ''Willie Boy'' is an exciting western chase story. One of the few major Hollywood films that has dealt sensitively with the question of the white man's treatment of the Indian. Set in '09 during the presidency of Taft, sheriff Redford hunts down a young Paiute Indian. (96 mins.)†

Tempest (1928)***½ John Barrymore, Camilla Horn, Louis Wolheim, Boris De Fas, George Fawcett. Terrific Russian Revolution adventure-romance, with Barrymore as an officer who has risen from the ranks in love with a princess, although she scorns him; when the Revolution comes, he saves her from the rage of the Bolsheviks. Superb decor by William Cameron Menzies. (Dir: Sam Taylor, 102 mins.)†

Tempest (Italy-Yugoslavia-France, 1958) *** Van Heflin, Silvana Mangano, Viveca Lindfors, Geoffrey Horne, Agnes Moorehead, Vittorio Gassman. Impressively produced drama of old Russia, as a rebel leader sacrifices his life to protect a soldier who had once saved his own. (Dir: Alberto Lattuada, 125 mins.)

Tempest (1982)*** John Cassavetes, Gena Rowlands, Susan Sarandon, Vittorio Gassman, Raul Julia, Molly Ringwald. Entertaining performances, superb photography in Greece, and some absorbing observations make this an unusual, enjoyable experience with flaws easily overlooked. A New York architect feels he must get away from work and marriage and runs away to Greece with his daughter and a girlfriend he meets on the way. (Dir: Paul Mazursky, 140 mins.)†

Temptation (1946)**½ Merle Oberon, George Brent, Charles Korvin, Paul Lukas. A silky-textured fallen woman flick. Married to an archaeologist, fickle Merle tries to excavate some romance with a lover. When that presents complications, she decides to get rid of both her spouse and her playmate. (Dir: Irving Pichel, 92 mins.)

Tempter, The (Italy-Great Britain, 1974)*** Glenda Jackson, Claudio Casinelli, Lisa Harrow, Adolfo Celi, Francisco Rabal. Interesting variation on the theme of institutional life versus the "real world." In this case, the maladjusted aren't mental patients but religious exiles who dwell in a convent run by Jackson. Taken on an outing, they are forced to choose between perilous freedom and communal security. (Dir: Damiano Damiani, 105 mins.)

Temptress, The (1926)*** Greta Garbo, Antonio Moreno. Heavy-breathing silent melodrama with Greta playing a femme fatale who winds up as an impoverished Parisian prostitute. (Dirs: Mauritz Stiller, Fred Niblo, 117 mins.)

"10" (1979)*** Dudley Moore, Julie Andrews, Bo Derek, Robert Webber, Sam Jones, Dee Wallace. Blake Edwards's mid-life-crisis comedy about a self-absorbed man searching desperately for romantic fulfillment when we know it's to be found in his own backyard (or bedroom). Edwards's direction is marred by sporadic clumsiness and a streak of vulgarity, but Moore plays the bumbling hero with great charm. (112 mins.)†

Tenant, The (France-U.S., 1976)*** Roman Polanski, Isabelle Adjani, Jo Van Fleet, Melvyn Douglas, Shelley Winters, Lila Kedrova. An uneven but fascinating black comedy. A Polish man moves into a Parisian apartment building and has difficulty interacting with his neighbors. Inexorably, his personality disintegrates as he takes on the personality of the previous tenant. The urban paranoia is rendered with great force, but director Polanski miscast himself as the tyrannized tenant. (125 mins.)†

Ten Cents a Dance (1931)*** Barbara Stanwyck, Ricardo Cortez, Sally Blane. A tough, sexy, Stanwyck vehicle, directed by the usually stodgy Lionel Barrymore. Uneven, but often remarkable. (80 mins.)

Ten Commandments, The (1923)***½ Theodore Roberts, Charles de Roche, Estelle Taylor, Rod LaRocque, Richard Dix. Epic silent film mixes Biblical tale of the Israelites' flight from Egypt with a contemporary parable about two brothers, one evil, one angelic. Terrific special effects and production values highlight Cecil B. DeMille's grand movie, some of which was shot in two-color process. (146 mins.)†

Ten Commandments, The (1956)***½ Charlton Heston, Edward G. Robinson, Yul Brynner, Sir Cedric Hardwicke, Debra Paget, John Derek, Anne Baxter. Cecil B. DeMille's spectacular film of Moses and his people and their exodus from Egypt combines a fine mixture of pageantry and drama. It's bolstered by an all-star cast, and the parting of the Red Sea is still thrilling. (219 mins.)†

Ten Days That Shook the World (U.S.S.R., 1928)**** Nikandrov, Vladimir Popov, Boris Livanov, the soldiers of the Red Army, the sailors of the Red Navy, the citizens of Leningrad. Epic masterpiece about the events of October 1917 when the Bolsheviks toppled the Russian leadership that ruled after the fall of the Czar. With magnificent use of montage, this is one of the great examples of the silent cinema. Reissued in 1967 with an original score by Dimitri Shostakovich. There are prints that run 103 mins. and 120 mins. AKA: **October.** (Dir: Sergei Eisenstein, 164 mins.)†

Ten Days to Tulara (1958)**½ Sterling Hayden, Grace Raynor, Rodolfo Hoyos, Carlos Muzquiz, Tony Caravajal. Cutthroat crooks led by Hoyos hold the son of pilot Hayden hostage, in order to get the airman to fly them to safety. Run-of-the-mill action drama, with Hayden a commanding, heroic presence. (Dir: George Sherman, 77 mins.)

Ten Days' Wonder (France, 1972)*½ Orson Welles, Anthony Perkins, Michel Piccoli. Absurd mess about a boy (Perkins) who falls in love with his stepmother who is married to Welles, a rich eccentric. Based on an Ellery Queen story. (Dir: Claude Chabrol, 105 mins.)†

Tender Comrade (1943)**½ Ginger Rogers, Robert Ryan. Young wife carries on bravely while her husband goes off to war. Drama pushes the sticky sentiment too much. (Dir: Edward Dmytryk, 102 mins.)

Tender Flesh—See: **Welcome to Arrow Beach**

Tenderfoot, The (1932)**½ Joe E. Brown, Ginger Rogers, Lew Cody, Vivien Oakland, Robert Greig, Spencer Charters. Nifty comedy for Brown as an innocent westerner who comes to New York and gets involved with a failing Broadway show and some gangsters. (Dir: Ray Enright, 70 mins.)

Tender Hearts (1955)**½ Hugo Hass, Francesca de Scaffa, June Hammerstein, Jeffery Stone, Ken Carlton, John Vosper. Low-low-budget effort has its share of effective moments; the plot concerns a poor old man's sad parting with his dog. (Dir: Hugo Hass, 78 mins.)

Tender Is the Night (1962)**½ Jennifer Jones, Jason Robards, Jr., Joan Fontaine, Tom Ewell. Adaptation of F. Scott Fitzgerald's novel about a psychiatrist who marries one of his patients and enters into the mad whirl of the twenties, eventually finding the marriage will destroy them both. Overlong and superficial. (Dir: Henry King, 146 mins.)

Tender Mercies (1983)*** Robert Duvall, Tess Harper. In this drama set in the Southwest, Oscar-winner Duvall convincingly plays a one-time country music star who is trying to rebound from his down-and-out psychological state. The director, Australian Bruce Beresford (*Breaker Morant*), has captured the Texas atmosphere of rural life and relationships with great conviction. (90 mins.)†

Tenderness of Wolves (West Germany, 1973)***½ Kurt Raab, Jeff Roden, Margit Carstensen, Hannelore Tiefenbrunner, Rainer Werner Fassbinder. Extraordinary drama, magnificently acted and directed, about the "Vampire of Dusseldorf," the heinous murderer of twenty-five boys whose bodies he sold as meat. True story was inspiration for Fritz Lang's *M*. Chillingly explicit film produced by Fassbinder. (Dir: Ulli Lommel, 83 mins.)

Tender Scoundrel (France-Italy, 1966)** Jean-Paul Belmondo, Nadja Tiller, Robert Morley, Stefania Sandrelli. Frenchman subsists on his attractiveness to women, is worn out by the "demands" of his vocation. (Dir: Jean Becker, 94 mins.)

Tender Trap, The (1955)*** Frank Sinatra, Debbie Reynolds, David Wayne, Celeste Holm. Broadway comedy is brought to the screen with a great deal of savoir faire. Sinatra is perfect as the footloose bachelor who avoids cute Debbie's inviting "trap" of marriage for most of the film's running time. (Dir: Charles Walters, 111 mins.)

Tender Warrior (1971)** Dan Haggerty, Charles Lee, Liston Elkins. An unfriendly moonshiner eventually takes a shine to Lee, a young man who lives with a menagerie of playful animals. (Dir: Stewart Raffill, 77 mins.)

Tender Years, The (1947)**½ Joe E. Brown, Richard Lyon, Noreen Nash, Josephine Hutchinson. Mistreated dog escapes from his owner and is taken in by the son of a small-town parson. Enjoyable heartwarmer. (Dir: Howard Schuster, 83 mins.)†

$10 Raise (1935)** Edward Everett Horton, Karen Morley, Alan Dinehart, Glen Boles, Berton Churchill. Character actor Horton had a rare starring role in this predictable comedy as an accountant who's too timid to ask for an increase in salary. (Dir: George Marshall, 70 mins.)

Tenebrae—See: **Unsane**

Tenement (1985)½ Joe Lynn, Martha de la Cruz, Enrique Sandino, Corrine Chateau. Nauseatingly violent tale of inner city scuzzoids out for revenge. (Dir: Roberta Findlay, 94 mins.)†

Ten from "Your Show of Shows" (1973)***½ Sid Caesar, Imogene Coca, Carl Reiner, Howard Morris, Louis Nye. Sketches from the famed TV comedy series of the early fifties. The stars are marvelous in some of their best-remembered routines, including hilarious takeoffs on *From Here to Eternity* and "This Is Your Life." (Dir: Max Leibman, 92 mins.)†

Ten Gentlemen from West Point (1942)*** Laird Cregar, George Montgomery, Maureen O'Hara. Good juvenile drama of the beginning of the USMA at West Point. (Dir: Henry Hathaway, 102 mins.)

Ten Little Indians (Great Britain, 1966)**½ Hugh O'Brian, Shirley Eaton, Stanley Holloway, Dennis Price, Daliah Lavi, Fabian, Wilfrid Hyde-White. A second version of the marvelous 1945 film *And Then There Were None*, not as suspenseful. (Dir: George Pollock, 92 mins.)

Ten Little Indians (Italy-France-Spain-West Germany, 1975)** Oliver Reed, Elke Sommer, Richard Attenborough, Gert Frobe. Third version of Agatha Christie's suspense classic. Ten people are stranded in a hotel in the Iranian desert, while one is doing away with his fellow guests. (Dir: Peter Collinson, 98 mins.)†

Ten Little Indians (Britain-U.S., 1989)** Donald Pleasence, Brenda Vaccaro, Frank Stallone, Sarah Maur Thorp, Herbert Lom. Unnecessary fourth adaptation of Agatha Christie's classic *And Then There Were None* lacks the requisite thrills. The setting this time is an African safari where the odd assortment of guests are picked off, one by one, by a calculating phantom avenger. (Dir: Alan Birkinshaw, 98 mins.)†

Tennessee Champ (1954)**½ Shelley Winters, Dewey Martin, Keenan Wynn, Earl Holliman. Entertaining tale about the fight game and the various people associated with it. (Dir: Fred M. Wilcox, 73 mins.)

Tennessee Johnson (1942)***½ Van Heflin, Lionel Barrymore, Ruth Hussey. Interesting biography of the man who became President when Lincoln was shot and missed being impeached by one vote. Van Heflin is superb in the title role. (Dir: William Dieterle, 102 mins.)

Tennessee's Partner (1955)*** John Payne, Ronald Reagan, Rhonda Fleming. Stranger steps into the middle of an argument and becomes the friend of a gambler. Entertaining action drama with a good cast. (Dir: Allan Dwan, 87 mins.)†

Ten North Frederick (1958)*** Gary Cooper, Diane Varsi, Suzy Parker, Geraldine Fitzgerald, Stuart Whitman. A good cast enlivens this script based on John O'Hara's novel about politics, infidelity, and the

struggle between the weak and the strong. (Dir: Philip Dunne, 102 mins.)†

10 Rillington Place (Great Britain, 1971)*** Richard Attenborough, Judy Geeson. Absorbing crime film; Attenborough is superb as the mild-mannered man who is in reality a demented murderer of women and children. (Dir: Richard Fleischer, 102 mins.)†

Ten Seconds to Hell (1959)** Jack Palance, Jeff Chandler, Martine Carol. Slow moving adventure yarn about a couple of he-men who pit their strength at work in Europe. (Dir: Robert Aldrich, 93 mins.)

Tension (1949)**½ Richard Basehart, Audrey Totter, Cyd Charisse, Barry Sullivan. Well-acted murder mystery thriller. Basehart plays the henpecked husband whose wife leaves him for another man. He quietly plans to get even with her, but his scheme backfires. (Dir: John Berry, 91 mins.)

Tension at Table Rock (1956)**½ Richard Egan, Dorothy Malone, Cameron Mitchell. An adult western in which a man must prove he has been unjustly labeled a coward. Good performances. (Dir: Charles Marquis Warren, 93 mins.)

Tenspeed and Brown Shoe (MTV 1980) **½ Ben Vereen, Jeff Goldblum, Robert Webber, Jayne Meadows. Tenspeed is a slippery dude who maneuvers a superheist of a million dollars. He eventually teams up with a young stockbroker, Brown Shoe, who's an innocent bystander at first. (Dir: E. W. Swackhamer, 104 mins.)

Tentacles (Italy, 1977)* John Huston, Shelley Winters, Henry Fonda, Bo Hopkins. An enormous octopus uses a seaside resort as a take-out seafood restaurant until killer whales save the day. (Dir: "Oliver Hellman" [Ovidio Assonitis], 102 mins.)†

Ten Tall Men (1951)*** Burt Lancaster, Jody Lawrance, Gilbert Roland. A merry spoof on the Foreign Legionnaires and their escapades with harem girls, etc. Lots of fun—played in great tongue-in-cheek style. (Dir: Willis Goldbeck, 97 mins.)

Tenth Avenue Angel (1948)*½ Margaret O'Brien, Angela Lansbury, George Murphy. Little girl plays Cupid to her aunt and an ex-convict. Poor slushy drama. (Dir: Roy Rowland, 74 mins.)

10:30 PM Summer (U.S.-Spain, 1966)*** Melina Mercouri, Romy Schneider, Peter Finch, Julian Mateos. Schneider joins her lover Finch and his family for a road trip through Spain in this esoteric, often erotic, account of the outside forces affecting a failing marriage. Co-scripted by novelist Marguerite Duras. (Dir: Jules Dassin, 85 mins.)

Tenth Man, The (MTV, 1988)**** Anthony

Hopkins, Derek Jacobi, Kristin Scott Thomas, Cyril Cusack. First-rate production of Graham Greene's novel about the lengths a man will go to preserve his life. Hopkins is excellent as a wealthy Parisian lawyer imprisoned by the Nazis who offers another man everything he owns to take his place. The bitter aftermath offers many plot surprises that will keep viewers mesmerized. (Dir: Jack Gold, 96 mins.)

Tenth Month, The (MTV 1979)**½ Carol Burnett, Keith Michell, Dina Merrill, Cristina Raines. This soapy but touching story of a middle-aged divorced woman who finds she is pregnant for the first time will appeal to Burnett fans. (Dir: Joan Tewkesbury, 124 mins.)†

Ten Thousand Bedrooms (1957)**½ Dean Martin, Anna Maria Alberghetti, Walter Slezak. Dean's a hotel tycoon, Anna Maria's a stenographer, and after two hours of songs, comedy, and four writers trying to make a script out of nothing, all the right people get together. Harmless fun. (Dir: Richard Thorpe, 114 mins.)

Tenth Victim, The (Italy, 1965)***½ Marcello Mastroianni, Ursula Andress. Nightmarish tale of the next century, wherein trained men and women have a license to kill each other for sport. Fantasy is a mixture of suspense thriller and satire, frequently effective because of the unusual sets, photography. (Dir: Elio Petri, 92 mins.)†

Ten to Midnight (1983)** Charles Bronson, Andrew Stevens, Lisa Eilbacher. Another Bronson vigilante flick, in which Chuck steps outside the law to nab a woman-hating psychopath. Chuck even goes so far as to plant evidence on the suspect, who retaliates by stalking Bronson's daughter, a nurse, in a subplot reminiscent of the real-life Richard Speck slayings. (Dir: J. Lee Thompson, 101 mins.)†

10 Violent Women (1982)½ Sherri Vernon, Dixie Lauren, Sally Alice Gamble, Georgia Morgan, T. V. Mikels. Enjoyable schlock with a group (somewhat smaller than ten) of nasty gals involved in a jewel robbery, drug deals, and even a prison run by the usual sadistic warden from central casting. Director Mikels has a memorable role as a fence whose criminal days are ended by a strategically placed high heel. (95 mins.)†

Ten Wanted Men (1955)**½ Randolph Scott, Richard Boone, Jocelyn Brando. Randolph Scott is a cattle baron in Arizona who wants only peace but the desperadoes see it another way. (Dir: H. Bruce Humberstone, 80 mins.)†

Ten Who Dared (1960)*½ Brian Keith, John Beal. You'll wish they hadn't! Ten men embark on an expedition to chart the Colorado River, an attempt that is wracked by disputes. Surprisingly directionless and dull. (Dir: William Beaudine, 92 mins.)†

Tequila Sunrise (1988)**½ Mel Gibson, Kurt Russell, Michelle Pfeiffer, Raul Julia. Seemingly endless melodrama about coke dealer Gibson and cop Russell, boyhood pals now on opposite sides of the law and in competition for the same woman (Pfeiffer). Star power and a late appearance by scene stealer Julia are the only assets of this muddled bore. (Dir: Robert Towne, 116 mins.)†

Teresa (1951)***½ Pier Angeli, Ralph Meeker, Patricia Collinge. An exceptionally good film about a mixed-up lad (Ericson) who marries an Italian girl (Angeli) during WWII and brings her home to New York City. (Dir: Fred Zinnemann, 102 mins.)

Teresa the Thief (Italy, 1973)***½ Monica Vitti, Valeriano Vallone, Michele Placido, Stefano Satta Flores, Isa Danieli. Vitti is sensational as Teresa, a woman for whom nothing—not family, not adulthood, not love, not anything—goes right. An endearing film, marvelously written. (Dir: Carlo Di Palma, 111 mins.)

Teresa Venerdi (Italy, 1941)*** Vittorio De Sica, Anna Magnani, Brasema Dellian, Adriana Benedetti. One of De Sica's first films as director, this is a romantic comedy of mistaken identity. The mood could not be farther from that of his neorealistic period. Comedy about a man up to his neck in financial difficulties and romantic entanglements with his mistress, his unexpected fiancée, and a fetching young convent girl. (71 mins.)

Terminal Choice (Canada, 1985)*½ Joe Spano, Diane Venora, David McCallum, Robert Joy. Doctors and nurses at a clinic bet on their patients' recovery rates, but one greedy gambler begins to hedge his wagers by using the infirmary's computer system to knock off patients—and anyone else who disagrees with the gambling. A gory, unsuspenseful thriller. Made in 1982. AKA: **Critical List**. (Dir: Sheldon Larry, 97 mins.)†

Terminal Entry (1987)* Edward Albert, Yaphet Kotto, Paul Smith, Heidi Helmer, Patrick Labyorteaux. Teenage computer nerds hack their way into a system and start playing a spy game on it, not knowing that they've accessed a terrorist network and are instructing the bad guys to start destroying U.S. targets. Interesting idea, lousy execution. Terminate it. (Dir: John Kinkade, 95 mins.)†

Terminal Exposure (1987)**½ (1987) Mark Hennessy, Scott King, Hope Marie Carlton, John Vernon. Two aspiring Venice Beach photographers seek fame and glory by solving a murder that they

1053

accidentally photographed. The inevitable chases are redeemed by some likably humorous touches. AKA: **Double Exposure**. (Dir: Nico Mastorakis, 100 mins.)†

Terminal Force (1990)* Richard Harrison, Troy Donahue. An actor gets involved with the mob in this technically atrocious gangster film featuring seminudity and lots of stupidity. Released directly to video without a theatrical run. No wonder. (Dir: Fred Olen Ray, 80 mins.)†

Terminal Island (1973)*½ Don Marshall, Phyllis Elizabeth Davis, Barbara Leigh, Sean Kenney, Roger Mosley, Tom Selleck. Southern California prison colony where male cons are sent in place of capital punishment starts swinging when it suddenly turns coed. Standard violence with a dose of heavy breathing. (Dir: Stephanie Rothman, 88 mins.)†

Terminal Man, The (1974)*½ George Segal, Jill Clayburgh, Joan Hackett. Muddled movie has a terrific sequence detailing the steps of an operation in which a small computer is placed in the brain of a paranoid psychotic. The rest is mush, with the operation going bad and Segal turning into a rampaging killer. (Dir: Mike Hodges, 104 mins.)†

Terminal Station—See: **Indiscretion of an American Wife**

Terminator, The (1984)*** Arnold Schwarzenegger, Linda Hamilton, Michael Biehn, Lance Henriksen, Paul Winfield. Director James Cameron's pulse-pounding sci-fi thriller is as cold and efficient as gunmetal, thanks to a clever, inventive story and direction that never lets up on the action or suspense. The perfectly cast Schwarzenegger plays a death-dealing android sent back from the 21st century to assassinate a young woman (Hamilton), but there's a determined foot soldier from the future (Biehn) who's hot on his trail. The film is given a dark, high-tech look that sets it apart from others of its kind. (105 mins.)†

Term of Trial (Great Britain, 1962)***½ Laurence Olivier, Simone Signoret, Terence Stamp, Sarah Miles. Just for Laurence Olivier's remarkable ability to submerge himself into a character, even so seedy a one as the schoolteacher he plays here, this film is worth your while. The cast of this downbeat tale about a British teacher in a slum school, victimized by a student (a sixteen-year-old girl), are all excellent. (Dir: Peter Glenville, 113 mins.)

Terms of Endearment (1983)*** Shirley MacLaine, Jack Nicholson, Debra Winger, Danny DeVito, Jeff Daniels, John Lithgow. Superbly acted, hugely popular comedy-drama about a mother-daughter relationship and its ups and downs over the years. Academy Awards for Best Film,

Director, Actress (MacLaine), Screenplay, and Supporting Actor (Nicholson). (Dir: James L. Brooks, 132 mins.)†

Terraces (MTV 1977)*** Lloyd Bochner, Lola Albright, Kit McDonough, Julie Newmar. Pilot for a series about tenants in a high-rise apartment building whose only connection is their "terraces" which touch. McDonough is enchanting as the ugly duckling who just moves in. (Dir: Lila Garrett, 72 mins.)†

Terrible Beauty, A—See: **Night Fighters**

Terrible Joe Moran (MTV 1984)** James Cagney, Art Carney, Peter Gallagher, Ellen Barkin. Cagney is back, and that's reason enough for his fans to tune in this sentimental yarn about a grand-daughter (Barkin) finding a place in the life of her estranged grandfather (Cagney). (Dir: Joseph Sargent, 104 mins.)

Terror, The (1963)* Boris Karloff, Jack Nicholson, Sandra Knight, Dick Miller, Jonathan Haze. One of those Roger Corman films shot in four days on left-over sets. Nicholson tracks a lost girl to the castle of Karloff, who's been mourning the death of his wife for twenty years. Take it from us—it's not worth it. (81 mins.)†

Terror Among Us (MTV 1981)** Don Meredith, Sarah Purcell, Jennifer Salt, Ted Shackelford. Routine, occasionally suspenseful drama about a rapist and the judicial system that keeps him out on the streets. (Dir: Paul Krasny, 104 mins.)

Terror at Alcatraz (MTV 1982)½ Dick Smothers, Tommy Smothers, Lynette Mettey, Diana Muldaur, Jack Albertson. Dismal pilot for the short-lived "Fitz and Bones" series. Dick and Tom Smothers play a TV newsman and cameraman out to uncover a hidden Al Capone treasure at Alcatraz. (Dir: Richard T. Heffron, 104 mins.)

Terror at the Opera—See: **Opera**

Terror at Red Wolf Inn (1972)**½ Linda Gillin, Arthur Space, John Neilson, Mary Jackson. Here's a rarity—a horror comedy that is not only funny, but intelligently made as well. A sweet old couple of cannibals lure victims to their inn with letters telling them they've won a free vacation. AKA: **The Folks at Red Wolf Inn**. (Dir: Bud Townsend, 90 mins.)†

Terror by Night (1946)**½ Basil Rathbone, Nigel Bruce, Renee Godfrey. Sherlock Holmes movie made after the series had fallen to B movie status. Here he investigates the murder of the owner of the "Star of Rhodesia" jewel, aboard a moving train. (Dir: Roy William Neill, 60 mins.)†

Terror Creatures from the Grave (U.S.-Italy 1965)**½ Barbara Steele, Richard Garret, Walter Brandt, Marilyn Mitchell.

More spaghetti scares with Steele, the queen of '60s Eurohorror. She plays a widow whose dead hubby, whom she helped murder, keeps returning, bringing some new friends—resurrected victims of the Black Death. Grisly doings, with Steele an impeccable victimizer-victim. (Dir: "Ralph Zucker" [Massimo Pupillo], 85 mins.)†

Terror From the Year 5,000 (1958)** Ward Costello, Joyce Holden, Salome Jens. Female monster comes from the past to kill. Farfetched horror tale has some scary scenes. (Dir: Robert J. Gurney, Jr., 68 mins.)

Terror From Under the House—See: **Revenge** (Great Britain, 1971)

Terror House—See: **The Night Has Eyes**

Terror in a Texas Town (1958)*** Sterling Hayden, Sebastian Cabot, Carol Kelly, Eugene Martin, Ned Young. A wayfaring sailor's visit back home proves turbulent for him and troublesome for a greedy land-baron who's been gobbling up the local farmlands. Exciting and off-the-beaten-track. (Dir: Joseph H. Lewis, 80 mins.)

Terror in the Aisles (1984)*½ A sloppily assembled hodgepodge of horror movie clips. The sequences included are often famous items, but they aren't scary out of context and the narration is as inspired as a high school drivers' education film. (Dir: Andrew J. Kuehn, 84 mins.)†

Terror in the City (1966)*½ Lee Grant, Richard Bray, Sylvia Miles. When a boy runs away from home, he befriends a prostitute, a gang of kids, and other colorful street people. (Dir: Allen Baron, 86 mins.)

Terror in the Crypt (Spain-Italy, 1963)** Christopher Lee. A strange nobleman, fearing for his daughter's life according to an ancient legend, has a group of scientists come to his home to see what they can do to help. (Dir: Camillo Mastrocinque, 84 mins.)

Terror in the Haunted House (1958)** Gerald Mohr, Cathy O'Donnell. A house on a hill, a newlywed couple spending the night, and lightning all over the place. (Dir: Harold Daniels, 80 mins.)†

Terror in the Sky (MTV 1971)** Leif Erickson, Doug McClure, Roddy McDowall, Lois Nettleton. When food poisoning strikes the pilot and passengers on a charter flight, a Vietnam chopper pilot is the only passenger with any experience who can take over the controls. Occasionally suspenseful remake of *Zero Hour*. (Dir: Bernard Kowalski, 78 mins.)

Terror in the Wax Museum (1973)** Maurice Evans, John Carradine, Ray Milland, Elsa Lanchester, Louis Hayward. Amiable but silly mystery thriller with a top cast. The museum is filled with wax figures of infamous murderers who have a strange way of coming to life. (Dir: Georg Fenady, 93 mins.)†

Terror Is a Man (1959)**½ Francis Lederer, Greta Thyssen, Richard Derr. Above-average horror film; mad doctor experiments on turning panthers into humans, is thwarted by a survivor of a shipwreck. AKA: **Blood Creature**. (Dir: Gerry DeLeon, 89 mins.)†

Terrorist on Trial: The United States vs. Salim Ajami (MTV 1988)*** Sam Waterson, Ron Leibman, Robert Davi, Joe Morton. Teledrama about a Palestinian terrorist extradited to the U.S. to stand trial for murderous acts. Script by "Columbo's" Levinson and Link, and fine acting make this above-average dramatic fare. (Dir: Jeff Bleckner, 96 mins.)

Terrorists, The (Great Britain, 1975)** Sean Connery, Ian McShane, Norman Bristow, John Cording, Isabel Dean. Imagine Connery playing a Scandinavian (named Nils Tahlvik) with his usual Scottish accent, contemplative Bergman cinematographer Sven Nyqvist photographing tense action scenes, and a cockpit full of unlikely plot twists, and you have this British attempt at a *Skyjacked* suspense picture. Connery does his best, but this one's doomed from the start. (Dir: Casper Wrede, 100 mins.)

Terrornauts, The (Great Britain, 1967)*½ Patricia Hayes, Stanley Meadows, Simon Oates. Scientists, skeptical that there is life on other worlds, are sucked up by green savages from a distant planet. Serves them right. (Dir: Montgomery Tully, 75 mins.)†

Terror of Godzilla, The—See: **Terror of Mechagodzilla, The**

Terror of Mechagodzilla, The (Japan, 1978)** Katsuhiko Sasaki, Tomoke Ai. Godzilla's evil mechanical double returns in this, the last film to feature the giant monster until *Godzilla 1985*. AKA: **The Terror of Godzilla**. (Dir: Ishiro Honda, 80 mins.)†

Terror of Rome Against the Son of Hercules, The (Italy-France, 1960)*½ Mark Forrest, Marilu Tolo. Roman gladiator Maciste becomes Caesar's favorite by defeating four gladiators at once and battling the "terror" (a scrawny ape). But when he loses his heart to a Christian girl, he becomes the champion of her people against Rome. Average muscleman tale, for fans of the genre only. (Dir: Mario Caiano, 100 mins.)†

Terror of the Tongs, The (Great Britain, 1961)** Christopher Lee, Yvonne Monlaur, Geoffrey Toone. Sea captain sets out to smash a terrorist Tong society when his daughter is killed. (Dir: Anthony Bushell, 80 mins.)

Terror of Tiny Town, The (1938) ½ Billy

Curtis, Yvonne Moray, Little Billy, John Bambury. A film best viewed with a magnifying glass; this all-midget western must be seen in all its tiny glory to be believed! A minuscule range war breaks out when a nefarious half-pint turns two teensy-weensy cattlemen against each other. (Dir: Sam Newfield, 63 mins.)†

Terror on a Train (1953)**½ Glenn Ford, Anne Vernon. Rather fast-paced western. Ford plays an armament expert who is called upon to disarm a hidden bomb on a train carrying explosives. (Dir: Ted Tetzlaff, 72 mins.)

Terror on Highway 91 (MTV 1989)**½ Ricky Schroder, George Dzundza, Matt Clark, Brad Dourif. In his first adult role, Schroder plays an idealistic rookie cop who finds corruption on the force. Nothing special, but Dzundza makes a good villain. (Dir: Jerry Jameson, 96 mins.)

Terror on the Beach (MTV 1973)**½ Dennis Weaver, Estelle Parsons, Susan Dey. Hoodlums aboard dune buggies and an old fire truck terrorize a vacationing family camping on an isolated beach. The slow buildup of pranks produces the desired suspense. (Dir: Paul Wendkos, 73 mins.)

Terror on the 40th Floor (MTV 1974)*½ John Forsythe, Anjanette Comer, Joseph Campanella. TV disaster flick in which office workers, trapped by fire on a skyscraper's top floor, take turns at high-level histrionics. Result— low-level drama. (Dir: Jerry Jameson, 72 mins.)†

Terror on Tour (1980)* Rick Styles, Dave Galluzzo, Rich Pemberton, Chip Greenman. The violent aspects of rock music are exploited, not explored, in this sick film about a madman who murders the groupies of a band called The Clowns. Often bloody and distasteful, but never scary. (Dir: Don Edmonds, 88 mins.)†

Terror out of the Sky (MTV 1978)** Efrem Zimbalist, Jr., Tovah Feldshuh, Dan Haggerty. Zimbalist is the head of the National Bee Center and it appears that some killer queen bees have infiltrated a hive and the bees have been shipped to beekeepers. (Dir: Lee H. Katzin, 104 mins.)†

Terror Squad (1987)*½ Chuck Connors, Bill Calvert, Jill Sanders, Kavi Raz. Libyan terrorists invade Kokomo, Indiana. Actually, they were planning to destroy a local nuclear power plant, but things got screwed up. Like *Red Dawn* without the asinine right-wing theology, not bad for action fans. (Dir: Peter Maris, 90 mins.)†

Terror Train (Canada, 1980)** Ben Johnson, Jamie Lee Curtis, David Copperfield, Hart Bochner. Horror queen Jamie Lee is the object of a knife-wielding, clown-masked madman in this implausible,

nonterrifying effort about a masquerade party held aboard a moving train. Grand Guignol on the Orient Express? (Dir: Roger Spottiswoode, 97 mins.)†

Terrorvision (1986)* Jennifer Richards, Diane Franklin, Chad Allen, Gerrit Graham, Mary Woronov, Bert Remsen. When the Puttermans install their nifty satellite dish, they not only pick up signals, they also start receiving extraterrestrials. Drenched with gross-out special effects and suffused with overblown black comedy bits. (Dir: Ted Nicolaou, 83 mins.)†

Terror Within, The (1989)** George Kennedy, Andrew Stevens, Starr Andreeff, Terri Treas. Competent end-of-the-world monster movie from the Roger Corman factory, with scientists at an underground lab the only survivors of a plague that has wiped out most of mankind and turned the rest into murderous mutants. (Dir: Thierry Notz, 86 mins.)†

Terry Fox Story, The (MCTV 1983)*** Eric Fryer, Robert Duvall, Chris Makepeace. The true-life story of the young Canadian athlete who lost his leg to cancer and embarked on a marathon trek across Canada that attracted national attention. This biographical film could have easily become another "victim rising above his tragedy" yarn but the screenplay avoids glorification and even shows Fox to be a difficult person. (Dir: Ralph L. Thomas, 118 mins.)†

Tess (Great Britain, 1980)***½ Nastassia Kinski, Peter Firth, Leigh Lawson, John Collin. Director Roman Polanski's faithful rendition of Thomas Hardy's novel exhibits great refinement. Kinski reacts with eloquence and stubbornness as the hapless Tess, wedded truly only to her own sense of doom as she is seduced by one man and treated unfairly by another. The ironies, romanticism, and social determinism are dramatized with precision and effectiveness. (170 mins.)†

Tess of the Storm Country (1960)** Diane Baker, Lee Philips, Jack Ging. Young girl arrived from Scotland finds herself involved in a feud between the townspeople and a Mennonite family. Leisurely, pleasing costume drama on the old-fashioned side. (Dir: Paul Guilfoyle, 84 mins.)

Testament (1983)*** Jane Alexander, William Devane, Roxana Zal, Lukas Haas. Compellingly what-if movie about the effects of a nuclear war's aftermath on one family. By dwelling on intimate day-to-day events and allowing us to know the family involved, *Testament* makes us perceive the tragedy in personal terms. (Dir: Lynne Litman, 89 mins.)†

Testament of Dr. Mabuse, The (Germany, 1932)*** Rudolf Klein-Rogge, Karl Meixner, Theodor Loos, Oskar Beregi.

Neither commitment to an insane asylum nor death itself can deter supervillain Dr. Mabuse from running his criminal empire. Fritz Lang's last German film (he fled the country when he realized the Nazis saw themselves criticized in it) shows the director at the peak of his powers. (122 mins.)†

Testament of Dr. Mabuse, The (West Germany, 1960)** Gert Frobe, Alan Dijon. Notorious mad doctor-criminal hypnotizes the head of a sanitarium into carrying out his plans for crime. Remake of the famous old Fritz Lang thriller doesn't compare with the original. (Dir: Werner Klinger, 87 mins.)†

Testament of Orpheus (France, 1959)***½ Jean Cocteau, Edouard Dermithe, Maria Casares, Yul Brynner, Jean Marais, Jean-Pierre Leaud, Pablo Picasso, François Perier, Charles Aznavour. Fascinating surrealist film, the last of director-writer-star Cocteau (a continuation of *The Blood of a Poet* and *Orpheus*) in which he travels into a bizarre landscape filled with magic and wonderment. Personal filmmaking at its best, worth seeing for the cast alone. (83 mins.)

Testimony (Great Britain, 1988)** Ben Kingsley, Sherry Bains, Mark Asquith. Lengthy biography of the Russian composer Shostakovich is more concerned with indicting the horrors of totalitarianism. Even worse, this pretentiously arty film makes little use of his music. (Dir: Tony Palmer, 157 mins.)

Test of Donald Norton, The (1926)**½ George Walsh, Tyrone Power, Sr., Robert Graves, Eugenie Gilbert, Evelyn Selbie, Mickey Moore. A fine western melodrama about a youth raised by Indians, thinking himself a half-breed, who goes to work for the Hudson's Bay Company and begins to rise in the world, only to be pursued by questions about his real parentage. First-class actioner. (Dir: B. Reeves Eason, 99 mins.)†

Test of Love, A (Australia, 1985)*** Angela Punch McGregor, Drew Forsythe, Liddy Clark. A rewarding true-life story of a severely handicapped cerebral palsy victim who spent much of her life misdiagnosed as retarded in an institution. (Dir: Gil Brealey, 93 mins.)†

Test Pilot (1938)*** Clark Gable, Myrna Loy, Spencer Tracy, Lionel Barrymore. Story of men who risk their lives testing aircraft should be remade today with jets. You'll find the planes funny but good acting makes this a pretty rousing drama. (Dir: Victor Fleming, 120 mins.)

Test Tube Babies (1948)½ Dorothy Dube, William Thomason, Timothy Farrell. Monumentally campy artifact attempts to promote artificial insemination with the story of a childless couple who sink into despair until they learn about the procedure. The fun comes from the bad acting and the unabashedly exploitative depiction of the couple's moral slide. Rereleased in 1967 as *The Pill* with additional scenes featuring Monica Davis and John Maitland. (Dir: W. Merle Connell, 52 mins.)

Tevya (1939)*** Maurice Schwartz, Leon Liebgold, Mirim Riselle, Rebecca Weintraub. One of the last and best of actor-director Schwartz's Yiddish productions, in which the Jewish patriarch Tevya is faced with the prospect of his daughter marrying a gentile. Beautifully staged film is a fascinating cinematic artifact. (93 mins.)

Tex (1982)*** Matt Dillon, Jim Metzler, Meg Tilly, Bill McKinney, Frances Lee McCain, Ben Johnson, Emilio Estevez. Young brothers growing up with an absent father in the Southwest must learn to take responsibility and solve their differences, thereby strengthening their relationship. Exceptionally well played by Matt Dillon. Good screenplay by Tim Hunter and Charlie Haas based on the novel by S. E. Hinton. (Dir: Tim Hunter, 103 mins.)†

Texans, The (1938)** Joan Bennett, Randolph Scott, May Robson, Walter Brennan, Robert Cummings. Pretentious class A western. Story of Texas after the Civil War hasn't got too much action or entertainment value. (Dir: James Hogan, 93 mins.)

Texas (1941)*** William Holden, Glenn Ford, Claire Trevor, Edgar Buchanan. Two wandering cowpokes take different trails; one with a pretty ranch girl, the other with an outlaw band. Fine lusty western, with some hilarious comedy sequences, good actors. (Dir: George Marshall, 93 mins.)†

Texas Across the River (1966)** Dean Martin, Alain Delon, Rosemary Forsyth. This western is geared for belly laughs, but only achieves grins. Martin is a gun runner who befriends Delon, playing a Spanish nobleman who's having romantic problems. (Dir: Michael Gordon, 101 mins.)

Texas, Brooklyn, and Heaven (1948)**½ Guy Madison, Diana Lynn, Lionel Stander, James Dunn, Florence Bates. Second-string comedy with a city girl and a country boy overcoming their differences by means of their mutual affection for horses. Engagingly played; Lynn is particularly charming. (Dir: William Castle, 76 mins.)

Texas Carnival (1951)*** Red Skelton, Esther Williams, Howard Keel, Ann Miller. Carnival barker and a chorus girl become involved in mixups at a swank desert resort. Fast-moving musical comedy. (Dir: Charles Walters, 77 mins.)

Texas Chainsaw Massacre, The (1975)*½ Marilyn Burns, Allen Danzinger, Paul A. Partain. A group of young people venturing into the Texas desert run afoul of a demented family who use human flesh in the meats that they eat and sell. (Dir: Tobe Hooper, 83 mins.)†

Texas Chainsaw Massacre Part 2, The (1986)*½ Dennis Hopper, Caroline Williams, Jim Siedow, Bill Johnson, Bill Moseley. This time, the chainsaw family operates a "Rolling Grill" that serves prize chili; guess what the secret ingredient is. An unpleasant, unscary sequel. (Dir: Tobe Hooper, 99 mins.)†

Texas Chainsaw Massacre III, The—See: **Leatherface: Texas Chainsaw Massacre III**

Texas Detour (1978)* Patrick Wayne, Cameron Mitchell, Priscilla Barnes. Detour to another movie. Low-budget, low-action adventure about a stuntman and his family encountering danger when their van is ripped off. (Dir: Hikmet Avedis, 92 mins.)†

Texas Lady (1955)** Claudette Colbert, Barry Sullivan. Colbert, always a lady to her fingertips on the screen, finds herself miscast as a crusading newspaper lady of the Old West. (Dir: Tim Whelan, 86 mins.)†

Texas Layover (1975)½ Yvonne De Carlo, Bob Livingston, Don "Red" Barry, Connie Hoffman, Regina Carrol, Jimmy Ritz, Harry Ritz. Nearly plotless mix of old-fashioned western adventure (with appropriate music), sleazy exploitation from a quartet of stewardesses, and embarrassing clowning from the two surviving Ritz Brothers. AKA: **Blazing Stewardesses**. (Dir: Al Adamson, 88 mins.)†

Texas Lightning (1981)** Cameron Mitchell, Channing Mitchell, Maureen McCormick, Peter Jason, Danone Camden. A pair of father and son truck drivers suffer domestic difficulties; pretty harmless. (Dir: Gary Graver, 93 mins.)

Texas Rangers, The (1936)**½ Fred MacMurray, Jack Oakie, Jean Parker, Lloyd Nolan, Edward Ellis, Gabby Hayes. Above-average historical western, tied in to the Texas Centennial celebration in 1935. Story of outlaws MacMurray and Oakie, who reform and join the fledgling organization, is based on fact. Fine, dusty, frontier atmosphere. (Dir: King Vidor, 95 mins.)

Texas Rangers, The (1951)**½ George Montgomery, Gale Storm, Jerome Courtland, Noah Beery, Jr. A band of notorious outlaws get together to fight the Texas Rangers. Enough gunplay for a dozen westerns. (Dir: Phil Karlson, 68 mins.)

Texas Rangers Ride Again (1940)**½ Ellen Drew, John Howard, Akim Tamiroff,

May Robson, Broderick Crawford, Charley Grapewin, Anthony Quinn, Eddie Foy, Jr. Muscular western, with two Rangers going undercover to foil a mob of rustlers, finding romance along the way. (Dir: James Hogan, 68 mins.)

Texasville (1990)*** Jeff Bridges, Cybill Shepherd, Annie Potts, Timothy Bottoms, Cloris Leachman, Randy Quaid, Angie Bolling, Su Hyatt. Disappointing sequel to *The Last Picture Show* doesn't have the exuberant sense of discovery that the original had, but the follies and foibles of the residents of Anarene, Texas, are still sassy enough to make for interesting viewing. The horny teens of the earlier film are grown up, with horny teens of their own. The movie is lovingly crafted; the main problem is the silliness inherent in Larry McMurtry's source novel. (Dir: Peter Bogdanovich, 123 mins.)†

Texican, The (USA-Spain, 1966)** Audie Murphy, Broderick Crawford, Diana Lorys. Unjustly framed and hounded by a powerful frontier boss, a Texan seeks revenge when his brother gets killed. OK western adventure. (Dir: Lesley Selander, 86 mins.)

Thaddeus Rose and Eddie (MTV 1978)**½ Johnny Cash, Bo Hopkins. Cash works without his guitar in Texas writer William D. Wittliff's story of a pair of country boys who don't want to grow up. (Dir: Jack Starrett, 104 mins.)

Thank God It's Friday (1978)*½ Jeff Goldblum, Valerie Landsburg. An episodic comedy with music interludes. It won the Best Song Oscar for "Last Dance," and, if you like loud disco music, tune in. Otherwise you'll have to wade through until it's over. (Dir: Robert Klane, 100 mins.)†

Thanks a Million (1935)*** Fred Allen, Dick Powell, Ann Dvorak, Patsy Kelly, Paul Whiteman and orchestra. Dated but often amusing musical about a crooner who runs for governor. Fred Allen steals the picture as the campaign manager. (Dir: Roy Del Ruth, 87 mins.)

Thanks for Everything (1938)*** Jack Haley, Jack Oakie, Adolphe Menjou, Tony Martin, Arleen Whelan. Very cute comedy about an advertising agency that discovers the perfect average American. Haley is perfect in the role. (Dir: William A. Seiter, 72 mins.)

Thanks for the Memory (1938)** Bob Hope, Shirley Ross, Charles Butterworth, Otto Kruger, Hedda Hopper, Roscoe Karns, Eddie "Rochester" Anderson. Slim vehicle for Hope finds him playing the role of house-husband and not liking it one bit. Forgettable gags, but two memorable songs: the title tune (originally sung in *The Big Broadcast of 1938*) and "Two Sleepy People." (Dir: George Archainbaud, 77 mins.)

Thanksgiving Day (MTV 1990)**½ Mary Tyler Moore, Tony Curtis, Jonathon Brandmeier, Kelly Curtis, Joseph Bologna, Jean Hale. Moore is celebrating Thanksgiving with her wealthy husband (Curtis) and her spoiled children when hubby suddenly drops dead. Wacky fun is a mixed bag of surprises and strained humor. (Dir: Gino Tanasescu, 96 mins.)

Thanksgiving Promise (MTV 1986)**½ Beau Bridges, Lloyd Bridges, Jordan Bridges, Millie Perkins. A homey holiday drama, overstuffed with sentiment. A boy who's agreed to nurse and fatten up a wounded goose in time for Thanksgiving grows too attached to his feathered friend to readily honor his commitment. (Dir: Beau Bridges, 104 mins.)

Thank You All Very Much (Great Britain, 1969)*** Sandy Dennis, Eleanor Bron, Ian McKellen. Rosamund (Sandy Dennis), a Ph.D. candidate, finds herself pregnant after her first affair, and decides to have and keep her baby. Touching, unsentimental. (Dir: Waris Hussein, 107 mins.)

Thank You, Jeeves (1936)**½ Arthur Treacher, David Niven. You'll love Mr. Treacher as P. G. Wodehouse's butler and David Niven as his tolerant employer. (Dir: Arthur Greville Collins, 68 mins.)

Thank You, Mr. Moto (1937)*** Peter Lorre, Pauline Frederick, Sidney Blackmer, Sig Ruman, John Carradine. That wily Oriental sleuth tries to dig up a map that may lead to buried treasure. Crisply efficient B movie-making. (Dir: Norman Foster, 67 mins.)

Thank Your Lucky Stars (1943)***½ Eddie Cantor, Dinah Shore, Bette Davis, Joan Leslie, Dennis Morgan, Ann Sheridan, Humphrey Bogart, Errol Flynn, John Garfield, Alan Hale, Jack Carson, Hattie McDaniel. Warner Bros.' contribution to the WWII all-star extravaganza. Davis sings "They're Either Too Young or Too Old." Other highlights include Sheridan's rendition of "Love Isn't Born, It's Made" and Carson and Hale duetting on "I'm Going North." (Dir: David Butler, 127 min.)†

That Certain Age (1938)** Deanna Durbin, Melvyn Douglas, Jackie Cooper, Irene Rich, Nancy Carroll. Comic treacle has Deanna falling for a reporter friend of her parents (Douglas); waiting in the wings are boyfriend Cooper and the inevitable "big show." The script for this horrifyingly nice, wholesome outing is co-credited to Billy Wilder! (Dir: Edward Ludwig, 95 mins.)

That Certain Feeling (1956)*** Bob Hope, Eva Marie Saint, George Sanders, Pearl Bailey. Artist is hired by a famous syndicated cartoonist to "ghost" a famous comic strip, falls for a secretary. In the better class of Hope comedies with bright lines, witty situations, delightful performances. (Dir: Norman Panama, 103 mins.)

That Certain Summer (MTV 1972)***½ Hal Holbrook, Hope Lange, Scott Jacoby, Martin Sheen. Holbrook gives a touching performance as a homosexual who is confronted with the torment of discovering that his fourteen-year-old son has found out about him. Tasteful and honest. (Dir: Lamont Johnson, 73 mins.)

That Certain Woman (1937)** Bette Davis, Henry Fonda. Maudlin, sentimental drama of a woman trying desperately to live down her past. Too heavy for modern tastes. Remake of *The Trespasser*. (Dir: Edmund Goulding, 93 mins.)

That Championship Season (1982)*** Robert Mitchum, Bruce Dern, Paul Sorvino, Stacy Keach. This drama, set in Scranton, Pa., is a sad examination of the collapse of the American dream, as expressed in the reunion of a coach and four of his players from a championship high school basketball team whose lives have gone awry. (Dir: Jason Miller, 110 mins.)†

That Cold Day in the Park (U.S.-Canada, 1969)*** Sandy Dennis, Michael Burns, John Garfield, Jr., Luana Anders, Michael Murphy. Unsettling early Robert Altman film about a mature spinster who takes in a rain-soaked, silent boy from the street and becomes obsessed with him while he milks her for material comforts. (112 mins.)†

That Darn Cat! (1965)**½ Dean Jones, Hayley Mills, Dorothy Provine, Elsa Lanchester, Roddy McDowall, William Demarest. Jones, Mills, and an independent Siamese cat romp through this amusing Disney opus, as the feline thwarts kidnappers. (Dir: Robert Stevenson, 116 mins.)†

That Forsyte Woman (1949)**½ Greer Garson, Errol Flynn, Janet Leigh, Robert Young, Walter Pidgeon. Rather long and on the dull side, but handsomely produced. Greer Garson falls in love with the man who is engaged to her niece. Acting is good. Based on Galsworthy's *A Man of Property*. (Dir: Compton Bennett, 114 mins.)

That Funny Feeling (1965)**½ Sandra Dee, Bobby Darin, Donald O'Connor. Girl who has been working as a maid meets a young executive, gives him her working address as a cover-up, and it's his apartment. Amusing comedy has occasional bright dialogue, pleasant performers. (Dir: Richard Thorpe, 93 mins.)

That Gang of Mine (1940)** East Side Kids, Joyce Bryant, Clarence Muse. Muggs wants to be a jockey and is given his chance when the Kids discover a poor black man and his thoroughbred horse in a barn. (Dir: Joseph H. Lewis, 62 mins.)

That Girl from Paris (1936)*** Lily Pons, Gene Raymond, Jack Oakie, Lucille Ball, Mischa Auer, Herman Bing, Frank Jenks. Fast-paced musical comedy features French girl Pons, ready to marry, getting cold feet and lamming it to the U.S.A. Lively tunes and terrific cast, a fun-filled example of what the Hollywood studio system did best. (Remake of *Street Girl*, remade again as *Four Jacks and a Jill*.) (Dir: Leigh Jason, 105 mins.)†

That Hagen Girl (1947)* Ronald Reagan, Shirley Temple. Rory Calhoun, Lois Maxwell. Shirley's adopted, supposedly illegitimate, plagued by gossip, but Ron comes to her rescue. (Dir: Peter Godfrey, 83 mins.)

That Hamilton Woman (1941)*** Vivien Leigh, Laurence Olivier, Gladys Cooper, Alan Mowbray. The romantic story of the love of Lord Nelson, British naval hero, for the beautiful Lady Hamilton, with its tragic outcome. Two fine stars in a long, but interesting costume drama. (Dir: Alexander Korda, 128 mins.)†

That Kind of Woman (1959)** Sophia Loren, Tab Hunter, George Sanders. Despite some excellent New York location shots and the directorial talents of Sidney Lumet, the tale about a beautiful woman who makes an attempt to find true love with a young soldier (Tab Hunter) adds up to glossy soap opera. (92 mins.)

That Lady (Great Britain, 1955)** Olivia de Havilland, Gilbert Roland, Paul Scofield. Love of a princess for a commoner is thwarted by the king's love for her and court intrigue. Stodgy costume drama moves slowly. (Dir: Terence Young, 100 mins.)

That Lady in Ermine (1948)*** Betty Grable, Cesar Romero, Douglas Fairbanks, Jr. A mish-mash of dreams and ancestors stepping out of their portraits makes for an entertaining little sophisticated musical comedy. (Dirs: Otto Preminger, Ernst Lubitsch, 89 mins.)

That'll Be the Day (Great Britain, 1973)*** David Essex, Ringo Starr, Rosemary Leach. Essex leaves home, learns the ropes, and dead-end-jobs it until he can spring for his first guitar. Finely observed example of kitchen sink realism. (Dir: Claude Whatham, 90 mins.)†

That Lucky Touch (Great Britain, 1976)** Roger Moore, Susannah York, Lee J. Cobb, Shelley Winters, Raf Vallone. Roger Moore plays one of his patented characters, a suave ladies' man with international dealings, in this lightweight story about a determined reporter (York) who wants to get the scoop on upcoming NATO war games. (Dir: Christopher Miles, 93 mins.)†

That Man Bolt (1973)* Fred Williamson, Byron Webster, Miko Mayama. Inane black-exploitation movie. Williamson is a courier whose cargo is a million bucks and it appears just everyone is after him for the loot. (Dirs: Henry Levin, David Lowell Rich, 102 mins.)

That Man From Rio (France-Italy, 1964)*** Jean-Paul Belmondo, Françoise Dorleac, Jean Servais. Pleasant enough spy spoof, aided by the engaging anarchic presence of Belmondo, hampered by the strenuousness of Philippe de Broca's direction. Filmed in Rio, Paris, Brasilia. (114 mins.)

That Man in Istanbul (France-Spain, 1965)*½ Horst Buchholz, Sylva Koscina, Klaus Kinski. Meandering espionage yarn. Buchholz makes an attractive playboy nightclub owner who is pressed into spy duty by a curvaceous Sylva Koscina, the Italian sexpot who mysteriously plays a U.S. agent in this dim-witted opus. (Dir: Anthony Isasi, 117 mins.)

That Midnight Kiss (1949)**½ Kathryn Grayson, Mario Lanza, Ethel Barrymore. Mario Lanza's debut film. Light and romantic story about a patroness of the arts (Barrymore) and her singing discoveries. (Dir: Norman Taurog, 96 mins.)

That Night (1957)*** John Beal, Augusta Dabney. Dramatic tale of a man suffering a heart attack, the consequences of its aftermath. (Dir: John Newland, 88 mins.)

That Night in Rio (1941)**½ Alice Faye, Don Ameche, S.Z. Sakall, Curt Bois, Carmen Miranda. Lavish but routine screen musical employing the old mistaken identity plot. Carmen is great in her numbers. (Dir: Irving Cummings, 94 mins.)†

That Night With You (1945)** Franchot Tone, Susanna Foster, Louise Allbritton, David Bruce, Jacqueline De Wit, Buster Keaton, Irene Ryan, Anthony Caruso. Light musical vehicle for soprano Foster, starring as an ambitious singer who convinces a big producer that she's his long-lost daughter so he'll support her career. (Dir: William A. Seiter, 84 mins.)

That Obscure Object of Desire (Spain-France, 1977)***½ Fernando Rey, Angela Molina, Carole Bouquet. This often-filmed tale of the femme fatale who ruins the lives of her admirers, especially an aging count who can't tear himself away, remains an effective melodrama. In the thirties, Josef von Sternberg turned this escapade into an ideal vehicle for Marlene Dietrich in *The Devil Is a Woman*. Buñuel splits the angel/whore aspects of the temptress's personality so that a different actress plays each facet. It's a bit confusing, but once you catch the spirit of the film it becomes provocative entertainment from a master director. (100 mins.)†

That's Dancing (1985)**½ This dazzling

collection of film clips from great dance musicals may have some musical-lovers dancing in the aisles. Unfortunately, not much imagination has filtered into the narration or linking devices, but it's still an occasionally ebullient experience. (Dir: Jack Haley, Jr., 105 mins.)†

That Secret Sunday (MTV 1986)**½ James Farentino, Parker Stevenson, Daphne Ashbrook. A veteran reporter/detective teaches a young team of journalists how to investigate a cop cover-up. Farentino is exceptionally good as the ethical reporter, but this one runs out of steam. (Dir: Richard Colla, 104 mins.)

That's Entertainment (1974)***½ Judy Garland, Fred Astaire, Frank Sinatra, Gene Kelly, Esther Williams. The title is right. It is marvelous entertainment: scenes from some of the greatest MGM musicals released from '29 to '58. Tune in if you're nostalgic or in search of wonderful entertainers struttin' their stuff. Written and directed by Jack Haley, Jr. (135 mins.)†

That's Entertainment, Part 2 (1976)*** Fred Astaire, Gene Kelly, Judy Garland, Katharine Hepburn, Frank Sinatra, Spencer Tracy. The MGM studio's archives have delivered a spectacular sequel. The seventy-five films culled are interwoven with new footage of Astaire and Kelly dancing together for the first time in thirty years. Gene Kelly directed the new sequences. (133 mins.)†

That Sinking Feeling (1979)*** Robert Buchanan, John Hughes, Billy Greenlees. A character comedy that is full of unexpected insights. After an unusual heist—ninety stainless steel sinks for fun and profit—an unemployed Scot finds himself beseiged with a growing number of accomplices. (Dir: Bill Forsyth, 82 mins.)†

That's Life (1986)*½ Jack Lemmon, Julie Andrews, Sally Kellerman, Robert Loggia, Chris Lemmon, Jennifer Edwards, Emma Walton, Felicia Farr. Set against a backdrop of Lemmon's hypochondriacal tirades, this sour comedy-drama cruelly keeps the audience on tenterhooks as they wonder whether Julie's biopsy for throat cancer is going to be malignant. Experiencing this film is like being trapped in a home movie belonging to people you detest. (Dir: Blake Edwards, 102 mins.)†

That's My Baby (Canada, 1985)** Timothy Weber, Sonja Smits, Joann McIntyre, Derek McGrath. Occasionally cute gender-reversal comedy of a man pleading with his career-conscious wife to get pregnant; mostly straight from sit-com land. (Dir: John Bradshaw, 98 mins.)†

That's My Boy (1932)*½ Richard Cromwell, Dorothy Jordon, Mae Marsh, Arthur Stone, Douglas Dumbrille. Dated pigskin drama with a college football star

tricked into working a phony stock scam. Not much to get excited over, unless you're a big fan of the Stone Age of football. Script by Norman Krasna. (Dir: Roy William Neill, 71 mins.)

That's My Boy (1951)** Dean Martin, Jerry Lewis, Eddie Mayehoff, Polly Bergen. Blustering former athletic hero wants his anemic son to follow in his footsteps. Early Martin and Lewis comedy suffers from repetition of gags. (Dir: Hal Walker, 98 mins.)

That's My Man (1947)**½ Don Ameche, Catherine McLeod. Gambler starts with a colt and a girl, becomes wealthy stable owner but a flop as a husband. Lengthy racing drama has good acting to see it through. (Dir: Frank Borzage, 98 mins.)

That's Right—You're Wrong (1939)**½ Kay Kyser, Lucille Ball, Dennis O'Keefe, Adolphe Menjou. Kyser's orchestra goes to Hollywood to make a picture, where the moguls try to change him. Amusing musical. (Dir: David Butler, 88 mins.)

That's the Spirit (1945)**½ Peggy Ryan, Jack Oakie, June Vincent, Gene Lockhart, Johnny Coy, Andy Devine, Arthur Treacher, Irene Ryan, Buster Keaton. Fantasy-musical of a deceased song-and-dance man who returns as an angel to aid his daughter's career. Nothing earth-shaking, but a good score and Keaton has an excellent bit. (Dir: Charles Lamont, 93 mins.)

That's the Way of the World (1975)*½ Harvey Keitel, Ed Nelson, Cynthia Bostick, Bert Parks, Jimmy Boyd. Energy is sorely lacking in this behind-the-scenes exposé of the record industry. That dynamite pop group Earth, Wind, and Fire enlivens the proceedings with their vocalizing, but that's the only grace note. AKA: **Shining Star** (Dir: Sig Shore, 100 mins.)†

That Summer (Great Britian, 1979)**½ Ray Winston, Tony London, Emily Moore, Julie Shipley. Standard coming-of-age film, with Winston and three pals journeying to the shore. Soundtrack is loaded with fine New Wave music by Elvis Costello, Patti Smith, the Boomtown Rats, Nick Lowe, and Ian Dury. (Dir: Harley Cokliss, 93 mins.)

That Tennessee Beat (1966)*½ Merle Travis, Minnie Pearl. Ambitious country singer robs to get ahead, is reformed under sympathetic guidance of a lady preacher after being mugged. Trite, slushy cornball; music is OK. (Dir: Richard Brill, 84 mins.)

That Touch of Mink (1962)*** Cary Grant, Doris Day, Audrey Meadows, Gig Young. A business tycoon makes a play for an unemployed damsel, and vice versa. Enjoyable comedy, lightly spicy, with some beautiful people romping in beautiful settings. (Dir: Delbert Mann, 99 mins.)†

That Uncertain Feeling (1941)*½ Merle Oberon, Burgess Meredith, Melvyn Douglas, Eve Arden. Anemic, whimsical comedy about a marriage headed for the rocks when the wife stirs things up with her infatuation with a temperamental pianist. (Dir: Ernst Lubitsch, 89 mins.)†

That Was Then...This Is Now (1985)*½ Emilio Estevez, Craig Sheffer, Kim Delaney, Frank Howard, Morgan Freeman. This exercise in vapidity written by Estevez concerns that burning question—what happens when your buddy grows up and you stay wedged in teenhood, or vice versa. (Dir: Christopher Cain, 103 mins.)†

That Way With Women (1947)**½ Dane Clark, Martha Vickers, Sydney Greenstreet, Alan Hale, Craig Stevens, Barbara Brown. Second screen adaptation of Earl Derr Biggers's *The Millionaire* with Greenstreet as the philanthropist who helps out gas station owner Clark and his girlfriend Vickers. The cast bring some charm to this familiar tale. (Dir: Frederick de Cordova, 84 mins.)

That Woman Opposite (Great Britain, 1957)** Phyllis Kirk, Dan O'Herlihy. Insurance investigator solves murder at a French resort. Slow mystery relies upon dialogue at the sacrifice of action. (Dir: Compton Bennett, 84 mins.)

That Wonderful Urge (1948)**½ Tyrone Power, Gene Tierney. Glamour girl has her revenge upon a reporter who's been writing nasty articles about her. Mildly pleasant romantic comedy. Remake of Power's *Love Is News*. (Dir: Robert B. Sinclair, 82 mins.)

Theatre of Blood (Great Britain, 1973)*** Vincent Price, Diana Rigg, Robert Morley. Fine black comedy with Price as a Shakespearean actor seeking revenge on critics who he believes denied him a best-acting prize. (Dir: Douglas Hickox, 104 mins.)†

Theatre of Death (Great Britain, 1966)*** Christopher Lee, Lelia Goldoni. Not a horror flick, but a neat, complex whodunit set in the Grand Guignol theater in Paris. A perverse director has a strange hold on two girls—when he is murdered the police must decide who did, in fact, do it. AKA: **Blood Fiend.** (Dir: Samuel Gallu, 90 mins.)†

Thelma and Louise (1991)***½ Susan Sarandon, Geena Davis, Harvey Keitel, Michael Madsen, Christopher McDonald, Brad Pitt. Outstanding road movie about two women (Sarandon and Davis) who murder a would-be rapist and flee the law through the Southwestern United States. Fresh and exhilarating with great music and dialogue, and wonderful acting, especially by Pitt as a country kid on the make. (Dir: Ridley Scott, 128 mins.)†

Thelonious Monk: Straight, No Chaser (1989)***½ Outstanding documentary about the late jazz piano genius includes footage of his concerts, rare interviews with him, his family, and friends, as well as more than 20 brilliant performances of Monk's original music. (Dir: Charlotte Zwerin, 90 mins.)†

Them (1954)***½ James Whitmore, Edmund Gwenn, James Arness, Fess Parker, Joan Weldon. Entertaining science fiction thriller about strange creatures who appear suddenly near the Mojave Desert. (Dir: Gordon Douglas, 94 mins.)†

Themroc (France, 1972)***½ Michel Piccoli, Beatrice Romand, Marilu Tolo, Francesca R. Coluzzi. Raging satire about a man whose life is in a rut. He lives with his mother and sister in a dreary flat, has a wretched job, and one day snaps. (Dir: Claude Faraldo, 110 mins.)

Then Came Bronson (MTV 1969)** Michael Parks, Bonnie Bedelia, Akim Tamiroff. Pilot for a TV series. Michael Parks stars as Bronson, a young reporter who chucks it all when his friend commits suicide, leaving him his motorcycle. (Dir: William Graham, 100 mins.)

Then There Were Three (Italy, 1962)**½ Frank Latimore, Alex Nicol. German officer infiltrates the American lines to kill an Italian partisan. Neat little combination of WWII and mystery yarn, filmed in Italy. No epic, but well done. (Dir: Alex Nicol, 82 mins.)

Theodora Goes Wild (1936)*** Irene Dunne, Melvyn Douglas, Thomas Mitchell, Spring Byington. Dunne's big comedic breakthrough as a modest small-town librarian who writes a steamy best-seller about the secret life of small towns. (Dir: Richard Boleslawski, 94 mins.)

There Goes My Girl (1937)*** Gene Raymond, Ann Sothern. Boy and girl reporters love each other, but are bitter rivals when a murder story breaks. Well-done comedy, light and amusing. (Dir: Ben Holmes, 74 mins.)

There Goes My Heart (1938)**½ Fredric March, Virginia Bruce. Spoiled heiress skips home and becomes a salesgirl, where a reporter discovers her secret. Pleasant, amusing comedy. (Dir: Norman Z. McLeod, 82 mins.)

There Goes the Bride (Great Britain, 1980)** Tom Smothers, Twiggy, Martin Balsam, Sylvia Syms, Michael Whitney, Hermione Baddeley, Jim Backus, Phil Silvers, Broderick Crawford, Gonzales Gonzales. Cute but forgettable comedy starring Smothers as a man who can't concentrate on his daughter's wedding because he's too busy having an imaginary affair with a '20s flapper (Twiggy). (Dir: Terence Marcel, 88 mins.)

There Goes the Groom (1937)**½ Burgess Meredith, Ann Sothern. Man blessed with sudden riches marries, and has in-law trouble. Diverting comedy. (Dir: Joseph Santley, 70 mins.)

There Must Be a Pony (MTV 1986)**½ Elizabeth Taylor, Robert Wagner, James Coco, William Windom. The potent casting of Elizabeth Taylor makes this a must for her fans. Elizabeth is an actress attempting a comeback in a prime time TV soap, while sorting out her personal life in the process. Based on James Kirkwood's memoirs, the film's script seems slapped together, but Taylor's star power fills in the gaps. (Dir: Joseph Sargent, 104 mins.)

There's a Girl in My Soup (Great Britain, 1970)*** Peter Sellers, Goldie Hawn, Tony Britton. The delightful combination of confident Sellers as a TV gourmet and scatterbrained Hawn as a girl who disrupts his free-wheeling lifestyle. Based on the London and Broadway stage comedy, the screen version is better. (Dir: Roy Boulting, 96 mins.)†

There's Always a Woman (1938)*** Joan Blondell, Melvyn Douglas, Mary Astor. Private eye returns to the DA's office and gives his agency to his wife; then they find themselves working on the same murder case. Entertaining comedy-mystery. (Dir: Alexander Hall, 81 mins.)

There's Always Tomorrow (1956)*** Barbara Stanwyck, Fred MacMurray, Joan Bennett. MacMurray is a disaffected toy manufacturer afflicted with a self-absorbed wife (Bennett) and ratty kids. Then old flame Stanwyck re-enters his life. Mordant, intelligent soaper. (Dir: Douglas Sirk, 84 mins.)

There's Always Vanilla (1972)**½ Ray Laine, Judith Streiner, Johanna Lawrence, Richard Ricci, Roger McGovern. Dated relationship drama that its director, horror specialist George A. Romero, would probably like to forget. Laine is a drifter who moves in with a pretty model (Streiner); when she becomes pregnant, their hip, swinging love affair quickly begins to crumble. (91 mins.)

Therese (France, 1986)***½ Catherine Mouchet, Aurore Prieto, Sylvie Habault, Ghislane Mona. Powerfully stylized vision of the life of St. Therese, a young woman whose near-romantic passion for Christ sustained her throughout her life, even when she was dying from tuberculosis. The film is comprised of beautifully composed tableaux which take us through Therese's induction into the Carmelite order, her poignant relationships with her sister nuns, and her even-

tual tragic demise. A strong aesthetic accomplishment for the director. (Dir: Alain Cavalier, 96 mins.)†

Thérèse and Isabelle (France, 1968)*** Essy Persson, Anna Gael, Remy Longa, Anne Vernon. Lavish soft-core fantasy film about women in love with each other, noted more for its lush, lyrical photography and gorgeous design than for its acts of passion. One of the many films directed by Radley Metzger in a dreamier era of porno chic. (118 mins.)

There's Magic in Music (1941)** Allan Jones, Susanna Foster, Margaret Lindsay, Lynne Overman, Grace Bradley, William Collier, Sr., Esther Dale. Mild vehicle for soprano Foster, unconvincing as a burlesque singer who discovers classical music at the National Music Camp. AKA: **The Hard-Boiled Canary.** (Dir: Andrew L. Stone, 80 mins.)

There's No Business Like Show Business (1954)*** Ethel Merman, Marilyn Monroe, Donald O'Connor, Dan Dailey, Mitzi Gaynor, Johnnie Ray. Overproduced show biz story about a trouping family and their plights on and off the stage. Many Irving Berlin songs make the film worthwhile. (Dir: Walter Lang, 117 mins.)†

There Was a Crooked Man (1970)*** Kirk Douglas, Henry Fonda, Hume Cronyn, Lee Grant, Burgess Meredith. Douglas, as a robber serving time in prison (circa 1880s), and Fonda, as a reform-oriented warden, spark this western tale. Although the script may get too talky at times, director Joseph L. Mankiewicz directs the action with a knowing hand, leading to the film's final confrontation between the two flinty leads. (118 mins.)†

These Are the Damned (Great Britain, 1963)*** Macdonald Carey, Oliver Reed, Shirley Anne Field, Viveca Lindfors, Alexander Knox, James Villiers. Dark, steely cross between a youth-gang picture and science fiction. Carey, Reed, and Field are involved in a rather conventional juvenile delinquent wrangle when they come upon a cave inhabited by strangely cold children, loosing a hideous doom. Film was drastically recut by the studio, but it's still an unusual, compelling (if basically over-emotional) vision. Sequel: *Children of the Damned.* (Dir: Joseph Losey, 77 mins.)

These Glamour Girls (1939)*** Lana Turner, Lew Ayres, Anita Louise, Richard Carlson. Good satirical comedy about college life although the film's social implications have lost their bite. (Dir: S. Sylvan Simon, 80 mins.)

These Thousand Hills (1959)**½ Don Murray, Richard Egan, Lee Remick, Patricia Owens, Stuart Whitman. Occasionally interesting, frequently meandering western about a young cowpoke who becomes prosperous in the Old West, and the troubles that beset him. (Dir: Richard Fleischer, 96 mins.)

These Three (1936)***½ Merle Oberon, Joel McCrea, Miriam Hopkins, Bonita Granville. A watered-down version of Lillian Hellman's provocative play *The Children's Hour* about a scandal which ruins the lives of three people. Granville is excellent as a school girl who sets the fuse of scandal about her two schoolteachers. (Dir: William Wyler, 90 mins.) †

These Wilder Years (1956)**½ James Cagney, Barbara Stanwyck, Walter Pidgeon. Steel magnate searches for his illegitimate son of twenty, runs into unexpected opposition. (Dir: Roy Rowland, 91 mins.)

They All Kissed the Bride (1942)**½ Joan Crawford, Melvyn Douglas. Career girl learns the importance of love in this familiar, but mildly amusing film. (Dir: Alexander Hall, 87 mins.)

They All Laughed (1981)*½ Audrey Hepburn, Ben Gazzara, John Ritter, Dorothy Stratten, Colleen Camp, Patti Hansen. Intended as a valentine to Manhattan, this amorphous light romance appears to have been improvised on the streets of New York, but not one of the insubstantial vignettes about private eyes tracking down romance seems fresh or involving. Contributing to the pall cast over the film is the fact that the promising Stratten was murdered before the film was released. (Dir: Peter Bogdanovich, 115 mins.) †

They Call Her One Eye (Sweden, 1974)* Christina Lindberg, Heinz Hopf, Despina Tomazini. If you thought *I Spit on Your Grave* was foul, check out this unpleasant Scandinavian exploitation flick. Lindberg is sold into white slavery, undergoing beatings and sexual attacks until she gathers her strength to take revenge against the scum who did her wrong. (Dir: Alex Fridolinski, 89 mins.)

They Call It Murder (MTV 1971)** Jim Hutton, Lloyd Bochner, Jessica Walter. Average murder mystery, as the DA finds a corpse in a swimming pool and tries to link the victim to an insurance claim and a car crash. Based on an Erle Stanley Gardner novel. (Dir: Walter Grauman, 97 mins.)

They Call It Sin (1932)** Loretta Young, George Brent, David Manners, Louis Calhern, Una Merkel, Helen Vinson. Simple soap opera about a chorus girl (Young) searching for true love among her many suitors, who include producer Calhern and doctor Brent. Unexciting but competent. (Dir: Thornton Freeland, 68 mins.)

They Call Me Bruce? (1982)*½ Johnny Yune, Margaux Hemingway, Ralph Mauro, Pam Huntington. A kung fu comic strip based on the unlikely proposition that a chef could be constantly mistaken for Bruce Lee. A chop suey comedy that will leave you hungry for more laughs. Sequel: *They Still Call Me Bruce?* AKA: **A Fistful of Chopsticks**. (Dir: Elliot Hong, 88 mins.) †

They Call Me Mr. Tibbs (1970)** Sidney Poitier, Martin Landau, Barbara McNair, Juano Hernandez, Norma Crane. Inferior sequel to the first-rate *In the Heat of the Night*. Sidney's Virgil Tibbs again, but this time the locale moves from the deep South, and a lot's been lost in the trek to San Francisco, with Poitier looking and acting, quite understandably, very bored. (Dir: Gordon Douglas, 108 mins.) †

They Call Me Trinity (Italy, 1972)** Terence Hill, Bud Spencer, Farley Granger. Uneven spaghetti western with tongue-in-cheek comedy. Plot concerns an involved scheme to rustle cattle, dreamed up by bogus sheriff Bambino and freewheeling Trinity. (Dir: E. B. Clucher, 110 mins.) †

They Came From Beyond Space (Great Britain, 1967)* Robert Hutton, Jennifer Jayne, Zia Mohyeddin, Bernard Kay, Michael Gough. This unpleasant-looking retread of *It Came from Outer Space* features Hutton as the only human capable of battling against aliens who assume human form in order to carry out repairs on their space ship. (Dir: Freddie Francis, 85 mins.) †

They Came From Within (Canada, 1975)*** Paul Hampton, Joe Silver, Lynn Lowry, Barbara Steele. Cronenberg's obsession with all the ills that human flesh is heir to reaches its apogee (or nadir, if you're squeamish) in this upsetting thriller. A mysterious plague strikes a swinging singles complex, causing the residents to attack each other even as their sexual appetites increase to the point of frenzy. Terrifying and stomach-churning. AKA: **Shivers, and Frissons**. (87 mins.) †

They Came to Blow Up America (1943)**½ George Sanders, Anna Sten, Ward Bond, Dennis Hoey, Sig Ruman, Ludwig Stossel. Double agent Sanders infiltrates Nazi saboteurs operating in the U.S. Tense and capably done. (Dir: Edward Ludwig, 73 mins.)

They Came to Cordura (1959)** Gary Cooper, Rita Hayworth, Van Heflin, Tab Hunter. Slow-moving tale about six soldiers (circa 1916) and one woman who make an arduous trek across impossible terrain to reach Cordura, a military outpost. The personal feelings of the seven are bared during the interminable journey. (Dir: Robert Rossen, 123 mins.) †

They Came to Rob Las Vegas (Spain-France-West Germany-Italy, 1968)* Gary Lockwood, Elke Sommer, Lee J. Cobb, Jack

Palance. Trivial crime drama in the Nevada desert as criminals rob an armored truck filled with gold. (Dir: Antonio Isasi, 130 mins.)

They Can't Hang Me (Great Britain, 1955)**½ Terence Morgan, Yolande Donlan. Condemned murderer bargains his freedom for information about a vital security leak. Unimportant but fast-moving mystery. (Dir: Val Guest, 75 mins.)

They Died With Their Boots On (1941)*** Errol Flynn, Olivia de Havilland, Arthur Kennedy, Anthony Quinn, Sydney Greenstreet. Flynn makes a dashing Gen. Custer, maturing from the light romantic comedian of his cadet days to the tragically betrayed figure of Little Big Horn. It's historical nonsense, but the visual style of director Raoul Walsh triumphs over every improbability in this long, expert epic that never drags despite its length. (138 mins.)†

They Don't Wear Black Tie (Brazil, 1982)**** Gianfrancesco Guarnieri, Fernanda Montenegro, Carlos Alberto Ricelli. Director Leon Hirszman uses one family's conflict regarding workers' solidarity to illuminate the political unrest in a local factory and to offer a larger criticism of Brazil's repressive military regime. A powerful and engrossing drama. (122 mins.)

They Drive by Night (1940)*** Ida Lupino, George Raft, Humphrey Bogart, Ann Sheridan. For its first half this is a social drama about trucking—fast, hard, bitter, brilliantly realized. Then the creaky murder-and-adultery plot gets under way and the rest is Lupino overacting. Half a masterpiece is better than none. (Dir: Raoul Walsh, 93 mins.)†

They Gave Him a Gun (1937)*** Spencer Tracy, Franchot Tone, Gladys George, Edgar Dearing, Charles Trowbridge. Strong, extremely well acted drama of doughboy buddies Tone and Tracy both in love with George during WWI; when Tracy is presumed killed, she marries Tone. Years later Tracy returns to find Tone involved with gangsters without George's knowledge. Forceful, moving, well-written story. (Dir: W. S. Van Dyke, 94 mins.)

They Got Me Covered (1943)*** Bob Hope, Dorothy Lamour, Otto Preminger, Lenore Aubert, Eduardo Ciannelli. A typical Hope vs. the German enemy agents chase film, which means it's fun all the way. (Dir: David Butler, 95 mins.)†

They Knew What They Wanted (1940)***½ Charles Laughton, Carole Lombard, William Gargan, Frank Fay, Harry Carey. Italian grape-grower takes a lonely waitress as a bride, with tragedy following. Powerful, finely acted drama. Basis for the musical *The Most Happy Fella*. (Dir: Garson Kanin, 96 mins.)†

They Live (1988)*** Roddy Piper, Keith David, Meg Foster, Raymond St. Jacques. Writer-director John Carpenter has a great idea for a sci-fi movie—what if Yuppies and Republicans were really alien monsters?—but doesn't take it far enough. Fun anyway as ex-wrestler "Rowdy" Roddy Piper plays a homeless laborer who discovers the secret and sets out to kick alien butt. (95 mins.)†

They Live by Night (1949)**** Farley Granger, Cathy O'Donnell, Howard da Silva, Helen Craig, Jay C. Flippen. Director Nicholas Ray's first film is possibly the most romantic crime film ever made. Granger and O'Donnell beguilingly portray an awkward young couple who are forced into becoming "lovers on the run" when Granger cannot escape his criminal past. Their sympathetic relationship is depicted with sensitivity and touching detail, and the performances are remarkably intense. Remade as *Thieves Like Us*. (95 mins.)†

They Made Me a Criminal (1939)*** John Garfield, Ann Sheridan, Dead End Kids, Claude Rains. Garfield's dynamic, yet sensitive, portrayal of a fugitive boxer who thinks he has murdered a man is so stirring that it lifts this commonplace story to the level of entertainment. Remake of *The Life of Jimmy Dolan*. (Dir: Busby Berkeley, 92 mins.)†

They Made Me a Killer (1946)**½ Robert Lowery, Barbara Britton. Young man is forced to join some bank robbers, but finally outwits them. Fast-moving melodrama with plenty of action. (Dir: William C. Thomas, 64 mins.)

They Meet Again (1941)** Jean Hersholt, Dorothy Lovett. Mystery gets injected into the series as Dr. Christian tries to clear an innocent man and locate the culprit. (Dir: Erle C. Kenton, 69 mins.)†

They Met in Bombay (1941)**½ Clark Gable, Rosalind Russell, Peter Lorre. Routine adventure story about a couple of jewel thieves who fall in love and in order to clear his name before the dashout he joins forces with the English in a battle against the Japanese. (Dir: Clarence Brown, 86 mins.)

They Might Be Giants (1971)*** George C. Scott, Joanne Woodward, Jack Gilford. Bizarre, sentimental fable with Scott as a retired judge who believes himself to be Sherlock Holmes. The judge's brother calls on a female Dr. Watson (Woodward) to have Scott committed so he can inherit the family fortune. Sometimes muddled, often appealing, and Scott and Woodward are splendid. Screenplay by James Goldman. Restored on TV and video to its full length, which had been trimmed to 88 mins. before it was released to theaters. (Dir: Anthony Harvey, 98 mins.)†

They Only Come Out at Night (MTV 1975)** Jack Warden, Tim O'Connor, Madeline Sherwood, Joe Mantell. Warden is better than his material in this routine police drama about a seasoned LAPD detective investigating the robbery-murders of old women. (Dir: Daryl Duke, 72 mins.)

They Only Kill Their Masters (1972)**½ James Garner, June Allyson, Peter Lawford, Hal Holbrook, Katharine Ross. James Garner's casual approach to his role as a California town police chief enhances this offbeat murder mystery about a swinger who's found dead on the beach. (Dir: James Goldstone, 97 mins.)

They Ran for Their Lives (1965)* John Payne, Jim Davis, Luana Patten. Boring chase film starring and directed by John Payne. He plays a man who helps a young woman evade her pursuers. (92 mins.)

They're Playing With Fire (1984)½ Sybil Danning, Andrew Prine, Eric Brown, Paul Clemens, K. T. Stevens. This is teen-titillation-cum-slasherama. Danning entices a student into helping her kill so she can get her greedy paws on an inheritance. Danning's chest continues to be the most expansive weapon in her arsenal of acting tricks, but even lip-smacking chauvinists will be disappointed by this cheesy display of violence and pinup porn. (Dir: ''Howard'' [Hikmet] Avedis, 96 mins.)†

They Rode West (1954)*** Robert Francis, Donna Reed, May Wynn, Phil Carey. Better-than-average western drama dealing with the efforts of a courageous young doctor to maintain peace with the Kiowa Indians. (Dir: Phil Karlson, 84 mins.)

They Saved Hitler's Brain (1963)½ Walter Stocker, Audrey Claire. Hitler's brain has been kept alive in the Caribbean and continues to issue orders to its loyal followers. Cutting footage together from a fifties schlocker with new sixties footage, this mishmash deserves a half-a-swastika rating. AKA: **Madmen of Mandoras.** (Dir: David Bradley, 74 mins.)†

They Shall Have Music (1939)**½ Joel McCrea, Walter Brennan, Marjorie Main, Andrea Leeds. A moderately successful drama about an East Side settlement house for young musicians. The highlight of the film is the violin artistry of Jascha Heifetz. (Dir: Archie Mayo, 100 mins.)†

They Shoot Horses, Don't They? (1969) **** Jane Fonda, Michael Sarrazin, Gig Young, Susannah York, Red Buttons, Bruce Dern, Bonnie Bedelia, Allyn Ann McLerie. Excellent film depicting the madness and desperation of the Depression era's marathon dance contests. Based on the '35 novel by Horace McCoy. The cast is perfect, the dance sessions are magnificently staged by director Sydney Pollack, and the film emerges as a haunting evocation of the thirties. (121 mins.)†

1066

They Still Call Me Bruce (1987)½ Johnny Yune, David Mendenhall, Robert Guillaume, Pat Paulsen. Seoul-less farce with Korean comic Yune playing a bumbling black belt, who gets involved with numerous baddies, an orphan boy, and a magic sock(?). (Dir: Johnny Yune, 91 mins.)†

They Went That-a-Way and That-a-Way (1978)** Tim Conway, Chuck McCann, Reni Santoni. Dopey comedy about cops and escaped convicts, written by Conway. (Dirs: Edward Montagne, Stuart E. McGowan, 106 mins.)†

They Were Expendable (1945)***½ John Wayne, Robert Montgomery, Donna Reed, Jack Holt. Exciting adventure story dedicated to the Navy men who fought Japanese vessels in small PT boats. A top-drawer war picture. (Dir: John Ford, 135 mins.)†

They Were Sisters (Great Britain, 1945)*** James Mason, Phyllis Calvert. The love affairs and marital mishaps of three devoted sisters are related. Well-acted drama. (Dir: Arthur Crabtree, 108 mins.)

They Were So Young (West Germany, 1955)*** Scott Brady, Johanna Matz, Raymond Burr. Innocent girls are sent to South America as entertainers and killed if they resist. Rather lurid but well-made melodrama with a good cast. (Dir: Kurt Neumann, 80 mins.)

They Who Dare (Great Britain, 1954)*** Dirk Bogarde, Akim Tamiroff. Six Englishmen and four Greek soldiers are assigned to blow up air fields in Rhodes when Allied communication lines are being hampered. Well-made, frequently exciting drama of WWII. (Dir: Lewis Milestone, 101 mins.)

They Won't Believe Me (1947)***½ Robert Young, Susan Hayward, Rita Johnson, Jane Greer. Man intending to kill his wife doesn't succeed, but through a quirk of fate goes on trial anyway. Absorbing ironic melodrama. (Dir: Irving Pichel, 95 mins.)†

They Won't Forget (1937)***½ Claude Rains, Allyn Joslyn, Lana Turner, Otto Kruger, Edward Norris. An exceptional drama about a prosecutor in a southern town who turns a murder case into a political stepping stone. Good writing, superb acting, and Mervyn LeRoy's expert direction make this a compelling film. (94 mins.)

Thief, The (1952)*** Ray Milland, Rita Gam, Martin Gabel. Story of how a Communist spy is forced to kill an FBI agent, and how his conscience causes him to give himself up. Unusual in that there is no dialogue; the only sounds are the musical score, and background noises. As such, a novelty; otherwise, the effect is forced, the melodrama routine. (Dir: Russell Rouse, 85 mins.)

Thief (MTV 1971)**½ Richard Crenna, Angie Dickinson, Cameron Mitchell, Hurd Hatfield. Writer John D. F. Black combines suspense with interesting character development as half-hero, half-heel Crenna is in a solid bind when he must rob to pay a gambling debt. (Dir: William Graham, 72 mins.)

Thief (1981)*** James Caan, Tuesday Weld, Willie Nelson, James Belushi, Robert Prosky, Tom Signorelli. This cold, technology-obsessed thriller features Caan as a thief with a heart of gold caught between the corrupt cops and the businesslike mob. Jangling music, controlled mayhem, and extraordinary night photography create the atmosphere others have sought, but few have found, in this much-trod caper flick territory. (Dir: Michael Mann, 126 mins.)†

Thief of Bagdad, The (1924)**** Douglas Fairbanks, Julanne Johnson, Snitz Edwards, Charles Belcher, Anna May Wong, Noble Johnson. Gorgeous, enthralling fantasy-adventure, one of Fairbanks' best movies, with a huge cast, great special effects, and enormous, astonishing sets by William Cameron Menzies. Still as exciting and wondrous as it was when it was made. (Dir: Raoul Walsh, 155 mins.)†

Thief of Bagdad, The (Great Britain, 1940)**** Sabu, John Justin, Rex Ingram, June Duprez, Conrad Veidt. One of the most popular screen fantasies, and deservedly so, this work reflects the flamboyant personality of its producer, Alexander Korda. Enchanting, with superb early Technicolor. Won four Oscars. (Dirs: Michael Powell, Tim Whelan, Ludwig Berger, 106 mins.)†

Thief of Bagdad, The (MTV 1978)**½ Peter Ustinov, Roddy McDowall, Pavla Ustinov, Kabir Bedi. Easy-to-take European-produced version of the Arabian Nights tale. Ustinov helps make things move along as the wily caliph of Baghdad, trying to marry off his daughter, Princess Yasmine, played by Ustinov's real-life daughter Pavla Ustinov. (Dir: Clive Donner, 104 mins.)†

Thief of Baghdad (France-Italy, 1961)** Muscle man Steve Reeves in the Arabian Nights adventure epic—colorful, but on a juvenile level. (Dir: Arthur Lubin, 89 mins.)

Thief of Hearts (1984)**½ Steve Bauer, Barbara Williams, John Getz, Christine Ebersole, George Wendt. Drenched in a modish Giorgio Moroder score and bathed in glittery colors, "Thief" nearly drowns in its own production values. What we're left with is a sleek, sexy romance about an upwardly mobile burglar who purloins a woman's diary during a break-in and next schemes to steal her heart. (Dir: Douglas Day Stewart, 100 mins.)†

Thief of Paris, The (France, 1967)***½ Jean-Paul Belmondo, Genevieve Bujold, Marie Dubois, Julien Guiomar, Françoise Fabian, Charles Denner. Dazzling thriller with Belmondo as a young man conned out of his inheritance by a devious uncle. He turns to crime and becomes a master thief. Strong acting, lavish production, and Louis Malle's exceptional direction energize powerful look at the politics and causes of crime. (120 mins.)

Thief Who Came to Dinner, The (1973)**½ Ryan O'Neal, Jacqueline Bisset, Warren Oates, Jill Clayburgh. Comedy about a computer programmer who happens to be a cat burglar on the side. Some of the plot gets too involved, but you'll enjoy the characters. (Dir: Bud Yorkin, 103 mins.)†

Thieves (1977)** Marlo Thomas, Charles Grodin, Irwin Corey, Hector Elizondo, Gary Merrill, Mercedes McCambridge. In this overly familiar slice of urban angst, Thomas and Grodin play native New Yorkers who split up and try to rediscover their sanity in this comedy whose greatest asset is some wonderful dialogue from playwright Herb Gardner. (Dir: John Berry, 92 mins.)

Thieves' Highway (1949)*** Richard Conte, Valentina Cortese, Lee J. Cobb, Jack Oakie. Action-melodrama concerning truckers, trollops, and thugs, on the long haul delivering fresh vegetables to market. (Dir: Jules Dassin, 94 mins.)

Thieves' Holiday—See: **Scandal in Paris, A**

Thieves Like Us (1974)**** Keith Carradine, Shelley Duvall, John Schuck, Louise Fletcher, Bert Remsen, Tom Skerritt. A marvelous version, directed beautifully by Robert Altman, of the '37 novel by Edward Anderson, first filmed as *They Live by Night*. Story of a pair of doomed lovers during the Depression is skillfully adapted by Calder Willingham, Joan Tewkesbury, and Altman. The performances are excellent, especially Carradine and Duvall, who give sensitive, touching performances as the doomed young lovers. (123 mins.)

Thieves of Fortune (1989)* Michael Nouri, Lee Van Cleef, Shawn Weatherly, Craig Gardner, Russel Savadier. Weak adventure about a girl who has to pretend she's tough in order to inherit a fortune, and then revert to femininity to marry the man of her dreams. Resolutely awful script includes stereotypical Mexican bandits out of another era. (Dir: Michael McCarthy, 100 mins.)†

Thin Air (U.S.-Great Britain, 1969)* George Sanders, Maurice Evans, Robert Flemyng, Patrick Allen, Neil Connery. Parachutists vanish, extraterrestrial beings are blamed. Unsteady sci-fi. (Dir: Gerry Levy, 91 mins.)

Thin Blue Line, The (1988)*** Chilling documentary about a tragic miscarriage of justice. In 1976, Randall Adams was convicted of the murder of a Texas policeman and sentenced to life imprisonment; subsequent revelations showed that a young man he met on the day of the murder was the more likely suspect. Filmmaker Earl Morris's collage approach (utilizing interviews, newspaper articles, documents, photographs and reenactments of the crime) effectively conveys the nightmarish quality of an innocent man condemned. Adams was finally released—several years after this film raised a public outcry. (106 mins.)†

Thing, The (1951)***½ Kenneth Tobey, Margaret Sheridan, James Arness. Scientific research station in the Arctic comes across a monster from another world. A terrifying thriller about a hostile visitor who regards human beings not as brothers but as sustenance. Also known as *The Thing From Another World*, this skillfully directed chiller remains one of the great sci-fi films. Some prints are 81 mins. Reputedly worked on by Howard Hawks. (Dir: Christian Nyby, 87 mins.)†

Thing, The (1983)** Kurt Russell, A. Wilford Brimley, Richard Dysart, Richard Masur. John Carpenter's dour remake of the fifties sci-fi classic is more faithful to its source material, *Who Goes There?*, but is not as entertaining as the first film. An isolated outpost in the Antarctic makes the chilling discovery that a creature from outer space has landed and can transform itself into an exact replica of any of the human scientists. Unfortunately, the movie is too much of an exercise in special effects that sicken rather than frighten us. (Dir: John Carpenter, 109 mins.)†

Things Are Tough All Over (1982)** Cheech Marin, Tommy Chong, Rikki Marin, Shelby Chong, Rip Taylor. C&C have taken a momentary respite from the drug culture and turned to more ambitious prospects—money and sex (and not always in that order!). They play dual roles as themselves and also as two rich Arabs. The Arabs dupe C&C into transporting tainted money to Las Vegas to be laundered. (Dir: Thomas K. Avildsen, 92 mins.)†

Things Change (1988)*** Don Ameche, Joe Mantegna, Robert Prosky, J. J. Johnston, Ricky Jay. Charming gangster piece has a low-ranking Mafioso (Mantegna) taking an innocent old Italian shoemaker (Ameche), who's been recruited to be the fall guy in a murder case, out for a weekend on the town in Reno. Brilliant, hard-edged playwright David Mamet does show signs here of mellowing out; otherwise, his direction is taut, the leads are 100 percent loveable, and the script, by director Mamet and songwriter/
1068

humorist Shel Silverstein, has a beguiling, old-fashioned feel to it. (100 mins.)†

Things in Their Season (MTV 1974)*** Patricia Neal, Meg Foster, Marc Singer, Ed Flanders. Touching drama of how a tight-knit family copes with the revelation that their mother is dying of leukemia. (Dir: James Goldstone, 75 mins.)

Things to Come (Great Britain, 1936)*** Raymond Massey, Ralph Richardson, Ann Todd, Cedric Hardwicke. A preview of the future by H. G. Wells who, although wildly wrong, had at least the courage to look foolish. Director William Cameron Menzies's camera work is less successful than his intriguingly designed sets. (113 mins.)

Thing That Couldn't Die, The (1958)* Andra Martin, William Reynolds, Carolyn Kearney, Jeffrey Stone. Deadly horror flick about a centuries-old head seeking to control the living while he tries to locate his missing bottom half. Maybe he should have spent his time mating with the female head from *The Brain That Wouldn't Die*. (Dir: Will Cowan, 69 mins.)

Thing with Two Heads, The (1972) ½ Ray Milland, Rosey Grier. Rubbish about grafted heads must have been made by people with a botched frontal lobotomy. Milland's head is grafted onto Grier's body and. . . . (Dir: Lee Frost, 90 mins.)

Thin Ice (1937)*** Sonja Henie, Tyrone Power, Jr., Arthur Treacher, Raymond Walburn, Joan Davis, Alan Hale, Sig Ruman, Melville Cooper. Henie's best picture, with Power as a European prince traveling incognito, visiting the resort where she teaches and falling for her. A fine score, good supporting cast, and excellent skating numbers make this better than average. (Dir: Sidney Lanfield, 78 mins.)

Thin Ice (MTV 1981)** Kate Jackson, Gerald Pendergast, Lillian Gish. A blond boy falls for his pretty teacher against a background of high school classrooms and afternoon sails, in a warm, earnest, and boring yarn about young love and small-town priggery. (Dir: Paul Aaron, 104 mins.)

Think Big (1990)**½ Peter Paul, David Paul, Ari Meyers, Martin Mull, David Carradine, Claudia Christian, Richard Kiel, Richard Moll, Michael Winslow, Tony Longo, Peter Lupus, Tiny Lister, Jr., Rafer Johnson. Dumbbell twin truckers (former wrestlers the Pauls) pick up a genius teenage hitchhiker on the run from bad guys who want her invention. Cheerfully dopey comedy. (Dir: Jon Turteltaub, 86 mins.)†

Think Dirty (Great Britain, 1970)*½ Marty Feldman, Shelley Berman, Judy Cornwell, Julie Ege, Patrick Cargill, Penelope Keith. Feldman, who at his best was riotously funny, is barely amusing in this insipid vehicle that seems to have been intended as a British version of *Putney Swope*. He plays a clever ad agency worker who decides to sell porridge with overtly sexy commercials. (Dir: Jim Clark, 94 mins.)

Think Fast, Mr. Moto (1937)**½ Peter Lorre, Sig Ruman, Murray Kinnell, Virginia Field. The first entry in the B movie series about the resourceful Asian detective who knew some mean ju jitsu, in addition to his sleuthing capabilities. Here, this Charlie Chan-derived detective is in hot pursuit of diamond smugglers who take their wares from Chinatown to Shanghai. (Dir: Norman Foster, 66 mins.)

Thin Line, The (Israel, 1980)*** Gila Alagor, Alex Peleg, Liat Panski. Sensitive, almost lyrical, depiction of a woman's horrifying descent into madness as witnessed by her shocked and saddened daughter. A beautifully realized film, superbly acted, and directed with serene grace by Michal Bat-Adam. (90 mins.)

Thin Man series. Everyone's favorite sophisticated couple (based on characters by Dashiell Hammett) combines marriage with mayhem through six features that were first-class items all the way. Droll and sophisticated, Powell and Loy made homicide-solving seem as natural as walking the dog (in this case, Asta). A TV series with Phyllis Kirk and Peter Lawford was also much admired. If you want to watch the screen's perfect couple combine romantic and detective teamwork, you should catch the following films in addition to those reviewed here: *After the Thin Man, Another Thin Man, Shadow of the Thin Man,* and *Song of the Thin Man.*

Thin Man, The (1934)***½ William Powell, Myrna Loy, Maureen O'Sullivan, Nat Pendleton, Minna Gombell, Porter Hall. Nick and Nora Charles, the screen's foremost practitioners of wit and urbanity, made their debuts in this sparkling whodunit. The plot, about the search for a certain "Thin Man" who bumped off an inventor, isn't the actual focus (that's proven by its quick summation at the film's end); what really matters is the bright repartee between Powell and Loy, a screen couple made in heaven. Writer Dashiell Hammett claimed he originally created the Charleses as a sort of negative vision of wealth during the Depression; what arrived on screen, thanks to fine scripting and inspired casting, was instead so delightful that decades later, the film's a cult favorite. (Dir: W. S. Van Dyke, 93 mins.)†

Thin Man Goes Home, The (1944)**½ William Powell, Myrna Loy, Lucile Watson, Anne Revere. Series returns after a three-year hiatus and is off standard. There's a murder, some good dialogue but it's lacking in the usual fast-paced witticisms. (Dir: Richard Thorpe, 101 mins.)†

Thin Red Line, The (1964)**½ Keir Dullea, Kleron Moore, Jack Warden. James Jones's fine novel of the men who fought and died at Guadalcanal with some fine rugged battle scenes, but a story treatment that never quite jells. (Dir: Andrew Marton, 99 mins.)

Third Day, The (1965)**½ George Peppard, Elizabeth Ashley, Roddy McDowall. Fairly engrossing tale about an amnesiac who has to piece together many events in his past after an auto crash and a possible murder. (Dir: Jack Smight, 119 mins.)

Third Finger, Left Hand (1940)** Melvyn Douglas, Myrna Loy. Not funny in spite of good acting is this sophisticated comedy about a cold cookie who falls for a guy but plays hard to get. (Dir: Robert Z. Leonard, 96 mins.)

Third Generation, The (West Germany, 1979)***½ Volker Spengler, Bulle Ogier, Hanna Schygulla, Udo Kier, Harry Baer, Eddie Constantine. Director Rainer Werner Fassbinder once said "I don't throw bombs, I make films." This outrageously funny and explosive thriller is his own jaundiced view of terrorism, the story of a group of middle-class radicals, emotional cripples desperate to be taken seriously as enemies of the state. (111 mins.)

Third Girl From the Left, The (MTV 1973)**½ Kim Novak, Tony Curtis, Michael Brandon. Familiar story about an over-the-hill New York chorine who's reached the crossroads in her life—she loses her front row spot in the chorus; terminates her thirteen-year engagement to her nightclub singer-comic boyfriend; and finds herself attracted to a very attentive and winning younger man. (Dir: Peter Medak, 74 mins.)

Third Key, The (Great Britain, 1956)***½ Jack Hawkins, Dorothy Alison. Police search for a safecracker, and the chase leads them to murder. Exciting crime drama. (Dir: Charles Frend, 96 mins.)

Third Lover, The (France, 1962)*** Jacques Charrier, Stephane Audran, Walther Reyer, Daniel Boulanger. Voyeuristic and fascinating study of a journalist who becomes friends with a happily married couple. He slowly becomes obsessed with their lives, and makes advances to the wife, which results in tragic consequences for the three of them. (Dir: Claude Chabrol, 80 mins.)

Third Man, The (Great Britain, 1949)**** Joseph Cotten, Orson Welles, Alida Valli, Trevor Howard. A classic from start to finish. Pulp writer Holly Martins (Cotten) searches through the intrigue-filled streets of postwar Vienna for traces of his old friend Harry Lime (Welles) in this taut thriller. Much has been said about Welles's stealing the picture with his portrayal of Lime, the most charismatic heel in movie history. Praise should also be lavished, however, on Cotten and Valli and the inventive visuals created by Carol Reed and cinematographer Robert Krasker (who won an Oscar). Who can forget the climactic sewer chase scene, with its strikingly tilted camera angles, or the haunting zither music played by Anton Karas? (100 mins.)†

Third Man on the Mountain (1959)*** Michael Rennie, James MacArthur, Janet Munro, Herbert Lom. Inspired by the first ascent of the Matterhorn in 1865, this movie concerns a Swiss youth joining a British expedition attempting a new peak. Typical, scenic Disney tale—a boy matures, the British play fair. (Dir: Ken Annakin, 105 mins.)†

Third Secret, The (Great Britain, 1964)*** Stephen Boyd, Pamela Franklin, Diane Cilento, Richard Attenborough. Uneven but often interesting psychological drama. When a leading British psychiatrist dies and the coroner's verdict is suicide, his teenage daughter convinces a TV commentator to investigate further. (Dir: Charles Crichton, 103 mins.)

Third Voice, The (1960)*** Edmond O'Brien, Laraine Day, Julie London. Fine suspense thriller made economically but excellently about an impostor hired to pose as a murdered financier by his private secretary. (Dir: Hubert Cornfield, 79 mins.)

Third Walker, The (Canada, 1979)*** Colleen Dewhurst, William Shatner, Frank Moore, David and Tony Meyer. The feature debut of director Teri McLuhan, daughter of Marshall McLuhan. The main plot concerns twins who are mixed up at birth and raised by different mothers. Interesting offbeat entry. (83 mins.)†

Thirst (Australia, 1979)*** David Hemmings, Chantal Contouri, Henry Silva. Better than *The Hunger*. A girl is taken to a vampire farm where some people are raised to be victims, while other clients drop by to drink up. Refreshingly different. (Dir: Rod Hardy, 98 mins.)†

Thirsty Dead, The (Philippines, 1974)* John Considine, Jennifer Billingsley, Judith McConnell, Tani Guthrie. Vampires in the jungle, amateurishness on the screen, and boredom in the audience. (Dir: Terry Becker, 96 mins.)†

13 at Dinner (MTV 1985)*** Faye Dunaway, Peter Ustinov, Jonathan Cecil, Lee Horsley, Bill Nighy, David Suchet. The presence of Ustinov as Hercule Poirot, is irresistible here. Alibis abound when Lord Edgware is murdered and his less-than-grieving widow (Dunaway) is the prime suspect. AKA: **Agatha Christie's 13 at Dinner.** (Dir: Lou Antonio, 104 mins.)

Thirteen Chairs, The—See: **12 + 1**

1070

13 Frightened Girls (1963)½ Murray Hamilton, Joyce Taylor, Hugh Marlowe, Khigh Dhiegh. Absurd, obvious Cold War intrigues. Young teenager capitalizes on her age to engage in some reckless spying, aiding her idol, a CIA agent. (Dir: William Castle, 89 mins.)

Thirteen Ghosts (1960)** Charles Herbert, Jo Morrow. A thoroughly gimmicked horror film. Mild entertainment, as a professor and family move into a haunted house. (Dir: William Castle, 88 mins.)†

Thirteen Hours by Air (1936)**½ Fred MacMurray, Joan Bennett, ZaSu Pitts. Dated but high-flying tale about adventure on board a flight hijacked by an ex-con. (Dir: Mitchell Leisen, 80 mins.)

13 Rue Madeleine (1946)*** James Cagney, Annabella, Walter Abel, Sam Jaffe, Frank Latimore, Richard Conte. Semidocumentary espionage thriller stars Cagney as the leader of a group of secret agents; he goes to France to complete a mission when one of his men is killed by the Nazis. One of a series of *March of Time*-inspired films produced by Louis de Rochemont. (Dir: Henry Hathaway, 95 mins.)†

Thirteenth Guest, The (1932)** Ginger Rogers, Lyle Talbot, J. Farrell MacDonald, Paul Hurst. Dated comedy mystery. The thirteenth guest is a mystery man, who inherited a fortune from a man who suddenly croaked at a dinner party thirteen years ago. The number thirteen continues to prove unlucky for several people probing the mystery in the mandatory old dark house. (Dir: Albert Ray, 69 mins.)†

13th Letter, The (1951)*** Charles Boyer, Linda Darnell, Constance Smith, Michael Rennie. Small town in Canada is in turmoil when a series of incriminating letters appear. Suspense, fine performances and direction (by Otto Preminger). Based on the French film *Le Corbeau*. (85 mins.)

13 West Street (1962)**½ Alan Ladd, Rod Steiger, Michael Callan, Dolores Dorn. Man beaten by a gang of teenagers refuses to cooperate with the police, seeks his own revenge. Tough little crime drama. (Dir: Philip Leacock, 80 mins.)

Thirteen Women (1932)**½ Myrna Loy, Irene Dunne, Ricardo Cortez, Jill Esmond, Florence Eldredge, Kay Johnson, Julie Haydon, Wally Albright, C. Henry Gordon, Ed Pawley. Intriguing mystery, with exotic oriental Loy taking murderous revenge on schoolmates who snubbed her. Fanciful and not really convincing, but fun. (Dir: George Archainbaud, 74 mins.)

30 (1959)** Jack Webb, William Conrad, David Nelson. "Thirty" is a journalist's way of saying "the end"; if only this film had reached that point sooner. It's the story of a night's work on a metropolitan newspaper told in a semidocumentary style. (Dir: Jack Webb, 96 mins.)

Thirty-Day Princess (1934)*** Sylvia Sidney, Cary Grant, Edward Arnold. A young actress is hired to take the place of a princess who has come down with mumps on a tour of New York City. Naturally, the ordinary girl falls in love with someone who thinks she is a princess. Fine light entertainment. Good script by Preston Sturges. (Dir: Marion Gering, 73 mins.)

'38: Vienna Before the Fall (Austria, 1986)**½ Tobias Engel, Sunnyi Melles, Heinz Trixner, Lotte Ledl. In the months before Hitler's march into Austria, a successful Jewish playwright and his Aryan lover blind themselves to the coming persecution. This attempt to probe the roots of Austrian anti-Semitism and to understand a dark episode in the country's history would be better had it been more fully thought through and dramatized. (Dir: Wolfgang Glück, 96 mins.)†

30 Foot Bride of Candy Rock, The (1959)*½ Lou Costello, Dorothy Provine. Corny, one-joke idea. Lou Costello falls in love with an outsized beauty, Miss Provine blown up to 30 feet. (Dir: Sidney Miller, 75 mins.)†

30 Is a Dangerous Age, Cynthia (Great Britain, 1968)*** Dudley Moore, Suzy Kendall, Eddie Foy, Jr. Moore attempts to attain success and marriage by age thirty (he's got six weeks to go) in this bewitching and eccentric release. (Dir: Joseph McGrath, 85 mins.)†

39 Steps, The (Great Britain, 1935)**** Robert Donat, Madeleine Carroll. Adaptation of the John Buchan spy thriller, with delightful work by Donat and Carroll, who spend much of the film handcuffed together, with the police and the real spies after them. The suspense is terrific, though the plot resolution is bald contrivance. The fundamental theme of director Alfred Hitchcock—an innocent man plunged into a world of deception, doubt, and chaos—is festooned with more action, humor, suspense, and visual artistry than anyone would have a right to expect. (89 mins.)†

39 Steps, The (Great Britain, 1959)**½ Kenneth More, Taina Elg. This remake doesn't measure up to Hitchcock, but suspense fans unfamiliar with the original will find enough here to sustain their interest. (Dir: Ralph Thomas, 93 mins.)

Thirty-Nine Steps, The (Great Britain, 1978)**½ Robert Powell, John Mills, Karen Dotrice. Third version proves you can't top Alfred Hitchcock's classic, although you can still get some mileage out of the plot. (Dir: Don Sharp, 102 mins.)†

Thirty Seconds Over Tokyo (1944)*** Van Johnson, Spencer Tracy, Robert Walker, Robert Mitchum, Phyllis Thaxter. An exciting war film which chronicles the story of our first raid on Japan. Slightly dated but still good entertainment. (Dir: Mervyn LeRoy, 138 mins.)†

Thirty Years of Fun (1963)*** One of Robert Youngson's fine comedy compilations, with material by Buster Keaton, Charlie Chaplin, Laurel and Hardy, Harry Langdon, Charley Chase, and Sydney Chaplin. Some priceless moments, and a good introduction to the lesser known performers. (85 mins.)

36 Fillette (France, 1988)*** Delphine Zentout, Etienne Chicot, Jean-Pierre Léaud. A maladjusted fourteen-year-old girl learns that her prematurely developed woman's body gives her control over adult men. Unsentimental, finely observed study of adolescent sexuality. (Dir: Catherine Breillat, 92 mins.)†

36 Hours (1964)*** James Garner, Rod Taylor, Eva Marie Saint. Army officer is abducted by the Nazis and made to believe the war has ended, so they can pry secrets from him. As soon as the plot becomes clear, it gradually deteriorates into a routine WWII spy thriller. (Dir: George Seaton, 115 mins.)

This Above All (1942)*** Tyrone Power, Joan Fontaine. Eric Knight's novel of the romance between a disillusioned British soldier and a patriotic girl is a powerful love story minus many of the book's values. Superbly directed, it is a bit too slow-moving to hold sustained interest. (Dir: Anatole Litvak, 110 mins.)

This Angry Age (1958)*½ Anthony Perkins, Silvana Mangano, Jo Van Fleet, Richard Conte, Alida Valli. An attempt to make an American film with a foreign flavor just doesn't come off. Perkins and Mangano are brother and sister and they've just about had it with Mama Van Fleet's insane determination to make their poor rice plantation a going thing. (Dir: René Clement, 111 mins.)

This Child Is Mine (MTV 1985)** Lindsay Wagner, Nancy McKeon, Chris Sarandon, Michael Lerner, John Philbin, Kathleen York. Standard fare. Who gets to keep the infant—the childless adoptive parents or the teenage mom who wants her baby back? (Dir: David Greene, 96 mins.)

This Could Be the Night (1957)*** Jean Simmons, Anthony Franciosa, Paul Douglas, Joan Blondell, Julie Wilson. Entertaining comedy about a schoolteacher charmingly played by Jean Simmons, who takes a part-time job as a secretary to a night club owner and ends up changing lives left and right. (Dir: Robert Wise, 103 mins.)

This Day and Age (1933)*** Charles Bickford, Judith Allen, Richard Cromwell. Slam-bang vigilante pic, about adolescents who pursue a murderer. Pow-

This Earth Is Mine (1959)**½ Rock Hudson, Jean Simmons, Claude Rains, Dorothy McGuire, Anna Lee. Sprawling family dynasty film set in the Napa Valley wine country. (Dir: Henry King, 125 mins.)

This Girl for Hire (MTV 1983)**½ Bess Armstrong, Roddy McDowall, José Ferrer, Howard Duff, Cliff De Young, Celeste Holm, Hermione Baddeley. A girl detective is hired by a mean-spirited mystery writer; moderately entertaining fare. (Dir: Jerry Jameson, 104 mins.)

This Gun for Hire (1942)***½ Alan Ladd, Veronica Lake. Exciting, tense tale of a hired killer who is double-crossed and seeks revenge. Ladd's portrayal of the killer made him a star. Based on the Graham Greene novel. (Dir: Frank Tuttle, 80 mins.)†

This Gun for Hire (MCTV 1991)**½ Robert Wagner, Nancy Everhard, John Harkins, Frederick Lehne. Wagner is a hired assassin on the run as he searches for of the men who framed him in this moderately entertaining tale of deception and murder. Based on a popular Graham Greene novel, this leisurely paced, stylish remake of the 1942 movie, which starred Alan Ladd and Veronica Lake, attempts the difficult task of recreating the feel of the *film noir* thrillers of the '40s. (Dir: Lou Antonio, 96 mins.)

This Happy Breed (Great Britain, 1944)***½ Robert Newton, Celia Johnson, John Mills, Stanley Holloway. Noel Coward's panoramic story of a family and of the house in which they live through two wars. Fine drama captures the spirit of England itself; exemplary in all departments. (Dir: David Lean, 114 mins.)†

This Happy Feeling (1958)*** Debbie Reynolds, Curt Jurgens, John Saxon, Mary Astor, Alexis Smith. Charming comedy about a young girl who fancies herself in love with a dashing older man. (Dir: Blake Edwards, 92 mins.)†

This House Possessed (MTV 1981)** Parker Stevenson, Lisa Eilbacher, Joan Bennett. Some chills in this predictable thriller with Stevenson as a rock star on the verge of a breakdown who takes some time off in a secluded mountain retreat. (Dir: William Wiard, 104 mins.)

This Is a Hijack (1973)** Adam Roarke, Neville Brand, Jay Robinson, Lynn Borden, Milt Kamen, John Alderman. Low-budget tale of airline terror has Roarke hijacking a plane to pay off his massive gambling debts. The tense moments only produce yawns. (Dir: Barry Pollack, 90 mins.)

This Is Elvis (1981)** Rhonda Lyn, David Scott, Johnny Harra, Lawrence Koller. Exploitative documentary that mixes real footage with dramatizations of events from the rock 'n' roll king's life. Not without interest, but the combination of fact and fancy obfuscates rather than enlightens our perception of Elvis. (Dirs: Malcolm Leo, Andrew Solti, 101 mins.)†

This Is Kate Bennett (MTV 1982)** Janet Eilber, David Haskell, Greg Mullavey, Kyle Richards, Granville Van Dusen. A woman struggles with the demands of being a TV news reporter and a single parent. (Dir: Harvey Hart, 78 mins.)

This Island Earth (1955)**½ Jeff Morrow, Faith Domergue, Rex Reason. Sci-fi with more intelligent plot and better special effects than usual. Earthlings become involved in space wars on a planet under heavy attack by meteors being directed at it by an enemy planet. (Dir: Joseph M. Newman, 87 mins.)†

This Is My Affair (1937)**½ Robert Taylor, Barbara Stanwyck, Victor McLaglen. Taylor is a secret agent assigned by President McKinley to investigate a band of train robbers. (Dir: William A. Seiter, 99 mins.)

This Is My Love (1954)** Linda Darnell, Rick Jason, Dan Duryea, Faith Domergue, Hal Baylor, Jerry Mathers. Rather bizarre '50s thriller, with Domergue and Darnell as sisters, one of whom murders her own husband and frames the other out of love for another man. (Dir: Stuart Heisler, 91 mins.)

This Is Not a Test (1962)**½ Mary Morlas, Seamon Glass. Tough state trooper takes charge when word comes of an impending nuclear attack, joins a group held up by a roadblock. Grim little drama occasionally whips up some powerful scenes. (Dir: Frederic Gadette, 72 mins.)†

This Is Spinal Tap (1984)***½ Rob Reiner, Christopher Guest, Michael McKean, Harry Shearer. Outrageous send-up of rock bands, cleverly using a documentary technique. We follow this fictitious group, Spinal Tap, from their post-Beatles influence days to their current U.S. tour, many of the foibles of the music business and public taste are lovingly satirized. Lots of cameos for the quick-eyed. (Dir: Rob Reiner, 82 mins.)†

This Is the Army (1943)*** George Murphy, Ronald Reagan, Joan Leslie, Kate Smith, Joe Louis. Pleasant Irving Berlin extravaganza is a forties artifact. The Broadway show was entirely cast with men in uniform; some of them appear in the film. Berlin appears at the piano to play his "Oh How I Hate to Get Up in the Morning"; you can tell he's dubbed, since the only key he could play in was F-sharp major, and he's not hitting the black keys. (Dir: Michael Curtiz, 121 mins.)†

This Is the Life (1944)**½ Donald

O'Connor, Susanna Foster, Peggy Ryan, Louise Allbritton, Patric Knowles, Eddie Quillan, Martha Vickers, Mantan Moreland. Comedy about a soldier in love with a flighty girl who has a crush on an older man. Several nice songs highlight Foster's singing and O'Connor's dancing. (Dir: Felix Feist, 85 mins.)

This Is the Night (1932)*** Lili Damita, Charlie Ruggles, Roland Young, Thelma Todd, Cary Grant, Claire Dodd. Delectable musical comedy, with a spirited and expert cast, including Grant in his first feature film. A fun-loving bachelor, pursuing a married lady, hires an alluring actress to pose as his wife to deceive her husband. Skillful, sexy, and charming. (Dir: Frank Tuttle, 78 mins.)

This Is the West That Was (MTV 1974)*½ Ben Murphy, Kim Darby, Jane Alexander, Tony Franciosa, Matt Clark. Ben Murphy is Wild Bill Hickok, Kim Darby is Calamity Jane, and Matt Clark is Buffalo Bill in this piece of nonsense that depicts Hickok as a hot-shot gunfighter whose deeds of gunplay stem from the lively imagination of Calamity Jane. (Dir: Fielder Cook, 100 mins.)

This Land Is Mine (1943)***½ Charles Laughton, Maureen O'Hara, Walter Slezak, George Sanders, Kent Smith. A timid schoolteacher becomes a hero when his country is overrun by Nazis. Fine performance by Laughton in this compelling drama. (Dir: Jean Renoir, 103 mins.)

This Love of Ours (1945)**½ Merle Oberon, Claude Rains, Charles Korvin. Maudlin soap opera about an unfaithful wife and mother who returns to her husband's home after twelve years to find resentment and finally love. Remade as *Never Say Good-bye*. (Dir: William Dieterle, 90 mins.)

This Man Is Mine (1934)**½ Irene Dunne, Ralph Bellamy, Constance Cummings, Kay Johnson, Charles Starrett, Sidney Blackmer. Glossy soap opera of two sisters fighting over the same man, who just happens to be the husband of one of them; well done, but with an undeveloped script. (Dir: John Cromwell, 76 mins.)

This Man Is News (Great Britain, 1938)*** Barrie K. Barnes, Valerie Hobson, Alastair Sim, John Warwick, Garry Marsh. Fast-moving British comedy-mystery, with wisecracking reporter Barnes investigating a gangland killing with the help of his clever wife Hobson. Pretty good attempt to model a team after *The Thin Man*'s Nick and Nora Charles, helped by a savvy script and a good supporting cast. (Dir: David MacDonald, 63 mins.)

This Man Must Die (France-Italy, 1969)***½ Michel Duchaussoy, Jean Yanne.

Director Claude Chabrol has fashioned another stunning crime tale. This time his main character is a man who vows to take revenge on the hit-and-run driver who killed his son. Duchaussoy plays the father, and Yanne plays the insidious and much-hated killer. (115 mins.)†

This Man's Navy (1945)*** Wallace Beery, Tom Drake, Jan Clayton. Veteran officer in the balloon service "adopts" a lad and urges him to make good in the Navy. Familiar but well-done melodrama. (Dir: William Wellman, 100 mins.)

This Man Stands Alone (MTV 1979)** Louis Gossett, Jr., Clu Gulager, Lonny Chapman. Gossett is the only reason to watch this pilot film about a minister who becomes the sheriff of a small Alabama town. (Dir: Jerrold Freedman, 104 mins.)

This Modern Age (1931)**½ Joan Crawford, Pauline Frederick, Neil Hamilton, Monroe Owsley, Hobart Bosworth. Pretty good soap opera, with debutante Crawford reunited with her glamorous mother, who lives in Paris, and discovering that she's not exactly respectable. Stylish emoting brings life to the hackneyed story. (Dir: Nick Grinde, 76 mins.)

This Property Is Condemned (1966)**½ Natalie Wood, Robert Redford, Charles Bronson. The allure of stars Redford and Wood, plus the characters created by Tennessee Williams in a one-act play, are the chief inducements in this soap opera about a free spirit of a girl longing for adventure and true love. (Dir: Sydney Pollack, 110 mins.)†

This Rebel Age—See: *Beat Generation, The*

This Rebel Breed (1960)** Rita Moreno, Mark Damon, Gerald Mohr, Diane (later Dyan) Cannon. Undercover cops deal with narcotics and racial tensions in high school. (Dir: Richard L. Bare, 90 mins.)

This Savage Land (MTV 1968)** Barry Sullivan, Glenn Corbett, Kathryn Hays, George C. Scott. Sullivan stars as an Ohio widower heading out West with his family to start again in the 19th century. (Dir: Vincent McEveety, 97 mins.)

This Side of the Law (1950)** Viveca Lindfors, Kent Smith, Janis Paige. Contrived plot has Smith hired by a shady lawyer to impersonate a missing wealthy man. (Dir: Richard L. Bare, 74 mins.)

This Special Friendship (France, 1964)**½ Francis Lacombrade, Didier Haudepin, Lucien Nat. Gallic insights into the delicacy of youthful homoerotic bonds, set of course in a Catholic boarding school and smothering with the requisite sensitivity. Based on Roger Peyrefitte's novel, the film was directed by hack sentimentalist Jean Delannoy. (99 mins.)†

This Sporting Life (Great Britain, 1963)***½ Richard Harris, Rachel Roberts, Alan Badel. Strong drama about a bastard of a rugby player, played by Harris, the most mannered of his generation of working-class heroes, as well as the most histrionic—it's still his best performance. Kitchen sink realism featuring brutal sexuality. (Dir: Lindsay Anderson, 134 mins.)†

This Stuff'll Kill Ya! (1971)*½ Jeffrey Allen, Tim Holt, Gloria King. Oddball moonshine comedy courtesy of the guru of gore, director Herschell Gordon Lewis. Allen plays a demented Holy Roller who has every ''likker'' store in town selling his brew until a federal agent (Holt, in his last, very weary, screen appearance) begins to look into the matter. The 'shine inspires several violent episodes, including one bizarre crucifixion incident. (100 mins.)

This, That, and the Other (Great Britain, 1970)**½ Victor Spinetti, Vanessa Howard, Vanda Hudson, John Bird. Different tales of romance and duplicity are interwoven here, with the brightest moments coming when Spinetti takes center stage. He plays a down-in-the-mouth gentleman whose life begins again when he meets a carefree woman (Howard). No big laughs, but not a total loss, either. (Dir: Derek Ford, 85 mins.)

This Thing Called Love (1941)*** Rosalind Russell, Melvyn Douglas, Lee J. Cobb. Newlyweds agree to a three-month platonic arrangement to test their marriage. Nicely played, amusing, adult comedy. (Dir: Alexander Hall, 98 mins.)

This Time for Keeps (1947)** Esther Williams, Johnnie Johnston, Lauritz Melchior, Jimmy Durante, Xavier Cugat and his orchestra. Lamentable Williams musical. (Dir: Richard Thorpe, 105 mins.)

This Wife for Hire (MTV 1985)**½ Pam Dawber, Robert Klein, Laraine Newman, Dick Gautier, Sal Viscuso, Sam Jones, Ann Jillian. Dawber is married to Klein, but she offers her services as an all-around housewife (minus bedroom duties, of course) to a number of clients, including some very amorous bachelors. (Dir: James R. Drake, 104 mins.)

This Woman Is Dangerous (1952)**½ Joan Crawford, Dennis Morgan, David Brian. A must for Miss Crawford's legion of fans. She plays a typical Crawford role, that of a woman who finds love after she's been through the mill. Brian is quite good as a big-time mobster who can't let Joan go. (Dir: Felix E. Feist, 97 mins.)

This Woman Is Mine (1941)** Franchot Tone, John Carroll, Walter Brennan, Carol Bruce, Nigel Bruce, Paul Hurst, Leo G. Carroll. Uninvolving historical melodrama of a fur-trading voyage. Eventful but unmoving due to the emphasis on a romantic triangle. (Dir: Frank Lloyd, 91 mins.)

This Wonderful Crook (Switzerland, 1974) *** Gerard Depardieu, Marlene Jobert, Dominique Labourier, Philippe Léotard. Depardieu (in a sublime performance) takes over his ailing father's business only to discover it's nearly bankrupt. He begins robbing post offices and banks to raise cash, and soon finds himself in love with one of his victims. Absorbing drama about desperation and regret. (Dir: Claude Goretta, 110 mins.)

This Year's Blonde (MTV 1980)*½ Lloyd Bridges, Constance Forslund, Norman Fell, Vic Tayback, Michael Lerner, John Marley. Another segment from the miniseries *Moviola*, this examination of the picked-over corpse of poor Marilyn Monroe deals with her early starlet days under the aegis of Johnny Hyde, her agent. (Dir: John Erman, 104 mins.)

Thomas Crown Affair, The (1968)*** Steve McQueen, Faye Dunaway, Paul Burke, Jack Weston. Ingenious caper film with McQueen as the cool operator who masterminds a bank heist which is fascinating to follow. Dunaway, gorgeously costumed, plays an efficient insurance company investigator who falls prey to McQueen's charm. (Dir: Norman Jewison, 102 mins.)†

Thomasine and Bushrod (1974)*** Max Julien, Vonetta McGee, George Murdock, Glynn Turman, Juanita Moore. A tangy comedy-adventure about a black outlaw duo cutting a swath through Texas in the early 1900s. Above average blaxploitation. (Dir: Gordon Parks, Jr., 95 mins.)

Thompson's Last Run (MTV 1986)** Robert Mitchum, Wilford Brimley, Kathleen York, Guy Boyd, Royce Wallace, Tony Frank. In this opus, Mitchum is serving a life sentence and jumps at his niece's plan to spring him. Standard cops and convicts. (Dir: Jerrold Freedman, 104 mins.)†

Thornwell (MTV 1981)**½ Glynn Turman, Vincent Gardenia, Craig Wasson, Todd Susman, Julius Harris. This movie, based on a real-life case, deals with the U.S. Army's use of LSD on James Thornwell and the results of the experiment. Thornwell's case, which was taken up by ''60 Minutes'' and gained national attention, is well suited to the TV movie genre. (Dir: Harry Moses, 104 mins.)

Thoroughbreds Don't Cry (1937)**½ Mickey Rooney, Judy Garland, Sophie Tucker. Fairly good racetrack drama thanks to Rooney's expert playing of a jockey. (Dir: Alfred E. Green, 80 mins.)

Thoroughly Modern Millie (1967)*** Julie Andrews, James Fox, Mary Tyler Moore, Carol Channing, Beatrice Lillie. Musical extravaganza with songs, dances, and marvelous comedy sequences. Andrews is a delight as the heroine who finds true love in the person of Fox, but not until she dances and warbles her way through many imaginative production numbers. Channing and Lillie are wonderful in the film's chief supporting roles. Oscar: Best Scoring. (Dir: George Roy Hill, 138 mins.)†

Those Calloways (1965)*** Brian Keith, Vera Miles, Brandon De Wilde, Linda Evans. Homespun, rustic drama with a good cast. The Calloways are good people who dream of building a bird sanctuary near a lake, but the townspeople have different ideas and thwart the enterprise all the way down the line. (Dir: Norman Tokar, 131 mins.)†

Those Daring Young Men in Their Jaunty Jalopies (Italy-France-Great Britain, 1969)** Tony Curtis, Susan Hampshire, Peter Cook, Terry-Thomas. A lumbering, disappointing effort to duplicate *Those Magnificent Men in Their Flying Machines*. About a 1,500-mile endurance race in the twenties, all heading for Monte Carlo but starting at five different locales. (Dir: Ken Annakin, 93 mins.)

Those Endearing Young Charms (1945)**½ Robert Young, Laraine Day, Bill Williams, Ann Harding, Marc Cramer, Anne Jeffreys, Glenn Vernon. Weightless romantic comedy with a triangle between Young, Williams, and Day. OK of this kind, but nothing spectacular. (Dir: Lewis Allen, 81 mins.)

Those Fantastic Flying Fools (Great Britain, 1967)** Burl Ives, Troy Donahue, Gert Frobe, Hermione Gingold, Lionel Jefferies, Daliah Lavi, Stratford Johns, Terry-Thomas. Farcical sci-fi *very* loosely adapted from Jules Verne's *Rocket to the Moon*. Circus master Ives wants to send "General Tom Thumb" into lunar orbit, but can't find any way to make the voyage a round-trip. Too many stars and too few laughs. (Dir: Don Sharp, 95 mins.)

Those Glory, Glory Days (Great Britain, 1985)** Julia McKenzie, Elizabeth Spriggs, Julia Goodman, Rachael Meidman. A small-scale tale of adolescent passage. A thirteen-year-old girl who's mad about soccer drives parents and teachers buggy, so she grows up to be a noted sports reporter. So what? (Dir: Philip Saville, 91 mins.)†

Those Lips, Those Eyes (1980)*** Frank Langella, Glynnis O'Connor, Thomas Hulce. All the clichés about coming of age and about the life of the theater are on display in this sappily sensitive saga of a college junior's summer love affair with a stock operetta company. Langella is the fading matinee lead waiting for the big break that will never come. (Dir: Michael Pressman, 107 mins.)†

Those Magnificent Men in Their Flying Machines (Great Britain, 1965)*** Stuart Whitman, Sarah Miles, Terry-Thomas, James Fox, Robert Morley. A lavish, wonderfully photographed comedy-adventure about an air race from London to Paris during the early days of aviation. International cast finds Whitman as an American cowboy swapping his horse for an airplane, and Terry-Thomas is one of the most lovable villains movies have ever served up. (Dir: Ken Annakin, 133 mins.)†

Those Redheads from Seattle (1953)** Rhonda Fleming, Gene Barry, Teresa Brewer, Guy Mitchell. Music and murder try but don't mix in this tale about the Gold Rush. (Dir: Lewis R. Foster, 90 mins.)

Those She Left Behind (MTV 1989)**½ Gary Cole, Colleen Dewhurst, Joanna Kerns. Cole plays a bewildered young dad left with an infant son after his wife dies in childbirth. Soft story heavy on sentiment about a man unable to cope with childhood and hating himself for it. Hurt by a pat ending. (Dir: Waris Hussein, 96 mins.)

Those Were the Days (1940)**½ Bill Holden, Bonita Granville, Ezra Stone. Silly, but often amusing comedy about college back in the horse and buggy days. (Dir: Theodore Reed, 76 mins.)

Those Wonderful Men With a Crank (Czechoslovakia, 1978)*** Rudolf Hrusinsky, Jiri Menzel, Blazena Holisova, Vlasta Fabianova, Vladimir Mensik. Beguiling and endearing comedy-drama set in 1907 about a man who travels to small towns to show one-reel movies to residents until he makes enough money to build the first cinema in Prague. Loving, atmospheric tribute to movies. (Dir: Jiri Menzel, 90 mins.)

Thousand and One Nights, A (1945)**½ Cornel Wilde, Evelyn Keyes, Phil Silvers, Adele Jergens. A lush studio fantasy that takes a slightly dated, tongue-in-cheek approach to its material. Wilde is Aladdin, a singer who gets to hook up with a princess (Jergens) through the graces of a voluptuous genie (Keyes). (Dir: Alfred E. Green, 92 mins.)

Thousand Clowns, A (1965)***½ Jason Robards, Jr., Barbara Harris, Martin Balsam, Barry Gordon, Gene Saks. A touching, wacky comedy based on Herb Gardner's Broadway hit. Robards winningly re-creates his role of the nonconformist writer, determined to make his teenage nephew charge (Gordon) wise before his time. The supporting characters are beautifully played. (Dir: Fred Coe, 118 mins.)†

Thousand Eyes of Dr. Mabuse, The (France-Italy-West Germany, 1960)*** Peter Van Eyck, Gert Frobe, Dawn Addams. The final part of director Fritz Lang's trilogy about Dr. Mabuse. In the comic book story, the criminal genius has come to life again and detective Frobe is after him. AKA: **The Secret of Dr. Mabuse.** (103 mins.)

Thousand Plane Raid, The (1969)* Christopher George, Laraine Stephens, J. D. Cannon, Michael Evans, Gary Marshall. A dangerous mission, led by George, attempts to destroy Germany's main airplane factory. (Dir: Boris Sagal, 84 mins.)

Thousands Cheer (1943)*** Gene Kelly, Kathryn Grayson, Mary Astor, José Iturbi, Kay Kyser and his orchestra, Lionel Barrymore, Margaret O'Brien, Judy Garland, Mickey Rooney, June Allyson, Red Skelton, Lena Horne. Another all-star WWII musical, glossy and patriotic, full of snappy tunes. (Dir: George Sidney, 126 mins.)†

Thou Shalt Not Commit Adultery (MTV 1978)** Louise Fletcher, Robert Reed, Wayne Rogers. Fletcher's character is encouraged by her husband (Reed), after he is incapacitated in an automobile accident, to seek a sexual outlet elsewhere, and the lady picks a golf pro (Rogers). (Dir: Delbert Mann, 104 mins.)

Thou Shalt Not Kill (MTV 1982)* Lee Grant, Michael Gwynne, Lane Smith, Albert Salmi, Diana Scarwid. Ponderous, boring drama concerns a lady lawyer (Lee Grant) determined to clear an innocent young mechanic (Gary Graham) on two murder raps. (Dir: I. C. Rapaport, 104 mins.)

Thou Shalt Not Kill...Except (1987)* Brian Schulz, John Manfredi, Robert Rickman, Tim Quill, Sam Raimi. Incompetent, gory horror movie about a Manson-like cult of cannibalistic killers. Would the *Evil Dead* director Raimi, who plays the cult's leader, had been behind the camera rather than in front of it. (Dir: Josh Becker, 94 mins.)

Thrashin' (1986)½ Josh Brolin, Pamela Gidley, Chuck McCann. Professional skateboarding enthusiasts will be the only interested viewers for this asinine outing about a California kid newly arrived in L.A. battling a nasty group of leather-and-chains-clad street skaters. (Dir: David Winters, 92 mins.)†

Threads (Great Britain, MTV 1985)**** Reece Dinsdale, Karen Meagher. A powerful drama dealing with the horrible aftereffects in the thirteen years following a fictional nuclear war between the Soviet Union and the U.S. Set in Sheffield, England, *Threads* pulls no punches in depicting the deterioration of civilization in the nuclear winter that devastates mankind. Told from the vantage points of both a working-class and middle-class family, the scenario is the most

convincing anti-nuclear drama to date. (Dir: Mick Jackson, 125 mins.)†

Threat, The (1949)*** Charles McGraw, Michael O'Shea, Virginia Grey. An escaped killer plans to avenge himself on those who sent him up. Fast, violent melodrama. (Dir: Charles R. Rondeau, 66 mins.)

Three Ages, The (1923)** Buster Keaton, Wallace Beery, Margaret Leahy, Joe Roberts, Lilian Lawrence, Oliver Hardy. Keaton's first feature-length film is a parody of the historical epics of Griffith and DeMille with three stories, one of a hapless caveman, one set in Roman times, and one contemporary. All are hilariously funny, if not quite as elegantly brilliant as Keaton's later features. (Dirs: Buster Keaton, Eddie Cline, 85 mins.)†

Three Amigos (1986)**½ Chevy Chase, Steve Martin, Martin Short, Patrice Martinez, Jon Lovitz. Despite the overproduction, this is an endearing spoof of Mexican bandit movies. Given those built-in limitations, and the fact that this plays like an overelaboration on a Three Stooges short subject (only the Stooges would have been funnier), this is a colorful send-up with some inspired moments, although the comedy eventually runs out of steam. (Dir: John Landis, 103 mins.)†

Three Bad Men (1926)*** George O'Brien, Lou Tellegen, J. Farrell MacDonald, Tom Santschi. An early version of the sentimental Peter B. Kyle fable about three outlaws who find a baby in the desert and adopt it. This heartwarming tale was remade as a talkie by Ford as *Three Godfathers,* and its lovely qualities have survived several remakes. (Dir: John Ford, 92 mins.)

Three Bad Sisters (1956)** Marla English, Kathleen Hughes, Sara Shane, John Bromfield. Campy fun. A woman schemes to bump off her two sisters in order to inherit all of her late father's estate. A good-looking pilot throws a monkey wrench into her plans, though, and the results are high-pitched, sex-ridden melodrama. (Dir: Gilbert L. Kay, 76 mins.)

Three Bites of the Apple (1967)** David McCallum, Tammy Grimes, Sylvia Koscina, Harvey Korman. A hokey story about tour guide (McCallum) winning a fortune at the gambling casino and becoming prey for an adventuress (Koscina). (Dir: Alvin Ganzer, 105 mins.)

Three Blind Mice (1938)**½ Loretta Young, Joel McCrea, David Niven. Pretty good comedy with the all too familiar plot about three girls who try to marry millionaires. (Dir: William A. Seiter, 76 mins.)

Three Brave Men (1957)**½ Ray Milland, Ernest Borgnine, Frank Lovejoy, Nina Foch. Borgnine portrays a government employee who is asked to resign after years of loyal service because he has been labeled a "security risk." How this affects his life and family and the fight he puts up for reinstatement constitutes the bulk of the plot. (Dir: Philip Dunne, 88 mins.)

Three Broadway Girls—See: **Greeks Had a Word for Them, The**

Three Brothers (Italy, 1980)**** Philippe Noiret, Charles Vanel, Michele Placido. Extraordinary film follows three brothers as they return to their family homestead for their mother's funeral. Expressing different walks of life, the three men's contemplations about their personal lives and their country's political future are juxtaposed with their father's remembrances of his wedding day. The film skillfully expresses both political and social concerns, as well as examining the family relationships. (Dir: Francesco Rosi, 111 mins.)†

Three Caballeros, The (1945)***½ Dora Luz, Aurora Miranda, Carmen Molina, Donald Duck, Jose Carioca, Panchito, voices of Sterling Holloway, Clarence Nash, Jose Oliveira, Joaquin Garay. Spectacular, greatly underrated, Walt Disney tribute to Latin America made at the behest of the U.S. State Department. Colorful film combines live action with animation and foot-tapping musical numbers including: "You Belong to My Heart," "Baia," and "Os Quindins de Ya Ya," sung by Aurora Miranda, Carmen's sister. (Dir: Norman Ferguson, 72 mins.)

Three Came Home (1950)*** Claudette Colbert, Patric Knowles, Sessue Hayakawa. Good drama concerns the tortures undergone by captive women in a Japanese internment camp. Performances effective, particularly Hayakawa as the commandant. (Dir: Jean Negulesco, 106 mins.)†

Three Cases of Murder (Great Britain, 1954)*** Orson Welles, Alan Badel, Elizabeth Sellars. A trio of tales: (1) Ghostly doings in an art gallery. (2) Two suspects when a girl is murdered. (3) A powerful lord is plagued by the memory of a House member he has publicly humiliated. All in all, above average. (Dirs: Wendy Toye, David Eady, and George More O'Ferrall, 99 mins.)

Three Charlies and One Phoney! (1914–18) *** Video compilation featuring three rare Charlie Chaplin comedies and an even rarer short featuring one of the many Chaplin imitators of the day. The improvised *Recreation* has Charlie getting in trouble for talking to the girlfriend of a sleeping sailor. *His Musical Career* features Chaplin and Charles Parrott (before he changed his name to Charley Chase) in an early version of the script later filmed as *The Music Box* with Laurel and Hardy. Brother Syd and Edna Purviance help Chaplin sell war bonds in *The Bond*. Finally, Billy West offers

an exacting Chaplin impersonation in *His Day Out*. Recommended more for serious Chaplinophiles than for general audiences. (69 mins.)†

Three Cheers for the Irish (1940)**½ Thomas Mitchell, Dennis Morgan, Priscilla Lane, Irene Hervey. Entertaining little film about an Irish cop who is honored after his retirement from the force by being elected alderman. (Dir: Lloyd Bacon, 100 mins.)

Three Coins in the Fountain (1954)**½ Clifton Webb, Louis Jourdan, Dorothy McGuire, Jean Peters, Maggie McNamara. Romance is the keynote in this pleasant comedy drama about three American secretaries in the Eternal City, Rome. (Dir: Jean Negulesco, 102 mins.)†

Three Comrades (1938)***½ Robert Taylor, Robert Young, Margaret Sullavan, Franchot Tone, Lionel Atwill. Erich Remarque's novel about post-WWI Germany is turned into a sensitive film. Not much on plot but deep in mood and character study. Margaret Sullavan is superb as a girl in love with an unsettled, sick veteran of the losing side. (Dir: Frank Borzage, 98 mins.)

Three-Cornered Moon (1933)** Claudette Colbert, Richard Arlen, Mary Boland, Wallace Ford, Lyda Roberti. In this wacky Depression-era comedy, a once-rich family is forced to earn a living. Being based upon a play restricts its scope, and some of the jokes are quite dated. Zany without being funny. (Dir: Elliot Nugent, 77 mins.)

Three Daring Daughters (1948)**½ Jeanette MacDonald, Jane Powell, José Iturbi, Edward Arnold. Daughters of a lady magazine editor have trouble adjusting themselves to her new husband. (Dir: Fred M. Wilcox, 115 mins.)

Three Days of the Condor (1975)*** Robert Redford, Faye Dunaway, Cliff Robertson, Max von Sydow, John Houseman. An intriguing, suspenseful spy story involving double agents, all of them, supposedly working for the CIA. Redford plays a CIA agent paid to read books while working for a covert operation in New York. All Redford's colleagues are murdered one afternoon. Surprising plot twists along the way before "Condor" finds out who was trying to kill him and why. (Dir: Sydney Pollack, 118 mins.)†

Three Desperate Men (1951)**½ Preston Foster, Jim Davis, Virginia Grey. Two deputies ride to save their brother from unjust punishment, but circumstances force all three outside the law. Above average western drama with good characterizations. (Dir: Sam Newfield, 71 mins.)

Three Faces East (1930)***½ Constance Bennett, Erich von Stroheim, William Courtenay, Charlotte Walker, Anthony Bushell, William Holden. Little-known early sound gem about a German spy (Bennett, in a grand performance) who infiltrates a British war minister's home in order to learn of invasion plans during WWI. Von Stroheim is sensational as a butler who may also be a spy. Technically outstanding, with magnificent production values and solid direction by Roy Del Ruth. (71 mins.)

Three Faces of Eve, The (1957)** Joanne Woodward, David Wayne, Lee J. Cobb, Nancy Kulp, Vince Edwards. Heavily meaningful foray into psychology (it even boasts narration by Alistair Cooke) that seemed interesting to audiences of the fifties, but now seems shallow. Woodward plays a woman with three distinct personalities. (Dir: Nunnally Johnson, 91 mins.)†

Three Faces West (1940)**½ John Wayne, Sigrid Gurie, Charles Coburn, Spencer Charters, Roland Varno. The Duke takes charge of Austrian refugees headed for resettlement in Oregon during WWII. Unusual frontier tale, a combination of western action and anti-Nazi propaganda that works intermittently. (Dir: Bernard Vorhaus, 79 mins.)

3:15—The Moment of Truth (1984)** Adam Baldwin, Deborah Foreman, Danny De La Paz, René Auberjonois, Ed Lauter, Mario Van Peebles, Wings Hauser. Tired of their violent ways, high schooler Baldwin quits the gang he belonged to, but gangleader De La Paz isn't about to let him go back to being an average student. From the public-school-as-urban-nightmare genre, none too deep. (Dir: Larry Gross, 86 mins.)†

Three for Bedroom C (1952)** Gloria Swanson, James Warren, Fred Clark. A glamorous screen star romances a scientist aboard a transcontinental train. Labored comedy never is as funny as it should be. (Dir: Milton Bren, 74 mins.)†

Three for Jamie Dawn (1956)** Laraine Day, Ricardo Montalbán, Richard Carlson, June Havoc. Ho-hum drama of jury members having the screws turned on them to free a defendant after three of the jurors are bribed. (Dir: Thomas Carr, 81 mins.)

Three for the Road (MTV 1975)** Alex Rocco, Julie Sommars, Vincent Van Patten, Leif Garrett. Sentimental yarn of the photographer-father of two sons who takes to the road after the death of his wife. (Dir: Boris Sagal, 78 mins.)

Three for the Road (1987)*½ Charlie Sheen, Kerri Green, Alan Ruck. Ridiculous teen road-pic featuring three misfits out on a spree. Congressional aide (Sheen) is selected to deposit a senator's daughter in a school for troubled teens; instead, he, his pal, and the girl tear off down life's highway. (Dir: B. W. L. Norton, 90 mins.)†

Three for the Show (1955)** Betty Grable,

Jack Lemmon, Marge and Gower Champion. Downright foolish musical comedy about a Broadway star who believes her first husband dead in the war and marries his best friend. Hubby No. 1 shows up intact and the mad whirl begins. (Dir: H. C. Potter, 93 mins.)

Three Fugitives (1989)**½ Nick Nolte, Martin Short, James Earl Jones, Kenneth McMillan. Reformed thief Nolte, just out of prison, finds himself back on the lam when he's taken "hostage" by bumbling bank robber Short. Knockabout comedy is best when going for slapstick laughs, weaker when it switches to sticky sentiment. (Dir: Francis Veber, 96 mins.)†

Three Girls About Town (1941)**½ Joan Blondell, Binnie Barnes, Janet Blair. Three wise girls try to hide a body found in a hotel, to save the hotel's reputation. Amusing farce. (Dir: Leigh Jason, 73 mins.)

Three Godfathers (1936)**½ Chester Morris, Lewis Stone, Walter Brennan, Irene Hervey. A western that shows bad guys transformed into good guys as they care for an infant in the desert. Although the story line wanders, the second half is quite moving, and the plot is sturdy enough to have been remade and revamped several times. (Dir: Richard Boleslawski, 82 mins.)

Three Godfathers (1948)**** John Wayne, Pedro Armendariz, Harry Carey, Jr., Ward Bond, Jane Darwell, Mildred Natwick. Ford cuts past the postcard plot to integrate with his notions of how society functions with his view of religion in that scheme of things. The Christmas charm is never cloying, the sense of mortality always palpable, and the film is a masterpiece. Three bad (wise) men, the apostles of civilization, and Natwick in an impressive turn as the not-so-virgin Mary consigned to a dusty fate, are all delicately, movingly acted. (Dir: John Ford, 105 mins.)†

Three Guns for Texas (1968)**½ Neville Brand, Peter Brown, Bill Smith, Martin Milner, Philip Carey. Theatrical feature comprised of three episodes of the TV series "Laredo," strung together to make a passable comedy-western. (Dirs: David Lowell Rich, Paul Stanley, Earl Bellamy, 99 mins.)

Three Guys Named Mike (1951)**½ Jane Wyman, Van Johnson, Howard Keel, Barry Sullivan. Small town girl finds herself the object of assorted Romeos when she becomes an airline stewardess. Pleasing comedy. (Dir: Charles Walters, 90 mins.)

Three Hearts for Julia (1942)** Ann Sothern, Melvyn Douglas. Well-played, but nonsensical farce about a man courting his wife while they're getting a divorce. (Dir: Richard Thorpe, 89 mins.)

Three Hours to Kill (1954)*** Dana Andrews, Donna Reed, Dianne Foster, Carolyn Jones. Andrews rides into town to find the man who killed his former sweetheart's brother. He has three hours to do so. Tight and tense western with good performances. (Dir: Alfred L. Werker, 77 mins.)

300 Miles for Stephanie (MTV 1981)** Tony Orlando, Peter Graves, Edward James Olmos, Pepe Serna, Julie Carmen, Gregory Sierra. Tony Orlando makes his dramatic TV movie debut as a father of a stricken girl. He runs a 300-mile marathon as a promise to God to help his little girl. (Dir: Clyde Ware, 104 mins.)

300 Spartans, The (1962)**½ Richard Egan, Diane Baker, Ralph Richardson. Relatively small band of soldiers stand against a mighty army of Persia in a fight for free Greece. (Dir: Rudolph Maté, 114 mins.)

Three Husbands (1950)*** Emlyn Williams, Eve Arden, Vanessa Brown. A recently deceased playboy leaves a note saying he was intimate with one of three wives, and their husbands intend to find out which one. Bright, well-acted sophisticated comedy. (Dir: Irving Reis, 78 mins.)

Three in the Attic (1969)* Christopher Jones, Yvette Mimieux, Nan Martin. College womanizer Jones meets his waterloo in the person of three of his conquests who team up to teach him a lesson. (Dir: Richard Wilson, 92 mins.)†

Three in the Cellar (1970)** Wes Stern, Larry Hagman, Joan Collins. Dated but occasionally witty tale of young poet Stern seeking revenge on politically ambitious college president Hagman by seducing his wife, daughter, and mistress. AKA: **Up in the Cellar**. (Dir: Theodore J. Flicker, 92 mins.)†

Three Into Two Won't Go (Great Britain, 1969)*** Rod Steiger, Claire Bloom, Judy Geeson, Peggy Ashcroft. Familiar tale of the man approaching forty who finds his marriage difficult and seeks ego fulfillment with a cooperative young lady. (Dir: Peter Hall, 93 mins.)

Three Is a Family (1944)*** Charlie Ruggles, Fay Bainter, Marjorie Reynolds, Helen Broderick, Arthur Lake. Eventful domestic comedy, with plenty of laughs. (Dir: Edward Ludwig, 81 mins.)

Three Kinds of Heat (1987)**½ Robert Ginty, Victoria Barrett, Shakti. U.S. agent Ginty and two Amazonian aides, New York cop Barrett and Mongolian officer Shakti, track international terrorists in this enjoyably tongue-in-cheek actioner. (Dir: Leslie Stevens, 87 mins.)†

Three Kings, The (MTV 1987)**½ Jack Warden, Stan Shaw, Lou Diamond Phillips, Jane Kaczmarek. Christmas fable

about three mental patients who believe they are the three wise men of the Bible. Pleasant holiday sentiment, with Warden a standout. (Dir: Mel Damski, 96 mins.)

Three Little Girls in Blue (1946)**½ June Haver, Vivian Blaine, Vera-Ellen, George Montgomery. A tuneful score, attractive cast and a good production make up for the flimsy tale of the girls in search of millionaires. (Dir: H. Bruce Humberstone, 90 mins.)

Three Little Words (1950)*** Fred Astaire, Debbie Reynolds, Red Skelton, Vera-Ellen, Arlene Dahl. If you like musicals with many production numbers, good dancing, pretty girls, and very little plot, this is right up your alley. The stars play tunesmiths Bert Kalmar and Harry Ruby and this is their story of how they made the big time. (Dir: Richard Thorpe, 102 mins.)†

Three Lives of Thomasina, The (U.S.-Great Britain, 1963)**½ Patrick McGoohan, Susan Hampshire, Karen Dotrice. Disney story of a veterinarian's daughter who loses her will to live after her cat has been put to sleep, has a nice fairy tale quality. (Dir: Don Chaffey, 97 mins.)†

Three Loves Has Nancy (1938)**½ Janet Gaynor, Robert Montgomery, Franchot Tone. Two bachelor friends and a girl between them is the focus of this pleasant, well-written, and played little comedy. (Dir: Richard Thorpe, 70 mins.)

Three Men and a Baby (1987)** Ted Danson, Tom Selleck, Steve Guttenberg, Nancy Travis, Margaret Colin. Three successful bachelors find themselves with an unwanted baby; smash hit is bogged down by a banal plot that drags the viewer through little more than a handful of funny moments. Remake of *Three Men and a Cradle*. Sequel: *Three Men and a Little Lady*. (Dir: Leonard Nimoy, 99 mins.)†

Three Men and a Cradle (France, 1985)**½ Roland Giraud, Michel Boujenah, Andrew Dussolier, Philippine Leroy Beaulieu. Winner of several French Academy Awards, this is a slight, bittersweet comedy about three bachelors into whose carefree lives a baby falls; soon they prove there's a little bit of the mother instinct in us all. (Dir: Coline Serreau, 100 mins.)†

Three Men and a Little Lady (1990)* Tom Selleck, Steve Guttenberg, Ted Danson, Nancy Travis, Sheila Hancock, Fiona Shaw. Fey and tediously unfunny sequel to *Three Men and a Baby*. The kid's a bit older, the men still aren't married, and mommy's in love with a possessive British theater director. (Dir: Emile Ardolino, 100 mins.)†

Three Men in a Boat (Great Britain, 1956)***

Laurence Harvey, Martita Hunt, Shirley Eaton, Jill Ireland. Bright British comedy about three young men who have a field day on a happy excursion up the Thames. (Dir: Ken Annakin, 84 mins.)

Three Men In White (1944)** Lionel Barrymore, Van Johnson, Keye Luke, Ava Gardner. Routine Dr. Gillespie film with the old boy looking for an assistant and trying to decide between Keye Luke and Van. (Dir: Willis Goldbeck, 85 mins.)

Three Men on a Horse (1936)***½ Sam Levene, Joan Blondell, Teddy Hart, Frank McHugh. One of our comedy classics. Story of the mild-mannered chap who can pick winners and the characters who try and use him is always good for laughs. (Dir: Mervyn LeRoy, 85 mins.)

Three Musketeers, The (1935)*** Walter Abel, Ian Keith, Onslow Stevens, Paul Lukas. Dumas's classic of the dashing D'Artagnan who joins the King's Musketeers. Acceptable version of famous adventure tale. (Dir: Rowland V. Lee, 96 mins.)

Three Musketeers, The (1939)** Don Ameche, Lionel Atwill, Ritz Brothers. Dumas's famous adventure novel, faithfully adapted except that the Ritzes appear in the title role. Mixture isn't good comedy or drama. (Dir: Allan Dwan, 73 mins.)

Three Musketeers, The (1948)*** Lana Turner, Gene Kelly, June Allyson. Dumas's classic as presented here is good juvenile action film set in France at the time of Louis XIII. (Dir: George Sidney, 125 mins.)†

Three Musketeers, The (Great Britain 1974)***½ Oliver Reed, Michael York, Raquel Welch, Richard Chamberlain, Faye Dunaway, Charlton Heston. A joyous whirlwind of an adventure comedy. In between there is a slew of fabulous sight gags from inventive director Richard Lester and his international cast, with big-name stars playing bit parts. Heston is Cardinal Richelieu and York is D'Artagnan, who understandably wants to seduce the married neighborhood seamstress (Welch). Gorgeous period costumes. Sequel: *The Four Musketeers*. (105 mins.)†

3 Nuts in Search of a Bolt (1964)* Mamie Van Doren, Tommy Noonan, Paul Gilbert, T. C. Jones, Alvy Moore. Sitcom farce with unemployed actor Noonan hired by three neurotics so that he can visit a psychiatrist and obtain cures for all of them at a discount. Originally an "adults only" feature because of a few inserted scenes with Van Doren as a stripper, but it's nothing you couldn't let the kids watch now (not that they'd laugh at it either). (Dir: Tommy Noonan, 80 mins.)†

Three O'Clock High (1987)*½ Casey Siemaszko, Anne Ryan, Stacey Glick, Jeffrey Tambor. A slight tale is given flashy but empty direction by Spielberg protege Phil Joanou. A nerdy kid upsets a new bully in school and spends the day in terror since the bully has threatened to settle up with him after class. (90 mins.)†

3 on a Couch (1966)* Jerry Lewis, Janet Leigh, Mary Ann Mobley. Remember the witty quip to a psychiatrist, "If I'm late start without me"? Well, Jerry started and finished this one without a script while trying to persuade *his* psychiatrist (Janet Leigh) to marry him. (Dir: Jerry Lewis, 109 mins.)

Three on a Date (MTV 1978)** June Allyson, Ray Bolger, Rick Nelson, Forbesy Russell. Adaptation of a book by Stephanie Buffington (played by Russell), a real-life chaperone to winning couples on TV's "The Dating Game," spruced up with guest stars and silly subplots. (Dir: Bill Bixby, 104 mins.)

Three on a Match (1932)** Joan Blondell, Bette Davis, Ann Dvorak, Edward Arnold, Humphrey Bogart. Three schoolmates take different paths—one a chorine, one a stenographer, the third a millionaire's wife. Interesting melodrama. Remade as *Broadway Musketeers*. (Dir: Mervyn LeRoy, 64 mins.)†

Three on a Match (MTV 1987)*½ Patrick Cassidy, David Hemmings, Bruce A. Young. Three convicts go on the lam after escaping from a Southern prison. The numerous good deeds they do help to feed the film's unbelievability; lame vehicle for Cassidy. (Dir: Don Bellisario, 96 mins.)

Three on a Meat Hook (1972)** Charles Kissinger, James Pickett, Sherry Steiner, Madelyn Buzzard. Horror movie about backwoods cannibals, a cross between *Texas Chainsaw Massacre* and *Psycho* (and derived from the same true case as those two films). A low-budget, amateurish effort that gets a creepy atmosphere from those limitations. Plenty of fake-looking gore effects by H. G. Lewis associate Pat Patterson. (Dir: William Girdler, 79 mins.)†

Threepenny Opera, The (Germany, 1931)*** Rudolf Forster, Vladimir Sokoloff, Lotte Lenya, Valeska Gert, Reinhold Schunzel. Film of Bertolt Brecht's musical play, which was inspired by John Gay's *The Beggar's Opera*. Brecht strongly disapproved of this version directed by G. W. Pabst, and it's easy to see why: it isn't very pointed, and the mounting is undynamic. Still, the cast is good and the design rich in atmospheric detail. (111 mins.)†

Three Ring Circus (1954)** Dean Martin,

Jerry Lewis, Zsa Zsa Gabor. Dean and Jerry join the circus for a mild amount of fun. Not their best, nor their worst. (Dir: Joseph Pevney, 103 mins.)

Three's a Crowd (MTV 1969)**½ Larry Hagman, Jessica Walter, E. J. Peaker. Made-for-TV comedy about bigamy. You'll probably stay with it to see whether husband Larry Hagman chooses wife #1 (E. J. Peaker) or wife #2 (Jessica Walter). (Dir: Harry Falk, 75 mins.)

Three Sailors and a Girl (1953)**½ Jane Powell, Gordon MacRae, Gene Nelson, Jack E. Leonard. Not to be confused with *Two Girls and a Sailor, Three Gobs and a Gal,* or *Two Sailors and Two Girls,* but if you do, it won't matter. It's all the same, anyway. (Dir: Roy Del Ruth, 95 mins.)

Three Secrets (1950)*** Eleanor Parker, Ruth Roman, Patricia Neal. Good soaper. Through flashbacks it tells the story of the three women as they wait word of their loved ones involved in a fatal air crash on a mountain. (Dir: Robert Wise, 99 mins.)†

Three Sisters, The (1965)**½ Kim Stanley, Geraldine Page, Sandy Dennis, Shelley Winters. A taped version of Anton Chekhov's play as performed in cooperation with the Actors' Studio. The drama of loneliness and frustration receives uneven treatment, with some brilliantly acted bits. (Dir: Lee Strasberg, 168 mins.)

Three Sisters, The (Great Britain, 1970) ***½ Laurence Olivier, Joan Plowright, Alan Bates, Jeanne Watts, Louise Purnell. Probably Olivier's best job of direction (with John Sichel). The performances, while shy of lusty, are impeccable, superbly modulated, and very moving. (165 mins.)

Three Smart Girls (1936)*** Deanna Durbin, Charles Winninger, Ray Milland. Delightful comedy about three sisters trying to keep their father away from a scheming woman. Durbin's voice is an asset. (Dir: Henry Koster, 90 mins.)

Three Smart Girls Grow Up (1939)*** Deanna Durbin, Robert Cummings, Charles Winninger. Light comedy about family involvements, notably the gay romances of three sisters. Charming Deanna is a delight. (Dir: Henry Koster, 73 mins.)

Threesome (MTV 1984)**½ Stephen Collins, Deborah Raffin, Joel Higgins. An attractive trio—Collins, Raffin, and Higgins—are caught up in a New York love triangle. This is supposed to be light-hearted romance but, despite the scenery, style, and easygoing acting, *Threesome* gets tiresome. (Dir: Lou Antonio, 104 mins.)

Three Sovereigns for Sarah (MTV 1985)**½ Vanessa Redgrave, Phyllis Thaxter, Kim Hunter, Patrick McGoohan. Originally presented as a three-episode series on PBS's "American Playhouse," this drama about the Salem witch hunt improves as it goes along. Redgrave plays Sarah, who goes to a magistrate looking to clear the names of her two sisters, who were hanged as witches. The production is severely lackluster at times, but Redgrave, as ever, is splendid. (Dir: Philip Leacock, 152 mins.)†

Three Stooges Go Around the World in a Daze, The (1963)* Three Stooges, Jay Sheffield, Joan Freeman. Slapstick Stooges team up with Fogg's descendant for a modern-day attempt. (Dir: Norman Maurer, 94 mins.)

Three Stooges in Orbit, The (1962)** The Three Stooges, Carol Christensen. The boys run across a Martian agent after a professor's new invention. (Dir: Edward Bernds, 87 mins.)

Three Stooges Meet Hercules, The (1962)** The Three Stooges, Vicki Trickett. The boys land in a time machine which takes them back to the days of kings and slaves. (Dir: Edward Bernds, 89 mins.)†

Three Strangers (1946)*** Sydney Greenstreet, Geraldine Fitzgerald, Peter Lorre. Interesting, well-played but contrived melodrama about three strangers who become partners on a sweepstakes ticket and the intrigue of their individual lives. (Dir: Jean Negulesco, 92 mins.)

Three Stripes in the Sun (1955)**½ Aldo Ray, Dick York, Phil Carey, Chuck Connors. Formerly prejudiced against the Japanese, a GI Sergeant falls in love with a Japanese translator and is torn by his old beliefs. Reasonably interesting. (Dir: Richard Murphy, 93 mins.)

3:10 to Yuma (1957)***½ Glenn Ford, Van Heflin, Felicia Farr. One of the best western dramas, almost in the league of *Shane* and *High Noon.* A farmer takes the job of bringing a notorious killer into Yuma because he needs the money. They have to wait together in a hotel room until the train for Yuma arrives. (Dir: Delmer Daves, 92 mins.)†

Three the Hard Way (1974)**½ Jim Brown, Fred Williamson, Jim Kelly, Sheila Frazier, Jay Robinson. A surprisingly unviolent thriller, highly implausible but well constructed at a pulsating pace. Robinson plays a white supremacist out to exterminate blacks by putting a serum in the water supply; Brown, Williamson, and Kelly are the dudes out to stop him. (Dir: Gordon Parks, Jr., 93 mins.)†

3,000 Mile Chase, The (MTV 1977)* Cliff De Young, Glenn Ford, Blair Brown, David Spielberg. Pilot with De Young cast as a courier with many identities, dispatched to bring back Ford (a star witness in a trial of a Mafia hit man). (Dir: Russ Mayberry, 104 mins.)

Three Violent People (1956)**½ Charlton Heston, Anne Baxter, Gilbert Roland, Tom Tryon. An action-filled western yarn for horse opera fans. Heston is appropriately cast in the role of a rancher who puts up a valiant fight against the illegal land grabbers. (Dir: Rudolph Maté, 100 mins.)

Three Wise Fools (1946)**½ Margaret O'Brien, Lionel Barrymore, Lewis Stone, Edward Arnold, Thomas Mitchell, Ray Collins, Jane Darwell, Henry O'Neill, Cyd Charisse. Trying to get their hands on her inheritance, three businessmen adopt a little girl (O'Brien); of course, they're soon won over by her. Oversentimental at times, this still has charm, and watching the contest between the three old pros is a treat in itself. (Dir: Edward Buzzell, 90 mins.)

Three Wise Girls (1931)** Jean Harlow, Mae Clarke, Marie Prevost, Walter Byron, Andy Devine, Natalie Moorhead. Pert, pre-Code comedy of a small-town girl coming to New York, making it as a fashion model, and falling for a shifty man-about-town who's already married; rather episodic script and pedestrian direction, but Harlow is Harlow. (Dir: William Beaudine, 68 mins.)

Three Wishes of Billy Grier, The (MTV 1984)*½ Ralph Macchio, Betty Buckley, Jeffrey Tambor, Hal Holbrook, Season Hubley. There is a rare blood disease that ages its victims rapidly in this silly, over-sentimental and ultimately boring drama. Macchio plays the victim, and his aging makeup and performance belong in a high-school production. (Dir: Corey Blechman, 104 mins.)

Three Women (1977)***½ Shelley Duvall, Sissy Spacek, Janice Rule, John Cromwell, Robert Fortier. A fascinating, daring film written, produced, and directed by Robert Altman. An audacious attempt to create a rich, textured film about two vapid leading characters is rewarded by extraordinarily varied and subtle performances by Duvall and Spacek, playing roommates in a Palm Springs, Calif., motel. Duvall is a self-assured physical therapist modeling her life on the inspirations she finds in "Good Housekeeping." A remarkable work of art. (125 mins.)

Three Word Brand (1921)***½ William S. Hart, Jane Novak, S. J. Bingham, Gordon Russell, Ivor McFadden. In another strong, original western, Hart is a rancher fighting off crooked politicians trying to gain control of water rights in Utah; filmed with a clear-eyed lyricism that was an inspiration to later directors like John Ford and Howard Hawks. (Dir: Lambert Hillyer, 65 mins.)†

Three Worlds of Gulliver, The (Great Britain, 1960)*** Kerwin Mathews, Jo Morrow. Fast-paced adventure fantasy aimed for the juvenile trade. (Dir: Jack Sher, 100 mins.)†

Three Young Texans (1954)** Mitzi Gaynor, Jeffrey Hunter, Keefe Brasselle. Cowboy tries to save his father, in the clutches of crooks, from robbing a train by doing it himself. (Dir: Henry Levin, 78 mins.)

Threshold (Canada, 1981)*** Donald Sutherland, John Marley, Sharon Ackerman, Mare Winningham, Jeff Goldblum. Riveting hospital drama about the implanting of a compact artificial heart. Especially fine performance by Sutherland as a top heart surgeon who tries the operation on a young woman who otherwise would die in the course of corrective open-heart surgery. (Dir: Richard Pearce, 106 mins.)†

Thrilled to Death (1989)*½ Blake Bahner, Rebecca Lynn [Krista Lane], Richard Maris [Rick Savage], Christine More. Doing research for a book, a writer and his wife befriend a jaded couple at a swingers' resort who lead them into all kinds of nasty doings. Low-budget, low-interest thriller. (Dir: Chuck Vincent, 92 mins.)†

Thrill Killers, The (1965)*½ Cash Flagg, Liz Renay, Brick Bardo, Carolyn Brandt, Herb Robbins. A homicidal nut and three escaped maniacs who like to decapitate strangers torment customers at a roadside cafe. Pretty dull stuff, considering that it came from the creator of *The Incredibly Strange Creatures Who Stopped Living and Became Mixed-Up Zombies*. (Dir: Ray Dennis Steckler, 72 mins.)†

Thrill of a Romance (1945)** Van Johnson, Esther Williams, Lauritz Melchior, Tommy Dorsey and orchestra. Air Corps hero romances a pretty swimming instructress at a mountain resort. Cloying musical comedy. (Dir: Richard Thorpe, 104 mins.)

Thrill of It All, The (1963)*** Doris Day, James Garner, Arlene Francis. Some bright moments in this amusing comedy about an obstetrician's wife who becomes a star of television commercials. Carl Reiner's script pokes fun at TV huckstering. (Dir: Norman Jewison, 108 mins.)†

Throne of Blood (Japan, 1957)*** Toshiro Mifune, Isuzu Yamada. Director Akira Kurosawa has steeped this adaptation of *Macbeth* so thoroughly in Japanese motifs that it bears little relationship to its source beyond the basic story. The result is Shakespeare without Shakespeare, a *sui generis* masterwork in which vision replaces the Western core of Shakespearean tragedy, voice. The camerawork transports the viewer to the heart of feudal Japan, but the linguistic barriers, the mundane subtitles that eschew poetry for expedient idiomatic translation, may keep some Westerners detached from the film. (109 mins.)†

Through a Glass Darkly (Sweden, 1961)*** Harriet Andersson, Max von Sydow, Gunnar Björstrand. Academy Award winner for Best Foreign Film. A dark and disturbing film about a woman who's released from a sanitarium and has to cope with her family's reactions to her illness on a remote island. Still not well, her grasp on reality is tenuous, but she struggles to piece her life back together. (Dir: Ingmar Bergman, 91 mins.)†

Through Naked Eyes (MTV 1983)**½ David Soul, Pam Dawber, Dick Anthony Williams, Gerald Castillo. A shy flutist (Soul) proves to be an innocent voyeur spying on a woman across the way. The lady (Dawber) being spied on shares his pastime, which leads to a love affair and involves them in a murder. (Dir: John Llewellyn Moxey, 104 mins.)

Throw Momma from the Train (1987)*** Danny DeVito, Billy Crystal, Kim Greist, Anne Ramsey. Director-star DeVito cleverly borrows Hitchcock's cross-murder plot (*Strangers on a Train*) and creates an amusing, entertaining whirlwind comedy. Crystal puts his comedic talents to work as the frustrated writer persuaded to cooperate in DeVito's scheme, and "Momma" (Ramsey) steals the film by reminding you of that relative you pray you'll never have. (88 mins.)†

Thumb Tripping (1972)**½ Michael Burns, Meg Foster, Marianne Hill, Burke Burns, Mike Conrad, Bruce Dern, Joyce Van Patten. Burns and Foster are wandering soul-searchers who hitchhike across California and encounter various familiar faces as characters in transition. Well-meaning but dated drama, with another splendid psycho performance from Dern. (Dir: Quentin Masters, 94 mins.)

Thunder Afloat (1939)**½ Wallace Beery, Chester Morris. Good comedy-drama about WWI campaign against subs by Naval Reserve. (Dir: George B. Seitz, 100 mins.)

Thunder Alley (1967)* Annette Funicello, Fabian, Jan Murray, Diane McBain, Maureen Arthur, Warren Berlinger. Fabian plays a stock car racer prone to blacking out behind the wheel. Unconvincing, woodenly acted. (Dir: Richard Rush, 90 mins.)†

Thunder Alley (1985)** Roger Wilson, Jill Schoelen, Scott McGinnis, Cynthia Eilbacher, Clancy Brown, Leif Garrett. Clichéd rise-to-fame story of teens in a rock 'n' roll band. Performers are all OK, and the movie is watchable, but the music is synthetic and there's no reason to go through this story again. (Dir: J. S. Cardone, 92 mins.)†

Thunder and Lightning (1977)** David Carradine, Kate Jackson, Roger C. Carmel. Rubbish about moonshiners a-cussin' 'n'a-fightin' in the Everglades. (Dir: Corey Allen, 95 mins.)†

Thunderball (Great Britain, 1965)*** Sean Connery, Claudine Auger, Adolfo Celi, Bernard Lee, Luciana Paluzzi. An exciting James Bond adventure. This time out, the ominous enemy organization, SPECTRE, is out to destroy the city of Miami if SPECTRE is not paid a ransom of 100 million pounds sterling—and super-hero Bond is not about to let all those tourists down. (Dir: Terence Young, 132 mins.)†

Thunder Bay (1953)**½ James Stewart, Joanne Dru, Dan Duryea, Gilbert Roland. High-spirited adventure yarn about oil prospectors and their run-in with shrimp fishermen in Louisiana when an offshore drilling operation interferes with the routine of a small fishing community. (Dir: Anthony Mann, 102 mins.)†

Thunder Below (1932)**½ Tallulah Bankhead, Charles Bickford, Paul Lukas. Heavy-breathing but undistinguished melodrama about Tallulah falling for her husband's best buddy. (Dir: Richard Wallace, 67 mins.)

Thunder Birds (1942)**½ Gene Tierney, Preston Foster, John Sutton, Jack Holt, Dame May Whitty, George Barbier, Richard Haydn, Reginald Denny. Routine wartime melodrama, with flight instructor Foster kept away from combat by his duties training new pilots; director William Wellman was forced to make several fairly low-budget programmers in exchange for being allowed to make *The Ox-bow Incident* at 20th Century Fox, and this was one of them. (78 mins.)

Thunder Boat Row (MTV 1989)** Chad Everett, Jason Adams, Nicki Corri, Robert Estes, Anthony Jones. Unsold pilot for an action series about a special corp of seagoing cops battling drug smugglers off the coast of Florida. Predictable. (Dir: Tom Wright, 96 mins.)

Thunderbolt and Lightfoot (1974)*** Clint Eastwood, Jeff Bridges, Geoffrey Lewis, Gary Busey, George Kennedy. Caper yarn set in the hill country of Montana. Clint, a Vietnam vet with a hankering to pull a big armory robbery and retire forever, teams up with young drifter Bridges. (Dir: Michael Cimino, 115 mins.)†

Thundercloud (1950)**½ Randolph Scott, Ruth Roman, Zachary Scott. Fast-paced western drama with the stress on action. Scott is a gun salesman whose merchandise (Colt .45s) is stolen and used to arm a band of outlaws. (Dir: Edwin L. Marin, 74 mins.)

Thundercrack (1976)**½ Marion Eaton, George Kuchar, Melinda McDowell. A bizarre black comedy supercharged with an astonishing variety of sexual perversions. It's a Freudian remake of one of those "old dark house" mysteries; only instead of being terrorized by mad scientists and hunchbacks, the unfortunate wayfarers in this eerie farmhouse suffer a more sexual brand of torment. (Dir: Curt McDowell, 150 mins.)

Thunderhead—Son of Flicka (1945)**½ Roddy McDowall, Preston Foster. Good juvenile film about a boy and a horse. A fair outdoor adventure with little of the fine qualities of *My Friend Flicka*. (Dir: Louis King, 78 mins.)

Thunder in the City (Great Britain, 1937)*** Edward G. Robinson, Luli Deste, Nigel Bruce, Constance Collier, Ralph Richardson, Arthur Wontner. Fascinating British-made comedy of a go-getting American promoter (Robinson) making a fortune in a stock exchange scam; good script (one of the writers was Robert Sherwood) and strong performances. Perhaps even more interesting today for the attitudes it reveals. (Dir: Marion Gering, 76 mins.)

Thunder in the East (1953)**½ Deborah Kerr, Alan Ladd, Charles Boyer, Corinne Calvet. Contrived but moderately entertaining film about a group of displaced persons and an American adventurer caught up in the new-found independence fever in India. (Dir: Charles Vidor, 98 mins.)

Thunder in the Sun (1959)** Susan Hayward, Jeff Chandler. Routine western. Wagon train of Basque settlers going to California to cultivate vineyards passes through hostile Indian territory. (Dir: Russell Rouse, 81 mins.)

Thunder in the Valley (1947)**½ Lon McCallister, Edmund Gwenn, Peggy Ann Garner. Good juvenile drama about a boy's love for his dog. (Dir: Louis King, 103 mins.)

Thunder Island (1963)** Gene Nelson, Fay Spain, Brian Kelly, Miriam Colon, Art Bedard. Low-budget suspense tale of an assassination plot against an out-of-power South American dictator, directed with gusto but hampered by indifferent performances. Co-written by Jack Nicholson. (Dir: Jack Leewood, 65 mins.)

Thunder of Drums, A (1961)**½ Richard Boone, George Hamilton, Luana Patten, Richard Chamberlain. Newly commissioned lieutenant, son of a former general, is treated rough by the captain of a western fort until he can prove he's a soldier. Familiar Cavalry vs. Indians actioner benefits from good performances. (Dir: Joseph M. Newman, 97 mins.)

Thunder on the Hill (1951)*** Ann Blyth, Claudette Colbert, Robert Douglas. Mystery yarn set in a British convent during a rainstorm makes absorbing drama when handled as well as it is here. Blyth plays a condemned murderess who is detained at the convent due to the storm, and Colbert plays a nun who sets out to prove her innocence. (Dir: Douglas Sirk, 84 mins.)

Thunder Over the Plains (1953)**½ Randolph Scott, Lex Barker, Phyllis Kirk, Charles McGraw, Henry Hull, Elisha Cook, Jr., Fess Parker. Straightforward, colorful western set in the immediate post-Civil War period, with Scott a cavalryman trying to restore order to an outpost torn by partisan strife; fine ensemble and tight direction. (Dir: Andre De Toth, 82 mins.)

Thunder Pass (1954)**½ Dane Clark, Dorothy Patrick, Andy Devine, Raymond Burr. Cavalry captain attempts to lead settlers to safety before the Indians go on the warpath. (Dir: Frank McDonald, 76 mins.)†

Thunder Road (1958)** Robert Mitchum, Keely Smith, Gene Barry. Uneven drama about a group of people in the Kentucky hills who make moonshine whiskey and sell it. (Dir: Arthur Ripley, 92 mins.)†

Thunder Rock (Great Britain, 1942)***½ Michael Redgrave, Lilli Palmer, James Mason. The keeper of an isolated lighthouse hates his fellow man, but is persuaded to return to society by spirits from the past. Thoughtful, excellently acted drama. (Dirs: John and Roy Boulting, 95 mins.)

Thursday's Child (MTV 1983)**½ Gena Rowlands, Don Murray, Jessica Walter, Rob Lowe, Larry Poindexter. True tale of a seventeen-year-old boy in desperate search of a transplant donor for his chronically diseased heart. (Dir: David Lowell Rich, 104 mins.)

Thursday's Game (MTV 1974)***½ Gene Wilder, Bob Newhart, Ellen Burstyn, Cloris Leachman, Valerie Harper, Nancy Walker, Rob Reiner. A cast of top comedy actors adds spark to this tale about two friends (Wilder and Newhart) who decide to lie and continue their weekly night out after their poker game is disbanded. It's a satirical look at marriage and male friendships. (Dir: Robert Moore, 74 mins.)†

THX-1138 (1971)** Robert Duvall, Maggie McOmie, Donald Pleasence. This was originally filmed as a short film at USC. Francis Ford Coppola was so impressed he took director George Lucas to Warner Brothers, who financed this full-length version. A man tries to escape the restrictions of a futuristic totalitarian state, which imposes its will on its citizens. Maybe it was better at a shorter length. (88 mins.)†

Thy Kingdom Come, Thy Will Be Done (MTV

1987)*** A hard-hitting two-part documentary which was co-produced by PBS and Britain's Central Television and shown in theaters before being broadcast. The focus is on the Christian fundamentalist movement in the South, with the first half exploring the "televangelist" phenomenon and the second centering on the First Baptist Church in Dallas, the biggest and richest Protestant congregation in America. (Dir: Antony Thomas, 107 mins.)

Thy Neighbor's Wife (1953)**½ Cleo Moore, Hugo Haas, Ken Carlton, Kathleen Hughes. Once again, Haas plays an elderly man deceived by a young, vivacious woman. Only this time, the setting is a 19th-century village, and Hugo's an unlikeable judge who discovers his wife's infidelities with a man charged with murder. (Dir: Hugo Haas, 73 mins.)

Tiara Tahiti (Great Britain, 1962)**½ James Mason, John Mills, Claude Dauphin. Pompous former officer lands in Tahiti to build a modern hotel, but finds unexpected opposition in the form of an old army enemy, living a life of ease on the isle. Leisurely in pace as befits the climate, this tropical comedy gets its chief lift from the able performances of the leading players. (Dir: William [Ted] Kotcheff, 100 mins.)†

Ticket of No Return (West Germany, 1979)***½ Tabea Blumenchein, Lutze, Magdalena Montezuma, Nina Hagen, Kurt Rabbe, Eddie Constantine, Volker Spengler. Extraordinary film about two female alcoholics, one wealthy and mute who consciously wants to drink herself to death, the other a bag lady who talks to herself and isn't aware of her problem. Heartbreaking film shows how alcohol can dissolve class distinctions but won't allow for honest communication. (Dir: Ulrike Ottinger, 108 mins.)

Ticket to Heaven (Canada, 1981)*** Nick Mancuso, Meg Foster, Kim Cattrall. An underrated, unsettling drama about religious cult activities. A vulnerable young man is seduced into a San Francisco-based cult and reduced to a hollow-eyed automaton before his friend can—and just barely does—kidnap and deprogram him. (Dir: Ralph L. Thomas, 107 mins.)†

Ticket to Tomahawk, A (1950)**½ Dan Dailey, Anne Baxter, Rory Calhoun, Walter Brennan. Small-time theatrical group invades the West. Marilyn Monroe has a bit role in this fairly amusing western spoof. (Dir: Richard Sale, 90 mins.)

Tickle Me (1965)** Elvis Presley, Jocelyn Lane, Julie Adams. Elvis as a rodeo star who winds up at a girls' health resort and helps uncover a hidden treasure. (Dir: Norman Taurog, 90 mins.)†

Ticklish Affair, A (1963)** Gig Young, Shirley Jones, Red Buttons, Carolyn Jones. Naval officer investigating an SOS encounters a widow and her children, and romance blossoms. Watery little comedy. (Dir: George Sidney, 89 mins.)

…tick…tick…tick (1970)**½ Jim Brown, Fredric March, George Kennedy. Fairly interesting drama about a Southern town's sudden shift from a peaceful community to a veritable powder keg. The incident which sets off the situation is the election of the town's first black sheriff, played by Jim Brown. (Dir: Ralph Nelson, 100 mins.)

Tidal Wave (Japan, 1975)* Lorne Greene, Keiju Kobayashi, Rhonda Leigh Hopkins. Really two films in one—Roger Corman acquired some classy footage of Japan going underwater done by a Japanese special effects team and intercut it with slapdash scenes of Green as the U.S. Ambassador to the UN, who tries to convince the Assembly to send aid to the stricken country. (Dir: Andrew Meyer, 90 mins.)

Tiefland (West Germany, 1954)*** Leni Riefenstahl, Bernhard Minetti, Aribert Wascher, Franz Eichberger. Director-writer Riefenstahl plays a flamenco dancer who is the mistress of a Spanish nobleman on the skids. He weds a wealthy official's daughter but won't give up his lover. Using stunning black and white images, Riefenstahl tells her romantic tragedy in melodramatic style, its spectacular beauty compensating for a rigid dramatic tone. Filmed in 1935, not completed until '54. (98 mins.)

Tie Me Up! Tie Me Down! (Spain, 1990)*** Victoria Abril, Antonio Banderas, Loles Leon, Francisco Rabal. Young man, recently released from a mental institution, invades the apartment of a movie actress and keeps her tied up while waiting for her to fall in love with him. Only in the hands of outrageous writer-director Pedro Almodóvar would material like this become the basis for a comedy. Fans may feel let down by Almodóvar's relatively subdued approach, though by any other yardstick this is fresh and original. AKA: **Atame!** (101 mins.)†

Tiger and the Pussycat, The (U.S.-Italy, 1967)** Ann-Margret, Vittorio Gassman, Eleanor Parker. This sex drama with comedy doesn't make good use of Gassman's dazzling talent. Gassman is approaching middle age, and he is taken over the coals by Ann-Margret. (Dir: Dino Risi, 105 mins.)†

Tiger Bay (Great Britain, 1959)**** Horst Buchholz, Hayley Mills, Yvonne Mitchell, Megs Jenkins, John Mills. Superb suspense yarn with a great plot twist. Hayley Mills is perfect in the role of a little girl who witnesses a murder and ends up protecting the young killer (effectively portrayed by Buchholz) from the authorities. (Dir: J. Lee Thompson, 105 mins.)†

Tiger by the Tail (1968)** Christopher George, Tippi Hedren, Dean Jagger, Charo, Lloyd Bochner, Glenda Farrell, Alan Hale, Skip Homeier. Routine action-pic about a returned Vietnam vet battling the men who murdered his brother to appropriate his race track. What a cast! (Dir: R. G. Springsteen, 99 mins.)

Tiger Makes Out, The (1967)***½ Eli Wallach, Anne Jackson, Charles Nelson Reilly, Elizabeth Wilson. If you pay attention you'll catch Dustin Hoffman in a tiny part. There are other good reasons to watch this wacky tale of a Greenwich Village bachelor who can't cope with the world and, therefore, turns to kidnapping, the major one being the delicious performances of husband-and-wife team Wallach and Jackson. (Dir: Arthur Hiller, 94 mins.)

Tiger Shark (1932)*** Edward G. Robinson, Richard Arlen, Zita Johann. Interesting Hawks antique in which a big-hearted fisherman sees his wayward wife fall in love with his best friend. (Dir: Howard Hawks, 80 mins.)

Tiger's Tale, A (1988)** Ann-Margret, C. Thomas Howell, Charles Durning. With dozens of bright and willing young men available, why would lovely A-M choose to enter into a romance with an arrogant adolescent named Bubber (played by the insufferable Howell)? Even after viewing this slender "May-December" romance, set in a sleepy Texas town, you still won't be able to answer. (Dir: Peter Douglas, 97 mins.)†

Tiger Town (MCTV 1983)*** Roy Scheider, Justin Henry, Bethany Carpenter, Noah Moazezi. Could the success of the Detroit Tigers and an aging ballplayer rest in the hands of an eleven-year-old boy? That is the question that is beautifully handled in this first made-for-cable movie for the Disney Channel. Compared to the usual sugary kiddie fare, this young baseball fan's devotion to a down-and-out legend (Scheider) is subtle in its warmth and humor. (Dir: Alan Shapiro, 93 mins.)†

Tiger Walks, A (1964)**½ Pamela Franklin, Brian Keith, Vera Miles, Sabu. When a circus tiger escapes, an animal-loving youngster organizes a campaign to find the Bengal a home at the zoo rather than have it destroyed. What's unusual here is the bitter portrait of the local community. The cynicism and the sap content are at odds with each other, but this is worth a look. (Dir: Norman Tokar, 91 mins.)†

Tiger Warsaw (1988)*½ Patrick Swayze, Piper Laurie, Lee Richardson, Mary McDonnell. A prodigal son (Swayze), who shot (but didn't kill) his dad years ago in a nasty argument, returns to his hometown to try to heal old wounds. Middling melodrama, with the audience sharing the character's confusion. (Dir: Amin Q. Chaudhri, 92 mins.)†

Tight Little Island (Great Britain, 1949)**** Basil Radford, Joan Greenwood. Scottish islanders low on spirits take drastic steps when a cargo of whiskey is marooned off their shore. This British joy is one of the drollest films you can hope to see. AKA: Whisky Galore. (Dir: Alexander Mackendrick, 81 mins.)

Tightrope (1984)*** Clint Eastwood, Geneviève Bujold, Alison Eastwood, Dan Hedaya, Jennifer Beck. Flawed but occasionally riveting thriller about a homicide investigator (Eastwood) who goes off the sexual deep end when his wife dumps him. As he explores the darker side of his sexuality, a psychopath is terrorizing the city with sex crimes. Eastwood's most ambitious and daring film to date. (Dir: Richard Tuggle, 114 mins.)†

Tight Shoes (1941)*** Broderick Crawford, John Howard, Binnie Barnes. A gangster gets a shoe clerk started on his way in a political career. Surprisingly funny Damon Runyon comedy has a fast pace, good situations. (Dir: Albert S. Rogell, 68 mins.)

Tight Spot (1955)*** Ginger Rogers, Edward G. Robinson, Brian Keith, Lorne Greene, Kathryn Grant. Well-acted crime drama about a girl set up by the police as a trap for a big-time gang leader. (Dir: Phil Karlson, 97 mins.)

Tijuana Story, The (1957)** James Darren, Joy Stoner. A predictable drama about a youth's involvement with the "drug traffic" in the open city of Tijuana. (Dir: Leslie Kardos, 72 mins.)

Till Death (1978)**½ Keith Atkinson, Belinda Balaski. Basically a two-character, one-set film: Atkinson, distraught over the death of wife Balaski on their wedding night, resurrects her from a crypt. Still an OK horror pic. (Dir: Walter Stocker, 89 mins.)

Tillie and Gus (1933)*** W. C. Fields, Alison Skipworth, Jacqueline Wells (Julie Bishop), Baby LeRoy. A great team, perfectly cast as crooked gamblers, in a generally routine film. (Dir: Francis Martin, 61 mins.)

Tillie's Punctured Romance (1914)**½ Marie Dressler, Charlie Chaplin, Mabel Normand, Charley Chase. Historically significant as the first full-length silent comedy, this is otherwise an unexceptional farce with Chaplin out of his Little Tramp character. He plays a fortune hunter with his eyes on rich but naïve Dressler, the star of the show. (Dir: Mack Sennett, 39 mins.)†

Till Marriage Do Us Part (Italy, 1976)*** Laura Antonelli, Jean Rochefort, Michele Placido. In early 20th-century Italy, Antonelli discovers on her wedding night that she has unknowingly married her illegitimate brother, and she seeks her release and fulfillment as she can. Uneven but frequently funny and poignant. (Dir: Luigi Comencini.)†

Till the Clouds Roll By (1946)**½ Robert Walker, Judy Garland, Dinah Shore, Van Johnson, Lena Horne, Frank Sinatra. Star-studded but uninspired musical biography of Jerome Kern. Garland's numbers are the highlights. (Dir: Richard Whorf, 137 mins.)†

Till the End of Time (1946)*** Dorothy McGuire, Guy Madison, Robert Mitchum, Bill Williams. Returned GI tries to readjust himself to civilian life, finds he has changed, falls for a flyer's widow. Potent, excellently produced drama. (Dir: Edward Dmytryk, 105 mins.)†

Till We Meet Again (1944)** Ray Milland, Barbara Britton, Walter Slezak, Lucille Watson, Vladimir Sokoloff, Mona Freeman, Konstantin Shayne, Marguerite D'Alvarez. Overwrought but moderately effective wartime romance has a downed pilot being aided by a young nun, who poses as his wife to help him travel to safety; pretty heavy going. (Dir: Frank Borzage, 88 mins.)

Till We Meet Again (MTV 1989)* Michael York, Courtney Cox, Mia Sara, Lucy Gutteridge, Hugh Grant, Charles Shaughnessy, Maxwell Caulfield, Barry Bostwick, Bruce Boxleitner, Juliet Mills, Michael Sarne. More tiresome twaddle from the pen of Judith Krantz, a family saga set in France and L.A. during WWII. (Dir: Charles Jarrott, 240 mins.)

Tilt (MTV 1979)*½ Brooke Shields, Ken Marshall, Charles Durning, John Crawford, Karen Lamm. Brooke Shields plays a pinball expert who is hustled by a desperate and unscrupulous would-be rock singer. (Dir: Rudy Durand, 104 mins.)†

'Til We Meet Again (1940)*** Merle Oberon, George Brent, Pat O'Brien, Geraldine Fitzgerald. Remake of *One Way Passage*. Story of the criminal and the dying girl is still worthwhile if you like to cry. (Dir: Edmund Goulding, 99 mins.)

Tim (Australia, 1979)**½ Piper Laurie, Mel Gibson. A predictable but engrossing love story set in Australia. Piper Laurie plays a woman who becomes physically attracted to her gardener, a young, muscular, handsome fellow who happens to also be slightly retarded. The ramifications of this unusual union make up the bulk of the drama. (Dir: Michael Pate, 108 mins.)†

Time After Time (1979)***½ Malcolm McDowell, David Warner, Mary Steenburgen, Charles Cioffi. The notion of H. G. Wells pursuing Jack the Ripper to modern-day San Francisco via time machine is a supremely viable concept, and this imaginative film is notable for its edge-of-your-seat suspense and for the tenderness between McDowell (a charming Wells) and Steenburgen. (Dir: Nicholas Meyer, 112 mins.)†

Time Bandits (1981)** John Cleese, Sean Connery, Shelley Duvall, Katherine Helmond, Ian Holm, Sir Ralph Richardson, Craig Warnock, David Rappaport. A fantasy film in the heavy-handed vein of *Dark Crystal* and *The Neverending Story*. Modeled in part on C. S. Lewis's *Narnia Chronicles*, the film features a military-minded boy through whose bedroom window passes a time-hole, by which some would-be thieves plan to escape. (Dir: Terry Gilliam, 116 mins.)†

Time Bomb (France-Italy, 1959)**½ Curt Jurgens, Mylene Demongeot. A French film with some suspense and good production values to recommend it. Curt Jurgens is the captain of a vessel which becomes an important part of a plot of intrigue. (Dir: Yves Ciampi, 92 mins.)

Time Bomb (MTV 1984)** Morgan Fairchild, Merlin Olsen, Billy Dee Williams, Joseph Bottoms. Leading a pack of international terrorists, Fairchild uses her wiles to attempt the theft of some deadly plutonium. Mildly explosive entertainment. (Dir: Paul Krasny, 104 mins.)

Time Flyers—See: **Blue Yonder, The**

Time for Killing, A—See: **Long Ride Home, The**

Time for Love, A (MTV 1973)**½ John Davidson, Lauren Hutton, Chris Mitchum, Jack Cassidy, Bonnie Bedelia. Two introspective, visually handsome love stories written by Stirling Silliphant. Davidson's straight-arrow junior exec learns to buck the patterned corporate-life groove from a questioning beauty in "No Promises, No Pledges." In "Go Sing the Songs, Mark," a sad-faced rock singer loves a teacher of deaf children, but won't relinquish his frenzied lifestyle. (Dirs: George Schaefer, Joseph Sargent, 99 mins.)

Time for Miracles, A (MTV 1980)** Kate Mulgrew, Jean-Pierre Aumont, Rossano Brazzi, John Forsythe, Lorne Greene. Melodramatic story of Elizabeth Seton later known as Mother Seton, the first native-born American to become a saint. (Dir: Michael O'Herlihy, 104 mins.)†

Time for Revenge, A (Argentina, 1981)***½ Federico Luppi, Haydee Padilla, Julio De Grazia, Rudolfo Ranni. Exciting political thriller, filmed while a repressive regime was in power, about a worker who loses his job because of his radical union activities, and decides to fight a system that exploits and corrupts both its people and its own country. (Dir: Adolfo Aristarain, 112 mins.)

Time Limit (1957)***½ Richard Widmark, Richard Basehart, June Lockhart, Martin Balsam. The provocative war drama presented on B'way has been brought to the screen with taste and skill. Story concerns the issue of collaboration with the enemy during the Korean campaign. Strong drama with excellent performances. (Dir: Karl Malden, 96 mins.)

Timelock (Great Britain, 1957)**½ Robert Beatty, Betty McDowall. Tight British drama about a bank official who accidentally locks his son in the vault, which is set to open sixty-three hours later. The inevitable gimmick about the race against time is used to the breaking point. (Dir: Gerald Thomas, 73 mins.)

Time Lost and Time Remembered (Great Britain, 1966)**½ Sarah Miles, Cyril Cusack. If the screenplay of this tale about a young girl's awakening to life and love matched its sensitive photography and splendid acting by Sarah Miles in the leading role, this would be a winner. But it turns out to be just an average tale, beautifully acted and photographed. (Dir: Desmond Davis, 91 mins.)

Time Machine, The (1960)*** Rod Taylor, Yvette Mimieux, Alan Young, Whit Bissell, Tom Helmore, Sebastian Cabot. Imaginative tale based on the H. G. Wells story of a young inventor who constructs a machine enabling him to travel to the future, and the strange adventures he meets in doing so. Trick work is excellent, the story continually interesting and well acted. Oscar, Best Special Effects. (Dir: George Pal, 103 mins.)†

Time Machine, The (MTV 1978)*½ John Beck, Priscilla Barnes, Andrew Duggan, Rosemary DeCamp. From the story by H. G. Wells. This time, the celebrated machine seems creaky. (Dir: Henning Schellerup, 104 mins.)†

Time of Destiny, A (1988)*½ William Hurt, Timothy Hutton, Melissa Leo, Stockard Channing, Megan Follows, Francisco Rabal. If you've ever thought that they can't make 'em like they used to, check out this corny melodrama which resurrects all the hallmarks of the grade Z romances and war movies of yesteryear. Hurt stars as a man obsessed by a ridiculous vendetta: He's out to kill brother-in-law Hutton, whom he believes (wrongly) intentionally caused his late father's fatal car crash. Hurt's career will recover from this rank misstep, but will Tim's? (Dir: Gregory Nava, 118 mins.)†

Time of Indifference (France-Italy, 1964)** Shelley Winters, Rod Steiger, Paulette Goddard, Claudia Cardinale. Grim, unpleasantly executed and played drama

1088

about the disintegration of a family in the late '20s. (Dir: Francisco Maselli, 84 mins.)

Time of Their Lives, The (1946)*** Bud Abbott, Lou Costello, Marjorie Reynolds, Binnie Barnes. A better than average A & C comedy with less stress on slapstick and more on story. Good supporting performances. (Dir: Charles Barton, 82 mins.)†

Time of Your Life, The (1948)**** James Cagney, Wayne Morris, Broderick Crawford, Jeanne Cagney, James Barton. A little San Francisco saloon, and the characters who frequent it. From William Saroyan's prize-winning play. Expertly handled. (Dir: H. C. Potter, 109 mins.)†

Time Out for Love (1962)*½ Jean Seberg, Maurice Ronet, Micheline Presle. American girl in France falls in with a trio of sophisticated modernists. Meandering romantic drama dubbed in English. (Dir: Philippe de Broca, 91 mins.)

Time Raiders—See: **Warriors of the Apocalypse**

Timerider (1983)½ Peter Coyote, Belinda Bauer, Richard Masur, Fred Ward, Ed Lauter. More like timewaster, this misguided sci-fi flick follows the adventures of a biker who, while running a desert race, is transported back to Mexico circa 1877. (Dir: William Dear, 93 mins.)†

Time Running Out (France-U.S., 1950)** Dane Clark, Simone Signoret. Run-of-the-mill cops and robbers yarn set in France. Signoret, as one of Clark's past mistresses, is totally wasted in a thankless role. (Dirs: Frank Tuttle, Boris Lewin, 90 mins.)

Times of Harvey Milk, The (1984)*** Extremely moving documentary about Harvey Milk, a gay politician who was assassinated along with Mayor George Moscone by Supervisor Dan White in 1978. This film works both as a biography of a charismatic figure and as an examination of the gay rights movement. (Dir: Robert Epstein, 87 mins.)†

Times Square (1980)*½ Tim Curry, Trini Alvarado, Robin Johnson, Peter Coffield, Herbert Berghof. Times Square itself has more drama going on on every corner, at any hour of the day or night, than is contained in this film about two teenyboppers who escape from a psychiatric hospital and later become celebrities with the help of a disc jockey. (Dir: Alan Moyle, 111 mins.)†

Timestalkers (MTV 1987)**½ Lauren Hutton, William Devane, Forrest Tucker, Klaus Kinski, Gail Youngs, John Ratzenberger, John Considine, Tracey Walter. A bizarre, somewhat entertaining, time-travel adventure. Covering the time span between the years 2586 and 1886, this saga concerns a demented scientist who journeys back to the Old West in order to reshape history to his own advantage. (Dir: Michael Schultz, 104 mins.)†

Time Stands Still (Hungary, 1982)**½ Stvan Znamenak, Henrik Pauer, Sandor Soth, Aniko Ivan, Peter Galfy. Informative, slow-moving social problem drama. Set in a boys' school, it details the difficulties of teenagers growing up in Budapest after the 1956 revolution. The director and cameraman create stylized vignettes about rebellion in an oppressive society. (Dir: Peter Gothar, 99 mins.)†

Time Stood Still (Italy, 1959)*** Natale Rossi, Roberto Seveso, Paolo Quadrubbi. Beautiful first film by Ermanno Olmi about two men, one old and one young, who are hired to guard an unfinished dam project through a harsh winter and how their friendship grows during the period of isolation. Confined-space film never seems dull or slow as it unspools with rare depth and warm good humor. (80 mins.)

Timetable (1956)*** Mark Stevens, Felicia Farr. A streamline train is robbed in a daringly intricate holdup. Neat crime melodrama has many twists. (Dir: Mark Stevens, 79 mins.)

Time, the Place and the Girl, The (1946)*½ Janis Paige, Dennis Morgan, Jack Carson. Middlin' musical comedy about a retired opera singer at cross-purposes with her hubby, who's helping two nightclub owners mount a musical extravaganza. (Dir: David Butler, 105 mins.)

Time to Kill (1942)** Lloyd Nolan, Heather Angel. Detective Michael Shayne on the trail of rare coin counterfeiters. Routine film is supported by Nolan's characterization. (Dir: Herbert I. Leeds, 61 mins.)

Time to Live, A (MTV 1985)*** Liza Minnelli, Corey Haim, Jeffrey DeMunn, Swoozie Kurtz. Inspirational true-life drama. Minnelli plays a mother coping with her bright young son's struggle with muscular dystrophy. Pulls the audience's heartstrings without insulting its intelligence. (Dir: Rick Wallace, 104 mins.)

Time to Love and a Time to Die, A (1958)*** John Gavin, Lilo Pulver, Jock Mahoney, Keenan Wynn. Erich Maria Remarque's novel about young romance during WWII in Nazi Germany comes off well in this screen adaptation. Although the film eventually becomes soap opera, it has some good moments in the earlier scenes. (Dir: Douglas Sirk, 133 mins.)†

Time to Triumph, A (MTV 1986)** Patty Duke, Joe Bologna, Denise Mickelbury, Dara Modglin. Join the Army with Patty Duke and become a chopper pilot. You know the plot; Patty taking guff from a drill sergeant, being jittery before she solos, etc. Uncle Sam wants better TV movies. (Dir: Noel Black, 104 mins.)

Time Travelers, The (1964)**½ Preston Foster, Philip Carey, Merry Anders, Joan Woodbury. Scientific team experimenting with time is projected into the future, don't exactly like what they find there. Intriguing scientific idea. (Dir: Ib Melchior, 82 mins.)

Time Travelers (MTV 1976)** Sam Groom, Tom Hallick, Richard Basehart. Tepid pilot film for another series about scientists who travel through time. It's kid stuff basically as two stalwart men (Groom, Hallick) go back to Chicago on the eve of the famous fire to obtain a cure for "Wood's fever." (Dir: Alexander Singer, 74 mins.)

Time Walker (1983)*½ Ben Murphy, Nina Axelrod, Kevin Brophy, James Karen. A hybrid of old-fashioned mummy-thrillers and newfangled science fiction; would you believe an alien entombed with King Tut? Naturally, it comes to life again and stalks a college campus, searching for crystals stolen from its coffin by a student. (Dir: Tom Kennedy, 84 mins.)†

Time Without Pity (Great Britain, 1957)** Michael Redgrave, Ann Todd, Joan Plowright, Peter Cushing, Lois Maxwell. A father has twenty-four hours to save his son from the death sentence. Despite the fine cast, this suspense drama never quite clarifies itself. (Dir: Joseph Losey, 88 mins.)

Tin Drum, The (West Germany-France, 1979)**** Angela Winkler, Mario Adorf, Daniel Olbrychski, David Bennent. Director Volker Schlöndorff's faithful adaptation of the Günter Grass masterpiece is assisted by the casting coup of young Bennent as the dwarf Oskar, who—from the age of three—refuses to grow. A substantial, entertaining, extraordinary film. Oscar for Best Foreign Language Film. (142 mins.)†

Tingler, The (1959)*** Vincent Price, Darryl Hickman, Patricia Cutts, Philip Coolidge, Judith Evelyn. A gimmicked horror film that works. Vincent Price bones up on research involving a creature that grows on the spinal cord when people are terrified. For the most part, spine-tingling. (Dir: William Castle, 80 mins.)

Tin Man, The (1983)**½ Timothy Bottoms, John Phillip Law, Troy Donahue, Deana Jurgens. A touching, muted "overcoming-the-obstacles" drama about a deaf auto mechanic who invents a computer that will benefit deaf people, and then must learn to deal with the upheaval his invention brings to his life. (Dir: John G. Thomas, 95 mins.)†

Tin Men (1987)*** Richard Dreyfuss, Danny DeVito, Barbara Hershey, Jackie Gayle, Bruno Kirby, Seymour Cassel. Screenwriter-director Barry Levinson returns to the territory of his coming-of-age hit *Diner*, viewing it this time from the vantage point of two who have come of age: Dreyfuss and DeVito, two aluminum-siding salesmen who are rapidly becoming disillusioned with their lives. If you can get past the "revenge" story line, where the two "Tin Men" engage in a serious case of one-upmanship (primarily involving DeVito's wife), you'll find that Levinson's eye for period detail and his ear for genuine dialogue are in evidence throughout. (110 mins.)†

Tin Pan Alley (1940)**½ Alice Faye, Betty Grable, Jack Oakie, John Payne. Undistinguished, pastiche Fox musical does, however, have a winning performance by Oakie, a memorable production number of "The Sheik of Araby" with Billy Gilbert as the sheik, and the amazing Nicholas Brothers. (Dir: Walter Lang, 94 mins.)

Tin Star, The (1957)***½ Henry Fonda, Anthony Perkins, Betsy Palmer. Expertly made western mixes humor with suspense, and a standout performance by Fonda as a wily bounty hunter who helps a young sheriff clean up a town. Superior of its type. (Dir: Anthony Mann, 93 mins.)

Tintorera (Mexico, 1978)* Susan George, Fiona Lewis, Hugo Stiglitz, Priscilla Barnes. A tiger shark munches on buxom beauties while two shark-hunters try to curb his appetite. Sort of a soft-core version of *Jaws* (without the suspense and thrills). (Dir: Rene Cardona, Jr., 91 mins.)†

Tip Off, The (1931)**½ Eddie Quillan, Robert Armstrong, Ginger Rogers, Joan Peers, Ralfe Harolde. Entertaining comedy of a naïve guy who inadvertently becomes involved with a gangster's moll, and is saved from the consequences by a tough boxer who befriends him. Quillan is nominally the star, but Rogers and Armstrong are the best things about the picture, with a breezy, wisecracking relationship that is still sexy. (Dir: Albert Rogell, 70 mins.)

Tip on a Dead Jockey (1957)*** Robert Taylor, Dorothy Malone, Jack Lord, Martin Gabel, Gia Scala. Irwin Shaw's crime story makes a good film with Taylor giving one of his better screen portrayals as a pilot involved with smugglers. (Dir: Richard Thorpe, 99 mins.)

Titanic (1953)*** Clifton Webb, Barbara Stanwyck, Robert Wagner, Thelma Ritter, Brian Aherne. Hollywood's version of the famous tragic event, the sinking of the sink-proof Titanic. Personal dramas are unfolded before the climax arrives when the ship hits the inevitable iceberg. Oscar: Best Story and Screenplay. (Dir: Jean Negulesco, 98 mins.)†

Titfield Thunderbolt, The (Great Britain, 1953)**** Stanley Holloway, George Relph, Hugh Griffith. Villagers resent the closing of their railway line by the government, take over the train themselves. Rollicking, completely delightful comedy, great fun. (Dir: Charles Crichton, 84 mins.)

Titicut Follies (1967)**** Brilliant, harrowing, devastating documentary about horrendous conditions at an institution for the criminally insane in Massachusetts. Frederick Wiseman got his camera into the center and filmed scenes of unrelenting filth, abuse, madness, ignorance, and tragedy. Movie was banned in Massachusetts and shocked a stunned nation. (85 mins.)

T-Men (1947)***½ Dennis O'Keefe, Alfred Ryder, June Lockhart. Documentary-type story of how Treasury agents broke up a gang of counterfeiters. One of the best of its kind, with special mention for a tight script. (Dir: Anthony Mann, 96 mins.)†

To All My Friends on Shore (MTV 1972)*** Bill Cosby, Gloria Foster. Strong performances and a believable script make this film about a hard-working black man, his sacrificing wife, and their doomed son worthwhile. Cosby plays a man determined to get his family out of the small Connecticut ghetto and buy a modest home of their own. (Dir: Gilbert Cates, 74 mins.)

Toast of New Orleans, The (1950)**½ Mario Lanza, Kathryn Grayson, David Niven. This was Mario Lanza's second film and the one in which he sang the popular "Be My Love." He plays a fisherman who is converted into an opera star. (Dir: Norman Taurog, 97 mins.)†

Toast of New York, The (1937)*** Edward Arnold, Cary Grant, Frances Farmer, Jack Oakie. Story of Jim Fisk, who rose from peddler to a Wall Street tycoon. Interesting biographical drama, well made. (Dir: Rowland V. Lee, 109 mins.)†

Tobacco Road (1941)**½ Charley Grapewin, Marjorie Rambeau, Gene Tierney, Dana Andrews, Ward Bond. Long-run Broadway play has been cleaned up for the screen and emerges as a fair tragicomedy of depravity in the impoverished Georgia farmland. (Dir: John Ford, 84 mins.)†

To Bed or Not to Bed (Italy, 1963)*** Alberto Sordi, Bernhard Tarschys, Inger Sjostrand, Ulf Palms. Very funny satire on the Latin "machismo," about an Italian family man who travels to Sweden on business, and en route lets his imagination balloon with visions of his sexual irresistibility. (Dir: Gian Luigi Polidoro, 103 mins.)

To Begin Again (Spain, 1983)**½ Antonio Ferrandis, Encarna Paso, Jose Bodalo.

Two lovers torn apart by the Spanish Civil War meet again in 1981 . . . will their romance be rekindled? Highly sentimental; best for die-hard romanticists. (Dir: José Luis Garci, 93 mins.)

To Be or Not to Be (1942)**** Jack Benny, Carole Lombard, Robert Stack, Sig Ruman, Stanley Ridges, Lionel Atwill. This story of a Shakespearean troupe in Poland fleeing from the Nazis is one of the greatest film comedies. Benny leads the troupe, and he is as funny impersonating Hamlet as he is impersonating Hitler. Lombard, who died shortly after the completion of the film, has one of her richest roles as his wife. (Dir: Ernst Lubitsch, 99 mins.)†

To Be or Not To Be (1984)*** Mel Brooks, Anne Bancroft, Tim Matheson, Charles Durning, José Ferrer. While this remake lacks the sophistication of the 1942 Ernst Lubitsch classic, it's agreeably sunny. A Polish acting troupe headed by the hammy Mr. Bronski (Brooks) helps a freedom fighter stop a counteragent from killing off the Polish underground. (Dir: Alan Johnson, 108 mins.)†

Tobruk (1967)** Rock Hudson, George Peppard, Nigel Green, Guy Stockwell. Routine WWII adventure with Hudson and Peppard cast as the heroes assigned to destroy Rommel's fuel supply. (Dir: Arthur Hiller, 110 mins.)†

Toby Tyler (1960)*** Kevin Corcoran, Henry Calvin, Bob Sweeney, Mr. Stubbs (the monkey). Popular kids' tale about a boy who runs away to join the circus and finds good pals—animal and people—and success there, is tailor-made for the Disney Studios. A touching, pleasant film. (Dir: Charles Barton, 96 mins.)†

To Catch a King (MCTV 1984)** Robert Wagner, Teri Garr, Barbara Parkins, Barry Foster, Jane Laportaire. Wagner is a Humphrey Bogart clone, running a nightspot in Lisbon and wearing a white dinner jacket, and Garr is a nightclub singer who becomes involved in a Nazi plot to kidnap the Duke of Windsor in 1940. (Dir: Clive Donner, 114 mins.)†

To Catch a Thief (1955)*** Cary Grant, Grace Kelly, Jessie Royce Landis, John Williams. Ex-jewel thief on the Riviera romances an American girl while trying to prove he's innocent of a series of robberies. Hitchcock comedy-thriller has spectacular scenery and popular players. Although the plot frequently dawdles, Grant and Kelly ignite fireworks. (Dir: Alfred Hitchcock, 97 mins.)†

To Commit a Murder (France-Italy-West Germany, 1967)** Louis Jourdan, Edmond O'Brien, Senta Berger, Bernard Blier, Fabrizzio Capucci. Routine spy-thriller. Louis Jourdan, a devil-may-care writer, gets inadvertently mixed up in

the kidnapping of a nuclear scientist. (Dir: Edouard Molinaro, 91 mins.)

Today's FBI (MTV 1981)*½ Mike Connors, Joseph Cali, Carol Potter, Rich Hill, Charles Brown. The same old federal agent stuff, updated, and given more pace to fit in with today's TV action shows. The cases are from the files of the FBI. (Dir: Virgil Vogel, 104 mins.)

Today We Live (1933)** Joan Crawford, Gary Cooper, Franchot Tone, Robert Young. This adaptation of a William Faulkner war story is so loaded with individual heroism and sacrifice that it will strike modern audiences as contrived. (Dir: Howard Hawks, 110 mins.)

Todd Killings, The (1971)*½ Robert F. Lyons, Richard Thomas, Ed Asner, Barbara Bel Geddes, Sherry Miles, Gloria Grahame. Lurid, squalid, and depressing. A boy hero-worships a pal who turns out to be a lady-killer, literally. The kind of film that makes you want to take a shower afterward. AKA: **A Dangerous Friend**. (Dir: Barry Shear, 93 mins.)†

To Die In Madrid (France, 1963)**** A superb documentary of the Spanish Civil War using newsreel footage from the archives of six different countries. Documents the beginning of the struggle in 1931 to Franco's assumption of complete power in 1939. Narrated by John Gielgud, Irene Worth, and others. (Dir: Frederic Roussif, 85 mins.)

To Die In Paris (MTV 1968)**½ Louis Jourdan, Kurt Krueger, Philippe Forquet, Robert Ellenstein. Fair suspense tale of French WWII Underground, casts Jourdan as Underground leader jailed by the Nazis who faces two enemies after his escape: Nazi agents and the Underground itself. (Dirs: Charles Dubin, Allen Reisner, 100 mins.)

To Each His Own (1946)***½ Olivia de Havilland, John Lund, Philip Terry, Mary Anderson, Roland Culver. Superb melodrama about a mother of an illegitimate son who meets him during WWII when he is a soldier (and his father's spitting image). Skillfully crafted in high style by director Mitchell Leisen. (100 mins.)

To Find a Man (1972)*** Pamela Martin, Lloyd Bridges, Phyllis Newman, Darren O'Conner. Interesting and occasionally perceptive tale of a young girl in quest of an abortion and the young boy who matures by helping her. AKA: **The Boy Next Door**. (Dir: Buzz Kulik, 94 mins.)

To Find My Son (MTV 1980)**½ Richard Thomas, Justin Dana, Allyn Ann McLerie, Steve Kanaly, Julie Cobb. Well-meaning drama written by Sandor Stern. Thomas is a young, single man of twenty-three who faces prejudices and obstacles in his efforts to adopt an orphan boy with a speech defect. (Dir: Delbert Mann, 104 mins.)

To Forget Venice (Italy, 1979)*** Erland Josephson, Mariangela Melato, Eleanora Giorgi, David Pontremoli. Effulgent melodrama of two homosexual couples engaged in reevaluating their relationship as they guest at the palazzo of a dying opera star. (Dir: Franco Brusati, 110 mins.)†

Together Again (1944)*** Charles Boyer, Irene Dunne. Straitlaced lady mayor of a small Vermont town falls for a dashing New York sculptor. Amusing, well-acted romantic comedy. (Dir: Charles Vidor, 94 mins.)

Together Brothers (1974)*** Anthony Wilson, Glynn Turman, Richard Yniguez. Acceptable action film about five black youths who stalk the ghetto to revenge the killer of their policeman friend. (Dir: William A. Graham, 94 mins.)

Togetherness (1970)** George Hamilton, Peter Lawford, Olinka Berova. Romantic comedy with a contrived plot. Hamilton stars as an American playboy in Greece masquerading as a Mexican journalist so he can trap the woman he loves. (Dir: Arthur Marks, 98 mins.)

To Have and Have Not (1944)*** Humphrey Bogart, Lauren Bacall (film debut), Walter Brennan, Marcel Dalio, Dan Seymour, Hoagy Carmichael. This is when the two lovebirds met and the picture has a good romance and plenty of intrigue to boot. Bogey is a fisherman in this one and between fishing for Nazis he manages to hook Lauren. Adapted from a Hemingway story but not too faithfully. (Dir: Howard Hawks, 100 mins.)†

To Heal a Nation (MTV 1988)**½ Eric Roberts, Glynnis O'Connor, Scott Paulin, Laurence Luckinbill. The story of how one dedicated veteran, Jan Scruggs (Roberts), spearheaded the movement to build the Vietnam Veterans Memorial in Washington, D.C. Roberts reproduces Scruggs' drive and sincerity quite well, but the rest is self-righteous melodrama. (Dir: Michael Pressman, 96 mins.)

To Hell and Back (1955)*** Audie Murphy, Susan Kohner, Charles Drake, David Janssen, Jack Kelly. Good screen adaptation of Audie Murphy's true heroic war adventures, which earned him the title of the most decorated soldier of WWII. Murphy plays himself with a surprising absence of arrogance. (Dir: Jesse Hibbs, 106 mins.)†

To Joy (Sweden, 1950)**½ Maj-Britt Nilson, Stig Olin, Burger Malmsten, John Ekman, Victor Sjostrom. An early film by Bergman. In flashbacks, the stormy courtship and marriage of an ambitious violinist and his music-loving mate pour out dramatically, along with generous samplings of classical music. After his wife's death, only music can lift the musician out of his grief. (Dir: Ingmar Bergman, 93 mins.)†

To Kill a Clown (1972)**½ Alan Alda, Blythe Danner, Heath Lamberts, Eric Clavering. In this thriller along the lines of *The Most Dangerous Game,* a couple is trapped on an island with a disturbed, disabled veteran. The political overtones are not completely worked out, but the basic horror-film plot remains an effective one. (Dir: George Bloomfield, 104 mins.)†

To Kill a Cop (MTV 1978)*** Joe Don Baker, Lou Gossett, Jr., Desi Arnaz, Jr., Christine Belford. Fine blend of New York street action mixed with backstage political maneuvering in the police department. Baker is thoroughly convincing as a harried chief of detectives, and Gossett is properly menacing as a black intellectual revolutionary. (Dir: Gary Nelson, 208 mins.)

To Kill a Mockingbird (1962)***½ Gregory Peck, Mary Badham, Philip Alford, Brock Peters. Excellent production of Harper Lee's novel about an Alabama lawyer bringing up his two motherless children. Peck (who won an Oscar) was never better, and the two children are most affecting. Superb script (Horton Foote) and direction (Robert Mulligan) make this, in its own quiet way, one of the best movies dealing with race relations that the American film industry has ever made. (129 mins.)†

To Kill a Priest (France-U.S., 1988)**½ Christophe Lambert, Ed Harris, Joanne Whalley, Joss Ackland. Exiled Polish director Agnieszka Holland (*Bitter Harvest*) recounts the story of a priest, sympathetic to the Solidarity movement, who was murdered by Polish security police in 1984. Harris's portrayal of the officer who engineered the assassination as a semilunatic weakens the film's political power. (116 mins.)†

To Kill a Stranger (1982)** Angelica Maria, Dean Stockwell, Donald Pleasence, Aldo Ray, Sergio Argones. In a Latin American country under military rule, a woman kills an attacker in self-defense. She and her husband try to cover it up, but the dead man was a war hero and the government is out for blood. Given the setting and the work of five writers, this should have been more compelling. (Dir: Juan Lopez-Moctezuma, 88 mins.)†

Tokyo After Dark (1959)** Richard Long, Michi Kobi. Military policeman accidentally kills a Tokyo teenager, breaks jail when he learns he's to be tried in a Japanese court. Fair drama of postwar Japan. (Dir: Norman Herman, 80 mins.)

Tokyo Joe (1949)** Humphrey Bogart, Florence Marly, Sessue Hayakawa. Not one of Bogart's better films. Slow-moving story of adventure and intrigue in Japan. (Dir: Stuart Heisler, 88 mins.)†

Tokyo Olymplad (Japan, 1965)*** The 1964 Olympics—in one of the finest photographic monuments to athletics ever made. Though this film was originally more comprehensive, a wide-ranging view of athletic endeavor and personal triumphs, it has been edited by its American distributors to focus on events of interest in this country, making it appear to be more newsreel reportage than documentary overview. It is still a magnificent job. (The original version is now on video.) (Dir: Kon Ichikawa, 93 mins.)†

Tokyo Pop (1988)** Carrie Hamilton, Yutaka Tadokoro, Taiji Tonoyoma. An airy, cross-cultural romance that's way too cute for its own good. Affable Hamilton plays an American rocker who journeys to Japan to check out the scene and winds up in love with a local talent. (Dir: Fran Rubel Kuzui, 97 mins.)†

Tokyo Senso Sengo Hiwa—See: **Man Who Left His Will on Film, The**

Tokyo Story (Japan, 1953)**** Chisu Ryu, Setsuko Hara, Chiyeko Higashiyama, Haruko Sugimura, So Yamamura, Kyoko Kagawa, Nobuo Nakamura. An elderly couple travel from a small village to Tokyo to visit their married children for the first time. Their son, a doctor, and their daughter, a beautician, feign delight at seeing them, but soon a sad resentment rises and the aged couple return home despondent, only to face a greater tragedy. Powerful, emotion-packed drama is a true masterpiece. (Dir: Yasujiro Ozu, 134 mins.)

Tokyo Twilight (Japan, 1957)*** Setsuko Hara, Isuzu Yamada, Ineko Arima, Chishu Ryu. A powerful script and stunning performances highlight this moody drama about two daughters living with their widowed father who discover that their mother may not be dead after all. Intensely depressing film. (Dir: Yasujiro Ozu, 141 mins.)

Tol'able David (1921)**** Richard Barthelmess, Gladys Hulette, Walter P. Lewis, Ernest Torrence. This exemplary rural drama, beautifully directed by Henry King, tells the story of a teenage mountain boy, his family, and the troubles that beset them when a family of criminals takes over their neighbor's farm. (80 mins.)†

Tol'able David (1930)** Richard Cromwell. An OK remake of the silent film classic with Richard Barthelmess. Cromwell isn't a charismatic star, but this saga of the backwoods boy who proves his manhood against mountain men is still entertaining. (Dir: John G. Blystone, 82 mins.)

To Live and Die in L.A. (1985)**½ William L. Petersen, Willem Dafoe, John Pankow, Debra Feuer, Darlanne Fluegel, John Turturro, Dean Stockwell. A brutal thriller from the director of *The French Connection* and *The Exorcist*. A reckless Secret Service agent stops at nothing in his attempt to nab the counterfeiter who killed his partner. Plenty of violent action and car chases, but it's the convincing depiction of the sleazy L.A. criminal elements that keeps the story line simmering. (Dir: William Friedkin, 116 mins.)†

Toll Gate, The (1920)***½ William S. Hart, Anna Q. Nilsson, Jack Richardson, Joseph Singleton, Master Richard Headrick. One of Hart's best films; here he stars as Black Deering, a reformed outlaw who falls in love with a woman married to a harsh, indifferent husband. Forthright story, told with stark simplicity and few frills, relying on sweeping scenery to impart a sense of grandeur. (Dir: Lambert Hillyer, 59 mins.)†

To Love a Vampire—See: **Lust for a Vampire**

Toma (1973)**½ Tony Musante, Susan Strasberg. Good police story and pilot for the TV series. Musante is fine as Dave Toma, real-life Newark, N.J., police detective, whose unique approach to his work helped him to crack, almost single-handedly, a big numbers operation connected to the syndicate. (Dir: Richard T. Heffron, 73 mins.)

Tomahawk (1951)** Van Heflin, Yvonne De Carlo, Jack Oakie, Rock Hudson. Just another Indian and cowboy film. This time the plot is involved with Indian Affairs treaties and those who fight to protect the enforcement of said treaties. (Dir: George Sherman, 82 mins.)

To Mary—With Love (1936)**½ Warner Baxter, Myrna Loy, Ian Hunter, Jean Dixon, Pat Somerset, Claire Trevor, Franklin Pangborn. The married life of one couple is contrasted with what was happening in the world at large, from 1925 to 1935; they have their ups and downs, and so does the country. Interesting idea could have been more fully developed, but this is skillfully done by real troupers. (Dir: John Cromwell, 87 mins.)

Tomb, The (1986)**½ Cameron Mitchell, John Carradine, Sybil Danning. Campy terror-pic spiced with some veteran ham actors. Loosely modeled after Bram Stoker's *Jewel of the Seven Stars* (already filmed as *The Awakening*), this shocker deals with an Egyptian princess who reincarnates so she can acquire amulets needed to keep her revivable. (Dir: Fred Olen Ray, 84 mins.)†

Tomb of Ligeia (Great Britain, 1965)*** Vincent Price, Elizabeth Shepherd, John Westbrook, Richard Johnson. This visually rich presentation of the Edgar Allan Poe story shows the spirit of Price's dead wife turning up as a cat and as his new wife (Shepherd). A stylish, spooky film written by Robert Towne. (Dir: Roger Corman, 81 mins.)†

Tomboy (1985)* Betsy Russell, Jerry Dinome, Richard Erdman, Kristi Somers. A curvaceous car-buff wants to be first on the track and in the sack with her chosen Romeo. An ordeal. (Dir: Herb Freed, 92 mins.)†

Tomboy and the Champ (1961)* Candy Moore, Ben Johnson, Jessie White, Jess Kirkpatrick, Rex Allen. While echoes of *The Yearling* ring in our ears, a plucky youngster sets out to prove that her music-loving calf will grow up to be a prize-winning side of beef. Don't miss the finale, in which the lovable steer lumbers into the little girl's hospital room and weeps while the song "Who Says Animals Can't Cry" is sung in the background. (Dir: Francis D. Lyon, 92 mins.)†

Tom Brown of Culver (1932)**½ Tom Brown, H. B. Warner, Slim Summerville, Richard Cromwell, Ben Alexander, Sidney Toler, Tyrone Power, Jr., Alan Ladd. Realistic schoolboy melodrama, with a youth attending Culver Military Academy being transformed from nonconformist to prize student; well done of this kind. (Dir: William Wyler, 82 mins.)

Tom Brown's School Days (1940)*** Cedric Hardwicke, Freddie Bartholomew, Gale Storm. Engrossing saga of Tom's exploits in a boys' school that seems like a hell-house until he improves things. The Victorian atmosphere is rendered with aplomb by a mixed bag of Brits and Hollywood reliables. (Dir: Robert Stevenson, 86 mins.)†

Tom Brown's School Days (Great Britain, 1951)***½ Robert Newton, Diana Wynyard. The adventures of a lad at an exclusive boys' school. Well-done version of classic story. (Dir: Gordon Parry, 93 mins.)

Tombs of the Blind Dead—See: **Night of the Death Cult**

Tombstone, the Town Too Tough to Die (1942)*** Richard Dix, Frances Gifford. This western rises way above the average thanks to slick production. Story of Wyatt Earp (again), and the infamous duel with the outlaws at Tombstone, Arizona. (Dir: William McGann, 80 mins.)

Tom, Dick and Harry (1941)***½ Ginger Rogers, George Murphy, Burgess Meredith, Alan Marshal. Telephone operator dreams what life would be like with three eligible suitors. Completely charming, novel comedy, excellent. Remade as *The Girl Most Likely*. (Dir: Garson Kanin, 86 mins.)†

Tom Horn (1980)** Steve McQueen, Linda Evans, Slim Pickens. McQueen plays a former Indian fighter, drifting through a settled West, who falls into a job collaring rustlers for a combine of ranchers.

Unsatisfying western. (Dir: William Wiard, 98 mins.)†

Tom Jones (Great Britain, 1963)**** Albert Finney, Susannah York, Diane Cilento, Joan Greenwood, Hugh Griffith, Joyce Redman, Edith Evans. Free-wheeling, hilarious comedy about a lusty rake in 18th-century England. The remarkable screenplay by John Osborne, based on Henry Fielding's classic novel of life in England, catches the infectious spirit of the novel. Rollicking, bawdy, beautiful England of two centuries ago is brilliantly captured by director Tony Richardson. Finney portrays the rambunctious country boy wenching and winning his way through life. The famous eating scene with Joyce Redman is one of the most riotous and sexy scenes ever filmed. (Won four Oscars.) (131 mins.)†

Tom Mix and Bill Hart (1915–16)**** A collection of classic early western two-reelers by two of the movies' most famous cowboys. First up is William S. Hart, in *Every Inch a Man*, 1915, directed by himself; here a hell-raising gambler is reformed by the love of the parson's daughter. This theme was repeated often throughout Hart's career. Next is a western comedy starring Tom Mix, *Local Color*, 1916, where some unruly cowboys hoodwink an eastern author who's come out west for authentic settings by exaggerating their exploits. Third is *An Arizona Wooing*, 1915, another Mix starrer, with our hero as a sheep rancher in trouble with cattlemen as well as Mexican bandits. All three are action packed and enthralling, though the two stars are very different. (51 mins.)†

Tommy (Great Britain, 1975)*** Ann-Margret, Oliver Reed, Jack Nicholson, Roger Daltrey, Elton John, Eric Clapton. A wildly uneven, often visually stunning musical of the Who's rock opera written by composer-guitarist Pete Townshend. Director Ken Russell wrote the screenplay, but the sung dialogue takes a back seat to the music and some crazed, hallucinatory images. Russell's flamboyant style is well suited to this garish material. (110 mins.)†

Tommy Steele Story, The—See: **Rock Around the World**

Tomorrow (1972)* Robert Duvall, Sudie Bond, Olga Bellin. A grim screen version of a Faulkner story. Duvall plays a sawmill laborer who befriends a pregnant woman who pleads with him to raise her child if she dies in childbirth. The film pushes its naturalistic style at you relentlessly, resulting in tedium. (Dir: Jospeh Anthony, 103 mins.)†

Tomorrow at 10 (Great Britain, 1962)**½ John Gregson, Robert Shaw, Helen Cherry. Kidnapper leaves his victim in a room with a time bomb, asks for ransom as the police race against time to nab him. Competent crime melodrama has quite a bit of suspense. (Dir: Lance Comfort, 80 mins.)

Tomorrow Is Another Day (1951)*** Ruth Roman, Steve Cochran. Fast-paced action drama about hoodlums and their women. Roman tries to start a new life but her past proves too strong an obstacle. Good performances. (Dir: Felix E. Feist, 90 mins.)

Tomorrow Is Forever (1946)**½ Claudette Colbert, Orson Welles, George Brent, Natalie Wood. Twenty years after he supposedly was killed, a disfigured and crippled chemist comes back to his wife, who remarried. Well-produced but slow drama with an Enoch Arden theme. (Dir: Irving Pichel, 105 mins.)

Tomorrow Is My Turn (France, 1960)*** Charles Aznavour, Georges Riviere, Nicole Courcel, Cordula Trantow. A pair of French POWS in WWII escape separately from German work farms, and after a series of adventures, both make their way to Paris and find each other. Aznavour is excellent as one of the prisoners, a baker by trade, who so yearns to return to his beloved city that he risks his life and dares the treacherous journey to be free. (Dir: Andre Cayatte, 125 mins.)

Tomorrow's Child (MTV 1982)**½ Stephanie Zimbalist, Ed Flanders, William Atherton, Bruce Davison, Arthur Hill. A mixture of science fiction and personal drama, with a story line about murders thrown in. A young wife agrees to be part of an experiment, which would involve a test-tube baby brought to term in a lab. (Dir: Joseph Sargent, 104 mins.)†

Tomorrow's Children (1934)* Diana Sinclair, Sarah Padden, Donald Douglas, Sterling Holloway. Though not as hysterical as *Reefer Madness*, this exploitation feature about sterilization will still astound modern audiences. A judge decides that a nice young girl, about to be married, should be sterilized because her family members are all drunks, feebleminded, and/or degenerates. (Dir: Crane Wilbur, 55 mins.)

Tomorrow the World (1944)***½ Fredric March, Betty Field, Skip Homeier. An American family adopts a German boy, discovers the Nazi influence has warped the child's mind. Excellent drama, thoughtful, gripping. (Dir: Leslie Fenton, 86 mins.)

Tom Sawyer (1930)**½ Jackie Coogan, Mitzi Green, Junior Durkin. Slightly static but engaging attempt to transfer Twain to the screen, with a modicum of Hollywoodization. More spunk than the later versions, but not definitive. (Dir: John Cromwell, 86 mins.)

Tom Sawyer (MTV 1973)** Josh Albee, Jeff Tyler, Jane Wyatt, Buddy Ebsen, Vic Morrow, John McGiver. Twain without the tartness, remade for TV; a classic story shines through nonetheless. (Dir: James Neilson, 104 mins.)

Tom Sawyer (1973)** Johnny Whitaker, Celeste Holm, Warren Oates, Jeff East, Jodie Foster. Strictly for the kids; the adults will be annoyed by this scrubbed-clean musical version of the Mark Twain classic. Shot entirely on location in Missouri (a plus), the film contains most of the familiar incidents, from the fence whitewashing to the scary chase through the caves. (Dir: Don Taylor, 104 mins.)†

Tom Sawyer, Detective (1938)**½ Billy Cook, Donald O'Connor, Porter Hall, Phillip Warren, Janet Waldo, Elisabeth Risdon, William Haade, Clem Bevans, Clara Blandick, Etta McDaniel. Affable family comedy-adventure has Mark Twain's characters Tom and Huck coming to the aid of a minister unjustly accused of murder; not exactly Twain, but harmlessly enjoyable. (Dir: Louis King, 68 mins.)

tom thumb (Great Britain, 1958)*** Russ Tamblyn, Terry-Thomas, Peter Sellers, Alan Young. Grimm's fairy tale brought to life using real actors, puppets, and animation, all cleverly arranged together. Concerns tiny five-inch tom who is forced to help robbers, and then later to capture them. Exemplary family fare. Oscar: Best Special Effects. (Dir: George Pal, 98 mins.)†

To My Daughter (MTV 1990)** Rue McClanahan, Michele Greene, Ty Miller, Samantha Mathis, George Coe. Adequate soap opera fare. McClanahan turns on the anguish as a mother who loses her oldest daughter. (Dir: Larry Shaw, 96 mins.)

Toni (France, 1935)***½ Charles Blavette, Jenny Helia, Celia Montalvan, Edouard Delmont. Lyrical melodrama about star-crossed lovers who part, only to meet again years later, both married to partners they hate and want to murder. Director Jean Renoir shot this magnificent film in actual locations, using direct sound and regional actors. (95 mins.)

Tonight and Every Night (1945)*** Rita Hayworth, Lee Bowman, Janet Blair, Leslie Brooks. The show must go on despite the London blitz, in this light musical about a gang of troupers who never miss a performance, going down into the underground if they have to. Not very authentic, but pleasant, with a dash of bracing wartime sentiment. (Dir: Victor Saville, 92 mins.)†

Tonight at 8:30 (Great Britain, 1952)**** Valerie Hobson, Nigel Patrick, Stanley Holloway. Three of Noel Coward's short plays, all comic gems, sophisticated, worthwhile, stylishly performed for civilized viewers. (Dir: Anthony Pelissier, 81 mins.)

Tonight for Sure! (1961)* Don Kenney, Karl Schanzer, Virginia Gordon, Marli Renfro. It doesn't always show up in his credits, but this nudie-cutie flick was Francis Ford Coppola's first movie. (He's credited as producer, writer, and director, all while he was still a student at UCLA!) The thin plot has two prudes planning to blow up a burlesque house, spinning tales of how naked women caused trouble in their lives. (66 mins.)†

Tonight Is Ours (1933)** Claudette Colbert, Fredric March, Alison Skipworth. Sparkling star chemistry saves this old-fashioned romance about a princess falling for a commoner in the City of Lights. Based on a forgettable Noel Coward play. (Dir: Stuart Walker, 76 mins.)

Tonight's the Night (Great Britain, 1954)** David Niven, Yvonne De Carlo, Barry Fitzgerald. A whimsical comedy filmed in Ireland with authentic settings (including an alleged haunted house) bolstering the film's appeal. (Dir: Mario Zampi, 88 mins.)

Tonight's the Night (MTV 1987)** Ed Marinaro, Ken Olin, Max Gail, Robert Rusler, Belinda Bauer, Tracy Nelson, Janet Margolin, Gerrit Graham. A silly comedy-drama of vignettes that attempts to do for nightclubs what *Single Bars, Single Women* did for bars. The setting is Los Angeles, where lovelorn yuppies flock to the club to look for one-night stands or long-term relationships. (Dir: Bobby Roth, 104 mins.)

Tonight We Raid Calais (1943)**½ Annabella, John Sutton, Lee J. Cobb. Another of those wartime espionage films. This one is the well-acted, improbable tale of a British agent in France to find a factory the RAF wants to bomb. (Dir: John Brahm, 70 mins.)

Tonight We Sing (1953)** David Wayne, Ezio Pinza, Anne Bancroft, Roberta Peters, Jan Peerce, Isaac Stern. The life of Sol Hurok provides the pretext for a hodgepodge of artsy production numbers. (Dir: Mitchell Leisen, 109 mins.)

Tonio Kroger (West Germany-France, 1964)**½ Jean-Claude Brialy, Nadja Tiller, Gert Frobe. An academic, fairly literal version of Thomas Mann's autobiographical novella about growing up in Germany in the late 19th century. As a film experience, it's stodgy, picturesque, with some lovely narration directly from the original. (Dir: Rolf Thiele, 90 mins.)†

Tonka—See: **Horse Named Comanche, A**

Tony Draws a Horse (Great Britain, 1950) **½ Anne Crawford, Cecil Parker. A psychiatrist and his wife disagree over the treatment of their son, and as a result a happy marriage is nearly terminated. Mildly amusing comedy has some good moments. (Dir: John Paddy Carstairs, 90 mins.)

Tony Rome (1967)** Frank Sinatra, Jill St. John, Richard Conte, Gena Rowlands. Slick production values, tough dialogue, a parade of feminine pulchitrude plus Sinatra as a private eye add up to not a hell of a lot. Rome is involved in a series of confrontations with an assortment of sordid characters, as he tries to solve a jewel theft and murder. (Dir: Gordon Douglas, 110 mins.)†

Too Bad She's Bad (Italy, 1955)**½ Sophia Loren, Vittorio De Sica, Marcello Mastroianni. Taxi driver gets involved with a band of crooks, but falls for one of the pretty ones. Mildly amusing dubbed comedy. (Dir: Alessandro Blasetti, 95 mins.)

Too Beautiful for You (France, 1989)*** Gerard Depardieu, Josiane Balski, Carole Bouquet. Sweet, intelligent bedroom farce with a twist; the husband is married to a classically beautiful woman, while his mistress is a frump. Writer-director Bertrand Blier has created such sensitive, caring people that it's easy to overlook the complexities of the romantic dilemma. The performances from the three stars are richly textured in a film that celebrates love, disappointment, and the comedy of expectations. (91 mins.)†

Too Early, Too Late (West Germany, 1981)***½ Another extraordinary work from the husband-wife filmmaking team of Jean-Marie Straub and Daniele Huillet. In this exquisite work the directors depict land and desertscapes in France and Egypt, shot in vivid color and enhanced by an appreciation of the power of nature and the serene passage of time. Groundbreaking and radiant. (105 mins.)

Too Far to Go (MTV 1979)***½ Blythe Danner, Michael Moriarty, Kathryn Walker. One of the standout TV films of the decade. Skillful adaptation by William Hanley of seventeen short stories by John Updike, about the dissolution of a twenty-year marriage. Danner is poignant and vulnerable as she both receives and hurls soft-spoken but nonetheless hurtful barbs at her embattled mate. (Dir: Fielder Cook, 98 mins.)

Too Hot to Handle (1938)*** Clark Gable, Myrna Loy, Walter Pidgeon, Leo Carrillo, Johnny Hines. Rival newsreel companies vie with each other for hot news. Big, exciting action melodrama, a most enjoyable show. (Dir: Jack Conway, 107 mins.)

Too Hot to Handle (Great Britain, 1960)*½ Jayne Mansfield, Leo Genn. Trashy crime melodrama about a nightclub entertainer trying to protect her boss from a murder frameup. (Dir: Terence Young, 92 mins.)

Too Hot to Handle (1976)½ Cheri Caffaro, Aharon Ipale, Corinne Calvet, John Van Dreelen, Vic Diaz. Perpetually half-clad Cheri plays "Samantha Fox," an inscrutable hit woman carrying on a romance with the very police detective who's hot on her trail. (Dir: Don Schain, 84 mins.)†

Too Late Blues (1961)** Bobby Darin, Stella Stevens. Glum, unpleasant story of a jazz musician who steals the affections of a blonde from his friend. (Dir: John Cassavetes, 100 mins.)

Too Late for Tears (1949)*** Lizabeth Scott, Don DeFore, Dan Duryea, Arthur Kennedy, Kristine Miller, Barry Kelley, Denver Pyle. An innocent couple is accidentally involved with a sum of money stolen by mobsters; the possession of the loot leads the acquisitive wife (Scott) to turn to crime herself. Strong performances and a cynical, uncompromising story. (Dir: Byron Haskin, 99 mins.)

Too Late the Hero (1970)***½ Cliff Robertson, Michael Caine, Henry Fonda. Rugged, complex war story. Caine and Robertson are reluctant men on a mission to a South Pacific island occupied by the Japanese in WWII. AKA: **Suicide Run**. (Dir: Robert Aldrich, 133 mins.)†

Toolbox Murders, The (1978)* Cameron Mitchell, Pamelyn Ferdin, Wesley Eure, Nicholas Beauvy. Nuts-and-bolts assortment of killings, most of them performed by Mitchell in a ski mask. (Dir: Dennis Donnelly, 93 mins.)†

Too Many Crooks (Great Britain, 1959)*** Terry-Thomas, George Cole. Thickheaded gang of crooks try to extort from a businessman. Amusingly daffy comedy. (Dir: Mario Zampi, 85 mins.)†

Too Many Girls (1940)*** Lucille Ball, Richard Carlson, Ann Miller, Desi Arnaz, Eddie Bracken. Small college with ten coeds to every boy wants badly to win a football game. Entertaining musical comedy. (Dir: George Abbott, 85 mins.)†

Too Many Husbands (1940)*** Jean Arthur, Fred MacMurray, Melvyn Douglas. About to marry again, a woman finds her first husband, believed dead, has returned. Pleasing sophisticated comedy. (Dir: Wesley Ruggles, 84 mins.)

Too Many Suspects—See: **Ellery Queen** (MTV 1975)

Too Many Thieves (1966)** Peter Falk, Britt Ekland, David Carradine. Moderately entertaining caper film with Falk playing an American lawyer who is hired by thieves who stole an art treasure from a Macedonian shrine. The character Falk plays is the same one he played in the short-lived TV series "The Trials of O'Brien." (Dir: Bob Hayes, 95 mins.)

Too Much (1987)* Bridgette Andersen. Children's film set in Japan about a young American girl who befriends her uncle's invention, a robot programmed to increase its own intelligence, then runs away with it when he tries to take it back. (Dir: Eric Rochat, 90 mins.)

Too Much Harmony (1933)**½ Bing Crosby, Jack Oakie, Grace Bradley, Judith Allen, Lilyan Tashman, Ned Sparks. A harmonic, diverting Crosby tuner, although there aren't enough songs to go around. (Dir: A. Edward Sutherland, 76 mins.)

Too Much Sun (1991)*** Robert Downey, Jr., Howard Duff, Laura Ernst, Jim Haynie, Eric Idle, Ralph Macchio, Andrea Martin, Leo Rossi, Jennifer Rubin. Delicious satire about a man whose son is gay and whose daughter is a lesbian; one of them must produce an heir or their inheritance will go to a conniving priest. Well acted by all, with Los Angeles settings that add spice to the comedy. (Dir: Robert Downey, Sr., 100 mins.)†

Too Much, Too Soon (1958)**½ Dorothy Malone, Errol Flynn, Martin Milner. Flynn is nothing short of brilliant playing his own late, beloved crony, John Barrymore. His performance alone is worth seeing in this film, but his scenes are unfortunately few and short. Otherwise, this is a cheap, maudlin adaptation of the cheap, maudlin book about John's daughter Diana Barrymore, whose life was apparently one long drunken binge of self-destruction. (Dir: Art Napoleon, 121 mins.)

Too Outrageous! (Canada, 1987)**½ Craig Russell, Hollis McLaren, David McIlwraith, Ron White. This entertaining sequel to the cult classic *Outrageous* follows the exploits of schizo writer Liza (McLaren) and Robin (Russell), the quippy female impersonator. (Dir: Richard Benner, 100 mins.)

Too Scared to Scream (1985)*½ Mike Connors, Anne Archer, Leon Isaac Kennedy, Ian McShane, John Heard, Maureen O'Sullivan. Inferior scare-job about a cop and two assistants trying to nab a crazed killer who's decimating the residents of a plush high-rise apartment building. (Dir: Tony Lo Bianco, 99 mins.)†

Tootsie (1982)**** Dustin Hoffman, Teri Garr, Jessica Lange, Sydney Pollack, Bill Murray. It's been a long time since we've had such an uproarious comedy and such a wonderful, poignant drama. Dustin Hoffman's portrayal is no in-drag impersonation but a subtle, well-conceived comedy coup. He plays Michael Dorsey, an actor who knows he's terrific but can't get a job. When his agent, played with great comic flair by the film's director, Sydney Pollack, tells him he is unemployable, Hoffman dresses as a woman and gets a job playing a tough, liberation-minded administrator of a hospital in a television soap opera. Screenwriters Larry Gelbart, Murray Schisgal, and uncredited Elaine May, have penned a yarn that is tasteful, insightful, and hilarious. (110 mins.)†

Too Young the Hero (MTV 1988)*½ Ricky Schroder, John DeVries, Ricky Warner. Incredible, true-life story of a twelve-year-old who served in the navy during WWII. The plot line contains many harrowing moments—among them the boy's first exposure to the life-and-death reality of war, and a vicious sexual attack in prison—but Schroder is all cute looks, and no conviction. (Dir: Buzz Kulik, 96 mins.)

Too Young to Die? (MTV 1990)**½ Juliette Lewis, Michael Tucker, Brad Pitt, Michael O'Keefe, Yvette Hayden, Emily Longstreth. Depressing but convincing story of a fifteen-year-old girl, abandoned by her family and reduced to life on the streets, who ends up on Death Row. Tucker is effective as the girl's lawyer, a man out of his depth, but the show belongs to young stars Lewis and Pitt. (Dir: Robert Markowitz, 96 mins.)

Too Young to Kiss (1951)*** Van Johnson, June Allyson, Gig Young. Young pianist can't get in to see a concert manager, so she poses as a thirteen-year-old. Bright comedy with plenty of laughs along the way. (Dir: Robert Z. Leonard, 91 mins.)

To Paris With Love (Great Britain, 1955)**½ Alec Guinness. Sometimes witty comedy about a father's lessons in love to his son. Alec Guinness scores again as the fun-loving father. (Dir: Robert Hamer, 78 mins.)†

Topaz (1969)**½ John Forsythe, Frederick Stafford. An espionage tale which has agents and double agents jumping around the globe when it is discovered that the Russians have infiltrated into high French government positions. Although Alfred Hitchcock directed this tale, it doesn't have his usual stamp of excitement, but the narrative itself should keep spy fans intrigued. (126 mins.)†

Topaze (1933)***½ John Barrymore, Myrna Loy, Albert Conti, Reginald Mason, Luis Alberni. Marcel Pagnol's stage play about a shy professor who turns the tables on sharks of industry seeking to exploit his ideas gives Barrymore an opportunity to turn in an irresistibly charming performance. (Dir: Harry d'Arrast, 78 mins.)†

Top Banana (1954)*** Phil Silvers, Rose Marie. A loud burlesque comic becomes a TV star and aids a young romance. From the Broadway stage hit, filmed as it was presented, this has nothing production-wise, but Silvers's yeoman

1098

service turns it into a funny show and you will see those wild sketches that made burlesque such a good training ground years ago for comedians. (Dir: Alfred E. Green, 100 mins.)

Topeka (1953)**½ Bill Elliott, Phyllis Coates. Outlaw is offered the job of sheriff, calls in his former gang members to help him clean up the territory. Lively western has plenty of action. (Dir: Thomas Carr, 69 mins.)

Top Gun (1955)**½ Sterling Hayden, William Bishop, Karen Booth, James Millican, Regis Toomey, John Dehner, Rod Taylor. Taut western, with a hired gunman warning the people of his hometown about a forthcoming raid by bandits; they won't listen to him, and he stays to help defend them. Gritty, muscular, capably done actioner. (Dir: Ray Nazarro, 73 mins.)

Top Gun (1986)** Tom Cruise, Kelly McGillis, Anthony Edwards, Tom Skerritt, Val Kilmer, Michael Ironside, Barry Tubb, John Stockwell. Surely one of the most vapid films to ever gross over 150 million dollars. Cruise is the arrogant individualist who strives to be the Navy's No. 1 pilot, and the romantic interest is McGillis, shoehorned pointlessly into the plot as a gorgeous astrophysicist. Shot like a high-gloss TV recruitment commercial, the film presents its young pilots as if they were handsome mannequins posing for a cologne ad. (Dir: Tony Scott, 109 mins.)†

Top Hat (1935)**** Fred Astaire, Ginger Rogers, Edward Everett Horton, Eric Blore, Erik Rhodes, Helen Broderick. Universally regarded as the Astaire-Rogers peak. Portraying a romantically inclined stage star, Astaire pursues Ginger from London to the Riviera, even though she proves unreceptive after mistaking Fred for her best friend's husband. There's an abundance of riches here, but our favorite number is the courtship dance in the pavilion during a rain storm, "Isn't This a Lovely Day?" Perfection. (Dir: Mark Sandrich, 99 mins.)†

Topkapi (1964)***½ Melina Mercouri, Maximilian Schell, Robert Morley, Peter Ustinov. An exciting jewel of a film about an ingenious theft of a jewel-encrusted dagger from the Topkapi Museum in Istanbul. The big heist scene may strike you as a more elaborate reshooting of the classic scene in *Rififi*, and you'll be right, because they're both the work of ace director Jules Dassin. He has assembled a flawless cast of charming rogues and charlatans. Oscar: Ustinov, Best Supporting Actor. (119 mins.)†

To Please a Lady (1950)**½ Clark Gable, Barbara Stanwyck. A romantic comedy-drama about a racing car enthusiast and his lady love, who objects to his risking his neck. (Dir: Clarence Brown, 91 mins.)

Top Man (1943)**½ Donald O'Connor, Richard Dix, Susanna Foster, Lillian Gish, Noah Beery, Jr. Corny dated comedy about a young man's taking over as head of the family while his father goes to war (WWII). (Dir: Charles Lamont, 74 mins.)

Top of His Head, The (Canada, 1989)***½ Stephen Ouimette, Christine MacFadyen, Gary Reineke. Avant-garde satire about a satellite dish salesman who falls in love with an alluring woman sought by the police for her pro-environmental actions. Director Peter Mettler's innovative methods break new ground in the way movies can be seen. (110 mins.)

Top of the Form (Great Britain, 1953)**½ Ronald Shiner, Jacqueline Pierreux, Anthony Newley. A race track tipster becomes the head of a boys' school by accident. Mildly amusing comedy. (Dir: John Paddy Carstairs, 75 mins.)

Top of the Hill, The (MTV 1980)*½ Wayne Rogers, Elke Sommer, Adrienne Barbeau, Sonny Bono, Mel Ferrer, Paula Prentiss. Macho guys and ski bunnies hop around at Mount Placid, handily capitalizing on the publicity from the 1980 Winter Olympics. (Dir: Walter Grauman, 200 mins.)

Top of the Hill (MTV 1989)** William Katt, Dick O'Neill, Jordan Baker, Tony Edwards, Kenneth McMillian, Corinne Bohrer, Kelsey Grammer. Pilot for the series starring Katt as a young California nonconformist who takes over his ailing father's congressional seat. Writer-producer Stephen J. Cannell doesn't seem to know if he wants this to be an updated *Mr. Smith Goes to Washington* or a more cynical story and the result shifts erratically between the two poles. (Dir: Alan Metzger, 96 mins.)

Top of the World (1955)**½ Dale Robertson, Evelyn Keyes, Frank Lovejoy. Jet pilot is assigned to an Alaskan observation unit. Typical service melodrama, enlivened by some good scenes in the frozen North. (Dir: Lewis R. Foster, 90 mins.)

Top o' the Morning (1949)**½ Bing Crosby, Barry Fitzgerald, Ann Blyth. Bing on the Emerald Isle, as he plays an insurance agent out to find who stole the Blarney Stone. Lazily amusing comedy with Bing crooning the songs. (Dir: David Miller, 100 mins.)

Topper (1937)*** Cary Grant, Roland Young, Constance Bennett. Gossamer fantasy-comedy about two ghosts interfering in the life of a milquetoast. Grand fantastic comedy, the original in the *Topper* series. (Dir: Norman Z. McLeod, 96 mins.)†

Topper (MTV 1979)* Kate Jackson,

Andrew Stevens, Jack Warden. Jackson and Stevens inadequately play those mischievous ghosts who make Cosmo Topper's life a comic shambles. (Dir: Charles Dubin, 104 mins.)

Topper Returns (1941)***½ Roland Young, Joan Blondell, Eddie ''Rochester'' Anderson, Dennis O'Keefe, Carole Landis. Mr. Cosmo Topper and his ghostly friends are involved in a spooky murder mystery. The best of the Toppers. Hilarious, loaded with laughs, thrills, tip-top performers! The colorized version should be avoided if possible. (Dir: Roy Del Ruth, 87 mins.)†

Topper Takes a Trip (1938)*** Roland Young, Constance Bennett. Mr. Topper goes to the Riviera for a holiday, only to find the spirit of Marion Kirby in hot pursuit. Amusing comedy. (Dir: Norman Z. McLeod, 87 mins.)

Top Secret (Great Britain, 1952)*** George Cole, Oscar Homolka. Sanitary engineer accidentally walks off with atomic secrets, is branded a traitor. Highly amusing topical comedy, good fun. AKA: **Mr. Potts Goes to Moscow.** (Dir: Mario Zampi, 94 mins.)

Top Secret (MTV 1978)*½ Bill Cosby, Tracy Reed, Sheldon Leonard, Gloria Foster. Cosby plays a special agent for Uncle Sam in Italy. (Dir: Paul Leaf, 104 mins.)

Top Secret (1984)**½ Val Kilmer, Lucy Gutteridge, Omar Sharif, Michael Gough, Christopher Villiers. The creators of *Airplane* don't take off quite so high this time, with this scattershot take-off of espionage thrillers. Plot concerns an American pop idol (Kilmer) en route to a Communist culture festival, where he sings and dances his way into resistance activities. (Dirs: Jim Abrahams, David Zucker, Jerry Zucker, 90 mins.)†

Top Secret Affair (1957)** Kirk Douglas, Susan Hayward. A tough major general and a crusading lady publisher slug it out in a slight comedy about Washington politics and the diplomatic service. From John P. Marquand's *Melville Goodwin, Esq.* (Dir: H. C. Potter, 90 mins.)

Tops Is the Limit—See: **Anything Goes (1936)**

To Race the Wind (MTV 1980)*** Steve Guttenberg, Randy Quaid, Mark Taylor. Blind Harold Krents went to Harvard and became a top-drawer law student; his story became the hit play and movie *Butterflies Are Free.* This good-humored film adapted from Krents's autobiography retains the same light touch. (Dir: Walter Grauman, 104 mins.)†

Tora! Tora! Tora! (1970)** Jason Robards, Jr., Martin Balsam, Joseph Cotten. You'll seldom see a more detailed or expensively mounted battle sequence than the bombing of Pearl Harbor which takes up a good part of the last half of the WWII film. This re-creation of the events leading up to and just after that "day of infamy" has a cast of familiar faces, as well as many Japanese actors. (Dirs: Richard Fleischer, Toshio Masuda, Kinji Fukasaku, 142 mins.)†

Torchlight (1985)*½ Pamela Sue Martin, Steve Railsback, Ian McShane, Al Corley. A well-meaning but preachy film, which depicts a perfect marriage's downfall when the bored husband becomes addicted to cocaine. Clichés and overacting turn this antidrug picture into a cocaine cartoon. (Dir: Tom Wright, 91 mins.)†

Torch Song (1953)*** Joan Crawford, Michael Wilding, Gig Young, Marjorie Rambeau, Harry Morgan, Dorothy Patrick. Crawford plays a brusque Broadway musical star (her singing is dubbed and her dancing should have been). Complications arise when a blind pianist offers Joan true love. Enjoyable melodrama; what's most amusing, in light of *Mommie Dearest*, is Joan's portrayal of a temperamental war-horse obsessed with controlling everyone around her. (Dir: Charles Walters, 90 mins.)†

Torch Song Trilogy (1988)*** Harvey Fierstein, Anne Bancroft, Matthew Broderick, Brian Kerwin. Adaptation of Fierstein's semi-autobiographical play about the life and loves of a gay drag queen occasionally sinks into bathos, but is worthy viewing for a bevy of strong performances, especially the hilarious Fierstein. (Dir: Paul Bogart, 121 mins.)†

Torment (Sweden, 1944)***½ Stig Jarrel, Alf Kjellin, Mai Zetterling, Olof Winnerstrand, Gunnar Björnstrand, Marta Arbin. Compelling drama about a sadistic teacher who viciously abuses a sensitive student and the girl he loves. Stark film relentlessly presents its theme of jealousy and cruelty, with stylized direction by Alf Sjoberg, a superb first screenplay by Ingmar Bergman, and an exquisite, attention-getting performance by Zetterling. (100 mins.)†

Torment (1986)** Taylor Gilbert, William Witt, Eve Brenner, Warren Lincoln, Stan Weston. Improbable scripting weakens this handsome-looking psychological thriller. A crazed killer fond of offing young lovers pursues the detective tracking him and the cop's girlfriend, too. (Dirs: Samson Aslanian, John Hopkins, 85 mins.)†

Torn Apart (1990)** Adrian Pasdar, Cecilia Peck, Machram Huri, Arnon Zadok, Barry Primus. Teen who returns to Israel to serve in the army after six years in the United States falls in love with an Arab girl he has known since childhood, setting off a feud among the two factions. Well-intentioned story is too melodramatic to accomplish its goals. (Dir: Jack Fisher, 96 mins.)†

Torn Between Two Lovers (MTV 1979)**½ Lee Remick, George Peppard, Joseph Bologna. A happily but unexcitingly married woman is accidentally thrown into the company of a divorced, handsome, sophisticated architect who falls in love with her. (Dir: Delbert Mann, 104 mins.)†

Torn Curtain (1966)** Paul Newman, Julie Andrews, Lila Kedrova. Substandard Alfred Hitchcock spy thriller. Newman plays a scientist who gets involved in an espionage mission while attending a convention in Denmark. (128 mins.)†

Torpedo Alley (1953)*** Mark Stevens, Dorothy Malone, Charles Winninger, Bill Williams. Well-paced, action-filled war movie about a former navy pilot who seeks to assuage his guilt over the death of his crew by volunteering for a dangerous submarine mission. Sincerely romantic and patriotically foursquare. (Dir: Lew Landers, 84 mins.)†

Torpedo Bay (France-Italy, 1963)**½ James Mason, Lilli Palmer, Gabriele Ferzeti, Alberto Lupo. When an Italian sub surfaces in neutral waters during WWII, it is met by the crew of a British antisub craft in Tangiers, and the sailors learn to like each other despite their nations' enmity. (Dirs: Bruno Vailati, Charles Frend, 91 mins.)

Torpedo of Doom, The (1938)*** Lee Powell, Herman Brix [Bruce Bennett], Eleanor Stewart. Feature version of serial *The Fighting Devil Dogs*. Two Marines combat a mysterious hooded figure who wants to rule the world. (Dirs: William Witney, John English, 100 mins.)

Torpedo Run (1958)**½ Glenn Ford, Ernest Borgnine, Dean Jones. Moderately interesting but slow moving submarine drama. Glenn Ford plays the commander of the sub, whose mission is to sink a transport on which his family are passengers. (Dir: Joseph Pevney, 98 mins.)

Torrent, The (1926)**½ Greta Garbo, Ricardo Cortez, Gertrude Olmsted, Edward Connelly, Lucien Littlefield, Martha Mattox, Tully Marshall, Mack Swain. Soapy vehicle for Garbo, in her first American picture, as a poor-but-honest Spanish peasant girl who flees to Paris to escape the attentions of a young nobleman. (Dir: Monta Bell, 68 mins.)

Torrent of Spring (Italy-France-Czechoslovakia, 1989)** Timothy Hutton, Nastassja Kinski, Valeria Golino, William Forsythe, Urbano Barberini. Good-looking but dull period piece adapted from a Turgenev novel casts Hutton (with a varying accent) as a Russian aristocrat torn between two loves—innocent Golino and scheming, married seductress Kinski. (Dir: Jerzy Skolimowski, 105 mins.)

Torrid Zone (1940)*** Pat O'Brien, Ann Sheridan, James Cagney, Andy Devine, Jerome Cowan. Good racy dialogue and the acting of the principals combine to make this a torrid picture. Jim is a no-good, Pat is his foreman, and Ann gives out with plenty of oomph as a night club girl. (Dir: William Keighley, 88 mins.)

Tortilla Flat (1942)** Spencer Tracy, John Garfield, Hedy Lamarr, Frank Morgan. Stale adaptation from the John Steinbeck novel about tramps on the California coast, with some unfortunate set design. Tracy does a good job, but is hopelessly miscast. (Dir: Victor Fleming, 105 mins.)

Torture Chamber of Baron Blood—See: **Baron Blood**

Torture Chamber of Dr. Sadism, The (West Germany, 1967)** Christopher Lee, Lex Barker, Karin Dor. In Blood Castle an evil count holds a baroness captive in an effort to gain immortality. For Lee enthusiasts only. AKA: **The Blood Demon.** (Dir: Harald Reinl, 85 mins.)†

Torture Garden (Great Britain, 1967)**½ Peter Cushing, Jack Palance, Burgess Meredith, Beverly Adams. Some eerie tales are spun by a sinister doctor (Burgess Meredith) at a sideshow. Best: the first one, about a cat's evil presence. Worst: the last, with a hammy Jack Palance performance. (Dir: Freddie Francis, 93 mins.)†

Torture Zone—See: **Chamber of Fear**

Toscanini: The Maestro (MTV 1988)*** Superbly researched and well-mounted documentary about the master conductor. Vintage home-movie footage and newsreel clips supply a continuity to a career that spanned more than seventy years and amassed enough accolades for a dozen great musical figures. (Dir: Peter Rosen, 90 mins.)

To Sir, With Love (Great Britain, 1967)*** Sidney Poitier, Judy Geeson, Suzy Kendall. A good humored, touching story of an idealistic ex-engineer (Poitier, of course) and his experiences in teaching a group of rambunctious white high school students from the slums of London's East End. Poitier is particularly appealing in this film skillfully produced, adapted, and directed by James Clavell. (105 mins.)†

To Sleep So as to Dream (Japan, 1986)*** Moe Kamura, Shiro Sano, Kojji Otake. Delightful and surreal comedy-drama about a pair of detectives investigating a bizarre case that leads to a reality-shattering adventure in an unfinished silent movie serial. (Dir: Kaizo Hayashi, 81 mins.)

To Sleep With Anger (1990)*** Danny Glover, Richard Brooks, Paul Butler, Mary Alice, Carl Lumbly, Vonetta McGee, Wonderful Smith. A seemingly peaceful Los Angeles household receives a visitor from the Deep South, who stirs up the tensions resting under the family's surface. Carefully constructed story builds slowly but evenly, providing choice parts for an able cast. (Dir: Charles Burnett, 95 mins.)†

Total Recall (1990)**½ Arnold Schwarzenegger, Rachel Ticotin, Sharon Stone, Michael Ironside, Ronny Cox. There's a lot to like in this sci-fi thriller about Schwarzenegger going to the Martian mining colonies to find out why someone wiped out his memory: state of the art special effects, clever plot twists, and a pair of actresses (Ticotin and Stone) who match Arnold in action scenes. But director Paul Verhoeven continually pounds the viewer with endless, numbing violence, and an interesting political subtext is abandoned for senseless action. Disappointing. (113 mins.)†

To the Devil...a Daughter (Great Britain, 1976)**½ Richard Widmark, Christopher Lee, Nastassia Kinski, Honor Blackman, Denholm Elliott. Satanist Lee earmarks Kinski to become the devil's daughter on her eighteenth birthday. Her distraught father, Elliott, enlists the aid of occult expert Widmark. Based on the Dennis Wheatley novel. (Dir: Peter Sykes, 93 mins.)†

To the Ends of the Earth (1948)***½ Dick Powell, Signe Hasso. Government agent chases a narcotic ring around the world. Intricate plotting keeps interest on high in this thrilling melodrama. Excellent. (Dir: Robert Stevenson, 109 mins.)

To the Shores of Hell (1965)* Marshall Thompson, Kiva Lawrence, Richard Arlen. Marine major struggles to rescue his doctor brother from the Vietcong in an awkward war saga that huffs and puffs in between bazooka bursts. (Dir: Will Zens, 81 mins.)

To the Victor (1948)**½ Dennis Morgan, Viveca Lindfors, Dorothy Malone, Denise Darcel. This romance of a black marketeer and a French girl collaborator in postwar Paris never gets off the ground. (Dir: Delmer Daves, 99 mins.)

To Trap a Spy (MTV 1966)** Robert Vaughn, Patricia Crowley, David McCallum. Pilot show for TV's "Man from U.N.C.L.E.," lengthened by some added lovemaking footage, yielding an instant movie. (Dir: Don Medford, 92 mins.)

Touch, The (Sweden-U.S., 1971)*** Elliott Gould, Bibi Andersson, Max von Sydow. A deeply moving melodrama directed in English, by Ingmar Bergman. The film is quiet and subtle, with a visual expressiveness unusual for the dour Swede. Andersson gives one of the most full-bodied emotional performances ever seen onscreen, as the woman who leaves von Sydow for Gould. (113 mins.)

Touchables, The (Great Britain, 1968)* Judy Huxtable, Esther Anderson, Marilyn Richard, Kathy Simmonds, David Anthony. Tasteless nonsense about four screwy London mods who kidnap a popular singing idol to satisfy their sexual appetites. (Dir: Robert Freeman, 97 mins.)

Touch and Go (Great Britain, 1955)*** Jack Hawkins, Margaret Johnston. Funny, sometimes hilarious comedy of a family's decision to pull up stakes and move to Australia. (Dir: Michael Truman, 84 mins.)

Touch and Go (1987)**½ Michael Keaton, Maria Conchita Alonso, Ajay Naidu. Making a statement about commitment with a sporadically effective mix of humor and sentimental drama, the movie stars Keaton as an emotionally isolated hockey player who grows to love Alonso, the mother of the eleven-year-old delinquent-in-training with whom he locks horns. (Dir: Robert Mandel, 101 mins.)†

Touched (1983)** Robert Hays, Kathleen Beller, Ned Beatty, Gilbert Lewis, Lyle Kessler. The acting doesn't save this story of two mental patients who escape from their institution and try to live normal lives. (Dir: John Flynn, 93 mins.)†

Touched by Love (1980)**½ Deborah Raffin, Diane Lane, Michael Learned, Clu Gulager, Mark Wickes. A sentimental yarn based on a true story. Raffin plays a teacher-nurse who works with children afflicted with cerebral palsy. One particular girl (Lane) is uncommunicative until Raffin hits upon a way to bring her out . . . writing to her idol Elvis Presley. (Dir: Gus Trikonis, 95 mins.)

Touch of Class, A (Great Britain, 1972)*** Glenda Jackson, George Segal. A delightful bittersweet romantic comedy about a pair of clandestine lovers in a London-Spain tryst. Despite lapses in this script about a married man eager to extend a brief encounter, Jackson and Segal are enormously appealing together. Best Actress Oscar for Jackson. (Dir: Melvin Frank, 106 mins.)†

Touch of Evil (1958)**** Orson Welles, Charlton Heston, Janet Leigh, Joseph Calleia, Dennis Weaver, Akim Tamiroff, Marlene Dietrich, Zsa Zsa Gabor, Joseph Cotten. The greatest masterpiece of all sleaze movies, director Orson Welles's baroque thriller was his last Hollywood film. Welles stars as a corrupt sheriff in a seedy border town who matches wits with a Mexican narcotics cop (Heston, on honeymoon with Leigh). Acting honors to Calleia's loyal lieutenant, whose moral quandaries give the drama heart. (108 mins.)†

Touch of Larceny, A (Great Britain, 1959)*** James Mason, Vera Miles, George Sanders. Lothario-like military man dreams

up a scheme to make it appear that he has defected to the Russians with secrets—so he can sell his memoirs and obtain money to marry. Mason is charming in this clever little comedy with a good portion of sly humor. (Dir: Guy Hamilton, 94 mins.)

Touch of Scandal, A (MTV 1984)** Angie Dickinson, Tom Skerritt, Jason Miller. Dickinson plays a liberal politician bucking blackmail, a dull husband, and a power-crazy minister. Political issues become a sidebar to the seamy action in the streets. (Dir: Ivan Nagy, 104 mins.)

Tough as They Come (1942)*½ Dead End Kids, Helen Parrish, Virginia Brissac. Billy Halop is a law student (sure!) who takes a job with a crooked finance company. His former friends help him see the error of his ways. (Dir: William Nigh, 61 mins.)

Tough Enough (1983)* Dennis Quaid, Stan Shaw, Pam Grier. Trite and tedious *Rocky* rip-off. Country-western singer Art Long (Dennis Quaid) wins "Toughman" boxing competition and works his way up to title fight and recording contract. (Dir: Richard O. Fleischer, 106 mins.)†

Tougher Than Leather (1988)* Run-DMC (Joseph Simmons, Darryl McDaniels, Jason Mizell), Richard Edson, Jenny Lumet. The rap group Run-DMC, who have always maintained an antiviolence stance, make their starring debut in this gratuitously brutal, misogynist action flick, with student-film level production values. Run-D other way! (Dir: Rick Rubin, 86 mins.)†

Toughest Gun in Tombstone (1958)** George Montgomery, Beverly Tyler, Jim Davis. Dull saga of a cowboy out to avenge the murder of his wife and bring to justice the villainous outlaw, Johnny Ringo. (Dir: Earl Bellamy, 72 mins.)

Toughest Man Alive (1955)**½ Dane Clark, Lita Milan. Government agent poses as a gun runner to break up a smuggling ring. Fast-moving melodrama. (Dir: Sidney Salkow, 72 mins.)

Toughest Man in the World, The (MTV 1984)**½ Mr. T., Dennis Dugan, Peggy Pope, Lynne Moody. It's tailor-made for Mr. T; he's a nightclub bouncer running a Chicago youth center that faces extinction unless he wins the "Toughest Man in the World" contest. (Dir: Dick Lowry, 104 mins.)

Tough Guys (1986)**½ Burt Lancaster, Kirk Douglas, Charles Durning, Alexis Smith, Dana Carvey, Darlanne Fluegel, Eli Wallach. Lancaster and Douglas are splendid as a pair of gentlemanly thieves who, released after thirty years in prison, are unprepared for the treatment that the elderly receive. Their rebellious activities and encounters with 1980s society are often hilarious, and only the conventionality of the last half hour keeps the film short of first-rate. (Dir: Jeff Kanew, 104 mins.)†

Tough Guys Don't Dance (1987)**½ Ryan O'Neal, Isabella Rossellini, Debra Sandlund, Wings Hauser, John Bedford Lloyd, Lawrence Tierney. Norman Mailer's savagely funny mystery is an odd artifact, one that will hopefully attract a cult following. The plot of the best-selling novel is left intact: O'Neal plays a writer who can clear himself of murder charges only by finding out who actually did kill his wife and mistress, and then put their decapitated heads in his secret marijuana patch. The film's real treat is its demented dialogue, which gives one pause to wonder what was going on in Mailer's mind; there are intentionally funny moments like Hauser's volatile kiss-off scene, and there are others that could have only been conceived in a camp state of grace, such as the scene where O'Neal stands on a rock, his heart broken, repeating "Oh man Oh god, Ohman Ohgod, Ohmanogod. . . ." (Dir: Norman Mailer, 110 mins.)†

Toughlove (MTV 1985)**½ Bruce Dern, Lee Remick, Eric Schiff, Jason Patric. Overwrought 'message' drama. Remick and Dern play the desperate parents of a drug-taking liar who manipulates them, so they join Toughlove, a support group that believes parents shouldn't allow their kids to ride roughshod over their lives. (Dir: Glenn Jordan, 104 mins.)†

Tourist (MTV 1980)*½ Lee Meriwether, Bradford Dillman, Lois Nettleton, Adrienne Barbeau, David Groh, Bonnie Bedelia. Unmistakably TV-ized product. Couples tour Europe and experience romantic dilemmas whose resolutions are too easily arrived at. (Dir: Jeremy Summers, 104 mins.)

Tourist Trap (1979)*½ Chuck Connors, Tanya Roberts, Jocelyn Jones. Not very good, but there are a few jolts provided. Hammy Connors treats the unwary visitors to his remote museum like dummies. (Dir: David Schmoeller, 90 mins.)†

Tout Va Bien (France, 1972)*** Jane Fonda, Yves Montand, Vittorio Caprioli, Anne Wiazemsky, Jean Pignol. At the peak of her political involvement, Fonda starred as an American reporter covering a takeover of a French factory by workers who have imprisoned their bosses. Surprisingly straightforward telling of radical action, highlighted by an extraordinary multilevel set and expressive camerawork. (Dirs: Jean-Luc Godard, Jean-Pierre Gorin, 95 mins.)

Tovarich (1937)*** Claudette Colbert, Charles Boyer, Basil Rathbone. Amusing comedy about two royal paupers who are carrying forty billion francs for the czar but would rather starve than spend it. Translated from Jacques Deval's play by Robert E. Sherwood. (Dir: Anatole Litvak, 98 mins.)

Toward the Unknown (1956)**½ William Holden, Lloyd Nolan, Virginia Leith, James Garner. Fairly interesting drama about the jet test pilots and their personal involvements. Holden plays a nervous major whose past record makes him over-zealous in the performance of his duty. (Dir: Mervyn LeRoy, 115 mins.)

Towering Inferno, The (1974)*** Paul Newman, Steve McQueen, Faye Dunaway, Fred Astaire, Jennifer Jones, Richard Chamberlain, Robert Vaughn, William Holden. A multimillion-dollar disaster epic that delivers the goods. Newman is the architect of one of the tallest buildings in the world, erected in San Francisco, and it's grand opening time. But Holden's greedy, selfish son-in-law (Chamberlain) has cut some corners, resulting in unsafe wiring and a big fire which endangers the lives of the guests at the swank opening. (Dir: Irwin Allen, 165 mins.)†

Tower of Evil—See: **Horror on Snape Island**

Tower of London (1939)*** Basil Rathbone, Boris Karloff, Vincent Price, Nan Grey. Atmospheric, witty drama about the rise of the (supposedly) wicked King Richard III, and the various and imaginative murders he committed to gain the British throne. (Dir: Rowland V. Lee, 92 mins.)

Tower of London (1962)** Vincent Price, Michael Pate, Joan Freeman. Melodramatic, lurid retelling of the story of King Richard III. Not as good as the '39 film of the same name. Vince really hams it up. (Dir: Roger Corman, 73 mins.)

Tower of Terror (Great Britain, 1941)** Michael Rennie, Movita, Wilfrid Lawson. OK WWII tale about a lighthouse off the German coast. Its half-mad keeper, Lawson, plays unwitting host to French concentration camp escapee Movita and British spy Rennie, who fall in love. (Dir: Lawrence Huntington, 80 mins.)†

Town Bully (MTV 1988)*½ Bruce Boxleitner, Pat Hingle, David Graf. Senseless drama featuring Graf as a mean, vicious type who beats up his fellow townspeople and rapes the women. Once they get up enough courage to kill him, it's time for special prosecutor Boxleitner to find the culprit. (Dir: Noel Black, 96 mins.)

Town Like Alice, A (Great Britain, 1956)*** Virginia McKenna, Peter Finch. Powerful film about the tragedy of a group of women who miss being evacuated from Malaya at the outbreak of WWII and suffer indignities in the hands of the conquering Japanese Army. The acting is first-rate. (Dir: Jack Lee, 107 mins.)

Town Like Alice, A (Australia, 1981)*** Helen Morse, Bryan Brown, Gordon Jackson. Television adaptation of Nevil Shute's novel, encompassing both the struggles of the women prisoners held in Malaysia by the Japanese and the lead characters' struggle to adjust after the war. Long but engrossing. (Dir: David Stevens, 300 mins.)†

Town on Trial (Great Britain, 1957)*** John Mills, Charles Coburn. Well-done tale of a murder investigation in a town loaded with secrets. (Dir: John Guillermin, 94 mins.)

Town Tamer (1965)* Dana Andrews, Terry Moore, Pat O'Brien, Lon Chaney. Lawyer, avenging his wife's death, corrals the lawless in western towns. (Dir: Lesley Selander, 89 mins.)

Town that Dreaded Sundown, The (1977)*½ Ben Johnson, Andrew Prine, Dawn Wells, Charles B. Pierce. Real-life tale of a lone-star looney terrorizing a town in Texas. (Dir: Charles Pierce, 90 mins.)†

Town Went Wild, The (1944)** Low-budget family comedy about two feuding families whose offspring fall in love; but it turns out that the boy might be the girl's brother, after a mix-up at the hospital. Mildly entertaining. (Dir: Ralph Murphy, 77 mins.)

Town Without Pity (U.S.-Switzerland-West Germany, 1961)** Kirk Douglas, E. G. Marshall, Christine Kaufmann, Robert Blake, Richard Jaeckel. Army major in Germany is assigned to defend a quartet of GIs accused of attacking a young girl. Downbeat, grim drama. (Dir: Gottfried Reinhardt, 105 mins.)

Toxic Avenger, The (1986)** Andree Maranda, Mitchell Cohen, Pat Ryan, Jr. Nerdy janitor at a small-town spa falls into a barrel of toxic waste and becomes a hulking superhero who sets out to clean up the corrupt town. (Dirs: Michael Herz, Samuel Weil, 82 mins.)†

Toxic Avenger, Part II, The (1989)* Ron Fazio, John Altamura, Phoebe Legere, Rick Collins. Dumb sequel that finds Tox going to Japan in search of his father. (Dirs: Lloyd Kaufman, Michael Herz, 95 mins.)†

Toxic Avenger III, The: The Last Temptation of Toxie (1989)* Ron Fazio, John Altamura, Phoebe Legere. Having rid Tromaville of crime and needing to raise money for an operation to cure his sightless girlfriend, Toxie takes a job with a corporation run by the Devil himself. (Dirs: Lloyd Kaufman, Michael Herz, 89 mins.)†

Toxic Zombies (1980)* Charles Austin, John Amplas. Marijuana farmers become murderous zombies. Just say no to this amateurish effort. AKA: **Blood-**

eaters. (Dir: Charles McCrann, 85 mins.)†

Toy, The (France, 1976)*** Pierre Richard, Michel Bouquet, Fabrice Greco. Engaging, heartwarming comedy about a schnook (Richard) who is hired to be a living "toy" for the spoiled son (Greco) of a wealthy businessman (Bouquet). Richard combines pathos and slapstick to good effect. (Dir: Francis Veber, 90 mins.)

Toy, The (1982)* Richard Pryor, Jackie Gleason, Ned Beatty, Scott Schwartz. Asinine remake of the charming French film. Even Pryor playing a man beseiged by debts can't save this slapstick mess about a tycoon (Gleason) who buys Pryor to amuse his spoiled child. (Dir: Richard Donner, 100 mins.)†

Toys in the Attic (1963)**½ Dean Martin, Geraldine Page, Wendy Hiller, Yvette Mimieux, Gene Tierney. A no-good rover returns to his New Orleans home with his childlike bride, brings trouble for his spinster sisters. Lillian Hellman's drama arrives onscreen with capable performers, but the result is disappointing. (Dir: George Roy Hill, 90 mins.)†

Toy Soldiers (1983)*½ Cleavon Little, Jason Miller, Rodolfo De Anda, Terri Garber. College kids get a liberal education in guerilla warfare when they're kidnapped by revolutionaries in Central America and must save their own necks. (Dir: David Fisher, 85 mins.)

Toy Soldiers (1991)*** Sean Astin, Wil Wheaton, T. E. Russell, George Perez, Keith Coogan, Andrew Divoff, Louis Gossett, Jr., Denholm Elliott, Mason Adams. *Dead Poets Society* meets *Die Hard* and the result is a disaster. It's about a prep school for incorrigibles that is taken over by terrorists seeking the release of a jailed drug baron. Generally poor acting and a dismal script. (Dir: Daniel Petrie, Jr., 112 mins.)†

Toy Tiger (1956)**½ Jeff Chandler, Laraine Day, Tim Hovey, David Janssen. Pleasant comedy about a neglected child who plays cupid for his career Mom and selects her new husband, one of her staff of commercial artists. (Dir: Jerry Hopper, 88 mins.)

Toy Wife, The (1938)**½ Melvyn Douglas, Luise Rainer, Robert Young, Barbara O'Neil, H. B. Warner. Comedy-drama of a spoiled southern belle who can't decide between two suitors; when she does marry, her husband finds that the childishness that was charming before is no longer appropriate. Rather a good concept not clearly thought out; and light comedy is not Rainer's forte. Elaborately set and costumed. (Dir: Richard Thorpe, 95 mins.)

Trackdown (1976)* Cathy Lee Crosby, Jim Mitchum, Anne Archer, Karen Lamm,

Erik Estrada. A girl runs away from home and into the L.A. call girl rackets. (Dir: Richard T. Heffron, 98 mins.)

Trackdown: Finding the Goodbar Killer (MTV 1983)** George Segal, Shelley Hack, Alan North. This TV sequel to *Looking for Mr. Goodbar* picks up with the investigation after the brutal murder of the young New York schoolteacher. A routine detective story. (Dir: Bill Persky, 104 mins.)

Tracker, The (MCTV 1988)** Kris Kristofferson, Scott Wilson, Mark Moses. Kris's sagebrush charisma is the only distinguishing element of this standard oater. He's the title "tracker" who's out to catch a demented Mormon gunman (house psycho Wilson) with the aid of a sheriff and his citified, law student son. (Dir: John Guillerman, 101 mins.)

Trackers, The (MTV 1971)*½ Sammy Davis, Jr., Ernest Borgnine, Julie Adams. Mundane western, with Borgnine seeking vengeance against his son's murderers and arguing with Sammy the deputy marshall who's tracking Ernest's kidnapped daughter. (Dir: Earl Bellamy, 73 mins.)

Track of the Cat (1954)** Robert Mitchum, Teresa Wright, Diana Lynn, Tab Hunter. A cougar hunt amid family squabbles makes up the action of this otherwise slow-paced movie. Best feature is the fine photography. (Dir: William Wellman, 102 mins.)

Track of the Vampire (1966)*½ William Campbell, Sandra Knight. Mad artist-vampire paints beautiful girls, then does them in. Gruesome thriller. AKA: **Blood Bath**. (Dir: Stephanie Rothman, 80 mins.)

Tracks (1976)***½ Dennis Hopper, Dean Stockwell, Taryn Power. Stream-of-consciousness tale about a Vietnam vet (Hopper) who is accompanying his dead buddy's body on a train. Hopper gives one of his strongest performances ever in this, one of the first American films to tackle the way the war psychologically crippled its soldiers. Without showing a single battle scene, director Henry Jaglom has conjured up the terror felt by a mind inflicted with tunnel vision, and provided some very fine comic material in the film's first half, with the confused Hopper encountering a gallery of amiable eccentrics. (90 mins.)†

Track the Man Down (Great Britain, 1955)**½ Kent Taylor, Petula Clark, Renée Houston, Walter Rilla, George Rose, Kenneth Griffith, Ursula Howells. Intriguing British-made mystery of a reporter tracing illegal dog-racing winnings; convoluted and novel setting. (Dir: R. G. Springsteen, 75 mins.)

Track 29 (1988)** Theresa Russell, Gary Oldman, Christopher Lloyd, Colleen Camp, Sandra Bernhard, Seymour Cassel. Erratic satire-*cum*-psychodrama from screenwriter Dennis Potter (*The Singing Detective*) and director Nicolas Roeg (*Bad Timing*). Russell plays a woman haunted by a young man who claims to be her long-lost son (Oldman). Like her character, we're kept uncertain of the reality of the situation. Make of it what you will. (90 mins.)†

Trader Horn (1931)**½ Harry Carey, Edwina Booth, Duncan Renaldo. This exciting jungle thriller scared the daylights out of 1931 audiences. You may find it funny but it was a step forward in realistic movie making. (Dir: W. S. Van Dyke, 120 mins.)

Trader Horn (1973)* Rod Taylor, Anne Heywood, Jean Sorel, Don Knight, Ed Bernard. Into the wilds of Africa, a world-famous Bwana and his intrepid party run up against some obviously studio-bound dangers. Even the dated thrills of the original surpass this remake. (Dir: Reza Badiyi, 105 mins.)

Trader Hornee (1970)* Elisabeth Monica, John Alderman, Christine Murray, Buddy Pantsari, Brandon Duffy, Lisa Grant, Deek Sills. Outrageous soft-core porn spoof of jungle movies is so bad, it's good. Jammed with big breasts, lousy acting, and every safari film cliché imaginable. (Dir: "Tsanusdi" [David Friedman], 105 mins.)†

Trade Winds (1938)***½ Fredric March, Joan Bennett, Ann Sothern, Ralph Bellamy, Thomas Mitchell. Director Tay Garnett had made a trip around the world, and came home with some dynamite travel footage he just *had* to use somehow. So he and co-writer Frank R. Adams concocted this wild, delightful chase around the globe, as wisecracking detective with a heart-of-gold March trails murder-suspect Bennett. Naturally this becomes a love story, by turns hilarious, suspenseful, and delicately affecting. Wonderful entertainment. (95 mins.)

Trading Places (1983)*** Dan Aykroyd, Eddie Murphy, Ralph Bellamy, Don Ameche, Denholm Elliott, Jamie Lee Curtis, Paul Gleason. An uneven but often hilarious tale of a millionaire and a pauper who switch roles. The old-hat plot is enlivened by fine acting all around, with Bellamy and Ameche especially notable as two conniving old men. (Dir: John Landis, 106 mins.)†

Traffic (France-Italy, 1971)*** Jacques Tati, Maria Kimberly. Virtually plotless free-form series of running gags about Paris, its traffic, and automobile drivers. Tati directed and wrote this slight but inventive satire about transporting a model camping car to an automobile show in Holland. (89 mins.)

Tragedy of a Ridiculous Man (Italy, 1981)**

Ugo Tognazzi, Anouk Aimée, Laura Morante, Victor Cavallo, Riccardo Tognazzi. Prolix tale about a man with mixed feelings about raising ransom money after his son is kidnapped remains an intellectual exercise. (Dir: Bernardo Bertolucci, 116 mins.)†

Tragedy of Flight 103, The: The Inside Story (MCTV 1990)**½ Ned Beatty, Peter Boyle, Vincent Gardenia, Timothy West, Michael Wincott. Grim, exploitative docudrama explores the events leading up to that tragic day of December 21, 1988, when Pan Am Flight 103 exploded over Lockerbie, Scotland. This disturbing investigative re-enactment focuses on the financially troubled Pan Am corporation, which was more concerned about saving dollars than developing a safer security program. (Dir: Leslie Woodhead, 86 mins.)†

Trail of the Lonesome Pine, The (1936)** Fred MacMurray, Henry Fonda, Sylvia Sidney. Now dated outdoor adventure about feuding and fighting in the backwoods when the railroad first came through. (Dir: Henry Hathaway, 102 mins.)

Trail of the Pink Panther (1982)** Peter Sellers, Joanna Lumley, Herbert Lom, David Niven, Richard Mulligan, Capucine. Director Blake Edwards, after Peter Sellers's death, assembled outtakes from the Pink Panther series, and concocted a flimsy storyline about Clouseau's associates' memories of him. (97 mins.)†

Trail of the Vigilantes (1940)*** Franchot Tone, Broderick Crawford, Peggy Moran, Warren William. Easterner is sent west to break up an outlaw gang. Entertaining western, with emphasis on some hilarious comedy. (Dir: Allan Dwan, 78 mins.)

Trail Street (1947)*** Randolph Scott, Robert Ryan, Anne Jeffreys, Gabby Hayes, Madge Meredith, Steve Brodie. Dynamic, colorful western, with stalwart Scott as Bat Masterson, engaged by a government land agent to help clean up a wide-open town. (Dir: Ray Enright, 84 mins.)

Train, The (U.S.-France-Italy, 1964)***½ Burt Lancaster, Paul Scofield, Michel Simon, Jeanne Moreau. An exciting WWII drama set in Paris during the German occupation. A railroad boss seeks the aid of the powerful French Resistance fighters when it becomes known that France's art treasures are going to be transported by train to Germany. (Dirs: Arthur Penn, John Frankenheimer, 133 mins.)

Train of Events (Great Britain, 1949)**½ Valerie Hobson, John Clements, Joan Dowling. Episodic film about people aboard a train whose problems are resolved in one way or another when the train is involved in an accident. (Dirs: Sidney Cole, Charles Crichton, Basil Dearden, 89 mins.)

Train Ride to Hollywood (1975)** Guy Marks, Michael Payne, Charles Love, Harry Williams, Charles McCormick. A silly film you might enjoy if you're in the mood. A black rock singer dreams he's a porter on a train heading for Hollywood, on which many stars turn out to be traveling. (Dir: Charles Rondeau, 85 mins.)

Train Robbers, The (1973)*½ John Wayne, Ann-Margret. Dull western which finds Wayne helping the helpless widow-lady Ann-Margret get her rightful share of the gold stashed away by her late husband. (Dir: Burt Kennedy, 92 mins.)†

Tramp, The (1915) and **A Woman** (1915)**** Two great short comedies written and directed by Charlie Chaplin. First, *The Tramp* establishes Chaplin's most renowned character, as he rescues country girl Edna Purviance from some toughs and remains to get a job on her parents' farm. The second film, *A Woman*, is a society spoof, as Chaplin woos Purviance and disposes of her other suitors—at one point he also removes his mustache and dresses up as a very convincing lady! Two real classics. (57 mins.)†

Tramplers, The (Italy, 1966)** Gordon Scott, Joseph Cotten, Jim Mitchum. Confederate soldier returns home to encounter trouble from his father and the problems left by war's aftermath. (Dirs: "Anthony Wileys" [Mario Sequi], Albert Band, 105 mins.)†

Trancers (1985)**½ Tim Thomerson, Helen Hunt, Michael Stefani, Art La Fleur. A gruff 22nd-century cop journeys to present-day L.A. to stop a zombie master from changing the future. (Dir: Charles Band, 85 mins.)†

Transatlantic (1931)**½ Edmund Lowe, Lois Moran, Myrna Loy. Atmospheric shipboard intrigue. Lowe is top-billed and suave, but the real stars are designer Gordon Wiles and cameraman James Wong Howe. (Dir: William K. Howard, 78 mins.)

Transatlantic Merry-Go-Round (1934)**½ Jack Benny, Nancy Carroll, Gene Raymond, Patsy Kelly, Sidney Blackmer, Mitzi Green. Whodunit matters less than whosingsit in this airy concoction about a collection of double-crossers suspected of murder at sea. (Dir: Ben Stoloff, 92 mins.)†

Transatlantic Tunnel (Great Britain, 1935)** Richard Dix, Madge Evans, Walter Huston, Leslie Banks, George Arliss. Only the sets retain some interest in this saga. (Dir: Maurice Elvey, 94 mins.)†

Trans-Europ-Express (France, 1966)*** Jean-Louis Trintignant, Christine Barbier, Marie-France Pisier, Nadine Verdier,

Alain Robbe-Grillet. Complex, fascinating drama about a film director aboard the titular train, writing a script about double murders and double agents. (Dir: Alain Robbe-Grillet, 90 mins.)

Transformers, the Movie (1986)* Voices of Eric Idle, Judd Nelson, Robert Stack, Leonard Nimoy, Orson Welles. The Autobots must battle the Decepticons over a medallion. Animated toy commercial for kids only; adults intrigued by the voice credits should note that all are so filtered as to be unrecognizable. (Dir: Nelson Shin, 86 mins.)†

Transmutations—See: **Underworld**

Transplant (MTV 1979)**½ Kevin Dobson, Granville Van Dusen, Ronny Cox, Melinda Dillon. Story of a heart attack victim—a highly charged man of thirty-five who smokes like a chimney, drinks like a fish—and his wife, a vigorous young woman, enormously appealing and supportive no matter how desperate the situation. (Dir: William A. Graham, 104 mins.)

Transylvania 6-5000 (1985)* Jeff Goldblum, Joseph Bologna, Ed Begley, Jr., Carol Kane, Jeffrey Jones, John Byner, Geena Davis. Two dopey newshounds (Goldblum and Begley, Jr.) visit Transylvania on a search for Frankenstein and headlines. Instead, they find vampires and mad scientists, all of whom have seen better days as foils for Abbott and Costello. (Dir: Rudy DeLuca, 90 mins.)†

Transylvania Twist (1989)**½ Robert Vaughn, Teri Copley, Steve Altman, Ace Mask, Angus Scrimm, Jay Robinson, Steve Franken, Howard Morris. Scattershot horror comedy from the Roger Corman factory, with ditzy Copley visiting the Transylvanian castle of Lord Bryon Orlock (Vaughn hamming it up effectively). Lots of in-jokes and references will endear it to horror fans; others should find a few chuckles. (Dir: Jim Wynorski, 82 mins.)†

Trap, The (1947)—See: **Charlie Chan and the Trap**

Trap, The (1959)**½ Richard Widmark, Tina Louise, Lee J. Cobb, Earl Holliman. Head of a crime syndicate trying to flee the country isolates a small desert town. (Dir: Norman Panama, 84 mins.)

Trap, The (Great Britain-Canada, 1966)*** Rita Tushingham, Oliver Reed. A raw, tough, unusual movie; a fur trapper and the mute girl he has bartered for as wife struggle in the wilderness of 19th-century Canada. (Dir: Sidney Hayers, 106 mins.)

Trapeze (1956)*** Burt Lancaster, Tony Curtis, Gina Lollobrigida, Katy Jurado, Thomas Gomez. Corny but colorful circus drama. Lancaster plays a former aerialist who helps a young acrobat achieve fame. Good European locations, exciting camera work are added assets. (Dir: Carol Reed, 105 mins.)†

Trapped (1949)***½ Barbara Payton, Lloyd Bridges, John Hoyt. T-men release a counterfeiter from jail, hoping he will lead them to a big money ring. Excellent documentary-type crime melodrama. (Dir: Richard Fleischer, 78 mins.)

Trapped (MTV 1973)*½ James Brolin, Susan Clark, Earl Holliman, Robert Hooks. How far can a movie go with a story line that locks a victim of teenaged muggers in a department store men's room, and then confronts him with killer dogs? (Dir: Frank De Felitta, 72 mins.)

Trapped (MTV 1989)*** Kathleen Quinlan, Bruce Abbott, Katy Boyer. A taut and quite suspenseful reinvention of a familiar plotline—a woman relentlessly pursued through an abandoned building. In this case, the building is a newly erected highrise, run entirely on electricity, and the woman is an agoraphobe working for the building's management. (Dir: Fred Walton, 96 mins.)†

Trapped Beneath the Sea (MTV 1974)**½ Lee J. Cobb, Martin Balsam. Well-made drama about the rescue of an experimental submarine. Good performances and realistic underwater sequences lift this disaster film above the average. (Dir: William Graham, 72 mins.)

Trapped by Boston Blackie (1948)** Chester Morris, June Vincent, Richard Lane. Standard B.B. adventure, with Blackie accused of pilfering a pearl necklace and forced to solve the case himself after an investigating detective is bumped off. (Dir: Seymour Friedman, 67 mins.)

Trapped in Silence (MTV 1986)*** Marsha Mason, Kiefer Sutherland, Ron Silver, John Mahoney. Moving drama portraying the aftermath of child mutism. Mason is given charge of a supposed lost cause who eventually learns to speak, and tells her of the horrors that have happened to him. (Dir: Michael Tuchner, 104 mins.)

Tras el Cristal—See: **In a Glass Cage**

Trash (1970)*** Joe Dallesandro, Holly Woodlawn, Geri Miller, Bruce Pecheur, Michael Sklar, Jane Forth. Tongue-in-cheek comedy from the Andy Warhol factory about junkie-thief Dallesandro living with transvestite Woodlawn, who wants to move up in the world by getting on welfare. Bizarre, often hilarious account of good-hearted social outcasts in New York City. (Dir: Paul Morrisey, 103 mins.)†

Traveling Executioner, The (1970)** Stacy Keach, Marianna Hill, Bud Cort. Keach's performance in the title role (with a portable electric chair, circa 1918) is better than this cheap, contrived movie deserves. (Dir: Jack Smight, 95 mins.)

Traveling Man (MTV 1989)**½ John Lithgow, Jonathan Silverman, Margaret Colin, John Glover, John M. Jackson.

Downbeat comedy-drama about a veteran traveling salesman assigned a trainee, not knowing that the younger man is to take over his route once he learns the ropes. Realistic depiction of road life until it changes course to set up the obligatory happy ending. (Dir: Irvin Kershner, 105 mins.)†

Traveling North (Australia, 1988)*** Leo McKern, Julia Blake, Graham Kennedy, Henri Szeps. Crusty, cockeyed old Leo gives a smashing performance as a crabby retiree whose dream of living undisturbed "up north" in Queensland with his middle-aged girlfriend is complicated by a talkative neighbor, the lady's dissatisfied daughters, and some nasty angina trouble. An endearing, sharply executed character study. (Dir: Carl Schultz, 98 mins.)†

Traveling Saleslady (1935)*** Joan Blondell, Glenda Farrell, Hugh Herbert, Grant Mitchell, William Gargan. This bright comedy stars Blondell as a girl who goes into direct competition with her father's business. Naturally her toothpaste sells better—it tastes like hootch. (Dir: Ray Enright, 75 mins.)

Traveling Saleswoman, The (1950)** Joan Davis, Andy Devine, Adele Jergens. Davis and Devine vie for laughs in this cornball western about a soap saleswoman and her rotund fiancé. (Dir: Charles F. Reisner, 75 mins.)

Travels with My Aunt (1972)*** Maggie Smith, Alec McCowen, Lou Gossett, Robert Stephens, Cindy Williams. Mostly delightful, sophisticated fare, immeasurably aided by Maggie Smith's glowing performance as Aunt Augusta out to ransom her old lover and, in the process, liberate her nephew Henry (McCowen). Screenwriters Jay Presson Allen and Hugh Wheeler scaled down Graham Greene's novel and added a few not very felicitous plot twists. (Dir: George Cukor, 109 mins.)

Travis Logan, D.A. (MTV 1971)**½ Vic Morrow, Hal Holbrook, Brenda Vaccaro, Chris Robinson, James Callahan, Brooke Bundy, George Grizzard, Edward Andrews, Ed Flanders. Another pilot for a TV series about a lawyer. Morrow plays a low-key small-town district attorney who puzzles out another one of those "perfect" murders. (Dir: Paul Wenkos, 100 mins.)

Travis McGee (MTV 1983)* Sam Elliott, Katharine Ross, Barry Corbin, Vera Miles. Fans of John MacDonald's novels would do better to read the book than watch this tiresome detective hunt for a missing husband who has allegedly died in a boating accident. (Dir: Stirling Silliphant, 104 mins.)

Traxx (1987)* Shadoe Stevens, Priscilla Barnes, Willard E. Pugh. Ever wonder just what it is that "Hollywood Squares" panelist Stevens *does*? Well, this cartoonish action movie shows what he's not—an actor. As an ex-mercenary who hires on to clean up a corrupt town, he's good at shooting lots of guns but that's about it. (Dir: Jerome Gary, 84 mins.)†

T. R. Baskin (1971)**½ Candice Bergen, James Caan, Peter Boyle. A romantic view of a working girl's life and loves. Bergen gives a subdued, thoroughly appealing performance as a young woman searching for answers in her formless life. (Dir: Herbert Ross, 104 mins.)

Treasure Island (1934)**½ Wallace Beery, Jackie Cooper, Lionel Barrymore, Lewis Stone, Nigel Bruce. Beery chews the scenery as Long John Silver in this generally enjoyable, visually stodgy MGM-version of Robert Louis Stevenson's adventure story. Cooper is Jim Hawkins and Barrymore has a memorable bit as the black-spotted Billy Bones. (Dir: Victor Fleming, 105 mins.)†

Treasure Island (1950)*** Bobby Driscoll, Robert Newton, Basil Sidney, Walter Fitzgerald, Denis O'Dea, Finlay Currie. Not a bull's-eye, but generally on target, this is the Disney version of the classic about a young boy's encounters with some salty buccaneers sailing the seven seas for treasure. (Dir: Byron Haskin, 96 mins.)†

Treasure Island (Great Britain, 1972)*** Orson Welles, Kim Burfield, Walter Slezak, Lionel Stander. Welles as Long John Silver eschews the emphasis on roguish charm which Robert Newton and Wallace Beery brought to the role, instead conveying the dangerous, ominous side of the pirate—more what Stevenson intended and dramatically more impressive. An entertaining version of the absorbing tale. (Dir: John Hough, 94 mins.)

Treasure Island (MTV 1990)*** Charlton Heston, Christian Bale, Oliver Reed, Christopher Lee, Julian Glover, Richard Johnson, Clive Woods, Michael Thoma. Heston has a good time playing the inscrutable and infamous pirate Long John Silver in this splendid adaptation of the classic tale, written, produced, and directed by his son Fraser. Bale is a bit wan as young Jim Hawkins, but Reed as Captain Bones and Lee as Blind Pew more than compensate. (131 mins.)†

Treasure of Fear—See: **Scared Stiff** (1945)

Treasure of Jamaica Reef (1974)** Stephen Boyd, Chuck Woolery, David Ladd, Cheryl Stoppelmoor [Cheryl Ladd], Roosevelt Grier. Fun cast saves this diving adventure, about a quest for gold at the bottom of the Caribbean Sea, from being a total disaster. AKA: **Evil in the Deep**. (Dir: Virginia Stone, 96 mins.)†

Treasure of Lost Canyon, The (1952)*½ William Powell, Julie Adams. Dull tale of buried treasure and how it changes lives. (Dir: Ted Tetzlaff, 82 mins.)

Treasure of Matecumbe, The (1976)**½ Johnny Doran, Billy Attmore, Peter Ustinov, Joan Hackett. Though geared to the young, this Disney film is rather entertaining for the whole family. The plot involves two small boys—one black, one white—who are searching for a treasure chest in the Florida Keys some time after the Civil War. (Dir: Vincent McEveety, 104 mins.)†

Treasure of Monte Cristo (1949)**½ Glenn Langan, Adele Jergens, Sid Melton, Steve Brodie, Michael Whelan, Robert Jordan. Gold-digging woman marries a sailor (who's a direct descendant of the Count of Monte Cristo!) strictly for the cash, then realizes she really loves him. Entertaining melodrama plays better than it sounds. (Dir: William Berke, 80 mins.)

Treasure of Monte Cristo (Great Britain, 1960)**½ Monty Berman, Rory Calhoun, Peter Arne, Gianna Maria Canale. Action adventure about a treasure hunt, loosely inspired by characters and settings in Dumas's *The Count of Monte Cristo*. (Dir: Robert S. Baker, 95 mins.)

Treasure of Pancho Villa, The (1955)** Rory Calhoun, Shelley Winters, Gilbert Roland. American adventurer plots a train robbery with the intention of delivering the gold to Villa's forces. (Dir: George Sherman, 96 mins.)

Treasure of Ruby Hills (1955)** Zachary Scott, Carole Mathews. Rancher steps in the middle of a fight to control range land. (Dir: Frank McDonald, 71 mins.)

Treasure of San Gennaro (Italy-Germany-France, 1966)** Harry Guardino, Senta Berger, Nino Manfredi, Toto, Claudine Auger. Naples's patron saint temporarily loses its treasure to the squabbling heisters of this weak comedy. (Dir: Dino Risi, 102 mins.)

Treasure of San Teresa (Great Britain-West Germany, 1957)** Dawn Addams, Eddie Constantine, Christopher Lee. A predictable espionage yarn with more narrow escapes than you can keep straight. (Dir: Alvin Rakoff, 81 mins.)

Treasure of Tayopa (1974)* Rena Winters, Phil Trapani, Andrew Farnsworth. Violent western about a trek into remote Mexican hills to find hidden treasure, supposedly buried there centuries before. Dusty, dumb, and derivative. Gilbert Roland appears in a silly prologue/epilogue to relate the history of the supposed Tayopa legend. (Dir: Bob Cawley, 90 mins.)

Treasure of the Amazon (1983)** Stuart Whitman, Bradford Dillman, Ann Sydney, Donald Pleasence, John Ireland. Low-budget story about a group of fortune hunters searching for a cache of diamonds hidden in the wilds of the Amazon. (Dir: Rene Cardona, Jr., 80 mins.)†

Treasure of the Four Crowns (Spain, 1983)* Tony Anthony, Ana Obregon, Gene Quintano, Francisco Rabal. A true 3-D film: the characters are dumb and dimensionless, and the caper they're involved in is dim-witted. International escapaders try to secure crystals with magical properties. (Dir: Ferdinando Baldi, 97 mins.)†

Treasure of the Golden Condor (1953)** Cornel Wilde, Constance Smith, Anne Bancroft, Fay Wray. Predictable costume adventure film which traps its stars in an 18th-century melodrama. Wilde plays the rightful heir to a noble fortune who is cheated and forced to live as a fugitive. (Dir: Delmer Daves, 93 mins.)†

Treasure of the Moon Goddess (1988)* Asher Brauner, Don Calfa, Linnea Quigley, Jo-Ann Ayres. Adventure-comedy with singer Quigley thought to be the reincarnation of a deity by jungle residents, rescued by hero-type Brauner. As Quigley's agent, Calfa steals some scenes, which barely qualifies as petty larceny. (Dir: Joseph Louis Agraz, 89 mins.)†

Treasure of the Sierra Madre, The (1948) **** Humphrey Bogart, Walter Huston, Tim Holt. A group of down-and-outs search the hills for gold only to be undone by their weaknesses of character. The grizzled prospector of Walter Huston is the capstone of his great and varied career. Bogart brings a conviction to his pathological role that few other actors could supply. Oscars to John Huston, Best Director and Best Adapted Screenplay; Walter Huston, Best Supporting Actor. (124 mins.)†

Tree Grows in Brooklyn, A (1945)**** Dorothy McGuire, James Dunn, Joan Blondell, Lloyd Nolan, Peggy Ann Garner. Magnificent rendition of Betty Smith's novel, moving and dramatically authentic, though it never leaves the studio sets. McGuire is brilliant as the mother, as are Blondell, Dunn as the alcoholic father (Oscar-winner), and the rest of the cast. (Dir: Elia Kazan, 128 mins.)†

Tree Grows in Brooklyn, A (MTV 1974)** Cliff Robertson, Diane Baker, Nancy Malone, Pamelyn Ferdin. Labored remake. Robertson, as the hard-drinking singing waiter and occasional breadwinner of the Nolan family, somehow slips into caricature rather than characterization. (Dir: Joel Hardy, 74 mins.)

Tree of the Wooden Clogs, The (Italy, 1978) **** Luigi Ornaghi, Francesca Moriggi, Omar Brignoli. A turn-of-the-century peasant epic told through the eyes of a young boy in Bergamo. Director Ermanno

Olmi is so close to his subject that he is incapable of sentimentality and untruth in art and observation. The pace is measured and the depth of observation is astonishing. (186 mins.)†

Tremors (1989)**½ Kevin Bacon, Fred Ward, Finn Carter, Michael Gross, Reba McEntire, Victor Wong, Bibi Besch. Silly, trashy, and heavily derivative, chiller about deadly wormlike creatures menacing a tiny desert community has the virtue of never taking itself seriously. The suspense is there, all right, as are all of the stock clichés. Not exactly memorable, but fun while it lasts. (Dir: Ron Underwood, 95 mins.)†

Trenchcoat (1983)** Margot Kidder, Robert Hays, Ronald Lacey. A stenographer (Kidder), who feels that to write a novel one must live a novel, goes to Malta, where she hopes to find intrigue. And, surprise, she does. A scatterbrained mystery spoof. (Dir: Michael Tuchner, 91 mins.)

Trenchcoat in Paradise (MTV 1989)** Dirk Benedict, Bruce Dern, Catherine Oxenberg, Kim Zimmer, Sydney Walsh, Michelle Phillips. After a run-in with the local crime boss, '40s-style New Jersey gumshoe Benedict is transplanted to Hawaii. Offbeat premise yields mildly comic results before giving way to the usual TV detective stuff. (Dir: Martha Coolidge, 96 mins.)

Trent's Last Case (Great Britain, 1952)*** Margaret Lockwood, Michael Wilding, Hugh McDermott, Miles Malleson, Orson Welles. Film version of the classic by E. C. Bentley. A sleuth is called to investigate the mysterious death of a tycoon (played exotically in flashback by Welles, with a nice fake nose). Was it murder, or suicide? And what did the beautiful widow have to do with it? The intricate plot is all talk, but for traditional mystery fans it is most absorbing. (Dir: Herbert Wilcox, 90 mins.)

Trespasses (1986)**½ Robert Kuhn, Mary Pillot, Van Brooks. Tale of murder and sex in a small Texas town was obviously inspired by the success of *Blood Simple*, and although it's not in that league, it's a worthwhile excursion nonetheless. (Dirs.: Loren Bivens, Adam Rourke, 90 mins.)†

Trial, The (Austria, 1948)***½ Ewald Balser, Ernst Deutsch, Heinz Moog, Gustav Diessl. Powerful courtroom drama about a group of Jews accused of a ritualistic murder in 1882 Hungary. Balser is outstanding as the lawyer who defends the men in this eloquent drama, based on an actual incident. (Dir: G. W. Pabst, 108 mins.)

Trial (1955)***½ Glenn Ford, Dorothy McGuire, Arthur Kennedy, John Hodiak, Katy Jurado. Absorbing drama about

the murder trial of a Mexican boy which is fantastically exploited by a Communist-backed organization for their own underhanded purposes. The cast is topnotch. (Dir: Mark Robson, 109 mins.)

Trial, The (1963)*** Anthony Perkins, Jeanne Moreau, Romy Schneider, Orson Welles. Kafka's frightening allegory of a nameless man accused of a crime without being informed of what it was. Orson Welles as producer and director gives it the Wellesian treatment, meaning some inspired scenes and good performances. (118 mins.)†

Trial and Error (Great Britain, 1962)**½ Peter Sellers, Beryl Reid, Roger Attenborough, David Lodge. A study in character acting from Sellers and Attenborough, as a bungling barrister and an accused murderer. They're fine, but the film becomes a thespic exhibition at the expense of the narrative, which is thin indeed. (Dir: James Hill, 88 mins.)

Trial of Billy Jack, The (1974) ½ Tom Laughlin, Delores Taylor, William Wellman, Jr. Simpleminded rubbish. Laughlin is again the crusading Indian half-breed fighting corruption in government, business, etc. (Dir: Frank Laughlin, actually directed by Tom Laughlin, 170 mins.)

Trial of Chaplain Jensen, The (MTV 1975)**½ James Franciscus, Charles Durning, Joanna Miles, Lynda Day George, Harris Yulin. A strange true-life tale gets a good mounting here. Franciscus is well cast as the devout Navy chaplain who is court-martialed when two Navy wives accuse him of adultery. (Dir: Robert Day, 72 mins.)

Trial of Joan of Arc (France, 1962)***½ Florence Carrez, Jean-Claude Fourneau, Roger Honorat, Jean Gillibert. Brilliant Robert Bresson film based on actual transcripts of the trial that aroused France. Carrez is magnificent as the martyred Joan, and her death is extraordinarily filmed by Bresson in a scene that is astonishing for its emotional simplicity and horrific brutality. (65 mins.)

Trial of Lee Harvey Oswald, The (MTV 1977)*** Ben Gazzara, Lorne Greene, Frances Lee McCain, John Pleshette, Lawrence Pressman. What if Lee Harvey Oswald, President Kennedy's accused assassin, hadn't been shot by Jack Ruby and actually stood trial? Ambitious TV drama painstakingly recreates the fatal day in Dallas and assumes the fictional events which might have followed. (Dir: David Greene, 208 mins.)†

Trial of the Catonsville Nine, The (1972) ***½ Ed Flanders, Richard Jordan, Peter Strauss, Douglas Watson, Nancy Malone. Flawed but often moving filmed record of a play by Daniel Berrigan about the trial of a group of anti-Vietnam War protesters, who raided the offices of the draft board in Catonsville, Md., and burned some of the files in May '68. (Dir: Gordon Davidson, 85 mins.) †

Trial Run (MTV 1968)**½ Leslie Nielsen, James Franciscus, Janice Rule, Diane Baker. Familiar fare about the machinations of a young, and somewhat ruthless lawyer (Franciscus) who gets his big chance when he's scheduled to defend a man who murdered his unfaithful wife. (Dir: William Graham, 98 mins.)

Trials of Alger Hiss, The (1980)***½ Alger Hiss, Richard M. Nixon, Whittaker Chambers. Illuminating, chilling documentary about blacklisting and McCarthyism. (Dir: John Lowenthal, 166 mins.)

Trials of Oscar Wilde, The (Great Britain, 1960)*** Peter Finch, James Mason, Nigel Patrick, Lionel Jeffries, Yvonne Mitchell. Handsome-looking film about Wilde's ill-fated libel suit against the Marquis of Queensbury and subsequent trial for sodomy. Finch's portrait of the playwright is multileveled, capturing the vanity and pomposity along with his sublime incomprehension of how fatally he is going to do himself in. (Dir: Ken Hughes, 123 mins.)

Triangle Factory Fire Scandal, The (MTV 1979)**½ Tom Bosley, Tovah Feldshuh, Stephanie Zimbalist, Ted Wass, Stacey Nelkin. Based on the real-life sweatshop fire in New York which killed 145 garment workers, this drama stars Bosley as a harsh, driving foreman, cracking the whip on immigrant employees in crowded, unsafe conditions. (Dir: Mel Stuart, 104 mins.) †

Tribes (MTV 1970)*** Jan-Michael Vincent, Darren McGavin, Earl Holliman. Absorbing, well-made film about a drafted hippie in Marine boot camp. The hippie (Vincent) can't be broken, and his survival methods are adopted by his barracks mates to the consternation of drill instructor McGavin. (Dir: Joseph Sargent, 74 mins.) †

Tribute (Canada-U.S., 1980)** Jack Lemmon, Robby Benson, Lee Remick, Colleen Dewhurst, Kim Cattrall. Glib, synthetic soap opera about a New York celebrity (Lemmon) who discovers he is dying of a rare blood disease and wants to patch things up with his estranged wife (Remick). (Dir: Bob Clark, 125 mins.) †

Tribute to a Bad Man (1956)*** James Cagney, Irene Papas, Don Dubbins. A powerful performance by James Cagney as a big horse breeder whose ruthless tactics alienate those closest to him is the bulwark of this underrated western drama. (Dir: Robert Wise, 95 mins.)

Tricheurs (France, 1986)**½ Jacques Dutronc, Bulle Ogier, Kurt Raab, Virgilio Teixeira, Steve Baes. A detached examination of compulsive gamblers. The film circles around the desperate lifestyles of a trio on the verge of disaster as they prowl the casinos and eventually stoop to cheating. (Dir: Barbet Schroeder, 94 mins.)

Trick Baby—See: **Double Con, The**

Trick or Treat (1986)**½ Marc Price, Tony Fields, Lisa Orgolini, Gene Simmons, Ozzy Osbourne. A teenager, frequently picked on for his obsession with hard rock music, gets revenge with the help of a heavy metal star that he raises from the dead. Naturally, things get out of control. More clever than scary. (Dir: Charles Martin Smith, 97 mins.) †

Trick or Treats (1982)* Jackelyn Giroux, Peter Jason, Chris Graver, David Carradine, Carrie Snodgress. When a baby-sitter is left to tend a boy with a bent for gruesome practical jokes, little does she know that the boy's psychopathic father has just escaped from an asylum and is on his way home. (Dir: Gary Graver, 91 mins.) †

Tricks of the Trade (MTV, 1988)** Cindy Williams, Markie Post, Scott Paulin, Chris Mulkey. Williams's husband is killed while visiting hooker Post's apartment, and the two team up to find the murderer. Starts out promisingly but bogs down in convoluted plot. (Dir: Jack Bender, 96 mins.)

Trilogy (MTV 1969)***½ Maureen Stapleton, Martin Balsam, Geraldine Page, Mildred Natwick. Three short stories by Truman Capote, originally produced for TV, are combined in this rewarding, magnificently acted collection. All three stories were adapted by Capote and writer Eleanor Perry, and directed by Frank Perry. The last story, "A Christmas Memory," is narrated by Capote and features a lovely performance by Page preparing for the Christmas season. (110 mins.)

Trilogy of Terror (MTV 1975)*** Karen Black, Robert Burton, John Karlen, George Gaynes. Karen Black has a field day playing four tormented women in three bizarre, offbeat short stories by Richard Matheson. Best is the last, as she battles a weird doll come to life. (Dir: Dan Curtis, 72 mins.) †

Trio (Great Britain, 1950)*** Michael Rennie, Jean Simmons, Wilfrid Hyde White. Second anthology of Somerset Maugham short stories is graced with memorable acting. Of the three basically solid yarns, the last, perhaps the most clichéd yet the most affecting, stars Rennie and Simmons as two sanitarium patients. (Dirs: Ken Annakin, Harold French, 91 mins.)

Trip, The (1967)**½ Peter Fonda, Susan

Strasberg, Bruce Dern. The quintessential sixties drug movie. Druggie neophyte Fonda drops acid with guidance from veteran "head" Dern, and experiences a psychedelic journey, with the best moment being a bizarre visit to the local laundromat! Scripted by Jack Nicholson. (Director: Roger Corman, 85 mins.)†

Triple Cross (France-Great Britain, 1966)**½ Christopher Plummer, Romy Schneider, Trevor Howard, Yul Brynner. A no-holds-barred WWII espionage yarn. Plummer plays a double agent who pulls out all stops in his dangerous missions crossing from Germany to England. Based on the real WWII exploits of famed British double-spy Eddie Chapman. (Dir: Terence Young, 126 mins.)

Triple Cross (MTV 1986)** Ted Wass, Markie Post, Gary Swanson. Three millionaires happen to be private investigators too. When another rich person dies in a mysterious fire, the trio is hired to solve the crime. (Dir: David Greene, 120 mins.)

Triple Deception (Great Britain, 1956)*** Michael Craig, Brenda De Banzie. Sailor poses as a member of a gold smuggling gang to get the goods on them. Rattling good melodrama, heavy on suspense. (Dir: Guy Green, 86 mins.)

Triple Echo (Great Britain, 1973)** Glenda Jackson, Oliver Reed, Brian Deacon, Jenny Lee Wright. An offbeat wartime romance turned tragedy, as a burly sergeant falls for a war widow's AWOL boyfriend, whom the woman has disguised as her younger sister. Given the unusual situation, the sexual tension somehow never builds. AKA: **Soldier in Skirts.** (Dir: Michael Apted, 90 mins.)†

Triple Trouble (1918) and **Easy Street** (1917)**** Two more hilarious Charlie Chaplin comedies. *Triple Trouble* is a madcap farce about a handyman working for an inventor who has developed a new kind of explosive—the obvious mayhem ensues. Next is *Easy Street*, one of Chaplin's best short films, in which the Little Tramp decides to change his ways and get a job—as a policeman, cleaning up a crime-ridden district and capturing an enormous villain through sheer cunning. Written and directed by Chaplin. (60 mins.)†

Triple Trouble (1950*½ Bowery Boys, Pat Collins, Richard Benedict. In an effort to find the real perpetrators of the crimes of which the Boys have been accused, Sach and Slip plead guilty in order to search for the mastermind behind prison walls. (Dir: Jean Yarbrough, 66 mins.)

Tripods, The (Great Britain, MTV 1986)*½ John Shockley, Jim Baker, Roderick Horn, Ceri Seel. Cheesy sci-fi made for British TV set in 2089 A.D., when the human race

has been conquered by mind-enslaving aliens. But of course there's a hardy band of young rebels. . . . (Dirs: Graham Theakston, Christopher Barry, 150 mins.)†

Tripoli (1950)** Maureen O'Hara, John Payne, Howard da Silva. The year is 1805 and the Marine Forces headed by John Payne defeat the Tripoli pirates but not until Countess Maureen O'Hara gets her man. (Dir: Will Price, 95 mins.)

Trip to Bountiful, The (1985)**½ Geraldine Page, John Heard, Carlin Glynn, Richard Bradford, Rebecca DeMornay, Kevin Cooney. This homespun, old-fashioned drama about life's little people is memorably enacted by Page, who won a long-overdue Oscar for Best Actress for her work here. Hemmed in by life with her weak-willed son and his high-strung wife, a feisty old lady dreams of revisiting the family home. Although she only finds ruins there, everyone's lives are changed for the better. (Dir: Peter Masterson, 106 mins.)†

Tripwire (1990)*½ Terence Knox, David Warner, Isabella Hoffman, Charlotte Lewis, Andras Jones, Sy Richardson. FBI agent Knox carries on a personal vendetta against terrorist Warner after the latter murders his wife, refusing to quit even after he is removed from active duty. (Dir: James Lemmo, 91 mins.)†

Tristana (France-Italy-Spain, 1970)**** Catherine Deneuve, Fernando Rey, Franco Nero. Dazzling adaptation of the novel by Benito Pérez Galdós about a woman who seeks what little independence is available to a young unmarried woman in turn-of-the-century Spain. The director's touch can be seen when the aging roué of an uncle (Rey) attempts to console the girl after her leg has been amputated by saying she shouldn't despair, some men will find her even more attractive now. (Dir: Luis Buñuel, 105 mins.)

Triumph of Sherlock Holmes, The (Great Britain, 1935)*** Arthur Wontner, Ian Fleming, Lyn Harding. Low-budget film stars Wontner as Holmes and Fleming as Dr. Watson in an adaptation of *The Valley of Fear*, a neglected novel in the Arthur Conan Doyle canon. (Dir: Leslie Hiscott, 84 mins.)†

Triumph of the Heart: The Ricky Bell Story (MTV 1991)**½ Mario Van Peebles, Lane Davis, Susan Ruttan, Lynn Whitfield, Polly Holliday. Overly sentimental, occasionally affecting story about a football player who helps a disabled lad overcome his difficulties. Then, in return, the boy proves invaluable when the football player finds he has a rare muscle disease that might end his career as an athlete. (Dir: Richard Michaels, 96 mins.)

Triumph of the Spirit (1989)** Willem Dafoe, Edward James Olmos, Robert Loggia, Wendy Gazelle, Kelly Wolf, Costas Mandylor. Disappointing film based on the true story of Greek boxer Salamo Arouch, taken with his family to Auschwitz during WWII where he was forced to fight other prisoners for the amusement of his captors. Even location filming at the sites of the Auschwitz and Birkenau camps fails to evoke much feeling, and the actors struggle with underwritten parts. (Dir: Robert M. Young, 120 mins.)†

Triumph of the Will (Germany, 1935)*** Infamous propaganda film that was banned after WWII because it was used by the Nazi party as a recruiting device. Today, the effect of this documentary about Hitler's rallies is alternately powerful and heavy-going. (Dir: Leni Riefenstahl, 110 mins.)†

Triumphs of a Man Called Horse (U.S.-Mexico, 1983)** Richard Harris, Michael Beck, Ana De Sade, Vaughn Armstrong. That a sequel is seldom as good as the original is proved by this third movie, a spin-off featuring Koda (Beck), the son of Man Called Horse. Teamed with a lovely Indian maiden, Koda fights to keep the Sioux land from the white settlers. (Dir: John Hough, 86 mins.)†

Trog (Great Britain, 1970)* Joan Crawford, Michael Gough, Kim Braden. Crawford's an anthropologist who has come across what she believes to be the missing link. The only thing missing here is credibility. Crawford's last film. (Dir: Freddie Francis, 91 mins.)

Trojan Women, The (1971)**½ Katharine Hepburn, Vanessa Redgrave, Genevieve Bujold, Irene Papas. Director Michael Cacoyannis's stage production of Euripides' play at New York's Circle in the Square in the early sixties was justly famous, but he has no flair for cinema. Here the poetry, aided greatly by splendid performances by Hepburn as ravaged queen mother Hecuba, and Redgrave as Andromache, is sunk by hyperactive cutting. Filmed in Spain. (102 mins.)†

Troll (1986)** Michael Moriarty, June Lockhart, Shelley Hack, Sonny Bono, Gary Sandy, Brad Hall, Julia Louis-Dreyfuss. The imaginative but sloppily executed screenplay involves a new family who move into an apartment building that houses a resident troll, who wants to remake the world in his own image. The more time the trolls spend on screen, the less time the cast has to embarrass themselves. (Dir: John Buechler, 86 mins.)†

Trollenberg Terror, The—See: **Crawling Eye, The**

Troma's War (1988)**½ Carolyn Beauchamp, Sean Bowen, Michael Ryder. Tongue-in-cheek, violent exploitation movie about survivors of an airliner crash in the jungle who must battle a gang of murderous terrorists as well as the elements. Fans of the production team of Lloyd Kaufman and Michael Herz, who regularly crank out this schlock, will love it. Others beware! Directed by Herz and Kaufman under the pseudonym Samuel Weil. Also available in an unrated 105 min. version. (90 mins.)†

Tron (1982)** Jeff Bridges, Cindy Morgan, Bruce Boxleitner, Barnard Hughes, David Warner. This sci-fi adventure inside a computer is technically effective, but weak in narrative content. Bridges stars as the computer whiz who seeks revenge for his stolen computer programs with the help of Boxleitner—from within the machine! (Dir: Steven Lisberger, 96 mins.)†

Troop Beverly Hills (1989)*** Shelley Long, Craig T. Nelson, Betty Thomas, Mary Gross. Long finally gets a good vehicle in this comedy about a Beverly Hills wife who teaches her girl scout troop the things that really matter in the big city. Writing and direction are only adequate, but Shelley shines. (Dir: Jeff Kanew, 105 mins.)†

Trooper Hook (1957)**½ Joel McCrea, Barbara Stanwyck, Susan Kohner, John Dehner, Earl Holliman. Good western drama bolstered by the stars. There are Indian raids and plenty of action sequences for adventure-seeking fans. (Dir: Charles Marquis Warren, 81 mins.)

Tropical Snow (1986)** Nick Corri, Madeline Stowe, David Carradine, Argermiro Catiblanco. Competently made but predictable drama about a Colombian couple who long to emigrate to the U.S., offered a chance by drug lord Carradine—if they'll agree to be his couriers. Filmed in Bogotá and other Colombian locations. (Dir: Ciro Duran, 88 mins.)†

Tropic Holiday (1938)** Dorothy Lamour, Ray Milland, Martha Raye. Romantic comedy set in Mexico is weak entertainment. (Dir: Theodore Reed, 80 mins.)

Tropici (Italy-Brazil, 1967)*** Janira Santiago, Joel Barcelos, Gracieli Campos, Batista Campos. Shot in documentary style, director Gianni Amico's vibrant little film follows an impoverished family from the cattle country of rural Brazil to the metropolis of São Paulo with its energy, excitement, drama, and dread. The family's anticipation of the journey and the trek itself is shaded by a unique mix of Mozart and Brazilian folk music and depicted with realistically photographed images. (87 mins.)

Tropic of Cancer (1970)*** Rip Torn, Ginette Le Clerc, James Callahan, Phil Brown. A series of good-natured sexual vignettes and escapades photographed in Paris in the late sixties, but ostensibly taking place during the 1930s. Based on Henry Miller's celebrated underground classic. (Dir: Joseph Strick, 87 mins.)

Tropic Zone (1953)** Ronald Reagan, Rhonda Fleming. Ho-hum adventure film. The independent banana plantation owners are plagued by a villainous shipping magnate who wants control of the whole works. (Dir: Lewis R. Foster, 94 mins.)

Trottie True—See: **Gay Lady, The**

Trouble Along the Way (1953)** John Wayne, Donna Reed. Wayne plays a football coach with a two-fisted approach to the game and life. Sentimental and sticky. (Dir: Michael Curtiz, 110 mins.)

Trouble at 16—See: **Platinum High School**

Trouble Comes to Town (MTV 1974)**½ Lloyd Bridges, Thomas Evans, Pat Hingle. The film tells the story of a black Chicago youngster who goes South to live with a white sheriff, and it's surprisingly effective at times. (Dir: Daniel Petrie, 73 mins.)

Trouble for Two (1936)*** Robert Montgomery, Rosalind Russell, Frank Morgan, Louis Hayward. Exciting adventure tale loosely based on Robert Louis Stevenson's *Suicide Club*. Scene about the club is as chilling a bit of business as you'll ever see. (Dir: J. Walter Ruben, 75 mins.)

Trouble in Mind (1985)*** Kris Kristofferson, Genevieve Bujold, Keith Carradine, Lori Singer, Divine. Director Alan Rudolph works his sleek, erotic magic in this stylish but failed *film noir* fable. Kristofferson is excellent as an ex-cop who tries to prevent a hick hood from being swallowed up in a metropolis's underworld, and also endeavors to win the hand of this fledgling crook's neglected wife. (111 mins.)†

Trouble in Paradise (1932)**** Miriam Hopkins, Herbert Marshall, Kay Francis. Exquisite, elegant comedy about jewel thieves as proficient at lifting hearts as purses. Hilarious from the opening sight gag of a crooning gondolier tenor on a garbage scow. (The voice is that of the legendary Enrico Caruso.) (Dir: Ernst Lubitsch, 83 mins.)

Trouble in Paradise (MTV 1989)**½ Raquel Welch, Jack Thompson, Anthony Wong, Ralph Cotterill, Adrian Brown. Grieving widow Welch is shipwrecked on a desert island with boisterous Australian sailor Thompson. (Dir: Di Drew, 96 mins.)

Trouble in the Glen (Great Britain, 1954)** Orson Welles, Margaret Lockwood, Forrest Tucker, Victor McLaglen. Scottish laird returns from South America to land in the middle of a feud over a closed road. Draggy pace and a script that misfires undermines a promising comedy idea. (Dir: Herbert Wilcox, 91 mins.)†

Trouble in the Sky (Great Britain, 1960)**½ Michael Craig, Peter Cushing, Bernard Lee, George Sanders, Elizabeth Seal. When her father is accused of causing the crash of a plane he was piloting, a woman enlists the aid of an expert to prove it was a mechanical error. Slight mystery-drama. AKA: **Code of Silence**. (Dir: Charles Frend, 76 mins.)

Trouble With Angels, The (1966)** Rosalind Russell, Hayley Mills, June Harding, Gypsy Rose Lee. Two high-spirited young students at St. Francis Academy keep things hopping for the understanding Mother Superior (Russell) and her staff of bewildered Sisters. Some of the intended comedy is strained, but the two teenage girls and their pranks have a modest, mindless appeal. (Dir: Ida Lupino, 112 mins.)†

Trouble With Girls, The (1969)**½ Elvis Presley, Marlyn Mason, Nicole Jaffe, Sheree North, Edward Andrews. Elvis in the Roaring Twenties and, believe it or not, this is a notch or two above most of his films. He heads a combination entertainment-education traveling show. (Dir: Peter Tewksbury, 105 mins.)†

Trouble With Harry, The (1955)*** John Forsythe, Shirley MacLaine (film debut), Mildred Natwick, Edmund Gwenn. When a body is discovered in the Vermont woods, various people have a hard time disposing of it. Director Alfred Hitchcock's macabre comic touch deftly makes this kooky little comedy worthwhile. (99 mins.)†

Trouble With Spies, The (MTV 1987)* Donald Sutherland, Ned Beatty, Ruth Gordon. Cloak-and-dagger shenanigans with Sutherland as a bumbling secret agent. Made in 1984 for HBO but not shown until three years later; that should give you an idea. (Dir: Burt Kennedy, 91 mins.)†

Trouble With Women, The (1947)** Ray Milland, Teresa Wright, Brian Donlevy. Psychology professor has his theories on women tested by an enterprising female reporter in this mild comedy. (Dir: Sidney Lanfield, 80 mins.)

Trout, The (France, 1982)**½ Isabelle Huppert, Jacques Spiesser, Jeanne Moreau, Jean-Pierre Cassel, Alexis Smith, Craig Stevens, Ruggero Raimondi. Glossy, complex drama about a beautiful young woman embroiled in the intriguing world of high finance, corporate backstabbing and a vast variety of sexual and asexual liaisons. AKA: **La Truite**. (Dir: Joseph Losey, 110 mins.)

Truck Stop Women (1974)**½ Claudia Jennings, Lieux Dressler, Dennis Fimple, Jennifer Burton. The title says it all; tawdry tale of shady ladies who use their truck stop as a sexual service station. (Dir: Mark Lester, 88 mins.)†

Truck Turner (1974)**½ Isaac Hayes,

Scatman Crothers, Yaphet Kotto, Annazette Chase. Blaxploitation film features Hayes as a skip tracer, and it has wit, speed, and sharply handled violence. (Dir: Jonathan Kaplan, 91 mins.)†

True Believer (1989)*** James Woods, Robert Downey, Jr., Margaret Colin, Kurtwood Smith. Woods, a burnt-out ex-radical lawyer, regains his spark when his hero-worshiping new assistant persuades him to take on the case of an unjustly imprisoned Asian youth. Woods is fine in a tailor-made part in this taut thriller. (Dir: Joseph Ruben, 102 mins.)†

True Blue (MTV 1989)** John Bolger, Nestor Serrano, Darnell Williams, Dick Latessa, Eddie Velez, Leo Burmeister. Pilot for a series about New York City's Emergency Services unit. Strictly formula. (Dir: William A. Graham, 96 mins.)

True Colors (1991)**½ John Cusack, James Spader, Imogen Stubbs, Mandy Patinkin, Richard Widmark, Dina Merrill, Philip Bosco, Paul Guilfoyle. The talented cast can't rescue this pompous story about political ambition and dirty tricks. Cusack is a law school dropout, now working for a U.S. Senator, who has no qualms about compromising his friendship with a Justice Department employee (Spader), and using a little blackmail. (Dir: Herbert Ross, 111 mins.)†

True Confession (1937)*** Carole Lombard, Fred MacMurray, John Barrymore. Fast moving, superbly played farce about a girl on trial for murder. Some of it may strike you as dated, but the method has been borrowed for many of our modern film comedies. (Dir: Wesley Ruggles, 85 mins.)

True Confessions (1981)*** Robert De Niro, Robert Duvall, Charles Durning, Ed Flanders, Burgess Meredith, Rose Gregorio, Cyril Cusack, Kenneth McMillan. Outstanding performances by De Niro as a priest and Duvall as his brother, a cop, make this an exciting drama entwining police work and the Church. In the late 1940s. (Dir: Ulu Grosbard, 108 mins.)†

True Grit (1969)*** John Wayne, Glen Campbell, Kim Darby, Jeremy Slate, Jeff Corey, Robert Duvall, Dennis Hopper. John Wayne's Academy Award-winning role as Rooster Cogburn, a one-eyed crotchety U.S. marshall who can still shoot straight. This delightful western chase-down of the bad guys features an appealing performance from Darby as a fourteen-year-old tomboy out to avenge her murdered father. (Dir: Henry Hathaway, 128 mins.)†

True Grit (MTV 1978)**½ Warren Oates, Lisa Pelikan, Lee Meriwether. Not a remake, but a sequel to the '69 *True Grit*. Oates is pretty good in the impossible job of filling John Wayne's shoes as Rooster Cogburn, and Pelikan, a talented and charming redhead, plays the Kim Darby role. (Dir: Richard T. Heffron, 104 mins.)

True Heart Susie (1919)**** Lillian Gish, Robert Harron, Loyola O'Connor, Walter Higby, Clarine Seymour, Kate Bruce. A lovely little rural romance from the great director D. W. Griffith, about an honest country girl who devotedly loves a young man, although he wants another. Simple, intelligent, heartfelt performances and strikingly beautiful photography of the disappearing pastoral scene by Billy Bitzer make this an American classic. (106 mins.)†

True Love (1989)*½ Annabella Sciorra, Ron Eldard, Aida Turturro, Roger Rignack. Slice-of-life look at a young Bronx couple preparing for their wedding. (Dir: Nancy Savocca, 104 mins.)†

True Stories (1986)** David Byrne, Swoosie Kurtz, Spalding Gray, John Goodman. An oddball view of life in a small Texas community. In and out of all these vignettes wanders David Byrne like the New Wave Mister Rogers. As could be expected, the music, by Byrne and the Talking Heads, is excellent. (Dir: David Byrne, 111 mins.)†

True Story of Jesse James, The (1957)**½ Robert Wagner, Jeffrey Hunter, Hope Lange, Agnes Moorehead. Director Nicholas Ray injects the vitality that is evident throughout this umpteenth rehashing of the legend of the James brothers. (92 mins.)

True Story of Lynn Stuart, The (1958)*½ Betsy Palmer, Jack Lord, Barry Atwater, Kim Spaulding. Good actors are wasted in this trite melodrama about a woman who works undercover for the cops. (Dir: Lewis Seiler, 78 mins.)

True to Life (1943)**½ Mary Martin, Dick Powell, Victor Moore, Franchot Tone. Cute little comedy about a soap opera writer who goes to live with a nice family and uses their conversations and actions in his scripts. (Dir: George Marshall, 94 mins.)

True to the Navy (1930)** Clara Bow, Fredric March, Harry Green, Rex Bell, Eddie Fetherston. Uneven service comedy, with soda jerk Bow falling for happy-go-lucky sailor March. (Dir: Frank Tuttle, 71 mins.)

True West (MTV 1984)*** John Malkovich, Gary Sinise. The Steppenwolf theater company's riotous, raucous adaptation of Sam Shepard's play about two mismatched brothers, Austin, a writer frantically trying to finish a screenplay, and the out-of-control Lee. (Dir: Allan Goldstein, 110 mins.)†

Truly, Madly, Deeply (Great Britain, 1990)

***½ Juliet Stevenson, Alan Rickman, Bill Paterson, Michael Maloney. An absurdist love story that's both truly funny and deeply moving. This impeccable little film chronicles the peculiar complications that develop when a young woman is rejoined by her dead lover. First-time director Minghella (he also scripted) fills the picture with several memorable bits of business, fashioning something very rare: a realistic fantasy. (Dir: Anthony Minghella, 107 mins.)

Trunk to Cairo (Israel-West Germany, 1966)* Audie Murphy, George Sanders, Marianne Koch. Ludicrous spy chase. German scientist's moon-rocket plans are sought by both Israelis and Egyptians. (Dir: Menahem Golem, 80 mins.)

Trust (1990)***½ Adrienne Shelly, Martin Donovan, Merritt Nelson, John MacKay. Provocative black comedy about two lost souls—a pregnant suburban teenager and a brooding television repairman —both escaping abusive relationships with family and friends. They meet and vow to live a normal, domestic life with unsettling results. Well acted, wonderfully written and directed, and completely absorbing. (Dir: Hal Hartley, 91 mins.)

Trust Me (1989)** Adam Ant, David Packer, Talia Balsam, William DeAcutis, Joyce Van Patten, Barbara Bain. Pleasant but insubstantial comedy. Gallery owner Ant trying to boost the chances for success of unconventional artist Packer by having him killed. (Dir: Bobby Houston, 94 mins.)†

Truth, The (France-Italy, 1960)**½ Brigitte Bardot, Charles Vanel, Paul Meurisse. An interesting film; an exploration of justice under France's outdated Napoleonic Code, using as vehicle and foil the uncontrollable sexuality of Miss Bardot, on trial for a murder which her defense claims was one of passion. (Dir: Henri-Georges Clouzot, 127 mins.)

Truth About Spring, The (1965)**½ Hayley Mills, John Mills, James MacArthur. Daughter of a rascally seaman experiences her first pangs of love when she meets a wealthy young man. Leisurely but entertaining romantic tale. (Dir: Richard Thorpe, 102 mins.)

Truth About Women, The (Great Britain, 1958)**½ Laurence Harvey, Julie Harris, Diane Cilento, Eva Gabor, Mai Zetterling. A fine cast does what it can to make this somewhat contrived comedy-romance workable. (Dir: Muriel Box, 98 mins.)

Truth Is Stranger—See: **When Ladies Meet** (1933)

Truth or Dare (1991)***½ This wild cinematic ride through pop singer Madonna's libido is part grand concert and part psychotherapy. The sound and visuals are extraordinary, and the singer-actress offers astonishing insights into life on the rock and roll road, her views on religion and family, and her own uninhibited sexuality. Wonderfully bawdy and fascinatingly watchable. AKA: **Madonna Truth or Dare**. (Dir: Alek Keshishian, 118 mins.)†

Try and Get Me (1950)*** Frank Lovejoy, Lloyd Bridges, Richard Carlson. Two kidnappers murder their victim, and are themselves victimized by mob violence upon their capture. Dramatic thunderbolt pulls no punches. (Dir: Cyril Endfield, 85 mins.)

Trygon Factor, The (Great Britain, 1967)** Stewart Granger, Susan Hampshire, Robert Morley. Scotland Yard mystery film. Granger is all British cool as the superintendent in charge of a murder investigation. (Dir: Cyril Frankel, 87 mins.)

Tucker: The Man and His Dream (1988)** Jeff Bridges, Joan Allen, Martin Landau, Frederic Forrest, Mako, Dean Stockwell, Lloyd Bridges. Disappointing slice of wholesome American pie from Francis Ford Coppola. Bridges plays Preston Tucker, the real-life inventor who wanted to revolutionize the automobile industry (he conceived the seatbelt), but faced overwhelming opposition from big corporate concerns. (110 mins.)†

Tuck Everlasting (1980)***½ Margaret Chamberlain, Paul Flessa, Fred Keller, James McGuire. A joyous treat that's must family viewing. Based on a prizewinning children's book, this tale of a girl who encounters a mysterious family of "immortals" is invigorating screen fare; not a bit patronizing to kids. (Dir: Frederick King Keller, 100 mins.)†

Tuff Turf (1985)** James Spader, Kim Richards, Paul Mones, Claudette Nevins, Matt Clark. A routine teen tale about a transplanted Easterner who has trouble adjusting to an inner-city California high school. (Dir: Fritz Kiersch, 112 mins.)†

Tugboat Annie (1933)*** Marie Dressler, Wallace Beery, Robert Young, Maureen O'Sullivan. Two old sots on the waterfront; a perfect vehicle to reteam Dressler and Beery after their successful *Min and Bill*. (Dir: Mervyn LeRoy, 87 mins.)

Tugboat Annie Sails Again (1940)** Marjorie Rambeau, Jane Wyman, Ronald Reagan, Alan Hale, Chill Wills. Misguided attempt to replace Marie Dressler in the title role with Rambeau, who was a fine actress, but unsuited to the role. (Dir: Lewis Seiler, 77 mins.)

Tulips (Canada, 1981)* Gabe Kaplan, Bernadette Peters, Henry Gibson. A weak romance between two perennial losers who keep attempting suicide. After viewing this, you'll wish they'd succeeded. (Dir: Stan Ferris, 92 mins.)†

Tulsa (1949)*** Susan Hayward, Robert

Preston. A fiery redhead battles for an oil empire in the early thirties, only to lose it all and become poorer but wiser. Good melodrama, with plenty of action. (Dir: Stuart Heisler, 90 mins.)†

Tumbleweed (1953)**½ Audie Murphy, Lori Nelson, Chill Wills, Roy Roberts, Russell Johnson, Lee Van Cleef, Lyle Talbot. Colorful western vehicle for Murphy, as shotgun rider on a wagon train wrongly accused of setting it up for a raid. Trim and fairly vigorous; Murphy acts with great authority, as usual. (Dir: Nathan Juran, 79 mins.)

Tumbleweeds (1925)**** William S. Hart, Barbara Bedford, Lucien Littlefield, J. Gordon Russell, George F. Marion. Hart's last picture, a thrilling and deeply felt saga. He plays a roving cowhand who decides to settle down on a patch of land he's picked out with the daughter of another homesteader. The extraordinary scene of the land rush, with every kind of horse-drawn vehicle precariously speeding toward open country, has yet to be matched. (Dirs: William S. Hart, King Baggot, 81 mins.)†

Tune In Tomorrow . . . (1990)** Barbara Hershey, Keanu Reeves, Peter Falk, Peter Gallagher, Buck Henry, Hope Lange, Elizabeth McGovern, Danny Aiello III, Patricia Clarkson. Failed comedy set in New Orleans in 1951 about the players who perform radio soap operas, and their private and public misadventures. Based on the novel *Aunt Julia and the Scriptwriter* by Mario Vargas Llosa. (Dir: Jon Amiel, 105 mins.)†

Tunes of Glory (Great Britain, 1960)**** John Mills, Alec Guinness. A beautiful film, recommended for the magnificent performances of its two stars. Story about the bitter struggle between a vicious, goldbricking colonel (Guinness) and the intelligent, disciplined young officer (Mills) who supersedes him in command. (Dir: Ronald Neame, 106 mins.)†

Tunnel of Love, The (1958)*** Richard Widmark, Doris Day, Gig Young, Gia Scala. Pleasantly performed comedy about a suburban couple who go through all sorts of red tape to adopt a child. (Dir: Gene Kelly, 98 mins.)

Tunnelvision (1976)** Chevy Chase, Laraine Newman, Brad Smirnoff, Howard Hesseman, Gerrit Graham, Al Franken. Following the *Groove Tube* and predating *Airplane*, and not as good as either. (Dir: Neal Israel, 75 mins.)†

Turk 182 (1985)** Timothy Hutton, Kim Cattrall, Robert Culp, Peter Boyle, Darren McGavin, Robert Urich. Hutton plays a vigilante graffiti artist who avenges his drunken fireman brother (Urich). A preposterous little guy vs. the Establishment flick! (Dir: Bob Clark, 97 mins.)†

Turkish Delight (Netherlands, 1973)***½ Rutger Hauer, Monique Van De Ven. Energetic, erotic drama about an iconoclastic sculptor (Hauer) who marries into a bourgeois family, only to have a variety of problems with the relationship. (Dir: Paul Verhoeven, 106 mins.)

Turnabout (1940)**½ Adolphe Menjou, John Hubbard, Carole Landis, Mary Astor. Through a mysterious power, husband and wife have a chance to change sexes, with the natural confusion resulting. Risqué comedy has a fair share of laughs. (Dir: Hal Roach, 83 mins.)

Turn Back the Clock (1933)*** Lee Tracy, Mae Clarke, Otto Kruger, George Barbier, Peggy Shannon. Provocative comedy-drama, from a story by Ben Hecht, about a businessman who mysteriously gets a chance to live his life over again. Intelligent, cleverly written, and sharply played, an unsung gem. (Dir: Edgar Selwyn, 80 mins.)

Turn Back the Clock (MTV 1989)**½ Connie Selleca, David Dukes, Wendy Kilbourne, Jere Burns, Gene Barry, Joan Leslie, Dina Merrill. Woman who has just capped a bad year by murdering her husband gets her wish to be able to live the past twelve months over again. Remake of the 1947 *Repeat Performance*. (Dir: Larry Elikann, 96 mins.)

Turner and Hooch (1989)*** Tom Hanks, Mare Winningham, Scott Paulin, Craig T. Nelson. Fastidious yuppie detective Hanks is forced to take care of the only witness to a puzzling murder—the dead man's dog. The memorably ugly mutt, all skin and slobber, seems determined to eat everything Hanks owns (car included) before the case is solved. (Dir: Roger Spottiswoode, 100 mins.)†

Turning Point, The (1952)**½ William Holden, Alexis Smith, Edmond O'Brien. Reporter learns that the father of the chairman of a crime investigating committee is mixed up with the crooks himself. (Dir: William Dieterle, 85 mins.)

Turning Point, The (1977)*** Anne Bancroft, Shirley MacLaine, Mikhail Baryshnikov, Leslie Browne, Tom Skerritt. Aging ballet star Bancroft rekindles an old friendship and rivalry with former colleague MacLaine who, long ago, abandoned her career for marriage. (Dir: Herbert Ross, 119 mins.)†

Turning Point of Jim Malloy, The (MTV 1975)** John Savage, Gig Young, Biff McGuire, Janis Paige, Kathleen Quinlan. John O'Hara's "Gibbsville" stories are the basis for this adaptation by Frank D. Gilroy, who also directed. A young man returns to his hometown in Pennsylvania after being expelled from Yale and gets a job on the local newspaper. (72 mins.)

Turnover Smith (MTV 1980)** William Conrad, Belinda Montgomery, Hilly Hicks. Predictable pilot film starring Conrad as a criminologist, based in San Francisco, who makes the breakthrough in a series of murders of young women. (Dir: Bernard L. Kowalski, 78 mins.)

Turn the Key Softly (Great Britain, 1953)*** Yvonne Mitchell, Joan Collins, Terence Morgan. Concerning the adventure of three women recently released from prison, their attempts to adjust themselves to society. Excellent performances give this drama a lift. (Dir: Hal Roach, 83 mins.)

Turtle Diary (Great Britain, 1986)*** Glenda Jackson, Ben Kingsley, Richard Johnson, Jeroen Krabbé, Eleanor Bron, Michael Gambon. A wistful talkfest splendidly adapted by Harold Pinter from a subtle novel by Russell Hoban and superlatively acted by the leads. Jackson's a writer of children's books; Kingsley's a clerk in a bookstore; these two smaller-than-life figures experience the grand adventure of freeing some sea turtles from an aquarium. (Dir: John Irvin, 97 mins.)†

Tuttles of Tahiti, The (1942)*** Charles Laughton, Jon Hall, Peggy Drake. The easygoing head of a large tropic family takes life as it comes, as long as it doesn't involve work. Pleasing story of the South Seas. (Dir: Charles Vidor, 91 mins.)†

Twelve Angry Men (1957)***½ Henry Fonda, Lee J. Cobb, Martin Balsam, Ed Begley, E. G. Marshall, Jack Klugman, Jack Warden, Robert Webber. As a period piece of liberal melodrama, this is rousing good fun. Fonda plays the sole holdout on a hanging jury who by dint of sweet reason and native guile turns the case around for the defendant, a boy accused of killing his father. (Dir: Sidney Lumet, 95 mins.)†

Twelve Chairs, The (1970)*** Mel Brooks, Dom DeLuise, Frank Langella, Ron Moody. Remember the Fred Allen starrer *It's in the Bag*? Well, this romp, filmed in Yugoslavia, written and directed by Mel Brooks, is based on the same Russian comedy-fable, and some of it is quite funny, as an impoverished nobleman (Moody) tries to track down some precious jewel-filled chairs. (94 mins.)†

Twelve O'Clock High (1949)*** Gregory Peck, Gary Merrill, Hugh Marlowe, Dean Jagger. Peck is a WWII flight commander cracking up under the strain of mission after mission. The film is intelligent and well produced, but Henry King's direction is too impersonal. Superb work by cameraman Leon Shamroy. (132 mins.)†

12 + 1 (1970)** Sharon Tate, Orson Welles, Vittorio Gassman, Vittorio De Sica, Terry-Thomas. Primarily notable for containing the last performance of the late Sharon Tate, this is another version of the novel *The Twelve Chairs* (Mel Brooks's version was released later in the same year); this time, Gassman is the heir who finds that the chairs he has traded away contain a hidden fortune. AKA: **The Thirteen Chairs**. (Dir: Nicolas Gessner, 95 mins.)†

Twentieth Century (1934)***½ John Barrymore, Carole Lombard, Walter Connolly, Roscoe Karns. Barrymore's Oscar Jaffe is a superb comic incarnation of a demented producer-director, and Lombard, playing his discovery who's become a big star, emerges as the wackiest comedienne as well as the most beautiful. Set aboard the famous New York-Chicago express train. (Dir: Howard Hawks, 91 mins.)

28 Up (Great Britain, MTV 1985)***½ Fascinating documentary (originally shown in four installments) that contains interviews of English children early in their lives (age seven), and then at the ages of fourteen, twenty-one, and twenty-eight. What has happened to these kids, and what hasn't happened to their dreams, is instructive and heartbreaking. (Dir: Michael Apted, 136 mins.)

25 Fireman's Street (Hungary, 1973)***½ Rita Bekes, Peter Muller, Lucyna Winnicka, Mari Szemes, Andras Balint. Haunting drama depicts thirty years of Hungarian history as recalled by the inhabitants of a deteriorated house on the night before its scheduled demolition. Stylized film is filled with warm characters and beautiful imagery. (Dir: Istvan Szabo, 97 mins.)†

25th Hour, The (France-Italy-Yugoslavia, 1967)*** Anthony Quinn, Virna Lisi, Michael Redgrave, Alexander Knox. Sometimes implausible but often affecting drama about Rumanian participation in WWII, and shortly thereafter. (Dir: Henri Verneuil, 119 mins.)

Twenty-Four Hours in a Woman's Life (France, 1968)*** Danielle Darrieux, Robert Hoffman, Marthe Alycia, Lena Skerla. An elegant society widow falls in love with a young man, who turns out to be a deserter from the Austrian military and a compulsive gambler. Subtle film captures the 1914 period and offers a wonderful look at sudden love, with Darrieux a treasure. (Dir: Dominique Delouche, 84 mins.)

24 Hours to Kill (Great Britain, 1965)* Mickey Rooney, Lex Barker, Walter Slezak. Espionage, junior grade. Mickey Rooney is a purser on a plane that has a twenty-four-hour layover in Beirut. Before too long, he's kidnapped. (Dir: Peter Bezencenet, 92 mins.)

Twenty Million Miles to Earth (1957)**½ William Hopper, Joan Taylor. Science-fiction rides again! This opus has a "gelatinous mass" which duplicates its size overnight. The army is called in and eventually destroys it atop the Colosseum in Rome. (Dir: Nathan Juran, 82 mins.)

Twenty Million Sweethearts (1934)**½ Dick Powell, Ginger Rogers, Pat O'Brien, Allen Jenkins, Grant Mitchell. Mildly satiric musical comedy with Powell as a singing waiter, who dreams of warbling his way to radio stardom. Remade as *My Dream Is Yours,* and featuring the beautiful ballad, "I'll String Along with You." Slight, but engaging. (Dir: Ray Enright, 89 mins.)

Twenty Mule Team (1940)*** Wallace Beery, Leo Carillo, Marjorie Rambeau, Anne Baxter, Douglas Fowley, Noah Beery, Jr., Arthur Hohl. One of Beery's best vehicles, this has him playing a rough, rowdy mule team driver transporting borax across the desert, with the assistance of his half-Indian partner Carillo. Burly, vigorous action, with an interesting and unusual historical theme. (Dir: Richard Thorpe, 82 mins.)

Twenty-one (1991)** Patsy Kensit, Jack Shepherd, Patrick Ryecart, Rufus Sewell, Sophie Thompson, Maynard Eziashi. Familiar story of a sassy British lass (Kensit), lacking common sense and good judgment, who travels to New York City to begin a new life. Starts out promisingly, but soon becomes dull and uninteresting. (Dir: Don Boyd, 101 mins.)

21 Days (Great Britain, 1938)**½ Laurence Olivier, Vivien Leigh, Leslie Banks, Robert Newton. Young lawyer has committed murder, finds he has three weeks with his love before justice intervenes. Lot of talent stuck in a drama that doesn't come off. (Dir: Basil Dean, 72 mins.)

Twenty-one Hours at Munich (MTV 1976)*** William Holden, Shirley Knight, Franco Nero. A fine re-creation of the dramatic, unforgettable, and terrifying slaughter of the Israeli athletes by Arab terrorists during the 1972 Olympics. The film has been impeccably produced using the actual Munich locations, and the cast is very good. (Dir: William A. Graham, 105 mins.)

Twenty Plus Two (1961)** David Janssen, Jeanne Crain, Dina Merrill, Agnes Moorehead, Brad Dexter. Routine murder-investigation film sparked by Janssen's portrayal of a hard-boiled private investigator not taking any guff from the colorful supporting cast. (Dir: Joseph M. Newman, 102 mins.)

27th Day, The (1957)**½ Gene Barry, Valerie French. A science-fiction tale with a few novel twists—at least there are no prehistoric monsters in this one.

A selected group of earth people are given capsules which can destroy mankind and our hero has to track them down. (Dir: William Asher, 75 mins.)

20,000 Leagues Under the Sea (1954)***½ Kirk Douglas, Paul Lukas, James Mason, Peter Lorre. Walt Disney's entertaining epic version of Jules Verne's nautical tale. Douglas is the robust harpooner who, along with shipmates Lukas and Lorre, is plunged into a series of exciting events aboard Captain Nemo's (Mason's) cosmic-powered submarine, circa 1860s. Oscars: Best Special Effects; Best Art Direction. (Dir: Richard Fleischer, 127 mins.)†

20,000 Years in Sing Sing (1933)*** Spencer Tracy, Bette Davis, Lyle Talbot, Louis Calhern, Grant Mitchell. Tracy and Davis only made one film together, this engrossing prison melodrama of a criminal and his self-sacrificing girlfriend. Powerful performances lift this one out of the ordinary. Remade with John Garfield as *Castle on the Hudson.* (Dir: Michael Curtiz, 81 mins.)

23 Paces to Baker Street (Great Britain, 1956)*** Van Johnson, Vera Miles. Neat mystery keeps the attention, as a blind man attempts to solve a murder. (Dir: Henry Hathaway, 103 mins.)†

2020 Texas Gladiators (Italy, 1985)* Harrison Muller, Al Cliver, Sabrina Siani, Daniel Stephen. More post-nuke non-thrills, even more muddled than usual, with bikers, neo-Nazis, and cowboys with bazookas. (Dir: Kevin Mancuso, 91 mins.)†

Twice Dead (1988)* Tom Breznahan, Jill Whitlow, Todd Bridges. Awful teenagers-in-jeopardy movie features Breznahan and Whitlow as brother and sister who have ghosts in their house and a gang of punks at the door with trouble in mind. (Dir: Bert Dragin, 87 mins.)†

Twice in a Lifetime (1985)*** Gene Hackman, Ann-Margret, Ellen Burstyn, Amy Madigan, Ally Sheedy, Brian Dennehy. Well-acted domestic soap opera. Steelworker Hackman, feeling bored and lifeless on his fiftieth birthday, begins an affair with widow Ann-Margret. Although there are gaps in continuity, this develops some real resonance on occasion. (Dir: Bud Yorkin, 117 mins.)†

Twice-Told Tales (1963)*** Vincent Price, Sebastian Cabot, Mari Blanchard, Brett Halsey, Richard Denning. Three Hawthorne tales, "Rapacinni's Daughter," "House of the Seven Gables," and "Dr. Heidegger's Experiment" are unveiled in shuddery interpretations in this bonanza for fright-night fans. (Dir: Sidney Salkow, 119 mins.)†

Twice Under (1990)*½ Ian Borger, Ron Spencer, Amy Lacy, Jack O'Hara. Insane Vietnam veteran stalks sewer tunnels, killing public works laborers. (Dir: Dean Crow, 90 mins.)

Twilight for the Gods (1958)** Rock Hudson, Cyd Charisse, Arthur Kennedy. Ernest Gann's novel is brought to the screen with a strange mixture of miscasting and overdrawn characterizations. The setting is a tramp steamer and the drama unfolds as the passengers begin to distrust each other's reasons for the voyage. (Dir: Joseph Pevney, 120 mins.)

Twilight of Honor (1963)** Richard Chamberlain, Claude Rains, Joey Heatherton, Nick Adams. Chamberlain plays a sincere young lawyer defending a murder suspect. Should have been tightly knit, but isn't. (Dir: Boris Sagal, 115 mins.)

Twilight of the Dead—See: Gates of Hell

Twilight's Last Gleaming (1977)**½ Burt Lancaster, Richard Widmark, Charles Durning, Melvyn Douglas. An antiwar statement gets muddled in this plot line about a former army general and three other inmates of death row who escape from prison, take over a SAC missile silo, and threaten to launch bombs on Russia and start WWIII if their political grievances are not settled. (Dir: Robert Aldrich, 146 mins.) †

Twilight Time (1983)**½ Karl Malden, Jodi Thelen, Mia Roth, Damien Nash. Malden's performance as a man who has toiled in the United States for many years and chooses to return to his native village in Yugoslavia for his twilight years, makes the film seem better than it is. (Dir: Goran Paskaljevic, 112 mins.)

Twilight Zone—The Movie (1983)**½ Vic Morrow, Scatman Crothers, Kathleen Quinlan, Patricia Barry, Abbe Lane, John Lithgow, Dan Aykroyd. Disappointing salute to Rod Serling's TV cult classic. The final sequence, directed by George Miller, is a must-see, however, a scary episode about a neurotic passenger who spots a gremlin destroying his airplane in midflight. (Dirs: John Landis, Steven Spielberg, Joe Dante, George Miller, 100 mins.) †

Twin Beds (1942)** George Brent, Joan Bennett, Mischa Auer, Una Merkel, Glenda Farrell, Margaret Hamilton. Mild bedroom farce about a couple whose lives are disrupted by their flamboyant neighbor, a Russian concert singer attracted to the wife; Bennett and Brent just aren't funny enough on their own to carry this kind of comedy, and Auer steals it handily. (Dir: Tim Whelan, 85 mins.)

Twin Detectives (MTV 1976)* Jim Hager, Jon Hager, Lillian Gish, Patrick O'Neal, David White. Identical twin detectives fool the culprits by appearing to be in two places at once. (Dir: Robert Day, 72 mins.)

Twinkle in God's Eye, The (1955)** Mickey Rooney, Coleen Gray, Hugh O'Brian. Parson arrives in a lawless frontier town to build a church. Offbeat role for Rooney, but still a maudlin drama. (Dir: George Blair, 73 mins.)

Twinkle, Twinkle, Killer Kane (1980)*** Stacy Keach, Scott Wilson, Jason Miller. Surrealistic thriller, shot in Hungary, about a new "doctor" in an institution for disturbed military men. Uneven but truly original film that moves from comedy to tragedy in disturbing ways. Available in several different running times. (Dir: William Peter Blatty, 105 mins.)

Twins (1988)** Arnold Schwarzenegger, Danny DeVito, Kelly Preston, Chloe Webb. Casting muscleman Arnold and runty DeVito as twin brothers, separated at birth, who meet for the first time is a funny idea. But this wan comedy misses its potential, wasting time instead on a gangster subplot and a lot of dewy sentimentality. Preston and Webb, as the duo's love interests, add the only spark. (Dir: Ivan Reitman, 103 mins.) †

Twins of Evil (1971)**½ Madeleine Collinson, Mary Collinson, Peter Cushing. Hammer Studios horror film about a pair of amply bosomed twins, one of whom is afflicted by an ancient vampiric curse. (Dir: John Hough, 87 mins.) †

Twirl (MTV 1981)* Erin Moran, Lisa Whelchel, Charles Haid, Stella Stevens. Only for devotees of baton twirling. Haid and Stevens play obsessed parents and bitter rivals who plague their kids with the "winning is everything" doctrine. (Dir: Gus Trikonis, 104 mins.) †

Twist, The (France, 1976)*½ Ann-Margret, Stephane Audran, Bruce Dern, Charles Aznavour, Curt Jurgens, Maria Schell. A stellar cast can do little to instill excitement into this tedious film by Claude Chabrol depicting the anxieties besetting some bored and boring upper-class Parisians. (Dir: Claude Chabrol, 105 mins.) †

Twist All Night (1961)* Louis Prima, June Wilkinson, Gertrude Michael, David Whorf. Sloppy musical showcase for Prima, the twist craze, busty June Wilkinson, and Sam Butera and the Witnesses. (Dir: William Hole, Jr., 78 mins.)

Twist and Shout (Denmark, 1984)*** Adam Tonsberg, Lars Simonsen, Camilla Soeberg, Ulrikke Juull Bondo. A teenage-trauma movie set among the Beatles-crazed kids of sixties Denmark. Thanks to good acting by the young stars and observant writing and direction, this is more sensitive than most of its American counterparts in its depiction of first love, generation gap battles, disillusionment with one's parents, and all other youth film rites of passage. (Dir: Bille August, 100 mins.) †

Twist Around the Clock (1962)**½ Chubby Checker, Dion, Clay Cole. Average musical about the origins of the revolu-

1120

tionary dance and chock-full of early rock standards like "The Wanderer" and "Runaround Sue." (Dir: Oscar Rudolph, 86 mins.)

Twisted Brain (1974)* Pat Cardi, Rosie Holotik, John Niland, Austin Stoker, Joyce Hash. Horror pic about a high school boy who discovers a secret formula and takes revenge on all the kids who were mean to him. (Dir: Larry N. Stouffer, 85 mins.)†

Twisted Justice (1990)* David Heavener, Erik Estrada, Karen Black, Shannon Tweed, Jim Brown, James Van Patten, Don Stroud. In 2020 Los Angeles, where even the police are forbidden to have guns, one rebel cop insists on using his outlawed weapon. (Dir: David Heavener, 90 mins.)†

Twisted Nerve (Great Britain, 1968)** Hayley Mills, Hywel Bennett, Billie Whitelaw, Frank Finlay, Barry Foster. A grotesque psycho-thriller about a chromosome-damaged psychopath. The film makes an unfortunate error in judgment by likening the killer's madness to the problem of mental retardation. (Dir: Roy Boulting, 118 mins.)

Twisted Obsession (Spain-France, 1990)* Jeff Goldblum, Dexter Fletcher, Miranda Richardson, Daniel Ceccaldi, Liza Walker. A screenwriter gets more than he bargains for when he falls in love with his producer's daughter. He soon realizes not everything is as it seems in this dull psychological melodrama, which never lives up to its kinky premise. (Dir: Fernando Trueba, 109 mins.)†

Twister (1988)* Suzy Amis, Crispin Glover, Harry Dean Stanton, Dylan McDermot, Jenny Wright, Charlaine Woodard, Lois Chiles, Tim Robbins, William Burroughs. Utterly pointless comedy-drama of a few days in the life of an odd family. (Dir: Michael Almereyda, 93 mins.)†

Twist of Fate (Great Britain, 1954)** Ginger Rogers, Herbert Lom, Stanley Baker, Jacques Bergerac. Ex-actress on the Riviera learns her husband-to-be is a dangerous criminal. Overdone melodrama. (Dir: David Miller, 89 mins.)

Twist of Fate (MTV, 1989)** Ben Cross, John Glover, Sarah Jessica Parker, Bruce Greenwood, Larry Lamb, Veronica Hamel. Nazi SS officer Cross has plastic surgery and passes himself off as a Jew to escape criminal charges. His plan backfires when he ends up in a concentration camp. (Dir: Ian Sharp, 192 mins.)

Twitch of the Death Nerve—See: **Bay of Blood**

Two Against the World (1936)** Humphrey Bogart, Beverly Roberts, Carlyle Moore, Jr., Linda Perry, Henry O'Neill, Claire Dodd. Not altogether successful attempt to redo *Five Star Final* in a radio studio setting. (Dir: William McGann, 64 mins.)

Two Cents Worth of Hope (Italy, 1952)*** Vincenzo Musolino, Filumena Russo, Maria Fiore, Luigi Astarita. Enjoyable neo-realist film about a man back from WWII trying to impress his fiancée's father by working a number of odd jobs. The conclusion of director Renato Castellani's trilogy of Italian life begun with *Under the Sun of Rome* and *It's Forever Springtime*. (98 mins.)

Two Daughters (India, 1962)***½ Anil Chatterjee. Two stories about young women in love. The first, "The Postmaster," is about a young servant girl's devotion to her postmaster employer; the other, "The Conclusion," is a charming tale about a young bride who runs away from her forced marriage to a nice man. (Dir: Satyajit Ray, 114 mins.)

Two Dollar Bettor (1951)**½ John Litel, Marie Windsor, Steve Brodie, Barbara Logan, Robert Sherwood, Walter Kingsford. Low-budget but effective story of an ordinary middle-class businessman becoming a compulsive gambler. Grim, no-frills production is suited to the subject. (Dir: Edward L. Cahn, 72 mins.)

Two English Girls (France, 1971)***½ Jean-Pierre Léaud, Kika Markham, Stacey Tendeter. Tender story of two English sisters in love with a young Frenchman (Léaud) in Paris before WWI. Based on a novel by Henri-Pierre Roche. (Dir: François Truffaut, 132 mins.)†

Two Evil Eyes (U.S.-Italy, 1990)*** Adrienne Barbeau, E. G. Marshall, Harvey Keitel, Martin Balsam. A pair of stories by Edgar Allan Poe are updated and given quality productions by masters of the genre in this two-part horror film, that will thrill fans of the form. George Romero superbly directs "The Truth About the Valdemar Case" and Dario Argento brings "The Black Cat" to wonderfully creepy life. (Dirs: George Romero, Dario Argento, 105 mins.)†

Two-Faced Woman (1941)*** Greta Garbo, Melvyn Douglas, Constance Bennett, Roland Young, Ruth Gordon, Robert Sterling. Sharp bedroom farce starring Garbo as a ski instructor who weds Douglas after a brief courtship. He returns to N.Y.C.; she stays behind. When she goes east, she pretends to be her own wicked twin sister. (Dir: George Cukor, 94 mins.)†

Two Faces of Dr. Jekyll, The (Great Britain, 1960)** Paul Massie, Christopher Lee. Still another version of the Stevenson story about the tormented Dr. Jekyll whose split personality makes him lead a double life. (Dir: Terence Fisher, 89 mins.)

Two Fathers' Justice (MTV 1985)** Robert

Conrad, George Hamilton, Brooke Bundy, Greg Terrell. Clumsy TV movie about vigilantism. Conrad and Hamilton join forces as a steelworker and a Boston blueblood, taking the law into their own hands to nail the killers of their kids. (Dir: Rod Holcomb, 104 mins.)†

Two-Five, The (MTV 1978)** Don Johnson, Joe Bennett, George Murdock, Michael Durrell, John Crawford. Unsold pilot for a TV show about two unorthodox cops, here resorting to odd subterfuges in order to bring down a major drug dealer. (Dir: Bruce Kessler, 73 mins.)

Two Flags West (1950)** Joseph Cotten, Linda Darnell, Jeff Chandler, Cornel Wilde, Dale Robertson. Spectacular battle scenes provide excitement in this Civil War western. (Dir: Robert Wise, 92 mins.)

Two for the Money (MTV 1972)**½ Robert Hooks, Stephen Brooks, Walter Brennan, Mercedes McCambridge. About ex-cops, one black (Hooks) and one white (Brooks), who open a private detective office. Case involves the search for a mass murderer, at large for over a decade. (Dir: Bernard L. Kowalski, 73 mins.)

Two for the Road (U.S.-Great Britain, 1967)***½ Audrey Hepburn, Albert Finney. Refreshing, sophisticated comedy-drama. Audrey Hepburn gives a convincing portrayal of a woman who loves the man she married and hates what he has become. Albert Finney is great as the husband who has a roving eye but still wants his wife. Directed with great flair by Stanley Donen. (112 mins.)†

Two for the Seesaw (1962)*** Shirley MacLaine, Robert Mitchum. Essentially a two-character comedy-drama about a disillusioned lawyer from Omaha who meets and loves a tough-tender New York girl. Humorous and poignant. (Dir: Robert Wise, 120 mins.)

Two for Tonight (1935)**½ Bing Crosby, Joan Bennett, Mary Boland, Lynne Overman, Thelma Todd. A tangy vehicle for Bing that coasts over its contrived plot with liberal samplings of comedy and song. (Dir: Frank Tuttle, 61 mins.)

240-Robert (MTV, 1979)½ Mark Harmon, Joanna Cassidy, John Bennett Perry. Another cop show pilot with gimmicks? Ingredients include speeding trucks, whirling choppers, a beautiful lady cop, and two rugged young officers of the rescue squad. (Dir: Paul Krasny, 78 mins.)

Two Gentlemen Sharing (Great Britain, 1969)** Robin Phillips, Judy Geeson, Hal Frederick, Esther Anderson. Rather ordinary race relations tale about a black and white man becoming roommates and their various tangled love affairs. (Dir: Ted Kotcheff, 92 mins.)

Two Girls and a Sailor (1944)*** Van

Johnson, June Allyson, Jimmy Durante, Gloria De Haven. One of those entertaining musicals that MGM became famous for. June and Gloria both love Van, and Jimmy is around for plenty of laughs. (Dir: Richard Thorpe, 124 mins.)†

Two Girls on Broadway (1940)** Lana Turner, George Murphy, Joan Blondell. A young singing and dancing Turner makes this back-stage yarn about a dancer who breaks up a sister act worth a look. (Dir: S. Sylvan Simon, 71 mins.)

Two Guys From Milwaukee (1946)**½ Dennis Morgan, Jack Carson, Joan Leslie, Janis Paige, S. Z. Sakall, Patti Brady. Formulaic musical about a prince in disguise (Morgan) learning about life in the U.S. from a charismatic cabbie (Carson); simple, but very deftly done and enjoyable. (Dir: David Butler, 90 mins.)

Two Guys From Texas (1948)**½ Jack Carson, Dennis Morgan, Dorothy Malone. Stranded vaudeville team outwits city thugs down in Texas. (Dir: David Butler, 86 mins.)

Two-Headed Spy, The (Great Britain, 1959)*** Jack Hawkins, Gia Scala. Highly suspenseful spy yarn with good performances by Hawkins and Scala as a couple of British agents working inside the German lines. (Dir: André de Toth, 93 mins.)

200 Motels (Great Britain, 1971)**½ Ringo Starr, Frank Zappa, Theodore Bikel. Rock film that follows the exploits of the Mothers of Invention, who are stranded in groupie-laden Centerville. (Dirs: Frank Zappa, Tony Palmer, 98 mins.)†

Two in a Crowd (1936)** Joan Bennett, Joel McCrea, Henry Armetta, Alison Skipworth, Nat Pendleton, Reginald Denny, Andy Clyde, Donald Meek. Dopey racetrack comedy, with thoroughbred owner McCrea innocently finding some loot from a bank robbery and spending it, only to have the thieves return for it. Meandering direction and bland script defeat a fine cast. (Dir: Alfred E. Green, 85 mins.)

Two Jakes, The (1990)** Jack Nicholson, Harvey Keitel, Meg Tilly, Madeleine Stowe, Eli Wallach, Rubén Blades, Frederic Forrest, David Keith, Richard Farnsworth. Land developers have replaced water seekers, and infidelity, rather than incest, rules in this complex, disappointing follow-up to *Chinatown*. Detective J.J. (Jake) Gittes, a golf-playing war hero in 1948 Los Angeles, investigates dirty dealings and double-crosses. Beautifully photographed by Vilmos Zsigmond. (Dir: Jack Nicholson, 137 mins.)†

Two Kinds of Love (MTV 1983)**½ Ricky Schroder, Peter Weller, Lindsay Wagner. Deeply involving tale of a boy trying to cope with the death of his mom, the one person he loved. (Dir: Jack Bender, 104 mins.)

Two-Lane Blacktop (1971)***½ Warren Oates, James Taylor, Dennis Wilson, Laurie Bird. Although it deals with car freaks, this lean drama is anything but souped-up. Monte Hellman's low-key, rigorously restrained direction is unsentimental about his heroes, who travel a lot but go nowhere. Along the way, they pick up a girl who gradually replaces the cars as the stakes in a race. (Dir: Monte Hellman, 101 mins.)

Two Little Bears, The (1961)** Eddie Albert, Brenda Lee, Jane Wyatt, Soupy Sales. Grammar school principal finds his children can turn themselves into bears. Mild fantasy should be enjoyed best by the younger set. (Dir: Randall Hood, 81 mins.)

Two Lives of Carol Letner, The (MTV 1981) ** Meredith Baxter Birney, Don Johnson, Robert Webber, Dolph Sweet, Salome Jens. An ex-call girl turned college student is forced by police to participate in a garment business-syndicate payoff scheme. Standard action show. (Dir: Philip Leacock, 104 mins.)

Two Lost Worlds (1950)** Laura Elliot, Jim Arness. A colony from Australia lands on a mysterious isle where prehistoric monsters roam. Low-grade thriller; you'll spot stock footage from *Captain Fury*, *One Million B.C.*, and *Captain Caution* used to stretch the budget. (Dir: Norman Dawn, 61 mins.)†

Two Loves (1961)** Shirley MacLaine, Laurence Harvey, Jack Hawkins. Miscasting and mis-scripting combine to throw this drama for a loss. About a teacher in New Zealand and her problems with a mixed-up young fatalist who nevertheless brings love to her spinsterish life. (Dir: Charles Walters, 99 mins.)

Two-Minute Warning (1976)* Charlton Heston, John Cassavetes, Martin Balsam, Gena Rowlands. Mindless claptrap about a mad sniper in a jammed football stadium. When it first aired on TV, much of the violence was cut and entirely new scenes were added; either version is a time-waster. (Dir: Larry Peerce, 112 mins.)

Two Moon Junction (1988)* Sherilyn Fenn, Richard Tyson, Louise Fletcher, Burl Ives, Kristy McNichol. Really dumb Southern-fried romance involving a wealthy young belle and a muscular carnival worker. (Dir: Zalman King, 104 mins.)†

Two Mrs. Carrolls, The (1947)** Humphrey Bogart, Barbara Stanwyck, Alexis Smith. Story of a nut who likes to bump off his wives after he paints their portraits is so melodramatic it may make you laugh. (Dir: Peter Godfrey, 99 mins.)

Two Mrs. Grenvilles, The (MTV 1987)*** Claudette Colbert, Ann-Margret, Stephen Collins, Penny Fuller, John Rubinstein. A '40s showgirl snares a millionaire, but her efforts to be accepted in high society finally cause the dream to become a nightmare. Based on Dominick Dunne's best-seller which fictionalized a real high society murder case. (Dir: John Erman, 208 mins.)

Two Mules for Sister Sara (1970)*** Clint Eastwood, Shirley MacLaine, Alberto Morin. Good action tale smashingly directed by Don Siegel, with visual verve and a command of storytelling. Eastwood is the drifter who picks up nun MacLaine in the desert and finds himself drawn into a local war of liberation in Mexico. (104 mins.)†

Two Nights with Cleopatra (Italy, 1954)* Sophia Loren, Ettore Manni, Alberto Sordi, Rolf Tasna. Ettore Scola co-wrote this silly comedy about Cleopatra setting up a double in her palace so she can sneak out to spend the night with Mark Antony. Originally famous for a nude scene with the twenty-year-old Loren, but it was deleted from the video version we saw. Originally 90 mins. (Dir: Mario Mattoli, 77 mins.)†

Twonky, The (1953)** Hans Conried, Gloria Blondell, Trilby Conried. Hans Conried's TV set becomes possessed by a spirit from the future in this lackluster sci-fi satire. (Dir: Arch Oboler, 72 mins.)

Two of a Kind (1951)** Lizabeth Scott, Edmond O'Brien, Alexander Knox. The usual femme fatale rigmarole, with Scott leading O'Brien about by the nose as she plans to fleece an old couple out of money. (Dir: Henry Levin, 75 mins.)

Two of a Kind (MTV 1982)**½ George Burns, Robby Benson, Cliff Robertson, Barbara Barrie. Burns is cast as an old man waiting to die in an old folks' home until his retarded grandson (Benson) gives him a new lease on life. (Dir: Roger Young, 104 mins.)†

Two of a Kind (1983)½ John Travolta, Olivia Newton-John, Beatrice Straight, Scatman Crothers, Charles Durning, Oliver Reed. God's about to end the world when three angels make a bet with him—if two self-centered earthlings can redeem their shallowness in a week's time the world will be saved. (Dir: John Herzfeld, 87 mins.)†

Two of Them (Women) (Hungary, 1977)*** Marina Vlady, Lili Monori, Miklos Tolnay, Jan Nowicki, Zsuzsa Cznocky. Complex film studies the friendship of a married, middle-aged woman and a rebellious young lady. Using a framework of feminist sensibilities, director Marta Meszaros tackles the issue of women in a communist society with an unabashedly passionate touch. (94 mins.)

Two of Us, The (France, 1967)**** Michel Simon, Alain Cohen, Luce Fabiole. A beautiful, touching, moving film about racial prejudice and anti-Semitism, featuring two near perfect performances from a crusty old bigot (Simon) and the young Jewish boy (Cohen) who comes to board in rural France during the Nazi occupation of Paris during WWII. Wonderfully written and directed by Claude Berri. (86 mins.)†

Two on a Bench (MTV 1971)** Patty Duke, Ted Bessell, John Astin. Gifted Patty turns to light comedy as she and Bessell play two young people who are under suspicion of trafficking with spies, and they're incarcerated for twenty-four hours. (Dir: Jerry Paris, 78 mins.)

Two on a Guillotine (1965)* Connie Stevens, Dean Jones, Cesar Romero. Silly horror film about a haunted house, an heiress (Stevens), a reporter (Jones) and a mad magician (Romero) whose big act was a guillotine bit which he plans to revive. (Dir: William Conrad, 107 mins.)

Two or Three Things I Know About Her (France, 1966) ***½ Anny Duperey, Marina Vlady, Roger Montsoret, Raoul Levy, Jean Narboni. Rich social satire from director Jean-Luc Godard presents the human body as the ultimate consumer good in this eclectic look at housewives who, bored and broke, turn to prostitution. Godard creates wonderful images and commentary about products and services the bourgeoisie has been conditioned to believe—through advertising—that it can't live without. (95 mins.)

Two People (1973)*½ Peter Fonda, Lindsay Wagner, Estelle Parsons. Fonda is a wandering Vietnam deserter on his way home to turn himself in. Wagner is a drifting high fashion model going back to her illegitimate son. Naturally they find each other irresistible! (Dir: Robert Wise, 100 mins.)

Two Rode Together (1961)**½ James Stewart, Richard Widmark, Shirley Jones. A Texas marshal and a cavalry lieutenant lead a wagon train into Comanche territory to rescue captives of the Indians. (Dir: John Ford, 109 mins.)†

Two Seconds (1932)**½ Edward G. Robinson, Vivienne Osborne, Preston Foster. Engrossing melodrama about a condemned man whose life flashes before him in the last two seconds of his life. His life-in-review shows us how he ended up walking the last mile. (Dir: Mervyn LeRoy, 68 mins.)

Two Sisters from Boston (1946)*** Kathryn Grayson, June Allyson, Peter Lawford.

A lot to like in this cute musical set at the turn of the century about two well-bred Boston girls who go to work in a joint on New York's Bowery. (Dir: Henry Koster, 112 mins.)

Two Smart People (1946)*½ Lucille Ball, John Hodiak. Crime pays until just about the end of this miserable hokum about some thieves and a friendly detective. (Dir: Jules Dassin, 93 mins.)

2,000 Maniacs (1964)** Thomas Wood, Connie Mason, Jeffrey Allen, Shelby Livingston, The Pleasant Valley Boys. A group of young swingers is held captive and tortured by a warped Southern ghost town, which comes alive every hundred years to avenge the sacking of their village during the Civil War. Hard going for viewers who aren't fans of creative bloodletting and bad acting. (Dir: Herschell Gordon Lewis, 75 mins.)†

2001: A Space Odyssey (U.S.-Great Britain, 1968)**** Keir Dullea, Gary Lockwood. Brilliant film; the plot and explanation exist on an almost subliminal level in this tracing of man's history and his contact with new life. In the beginning, the earth heated; the earth cooled; apes gave way to man; man to superman and beyond; a space voyage to Jupiter manned by astronauts Bowman (Dullea) and Poole (Lockwood) and computer HAL. (Dir: Stanley Kubrick, 138 mins.)†

2010 (1984)** Roy Scheider, John Lithgow, Bob Balaban, Helen Mirren, Keir Dullea, Douglas Rain (voice of HAL). This disappointing follow-up to the magisterial 2001 suffers from an overexplanation of events better left shrouded in mystery. Putting aside their differences, the U.S. and Russia team up to probe the unexplained events of the Jupiter voyage from 2001. (Dir: Peter Hyams, 114 mins.)†

Two Thousand Women (Great Britain, 1944)***½ Phyllis Calvert, Flora Robson, Patricia Roc. Nazis intern British women, but they turn the tables and secretly help downed RAF fliers to escape occupied territory. Suspenseful melodrama. (Dir: Frank Launder, 97 mins.)

Two Tickets to Broadway (1951)**½ Janet Leigh, Tony Martin, Ann Miller, Eddie Bracken, Smith and Dale. Small-town girl and a singer arrange a hoax to get them on a TV show. Fairly pleasing musical comedy. (Dir: James V. Kern, 106 mins.)

Two Tickets to London (1943)** Michele Morgan, Alan Curtis, Barry Fitzgerald. Espionage and love don't mix as the hero finds out in this WWII tale of German U-boats and admiralty dragnets. (Dir: Edwin L. Martin, 79 mins.)

Two to Tango (U.S.-Argentina, 1988)**½ Don Stroud, Adrienne Sachs, Duilo Marzio, Michael Cavanaugh. A hit man, tired of his wasteful life, yearns for peace and quiet, happiness and love. A beautiful tango dancer in Buenos Aires teaches him a few steps, but his past still haunts him in this moderately interesting thriller with a few good plot twists. (Dir: Hector Olivera, 87 mins.)

Two-Way Stretch (Great Britain, 1960)***½ Peter Sellers, Lionel Jeffries, Wilfred Hyde-White, Bernard Cribbins, Beryl Reid. Classic comedy of cons breaking in and out of prison. (Dir: Robert Day, 87 mins.)†

Two Weeks In Another Town (1962)**½ Kirk Douglas, Edward G. Robinson, Cyd Charisse, Claire Trevor, George Hamilton. The sensational best-seller about American filmmakers in Rome makes a flashy but empty film. Kirk Douglas does what he can in the complex role of a has-been actor who attempts a comeback in the Roman film capital. (Dir: Vincente Minnelli, 107 mins.)

Two Weeks in September (France, 1967)*½ Brigitte Bardot, Laurent Terzieff, Michael Sarne, James Robertson Justice. Bardot sweeps across the Scottish moors in this dreary tale of a model dallying with two lovers, her older sugar daddy and a new young man. (Dir: Serge Bourguignon, 96 mins.)

Two Weeks With Love (1950)**½ Jane Powell, Ricardo Montalban, Debbie Reynolds. Daughter's growing up, parents refuse to realize it. She makes them see the light while on a Catskill vacation. Mildly amusing comedy of the early 1900s. (Dir: Roy Rowland, 92 mins.)†

Two Women (France-Italy, 1960)**** Sophia Loren, Raf Vallone, Eleanora Brown, Jean-Paul Belmondo. Miss Loren deservedly won an Oscar for Best Actress for her performance as an Italian mother who faces tragedy with her daughter during WWII. Deeply moving, realistic, well directed. (Dir: Vittorio De Sica, 99 mins.)†

Two Worlds of Jennie Logan, The (MTV 1979)*** Lindsay Wagner, Alan Feinstein, Marc Singer, Linda Gray. Entertaining supernatural yarn. Wagner discovers a 19th-century dress in the attic of the old house she and her husband have bought; whenever she puts it on it transports her back in time. (Dir: Frank DeFelitta, 104 mins.)†

Two Wrongs Make a Right (1989)**½ Ivan Rogers, Eva Wu, Rich Komenich, R. Michael Pyle. Nightclub owner Rogers resists the efforts of gangsters to buy him out, but fights back when they start playing dirty. Comparatively low-key, almost thoughtful action picture, a change of pace from the usual punch-outs. (Dir: Robert Brown, 83 mins.)†

Two Yanks in Trinidad (1942)*** Pat

O'Brien, Brian Donlevy, Janet Blair. Two racketeers enlist in the Army, get patriotism after Pearl Harbor. Breezy comedy-drama has some bright dialogue, amusing situations. (Dir: Gregory Ratoff, 88 mins.)

Two Years Before the Mast (1946)** Alan Ladd, William Bendix, Brian Donlevy, Barry Fitzgerald. A shanghaied crew on a trip around the Horn in the 1880s is the salty background for this lackluster version of the famous tale of the sea. (Dir: John Farrow, 98 mins.)

Tycoon (1947)*** John Wayne, Laraine Day, Anthony Quinn, Cedric Hardwicke. Young railroad builder meets with many obstructions before he achieves his goal. Nicely made, well-acted but overlong melodrama. (Dir: Richard Wallace, 128 mins.)†

Typhoon (1940)*** Dorothy Lamour, Robert Preston, Lynne Overman, J. Carrol Naish, Jack Carson. A savvy sarong epic. Two sailors discover Lamour on a deserted isle in an enjoyable adventure full of silly contrivances, pidgin English, and old-movie escapism. (Dir: Louis King, 70 mins.)

UFOria (1981)*** Cindy Williams, Harry Dean Stanton, Fred Ward, Robert Gray, Darrell Larson. A humorous, quirky science-fiction spoof. Williams is a nutty cashier who foretells the coming of a flying saucer, and finds a bunch of lunatics and con artists who are more than happy to jump on her cosmic bandwagon. (Dir: John Binder, 100 mins.)†

Ugetsu (Japan, 1953)***½ Machiko Kyo, Masayuki Mori, Kinyo Tanaka. This mysterious, haunting drama centers on two friends who go their separate ways in their search for fulfillment in 16th-century Japan. (Dir: Kenji Mizoguchi, 96 mins.)†

Ugly American, The (1963)*** Marlon Brando, Eiji Okada, Arthur Hill, Jocelyn Brando. Brando is memorable in the role of a distinguished American ambassador to an Asian country whose failure to understand differences in policy brings personal and political disaster. (Dir: George H. Englund, 120 mins.)†

Ugly Dachshund, The (1966)**½ Dean Jones, Suzanne Pleshette. A cute Disney about a married couple competing in dog shows with their respective pets. Their family circle is extended when their dachshund rears a lunky Great Dane as one of her own. (Dir: Norman Tokar, 93 mins.)†

Ugly, Dirty and Mean—See: **Down and Dirty**

UHF (1989)*** Weird Al Yankovic, Victoria Jackson, Michael Richards, Kevin McCarthy, David Bowe, Anthony Geary, Sue Ane Langdon. Story about goofball Yankovic given the management of bottom-of-the-barrel Channel 62 is mostly an excuse for some funny parodies of bad TV. (Dir: Jay Levey, 96 mins.)†

Ultimate Chase, The (1974)** Barry Brown, Britt Ekland, Eric Braeden. Two lengthy ski chases lift this thriller above the ordinary, as ruthless Braeden pursues wife Britt's lovers to the death. AKA: **The Ultimate Thrill**. (Dir: Robert Butler, 80 mins.)

Ultimate Impostor, The (MTV 1979)** Joseph Hacker, Keith Andes. A secret agent is chemically brainwashed by the Communists and submits to an experiment that feeds him data through a computer. (Dir: Paul Stanley, 104 mins.)

Ultimate Solution of Grace Quigley, The— See: **Grace Quigley**

Ultimate Thrill, The—See: **Ultimate Chase, The**

Ultimate Warrior, The (1974)** Yul Brynner, Max von Sydow, Joanna Miles, William Smith. Not quite the ultimate in low-budget potboilers. Yul is a lone gladiator in the 21st-century wasteland run by warlord Max. (Dir: Robert Clouse, 94 mins.)†

Ulysses (Italy, 1955)*** Kirk Douglas, Silvana Mangano, Anthony Quinn, Rossana Podesta. Lavishly produced version of some of the adventures of Homer's King of Ithaca. Douglas is an excellent choice for the title character, who is both vain and glorious. (Dir: Mario Camerini, 104 mins.)†

Ulysses (1967)**½ Milo O'Shea, Barbara Jefford, T. P. McKenna, Maurice Roeves. James Joyce's masterpiece made it to the screen in this brave but flawed production. The acting is excellent, and the Irish atmosphere helps, but the book remains unfilmable. (Dir: Joseph Strick, 140 mins.)†

Ulzana's Raid (1972)*** Burt Lancaster, Bruce Davison. Deceptively ordinary Indian vs. Cavalry yarn turns into a tense, well-acted, and ultimately absorbing film. Lancaster is cast as an Indian scout who assists an inexperienced cavalry officer (Davison) in trying to roust renegade Apache Ulzana. (Dir: Robert Aldrich, 93 mins.)†

Umberto D (Italy, 1955)**** Carlo Battisti, Maria Pia Casilio. Italian director Vittorio De Sica's masterpiece; shattering study of a lonely old man, succumbing to the ravages of age. One of the most remarkable European films of the decade. (89 mins.)†

Umbrellas of Cherbourg, The (France-West Germany, 1964)***½ Catherine Deneuve, Nino Castelnuovo, Anne Vernon. A bittersweet film opera. Director Jacques Demy wrote the lyrics, Michel Legrand the music. The story of simple love thwarted is not as saccharine as con-

temporary reviews claimed. (95 mins.)†

UMC (MTV 1969)** James Daly, Richard Bradford, Maurice Evans, Kim Stanley, Edward G. Robinson. Routine drama, which served as the pilot for "Medical Center." (Dir: Boris Sagal, 100 mins.)

Unbearable Lightness of Being, The (1988) **** Daniel Day-Lewis, Juliette Binoche, Lena Olin, Derek de Lint. Day-Lewis is the doctor whose romantic interludes with the fragile Binoche and the assertive Olin are placed in delicate counterpoint to the '68 Russian invasion of Czechoslovakia. Provocative and at times difficult to follow (especially if you haven't read Milan Kundera's novel), but well worth the work. (Dir: Philip Kaufman, 171 mins.)†

Unbelievable Truth, The (1990)*** Adrienne Shelly, Robert Burke, Christopher Burke, Julia McNeal. Rich satire about the ennui of suburban living tells the story of a young man, released from prison, who returns home for a period of self-reflection, self-improvement, and self-discovery. Filled with wonderful characters, quirky dialogue, and romantic insights. A little gem of a movie. (Dir: Hal Hartley, 85 mins.)

Unborn, The (1991)*½ Brooke Adams, Jeff Hayenga, James Karen, K Callen. A bizarre horror film ultimately defeated by gratuitous gore. A childless couple (Adams and Hayenga) receive assistance from a not-so-normal doctor (Karen), whose unethical fertilization process creates homicidal infants. Adams manages to shine above the mayhem. (Dir: Rodman Flender, 87 mins.)†

Uncanny, The (Great Britain-Canada, 1977)** Peter Cushing, Ray Milland, Donald Pleasence. Cheapie horror flick. Horror ace Cushing documents a feline conspiracy to dominate the human race. (Dir: Denis Heroux, 85 mins.)†

Uncertain Glory (1944)** Errol Flynn, Paul Lukas, Faye Emerson, Jean Sullivan. Errol is a French crook but he's willing to pretend to be a saboteur and die if it will help France. Hackneyed. (Dir: Raoul Walsh, 102 mins.)

Uncertain Lady (1934)** Edward Everett Horton, Genevieve Tobin, Renée Gadd, Paul Cavanagh, Mary Nash, George Meeker. Low-budget comedy with some very familiar plot twists. Horton is cheating on his businesswoman wife (Tobin) who, in turn, decides to make him jealous. An odd assignment for director Karl Freund, better known for his work as director or cinematographer of several horror-fantasy classics (*Dracula, The Mummy, Metropolis*). (65 mins.)

Unchained (1955)*** Elroy Hirsch, Chester Morris, Barbara Hale. Warden of an honor prison tames unruly convicts. Based on fact, this is an excellent prison film. (Dir: Hall Bartlett, 75 mins.)

Uncle Buck (1989)** John Candy, Jean Louisa Kelly, Amy Madigan, Gaby Hoffman, Laurie Metcalf. Peculiar, uncertain mix of dark and light humor about family black sheep Candy called on to mind his brother's kids for a week. His sitcom inabilities to cook and clean are predictable; less so (at least in a John Hughes movie) is a menacing subtext about his niece's flirtation with losing her virginity that depicts teenagers as predatory and thoroughly dislikable. Kelly is unbearable as the snotty niece. (100 mins.)†

Uncle Harry (1945)*** George Sanders, Ella Raines, Geraldine Fitzgerald. Henpecked by his two sisters, a man takes drastic steps when they begin to interfere with his romance. Excellent performances and a suspenseful atmosphere atone for the poor conclusion to this drama. AKA: **The Strange Case of Uncle Harry.** (Dir: Robert Siodmak, 80 mins.)

Uncle Joe Shannon (1978)* Burt Young, Doug McKeon, Madge Sinclair. Overtly sentimental hogwash about a skid row trumpet player and the orphaned kid who attaches himself to the loser. It turns out the lad has cancer, as the downbeat film slips into self-indulgent pathos. (Dir: Joseph Hanwright, 115 mins.)

Uncle Scam (1981)** Tom McCarthy, Maxine Greene, John Russell, James E. Myers, Sharon Victoria, David Cassling, Pat Cooper, Joan Rivers. Graft is the subject of a federal probe in this bargain basement comedy that tosses in some sex when the going gets really dull. Few things age as badly as political comedies; this one seems to sprout wrinkles while you're watching it. (Dirs: Tom Pileggi, Micjale Levanios, Jr., 105 mins.)

Uncle Silas—See: **Inheritance, The** (1947)

Uncle Tom's Cabin (West Germany-France-Italy-Yugoslavia, 1965)* John Kitzmiller, Herbert Lom, O. W. Fisher, Eleonora Rossi-Drago, Eartha Kitt. Expensive but dull, badly dubbed version of the classic story dwells on the melodramatic elements. Originally released at 170 mins. in widescreen 70mm; the U.S. print was handled by the legendary Kroger Babb. (Dir: Geza Radvanyi, 118 mins.)†

Uncle Tom's Cabin (MCTV 1987)**½ Avery Brooks, Phylicia Rashad, Edward Woodward, Bruce Dern, Frank Converse. Well-made adaption of the legendary novel. Brooks, as Uncle Tom, gives great depth to his portrayal. The rest of the cast help to round out a story that, even a century later, still has social significance. (Dir: Stan Lathan, 108 mins.)

Uncle Vanya (Great Britian, 1963)*** Sybil Thorndike, Laurence Olivier, Michael Redgrave, Lewis Casson, Joan Plowright, Rosemary Harris, Fay Compton. Minimalist, often claustrophobic, film of a production of the Chekhov play staged for the Chichester Festival in England and directed by Olivier himself. Though the film has an unpleasant static quality to it, the performances are all, as could be expected, top flight. Not released until 1972. (Dir: Stuart Burge, 120 mins.)

Uncle Was a Vampire (Italy, 1961)**½ Renato Rascel, Christopher Lee, Sylva Koscina. Former baron now working as a hotel porter has trouble on his hands when his uncle turns up in vampire form. Amusing spoof of horror films. (Dir: Stefano Steno, 95 mins.)

Uncommon Love, An (MTV 1983)*½ Barry Bostwick, Kathryn Harrold, Holly Hunter, Ed Begley, Jr. Bostwick is a junior-college marine biology teacher hooked on a pretty student (Harrold), who turns out to be a hooker on the side. A common TV movie. (Dir: Steven Hilliard Stern, 104 mins.)

Uncommon Valor (MTV 1983)* Mitchell Ryan, Ben Murphy, Rick Lohman, Barbara Parkins. Contrived, poorly acted action-drama about a fire in a Salt Lake City hospital. (Dir: Rod Amateau, 104 mins.)†

Uncommon Valor (1983)**½ Gene Hackman, Fred Ward, Tim Thomerson, Robert Stack. Standard action pic following some misfits as they endeavor to locate and free some soldiers missing in action. Awash in clichés, but there is some suspense as we wonder which members of this privately financed commando mission will return. (Dir: Ted Kotcheff, 105 mins.)†

Unconquered (1947)**½ Gary Cooper, Paulette Goddard, Howard Da Silva, Boris Karloff. White man vs. Indian in 1763, tons of action, plenty of movement, and colorful acting are the total assets of this mammoth production. (Dir: Cecil B. DeMille, 146 mins.)

Unconquered (MTV, 1989)*** Peter Coyote, Dermot Mulroney, Tess Harper. True story set in fifties Alabama of high school athlete Richmond Flowers, Jr., who had to overcome both a physical handicap and his peers' hatred of his father, the state's attorney general and a supporter of the civil rights movement. A telling portrait of life in the South, well acted by the two stars. (Dir: Dick Lowry, 119 mins.)

Undead, The (1957)**½ Richard Garland, Pamela Duncan, Allison Hayes, Mel Welles. Slow-going but interesting tale of a prostitute sent back to the Middle Ages, where she was burned at the stake in a previous life. When the scientist and his subject tamper with fate, chaos spans the centuries. (Dir: Roger Corman, 75 mins.)

Undefeated, The (1969)**½ John Wayne, Rock Hudson, Lee Meriwether, Bruce Cabot. Routine western, bolstered somewhat by the presence of Wayne and Hudson. Wayne is an ex-Union officer who is on his way to sell horses to Mexico's emperor and meets up with his former enemy, Confederate officer Hudson. (Dir: Andrew V. McLaglen, 118 mins.)†

Underachievers, The (1987)*½ Edward Albert, Barbara Carrera, Michael Pataki, Susan Tyrrell, Mark Blankfield, Garrett Morris, Vic Tayback. Lame comedy set at a night school populated by various rejects from society. Brassy Tyrrell is the highlight, but don't expect much. (Dir: Jackie Kong, 90 mins.)

Under Capricorn (Great Britain, 1949)**½ Ingrid Bergman, Joseph Cotten, Michael Wilding, Margaret Leighton. Not one of Alfred Hitchcock's best efforts; the script is much too talky in this stuffy costume drama set in 19th-century Australia. Bergman is splendid as a dipsomaniac driven crazy by husband Cotten, with Wilding as a visitor who upsets Cotten's rotten applecart. The performances make it worth watching. (117 mins.)†

Under Capricorn (Australia, 1982)** Lisa Harrow, John Hallam, Peter Cousens. Atmospheric but unnecessary remake of a lesser Hitchcock film about an alcoholic woman whose life is in danger. (Dir: Rod Hardy, 150 mins.)†

Undercover (1987)*½ David Neidorf, Jennifer Jason Leigh, Kathleen Wilhoite. Baltimore cop poses as a high school student in order to infiltrate a drug ring in a Louisiana school. Interesting idea is poorly exploited. (Dir: John Stockwell, 95 mins.)†

Undercover Girl (1950)** Alexis Smith, Scott Brady, Gladys George, Richard Egan. A girl aids the police by infiltrating the gang that killed her father; nothing special, but good of this kind. (Dir: Joseph Pevney, 83 mins.)

Undercover Maisie (1947)** Ann Sothern, Barry Nelson. Blonde chorus girl becomes an undercover investigator for the police. (Dir: Harry Beaumont, 90 mins.)

Under-Cover Man, The (1932)**½ George Raft, Nancy Carroll, Roscoe Karns, Lew Cody. Unpretentious crime thriller has tough guy with a heart of gold Raft diligently searching out his father's murderer. Raft's spirited performance shows why he became a star. (Dir: James Flood, 70 mins.)

Undercover Man, The (1949)*** Glenn Ford, Nina Foch, James Whitmore. Tax experts try to pin the goods on a notorious gangster by legal means. Different sort

of G-man melodrama with a nice style, some suspenseful moments. (Dir: Joseph H. Lewis, 89 mins.)

Undercovers Hero (Great Britian, 1973)** Peter Sellers, Lila Kedrova, Curt Jurgens, Beatrice Romand, Rula Lenska. Disappointing Sellers vehicle (made before he returned to the Pink Panther series) about the contributions of a Parisian brothel to the Allied effort in WWII. Even though he plays six different roles, there's not a single decent line of dialogue. AKA: **Soft Beds, Hard Battles.** (Dir: Roy Boulting, 95 mins.)

Undercover with the KKK (MTV 1979)**½ Don Meredith, James Wainwright. Real-life story of an Alabama redneck (Meredith) who infiltrates the Ku Klux Klan for the FBI. (Dir: Barry Shear, 104 mins.)

Undercurrent (1946)**½ Katharine Hepburn, Robert Taylor, Robert Mitchum. The acting is good but the story of a girl who slowly discovers she has married a villain is not new and, in this case, not too well told. (Dir: Vincente Minnelli, 116 mins.)

Under Fire (1983)***½ Nick Nolte, Gene Hackman, Joanna Cassidy, Jean-Louis Trintignant, Ed Harris. A modern-day version of forties political melodramas in which the uncommitted outsider becomes a hero through his involvement in a cause. A magazine reporter (Hackman) and his lover, a radio correspondent (Cassidy), are on the verge of breaking up as the action shifts from Chad to Nicaragua. A romance develops between the girl and Nolte, a photojournalist who previously viewed the revolution as just another backdrop for his photographs. Well directed and acted. (Dir: Roger Spottiswoode, 130 mins.)†

Undergrads, The (MTV 1986)*** Art Carney, Chris Makepeace, Len Birman, Dawn Green Hall, Lesleh Donaldson, Kim Barrett, Jackie Burroughs. A Disney film about a grandfather going back to college with his grandson. It's a bright generational comedy about Carney's estrangement from his tradition-minded son and how the grandkid closes the breach. (Dir: Steven Hilliard Stern, 104 mins.)†

Underground (1941)*** Jeffrey Lynn, Philip Dorn. Exciting melodrama about the underground in Nazi Germany. All involved turn in A work in this story of people risking their lives to create secret broadcasts under the Germans' noses. (Dir: Vincent Sherman, 95 mins.)

Underground (Great Britain, 1970)** Robert Goulet, Daniele Gaubert, Lawrence Dobkin, Carl Duering, Joachim Hansen, Roger Delgado. Routine WWII race-against-time with singer Goulet in his starring dramatic debut as an Army intelligence agent out to capture a ruthless Nazi general. (Dir: Arthur H. Nadel, 100 mins.)

Underground (1976)**½ This documentary about the goals and philosophies of the Weather Underground features interviews with five of the Weathermen, all of whom were wanted by the FBI at the time. An informative discussion of issues central to radical politics of the sixties, (Dirs: Emile De Antonio, Mary Lampson, Haskell Wexler, 88 mins.)†

Underground Man, The (MTV 1974)**½ Peter Graves, Jack Klugman, Sharon Farrell, Vera Miles, Jim Hutton. Ross Macdonald's best-seller is adapted with care and attention. Graves makes a fairly convincing Lew Archer, Macdonald's laconic, compassionate sleuth, as he delves into the murder of a man investigating his father's disappearance. (Dir: Paul Wendkos, 100 mins.)

Underground U.S.A. (1980)**½ Patti Astor, Eric Mitchell, Rene Ricard, Tom Wright, Jackie Curtis, Cookie Mueller, Taylor Mead, John Lurie. Offbeat version of the kind of self-conscious filmmaking pioneered by Andy Warhol, with some serious Lower East Side posing thrown in for good measure. Producer-scripter-director Mitchell plays a male hustler who parties with washed-up actress Astor while encountering various Village "personalities." (85 mins.)

Under Milk Wood (Great Britain, 1971) **½ Richard Burton, Elizabeth Taylor, Peter O'Toole, Glynis Johns, Sian Phillips. The pictures make the great, glorious language of the classic Dylan Thomas radio play seem peripheral, where it should be central. The readings, nonetheless, are first-rate. (Dir: Andrew Sinclair, 90 mins.)†

Under My Skin (1950)** John Garfield, Micheline Presle, Luther Adler. An Ernest Hemingway yarn about the racing game and a one-time crooked jockey's efforts to go straight. Involved drama, spottily acted. (Dir: George Blair, 90 mins.)

Under Secret Orders (Great Britain, 1943)*** Erich von Stroheim, Dita Parlo, Clare Luce. Dated but delightful spy nonsense about a foreign agent's girlfriend (Parlo) who drifts into espionage after he's murdered. Even though she uses her wiles against the good guys, we root for her because she's so ineffably glamorous. (Dir: Edmond Greville, 66 mins.)

Under Siege (MTV, 1986)** Peter Strauss, Hal Holbrook, E. G. Marshall, George Grizzard, Paul Winfield, Mason Adams. A tendentious and implausible scare-movie on what might happen if terrorists attacked America. (Dir: Roger Young, 126 mins.)

Understudy, The: Graveyard Shift II (1989)*½

Wendy Gazelle, Mark Soper, Silvio Oliverio, Ilse Von Glatz. The vampire anti-hero of *Graveyard Shift* gets a job as the leading man in a horror movie about—you guessed it—a vampire. This one's almost entirely devoted to style in place of anything of interest in the plot. (Dir: Gerard Cicoritti, 88 mins.)†

Undertaker and His Pals, The (1966)½ Ray Dannis, Warrene Ott, Rad Fulton, Robert Lowery. Early gore comedy about funeral parlor employees who drum up work when business is slow by running over strangers with their motorcycles. Badly acted and cheaply made, but that's what fans of this stuff look for. (Dir: David C. Graham, 60 mins.)

Under Ten Flags (U.S.-Great Britain-Italy, 1960)** Van Heflin, Charles Laughton, Mylene Demongeot, John Ericson. German raider commanded by a humane captain cleverly thwarts British efforts to capture it. (Dir: Duilio Coletti, 92 mins.)

Under the Biltmore Clock (MTV 1984)**½ Sean Young, Lenny Von Dohlen, Barnard Hughes. Jazz Age comedy about the sparks that fly when quiet heir Von Dohlen takes his new bride Young home to meet his weird family. Based on F. Scott Fitzgerald's story "Myra Meets the Family." (Dir: Neal Miller, 70 mins.)†

Under the Boardwalk (1988)*½ Keith Coogan, Danielle von Zerneck, Richard Joseph Paul, Tracey Walter, Dick Miller, Sonny Bono. Forgettable surf epic with all the usual teen clichés filling in the spaces between the big waves. Like sixties beach party movies, the only amusement in this one is the brief appearances of character actors in tiny parts. (Dir: Fritz Kiersch, 100 mins.)†

Under the Cherry Moon (1986)* Prince, Jerome Benton, Kristin Scott-Thomas, Francesca Annis, Alexandra Stewart, Steven Berkoff. A great title for an unprincely flick. Playing a moist-lipped gigolo specializing in jaded ladies, Prince combines business with pleasure when he pursues a rich, beautiful young lady and (surprise) falls head over heels for her. The film was shot in color but released in black and white under the star's orders. (Dir: Prince, 98 mins.)†

Under the Glacier (Iceland, 1989)***½ Sigurour Sigurjonsson, Margret Helga Johannsdottir, Bladvin Halldorsson. Mesmerizing tale of a geology student who travels to a village near a famous glacier to investigate the odd behavior of the residents. Uniquely weird film creates a haunting atmosphere of dread. (Dir: Gundy Halldorsdottir, 81 mins.)

Under the Gun (1988)*½ Sam Jones, Vanessa Williams, John Russell, Michael Halsey, Nick Cassavetes. St. Louis cop recruits lawyer Williams as his less-than-willing partner while he hunts for the evil dudes who had his brother killed. Familiar stuff. (Dir: James Sbardellati, 90 mins.)†

Under the Influence (MTV 1986)**** Andy Griffith, Joyce Van Patten, Season Hubley, Paul Provenza, William Schallert, Dana Anderson, Keanu Reeves. The devastation of alcoholism on a middle class family is distilled into exceptional TV drama. Griffith, a businessman who denies his drinking problem, wreaks havoc on his entire family, particularly his youngest boy (Reeves), who is starting to emulate his father's destructive habits. Towers above most other TV films, with Hubley and Griffith doing brilliant work. (Dir: Thomas Carter, 104 mins.)

Under the Rainbow (1981) *½ Chevy Chase, Carrie Fisher, Eve Arden, Joseph Maher, Pat McCormick, Mako, Billy Barty. A funny comedy might have been made about the notorious shenanigans carried out by the Munchkin cast during the making of *The Wizard of Oz*, but this one throws in the excess baggage of a story line about spies. (Dir: Steve Rash, 98 mins.)†

Under the Red Robe (Great Britain, 1937)*** Conrad Veidt, Annabella, Raymond Massey, Romney Brent. Unusual swashbuckler set in 17th-century France. A poverty-stricken soldier of fortune is forced to serve the wicked Cardinal Richelieu; he must risk his life to save the girl he loves. (Dir: Victor Seastrom [Sjostrom], 82 mins.)†

Under the Roofs of Paris (France, 1930)*** Albert Prejean, Gaston Modot, Pola Illery, Edmond Gréville. Marvelous early French talkie, a wistful tale of love found and love lost. Simple story of the romance between a handsome street singer and a beautiful girl is filmed without a trace of melodrama, using sound effects to create much of the mood. (Dir: René Clair, 86 mins.)

Under the Volcano (1984)*** Albert Finney, Jacqueline Bisset, Anthony Andrews, Katy Jurado. Malcolm Lowry's harrowing novel, set in 1938, about the last day in the life of an alcoholic ex-consul in Mexico, translated to the screen with remarkable clarity by John Huston. The British diplomat's alcoholism, aggravated by his wife's infidelity with his half-brother, becomes the device that drives this haunted man into a personal abyss that is paralleled by the world's deteriorating political situation. (112 mins.)†

Under the Yum Yum Tree (1963)**½ Jack Lemmon, Carol Lynley, Dean Jones, Edie Adams, Imogene Coca. Good fun. Broadway comedy transfers to the screen with ease, thanks to Jack Lemmon's energetic performance as an amorous landlord. (Dir: David Swift, 110 mins.)

Undertow (1950)**½ Scott Brady, Peggy Dow, John Russell. Fast-moving, routine chase melodrama about a man who is wrongly accused of murder and has to prove his innocence. (Dir: William Castle, 71 mins.)

Under Two Flags (1936)**½ Ronald Colman, Claudette Colbert, Rosalind Russell, Victor McLaglen. Creaky, perennial story of love and adventure in the Foreign Legion gets new life in this film but still falls short of top-notch entertainment. (Dir: Frank Lloyd, 105 mins.)

Underwater (1955)**½ Jane Russell, Gilbert Roland, Richard Egan, Lori Nelson, Jayne Mansfield. Two skin divers brave the perils of the deep to locate sunken treasure. Passable melodrama has good underwater photography. (Dir: John Sturges, 99 mins.)†

Underwater City, The (1962)* William Lundigan, Julie Adams, Roy Roberts, Carl Benton Reid. Engineer designs a prefab submerged city in anticipation of nuclear war. More speculative about the possibility of living underwater than dramatic; unfortunately, pretty dull for that, though it's always nice to see Ms. Adams. (Dir: Frank McDonald, 78 mins.)

Underwater Warrior (1958)** Dan Dailey, James Gregory, Claire Kelly. Song-and-dance man Dailey is defeated by this shallow water script as he goes dramatic and dons an underwater diving outfit to play a naval commander in the Korean War. (Dir: Andrew Marton, 90 mins.)

Underworld (Britain, 1985)*½ Denholm Elliott, Larry Lamb, Nicola Cowper. Clive Barker adaptation is more mystery than horror, and boring to boot. Ex-gangster searching for a missing prostitute finds a doctor producing mutants through drug experiments. AKA: **Transmutations**. (Dir: George Pavlou, 103 mins.)†

Underworld Story, The (1950)*** Dan Duryea, Gale Storm, Herbert Marshall. Reporter buys an interest in a small-town newspaper and starts things humming by exposing corruption in back of a murder case. Tightly knit drama. (Dir: Cy Endfield, 90 mins.)†

Underworld, USA (1961)*** Cliff Robertson, Dolores Dorn, Beatrice Kay. Kid who has had a hard road in life grows up determined to get the men who murdered his father in a gang slaying. Crime drama covers familiar ground, but does so expertly. (Dir: Samuel Fuller, 98 mins.)†

Under Your Spell (1936)** Lawrence Tibbett, Wendy Barrie, Gregory Ratoff, Arthur Treacher, Gregory Gaye. Tibbet is cast to type as a famous vocalist who decides to get away from it all and hides in Mexico. The arrival of debutante Barrie sets his plans awry. Limp vehicle is notable as the first American film directed by Otto Preminger. (62 mins.)

Undying Monster, The (1942)**½ James Ellison, Heather Angel, John Howard, Bramwell Fletcher, Heather Thatcher, Aubrey Mather. Slick monster movie about an upper-class werewolf (Howard), with a stylish, spooky atmosphere created by studio sets and lighting, and a much better cast than usual. (Dir: Bryan Foy, 63 mins.)

Unearthly, The (1957)*½ John Carradine, Allison Hayes. Two stalwarts of grade Z sci-fi, Carradine and Hayes, in a mad scientist flick about some innovative experimentation being done on human beings. (Dir: Brooke L. Peters, 73 mins.)†

Unearthly Stranger, The (1964)** John Neville, Gabriella Licudi, Philip Stone, Jean Marsh, Patrick Newell. Oddball sci-fi about an alien who falls for the man her planet sent her to Earth to destroy. (Dir: John Krish, 68 mins.)

Une Femme Douce (France, 1969)*** Dominique Sanda, Guy Frangin. Based on Dostoyévski's novella *A Gentle Creature*, the film begins with a young wife's suicide and ends with the lid of her coffin being screwed into place. In between is an exposition by the husband of what led up to the suicide. Ultimately quite moving. (Dir: Robert Bresson, 87 mins.)

Une Partie de Plaisir (France, 1975)*** Paul Gegauff, Danielle Ester, Paula Moore, Pierre Santini, Michel Vaiette. Strong, earnestly realistic drama of the disintegration of a marriage due to the domineering husband's unfaithfulness. Gegauff was better known as the writer of most of director Claude Chabrol's greatest films; he and Chabrol collaborated on this unique film as well. Gegauff and Ester were formerly married in real life; he was later killed by his second wife. (105 mins.)

Unexpected Uncle (1941)**½ Charles Coburn, Anne Shirley, James Craig. Old reprobate aids a shopgirl in her romance with a rich man. Mildly amusing comedy. (Dir: Peter Godfrey, 67 mins.)

Unfaithful, The (1947)*** Ann Sheridan, Zachary Scott, Lew Ayres, Eve Arden. Ann Sheridan, that most underappreciated of forties stars, goes dramatic with considerable éclat here. In this uncredited, loose remake of *The Letter*, Ann gets mixed up in the murder of a man who'd been her inamorato when her hubby was away at war. (Dir: Vincent Sherman, 109 mins.)

Unfaithfully Yours (1948)***½ Rex Harrison, Linda Darnell, Rudy Vallee. Director Preston Sturges's devilish conceit in which an egotistical symphony conductor (limned by Harrison in a parody of Thomas Beecham) imagines the jealous murder of his wife (Darnell) to the strains of the three classical works that are on his program of the evening. (105 mins.)†

Unfaithfully Yours (1984)*** Dudley Moore, Armand Assante, Nastassia Kinski. An amusing crime-of-passion comedy. A symphony conductor in the throes of male menopause is driven to desperation by jealousy. Not as droll as Preston Sturges's original, but briskly directed and smartly acted. (Dir: Howard Zieff, 97 mins.)†

Unfinished Business (1941)** Irene Dunne, Robert Montgomery. Irene Dunne, a small town girl, goes to the big city to find adventure and love in this silly comedy-romance. (Dir: Gregory La Cava, 96 mins.)

Unfinished Dance, The (1947)**½ Cyd Charisse, Danny Thomas, Margaret O'Brien. Some nice ballet sequences for fans of the dance, but story of a little girl who worships a ballerina and tries to stop another dancer from taking her place is not convincingly played or written. (Dir: Henry Koster, 101 mins.)

Unfinished Piece for Player Piano, An (U.S.S.R., 1982)***½ Aleksandr Kalaigin, Yelena Solovei. Stately, moving adaptation of the early Chekhov play *Platonov*, about a large family which gathers at a remote country house to sort out all of their petty jealousies and unresolved relationships. (Dir: Nikita Mikhalkov, 100 mins.)

Unforgettable Nat King Cole, The (1989)***½ Maria Cole, Natalie Cole, Mel Torme, Ella Fitzgerald, George Shearing, Oscar Peterson, Harry Belafonte, Frank Sinatra. Revealing and affectionate documentary about Cole's life and music, filled with stories about his family and career as told by those who knew him best. (Dir: Alan Lewens, 90 mins.)†

Unforgiven, The (1960)*** Audrey Hepburn, Burt Lancaster, Audie Murphy, Lillian Gish, Charles Bickford, Joseph Wiseman, Albert Salmi, John Saxon, Doug McClure. Huston's career probably hit its critical nadir with this hysterical western with racial overtones (Hepburn is suspected of being a halfbreed), but if it's viewed in the context of this subgenre of the forties, the film becomes a satisfying and stimulating work. (Dir: John Huston, 125 mins.)†

Unguarded Hour, The (1936)**½ Loretta Young, Franchot Tone, Roland Young, Lewis Stone, Dudley Digges, Henry Daniell, Jessie Ralph. Unusual courtroom melodrama with a British prosecutor finding that the case he's trying will draw attention to entanglements in his own private life. (Dir: Sam Wood, 90 mins.)

Unguarded Moment (1956)** Esther Williams, John Saxon, George Nader. Williams plays a high school teacher who's the object of unwanted attention by one of her pupils. Flimsy story (scripted by

Rosalind Russell) and unconvincing performances. (Dir: Harry Keller, 95 mins.)

Unheard Music, The—See **X: The Unheard Music**

Unholy, The (1988)** Ben Cross, Ned Beatty, Jill Carroll, William Russ, Hal Holbrook, Trevor Howard. When a priest who has miraculously survived a fall is assigned to a New Orleans church, he begins to unravel the mystery of two murders that occurred there. Confusing, overwrought horror tale. (Dir: Camilo Vila, 104 mins.)†

Unholy Garden, The (1931)*** Ronald Colman, Fay Wray, Estelle Taylor, Tully Marshall. Script by Ben Hecht and Charles MacArthur. Colman is sexy, wistful, and charming in this entertaining if slight melodrama about a gentleman thief, living in exile in the mysterious desert. (Dir: George Fitzmaurice, 74 mins.)

Unholy Matrimony (MTV 1988)** Patrick Duffy, Charles Durning, Michael O'Keeffe, Lisa Blount. A complicated murder mystery that benefits from the agile performance by O'Keefe as a self-ordained reverend with a dark secret in his past. (Dir: Jerrold Freedman, 96 mins.)

Unholy Night, The (1929)**½ Ernest Torrance, Roland Young, Dorothy Sebastian, Natalie Moorhead, John Loder, Boris Karloff. Traditional mystery set in London, where veterans of a regiment are being murdered one by one, and the survivors band together to catch the killer. The story, by Ben Hecht, has clues liberally scattered throughout and a high body count. (Dir: Lionel Barrymore, 92 mins.)

Unholy Partners (1941)**½ Edward G. Robinson, Edward Arnold, Laraine Day, Marsha Hunt. Well-acted, contrived drama of an editor who is in partnership with a racketeer and decides to expose him in their own paper. (Dir: Mervyn LeRoy, 94 mins.)

Unholy Rollers (1972)**½ Claudia Jennings, Louis Quinn, Betty Anne Rees, Roberta Collins. Tawdry tale of a hell-on-wheels Roller Derby queen who rolls all over her team-mates. (Dir: Vernon Zimmerman, 88 mins.)†

Unholy Three, The (1925)*** Lon Chaney, Mae Busch, Matt Moore, Victor McLaglen, Harry Earles, Harry Betz. Eerie silent thriller about four ex-carnival performers who plan a clever con game using a pet shop as a front for a burglary racket. Chaney disguises himself as a sweet, harmless old lady throughout the film. An individualistic, completely engrossing classic. (Dir: Tod Browning, 86 mins.)

Unholy Three, The (1930)*** Lon Chaney, Lila Lee, Elliott Nugent, Harry Earles, Ivan Linow, John Miljan, Clarence

Burton. Talkie version of the silent classic is as good as the original. Chaney's characterization of the clever, vindictive ventriloquist is even more effective with sound, and he adapted easily to sound in his only nonsilent movie. A unique, compelling thriller. (Dir: Jack Conway, 90 mins.)

Unholy Wife (1957)** Diana Dors, Rod Steiger, Tom Tryon, Marie Windsor. Steiger chews up the scenery in this muddled story of a wealthy wife's infidelity and plans for murder. (Dir: John Farrow, 94 mins.)†

Unidentified Flying Oddball (Great Britain, 1979)**½ Dennis Dugan, Jim Dale, Ron Moody. This Disney feature is a space-age version of Twain's *A Connecticut Yankee in King Arthur's Court*. (Dir: Russ Mayberry, 93 mins.)†

Uninhibited, The (Spain-France-Italy, 1965)** Melina Mercouri, James Mason, Hardy Kruger. Incoherent melodrama about a worldly wise woman, a besotted novelist, and a searching youth in a small Spanish fishing village. (Dir: Juan Antonio Bardem, 104 mins.)

Uninvited, The (1944)*** Ray Milland, Ruth Hussey, Cornelia Otis Skinner, Gail Russell. Ghost fans will love this well-told chiller about a young couple (brother and sister) who buy a house in England that is haunted. (Dir: Lewis Allen, 98 mins.)

Uninvited, The (1988)½ Alex Cord, George Kennedy, Clu Gulager, Toni Hudson, Sharri Shattuck. Passengers on a cruise ship heading to the Cayman Islands are terrorized by a stowaway: a radiation-crazed killer kitty! Don't invite this one home, unless you're in the mood for a few laughs at the cast's expense. (Dir: Greydon Clark, 89 mins.)†

Union City (1980)**½ Deborah Harry, Dennis Lipscomb, Irina Maleeva, Pat Benatar. Offbeat, *film noir* spoof with spacy Harry as a bored housewife whose husband commits a murder after someone steals their milk. (Dir: Mark Reichert, 87 mins.)†

Union Depot (1932)*** Douglas Fairbanks, Jr., Joan Blondell, Guy Kibbee, Alan Hale, Dickie Moore, Frank McHugh. Snazzy comedy-drama of the people passing through a major train station and how their lives intersect. Crackling dialog, stylish direction, and vigorous acting make this entertaining all the way. (Dir: Alfred E. Green, 75 mins.)

Union Pacific (1939)*** Joel McCrea, Barbara Stanwyck, Akim Tamiroff, Robert Preston, Brian Donlevy. Grandiose western. Saga of linking the east and west by rails is well acted and loaded with action. (Dir: Cecil B. DeMille, 135 mins.)

Union Station (1950)*** William Holden, Barry Fitzgerald, Nancy Olson, Jan Sterling. Police join in a manhunt for the kidnapper of a blind girl. Suspenseful crime drama. (Dir: Rudolph Maté, 80 mins.)

Unkissed Bride, The (1966)* Tom Kirk, Anne Helm, Jacques Bergerac, Joe Pyne, Henny Youngman. What did Walt Disney think when he saw former child star Tommy Kirk in this adults-only comedy as a bridegroom unable to perform his "marital duties"? The cure prescribed by a lady psychiatrist involves spraying LSD over him while he sleeps (it was still legal then) so he can hallucinate about the fairy tales that he fantasizes about. AKA: Mother Goose a Go-Go. (Dir: Jack H. Harris, 82 mins.)†

Unknown Guest, The (1943)*** Victor Jory, Pamela Blake. A stranger stops in a small village, and is suspected to be an escaped criminal. Tense, exciting melodrama, well acted. (Dir: Kurt Neumann, 64 mins.)

Unknown Man, The (1951)**½ Walter Pidgeon, Ann Harding, Keefe Brasselle, Barry Sullivan. Honest lawyer defends a murder suspect, finds afterwards his client really was guilty. Involved crime melodrama, with the twists and turns of the plot sustaining interest most of the way. (Dir: Richard Thorpe, 86 mins.)

Unknown World (1951)*½ Bruce Kellogg, Marilyn Nash, Victor Killian, Jim Bannon. Not unknown enough—someone dug this moldy oldie out and put it on video. A sci-fi classic it's not, but this odd cheapie about scientists looking for a haven from nuclear radiation who burrow into the Earth with their molemobile is at least unusual. (Dir: Terrell O. Morse, 73 mins.)†

Unman, Wittering, and Zigo (Great Britain, 1971)**½ David Hemmings, Carolyn Seymour. Hemmings plays a schoolteacher at a boys' school who takes over at midterm after his predecessor has taken a suspicious tumble on the stairs. (Dir: John MacKenzie, 100 mins.)

Unmarried Woman, An (1978)***½ Jill Clayburgh, Alan Bates, Pat Quinn, Cliff Gorman, Michael Murphy. Poignant, observant, and funny, with a knockout performance by Clayburgh as a woman who seems to be doing all the right things until the day her husband (Murphy) announces he's leaving for another woman. Clayburgh's realignment of her priorities is fascinating, and the film doesn't take preachy stands or offer pat solutions. (Dir: Paul Mazursky, 124 mins.)†

Unmasked Part 25 (Great Britain, 1989)*½ Gregory Cox, Fiona Evans, Edward Brayshaw, Debbie Lee London. Parody of the endless series of *Friday the 13th* movies has a few laughs for horror fans, but not enough to fill a feature film. AKA: Hand of Death Part 25. (Dir: Anders Palm, 85 mins.)†

Unnamable, The (1988)*½ Charles King, Mark Kinsey Stephenson, Alexandra Durrell, Laura Albert. Adaptation of a H. P. Lovecraft tale (you can tell because the *Necronomicon* pops up) sets college students in an old, dark house rumored to have been sealed up because of a monster in the attic. Fast-forward to the monster's appearance at the end and skip the rest of it. (Dir: Jean-Paul Ouelette, 87 mins.)†

Unnatural Causes (MTV 1986)*** John Ritter, Alfre Woodard, Patti LaBelle, Dee McCafferty. Powerhouse drama about how a Vietnam vet and Veterans Administration counselor forced the government to admit that Agent Orange chemical did damage to our troops. Ritter is moving as the dying vet determined to prove that Agent Orange caused his illness, and Woodard is superb as the VA counselor who bucks superiors for a cause. (Dir: Lamont Johnson, 104 mins.)†

Unremarkable Life, An (1989)**½ Patricia Neal, Shelley Winters, Mako, Rochelle Oliver. Neal and Winters get a chance to display their acting skills in this examination of two sisters, one widowed and one never married, who share a house. Not much on plot, but the actresses make their characters live on screen. (Dir: Amin Q. Chaudhri, 98 mins.)†

Unsane (Italy, 1984)*** Anthony Franciosa, Daria Nicolodi, John Saxon. Fans of Italian horror maestro Dario Argento will recognize all of his trademarks here —bloody murders, a confusing but involving plot, and a deafening, droning synthesizer score. Mystery novelist learns that a spree of murders are based on his latest book. AKA: Tenebrae. Cut from 100 mins. (92 mins.)†

Unseen, The (1945)**½ Joel McCrea, Gail Russell, Herbert Marshall, Phyllis Brooks, Isobel Elsom, Norman Lloyd. Enjoyable gothic mystery-romance, with governess Russell wondering if her appealing employer (McCrea) is a murderer, or just misunderstood. Well-established atmosphere of repressed hysteria suitable to the genre; one of the scriptwriters was Raymond Chandler. (Dir: Lewis Allen, 81 mins.)

Unseen, The (1980)**½ Barbara Bach, Sidney Lassick, Stephen Furst, Karen Lamm, Lelia Goldoni. Three women shooting a news program on location in Solvag, California, pick the wrong house to stay in. Frightening and bizarre although it's nearly wrecked by a climax that gets out of control. (Dir: Peter Foleg, 89 mins.)†

Unsinkable Molly Brown, The (1964)*** Debbie Reynolds, Harve Presnell, Ed Begley, Hermione Baddeley. Rowdy, raucous Meredith Willson musical entertainment for the whole family. Reynolds is all hustle and bustle as Molly, the tough backwoods girl who goes after money, social position, and love with nonstop energy. (Dir: Charles Walters, 128 mins.)†

Unspeakable Acts (MTV 1990)** Jill Clayburgh, Brad Davis, Sam Behrens, Gary Frank, James Handy, Mark Harelik, Season Hubley, Terence Knox, Bebe Neuwirth, Gregory Sierra. Dramatization of a 1984 trial of workers at a Miami day-care center for child abuse, centering on efforts of psychologists to gather evidence using the testimony of the young victims. As in most such TV movies, this is more concerned with exploiting the pain of the victims than delving into the causes of such crimes. (Dir: Linda Otto, 96 mins.)

Unsuitable Job for a Woman, An (Great Britain, 1981)**½ Pippa Guard, Billie Whitelaw, Paul Freeman. Based on a thriller by P. D. James, this clever, unnecessarily arty film centers on Cordelia Gray (Guard) who, following the death of her employer, takes over his gumshoe activities. (Dir: Christopher Petit, 94 mins.)†

Unsuspected, The (1947)*** Claude Rains, Joan Caulfield, Audrey Totter, Constance Bennett, Michael North. This engrossing *film noir* has Claude Rains playing a debonair radio crime-drama announcer who is himself a murderer. The tension grows as we wait to see if he can be unmasked before he kills again. (Dir: Michael Curtiz, 103 mins.)

Untamed (1929)** Joan Crawford, Robert Montgomery, Ernest Torrence, Holmes Herbert, John Miljan. One of Crawford's dopey shopgirl romances, with the star as an uninhibited heiress brought up in the jungle (!) who comes to New York and falls for sophisticated Montgomery; he refuses to marry her because she's rich and he's not. Awful tripe, though Crawford is gorgeous. (Dir: Jack Conway, 88 mins.)

Untamed (1955)** Tyrone Power, Susan Hayward, Richard Egan, Rita Moreno, Agnes Moorehead. Overly romantic adventure yarn about the he-men who pioneered the Zulu territory of Africa. (Dir: Henry King, 111 mins.)

Untamed Frontier (1952)**½ Joseph Cotten, Shelley Winters, Scott Brady. Sprawling western. Concerns the Texas frontier when cattle barons ran things and range wars were commonplace. (Dir: Hugo Fregonese, 75 mins.)

Untamed Women (1952)½ Mikel Conrad, Doris Merrick, Richard Monahan. Air Force bomber crew stranded on an island inhabited by daughters of the Druids. An active volcano and a band of marauding "hairy men" make life interesting for the untamed women. Untamed camp, and dig those dance steps. (Dir: W. Merle Connell, 70 mins.)

Untamed Youth (1957)*½ Mamie Van Doren, Lori Nelson, John Russell. Low-grade sex drama set on a correction farm with both male and female inmates. (Dir: Howard W. Koch, 80 mins.)

Until September (1984)** Karen Allen, Thierry L'hermitte, Johanna Pavlis. In France, everyone goes on vacation in August, except for certain married men who hang around to fall in love with young American women like Allen who miss their flights back home. If you're a sucker for romance, this is painless, but you may end up wondering what's a nice city like Paris doing in a movie like this? (Dir: Richard Marquand, 110 mins.)†

Until They Sail (1957)*** Paul Newman, Jean Simmons, Joan Fontaine, Piper Laurie, Sandra Dee (film debut). Soap opera made palatable by a good all-star cast. Plot revolves around the events in the lives of four sisters living in New Zealand during WWII. (Dir: Robert Wise, 95 mins.)

Untouchables, The (1987)***½ Kevin Costner, Sean Connery, Charles Martin Smith, Andy Garcia, Robert De Niro, Richard Bradford, Jack Kehoe. Flawlessly produced gangster epic about Eliot Ness and his creation of the Untouchable team, who cleaned up the corruption-riddled city of Chicago. With prohibition and bootlegging battling each other at full force, Ness (Costner), a seasoned policeman (Oscar-winner Connery), a rookie (Garcia), and an accountant (Smith) band together to put a dent in Al Capone's violent reign of terror. Despite some slowness in unwinding the introductory exposition, the film is masterfully directed, tangily written (by David Mamet), and memorably acted. (Dir: Brian De-Palma, 119 mins.)†

Unvanquished, The—See: **Aparajito**

Unwed Father (MTV 1974)**½ Joseph Bottoms, Kay Lenz, Beverly Garland, Kim Hunter, Joseph Campanella. Despite the silly title, this has some credible moments. A principled young man fights for the custody of his illegitimate child, going against the wishes of his girl friend who wants to put the baby up for adoption. (Dir: Jeremy Kagan, 74 mins.)

Unwed Mother (1958)** Norma Moore, Robert Vaughn, Diana Darrin. Attractive girl gets involved with a lady killer, finds herself pregnant, refuses to give her baby up for adoption. (Dir: Walter Doniger, 74 mins.)

Up! (1976)**½ Robert McLane, Janet Wood, Raven de la Croix, Monte Bane, Foxy Lae, Francesca "Kitten" Natividad. Mock-Shakespearean murder mystery about some Nazis, a Southern sheriff, a pilgrim, trucker lesbians, killer piranha, and a big-chested, one-woman Greek chorus (Natividad), who runs around the forest in the nude. Not for a moment to be taken seriously. (Dir: Russ Meyer, 80 mins.)†

Up Against the Wall (1991)** Maria Gibbs, Ron O'Neal, Stoney Jackson, Catero Alain Colbert, Oscar Brown, Jr. Ambitious independent black film's intentions are far better than the results. A mother (Gibbs) wants her naive teen son (Colbert) to attend a suburban high school for a better education. He moves in with his older brother (Jackson) for the convenience and gets caught up in the corruption. Earnest performances. (Dir: Ron O'Neal, 100 mins.)†

Up from the Beach (1965)*** Cliff Robertson, Irina Demick, Broderick Crawford, Red Buttons. Interesting WWII story about a group of American soldiers who liberate a small French village on the day after D-Day. The group takes over a farmhouse where three German SS soldiers are holding hostages. (Dir: Robert Parrish, 98 mins.)

Up from the Depths (1979)* Sam Bottoms, Susanne Reed, Virgil Frye, Kedric Wolfe. The manager of a hotel runs a contest to see who can kill the prehistoric fish-monster that is wrecking seaside business. Addle-headed *Jaws* rip-off. (Dir: Charles B. Griffith, 75 mins.)†

Up Front (1951)*** David Wayne, Tom Ewell. Bill Mauldin's zany cartoon characters, Willie and Joe, are brought to life by Wayne and Ewell in this amusing film about GI's fighting in Italy during WWII. (Dir: Alexander Hall, 92 mins.)

Up Goes Maisie (1946)**½ Ann Sothern, George Murphy. The usual hijinks for series fans as Maisie faces the post-WWII period with a new job. She's up on cloud nine over her aviation-whiz boss, Murphy. (Dir: Harry Beaumont, 89 mins.)

Uphill All the Way (1986)* Roy Clark, Mel Tillis, Glen Campbell, Trish Van Devere. Country comedy about two con men mistaken for bank robbers and chased around turn-of-the-century Texas. Burt Reynolds makes a cameo appearance. (Dir: Frank Q. Dobbs, 86 mins.)†

Up In Arms (1944)*** Danny Kaye, Dinah Shore, Dana Andrews. Kaye made his feature film debut, as a hypochondriac who gets drafted, in this splashy Goldwyn musical designed to showcase his talents. (Dir: Elliott Nugent, 106 mins.)†

Up In Central Park (1948)** Deanna Durbin, Dick Haymes, Vincent Price. Film version of stage musical with Durbin as a young Irish colleen at the turn of the century. (Dir: William A. Seiter, 88 mins.)

Up In Mabel's Room (1944)**½ Dennis O'Keefe, Marjorie Reynolds, Mischa

Auer, Charlotte Greenwood, Gail Patrick. A flustered husband tries to retrieve a memento given innocently to his old flame. Farce gets pretty funny at times. (Dir: Allan Dwan, 76 mins.)

Up In Smoke (1957)*½ Huntz Hall, Stanley Clements, David Gorcey, Byron Foulger, Judy Bamber. One of the Bowery Boys sells his soul to the Devil (Foulger) in exchange for racing tips in an effort to replenish charity funds that he's lost. (Dir: William Beaudine, 61 mins.)

Up In Smoke (1978)**½ Cheech and Chong, Tom Skerritt, Stacy Keach. Two free-spirited bums decide to join forces in their endless search for substances to snort, smoke, or drop. The first and best of their films. (Dir: Lou Adler, 85 mins.)†

Up In the Cellar—See: Three In the Cellar

Up Periscope (1959)**½ James Garner, Edmond O'Brien. Routine submarine drama. Garner deserved better material as his later career proved. For action fans. (Dir: Gordon Douglas, 111 mins.)

Uprising, The (West Germany, 1980)*** Agustin Pereira, Carlos Catania, Maria De Zelaya, Oscar Castillo. Political film tells the story of a young man in Nicaragua who sides with the Sandinistas during the last days of dictator Somoza's rule. Director Peter Lilienthal, who lived in Latin America for most of his life, made this rousing film in Nicaragua immediately after the revolution, giving it an exciting immediacy. (96 mins.)

Upstairs and Downstairs (Great Britain, 1959)*** Michael Craig, Anne Heywood, Mylene Demongeot, Claudia Cardinale. Charming domestic comedy about a young married couple and their problems in obtaining the right servant girl. Good fun. (Dir: Ralph Thomas, 100 mins.)

Up the Academy (1980)** Ron Leibman, Wendell Brown, Tom Citera. The first, and probably last, *Mad* magazine movie, set in a boys' military school, is uneven, occasionally inventive. (Dir: Robert Downey, 96 mins.)†

Up the Creek (Great Britain, 1958)**½ Wilfred Hyde-White, Peter Sellers, David Tomlinson. Not as funny as other British naval comedies, but occasionally lively due to the antics of Tomlinson as an ingenious lieutenant. (Dir: Val Guest, 83 mins.)

Up the Creek (1984)** Tim Matheson, Stephen Furst, Dan Monahan, James B. Sikking. It's teen-sex time again during a river-rafting contest where all of the girls naturally end up losing their tops. (Dir: Robert Butler, 95 mins.)†

Up the Down Staircase (1967)*** Sandy Dennis, Patrick Bedford, Eileen Heckart, Jean Stapleton. Bel Kaufman's perceptive best-selling novel about the experiences of a young teacher in a New York high school is transferred to the screen with taste and skill by director Robert Mulligan and screenwriter Tad Mosel. (124 mins.)

Up the River (1930)** Spencer Tracy, Warren Hymer, Clare Luce, Humphrey Bogart. A throwaway comedy, intriguing for the casting of Bogart and Tracy. An ex-con tries desperately to cover up his past; two of his prison pals think enough of him to break out just to lend him a helping hand. (Dir: John Ford, 80 mins.)

Up the Sandbox (1972)*** Barbra Streisand, David Selby, Ariane Heller. A funny, wry, and often genuinely touching story about a New York housewife living on Riverside Drive. Streisand gives an observant, restrained performance as a young mother questioning her lot in life. (Dir: Irvin Kershner, 97 mins.) †

Up Tight (1968)** Raymond St. Jacques, Frank Silvera, Ruby Dee, Julian Mayfield, Roscoe Lee Browne, Max Julien. A sporadically exciting but fussed-over all-black revamp of the classic, *The Informer* (1935). After a street cleaner informs on his activist friends, they get uptight and seek redress. (Dir: Jules Dassin, 104 mins.)

Up to a Certain Point (Cuba, 1984)***½ Oscar Alvarez, Mirta Ibarra, Coralia Veloz, Rogelio Blain, Omar Valdes, Ana Vinba. Middle-aged man who prides himself as being sexually liberated finds that he is more "macho" than the less-educated working-class associates of a woman with whom he has become enchanted. Well-acted comedy mixes taped interviews of actual workers with a fictional plot filled with anger and bitterness. (Dir: Tomas Gutierrez Alea, 72 mins.)

Up to His Ears (France, 1965)*** Jean-Paul Belmondo, Valery Inkijinoff, Ursula Andress, Jean Rochefort. Belmondo is a wealthy man so bored that he arranges for a hit man to kill him. After he meets a stunning stripper he has second thoughts, but the assassin is already on his trail. Lots of fun, with wildly comic chases and plot twists. (Dir: Philippe DeBroca, 110 mins.)

Up to His Neck (Great Britain, 1954)** Ronald Shiner, Laya Raki, Anthony Newley, Bryan Forbes. Wacky, mixed-up farce with only a few funny moments. (Dir: John Paddy Carstairs, 89 mins.)

Uptown New York (1932)**½ Jack Oakie, Shirley Grey, Leon Ames, George Cooper, Raymond Hatton, Henry Armetta. Unpretentious soap opera, with an unusual interfaith theme; a loyal Jewish girl's upwardly mobile doctor boyfriend rejects her, so she marries happy-go-lucky Irishman Oakie. Warm and unselfconscious, nicely done. (Dir: Victor Schertzinger, 80 mins.)

Uptown Saturday Night (1974)*** Sidney Poitier, Bill Cosby, Harry Belafonte, Flip Wilson, Calvin Lockhart, Richard Pryor, Roscoe Lee Browne. High-spirited fun as Cosby and Poitier play a pair of innocents whose night on the town is interrupted when they're held up at an illegal after-hours nightclub. (Dir: Sidney Poitier, 104 mins.) †

Upturned Glass, The (Great Britain, 1947)**½ James Mason, Rosamund John, Pamela Kellino, Ann Stephens, Morland Graham, Maurice Denham. Moody, suspenseful thriller about a brilliant surgeon revenging his beloved mistress's murder by committing the perfect crime himself, with the murderer now his victim. Tense and controlled. (Dir: Lawrence Huntington, 87 mins.)

Up Your Alley (1989)* Linda Blair, Murray Lanston, Bob Zany, Ruth Buzzi, Johnny Dark, Yakov Smirnoff. Ex-"Unknown Comic" Langston produced and co-wrote this feeble comedy about reporter Blair getting a story on the homeless by pretending to be one of them. Not as tasteless as it sounds—actually, it was made to promote awareness of the homeless—but pretty poor just the same. (Dir: Bob Logan, 88 mins.) †

Up Your Teddy Bear (1970)*½ Wally Cox, Julie Newmar, Victor Buono, Claire Kelly, Angelique Pettyjohn, Thordis Brandt. Sadly misguided farce squanders the talents of its three leads. It also curiously blunts Newmar's sultry sexuality by making her Cox's no-nonsense boss, a toy-making businesswoman who wants him to surrender his homemade dolls, but whom he looks up to only as a mother. (Dir: Don Joslyn, 89 mins.)

Urban Cowboy (1980)*** John Travolta, Debra Winger, Scott Glenn, Madolyn Smith, Barry Corbin. A sultry Texas romance with a core of gritty intelligence. Travolta plays a young oil field worker who goes looking for love in Gilley's country-and-western bar and falls hard for Winger, only to find the romance fading as their marriage begins. In many ways a honky-tonk revision of *Saturday Night Fever*, the film features one of Travolta's most appealing performances, and a stunningly sexy, emotionally raw turn by Winger, as the young woman who can't stop competing with and fighting against her husband. (Dir: James Bridges, 135 mins.) †

Urgh! A Music War (Great Britain, 1981)*** Quite thorough documentary showing concert performances of a number of "New Wave" rock bands. The film runs a bit too long, but it does offer fascinating glimpses at such exciting acts as The

Police, X, The Dead Kennedys, Joan Jett, UB40, Devo, The Cramps, OMD, The Fleshtones, and Gary Numan (there are over thirty acts in all). (Dir: Derek Burbidge, 124 mins.)†

Urinal (Canada, 1988)*** Pauline Carey, Paul Bettis, Mark Gomes, Lance Eng. Fascinating film about the ghosts of deceased homosexuals appearing in a Toronto garden and commenting on government-sanctioned acts of bias, violence, and oppression against gays. (Dir: John Greyson, 100 mins.)

Us Against the World (MTV 1975)**½ Meredith Baxter Birney, Linda Purl. Interesting but uneven drama about the difficulties young women interns face in the rigorous medical world. (Dir: William Asher, 122 mins.)

Used Cars (1980)**½ Kurt Russell, Jack Warden, Gerrit Graham. This nasty comedy veers into the grotesque too often to be consistently funny, but it has its moments. The zany plot concerns a young go-getter trying to make it to the top any way he can. (Dir: Robert Zemeckis, 113 mins.)†

Users, The (MTV 1978)** Jaclyn Smith, Tony Curtis. Gossip columnist Joyce Haber's sex-ridden book about sinful Tinsel Town becomes an overproduced, dramatically underdressed film. Smith plays an ex-prostitute who climbs up the social ladder until she marries a multimillionaire. (Dir: Joseph E. Hardy, 104 mins.)

Utamaro and His Five Women (Japan, 1946)***½ Minosule Bando, Kinuyo Tanaka, Hiroko Kawsaki, Kotaro Bando. Fascinating account of the life of master Japanese printmaker Utamaro examines the problems of great artists and presents a vivid account of the underworld of Tokyo in the late 18th century. (Dir: Kenji Mizoguchi, 95 mins.)

Utilities (Canada, 1981)*½ Robert Hays, Brooke Adams, John Marley, James Blendick. Lame comedy about a disgruntled man who takes on the utility companies to prove a point. Made from the wrong bits of Frank Capra movies. (Dir: Harvey Hart, 91 mins.)†

Utopia (France, 1950)*½ Stan Laurel, Oliver Hardy, Suzy Delair. Stan and Ollie inherit a Pacific island, where uranium is discovered. Last L&H effort, and a sad farewell it is. AKA: Atoll K. (Dir: Leo Joannon, 80 mins.)†

Utu (New Zealand, 1984)*** Anzac Wallace, Bruno Lawrence, Tim Elliott. A New Zealand western, circa 1870, about the retribution of the Maoris after the colonials attack, squeezing them out the way the American settlers forced out the Indians. (Dir: Geoff Murphy, 104 mins.)†

U-Turn—See: **Girl in Blue, The**

U2 Rattle and Hum (1988)*** Documentary of the rousing Irish rock band's 1987 U.S. tour captures their powerful stage presence to good effect, though the direction by Spielberg protégé Phil Joanou is often hopelessly pretentious. Highlight is an appearance by B.B. King on "When Love Came to Town." (99 mins.)†

V (MTV 1983)*** Marc Singer, Faye Grant, Jane Badler. Entertaining sci-fi about an alien invasion of Earth. Intelligent strangers arrive seeking chemicals and a refuge. They profess to be peaceful, but have other motives as Marc Singer's TV news-cameraman finally discovers. Followed by V: the Final Battle, a mini-series and then a weekly series. (Dir: Kenneth Johnson, 208 mins.)

Vacation, The (Italy, 1971)** Vanessa Redgrave, Franco Nero, Leopoldo Trieste, Corin Redgrave, Osiride Pevarello, Countessa Veronica. Allegorical tale of nonconformity is at once symbolic of everything and, ultimately, nothing. Redgrave is an asylum inmate who is set free for awhile to see if she can adjust to the real world. (Dir: Tinto Brass, 101 mins.)

Vacation from Marriage (Great Britain, 1945)*** Robert Donat, Deborah Kerr, Ann Todd, Glynis Johns. Cute little "sleeper" about a mild little English couple who go into service during the war and have their personalities overhauled. (Dir: Alexander Korda, 92 mins.)

Vacation in Hell (MTV 1979)** Michael Brandon, Priscilla Barnes, Barbara Feldon. Four vacationing women and the obligatory male flee for their lives in a dense jungle on the outskirts of a posh tropical resort. (Dir: David Greene, 104 mins.)

Vagabond (France, 1985)***½ Sandrine Bonnaire, Macha Meril, Elaine Cortadellas, Stephane Freiss. Disturbing tale of the tragic life of a young female vagrant struggling to survive in the south of France. Mona (Bonnaire) is a young drifter, whose obsession with freedom prevents her from accepting help from those she meets during her lonely travels. (Dir: Agnes Varda, 105 mins.)†

Vagabond King, The (1956)** Kathryn Grayson, Oreste, Rita Moreno. Operetta about Francois Villon, poet and vagabond, and the revolt in Paris. (Dir: Michael Curtiz, 86 mins.)

Vagabond Lover, The (1929)**½ Rudy Vallee, Marie Dressler, Charles Sellon, Sally Blane. Get out your megaphone. Filmed at a time when Rudy made women swoon with his singing. He plays an orchestra leader smitten with a wealthy dowager's niece. (Dir: Marshall Neilan, 69 mins.)

Valachi Papers, The (France-Italy, 1972)** Charles Bronson, Lino Ventura, Joseph Wiseman. Violent saga of the Cosa Nostra based on Peter Maas's bestseller. Bronson plays the dim-witted Joe Valachi, a Mafia soldier who turned informer. (Dir: Terence Young, 125 mins.)

Valdez Is Coming (1971)**½ Burt Lancaster, Susan Clark, Jon Cypher. A lot of Lancaster to watch here, and that's the nimblest aspect of this western-type tale of a Mexican lawman who, after being forced to kill a suspect, tries to provide for his pregnant widow. (Dir: Edwin Sherin, 90 mins.)

Valentine (MTV 1979)*** Jack Albertson, Mary Martin, Loretta Swit. Albertson and Martin are lovely as a pair of senior citizens who find romance at an offbeat old-folks' home in Venice, Calif. (Dir: Lee Philips, 104 mins.)

Valentine Magic on Love Island (MTV 1980)* Janis Paige, Howard Duff, Adrienne Barbeau, Lisa Hartman. More trashy romantic vignettes from a tropical island locale. (Dir: Earl Bellamy, 104 mins.)

Valentino (1951)** Anthony Dexter, Eleanor Parker, Patricia Medina, Richard Carlson. A romanticized version of the Valentino legend; produced in elaborate style. Anthony Dexter bears a striking physical resemblance to the original Sheik of the Silver Screen, but that's where the resemblance ends. (Dir: Lewis Allen, 102 mins.)

Valentino (1977)*½ Rudolf Nureyev, Leslie Caron, Michelle Phillips, Carol Kane, Felicity Kendall, Huntz Hall. Another lurid biopic from director Ken Russell. Nureyev's dancing charisma doesn't translate into a sexy screen presence. As the legendary Latin Lover, he has two left feet. A parade of famous names from the past drift through this overblown kiss-and-tell screenplay with little impact. (127 mins.)

Valerie (1957)** Sterling Hayden, Anita Ekberg, Anthony Steel, Peter Walker. Dull quasi-mystery about murder and romance, worth watching only for Hayden's usual good performance and the sultry, sexy Ekberg. (Dir: Gerd Oswald, 81 mins.)

Valerie and Her Week of Wonders (Czechoslovakia, 1970)*** Jaroslava Schallerova, Helena Anyzkova, Petr Kopriva, Jan Klusak. Visually spectacular fantasy filled with nightmarish Gothic images. A sweet thirteen-year-old girl who lives with her grandmother has the most incredible dreams imaginable, including one about a magic pair of earrings, given to her by a man who might be her brother. (Dir: Jaromil H. Jires, 77 mins.)

Valet Girls (1986)* Meri D. Marshall, April Stewart, Mary Kohnert, Christopher Weeks, John Terlesky. Insipid comedy about California gals parking cars for the rich and famous while waiting for that big break as singers. Only for those with an affinity for cocaine jokes. (Dir: Rafal Zielinski, 82 mins.)†

Valiant Is the Word for Carrie (1936)**½ Gladys George, Arline Judge, John Howard. George rarely got the roles that would have put her in the big league. Here, playing a woman unselfishly caring for orphans, she got such a part, played it to the hilt, and received an Oscar nomination for Best Actress. (Dir: Wesley Ruggles, 110 mins.)

Valley Girl (1983)**½ Deborah Foreman, Nicolas Cage, Frederic Forrest, Colleen Camp. Romeo and Juliet at the shopping mall: Valley Girl goes out with Hollywood punk and is rejected by her peers. Not as bad as you might think, thanks to some solid acting and a few genuinely funny scenes. (Dir: Martha Coolidge, 107 mins.)†

Valley of Decision, The (1945)*** Greer Garson, Gregory Peck, Donald Crisp, Marsha Hunt, Lionel Barrymore. Story of a girl who became a servant in a Pittsburgh industrialist's home and spent the rest of her life there—as a maid and then married to the son. Not a great film but, thanks to cast and production, top screen entertainment. (Dir: Tay Garnett, 111 mins.)

Valley of Gwangi (1969)*½ James Franciscus, Gila Golan, Richard Carlson. Science-fiction western about a prehistoric world hidden in the Forbidden Valley located in the Mexico of 1912. (Dir: James O'Connolly, 95 mins.)

Valley of Mystery (1967)*½ Richard Egan, Peter Graves, Lois Nettleton, Joby Baker, Harry Guardino. Clichéd story of a group of airline passengers forced to land in a South American jungle fighting for survival. (Dir: Josef Leytes, 90 mins.)

Valley of the Dolls (1967)½ Barbara Parkins, Patty Duke, Sharon Tate, Susan Hayward, Paul Burke, Martin Milner, Lee Grant, Tony Scotti. Three show-biz hopefuls ascend to dizzying career heights only to plummet into the valley of quick-fix tranquilizers. Tate is touching as the ill-fated showgirl, and Hayward is memorable, but everything and everyone else is a laughable mess. (Dir: Mark Robson, 123 mins.)†

Valley of the Dolls (MTV 1981)**½ Catherine Hicks, Lisa Hartman, Veronica Hamel, David Birney, Jean Simmons, James Coburn, Bert Convy. Glossy account of ladies climbing up Hollywood's success ladder is an improvement over the 1967 original. (Dir: Walter Grauman, 196 mins.)

Valley of the Dragons (1961)½ Sean McClory, Cesare Danova, Joan Staley, Roger Til, I. Stanford Jolley. Supposedly based on a Jules Verne story, this rip-off is little more than stock footage from the oft-plundered *One Million B.C.* (1940) padded out with a few new scenes. (Dir: Edward Bernds, 79 mins.)

Valley of the Eagles (Great Britain, 1951)**½ Jack Warner, John McCallum, Nadia Gray. Young scientist has his invention stolen, follows the culprits together with a police inspector to the wastes of Lapland. Up-to-par melodrama. (Dir: Terence Young, 83 mins.)

Valley of the Giants (1938)*** Wayne Morris, Claire Trevor, Charles Bickford, Frank McHugh, Donald Crisp, Jack LaRue, John Litel. Back in the '30s, this little adventure pix was considered environmentally correct. Morris puts up a valiant fight to keep Bickford from logging northern California's beautiful redwood trees. Trevor is delightful as a bar girl. (Dir: William Keighley, 79 mins.)

Valley of the Headhunters (1953)** Johnny Weissmuller, Christine Larson. Jungle Jim helps the government make peace with tribal bigwigs in order to clear the way for obtaining important minerals. (Dir: William Berke, 67 mins.)

Valley of the Kings (1954)**½ Robert Taylor, Eleanor Parker, Carlos Thompson. Passable adventure set in Egypt. Taylor plays an archeologist who accompanies Eleanor Parker and her villainous husband on an expedition to the tombs of Pharaoh Rahotep. (Dir: Robert Pirosh, 86 mins.)

Valley of the Redwoods (1960)**½ John Hudson, Lynn Bernay, Ed Nelson, Robert Shayne, Michael Forest. Standard adventure tale of thieves hitting an armored car and trying to flee across the border to Canada. Not bad, with some young faces trying hard to make their mark in the movies. (Dir: William Witney, 65 mins.)

Valley of the Sun (1942)*** Lucille Ball, James Craig, Dean Jagger. Frontiersman finally exposes a crooked Indian agent. Exciting, fast-moving western with a good cast. (Dir: George Marshall, 79 mins.)†

Valley of the Zombies (1946)* Robert Livingston, Adrian Booth, Thomas Jackson, LeRoy Mason, Ian Keith. Crummy horror tale about a mad doctor who comes back as a zombie and seeks revenge on those who irked him during his life. Resolutely awful. (Dir: Philip Ford, 60 mins.)

Valmont (1989)***½ Colin Firth, Annette Bening, Meg Tilly, Fairuza Balk, Sian Phillips, Jeffrey Jones, Henry Thomas, Vincent Schiavelli. Light, funny, and sexy, this loose adaptation of DeLaclos's *Les Liaisons Dangereuses* was swept under the rug as a result of being released after the more mainstream *Dangerous Liaisons*. Director Milos Forman goes for period detail, ripe sexuality, and amusing portrayals of the two "puppet master" characters who manipulate the love lives of the rest of the ensemble. (137 mins.)†

Vals, The (1983)* Jill Carroll, Elena Stratheros, Michaelle Laurita, Chuck Connors, Tiffany Bolling, Sue Ane Langdon, Sonny Bono, John Carradine. The whole "valley girl" craze ran its course pretty quickly. Unfortunately, it was around long enough to prompt this turkey about four bubbleheads trying to raise money to save an orphanage. (Dir: James Polakof, 99 mins.)†

Value for Money (Great Britain, 1955)*** John Gregson, Diana Dors, Donald Pleasence, Ernest Thesiger, Derek Farr, Cyril Smith. Bright, typical British '50s comedy about a young man who inherits his father's vast wealth and has a perfectly marvelous time spending it all. Dors is tantilizingly at the peak of her sashaying flamboyance. (Dir: Ken Annakin, 89 mins.)

Vamp (1986)**½ Chris Makepeace, Robert Rusler, Sandy Baron, Gedde Watanabe, Grace Jones. Jones is stunning as a vampire queen who works in a strip club where all the workers are bloodsuckers. When a trio of students show up to find a stripper for a frat party, the stage is set for a few good laughs and some genuine scares. (Dir: Richard Wenk, 93 mins.)†

Vamping (1984)**½ Patrick Duffy, Catherine Hyland, Rod Arrants, Fred A. Keller. Atmospheric melodrama about a musician who moonlights as a burglar, only to fall in love with his alluring victim. (Dir: Frederick King Keller, 107 mins.)†

Vampire, The—See: Mark of the Vampire (1957)

Vampire (MTV 1979)*** Richard Lynch, Jason Miller, E. G. Marshall, Jessica Walter, Barrie Youngfellow. A long-dead vampire is revived by construction on the site of his grave. A little slow-moving, but fairly well done. (Dir: E. W. Swackhamer, 104 mins.)

Vampire at Midnight (1988)**½ Jason Williams, Gustav Vintas, Leslie Milne. Erotic horror tale about a modern-day vampire stalking its victims in Los Angeles, with cop Williams on its trail. The ending is a trifle disappointing in this otherwise solid spooker. (Dir: Gregory McClatchy, 93 mins.)†

Vampire Bat, The (1933)**½ Melvyn Douglas, Fay Wray, Lionel Atwill, Dwight Frye, Maude Eburne. Mad doctor terrorizes a small village with a series of wanton murders. Dated but crisply played horror thriller. (Dir: Frank Strayer, 71 mins.)†

Vampire Circus (Great Britain, 1971)*** John Moulder Brown, Adrienne Corri. Intriguing Hammer Studios' horror-thon about a touring show whose performers are vampires, and their constant travelling gives them a new bloodbank wherever they go. (Dir: Robert Young, 87 mins.)

Vampire Hookers (1979)½ John Carradine, Lenka Novak, Karen Stride, Bruce Fairbairn, Trey Wilson, Vic Diaz. A bloodsucker sends out his pulchritudinous minions to do his dirty work. Truly awful. (Dir: Cirio H. Santiago, 82 mins.)†

Vampire Lovers, The (Great Britain, 1971)*** Ingrid Pitt, Pippa Steele, Madeline Smith, Peter Cushing, George Cole. Sexy bloodsucking saga about toothsome women who nibble their dates' necks too deeply. Based on Le Fanu's *Camilla*. (Dir: Roy Ward Baker, 88 mins.)†

Vampire Men of the Lost Planet—See: Horror of the Blood Monsters

Vampires, The (Italy, 1965)* Gordon Scott, Gianna Maria Canale. A gladiatorial creature feature as band of androids led by the Vampire kidnap young women to sell them as slaves. AKA: **Goliath and the Vampires.** (Dirs: Giacomo Gentilomo, Sergio Corbucci, 91 mins.)

Vampire's Coffin, The (Mexico, 1959)* Abel Salazar, Ariadne Welter, German Robles. Vampire is revived from the dead, menaces a young girl. Inept horror thriller dubbed in English. (Dirs: Fernando Mendez, Paul Nagle, 81 mins.)

Vampires in Havana (Cuba, 1985)*** Clever adult cartoon spoofs everything in sight in a story of gangster vampires in Chicago and Germany battling over an elixir that will enable them to survive in the sunlight. Writing and design are stressed over technical niceties of the animator's art, making this less showoffy than most such American efforts. (Dir: Juan Padron, 80 mins.)

Vampire's Kiss (1989)***½ Nicolas Cage, Maria Conchita Alonso, Elizabeth Ashley, Jennifer Beals. Bizarre satire with Cage as an arrogant, pretentious yuppie who believes that he has been bitten by a vampire and is becoming one himself. Cage's demented performance is a knockout; Alonso is also excellent as the meek secretary whom he torments. (Dir: Robert Bierman, 111 mins.)†

Vampyr (Germany, 1932)**** Julian West, Sybille Schmitz, Harriet Gerard. A chilling, impeccably photographed mood piece. Continuously eerie, the film portrays vampirism as an unearthly plague, almost a sickness of the soul, as an outsider visits a fear-ridden community and fights the dominance of the local Mephistophelian doctor. (Dir: Carl Dreyer, 60 mins.)†

Vampyres (Great Britain, 1974)**½ Marianne Morris, Anulka, Murray Brown. Considered pornographic in its time, this tale of two female vampires who lust for more than just their victims' blood is tame now, slow-moving but occasionally erotic. (Dir: Joseph Larraz, 87 mins.)†

Van, The (1976)** Stuart Getz, Deborah White, Stephen Oliver, Danny DeVito. Bashful California dude foregoes college to buy an elaborate van that he hopes will work as a homing device to pick up girls. (Dir: Sam Grossman, 92 mins.)†

Vanessa, Her Love Story (1935)**½ Helen Hayes, Robert Montgomery, May Robson, Lewis Stone, Otto Kruger. Romantic escapade features Hayes in love with rapscallion Montgomery. Well acted '30s melodrama. (Dir: William K. Howard, 75 mins.)

Vanina Vanini (Italy, 1961)***½ Sandra Milo, Martine Carol, Paolo Stoppe, Laurent Terzieff. Court politics are the subject of this romantic period adventure about an Italian revolutionary who goes to Rome to assassinate a traitor and is given shelter by a countess. Director Roberto Rossellini blends a tale of inequity, corruption, and dangerous love with allusions to 20th-century governmental intrigue in this well-acted, complexly written film. (130 mins.)

Vanished (MTV 1971)*** Richard Widmark, James Farentino, Robert Young, Eleanor Parker. Suspenseful version of the best-selling novel by Fletcher Knebel. Widmark is effective as the President of the United States who faces a major crisis when one of his top advisers is allegedly kidnapped by what appears to be a foreign power. (Dir: Buzz Kulik, 196 mins.)

Vanishing, The (Netherlands, 1988)***½ Bernard-Pierre Donnadieu, Gene Bervoets, Johanna ter Steege, Gwen Eckhaus. Chilling, intellectual horror tale about the disappearance of a woman and the evil that lurks in every person's heart. A great film about obsessive-compulsive behavior: well scripted, with fine performances. As fascinating as a disturbing nightmare. (Dir: George Sluizer, 105 mins.)

Vanishing Act (MTV 1986)*** Mike Farrell, Margot Kidder, Elliott Gould, Fred Gwynne, Graham Jarvis. Slick mystery with wry humor and enough twists to keep fans off balance. A good cast has fun with this tale of a missing bride who turns out to be a stranger to her new husband. (Dir: David Greene, 104 mins.)†

Vanishing American, The (1925)***½ Richard Dix, Lois Wilson, Noah Beery, Malcolm McGregor, Nocki. Epic western, based on a Zane Grey novel, about a young Navajo leader who serves in WWI, and returns to the reservation to fight injustices against his people. Unusual for its uncompromising account of the Indians' betrayal at the hands of the U.S. government and its agents. (Dir: George B. Seitz, 153 mins.)†

Vanishing American, The (1955)**½ Scott Brady, Forrest Tucker, Jay Silverheels, Gene Lockhart, Audrey Totter, Jim Davis. Native Americans battle an attempt to seize more territory belonging to the Navajos. Interesting adventure tries but fails to address the issue of the rights of America's earliest settlers. (Dir: Joseph Kane, 90 mins.)

Vanishing Point (1971)** Barry Newman, Dean Jagger, Robert Donner, Cleavon Little. Odd thriller about a man determined to go from Denver to San Francisco in fifteen hours. Charlotte Rampling is in the complete 107-minute version of Newman's drive from Colorado to California. (Dir: Richard C. Sarafian, 99 mins.)†

Vanishing Prairie (1954)*** An absorbing, educational Disney documentary; the second in their True-Life series; it deals with the great American prairie bounded by the Rockies and the Mississippi. Academy Award for Best Documentary. (Dir: James Algar, 75 mins.)†

Vanishing Virginian, The (1941)** Frank Morgan, Kathryn Grayson. Sentimental, sugary little story which is set back at the beginning of the fight for women's suffrage. (Dir: Frank Borzage, 97 mins.)

Vanishing Wilderness (1973)*** Excellent documentary footage makes this family entertainment appealing. The cameras travel across North America, focusing on wildlife, from the polar bears of the Arctic to pelicans, alligators, buffaloes, and whooping cranes. (Dirs: Arthur Dubs, Heinz Seilmann, 93 mins.)†

Van Nuys Boulevard (1979)** Bill Adler, Cynthia Wood, Dennis Bowen, Melissa Prophet, David Hayward, Tara Strohmeier. And . . . they're off! Not the cars, but the viewing audience when they find that this melange of drag racing, spicy women and disco dancing is simply a dreary update of all the small-town-boy-makes-good-in-fast-car sagas that have spun out of control since time immemorial. (Dir: William Sachs, 93 mins.)

Vanquished, The (1953)**½ John Payne, Jan Sterling, Ellen Corby, Coleen Gray, Lyle Bettger. Formula western about evil varmints taking over a cowtown and the good citizens trying to clean up the place. Better acted than most of its genre, with a few nice directorial touches. (Dir: Edward Ludwig, 84 mins.)

Varan, the Unbelievable (U.S.-Japanese, 1962)* Myron Healey, Tsuruko Kobayashi. Japanese horror about a monster on the loose with some American footage tacked on—a cheapie-creepie. (Dirs: Jerry Baerwitz, Inoshiro Honda, 70 mins.)†

Variety (Germany, 1925)***½ Emil Jannings, Maly Delschaft, Lya De Putti, Warwick Ward. Innovative film, told in flashback, of the fall of a famous circus aerialist when he becomes entangled with an amoral vamp. More important than the plot is the dazzling, stylized camerawork by Karl Freund which influenced generations of directors. (Dir: E. A. Dupont, 94 mins.)†

Variety (1983)*½ Sandy McLeod, Will Patton, Richard Davidson, Luiz Guzman. An independently made film that introduces a fascinating premise and then fails to explore it to the fullest. McLeod plays a young woman who works as a ticket-taker at the Variety Photoplays—one of N.Y.'s oldest movie theaters, now an adult grind house. The young woman's aversion to porn films quickly turns into a fascination with their patrons. (Dir: Bette Gordon, 100 mins.)†

Variety Girl (1947)**½ Mary Hatcher, Olga San Juan, and an all-star cast. Big mass of stars show their mugs and make this thing passable. Crosby and Hope have the best lines. (Dir: George Marshall, 93 mins.)

Variety Lights (Italy, 1950)**½ Peppino de Fillipo, Carla del Poggio, Giulietta Masina. Fellini made his directorial debut with this charming but meandering comedy about a troupe of traveling players. (Dir: Federico Fellini, 93 mins.)†

Varsity Show (1937)*** Dick Powell, Priscilla Lane, Fred Waring. A Broadway big shot helps out his alma mater when the annual college revels experience setbacks. Choreographer Busby Berkeley's staging keeps this musical brew bubbling merrily along for the most part. The longer version is more fun. (Dir: William Keighley, 81 mins.) (Originally 121 mins.)

Vasectomy: A Delicate Matter (1986) ½ Paul Sorvino, Cassandra Edwards, Abe Vigoda, Ina Balin, June Wilkinson, Lorne Greene. Several cuts below average. Broad comedy about a man whose wife wants him to have the titular operation. (Dir: Robert Burge, 90 mins.)†

Vassa (Russia 1982)*** Irina Churikova, Vadim Med. This adaptation of Maxim Gorky's play is engrossing despite its stagy presentation. Worth seeing for Irina's spellbinding performance as a ruthless heiress who dominates the lives of her family. (Dir: Gleb Panfilov, 106 mins.)

Vatican Affair, The (1970)*½ Walter Pidgeon, Ira Furstenberg, Klaus Kinski, Tino

Carraro. Shoddy caper film involving the Vatican treasures. Pidgeon is a blind man with an obsessive interest in the Vatican's collection of jewels and artifacts, so he sets up a team to steal them. (Dir: Emilio Miraglia, 94 mins.)

Vault of Horror (Great Britain, 1973)**½ Daniel Massey, Anna Massey, Terry-Thomas, Glynis Johns, Curt Jurgens, Dawn Addams, Tom Baker, Denholm Elliott. Five tales of terror adapted from the legendary E. C. comic book of the fifties. (Dir: Roy Ward Baker, 93 mins.)†

Vegas (MTV 1978)**½ Robert Urich, June Allyson, Tony Curtis, Red Buttons. Las Vegas is again a backdrop for a tale of mystery and murder. In this pilot film Urich is the attractive ex-cop hired to find a runaway teenage girl involved with the underbelly of corruption in the glittering city. (Dir: Richard Lang, 104 mins.)†

Vegas Strip Wars, The (MTV 1984)**½ Rock Hudson, Pat Morita, James Earl Jones, Sharon Stone. Steady drama of struggling casino-owner Hudson, who faces an uphill battle to succeed on the Las Vegas strip. (Dir: George Englund, 104 mins.)†

Veils of Bagdad (1953)** Victor Mature, Mari Blanchard, Virginia Field, James Arness. Mature seems very much at home in his 16th-century costumes of a palace guard in Bagdad. Action fans will get more than their share in this typical Arabian Nights adventure. (Dir: George Sherman, 82 mins.)

Velvet (MTV 1984)** Polly Bergen, Shari Belafonte-Harper, Leah Ayres, Sheree Wilson, Mary-Margaret Humes. Slick, sexy pilot for a proposed series which has four gorgeous ladies posing as aerobic instructors as a cover for their real jobs—American spies. (Dir: Richard Lang, 104 mins.)

Velvet Touch, The (1948)**½ Rosalind Russell, Leo Genn, Claire Trevor, Sydney Greenstreet. Famous stage actress is involved in a murder case. Slick but conventional mystery drama. (Dir: John Gage, 98 mins.)†

Velvet Vampire, The (1971)**½ Michael Blodgett, Celeste Yarnall, Sherry Miles. Velvety vampire Yarnall invites a couple (Miles and Blodgett) to her desert home for a picnic—and they're the beverage! A rather stylish bloodletter, stronger on atmosphere than characterizations. (Dir: Stephanie Rothman, 80 mins.)†

Vendetta (1950)*½ Faith Domergue, George Dolenz, Hillary Brooke, Nigel Bruce, Joseph Calleia, Hugo Haas. The extremely tangled production history of this film, caused by Howard Hughes's fussy intervention, did not result in a worthwhile film. It's a lush-looking period melodrama about an Italian girl obsessed with avenging the murder of her father. The other directors who had a hand in this mess include Max Ophuls, Preston Sturges, and Hughes himself. (Dir: Mel Ferrer, 84 mins.)

Vendetta (1986)**½ Karen Chase, Sandy Martin, Durga McBroom, Kin Shriner. Sexploitation filmmakers never run out of reasons for putting women behind bars; this time it's a Hollywood stuntwoman who goes willingly into the slammer to investigate her sister's death. Satisfyingly souped-up revenge drama. (Dir: Bruce Logan, 89 mins.)†

Venetian Affair, The (1967)*½ Robert Vaughn, Boris Karloff, Elke Sommer, Felicia Farr. Reporter (Vaughn) works for the CIA and imperils his life. Tedious, jumbled. (Dir: Jerry Thorpe, 92 mins.)

Venetian Woman, The (Italy, 1986)*** Laura Antonelli, Jason Connery, Claudio Amendola, Monica Guerritore. Delightfully sexy comedy romp about young Connery in 16th-century Venice who beds love-starved older women. Well acted, enjoyable script filmed with lavish sets and costumes and a sprightly Ennio Morricone score. Underrated gem, well worth a look. (Dir: Mauro Bolognini, 85 mins.)

Vengeance (1937)** Lyle Talbot, Wendy Barrie, Wally Albright, Marc Lawrence. Low-budget, original gangster film about an ex-police officer who joins up with a vicious mob to get the goods on them; good plot, neatly done by a competent Grade B cast. (Dir: Del Lord, 61 mins.)

Vengeance Is Mine (Japan, 1980)***½ Ken Ogata, Rentaro Mikuni, Chocho Miyako. Fascinating character study of a psychopath, immaculately incarnated by Ogata. Through a series of chronological jumps, we view his infamous deeds, and his slightly skewed motivation-contempt for his weak-willed pious father, who has designs on Ogata's wife. The sex and violence aren't as explicit as can be found elsewhere, but the force with which they are delivered makes this a highly disturbing and involving work. (Dir: Shohei Imamura, 128 mins.)†

Vengeance of Fu Manchu, The (British, 1967)* Christopher Lee, Douglas Wilmer, Tony Ferrer, Tsai Chin. The mad Oriental tyrant is out to set up an international crime syndicate. Sequel: *Blood of Fu Manchu, The.* (Dir: Jeremy Summers, 91 mins.)

Vengeance of She, The (British, 1968)*½ Olinka Berova, John Richardson, Edward Judd, Colin Blakely. Young woman is thought to be the reincarnation of the queen of a lost city, which means danger for her. (Dir: Cliff Owens, 100 mins.)

Vengeance: The Story of Tony Cimo (MTV 1986)** Brad Davis, Roxanne Hart, Brad

Dourif, William Conrad. Fact-based drama with Davis well cast as an ordinary guy who vows vengeance when his mother and stepfather are slain during a robbery. (Dir: Marc Daniels, 104 mins.)

Vengeance Valley (1951)*** Burt Lancaster, Robert Walker, Joanne Dru. Two-fisted western adventure with Lancaster the tall man in the saddle. Walker plays Burt's young brother with a penchant for trouble. (Dir: Richard Thorpe, 83 mins.)†

Venom (1982)* Klaus Kinski, Oliver Reed, Nicol Williamson, Sterling Hayden, Sarah Miles. Rubbish about a black mamba menacing a kidnapped boy and his captors. (Dir: Piers Haggard, 93 mins.)†

Venusian, The—See: **Stranger from Venus**

Venus in Furs (Great Britain-Italy-Germany, 1970)** James Darren, Barbara McNair, Maria Rohm, Klaus Kinski. Sexed-up tale about a femme fatale, possibly immortal and definitely dangerous to the men who find her irresistible. (Dir: Jess Franco, 86 mins.)†

Vera (Brazil, 1987)***½ Beatriz Nogueira, Raul Cortez, Aida Leiner, Carlos Kroeber. Sensitive, moving drama with a brilliant performance by Nogueira as an orphan girl who finds work at an important research center which frowns on controversy. Troubled by her uncertain sexual identity, she begins a relationship with another woman, while fearing for her career. (Dir: Sergio Toledo, 87 mins.)

Vera Cruz (1954)**½ Gary Cooper, Burt Lancaster, Cesar Romero, Ernest Borgnine, Charles Bronson. The often used western plot of two opportunistic adventurers is on hand once again. This time it's Mexico during the Revolution of 1866. (Dir: Robert Aldrich, 94 mins.)†

Verboten (1959)*** James Best, Susan Cummings, Tom Bittman, Steven Geray. An intense postwar love story about a disillusioned German girl romanced by a Yank GI in occupied Germany, after WWII. Fuller's frenzied direction piles on as much visual excitement as the story line can support. (Dir: Sam Fuller, 94 mins.)

Verdict, The (1946)***½ Sydney Greenstreet, Peter Lorre, Rosalind Ivan, Joan Lorring, George Coulouris. Donald Siegel directs probably the most enjoyable of the Greenstreet-Lorre vehicles, an amiable Victorian murder mystery where, for once, Greenstreet is on the side of the law. Impressive moviemaking. (86 mins.)

Verdict, The (1982)*** Paul Newman, Charlotte Rampling, Jack Warden, James Mason, Milo O'Shea, Edward Binns, Julie Bovasso. Smart, crackling performances and astute direction by veteran Sidney Lumet make this an entertaining courtroom drama with Newman as a lawyer given one last shot at integrity and solvency. Opposing Newman is the suave, ruthless lawyer of one of Boston's top law firms, played with great style by Mason in one of his best performances. Screenplay by playwright David Mamet. (129 mins.)†

Verne Miller (1987)**½ Scott Glenn, Barbara Stock, Andrew Robinson, Diane Salinger. Interesting adventure drama features laconic Glenn as an infamous gangster who became a minor legend in the 1920s and 1930s. A strong sense of the criminal element of the times is nicely captured in this moody tale. (Dir: Rod Hewitt, 92 mins.)†

Vernon, Florida (1981)*** Documentarian Errol Morris's sympathetic and strangely serene look at the eccentrics and crackpots that populate small-town America. Lovingly directed with an affectionate distance from his subjects, Morris's portraits are a mesmerizing look into the bizarre soul of a nation. (65 mins.)†

Veronika Voss (West Germany, 1982)*** Rosel Zech, Hilmer Thate, Annemarie Duringer, Cornelia Frafoess. The last completed work of the late Rainer Werner Fassbinder, this depressing film is a morbid account of an aging, yet still seductive movie star whose career has deteriorated due to addiction to morphine. She is held prisoner to the drug by a sinister doctor who wishes her irreversible harm. (104 mins.)

Vertigo (1958)**** Kim Novak, James Stewart, Tom Helmore, Barbara Bel Geddes, Ellen Corby, Raymond Bailey, Lee Patrick, Henry Jones. This complex Alfred Hitchcock mystery is a romantic film in the fullest sense of that word. The film's story line involves a cop whose vertigo seems to have caused not only the death of a fellow policeman but also that of a patrician beauty whom he had been hired to follow. Feeling responsible for her death, the detective withdraws from life until he chances upon a shopgirl whom he cruelly tries to remake in the image of the dead woman he had fallen in love with. As his obsession grows, the film builds to a dizzying crescendo of duplicity, derangement, and folie à deux. A spellbinding work, graced with a mesmerizing score by Bernard Herrmann and Novak's haunting embodiment of the mystery woman (a role Hitchcock originally intended for Vera Miles). (128 mins.)†

Very Close Quarters (1986)** Shelley Winters, Farley Granger, Paul Sorvino, Theodore Bikel. Crude comedy about a housing shortage in Moscow. Filmed in 1983. (Dir: Vladimir Rif, 101 mins.)†

Very Curious Girl, A (France, 1969)*** Bernadette Lafont, Georges Geret, Julien

Guiomar, Claire Maurier, Michel Constantin, Jean Paredes. Lively social satire about woman who becomes a prostitute in order to gain revenge on villagers who treated her badly. (Dir: Nelly Kaplan, 106 mins.)†

Very Edge, The (Great Britain, 1962)*** Richard Todd, Anne Heywood, Jack Hedley, Jeremy Brett, Patrick Magee, Maurice Denham. Nasty little thriller with Heywood good as a pregnant woman attacked by a sex maniac. Crisp black and white photography gives a brooding, nightmarish quality to this creepy film. (Dir: Cyril Frankel, 82 mins.)†

Very Honorable Guy, A (1934)**½ Joe E. Brown, Alice White, Robert Barrat, Alan Dinehart, Irene Franklin, Harold Huber, Hobart Cavanaugh. Gangster comedy vehicle for Brown, from a Damon Runyon story, has a gambler selling his body to a mad scientist in an attempt to pay off on his markers. (Dir: Lloyd Bacon, 62 mins.)

Very Missing Person, A (MTV 1972)** Eve Arden, James Gregory, Ray Danton, Julie Newmar. Eve plays Hildegarde Withers, spinster sleuth; Hildegarde picks locks with a hatpin and wards off assailants by swinging her handbag, while tracing a wealthy youngster. (Dir: Russell Mayberry, 73 mins.)

Very Natural Thing, A (1974)*** Robert Joel, Curt Gareth, Bo White, Jay Pierce. Drama about a man who leaves the monastic life and settles down in New York City, hoping to meet a man to love and share life with. Honest, well-acted film tackles sensitive subject without prurience. (Dir: Christopher Larkin, 80 mins.)

Very Private Affair, A (France-Italy, 1962)*½ Brigitte Bardot, Marcello Mastroianni, Louis Malle. Early film by Louis Malle details the thirst for privacy of a successful movie idol (Bardot). This portrait of the misery, nonfulfillment of stardom is superficial and tedious. (95 mins.)†

Very Special Favor, A (1965)**½ Rock Hudson, Leslie Caron, Charles Boyer. French lawyer persuades Rock, as a favor, to romance his daughter to help her find herself as a woman. Glossy comedy with a pretty production and familiar players. (Dir: Michael Gordon, 104 mins.)

Very Thought of You, The (1944)*** Eleanor Parker, Dennis Morgan, Faye Emerson, Dane Clark, Beulah Bondi. Tense romantic drama about a man and a woman marrying during WWII, returning home and discovering an ugly antagonism against their union. Parker and Morgan lead a strong cast. (Dir: Delmer Daves, 99 mins.)

Vestige of Honor (MTV 1990)*** Gerald McRaney, Michael Gross, Season Hubley,

Kenny Lao, Cliff Gorman. Gross stars as real-life Don Scott, an American soldier who, along with a caustic captain (McRaney), swore to help the Montagnard soldiers of Vietnam, and met with insurmountable odds. Touching, beautifully acted piece of personal history involving a tragic footnote to the unpopular war. (Dir: Jerry London, 96 mins.)

Vibes (1988)**½ Cyndi Lauper, Jeff Goldblum, Peter Falk, Julian Sands. Silly adventure comedy brightened by its three colorful leads. Lauper makes a beguiling screen debut as a kooky psychic who joins with fellow mentalist Goldblum and con-man Falk to find a lost South American treasure. (Dir: Ken Kwapis, 99 mins.)†

Vice and Virtue (Italy-France, 1963)** Annie Girardot, Robert Hossein, Catherine Deneuve. Misguided attempt to update two novels by de Sade (*Juliette, Justine*) and make a relevant comment about contemporary society. Two sisters, one virtuous, one decadent, cope with the Nazi occupation of France. (Dir: Roger Vadim, 108 mins.)

Vice Raid (1960)* Mamie Van Doren, Richard Coogan, Brad Dexter. Sleazy crime drama of call-girl-racket crackdown uses TV-cop techniques. (Dir: Edward L. Cahn, 71 mins.)

Vice Squad (1931)*** Paul Lukas, Kay Francis, Esther Howard, William B. Davidson, Helen Johnson. Well-acted, hard-hitting crime drama about a corrupt police vice squad. Tough-minded, sharp script. (Dir: John Cromwell, 81 mins.)†

Vice Squad (1953)**½ Edward G. Robinson, Paulette Goddard. A day in the life of a cop, with more plot than you can count on your fingers and toes. Robinson is tough, Goddard is pseudo-sultry, and the result is haphazard. (Dir: Arnold Laven, 87 mins.)

Vice Squad (1982)** Wings Hauser, Season Hubley, Gary Swanson. A film that redefines the word "sleaze." This expose of L.A.'s underbelly involves a whore who's badgered by police to help ensnare a vicious wire-hanger wielding pimp. No wire hangers, please! (Dir: Gary A. Sherman, 97 mins.)†

Vice Versa (Great Britain, 1948)**½ Roger Livesey, Kay Walsh, David Hutcheson. Years before it became a familiar plot, this amusing comedy introduced the concept of a father and son switching identities. The transformation is caused by a magic stone, and the resulting complications are quite witty, especially the scenes where "Father" attends school. (Dir: Peter Ustinov, 111 mins.)

Vice Versa (1987)*½ Judge Reinhold, Fred

Savage, Corinne Bohrer, Swoozie Kurtz, David Proval. Of all the recent movies about pubescent boys magically exchanging bodies with adults, this is the worst. Overworked executive Reinhold and son Savage are brought closer together after they walk a mile in each other's shoes (literally), but the message is so trite, and the comedy so flat, that the viewer will have long since walked out. (Dir: Brian Gilbert, 97 mins.)†

Vicious (Australia, 1988)* Tamblyn Lord, Craig Pearce, Tiffiny Dowe, Ralph Cotterill. Spoiled teenager joins up with three blatent psychotics who bring out the sadist in him. Arch, annoying, and senseless. (Dir: Karl Zwicky, 88 mins.)†

Vicious Circle, The (Great Britain, 1957)*** John Mills, Noelle Middleton. Surgeon is suspected of murder when a film star is found dead in his flat. Suspenseful, compact mystery. (Dir: Gerald Thomas, 84 mins.)

Vicki (1953)** Jeanne Crain, Richard Boone, Jean Peters. Dogged detective tries to pin murder of a local glamour girl on her suitor. This was better as *I Wake Up Screaming* with Grable and Mature. (Dir: Harry Horner, 85 mins.)

Victim (Great Britain, 1961)***½ Dirk Bogarde, Sylvia Syms, Dennis Price. When a lawyer (Bogarde) becomes involved in a case with homosexual implications, his own past jeopardizes his career. Thoughtful effort, and one of the earliest movies to deal with the heretofore forbidden subject of homosexuality. (Dir: Basil Dearden, 100 mins.)†

Victim, The (MTV 1972)** Elizabeth Montgomery. Tepid thriller about a woman trapped in a remote house during a violent storm. (Dir: Herschel Daugherty, 73 mins.)

Victims (MTV 1982)*** Kate Nelligan, Madge Sinclair, Ken Howard, Howard Hesseman, Jonelle Allen, Amy Madigan. A provocative subject well handled for the most part. Kate Nelligan gives a fine performance as a rape victim who, along with other rape victims, take it upon themselves to haunt the rapist, who beats the rap on a technicality. (Dir: Jerrold Freedman, 104 mins.)

Victims for Victims: The Theresa Saldana Story (MTV 1984)*** Theresa Saldana, Adrian Zmed, Laurence Pressman. Actress Saldana was attacked and stabbed in the street by a crazed fan in real life. She plays herself in this sad and agonizing tale of a victim, and it's not easy to take. Her point that the victim suffers while the criminal is protected by law is made in a dramatic, forceful way. (Dir: Karen Arthur, 104 mins.)

Victoria the Great (Great Britain, 1937)*** Anna Neagle, Anton Walbrook, Walter

Rilla. Slow-moving but interesting film about the reign of Queen Victoria. (Dir: Herbert Wilcox, 112 mins.)

Victors, The (1963)*** George Peppard, George Hamilton, Eli Wallach, Jeanne Moreau, Melina Mercouri. Curious, sprawling saga of a squad of American soldiers, following them through Europe during WWII. Uneven results, but done on a broad canvas, commendable in intent. (Dir: Carl Foreman, 175 mins.)

Victor/Victoria (1982)***½ Julie Andrews, Robert Preston, James Garner, Lesley Ann Warren, Alex Karras, John Rhys-Davies, Graham Stark. Bright, often extremely funny farce about sexual attitudes. Andrews is delightful as a down-and-out singer in 1934 Paris who gains stardom by pretending to be a gay Polish count who is a female impersonator. The complications arise when a macho gangster from Chicago, engagingly played by Garner, falls in love with him/her. Preston is amusing as Andrew's gay pal. (Dir: Blake Edwards, 133 mins.)†

Victory (1940)**½ Fredric March, Betty Field, Cedric Hardwicke. A fatally bowdlerized adaptation of the Joseph Conrad novel, though many points of interest linger. (Dir: John Cromwell, 78 mins.)

Victory (1981)*** Michael Caine, Sylvester Stallone, Max von Sydow, Pele, Daniel Massey, Carol Laure. Canny adventure film that should especially delight soccer fans. Any resemblance between this film and the real WWII is coincidental, but the fighting spirit is there. For propaganda purposes, the Germans organize a soccer game between their team and Allied war prisoners in order to show their superiority, and an escape plan is hatched. (Dir: John Huston, 110 mins.)†

Victory at Entebbe (MTV 1976)** Elizabeth Taylor, Kirk Douglas, Linda Blair, Burt Lancaster, Helen Hayes. This recreation of the dramatic Israeli rescue of the hostages at Uganda's Entebbe Airport was hastily put together, and it shows! (Dir: Marvin Chomsky, 104 mins.)

Victory at Sea (1954)**** Now-classic documentary, drawn from the successful television show, about Allied forces battling for control of the seas during WWII. Exciting and well-written film uses amazing archival footage, set to a brilliant symphonic musical score by Richard Rodgers. Magnificently narrated by Alexander Scourby and superbly produced by Henry Salomon. (108 mins.)†

Vidas Secas (Brazil, 1963)***½ Atila Iorio, Maria Ribiero, Jofre Soares, Gilvan Lima. Considered *the* formative work of Brazil's *Cinema Novo*, the story of an impoverished family of herders forced to wander the harsh, dry Brazilian flatlands trying to make a living. Filmed with compassion and rage at the injustices carried out against the poor. The photography is sublime. AKA: **Barren Lives.** (Dir: Nelson Pereira Dos Santos, 115 mins.)

Video Dead, The (1987)* Roxanna Augesen, Rocky Duvall, Vickie Bastel, Jennifer Miro. A haunted television set stops playing *Zombie Blood Nightmare* just long enough to spew forth real zombies to terrorize the peaceful town of Shady Lane. As dumb as it sounds; only some especially (if unbelievably) gory effects are likely to keep you awake. (Dir: Robert Scott, 91 mins.)†

Videodrome (Canada, 1983)** James Woods, Deborah Harry, Peter Dvorsky, Les Carlson. The owner of a cable TV station programs soft-core porn, with surprising results. You can get too much of a good thing, apparently, for he discovers that porning-out can cause hallucinations. A good premise is botched because we don't care what happens to this man or anyone else in the film. (Dir: David Cronenberg, 88 mins.)†

Video Murders (1987)*½ Eric Brown, Virginia Lorridans, John Feritta, Lee Larrimore. Psycho killer with a penchant for videotaping his victims kidnaps a young woman and holds her captive. Not unwatchable, but hardly compelling, either. (Dir: Jim McCullough, Jr., 90 mins.)†

Video Violence (1987)½ Art Neill, William Toddie, Uke, Bart Sumner. The new owner of a small-town video shop discovers that his customers, bored with tame Hollywood horror movies, have taken to rolling their own. Shot-on-video movie has little plot, just lots of phony-looking dismemberments and bloodletting. (Dir: Gary Cohen, 90 mins.)†

Vietnam, Texas (1990)*½ Robert Ginty, Haing S. Ngor, Tim Thomerson, Kieu Chinh, Bert Remsen. Priest Ginty tracks down the woman he abandoned (while pregnant) in Vietnam, finds her in the Texas Vietnamese community married to drug lord Ngor. Film's social conscience doesn't mesh with the shoot-'em-up style. (Dir: Robert Ginty, 85 mins.)†

Vietnam—Year of the Pig—See: **In the Year of the Pig**

View from Pompey's Head, The (1955)**½ Richard Egan, Dana Wynter, Cameron Mitchell. Full-blown soap opera played in the Southern social set. Egan plays an executive who goes back home to investigate a claim of money due by an aging author who lives in an air of mystery. (Dir: Philip Dunne, 97 mins.)

View from the Bridge, A (France-Italy-U.S., 1962)*** Raf Vallone, Maureen Stapleton, Carol Lawrence, Jean Sorel, Raymond Pellegrin. Screen version of Arthur Mill-

er's play about an Italian longshoreman and his eruptive relationships with his wife and niece. The performances are individually exciting and perfectly blended for full dramatic effect. Another fine directing job from Sidney Lumet. (114 mins.)

View To A Kill, A (1985)**½ Roger Moore, Christopher Walken, Grace Jones. Sixteenth Bond outing has Agent 007 fighting a psychopathic industrialist who wants to corner the microchip market by sinking part of California. One of the more protracted Bonds, but there's a smashing climax atop the Golden Gate Bridge. (Dir: John Glen, 133 mins.)†

Vigilante (1983)*½ Robert Forster, Rutanya Alda, Carol Lynley. Exploitation flick goes to even more ridiculous lengths than usual to demonstrate how ineffective the police and the courts are in keeping us safe from crime. (Dir: William Lustig, 93 mins.)†

Vigilante Force (1976)**½ Jan-Michael Vincent, Kris Kristofferson, Bernadette Peters, Victoria Principal, David Doyle, Andrew Stevens. A sweaty, violent vigilante adventure about a California village that hires Vietnam veterans for protection, only to end up needing protection from their protectors. You won't be bored. (Dir: George Armitage, 89 mins.)

Vigilantes Return, The (1947)** Jon Hall, Paula Drew, Margaret Lindsay, Andy Devine, Jack Lambert. Fun western about Hall as marshall hired to clean up a wild town. Standard plot enhanced by Devine's gravelly-voiced acting and colorful vistas. (Dir: Ray Taylor, 68 mins.)

Vigil in the Night (1940)*** Carole Lombard, Brian Aherne, Anne Shirley. A young nurse in an English hospital makes a fatal mistake, for which her sister takes the blame. Grim but excellently done drama. (Dir: George Stevens, 96 mins.)

Viking Massacre (Italy, 1967)** Cameron Mitchell, Fausto Tozzi, Luciano Polletin, Elisa Mitchell. Mysterious stranger Mitchell protects the wife and family of an absent Viking chief from attempts to take over the kingdom. Not unlike a spaghetti western in animal skins and helmets, if that's your idea of a good time. AKA: **Knives of the Avenger.** (Dir: "John Hold" [Mario Bava], 86 mins.)†

Viking Women and the Sea Serpent (1957)* Abby Dalton, Brad Jackson, Susan Cabot, Richard Devon. Typical Roger Corman schlock about Viking women imprisoned on an island with a hungry horny sea serpent for company. Efficiently made cult favorite's original title was *The Voyage of the Viking Women to the Waters of the Great Sea Serpent*. (67 mins.)

Viking Queen, The (Great Britain, 1967)** Don Murray, Carita, Donald Houston,

Andrew Keir. A costumed period piece about the Roman occupation of Britain, and the love that was not meant to be between the Roman military governor and the queen of the local tribe. (Dir: Don Chaffey, 91 mins.)

Vikings, The (1958)**½ Kirk Douglas, Janet Leigh, Tony Curtis, Ernest Borgnine. An all-star cast enhances this elaborately mounted adventure epic which places the stress on action. The battle sequences are the highlights of the film which tells the story of the Vikings' invasion of England. (Dir: Richard Fleischer, 114 mins.)†

Viktor und Viktoria (Germany, 1933)*** Renate Muller, Hermann Thimig, Hilde Hildebrand, Fritz Odeman. The source film for Blake Edwards's *Victor/Victoria*, this German original is every bit as good, maybe even better. Deftly directed, wonderfully atmospheric comedy. (Dir: Reinhold Schunzel, 101 mins.)

Villa! (1958)** Brian Keith, Cesar Romero, Margia Dean, Rodolfo Hoyos, Rosenda Monteros, Carlos Muzquiz. Hoyos is the legendary peasant leader-turned-bandit Pancho Villa in this sentimentalized biography. Keith is his gun-running friend, whom he also introduces to the righteousness of the peasant rebellion. Works better as a standard sagebrush drama than as political history. (Dir: James B. Clark, 72 mins.)

Village, The (Switzerland, 1954)*** John Justin, Eva Dahlbeck. Two teachers at the Pestalozzi school for children of postwar displaced persons fall in love, but she is from behind the Iron Curtain. Frequently touching drama. (Dir: Leopold Lindtberg, 98 mins.)

Village Barn Dance (1940)** Richard Cromwell, Don Wilson. Diverting escapism as two youngsters attempt to open a radio station to gain their town national recognition. (Dir: Frank McDonald, 72 mins.)

Village in the Mist (South Korea, 1983)***½ Chong Yun-Hee, Ahn Song-Ki, Lee Yea-Min, Choi Dong-Jun. A young teacher from the city takes her first job (away from her fiancé) in a remote village and encounters strange customs and mysterious residents which both attract and repel her. Expressively filmed, with majestic performances by a strong ensemble cast. (Dir: Lim Kwon-Taek, 90 mins.)

Village of the Damned (Great Britain, 1960)***½ George Sanders, Barbara Shelley, Martin Stephens. Outstanding low-budget, high-shudder shocker. Fine direction from Wolf Rilla in this chiller about strange kids trying to conquer a village. (78 mins.)†

Village of the Giants (1965)* Tommy Kirk, Johnny Crawford, Beau Bridges. Inept and tasteless fantasy about a group of teenagers out for kicks who stumble across a potion that will make them huge. (Dir: Bert I. Gordon, 80 mins.)†

Villain (Great Britain, 1971)**½ Richard Burton, Ian McShane. Uneven crime melodrama with a heavy accent on violence. Burton gives a good account of himself in the offbeat role of a sadistic thief who stops at nothing to get his job done. Burton's character is also a jealous homosexual, which adds some bite to the already heavily plotted film. (Dir: Michael Tuchner, 97 mins.)

Villain, The (1979)** Kirk Douglas, Ann-Margret, Arnold Schwarzenegger. Clumsy western farce which finds cowpoke Douglas caught between the overwhelming chests of Schwarzenegger and Ann-Margret. The film does contain some fancy stunts, courtesy of director Hal Needham, but the characters are slim and the humor is sophomoric. (93 mins.)

Villain Still Pursued Her, The (1940)**½ Hugh Herbert, Anita Louise, Alan Mowbray, Buster Keaton, Richard Cromwell, Billy Gilbert, Margaret Hamilton, William Farnum. Amusing curiosity is a version of a traditional temperance melodrama, *The Fallen Saved*, with an all-star cast of farceurs engaging in a deadpan parody of this time-honored form. Louise is a lovely, almost idiotically innocent heroine, Mowbray a mustache-twirling villain, Cromwell a true-blue hero, and Keaton his staunch ally. A fascinating experiment. (Dir: Edward F. Cline, 65 mins.)†

Villa Rides (1968)**½ Yul Brynner, Robert Mitchum, Charles Bronson, Herbert Lom. Action-packed adventure stars Brynner as rebel leader Pancho Villa, and Mitchum as a gun-running aviator who joins forces with Villa to further the revolution in Mexico. (Dir: Buzz Kulik, 122 mins.)

Vincent and Theo (Great Britain-France, 1990)*** Tim Roth, Paul Rhys, Jip Wijngaarden, Johanna Ter Steege, Wladimir Yordanoff, Jean-Pierre Cassel. Exemplary biography of Vincent van Gogh concentrates on his poverty-stricken later years and his relationship with his brother Theo, an art dealer who struggled but failed to bring Vincent's work the attention it deserved. Director Robert Altman approaches the script with a surprising degree of control and realism; ironically, one of his least typical films is probably the most personal, offering a parable of all artists (including himself) whose rejected work proves to be ahead of its time. (138 mins.)†

Vincent, François, Paul and the Others (France, 1975)***½ Yves Montand, Michel Piccoli, Gerard Depardieu, Serge Reggiani, Stephane Audran. Three old friends—a doctor, a novelist, and a boxer—

support each other through a variety of mid-life, vocational, and marital problems. Powerfully acted, richly rewarding look at life from men's perspectives. (Dir: Claude Sautet, 118 mins.)†

Vincent: The Life and Death of Vincent van Gogh (Australia, 1987)*** The art and the artist receive equal attention in this thoughtful biographical essay about van Gogh's life and death. As the camera examines many of his masterpieces and early works, excerpts from his letters are read offscreen by John Hurt. The acted-out artistic tableaux are, however, a big mistake. (Dir: Paul Cox, 105 mins.)

Vindicator, The (Canada, 1985)* Terri Austin, Richard Cox, David McIlwraith, Maury Chaykin, Pam Grier. Scientist fatally injured in a lab explosion is revived as a murderous cyborg. Problem is, the guy doesn't *want* to kill, so he re-programs himself and sets off after his creators. Better than you'd think, in a Saturday afternoon matinee kinda way. AKA: **Frankenstein '88**. (Dir: Jean-Claude Lord, 92 mins.)†

Vintage, The (1957)**½ Pier Angeli, John Kerr, Michele Morgan, Mel Ferrer, Leif Erickson, Theodore Bikel. Powerhouse '50s cast does well in this family drama about brothers hiding out from the law in a French vineyard. Colorful melodrama plays like a page out of TV's "Falcon Crest." (Dir: Jeffrey Hayden, 92 mins.)

Vinyl (1965)*** Gerard Malanga, Edie Sedgwick, John MacDermott, Ondine, Tosh Carillo, Larry Latrae, Jacques Potin. Bizarre black comedy directed by Andy Warhol loosely based on Anthony Burgess's novel *A Clockwork Orange*. Contains scenes of sadomasochistic torture and weird peripheral characters who seem to have been selected for both their shock and comic value. (70 mins.)

Violated (1984)*½ J. C. Quinn, April Daisy White, John Heard, D. Balin, Elizabeth Kaitan, Samantha Fox. Overpopulated crime drama about a young actress abused by gangsters and discredited in court who fights back with the help of friendly cop Quinn. Pretty dull, though there's a lively ending if you last that long. (Dir: Richard Cannistraro, 88 mins.)†

Violation of Sarah McDavid, The (MTV 1981) *** Patty Duke, Ned Beatty, James Sloyan. Frightening depiction of violence in the high school system. When a caring teacher is brutally attacked in her classroom, her principal tries to hush up the incident so his own reputation won't suffer. (Dir: John Llewellyn Moxey, 104 mins.)

Violent Breed, The (Italy, 1983)* Henry Silva, Harrison Muller, Woody Strode, Carole Andre. Top-billed Silva appears only briefly in this confusing tale of revenge and drug running in Southeast Asia, involving the CIA, the KGB, the Mafia, and agents who don't seem to know whose side they're on. (Dir: Fernando DiLeo, 91 mins.)†

Violent Enemy, The (Great Britain, 1968)*** Tom Bell, Susan Hampshire, Jon Laurimore, Ed Begley, Noel Purcell. Effective thriller about an IRA plot to destroy a British power plant. Tense, well-acted film weakened by heavy-handed foray into the political side of the struggle for Irish civil rights. Still, worth a look. (Dir: Don Sharp, 95 mins.)

Violent Four, The (Italy, 1968)*** Gian Maria Volonte, Margaret Lee, Tomas Milian, Don Backy. Exciting crime thriller about a gang of Italian bank robbers noted for their headline-making heists, and the gigantic effort by the police to thwart their schemes. Plenty of action and energy throughout. (Dir: Carlo Lizzani, 98 mins.)

Violent Men, The (1955)**½ Glenn Ford, Barbara Stanwyck, Edward G. Robinson, Brian Keith. A large, sprawling western drama about a ruthless land baron who loses his grip on things due to violent forces opposing him. (Dir: Rudolph Maté, 96 mins.)

Violent Ones, The (1967)* Fernando Lamas, Aldo Ray, David Carradine, Lisa Gaye. Sheriff (Lamas) tries to save murder suspects from a lynch mob. Because Fernando also directed, he takes a double rap for this junk. (Dir: Fernando Lamas, 84 mins.)†

Violent Playground (Great Britain, 1958)*** Stanley Baker, Peter Cushing, David McCallum, Anne Heywood. Policeman tries to prevent crime in a tenement area of Liverpool. Gripping, well-acted drama of juvenile delinquents. (Dir: Basil Dearden, 106 mins.)

Violent Professionals, The (Italy, 1973)*** Richard Conte, Luc Merenda, Steffan Zaccharias, Silvana Tranquilli. Action-packed, bloody thriller about a disgraced policeman who, determined to clear his name, infiltrates organized crime in order to bring a vicious gang leader to justice. (Dir: Sergio Martino, 92 mins.)

Violent Road (1958)** Brian Keith, Efrem Zimbalist, Jr. Average drama about the truck drivers who transport highly explosive rocket fuel to a newly built missile base and the dangers they encounter. (Dir: Howard W. Koch, 86 mins.)

Violent Saturday (1955)*** Victor Mature, Richard Egan, Sylvia Sidney, Ernest Borgnine, Stephen McNally, Lee Marvin. A good cast bolsters this episodic yarn about a planned bank robbery by a trio of hoods. Many of the townspeople's stories come into focus as the thieves stake out the town before the heist. (Dir: Richard Fleischer, 91 mins.)

Violent Stranger (Great Britain, 1957)**½ Zachary Scott, Faith Domergue, Peter Illing, Gordon Jackson. Straightforward thriller with the wife of a man unjustly convicted of murder going after the real killer. Fast-paced, full of twists. (Dir: Montgomery Tully, 83 mins.)

Violent Summer (France-Italy, 1959)*** Eleonora Rossi-Drago, Jean-Louis Trintignant, Jacqueline Sassard. Quiet, perceptive film despite that title. About a frivolous romance solidifying into a passionate, mature affair, set against the upheaval of Mussolini's rotting fascist regime. (Dir: Vallerio Zurlini, 95 mins.)

Violent Women (1959)½ Jennifer Statler, Jo-Ann Kelly, Pamela Perry, Sandy Lyn. Grade Z women's prison picture that, despite the title, contains no violence until the final sequences. (Dir: Barry Mahon, 60 mins.)

Violent Years, The (1956)½ Jean Moorhead, Barbara Weeks. A sizzling story of teenage girl delinquents told in an atrociously bad '50s low-budget style. Screenplay by Ed (Plan 9 From Outer Space) Wood. (Dir: Franz Eichorn, 75 mins.)†

Violets Are Blue (1986)**½ Sissy Spacek, Kevin Kline, John Kellogg, Bonnie Bedelia. A sweet but silly fairy tale about adultery between globetrotting photojournalist Spacek and small-town editor Kline, her high-school boyfriend. The film clings to old movie traditions even as it throws relevant modern character motivations at the audience. (Bedelia steals the film). (Dir: Jack Fisk, 88 mins.)†

Violette (France-Canada, 1978)*** Isabelle Huppert, Stéphane Audran, Jean Carmet, Bernadette Lafont. The real-life story of a self-centered teenager who poisoned her parents in '33, brilliantly played by Huppert. Well done, but too long. (Dir: Claude Chabrol, 123 mins.)

V.I.P.'s, The (Great Britain, 1963)*** Elizabeth Taylor, Richard Burton, Louis Jourdan, Margaret Rutherford, Orson Welles. A sort of *Grand Hotel* located at a London airport, as passengers waiting for a delayed flight intercross each other's lives. An Oscar-winning performance by Rutherford. (Dir: Anthony Asquith, 119 mins.)

Virgin Among the Living Dead—See: Among the Living Dead

Virgin and the Gypsy, The (Great Britain, 1970)*** Franco Nero, Joanna Shimkus, Honor Blackman. Shimkus swelters under the Victorian burden of her clerical dad, while the libidinous gypsy clues her in. Well handled by director Christopher Miles. From the D. H. Lawrence novella. (92 mins.)

Virgin High (1990)* Burt Ward, Linnea Quigley, Traci Dali, Richard Gabai, Kent Burden. Tiresome teen sex comedy set in a Catholic girls school that never quite gets into high gear. The boys are naughty and the girls giggle a lot. Ward, television's Robin (of "Batman") is now playing dad roles. (Dir: Richard Gabai, 89 mins.)†

Virginia (1941)** Madeleine Carroll, Fred MacMurray, Helen Broderick, Sterling Hayden, Marie Wilson. A magnolia-drenched heroine is forced to give up her plantation in order to make ends meet. (Dir: Edward H. Griffith, 110 mins.)

Virginia City (1940)*** Errol Flynn, Miriam Hopkins, Randolph Scott, Humphrey Bogart. Just from the cast you know this is a virile, action-packed western. Loaded with clichés and contrivances, it still comes out entertainment. (Dir: Michael Curtiz, 121 mins.)†

Virginia Hill Story, The (MTV 1974)** Dyan Cannon, Harvey Keitel, Allen Garfield, Robby Benson. Cannon stars in this true-life tale about a poor Southern girl who hits the big time as the girlfriend of Bugsy Siegel, who was murdered in Beverly Hills in 1947. (Dir: Joel Schumacher, 72 mins.)

Virginian, The (1929)*** Gary Cooper, Richard Arlen, Walter Huston, Mary Brian. Sterling film version of Owen Wister's Western classic. Cooper is perfectly cast as the laconic noble cowboy; Arlen is his pal who runs afoul of the law, and Brian is the sweet girl who loves him. But best of all is Huston as the varmint of a villain, complete with black mustache. (Dir: Victor Fleming, 90 mins.)†

Virginian, The (1946)*** Joel McCrea, Brian Donlevy, Sonny Tufts, Barbara Britton, Fay Bainter. Not exactly powerful, but fairly interesting western about the age-old struggle between ranchers and rustlers. (Dir: Stuart Gilmore, 87 mins.)

Virgin Island (Great Britain, 1958)** John Cassavetes, Virginia Maskell, Sidney Poitier, Ruby Dee. Young writer and his bride buy an island in the Caribbean, live there with the help of a local fisherman. Romantic comedy. (Dir: Pat Jackson, 94 mins.)

Virgin Machine (West Germany, 1988)*** Ina Blum, Dominique Caspar, Susie Bright. German journalist, bored with her life, comes to San Francisco to do research and discovers the lesbian scene. Lighthearted exploration of alternate lifestyles should appeal to all adult audiences. Bright is hilarious as "Susie Sexpert." (Dir: Monika Treut, 85 mins.)

Virgin President, The (1968)**½ Severn Darden, Andrew Duncan, Richard Schaal,

Paul Benedict, Sudie Bond, Peter Boyle. Clever, lighthearted satire about a young U.S. president named Fillard Millmore. Spoof aims high, and sometimes hits the bull's-eye, but much of the improvised dialogue falls wide of the mark. (Dir: Graeme Ferguson, 72 mins.)

Virgin Queen, The (1955)*** Bette Davis, Richard Todd, Joan Collins, Herbert Marshall, Dan O'Herlihy. Davis fans will not want to miss their favorite in the flashy role of the aging Queen Elizabeth sparring with Sir Walter Raleigh. Davis gives a flamboyant performance as the British Queen and the supporting cast is more than competent. (Dir: Henry Koster, 92 mins.)†

Virgin Queen of St. Francis High, The (Canada, 1987)* Joseph R. Straface, Stacey Christensen, J. T. Wotton. Mild teen fare about an innocent girl and a boy who bets a loudmouthed friend that he can bed her. Tries to be uplifting rather than sleazy, but it's as dull as a Sunday school lesson. (Dir: Francesco Lucente, 89 mins.)†

Virgin Soldiers, The (Great Britain, 1969)*** Hywel Bennett, Nigel Patrick, Lynn Redgrave, Rachel Kempson, Tsai Chin, Jack Shepherd. Competently acted, sharply observant film about raw English recruits stationed in Singapore and their adventures in the field of battle and in the boudoir. David Bowie has a bit part. (Dir: John Dexter, 96 mins.)†

Virgin Spring, The (Sweden, 1960)**** Max von Sydow, Brigitta Valberg, Gunnel Lindblom, Brigitta Pettersson. Ingmar Bergman's quietly chilling morality play, set in the Swedish countryside of the 14th century, about pagan lusts, Christian renewal. Based on a Swedish legend, a young virgin girl is brutally despoiled and murdered after her sister invokes a pagan curse. Bergman has captured the quality of ancient legends: their primitive passions; human sorrows; abrupt beauty, for one of his most powerful films. Oscar: Best Foreign Film. (88 mins.)†

Virgin Witch (Great Britain, 1970)** Anne Michelle, Vicky Michelle, Keith Buckley, Patricia Haines. Twin sisters come to London looking for work as models, but make the mistake of signing up with an agency headed by a lesbian Satan-worshipper. Heavy-breathing horror. (Dir: Ray Austin, 89 mins.)†

Viridiana (Mexico-Spain, 1962)**** Silvia Pinal, Francisco Rabal, Fernando Rey. A chaste, charitable girl, Viridiana (Pinal) is about to become a nun. She visits her lovable uncle, who dresses her up in his dead wife's wedding gown, drugs her, and failing to rape her, hangs himself with a child's jump rope. And that's just the first reel of this masterful work directed by Luis Buñuel. (90 mins.)†

Virtue's Revolt (1925)½ Edith Thornton, Crauford Kent, Charles Cruz, Niles Welch. Entertainingly awful silent melodrama about a girl from the sticks who comes to New York, hoping to make it on Broadway. She gets an offer from a producer, provided she makes a pit stop at his (gasp!) casting couch. (Dir: James Chapin, 52 mins.)†

Virtuous Sin, The (1930)**½ Kay Francis, Walter Huston, Kenneth MacKenna. Strange, melodramatic romance, set during WWI just before the Russian Revolution, has the devoted wife of a cowardly officer having an affair with his commanding officer to try and influence him in favor of her husband. Plot makes little sense, but Francis and Huston are oddly compelling. (Dirs: George Cukor, Louis Gasnier, 80 mins.)

Virus (Japan, 1980)*½ Glenn Ford, Olivia Hussey, Robert Vaughn, Sonny Chiba. Curiously nihilistic Japanese disaster film that shows a bacterium's catastrophic effect on the earth's populace, and the efforts of 858 survivors in Antarctica to rebuild civilization. Marred by grainy photography and incomprehensible editing (from an original 2½ hours). (Dir: Kinji Fukasaku, 106 mins.)†

Virus Knows No Morals, A (West Germany, 1986)*** Rosa von Praunheim, Christian Kesten, Eva Kurz, Dieter Dicken. Funny, campy satire of society's attitudes toward homosexuals and AIDS starring producer-writer-director von Praunheim (actually a chap named Holger Mischwitzki) as a gay bathhouse owner who finds AIDS an annoyance and a drag on business. (82 mins.)

Viscount, The (France-Italy-Spain, 1967)*½ Kerwin Mathews, Edmond O'Brien, Jane Fleming, Fernando Rey, Jean Yanne. Spy thriller has cult status in Europe due to eclectic cast and odd hero (an insurance investigator); maybe it just didn't translate well. (Dir: Maurice Cloche, 98 mins.)

Vision Quest (1985)*** Matthew Modine, Ronny Cox, Linda Fiorentino. Teen (Modine) loses his virginity and enters the world of manhood via the wrestling mat. The sensitive-young-man clichés abound. (Dir: Harold Becker, 102 mins.)†

Visions (MTV 1972)** Monte Markham, Telly Savalas, Barbara Anderson. Clairvoyant professor warns police about impending bombing in Denver. When a building is dynamited, police first suspect the professor. (Dir: Lee Katzin, 73 mins.)

Vision Shared, A: A Tribute to Woody Guthrie and Leadbelly (1988)***½ Pete Seeger, Arlo Guthrie, Bruce Springsteen, Willie

Nelson, Bob Dylan, Emmylou Harris, Little Richard, John Cougar Mellencamp. Sweet Honey in the Rock, Taj Mahal, U2. Narrated by Robbie Robertson. Powerful documentary pays tribute to Guthrie and Leadbelly, two of the U.S.'s greatest folk music geniuses, interweaving stories of their lives with performances of their songs by themselves and by an impressive roster of musicians. (Dir: Jim Brown, 72 mins.)†

Visions of Eight (1973)***½ A documentary about the 1972 Olympics in Munich lets each of eight of the best directors in the world film his or her vision of one event. (Dirs: Arthur Penn, Kon Ichikawa, Claude Lelouch, John Schlesinger, Miloš Forman, Judi Ozerov, Michael Pfleghar, Mai Zetterling, 110 mins.)

Visit, The (U.S.-West Germany-France-Italy, 1964)** Anthony Quinn, Ingrid Bergman, Irina Demick, Eduardo Ciannelli, Valentina Cortese. It took the efforts of four countries to dilute the fascinating play by Swiss playwright Friedrich Durrenmatt. Bergman is miscast as a strong-willed woman who goes to great lengths to wreak vengeance on her former lover. (Dir: Bernhard Wicki, 100 mins.)

Visiting Hours (Canada 1982)½ Lee Grant, Michael Ironside, Linda Purl, William Shatner. In addition to the usual gore, this film touches on women's rights and violence in an exploitative manner. The misogynist villain gets his kicks stalking a crusader for women's rights at home and in the hospital, after he has already attacked her once. (Dir: Jean Claude Lord, 106 mins.)†

Visitor, The (1980)* Mel Ferrer, Glenn Ford, Lance Henriksen, John Huston, Sam Peckinpah, Shelley Winters, Paige Conner. Ferrer and his extraterrestrial progeny (Conner) run amok in this wretched rip-off of *The Exorcist, The Omen,* and just about every other horror hit of the '70s. The director's showy camerawork and a cast of (pandering) old pros fill in the gaps. (Dir: Michael J. Paradise, 90 mins.)†

Visitors, The (1972)*** Patrick McVey, James Woods, Patricia Joyce. Low-budget (less than $200,000) psychological thriller, often quite moving. Two ex-cons "visit" the home of a prosecution witness who helped send them up. Director Elia Kazan, as always, has a remarkable flair for dealing with actors. (88 mins.)

Visit to a Chief's Son (1974)*** Richard Mulligan, Johnny Sekka, Jesse Kinaru, Steve Railsback. Pleasant adventure of a father and son, at odds with each other, who renew ties during a journey into the African plains. Gorgeous scenery and strong acting enhance the drama. (Dir: Lamont Johnson, 93 mins.)

Visit to a Small Planet (1960)** Jerry Lewis, Joan Blackman, Fred Clark, John Williams, Earl Holliman. Impish creature from outer space lands on earth to study the ways of us earthlings. Jerry as a spaceman might bring some laughs, but the satiric point of the original Broadway play by Gore Vidal is blunted with slapstick. (Dir: Norman Taurog, 85 mins.)

Vital Signs (MTV 1986)** Edward Asner, Gary Cole, Kate McNeil, Barbara Barrie. Asner is the respected doctor with a drinking problem, and Cole is his son (also an M.D.), who is battling a drug habit. Done in by fraying plot mechanics and under-written characters. (Dir: Stuart Millar, 104 mins.)

Vital Signs (1990)** Adrian Pasdar, Diane Lane, Jimmy Smits, Jane Adams, Tim Ransom, Laura San Giacomo, Norma Aleandro, William Devane. Updated version of one of those innocuous medical-themed melodramas of the '50s. Five concerned, romantically troubled med students compete for a coveted internship, though it's clear from the start that it'll come down to a surgical showdown between the hunky hero and his resentful rival. Some unintentionally hilarious moments as the clichés are trotted out. (Dir: Marisa Silver, 103 mins.)†

Vivacious Lady (1938)*** Ginger Rogers, James Stewart, James Ellison, Beulah Bondi, Charles Coburn. Delectable comedy directed by George Stevens in a deliberate, measured style that elicits much charm. Professor Stewart goes to Manhattan to rescue his prodigal brother from a chorine. Of course, he stays out all night and marries the self-same chorine the next morning. (90 mins.)†

Viva Italia! (Italy, 1979)*** Vittorio Gassman, Ugo Tognazzi, Alberto Sordi, Ornella Muti. Sketchy film, necessarily uneven, directed in corporate-collective style by Ettore Scola, Mario Monicelli, and Dino Risi. (111 mins.)

Viva Knievel (1977)** Evel Knievel, Gene Kelly, Marjoe Gortner, Lauren Hutton, Red Buttons. The irrepressible Knievel battles drug smugglers and syndicate hit men while trying to sober up his mechanic (Kelly). (Dir: Gordon Douglas, 104 mins.)†

Viva La Muerte (France-Tunisia, 1971)*** Nuria Espert, Anouk Ferjac, Mahdi Chaouch, Ivan Henriques. Strange cult classic about a young boy's search for his missing father. Directed by avant-garde writer Fernando Arrabal, this mesmerizing, uncomfortable film is filled with images of animal cruelty, sadomasochism, and self-cannibalism, presenting a powerful vision of hopelessness and attacking the grotesque brutality of oppression. (90 mins.)

Viva La Republica (Cuba, 1973)*** Cynical documentary blends old still photos and archival footage to tell the history of Cuba's so-called "Republic" period, the U.S.-dominated era of the early twentieth century. Socialist-sponsored film whose strident anti-Americanism lessens the impact of its presentation of the true reasons behind Cuba's bitterness towards the U.S. (Dir: Pastor Vega, 92 mins.)

Viva Las Vegas (1964)*** Elvis Presley, Ann-Margret, Cesare Danova. This quintessential Presley vehicle benefits from the inspired pairing of the King and Ann-Margret. To pay for the motor he needs to race in the "Las Vegas Grand Prix" against Danova, Elvis has to win a hotel employees' talent contest against A-M. Glossy, colorful entertainment. (Dir: George Sidney, 85 mins.)†

Viva Maria! (France-Italy, 1965)**½ Jeanne Moreau, Brigitte Bardot, George Hamilton. The place is Central America and the two gals, both named Maria, are dancers who become involved with the cause of the local revolutionaries when they fall for the charms of the leading revolutionary (Hamilton). Most of the comedy is tongue-in-cheek, and some of it works. (Dir: Louis Malle, 119 mins.)

Viva Max! (1969)**½ Peter Ustinov, Jonathan Winters, Pamela Tiffin, Keenan Wynn. A funny premise never quite takes hold. In any case, there are plenty of laughs as Ustinov, playing a modern-day Mexican general with a thick accent, leads a scraggly group of men over the border and into the Alamo, reclaiming the tourist attraction for his homeland. (Dir: Jerry Paris, 92 mins.)†

Viva Villa (1934)***½ Wallace Beery, Stuart Erwin, Fay Wray, Leo Carrillo, Joseph Schildkraut, Katherine De Mille. Excellent historical drama of the Mexican bandit-revolutionary. Fast moving screenplay with colorful dialogue, lots of action, and a point; it tries to understand something of the process of revolution, which degenerates so easily into mere power politics. Beery gives one of his best performances as the endearing, ruthless and ultimately uncomprehending Villa. (Dirs: Jack Conway, Howard Hawks, 115 mins.)

Viva Zapata! (1952)***½ Marlon Brando, Jean Peters, Joseph Wiseman, Anthony Quinn. Follows the rise of Mexican revolutionary Emiliano Zapata from peon to the presidency. Brando is magnificent as Zapata, and Quinn won a Best Supporting Actor Oscar for a superb depiction of Zapata's brother. John Steinbeck wrote the screenplay. (Dir: Elia Kazan, 113 mins.)†

Vivre Sa Vie—See: **My Life to Live**

Vixen (1968)*** Erica Gavin, Harrison Page, Garth Pillsbury, Michael O'Donnell, Vincent Wallace. One of the high points in the career of Russ Meyer—a film that combines humor and eroticism in a very original way. Gavin gives a mesmerizing, high-camp performance as "Vixen," the buxom wife of a bush pilot who seduces everyone in sight, including a stud fisherman, his dissatisfied wife, and even her own brother. (Dir: Russ Meyer, 71 mins.)†

Vladmir Horowitz, The Last Romantic (1985)*** Classical music fans will be in seventh heaven watching this perceptive portrait of the master pianist; numerous selections are played, and the artist's lighter side is shown through interviews and practice sessions. (Dir: David and Albert Maysles, 90 mins.)†

Vogues of 1938 (1937)*** Warner Baxter, Joan Bennett, Mischa Auer, Alan Mowbray, Helen Vinson, Jerome Cowan, Hedda Hopper. Enjoyable musical-comedy with the always wonderful Bennett as a wealthy lass who wants to become a fashion model, to the annoyance of fiancé Baxter. Typical '30s time-waster, no surprises but as cosmopolitan, witty, and tuneful now as it was then. (Dir: Irving Cummings, 108 mins.)†

Voice in the Mirror (1958)*** Richard Egan, Julie London, Arthur O'Connell, Walter Matthau, Troy Donahue. With a little more work on the script, this drama about alcoholism and the long road back could have been a very good film. As it is, it's worth your attention. (Dir: Harry Keller, 102 mins.)

Voice in the Wind (1943)*** Francis Lederer, Sigrid Gurie. Tragic drama of a mentally shattered refugee pianist who finds his lost love on a tropical isle. Strange, moody, well acted. (Dir: Arthur Ripley, 85 mins.)

Voice of Bugle Ann, The (1936)*** Lionel Barrymore, Maureen O'Sullivan, Spring Byington, Dudley Digges, Charles Grapewin, Eric Linden. Wonderfully acted, moving story about the owner of a murdered dog getting revenge on the killer. Little gem of a movie is a terrific example of '30s melodrama. Only the coldest of heart won't be touched by this well-written tale. (Dir: Richard Thorpe, 70 mins.)

Voice of Terror: The Achille Lauro Affair (MTV 1990)*** Burt Lancaster, Eva Marie Saint, Robert Culp, Renzo Montagnani, Joseph Nasser, Dominique Sanda, Rebecca Schaeffer. Story of the American cruise ship hijacked by terrorists in the Mediterranean is a cut above the other TV version of the story, *The Hijacking of the Achille Lauro*, thanks to a more in-depth script and equally fine performances. (Dir: Alberto Negrin, 192 mins.)

Voice of the Heart (MTV 1990)** Lindsay Wagner, James Brolin, Victoria Tennant, Honor Blackman, Richard Johnson, Pip Torrens, Leigh Lawson. Romantic nonsense, based on a Barbara Taylor Bradford story, centers around the manipulations and seductions going on behind the scenes of a film. (Dir: Tony Whamby, 192 mins.)

Voice of the Turtle (1947)*** Ronald Reagan, Eleanor Parker, Eve Arden, Wayne Morris. Broadway play about a weekend romance in a New York apartment between a budding actress and a soldier on leave is amusing and well played by the cast. (Dir: Irving Rapper, 103 mins.)

Voice of the Water, The (Netherlands, 1966)*** Acclaimed documentary about the relationship of the Dutch people to the seas that provide their lifeblood and endanger their very existence. Charming. (Dir: Bert Haanstra, 82 mins.)

Voice of the Whistler (1945)** Richard Dix, Lynn Merrick. Twists and turns galore, but no real thrills in this ironic tale of a terminally ill tycoon who persuades his already engaged nurse to marry him. (Dir: William Castle, 60 mins.)

Voices (1979)**½ Amy Irving, Michael Ontkean, Viveca Lindfors, Herbert Berghof. Sentimental love story in which Ontkean can't break away from the family business, though he wants to be a singer. Irving yearns to be a dancer, but she's deaf. (Dir: Robert Markowitz, 107 mins.)

Voices of Sarafina (1988)***½ Miriam Makeba, Mbongeni Ngema. Energetic documentary about the Broadway production of the musical drama, *Sarafina*, which tells the story of the children involved in the Soweto uprising of 1976, set to the exciting street music, Mbaqanga (co-written by Ngema and Hugh Masekela), of the black townships. (Dir: Nigel Nobel, 85 mins.)

Voices Within: The Lives of Truddi Chase (MTV 1990)*** Shelley Long, Tom Conti, John Rubinstein, Alan Fudge, Jamie Rose, Christine Healy. Sometimes powerful drama about a woman who submerges the horrific abuse she experienced as a child by adopting multiple personalities in order to cope as an adult. Long pulls out all stops as a woman obsessed with seeking revenge against her stepfather, who sexually abused her during childhood. (Dir: Lamont Johnson, 192 mins.)

Volcano (Italy, 1953)**½ Anna Magnani, Rossano Brazzi, Eduardo Ciannelli, Geraldine Brooks. Melodramatic adventure of sisters involved with an unscrupulous deep sea diver. (Dir: William Dieterle, 106 mins.)

Volcano (1969)—See: **Krakatoa, East of Java**

Volpone (France, 1940)*** Harry Baur, Louis Jouvet, Fernand Ledoux, Marion Dorian. Lavish version of Ben Jonson's comedy about a wealthy Venetian who pretends to be dying in order to watch his friends position themselves to inherit his vast wealth. Well played, especially by Baur and Jouvet, with magnificently dreamy sets and superb camerawork. (Dir: Maurice Tourneur, 98 mins.)†

Voltaire (1933)*** George Arliss, Doris Kenyon, Margaret Lindsay, Theodore Newton, Reginald Owen, Alan Mowbray. One of Arliss's best vehicles, adapted from a popular fictionalized biography of the great French philosopher. The fast-paced plot involves the famous writer in rather more derring-do than is strictly factual, but Arliss is in his element, adeptly spinning sly epigrams suitable for every occasion. (Dir: John G. Adolphi, 72 mins.)

Volunteers (1985)**½ Tom Hanks, John Candy, Rita Wilson, Tim Thomerson, Gedde Watanabe, George Plimpton. Outlandish but moderately amusing comedy about a sarcastic playboy who finds himself drafted into the Peace Corps, and consigned into building a bridge in an isolated Thailand community. (Dir: Nicholas Meyer, 106 mins.)†

Von Richthofen and Brown (1971)***½ John Phillip Law, Don Stroud, Hurd Hatfield, Corin Redgrave. The serial dogfights of WWI are poignantly counterpointed with some good dialogue about the changing nature of war; the aristocrat von Richthofen is contrasted with the modern man, the reluctant Brown. (Dir: Roger Corman, 96 mins.)

Von Ryan's Express (1965)*** Frank Sinatra, Trevor Howard. Exciting WWII adventure yarn with Frank Sinatra giving a fine performance as an American Army colonel who goes from heel to hero. Trevor Howard is also excellent as the British officer who is the prisoners' unofficial leader until Ryan takes over. The last quarter of the film follows the escaping prisoners as they commandeer a German train, and you can't ask for a more exciting sequence. (Dir: Mark Robson, 117 mins.)†

Voodoo Blood Bath—See: **Zombies**

Voodoo Dawn (1990)** Raymond St. Jacques, Theresa Merritt, Gina Gershon, Kirk Baily, Billy (Sly) Williams. A college chap out to write a thesis about a southern plantation is zapped by a witch doctor. Passable supernatural thriller for the undiscriminating. (Dir: Steven Fierberg, 83 mins.)†

Voodoo Island (1957)** Boris Karloff, Beverly Tyler, Murvyn Vye. Horror fans will be a bit disappointed by this slow moving tale of witchcraft and monsters. (Dir: Reginald Le Borg, 76 mins.)

Voodoo Man (1944)* Bela Lugosi, John Carradine, George Zucco, Michael Ames. Bela kidnaps unsuspecting young femmes and tries transferring their minds into the zombielike body of his wife. (Dir: William Beaudine, 62 mins.)

Voodoo Tiger (1952)**½ Johnny Weissmuller, Jean Byron. Jungle Jim knocks the heck out of Nazis and headhunters as he gets involved in a search for art-thieving Hitlerians. (Dir: Spencer Bennet, 67 mins.)

Voodoo Woman (1957)*½ Marla English, Tom Conway, Michael Connors, Lance Fuller. A doctor seeks gorgeous women for zombiedom and the possible start of a sexy super race. (Dir: Edward L. Cahn, 77 mins.)

Vortex (1982)** Lydia Lunch, James Russo, Bill Rice. Standard New York underground fare with extremely stylized sets, botched lines, moody cinematography, and eerie synthesized music. A trashy private eye, Lydia Lunch, is on the trail of a fascistic nuclear weapons manufacturer (Bill Rice). (Dirs: Scott and Beth B, 90 mins.)

Voyage, The (Italy, 1973)*** Sophia Loren, Richard Burton, Barbara Pilavin, Ian Bannen. Beautifully photographed drama about lovers Loren and Burton who are barred from marrying and seem to be living under a curse as tragedy stalks their lives. Strong cast delivers solid performances, although the melodramatics get heavy at times. Based on a short story by Luigi Pirandello. (Dir: Vittorio De Sica, 95 mins.)

Voyage en Douce (France, 1979)*** Dominique Sanda, Geraldine Chaplin. Compelling drama stars Chaplin and Sanda as two dissatisfied women who share a Provençal country house, telling stories about their relationships with men and weaving erotic fantasies. Superbly acted film creating a powerful aura of friendship and sensuality. (Dir: Michel Deville, 97 mins.)

Voyage of the Damned (Great Britain-Spain, 1976)**½ Faye Dunaway, Orson Welles, Oskar Werner, James Mason, Max von Sydow, Lee Grant. Fairly engrossing WWII shipboard drama. Jewish refugees are adrift on an ocean liner, and no country is willing to take them in. Some of the stars aboard (Dunaway, Werner) are memorable, even if this vehicle threatens to sink under the weight of heavy overacting (particularly from Grant). (Dir: Stuart Rosenberg, 134 mins.)†

Voyage of the Rock Aliens (1985)* Pia Zadora, Tom Nolan, Craig Sheffer, and Ruth Gordon as the sheriff. (You know we're in trouble already, don't you?)

Besides the slick (and superfluous) opening rock video starring Pia and Jermaine Jackson, the only notable thing about this sci-fi musical comedy is the starring turn from the diva of camp, Ms. Zadora. The antics of the title characters, a group of nerdish alien musicians, are on a par with the "New Monkees." (Dir: James Fargo, 97 mins.)†

Voyage of the Viking Women to the Waters of the Great Sea Serpent, The—See: **Viking Women and the Sea Serpent**

Voyage of the Yes, The (MTV 1972)** Desi Arnaz, Jr., Mike Evans, Beverly Garland, Skip Homeier, Della Reese. Another opus about whites learning to live with blacks. A rich California youngster sails off to Hawaii with an inexperienced Chicago black on the lam. (Dir: Lee Katzin, 73 mins.)

Voyage Round My Father, A (Great Britain MTV 1982)**** Laurence Olivier, Alan Bates, Elizabeth Sellars, Jane Asher. A television film of unusual beauty and merit, splendidly adapted by John Mortimer from his long-running stage play. His semi-autobiographical remembrance of the stormy yet always loving relationship between him and his father, an opinionated, eccentric barrister, contains humor, drama, and unerring emotional resonance. (Dir: Alvin Rakoff, 90 mins.)†

Voyage Surprise (France, 1946)***½ Sinoel, Martine Carol, Maurice Baquet, Jacques Henri Duval. Delightful comedy, directed by co-star Prevert (and co-written by him with his brother Jacques), about an old man living his dream to organize a grand mystery tour. He gathers his eccentric family and friends for an adventure that ends in a comic explosion of plotting villains, mad anarchists, and goofy cops. (85 mins.)

Voyage to the Bottom of the Sea (1961)**½ Walter Pidgeon, Joan Fontaine, Barbara Eden, Frankie Avalon, Peter Lorre. Submarine speeds to explode a radiation belt threatening earth, is hampered by dirty work aboard. Sci-fi melodrama on the juvenile side, enhanced by superb trick photography and special effects. Inspired a TV series of the same name. (Dir: Irwin Allen, 105 mins.)†

Voyage to the End of the Universe (Czechoslovakia, 1963)*** Dennis Stephans, Francis Smolen, Dana Meredith, Otto Lack. Intellectual sci-fi film about the crew of a 25th-century space probe under attack by enigmatic radioactive forces emanating from a black star in the solar system. More talk than action, but still interesting. (Dir: "Jack Pollack" [Jindrich Polak], 81 mins.)

Voyage to the Planet of Prehistoric Women (1968)½ Mamie Van Doren, Mary Marr,

Paige Lee, Aldo Roman. A misbegotten film using footage from a Russian sci-fi flick. The new and old footage knock against each other in this cloddish thriller about U.S. space heroes putting a Venusian monster out of commission. Peter Bogdanovich was reputedly the director; maybe he should have put Mamie Van Doren in his film version of *Daisy Miller*. (Dir: Derek Thomas, 80 mins.)

Voyage to the Prehistoric Planet (1965)½ Basil Rathbone, Faith Domergue, Marc Shannon. Roger Corman returned to the same Soviet film he cannibalized for *Voyage to the Planet of Prehistoric Women* to get footage for this sci-fi cheapie. This time Curtis Harrington (pseudonymously credited as "John Sebastian," no relation to the singer) did the cut-and-paste job, with Rathbone looking tired as the ground-based scientist advising the astronauts. What plot remains is strictly by default. (92 mins.)†

Vulture, The (U.S.-Great Britain-Canada, 1967)** Robert Hutton, Akim Tamiroff, Broderick Crawford. Atomic scientist uses nuclear energy to reincarnate rampaging composite of a sea captain and gigantic, vulturous bird, both buried alive a century earlier. (Dir: Lawrence Huntington, 91 mins.)†

Vulture, The (Israel, 1981)*** Shraga Harpaz, Shimon Finkel, Ilana Morgan. Sharp satire about an Israeli veteran who decides to get rich and earn fame and respect in the "hero business." Director Yaky Yosha's comedy is comparable to the topical, adult humor of Blake Edwards and Billy Wilder. (93 mins.)

Vultures (1984)* Yvonne De Carlo, Stuart Whitman, Meredith MacRae, Aldo Ray. This carcass of a mystery plot is propped on its death-bed pillows as a dying man's relatives can't wait for him to kick the bucket. (Dir: Paul Leder, 101 mins.)†

W (1974)* Twiggy, Dirk Benedict, Michael Witney. Deadly dull thriller in which Twiggy and her new hubby are threatened by her crazy former husband. AKA: I Want Her Dead (Dir: Richard Quine, 109 mins.)†

Wabash Avenue (1950)*** Betty Grable, Victor Mature, Phil Harris. Typical Betty Grable musical set at the turn of the century. She sings, dances, throws vases at Mature, sings some more, dances some more, and ends up in Mature's arms. Remake of *Coney Island*. (Dir: Henry Koster, 92 mins.)

WAC from Walla Walla, The (1952)*½ Judy Canova, Stephen Dunne, Irene Ryan, Allen Jenkins. Slight comedy of a small-town girl turned WAC who captures foreign agents attempting to steal missile secrets. (Dir: William Witney, 83 mins.)

Wackiest Ship in the Army, The (1960)*** Jack Lemmon, Ricky Nelson, Chips Rafferty, John Lund. Slightly different mixture of war heroics and comedy blended into an entertaining film about a sailing expert who's tricked into commanding an aged hulk disguised as a sailing vessel which will secretly land a scout in enemy territory. (Dir: Richard Murphy, 99 mins.)†

Wacky World of Wills and Burke, The (Australia, 1985)** Garry McDonald, Kim Gyngell, Jonathan Hardy, Nicole Kidman. Monty Python-ish parody of the story of the failed 1860 expedition (more reverently depicted the same year in *Burke and Wills*). Some laughs, though the story needed to be firmer and blacker—a lighthearted goof on such a tragic story seems merely petty. (Dir: Bob Weis, 97 mins.)†

Waco (1966)* Howard Keel, Jane Russell, Brian Donlevy. Routine western with Keel in the title role of a gunfighter who cleans up a small town steeped in corruption. (Dir: R. G. Springsteen, 85 mins.)

Waco and Rinehart (MTV 1987)*½ Charles C. Hill, Justin Deas, William Hootkins, Bob Tzudiker. Two U.S. marshals go looking for the killer of a colleague. Dismal action fare. (Dir: Christian I. Nyby II, 104 mins.)

Wages of Fear, The (France, 1955)**** Yves Montand, Peter Van Eyck, Vera Clouzot. This existentialist melodrama about four men trucking nitro across the Andes is compelling and exciting as it delivers nail-biting suspense. Remade as *Sorceror*. (Dir: Henri-Georges Clouzot, 105 mins.)†

Wagner (Great Britain, MTV 1985)*½ Richard Burton, John Gielgud, Ralph Richardson, Laurence Olivier. Originally nine hours, coherence apparently ended up on the cutting room floor; this international production is a lavishly produced compendium of great moments from Wagner's life, smothered with generous outpourings of his music. Everyone acts as if dazed by the importance of the task at hand, except for Burton, who looks like a ravaged specter, a ghost of a once-great actor. (Dir: Tony Palmer, 208 mins.)†

Wagonmaster (1950)***½ Ben Johnson, Harry Carey, Jr., Joanne Dru, Ward Bond. Eloquent western, directed by John Ford, that eschews pomposity, self-consciousness, and even movie stars. Two drifters (Johnson and Carey) sign on to guide a Mormon wagon train (led by Bond) to the Utah frontier. (86 mins.)†

Wagons Roll at Night, The (1941)**½ Eddie

Albert, Joan Leslie, Anthony Quinn, Humphrey Bogart, Sylvia Sidney. Carnival comedy gets a big assist from Albert as a fledgling lion tamer but help from other sources, mainly the script, never arrives. (Dir: Ray Enright, 84 mins.)

Walkiki (MTV 1980)** Dack Rambo, Steve Marachuck, Donna Mills, Darren McGavin. Two young detectives take on a complicated case, the "cane-field murders." (Dir: Ron Satloff, 104 mins.)†

Walkiki Wedding (1937)*** Bing Crosby, Shirley Ross, Martha Raye. Pleasant musical about a pineapple queen's experiences in Hawaii. As Bing is the press agent for the pineapples, we get a nice mixture of romance and comedy. (Dir: Frank Tuttle, 88 mins.)

Wait for the Dawn (1960)**½ Leo Genn. One of director Roberto Rosellini's lesser efforts but worth watching. Genn plays an Englishman who keeps one step ahead of the Nazis in war-torn Italy. (82 mins.)

Waiting for the Light (1990)***½ Shirley MacLaine, Teri Garr, Hillary Wolf, Colin Baumgartner, Clancy Brown, Vincent Schiavelli, Jeff McCracken. Set against the backdrop of the Cuban missile crisis of 1962, this delightful comedy features a star turn by MacLaine as an eccentric ex-vaudeville magician who helps her niece (Garr in a lovely performance) start a new life when they reopen a run-down diner. Complications arise! (Dir: Christopher Monger, 94 mins.)

Waiting for the Moon (1987)**½ Linda Hunt, Linda Bassett, Bernadette Lafont, Bruce McGill, Andrew McCarthy. A convincing but slow-moving re-creation of the lives of Alice B. Toklas and Gertrude Stein. Hunt makes a striking Toklas. (Dir: Jill Godmilow, 88 mins.)†

Wait Till Your Mother Gets Home (MTV 1983)**½ Dee Wallace, Paul Michael Glaser. A true story about a high school coach taking over the household while his wife (Wallace) enters the work force. (Dir: Bill Persky, 104 mins.)†

Wait 'Til the Sun Shines, Nellie (1952)***½ David Wayne, Jean Peters. Fine piece of Americana. Tender story of a small-town barber, his hopes and disappointments through the early part of the 20th century. Wayne is superb, as is the rest of the cast. Catch this much underrated film. (Dir: Henry King, 108 mins.)

Wait Until Dark (1967)*** Audrey Hepburn, Alan Arkin, Jack Weston, Richard Crenna, Efrem Zimbalist, Jr. Tense suspense involving a blind woman (Hepburn) who has inadvertently obtained an antique doll full of heroin which Arkin must retrieve. The film is based on Frederick Knott's stage play, and one hardly notices that the action rarely moves from the interior of the house—especially when

the lights go out and the pursuer becomes the blind. Arkin is genuinely frightening in his evilness and charm. (Dir: Terence Young, 108 mins.)†

Wake Island (1942)*** Brian Donlevy, William Bendix, Robert Preston, Macdonald Carey. Dramatic saga of the glorious but bitter defeat suffered by the Marines at Wake Island early in the war. (Dir: John Farrow, 78 mins.)†

Wake Me When It's Over (1960)** Dick Shawn, Ernie Kovacs, Jack Warden, Don Knotts. Mildly amusing service comedy with Shawn working hard as a WWII vet who gets drafted all over again due to an error. (Dir: Mervyn LeRoy, 126 mins.)

Wake Me When the War Is Over (MTV 1969)*½ Ken Berry, Eva Gabor, Werner Klemperer. Inept, silly comedy about an American lieutenant who is kept prisoner in a lush mansion during WWII, not by the enemy but by Baroness Eva Gabor. (Dir: Gene Nelson, 73 mins.)

Wake of the Red Witch (1948)**½ John Wayne, Gail Russell, Luther Adler, Gig Young, Henry Daniell, Adele Mara. A few good action scenes in this confused sea story about a rivalry between a ship's owner and its captain over pearls and a gal. (Dir: Edward Ludwig, 106 mins.)†

Wake Up and Dream (1946)** John Payne, June Haver, Charlotte Greenwood. Story of a strange voyage in search of a missing sailor fails long before the fadeout. Confusing adaptation of a Robert Nathan novel. (Dir: Lloyd Bacon, 92 mins.)

Wake Up and Live (1937)**½ Walter Winchell, Ben Bernie, Alice Faye. This film was made to exploit the feud between Winchell and Bernie, but even now it's an OK musical film, with Jack Haley stealing the show as a crooner with mike fright. (Dir: Sidney Lanfield, 100 mins.)

Walkabout (Australia, 1971)***½ Jenny Agutter, Lucien John, David Gumpilil. Stimulating adventure with disturbing social overtones. Two white Australian children are stranded in the Outback, and must negotiate their way across the desert. They adapt to the harsh conditions with the help of an aborigine familiar with the terrain. Directed and photographed on location in Australia by Nicolas Roeg. (95 mins.)

Walk a Crooked Mile (1948)** Louis Hayward, Dennis O'Keefe, Louise Albritton, Carl Esmond, Onslow Stevens, Raymond Burr. Procedural police drama has a joint operation by the FBI and Scotland Yard to capture spies seeking atomic secrets; tense atmosphere hampered by a mundane script. (Dir: Gordon Douglas, 91 mins.)

Walk, Don't Run (1966)**½ Cary Grant, Samantha Eggar, Jim Hutton. Pedestrian remake of *The More the Merrier*. The housing situation is crowded during the 1964 Tokyo Olympics, and Grant plays the kindly older man who gets the youngsters (Hutton and Eggar) together. (Dir: Charles Walters, 114 mins.)†

Walk East on Beacon (1952)*** George Murphy, Virginia Gilmore. FBI cracks a Red spy ring. Documentary-style; earnest, but rather commonplace. (Dir: Alfred L. Werker, 98 mins.)

Walker (1987)* Ed Harris, Rene Auberjonois, Peter Boyle, Marlee Matlin, Joe Strummer. An absurdist misfire from cult director Alex Cox (*Repo Man*) which takes a piece of American history and transforms it into an anarchic farce. Harris is Walker, an American soldier of fortune whose keen belief in Manifest Destiny led him to declare himself President of Nicaragua in the mid-19th century. Cox delivers this stunning parable for America's current Central American policies as a comedy, complete with anachronisms popping up in a "period" context. Harris has no opportunity to lend depth to the role, with the exception of the scenes where Walker deals with his militant deaf girlfriend (Matlin), who dies early on. (Dir: Alex Cox, 95 mins.)†

Walking After Midnight (Canada, 1988)** Martin Sheen, k.d. Lang, Willie Nelson, James Coburn, Helen Shaver, and other celebrities discuss near-death and past life experiences. Presented with solemnity, it too often lapses into silliness; narration by the irony-laden voice of Ringo Starr doesn't help. (Dir: Jonathon Kay, 92 mins.)

Walking Dead, The (1936)*** Boris Karloff, Ricardo Cortez, Warren Hull, Barton MacLane, Edmund Gwenn. Chilling thriller in which Boris is resurrected from the dead. (Dir: Michael Curtiz, 66 mins.)

Walking Hills, The (1949)*** Randolph Scott, Ella Raines, John Ireland, Arthur Kennedy. Ill-assorted group of adventurers seek a lost gold mine. Better-than-average western with a good script. (Dir: John Sturges, 78 mins.)

Walking My Baby Back Home (1953)**½ Donald O'Connor, Janet Leigh, Buddy Hackett. If you forget the plot in this muddled musical comedy, you'll enjoy the musical numbers and Buddy Hackett's comedy routines. (Dir: Lloyd Bacon, 95 mins.)

Walking Stick, The (Great Britain, 1970)**½ Samantha Eggar, David Hemmings, Emlyn Williams, Phyllis Calvert. An outstanding, finely etched performance by Eggar makes this otherwise predictable drama worthwhile. She's a cripple, stricken by polio in childhood, who is befriended by artist-thief Hemmings. (Dir: Eric Till, 101 mins.)

Walking Tall (1973)**½ Joe Don Baker, Elizabeth Hartman, Gene Evans, Rosemary Murphy. A real Tennessee sheriff, Buford Pusser, did take a stand against his hometown syndicate-owned gambling operations, and one brutal beating from the mobsters almost cost him his life. Hartman plays Pusser's wife who gets killed by the local mobsters. (Dir: Phil Karlson, 126 mins.)†

Walking Tall, Part 2 (1975)** Bo Svenson, Luke Askew, Noah Beery. Lawman-extraordinaire Pusser, now played by Svenson, attempts to track down the man who killed his wife in an ambush which left him severely wounded. (Dir: Earl Bellamy, 109 mins.)†

Walking Tall—Final Chapter—See: **Final Chapter—Walking Tall**

Walking the Edge (1985)*½ Robert Forster, Nancy Kwan, Joe Spinell, A Martinez. Forster is better than his material in this formula vengeance yarn about an L.A. cabbie who gets in the bad graces of a particularly nasty street gang. (Dir: Norbert Meisel, 94 mins.)†

Walking Through the Fire (MTV 1979)*** Bess Armstrong, Tom Mason, Richard Masur. Uplifting and engrossing. Armstrong gives a sensitive performance as Laurel Lee, who discovers she has Hodgkins's disease while carrying her third child, and risks her life to have her baby. (Dir: Robert Day, 104 mins.)

Walk in the Shadow (Great Britain, 1962)**½ Michael Craig, Patrick McGoohan, Janet Munro. Incisive, refined soap opera; a man who allows his daughter to die because of his inflexible religious beliefs begins to loosen up as grief and realities take hold. Understated, intelligent, well acted. (Dir: Basil Dearden, 93 mins.)

Walk in the Spring Rain, A (1970)**½ Ingrid Bergman, Anthony Quinn, Fritz Weaver. Star-powered postmenopausal romance in which a lecturer's wife finds fulfillment while vacationing in the boondocks. (Dir: Guy Green, 100 mins.)†

Walk in the Sun, A (1945)***½ Dana Andrews, Richard Conte, John Ireland. War story of a platoon of Texas Division infantrymen in Italy, whose task it is to clear a farmhouse of Germans entrenched there. One of the best WWII dramas. Realistic, well acted. (Dir: Lewis Milestone, 117 mins.)†

Walk Like a Dragon (1960)**½ James Shigeta, Nobu McCarthy, Jack Lord, Mel Torme. Saving a Chinese girl from the San Francisco slave market, a man brings her to his hometown, along with a young Chinese immigrant. Drama of racial problems in the early west has the advantage of a different sort of plot and sincere performances. (Dir: James Clavell, 95 mins.)

Walk Like a Man (1987) ½ Howie Mandel, Amy Steel, Christopher Lloyd, Cloris Leachman, Colleen Camp. Mandel's lack of talent continues to hound moviegoers in this mangy comedy about a boy raised by wolves. Can the feral creature make it in society as an upright human being? Can Mandel? (Dir: Melvin Frank, 86 mins.)†

Walk on the Wild Side (1962)**½ Laurence Harvey, Capucine, Jane Fonda, Anne Baxter, Barbara Stanwyck. A man finds his childhood love working in a New Orleans brothel during the Depression. Tawdry adaptation of Nelson Algren's novel. (Dir: Edward Dmytryk, 114 mins.)

Walkover (Poland, 1965)***½ Jerzy Skolimowski, Krzystof Chamiec, Andrzej Herder, Aleksandra Zawieruszanka. Sequel to director-star Skolimowski's *Identification Marks: None*, film follows amateur boxer Andrzej, on the eve of his 30th birthday, as he meets a beautiful girl from his past and enters a fight tournament at a local factory. Challenging study of the rootless outsider and of loss of talent is noteworthy for its prowling camera and very long takes. (78 mins.)

Walk Proud (1979)** Robby Benson, Sarah Holcomb, Henry Darrow. Can you believe boyish Benson as a Chicano who falls in love with well-off WASP Holcomb? Contrived story of a gang member and his conflicts in the Los Angeles barrio, written by Evan Hunter. (Dir: Robert Collins, 102 mins.)

Walk Softly, Stranger (1950)*** Joseph Cotten, Valli. A small-time crook is reformed by the love of a crippled girl. Well-written, deftly acted melodrama. (Dir: Robert Stevenson, 81 mins.)†

Walk the Proud Land (1956)*** Audie Murphy, Anne Bancroft, Pat Crowley. Better-than-average Audie Murphy western. He plays an Indian agent who wins the Apache's friendship and loses the white man's trust in the process. (Dir: Jesse Hibbs, 88 mins.)

Walk with Love and Death, A (1969)**½ Anjelica Huston, Assaf Dayan. Back in medieval France, two star-crossed lovers try to find peace amidst the carnage of war. One wishes the leads had the movie-star presence to carry off a project so dependent on the dynamism that stars can generate. Still, this romance has darkly appealing scenic backgrounds, and the love story is conveyed with some conviction. (Dir: John Huston, 90 mins.)

Wall, The (MTV 1982)*** Lisa Eichhorn, Tom Conti, Eli Wallach, Gerald Hiken, Rachel Roberts, Philip Sterling. John Hersey's novel about the valiant resistance staged by a small group of Jews in the Warsaw Ghetto against their Nazi oppressors during WWII certainly has all the ingredients for a gripping film. However, this beautifully acted adaptation comes to life only sporadically. (Dir: Robert Markowitz, 156 mins.)

Wall, The (1982)—See: **Pink Floyd—The Wall**

Wall, The (Turkey, 1985)***½ Tuncel Kuritz, Ayse Emel Mesci, Malik Berrichi, Nicolas Hossein. Brutal filmic descent into the bowels of a Turkish prison. Made by the director of *Yol*, this moving plea for better conditions was created out of the true-life experience of the filmmaker, a one-time political prisoner, who died in 1984, only three years after breaking out of a Turkish jail. (Dir: Yilmaz Guney, 117 mins.)

Wallenberg: A Hero's Story (MTV, 1985)*** Richard Chamberlain, Alice Krige, Bibi Andersson, Melanie Mayron. Chamberlain stars as Raoul Wallenberg, a Swedish aristocrat, who saved many Budapest Jews from Nazi Colonel Adolph Eichmann at the tail end of WWII. It's a grim but uplifting story, made up of memorable vignettes; and Chamberlain is exceptional. (Dir: Lamont Johnson, 196 mins.)

Wallflower (1948)*** Robert Hutton, Joyce Reynolds, Janis Paige. Pleasant little comedy about a "wallflower" who blossoms out very neatly and gets involved in a scandal. (Dir: Frederick de Cordova, 77 mins.)

Wall of Noise (1963)**½ Suzanne Pleshette, Ty Hardin, Dorothy Provine, Ralph Meeker, Murray Matheson, Simon Oakland. A tough look at horse racing and the people who are closely involved with it. (Dir: Richard Wilson, 112 mins.)

Walls Came Tumbling Down, The (1946)*** Lee Bowman, Marguerite Chapman. Columnist investigates the death of a priest, becomes involved in murder and stolen paintings. Well-written, entertaining mystery. (Dir: Lothar Mendes, 82 mins.)

Walls of Glass—See: **Flanagan**

Walls of Gold (1933)*½ Sally Eilers, Norman Foster, Ralph Morgan, Rosita Moreno, Rochelle Hudson, Marjorie Gateson. Dopey soap-opera concerns the unbelievable romantic entanglements of two sisters; one marries the other's fiancé, leading the first to marry the fiancé's rich uncle. Got that? Not worth bothering about. (Dir: Kenneth MacKenna, 74 mins.)

Walls of Jericho, The (1948)**½ Cornel Wilde, Linda Darnell, Anne Baxter, Kirk Douglas, Ann Dvorak, Marjorie Rambeau, Henry Hull, Barton MacLane. A newspaper man wants to go places beyond Jericho, Kansas, but his millstone of a wife is determined to keep him under her thumb. The performances and the black and white photography deserve kudos. (Dir: John Stahl, 106 mins.)

Walls of Malapaga (France, 1949)***½ Jean Gabin, Isa Miranda, Andrea Checchi, Vera Talchi, Robert Dalban. Eloquent drama about a French fugitive from justice (Gabin) and a sad Italian waitress (Miranda) who meet in bombed-out post-WWII Genoa and bring much-needed happiness to each other's dreary lives. A beautiful love story, simple and sublimely acted. (Dir: René Clement, 91 mins.)

Wall Street (1987)***½ Charlie Sheen, Michael Douglas, Daryl Hannah, Martin Sheen, Terence Stamp, Hal Holbrook, James Spader, James Karen, Sean Young. The director and star of *Platoon* reunite to explore another dangerous and cutthroat world—that of Wall Street, where the injuries sustained are emotional rather than physical. Sheen plays a corruptible innocent adrift in an uncertain moral climate. This time around, however, he capitulates to the dark side, embodied by a vicious, amoral trader (brilliantly played by Best Actor Oscar winner Douglas). Oliver Stone's direction is flawless, eliciting both anger and tears. (125 mins.)†

Waltz Across Texas (1982)** Terry Jastrow, Anne Archer, Noah Beery, Mary Kay Place, Josh Taylor, Richard Farnsworth, Ben Piazza. Unexceptional romance between an oil man and a fetching geologist. (Dir: Ernest Day, 99 mins.)†

Waltz King, The (MTV 1963)**½ Kerwin Mathews, Brian Aherne, Senta Berger, Peter Kraus, Fritz Eckhardt. A schmaltzy musical biography of the composer Johann Strauss has enough hummable tunes and charming moments to make it likable family fare in the Disney manner. (Dir: Steve Previn, 95 mins.)†

Waltz of the Toreadors (Great Britain, 1962)*** Peter Sellers, Margaret Leighton, Dany Robin. Sellers is oddly cast as the lascivious colonel in the Jean Anouilh play, but is credible, as is everything else in this determinedly adequate film adaptation. (Dir: John Guillermin, 105 mins.)†

Wanda (1971)***½ Barbara Loden, Michael Higgins. Perceptive, poignant story written and directed by Barbara Loden about a hapless, ill-educated young woman from coal mining country who goes through a series of brutalizing relationships with itinerant men. (101 mins.)

Wanda Nevada (1979)** Brooke Shields, Peter Fonda, Henry Fonda, Fiona Lewis. A drifting cowboy is forced to care for a young girl. Among the odd characters along the trail is an unrecognizable Henry Fonda as a bearded old prospector. (Dir: Peter Fonda, 105 mins.)†

Wanderers, The (1979)**½ Ken Wahl, John Friedrich, Karen Allen, Toni Kalem. Visually impressive saga of teenagers in a Bronx high school, circa 1963. The violent sequences are overly brutal, but genuine period atmosphere gets captured here. (Dir: Philip Kaufman, 113 mins.)†

Wannsee Conference, The (West Germany, 1987)*** Robert Artzhorn, Gerd Bockmann, Dietrich Mattausch. On January 20, 1942, high officials of the Nazi regime gathered in Wannsee for a meeting that decided the "final solution" to the Jewish question. This is a reconstruction of that infamous meeting in all its petty detail, with the participants discussing logistics, quotas, and goals. Terrifying in its inhuman matter-of-fact approach to mass murder. (Dir: Heinz Schirk, 85 mins.)†

Wanted Dead or Alive (1987)** Rutger Hauer, Gene Simmons, Robert Guillaume, Mel Harris. Unofficial spin-off of the old Steve McQueen series finds bounty hunter Hauer on the trail of terrorists led by Simmons. A few good action sequences. (Dir: Gary Sherman, 106 mins.)†

Wanted for Murder (Great Britain, 1946)**½ Eric Portman, Roland Culver, Dulcie Gray, Kieron Moore, Stanley Holloway. While Scotland Yard searches for a demented strangler, a girl falls for him. Competent thriller. (Dir: Lawrence Huntington, 95 mins.)

Wanted: The Sundance Woman (MTV 1976)**½ Katharine Ross, Stella Stevens. Ms. Ross is quite good as Sundance's woman, Etta Place, who has to revert to the life of a fugitive every time a Pinkerton detective gets wind of her trail. (Dir: Lee Philips, 105 mins.)

Wanton Contessa, The—See: Senso

War Against Mrs. Hadley, The (1942)** Fay Bainter, Richard Ney, Sara Allgood, Spring Byington, Jean Rogers, Frances Rafferty. Dated propaganda about a Washington lady who wishes WWII would go away so she can get on with her life. (Dir: Harold Bucquet, 86 mins.)

War and Love (1985)** Sebastian Keneas, Kyra Sedgwick, David Spielberg. Based on the producer Jack Eisner's own experiences, chronicled in the book *The Survivor*. This filmization about a young man who lived to write about the horrendous suffering he and others endured in the Warsaw Ghetto and concentration camps is well meaning but underdramatized. (Dir: Moshe Mizrahi, 112 mins.)†

War and Peace (1956)*** Audrey Hepburn, Henry Fonda, Mel Ferrer, Vittorio Gassman, John Mills, Oscar Homolka, Herbert Lom. King Vidor's mounting of the Tolstoy novel (with Mario Soldati) has some spectacularly effective sequences, notably on the battlefield and whenever Hepburn is incandescently on-screen. Filmed in Italy. (208 mins.)†

War and Peace (U.S.S.R., 1967)****
Lyudmila Savelyeva, Sergei Bondarchuk.
Here's the epic, multimillion-dollar
Russian film adaptation of the great
Tolstoy novel. Russia's most popular
director, Bondarchuk, also plays one of
the leading roles, that of Pierre, and
Natasha Rostov is played by Savelyeva.
As an epic, few films can even touch it.
Oscar: Best Foreign Film. (373 mins.)†

War and Peace (West Germany, 1982)**½
Jurgen Prochnow, Gunther Kaufman,
Manfred Zapatka. Examining the proba-
bility of nuclear Armageddon, this documentary deals with the possible role
Germany would play in a U.S./U.S.S.R.
nuclear conflict. Using newsreel clips
and fictional footage, the film makes an
important statement about nuclear madness; its primary flaw is that it lacks
cohesiveness. (Dirs: Heinrich Boll, Volker
Schlondorff, Alexander Kluge, Stefan
Anst, Axel Engstfeld, 85 mins.)

War Arrow (1953)** Maureen O'Hara, Jeff
Chandler. Chandler arrives at a Texas
cavalry garrison to train Seminole Indians
for the purpose of quieting a Kiowa
uprising. In between drilling the Red-
skins, he falls for redheaded O'Hara.
(Dir: George Sherman, 78 mins.)

War Between Men and Women, The (1972)
**½ Jack Lemmon, Barbara Harris, Jason
Robards. Named after a cartoon sequence
by humorist James Thurber, this overly
sentimental comedy-drama relies on heavy-
handed vignettes rather than the excellence of its cast. Lemmon is better than
his material playing the Thurber role, as
a sardonic but sensitive man who is losing his eyesight. He meets, courts, and
marries the wonderful Harris, inheriting
her three kids, dog, and ex-husband. (Dir:
Melville Shavelson, 104 mins.)

War Between the Planets (Italy, 1965)* Peter Martell, Amber Collins, Jack Stuart,
Alina Zalewska. Earth faces disaster as
a rogue planet hurtles toward it from
outer space. Scientists scramble to save
mankind. Viewers scramble for the remote control. AKA: **Planet On The Prowl**.
(Dir: "Anthony Dawson" [Antonio
Margheriti], 80 mins.)†

War Between the Tates, The (MTV 1977)**½
Elizabeth Ashley, Richard Crenna, Annette
O'Toole. Elizabeth Ashley is unquestion-
ably the star of this film adaptation of
Alison Lurie's novel about Mrs. Tate and
her war with Mr. Tate over his ridiculous
affair with Wendy, a flower child of the
'60s. (Dir: Lee Philips, 104 mins.)

War Birds (1989)*½ Jim Eldert, Timothy
Hicks, Bill Brinsfield, Cully Hollan.
Iron Eagle clone: a special squad of
U.S. air boys are assigned to put down
an Arab uprising in a fictitious Middle
Eastern country. Too little action for

dogfight devotees, the only conceivable
market for this programmer. (Dir: Ulli
Lommel, 88 mins.†

War Boy, The (Canada, 1985)** Helen Shaver, Jason Hopely, Kenneth Welsh. Low-
key WWII drama contrasts the brutality
of life under the Nazis with the family
life of a Canadian boy being raised in
Central Europe by his father and unfaithful stepmother. Not in the class of
Hope and Glory or *Empire of the Sun*,
both of which it preceded. (Dir: Allan
Eastman, 86 mins.)†

War Bus Commando (Italy, 1989)*½ Mark
Gregory, John Vernon, Savina Gersak.
U.S. soldier is sent on a nigh-impossible
mission into Afghanistan to rescue prisoners and retrieve a top-secret "war
bus." Wait a minute—wasn't that the
plot of *Stripes*? Unfortunately, they're
dead serious here. (Dir: Frank Valenti,
87 mins.)†

WarCat (1987)*½ Jannina Poynter, David
O'Hara, Macka Foley, Carl Erwin. Female journalist is captured by a crazy
bunch of desert survivalists, who let her
loose so they can hunt her down. That
this pen-pusher manages to hold her
own is only one of many ridiculous
elements of this silly potboiler. AKA:
Angel of Vengeance. (Dir: T. V. Mikels,
78 mins.)†

War Dogs (Sweden, 1987)*½ Tim Earle,
Bill Redvers, Sidney Livingstone,
Catherine Jeppson. Refusing to believe
that his brother was killed in Vietnam, a
man investigates and uncovers a government plot to turn soldiers into drug-
controlled killing machines. Poor acting
and an abundance of violence wreck a
good premise. (Dir: Bjorn Carlstrom,
Daniel Hubenbecker, 96 mins.)†

War Drums (1957)** Lex Barker, Joan
Taylor, Ben Johnson. Apache chief takes
a Mexican girl for his wife. Meandering
western drama. (Dir: Reginald Le Borg,
75 mins.)

Ward 13—See: **Hospital Massacre**

War Game, The (Great Britain, 1965)****
Enormously powerful "staged" documentary about the horrors of nuclear
war after a missile attack. Cleverly, perhaps manipulatively, combines simulated newsreels and various street interviews with a bland narrative. (Dir: Peter
Watkins, 50 mins.)†

WarGames (1983)***½ Matthew Broderick, Ally Sheedy, Dabney Coleman, John
Wood, Barry Corbin. A funny, suspenseful, and timely adventure about a teenage computer whiz who, believing he's
playing an advanced new video game,
accidentally taps into the United States
nuclear defense system and nearly causes
WWIII. Director John Badham has made
a film that succeeds as thrill-a-minute

action, cautionary political satire, and intricate suspense. (113 mins.)†

War Games—See: **Suppose They Gave a War and Nobody Came**

War Gods of the Deep (1965)*** Vincent Price, Tab Hunter, David Tomlinson, Susan Hart. Edgar Allan Poe's *City Under the Sea* is beautifully translated to film by director Tourneur in his last production. Price has one of his most effective roles as the ruler of an ancient underwater domain who sacrifices the local villagers and sends his gill-men to capture a woman who reminds him of a long-lost love. (Dir: Jacques Tourneur, 85 mins.)

War Hunt (1962)*** John Saxon, Robert Redford (film debut). An offbeat war film. John Saxon does very well as a young soldier in the Korean war who loses his perspective and begins to enjoy killing. Robert Redford is also effective as a young private who sees through Saxon's heroics. (Dir: Denis Sanders, 81 mins.)

War Is Hell (1964)**½ Tony Russel, Baynes Barron. Soldier on Korea patrol stops at nothing, including murder, to grab his share of glory. Grim and violent war drama. (Dir: Burt Topper, 81 mins.)

War Italian Style (Italy, 1965)*½ Buster Keaton, Martha Hyer, Fred Clark. The great Keaton as a bumbling German general who allows two American Marines to escape with secret battle plans. Keaton's genius is wasted in this, his last film. (Dir: Luigi Scattini, 84 mins.)

Warlock (1959)*** Richard Widmark, Henry Fonda, Anthony Quinn, Dorothy Malone. Gunfighter is hired by a town to wipe out outlaws; afterward his own rule is challenged by a cowboy who helped him clean up. Sprawling western. (Dir: Edward Dmytryk, 123 mins.)†

Warlock (1991)**½ Julian Sands, Lori Singer, Richard E. Grant, Mary Woronov, Kevin O'Brien, Richard Kuss. A male witch from 1691 Massachusetts materializes in contemporary U.S.A. in search of a book that will reveal God's true name and lead to the destruction of life on earth. Interesting, with fair special effects, but not as scary as it could have been. (Dir: Steve Miner, 103 mins.)†

War Lord, The (1965)*** Charlton Heston, Richard Boone, Rosemary Forsyth, Maurice Evans. Governor of a coastal village in 11th-century England falls in love with a local girl, which starts many conflicts, leading to tragedy. Costume spectacle with some intelligence in production, direction, and script—for a change. (Dir: Franklin Schaffner, 123 mins.)

Warlords (1989)*½ David Carradine, Dawn Wildsmith, Sid Haig, Ross Hagen, Fox Harris, Robert Quarry, Michelle Bauer.

Carradine's back in the future as a warrior trying to rescue his wife from Haig, nasty ruler of this post-nuke land. It's all pretty dismal. (Dir: Fred Olen Ray, 85 mins.)†

Warlords of Atlantis (Great Britain, 1978)** Doug McClure, Cyd Charisse, Daniel Massey. Stupid adventure has a diving bell falling to the ocean floor, its researcher passengers discovering Atlantis. (Dir: Kevin Connor, 96 mins.)

Warlords of the 21st Century (1982)* Michael Beck, Annie McEnroe. The usual outer space-y violence occurs as Beck and McEnroe contend with a desperate fuel shortage as they fight to survive in the 21st century. AKA: **Battletruck.** (Dir: Harley Cokliss, 91 mins.)†

War Lover, The (Great Britain, 1962)**½ Steve McQueen, Robert Wagner, Shirley Anne Field. While it stays in the air, this story of a reckless and unlikable hotshot pilot is graphically absorbing. On the ground, the trite love story involving pilot, copilot, and an English girl is for the birds. (Dir: Philip Leacock, 105 mins.)†

Warm December, A (Great Britain–U.S., 1972)*½ Sidney Poitier, Esther Anderson, Yvette Curtis. A black *Love Story*, and the fatal illness is sickle-cell anemia. The film is a let-down for romantics everywhere. (Dir: Sidney Poitier, 103 mins.)

Warm Hearts, Cold Feet (MTV, 1987)**½ Tim Matheson, Margaret Colin, Elizabeth Ashley, Barry Corbin, George DiCenzo. A fairly winning comedy about the problems of a working woman having a baby. (Dir: James Frawley, 104 mins.)

Warm Nights on a Slow Moving Train (Australia, 1987)** Wendy Hughes, Colin Friels, Norman Kaye, John Clayton. Prostitute Hughes entices men on a train by appealing to their fantasies, but has the tables turned on her when she lets herself become involved with one of the men she meets. Originally 130 mins. (Dir: Bob Ellis, 92 mins.)†

Warning from Space (Japan, 1956)*½ Creatures from space warn Earth of a collision with another planet, but get a cold reception. (Dir: Koji Shima, 87 mins.)†

Warning Shadows (Germany, 1923)***½ Fritz Kortner, Ruth Weyher, Alexander Granach, Fritz Rasp. Extremely stylized expressionist film, one of many directly influenced by *The Cabinet of Dr. Caligari.* A travelling showman hypnotizes a group of guests at a dark, shadowy (of course) house into acting out their deepest emotions. Perfectly described by its subtitle—"A Nocturnal Hallucination." AKA: **Schatten.** (Dir: Arthur Robison, 93 mins.)†

Warning Shot (1967)*** David Janssen, Lillian Gish, Eleanor Parker, Joan Collins, Walter Pidgeon, George Sanders,

Stefanie Powers, Steve Allen, Carroll O'Connor, George Grizzard. Tough, slick, hard-hitting detective yarn. Janssen's a police detective who shoots a seemingly respectable doctor in the line of duty and finds himself in hot water up to his badge. (Dir: Buzz Kulik, 100 mins.)

Warning Sign (1985)*** Sam Waterston, Kathleen Quinlan, Yaphet Kotto, Jeffrey De Munn, Richard Dysart. A germ-warfare experiment goes awry and turns those exposed into *Night of the Living Dead*–like monsters. While the film has some merit as a cautionary warning tale hinting at governmental responsibility for dangerous experimentation, this stylish sci-fi flick works best as a gadget-laden scare-a-thon. (Dir: Hal Barwood, 99 mins.)†

War of Children, A (MTV 1972)*** Vivien Merchant, Anthony Andrews, Jenny Agutter. Often poignant drama on the agonizing war between Catholics and Protestants in northern Ireland. James Costigan writes about the emergence of blind hate and the departure of all reason from a sweet Catholic Belfast housewife, after her husband is carted off to prison for a small act of friendship. Made in Ireland. (Dir: George Schaefer, 73 mins.)

War of the Buttons, The (France, 1962)***½ Andre Treton, Michel Isella, Martin Lartigue, Jean Richard. Delightful satire about two groups of young boys who play "war games" in which belts, suspenders, or buttons are removed from each "prisoner." The leader of one team comes up with the idea of going into war stark naked, which brings the kids' parents onto the scene. (Dir: Yves Robert, 95 mins.)

War of the Colossal Beast (1958)* Sally Fraser, Roger Pace, Dean Parkin, Russ Bender. Unmemorable sequel to *The Amazing Colossal Man*. The Big Boy returns to destroy property and to experience king-size Excedrin headaches, which might have been cured by the invention of oversized aspirin or a roll in the hay with the fifty-foot woman. (Dir: Bert Gordon, 68 mins.)

War of the Gargantuas, The (Japan, 1970)*½ Russ Tamblyn, Kumi Mizuno, Kipp Hamilton, Yu Fujiki. Two huge, half-human monsters—one good, one evil, both destructive—battle it out using Tokyo as a ring. (Dir: Inoshiro Honda, 89 mins.)

War of the Monsters (Japan, 1966)* Kojiro Hongo, Kyoko Enami. Revel in camp as a stolen opal turns into Barugon, the 130-foot monster who is afraid of the

1162

water. Enter Gamera, just returned from Mars. Exit viewers, gone to sleep. AKA: **Gamera vs. Barugon.** (Dir: Shigeo Tanaka, 95 mins.)†

War of the Roses, The (1989)**** Michael Douglas, Kathleen Turner, Danny DeVito, Marianne Sagebrecht, Sean Astin, Heather Fairfield, G. D. Spradlin. Extremely black comedy about an affluent couple (Douglas and Turner in roles completely different from their two *Romancing the Stone* teamings) who destroy everything they have in an escalatingly ugly divorce. The impact of this dark fable is softened somewhat by framing it as a tale told by divorce lawyer DeVito to discourage a client, but otherwise this is an unrelenting attack on the materialism and lack of values of the modern middle class. DeVito directed with both flash and skill that amplifies the story's bitter lessons. The ballsiest comedy to come out of Hollywood in years. (116 mins.)†

War of the Wildcats (1943)*** John Wayne, Martha Scott, Albert Dekker, Gabby Hayes. Ex-cowpuncher fights an oil tycoon for the oil rights to Indian lands. Good melodrama of the oil boom days; plenty of action. (Dir: Albert S. Rogell, 102 mins.)†

War of the Worlds, The (1953)*** Gene Barry, Ann Robinson, Les Tremayne. Workmanlike, entertaining sci-fi thriller that highlights the wasting of L.A. by Martians. Good show. Oscar winner, Best Special Effects. Produced by George Pal. Based on an H. G. Wells story. (Dir: Byron Haskin, 85 mins.)†

War of the Zombies, The (Italy, 1965)** John Drew Barrymore, Susi Anderson, Ettore Mani, Ida Galli. Overwrought gladiator spectacle about a highly disturbed high priest with plans for world conquest that involve activating an army of dead soldiers, since he can't find enough living recruits. (Dir: Giuseppe Vari, 85 mins.)

War Paint (1953)*** Robert Stack, Joan Taylor, Peter Graves. Cavalry detachment experiences treachery and danger when they try to deliver a peace treaty to an Indian chief. Exciting outdoor drama. (Dir: Lesley Selander, 89 mins.)

War Party (1988)** Kevin Dillon, Billy Wirth, Tim Sampson, M. Emmet Walsh. After a white man is killed during a holiday re-enactment of a 19th-century Indian massacre, four Indian youths head for the hills, pursued by state troopers and a mob of redneck vigilantes. Intended as an examination of the treatment of Native Americans by modern society, the film is so stacked in their favor that it's impossible to take seriously. (Dir: Franc Roddam, 100 mins.)†

Warpath (1951)** Edmond O'Brien, Polly

Bergen, Dean Jagger. O'Brien rides a trail of revenge for the murder of his fiancée. The big scene comes at the finale when the Sioux attack the fort. (Dir: Byron Haskin, 95 mins.)

Warrendale (Canada, MTV 1967)**** Powerful documentary about the unique treatment offered to emotionally disturbed teenagers at an innovative treatment center in Warrendale, Ont. Produced and directed by Allan King. Remarkable early cinema verité entry. (100 mins.)

Warrior Queen (1987)½ Sybil Danning, Donald Pleasence, Richard Hill. Another grind-house exploration of Roman decadence, featuring the irrepressible Sybil. Sotted emperor Pleasence eats up the scenery with a vengeance (that's not too hard when it's cardboard), and Mt. Vesuvius erupts in response. (Dir: Chuck Vincent, 69 mins.)†

Warriors, The (Great Britain, 1955)**½ Errol Flynn, Joanne Dru, Peter Finch. Flynn swashbuckles his way to lovely Joanne Dru's boudoir and kills many tyrants on the way. Lavish sets and costumes make things easier to watch. (Dir: Henry Levin, 85 mins.)†

Warriors, The (1979)*** Michael Beck, Thomas Waites, Deborah Van Valkenburgh, James Remar. A disturbing, reckless, but powerful drama. A Coney Island gang is trying to return home safely while being besieged by heavily armed rival gangs out to avenge an assassination. Much of the film is so artfully posed and choreographed that it looks more like a ballet than street warfare. (Dir: Walter Hill, 94 mins.)†

Warriors Five (Italy, 1962)** Jack Palance, Giovanna Ralli, Serge Reggiani. Four liberated Italian prisoners aid an American paratrooper in carrying out sabotage during WWII. OK war story. (Dir: Leopoldo Savona, 95 mins.)

Warriors of the Apocalypse (1985)* Michael James, Deborah Moore, Franco Guerrero, Ken Metcalfe. In 2135 A.D., 50 years after civilization was wiped out by war, a roving band of survivors search for a mountain rumored to hold the key to eternal life. What they find instead is a jungle civilization of Amazons and immortal warriors. Pretty dreary. AKA: **Searchers of the Voodoo Mountain** and **Time Raiders**. (Dir: Bobby A. Suarez, 96 mins.)†

Warriors of the Wasteland (Italy, 1983)* Fred Williamson, Timothy Brent, Anna Kanakis, Venantino Venantini. In 2019, nine years after the ever-popular nuclear devastation, two good guys protect the meek from a group of violent homosexual villains. Silly and barbaric. (Dir: Enzo Castellari, 87 mins.)†

War Wagon, The (1967)*** John Wayne, Kirk Douglas, Howard Keel. Good, action-filled western with John Wayne playing an ex-con who is bent on revenge for being framed and robbed of his gold-yielding land. The ingredients are familiar for western fans and they won't be disappointed when Wayne teams up with two-fisted Kirk Douglas to steal the gold shipment being transported in a specially armored stage known as the War Wagon. (Dir: Burt Kennedy, 101 mins.)†

Wash, The (1988)***½ Mako, Nobu McCarthy, Patty Yasutake. Compelling drama about the breakup of a Japanese-American couple's forty-year marriage. Fleshed out by an excellent cast and a screenplay attentive to the cultural and sociological pressures on this family. (Dir: Michael Toshiyuki Uno, 94 mins.)†

Washington Merry-Go-Round (1932)**½ Lee Tracy, Constance Cummings, Alan Dinehart, Walter Connolly, Clarence Muse, Arthur Hoyt. Timely social comedy-drama of an honest freshman congressman finding corruption and influence-peddling permeating the Washington scene; punchy dialogue and vital performances make it extremely entertaining. (Dir: James Cruze, 79 mins.)

Washington Mistress (MTV 1982)** Lucie Arnaz, Richard Jordan, Pat Hingle, Tony Bill, Tarah Nutter. A congressional aide with a future falls for a married man with a reputation to protect, so naturally mum's the word. The stars disport themselves charmlessly. (Dir: Peter Levin, 104 mins.)†

Washington Story (1952)** Van Johnson, Patricia Neal, Louis Calhern. Writer is assigned to do a hatchet job on the capital and selects a sincere young Congressman as her target. Well-meant but mild, rather dry drama. (Dir: Robert Pirosh, 81 mins.)

Wasn't That a Time!—See: **Weavers, The: Wasn't That a Time!**

Wasp Woman, The (1960)* Susan Cabot, Anthony Eisley. Ridiculous horror film about a cosmetic firm head who turns into the wasp woman. Grade Z film fare. (Dir: Roger Corman, 73 mins.)†

Wastrel, The (Italy-Greece, 1962)*½ Van Heflin, Ellie Lambetti. Good acting but an inept script about the life of a man relived as he struggles for survival after a shipwreck. (Dir: Michael Cacoyannis, 84 mins.)

Watched (1972)** Stacey Keach, Harris Yulin, Brigid Polk. In this meandering drama, Keach plays a lawyer who tries to help the dope generation while a government man keeps a watchful eye on his activities with the stoned subculture. (Dir: John Parsons, 95 mins.)†

Watcher in the Woods, The (Great Britain, 1980)**½ Bette Davis, Carroll Baker,

Lynn-Holly Johnson, Kyle Richards, David McCallum. Young children may have trouble sleeping after seeing this spooky movie about a young girl's ghost returning to an English manor house after disappearing thirty years earlier. Interesting ghost tale re-edited by Disney studios; one version runs 84 mins. (Dir: John Hough, 108 mins.)†

Watchers (Canada, 1988)*½ Corey Haim, Barbara Williams, Michael Ironside. Sloppy adaptation of Dean R. Koontz novel about government-created monsters that escape from the lab and start killing innocent taxpayers instead of evil Commies. Don't watch. (Dir: Jon Hess, 92 mins.)†

Watch on the Rhine (1943)*** Paul Lukas, Bette Davis, Beulah Bondi, George Coulouris, Lucile Watson. Lillian Hellman's agitprop play is a relic of its time. Lukas, who won an Oscar, is outstanding as an underground patriot, with Coulouris and Watson in effective support as the slimy amoralist and the complacent bystander. (Dir: Herman Shumlin, 114 mins.)†

Watch the Birdie (1950)**½ Red Skelton, Arlene Dahl, Ann Miller. Red's fans will enjoy his crazy antics as a photographer who focuses on trouble. There's a wild chase sequence at the end that makes up for any shortcoming the film might have. (Dir: Jack Donohue, 71 mins.)

Watch Your Stern (Great Britain, 1960)*½ Kenneth Connor, Eric Barker. Farcical takeoff on the British Navy; two "limeys" become quick-change con artists when they bungle an official mission. (Dir: Gerald Thomas, 88 mins.)

Water (Great Britain, 1985)** Michael Caine, Valerie Perrine, Brenda Vaccaro, Jimmie Walker, Dennis Dugan, Leonard Rossiter. Semi-amusing, semi-irritating everything-but-the-kitchen-sink satire about the discovery of a delicious mineral water in a British colony. The alleged hilarity won't quench your thirst for laughter. (Dir: Dick Clement, 91 mins.)†

Water Babies (Great Britain–Poland, 1978)*½ James Mason, Billie Whitelaw, Bernard Cribbins, Joan Greenwood, David Tomlinson. Based on the beloved Kingsley classic, this is a disheartening blend of live action and animation. In 1850, a chimney sweep escapes his difficulties by diving into an enchanted underwater world. (Dir: Lionel Jeffries, 92 mins.)†

Waterfront (1944)** John Carradine, J. Carrol Naish, Maris Wrixon, Edwin Maxwell. Nazi spies try to take over the San Francisco waterfront area, but end up fighting among themselves for ultimate power in this low-budget, enjoyably acted espionage thriller. (Dir: Steve Sekely, 65 mins.)

Waterhole No. 3 (1967)*** James Coburn, Carroll O'Connor, Joan Blondell, James Whitmore, Bruce Dern. An attempt to make a zany western that succeeds more than half the time. Coburn is a roguish adventurer who is after a hidden cache of gold. He isn't the only one, as it turns out. (Dir: William Graham, 95 mins.)†

Waterloo (Italy-U.S.S.R., 1970)*½ Rod Steiger, Christopher Plummer, Jack Hawkins, Orson Welles, Virginia McKenna. Despite a lavish budget, this production of Napoleon's escape from exile, rise to power, and subsequent defeat is a Waterloo for everyone except Christopher Plummer. (Dir: Sergei Bondarchuk, 123 mins.)

Waterloo Bridge (1931)**½ Mae Clarke, Douglass Montgomery, Bette Davis. Robert Sherwood's dramatic situations have aged badly, and director James Whale's command of the medium was shaky. Love story about a prostitute and a naive soldier of genteel background. (81 mins.)

Waterloo Bridge (1940)*** Vivien Leigh, Robert Taylor, Lucile Watson, Virginia Field. Tearjerker about a back-row ballerina who has an affair with an upper-class young officer works well. Remade as *Gaby*. (Dir: Mervyn LeRoy, 103 mins.)

Waterloo Road (Great Britain, 1945)*** John Mills, Stewart Granger, Alastair Sim. An Army private leads everyone a merry chase when he goes AWOL after learning his wife has been seeing an oily rogue. Fast, suspenseful comedy-drama. (Dir: Sidney Gilliat, 77 mins.)

Watermelon Man (1970)**½ Godfrey Cambridge, Estelle Parsons, Howard Caine. White insurance salesman wakes up in his suburban home, finds he's turned black overnight. The laughs are broad, but the energies of Melvin Van Peebles, who directed, scored the music, and produced, shine through. (97 mins.)†

Watership Down (Great Britain, 1978)*** Voices of John Hurt, Harry Andrews, Ralph Richardson, Michael Hordern, Denholm Elliott, Zero Mostel. Darwinian animated tale, from the Richard Adams novel. The problem of reconciling animation, dramatic forms, and realistic drawing of rabbit protagonists is nearly solved. (Dir: Martin Rosen, 97 mins.)†

Watts Monster, The (1976)** Bernie Casey, Rosalind Cash, Marie O'Henry, Ji-tu Cumbuka. A low-wattage, low-budget chiller about a black doctor who fools with chemicals and turns into a beast. Casey's terrific; the film itself will leave you asking "So Watts?" AKA: **Dr. Black and Mr. Hyde** (Dir: William Crain, 87 mins.)

Watusi (1959)** George Montgomery, Taina Elg, David Farrar. Slightly altered remake of the African adventure *King*

Solomon's Mines. (Dir: Kurt Neumann, 85 mins.)

Wavelength (1983)** Robert Carradine, Keenan Wynn, Cherie Currie. Fairly interesting sci-fi time-waster about three visiting creatures from the furthest reaches of space. As the U.S. Air Force tracks them down, they find some unlikely allies in the persons of a rock musician, his girl, and a cantankerous old prospector. (Dir: Mike Gray, 87 mins.)†

Waxwork (1988)**½ Zach Galligan, Deborah Foreman, Miles O'Keeffe, Michelle Johnson, David Warner. Teens on a midnight visit to a wax museum's chamber of horrors discover that the museum is a gateway to another dimension, where they become victims in the crimes displayed. The script and director show affection for the genre, which helps. (Dir: Anthony Hickox, 97 mins.)†

Way Ahead, The (Great Britain, 1944)***½ David Niven, Stanley Holloway. A group of civilians are drafted into the infantry during WWII, serve bravely in North Africa. Excellently acted, authentic war drama. (Dir: Carol Reed, 91 mins.)

Way Down East (1920)**** Lillian Gish, Richard Barthelmess, Lowell Sherman. A masterpiece; an outrageously hoary melodrama is transformed by screen artists Gish and Griffith. Gish is seduced by a rake into a pretended marriage. When her disgrace is discovered, she is sent into the frozen wastes by her New England community. Recently reconstructed to its full 165 minutes; some prints run 148 minutes.(Dir: D. W. Griffith, 119 mins.)†

Way Down East (1935)** Henry Fonda, Rochelle Hudson. The D. W. Griffith silent film was far, far better. (Dir: Henry King, 80 mins.)

Way Down South (1939)**½ Bobby Breen, Alan Mowbray, Ralph Morgan, Clarence Muse, Stymie Beard. Pre-Civil War tale written by Langston Hughes and Clarence Muse about a young boy (Breen) who rescues his family's plantation and slaves from a cruel, crooked lawyer. The tremendous Hall Johnson Choir performs several traditional spirituals. Altogether an odd curio, well worth seeing. (Dir: Bernard Vorhaus, 62 mins.)

Way for a Sailor (1930)**½ John Gilbert, Wallace Beery, Leila Hyams, Polly Moran, Jim Tully, Doris Lloyd, Sojin, Raymond Milland. Gilbert and Beery are excellent as rollicking sailors, but the sappy story of this effort does it in; happy-go-lucky Gilbert falls in love with a snooty girl who doesn't like sailors, so he pretends to have a regular job. (Dir: Sam Wood, 83 mins.)

Way It Is, The (1986)* Kai Eric, Boris Major, Steve Buscemi, Jessica Stutchbury,

Rockets Redglare. A sleep-inducing brush with cult filmmaking. Some East Villagers put on a production of Cocteau's *Orpheus* in this film, which puts down the pretensions of art house movie styles. (Dir: Eric Mitchell, 80 mins.)

Way of a Gaucho (1952)** Rory Calhoun, Gene Tierney, Richard Boone, Hugh Marlowe. A slow-moving tale of the people who live in the untamed Argentine territory during the end of the 19th century. (Dir: Jacques Tourneur, 91 mins.)

Way of All Flesh, The (1940)** Akim Tamiroff, Gladys George, William Henry, John Hartley, Marilyn Knowlden, Darryl Hickman, Berton Churchill, Fritz Leiber. Maudlin story of a European businessman who loses everything and lets his family believe he is dead; when he returns he finds that they haven't forgotten him. Pointlessly sentimental. (Dir: Louis King, 86 mins.)

Way of Youth, The (France, 1960)**½ Francoise Arnoul, Bourvil, Alain Delon. During the Occupation, a father finds his son has been having an affair with a woman whose husband is a prisoner of war. Slow, interesting drama of wartime moral problems. (Dir: Michel Boisrond, 81 mins.)

Way Out West (1936)***½ Stan Laurel, Oliver Hardy. This is the great slapstick pair's version of a western, as Stan and Ollie help a young girl who is being cheated out of her inheritance. Lots of funny gags, better direction than usual. (Dir: James W. Horne, 65 mins.)†

Way to Love, The (1933)*** Maurice Chevalier, Ann Dvorak, Edward Everett Horton, Arthur Pierson, Douglas Dumbrille, John Miljan. Musical comedy vehicle for Chevalier, as a sandwich-board man who falls for carnival performer Dvorak. (Dir: Norman Taurog, 80 mins.)

Way to the Gold, The (1957)** Barry Sullivan, Sheree North, Jeffrey Hunter. Moderately suspenseful chase drama concerning a young convict who knows where a fortune in stolen gold is hidden. (Dir: Robert D. Webb, 94 mins.)

Way to the Stars, The—See: *Johnny in the Clouds*

Wayward Bus, The (1957)**½ Joan Collins, Jayne Mansfield, Dan Dailey, Rick Jason. John Steinbeck's novel about a group of people who take a short bus ride in California makes an occasionally interesting film. Miss Mansfield plays it straight for a change as a former bubble dancer who wants to go legit and she's not bad. (Dir: Victor Vicas, 89 mins.)

Wayward Wife, The (Italy, 1952)*½ Gina Lollobrigida, Gabriele Ferzetti, Franco Interlenghi. A young Lollobrigida is the only reason to watch this run-of-the-mill drama about a wife threatened with blackmail. (Dir: Mario Soldati, 91 mins.)

Way, Way Out (1966)½ Jerry Lewis, Connie Stevens, Robert Morley, Dick Shawn. Jerry goes to the moon with Connie, and you'll be lucky to last past lift-off. (Dir: Gordon Douglas, 106 mins.)

Way West, The (1967)** Kirk Douglas, Robert Mitchum, Richard Widmark, Lola Albright, Sally Field, William Lundigan. The fine novel by A. B. Guthrie, Jr., has been turned into a hackneyed, disappointing saga of a wagon train on the great trek to Oregon in the 1840s. (Dir: Andrew V. McLaglen, 122 mins.)

Way We Were, The (1973)*** Barbra Streisand, Robert Redford, Patrick O'Neal, Murray Hamilton, Bradford Dillman, Lois Chiles. The charismatic appeal of the stars makes this film an appealing love story, despite a lot of flaws in the script. (Dir: Sydney Pollack, 118 mins.)†

W. C. Fields and Me (1976)*** Rod Steiger, Valerie Perrine, John Marley, Paul Stewart, Jack Cassidy, Billy Barty, Bernadette Peters. Based on the memoir by Carlotta Monti, the woman who served as Fields's "secretary" and lover for the last years of his life. Steiger is remarkably restrained. (Dir: Arthur Hiller, 110 mins.)

We All Loved Each Other So Much (Italy, 1977)**** Vittorio Gassman, Nino Manfredi, Stefania Sandrelli, Giovanna Ralli. Moving story of three friends who spend the years mostly apart, meeting occasionally, paralleled by the history of Italian cinema during those years. (Dir: Ettore Scola, 124 mins.)†

Weapon, The (Great Britain, 1956)**½ Steve Cochran, Lizabeth Scott, Herbert Marshall, Jon Whiteley. Boy flees after accidentally shooting a playmate. Fairly suspenseful melodrama. (Dir: Hal E. Chester, 80 mins.)

We Are All Murderers (France, 1957)***½ Raymond Pellegrin, Mouloudji. Youth with three strikes against him is tried and convicted for murder. Moving plea against capital punishment, extremely well directed. (Dir: André Cayatte, 113 mins.)

We Are in the Navy Now (Great Britain, 1962)*** Kenneth More, Lloyd Nolan, Joan O'Brien. Wacky comedy about a naval officer who continually gets himself into hot water, is bounced from post to post, finally winds up hero of a revolution. (Dir: Wendy Toye, 102 mins.)

We Are Not Alone (1939)***½ Paul Muni, Jane Bryan, Flora Robson, Una O'Connor, Cecil Kellaway, Henry Daniell, Alan Napier. Beautiful, sensitive adaptation of the James Hilton novel superbly played by the cast. (Dir: Edmund Goulding, 112 mins.)

We Are the Children (MTV 1987)** Ted Danson, Ally Sheedy, Judith Ivey. The Ethiopian famine placed in a dramatic, romantic context. Danson plays a TV-documentary maker who falls for the newly arrived doctor. (Dir: Robert M. Young, 104 mins.)

Weary River (1929)*** Richard Barthelmess, Betty Compson, William Holden, Louis Natheaux, George Stone, Raymond Turner. Ingenious early sound melodrama combines the gangster and musical genres. Barthelmess plays a bootlegger who reforms in prison when he discovers his talent for music; he becomes a radio star, but can't handle his new success. (Dir: Frank Lloyd, 84 mins.)

Weavers, The: Wasn't That a Time! (1982) **** Pete Seeger, Lee Hays, Ronnie Gilbert, Fred Hellerman. Glorious and exciting reunion of, and tribute to, the seminal folk-singing group with music as fresh as ever and the four personalities shining as individuals and as group members. AKA: **Wasn't That a Time!** (Dir: Jim Brown, 78 mins.)†

Web, The (1947)*** Edmond O'Brien, Ella Raines, William Bendix, Vincent Price. Tight and exciting melodrama about a bodyguard who kills his boss's archenemy only to find himself involved in a double-cross. (Dir: Michael Gordon, 87 mins.)

Web of Deceit (MCTV 1990)** Linda Purl, James Read, Paul de Souza, Larry Black, Barbara Rush. Standard courtroom drama about a defense attorney who returns to her Southern hometown to defend a young auto mechanic unjustly accused of rape and murder. (Dir: Sandor Stern, 96 mins.)

Web of Evidence (Great Britain, 1959)**½ Van Johnson, Vera Miles, Emlyn Williams, Bernard Lee. A man's search to find out about his father. Good performances by the American stars and a competent supporting cast add to the film's interest. (Dir: Jack Cardiff, 88 mins.)

Web of Passion (France-Italy, 1959)**½ Madeleine Robinson, Jean-Paul Belmondo, Antonella Lualdi. Mysterious girl next door threatens to disrupt an unhappy family until she's suddenly murdered. Intricate whodunit is visually dazzling, obscure in plot, unsympathetic in characterization. (Dir: Claude Chabrol, 101 mins.)

Wedding, A (1978)***½ Carol Burnett, Desi Arnaz, Jr., Mia Farrow, Lauren Hutton, Paul Dooley, Lillian Gish, Howard Duff, Pat McCormick, Dina Merrill, Dennis Christopher, John Considine. Altman's kaleidoscopic portrait of a wedding party. Although it does spread itself a bit thin with twenty-four major characters, the overall effect is that of an exhilarating carnal comedy in which a nuptial ceremony is turned into a three-ring circus where everyone wants to be in the center ring. (Dir: Robert Altman, 125 mins.)†

Wedding Band (1990)** William Katt, Joyce Hyser, Tino Insana, Lance Kinsey, David Rasche. Title refers to a rock'n'roll band, the kind that plays popular songs at weddings. The band's performances at a series of peculiar ceremonies is the basis of this amiable but wan episodic comedy. Joe Flaherty, Tim Kazurinsky, Jim Belushi, and Penelope Spheeris have cameo appearances. (Dir: Daniel Raskov, 82 mins.)†

Wedding in Blood (France-Italy, 1973)**** Stéphane Audran, Michel Piccoli, Claude Pieplu, Clothilde Joana. Two lovers, married to other people, engage in an illicit affair destined to end in murder. A perfect marriage of mystery and keen social observation. Based on a real case, suggesting an upper-class version of *The Postman Always Rings Twice.* (Dir: Claude Chabrol, 98 mins.)†

Wedding in Galilee, A (France-Belgium, 1987)*** Ali M. El Akili, Nazih Akleh, Anna Achdian. Palestine-born filmmaker Michel Khleifi has fashioned an overlong but entrancing story whose theme, the conflict of present-day Palestinian Arabs with both their own pasts and Israeli occupation, unfolds against the backdrop of a traditional wedding. Provocative. (116 mins.)

Wedding in White (Canada, 1972)**½ Carol Kane, Donald Pleasence, Doris Petrie. When their daughter becomes pregnant, a Canadian family closes ranks to still the wagging tongues of the local gossips. Fine acting makes this mournful tale fairly affecting. (Dir: William Fruet, 106 mins.)†

Wedding March, The (1927)**** Erich von Stroheim, Fay Wray, George Fawcett, ZaSu Pitts, Matthew Betz, George Nichols. One of director von Stroheim's most romantic and least cynical films; he plays a far more sympathetic character than usual, a dissolute, poverty-stricken young nobleman who is forced to marry for money, even though he loves a lovely peasant girl. (113 mins.)†

Wedding Night, The (1935)*** Gary Cooper, Anna Sten, Ralph Bellamy. Tenderly played drama about a cosmopolitan gentleman who falls in love with a simple Connecticut farm girl, very well-defined by Anna Sten. (Dir: King Vidor, 90 mins.)

Wedding on Walton's Mountain, A (MTV 1982)**½ Ralph Waite, Jon Walmsley, Judy Norton-Taylor, Eric Scott. The homey Waltons keep rolling along. Set after WWII, the story concerns Erin's wedding to Paul Northridge and her feelings for her old beau Ashley who appears in the nick of time. (Dir: Lee Philips, 104 mins.)

Wedding Party, The (1969)*½ Charles Pfluger, Jill Clayburgh, Valda Satterfield, Jennifer Salt, John Braswell, William Finley, Robert De Niro. Tiresome comedy about a groom who gets connubial cold feet after being exposed to his bride-to-be's family. Notable only for the debut appearances of Clayburgh and De Niro. Shot in 1963. (Dirs: Cynthia Munroe, Wilford Leach, Brian DePalma, 92 mins.)†

Wedding Present (1936)*** Cary Grant, Joan Bennett, George Bancroft, Conrad Nagel, Gene Lockhart. Two newspaper reporters have a ball off the job; and so will you, because Grant and Bennett always had such easygoing rapport. They should have reteamed more often. (Dir: Richard Wallace, 81 mins.)

Weddings and Babies (1958)*** Viveca Lindfors, John Myhers. Momentary, moody affair involving a photographer and a model, both past the age of tender young love. This neglected feature is worth seeing. (Dir: Morris Engel, 81 mins.)

We Dive at Dawn (Great Britain, 1943)*** John Mills, Eric Portman, Niall MacGinnis, Reginald Purdell, Louis Bradfield. Expert psychological study of submarine stress, a sort of English *Das Boot* for its time. The film's an involving study of the seamen who brave the ocean depths, even though their personal problems and fears aren't so easily submerged. (Dir: Anthony Asquith, 98 mins.)

Wednesday's Child (Great Britain, 1971) ***½ Sandy Ratcliff, Bill Dean, Grace Cave, Malcolm Tierney. A harrowing, deeply moving film that is directed like a documentary about a mentally disturbed young woman and her family. Superbly directed by Ken Loach. (108 mins.)

Weeds (1987)*** Nick Nolte, Lane Smith, William Forsythe, Joe Mantegna, Ernie Hudson. Entertaining prison drama dealing with a lifer who cultivates a love of the theater; after winning a pardon he forms a group of traveling actors who perform in prisons. Offbeat and immensely likable. (Dir: John Hancock, 115 mins.)†

Wee Geordie (Great Britain, 1955)***½ Bill Travers, Alastair Sim. Charming comedy about a skinny Scottish boy who grows up into a big, brawny man after sending for a "British Charles Atlas" bodybuilding correspondence course. (Dir: Frank Launder, 93 mins.)

Weekend (France-Italy, 1967)***½ Mireille Darc, Jean-Pierre Kalfon, Jean-Pierre Léaud, Jean Yanne. One of writer-director Jean-Luc Godard's most daring and disturbing diatribes against the capitalist societies of the West. Focuses on a car ride of a couple heading for the countryside and the apathy, anger, and violence they see along the way. (103 mins.)

Weekend at Bernie's (1989)*** Andrew McCarthy, Jonathan Silverman, Catherine Mary Stewart, Terry Kiser, Don Calfa. Raucous slapstick with Silverman and McCarthy spending a weekend at a summer resort trying to fool a mob hit man into thinking that his most recent victim, their boss, is still alive. Kiser is hilarious as the dead Bernie in this comedy written by Robert Klane (*Where's Poppa?*) (Dir: Ted Kotcheff, 97 mins.)†

Weekend at the Waldorf (1945)*** Ginger Rogers, Lana Turner, Walter Pidgeon, Van Johnson, Robert Benchley, Keenan Wynn. A fun reworking of *Grand Hotel*, set, obviously, at the Waldorf Hotel in N.Y.C. The various characters are cleverly updated—the ballerina is a movie star, the Baron a trenchcoated war correspondent; the previous film is slyly mentioned. In fact, some of the subordinate players are better than in the original. (Dir: Robert Z. Leonard, 130 mins.)

Weekend for Three (1941)*** Dennis O'Keefe, Jane Wyatt, Philip Reed. Newlyweds are troubled by a weekend guest who is attracted to the wife. Amusing comedy has good dialogue, pleasant players. (Dir: Irving Reis, 66 mins.)

Weekend in Havana (1941)**½ Alice Faye, Carmen Miranda, Cesar Romero. Another musical made at the time Latin American music was catching on. Routine, passable musical. (Dir: Walter Lang, 80 mins.)

Week-end Marriage (1932)** Loretta Young, Norman Foster, George Brent, Aline MacMahon, Vivienne Osborne, J. Farrell MacDonald. Silly depression comedy of a working wife going back to the kitchen to keep her whiny husband, on the theory that any husband is better than none. Young wasn't really a very accomplished comedienne at this point. (Dir: Thornton Freeland, 66 mins.)

Weekend Nun, The (MTV 1972)**½ Joanna Pettet, Vic Morrow, Ann Sothern, Beverly Garland. Based on a true story about Joyce Duco, a former nun who served in an experimental program in which she donned civilian clothes and functioned as a juvenile probation officer by day, returning to the convent each night. (Dir: Jeannot Szwarc, 78 mins.)

Weekend of Terror (MTV 1970)** Lee Majors, Robert Conrad, Lois Nettleton, Carol Lynley, Jane Wyatt. Conrad and Majors play a couple of desperate criminals whose kidnap victim accidentally dies, forcing them to snatch a substitute in order to collect the ransom. (Dir: Jud Taylor, 73 mins.)

Weekend Pass (1984)** D. W. Brown, Peter Ellenstein, Patrick Hauser, Chip

McAllister, Pamela G. Kay. Four sailors spend a weekend in L.A. looking for fun and romance. Nothing special. (Dir: Lawrence Bassoff, 92 mins.)†

Weekend War (MTV 1988)** Stephen Collins, Daniel Stern, Evan Mirand. An intriguing premise explored in static fashion, as a group of National Guardsman venture to Honduras to repair an airstrip and instead become involved in a *River Kwai*-like dilemma over a bridge that links Honduras to Nicaragua. (Dir: Steven Hilliard Stern, 96 mins.)

Weekend Warriors (1986)*½ Chris Lemmon, Vic Tayback, Lloyd Bridges, Graham Jarvis, Daniel Greene, Marty Cohen. Goofball service comedy about draft-conscious guys who join the National Guard to avoid active duty. Bert Convy's directorial debut. (85 mins.)†

Weekend with Father (1951)*** Van Heflin, Patricia Neal, Gigi Perreau, Richard Denning, Virginia Field. A widower and widow combine families, get situation comedy responses from the two sets of offspring. (Dir: Douglas Sirk, 83 mins.)

Weekend with Kate (Australia, 1990)*** Colin Friels, Catherine McClements, Jerome Ehlers, Helen Mutkins. Sophisticated comedy of adultery set in a beach house where promoter Friels, mistress Mutkins, wife McClements, and client Ehlers engage in sexual perfidy and confusion. Sunny farce with well-balanced characters. (Dir: Arch Nicholson, 95 mins.)

Week's Vacation, A (France 1980)***½ Nathalie Baye, Gerard Lanvin. A young Lyon schoolteacher is seized with a sudden feeling of frustrated alienation and self-doubt. Her sympathetic doctor recommends that she take a week off from work during which time she tries to re-evaluate her role as a teacher, as a lover, as a woman, and as a product of the educational changes wrought in the sixties. Intimate and emotional, many of the images and moments of confrontation linger in the mind. (Dir: Bertrand Tavernier, 102 mins.)

Wee Willie Winkie (1937)*** Shirley Temple, Victor McLaglen, June Lang, Cesar Romero. Shirley practically stops a war in India's Khyber Pass as part of the plot in this overly sentimental tale of garrison life in India. Shirley's fans will love it—others beware. (Dir: John Ford, 75 mins.)†

Weirdo (1986)½ Steve Burington, Jessica Straus, Naomi Sherwood, Lynne Agnus, Lynne Caryl. Slow-witted youth spends most of the movie enduring bullies, cycle sluts, and even his own mother's plans to sell him into slavery, before breaking out in a spree of murderous revenge. Staten Island filmmaker Andy Milligan has been making these no-budget horror turkeys for three decades; so much for practice making perfect. (91 mins.)†

Weird Science (1985)* Anthony Michael Hall, Kelly LeBrock, Bill Paxton, Ilan Mitchell-Smith, Suzanne Snyder. Two sexually desperate youths use their home computer to create the ideal woman, an independent creature who overturns their lives. (Dir: John Hughes, 91 mins.)†

Weird Woman (1944)**½ Lon Chaney, Evelyn Ankers. Chaney comes home with a tropic bride, raised in the South Seas, and finds himself in trouble with an old girl friend. OK melodrama. (Dir: Reginald Le Borg, 64 mins.)

Welcome Home (1989)** Kris Kristofferson, JoBeth Williams, Brian Keith, Sam Waterston, Trey Wilson, J.J. After seventeen years hiding from the Khmer Rouge in Cambodia, Kristofferson returns home to a wife who thought him dead and a son he never knew he had. Drama has some affecting moments but far too little plot. (Dir: Franklin J. Schaffner, 87 mins.)†

Welcome Home, Bobby (MTV 1986)** Tony LoBianco, Timothy Williams, Gisela Caldwell, Nan Woods. Well-intentioned but muddled story of a young teen who is unable to readjust to his former life after he runs away from home and has a brief homosexual relationship with an older man. (Dir: Herbert Wise, 104 mins.)

Welcome Home, Johnny Bristol (MTV 1972)**½ Martin Landau, Jane Alexander, Pat O'Brien, Martin Sheen, Brock Peters. Landau is very good as Johnny Bristol, an Army captain who returns to the U.S. after having been a prisoner in Vietnam for two years and discovers there's no trace of the town in Vermont where he grew up. (Dir: George McCowen, 99 mins.)

Welcome Home, Roxy Carmichael (1990)**½ Winona Ryder, Jeff Daniels, Laila Robins, Dinah Manoff, Thomas Wilson Brown, Frances Fisher, Sachi Parker. Sweet, sentimental comedy about the return of a hometown-girl-made-good and the influence the event has on the residents of Clyde, Ohio, especially the iconoclastic, young Dinki Bossetti (Ryder). Worth a look. (Dir: Jim Abrahams, 97 mins.)†

Welcome Home, Soldier Boys (1972)*½ Joe Don Baker, Paul Koslo, Alan Vint, Elliott Street, Billy Green Bush, Francine York, Geoffrey Lewis. An exploitative look at post-Vietnam adjustment crises. Four ex-Green Berets have trouble adapting themselves to peacetime. (Dir: Richard Compton, 91 mins.)

Welcome Stranger (1947)*** Bing Crosby, Barry Fitzgerald, Joan Caulfield, Wanda Hendrix. Young carefree doctor arrives to take over practice of conservative country doctor. The fine performances make for delightful entertainment. (Dir: Elliott Nugent, 107 mins.)

Welcome to Arrow Beach (1974)**½ Laurence Harvey, Stuart Whitman, Joanna Pettet, John Ireland, Meg Foster. Harvey's last film. Eerie psycho-chiller; a returning war vet enjoys battle carnage so much he has to keep killing to satisfy his blood-lust. AKA: **Tender Flesh.** (Dir: Laurence Harvey, 99 mins.)

Welcome to 18 (1986)** Courtney Thorne-Smith, Mariska Hargitay, Jo Ann Wilette. Over the summer, some teenage girls learn to cope with the cold, cruel world of adult employment. (Dir: Terry Carr, 89 mins.)†

Welcome to Hard Times (1967)**½ Henry Fonda, Janice Rule, Aldo Ray, Janis Paige, Lon Chaney, Jr. Interesting western; Fonda plays a leading citizen of Hard Times who doesn't stand up to a crazed gunman, played with dripping evil by Ray. (Dir: Burt Kennedy, 104 mins.)

Welcome to L.A. (1976)*** Keith Carradine, Sally Kellerman, Harvey Keitel, Geraldine Chaplin, Lauren Hutton, Sissy Spacek. Fragmented and flawed, but one of the most illuminating films ever made about Hollywood and the mystique of Lotus Land. An innovative, ambitious film. (Dir: Alan Rudolph, 106 mins.)†

Welcome to Oblivion (1990)½ Dack Rambo, Clare Beresford, Meshach Taylor. Dreadful end-of-the-world effort with cheesy heavy metal scenery and costumes, absurd mutants, and a boring script. Only the Peruvian settings get half a star. (Dir: Augusto Tamayo, 80 mins.)†

We Live Again (1934)*** Fredric March, Anna Sten, Sam Jaffe, Jane Baxter, C. Aubrey Smith. From Tolstoy's novel *Resurrection*. March is extraordinary in this weighty 19th-century drama. He plays a Russian aristocrat who comes to realize that his life is empty, and that he truly loves a good peasant girl. (Dir: Rouben Mamoulian, 82 mins.)

Well, The (1951)**** Richard Rober, Barry Kelley, Harry Morgan. Mob violence flares when a child disappears; however, the town bands together when she is discovered trapped in a well. Breathless, gripping drama, excellent in all departments. (Dirs: Leo Popkin, Russell Rouse, 85 mins.)

We'll Bury You (1961)**½ OK documentary tells of the rise of Communism. (Producers: Jack Leewood, Jack Thomas, 72 mins.)

Well-Digger's Daughter, The (France, 1941)**** Fernandel, Raimu, Josette Day Charpin, George Grey. Warm human story of a working-class girl who falls in love with the son of an upper-class

1169

family. When he goes off to war and is missing in action, she's left pregnant and alone. How her family and neighbors cope with the situation is uniquely French, and hugely enjoyable. Fernandel, as the well-digger's assistant who loves the girl, is marvelous. (Dir: Marcel Pagnol, 122 mins.)†

Well-Groomed Bride, The (1946)** Olivia de Havilland, Ray Milland, Sonny Tufts. Silly postwar comedy about a bride who wants champagne for her wedding and a naval officer who needs it to launch a ship. (Dir: Sidney Lanfield, 75 mins.)

Wells Fargo (1937)*** Joel McCrea, Bob Burns, Frances Dee, Lloyd Nolan, Robert Cummings. This is a super western about the beginnings of the famous company that transports money. (Dir: Frank Lloyd, 116 mins.)

We of the Never Never (Australia, 1982)*** Angela Punch McGregor, Arthur Dignam, Tommy Lewis. The true story of a young woman who leaves Melbourne at the turn of the century (1900) and, with her new husband, settles in the remote outback of Australia. There she struggles bravely for her own rights as an equal in a man's country, and for better understanding between the white man and the aborigines. (Dir: Igor Auzins, 132 mins.)†

We're Fighting Back (MTV 1981)** Kevin Mahon, Paul McCrane, Elgin Jones, Ellen Barkin. New York's ''Guardian Angels,'' the self-styled youth patrol riding the subways to deter crime, inspired this well-intentioned film. It would have been better if the film told the real story of Curtis Sliwa, and his band of streetwise ''Angels.'' (Dir: Lou Antonio, 104 mins.)

We're Going to Be Rich (Great Britain, 1938)**½ Gracie Fields, Victor McLaglen, Brian Donlevy, Coral Browne, Ted Smith. Charming, unusual period musical, set in 1890s South Africa, of a prospector and his wife trying to hit it big in the gold fields. (Dir: Monty Banks, 80 mins.)

We're in the Legion Now (1937)** Reginald Denny, Esther Ralston, Eleanor Hunt, Vince Barnett. Pair of petty gangsters hiding out in Paris are tracked by their enemies, so they take the last place left to hide—they join the Foreign Legion. Pleasant slapstick. (Dir: Crane Wilbur, 56 mins.)†

We're No Angels (1955)**½ Humphrey Bogart, Aldo Ray, Peter Ustinov, Joan Bennett, Basil Rathbone. Three escaped convicts from Devil's Island take over the store of a French shopkeeper, right some wrongs. Comedy has its amusing scenes, but the stage origin is too evident in its talkiness, lack of movement. (Dir: Michael Curtiz, 106 mins.)†

We're No Angels (1989)*** Robert De Niro, Sean Penn, Demi Moore, Hoyt Axton, Bruno Kirby, Ray McAnallay, James Russo, Wallace Shawn. In-name-only remake of the Bogart movie casts De Niro and Penn as dimwitted escaped convicts hiding out in a small New England town disguised as priests. Fans of the two stars will enjoy seeing them as a comedy team. Endearing and low-key. (Dir: Neil Jordan, 110 mins.)†

We're Not Dressing (1934)*** Bing Crosby, Carole Lombard, George Burns, Gracie Allen, Ethel Merman, Leon Errol, Ray Milland. Silly but tuneful rehash of James Barrie's *The Admirable Crichton*, about a screwball debutante tamed by a sailor when they're cast away on a deserted isle. (Dir: Norman Taurog, 80 mins.)

We're Not Married (1952)*** Ginger Rogers, Fred Allen, Marilyn Monroe, Mitzi Gaynor, David Wayne. Five couples are informed that their marriages are not legal. Episodic comedy with some sequences better than others—but the Fred Allen–Ginger Rogers section is a comedy gem. (Dir: Edmund Goulding, 85 mins.)

We're Rich Again (1934)** Edna May Oliver, Billie Burke, Marion Nixon, Reginald Denny, Joan Marsh, Buster Crabbe, Grant Mitchell, Edgar Kennedy. A silly script doesn't provide enough real wit to keep these characters going, as stuffy Denny marries nouveau-poor Marsh and puts up with her nutty family; good players are wasted. (Dir: William A. Seiter, 73 mins.)

Werewolf, The (1956)** Steven Ritch, Don Megowan, Joyce Holden, Eleanore Tanin. Extremely low-budget monster movie, with scientists trying out a cure for radiation poisoning that accidentally turns an ordinary guy into a werewolf. Unusually dopey, even for the '50s. (Dir: Fred F. Sears, 83 mins.)

Werewolf (MTV 1987)** Lance Le Gault, Chuck Connors, Raphael Sbarge. Non-hairraising tale of teen wolf trauma. That a guy's best friend is not his werewolf is the lesson learned by our hero after he's attacked by his best buddy. (Dir: David Hemmings, 90 mins.)

Werewolf in a Girl's Dormitory (Italy-Austria, 1963)* Barbara Lass, Carl Schell. Members of the staff of a school are suspected when a series of murders occur. English-dubbed horror flub. (Dir: ''Richard Benson'' [Paolo Heusch], 84 mins.)†

Werewolf of London (1935)**½ Henry Hull, Warner Oland, Valerie Hobson, Spring Byington. Leisurely but interesting chiller. A doctor, bitten by a werewolf, turns into a fiend. (Dir: Stuart Walker, 75 mins.)

Werewolf of Washington, The (1973)* Dean Stockwell, Biff McGuire, Clifton James, Beeson Carroll, Thayer David. Cheapjack werewolf flick that's a klutzy blend of political parody and wolfman chills. (Dir: Milton Moses Ginsberg, 90 mins.)†

Werewolves on Wheels (1971)½ Stephen Oliver, Severn Darden, D. J. Anderson, Duece Berry, Billy Gray, Barry McGuire. Comic-horror-biker picture that has cyclists turning into lycanthropes at the behest of high priest Darden. Almost unwatchable. (Dir: Michael Levesque, 85 mins.)†

Westbound (1959)** Randolph Scott, Virginia Mayo. Leather-faced Scott gives another tight-lipped performance in this predictable western. Virginia Mayo is a notch above the usual Scott leading lady. (Dir: Budd Boetticher, 72 mins.)

West-Bound Limited, The (1923)**½ Ralph Lewis, Claire McDowell, Ella Hall, Johnny Harron. One of a series of popular silent railroad melodramas, this concerns a hard working engineer and his family; he rescues the daughter of the president of the company he works for from an accident, and becomes involved in financial intrigue. Played for thrills rather than drama; a fascinating curio. (Dir: Emory Johnson, 65 mins.)†

Westerner, The (1940)*** Gary Cooper, Walter Brennan, Doris Davenport, Forrest Tucker, Dana Andrews. Brennan's ornery, many-layered performance as Judge Roy Bean dominates the picture, although Cooper is the nominal star. William Wyler's direction is too meticulous, and his comedy relief doesn't play well. (100 mins.)†

Western Union (1941)*** Randolph Scott, Robert Young, Dean Jagger. A good western based on the laying of the first transcontinental Western Union wire in 1861. (Dir: Fritz Lang, 94 mins.)†

We Still Kill the Old Way (Italy, 1967)*** Irene Papas, Gian Maria Volonte, Luigi Pistilli. Thrilling melodrama about the psychology of the Mafia and how the locals take care of their own, Sicilian-style. (Dir: Elio Petri, 92 mins.)

West of Shanghai (1937)**½ Boris Karloff, Beverly Roberts, Ricardo Cortez, Gordon Oliver, Sheila Bromley, Vladimir Sokoloff, Richard Loo. Exotic melodrama of Chinese warlord Karloff who comes to the aid of American oilman Oliver when renegade profiteers threaten his contracts. OK actioner, with good, colorful decor. AKA: **The Warlord.** (Dir: John Farrow, 65 mins.)

West of the Pecos (1945)**½ Robert Mitchum, Barbara Hale, Bill Williams. Zane Grey story of a cowboy who saves a meat packer's daughter, disguised as a boy, from bandits. Pleasing, well-made western. (Dir: Edward Killy, 68 mins.)

West of Zanzibar (1928)*** Lon Chaney, Lionel Barrymore, Warner Baxter, Mary Nolan. Intense story with Chaney outstanding as the crippled ruler of a jungle kingdom who thirsts for revenge against the man who wronged him, and exacts it upon his daughter. This is one of several teamings of Chaney and the eccentric horror director Tod Browning, which range from the bizarre to the actively unpleasant. Re-made as *Kongo*. (63 mins.)†

West of Zanzibar (Great Britain, 1954)** Anthony Steel, Sheila Sim, William Simons, Orlando Martins. Hackneyed British drama, with game warden Steel foiling ivory poachers; a good cause in itself, but very paternalistically portrayed. Dull, despite the scenery. (Dir: Harry Watt, 94 mins.)

West Point of the Air (1935)**½ Wallace Beery, Robert Young, Maureen O'Sullivan, Lewis Stone, James Gleason, Rosalind Russell. Typical military melodrama, with Beery as an aviation veteran trying to force his happy-go-lucky son to follow in his footsteps. Formulaic, but effective, with a cast of MGM professionals. (Dir: Richard Rosson, 100 mins.)

West Point Story, The (1950)** James Cagney, Doris Day, Gordon MacRae, Virginia Mayo. Corny musical comedy about a Broadway director who stages a big revue at West Point. It's a delight though to see James Cagney hoofing again. (Dir: Roy Del Ruth, 107 mins.)

West Point Widow (1941)**½ Anne Shirley, Richard Carlson. Nurse marries an Army football star, but the secret union is in jeopardy when she is about to become a mother. (Dir: Robert Siodmak, 64 mins.)

West Side Story (1961)***½ Natalie Wood, Rita Moreno, Richard Beymer, George Chakiris, Russ Tamblyn. The Broadway musical masterpiece about rival white and Puerto Rican gangs in a New York ghetto becomes a spectacular movie musical. Jerome Robbins's choreography in this modern Romeo and Juliet story is enhanced greatly by the magnificent New York City location photography. The familiar score by Leonard Bernstein and Stephen Sondheim hasn't diminished in quality. (Dirs: Robert Wise, Jerome Robbins, 155 mins.)†

Westward Ho the Wagons (1956)** Fess Parker, Kathleen Crowley, Jeff York, David Stollery, Sebastian Cabot. The classic Disney production values are about the only things worth tuning in for in this scenic, vapid western. (Dir: William Beaudine, 90 mins.)†

Westward Passage (1932)*** Ann Harding, Laurence Olivier, ZaSu Pitts, Irving

Pichel, Juliette Compton, Bonita Granville. Delightful romantic comedy-drama; Olivier is an egotistical writer who leaves his wife and daughter to pursue his career. A few years later, after his wife has remarried, they meet and fall in love again. Frank, engaging, and spirited. (Dir: Robert Milton, 72 mins.)

Westward the Women (1951)**½ Robert Taylor, Denise Darcel, John McIntire. All the elements seem in place in this long, handsome western about 150 Chicago women being led to California in the 1850s to find husbands. (Dir: William A. Wellman, 118 mins.)

Westworld (1973)*** Richard Benjamin, Yul Brynner, James Brolin. An original sci-fi story about a vacation spot where the guests can act out their biggest fantasies with the aid of programmed robots. Two guests find themselves in an "Old West" nightmare when the robots run amok. (Dir: Michael Crichton, 88 mins.) †

Wet Gold (MTV 1984)**½ Brooke Shields, Burgess Meredith, Brian Kerwin, Tom Byrd. The notable things about this routine 'treasure hunt' drama are: the picturesque scenery, the number of times Shields changes swimming togs, and the rather nasty end met by the villain. (Dir: Dick Lowry, 104 mins.)†

We the Living (Italy, 1941)*** Rossano Brazzi, Alida Valli, Fosco Giachetti. Suppressed by the Mussolini government and thought lost until recently, this restored adaptation of Ayn Rand's novel is tame as anticommunist propaganda, though a fine romantic melodrama. In the post-Revolutionary U.S.S.R., a headstrong young woman becomes the mistress of an aristocrat's son while resisting the attentions of a young Communist Party official. (Dir: Goffredo Alessandrini, 170 mins.) †

Wetherby (Great Britain, 1985)***½ Vanessa Redgrave, Ian Holm, Judi Dench. Redgrave, a spinster schoolmarm, is jolted into re-examining her relationships when a young stranger calmly kills himself in her presence. A stimulating screenplay by playwright David Hare (who also directed), provides a moving experience. (102 mins.)†

We Think the World of You (Great Britain, 1988)** Alan Bates, Gary Oldman, Liz Smith. While bisexual Oldman is in jail, his older lover (Bates) transfers his affections to Oldman's dog. Peculiar tale is too indifferently made to have much impact. (Dir: Colin Gregg, 94 mins.)†

We Three (Italy, 1985)**½ Christopher Davidson, Lino Capolicchio, Gianni Cavina. Biographical film dramatizes an incident in the youth of Mozart, a prodigy denied a normal childhood. What could have turned into *Young Amadeus* is a bit more interesting thanks to the sensibility of odd Italian director Pupi Avati. (90 mins.)

Wet Parade, The (1932)** Myrna Loy, Jimmy Durante, Walter Huston, Robert Young. Prohibition comedy-drama based on Upton Sinclair material, powerhouse cast, and a dog from the word go. (Dir: Victor Fleming, 120 mins.)

We've Never Been Licked (1943)*** Richard Quine, Anne Gwynne, Martha O'Driscoll, Noah Beery, Jr., William Frawley, Robert Mitchum. Patriotic WWII melodrama concerns a youth who was brought up in Japan unjustly accused of espionage and becoming a counterspy for the Allies. Outlandish heroics take over towards the end. (Dir: John Rawlins, 103 mins.)

We Were Dancing (1941)** Norma Shearer, Melvyn Douglas. Contrived rehash of some Noel Coward one-act plays has flashes of wit, is well played but not entertaining. (Dir: Robert Z. Leonard, 94 mins.)

We Were One Man (France, 1980)*** Serge Avedikian, Piotr Stanislas, Catherine Albin. During WWII, a quiet young Frenchman and a wounded German soldier overcome the differences of language and political enmity to develop a loving, fulfilling relationship. A subtle and moving film. (Dir: Philippe Vallois, 90 mins.)

We Were So Beloved (1986)***½ Questions of conscience generated by the Holocaust are examined from a unique angle in a series of interviews with German-Jewish immigrants who left Nazi Germany just prior to the start of WWII. (Dir: Manfred Kirchheimer, 145 mins.)

We Were Strangers (1949)**½ Jennifer Jones, John Garfield, Pedro Armendariz. Despite the powerhouse cast, this movie about political intrigue and revolution in Cuba during the thirties is a disappointment. (Dir: John Huston, 106 mins.)

We Who Are Young (1940)**½ Lana Turner, John Shelton, Gene Lockhart, Jonathan Hale, Ian Wolfe. Star-making vehicle for Turner as an honest working girl who falls in love with a young man who works for the same company, but whom corporate policy forbids her to marry. Capable populist drama, and Turner is excellent. Story by Dalton Trumbo. (Dir: Harold S. Bucquet, 80 mins.)

We Will Not Grow Old Together (France, 1972)***½ Marlene Jobert, Jean Yanne, Macha Meril, Jacques Galland. Standout drama about a vain married man who has an affair with a much younger woman. The relationship crumbles, devastating the woman and drawing her family and friends into the maelstrom. Yanne and Jobert are brilliant in this painful film. (Dir: Maurice Pialat, 107 mins.)

Whale for the Killing, A (MTV 1981)** Peter Strauss, Dee Wallace, Bill Calvert, Richard Widmark. Well-intentioned script gets bogged down in platitudes and rhetoric. Strauss spearheads the battle against townspeople who want to sell a beached whale to a Russian trawler. (Dir: Richard T. Heffron, 156 mins.)†

Whales of August, The (Great Britain, 1987)**** Lillian Gish, Bette Davis, Ann Sothern, Vincent Price, Harry Carey, Jr. Superb film about two elderly sisters who bravely face the vicissitudes of aging together in different ways. Gish is ineffably moving as the gentle caretaker who looks after her blind sister, and Davis is magnificent as the embittered, blind Libby, forever passing judgment and clearly thriving on her querulousness. (Dir: Lindsay Anderson, 90 mins.)†

What! (Italy–France–Great Britain, 1963)** Daliah Lavi, Christopher Lee, Tony Kendall. Grisly murders begin when a dastardly brother returns to his castle after a long absence. Gothic horror thriller with some chilling moments. (Dir: "John M. Old" [Mario Bava], 92 mins.)

What? (Italy, 1973)* Sydne Rome, Marcello Mastroianni, Hugh Griffith, Romolo Valli, Guido Alberti. Self-indulgent comedy from Roman Polanski; a sweet young thing stays at the manse of an Italian millionaire where she's subjected to bizarre humiliations. AKA: **Diary of Forbidden Dreams.** (112 mins.)†

What About Bob? (1991)**½ Bill Murray, Richard Dreyfuss, Julie Hagerty, Charlie Korsmo, Kathryn Erbe, Tom Aldredge, Susan Willis. Wacky, but ultimately tedious, reshaping of *The Man Who Came to Dinner* stars Murray as a simple-minded goofball with myriad problems who follows his psychiatrist (Dreyfuss) on his vacation and won't go away. The film collapses under the weight of Bob's annoyance factor, but the first half is fun. (Dir: Frank Oz, 97 mins.)†

What a Life (1939)*** Jackie Cooper, Betty Field (film debut), Hedda Hopper. The original Henry Aldrich story about the high school boy who can't stay out of trouble. Screen adaptation by Billy Wilder and Charles Brackett. Good fun. (Dir: Theodore Reed, 79 mins.)

What Are Best Friends For? (MTV 1973)** Lee Grant, Larry Hagman, Ted Bessell, Barbara Feldon. Wacky, implausible comedy about an immature cuckold (Bessell) who finds a sanctuary with his best friends during his period of adjustment. (Dir: Jay Sandrich, 74 mins.)

What a Way to Go (1964)**½ Shirley MacLaine, Paul Newman, Dick Van Dyke, Robert Mitchum, Gene Kelly, Dean Martin, Bob Cummings. Overproduced black comedy with some good musical numbers. MacLaine plays a simple country girl who marries a succession of wealthy men. (Dir: J. Lee Thompson, 111 mins.)

What a Woman! (1943)**½ Rosalind Russell, Brian Aherne, Ann Savage, Willard Parker, Alan Dinehart. What a comedienne! Roz plays a buttinski literary agent who charms the pants off her clients, including a milquetoast whom she breathes life into. (Dir: Irving Cummings, 94 mins.)

What Changed Charley Farthing—See: **Bananas Boat, The**

What Comes Around (1986)* Jerry Reed, Barry Corbin, Bo Hopkins, Arte Johnson. Reed executive-produced and directed this feature starring himself as a famous burnt-out country singer who's been ripped off for millions of dollars by his manager. Surprisingly humorless tale is unlikely to appeal to those looking for another *Smokey and the Bandit.* (86 mins.)†

What Did You Do in the War, Daddy? (1966)* James Coburn, Dick Shawn, Harry Morgan. Another Hollywood reminder—and a vulgar, distasteful one at that—that war, this time WWII in Sicily, is just a hilarious bunch of chuckles and good clean fun for everyone concerned. (Dir: Blake Edwards, 119 mins.)

What Do You Say to a Naked Lady? (1970)** Director Allen (*Candid Camera*) Funt's idea of a joke: the title adequately summarizes the premise of this feature-length stunt. Some funny vignettes. (92 mins.)†

Whatever Happened to Aunt Alice? (1969)**½ Geraldine Page, Rosemary Forsyth, Ruth Gordon, Mildred Dunnock. Another in the line of Grand Guignol melodramas starring veteran actresses. Gordon, as dotty as ever, is the prime victim of crazy Page, whose housekeepers keep disappearing after they are hired. (Dir: Lee H. Katzin, 101 mins.)†

What Ever Happened to Baby Jane? (1962)***½ Bette Davis, Joan Crawford, Victor Buono, Anna Lee, Marjorie Bennett, Maidie Norman. Grand Guignol in the grand manner, with a chilling performance by Davis as a faded former child movie star who lives in seclusion and gets kicks by mentally torturing her crippled sister. Virtuoso direction by Robert Aldrich, good performances by the stars, and admirably nasty acting by Victor Buono. (132 mins.)†

What Ever Happened to Baby Jane? (MTV 1991)*** Vanessa Redgrave, Lynn Redgrave, John Glover, Bruce Young, Amy Steel. The first question most filmgoers will ask is: "Who needs a remake of the *classic* cult film that starred Bette Davis and Joan Crawford?" There's only one reason why this was remade and that is to topline real-life sisters,

Vanessa and Lynn Redgrave, as the former movie stars living out their final years together in a love-hate relationship. Lynn has the flashier role as the warped Jane, a former child star who hopes to stage a comeback. Vanessa, as the crippled sister Blanche, manages to keep the story from becoming a totally Grand Guignol horror show. There's life in the old Guignol yet! (Dir: David Greene, 96 mins.)

Whatever It Takes (1986)*½ Tom Mason, Martin Balsam, Chris Weatherhead. Muddled character study of a cartoonist trying to scribble his way to syndicated glory. (Dir: Bob Demchuk, 93 mins.)

What Every Woman Knows (1934)***½ Helen Hayes, Brian Aherne, Lucile Watson, Madge Evans, Donald Crisp. Hayes is charming as she pulls the strings and keeps her handsome but bumbling politician hubby from making a fool of himself. (Dir: Gregory La Cava, 92 mins.)

What Happened to Kerouac? (1986)**½ William Burroughs, Neal Cassady, Carolyn Cassady, Lawrence Ferlinghetti, Jack Kerouac, Jan Kerouac. A rather affecting documentary about the Beat Generation figurehead. (Dirs: Richard Lerner, Lewis MacAdams, 96 mins.)†

What Have I Done to Deserve This? (Spain, 1984)***½ Carmen Maura, Veronica Forque. A bizarre but liberating comic exploration about a woman under the influence of modern times in Spain. Wacky and irreverent. (Dir: Pedro Almodovar, 100 mins.)†

What Next, Corporal Hargrove? (1945)**½ Robert Walker, Keenan Wynn. Weak follow-up to the original. This is pure slapstick with Hargrove over in France romancing some French cuties. (Dir: Richard Thorpe, 95 mins.)

What! No Beer? (1933)** Buster Keaton, Jimmy Durante, Roscoe Ates, Phyllis Barry, John Miljan, Henry Armetta, Edward Brophy. One of Keaton's poorest sound vehicles, this has two brewers trying to set up in business a few months before Prohibition is repealed. (Dir: Edward Sedgwick, 70 mins.)

What Price Glory? (1926)**** Victor McLaglen, Edmund Lowe, Dolores Del Rio. Classic silent film based on the play by Laurence Stallings and Maxwell Anderson. Eloquent antiwar drama with outstanding performances by McLaglen and Lowe as two tough but human Marines fighting in the trenches of WWI, and Del Rio as the French country girl who sparks their intense rivalry. The battle scenes are surreal, stark, and used sparingly. (Dir: Raoul Walsh, 120 mins.)

What Price Glory (1952)**½ James Cagney, Dan Dailey, Corinne Calvet, Robert Wagner. Although not as successful as the original silent film classic of the same title, this remake is greatly aided by the robust performances of Cagney and Dailey as hard-drinking, two-fisted soldiers stationed in France during WWI. (Dir: John Ford, 111 mins.)†

What Price Hollywood? (1932)**** Constance Bennett, Lowell Sherman, Neil Hamilton, Gregory Ratoff. Splendid Hollywood drama about an aspiring actress discovered by a famous director. As her career progresses, his is shattered by drink and dissolution. Bennett is clever and beautiful, and veteran actor-director Sherman is brilliant as a talented man who sees his life destroyed by indulgence. (Dir: George Cukor, 88 mins.)†

What Price Victory? (MTV 1988)*½ Mac Davis, George Kennedy, Robert Culp, Brian Wimmer. Run-of-the-mill sports drama about "Desert State University" and its efforts to get a successful football team. (Dir: Kevin Connor, 96 mins.)

What's a Nice Girl Like You...? (MTV 1971)** Brenda Vaccaro, Jack Warden, Vincent Price, Roddy McDowall, Edmond O'Brien. Passable comedy about a Bronx girl who poses as a socialite in an elaborate extortion plot. (Dir: Jerry Paris, 72 mins.)

What's New, Pussycat? (U.S.-France, 1965)** Peter Sellers, Peter O'Toole, Woody Allen, Romy Schneider, Ursula Andress, Paula Prentiss, Capucine. Occasionally funny comedy that rambles all over the place. Sellers is a wacky psychiatrist; O'Toole is a tireless ladies' man who seeks Sellers' advice; Woody is O'Toole's bumbling buddy. (Dir: Clive Donner, 108 mins.)†

What's So Bad About Feeling Good? (1968)** George Peppard, Mary Tyler Moore, Dom DeLuise, Don Stroud, Thelma Ritter, Susan St. James. Silly, harmless little comedy about a bird which spreads a strange virus resulting in "instant happiness." (Dir: George Seaton, 94 mins.)

What's the Matter with Helen? (1971)*** Debbie Reynolds, Shelley Winters, Dennis Weaver, Agnes Moorehead. A thriller in the *Baby Jane* vein. In the 1930s, two women flee from their past (which includes murders committed by their sons) and open up a dance school in Hollywood, but they feel the past catching up with them. Flashily directed and eerily on target. (Dir: Curtis Harrington, 101 mins.)

What's Up Doc? (1972)** Barbra Streisand, Ryan O'Neal, Madeline Kahn. Director Peter Bogdanovich resurrects the screwball comedy and tries to invest it with new meanings for our time. O'Neal is an absentminded professor who has many a misadventure with Streisand, ending in an outlandish car chase. (90 mins.)†

What's Up Front (1964)* Tommy Holden, Marilyn Manning, Carolyn Walker, William Watters [Arch Hall, Sr.]. Presexual revolution comedy about a salesman who discovers a way to save a failing brassiere company—by selling door to door. (Dir: Bob Wehling, 83 mins.)†

What's Up, Hideous Sun Demon (1989)*** Voices of Jay Leno, Susan Tyrell, Barbara Goodson. 1959's *Hideous Sun Demon* is given campy new dialogue in this generally funny parody. Fortunately it's a short film, as this type of humor tends to wear thin quickly. (Dir: Craig Mitchell, 71 mins.)†

What's Up, Tiger Lily? (U.S.-Japan, 1966) *** Woody Allen, Lovin' Spoonful. The zany Mr. Allen wrote some incongruous English dialogue to accompany a magnificently photographed Japanese ('64) spy story which just happened to be a terrible film without any prospect of a profitable release in the U.S. This juxtaposition of original footage with a new soundtrack has been done before, but a lot of this is quite wild, if you're in the mood for this kind of a romp. (Dirs: Woody Allen, Senkichi Taniguchi, 80 mins.)†

What the Peeper Saw (Great Britain, 1971)** Mark Lester, Britt Ekland, Hardy Kruger, Lilli Palmer, Harry Andrews. An angelic-looking twelve-year-old (Lester) is not quite right in the head and may have killed his mother. A lip-smacking psycho-thriller. AKA: **Night Hair Child**. (Dir: James Kelly, 89 mins.)†

What Waits Below (1984)** Robert Powell, Lisa Blount, Timothy Bottoms, Anne Heywood, Richard Johnson. Scientists trying to install a listening device in an underground cavern discover an alien civilization, along with a few nasty beasties. (Dir: Don Sharp, 88 mins.)†

Wheeler and Murdock (MTV 1972)*½ Jack Warden, Christopher Stone. Warden is the older and firmer half of a detective partnership, and younger, swinging Stone fills the bill as the other half. The plot deals with some Mafia money. (Dir: Joseph Sargent, 73 mins.)

Wheeler Dealers, The (1963)*** James Garner, Lee Remick, Chill Wills, Shelley Berman. Zany comedy about an oil tycoon who comes to New York to raise money for some drilling, runs across a pretty stock analyst. Witty dialogue, performances by a cast filled with funsters like Jim Backus, Phil Harris, John Astin, Louis Nye. (Dir: Arthur Hiller, 106 mins.)

Wheels of Terror (MCTV 1990)** Joanna Cassidy, Marcie Leeds, Arlen Dean Snyder. Tacky, exploitative chase tale. A peaceful Arizona community is abruptly thrown into pandemonium when a monstrous black sedan, driven by an unseen force, preys upon unsuspecting children. A strong performance by Ms. Cassidy, who single-handedly battles the demonic car. (Dir: Chris Cain, 96 mins.)

When a Stranger Calls (1979)*** Carol Kane, Rachel Roberts, Tony Beckley, Charles Durning, Colleen Dewhurst. A brilliant, short horror film, trapped inside an interesting but unexceptional longer one. The first twenty minutes are a terrifying, virtual self-contained mini-movie in which a babysitter (Kane) is tormented by phone calls from an unseen maniac who's threatening to murder the children in her charge. After the fear reaches an almost unbearable pitch, the filmmakers loosen their grip a little, and the film never fully regains its momentum. (Dir: Fred Walton, 97 mins.)†

When a Woman Ascends the Stairs (Japan, 1960)*** Hideko Takamine, Masayuki Mori, Daisuke Kato. Tense, disturbing drama about bar girls in Tokyo, some of whom practice prostitution because of family pressures. Unusual look at a side of gleaming, modern Tokyo that's not in the travel brochures. (Dir: Mikio Naruse, 110 mins.)

When Comedy Was King (1960)*** Robert Youngson's second compilation movie featuring scenes from classic silent movie comedies. Many of the great film pioneers appear in this joyful collection, including Buster Keaton, Gloria Swanson, Ben Turpin, Charlie Chaplin, Fatty Arbuckle, the Keystone Kops, Charley Chase, Laurel and Hardy, and Wallace Beery. (81 mins.)†

When Dinosaurs Ruled the Earth (1970)** Victoria Vetri, Robin Hawdon, Patrick Allen, Drewe Henley. Simple-minded plot about a cavewoman (Vetri) who links up with fishermen from a neighboring tribe after she's been banished from hers for being a blonde. (Dir: Val Guest, 100 mins.)

When Dreams Come True (MTV 1985)*½ Lee Horsley, Cindy Williams, David Morse, Jessica Harper, Stan Shaw, Jeanne Cairns. Cindy Williams and detective Lee Horsley are lovers but Cindy has been dreaming about a fascinating man who materializes in her real life. Meanwhile, her boyfriend is hot on a case involving a multiple murderer. Can you guess the rest? (Dir: John Llewellyn Moxey, 104 mins.)

When Eight Bells Toll (Great Britain,

1971)** Anthony Hopkins, Robert Morley, Jack Hawkins. Features a plodding script by Alistair MacLean, and the waste of a superb British cast. Clichés center on Hopkins's underwater search for stolen bullion. (Dir: Étienne Perier, 94 mins.)

When Every Day Was the Fourth of July (MTV 1978)**½ Dean Jones, Louise Sorel. Based on recollections of producer-director Dan Curtis's childhood, this murder mystery offers a solid yarn, with good characters and a suspenseful plot. In '37 in Bridgeport, Conn., a candy store owner is murdered. Though the crime is pinned on a slightly retarded, mute handyman, the efforts of a young girl, her brother, and his friends result in justice. (104 mins.)†

When Father Was Away on Business (Yugoslavia, 1985)*** Moreno D'E Bartoli, Miki Manojlovic, Mira Furlan, Mirjana Karanovic. A critically overpraised but worthwhile film set in Yugoslavia in the 1950s. Although the film takes too much time to unveil this memory play about how the mechanics of domestic life operate and how the political machinery of the bureaucracy is oiled by lies, it is undeniably poignant, especially since the events are viewed through a child's memory. (Dir: Emil Kusturica, 124 mins.)

When Harry Met Sally (1989)*** Billy Crystal, Meg Ryan, Carrie Fisher. When a wonderfully funny and witty screenplay meets both a top flight cast and a gifted director, the result is a fine romantic comedy in the style of *Annie Hall*. Nora Ephron's original screenplay is knowing, poignant, and hilarious, and Crystal is vulnerable, tender, and adorable. This marvelous comedy manages to look at the serious and the farcical side of love in the 1980s. (Dir: Rob Reiner, 95 mins.)†

When Hell Broke Loose (1958)** Charles Bronson, Violet Rensing. Racketeer in the army has a rough time until the love of a German girl reforms him. Good performance by Bronson in an ordinary war drama. (Dir: Kenneth Crane, 78 mins.)

When Hell Was in Session (MTV 1979) ***½ Hal Holbrook, Eva Marie Saint, Mako, Ronny Cox. A moving study of one man's courage and stubbornness, based on the experiences of a navy commander who spent 7½ years as a tortured POW in Vietnam. (Dir: Paul Krasny, 100 mins.)

When He's Not a Stranger (MTV 1989)**½ Annabeth Gish, Kevin Dillon, John Terlewsky, Kay Meyers, Paul Dooley. The subject of date rape is treated with care and candor in this telefilm starring Gish as a college girl who is raped by her best friend's boyfriend, the school's star jock. (Dir: John Gray, 96 mins.)

When I Grow Up (1951)***½ Robert Preston,
1176

Martha Scott, Bobby Driscoll, Charley Grapewin. His parents fail to understand a mischievous youngster, until the grandfather takes a hand and straightens things out. Very good drama of a boy's problems, handled with insight and care. (Dir: Michael Kanin, 80 mins.)

When in Rome (1952)**½ Van Johnson, Paul Douglas. During the Holy Year 1950, a con man swipes a priest's clothes, finds the outfit beginning to get him. Dated but fairly amusing comedy-drama. (Dir: Clarence Brown, 78 mins.)

When Joseph Returns (Hungary, 1976)*** Lili Monori, Gyorgy Pogany, Maria Ronyecz, Eva Ruttkai. New bride Monori is left frightened and alone when her sailor husband returns to his ship. When her recently divorced mother-in-law begins sleeping around, she follows suit. Superbly photographed melodrama creates a touching world of a bewildered and saddened young woman. (Dir: Zsolt Kezdi-Kovacs, 92 mins.)

When Knights Were Bold (Great Britain, 1936)**½ Jack Buchanan, Fay Wray, Garry Marsh, Kate Cutler, Martita Hunt, Robert Horton. Sprightly British comedy about a nonconformist peer who causes social havoc by preferring the company of local villagers to that of upper class snobs. (Dir: Jack Raymond, 76 mins.)†

When Ladies Meet (1933)*** Ann Harding, Myrna Loy, Robert Montgomery, Frank Morgan, Alice Brady. Interesting, clever romantic comedy about an authoress and a publisher's wife finding their own rivalry parallels the plot of a novel. High-powered cast, glossy production, and deft direction. AKA: Truth Is Stranger. (Dir: Harry Beaumont, 73 mins.)

When Ladies Meet (1941)**½ Joan Crawford, Robert Taylor, Greer Garson, Herbert Marshall, Spring Byington. A love quadrangle, played by superprofessionals. Some once-serious discussion of "women's rights" that has dated badly, but on the whole it's an oddly attractive picture. AKA: Strange Skirts. (Dir: Robert Z. Leonard, 108 mins.)

When Michael Calls (MTV 1971)*½ Elizabeth Ashley, Ben Gazzara, Michael Douglas. Limp thriller which has Miss Ashley receiving phone calls from a child who is supposedly dead, but who insists on avenging the murder of his mother. (Dir: Philip Leacock, 73 mins.)

When My Baby Smiles at Me (1948)**½ Betty Grable, Dan Dailey, James Gleason, Jack Oakie, June Havoc. Burlesque, the play about a comic and his wife, has been set to music for this routine film. Routine. (Dir: Walter Lang, 98 mins.)

When Nature Calls (1985)*½ David Orange, Barbara Marineau, Nickey Beim, G. Gordon Liddy. The plot, about a city family "getting back to nature," is merely an excuse for a scattershot collection of ineffective gags about everything under the sun. However, the telethon raising funds for a cure for Jerry Lewis disease is a satiric idea worthy of praise. (Dir: Charles Kaufman, 76 mins.)†

When She Says No (MTV 1984)** Kathleen Quinlan, Jane Alexander, Jeffrey DeMunn, David Huffman, Kenneth McMillan, Rip Torn. College professor (Quinlan) invites three male colleagues to her room during a convention weekend. She claims they raped her, and that's the crux of the story. (Dir: Paul Aaron, 104 mins.)

When She Was Bad (MTV 1979)**½ Robert Urich, Cheryl Ladd, Eileen Brennan, Dabney Coleman. Ladd plays a troubled wife and mother who lashes out at her young daughter whenever she feels the pressures building. (Dir: Peter Hunt, 104 mins.)

When Strangers Marry—See: Betrayed (1944)

When the Bough Breaks (MTV 1986)** Ted Danson, Richard Masur, Kim Miyori, Rachel Ticotin. This downbeat, tasteless mystery tale concerns a group of successful businessmen who mistreat children. Ted Danson stars as the psychologist turned detective bent on unraveling two murders; his investigation leads him to a fraternity of very sick men. (Dir: Waris Hussein, 104 mins.)

When the Boys Meet the Girls (1965)** Connie Francis, Harve Presnell, Herman's Hermits. The best thing about this remake of the Judy Garland-Mickey Rooney musical *Girl Crazy* is the songs, such as "I Got Rhythm," "Bidin' My Time," and "Embraceable You." The thin plot about a ranch on the verge of bankruptcy which is turned into a dude ranch, serves as a stage wait between musical numbers. (Dir: Alvin Ganzer, 110 mins.)

When the Circus Came to Town (MTV 1981)*** Elizabeth Montgomery, Christopher Plummer, Eileen Brennan, Gretchen Wyler, Timothy Hill. Plummer and Montgomery are perfectly suited in this romantic yarn about a woman who gives into a lifelong ambition to run away and join the circus. (Dir: Boris Sagal, 104 mins.)

When the Daltons Rode (1940)*** Randolph Scott, Kay Francis, Brian Donlevy, Broderick Crawford, George Bancroft. Good old-fashioned western, plenty of action. (Dir: George Marshall, 80 mins.)

When the Legends Die (1972)*** Richard Widmark, Frederic Forrest, Luana Anders. Lovely, understated, perceptive story about a young Indian boy who leaves his reservation to try his luck on the rodeo circuit under the aegis of his hard-drinking guardian (Widmark). (Dir: Stuart Miller, 105 mins.)†

When the Mountains Tremble (1983)*** Zealous documentary details the struggles of the peasant class of Guatemala against seemingly endless domination and repression by state, regional, and foreign interests. Determined film doesn't shy from attacking perceived enemies of the people, including corporate exploiters. (Dirs: Pamela Yates, Thomas Sigel, 83 mins.)

When the North Wind Blows (1974)** Dan Haggerty, Henry Brandon. In this nature drama an old trapper hides in the wilderness and befriends wild animals, after accidentally wounding a young boy. Haggerty plays a villager who tries to convince him to come back. (Dir: Stewart Raffill, 108 mins.)†

When the Time Comes (MTV 1987)*** Bonnie Bedelia, Brad Davis, Terry O'Quinn. Bedelia shines as a thirty-four-year-old woman who discovers that she's facing a protracted and painful decline from cancer and meets resistance when she decides to take her own life. (Dir: John Erman, 104 mins.)

When the West Was Young (1933)**½ Randolph Scott, Sally Blane, J. Farrell MacDonald, Guinn Williams. One of three versions of Zane Grey's novel *Heritage of the Desert* (the film's original release title) stars a young Scott as an Eastern surveyor who comes west and gets caught up in a land war. Solid western was director Henry Hathaway's first film. (53 mins.)†

When the Whales Came (Great Britain, 1989)**½ Helen Mirren, Paul Scofield, David Threfall, David Suchet, Helen Pearce. Picturesque scenery and an unusual atmosphere; two children on a small British isle ignore their fellow islanders' prejudices about old hermit Scofield. (Dir: Clive Rees, 100 mins.)†

When the Wind Blows (Great Britain, 1988)**½ Voices of Peggy Ashcroft, John Mills. Animated black comedy about two elderly Brits who make the mistake of following their government's advice on surviving a nuclear attack. A brutal bit of satire, though the subject deserves it. (Dir: Jimmy T. Murakami, 81 mins.)†

When Time Ran Out (1980)* Paul Newman, Jacqueline Bisset, William Holden, Red Buttons, Ernest Borgnine, James Franciscus. Irwin Allen has churned out another disaster epic filled with high-priced stars. Just plug in a tropical island, a tidal wave, a volcano, and the rest is easy. AKA: Earth's Final Fury. (Dir: James Goldstone, 118 mins.)†

When Tomorrow Comes (1939)**½ Irene Dunne, Charles Boyer, Barbara O'Neil. A tearjerker. Boyer falls in love with

1177

Dunne and understandably asks her to go to Paris with him despite the fact that he is already married. (Dir: John M. Stahl, 82 mins.)

When Will I Be Loved? (MTV 1990)*½ Stefanie Powers, Katherine Helmond. Sentimental tripe. Three divorced women meet in a lawyer's office and learn how to survive divorce. Soap opera shenanigans. (Dir: Michael Tuchner, 96 mins.)

When Willie Comes Marching Home (1950) *** Dan Dailey, Mae Marsh, William Demarest, Corinne Calvet. Delightful and somewhat touching film about a West Virginian lad who goes into the Army (WWII) and has a series of adventures including an interlude with a beautiful French underground leader. (Dir: John Ford, 81 mins.)

When Wolves Cry—See: Christmas Tree, The

When Women Had Tails (Italy, 1970)*½ Senta Berger, Guiliano Gemma, Frank Wolff, Lando Buzzanca. A silly, sexed-up, prehistoric version of Snow White, in which a comely cavewoman is pursued by seven perpetually tumescent cavemen. Co-written by Lina Wertmuller of all people. Sequel: *When Women Lost Their Tails.* (Dir: Pasquale Festa Campanile, 110 mins.)†

When Worlds Collide (1951)*** Richard Derr, Barbara Rush, Peter Hanson. Good effects and premise sustain this sci-fi piece about choosing the survivors of an impending collision with a planetoid. Oscar to Gordon Jennings for Best Special Effects. (Dir: Rudolph Maté, 81 mins.)†

When You Comin' Back, Red Ryder? (1979) *½ Marjoe Gortner, Lee Grant, Peter Firth, Candy Clark, Pat Hingle. Bombastic screen version of a play about a disparate group being terrorized in a diner in the Southwest by a mentally disturbed Vietnam vet. (Dir: Milton Katselas, 118 mins.)

When You're in Love (1937)**½ Grace Moore, Cary Grant, Aline MacMahon, Thomas Mitchell, Emma Dunn. Dated, but still watchable comedy with music in which Gracie entices Cary to pose as her hubby. Kittenish Moore trills arias and pop music, while Grant and the supporting cast deliver the comedy. (Dir: Robert Riskin, 104 mins.)

When You Remember Me (MTV 1990)**½ Fred Savage, Ellen Burstyn, Kevin Spacey, Lee Garlington, Dwier Brown. Uneven drama loosely based on the life of Michael Patrick Smith, a child who had muscular dystrophy. Savage invests him with a spunky dignity as he takes on the establishment, fighting for nursing home patients' rights. (Dir: Harry Winer, 96 mins.)

When You're Smiling (1950)**½ Frankie

Laine, Jerome Courtland, Lola Albright, Bob Crosby, Billy Daniels, Mills Brothers, Kay Starr. Fairly amusing musical comedy about the ups and downs of the record business. (Dir: Joseph Santley, 75 mins.)

When Your Lover Leaves (MTV 1983)** Valerie Perrine, Betty Thomas, David Ackroyd. A slight show about a rejected lady who learns to roll with the punches and enjoy life. (Dir: Jeff Bleckner, 104 mins.)

Whereabouts of Jenny, The (MTV 1991)*** Ed O'Neill, Deborah Farentino, Mike Farrell. A desperate father is pitted against an insensitive bureaucracy after his daughter has been moved around by the Federal Witness Relocation Program. Realistic subject matter and a good script by John Maglis make this worth watching. (Dir: Gene Reynolds, 96 mins.)

Where Angels Go—Trouble Follows! (1968)** Rosalind Russell, Stella Stevens, Robert Taylor, Van Johnson, Arthur Godfrey. A sequel to *The Trouble With Angels.* This second outing has Russell playing a Mother Superior, opposing new ideas in the person of young nun, Stevens. (Dir: James Neilson, 95 mins.)

Where Are the Children? (1986)**½ Jill Clayburgh, Frederic Forrest, Max Gail. A woman, previously cleared on charges of murdering her kids, relives the nightmare when her former mate kidnaps her children from her current marriage. (Dir: Bruce Malmuth, 92 mins.)†

Where Are Your Children? (1943)** Jackie Cooper, Gale Storm, Patricia Morison, John Litel, Gertrude Michael, Betty Blythe. Teenager Storm is led astray by a gang of ne'er-do-well kids in this well-intentioned melodrama, and Cooper helps her go straight. OK of this kind. (Dir: William Nigh, 73 mins.)

Where Danger Lives (1950)*** Robert Mitchum, Faith Domergue, Claude Rains, Maureen O'Sullivan, Charles Kemper. Perverse "lovers-on-the-run" yarn that has an upstanding doctor (Mitchum) falling under the spell of a disturbed femme fatale. (Dir: John Farrow, 84 mins.)

Where Does It Hurt? (1972)** Peter Sellers, Jo Ann Pflug, Rick Lenz, Pat Morita. Even Sellers, as the corrupt head of a hospital staffed by incompetents, can't save this stumbling slapstick. (Dir: Rod Amateau, 95 mins.)

Where Do We Go from Here? (1945)*** Fred MacMurray, June Haver, Joan Leslie. Fred takes us through a cavalcade of American history as a genie grants his request to be in the Army but puts him in the wrong one. Score by Kurt Weill and Ira Gershwin helps. (Dir: Gregory Ratoff, 77 mins.)

Where Do You Work-a, John? (1921–25)***

Eddie Boland, Martha Sleeper, Paul Parrott, Jobyna Ralston. A collection of three specifically working-class silent comedies. First is *Prince Pistacio*, an absurd fantasy of a demolition man mistaken for a prince. Next, *Sure-Mike* takes us into a department store and the highjinks of its workers. In *Take Next Car*, a trolley-car conductor contends with troublesome passengers. Fascinating social documents. (54 mins.)†

Where Eagles Dare (Great Britain, 1969)*** Richard Burton, Clint Eastwood, Mary Ure. Adventure yarn about a dangerous mission during WWII. Agents Burton and Eastwood attempt to free an important American officer being held prisoner in one of those supposedly escape-proof prisons. (Dir: Brian G. Hutton, 158 mins.)†

Where Have All the People Gone? (MTV 1974)** Peter Graves, Verna Bloom, Michael-James Wixted, Kathleen Quinlan. A radioactive explosion causes a virus, decimating the population and leaving only a few survivors. (Dir: John Llewellyn Moxey, 72 mins.)†

Where Is My Child? (1937)** Celia Adler, Samuel Steinberg, Morris Silberkasten, Anna Lillian. Weak example of Yiddish movie-making, the excruciating story of a woman who, decades earlier, gave up her son as a baby. If they gave out Oscars for crying, Adler would have retired the award, hands down. (Dir: Abraham Leff, 95 mins.)

Where It's At (1969)**½ David Janssen, Robert Drivas, Rosemary Forsyth, Don Rickles. Entertaining comedy examining a father-son relationship. Dad is Janssen, who runs a Las Vegas casino-hotel, and his son (Drivas) is a college student with a different set of moral and ethical standards. (Dir: Garson Kanin, 97 mins.)

Where Love Has Gone (1964)*½ Susan Hayward, Bette Davis, Joey Heatherton, Mike Connors. Tacky sex drama based on Harold Robbins's novel about a famous sculptress whose lover is stabbed to death. (Dir: Edward Dmytryk, 114 mins.)

Where Pigeons Go to Die (MTV 1990)**½ Art Carney, Cliff De Young, Robert Hy Gorman, Ronne Troup, Michael Landon, Richard Bull, Michael Faustino. Sentimental story set in 1950 of a ten-year-old boy and his grandfather, joined by their love of racing pigeons. Not recommended for cynics. (Dir: Michael Landon, 96 mins.)

Where's Charley? (Great Britain, 1952)**** Ray Bolger, Allyn Ann McLerie, Robert Shackleton. The musical version of the classic British farce *Charley's Aunt*. Broadway hit boasts music and lyrics by Frank Loesser, and old and young alike will enjoy catching Ray Bolger in his show-stopper "Once in Love with Amy." (Dir: David Butler, 97 mins.)

Where's Picone? (Italy, 1984)*** Giancarlo Giannini, Lina Sastri, Clelia Rondinella, Carol Croccolo. Giannini is hilarious as a bum who gets caught up in the search for a missing businessman in this fast-paced Italian farce. The slapstick sometimes gets out of hand, but overall a good bet for fans of continental comedy. (Dir: Nanni Loy, 110 mins.)†

Where's Poppa? (1970)*** George Segal, Ruth Gordon, Ron Leibman, Vincent Gardenia, Trish Van Devere. Wild, imaginative black comedy about a bachelor (Segal) who schemes to eliminate his aging mother. Director Carl Reiner is a deft hand with sight gags, and septuagenarian scene stealer Gordon is a joy. (84 mins.)†

Where the Boys Are (1960)*** Dolores Hart, George Hamilton, Connie Francis, Paula Prentiss, Jim Hutton, Yvette Mimieux, Frank Gorshin, Barbara Nichols, Chill Wills. A breezy comic romp that's a real nostalgia wallow. Four red-blooded American girls spend their spring break in Fort Lauderdale trying to lose their hearts but not their virginity. (Dir: Henry Levin, 99 mins.)†

Where the Boys Are (1984)* Lisa Hartman, Lorna Luft, Russell Todd, Wendy Schaal. A senseless remake of the popular 1960 film. (Dir: Hy Averback, 93 mins.)†

Where the Buffalo Roam (1980)*½ Bill Murray, Peter Boyle, Bruno Kirby, Mark Metcalf, Craig T. Nelson. Not very funny account of the life of Dr. Hunter S. Thompson, a gonzo journalist, that is, one who participates in the events he is recording and changes their outcome. (Dir: Art Linson, 98 mins.)†

Where the Bullets Fly (Great Britain, 1966)*½ Tom Adams, Dawn Addams. Inept spy spoof with Tom Adams playing a James Bond type of superagent who is super-cool. (Dir: John Gilling, 88 mins.)

Where the Green Ants Dream (Germany, 1984)*** Bruce Spence, Wandjuk Marika, Roy Marika. An understated film about Australian miners moving out the local aborigines to get at the valuable minerals underneath their sacred land. A poignant statement about modern society's ecological abuses. (Dir: Werner Herzog, 100 mins.)†

Where the Heart Is (1990)*½ Dabney Coleman, Uma Thurman, Joanna Cassidy, Crispin Glover, Suzy Amis, Christopher Plummer, David Hewlett, Maury Chaykin. Self-made millionaire Coleman, tired of supporting his spineless adult children, carts them off to a Brooklyn slum to make something of themselves. Dated comedy is a major misfire from

1179

director John Boorman, who co-wrote this with his daughter Telsche. (94 mins.)†

Where the Heart Roams (1987)**½ The world of paperback romance novels, their authors, and their fans is amusingly unveiled in this perceptive documentary. Highlights: an inadvertently hilarious interview with genre queen Barbara Cartland, and a look at the Love Train, where readers and writers can mingle. (Dir: George Paul Csicsery, 81 mins.)

Where the Hot Wind Blows (France–Italy, 1960)** Melina Mercouri, Gina Lollobrigida, Marcello Mastroianni, Yves Montand. A melodrama about the decadence of a small town from the peasants to the aristocracy. (Dir: Jules Dassin, 126 mins.)†

Where the Ladies Go (MTV 1980)**½ Earl Holliman, Karen Black, Candy Clark, Lisa Hartman. Clever little yarn about housewives and an assorted collection of men who go to a bar which opens at 9 a.m. and closes at 3 p.m. (Dir: Theodore Flicker, 104 mins.)

Where the Lilies Bloom (1974)*** Julie Gholson, Jan Smithers, Harry Dean Stanton. A lovely, gentle film about four children orphaned when their father dies. The plucky fourteen-year-old daughter assumes command and conspires to keep the news of her father's passing from her neighbors. (Dir: William A. Graham, 97 mins.)

Where the Red Fern Grows (1974)**½ James Whitmore, Beverly Garland, Jack Ging, Stewart Petersen. Petersen is a young lad who wants nothing more than to own and train redbone hounds to be the best coon hunters in the county. (Dir: Norman Tokar, 108 mins.)†

Where There's Life (1947)*** Bob Hope, Signe Hasso, William Bendix. Disc jockey becomes ruler of foreign kingdom in this zany Hope film. (Dir: Sidney Lanfield, 75 mins.)

Where the River Runs Black (1986)*** Charles Durning, Alessandro Rabelo, Divana Brandao, Peter Horton, Castulo Guerra. Leisurely paced, stunningly photographed children's film about a jungle boy; a fatherly priest brings him to an orphanage, where the feral child must grapple with civilization. (Dir: Christopher Cain, 100 mins.)†

Where the Sidewalk Ends (1950)***½ Dana Andrews, Gene Tierney, Gary Merrill, Karl Malden. A sizzling, brutal melodrama; Andrews is a hotheaded cop whose temper gets him into trouble when he kills a suspect. He then tries to frame a gangland figure for the crime. (Dir: Otto Preminger, 95 mins.)

Where the Spies Are (Great Britain, 1965)*** David Niven, Françoise Dorleac. Diverting and frequently clever spy tale with a rather good performance by Niven as a doctor recruited for espionage service. (Dir: Val Guest, 110 mins.)

Where Were You When the Lights Went Out? (1968)* Doris Day, Robert Morse, Terry-Thomas, Steve Allen. Someone was bound to make a film based on the big Eastern Seaboard blackout in 1965, and it's been turned into another vapid Doris Day comedy. Bad boudoir burlesque. (Dir: Hy Averback, 95 mins.)

Which Way Home (MCTV 1991)** Cybill Shepherd, John Waters, John Ewart, Marc Gray. Disappointing tale about the brutality of war and the ramifications it has on civilians. Shepherd stars as a courageous American nurse—working in Phnom Penh, Cambodia, during 1979—who risks her life to save refugee children. Compassionate at its core, the tale is ultimately defeated by a wandering storyline. (Dir: Carl Schultz, 140 mins.)†

Which Way Is Up? (1977)** Richard Pryor, Lonette McKee, Margaret Avery. Pryor plays three roles in this loose remake of the Italian comedy *The Seduction of Mimi*, now transplanted to the orange groves of Southern California. (Dir: Michael Schultz, 84 mins.)†

Which Way to the Front? (1970)** Jerry Lewis. Director Jerry Lewis grinds these slapstick efforts out like hamburger. The comedy was left in the trenches. (96 mins.)†

Whiffs (1975) ½ Elliott Gould, Jennifer O'Neill, Eddie Albert, Harry Guardino, Godfrey Cambridge, Howard Hesseman. Dreary spoof of army chemical warfare testing, with Gould as a guinea pig who gets discharged for disability. (Dir: Ted Post, 92 mins.)†

While the City Sleeps (1956)*** Rhonda Fleming, Dana Andrews, Ida Lupino, Vincent Price, Thomas Mitchell, Howard Duff, George Sanders. This bizarre newspaper drama has an intriguing plot. Whoever captures a sex maniac who's been eluding the police will garner the plum job of city editor. Not a sympathetic portrait of the news media, but the director Fritz Lang has conveyed the vitriolic expose with his customary forcefulness. (Dir: Fritz Lang, 100 mins.)†

Whip Hand, The (1951)*½ Carla Balenda, Elliott Reid, Edgar Barrier, Raymond Burr, Otto Waldis, Lurene Tuttle. Inane anti-Communist melodrama from Howard Hughes had an entire town of Reds plotting to produce biological weapons and take over the U.S. (Dir: William Cameron Menzies, 82 mins.)

Whiplash (1948)**½ Dane Clark, Alexis Smith, Zachary Scott, Eve Arden, Jeffrey Lynn. Hackneyed romantic melodrama, with an unsuccessful painter becoming a champion boxer and getting involved with a crippled nightclub owner's glamorous wife. Compelling *noir* atmosphere makes it more interesting than it would otherwise appear. (Dir: Lewis Seiler, 91 mins.)

Whipsaw (1935)*** Myrna Loy, Spencer Tracy, Harvey Stephens, William Harrigan, John Qualen. Appealing gangster-romance, with one gang of jewel thieves tangling with another gang; the whole mob is infiltrated by sharp undercover G-man Tracy. Neat and classy, with Loy and Tracy making a great team. (Dir: Sam Wood, 78 mins.)

Whirlpool (1949)*** Gene Tierney, Richard Conte, Jose Ferrer. Suspenseful drama dealing with blackmail, hypnosis, and murder. (Dir: Otto Preminger, 97 mins.)

Whisky Galore—See: Tight Little Island

Whisperers, The (Great Britain, 1966)*** Edith Evans, Eric Portman, Nanette Newman, Leonard Rossiter, Gerald Sim, Ronald Fraser. Slow-moving, heartwrenching tale of a lonely old woman who is bilked of her fortune. Poignant and beautifully acted; Dame Edith gives a towering performance. (Dir: Bryan Forbes, 106 mins.)

Whispering Footsteps (1943)*** John Hubbard, Rita Quigley. A bank clerk fits the description of a mad killer, and his friends turn against him in fear and distrust. Engrossing suspense melodrama. (Dir: Howard Bretherton, 54 mins.)

Whispering Ghosts (1942)** Milton Berle, Brenda Joyce, John Carradine. Milton gets a few laughs out of this film but not enough for success. He's out to solve a sea captain's murder and recover some buried treasure. (Dir: Alfred L. Werker, 75 mins.)

Whispering Smith (1948)*** Alan Ladd, Robert Preston, Brenda Marshall. Railroad detective finds his best friend is in with bandits. Good western is nicely made, full of action. (Dir: Leslie Fenton, 88 mins.)

Whisper Kills, A (MTV 1988)*½ Loni Anderson, Joe Penny, June Lockhart. The tranquillity of a small California town is disturbed when a series of murders occurs, with the murderer calling his victims prior to killing them. (Dir: Christian I. Nyby II, 96 mins.)

Whispers (Canada, 1990)***½ Victoria Tennant, Jean Leclerc, Chris Sarandon, Peter MacNeill. Exceptional, well-acted, cleverly scripted thriller, drawn from Dean R. Koontz's novel, about a writer (Tennant) attacked by a psychotic (Leclerc) who repeatedly returns to terrorize his victim. A definite must-see! (Dir: Douglas Jackson, 93 mins.)†

Whisper to a Scream, A (Canada, 1989)**

Nadia Capone, Silvio Oliviero, Yaphet Kotto, Lawrence Bayne. Psycho tracks and kills strippers. Some suspenseful elements. (Dir: Robert Bergman, 96 mins.)†

Whistle at Eaton Falls (1951)**½ Lloyd Bridges, Dorothy Gish, Anne Francis, Murray Hamilton, Ernest Borgnine. Union leader suddenly finds himself as manager of a plant, with the necessity of laying off men. Sincere but talky, rather slow drama. (Dir: Robert Siodmak, 96 mins.)

Whistle Blower, The (Great Britain, 1987)*** Michael Caine, Nigel Havers, Barry Foster, John Gielgud, James Fox. An engrossing espionage yarn which deals with the little men who work for government agencies and come across information which could blow the whistle on high officials. Havers works for just such an agency and when he decides to do the right thing, he is killed. His father, Caine, looks into his death and picks up where his son left off in the investigation. (Dir: Simon Langton, 100 mins.)†

Whistle Down the Wind (Great Britain, 1962)**** Hayley Mills, Alan Bates, Bernard Lee, Norman Bird. An almost perfect film about a trio of children who find an escaped criminal in their barn and mistake him for Christ. Mills and Bates, as the convict, give excellent performances. Touching, honest, wonderfully directed, and altogether recommended. (Dir: Bryan Forbes, 98 mins.)†

Whistler series. Based on the popular radio anthology, "The Whistler" differs from other series in that the character of the Whistler—a symbol of fate—drifts in and out of the action, providing basic continuity (but not starring in adventures). The series starred Richard Dix, who was sometimes a hero, sometimes a villain in these ironic suspense features. Fans should see *The Whistler, Mark of the Whistler, Power of the Whistler, Voice of the Whistler,* and *Return of the Whistler.*

Whistler, The (1944)**½ Richard Dix, J. Carrol Naish, Gloria Stuart, Alan Dinehart. This fairly suspenseful tale concerns a man so distraught over the drowning of his wife that he hires a hit man for himself. When the wife turns up alive, he tries desperately to cancel the contract on his life. (Dir: William Castle, 59 mins.)

Whistle Stop (1946)** George Raft, Ava Gardner, Victor McLaglen. Rather glum melodrama with Gardner trying to help ne'er-do-well Raft while fighting off villainous nightclub owner McLaglen. (Dir: Leonide Moguy, 84 mins.)

Whistling in Brooklyn (1943)**½ Red

Skelton, Ann Rutherford. Another in the fairly amusing comic detective series with Red again playing "The Fox." (Dir: S. Sylvan Simon, 87 mins.)

Whistling in Dixie (1942)**½ Red Skelton, Ann Rutherford. Red's fans and the kids will like this mystery-comedy set in some old southern mansions and abandoned forts. (Dir: S. Sylvan Simon, 74 mins.)

Whistling in the Dark (1941)*** Red Skelton, Ann Rutherford. Red's first starring film and his fans will have a lot of fun with it. He's in the hands of killers and imprisoned in a big mansion. (Dir: S. Sylvan Simon, 77 mins.)

White Angel, The (1936)** Kay Francis, Ian Hunter, Donald Woods, Nigel Bruce, Donald Crisp, Henry O'Neill. Expensively mounted life story of Florence Nightingale; this could have been interesting, but a poor script and oddly flat, unfeeling direction do it in. (Dir: William Dieterle, 75 mins.)

White Banners (1938)*** Claude Rains, Fay Bainter, Jackie Cooper, Bonita Granville. Miss Bainter's magnificent acting makes something out of this Lloyd C. Douglas morality fable. Very talky. (Dir: Edmund Goulding, 96 mins.)

White Buffalo (1977)** Charles Bronson, Jack Warden, Kim Novak. A wild west adventure with allegorical overtones; Wild Bill Hickock and Crazy Horse both hunt a mysterious albino bison. (Dir: J. Lee Thompson, 97 mins.)

White Cargo (1942)** Hedy Lamarr, Walter Pidgeon, Frank Morgan. Boring tale of an Englishman who succumbs to a lovely native girl. Hedy is gorgeous. (Dir: Richard Thorpe, 88 mins.)

White Christmas (1954)*** Bing Crosby, Danny Kaye, Dean Jagger, Rosemary Clooney, Vera-Ellen. Colorful package of holiday entertainment for the whole family—songs, dances, clowning, plus Irving Berlin's title tune. The cast fits perfectly into the lightweight story which merely serves as a framework for the fifteen musical numbers. Reworking of Bing's *Holiday Inn*. (Dir: Michael Curtiz, 120 mins.)†

White Cliffs of Dover, The (1944)*** Irene Dunne, Van Johnson. Well acted, occasionally slow, but moving story of an American girl who marries an English lord in 1914. He dies in 1918, and the story follows his life in England. (Dir: Clarence Brown, 126 mins.)

White Corridors (Great Britain, 1951)*** Googie Withers, James Donald, Barry Jones, Petula Clark. Researcher is accidentally infected with disease germs, asks a lady doctor to try a new test on him. Behind-the-scenes medical drama showing routine in a hospital is well done. (Dir: Pat Jackson, 82 mins.)

1182

White Dawn, The (1974)*** Warren Oates, Timothy Bottoms, Louis Gossett, Jr. In 1896, three whalers are saved by some Eskimos after their boat fails them. Based on fact, the story remains intriguing and is blessedly free of melodramatics. (Dir: Philip Kaufman, 109 mins.)†

White Dog (1982)**½ Kristy McNichol, Paul Winfield, Burl Ives, Jameson Parker, Lynne Moody. Based on Romain Gary's metaphorical story, the film is about a dog trained to attack blacks and the efforts of scientist Winfield to cure it. Despite the lack of nail-biting suspense, this remains a disturbing creation. (Dir: Samuel Fuller, 90 mins.)

White Fang (1991)*** Ethan Hawke, Klaus Maria Brandauer, Seymour Cassel, Susan Hogan, James Remar. Exciting adventure based on Jack London's novel, about a young man who journeys to Alaska during the gold rush and faces the challenges of nature and human greed while befriending a wolf-dog. With gorgeous scenery and plenty of colorful action, this is a fine family film. (Dir: Randal Kleiser, 107 mins.)†

White Feather (1955)** Robert Wagner, Debra Paget, Jeffrey Hunter, John Lund, Hugh O'Brian. Wagner plays a government man who tries to get a tribe of Cheyenne to move to a reservation. Debra Paget and blue-eyed Jeff Hunter play Indians. (Dir: Robert D. Webb, 102 mins.)

White Flame, The (1921) and **Sacred Mountain, The** (Germany, 1926)*** Video compilation with two examples of the German mountain-climbing melodrama, an extremely popular genre in Europe between the wars. Each dramatic adventure stars Leni Riefenstahl, who later became a groundbreaking director. (Dir: Dr. Arnold Fanck, 60 mins.)†

White Gold (1927)*** Jetta Goudal, Kenneth Thomson, George Bancroft, George Nichols. A remarkable silent western about a vibrant Mexican girl whose marriage to an Arizona sheep rancher is ruined by his embittered father. An involving drama, thought to have been lost but recently rediscovered. (Dir: William K. Howard, 68 mins.)†

White Heat (1949)**** James Cagney, Virginia Mayo, Edmond O'Brien, Steve Cochran, Margaret Wycherly. Brutal, brilliant gangster saga with Cagney in his most flamboyant role, as mother-loving Cody Jarrett, the man with the cinema's strongest Oedipus complex. (Dir: Raoul Walsh, 114 mins.)†

White Hot (1988)*½ Robby Benson, Tawny Kitaen, Danny Aiello, Tony Gillan. Two yuppies are seduced into the easy money of cocaine dealing in this unconvincing, hysterical antidrug diatribe. (Dir: Robby Benson, 95 mins.)†

White Hunter, Black Heart (1990)*** Clint Eastwood, Jeff Fahey, George Dzundza, Marisa Berenson, Timothy Spall, Mel Martin. Uneven but involving adaptation of Peter Viertel's novel based on his actual experiences polishing up James Agee's script for the movie classic *The African Queen*. Eastwood plays a John Huston-type director, but he never fully captures Huston's larger-than-life character. Berenson's Katharine Hepburn imitation is hopelessly inadequate, but Fahey, as the young writer, stands out. (Dir: Clint Eastwood, 112 mins.)†

White Lightning (1973)**½ Burt Reynolds, Jennifer Billingsley, Ned Beatty, Louise Latham, Bo Hopkins. Fast-paced melodrama about murder, revenge, and moonshine in the new South. (Dir: Joseph Sargent, 101 mins.)†

White Line Fever (1975)*** Jan-Michael Vincent, Kay Lenz, Slim Pickens, L. Q. Jones. Sensitive treatment of a young trucker's troubles at fighting corruption in his profession. Forced to smuggle contraband goods, Air Force vet-turned-independent-trucker Vincent rebels. (Dir: Jonathan Kaplan, 89 mins.)†

White Mama (MTV 1980)**½ Bette Davis, Ernest Harden, Jr., Virginia Capers, Lurene Tuttle, Eileen Heckart. The indomitable Davis as a poor widow forced to take in a young black street thief to make ends meet. (Dir: Jackie Cooper, 104 mins.)†

White Mischief (Great Britain, 1988)** Charles Dance, Greta Scacchi, Joss Ackland, Sarah Miles, John Hurt, Geraldine Chaplin. Dreary tale of civilized decadence among the British upper crust in Kenya, circa 1940. Based on real events, it tells of the suspected murder of a notorious playboy (Dance) by a jealous husband. (Dir: Michael Radford, 105 mins.)†

White Nights (Italy, 1957)*** Maria Schell, Marcello Mastroianni, Jean Marais, Clara Calamai. From Dostoevsky's story, this is a lushly filmed tale of a young man who becomes enchanted with a mysterious girl who talks only of her absent lover. (Dir: Luchino Visconti, 107 mins.)

White Nights (U.S.S.R., 1959)*** Oleg Strizhenov, Ludmila Marchenko, U. N. Popova. Russian version of Dostoevsky's story retains the original 19th-century setting for the haunting tale of a strange and lonely man who meets a beautiful woman. (Dir: Ivan Pyriev, 97 mins.)

White Nights (1985)**½ Mikhail Baryshnikov, Gregory Hines, Isabella Rossellini, Geraldine Page, Jerzy Skolimowski. Great dance sequences submerged in a plot rife with twists. Baryshnikov plays a ballet star whose plane crashes in the Soviet Union; Hines portrays an American tap dancer who defected to Russia in order to protest America's involvement in Vietnam. (Dir: Taylor Hackford, 135 mins.)†

White of the Eye (1988)*** David Keith, Cathy Moriarty, Art Evans. Disturbing, effective thriller. Moriarty is riveting as the jaded New Yorker who thinks she's found suburban tranquility in Tucson, and she's matched by Keith as the husband and father who views his murders as a minor sideline. (Dir: Donald Cammell, 111 mins.)†

White Palace (1990)*** Susan Sarandon, James Spader, Eileen Brennan, Jason Alexander, Rachel Levin, Kathy Bates, Renee Taylor. A successful, under-thirty yuppie (Spader), who's repressed and unlucky in the life-lived department, meets an earthy, over-forty waitress (Sarandon), sexually hip and willing to nurture. They attempt to overcome the problems of class, family objections, and inhibitions. This intimate romantic drama succeeds in rejecting the clichés endemic to the genre, and presents a mature relationship that isn't fairy tale perfect. Well acted, with a completely believable portrait of love and hope. (Dir: Luis Mandoki, 103 mins.)†

White Room (Canada, 1990)**½ Kate Nelligan, Maurice Godin, Margot Kidder, Sheila McCarthy. Unusual mystery involves the plight of a young man, eagerly seeking fame as a writer, whose life is forever changed when he witnesses the murder of a popular singer. (Dir: Patricia Rozema, 91 mins.)†

White Rose, The (West Germany, 1982)**½ Lena Stolze, Wulf Kessler. True story of a group of college students in World War II Germany who banded together in an underground group to condemn the Nazi government. (Dir: Michael Verhoeven, 108 mins.)†

White Savage (1943)** Jon Hall, Maria Montez, Sabu, Turhan Bey, Don Terry, Sidney Toler, Thomas Gomez, Pedro de Cordoba. Montez, the princess of exotic Temple Island (also inhabited by Sabu and Bey), falls in love with an American fisherman. Good, campy fun. (Dir: Arthur Lubin, 75 mins.)

White Sheik, The (Italy, 1951)*** Alberto Sordi, Brunella Bora, Leopoldo Trieste. A newlywed couple runs into trouble on their honeymoon when the wife meets her idol, the "white sheik," a hero from the pages of the *fumetti* (comic strips done with photographs). (Dir: Federico Fellini, 88 mins.)†

White Sister, The (1933)**½ Helen Hayes, Clark Gable, Louise Closser Hale, Lewis Stone, May Robson. From a bestseller by F. Marion Crawford, this concerns a girl who takes the veil when she believes her fiancé dead. (Dir: Victor Fleming, 110 mins.)

White Sister (Italy, 1973)** Sophia Loren, Adriana Celentano, Fernando Rey. A love story that never ignites. A nun tries to submerge her feelings for a worker at the hospital she runs. (Dir: Alberto Lattuada, 104 mins.)

White Slave (Italy, 1985)** Elvie Audray, Will Gonzales, Dick Marshall, Andrew Louis Coppola. This is a supposedly true story about a young woman taken in by natives of the Amazon after her plantation-owning parents are murdered. Pretty lurid, but not dull. (Dir: ''Roy Garrett'' [Mario Gariazzo], 89 mins.)†

White Slave Ship (France-Italy, 1962)** Pier Angeli, Edmund Purdom. Mutiny on a prison ship carrying girls from London jails en route to the colonies. (Dir: Silvio Amadio, 92 mins.)

White Star—See: **Let It Rock**

White Tie and Tails (1946)**½ Dan Duryea, Ella Raines, William Bendix. A screwy comedy about a butler who takes charge of his employer's mansion when his employer goes on vacation. (Dir: Charles Barton, 81 mins.)

White Tower, The (1950)*** Glenn Ford, Valli, Claude Rains, Lloyd Bridges. Six people risk their lives to scale the Swiss Alps. Thrilling mountain-climbing melodrama. (Dir: Ted Tetzlaff, 98 mins.)†

White Wall, The (Sweden, 1975)**** Harriet Andersson, Lena Nyman, Tomas Ponten. Insightful study of the female psyche, directed, written, and co-edited by Stig Bjorkman. A thirty-five-year-old divorced housewife searches for a job, male companionship, and affection. Andersson is profoundly touching. (80 mins.)

White Warrior, The (Italy, 1959)*½ Steve Reeves, Georgia Moll. Brave tribal chieftain fights against the Czar's troops and battles treachery within his own ranks—and a silly plot, bad English-dubbing, stilted acting, etc. (Dir: Riccardo Freda, 86 mins.)

White Water Rebels (MTV 1983)* Catherine Bach, James Brolin, Pepe Serna, Kai Wulff, Michael Gwynne. Outdoor telefilm concerns intrepid river kayakers, unscrupulous land developers, and a lady photojournalist, if anyone cares. (Dir: Reza S. Badiyi, 104 mins.)

White Water Summer (1987)*½ Kevin Bacon, Sean Astin, Jonathan Ward, K. C. Martel. Muddled drama about a gung ho outdoorsman guiding some unwilling kids on a wilderness expedition. When he's injured, the least likely youngster becomes responsible for his safety. (Dir: Jeff Bleckner, 90 mins.)†

White Wilderness (1958)*** One of the better Disney ''True-Life Adventures.''

Records animal life in the Arctic regions of North America. (Dir: James Algar, 73 mins.)

White Witch Doctor (1953)**½ Robert Mitchum, Susan Hayward, Timothy Carey, Walter Slezak. Sweet Susan is guided into hostile African territory to bring modern medicine to the natives, but Bad Bob and Wicked Walter are more interested in finding a hidden treasure of gold. (Dir: Henry Hathaway, 96 mins.)

White Zombie (1932)*** Bela Lugosi, Madge Bellamy. Sinister Lugosi wants beautiful Bellamy for himself, so they can rule the zombie jungle empire together. Extremely atmospheric, although laughable at times, this archetypical horror thriller still holds some interest. (Dir: Victor Halperin, 73 mins.)†

Whity (West Germany, 1970)*** Gunter Kaufmann, Hanna Schygulla, Ulli Lommel, Harry Baer, Rainer Werner Fassbinder, Ron Randall. Bizarre western from director-co-star Fassbinder about a half-black slave who, influenced by a sexually abused barmaid, plans the murder of his exploitative masters. Strange little film filled with personal inside jokes. (95 mins.)

Who? (Great Britain, 1974)**½ Elliott Gould, Trevor Howard, Joe Bova, Ed Grover. American scientist Bova has a near-fatal accident in East Berlin, where doctors save his life by replacing his face. At least that's what the man who returns says happened; FBI agent suspects he may be a Communist agent sent to infiltrate U.S. security. Nifty little drama of paranoia and identity wasn't released until '82. AKA: **Roboman**. (Dir: Jack Gold, 93 mins.)†

Who Am I This Time? (MTV 1982)*** Christopher Walken, Susan Sarandon, Robert Ridgely, Dorothy Patterson. Charming romantic comedy about a schlemiel who can only function when he's playing a role in the local community theater, and the woman who wants to bring him out of his shell. Based on a Kurt Vonnegut, Jr., story. (Dir: Jonathan Demme, 60 mins.)†

Who Done It? (1942)*½ Bud Abbott & Lou Costello, Patric Knowles, William Bendix, Don Porter. For Abbott & Costello fans only; trite murder mystery about a real murder occurring during a mystery show broadcast. (Dir: Erie C. Kenton, 75 mins.)†

Who Done It? (Great Britain, 1956)**½ Benny Hill, Belinda Lee, David Kossoff, Garry Marsh. A spry mystery-comedy as an ice-rink worker sleuths in his spare time and becomes a spy-catcher. (Dir: Basil Dearden, 85 mins.)

Whoever Says the Truth Shall Die (Netherlands, 1981)*** Documentary explores the mystery of Italian director Pier Paolo Pasolini's murder (the courts decided he was a "victim of a homosexual encounter gone sour"), and examines his life as a writer, poet, and filmmaker, including his thirty-three trials on charges of obscenity, corruption of minors, and blasphemy (he was always acquitted). (Dir: Philo Bregstein, 65 mins.)†

Who Framed Roger Rabbit? (1988)***½ Bob Hoskins, Christopher Lloyd, Joanna Cassidy, Stubby Kaye, voice of Kathleen Turner (uncredited). Hoskins plays straight man to an assortment of cartoon characters in this magical movie that combines live action and animation with unparalleled perfection. Someone's murdered a practical joker with clout (Kaye), and private eye Eddie Valiant (Hoskins) is out to find the culprit. Accompanying him on his search is "Roger Rabbit," a cartoon star who has a motivation for the killing (his wife was "playing pat-a-cake" with the victim). "Roger" may just be a slaphappy version of Bugs Bunny, but his cartoon compatriots are plentiful, and they include some of the biggest names in "Toon" history (including characters from the Disney, Warner Bros., and Fleischer studios). The interaction among these characters is so enchanting that you won't want to return to the main plot line (which bogs down in the middle). However, how often can you see Daffy and Donald Duck attempt a piano duet? (Dir: Robert Zemeckis, 96 mins.)†

Who Gets the Friends? (MTV 1988)*½ Jill Clayburgh, James Farentino, Lucie Arnaz, Leigh Taylor-Young. Clayburgh plays another *Unmarried Woman*, in this made-for-TV comedy which·has more than its share of unhappy moments. Things look pretty grim until the totally unrealistic happy ending. (Dir: Lila Garrett, 96 mins.)

Who Has Seen the Wind (Canada, 1977)**½ Jose Ferrer, Doug Junor, Brian Painchaud. Slow, understated movie about two boys growing up in a small Saskatchewan town. (Dir: Allan King, 105 mins.)†

Who Is Harry Kellerman and Why Is He Saying Those Terrible Things About Me? (1971)*** Dustin Hoffman, Barbara Harris, Jack Warden. Hoffman is wonderful as a pop composer who is bedeviled by an unknown man who is out to ruin his reputation—or is he? Uneven but often acerbic and funny. (Dir: Ulu Grosbard, 108 mins.)

Who Is Julia? (MTV 1986)** Mare Winningham, Jameson Parker, Jeffrey De Munn, Jonathan Banks, Mason Adams, Bert Remsen. The hokiest of sci-fi B-movie concepts—a brain transplant—gets the kind of sober treatment here that TV movies usually reserve for terminal diseases or social issues. Winningham plays a young mother, brain-dead after a hemorrhage, who receives the brain of a gorgeous model just killed in an accident. (Dir: Walter Grauman, 100 mins.)

Who Is Killing the Great Chefs of Europe? (Great Britain, 1978)*** George Segal, Jacqueline Bisset, Robert Morley. Segal is a fast-food businessman in constant pursuit of his lovely master dessert chef ex-wife, while murders on the international cuisine set multiply. As a mystery it's so-so, but as a romantic escapade it's quite digestible. (Dir: Ted Kotcheff, 115 mins.)

Who Is Killing the Stuntmen?—See: **Stunts**

Who Is the Black Dahlia? (MTV 1975)**½ Lucie Arnaz, Efrem Zimbalist, Jr., Macdonald Carey, Donna Mills. Sensational 1947 Los Angeles murder is exhumed and receives fairly interesting treatment. Lucie Arnaz stars as the mixed-up, movie-struck girl who ends up a corpse in a vacant lot. (Dir: Joseph Pevney, 96 mins.)

Who Killed Gail Preston? (1938)**½ Rita Hayworth, Don Terry, Robert Paige, Wyn Cahoon. Clever murder-mystery set in a night spot (made before Hayworth became the Love Goddess of the forties). Smoothly done. (Dir: Leon Barsha, 60 mins.)

Who Killed Mary Whats'er'name? (1971)** Red Buttons, Sylvia Miles, Alice Playten. The murder of a Greenwich Village prostitute leads former lightweight champion, now diabetic Red Buttons, out of the boredom of retirement to play amateur sleuth. Good cast is wasted on a screenplay whose main ingredient is plot loopholes. (Dir: Ernie Pintoff, 90 mins.)†

Who Killed Teddy Bear? (1965)** Sal Mineo, Juliet Prowse, Jan Murray, Elaine Stritch. Sexually psychotic busboy preys on disco dancer, as cop trails. Low-key direction creates a portrait of obsession, with some suspense. (Dir: Joseph Cates, 91 mins.)

Whole Shootin' Match, The (1978)** Lou Perry, Sonny Davis, Doris Hargrave, Eric Henshaw. A low-key, lone star slice of life, a bit on the tedious side. Two pals look for the silver lining, even though their lives seem to be perpetually cloud-filled and worrisome as they grow older. (Dir: Eagle Pennell, 101 mins.)

Whole Town's Talking, The (1935)*** Edward G. Robinson, Wallace Ford, Jean Arthur. Meek, white collar worker is mistaken for Public Enemy No. 1. Excellent comedy-drama is still fairly entertaining. (Dir: John Ford, 90 mins.)

Whole Truth, The (Great Britain, 1958)** Stewart Granger, Donna Reed, George

1185

Sanders. A whodunit with very little suspense. Plot concerns an actress's murder which is pinned on an American producer whose wife refuses to believe he did it. (Dir: John Guillermin, 84 mins.)

Whole Truth, The—See: Blind Justice

Whole World Is Watching, The (MTV 1969) ** Burl Ives, Joseph Campanella, James Farentino, Hal Holbrook. Ives, Campanella, and Farentino play a trio of lawyers, who take on the defense of a leader of a college student uprising arrested for the murder of a campus policeman. (Dir: Richard Colla, 97 mins.)

Who'll Save Our Children? (MTV 1978)*** Shirley Jones, Len Cariou. A childless couple raise two deserted youngsters in this tale of adjustment. After they fall in love with the kids, they must face the trauma of losing them. (Dir: George Schaefer, 104 mins.)

Who'll Stop the Rain (1978)**½ Michael Moriarty, Tuesday Weld, Nick Nolte. Based on Robert Stone's *Dog Soldiers*, the plot concerns a war correspondent with psychological hang-ups about Vietnam. When he returns to America, he finds that his mainstream homeland is just as violent as the land he just left. (Dir: Karel Reisz, 126 mins.)†

Wholly Moses (1980)** Dudley Moore, Richard Pryor, John Houseman, Laraine Newman, Dom DeLuise. Soporific biblical parody that wastes many fine comedians. (Dir: Gary Weis, 104 mins.)†

Whoopee (1930)*** Eddie Cantor, Eleanor Hunt. Potent combination of Samuel Goldwyn and Florenz Ziegfeld (producers), Busby Berkeley (dance director), and Cantor (in his original Broadway role) will seem awful to some, a lot of fun to others. Remade as *Up in Arms*. (Dir: Thornton Freeland, 92 mins.)†

Whoopee Boys, The (1986)* Michael O'Keeffe, Paul Rodriguez, Denholm Elliott, Carole Shelley. Exercise in bad taste specializes in ethnic and sex jokes while following two New York street hustlers trying to con their way into high society in Palm Beach. (Dir: John Byrum, 88 mins.)†

Whoops Apocalypse (1986)** Loretta Swit, Peter Cook, Ian Richardson, Herbert Lom. Hyperactive parody of nuclear-disaster movies, with U.S. president Swit trying to prevent British Prime Minister Cook from launching a first strike in Latin America. (Dir: Tom Bussman, 93 mins.)†

Whore (1991)**½ Theresa Russell, Benjamin Mouton, Antonio Fargas. Gritty, depressing, but fascinating look at the world of prostitution as seen by one Los Angeles hooker (Russell in a scenery-chewing performance). Based on a British

play by David Hines. (Dir: Ken Russell, 84 mins.)†

Who's Afraid of Virginia Woolf? (1966)**** Elizabeth Taylor, Richard Burton, Sandy Dennis, George Segal. Edward Albee's brilliant, biting play about the love-hate relationship between a middle-aged, resigned college professor and his vitriolic, denigrating, yet seductive wife is turned into a movie experience to be cherished. It's a cinematic feast thanks to Mike Nichols's astute debut as director; Taylor's towering portrayal as the foul-mouthed Martha (Academy Award); Burton's magnificent portrait of the tortured professor; Dennis's Oscar-winning performance as the nervous young wife. (129 mins.)†

Who Says I Can't Ride a Rainbow? (1971) *** Jack Klugman, Nancy French, Reuben Figueroa, Kevin Riou, Val Avery, Morgan Freeman. Poignant family fare; a little padded, but brimming with unexpected depth. When an animal lover is thrown off his land, he's got to find homes for his menagerie. (Dir: Edward Mann, 85 mins.)

Who's Been Sleeping In My Bed? (1963)**½ Dean Martin, Elizabeth Montgomery, Carol Burnett, Martin Balsam, Jill St. John. TV idol's fiancée wants to get him hitched before his affinity for the girls becomes too strong. Frequently amusing. (Dir: Daniel Mann, 103 mins.)

Whose Life Is It Anyway? (1981)*** Richard Dreyfuss, John Cassavetes, Christine Lahti, Bob Balaban, Kenneth McMillan, Kaki Hunter. Dreyfuss is brilliant as the artist cut down in his prime and not willing to live as a vegetable. His arguments are valid and touching. Moving story about the right to die with dignity. (Dir: John Badham, 118 mins.)†

Who's Got the Action? (1962)**½ Dean Martin, Lana Turner, Walter Matthau, Eddie Albert. All the familiar jokes and characters involved in the world of a compulsive horseplayer are trotted out in this occasionally diverting comedy. The plot has Turner trying to curtail hubby Martin's out-of-hand betting habits by secretly joining forces with a bookie. (Dir: Daniel Mann, 93 mins.)

Who's Harry Crumb? (1989)*½ John Candy, Jeffrey Jones, Annie Potts, Tim Thomerson. Candy's hefty talents are wasted in this crumby comedy; he plays an arrogant but incompetent private eye. (Dir: Paul Flaherty, 87 mins.)†

Who Slew Auntie Roo? (U.S.–Great Britain, 1971)**½ Shelley Winters, Mark Lester, Ralph Richardson, Hugh Griffith, Lionel Jeffries. Another in the line of films casting flamboyant actresses as macabre, slightly mad ladies in gothic tales. Winters as an American widow living in a large house in England, takes her cue from the wicked witch in "Hansel and Gretel" and tries to lure young children into her lair. (Dir: Curtis Harrington, 91 mins.)†

Who's Minding the Mint? (1967)*** Milton Berle, Joey Bishop, Jack Gilford, Walter Brennan, Dorothy Provine, Jim Hutton. A zany, spirited romp. Hutton plays a charming young man who works in the U.S. Mint. When he accidentally burns a large batch of new bills, he sets up an operation to replace them. (Dir: Howard Morris, 97 mins.)†

Who's Minding the Store? (1963)*½ Jerry Lewis, Jill St. John, John McGiver. Jerry's uncritical fans will get a few forced laughs from his antics as a department store flunky who's in love with the boss's daughter. (Dir: Frank Tashlin, 90 mins.)

Who's That Girl (1987)* Madonna, Griffin Dunne, Haviland Morris, John McMartin. Screwy comedy about a falsely accused woman who wins parole and seeks out the louse who framed her. Energetically performed and directed, but few laughs. (Dir: James Foley, 92 mins.)†

Who's That Knocking at My Door? (1968)*** Harvey Keitel, Zina Bethune, Anne Collette. Martin Scorsese's first feature covers the same territory as *Mean Streets,* with a more experimental outlook. Keitel is a young Italian Catholic whose "Madonna complex" and rigid views on sexuality prevent him from making a commitment with his girlfriend, who's been the victim of a rape. (90 mins.)†

Who Was That Lady? (1960)**½ Tony Curtis, Dean Martin, Janet Leigh, James Whitmore, Barbara Nichols. Fast-paced comedy romp that fizzles out before the finale. Tony Curtis and Dean Martin play men-about-town, one married and one not, and their adventures lead to complications found only in French farces. (Dir: George Sidney, 115 mins.)

Who Will Love My Children? (MTV 1983)*** Ann-Margret, Frederic Forrest, Cathryn Damon, Donald Moffat, Lonny Chapman. Ann-Margret is effective as a terminally ill mother who decides to find homes for her ten children after she realizes that her alcoholic husband won't be able to handle them. (Dir: John Erman, 104 mins.)

Why? (Italy, 1971)*** Alberto Sordi, Elga Andersen, Lino Banfi, Giuseppe Anatrelli, Tano Cimarosa. Powerful drama about horrifying conditions and corruption in Italian prisons focuses on a civil engineer who, upon returning to Italy after a trip to Sweden, is unjustly arrested at customs. Comic actor Sordi is magnificent as the wrong man. (Dir: Nanni Loy, 102 mins.)

Why Bother to Knock? (Great Britain, 1961)* Elke Sommer, Richard Todd, Judith Anderson, Nicole Maurey. Don't bother to watch. Young man on the make indiscriminately gives out keys to his apartment to young ladies—all of whom show up at the same time. Lumbering sex comedy wasn't funny then, and it's even less so now. (Dir: Cyril Frankel, 88 mins.)

Why Does Herr R. Run Amok? (West Germany, 1969)***½ Kurt Raab, Lilith Ungerer, Hanna Schygulla, Amadeus Fengler, Franz Maron. An ordinary man calmly murders his family and a visiting neighbor, using a decorative lamp as the tool of destruction. Director Rainer Werner Fassbinder's gripping look at hidden madness and sudden murder based on a true incident; one of his most provocative and enlightening films. (88 mins.)

Why Me? (MTV 1984)*** Glynnis O'Connor, Armand Assante, Michael Sacks, Craig Wasson, Annie Potts. A true story about a woman who was disfigured in an auto accident and had to undergo forty operations to rebuild her face. (Dir: Fielder Cook, 104 mins.)

Why Me? (1990)**½ Christophe Lambert, Christopher Lloyd, Kim Greist, J. T. Walsh, Michael J. Pollard, Tony Plana, John Hancock. Caper comedy about crooks heisting a valuable ruby from its Middle Eastern owners, setting off an international crisis and putting the gang in trouble with everyone in the city of New York. Adapted by Donald E. Westlake from one of his popular Dortmunder novels (Hollywood previously raided the series for *The Hot Rock, Bank Shot,* and *Jimmy the Kid*), film is miscast and never captures the proper tone, substituting slapstick for wit. (Dir: Gene Quintano, 88 mins.)†

Why Must I Die? (1960)** Terry Moore, Debra Paget, Bert Freed, Julie Reding. Well-intentioned but melodramatic, overwrought plea for the abolishment of the death penalty, with Moore as an innocent woman sentenced to Death Row on flimsy evidence. (Dir: Roy Del Ruth, 86 mins.)

Why Not? (France, 1979)***½ Sami Frey, Christine Murillo, Mario Gonzalez, Michel Aumont, Nicole Jamet. A lovely, original comedy-drama about three social misfits exploring their sexuality, but experiencing static when their ménage à trois expands to include a new member. (Dir: Coline Serreau, 93 mins.)

Why Shoot the Teacher (Canada, 1976)*** Bud Cort, Samantha Eggar, Kenneth Griffith. Entertaining Depression tale about a teacher who arrives in a tiny, freezing town and meets with an equally chilly reception from the townspeople. (Dir: Silvio Narizzano, 99 mins.)†

Why Worry? (1923)**** Harold Lloyd, Jobyna Ralston, John Aasen, Leo White.

Another comic masterpiece from Lloyd, here a wealthy hypochondriac who journeys to a South American nation—for his health—just as a revolution breaks out. An endless stream of hilarious gags. (Dirs: Fred Newmeyer, Sam Taylor, 55 mins.)

Why Would I Lie? (1980)** Treat Williams, Lisa Eichhorn, Jocelyn Brando. A charmless romantic comedy. When social worker Williams isn't fibbing colorfully, he's romancing a women's libber and espousing his half-baked philosophical ideas. (Dir: Larry Peerce, 105 mins.)

Wichita (1955)**½ Joel McCrea, Vera Miles, Lloyd Bridges. Wyatt Earp is once again the lawman who brings law and order to a small western town which is overrun with outlaws. Good action. (Dir: Jacques Tourneur, 81 mins.)

Wicked As They Come (Great Britain, 1957)** Arlene Dahl, Phil Carey, Herbert Marshall, David Kossoff. Dahl is ravishing as a bad girl with a heart of gold trying to make it big and getting entangled with gangsters during her rise, though this B picture lacks class otherwise. AKA: Portrait in Smoke. (Dir: Ken Hughes, 94 mins.)

Wicked City, The (France, 1950)** Maria Montez, Lili Palmer, Jean-Pierre Aumont, Marcel Dalio. Amoral woman seduces a young sailor into her sordid criminal life. Unfortunately she also takes the audience along for the ride. Too-familiar bad-girl routine made worse by camp queen Montez's overacting. (Dir: Francois Villiers, 77 mins.)

Wicked Dreams of Paula Schultz, The (1968)* Elke Sommer, Bob Crane, Werner Klemperer. Tasteless, claptrap comedy in which Sommer stars as an Olympic athlete who finds herself the object of a cold-war ploy. (Dir: George Marshall, 113 mins.)

Wicked Lady, The (Great Britain, 1945)**½ Margaret Lockwood, James Mason, Michael Rennie, Patricia Roc. Scheming woman takes over all the men who cross her path, eventually joins a highwayman as his aide. Theatrical costume drama is lifted a bit by Mason's tongue-in-cheek portrayal of a bandit. (Dir: Leslie Arliss, 98 mins.)†

Wicked Lady (Great Britain, 1983)** Faye Dunaway, Alan Bates, John Gielgud, Denholm Elliott. A high-spirited but disappointing romp through *Tom Jones* country. Dunaway camps it up outrageously as a female highwayman. (Dir: Michael Winner, 98 mins.)†

Wicked Stepmother (1989)* Bette Davis, Barbara Carrera, Colleen Camp, David Rasche, Lionel Stander, Tom Bosley, Richard Moll. When Bette Davis and writer-producer-director Larry Cohen fought over the direction of this movie, she left and he replaced her with Barbara Carrera. That's one reason why this sto-

ry about a modern-day witch is such a mess, though from the evidence presented here it would have been a mess anyway. Not so much wicked as rotten. (92 mins.)

Wicked, Wicked (1973)* Scott Brady, Tiffany Bolling, Edd Byrnes, David Bailey. Crummy mystery-thriller with a gimmick: the entire movie is filmed in split screen, showing the simultaneous actions of both a killer stalker and his intended victim. It doesn't help. (Dir: Richard L. Bare, 95 mins.)

Wicked Woman (1954)** Richard Egan, Beverly Michaels, Evelyn Scott, Percy Helton. This sultry street-smart female is a waitress who serves up a bad attitude. Predictable '50s raunch is arch and harmless. (Dir: Russell Rouse, 77 mins.)

Wicker Man, The (1973)*** Edward Woodward, Christopher Lee, Britt Ekland, Ingrid Pitt. Anthony Shaffer (*Sleuth*) wrote this disturbing sexual parable that has since developed cult status. A puritanical police officer goes to the Scottish Isles to investigate a child's disappearance, and discovers a pagan society whose inhabitants believe that lovemaking is the best way to fertilize the earth. Provocative and bizarre. (Dir: Robin Hardy, 102 mins.)†

Wide Open Faces (1938)**½ Joe E. Brown, Jane Wyman, Alison Skipworth, Lyda Roberti, Alan Baxter, Lucien Littlefield, Sidney Toler. Lively vehicle for Brown as a soda jerk who foils the gangsters who threaten his girl (Wyman) and her aunt (Skipworth). Slender but enjoyable, with wonderful supporting players. (Dir: Kurt Neumann, 67 mins.)

Widow (MTV 1976)**½ Michael Learned, Bradford Dillman, Farley Granger, Robert Lansing. Moderately absorbing drama based on Lynn Caine's autobiographical best-seller. Learned plays the withdrawn widow attempting to cope with two young children, a lack of money, and a new suitor. (Dir: J. Lee Thompson, 98 mins.)

Widow from Chicago, The (1930)**½ Alice White, Edward G. Robinson, Neil Hamilton, Frank McHugh, Lee Shumway. Sister of a slain cop swears to see his killer caught; in the process she teams up with a rival hood. Stone-faced melodrama whose soap-opera overtones don't do White justice; she was much better at suggestive comedy. (Dir: Edward L. Cline, 64 mins.)

Wife, Doctor and Nurse (1937)*** Loretta Young, Warner Baxter, Virginia Bruce, Sidney Blackmer, Jane Darwell. Spiffy triangular comedy sparked by the cast. Will Warner choose Loretta or Virginia or both? (Dir: Walter Lang, 85 mins.)

Wife, Husband and Friend (1939)*** Loretta Young, Warner Baxter, Binnie Barnes, George Barbier, Cesar Romero. Huggable comedy about a perturbed hubby who throws a monkey wrench into his wife's plans for a professional singing career by becoming a singer himself. Based on a novella by James M. Cain. (Dir: Gregory Ratoff, 80 mins.)

Wifemistress (Italy, 1977)*** Laura Antonelli, Marcello Mastroianni, Leonard Mann. A woman confines herself to bed with psychosomatic paralysis while her enlightened husband finances radical causes and writes suffragist pamphlets. She comes into her own after he goes underground after a political murder. (Dir: Marco Vicario, 106 mins.)†

Wife Takes a Flyer, The (1942)** Joan Bennett, Franchot Tone, Allyn Joslyn, Cecil Cunningham, Lloyd Corrigan. Wartime comedy misfire, with Tone a downed flyer in Holland sheltered by a beautiful woman, and deceiving the Nazis into thinking he's her mad husband. (Dir: Richard Wallace, 86 mins.)

Wife vs. Secretary (1936)***½ Clark Gable, Jean Harlow, Myrna Loy, May Robson, James Stewart, Hobart Cavanaugh. Title tells it all in this skillful story of high-powered businessman Gable, whose wife Loy becomes suspicious of his relationship with his devoted secretary Harlow. What could have been a pretty low-grade soap opera is intelligent and sensitively done. (Dir: Clarence Brown, 88 mins.)

Wife Wanted (1946)** Kay Francis, Paul Cavanagh, Robert Shayne, Veda Ann Borg. Low-budget melodrama has an ex-movie star tangled up with a lonelyhearts racket; Francis's last film, and she deserved better. (Dir: Phil Karlson, 73 mins.)

Wilby Conspiracy, The (1975)**½ Michael Caine, Sidney Poitier, Nicol Williamson, Persis Khambatta. Much of this adventure drama set in Africa is predictable, but Caine and Poitier are fine. (Dir: Ralph Nelson, 104 mins.)†

Wild and the Free, The (MTV 1980)** Granville Van Dusen, Linda Gray. Light entertainment in which scientists save research chimps from radiation experiments by returning them to Africa. (Dir: James Hill, 104 mins.)†

Wild and the Innocent, The (1959)**½ Audie Murphy, Sandra Dee, Gilbert Roland, Joanne Dru. Slightly offbeat story of a fur trader, a wild mountain waif, and their misadventures in town during a Fourth of July celebration. (Dir: Jack Sher, 84 mins.)

Wild and the Willing, The—See: **Young and the Willing, The**

Wild and Wonderful (1964)** Tony Curtis, Christine Kaufmann, Larry Storch, Marty Ingels. A French poodle with a thirst for liquor is found by an American in Europe, and the owner's pretty daughter goes looking for the pooch. Uninspired light comedy. (Dir: Michael Anderson, 88 mins.)

Wild and Woolly (1917)***½ Douglas Fairbanks, Eileen Percy, Sam De Grasse, Walter Bytell, Joseph Singleton. Hilarious vehicle for Fairbanks, as the son of a railroad magnate crazy about the Wild West; his father sends him to Arizona on business, and westerners take him for a foolish eastern dude. The scenario, by Anita Loos, combines slam-bang action and wit; Fairbanks is breathtaking. (Dir: John Emerson, 90 mins.)†

Wild and Wooly (MTV 1979)** Chris DeLisle, Susan Bigelow, Elyssa Davalos. Set in old frontier days, three lovelies parlay their talents to stem the tide of villainy. (Dir: Philip Leacock, 104 mins.)

Wild Angels, The (1966)**½ Peter Fonda, Nancy Sinatra, Bruce Dern, Michael J. Pollard, Diane Ladd. Low-budget cyclesaga used real members of the California Hell's Angels in its cast; Fonda plays Heavenly Blues, a biker chieftain whose friend is shot fleeing from the cops. Blues arranges his "rescue" from the confines of a hospital, and his subsequent funeral service. (Dir: Roger Corman, 83 mins.)†

Wild at Heart (1990)*** Nicolas Cage, Laura Dern, Diane Ladd, Harry Dean Stanton, Isabella Rossellini, Willem Dafoe. Disturbing road movie follows a contemporary outlaw (Cage) and his feverishly adoring lover (Dern) through an American hell, down a sordid, murderstrewn path filled with eroticism, insanity, fantasy, and mayhem, ending in a deranged bath of self-redemption. You'll never forget Ladd's completely mad mom, who seems willing to devour humans to achieve her goals. (Dir: David Lynch, 124 mins.)†

Wild Blue Yonder, The (1951)** Wendell Corey, Vera Ralston, Forrest Tucker, Phil Harris, Walter Brennan, Ruth Donnelly. Just another up-in-the-clouds aviationpic celebrating male bonding, which receives its severest test when two buddies fall for the same gal. (Dir: Allan Dwan, 98 mins.)

Wild Boys of the Road (1933)***½ Frankie Darro, Dorothy Coonan, Edwin Phillips, Rochelle Hudson, Ann Hovey, Grant Mitchell, Sterling Holloway. The effect of the Depression on ordinary American families is grimly delineated in this still-relevant drama from director William Wellman; two teenage boys leave home when their unemployed fathers can no longer support them. (77 mins.)

Wild Bunch, The (1969)***½ William Holden, Ernest Borgnine, Edmond O'Brien,

Warren Oates, Robert Ryan. Director Sam Peckinpah delivers violence on the Texas-Mexican border in '13 with a cynical band of outlaws joining a rebel Mexican general against law, order, and the Mexican army. Holden incarnates weary, honorable cutthroatery, while Ryan plays the consummate man-who-watches. Outstanding western. (135 mins.)†

Wildcat, The (Germany, 1921)*** Pola Negri, Viktor Janson, Wilhelm Diegelmann, Herman Thimig, Paul Heidemann. Grand example of director Ernst Lubitsch's German comedies tells the story of the independent-minded daughter of the chief of a gang of thieves who wants to marry a lieutenant in the military. Wonderful satire is graced by Negri's performance, stupendous sets, and a fun mix of silent movie villains and heroes. (80 mins.)

Wildcat (1942)** Richard Arlen, Arline Judge, William Frawley, Buster Crabbe, Arthur Hunnicutt, Elisha Cook, Jr. Ordinary adventure yarn, concerning not felines but oilmen. Two rival drillers compete for the rights to a rich field; burly but unspectacular. (Dir: Frank Mcdonald, 73 mins.)

Wildcats (1986)** Goldie Hawn, Bruce McGill, James Keach, Brandy Gold, Swoosie Kurtz, Jan Hooks, Nipsey Russell. A formula movie that counts way too much on audience goodwill toward Hawn, who works her cute pout overtime. This predictable comedy is a stale blend of feminism and Stallone-ian sentiments about being able to overcome the odds. When Goldie's shunted off to coach a ghetto high school football team, everyone foolishly expects her to fall on her face. (Dir: Michael Ritchie, 107 mins.)

Wildcats on the Beach (Italy, 1962)** Alberto Sordi, Rita Gam, Elsa Martinelli, Georges Marchal. Four separate stories taking place on the Côte d'Azur, European playground. (Dir: Vittorio Sala, 85 mins.)

Wild Child, The (France, 1970)***½ Jean-Pierre Cargol, Jean Daste, François Truffaut. A beautiful essay on teaching, giving, and eventual receiving, of love. "The Wild Child" is a baby abandoned in the woods of France and discovered years later, around 1797, by a local farmer. Director François Truffaut himself portrays the dedicated Dr. Jean Itard, a Frenchman who undertook the formidable task of training the brutish child. (90 mins.)

Wild Company (1930)** Frank Albertson, H. B. Warner, Sharon Lynn, Joyce Compton, Claire Mcdowell, Bela Lugosi. A wild-living youth hangs out in nightclubs until he is framed for murder and sees the error of his ways. Like all

movie warnings to the younger generation, then and now, the plot is unconvincing and the moralizing dull. (Dir: Leo McCarey, 71 mins.)

Wild Duck, The (Australia, 1985)*½ Jeremy Irons, Liv Ullmann, Lucinda Jones. A senseless update of Ibsen that's a thudding bore. Irons gives a fussy, actory performance that does not illuminate the text; Ullmann is so understated she recedes into the over-stuffed set decoration; and there's a dewy-eyed Pollyanna of a child actress (Jones) who's hard to take as Henrietta. (Dir: Henry Safran, 96 mins.)†

Wilderness Family, Part 2, The (1978)*** Robert Logan, Susan Damante Shaw, Heather Rattray. Sequel to *Adventures of the Wilderness Family*, one of the more successful independent features of the seventies. In part two the family, all sunshine and wholesomeness, survive a bitter winter. (Dir: Frank Zuniga, 104 mins.)†

Wildest Dreams (1987)*½ James Davies, Heidi Paine, Deborah Blaisdell [Tracey Adams], Ruth Collins, Jane Hamilton. Nerd finds a magic bottle, asks the obligatory genie to help him find true love. Of course, it doesn't work out the way it's supposed to in this sexed-up comedy in which love nevertheless wins out in the end (and none too soon, either). (Dir: Chuck Vincent, 80 mins.)†

Wild for Kicks—See: Beat Girl

Wild Game (West Germany, 1972)*** Jorge Von Liebenfels, Ruth Drexel, Eva Mattes, Kurt Raab, Harry Baer. Director Rainer Werner Fassbinder's adaptation of Franz Kroetz's drama captures the powerful social aspects of this tense story of a fourteen-year-old girl who urges her nineteen-year-old lover to kill her brutalizing father. (102 mins.)

Wild Geese, The (Great Britain, 1978)** Richard Burton, Richard Harris, Roger Moore, Hardy Kruger. Based on a true-story novel, the film is shallow, romanticized, and oversensationalized. The leads are four officers hired by a British banker (Stewart Granger) to command a mercenary force attempting to rescue the president of an emerging African nation. Sequels: *Wild Geese II* and *Codename: Wild Geese* (Dir: Andrew V. McLaglen, 135 mins.)†

Wild Geese II (Great Britain, 1985)** Scott Glenn, Barbara Carrera, Edward Fox, Laurence Olivier, Robert Webber, Robert Freitag. The garbled plot involves an attempt to kidnap imprisoned Nazi biggie, Rudolph Hess. Mindless action punctuated with the usual terrorists, assassination attempts, and colorful carnage. Followed by *Codename: Wild Geese*. (Dir: Peter Hunt, 125 mins.)†

Wild Geese Calling (1941)** Henry Fonda, Joan Bennett, Warren William. Set in 1890, this story of a man with the wanderlust is sensitively told but is a dull film. (Dir: John Brahm, 77 mins.)

Wild Gold (1934)** John Boles, Claire Trevor, Harry Green, Roger Imhof, Ruth Gillette. A gold prospector (a miscast Boles) falls in love with dance hall girl Trevor, on the run from her crooked husband. Humdrum adventure-romance enlivened by songs and a climactic flood, but it's quite heavy going nevertheless. (Dir: George Marshall, 75 mins.)

Wild Guitar (1962)½ Arch Hall, Jr., Nancy Czar, William Watters (Arch Hall, Sr.), Cash Flagg (Ray Dennis Steckler.) A twist-crazy turkey about a pompadoured rock n' roller whom a record producer takes advantage of. (Dir: Ray Dennis Steckler, 87 mins.)†

Wild Harvest (1947)*½ Dorothy Lamour, Alan Ladd, Robert Preston, Lloyd Nolan, Richard Erdman. Dreary tale of itinerant farm workers who take time out from harvesting in order to fight for Dottie's hand. A lot of threshing and thrashing for naught. (Dir: Tay Garnett, 92 mins.)

Wild Heart, The—See: **Gone to Earth**

Wild Heritage (1958)**½ Will Rogers, Jr., Maureen O'Sullivan, Troy Donahue, Rod McKuen. Two pioneer families trek west to make their home in a new land, meet with many adventures along the way. Refreshing change from ordinary western fare moves leisurely but pleasantly. (Dir: Charles Haas, 78 mins.)

Wild Horse Hank (1978)**½ Linda Blair, Michael Wincott, Al Waxman, Richard Crenna. A good kid's story starring Blair as a spirited young lady who takes on mercenary herders intent on bringing a pack of wild horses to food-processing plants. (Dir: Eric Tell, 94 mins.)†

Wild Horses (MTV 1985)**½ Kenny Rogers, Pam Dawber, Ben Johnson, David Andrews, Richard Masur, Karen Carlson. Kenny Rogers stars as an ex-rodeo champion looking for a way out of his mundane life. With Dawber's help, he foils a crooked government agent's plan involving the wild horses and finds his place in life in the process. (Dir: Dick Lowry, 104 mins.)

Wild in the Country (1961)** Elvis Presley, Hope Lange, Tuesday Weld, Millie Perkins, John Ireland. Rural boy is saved from delinquency by a female social worker, who encourages him in his writing talent. Wild in the country is boring at home. (Dir: Philip Dunne, 114 mins.)†

Wild in the Sky—See: **Black Jack**

Wild in the Streets (1968)*** Shelley Winters, Christopher Jones, Diane Varsi, Hal Holbrook, Bert Freed, Millie Perkins,

Richard Pryor. A tongue-in-cheek paranoid fantasy about the ultimate youth revolution. Rock star Jones spearheads a movement to lower the voting age to fourteen, and becomes the youngest president in U.S. history. Once elected, he puts everyone over thirty in internment camps, where they're force-fed LSD. The scripting for this "head"-y farce is impeccable, and the acid-in-the-water stream sequence was so frightening to the establishment that the Yippies borrowed the concept for the '68 Democratic Convention. (Dir: Barry Shear, 97 mins.)†

Wild Is the Wind (1957)*** Anna Magnani, Anthony Quinn, Anthony Franciosa. Familiar triangle (Magnani is to marry Quinn, but she and his ward, Franciosa, are attracted) is deftly handled by director George Cukor. (114 mins.)

Wild Life, The (1984)* Christopher Penn, Ilan Mitchell-Smith, Eric Stoltz, Rick Moranis. A mere shadow of a follow-up to the film *Fast Times at Ridgemont High.* The characters are different, but the humor is on the same sophomoric level. (Dir: Art Linson, 95 mins.)†

Wild Man (1989)* Don Scribner, Michelle Bauer, Kathleen Middleton, Dawn Lynn Allen. A Las Vegas casino owner moonlights for Uncle Sam by battling a drug lord. His advantage: a magic ring that renders him invulnerable. The viewer's advantage: the "off" button. (Dir: Fred J. Lincoln, 117 mins.)†

Wild Man of Borneo, The (1941)**½ Frank Morgan, Mary Howard, Billie Burke, Donald Meek, Marjorie Main, Connie Gilchrist, Bonita Granville. A rascally carny barker returns to his long-lost daughter, and they decide to try a con game together. Based on a play by Herman Mankiewicz and Marc Connolly, this is a slight but warmly played comedy. Morgan steals the show, but he has some great competition. (Dir: Robert B. Sinclair, 78 mins.)

Wild McCullochs, The—See: **McCullochs, The**

Wild 90 (1969)*½ Norman Mailer, Buzz Farber, Mickey Knox. If the sight of Norman Mailer struggling hard in a new medium and falling flat on his talented face is your idea of a good time, you might have fun with this self-indulgent item. (Dir: Norman Mailer, 90 mins.)

Wild North, The (1952)** Stewart Granger, Cyd Charisse, Wendell Corey. Heman adventure drama about fur trappers and their many fights with nature. (Dir: Andrew Marton, 97 mins.)

Wild One, The (1954)***½ Marlon Brando, Mary Murphy, Lee Marvin. Brando gives a powerful performance as Johnny, leader of a motorcycle gang that invades a small town and raises havoc. Inspired dozens of would-be bikers and one classic pop poster. (Dir: Laslo Benedek, 79 mins.)†

Wild on the Beach (1965)* Frankie Randall, Sherry Jackson, Sonny and Cher. Girls and boys romp in a beach house to beat the housing shortage on campus. (Not a sequel to Stanley Kramer's *On the Beach*, either.) (Dir: Maury Dexter, 77 mins.)

Wild Orchid (1990)* Mickey Rourke, Jacqueline Bisset, Carre Otis, Bruce Greenwood, Assumpta Serna. Overheated, dreadfully acted romantic fantasy about rookie lawyer Otis on her first big job as an assistant to Bisset in Rio de Janeiro; there she meets Rourke, who is wealthy, mysterious, overtanned, and prone to speaking in pained clichés. The much-ballyhooed climactic sex scene is about as erotic as earwax. (Dir: Zalman King, 103 mins.)†

Wild Orchids (1929)*** Greta Garbo, Nils Asther, Lewis Stone. Garbo is glamorous in this exotic soap opera of a married woman who dallies with a seductive Javanese prince (Asther), but returns to her husband (Stone) in the end. Dopey story, but lovely photography, sets, costumes, and lighting make the best of the star. (Dir: Sidney Franklin, 102 mins.)†

Wild Pair, The (1987)* Beau Bridges, Bubba Smith, Lloyd Bridges, Gary Lockwood, Raymond St. Jacques. Unlikely partners Beau and Bubba go after a right-wing crazy (played with verve by Bridges, Sr.) and an evil drug dealer (St. Jacques). As a director, Beau shows a penchant for car chases, violent confrontations, and hollow sentiment. (86 mins.)†

Wild Party, The (1929)*** Clara Bow, Fredric March, Jack Oakie. Bow is a headstrong college girl out to snag a professor (March), with or without marriage. (Dir: Dorothy Arzner, 78 mins.)†

Wild Party, The (1956)** Anthony Quinn, Carol Ohmart, Kathryn Grant. Former football hero on the skids joins a group of beatniks and holds a couple captive. Way-out drama features some hipster dialogue that's practically unintelligible but has some suspense. (Dir: Harry Horner, 81 mins.)

Wild Party, The (1974)**½ James Coco, Raquel Welch, Perry King. Coco stars as a silent movie star down on his luck, trying for a comeback by giving a party at which he plans to show his latest movie. The party turns into a wild, sexual free-for-all, ending in murder. Loosely based on the Fatty Arbuckle scandal. (Dir: James Ivory, 100 mins.)†

Wild Racers, The (1968)* Fabian, Mimsy Farmer, Judy Cornwall, David Landers. A racing-car driver dallies with tender love, then discards it. Fabian flopped; Farmer fled to Europe. (Dir: Daniel Haller, 79 mins.)

Wild Ride, The (1960)* Jack Nicholson, Georgianna Carter. Rebellious hot-rodder tries to break up a romance and brings tragedy to all concerned. Nasty little low-budget melodrama not worth the ride. (Dir: Harvey Berman, 63 mins.)†

Wild River (1960)***½ Montgomery Clift, Lee Remick, Jo Van Fleet. An excellent film about the dramatic conflicts surrounding the Tennessee Valley Authority's efforts to install dams during the tail end of the Depression years. Director Elia Kazan and a superb cast bring this period of recent history graphically to life. A vastly underrated film when it was first released. (110 mins.)

Wildrose (1985)**½ Lisa Eichhorn, Tom Bower, Jim Cada, Cinda Jackson. A commendable drama that creates flesh-and-blood characters. Recently divorced Eichhorn, still trying to put her life together after an abusive marriage, gets even more flak at the strip mine where she works when she is transferred to an otherwise all-male crew. Effectively filmed on location in the Midwest. (Dir: John Hanson, 96 mins.)†

Wild Rovers (1971)*** William Holden, Ryan O'Neal, Karl Malden, Joe Don Baker, Rachel Roberts. Holden's crisp, strong performance as a cowboy on the shady side of fifty makes this unusual western drama interesting. He and O'Neal make an unlikely pair as they team up for a bank robbery and the inevitable getaway trek to Mexico. (Dir: Blake Edwards, 109 mins.)†

Wild Seed, The (1965)** Michael Parks, Celia Kaye. Young drifter befriends a teenage girl running away from her foster parents; together they seek happiness. Slow-moving drama uses younger players to advantage, but the story's no help. (Dir: Brian Hutton, 99 mins.)

Wild Side, The—See: *Suburbia*

Wild Stallion (1952)**½ Ben Johnson, Edgar Buchanan, Martha Hyer. Orphan grows up obsessed with the idea of recapturing a wild stallion he lost as a boy. Pleasant outdoor drama, a welcome relief from the usual western. (Dir: Lewis D. Collins, 72 mins.)

Wild Strawberries (Sweden, 1957)***½ Victor Sjostrom (Seastrom), Ingrid Thulin, Bibi Andersson. Director Ingmar Bergman's landmark film. Valedictory performance of Sweden's first great director and star (Sjostrom) as an old professor taking stock of his life as he rides in a car to get an honorary degree. (90 mins.)†

Wild Style (1982)** Lee George Quinones, Patti Astor. A spirited semidocumentary featuring rap singing and breakdancing. A promoter helps a graffiti artist to break out of the ghetto and earn his niche in the trendy art world. (Dir: Charlie Ahearn, 82 mins.)†

Wild Thing (1987)* Rob Knepper, Kathleen Quinlan, Robert Davi, Betty Buckley. A ragged social satire, with script by John Sayles that's best left in the sewers. After his family is rubbed out, a youngster escapes a similar fate and stays alive by hiding out in a metropolitan sewer system. He eventually emerges as a subcultural hero. (Dir: Max Reid, 92 mins.)†

Wild, Wild Planet (Italy, 1966)** Tony Russel, Lisa Gastoni, Franco Nero. Complicated science-fiction about a mad scientist. The deranged man likes to spend his time kidnapping specimens from Earth. (Dir: Anthony Dawson, 93 mins.)

Wild Wild West Revisited, The (MTV 1979)**½ Robert Conrad, Ross Martin, Harry Morgan, René Auberjonois. Return to the old TV series starring Conrad and Martin as a wily, unorthodox pair of 19th-century government secret agents. (Dir: Burt Kennedy, 104 mins.)

Wild, Wild World of Jayne Mansfield, The (1968)* This "Mondo"-type documentary with Mansfield taking viewers on a tour of her life and hobbies (most of which involve her or someone else in some form of undress) was unfinished at the time of her death. In appropriately sleazy fashion, footage of her fatal automobile wreck was added to complete the film! Tasteless, but isn't that what you were expecting? (Dir: Arthur Knight, 120 mins.)†

Wild Women (MTV 1970)*½ Hugh O'Brian, Anne Francis, Marilyn Maxwell, Marie Windsor, Sherry Jackson, Cynthia Hall. Brave O'Brian, women stockade prisoners, and U.S. Army Engineers fight off Indians and Mexicans in this comedy-western, which leans heavily on comedy. (Dir: Don Taylor, 73 mins.)†

Wild Women of Chastity Gulch, The (MTV 1982)*½ Priscilla Barnes, Joan Collins, Donny Osmond, Lee Horsley, Howard Duff, Lisa Whelchel, Phyllis Davis, Pamela Bellwood. A sinful town is redeemed by a pretty, Eastern-educated doctor (Barnes) as the women battle evil renegade soldiers. (Dir: Philip Leacock, 104 mins.)

Wild Women of Wongo (1958)* Ed Fury, Adrienne Bourbeau. A colorful, badly acted bit of camp trash. A tribe of beautiful babes in loincloths shed their pug-ugly hubbies for the muscle-bound tribe across the river. The Bourbeau listed in the credits is not the similar-sounding actress who starred on TV's "Maude." (Dir: James Wolcott, 72 mins.)

Wild World of Batwoman, The (1966)½ Katherine Victor, George Andre, Steve Brodie, Lloyd Nelson. Oddball parody with the statuesque Victor as a female masked avenger with a band of go-go dancing followers. When DC Comics sued over unauthorized use of the "bat" name, producer-director Jerry Warren retitled it She Was a Hippy Vampire and added an inane new opening sequence (included on the video version) showing the crimefighters drinking fake "blood" as part of their initiation rites! (68 mins.)†

Wild Youth—See: **Cruel Story of Youth**

Willa (MTV 1979)*** Deborah Raffin, Clu Gulager, Diane Ladd, Nancy Marchand. Willa (Raffin), a waitress at a hash joint, single mother of two young children with a third on the way and an alcoholic mother, is going to be a trucker come hell or high water. (Dirs: Joan Darling, Claudio Guzman, 104 mins.)†

Willard (1971)** Bruce Davidson, Ernest Borgnine, Sondra Locke. The hit movie about a young man who trains rats as agents of revenge. For hard-core rat fans only. (Dir: Daniel Mann, 95 mins.)†

Will, G. Gordon Liddy (MTV 1982)**½ Robert Conrad, Kathy Cannon, Gary Bayer. Based upon Liddy's best-selling autobiography, the highly compressed and sanitized TV movie is most effective in the latter part covering Liddy's time in prison. (Dir: Robert Lieberman, 104 mins.)†

Willie and Phil (1980)*** Margot Kidder, Michael Ontkean, Ray Sharkey. Writer-director Paul Mazursky attempts an American update of Truffaut's Jules and Jim, with enchanting results. Two men fall in love with the same woman, and they try to live as a threesome, but complications develop. (115 mins.)

Willow (1988)**½ Val Kilmer, Joanne Whalley, Warwick Davis, Jean Marsh, Billy Barty. In a mythical kingdom, an elf named Willow (Davis) is assigned to protect a baby destined to end the black-magic reign of evil Queen Bavmorda. Director Ron Howard and executive producer George Lucas succeed about halfway in their attempt to resuscitate the moribund fantasy genre by offering a nonstop procession of cleverly conceived stunt work, action, and special effects. But the plot grinds toward its inevitable resolution so mechanically that every event seems preordained. (121 mins.)†

Will Penny (1968)***½ Charlton Heston, Joan Hackett, Donald Pleasence, Lee Majors, Bruce Dern. A quiet western with action, not for action's sake, but growing out of the character development. A saga of a saddle-worn cowboy (Heston) who tries to stay uninvolved and peaceful despite interfering circumstances. Hackett registers strongly as a young frontier woman who wants to build a new life for her son and herself. Written and directed by Tom Gries. (109 mins.)†

Will Success Spoil Rock Hunter (1957)***½ Tony Randall, Jayne Mansfield, Betsy Drake, Joan Blondell, John Williams, Henry Jones, Mickey Hargitay. A hilarious sex comedy based on the farcical play about an ad man playing lapdog to a glamorous client. Performing flamboyantly, as if the film were a live-action cartoon, Mansfield (recreating her Broadway role) bounces beautifully off Randall's beleaguered straight man. Coarse, but fast-paced and funny. (Dir: Frank Tashlin, 94 mins.)

Will There Really Be a Morning? (MTV 1983)** Susan Blakely, Lee Grant, Royal Dano, Joe Lambie, John Heard. A lengthy adaptation of the biography of film star Frances Farmer. Certain incidents (including Farmer's dealings with the Group Theater) are truthfully depicted, but the central relationship between Frances and her domineering mother (Grant) is distorted, to the point where the scripters have concocted a fictional happy ending for Farmer's tragic existence. (Dir: Fielder Cook, 156 mins).

Willy/Milly—See: *Something Special*

Willy Wonka & The Chocolate Factory (1971)*** Gene Wilder, Jack Albertson. An uneven but amusing and unconventional kids film with Wilder's nutty charm as a madcap Candyman a big asset. Based on Roald Dahl's book *Charlie and the Chocolate Factory*. (Dir: Mel Stuart, 94 mins.)†

Wilma (MTV 1977)*** Cicely Tyson, Shirley Jo Finney. Involving TV biopic about Wilma Rudolph, triple Olympic gold-medal winner in 1960, who overcame crippling cases of pneumonia and scarlet fever as a child. (Dir: Bud Greenspan, 104 mins.)†

Wilmar 8 (1980)***½ Documentary about eight brave women who staged and lost the first bank strike in Minnesota history when they were told they would never earn as much as their male counterparts "because they were women." (Dir: Lee Grant, 55 mins.)

Wilson (1944)***½ Alexander Knox, Geraldine Fitzgerald, Charles Coburn, Vincent Price. Biography of our WWI President is a powerful story, superbly performed and graphically proving his great philosophy and foresight. (Dir: Henry King, 154 mins.)

Wimps (1986)**½ Louie Bonanno, Deborah Blaisdell, Jim Abele. Update of the *Cyrano de Bergerac* story, set on a college campus, where shy, studious Francis ghostwrites love letters to help his frat brother win the heart of librarian Roxanne. Sweet story marred by unnecessary raunchiness and nudity. (Dir: Chuck Vincent, 94 mins.)†

Winchester 73 (1950)*** James Stewart, Shelley Winters, Dan Duryea. Better-than-average western drama about a man who trails a man and a gun through a series of adventures until an old score is settled. Good performances by the entire cast. (Dir: Anthony Mann, 92 mins.)†

Winchester 73 (MTV 1967)** Tom Tryon, John Saxon, Joan Blondell. Remake lacks the tautness of the original. Story of a renegade after a valuable rifle moves sluggishly, is just another routine western. (Dir: Herschel Daugherty, 97 mins.)

Wind, The (1928)**** Lillian Gish, Lars Hanson, Montagu Love. A silent movie masterwork. This stirring film starring the incomparable Lillian Gish as a sheltered city woman who heads out to the frontier, where the harsh, omnipotent wind is a metaphor for her fear and insecurity achieves a level of emotional intensity that few films have ever matched. (Dir: Victor Seastrom (Sjostrom), 75 mins.)†

Wind, The (Mali, 1982)*** Fousseyni Sissoko, Goundo Guisse, Balla Moussa Keita, Ismaila Sarr, Oumou Diarra. Brave satire about two college students from diverse backgrounds who meet, fall in love, and share experiences, including joining a student movement fighting for equality against a military regime.(Dir: Souleymane Cisse, 100 mins.)

Wind, The (1986)*** Meg Foster, Wings Hauser, David McCallum, Steve Railsback, Robert Morley. Gripping suspense film that develops characterizations with unexpected depth and even works in some humor, all within the boundaries of the genre. Novelist is stranded during a storm in an island mansion with a killer. (Dir: Nico Mastorakis, 93 mins.)†

Wind Across the Everglades (1958)*** Burl Ives, Christopher Plummer, Gypsy Rose Lee, George Voskovec, Emmett Kelly. Plummer is a Wildlife Service investigator, and Ives is the enigmatic king of the swamps in director Nicholas Ray's strange film about Plummer's attempts to save the natural beauty of the Florida wilds in the early part of the century. Screenplay by Budd Schulberg. (93 mins.)

Wind and the Lion, The (1975)*** Sean Connery, Candice Bergen, Brian Keith, John Huston. Old-fashioned excursion into America's protoimperialist era ('04). Bergen is an American lady abducted by Berber bandit, autodidact, and self-proclaimed deity Connery, while Teddy Roosevelt (Keith) dispatches the Marines to get her back. (Dir: John Milius, 119 mins.)†

Wind Cannot Read, The (Great Britain, 1958)**½ Dirk Bogarde, Yoko Tani,

Ronald Lewis. Far Eastern color highlights uneven tale of British pilot in WWII and his romance with a Japanese woman training him for language duty. (Dir: Ralph Thomas, 115 mins.)

Wind in the Willows—See: Adventures of Ichabod and Mister Toad, The

Windmills of the Gods (MTV 1988)** Jaclyn Smith, Robert Wagner, Franco Nero. Yet another miniseries based on a bestseller by Sidney ("I Dream of Jeannie") Sheldon. Smith becomes the ambassador to Romania and winds up the target of an assassination plot. More glamorous pap. (Dir: Lee Phillips, 192 mins.)

Windom's Way (Great Britain, 1957)*** Peter Finch, Mary Ure. Doctor in a remote Malay village tries to prevent the oppressed natives from going Communist. Absorbing drama. (Dir: Ronald Neame, 108 mins.)†

Window, The (1949)***½ Bobby Driscoll, Arthur Kennedy, Ruth Roman, Barbara Hale. Child witnesses a murder, but no one will believe him. Terrifically tense, suspenseful melodrama. Special Oscar, Driscoll. (Dir: Ted Tetzlaff, 73 mins.)

Windows (1980)½ Talia Shire, Elizabeth Ashley, Joseph Cortese. Celebrated cinematographer Gordon Willis fails dismally in his debut as director. A morose, distasteful, and boring chiller about a vulnerable young woman who becomes the target of a predatory lesbian who doesn't like being spurned. (96 mins.)†

Window to the Sky, A—See: Other Side of the Mountain, The

Winds of Jarrah, The (Australia, 1983)*½ Terence Donovan, Susan Lyons, Harold Hopkins. Paint-by-numbers dimestore romance: woman on the run from a bad love affair takes a job as nanny for the children of a bitter, lonely man. Film offers nice photography of the Australian countryside, and the actors manage not to yawn, which puts them one up on the audience. (Dir: Mark Egerton, 78 mins.)†

Winds of Kitty Hawk, The (MTV 1978)***½ Michael Moriarty, David Huffman. A loving tribute to the Wright Brothers' first flight. The drama succeeds in recreating the wonder of the Wrights flying like birds in their flimsy craft. (Dir: E.W. Swackhamer, 104 mins.)†

Windwalker (1980)***½ Trevor Howard, Nick Ramus, James Remar. An authentic drama of American Indians before the whites came. Set in the late 18th century with only Indian characters (and actors, except Howard in the title role) and dialogue in Crow and Cheyenne (with English subtitles and narration). Director Keith Merrill has made an attractive, intelligent low-budget independent film. (Dir: Keith Merrill, 108 mins.)†

Windy City (1984)** John Shea, Kate Capshaw, Josh Mostel. When a struggling writer and his dying childhood buddy were growing up, they wanted to be pirates. Now, they set sail on a sea of ideas drawn from old movies. Their sailboat is no doubt propelled by the hot air from this screenplay. (Dir: Armyan Bernstein, 105 mins.)†

Wine, Women and Horses (1937)*½ Barton MacLane, Ann Sheridan, Dick Purcell, Peggy Bates. Inferior remake of Dark Hazard, with MacLane in the Edward G. Robinson role of an inveterate horse player whose addiction causes trouble in his marriage (though in this version, that's all to the good, because Sheridan's waiting in the wings). (Dir: Louis King, 64 mins.)

Wing and a Prayer, A (1944)*** Don Ameche, Dana Andrews. Story of Navy pilots aboard a carrier and their wartime heroism is a good action drama, well acted and directed. (Dir: Henry Hathaway, 97 mins.)

Winged Victory (1944)***½ Lon McCallister, Jeanne Crain, Edmond O'Brien, Judy Holliday. Moss Hart's stirring tribute to the Air Corps is a well-done and entertaining film. Watch for Peter Lind Hayes, Red Buttons, Gary Merrill, Barry Nelson, and Lee J. Cobb. (Dir: George Cukor, 130 mins.)

Wings (1927)**** Clara Bow, Charles Rogers, Richard Arlen, Gary Cooper, Hedda Hopper. One of the most exciting silent dramas, featuring some of the best aerial photography and dogfighting to be seen. About American pilots in WWI. Winner of the first Oscar as Best Picture. (Dir: William A. Wellman, 130 mins.)†

Wings and the Woman (Great Britain, 1942)*** Anna Neagle, Robert Newton. Story of Jim and Amy Mollison, renowned airplane pilots. Good biographical drama. (Dir: Herbert Wilcox, 94 mins.)

Wings for the Eagle (1942)**½ Ann Sheridan, Dennis Morgan, Jack Carson, George Tobias, Russell Arms, Don DeFore, Tom Fadden. Fine patriotic wartime drama, with comic overtones, of the workers at a Lockheed Aircraft plant in California. Engaging performances by the leads, supported by the Warner Bros. stock company. (Dir: Lloyd Bacon, 85 mins.)

Wings in the Dark (1935)**½ Cary Grant, Myrna Loy, Roscoe Karns. Corny but well-acted melodrama about a test pilot who is accidentally blinded. (Dir: James Flood, 75 mins.)

Wings of Desire (West Germany, 1987)**** Bruno Ganz, Solveig Dommartin, Otto Sander, Curt Bois, Peter Falk. Wim Wenders' exquisite vision of the angels who watch over the city of Berlin is a rare combination of fantasy and sentiment that eschews the tenderhearted excesses of Capra for the crisp humanism of Renoir and Truffaut. Ganz is our protagonist, a heaven-sent guardian who becomes entranced by human existence and infatuated with a dreamy circus aerialist (Dommartin). Cinematographer Henri Alekan aids Wenders in realizing an exceptional black-and-white look which fades to color as Ganz gets closer to humanity. The film's opening section, presenting the angel's perspective on daily West German existence, is mesmerizing in its beauty; the rest, detailing Ganz's yearning to be earthbound, is equally impressive, with Falk (playing himself) stealing the picture with a thoroughly brilliant supporting performance. (130 mins.)†

Wings of Eagles, The (1957)**½ John Wayne, Dan Dailey, Maureen O'Hara, Ward Bond, Edmund Lowe. He-man Wayne brawls and grins his way through this robust comedy-drama about Commander ''Spig'' Wead, who started as a barnstormer and ended up a war hero. (Dir: John Ford, 110 mins.)†

Wings of Fire (MTV 1967)*½ Suzanne Pleshette, James Farentino, Ralph Bellamy, Lloyd Nolan, Juliet Mills. Hopelessly cluttered, pretentious drama of a lady pilot, the war hero with a hangup who married someone else, and assorted dull clichés peculiar to inferior magazine fiction. (Dir: David Lowell Rich, 100 mins.)

Wings of the Hawk (1953)** Van Heflin, Julia Adams, Abbe Lane. Predictable adventure set in Mexico involving renegades and their efforts to take over the government. (Dir: Budd Boetticher, 81 mins.)

Wings of the Morning (Great Britain, 1937)**½ Henry Fonda, Annabella. Gypsies, romance and horsemanship in modern Ireland. Studied, often captivating romantic drama. First British film in Technicolor. (Dir: Harold D. Schuster, 89 mins.)

Wings of the Navy (1939)** George Brent, Olivia de Havilland, John Payne, Frank McHugh, John Litel, Victor Jory. OK melodrama of pilots in training competing in the air and on the ground for the love of the fair De Havilland. Good aerial photography, but otherwise nothing special. (Dir: Lloyd Bacon, 89 mins.)

Winner Never Quits, A (MTV 1986)*** Keith Carradine, Mare Winningham, Dennis Weaver, Huckleberry Fox, Fionnula Flanagan. A true story that can't help but touch your emotions. Pete Gray played pro baseball in the forties; what set him apart from the other players was the fact that he had only one arm. (Dir: Mel Damski, 104 mins.)

Winners Take All (1986)** Don Michael Paul, Kathleen York, Robert Krantz, Deborah Richter. After his old friend becomes a motocross star, a California teen decides to compete in the Dallas Supercross competition. All the sports movie clichés are there, but it picks up momentum as it goes along. (Dir: Fritz Kiersch, 103 mins.)†

Winner Take All (1932)**½ James Cagney, Marion Nixon, Virginia Bruce, Guy Kibbee, Alan Mowbray, Dickie Moore. Breezy Cagney vehicle is more like shadowboxing than a clean knockout, but he's as charismatic as ever, playing a punchy prize fighter torn between two women. (Dir: Roy Del Ruth, 68 mins.)

Winner Take All (MTV 1975)**½ Shirley Jones, Laurence Luckinbill, Joan Blondell, Sylvia Sidney. Director Paul Bogart deserves credit for his handling of this story about a compulsive gambler—a housewife attempting to raise the money she has gambled away out of her husband's savings. (100 mins.)

Winning (1969)*** Paul Newman, Joanne Woodward, Robert Wagner, Richard Thomas. A credible drama of professional car racing. Newman, a winner on the track, is less heroic in his personal life after he meets and weds divorcée Woodward. The racing sequences leading to the Indianapolis 500 are superbly staged, and the cast are first-rate. (Dir: James Goldstone, 123 mins.)†

Winning Team, The (1952)**½ Doris Day, Ronald Reagan, Frank Lovejoy. Baseball pitcher Grover Cleveland Alexander's biography. Both Day and Reagan have trouble in this not-too-convincing film. (Dir: Lewis Seiler, 98 mins.)

Winslow Boy, The (British, 1949)**** Robert Donat, Margaret Leighton, Cedric Hardwicke. A noted lawyer is engaged to defend a boy accused of stealing at school. Literate, wonderfully well-acted drama, excellent. (Dir: Anthony Asquith, 97 mins.)†

Winter a Go-Go (1965)*½ James Stacy, Jill Donohue, Beverly Adams, William Wellman, Jr. Ski resort for rich set, and strictly from hunger. (Dir: Richard Benedict, 88 mins.)

Winter Carnival (1939)**½ Ann Sheridan, Richard Carlson. An on-again-off-again romance between a professor and a glamor girl is played against the background of the famous winter carnival at Dartmouth University. (Dir: Charles F. Reisner, 100 mins.)

Winterkill (MTV 1974)**½ Andy Griffith, Sheree North, Joyce Van Patten. Andy Griffith as a chief of police in a mountain resort area. It's a pretty sound murder yarn with a killer on the loose and a guest star lineup of victims and suspects. (Dir: Jud Taylor, 100 mins.)

Winter Kills (1979)*** Jeff Bridges, John Huston, Belinda Bauer, Anthony Perkins, Richard Boone, Sterling Hayden, Toshiro Mifune, Eli Wallach, Dorothy Malone, Elizabeth Taylor. This striking black comedy is a baroque, paranoid fairy tale about political power—you don't have to be a conspiracy theory buff to appreciate its tangled rendition of history. Bridges plays the young brother of a slain U.S. president who enters the corridors of power to find out the truth behind the murder, and discovers a labyrinthine, long-hidden plot. The satirical screenplay is uneven, but there are great moments and performances, especially from Huston as a randy old tycoon. (Dir: William Richert, 97 mins.)†

Winter Light (Sweden, 1963)***½ Ingrid Thulin, Gunnar Bjornstrand, Max von Sydow. Disillusioned pastor watches his congregation crumble along with his faith. Director Ingmar Bergman's chilling exploration of man's spiritual debasement, the poverty of humanity, Christian interdependence, and the relation of love to God. A lean, powerful film. Second in the trilogy with *Through a Glass Darkly* and *The Silence*. (80 mins.)†

Winter Meeting (1948)**½ Bette Davis, Jim Davis, John Hoyt, Janis Paige. Bette is in love with a man who wants to be a priest. Terribly talky script bogs down a potentially dramatic situation. (Dir: Bretaigne Windust, 104 mins.)

Winter of Our Discontent, The (MTV 1983)**½ Donald Sutherland, Tuesday Weld, Teri Garr, E. G. Marshall, Richard Masur. John Steinbeck's novel about the sacrifices a man will make in order to achieve his life's ambition is faithfully adapted, though something is lost in translation. Sutherland is about to go get back the family business, but he must convince a friend to sell his cherished home to clinch the deal. (Dir: Waris Hussein, 104 mins.)

Winter People (1988)**½ Kelly McGillis, Kurt Russell, Lloyd Bridges. Low-key romantic drama set during the Depression. Clockmaker Russell arrives in an Appalachian town and falls in love with single mother McGillis, unwittingly setting off an old family rivalry. (Dir: Ted Kotcheff, 110 mins.)†

Winterset (1936)**** Burgess Meredith (film debut), Margo, Stanley Ridges, Eduardo Ciannelli, John Carradine. Twenty years after his father was executed for a crime he didn't commit, his son searches for the real criminal. Fine version of Maxwell Anderson's play; poetic, dramatic, powerful. (Dir: Alfred Santell, 80 mins.)†

Wintertime (1943)** Sonja Henie, Jack Oakie, Cesar Romero, Carole Landis, Cornel Wilde. Extremely mild vehicle for ice-skating Henie, boosted by an appearance by Woody Herman and his Orchestra; otherwise, forgettable. (Dir: John Brahm, 82 mins.)

Wired (1989)* Michael Chiklis, Ray Sharkey, J. T. Walsh, Patti D'Arbanville, Gary Groomes, Alex Rocco. A biographical atrocity that doesn't just alter events in the life of its subject; it fabricates entirely new ones. Conceived as a fantasy meditation on the life of comic actor John Belushi, and remotely based on the book by Bob Woodward, the film turns a tale of self-destruction in the fast lane into a bizarre but unfunny antidrug comedy. (Dir: Larry Peerce, 109 mins.)†

Wired to Kill (1986)*½ Emily Longstreth, Devin Hoelscher, Merritt Butrick, Frank Collinson. It's 1998 and most of America has been wiped out by a vague sort of plague—the survivors have to endure rampant lawlessness. After a teen's family is beseiged and brutalized, he ingeniously builds a remote-controlled erector set programmed for revenge. (Dir: Franky Schaeffer, 96 mins.)†

Wisdom (1986)* Emilio Estevez, Demi Moore, Tom Skerritt, Veronica Cartwright, William Allen Young. Because of a youthful indiscretion, John Wisdom (Estevez) can't find meaningful employment and decides to become a Reagan-era Robin Hood. (Estevez was the youngest person to star in, write, and direct a major film, but the result is nothing to brag about). (109 mins.)†

Wise Blood (1979)*** Brad Dourif, Amy Wright, Harry Dean Stanton. Sagacious version of Flannery O'Connor's novella. Dourif is a searingly intense, bedeviled psychotic who preaches a gospel of the Church of Jesus Christ Without Christ. Only John Huston could direct a film so simultaneously hilarious and depressing. (108 mins.)†

Wise Girl (1937)**½ Miriam Hopkins, Ray Milland, Walter Abel, Guinn Williams, Henry Stephenson. An eccentric artist (Milland) raises some orphans, and their wealthy aunt (Hopkins) poses as a working girl to get to know him; nice romantic comedy, with good chemistry between the leads. (Dir: Leigh Jason, 70 mins.)

Wise Guys (1986)*** Danny DeVito, Joe Piscopo, Harvey Keitel, Dan Hedaya, Captain Lou Albano, Patti LuPone, Ray Sharkey. This is not a typical DePalma scare-fest, but a funny tale about organized crime in Newark. DeVito and Piscopo are two bumbling Laurel and Hardy types, irresistibly comical as they try to bilk their sadistic boss out of a bundle of money in a gambling scheme, only to become his target after they lose it all. (Dir: Brian DePalma, 92 mins.)†

Wishing Well (Great Britain, 1954)**½ Brenda De Banzie, Donald Houston, Petula Clark. Three women use a wishing well to make their dreams come true. Leisurely little comedy-drama, but well acted. (Dir: Maurice Elvey, 78 mins.)

Wish You Were Here (Great Britain, 1987)***½ Emily Lloyd, Tom Bell, Jesse Birdsall, Geoffrey Hutchings. Lloyd made a triumphant debut in this character study of a nonconformist teenager whose disapproving dad and stifling community try, but fail to rein in. Set during post-WWII, the film is based loosely on the early life of Cynthia Paine, whose later years were covered in the film *Personal Services*. (Dir: David Leland, 92 mins.)†

Wistful Widow of Wagon Gap, The (1947)** Bud Abbott, Lou Costello, Marjorie Main. A&C on the range this time with Marjorie Main as the ''wishful and willing widow.'' Not one of the comedy team's best. (Dir: Charles Barton, 78 mins.)

Witchboard (1987)**½ Todd Allen, Tawny Kitaen, Stephen Nichols, Kathleen Wilhoite, Rose Marie. Watchable low-budget thriller about a girl who attracts the interest of the spirit inside a Ouija board. (Dir: Kevin S. Tenney, 98 mins.)†

Witchcraft (1988)** Anat-Topol Barzilai, Gary Sloan, Lee Kisman, Deborah Scott. New mother is persuaded by her husband to visit her mother-in-law, who lives in one of those houses that anyone who wasn't already suffering from postnatal depression would know enough to avoid. Even if you've never seen *Rosemary's Baby*, you'll guess the ending. (Dir: Robert Spera, 90 mins.)†

Witch Doctor—See: **Men of Two Worlds**

Witchery (Italy, 1988)** Linda Blair, David Hasselhoff, Catherine Hickland, Annie Ross, Hildegarde Knef. Travelers stuck on an island off the Massachusetts coast are stalked by ghostly Knef. Gory Italo horror, with lots of in-jokes for genre buffs. (Dir: ''Martin Newlin'' [Fabrizio Laurenti], 95 mins.)†

Witches, The (Great Britain, 1990)***½ Anjelica Huston, Mai Zetterling, Jasen Fisher, Bill Paterson, Brenda Blethyn, Rowan Atkinson. Grandly entertaining film about a witch (Huston in a wickedly funny performance) and her nefarious plot to eliminate the children of England by turning them into mice. The special effects are top-notch, the photography is superb, and the script is thrilling. Expert family movie-making. From a book by Roald Dahl. Executive produced by Jim
1198

Henson. (Dir: Nicolas Roeg, 92 mins.)†

Witches' Brew (1983)**½ Richard Benjamin, Teri Garr, Lana Turner, Kathryn Leigh Scott, Jordan Charney. College professor Benjamin is nonplussed when wife Garr begins dabbling in witchcraft, eventually involving him in supernatural perils. Fantasy-comedy often resembles a TV-movie. (Dirs: Richard Shorr, Herbert L. Strock, 99 mins.)†

Witches of Eastwick, The (1987)**½ Jack Nicholson, Cher, Susan Sarandon, Michelle Pfeiffer, Veronica Cartwright. Although it lacks the flair and subtlety of the John Updike novel on which it is based, this devilish comedy has its moments, particularly whenever Nicholson is hamming it up. With great relish he plays a devil, and he's been conjured up by three amateur witches who are tired of the shortage of available men in their sleepy vale. The trio prove more than a match for him in this supernatural battle of the sexes that loses its balance whenever it concentrates on special effects at the expense of character development. (Dir: George Miller, 122 mins.)†

Witches of Salem—See: **Crucible, The**

Witchfinder General (Great Britain, 1968)*** Ian Ogilvy, Hilary Dwyer, Vincent Price. Vincent Price plays a nasty 17th-century tyrant callously destroying lives while serving as a self-appointed witchhunter. Gruesome but compelling shocker. AKA: **The Conqueror Worm**. (Dir: Michael Reeves, 98 mins.)

Witchfire (1986)* Shelley Winters, Gary Swanson, Francesca De Sapio, David Mendenhall. Winters-watchers will have a field day with this overheated thriller that has three mental patients setting up house in the woods after their doctor is killed in a car crash and conducting seances to contact his host. (Dir: Vincent J. Privitera, 100 mins.)†

Witchmaker, The (1969)*½ John Lodge, Alvy Moore, Anthony Eisley. A party of students and their professor get more than they bargained for when they investigate witchcraft in a Louisiana swamp. Nothing new here. (Dir: William O. Brown, 99 mins.)†

Witchtrap (1988)** James W. Quinn, Kathleen Bailey, Judy Tatum, Rob Zapple, Linnea Quigley. A group of paranormal experts are hired to free a house from the evil spirit of a former owner. Seeing smart people on screen instead of the usual horror movie bimbos is a nice change of pace, even if the movie as a whole isn't. Several conspicuously awful performances drag this otherwise competent fright flick down a notch. (Dir: Kevin S. Tenney, 90 mins.)†

Witch Without a Broom, A (U.S.-Spain, 1966)*½ Jeffrey Hunter, Maria Perschy,

Gustavo Rojo, Perla Cristal. Incompetent witch involves herself and American professor in wide-ranging exploits through time and space. Cheaply made, unpersuasive comedy. (Dirs: Joe Lacy, Jose E. Lorrieta, 78 mins.)

With a Song in My Heart (1952)*** Susan Hayward, David Wayne, Rory Calhoun, Thelma Ritter, Robert Wagner. Good biopic of singer Jane Froman and her comeback after an air crash which left her almost completely crippled. Hayward gives a strong performance with a stress on the dramatics. Many songs are sung by Miss Froman with Hayward doing an admirable miming job. Oscar: Alfred Newman, Best Scoring. (Dir: Walter Lang, 117 mins.)

With Buffalo Bill on the U. P. Trail (1925)**½ Roy Stewart, Kathryn McGuire, Cullen Landis, Sheldon Lewis, Earl Metcalf. Interesting early western with Buffalo Bill rescuing a wagon train, foiling land speculators, and demonstrating truth, justice, and the American way. Film displays a sympathetic attitude toward Indians that was all too rare. AKA: **Buffalo Bill on the U.P. Trail.** (Dir: Frank S. Mattison, 89 mins.)†

With Intent to Kill (MTV 1984)**½ Karl Malden, Alex McArthur, Holly Hunter. Earnest drama about a young man who returns to his small town after serving four years in a mental institution for slaying his high-school sweetheart. (Dir: Mike Robe, 104 mins.)

Within These Walls (1945)** Thomas Mitchell, Mary Anderson, Edward Ryan, Mark Stevens. Contrived, low-energy prison melodrama, with warden Mitchell supervising his prisoner son; dank and quite cliché-ridden. (Dir: H. Bruce Humberstone, 71 mins.)

With Kit Carson over the Great Divide (1925)**½ Roy Stewart, Henry B. Walthall, Marguerite Snow, Sheldon Lewis. In this recently re-discovered silent western, a family traveling west crosses the path of John C. Fremont's historic expedition to survey the Great Divide in Colorado, for which frontiersman Kit Carson served as a guide. Exciting historical drama, with breathtaking scenery. (Dir: Frank S. Mattison, 72 mins.)†

Withnail and I (Great Britain, 1987)**** Richard E. Grant, Paul McGann, Richard Griffiths, Ralph Brown, Michael Elphick. Acerbic comedy that provides a bitterly funny remembrance of things past for the period of the late sixties. Two struggling actors share drugs, liquor, and failure in a seedy flat. They decide to escape to a recuperative weekend in the country which proves just as taxing and terrifying as life in the big city. A brilliant directorial debut for Bruce Robinson,

a former actor who wrote the screenplay for *The Killing Fields*. (108 mins.)†

Without a Clue (Great Britain-U.S., 1988)*** Michael Caine, Ben Kingsley, Jeffrey Jones, Lysette Anthony, Paul Freeman. Delightful comedy that proposes that Dr. Watson (Kingsley) was actually the mastermind detective, and Sherlock Holmes was simply an actor (Caine) he hired to play the role of the master sleuth. The impeccable Kingsley and Caine keep this high-spirited farce moving along nicely, and convincingly do away with years of Rathbone-Bruce whodunit mythology. (Dir: Thom Eberhardt, 107 mins.)†

Without Anesthesia (Poland, 1978)***½ Zbigniew Zapasiewicz, Ewa Dalkowska, Andrzej Seweryn, Krystyna Janda. Andrzej Wajda's painfully intimate study of a well-known Polish foreign correspondent whose personal and professional life suddenly start to disintegrate. (130 mins.)

Without a Trace (1983)** Kate Nelligan, Judd Hirsch, David Dukes, Stockard Channing, Daniel Bryan Corkill. Screenwriter Beth Gutcheon, whose book *Still Missing*, is the basis for this film, and director Stanley R. Jaffe give us a set of characters who are more formula than fascinating. Nelligan and Dukes struggle to bring their characters to life, as an estranged couple whose young son disappears, but neither is especially interesting. (120 mins.)†

Without Her Consent (MTV 1990)* Melissa Gilbert, Barry Tubb, Scott Valentine, Bebe Neuwirth, Crystal Bernard. Gilbert pulls out all the stops in yet another TV rape drama that asks the question: If a woman knows her attacker, has a crime been committed? We ask: If viewers keep tuning into these exploitative melodramas, can they complain that they're such garbage? (Dir: Sandor Stern, 96 mins.)

Without Love (1945)*** Spencer Tracy, Katharine Hepburn, Lucille Ball, Gloria Grahame, Keenan Wynn. Talky, often amusing comedy about a scientist and a widow who get married just for convenience. (Dir: Harold S. Bucquet, 111 mins.)

Without Pity (Italy, 1949)*** Carla Del Poggio, John Kitzmiller, Pierre Claude, Giulietta Masina. Terrific *noir* about a prostitute who falls in love with an AWOL American soldier; they plot to rob her pimp to get money to flee to America. Federico Fellini co-wrote this tense thriller which helped provide a bridge between Italy's neo-realism and New Wave movements. (Dir: Alberto Lattuada, 94 mins.)

Without Reservations (1946)**½ Claudette Colbert, John Wayne, Don DeFore. Couple of Marines out for fun and romance encounter a lady novelist on a Hollywood-bound train. Amusing romantic comedy. (Dir: Mervyn LeRoy, 107 mins.)†

Without Warning (1952)*** Adam Williams, Meg Randall. Police search for a mad killer who strangles blondes without reason. Sordid tale is surmounted by fine direction of Arnold Laven. (75 mins.)

Without Warning (1980)* Martin Landau, Jack Palance. Be warned. Space invaders attack a small town and the townspeople are overtaken by leech-like creatures. (Dir: Greydon Clark, 89 mins.)

Without You I'm Nothing (1990)*** Sandra Bernhard, Steve Antin, John Doe, Lu Leonard, Cynthia Bailey, Ken Foree, Robin Byrd. This adaptation of Bernhard's one-woman stage show crackles with nervous energy as the actress-singer-comedienne leads the viewer on an expertly filmed, musically exciting, sometimes strident, almost erotic, often hilarious look at the influences that pop, rock, and rhythm and blues have on American culture. Bernhard's detractors will hate it, but no one can deny her originality and talent. Satire and sarcasm don't get any better than this. (Dir: John Boskovich, 99 mins.)†

With Six You Get Eggroll (1968)** Doris Day, Brian Keith, Barbara Hershey. One of those bumbling affairs which casts Day as a widow with three kids who teams up with widower Keith who has only one daughter. (Dir: Howard Morris, 99 mins.)†

With This Ring (MTV 1978)**½ Dick Van Patten, Betty White, John Forsythe. Comical if predictable vignettes about weddings. Van Patten is well cast as a harried father of the bride worrying about how he's going to pay for the nuptials. White also scores as a social-climbing mother who goes all out for her daughter's wedding and is reunited with her estranged husband (Forsythe). (Dir: James Sheldon, 104 mins.)

Witness (1985)***½ Harrison Ford, Kelly McGillis, Alexander Godunov, Lukas Haas, Danny Glover, Josef Sommer. An atmospheric thriller that's rich in characterization. Using locations effectively, Witness spins a tale about a small Amish boy who witnesses a murder scene. Ford gives a fine performance as the detective who becomes involved with both the case and with the boy's mother as he and the boy hide out in this child's home. (Dir: Peter Weir, 112 mins.)†

Witness Chair, The (1936)**½ Ann Harding, Walter Abel, Douglas Dumbrille, Frances Sage, Moroni Olsen. Atmospheric courtroom drama, with a devoted secretary trying to save her employer from a spurious charge; well acted, with surprising twists. (Dir: George Nicholls, 64 mins.)

Witness for the Prosecution (1957)**** Tyrone Power, Charles Laughton, Marlene Dietrich, John Williams, Elsa Lanchester. Agatha Christie's clever and suspenseful play about a sensational London murder trial is excellently recreated on the screen. The cast is uniformly brilliant. Laughton, as an aging barrister, is a standout; Power gives one of his best performances. (Dir: Billy Wilder, 116 mins.)†

Witness for the Prosecution (MTV 1982)*** Ralph Richardson, Deborah Kerr, Beau Bridges, Donald Pleasence, Diana Rigg. The Agatha Christie play-turned-movie works both as a mystery and a courtroom drama, and audiences unfamiliar with the plot will relish every minute of it. The wondrous Richardson is splendid as the barrister who takes on the murder case of a man (Bridges) accused of killing an old woman for her money. (Dir: Alan Gibson, 104 mins.)

Witness to Murder (1954)*** Barbara Stanwyck, Gary Merrill, George Sanders. Well-acted, minor little suspense tale. Barbara sees the murder. George commits it and Gary is the cop. (Dir: Roy Rowland, 83 mins.)

Wives and Lovers (1963)*** Van Johnson, Janet Leigh, Shelley Winters, Martha Hyer. A sparkling sophisticated comedy with brittle dialogue and stylish performances. It's all about a "nice-guy" writer whose sudden success changes him into a silly strutting egomaniac, and almost destroys his happy marriage. (Dir: John Rich, 103 mins.)

Wives Never Know (1936)**½ Charlie Ruggles, Mary Boland, Adolphe Menjou, Vivienne Osborne, Fay Holden. Frolicsome marital comedy vehicle for the wonderful team of Ruggles and Boland, as a husband and wife putting romance back into their marriage; good supporting players help, as does deft direction by Elliott Nugent. (75 mins.)

Wives under Suspicion (1938)**½ Warren William, Gail Patrick, Constance Moore, Ralph Morgan, William Lundigan. Selfish attorney William takes notice when he thinks his neglected wife loves another man. Pointless remake of *The Kiss Before the Mirror*, also directed by James Whale, though the material is still good, and so is the cast. (69 mins.)

Wiz, The (1978)½ Diana Ross, Nipsey Russell, Ted Ross, Mabel King, Michael Jackson, Richard Pryor, Lena Horne. Hyperextended musical derivative of *The Wizard of Oz*. With the usual dark disco lighting and romanticizing of urban rubble, it's chipper yet depressing. The casting of Ross (instead of using a little girl) wrecks whatever chance this ill-conceived musical had for success. (Dir: Sidney Lumet, 133 mins.)†

Wizard, The (1989)** Fred Savage, Jenny Lewis, Luke Edwards, Beau Bridges,

Christian Slater. Vapid kiddie version of *Rain Man* is actually a blatant ad for Nintendo video games and the Universal Studios tour. Savage and his introverted brother, a genius at video games, journey cross-country to a national video championship and an impromptu reunion with the past. In one irresponsible scene, Lewis, the boys' travel companion, falsely accuses an older man of fondling her, simply to get away from him. (Dir: Todd Holland, 100 mins.)†

Wizard of Babylon, The (West Germany, 1982)***½ Powerful documentary about eclectic director Rainer Werner Fassbinder, focusing on the shooting of his film *Querelle* and including an illuminating interview with him given hours before his tragic death. The essence of his genius and the freshness and excitement of his work are captured in this superb film. (Dir: Dieter Schidor, 83 mins.)

Wizard of Baghdad, The (1960)*½ Dick Shawn, Diane Baker. Genie without much talent is ordered to settle down in his work, is assigned to Baghdad. (Dir: George Sherman, 92 mins.)

Wizard of Loneliness, The (1988)**½ Lukas Haas, Lea Thompson, Jeremiah Warner, John Randolph, Dylan Baker. Downbeat story of an intelligent young boy (Haas) with a severe attitude problem. The episodic nature of the storyline allows for some deliberately understated moments (with Thompson, who never looked better), and others which fall flat (involving psycho war veteran Baker). (Dir: Jenny Bowen, 110 mins.)

Wizard of Mars, The (1964)* John Carradine, Roger Gentry, Vic McGee. Four astronauts crash-land on Mars where Carridine is the sole survivor of a long-dead civilization. The concept—*The Wizard of Oz* on Mars—is much cleverer than the execution. AKA: **Alien Massacre** and **Horrors of the Red Planet**. (Dir: David L. Hewitt, 81 mins.)†

Wizard of Oz, The (1925)**½ Larry Semon, Bryant Washburn, Dorothy Dwan, Virginia Pearson, Charles Murray, Oliver Hardy, G. Howe Black. Typically wacky silent Oz adventure, under the direction of slapstick comedian Larry Semon, who also plays the Scarecrow; quite close to the original book, but in this one, Dorothy is eighteen instead of eight! Agreeable children's entertainment. (93 mins.)†

Wizard of Oz, The (1939)**** Judy Garland, Frank Morgan, Ray Bolger, Bert Lahr, Margaret Hamilton, Billie Burke, Jack Haley. This musical fantasy about the farm girl whisked to the incredible land of Oz and her adventures with the scarecrow, the tin woodman, and the cowardly lion has become a TV classic over the years. Just to hear "Over the Rainbow" once again is worth tuning in. Oscars: Special Award to Judy; Best Original Score (Herbert Stothart); Best Song, "Over the Rainbow." From the book by L. Frank Baum. (Dir: Victor Fleming, 102 mins.)†

Wizard of Speed and Time, The (1988)*** Mike Jittlov, Richard Kaye, Paige Moore, David Conrad, Philip Michael Thomas, Angelique Pettyjohn. Special effects whiz Mike Jittlov uses a frame plot about how difficult it is for an outsider to work in Hollywood as a basis for plenty of his invigorating trick-photography work. Jittlov's joy in his craft is infectious. (Dir: "The Guy in the Green Jacket" [Jittlov], 92 mins.)†

Wizards (1977)*** Ace animator Ralph Bakshi spins a tale of a future civilization where an aged wizard battles his fascist brother. State-of-the-art (for its time) animation and some humorous plot twists. (Dir: Ralph Bakshi, 81 mins.)†

Wizards of the Lost Kingdom (U.S.-Argentina, 1985)*½ Bo Svenson, Vidal Peterson, Thom Christopher, Barbara Stock. Sword-'n'-sorcery saga with wandering warrior Svenson aiding young prince Peterson in regaining his kingdom from the control of evil magician Christopher. No sex, very little violence make this OK for kids but pretty dull for grown-ups. Filmed in 1983. (Dir: Hector Olivera, 76 mins.)†

Wizards of the Lost Kingdom II (1989)*½ David Carradine, Bobby Jacoby, Lana Clarkson, Mel Welles, Susan Lee Hoffman, Sid Haig. In-name-only sequel has warrior "Dark One" helping wizard Welles combat evil in a mystical kingdom. Of interest only to Roger Corman completists, who will recognize many names in the credits. (Dir: Charles B. Griffith, 79 mins.)†

Wolf at the Door, The (Denmark-France, 1987)** Donald Sutherland, Max von Sydow. This unilluminating biography of Paul Gauguin focuses on a period late in this life, when he returned from Tahiti but still couldn't find success or happiness in Paris. Sutherland's passionate turn is unsupported by any insight or drama in the script, which somehow wedges in August Strindberg (von Sydow) for a few aimless exchanges. (Dir: Henning Carlsen, 90 mins.)†

Wolfen (1981)**½ Albert Finney, Diane Venora, Tom Noonan, Gregory Hines. This high-budget, high-tech thriller concerns a pack of superwolves living in the South Bronx. Eating only the dregs of society, they keep to themselves until threatened. Then they become a bunch of murderous animals. (Dir: Michael Wadleigh, 114 mins.)†

Wolf Larsen (1958)** Barry Sullivan, Peter Graves. Brutal sea captain meets his match. If this looks like *The Sea Wolf* it's a remake—in other words, warmed over. (Dir: Harmon Jones, 83 mins.)

Wolf Man, The (1941)*** Lon Chaney, Jr., Claude Rains, Evelyn Ankers, Maria Ouspenskaya, Ralph Bellamy, Bela Lugosi. "Even a man who is pure in heart/ And says his prayers by night/Can become a wolf when the wolfbane blooms/ And the autumn moon is bright" —poor guy! Lon is bitten by a werewolf, which gives him paws. Suddenly he starts to feel all funny in the moonlight, and for some reason his father thinks he's crazy. There's also a pretty snappy love story with Ankers, queen of the screamers, good effects, and mist-laden scenery full of those Universal Studios trees that grow straight into the ground—or floor—without any roots. Consistently enjoyable. (Dir: George Waggner, 71 mins.)†

Woman and the Hunter, The (1957)*½ Ann Sheridan, David Farrar, John Loder. The pace of this safari-drama is so slow even the animals look sleepy, and the jungle vegetation looks as if it were drooping. (Dir: George Breakston, 79 mins.)

Woman Called Golda, A (MTV 1980)***½ Ingrid Bergman, Leonard Nimoy, Ned Beatty, Judy Davis. Former prime minister of Israel, Golda Meir, was assuredly one of the most remarkable women of this century. The wonderful Australian actress, Davis, plays Golda as a young woman; and Bergman plays Golda in her middle and late years. A compelling and historically accurate docudrama. (Dir: Alan Gibson, 208 mins.)†

Woman Called Moses, A (MTV 1978)***½ Cicely Tyson, Dick Anthony Williams, John Getz. Tyson gives a sparkling, luminous performance as Harriet Ross Tubman, one of the most famous black women in history. Beginning deals with Harriet's early life and her relentless drive to work hard and long in order to save up enough money to buy her freedom. (Dir: Paul Wendkos, 208 mins.)

Woman Chases Man (1937)*** Joel McCrea, Miriam Hopkins, Broderick Crawford. Vastly entertaining screwball comedy about love among the rich. (Dir: John G. Blystone, 71 mins.)

Woman Eater, The (Great Britain, 1957)½ George Coulouris, Robert MacKenzie, Norman Claridge, Marissa Dawn, Joy Webster. A cheesy horror-pic about a ravenous tree that has a yen for zoftig girls, and the mad scientist who sees that it's supplied with a steady stream of well-stacked tree food. (Dir: Charles Saunders, 70 mins.)

Woman for Charley, A—See: Cockeyed Cowboys of Calico County, The

Woman Hater (Great Britain, 1949)**½

Stewart Granger, Edwige Feuillere, Ronald Squire. Hackneyed but fairly pleasant romantic comedy of a determined bachelor pursued by an enticing girl. Carried by Granger's charm; without him, it would be nothing special. (Dir: Terence Young, 70 mins.)†

Woman He Loved, The (MTV 1988)**½ Jane Seymour, Anthony Andrews, Olivia de Havilland. A fine drama recounting the famous love story of England's King Edward VIII and Wallis Simpson. Both lead performers provide interesting portraits of these two fabled romantics, and the first-class script by William Luce underscores their fine work. (Dir: Charles Jarrott, 96 mins.)

Woman in a Dressing Gown (Great Britain, 1957)***½ Yvonne Mitchell, Sylvia Syms, Anthony Quayle. Touching adult story about a married couple who get too used to one another and decide on a divorce. Extremely well directed by J. Lee Thompson. (93 mins.)

Woman in Bondage (1943)** Gail Patrick, Nancy Kelly, Gertrude Michael, H. B. Warner, Anne Nagel, Tala Birch. Sensationalistic anti-Nazi WWII propaganda, with occupying Germans brutalizing local women; low-budget melodrama, competently done. (Dir: Steve Sekely, 70 mins.)

Woman in Flames, A (Germany, 1984)*** Gudrun Landgrebe, Mathieu Carriere, Gabriele Lafari. Heralded as Fassbinder's successor, Robert Van Ackeren has helmed an outlandishly plotted tale of romantic obsessiveness and moral righteousness. Bored with her bourgeois husband, a women flees convention to become a hooker and ends up falling for a male prostitute. (106 mins.)†

Woman in Green, The (1945)**½ Basil Rathbone, Nigel Bruce, Hillary Brooke. Holmes and Watson are on the trail of a blackmail outfit that utilizes a shady lady hypnotist. Blackmail soon leads to murder, and Sherlock goes into his trance to solve the mystery. (Dir: Roy William Neill, 68 mins.)†

Woman in Hiding (1949)** Ida Lupino, Howard Duff, Peggy Dow. Contrived drama about a ruthless man who stops at nothing, from marriage to murder, to get control of a prosperous mill. (Dir: Michael Gordon, 92 mins.)

Woman in Question, The (Great Britain, 1950)*** Jean Kent, Dirk Bogarde. When a questionable fortune teller is found murdered, a police investigation reveals many sides of her character. Neat mystery. (Dir: Anthony Asquith, 88 mins.)

Woman in Red, The (1935)** Barbara Stanwyck, Gene Raymond, Genevieve Tobin, John Eldredge, Philip Reed. Courtroom drama about Barbara's marriage being damaged by accusations that she's an adulteress. (Dir: Robert Florey, 68 mins.)

Woman in Red, The (1984)*½ Gene Wilder, Joe Bologna, Gilda Radner, Charles Grodin, Judith Ivey, Kelly LeBrock. Happily married Wilder gets the seven-year itch in this passable farce about a mild-mannered man's pursuit of a scrumptious model. This remake of the effervescent *Pardon Mon Affaire*, flattens that bubbly champagne film into a slightly flat romantic comedy, domestic vintage. (Dir: Gene Wilder, 87 mins.)†

Woman Inside, The (1979)*½ Gloria Manon, Dane Clark, Joan Blondell, Michael Champion. Those expecting another *Glen or Glenda?* will be disappointed at this tale of Vietnam veteran Hollis who longs to become Holly, and gets his/her wish through the miracle of modern surgery. On the other hand, even the most open minds are going to have some trouble taking this overly corny drama seriously. Blondell's last film, sadly enough. (Dir: Joseph Van Winkle, 94 mins.)

Woman in the Dunes (Japan, 1964)**** Eiji Okada, Kyoko Kishida. A haunting, engrossing allegory about a man and a woman trapped in a shack at the bottom of a desolate sand pit amidst isolated dunes. Based on the critically acclaimed Japanese novel by Kobo Abé, who adapted it for the screen. But the impact of the film is due principally to the camerawork of Hiroshi Segawa, and to the extraordinary direction of Hiroshi Teshigahara. (123 mins.)†

Woman in the Moon, The (Germany, 1929)*** Gerda Maurus, Fritz Rasp, Willy Fritsch. Fascinating silent film from director Fritz Lang, a follow-up to *Metropolis*, details the first rocket launched to the moon, sponsored by greedy bankers in search of gold. Lang researched the notion of space travel thoroughly, and predicted what it would be like with surprising accuracy (as well as some misfires). (146 mins.)†

Woman in the Window, The (1944)***½ Edward G. Robinson, Joan Bennett, Raymond Massey, Dan Duryea. His family on holiday, a professor makes a chance acquaintance with a beautiful woman, becomes involved in murder. Despite a weak ending, this remains a superbly thrilling, tense melodrama. Fine Fritz Lang direction, good performances. (99 mins.)

Woman in White, The (1948)**½ Eleanor Parker, Alexis Smith, Sydney Greenstreet, Gig Young, Agnes Moorehead. From the gothic novel by Wilkie Collins. Stormy melodrama about an eccentric household, an emotionally tormented heiress, and the young man who arrives to

untangle her problems. (Dir: Peter Godfrey, 109 mins.)

Woman Is a Woman, A (France, 1961)***½ Jean-Paul Belmondo, Anna Karina, Marie Dubois, Jean-Claude Brialy. Director Jean-Luc Godard's first color and Cinemascope film is a joyous ode to Hollywood musicals. Karina is breathtaking as a stripper who wants to settle down with her lover and have a baby. When he says no, she asks his best friend to take on the task. The interplay among the three main characters is wonderful, and Legrand's music is fresh and charming. (85 mins.)

Woman Next Door, The (France, 1981)*** Gerard Depardieu, Fanny Ardant, Michele Baumgartner. François Truffaut's contemporary tale of a married man whose passions rise uncontrollably to the surface when an old flame becomes his neighbor, shifts from bourgeois comedy to dark romantic drama with surprising, though not complete, success. (106 mins.)†

Woman Obsessed (1959)** Susan Hayward, Stephen Boyd. Woman finds love again after her husband is accidentally killed. Soapy drama. (Dir: Henry Hathaway, 102 mins.)

Woman Obsessed, A (1989)½ Ruth Raymond [Georgina Spelvin], Gregory Patrick, Carolyn Van Bellinghen, Troy Donohue, Linda Blair. Just as over-the-hill actresses like Bette Davis and Joan Crawford did in the '60s, ex-porn star Spelvin (under the pseudonym "Ruth Raymond") stars in a gothic story of a neurotic woman driven over the edge when she discovers her long-lost son. Hilariously awful melodrama, played straight-faced by all, has many scenes sure to become camp classics, but our favorite was the nasty new variation on that old favorite, "This Little Piggy." (Dir: Chuck Vincent, 103 mins.)†

Woman of Affairs, A (1928)*** Greta Garbo, John Gilbert, Douglas Fairbanks, Jr., Dorothy Sebastian, Lewis Stone, Johnny Mack Brown. A heavily censored version of Michael Arlen's then-shocking novel, *The Green Hat*, this emerged as a glossy, emotionally fraught soap opera. However, the whole cast is superb, especially Fairbanks and Garbo. (Dir: Clarence Brown, 108 mins.)†

Woman of Distinction, A (1950)**½ Ray Milland, Rosalind Russell, Edmund Gwenn, Janis Carter. A woman dean of a college finds that she must choose between her career and love. Old stuff nicely played. (Dir: Edward Buzzell, 85 mins.)†

Woman of Dolwyn, The (Great Britain, 1949)***½ Hugh Griffith, Anthony James, Edith Evans, Richard Burton (film debut). The story of the last days of a

Welsh village, which is wiped away by flood at the conclusion. Fine cast includes Emlyn Williams (who also wrote and directed). (95 mins.)

Woman of Paris, A (1924) and **Sunnyside** (1919)****** Two Charles Chaplin-directed classics are included in this compilation. *A Woman of Paris* is his only dramatic film, starring Edna Purviance and Adolphe Menjou (Chaplin does not appear). It's a simple yet throroughly sophisticated tale of a French girl's life as the mistress of a man-about-town, without moralizing or heavy histrionics—a remarkable film, brilliantly directed. *Sunnyside* is more conventional Chaplin, with the star in high comic form as a hotel handyman getting into mischief. A fine collection. (111 mins.)†

Woman of Straw (Great Britain, 1964)****½** Gina Lollobrigida, Sean Connery, Ralph Richardson. You may enjoy this well-dressed murder mystery starring sex symbols Lollobrigida and Connery. However, the two smoldering stars are completely upstaged by veteran pro Richardson, who plays the stuffings out of some eccentric views on life. (Dir: Basil Dearden, 117 mins.)

Woman of the Town, The (1943)*****½** Claire Trevor, Albert Dekker, Barry Sullivan. Good western about Bat Masterson, frontier marshal whose love for dance hall girl Dora Hand ended tragically when he cleaned up the town. (Dir: George Archainbaud, 89 mins.)

Woman of the Year (1941)*****½** Spencer Tracy, Katharine Hepburn, Roscoe Karns, William Bendix. Wonderful comedy about the marriage of a nonchalant sportswriter and a charming international reporter. Funny, witty, brilliantly played and a must-see. (Dir: George Stevens, 112 mins.)†

Woman of the Year, The (MTV 1976)***½** Renee Taylor, Joseph Bologna, Dick O'Neill, Anthony Holland. Taylor and Bologna are overbearing in the roles of romantically sparring sportswriter and society columnist. (Dir: Jud Taylor, 104 mins.)

Woman on Pier 13, The (1949)***** Laraine Day, Robert Ryan, Janis Carter. An ultra-patriotic saga about a Communist who sees the light of capitalism and tries to reform himself. AKA: **I Married a Communist.** (Dir: Robert Stevenson, 73 mins.)

Woman on the Beach (1947)******* Joan Bennett, Robert Ryan, Charles Bickford. Nightmarish, elusive tale of a coast guard officer (Ryan) and his near-tragic dalliance with the fetching wife of a painter (Bennett). (Dir: Jean Renoir, 71 mins.)

Woman on the Run (1950)******* Ann Sheridan, Dennis O'Keefe. When her husband witnesses a murder and flees, his

1204

wife and the police try to catch up with him before the real killer does. Compact melodrama, suspenseful. (Dir: Norman Foster, 77 mins.)

Woman Rebels, A (1936)******* Katharine Hepburn, Herbert Marshall, Elizabeth Allan, Van Heflin (film debut). A feminist story given a less than compelling treatment. Hepburn is a rebellious Victorian girl who flaunts convention and becomes a pamphleteer for women's rights. (Dir: Mark Sandrich, 88 mins.)

Woman's Decision, A (Poland, 1974)*****½** Maya Komorowska, Piotr Franczewski, Marek Piwowski. Penetrating drama about a seemingly successful woman confronting reality when she must decide between her suddenly fragmenting marriage and the allure of her lover. With a strong performance by Komorowska as the woman, and sentient direction by Krzysztof Zanussi. (99 mins.)

Woman's Devotion, A (1956)****** Ralph Meeker, Janice Rule, Paul Henreid. Artist and his wife in Mexico are implicated in murder. Uneven, confused mystery melodrama. AKA: **Battleshock.** (Dir: Paul Henreid, 88 mins.)

Woman's Face, A (1941)*****½** Joan Crawford, Melvyn Douglas, Conrad Veidt. Crawford is an evil woman with a facial scar, and Veidt is her epicene manipulator. When plastic surgery restores her face, her personality improves and she resists her former bad habits. Hard-edged and suspenseful. (Dir: George Cukor, 105 mins.)†

Woman's Secret, A (1949)******* Maureen O'Hara, Melvyn Douglas, Bill Williams, Gloria Grahame. Police investigate why a singer should be shot by the woman who made her a success. Interesting melodrama. (Dir: Nicholas Ray, 85 mins.)

Woman's Vengeance, A (1947)*****½** Charles Boyer, Ann Blyth, Jessica Tandy. Married man having an affair with a younger woman is placed on trial when his wife is found to have been poisoned. Great performances in this absorbing drama written by Aldous Huxley. (Dir: Zoltan Korda, 96 mins.)

Woman's World, A (1954)****½** June Allyson, Lauren Bacall, Van Heflin, Fred MacMurray, Cornel Wilde, Clifton Webb, Arlene Dahl. This glossy and ultra-sophisticated glimpse into the leather-lined world of big business may not be an accurate one, but it provides the background for some chic fashions worn by the trio of female stars, and some slick dialogue by the male contingent. (Dir: Jean Negulesco, 94 mins.)

Woman Times Seven (U.S.-France-Italy, 1967)****½** Shirley MacLaine, Michael Caine, Peter Sellers, Alan Arkin, Rossano Brazzi. Shirley MacLaine has an actress's dream in this uneven film—she plays seven different roles with seven different leading men in as many episodes. (Dir: Vittorio De Sica, 99 mins.)†

Woman Under the Influence, A (1974)***½ Gena Rowlands, Peter Falk, Fred Draper. An ambitious, harrowing drama focusing on a mad lower-middle-class housewife (quite devastatingly acted by Rowlands) who is searching for her identity. Writer-director John Cassavetes achieves a remarkable sense of improvisation with his acting troupe. (155 mins.)

Woman Wanted (1935)**½ Joel McCrea, Maureen O'Sullivan, Lewis Stone, Louis Calhern, Adrienne Ames, Edgar Kennedy. Neat crime melodrama, with O'Sullivan an innocent girl unjustly suspected of involvement with criminals, and pursued by gangsters and the law; nothing extra-special, but competent and unpretentious. (Dir: George B. Seitz, 68 mins.)

Woman Who Came Back, The (1945)** Nancy Kelly, John Loder, Otto Kruger, Ruth Ford. A fine cast struggles under the curse of indifferent writing and direction in this yarn about a woman terrified that she's under a centuries-old curse. (Dir: Walter Colmes, 68 mins.)†

Woman Who Wouldn't Die, The (U.S.–Great Britain, 1965)* Gary Merrill, Georgina Cookson. Merrill is the husband of a rich, overbearing woman who makes his life and that of her male secretary unbearable. So, they conspire to do her in! (Dir: Gordon Hessler, 84 mins.)

Woman Without Love, A (Mexico, 1951)*** Julio Villareal, Rosario Granados, Tito Junco, Javier Loya. Exquisite drama takes place in a mansion belonging to an antiques dealer whose wife has a short secret affair that returns to haunt her years later. Visually rich melodrama based on a Guy de Maupassant novel was one of director Luis Buñuel's movies-for-hire, though it bears his usual tweaking of bourgeois values. (91 mins.)†

Women, The (1939)**** Joan Crawford, Norma Shearer, Rosalind Russell, Mary Boland, Paulette Goddard, Joan Fontaine. Another all-star comedy invigorated by George Cukor's sophisticated touch and a brilliant cast of fire-breathing actresses. Not exactly an expression of feminist solidarity, it shows us how the fur flies at a posh dude ranch for incipient divorcées waiting for their decrees in this vast improvement on the theatrical bitch-fest by Clare Boothe Luce. With a color fashion show thrown in but often cut for TV showings; capably remade as a part-musical as *The Opposite Sex*. (132 mins.)†

Women Are Like That (1938)**½ Kay Francis, Pat O'Brien, Melville Cooper, Ralph Forbes. Star chemistry lifts this romantic comedy of a brash advertising man and his love for the boss's chic daughter; enjoyable and weightless. (Dir: Stanley Logan, 78 mins.)

Women at West Point (MTV 1979)*** Linda Purl, Andrew Stevens, Jameson Parker. Purl, as the young, feisty, determined plebe who is the focus of the movie, gives a thoroughly believable performance. (Dir: Vincent Sherman, 104 mins.)

Women in Cell Block 7 (Italy-U.S., 1977)* Anita Strinberg, Eva Czemeys, Olga Bisera, Jane Avril. To clear her father's name, a mobster's daughter volunteers to be put in a women's prison in this tawdry sleaze melodrama. There's a welcome tone of fatalism, but an overly developed plot bogs the movie down. (Dir: Rino Di Silvestro, 81 mins.)†

Women in Chains (MTV 1972)*½ Lois Nettleton, Belinda Montgomery, Ida Lupino. You've seen all those prison shows about the sadistic guard playing games with male inmates—well, here's the same plot in a women's institution with veteran film actress Lupino cast as the sadistic matron. (Dir: Bernard Kowalski, 104 mins.)

Women in Limbo—See: **Limbo**

Women in Love (Great Britain, 1970)***½ Alan Bates, Glenda Jackson, Oliver Reed, Jennie Linden, Eleanor Bron. Jackson won an Oscar for her multi-edged portrayal in this film version of the D. H. Lawrence novel. The film is sensuously shot and dramatized more for mood and effect than plot and action. Bates and Reed co-star and they read the tricky dialogue with spectacular skill. (Dir: Ken Russell, 129 mins.)†

Women in Revolt (1972)*** Candy Darling, Jackie Curtis, Holly Woodlawn. Funny spoof of Hollywood soap operas features three stories about women's liberation, from the fertile mind and camera of Andy Warhol, who directed along with Paul Morrissey. Each of the film's stars blurs the fine line between male and female. AKA: **Andy Warhol's Women and Sex.** (87 mins.)

Women of Brewster Place, The (MTV 1989)*** Oprah Winfrey, Robin Givens, Jackee, Paula Kelly, Lonette McKee, Cicely Tyson. Melodramatic male-bashing that provides many talented black actresses with juicy roles. Winfrey heads the cast in a story set in an urban ghetto during the 1960s. (Dir: Donna Deitch, 192 mins.)†

Women of Pitcairn Island (1957)*½ James Craig, Lynn Bari. In case you didn't know, Gable and Laughton left some exciting gals on the island after the Bounty mutiny. This contrived mess tells all about them and their kids. (Dir: Jean Yarbrough, 72 mins.)

Women of San Quentin (MTV 1983)** Stella Stevens, Amy Steel. Sensationalized prison yarn focusing on the female prison guards in the all-male detention facility of San Quentin. (Dir: William Graham, 104 mins.)

Women of the Prehistoric Planet (1966)* Wendell Corey, Keith Larsen, John Agar. Studio-bound science fictioner about a spaceship overpowered by alien hostages and crash-landing on an unknown world. (Dir: Arthur C. Pierce, 87 mins.)†

Women of Valor (MTV 1986)**½ Susan Sarandon, Kristy McNichol, Alberta Watson. Those who've missed WWII propaganda films will no doubt be gladdened by this old-fashioned, well-acted TV film. Others will wonder whether it is particularly edifying to see these captive nurses being raped, starved, and brutalized in a Japanese prison camp in the Philippines. (Dir: Buzz Kulik, 104 mins.)†

Women on the Verge of a Nervous Breakdown (Spain, 1988)*** Carmen Maura, Antonio Banderas, Julieta Serrano. Farce involving an actress trying to contact her recently departed lover, only to uncover a slew of tangential romantic disasters. Writer-director Pedro Almodovar's film is fast and funny, but lacks the depth of his previous work. (98 mins.)†

Women's Club, The (1987)* Michael Paré, Maud Adams, Eddie Velez. Thicktongued Paré is improbably cast as an aspiring Hollywood screenwriter who finds that a wealthy benefactress (Adams) is more interested in his horizontal talents; she soon begins brokering him to her friends. Neither sexy nor funny—this is just the kind of film the main character would write. (Dir: Sandra Weintraub, 85 mins.)†

Women's Prison (1955)** Ida Lupino, Jan Sterling, Phyllis Thaxter, Howard Duff, Cleo Moore. Unbelievable account of conditions in a women's prison presided over by a ruthless superintendent. (Dir: Lewis Seiler, 80 mins.)

Women's Prison Massacre (Italy, 1985)½ Laura Gemser, Gabriele Truti, Ursula Flores. Don't even bother with this badly dubbed exploitation film about four male killers who set off a riot in a female prison. The most pressing question is: how did these men get put in a women's prison? (Dir: Gilbert Rousel, 89 mins.)†

Women's Room, The (MTV 1980)**½ Lee Remick, Colleen Dewhurst, Patty Duke Astin, Gregory Harrison, Tyne Daly. Dramatization of Marilyn French's provocative best-seller, with Remick going through the familiar cycle of fifties college girl, blushing bride, harried mother, and divorcee. Then she goes back to college

and finds a whole new awareness has sprung up. (Dir: Glenn Jordan, 132 mins.)

Wonder Bar (1934)** Al Jolson, Dick Powell, Kay Francis, Dolores Del Rio. Bizarre Jolson musical mixes murder with a nightclub milieu. (Dir: Lloyd Bacon, 84 mins.)

Wonderful Country, The (1959)**½ Robert Mitchum, Julie London, Jack Oakie, Gary Merrill. Fast action western tale with Mitchum cast as a Texan who has a strange allegiance to the Mexicans and consents to buy arms to be used in the revolution. (Dir: Robert Parrish, 96 mins.)

Wonderful World of the Brothers Grimm, The (1962)*** Laurence Harvey, Claire Bloom, Barbara Eden. Children's picture with some biography of Jacob and Wilhelm and versions of their fairy tales. (Dirs: Henry Levin, George Pal, 129 mins.)†

Wonderland (Great Britain, 1988)*** Emile Charles, Tony Forsyth, Robert Stephens, Robbie Coltrane, Claire Higgins. Two gay Liverpool teenagers witness a gangland killing and are forced to run for their lives. Fresh take on a familiar theme in this well-written film that's as much about friendship as it is about fear. (Dir: Philip Saville, 103 mins.)†

Wonder Man (1945)*** Danny Kaye, Virginia Mayo, Vera-Ellen, Steve Cochran. One of Kaye's best performances—he plays a dual role as twins: one is the bookish type while the other is a fast-talking nightclub entertainer. When the gangsters bump off the wrong twin, the bookish Kaye steps in and the fun begins. (Dir: H. Bruce Humberstone, 99 mins.)†

Wonders of Aladdin (France-Italy, 1961)** Donald O'Connor, Noelle Adam, Vittorio De Sica. Strictly for the youngsters—a comedy version of Arabian Nights' adventure complete with magic lamps, genies, and flying carpets. (Dir: Henry Levin, 93 mins.)†

Wonderwall (Great Britain, 1968)*½ Jack MacGowran, Jane Birkin, Irene Handl, Richard Wattis. A professor discovers a mysterious hole in his wall that allows him to watch the young woman next door, opening up a world of fantasy for him. Relic of the psychedelic sixties is remembered (if at all) for George Harrison's experimental music score. Originally 93 mins. (Dir: Joe Massot, 80 mins.)†

Wonder Woman (MTV 1974)** Cathy Lee Crosby, Ricardo Montalban. Crosby doesn't make a convincing Amazonian superhero, her stars-and-stripes frock doesn't compare to the original, and the villain she's faced with—the ultra-hammy Montalban—would've been laughed off the old "Batman" series. (Dir: Vincent McEveety, 75 mins.)

Won Ton Ton, the Dog Who Saved Hollywood (1976)*½ Bruce Dern, Madeline Kahn, Art Carney, Phil Silvers, Teri Garr, Ron Leibman. Sadly awful spoof of silent-moviemaking days—sad because, with dozens of cameo appearances from stars of the '30s and '40s, from Joan Blondell to Stepin Fetchit, old-movie buffs will feel compelled to watch it anyway. (Dir: Michael Winner, 92 mins.)

Wooden Horse, The (Great Britain, 1950) **½ Leo Genn, David Tomlinson, Anthony Dawson, Bryan Forbes, Anthony Steel, Peter Finch. Taut, detailed thriller of British officers planning an escape from a German P.O.W. camp. The clever scheme involves the wooden horse of the title. (Dir: Jack Lee, 101 mins.)

Woodstock (1970)**** Jimi Hendrix, Joan Baez, Joe Cocker, Arlo Guthrie, Richie Havens, The Who. An incredible array of rock stars are filmed live at the historic four-day celebration. Jimi Hendrix's closing rendition of "The Star-Spangled Banner" is an awesome redefinition of American ideals through the spirituality of music. (Dir: Michael Wadleigh, 184 mins.)†

Word Is Out: Stories of Some of Our Lives (1978)*** Documentary reveals the thoughts, moods, and life histories of twenty-six gay men and women as they talk about their lifestyles. Most of the participants are older couples who have been together for decades; their shared experiences provide lessons for everyone. (Dirs: Peter Adair, Nancy Adair, Andrew Brown, Robert Epstein, Lucy Massie Phenix, Veronica Selver, 130 mins.)

Word of Honor (MTV 1981)*** Karl Malden, Rue McClanahan, Ron Silver. A small-town newspaper reporter's world changes when he refuses to name a source in the trial of a leading citizen accused of murder. (Dir: Mel Damski, 104 mins.)

Words and Music (1948)*** Mickey Rooney, Tom Drake, Gene Kelly, Vera-Ellen, Mel Tormé, June Allyson, Ann Sothern, Betty Garrett, Lena Horne, Perry Como, Allyn Ann McLerie, Cyd Charisse, Janet Leigh. Drake as Richard Rodgers and Rooney as Lorenz Hart in a not-too-accurate biographical pic which is mostly an excuse for musical numbers. (Dir: Norman Taurog, 119 mins.)†

Work (1915) and **Police** (1916)**** Video compilation of great Charlie Chaplin comedies. In *Work*, co-starring with Edna Purviance and Billy Armstrong, a family makes the mistake of hiring slapstick comics as wallpaper-hangers. *Police*, with Chaplin, Purviance, Armstrong, and Wesley Ruggles, has the Little Tramp

getting out of prison and *trying* to go straight, with no help from his former cronies. Classic buffoonery. (Dir: Charles Chaplin, 81 mins.)†

Working Class Goes to Heaven, The (Italy, 1972)***½ Gian Maria Volonte, Mariangela Melato, Salvo Randone, Gino Pernice. Complex drama about a factory worker who strives to be the best at his job, incurring the wrath of his fellow employees who are struggling for better conditions at the plant. Provocative and imaginative. (Dir: Elio Petri, 126 mins.)

Working Girl (1988)***½ Melanie Griffith, Harrison Ford, Sigourney Weaver, Joan Cusack, Alec Baldwin. Delightful, insightful comedy with ambitious but frustrated secretary Griffith taking advantage of her boss's skiing accident to advance her own career. (Dir: Mike Nichols, 114 mins.)†

Working Girls (1987)*** A documentary-flavored film about some call girls who make the prostitution racket work for them. An interesting examination of sexual politics. (Dir: Lizzie Borden, 90 mins.)†

Working Man, The (1933)**½ George Arliss, Bette Davis, Hardie Albright, Theodore Newton, Gordon Westcott. Deft comedy with zealous businessman Arliss softening towards his rival's congenial offspring; unusual and stylish. (Dir: John G. Adolfi, 75 mins.)

Working Trash (MTV 1990)** George Carlin, Ben Stiller, Buddy Ebsen, Michael J. Pollard. Clumsy comedy about a pair of janitors (Carlin and Stiller) in a brokerage firm who stumble upon some information that prompts them to play the market. Carlin is appealing as the working class stiff who finally collects on his dreams. (Dir: Alan Metter, 96 mins.)

Work Is a Four-Letter Word (Great Britain, 1968)**½ David Warner, Cilla Black, Zia Mohyeddin. Giant mushrooms make the characters euphoric in this film—you will be less so. Mildly antic fun. (Dir: Peter Hall, 87 mins.)

World According to Garp, The (1982)***½ Robin Williams, Glenn Close, John Lithgow, Mary Beth Hurt, Hume Cronyn, Jessica Tandy, Swoosie Kurtz. Fine adaptation of John Irving's complicated novel; Williams is a delightful surprise as an actor, playing Garp with a combination of tenderness and humor. Close is wonderful as his mother, feminist Jenny Fields; Lithgow is hilarious but always believable as Roberta, the former football player who has undergone a sex change; and Hurt is excellent as Garp's wife. (Dir: George Roy Hill, 136 mins.)†

World and the Flesh (1932)**½ Miriam

Hopkins, George Bancroft, Alan Mowbray, George E. Stone. Russian countess Hopkins sacrifices herself to a fate worse than death in this melodrama of the Russian revolution. Strongly atmospheric, but deliberately paced. (Dir: John Cromwell, 75 mins.)

World Apart, A (Great Britain, 1988)***½ Barbara Hershey, Jodhi May, David Suchet, Jeroen Krabbé, Linda Mvusi. Personalized view of the South African apartheid issue. The film follows the activities of a journalist who was imprisoned for her political views. Chris Menges's absorbing direction and the sensitive details in the screenplay by Shawn Slovo (the daughter of the real-life heroine) make up for any lapses. (113 mins.)†

World Changes, The (1933)**½ Paul Muni, Mary Astor, Aline MacMahon. A striking performance by Muni (before he took up George Arliss's fustian mantle at Warner Bros.) highlights this conventional cautionary tale about a farmer who can't cope with his personal life after he finds success in the business world. (Dir: Mervyn LeRoy, 90 mins.)

World for Ransom (1954)**½ Dan Duryea, Gene Lockhart. Adventurer matches wits with a gang of criminals. A few twists help this one. (Dir: Robert Aldrich, 82 mins.)

World Gone Mad, The (1933)**½ Pat O'Brien, Evelyn Brent, Neil Hamilton, Mary Brian, Louis Calhern. Snazzy white-collar-crime drama of a D.A. going after crooked Wall Street brokers; fast, lively, and extremely topical in the Depression years—and perhaps today. (Dir: Christy Cabanne, 73 mins.)†

World Gone Wild (1988)*½ Bruce Dern, Michael Paré, Catherine Mary Stewart, Adam Ant, Rick Podell. After the apocalypse—perhaps the favorite setting for late-'80s exploitation films—the leader of a makeshift community tries to protect his people against a brutal invader (Ant). Violent exploitation with elements of parody that in no way redeem it. (Dir: Lee H. Katzin, 94 mins.)†

World in His Arms, The (1952)*** Gregory Peck, Ann Blyth, Anthony Quinn. Rugged romantic adventure with old-fashioned escapes, rescues, brawls, and love scenes set amid the raucous, lawless period when fur traders brought cargoes to San Francisco. (Dir: Raoul Walsh, 104 mins.)

World in My Corner (1956)**½ Audie Murphy, Barbara Rush. Familiar boxing story about the kid from the slums who tastes luxury by fighting in the ring and becomes addicted until it almost ruins his life. (Dir: Jesse Hibbs, 82 mins.)

World in My Pocket (France-Italy-West Germany, 1961)** Rod Steiger, Nadia Tiller, Ian Bannen, Jean Servais. Another payroll robbery, masterminded by a dame (Tiller). Some suspense. (Dir: Alvin Rakoff, 93 mins.)

World Moves On, The (1934)**½ Madeleine Carroll, Franchot Tone, Reginald Denny, Louise Dresser, Stepin Fetchit, Raul Roulien. Historical drama of one Louisiana family rising in the world during the period from the Civil War to WWI. Engrossing and different, with a strong cast. An unusual effort from direcror John Ford. (90 mins.)

World of Abbott and Costello, The (1965)**½ Bud Abbott, Lou Costello. Documentary of highlights from the comedy duo's career. (Dir: Sidney Meyers, 75 mins.)

World of Apu, The (India, 1959)**** Soumitra Chatterjee, Sharmila Tagore. The last part of director Satyajit Ray's great trilogy (with *Pather Panchali* and *Aparajito*), certainly the masterpiece of the series. Apu (Chatterjee) marries a young girl (Tagore) through a fluke and grows to love her; when she dies, he undergoes a period of despair and gradual spiritual regeneration. (117 mins.)

World of Henry Orient, The (1964)***½ Peter Sellers, Tippy Walker, Merrie Spaeth, Phyllis Thaxter, Bibi Osterwald, Tom Bosley, Angela Lansbury, Paula Prentiss. A rare combination of humor and sensitivity makes this comedy special. It tells a wacky story about a madly egocentric and overly amorous concert pianist (Sellers), who is hilariously pursued around New York City by two teenage fans, brilliantly portrayed by Walker and Spaeth. (Dir: George Roy Hill, 106 mins.)†

World of Suzie Wong, The (Great Britain, 1960)** William Holden, Nancy Kwan. Drama of an American artist and his love for a girl of the streets in Hong Kong. Tries to be daring, emerges as soap opera. (Dir: Richard Quine, 129 mins.)†

World of Tomorrow (1984)*** A well-researched documentary about the 1939 World Fair. An enthralling essay on the great expectations of the times. (Dirs: Tom Johnson, Lance Bird, 78 mins.)

World Premiere (1941)*** John Barrymore, Frances Farmer. Daffy satire on Hollywood openings involves some Nazis assigned to see that producer Barrymore's film never opens. Silly, somewhat dated but fun. (Dir: Ted Tetzlaff, 70 mins.)

World's Greatest Athlete, The (1973)* Jan-Michael Vincent, Tim Conway, John Amos, Howard Cosell. Witless drivel from the Disney Studios about a white youth, raised in Africa Tarzan-style, who is brought to America. (Dir: Robert Scheerer, 92 mins.)†

World's Greatest Lover, The (1977)*** Gene Wilder, Carol Kane, Carl Ballantine, Dom DeLuise. Not all the sight gags work, but a great many of them are funny in this maniacal romp which not only stars Wilder but is written, produced, and directed by him. Wilder plays Rudi Valentine—a baker from Milwaukee in the mid-twenties who sets out to achieve recognition as the WGL. (89 mins.)†

World's Oldest Living Bridesmaid, The (MTV 1990)** Donna Mills, Brian Wimmer, Winston Rekert, Art Hindle, Laura Press, Beverly Garland. Donna Mills is perfectly cast as a beautiful, 40-plus, successful attorney whose secretaries keep quitting to get married. London locations help this labored romantic comedy. (Dir: Joseph L. Scanlon, 96 mins.)

World, the Flesh and the Devil, The (1959)*** Harry Belafonte, Inger Stevens, Mel Ferrer. Belafonte spends the first part of the film alone on screen, supposedly the last survivor on earth after poisonous gasses have destroyed humanity. These early scenes are skillfully handled. Enter Stevens and Ferrer and conflicts begin, most of which are obvious and pat. (Dir: Ranald MacDougall, 95 mins.)

World War III (MTV 1982)*** David Soul, Rock Hudson, Brian Keith, Robert Prosky, Jeroen Krabbé, Cathy Lee Crosby. A terrifying, fictionalized confrontation between the U.S. and Russia over a secret Soviet incursion in Alaska to seize an oil pipeline. Guerrilla warfare escalates into a nuclear alert when the U. S. President and the Soviet Secretary refuse to back down. (Dir: David Greene, 240 mins.)

World Without End (1956)** Hugh Marlowe, Nancy Gates, Rod Taylor. A space flight intended for Mars goes through the time barrier and ends up on Earth during the 26th century. Absorbing sci-fi. (Dir: Edward Bernds, 80 mins.)

World Without Sun (France-Italy, 1964)**** Excellent French documentary, showing the experiments of Jacques-Yves Cousteau and his men under the Red Sea. Oscar: Best Documentary. (Dir: Jacques-Yves Cousteau, 93 mins.)

Worm Eaters, The (1977)½ Herb Robins, Barry Hostetler, Lindsay Armstrong Black. You can't get any grosser than this horror-comedy about a clubfooted hermit who turns his neighbors into "worm people" by sneaking live worms into their food. (Dir: Herb Robins, 75 mins.)†

Worm's Eye View (Great Britain, 1951)**½ Ronald Shiner, Diana Dors. Comic complications when five RAF men are billeted in a suburban villa during WWII. (Dir: Jack Raymond, 77 mins.)

Worst Woman in Paris?, The (1933)**½ Benita Hume, Adolphe Menjou, Helen Chandler, Harvey Stephens. Spirited romantic comedy of a neglected French wife who runs away from her blasé husband and takes up with a young American; chic and irreverent, good fun. (Dir: Monta Bell, 78 mins.)

Worth Winning (1989)** Mark Harmon, Madeleine Stowe, Lesley Ann Warren, Maria Holvoe, Mark Blum, Andrea Martin, Tony Longo, David Brenner. A self-confident TV weatherman who makes a bet with unctuous friend Blum that he can get three lovely women to accept his proposal of marriage. (Dir: Will Mackenzie, 103 mins.)†

Woyzeck (West Germany, 1979)*** Klaus Kinski, Eva Mattes, Wolfgang Reichmann. Kinski gives a riveting performance as the orderly driven to murder as a result of mistreatment from his superiors and his wife's flagrant infidelity. This screen adaptation of Georg Buchner's theater piece gains much from director Werner Herzog's unique visual approach, in which the camera's confined view of the action communicates the feeling of enclosure and confusion that Woyzeck is experiencing. (81 mins.)†

Wraith, The (1986)*½ Charlie Sheen, Nick Cassavetes, Clint Howard, Randy Quaid, Griffin O'Neal. A gang of vicious "road pirates" in a small Southwestern town find themselves menaced by the strange, leather-clad driver of a very fast car. A supernatural action film with a ridiculous script. (Dir: Mike Marvin, 91 mins.)†

Wrath of God, The (1972)*½ Robert Mitchum, Frank Langella, Rita Hayworth, Ken Hutchinson, Victor Buono. Mitchum walks through this puzzling yarn about a defrocked priest-adventurer who finds himself in an unspecified Latin American country in the throes of revolution during the 1920s. (Dir: Ralph Nelson, 111 mins.)

Wrecking Crew, The (1969)** Dean Martin, Elke Sommer, Nancy Kwan, Sharon Tate. Dean plays swinging sleuth Matt Helm again. This time, Matt has to almost single-handedly save the American and British economies by making certain a gold shipment, en route to London via Denmark, arrives safely. (Dir: Phil Karlson, 104 mins.)

Wreck of the Hesperus, The (1948)**½ Willard Parker, Patricia White, Edgar Buchanan. Low-budget melodrama based on the famous Longfellow poem about a disastrous shipwreck; interesting, but hampered by poor production values. (Dir: John Hoffman, 70 mins.)

Wreck of the Mary Deare, The (U.S.-Great Britain, 1959)**½ Charlton Heston, Gary Cooper, Richard Harris. Rather slow-moving mystery-adventure yarn. The plot concerns the strange circumstances surrounding the wreck of the freighter called the Mary Deare. (Dir: Michael Anderson, 105 mins.)

Wrestling Queen (1973)** Vivian Vachon,

Maurice "Mad Dog" Vachon, Waldek "Killer" Kowalski, Paul "Butcher" Vachon, Jean Ferre (Andre the Giant). Documentary focusing on die-hard wrestling fans, the ones who actually believe in the sport's choreographed excesses. Includes some cursory interviews with the grapplers themselves, providing a good view of the sport in the "dark ages" between Gorgeous George and Hulk Hogan. (No director credited, 72 mins.)

Wrestling Women Vs. The Aztec Ape— See: Doctor of Doom

Wrestling Women vs. the Aztec Mummy (Mexico, 1965)½ Lorena Velazquez, Armand Silvestre. Outlandish horror thriller about a mummy, returned from the dead, who just wants the lady wrestlers to return a necklace they helped remove from his crypt. (Dir: Rene Cardona, 88 mins.)†

Written on the Wind (1956)***½ Rock Hudson, Robert Stack, Lauren Bacall, Dorothy Malone. A flashy melodrama enhanced by the director's stylized use of color. Examining the decline and fall of the oil aristocracy, the film focuses on the sexual problems of a doomed family: the scion, who's suffering from infertility and coping with suspicions about his wife's fidelity, and the sister, a nymphomaniac who, having failed to get the man she loves, proceeds to sleep with every other man in Texas. Provocative and supercharged; Malone deserved her Oscar for Best Supporting Actress. (Dir: Douglas Sirk, 99 mins.)

WR: Mysteries of the Organism (Yugoslavia–West Germany, 1971)*** Milena Dravic, Jagoda Kaloper, Zoran Radmilovic, Tuli Kupferberg, Jackie Curtis. A cockeyed collage mixes interviews with disciples of Wilhelm Reich with a zany story of a sexually liberated Yugoslav Communist party member who preaches political freedom through sexual energy. (Dir: Dusan Makavejev, 86 mins.)†

Wrong Arm of the Law, The (Great Britain, 1961)***½ Peter Sellers, Bernard Cribbins, Lionel Jeffries, Nanette Newman. Another British spoof of crime films, with Sellers the Brain planning a very elaborate robbery. (Dir: Cliff Owen, 91 mins.)†

Wrong Box, The (Great Britain, 1966)**** John Mills, Ralph Richardson, Michael Caine, Peter Cook, Dudley Moore. Merry, nimble farce, based on a tale co-authored by Robert Louis Stevenson, about Victorian inheritance intrigues and a migratory body, which tumbles between slapstick, black humor, and beguiling absurdity, and is played with vigor by an incomparable cast. (Dir: Bryan Forbes, 98 mins.)†

Wrong Guys, The (1988)* Louie Anderson,

Richard Lewis, Richard Belzer, Franklyn Ajaye, Tim Thomerson, John Goodman. Putting a cast of hot stand-up comics together was a good idea; burdening them with a tired screenplay full of pratfalls and dumb gags was not. As a reunited Cub Scout pack on a camping trip battling an escaped convict (Goodman) who thinks they're the CIA, none of these funny men gets to display his particular talents. (Dir: Danny Bilson, 86 mins.)†

Wrong Is Right (1982)**½ Sean Connery, George Grizzard, Robert Conrad, Katharine Ross, G. D. Spradlin, John Saxon. Satirical, gallows comedy spoofing our preoccupation with violence and the cynical efforts of the government to use violence for its ends and to hide the truth from the public (and often from those within the government itself). The screenplay, written by director Richard Brooks, is not nearly funny or imaginative enough. (117 mins.)†

Wrong Man, The (1957)***½ Henry Fonda, Vera Miles, Harold J. Stone, Anthony Quayle. Frightening account of what happens to a man and his wife when he is wrongly accused of being the man who has performed a series of hold-ups. This story is based on fact. Directed with his customary skill by Alfred Hitchcock. (105 mins.)†

Wrong Move, The (West Germany, 1973)***½ Rudiger Vogler, Hanna Schygulla, Marianne Hoppe, Hans-Christian Blech, Nastassja Kinski. Second film in Wim Wenders "road" trilogy (between *Alice in the Cities* and *Kings of the Road*) follows a dissatisfied writer who journeys through Germany, meeting an assortment of alluring and bizarre characters. Engrossing allegorical film written by Peter Handke. Kinski's debut. (103 mins.)†

WUSA (1970)* Paul Newman, Joanne Woodward, Laurence Harvey, Anthony Perkins. A pretentious film with unfulfilled aspirations to dissect the Southern right-wing political ideology. Newman, miscast, plays an ex-drunk who gets a job as a disc jockey on WUSA, an all-the-way-to-the-right radio station in New Orleans. (Dir: Stuart Rosenberg, 115 mins.)

Wuthering Heights (1939)**** Laurence Olivier, Merle Oberon, David Niven, Geraldine Fitzgerald. Emily Brönte's hypnotic, romantic novel is tastefully brought to the screen with the perfect cast. Olivier is the epitome of the mysterious, dashing Heathcliff and Oberon registers in the role of his love, Cathy. William Wyler directed with his usual sure hand. (110 mins.)†

Wuthering Heights (Mexico, 1954)**½

Iraseme Dilian, Jorge Mistral, Lilia Prado, Ernesto Alonso. Not one of Buñuel's finest hours, this brooding film follows the famous tale of the vengeful former servant who reappears in his beloved's life as a wealthy man. Lesser Buñuel is still fascinating. AKA: **Abismos de Pasion**. (90 mins.)†

Wuthering Heights (Great Britain, 1970) *** Timothy Dalton, Anna Calder-Marshall. This remake falls short of the 1939 version. However, the physical production is handsome, the leads are well-cast, and the tale remains interesting. (Dir: Robert Fuest, 105 mins.)

W.W. and the Dixie Dancekings (1975)*** Burt Reynolds, Art Carney, Ned Beatty, James Hampton, Jerry Reed, Conny Van Dyke. Burt stars in this fast-paced, down-home story of a 1950s con man who becomes the manager of a third-rate country and western group. (Dir: John Avildsen, 104 mins.)

Wyoming (1940)** Wallace Beery, Ann Rutherford. Typical Beery western which will appeal to his legions of fans. They'll particularly like his "Aw, shucks" romance with Marjorie Main. (Dir: Richard Thorpe, 89 mins.)

Wyoming Kid, The (1947)** Dennis Morgan, Jane Wyman, Janis Paige, Arthur Kennedy. Gambler is hired to capture a notorious stagecoach robber, falls for the outlaw's wife. Routine western. (Dir: Raoul Walsh, 100 mins.)

Xala (Senegal, 1974)***½ Tierno Leye, Seune Samb, Younouss Seye, Miriam Niang, Dieynaba Niang, Fatim Diagne. An important businessman planning to wed his third wife becomes the victim of a curse that renders him impotent. Director Ousmane Sembene's satire (adapted from his novel) on Senegalese who desire a colonial era-style class system in order to sustain their wealth and power. (123 mins.)

Xanadu (1980)* Olivia Newton-John, Gene Kelly, Michael Beck, James Sloyan. An updated rip-off of the Rita Hayworth film *Down to Earth*. A muse (Newton-John) takes a vacation from her place in a mural in order to inspire two men to make their dreams come true. (Dir: Robert Greenwald, 96 mins.)†

X-15 (1961)** Charles Bronson, Kenneth Tobey, Mary Tyler Moore. Stilted semi-documentary about test pilots on the X-15 missile project. This one is grade B movie fare with all the clichés. Narrated by James Stewart. (Dir: Richard Donner, 105 mins.)

X from Outer Space, The (Japan, 1967)* Eiji Okada, Toshiya Wazake. FAFC (Fupi-Astro Flying Center) launches a spaceship to Mars which returns with a slimy spore which grows into the devastating Guilula monster. (Dir: Nazui Nihomatsu, 85 mins.)†

Xica (Brazil, 1983)** Zeze Motta, Walmor Chagos. Xica, a real-life black slave in 19th-century Brazil, achieves freedom, power, and riches in this comedy-drama as the mistress of a white Portuguese contractor. The film's mannered, folksy style emphasizes Xica's sensual, comic flamboyance, and also examines the deeper theme of racism in a colonial setting. (Dir: Carlos Diegues, 100 mins.)

X-Ray—See: Hospital Massacre

"X": The Man with the X-Ray Eyes (1963)*** Ray Milland, John Hoyt, Diana Van Der Vlis. Science fiction-horror film about a scientist who is cursed with the ability to see through things. Director Roger Corman demonstrates his special ability to extract maximum mileage from low-cost visuals. (80 mins.)†

X: The Unheard Music (1986)*** Bright docu-musical about the talented musical group X. Featuring a refreshing examination of the L.A. New Wave scene that spawned the group as well. AKA: **The Unheard Music**, (Dir: W. T. Morgan, 86 mins.)†

X—The Unknown (Great Britain, 1957)*½ Dean Jagger, Edward Chapman. This science fiction tale centers around a creature or thing that cannot be defined—well, neither can this plot. (Dir: Leslie Norman, 80 mins.)

Xtro (Great Britain, 1983)*½ Philip Sayer, Bernice Stegers, Danny Brainin, Simon Nash, Maryam D'Abo. Interesting premise, of a man returning to his family after being kidnapped for three years by aliens, falls apart when the story goes off in too many directions. (Dir: Harry Bromley Davenport, 80 mins.)†

X, Y and Zee (Great Britain, 1972)*** Elizabeth Taylor, Michael Caine, Susannah York, Margaret Leighton. Three troupers put soap opera through the wringer with intelligent dialogue by novelist Edna O'Brien. Taylor and Caine are married; York interferes. Brian G. Hutton, known for mindless action and such, directed this change of pace. (110 mins.)†

Yaaba (Burkina Faso, 1989)***½ Fatimata Sanga, Noufou Ouedraogo, Roukietou Barry. Stimulating tale of an independent twelve-year-old boy's friendship with an old woman who has been shunned by her neighbors as a witch. Much of this serene film is wordless, but the boy's warmth for the woman he calls "yaaba" (grandmother) is revealed in powerful and cinematically pure terms. (Dir: Idrissa Ouedraogo, 90 mins.)

Yakuza, The (1975)****½** Robert Mitchum, Brian Keith, Keiko Kishi. The yakuza represent Japan's idea of honor among thieves. American tough guy Mitchum runs afoul of these Nipponese Mafioso in a violent but exotic adventure film. (Dir: Sydney Pollack, 99 mins.)†

Yank at Eton, A (1942)****** Mickey Rooney, Ian Hunter, Edmund Gwenn, Peter Lawford. Brash Mickey goes to school in England and the result is forced, not too funny, comedy. (Dir: Norman Taurog, 88 mins.)

Yank at Oxford, A (U.S.-Great Britain, 1938)****** Robert Taylor, Vivien Leigh, Maureen O'Sullivan, Lionel Barrymore. The mutual chauvinistic attitudes of the film have become shopworn. Taylor is the brash youth who encounters an alien culture at the British university. (Dir: Jack Conway, 100 mins.)

Yankee Buccaneer (1952)****** Jeff Chandler, Scott Brady, Suzan Ball, David Janssen. Chandler climbs the mast and commands a decoy U.S. naval ship which is rigged as a private vessel in order to dupe the thieves of the high seas. (Dir: Frederick de Cordova, 86 mins.)

Yankee Clipper, The (1927)****½** William Boyd, Elinor Fair, Junior Coghlan, John Miljan, Walter Long, Burr McIntosh. Historical adventure with sea captain Boyd (long before Hopalong Cassidy) outracing his business rival in his clipper ship to win an important trading contract with China. Exciting seagoing action. (Dir: Rupert Julian, 81 mins.)†

Yankee Doodle Dandy (1942)*****½** James Cagney, Walter Huston, Joan Leslie, Jeanne Cagney, Richard Whorf, Rosemary De Camp. Cagney won an Oscar playing Broadway entertainer George M. Cohan in this spirited musical biography. A nice blend of flag waving, family melodrama, and musical numbers (impressively danced by Cagney). Avoid the colorized version. (Dir: Michael Curtiz, 126 mins.)†

Yankee Pasha (1954)****½** Jeff Chandler, Rhonda Fleming, Lee J. Cobb, Mamie Van Doren, Hal March. Edison Marshall's bestselling novel about a man who fights pirates, sultans, harem girls, and other obstacles in order to win his lady fair, is elaborately brought to the screen. (Dir: Joseph Pevney, 84 mins.)

Yank in the R.A.F., A (1941)******* Tyrone Power, Betty Grable. Dated but exciting story of a Yank who joins the RAF just to be near an old girl friend and has some of the cockiness knocked out of him by the RAF spirit. (Dir: Henry King, 97 mins.)

Yank in Vietnam, A (1964)****** Marshall

Thompson, Enrique Magalona. Marine officer is freed from the Communist forces and joins with a soldier to free a kidnapped doctor. (Dir: Marshall Thompson, 80 mins.)

Yanks (U.S.-Great Britain, 1979)******* Richard Gere, Vanessa Redgrave, William Devane, Chick Vennera, Lisa Eichhorn. Boy meets girl in this story of American GIs in WWII Britain. John Schlesinger's direction is a bit studied, but the performances are fine, and the film has a romantic glow about it. (140 mins.)

Yaqui Drums (1956)****** Rod Cameron, J. Carrol Naish, Robert Hutton, Mary Castle. Tired western features an honest rancher going against a plum ornery saloon owner who wants to own the town and buy up the surrounding land. Pass the red eye or change the channel. (Dir: Jean Yarbrough, 72 mins.)

Yearling, The (1946)******** Gregory Peck, Jane Wyman, Claude Jarman, Jr. Heart wrenching presentation of a simple story of a boy's love for a pet fawn which his father must destroy. The emotions involved are complex and real, yet this picture has captured all the feelings and depth of the bestselling novel without ever employing Hollywood tricks. A must for the whole family. (Dir: Clarence Brown, 128 mins.)†

Year My Voice Broke, The (Australia, 1988)****½** Noah Taylor, Loene Carmen, Ben Mendelsohn. A trio of young talented novice actors carry this glum and rather predictable saga of teen love. A gangly boy falls in love with his childhood playmate and carries the torch nobly through her ill-fated romance with an older, wilder youth. Frank and explicit, somewhat sad, and not very enjoyable. (Dir: John Duigan, 103 mins.)†

Year of Living Dangerously, The (1983)******* Mel Gibson, Sigourney Weaver, Linda Hunt, Michael Murphy. *The Year of Living Dangerously* unfolds in Indonesia during the 1965 civil strife, and is long on atmosphere enlivened by a good cast, and weakened by a script that lacks believability. Gibson plays a TV journalist who finds himself in danger when he becomes privy to some vital military information. (Dir: Peter Weir, 114 mins.)†

Year of the Dragon (1985)****½** Mickey Rourke, John Lone, Ariane. An entertaining but silly movie, whose racist attitudes, sexism, and slippery grasp on logic can often be overlooked by the sheer force of the film's kinetic action. Hard-boiled detective Rourke decides to clean up his new beat in Chinatown by putting an end to the Chinese Mafia. His actions defy human description outside of institutions for the criminally insane, but the director does create a memorable vision of Chinatown as a tourist trap on the outskirts of Hell. (Dir: Michael Cimino, 126 mins.)†

Year of the Quiet Sun, A (Poland, 1985)*** Scott Wilson, Maja Komorowska, Hanna Skarzanka, Ewa Dalkowska. A beautifully controlled wartime love story about a Polish widow and a shell-shocked American POW. As a study of the rehabilitatory power of love, this deeply felt romance merits consideration from serious moviegoers. (Dir: Krzysztof Zanussi, 106 mins.)†

Years Between, The (Great Britain, 1946)**½ Michael Redgrave, Valerie Hobson. Believed dead, a prisoner of war returns to find his wife remarried. Occasionally interesting drama, despite some lags. (Dir: Compton Bennett, 98 mins.)

Yellow Balloon (Great Britain, 1952)*** Andrew Ray, Kenneth More, William Sylvester. Small boy, shocked by the accidental death of a playmate, is used for evil purposes by a petty crook. Gripping suspense melodrama, well done. (Dir: J. Lee Thompson, 80 mins.)

Yellowbeard (1983)** Graham Chapman, Marty Feldman, Eric Idle, Madeline Kahn, Peter Boyle, Martin Hewitt, James Mason. A disappointing send-up of pirate films. In the 17th century, Yellowbeard tries to recover some ill-gotten booty with the aid of his would-be son, who has the treasure map tatooed on his head. (Dir: Mel Damski, 101 mins.)†

Yellow Cab Man, The (1950)**½ Red Skelton, Gloria De Haven, Walter Slezak. Red's a cab driver who goes out of his way to pick up pretty girls and trouble. Hilarious, slapstick chase is the climax. (Dir: Jack Donohue, 85 mins.)

Yellow Canary (Great Britain, 1943)**½ Anna Neagle, Richard Greene, Margaret Rutherford. English girl poses as a Nazi sympathizer to track down spies. Fairly good espionage melodrama. (Dir: Herbert Wilcox, 84 mins.)

Yellow Canary, The (1963)**½ Pat Boone, Barbara Eden, Steve Forrest, Jack Klugman. Dramatically tight mystery-suspense tale, scripted by Rod Serling, about a singer whose infant son is kidnapped, falls short on characterization. (Dir: Buzz Kulik, 93 mins.)

Yellow Fin (1951)*** Wayne Morris, Adrian Booth. Young owner of fishing boat is beset by troubles in the form of a rascally rival and a grasping dame. Good action melodrama. (Dir: Frank McDonald, 74 mins.)

Yellow Hair and the Fortress of Gold (U.S.-Spain, 1984)** Laurene Landon, Ken Roberson, John Ghaffari, Luis Lorento. Mild parody-tribute to old-time western adventures, with part-Indian heroine Landon and her partner the Pecos Kid (Roberson) fighting the bad guys while searching for an ancient treasure. AKA: **Yellow Hair and the Pecos Kid.** (Dir: Matt Cimber, 102 mins.)†

Yellow Hair and the Pecos Kid—See: **Yellow Hair and the Fortress of Gold**

Yellow Jack (1938)**½ Robert Montgomery, Virginia Bruce, Lewis Stone, Henry Hull, Buddy Ebsen, Stanley Ridges, Andy Devine, Charles Coburn, Sam Levene, Henry O'Neill, William Henry, Alan Curtis. Great cast deserves better in this stagy biography about Dr. Walter Reed's search for a cure for yellow fever. About as dramatic as . . . well, as watching lab work. Drawn from Sidney Howard's successful play. (Dir: George B. Seitz, 84 mins.)

Yellow Mountain (1955)*½ Lex Barker, Mala Powers, Howard Duff. Dull western about a couple of two-fisted men who take on all comers in their efforts to strike it rich in gold. (Dir: Jesse Hibbs, 78 mins.)

Yellowneck (1955)*** Lin McCarthy, Stephen Courtleigh. Civil War deserters try to make their way through the Florida Everglades to freedom. Strong drama. (Dir: R. John Hugh, 83 mins.)

Yellow Rolls Royce, The (Great Britain, 1964)*** Rex Harrison, Ingrid Bergman, Shirley MacLaine, Omar Sharif, George C. Scott. Most audiences will enjoy the star-studded cast in this film about the adventures of a fancy Rolls Royce and the various people who own it. With so much talent before and behind the cameras, it should have been far better than it is. (Dir: Anthony Asquith, 122 mins.)

Yellow Rose of Texas, The (1944)** Roy Rogers, Dale Evans, Grant Withers, Harry Shannon. Insurance investigator Roy sings the title tune while posing as a showboat entertainer in order to find the thieves who stole a fat payroll five years ago. Bob Nolan and the Sons of the Pioneers contribute a few songs to one of Rogers's more memorable vehicles. (Dir: Joseph Kane, 79 mins.)†

Yellow Sky (1948)*** Gregory Peck, Richard Widmark, Anne Baxter, James Barton, Harry Morgan. Offbeat, arty western, loosely based on Shakespeare's *The Tempest*. Not a total success. (Dir: William A. Wellman, 98 mins.)

Yellowstone (1936)** Andy Devine, Ralph Morgan, Alan Hale, Judith Barrett. Modest adventure of disparate people searching for buried treasure in the national park. Brightly paced and straightforward. (Dir: Arthur Lubin, 65 mins.)

Yellowstone Kelly (1959)**½ Clint Walker, John Russell, Edd Byrnes, Ray Danton. Routine western, with most of the Warner Bros. stable of TV western stars. (Dir: Gordon Douglas, 91 mins.)

Yellow Submarine (Great Britain, 1968) **** A film treat which shouldn't be missed. It's the delightful, engaging animated fantasy in which the Beatles fight off the Blue Meanies, who have the audacity to disrupt the tranquil amiability of the mythical kingdom of Pepperland. (Dir: George Dunning, 85 mins.)†

Yellow Ticket (1931)*** Elissa Landi, Laurence Olivier, Lionel Barrymore, Walter Byron, Boris Karloff. A great cast in a zesty melodrama about a wide-eyed Russian lass whom a roguish officer wants to take for a troika ride in the country. Vigorous pacing, top-notch script, and a chance to see the early Sir Laurence. (Dir: Raoul Walsh, 81 mins.)

Yellow Tomahawk, The (1954)* Rory Calhoun, Peggie Castle, Warner Anderson, Noah Beery. Native American turns against his own people to warn encroaching white settlers about impending attacks by his brother warriors. Lame and insulting. Pick a stereotype—it's here! (Dir: Lesley Selander, 82 mins.)

Yentl (1983)**½ Barbra Streisand, Mandy Patinkin, Amy Irving, Nehemiah Persoff. Barbra plays a pre-WWI Jewish woman who disguises herself as a male scholar in order to study the Talmud. When she becomes engaged to the beloved of the man she's fallen for during her masquerade, the romantic scenes are charmingly played. This Funny Boy film may, however, make some yearn for *Funny Girl*, when more disciplined filmmakers had Streisand's ego in control. Based on Isaac Bashevis Singer's *Yentl, the Yeshiva Boy*. (Dir: Barbra Streisand, 134 mins.)†

Yes Giorgio (1982)* Luciano Pavarotti, Kathryn Harrold, Eddie Albert. This story of a famous opera star who falls in love with a woman doctor even though he's a committed family man is foolish. But he does get to sing—and how! (Dir: Franklin J. Schaffner, 113 mins.)†

Yes, My Darling Daughter (1939)**½ Fay Bainter, Roland Young, Priscilla Lane, May Robson, Jeffrey Lynn, Genevieve Tobin, Ian Hunter. Light romantic comedy of a young couple delighting their unconventional families by deciding to elope. Fine supporting cast of experts makes this better than average. (Dir: William Keighley, 86 mins.)

Yes Sir, That's My Baby (1949)**½ Donald O'Connor, Gloria De Haven, Charles Coburn, Jim Davis. Silly but entertaining comedy-musical about the campus life of ex-GI's going to college on the GI Bill of Rights. (Dir: George Sherman, 82 mins.)

Yesterday (Canada, 1980)** Vincent Van Patten, Claire Pimpare, Eddie Albert,

Cloris Leachman, Nicholas Campbell. Trite Vietnam-era love story about an American guy who falls hard for a French-Canadian gal. Young love, old hat. (Dir: Larry Kent, 97 mins.)

Yesterday Girl (West Germany, 1966)*** Alexandra Kluge, Hans Korte, Eva Marie Neinecke, Gunther Mack. Groundbreaking film of the German New Wave tells the story of an antisocial East German girl who escapes to the West, only to be at loggerheads with aspects of the new society. First feature by Alexander Kluge, based on a true incident. His sister is superb as the angry young woman. (90 mins.)

Yesterday Machine, The (1963)* James Britton, Tim Holt, Jack Herman. Nazi scientist tries to revive Adolph you-know-who with the aid of a time machine. Fortunately, this is America where we don't cotton to that kinda stuff, or to boring, preposterous movies like this. (Dir: Russ Marker, 85 mins.)†

Yesterday's Child (MTV 1977)**½ Shirley Jones, Geraldine Fitzgerald. A seventeen-year-old girl is brought to her wealthy mother and grandmother's house claiming to be the little girl who was kidnapped and believed killed many years before. (Dirs: Corey Allen, Bob Rosenbaum, 106 mins.)

Yesterday's Enemy (Great Britain, 1959)**½ Stanley Baker, Guy Rolfe, Bryan Forbes, Philip Ahn. Moderately interesting British war film about a small group of soldiers who take over a Burmese jungle village. (Dir: Val Guest, 95 mins.)

Yesterday's Hero (Great Britain, 1979)* Ian McShane, Suzanne Somers, Paul Nichols. Washed-up soccer star McShane is spurred to make a comeback when pop star Nichols signs him up for the team he owns. Added incentive is provided by Somers, Nichols's partner and McShane's ex-lover. Mediocre sports drama made completely unwatchable by the wretched Nichols-Somers disco songs. (Dir: Neil Leifer, 95 mins.)†

Yesterday, Today and Tomorrow (Italy-France, 1963)***½ Sophia Loren, Marcello Mastroianni. Three spicy stories tailored for the talents of the two stars, especially Loren; in one, she's a black marketeer who takes an unusual method of avoiding the law; in another, she's the flirtatious wife of an industrialist; in the last, she's a call girl whom a seminary student tries to reform. Funny adult fare. (Dir: Vittorio De Sica, 119 mins.)†

Yin and Yang of Mr. Go, The (1970)½ James Mason, Jeff Bridges, Burgess Meredith, Peter Lind Hayes, Broderick Crawford. Meredith will pick up some bad karma for writing and directing this garbled adventure about a super criminal who mends his ways and doesn't sell an advanced weapons system to the highest bidder. Oriental spoof seems like the product of people who've spent too much time in an opium den. (89 mins.) †

Yog—Monster from Space (1971)* Akira Kubo, Atsuko Takahashi, Yoshio Tsuchiya. Earth animals are possessed by alien forces who beef the critters up to giant size. (Dir: Inoshiro Honda, 84 mins.) †

Yojimbo (Japan, 1963)**** Toshiro Mifune, Eijiro Tono, Isuzu Yamada, Seizaburo Kawazu. Superior samurai film with a large twist of black humor. The great Japanese actor Mifune is magnificent in the title role of a wandering samurai. Yojimbo swaggers into a town that is in the midst of a fighting feud between two corrupt factions—he hires himself out to both sides and proceeds to help them destroy most of the town. Directed by Akira Kurosawa with a good deal of style and authority. (112 mins.) †

Yokel Boy (1942)*** Albert Dekker, Joan Davis, Eddie Foy, Jr. A hick idea man for a Hollywood studio suggests the life of a notorious gangster—with the gangster himself in the lead. Highly amusing comedy. (Dir: Joseph Santley, 69 mins.)

Yol (Turkey, 1981)***½ Tarik Akan, Halil Ergun, Serif Sezer. A devastating drama dealing with political, ethnic, and cultural repression in contemporary Turkey. Written and directed by Yilmaz Guney, and filmed secretly in Turkey at great risk to those involved. (111 mins.) †

Yolanda and the Thief (1945)*** Fred Astaire, Lucille Bremer, Frank Morgan, Leon Ames, Mildred Natwick, Mary Nash. A sugar-coated fantasy. Minnelli crams the frame with so much Crayola-box color, you overdose. Still, musical-comedy lovers will be impressed by this whimsy about an ersatz guardian angel who falls for the convent lass he sets out to con. One of MGM's lushest romantic musicals with the production numbers ladled lovingly over the fantasy's script deficiencies. (Dir: Vincente Minnelli, 108 mins.) †

Yongary, Monster from the Deep (South Korea, 1967) Oh Young Il, Nam Chung-Im. Probably your only chance to see a *Korean* giant monster movie, as opposed to the usual Japanese variety, not that there's any discernible difference: stunt man in a rubber dragon suit knocks over miniature buildings. (Dir: Kim Ki-Duk, 79 mins.) †

Yor: The Hunter from the Future (1983)** Reb Brown, Corinne Clery. "Yor" going to believe this one! This primitive tale is set not in the caveman era but after a nuclear holocaust. Despite the pervasive silliness, *Yor* is entertaining in the manner of a cheap 1940s action serial. (Dir: Anthony M. Dawson, 89 mins.) †

You and Me (1938)*** Sylvia Sidney, George Raft, Robert Cummings. Unusual drama with songs by Kurt Weill. A girl overcoming a checkered past pairs up with an ex-con. (Dir: Fritz Lang, 90 mins.)

You Are What You Eat (1969)** Tiny Tim, Peter Yarrow, Father Malcolm Boyd, Super Spade, Harper's Bizarre, Paul Butterfield, Barry McGuire. One of the first of the rock concert films; only for those itching to relive the late sixties music scene. (Dir: Barry Feinstein, 75 mins.)

You Belong to Me (1941)**½ Barbara Stanwyck, Henry Fonda, Edgar Buchanan, Roger Clark, Ruth Donnelly, Maude Eburne. Snappy tale about marital mix-ups. Hank's jealousy gets the better of him every time his wife, the doctor, sees a new male patient. (Dir: Wesley Ruggles, 94 mins.)

You Better Watch Out (1980)** Brandon Maggart, Dianne Hull, Joe Jamrog, Peter Friedman, Scott McKay. Crummy thriller about a disturbed man who ruins Christmas by dressing up as Santa Claus and killing people. Not original enough to make anyone's list of psycho goodies. AKA: **Christmas Evil.** (Dir: Lewis Jackson, 100 mins.) †

You Came Along (1945)**½ Lizabeth Scott, Robert Cummings, Charles Drake, Don DeFore, Julie Bishop. Interesting but odd combination of comedy and heavy romance in which three servicemen pursue the same girl during a war bond tour. (Dir: John Farrow, 103 mins.)

You Can't Beat Love (1937)**½ Preston Foster, Joan Fontaine, William Brisbane, Paul Hurst, Berton Churchill, Milburn Stone. Charming romantic comedy about political man-about-town who casts his love ballot for the mayor's beautiful daughter. Endearing. (Dir: Christy Cabanne, 83 mins.)

You Can't Cheat an Honest Man (1939)*** W. C. Fields, Grady Sutton, Edgar Bergen. Fields runs a traveling show, can't make a buck or stay ahead of the sheriff. Deft performances make this nonsense entertaining. (Dir: George Marshall, 79 mins.) †

You Can't Fool Your Wife (1940)** Lucille Ball, James Ellison, Robert Coote, Emma Dunn. Typical marital comedy of a wife getting back at her husband when he romances another woman. Enlivened by Ball; otherwise, nothing special. (Dir: Ray McCarey, 68 mins.) †

You Can't Get Away with Murder (1939)*** Humphrey Bogart, Gale Page, Billy Halop. This was made while Bogey was playing crooks and his performance as a killer is so good that it's no wonder he was typed. It's a familiar death-house drama but engrossing and well acted. (Dir: Lewis Seiler, 78 mins.)

You Can't Go Home Again (MTV 1979)*** Lee Grant, Chris Sarandon, Hurd Hatfield. Thomas Wolfe's last long, thinly disguised autobiographical novel is carefully brought to the screen. Sarandon's sharply defined portrait of the writer-hero makes it worthwhile. (Dir: Ralph Nelson, 104 mins.)

You Can't Have Everything (1937)*** Alice Faye, Don Ameche, Ritz Brothers, Tony Martin. The Ritz Brothers supply the comedy and almost succeed in supporting the frail backstage plot. (Dir: Norman Taurog, 99 mins.)

You Can't Hurry Love (1988)*½ David Packer, Scott McGinnis, Bridget Fonda, David Leisure, Charles Grodin, Sally Kellerman, Kristy McNichol. The old saw about the boy from a small town (in Ohio) who comes to the big city (L.A.) and goes looking for love. (Dir: Richard Martini, 92 mins.)†

You Can't Run Away from It (1956)** June Allyson, Jack Lemmon. Uninspired remake of classic *It Happened One Night* with music, no less. (Dir: Dick Powell, 96 mins.)

You Can't Sleep Here—See: **I Was a Male War Bride**

You Can't Take It with You (1938)***½ Jean Arthur, Lionel Barrymore, James Stewart, Edward Arnold, Mischa Auer, Ann Miller, Spring Byington, Samuel S. Hinds, Donald Meek, H. B. Warner. Charming Broadway comedy by George S. Kaufman and Moss Hart about the eccentric Sycamore family is transposed to the screen in director Frank Capra's wonderfully acted, marvelously framed production. Oscar winner for best picture and director. (127 mins.)†

You Can't Win 'Em All (1970)*½ Tony Curtis, Charles Bronson, Michele Mercier, Gregoire Aslan, Patrick Magee. Feeble-minded adventure. Curtis and Bronson play WWI adventurers out to make a big financial killing as the Ottoman Empire is collapsing all around them. (Dir: Peter Collinson, 97 mins.)

You Elvis, Me Monroe (Germany, 1990)*** Barduri, Nigun Taifun, Inga Schrader. A young Arab living in Berlin becomes an object of fascination for his neighbors when he becomes involved with members of both sexes. Vibrant example of minimalist cinema. (Dir: Lothar Lambert, 72 mins.)

You for Me (1952)**½ Peter Lawford, Jane Greer, Gig Young. Two of Hollywood's most suave leading men, Lawford and Young, save this otherwise lightweight romantic comedy from total boredom. (Dir: Don Weis, 71 mins.)

You Gotta Stay Happy (1948)**½ James Stewart, Joan Fontaine, Eddie Albert. This could easily be called "The Flier Takes a Lady"; the lady is Fontaine and the flier, none other than Stewart. Fast but disappointing comedy. (Dir: H. C. Potter, 99 mins.)

You Know What Sailors Are (Great Britain, 1954)**½ Akim Tamiroff, Donald Sinden, Sarah Lawson, Naughton Wayne. Jokey service comedy about a sailor who convinces shipmates that some scrap metal is actually a top secret weapon. Droll British humor makes the cornball plot fun. (Dir: Ken Annakin, 89 mins.)

You Light Up My Life (1977)*½ Didi Conn, Joe Silver, Michael Zaslow. This tale of an aspiring songwriter with a propensity for falling for guys who reject her (someone in the film has taste) is filled with platitudes like "Be your own person." (Dir: Joseph Brooks, 90 mins.)†

You'll Find Out (1940)**½ Kay Kyser, Bela Lugosi, Peter Lorre, Boris Karloff. A bouncy, entertaining mish-mash of music and mystery, as Kay's hired to play at a rich girl's twenty-first birthday bash. However, Bela, Boris, and Peter are out to make sure that she doesn't live to celebrate her twenty-second. (Dir: David Butler, 97 mins.)†

You'll Like My Mother (1972)**½ Patty Duke, Rosemary Murphy, Sian Barbara Allen, Richard Thomas. Good performances save an awkward screenplay. Miss Duke, pregnant with her dead husband's child, comes to stay with her cold mother-in-law (Murphy) and retarded sister-in-law (Allen), with an evil villain lurking about. (Dir: Lamont Johnson, 92 mins.)

You'll Never Get Rich (1941)*** Fred Astaire, Rita Hayworth, Robert Benchley. Enjoyable musical features Astaire as a hoofer who knows the show must go on even if he's drafted. Great Cole Porter score. (Dir: Sidney Lanfield, 88 mins.)†

You'll Never See Me Again (MTV 1973)** David Hartman, Jane Wyatt, Ralph Meeker. Suspense thriller. A newly married husband is accused of murder after his spouse disappears. From a story by Cornell Woolrich. (Dir: Jeannot Szwarc, 73 mins.)

You Must Be Joking! (Great Britain, 1965)**½ Michael Callan, Lionel Jeffries, Terry-Thomas, Denholm Elliott. Terry-Thomas is a wacky army psychiatrist who drafts five equally zany officers to perform a forty-eight-hour "initiative test." (Dir: Michael Winner, 100 mins.)

You Never Can Tell (1951)*** Dick Powell, Peggy Dow, Joyce Holden. Wacky film about the reincarnation of a dog and a horse into a private detective (Powell) and a blond secretary (Holden), respectively, who come to earth to settle an old score concerning murder. (Dir: Lou Breslow, 78 mins.)

Young Americans, The (1969)** Milton C. Anderson, Judy Thomas. A saccharine display of flag-waving. Semidocumentary about a group of wholesome, well-groomed kids who sing stirring, heartfelt songs and live unblemished lives. Imagine a whole world populated by Osmonds, and you'll get the feel of this movie. (Dir: Alex Grasshoff, 104 mins.)

Young and Dangerous (1957)** Mark Damon, Lili Gentle, Connie Stevens, Edward Binns, Ann Doran. Typical teen chameleon drama about nasty boy Damon turning over a new leaf for love of the perfect girl. Say no to crime; say yes to sex. (Dir: William Claxton, 78 mins.)

Young and Innocent (Great Britain, 1937)***½ Nova Pilbeam, Derrick de Marney, Percy Marmont, Edward Rigby, Mary Clare, Basil Radford. One of the best of director Alfred Hitchcock's early films. A writer is wrongly suspected of murder; he enlists the unwilling aid of a detective's daughter to prove his innocence. Of course they fall in love. (82 mins.)†

Young and the Damned, The—See: **Los Olvidados**

Young and the Immoral, The—See: **Sinister Urge, The**

Young and the Willing, The (Great Britain, 1962)**½ Ian McShane, Samantha Eggar, John Hurt. Interesting tale of a potentially gifted boy (McShane) whose scholastic career is jeopardized by the attentions of his professor's wife (Maskell). AKA: **The Wild and the Willing.** (Dir: Ralph Thomas, 113 mins.)

Young and Wild (1958)* Gene Evans, Scott Marlowe, Carolyn Kearney, Robert Arthur. Baaaaaddddd teenagers romp and roll in a stolen auto in this ideal example of fifties juvenile delinquent "out of the headlines and onto the screen" moviemaking. Greased hair, tight sweaters, and loads of unintentional laughs. (Dir: William Witney, 69 mins.)

Young and Willing (1942)** William Holden, Eddie Bracken, Susan Hayward, Robert Benchley, Barbara Britton. Some struggling young actors try to interest a big theatrical producer. Mildly amusing comedy. (Dir: Edward Griffith, 82 mins.)†

Young Aphrodites (Greece, 1966)**½ Takis Emmanouel, Vangelis Joannides, Cleopatra Rota, Eleni Prokopiou. Young shepherds in ancient Greece discover a fishing village inhabited entirely by women. Their experiments in sensuality bring tragic results in this moodily seductive but slow-moving film. Originally 98 mins. (Dir: Nikos Koundouros, 87 mins.)†

Young April (1925)*** Bessie Love, Joseph Schildkraut, Rudolph Schildkraut, Bryant Washburn. Charming comedy of a crown prince running away for a fling to Paris, where he falls in love with a headstrong American girl who's there for the same reason. Naturally, his father objects strongly. The elder Schildkraut gives a rich performance as the king. Most entertaining. (Dir: Donald Crisp, 65 mins.)†

Young at Heart (1954)*** Frank Sinatra, Doris Day, Gig Young, Ethel Barrymore, Dorothy Malone. This musical remake of Fannie Hurst's *Four Daughters* hasn't the classy patina of the '38 original, but has charm and professionalism. (Dir: Gordon Douglas, 117 mins.)†

Young Bess (1953)***½ Jean Simmons, Charles Laughton, Deborah Kerr, Stewart Granger. Handsomely mounted historical drama with two excellent performances by Jean Simmons as the high-spirited Bess, and Charles Laughton as her father, Henry VIII. (Dir: George Sidney, 112 mins.)

Young Billy Young (1969)* Robert Mitchum, Angie Dickinson, Robert Walker. A dull western from fade-in to fade-out. Mitchum is the stone-faced lawman who tries to bring young Billy Young (Walker) to justice but finds a hostile town standing in his way. (Dir: Burt Kennedy, 90 mins.)

Youngblood (1978)** Lawrence-Hilton Jacobs, Bryan O'Dell, Ren Woods. Black exploitationer about a ghetto youth gang, the Kingsmen, who war on a local drug ring. Rather well done of its type with a good cast and authentic L.A. ghetto locales. (Dir: Noel Nosseck, 90 mins.)

Youngblood (1986)** Rob Lowe, Patrick Swayze, Cynthia Gibb. Lowe skates on thin ice as a hockey neophyte who must undergo a baptism by fire in order to be accepted by his teammates. A passable vehicle for Lowe. (Dir: Peter Markle, 110 mins.)†

Youngblood Hawke (1964)*½ James Franciscus, Suzanne Pleshette, Genevieve Page. Inept screen treatment of Herman Wouk's best-seller about a young author caught in the web of the big city's publishing world. (Dir: Delmer Daves, 137 mins.)

Young Captives, The (1959)**½ Steven Marlo, Luana Patten, Ed Nelson. Teenage couple eloping to Mexico run afoul of a crazed killer who holds them captive. Tight little suspense drama. (Dir: Irvin Kershner, 61 mins.)

Young Cassidy (U.S.-Great Britain, 1965)*** Rod Taylor, Maggie Smith, Julie Christie, Michael Redgrave, Flora Robson, Edith Evans. Interesting, if uneven, biographical drama about the early life of playwright Sean O'Casey, depicting his rise from the Dublin slums to the celebrated openings of his early

1217

plays. (Dirs: John Ford, Jack Cardiff, 110 mins.)

Young Catherine (MCTV 1991)*** Vanessa Redgrave, Julia Ormond, Christopher Plummer, Franco Nero, Marthe Keller, Maximilian Schell, Mark Frankel. Entertaining story of the rise of Russia's Catherine the Great. A truly lavish production that benefits greatly from the location shooting in the U.S.S.R. Sweeping saga of royal court intrigues, arranged marriages, clandestine affairs, illegitimate heirs, and attempted murder. Vanessa Redgrave savors every line as Elizabeth, empress of all the Russias. (Dir: Michael Anderson, 192 mins.)†

Young Country, The (MTV 1970)**½ Roger Davis, Joan Hackett, Peter Deuel, Walter Brennan, Wally Cox. Comic western with Roger Davis as a bewildered hero who gets into trouble trying to earn his keep playing cards. (Dir: Roy Huggins, 73 mins.)

Young Daniel Boone (1950)* David Bruce, Kristine Miller, Don Beddoe, Mary Treen. Dan'l learns early on how to shoot Indians and 'rassle a bear. Hokey, banal and boring. (Dir: Reginald LeBorg, 71 mins.)

Young Dillinger (1965)*½ Nick Adams, Robert Conrad, Mary Ann Mobley. A highly fictionalized account of the life of criminal John Dillinger and his cohorts. (Dir: Terry Morse, 102 mins.)

Young Doctors, The (1961)*** Fredric March, Ben Gazzara, Eddie Albert, George Segal (debut), Dick Clark. Routine hospital soap opera elevated to good drama by the earnest playing of a fine cast. (Dir: Phil Karlson, 102 mins.)

Young Doctors in Love (1982)**½ Michael McKean, Sean Young, Harry Dean Stanton, Patrick Macnee, Hector Elizondo. Madcap satire of goings-on in a hospital, where a group of unlikely prospects become resident surgeons in training. Many gags fall flat, but there's some outlandish, rib-tickling comedy performed by an expert cast. (Dir: Garry Marshall, 95 mins.)†

Young Don't Cry, The (1957)** Sal Mineo, James Whitmore. Confused melodrama about a badly run Georgia orphanage and one teenager in particular who gets involved with an escaped convict. (Dir: Alfred L. Werker, 89 mins.)

Young Dr. Kildare (1938)*** Lew Ayres, Lionel Barrymore. Good, sensitive story of intern's problems in a big-city hospital. First of the MGM series and well played by Ayres and Barrymore. (Dir: Harold S. Bucquet, 82 mins.)

Young Einstein (Australia, 1988)**½ Yahoo Serious, Odile Le Clezio, John Howard, Peewee Wilson, Su Cruickshank. Lushly photographed farce has New Zealand farm lad Einstein discovering various physics theorems while inventing surfing and rock'n'roll, romancing Marie Curie, and trying to retrieve his nuclear brewery from an evil entrepreneur before he blows up the world with it! (Dir: Yahoo Serious, 90 mins.)†

Younger Brothers, The (1949)*** Wayne Morris, Bruce Bennett, Robert Hutton, Janis Paige, Geraldine Brooks, Fred Clark, Alan Hale. Thoughtful western about the infamous Younger brothers gang and the motivation for their reign of crime and violence. (Dir: Edwin L. Martin, 77 mins.)

Younger Generation, The (1929)*** Jean Hersholt, Lina Basquette, Ricardo Cortez, Rosa Rosanova, Rex Lease. Well-made Fannie Hurst tearjerker about a young Jewish man's ambition to leave his roots and make his way in New York City's high society. Filmed as a silent, with some talking sequences. (Dir: Frank Capra, 88 mins.)

Youngest Profession, The (1943)**½ Virginia Weidler, Jean Porter, Edward Arnold, John Carroll, Scotty Beckett, Agnes Moorhead. Cute teen movie about two indefatigable autograph hunters and the trouble they get into, with cameos by lots of MGM stars. Enjoyable fluff. (Dir: Edward Buzzell, 82 mins.)

Youngest Spy, The (U.S.S.R., 1962)*** Kolya Burlyayev. Story of a Soviet lad whose parents were killed by the Nazis and became a spy behind the enemy lines. Good observation of child's thoughts, some poetic sequences. English-dubbed. (Dir: Andrei Tarkovsky, 94 mins.)

Young Frankenstein (1974)***½ Gene Wilder, Peter Boyle, Marty Feldman, Madeline Kahn, Gene Hackman, Teri Garr. Inspired lunacy. Wilder is the grandson of the nefarious Baron Frankenstein; he visits the old family homestead in Transylvania and decides to make a living creature himself. Some incredibly funny sight gags strewn along the way. (Dir: Mel Brooks, 98 mins.)†

Young Fugitives (1938)**½ Harry Davenport, Robert Wilcox, Dorothea Kent, Larry Blake. An old codger gets $50,000 and uses the dough to help put a troubled lad and a runaway girl back on the right track. Heartwarming, modest B movie. (Dir: George Robinson, 67 mins.)

Young Fury (1965)*½ Rory Calhoun, Virginia Mayo, Lon Chaney, Richard Arlen, John Agar, Jody McCrea, William Bendix. Top cast of old-time western stars aids floundering plot about a weary gunslinger returning home to find his son is leader of a terrorist band of young gunmen. (Dir: Christian Nyby, 80 mins.)

Young Girls of Rochefort, The (France,

1967)** Catherine Deneuve, Francoise Dorleac, Gene Kelly, Danielle Darrieux, George Chakiris. A charming score by Michel Legrand and the lovely Deneuve and her sister, Dorleac, are the best things about this overly sweet musical. It's a tale about a fair in the quaint French village of Rochefort-sur-Mer where everyone falls in and out of love at the drop of a song cue. (Dir: Jacques Demy, 126 mins.)

Young Graduates, The (1971)*½ Tom Stewart, Gary Rist, Patricia Wymer, Dennis Christopher, Jennifer Rist. High school girl is smitten with a teacher while geeks and goofballs cavort in the halls. Tedious and trite. (Dir: Robert Anderson, 99 mins.)†

Young Guns, The (1956)**½ Russ Tamblyn, Gloria Talbott, Scott Marlowe. Well-acted, but routine western about a boy who has to make a choice between becoming a gunslinger or a law-abiding citizen. (Dir: Albert Band, 84 mins.)

Young Guns (1988)** Emilio Estevez, Kiefer Sutherland, Casey Siemaszko, Lou Diamond Phillips, Charlie Sheen, Terry O'Quinn, Jack Palance, Terence Stamp. Dopey western, full of careless anachronisms, but enjoyable if you approach it with low expectations; Estevez (as a gleefully sociopathic Billy the Kid) and Siemaszko come off best. (Dir: Christopher Cain, 97 mins.)†

Young Guns II (1990)** Emilio Estevez, Kiefer Sutherland, Lou Diamond Phillips, William Petersen, Christian Slater, Balthazar Getty, James Coburn. Fans of the Brat Pack won't be disappointed by the escapades of Billy the Kid (Estevez) and his gang as they flee Old Mexico, with Pat Garrett (Petersen) in hot pursuit. Harmless sequel geared for teens includes Jon Bon Jovi's Oscar-nominated song "Blaze of Glory." (Dir: Geoff Murphy, 105 mins.)†

Young Guns of Texas (1962)** James Mitchum, Alana Ladd, Jody McCrea, Chill Wills. The chase is on after a group of Confederates as the Civil War ends, with Apaches on the warpath complicating matters. So-so western whose only novelty is the offspring of famous actors in leading roles. (Dir: Maury Dexter, 78 mins.)

Young Harry Houdini (MTV 1987)*** Jose Ferrer, Wil Wheaton, Jeffrey DeMunn. Fictional musing about how Houdini, the master illusionist, may have first picked up the tricks of his trade. (Dir: James Orr, 104 mins.)

Young Hellions—See: **High School Confidential**

Young Ideas (1943)** Susan Peters, Herbert Marshall, Mary Astor, Richard Carlson. Silly family comedy about a girl who secretly marries a boy her parents disapprove of. (Dir: Jules Dassin, 77 mins.)

Young In Heart, The (1938)***½ Douglas Fairbanks, Jr., Janet Gaynor, Paulette Goddard, Billie Burke, Roland Young, Richard Carlson. A dizzy family of card-sharps and fortune hunters is reformed by the kindness of a sweet old lady, whom they vow to help by leading better lives. Delightful comedy. (Dir: Richard Wallace, 91 mins.)

Young Jesse James (1960)** Ray Stricklyn, Robert Dix, Willard Parker. Still another version of how Jesse went bad—this time he joined Quantrill's Raiders because Union soldiers killed his father. (Dir: William Claxton, 73 mins.)

Young Joe, the Forgotten Kennedy (MTV 1977)**½ Peter Strauss, Barbara Parkins, Simon Oakland. Peter Strauss stars as Joseph Kennedy, Jr., the handsome eldest son of the Kennedy clan, groomed from childhood to be the heir of the family's political dynasty. (Dir: Richard T. Heffron, 104 mins.)

Young Ladies of Wilko, The (Poland, 1979)***½ Daniel Olbrychski, Christine Pascal, Maja Komorowska, Stanislawa Celinska. Witty and romantic tale of an aging bachelor visiting relatives who live next door to an estate belonging to five sisters. His return rekindles memories and brings new hope. Beautifully acted and gorgeously photographed. (Dir: Andrzej Wajda, 116 mins.)

Young Lady Chatterley (1977)*½ Harlee McBride, Peter Ratray, William Beckley, Ann Michelle. A descendant of the original Lady C. inherits the family estate and explores her inhibitions with the hired help. (Dir: Alan Roberts, 100 mins.)†

Young Lady Chatterley II (1985)* Harlee McBride, Brett Clark, Adam West, Sybil Danning. Having turned the family manse into a palace of non-stop carnality, Lady C. has to ward off developers who want to build a nuclear power plant on the premises! (Dir: Alan Roberts, 86 mins.)†

Young Land, The (1959)** Pat Wayne, Yvonne Craig, Dan O'Herlihy, Dennis Hopper. In early California, an American is placed on trial for killing a Mexican. Racial problems in the old West—film pleads for tolerance but becomes a western minus action. (Dir: Ted Tetzlaff, 89 mins.)

Young Lawyers, The (MTV 1969)*** Jason Evers, Keenan Wynn, Michael Parks. Well produced, well acted, and interesting. A new organization, the Boston Neighborhood Law Office, gives student lawyers the opportunity to try cases in court. (Dir: Harvey Hart, 74 mins.)

Young Lions, The (1958)**½ Marlon Brando, Montgomery Clift, Dean Martin,

Maximilian Schell, Hope Lange, Mai Britt. Irwin Shaw's big novel of WWII sprawls across the screen. Director Edward Dmytryk fails to command the material. What merit the film has is in Joe MacDonald's cinematography and the performances. (167 mins.)†

Young Love, First Love (MTV 1979)** Timothy Hutton, Valerie Bertinelli, Arlen Dean Snyder. Sudsy telefilm about two teenagers awakening to love, with the girl (Bertinelli) the aggressor and the boy (Hutton) shy and old-fashioned. Awfully familiar, despite the pleasant cast. AKA: **A Girl and a Boy: The First Time.** (Dir: Steven Hilliard Stern, 96 mins.)

Young Lovers, The (1949)***½ Sally Forrest, Keefe Brasselle, Hugh O'Brian. The ravages of polio cause a young dancer to readjust herself both physically and mentally. Gripping drama, sensitively directed by Ida Lupino, well acted. (85 mins.)

Young Lovers, The (1964)* Peter Fonda, Sharon Hugueny, Nick Adams, Deborah Walley. The pangs of first love, Hollywood-style. (Dir: Samuel Goldwyn, Jr., 105 mins.)

Young Man with a Horn (1950)*** Kirk Douglas, Lauren Bacall, Doris Day, Juano Hernandez, Hoagy Carmichael, Mary Beth Hughes. Douglas gives an excellent performance as a trumpet player who lived exclusively for his music until it was almost too late. Day acts (not too well) and sings (very well). (Dir: Michael Curtiz, 112 mins.)†

Young Man with Ideas (1952)**½ Glenn Ford, Ruth Roman, Denise Darcel, Nina Foch, Donna Corcoran. Lawyer moves his family to California and gets a job as a bill collector, which leads to complications. Story never hits any great heights, but the players are pleasant. (Dir: Mitchell Leisen, 84 mins.)

Young Mr. Lincoln (1939)*** Henry Fonda, Alice Brady, Richard Cromwell, Donald Meek, Marjorie Weaver. Story of Abe as a lawyer is not the greatest of Lincoln stories but John Ford's direction and fine acting by Fonda and Brady make it good entertainment. (100 mins.)†

Young Mr. Pitt, The (Great Britain, 1942)**½ Robert Donat, Robert Morley, Phyllis Calvert, John Mills. Well-acted but basically boring historical biography of one of England's greatest prime ministers; Donat is compelling, but the script generally lacks drama. Morley, however, is a standout as a dissolute Liberal MP. (Dir: Carol Reed, 118 mins.)

Young Nowheres (1929)*** Richard Barthelmess, Marion Nixon, Bert Roach, Raymond Turner, Anders Randolf. Charming story of two young working people who can't afford to get married, borrow a rich man's apartment while he's away

and find themselves in hot water. Well-wrought script tells the story in flashbacks, paying careful attention to point of view. (Dir: Frank Lloyd, 70 mins.)

Young Nurses, The (1973)** Jean Mason, Ashley Porter, Angela Gibbs, Zack Taylor, Jack LaRue, Jr., Dick Miller, Sally Kirkland, Allan Arbus, Mantan Moreland. Interesting cast is the only highlight of producer Roger Corman's fourth nurses drive-in special. Plot centers around hospital drug ring with legendary director Sam Fuller giving his all in a cameo as the villain. (Dir: Clinton Kimbrough, 77 mins.)†

Young Nurses in Love (1986)** Jeanne Marie, Alan Fisher, Jane Hamilton, Jamie Gillis. Sexy hospital hijinks set in motion by a Russian plot to raid a sperm bank containing samples from American geniuses. Blandly goofy comedy. (Dir: Chuck Vincent, 76 mins.)†

Young One, The (Mexico, 1960)** Zachary Scott, Bernie Hamilton, Key Meersman. Black musician fleeing the law is drawn into a web of danger when he lands on an island inhabited by a young girl and a lecherous older man. Unpleasant mixture of racial theme, *Lolita*, and assorted violence. (Dir: Luis Buñuel, 96 mins.)

Young People (1940)** Shirley Temple, Jack Oakie, Charlotte Greenwood. Temple vehicle directed by veteran Allan Dwan, who makes it at least a persuasive sow's ear. (78 mins.)

Young Philadelphians, The (1959)*** Paul Newman, Barbara Rush, Alexis Smith, Brian Keith, Billie Burke, Robert Vaughn, John Williams. Rather long film based on the best-seller about people from different levels of Philadelphia society. (Dir: Vincent Sherman, 136 mins.)†

Young Pioneers, The (MTV 1976)**½ Linda Purl, Roger Kern. Quality on-location production and two appealing young stars bolster this tale about two young newlyweds who trek to the wilds of Dakota to homestead land given to settlers in the 1870s. (Dir: Michael O'Herlihy, 98 mins.)

Young Pioneers' Christmas (MTV 1976)**½ Linda Purl, Roger Kern, Robert Hays. Holiday film about rugged pioneer days in the wilds of Dakota in the 1870s. (Dir: Michael O'Herlihy, 104 mins.)

Young Racers, The (1963)** Mark Damon, William Campbell, Luana Anders, Patrick Magee. Former racer turned writer intends to expose a reckless road ace in a book but grows to like him. (Dir: Roger Corman, 87 mins.)

Young Runaways, The (1968)** Brooke Bundy, Kevin Coughlin, Lloyd Bochner, Patty McCormack, Lynn Bari. Predictable, if earnest, attempt to focus on the kids who run away to Chicago's hippie section, in order to find themselves, circa

1968. (Dir: Arthur Dreifuss, 91 mins.)

Young Savages, The (1961)*** Burt Lancaster, Dina Merrill, Shelley Winters, Telly Savalas. Hard-hitting crime drama with Burt Lancaster playing a determined assistant DA engaged in the battle against juvenile delinquency. (Dir: John Frankenheimer, 103 mins.)

Young Scarface (Great Britain, 1947)**½ Richard Attenborough, Hermione Baddeley, William Hartnell. A brave young woman whose reporter fiancé has been killed investigates organized gang violence. A shocker in its day. Script by Graham Greene, from his novel *Brighton Rock*. (Dir: John Boulting, 91 mins.)

Young Sherlock Holmes (1985)**½ Nicholas Rowe, Alan Cox, Sophie Ward, Anthony Higgins, Michael Hordern, Freddie Jones. The concept of Holmes and Watson meeting as teenagers at school in Victorian London might have been interesting had it delved into the psychological underpinnings of the great, but neurotic detective as a young man. Unfortunately, this is merely another product of the Spielberg factory, almost a remake of *Indiana Jones and the Temple of Doom* in its latter half. (Dir: Barry Levinson, 110 mins.)†

Young Sinner, The (1965)*½ Tom Laughlin, Stefanie Powers. Early film by "Billy Jack" Laughlin about a young carouser who repents. (Dir: Tom Laughlin, 82 mins.)

Young Stranger (1957)*** James MacArthur, James Daly, Kim Hunter. A moving story of a boy and his relationship with his father, who doesn't take time from his busy schedule to try and understand his son. Based on a TV play and debut film direction by John Frankenheimer. (84 mins.)

Young Swingers (1963)** Molly Bee, Rod Lauren, Gene McDaniels, Jack Larsen, Jo Helton. They're young and they swing—and sing—in this throwaway drama about nightclub owner who faces eviction from cruel landlord. (Dir: Maury Dexter, 71 mins.)

Young, the Evil and the Savage, The (Italy, 1968)** Michael Rennie, Mark Damon, Eleanora Brown. English girls' school provides setting for an unoriginal but painless murder mystery. (Dir: Antonio Margheriti, 82 mins.)

Young Tom Edison (1940)*** Mickey Rooney, Fay Bainter. Good biography of the youth of the great inventive genius. Mickey is in rare form and the whole family will enjoy this. (Dir: Norman Taurog, 86 mins.)

Young Torless (West Germany, 1966)***½ Matthieu Carriere, Marian Seidowsky, Bernd Fischer, Barbara Steele. A sensitive boarding school student who witnesses the terrible verbal and physi-

cal abuse of his friend by two other pupils at the school, must decide whether or not to turn them into the authorities. First feature by director Volker Schlondorff offers a brave interpretation of moral responsiblity and the seeds of Nazism. (87 mins.)

Young Warriors, The (1967)** James Drury, Steve Carlson, Norman Fell. An average WWII tale which tries to analyze the effect killing has on a professional soldier and a young newcomer. (Dir: John Peyser, 93 mins.)

Young Warriors (1983)*½ Ernest Borgnine. Richard Roundtree, Lynda Day George, James Van Patten, Anne Lockhart. Schizophrenic exploitation movie starts off like a college sex comedy and ends up as a teenage vigilante thriller. Mix in some weird animation sequences and a preachy message against the use of private justice and you've got one bizarre, skippable film. (Dir: Lawrence D. Foldes, 103 mins.)†

Young Widow (1946)**½ Jane Russell, Marie Wilson, Louis Hayward, Faith Domergue, Kent Taylor, Penny Singleton, Cora Witherspoon. Emotional WWII story with Russell as a widow saddened by the loss of her husband. Tears flow and hearts break in this well-acted little drama, with some wonderful character performers giving their all. (Dir: Edwin L. Marin, 100 mins.)

Young Winston (Great Britain, 1972)*** Simon Ward, Anne Bancroft, Robert Shaw, John Mills, Patrick Magee, Ian Holm, Jack Hawkins. Interesting, highly enjoyable biography of Winston Churchill as a young man. Ward plays Churchill with power, and Bancroft and Shaw are moving as Churchill's inattentive parents. (Dir: Richard Attenborough, 157 mins.)†

Young Wives' Tale (Great Britain, 1951)** Joan Greenwood, Nigel Patrick, Audrey Hepburn, Derek Farr. A housing shortage in Great Britain causes comical complications for a number of couples, including a bohemian pair forced to share digs with a straightlaced couple. (Dir: Henry Cass, 78 mins.)

Young Wolves, The (France, 1968)*** Haydee Politoff, Roland Lesaffre, Christian Hay, Yves Benyeton. Drama about a gigolo who uses wealthy older women, but falls in love with an attractive young girl. When a man offers him a job in his mansion, he passes the girl off as his sister so the two can be together, but problems arise. Interesting comment on French youth from the political and cultural watershed year of 1968. (Dir: Marcel Carne, 11 mins.)

You Only Live Once (1937)***½ Henry Fonda, Sylvia Sidney. Circumstances cause an innocent man to be sent to prison, there to be turned into a killer. Gripping drama, excellently directed by Fritz Lang. (90 mins.)†

You Only Live Twice (Great Britain, 1967)**½ Sean Connery, Donald Pleasence, Tetsuro Tamba, Karin Dor. Drawn-out James Bond adventure set in Japan. The evil SPECTRE organization is out to start a war. (Dir: Lewis Gilbert, 116 mins.)†

Your Cheatin' Heart (1964)*** George Hamilton, Susan Oliver, Red Buttons, Arthur O'Connell. Hamilton manages to overcome his handsome playboy image to create a solid characterization of the ill-fated country-western singer Hank Williams. Tunes associated with the singer are mouthed by Hamilton in excellent fashion, and recorded for the soundtrack by Hank Williams, Jr. (Dir: Gene Nelson, 199 mins.)

You're a Big Boy Now (1967)*** Peter Kastner, Elizabeth Hartman, Geraldine Page, Julie Harris, Karen Black. A fast-paced, inventive comedy about a youth (Kastner) who is on the brink of becoming an adult. His escapade with a man-hating go-go dancer, well played by Hartman, leads to some wildly funny scenes. An impressive early effort from director Francis Ford Coppola, who also wrote the screenplay. Music by the Lovin' Spoonful. (96 mins.)†

You're a Sweetheart (1937)*** Alice Faye, George Murphy, Andy Devine, William Gargan. Faye's throaty voice and puff-cheeked charm are seen to good advantage here. In order to launch Faye's career properly, Murphy lets his imagination run riot and dreams up all sorts of publicity gimmicks. (Dir: David Butler, 96 mins.)

You're in the Army Now (1941)**½ Jimmy Durante, Phil Silvers, Jane Wyman. You'll watch it just to see Phil and Jimmy but don't expect miracles from this frail comedy about two vacuum cleaner salesmen who get into the army by mistake. (Dir: Lewis Seiler, 79 mins.)

You're in the Navy Now (1951)** Gary Cooper, Jane Greer, Eddie Albert, Jack Webb. A group of misfits led by Cooper (a green officer) are chosen to experiment with a craft outfitted with a steam turbine instead of the conventional diesel engine. The results are supposed to be uproariously funny. (Dir: Henry Hathaway, 93 mins.)

You're Jinxed, Friend, You've Met Sacramento (Italy, 1970)** Ty Hardin, Christian Hay, Jenny Atkins. Silly spaghetti western-comedy. Rancher Hardin bets on himself as a barroom brawler when he's not trying to whip his heirs into line. Not very funny, and the action is bland. (Dir: Giorgio Cristallini, 99 mins.)†

You're My Everything (1949)*** Dan Dailey, Anne Baxter, Shari Robinson, Buster Keaton. When this film is poking fun at the Hollywood heyday of the twenties and thirties it borders on being great, but when it reverts to the cornball sentiment of the tragic backstage life of the stars, it is only average entertainment. (Dir: Walter Lang, 94 mins.)

You're Never Too Young (1955)** Dean Martin, Jerry Lewis, Diana Lynn, Raymond Burr. Jerry as a wacky barber who is forced to pose as a child, with a thief and murderer on his trail. Reworking of *The Major and the Minor* to suit the talents of Martin and Lewis; not one of the team's better comedies. (Dir: Norman Taurog, 102 mins.)

You're Not So Tough (1940)** The Dead End Kids. Billy Halop is the leader of the Boys at this point in the series, and his leadership lands them a job on Mama Posita's Ranch, trying to save the crops! Not so bad. (Dir: Joe May, 65 mins.)

You're Only Young Once (1937)**½ Lewis Stone, Mickey Rooney. First in the Stone-Rooney group and a good example of wholesome family comedy which made the Hardy series so popular. (Dir: George B. Seitz, 77 mins.)

You're Telling Me (1934)***½ W. C. Fields, Buster Crabbe, Joan Marsh, Louise Carter, Kathleen Howard. The "master" appears in almost every hilarious scene of this film and he, and you, have a field day. He's an inventor and you'll hurt your sides laughing at his inventions. (Dir: Erle C. Kenton, 70 mins.)

Your Money or Your Wife (MTV 1972)*½ Ted Bessell, Elizabeth Ashley, Jack Cassidy. Out-of-work TV writer concocts a kidnapping plot and is talked into using his game plan on a nasty TV performer. (Dir: Allen Reisner, 104 mins.)

Your Past Is Showing (Great Britain, 1957) *** Peter Sellers, Terry-Thomas, Dennis Price, Shirley Eaton, Peggy Mount. Price is a blackmailing publisher of a tawdry exposé magazine; Sellers, a nasty TV personality; Terry-Thomas, a racketeering peer; Eaton, a model. The bits are pungently etched and the comedy is pleasantly oddball. (Dir: Mario Zampi, 92 mins.)

Your Place or Mine (MTV 1983)** Bonnie Franklin, Robert Klein, Peter Bonerz, Tyne Daly, Penny Fuller. Can a bright, single woman find Mr. Right in the city by the bay? Bonnie Franklin plays a psychiatrist on the lookout for a suitable mate. (Dir: Robert Day, 104 mins.)†

Yours, Mine and Ours (1968)** Henry Fonda, Lucille Ball, Van Johnson, Tom Bosley. You have to love the stars in order to tolerate this farce which has Lucy playing a widow with eight kids who marries widower Fonda, who has ten. (Dir: Melville Shavelson, 111 mins.)†

Your Three Minutes Are Up (1973)*** Beau Bridges, Kathleen Freeman, Janet Margolin, Ron Leibman. Well-acted little gem about two guys—one a hellraiser always looking to run a scam, and the other a straight arrow in awe of his friend's carefree aplomb. Intelligent comedy probes America's twisted value system. (Dir: Douglas N. Schwartz, 92 mins.)

Your Ticket Is No Longer Valid (Canada, 1979)** Richard Harris, George Peppard, Jeanne Moreau, Jennifer Dale, Alexandra Stewart, Winston Rekert. Highbrow Romain Gary trash about an impotent man trying to revive his business and haunted by erotic dreams of a young male gypsy. (Dir: George Kaczender, 91 mins.)†

Your Turn, Darling (France, 1963)*½ Eddie Constantine. Constantine, portraying FBI agent Lemmy Caution, two-fists his way through another fast-paced grade B crime film with all the predictable plot twists. (Dir: Bernard Borderie, 93 mins.)

Your Turn, My Turn (France, 1978)*** Marlene Jobert, Philippe Léotard, Micheline Presle. Bright comedy about a neglected wife and a divorced building contractor who literally meet by accident (in a minor traffic collision) and carry on an affair while somehow seeing to their respective children's needs. (Dir: François Leterrier, 95 mins.)

You Said a Mouthful (1932)*** Joe E. Brown, Ginger Rogers, Preston Foster, Guinn Williams. Delightful Brown comedy, in which the acrobatic comic plays an eccentric inventor who comes up with a swimsuit that floats! One of his best. (Dir: Lloyd Bacon, 75 mins.)

You Talkin' to Me? (1987)½ Jim Youngs, James Noble, Mykel T. Williamson, Faith Ford, Bess Motta. Two bad things have been associated with Scorsese's brilliant *Taxi Driver*—the first was John Hinckley, the second was this incredibly awful comedy. However, with luck, no one will remember this atrocity about a De Niro fan and aspiring actor (Youngs) who goes to Southern California and confronts a white supremacy group intent on getting his black model friend. (Dir: Charles Winkler, 97 mins.)†

Youth Runs Wild (1944)**½ Bonita Granville, Kent Smith, Tessa Brind. In frustration, neglected adolescents strike back at their parents and the authorities. Their parents are so busy with the war effort that their offspring become casualties of WWII on the homefront. An intelligently scripted, if undynamic, message-movie. (Dir: Mark Robson, 67 mins.)

Youth Takes a Fling (1938)** Joel McCrea, Andrea Leeds, Isobel Jeans, Frank Jenks, Virginia Grey. The romantic entanglements of a girl and a sailor aren't really enough to fill out a whole movie, and Leeds never developed enough sparkle to carry something like this by herself, anyway. (Dir: Archie Mayo, 79 mins.)

You've Got to Walk It Like You Talk It or You'll Lose That Beat (1971)*** Zalman King, Richard Pryor, Bob [Robert] Downey, Liz Torres, Roz Kelly, Allen Garfield, Steve Landisberg. Sharp satire, filmed in 1968, takes a solid look at the youth culture of the sixties as it examines the lifestyle of an aimless young man caught up in the countercultural emotions and excitement of the era. (Dir: Peter Locke, 85 mins.)

You Were Meant for Me (1948)*** Jeanne Crain, Dan Dailey. A nice score of popular standards, pleasing performances, and a routine story of a girl who marries a bandleader. (Dir: Lloyd Bacon, 92 mins.)

You Were Never Lovelier (1942)***½ Rita Hayworth, Fred Astaire, Adolphe Menjou, Leslie Brooks. Jerome Kern's music, Fred's dancing and Rita's charm combine with delightful results in this tuneful tale of a father who invents a fictitious Lochinvar for his daughter and then has to produce him in the flesh. (Dir: William A. Seiter, 97 mins.)†

Yoyo (France, 1965)*** Luce Klein, Pierre Etaix, Claudine Auger, Philippe Dionnet. Salute to the techniques of silent film tells two stories, of a millionaire who loses his fortune but reclaims a lost love and joins a circus troupe, and of his son, grown to be the circus's star clown, trying to restore his father's deteriorated mansion. Wistful comedy-drama features star-director Etaix playing the wealthy man and Yoyo as an adult. (97 mins.)

Yuma (MTV 1971)*½ Clint Walker, Barry Sullivan. That tree of a man, Clint Walker, rides again in a western packed with traditional ingredients. Walker is a cool, unflustered new sheriff who tames a wild town. (Dir: Ted Post, 73 mins.)†

Yum-Yum Girls, The (1976)**½ Judy Landers, Tanya Roberts, Michelle Dawn, Carey Poe, Stan Bernstein. Breezy take on standard "two girls agog in the big city" story as young lasses arrive in Manhattan to become fashion models. Filled with peppy people and diverting inside jokes. (Dir: Barry Rosen, 93 mins.)†

Yuri Nosenko, KGB (MCTV 1986)*** Tommy Lee Jones, Ed Lauter, Oleg Rudnik, Josef Sommer. When Yuri defects from the U.S.S.R., the CIA has visions of obtaining all sorts of info about the KGB (in addition to possible proof of a conspiracy in the Kennedy assassination). Unfortunately, he may be a plant. Jones plays the U.S. agent who damages his career in his zeal to break down Nosenko's story. No thrills, but a sharp appraisal of how secret agents operate. (Dir: Mick Jackson, 90 mins.)†

Z (France-Algeria, 1969)**** Yves Montand, Irene Papas, Charles Denner, Georges Geret, Jean-Louis Trintignant. This marvelous political film is based on the killing of a peace movement leader in Greece in 1963, the subsequent investigation, which uncovered a right-wing terrorist organization with government connections, and the military coup that destroyed democracy. Put in the frame of a thriller, what follows is not only a fine social protest, but exciting movie-making. Oscar: Best Foreign Film (Dir: Costa-Gavras, 127 mins.)†

Zabriskie Point (1970)* Mark Frechette, Daria Halprin, Rod Taylor, Harrison Ford, Kathleen Cleaver. A jumbled Antonioni essay about desolation and alienation and it's appropriate that one of the locations used in this, Antonioni's first feature shot in America, is Death Valley. (110 mins.)†

Zachariah (1971)** John Rubinstein, Pat Quinn, Don Johnson, Elvin Jones, Dick Van Patten, Country Joe and the Fish, The Doug York Rock Ensemble. Dated western with rock music overtones; different and sometimes amusing, but more often listless. (Dir: George Englund, 93 mins.)†

Zamba (1949)*½ Jon Hall, June Vincent, George Cooper, George O'Hanlon, Jane Nigh. Sub-standard Hollywood adventure about a boy raised by gorillas. What makes it different from Tarzan movies is that it isn't any good. (Dir: William Berke, 76 mins.)

Zandy's Bride—See: For Better, for Worse

Zany Adventures of Robin Hood (MTV 1984)** George Segal, Morgan Fairchild, Janet Suzman, Roddy McDowall, Tom Baker, Roy Kinnear. Mel Brooks did a spoof series years ago about Robin Hood and his Merry Men titled "When Things Were Rotten," and any half-hour is five times as funny as this. Segal looks ridiculous in tights, and Fairchild plays it so tongue-in-cheek that she can hardly articulate. (Dir: Ray Austin, 104 mins.)†

Zapped! (1982)** Willie Aames, Scott Baio, Heather Thomas, Felice Schachter. Baio is a high school student with a bent for science, who comes up with a formula that gives him certain powers, like lifting girls' skirts at will. He and his horny buddy (Aames) go on an innocent rampage satisfying all their fantasies, and in the process those of their fans. (Dir: Robert Rosenthal, 96 mins.)†

Zapped Again (1990)* Todd Eric Andrews, Kelli Williams, Reed Rudy, Maria

McCann, Karen Black, Linda Blair, Sue Ane Langdon, Lyle Alzado. New kid at Emerson High discovers the magical elixir that confers telekinetic powers and puts them to the same uses—namely, getting even with bullies and causing girls' clothing to fall up, down, and off. We'd be embarrassed to be seen renting this. (Dir: Doug Campbell, 93 mins.)†

Zarak (Great Britain, 1957)** Victor Mature, Michael Wilding, Anita Ekberg. Vic becomes an outlaw leader when he's driven from his village, with the British on his trail. Standard adventure opus. (Dir: Terence Young, 99 mins.)

Zardoz (Great Britain, 1974)** Sean Connery, Charlotte Rampling, Sara Kestelman. Science fiction head trip set in 2293. Immortality has led to overrationalization and boredom. Correction is needed from Connery, who plays a savage. The film examines ideas as if they were to be looked at but not touched. (Dir: John Boorman, 105 mins.)†

Zatoichi vs. Yojimbo (Japan, 1970)***½ Toshiro Mifune, Shintaro Katsu, Osamu Takizawa, Ayako Wakao. After more than twenty-five separate samurai epics, Zatoichi, the blind warrior swordsman, finally meets Yojimbo, the crude wandering samurai without a master, in a town run by gangsters. When these two perfectionists meet, the action and excitement sear the screen. (Dir: Kihachi Okamoto, 116 mins.)†

Zaza (1939)** Claudette Colbert, Herbert Marshall, Helen Westley. George Cukor and Colbert should have added up to more than this perfunctory tale of a cabaret performer in love with a married nobleman. Overstuffed production with Claudette uncomfortable in the role. (80 mins.)

Zazie dans le Metro (France, 1960)***½ Catherine Demonget, Philippe Noiret, Carla Marlier, Hubert Deschamps. Foulmouthed, sophisticated eleven-year-old Zazie spends a day and a half in Paris with her female-impersonator uncle. The highlight is to be a ride on the subway, but a series of hilarious sidetrips and meetings with bizarre Parisians keep delaying them. Ingenious comedy filled with outrageous sightgags, visual puns, and spoofs of other films. One of the best of the French New Wave movies. (Dir: Louis Malle, 92 mins.)†

Zebra Force (1977)*½ Mike Lane, Richard X. Slattery, Anthony Caruso, Rockne Tarkington, Glenn Wilder. Gang of Vietnam war veterans use tactics learned at the front to battle mobsters and get rich while doing the killing. Crude exploitation flick. (Dir: Joe Tornatore, 100 mins.)†

Zebra in the Kitchen (1965)**½ Jay North,

Marshall Thompson, Martin Milner, Jim Davis, Andy Devine. North stars as the boy who causes an uproar when he frees all the animals from a zoo. The animals are the scene stealers here and the kids will enjoy their antics. (Dir: Ivan Tors, 93 mins.)

Zed and Two Noughts, A (Great Britain, 1986)*** Andrea Ferreol, Brian Deacon, Eric Deacon, Frances Barber, Joss Ackland. A perverse, elegant puzzle of a movie for avant-garde enthusiasts only. The mazelike plot concerns two brothers, the curators of a European zoo, who begin to lose their minds after both of their wives are killed in a freak car crash. When they enter a ménage à trois with the accident's sole survivor, the truth about their strange relationship begins to come to the surface. (Dir: Peter Greenaway, 114 mins.)†

Zelig (1983)**** Woody Allen, Mia Farrow. Audacious satire of the media and a witty send-up of the newsreel format. Allen plays Leonard Zelig, a neurotic conformist who becomes famous for his chameleonlike ability to physically and mentally adapt to any crowd by changing his appearance at will. The film's cinematic cleverness provides a lot of the humor as we see faked newsreel footage of Zelig with Chaplin, Babe Ruth, and even Hitler. (Dir: Woody Allen, 79 mins.)†

Zelly and Me (1987)*** Isabella Rossellini, Glynis Johns, David Lynch, Alexandra Johnes. Tender, sometimes painful story of the special friendship between a lonely rich girl and her understanding governess. The girl's devotion to her idol, Joan of Arc, is helped along by the incredibly strict punishments she receives from her grandmother, who wants to be the girl's only loved one. The punishment sequences are somewhat hard to weather (they're not graphic, just downright mean), but the radiant Isabella sets it all right with her best screen work to date as Mademoiselle, whose awkward suitor is played (awkwardly) by Lynch. (Dir: Tina Rathborne, 87 mins.)†

Zenobia (1939)** Oliver Hardy, Harry Langdon, Billie Burke, Alice Brady, James Ellison, June Lang. A Langdon and Hardy comedy (Stan Laurel was lucky to be out of it). In a sleepy vale, the local medic (Hardy) becomes personal physician to a performing pachyderm. Genial, but not exactly brimming with hilarity. (Dir: Gordon Douglas, 71 mins.)

Zeppelin (Great Britain, 1971)** Michael York, Elke Sommer. A rather ridiculous World War I adventure spy epic which relies on superheroics and a big dirigible which is used in a mission to obtain valuable English documents and thereby destroy British morale. (Dir: Etienne Perier, 101 mins.)

Zero Boys, The (1985)*½ Daniel Hirsch, Kelli Maroney, Tom Shell, Nicole Rio. Teen champions at a survivalist game take a wrong turn in the woods and run afoul of the real thing in a pair of mass murderers. Underdeveloped and rather nasty. (Dir: Nico Mastorakis, 89 mins.)†

Zero de Conduite (France, 1933)**** Henri Storck. Charts the rebellion of three young boys in a provincial boarding school. On graduation day the boys dump garbage on the assembled dignitaries (some of whom are cardboard cutouts). Director Jean Vigo's grasp of the relationship between the real and the farcical makes this memorable. AKA: **Zero for Conduct.** (Dir: Jean Vigo, 47 mins.)†

Zero Hour (1957)** Dana Andrews, Linda Darnell, Sterling Hayden. Predictable tale about a man who was a fighter pilot (WWII). Dana Andrews strikes the right note as the troubled ex-pilot. The inspiration for *Airplane.* (Dir: Hall Barlett, 81 mins.)

Zero to Sixty (1978)* Darren McGavin, Sylvia Miles, Denise Nickerson, Lorraine Gray, Joan Collins, The Hudson Brothers. Preposterous comedy-adventure about recently divorced loser McGavin and street-wise teen Nickerson, who makes a living repossessing cars. (Dir: Don Weis, 96 mins.)†

Zeta One—See: **Alien Women**

Ziegfeld Follies (1945)***½ Fred Astaire, Lucille Ball, Gene Kelly, Judy Garland, Lucille Bremer. This *Follies* imitation has a specialty number by everyone at MGM and is certainly better than most TV spectaculars. (Dir: Vincente Minnelli, 110 mins.)†

Ziegfeld Girl (1941)*** James Stewart, Judy Garland, Hedy Lamarr, Tony Martin, Ian Hunter, Lana Turner. Lavish musical about the girls who were glorified by Ziegfeld is generally routine musical entertainment boasting a lot of stars. (Dir: Robert Z. Leonard, 131 mins.)

Ziegfeld: The Man and His Women (MTV 1978)**½ Paul Shenar, Valerie Perrine, Samantha Eggar, Barbara Parkins, Pamela Peadon. A valentine to those Hollywood movie musical biographies of the thirties and forties, but the lace on the satin heart is a bit tattered. Story of Florenz Ziegfeld, perhaps the most publicized Broadway entrepreneur of all time, is told through the eyes of the women in his life. (Dir: Buzz Kulik, 156 mins.)

Ziggy Stardust and the Spiders from Mars (1983)* Cinema verité documentarian D. A. Pennebaker's film of a 1973 David Bowie concert went unseen for ten years, and it's clear why. The show, Bowie's last from his glam-rock "Ziggy Stardust'' phase, is of historical interest to fans, but the poor sound quality and what looks like 8 mm footage produce more headaches than nostalgia. (91 mins.)†

Zigzag (1970)**½ George Kennedy, Anne Jackson, Eli Wallach. Another variation on a murder-for-insurance theme has Kennedy as a terminally ill man who frames himself for a murder to get insurance for his wife. (Dir: Richard A. Colla, 104 mins.)

Zita (France, 1968)*** Joanna Shimkus, Katina Paxinou, Jose Maria Flotats. Unusual, appealing film, about a young girl maturing after the experiences of a loved aunt's death and her own first tastes of love and different sorts of living. (Dir: Robert Enrico, 92 mins.)

Zodiac Killer, The (1971)*½ Hal Reed, Bob Jones, Ray Lynch, Tom Pittman. No-budget account of the never-found killer who terrorized San Francisco in the late '60s. Has a few effective moments, but it's too factual to work as a horror film and too cheap for anything else. Doodles Weaver makes a guest appearance (!). (Dir: Tom Hanson, 87 mins.)†

Zombie (1964)—See: Zombies

Zombie (1979) ½ Tisa Farrow, Ian McCulloch, Richard Johnson, Al Cliver. Gruesome chiller about the living dead doing their thing in the Caribbean. Cast looks half-dead; maybe they're real zombies. (Dir: Lucio Fulci, 91 mins.)†

Zombie High (1987)* Virginia Madsen, Richard Cox. Vague mix of social satire and horror set at a prep school renowned for making even the most troublesome students models of good behavior. Never establishes a consistent direction. AKA: The School that Ate My Brain. (Dir: Ron Link, 91 mins.)†

Zombie Island Massacre (1985)* Rita Jenrette, David Broadnax, Tom Cantrell. See Abscam wife, Jenrette, take off all her clothes! See her and several other actors take a tour into an eerie jungle and get killed off one by one by strange creatures! Atrocious would-be shocker. (Dir: John N. Carter, 85 mins.)†

Zombie Nightmare (Canada, 1986)*½ Jon-Mikl Thor, Adam West, Tia Carrere, Manuska Rigaud. Teenager killed in a hit-and-run accident is resurrected as a zombie by his mother so he can seek revenge. Surprise ending raises a little interest, but otherwise this one's as dead as its hero. (Dir: Jack Bravman, 89 mins.)†

Zombies (1964) ½ William Joyce, Heather Hewitt, Betty Hyatt Linton, Dan Stapleton. Del Tenney, the director of the immortal *The Horror of Party Beach* is at it again in *Zombies*, which offers startling evidence on the dangers of cancer research; it can result in zombiedom! A writer doing research in a tropical

paradise discovers that native voodoo rituals combined with out-of-control laboratory research have created an army of the living dead. It's hard to say which is scarier—the zombies on a murderous spree or the film's comic relief. AKA: Voodoo Blood Bath, Zombie, and I Eat Your Skin, which is its title on video. (82 mins.)†

Zombies of Mora Tau (1957)*½ Gregg Palmer, Allison Hayes, Joel Ashley, Autumn Russell. Dim-witted chiller about the living dead guarding a sunken treasure while mercenary types try to figure out a way to get the loot. Zombiesque. (Dir: Edward L. Cahn, 70 mins.)†

Zombies of Sugar Hill, The—See: Sugar Hill

Zombies on Broadway (1945)**½ Bela Lugosi, Wally Brown, Alan Carney, Sheldon Leonard, Ann Jeffreys. Not as bad as you'd expect. This amiable, ramshackle comedy is about two overzealous press agents who visit Voodoo Island and try to give the living dead their first break in show business. Zany and modestly amusing. (Dir: Gordon Douglas, 68 mins.)

Zone Troopers (1986)**½ Tim Thomerson, Timothy Van Patten. A gimmicky adventure film. Back in WWII, the Allies are trapped behind enemy lines, until they receive help from outer space creatures. A solid action pic about the Yanks beating the Germans, so who needed the aliens? (Dir: Danny Bilson, 88 mins.)†

Zontar, the Thing from Venus (1966)½ John Agar, Anthony Huston, Warren Hammack. A sci-fi film from the depths of American-International Pictures, and you can't go much deeper than that. Agar, the stalwart star of many an horrific horror film, battles alien fiends capable of dominating the human mind. "SCTV" did a popular spoof on this film, but even they couldn't match the original for hilarity. (Dir: Larry Buchanan, 68 mins.)†

Zoo Gang, The (1985)** Jackie Earle Haley, Eric Gurry, Tiffany Helm, Jason Gedrick, Ben Vereen. Sort of a Junior Chamber of Commerce comedy. Some adolescents want to launch their own nightclub, but some terrible teens decide to spoil their enterprising dreams. (Dirs: John Watson, Pen Densham, 90 mins.)†

Zoo in Budapest (1933)***½ Gene Raymond, Loretta Young, O. P. Heggie, Paul Fix. A romantic film with a shimmery glow to it. A homeless girl finds a home and heart's desire with a zookeeper. That plot description doesn't do justice to the radiant romanticism here; the photography is stunning, as if the film were suffused with a belief in the power of love to transform everyday realities. (Dir: Rowland V. Lee, 85 mins.)

Zoot Suit (1982)** Daniel Valdez, Edward James Olmos, Charles Aidman, Tyne Daly. This real-life happening (the 1942 Los Angeles trial of a group of Chicanos for the murder of an opposing gang member) made a good stage play, but as a film, it fails. (Dir: Luis Valdez, 103 mins.)

Zorba the Greek (U.S.-Greece, 1964)***½ Anthony Quinn, Irene Papas, Lila Kedrova, Alan Bates. A marvelous rousing drama set in Crete about a lusty individualist determined to live his own life, free of any restrictions imposed upon him by an unyielding and unchanging Greek society. Noteworthy performance from Quinn, whose magnetism and vitality are perfectly suited to the part. Lila Kedrova won an Oscar for her supporting performance as an aging courtesan who dwells in the past. (Dir: Michael Cacoyannis, 142 mins.)†

Zorro (France-Italy, 1975)** Alain Delon, Stanley Baker. European version of the popular story of the masked Mexican crusader (Delon) vs. the corrupt aristocracy, presided over by Colonel Huerta (well played by Baker). (Dir: Duccio Tessari, 120 mins.)

Zorro, The Gay Blade (1981)*** George Hamilton, Lauren Hutton, Ron Leibman, Brenda Vaccaro. Despite the title, this is not an offensive "swishbuckler" aiming for cheap laughs. This loving send-up of Mr. Z. films delivers chuckles and dashing heroics due to Hamilton's persuasive performance. (Dir: Peter Medak, 93 mins.)†

Zotz! (1962)** Tom Poston, Julia Meade, Jim Backus, Fred Clark. Professor finds an old coin with the magical power to make people move in slow motion, becomes a target for spies after the coin. Moderate comedy doesn't have the sparkle necessary to bring it off. (Dir: William Castle, 87 mins.)†

Zouzou (France, 1934)*** Josephine Baker, Jean Gabin, Yvette Leblon, Illa Meery. Peachy French backstage musical vehicle for the wonderful Baker as an unassuming laundress who becomes a glamorous stage star. Extravagantly produced numbers set off Baker's talent and charm to perfection, as do her costumes. (Dir: Marc Allegret, 92 mins.)†

Z.P.G. (Great Britain, 1972)**½ Oliver Reed, Geraldine Chaplin, Diane Cilento, Don Gordon. Interesting sci-fi story of future society in which reproduction is a crime punishable by death. Cerebral tale avoids pyrotechnics, but weak script causes it to come up short in the entertainment department. (Dir: Michael Campus, 95 mins.)

Zulu (Great Britain, 1964)*** Stanley Baker, Jack Hawkins, James Booth, Michael Caine. An exciting adventure based on a real-life incident in African history, the massacre in 1879 of a British mission by Zulu warriors. The events leading to the epic battle are depicted in personal terms involving a missionary, his daughter, the mission's commander and his men. (Dir: Cy Endfield, 138 mins.)†

Zulu Dawn (U.S.–Netherlands, 1979)**½ Peter O'Toole, Burt Lancaster, Simon Ward, John Mills. A violent, historic epic on the massacre of British troops by Zulu warriors, with film stars Lancaster and O'Toole as a general and colonialist, respectively. (Dir: Douglas Hickox, 121 mins.)†

Zuma Beach (MTV 1978)*½ Suzanne Somers, P. J. Soles, Steven Keats. Routine comedy-drama, used to showcase Somers, relies too heavily on her modest charms. (Dir: Lee H. Katzin, 104 mins.)

We Deliver!
And So Do These Bestsellers.

DON'T MISS YOUR FAVORITE
MOVIES IN PRINT!

- ❑ **BONFIRE OF THE VANITIES**, Tom Wolfe 27597-6 $5.95
- ❑ **THE RUSSIA HOUSE**, John LeCarre 28534-3 $5.95
- ❑ **THE LITTLE DRUMMER GIRL**,
  John LeCarre 26757-4 $5.95
- ❑ **AN INCONVENIENT WOMAN**,
  Dominick Dunne 28906-3 $5.99
- ❑ **PEOPLE LIKE US**, Dominick Dunne 27891-6 $5.95
- ❑ **DICK TRACY**, Max Allan Collins 28528-9 $4.95
- ❑ **HAMLET**, William Shakespeare 21292-3 $2.95
- ❑ **THE TERMINATOR**, Frakes and Wisher 25317-4 $4.99
- ❑ **TERMINATOR 2: JUDGEMENT DAY**,
  Randall Frakes 29169-6 $4.99
- ❑ **CONAGHER**, Louis L'Amour 28101-1 $3.99
- ❑ **VOICE OF THE HEART**,
  Barbara Taylor Bradford 26253-X $5.95
- ❑ **WHITE PALACE**, Glenn Savan 27659-X $4.95
- ❑ **SOPHIE'S CHOICE**, William Styron 27749-9 $5.95
- ❑ **CALL OF THE WILD/WHITE FANG**,
  Jack London 21233-8 $2.95
- ❑ **THE BOURNE IDENTITY**, Robert Ludlum ... 26011-1 $5.95
- ❑ **LOVE STORY**, Erich Segal 27528-3 $4.95
- ❑ **THE PRINCE OF TIDES**, Pat Conroy 26888-0 $5.99
- ❑ **BALLAD OF THE SAD CAFE**,
  Carson McCullers 27254-3 $3.95